W9-CGS-593

.for.

Sharry
.from.
Mary Jo
- 2000 -

For Bill

Copyright © 1997
Peter Pauper Press, Inc.
202 Mamaroneck Avenue
White Plains, NY 10601
All rights reserved
ISBN 0-88088-811-3
Printed in China
7   6   5   4   3   2   1

So Many Candles
So Little Cake

Age is a number,
and mine is unlisted.

You know you're
getting older when an
"organ recital" refers to
the state of your insides,
and not to a musical event.

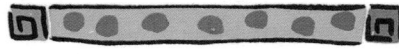

With the grace of God
and a good lighting director,
I plan to stick around
for a good long time.

BARBARA WALTERS

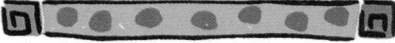

Most people my age are dead.
You could look it up.

CASEY STENGEL

By the time we reach
greener pastures, we can't
climb the fence.

Age is all in your mind.
The trick is to keep it
from creeping down into
your body.

Maturity is the time of
life when, if you had
the time, you'd have the
time of your life.

You know you're getting older when people stop *telling* you about the good old days and start *asking* you about them.

You can live to be a hundred
if you give up all the things
that make you want to live
to be a hundred.

WOODY ALLEN

You know you're getting older when your pharmacist starts to call you by your first name.

You know you're getting
older when your car battery
goes dead because the
turn signal was on for
two weeks straight.

Let's do it while we're still ambulatory.

DR. JANE KATZ,
age 52, about marrying
Dr. Herbert L. Erlanger, age 70

You're not getting older,
you're getting better—
discounts.
*heard on Garrison's Keillor's
radio program*

What would I like to be at seventy? At seventy I confidently hope I will have had at least eight more wives, have grown a stomach that I can regard with respect, and can still walk upstairs to the bedroom without aching or groaning.

ERROL FLYNN,
at 46

I'd go out with women my age, but there aren't any women my age.

GEORGE BURNS,
nearing 100

The most conservative
persons I ever met are
college undergraduates.
The radicals are the men
past middle life.

WOODROW WILSON

When we asked [an 85-year-old] how he felt . . . , he said, "I feel *good*. In fact, I feel like I did when I was thirty-five. As long as I don't *do* what I did when I was thirty-five."

HUGH DOWNS,
Thirty Dirty Lies about Old

I'm 71, and I can still dance.
I can't do a whole number,
but I'm terrific for 16 bars.

GWEN VERDON

People nowadays are living longer; they aren't getting old—they're adding more years to the middle! . . . I have often observed handsome, active and athletic people in their 70s and 80s who ignore the obvious mathematical impossibility and refer to themselves as "middle-aged."

FAYE MENKEN SCHNEIER

Nobody's "old" anymore—
they've just been around for
a long time.

ABIGAIL VAN BUREN

When Bob Dole stands next
to Strom Thurmond, he looks
like the new lifeguard
on Baywatch.

JAY LENO

You know you're growing
older when your eye doctor
asks you to read the chart
on the wall and you can't
see the wall.

You're only old once!

Dr. Seuss (Theodor Geisel)

Fame is a mixed blessing. When you're 40 you can always say, "I'll finish that novel when I'm 50 or 60." But at my age, you run out of excuses.

DOROTHY WEST,
age 88

I don't bleach my hair, and I
don't wear high heels and
I don't see why I should
bleach my teeth.

CAROLYN HEILBRUN,
age 70

[I've survived to age 102 because] God doesn't need me, and the Devil doesn't want me.

MICHAEL MAKOWSKI

The best part of reaching 100:
"You begin to be able to shirk
responsibility."

BILL STERICO,
age 100

In my heart, in my head,
I still feel energetic, young.
At the same time, the passage
of the years leaves its marks,
and one's appearance is
no longer in tune with
one's feelings . . .

CATHERINE DENEUVE,
age 52

I don't have too much work.
Once you're 90, people
don't tie you up for
long-term projects.

PHILIP JOHNSON

Every year I get richer—
I have one year less to
live on my money.

HARRIET PINOVER

There's no fool like an old fool. You can't beat experience.

JACOB M. BRAUDE

The hardest years in life
are those between ten
and seventy.

HELEN HAYES,
at 83

I'm only 88. When I get to
be 150, I may be slowing
down a little.

MELVIN BELLI

George Bernard Shaw . . . said
he had lived so long because
he never drank and was a
vegetarian. Then Winston
Churchill, who was the same
age, said he drank a bottle of
brandy a day, and ate steak.
I thought: "They're both
idiots." . . . It's all in the genes.

AL HIRSCHFELD

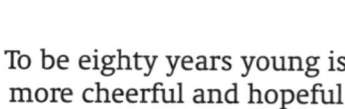

To be eighty years young is
more cheerful and hopeful
than forty years old.

FORTUNE COOKIE LEGEND

My health is good;
it's my age that's bad.

ROY ACUFF,
age 83

Old men and comets have been reverenced for the same reason: their long beards, and pretenses to foretell events.

JONATHAN SWIFT

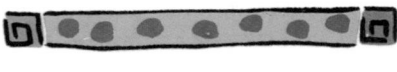

They tell you that you'll
lose your mind when you
grow older. What they don't
tell you is that you won't
miss it very much.

MALCOLM COWLEY

I don't want to achieve
immortality by being inducted
into baseball's Hall of Fame.
I want to achieve immortality
by not dying.

LEO DUROCHER,
at 81

We're not over the hill yet,
but we're probably high
enough to get nosebleeds.

No part of aging is more
dismaying than losing your
references, than getting
a blank look from a young
person to whom you have
just mentioned the name
of someone obscure,
like Paul McCartney.

BILL COSBY

It's not the age that counts.
It's your performance
that counts.

Strom Thurmond,
at 93

When Jeanne Calment, the oldest documented person alive, was asked at age 120 how she would feel about living to 125, she answered, "Why be pessimistic?"

At my age [70], I only
remember two things:
Ladies are pretty and
money pays the bills
if you can get it.

B. B. KING

It is not all bad, this getting old, ripening. After the fruit has got its growth it should juice up and mellow. God forbid I should live long enough to ferment and rot and fall to the ground in a squash.

EMILY CARR

You know you're getting
older when the free
insurance company
calendar starts coming
to you one month
at a time.

The best thing about getting
old is that all those things
you couldn't have when
you were young you
no longer want.

L. S. MCCANDLESS

You know you're getting
older when a postage
stamp costs more than
a movie ticket did when
you were young.

I'm saving that rocker for
the day when I feel as old
as I really am.

DWIGHT D. EISENHOWER

Old age is when the liver spots
show through your gloves.

PHYLLIS DILLER

You're never too old
to become younger.

MAE WEST

People who say you're just
as old as you feel are
all wrong, fortunately.

RUSSELL BAKER

The first half of our lives is
ruined by our parents and the
second half by our children.

CLARENCE DARROW

If you don't hear your
older friends complain
about their age, perhaps
the problem is in
your hearing.

The years between fifty
and seventy are the hardest.
You are always being asked
to do things, and yet you
are not decrepit enough
to turn them down.

T. S. Eliot

I'm a late bloomer.
My mind and my
experience have caught
up to my body.

RAQUEL WELCH

Society conditions us to think of 50 as "over the hill," even though at that age most people still have about half of their adult lives ahead of them. Besides, people don't want to believe they're past their peak; I know I don't, and I'm 76.

EUGENE I. LEHRMANN,
President, AARP

You can't be rigid. There is no one way to do things. You have to be able to change and meet and deal with each situation as you see it.

HAROLD GOLDSTEIN,
age 100

What happens to you in that new third to half of life [middle to old age] varies more from individual to individual, and depends more on what you do and don't do, than in any other period of life.

BETTY FRIEDAN

Never have I enjoyed youth
so thoroughly as I have in
my old age. . . . Nothing is
inherently and invincibly
young except spirit. And
spirit can enter a human
being perhaps better in the
quiet of old age and dwell
there more undisturbed than
in the turmoil of adventure.

GEORGE SANTAYANA

I think [at age 81] I am finally learning how to conduct.

DAVID RANDOLPH,
choral and orchestral conductor

It's nice to be here. When
you're 100 years old, it's nice
to be anywhere.

GEORGE BURNS

You only live once, but once is enough if you play it right.

WOODY ALLEN,
line from Interiors

No one grows old by living—
only by losing interest
in living.

MARIE RAY

People are largely responsible
for their own old age.

DR. JOHN W. ROWE,
Director, MacArthur Foundation
Consortium on Successful Aging

You know you're getting
old when the candles cost
more than the cake.

BOB HOPE

2005
ESPN
SPORTS
ALMANAC

With Exclusive Year in Review Commentary from ESPN Anchors and Analysts

Chris Berman
on Pro Football

Dan Patrick
on Top Personalities

Steve Levy
on Hockey

Linda Cohn
on Top Personalities

Stuart Scott
on Top Moments

Karl Ravech
on Baseball

Chris Fowler
on College Football

Trey Wingo
on Top Moments

ALSO CONTRIBUTING

Dick Vitale
on College Basketball

Andy Katz
on College Basketball

Lee Corso
on College Football

Seth Wickersham
on the Summer Olympics

Jerry Bembry
on Pro Basketball

Scott Van Pelt
on Golf

The Champions of 2004

Auto Racing
For all the statistics, see the Auto Racing section.

NASCAR Circuit
Daytona 500 . . . . Dale Earnhardt Jr.
Coca-Cola 600 . . . . Jimmie Johnson
Brickyard 400 . . . . Jeff Gordon
EA Sports 500 . . . . Dale Earnhardt Jr.
Mountain Dew Southern 500 . . . . Nov. 14
Nextel Cup Points Leader . . . . Kurt Busch, 6015 pts
(through Oct. 31)

Champ Car World Series Circuit
Points Championship . . . . . Sebastien Bourdais, 335 pts
(through Oct. 24)

Indy Racing League Circuit
Indianapolis 500. . . . . Buddy Rice
IndyCar Championship . . . . Tony Kanaan, 618 pts

Formula One Circuit
U.S. Grand Prix. . . . . Michael Schumacher
World Driving Champion. . Michael Schumacher, 148 pts

Baseball
For all the statistics, see the Baseball section.

World Series . . . . . . Boston def. St. Louis, 4 games to 0
MVP . . . . Manny Ramirez, Boston, OF
ALCS . . . . Boston def. New York, 4 games to 3
NLCS . . . . St. Louis def. Houston, 4 games to 3
All-Star Game . . American League 9, National League 4
MVP . . . . Alfonso Soriano, AL (Texas), 2B
Coll. World Series CS-Fullerton def. Texas, 2 games to 0
MVP. . . . . Jason Windsor, CS-Fullerton, P

College Basketball
For all the statistics, see the College Basketball section.

Men's NCAA Tournament
Championship. . . . . . . Connecticut 82, Georgia Tech 73
MVP . . . . Emeka Okafor, Connecticut, F/C

Women's NCAA Tournament
Championship . . . . Connecticut 70, Tennessee 61
MVP . . . . Diana Taurasi, Connecticut, G

Pro Basketball
For all the statistics, see the Pro Basketball section.

NBA Finals . . . . Detroit def. LA Lakers, 4 games to 1
MVP . . . . Chauncey Billups, Detroit, G
Eastern Final . . . . . . Detroit def. Indiana, 4 games to 2
Western Final . . LA Lakers def. Minnesota, 4 games to 2
All-Star Game . . . . West 136, East 132
MVP . . . . Shaquille O'Neal, West (LA Lakers), C

Bowling
For all the statistics, see the Bowling section.

Men's Major Championships
Tournament of Champions (2003). . . . . Patrick Healey Jr.
ABC Masters . . . . Walter Ray Williams Jr.
U.S. Open. . . . . Pete Weber
PBA World Championship . . . . Tom Baker

Women's Major Championships
WIBC Queens . . . . Marianne DiRupo

College Football (2003)
For all the statistics, see the College Football section.

National Champions
AP . . . . USC (12-1)
ESPN/USA Today Coaches' . . . . LSU (13-1)

Major Bowls
Rose . . . . USC 28, Michigan 14
Sugar . . . . LSU 21, Oklahoma 14
Fiesta . . . . Ohio St. 35, Kansas St. 28
Orange. . . . . Miami-FL 16, Florida St. 14
Heisman Trophy . . . . Jason White, Oklahoma, QB

Pro Football (2003)
For all the statistics, see the Pro Football section.

Super Bowl XXXVIII . . . New England 32, Carolina 29
MVP . . . . Tom Brady, New England, QB
AFC Championship . New England 24, Indianapolis 14
NFC Championship . . . . . . Carolina 14, Philadelphia 3
Pro Bowl. . . . . NFC 55, AFC 52
MVP. . . . . Marc Bulger, St. Louis, QB
CFL Grey Cup Final . . . . . . Edmonton 34, Montreal 22
MVP . . . . Jason Tucker, Edmonton, WR

Golf
For all the statistics, see the Golf section.

Men's Major Championships
Masters . . . . Phil Mickelson
U.S. Open . . . . Retief Goosen
British Open. . . . . Todd Hamilton
PGA Championship . . . . Vijay Singh

Champions (Seniors) Major Championships
The Tradition . . . . Craig Stadler
Senior PGA Championship . . . . Hale Irwin
U.S. Senior Open. . . . . Peter Jacobsen
Senior Players Championship . . . . Mark James
Senior British Open . . . . Pete Oakley

Women's Major Championships
Kraft Nabisco Championship . . . . Grace Park
LPGA Championship . . . . Annika Sorenstam
U.S. Women's Open . . . . Meg Mallon
Women's British Open . . . . Karen Stupples

National Team Competition
Ryder Cup. . . . . Europe 18½, United States 9½

Hockey
For all the statistics, see the Hockey section.

Stanley Cup . . . . Tampa Bay def. Calgary, 4 games to 3
MVP . . . . Brad Richards, Tampa Bay, C
Eastern Final Tampa Bay def. Philadelphia, 4 games to 3
Western Final . . . . Calgary def. San Jose, 4 games to 2
All-Star Game . . . . East 6, West 4
MVP . . . . Joe Sakic, Colorado, C

Horse Racing
For all the statistics, see the Horse Racing section.

Triple Crown Champions
Kentucky Derby . . . . Smarty Jones (Stewart Elliott)
Preakness Stakes . . . . Smarty Jones (Stewart Elliott)
Belmont Stakes . . . . Birdstone (Edgar Prado)

Harness Racing
Hambletonian . Windsong's Legacy (Trond Smedshammer)
Little Brown Jug . . . . . Timesarechanging (Ron Pierce)

Soccer
For all the statistics, see the Soccer section.

MLS Cup 2003 . . . . San Jose 4, Chicago 2
MVP . . . . Landon Donovan, San Jose, F

Tennis
For all the statistics, see the Tennis section.

Men's Grand Slam Championships
Australian Open . . . . Roger Federer
French Open . . . . Gaston Gaudio
Wimbledon . . . . Roger Federer
U.S. Open . . . . Roger Federer

Women's Grand Slam Championships
Australian Open . . . . Justine Henin-Hardenne
French Open . . . . Anastasia Myskina
Wimbledon . . . . Maria Sharapova
U.S. Open . . . . Svetlana Kuznetsova

Miscellaneous Champions
For more, see the Miscellaneous & Int'l Sports sections.

Little League World Series . . . . . Willemstad, Curacao
Tour de France . . . . Lance Armstrong (USA)
Iditarod . . . . Mitch Seavey
World Series of Poker . . . . Greg Raymer

2005 ESPN® SPORTS ALMANAC

Gerry Brown
Michael Morrison
EDITORS

HYPERION
ESPN® BOOKS

Editors
Gerry Brown
Michael Morrison

Technical Support
Sean Dessureau
Mike Leary
Adam Polgreen

Comments and suggestions from readers are invited. Because of the many letters received, however, it is not possible to respond personally to every correspondent. Nevertheless, all letters are welcome and each will be carefully considered. The **ESPN Sports Almanac** does not rule on bets or wagers. Address all correspondence to: Sports Almanac, Inc., P.O. Box 542281, Lake Worth, FL 33454-2281. Email: info@espnalmanac.com.

ISBN 0–7868–8893–8

FIRST EDITION

10 9 8 7 6 5 4 3 2 1

CONTENTS

6   CONTENTS

The future can be a scary thing, but the past has been downright frightening for some of us—most specifically, those of us who were born and bred Red Sox fans. If it's true that the past is prologue, then the story began in 1918. After teasing and torturing our grandfathers and fathers for decades, the Olde Town Team once again buckled our knees in 1978 and 1986, before giving us a final parting shot below the belt in 2003. Finally, after 86 years, that's all behind us and wherever the future brings us, we won't have to listen to that lousy "19-18" chant anymore.

One thing we don't get sick of hearing is the guidance, advice and assistance of the following fine folks, even if some of them listed below (they shall remain nameless) are Yankee fans.

At ESPN Books, thanks to Chris Raymond for leading the way and keeping us on course, and to Maria Delgado for getting all the paperwork straightened out.

Connecticut basketball had a big year, and while Emeka and Diana may have been their team's MVPs and Jim Calhoun and Geno Auriemma are big wheels down there, our favorite folks from the Nutmeg State are as follows:

In Waterbury, our everlasting gratitude goes to Almanac Editor Emeritus Mike Meserole for continuing to care so much and for the reliable crunch-time shipment of Peggy Lawtons. In Bristol, thanks to former editor John Hassan for always coming through in the clutch, along with Russell Baxter and all of the essay and list contributors.

Also further south in New Jersey, big thanks go to the guys who put ink to paper: Rick Sommers of Command Web and Rob Conte and Paul Morgan from SCI for their bottomless well of patience.

As always, thanks to Gretchen Young, Zareen Jaffrey and David Lott at Hyperion. Also, Ed Macedo and Paul Kinney from ESPN research for their usual top-notch work, SportsNation gurus Royce Webb, Marc Appleman, Daniel Dodd, Mary Buckheit and Graham Hays, Barbara Zidovsky from Nielsen Media Research and Yvette Reyes from AP/Wide World Photos.

We'd be nowhere without the timely technical help from Adam Polgreen, Sean Dessureau and Mike Leary. That dinner we owe you is coming, we promise.

Thanks once again to Rick Campbell and Gary Johnson at the NCAA, U.S. Trotting's Paul Ramlow, the PBA Tour's Jason Carr, Joan Lawrence from the NTRA and Cadillac Bill Magrath from the *Sports Business Daily*.

Also, our continued appreciation goes out to the innumerable gracious pro and college sports media relations folks from coast to coast that actually answered and/or returned our calls and emails. Thanks also to Jay Lind at Miller Wachman and to expert proofreader Bob "Page-a-Day" Kerler, and a big low five to Nelson de la Rosa, wherever you are.

Lastly, we can't forget our wives, Lisa and Lori, for their understanding about why sports matters so much, even when we're not sure sometimes.

Gerry Brown
Michael Morrison

October 29, 2004

Major League Cities & Teams

As of Oct. 31, 2004, there were 134 major league teams playing or scheduled to play men's baseball, men's basketball, NFL football, hockey and men's soccer in 52 cities in the United States, Canada and Puerto Rico. Listed below are the cities and the teams that play there.

Anaheim
AL	Angels
NHL	Mighty Ducks of Anaheim

Atlanta
NL	Braves
NBA	Hawks
NFL	Falcons
NHL	Thrashers

Baltimore
AL	Orioles
NFL	Ravens

Boston
AL	Red Sox
NBA	Celtics
NFL	N.E. Patriots (Foxboro)
NHL	Bruins
MLS	N.E. Revolution (Foxboro)

Buffalo
NFL	Bills (Orchard Park)
NHL	Sabres

Calgary
NHL	Flames

Charlotte
NBA	Bobcats
NFL	Carolina Panthers

Chicago
AL	White Sox
NL	Cubs
NBA	Bulls
NFL	Bears
NHL	Blackhawks
MLS	Fire

Cincinnati
NL	Reds
NFL	Bengals

Cleveland
AL	Indians
NBA	Cavaliers
NFL	Browns

Columbus
NHL	Blue Jackets
MLS	Crew

Dallas
AL	Texas Rangers (Arlington)
NBA	Mavericks
NFL	Cowboys (Irving)
NHL	Stars
MLS	FC Dallas

Denver
NL	Colorado Rockies
NBA	Nuggets
NFL	Broncos
NHL	Colorado Avalanche
MLS	Colorado Rapids

Detroit
AL	Tigers
NBA	Pistons (Auburn Hills)
NFL	Lions
NHL	Red Wings

East Rutherford
NBA	New Jersey Nets
NFL	New York Giants
NFL	New York Jets
NHL	New Jersey Devils
MLS	MetroStars

Edmonton
NHL	Oilers

Green Bay
NFL	Packers

Houston
NL	Astros
NBA	Rockets
NFL	Texans

Indianapolis
NBA	Indiana Pacers
NFL	Colts

Jacksonville
NFL	Jaguars

Kansas City
AL	Royals
NFL	Chiefs
MLS	Wizards

Los Angeles
NL	Dodgers
NBA	Clippers
NBA	Lakers
NHL	Kings
MLS	Galaxy (Carson)
MLS	Club Chivas USA (Carson)

Memphis
NBA	Grizzlies

Miami
NL	Florida Marlins
NBA	Heat
NFL	Dolphins
NHL	Florida Panthers (Sunrise)

Milwaukee
NL	Brewers
NBA	Bucks

Minneapolis
AL	Minnesota Twins
NBA	Minnesota Timberwolves
NFL	Minnesota Vikings

Montreal
NHL	Canadiens

Nashville
NFL	Tennessee Titans
NHL	Predators

New Orleans
NBA	Hornets
NFL	Saints

New York
AL	Yankees
NL	Mets (Flushing)
NBA	Knicks
NHL	Rangers
NHL	Islanders (Uniondale)

Oakland
AL	Athletics
NBA	Golden St. Warriors
NFL	Raiders

Orlando
NBA	Magic

Ottawa
NHL	Senators (Kanata)

Philadelphia
NL	Phillies
NBA	76ers
NFL	Eagles
NHL	Flyers

Phoenix
NL	Arizona Diamondbacks
NBA	Suns
NFL	Arizona Cardinals (Tempe)
NHL	Coyotes

Pittsburgh
NL	Pirates
NFL	Steelers
NHL	Penguins

Portland
NBA	Trail Blazers

Raleigh
NHL	Carolina Hurricanes

Sacramento
NBA	Kings

St. Louis
NL	Cardinals
NFL	Rams
NHL	Blues

St. Paul
NHL	Minnesota Wild

Salt Lake City
NBA	Utah Jazz
MLS	Real Salt Lake

San Antonio
NBA	Spurs

San Diego
NL	Padres
NFL	Chargers

San Francisco
NL	Giants
NFL	49ers

San Jose
NHL	Sharks
MLS	Earthquakes

Seattle
AL	Mariners
NBA	SuperSonics
NFL	Seahawks

Tampa
AL	T.B. Devil Rays (St. Petersburg)
NFL	T.B. Buccaneers
NHL	T.B. Lightning

Toronto
AL	Blue Jays
NBA	Raptors
NHL	Maple Leafs

Vancouver
NHL	Canucks

Washington
NL	Expos
NBA	Wizards
NFL	Redskins (Raljon, Md.)
NHL	Capitals
MLS	D.C. United

Updates

Ghostzapper and jockey **Javier Castellano** won the $4 million Breeders' Cup Classic.

AP/Wide World Photos

AUTO RACING

Late 2004 Results
NASCAR
Chase for the Nextel Cup

Date	Event	Location	Winner (Pos)	Avg.mph	Earnings	Pole	Qual.mph
Oct. 16	UAW-GM 500	Charlotte	Jimmie Johnson (9)	130.214	$191,450	R. Newman	188.877
Oct. 24	Subway 500	Martinsville	Jimmie Johnson (18)	66.103	157,440	R. Newman	97.043
Oct. 31	Bass Pro Shops MBNA 500 Atlanta		Jimmie Johnson (8)	145.847	298,250	R. Newman	191.575

Winning Cars: CHEVROLET (3)—Johnson 3.
Remaining Races (3): Checker Auto Parts 500 in Phoenix (Nov. 7); Mountain Dew Southern 500 in Darlington (Nov. 14); Ford 400 in Homestead-Miami (Nov. 21).

Champ Car World Series

Date	Event	Location	Winner	Time	Avg.mph	Pole	Qual.mph
Oct. 26	Lexmark Indy 300 . . .	Queensland	Bruno Junqueira	1:46:45.941	89.532	P. Tracy	107.551

Winning Cars: FORD/LOLA (1)—Junqueira.
Remaining Race: season complete.

Formula One

Date	Event	Location	Winner	Time	Avg.mph	Pole
Oct. 24	Brazilian Grand Prix . . .	Sao Paolo	Juan Montoya	1:28:01.451	129.570	R. Barrichello

Winning Cars: WILLIAMS-BMW (1)—Montoya.
Remaining Race: season complete.

Indy Racing League

Date	Event	Location	Winner	Time	Avg.mph	Pole	Qual.mph
Oct. 17	Chevy 500	Ft. Worth	H. Castroneves	1:49:32.2547	159.397	H. Castroneves	215.996

Winning Cars: DALLARA-TOYOTA (1)—Castroneves.
Remaining Race: season complete.

NHRA

Date	Event	Winner	Time	MPH	2nd Place	Time	MPH
Oct. 31 Las Vegas Nationals . . .	Top Fuel	Doug Kalitta	4.530	329.02	Morgan Lucas	4.612	306.40
	Funny Car	Gary Scelzi	4.790	326.32	John Force	4.754	322.81
	Pro Stock	Greg Anderson	6.796	202.52	Jason Line	6.822	201.85

Remaining Event (1): Automobile Club of Southern California NHRA Finals in Pomona, Cal. (Nov. 11-14).

GOLF

Late 2004 Tournament Results
PGA Tour

Last Rd Tournament	Winner	Earnings	Runner-Up
Oct. 10 Michelin Championship at Las Vegas . . .	Andre Stolz (266)	$720,000	3-way tie (267)
Oct. 17 Chrysler Classic of Greensboro	Brent Geiberger (270)	828,000	3-way tie (267)
Oct. 24 Funai Classic at Walt Disney World . . .	Ryan Palmer (266)	756,000	B. Baird & V. Singh (269)
Oct. 31 Chrysler Championship	Vijay Singh (266)	900,000	J. Parnevik & T. Armour III (271)

Second place ties (three players or more): **Michelin** (H. Frazar, T. Ridings and T. Lehman).
Remaining Events (8): The Tour Championship (Nov. 4-7); Franklin Templeton Shootout (Nov. 11-14); World Golf Championships: World Cup (Nov. 18-21); Merrill Lynch Skins Game (Nov. 27-28); Korea Golf Championships (Nov. 22-28); Target World Challenge (Dec. 9-12); Wendy's Three-Tour Challenge (Dec. 19); Tommy Bahama Challenge (Jan. 1).
Note: The Tour Championship (Nov. 4-7) is the final official PGA Tour event of 2004.

European PGA Tour

Last Rd Tournament	Winner	Earnings	Runner-Up
Oct. 10 Dunhill Links Championship	Stephen Gallacher (269)*	£ 645,162	G. McDowell (269)
Oct. 17 World Match Play Championship	Ernie Els (2&1)	£1,000,000	L. Westwood
Oct. 17 Mallorca Classic	Sergio Garcia (268)	166,660	S. Khan (272)
Oct. 24 Open de Madrid	Richard Sterne (266)	166,660	A. Hansen (268)
Oct. 31 Volvo Masters Andalucia	Ian Poulter (277)*	625,000	S. Garcia (277)

*Playoffs: Dunhill—Gallacher won on the first playoff hole; **Andalucia**—Poulter won on the first playoff hole.
Remaining Event: World Golf Championships: World Cup (Nov. 18-21).

Champions Tour

Last Rd Tournament	Winner	Earnings	Runner-Up
Oct. 10 Administaff Classic	Larry Nelson (202)*	$240,000	H. Irwin (202)
Oct. 17 SBC Championship	Mark McNulty (195)	225,000	G. McCord (203)
Oct. 24 Charles Schwab Cup Championship . . .	Mark McNulty (277)	440,000	T. Kite (278)

*Playoffs: Administaff—Nelson won on the first playoff hole.
Remaining Events (3): UBS Cup (Nov. 20-22); Office Depot Father-Son Challenge (Dec. 3-5); Wendy's Three-Tour Challenge (Dec. 19).

LPGA Tour

Last Rd	Tournament	Winner	Earnings	Runner-Up
Oct. 10	Asahi Ryokuken Int'l Championship	Liselotte Neumann (273)	$150,000	G. Park (276)
Oct. 17	Samsung World Championship	Annika Sorenstam (270)	206,250	G. Park (273)
Oct. 31	CJ Nine Bridges Classic	Grace Park (200)	202,500	A. Sorenstam & C. Koch (205)

Remaining Events (4): Mizuno Classic (Nov. 5-7); Mitchell Company Tournament of Champions (Nov. 11-14); ADT Championship (Nov. 18-21); Wendy's Three-Tour Challenge (Dec. 19).

TENNIS

Late 2004 Tournament Results

Men's Tour

Finals	Tournament	Winner	Earnings	Loser	Score
Oct. 3	International Championships (Palermo)	Tomas Berdych	$63,844	F. Volandri	63 63
Oct. 3	Thailand Open (Bangkok)	Roger Federer	76,500	A. Roddick	64 60
Oct. 3	Shanghai Open	Guillermo Canas	52,000	L. Burgsmuller	61 60
Oct. 10	Japan Open (Tokyo)	Jiri Novak	118,000	T. Dent	57 61 63
Oct. 10	Grand Prix of Tennis (Lyon)	Robin Soderling	138,676	X. Malisse	62 36 64
Oct. 17	Kremlin Cup (Moscow)	Nikolay Davydenko	142,000	G. Rusedski	36 63 75
Oct. 17	Open De Moselle (Metz)	Jerome Haehnel	64,200	R. Gasquet	76 64
Oct. 17	BA-CA Tennis Trophy (Vienna)	Feliciano Lopez	157,950	G. Canas	64 16 75 36 75
Oct. 24	TMS—Madrid	Marat Safin	565,384	D. Nalbandian	62 64 63
Oct. 31	St. Petersburg Open	Mikhail Youzhny	142,000	K. Beck	62 62
Oct. 31	Stockholm Open	Thomas Johansson	115,329	A. Agassi	36 63 76
Oct. 31	Swiss Indoors (Basel)	Jiri Novak	187,545	D. Nalbandian	57 63 64 16 62

Remaining Events (3): Paris Masters (Nov. 7); Tennis Masters Cup Houston (Nov. 14); Davis Cup Final-Australia (Dec. 5).

Women's Tour

Finals	Tournament	Winner	Earnings	Loser	Score
Oct. 3	Gaz De France Stars (Hasselt, Belgium)	Elena Dementieva	$27,000	E. Bovina	06 60 64
Oct. 3	Guangzhou International	Na Li	27,000	M. Sucha	63 64
Oct. 10	Japan Open (Tokyo)	Maria Sharapova	27,000	M. Washington	60 61
Oct. 10	Porsche Tennis Grand Prix (Filderstadt)	Lindsay Davenport	98,500	A. Mauresmo	62 retired
Oct. 17	Tashkent Open (Uzbekistan)	Nicole Vaidisova	22,000	V. Razzano	57 63 62
Oct. 24	Swisscom Challenge (Zurich)	Alicia Molik	189,000	M. Sharapova	26 62 63
Oct. 31	Generali Open (Linz)	Amelie Mauresmo	93,000	E. Bovina	62 60
Oct. 31	Seat Open (Luxembourg)	Alicia Molik	35,000	D. Safina	63 64

Remaining Events (5): Advanta Championships (Nov. 7); Bell Challenge (Nov. 7); Volvo Open (Nov. 14); WTA Tour Championships (Nov. 15); Fed Cup Final (Nov. 28).

THOROUGHBRED RACING

Late 2004 Major Stakes Races

Date	Race	Location	Miles	Winner	Jockey	Purse
Oct. 2	Vosburgh Stakes	Belmont	6 F	Pico Central (BRZ)	Victor Espinoza	$490,000
Oct. 2	Flower Bowl Invitational	Belmont	1¼ (T)	Riskaverse	Carnelio Velasquez	750,000
Oct. 2	Turf Classic Invitational	Belmont	1½ (T)	Kitten's Joy	John Velazquez	750,000
Oct. 2	Jockey Club Gold Cup	Belmont	1¼	Funny Cide	Jose Santos	1,000,000
Oct. 2	Yellow Ribbon Stakes	Santa Anita	1¼ (T)	Light Jig (GB)	Rene Douglas	500,000
Oct. 2	Goodwood B.C. Handicap	Santa Anita	1⅛	Lundy's Liability	David Romero Flores	480,000
Oct. 2	Oak Leaf Stakes	Santa Anita	1¹⁄₁₆	Sweet Catomine	Corey Nakatani	200,000
Oct. 3	Lady's Secret BC Handicap	Santa Anita	1¹⁄₁₆	Island Fashion	Kerwin John	300,000
Oct. 3	Clement L. Hirsch Turf Championship Stakes	Santa Anita	1¼ (T)	Star Over the Bay	Tyler Baze	250,000
Oct. 3	Prix de l'Arc de Triomphe*	Longchamp	1½ (T)	Bago	T. Gillet	E1,600,000
Oct. 5	Norfolk Stakes	Santa Anita	1¹⁄₁₆	Roman Ruler	Corey Nakatani	196,000
Oct. 5	Beldame Stakes	Belmont	1⅛	Sightseek	Javier Castellano	735,000
Oct. 5	Kelso Handicap	Belmont	1 (T)	Mr O'Brien (IRE)	Eibar Coa	270,000
Oct. 8	Phoenix B.C. Stakes	Keeneland	6 F	Champali	Rafael Bejarano	271,250
Oct. 8	Darley Alcibiades Stakes	Keeneland	1¹⁄₁₆	Runway Model	Rafael Bejarano	400,000
Oct. 9	Frizette Stakes	Belmont	1¹⁄₁₆	Balletto (UAE)	Corey Nakatani	500,000
Oct. 9	Champagne Stakes	Belmont	1¹⁄₁₆	Proud Accolade	John Velazquez	500,000
Oct. 9	Oak Tree B.C. Mile	Santa Anita	1 (T)	Musical Chimes	Kent Desormeaux	246,000
Oct. 9	Lane's End Futurity Stakes	Keeneland	1¹⁄₁₆	Consolidator	Rafael Bejarno	500,000
Oct. 9	Shadwell Turf Mile	Keeneland	1 (T)	Nothing to Lose	Robby Albarado	600,000
Oct. 10	Ancient Title B.C. Handicap	Santa Anita	6 F	Pt's Grey Eagle	Alex Bisono	213,000
Oct. 10	WinStar Galaxy Stakes	Keeneland	1³⁄₁₆	Stay Forever	Eddie Castro	500,000
Oct. 10	Spinster Stakes	Keeneland	1⅛	Azeri	Pat Day	500,000

Thoroughbred Racing (Cont.)

Date	Race	Location	Miles	Winner	Jockey	Purse
Oct. 12	TC of America Stakes	Keeneland	6 F	Molto Vita	Rafael Bejarano	$125,000
Oct. 15	Raven Run Stakes	Keeneland	7 F	Josh's Madelyn	Justin Shepherd	224,200
Oct. 16	QE II Challenge Cup	Keeneland	1⅛ (T)	Ticker Tape (GB)	Kent Desormeaux	500,000
Oct. 17	Oak Tree Derby	Santa Anita	1⅛	Greek Sun	Edgar Prado	150,000
Oct. 19	Canadian International* . . .	Woodbine	1½ (T)	Sulamani (IRE)	Lanfranco Dettori	1,500,000
Oct. 23	Empire Classic Handicap . . .	Belmont	1⅛	Spite the Devil	Javier Castellano	250,000
Oct. 23	My Dear Girl Stakes	Calder	1¹⁄₁₆	Aclassysassylassy	Manuel Aguilar	400,000
Oct. 23	Calder Oaks.	Calder	1⅛ T	Hoplessly Devoted	Cornelio Velasquez	200,000
Oct. 23	In Reality Stakes	Calder	1¹⁄₁₆	B.B. Best	Eddie Castro	400,000
Oct. 24	E.P. Taylor Stakes	Woodbine	1¼ (T)	Commercante (FR)	John Velazquez	750,000
Oct. 24	Nearctic Handicap	Woodbine	6 F	I Thee Wed	James McAleney	282,750
Oct. 30	Breeders' Cup - Distaff.	Lone Star Park	1⅛	Ashado	John Velazquez	1,834,000
Oct. 30	Breeders' Cup - Juv. Fillies . .	Lone Star Park	1¹⁄₁₆	Sweet Catomine	Corey Nakatani	1,000,000
Oct. 30	Breeders' Cup - Mile	Lone Star Park	1 (T)	Singletary	David Flores	1,540,560
Oct. 30	Breeders' Cup - Sprint	Lone Star Park	6 F	Speightstown	John Velazquez	1,060,000
Oct. 30	Breeders' Cup - F&M Turf. . .	Lone Star Park	1¼ (T)	Ouija Board (GB)	Kieren Fallon	1,000,000
Oct. 30	Breeders' Cup - Juvenile. . . .	Lone Star Park	1⅛	Wilko	Frankie Dettori	1,375,500
Oct. 30	Breeders' Cup - Turf*	Lone Star Park	1½ (T)	Better Talk Now	Ramon Dominguez	2,000,000
Oct. 30	Breeders' Cup - Classic*	Lone Star Park	1¼ .	Ghostzapper	Javier Castellano	4,000,000

*World Series Racing Championship race.

HARNESS RACING

Late 2004 Major Stakes Races

Date	Race	Raceway	Winner	Driver	Purse
Oct. 9	**Kentucky Futurity**	Lexington	Windsong's Legacy	Trond Smedshammer	$393,300

Note: *Wingsong's Legacy* became the first Trotting Triple Crown winner since Super Bowl in 1972, following up wins in the Hambletonian and Yonkers Trot with a win in the Kentucky Futurity.

BOWLING

Late 2004 Results

PBA

Final	Event	Winner	Earnings	Final	Runner-Up
Sept. 20	Japan Cup.	Tommy Jones	$ 50,000	195-169	Minoru Sendan
Oct. 31	PBA Miller High Life Masters	Danny Wiseman	100,000	268-183	Patrick Allen

Remaining 2004 Events: see the 2004-05 PBA Tour schedule on page 767.

SOCCER

Major League Soccer Playoffs

Eastern Conference
Semifinals (Total Goals)

New England Revolution vs. Columbus Crew
Oct. 23　Columbus 0 . . . . .at New England 1
Oct. 31　New England 1 . . . . .at Columbus 1
　　　　Revolution advances on aggregate, 2-1

D.C. United vs. MetroStars
Oct. 23　D.C. United 2 . . . . .at MetroStars 0
Oct. 30　MetroStars 0 . . . . .at D.C. United 2
　　　　D.C. United advances on aggregate, 4-0

Finals (Single Elimination)
New England vs. D.C. United

Western Conference
Semifinals (Total Goals)

Kansas City Wizards vs. San Jose Earthquakes
Oct. 24　Kansas City 0 . . . . .at San Jose 2
Oct. 30　San Jose 0 . . . . .at Kansas City 3
　　　　Kansas City advances on aggregate, 3-2

Los Angeles Galaxy vs. Colorado Rapids
Oct. 22　Los Angeles 0 . . . . .at Colorado 1
Oct. 30　Colorado 0 . . . . .at Los Angeles 2
　　　　Los Angeles advances on aggregate, 2-1

Finals (Single Elimination)
Kansas City vs. Los Angeles

MLS Cup 2004
Nov. 14 at The Home Depot Center
Carson, Calif.

Personalities

LeBron James proved he was worth all the hype as the Cavs more than doubled their win total.

AP/Wide World Photos

Top 20 Sports Personalities of 2004

Dan and Linda salute their top newsmakers of the year.

*by **Dan Patrick** and **Linda Cohn***

Michael Phelps

It wasn't necessarily the medals Phelps won that put him on this list, but rather the medal that he gave to his teammate. When he ceded his spot to Ian Crocker for the finals of the medley relay, Phelps showed what a true champion is.

He had faith in his teammates, and he wanted to give Crocker an opportunity to make up for his sub-par performance in the 4x100 freestyle relay. Behind Crocker, the U.S. cruised to victory. Phelps was awarded a gold as well for swimming in the prelims, and it's perhaps the most meaningful of his six.

Pat Tillman

The last thing he'd want is any recognition for what he did. We all know the story by now. Tillman spurned millions from the NFL because he felt it was his duty as an American to defend his country. It was his calling. In doing so, he lost his life, but he also may have put a national face on the war.

As great as his sacrifice was, Tillman was always quick to point out that there are hundreds of thousands of other young men and women who have made the same sacrifice, though sometimes they may be overlooked because they weren't celebrities. Tillman never saw himself as different than any of them.

Ichiro Suzuki

In 2004 Ichiro smacked 262 hits to break George Sisler's record that had

Dan Patrick *is a co-anchor on ESPN's SportsCenter and hosts The Dan Patrick Show from 1-4 p.m. EST, M-F, on ESPN Radio.*

AP/Wide World Photos

Michael Phelps *celebrates one of his eight medals (six gold and two bronze) at the 2004 Summer Olympics in Athens.*

stood since 1920. There seemed to be a sort of negative backlash because he's primarily a singles hitter, but in my opinion, what he did is amazing.

Home runs might grab the ratings and hefty contracts, and chicks might dig the long ball, but getting on base is the name of the game. Tony Gwynn sure made a nice career out of it. *Baseball Tonight* analyst John Kruk may have said it best when he argued that Ichiro could win the Home Run Derby, if he wanted to.

Maria Sharapova

Okay so this one's admittedly a little unfair. Sure, Sharapova was terrific in 2004, winning two tournaments through September, including an impressive straight-set victory over Serena Williams in the Wimbledon finals.

But Russians Anastasia Myskina and Svetlana Kuznetsova also won grand slam events this year too. So why should Sharapova get the headline? Her model looks and growing popularity don't hurt. We can't help

AP/Wide World Photos

Ricky Williams dealt a stiff-arm to his own team in 2004, retiring from the NFL with less than a week to go before Dolphins training camp.

but draw similarities between Sharapova and another statuesque blonde Russian who's been known to grace magazine covers. But unlike Anna Kournikova, this one can actually win tournaments.

LeBron James

It would be so easy for people to look at LeBron as a model for what might be wrong with the NBA these days. But they'd be wrong. On the surface, some might just see the multi-million dollar marketing deals and the highlight reel dunks, but after just one year it's blatantly apparent what made this kid so attractive coming out of high school. Like Michael, Larry and Magic before him, he just understands the game. He has an innate ability to find the open man. And it's refreshing to see, especially from someone who didn't go to college.

Kobe Bryant

In the middle of jury selection in the most anticipated case since the O.J trial, the prosecution abruptly dropped all criminal charges against Kobe, evidently because the accuser had had enough. So we may really never know what happened in that Colorado hotel room, but what we do know is, Kobe is a free man.

Or is he? While he gained his freedom, he lost so much during this saga. You can put a price on the lost endorsements. But the blow to his reputation is incalculable.

Ricky Williams

Let's call this entry "The Passion of the Ricky." Claiming he lost his passion for football, the talented but enigmatic running back retired in late July, leaving the Dolphins scrambling for a replacement that as I write this, they still haven't found.

Reasons were numerous. He couldn't take the weekly pounding. He wanted to travel the world. He failed a drug test. Whatever, by September he was exploring ways to get back into the league. Maybe this story is worthy of a Mel Gibson movie too.

The Detroit Pistons

Without one player that would be considered a superstar, the Pistons completely dismantled a heavily favored Lakers team laced with surefire, first-ballot hall of famers. With stifling defense and unmatched hustle, the Pistons taught the Lakers what it's like to play as a team, rather than a collection of individuals.

Sure Chauncey Billups took home the Finals MVP award, but is there anyone in that starting lineup that wasn't deserving?

Tom Brady

The difference between Tom Brady and the other top NFL quarterbacks is the difference between fantasy and reality. In this day and age, football fans seem to define greatness based on what a player can do for their fantasy football team. Well Brady will never be the first quarterback taken in your draft. But he has certainly won his share of big games, and in the end, that's what it's really all about.

Michael Schumacher

Like soccer, Formula One racing may never be as big a deal in the United States as it is in the rest of the world. But that doesn't diminish what Schumacher accomplished in 2004. The F-1 circuit boasts the best drivers in the world. In fact, historically many of the other series' top open-wheel racers have defected to F-1 to challenge themselves against the best. Now consider this. There were 17 Formula One races through mid-October. Schumacher won a record 13 of them. You don't have to be a racing fan to know that's good.

Curt Schilling

Forget, for a minute, about the 21 wins he had in the regular season. The regular season isn't why the Red Sox courted him so hard in the offseason. They wanted him, needed him, for the playoffs, and specifically, for the ALCS against the Yankees.

When a dislocated ankle tendon rendered him ineffective in Game 1 and doubtful for the rest of the series, Schilling turned into Superman. Stitched up, with blood seeping through his sock, he fought through the agony and gave the Red Sox what they desperately needed – a Game 6 ALCS win, and then another in the World Series.

Dale Earnhardt Jr.

The 2004 NASCAR season began exactly the way it was supposed to. An Earnhardt won the sport's biggest race. Dale Jr. was flooded with emotion after his victory at the Daytona 500, where his father was killed three years ago. "He was over in the passenger side with me," he said. Five months later, he would call upon his father again. After escaping a fiery crash at an American

Linda Cohn is a co-anchor on ESPN's SportsCenter

Le Mans Series race with minor burns, Earnhardt Jr. told *60 Minutes'* Mike Wallace that his father helped him climb out of the burning car.

Diana Taurasi

As the clock wound down in New Orleans, Taurasi drop-kicked the ball into the stands, and with that, her illustrious college career was over. She had won her third straight Division I national title with Connecticut and earned her second Most Outstanding Player Award. She was the leader of a team that went 22-1 in Tournament games and 139-8 overall, one of the most impressive runs in women's college history.

Paul Hamm

On August 18, after nearly tumbling into the judges' table on a vault attempt, Hamm recovered beautifully to win the gold in men's gymnastics all-around competition. Or so he thought. On October 21, a full two months later, his medal finally became official, decided on not by a panel of judges, but by the Court of Arbitration for Sport. When the court denied South Korea's Yang-Tae Young's final appeal, the messy saga mercifully came to a conclusion.

AP/Wide World Photos

*Gymnast **Paul Hamm** grimaces during his rings routine at the Summer Olympics in Athens. That expression stayed with him until October, when a court finally made his all-around gold official.*

USA Softball

The U.S. women would not be denied at the Summer Olympics in Athens, playing inspired ball after the death of head coach Mike Candrea's wife Sue to a brain aneurysm just weeks before the start of the tournament.

With one goal in mind, this team was flawless and merciless. They went 9-0 en route to the gold medal and outscored the best the world had to offer, 51-1. Look at that score again. Who said the U.S. didn't have a dream team?

Phil Mickelson

With the boisterous Augusta National crowd pulling for him, Mickelson strolled up to the 72nd hole at the Masters, and calmly sank a 20-foot birdie putt to eke out a dramatic one-stroke victory over South African Ernie Els.

Possibly the only sound that could be made out over the roar of the crowd was the huge sigh of relief from Mickelson. Best golfer to never win a major? Give that title to some one else. After 47 tries, Mickelson finally got his.

AP/Wide World Photos

*Mike Weir, 2003 Masters champ, helps **Phil Mickelson** with his new green jacket after Lefty's dramatic Masters win in April. Mickelson then leaves it on for the entire month.*

Barry Bonds

In 2004, he turned 40 and yet he continues to get better with age. With another 45 home runs added to his resume (including his 700th in September), a National League-leading .362 batting average and an eye-popping 232 walks, Bonds had the San Francisco Giants playing for the division crown right up until the last weekend of the season.

With Major League Baseball's new steroid policy and BALCO investigation hovering, Bonds' name consistently surfaces. His involvement is unclear, however, one thing's for sure – the man never, EVER swings at a pitch outside the strike zone, and on the rare occasion he gets a pitch to hit, he hits it solidly. Is there a steroid that can do *that*?

Lance Armstrong

I'm starting to run out of adjectives to describe him. Astonishing? Breathtaking? Inspiring? Sure, those all work. There aren't many sure things in life but Lance Armstrong winning the Tour de France has become one. How can that be? It's arguably the most grueling athletic event in the world! For that reason, only four men had ever won more than three of them since the Tour began in 1901. And then came Lance. This year, he won his record sixth in a row. And it was probably his most dominant yet. He had to compete while fighting off relentless doping accusations and dodging spit from classless spectators on the side of the road.

Roger Federer

How times have changed. While now it's the women that grab most of the tennis headlines, men's tennis has a budding superstar of its own in Federer. In 2004 he won three Grand Slam events – the Australian Open, Wimbledon and the U.S. Open – a feat that hasn't been accomplished in 16 years.

His nine victories through mid-October helped him snatch the top ranking away from American Andy Roddick. The pair have developed quite a rivalry, though as Roddick says, "I'm going to have to start winning some of them to call it a rivalry."

Vijay Singh

With a quiet demeanor and an intense focus that some might see as moody, he'll likely never get the endorsement dollars that Tiger Woods gets.

AP/Wide World Photos

*Switzerland's **Roger Federer** smiles after winning the U.S. Open, his third major of the year.*

But his legendary tireless work ethic has paid off. In Sept. 2004, after beating Tiger in a mano-a-mano showdown at the Deutsche Bank Classic in Norton, Mass., he officially replaced him as the No. 1-ranked golfer in the world, a position Tiger had held for over five years. Through October he had already broken Tiger's record for single-season earnings on the PGA Tour with over $10 million. And he won nine tournaments, including a three-way playoff at the PGA Championship that was never really in doubt.

Personalities of the Year from SPORTSNATION

Archie Manning runs the NFL draft by making sure Eli is not a Charger.

— **Pamonyok** from Bristol

Emeka Okafor and Diana Taurasi leading the 2004 University of Connecticut men's and women's basketball teams to national championships in the same year.

— **Silverspree8** from Shrub Oak, N.Y.

Lance Armstrong — enough said.

— **der180** from Penn State

1. Paul Hamm 2. Shaquille O'Neal 3. Kobe Bryant 4. David Ortiz.

— **Lamonte** from Columbus, Ohio

Kevin Garnett wins the MVP award and the T-Wolves finally get out of the first round of the playoffs.

— **Steven** from Minneapolis

The Calgary Flames and Jarome Iginla. Hadn't won a series since Cup final in '89. Non-existent payroll. Too bad they couldn't finish it in Game 6.

— **Jeff** from Royal Oak, Mich.

At the 1998 NFL draft all the hype surrounded Ryan Leaf, but I knew then that the better pick was Peyton Manning. Peyton turned out to be the Golden Boy and was surrounded with players such as Marvin and Edgerrin. Unfortunately, I think he's in for a rude awakening when the team can't afford to keep players. Peyton, I love ya but 45 million?

— **Debbie** from Richmond, Ind.

Thank you! Mr. Henry's purchase; Theo's mastery; Terry's decisions; Tek's leadership; Pedro's dominance; Curt's tenacity; Ortiz's heroics; Manny's consistency; Johnny's infallibility; Orlando's grace; Mueller's recovery; Trot's dedication; D-Lowe's timing; Bellhorn's patience; Millar's enthusiasm; Roberts' steal; Wake's unselfishness; Bronson's flexibility; Foulke's toughness; Timlin and Embree's reliability. From the bottom of my heart, thank you!

— **H** from Boston

Check out SPORTSNATION at ESPN.com

Moments

Red Sox slugger **David Ortiz** delivered plenty of memorable moments in October, including this homer in Game 7 of the ALCS.

AP/Wide World Photos

Top 20 Sports Moments of 2004

Stuart Scott and Trey Wingo give us their picks for the biggest moments of the year in sports.

by **Stuart Scott** and **Trey Wingo**

Triple Threat

You always hear, "this is the horse that's gonna win the Triple Crown." Well since 1978, when Affirmed ran the table, many had tried but none had been able to get it done. Nine horses had won the first two, then failed in the final challenge at the Belmont. But it was a horse that was the most popular athlete from the city of Philadelphia, Smarty Jones, that was going to end the drought. He hadn't even really been challenged and won the Preakness like Secretariat won the Belmont, in a rout. But sad, sad, sad day...again...the horse failed. So what? He's *still* the most popular athlete in Philly.

Stuart Scott *is an anchor/reporter on ESPN's SportsCenter.*

Red Sox Nation

The sad thing is, if Red Sox fans were honest, 98 percent would take a win over the Yankees in the ALCS and a World Series LOSS over a win against the Twins in the ALCS and a World Series WIN. The thing is to BEAT THE YANKEES. After three games of the ALCS there was no way possible it was going to happen this year. Babe Ruth couldn't have risen from his grave, donned a Red Sox uniform and done that. No team in baseball, or basketball history for that matter, had ever come back from 3-0. I see, so *that's* what it was all about: making history and beating the hated evil empire. "Sweet" needed a new definition. Oh, and yeah, they also won the World Series. Finally.

AP/Wide World Photos

*San Francisco Giant **Barry Bonds** reached an historic plateau in his climb up the all-time home run rankings in 2004. He could reach the top of the heap next year.*

Roy Jones Jr.

He was, pound-for-pound, the best boxer in the world. In fact, after moving up and winning a piece of the heavyweight title last year, you could forget the "pound-for-pound" business. Roy Jones Jr., the man who was not supposed to lose, the man whose only loss occurred when he was controversially disqualified, shocks the world. He goes down. Twice! Hey, he still looks good in those HBO tuxedos.

700 Club

They didn't need to stop the game for home runs number 660 or 661. No disrespect to Willie Mays or Barry Bonds but the 660 milestone just wasn't as huge as 700. This man, this freak of nature, who's only gone and turned into, perhaps, the greatest baseball player ever, cruised past 700 home runs and (likely) cruised into his seventh MVP award. Did I mention he's over 40 years old? The once unthinkable number of 755 is in serious jeopardy.

AP/Wide World Photos

The **Tampa Bay Lightning** captured the Stanley Cup in seven games against the Calgary Flames in 2004. They could be reigning champs for some time.

Cup Crazy

If the Tampa Bay Lightning win the Stanley Cup finals and no league is around to hear it at the beginning of next season...does it make a sound? They certainly made noise in their seven-game war with the Calgary Flames. Conn Smythe winner Brad Richards, Martin St. Louis and Nikolai Khabibulin were the noisiest, leading the way for the Lightning.

Golden Good-bye

She is the most prolific scorer in the history of international soccer. She's the best athlete in her family, which is saying a lot since she recently married All-Star shortstop Nomar Garciaparra. If it were a Hollywood script, it would have been tossed out because it's too syrupy, too hokey and too beautifully neat. But there she was about to retire. Mia Hamm led Team USA into the Olympics, won gold and walked away from her sport the way she spent most of her time as a player: as a champion.

Team Win

Team. Team. Larry Brown preached it. He convinced his players to live it. And they not only beat the Lakers to win the NBA championship but beat them *badly*. One observer said it was the first five-game sweep in the history of sports. One hand: five individual fingers but one hand. One team: Rip, 'Sheed, Big Ben, a Prince and what's his name? You know. The Finals MVP...Oh yeah...Chauncey Billups. It may be hard to remember their names, but it's easy to see what they did. Win together.

Dale Jr. Does it for Dad

It was the racetrack where his dad won more races than anyone, but couldn't win the big one, the Daytona 500, until late in his career. It was the track where his dad died. In 2004, Dale Earnhardt Jr. completed the family circle. On an emotional February day he won NASCAR's biggest race, the Daytona 500, with his dad in his heart every lap of the oval.

Coed School

Ladies and gentlemen, please come up together and receive your trophies! Little Storrs, Connecticut. There resides the best program in college basketball. With Diana and Emeka, UConn became the first school to win both the men's and women's national titles in the same year. The guy Okafor who's so smart and the girl Taurasi whose jumper looks like a guy's. Now if we could only get their two coaches to be buddies.

Fall of a Hero

I apologized to Pat Tillman's brother for his loss, but thanked him. I said, "because of your brother Pat, I got a chance to teach my nine-year-old daughter about heroes." Pat Tillman gave up the luxury of a rich NFL life. Simply because he felt like he wasn't doing what he should have been. September 11th affected him like that. So, good-bye NFL. Hello Army Rangers. What he did was give his life. No longer are sports stars heroes. They can't be. Because then, they'd be in Tillman's class and nobody is. Pat, thank you, and we'll miss you.

Trey Wingo's Moments of the Year

Ricky Sinks a Franchise

The Miami Dolphins found out the hard way how important one player was to their team. When Ricky Williams left right before camp—leaving the team high and dry—we all saw what happens when the one player you plan your season around isn't there. With all the hurricanes this fall, I'm not sure what was worse about South Beach, the weather or the Dolphins.

Breakup of the Lakers

Let's get one thing straight. L.A. didn't have to trade Shaq. They chose to. And when it's all said and done, they may regret putting the entire team squarely behind #8. Yes, Kobe Bryant is a terrific player. But nobody can do what Shaq can do, because he's the world's largest sports-playing mammal. And considering the bitter way these two parted, look for Shaq to come back strong and dominate the Lakers the two times they play each other this season.

Trey Wingo *is a co-anchor on ESPN's SportsCenter*

Mickelson's Masters Moment

Phil Mickelson's win at Augusta proved two things for sure in 2004: he has what it takes to win a major and white men most definitely can't jump. But the win—as satisfying as it must have been for Phil—still shows you why Lefty can be so maddening. You'd think after his breakthrough he'd keep it going. Instead? A three jack on the 17th green that all but handed the U.S. Open to Retief Goosen and then his sudden change of equipment right before the Ryder Cup, in which he played awful. He can be so good. But he always leaves us wanting more.

BALCO Questions

Nobody escapes from the tentacles of this story clean. Whether it's Marion Jones' disappearing act, Barry's question marks, or Jason Giambi's injury plagued summer. Anyone touched by the one time "supplement pumping lab to the stars" has got to come under major scrutiny. How much did they know and how much did they take? Does every sports record from home runs to 100 meter times now deserve to be under suspicion?

AP/Wide World Photos

*The **European Team** celebrated another win on American sod at the Ryder Cup. Despite dominating the world golf rankings, the American Team was dominated in the tournament.*

Roger, Roger. Over, Under.

Greatness, thy name is Federer. Thundering through three of the four majors in tennis, Switzerland's Roger Federer left little doubt who the king of the courts was in 2004. None other than the great Rod Laver said he believes Federer can win them all in one year. But don't take his word for it. Take it from the players with yellow felt embedded in their foreheads. They're the unlucky victims that had to actually play Roger this year.

Another Ryder Cup Meltdown

I understand that having to play the President's Cup every other year takes some of the passion out of the U.S. squad. But come on! Players like Ian Poulter and Miguel Angel Jimenez come into our country and kick our butts? Please. It's time to take pride in what is arguably the greatest sporting event going: millionaires playing for free. Outside of the play of the U.S. squad in three out of the last four tournaments, the Ryder Cup represents all that is right about sports. Now we need to start holding up our end of the deal.

AP/Wide World Photos

*New England's clutch kicker **Adam Vinatieri** won another big game—the Super Bowl—with a pressure-packed late field goal in 2004.*

The Streak

The Patriots' record for consecutive victories in the NFL is really a testament to how hard it is to do what New England is doing: win on a consistent basis. Outside of quarterback Tom Brady, there aren't a lot of stars on this team. Yet the front office and coaching staff continue to find ways to get players that can help them win. And the Pats ripped off 21 straight before finally losing to the Steelers on the road.

Hamm on Wait

American Paul Hamm had a golden moment taken away. Because of the atrocious scoring at the Olympic gymnastics venue in Athens the men's all-around champion had to wait to find out if he got to keep the gold medal he won. Seriously, the entire meet was a joke and everyone was in on it except Moe, Larry and Curly who were handing out numbers that made no sense. I've never seen anything like the men's high bar final. The crowd went nuts for 20 minutes about how ridiculous the scoring was. It *almost* made me feel like I was at an actual sporting event.

Ichiro Makes History

Obviously Barry Bonds hitting his 700th homer is a huge deal. But what Ichiro Suzuki did in 2004 is, for my money, one of the greatest things we've ever seen. On an absolutely awful Mariners team, Ichiro just kept hitting. The fundamental principle of anyone who steps into the batter's box with a piece of wood is to get a hit. Not to hit a home run, but to get a hit. And in 2004, Ichiro took that to a whole new level, breaking George Sisler's 84-year run as the hit king. Hitters hit. And nobody has done that more often than Ichiro in 2004.

Vinatieri's Kick, the Sequel

Football players, especially kickers, live for the chance to make the one play that wins them a championship. The Patriots' Adam Vinatieri has now done it twice. His second Super Bowl-winning kick in three years not only gave the Pats their second Lombardi trophy under head coach Bill Belichick, it also firmly established Vinatieri as the most consistent pressure kicker the game has ever seen. Don't forget his two field goals in the snow two years ago and a 46-yarder in the 2003 postseason against the Titans when it was about 300 degrees below zero. Kicking in that game was like kicking a rock. Yet he delivered again.

BONUS MOMENT!

Lance in France, Again

Look, it's getting repetitive. But it's not getting old. Unless you're one of the 50 or so elite cyclists in the world who do nothing but stare at Lance Armstrong's butt every summer in France. Six straight Tour titles. And this one may have been his most dominant yet. In the stages he won, Lance seemed to toy with his closest pursuers. The way a predator will let his kill get away for a second before squashing their hopes of survival. Why should it end here? He's clearly the best in the biz by a long shot. At this point, winning the Powerball seems like a surer bet that beating Lance in France. Live strong, indeed.

Moments of the Year from SPORTSNATION

During Game 7 of the ALCS, I was in northern Wisconsin, where it can be very hard to pick up radio signals. I'll never forget moving my radio around my room and hearing a Johnny Damon home run or some other Red Sox scoring play just about every time the static cleared. Hearing Boston stomp my be-hated Yanks made my 2004 great. — **Kirke** from Madison.

The Detroit Pistons literally obliterating the face of Los Angeles. From their team, to their coach, to even their network of fans, all were broken up and crying. Best five game sweep that I consider a big part of NBA history. — **ahickman** from Detroit.

Without a doubt it was when the Boston Red Sox came back to defeat the New York Yankees and they celebrated right on the mound at the Stadium with Boston fans screaming "Who's your daddy." I went to Game 1 but that doesn't even match watching the Sox celebrating on the field...and getting to see A-Rod's face in disappointment! — **Richard** from Cranston, R.I.

Brett Favre's amazing game on Monday night versus the Raiders was outstanding and I'll remember that game for the rest of my life.

— **Chris** from Nashville.

Nebraska signing Bill Callahan. USA wins softball gold. Paul Hamm winning the gold. David Ortiz's walk-off home runs. — **Jake** from Lincoln.

What a year, the BCS goes bust once again and gets it wrong, the Patriots become the next great dynasty, the Lakers create a dream team and lose to a real team, and the U.S. dream team, well, that's all that needs to be said... Tampa has a Stanley Cup...and Boston vs. New York still is the greatest rivalry in all of sports. And Lance is Lance. All of that is great and wild but the best of the best is Lefty. Yes the big goat of golf finally vanquished his demons and ended a horrid life of misery for his fans. Phil Mickelson won the Masters and removed the title of world's greatest golfer never to win a major. — **Patrick** from Pensacola.

Check out SPORTSNATION at ESPN.com

Calendar

Now was that a left at the giant arch or a right?
Lance Armstrong found his way to a sixth
straight Tour de France win in July.

AP/Wide World Photos

November 2003

Sun	Mon	Tue	Wed	Thu	Fri	Sat
						1
2	3	4	5	6	7	8
9	10	11	12	13	14	15
16	17	18	19	20	21	22
23/30	24	25	26	27	28	29

Quote of the Month

"It's a complete and utter joke. You can test positive for steroids five times, then they think of booting you out for a year? Give me a break."

Dick Pound, chairman of the World Anti-Doping Agency, responding to Major League Baseball's new steroid policy, announced on Nov. 13.

SPORTSNATION Polls

Is our national pastime juiced?

What percentage of MLB players do you think use steroids?

46.6% —	0-25 percent of all players
40.6% —	26-50
10.7% —	51-75
2.1% —	76-100

Do you believe that Barry Bonds has used steroids in the past?

83.7% —	Yes
12.7% —	No

Would you use steroids if it meant you could lead the league in HRs and make $15 million per year?

54.4% —	No
45.6% —	Yes

Total Votes: 33,080

1 **Arkansas beats Kentucky, 71-63,** in an NCAA football record-tying seven overtimes. Tied, 24-24, after regulation, the teams combined for 86 overtime points.

2 **Kenyan Margaret Okayo** breaks her own course record by almost two minutes to win the women's division of the New York Marathon in 2:22:31. Fellow countryman Martin Lel wins the men's title in 2:10:30.

3 **Ozzie Guillen is named** the new manager of the Chicago White Sox. It's the first managerial post for Guillen, the former White Sox shortstop.

Five-time Stanley Cup winner Grant Fuhr and 468-goal scorer Pat LaFontaine are among four inducted into the Hockey Hall of Fame.

Patriots' coach Bill Belichick's decision to take an intentional safety with under three minutes remaining sparks his team to a 30-26 come-from-behind win over the Denver Broncos on Monday Night Football.

4 **NY Rangers' Mark Messier** scores two goals in a 3-0 win over Dallas to pass Gordie Howe and move into 2nd place on the NHL all-time points list with 1,851.

7 **America's pastime?** The defending Olympic champion United States baseball team falls to Mexico, 2-1, ousting them from their qualifying tournament and from participating in the upcoming Athens Olympics.

Yankees first base coach Lee Mazzilli is hired as the manager of the Baltimore Orioles.

8 **Roy Jones Jr. struggles** but wins a controversial majority decision over Antonio Tarver to regain the light heavyweight title he had vacated upon moving up to the heavyweight class earlier in the year.

Division III St. John's (Minn.) beats Bethel, 29-26, giving head coach John Gagliardi his 409th career victory, making him the NCAA all-time leader. The 77-year-old passes Grambling legend Eddie Robinson who retired in 1997 with 408 wins.

Top-ranked Oklahoma annihilates Texas A&M, 77-0. It is A&M's most lopsided loss in its 108-year football history. In other major I-A action, Clemson defeats No. 3 Florida St., 26-10, for head coach Tommy Bowden's first victory over his father, Bobby, in five chances.

9 **Matt Kenseth places fourth** at the Pop Secret 400 in Rockingham which is enough for the Wisconsin native to clinch the season-long Winston Cup points championship.

Three-time Top Fuel champ Shirley Muldowney retires, ending her illustrious 30-year racing career. She was the first female to win a major motor sports championship.

Florida Panthers coach Mike Keenan is fired after a 5-8-2-0 start and replaced by GM Rick Dudley.

Chad Campbell cards a final-round 68 to win the PGA Tour Championship with a tournament record (in relation to par) 16-under 268. Tiger Woods wins his fifth straight Vardon Trophy (lowest season-long scoring avg.) while Vijay Singh captures his first PGA season money title.

10 **Kansas City Royals shortstop Angel Berroa** wins the A.L. Rookie of the Year Award over Yankees outfielder and 10-year Japanese leaguer Hideki Matsui in the closest vote (four-point margin) since 1980. Pitcher Dontrelle Willis of the Florida Marlins wins the N.L. award.

11 **Four U.S. track athletes** — middle distance runner Regina Jacobs, shot putter Kevin Toth, hammer thrower John McEwen and an unnamed athlete — test positive for designer steroid THG and face a two-tear ban from competition.

Toronto Blue Jays ace Roy Halladay wins the A.L. Cy Young Award over runner-up Esteban Loaiza of Chicago.

12 **World Series champ** Jack McKeon of the Florida Marlins and Kansas City skipper Tony Pena are voted N.L. and A.L. managers of the year, respectively.

AP/Wide World Photos

*Montreal Canadiens goalie **Jose Theodore**, playing with a ski cap over his mask, exhales during the Heritage Classic on Nov. 22 in Edmonton. The game, in which the Canadiens beat Edmonton, 4-3, was played outdoors in temperatures hovering near zero degrees.*

13 Major League Baseball announces its new plan beginning in 2004 to penalize players who test positive for steroids. The plan is triggered by a 2003 test which produced between 5 and 7 percent positive results. Punishments range from "treatment only" for a first offense to a one-year suspension and/or $100,000 fine for a fifth offense.

Dodgers closer Eric Gagne wins the N.L. Cy Young Award after going 55-for-55 in save opportunities.

16 Jason Tucker catches two TD passes to lead the Edmonton Eskimos to a 34-22 victory over the Montreal Alouettes in the 91st Grey Cup. It is Edmonton's 12th title.

The Cincinnati Bengals make good on WR Chad Johnson's guarantee, handing the Kansas City Chiefs (9-1) their first loss of the season, 24-19.

Roger Federer beats Andre Agassi, 6-3, 6-0, 6-4 in the Tennis Masters Cup final, the last event of the ATP season.

17 Texas shortstop Alex Rodriguez wins his first A.L. MVP award, besting runner-up Carlos Delgado of Toronto.

NBA realignment gets the OK as owners approve a plan to split the league into two conferences, each with three five-team divisions, beginning with the 2004-05 season.

Doc Rivers is fired as coach of the Orlando Magic after a 1-10 start and replaced by assistant Johnny Davis.

18 WR Keyshawn Johnson is deactivated by the Tampa Bay Buccaneers due to his "disruptive attitude." He will sit out the rest of the season, but continue to be paid.

San Francisco Giants Barry Bonds wins his unprecedented sixth N.L. MVP award. He also becomes the first player in history to win three consecutive MVP awards.

High schooler Freddy Adu, 14, is signed by the MLS' DC United to a four-year contract. He becomes the youngest U.S. professional team athlete in over 100 years.

21 The U.S. short track speedskating team pulls out of next week's World Cup event in South Korea after team member Apolo Anton Ohno receives numerous death threats.

22 More than 57,000 spectators brave below-zero temperatures to watch the Montreal Canadiens beat the Edmonton Oilers, 4-3, in the first outdoor game in NHL history.

England defeats defending champ Australia, 20-17, to win its first Rugby World Cup in Sydney.

23 Presidents Cup captains Jack Nicklaus (USA) and Gary Player (International) agree to end the four-day tournament in a tie due to darkness. It is the first draw in the Cup's nine-year existence. Both teams agreed to share the Cup.

The San Jose Earthquakes win MLS Cup 2003 with a 4-2 win over the Chicago Fire. Landon Donovan nets two goals for the Earthquakes and is named game MVP.

24 Nets center Alonzo Mourning abruptly retires upon learning his kidney disease is worsening and he'll need a kidney transplant over the next few months.

Hall of Fame pitcher Warren Spahn dies at his home in Oklahoma at the age of 82.

Bill Cartwright is fired as coach of the 4-10 Chicago Bulls. Scott Skiles is hired as his replacement two days later.

27 The Miami Dolphins rout Dallas, 40-21, while the Detroit Lions shock the Green Bay Packers, 22-14, in NFL Thanksgiving Day action.

28 Curt Schilling is traded from the Diamondbacks to the Red Sox for Casey Fossum and three other players.

30 In a compelling interview with *60 Minutes*, former linebacker Lawrence Taylor candidly speaks about, among other things, the thousands of dollars a day he spent on drugs and women during his playing days.

Nebraska football coach Frank Solich is fired.

December 2003

Sun	Mon	Tue	Wed	Thu	Fri	Sat
	1	2	3	4	5	6
7	8	9	10	11	12	13
14	15	16	17	18	19	20
21	22	23	24	25	26	27
28	29	30	31			

Quote of the Month

"I see a lot of the 'Bubbas' who work in my administration have shown up."

George W. Bush, United States President and racing fan, while honoring the top NASCAR drivers at the White House on Dec. 2.

SPORTSNATION Polls

BCS Mess

Which two teams should play for the College National Football Championship?

61.1% —	USC vs LSU
26.2% —	USC vs Oklahoma
12.6% —	Oklahoma vs LSU

Total Votes: 393,893

What's your opinion of the BCS system?

55.3% —	Needs to be tweaked.
27.1% —	Fouled up beyond all repair.
17.6% —	Working how it's supposed to.

Given the current system, who should be voted No. 1?

69.7% —	LSU
30.3% —	USC

If they were to play on a neutral field, who would win?

66.1% —	LSU
33.9% —	USC

Total Votes: 174,145

---

1 **Green Bay Packers asst. Sylvester Croom** is hired as head football coach at Mississippi State, becoming the first black head coach in the 71-year history of the SEC.

3 **Oft-troubled forward Bonzi Wells** is dealt from the Portland Trail Blazers to the Memphis Grizzlies on the same day Blazers forward Zach Randolph publicly apologizes after being charged with driving under the influence.

4 **The Boston Red Sox name** former Philadelphia Phillies manager Terry Francona as their new manager. Also, the Cincinnati Reds remove the "interim" tag from manager Dave Miley by offering him a one-year contract.

The New York Yankees answer the Red Sox moves by acquiring talented pitcher Javier Vazquez from the Montreal Expos for Nick Johnson and two additional players.

6 **No. 1 Oklahoma is trounced,** 35-7, by No. 13 Kansas State in the Big 12 championship game for their first loss of the year. Elsewhere, No. 2 USC beats Oregon State for the Pac-10 crown, third-ranked LSU whips Georgia to win the SEC and Navy beats Army, 34-6, in their 104th meeting.

7 **Despite a new No. 1 ranking** in the "human" polls, USC is denied a spot in the BCS Championship Game, the Nokia Sugar Bowl, on Jan. 4. The Trojans will play No. 4 Michigan in the Rose Bowl while No. 2 LSU will battle No. 3 Oklahoma in the Sugar Bowl.

Redskins DE Bruce Smith wraps up Giants QB Jesse Palmer for a seven-yard loss to pass Reggie White and become the NFL's all-time sack leader with 199.

Denver RB Clinton Portis scampers for 218 yards and scores five rushing touchdowns in the Broncos' 45-27 win over Kansas City.

Big men Tim Duncan and David Robinson are named *Sports Illustrated's* Sportsmen of the Year for leading the San Antonio Spurs to the 2003 NBA title.

8 **What slump?** Tiger Woods is voted by his peers as PGA Tour Player of the Year for the fifth straight year.

The Orlando Magic beat the Phoenix Suns, 105-98, to avoid becoming the sixth team in NBA history to lose 20 consecutive games. It was the longest streak since Denver's 23-game losing streak in 1997-98.

Brett Hull scores the 732nd goal of his career in the Red Wings' 3-2 OT win over the Kings to pass Marcel Dionne and move into third place on the NHL all-time goals list.

9 **Legendary coach Norm Sloan,** who coached at Florida and guided N.C. State to the 1974 NCAA basketball title, dies at the age of 77.

10 **The New York Mets sign** Japanese star shortstop Kaz Matsui to a three-year deal worth $20.1 million.

On a tough day for professional coaches, Dan Reeves is let go by the Atlanta Falcons with three games left and replaced by Wade Phillips, Bruce Cassidy is fired as coach of the 8-18-1-1 Washington Capitals and replaced by assistant Glen Hanlon and in the NBA, the Phoenix Suns (8-13) fire Frank Johnson and replace him with Mike D'Antoni.

12 **The Yankees deal** pitcher Jeff Weaver to the Dodgers for Kevin Brown in an attempt to reduce the impact of lefty Andy Pettitte's departure to the Houston Astros a day earlier.

13 **Oklahoma QB Jason White wins** the 2003 Heisman Trophy, beating runner-up Larry Fitzgerald of Pittsburgh. Mississippi's Eli Manning and Michigan's Chris Perry finish third and fourth, respectively.

In front of a world-record crowd at Detroit's Ford Field, No. 8 Kentucky defeats No. 21 Michigan State, 79-74. The crowd of 78,129 breaks the previous basketball record (75,000) set in 1951 by the Harlem Globetrotters.

The Quiet Man John Ruiz clutches and grabs his way to a decision over Hasim Rahman in their heavyweight bout, while Cory Spinks (son of Leon) upsets Ricardo Mayorga in a majority decision for the undisputed welterweight title.

*New Orleans Saints wide receiver **Joe Horn** pretends to make a call after pulling a cell phone out of the goalpost padding in celebration of a touchdown against the Giants on Dec. 14. He was penalized for unsportsmanlike conduct and later fined $30,000.*

14 Joe Horn scores four touchdowns in the Saints' 45-7 victory over the NY Giants, but it's his celebration after the second one that attracts the most attention. Horn grabs a hidden cell phone out of the padding on the goalpost and pretends to make a call as he walks back to the bench. Two days later he is fined $30,000 for the stunt, making it the most expensive call of his life.

The Baltimore Orioles sign premier shortstop and 2002 AL MVP Miguel Tejada to a six-year, $72 million deal.

15 The Carolina Hurricanes fire longtime coach Paul Maurice and replace him with Peter Laviolette. Maurice had been coach of the Hurricanes/Whalers since 1995.

French soccer player Zinedine Zidane wins his third FIFA Player of the Year award, beating runner-up Thierry Henry and Real Madrid teammate Ronaldo. Germany's Birgit Prinz wins the women's award over Mia Hamm.

17 A proposed deal that would send Alex Rodriguez from the Rangers to the Red Sox is nixed when the players' union rejects Boston's attempts to restructure Rodriguez's contract.

Hall of Fame QB Otto Graham, who led the Browns to four AAFC titles and three NFL championships, dies at the age of 82.

The 4-10 NY Giants fire head coach Jim Fassel, effective at the end of the season.

19 Harry Caray's Restaurant group purchases "the Bartman ball" for $106,000 with the intentions of blowing it up in a ceremony in late February.

Delaware pounds Colgate, 40-0, to capture its first Division I-AA national championship.

20 Coach John Gagliardi's St. John's (Minn.) snaps Mt. Union's 55-game winning streak with a 24-6 win in the NCAA Division III championship game.

21 In a play reminiscent of Cal-Stanford, the New Orleans Saints use an Aaron Brooks pass to Donte' Stallworth and multiple laterals to score with no time left on the clock and come within one point (20-19) of the Jacksonville Jaguars. Usually sure-footed veteran John Carney then misses the extra point to give the Jags the win.

22 Just one day after his father died, an emotional Brett Favre throws for 399 yards and four TDs to lead the Packers to a 41-7 win over the Raiders on Monday Night Football.

Isiah Thomas is hired as president of basketball operations of the New York Knicks, replacing Scott Layden.

23 Only in New York. Between periods of the Islanders-Flyers game on Long Island, a seemingly harmless Christmas promotion went wrong when one of the 1,000 fans permitted to stroll across the ice in Santa suits removed his red jacket to reveal a NY Rangers shirt. A six-minute melee ensued.

25 LeBron James and Tracy McGrady put on a Christmas day show in the Magic's 113-101 win over the Cavaliers. James nets 34 points while McGrady in 41.

28 Cyclist Lance Armstrong is named AP male athlete of the year for the second consecutive year. Golfer Annika Sorenstam wins the women's award the following day.

Jamal Lewis rushes for 114 yards against Pittsburgh, giving him 2,066 for the season. He falls 39 yards short of Eric Dickerson's single-season mark but becomes the fifth member of the 2,000-yard club.

Josh McCown's 28-yard pass to Nathan Poole with no time left gives the Cardinals an 18-17 win over the Vikings and sends the Packers to the playoffs.

29 The day after the end of the NFL regular season brings multiple firings as Buffalo's Gregg Williams, Arizona's Dave McGinnis and Chicago's Dick Jauron are sent packing.

January 2004

Sun	Mon	Tue	Wed	Thu	Fri	Sat
				1	2	3
4	5	6	7	8	9	10
11	12	13	14	15	16	17
18	19	20	21	22	23	24
25	26	27	28	29	30	31

Quote of the Month

"We want the ball and we're going to score."

Matt Hasselbeck, quarterback of the Seattle Seahawks, after winning the coin toss at the beginning of overtime of the Packers-Seahawks playoff game on Jan. 5. On that opening drive, Hasselbeck threw an interception which Packers cornerback Al Harris returned for the game-winning touchdown.

SPORTSNATION Polls

Rose in the Hall?

Should Pete Rose be allowed into the Baseball Hall of Fame?

45.2%	—	No, he bet on baseball and his own team
40.8%	—	Yes, as soon as possible
13.1%	—	Yes, after his death
0.9%	—	No, he didn't earn it on the field

Total Votes: 42,867

Michelle on the men's tour?

Do you think Michelle Wie will play on the PGA Tour someday?

46.9%	—	Yes
34.9%	—	Only part-time
18.1%	—	No

Total Votes: 14,907

1 **USC does its job,** whipping Michigan, 28-14, in the Rose Bowl. Quarterback Matt Leinart powers the Trojans with 327 yards passing. Elsewhere, Miami-FL edges Florida, 16-14, in the Orange Bowl after Florida St. misses yet another field goal in the closing minutes.

2 **Indianapolis QB Peyton Manning** and Tennessee QB Steve McNair are named co-winners of the Associated Press NFL MVP award.

Ohio State's Craig Krenzel tosses four touchdown passes to lead the Buckeyes to a 35-28 win over Kansas State in the Fiesta Bowl.

3 **New England's Bill Belichick** is named Associated Press Coach of the Year after leading the Patriots to 12 straight wins and a 14-2 regular season record.

4 **Setting up a nightmare scenario for the BCS,** the LSU Tigers roll to a 21-14 win over Jason White and the Oklahoma Sooners in the Sugar Bowl to claim half the national championship. It's LSU's first national championship since 1958. They split the title with USC, who won the Rose Bowl three days earlier.

5 **Just a day before** the annual Baseball Hall of Fame induction announcements, Pete Rose grabs the spotlight by finally coming clean and confessing to betting on baseball. Rose's admission comes on ABC's Good Morning America and is also prominent in his upcoming book, *My Prison Without Bars.*

Colorful former reliever Tug McGraw dies of brain cancer at the age of 59.

Guard Stephon Marbury is dealt to his hometown NY Knicks along with Penny Hardaway in an eight-player deal that sends Antonio McDyess to the Phoenix Suns.

6 **Dennis Eckersley and Paul Molitor** are elected by the BWAA to the Baseball Hall of Fame.

Fiery Tom Coughlin is named head coach of the New York Giants.

7 **NASCAR officials** propose their new playoff system (later called the Chase for the Nextel Cup) that will add drama to the end of the season. The details still need to be worked out, but the final 10 races of the season will decide the points champion and the top 10 points leaders at that time will be eligible. Many purists are against the decision.

Joe Gibbs, who led the Washington Redskins to three Super Bowl wins in 1982, 1987 and 1991, is back in the saddle after being hired as coach and president of the team. Additionally, Dennis Green is hired as coach of the perennially struggling Arizona Cardinals.

9 **Phoenix Coyotes goalie Brian Boucher** shuts out the Minnesota Wild for his fifth consecutive shutout. He breaks Bill Durnan's mark of 309 minutes, 21 seconds, set in 1949 as a member of the Montreal Canadiens. The streak ultimately ends two days later at 332 minutes, one second.

10 **The New England Patriots** extend their winning streak to 13 win a 17-14 win over the Titans in chilly Foxboro. Also, the Carolina Panthers upset the St. Louis Rams, 29-23, in double OT on a 69-yd touchdown pass from Jake Delhomme to Steve Smith.

Michelle Kwan wins her eighth national title at the U.S. Figure Skating Championships, behind seven perfect 6.0s. It is her seventh straight U.S. title. Delaware's Johnny Weir wins his first men's national title over second-place finisher Michael Weiss.

11 **Philadelphia edges Green Bay,** 20-17, in overtime while Indianapolis conquers the Kansas City Chiefs, 38-31, to advance to the NFC and AFC Championship games, respectively.

Coveted free agent Vladimir Guerrero signs with the Anaheim Angels. Terms are not disclosed but are estimated at $70 million over five years.

AP/Wide World Photos

Pete Rose signs copies of his new book, Pete Rose: My Prison Without Bars, on Jan. 9 in New York. Just days before the book was to hit stores, and one day before the annual Baseball Hall of Fame inductions, Rose admitted to betting on baseball.

12 **Less than three months** after announcing his retirement from Major League Baseball, Roger Clemens opts to join his friend and former teammate Andy Pettitte as a member of his hometown Houston Astros.

13 **Coaching Carousel.** The Buffalo Bills hire Steelers offensive coordinator Mike Mularkey as their new head coach. The Chicago Bears then name St. Louis Rams defensive coordinator Lovie Smith as theirs. In the NBA, the N.Y. Knicks tab 66-year-old Lenny Wilkens, the all-time winningest coach in league history, to lead their team.

15 **Michelle Wie** falls just one stroke short of making the cut at the PGA Tour's Sony Open in Honolulu. The 14-year-old cards a 2-under-par 68 (after a 72 the day before) which is the lowest score ever by a female competing against men.

One step forward, one step back. FIFA president Sepp Blatter says women should consider wearing tighter shorts to bring more attention to women's soccer.

18 **Peyton Manning is picked off** four times in the snow by the relentless Patriots defense as the Pats beat the Colts, 24-14, in the AFC Championship game. In the NFC, the Carolina Panthers stop Philly's Donovan McNabb and roll to a 14-3 win to set up the Super Bowl matchup. It's the Eagles' third straight loss in the NFC Championship game.

21 **The Champions Tour,** formerly the Senior PGA Tour (for golfers age 50 and up), announces its plans to eliminate the use of carts beginning with the 2005 season.

New York real estate developer Bruce Ratner agrees in principle to a $300 million deal to purchase the New Jersey Nets with hopes of moving the team to Brooklyn.

23 **All-star right wing Jaromir Jagr** is dealt from the Washington Capitals to the free-spending New York Rangers for Anson Carter.

24 **Arturo Gatti,** fighting with a broken hand, floors Gianluca Branco with a nasty left in Round 10 and goes on to win a unanimous decision to capture the vacant junior welterweight title.

Lakers forward Karl Malone is upset by a tasteless halftime skit put on by his former team, the Utah Jazz, that mocked him and his teammate Kobe Bryant.

26 **Miami Dolphins offensive coordinator** Norv Turner is selected to be the head coach of the Oakland Raiders.

Mineshaft is named Horse of the Year at the annual Eclipse Awards ceremony in Hollywood. Funny Cide (three-year-old male), Jerry Bailey (jockey) and Bobby Frankel (trainer) highlight the other winners.

Byron Scott is fired from the Atlantic Division-leading New Jersey Nets in the midst of a 4-6 run, and replaced by assistant Lawrence Frank.

27 **Jim O'Brien adds to the** NBA's list of coaching casualties after resigning from the Celtics over "philosophical differences" with head of basketball operations Danny Ainge. Asst. John Carroll is promoted to replace him.

28 **Dany Heatley returns** to the ice (in a 1-1 tie) for the first time since his car crash four months ago that took the life of his Atlanta Thrashers teammate Dan Snyder.

Temple hoops coach John Chaney gets his 700th career victory, a 76-57 thrashing of St. Bonaventure.

29 **The Los Angeles Dodgers sale** to Boston developer Frank McCourt is approved (30-0) by MLB owners.

30 **Justine Henin-Hardenne** wins her third Grand Slam title with a 6-3, 4-6, 6-3 win over countrywoman Kim Clijsters.

31 **John Elway, Barry Sanders,** Carl Eller and tackle Bob Brown are the newest inductees to the Pro Football Hall of Fame.

February 2004

Sun	Mon	Tue	Wed	Thu	Fri	Sat
1	2	3	4	5	6	7
8	9	10	11	12	13	14
15	16	17	18	19	20	21
22	23	24	25	26	27	28
29						

Quote of the Month

"The only thing I'm upset about is that the French judges only gave me a 5.6"

Pro snowboarder **Tara Dakides,** after flying 25 feet off a ramp and crashing to the pavement during a stunt on *Late Show with David Letterman.* After a night's stay in the hospital and several stitches, Dakides was back in action.

SPORTSNATION Polls

Wardrobe malfunction, huh?

What's your take on Janet Jackson's half-time exposure?

60.9%	—	It was intentional.
22.0%	—	What's the big deal?
9.4%	—	What happened?
7.4%	—	It was unintentional.

Total Votes: 237,207

What was the best part of Super Bowl XXVIII?

42.2%	—	The big plays back and forth.
30.6%	—	Janet Jackson's halftime show.
11.9%	—	Adam Vinatieri's game-winning field goal.
10.9%	—	The longest pass play in Super Bowl history.
4.1%	—	The commercials.

Total Votes: 40,182

1   **The New England Patriots win** their second Super Bowl in the last three years with a 32-29 victory over the resilient Carolina Panthers. Like he had two years prior, quarterback and game MVP Tom Brady leads his team downfield as the clock winds down to set up a game-winning Adam Vinatieri field goal (of 41 yards).

In a racy halftime show at the Super Bowl, singer Justin Timberlake rips off part of Janet Jackson's costume to reveal her bejeweled, but otherwise naked right breast. She later referred to the stunt as a "wardrobe malfunction." Both performers, CBS, Viacom, MTV and the FCC immediately begin damage control and ultimately results in numerous fines and live TV delays.

Roger Federer rolls to his first Grand Slam title of the year with a 7-6, 6-4, 6-2 win over Marat Safin at the Australian Open.

2   **Marlins catcher Pudge Rodriguez** goes from first to worst, signing a four-year, $40 million contract with the Detroit Tigers.

3   **Former Dolphins great Dan Marino** resigns from the club's senior vice president post he had accepted three weeks prior to remain a TV studio analyst.

Texas Tech basketball coach Bobby Knight is reprimanded, but not suspended, after a public verbal confrontation with Chancellor David Smith at the salad bar of an upscale grocery store.

5   **UConn easily handles** No. 1-ranked Tennessee, 81-67, in Knoxville in a battle of women's college basketball powerhouses. The Huskies are led by All-American Diana Taurasi with 18 points.

6   **Andy Roddick blasts** a 150-mph serve, the fastest ever recorded, during his straight-set Davis Cup victory over Austrian Stefan Koubek.

7   **Stanford's Nick Robinson** sinks a desperation three-pointer from about 35 feet at the buzzer to give the Cardinal a thrilling 80-77 win over Pac-10 rival Arizona. The win keeps Stanford undefeated as they join St. Joe's at 20-0.

Heavyweight champion Lennox Lewis makes it official, announcing his retirement after 14 years as a pro.

8   **Down 31-13 at halftime, the NFC** makes a stunning second-half comeback to edge the AFC, 55-52, at the Pro Bowl in Honolulu. Rams quarterback Marc Bulger throws for a Pro Bowl record four touchdown passes to lead the charge and is named MVP.

The East defeats the West, 6-4, in the 54th NHL All-Star Game in Minnesota, despite three goals from Colorado center and game MVP Joe Sakic.

The Golden State Warriors tie an NBA record for futility by scoring just two points in the fourth quarter of their 84-81 overtime loss to Toronto. The team goes 1-for-13 from the field during the 12-minute span.

9   **Racecar driver Bobby Labonte** unveils the car he'll be driving at the upcoming Daytona 500 that displays an advertisement on the hood for Mel Gibson's controversial film, *The Passion of the Christ.*

10   **Josh, a shiny, black 155-pound** Newfoundland, edges Coco, Les and Miki to be named Best in Show at the Westminster Dog Show at Madison Square Garden.

Head coach Randy Ayers is fired by the Philadelphia 76ers and replaced by veteran Chris Ford.

12   **Arthur Levitt Jr.,** the former chairman of the Securities Exchange Commission, releases a report that shows NHL teams losing $273 million during the 2002-03 season. He claims the league is on a "treadmill to obscurity."

14   **Popular Italian cyclist** Mario Pantani is found dead of cocaine poisoning in his hotel room in Rimini, Italy. Pantani, known as "Pirate," won the 1998 Tour de France, the last one not won by Lance Armstrong.

AP/Wide World Photos

Air Force One rises above the grandstands of the Daytona International Speedway on Feb. 15. President Bush arrived before the Daytona 500, spoke with drivers and then gave the command for drivers to start their engines.

Indiana's Fred Jones wins the NBA Slam Dunk contest, dethroning former champ Jason Richardson, who missed on his final two dunks. Denver's Voshon Lenard wins the three-point contest over Peja Stojakovic.

15 Dale Earnhardt Jr. wins his first Daytona 500, finishing just ahead of Tony Stewart. It is an emotional victory for him as he remembered his father who died in a last-lap crash at Daytona in 2001.

Surprise! The New York Yankees finalize their trade with Texas for superstar shortstop Alex Rodriguez. The Yankees trade second baseman Alfonso Soriano for Rodriguez and move the league MVP to third base. Red Sox fans everywhere immediately feel nauseous.

Lakers center Shaquille O'Neal pours in 24 points and grabs 11 rebounds to lead the West to a 136-132 win over the East in the NBA All-Star Game in Los Angeles.

Fan-favorite John Daly wins a three-man playoff at the Buick Invitational for his first win in almost nine years. He had fallen to No. 299 in the Official World Ranking.

16 Paul DePodesta, 31, is named general manager of the Los Angeles Dodgers, making him the third-youngest GM in history (Theo Epstein, 28, hired by Boston in 2002 and Randy Smith, 29 by San Diego in 1993).

17 Former Colorado kicker Katie Hnida tells *Sports Illustrated* she was raped by a teammate four years ago, but was too frightened at that time to come forward. Head coach Gary Barnett would later offer the following statement, "Katie was a girl. Not only was she a girl, she was terrible."

18 The New Jersey Nets win their 11th consecutive and 10th behind new head coach Lawrence Frank, 98-92, over the Atlanta Hawks. The 33-year-old breaks the NBA record for wins to start a coaching career.

18 Talented but volatile forward Rasheed Wallace, who was just traded from Portland to Atlanta a week ago, is dealt to the Detroit Pistons in a three-team deal with the Boston Celtics. Two days later he would be pulled from his Piston debut after 12 minutes because the proper paperwork had not been filed.

20 The St. Louis Cardinals lock up slugger Albert Pujols for the foreseeable future, inking him to a $100 million deal (with an option) over seven years.

22 Matt Kenseth edges rookie Kasey Kahne by .01 seconds in Rockingham, the fourth-closest finish since NASCAR introduced electronic scoring in 1993.

24 Two more NHL coaches, St. Louis' Joel Quenneville and Phoenix Coyotes' Bob Francis are fired. Both are former coaches of the year—Francis in 2003, Quenneville in 2000. The following day, Glen Sather would quit as coach of the Rangers, handing the reins to Tom Renney.

25 The Minnesota Timberwolves take down the New Jersey Nets, 81-68, stopping the Nets' winning streak at 14.

Ravens running back Jamal Lewis is indicted on charges of conspiring to possess and distribute approximately 11 pounds of cocaine in the spring of 2000. He enters a plea of not guilty.

26 The infamous Steve Bartman ball is blown up in front of Harry Caray's Restaurant in Chicago. It had been purchased by the restaurant partners for $106,000.

29 At the Accenture Match Play Championship in California, Davis Love III becomes infuriated with a heckler during his match with Tiger Woods and threatens to stop playing unless he is identified. The fan had evidently cheered when Love missed a putt, then yelled, "No Love!" at the tee box a few holes later.

March 2004

Sun	Mon	Tue	Wed	Thu	Fri	Sat
	1	2	3	4	5	6
7	8	9	10	11	12	13
14	15	16	17	18	19	20
21	22	23	24	25	26	27
28	29	30	31			

Quote of the Month

"I never saw him put it into his body. But look, Barry went to the bank with the robber, he drove the car, he got money in his pocket from the bag that came out of the bank. Come to your own conclusion. Did he spend the money? You decide."

Andy Van Slyke, former Pittsburgh teammate of Barry Bonds, in a radio interview discussing whether he believes Bonds ever took an illegal substance.

SPORTSNATION Polls

Hockey Brutality

What punishment should Todd Bertuzzi receive?

59.8% —	One year suspension.
25.4% —	Suspended for regular season and playoffs.
8.4% —	11-20 games suspension.
4.8% —	1-10 game suspension.
1.6% —	No punishment.

Total Votes: 191,076

What's your fantasy?

Which hitter will have the best fantasy baseball season in 2004?

60.0% —	Albert Pujols
28.7% —	Alex Rodriguez
11.1% —	Barry Bonds

Total Votes: 216,604

2 **Clinton Portis agrees** to an eight-year, $50.5 million contract with the Washington Redskins, paving the way for a blockbuster deal that sends cornerback Champ Bailey and a second-round pick to Denver.

Marge Schott, the controversial longtime Cincinnati Reds owner dies at the age of 75.

The Indianapolis Colts make quarterback Peyton Manning the highest-paid player in NFL history, inking him to a $98 million deal with a $34.5 million signing bonus.

The San Francisco Chronicle **reports** that Barry Bonds was given steroids and human growth hormone by BALCO and also accuses Jason Giambi, Gary Sheffield, three other major leaguers and an NFL player of receiving steroids.

3 **The New York Rangers,** looking as though they will miss the playoffs, deal 1994 Conn Smythe Award and two-time Norris Trophy-winning defenseman Brian Leetch to the Toronto Maple Leafs for two players and two picks. Elsewhere, the Boston Bruins land coveted defenseman Sergei Gonchar from the Capitals to bolster their playoff run.

Mianne Bagger becomes the first transsexual to play in a professional golf tournament when she tees it up at the Women's Australian Open.

6 **Ted Williams' son, John Henry,** who was at the center of the controversy surrounding his father's remains, dies of leukemia at the age of 35. According to family members, his remains will be delivered to the same cryogenics lab where the body of his father is kept.

Washington defeats Stanford, 75-62, in men's basketball, to put an end to the Cardinal's 26-game winning streak, leaving St. Joe's (27-0) as the only unbeaten team.

8 **Vancouver Canucks Todd Bertuzzi** levels Colorado Avalanche forward Steve Moore with a sucker punch from behind in apparent retaliation for a hit Moore laid on Vancouver's Markus Naslund a month earlier. Moore is transported to the hospital with a broken neck, concussion and deep cuts to his face. Bertuzzi is later suspended for the remaining 13 games of the regular season, plus the playoffs, and loses $500,000 in salary. The Canucks were also fined $250,000.

10 **Orlando Magic's Tracy McGrady** scores a career and team-high 62 points in a 108-99 win over the Wizards. It's the first 60-point NBA game since Lakers center Shaquille O'Neal dropped 61 on the Clippers in 2000.

11 **And then there were none.** St. Joe's is pounded by Xavier, 87-67, in the quarterfinals of the Atlantic 10 Tournament for the Hawks' first loss of the year after 27 straight wins.

12 **Detroit Red Wings goalie Dominik Hasek,** out for the remainder of the season with a groin injury, refuses to accept his $3 million salary because he doesn't feel like he's earned it.

13 **Austrian Hermann Maier completes** his amazing recovery from a motorcycle accident that nearly claimed his leg, by winning his fourth World Cup overall title. Sweden's Anja Paerson wins the women's overall title, while American Bode Miller grabs the Giant Slalom championship.

Winky Wright works over 154-pound champ and heavy favorite Shane Mosley and is awarded a unanimous decision to become the undisputed super welterweight champion of the world.

14 **Philadelphia guard Allen Iverson** refuses to come off the bench in the 76ers loss to Detroit after coach Chris Ford told him he wouldn't start. "I'm a starter," Iverson said. "I've been a starter here for eight years. I'm not a sixth man."

Brackets for the NCAA basketball tournaments are set, with Kentucky, St. Joseph's, Duke and Stanford grabbing No. 1 men's seeds and Penn St., Duke, Tennessee and Texas earning the top spots for the women's tourney.

AP/Wide World Photos and Rogers Sportsnet

In this television image, Vancouver Canucks' **Todd Bertuzzi** *lands on Colorado's Steve Moore after punching him during their game on March 8. Moore suffers a broken neck and a concussion while Bertuzzi is suspended, fined and later brought up on assault charges.*

16 Terrell Owens finally gets his wish to play for the Philadelphia Eagles, signing a seven-year, $42 million deal after an arbitrator agreed that he should become a free agent. Eleven days earlier, Owens was traded from the 49ers to the Baltimore Ravens for a second-round draft pick after a paperwork mix-up had apparently prevented his free agency. The Ravens were awarded a fifth-rounder and the 49ers received defensive end Brandon Whiting as compensation.

17 Alaskan Mitch Seavey wins the annual Iditarod Trail Sled Dog Race, mushing 1,100 miles from Anchorage to Nome in nine days, 12 hours, 20 minutes and 22 seconds. It's his first win after 11 tries.

18 The NCAA Division I hoops tournament tips off with most of the high seeds advancing. No. 5 seed Florida, however, is upset by No. 12 Manhattan, 75-60, while tenth-seeded Nevada upends Michigan State, 72-66.

The Tampa Bay Buccaneers and Dallas Cowboys swap wide receivers with Keyshawn Johnson heading to Dallas and Bill Parcells in exchange for veteran Joey Galloway.

The Champ Car World Series, formerly CART, suffers another defection when team owner Bobby Rahal leaves to focus on the rival Indy Racing League.

20 Stanford, the No. 1 seed in the West, is ousted from the men's tournament, falling to Alabama, 70-67. Elsewhere, Nevada continues its Cinderella run, beating former Cinderellas but now No. 2 seeded Gonzaga, 91-72.

Seven-time Pro Bowl defensive tackle Warren Sapp signs a seven-year, $36.6 million deal with the Raiders.

21 In another bracket-buster, ninth-seeded Alabama-Birmingham shocks top-seeded Kentucky, 76-75, on Mo Finley's jumper with 13 seconds left to advance to the Sweet 16.

23 Connecticut's Diana Taurasi and St. Joseph's Jameer Nelson are selected as the 2004 Naismith college basketball players of the year. It is Taurasi's second straight.

25 Greek actress Thalia Prokopiou lights the Olympic flame at the sanctuary where the Olympics were born 2,780 years ago.

Two quadruple jumps and a triple axel-triple flip in his long routine carry Russian Evgeni Plushenko to his third men's title at the World Figure Skating Championships.

27 Japan's Shizuka Arakawa wins her first title at the World Figure Skating Championships while Americans Sasha Cohen and Michelle Kwan take second and third, respectively.

28 Georgia Tech beats Kansas, 79-71 in overtime, while Duke takes care of Xavier, 66-63, to fill out the rest of the men's Final Four after Connecticut and Oklahoma State punched their tickets a day before. Oklahoma State knocked out St. Joseph's, 64-62, on a three-pointer by John Lucas III with 6.9 seconds left.

Grace Park wins the Kraft Nabisco Championship, the first major event on the 2004 LPGA Tour, with an 11-under 277. She holds off teenagers Aree Song (second place) and Michelle Wie (fourth) for her first major.

29 The sale of the Atlanta Hawks and Atlanta Thrashers to Atlanta Spirit LLC, a partnership with nine investors, is finalized when the NHL gives its stamp of approval. The deal is worth approximately $250 million.

30 The 2004 Major League Baseball Season officially gets underway as the Tampa Bay Devil Rays whip the New York Yankees, 8-3, in Tokyo, souring Alex Rodriguez's much-anticipated debut in pinstripes.

April 2004

Sun	Mon	Tue	Wed	Thu	Fri	Sat
				1	2	3
4	5	6	7	8	9	10
11	12	13	14	15	16	17
18	19	20	21	22	23	24
25	26	27	28	29	30	

Quote of the Month

"While many of us will be blessed to live a longer life, few of us will ever live a better one."

Sen. John McCain, R-Ariz., at a gathering in San Jose, Calif. in honor of Pat Tillman, who gave up millions playing football to join the Army Rangers. Tillman was killed in battle in Afghanistan on April 22.

SPORTSNATION Polls

It's finally Phil

What's your most memorable golf moment of the past 25 years?

41.8%	—	Mickelson wins first major in dramatic fashion.
28.1%	—	Nicklaus wins Masters at 46.
19.7%	—	Justin Leonard's Ryder Cup putt.
10.2%	—	Tom Watson's birdie chip.

Total Votes: 557

Who is Tiger Woods' biggest rival?

48.8%	—	Himself (boredom, married life)
33.6%	—	Vijay Singh
8.6%	—	Phil Mickelson
7.4%	—	Ernie Els
1.2%	—	Sergio Garcia

Total Votes: 2,314

1 **The Michigan Wolverines,** who in September successfully appealed NCAA sanctions that would have barred them from the postseason, defeat Rutgers, 62-55, to win the NIT Championship in New York.

3 **Down by eight late in the game, UConn** rips off a 12-3 run to edge Duke, 79-78, and advance to the NCAA men's championship game. In the other semifinal, Georgia Tech eliminates Oklahoma State, 67-65, on guard Will Bynum's layup with 1.5 seconds left.

Soccer prodigy Freddy Adu, 14, makes his MLS debut with the D.C. United. He enters the game in the 61st minute of the 2-1 win over San Jose but doesn't register a shot. The game is sold out (24,603 fans).

The St. Louis Blues defeat the Nashville Predators, 4-1, to clinch a playoff spot for the 25th consecutive year, the longest such streak in major league sports.

4 **Tennessee nips LSU,** 52-50 while UConn disposes of Minnesota, 67-58, to set up the championship game most women's hoops fans wanted to see. The Huskies and Vols have combined for seven of the last 10 national titles.

Hall of famer Annika Sorenstam wins the Office Depot Championship in Los Angeles by three strokes for her 50th LPGA Tour title.

5 **MVP Emeka Okafor dominates** the boards with 15 rebounds and adds 24 points to lead UConn to the NCAA Division I men's basketball championship with an 82-73 victory over Georgia Tech. Ben Gordon adds 21 points for the Huskies and B.J. Elder leads the Yellow Jackets with 14. It is the second title for Jim Calhoun's squad and second in the last six years.

Clyde "The Glide" Drexler heads a class of six elected to the Basketball Hall of Fame in Springfield, Mass.

6 **The Connecticut women** beat rival Tennessee, 70-61 in the NCAA Division I championship game for their third straight title and fifth overall. Naismith Player of the Year Diana Taurasi leads the Huskies with 17 points and is named tournament MVP for the second consecutive year. It is the first time in Division I basketball history that a school has won both the men's and women's titles.

8 **The 2004 Masters** gets underway at Augusta. Justin Rose jumps out to an early two-stroke lead while favorite Tiger Woods can't find his swing and shoots a 4-over 76. A distraught Tom Watson also shoots a 76 after learning that his longtime caddie and friend Bruce Edwards died from ALS earlier in the morning.

10 **Goaltender Adam Berkhoel** stops 24 shots to lead Denver to a 1-0 victory over Maine in the NCAA Division I men's hockey championship game. Gabe Gauthier nets the only goal of the game and the Denver defense withstands a 6-on-3 Maine advantage in the final minute.

11 **After 46 majors without a win,** Phil Mickelson finally breaks through with a dramatic one-stroke victory over Ernie Els at the Masters. Mickelson sinks a 20-footer on the 18th hole to clinch the win and the green jacket, then leaps for joy along with his throngs of supporters.

12 **The Philadelphia Phillies** christen brand new Citizens Bank Park with a sluggish 4-1 loss to Cincinnati. The team had been in Veterans Stadium since 1971.

13 **Barry Bonds launches** home run No. 661 in the seventh inning of the Giants' 4-2 win over Milwaukee, vaulting him over his godfather Willie Mays and into third place on the all-time home run list.

Michael Phelps wins the Sullivan Award as the nation's top amateur athlete. He is the first swimmer to win the award since Janet Evans in 1989.

16 **St. Louis Blues winger** Mike Danton is arrested and charged with attempting to hire someone to murder an unnamed male acquaintance.

Arnold Palmer walks over the Hogan Bridge on the 12th hole at Augusta National for the final time in Masters competition on April 9. The four-time Masters champion had earlier announced that this year's would be his last.

17 The Phoenix Mercury make guard Diana Taurasi the top overall pick in the WNBA draft.

Chris Byrd retains his IBF heavyweight crown with a draw against Andrew Golota in Madison Square Garden. Also, the "Quiet Man," John Ruiz, registers a TKO over Fres Oquendo in the 11th round of a lackluster bout to keep his WBA heavyweight belt.

19 A federal appeals court suspends a previous ruling that allowed high school players or anyone less than three years removed from high school to enter the NFL draft. What this mean is, Maurice Clarett and USC wide receiver Mike Williams are ineligible for the upcoming NFL draft. The case is then ruled on three days later by the Supreme Court but the decision is unchanged.

Longtime Cincinnati Bengals running back Corey Dillon is traded to the Super Bowl champion New England Patriots for a second-round pick in the upcoming draft.

The Montreal Canadiens overcome a 3-1 series deficit to beat the Boston Bruins and advance to the Eastern Conference semifinals.

In unseasonably hot temperatures that rise well into the 80s, Kenyans Timothy Cherigat (2:10:37) and Catherine Ndereba (2:24:27) win the 108th Boston Marathon. It is Ndereba's third Boston crown.

20 LeBron James wins the NBA Rookie of the Year award after helping the Cleveland Cavaliers boost their win total from 17 in 2002-03 to 35. At 19, he is the youngest to win the award. James totaled 508 votes to 430 for Denver's Carmelo Anthony.

21 Hubie Brown, who led the Memphis Grizzlies to their first playoff berth, is selected as NBA Coach of the Year, edging Utah's Jerry Sloan, 466-424.

22 Eli Manning and his family asks the San Diego Chargers to either trade the top pick in the NFL draft or select someone other than him.

Charlie Sifford becomes the first African-American player to be selected for induction into the World Golf Hall of Fame. He is joined by Tom Kite, Isao Aoki and Marlene Stewart Streit.

Pat Tillman, who pushed aside a multi-million dollar NFL contract to join the Army Rangers and fight for his country, is killed in Afghanistan at the age of 27.

24 The San Diego Chargers honor Eli Manning's request by drafting the quarterback from Mississippi, then trading him to the New York Giants for quarterback Philip Rivers of N.C. State (taken fourth overall by the Giants) and three additional draft picks.

Heavyweight Vitali Klitschko beats Corrie Sanders at 2:46 of the eighth round to win the WBC title vacated by the retirement of Lennox Lewis.

25 Jeff Gordon wins under caution at the Aaron's 499 at Talladega, prompting Dale Earnhardt Jr. fans to throw beer cans and other debris onto the track in protest.

27 Australian world record holder Ian Thorpe accepts teammate Craig Stevens' offer to take his spot in the 400-meter freestyle in the Athens Games. Thorpe was originally disqualified for a false start at his country's trials.

28 The Cincinnati Reds jump out to an early 9-0 lead against the Milwaukee Brewers only to see their lead vanish and lose, 10-9, in 10 innings.

30 Former NBA player Jayson Williams is acquitted on manslaughter charges after the shotgun slaying of his limo driver, Gus Christofi. He was convicted, however, of four lesser charges related to tampering with evidence.

May 2004

Sun	Mon	Tue	Wed	Thu	Fri	Sat
						1
2	3	4	5	6	7	8
9	10	11	12	13	14	15
16	17	18	19	20	21	22
23/30	24/31	25	26	27	28	29

Quote of the Month

"I notice guys don't want to shake hands with him. Everybody just gives him the fist."

Dusty Baker, Chicago Cubs manager, upon learning that left fielder Moises Alou occasionally urinates on his hands to condition his skin.

SPORTSNATION Polls

Perfect Unit

Which was the most dominating pitching performance?

29.8% —	Kerry Wood fans 20 Astros.
18.6% —	Nolan Ryan's 7th no-hitter.
14.4% —	Randy Johnson's perfect game.
10.8% —	Jack Morris, 1991 WS, Game 7
25.9% —	Other

Total Votes: 30,172

Things I would rather do instead of batting lefty against Randy Johnson:

40.5% —	Cut class, then be late for a Bobby Knight practice.
25.1% —	Box Mike Tyson with hot-wing sauce on my ears.
12.7% —	Bat vs. Roger Clemens after a teammate showboats.
10.7% —	Take a Shaq charge after keying his SUV.
10.7% —	Go across the middle vs. Ray Lewis, wearing a T.O. jersey.

Total Votes: 3,845

1 Smarty Jones, a 4-1 racetime favorite under jockey Stewart Elliott, takes the lead down the stretch and powers to a 2¾-length win at the 130th Kentucky Derby at Churchill Downs. He earns not only the million dollar first-place prize, but also an additional $5 million bonus for also having previously won the Arkansas Derby and the Rebel Stakes. It's quite a comeback for a horse who nearly died after fracturing his skull in July 2003.

A fire breaks out at a hotel in Rome where tennis players Andy Roddick, Marat Safin and others are staying for the Italian Open. Three people are killed but the players escape unharmed. Roddick reportedly helps officials with the rescue efforts.

3 Minnesota Timberwolves forward Kevin Garnett is the runaway selection as NBA MVP. Garnett receives 120 of the 123 first-place votes. Spurs center Tim Duncan is a distant second while Indiana's Jermaine O'Neal, with two first-place votes, takes third.

5 Major League Baseball announces it will be placing advertisements for the movie Spider-Man 2 on bases at select parks. Several teams, including the New York Yankees complain, causing officials to rethink their idea and scrap the plan a day later.

Just over three months before the start of the Olympics, three bombs explode in the Athens suburb of Kalithea.

7 Head coaches Tim Floyd (New Orleans) and Terry Stotts (Atlanta) are both fired, meaning all 15 Eastern Conference teams have changed coaches at least once since the end of the 2002-03 season.

8 The Texas Rangers and Detroit Tigers combine for 18 runs in the fifth inning of the Rangers' 16-15 10-inning victory. It is one run shy of the major league record. After scoring eight, Detroit holds a 14-4 lead in the top of the fifth before the Rangers put up a 10-spot to tie. Alfonso Soriano goes 6-for-6 in the game.

9 Se Ri Pak wins the Michelob Ultra Open, the 22nd victory of her career, which qualifies her for entry into the LPGA Hall of Fame. She now needs to play just three more years to satisfy the hall's 10-year requirement.

Michael Schumacher wins his fifth straight Formula One race to start the season at the Spanish Grand Prix and ties the record for best start to the season set by Nigel Mansell in 1992.

11 Officials from Pittsfield, Mass. release a document they uncovered from a library vault that shows baseball was being played there in the late 1700s. The document, from 1791, was written to protect the windows of the town meeting house by banning anyone from playing baseball within 80 yards of the house. The game is long thought to have been invented by Abner Doubleday in 1839 in Cooperstown, N.Y.

12 By beating Saudi Arabia, 3-1, and then watching Kuwait and Oman tie, the Iraqi national soccer team qualifies for the upcoming Olympic Games in Athens.

13 Guard Derek Fisher hits an off-balance, fall-away 16-footer with 0.4 seconds remaining to give the Los Angeles Lakers a 74-73 win over the San Antonio Spurs and a 3-2 series lead in the Western Conference semifinals. Just a moment before, Spurs center Tim Duncan hit a clutch jumper from the top of the key to give the Spurs what they thought was the lead for good.

Penn State extends football coach Joe Paterno's contract an additional four years, which would make the 77-year-old coach of the Nittany Lions through 2008.

14 The New Jersey Nets beat the Detroit Pistons, 127-120, in triple overtime to take a 3-2 series lead in the Eastern Conference semis.

AP/Wide World Photos

The "Big Unit," **Randy Johnson** *salutes the crowd in Atlanta after throwing the 17th perfect game in Major League Baseball history on May 18. The 40-year-old retired 27 straight Braves batters, while striking out 13 of them, in the Diamondbacks' 2-0 win.*

15 **Smarty Jones cruises** to a Preakness-record 11½-length romp at Pimlico for his eighth consecutive win. The victory pushes him to fourth place on thoroughbred racing's all-time earnings list and sets up the possibility for the first Triple Crown winner since Affirmed in 1978. It is the sixth time in the last eight years that a horse has won the Kentucky Derby and the Preakness.

According to unidentified sources, Dolphins running back Ricky Williams tests positive for marijuana, his second violation of the NFL's substance abuse policy, and faces a $650,000 fine.

Antonio Tarver gets his revenge, knocking out Roy Jones Jr. at 1:41 of the second round with a devastating shot to the chin to take Jones' light heavyweight title.

16 **Milwaukee's Ben Sheets** strikes out a franchise record 18 batters in the Brewers' 4-1 victory over the Atlanta Braves.

Sacramento guard Anthony Peeler delivers a forearm shiver to the head of Timberwolves' forward Kevin Garnett in the Kings' 104-87 Game 6 win. He is subsequently suspended for two games, meaning he'll miss the all-important Game 7.

17 **Ashley McElhiney, 22,** former guard at Vanderbilt, is introduced as coach of the American Basketball Association's Nashville Rhythm. She becomes the first female to coach a professional men's team.

18 **Arizona flamethrower Randy Johnson** records the 17th perfect game in major league history, retiring 27 consecutive Atlanta batters and whiffing 13 in a 2-0 win. It is his second career no-hitter. At age 40, he is the oldest pitcher to throw a perfect game and the first since David Cone in 1999 to accomplish the feat.

19 **American sprinter Kelli White** accepts a two-year ban from competition after testing positive for a stimulant during the 2003 World Championships and U.S. Nationals. She loses every medal she had won over the last four years.

Vicente Rodriguez and Mista Ferrer each score to lead Spain's Valencia to a 2-0 victory over Marseille in European soccer's UEFA Cup in Goteborg.

20 **The Detroit Pistons** stifle the New Jersey Nets, 90-69, in Game 7 to complete the matchups for the Conference Finals. The Pistons will take on the Pacers in the East, while the Lakers take on the Timberwolves in the West.

22 **The Tampa Bay Lightning** edge the Philadelphia Flyers, 2-1, in Game 7 to set up the Stanley Cup finals with the Calgary Flames, who had advanced by beating the San Jose Sharks.

23 **Talk about an expensive publicity stunt.** To promote a gem firm, F-1 driver Christian Klien's car for the Monaco Grand Prix is fitted with a $322,000, 108-carat diamond in the nose. He then crashes on the first lap, sending debris everywhere. The diamond is nowhere to be found.

24 **Mike Keenan** and Jacques Martin are hired as general manager and coach of the Florida Panthers, respectively.

Tayshaun Prince comes out of nowhere to swat Reggie Miller's layup to help the Detroit Pistons beat the Indiana Pacers, 72-67, in Game 2 of the Eastern Conference finals.

27 **Marat Safin inexplicably** pulls down his shorts after winning a shot during his five-set win over Felix Mantilla at the French Open.

30 **Buddy Rice, driving** for team owners David Letterman and Bobby Rahal, wins the rain-shortened Indianapolis 500, while Jimmy Johnson captures NASCAR's Coca-Cola 600 at Lowe's Motor Speedway.

June 2004

Sun	Mon	Tue	Wed	Thu	Fri	Sat
		1	2	3	4	5
6	7	8	9	10	11	12
13	14	15	16	17	18	19
20	21	22	23	24	25	26
27	28	29	30			

Quote of the Month

"...as we all know, the majority of fans are white America. And if you just had a couple of white guys in there, you might get them a little excited. But it's a black man's game and it will be forever. I mean, the greatest athletes in the world are African-American."

Larry Bird, Indiana Pacers president and hall of famer, commenting on the state of the NBA in a discussion with Jim Gray, Magic Johnson, LeBron James and Carmelo Anthony.

SPORTSNATION Polls

White players in the NBA

Do you think the NBA would benefit from more white stars?

64.5%	—	Yes
35.4%	—	No

Total Votes: 68,185

What does the NBA need most?

43.2%	—	Minimum age requirement.
20.2%	—	More scoring.
19.8%	—	More white superstars.
12.1%	—	Realignment.
4.5%	—	International expansion.

Total Votes: 2,685

1 **The Williams sisters are dispatched** in the quarterfinals of the French Open within 30 minutes of each other. Serena loses to American Jennifer Capriati, 6-2, 2-6, 6-3, and then Venus is taken down by Anastasia Myskina of Russia, 6-3, 6-4.

4 **Paul Hamm**, the defending world champion, wins his third straight national title at the U.S. Gymnastics Championships in Nashville, followed by Brett McClure, Hamm's twin brother Morgan and Todd Thornton.

5 **Nick Zito's Birdstone edges** Smarty Jones by one length to win the 136th Belmont Stakes and ruin his bid to become the first Triple Crown winner since 1978. While obviously thrilled with their win, all of Birdstone's handlers, from owner/breeder Marylou Whitney to jockey Edgar Prado, apologize for spoiling the party.

Martin St. Louis scores 33 seconds into the second overtime to give the Tampa Bay Lightning a 3-2 win over the Calgary Flames and tie their best-of-seven Stanley Cup finals at three games apiece.

Anastasia Myskina wipes out countrywoman Elena Dementieva, 6-1, 6-2, in just 58 minutes to win the women's French Open singles title.

Carly Patterson and Courtney Kupets each finish with a 76.45 points and share the title at the U.S. Gymnastics Championships.

Harvard's crew stays undefeated for the season, cruising to victory in the Varsity Eights final at the annual Intercollegiate Rowing Association Championship on the Cooper River in New Jersey. Washington finishes runner-up while California places third.

6 **The men's French Open final** is an all-Argentine affair as unseeded Gaston Gaudio storms back from two sets down to beat Guillermo Coria, 0-6, 3-6, 6-4, 6-1, 8-6. Just two points away from victory, Coria's right leg cramps, setting the stage for the comeback.

Despite 34 points from Shaquille O'Neal and 25 from Kobe Bryant, the Detroit Pistons march into Los Angeles and beat the Lakers, 87-75, in Game 1 of the NBA Finals.

7 **Ruslan Fedotenko scores** two goals and goalie Nikolai "The Bulin Wall" Khabibulin shuts down Jarome Iginla and the rest of the Flames offense as the Tampa Bay Lightning win Game 7 of the Stanley Cup Finals, 2-1. It is the Lightning's first title. Forward Brad Richards earns the Conn Smythe Trophy for playoff MVP with 12 goals, including seven game winners.

The San Diego Padres select shortstop/pitcher Matt Bush from nearby Mission Bay, Calif. with the top overall pick in the annual major league first-year player draft. Highly-touted Stephen Drew, a client of Scott Boras, falls to 14th (Arizona) due to potential signability issues.

8 **Kobe Bryant's** clutch three-pointer with 2.1 seconds on the clock sends the game into overtime, where the Lakers win Game 2 of the NBA Finals, 99-91. Bryant finishes with 33 points. The Pistons had led, 89-83, with under a minute left in regulation.

Jim O'Brien is fired as head basketball coach at Ohio State after disclosing that in 1999 he gave $6,000 to a recruit that never played for the Buckeyes.

10 **In a controversial roundtable discussion** with Jim Gray, Pacers president and former Celtics great Larry Bird claims, among other things, that the NBA needs more white star players and that he "really got irritated" when a white player tried to guard him. Magic Johnson downplays the comments, saying, "We need some more Larry Birds."

Three days after winning the Stanley Cup, the Lightning clean up at the NHL Awards as Martin St. Louis wins the Hart Trophy (MVP), John Tortorella wins the Jack Adams (coach) and Brad Richards wins the Lady Byng.

AP/Wide World Photos

Detroit Pistons' head coach **Larry Brown** *waves during the team's championship parade on the streets of Detroit on June 17. The Pistons shocked the Los Angeles Lakers with a dominating 4-1 series victory in the NBA Finals.*

11 **Andy Roddick breaks** his own record for the fastest serve ever recorded, hammering a 153-mph rocket during his win over Paradorn Srichaphan at the Queen's Club Tournament in London.

13 **Annika Sorenstam wins her** seventh major tournament, a three-shot victory over Shi Hyun Ahn at the LPGA Championship in Wilmington, Del.

Ralph Wiley, columnist for ESPN.com and former writer for *Sports Illustrated,* dies of heart failure at 52.

14 **Lance Armstrong is forced** to defend himself yet again, after a recently published book, *L.A. Confidential, the Secrets of Lance Armstrong* accuses him of asking a staff member to throw away syringes and supply him with make-up to cover up needle marks. Armstrong denies all charges.

15 **With a total team effort,** the Detroit Pistons shock the Los Angeles Lakers, 100-87, to win Game 5 of the NBA Finals and their first championship since 1990. Chauncey Billups is the Finals MVP and Larry Brown becomes the first coach to win titles at the pro and college level. The win makes team owner Bill Davidson a four-time winner over the past year, as he also owns the NHL's Tampa Bay Lightning, WNBA's Detroit Shock and is part owner of the Arena Football League's Tampa Bay Storm.

16 **And now it's Marion Jones'** turn to dispute drug allegations levied against her by the U.S. Anti-Doping Agency. She calls the organization a "kangaroo court" and reminds the public that she has taken over 160 drug tests and never failed one of them.

A Texas Rangers fan who jumped over a row of seats and knocked over a 4-year-old boy to get a baseball agrees to send the baseball, a letter of apology and tickets to another game to the boy and his family.

20 **A cool, collected Retief Goosen** cards a final round 1-over-par 71 to win the U.S. Open by two strokes over Phil Mickelson. The story of the tournament, however, may have been what many consider unfair conditions at Shinnecock Hills that led to only two golfers breaking par.

Ken Griffey Jr. swats a fastball into the rightfield stands off Cardinals pitcher Matt Morris to give him 500 for his career. The Reds beat the Cardinals, 6-0.

Wimbledon gets underway as 47-year-old legend Martina Navratilova crushes Colombia's Catalina Castano, 6-0, 6-1, ten years after her last Wimbledon singles match.

22 **Yankees pitcher Jose Contreras** is reunited with his wife and daughters after they make a daring nighttime escape from Cuba in a crowded smugglers boat.

24 **The Orlando Magic select 6-11** Atlanta high school senior Dwight Howard with the first overall pick in the NBA draft. He is followed by two Connecticut Huskies, Emeka Okafor, chosen second by expansion Charlotte, and Ben Gordon, chosen third by the Chicago Bulls.

Prized outfielder Carlos Beltran is traded from the Kansas City Royals to the Houston Astros as part of a three-way deal that also sends closer Octavio Dotel to Oakland.

England loses to Portugal in the European Championship soccer tournament in Lisbon when star David Beckham's penalty kick sails high and into the crowd.

26 **Russian wing Alexander Ovechkin** is chosen first overall by the Washington Capitals in the NHL entry draft.

27 **Cal State-Fullerton** wins the College Baseball World Series for the fourth time with a 3-2 win over Texas.

29 **Orlando's Tracy McGrady is traded** to the Houston Rockets for guard Steve Francis.

July 2004

Sun	Mon	Tue	Wed	Thu	Fri	Sat
				1	2	3
4	5	6	7	8	9	10
11	12	13	14	15	16	17
18	19	20	21	22	23	24
25	26	27	28	29	30	31

Quote of the Month

"I didn't quit football because I failed a drug test. I failed a drug test because I was ready to quit football."

Ricky Williams, Miami Dolphins running back, as quoted in an interview with the *Miami Herald*. Williams abruptly retired from football on July 25, citing various reasons ranging from a lack of passion for the game to his desire to freely use recreational drugs.

SPORTSNATION Polls

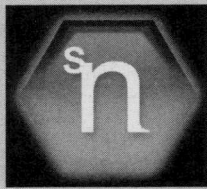

Ricky Runs

Without Ricky Williams, how many wins will the Dolphins have in 2004 (poll posted in the preseason)?

52.3%	—	6 or 7
27.4%	—	5 or fewer
16.9%	—	8 or 9
3.2%	—	10 or more

Total Votes: 167,074

What do you think of Ricky Williams' decision to retire from the NFL?

40.4%	—	He should be admired for following his own path in life.
38.3%	—	He's a quitter.
21.3%	—	He's not really retiring.

Total Votes: 52,719

1 Ex-NBA center **Manute Bol** is critically injured when the cab he is riding in flips over on a Connecticut road. The driver, Neville Robinson, is killed.

The New York Yankees defeat the Boston Red Sox, 5-4, on a single by pinch-hitter John Flaherty in the bottom of the 13th inning. The game is highlighted by shortstop Derek Jeter's fearless dive into the stands to catch Trot Nixon's foul pop-up. Jeter is bruised and bloodied but returns to play the following night.

2 **Bob Brenly is fired** as manager of the last-place Arizona Diamondbacks and replaced by third base coach Al Pedrique. Brenly won a World Series with the team in 2001.

3 **Maria Sharapova, 17,** downs top-seeded Serena Williams in straight sets, 6-1, 6-4, to win the women's singles Wimbledon championship for her first major title. She is the fourth-youngest female Grand Slam champion.

4 **Roger Federer wins** the men's singles Wimbledon title for the second year in a row, with a hard-fought 4-6, 7-5, 7-6, 6-4 victory over Andy Roddick. It's Federer's 24th consecutive on grass, passing Pete Sampras for the longest streak.

Meg Mallon wins the U.S. Women's Open in South Hadley, Mass. by two strokes over Annika Sorenstam. It's her second U.S. Open title, the first one coming 13 years ago.

5 **Los Angeles Dodgers closer** Eric Gagne's major league leading streak of 84 consecutive saves ends when he gives up two runs to the Arizona Diamondbacks to blow a 5-3 lead. The Dodgers win the game, 6-5, in the 10th. He had not blown a save since Aug. 26, 2002.

6 **Goaltender Dominik Hasek signs** a one-year, $2 million deal with incentives to play for the Ottawa Senators.

7 **In the rain-soaked fourth stage** team trial of the Tour de France, U.S. Postal Service team's Lance Armstrong earns his familiar yellow shirt by claiming the overall Tour lead. Lance and his team average 33.36 mph over the 40.1-mile stage.

8 **Carlos Boozer agrees** to a six-year, $68 million deal with the Utah Jazz, apparently changing his mind and going back on the promise he made a few days earlier to re-sign with the Cleveland Cavaliers.

10 **Rudy Tomjanovich,** who led the Houston Rockets to the NBA Championship in 1994 and '95, is chosen to replace Phil Jackson as coach of the Los Angeles Lakers.

11 **Steffi Graf is inducted** into the International Tennis Hall of Fame in Newport, R.I., and presented by her husband Andre Agassi, who will someday have his own day in Newport. Stefan Edberg and Dodo Cheney are also inducted.

Tony Stewart wins the NASCAR Tropicana 400 in Joliet, but not before inciting a little controversy. Stewart bumps race leader Kasey Kahne at the race's half-way point, sparking a brawl between the two drivers' pit crews.

12 **Baltimore shortstop Miguel Tejada** wins Major League Baseball's annual Home Run Derby in Houston, edging hometown favorite Lance Berkman of the Astros, 5-4, in the finals. The night is also highlighted by a reunion of the 14 living 500-home run hitters.

13 **National League starter** Roger Clemens is touched for six runs in the first inning, including a three-run homer by game MVP Alfonso Soriano and a solo shot by Manny Ramirez, as the American League wins the 75th Major League Baseball All-Star Game, 9-4. Immediately rumors swirl (mostly jokingly) that N.L. catcher and Clemens-rival Mike Piazza may have been tipping pitches.

Long Beach State hurler Jered Weaver wins the Golden Spike Award as the nation's top college baseball player. Weaver, whose brother Jeff is already in the big leagues, went 15-1 in 2004.

Lance Armstrong *spent the month of July the same way he has for the past five years — by thoroughly dominating the best cyclists in the world at the Tour de France. Armstrong won number six in 2004, more than any rider in Tour history.*

14 **The long-awaited trade** of Shaquille O'Neal becomes official as the seven-footer is dealt from the Lakers to the Miami Heat for Lamar Odom, Caron Butler, Brian Grant and a first-round pick. The trade successfully separates Shaq and Kobe, two immensely talented but constantly bickering superstars.

Major League Soccer announces its plans to expand to 12 teams beginning in 2005, by adding clubs in Salt Lake City and a second in Los Angeles (announced at a later date).

Houston Astros manager Jimy Williams is fired and replaced by former Astros player and Detroit and Milwaukee manager Phil Garner.

Oakland Raiders' Chris Cooper and Barret Robbins, along with Dana Stubblefield, are fined after testing positive for the steroid THG.

15 **Kobe Bryant inks** a seven-year deal worth more than $136 million to stay with the Lakers, while New Jersey's Kenyon Martin is dealt to the Denver Nuggets for three future first-round draft picks.

18 **PGA Tour rookie Todd Hamilton**, 38, wins a four-hole playoff with Ernie Els to capture the British Open title at Royal Troon. Phil Mickelson finishes one shot back of the pair.

Dale Earnhardt Jr. escapes with "moderate-sized burns" after a crash at the American Le Mans Series race in Sonoma, Calif. turns his car into a giant fireball. He walks away with second-degree burns on his legs and his chin.

20 **After a thrilling Stage 15 battle** with rider Ivan Basso in the mountains, Lance Armstrong grabs the yellow jersey once again, turning a 22-second deficit into a one minute and 25 second lead.

23 **Italian rider Filippo Simeoni**, who had testified about drug use in cycling, is chased down by a furious Lance Armstrong and denied a chance to win Stage 18 of the Tour

24 **The Red Sox and Yankees play** another thriller as Bill Mueller wins it for Boston with a home run in the bottom of the ninth off Mariano Rivera. The game features a bench-clearing brawl as Alex Rodriguez and Jason Varitek go at it after Rodriguez is plunked by Sox pitcher Bronson Arroyo.

25 **Miami Dolphins running back** Ricky Williams stuns his team, the NFL and fantasy football players everywhere by announcing his retirement from the game less than a week before the opening of training camp.

Lance Armstrong, as we all knew he would, coasts down the Champs-Elysees wearing a yellow jersey and holding a glass of champagne. He beats his nearest rival by six minutes, 19 seconds and sets an all-time record with his sixth consecutive Tour de France win.

30 **Fan favorite Paul Lo Duca** is traded, along with reliever Guillermo Mota and outfielder Juan Encarnacion, from the Los Angeles Dodgers to the Florida Marlins for pitcher Brad Penny and infielder Hee Sop Choi. Also, the New York Mets acquire pitchers Kris Benson and Victor Zambrano.

Mike Tyson is pummeled in the fourth round by unheralded British heavyweight Danny Williams.

31 **Nomar Garciaparra**, once considered the heart and soul of the Boston Red Sox but disenchanted after the team's offseason pursuit of Alex Rodriguez, is traded to the Chicago Cubs in a four-team deal that sends Orlando Cabrera and Doug Mientkiewicz to the Red Sox, shortstop Alex Gonzalez, pitcher Francis Beltran and infielder Brendan Harris to the Expos and minor leaguer Justin Jones to the Twins.

August 2004

Sun	Mon	Tue	Wed	Thu	Fri	Sat
1	2	3	4	5	6	7
8	9	10	11	12	13	14
15	16	17	18	19	20	21
22	23	24	25	26	27	28
29	30	31				

Quote of the Month

"I personally feel in my heart I was the Olympic champion that night. I would be a little bit upset if another gold medal was awarded because I really felt I won the event."

Paul Hamm, United States gymnast and all-around gold medalist, explaining his thoughts regarding the controversial decision to award him the gold.

SPORTSNATION Polls

Paul Hamm's all-around fiasco

Which of these statements is closest to your point of view?

44.6% —	Judging in gymnastics is always suspect.
34.3% —	This was just an honest mistake in an upright sport.
21.2% —	Gymnastics is not a sport because it relies on judging.

What outcome would you like to see?

35.5% —	Paul Hamm keeps the gold and Yang Tae Young is awarded a second gold.
35.4% —	Paul Hamm keeps the gold and Yang Tae Young keeps the bronze.
29.1% —	Yang Tae Young is awarded the gold and Paul Hamm is given the silver.

Total Votes: 58,385

1 **Karen Stupples becomes** the first English winner of the Weetabix Women's British Open since 1991. She cards a record-tying 19-under 269 to capture her first major.

Yankees first baseman Jason Giambi, who has been sick and fatigued for a good part of the season, is diagnosed with a benign tumor but is expected to return this year.

Nomar Garciaparra is welcomed with a standing ovation at Wrigley, then goes 1-for-4 with an RBI in his Cubs debut, a 6-3 win over the Phillies.

2 **Smarty Jones,** who missed out on the Triple Crown by one length at the Belmont Stakes, is forced into an early retirement with bones bruises in all four of his hooves.

Tiger Woods and Hank Kuehne win the made-for-TV "Battle at the Bridges," defeating John Daly and Phil Mickelson by a score of 2&1.

3 **The U.S. men's basketball team** receives a much-needed wake-up call with a humbling loss to Italy in a pre-Olympic exhibition, 95-78. A day later, Allen Iverson hits a jumper at the buzzer to give the team an 80-77 win over Germany, a team that failed to qualify for the Athens Games.

6 **The Miami Dolphins are dealt** another huge blow when their top offseason acquisition, wide receiver David Boston, is lost for the season with a torn knee ligament.

The St. Louis Cardinals acquire veteran Larry Walker from the Colorado Rockies to bolster their already impressive lineup for the stretch run and postseason.

7 **Chicago Cubs starter Greg Maddux** becomes the 22nd pitcher to win 300 games with an 8-4 victory over the San Francisco Giants. Maddux is far from sharp, allowing four runs and seven hits in five-plus innings, but the Cubs bullpen and offense make sure he reaches his milestone.

8 **Driver Jeff Gordon wins** the Brickyard 400 for the fourth time in his career, outgunning the rest of the field in a two-lap sprint.

9 **Classy Seattle Mariners DH** Edgar Martinez announces his retirement from Major League Baseball at the end of the season, after 18 seasons, two American League batting titles and 10 seasons batting over .300.

10 **New York Mets pitcher** Tom Glavine loses two front teeth in a car accident while going from LaGuardia Airport to Shea Stadium in a taxi. He misses one scheduled start.

11 **American sprinter Torri Edwards,** a hopeful for at least one medal at the Olympics, is suspended for two years after testing positive for a banned stimulant. Gail Devers will take her spot in the women's 100-meter dash.

13 **The 2004 Summer Olympics** in Athens officially begins with a spectacular opening ceremony. Greek windsurfer Nikolaos Kaklamanakis lights the Olympic cauldron in front of 72,000 fans.

14 **The first full day** of Olympic competition begins as predicted, with American swimmer Michael Phelps winning his first gold medal in the 400-meter individual medley. Australian Ian Thorpe takes gold in the 400-meter freestyle.

The preseason Associated Press College Football Poll is released with last season's co-champion USC grabbing the top spot, followed by Oklahoma, Georgia and LSU.

15 **After a final round 4-over 76,** Vijay Singh picks the best time for his first birdie of the tournament — on the first hole of the three-hole playoff with Chris DiMarco and Justin Leonard at the PGA Championship. Singh follows the birdie with two pars to clinch his fifth win of the season and the third major tournament victory of his career.

Poor shooting, a lazy attitude and poor team play is enough to do in the U.S. men's basketball team as they are embarrassed by Puerto Rico, 92-73.

The Iraqi soccer team tops Costa Rica, 2-0, to gain a berth in the Olympic quarterfinals.

AP/Wide World Photos

*Defrocked Irish priest **Cornelius Horan** grabs **Vanderlei de Lima** of Brazil and knocks him into the crowd with three miles remaining in the men's Olympic marathon in Athens on Aug. 29. De Lima had been leading until the incident but finished third.*

16 **The U.S. men's gymnastics team** wins just its third medal in Olympic history, taking the silver behind fantastic efforts by the Hamm twins, Jason Gatson and Blaine Wilson. Japan wins the gold while Romania takes the bronze.

Ian Thorpe wins the anticipated 200-meter freestyle head-to-head showdown ahead of the Netherlands' Pieter van den Hoogenband and bronze medalist Michael Phelps.

17 **The NCAA rules against** Colorado's Jeremy Bloom in his request to play football for the Buffaloes after accepting endorsement money to finance his freestyle skiing career.

Klete Keller holds off a charging Ian Thorpe to give the U.S. 4x200-meter freestyle team the gold over Australia.

The U.S. women's gymnastics team is upset by Romania, but still takes the silver.

18 **American gymnast Paul Hamm** bounces back from a nasty fall into the scorers' table during his vault to deliver an amazing high bar routine and win the men's all-around gold medal by .012 points. Bronze medalist Yang Tae Young of South Korea complains of a scoring error but the gold is still awarded to Hamm. The decision triggers the most Olympic-related controversy and discussion since Tonya's henchmen whacked Nancy in 1994.

The U.S. women's 4x200-freestyle relay team wins the gold and smashes the 17-year-old world record held by East Germany.

19 **Carly Patterson becomes** the first American woman since Mary Lou Retton in 1984 to win the all-around gold in women's gymnastics. Russian diva Svetlana Khorkina wins the silver.

21 **Michael Phelps gives up** his spot on the 400-meter medley relay to teammate Ian Crocker. The squad wins gold and Phelps finishes with six gold and two bronze medals.

22 **American Justin Gatlin** can now call himself the fastest man in the world after winning Olympic gold in the 100-meter dash. Teammate Maurice Greene takes third.

Hockey fans everywhere gasp as the Stanley Cup is lost in transit on a flight from Vancouver to Fort St. John, B.C. It was found later, back in Vancouver.

23 **The U.S. women's softball team,** led by head coach Mike Candrea who lost his wife to a brain aneurysm just a month earlier, beats Australia, 5-1, in the gold medal game. It's the first run the team had given up all tournament, as they go 9-0 and outscore their opponents 51-1.

24 **Top-seeded women's beach volleyballers** Kerri Walsh and Misty May win the gold medal over Brazil.

25 **Rulon Gardener,** surprise winner of the 2000 Greco-Roman gold over undefeated Alexander Karelin, wins the bronze in Athens then removes his wrestling shoes and walks off the mat for good.

Windsurfer Gal Fridman wins the first-ever Israeli gold medal and dedicates it to the 11 athletes killed at the 1972 Games in Munich.

The Greek crowd goes wild as one of their own, Fani Halkia wins gold in the 400-meter hurdles.

26 **Mia Hamm, Brandi Chastain, Julie Foudy** and co. go out on top as they lead the U.S. women's soccer team to a 2-1 OT victory over Brazil in the gold medal game.

27 **The NCAA refuses** to restore eligibility to USC wide receiver Mike Williams, who was denied entry into the NFL draft by a court ruling.

The U.S. men's basketball team is ousted by eventual gold medalist Argentina, 89-81, and goes on to win a disappointing bronze medal. The women's team, however, wins gold the following day with a 74-63 win over Australia.

September 2004

Sun	Mon	Tue	Wed	Thu	Fri	Sat
			1	2	3	4
5	6	7	8	9	10	11
12	13	14	15	16	17	18
19	20	21	22	23	24	25
26	27	28	29	30		

Quote of the Month

"Even with wings you never as fly as me...you remind me of Kobe Bryant trying to be high as me...but you can't...even if you get me traded...wherever I'm at, I'm Puffy; you Mase and you're still hated."

Shaquille O'Neal, Miami Heat center, taking a shot at former Lakers teammate Kobe Bryant on his new CD.

SPORTSNATION Polls

Frank Francisco's chair throw

Who is most responsible for the incident escalating out of control?

38.5% —	Frank Francisco
33.7% —	Ballpark security
21.2% —	Fans
6.6% —	Other Texas players

Which was the worst incident between fans and on-field personnel?

68.3% —	Kansas City's Tom Gamboa attacked at Comiskey.
21.6% —	Frank Francisco throws a chair into the stands.
7.1% —	Karim Garcia-Jeff Nelson brawl with Boston groundskeeper.
3.0% —	Dodgers pursue stolen cap into Wrigley stands.

Total Votes: 122,864

1 **"Neon" Deion Sanders** leaves the TV studio and comes out of retirement to join what already appears to be the best defense in the NFL, the Baltimore Ravens.

The trial date for Vancouver's Todd Bertuzzi's assault on Colorado Avalanche center Steve Moore is slated to begin Jan. 17. Last week he appeared in court and pleaded not guilty.

2 **The mother of Tigers reliever** Ugueth Urbina is kidnapped from her home in Venezuela by four men disguised as police officers.

3 **Yankees hurler Kevin Brown** breaks his left hand when he punches a wall in the Yankee Stadium clubhouse during a 3-1 loss to Baltimore.

4 **Hurricane Frances wreaks havoc,** canceling various events all over the southeastern United States.

6 **Vijay Singh shoots a** final round 69 at the Deutsche Bank Classic in Norton, Mass. to not only beat Tiger Woods for the tournament win, but to also replace him as the No. 1 ranked golfer in the world. Woods had held the top spot in the official World Golf Rankings for more than five years, a record 264 weeks.

7 **Serena Williams is eliminated** by Jennifer Capriati in the quarterfinals of the U.S. Open, 2-6, 6-4, 6-4. The match gets a little testy in the first game of the final set when a questionable overruling goes in favor of Capriati. Williams argues her case but to no avail.

Iranian officials give $125,000 to Arash Miresmaeili, the judo champ who refused to fight Israeli Ehud Vaks in the Olympics because Iran does not recognize Israel. The amount is what he would have won had he won the gold.

9 **The Kansas City Royals** crush the Detroit Tigers, 26-5 in the opening game of their doubleheader. In Game 2, they're shut out, 8-0.

The New England Patriots pick up where they left off, frustrating Colts quarterback Peyton Manning and beating the Colts, 27-24, in the first NFL game of the 2004 season. Kicker Mike Vanderjagt misses a game-tying 48-yard field goal with 19 seconds left.

10 **Now ACC foes,** Florida State and Miami play another instant classic with Miami winning its sixth straight, 16-10, in overtime on an 18-yard Frank Gore touchdown.

The United States falls, 2-1, to Finland in the semifinals of the World Cup of Hockey and is eliminated, ruining their bid to defend their 1996 title.

11 **Notre Dame,** led by freshman running back Darius Walker's 115 yards rushing and two touchdowns, upsets eighth-ranked Michigan, 28-20, in South Bend.

In an all-Russian U.S. Open women's final, Svetlana Kuznetsova beats Elena Dementieva, 6-3, 7-5, for her first grand slam title.

Jeremy Mayfield's win at Richmond allows him to slip into the top 10 in the point standings, making him eligible for the NASCAR points championship. The field for the "Chase for the Nextel Cup" is now set, with Jeff Gordon starting the final 10 races in first place.

12 **In the first full slate** of NFL games, Joe Gibbs' return to the Redskins is a successful one as Washington beats Tampa Bay, 16-10, while Terrell Owens makes an impressive debut with the Eagles, hauling in three touchdowns from Donovan McNabb in a 31-17 win over the Giants.

Roger Federer becomes the first man since Mats Wilander in 1988 to win three Grand Slam events in one year with a dominating 6-0, 7-6, 6-0 victory over Australian Lleyton Hewitt.

13 **During an ugly brawl** between Oakland A's fans and the Rangers' bullpen, reliever Frank Francisco inexplicably hurls a chair into the crowd, breaking a woman's nose.

AP/Wide World Photos

Oakland A's fans develop their own creative, protective headgear a day after a nasty brawl between the Texas Rangers bullpen and the surrounding fans ends with reliever Frank Francisco hurling a chair into the crowd.

14 Canada wins the 2004 World Cup of Hockey with a tightly contested 3-2 victory over Finland at the Air Canada Centre in Toronto. Shane Doan scores the go-ahead goal on a pretty feed from Joe Thornton 34 seconds into the third period. The win is bittersweet, however, because...

The dreaded NHL lockout begins at midnight when the collective bargaining agreement expires. With the owners and the Players Association so far apart on the important issues, it's expected that the lockout could be a prolonged one. Owners are demanding a "cost certain" economic system, which the players see as a euphemism for a salary cap.

15 Art Howe is fired as manager of the New York Mets, but is allowed to finish out the season.

16 Dodgers fan and entrepreneur Michael Mahan buys an entire section of seats in the rightfield stands for $25,000 for two of the final three games of the season with San Francisco, hoping that Barry Bonds' 700th home run might land there. Problem is, Bonds is way ahead of Mahan's schedule, however Mahan is still selling the tix for a profit.

17 Barry Bonds cracks home run No. 700 off San Diego's Jake Peavy, joining Hank Aaron (755) and Babe Ruth (714) as exclusive members of that club.

Europe takes a commanding 6½-1½ lead on the first day of the 35th Ryder Cup at Bloomfield Hills, Mich. The curious pairing of Tiger Woods and Phil Mickelson goes 0-2 on the day.

Texas reliever Frank Francisco is suspended for the remainder of the season for tossing a chair into the stands in Oakland earlier this week during a battle with hecklers.

18 Bernard Hopkins lands a devastating shot to the midsection of Oscar De La Hoya, knocking him out in the ninth round of their middleweight title fight, as he had promised.

19 The massacre is over as Europe retains the Ryder Cup with an impressive 18½-9½ victory over the U.S. It's the worst loss for a U.S. team in Ryder Cup history.

20 NASCAR driver Robby Gordon apologizes for purposefully spinning out Greg Biffle at the New Hampshire International Speedway the day before. The crash also takes out Tony Stewart and Jeremy Mayfield, who are part of the Chase for the Nextel Cup.

23 Tyler Hamilton, who won a cycling gold medal for the U.S. but has recently come under fire over a failed blood test, will be allowed to keep his gold due to a laboratory foul-up.

Cubs hurler Greg Maddux reaches the 15-win plateau for a major league record 17th consecutive year.

24 A judge rules that retired Dolphins running back Ricky Williams must reimburse the team $8.6 million that he had earned playing football. The total includes $5.3 million paid by the Dolphins and $3.3 million in signing bonus paid by New Orleans in 1999.

26 Vijay Singh wins the 84 Lumber Classic in Pennsylvania and in the process, breaks the all-time PGA Tour mark for earnings in one season ($9,188,321) set by Tiger Woods in 2000.

28 San Francisco's Candlestick Park acquires a new sponsor (Monster Cable) in a deal worth an reported $6 million and will now be known as Monster Park.

29 Major League Baseball officially announces what had been rumored for some time — the Montreal Expos will relocate to Washington, D.C. for the 2005 season. The deal is contingent on the proper financing for a new ballpark, but it is expected that the details will be worked out. Until the new park is finished, the team will play its home games at RFK Stadium.

October 2004

Sun	Mon	Tue	Wed	Thu	Fri	Sat
					1	2
3	4	5	6	7	8	9
10	11	12	13	14	15	16
17	18	19	20	21	22	23
24/31	25	26	27	28	29	30

Quote of the Month

"It's awesome, dude. You can launch a wiener in there."

Tommy Lee, Motley Crue drummer and now a member of the University of Nebraska marching band, explaining how cool it is to control the school's hand-held air cannon that shoots hot dogs into the crowd. Lee enrolled in the school for the filming of a possible reality TV show.

SportsNation Polls

ALCS Comeback

Where does this season's ALCS rank in post-season history?

47.0%	—	The best series
42.0%	—	Top 5
6.0%	—	Top 10
5.0%	—	Good but not great

Total Votes: 110,819

Ichiro hits record

Ichiro's chase of George Sisler's 84-year-old hits record never exactly became a media circus. Why?

33.8%	—	People dig the long ball.
23.0%	—	Mariners miss the postseason.
22.9%	—	I have no idea but it's a shame.
20.4%	—	People aren't familiar with George Sisler.

Total Votes: 7,114

1   **Seattle Mariners right fielder Ichiro Suzuki** slaps a ground ball up the middle in the third inning against the Rangers for his second hit of the game and the 258th of the season, thus breaking George Sisler's 84-year-old record (257). For good measure, he adds two 259th three innings later and in the coming days would add three more to establish the mark at 262.

2   **On the penultimate day** of the Major League Baseball season, the Los Angeles Dodgers clinch the National League West on Steve Finley's ninth-inning walk-off grand slam against the San Francisco Giants. Elsewhere, the Cubs are eliminated from contention, adding to their historic woes, and the Anaheim Angels rally in the eighth to defeat the Oakland A's and clinch the American League West.

Larry Bowa is fired as manager of the disappointing Philadelphia Phillies.

Felix "Tito" Trinidad, in his first fight in two years, knocks down Richard Mayorga three times in the eighth round before the fight is finally stopped.

3   **Ernie Els wins** the American Express Championship in Ireland and in the process, supplants Tiger Woods as the No. 2-ranked golfer in the world behind Vijay Singh.

Dale Earnhardt Jr. passes Kevin Harvick with two laps remaining to win the EA Sports 500 at Talladega. After the race his enthusiasm gets the best of him and he utters one of George Carlin's "seven dirty words" in a TV interview. He is docked 25 points in the standings and fined $10,000.

Brandon Backe pitches the Houston Astros to a 5-3 win over Rockies on the final day of the regular season, to send them to the postseason with a wildcard berth.

Roger Federer beats Andy Roddick, 6-4, 6-0, in the finals of the Thailand Open. He joins John McEnroe and Bjorn Borg as the only men in the last 25 years to win 12 straight ATP finals.

Adrian Fernandez wins the Indy Racing League's Toyota 400 in Fontana, Calif., but Tony Kanaan's runner-up finish clinches him the overall IRL season-long points title.

4   **After a 99-loss season,** manager Bob Melvin is canned by the Seattle Mariners.

5   **Scottie Pippen,** six-time champion with the Chicago Bulls and one of the NBA's Top 50 Players, retires.

6   **With a guest list that** includes Charles Barkley, Michael Jordan and Oprah Winfrey, the long-rumored wedding of Tiger Woods and Swedish model/nanny Elin Nordgren takes place at a swanky resort in Barbados. Estimated cost of the affair is $1.5 million.

7   **Volatile Dodgers outfielder** Milton Bradley is under fire again, a day after calling *Los Angeles Times* reporter Jason Reid an "Uncle Tom" in a postgame confrontation. It is Bradley's first game back from a suspension caused by a bottle-throwing incident.

8   **David Ortiz'** walk-off 10th inning home run off Jarrod Washburn gives the Red Sox a 3-0 series win over Anaheim, sending them to the ALCS against...

9   **The New York Yankees,** down 5-1 in the eighth, bounce back to beat the Minnesota Twins, 6-5, in 11 innings and win their series 3 games to 1.

Nebraska falls, 70-10, to Texas Tech, its worst loss in the 114-year history of the program. Also, Tennessee puts themselves in the driver's seat in the SEC-East with a 19-14 win over third-ranked Georgia.

10   **The New England Patriots** set an (unofficial) NFL record by winning its 19th consecutive game, including the postseason, with a 24-10 victory over the Miami Dolphins.

Michael Schumacher, who had already clinched his seventh Formula One points title, wins his record 13th race of the season at the Japanese Grand Prix.

AP/Wide World Photos

Fan **Jim Sarkisian** holds up a sign at the Patriots-Dolphins game on Oct. 10, celebrating both the New England Patriots' record 19-game winning streak and his hope for Red Sox postseason success.

Former National League MVP Ken Caminiti is found dead of a drug overdose in the Bronx at age 41.

11 **The Houston Astros** defeat the Atlanta Braves, 12-3, for its first postseason series victory in 43 years and will face the St. Louis Cardinals in the NLCS.

12 **Betty Lennox pours in 23 points** in Game 3 of the WNBA Finals to carry the Seattle Storm to a 74-60 victory over the Connecticut Sun and its first league title. For her efforts, Lennox takes home the Finals MVP award.

14 **Lindsay Davenport** regains the WTA No. 1 ranking for the first time in two years with her second-round victory at the Kremlin Cup in Moscow.

Retief Goosen sets an all-time record for margin of victory at a match play event, trouncing Jeff Maggert, 12&11, at the World Match Play Championship.

16 **The New York Yankees** pound pitcher Bronson Arroyo and any other pitcher Boston tries, and thrash the Red Sox, 19-8, in Fenway to take a seemingly insurmountable 3-0 series lead in the ALCS.

17 **Ernie Els edges** Lee Westwood, 2&1, to win the World Match Play Championship and the accompanying $1.8 million first-place prize. It is the record sixth World Match play title for Els.

The Indy Racing League season comes to a close with Helio Castroneves winning the Chevy 500, but perhaps more impressively, Tony Kanaan becomes the first driver to complete every lap in every race of the season, 3,305 in all.

18 **Jeff Kent's walk-off home run** gives the Astros a 3-0 win over the Cardinals and a 3-2 series lead in the NLCS.

Minnesota's Daunte Culpepper throws for five touchdowns for the third time in his first five games of the season in a Monday night win over New Orleans.

19 **Pitching with a stitched-up, bloody right ankle,** Boston ace Curt Schilling bounces back from a rough start in Game 2 to propel the Red Sox to a 4-2 victory over the Yankees to tie the ALCS at three games apiece. The game features two overturned umpire decisions. The first one awards Mark Bellhorn a home run after his ball clearly strikes a fan over the leftfield wall, and on the other, Alex Rodriguez is called out for slapping the ball out of pitcher Bronson Arroyo's glove in the first base line.

Disgruntled Raiders receiver Jerry Rice is shipped to the Seattle Seahawks, where he will likely (and hopefully) close out his Hall of Fame career.

20 **The Red Sox' impossible comeback** is complete as Derek Lowe shuts down the powerful Yankee offense in a 10-3 Boston win. Johnny Damon smacks two home runs (including a grand slam) as the Red Sox advance to the World Series and become the first team in major league history to come back from a 3-0 series deficit in the postseason.

21 **The St. Louis Cardinals** get to Houston's Roger Clemens as Scott Rolen's sixth-inning, two-run shot leads their team to a 5-2 win in Game 7 of the NLCS.

Two months after his performance in Athens, gymnast Paul Hamm is officially and definitively awarded the men's all-around gold medal by the Court of Arbitration for Sport.

24 **Tragedy strikes NASCAR** when an airplane belonging to Hendrick Motorsports crashes on its way to the race in Martinsville, Va., killing 10 people including several members of team owner Rick Hendrick's family.

27 **The legendary drought is over!** The Boston Red Sox defeat the St. Louis Cardinals, 3-0, to complete a four game sweep and win the team's first World Series title since 1918. Manny Ramirez wins the Series' MVP award.

Preview 2005

A brief look at the sports world's major question marks for 2005.

AP/Wide World Photos

*Can **Barry Bonds** hit 53 home runs to pass Hank Aaron as the all-time home run king?*

AP/Wide World Photos

*Will we ever see **NHL hockey** again? And if so, how many teams will be left standing?*

AP/Wide World Photos

*Can **Tiger Woods** rebound from a subpar year (by his standards) and return to winning majors?*

AP/Wide World Photos

*Will New York City be successful in its bid for the **2012 Summer Olympics**?*

Baseball

Boston hero **Curt Schilling** fought through an injured ankle to give the Red Sox much-needed wins in the ALCS and World Series.

AP/Wide World Photos

1918-2004

The Boston Red Sox exorcise their demons and win the World Series for the first time in 86 years.

Karl Ravech
is an analyst for ESPN's baseball coverage.

In the end, the 2004 edition of the Boston Red Sox turned out to be a bunch of idiot savants, not merely the idiots they had labeled themselves during the most magical baseball season Boston had seen in almost a century. The Red Sox may not have been the most learned or clean-cut class of ball player but they were acutely aware of their roles. And when collectively taken between the white lines, they were the best team in the major leagues.

The difference between the 2004 Red Sox and other editions of Boston's home-town team is that this team actually won the World Series. The 86-year-old Curse, born the day the Red Sox sold Babe Ruth to the Yankees, was officially killed when Edgar Renteria of the St. Louis Cardinals, wearing the same number 3 made most famous by the Babe himself, grounded out to Red Sox reliever Keith Foulke, thus closing out one of the

most lopsided and anti-climactic World Series in recent memory.

Boston dusted St. Louis, four games to none. The Red Sox starting pitching, featuring Curt Schilling, Pedro Martinez and Derek Lowe, proved superior to the vaunted Cardinals offense, which during the regular season helped contribute to a major league high 105 wins. This was the Series that never was a series. Instead the argument could be made that the *real* World Series was actually played the week before.

The greatest rivalry in baseball has long been the Red Sox and Yankees. The teams met in the 2003 American League Championship Series and it wasn't decided until the 11th inning of Game 7, when Aaron Boone hit a home run off Red Sox reliever Tim Wakefield. As the teams advanced again to the 2004 ALCS, the prevailing thought was that there was no way in Red Sox Hell (a constant state of mind for Boston's baseball fans) that the

AP/Wide World Photos

Pedro Martinez, Curt Schilling and David Ortiz were instrumental in leading the Red Sox to the promised land for the first time since 1918.

two teams could top the drama of '03. It turned out everyone was wrong.

For the first time in the history of Major League Baseball, a team blew a three-games-to-none lead in the best-of-seven playoff format. This wasn't just any team, it was the 26-time World Champion New York Yankees. The team with history on its side. Their opponent was their most fierce competitor—some would say rival, but if you adhere to the notion that a rival actually wins as often as the opponent, then you know these teams aren't rivals, they're competitors. The Yankees always win.

New York won the first two games of the Series at home, then traveled to Boston and won Game 3 by the hideously one-sided score of 19-8. The Yankees were one game away, in fact three outs away, when manager Joe Torre brought in the most automatic thing in pinstripes, closer Mariano Rivera. It didn't work. In fact it blew up, or at the very least it lit the fuse which ignited the charge that blew up the record books. The Red Sox won Game 4 of the ALCS and never lost again.

Their dramatic and historic comeback was followed by a ho-hum four-game sweep of the Cardinals, who as it turned

AP/Wide World Photos

*Mariners rightfielder **Ichiro Suzuki** set a new MLB record for hits an a season in 2004 (262), breaking George Sisler's mark that had stood since 1920.*

out were nothing more than a bunch of pavers on the Red Sox walk into history. Eight straight postseason wins.

Boston's heroes were many: World Series Most Valuable Player Manny Ramirez, longhaired centerfielder Johnny Damon, who authored the, "we're just a bunch of idiots" mantra. Power-hitting David Ortiz, nicknamed "Papi." When the Red Sox needed a home run, he hit one. Curt Schilling, who pitched with blood seeping through his white sock, literally turning it into a red sock because of some experimental surgery he needed before taking the mound so that the pain in his ankle would be reduced enough for him to

throw. It sounds like the stuff the Yankees have been made of for so long...but this time it was the Red Sox.

Boston was a brilliantly built team, and the architect was a 30-year-old Yale grad who got his baseball education in places like Baltimore and San Diego. Theo Epstein understood the value of pitching and defense. He traded the team's most popular player, shortstop Nomar Garciaparra, at the trading deadline and for weeks couldn't walk the streets of Boston without someone cursing him out. Who knew his devotion to those disciplines, pitching and defense, would eventually silence all curses?

continued on page 64 ▶

The Ten Biggest Stories of the Year in Baseball

10 Roger Clemens gives back his gold Rolex and comes out of retirement to pitch for his hometown Houston Astros. "The Rocket" still has plenty of fuel left in the tank, registering an 18-4 record, 2.98 ERA and yet another 200-strikeout season. Most importantly, he pitches the Astros into the NLCS where they'd lose in seven.

9 During an ugly brawl between the Rangers' bullpen and heckling fans at Oakland's Network Associates Coliseum, reliever Frank Francisco throws a chair into the crowd, breaking a fan's nose. He is suspended for the remainder of the season and charged with aggravated battery.

8 On July 5, the Diamondbacks score two runs in the ninth inning to come from behind and tie the Los Angeles Dodgers, 5-5. What makes this rally different than most, however, is that it's off Eric Gagne, putting an end to the closer's consecutive saves streak at 84. The Dodgers win, 6-5, in the 10th.

7 Barry Bonds continues his rapid ascent up the all-time home run list, first passing his godfather Willie Mays, then becoming the third member of the exclusive 700 Club. He does this while rarely getting a pitch to hit, as evidenced by his record-shattering 232 walks.

6 The Montreal Expos become Major League Baseball's first team to change cities since 1972, leaving their home north of the border for Washington, D.C. beginning in 2005.

5 Randy Johnson issues Major League Baseball's 17th official perfect game, retiring all 27 Atlanta Braves hitters in a 2-0 Arizona win on May 18. It is the second career no-hitter for the "Big Unit" and at age 40, he becomes the oldest pitcher to throw a perfect game.

4 Tony La Russa's St. Louis Cardinals record a major league high 105 regular season wins, then defeat the Dodgers and Astros to reach the World Series. The Cards' 3-4-5 hitters (Albert Pujols, Scott Rolen and Jim Edmonds) combine for 122 home runs and 358 RBI.

3 Seattle Mariners rightfielder Ichiro Suzuki slaps 262 hits to break George Sisler's 84-year-old single-season record (257). He finishes the season with a .372 batting average.

2 The Boston Red Sox become the first team in major league history to come back from an 3-0 deficit in a best-of-seven series, shocking the New York Yankees in the ALCS to advance to the World Series. Pitcher Curt Schilling gives one of the grittier performances in recent memory in Game 6, throwing seven strong innings on a bloody ankle.

1 Pigs fly. Hell freezes over. And the Curse of the Bambino is no more. The Boston Red Sox win their first World Series in 86 years with a 4-0 series sweep of the St. Louis Cardinals.

When the final out of the World Series was recorded in St. Louis, Red Sox players acted like complete idiots. Running around with their arms out looking for anyone and anything to grab a hold of. There were high-fives and head butts. There were tears of joy when first year manager Terry Francona bear hugged David Ortiz.

There was Manny, who in spite of the significance of his team's giant accomplishment, chose to point out was that he was, "going to Disney World."

Dreams do come true, even the impossible ones.

It Ain't Over till it's Over

In the ALCS against the Yankees, the Boston Red Sox became the first team in MLB history, and third in any major North American professional sport, to win a series after falling behind, three games to none.

Sport	3-0 Deficits	Comebacks
MLB	26	1
NBA	73	0
NHL	140	2
TOTAL	239	3

Note: The two NHL teams to accomplish the feat are the 1975 New York Islanders (Stanley Cup quarterfinals against Pittsburgh) and the 1942 Toronto Maple Leafs (Stanley Cup finals against Detroit).

Source: Elias Sports Bureau

Perfecto!

Randy Johnson's perfect game on May 18 was the second no-hitter of his Hall of Fame career, the first coming against the Detroit Tigers in 1990 as a member of the Seattle Mariners. The span of 14 years between no-no's is the longest in MLB history.

Pitcher	Years	Span (in yrs.)
Randy Johnson	1990-2004	14
Nolan Ryan	1981-1990	9
Cy Young	1897-1904	7
Nolan Ryan	1975-1981	6
Bob Feller	1940-1946	6
Jim Bunning	1958-1964	6

In 2004, Seattle's Ichiro Suzuki and San Francisco's Barry Bonds led the American League and National League, respectively, in batting average.

Did you know, the 127-hit differential between the league leaders (262 for Ichiro, 135 for Bonds) is the largest in MLB history? It eclipses the 1911 margin of 90 (Ty Cobb 248, Honus Wagner 158).

2004
Season in Review

SPORTS ALMANAC

Final Major League Standings

Division champions (*) and Wild Card (†) winners are noted. Number of seasons listed after each manager refers to current tenure with club.

American League
East Division

	W	L	Pct	GB	Home	Road
*New York	101	61	.623	—	57-24	44-37
†Boston	98	64	.605	3	55-26	43-38
Baltimore	78	84	.481	23	38-43	40-41
Tampa Bay	70	91	.435	30½	41-39	29-52
Toronto	67	94	.416	33½	40-41	27-53

2004 Managers: NY–Joe Torre (9th season); **Bos**– Terry Francona (1st); **Bal**–Lee Mazzilli (1st); **TB**–Lou Piniella (2nd); **Tor**–Carlos Tosca (3rd, 47-64) was fired on Aug. 8 and replaced by first base coach John Gibbons (20-30). **2003 Standings:** 1. New York (101-61); 2. Boston (95-67); 3. Toronto (86-76); 4. Baltimore (71-91); 5. Tampa Bay (63-99).

Central Division

	W	L	Pct	GB	Home	Road
*Minnesota	92	70	.568	—	49-32	43-38
Chicago	83	79	.512	9	46-35	37-44
Cleveland	80	82	.494	12	44-37	36-45
Detroit	72	90	.444	20	38-43	34-47
Kansas City	58	104	.358	34	33-47	25-57

2004 Managers: Min–Ron Gardenhire (3rd season); **Chi**–Ozzie Guillen (1st); **Cle**–Eric Wedge (2nd); **Det**–Alan Trammell (2nd); **KC**–Tony Pena (3rd). **2003 Standings:** 1. Minnesota (90-72); 2. Chicago (86-76); 3. Kansas City (83-79); 4. Cleveland (68-94); 5. Detroit (43-119).

West Division

	W	L	Pct	GB	Home	Road
*Anaheim	92	70	.568	—	45-36	47-34
Oakland	91	71	.562	1	52-29	39-42
Texas	89	73	.549	3	51-30	38-43
Seattle	63	99	.389	29	38-44	25-55

2004 Managers: Ana–Mike Scioscia (5th season); **Oak**–Ken Macha (2nd); **Tex**–Buck Showalter (2nd); **Sea**–Bob Melvin (2nd). **2003 Standings:** 1. Oakland (96-66); 2. Seattle (93-69); 3. Anaheim (77-85); 4. Texas (71-91).

National League
East Division

	W	L	Pct	GB	Home	Road
*Atlanta	96	66	.593	—	49-32	47-34
Philadelphia	86	76	.531	10	42-39	44-37
Florida	83	79	.512	13	42-38	41-41
New York	71	91	.438	25	42-39	29-52
Montreal	67	95	.414	29	35-45	32-50

2004 Managers: Atl–Bobby Cox (15th season); **Phi**–Larry Bowa (4th); **Fla**–Jack McKeon (2nd); **NY**–Art Howe (2nd); **Mon**– Frank Robinson (3rd). **2003 Standings:** 1. Atlanta (101-61); 2. Florida (91-71); 3. Philadelphia (86-76); 4. Montreal (83-79); 5. New York (66-95).

Central Division

	W	L	Pct	GB	Home	Road
*St. Louis	105	57	.648	—	53-28	52-29
†Houston	92	70	.568	13	48-33	44-37
Chicago	89	73	.549	16	45-37	44-36
Cincinnati	76	86	.469	29	40-41	36-45
Pittsburgh	72	89	.447	32½	39-41	33-48
Milwaukee	67	94	.416	37½	36-45	31-49

2004 Managers: St.L–Tony La Russa (9th season); **Hou**–Jimy Williams (3rd, 44-44) was fired on July 14 and replaced by Phil Garner (48-26); **Chi**–Dusty Baker (2nd); **Cin**–Dave Miley (2nd); **Pit**–Lloyd McClendon (4th); **Mil**–Ned Yost (2nd). **2003 Standings:** 1. Chicago (88-74); 2. Houston (87-75); 3. St. Louis (85-77); 4. Pittsburgh (75-87); 5. Cincinnati (69-93); 6. Milwaukee (68-94).

West Division

	W	L	Pct	GB	Home	Road
*Los Angeles	93	69	.574	—	49-32	44-37
San Francisco	91	71	.562	2	47-35	44-36
San Diego	87	75	.537	6	42-39	45-36
Colorado	68	94	.420	25	38-43	30-51
Arizona	51	111	.315	42	29-52	22-59

2004 Managers: LA–Jim Tracy (4th season); **SF**–Felipe Alou (2nd); ; **SD**–Bruce Bochy (10th); **Col**– Clint Hurdle (3rd); **Ari**–Bob Brenly (4th, 29-50) was fired on July 2 and replaced by third base coach Al Pedrique (22-61). **2003 Standings:** 1. San Francisco (100-61); 2. Los Angeles (85-77); 3. Arizona (84-78); 4. Colorado (74-88); 5. San Diego (64-98).

Interleague Play Standings

American League

	W-L	Pct		W-L	Pct
Tampa Bay	15-3	.833	Seattle	9-9	.500
Minnesota	11-7	.611	Chicago	8-10	.444
New York	10-8	.556	Toronto	8-10	.444
Cleveland	10-8	.556	Anaheim	7-11	.389
Oakland	10-8	.556	Kansas City	6-12	.333
Texas	10-8	.556	Baltimore	5-13	.278
Boston	9-9	.500	**Totals**	**127-125**	**.504**
Detroit	9-9	.500			

National League

	W-L	Pct		W-L	Pct
St. Louis	11-1	.917	Colorado	8-10	.444
Chicago	8-4	.667	San Diego	8-10	.444
Milwaukee	8-4	.667	Cincinnati	5-7	.417
San Francisco	11-7	.611	Florida	7-11	.389
Houston	7-5	.583	Montreal	7-11	.389
Los Angeles	10-8	.556	Arizona	6-12	.333
New York	10-8	.556	Pittsburgh	2-10	.167
Philadelphia	9-9	.500	**Totals**	**125-127**	**.496**
Atlanta	8-10	.444			

Seattle Mariners
Ichiro Suzuki
Batting Avg., Hits

Anaheim Angels
Vladimir Guerrero
Runs, Total Bases

Minnesota Twins
Johan Santana
ERA, Opp. BA, WHIP, K

New York Yankees
Mariano Rivera
Saves

American League Leaders
(*) indicates rookie.

Batting

	Bat	Gm	AB	R	H	Avg	TB	2B	3B	HR	RBI	BB	SO	SB	Slg Pct	OBP
Ichiro Suzuki, Sea	L	161	704	101	262	.372	320	24	5	8	60	49	63	36	.455	.414
Melvin Mora, Bal	R	140	550	111	187	.340	309	41	0	27	104	66	95	11	.562	.419
Vladimir Guerrero, Ana	R	156	612	124	206	.337	366	39	2	39	126	52	74	15	.598	.391
Ivan Rodriguez, Det	R	135	527	72	176	.334	269	32	2	19	86	41	91	7	.510	.383
Erubiel Durazo, Oak	L	142	511	80	164	.321	267	35	1	22	88	56	104	3	.523	.396
Carlos Guillen, Det	S	136	522	97	166	.318	283	37	10	20	97	52	87	12	.542	.379
Javy Lopez, Bal	R	150	579	83	183	.316	291	33	3	23	86	47	97	0	.503	.370
Mark Kotsay, Oak	L	148	606	78	190	.314	278	37	3	15	63	55	70	8	.459	.370
Michael Young, Tex	R	160	690	114	216	.313	333	33	9	22	99	44	89	12	.483	.353
Travis Hafner, Cle	L	140	482	96	150	.311	281	41	3	28	109	68	111	3	.583	.410
Miguel Tejada, Bal	R	162	653	107	203	.311	349	40	2	34	150	48	73	4	.534	.360
Aaron Rowand, Chi	R	140	487	94	151	.310	265	38	2	24	69	30	91	17	.544	.361
Manny Ramirez, Bos	R	152	568	108	175	.308	348	44	0	43	130	82	124	2	.613	.397
Carlos Lee, Chi	R	153	591	103	180	.305	310	37	3	31	99	54	86	11	.525	.366
Johnny Damon, Bos	L	150	621	123	189	.304	296	35	6	20	94	76	71	19	.477	.380

Note: Batters must have 3.1 plate appearances per their team's games played to qualify.

Home Runs
Ramirez, Bos 43
Konerko, Chi 41
Ortiz, Bos 41
Guerrero, Ana 39
Teixeira, Tex 38
Rodriguez, NY 36
Sheffield, NY 36
Tejada, Bal 34
Blalock, Tex 32
Delgado, Tor 32

Triples
Crawford, TB 19
Figgins, Ana 17
Guillen, Det 10
Infante, Det 9
M. Young, Tex 9
Cruz, TB 8
Five tied with 7 each.

On Base Pct.
Mora, Bal .... .419
Suzuki, Sea ...... .414
Hafner, Cle ...... .410
Posada, NY .... .400
Chavez, Oak ...... .397
Ramirez, Bos ..... .397
Durazo, Oak ...... .396
Sheffield, NY .... .393

Runs Batted In
Tejada, Bal 150
Ortiz, Bos 139
Ramirez, Bos 130
Guerrero, Ana 126
Sheffield, NY 121
Konerko, Chi 117
Teixeira, Tex 112
Blalock, Tex 110
Hafner, Cle 109
Martinez, Cle. 108
Matsui, NY 108

Doubles
Roberts, Bal. 50
Belliard, Cle 48
Ortiz, Bos 47
Jeter, NY 44
Ramirez, Bos 44
Three tied with 41 each.

Slugging Pct.
Ramirez, Bos ...... .613
Ortiz, Bos .... .603
Guerrero, Ana ..... .598
Hafner, Cle .... .583
Mora, Bal .... .562
Teixeira, Tex ..... .560
Rowand, Chi .... .544
Guillen, Det ...... .542

Hits
Suzuki, Sea 262
M. Young, Tex 216
Guerrero, Ana 206
Tejada, Bal 203
Kotsay, Oak 190
Damon, Bos 189
Jeter, NY 188
Mora, Bal 187
Crawford, TB 185

Runs
Guerrero, Ana 124
Damon, Bos 123
Sheffield, NY 117
M. Young, Tex 114
Rodriguez, NY 112
Jeter, NY 111
Mora, Bal 111
Lawton, Cle 109
Matsui, NY 109

Walks
Chavez, Oak 95
Sheffield, NY 92
Bellhorn, Bos 88
Matsui, NY 88
Posada, NY 88
Palmeiro, Bal 86
Williams, NY 85

Stolen Bases
	SB	CS
Crawford, TB	.59	15
Suzuki, Sea	.36	11
Figgins, Ana	.34	13
Roberts, Bal	.29	12
Rodriguez, NY	...28	4
Jeter, NY	.23	4
Lawton, Cle	.23	9

Total Bases
Guerrero, Ana 366
Ortiz, Bos 351
Tejada, Bal 349
Ramirez, Bos 348
M. Young, Tex 333
Suzuki, Sea 320
Blalock, Tex 312
Lee, Chi 310
Mora, Bal 309

Strikeouts
Bellhorn, Bos 177
Blalock, Tex 149
Pena, Det 146
Crosby*, Oak 141
Blake, Cle 139
Valentin, Chi 139
Boone, Sea 135

Pitching

	Arm	W	L	ERA	Gm	GS	CG	ShO	Sv	IP	H	R	ER	HR	HB	BB	SO	WP
Johan Santana, Min	L	20	6	2.61	34	34	1	1	0	228.0	156	70	66	24	9	54	265	7
Curt Schilling, Bos	R	21	6	3.26	32	32	3	0	0	226.2	206	84	82	23	5	35	203	3
Jake Westbrook, Cle	R	14	9	3.38	33	30	5	0	0	215.2	208	95	81	19	5	61	116	4
Brad Radke, Min	R	11	8	3.48	34	34	1	1	0	219.2	229	92	85	23	6	26	143	2
Tim Hudson, Oak	R	12	6	3.53	27	27	3	2	0	188.2	194	82	74	8	12	44	103	4
Rodrigo Lopez, Bal	R	14	9	3.59	37	23	1	1	0	170.2	164	71	68	21	2	54	121	4
Freddy Garcia, Sea-Chi	R	13	11	3.81	31	31	1	0	0	210.0	192	92	89	22	7	64	184	8
Mark Buehrle, Chi	L	16	10	3.89	35	35	4	1	0	245.1	257	119	106	33	8	51	165	0
Pedro Martinez, Bos	R	16	9	3.90	33	33	1	1	0	217.0	193	99	94	26	16	61	227	2
Kelvim Escobar, Ana	R	11	12	3.93	33	33	0	0	0	208.1	192	91	91	21	7	76	191	9
Rich Harden, Oak	R	11	7	3.99	31	31	0	0	0	189.2	171	90	84	16	3	81	167	4
Bronson Arroyo, Bos	R	10	9	4.03	32	29	0	0	0	178.2	171	99	80	17	20	47	142	5
Ted Lilly, Tor	L	12	10	4.06	32	32	2	1	0	197.1	171	92	89	26	6	89	168	6
C.C. Sabathia, Cle	L	11	10	4.12	30	30	1	0	0	188.0	176	90	86	20	7	72	139	1
Ryan Drese, Tex	R	14	10	4.20	34	33	2	0	0	207.2	233	104	97	16	11	58	98	1

Note: Pitchers must have one inning pitched per their team's games played to qualify.

Wins

Schilling, Bos 21-6
Santana, Min 20-6
Rogers, Tex 18-9
Colon, Ana 18-12
Mulder, Oak 17-8
Martinez, Bos 16-9
Buehrle, Chi 16-10
Nine tied with 14 each.

Appearances

Quantrill, NY 86
Gordon, NY 80
Rincon, Min 77
Ryan, Bal 76
Timlin, Bos 76
Myers, Sea-Bos 75
Marte, Chi 74
Rivera, NY 74
Romero, Min 74

Complete Games

Mulder, Oak 5
Ponson, Bal 5
Westbrook, Cle 5
Buehrle, Chi 4
Hudson, Oak 3
May, KC 3
Schilling, Bos 3
Twelve tied with 2 each.

Shutouts

Bonderman, Det 2
Hudson, Oak 2
Ponson, Bal 2
27 tied with 1 each.

Losses

May, KC 9-19
Franklin, Sea 4-16
Johnson, Det 8-15
Ponson, Bal 11-15
Hendrickson, TB . . 10-15
Moyer, Sea 7-13
Batista, Tor 10-13
Lohse, Min 9-13
Maroth, Det 11-13
Lackey, Ana 14-13
Bonderman, Det . . 11-13

Innings

Buehrle, Chi 245.1
Santana, Min 228.0
Schilling, Bos 226.2
Mulder, Oak 225.2
Radke, Min 219.2
Garland, Chi 217.0
Maroth, Det 217.0
Martinez, Bos 217.0
Ponson, Bal 215.2
Westbrook, Cle . . . 215.2

Saves

	SV	BS
Rivera, NY	.53	4
Cordero, Tex	.49	5
Nathan, Min	.44	3
Percival, Ana	.33	5
Foulke, Bos	.32	7
Baez, TB	.30	3
Dotel, Oak	.22	6
Julio, Bal	.22	4
Urbina, Det	.21	3
Takatsu, Chi	.19	1

Walks

Batista, Tor 96
Zambrano, TB 96
Lilly, TB 89
Cabrera*, Bal 89
Contreras, NY-Chi . . . 84
Mulder, Oak 83
Three tied with 81 each.

HRs Allowed

Moyer, Sea 44
May, KC 38
Colon, Ana 38
Garland, Chi 34
Anderson, KC 33
Vazquez, NY 33
Franklin, Sea 33
Buehrle, Chi 33

Wild Pitches

Contreras, Chi 17
Gregg*, Ana 13
Batista, Tor 12
Cabrera*, Bal 12
Vazquez, NY 12
Knotts, Det 11
Lackey, Ana 11

Hit Batters

Arroyo, Bos 20
Martinez, Bos 16
Wakefield, Bos 16
Zambrano, TB 16
Park, Tex 13
Villone, Sea 12
Hudson, Oak 12
Mulder, Oak 12

Strikeouts

Santana, Min 265
Martinez, Bos 227
Schilling, Bos 203
Escobar, Ana 191
Garcia, Sea-Chi 184
Bonderman, Det 168
Lilly, Tor 168
Harden, Oak 167
Buehrle, Chi 165
Zito, Oak 163

Opp. Batting Average

Santana, Min 192
Lilly, Tor 230
Martinez, Bos 238
Schilling, Bos 239
Bonderman, Det 242
Garcia, Sea-Chi 242
Harden, Oak 242
Escobar, Ana 244
Arroyo, Bos 249
Lopez, Bal 252

WHIP

(Walks + Hits/IP)

Santana, Min 0.92
Schilling, Bos 1.06
Radke, Min 1.16
Martinez, Bos 1.17
Arroyo, Bos 1.22
Garcia, Sea-Chi 1.22
Westbrook, Cle 1.25
Buehrle, Chi 1.26
Hudson, Oak 1.26
Lopez, Bal 1.28

Fielding

Put Outs

Hatteberg, Oak 1281
Teixeira, Tex 1210
Konerko, Chi 1149
Pena, Det 1142
Palmeiro, Bal 1089
Delgado, Tor 1041
Broussard, Cle 991
Erstad, Ana 986
Mientkiewicz, Min-Bos 926
Olerud, Sea-NY 917

Assists

Tejada, Bal 526
Crosby*, Oak 505
Hudson, Tor 449
Guzman, Min 440
Belliard, Cle 427
Roberts, Bal 426
M. Young, Tex 423
Lugo, TB 422
Soriano, Tex 418
Guillen, Det 417

OF Assists

Guerrero, Ana 13
Higginson, Det 13
Suzuki, Sea 12
Lee, Chi 11
Kotsay, Oak 11
Baldelli, TB 11
Sheffield, NY 11
Rios*, Tor 11
Byrnes, Oak 11
Three tied with 10 each.

Errors

Berroa, KC 28
Blake, Cle 26
Lugo, TB 25
Tejada, Bal 24
Soriano, Tex 23
Mora, Bal 21
Valentin, Chi 20
M. Young, Tex 19
Crosby*, Oak 19
Two tied with 17 each.

San Francisco Giants
Barry Bonds
BA, SLG, OBP, Walks

St. Louis Cardinals
Albert Pujols
Runs, Total Bases

San Diego Padres
Jake Peavy
ERA

Arizona Diamondbacks
Randy Johnson
K, WHIP, Opp. BA

National League Leaders

(*) indicates rookie.

Batting

	Bat	Gm	AB	R	H	Avg	TB	2B	3B	HR	RBI	BB	SO	SB	Slg Pct	OBP
Barry Bonds, SF	L	147	373	129	135	.362	303	27	3	45	101	232	41	6	.812	.609
Todd Helton, Col	L	154	547	115	190	.347	339	49	2	32	96	127	72	3	.620	.469
Mark Loretta, SD	R	154	620	108	208	.335	307	47	2	16	76	58	45	5	.495	.391
Adrian Beltre, LA	R	156	598	104	200	.334	376	32	0	48	121	53	87	7	.629	.388
Albert Pujols, St.L	R	154	592	133	196	.331	389	51	2	46	123	84	52	5	.657	.415
Juan Pierre, Fla	L	162	678	100	221	.326	276	22	12	3	49	45	35	45	.407	.374
Sean Casey, Cin	L	146	571	101	185	.324	305	44	2	24	99	46	36	2	.534	.381
Jason Kendall, Pit	R	147	574	86	183	.319	224	32	0	3	51	60	41	11	.390	.399
Aramis Ramirez, Chi	R	145	547	99	174	.318	316	32	1	36	103	49	62	0	.578	.373
Lance Berkman, Hou	S	160	544	104	172	.316	308	40	3	30	106	127	101	9	.566	.450
Scott Rolen, St.L	R	142	500	109	157	.314	299	32	4	34	124	72	92	4	.598	.409
Johnny Estrada, Atl	S	134	462	56	145	.314	208	36	0	9	76	39	66	0	.450	.378
Shea Hillenbrand, Ari	R	148	562	68	174	.310	261	36	3	15	80	24	49	2	.464	.348
Jack Wilson, Pit	R	157	652	82	201	.308	299	41	12	11	59	26	71	8	.459	.335
Tony Womack, St.L	L	145	553	91	170	.307	213	22	3	5	38	36	60	26	.385	.349

Note: Batters must have 3.1 plate appearances per their team's games played to qualify.

Home Runs

Beltre, LA	48
Dunn, Cin	46
Pujols, St.L	46
Bonds, SF	45
Edmonds, St.L	42
Thome, Phi	42
Alou, Chi	39
Burnitz, Col	37
Finley, Ari-LA	36
Ramirez, Chi	36

Triples

Pierre, Fla	12
Rollins, Phi	12
J. Wilson, Pit	12
Izturis, LA	9
Four tied with 8 each.	

On Base Pct.

Bonds, SF	.609
Helton, Col	.469
Berkman, Hou	.450
Drew, Atl	.436
Abreu, Phi	.428
Edmonds, St.L	.418
Pujols, St.L	.415
Rolen, St.L	.409
Kendall, Pit	.399

Runs Batted In

Castilla, Col	131
Rolen, St.L	124
Pujols, St.L	123
Beltre, LA	121
Cabrera, Fla	112
Edmonds, St.L	111
Batista, Mon	110
Burnitz, Col	110
Kent, Hou	107

Doubles

Overbay, Mil	53
Pujols, St.L	51
Helton, Col	49
Abreu, Phi	47
Biggio, Hou	47
Loretta, SD	47
Casey, Cin	44
Lowell, Fla	44

Slugging Pct.

Bonds, SF	.812
Pujols, St.L	.657
Edmonds, St.L	.643
Beltre, LA	.629
Helton, Col	.620
Rolen, St.L	.598
Thome, Phi	.581

Hits

Pierre, Fla	221
Loretta, SD	208
J. Wilson, Pit	201
Beltre, LA	200
Pujols, St.L	196
Izturis, LA	193
Helton, Col	190
Rollins, Phi	190
Casey, Cin	185

Runs

Pujols, St.L	133
Bonds, SF	129
Rollins, Phi	119
Abreu, Phi	118
Drew, Atl	118
Helton, Col	115
Wilkerson, Mon	112
Rolen, St.L	109

Walks

Bonds, SF	232
Abreu, Phi	127
Berkman, Hou	127
Helton, Col	127
Drew, Atl	118
Dunn, Cin	108
Wilkerson, Mon	106

Stolen Bases

	SB	CS
Podsednik, Mil	70	13
Pierre, Fla	45	24
Abreu, Phi	40	5
Freel, Cin	37	10
Roberts, LA	33	1
Chavez, Mon	32	7
Patterson, Chi	32	9
Rollins, Phi	30	9

Total Bases

Pujols, St.L	389
Beltre, LA	376
Helton, Col	339
Alou, Chi	335
Dunn, Cin	323
Edmonds, St.L	320
Ramirez, Chi	316
Abreu, Phi	312
Castilla, Col	312

Strikeouts

Dunn, Cin	195
C. Wilson, Pit	169
Patterson, Chi	168
Jenkins, Mil	152
Wilkerson, Mon	152
Edmonds, St.L	150

Pitching

	Arm	W	L	ERA	Gm	GS	CG	ShO	Sv	IP	H	R	ER	HR	HB	BB	SO	WP
Jake Peavy, SD	R	15	6	2.27	27	27	0	0	0	166.1	146	49	42	13	11	53	173	1
Randy Johnson, Ari	L	16	14	2.60	35	35	4	2	0	245.2	177	88	71	18	10	44	290	3
Ben Sheets, Mil	R	12	14	2.70	34	34	5	0	0	237.0	201	85	71	25	4	32	264	8
Carlos Zambrano, Chi	R	16	8	2.75	31	31	1	1	0	209.2	174	73	64	14	20	81	188	6
Roger Clemens, Hou	R	18	4	2.98	33	33	0	0	0	214.1	169	76	71	15	6	78	218	5
Oliver Perez, Pit	L	12	10	2.98	30	30	2	1	0	196.0	145	71	65	22	9	81	239	2
Carl Pavano, Fla	R	18	8	3.00	31	31	2	2	0	222.1	212	80	74	16	11	49	139	2
Jason Schmidt, SF	R	18	7	3.20	32	32	4	3	0	225.0	165	84	80	18	3	77	251	7
Al Leiter, NY	L	10	8	3.21	30	30	0	0	0	173.2	138	65	62	16	11	97	117	1
Odalis Perez, LA	L	7	6	3.25	31	31	0	0	0	196.1	180	76	71	26	4	44	128	2
Jaret Wright, Atl	R	15	8	3.28	32	32	0	0	0	186.1	168	79	68	11	3	70	159	3
Doug Davis, Mil	L	12	12	3.39	34	34	0	0	0	207.1	192	84	78	14	7	79	166	4
Chris Carpenter, St.L	R	15	5	3.46	28	28	1	0	0	182.0	169	75	70	24	8	38	152	4
Roy Oswalt, Hou	R	20	10	3.49	36	35	2	0	0	237.0	233	100	92	17	11	62	206	5
Brandon Webb, Ari	R	7	16	3.59	35	35	1	0	0	208.0	194	111	83	17	11	119	164	17

Note: Pitchers must have one inning pitched per their team's games played to qualify.

Wins

Oswalt, Hou	20-10
Clemens, Hou	18-4
Schmidt, SF	18-7
Pavano, Fla	18-8
Zambrano, Chi	16-8
Suppan, St.L	16-9
Maddux, Chi	16-11
Johnson, Ari	16-14

Eight tied with 15 each.

Losses

Webb, Ari	7-16
Fossum, Ari	4-15
Hernandez, Mon	11-15
Glavine, NY	11-14
Eaton, SD	11-14
Sheets, Mil	12-14
Lawrence, SD	15-14
Johnson, Ari	16-14

Walks

Webb, Ari	119
Ortiz, Atl	112
Estes, Col	105
Jennings, Col	101
Ishii, LA	98
Leiter, NY	97
Trachsel, NY	83
Hernandez, Mon	83

Strikeouts

Johnson, Ari	290
Sheets, Mil	264
Schmidt, SF	251
Perez, Pit	239
Clemens, Hou	218
Oswalt, Hou	206
Clement, Chi	190
Zambrano, Chi	188
Hernandez, Mon	186
Peavy, SD	173

Appearances

Brower, SF	89
King, St.L	86
Cormier, Phi	84
Reitsma, Atl	84
Torres, Pit	84
Eyre, SF	83
Stanton, NY	83
Ayala, Mon	81

Innings

Hernandez, Mon	255.0
Johnson, Ari	245.2
Oswalt, Hou	237.0
Sheets, Mil	237.0
Schmidt, SF	225.0
Pavano, Fla	222.1
Weaver, LA	220.0
Clemens, Hou	214.1
Maddux, Chi	212.2
Glavine, NY	212.1

HR Allowed

Milton, Phi	43
Maddux, Chi	35
Morris, St.L	35
Lima, LA	33
Valdez, SD-Fla	33
Fossum, Ari	31
Myers, Phi	31

Two tied with 30 each.

Opp. Batting Average

Johnson, Ari	.197
Schmidt, SF	.202
Perez, Pit	.207
Clemens, Hou	.217
Leiter, NY	.218
Zambrano, Chi	.225
Sheets, Mil	.226
Clement, Chi	.229
Peavy, SD	.236
Wright, Atl	.242

Complete Games

Hernandez, Mon	9
Lidle, Cin-Phi	5
Sheets, Mil	5
Johnson, Ari	4
Schmidt, SF	4
Morris, St.L	3

Ten tied with 2 each.

Saves

	SV	BS
Benitez, Fla	.47	4
Isringhausen, St.L	.47	7
Gagne, LA	.45	2
Smoltz, Atl	.44	5
Mesa, Pit	.43	5
Graves, Cin	.41	9
Hoffman, SD	.41	4
Kolb, Mil	.39	5
Chacon, Col	.35	9
Looper, NY	.29	5
Lidge, Hou	.29	4

Wild Pitches

Webb, Ari	17
Clement, Chi	14
Williams, St.L	12
Tomko, SF	10
Brower, SF	10

Three tied with 9 each.

Hit Batters

Zambrano, Chi	20
Williams, SF	17
Weaver, LA	14
Kim, Mon	13
Clement, Chi	12

Seven tied with 11 each.

WHIP

(Walks + Hits/IP)

Johnson, Ari	0.90
Sheets, Mil	0.98
Schmidt, SF	1.08
Carpenter, St.L	1.14
Wells, SD	1.14
Perez, LA	1.14
Perez, Pit	1.15
Clemens, Hou	1.16

Shutouts

Schmidt, SF	3
Lidle, Cin-Phi	3

Six tied with 2 each.

Fielding

Put Outs

Pujols, St.L	1458
Helton, Col	1356
Overbay, Mil	1309
Lee, Chi	1259
Casey, Cin	1233
Bagwell, Hou	1190
Nevin, SD	1132
Hillenbrand, Ari	1127
Thome, Phi	1090
Barrett, Chi	1035

Assists

J. Wilson, Pit	492
Loretta, SD	451
Gonzalez, Fla	425
Renteria, St.L	419
Clayton, Col	418
Furcal, Atl	411
Castillo, Fla	406
Rollins, Phi	399
Womack, St.L	391
Jimenez, Cin	389

OF Assists

Rivera, Mon	14
Hidalgo, Hou-NY	14
Cabrera, Fla	13
Abreu, Phi	13
Drew, Atl	12
Payton, SD	11
Edmonds, St.L	11
Bonds, SF	11
Berkman, Hou	11

Four tied with 10 each.

Errors

Tracy,* Ari	25
Bell, Phi	24
Furcal, Atl	24
Matsui*, NY	23
Greene*, SD	20
Batista, Mon	19
Wigginton, NY-Pit	18
J. Wilson, Pit	17

Three tied with 16 each.

Team Batting Statistics

American League

Team	Avg	AB	R	H	HR	RBI	SB
Anaheim	.282	5675	836	1603	162	783	143
Boston	.282	5720	949	1613	222	912	68
Baltimore	.281	5736	842	1614	169	803	101
Cleveland	.276	5676	858	1565	184	820	94
Detroit	.272	5623	827	1531	201	800	86
Seattle	.270	5722	698	1544	136	658	110
Oakland	.270	5728	793	1545	189	752	47
New York	.268	5527	897	1483	242	863	84
Chicago	.268	5534	865	1481	242	823	78
Texas	.266	5615	860	1492	227	825	69
Minnesota	.266	5623	780	1494	191	735	116
Toronto	.260	5531	719	1438	145	680	58
Kansas City	.259	5538	720	1432	150	675	67
Tampa Bay	.258	5483	714	1416	145	685	132

National League

Team	Avg	AB	R	H	HR	RBI	SB
St. Louis	.278	5555	855	1544	214	817	111
Colorado	.275	5577	833	1531	202	795	44
San Diego	.273	5573	768	1521	139	722	52
San Francisco	.270	5546	850	1500	183	805	43
Atlanta	.270	5570	803	1503	178	767	86
Chicago	.268	5628	789	1508	235	755	66
Philadelphia	.267	5643	840	1505	215	802	100
Houston	.267	5468	803	1458	187	756	89
Florida	.264	5486	718	1447	148	677	96
Los Angeles	.262	5542	761	1450	203	731	102
Pittsburgh	.260	5483	680	1428	142	648	63
Arizona	.253	5544	615	1401	135	582	53
Cincinnati	.250	5518	750	1380	194	713	77
New York	.249	5532	684	1376	185	658	107
Montreal	.249	5474	635	1361	151	605	109
Milwaukee	.248	5483	634	1358	135	601	138

Team Pitching Statistics

American League

Team	ERA	W	Sv	CG	ShO	HR	BB	SO
Minnesota	4.03	92	48	4	9	167	431	1123
Oakland	4.17	91	35	10	8	164	544	1034
Boston	4.18	98	36	4	12	159	447	1132
Anaheim	4.28	92	50	2	11	170	502	1164
Texas	4.53	89	52	5	9	182	547	979
New York	4.69	101	59	1	5	182	445	1058
Baltimore	4.70	78	27	8	10	159	687	1090
Seattle	4.76	63	28	7	7	212	575	1036
Tampa Bay	4.81	70	35	3	5	192	580	923
Cleveland	4.81	80	32	8	8	201	579	1115
Toronto	4.91	67	37	6	11	181	608	956
Chicago	4.91	83	34	8	8	224	527	1013
Detroit	4.93	72	35	7	9	190	530	995
Kansas City	5.15	58	25	6	3	208	518	887

National League

Team	ERA	W	Sv	CG	ShO	HR	BB	SO
Atlanta	3.74	96	48	4	13	154	523	1025
St. Louis	3.75	105	57	4	12	169	440	1041
Chicago	3.81	89	42	3	6	169	545	1346
Los Angeles	4.01	93	51	2	6	178	521	1066
San Diego	4.03	87	44	3	8	184	422	1079
Houston	4.05	92	47	2	13	174	525	1282
New York	4.09	71	31	2	6	156	592	977
Florida	4.10	83	53	6	14	166	513	1116
Milwaukee	4.24	67	42	6	10	164	476	1098
Pittsburgh	4.29	72	46	3	8	149	576	1079
San Francisco	4.29	91	46	8	8	161	548	1020
Montreal	4.33	67	31	11	11	191	582	1032
Philadelphia	4.45	86	43	4	5	214	502	1070
Arizona	4.98	51	33	5	6	197	668	1153
Cincinnati	5.19	76	47	5	8	236	572	992
Colorado	5.54	68	36	3	2	198	697	947

Team Fielding Statistics

American League

Team	Pct	TC	E	PO	A	DP	TP
Oakland	.986	6315	91	4414	1810	172	0
Anaheim	.985	5965	90	4363	1512	126	0
Toronto	.985	5985	91	4263	1631	150	0
Minnesota	.984	6187	101	4428	1658	158	0
Chicago	.984	6066	100	4297	1669	167	1
New York	.984	6002	99	4331	1572	148	0
Cleveland	.983	6182	106	4400	1676	152	0
Seattle	.983	5955	103	4378	1474	140	0
Baltimore	.982	6159	110	4366	1683	161	0
Boston	.981	6122	118	4354	1650	129	0
Texas	.981	6042	117	4319	1606	152	0
Tampa Bay	.980	5900	119	4251	1530	139	0
Kansas City	.978	6028	131	4261	1636	169	0
Detroit	.977	6174	144	4319	1711	160	0

National League

Team	Pct	TC	E	PO	A	DP	TP
Los Angeles	.988	6099	73	4360	1666	145	0
Philadelphia	.987	6098	81	4388	1629	142	0
Chicago	.986	6061	86	4396	1579	126	0
Colorado	.986	6219	89	4306	1824	161	0
Florida	.986	6007	86	4317	1604	153	0
St. Louis	.985	6292	97	4361	1834	154	0
Montreal	.984	6140	99	4341	1700	172	0
San Francisco	.984	6211	101	4371	1739	153	0
Houston	.983	6050	101	4329	1620	136	1
Pittsburgh	.983	6080	103	4284	1693	189	0
San Diego	.982	6032	108	4823	1601	146	0
Atlanta	.981	6258	116	4350	1792	171	1
Cincinnati	.981	6085	113	4331	1641	123	0
Milwaukee	.981	6035	117	4326	1592	132	0
New York	.978	6231	137	4347	1747	144	0
Arizona	.977	6164	139	4308	1717	144	0

Pct—Fielding Percentage; **TC**—Total Chances; **E**—Errors; **PO**—Put Outs; **A**—Assists; **DP**—Double Plays; **TP**—Triple Plays.

2004 All-Star Game

75th Baseball All-Star Game. Date: July 13 at Minute Maid Park, Houston, Texas; **Managers:** Joe Torre, NY Yankees (AL) and Jack McKeon, Florida (NL); **Ted Williams MVP Award:** Alfonso Soriano (AL): 2-for-3 with a HR and 3 RBI.

Note: The league that wins the All-Star Game also secures home-field advantage for the World Series.

American League

	AB	R	H	BI	BB	SO	Avg
Ichiro Suzuki, Sea, cf	4	1	1	0	0	0	.250
Ronnie Belliard, 2b	1	0	0	0	0	1	.000
Ivan Rodriguez, Det, c	4	1	2	1	0	0	.500
Victor Martinez, Cle, c	1	0	0	0	0	0	.000
Vladimir Guerrero, Ana, rf	4	1	1	0	0	0	.250
Miguel Tejada, Bal, ss	1	0	0	0	0	0	.000
Manny Ramirez, Bos, lf	2	1	1	2	0	0	.500
David Ortiz, Bos, ph-1b	1	2	1	2	2	0	1.000
Alex Rodriguez, NY, 3b	3	0	1	1	0	1	.333
Hank Blalock, Tex, ph-3b	2	0	0	0	0	0	.000
Jason Giambi, NY, 1b	2	1	1	0	0	0	.500
Carl Crawford, TB, ph-lf	2	0	0	0	0	1	.000
Hideki Matsui, NY, ph-lf	1	0	0	0	0	1	.000
Derek Jeter, NY, ss	3	1	3	0	0	0	1.000
Matt Lawton, Cle, cf	2	0	1	0	0	1	.500
Alfonso Soriano, Tex, 2b	3	1	2	3	0	1	.667
Gary Sheffield, NY, rf	1	0	0	0	0	0	.000
Mark Mulder, Oak, p	1	0	0	0	0	1	.000
Ken Harvey, KC, ph	1	0	0	0	0	1	.000
Michael Young, Tex, ph-ss	2	0	0	0	0	0	.000
TOTALS	41	9	14	9	2	8	.341

National League

	AB	R	H	BI	BB	SO	Avg
Edgar Renteria, St.L, ss	3	1	1	1	0	0	.333
Jack Wilson, Pit, ss	2	0	0	0	0	0	.000
Albert Pujols, St.L, 1b	3	1	2	2	0	0	.667
Jim Thome, Phi, 1b	2	0	0	0	0	1	.000
Barry Bonds, SF, lf	2	0	0	0	1	0	.000
Bobby Abreu, Phi, ph	1	0	0	0	0	1	.000
Scott Rolen, St.L, 3b	1	0	1	0	0	0	1.000
Mike Lowell, Fla, ph-3b	2	0	0	0	0	1	.000
Sammy Sosa, Chi, rf	2	0	1	1	0	0	.500
Miguel Cabrera, Fla, rf	2	0	0	0	0	1	.000
Mike Piazza, NY, c	2	0	0	0	0	1	.000
Johnny Estrada, Atl, c	2	0	0	0	0	1	.000
Lance Berkman, Hou, cf	2	0	0	0	0	0	.000
Moises Alou, Chi, lf	2	0	1	0	0	0	.500
Jeff Kent, Hou, 2b	2	1	1	0	0	0	.500
Mark Loretta, SD, ph-2b	2	0	1	0	0	0	.500
Roger Clemens, Hou, p	0	0	0	0	0	0	.000
Barry Larkin, Cin, ss	1	0	0	0	0	0	.000
Carlos Beltran, Hou, ph-cf	2	1	1	0	0	0	.500
Todd Helton, Col, ph	1	0	0	0	0	1	.000
TOTALS	36	4	9	4	1	6	.250

	1	2	3	4	5	6	7	8	9		R	H	E
American League	6	0	0	1	0	2	0	0	0	–	9	14	0
National League	1	0	0	3	0	0	0	0	0	–	4	9	1

E—Kent (NL, ground ball). **DP**—NL (Wilson-Loretta-Thome). **LOB**—American 7, National 7. **2B**—Suzuki (AL), Pujols 2, Renteria (NL). **3B**—I. Rodriguez, A. Rodriguez (AL). **HR**—Ramirez (AL, off Clemens, 1 on), Soriano (AL, off Clemens, 2 on), Ortiz (AL, off Pavano 1 on). **SB**—none. **SF**—none. **GIDP**—Sheffield (AL).

AL Pitching	IP	H	R	ER	BB	SO
Mark Mulder, Oak (W, 1-0)	2.0	2	1	1	0	1
Esteban Loaiza, Chi	1.0	1	0	0	1	0
C.C. Sabathia, Cle	1.0	4	3	3	0	0
Javier Vazquez, NY	1.0	0	0	0	0	2
Ted Lilly, Tor	1.0	2	0	0	0	1
Joe Nathan, Min	1.0	0	0	0	0	0
Tom Gordon, NY	0.1	0	0	0	0	0
Francisco Rodriguez, Ana	0.2	0	0	0	0	0
Mariano Rivera, NY	1.0	0	0	0	0	0
TOTALS	9.0	9	4	4	1	6

NL Pitching	IP	H	R	ER	BB	SO
Roger Clemens, Hou (L, 0-1)	1.0	5	6	3	0	2
Danny Kolb, Mil	1.0	1	0	0	0	0
Randy Johnson, Ari	1.0	3	0	0	0	1
Carlos Zambrano, Chi	1.0	1	1	1	1	1
Carl Pavano, Fla	2.0	3	2	2	0	1
Tom Glavine, NY	1.0	1	0	0	0	0
Ben Sheets, Mil	1.0	0	0	0	0	1
Eric Gagne, LA	1.0	0	0	0	1	2
TOTALS	9.0	14	9	6	2	8

HBP—by Mulder (Rolen). **WP**—none. **Umpires**—Ed Montague (plate); John Hirschbeck (1b); Doug Eddings (2b); Jim Reynolds (3b); Marvin Hudson (lf); Sam Holbrook (rf). **Attendance**—41,886 (40,950 cap.). **Time**—2:59. **TV Rating**—8.8/15 share (FOX).

Home Run Derby

Results of the 2004 All-Star Home Run Derby held at Minute Maid Park in Houston, Texas on July 12.

First Round

	No.	Long (ft)
Rafael Palmeiro, Baltimore	9	425
Barry Bonds, San Francisco	8	483
Miguel Tejada, Baltimore	7	424
Lance Berkman, Houston	7	454
Sammy Sosa, Chicago Cubs	5	450
Jim Thome, Philadelphia	4	430
Hank Blalock, Texas	3	453
David Ortiz, Boston	3	419

(Top four advance to second round)

Second Round

	No.	Long (ft)
Miguel Tejada, Baltimore	15	497
Lance Berkman, Houston	10	493
Rafael Palmeiro, Baltimore	5	445
Barry Bonds, San Francisco	3	462

(Top two advance to Finals)

Finals

	No.	Long (ft)
Miguel Tejada, Baltimore	5	451
Lance Berkman, Houston	4	461

(Tejada hit the winning HR with 5 outs remaining)

AL Team by Team Statistics

At least 135 at bats or 40 innings pitched during the regular season, unless otherwise indicated. Players who competed for more than one AL team are listed with their final club. Players traded from the NL are listed with AL team only if they have 135 AB or 40 IP. Note that (*) indicates rookie and PTBN indicates player to be named.

Anaheim Angels

Batting (135 AB)	Avg	AB	R	H	HR	RBI	SB
Robb Quinlan*	.344	160	23	55	5	23	3
Vladimir Guerrero ..	.337	612	124	206	39	126	15
Garret Anderson ...	.301	442	57	133	14	75	2
Chone Figgins	.296	577	83	171	5	60	34
Darin Erstad	.295	495	79	146	7	69	16
Jose Guillen	.294	565	88	166	27	104	5
Adam Kennedy	.278	468	70	130	10	48	15
Jeff DaVanon	.277	285	41	79	7	34	18
Bengie Molina	.276	337	36	93	10	54	0
David Eckstein	.276	566	92	156	2	35	16
Jose Molina	.261	203	26	53	3	25	4
Tim Salmon	.253	186	15	47	2	23	1
Troy Glaus	.251	207	47	52	18	42	2

Pitching (40 IP)	ERA	W-L	Gm	IP	BB	SO
Francisco Rodriguez .	1.82	4-1	69	84.0	33	123
Troy Percival.......	2.90	2-3	52	49.2	19	33
Brendan Donnelly....	3.00	5-2	40	42.0	15	56
Scot Shields	3.33	8-2	60	105.1	40	109
Kelvim Escobar	3.93	11-12	33	208.1	76	191
Kevin Gregg*.......	4.21	5-2	55	87.2	28	84
Ramon Ortiz.......	4.43	5-7	34	128.0	38	82
Jarrod Washburn ...	4.64	11-8	25	149.1	40	86
John Lackey	4.67	14-13	33	198.1	60	144
Bartolo Colon	5.01	18-12	34	208.1	71	158
Aaron Sele........	5.05	9-4	28	132.0	51	51

Saves: Percival (33), Rodriguez (12), Shields (4), Gregg (1). **Complete games:** Washburn and Lackey (1). **Shutouts:** Washburn and Lackey.

Baltimore Orioles

Batting (135 AB)	Avg	AB	R	H	HR	RBI	SB
Melvin Mora	.340	550	111	187	27	104	11
Javy Lopez........	.316	579	83	183	23	86	0
David Newhan	.311	373	66	116	8	54	11
Miguel Tejada	.311	653	107	203	34	150	4
B.J. Surhoff	.309	343	49	106	8	50	2
Jerry Hairston Jr...	.303	287	43	87	2	24	13
Larry Bigbie.......	.280	478	76	134	15	68	8
Brian Roberts	.273	641	107	175	4	53	29
Rafael Palmeiro ...	.258	550	68	142	23	88	2
Jay Gibbons	.246	346	36	85	10	47	1
Luis Matos	.224	330	36	74	6	28	12

Acquired: P Chen from Tor. for PTBN on May 3; P Grimsley from KC for P Denny Bautista (June 21)I P DeJean from NYM for OF Karim Garcia (July 19).

Pitching (35 IP)	ERA	W-L	Gm	IP	BB	SO
B.J. Ryan	2.28	4-6	76	87.0	35	122
Bruce Chen	3.02	2-1	8	47.2	16	32
John Parrish	3.46	6-3	56	78.0	55	71
Rodrigo Lopez	3.59	14-9	37	170.2	54	121
Jason Grimsley	3.86	5-7	73	63.0	35	39
Jorge Julio	4.57	2-5	65	69.0	39	70
Erik Bedard*	4.59	6-10	27	137.1	71	121
Rick Bauer	4.70	2-1	23	53.2	20	37
Eddy Rodriguez* ...	4.78	1-0	29	43.1	30	37
Buddy Groom	4.78	4-1	60	52.2	16	32
Daniel Cabrera*....	5.00	12-8	28	147.2	89	76
Dave Borkowski	5.14	3-4	17	56.0	15	45
Sidney Ponson	5.30	11-15	33	215.2	69	115
Matt Riley*........	5.63	3-4	14	64.0	44	60
Mike DeJean	6.13	0-5	37	39.2	28	36
Eric DuBose	6.39	4-6	14	74.2	44	48

Saves: Julio (22), Ryan (3), Parrish and Cabrera (1). **Complete games:** Ponson (5), Chen, Lopez and Cabrera (1). **Shutouts:** Ponson (2), Lopez and Cabrera (1).

Boston Red Sox

Batting (165 AB)	Avg	AB	R	H	HR	RBI	SB
Manny Ramirez	.308	568	108	175	43	130	2
Johnny Damon	.304	621	123	189	20	94	19
David Ortiz.......	.301	582	94	175	41	139	0
Kevin Millar.......	.297	508	74	151	18	74	1
Jason Varitek	.296	463	67	137	18	73	10
Orlando Cabrera ...	.294	228	33	67	6	31	4
Bill Mueller	.283	399	75	113	12	57	2
Gabe Kapler	.272	290	51	79	6	33	5
Mark Bellhorn	.264	523	93	138	17	82	6
Kevin Youkilis*....	.260	208	38	54	7	35	0
Doug Mientkiewicz..	.238	391	47	93	6	35	2
Pokey Reese.......	.221	244	32	54	3	29	6

Acquired: P Adams from Tor. for a minor leaguer (July 24); IF Cabrera from Mon. and IF Mientkiewicz from Min. in a 4-team deal that sent IF Nomar Garciaparra and OF Matt Murton to ChC (July 31).

Pitching (45 IP)	ERA	W-L	Gm	IP	BB	SO
Keith Foulke	2.17	5-3	72	83.0	15	79
Curt Schilling	3.26	21-6	32	226.2	35	203
Pedro Martinez	3.90	16-9	33	217.0	61	227
Bronson Arroyo	4.03	10-9	32	178.2	47	142
Mike Timlin	4.13	5-4	76	76.1	19	56
Alan Embree	4.13	2-2	71	52.1	11	37
Terry Adams......	4.76	6-4	61	70.0	28	56
Tim Wakefield	4.87	12-10	32	188.1	63	116
Derek Lowe	5.42	14-12	33	182.2	71	105

Saves: Foulke (32), Leskanic (4), Adams (3), Timlin and Scott Williamson (1). **Complete games:** Schilling (3), Martinez (1). **Shutouts:** Martinez (1).

Chicago White Sox

Batting (160 AB)	Avg	AB	R	H	HR	RBI	SB
Ross Gload*	.321	234	28	75	7	44	0
Aaron Rowand	.310	487	94	151	24	69	17
Carlos Lee	.305	591	103	180	31	99	11
Magglio Ordonez ...	.292	202	32	59	9	37	0
Juan Uribe	.283	502	82	142	23	74	9
Paul Konerko	.277	563	84	156	41	117	1
Frank Thomas	.271	240	53	65	18	49	0
Willie Harris	.262	409	68	107	2	27	19
Timo Perez	.246	293	38	72	5	40	3
Joe Crede	.239	490	67	117	21	69	1
Jose Valentin	.216	450	73	97	30	70	8
Ben Davis	.207	193	22	40	6	18	1
Joe Borchard*	.174	201	26	35	9	20	1

Acquired: P Garcia, C Davis and cash from Sea. for C Miguel Olivo and 2 minor leaguers (June 27); P Contreras from NYY for P Esteban Loaiza (July 31).

Pitching (40 IP)	ERA	W-L	Gm	IP	BB	SO
Shingo Takatsu* ...	2.31	6-4	59	62.1	21	50
Damaso Marte	3.42	6-5	74	73.2	34	68
Freddy Garcia	3.81	13-11	31	210.0	64	184
Mark Buehrle	3.89	16-10	35	245.1	51	165
Cliff Politte	4.38	0-3	54	51.1	22	48
Jon Adkins*	4.65	2-3	50	62.0	20	44
Jon Garland	4.89	12-11	34	217.0	76	113
Mike Jackson	5.01	2-0	45	46.2	15	26
Jose Contreras	5.50	13-9	31	170.1	84	150
Scott Schoeneweis ..	5.59	6-9	20	112.2	49	69
Neal Cotts*	5.65	4-4	56	65.1	30	58
Felix Diaz*	6.75	2-5	18	49.1	16	33
Jason Grilli*	7.40	2-3	8	45.0	20	26

Saves: Takatsu (19), Billy Koch (8), Marte (6), Politte (1). **Complete games:** Buehrle (4); Garcia, Garland and Grilli (1). **Shutouts:** Buehrle (1).

Cleveland Indians

Batting (100 AB)	Avg	AB	R	H	HR	RBI	SB
Travis Hafner	.311	482	96	150	28	109	3
Coco Crisp	.297	491	78	146	15	71	20
Omar Vizquel	.291	567	82	165	7	59	19
Lou Merloni	.289	190	25	55	4	28	1
Victor Martinez	.283	520	77	147	23	108	0
Ronnie Belliard	.282	599	78	169	12	70	3
Matt Lawton	.277	591	109	164	20	70	23
Ben Broussard	.275	418	57	115	17	82	4
Casey Blake	.271	587	93	159	28	88	5
Jody Gerut	.252	481	72	121	11	51	13
Josh Phelps	.251	371	51	93	17	61	0
Grady Sizemore*	.246	138	15	34	4	24	2
Tim Laker	.214	117	12	25	3	17	0

Acquired: IF Phelps from Tor. for a minor leaguer (Aug. 6). **Signed:** free agent P Elarton (May 25). **Waived:** P Durbin (Aug. 28).

Pitching (30 IP)	ERA	W-L	Gm	IP	BB	SO
Bob Howry	2.74	4-2	37	42.2	12	39
Matt Miller*	3.09	4-1	57	55.1	23	55
Jake Westbrook	3.38	14-9	33	215.2	61	116
David Riske	3.72	7-3	72	77.1	41	78
Rafael Betancourt*	3.92	5-6	68	66.2	18	76
C.C. Sabathia	4.12	11-10	30	188.0	72	139
Scott Elarton	4.53	3-5	21	117.1	42	80
Kazuhito Tadano*	4.65	1-1	14	50.1	18	39
Rick White	5.29	5-5	59	78.1	29	44
Cliff Lee	5.43	14-8	33	179.0	81	161
Jason Davis	5.51	2-7	26	114.1	51	72
Chad Durbin	6.66	5-6	17	51.1	24	38
Jeff D'Amico	7.63	1-2	7	30.2	6	16
Jose Jimenez	8.42	1-7	31	36.1	14	21

Saves: Bob Wickman (13), Jose Jimenez (8), Riske (5), Betancourt (4), Miller and White (1). **Complete games:** Westbrook (5), Sabathia, Elarton and Durbin (1). **Shutouts:** Westbrook, Sabathia and Elarton (1).

Detroit Tigers

Batting (135 AB)	Avg	AB	R	H	HR	RBI	SB
Ivan Rodriguez	.334	527	72	176	19	86	7
Alex Sanchez	.322	532	41	107	2	26	19
Carlos Guillen	.318	522	97	166	20	97	12
Craig Monroe	.293	447	65	131	18	72	3
Brandon Inge	.287	408	43	117	13	64	5
Dmitri Young	.272	389	72	106	18	60	0
Rondell White	.270	448	76	121	19	67	1
Omar Infante	.264	503	69	133	16	55	13
Marcus Thames*	.255	165	24	42	10	33	0
Bobby Higginson	.246	448	63	110	12	64	5
Carlos Pena	.241	481	89	116	27	82	7
Jason Smith*	.239	155	20	37	5	19	1
Eric Munson	.212	321	36	68	19	49	1

Pitching (40 IP)	ERA	W-L	Gm	IP	BB	SO
Jamie Walker	3.20	3-4	70	64.2	12	53
Esteban Yan	3.83	3-6	69	87.0	32	69
Mike Maroth	4.31	11-13	33	217.0	59	108
Wilfredo Ledezma	4.39	4-3	15	53.1	18	29
Ugueth Urbina	4.50	4-6	54	54.0	32	56
Al Levine	4.58	3-4	65	70.2	24	32
Danny Patterson	4.75	0-4	37	41.2	16	24
Jeremy Bonderman	4.89	11-13	33	184.0	73	168
Nate Robertson	4.90	12-10	34	196.2	66	155
Jason Johnson	5.13	8-15	33	196.2	60	125
Gary Knotts	5.25	7-6	36	135.1	58	81

Saves: Urbina (21), Yan (7), Patterson and Knotts (2), Walker, Robertson and John Ennis (1). **Complete games:** Maroth, Bonderman and Johnson (2), Robertson (1). **Shutouts:** Bonderman (2), Maroth and Johnson (1).

Kansas City Royals

Batting (135 AB)	Avg	AB	R	H	HR	RBI	SB
Ken Harvey	.287	456	47	131	13	55	1
Mike Sweeney	.287	411	56	118	22	79	3
Joe Randa	.287	485	65	139	8	56	0
David DeJesus*	.287	363	58	104	7	39	8
Carlos Beltran	.278	266	51	74	15	51	14
Benito Santiago	.274	175	15	48	6	23	1
Ruben Gotay*	.270	152	17	41	1	16	0
Matt Stairs	.267	439	48	117	18	66	1
Tony Graffanino	.263	278	37	73	3	26	10
Angel Berroa	.262	512	72	134	8	43	14
Dee Brown	.251	195	19	49	4	24	2
John Buck*	.235	238	36	56	12	30	1
Abraham Nunez	.226	221	31	50	5	29	0
Desi Relaford	.221	380	45	84	6	34	5
Aaron Guiel	.156	135	15	21	5	13	1

Acquired: C Buck from Hou., P Wood and a minor leaguer from Oak. in a 3-team deal that sent OF Beltran to Hou. and P Octavio Dotel from Hou. to Oak. (June 24); OF Nunez from Fla. for P Rudy Seanez (July 31).

Pitching (40 IP)	ERA	W-L	Gm	IP	BB	SO
Jaime Cerda	3.15	1-4	53	45.2	30	33
Shawn Camp	3.92	2-2	42	66.2	16	51
Zack Greinke*	3.97	8-11	24	145.0	26	100
Nate Field*	4.26	2-3	43	44.1	19	30
Dennys Reyes	4.75	4-8	40	108.0	50	91
Scott Sullivan	4.77	3-4	49	60.1	24	45
Jeremy Affeldt	4.95	3-4	38	76.1	32	49
Jimmy Gobble	5.35	9-8	25	148.0	43	49
Darrell May	5.61	9-19	31	186.0	55	120
Brian Anderson	5.64	6-12	35	166.0	53	70
Mike Wood*	5.94	3-8	17	100.0	28	54
Chris George	7.23	1-2	10	42.1	25	15

Saves: Affeldt (13), Field (3), Cerda and Camp (2), Ryan Bukvich, Mike MacDougal and Justin Huisman (1). **Complete games:** May (3), Anderson, Gobble (1). **Shutouts:** May and Anderson (1).

Minnesota Twins

Batting (100 AB)	Avg	AB	R	H	HR	RBI	SB
Joe Mauer*	.308	107	18	33	6	17	1
Shannon Stewart	.304	378	46	115	11	47	6
Lew Ford*	.299	569	89	170	15	72	20
Cristian Guzman	.274	576	84	158	8	46	10
Justin Morneau*	.271	280	39	76	19	58	0
Torii Hunter	.271	520	79	141	23	81	21
Matt LeCroy	.269	264	25	71	9	39	0
Michael Cuddyer	.263	339	49	89	12	45	5
Luis Rivas	.256	336	44	86	10	34	15
Jose Offerman	.256	172	22	44	2	22	1
Jacque Jones	.254	555	69	141	24	80	13
Corey Koskie	.251	422	68	106	25	71	9
Henry Blanco	.206	315	36	65	10	37	0

Pitching (35 IP)	ERA	W-L	Gm	IP	BB	SO
Joe Nathan	1.62	1-2	73	72.1	23	89
Johan Santana	2.61	20-6	34	228.0	54	265
Juan Rincon	2.63	11-6	77	82.0	32	106
Brad Radke	3.48	11-8	34	219.2	26	143
J.C. Romero	3.51	7-4	74	74.1	38	69
Carlos Silva	4.21	14-8	33	203.0	35	76
Grant Balfour*	4.35	4-1	36	39.1	21	42
Joe Roa	4.50	2-3	48	70.0	24	47
Aaron Fultz	5.04	3-3	55	50.0	23	37
Terry Mulholland	5.18	5-9	39	123.1	33	60
Kyle Lohse	5.34	9-13	35	194.0	76	111
Seth Greisinger	6.18	2-5	12	51.0	15	36

Saves: Nathan (44), Rincon (2), Romero and Fultz (1). **Complete games:** Santana, Radke, Silva and Lohse (1). **Shutouts:** Santana, Radke, Silva and Lohse (1).

New York Yankees

Batting (135 AB)

	Avg	AB	R	H	HR	RBI	SB
Hideki Matsui	.298	584	109	174	31	108	3
Derek Jeter	.292	643	111	188	23	78	23
Miguel Cairo	.292	360	48	105	6	42	11
Gary Sheffield	.290	573	117	166	36	121	5
Alex Rodriguez	.286	601	112	172	36	106	28
Kenny Lofton	.275	276	51	76	3	18	7
Jorge Posada	.272	449	72	122	21	81	1
Bernie Williams	.262	561	105	147	22	70	1
John Olerud	.259	425	45	110	9	48	0
John Flaherty	.252	127	11	32	6	16	0
Ruben Sierra	.244	307	40	75	17	65	1
Tony Clark	.221	253	37	56	16	49	0
Enrique Wilson	.213	240	19	51	6	31	1
Jason Giambi	.208	264	33	55	12	40	0

Acquired: P Sturtze from LA for a minor leaguer (May 15); P Loaiza from ChW for P Jose Contreras (July 31). **Signed:** free agent Olerud (Aug. 2).

Pitching (30 IP)

	ERA	W-L	Gm	IP	BB	SO
Mariano Rivera	1.94	4-2	74	78.2	20	66
Tom Gordon	2.21	9-4	80	89.2	23	96
Orlando Hernandez	3.30	8-2	15	84.2	36	84
Kevin Brown	4.09	10-6	22	132.0	35	83
Jon Lieber	4.33	14-8	27	176.2	18	102
Mike Mussina	4.59	12-9	27	164.2	40	132
Paul Quantrill	4.72	7-3	86	95.1	20	37
Javier Vazquez	4.91	14-10	32	198.0	60	150
Tanyon Sturtze	5.47	6-2	28	77.1	33	56
Esteban Loaiza	5.70	10-7	31	183.0	71	117
Felix Heredia	6.28	1-1	47	38.2	20	25
Brad Halsey*	6.47	1-3	8	32.0	14	25

Saves: Rivera (53), Gordon (4), Quantrill and Sturtze (1). **Complete games:** Loaiza (2), Mussina (1). **Shutouts:** Loaiza (1).

Oakland Athletics

Batting (135 AB)

	Avg	AB	R	H	HR	RBI	SB
Erubiel Durazo	.321	511	80	164	22	88	3
Mark Kotsay	.314	606	78	190	15	63	8
Scott Hatteberg	.284	550	87	156	15	82	0
Eric Byrnes	.283	569	91	161	20	73	17
Eric Chavez	.276	475	87	131	29	77	6
Marco Scutaro*	.273	455	50	124	7	43	0
Damian Miller	.272	397	39	108	9	58	0
Jermaine Dye	.265	532	87	141	23	80	4
Adam Melhuse	.257	214	23	55	11	31	0
Mark McLemore	.248	250	29	62	2	21	0
Bobby Crosby*	.239	545	70	130	22	64	7
Bobby Kielty	.214	238	29	51	7	31	1

Acquired: P Dotel from Hou. in a 3-team deal that sent P Mike Wood and a minor leaguer to KC, C John Buck from Hou. to KC and OF Carlos Beltran from KC to Hou. (June 24).

Pitching (40 IP)

	ERA	W-L	Gm	IP	BB	SO
Chris Hammond	2.68	4-1	41	53.2	13	34
Justin Duchscherer*	3.27	7-6	53	96.1	32	59
Tim Hudson	3.53	12-6	27	188.2	44	103
Jim Mecir	3.59	0-5	65	47.2	19	49
Ricardo Rincon	3.68	1-1	67	44.0	22	40
Rich Harden	3.99	11-7	31	189.2	81	167
Octavio Dotel	4.09	6-4	45	50.2	18	72
Chad Bradford	4.42	5-7	68	59.0	24	34
Mark Mulder	4.43	17-8	33	225.2	83	140
Barry Zito	4.48	11-11	34	213.0	81	163
Mark Redman	4.71	11-12	32	191.0	68	102

Saves: Dotel (22), Arthur Rhodes (9), Mecir (2), Hammond and Bradford (1). **Complete games:** Mulder (5), Hudson (3), Redman (1). **Shutouts:** Hudson (2), Mulder (1).

Seattle Mariners

Batting (135 AB)

	Avg	AB	R	H	HR	RBI	SB
Ichiro Suzuki	.372	704	101	262	8	60	36
Raul Ibanez	.304	481	67	146	16	62	1
Randy Winn	.286	626	84	179	14	81	21
Bucky Jacobsen*	.275	160	17	44	9	28	0
Jolbert Cabrera	.270	359	38	97	6	47	10
Edgar Martinez	.263	486	45	128	12	63	1
Bret Boone	.251	593	74	149	24	83	10
Dan Wilson	.251	319	23	80	2	33	0
Willie Bloomquist	.245	188	27	46	2	18	13
Rich Aurilia	.241	261	27	63	4	28	1
Miguel Olivo	.233	301	46	70	13	40	7
Jose Lopez*	.232	207	28	48	5	22	0
Scott Spiezio	.215	367	38	79	10	41	4

Acquired: C Olivo and 2 minor leaguers from ChW for P Freddy Garcia, C Ben Davis and cash (June 27). **Traded:** IF Aurilia to SD for PTBN or cash (July 19).

Pitching (35 IP)

	ERA	W-L	Gm	IP	BB	SO
Eddie Guardado	2.78	2-2	41	45.1	14	45
Bobby Madritsch*	3.27	6-3	15	88.0	33	60
Ron Villone	4.08	8-6	56	117.0	64	86
Joel Pineiro	4.67	6-11	21	140.2	43	111
Julio Mateo	4.68	1-2	45	57.2	16	43
J.J. Putz*	4.71	0-3	54	63.0	24	47
Ryan Franklin	4.90	4-16	32	200.1	61	104
Gil Meche	5.01	7-7	23	127.2	47	99
Shigetoshi Hasegawa	5.16	4-6	68	68.0	31	46
Jamie Moyer	5.21	7-13	34	202.0	63	125
Clint Nageotte*	7.36	1-2	12	36.2	27	24

Saves: Guardado (18), Putz (9), Mateo (1). **Complete games:** Franklin (2), Madritsch, Pineiro, Meche and Moyer (1). **Shutouts:** Franklin and Meche (1).

Tampa Bay Devil Rays

Batting (135 AB)

	Avg	AB	R	H	HR	RBI	SB
Jorge Cantu*	.301	173	25	52	2	17	0
Aubrey Huff	.297	600	92	178	29	104	5
Carl Crawford	.296	626	104	185	11	55	59
Rocco Baldelli	.280	518	79	145	16	74	17
Julio Lugo	.275	581	83	160	7	75	21
Tino Martinez	.262	458	63	120	23	76	3
B.J. Upton*	.258	159	19	41	4	12	4
Toby Hall	.255	404	35	103	8	60	0
Rey Sanchez	.246	285	23	70	2	26	0
Jose Cruz Jr.	.242	545	76	132	21	78	11
Geoff Blum	.215	339	38	73	8	35	2
Brook Fordyce	.205	151	14	31	2	9	0
Robert Fick	.201	214	12	43	6	26	0

Traded: P Zambrano and P Bartolome Fortunato to NYM for P Scott Kazmir and a minor leaguer (July 30). **Released:** P Abbott (June 3); IF Fick (Aug. 13).

Pitching (40 IP)

	ERA	W-L	Gm	IP	BB	SO
Trever Miller	3.12	1-1	60	49.0	15	43
Jesus Colome	3.27	2-2	33	41.1	18	40
Lance Carter	3.47	3-3	56	80.1	23	36
Danys Baez	3.57	4-4	62	68.0	29	52
Travis Harper	3.89	6-2	52	78.2	23	59
Victor Zambrano	4.43	9-7	23	128.0	96	109
Rob Bell	4.46	8-8	24	123.0	41	57
John Halama	4.70	7-6	34	118.2	27	59
Dewon Brazelton	4.77	6-8	22	120.2	53	64
Mark Hendrickson	4.81	10-15	32	183.1	46	87
Chad Gaudin*	4.85	1-2	26	42.2	16	30
Jorge Sosa	5.53	4-7	43	99.1	54	94
Doug Waechter*	6.01	5-7	14	70.1	33	36
Paul Abbott	6.70	2-5	10	47.0	27	25
Jeremi Gonzalez	6.97	0-5	11	50.1	20	22

Saves: Baez (30), Colome (5), Miller and Sosa (1). **Complete games:** Hendrickson (2), Bell (1). **Shutouts:** none.

Texas Rangers

Batting (130 AB)	Avg	AB	R	H	HR	RBI	SB
Michael Young	.313	690	114	216	22	99	12
Eric Young	.288	344	55	99	1	27	14
Mark Teixeira	.281	545	101	153	38	112	4
Alfonso Soriano	.280	608	77	170	28	91	18
Kevin Mench	.279	438	69	122	26	71	0
Hank Blalock	.276	624	107	172	32	110	2
Gary Matthews Jr.	.275	280	37	77	11	36	5
Rod Barajas	.249	358	50	89	15	58	0
Laynce Nix	.248	371	58	92	14	46	1
Dave Dellucci	.242	331	59	80	17	61	9
Brad Fullmer	.233	258	41	60	11	33	1
Gerald Laird*	.224	147	20	33	1	16	0
Herbert Perry	.224	134	13	30	5	17	0
Brian Jordan	.222	212	27	47	5	23	2

Pitching (20 IP)	ERA	W-L	Gm	IP	BB	SO
Ricardo Rodriguez	2.03	3-1	5	26.2	12	15
Francisco Cordero	2.13	3-4	67	71.2	32	79
Brian Shouse	2.23	2-0	53	44.1	18	34
Ron Mahay	2.55	3-0	60	67.0	29	54
Frank Francisco	3.33	5-1	45	51.1	28	60
Jay Powell	3.38	1-1	23	24.0	11	17
Carlos Almanzar	3.72	7-3	67	72.2	19	44
Juan Dominguez*	3.91	1-2	4	23.0	5	14
Doug Brocail	4.13	4-1	43	52.1	20	43
Ryan Drese	4.20	14-10	34	207.2	58	98
Erasmo Ramirez*	4.29	5-3	34	35.2	7	21
Chris Young*	4.71	3-2	7	36.1	10	27
Kenny Rogers	4.76	18-9	35	211.2	66	126
Jeff Nelson	5.32	1-2	29	23.2	19	22
Chan Ho Park	5.46	4-7	16	95.2	33	63
R.A. Dickey	5.61	6-7	25	104.1	33	57
Joaquin Benoit	5.68	3-5	28	103.0	31	95
John Wasdin	6.78	2-4	15	65.0	23	36

Saves: Cordero (49), Brocail, Dickey and Jeff Nelson (1).
Complete games: Drese and Rogers (2), Ricardo Rodriguez (1). **Shutouts:** Rodriguez and Rogers (1).

Toronto Blue Jays

Batting (115 AB)	Avg	AB	R	H	HR	RBI	SB
Frank Catalanotto	.293	249	27	73	1	26	1
Alexis Rios*	.286	426	55	122	1	28	15
Chris Gomez	.282	341	41	96	3	37	3
Frank Menechino	.275	269	40	74	9	26	0
Vernon Wells	.272	536	82	146	23	67	9
Reed Johnson	.270	537	68	145	10	61	6
Orlando Hudson	.270	489	73	132	12	58	7
Gregg Zaun	.269	338	46	91	6	36	0
Carlos Delgado	.269	458	74	123	32	99	0
Dave Berg	.253	154	13	39	3	23	0
Eric Hinske	.246	570	66	140	15	69	12
Chris Woodward	.235	213	21	50	1	24	1
Howie Clark*	.217	115	17	25	3	12	0
Gabe Gross*	.209	129	18	27	3	16	2
Kevin Cash*	.193	181	18	35	4	21	0

Acquired: IF Menechino from Oak. for future considerations (May 12).

Pitching (25 IP)	ERA	W-L	Gm	IP	BB	SO
David Bush*	3.69	5-4	16	97.2	25	64
Justin Speier	3.91	3-8	62	69.0	25	52
Ted Lilly	4.06	12-10	32	197.1	89	168
Jason Frasor*	4.08	4-6	63	68.1	36	54
Roy Halladay	4.20	8-8	21	133.0	39	95
Vinnie Chulk*	4.66	1-3	47	56.0	27	44
Miguel Batista	4.80	10-13	38	198.2	96	104
Bob File	4.81	1-0	24	33.2	12	.15
Josh Towers	5.11	9-9	21	116.1	26	51
Justin Miller	6.06	3-4	19	81.2	42	47
Sean Douglass	6.28	0-2	14	38.2	28	36
Kerry Ligtenberg	6.38	1-6	57	55.0	25	49
Kevin Frederick*	6.59	0-2	22	28.2	16	22
Pat Hentgen	6.95	2-9	18	80.1	42	33
Mike Nakamura*	7.36	0-3	19	25.2	7	24

Saves: Frasor (17), Speier (7), Batista (5), Ligtenberg (3), Chulk (2). **Complete games:** Lilly and Batista (2), Bush and Halladay (1). **Shutouts:** Bush, Lilly and Batista (1).

Home Attendance

Overall 2004 MLB regular season attendance (based on tickets sold) was 73,022,969, the highest total in history. The average per game crowd of 30,401 was the third-highest in history. Numbers in parentheses indicate ranking in 2002. HD indicates home dates. **Note:** Philadelphia and San Diego moved to new home parks in 2004.

American League

		Attendance	HD	Average
1	New York (1)	3,775,292	79	47,788
2	Anaheim (3)	3,375,677	81	41,675
3	Seattle (2)	2,940,731	81	36,305
4	Boston (4)	2,837,304	81	35,028
5	Baltimore (5)	2,747,573	80	34,300
6	Texas (7)	2,513,685	79	31,818
7	Oakland (6)	2,201,516	81	27,179
8	Chicago (9)	1,930,537	79	24,437
9	Detroit (13)	1,917,004	80	23,962
10	Minnesota (8)	1,911,418	81	23,598
11	Toronto (11)	1,900,041	81	23,457
12	Cleveland (12)	1,814,401	81	22,400
13	Kansas City (10)	1,661,478	79	21,031
14	Tampa Bay (14)	1,275,011	79	16,139
	TOTALS	32,801,668	1122	29,235

National League

		Attendance	HD	Average
1	Los Angeles (2)	3,488,283	81	43,065
2	Philadelphia (9)	3,250,092	80	40,626
3	San Francisco (1)	3,256,858	81	40,208
4	Chicago (3)	3,170,184	81	39,138
5	Houston (5)	3,087,872	81	38,121
6	St. Louis (4)	3,048,427	81	37,635
7	San Diego (12)	3,016,752	81	37,244
8	Arizona (7)	2,519,560	81	31,105
9	Colorado (10)	2,338,069	79	29,595
10	Atlanta (6)	2,322,565	79	29,399
11	New York (11)	2,318,321	80	28,979
12	Cincinnati (8)	2,287,250	81	28,237
13	Milwaukee (13)	2,062,382	81	25,461
14	Florida (15)	1,723,105	78	22,091
15	Pittsburgh (14)	1,583,031	75	21,107
16	Montreal (16)	748,550	80	9,356
	TOTALS	40,221,301	1280	31,423

NL Team by Team Statistics

At least 135 at bats or 40 innings pitched during the regular season unless otherwise indicated. Players who competed for more than one NL team are listed with their final club. Players traded from the AL are listed with NL team only if they have 135 AB or 40 IP. Note that (*) indicates rookie and PTBN indicates player to be named.

Arizona Diamondbacks

Batting (135 AB)

	Avg	AB	R	H	HR	RBI	SB
Shea Hillenbrand . . .	.310	562	68	174	15	80	2
Quinton McCracken . .	.288	156	20	45	2	13	2
Danny Bautista	.286	539	64	154	11	65	6
Chad Tracy*	.285	481	45	137	8	53	2
Alex Cintron	.262	564	56	148	4	49	3
Luis Gonzalez	.259	379	69	98	17	48	2
Scott Hairston*	.248	339	39	84	13	29	3
Matt Kata	.247	162	17	40	2	13	4
Luis Terrero*	.245	229	21	56	4	14	10
Robby Hammock	.241	195	22	47	4	18	3
Juan Brito*	.205	171	17	35	3	12	1

Signed: free agent P Fassero (Sept. 29).

Pitching (40 IP)

	ERA	W-L	Gm	IP	BB	SO
Randy Johnson	2.60	16-14	35	245.2	44	290
Brandon Webb	3.59	7-16	35	208.0	119	164
Mike Koplove	4.05	4-4	24	86.2	37	55
Randy Choate	4.62	2-4	74	50.2	28	49
Andrew Good	5.31	1-2	10	40.2	13	26
Jeff Fassero	5.46	3-8	41	112.0	44	60
Stephen Randolph	5.51	2-5	45	81.2	76	62
Steve Sparks	6.04	3-7	29	120.2	45	57
Casey Fossum	6.65	4-15	27	142.0	63	117
Casey Daigle*	7.16	2-3	10	49.0	27	17
Lance Cormier*	8.14	1-4	17	45.1	25	24
Edgar Gonzalez*	9.32	0-9	10	46.1	18	31

Saves: Greg Aquino (16), Jose Valverde (8), Matt Mantei (4), Koplove (2), Mike Fetters (1). **Complete games:** Johnson (4), Webb (1). **Shutouts:** Johnson (2).

Atlanta Braves

Batting (135 AB)

	Avg	AB	R	H	HR	RBI	SB
Eli Marrero	.320	250	37	80	10	40	4
Johnny Estrada	.314	462	56	145	9	76	0
Marcus Giles	.311	379	61	118	8	48	17
Julio Franco	.309	320	37	99	6	57	4
J.D. Drew	.305	518	118	158	31	93	12
Charles Thomas*	.288	236	35	68	7	31	3
Rafael Furcal	.279	563	103	157	14	59	29
Adam LaRoche*	.278	324	45	90	13	45	0
Nick Green*	.273	264	40	72	3	26	1
Andruw Jones	.261	570	85	149	29	91	6
Chipper Jones	.248	472	69	117	30	96	2
Mark DeRosa	.239	309	33	74	3	31	1
Eddie Perez	.229	170	14	39	3	13	0
Dewayne Wise	.228	162	24	37	6	17	6

Acquired: P Martin and cash from LA for (July 31).

Pitching (40 IP)

	ERA	W-L	Gm	IP	BB	SO
Horacio Ramirez	2.39	2-4	10	60.1	30	31
Antonio Alfonseca . . .	2.57	6-4	79	73.2	28	45
Juan Cruz	2.75	6-2	50	72.0	30	70
John Smoltz	2.76	0-1	73	81.2	13	85
Kevin Gryboski	2.84	3-2	69	50.2	23	24
Jaret Wright	3.28	15-8	32	186.1	70	159
John Thomson	3.72	14-8	33	198.1	52	133
Paul Byrd	3.94	8-7	19	114.1	19	79
Tom Martin	3.97	0-2	76	45.1	19	30
Chris Reitsma	4.07	6-4	84	79.2	20	60
Russ Ortiz	4.13	15-9	34	204.2	112	143
Mike Hampton	4.28	13-9	29	172.1	65	87
Travis Smith	6.20	2-3	16	40.2	12	26

Saves: Smoltz (44), Gryboski and Reitsma (2), Martin (1). **Complete games:** Ortiz (2), Ramirez and Hampton (1). **Shutouts:** Ortiz (1).

Chicago Cubs

Batting (140 AB)

	Avg	AB	R	H	HR	RBI	SB
Aramis Ramirez	.318	547	99	174	36	103	0
Todd Hollandsworth . . .	.318	148	28	47	8	22	1
Mark Grudzielanek . .	.307	257	32	79	6	23	1
Nomar Garciaparra . .	.297	165	28	49	4	20	2
Moises Alou	.293	601	106	176	39	106	3
Michael Barrett	.287	456	55	131	16	65	1
Derek Lee	.278	605	90	168	32	98	12
Todd Walker	.274	372	60	102	15	50	0
Jose Macias	.268	194	23	52	3	22	4
Corey Patterson	.266	631	91	168	24	72	32
Ben Grieve	.260	250	30	65	8	35	0
Neifi Perez	.255	381	40	97	4	39	1
Sammy Sosa	.253	478	69	121	35	80	0
Ramon Martinez	.246	260	22	64	3	30	1

Acquired: IF Garciaparra and OF Matt Murton from Bos. in a 4-team deal that sent IF Alex Gonzalez, P Francis Beltran and IF Brendan Harris to Mon. (July 31); OF Grieve from Mil. for P Andy Pratt (Aug. 31). **Signed:** free agent IF Perez (Aug. 19).

Pitching (45 IP)

	ERA	W-L	Gm	IP	BB	SO
Kent Mercker	2.55	3-1	71	53.0	27	51
LaTroy Hawkins	2.63	5-4	77	82.0	14	69
Carlos Zambrano	2.75	16-8	31	209.2	81	188
Glendon Rusch	3.47	6-2	32	129.2	33	90
Matt Clement	3.68	9-13	30	181.0	77	190
Kerry Wood	3.72	8-9	22	140.1	51	144
Mark Prior	4.02	6-4	21	118.2	48	139
Greg Maddux	4.02	16-11	33	212.2	33	151
Kyle Farnsworth	4.73	4-5	72	66.2	33	78
Sergio Mitre*	6.62	2-4	12	51.2	20	37

Saves: Hawkins (25), Joe Borowski (9), Rusch, Mike Remlinger and Ryan Dempster (2), Michael Wuertz and Jimmy Anderson (1). **Complete games:** Maddux (2), Zambrano (1). **Shutouts:** Zambrano and Maddux (1).

Cincinnati Reds

Batting (135 AB)

	Avg	AB	R	H	HR	RBI	SB
Sean Casey	.324	571	101	185	24	99	2
Barry Larkin	.289	346	55	100	8	44	2
Ryan Freel	.277	505	74	140	3	28	37
D'Angelo Jimenez . .	.270	563	76	152	12	67	13
Adam Dunn	.266	568	105	151	46	102	6
Wily Mo Pena	.259	336	45	87	26	66	5
Ken Griffey Jr.	.253	300	49	76	20	60	1
Jason LaRue	.251	390	46	98	14	55	0
Juan Castro	.244	299	36	73	5	26	1
Felipe Lopez	.242	264	35	64	7	31	1
Javier Valentin	.233	202	18	47	6	20	0
Austin Kearns	.230	217	28	50	9	32	2
Jacob Cruz	.224	147	22	33	3	28	0

Acquired: P Hancock and a minor leaguer from Phi. for P Todd Jones and a minor leaguer (July 30).

Pitching (40 IP)

	ERA	W-L	Gm	IP	BB	SO
Luke Hudson*	2.42	4-2	9	48.1	25	38
Danny Graves	3.95	1-6	68	68.1	13	40
Paul Wilson	4.36	11-6	29	183.2	63	117
Ryan Wagner*	4.70	3-2	49	51.2	27	37
Aaron Harang	4.86	10-9	28	161.0	53	125
Phil Norton*	5.07	2-0	69	65.2	38	48
Josh Hancock*	5.09	5-2	16	63.2	28	36
John Riedling	5.10	5-3	70	77.2	40	46
Jose Acevedo	5.94	5-12	39	157.2	45	117
Todd Van Poppel . . .	6.09	4-6	48	115.1	32	72
Brandon Claussen* . .	6.14	2-8	14	66.0	35	45

Saves: Graves (41), Joe Valentine (4), Gabe White (1). **Complete games:** Wilson and Harang (1). **Shutouts:** Harang (1).

Colorado Rockies

Batting (100 AB)	Avg	AB	R	H	HR	RBI	SB
Todd Helton	.347	547	115	190	32	96	3
J.D. Closser*	.319	113	5	36	1	10	0
Aaron Miles*	.293	522	75	153	6	47	12
Luis Gonzalez*	.292	322	42	94	12	40	1
Matt Holliday*	.290	400	65	116	14	57	3
Jeromy Burnitz	.283	540	94	153	37	110	5
Todd Greene	.282	195	23	55	10	35	0
Royce Clayton	.279	574	95	160	8	54	10
Vinny Castilla	.271	583	93	158	35	131	0
Mark Sweeney	.266	177	25	47	9	40	1
Brad Hawpe*	.248	105	12	26	3	9	1
Preston Wilson	.248	202	24	50	6	29	2
Kit Pellow*	.240	121	15	29	2	10	1
Charles Johnson	.236	305	42	72	13	47	2

Waived: P Elarton (May 20).

Pitching (40 IP)	ERA	W-L	Gm	IP	BB	SO
Joe Kennedy	3.66	9-7	27	162.1	67	117
Steve Reed	3.67	3-8	65	66.0	17	38
Scott Dohmann*	4.11	0-3	41	46.0	19	49
Jamey Wright	4.12	2-3	14	78.2	45	41
Aaron Cook	4.28	6-4	16	96.2	39	40
Tim Harikkala*	4.74	6-6	55	62.2	23	30
Jason Jennings	5.51	11-12	33	201.0	101	133
Brian Fuentes	5.64	2-4	47	44.2	19	48
Shawn Estes	5.84	15-8	34	202.0	105	117
Shawn Chacon	7.11	1-9	66	63.1	52	52
Javier Lopez	7.52	1-2	64	40.2	26	20
Scott Elarton	9.80	0-6	8	41.1	20	23

Saves: Chacon (35), Chin-hui Tsao (1). **Complete games:** Kennedy, Cook and Estes (1). **Shutouts:** none.

Florida Marlins

Batting (135 AB)	Avg	AB	R	H	HR	RBI	SB
Juan Pierre	.326	678	100	221	3	49	45
Miguel Cabrera	.294	603	101	177	33	112	5
Mike Lowell	.293	598	87	175	27	85	5
Luis Castillo	.291	564	91	164	2	47	21
Paul Lo Duca	.286	535	68	153	13	80	4
Jeff Conine	.280	521	55	146	14	83	5
Mike Remond	.256	246	19	63	2	25	1
Damion Easley	.238	223	26	53	9	43	4
Juan Encarnacion	.236	484	63	114	16	62	5
Alex Gonzalez	.232	561	67	130	23	79	3

Acquired: C Lo Duca, P Mota and OF Encarnacion from LA for P Brad Penny, IF Hee Sop Choi and a minor leaguer (July 30); P Valdez from SD for a minor leaguer (July 31). **Signed:** free agent P Weathers (Sept. 8).

Pitching (30 IP)	ERA	W-L	Gm	IP	BB	SO
Armando Benitez	1.29	2-2	64	69.2	21	62
Carl Pavano	3.00	18-8	31	222.1	49	139
Guillermo Mota	3.07	9-8	78	96.2	37	85
A.J. Burnett	3.68	7-6	20	120.0	38	113
Josh Beckett	3.79	9-9	26	156.2	54	152
Dontrelle Willis	4.02	10-11	32	197.0	61	139
David Weathers	4.15	7-7	66	82.1	35	61
Matt Perisho	4.40	5-3	66	47.0	26	42
Tommy Phelps	4.76	1-1	19	34.0	12	28
Nate Bump*	5.01	2-4	50	73.2	32	44
Ismael Valdez	5.19	14-9	34	170.0	49	67
Ben Howard*	5.50	1-1	31	37.2	21	33
Justin Wayne*	5.79	3-3	19	32.2	18	20
Josias Manzanillo	6.12	3-3	26	32.1	15	27

Saves: Benitez (47), Mota (4), Bump, Manzanillo and Franklyn Gracesqui (1). **Complete games:** Pavano and Willis (2), Burnett, Beckett and Valdez (1). **Shutouts:** Pavano (2), Beckett and Valdez (1).

Houston Astros

Batting (140 AB)	Avg	AB	R	H	HR	RBI	SB
Lance Berkman	.316	544	104	172	30	106	9
Jeff Kent	.289	540	96	156	27	107	7
Mike Lamb	.288	278	38	80	14	58	1
Craig Biggio	.281	633	100	178	24	63	7
Morgan Ensberg	.275	411	51	113	10	66	6
Jose Vizcaino	.274	358	34	98	3	33	1
Adam Everett	.273	384	66	105	8	31	13
Jeff Bagwell	.266	572	104	152	27	89	6
Carlos Beltran	.258	333	70	86	23	53	28
Brad Ausmus	.248	403	38	100	5	31	2
Raul Chavez	.210	162	9	34	0	23	0

Acquired: P Harville from Oak. for P Kirk Saarloos (Apr. 16); OF Beltran from KC in a 3-team deal that sent C John Buck to KC, P Octavio Dotel to Oak. and P Mike Wood and a minor leaguer from Oak. to KC (June 24); P Oliver from Fla. for PTBN or cash (July 23); P Wheeler from NYM for a minor leaguer (Aug. 27).

Pitchers (50 IP)	ERA	W-L	Gm	IP	BB	SO
Brad Lidge	1.90	6-5	80	94.2	30	157
Roger Clemens	2.98	18-4	33	214.1	79	218
Wade Miller	3.35	7-7	15	88.2	44	74
Roy Oswalt	3.49	20-10	36	237.0	62	206
Dan Miceli	3.59	6-6	74	77.2	27	83
Andy Pettitte	3.90	6-4	15	83.0	31	79
Dan Wheeler	4.29	3-1	46	65.0	20	55
Brandon Backe	4.30	5-3	33	67.0	27	54
Chad Harville	4.75	3-2	56	53.0	26	46
Pete Munro	5.15	4-7	21	99.2	26	63
Tim Redding	5.72	5-7	27	100.2	43	56
Darren Oliver	5.94	3-3	37	72.2	21	46

Saves: Lidge (29), Octavio Dotel (14), Miceli (2), Chad Qualls and Kirk Bullinger (1). **Complete games:** Oswalt (2). **Shutouts:** Oswalt (1).

Los Angeles Dodgers

Batting (160 AB)	Avg	AB	R	H	HR	RBI	SB
Adrian Beltre	.334	598	104	200	48	121	7
Jose Hernandez	.289	211	32	61	13	29	3
Cesar Izturis	.288	670	90	193	4	62	25
Steve Finley	.271	628	92	170	36	94	9
Milton Bradley	.267	516	72	138	19	67	15
Shawn Green	.266	590	92	157	28	86	5
Alex Cora	.264	405	47	107	10	47	3
Jayson Werth*	.262	290	56	76	16	47	4
Dave Roberts	.253	233	45	59	2	21	33
Hee Sop Choi	.251	343	53	86	15	46	1
Brent Mayne	.221	190	14	42	0	15	1
Jason Grabowski*	.220	173	18	38	7	20	0
David Ross	.170	165	13	28	5	15	0

Acquired: P Penny, IF Choi and a minor leaguer from Fla. for C Paul Lo Duca, P Guillermo Mota and OF Juan Encarnacion (July 30); OF Finley and C Mayne from Ari. for 3 minor leaguers (July 31); P Dessens and cash from Ari. for a minor leaguer (Aug. 19). **Traded:** OF Roberts to Bos. for a minor leaguer (July 31).

Pitching (40 IP)	ERA	W-L	Gm	IP	BB	SO
Giovanni Carrara	2.18	5-2	42	53.2	20	48
Eric Gagne	2.19	7-3	70	82.1	22	114
Brad Penny	3.15	9-10	24	143.0	45	111
Odalis Perez	3.25	7-6	31	196.1	44	128
Duaner Sanchez*	3.38	3-1	67	80.0	27	44
Jeff Weaver	4.01	13-13	34	220.0	67	153
Wilson Alvarez	4.03	7-6	40	120.2	31	102
Jose Lima	4.07	13-5	36	170.1	34	93
Darren Dreifort	4.44	1-4	60	50.2	36	63
Elmer Dessens	4.46	2-6	50	105.0	31	73
Kazuhisa Ishii	4.71	13-8	31	172.0	98	99
Hideo Nomo	8.25	4-11	18	84.0	42	54

Saves: Gagne (45), Carrara and Dessens (2), Alvarez and Dreifort (1). **Complete games:** Ishii (2). **Shutouts:** Ishii (2).

Milwaukee Brewers

Batting (135 AB)	Avg	AB	R	H	HR	RBI	SB
Lyle Overbay	.301	579	83	174	16	87	2
Brady Clark	.280	353	41	99	7	46	15
Junior Spivey	.272	228	33	62	7	28	5
Geoff Jenkins	.264	617	88	163	27	93	3
Wes Helms	.263	274	24	72	4	28	0
Keith Ginter	.262	386	47	101	19	60	8
Scott Podsednik	.244	640	85	156	12	39	70
Craig Counsell	.241	473	59	114	2	23	17
Bill Hall	.238	390	43	93	9	53	12
Russell Branyan	.234	158	21	37	11	27	1
Gary Bennett	.224	219	18	49	3	20	1
Chad Moeller	.208	317	25	66	5	27	0

Acquired: IF Branyan from Cle. for cash (July 26). **Waived:** P Kinney (Aug. 6).

Pitching (40 IP)	ERA	W-L	Gm	IP	BB	SO
Ben Sheets	2.70	12-14	34	237.0	32	264
Danny Kolb	2.98	0-4	64	57.1	15	21
Doug Davis	3.39	12-12	34	207.1	79	166
Mike Adams*	3.40	2-3	46	53.0	14	39
Luis Vizcaino	3.75	4-4	73	72.0	24	63
Brooks Kieschnick	3.77	1-1	32	43.0	13	28
Matt Wise	4.44	1-2	30	52.2	15	30
Jeff Bennett*	4.79	1-5	60	71.1	26	45
Victor Santos	4.97	11-12	31	154.0	57	115
Chris Capuano*	4.99	6-8	17	88.1	37	80
Matt Kinney	5.78	3-4	32	62.1	23	52
Wes Obermueller	5.80	6-8	25	118.0	42	59
Ben Hendrickson*	6.22	1-8	10	46.1	20	29

Saves: Kolb (39), Vizcaino (1). **Complete games:** Sheets (5), Obermueller (1). **Shutouts:** Obermueller (1).

Montreal Expos

Batting (125 AB)	Avg	AB	R	H	HR	RBI	SB
Juan Rivera	.307	391	48	120	12	49	6
Jose Vidro	.294	412	51	121	14	60	3
Jamey Carroll	.289	218	36	63	0	16	5
Endy Chavez	.277	502	65	139	5	34	32
Termel Sledge*	.269	398	45	107	15	62	3
Brian Schneider	.257	436	40	112	12	49	0
Brad Wilkerson	.255	572	112	146	32	67	13
Carl Everett	.252	127	8	32	2	14	0
Nick Johnson	.251	251	35	63	7	33	6
Orlando Cabrera	.246	390	41	96	4	31	12
Tony Batista	.241	606	76	146	32	110	14
Einar Diaz	.223	139	9	31	1	11	2

Acquired: P Beltran, IF Alex Gonzalez and IF Brendan Harris from ChC in a four-team trade that sent IF Cabrera to Bos. (July 31). **Traded:** OF Everett to ChW for 2 minor leaguers (July 18).

Pitching (40 IP)	ERA	W-L	Gm	IP	BB	SO
Luis Ayala	2.69	6-12	81	90.1	15	63
Chad Cordero*	2.94	7-3	69	82.2	43	83
Joe Horgan*	3.15	4-1	47	40.0	22	30
Tomo Ohka	3.40	3-7	15	84.2	20	38
Livan Hernandez	3.60	11-15	35	255.0	83	186
T.J. Tucker	3.72	4-2	54	67.2	17	44
Zach Day	3.93	5-10	19	116.2	45	61
Sun-Woo Kim	4.58	4-6	43	135.2	55	87
Tony Armas	4.88	2-4	16	72.0	45	54
John Patterson	5.03	4-7	19	98.1	46	99
Scott Downs	5.14	3-6	12	63.0	23	38
Claudio Vargas	5.25	5-5	45	118.1	64	89
Francis Beltran*	5.47	2-2	45	49.1	27	48
Rocky Biddle	6.92	4-8	47	78.0	31	51

Saves: Cordero (14), Biddle (11), Ayala and Horgan (2), Beltran and Gary Majewski (1). **Complete games:** Hernandez (9), Day and Downs (1). **Shutouts:** Hernandez (2), Day and Downs (1).

New York Mets

Batting (140 AB)	Avg	AB	R	H	HR	RBI	SB
David Wright*	.293	263	41	77	14	40	6
Shane Spencer	.281	185	21	52	4	26	6
Vance Wilson	.274	157	18	43	4	21	1
Kazuo Matsui*	.272	460	65	125	7	44	14
Eric Valent	.267	270	39	72	13	34	0
Mike Piazza	.266	455	47	121	20	54	0
Cliff Floyd	.260	396	55	103	18	63	11
Jose Reyes	.255	220	33	56	2	14	19
Richard Hidalgo	.239	523	67	125	25	82	6
Karim Garcia	.234	192	24	45	7	22	3
Todd Zeile	.233	348	30	81	9	35	0
Mike Cameron	.231	493	76	114	30	76	22
Jason Phillips	.218	362	34	79	7	34	0

Acquired: OF Hidalgo from Hou. for P David Weathers and a minor leaguer (June 18); OF Garcia from Bal. for P Mike DeJean (July 19); P Benson and IF Jeff Keppinger from Pit. for IF Jose Bautista, IF Ty Wigginton and P Matt Peterson (July 30).

Pitching (40 IP)	ERA	W-L	Gm	IP	BB	SO
Braden Looper	2.70	2-5	71	83.1	16	60
Mike Stanton	3.16	2-6	83	77.0	33	58
Al Leiter	3.21	10-8	30	173.2	97	117
Ricky Bottalico	3.38	3-2	60	69.1	34	61
Tom Glavine	3.60	11-14	33	212.1	70	109
Steve Trachsel	4.00	12-13	33	202.2	83	117
Kris Benson	4.31	12-12	31	200.1	61	134
Matt Ginter	4.54	1-3	15	69.1	20	38
Jae Weong Seo	4.90	5-10	24	117.2	50	54
John Franco	5.28	2-7	52	46.0	24	36
Tyler Yates*	6.36	2-4	21	46.2	25	29

Saves: Looper (29), Orber Moreno and Bartolome Fortunato (1). **Complete games:** Glavine and Benson (1). **Shutouts:** Glavine and Benson (1).

Philadelphia Phillies

Batting (135 AB)	Avg	AB	R	H	HR	RBI	SB
Bobby Abreu	.301	574	118	173	30	105	40
Placido Polanco	.298	503	74	150	17	55	7
David Bell	.291	533	67	155	18	77	1
Jimmy Rollins	.289	657	119	190	14	73	30
Jason Michaels	.274	299	44	82	10	40	2
Jim Thome	.274	508	97	139	42	105	0
Mike Lieberthal	.271	476	58	129	17	61	1
Chase Utley	.266	267	36	71	13	57	4
Pat Burrell	.257	448	66	115	24	84	2
Marlon Byrd	.228	346	48	79	5	33	2
Tomas Perez	.216	176	22	38	6	21	0
Doug Glanville	.210	162	21	34	2	14	8

Acquired: P Jones and a minor leaguer from Cin. for P Josh Hancock (July 30); P Rodriguez from SF for OF Ricky Ledee (July 30); P Lidle from Cin. for two minor leaguers and a PTBN (Aug 2).

Pitchers (45 IP)	ERA	W-L	Gm	IP	BB	SO
Ryan Madson*	2.34	9-3	52	77.0	19	55
Billy Wagner	2.42	4-0	45	48.1	6	59
Felix Rodriguez	3.29	5-8	76	65.2	29	59
Rheal Cormier	3.56	4-5	84	81.0	26	46
Tim Worrell	3.68	5-6	77	78.1	21	64
Todd Jones	4.15	1-5	78	82.1	33	59
Randy Wolf	4.28	5-8	23	136.2	36	89
Amaury Telemaco	4.31	0-2	42	54.1	19	32
Vicente Padilla	4.53	7-7	20	115.1	36	82
Eric Milton	4.75	14-6	34	201.0	75	161
Roberto Hernandez	4.76	3-5	63	56.2	29	44
Kevin Millwood	4.85	9-6	25	141.0	51	125
Cory Lidle	4.90	12-12	34	211.1	61	126
Brett Myers	5.52	11-11	32	176.0	62	116
Paul Abbott	6.24	1-6	10	49.0	31	21

Saves: Wagner (21), Worrell (19), Jones (2), Madson and Rodriguez (1). **Complete games:** Lidle (5), Wolf and Myers (1). **Shutouts:** Lidle (3), Wolf and Myers (1).

Pittsburgh Pirates

Batting (135 AB)	Avg	AB	R	H	HR	RBI	SB
Jason Kendall	.319	574	86	183	3	51	11
Jack Wilson	.308	652	82	201	11	59	8
Jason Bay*	.282	411	61	116	26	82	4
Tike Redman	.280	546	65	153	8	51	18
Bobby Hill	.266	233	28	62	2	27	0
Craig Wilson	.264	561	97	148	29	82	2
Ty Wigginton	.261	494	63	129	17	66	7
Jose Castillo*	.256	383	44	98	8	39	3
Daryle Ward	.249	293	39	73	15	57	0
Rob Mackowiak	.246	491	65	121	17	75	13
Abraham O. Nunez	.236	182	17	43	2	13	1
Chris Stynes	.216	162	16	35	1	16	0
Randall Simon	.194	175	14	34	3	14	0

Acquired: IF Wigginton, IF Jose Bautista and P Matt Peterson from NYM for P Kris Benson and IF Jeff Keppinger (July 30). **Released:** IF Simon (Aug. 19).

Pitching (40 IP)	ERA	W-L	Gm	IP	BB	SO
Mike Gonzalez*	1.25	3-1	47	43.1	6	55
Salomon Torres	2.64	7-7	84	92.0	22	62
Oliver Perez	2.98	12-10	30	196.0	81	239
Jose Mesa	3.25	5-2	70	69.1	20	37
Brian Meadows	3.58	2-4	68	78.0	19	46
Kip Wells	4.55	5-7	24	138.1	66	116
Josh Fogg	4.64	11-10	32	178.1	66	82
Sean Burnett*	5.02	5-5	13	71.2	28	30
John Grabow*	5.11	2-5	68	61.2	28	64
Ryan Vogelsong	6.50	6-13	31	133.0	67	92

Saves: Mesa (43), Gonzalez, Meadows and Grabow (1). **Complete games:** Perez (2), Burnett (1). **Shutouts:** Perez and Burnett (1).

St. Louis Cardinals

Batting (135 AB)	Avg	AB	R	H	HR	RBI	SB
Albert Pujols	.331	592	133	196	46	123	5
Scott Rolen	.314	500	109	157	34	124	4
Tony Womack	.307	553	91	170	5	38	26
Jim Edmonds	.301	498	102	150	42	111	8
Larry Walker	.298	258	51	77	17	47	6
John Mabry	.296	240	32	71	13	40	0
So Taguchi*	.291	179	26	52	3	25	6
Edgar Renteria	.287	586	84	168	10	72	17
Yadier Molina*	.267	135	12	36	2	15	0
Roger Cedeno	.265	200	22	53	3	23	5
Reggie Sanders	.260	446	64	116	22	67	21
Ray Lankford	.255	200	36	51	6	22	2
Hector Luna*	.249	173	25	43	3	22	6
Mike Matheny	.247	385	28	95	5	50	0
Marlon Anderson	.237	253	31	60	8	28	6

Acquired: OF Walker from Col. for a minor leaguer and 2 PTBN (Aug. 6).

Pitching (40 IP)	ERA	W-L	Gm	IP	BB	SO
Steve Kline	1.79	2-2	67	50.1	17	35
Julian Tavarez	2.38	7-4	77	64.1	19	48
Ray King	2.61	5-2	86	62.0	24	40
Kiko Calero	2.78	3-1	41	45.1	10	47
Jason Isringhausen	2.87	4-2	74	75.1	23	71
Chris Carpenter	3.46	15-5	28	182.0	38	152
Jason Marquis	3.71	15-7	32	201.1	70	138
Cal Eldred	3.76	4-2	52	67.0	17	54
Jeff Suppan	4.16	16-9	31	188.0	65	110
Woody Williams	4.18	11-8	31	189.2	58	131
Danny Haren	4.50	3-3	14	46.0	17	32
Matt Morris	4.72	15-10	32	202.0	56	131

Saves: Isringhausen (47), Tavarez (4), Kline (3), Calero (2), Eldred (1). **Complete games:** Morris (3), Carpenter (1). **Shutouts:** Morris (2).

San Diego Padres

Batting (115 AB)	Avg	AB	R	H	HR	RBI	SB
Mark Loretta	.335	620	108	208	16	76	5
Sean Burroughs	.298	523	76	156	2	47	5
Terrence Long	.295	288	31	85	3	28	3
Ryan Klesko	.291	402	58	117	9	66	3
Phil Nevin	.289	547	78	158	26	105	0
Brian Giles	.284	609	97	173	23	94	10
Ramon Hernandez	.276	384	45	106	18	63	1
Khalil Greene*	.273	484	67	132	15	65	4
Jay Payton	.260	458	57	119	8	55	2
Miguel Ojeda	.256	156	23	40	8	26	0
Rich Aurilia	.254	138	22	35	2	16	0
Ramon Vazquez	.235	115	12	27	1	13	1
Alex Gonzalez	.225	285	36	64	7	27	2

Acquired: IF Aurilia from Sea. for PTBN or cash (July 19); IF Gonzalez from Mon. for PTBN or cash (Sept. 17). **Claimed:** P Stone off waivers from Hou. (June 18).

Pitching (35 IP)	ERA	W-L	Gm	IP	BB	SO
Akinori Otsuka*	1.75	7-2	73	77.1	26	87
Scott Linebrink	2.14	7-3	73	84.0	26	83
Jake Peavy	2.27	15-6	27	166.1	53	173
Trevor Hoffman	2.30	3-3	55	54.2	8	53
Antonio Osuna	2.45	2-1	31	36.2	11	36
Jay Witasick	3.21	0-1	44	61.2	26	57
David Wells	3.73	12-8	31	195.2	20	101
Blaine Neal	4.07	1-1	40	42.0	11	36
Brian Lawrence	4.12	15-14	34	203.0	55	121
Adam Eaton	4.61	11-14	33	199.1	52	153
Dennis Tankersley	5.14	0-5	9	35.0	17	29
Ricky Stone	6.45	2-2	43	51.2	16	38

Saves: Hoffman (41), Otsuka (2), Witasick (1). **Complete games:** Lawrence (2). **Shutouts:** Lawrence (1).

San Francisco Giants

Batting (135 AB)	Avg	AB	R	H	HR	RBI	SB
Barry Bonds	.362	373	129	135	45	101	6
J.T. Snow	.327	346	62	113	12	60	4
Deivi Cruz	.292	397	46	116	7	55	1
Edgardo Alfonzo	.289	519	66	150	11	77	1
Ray Durham	.282	471	95	133	17	65	10
Marquis Grissom	.279	562	78	157	22	90	3
Pedro Feliz	.276	503	72	139	22	84	5
Dustan Mohr	.274	263	52	72	7	28	0
A.J. Pierzynski	.272	471	45	128	11	77	0
Michael Tucker	.256	464	77	119	13	62	5
Ricky Ledee	.233	176	25	41	7	30	3
Yorvit Torrealba	.227	172	19	39	6	23	2

Acquired: OF Ledee from Phi for P Felix Rodriguez (July 30); Burba from Mil. for a minor leaguer (Sept. 2).

Pitching (35 IP)	ERA	W-L	Gm	IP	BB	SO
Jason Schmidt	3.20	18-7	32	225.0	77	251
Jim Brower	3.29	7-7	89	93.0	36	63
Noah Lowry*	3.82	6-0	16	92.0	28	72
Brett Tomko	4.04	11-7	32	194.0	64	108
Scott Eyre	4.10	2-2	83	52.2	27	49
Dave Burba	4.21	4-1	51	77.0	26	50
Tyler Walker*	4.24	5-1	52	63.2	24	48
Jerome Williams	4.24	10-7	22	129.1	44	80
Jason Christiansen	4.50	4-3	60	36.0	26	22
Dustin Hermanson	4.53	6-9	47	131.0	46	102
Kirk Rueter	4.73	9-12	33	190.1	66	56
Matt Herges	5.23	4-5	70	65.1	21	39
Wayne Franklin	6.39	2-1	43	50.2	22	40

Saves: Herges (23), Hermanson (17), Jason Christiansen (3), Burba (2), Brower, Eyre and Walker (1). **Complete games:** Schmidt (4), Lowry and Tomko (1). **Shutouts:** Schmidt (3), Lowry and Tomko (1).

BASEBALL PLAYOFFS

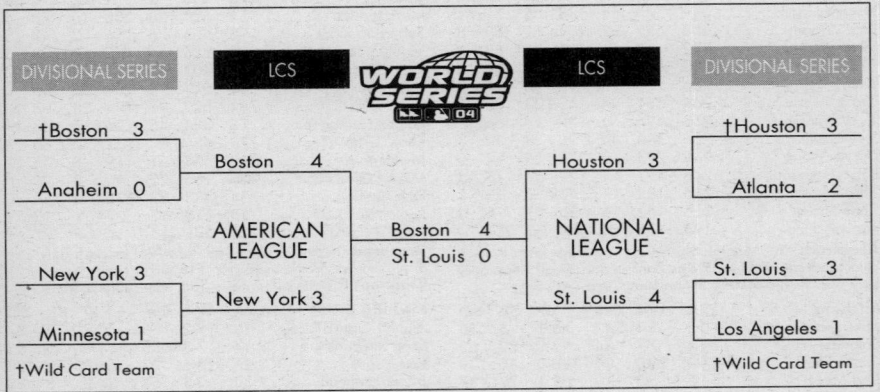

Divisional Series Summaries

AMERICAN LEAGUE

Yankees, 3-1

Date	Winner	Home Field
Oct. 5............	Twins, 2-0	at New York
Oct. 6..........	Yankees, 7-6 (12 inn.)	at New York
Oct. 8..........	Yankees, 8-4	at Minnesota
Oct. 9..........	Yankees, 6-5 (11 inn.)	at Minnesota

Game 1
Tuesday, Oct. 5, at New York

	1 2 3	4 5 6	7 8 9	R	H	E
Minnesota	. . . 0 0 1	0 0 1	0 0 0 -	2	7	0
New York	. . . 0 0 0	0 0 0	0 0 0 -	0	9	0

Win: Santana, Min. (1-0). **Loss:** Mussina, NY (0-1).
Save: Nathan, Min. (1).
2B: New York—Matsui (1), Cairo (1). **HR:** Minnesota—Jones (1, off Mussina, 0 on). **RBI:** Minnesota—Stewart (1), Jones (1). **SB:** Minnesota—Hunter (1).
Attendance: 55,749 (57,478). **Time:** 2:53.

Game 2
Wednesday, Oct. 6, at New York

	1 2 3	4 5 6	7 8 9 10 11 12	R	H	E
Minnesota	1 2 0	0 0 0	0 2 0 0 0 1 -	6	12	0
New York	1 0 2	0 1 0	1 0 0 0 0 2 -	7	9	0

Win: Quantrill, NY (1-0). **Loss:** Nathan, Min. (0-1).
2B: Minnesota—Morneau (1), Koskie (1); New York—Williams (1), Olerud (1), Rodriguez (1). **HR:** Minnesota—Hunter (1, off Sturtze, 0 on); New York—Jeter (1, off Radke, 0 on), Sheffield (1, off Radke, 1 on), Rodriguez (1, off Radke, 0 on). **RBI:** Minnesota—Morneau 2 (2), Cuddyer (1), Blanco (1), Koskie (1), Hunter (1); New York—Jeter (1), Sheffield 2 (2), Rodriguez 3 (3), Matsui (1). **SB:** Minnesota—Hunter (2); New York—Sierra (1).
Attendance: 56,354 (57,478). **Time:** 4:19.

Game 3
Friday, Oct. 8, at Minnesota

	1 2 3	4 5 6	7 8 9	R	H	E
New York	. . . 0 3 0	0 0 4	1 0 0 -	8	14	1
Minnesota	. . . 1 0 0	0 0 0	0 0 3 -	4	12	1

Win: Brown, NY (1-0). **Loss:** Silva, Min. (0-1).
2B: New York—Sheffield (1), Jeter (1); Minnesota—Hunter (1), Jones (1). **HR:** New York—Williams (1, off Silva, 1 on), Matsui (1, off Mulholland, 0 on); Minnesota—Jones (2, off Brown, 0 on). **RBI:** New York— Cairo (1), Lofton (1), Jeter 3 (4), Williams 2 (2), Matsui (2); Minnesota—Jones (2), Cuddyer (2), Offerman (1), Stewart (2). **SB:** New York—Jeter (1); Minnesota—Guzman (1). **E:** New York—Jeter (1); Minnesota—Guzman (1).
Attendance: 54,803 (45,423). **Time:** 3:02.

Game 4
Saturday, Oct. 9, at Minnesota

	1 2 3	4 5 6	7 8 9 10 11	R	H	E
New York	. 0 0 1	0 0 0	0 4 0 0 1 -	6	11	0
Minnesota	. . 1 0 0	1 3 0	0 0 0 0 0 -	5	12	1

Win: Rivera, NY (1-0). **Loss:** Lohse, Min. (0-1).
2B: New York—Olerud (2), Rodriguez 2 (3); Minnesota—Morneau (2), Ford (1), Kubel (1). **HR:** New York—Sierra (1, off Rincon, 2 on); Minnesota—Blanco (1, off Vazquez, 0 on). **RBI:** New York— Matsui (3), Williams (3), Sierra (3); Minnesota—Hunter (4), Koskie (2), Blanco (2), Ford 2 (2). **SB:** New York—Rodriguez 2 (2); Minnesota—Ford (1). **E:** Minnesota—Blanco (1).
Attendance: 52,498 (45,423). **Time:** 4:16.

Red Sox, 3-0

Date	Winner	Home Field
Oct. 5	Red Sox, 9-3	at Anaheim
Oct. 6	Red Sox, 8-3	at Anaheim
Oct. 8	Red Sox, 8-6 (10 inn.)	at Boston

Game 1

Tuesday, Oct. 5, at Anaheim

	1 2 3	4 5 6	7 8 9	R H E
Boston	1 0 0	7 0 0	0 1 0	- 9 11 1
Anaheim	. 0 0 0	1 0 0	2 0 0	- 3 9 1

Win: Schilling, Bos. (1-0). **Loss:** Washburn, Ana. (0-1).
2B: Boston—Ramirez (1), Damon (1); Anaheim—Glaus 2 (2). **HR:** Boston—Millar (1, off Washburn, 1 on), Ramirez (1, off Shields, 2 on); Anaheim—Glaus (1, off Schilling, 0 on), Erstad (1, off Schilling, 0 on). **RBI:** Boston—Ortiz (1), Millar 2 (2), Ramirez 3 (3), Mientkiewicz (1); Anaheim—Glaus 2 (2), Erstad (1). **SB:** Boston—Damon (1); Anaheim—Figgins (1). **E:** Boston—Schilling (1); Anaheim—Figgins (1).
Attendance: 44,608 (45,030). **Time:** 3:04.

Game 2

Wednesday, Oct. 6, at Anaheim

	1 2 3	4 5 6	7 8 9	R H E
Boston	0 1 0	0 0 2	1 0 4	- 8 12 0
Anaheim	0 1 0	0 2 0	0 0 0	- 3 7 0

Win: Martinez, Bos. (1-0). **Loss:** Rodriguez, Ana. (0-1).
Save: Foulke, Bos. (1).
2B: Boston—Ramirez (2), Cabrera (1). **HR:** Boston—Varitek (1, off Colon, 1 on). **RBI:** Boston—Ramirez 2 (5), Varitek 2 (2), Nixon (1), Cabrera 3 (3); Anaheim—McPherson (1), Guerrero 2 (2). **SB:** Boston—Damon (2).
Attendance: 45,118 (45,030). **Time:** 3:48.

Game 3

Friday, Oct. 8, at Boston

	1 2 3	4 5 6	7 8 9 10	R H E
Anaheim	. 0 0 0	1 0 0	5 0 0 0	- 6 8 2
Boston	. . . 0 0 2	3 1 0	0 0 0 2	- 8 12 0

Win: Lowe, Bos. (1-0). **Loss:** Rodriguez, Ana. (0-2).
2B: Anaheim—Erstad (1); Boston—Ortiz 2 (2). **HR:** Anaheim—Glaus (2, off Arroyo, 0 on), Guerrero (1, off Timlin, 3 on); Boston—Ortiz (1, off Washburn, 1 on). **RBI:** Anaheim—Glaus (3), Erstad (2), Guerrero 4 (6); Boston—Nixon (2), Millar 2 (4), Ramirez 2 (7), Ortiz 3 (4). **SB:** Boston—Damon (3). **E:** Anaheim—Figgins (2), Eckstein (1).
Attendance: 35,547 (35,095). **Time:** 4:11.

NATIONAL LEAGUE

Cardinals, 3-1

Date	Winner	Home Field
Oct. 5	Cardinals, 8-3	at St. Louis
Oct. 7	Cardinals, 8-3	at St. Louis
Oct. 9	Dodgers, 4-0	at Los Angeles
Oct. 10	Cardinals, 6-2	at Los Angeles

Game 1

Tuesday, Oct. 5, at St. Louis

	1 2 3	4 5 6	7 8 9	R H E
Los Angeles	. 0 0 0	0 1 1	0 0 1	- 3 9 1
St. Louis	. . . . . 1 0 5	1 0 0	1 0 x	- 8 9 0

Win: Williams, St.L (1-0). **Loss:** Perez, LA (0-1).
2B: Los Angeles—Izturis (1), Werth (1); St. Louis—Renteria (1). **HR:** Los Angeles—Wilson (1, off Isringhausen, 0 on); St. Louis—Pujols (1, off Perez, 0 on), Walker 2 (2, off Perez, 0 on; off Carrara, 0 on), Edmonds (1, off Perez, 1 on), Matheny (1, off Dessens, 0 on). **RBI:** Los Angles—Werth (1), Cora (1), Wilson (1); St. Louis—Pujols (1), Walker 2 (2), Renteria 2 (2), Edmonds 2 (2), Matheny (1). **SB:** Los Angeles—Bradley (1); St. Louis—Renteria (1). **E:** Los Angeles—Perez (1).
Attendance: 52,127 (50,345). **Time:** 3:11.

Game 2

Thursday, Oct. 7, at St. Louis

	1 2 3	4 5 6	7 8 9	R H E
Los Angeles	. 1 0 0	2 0 0	0 0 0	- 3 6 1
St. Louis	. . . . . 0 3 0	0 3 0	2 0 x	- 8 11 0

Win: Haren, St.L (1-0). **Loss:** Weaver, LA (0-1).
2B: Los Angeles—Bradley (1); St. Louis—Renteria (2), Walker (1). **3B:** St. Louis—Womack (1). **HR:** Los Angeles—Werth (1, off Marquis, 0 on), Green (1, off Marquis, 0 on), Bradley (1, off Marquis, 0 on). **RBI:** Los Angles—Werth (2), Green (1), Bradley (1); St. Louis—Womack (1), Walker (3), Renteria (3), Matheny 4 (5). **SB:** St. Louis—Sanders (1). **E:** Los Angeles—Weaver (1).
Attendance: 52,228 (50,345). **Time:** 3:36.

Game 3

Saturday, Oct. 9, at Los Angeles

	1 2 3	4 5 6	7 8 9	R H E
St. Louis	. . . . 0 0 0	0 0 0	0 0 0	- 0 5 0
Los Angeles	. 0 0 2	1 0 1	0 0 x	- 4 7 0

Win: Lima, LA (1-0). **Loss:** Morris, St.L (0-1).
2B: Los Angeles—Finley (1). **HR:** Los Angeles—Green 2 (3, off Morris, 0 on; off Morris, 0 on). **RBI:** Los Angeles—Finley 2 (2), Green 2 (3). **SB:** St. Louis—Womack (2).
Attendance: 55,992 (56,000). **Time:** 2:23.

Game 4

Sunday, Oct. 10, at Los Angeles

	1 2 3	4 5 6	7 8 9	R H E
St. Louis	. . . . 0 1 1	3 0 0	1 0 0	- 6 8 0
Los Angeles	. 1 0 1	0 0 0	0 2 x	- 2 3 1

Win: Suppan, St.L (1-0). **Loss:** Alvarez, LA (0-1).
HR: St. Louis—Sanders (1, off Perez, 0 on), Pujols (2, off Alvarez, 2 on); Los Angeles—Werth (2, off Suppan, 0 on). **RBI:** St. Louis—Sanders (1), Renteria (4), Pujols 4 (5); Los Angeles—Werth (3), Beltre (1). **SB:** St. Louis—Walker (1); Los Angeles—Bradley (2). **E:** Los Angeles—Ross (1).
Attendance: 56,268 (56,000). **Time:** 3:21.

Divisional Series Summaries (Cont.)

Astros, 3-2

Date	Winner	Home Field
Oct. 6	Astros, 9-3	at Atlanta
Oct. 7	Braves, 4-2 (11 inn.)	at Atlanta
Oct. 9	Astros, 8-5	at Houston
Oct. 10	Braves, 6-5	at Houston
Oct. 11	Astros, 12-3	at Atlanta

Game 1
Wednesday, Oct. 6, at Atlanta

	1 2 3	4 5 6	7 8 9	R H E
Houston	0 0 4	0 3 0	1 0 1	- 9 13 1
Atlanta	1 0 0	0 1 1	0 0 0	- 3 7 0

Win: Clemens, Hou. (1-0). **Loss:** Wright, Atl. (0-1).
2B: Houston—Bagwell (1), Kent (1). **3B:** Atlanta—Furcal (1).
HR: Houston—Ausmus (1, off Wright, 0 on), Berkman (1, off Wright, 1 on), Beltran (1, off Wright, 1 on), Lane (1, off Reitsma, 0 on). **RBI:** Houston—Ausmus (1), Bagwell (1), Berkman 2 (2), Beltran 2 (2), Kent (1), Ensberg (1), Lane (1); Atlanta—Estrada (1), A. Jones (1), Giles (1). **SB:** Houston—Beltran (1), Biggio (1); Atlanta—Giles (1). **E:** Houston—Berkman (1).
Attendance: 41,464 (50,091). **Time:** 3:08.

Game 2
Wednesday, Oct. 1, at Atlanta

	1 2 3	4 5 6	7 8 9 10 11	R H E
Houston	1 0 1	0 0 0	0 0 0 0 2	4 1
Atlanta	0 0 0	0 0 0	1 1 0 0 0	- 4 14 0

Win: Alfonseca, Atl. (1-0). **Loss:** Miceli, Hou. (0-1).
2B: Atlanta—Wise (1), LaRaoche (1). **HR:** Houston—Bagwell (1, off Hampton, 0 on), Chavez (1, off Hampton, 0 on); Atlanta—Furcal (1, off Miceli, 1 on). **RBI:** Houston—Bagwell (2), Chavez (1); Atlanta—Furcal 3 (3), LaRoche (1). **SB:** Atlanta—Furcal (1), Thomas (1). **E:** Houston—Chavez (1).
Attendance: 40,075 (50,091). **Time:** 3:27.

Game 3
Saturday, Oct. 9, at Houston

	1 2 3	4 5 6	7 8 9	R H E
Atlanta	0 0 0	2 0 0	0 3 0	- 5 8 0
Houston	0 0 2	0 2 3	1 0 x	- 8 11 0

Win: Backe, Hou. (1-0). **Loss:** Byrd, Atl. (0-1). **Save:** Lidge, Hou. (1). **2B:** Atlanta—A. Jones (1); Houston—Beltran (1), Bagwell (2), Kent (2), Ensberg (1). **HR:** Atlanta—Estrada (1, off Backe, 0 on), A. Jones (2, off Springer, 2 on); Houston—Beltran (2, off Byrd, 1 on). **RBI:** Atlanta—Estrada (2), Byrd (1), A. Jones 3 (4); Houston—Beltran 2 (4), Kent (2), Ensberg 3 (4), Berkman (3), Lamb (1). **SB:** Houston—Beltran (2).
Attendance: 43,547 (40,950). **Time:** 3:19.

Game 4
Sunday, Oct. 10, at Houston

	1 2 3	4 5 6	7 8 9	R H E
Atlanta	0 2 0	0 0 3	0 0 1	- 6 10 0
Houston	0 0 0	0 0 0	0 0 5	13 0

Win: Smoltz, Atl. (1-0). **Loss:** Springer, Hou. (0-1).
2B: Atlanta—A. Jones (2); Houston—Biggio (1), Beltran (1). **HR:** Atlanta—LaRoche (1, off Qualls, 2 on); Houston—Biggio (1, off Ortiz, 2 on). **RBI:** Atlanta—A. Jones (5), LaRoche 3 (4), Drew (1); Houston—Clemens (1), Biggio 3 (3), Bagwell (3). **SB:** Atlanta—Furcal 2 (3), A. Jones (1), Drew (1).
Attendance: 43,336 (40,950). **Time:** 3:24.

Game 5
Monday, Oct. 11, at Atlanta

	1 2 3	4 5 6	7 8 9	R H E
Houston	0 2 1	0 0 1	5 3 0	- 12 17 1
Atlanta	0 0 0	0 2 0	1 0 0	- 3 9 1

Win: Oswalt, Hou. (1-0). **Loss:** Wright, Atl. (0-2).
2B: Houston—Kent (3), Berkman (1), Ensberg (2), Biggio (2). **HR:** Houston—Beltran 2 (4, off Wright, 0 on; off Wright, 0 on), Bagwell (2, off Reitsma, 1 on); Atlanta—Furcal (2, off Oswalt, 0 on), Estrada (2, off Oswalt, 0 on). **RBI:** Houston—Ensberg (5), Vizcaino (1), Beltran 5 (9), Biggio (4), Bagwell 2 (5), Kent (3), Lane (2); Atlanta—Furcal (4), Estrada 2 (4). **E:** Houston—Bagwell (1); Atlanta—Drew (1).
Attendance: 54,068 (50,091). **Time:** 3:12.

American League Championship Series

Red Sox, 4-3

Date	Winner	Home Field
Oct. 12	Yankees, 10-7	at New York
Oct. 13	Yankees, 3-1	at New York
Oct. 16	Yankees, 19-8	at Boston
Oct. 17	Red Sox, 6-4 (12 inn.)	at Boston
Oct. 18	Red Sox, 5-4 (14 inn.)	at Boston
Oct. 19	Red Sox, 4-2	at New York
Oct. 20	Red Sox, 10-3	at New York

Game 1
Tuesday, Oct. 12, at New York

	1 2 3	4 5 6	7 8 9	R H E
Boston	0 0 0	0 0 0	5 2 0	- 7 10 0
New York	2 0 4	0 0 2	0 2 x	-10 14 0

Win: Mussina, NY (1-1). **Loss:** Schilling, Bos. (1-1). **Save:** Rivera, NY (1).
2B: Boston—Bellhorn (1), Millar (1); New York—Sheffield 2 (3), Matsui 2 (3), Williams (2). **3B:** Boston—Ortiz (1). **HR:** Boston—Varitek (2, off Sturtze, 1 on); New York—Lofton (1, off Wakefield, 0 on). **RBI:** Boston—Millar 2 (6), Nixon (3); New York—Matsui 5 (8), Williams 3 (6), Posada (1), Lofton (3).
Attendance: 56,135 (57,478). **Time:** 3:20.

Game 2
Wednesday, Oct. 13, at New York

	1 2 3	4 5 6	7 8 9	R H E
Boston	0 0 0	0 0 0	0 1 0	- 1 5 0
New York	1 0 0	0 0 2	0 0 x	- 3 7 0

Win: Lieber, NY (1-0). **Loss:** Martinez, Bos. (1-1). **Save:** Rivera, NY (2). **2B:** Boston—Varitek (1), Ramirez (3). **HR:** New York—Olerud (1, off Martinez, 1 on). **RBI:** Boston—Cabrera (4); New York—Sheffield (3), Olerud 2 (2). **SB:** New York—Jeter (2). **Attendance:** 56,136 (57,478). **Time:** 3:15.

Game 3
Saturday, Oct. 16, at Boston

	1 2 3	4 5 6	7 8 9	R H E
New York	3 0 3	5 2 0	4 0 2	-19 22 1
Boston	0 4 2	0 0 0	2 0 0	- 8 15 0

Win: Vazquez, NY (1-0). **Loss:** Mendoza, Bos. (0-1). **2B:** New York—Rodriguez 2 (5), Matsui 2 (5), Sheffield (4), Williams (3), Posada (3); Boston—Mueller (1), Millar (2), Cabrera 2 (3), Nixon (1). **3B:** New York—Sierra (1). **HR:** New York—Matsui 2 (4), Rodriguez (2), Sheffield (2); Boston—Nixon (1), Varitek (1). **RBI:** New York—Rodriguez 3 (6), Matsui 5 (13), Williams 3 (9), Sheffield 4 (7), Sierra 2 (5), Posada 2 (3); Boston—Nixon 2 (5), Damon (1), Cabrera 2 (6), Varitek 2 (6). **E:** New York—Jeter (2).
Attendance: 35,126 (35,095). **Time:** 4:20.

Game 4
Sunday, Oct. 17, at Boston

```
           1 2 3   4 5 6   7 8 9  10 11 12   R  H  E
N.Y.  ....0 0 2   0 0 2   0 0 0  - 4 12  1
Bos.  ....0 0 0   0 3 0   0 0 1   0 0 2  - 6  8  0
```

Win: Leskanic, Bos. (1-0). **Loss:** Quantrill, NY (1-1).
2B: New York—Matsui (6). **3B:** New York—Matsui (1). **HR:** New York—Rodriguez (3, off Lowe, 1 on); Boston—Ortiz (2, off Quantrill, 1 on). **RBI:** New York—Rodriguez 2 (8), Williams (10), Clark (1); Boston—Cabrera (7), Ortiz 4 (10), Mueller (1). **SB:** Boston—Roberts (1), Damon (4). **E:** New York—Clark (1).
Attendance: 34,826 (35,095). **Time:** 5:02.

Game 5
Monday, Oct. 18, at Boston

```
          1 2 3   4 5 6   7 8 9  10 11 12 13 14   R  H  E
N.Y.  ..0 1 0   0 0 3   0 0 0   0 0 0 0 0  - 4 12  1
Bos.  ..2 0 0   0 0 0   0 2 0   0 0 0 0 1  - 5 13  1
```

Win: Wakefield, Bos. (1-0). **Loss:** Loaiza, NY (0-1).
2B: New York—Jeter (2), Cairo (2), Clark (1); Boston—Bellhorn (2), Mientkiewicz (1). **HR:** New York—Williams (2, off Martinez, 0 on); Boston—Ortiz (3, off Gordon, 0 on). **RBI:** New York—Williams (11), Jeter 3 (7); Boston—Ortiz 3 (13), Varitek 2 (8). **E:** New York—Jeter (3); Boston—Ramirez (1).
Attendance: 35,120 (35,095). **Time:** 5:49.

Most Valuable Player
David Ortiz, Boston, DH

AVG	AB	R	H	HR	RBI	BB
.387	31	6	12	3	11	4

Game 6
Tuesday, Oct. 19, at New York

```
            1 2 3   4 5 6   7 8 9    R  H  E
Boston .....0 0 0   4 0 0   0 0 0  - 4 11  0
New York ..0 0 0   0 0 0   1 1 0  - 2  6  0
```

Win: Schilling, Bos. (2-1). **Loss:** Lieber, NY (1-1). **Save:** Foulke, Bos. (2).
2B: Boston—Millar (3); New York—Cairo 2 (4). **HR:** Boston—Bellhorn (1, off Lieber, 2 on); New York—Williams (3, off Schilling, 0 on). **RBI:** Boston—Varitek (9), Bellhorn 3 (3); New York—Williams (12), Jeter (8). **SB:** Boston—Cabrera (1).
Attendance: 56,128 (57,478). **Time:** 3:50.

Game 7
Wednesday, Oct. 20, at New York

```
            1 2 3   4 5 6   7 8 9    R  H  E
Boston .....2 4 0   2 0 0   0 1 1  -10 13  0
New York ..0 0 1   0 0 0   2 0 0  - 3  5  1
```

Win: Lowe, Bos. (2-0). **Loss:** Brown, NY (1-1).
2B: New York—Matsui (7), Williams (4). **HR:** Boston—Ortiz (4, off Brown, 1 on), Damon 2 (2, off Vazquez, 3 on; off Vazquez, 1 on), Bellhorn (2, off Gordon, 0 on). **RBI:** Boston—Ortiz 2 (15), Damon 6 (7), Bellhorn (4), Cabrera (8); New York—Jeter (9), Williams (13), Lofton (3). **SB:** Boston—Damon (5); New York—Cairo (1), Lofton (1). **E:** New York—Loaiza (1).
Attendance: 56,129 (57,478). **Time:** 3:31.

ALCS Composite Box Score

Boston Red Sox

Batting	LCS vs. New York								Overall AL Playoffs							
	Avg	AB	R	H	HR	RBI	BB	SO	Avg	AB	R	H	HR	RBI	BB	SO
Doug Mientkiewicz	.500	4	0	2	0	0	0	1	.500	8	0	4	0	1	0	1
David Ortiz	.387	31	6	12	3	11	4	7	.429	42	10	18	4	15	9	9
Orlando Cabrera	.379	29	5	11	0	5	3	5	.310	42	6	13	0	8	5	7
Gabe Kapler	.333	3	0	1	0	0	0	0	.250	8	2	2	0	0	0	0
Jason Varitek	.321	28	5	9	2	7	2	6	.275	40	8	11	3	9	4	11
Manny Ramirez	.300	30	3	9	0	0	5	4	.326	43	6	14	1	7	6	8
Bill Mueller	.267	30	4	8	0	1	2	1	.286	42	7	12	0	1	3	2
Kevin Millar	.250	24	4	6	0	2	5	4	.265	34	6	9	1	6	6	6
Trot Nixon	.207	29	4	6	1	3	2	4	.216	37	4	8	1	5	2	6
Mark Bellhorn	.192	26	5	5	2	4	5	11	.162	37	5	6	2	4	10	15
Johnny Damon	.171	35	5	6	2	7	2	8	.260	50	9	13	2	7	3	10
Doug Mirabelli	.000	1	0	0	0	0	0	0	.000	1	0	0	0	0	0	0
Pokey Reese	.000	1	0	0	0	0	0	1	.000	1	1	0	0	0	0	1
Dave Roberts	—	0	2	0	0	0	0	0	—	0	2	0	0	0	0	0
Kevin Youkilis	—	0	0	0	0	0	0	0	.000	2	0	0	0	0	0	1
TOTALS	.277	271	41	75	10	40	28	53	.387	66	110	14	63	48	76

Pitching	ERA	W-L	Sv	Gm	IP	H	BB	SO	ERA	W-L	Sv	Gm	IP	H	BB	SO
Keith Foulke	0.00	0-0	1	5	6.0	1	6	6	0.00	0-0	2	7	9.0	3	7	11
Derek Lowe	3.18	1-0	0	2	11.1	7	1	6	2.92	2-0	0	3	12.1	8	2	6
Alan Embree	3.86	0-0	0	6	4.2	9	1	2	3.18	0-0	0	8	5.2	9	2	2
Ramiro Mendoza	4.50	0-1	0	2	2.0	2	0	1	4.50	0-1	0	2	2.0	2	0	1
Mike Timlin	4.76	0-0	0	5	5.2	10	5	2	6.23	0-0	0	8	8.2	13	6	7
Pedro Martinez	6.23	0-1	0	3	13.0	14	9	14	5.40	1-1	0	4	20.0	20	11	20
Curt Schilling	6.30	1-1	0	2	10.0	10	2	5	4.86	2-1	0	3	16.2	19	4	9
Mike Myers	7.71	0-0	0	5	2.1	5	1	4	10.13	0-0	0	5	2.2	5	2	5
Tim Wakefield	8.59	1-0	0	3	7.1	9	5	3	8.59	1-0	0	3	7.1	9	5	3
Curtis Leskanic	10.13	1-0	0	3	2.2	3	3	2	10.13	1-0	0	3	2.2	3	3	2
Bronson Arroyo	15.75	0-0	0	4	4.0	8	1	4	8.10	0-0	0	4	10.0	11	4	10
TOTALS	5.87	4-3	1	7	69.0	78	33	51	5.20	7-3	2	10	97.0	102	44	79

ALCS Composite Box Score (Cont.)

New York Yankees

Batting	Avg	AB	R	H	HR	RBI	BB	SO	Avg	AB	R	H	HR	RBI	BB	SO
			LCS vs. Boston								Overall AL Playoffs					
Hideki Matsui	.412	34	9	14	2	10	2	4	.412	51	12	21	3	13	5	8
Gary Sheffield	.333	30	7	10	1	5	6	8	.292	48	9	14	2	7	9	9
Ruben Sierra	.333	21	1	7	0	2	3	8	.273	33	2	9	1	5	5	11
Bernie Williams	.306	36	4	11	2	10	0	5	.296	54	6	16	3	13	1	7
Kenny Lofton	.300	10	1	3	1	2	2	3	.286	14	1	4	1	3	2	4
Miguel Cairo	.280	25	4	7	0	0	2	4	.256	39	7	10	0	1	4	9
Jorge Posada	.259	27	4	7	0	2	7	1	.244	45	6	11	0	2	7	7
Alex Rodriguez	.258	31	8	8	2	5	4	6	.320	50	11	16	3	8	6	7
Derek Jeter	.200	30	5	6	0	5	6	2	.245	49	8	12	1	9	7	6
John Olerud	.167	12	1	2	1	2	1	1	.192	26	3	5	1	2	2	3
Tony Clark	.143	21	0	3	0	1	0	9	.136	22	0	3	0	1	0	10
Bubba Crosby	—	0	1	0	0	0	0	0	—	0	1	0	0	0	0	0
TOTALS	.282	277	45	78	9	44	33	51		431	66	121	15	64	48	81

Pitching	ERA	W-L	Sv	Gm	IP	H	BB	SO	ERA	W-L	Sv	Gm	IP	H	BB	SO
Felix Heredia	0.00	0-0	0	3	1.1	1	0	1	10.80	0-0	0	4	1.2	1	0	1
Mariano Rivera	1.29	0-0	2	5	7.0	6	2	6	0.71	1-0	2	9	12.2	8	2	8
Esteban Loaiza	1.42	0-1	0	2	6.1	5	3	5	1.08	0-1	0	3	8.1	9	3	5
Tanyon Sturtze	2.70	0-0	0	4	3.1	2	2	2	4.50	0-0	0	6	6.0	6	5	6
Jon Lieber	3.14	1-1	0	2	14.1	12	1	5	3.43	1-1	0	3	21.0	19	2	9
Mike Mussina	4.26	1-0	0	2	12.2	10	2	15	3.66	1-1	0	3	19.2	17	3	22
Orlando Hernandez	5.40	0-0	0	1	5.0	3	5	6	5.40	0-0	0	1	5.0	3	5	6
Paul Quantrill	5.40	0-1	0	4	3.1	8	0	2	3.38	1-1	0	6	5.1	10	0	3
Tom Gordon	8.10	0-0	0	6	6.2	10	2	3	6.97	0-0	0	9	10.1	12	2	6
Javier Vazquez	9.95	1-0	0	2	6.1	9	7	6	9.53	1-0	0	3	11.1	16	9	12
Kevin Brown	21.60	0-1	0	2	3.1	9	4	2	8.68	1-1	0	3	9.1	17	4	3
TOTALS	5.17	3-4	2	7	69.2	75	28	53	4.64	6-5	2	11	110.2	118	35	81

Score by Innings

	1	2	3	4	5	6	7	8	9	10	11	12	13	14		R	H	E
Boston	4	8	2	6	3	0	7	6	2	0	0	2	0	1	–	41	75	1
New York	6	1	10	5	2	9	7	3	2	0	0	0	0	0	–	45	78	4

E: Boston—Ramirez; New York—Jeter 2, Clark, Loaiza. **2B:** Boston—Millar 3, Cabrera 2, Bellhorn 2, Mientkiewicz, Varitek, Ramirez, Mueller, Nixon; New York—Matsui 6, Sheffield 3, Williams 3, Cairo 3, Rodriguez 2, Sierra, Posada, Jeter, Clark. **3B:** Boston—Ortiz; New York—Matsui, Sierra. **SB:** Boston—Damon 2, Cabrera, Roberts; New York—Lofton, Cairo, Jeter. **CS:** Boston—Ortiz, Damon. **S:** Boston—Mientkiewicz; New York—Jeter 2, Cairo. **SF:** Boston—Cabrera, Varitek; New York—Posada. **PB:** Boston—Varitek 4; New York—Posada. **HBP:** by Lieber (Mueller), by Mendoza (Cairo, Posada), by Martinez (Rodriguez 2, Cairo), by Foulke (Cairo), by Lowe (Cairo). **WP:** Boston—Timlin; New York—Brown, Gordon, Lieber. **Balk:** Boston—Mendoza. **LOB:** Boston—53; New York—69.
Umpires: Randy Marsh, Jeff Nelson, John Hirschbeck, Jim Joyce, Jeff Kellogg, Joe West.

National League Championship Series

Cardinals, 4-3

Date	Winner	Home Field
Oct. 13	Cardinals, 10-7	at St. Louis
Oct. 14	Cardinals, 6-4	at St. Louis
Oct. 16	Astros, 5-2	at Houston
Oct. 17	Astros, 6-5	at Houston
Oct. 18	Astros, 3-0	at Houston
Oct. 20	Cardinals, 6-4 (12 inn.)	at St. Louis
Oct. 21	Cardinals, 5-2	at St. Louis

Most Valuable Player
Albert Pujols, St. Louis, 1B

AVG	AB	R	H	HR	RBI	BB
.500	28	10	14	4	9	4

Game 1
Wednesday, Oct. 13, at St. Louis

	1	2	3	4	5	6	7	8	9		R	H	E
Houston	2	0	0	2	0	0	0	2	1	–	7	10	1
St. Louis	2	0	0	0	2	6	0	0	x	–	10	12	0

Win: Williams, St.L (2-0). **Loss:** Qualls, Hou. (0-1). **Save:** Isringhausen, St.L (1).

2B: Houston—Palmeiro (1), Biggio (3); St. Louis—Williams (1), Walker (2), Edmonds (1). **3B:** St. Louis—Walker (1). **HR:** Houston—Beltran (5, off Williams, 1 on), Kent (1, off Williams, 1 on), Berkman (2, off King, 1 on), Lamb (1, off Tavarez, 0 on); St. Louis—Pujols (3, off Backe, 1 on). **RBI:** Houston—Beltran 2 (11), Kent 2 (5), Berkman 2 (5), Lamb (2); St. Louis—Pujols 2 (7), Walker (2), Rolen (1), Cedeno (1), Womack (2), Edmonds 3 (5). **SB:** St. Louis—Womack (2). **E:** Houston—Vizcaino (1).
Attendance: 52,323 (50,345). **Time:** 3:15.

Game 2
Thursday, Oct. 14, at St. Louis

	1 2 3	4 5 6	7 8 9	R H E
Houston	1 0 0	1 1 0	1 0 0	- 4 10 1
St. Louis	0 0 0	0 4 0	0 2 x	- 6 9 0

Win: Tavarez, St.L (1-0). **Loss:** Miceli, Hou. (0-2). **Save:** Isringhausen, St.L (2). **2B:** Houston—Kent (4), Berkman (2); St. Louis—Edmonds (2). **HR:** Houston—Beltran (6, off Morris, 0 on), Ensberg (1, off Williams, 1 on), Berkman (2, off King, 1 on), Lamb (1, off Morris, 0 on); St. Louis—Walker (3, off Munro, 1 on), Rolen 2 (2, off Harville, 1 on; off Miceli, 0 on), Pujols (4, off Miceli, 0 on). **RBI:** Houston—Beltran (12), Enberg 2 (7), Berkman (6); St. Louis—Walker 2 (6), Rolen 3 (4), Pujols (8). **SB:** Houston—Berkman (1); St. Louis—Womack (3). **E:** Houston—Munro (1).
Attendance: 52,347 (50,345). **Time:** 3:02.

Game 3
Saturday, Oct. 16, at Houston

	1 2 3	4 5 6	7 8 9	R H E
St. Louis	1 1 0	0 0 0	0 0 0	- 2 5 0
Houston	3 0 0	0 0 0	2 x	- 5 8 0

Win: Clemens, Hou. (2-0). **Loss:** Suppan, St.L (1-1). **Save:** Lidge, Hou. (2). **2B:** Houston—Beltran (3). **HR:** St. Louis—Walker (4, off Clemens, 0 on), Edmonds (2, off Clemens, 0 on); Houston—Kent (2, off Suppan, 0 on), Beltran (7, off Haren, 0 on), Berkman (3, off King, 0 on). **RBI:** St. Louis—Walker (7), Edmonds (6); Houston—Berkman 2 (8), Kent 2 (7), Beltran (13).
Attendance: 42,896 (40,950). **Time:** 2:57.

Game 4
Sunday, Oct. 17, at Houston

	1 2 3	4 5 6	7 8 9	R H E
St. Louis	3 0 1	1 0 0	0 0 0	- 5 9 0
Houston	1 0 2	0 0 2	1 0 x	- 6 9 0

Win: Wheeler, Hou. (1-0). **Loss:** Tavarez, St.L (1-1). **Save:** Lidge, Hou. (3). **2B:** St. Louis—Rolen (1); Houston—Bagwell (3), Berkman (3), Vizcaino (1). **HR:** St. Louis—Pujols (5, off Oswalt, 1 on); Houston—Berkman (4, off Calero, 0 on), Beltran (8, off Tavarez, 0 on). **RBI:** St. Louis—Pujols 3 (11), Mabry (1), Edmonds (7); Houston—Bagwell (6), Berkman 3 (11), Chavez (2), Beltran (14).
Attendance: 42,760 (40,950). **Time:** 3:01.

Game 5
Monday, Oct. 18, at Houston

	1 2 3	4 5 6	7 8 9	R H E
St. Louis	0 0 0	0 0 0	0 0 0	- 0 1 0
Houston	0 0 0	0 0 0	0 0 3	- 3 3 0

Win: Lidge, Hou. (1-0). **Loss:** Tavarez (1-1). **HR:** Houston—Kent (3, off Isringhausen, 2 on). **RBI:** Houston—Kent 3 (10). **SB:** Houston—Beltran (3).
Attendance: 42,760 (40,950). **Time:** 3:01.

Game 6
Wednesday, Oct. 20, at St. Louis

	1 2 3	4 5 6	7 8 9	10 11 12	R H E
Houston	1 0 1	1 0 0	0 0 1	0 0 0	- 4 10 0
St. Louis	2 0 2	0 0 0	0 0 0	0 0 2	- 6 15 0

Win: Tavarez, St.L (2-1). **Loss:** Miceli, Hou. (0-3). **2B:** Houston—Bagwell (4), Kent (5); St. Louis—Pujols (1), Sanders 2 (2), Rolen (2). **HR:** Houston—Lamb (2, off Morris, 0 on); St. Louis—Pujols (6, off Munro, 1 on), Edmonds (3, off Miceli, 1 on). **RBI:** Houston—Berkman (12), Bagwell 2 (8), Lamb (2), Kent (11); St. Louis—Pujols 2 (13), Renteria 2 (6), Edmonds 2 (9). **SB:** Houston—Beltran 2 (5), Bagwell (1).
Attendance: 52,144 (50,345). **Time:** 3:54.

Game 7
Thursday, Oct. 21, at St. Louis

	1 2 3	4 5 6	7 8 9	R H E
Houston	1 0 1	0 0 0	0 0 0	- 2 3 0
St. Louis	0 0 1	0 0 3	0 1 x	- 5 9 1

Win: Suppan, St.L (2-1). **Loss:** Clemens, Hou. (2-1). **2B:** St. Louis—Womack (1), Pujols (2), Anderson (1). **HR:** Houston—Biggio (2, off Suppan, 0 on); St. Louis—Rolen (3, off Clemens, 1 on). **RBI:** Houston—Biggio (5); St. Louis—Suppan (1), Pujols (14), Rolen 2 (6), Walker (8). **SB:** Houston—Beltran (6).
Attendance: 52,140 (50,345). **Time:** 2:51.

NLCS Composite Box Score
St. Louis Cardinals

Batting		LCS vs. Houston								Overall NL Playoffs						
	Avg	AB	R	H	HR	RBI	BB	SO		Avg	AB	R	H	HR	RBI	BB	SO
Albert Pujols	.500	28	10	14	4	9	4	3		.442	43	14	19	6	14	7	3
Jason Marquis	.500	2	0	1	0	0	0	0		.333	3	0	1	0	0	0	0
Marlon Anderson	.333	3	1	1	0	0	1	0		.167	6	1	1	0	0	1	1
Scott Rolen	.310	29	6	9	3	6	2	9		.220	41	7	9	3	6	8	12
Jim Edmonds	.292	24	2	7	2	7	2	6		.282	39	3	11	3	9	3	15
Tony Womack	.269	26	5	7	0	1	1	3		.222	45	7	10	0	2	1	5
Woody Williams	.250	4	1	1	0	0	0	0		.167	6	1	1	0	0	0	0
Yadier Molina	.250	4	0	1	0	0	0	0		.250	4	0	1	0	0	0	0
Larry Walker	.241	29	6	7	2	5	3	8		.273	44	12	12	4	8	5	13
Reggie Sanders	.190	21	1	4	0	0	1	5		.229	35	4	8	1	1	1	7
Edgar Renteria	.167	24	1	4	0	2	2	6		.257	35	5	9	0	5	5	6
John Mabry	.167	6	0	1	0	1	0	0		.143	7	0	1	0	1	0	4
Roger Cedeno	.167	6	1	1	0	0	0	1		.250	8	1	2	0	0	0	1
Mike Matheny	.105	19	0	2	0	0	1	4		.182	33	1	6	1	5	1	10
So Taguchi	.000	2	0	0	0	0	0	0		.000	2	0	0	0	0	0	0
Matt Morris	.000	2	0	0	0	0	0	1		.000	4	0	0	0	0	0	1
Jeff Suppan	.000	2	0	0	0	1	0	0		.400	5	0	2	0	1	0	0
Hector Luna	.000	4	0	0	0	0	0	0		.000	4	0	0	0	0	0	0
Danny Haren	—	0	0	0	0	0	0	0		.000	1	0	0	0	0	0	0
TOTALS	.255	235	34	60	11	33	17	56			365	56	93	18	54	32	82

NLCS Composite Box Score (Cont.)

Pitching

Pitching	ERA	W-L	Sv	Gm	IP	H	BB	SO	ERA	W-L	Sv	Gm	IP	H	BB	SO
		LCS vs. Houston									Overall NL Playoffs					
Cal Eldred	0.00	0-0	0	1	0.1	0	1	0	0.00	0-0	0	3	1.0	1	3	0
Woody Williams	2.77	1-0	0	2	13.0	5	3	9	2.84	2-0	0	3	19.0	13	4	11
Jeff Suppan	3.00	1-1	0	2	12.0	8	4	9	2.84	2-1	0	3	19.0	10	7	11
Julian Tavarez	3.00	2-1	0	5	6.0	3	2	3	2.16	2-1	0	7	8.1	5	2	6
Kiko Calero	3.86	0-0	0	5	7.0	8	1	7	3.38	0-0	0	6	8.0	8	1	9
Jason Isringhausen	4.70	0-1	3	6	7.2	4	4	3	4.66	0-1	3	8	9.2	5	6	5
Matt Morris	5.40	0-0	0	2	10.0	11	8	6	5.29	0-1	0	3	17.0	17	10	11
Jason Marquis	6.75	0-0	0	1	4.0	5	2	2	7.36	0-0	0	2	7.1	9	6	2
Danny Haren	10.80	0-0	0	2	1.2	3	0	2	4.91	1-0	0	3	3.2	4	1	5
Ray King	10.80	0-0	0	4	1.2	4	0	1	4.50	0-0	0	7	4.0	4	0	2
Steve Kline	—	0-0	0	1	0.0	2	0	0	0.00	0-0	0	3	1.1	2	0	0
TOTALS	4.26	4-3	3	7	63.1	53	25	42	3.84	7-4	3	11	98.1	78	40	62

Houston Astros

Batting

Batting	Avg	AB	R	H	HR	RBI	BB	SO	Avg	AB	R	H	HR	RBI	BB	SO
		LCS vs. St. Louis									Overall NL Playoffs					
Carlos Beltran	.417	24	12	10	4	5	8	4	.435	46	21	20	8	14	9	8
Mike Lamb	.400	5	2	2	2	2	1	1	.250	8	2	2	2	3	1	1
Orlando Palmeiro	.333	6	0	2	0	0	0	0	.300	10	0	3	0	0	0	0
Lance Berkman	.292	24	7	7	3	9	5	4	.348	46	12	16	4	12	8	10
Jeff Bagwell	.259	27	1	7	0	3	4	5	.286	49	6	14	2	8	7	8
Raul Chavez	.250	4	0	1	0	1	0	1	.444	9	1	4	1	2	0	1
Jose Vizcaino	.250	28	1	7	0	0	1	1	.191	47	3	9	0	1	1	3
Jeff Kent	.240	25	3	6	3	7	3	5	.234	47	6	11	3	10	5	10
Craig Biggio	.188	32	3	6	1	1	0	4	.269	52	8	14	2	5	2	8
Morgan Ensberg	.136	22	2	3	1	2	1	3	.244	41	3	10	1	7	4	4
Brad Ausmus	.105	19	0	2	0	0	2	8	.179	28	3	5	1	1	5	11
Brandon Backe	.000	5	0	0	0	0	0	1	.000	6	0	0	0	0	0	3
Roger Clemens	.000	4	0	0	0	0	0	3	.000	7	0	0	0	1	1	4
Pete Munro	.000	2	0	0	0	0	1	0	.000	2	0	0	0	0	0	1
Eric Bruntlett	.000	2	0	0	0	0	0	0	.000	3	0	0	0	0	1	0
Roy Oswalt	.000	2	0	0	0	0	0	0	.000	5	0	0	0	0	1	0
Adam Everett	.000	1	0	0	0	0	0	0	.000	1	0	0	0	0	0	0
Jason Lane	.000	1	0	0	0	0	0	0	.500	6	2	3	1	2	0	1
TOTALS	.227	233	31	53	14	30	25	42	.269	413	67	111	25	66	46	72

Pitching

Pitching	ERA	W-L	Sv	Gm	IP	H	BB	SO	ERA	W-L	Sv	Gm	IP	H	BB	SO
Brad Lidge	0.00	1-0	2	4	8.0	1	2	14	0.73	1-0	3	7	12.1	5	3	20
Dan Wheeler	0.00	1-0	0	4	7.0	4	0	9	0.00	1-0	0	5	8.0	4	0	9
Brandon Backe	2.84	0-0	0	2	12.2	6	4	10	2.89	1-0	0	3	18.2	11	6	15
Roger Clemens	4.15	1-1	0	2	13.0	10	2	9	3.60	2-1	0	4	25.0	22	10	21
Roy Oswalt	6.75	0-0	0	2	8.0	11	4	2	4.19	1-0	0	4	19.1	26	8	10
Pete Munro	9.00	0-0	0	2	7.0	14	1	5	9.00	0-0	0	2	7.0	14	1	5
Chad Qualls	11.25	0-1	0	3	4.0	8	2	4	9.00	0-1	0	6	8.0	12	3	7
Chad Harville	13.50	0-0	0	3	1.1	3	1	3	9.00	0-0	0	4	2.0	3	1	3
Dan Miceli	27.00	0-2	0	2	1.1	3	1	0	11.57	0-3	0	5	4.2	5	2	2
Mike Gallo	—	0-0	0	1	0.0	0	0	0	4.50	0-0	0	3	2.0	3	1	4
Russ Springer	—	0-0	0	1	0.0	0	0	0	18.00	0-1	0	2	2.0	3	1	5
TOTALS	4.91	3-4	2	7	62.1	60	17	56	4.46	6-6	3	12	109.0	108	36	101

Score by Innings

	1	2	3	4	5	6	7	8	9	10	11	12		R	H	E
Houston	9	0	4	4	1	2	2	4	5	0	0	0	-	31	53	2
St. Louis	8	1	4	1	6	9	0	3	0	0	0	2	-	34	60	1

E: Houston—Vizcaino, Munro; St. Louis—Edmonds. **2B:** Houston—Berkman 2, Bagwell 2, Kent 2, Beltran, Palmeiro, Vizcaino, Biggio; St. Louis—Pujols 2, Rolen 2, Edmonds 2, Sanders 2, Anderson, Womack, Walker. **3B:** St. Louis—Walker. **SB:** Houston—Beltran 4, Berkman, Bagwell; St. Louis—Womack 2. **CS:** Houston—Bagwell, Vizcaino, Biggio, Ensberg. **S:** Houston—Bruntlett; St. Louis—Renteria 2, Matheny, Morris, Taguchi, Suppan. **SF:** Houston—Berkman; St. Louis—Edmonds. **PB:** Houston—Chavez. **HBP:** by Backe (Edmonds), by Lidge (Anderson), by Tavarez (Kent), by Williams (Ensberg), by Isringhausen (Ensberg), by Calero (Palmeiro), by Suppan (Kent). **WP:** Houston—Clemens; St. Louis—Morris 2, Tavarez. **Balk:** St. Louis—Morris. **LOB:** Houston—44; St. Louis—40.

Umpires: Tim Welke, Eric Cooper, Gary Darling, Mike Winters, Angel Hernandez, Ed Rapuano.

WORLD SERIES

Red Sox, 4-0

Date	Winner	Home Field	Date	Winner	Home Field
Oct. 23 . . . . Red Sox, 11-9		at Boston	Oct. 26 . . . . Red Sox, 4-1		at St. Louis
Oct. 24 . . . . Red Sox, 6-2		at Boston	Oct. 27 . . . . Red Sox, 3-0		at St. Louis

Game 1
Saturday, Oct. 23, at Boston

St. Louis	AB	R	H	RBI	Boston	AB	R	H	RBI
Renteria, ss	4	1	2	1	Damon, cf	6	1	2	1
Walker, rf	5	1	4	2	Cabrera, ss	4	2	1	1
Pujols, 1b	3	0	0	0	Ramirez, lf	5	0	3	2
Rolen, 3b	5	0	0	0	Ortiz, dh	3	1	2	4
Edmonds, cf	4	2	1	0	Millar, 1b	5	1	1	0
Sanders, dh	3	1	0	0	Mientk'wicz,1b	0	0	0	0
Womack, 2b	1	1	0	0	Nixon, rf	3	0	0	0
Anderson, 2b	2	0	1	0	Kapler, ph-rf	1	0	0	0
Matheny, c	2	0	1	2	Mueller, 3b	3	1	1	1
Marquis, pr	0	1	0	0	Mirabelli, c	3	1	1	0
Molina, c	1	0	0	0	Varitek, ph-c	2	1	0	0
Taguchi, lf	3	1	1	1	Bellhorn, 2b	3	3	2	2
Cedeno, ph-lf	2	1	1	0	Reese, 2b	0	0	0	0
Totals	**35**	**9**	**11**	**6**	**Totals**	**38**	**11**	**13**	**11**

									R	H	E
St. Louis	011	302	020	—					9	11	1
Boston	403	000	22x	—					11	13	4

E: St. Louis—Renteria (1); Boston—Ramirez 2 (2), Millar, Arroyo. **2B:** St. Louis—Walker 2 (2), Renteria (1), Anderson (1); Boston—Damon (1), Millar (1). **HR:** St. Louis—Walker (1, off Williams, 0 on); Boston—Ortiz (1, off Williams, 2 on), Bellhorn (1, off Tavarez, 1 on). **BB:** St. Louis—Sanders 2, Renteria, Pujols, Edmonds, Womack; Boston—Ortiz 2, Mueller 2, Bellhorn 2, Cabrera, Nixon. **S:** St. Louis—Womack. **SF:** St. Louis—Matheny.

St. Louis	IP	H	R	ER	BB	SO	HR	ERA
Williams	2⅓	8	7	7	3	1	1	27.00
Haren	3⅔	3	0	0	3	1	0	0.00
Calero	⅓	1	2	2	2	0	0	54.00
King	⅓	1	0	0	0	0	0	0.00
Eldred	1	0	0	0	0	1	0	0.00
Tavarez (L, 0-1)	1	1	2	1	0	1	1	9.00
Boston								
Wakefield	3⅔	3	5	5	5	2	1	12.27
Arroyo	2⅓	4	2	2	0	4	0	7.71
Timlin	1⅓	1	1	1	0	0	0	6.75
Embree	0	1	1	0	0	0	0	—
Foulke (W, 1-0)	1⅔	2	0	0	1	3	0	0.00

HBP: by Williams (Cabrera), by Wakefield (Pujols). **PB:** Mirabelli. **Attendance:** 35,035 (35,095). **Time:** 4:00.

Game 2
Sunday, Oct. 24, at Boston

St. Louis	AB	R	H	RBI	Boston	AB	R	H	RBI
Renteria, ss	3	1	0	0	Damon, cf	5	1	1	0
Walker, rf	4	0	0	0	Cabrera, ss	4	0	1	2
Pujols, 1b	4	1	3	0	Ramirez, lf	4	1	1	0
Rolen, 3b	3	0	0	1	Kapler, lf	0	0	0	0
Edmonds, cf	4	0	0	0	Ortiz, dh	3	1	0	0
Sanders, lf	3	0	0	0	Varitek, c	3	0	1	2
Womack, 2b	4	0	1	0	Millar, 1b	1	1	0	0
Matheny, c	4	0	1	0	Mientk'wicz,1b	0	0	0	0
Anderson, dh	2	0	0	0	Nixon, rf	4	1	1	0
Taguchi, ph-dh	1	0	0	0	Mueller, 3b	3	1	2	0
					Bellhorn, 2b	3	0	1	2
					Reese, 2b	1	0	0	0
Totals	**32**	**2**	**5**	**1**	**Totals**	**31**	**6**	**8**	**6**

									R	H	E
St. Louis	000	100	010	—					2	5	0
Boston	200	202	00x	—					6	8	4

E: Boston—Mueller 3 (3), Bellhorn (1). **2B:** St. Louis—Pujols 2 (2); Boston—Mueller (1), Bellhorn (1). **3B:** Boston—Varitek (1). **BB:** St. Louis—Renteria, Sanders; Boston—Millar 2, Cabrera, Ramirez, Ortiz, Mueller. **SF:** St. Louis—Rolen.

St. Louis	IP	H	R	ER	BB	SO	HR	ERA
Morris (L, 0-1)	4⅓	4	4	4	4	3	0	8.31
Eldred	1⅓	4	2	2	0	1	0	10.80
King	⅓	0	0	0	0	1	0	0.00
Marquis	1	0	0	0	2	0	0	0.00
Reyes	1	0	0	0	0	0	0	0.00
Boston								
Schilling (W, 1-0)	6	4	1	0	1	4	0	0.00
Embree	1	0	0	0	0	3	0	0.00
Timlin	⅔	1	1	1	1	0	0	9.00
Foulke	1⅓	0	0	0	0	2	0	0.00

HBP: by Morris (Millar), by Eldred (Varitek). **Attendance:** 35,001 (35,095). **Time:** 3:20.

World Series
Most Valuable Player
Manny Ramirez, Boston, OF

AVG	AB	R	H	HR	RBI	BB
.412	17	2	7	1	4	3

World Series (Cont.)

Game 3
Tuesday, Oct. 26, at St. Louis

Boston	AB	R	H	RBI	St. Louis	AB	R	H	RBI
Damon, cf	5	1	1	0	Renteria, ss	4	0	1	0
Cabrera, ss	4	1	2	0	Walker, rf	3	1	1	1
Ramirez, lf	4	1	2	2	Pujols, 1b	4	0	1	0
Ortiz, 1b	4	0	1	0	Rolen, 3b	3	0	0	0
Mientk'wicz,1b	0	0	0	0	Edmonds, cf	3	0	0	0
Varitek, c	3	0	0	0	Sanders, lf	3	0	0	0
Mueller, 3b	4	1	2	1	Womack, 2b	3	0	0	0
Nixon, rf	3	0	1	1	Matheny, c	2	0	0	0
Kapler, ph-rf	1	0	0	0	Cedeno, ph	1	0	0	0
Bellhorn, 2b	3	0	0	0	Tavarez, p	0	0	0	0
Reese, 2b	0	0	0	0	Suppan, p	1	0	1	0
Martinez, p	2	0	0	0	Reyes, p	0	0	0	0
Millar, ph	1	0	0	0	Anderson, ph	1	0	0	0
Timlin, p	0	0	0	0	Calero, p	0	0	0	0
Foulke, p	0	0	0	0	King, p	0	0	0	0
					Mabry, ph	1	0	0	0
					Molina, c	0	0	0	0
Totals	34	4	9	4	Totals	29	1	4	1

```
              R  H  E
Boston........100 120 000 —  4  9  0
St. Louis.....000 000 001 —  1  4  0
```

2B: Boston—Mueller (2), Damon (2), Cabrera (1); St. Louis—Renteria (2). **HR:** Boston—Ramirez (1, off Suppan, 0 on); St. Louis—Walker (2, off Foulke, 0 on). **BB:** Boston—Cabrera, Ramirez, Varitek, Martinez; St. Louis—Walker, Rolen.

Boston	IP	H	R	ER	BB	SO	HR	ERA
Martinez (W, 1-0)	7	3	0	0	2	6	0	0.00
Timlin	1	0	0	0	0	0	0	6.00
Foulke	1	1	1	1	0	2	1	2.25
St. Louis								
Suppan (L, 0-1)	4⅔	8	4	4	1	4	1	7.71
Reyes	⅓	0	0	0	0	0	0	0.00
Calero	1	1	0	0	2	0	0	13.50
King	2	0	0	0	1	0	0	0.00
Tavarez	1	0	0	0	1	0	0	4.50

HBP: by Suppan (Bellhorn).
Attendance: 52,015 (50,345). **Time:** 2:58.

Game 4
Wednesday, Oct. 27, at St. Louis

Boston	AB	R	H	RBI	St. Louis	AB	R	H	RBI
Damon, cf	5	1	2	1	Womack, 2b	3	0	1	0
Cabrera, ss	5	0	0	0	Luna, ph-2b	1	0	0	0
Ramirez, lf	4	0	1	0	Walker, rf	2	0	0	0
Ortiz, 1b	3	1	1	0	Pujols, 1b	4	0	1	0
Mientk'wicz,1b	1	0	0	0	Rolen, 3b	4	0	0	0
Varitek, c	5	1	1	0	Edmonds, cf	4	0	0	0
Mueller, 3b	4	0	1	0	Renteria, ss	4	0	2	0
Nixon, rf	4	0	3	2	Mabry, lf	3	0	0	0
Kapler, pr-rf	0	0	0	0	Isringhausen, p	0	0	0	0
Bellhorn, 2b	1	0	0	0	Molina, c	2	0	0	0
Reese, pr-2b	0	0	0	0	Cedeno, ph	1	0	0	0
Lowe, p	2	0	0	0	Matheny, c	2	0	0	0
Millar, ph	1	0	0	0	Marquis, p	1	0	0	0
Arroyo, p	0	0	0	0	Anderson, ph	1	0	0	0
Embree, p	0	0	0	0	Haren, p	0	0	0	0
Foulke, p	0	0	0	0	Sanders, lf	0	0	0	0
Totals	35	3	9	3	Totals	30	0	4	0

```
              R  H  E
Boston........102 000 000 —  3  9  0
St. Louis.....000 000 000 —  0  4  0
```

2B: Boston—Nixon 3 (3), Ortiz (1); St. Louis—Renteria (3). **3B:** Boston—Damon (1). **HR:** Boston—Damon (1, off Marquis, 0 on). **BB:** Boston—Bellhorn 3, Ramirez, Ortiz, Mueller; St. Louis—Walker, Sanders. **S:** Boston—Lowe; St. Louis—Walker. **SB:** St. Louis—Sanders (1).

Boston	IP	H	R	ER	BB	SO	HR	ERA
Lowe (W, 1-0)	7	3	0	0	1	4	0	0.00
Arroyo	⅓	0	0	0	1	0	0	6.75
Embree	⅔	0	0	0	0	1	0	0.00
Foulke (S, 1)	1	1	0	0	0	1	0	1.80
St. Louis								
Marquis (L, 0-1)	6	6	3	3	5	4	1	3.86
Haren	1	2	0	0	1	0	0	0.00
Isringhausen	2	1	0	0	1	2	0	0.00

WP: Lowe.
Attendance: 52,037 (50,345). **Time:** 3:14.

World Series Composite Box Score
Boston Red Sox

		WS vs. St. Louis								Overall Playoffs						
Batting	Avg	AB	R	H	HR	RBI	BB	SO	Avg	AB	R	H	HR	RBI	BB	SO
Bill Mueller	.429	14	3	6	0	2	4	0	.321	56	10	18	0	3	7	2
Manny Ramirez	.412	17	2	7	1	4	3	3	.350	60	8	21	2	11	9	11
Trot Nixon	.357	14	1	5	0	3	1	1	.255	51	5	13	1	8	3	7
Doug Mirabelli	.333	3	1	1	0	0	0	1	.250	4	1	1	0	0	0	1
David Ortiz	.308	13	3	4	1	4	4	1	.400	55	13	22	5	19	13	10
Mark Bellhorn	.300	10	3	3	1	4	5	2	.191	47	8	9	3	8	15	17
Johnny Damon	.286	21	4	6	1	2	0	1	.268	71	13	19	3	9	3	11
Orlando Cabrera	.235	17	3	4	0	3	0	0	.288	59	9	17	0	11	8	8
Jason Varitek	.154	13	2	2	0	2	1	4	.245	53	10	13	3	11	5	15
Kevin Millar	.125	8	2	1	0	0	2	2	.238	42	8	10	1	6	8	7
Derek Lowe	.000	2	0	0	0	0	0	1	.000	2	0	0	0	0	0	1
Gabe Kapler	.000	2	0	0	0	0	0	1	.200	10	2	2	0	0	0	1
Pedro Martinez	.000	2	0	0	0	0	1	2	.000	2	0	0	0	0	1	2
Pokey Reese	.000	1	0	0	0	0	0	0	.000	2	1	0	0	0	0	0
Doug Mientkiewicz	.000	1	0	0	0	0	0	0	.444	9	0	4	0	1	0	1
Kevin Youkilis	—	0	0	0	0	0	0	0	.000	2	0	0	0	0	0	1
Dave Roberts	—	0	0	0	0	0	0	0	.000	2	0	0	0	0	0	0
TOTALS	.283	138	24	39	4	24	24	20	.284	525	90	149	18	87	72	96

Pitching	ERA	W-L	Sv	Gm	IP	H	BB	SO	ERA	W-L	Sv	Gm	IP	H	BB	SO
Alan Embree	0.00	0-0	0	3	1.2	1	0	4	2.45	0-0	0	11	7.1	10	2	6
Derek Lowe	0.00	1-0	0	1	7.0	3	1	4	1.86	3-0	0	4	19.1	11	3	10
Curt Schilling	0.00	1-0	0	1	6.0	4	1	4	3.57	3-1	0	4	22.2	23	5	13
Pedro Martinez	0.00	1-0	0	1	7.0	3	2	6	4.00	2-1	0	5	27.0	23	13	26
Keith Foulke	1.80	1-0	1	4	5.0	4	1	8	0.64	1-0	3	11	14.0	7	8	19
Tim Wakefield	12.27	0-0	0	1	3.2	3	5	2	9.82	1-0	0	4	11.0	12	8	8
Mike Timlin	6.00	0-0	0	3	3.0	2	1	0	6.17	0-0	0	11	11.2	15	7	7
Bronson Arroyo	6.75	0-0	0	2	2.2	4	1	4	7.82	0-0	0	6	12.2	15	5	14
Ramiro Mendoza	—	0-0	0	0	0.0	0	0	0	4.50	0-1	0	2	2.0	2	0	1
Curtis Leskanic	—	0-0	0	0	0.0	0	0	0	10.13	1-0	0	3	2.2	3	3	2
Mike Myers	—	0-0	0	0	0.0	0	0	0	10.13	0-0	0	5	2.2	5	2	5
TOTALS	2.50	4-0	1	4	36.0	24	12	32	4.47	11-3	3	14	133.0	126	56	111

St. Louis Cardinals

Batting	Avg	AB	R	H	HR	RBI	BB	SO	Avg	AB	R	H	HR	RBI	BB	SO
Jeff Suppan	1.000	1	0	1	0	0	0	0	.500	6	0	3	0	1	0	0
Larry Walker	.357	14	2	5	2	3	2	2	.293	58	14	17	6	11	7	15
Edgar Renteria	.333	15	2	5	0	1	2	2	.280	50	7	14	0	7	7	8
Albert Pujols	.333	15	1	5	0	0	1	3	.414	58	15	24	6	14	8	6
Mike Matheny	.250	8	0	2	0	2	0	3	.195	41	1	8	1	7	1	13
Roger Cedeno	.250	4	1	1	0	0	0	1	.250	12	2	3	0	1	0	3
So Taguchi	.250	4	1	1	0	1	0	2	.167	6	1	1	0	1	0	3
Tony Womack	.182	11	1	2	0	0	1	2	.214	56	8	12	0	2	2	7
Marlon Anderson	.167	6	0	1	0	0	0	1	.167	12	1	2	0	0	1	2
Jim Edmonds	.067	15	2	1	0	1	6		.222	54	5	12	3	9	4	21
Scott Rolen	.000	15	0	0	0	1	1	1	.161	56	7	9	3	7	9	13
Reggie Sanders	.000	9	1	0	0	0	4	5	.182	44	5	8	1	1	5	12
John Mabry	.000	4	0	0	0	0	0	2	.091	11	0	1	0	1	0	6
Yadier Molina	.000	3	0	0	0	0	0	1	.143	7	0	1	0	0	0	0
Jason Marquis	.000	1	0	0	0	0	0	0	.250	4	1	1	0	0	0	0
Hector Luna	.000	1	0	0	0	0	0	1	.000	5	0	0	0	0	0	3
Woody Williams	—	0	0	0	0	0	0	0	.167	6	1	1	0	0	0	1
Matt Morris	—	0	0	0	0	0	0	0	.000	4	0	0	0	0	0	1
Danny Haren	—	0	0	0	0	0	0	0	.000	1	0	0	0	0	0	0
TOTALS	.000	126	12	24	2	8	12	32	.238	491	68	117	20	62	44	114

Pitching	ERA	W-L	Sv	Gm	IP	H	BB	SO	ERA	W-L	Sv	Gm	IP	H	BB	SO
Jason Isringhausen	0.00	0-0	0	1	2.0	1	1	2	3.86	0-1	3	9	11.2	6	7	7
Al Reyes	0.00	0-0	0	2	1.1	0	0	0	0.00	0-0	0	2	1.1	0	0	0
Ray King	0.00	0-0	0	3	2.2	1	1	1	2.70	0-0	0	10	6.2	5	1	3
Danny Haren	0.00	0-0	0	2	4.2	4	3	2	2.16	1-0	0	5	8.1	8	1	4
Cal Eldred	10.80	0-0	0	2	1.2	4	0	2	6.75	0-0	0	5	2.2	5	3	2
Kiko Calero	13.50	0-0	0	2	1.1	2	4	0	4.82	0-0	0	8	9.1	10	5	9
Jason Marquis	3.86	0-1	0	3	7.0	6	7	4	3.77	0-1	0	4	14.1	15	13	6
Woody Williams	27.00	0-0	0	1	2.1	8	3	1	5.48	2-0	0	4	21.1	21	7	12
Julian Tavarez	4.50	0-1	0	2	2.0	1	0	1	2.61	2-2	0	9	10.1	6	2	7
Jeff Suppan	7.72	0-1	0	1	4.2	8	1	4	3.80	2-2	0	4	23.2	18	4	8
Matt Morris	8.31	0-1	0	1	4.1	4	4	3	5.91	0-2	0	4	21.1	21	14	14
Steve Kline	—	0-0	0	1	0-0	0	0	0	0.00	0-0	0	3	1.1	2	0	0
TOTALS	6.09	0-4	0	4	34	39	24	20	4.42	7-8	3	15	132.1	117	64	82

Score by Innings

	1	2	3	4	5	6	7	8	9		R	H	E
St. Louis	0	1	1	4	0	2	0	3	1	—	12	24	1
Boston	8	0	5	3	2	2	2	0	—		24	39	8

E: St. Louis—Renteria; Boston—Mueller 3, Ramirez 2, Arroyo, Bellhorn, Millar. **2B:** St. Louis—Renteria 3, Walker 2, Pujols 2, Anderson; Boston—Nixon 3, Mueller 2, Damon 2, Ortiz, Bellhorn, Cabrera, Millar. **3B:** Boston—Damon, Varitek. **SB:** St. Louis— Sanders. **S:** St. Louis—Walker, Womack; Boston—Lowe. **SF:** St. Louis—Matheny 2, Rolen. **PB:** Boston—Mirabelli. **WP:** Boston—Lowe. **HBP:** by Wakefield (Pujols), by Williams (Cabrera), by Morris (Millar), by Eldred (Varitek), by Suppan (Bellhorn). **LOB:** St. Louis—24; Boston—41.
Umpires: Ed Montague, Dale Scott, Brian Gorman, Chuck Meriwether, Gerry Davis, Charlie Reliford.

COLLEGE

Final *Baseball America* Top 25

Final 2004 Division I Top 25, voted on by the editors of *Baseball America* and released after the NCAA CollegeWorld Series. Given are final records (excluding ties) and winning percentage (including all postseason games); records in College World Series and team eliminated by (DNP indicates team did not play in tourney); head coach (career years and four-year college record including 2004 postseason); preseason ranking and rank before start of CWS.

		Record	Pct	CWS Recap	Head Coach	Preseason Rank	Rank before CWS
1	CS-Fullerton	47-22	.681	5-1	George Horton (8 yrs: 357-154-1)	4	4
2	Texas	58-15	.795	3-2 (CS-Fullerton)	Augie Garrido (36 yrs: 1488-701-8)	8	2
3	South Carolina	53-17	.757	3-2 (CS-Fullerton)	Ray Tanner (17 yrs: 767-325-3)	7	3
4	Miami-FL	50-13	.794	1-2 (S. Carolina)	Jim Morris (23 yrs: 1026-422-2)	3	1
5	Georgia	45-23	.662	2-2 (Texas)	Dave Perno (3 yrs: 106-78)	NR	6
6	Arkansas	45-24	.652	0-2 (Arizona)	Dave Van Horn (11 yrs: 451-214)	NR	5
7	Louisiana St.	46-19	.708	0-2 (S. Carolina)	Smoke Laval (10 yrs: 376-222)	2	7
8	East Carolina	51-13	.797	DNP	Randy Mazey (5 yrs: 151-134-2)	NR	8
9	Stanford	46-14	.767	DNP	Mark Marquess (28 yrs: 1190-565-5)	6	9
10	Georgia Tech	44-21	.677	DNP	Danny Hall (17 yrs: 692-328)	5	10
11	Rice	46-14	.767	DNP	Wayne Graham (13 yrs: 582-238)	1	11
12	Arizona	36-27-1	.571	1-2 (Georgia)	Andy Lopez (22 yrs: 789-492-7)	16	12
13	Long Beach St	40-21	.656	DNP	Mike Weathers (5 yrs: 160-101)	9	13
14	Florida State	45-23	.662	DNP	Mike Martin (25 yrs: 1338-452-4)	22	14
15	Notre Dame	51-12	.810	DNP	Paul Mainieri (22 yrs: 774-459-2)	19	15
16	Florida	43-22	.662	DNP	Pat McMahon (12 yrs: 479-236-1)	20	16
17	Vanderbilt	45-19	.703	DNP	Tim Corbin (8 yrs: 178-185)	NR	17
18	Oral Roberts	50-11	.820	DNP	Rob Walton (1 yr: 50-11)	NR	18
19	Tulane	41-21	.661	DNP	Rick Jones (16 yrs: 641-287-1)	10	19
20	Texas A&M	42-22	.656	DNP	Mark Johnson (20 yrs: 846-406-2)	21	20
21	Washington	39-20-1	.661	DNP	Ken Knutson (12 yrs: 428-273-1)	NR	21
22	Arizona St.	41-18	.695	DNP	Pat Murphy (20 yrs: 772-369-3)	18	22
23	Mississippi	39-21	.650	DNP	Mike Bianco (7 yrs: 250-161-1)	17	23
24	Virginia	44-15	.746	DNP	Brian O'Connor (1 yr: 44-15)	NR	24
25	Oklahoma	38-24	.613	DNP	Larry Cochell (38 yrs: 1307-794-3)	NR	25

College World Series

CWS participants: Arizona (35-25-1); Arkansas (45-22); CS-Fulleron (42-21); Georgia (43-21); LSU (46-17); Miami-FL (49-11); South Carolina (50-15); Texas (55-13).

Bracket One

June 18—Georgia 8 . . . . Arizona 7
June 18—Texas 13 . . . . Arkansas 2
June 20—Arizona 7 . . . . Arkansas 2 (out)
June 20—Texas 9 . . . . Georgia 3
June 22—Georgia 3 . . . . Arizona 1 (out)
June 23—Texas 7 . . . . Georgia 6 (out)

Bracket Two

June 19—CS-Fullerton 2 . . . . South Carolina 0
June 19—Miami 9 . . . . LSU 5
June 21—South Carolina 15 . . . . LSU 4 (out)
June 21—CS-Fullerton 6 . . . . Miami-FL 3
June 22—South Carolina 15 . . . . Miami-FL 11 (out)
June 23—South Carolina 5 . . . . CS-Fullerton 3
June 24—CS-Fullerton 4 . . . . South Carolina 0 (out)

Championship Series

June 26—CS-Fullerton 6 . . . . Texas 4
June 27—CS-Fullerton 3 . . . . Texas 2 (out)

Most Outstanding Player

Jason Windsor, CS-Fullerton, P

IP	H	ER	BB	K	W-L	Sv	ERA
21.0	11	2	6	29	2-0	1	0.86

All-Tournament Team

C—Landon Powell, USC; **1B**—Steve Pearce, USC; **2B**—Seth Johnston, Texas; **3B**—Bryan Triplett, USC; **SS**—Roger Tomas, Miami-FL; **OF**—John Jay, Miami-FL; Trevor Crowe, Arizona; Brian Barton, Miami-FL; **DH**—Felipe Garcia, CS-Fullerton; **P**—Jason Windsor, CS-Fullerton; Ricky Romero, CS-Fullerton.

Annual Awards

Chosen by *Baseball America, Collegiate Baseball,* National Collegiate Baseball Writers Association, American Baseball Coaches Association and USA Baseball.

Player of the Year

Jered Weaver, Long Beach St., P . . . .*BA, CB,*
Dick Howser (NCBWA), ABCA,
Golden Spikes (USA Baseball)

Coach of the Year

George Horton, CS-Fullerton . . . .*CB,* ABCA
Dave Perno, Georgia . . . .*BA*

Consensus All-America Team

NCAA Division I players cited most frequently by the following four selectors: the American Baseball Coaches Assn. (ABCA), Baseball America, Collegiate Baseball and the National Collegiate Baseball Writers Assn. (NCBWA).

First Team

Pos		Cl	Avg	HR	RBI
C	Kurt Suzuki, CS-Fullerton	Jr.	.413	16	87
1B	Josh Brady, Texas Tech	Jr.	.362	20	90
2B	Warner Jones, Vanderbilt	So.	.414	11	74
SS	Dustin Pedroia, Arizona St.	Jr.	.393	9	49
3B	Alex Gordon, Nebraska	So.	.365	18	75
OF	Eddy Martinez-Esteve, Fla. St.	So.	.385	19	81
OF	Eric Nielsen, UNLV	Jr.	.402	16	87
OF	Chris Rahl, Wm. & Mary	So.	.389	20	70
UT	Ryan Jones, E. Carolina	Sr.	.400	19	69

Pos		Cl	W-L	Sv	ERA
P	J.P. Howell, Texas	Jr.	15-2	1	2.13
P	Jered Weaver, Long Beach St.	Jr.	15-1	0	1.62
P	Philip Humber, Rice	Jr.	13-4	1	2.27
P	Justin Hoyman, Florida	Jr.	11-2	0	2.71
P	Wade Townsend, Rice	Jr.	12-0	2	1.80
P	Huston Street, Texas	Jr.	6-1	12	1.58

Second Team

Pos		Cl	Avg	HR	RBI
C	Landon Powell, S. Carolina	Sr.	.330	19	66
1B	Mike Ferris, Miami-Ohio	Jr.	.361	21	62
2B	Jed Lowrie, Stanford	So.	.399	17	68
SS	Brian Bixler, Eastern Mich.	Jr.	.453	8	47
3B	Matt Macri, Notre Dame	Jr.	.367	14	56
OF	Jon Zeringue, LSU	Jr.	.384	12	57
OF	Marshall Hubbard, N. Carolina	Jr.	.352	17	83
OF	Richie Robnett, Fresno St.	Jr.	.384	13	51
UT	Stephen Head, Mississippi	So.	.346	13	53

Pos		Cl	W-L	Sv	ERA
P	Matt Fox, Central Florida	Jr.	14-2	0	1.85
P	Greg Bunn, E. Carolina	Jr.	10-1	0	2.70
P	Mike Pelfrey, Wichita St.	So.	11-2	0	2.18
P	Jason Windsor, CS-Fullerton	Sr.	13-4	1	1.72
P	Austin Tubb, Southern Miss.	Sr.	8-0	10	0.93
P	Chad Blackwell, S. Carolina	Jr.	4-3	20	2.57

NCAA Division I Leaders

Batting

Average

(At least 75 AB & 2.5/Gm)	Cl	Gm	AB	H	Avg
Caleb Moore, East Tenn. St.	Jr.	52	202	92	.455
Brian Bixler, Eastern Mich.	Jr.	59	243	110	.453
Stephen Carter, Eastern Ky.	Sr.	46	183	82	.448
Bryant Lange, Jackson St.	Jr.	49	164	72	.439
Jim Geldhof, Central Mich.	Jr.	56	227	97	.427
Trey Hendricks, Harvard	Sr.	38	143	61	.427
Bryant Jones, Tenn.-Martin	Sr.	54	226	96	.425
Kiel Thibault, Gonzaga	So.	51	205	87	.424
Corey Wimberley, Alcorn St.	Fr.	42	150	63	.420
Jonathan Woodard, Eastern Ky.	Sr.	51	184	77	.418

Runs Batted In (per game)

(At least 50 RBI)	Cl	Gm	RBI	Avg
Billy Becher, New Mexico St.	Sr.	59	90	1.53
Josh Brady, Texas Tech	Jr.	61	90	1.48
Jarrett Hoffpauir, Southern Miss.	Jr.	64	92	1.44
Eric Nielsen, UNLV	Jr.	61	87	1.43
Cameron Blair, Texas Tech	Jr.	58	81	1.40
Chris Looze, George Mason	Sr.	58	81	1.40
Andrew Toussaint, Southern	Jr.	40	54	1.35
Brent Johnson, UNLV	Sr.	54	72	1.33
Marshall Hubbard, N. Carolina	Jr.	64	83	1.30
Chris Rahl, Wm. & Mary	So.	54	70	1.30

Home Runs (per game)

(At least 15 HR)	Cl	Gm	HR	Avg
Billy Becher, New Mex. St.	Sr.	59	25	0.42
Drew Moffitt, Wichita St.	Sr.	62	26	0.42
P.J. Hiser, Pittsburgh	Sr.	53	21	0.40
Chris Rahl, Wm. & Mary	So.	54	20	0.37
Mike Ferris, Miami-OH	Jr.	57	21	0.37
Jared Greenwood, W. Carolina	Jr.	59	21	0.36
Chris O'Dell, Eastern Ky.	So.	43	15	0.35
Anthony Gressick, Ohio	So.	46	16	0.35
Mike Butia, James Madsion	Jr.	52	18	0.35
Ryan Frith, Southern Miss.	Sr.	64	22	0.34

Stolen Bases (per game)

	Cl	Gm	SB	CS	Avg
Carl Lipsey, Jackson St.	Jr.	47	49	8	1.04
Corey Wimberley, Alcorn St.	Fr.	42	40	6	0.95
Garrett Weir, Delaware St.	Sr.	48	41	5	0.85
Dennis Diaz, Florida Int'l	Jr.	62	49	4	0.79
Chris Monaco, Marshall	Jr.	51	40	12	0.78
Chris Rahl, Wm. & Mary	So.	54	42	4	0.78
Anthony Granato, VCU	Sr.	57	44	5	0.77
Eric Patterson, Georgia Tech	Jr.	65	48	7	0.74
Kyle Brown, Le Moyne	Sr.	57	42	7	0.74
Matt Vanderbosch, Oral Roberts	Sr.	61	44	4	0.72

Pitching

Earned Run Avg.

(At least 50 inn.)	Cl	Gm	IP	ERA
Nate Moore, Troy St.	Jr.	32	64.2	1.25
Jered Weaver, Long Beach St.	Jr.	19	144.0	1.63
Brad Kilby, San Jose St.	Jr.	25	58.0	1.71
Jason Windsor, CS-Fullerton	Sr.	22	162.2	1.71
Wade Townsend, Rice	Jr.	18	120.1	1.72
Matt Fox, Central Fla.	Jr.	17	111.2	1.85
Jon Wilson, Winthrop	Jr.	34	67.0	1.88
Derrick Gordon, Lamar	Fr.	18	65.2	1.92
Kyle Bono, Central Florida	So.	18	97.1	1.94
Taylor Tankersley, Alabama	Jr.	20	67.2	1.99

Wins

	Cl	Gm	IP	W-L
Jered Weaver, Long Beach St.	Jr.	19	144.0	15-1
J.P. Howell, Texas	Jr.	24	135.1	15-2
Matt Fox, Central Fla.	Jr.	17	111.2	14-2
Ricky Romero, CS-Fullerton	So.	22	155.0	14-4
Dennis Bigley, Oral Roberts	Jr.	16	117.2	13-1
Philip Humber, Rice	Jr.	20	115.0	13-4
Aaron Rawl, S. Carolina	Jr.	20	122.0	13-4
Dennis Robinson, Jacksonville	Jr.	18	120.0	13-4
Jason Windsor, CS-Fullerton	Sr.	22	162.7	13-4
Twelve tied with 12 wins each.				

Strikeouts (per 9 inn.)

(At least 50 inn.)	Cl	IP	SO	Avg
Jered Weaver, Long Beach St.	Jr.	144.0	213	13.3
Tim Lincecum, Washington	Fr.	112.1	161	12.9
Justin Verlander, Old Dominion	Jr.	105.2	151	12.9
Bill Bray, Wm. & Mary	Jr.	59.0	84	12.8
Chris Blazek, Vermont	So.	67.2	92	12.2
Josh Schmidt, Pacific	Jr.	54.0	73	12.2
Philip Humber, Rice	Jr.	115.0	154	12.1
Zachary Ward, Gardner-Webb	So.	79.2	106	12.0
Zach Zuercher, Rhode Island	So.	92.2	123	11.9
Nate Moore, Troy St.	Jr.	64.2	84	11.7

Saves

	Cl	Gm	IP	Sv
Chad Blackwell, S. Carolina	Jr.	37	63.0	20
Blair Erickson, UC-Irvine	Fr.	30	37.1	17
Shawn Ryan, Albany	Jr.	27	25.0	14
Ryan Schroyer, San Diego St.	Sr.	28	41.0	13
Justin Ramsey, Oral Roberts	Sr.	30	58.2	13
Anthony Rea, Santa Clara	Jr.	30	53.2	13
Brett Harker, Coll. of Charleston.	So.	33	50.2	13
Eight tied with 12 each.				

Other College World Series

Participants' final records in parentheses.

NCAA Div. II

at Montgomery, Ala. (May 22-29)

Participants: Bryant, R.I. (40-17); CS-Chico (42-21-1); Central Missouri St. (57-8); Columbus St., Ga. (40-21); Delta St., Miss. (54-11); Grand Valley St., Mich. (46-16); Kutztown, Penn. (37-16); Rollins, Fla. (48-12).

Championship: Delta St. def. Grand Valley St., 12-8.

NAIA

at Lewiston, Idaho (May 28-June 3)

Participants: Bellevue, Neb. (55-20); Concordia, Ore. (37-22); Cumberland, Tenn. (59-21); Embry-Riddle, Fla. (53-10); Jamestown, N.D. (46-10); Lewis-Clark St., Idaho (52-10); Mount Vernon Nazarene, Ohio (41-19); Oklahoma City (73-7); Pt. Loma Nazarene, Calif. (47-16); William Penn, Iowa (48-15).

Championship: Cumberland def. Oklahoma City, 10-3.

NCAA Div. III

at Appleton, Wis. (May 28-June 1)

Participants: Aurora, Ill. (28-19); Brockport St., N.Y. (34-15); Eastern Connecticut St. (43-11); George Fox, Ore. (40-10); Manchester, Ind. (35-12); Rowan, N.J. (41-8), Salisbury, Md. (36-13); Wis.-Whitewater (38-9).

Championship: George Fox def. Eastern Conn. St., 6-3.

NJCAA Div. I

at Grand Junction, Colo. (May 24-31)

Participants: Dixie St., Utah (51-14); Grayson County JC, Texas (45-18); Indian Hills CC, Iowa (36-33); Meridian CC, Miss. (46-14); Middle Georgia (45-19); Pensacola JC, Fla. (36-21); Potomac St., W. Va. (31-21); San Jacinto-North, Texas (41-22); Seminole St., Okla. (34-27); Seward County CC, Kan. (47-16).

Championship: Dixie St. def. San Jacinto-North, 4-3.

2004 MLB First-Year Player Draft

First round selections at the 40th First-Year Player Draft held June 7-8, 2004 in New York. Clubs select in reverse order of their standing from the preceding season. The worst National League team selects first in even years and the worst American League team goes first in odd years. Leagues then alternate picks throughout the rounds. Note that picks 31-41 are supplemental compensatory selections.

First Round

No		Pos
1	San Diego ...... Matt Bush, Mission Bay HS, San Diego, Calif.	SS
2	Detroit. ...... Justin Verlander, Old Dominion	RHP
3	NY Mets ...... Philip Humber, Rice	RHP
4	Tampa Bay ...... Jeff Niemann, Rice	RHP
5	Milwaukee .... Mark Rogers, Mount Ararat HS, Orr's Island, Maine	RHP
6	Cleveland ...... Jeremy Sowers, Vanderbilt	LHP
7	Cincinnati . . Homer Bailey, La Grange (Texas) HS	RHP
8	Baltimore ...... Wade Townsend, Rice	RHP
9	Colorado. Chris Nelson, Redan HS, Decatur, Ga.	SS
10	Texas ...... Thomas Diamond, New Orleans	RHP
11	Pittsburgh...... Neil Walker, Pine Richland HS, Gibsonia, Penn.	C
12	Anaheim ...... Jered Weaver, Long Beach St.	RHP
13	Montreal ...... Bill Bray, Wm. & Mary	LHP
14	Kansas City...... Billy Butler, Wolfson Sr. HS, Jacksonville, Fla.	3B
15	Arizona ...... Stephen Drew, Florida St.	SS
16	Toronto ...... David Purcey, Oklahoma	LHP
17	Los Angeles . . . Timothy Elbert, Seneca (Mo.) HS	LHP
18	Chicago-AL ...... Josh Fields, Oklahoma St.	3B
19	St. Louis ...... Chris Lambert, Boston College	RHP
20	Minnesota . . Trevor Plouffe, Crespi Carmelite HS, Northridge, Calif.	SS
21	Philadelphia ...... Greg Golson, Connally HS, Austin, Texas	CF

No		Pos
22	Minnesota ...... Glen Perkins, Minnesota	LHP
23	NY Yankees ...... Philip Hughes, Foothill HS, Santa Ana, Calif.	RHP
24	Oakland ...... Landon Powell, South Carolina	C
25	Minnesota ...... Kyle Waldrop, Farragut HS, Knoxville, Tenn.	RHP
26	Oakland ...... Richie Robnett, Fresno St.	CF
27	Florida ...... Taylor Tankersley, Alabama	LHP
28	Los Angeles . . Blake Dewitt, Sikeston (Mo.) HS	2B
29	Kansas City . . . .Matt Campbell, South Carolina	LHP
30	Texas ...... Eric Hurley, Wolfson Sr. HS, Jacksonville, Fla.	RHP
31	a-Kansas City ...... James Howell, Texas	LHP
32	b-Toronto ...... Zachary Jackson, Texas A&M	LHP
33	c-Los Angeles ...... Justin Orenduff, VCU	RHP
34	d-Chicago-AL ...... Tyler Lumsden, Clemson	LHP
35	e-Minnesota ...... Matthew Fox, Central Fla.	RHP
36	f-Oakland ...... Daniel Putnam, Stanford	CF
37	g-NY Yankees . . . . Jonathan Poterson, Chandler (Ariz) HS	C
38	h-Chicago-AL . . Giovany Gonzalez, Monsignor Edward Pace HS, Hialeah, Fla.	LHP
39	i-Minnesota Jay Rainville, Bishop Hendricken HS, Pawtucket, R.I.	RHP
40	j-Oakland ...... Huston Street, Texas	RHP
41	k-NY Yankees Jeffrey Marquez, Sacramento CC	RHP

Supplemental picks: a-for Raul Ibanez; **b-**for Kelvim Escobar; **c-**for Paul Quantrill; **d-**for Bartolo Colon; **e-**for Eddie Guardado; **f-**for Keith Foulke; **g-**for Andy Pettitte; **h-**for Tom Gordon; **i-**for LaTroy Hawkins; **j-**for Miguel Tejada; **k-**for David Wells.

Minor League Triple-A Final Standings

Division champions (*) and Wild Card (†) winners are noted.

International League

North Division	W	L	Pct	GB
*Buffalo (Indians)	83	61	.576	—
Rochester (Twins)	73	71	.507	10
Pawtucket (Red Sox)	73	71	.507	10
Scranton-Wilkes Barre (Phillies)	69	73	.486	13
Syracuse (Blue Jays)	66	78	.458	17
Ottawa (Orioles)	66	78	.458	17

South Division	W	L	Pct	GB
*Richmond (Braves)	79	62	.560	—
†Durham (Devil Rays)	77	67	.535	3½
Norfolk (Mets)	72	72	.500	8½
Charlotte (White Sox)	68	74	.479	11½

West Division	W	L	Pct	GB
*Columbus (Yankees)	80	64	.556	—
Louisville (Reds)	67	77	.465	13
Indianapolis (Brewers)	66	78	.458	14
Toledo (Tigers)	65	78	.455	14½

Playoffs
First Round (Best-of-Five)

Buffalo 3 . . . . Durham 2
Richmond 3 . . . . Columbus 2

Championship (Best-of-Five)
Richmond vs. Buffalo

Sept. 14	Richmond, 11-4	at Buffalo
Sept. 15	Buffalo, 4-3	at Buffalo
Sept. 16	Buffalo, 5-4	at Richmond
Sept. 17	Buffalo, 6-1	at Richmond

Buffalo wins Governors' Cup, 3-1

Pacific Coast League

American Conference

Eastern Division	W	L	Pct	GB
*Oklahoma (Rangers)	81	63	.563	—
Memphis (Cardinals)	73	71	.507	8
New Orleans (Astros)	66	78	.458	15
Nashville (Pirates)	63	79	.444	17

Central Division	W	L	Pct	GB
*Iowa (Cubs)	79	64	.552	—
Colorado Springs (Rockies)	78	65	.545	1
Omaha (Royals)	71	73	.493	8½
Albuquerque (Marlins)	67	77	.465	12½

Pacific Conference

Northern Division	W	L	Pct	GB
*Portland (Padres)	84	60	.583	—
Tacoma (Mariners)	79	63	.556	4
Edmonton (Expos)	69	74	.483	14½
Salt Lake (Angels)	56	88	.389	28

Southern Division	W	L	Pct	GB
*Sacramento (A's)	79	65	.549	—
Tucson (D'Backs)	74	70	.514	5
Las Vegas (Dodgers)	67	76	.469	11½
Fresno (Giants)	62	82	.431	17

Playoffs
Conference Finals (Best-of-Five)

Sacramento 3 . . . . Portland 1
Iowa 3 . . . . Oklahoma 2

Championship (Best-of-Five)
Sacramento vs. Iowa

Sept. 14	Sacramento, 10-5	at Iowa
Sept. 15	Sacramento, 5-4	at Iowa
Sept. 17	Sacramento, 4-3	at Sacramento

Sacramento wins PCL Championship, 3-0

2004 International League All-Star Team

As selected by IL managers, coaches and media.

Pos	Name/Team
C	Kelly Shoppach, Pawtucket
1B	Justin Morneau, Rochester
2B	Pete Orr, Richmond
SS	Jhonny Peralta, Buffalo
3B	Earl Snyder, Pawtucket
DH	Ernie Young, Buffalo
OF	Matt Diaz, Durham
OF	Adam Hyzdu, Pawtucket
OF	Jason Kubel, Rochester
UT	Jorge Cantu, Durham
SP	Ben Hendrickson, Indianapolis
REL	Matt Whiteside, Richmond

2004 Pacific Coast League All-Star Team

As selected by PCL managers and media representatives.

Pos	Name/Team
C	Mike Rose, Sacramento
1B	Dan Johnson, Sacramento
2B	Chris Burke, New Orleans
SS	Clint Barnes, Colorado
3B	Garrett Atkins, Colorado
DH	Calvin Pickering, Omaha
OF	Chad Allen, Oklahoma
OF	Ryan Church, Edmonton
OF	Adam Riggs, Salt Lake
RHP	Brian Sweeney, Portland
LHP	Scott Downs, Edmonton
REL	Al Reyes, Memphis

1876-2004
Through the Years

ESPN SPORTS ALMANAC

The World Series

The World Series began in 1903 when Pittsburgh of the older National League (founded in 1876) invited Boston of the American League (founded in 1901) to play a best-of-9 game series to determine which of the two league champions was the best. Boston was the surprise winner, 5 games to 3. The 1904 NL champion New York Giants refused to play Boston the following year, so there was no Series. Giants' owner John T. Brush and his manager John McGraw both despised AL president Ban Johnson and considered the junior circuit to be a minor league. By the following year, however, Brush and Johnson had smoothed out their differences and the Giants agreed to play Philadelphia in a best-of-7 game series. Since then the World Series has been a best-of-7 format, except from 1919-21 when it returned to best-of-9.

After surviving two world wars and an earthquake in 1989, the World Series was cancelled for only the second time in 1994 due to the players' strike.

In the chart below, the National League teams are listed in CAPITAL letters. Also, each World Series champion's wins and losses are noted in parentheses after the Series score in games.

Multiple champions: New York Yankees (26); Philadelphia-Oakland A's and St. Louis Cardinals (9); Boston Red Sox and Brooklyn-Los Angeles Dodgers (6); Cincinnati Reds, New York-San Francisco Giants and Pittsburgh Pirates (5); Detroit Tigers (4); Baltimore Orioles, Boston-Milwaukee-Atlanta Braves and Washington Senators-Minnesota Twins (3); Chicago Cubs, Chicago White Sox, Cleveland Indians, Florida Marlins, New York Mets and Toronto Blue Jays (2).

Year	Winner	Manager	Series	Loser	Manager
1903	Boston Red Sox	Jimmy Collins	5-3 (LWLLWWWW)	PITTSBURGH	Fred Clarke
1904	Not held				
1905	NY GIANTS	John McGraw	4-1 (WLWWW)	Philadelphia A's	Connie Mack
1906	Chicago White Sox	Fielder Jones	4-2 (LWLWLW)	CHICAGO CUBS	Frank Chance
1907	CHICAGO CUBS	Frank Chance	4-0-1 (TWWWW)	Detroit	Hughie Jennings
1908	CHICAGO CUBS	Frank Chance	4-1 (WWLWW)	Detroit	Hughie Jennings
1909	PITTSBURGH	Fred Clarke	4-3 (WLWLWLW)	Detroit	Hughie Jennings
1910	Philadelphia A's	Connie Mack	4-1 (WWWLW)	CHICAGO CUBS	Frank Chance
1911	Philadelphia A's	Connie Mack	4-2 (LWWWLW)	NY GIANTS	John McGraw
1912	Boston Red Sox	Jake Stahl	4-3-1 (WTLWWLLW)	NY GIANTS	John McGraw
1913	Philadelphia A's	Connie Mack	4-1 (WLWWW)	NY GIANTS	John McGraw
1914	BOSTON BRAVES	George Stallings	4-0	Philadelphia A's	Connie Mack
1915	Boston Red Sox	Bill Carrigan	4-1 (LWWWW)	PHILA. PHILLIES	Pat Moran
1916	Boston Red Sox	Bill Carrigan	4-1 (WWLWW)	BROOKLYN	Wilbert Robinson
1917	Chicago White Sox	Pants Rowland	4-2 (WWLLWW)	NY GIANTS	John McGraw
1918	Boston Red Sox	Ed Barrow	4-2 (WWLWLW)	CHICAGO CUBS	Fred Mitchell
1919	CINCINNATI	Pat Moran	5-3 (WWLWWLLW)	Chicago White Sox	Kid Gleason
1920	Cleveland	Tris Speaker	5-2 (WLLWWWW)	BROOKLYN	Wilbert Robinson
1921	NY GIANTS	John McGraw	5-3 (LLWLWWWW)	NY Yankees	Miller Huggins
1922	NY GIANTS	John McGraw	4-0-1 (WTWWW)	NY Yankees	Miller Huggins
1923	NY Yankees	Miller Huggins	4-2 (LWLWW)	NY GIANTS	John McGraw
1924	Washington	Bucky Harris	4-3 (LWLWLW)	NY GIANTS	John McGraw
1925	PITTSBURGH	Bill McKechnie	4-3 (LWLLWW)	Washington	Bucky Harris
1926	ST.L. CARDINALS	Rogers Hornsby	4-3 (LWWLLWW)	NY Yankees	Miller Huggins
1927	NY Yankees	Miller Huggins	4-0	PITTSBURGH	Donie Bush
1928	NY Yankees	Miller Huggins	4-0	ST.L. CARDINALS	Bill McKechnie
1929	Philadelphia A's	Connie Mack	4-1 (WWLWW)	CHICAGO CUBS	Joe McCarthy
1930	Philadelphia A's	Connie Mack	4-2 (WWLLWW)	ST.L. CARDINALS	Gabby Street
1931	ST.L. CARDINALS	Gabby Street	4-3 (LWLWLW)	Philadelphia A's	Connie Mack
1932	NY Yankees	Joe McCarthy	4-0	CHICAGO CUBS	Charlie Grimm
1933	NY GIANTS	Bill Terry	4-1 (WWLWW)	Washington	Joe Cronin
1934	ST.L. CARDINALS	Frankie Frisch	4-3 (WLWLLWW)	Detroit	Mickey Cochrane
1935	Detroit	Mickey Cochrane	4-2 (LWWWLW)	CHICAGO CUBS	Charlie Grimm
1936	NY Yankees	Joe McCarthy	4-2 (WLWWLW)	NY GIANTS	Bill Terry
1937	NY Yankees	Joe McCarthy	4-1 (WWWLW)	NY GIANTS	Bill Terry
1938	NY Yankees	Joe McCarthy	4-0	CHICAGO CUBS	Gabby Hartnett
1939	NY Yankees	Joe McCarthy	4-0	CINCINNATI	Bill McKechnie
1940	CINCINNATI	Bill McKechnie	4-3 (LWLWLWW)	Detroit	Del Baker
1941	NY Yankees	Joe McCarthy	4-1 (WLWWW)	BKLN. DODGERS	Leo Durocher
1942	ST.L. CARDINALS	Billy Southworth	4-1 (LWWWW)	NY Yankees	Joe McCarthy
1943	NY Yankees	Joe McCarthy	4-1 (WLWWW)	ST.L. CARDINALS	Billy Southworth

Year	Winner	Manager	Series		Loser	Manager
1944	ST.L. CARDINALS	Billy Southworth	4-2	(LWLWWW)	St. Louis Browns	Luke Sewell
1945	Detroit	Steve O'Neill	4-3	(LWLWWWLW)	CHICAGO CUBS	Charlie Grimm
1946	ST.L. CARDINALS	Eddie Dyer	4-3	(LWLWLWW)	Boston Red Sox	Joe Cronin
1947	NY Yankees	Bucky Harris	4-3	(WWLLWLW)	BKLN. DODGERS	Burt Shotton
1948	Cleveland	Lou Boudreau	4-2	(LWWWLW)	BOSTON BRAVES	Billy Southworth
1949	NY Yankees	Casey Stengel	4-1	(WLWWW)	BKLN. DODGERS	Burt Shotton
1950	NY Yankees	Casey Stengel	4-0		PHILA. PHILLIES	Eddie Sawyer
1951	NY Yankees	Casey Stengel	4-2	(LWLWWW)	NY GIANTS	Leo Durocher
1952	NY Yankees	Casey Stengel	4-3	(LWLWLWW)	BKLN. DODGERS	Charlie Dressen
1953	NY Yankees	Casey Stengel	4-2	(WWLLWW)	BKLN. DODGERS	Charlie Dressen
1954	NY GIANTS	Leo Durocher	4-0		Cleveland	Al Lopez
1955	BKLN. DODGERS	Walter Alston	4-3	(LLWWWLW)	NY Yankees	Casey Stengel
1956	NY Yankees	Casey Stengel	4-3	(LLWWWLW)	BKLN. DODGERS	Walter Alston
1957	MILW. BRAVES	Fred Haney	4-3	(LWLWWLW)	NY Yankees	Casey Stengel
1958	NY Yankees	Casey Stengel	4-3	(LLWWWLW)	MILW. BRAVES	Fred Haney
1959	LA DODGERS	Walter Alston	4-2	(LWWWLW)	Chicago White Sox	Al Lopez
1960	PITTSBURGH	Danny Murtaugh	4-3	(WLLWWLW)	NY Yankees	Casey Stengel
1961	NY Yankees	Ralph Houk	4-1	(WLWWW)	CINCINNATI	Fred Hutchinson
1962	NY Yankees	Ralph Houk	4-3	(WLWLWLW)	SF GIANTS	Alvin Dark
1963	LA DODGERS	Walter Alston	4-0		NY Yankees	Ralph Houk
1964	ST.L. CARDINALS	Johnny Keane	4-3	(WLWLWLW)	NY Yankees	Yogi Berra
1965	LA DODGERS	Walter Alston	4-3	(LLWWWLW)	Minnesota	Sam Mele
1966	Baltimore	Hank Bauer	4-0		LA DODGERS	Walter Alston
1967	ST.L. CARDINALS	Red Schoendienst	4-3	(WLWWLW)	Boston Red Sox	Dick Williams
1968	Detroit	Mayo Smith	4-3	(LWLLWWW)	ST.L. CARDINALS	Red Schoendienst
1969	NY METS	Gil Hodges	4-1	(LWWWW)	Baltimore	Earl Weaver
1970	Baltimore	Earl Weaver	4-1	(WWWLW)	CINCINNATI	Sparky Anderson
1971	PITTSBURGH	Danny Murtaugh	4-3	(LLWWWLW)	Baltimore	Earl Weaver
1972	Oakland A's	Dick Williams	4-3	(WWLWLLW)	CINCINNATI	Sparky Anderson
1973	Oakland A's	Dick Williams	4-3	(WLWWLLW)	NY METS	Yogi Berra
1974	Oakland A's	Alvin Dark	4-1	(LWWWW)	LA DODGERS	Walter Alston
1975	CINCINNATI	Sparky Anderson	4-3	(LWWWLW)	Boston Red Sox	Darrell Johnson
1976	CINCINNATI	Sparky Anderson	4-0		NY Yankees	Billy Martin
1977	NY Yankees	Billy Martin	4-2	(WLWWLW)	LA DODGERS	Tommy Lasorda
1978	NY Yankees	Bob Lemon	4-2	(LLWWWW)	LA DODGERS	Tommy Lasorda
1979	PITTSBURGH	Chuck Tanner	4-3	(LWLLWWW)	Baltimore	Earl Weaver
1980	PHILA. PHILLIES	Dallas Green	4-2	(WWLLWW)	Kansas City	Jim Frey
1981	LA DODGERS	Tommy Lasorda	4-2	(LLWWWW)	NY Yankees	Bob Lemon
1982	ST.L. CARDINALS	Whitey Herzog	4-3	(LWWLLWW)	Milwaukee Brewers	Harvey Kuenn
1983	Baltimore	Joe Altobelli	4-1	(LWWWW)	PHILA. PHILLIES	Paul Owens
1984	Detroit	Sparky Anderson	4-1	(WWLWW)	SAN DIEGO	Dick Williams
1985	Kansas City	Dick Howser	4-3	(LLWWLWW)	ST.L. CARDINALS	Whitey Herzog
1986	NY METS	Davey Johnson	4-3	(LLWWWLW)	Boston Red Sox	John McNamara
1987	Minnesota	Tom Kelly	4-3	(WWLLLWW)	ST.L. CARDINALS	Whitey Herzog
1988	LA DODGERS	Tommy Lasorda	4-1	(WWLWW)	Oakland A's	Tony La Russa
1989	Oakland A's	Tony La Russa	4-0		SF GIANTS	Roger Craig
1990	CINCINNATI	Lou Piniella	4-0		Oakland A's	Tony La Russa
1991	Minnesota	Tom Kelly	4-3	(WWLLLWW)	ATLANTA BRAVES	Bobby Cox
1992	Toronto	Cito Gaston	4-2	(LWWWLW)	ATLANTA BRAVES	Bobby Cox
1993	Toronto	Cito Gaston	4-2	(WLWWLW)	PHILA. PHILLIES	Jim Fregosi
1994	Not held					
1995	ATLANTA BRAVES	Bobby Cox	4-2	(WWLWLW)	Cleveland	Mike Hargrove
1996	NY Yankees	Joe Torre	4-2	(LLWWWW)	ATLANTA BRAVES	Bobby Cox
1997	FLORIDA	Jim Leyland	4-3	(WLWLWLW)	Cleveland	Mike Hargrove
1998	NY Yankees	Joe Torre	4-0		SAN DIEGO	Bruce Bochy
1999	NY Yankees	Joe Torre	4-0		ATLANTA BRAVES	Bobby Cox
2000	NY Yankees	Joe Torre	4-1	(WWLWW)	NY METS	Bobby Valentine
2001	ARIZONA	Bob Brenly	4-3	(WWLLLWW)	NY Yankees	Joe Torre
2002	Anaheim	Mike Scioscia	4-3	(LWLWLWW)	SF GIANTS	Dusty Baker
2003	FLORIDA	Jack McKeon	4-2	(WLLWWW)	NY Yankees	Joe Torre
2004	Boston	Terry Francona	4-0		ST. LOUIS	Tony La Russa

Walk-off HR to Win a Postseason Series

Year	Player	Team	Series, Game	Opponent	Final Score
2004	David Ortiz	Boston	ALDS Game 3	Anaheim	8-6 (10 inn.)
2003	Aaron Boone	NY Yankees	ALCS Game 7	Boston	6-5 (11 inn.)
1999	Todd Pratt	NY Mets	NLDS Game 4	Arizona	4-3 (10 inn.)
1993	Joe Carter	Toronto	WS, Game 6	Philadelphia	8-6
1976	Chris Chambliss	NY Yankees	ALCS, Game 5	Kansas City	7-6
1960	Bill Mazeroski	Pittsburgh	WS, Game 7	NY Yankees	10-9

The World Series (Cont.)
Most Valuable Players

Currently selected by media panel and World Series official scorers. Presented by *Sport* magazine from 1955-88 and by Major League Baseball since 1989. Winner who did not play for World Series champions is in **bold** type.

Multiple winners: Bob Gibson, Reggie Jackson and Sandy Koufax (2).

Year	Year	Year
1955 Johnny Podres, Bklyn, P	1974 Rollie Fingers, Oak., P	1991 Jack Morris, Min., P
1956 Don Larsen, NY, P	1975 Pete Rose, Cin., 3B	1992 Pat Borders, Tor., C
1957 Lew Burdette, Mil., P	1976 Johnny Bench, Cin., C	1993 Paul Molitor, Tor., DH/1B/3B
1958 Bob Turley, NY, P	1977 Reggie Jackson, NY, OF	1994 Series not held.
1959 Larry Sherry, LA, P	1978 Bucky Dent, NY, SS	1995 Tom Glavine, Atl., P
	1979 Willie Stargell, Pit., 1B	1996 John Wetteland, NY, P
1960 **Bobby Richardson**, NY, 2B		1997 Livan Hernandez, Fla., P
1961 Whitey Ford, NY, P	1980 Mike Schmidt, Phi., 3B	1998 Scott Brosius, NY, 3B
1962 Ralph Terry, NY, P	1981 Pedro Guerrero, LA, OF;	1999 Mariano Rivera, NY, P
1963 Sandy Koufax, LA, P	Ron Cey, LA, 3B;	
1964 Bob Gibson, St.L., P	& Steve Yeager, LA, C	2000 Derek Jeter, NY, SS
1965 Sandy Koufax, LA, P	1982 Darrell Porter, St.L., C	2001 Curt Schilling, Ari., P
1966 Frank Robinson, Bal., OF	1983 Rick Dempsey, Bal., C	& Randy Johnson, Ari., P
1967 Bob Gibson, St.L., P	1984 Alan Trammell, Det., SS	2002 Troy Glaus, Ana., 3B
1968 Mickey Lolich, Det., P	1985 Bret Saberhagen, KC, P	2003 Josh Beckett, Fla., P
1969 Donn Clendenon, NY, 1B	1986 Ray Knight, NY, 3B	2004 Manny Ramirez, Bos., OF
	1987 Frank Viola, Min., P	
1970 Brooks Robinson, Bal., 3B	1988 Orel Hershiser, LA, P	
1971 Roberto Clemente, Pit., OF	1989 Dave Stewart, Oak., P	
1972 Gene Tenace, Oak., C		
1973 Reggie Jackson, Oak., OF	1990 Jose Rijo, Cin., P	

All-Time World Series Leaders
CAREER

World Series leaders through 2004. Years listed indicate number of World Series appearances.

Hitting

Games

	Yrs	Gm
Yogi Berra, NY Yankees	14	75
Mickey Mantle, NY Yankees	12	65
Elston Howard, NY Yankees—Boston	10	54
Hank Bauer, NY Yankees	9	53
Gil McDougald, NY Yankees	8	53

At Bats

	Yrs	AB
Yogi Berra, NY Yankees	14	259
Mickey Mantle, NY Yankees	12	230
Joe DiMaggio, NY Yankees	10	199
Frankie Frisch, NY Giants-St.L. Cards	8	197
Gil McDougald, NY Yankees	8	190

Batting Avg. (minimum 50 AB)

	AB	H	Avg
Pepper Martin, St.L. Cards	55	23	.418
Paul Molitor, Mil. Brewers-Tor. Blue Jays	55	23	.418
Lou Brock, St. Louis	87	34	.391
Marquis Grissom, Atl-Cle	77	30	.390
Thurman Munson, NY Yankees	67	25	.373
George Brett, Kansas City	51	19	.373
Hank Aaron, Milw. Braves	55	20	.364

Hits

	AB	H	Avg
Yogi Berra, NY Yankees	259	71	.274
Mickey Mantle, NY Yankees	230	59	.257
Frankie Frisch, NYG-St.L. Cards	197	58	.294
Joe DiMaggio, NY Yankees	199	54	.271
Hank Bauer, NY Yankees	188	46	.245
Pee Wee Reese, Brooklyn	169	46	.272

Runs

	Gm	R
Mickey Mantle, NY Yankees	65	42
Yogi Berra, NY Yankees	75	41
Babe Ruth, Boston Red Sox-NY Yankees	41	37
Lou Gehrig, NY Yankees	34	30
Joe DiMaggio, NY Yankees	51	27
Derek Jeter, NY Yankees	32	27

Home Runs

	AB	HR
Mickey Mantle, NY Yankees	230	18
Babe Ruth, Boston Red Sox-NY Yankees	129	15
Yogi Berra, NY Yankees	259	12
Duke Snider, Brooklyn-LA	133	11
Lou Gehrig, NY Yankees	119	10
Reggie Jackson, Oakland-NY Yankees	98	10

Runs Batted In

	Gm	RBI
Mickey Mantle, NY Yankees	65	40
Yogi Berra, NY Yankees	75	39
Lou Gehrig, NY Yankees	34	35
Babe Ruth, Boston Red Sox-NY Yankees	41	33
Joe DiMaggio, NY Yankees	51	30

Stolen Bases

	Gm	SB
Lou Brock, St. Louis	21	14
Eddie Collins, Phi. A's-Chisox	34	14
Frank Chance, Chi. Cubs	20	10
Davey Lopes, Los Angeles	23	10
Phil Rizzuto, NY Yankees	52	10

Total Bases

	Gm	TB
Mickey Mantle, NY Yankees	.65	123
Yogi Berra, NY Yankees	.75	117
Babe Ruth, Boston Red Sox-NY Yankees	.41	96
Lou Gehrig, NY Yankees	.34	87
Joe DiMaggio, NY Yankees	.51	84

Slugging Pct. (minimum 50 AB)

	AB	Pct
Reggie Jackson, Oakland-NY Yankees	.98	.755
Babe Ruth, Boston Red Sox-NY Yankees	.129	.744
Lou Gehrig, NY Yankees	.119	.731
Al Simmons, Phi. A's-Cincinnati	.73	.658
Lou Brock, St. Louis	.87	.655

Pitching

Games

	Yrs	Gm
Whitey Ford, NY Yankees	.11	22
Mike Stanton, Atlanta-NY Yankees	.6	20
Mariano Rivera, NY Yankees	.6	20
Rollie Fingers, Oakland	.3	16
Jeff Nelson, NY Yankees	.5	16
Allie Reynolds, NY Yankees	.6	15
Bob Turley, NY Yankees	.5	15

Shutouts

	GS	CG	ShO
Christy Mathewson, NY Giants	.11	10	4
Three Finger Brown, Chi. Cubs	.7	5	3
Whitey Ford, NY Yankees	.22	7	3
Seven pitchers tied with 2 each.			

Innings Pitched

	Gm	IP
Whitey Ford, NY Yankees	.22	146.0
Christy Mathewson, NY Giants	.11	101.2
Red Ruffing, NY Yankees	.10	85.2
Chief Bender, Philadelphia A's	.10	85.0
Waite Hoyt, NY Yankees-Phi. A's	.12	83.2

Wins

	Gm	W-L
Whitey Ford, NY Yankees	.22	10-8
Bob Gibson, St. Louis	.9	7-2
Allie Reynolds, NY Yankees	.15	7-2
Red Ruffing, NY Yankees	.10	7-2
Lefty Gomez, NY Yankees	.7	6-0
Chief Bender, Philadelphia A's	.10	6-4
Waite Hoyt, NY Yankees-Phi. A's	.12	6-4

Complete Games

	GS	CG	W-L
Christy Mathewson, NY Giants	.11	10	5-5
Chief Bender, Philadelphia A's	.10	9	6-4
Bob Gibson, St. Louis	.9	8	7-2
Whitey Ford, NY Yankees	.22	7	10-8
Red Ruffing, NY Yankees	.10	7	7-2

ERA (minimum 25 IP)

	Gm	IP	ERA
Jack Billingham, Cincinnati	.7	25.1	0.36
Harry Brecheen, St. Louis	.7	32.2	0.83
Babe Ruth, Boston Red Sox	.3	31.0	0.87
Sherry Smith, Brooklyn	.3	30.1	0.89
Sandy Koufax, Los Angeles	.8	57.0	0.95

Strikeouts

	Gm	IP	SO
Whitey Ford, NY Yankees	.22	146.0	94
Bob Gibson, St. Louis	.9	81.0	92
Allie Reynolds, NY Yankees	.15	77.1	62
Sandy Koufax, Los Angeles	.8	57.0	61
Red Ruffing, NY Yankees	.10	85.2	61

Saves

	Gm	IP	Sv
Mariano Rivera, NY Yankees	.20	31.0	9
Rollie Fingers, Oakland	.16	33.1	6
Allie Reynolds, NY Yankees	.15	77.1	4
Johnny Murphy, NY Yankees	.8	16.1	4
John Wetteland, NY Yankees	.5	4.1	4
Robb Nen, Florida-SF	.7	7.2	4
Nine pitchers tied with 3 each.			

Losses

	Gm	W-L
Whitey Ford, NY Yankees	.22	10-8
Christy Mathewson, NY Giants	.11	5-5
Joe Bush, Phi. A's-Bosox-NY Yankees	.9	2-5
Rube Marquard, NY Giants-Brooklyn	.11	2-5
Eddie Plank, Philadelphia A's	.7	2-5
Schoolboy Rowe, Detroit	.8	2-5

World Series Appearances

In the 100 years that the World Series has been contested, American League teams have won 59 championships while National League teams have won 41.

The following teams are ranked by number of appearances through the 2004 World Series; (*) indicates AL teams.

	App	W	L	Pct.	Last Series	Last Title
NY Yankees*	.39	26	13	.667	2003	2000
Bklyn/LA Dodgers	.18	6	12	.333	1988	1988
NY/SF Giants	.17	5	12	.294	2002	1954
St.L. Cardinals	.16	9	7	.563	2004	1982
Phi/KC/Oak.A's*	.14	9	5	.643	1990	1989
Boston Red Sox*	.10	6	4	.600	2004	2004
Chicago Cubs	.10	2	8	.200	1945	1908
Cincinnati Reds	.9	5	4	.556	1990	1990
Detroit Tigers*	.9	4	5	.444	1984	1984
Bos/Mil/Atl.Braves	.9	3	6	.333	1999	1995
Pittsburgh Pirates	.7	5	2	.714	1979	1979
St.L/Bal.Orioles*	.7	3	4	.429	1983	1983
Wash/Min.Twins*	.6	3	3	.500	1991	1991
Cle. Indians*	.5	2	3	.400	1997	1948
Phi. Phillies	.5	1	4	.200	1993	1980
Chi. White Sox*	.4	2	2	.500	1959	1917
NY Mets	.4	2	2	.500	2000	1986
Fla. Marlins	.2	2	0	1.000	2003	2003
Tor. Blue Jays*	.2	2	0	1.000	1993	1993
KC Royals*	.2	1	1	.500	1985	1985
SD Padres	.2	0	2	.000	1998	—
Anaheim Angels*	.1	1	0	1.000	2002	2002
Ari. Diamondbacks	.1	1	0	1.000	2001	2001
Sea/Mil.Brewers*	.1	0	1	.000	1982	—

League Championship Series

Division play came to the major leagues in 1969 when both the American and National Leagues expanded to 12 teams. With an East and West Division in each league, League Championship Series (LCS) became necessary to determine the NL and AL pennant winners. In 1994, teams were realigned into three divisions, the East, Central, and West with division winners and one wildcard team playing a best-of-5 League Divisional Series (see following pages for LDS results) to determine the LCS competitors.

In the tables below, the East Division champions are noted by the letter E, the Central division champions by C and the West Division champions by W. Wildcard winners are noted by WC. Also, each playoff winner's wins and losses are noted in parentheses after the series score. The LCS changed from best-of-5 to best-of-7 in 1985. Each league's LCS was cancelled in 1994 due to the players' strike.

National League

Multiple champions: Atlanta, Cincinnati and LA Dodgers (5); NY Mets and St. Louis (4); Philadelphia (3); Florida, Pittsburgh, San Diego and San Francisco (2).

Year	Winner	Manager	Series		Loser	Manager
1969	E–New York	Gil Hodges	3-0		W–Atlanta	Lum Harris
1970	W–Cincinnati	Sparky Anderson	3-0		E–Pittsburgh	Danny Murtaugh
1971	E–Pittsburgh	Danny Murtaugh	3-1 (LWWW)		W–San Francisco	Charlie Fox
1972	W–Cincinnati	Sparky Anderson	3-2 (LWLWW)		E–Pittsburgh	Bill Virdon
1973	E–New York	Yogi Berra	3-2 (LWWLW)		W–Cincinnati	Sparky Anderson
1974	W–Los Angeles	Walter Alston	3-1 (WWLW)		E–Pittsburgh	Danny Murtaugh
1975	W–Cincinnati	Sparky Anderson	3-0		E–Pittsburgh	Danny Murtaugh
1976	W–Cincinnati	Sparky Anderson	3-0		E–Philadelphia	Danny Ozark
1977	W–Los Angeles	Tommy Lasorda	3-1 (LWWW)		E–Philadelphia	Danny Ozark
1978	W–Los Angeles	Tommy Lasorda	3-1 (WWLW)		E–Philadelphia	Danny Ozark
1979	E–Pittsburgh	Chuck Tanner	3-0		W–Cincinnati	John McNamara
1980	E–Philadelphia	Dallas Green	3-2 (WLLWW)		W–Houston	Bill Virdon
1981	W–Los Angeles	Tommy Lasorda	3-2 (WLLWW)		E–Montreal	Jim Fanning
1982	E–St. Louis	Whitey Herzog	3-0		W–Atlanta	Joe Torre
1983	E–Philadelphia	Paul Owens	3-1 (WLWW)		W–Los Angeles	Tommy Lasorda
1984	W–San Diego	Dick Williams	3-2 (LLWWW)		E–Chicago	Jim Frey
1985	E–St. Louis	Whitey Herzog	4-2 (LLWWWW)		W–Los Angeles	Tommy Lasorda
1986	E–New York	Davey Johnson	4-2 (LWWLWW)		W–Houston	Hal Lanier
1987	E–St. Louis	Whitey Herzog	4-3 (WLWLLWW)		W–San Francisco	Roger Craig
1988	W–Los Angeles	Tommy Lasorda	4-3 (LWLWLWW)		E–New York	Davey Johnson
1989	W–San Francisco	Roger Craig	4-1 (WLWWW)		E–Chicago	Don Zimmer
1990	W–Cincinnati	Lou Piniella	4-2 (LWWWLW)		E–Pittsburgh	Jim Leyland
1991	W–Atlanta	Bobby Cox	4-3 (LWWLLWW)		E–Pittsburgh	Jim Leyland
1992	W–Atlanta	Bobby Cox	4-3 (LWWLWLLW)		E–Pittsburgh	Jim Leyland
1993	E–Philadelphia	Jim Fregosi	4-2 (WLLWWW)		W–Atlanta	Bobby Cox
1994	Not held					
1995	E–Atlanta	Bobby Cox	4-0		C–Cincinnati	Davey Johnson
1996	E–Atlanta	Bobby Cox	4-3 (WLLLWWWW)		C–St. Louis	Tony La Russa
1997	WC–Florida	Jim Leyland	4-2 (WLWLWW)		E–Atlanta	Bobby Cox
1998	W–San Diego	Bruce Bochy	4-2 (WWWLLW)		E–Atlanta	Bobby Cox
1999	E–Atlanta	Bobby Cox	4-2 (WWWLLW)		WC–New York	Bobby Valentine
2000	WC–New York	Bobby Valentine	4-1 (WWLWW)		C–St. Louis	Tony La Russa
2001	W–Arizona	Bob Brenly	4-1 (WLWWW)		E–Atlanta	Bobby Cox
2002	WC–San Francisco	Dusty Baker	4-1 (WWLWW)		C–St. Louis	Tony La Russa
2003	WC–Florida	Jack McKeon	4-3 (WLLLWWW)		C–Chicago	Dusty Baker
2004	C–St. Louis	Tony La Russa	4-3 (WWLLLWW)		WC–Houston	Phil Garner

NLCS Most Valuable Players

Winners who did not play for NLCS champions are in **bold** type.

Multiple winner: Steve Garvey (2).

Year		Year		Year	
1977	Dusty Baker, LA, OF	1987	**Jeff Leonard,** SF, OF	1996	Javy Lopez, Atl., C
1978	Steve Garvey, LA, 1B	1988	Orel Hershiser, LA, P	1997	Livan Hernandez, Fla., P
1979	Willie Stargell, Pit., 1B	1989	Will Clark, SF, 1B	1998	Sterling Hitchcock, SD, P
1980	Manny Trillo, Phi., 2B	1990	Rob Dibble, Cin., P	1999	Eddie Perez, Atl., C
1981	Burt Hooton, LA, P		& Randy Myers, Cin., P	2000	Mike Hampton, NY, P
1982	Darrell Porter, St.L., C	1991	Steve Avery, Atl., P	2001	Craig Counsell, Ari., 2B
1983	Gary Matthews, Phi., OF	1992	John Smoltz, Atl., P	2002	Benito Santiago, SF, C
1984	Steve Garvey, SD, 1B	1993	Curt Schilling, Phi., P	2003	Ivan Rodriguez, Fla., C
1985	Ozzie Smith, St.L., SS	1994	LCS not held.	2004	Albert Pujols, St.L, 1B
1986	**Mike Scott,** Hou., P	1995	Mike Devereaux, Atl., OF		

American League

Multiple champions: NY Yankees (10); Oakland (6); Baltimore (5); Boston (3); Cleveland, Kansas City, Minnesota and Toronto (2).

Year	Winner	Manager	Series	Loser	Manager
1969	E–Baltimore	Earl Weaver	3-0	W–Minnesota	Billy Martin
1970	E–Baltimore	Earl Weaver	3-0	W–Minnesota	Bill Rigney
1971	E–Baltimore	Earl Weaver	3-0	W–Oakland	Dick Williams
1972	W–Oakland	Dick Williams	3-2 (WWLLW)	E–Detroit	Billy Martin
1973	W–Oakland	Dick Williams	3-2 (LWWLW)	E–Baltimore	Earl Weaver
1974	W–Oakland	Alvin Dark	3-1 (LWWW)	E–Baltimore	Earl Weaver
1975	E–Boston	Darrell Johnson	3-0	W–Oakland	Alvin Dark
1976	E–New York	Billy Martin	3-2 (WLWLW)	W–Kansas City	Whitey Herzog
1977	E–New York	Billy Martin	3-2 (LWLWW)	W–Kansas City	Whitey Herzog
1978	E–New York	Bob Lemon	3-1 (WLWW)	W–Kansas City	Whitey Herzog
1979	E–Baltimore	Earl Weaver	3-1 (WWLW)	W–California	Jim Fregosi
1980	W–Kansas City	Jim Frey	3-0	E–New York	Dick Howser
1981	E–New York	Bob Lemon	3-0	W–Oakland	Billy Martin
1982	E–Milwaukee	Harvey Kuenn	3-2 (LLWWW)	W–California	Gene Mauch
1983	E–Baltimore	Joe Altobelli	3-1 (LWWW)	W–Chicago	Tony La Russa
1984	E–Detroit	Sparky Anderson	3-0	W–Kansas City	Dick Howser
1985	W–Kansas City	Dick Howser	4-3 (LLWLWWW)	E–Toronto	Bobby Cox
1986	E–Boston	John McNamara	4-3 (LWWLLWW)	W–California	Gene Mauch
1987	W–Minnesota	Tom Kelly	4-1 (WWLWW)	E–Detroit	Sparky Anderson
1988	W–Oakland	Tony La Russa	4-0	E–Boston	Joe Morgan
1989	W–Oakland	Tony La Russa	4-1 (WWLWW)	E–Toronto	Cito Gaston
1990	W–Oakland	Tony La Russa	4-0	E–Boston	Joe Morgan
1991	W–Minnesota	Tom Kelly	4-1 (WLWWW)	E–Toronto	Cito Gaston
1992	E–Toronto	Cito Gaston	4-2 (LWWWLW)	W–Oakland	Tony La Russa
1993	E–Toronto	Cito Gaston	4-2 (WWLLWW)	W–Chicago	Gene Lamont
1994	Not held				
1995	C–Cleveland	Mike Hargrove	4-2 (LWLWWW)	W–Seattle	Lou Piniella
1996	E–New York	Joe Torre	4-1 (WLWWW)	WC–Baltimore	Davey Johnson
1997	C–Cleveland	Mike Hargrove	4-2 (LWWWLW)	E–Baltimore	Davey Johnson
1998	E–New York	Joe Torre	4-2 (WLLWWW)	C–Cleveland	Mike Hargrove
1999	E–New York	Joe Torre	4-1 (WWLWW)	WC–Boston	Jimy Williams
2000	E–New York	Joe Torre	4-2 (WWWLWL)	WC–Seattle	Lou Piniella
2001	E–New York	Joe Torre	4-1 (WWLWW)	W–Seattle	Lou Piniella
2002	WC–Anaheim	Mike Scioscia	4-1 (LWWWW)	C–Minnesota	Ron Gardenhire
2003	E–New York	Joe Torre	4-3 (LWWLWLW)	WC–Boston	Grady Little
2004	WC–Boston	Terry Francona	4-3 (LLLWWWW)	E–New York	Joe Torre

ALCS Most Valuable Players

Winner who did not play for ALCS champions is in **bold** type.

Multiple winner: Dave Stewart (2).

Year		
1980 Frank White, KC, 2B	1989 Rickey Henderson, Oak., OF	1998 David Wells, NY, P
1981 Graig Nettles, NY, 3B	1990 Dave Stewart, Oak., P	1999 Orlando Hernandez, NY, P
1982 **Fred Lynn,** Cal., OF	1991 Kirby Puckett, Min., OF	2000 Dave Justice, NY, OF
1983 Mike Boddicker, Bal., P	1992 Roberto Alomar, Tor., 2B	2001 Andy Pettitte, NY, P
1984 Kirk Gibson, Det., OF	1993 Dave Stewart, Tor., P	2002 Adam Kennedy, Ana., 2B
1985 George Brett, KC, 3B	1994 LCS not held.	2003 Mariano Rivera, NY, P
1986 Marty Barrett, Bos., 2B	1995 Orel Hershiser, Cle., P	2004 David Ortiz, Bos., DH
1987 Gary Gaetti, Min., 3B	1996 Bernie Williams, NY, OF	
1988 Dennis Eckersley, Oak., P	1997 Marquis Grissom, Cle., OF	

League Divisional Series

In 1994, leagues were realigned into three divisions, the East, Central, and West with division winners and one wildcard team playing a best-of-5 League Divisional Series to determine the LCS competitors. In the tables below, the East Division champions are noted by the letter E, the Central Division champions by C and the West Division champions by W. Wildcard winners are noted by WC. Also, each playoff winner's wins and losses are noted in parentheses after the series score. Each league's LDS was cancelled in 1994 due to the players' strike.

National League

Multiple champions: Atlanta (6); St. Louis (4); Florida and NY Mets (2).

Year	Winner	Manager	Series	Loser	Manager
1995	E–Atlanta	Bobby Cox	3-1 (WWLW)	WC–Colorado	Don Baylor
	C–Cincinnati	Davey Johnson	3-0	W–Los Angeles	Tommy Lasorda
1996	E–Atlanta	Bobby Cox	3-0	WC–Los Angeles	Bill Russell
	C–St. Louis	Tony La Russa	3-0	W–San Diego	Bruce Bochy
1997	E–Atlanta	Bobby Cox	3-0	C–Houston	Larry Dierker
	WC–Florida	Jim Leyland	3-0	W–San Francisco	Dusty Baker

League Divisional Series (Cont.)

Year	Winner	Manager	Series	Loser	Manager
1998	E–Atlanta	Bobby Cox	3-0	WC–Chicago	Jim Riggleman
	W–San Diego	Bruce Bochy	3-1 (WLWW)	C–Houston	Larry Dierker
1999	E–Atlanta	Bobby Cox	3-1 (LWWW)	C–Houston	Larry Dierker
	WC–New York	Bobby Valentine	3-1 (WLWW)	W–Arizona	Buck Showalter
2000	C–St. Louis	Tony La Russa	3-0	E–Atlanta	Bobby Cox
	WC–New York	Bobby Valentine	3-1 (LWWW)	W–San Francisco	Dusty Baker
2001	E–Atlanta	Bobby Cox	3-0	C–Houston	Larry Dierker
	W–Arizona	Bob Brenly	3-2 (WLWLW)	WC–St. Louis	Tony La Russa
2002	WC–San Francisco	Dusty Baker	3-2 (WLLWW)	E–Atlanta	Bobby Cox
	C–St. Louis	Tony La Russa	3-0	W–Arizona	Bob Brenly
2003	C–Chicago	Dusty Baker	3-2 (WLWLW)	E–Atlanta	Bobby Cox
	WC–Florida	Jack McKeon	3-1 (LWWW)	W–San Francisco	Felipe Alou
2004	C–St. Louis	Tony La Russa	3-1 (WWLW)	W–Los Angeles	Jim Tracy
	WC–Houston	Phil Garner	3-2 (WLWLW)	E–Atlanta	Bobby Cox

American League

Multiple champions: NY Yankees (7); Boston, Cleveland and Seattle (3); Baltimore (2).

Year	Winner	Manager	Series	Loser	Manager
1995	C–Cleveland	Mike Hargrove	3-0	E–Boston	Kevin Kennedy
	W–Seattle	Lou Piniella	3-2 (LLWWW)	WC–New York	Buck Showalter
1996	E–New York	Joe Torre	3-1 (LWWW)	W–Texas	Johnny Oates
	WC–Baltimore	Davey Johnson	3-1 (WWLW)	C–Cleveland	Mike Hargrove
1997	E–Baltimore	Davey Johnson	3-1 (WWLW)	W–Seattle	Lou Piniella
	C–Cleveland	Mike Hargrove	3-2 (LWLWW)	WC–New York	Joe Torre
1998	E–New York	Joe Torre	3-0	W–Texas	Johnny Oates
	C–Cleveland	Mike Hargrove	3-1 (LWWW)	WC–Boston	Jimy Williams
1999	E–New York	Joe Torre	3-0	W–Texas	Johnny Oates
	WC–Boston	Jimy Williams	3-2 (LLWWW)	C–Cleveland	Mike Hargrove
2000	E–New York	Joe Torre	3-2 (LWWLW)	W–Oakland	Art Howe
	WC–Seattle	Lou Piniella	3-0	C–Chicago	Jerry Manuel
2001	E–New York	Joe Torre	3-2 (LLWWW)	WC–Oakland	Art Howe
	W–Seattle	Lou Piniella	3-2 (LWLWW)	C–Cleveland	Charlie Manuel
2002	WC–Anaheim	Mike Scioscia	3-1 (LWWW)	E–New York	Joe Torre
	C–Minnesota	Ron Gardenhire	3-2 (WLLWW)	W–Oakland	Art Howe
2003	E–New York	Joe Torre	3-1 (LWWW)	C–Minnesota	Ron Gardenhire
	WC–Boston	Grady Little	3-2 (LLWWW)	W–Oakland	Ken Macha
2004	E–New York	Joe Torre	3-1 (LWWW)	C–Minnesota	Ron Gardenhire
	WC–Boston	Terry Francona	3-0	W–Anaheim	Mike Scioscia

Other Playoffs

Ten times since 1946, playoffs have been necessary to decide league or division championships or wild card berths when two teams were tied at the end of the regular season. Additionally, in the strike year of 1981 there were playoffs between the first and second half-season champions in both leagues.

National League

Year	NL	W	L	Manager
1946	Brooklyn	96	58	Leo Durocher
	St. Louis	96	58	Eddie Dyer
	Playoff: (Best-of-3) St. Louis, 2-0			
	NL	**W**	**L**	**Manager**
1951	Brooklyn	96	58	Charlie Dressen
	New York	96	58	Leo Durocher
	Playoff: (Best-of-3) New York, 2-1 (WLW)			
	NL	**W**	**L**	**Manager**
1959	Milwaukee	86	68	Fred Haney
	Los Angeles	86	68	Walter Alston
	Playoff: (Best-of-3) Los Angeles, 2-0			
	NL	**W**	**L**	**Manager**
1962	Los Angeles	101	61	Walter Alston
	San Francisco	101	61	Alvin Dark
	Playoff: (Best-of-3) San Francisco, 2-1 (WLW)			
	NL West	**W**	**L**	**Manager**
1980	Houston	92	70	Bill Virdon
	Los Angeles	92	70	Tommy Lasorda
	Playoff: (1 game) Houston, 7-1 (at LA)			

Year	NL East	W	L	Manager
1981	(1st Half) Philadelphia	34	21	Dallas Green
	(2nd Half) Montreal	30	23	Jim Fanning
	Playoff: (Best-of-5) Montreal, 3-2 (WWLLW)			
	NL West	**W**	**L**	**Manager**
1981	(1st Half) Los Angeles	36	21	Tommy Lasorda
	(2nd Half) Houston	33	20	Bill Virdon
	Playoff: (Best-of-5) Los Angeles, 3-2 (LLWWW)			
	NL Wild Card	**W**	**L**	**Manager**
1998	Chicago	89	73	Jim Riggleman
	San Francisco	89	73	Dusty Baker
	Playoff: (1 game) Chicago, 5-3 (at Chicago)			
	NL Wild Card	**W**	**L**	**Manager**
1999	Cincinnati	96	66	Jack McKeon
	New York	96	66	Bobby Valentine
	Playoff: (1 game) New York, 5-0 (at Cincinnati)			

Year	AL	W	L	Manager
1948	Boston	96	58	Joe McCarthy
	Cleveland	96	58	Lou Boudreau
	Playoff: (1 game) Cleveland, 8-3 (at Boston)			

	AL East	W	L	Manager
1978	Boston	99	63	Don Zimmer
	New York	99	63	Bob Lemon
	Playoff: (1 game) New York, 5-4 (at Boston)			

	AL East	W	L	Manager
1981	(1st Half) N.Y	34	22	Bob Lemon
	(2nd Half) Milw	31	22	Buck Rodgers
	Playoff: (Best-of-5) New York, 3-2 (WWLLW)			

Year	AL West	W	L	Manager
1981	(1st Half) Oakland	37	23	Billy Martin
	(2nd Half) Kan. City	30	23	Jim Frey
	Playoff: (Best-of-5), Oakland, 3-0			

	AL West	W	L	Manager
1995	Seattle	78	66	Lou Piniella
	California	78	66	M. Lachemann
	Playoff: (1 game) Seattle, 9-1 (at Seattle)			

Regular Season League & Division Winners

Regular season National and American League pennant winners from 1900-68, as well as West and East divisional champions from 1969-93. In 1994, both leagues went to three divisions, West, Central and East, and each league also sent a wild card (WC) team to the playoffs. Note that (*) indicates 1994 divisional champion is unofficial (due to the players' strike). Note that **GA** column indicates games ahead of the second place club.

National League

Year	Team	W	L	Pct	GA
1900	Brooklyn	82	54	.603	4½
1901	Pittsburgh	90	49	.647	7½
1902	Pittsburgh	103	36	.741	27½
1903	Pittsburgh	91	49	.650	6½
1904	New York	106	47	.693	13
1905	New York	105	48	.686	9
1906	Chicago	116	36	.763	20
1907	Chicago	107	45	.704	17
1908	Chicago	99	55	.643	1
1909	Pittsburgh	110	42	.724	6½
1910	Chicago	104	50	.675	13
1911	New York	99	54	.647	7½
1912	New York	103	48	.682	10
1913	New York	101	51	.664	12½
1914	Boston	94	59	.614	10½
1915	Philadelphia	90	62	.592	7
1916	Brooklyn	94	60	.610	2½
1917	New York	98	56	.636	10
1918	Chicago	84	45	.651	10½
1919	Cincinnati	96	44	.686	9
1920	Brooklyn	93	61	.604	7
1921	New York	94	59	.614	4
1922	New York	93	61	.604	7
1923	New York	95	58	.621	4½
1924	New York	93	60	.608	1½
1925	Pittsburgh	95	58	.621	8½
1926	St. Louis	89	65	.578	2
1927	Pittsburgh	94	60	.610	1½
1928	St. Louis	95	59	.617	2
1929	Chicago	98	54	.645	10½
1930	St. Louis	92	62	.597	2
1931	St. Louis	101	53	.656	13
1932	Chicago	90	64	.584	4
1933	New York	91	61	.599	5
1934	St. Louis	95	58	.621	2
1935	Chicago	100	54	.649	4
1936	New York	92	62	.597	5
1937	New York	95	57	.625	3
1938	Chicago	89	63	.586	2
1939	Cincinnati	97	57	.630	4½
1940	Cincinnati	100	53	.654	12
1941	Brooklyn	100	54	.649	2½
1942	St. Louis	106	48	.688	2
1943	St. Louis	105	49	.682	18
1944	St. Louis	105	49	.682	14½
1945	Chicago	98	56	.636	3
1946	St. Louis†	98	58	.628	2
1947	Brooklyn	94	60	.610	5
1948	Boston	91	62	.595	6½
1949	Brooklyn	97	57	.630	1
1950	Philadelphia	91	63	.591	2
1951	New York†	98	59	.624	1
1952	Brooklyn	96	57	.627	4½
1953	Brooklyn	105	49	.682	13
1954	New York	97	57	.630	5
1955	Brooklyn	98	55	.641	13½
1956	Brooklyn	93	61	.604	1
1957	Milwaukee	95	59	.617	8
1958	Milwaukee	92	62	.597	8
1959	Los Angeles†	88	68	.564	2
1960	Pittsburgh	95	59	.617	7
1961	Cincinnati	93	61	.604	4
1962	San Francisco†	103	62	.624	1
1963	Los Angeles	99	63	.611	6
1964	St. Louis	93	69	.574	1
1965	Los Angeles	97	65	.599	2
1966	Los Angeles	95	67	.586	1½
1967	St. Louis	101	60	.627	10½
1968	St. Louis	97	65	.599	9
1969	West—Atlanta	93	69	.574	3
	East—N.Y. Mets	100	62	.617	8
1970	West—Cincinnati	102	60	.630	14½
	East—Pittsburgh	89	73	.549	5
1971	West—San Francisco	90	72	.556	1
	East—Pittsburgh	97	65	.599	7
1972	West—Cincinnati	95	59	.617	10½
	East—Pittsburgh	96	59	.619	11
1973	West—Cincinnati	99	63	.611	3½
	East—N.Y. Mets	82	79	.509	1½
1974	West—Los Angeles	102	60	.630	4
	East—Pittsburgh	88	74	.543	1½
1975	West—Cincinnati	108	54	.667	20
	East—Pittsburgh	92	69	.571	6½
1976	West—Cincinnati	102	60	.630	10
	East—Philadelphia	101	61	.623	9
1977	West—Los Angeles	98	64	.605	10
	East—Philadelphia	101	61	.623	5
1978	West—Los Angeles	95	67	.586	2½
	East—Philadelphia	90	72	.556	1½
1979	West—Cincinnati	90	71	.559	1½
	East—Pittsburgh	98	64	.605	2
1980	West—Houston†	93	70	.571	1
	East—Philadelphia	91	71	.562	1
1981	West—Los Angeles$	63	47	.573	—
	East—Montreal$	60	48	.556	—
1982	West—Atlanta	89	73	.549	1
	East—St. Louis	92	70	.568	3

Regular Season League & Division Winners (Cont.)

Year		W	L	Pct	GA	Year		W	L	Pct	GA
1983	West—Los Angeles	91	71	.562	3	1997	West—San Francisco	90	72	.556	2
	East—Philadelphia	90	72	.556	6		Central—Houston	84	78	.519	5
1984	West—San Diego	92	70	.568	12		East—Atlanta	101	61	.623	9
	East—Chicago	96	65	.596	6½		WC—Florida	92	70	.568	—
1985	West—Los Angeles	95	67	.586	5½	1998	West—San Diego	98	64	.605	9½
	East—St. Louis	101	61	.623	3		Central—Houston	102	60	.630	12½
1986	West—Houston	96	66	.593	10		East—Atlanta	106	56	.654	18
	East—N.Y. Mets	108	54	.667	21½		WC—Chicago†	90	73	.552	—
1987	West—San Francisco	90	72	.556	6	1999	West—Arizona	100	62	.617	14
	East—St. Louis	95	67	.586	3		Central—Houston	97	65	.599	1½
1988	West—Los Angeles	94	67	.584	7		East—Atlanta	103	59	.636	6½
	East—N.Y. Mets	100	60	.625	15		WC—N.Y. Mets†	97	66	.595	—
1989	West—San Francisco	92	70	.568	3	2000	West—San Francisco	97	65	.599	11
	East—Chicago	93	69	.574	6		Central—St. Louis	95	67	.586	10
1990	West—Cincinnati	91	71	.562	5		East—Atlanta	95	67	.586	1
	East—Pittsburgh	95	67	.586	4		WC—N.Y. Mets	94	68	.580	—
1991	West—Atlanta	94	68	.580	1	2001	West—Arizona	92	70	.568	2
	East—Pittsburgh	98	64	.605	14		Central—Houston@	93	69	.574	—
1992	West—Atlanta	98	64	.605	8		East—Atlanta	88	74	.543	2
	East—Pittsburgh	96	66	.593	9		WC—St. Louis	93	69	.574	—
1993	West—Atlanta	104	58	.642	1	2002	West—Arizona	98	64	.605	2½
	East—Philadelphia	97	65	.599	3		Central—St. Louis	97	65	.599	13
1994	West—Los Angeles*	58	56	.509	3½		East—Atlanta	101	59	.631	19
	Central—Cincinnati*	66	48	.579	½		WC—San Francisco	95	66	.590	—
	East—Montreal*	74	40	.649	6	2003	West—San Francisco	100	61	.621	15½
1995	West—Los Angeles	78	66	.542	1		Central—Chicago	88	74	.543	1
	Central—Cincinnati	85	59	.590	9		East—Atlanta	101	61	.623	10
	East—Atlanta	90	54	.625	21		WC—Florida	91	71	.562	—
	WC—Colorado	77	67	.535	—	2004	West—Los Angeles	93	69	.574	2
1996	West—San Diego	91	71	.562	1		Central—St. Louis	105	57	.648	13
	Central—St. Louis	88	74	.543	6		East—Atlanta	96	66	.593	10
	East—Atlanta	96	66	.593	8		WC—Houston	92	70	.568	—
	WC—Los Angeles	90	72	.556	—						

†**Regular season playoffs:** See "Other Playoffs" on pages 100-101 for details.
$**Divisional playoffs:** See "Other Playoffs" on pages 100-101 for details.
@Houston (93-69) won the division over St. Louis (93-69) due to a better head-to-head record.

American League

Year		W	L	Pct	GA	Year		W	L	Pct	GA
1901	Chicago	83	53	.610	4	1930	Philadelphia	102	52	.662	8
1902	Philadelphia	83	53	.610	5	1931	Philadelphia	107	45	.704	13½
1903	Boston	91	47	.659	14½	1932	New York	107	47	.695	13
1904	Boston	95	59	.617	1½	1933	Washington	99	53	.651	7
1905	Philadelphia	92	56	.622	2	1934	Detroit	101	53	.656	7
1906	Chicago	93	58	.616	3	1935	Detroit	93	58	.616	3
1907	Detroit	92	58	.613	1½	1936	New York	102	51	.667	19½
1908	Detroit	90	63	.588	½	1937	New York	102	52	.662	13
1909	Detroit	98	54	.645	3½	1938	New York	99	53	.651	9½
1910	Philadelphia	102	48	.680	14½	1939	New York	106	45	.702	17
1911	Philadelphia	101	50	.669	13½	1940	Detroit	90	64	.584	1
1912	Boston	105	47	.691	14	1941	New York	101	53	.656	17
1913	Philadelphia	96	57	.627	6½	1942	New York	103	51	.669	9
1914	Philadelphia	99	53	.651	8½	1943	New York	98	56	.636	13½
1915	Boston	101	50	.669	2½	1944	St. Louis	89	65	.578	1
1916	Boston	91	63	.591	2	1945	Detroit	88	65	.575	1½
1917	Chicago	100	54	.649	9	1946	Boston	104	50	.675	12
1918	Boston	75	51	.595	2½	1947	New York	97	57	.630	12
1919	Chicago	88	52	.629	3½	1948	Cleveland†	97	58	.626	1
1920	Cleveland	98	56	.636	2	1949	New York	97	57	.630	1
1921	New York	98	55	.641	4½	1950	New York	98	56	.636	3
1922	New York	94	60	.610	1	1951	New York	98	56	.636	5
1923	New York	98	54	.645	16	1952	New York	95	59	.617	2
1924	Washington	92	62	.597	2	1953	New York	99	52	.656	8½
1925	Washington	96	55	.636	8½	1954	Cleveland	111	43	.721	8
1926	New York	91	63	.591	3	1955	New York	96	58	.623	3
1927	New York	110	44	.714	19	1956	New York	97	57	.630	9
1928	New York	101	53	.656	2½	1957	New York	98	56	.636	8
1929	Philadelphia	104	46	.693	18	1958	New York	92	62	.597	10

Year		W	L	Pct	GA
1959	Chicago	94	60	.610	5
1960	New York	97	57	.630	8
1961	New York	109	53	.673	8
1962	New York	96	66	.593	5
1963	New York	104	57	.646	10½
1964	New York	99	63	.611	1
1965	Minnesota	102	60	.630	7
1966	Baltimore	97	63	.606	9
1967	Boston	92	70	.568	1
1968	Detroit	103	59	.636	12
1969	West—Minnesota	97	65	.599	9
	East—Baltimore	109	53	.673	19
1970	West—Minnesota	98	64	.605	9
	East—Baltimore	108	54	.667	15
1971	West—Oakland	101	60	.627	16
	East—Baltimore	101	57	.639	12
1972	West—Oakland	93	62	.600	5½
	East—Detroit	86	70	.551	½
1973	West—Oakland	94	68	.580	6
	East—Baltimore	97	65	.599	8
1974	West—Oakland	90	72	.556	5
	East—Baltimore	91	71	.562	2
1975	West—Oakland	98	64	.605	7
	East—Boston	95	65	.594	4½
1976	West—KansasCity	90	72	.556	2½
	East—New York	97	62	.610	10½
1977	West—Kansas City	102	60	.630	8
	East—New York	100	62	.617	2½
1978	West—Kansas City	92	70	.568	5
	East—New York†	100	63	.613	1
1979	West—California	88	74	.543	3
	East—Baltimore	102	57	.642	8
1980	West—Kansas City	97	65	.599	14
	East—New York	103	59	.636	3
1981	West—Oakland$	64	45	.587	—
	East—New York$	59	48	.551	—
1982	West—California	93	69	.574	3
	East—Milwaukee	95	67	.586	1
1983	West—Chicago	99	63	.611	20
	East—Baltimore	98	64	.605	6
1984	West—Kansas City	84	78	.519	3
	East—Detroit	104	58	.642	15
1985	West—Kansas City	91	71	.562	1
	East—Toronto	99	62	.615	2
1986	West—California	92	70	.568	5
	East—Boston	95	66	.590	5½
1987	West—Minnesota	85	77	.525	2
	East—Detroit	98	64	.605	2
1988	West—Oakland	104	58	.642	13
	East—Boston	89	73	.549	1
1989	West—Oakland	99	63	.611	7
	East—Toronto	89	73	.549	2

Year		W	L	Pct	GA
1990	West—Oakland	103	59	.636	9
	East—Boston	88	74	.543	2
1991	West—Minnesota	95	67	.586	8
	East—Toronto	91	71	.562	7
1992	West—Oakland	96	66	.593	6
	East—Toronto	96	66	.593	4
1993	West—Chicago	94	68	.580	8
	East—Toronto	95	67	.586	7
1994	West—Texas*	52	62	.456	1
	Central—Chicago*	67	46	.593	1
	East—New York*	70	43	.619	6½
1995	West—Seattle†	79	66	.545	1
	Central—Cleveland	100	44	.694	30
	East—Boston	86	58	.597	7
	WC—New York	79	65	.549	—
1996	West—Texas	90	72	.556	4½
	Central—Cleveland	99	62	.615	14½
	East—New York	92	70	.568	4
	WC—Baltimore	88	74	.543	—
1997	West—Seattle	90	72	.556	6
	Central—Cleveland	86	75	.534	6
	East—Baltimore	98	64	.605	2
	WC—New York	96	66	.593	—
1998	West—Texas	88	74	.543	3
	Central—Cleveland	89	73	.549	9
	East—New York	114	48	.704	22
	WC—Boston	92	70	.568	—
1999	West—Texas	95	67	.586	8
	Central—Cleveland	97	65	.599	21½
	East—New York	98	64	.605	4
	WC—Boston	94	68	.580	—
2000	West—Oakland	91	70	.565	½
	Central—Chicago	95	67	.586	5
	East—New York	87	74	.540	2½
	WC—Seattle	91	71	.562	—
2001	West—Seattle	116	46	.716	14
	Central—Cleveland	91	71	.562	6
	East—New York	95	65	.594	13½
	WC—Oakland	102	60	.630	—
2002	West—Oakland	103	59	.636	4
	Central—Minnesota	94	67	.584	13½
	East—New York	103	58	.640	10½
	WC—Anaheim	99	63	.611	—
2003	West—Oakland	96	66	.593	3
	Central—Minnesota	90	72	.556	4
	East—New York	101	61	.623	6
	WC—Boston	95	67	.586	—
2004	West—Anaheim	92	70	.568	1
	Central—Minnesota	92	70	.568	9
	East—New York	101	61	.623	3
	WC—Boston	98	64	.605	—

†**Regular season playoffs:** See "Other Playoffs" on pages 100-101 for details.
$**Divisional playoffs:** See "Other Playoffs" on pages 100-101 for details.

The All-Star Game

Baseball's first All-Star Game was held on July 6, 1933, before 47,595 at Comiskey Park in Chicago. From that year on, the All-Star Game has matched the best players in the American League against the best in the National. From 1959-62, two All-Star Games were played. The only year an All-Star Game wasn't played was 1945, when World War II travel restrictions made it necessary to cancel the meeting. The NL leads the series, 40-33-2. In the chart below, the American League is listed in **bold** type.

Since 2002, the game's MVP award has been named the Ted Williams Award, after the Red Sox Hall of Famer. Beginning in 2003, the league that won the All-Star Game received home-field advantage in that season's World Series.

MVP Multiple winners: Gary Carter, Steve Garvey, Willie Mays and Cal Ripken Jr. (2).

Year	Host		AL Manager	NL Manager	MVP
1933	**American, 4-2**	Chicago (AL)	Connie Mack	John McGraw	No award
1934	**American, 9-7**	New York (NL)	Joe Cronin	Bill Terry	No award
1935	**American, 4-1**	Cleveland	Mickey Cochrane	Frankie Frisch	No award
1936	National, 4-3	Boston (NL)	Joe McCarthy	Charlie Grimm	No award
1937	**American, 8-3**	Washington	Joe McCarthy	Bill Terry	No award
1938	National, 4-1	Cincinnati	Joe McCarthy	Bill Terry	No award
1939	**American, 3-1**	New York (AL)	Joe McCarthy	Gabby Hartnett	No award
1940	National, 4-0	St. Louis (NL)	Joe Cronin	Bill McKechnie	No award
1941	**American, 7-5**	Detroit	Del Baker	Bill McKechnie	No award

The All-Star Game (Cont.)

Year		Host	AL Manager	NL Manager	MVP
1942	**American,** 3-1	New York (NL)	Joe McCarthy	Leo Durocher	No award
1943	**American,** 5-3	Philadelphia (AL)	Joe McCarthy	Billy Southworth	No award
1944	National, 7-1	Pittsburgh	Joe McCarthy	Billy Southworth	No award
1945	Not held				
1946	**American,** 12-0	Boston (AL)	Steve O'Neill	Charlie Grimm	No award
1947	**American,** 2-1	Chicago (NL)	Joe Cronin	Eddie Dyer	No award
1948	**American,** 5-2	St. Louis (AL)	Bucky Harris	Leo Durocher	No award
1949	**American,** 11-7	Brooklyn	Lou Boudreau	Billy Southworth	No award
1950	National, 4-3 (14)	Chicago (AL)	Casey Stengel	Burt Shotton	No award
1951	National, 8-3	Detroit	Casey Stengel	Eddie Sawyer	No award
1952	National, 3-2 (5, rain)	Philadelphia (NL)	Casey Stengel	Leo Durocher	No award
1953	National, 5-1	Cincinnati	Casey Stengel	Charlie Dressen	No award
1954	**American,** 11-9	Cleveland	Casey Stengel	Walter Alston	No award
1955	National, 6-5 (12)	Milwaukee	Al Lopez	Leo Durocher	No award
1956	National, 7-3	Washington	Casey Stengel	Walter Alston	No award
1957	**American,** 6-5	St. Louis	Casey Stengel	Walter Alston	No award
1958	**American,** 4-3	Baltimore	Casey Stengel	Fred Haney	No award
1959-a	National, 5-4	Pittsburgh	Casey Stengel	Fred Haney	No award
1959-b	**American,** 5-3	Los Angeles	Casey Stengel	Fred Haney	No award
1960-a	National, 5-3	Kansas City	Al Lopez	Walter Alston	No award
1960-b	National, 6-0	New York	Al Lopez	Walter Alston	No award
1961-a	National, 5-4 (10)	San Francisco	Paul Richards	Danny Murtaugh	No award
1961-b	TIE, 1-1 (9, rain)	Boston	Paul Richards	Danny Murtaugh	No award
1962-a	National, 3-1	Washington	Ralph Houk	Fred Hutchinson	Maury Wills, LA (NL), SS
1962-b	**American,** 9-4	Chicago (NL)	Ralph Houk	Fred Hutchinson	Leon Wagner, LA (AL), OF
1963	National, 5-3	Cleveland	Ralph Houk	Alvin Dark	Willie Mays, SF, OF
1964	National, 7-4	New York (NL)	Al Lopez	Walter Alston	Johnny Callison, Phi., OF
1965	National, 6-5	Minnesota	Al Lopez	Gene Mauch	Juan Marichal, SF, P
1966	National, 2-1 (10)	St. Louis	Sam Mele	Walter Alston	Brooks Robinson, Bal., 3B
1967	National, 2-1 (15)	California	Hank Bauer	Walter Alston	Tony Perez, Cin., 3B
1968	National, 1-0	Houston	Dick Williams	Red Schoendienst	Willie Mays, SF, OF
1969	National, 9-3	Washington	Mayo Smith	Red Schoendienst	Willie McCovey, SF, 1B
1970	National, 5-4 (12)	Cincinnati	Earl Weaver	Gil Hodges	Carl Yastrzemski, Bos., OF-1B
1971	**American,** 6-4	Detroit	Earl Weaver	Sparky Anderson	Frank Robinson, Bal., OF
1972	National, 4-3 (10)	Atlanta	Earl Weaver	Danny Murtaugh	Joe Morgan, Con., 2B
1973	National, 7-1	Kansas	Dick Williams	Sparky Anderson	Bobby Bonds, SF, OF
1974	National, 7-2	Pittsburgh	Dick Williams	Yogi Berra	Steve Garvey, LA, 1B
1975	National, 6-3	Milwaukee	Alvin Dark	Walter Alston	Bill Madlock, Chi. (NL), 3B & Jon Matlack, NY (NL), P
1976	National, 7-1	Philadelphia	Darrell Johnson	Sparky Anderson	George Foster, Cin., OF
1977	National, 7-5	New York (AL)	Billy Martin	Sparky Anderson	Don Sutton, LA, P
1978	National, 7-3	San Diego	Billy Martin	Tommy Lasorda	Steve Garvey, LA, 1B
1979	National, 7-6	Seattle	Bob Lemon	Tommy Lasorda	Dave Parker, Pit, OF
1980	National, 4-2	Los Angeles	Earl Weaver	Chuck Tanner	Ken Griffey, Cin., OF
1981	National, 5-4	Cleveland	Jim Frey	Dallas Green	Gary Carter, Mon., C
1982	National, 4-1	Montreal	Billy Martin	Tommy Lasorda	Dave Concepcion, Cin., SS
1983	**American,** 13-3	Chicago (AL)	Harvey Kuenn	Whitey Herzog	Fred Lynn, Cal., OF
1984	National, 3-1	San Francisco	Joe Altobelli	Paul Owens	Gary Carter, Mon., C
1985	National, 6-1	Minnesota	Sparky Anderson	Dick Williams	LaMarr Hoyt, SD, P
1986	**American,** 3-2	Houston	Dick Howser	Whitey Herzog	Roger Clemens, Bos., P
1987	National, 2-0 (13)	Oakland	John McNamara	Davey Johnson	Tim Raines, Mon., OF
1988	**American,** 2-1	Cincinnati	Tom Kelly	Whitey Herzog	Terry Steinbach, Oak., C
1989	**American,** 5-3	California	Tony La Russa	Tommy Lasorda	Bo Jackson, KC, OF
1990	**American,** 2-0	Chicago (NL)	Tony La Russa	Roger Craig	Julio Franco, Tex., 2B
1991	**American,** 4-2	Toronto	Tony La Russa	Lou Piniella	Cal Ripken Jr., Bal., SS
1992	**American,** 13-6	San Diego	Tom Kelly	Bobby Cox	Ken Griffey Jr., Sea., OF
1993	**American,** 9-3	Baltimore	Cito Gaston	Bobby Cox	Kirby Puckett, Min., OF
1994	National, 8-7 (10)	Pittsburgh	Cito Gaston	Jim Fregosi	Fred McGriff, Atl., 1B
1995	National, 3-2	Texas	Buck Showalter	Felipe Alou	Jeff Conine, Fla., PH
1996	National, 6-0	Philadelphia	Mike Hargrove	Bobby Cox	Mike Piazza, LA, C
1997	**American,** 3-1	Cleveland	Joe Torre	Bobby Cox	Sandy Alomar Jr., Cle., C
1998	**American,** 13-8	Colorado	Mike Hargrove	Jim Leyland	Roberto Alomar, Bal., 2B
1999	**American,** 4-1	Boston	Joe Torre	Bruce Bochy	Pedro Martinez, Bos., P
2000	**American,** 6-3	Atlanta	Joe Torre	Bobby Cox	Derek Jeter, NY (AL), SS
2001	**American,** 4-1	Seattle	Joe Torre	Bobby Valentine	Cal Ripken Jr., Bal., SS-3B
2002	TIE, 7-7 (11 inn.) *	Milwaukee	Joe Torre	Bob Brenly	No award
2003	**American,** 7-6	Chicago (AL)	Mike Scioscia	Dusty Baker	Garret Anderson, Ana., OF
2004	**American,** 9-4	Houston	Joe Torre	Jack McKeon	Alfonso Soriano, Tex., 2B

* Due to the depletion of both the AL and NL rosters, the 2002 game was called a tie after 11 innings.

Major League Franchise Origins

Here is what the current 30 teams in Major League Baseball have to show for the years they have put in as members of the National League (NL) and American League (AL). Pennants and World Series championships are since 1901.

National League

	1st Year	Pennants & World Series	Franchise Stops
Arizona Diamondbacks	..1998	1 NL (2001) 1 WS (2001)	• Phoenix (1998–)

Atlanta Braves	1876	9 NL (1914,48,57-58,91-92,95,96,99)
		3 WS (1914,57,95)
			• Boston (1876–1952)
			  Milwaukee (1953–65)
			  Atlanta (1966–)

Chicago Cubs	1876	10 NL (1906-08,10,18,29,32,35,38,45) 2 WS (1907-08)	• Chicago (1876–)
Cincinnati Reds	1876	9 NL (1919,39-40,61,70,72,75-76,90) 5 WS (1919,40,75-76,90)	• Cincinnati (1876–80) Cincinnati (1890–)
Colorado Rockies	1993	None	• Denver (1993–)
Florida Marlins	1993	2 NL (1997, 2003) 2 WS (1997, 2003)	• Miami (1993–)
Houston Astros	1962	None	• Houston (1962–)
Los Angeles Dodgers	1890	18 NL (1916,20,41,47,49,52-53,55-56, 59,63, 65-66,74,77-78, 81,88) 6 WS (1955,59,63,65,81,88)	• Brooklyn (1890-1957) Los Angeles (1958–)
Milwaukee Brewers	1969	1 AL (1982)	• Seattle (1969) Milwaukee (1970–)
New York Mets	1962	4 NL (1969,73,86,00) 2 WS (1969,86)	• New York (1962–)
Philadelphia Phillies	1883	5 NL (1915,50,80,83,93) 1 WS (1980)	• Philadelphia (1883–)
Pittsburgh Pirates	1887	7 NL (1903,09,25,27,60,71,79) 5 WS (1909,25,60,71,79)	• Pittsburgh (1887–)
St. Louis Cardinals	1892	16 NL (1926,28,30-31,34,42-44,46,64, 67-68,82,85,87,2004) 9 WS (1926,31,34,42,44,46,64,67,82)	• St. Louis (1892–)
San Diego Padres	1969	2 NL (1984,98)	• San Diego (1969–)
San Francisco Giants	1883	17 NL (1905,11-13,17,21-24,33,36-37,51, 54,62,89,2002) 5 WS (1905,21-22,33,54)	• New York (1883–1957) San Francisco (1958–)
Washington (unnamed as of Oct. 31, 2004)	1969	None	• Montreal (1969–2004) Washington, DC (2005–)

American League

	1st Year	Pennants & World Series	Franchise Stops
Anaheim Angels	1961	1 AL (2002) 1 WS (2002)	• Los Angeles (1961–65) Anaheim, CA (1966–)

Baltimore Orioles	1901	7 AL (1944,66,69-71,79,83)
		3 WS (1966,70,83)
			• Milwaukee (1901)
			  St. Louis (1902–53)
			  Baltimore (1954–)

Boston Red Sox	1901	10 AL (1903,12,15-16,18,46,67,75,86,2004) 6 WS (1903,12,15-16,18,2004)	• Boston (1901–)
Chicago White Sox	1901	4 AL (1906,17,19,59) 2 WS (1906,17)	• Chicago (1901–)
Cleveland Indians	1901	5 AL (1920,48,54,95,97) 2 WS (1920,48)	• Cleveland (1901–)
Detroit Tigers	1901	9 AL (1907-09,34-35,40,45,68,84) 4 WS (1935,45,68,84)	• Detroit (1901–)
Kansas City Royals	1969	2 AL (1980,85) 1 WS (1985)	• Kansas City (1969–)

Minnesota Twins	1901	6 AL (1924-25,33,65,87,91)
		3 WS (1924,87,91)
			• Washington, DC (1901–60)
			  Bloomington, MN (1961–81)
			  Minneapolis (1982–)

New York Yankees	1901	39 AL (1921-23,26-28,32,36-39,41-43,47, 49-53,55-58,60-64,76-78,81,96,98-01,03) 26 WS (1923,27-28,32,36-39,41,43,47, 49-53,56,58,61-62,77-78,96,98-00)	• Baltimore (1901–02) New York (1903–)

Oakland Athletics	1901	14 AL (1905,10-11,13-14,29-31,72-74,
		88-90)
		9 WS (1910-11,13,29-30,72-74,89)
			• Philadelphia (1901-54)
			  Kansas City (1955–67)
			  Oakland (1968–)

Seattle Mariners	1977	None	• Seattle (1977–)
Tampa Bay Devil Rays	...1998	None	• Tampa Bay (1998–)
Texas Rangers	1961	None	• Washington, DC (1961–71) Arlington, TX (1972–)
Toronto Blue Jays	1977	2 AL (1992-93) 2 WS (1992-93)	• Toronto (1977–)

The Growth of Major League Baseball

The National League (founded in 1876) and the American League (founded in 1901) were both eight-team circuits at the turn of the century and remained that way until expansion finally came to Major League Baseball in the 1960s. The AL added two teams in 1961 and the NL did the same a year later. Both leagues went to 12 teams and split into two divisions in 1969. The AL then grew by two more teams to 14 in 1977, but the NL didn't follow suit until adding its 13th and 14th clubs in 1993. The NL added two teams (making it 16) in 1998 when the expansion Arizona Diamondbacks entered the league and the Milwaukee Brewers moved over from the AL. The Tampa Bay Devil Rays joined the AL in 1998, keeping the AL at 14 teams.

Expansion Timetable (Since 1901)

1961—Los Angeles Angels (now Anaheim) and Washington Senators (now Texas Rangers) join AL; **1962**—Houston Colt .45s (now Astros) and New York Mets join NL; **1969**—Kansas City Royals and Seattle Pilots (now Milwaukee Brewers) join AL, while Montreal Expos and San Diego Padres join NL; **1977**—Seattle Mariners and Toronto Blue Jays join AL; **1993**—Colorado Rockies and Florida Marlins join NL; **1998**—Arizona Diamondbacks join NL and Tampa Bay Devil Rays join AL.

City and Nickname Changes
National League

1953—Boston Braves move to Milwaukee; **1958**—Brooklyn Dodgers move to Los Angeles and New York Giants move to San Francisco; **1965**—Houston Colt .45s renamed Astros; **1966**—Milwaukee Braves move to Atlanta; **2004**—Montreal Expos move to Washington, DC (no new nickname as of Oct. 31, 2004).

    Other nicknames: Boston (Beaneaters and Doves through 1908, and Bees from 1936-40); **Brooklyn** (Superbas through 1926, then Robins from 1927-31; then Dodgers from 1932-57); **Cincinnati** (Red Legs from 1944-45, then Redlegs from 1954-60, then Reds since 1961); **Philadelphia** (Blue Jays from 1943-44).

American League

1902—Milwaukee Brewers move to St. Louis and become Browns; **1903**—Baltimore Orioles move to New York and become Highlanders; **1913**—NY Highlanders renamed Yankees; **1954**—St. Louis Browns move to Baltimore and become Orioles; **1955**—Philadelphia Athletics move to Kansas City; **1961**—Washington Senators move to Bloomington, Minn., and become Minnesota Twins; **1965**—LA Angels renamed California Angels; **1966**—California Angels move to Anaheim; **1968**—KC Athletics move to Oakland and become A's; **1970**—Seattle Pilots move to Milwaukee and become Brewers; **1972**—Washington Senators move to Arlington, Texas, and become Rangers; **1982**—Minnesota Twins move to Minneapolis; **1987**—Oakland A's renamed Athletics; **1997**—California Angels renamed Anaheim Angels.

    Other nicknames: Boston (Pilgrims, Puritans, Plymouth Rocks and Somersets through 1906); **Cleveland** (Bronchos, Blues, Naps and Molly McGuires through 1914); **Washington** (Senators through 1904, then Nationals from 1905-44, then Senators again from 1945-60).

National League Pennant Winners from 1876-99

Founded in 1876, the National League played 24 seasons before the turn of the century and its eventual rivalry with the younger American League.

    Multiple winners: Boston (8); Chicago (6); Baltimore (3); Brooklyn, New York and Providence (2).

Year		Year		Year		Year	
1876	Chicago	1882	Chicago	1888	New York	1894	Baltimore
1877	Boston	1883	Boston	1889	New York	1895	Baltimore
1878	Boston	1884	Providence	1890	Brooklyn	1896	Baltimore
1879	Providence	1885	Chicago	1891	Boston	1897	Boston
1880	Chicago	1886	Chicago	1892	Boston	1898	Boston
1881	Chicago	1887	Detroit	1893	Boston	1899	Brooklyn

Champions of Leagues That No Longer Exist

A Special Baseball Records Committee appointed by the commissioner found in 1968 that four extinct leagues qualified for major league status—the American Association (1882-91), the Union Association (1884), the Players' League (1890) and the Federal League (1914-15). The first years of the American League (1900) and Federal League (1913) were not recognized.

American Association

Year	Champion	Manager	Year	Champion	Manager	Year	Champion	Manager
1882	Cincinnati	Pop Snyder	1886	St. Louis	Charlie Comiskey	1890	Louisville	Jack Chapman
1883	Philadelphia	Lew Simmons	1887	St. Louis	Charlie Comiskey	1891	Boston	Arthur Irwin
1884	New York	Jim Mutrie	1888	St. Louis	Charlie Comiskey			
1885	St. Louis	Charlie Comiskey	1889	Brooklyn	Bill McGunnigle			

Union Association

Year	Champion	Manager
1884	St. Louis	Henry Lucas

Players' League

Year	Champion	Manager
1890	Boston	King Kelly

Federal League

Year	Champion	Manager
1914	Indianapolis	Bill Phillips
1915	Chicago	Joe Tinker

Annual Batting Leaders (since 1900)
Batting Average
National League

Multiple winners: Tony Gwynn and Honus Wagner (8); Rogers Hornsby and Stan Musial (7); Roberto Clemente and Bill Madlock (4); Pete Rose, Larry Walker and Paul Waner (3); Hank Aaron, Richie Ashburn, Barry Bonds, Jake Daubert, Tommy Davis, Ernie Lombardi, Willie McGee, Lefty O'Doul, Dave Parker and Edd Roush (2).

Year		Avg	Year		Avg	Year		Avg
1900	Honus Wagner, Pit	.381	1935	Arky Vaughan, Pit	.385	1970	Rico Carty, Atl	.366
1901	Jesse Burkett, St.L	.382	1936	Paul Waner, Pit	.373	1971	Joe Torre, St.L	.363
1902	Ginger Beaumont, Pit	.357	1937	Joe Medwick, St.L	.374	1972	Billy Williams, Chi	.333
1903	Honus Wagner, Pit	.355	1938	Ernie Lombardi, Cin	.342	1973	Pete Rose, Cin	.338
1904	Honus Wagner, Pit	.349	1939	Johnny Mize, St.L	.349	1974	Ralph Garr, Atl	.353
1905	Cy Seymour, Cin	.377	1940	Debs Garms, Pit	.355	1975	Bill Madlock, Chi	.354
1906	Honus Wagner, Pit	.339	1941	Pete Reiser, Bklyn	.343	1976	Bill Madlock, Chi	.339
1907	Honus Wagner, Pit	.350	1942	Ernie Lombardi, Bos	.330	1977	Dave Parker, Pit	.338
1908	Honus Wagner, Pit	.354	1943	Stan Musial, St.L	.357	1978	Dave Parker, Pit	.334
1909	Honus Wagner, Pit	.339	1944	Dixie Walker, Bklyn	.357	1979	Keith Hernandez, St.L	.344
1910	Sherry Magee, Phi	.331	1945	Phil Cavarretta, Chi	.355	1980	Bill Buckner, Chi	.324
1911	Honus Wagner, Pit	.334	1946	Stan Musial, St.L	.365	1981	Bill Madlock, Pit	.341
1912	Heinie Zimmerman, Chi	.372	1947	Harry Walker, St.L-Phi	.363	1982	Al Oliver, Mon	.331
1913	Jake Daubert, Bklyn	.350	1948	Stan Musial, St.L	.376	1983	Bill Madlock, Pit	.323
1914	Jake Daubert, Bklyn	.329	1949	Jackie Robinson, Bklyn	.342	1984	Tony Gwynn, SD	.351
1915	Larry Doyle, NY	.320	1950	Stan Musial, St.L	.346	1985	Willie McGee, St.L	.353
1916	Hal Chase, Cin	.339	1951	Stan Musial, St.L	.355	1986	Tim Raines, Mon	.334
1917	Edd Roush, Cin	.341	1952	Stan Musial, St.L	.336	1987	Tony Gwynn, SD	.370
1918	Zack Wheat, Bklyn	.335	1953	Carl Furillo, Bklyn	.344	1988	Tony Gwynn, SD	.313
1919	Edd Roush, Cin	.321	1954	Willie Mays, NY	.345	1989	Tony Gwynn, SD	.336
1920	Rogers Hornsby, St.L	.370	1955	Richie Ashburn, Phi	.338	1990	Willie McGee, St.L	.335
1921	Rogers Hornsby, St.L	.397	1956	Hank Aaron, Mil	.328	1991	Terry Pendleton, Atl	.319
1922	Rogers Hornsby, St.L	.401	1957	Stan Musial, St.L	.351	1992	Gary Sheffield, SD	.330
1923	Rogers Hornsby, St.L	.384	1958	Richie Ashburn, Phi	.350	1993	Andres Galarraga, Col	.370
1924	Rogers Hornsby, St.L	.424	1959	Hank Aaron, Mil	.355	1994	Tony Gwynn, SD	.394
1925	Rogers Hornsby, St.L	.403	1960	Dick Groat, Pit	.325	1995	Tony Gwynn, SD	.368
1926	Bubbles Hargrave, Cin	.353	1961	Roberto Clemente, Pit	.351	1996	Tony Gwynn, SD	.353
1927	Paul Waner, Pit	.380	1962	Tommy Davis, LA	.346	1997	Tony Gwynn, SD	.372
1928	Rogers Hornsby, Bos	.387	1963	Tommy Davis, LA	.326	1998	Larry Walker, Col	.363
1929	Lefty O'Doul, Phi	.398	1964	Roberto Clemente, Pit	.339	1999	Larry Walker, Col	.379
1930	Bill Terry, NY	.401	1965	Roberto Clemente, Pit	.329	2000	Todd Helton, Col	.372
1931	Chick Hafey, Phi	.349	1966	Matty Alou, Pit	.342	2001	Larry Walker, Col	.350
1932	Lefty O'Doul, Bklyn	.368	1967	Roberto Clemente, Pit	.357	2002	Barry Bonds, SF	.370
1933	Chuck Klein, Phi	.368	1968	Pete Rose, Cin	.335	2003	Albert Pujols, St.L	.359
1934	Paul Waner, Pit	.362	1969	Pete Rose, Cin	.348	2004	Barry Bonds, SF	.362

American League

Multiple winners: Ty Cobb (12); Rod Carew (7); Ted Williams (6); Wade Boggs (5); Harry Heilmann (4); George Brett, Nap Lajoie, Tony Oliva and Carl Yastrzemski (3); Luke Appling, Joe DiMaggio, Ferris Fain, Jimmie Foxx, Nomar Garciaparra, Edgar Martinez, Pete Runnels, Al Simmons, George Sisler, Ichiro Suzuki and Mickey Vernon (2).

Year		Avg	Year		Avg	Year		Avg
1901	Nap Lajoie, Phi	.422	1924	Babe Ruth, NY	.378	1947	Ted Williams, Bos	.343
1902	Ed Delahanty, Wash	.376	1925	Harry Heilmann, Det	.393	1948	Ted Williams, Bos	.369
1903	Nap Lajoie, Cle	.355	1926	Heinie Manush, Det	.378	1949	George Kell, Det	.343
1904	Nap Lajoie, Cle	.381	1927	Harry Heilmann, Det	.398	1950	Billy Goodman, Bos	.354
1905	Elmer Flick, Cle	.306	1928	Goose Goslin, Wash	.379	1951	Ferris Fain, Phi	.344
1906	George Stone, St.L	.358	1929	Lew Fonseca, Cle	.369	1952	Ferris Fain, Phi	.327
1907	Ty Cobb, Det	.350	1930	Al Simmons, Phi	.381	1953	Mickey Vernon, Wash	.337
1908	Ty Cobb, Det	.324	1931	Al Simmons, Phi	.390	1954	Bobby Avila, Clev	.341
1909	Ty Cobb, Det	.377	1932	Dale Alexander, Det-Bos	.367	1955	Al Kaline, Det	.340
1910	Ty Cobb, Det	.383	1933	Jimmie Foxx, Phi	.356	1956	Mickey Mantle, NY	.353
1911	Ty Cobb, Det	.420	1934	Lou Gehrig, NY	.363	1957	Ted Williams, Bos	.388
1912	Ty Cobb, Det	.409	1935	Buddy Myer, Wash	.349	1958	Ted Williams, Bos	.328
1913	Ty Cobb, Det	.390	1936	Luke Appling, Chi	.388	1959	Harvey Kuenn, Det	.353
1914	Ty Cobb, Det	.368	1937	Charlie Gehringer, Det	.371	1960	Pete Runnels, Bos	.320
1915	Ty Cobb, Det	.369	1938	Jimmie Foxx, Bos	.349	1961	Norm Cash, Det	.361*
1916	Tris Speaker, Cle	.386	1939	Joe DiMaggio, NY	.381	1962	Pete Runnels, Bos	.326
1917	Ty Cobb, Det	.383	1940	Joe DiMaggio, NY	.352	1963	Carl Yastrzemski, Bos	.321
1918	Ty Cobb, Det	.382	1941	Ted Williams, Bos	.406	1964	Tony Oliva, Min	.323
1919	Ty Cobb, Det	.384	1942	Ted Williams, Bos	.356	1965	Tony Oliva, Min	.321
1920	George Sisler, St.L	.407	1943	Luke Appling, Chi	.328	1966	Frank Robinson, Bal	.316
1921	Harry Heilmann, Det	.394	1944	Lou Boudreau, Clev	.327	1967	Carl Yastrzemski, Bos	.326
1922	George Sisler, St.L	.420	1945	Snuffy Stirnweiss, NY	.309	1968	Carl Yastrzemski, Bos	.301
1923	Harry Heilmann, Det	.403	1946	Mickey Vernon, Wash	.353	1969	Rod Carew, Min	.332

Batting Average (Cont.)

Year		Avg	Year		Avg	Year		Avg
1970	Alex Johnson, Cal.	.329	1983	Wade Boggs, Bos.	.361	1996	Alex Rodriguez, Sea	.358
1971	Tony Oliva, Min	.337	1984	Don Mattingly, NY	.343	1997	Frank Thomas, Chi	.347
1972	Rod Carew, Min	.318	1985	Wade Boggs, Bos.	.368	1998	Bernie Williams, NY.	.339
1973	Rod Carew, Min	.350	1986	Wade Boggs, Bos.	.357	1999	Nomar Garciaparra, Bos.	.357
1974	Rod Carew, Min	.364	1987	Wade Boggs, Bos.	.363			
1975	Rod Carew, Min	.359	1988	Wade Boggs, Bos.	.366	2000	Nomar Garciaparra, Bos.	.372
1976	George Brett, KC	.333	1989	Kirby Puckett, Min.	.339	2001	Ichiro Suzuki, Sea.	.350
1977	Rod Carew, Min	.388				2002	Manny Ramirez, Bos	.349
1978	Rod Carew, Min	.333	1990	George Brett, KC	.329	2003	Bill Mueller, Bos.	.326
1979	Fred Lynn, Bos	.333	1991	Julio Franco, Tex	.341	2004	Ichiro Suzuki, Sea.	.372
1980	George Brett, KC	.390	1992	Edgar Martinez, Sea.	.343			
1981	Carney Lansford, Bos.	.336	1993	John Olerud, Tor.	.363			
1982	Willie Wilson, KC.	.332	1994	Paul O'Neill, NY	.359			
			1995	Edgar Martinez, Sea.	.356			

*Norm Cash later admitted to using a corked bat the entire season. He played 16 other seasons and never hit better than .286.

Home Runs
National League

Multiple winners: Mike Schmidt (8); Ralph Kiner (7); Gavvy Cravath and Mel Ott (6); Hank Aaron, Chuck Klein, Willie Mays, Johnny Mize, Cy Williams and Hack Wilson (4);Willie McCovey (3); Ernie Banks, Johnny Bench, Barry Bonds, George Foster, Rogers Hornsby, Tim Jordan, Dave Kingman, Eddie Mathews, Mark McGwire, Dale Murphy, Bill Nicholson, Dave Robertson, Wildfire Schulte, Sammy Sosa and Willie Stargell (2).

Year		HR	Year		HR	Year		HR
1900	Herman Long, Bos	12	1934	Rip Collins, St.L	35	1968	Willie McCovey, SF	36
1901	Sam Crawford, Cin	16		& Mel Ott, NY.	35	1969	Willie McCovey, SF	45
1902	Tommy Leach, Pit	6	1935	Wally Berger, Bos.	34	1970	Johnny Bench, Cin	45
1903	Jimmy Sheckard, Bklyn	9	1936	Mel Ott, NY.	33	1971	Willie Stargell, Pit.	48
1904	Harry Lumley, Bklyn	9	1937	Joe Medwick, St.L.	31	1972	Johnny Bench, Cin	40
1905	Fred Odwell, Cin.	9		& Mel Ott, NY.	31	1973	Willie Stargell, Pit.	44
1906	Tim Jordan, Bklyn	12	1938	Mel Ott, NY.	36	1974	Mike Schmidt, Phi.	36
1907	Dave Brain, Bos	10	1939	Johnny Mize, St.L	28	1975	Mike Schmidt, Phi.	38
1908	Tim Jordan, Bklyn	12	1940	Johnny Mize, St.L	43	1976	Mike Schmidt, Phi.	38
1909	Red Murray, NY	7	1941	Dolph Camilli, Bklyn.	34	1977	George Foster, Cin	52
1910	Fred Beck, Bos	10	1942	Mel Ott, NY.	30	1978	George Foster, Cin	40
	& Wildfire Schulte, Chi	10	1943	Bill Nicholson, Chi	29	1979	Dave Kingman, Chi	48
1911	Wildfire Schulte, Chi.	21	1944	Bill Nicholson, Chi	33	1980	Mike Schmidt, Phi.	48
1912	Heinie Zimmerman, Chi.	14	1945	Tommy Holmes, Bos	28	1981	Mike Schmidt, Phi.	31
1913	Gavvy Cravath, Phi.	19	1946	Ralph Kiner, Pit.	23	1982	Dave Kingman, NY.	37
1914	Gavvy Cravath, Phi.	19	1947	Ralph Kiner, Pit.	51	1983	Mike Schmidt, Phi.	40
1915	Gavvy Cravath, Phi.	24		& Johnny Mize, NY	51	1984	Dale Murphy, Atl.	36
1916	Cy Williams, Chi	12	1948	Ralph Kiner, Pit.	40		& Mike Schmidt, Phi.	36
	& Dave Robertson, NY.	12		& Johnny Mize, NY	40	1985	Dale Murphy, Atl.	37
1917	Gavvy Cravath, Phi.	12	1949	Ralph Kiner, Pit.	54	1986	Mike Schmidt, Phi.	37
	& Dave Robertson, NY.	12	1950	Ralph Kiner, Pit.	47	1987	Andre Dawson, Chi	49
1918	Gavvy Cravath, Phi.	8	1951	Ralph Kiner, Pit.	42	1988	Darryl Strawberry, NY.	39
1919	Gavvy Cravath, Phi.	12	1952	Ralph Kiner, Pit.	37	1989	Kevin Mitchell, SF	47
1920	Cy Williams, Phi.	15		& Hank Sauer, Chi	37	1990	Ryne Sandberg, Chi	40
1921	George Kelly, NY	23	1953	Eddie Mathews, Mil	47	1991	Howard Johnson, NY.	38
1922	Rogers Hornsby, St.L	42	1954	Ted Kluszewski, Cin	49	1992	Fred McGriff, SD	35
1923	Cy Williams, Phi.	41	1955	Willie Mays, NY.	51	1993	Barry Bonds, SF	46
1924	Jack Fournier, Bklyn	27	1956	Duke Snider, Bklyn	43	1994	Matt Williams, SF	43
1925	Rogers Hornsby, St.L.	39	1957	Hank Aaron, Mil.	44	1995	Dante Bichette, Col.	40
1926	Hack Wilson, Chi	21	1958	Ernie Banks, Chi.	47	1996	Andres Galarraga, Col	47
1927	Cy Williams, Phi.	30	1959	Eddie Mathews, Mil	46	1997	Larry Walker, Col	49
	& Hack Wilson, Chi	30	1960	Ernie Banks, Chi.	41	1998	Mark McGwire, St.L	70
1928	Jim Bottomley, St.L.	31	1961	Orlando Cepeda, SF.	46	1999	Mark McGwire, St.L.	65
	& Hack Wilson, Chi	31	1962	Willie Mays, SF	49	2000	Sammy Sosa, Chi	50
1929	Chuck Klein, Phi	43	1963	Hank Aaron, Mil.	44	2001	Barry Bonds, SF	73
1930	Hack Wilson, Chi	56		& Willie McCovey, SF.	44	2002	Sammy Sosa, Chi	49
1931	Chuck Klein, Phi	31	1964	Willie Mays, SF	47	2003	Jim Thome, Phi	47
1932	Chuck Klein, Phi	38	1965	Willie Mays, SF	52	2004	Adrian Beltre, LA	48
	& Mel Ott, NY.	38	1966	Hank Aaron, Atl	44			
1933	Chuck Klein, Phi	28	1967	Hank Aaron, Atl	39			

American League

Multiple winners: Babe Ruth (12); Harmon Killebrew (6); Home Run Baker, Harry Davis, Jimmie Foxx, Hank Greenberg, Ken Griffey Jr., Reggie Jackson, Mickey Mantle and Ted Williams (4); Lou Gehrig, Jim Rice and Alex Rodriguez (3); Dick Allen, Tony Armas, Jose Canseco, Joe DiMaggio, Larry Doby, Cecil Fielder, Juan Gonzalez, Mark McGwire, Wally Pipp, Al Rosen and Gorman Thomas (2).

Year		HR	Year		HR	Year		HR
1901	Nap Lajoie, Phi	14	1904	Harry Davis, Phi	10	1907	Harry Davis, Phi	8
1902	Socks Seybold, Phi	16	1905	Harry Davis, Phi	8	1908	Sam Crawford, Det.	7
1903	Buck Freeman, Bos	13	1906	Harry Davis, Phi	12	1909	Ty Cobb, Det	9

Year	HR
1910	Jake Stahl, Bos 10
1911	Home Run Baker, Phi 11
1912	Home Run Baker, Phi 10
	& Tris Speaker, Bos. 10
1913	Home Run Baker, Phi. 12
1914	Home Run Baker, Phi. 9
1915	Braggo Roth, Chi-Cle 7
1916	Wally Pipp, NY. 12
1917	Wally Pipp, NY 9
1918	Babe Ruth, Bos 11
	& Tilly Walker, Phi 11
1919	Babe Ruth, Bos 29
1920	Babe Ruth, NY 54
1921	Babe Ruth, NY 59
1922	Ken Williams, St.L. 39
1923	Babe Ruth, NY 41
1924	Babe Ruth, NY 46
1925	Bob Meusel, NY 33
1926	Babe Ruth, NY 47
1927	Babe Ruth, NY 60
1928	Babe Ruth, NY 54
1929	Babe Ruth, NY 46
1930	Babe Ruth, NY . .· 49
1931	Lou Gehrig, NY. 46
	& Babe Ruth, NY 46
1932	Jimmie Foxx, Phi 58
1933	Jimmie Foxx, Phi 48
1934	Lou Gehrig, NY. 49
1935	Jimmie Foxx, Phi 36
	& Hank Greenberg, Det. . . 36
1936	Lou Gehrig, NY. 49
1937	Joe DiMaggio, NY 46
1938	Hank Greenberg, Det. 58
1939	Jimmie Foxx, Bos. 35
1940	Hank Greenberg, Det. 41
1941	Ted Williams, Bos. 37
1942	Ted Williams, Bos 36

Year	HR
1943	Rudy York, Det. 34
1944	Nick Etten, NY 22
1945	Vern Stephens, St.L 24
1946	Hank Greenberg, Det. . . . 44
1947	Ted Williams, Bos. 32
1948	Joe DiMaggio, NY 39
1949	Ted Williams, Bos 43
1950	Al Rosen, Cle. 37
1951	Gus Zernial, Chi-Phi 33
1952	Larry Doby, Cle. 32
1953	Al Rosen, Cle. 43
1954	Larry Doby, Cle. 32
1955	Mickey Mantle, NY. 37
1956	Mickey Mantle, NY. 52
1957	Roy Sievers, Wash 42
1958	Mickey Mantle, NY. 42
1959	Rocky Colavito, Cle 42
	& Harmon Killebrew, Wash .42
1960	Mickey Mantle, NY. 40
1961	Roger Maris, NY. 61
1962	Harmon Killebrew, Min . . 48
1963	Harmon Killebrew, Min . . 45
1964	Harmon Killebrew, Min . . 49
1965	Tony Conigliaro, Bos. . . . 32
1966	Frank Robinson, Bal 49
1967	Harmon Killebrew, Min . . 44
	& Carl Yastrzemski, Bos. . 44
1968	Frank Howard, Wash. . . . 44
1969	Harmon Killebrew, Min . . 49
1970	Frank Howard, Wash. . . . 44
1971	Bill Melton, Chi 33
1972	Dick Allen, Chi. 37
1973	Reggie Jackson, Oak 32
1974	Dick Allen, Chi.· 32
1975	Reggie Jackson, Oak 36
	& George Scott, Mil 36

Year	HR
1976	Graig Nettles, NY 32
1977	Jim Rice, Bos 39
1978	Jim Rice, Bos 46
1979	Gorman Thomas, Mil 45
1980	Reggie Jackson, NY 41
	& Ben Oglivie, Mil 41
1981	Tony Armas, Oak 22
	Dwight Evans, Bos 22
	Bobby Grich, Cal 22
	& Eddie Murray, Bal. . . . 22
1982	Reggie Jackson, Cal. 39
	& Gorman Thomas, Mil. . . 39
1983	Jim Rice, Bos 39
1984	Tony Armas, Bos. 43
1985	Darrell Evans, Det. 40
1986	Jesse Barfield, Tor 40
1987	Mark McGwire, Oak 49
1988	Jose Canseco, Oak. 42
1989	Fred McGriff, Tor 36
1990	Cecil Fielder, Det 51
1991	Jose Canseco, Oak. 44
	& Cecil Fielder, Det. 44
1992	Juan Gonzalez, Tex. 43
1993	Juan Gonzalez, Tex. 46
1994	Ken Griffey Jr., Sea. 40
1995	Albert Belle, Cle 50
1996	Mark McGwire, Oak 52
1997	Ken Griffey Jr., Sea. 56
1998	Ken Griffey Jr., Sea. 56
1999	Ken Griffey Jr., Sea. 48
2000	Troy Glaus, Ana 47
2001	Alex Rodriguez, Tex 52
2002	Alex Rodriguez, Tex 57
2003	Alex Rodriguez, Tex 47
2004	Manny Ramirez, Bos. 43

Runs Batted In
National League

Multiple winners: Hank Aaron, Rogers Hornsby, Sherry Magee, Mike Schmidt and Honus Wagner (4); Johnny Bench, George Foster, Joe Medwick, Johnny Mize and Heinie Zimmerman (3); Ernie Banks, Jim Bottomley, Orlando Cepeda, Gavvy Cravath, Andres Galarraga, George Kelly, Chuck Klein, Willie McCovey, Dale Murphy, Stan Musial, Bill Nicholson, Sammy Sosa and Hack Wilson (2).

Year	RBI
1900	Elmer Flick, Phi 110
1901	Honus Wagner, Pit 126
1902	Honus Wagner, Pit 91
1903	Sam Mertes, NY. 104
1904	Bill Dahlen, NY 80
1905	Cy Seymour, Cin 121
1906	Jim Nealon, Pit. 83
	& Harry Steinfeldt, Chi. . . 83
1907	Sherry Magee, Phi 85
1908	Honus Wagner, Pit 109
1909	Honus Wagner, Pit 100
1910	Sherry Magee, Phi 123
1911	Wildfire Schulte, Chi. . . . 121
1912	Heinie Zimmerman, Chi. . 103
1913	Gavvy Cravath, Phi. 128
1914	Sherry Magee, Phi 103
1915	Gavvy Cravath, Phi. 115
1916	Heinie Zimmerman, Chi-NY .83
1917	Heinie Zimmerman, NY. . 102
1918	Sherry Magee, Cin. 76
1919	Hy Myers, Bklyn 73
1920	Rogers Hornsby, St.L. 94
	& George Kelly, NY 94
1921	Rogers Hornsby, St.L 126
1922	Rogers Hornsby, St.L 152
1923	Irish Meusel, NY. 125
1924	George Kelly, NY. 136

Year	RBI
1925	Rogers Hornsby, St.L 143
1926	Jim Bottomley, St.L. 120
1927	Paul Waner, Pit. 131
1928	Jim Bottomley, St.L. 136
1929	Hack Wilson, Chi. 159
1930	Hack Wilson, Chi. 191
1931	Chuck Klein, Phi 121
1932	Don Hurst, Phi. 143
1933	Chuck Klein, Phi 120
1934	Mel Ott, NY. 135
1935	Wally Berger, Bos. 130
1936	Joe Medwick, St.L. 138
1937	Joe Medwick, St.L. 154
1938	Joe Medwick, St.L. 122
1939	Frank McCormick, Cin . . 128
1940	Johnny Mize, St.L. 137
1941	Dolph Camilli, Bklyn 120
1942	Johnny Mize, NY 110
1943	Bill Nicholson, Chi 128
1944	Bill Nicholson, Chi 122
1945	Dixie Walker, Bklyn. 124
1946	Enos Slaughter, St.L. 130
1947	Johnny Mize, NY 138
1948	Stan Musial, St.L. 131
1949	Ralph Kiner, Pit. 127
1950	Del Ennis, Phi. 126
1951	Monte Irvin, NY 121

Year	RBI
1952	Hank Sauer, Chi. 121
1953	Roy Campanella, Bklyn . . 142
1954	Ted Kluszewski, Cin 141
1955	Duke Snider, Bklyn 136
1956	Stan Musial, St.L. 109
1957	Hank Aaron, Mil 132
1958	Ernie Banks, Chi. 129
1959	Ernie Banks, Chi. 143
1960	Hank Aaron, Mil 126
1961	Orlando Cepeda, SF. . . . 142
1962	Tommy Davis, LA 153
1963	Hank Aaron, Mil 130
1964	Ken Boyer, St.L. 119
1965	Deron Johnson, Cin. 130
1966	Hank Aaron, Atl 127
1967	Orlando Cepeda, St.L . . . 111
1968	Willie McCovey, SF 105
1969	Willie McCovey, SF 126
1970	Johnny Bench, Cin 148
1971	Joe Torre, St.L. 137
1972	Johnny Bench, Cin 125
1973	Willie Stargell, Pit. 119
1974	Johnny Bench, Cin 129
1975	Greg Luzinski, Phi. 120
1976	George Foster, Cin. 121
1977	George Foster, Cin. 149
1978	George Foster, Cin. 120

Runs Batted In (Cont.)

Year		RBI
1979	Dave Winfield, SD	118
1980	Mike Schmidt, Phi.	121
1981	Mike Schmidt, Phi.	91
1982	Dale Murphy, Atl	109
	& Al Oliver, Mon	109
1983	Dale Murphy, Atl	121
1984	Gary Carter, Mon.	106
	& Mike Schmidt, Phi.	106
1985	Dave Parker, Cin	125
1986	Mike Schmidt, Phi.	119

Year		RBI
1987	Andre Dawson, Chi	137
1988	Will Clark, SF	109
1989	Kevin Mitchell, SF.	125
1990	Matt Williams, SF.	122
1991	Howard Johnson, NY	117
1992	Darren Daulton, Phi.	109
1993	Barry Bonds, SF	123
1994	Jeff Bagwell, Hou	116
1995	Dante Bichette, Col.	128
1996	Andres Galarraga, Col	150

Year		RBI
1997	Andres Galarraga, Col	140
1998	Sammy Sosa, Chi.	158
1999	Mark McGwire, St.L.	147
2000	Todd Helton, Col	147
2001	Sammy Sosa, Chi.	160
2002	Lance Berkman, Hou	128
2003	Preston Wilson, Col	141
2004	Vinny Castilla, Col	131

American League

Multiple winners: Babe Ruth (6); Lou Gehrig (5); Ty Cobb, Hank Greenberg and Ted Williams (4); Albert Belle, Sam Crawford, Cecil Fielder, Jimmie Foxx, Jackie Jensen, Harmon Killebrew, Vern Stephens and Bobby Veach (3); Home Run Baker, Cecil Cooper, Harry Davis, Joe DiMaggio, Buck Freeman, Nap Lajoie, Roger Maris, Jim Rice, Al Rosen, and Bobby Veach (2).

Year		RBI
1901	Nap Lajoie, Phi.	125
1902	Buck Freeman, Bos.	121
1903	Buck Freeman, Bos.	104
1904	Nap Lajoie, Cle	102
1905	Harry Davis, Phi.	83
1906	Harry Davis, Phi.	96
1907	Ty Cobb, Det.	116
1908	Ty Cobb, Det.	108
1909	Ty Cobb, Det.	107
1910	Sam Crawford, Det.	120
1911	Ty Cobb, Det.	144
1912	Home Run Baker, Phi.	133
1913	Home Run Baker, Phi.	126
1914	Sam Crawford, Det.	104
1915	Sam Crawford, Det.	112
	& Bobby Veach, Det	112
1916	Del Pratt, St.L.	103
1917	Bobby Veach, Det.	103
1918	Bobby Veach, Det.	78
1919	Babe Ruth, Bos	114
1920	Babe Ruth, NY	137
1921	Babe Ruth, NY	171
1922	Ken Williams, St.L.	155
1923	Babe Ruth, NY	131
1924	Goose Goslin, Wash.	129
1925	Bob Meusel, NY.	138
1926	Babe Ruth, NY.	145
1927	Lou Gehrig, NY	175
1928	Lou Gehrig, NY	142
	& Babe Ruth, NY	142
1929	Al Simmons, Phi	157
1930	Lou Gehrig, NY	174
1931	Lou Gehrig, NY	184
1932	Jimmie Foxx, Phi.	169
1933	Jimmie Foxx, Phi.	163
1934	Lou Gehrig, NY	165
1935	Hank Greenberg, Det	170

Year		RBI
1936	Hal Trosky, Cle.	162
1937	Hank Greenberg, Det	183
1938	Jimmie Foxx, Bos	175
1939	Ted Williams, Bos.	145
1940	Hank Greenberg, Det	150
1941	Joe DiMaggio, NY.	125
1942	Ted Williams, Bos.	137
1943	Rudy York, Det	118
1944	Vern Stephens, St.L.	109
1945	Nick Etten, NY	111
1946	Hank Greenberg, Det	127
1947	Ted Williams, Bos.	114
1948	Joe DiMaggio, NY.	155
1949	Ted Williams, Bos.	159
	& Vern Stephens, Bos.	159
1950	Walt Dropo, Bos.	144
	& Vern Stephens, Bos.	144
1951	Gus Zernial, Chi-Phi.	129
1952	Al Rosen, Cle.	105
1953	Al Rosen, Cle.	145
1954	Larry Doby, Cle.	126
1955	Ray Boone, Det.	116
	& Jackie Jensen, Bos.	116
1956	Mickey Mantle, NY.	130
1957	Roy Sievers, Wash	114
1958	Jackie Jensen, Bos.	122
1959	Jackie Jensen, Bos.	112
1960	Roger Maris, NY	112
1961	Roger Maris, NY	142
1962	Harmon Killebrew, Min .	126
1963	Dick Stuart, Bos.	118
1964	Brooks Robinson, Bal	118
1965	Rocky Colavito, Cle	108
1966	Frank Robinson, Bal	122
1967	Carl Yastrzemski, Bos	121
1968	Ken Harrelson, Bos	109
1969	Harmon Killebrew, Min .	140

Year		RBI
1970	Frank Howard, Wash	126
1971	Harmon Killebrew, Min.	119
1972	Dick Allen, Chi.	113
1973	Reggie Jackson, Oak.	117
1974	Jeff Burroughs, Tex	118
1975	George Scott, Mil.	109
1976	Lee May, Bal	109
1977	Larry Hisle, Min	119
1978	Jim Rice, Bos	139
1979	Don Baylor, Cal	139
1980	Cecil Cooper, Mil.	122
1981	Eddie Murray, Bal.	78
1982	Hal McRae, KC.	133
1983	Cecil Cooper, Mil.	126
	& Jim Rice, Bos.	126
1984	Tony Armas, Bos.	123
1985	Don Mattingly, NY	145
1986	Joe Carter, Cle.	121
1987	George Bell, Tor	134
1988	Jose Canseco, Oak.	124
1989	Ruben Sierra, Tex	119
1990	Cecil Fielder, Det	132
1991	Cecil Fielder, Det	133
1992	Cecil Fielder, Det	124
1993	Albert Belle, Cle.	129
1994	Kirby Puckett, Min.	112
1995	Albert Belle, Cle.	126
	& Mo Vaughn, Bos.	126
1996	Albert Belle, Cle.	148
1997	Ken Griffey Jr., Sea.	147
1998	Juan Gonzalez, Tex.	157
1999	Manny Ramirez, Cle.	165
2000	Edgar Martinez, Sea.	145
2001	Bret Boone, Sea	141
2002	Alex Rodriguez, Tex.	142
2003	Carlos Delgado, Tor	145
2004	Miguel Tejada, Bal	150

Batting Triple Crown Winners

Players who led either league in Batting Average, Home Runs and Runs Batted In over a single season.

National League

	Year	Avg	HR	RBI
Paul Hines, Providence	1878	.358	4	50
Hugh Duffy, Boston	1894	.438	18	145
Heinie Zimmerman, Chicago	1912	.372	14	103
Rogers Hornsby, St. Louis	1922	.401	42	152
Rogers Hornsby, St. Louis	1925	.403	39	143
Chuck Klein, Philadelphia	1933	.368	28	120
Joe Medwick, St. Louis	1937	.374	31*	154

*Tied for league lead in HRs with Mel Ott, NY.

American League

	Year	Avg	HR	RBI
Nap Lajoie, Philadelphia	1901	.422	14	125
Ty Cobb, Detroit	1909	.377	9	115
Jimmie Foxx, Philadelphia	1933	.356	48	163
Lou Gehrig, New York	1934	.363	49	165
Ted Williams, Boston	1942	.356	36	137
Ted Williams, Boston	1947	.343	32	114
Mickey Mantle, New York	1956	.353	52	130
Frank Robinson, Baltimore	1966	.316	49	122
Carl Yastrzemski, Boston	1967	.326	44*	121

*Tied for league lead in HRs with Harmon Killebrew, Min.

Stolen Bases
National League

Multiple winners: Max Carey (10); Lou Brock (8); Vince Coleman and Maury Wills (6); Honus Wagner (5); Bob Bescher, Kiki Cuyler, Willie Mays and Tim Raines (4); Bill Bruton, Frankie Frisch, Pepper Martin and Tony Womack (3); George Burns, Luis Castillo, Frank Chance, Augie Galan, Marquis Grissom, Stan Hack, Sam Jethroe, Davey Lopes, Omar Moreno, Pete Reiser and Jackie Robinson (2).

Year		SB	Year		SB	Year		SB
1900	Patsy Donovan, St.L	45	1934	Pepper Martin, St.L	23	1970	Bobby Tolan, Cin	57
	& George Van Haltren, NY.	45	1935	Augie Galan, Chi	22	1971	Lou Brock, St.L	64
1901	Honus Wagner, Pit	49	1936	Pepper Martin, St.L	23	1972	Lou Brock, St.L	63
1902	Honus Wagner, Pit	42	1937	Augie Galan, Chi	23	1973	Lou Brock, St.L	70
1903	Frank Chance, Chi	67	1938	Stan Hack, Chi	16	1974	Lou Brock, St.L	118
	& Jimmy Sheckard, Bklyn.	67	1939	Stan Hack, Chi	17	1975	Davey Lopes, LA.	77
1904	Honus Wagner, Pit	53		& Lee Handley, Pit	17	1976	Davey Lopes, LA.	63
1905	Art Devlin, NY.	59				1977	Frank Taveras, Pit	70
	& Billy Maloney, Chi	59	1940	Lonny Frey, Cin	22	1978	Omar Moreno, Pit.	71
1906	Frank Chance, Chi	57	1941	Danny Murtaugh, Phi	18	1979	Omar Moreno, Pit.	77
1907	Honus Wagner, Pit	61	1942	Pete Reiser, Bklyn	20			
1908	Honus Wagner, Pit	53	1943	Arky Vaughan, Bklyn	20	1980	Ron LeFlore, Mon	97
1909	Bob Bescher, Cin	54	1944	Johnny Barrett, Pit	28	1981	Tim Raines, Mon.	71
			1945	Red Schoendienst, St.L	26	1982	Tim Raines, Mon.	78
1910	Bob Bescher, Cin	70	1946	Pete Reiser, Bklyn	34	1983	Tim Raines, Mon.	90
1911	Bob Bescher, Cin	81	1947	Jackie Robinson, Bklyn.	29	1984	Tim Raines, Mon.	75
1912	Bob Bescher, Cin	67	1948	Richie Ashburn, Phi.	32	1985	Vince Coleman, St.L	110
1913	Max Carey, Pit	61	1949	Jackie Robinson, Bklyn.	37	1986	Vince Coleman, St.L.	107
1914	George Burns, NY	62				1987	Vince Coleman, St.L	109
1915	Max Carey, Pit	36	1950	Sam Jethroe, Bos.	35	1988	Vince Coleman, St.L	81
1916	Max Carey, Pit	63	1951	Sam Jethroe, Bos.	35	1989	Vince Coleman, St.L	65
1917	Max Carey, Pit	46	1952	Pee Wee Reese, Bklyn.	30			
1918	Max Carey, Pit	58	1953	Bill Bruton, Mil.	26	1990	Vince Coleman, St.L	77
1919	George Burns, NY	40	1954	Bill Bruton, Mil.	34	1991	Marquis Grissom, Mon	76
			1955	Bill Bruton, Mil.	25	1992	Marquis Grissom, Mon	78
1920	Max Carey, Pit	52	1956	Willie Mays, NY.	40	1993	Chuck Carr, Fla.	58
1921	Frankie Frisch, NY	49	1957	Willie Mays, NY.	38	1994	Craig Biggio, Hou	39
1922	Max Carey, Pit	51	1958	Willie Mays, SF	31	1995	Quilvio Veras, Fla	56
1923	Max Carey, Pit	51	1959	Willie Mays, SF	27	1996	Eric Young, Col	53
1924	Max Carey, Pit	49				1997	Tony Womack, Pit	60
1925	Max Carey, Pit	46	1960	Maury Wills, LA.	50	1998	Tony Womack, Pit	58
1926	Kiki Cuyler, Pit.	35	1961	Maury Wills, LA.	35	1999	Tony Womack, Ari	72
1927	Frankie Frisch, St.L	48	1962	Maury Wills, LA.	104			
1928	Kiki Cuyler, Chi.	37	1963	Maury Wills, LA.	40	2000	Luis Castillo, Fla	62
1929	Kiki Cuyler, Chi.	43	1964	Maury Wills, LA.	53	2001	Juan Pierre, Col.	46
1930	Kiki Cuyler, Chi.	37	1965	Maury Wills, LA.	94		& Jimmy Rollins, Phi	46
1931	Frankie Frisch, St.L	28	1966	Lou Brock, St.L	74	2002	Luis Castillo, Fla	48
1932	Chuck Klein, Phi	20	1967	Lou Brock, St.L	52	2003	Juan Pierre, Fla.	65
1933	Pepper Martin, St.L	26	1968	Lou Brock, St.L	62	2004	Scott Podsednik, Mil	70
			1969	Lou Brock, St.L	53			

30 Homers & 30 Stolen Bases in One Season
National League

	Year	Gm	HR	SB
Willie Mays, NY Giants	1956	152	36	40
Willie Mays, NY Giants	1957	152	35	38
Hank Aaron, Milwaukee	1963	161	44	31
Bobby Bonds, San Francisco	1969	158	32	45
Bobby Bonds, San Francisco	1973	160	39	43
Dale Murphy, Atlanta	1983	162	36	30
Eric Davis, Cincinnati	1987	129	37	50
Howard Johnson, NY Mets.	1987	157	36	32
Darryl Strawberry, NY Mets.	1987	154	39	36
Howard Johnson, NY Mets.	1989	153	36	41
Ron Gant, Atlanta	1990	152	32	33
Barry Bonds, Pittsburgh	1990	151	33	52
Ron Gant, Atlanta	1991	154	32	34
Howard Johnson, NY Mets.	1991	156	38	30
Barry Bonds, Pittsburgh	1992	140	34	39
Sammy Sosa, Chicago	1993	159	33	36
Barry Bonds, San Francisco	1995	144	33	31
Sammy Sosa, Chicago	1995	144	36	34
Barry Bonds, San Francisco	1996	158	42	40
Ellis Burks, Colorado	1996	156	40	32
Dante Bichette, Colorado	1996	159	31	31
Barry Larkin, Cincinnati	1996	152	33	36
Larry Walker, Colorado	1997	153	49	33

	Year	Gm	HR	SB
Barry Bonds, San Francisco	1997	159	40	37
Raul Mondesi, Los Angeles.	1997	159	30	32
Jeff Bagwell, Houston	1997	162	43	31
Jeff Bagwell, Houston	1999	162	42	30
Raul Mondesi, Los Angeles.	1999	159	33	36
Preston Wilson, Florida	2000	161	31	36
Vladimir Guerrero, Montreal	2001	159	34	37
Bobby Abreu, Philadelphia.	2001	162	31	36
Vladimir Guerrero, Montreal	2002	161	39	40
Bobby Abreu, Philadelphia.	2004	159	30	40

American League

	Year	Gm	HR	SB
Kenny Williams, St. Louis	1922	153	39	37
Tommy Harper, Milwaukee	1970	154	31	38
Bobby Bonds, New York.	1975	145	32	30
Bobby Bonds, California.	1977	158	37	41
Bobby Bonds, Chicago-Texas.	1978	156	31	43
Joe Carter, Cleveland	1987	149	32	31
Jose Canseco, Oakland	1988	158	42	40
Alex Rodriguez, Seattle.	1998	161	42	46
Shawn Green, Toronto	1998	158	35	35
Jose Cruz Jr., Toronto.	2001	146	34	32
Alfonso Soriano, New York	2002	156	39	41
Alfonso Soriano, New York	2003	156	38	35

Note: In 2004, Carlos Beltran switched leagues mid-season. Combining his AL and NL totals, he hit 38 HR and stole 42 bases.

Stolen Bases (Cont.)
American League

Multiple winners: Rickey Henderson (12); Luis Aparicio (9); Bert Campaneris, George Case and Ty Cobb (6); Kenny Lofton (5); Ben Chapman, Eddie Collins and George Sisler (4); Bob Dillinger, Minnie Minoso and Bill Werber (3); Carl Crawford, Elmer Flick, Tommy Harper, Brian Hunter, Clyde Milan, Johnny Mostil, Bill North and Snuffy Stirnweiss (2).

Year		SB	Year		SB	Year		SB
1901	Frank Isbell, Chi	52	1936	Lyn Lary, St.L	37	1970	Bert Campaneris, Oak.	42
1902	Topsy Hartsel, Phi	47	1937	Ben Chapman, Wash-Bos	35	1971	Amos Otis, KC	52
1903	Harry Bay, Cle	45		& Bill Werber, Phi	35	1972	Bert Campaneris, Oak.	52
1904	Elmer Flick, Cle	42	1938	Frank Crosetti, NY	27	1973	Tommy Harper, Bos	54
1905	Danny Hoffman, Phi	46	1939	George Case, Wash.	51	1974	Bill North, Oak.	54
1906	John Anderson, Wash.	39	1940	George Case, Wash.	35	1975	Mickey Rivers, CA	70
	& Elmer Flick, Cle	39	1941	George Case, Wash.	33	1976	Bill North, Oak.	75
1907	Ty Cobb, Det	49	1942	George Case, Wash.	44	1977	Freddie Patek, KC	53
1908	Patsy Dougherty, Chi	47	1943	George Case, Wash.	61	1978	Ron LeFlore, Det	68
1909	Ty Cobb, Det	76	1944	Snuffy Stirnweiss, NY.	55	1979	Willie Wilson, KC.	83
1910	Eddie Collins, Phi	81	1945	Snuffy Stirnweiss, NY.	33	1980	Rickey Henderson, Oak.	100
1911	Ty Cobb, Det	83	1946	George Case, Cle	28	1981	Rickey Henderson, Oak.	56
1912	Clyde Milan, Wash.	88	1947	Bob Dillinger, St.L	34	1982	Rickey Henderson, Oak.	130
1913	Clyde Milan, Wash.	75	1948	Bob Dillinger, St.L	28	1983	Rickey Henderson, Oak.	108
1914	Fritz Maisel, NY	74	1949	Bob Dillinger, St.L	20	1984	Rickey Henderson, Oak.	66
1915	Ty Cobb, Det	96	1950	Dom DiMaggio, Bos.	15	1985	Rickey Henderson, NY.	80
1916	Ty Cobb, Det	68	1951	Minnie Minoso, Cle-Chi.	31	1986	Rickey Henderson, NY.	87
1917	Ty Cobb, Det	55	1952	Minnie Minoso, Chi	22	1987	Harold Reynolds, Sea	60
1918	George Sisler, St.L	45	1953	Minnie Minoso, Chi	25	1988	Rickey Henderson, NY.	93
1919	Eddie Collins, Chi.	33	1954	Jackie Jensen, Bos.	22	1989	R. Henderson, NY-Oak	77
1920	Sam Rice, Wash.	63	1955	Jim Rivera, Chi.	25	1990	Rickey Henderson, Oak.	65
1921	George Sisler, St.L	35	1956	Luis Aparicio, Chi.	21	1991	Rickey Henderson, Oak.	58
1922	George Sisler, St.L	51	1957	Luis Aparicio, Chi.	28	1992	Kenny Lofton, Cle	66
1923	Eddie Collins, Chi.	47	1958	Luis Aparicio, Chi.	29	1993	Kenny Lofton, Cle	70
1924	Eddie Collins, Chi.	42	1959	Luis Aparicio, Chi.	56	1994	Kenny Lofton, Cle	60
1925	Johnny Mostil, Chi	43	1960	Luis Aparicio, Chi.	51	1995	Kenny Lofton, Cle	54
1926	Johnny Mostil, Chi	35	1961	Luis Aparicio, Chi.	53	1996	Kenny Lofton, Cle	75
1927	George Sisler, St.L	27	1962	Luis Aparicio, Chi.	31	1997	Brian Hunter, Det	74
1928	Buddy Myer, Bos.	30	1963	Luis Aparicio, Bal	40	1998	Rickey Henderson, Oak.	66
1929	Charlie Gehringer, Det.	28	1964	Luis Aparicio, Bal	57	1999	Brian Hunter, Det-Sea.	44
1930	Marty McManus, Det	23	1965	Bert Campaneris, KC	51	2000	Johnny Damon, KC.	46
1931	Ben Chapman, NY.	61	1966	Bert Campaneris, KC	52	2001	Ichiro Suzuki, Sea.	56
1932	Ben Chapman, NY.	38	1967	Bert Campaneris, KC	55	2002	Alfonso Soriano, NY.	41
1933	Ben Chapman, NY.	27	1968	Bert Campaneris, Oak.	62	2003	Carl Crawford, TB	55
1934	Bill Werber, Bos	40	1969	Tommy Harper, Sea	73	2004	Carl Crawford, TB	59
1935	Bill Werber, Bos	29						

Consecutive Game Streaks
(Regular season games through 2004)

Games Played

Gm		Dates of Streak
2632	Cal Ripken Jr., Bal	5/30/82 to 9/19/98
2130	Lou Gehrig, NY	6/1/25 to 4/30/39
1307	Everett Scott, Bos-NY	6/20/16 to 5/5/25
1207	Steve Garvey, LA-SD.	9/3/75 to 7/29/83
1117	Billy Williams, Cubs	9/22/63 to 9/2/70
1103	Joe Sewell, Cle	9/13/22 to 4/30/30
895	Stan Musial, St.L	4/15/52 to 8/23/57
829	Eddie Yost, Wash	4/30/49 to 5/11/55
822	Gus Suhr, Pit	9/11/31 to 6/4/37
798	Nellie Fox, Chisox.	8/8/55 to 9/3/60
756	Miguel Tejada, Oak-Bal	6/1/00 to present
745	Pete Rose, Cin-Phi	9/2/78 to 8/23/83
740	Dale Murphy, Atl.	9/26/81 to 7/8/86
730	Richie Ashburn, Phi	6/7/50 to 4/13/55
717	Ernie Banks, Cubs.	8/28/56 to 6/22/61
678	Pete Rose, Cin	9/28/73 to 5/7/78

Others

Gm		Gm	
673	Earl Averill	565	Aaron Ward
652	Frank McCormick	546	Alex Rodriguez
648	Sandy Alomar Sr.	540	Candy LaChance
618	Eddie Brown	535	Buck Freeman
585	Roy McMillan	533	Fred Luderus
577	George Pinckney	511	Clyde Milan
574	Steve Brodie	511	Charlie Gehringer

Hitting

		Gm	Year
Joe DiMaggio, New York (AL)		56	1941
Willie Keeler, Baltimore (NL).		44	1897
Pete Rose, Cincinnati (NL)		44	1978
Bill Dahlen, Chicago (NL)		42	1894
George Sisler, St. Louis (AL)		41	1922
Ty Cobb, Detroit (AL)		40	1911
Paul Molitor, Milwaukee (AL)		39	1987
Tommy Holmes, Boston (NL)		37	1945
Billy Hamilton, Philadelphia (NL)		36	1894
Fred Clarke, Louisville (NL)		35	1895
Ty Cobb, Detroit (AL)		35	1917
Luis Castillo, Florida (NL).		35	2002
Ty Cobb, Detroit (AL)		34	1912
George Sisler, St. Louis (AL)		34	1925
George McQuinn, St. Louis (AL).		34	1938
Dom DiMaggio, Boston (AL)		34	1949
Benito Santiago, San Diego (NL)		34	1987
George Davis, New York (NL)		33	1893
Hal Chase, New York (AL)		33	1907
Rogers Hornsby, St. Louis (NL)		33	1922
Heinie Manush, Washington (AL).		33	1933
Ed Delahanty, Philadelphia (NL).		31	1899
Nap Lajoie, Cleveland (AL).		31	1906
Sam Rice, Washington, (AL)		31	1924
Willie Davis, Los Angeles (NL)		31	1969
Rico Carty, Atlanta (NL)		31	1970
Ken Landreaux, Minnesota (AL)		31	1980
Vladimir Guerrero, Montreal (NL)		31	1999

Annual Pitching Leaders (since 1900)
Winning Percentage
At least 15 wins, except in strike years of 1981 and 1994 (when the minimum was 10).

National League

Multiple winners: Ed Reulbach and Tom Seaver (3); Larry Benton, Harry Brecheen, Jack Chesbro, Paul Derringer, Freddie Fitzsimmons, Don Gullett, Claude Hendrix, Carl Hubbell, Randy Johnson, Sandy Koufax, Bill Lee, Greg Maddux, Christy Mathewson, Don Newcombe, Preacher Roe and John Smoltz (2).

Year		W-L	Pct	Year		W-L	Pct
1900	Jesse Tannehill, Pittsburgh	20-6	.769	1953	Carl Erskine, Brooklyn	20-6	.769
1901	Jack Chesbro, Pittsburgh	21-10	.677	1954	Johnny Antonelli, New York	21-7	.750
1902	Jack Chesbro, Pittsburgh	28-6	.824	1955	Don Newcombe, Brooklyn	20-5	.800
1903	Sam Leever, Pittsburgh	25-7	.781	1956	Don Newcombe, Brooklyn	27-7	.794
1904	Joe McGinnity, New York	35-8	.814	1957	Bob Buhl, Milwaukee	18-7	.720
1905	Christy Mathewson, New York	31-8	.795	1958	Warren Spahn, Milwaukee	22-11	.667
1906	Ed Reulbach, Chicago	19-4	.826		& Lew Burdette, Milwaukee	20-10	.667
1907	Ed Reulbach, Chicago	17-4	.810	1959	Roy Face, Pittsburgh	18-1	.947
1908	Ed Reulbach, Chicago	24-7	.774				
1909	Howie Camnitz, Pittsburgh	25-6	.806	1960	Ernie Broglio, St. Louis	21-9	.700
	& Christy Mathewson, New York	25-6	.806	1961	Johnny Podres, Los Angeles	18-5	.783
				1962	Bob Purkey, Cincinnati	23-5	.821
1910	King Cole, Chicago	20-4	.833	1963	Ron Perranoski, Los Angeles	16-3	.842
1911	Rube Marquard, New York	24-7	.774	1964	Sandy Koufax, Los Angeles	19-5	.792
1912	Claude Hendrix, Pittsburgh	24-9	.727	1965	Sandy Koufax, Los Angeles	26-8	.765
1913	Bert Humphries, Chicago	16-4	.800	1966	Juan Marichal, San Francisco	25-6	.806
1914	Bill James, Boston	26-7	.788	1967	Dick Hughes, St. Louis	16-6	.727
1915	Grover Alexander, Phila.	31-10	.756	1968	Steve Blass, Pittsburgh	18-6	.750
1916	Tom Hughes, Boston	16-3	.842	1969	Tom Seaver, New York	25-7	.781
1917	Ferdie Schupp, New York	21-7	.750				
1918	Claude Hendrix, Chicago	19-7	.731	1970	Bob Gibson, St. Louis	23-7	.767
1919	Dutch Ruether, Cincinnati	19-6	.760	1971	Don Gullett, Cincinnati	16-6	.727
				1972	Gary Nolan, Cincinnati	15-5	.750
1920	Burleigh Grimes, Brooklyn	23-11	.676	1973	Tommy John, Los Angeles	16-7	.696
1921	Bill Doak, St. Louis	15-6	.714	1974	Andy Messersmith, Los Angeles	20-6	.769
1922	Pete Donohue, Cincinnati	18-9	.667	1975	Don Gullett, Cincinnati	15-4	.789
1923	Dolf Luque, Cincinnati	27-8	.771	1976	Steve Carlton, Philadelphia	20-7	.741
1924	Emil Yde, Pittsburgh	16-3	.842	1977	John Candelaria, Pittsburgh	20-5	.800
1925	Bill Sherdel, St. Louis	15-6	.714	1978	Gaylord Perry, San Diego	21-6	.778
1926	Ray Kremer, Pittsburgh	20-6	.769	1979	Tom Seaver, Cincinnati	16-6	.727
1927	Larry Benton, Boston-NY	17-7	.708				
1928	Larry Benton, New York	25-9	.735	1980	Jim Bibby, Pittsburgh	19-6	.760
1929	Charlie Root, Chicago	19-6	.760	1981	Tom Seaver, Cincinnati	14-2	.875
				1982	Phil Niekro, Atlanta	17-4	.810
1930	Freddie Fitzsimmons, NY	19-7	.731	1983	John Denny, Philadelphia	19-6	.760
1931	Paul Derringer, St. Louis	18-8	.692	1984	Rick Sutcliffe, Chicago	16-1	.941
1932	Lon Warneke, Chicago	22-6	.786	1985	Orel Hershiser, Los Angeles	19-3	.864
1933	Ben Cantwell, Boston	20-10	.667	1986	Bob Ojeda, New York	18-5	.783
1934	Dizzy Dean, St. Louis	30-7	.811	1987	Dwight Gooden, New York	15-7	.682
1935	Bill Lee, Chicago	20-6	.769	1988	David Cone, New York	20-3	.870
1936	Carl Hubbell, New York	26-6	.813	1989	Mike Bielecki, Chicago	18-7	.720
1937	Carl Hubbell, New York	22-8	.733				
1938	Bill Lee, Chicago	22-9	.710	1990	Doug Drabek, Pittsburgh	22-6	.786
1939	Paul Derringer, Cincinnati	25-7	.781	1991	John Smiley, Pittsburgh	20-8	.714
					& Jose Rijo, Cincinnati	15-6	.714
1940	Freddie Fitzsimmons, Bklyn	16-2	.889	1992	Bob Tewksbury, St. Louis	16-5	.762
1941	Elmer Riddle, Cincinnati	19-4	.826	1993	Mark Portugal, Houston	18-4	.818
1942	Larry French, Brooklyn	15-4	.789	1994	Marvin Freeman, Colorado	10-2	.833
1943	Mort Cooper, St. Louis	21-8	.724	1995	Greg Maddux, Atlanta	19-2	.905
1944	Ted Wilks, St. Louis	17-4	.810	1996	John Smoltz, Atlanta	24-8	.750
1945	Harry Brecheen, St. Louis	14-4	.778	1997	Greg Maddux, Atlanta	19-4	.826
1946	Murray Dickson, St. Louis	15-6	.714	1998	John Smoltz, Atlanta	17-3	.850
1947	Larry Jansen, New York	21-5	.808	1999	Mike Hampton, Houston	22-4	.846
1948	Harry Brecheen, St. Louis	20-7	.741				
1949	Preacher Roe, Brooklyn	15-6	.714	2000	Randy Johnson, Arizona	19-7	.731
				2001	Curt Schilling, Arizona	22-6	.786
1950	Sal Maglie, New York	18-4	.818	2002	Randy Johnson, Arizona	24-5	.828
1951	Preacher Roe, Brooklyn	22-3	.880	2003	Jason Schmidt, San Francisco	17-5	.773
1952	Hoyt Wilhelm, New York	15-3	.833	2004	Roger Clemens, Houston	18-4	.818

Note: In 1984, Sutcliffe was also 4-5 with Cleveland for a combined AL-NL record of 20-6 (.769).

Winning Percentage (Cont.)

American League

Multiple winners: Lefty Grove (5); Chief Bender, Roger Clemens and Whitey Ford (3); Johnny Allen, Eddie Cicotte, Mike Cuellar, Lefty Gomez, Ron Guidry, Catfish Hunter, Randy Johnson, Walter Johnson, Pedro Martinez, Jim Palmer, Pete Vuckovich and Smokey Joe Wood (2).

Year		W-L	Pct	Year		W-L	Pct
1901	Clark Griffith, Chicago	24-7	.774	1954	Sandy Consuegra, Chicago	16-3	.842
1902	Bill Bernhard, Phila-Cleve	18-5	.783	1955	Tommy Byrne, New York	16-5	.762
1903	Cy Young, Boston	28-9	.757	1956	Whitey Ford, New York	19-6	.760
1904	Jack Chesbro, New York	41-12	.774	1957	Dick Donovan, Chicago	16-6	.727
1905	Andy Coakley, Philadelphia	20-7	.741		& Tom Sturdivant, New York	16-6	.727
1906	Eddie Plank, Philadelphia	19-6	.760	1958	Bob Turley, New York	21-7	.750
1907	Wild Bill Donovan, Detroit	25-4	.862	1959	Bob Shaw, Chicago	18-6	.750
1908	Ed Walsh, Chicago	40-15	.727	1960	Jim Perry, Cleveland	18-10	.643
1909	George Mullin, Detroit	29-8	.784	1961	Whitey Ford, New York	25-4	.862
1910	Chief Bender, Philadelphia	23-5	.821	1962	Ray Herbert, Chicago	20-9	.690
1911	Chief Bender, Philadelphia	17-5	.773	1963	Whitey Ford, New York	24-7	.774
1912	Smokey Joe Wood, Boston	34-5	.872	1964	Wally Bunker, Baltimore	19-5	.792
1913	Walter Johnson, Washington	36-7	.837	1965	Mudcat Grant, Minnesota	21-7	.750
1914	Chief Bender, Philadelphia	17-3	.850	1966	Sonny Siebert, Cleveland	16-8	.667
1915	Smokey Joe Wood, Boston	15-5	.750	1967	Joe Horlen, Chicago	19-7	.731
1916	Eddie Cicotte, Chicago	15-7	.682	1968	Denny McLain, Detroit	31-6	.838
1917	Reb Russell, Chicago	15-5	.750	1969	Jim Palmer, Baltimore	16-4	.800
1918	Sad Sam Jones, Boston	16-5	.762	1970	Mike Cuellar, Baltimore	24-8	.750
1919	Eddie Cicotte, Chicago	29-7	.806	1971	Dave McNally, Baltimore	21-5	.808
1920	Jim Bagby, Cleveland	31-12	.721	1972	Catfish Hunter, Oakland	21-7	.750
1921	Carl Mays, New York	27-9	.750	1973	Catfish Hunter, Oakland	21-5	.808
1922	Joe Bush, New York	26-7	.788	1974	Mike Cuellar, Baltimore	22-10	.688
1923	Herb Pennock, New York	19-6	.760	1975	Mike Torrez, Baltimore	20-9	.690
1924	Walter Johnson, Washington	23-7	.767	1976	Bill Campbell, Minnesota	17-5	.773
1925	Stan Coveleski, Washington	20-5	.800	1977	Paul Splittorff, Kansas City	16-6	.727
1926	George Uhle, Cleveland	27-11	.711	1978	Ron Guidry, New York	25-3	.893
1927	Waite Hoyt, New York	22-7	.759	1979	Mike Caldwell, Milwaukee	16-6	.727
1928	General Crowder, St. Louis	21-5	.808	1980	Steve Stone, Baltimore	25-7	.781
1929	Lefty Grove, Philadelphia	20-6	.769	1981	Pete Vuckovich, Milwaukee	14-4	.778
1930	Lefty Grove, Philadelphia	28-5	.848	1982	Pete Vuckovich, Milwaukee	18-6	.750
1931	Lefty Grove, Philadelphia	31-4	.886		& Jim Palmer, Baltimore	15-5	.750
1932	Johnny Allen, New York	17-4	.810	1983	Rich Dotson, Chicago	22-7	.759
1933	Lefty Grove, Philadelphia	24-8	.750	1984	Doyle Alexander, Toronto	17-6	.739
1934	Lefty Gomez, New York	26-5	.839	1985	Ron Guidry, New York	22-6	.786
1935	Eldon Auker, Detroit	18-7	.720	1986	Roger Clemens, Boston	24-4	.857
1936	Monte Pearson, New York	19-7	.731	1987	Roger Clemens, Boston	20-9	.690
1937	Johnny Allen, Cleveland	15-1	.938	1988	Frank Viola, Minnesota	24-7	.774
1938	Red Ruffing, New York	21-7	.750	1989	Bret Saberhagen, Kansas City	23-6	.793
1939	Lefty Grove, Boston	15-4	.789	1990	Bob Welch, Oakland	27-6	.818
1940	Schoolboy Rowe, Detroit	16-3	.842	1991	Scott Erickson, Minnesota	20-8	.714
1941	Lefty Gomez, New York	15-5	.750	1992	Mike Mussina, Baltimore	18-5	.783
1942	Ernie Bonham, New York	21-5	.808	1993	Jimmy Key, New York	18-6	.750
1943	Spud Chandler, New York	20-4	.833	1994	Jason Bere, Chicago	12-2	.857
1944	Tex Hughson, Boston	18-5	.783	1995	Randy Johnson, Seattle	18-2	.900
1945	Hal Newhouser, Detroit	25-9	.735	1996	Charles Nagy, Cleveland	17-5	.773
1946	Boo Ferriss, Boston	25-6	.806	1997	Randy Johnson, Seattle	20-4	.833
1947	Allie Reynolds, New York	19-8	.704	1998	David Wells, New York	18-4	.818
1948	Jack Kramer, Boston	18-5	.783	1999	Pedro Martinez, Boston	23-4	.852
1949	Ellis Kinder, Boston	23-6	.793	2000	Tim Hudson, Oakland	20-6	.769
1950	Vic Raschi, New York	21-8	.724	2001	Roger Clemens, New York	20-3	.870
1951	Bob Feller, Cleveland	22-8	.733	2002	Pedro Martinez, Boston	20-4	.833
1952	Bobby Shantz, Philadelphia	24-7	.774	2003	Roy Halladay, Toronto	22-7	.759
1953	Ed Lopat, New York	16-4	.800	2004	Curt Schilling, Boston	21-6	.778

Earned Run Average

Earned Run Averages were based on at least 10 complete games pitched (1900-49), at least 154 innings pitched (1950-60), and at least 162 innings pitched since 1961 in the AL and 1962 in the NL. In the strike years of 1981, '94 and '95, qualifiers had to pitch at least as many innings as the total number of games their team played that season.

National League

Multiple winners: Grover Alexander, Sandy Koufax and Christy Mathewson (5); Greg Maddux (4); Carl Hubbell, Randy Johnson, Tom Seaver, Warren Spahn and Dazzy Vance (3); Kevin Brown, Bill Doak, Ray Kremer, Dolf Luque, Howie Pollet, Nolan Ryan, Bill Walker and Bucky Walters (2).

Year		ERA	Year		ERA	Year		ERA
1900	Rube Waddell, Pit	2.37	1935	Cy Blanton, Pit	2.58	1970	Tom Seaver, NY	2.81
1901	Jesse Tannehill, Pit	2.18	1936	Carl Hubbell, NY	2.31	1971	Tom Seaver, NY	1.76
1902	Jack Taylor, Chi	1.33	1937	Jim Turner, Bos	2.38	1972	Steve Carlton, Phi	1.97
1903	Sam Leever, Pit	2.06	1938	Bill Lee, Chi	2.66	1973	Tom Seaver, NY	2.08
1904	Joe McGinnity, NY	1.61	1939	Bucky Walters, Cin	2.29	1974	Buzz Capra, Atl	2.28
1905	Christy Mathewson, NY	1.27	1940	Bucky Walters, Cin	2.48	1975	Randy Jones, SD	2.24
1906	Three Finger Brown, Chi	1.04	1941	Elmer Riddle, Cin	2.24	1976	John Denny, St.L	2.52
1907	Jack Pfiester, Chi	1.15	1942	Mort Cooper, St.L	1.78	1977	John Candelaria, Pit	2.34
1908	Christy Mathewson, NY	1.43	1943	Howie Pollet, St.L	1.75	1978	Craig Swan, NY	2.43
1909	Christy Mathewson, NY	1.14	1944	Ed Heusser, Cin	2.38	1979	J.R. Richard, Hou	2.71
1910	George McQuillan, Phi	1.60	1945	Hank Borowy, Chi	2.13	1980	Don Sutton, LA	2.21
1911	Christy Mathewson, NY	1.99	1946	Howie Pollet, St.L	2.10	1981	Nolan Ryan, Hou	1.69
1912	Jeff Tesreau, NY	1.96	1947	Warren Spahn, Bos	2.33	1982	Steve Rogers, Mon	2.40
1913	Christy Mathewson, NY	2.06	1948	Harry Brecheen, St.L	2.24	1983	Atlee Hammaker, SF	2.25
1914	Bill Doak, St.L	1.72	1949	Dave Koslo, NY	2.50	1984	Alejandro Peña, LA	2.48
1915	Grover Alexander, Phi	1.22	1950	Jim Hearn, St.L-NY	2.49	1985	Dwight Gooden, NY	1.53
1916	Grover Alexander, Phi	1.55	1951	Chet Nichols, Bos	2.88	1986	Mike Scott, Hou	2.22
1917	Grover Alexander, Phi	1.86	1952	Hoyt Wilhelm, NY	2.43	1987	Nolan Ryan, Hou	2.76
1918	Hippo Vaughn, Chi	1.74	1953	Warren Spahn, Mil	2.10	1988	Joe Magrane, St.L	2.18
1919	Grover Alexander, Chi	1.72	1954	Johnny Antonelli, NY	2.30	1989	Scott Garrelts, SF	2.28
1920	Grover Alexander, Chi	1.91	1955	Bob Friend, Pit	2.83	1990	Danny Darwin, Hou	2.21
1921	Bill Doak, St.L	2.59	1956	Lew Burdette, Mil	2.70	1991	Dennis Martinez, Mon	2.39
1922	Rosy Ryan, NY	3.01	1957	Johnny Podres, Bklyn	2.66	1992	Bill Swift, SF	2.08
1923	Dolf Luque, Cin	1.93	1958	Stu Miller, SF	2.47	1993	Greg Maddux, Atl	2.36
1924	Dazzy Vance, Bklyn	2.16	1959	Sam Jones, SF	2.83	1994	Greg Maddux, Atl	1.56
1925	Dolf Luque, Cin	2.63	1960	Mike McCormick, SF	2.70	1995	Greg Maddux, Atl	1.63
1926	Ray Kremer, Pit	2.61	1961	Warren Spahn, Mil	3.02	1996	Kevin Brown, Fla.	1.89
1927	Ray Kremer, Pit	2.47	1962	Sandy Koufax, LA	2.54	1997	Pedro Martinez, Mon	1.90
1928	Dazzy Vance, Bklyn	2.09	1963	Sandy Koufax, LA	1.88	1998	Greg Maddux, Atl	2.22
1929	Bill Walker, NY	3.09	1964	Sandy Koufax, LA	1.74	1999	Randy Johnson, Ari.	2.48
1930	Dazzy Vance, Bklyn	2.61	1965	Sandy Koufax, LA	2.04	2000	Kevin Brown, LA	2.58
1931	Bill Walker, NY	2.26	1966	Sandy Koufax, LA	1.73	2001	Randy Johnson, Ari.	2.49
1932	Lon Warneke, Chi	2.37	1967	Phil Niekro, Atl	1.87	2002	Randy Johnson, Ari.	2.32
1933	Carl Hubbell, NY	1.66	1968	Bob Gibson, St.L	1.12	2003	Jason Schmidt, SF	2.34
1934	Carl Hubbell, NY	2.30	1969	Juan Marichal, SF	2.10	2004	Jake Peavy, SD	2.27

Note: In 1945, Borowy had a 3.13 ERA in 18 games with New York (AL) for a combined ERA of 2.65.

American League

Multiple winners: Lefty Grove (9); Roger Clemens (6); Walter Johnson (5); Pedro Martinez (4); Spud Chandler, Stan Coveleski, Red Faber, Whitey Ford, Lefty Gomez, Ron Guidry, Addie Joss, Hal Newhouser, Jim Palmer, Gary Peters, Luis Tiant and Ed Walsh (2).

Year		ERA	Year		ERA	Year		ERA
1901	Cy Young, Bos	1.62	1919	Walter Johnson, Wash	1.49	1937	Lefty Gomez, NY	2.33
1902	Ed Siever, Det	1.91	1920	Bob Shawkey, NY	2.45	1938	Lefty Grove, Bos	3.08
1903	Earl Moore, Cle	1.77	1921	Red Faber, Chi	2.48	1939	Lefty Grove, Bos	2.54
1904	Addie Joss, Cle	1.59	1922	Red Faber, Chi	2.80	1940	Ernie Bonham, NY	1.90
1905	Rube Waddell, Phi	1.48	1923	Stan Coveleski, Cle	2.76	1941	Thornton Lee, Chi	2.37
1906	Doc White, Chi	1.52	1924	Walter Johnson, Wash	2.72	1942	Ted Lyons, Chi	2.10
1907	Ed Walsh, Chi	1.60	1925	Stan Coveleski, Wash	2.84	1943	Spud Chandler, NY	1.64
1908	Addie Joss, Cle	1.16	1926	Lefty Grove, Phi	2.51	1944	Dizzy Trout, Det.	2.12
1909	Harry Krause, Phi	1.39	1927	Wilcy Moore, NY	2.28	1945	Hal Newhouser, Det	1.81
1910	Ed Walsh, Chi	1.27	1928	Garland Braxton, Wash	2.51	1946	Hal Newhouser, Det	1.94
1911	Vean Gregg, Cle	1.81	1929	Lefty Grove, Phi	2.81	1947	Spud Chandler, NY	2.46
1912	Walter Johnson, Wash	1.39	1930	Lefty Grove, Phi.	2.54	1948	Gene Bearden, Cle	2.43
1913	Walter Johnson, Wash	1.09	1931	Lefty Grove, Phi.	2.06	1949	Mel Parnell, Bos	2.77
1914	Dutch Leonard, Bos	1.01	1932	Lefty Grove, Phi.	2.84	1950	Early Wynn, Cle	3.20
1915	Smokey Joe Wood, Bos	1.49	1933	Monte Pearson, Cle	2.33	1951	Saul Rogovin, Det-Chi	2.78
1916	Babe Ruth, Bos	1.75	1934	Lefty Gomez, NY	2.33	1952	Allie Reynolds, NY	2.06
1917	Eddie Cicotte, Chi	1.53	1935	Lefty Grove, Bos	2.70	1953	Ed Lopat, NY	2.42
1918	Walter Johnson, Wash	1.27	1936	Lefty Grove, Bos	2.81	1954	Mike Garcia, Cle	2.64

Earned Run Average (Cont.)

Year		ERA
1955	Billy Pierce, Chi	1.97
1956	Whitey Ford, NY	2.47
1957	Bobby Shantz, NY	2.45
1958	Whitey Ford, NY	2.01
1959	Hoyt Wilhelm, Bal.	2.19
1960	Frank Baumann, Chi	2.67
1961	Dick Donovan, Wash	2.40
1962	Hank Aguirre, Det.	2.21
1963	Gary Peters, Chi	2.33
1964	Dean Chance, LA	1.65
1965	Sam McDowell, Cle	2.18
1966	Gary Peters, Chi	1.98
1967	Joe Horlen, Chi	2.06
1968	Luis Tiant, Cle	1.60
1969	Dick Bosman, Wash	2.19
1970	Diego Segui, Oak.	2.56
1971	Vida Blue, Oak	1.82

Year		ERA
1972	Luis Tiant, Bos	1.91
1973	Jim Palmer, Bal	2.40
1974	Catfish Hunter, Oak	2.49
1975	Jim Palmer, Bal	2.09
1976	Mark Fidrych, Det.	2.34
1977	Frank Tanana, Cal	2.54
1978	Ron Guidry, NY	1.74
1979	Ron Guidry, NY	2.78
1980	Rudy May, NY	2.47
1981	Steve McCatty, Oak	2.32
1982	Rick Sutcliffe, Cle	2.96
1983	Rick Honeycutt, Tex	2.42
1984	Mike Boddicker, Bal	2.79
1985	Dave Stieb, Tor	2.48
1986	Roger Clemens, Bos	2.48
1987	Jimmy Key, Tor	2.76
1988	Allan Anderson, Min	2.45

Year		ERA
1989	Bret Saberhagen, KC	2.16
1990	Roger Clemens, Bos	1.93
1991	Roger Clemens, Bos	2.62
1992	Roger Clemens, Bos	2.41
1993	Kevin Appier, KC	2.56
1994	Steve Ontiveros, Oak	2.65
1995	Randy Johnson, Sea	2.48
1996	Juan Guzman, Tor.	2.93
1997	Roger Clemens, Tor	2.05
1998	Roger Clemens, Tor	2.65
1999	Pedro Martinez, Bos	2.07
2000	Pedro Martinez, Bos	1.74
2001	Freddy Garcia, Sea	3.05
2002	Pedro Martinez, Bos	2.26
2003	Pedro Martinez, Bos	2.22
2004	Johan Santana, Min	2.61

Strikeouts

National League

Multiple winners: Dazzy Vance (7); Grover Alexander (6); Steve Carlton, Randy Johnson, Christy Mathewson and Tom Seaver (5); Dizzy Dean, Sandy Koufax and Warren Spahn (4); Don Drysdale, Sam Jones and Johnny Vander Meer (3); David Cone, Dwight Gooden, Bill Hallahan, J.R. Richard, Robin Roberts, Nolan Ryan, Curt Schilling, John Smoltz and Hippo Vaughn (2).

Year		SO
1900	Rube Waddell, Pit	130
1901	Noodles Hahn, Cin	239
1902	Vic Willis, Bos	225
1903	Christy Mathewson, NY	267
1904	Christy Mathewson, NY	212
1905	Christy Mathewson, NY	206
1906	Fred Beebe, Chi-St.L.	171
1907	Christy Mathewson, NY	178
1908	Christy Mathewson, NY	259
1909	Orval Overall, Chi	205
1910	Earl Moore, Phi	185
1911	Rube Marquard, NY	237
1912	Grover Alexander, Phi	195
1913	Tom Seaton, Phi	168
1914	Grover Alexander, Phi	214
1915	Grover Alexander, Phi	241
1916	Grover Alexander, Phi	167
1917	Grover Alexander, Phi	201
1918	Hippo Vaughn, Chi	148
1919	Hippo Vaughn, Chi	141
1920	Grover Alexander, Chi	173
1921	Burleigh Grimes, Bklyn	136
1922	Dazzy Vance, Bklyn	134
1923	Dazzy Vance, Bklyn	197
1924	Dazzy Vance, Bklyn	262
1925	Dazzy Vance, Bklyn	221
1926	Dazzy Vance, Bklyn	140
1927	Dazzy Vance, Bklyn	184
1928	Dazzy Vance, Bklyn	200
1929	Pat Malone, Chi	166
1930	Bill Hallahan, St.L	177
1931	Bill Hallahan, St.L	159
1932	Dizzy Dean, St.L	191
1933	Dizzy Dean, St.L	199
1934	Dizzy Dean, St.L	195
1935	Dizzy Dean, St.L	190

Year		SO
1936	Van Lingle Mungo, Bklyn	238
1937	Carl Hubbell, NY	159
1938	Clay Bryant, Chi	135
1939	Claude Passeau, Phi-Chi	137
	& Bucky Walters, Cin	137
1940	Kirby Higbe, Phi	137
1941	John Vander Meer, Cin	202
1942	John Vander Meer, Cin	186
1943	John Vander Meer, Cin	174
1944	Bill Voiselle, NY	161
1945	Preacher Roe, Pit	148
1946	Johnny Schmitz, Chi.	135
1947	Ewell Blackwell, Cin.	193
1948	Harry Brecheen, St.L	149
1949	Warren Spahn, Bos	151
1950	Warren Spahn, Bos	191
1951	Don Newcombe, Bklyn	164
	& Warren Spahn, Bos	164
1952	Warren Spahn, Bos	183
1953	Robin Roberts, Phi	198
1954	Robin Roberts, Phi	185
1955	Sam Jones, Chi	198
1956	Sam Jones, Chi	176
1957	Jack Sanford, Phi	188
1958	Sam Jones, St.L	225
1959	Don Drysdale, LA	242
1960	Don Drysdale, LA	246
1961	Sandy Koufax, LA	269
1962	Don Drysdale, LA	232
1963	Sandy Koufax, LA	306
1964	Bob Veale, Pit	250
1965	Sandy Koufax, LA	382
1966	Sandy Koufax, LA	317
1967	Jim Bunning, Phi	253
1968	Bob Gibson, St.L	268
1969	Ferguson Jenkins, Chi	273

Year		SO
1970	Tom Seaver, NY	283
1971	Tom Seaver, NY	289
1972	Steve Carlton, Phi	310
1973	Tom Seaver, NY	251
1974	Steve Carlton, Phi	240
1975	Tom Seaver, NY	243
1976	Tom Seaver, NY	235
1977	Phil Niekro, Atl	262
1978	J.R. Richard, Hou	303
1979	J.R. Richard, Hou	313
1980	Steve Carlton, Phi	286
1981	F. Valenzuela, LA	180
1982	Steve Carlton, Phi	286
1983	Steve Carlton, Phi	275
1984	Dwight Gooden, NY	276
1985	Dwight Gooden, NY	268
1986	Mike Scott, Hou	306
1987	Nolan Ryan, Hou	270
1988	Nolan Ryan, Hou	228
1989	Jose DeLeon, St.L	201
1990	David Cone, NY	233
1991	David Cone, NY	241
1992	John Smoltz, Atl.	215
1993	Jose Rijo, Cin	227
1994	Andy Benes, SD	189
1995	Hideo Nomo, LA	236
1996	John Smoltz, Atl	276
1997	Curt Schilling, Phi	319
1998	Curt Schilling, Phi	300
1999	Randy Johnson, Ari	364
2000	Randy Johnson, Ari	347
2001	Randy Johnson, Ari	372
2002	Randy Johnson, Ari	334
2003	Kerry Wood, Chi	266
2004	Randy Johnson, Ari	290

American League

Multiple winners: Walter Johnson (12); Nolan Ryan (9); Bob Feller and Lefty Grove (7); Rube Waddell (6); Roger Clemens and Sam McDowell (5); Randy Johnson (4); Lefty Gomez, Mark Langston, Pedro Martinez and Camilo Pascual (3); Len Barker, Tommy Bridges, Jim Bunning, Hal Newhouser, Allie Reynolds, Herb Score, Ed Walsh and Early Wynn (2).

Year		SO	Year		SO	Year		SO
1901	Cy Young, Bos	.158	1937	Lefty Gomez, NY	.194	1971	Mickey Lolich, Det	.308
1902	Rube Waddell, Phi	.210	1938	Bob Feller, Cle	.240	1972	Nolan Ryan, Cal	.329
1903	Rube Waddell, Phi	.302	1939	Bob Feller, Cle	.246	1973	Nolan Ryan, Cal	.383
1904	Rube Waddell, Phi	.349	1940	Bob Feller, Cle	.261	1974	Nolan Ryan, Cal	.367
1905	Rube Waddell, Phi	.287	1941	Bob Feller, Cle	.260	1975	Frank Tanana, Cal	.269
1906	Rube Waddell, Phi	.196	1942	Tex Hughson, Bos	.113	1976	Nolan Ryan, Cal	.327
1907	Rube Waddell, Phi	.232		& Bobo Newsom, Wash	.113	1977	Nolan Ryan, Cal	.341
1908	Ed Walsh, Chi	.269	1943	Allie Reynolds, Cle	.151	1978	Nolan Ryan, Cal	.260
1909	Frank Smith, Chi	.177	1944	Hal Newhouser, Det	.187	1979	Nolan Ryan, Cal	.223
1910	Walter Johnson, Wash	.313	1945	Hal Newhouser, Det	.212	1980	Len Barker, Cle	.187
1911	Ed Walsh, Chi	.255	1946	Bob Feller, Cle	.348	1981	Len Barker, Cle	.127
1912	Walter Johnson, Wash	.303	1947	Bob Feller, Cle	.196	1982	Floyd Bannister, Sea	.209
1913	Walter Johnson, Wash	.243	1948	Bob Feller, Cle	.164	1983	Jack Morris, Det	.232
1914	Walter Johnson, Wash	.225	1949	Virgil Trucks, Det	.153	1984	Mark Langston, Sea	.204
1915	Walter Johnson, Wash	.203	1950	Bob Lemon, Cle	.170	1985	Bert Blyleven, Cle-Min	.206
1916	Walter Johnson, Wash	.228	1951	Vic Raschi, NY	.164	1986	Mark Langston, Sea	.245
1917	Walter Johnson, Wash	.188	1952	Allie Reynolds, NY	.160	1987	Mark Langston, Sea	.262
1918	Walter Johnson, Wash	.162	1953	Billy Pierce, Chi	.186	1988	Roger Clemens, Bos	.291
1919	Walter Johnson, Wash	.147	1954	Bob Turley, Bal	.185	1989	Nolan Ryan, Tex	.301
1920	Stan Coveleski, Cle	.133	1955	Herb Score, Cle	.245	1990	Nolan Ryan, Tex	.232
1921	Walter Johnson, Wash	.143	1956	Herb Score, Cle	.263	1991	Roger Clemens, Bos	.241
1922	Urban Shocker, St.L	.149	1957	Early Wynn, Cle.	.184	1992	Randy Johnson, Sea	.241
1923	Walter Johnson, Wash	.130	1958	Early Wynn, Chi.	.179	1993	Randy Johnson, Sea	.308
1924	Walter Johnson, Wash	.158	1959	Jim Bunning, Det	.201	1994	Randy Johnson, Sea	.204
1925	Lefty Grove, Phi	.116	1960	Jim Bunning, Det	.201	1995	Randy Johnson, Sea	.294
1926	Lefty Grove, Phi	.194	1961	Camilo Pascual, Min	.221	1996	Roger Clemens, Bos	.257
1927	Lefty Grove, Phi	.174	1962	Camilo Pascual, Min	.206	1997	Roger Clemens, Tor	.292
1928	Lefty Grove, Phi	.183	1963	Camilo Pascual, Min	.202	1998	Roger Clemens, Tor	.271
1929	Lefty Grove, Phi	.170	1964	Al Downing, NY	.217	1999	Pedro Martinez, Bos	.313
1930	Lefty Grove, Phi	.209	1965	Sam McDowell, Cle	.325	2000	Pedro Martinez, Bos	.284
1931	Lefty Grove, Phi	.175	1966	Sam McDowell, Cle	.225	2001	Hideo Nomo, Bos	.220
1932	Red Ruffing, NY	.190	1967	Jim Lonborg, Bos	.246	2002	Pedro Martinez, Bos	.239
1933	Lefty Gomez, NY	.163	1968	Sam McDowell, Cle	.283	2003	Esteban Loaiza, Chi	.207
1934	Lefty Gomez, NY	.158	1969	Sam McDowell, Cle	.279	2004	Johan Santana, Min	.265
1935	Tommy Bridges, Det	.163	1970	Sam McDowell, Cle	.304			
1936	Tommy Bridges, Det	.175						

Pitching Triple Crown Winners

Pitchers who led either league in Earned Run Average, Wins and Strikeouts over a single season.

National League

	Year	ERA	W-L	SO
Tommy Bond, Bos	1877	2.11	40-17	170
Hoss Radbourn, Prov	1884	1.38	60-12	441
Tim Keefe, NY	1888	1.74	35-12	333
John Clarkson, Bos	1889	2.73	49-19	284
Amos Rusie, NY.	1894	2.78	36-13	195
Christy Mathewson, NY	1905	1.27	31-8	206
Christy Mathewson, NY	1908	1.43	37-11	259
Grover Alexander, Phi	1915	1.22	31-10	241
Grover Alexander, Phi	1916	1.55	33-12	167
Grover Alexander, Phi	1917	1.86	30-13	201
Hippo Vaughn, Chi	1918	1.74	22-10	148
Grover Alexander, Chi	1920	1.91	27-14	173
Dazzy Vance, Bklyn	1924	2.16	28-6	262
Bucky Walters, Cin	1939	2.29	27-11	137
Sandy Koufax, LA	1963	1.88	25-5	306
Sandy Koufax, LA	1965	2.04	26-8	382
Sandy Koufax, LA	1966	1.73	27-9	317
Steve Carlton, Phi	1972	1.97	27-10	310
Dwight Gooden, NY	1985	1.53	24-4	268
Randy Johnson, Ari	2002	2.32	24-5	334

Ties: In 1894, Rusie tied for league lead in wins with Jouett Meekin, NY (36-10); in 1939, Walters tied for league lead in strikeouts with Claude Passeau, Phi-Chi; in 1963, Koufax tied for the league lead in wins with Juan Marichal, SF.

American League

	Year	ERA	W-L	SO
Cy Young, Bos	1901	1.62	33-10	158
Rube Waddell, Phi.	1905	1.48	26-11	287
Walter Johnson, Wash	1913	1.09	36-7	243
Walter Johnson, Wash	1918	1.27	23-13	162
Walter Johnson, Wash	1924	2.72	23-7	158
Lefty Grove, Phi	1930	2.54	28-5	209
Lefty Grove, Phi	1931	2.06	31-4	175
Lefty Gomez, NY	1934	2.33	26-5	158
Lefty Gomez, NY	1937	2.33	21-11	194
Hal Newhouser, Det	1945	1.81	25-9	212
Roger Clemens, Tor	1997	2.05	21-7	292
Roger Clemens, Tor	1998	2.65	20-6	271
Pedro Martinez, Bos	1999	2.07	23-4	313

Ties: In 1998, Clemens tied for league lead in wins with David Cone, NY (20-7) and Rick Helling, Tex (20-7).

Saves

The "save" was created by Chicago baseball writer Jerome Holtzman in the 1960's and accepted as an official statistic by the Official Rules Committee of Major League Baseball in 1969. From 1969-72, a save was credited to a pitcher who finished a game his team won. From 1973-74, a save was credited to a pitcher who finished a game his team won with the tying or winning run on base or at bat. Since 1975 a pitcher has been credited with a save when he meets all three of the following conditions:

(1) He is the finishing pitcher in a game won by his club; (2) He is not the winning pitcher; (3) He qualifies under one of the following conditions: (a) He enters the game with a lead of no more than three runs and pitches for at least one inning; (b) He enters the game with the potential tying run either on base, or at bat, or on deck; (c) He pitches effectively for at least three innings. No more than one save may be credited in each game.

National League

Multiple winners: Bruce Sutter (5); John Franco and Lee Smith (3); Rawly Eastwick, Rollie Fingers, Mike Marshall, Randy Myers and Todd Worrell (2).

Year		Svs	Year		Svs	Year		Svs
1969	Fred Gladding, Hou	.29	1981	Bruce Sutter, St.L	.25	1994	John Franco, NY	.30
1970	Wayne Granger, Cin	.35	1982	Bruce Sutter, St.L	.36	1995	Randy Myers, Chi	.38
1971	Dave Giusti, Pit	.30	1983	Lee Smith, Chi	.29	1996	Jeff Brantley, Cin	.44
1972	Clay Carroll, Cin.	.37	1984	Bruce Sutter, St.L	.45		& Todd Worrell, LA	.44
1973	Mike Marshall, Mon.	.31	1985	Jeff Reardon, Mon	.41	1997	Jeff Shaw, Cin	.42
1974	Mike Marshall, LA	.21	1986	Todd Worrell, St.L	.36	1998	Trevor Hoffman, SD	.53
1975	Rawly Eastwick, Cin	.22	1987	Steve Bedrosian, Phi.	.40	1999	Ugueth Urbina, Mon	.41
	& Al Hrabosky, St.L	.22	1988	John Franco, Cin	.39	2000	Antonio Alfonseca, Fla	.45
1976	Rawly Eastwick, Cin	.26	1989	Mark Davis, SD.	.44	2001	Robb Nen, SF	.45
1977	Rollie Fingers, SD	.35	1990	John Franco, NY	.33	2002	John Smoltz, Atl	.55
1978	Rollie Fingers, SD	.37	1991	Lee Smith, St.L	.47	2003	Eric Gagne, LA	.55
1979	Bruce Sutter, Chi	.37	1992	Lee Smith, St.L	.43	2004	Armando Benitez, Fla	.47
1980	Bruce Sutter, Chi	.28	1993	Randy Myers, Chi	.53		& Jason Isringhausen, St.L	.47

American League

Multiple winners: Dan Quisenberry (5); Rich Gossage and Mariano Rivera (3); Dennis Eckersley, Sparky Lyle and Ron Perranoski (2).

Year		Svs	Year		Svs	Year		Svs
1969	Ron Perranoski, Min	.31	1982	Dan Quisenberry, KC	.35	1995	Jose Mesa, Cle	.46
1970	Ron Perranoski, Min	.34	1983	Dan Quisenberry, KC.	.45	1996	John Wetteland, NY	.43
1971	Ken Sanders, Mil.	.31	1984	Dan Quisenberry, KC.	.44	1997	Randy Myers, Bal	.45
1972	Sparky Lyle, NY.	.35	1985	Dan Quisenberry, KC.	.37	1998	Tom Gordon, Bos	.46
1973	John Hiller, Det	.38	1986	Dave Righetti, NY	.46	1999	Mariano Rivera, NY	.45
1974	Terry Forster, Chi	.24	1987	Tom Henke, Tor	.34	2000	Todd Jones, Det.	.42
1975	Rich Gossage, Chi	.26	1988	Dennis Eckersley, Oak	.45		& Derek Lowe, Bos	.42
1976	Sparky Lyle, NY.	.23	1989	Jeff Russell, Tex	.38	2001	Mariano Rivera, NY.	.50
1977	Bill Campbell, Bos	.31	1990	Bobby Thigpen, Chi	.57	2002	Eddie Guardado, Min	.45
1978	Rich Gossage, NY	.27	1991	Bryan Harvey, Cal	.46	2003	Keith Foulke, Oak	.43
1979	Mike Marshall, Min	.32	1992	Dennis Eckersley, Oak	.51	2004	Mariano Rivera, NY.	.53
1980	Rich Gossage, NY	.33	1993	Jeff Montgomery, KC	.45			
	& Dan Quisenberry, KC	.33		& Duane Ward, Tor	.45			
1981	Rollie Fingers, Mil	.28	1994	Lee Smith, Bal	.33			

Perfect Games

Eighteen pitchers have thrown perfect games (27 up, 27 down) in major league history. However, the game pitched by Ernie Shore is not considered to be official.

National League

	Game	Date	Score
Lee Richmond	Wor. vs Cle.	6/12/1880	1-0
Monte Ward	Prov. vs Buf.	6/17/1880	5-0
Jim Bunning	Phi. at NY	6/21/1964	6-0
Sandy Koufax	LA vs Chi.	9/9/1965	1-0
Tom Browning	Cin. vs LA	9/16/1988	1-0
Dennis Martinez	Mon. at LA	7/28/1991	2-0
Randy Johnson	Ari. at Atl.	5/18/2004	2-0

Note: Pittsburgh's Harvey Haddix pitched 12 perfect innings against the Milwaukee Braves on May 26, 1959 before losing, 1-0, in the 13th. Braves' lead-off batter Felix Mantilla reached on a throwing error by Pirates 3B Don Hoak, Eddie Mathews sacrificed Mantilla to 2nd, Hank Aaron was walked intentionally, and Joe Adcock hit a 3-run HR. Adcock, however, passed Aaron on the bases and was only credited with a 1-run double.

Note: Montreal's Pedro Martinez pitched nine perfect innings against the San Diego Padres on June 3, 1995 before surrendering a leadoff double to Bip Roberts in the 10th. He was then relieved by Mel Rojas, who finished the game, which Montreal won, 1-0.

American League

	Game	Date	Score
Cy Young	Bos. vs Phi.	5/5/1904	3-0
Addie Joss	Cle. vs Chi.	10/2/1908	1-0
Ernie Shore	Bos. vs Wash.	6/23/1917	4-0*
Charlie Robertson	Chi. at Det.	4/30/1922	2-0
Catfish Hunter	Oak. vs Min.	5/8/1968	4-0
Len Barker	Cle. vs Tor.	5/15/1981	3-0
Mike Witt	Cal. at Tex.	9/30/1984	1-0
Kenny Rogers	Tex. vs Cal.	7/28/1994	4-0
David Wells	NY vs Min.	5/17/1998	4-0
David Cone	NY vs Mon.	7/18/1999	6-0

*Babe Ruth started for Boston, walking Senators' lead-off batter Ray Morgan, then was thrown out of game by umpire Brick Owens for arguing the call. Shore came on in relief. Morgan was caught stealing and Shore retired the next 26 batters in a row. While technically not a perfect game—since he didn't start—Shore gets credit anyway.

World Series

Pitcher	Game	Date	Score
Don Larsen	NY vs Bklyn	10/8/1956	2-0

No-Hit Games

Nine innings or more, including perfect games, since 1876. Losing pitchers in **bold** type. **Multiple no-hitters:** Nolan Ryan (7); Sandy Koufax (4); Larry Corcoran, Bob Feller and Cy Young (3); Jim Bunning, Steve Busby, Carl Erskine, Bob Forsch, Pud Galvin, Ken Holtzman, Randy Johnson, Addie Joss, Hub (Dutch) Leonard, Jim Maloney, Christy Mathewson, Hideo Nomo, Allie Reynolds, Warren Spahn, Bill Stoneman, Virgil Trucks, Johnny Vander Meer and Don Wilson (2).

National League

Year	Date	Pitcher	Result	Year	Date	Pitcher	Result
1876	7/15	George Bradley	St.L vs Har, 2-0	1961	4/28	Warren Spahn	Mil vs SF, 1-0
1880	6/12	Lee Richmond	Wor vs Cle, 1-0 (perfect game)	1962	6/30	Sandy Koufax	LA vs NY, 5-0
	6/17	Monte Ward	Prov vs Buf, 5-0 (perfect game)	1963	5/11	Sandy Koufax	LA vs SF, 8-0
	8/19	Larry Corcoran	Chi vs Bos, 6-0		5/17	Don Nottebart	Hou vs Phi, 4-1
	8/20	Pud Galvin	Buf at Wor, 1-0		6/15	Juan Marichal	SF vs Hou, 1-0
1882	9/20	Larry Corcoran	Chi vs Wor, 5-0	1964	4/23	**Ken Johnson**	Hou vs Cin, 0-1
1883	7/25	Old Hoss Radbourn	Prov at Cle, 8-0		6/4	Sandy Koufax	LA at Phi, 3-0
	9/13	Hugh Daily	Cle at Phi, 1-0		6/21	Jim Bunning	Phi at NY, 6-0 (perfect game)
1884	6/27	Larry Corcoran	Chi vs Prov, 6-0	1965	8/19	Jim Maloney	Cin at Chi, 1-0 (10)
	8/4	Pud Galvin	Buf at Det, 18-0		9/9	Sandy Koufax	LA vs Chi, 1-0 (perfect game)
1885	7/27	John Clarkson	Chi vs Prov, 4-0	1967	6/18	Don Wilson	Hou vs Atl, 2-0
	8/29	Charlie Ferguson	Phi vs Prov, 1-0	1968	7/29	George Culver	Cin at Phi, 6-1
1891	6/22	Tom Lovett	Bklyn vs NY, 4-0		9/17	Gaylord Perry	SF vs St.L, 1-0
	7/31	Amos Rusie	NY vs Bklyn, 6-0		9/18	Ray Washburn	St.L at SF, 2-0 (next day, same park)
1892	8/6	John Stivetts	Bos vs Bklyn, 11-0				
	8/22	Ben Sanders	Lou vs Bal, 6-2	1969	4/17	Bill Stoneman	Mon at Phi, 7-0
	10/15	Bumpus Jones	Cin vs Pit, 7-1 (1st major league game)		4/30	Jim Maloney	Cin vs Hou, 10-0
					5/1	Don Wilson	Hou at Cin, 4-0
1893	8/16	Bill Hawke	Bal vs Wash, 5-0		8/19	Ken Holtzman	Chi vs Atl, 3-0
1897	9/18	Cy Young	Cle vs Cin, 6-0		9/20	Bob Moose	Pit at NY, 4-0
1898	4/22	Ted Breitenstein	Cin vs Pit, 11-0	1970	6/12	Dock Ellis	Pit at SD, 2-0
	4/22	Jim Hughes	Bal vs Bos, 8-0		7/20	Bill Singer	LA vs Phi, 5-0
	7/8	Red Donahue	Phi vs Bos, 5-0	1971	6/3	Ken Holtzman	Chi at Cin, 1-0
	8/21	Walter Thornton	Chi vs Bklyn, 2-0		6/23	Rick Wise	Phi at Cin, 4-0
1899	5/25	Deacon Phillippe	Lou vs NY, 7-0		8/14	Bob Gibson	St.L at Pit, 11-0
1900	7/12	Noodles Hahn	Cin vs Phi, 4-0	1972	4/16	Burt Hooton	Chi vs Phi, 4-0
1901	7/15	Christy Mathewson	NY at St.L, 5-0		9/2	Milt Pappas	Chi vs SD, 8-0
1903	9/18	Chick Fraser	Phi at Chi, 10-0		10/2	Bill Stoneman	Mon vs NY, 7-0
1905	6/13	Christy Mathewson	NY at Chi, 1-0	1973	8/5	Phil Niekro	Atl vs SD, 9-0
1906	5/1	John Lush	Phi at Bklyn, 6-0	1975	8/24	Ed Halicki	SF vs NY, 6-0
	7/20	Mal Eason	Bklyn at St.L, 2-0	1976	7/9	Larry Dierker	Hou vs Mon, 6-0
1907	5/8	Frank Pfeffer	Bos vs Cin, 6-0		8/9	John Candelaria	Pit vs LA, 2-0
	9/20	Nick Maddox	Pit vs Bkn, 2-1		9/29	John Montefusco	SF vs Atl, 9-0
1908	7/4	Hooks Wiltse	NY vs Phi, 1-0 (10)	1978	4/16	Bob Forsch	St.L vs Phi, 5-0
	9/5	Nap Rucker	Bklyn vs Bos, 6-0		6/16	Tom Seaver	Cin vs St.L, 4-0
1912	9/6	Jeff Tesreau	NY at Phi, 3-0	1979	4/7	Ken Forsch	Hou vs Atl, 6-0
1914	9/9	George Davis	Bos vs Phi, 7-0	1980	6/27	Jerry Reuss	LA at SF, 8-0
1915	4/15	Rube Marquard	NY vs Bklyn, 2-0	1981	5/10	Charlie Lea	Mon vs SF, 4-0
	8/31	Jimmy Lavender	Chi at N.Y, 2-0		9/26	Nolan Ryan	Hou vs LA, 5-0
1916	6/16	Tom Hughes	Bos vs. Pit, 2-0	1983	9/26	Bob Forsch	St.L vs Mon, 3-0
1917	5/2	Fred Toney	Cin at Chi, 1-0 (10)	1986	9/25	Mike Scott	Hou vs SF, 2-0
1919	5/11	Hod Eller	Cin at St.L, 6-0	1988	9/16	Tom Browning	Cin vs LA, 1-0 (perfect game)
1922	5/7	Jesse Barnes	NY vs Phi, 6-0				
1924	7/17	Jesse Haines	St.L vs Bos, 5-0	1990	6/29	Fernando Valenzuela	LA vs St.L, 6-0
1925	9/13	Dazzy Vance	Bklyn vs Phi, 10-1		8/15	Terry Mulholland	Phi vs SF, 6-0
1929	5/8	Carl Hubbell	NY vs Pit, 11-0	1991	5/23	Tommy Greene	Phi at Mon, 2-0
1934	9/21	Paul Dean	St.L at Bklyn, 3-0		7/28	Dennis Martinez	Mon at LA, 2-0 (perfect game)
1938	6/11	Johnny Vander Meer	Cin vs Bos, 3-0		9/11	Mercker (6), Wohlers (2) & Peña (1)	Atl vs SD, 1-0 (combined no-hitter)
	6/15	Johnny Vander Meer	Cin at Bklyn, 6-0 (consecutive starts)				
				1992	8/17	Kevin Gross	LA vs SF, 2-0
1940	4/30	Tex Carleton	Bklyn at Cin, 3-0	1993	9/8	Darryl Kile	Hou vs NY, 7-1
1941	8/30	Lon Warneke	St.L at Cin, 2-0	1994	4/8	Kent Mercker	Atl at LA, 6-0
1944	4/27	Jim Tobin	Bos vs Bklyn, 2-0	1995	7/14	Ramon Martinez	LA vs Fla, 7-0
	5/15	Clyde Shoun	Cin vs Bos, 1-0	1996	5/11	Al Leiter	Fla vs Col, 11-0
1946	4/23	Ed Head	Bklyn vs Bos, 2-0		9/17	Hideo Nomo	LA at Col, 9-0
1947	6/18	Ewell Blackwell	Cin vs Bos, 6-0	1997	6/10	Kevin Brown	Fla at SF, 9-0
1948	9/9	Rex Barney	Bklyn at NY, 2-0		7/12	Francisco Cordova (9) Ricardo Rincon (1)	Pit vs. Hou, 3-0 (10 inn.) (combined no-hitter)
1950	8/11	Vern Bickford	Bos vs Bklyn, 7-0				
1951	5/6	Cliff Chambers	Pit at Bos, 3-0	1999	6/25	Jose Jimenez	St.L at Ari, 1-0
1952	6/19	Carl Erskine	Bklyn vs Chi, 5-0	2001	5/12	A.J. Burnett	Fla at SD, 3-0
1954	6/12	Jim Wilson	Mil vs Phi, 2-0		9/3	Bud Smith	St.L at SD, 4-0
1955	5/12	Sam Jones	Chi vs Pit, 4-0	2003	4/27	Kevin Millwood	Phi vs SF, 1-0
1956	5/12	Carl Erskine	Bklyn vs NY, 3-0		6/11	Oswalt (1), Munro (2.2) Saarloos (1.1), Lidge (2), Dotel (1) & Wagner (1)	Hou at NY-AL, 8-0 (combined no-hitter)
	9/25	Sal Maglie	Bklyn vs Phi, 5-0				
1960	5/15	Don Cardwell	Chi vs St.L, 4-0	2004	5/18	Randy Johnson	Ari at Atl, 2-0 (perfect game)
	8/18	Lew Burdette	Mil vs Phi, 1-0				
	9/16	Warren Spahn	Mil vs Phi, 4-0				

No-Hit Games (Cont.)
American League

Year	Date	Pitcher	Result
1902	9/20	Jimmy Callahan	Chi vs Det, 3-0
1904	5/5	Cy Young	Bos vs Phi, 3-0 (perfect game)
	8/17	Jesse Tannehill	Bos at Chi, 6-0
1905	7/22	Weldon Henley	Phi at St. L, 6-0
	9/6	Frank Smith	Chi at Det, 15-0
	9/27	Bill Dinneen	Bos vs Chi, 2-0
1908	6/30	Cy Young	Bos at NY, 8-0
	9/18	Dusty Rhoades	Cle vs Bos, 2-1
	9/20	Frank Smith	Chi vs Phi, 1-0
	10/2	Addie Joss	Cle vs Chi, 1-0 (perfect game)
1910	4/20	Addie Joss	Cle at Chi, 1-0
	5/12	Chief Bender	Phi vs Cle, 4-0
1911	7/29	Smokey Joe Wood	Bos vs St. L, 5-0
	8/27	Ed Walsh	Chi vs Bos, 5-0
1912	7/4	George Mullin	Det vs St. L, 7-0
	8/30	Earl Hamilton	St. L at Det, 5-1
1914	5/31	Joe Benz	Chi vs Cle, 6-1
1916	6/16	Rube Foster	Bos vs NY, 2-0
	8/26	Joe Bush	Phi vs Cle, 5-0
	8/30	Hub (Dutch) Leonard	Bos vs St. L, 4-0
1917	4/14	Ed Cicotte	Chi at St. L, 11-0
	4/24	George Mogridge	NY at Bos, 2-1
	5/5	Ernie Koob	St. L vs Chi, 1-0
	5/6	Bob Groom	St. L vs Chi, 3-0 (next day, same park)
	6/23	Babe Ruth (0) & Ernie Shore (9)	Bos vs Wash, 4-0 (combined no-hitter)
1918	6/3	Hub (Dutch) Leonard	Bos at Det, 5-0
1919	9/10	Ray Caldwell	Cle at NY, 3-0
1920	7/1	Walter Johnson	Wash at Bos, 1-0
1922	4/30	Charlie Robertson	Chi at Det, 2-0 (perfect game)
1923	9/4	Sam Jones	NY at Phi, 2-0
	9/7	Howard Ehmke	Bos at Phi, 4-0
1926	8/21	Ted Lyons	Chi at Bos, 6-0
1931	4/29	Wes Ferrell	Cle vs St. L, 9-0
	8/8	Bob Burke	Wash vs Bos, 5-0
1935	8/31	Vern Kennedy	Chi vs Cle, 5-0
1937	6/1	Bill Dietrich	Chi vs St. L, 8-0
1938	8/27	Monte Pearson	NY vs Cle, 13-0
1940	4/16	Bob Feller	Cle at Chi, 1-0 (Opening Day)
1945	9/9	Dick Fowler	Phi vs St. L, 1-0
1946	4/30	Bob Feller	Cle at NY, 1-0
1947	7/10	Don Black	Cle vs Phi, 3-0
	9/3	Bill McCahan	Phi vs Wash, 3-0
1948	6/30	Bob Lemon	Cle at Det, 2-0
1951	7/1	Bob Feller	Cle vs Det, 2-1
	7/12	Allie Reynolds	NY at Cle, 1-0
	9/28	Allie Reynolds	NY vs Bos, 8-0
1952	5/15	Virgil Trucks	Det vs Wash, 1-0
	8/25	Virgil Trucks	Det at NY, 1-0
1953	5/6	Bobo Holloman	St. L vs Phi, 6-0 (first major league start)
1956	7/14	Mel Parnell	Bos vs Chi, 4-0
	10/8	Don Larsen	NY vs Bklyn, 2-0 (perfect W. Series game)
1957	8/20	Bob Keegan	Chi vs Wash, 6-0
1958	7/20	Jim Bunning	Det at Bos, 3-0
	9/20	Hoyt Wilhelm	Bal vs NY, 1-0
1962	5/5	Bo Belinsky	LA vs Bal, 2-0
	6/26	Earl Wilson	Bos vs LA, 2-0
	8/1	Bill Monbouquette	Bos at Chi, 1-0
	8/26	Jack Kralick	Min vs KC, 1-0

Year	Date	Pitcher	Result
1965	9/16	Dave Morehead	Bos vs Cle, 2-0
1966	6/10	Sonny Siebert	Cle vs Wash, 2-0
1967	4/30	**Steve Barber** (8⅔) & **Stu Miller** (⅓)	Bal vs Det, 1-2 (combined no-hitter)
	8/25	Dean Chance	Min at Cle, 2-1
	9/10	Joel Horlen	Chi vs Det, 6-0
1968	4/27	Tom Phoebus	Bal vs Bos, 6-0
	5/8	Catfish Hunter	Oak vs Min, 4-0 (perfect game)
1969	8/13	Jim Palmer	Bal vs Oak, 8-0
1970	7/3	Clyde Wright	Cal vs Oak, 4-0
	9/21	Vida Blue	Oak vs Min, 6-0
1973	4/27	Steve Busby	KC at Det, 3-0
	5/15	Nolan Ryan	Cal at KC, 3-0
	7/15	Nolan Ryan	Cal at Det, 6-0
	7/30	Jim Bibby	Tex at Oak, 6-0
1974	6/19	Steve Busby	KC at Mil, 2-0
	7/19	Dick Bosman	Cle vs Oak, 4-0
	9/28	Nolan Ryan	Cal vs Min, 4-0
1975	6/1	Nolan Ryan	Cal vs Bal, 1-0
	9/28	Vida Blue (5), Glenn Abbott (1), Paul Lindblad (1), & Rollie Fingers (2)	Oak vs Cal, 5-0 (combined no-hitter)
1976	7/28	John Odom (5) & Francisco Barrios (4)	Chi at Oak, 2-1 (combined no-hitter)
1977	5/14	Jim Colborn	KC vs Tex, 6-0
	5/30	Dennis Eckersley	Cle vs Cal, 1-0
	9/22	Bert Blyleven	Tex at Cal, 6-0
1981	5/15	Len Barker	Cle vs Tor, 3-0 (perfect game)
1983	7/4	Dave Righetti	NY vs Bos, 4-0
	9/29	Mike Warren	Oak vs Chi, 3-0
1984	4/7	Jack Morris	Det at Chi, 4-0
	9/30	Mike Witt	Cal at Tex, 1-0 (perfect game)
1986	9/19	Joe Cowley	Chi at Cal, 7-1
1987	4/15	Juan Nieves	Mil at Bal, 7-0
1990	4/11	Mark Langston (7) & Mike Witt (2)	Cal vs Sea, 1-0 (combined no-hitter)
	6/2	Randy Johnson	Sea vs Det, 2-0
	6/11	Nolan Ryan	Tex at Oak, 5-0
	6/29	Dave Stewart	Oak at Tor, 5-0
	9/2	Dave Stieb	Tor at Cle, 3-0
1991	5/1	Nolan Ryan	Tex vs Tor, 3-0
	7/13	Bob Milacki (6), Mike Flanagan (1), Mark Williamson (1) & Gregg Olson (1)	Bal at Oak, 2-0 (combined no-hitter)
	8/11	Wilson Alvarez	Chi at Bal, 7-0
	8/26	Bret Saberhagen	KC vs Chi, 7-0
1993	4/22	Chris Bosio	Sea vs Bos, 7-0
	9/4	Jim Abbott	NY vs Cle, 4-0
1994	4/27	Scott Erickson	Min vs Mil, 6-0
	7/28	Kenny Rogers	Tex vs Cal, 4-0 (perfect game)
1996	5/14	Dwight Gooden	NY vs Sea, 2-0
1998	5/17	David Wells	NY vs Min, 4-0 (perfect game)
1999	7/18	David Cone	NY vs Mon, 6-0 (perfect game)
	9/11	Eric Milton	Min vs Ana, 7-0
2001	4/4	Hideo Nomo	Bos at Bal, 3-0
2002	4/27	Derek Lowe	Bos vs TB, 10-0

All-Time Major League Leaders
Through the 2004 regular season.
CAREER
Players active in 2004 in **bold** type.
Batting
Note that (*) indicates left-handed hitter and (†) indicates switch-hitter.

Batting Average
(Minimum 3,000 AB)

		Yrs	AB	H	Avg
1	Ty Cobb*	.24	11,434	4189	.366
2	Rogers Hornsby	.23	8,173	2930	.358
3	Joe Jackson*	.13	4,981	1772	.356
4	Ed Delahanty	.16	7,505	2596	.346
5	Tris Speaker*	.22	10,195	3514	.345
6	Ted Williams*	.19	7,706	2654	.344
7	Billy Hamilton*	.14	6,269	2159	.344
8	Dan Brouthers*	.19	6,711	2296	.342
9	Babe Ruth*	.22	8,399	2873	.342
10	Harry Heilmann	.17	7,787	2660	.342
11	Pete Browning	.13	4,820	1646	.341
12	Willie Keeler*	.19	8,591	2932	.341
13	Bill Terry*	.14	6,428	2193	.341
14	George Sisler*	.15	8,267	2812	.340
15	Lou Gehrig*	.17	8,001	2721	.340
16	**Todd Helton***	.8	4,051	1372	.339
17	Jesse Burkett*	.16	8,421	2850	.338
18	Tony Gwynn*	.20	9,288	3141	.338
19	Nap Lajoie	.21	9,589	3242	.338
20	Riggs Stephenson	.14	4,508	1515	.336
21	Al Simmons	.20	8,759	2927	.334
22	Paul Waner*	.20	9,459	3152	.333
23	Eddie Collins*	.25	9,949	3315	.333
24	Stan Musial*	.22	10,972	3630	.331
25	Sam Thompson*	.14	5,984	1979	.331

Hits

		Yrs	AB	H	Avg
1	Pete Rose†	.24	14,053	4256	.303
2	Ty Cobb*	.24	11,434	4189	.366
3	Hank Aaron	.23	12,364	3771	.305
4	Stan Musial*	.22	10,972	3630	.331
5	Tris Speaker*	.22	10,195	3514	.345
6	Carl Yastrzemski*	.23	11,988	3419	.285
7	Honus Wagner	.21	10,430	3415	.327
8	Paul Molitor	.21	10,835	3319	.306
9	Eddie Collins*	.25	9,949	3315	.333
10	Willie Mays	.22	10,881	3283	.302
11	Eddie Murray†	.21	11,336	3255	.287
12	Nap Lajoie	.21	9,589	3242	.338
13	Cal Ripken Jr	.21	11,551	3184	.276
14	George Brett*	.21	10,349	3154	.305
15	Paul Waner*	.20	9,459	3152	.333
16	Robin Yount	.20	11,008	3142	.285
17	Tony Gwynn*	.20	9,288	3141	.338
18	Dave Winfield	.22	11,003	3110	.283
19	Rickey Henderson	.25	10,961	3055	.279
20	Rod Carew*	.19	9,315	3053	.328
21	Lou Brock*	.19	10,332	3023	.293
22	Wade Boggs*	.18	9,180	3010	.328
23	Al Kaline	.22	10,116	3007	.297
24	Cap Anson	.22	9,108	3000	.329
	Roberto Clemente	.18	9,454	3000	.317

Players Active in 2004

		Yrs	AB	H	Avg
1	Todd Helton*	.8	4,051	1372	.339
2	Vladimir Guerrero	.9	4,375	1421	.325
3	Nomar Garciaparra	.9	4,133	1330	.322
4	Manny Ramirez	.12	5,572	1760	.316
5	Mike Piazza	.13	5,805	1829	.315
6	Derek Jeter	.10	5,513	1734	.315
7	Larry Walker*	.16	6,592	2069	.314
8	Edgar Martinez	.18	7,213	2247	.312
9	Frank Thomas	.15	6,851	2113	.308
10	Magglio Ordonez	.8	3,807	1167	.307
11	Ivan Rodriguez	.13	6,694	2051	.306
12	Jason Kendall	.9	4,606	1409	.306
13	Alex Rodriguez	.11	5,590	1707	.305

Players Active in 2004

		Yrs	AB	H	Avg
1	Rafael Palmeiro*	.19	10,103	2922	.289
2	Barry Bonds*	.19	9,098	2730	.300
3	Roberto Alomar†	.17	9,073	2724	.300
4	Craig Biggio	.17	9,221	2639	.286
5	Fred McGriff*	.19	8,757	2490	.284
6	Julio Franco	.20	8,189	2457	.300
7	Barry Larkin	.19	7,937	2340	.295
8	Steve Finley	.16	8,471	2336	.276
9	Andres Galarraga	.19	8,096	2333	.288
10	Jeff Bagwell	.14	7,697	2289	.297
11	B.J. Surhoff	.18	7,955	2248	.283
12	Edgar Martinez	.18	7,213	2247	.312
13	Marquis Grissom	.16	8,138	2222	.273

Games Played

1	Pete Rose	3562
2	Carl Yastrzemski	3308
3	Hank Aaron	3298
4	Rickey Henderson	3081
5	Ty Cobb	3035
6	Stan Musial	3026
	Eddie Murray	3026
8	Cal Ripken Jr.	3001
9	Willie Mays	2992
10	Dave Winfield	2973
11	Rusty Staub	2951
12	Brooks Robinson	2896
13	Robin Yount	2856
14	Al Kaline	2834
15	Harold Baines	2830
16	Eddie Collins	2826
17	Reggie Jackson	2820
18	Frank Robinson	2808
19	Honus Wagner	2792
20	Tris Speaker	2789

At Bats

1	Pete Rose	14,053
2	Hank Aaron	12,364
3	Carl Yastrzemski	11,988
4	Cal Ripken Jr.	11,551
5	Ty Cobb	11,434
6	Eddie Murray	11,336
7	Robin Yount	11,008
8	Dave Winfield	11,003
9	Stan Musial	10,972
10	Rickey Henderson	10,961
11	Willie Mays	10,881
12	Paul Molitor	10,835
13	Brooks Robinson	10,654
14	Honus Wagner	10,430
15	George Brett	10,349
16	Lou Brock	10,332
17	Luis Aparicio	10,230
18	Tris Speaker	10,195
19	Al Kaline	10,116
20	**Rafael Palmeiro**	10,103

Total Bases

1	Hank Aaron	6856
2	Stan Musial	6134
3	Willie Mays	6066
4	Ty Cobb	5854
5	Babe Ruth	5793
6	Pete Rose	5752
7	**Barry Bonds**	5556
8	Carl Yastrzemski	5539
9	Eddie Murray	5397
10	Frank Robinson	5373
11	**Rafael Palmeiro**	5223
12	Dave Winfield	5221
13	Cal Ripken Jr.	5168
14	Tris Speaker	5101
15	Lou Gehrig	5060
16	George Brett	5044
17	Mel Ott	5041
18	Jimmie Foxx	4956
19	Ted Williams	4884
20	Honus Wagner	4862

Home Runs

		Yrs	AB	HR	AB/HR
1	Hank Aaron	23	12,364	755	16.4
2	Babe Ruth*	22	8,399	714	11.8
3	**Barry Bonds***	19	9,098	703	12.9
4	Willie Mays	22	10,881	660	16.5
5	Frank Robinson	21	10,006	586	17.1
6	Mark McGwire	16	6,187	583	10.6
7	**Sammy Sosa**	16	8,021	574	14.0
8	Harmon Killebrew	22	8,147	573	14.2
9	Reggie Jackson*	21	9,864	563	17.5
10	**Rafael Palmeiro***	19	10,103	551	18.3
11	Mike Schmidt	18	8,352	548	15.2
12	Mickey Mantle†	18	8,102	536	15.1
13	Jimmie Foxx	20	8,134	534	15.2
14	Ted Williams*	19	7,706	521	14.8
	Willie McCovey*	22	8,197	521	15.7
16	Eddie Mathews*	17	8,537	512	16.7
	Ernie Banks	19	9,421	512	18.4
18	Mel Ott*	22	9,456	511	18.5
19	Eddie Murray†	21	11,336	504	22.5
20	**Ken Griffey Jr.***	16	7,379	501	14.7
21	Lou Gehrig*	17	8,001	493	16.2
	Fred McGriff*	19	8,757	493	17.8
23	Willie Stargell*	21	7,927	475	16.7
	Stan Musial*	22	10,972	475	23.1
25	Dave Winfield	22	11,003	465	23.7

Runs Batted In

		Yrs	Gm	RBI	P/G
1	Hank Aaron	23	3298	2297	.70
2	Babe Ruth*	22	2503	2213	.88
3	Lou Gehrig*	17	2164	1995	.92
4	Stan Musial*	22	3026	1951	.64
5	Ty Cobb*	24	3034	1938	.64
6	Jimmie Foxx	20	2317	1922	.83
7	Eddie Murray†	21	2980	1917	.64
8	Willie Mays	22	2992	1903	.64
9	Mel Ott*	22	2730	1860	.68
10	Carl Yastrzemski*	23	3308	1844	.56
11	**Barry Bonds***	19	2716	1843	.68
12	Ted Williams*	19	2292	1839	.80
13	Dave Winfield	22	2973	1833	.62
14	Al Simmons	20	2215	1827	.82
15	Frank Robinson	21	2808	1812	.65
16	**Rafael Palmeiro***	19	2721	1775	.65
17	Honus Wagner	21	2792	1732	.62
18	Cap Anson	22	2276	1715	.75
19	Reggie Jackson*	21	2820	1702	.60
20	Cal Ripken Jr.	21	3001	1695	.56
21	Tony Perez	23	2777	1652	.59
22	Ernie Banks	19	2528	1636	.65
23	Harold Baines*	22	2830	1628	.58
24	Goose Goslin*	18	2287	1609	.70
25	Nap Lajoie	21	2480	1599	.64

Players Active in 2004

		Yrs	AB	HR	AB/HR
1	Barry Bonds*	19	9,098	703	12.9
2	Sammy Sosa	16	8,021	574	14.0
3	Rafael Palmeiro*	19	10,103	551	18.3
4	Ken Griffey Jr.*	16	7,379	501	14.7
5	Fred McGriff*	19	8,757	493	17.8
6	Jeff Bagwell	14	7,697	446	17.3
7	Frank Thomas	15	6,851	436	15.7
8	Juan Gonzalez	16	6,555	434	15.1
9	Jim Thome*	14	5,726	423	13.5
10	Gary Sheffield	17	7,302	415	17.6
11	Andres Galarraga	19	8,096	399	20.3
12	Manny Ramirez	12	5,572	390	14.3
13	Alex Rodriguez	11	5,590	381	14.7
14	Mike Piazza	13	5,805	378	15.4
15	Larry Walker*	16	6592	368	17.9

Players Active in 2004

		Yrs	Gm	RBI	P/G
1	Barry Bonds*	19	2716	1843	.68
2	Rafael Palmeiro*	19	2721	1775	.65
3	Fred McGriff*	19	2460	1550	.63
4	Sammy Sosa	16	2138	1530	.72
5	Jeff Bagwell	14	2111	1510	.72
6	Ken Griffey Jr.*	16	1997	1444	.72
7	Frank Thomas	15	1925	1439	.75
8	Andres Galarraga	19	2257	1425	.63
9	Juan Gonzalez	16	1688	1404	.83
10	Gary Sheffield	17	2036	1353	.66
11	Ruben Sierra†	18	2111	1289	.61
12	Manny Ramirez	12	1535	1270	.83
13	Edgar Martinez	18	2055	1261	.61
14	Larry Walker*	16	1888	1259	.67
15	Tino Martinez	15	1892	1222	.65

Runs

1	Rickey Henderson	2295
2	Ty Cobb	2246
3	Babe Ruth	2174
	Hank Aaron	2174
5	Pete Rose	2165
6	**Barry Bonds**	2070
7	Willie Mays	2062
8	Stan Musial	1949
9	Lou Gehrig	1888
10	Tris Speaker	1882
11	Mel Ott	1859
12	Frank Robinson	1829
13	Eddie Collins	1821
14	Carl Yastrzemski	1816
15	Ted Williams	1798
16	Paul Molitor	1782
17	Charlie Gehringer	1774
18	Jimmie Foxx	1751
19	Honus Wagner	1736
20	Willie Keeler	1727

Extra Base Hits

1	Hank Aaron	1477
2	Stan Musial	1377
3	Babe Ruth	1356
4	**Barry Bonds**	1343
5	Willie Mays	1323
6	Lou Gehrig	1190
7	Frank Robinson	1186
8	**Rafael Palmeiro**	1161
9	Carl Yastrzemski	1157
10	Ty Cobb	1136
11	Tris Speaker	1131
12	George Brett	1119
13	Ted Williams	1117
	Jimmie Foxx	1117
15	Eddie Murray	1099
16	Dave Winfield	1093
17	Cal Ripken Jr.	1078
18	Reggie Jackson	1075
19	Mel Ott	1071
20	Pete Rose	1041

Slugging Percentage
(Minimum 3,000 AB)

1	Babe Ruth	.690
2	Ted Williams	.634
3	Lou Gehrig	.632
4	**Todd Helton**	.616
5	**Barry Bonds**	.611
6	Jimmie Foxx	.609
7	Hank Greenberg	.605
8	**Manny Ramirez**	.599
9	Mark McGwire	.588
10	**Vladimir Guerrero**	.589
11	Joe DiMaggio	.579
12	Rogers Hornsby	.577
13	**Alex Rodriguez**	.574
14	**Jim Thome**	.569
15	**Larry Walker***	.568
16	**Frank Thomas**	.567
17	Albert Belle	.564
18	Johnny Mize	.562
19	**Mike Piazza**	.562
20	**Juan Gonzalez**	.561

Stolen Bases

1	Rickey Henderson	1406
2	Lou Brock	938
3	Billy Hamilton	912
4	Ty Cobb	892
5	Tim Raines	808
6	Vince Coleman	752
7	Eddie Collins	745
8	Max Carey	738
9	Honus Wagner	722
10	Joe Morgan	689
11	Arlie Latham	679
12	Willie Wilson	668
13	Bert Campaneris	649
14	Tom Brown	627
15	Otis Nixon	620
16	George Davis	616
17	Dummy Hoy	594
18	Maury Wills	586
19	George Van Haltren	583
20	Ozzie Smith	580

Walks

1	**Barry Bonds**	2302
2	Rickey Henderson	2190
3	Babe Ruth	2062
4	Ted Williams	2019
5	Joe Morgan	1865
6	Carl Yastrzemski	1845
7	Mickey Mantle	1733
8	Mel Ott	1708
9	Eddie Yost	1614
10	Darrell Evans	1605
11	Stan Musial	1599
12	Pete Rose	1566
13	Harmon Killebrew	1559
14	Lou Gehrig	1508
15	Mike Schmidt	1507
16	Eddie Collins	1499
17	Willie Mays	1464
18	Jimmie Foxx	1452
19	**Frank Thomas**	1450
20	Eddie Mathews	1444

Strikeouts

1	Reggie Jackson	2597
2	**Sammy Sosa**	2110
3	**Andres Galarraga**	2003
4	Jose Canseco	1942
5	Willie Stargell	1936
6	Mike Schmidt	1883
7	**Fred McGriff**	1882
8	Tony Perez	1867
9	Dave Kingman	1816
10	Bobby Bonds	1757
11	Dale Murphy	1748
12	Lou Brock	1730
13	Mickey Mantle	1710
14	**Jim Thome**	1703
15	Harmon Killebrew	1699
16	Chili Davis	1698
17	Dwight Evans	1697
18	Rickey Henderson	1694
19	Dave Winfield	1686
20	Gary Gaetti	1602

Pitching

Note that (*) indicates left-handed pitcher. Active pitching leaders are listed for wins and strikeouts.

Wins

		Yrs	GS	W	L	Pct
1	Cy Young	22	815	**511**	316	.618
2	Walter Johnson	21	666	**417**	279	.599
3	Christy Mathewson	17	551	**373**	188	.665
	Grover Alexander	20	598	**373**	208	.642
5	Pud Galvin	15	688	**365**	310	.541
6	Warren Spahn*	21	665	**363**	245	.597
7	Kid Nichols	15	561	**361**	208	.634
8	Tim Keefe	14	594	**342**	225	.603
9	Steve Carlton*	24	709	**329**	244	.574
10	**Roger Clemens**	21	639	**328**	164	.667
	John Clarkson	12	518	**328**	178	.648
12	Eddie Plank*	17	529	**326**	194	.627
13	Don Sutton	23	756	**324**	256	.559
	Nolan Ryan	27	773	**324**	292	.526
15	Phil Niekro	24	716	**318**	274	.537
16	Gaylord Perry	22	690	**314**	265	.542
17	Tom Seaver	20	647	**311**	205	.603
18	Old Hoss Radbourn	12	503	**309**	195	.613
19	Mickey Welch	13	549	**307**	210	.594
20	**Greg Maddux**	19	604	**305**	174	.637
21	Lefty Grove*	17	456	**300**	141	.680
	Early Wynn	23	612	**300**	244	.551
23	Bobby Mathews	15	568	**297**	248	.545
24	Tommy John*	26	700	**288**	231	.555
25	Bert Blyleven	22	685	**287**	250	.534
26	Robin Roberts	19	609	**286**	245	.539
27	Tony Mullane	13	504	**284**	220	.563
	Ferguson Jenkins	19	594	**284**	226	.557
29	Jim Kaat*	25	625	**283**	237	.544
30	Red Ruffing	22	536	**273**	225	.548

Strikeouts

		Yrs	IP	SO	P/9
1	Nolan Ryan	27	5386.0	**5714**	9.55
2	**Roger Clemens**	21	4493.0	**4317**	8.65
3	**Randy Johnson***	17	3368.0	**4161**	11.12
4	Steve Carlton*	24	5217.1	**4136**	7.13
5	Bert Blyleven	22	4970.0	**3701**	6.70
6	Tom Seaver	20	4782.2	**3640**	6.85
7	Don Sutton	23	5282.1	**3574**	6.09
8	Gaylord Perry	22	5350.1	**3534**	5.94
9	Walter Johnson	21	5914.1	**3508**	5.34
10	Phil Niekro	24	5404.1	**3342**	5.57
11	Ferguson Jenkins	19	4500.2	**3192**	6.38
12	Bob Gibson	17	3884.1	**3117**	7.22
13	**Greg Maddux**	19	4181.1	**2916**	6.28
14	Jim Bunning	17	3760.1	**2855**	6.83
15	Mickey Lolich*	16	3638.1	**2832**	7.01
16	Cy Young	22	7356.0	**2803**	3.43
17	Frank Tanana*	21	4186.2	**2773**	5.96
18	**Curt Schilling**	17	2812.2	**2745**	8.78
19	David Cone	17	2898.2	**2668**	8.28
20	**Pedro Martinez**	13	2296.0	**2653**	10.40
21	Chuck Finley*	17	3197.1	**2610**	7.35
22	Warren Spahn*	21	5243.2	**2583**	4.43
23	Bob Feller	18	3827.0	**2581**	6.07
24	Tim Keefe	14	5049.2	**2564**	4.57
25	Jerry Koosman*	19	3839.1	**2556**	5.99
26	Christy Mathewson	17	4781.0	**2502**	4.71
27	Don Drysdale	14	3432.0	**2486**	6.52
28	Jack Morris	18	3824.2	**2478**	5.83
29	Mark Langston*	16	2962.2	**2464**	7.49
30	Jim Kaat*	25	4530.1	**2461**	4.89

Pitchers Active in 2004

		Yrs	GS	W	L	Pct
1	Roger Clemens	21	639	**328**	164	.667
2	Greg Maddux	19	604	**305**	174	.637
3	Tom Glavine*	18	570	**262**	171	.605
4	Randy Johnson*	17	479	**246**	128	.658
5	David Wells*	18	417	**212**	136	.609
6	Mike Mussina	14	413	**211**	119	.639
7	Kevin Brown	18	463	**207**	137	.602
8	Jamie Moyer*	18	453	**192**	145	.570
9	Curt Schilling	17	370	**184**	123	.599
10	Pedro Martinez	13	321	**182**	76	.705

Pitchers Active in 2004

		Yrs	IP	SO	P/9
1	Roger Clemens	21	4493.0	**4317**	8.65
2	Randy Johnson*	17	3368.0	**4161**	11.12
3	Greg Maddux	19	4181.1	**2916**	6.28
4	Curt Schilling	17	2812.2	**2745**	8.78
5	Pedro Martinez	13	2296.0	**2653**	10.40
6	John Smoltz	17	2699.2	**2398**	7.99
7	Kevin Brown	18	3183.0	**2347**	6.64
8	Mike Mussina	14	2833.1	**2258**	7.17
9	Tom Glavine*	18	3740.1	**2245**	5.40
10	Kevin Appier	16	2595.1	**1994**	6.91

Winning Pct.
(Minimum 100 wins)

		Yrs	W-L	Pct
1	Al Spalding	7	252-65	.795
2	Spud Chandler	11	109-43	.717
3	**Pedro Martinez**	13	182-76	.705
4	Dave Foutz	11	147-66	.690
5	Whitey Ford*	16	236-106	.690
6	Bob Caruthers	9	218-99	.688
7	Don Gullett*	9	109-50	.686
8	Lefty Grove*	17	300-141	.680
9	Smokey Joe Wood	11	117-57	.672
10	**Roger Clemens**	21	328-164	.667
	Vic Raschi	10	132-66	.667
12	Larry Corcoran	8	177-89	.665
13	Christy Mathewson	17	373-188	.665
14	Sam Leever	13	194-100	.660
15	**Randy Johnson***	17	246-128	.658

Losses

		Yrs	GS	W	L	Pct
1	Cy Young	22	815	511	**316**	.618
2	Pud Galvin	15	688	365	**310**	.541
3	Nolan Ryan	27	773	324	**292**	.526
4	Walter Johnson	21	666	417	**279**	.599
5	Phil Niekro	24	716	318	**274**	.537
6	Gaylord Perry	22	690	314	**265**	.542
7	Don Sutton	23	756	324	**256**	.559
8	Jack Powell	16	516	245	**254**	.491
9	Eppa Rixey*	21	552	266	**251**	.515
10	Bert Blyleven	22	685	287	**250**	.534
11	Bobby Mathews	15	568	297	**248**	.545
12	Robin Roberts	19	609	286	**245**	.539
	Warren Spahn*	21	665	363	**245**	.597
14	Early Wynn	23	612	300	**244**	.551
	Steve Carlton*	24	709	329	**244**	.574

Appearances

1	Jesse Orosco	1252
2	**John Franco**	1088
3	Dennis Eckersley	1071
4	Hoyt Wilhelm	1070
5	Dan Plesac	1064
6	Kent Tekulve	1050
7	Lee Smith	1022
8	**Mike Jackson**	1005
9	Rich Gossage	1002
10	Lindy McDaniel	987
11	**Mike Stanton**	968
12	Rollie Fingers	944
13	Gene Garber	931
14	Cy Young	906
15	Sparky Lyle	899

Innings Pitched

1	Cy Young	7356.0
2	Pud Galvin	6003.1
3	Walter Johnson	5914.1
4	Phil Niekro	5404.1
5	Nolan Ryan	5386.0
6	Gaylord Perry	5350.1
7	Don Sutton	5282.1
8	Warren Spahn	5243.2
9	Steve Carlton	5217.1
10	Grover Alexander	5190.0
11	Kid Nichols	5056.1
12	Tim Keefe	5049.2
13	Bert Blyleven	4970.0
14	Bobby Mathews	4956.0
15	Mickey Welch	4802.0

Earned Run Avg.
(Minimum 1500 IP)

1	Ed Walsh	1.82
2	Addie Joss	1.89
3	Al Spalding	2.04
4	Three Finger Brown	2.06
5	Monte Ward	2.10
6	Christy Mathewson	2.13
7	Rube Waddell	2.16
8	Walter Johnson	2.17
9	Orval Overall	2.23
10	Tommy Bond	2.25
11	Will White	2.28
12	Ed Reulbach	2.28
13	Jim Scott	2.30
14	Eddie Plank	2.35
15	Larry Corcoran	2.36

Shutouts

1	Walter Johnson	110
2	Grover Alexander	90
3	Christy Mathewson	79
4	Cy Young	76
5	Eddie Plank	69
6	Warren Spahn	63
7	Nolan Ryan	61
	Tom Seaver	61
8	Bert Blyleven	60
10	Don Sutton	58
11	Pud Galvin	57
	Ed Walsh	57
13	Bob Gibson	56
14	Three Finger Brown	55
	Steve Carlton	55

Walks Allowed

1	Nolan Ryan	2795
2	Steve Carlton	1833
3	Phil Niekro	1809
4	Early Wynn	1775
5	Bob Feller	1764
6	Bobo Newsom	1732
7	Amos Rusie	1704
8	Charlie Hough	1665
9	Gus Weyhing	1566
10	Red Ruffing	1541
11	**Roger Clemens**	1458
12	Bump Hadley	1442
13	Warren Spahn	1434
14	Earl Whitehill	1431
15	Tony Mullane	1408

HRs Allowed

1	Robin Roberts	505
2	Ferguson Jenkins	484
3	Phil Niekro	482
4	Don Sutton	472
5	Frank Tanana	448
6	Warren Spahn	434
7	Bert Blyleven	430
8	Steve Carlton	414
9	Gaylord Perry	399
10	Jim Kaat	395
11	Jack Morris	389
12	Charlie Hough	383
13	Tom Seaver	380
14	Catfish Hunter	374
15	Jim Bunning	372
	Dennis Martinez	372

Saves

1	Lee Smith	478
2	**John Franco**	424
3	**Trevor Hoffman**	393
4	Dennis Eckersley	390
5	Jeff Reardon	367
6	Randy Myers	347
7	Rollie Fingers	341
8	**Mariano Rivera**	336
9	John Wetteland	330
10	Roberto Hernandez	320
11	Rick Aguilera	318
12	**Troy Percival**	316
13	**Robb Nen**	314
14	Tom Henke	311
15	Rich Gossage	310
16	Jeff Montgomery	304
17	Doug Jones	303
18	Bruce Sutter	300
19	**Jose Mesa**	292
20	**Rod Beck**	286
21	Todd Worrell	256
22	Dave Righetti	252
23	**Billy Wagner**	246
24	Dan Quisenberry	244
	Armando Benitez	244
26	Sparky Lyle	238
27	Hoyt Wilhelm	227
	Ugueth Urbina	227
29	Gene Garber	218
30	Gregg Olson	217

SINGLE SEASON
Through 2004 regular season.
Batting

Home Runs

		Year	Gm	AB	HR
1	Barry Bonds, SF	2001	153	476	73
2	Mark McGwire, St.L	1998	155	509	70
3	Sammy Sosa, Chi-NL	1998	159	643	66
4	Mark McGwire, St.L	1999	153	521	65
5	Sammy Sosa, Chi-NL	2001	160	577	64
6	Sammy Sosa, Chi-NL	1999	162	625	63
7	Roger Maris, NY-AL	1961	162	590	61
8	Babe Ruth, NY-AL	1927	151	540	60
9	Babe Ruth, NY-AL	1921	152	540	59
10	Mark McGwire, Oak-St.L	1997	156	540	58
	Hank Greenberg, Det	1938	155	556	58
	Jimmie Foxx, Phi-AL	1932	154	585	58
13	Alex Rodriguez, Tex	2002	162	624	57
	Luis Gonzalez, Ari	2001	162	609	57
15	Hack Wilson, Chi-NL	1930	155	585	56
	Ken Griffey Jr., Sea	1997	157	608	56
	Ken Griffey Jr., Sea	1998	161	633	56
18	Babe Ruth, NY-AL	1920	142	458	54
	Mickey Mantle, NY-AL	1961	153	514	54
	Babe Ruth, NY-AL	1928	154	536	54
	Ralph Kiner, Pit	1949	152	549	54

Hits

		Year	AB	H	Avg
1	**Ichiro Suzuki**, Sea.	2004	704	**262**	.372
2	George Sisler, StL-AL	1920	631	**257**	.407
3	Bill Terry, NY-NL	1930	633	**254**	.401
	Lefty O'Doul, Phi-NL	1929	638	**254**	.398
5	Al Simmons, Phi-AL	1925	658	**253**	.384
6	Rogers Hornsby, StL-NL	1922	623	**250**	.401
	Chuck Klein, Phi-NL	1930	648	**250**	.386
8	Ty Cobb, Det	1911	591	**248**	.420
9	George Sisler, StL-AL	1922	586	**246**	.420
10	Ichiro Suzuki, Sea	2001	692	**242**	.350
11	Babe Herman, Bklyn	1930	614	**241**	.393
	Heinie Manush, StL-AL	1928	638	**241**	.378
13	Wade Boggs, Bos	1985	653	**240**	.368
	Darin Erstad, Ana	2000	676	**240**	.355
15	Rod Carew, Min	1977	616	**239**	.388
16	Don Mattingly, NY-AL	1986	677	**238**	.352
17	Harry Heilmann, Det	1921	602	**237**	.394
	Paul Waner, Pit	1927	623	**237**	.380
	Joe Medwick, StL-NL	1937	633	**237**	.374
20	Jack Tobin, StL-AL	1921	671	**236**	.352

Batting Average

From 1900-49

		Year	AB	H	Avg
1	Rogers Hornsby, StL-NL	1924	536	227	.424
2	Nap Lajoie, Phi-AL	1901	543	229	.422
3	George Sisler, StL-AL	1922	586	246	.420
4	Ty Cobb, Det	1911	591	248	.420
5	Ty Cobb, Det	1912	533	227	.410
6	Joe Jackson, Cle	1911	571	233	.408
7	George Sisler, StL-AL	1920	631	257	.407
8	Ted Williams, Bos-AL	1941	456	185	.406
9	Rogers Hornsby, StL-NL	1925	504	203	.403
10	Harry Heilmann, Det	1923	524	211	.403

Since 1950

		Year	AB	H	Avg
1	Tony Gwynn, SD	1994	419	175	.394
2	George Brett, KC	1980	449	175	.390
3	Ted Williams, Bos	1957	420	163	.388
4	Rod Carew, Min	1977	616	239	.388
5	Larry Walker, Col	1999	438	166	.379
6	Todd Helton, Col	2000	580	216	.372
7	Nomar Garciaparra, Bos	2000	529	197	.372
8	**Ichiro Suzuki**, Sea	2004	704	262	.372
9	Tony Gwynn, SD	1997	592	220	.372
10	Andres Galarraga, Col	1993	470	174	.370

Total Bases

From 1900-49

		Year	TB
1	Babe Ruth, New York-AL	1921	457
2	Rogers Hornsby, St. Louis-NL	1922	450
3	Lou Gehrig, New York-AL	1927	447
4	Chuck Klein, Philadelphia-NL	1930	445
5	Jimmie Foxx, Philadelphia-AL	1932	438
6	Stan Musial, St. Louis-NL	1948	429
7	Hack Wilson, Chicago-NL	1930	423
8	Chuck Klein, Philadelphia-NL	1932	420
9	Lou Gehrig, New York-AL	1930	419
10	Joe DiMaggio, New York-AL	1937	418

Since 1950

		Year	TB
1	Sammy Sosa, Chicago-NL	2001	425
2	Luis Gonzalez, Arizona	2001	419
3	Sammy Sosa, Chicago-NL	1998	416
4	Barry Bonds, San Francisco	2001	411
5	Larry Walker, Colorado	1997	409
6	Jim Rice, Boston	1978	406
7	Todd Helton, Colorado	2000	405
8	Todd Helton, Colorado	2001	402
9	Hank Aaron, Milwaukee	1959	400
10	Albert Belle, Chicago-AL	1998	399

Runs Batted In

From 1900-49

		Year	Avg	HR	RBI
1	Hack Wilson, Chi-NL	1930	.356	56	191
2	Lou Gehrig, NY-AL	1931	.341	46	184
3	Hank Greenberg, Det	1937	.337	40	183
4	Lou Gehrig, NY-AL	1927	.373	47	175
	Jimmie Foxx, Bos-AL	1938	.349	50	175
6	Lou Gehrig, NY-AL	1930	.379	41	174
7	Babe Ruth, NY-AL	1921	.378	59	171
8	Chuck Klein, Phi-NL	1930	.386	40	170
	Hank Greenberg, Det	1935	.328	36	170
10	Jimmie Foxx, Phi-AL	1932	.364	58	169

Since 1950

		Year	Avg	HR	RBI
1	Manny Ramirez, Cle	1999	.333	44	165
2	Sammy Sosa, Chi-NL	2001	.328	64	160
3	Sammy Sosa, Chi-NL	1998	.308	66	158
4	Juan Gonzalez, Tex	1998	.318	45	157
5	Tommy Davis, LA-NL	1962	.346	27	153
6	Albert Belle, Chi-AL	1998	.328	49	152
7	Andres Galarraga, Col	1996	.304	47	150
	Miguel Tejada, Bal	2004	.311	34	150
9	George Foster, Cin	1977	.320	52	149
10	Rafael Palmeiro, Tex	1999	.324	47	148
	Johnny Bench, Cin	1970	.293	45	148
	Albert Belle, Cle	1996	.311	48	148

Runs

		Year	Runs
1	Babe Ruth, New York-AL	1921	177
2	Lou Gehrig, New York-AL	1936	167
3	Babe Ruth, New York-AL	1928	163
	Lou Gehrig, New York-AL	1931	163
5	Babe Ruth, New York-AL	1920	158
	Babe Ruth, New York-AL	1927	158
	Chuck Klein, Philadelphia-NL	1930	158
8	Rogers Hornsby, Chicago-NL	1929	156
9	Kiki Cuyler, Chicago-NL	1930	155
10	Lefty O'Doul, Philadelphia-NL	1929	152
	Woody English, Chicago-NL	1930	152
	Al Simmons, Philadelphia-AL	1930	152
	Chuck Klein, Philadelphia-NL	1932	152
	Jeff Bagwell, Houston	2000	152
15	Babe Ruth, New York-AL	1923	151
	Jimmie Foxx, Philadelphia-AL	1932	151
	Joe DiMaggio, New York-AL	1937	151
18	Babe Ruth, New York-AL	1930	150
	Ted Williams, Boston-AL	1949	150
20	Lou Gehrig, New York-AL	1927	149
	Babe Ruth, New York-AL	1931	149

Walks

		Year	BB
1	**Barry Bonds**, San Francisco	2004	232
2	Barry Bonds, San Francisco	2002	198
3	Barry Bonds, San Francisco	2001	177
4	Babe Ruth, New York-AL	1923	170
5	Ted Williams, Boston-AL	1947	162
	Ted Williams, Boston-AL	1949	162
	Mark McGwire, St. Louis	1998	162
8	Ted Williams, Boston-AL	1946	156
9	Barry Bonds, San Francisco	1996	151
	Eddie Yost, Washington	1956	151

Extra Base Hits

		Year	EBH
1	Babe Ruth, New York-AL	1921	119
2	Lou Gehrig, New York-AL	1927	117
3	Chuck Klein, Philadelphia-NL	1930	107
	Barry Bonds, San Francisco	2001	107
5	Todd Helton, Colorado	2001	105
6	Chuck Klein, Philadelphia-NL	1932	103
	Hank Greenberg, Detroit	1937	103
	Stan Musial, St. Louis-NL	1948	103
	Albert Belle, Cleveland	1995	103
	Todd Helton, Colorado	2000	103
	Sammy Sosa, Chicago-NL	2001	103

Slugging Percentage
From 1900-49

		Year	Pct
1	Babe Ruth, New York-AL	1920	.847
2	Babe Ruth, New York-AL	1921	.846
3	Babe Ruth, New York-AL	1927	.772
4	Lou Gehrig, New York-AL	1927	.765
5	Babe Ruth, New York-AL	1923	.764
6	Rogers Hornsby, St. Louis-NL	1925	.756
7	Jimmie Foxx, Philadelphia-AL	1932	.749
8	Babe Ruth, New York-AL	1924	.739
9	Babe Ruth, New York-AL	1926	.737
10	Ted Williams, Boston-AL	1941	.735

Since 1950

		Year	Pct
1	Barry Bonds, San Francisco	2001	.863
2	**Barry Bonds**, San Francisco	2004	.812
3	Barry Bonds, San Francisco	2002	.799
4	Mark McGwire, St. Louis	1998	.752
5	Jeff Bagwell, Houston	1994	.750
6	Barry Bonds, San Francisco	2003	.749
7	Sammy Sosa, Chicago-NL	2001	.737
8	Ted Williams, Boston	1957	.731
9	Mark McGwire, Oakland	1996	.730
10	Frank Thomas, Chicago-AL	1994	.729

Doubles

		Year	2B
1	Earl Webb, Boston-AL	1931	67
2	George Burns, Cleveland	1926	64
	Joe Medwick, St. Louis-NL	1936	64
4	Hank Greenberg, Detroit	1934	63
5	Paul Waner, Pittsburgh	1932	62
6	Charlie Gehringer, Detroit	1936	60
7	Tris Speaker, Cleveland	1923	59
	Chuck Klein, Philadelphia-NL	1930	59
	Todd Helton, Colorado	2000	59
10	Three tied with 57 each.		

Triples
From 1900-49

		Year	3B
1	Chief Wilson, Pittsburgh	1912	36
2	Joe Jackson, Cleveland	1912	26
3	Sam Crawford, Detroit	1914	26
4	Kiki Cuyler, Pittsburgh	1925	26
5	Three tied with 25 each.		

Since 1950

		Year	3B
1	Willie Wilson, Kansas City	1985	21
	Lance Johnson, New York-NL	1996	21
3	Willie Mays, New York-NL	1957	20
	George Brett, Kansas City	1979	20
	Cristian Guzman, Minnesota	2000	20

Stolen Bases

		Year	SB
1	Rickey Henderson, Oakland	1982	130
2	Lou Brock, St. Louis	1974	118
3	Vince Coleman, St. Louis	1985	110
4	Vince Coleman, St. Louis	1987	109
5	Rickey Henderson, Oakland	1983	108
6	Vince Coleman, St. Louis	1986	107
7	Maury Wills, Los Angeles-NL	1962	104
8	Rickey Henderson, Oakland	1980	100
9	Ron LeFlore, Montreal	1980	97
10	Ty Cobb, Detroit	1915	96
	Omar Moreno, Pittsburgh	1980	96
12	Maury Wills, Los Angeles	1965	94
13	Rickey Henderson, New York-AL	1988	93
14	Tim Raines, Montreal	1983	90
15	Clyde Milan, Washington	1912	88

Strikeouts

		Year	SO
1	**Adam Dunn**, Cincinnati	2004	195
2	Bobby Bonds, San Francisco	1970	189
3	Jose Hernandez, Milwaukee	2002	188
4	Bobby Bonds, San Francisco	1969	187
	Preston Wilson, Florida	2000	187
6	Rob Deer, Milwaukee	1987	186
7	Pete Incaviglia, Texas	1986	185
	Jose Hernandez, Milwaukee	2001	185
	Jim Thome, Cleveland	2001	185
10	Cecil Fielder, Detroit	1990	182
	Jim Thome, Philadelphia	2003	182

Pinch Hits
Career pinch hits in parentheses.

		Year	PH	
1	John Vander Wal, Colorado	1995	28	(126)
2	Lenny Harris, Col-Ari	1999	26	(193)
3	Jose Morales, Montreal	1976	25	(123)
4	Dave Philley, Baltimore	1961	24	(93)
	Vic Davalillo, St. Louis	1970	24	(95)
	Rusty Staub, New York-NL	1983	24	(100)
	Gerald Perry, St. Louis	1993	24	(95)

Note: Harris (193) is the career leader.

Pitching
Wins

From 1900-49

		Year	W	L	Pct
1	Jack Chesbro, NY-AL	1904	41	12	.774
2	Ed Walsh, Chi-AL	1908	40	15	.727
3	Christy Mathewson, NY-NL	1908	37	11	.771
4	Walter Johnson, Wash	1913	36	7	.837
5	Joe McGinnity, NY-NL	1904	35	8	.814
6	Smokey Joe Wood, Bos-AL	1912	34	5	.872
7	Cy Young, Bos-AL	1901	33	10	.767
	Grover Alexander, Phi-NL	1916	33	12	.733
	Christy Mathewson, NY-NL	1904	33	12	.733
10	Cy Young, Bos-AL	1902	32	11	.744

Since 1950

		Year	W	L	Pct
1	Denny McLain, Det	1968	31	6	.838
2	Robin Roberts, Phi-NL	1952	28	7	.800
3	Bob Welch, Oak	1990	27	6	.818
	Don Newcombe, Bklyn	1956	27	7	.794
	Sandy Koufax, LA	1966	27	9	.750
	Steve Carlton, Phi	1972	27	10	.730
7	Sandy Koufax, LA	1965	26	8	.765
	Juan Marichal, SF	1968	26	9	.743

Note: 11 pitchers tied with 25 wins, including Marichal twice.

Earned Run Average

From 1900-49

		Year	ShO	ERA
1	Dutch Leonard, Bos-AL	1914	7	1.01
2	Three Finger Brown, Chi-NL	1906	10	1.04
3	Walter Johnson, Wash	1913	11	1.09
4	Christy Mathewson, NY-NL	1909	8	1.14
5	Jack Pfiester, Chi-NL	1907	3	1.15
6	Addie Joss, Cle	1908	9	1.16
7	Carl Lundgren, Chi-NL	1907	7	1.17
8	Grover Alexander, Phi-NL	1915	12	1.22
9	Cy Young, Bos-AL	1908	3	1.26
10	Three pitchers tied at 1.27			

Since 1950

		Year	ShO	ERA
1	Bob Gibson, St.L	1968	13	1.12
2	Dwight Gooden, NY-NL	1985	8	1.53
3	Greg Maddux, Atl	1994	3	1.56
4	Luis Tiant, Cle	1968	9	1.60
5	Greg Maddux, Atl	1995	3	1.63
6	Dean Chance, LA-AL	1964	11	1.65
7	Nolan Ryan, Cal	1981	3	1.69
8	Sandy Koufax, LA	1966	5	1.73
9	Sandy Koufax, LA	1964	7	1.74
10	Pedro Martinez, Bos	2000	4	1.74

Note: Koufax's ERA in 1964 was 1.735. Martinez' ERA in 2000 was 1.742. The Yankees' Ron Guidry narrowly missed the top 10 list with an ERA of 1.743 in 1978.

Winning Pct.

		Year	W-L	Pct
1	Roy Face, Pit	1959	18-1	.947
2	Rick Sutcliffe, Chi-NL*	1984	16-1	.941
3	Johnny Allen, Cle	1937	15-1	.938
4	Greg Maddux, Atl	1995	19-2	.904
5	Randy Johnson, Sea	1995	18-2	.900
6	Ron Guidry, NY-AL	1978	25-3	.893
7	Freddie Fitzsimmons, Bklyn	1940	16-2	.889
8	Lefty Grove, Phi-AL	1931	31-4	.886
9	Bob Stanley, Bos	1978	15-2	.882
10	Preacher Roe, Bklyn	1951	22-3	.880

*Sutcliffe began 1984 with Cleveland and was 4-5 before being traded to the Cubs; his overall winning pct. was .769 (20-6).

Strikeouts

		Year	SO	P/9
1	Nolan Ryan, Cal	1973	383	10.57
2	Sandy Koufax, LA	1965	382	10.24
3	Randy Johnson, Ari	2001	372	13.41
4	Nolan Ryan, Cal	1974	367	9.93
5	Randy Johnson, Ari	1999	364	12.06
6	Rube Waddell, Phi-AL	1904	349	8.20
7	Bob Feller, Cle	1946	348	8.43
8	Randy Johnson, Ari	2000	347	12.56
9	Nolan Ryan, Cal	1977	341	10.26
10	Randy Johnson, Ari	2002	334	11.56

Appearances

		Year	App	Sv
1	Mike Marshall, LA	1974	106	21
2	Kent Tekulve, Pit	1979	94	31
3	Mike Marshall, LA	1973	92	31
4	Kent Tekulve, Pit	1978	91	31
5	Wayne Granger, Cin	1969	90	27
	Mike Marshall, Min	1979	90	32
	Kent Tekulve, Phi	1987	90	3

Saves

		Year	App	Sv
1	Bobby Thigpen, Chi-AL	1990	77	57
2	John Smoltz, Atl	2002	75	55
	Eric Gagne, LA	2003	77	55
4	Randy Myers, Chi-NL	1993	73	53
	Trevor Hoffman, SD	1998	66	53
	Mariano Rivera, NY-AL	2004	74	53
7	Eric Gagne, LA	2002	77	52
8	Dennis Eckersley, Oak	1992	69	51
	Rod Beck, Chi-NL	1998	81	51
10	Mariano Rivera, NY-AL	2001	71	50

Innings Pitched (since 1920)

		Year	IP	W-L
1	Wilbur Wood, Chi-AL	1972	376.2	24-17
2	Mickey Lolich, Det	1971	376.0	25-14
3	Bob Feller, Cle	1946	371.1	26-15
4	Grover Alexander, Chi-NL	1920	363.1	27-14
5	Wilbur Wood, Chi-AL	1973	359.1	24-20

Shutouts

		Year	ShO	ERA
1	Grover Alexander, Phi-NL	1916	16	1.55
2	Jack Coombs, Phi-AL	1910	13	1.30
	Bob Gibson, St.L	1968	13	1.12
4	Christy Mathewson, NY-NL	1908	12	1.43
	Grover Alexander, Phi-NL	1915	12	1.22

Walks Allowed (since 1920)

		Year	BB	SO
1	Bob Feller, Cle	1938	208	240
2	Nolan Ryan, Cal	1977	204	341
3	Nolan Ryan, Cal	1974	202	367
4	Bob Feller, Cle	1941	194	260
5	Bobo Newsom, St.L-AL	1938	192	226

Home Runs Allowed

		Year	HRs
1	Bert Blyleven, Minnesota	1986	50
2	Jose Lima, Houston	2000	48
3	Robin Roberts, Philadelphia	1956	46
	Bert Blyleven, Minnesota	1987	46
5	**Jamie Moyer**, Seattle	2004	44

SINGLE GAME
Through 2003 regular season.

Batting

Home Runs

No		Date	Inn
4	Bobby Lowe, Boston-NL	5/30/1894	9
	Ed Delahanty, Philadelphia-NL	7/13/1896	9
	Lou Gehrig, New York-AL	6/3/1932	9
	Chuck Klein, Philadelphia-NL	7/10/1936	10
	Pat Seerey, Chicago-AL	7/18/1948	11
	Gil Hodges, Brooklyn	8/31/1950	9
	Joe Adcock, Milwaukee	7/31/1954	9
	Rocky Colavito, Cleveland	6/10/1959	9
	Willie Mays, San Francisco	4/30/1961	9
	Mike Schmidt, Philadelphia	4/17/1976	10
	Bob Horner, Atlanta	7/6/1986	9
	Mark Whiten, St. Louis	9/7/1993	9
	Mike Cameron, Seattle	5/2/2002	9
	Shawn Green, Los Angeles	5/23/2002	9
	Carlos Delgado, Toronto	9/25/2003	9

Runs

No		Date	Inn
7	Guy Hecker, Louisville	8/15/1886	9

Strikeouts

No		Date	Inn
21	Tom Cheney, Washington	9/12/1962	16
20	Roger Clemens, Boston	4/29/1986	9
	Roger Clemens, Boston	9/18/1996	9
	Kerry Wood, Chicago-NL	5/6/1998	9
	Randy Johnson, Arizona	5/8/2001	9*

*Johnson struck out 20 in nine innings and was removed with the game tied, 1-1. Arizona beat Cincinnati, 4-3, in 11 innings.

Hits

No		Date	Inn
9	Johnny Burnett, Cleveland (9-for-11)	7/10/1932	18
7	Wilbert Robinson, Baltimore (7-for-7)	6/10/1892	9
	Rennie Stennett, Pittsburgh (7-for-7)	9/16/1975	9
	Cesar Gutierrez, Detroit (7-for-7)	6/21/1970	12
	Rocky Colavito, Detroit (7-for-10)	6/24/1962	22

Runs Batted In

No		Date	Inn
12	Jim Bottomley, St. Louis-NL	9/16/1924	9
	Mark Whiten, St. Louis	9/7/1993	9

Pitching

Innings Pitched

No		Date
26	Leon Cadore, Brooklyn (tie, 1-1)	5/1/1920
	Joe Oeschger, Boston-NL (tie, 1-1)	5/1/1920

Unassisted Triple Plays

One of the rarest feats in baseball, the unassisted triple play has been accomplished only 12 times in major league history. Ironically, in what can only be described as a statistic anomaly, the trick was turned twice in two days in May of 1927.

Player, Position, Team	Date	Opponent
Paul Hines, OF, Providence	May 8, 1878	Boston-NL
Neal Ball, SS, Cleveland	July 19, 1909	Boston-AL
Bill Wambganss, 2B, Cleveland*	Oct. 10, 1920	Brooklyn
George Burns, 1B, Boston-AL	Sept. 14, 1923	Cleveland
Ernie Padgett, SS, Boston-NL	Oct. 6, 1923	Philadelphia
Glenn Wright, SS, Pittsburgh	May 7, 1925	St.Louis-NL
Jimmy Cooney, SS, Chicago-NL	May 30, 1927	Pittsburgh
Johnny Neun, 1B, Detroit	May 31, 1927	Cleveland
Ron Hansen, SS, Washington	July 30, 1968	Cleveland
Mickey Morandini, 2B, Philadelphia	Sept. 20, 1992	Pittsburgh
John Valentin, SS, Boston	July 8, 1994	Seattle
Randy Velarde, 2B, Oakland	May 29, 2000	NY Yankees
Rafael Furcal, SS, Atlanta	Aug. 10, 2003	St. Louis

* World Series game

Most Gold Gloves (by position)

Gold Gloves have been awarded since the 1957 season by Rawlings Sporting Goods to superior major league fielders at each position in both leagues. Voting has been conducted by a panel of sportswriters appointed by *The Sporting News* publisher J.G. Taylor Spink (1957), major league players (1958-1964) and managers and coaches (1965-present). Top 5 in each position are listed, through the 2003 season.

Pitchers	No	Catchers	No	First Basemen	No	Second Basemen	No
1 Jim Kaat	16	1 Johnny Bench	10	1 Keith Hernandez	11	1 Roberto Alomar	10
2 Greg Maddux	13	Ivan Rodriguez	10	2 Don Mattingly	9	2 Ryne Sandberg	9
3 Bob Gibson	9	3 Bob Boone	7	3 George Scott	8	3 Bill Mazeroski	8
4 Bobby Shantz	8	4 Jim Sundberg	6	4 Vic Power	7	Frank White	8
5 Mark Langston	7	5 Bill Freehan	5	Bill White	7	5 Joe Morgan	5
						Bobby Richardson	5

Third Basemen	No	Shortstops	No	Outfielders	No
1 Brooks Robinson	16	1 Ozzie Smith	13	1 Roberto Clemente	12
2 Mike Schmidt	10	2 Luis Aparicio	9	Willie Mays	12
3 Buddy Bell	6	Omar Vizquel	9	3 Ken Griffey Jr.	10
4 Robin Ventura	6	4 Mark Belanger	8	Al Kaline	10
5 Four tied with 5 each.		5 Dave Concepcion	5	5 Five tied with 8 each

All-Time Winningest Managers

Top 20 Major League career victories through the 2004 season. Career, regular season and postseason (playoffs and World Series) records are noted along with AL and NL pennants and World Series titles won. Managers active during 2004 season in **bold** type.

		Career			Regular Season			Postseason			
		Yrs	W	L	Pct	W	L	Pct	W	L	Pct	Titles
1	Connie Mack	.53	**3755**	3967	.486	3731	3948	.486	24	19	.558	9 AL, 5 WS
2	John McGraw	.33	**2866**	2012	.588	2840	1984	.589	26	28	.482	10 NL, 3 WS
3	Sparky Anderson	.26	**2228**	1855	.547	2194	1834	.545	34	21	.618	4 NL, 1 AL, 3 WS
4	Bucky Harris	.29	**2168**	2228	.493	2157	2218	.493	11	10	.524	3 AL, 2 WS
5	**Tony La Russa**	.26	**2157**	1885	.534	2114	1846	.534	43	39	.524	3 AL, 1 NL, 1 WS
6	Joe McCarthy	.24	**2155**	1346	.616	2125	1333	.615	30	13	.698	1 NL, 8 AL, 7 WS
7	Walter Alston	.23	**2063**	1634	.558	2040	1613	.558	23	21	.523	7 NL, 4 WS
8	Leo Durocher	.24	**2015**	1717	.540	2008	1709	.540	7	8	.467	3 NL, 1 WS
9	**Bobby Cox**	.23	**2067**	1594	.565	2002	1531	.567	65	63	.508	5 NL, 1 WS
10	Casey Stengel	.25	**1942**	1868	.510	1905	1842	.508	37	26	.587	·10 AL, 7 WS
11	Gene Mauch	.26	**1907**	2044	.483	1902	2037	.483	5	7	.417	—None—
12	Bill McKechnie	.25	**1904**	1737	.523	1896	1723	.524	8	14	.364	4 NL, 2 WS
13	**Joe Torre**	.23	**1853**	1611	.535	1781	1570	.531	72	41	.637	6 AL, 4 WS
14	Tommy Lasorda	.21	**1630**	1469	.526	1599	1439	.526	31	30	.508	4 NL, 2 WS
15	Ralph Houk	.20	**1627**	1539	.514	1619	1531	.514	8	8	.500	3 AL, 2 WS
16	Fred Clarke	.19	**1609**	1189	.575	1602	1181	.576	7	8	.467	4 NL, 1 WS
17	Dick Williams	.21	**1592**	1474	.519	1571	1451	.520	21	23	.477	3 AL, 1 NL, 2 WS
18	Earl Weaver	.17	**1506**	1080	.582	1480	1060	.583	26	20	.565	4 AL, 1 WS
19	Clark Griffith	.20	**1491**	1367	.522	1491	1367	.522	0	0	.000	1 AL (1901)
20	**Lou Piniella**	.18	**1475**	1346	523	1452	1325	.523	23	21	.523	1 NL, 1 WS

Notes: John McGraw's postseason record also includes two World Series tie games (1912,'22).

Where They Managed

Alston—Brooklyn/Los Angeles NL (1954-76); **Anderson**—Cincinnati NL (1970-78), Detroit AL (1979-95); **Clarke**— Louisville NL (1897-99), Pittsburgh NL (1900-15); **Cox**—Atlanta (1978-81, 1990–), Toronto (1982-85); **Durocher**—Brooklyn NL (1939-46,48), New York NL (1948-55), Chicago NL (1966-72), Houston (1972-73); **Griffith**—Chicago AL (1901-02), New York AL (1903-08), Cincinnati NL (1909-11), Washington AL (1912-20); **Harris**—Washington AL (1924-28,35-42,50-54), Detroit AL (1929-33,55-56), Boston AL (1934), Philadelphia NL (1943), New York AL (1947-48); **Houk**—New York AL (1961-63,66-73), Detroit AL (1974-78), Boston AL (1981-84); **La Russa**—Chicago AL (1979-86), Oakland (1986-95); St. Louis (1996–) **Lasorda**—Los Angeles NL (1976-96).

Mack—Pittsburgh NL (1894-96), Philadelphia AL (1901-50); **Mauch**—Philadelphia NL (1960-68), Montreal (1969-75), Minnesota (1976-80), California AL (1981-82,85-87); **McCarthy**—Chicago NL (1926-30), New York AL (1931-46), Boston AL (1948-50); **McGraw**—Baltimore NL (1899), Baltimore AL (1901-02), New York NL (1902-32); **McKechnie**—Newark FL (1915), Pittsburgh NL (1922-26), St. Louis NL (1928-29), Boston NL (1930-37), Cincinnati NL (1938-46); **Piniella**—New York AL (1986-88), Cincinnati (1990-92), Seattle (1993-2002), Tampa Bay (2003–); **Stengel**—Brooklyn NL (1934-36), Boston NL (1938-43), New York AL (1949-60), New York NL (1962-65); **Torre**—New York NL (1977-81), Atlanta (1982-84), St. Louis (1990-95), New York AL (1996–); **Weaver**—Baltimore AL (1968-82,85-86); **Williams**—Boston AL (1967-69), Oakland AL (1971-73), California AL (1974-76), Montreal NL (1977-81), San Diego NL (1982-85), Seattle (1986-88).

Regular Season Winning Pct.

Minimum of 750 victories.

		Yrs	W	L	Pct	Pen
1	Joe McCarthy	.24	2125	1333	**.615**	9
2	Charlie Comiskey	..12	838	541	**.608**	4
3	Frank Selee	.16	1284	862	**.598**	5
4	Billy Southworth	.13	1044	704	**.597**	4
5	Frank Chance	.11	946	648	**.593**	4
6	John McGraw	.33	2840	1984	**.589**	10
7	Al Lopez	.17	1410	1004	**.584**	2
8	Earl Weaver	.17	1480	1060	**.583**	4
9	Cap Anson	.20	1296	947	**.578**	5
10	Fred Clarke	.19	1602	1181	**.576**	4
11	**Bobby Cox**	.23	2002	1531	**.567**	5
12	Davey Johnson	..14	1148	888	**.564**	1
13	Steve O'Neill	.14	1040	821	**.559**	1
14	Walter Alston	.23	2040	1613	**.558**	7
15	Bill Terry	.10	823	661	**.555**	3
16	Miller Huggins	.17	1413	1134	**.555**	6
17	Billy Martin	.16	1253	1013	**.553**	2
18	Harry Wright	.18	1000	825	**.548**	3
19	Charlie Grimm	.19	1287	1067	**.547**	3
20	Sparky Anderson	.26	2194	1834	**.545**	5

World Series Victories

		App	W	L	T	Pct	WS
1	Casey Stengel	.10	**37**	26	0	.587	7
2	Joe McCarthy	..9	**30**	13	0	.698	7
3	John McGraw	..9	**26**	28	2	.482	3
4	Connie Mack	..8	**24**	19	0	.558	5
5	**Joe Torre**	..6	**21**	11	0	.656	4
6	Walter Alston	..7	**20**	20	0	.500	4
7	Miller Huggins	..6	**18**	15	1	.544	3
8	Sparky Anderson	...5	**16**	12	0	.571	3
9	Tommy Lasorda	...4	**12**	11	0	.522	2
	Dick Williams	...4	**12**	14	0	.462	2
11	Frank Chance	...4	**11**	9	1	.548	2
	Bucky Harris	...3	**11**	10	0	.524	2
	Billy Southworth	...4	**11**	11	0	.500	2
	Earl Weaver	...4	**11**	13	0	.458	1
	Bobby Cox	...5	**11**	18	0	.379	1
16	Whitey Herzog	...3	**10**	11	0	.476	1
17	Bill Carrigan	...2	**8**	2	0	.800	2
	Danny Murtaugh	...2	**8**	6	0	.571	2
	Cito Gaston	...2	**8**	6	0	.571	2
	Tom Kelly	...2	**8**	6	0	.571	2
	Ralph Houk	...3	**8**	5	0	.500	2
	Bill McKechnie	...4	**8**	14	0	.364	2

Active Managers' Records

Regular season games only; through 2004 (updated as of Oct. 26).

National League

		Yrs	W	L	Pct
1	Tony La Russa, St.L.	26	2114	1846	.534
2	Bobby Cox, Atl.	23	2002	1531	.567
3	Dusty Baker, Chi	12	1017	862	.541
4	Jack McKeon, Fla.	14	928	861	.519
5	Frank Robinson, Mon.	14	913	1004	.476
6	Felipe Alou, SF	12	882	849	.510
7	Bruce Bochy, SD	10	781	821	.488
8	Phil Garner, Hou.	12	756	828	.477
9	Jim Tracy, LA	4	356	292	.549
10	Lloyd McClendon, Pit.	4	281	365	.435
11	Clint Hurdle, Col	3	209	255	.450
12	Ned Yost, Mil	2	135	188	.418
13	Dave Miley, Cin	2	98	121	.447
14	Arizona				
	NY Mets				
	Philadelphia				

American League

		Yrs	W	L	Pct
1	Joe Torre, NY	23	1781	1570	.531
2	Lou Piniella, TB	18	1452	1325	.523
3	Mike Hargrove, Sea	13	996	963	.508
4	Buck Showalter, Tex.	9	723	668	.520
5	Mike Scioscia, Ana.	5	425	385	.525
6	Terry Francona, Bos.	5	383	427	.473
7	Ron Gardenhire, Min.	3	276	209	.569
8	Tony Pena, KC	3	190	260	.422
9	Ken Macha, Oak	2	187	137	.577
10	Eric Wedge, Cle.	2	148	177	.455
11	Alan Trammell, Det.	2	115	209	.355
12	Ozzie Guillen, Chi	1	83	79	.512
13	Lee Mazzilli, Bal	1	78	84	.481
14	John Gibbons, Tor.	1	20	30	.400

Annual Awards

MOST VALUABLE PLAYER

There have been three different Most Valuable Player awards in baseball since 1911—the Chalmers Award (1911-14), presented by the Detroit-based automobile company; the League Award (1922-29), presented by the National and American Leagues; and the Baseball Writers' Award (since 1931), presented by the Baseball Writers' Association of America. Statistics for winning players are provided below. Stats for winning pitchers before advent of Cy Young Award are in MVP Pitchers' Statistics table.

Multiple winners: NL—Barry Bonds (6); Roy Campanella, Stan Musial and Mike Schmidt (3); Ernie Banks, Johnny Bench, Rogers Hornsby, Carl Hubbell, Willie Mays, Joe Morgan and Dale Murphy (2). **AL**—Yogi Berra, Joe DiMaggio, Jimmie Foxx and Mickey Mantle (3); Mickey Cochrane, Lou Gehrig, Juan Gonzalez, Hank Greenberg, Walter Johnson, Roger Maris, Hal Newhouser, Cal Ripken Jr., Frank Thomas, Ted Williams and Robin Yount (2). **NL & AL**—Frank Robinson (2, one in each).

Chalmers Award

National League

Year		Pos	HR	RBI	Avg
1911	Wildfire Schulte, Chi	OF	21	121	.300
1912	Larry Doyle, NY	2B	10	90	.330
1913	Jake Daubert, Bklyn	1B	2	52	.350
1914	Johnny Evers, Bos	2B	1	40	.279

American League

Year		Pos	HR	RBI	Avg
1911	Ty Cobb, Det	OF	8	144	.420
1912	Tris Speaker, Bos	OF	10	98	.383
1913	Walter Johnson, Wash	P	—	—	—
1914	Eddie Collins, Phi	2B	2	85	.344

League Award

National League

Year		Pos	HR	RBI	Avg
1922	No selection				
1923	No selection				
1924	Dazzy Vance, Bklyn	P	—	—	—
1925	Rogers Hornsby, St.L	2B-Mgr	39	143	.403
1926	Bob O'Farrell, St.L	C	7	68	.293
1927	Paul Waner, Pit	OF	9	131	.380
1928	Jim Bottomley, St.L	1B	31	136	.325
1929	Rogers Hornsby, Chi	2B	39	149	.380

American League

Year		Pos	HR	RBI	Avg
1922	George Sisler, St.L	1B	8	105	.420
1923	Babe Ruth, NY	OF	41	131	.393
1924	Walter Johnson, Wash	P	—	—	—
1925	Roger Peckinpaugh, Wash	SS	4	64	.294
1926	George Burns, Cle	1B	4	114	.358
1927	Lou Gehrig, NY	1B	47	175	.373
1928	Mickey Cochrane, Phi	C	10	57	.293
1929	No selection				

Most Valuable Player
National League

Year		Pos	HR	RBI	Avg	Year		Pos	HR	RBI	Avg
1931	Frankie Frisch, St.L	2B	4	82	.311	1950	Jim Konstanty, Phi	P	—	—	—
1932	Chuck Klein, Phi	OF	38	137	.348	1951	Roy Campanella, Bklyn	C	33	108	.325
1933	Carl Hubbell, NY	P	—	—	—	1952	Hank Sauer, Chi	OF	37	121	.270
1934	Dizzy Dean, St.L	P	—	—	—	1953	Roy Campanella, Bklyn	C	41	142	.312
1935	Gabby Hartnett, Chi	C	13	91	.344	1954	Willie Mays, NY	OF	41	110	.345
1936	Carl Hubbell, NY	P	—	—	—	1955	Roy Campanella, Bklyn	C	32	107	.318
1937	Joe Medwick, St.L	OF	31	154	.374	1956	Don Newcombe, Bklyn	P	—	—	—
1938	Ernie Lombardi, Cin	C	19	95	.342	1957	Hank Aaron, Mil	OF	44	132	.322
1939	Bucky Walters, Cin	P	—	—	—	1958	Ernie Banks, Chi	SS	47	129	.313
1940	Frank McCormick, Cin	1B	19	127	.309	1959	Ernie Banks, Chi	SS	45	143	.304
1941	Dolf Camilli, Bklyn	1B	34	120	.285	1960	Dick Groat, Pit	SS	2	50	.325
1942	Mort Cooper, St.L	P	—	—	—	1961	Frank Robinson, Cin	OF	37	124	.323
1943	Stan Musial, St.L	OF	13	81	.357	1962	Maury Wills, LA	SS	6	48	.299
1944	Marty Marion, St.L	SS	6	63	.267	1963	Sandy Koufax, LA	P	—	—	—
1945	Phil Cavarretta, Chi	1B	6	97	.355	1964	Ken Boyer, St.L	3B	24	119	.295
1946	Stan Musial, St.L	1B-OF	16	103	.365	1965	Willie Mays, SF	OF	52	112	.317
1947	Bob Elliott, Bos	3B	22	113	.317	1966	Roberto Clemente, Pit	OF	29	119	.317
1948	Stan Musial, St.L	OF	39	131	.376	1967	Orlando Cepeda, St.L	1B	25	111	.325
1949	Jackie Robinson, Bklyn	2B	16	124	.342	1968	Bob Gibson, St.L	P	—	—	—

Year	Player	Pos	HR	RBI	Avg
1969	Willie McCovey, SF	1B	45	126	.320
1970	Johnny Bench, Cin	C	45	148	.293
1971	Joe Torre, St.L	3B	24	137	.363
1972	Johnny Bench, Cin	C	40	125	.270
1973	Pete Rose, Cin	OF	5	64	.338
1974	Steve Garvey, LA	1B	21	111	.312
1975	Joe Morgan, Cin	2B	17	94	.327
1976	Joe Morgan, Cin	2B	27	111	.320
1977	George Foster, Cin	OF	52	149	.320
1978	Dave Parker, Pit	OF	30	117	.334
1979	Keith Hernandez, St.L	1B	11	105	.344
	Willie Stargell, Pit	1B	32	82	.281
1980	Mike Schmidt, Phi	3B	48	121	.286
1981	Mike Schmidt, Phi	3B	31	91	.316
1982	Dale Murphy, Atl	OF	36	109	.281
1983	Dale Murphy, Atl	OF	36	121	.302
1984	Ryne Sandberg, Chi	2B	19	84	.314
1985	Willie McGee, St.L	OF	10	82	.353
1986	Mike Schmidt, Phi	3B	37	119	.290
1987	Andre Dawson, Chi	OF	49	137	.287
1988	Kirk Gibson, LA	OF	25	76	.290
1989	Kevin Mitchell, SF	OF	47	125	.291
1990	Barry Bonds, Pit	OF	33	114	.301
1991	Terry Pendleton, Atl	3B	22	86	.319
1992	Barry Bonds, Pit	OF	34	103	.311
1993	Barry Bonds, SF	OF	46	123	.336
1994	Jeff Bagwell, Hou	1B	39	116	.368
1995	Barry Larkin, Cin	SS	15	66	.319
1996	Ken Caminiti, SD	3B	40	130	.326
1997	Larry Walker, Col	OF	49	130	.366
1998	Sammy Sosa, Chi	OF	66	158	.308
1999	Chipper Jones, Atl	3B	45	110	.319
2000	Jeff Kent, SF	2B	33	125	.334
2001	Barry Bonds, SF	OF	73	137	.328
2002	Barry Bonds, SF	OF	46	110	.370
2003	Barry Bonds, SF	OF	45	90	.341

American League

Year	Player	Pos	HR	RBI	Avg
1931	Lefty Grove, Phi	P	—	—	—
1932	Jimmie Foxx, Phi	1B	58	169	.364
1933	Jimmie Foxx, Phi	1B	48	163	.356
1934	Mickey Cochrane, Det	C-Mgr	2	76	.320
1935	Hank Greenberg, Det	1B	36	170	.328
1936	Lou Gehrig, NY	1B	49	152	.354
1937	Charlie Gehringer, Det	2B	14	96	.371
1938	Jimmie Foxx, Bos	1B	50	175	.349
1939	Joe DiMaggio, NY	OF	30	126	.381
1940	Hank Greenberg, Det	OF	41	150	.340
1941	Joe DiMaggio, NY	OF	30	125	.357
1942	Joe Gordon, NY	2B	18	103	.322
1943	Spud Chandler, NY	P	—	—	—
1944	Hal Newhouser, Det	P	—	—	—
1945	Hal Newhouser, Det	P	—	—	—
1946	Ted Williams, Bos	OF	38	123	.342
1947	Joe DiMaggio, NY	OF	20	97	.315
1948	Lou Boudreau, Cle	SS-Mgr	18	106	.355
1949	Ted Williams, Bos	OF	43	159	.343
1950	Phil Rizzuto, NY	SS	7	66	.324
1951	Yogi Berra, NY	C	27	88	.294
1952	Bobby Shantz, Phi	P	—	—	—
1953	Al Rosen, Cle	3B	43	145	.336
1954	Yogi Berra, NY	C	22	125	.307
1955	Yogi Berra, NY	C	27	108	.272
1956	Mickey Mantle, NY	OF	52	130	.353
1957	Mickey Mantle, NY	OF	34	94	.365
1958	Jackie Jensen, Bos	OF	35	122	.286
1959	Nellie Fox, Chi	2B	2	70	.306
1960	Roger Maris, NY	OF	39	112	.283
1961	Roger Maris, NY	OF	61	142	.269
1962	Mickey Mantle, NY	OF	30	89	.321
1963	Elston Howard, NY	C	28	85	.287
1964	Brooks Robinson, Bal	3B	28	118	.317
1965	Zoilo Versalles, Min	SS	19	77	.273
1966	Frank Robinson, Bal	OF	49	122	.316
1967	Carl Yastrzemski, Bos	OF	44	121	.326
1968	Denny McLain, Det	P	—	—	—
1969	Harmon Killebrew, Min	3B-1B	49	140	.276
1970	Boog Powell, Bal	1B	35	114	.297
1971	Vida Blue, Oak	P	—	—	—
1972	Dick Allen, Chi	1B	37	113	.308
1973	Reggie Jackson, Oak	OF	32	117	.293
1974	Jeff Burroughs, Tex	OF	25	118	.301
1975	Fred Lynn, Bos	OF	21	105	.331
1976	Thurman Munson, NY	C	17	105	.302
1977	Rod Carew, Min	1B	14	100	.388
1978	Jim Rice, Bos	OF-DH	46	139	.315
1979	Don Baylor, Cal	OF-DH	36	139	.296
1980	George Brett, KC	3B	24	118	.390
1981	Rollie Fingers, Mil	P	—	—	—
1982	Robin Yount, Mil	SS	29	114	.331
1983	Cal Ripken Jr., Bal	SS	27	102	.318
1984	Willie Hernandez, Det	P	—	—	—
1985	Don Mattingly, NY	1B	35	145	.324
1986	Roger Clemens, NY	P	—	—	—
1987	George Bell, Tor	OF	47	134	.308
1988	Jose Canseco, Oak	OF	42	124	.307
1989	Robin Yount, Mil	OF	21	103	.318
1990	Rickey Henderson, Oak	OF	28	61	.325
1991	Cal Ripken Jr., Bal	SS	34	114	.323
1992	Dennis Eckersley, Oak	P	—	—	—
1993	Frank Thomas, Chi	1B	41	128	.317
1994	Frank Thomas, Chi	1B	38	101	.353
1995	Mo Vaughn, Bos	1B	39	126	.300
1996	Juan Gonzalez, Tex	OF-DH	47	144	.314
1997	Ken Griffey Jr., Sea	OF	56	147	.304
1998	Juan Gonzalez, Tex	OF	45	157	.318
1999	Ivan Rodriguez, Tex	C	35	113	.332
2000	Jason Giambi, Oak	1B	43	137	.333
2001	Ichiro Suzuki, Sea	OF	8	69	.350
2002	Miguel Tejada, Oak	SS	34	131	.308
2003	Alex Rodriguez, Tex	SS	47	118	.298

MVP Pitchers' Statistics

Pitchers have been named Most Valuable Player on 23 occasions, 10 times in the NL and 13 in the AL. Four have been relief pitchers—Jim Konstanty, Rollie Fingers, Willie Hernandez and Dennis Eckersley. For statistics of MVP pitchers since 1956, see Cy Young Award tables on following page.

National League

Year	Player	Gm	W-L	SV	ERA
1924	Dazzy Vance, Bklyn	35	28-6	0	2.16
1933	Carl Hubbell, NY	45	23-12	5	1.66
1934	Dizzy Dean, St.L	50	30-7	7	2.66
1936	Carl Hubbell, NY	42	26-6	3	2.31
1939	Bucky Walters, Cin	39	27-11	0	2.29
1942	Mort Cooper, St.L	37	22-7	0	1.78
1950	Jim Konstanty, Phi	74	16-7	22	2.66

American League

Year	Player	Gm	W-L	SV	ERA
1913	Walter Johnson, Wash	47	36-7	2	1.09
1924	Walter Johnson, Wash	38	23-7	0	2.72
1931	Lefty Grove, Phi	41	31-4	5	2.06
1943	Spud Chandler, NY	30	20-4	0	1.64
1944	Hal Newhouser, Det	47	29-9	2	2.22
1945	Hal Newhouser, Det	40	25-9	2	1.81
1952	Bobby Shantz, Phi	33	24-7	0	2.48

CY YOUNG AWARD

Voted on by the Baseball Writers Association of America. One award was presented from 1956-66, two since 1967. Pitchers who won the MVP and Cy Young awards in the same season are in **bold** type.
Multiple winners: NL—Steve Carlton, Greg Maddux and Randy Johnson (4); Sandy Koufax and Tom Seaver (3); Bob Gibson and Tom Glavine (2). **AL**—Roger Clemens (6); Jim Palmer (3); Pedro Martinez and Denny McLain (2). **NL & AL**—Randy Johnson (5, four in NL, one in AL), Pedro Martinez (3, two in AL, one in NL) and Gaylord Perry (2, one in each).

NL and AL Combined

Year	National League	Gm	W-L	SV	ERA	Year	American League	Gm	W-L	SV	ERA
1956	**Don Newcombe**, Bklyn	38	27-7	0	3.06	1958	Bob Turley, NY	33	21-7	1	2.97
1957	Warren Spahn, Mil	39	21-11	0	2.69	1959	Early Wynn, Chi	37	22-10	0	3.17
1960	Vernon Law, Pit	35	20-9	0	3.08	1961	Whitey Ford, NY	39	25-4	0	3.21
1962	Don Drysdale, LA	43	25-9	1	2.83	1964	Dean Chance, LA	46	20-9	4	1.65
1963	**Sandy Koufax**, LA	40	25-5	0	1.88						
1965	Sandy Koufax, LA	43	26-8	2	2.04						
1966	Sandy Koufax, LA	41	27-9	0	1.73						

Separate League Awards

Year	National League	Gm	W-L	SV	ERA	Year	American League	Gm	W-L	SV	ERA
1967	Mike McCormick,SF	40	22-10	0	2.85	1967	Jim Lonborg, Bos	39	22-9	0	3.16
1968	**Bob Gibson**, St.L	34	22-9	0	1.12	1968	**Denny McLain**, Det	41	31-6	0	1.96
1969	Tom Seaver, NY	36	25-7	0	2.21	1969	Denny McLain, Det	42	24-9	0	2.80
							Mike Cuellar, Bal	39	23-11	0	2.38
1970	Bob Gibson, St.L	34	23-7	0	3.12	1970	Jim Perry, Min	40	24-12	0	3.03
1971	Ferguson Jenkins, Chi	39	24-13	0	2.77	1971	**Vida Blue**, Oak	39	24-8	0	1.82
1972	Steve Carlton, Phi	41	27-10	0	1.97	1972	Gaylord Perry, Cle	41	24-16	1	1.92
1973	Tom Seaver, NY	36	19-10	0	2.08	1973	Jim Palmer, Bal	38	22-9	1	2.40
1974	Mike Marshall, LA	106	15-12	21	2.42	1974	Catfish Hunter, Oak	41	25-12	0	2.49
1975	Tom Seaver, NY	36	22-9	0	2.38	1975	Jim Palmer, Bal	39	23-11	1	2.09
1976	Randy Jones, SD	40	22-14	0	2.74	1976	Jim Palmer, Bal	40	22-13	0	2.51
1977	Steve Carlton, Phi	36	23-10	0	2.64	1977	Sparky Lyle, NY	72	13-5	26	2.17
1978	Gaylord Perry, SD	37	21-6	0	2.72	1978	Ron Guidry, NY	35	25-3	0	1.74
1979	Bruce Sutter, Chi	62	6-6	37	2.23	1979	Mike Flanagan, Bal	39	23-9	0	3.08
1980	Steve Carlton, Phi	38	24-9	0	2.34	1980	Steve Stone, Bal	37	25-7	0	3.23
1981	Fernando Valenzuela, LA	25	13-7	0	2.48	1981	**Rollie Fingers**,Mil	47	6-3	28	1.04
1982	Steve Carlton, Phi	38	23-11	0	3.10	1982	Pete Vuckovich, Mil	30	18-6	0	3.34
1983	John Denny, Phi	36	19-6	0	2.37	1983	LaMarr Hoyt, Chi	36	24-10	0	3.66
1984	Rick Sutcliffe, Chi	20*	16-1	0	2.69	1984	**Willie Hernandez**, Det	80	9-3	32	1.92
1985	Dwight Gooden, NY	35	24-4	0	1.53	1985	Bret Saberhagen, KC	32	20-6	0	2.87
1986	Mike Scott, Hou	37	18-10	0	2.22	1986	**Roger Clemens**, Bos	33	24-4	0	2.48
1987	Steve Bedrosian, Phi	65	5-3	40	2.83	1987	Roger Clemens, Bos	36	20-9	0	2.97
1988	Orel Hershiser, LA	35	23-8	1	2.26	1988	Frank Viola, Min	35	24-7	0	2.64
1989	Mark Davis, SD	70	4-3	44	1.85	1989	Bret Saberhagen, KC	36	23-6	0	2.16
1990	Doug Drabek, Pit	33	22-6	0	2.76	1990	Bob Welch, Oak	35	27-6	0	2.95
1991	Tom Glavine, Atl	34	20-11	0	2.55	1991	Roger Clemens, Bos	35	18-10	0	2.62
1992	Greg Maddux, Chi	35	20-11	0	2.18	1992	**Dennis Eckersley**, Oak	69	7-1	51	1.91
1993	Greg Maddux, Atl	36	20-10	0	2.36	1993	Jack McDowell, Chi	34	22-10	0	3.37
1994	Greg Maddux, Atl	25	16-6	0	1.56	1994	David Cone, KC	23	16-5	0	2.94
1995	Greg Maddux, Atl	28	19-2	0	1.63	1995	Randy Johnson, Sea	30	18-2	0	2.48
1996	John Smoltz, Atl	35	24-8	0	2.94	1996	Pat Hentgen, Tor	35	20-10	0	3.22
1997	Pedro Martinez, Mon	31	17-8	0	1.90	1997	Roger Clemens, Tor	34	21-7	0	2.05
1998	Tom Glavine, Atl	33	20-6	0	2.47	1998	Roger Clemens, Tor	33	20-6	0	2.65
1999	Randy Johnson, Ari	35	17-9	0	2.48	1999	Pedro Martinez, Bos	31	23-4	0	2.07
2000	Randy Johnson, Ari	35	19-7	0	2.64	2000	Pedro Martinez, Bos	29	18-6	0	1.74
2001	Randy Johnson, Ari	35	21-6	0	2.49	2001	Roger Clemens, NY	33	20-3	0	3.51
2002	Randy Johnson, Ari	35	24-5	0	2.32	2002	Barry Zito, Oak	35	23-5	0	2.75
2003	Eric Gagne, LA	77	2-3	55	1.20	2003	Roy Halladay, Tor	36	22-7	0	3.25

*NL games only, Sutcliffe pitched 15 games with Cleveland before being traded to the Cubs.

ROOKIE OF THE YEAR

Voted on by the Baseball Writers Assn. of America. One award was presented from 1947-48. Two awards (one for each league) have been presented since 1949. Winners who were also named MVP in the same season are in **bold** type.

NL and AL Combined

Year		Pos	Year		Pos
1947	Jackie Robinson, Brooklyn	1B	1948	Alvin Dark, Boston-NL	SS

National League

Year		Pos	Year		Pos	Year		Pos
1949	Don Newcombe, Bklyn	P	1951	Willie Mays, NY	OF	1953	Jim Gilliam, Bklyn	2B
1950	Sam Jethroe, Bos	OF	1952	Joe Black, Bklyn	P	1954	Wally Moon, St.L	OF

Year		Pos	Year		Pos	Year		Pos
1955	Bill Virdon, St.L	OF	1972	Jon Matlack, NY	P	1988	Chris Sabo, Cin	3B
1956	Frank Robinson, Cin	OF	1973	Gary Matthews, SF	OF	1989	Jerome Walton, Chi	OF
1957	Jack Sanford, Phi	P	1974	Bake McBride, St.L	OF	1990	David Justice, Atl	OF
1958	Orlando Cepeda, SF	1B	1975	John Montefusco, SF	P	1991	Jeff Bagwell, Hou.	1B
1959	Willie McCovey, SF	1B	1976	Butch Metzger, SD	P	1992	Eric Karros, LA	1B
1960	Frank Howard, LA	OF		& Pat Zachry, Cin	P	1993	Mike Piazza, LA	C
1961	Billy Williams, Chi	OF	1977	Andre Dawson, Mon	OF	1994	Raul Mondesi, LA	OF
1962	Ken Hubbs, Chi	2B	1978	Bob Horner, Atl	3B	1995	Hideo Nomo, LA	P
1963	Pete Rose, Cin	2B	1979	Rick Sutcliffe, LA	P	1996	Todd Hollandsworth, LA	OF
1964	Richie Allen, Phi	3B	1980	Steve Howe, LA	P	1997	Scott Rolen, Phi	3B
1965	Jim Lefebvre, LA	2B	1981	Fernando Valenzuela, LA	P	1998	Kerry Wood, Chi	P
1966	Tommy Helms, Cin	3B	1982	Steve Sax, LA	2B	1999	Scott Williamson, Cin	P
1967	Tom Seaver, NY	P	1983	Darryl Strawberry, NY	OF	2000	Rafael Furcal, Atl	SS
1968	Johnny Bench, Cin	C	1984	Dwight Gooden, NY	P	2001	Albert Pujols, St.L	OF-3B
1969	Ted Sizemore, LA	2B	1985	Vince Coleman, St.L	OF	2002	Jason Jennings, Col	P
1970	Carl Morton, Mon	P	1986	Todd Worrell, St.L	P	2003	Dontrelle Willis, Fla	P
1971	Earl Williams, Atl	C	1987	Benito Santiago, SD	C			

American League

Year		Pos	Year		Pos	Year		Pos
1949	Roy Sievers, St.L	OF	1968	Stan Bahnsen, NY	P	1986	Jose Canseco, Oak	OF
1950	Walt Dropo, Bos	1B	1969	Lou Piniella, KC	OF	1987	Mark McGwire, Oak	1B
1951	Gil McDougald, NY	3B	1970	Thurman Munson, NY	C	1988	Walt Weiss, Oak	SS
1952	Harry Byrd, Phi	P	1971	Chris Chambliss, Cle	1B	1989	Gregg Olson, Bal	P
1953	Harvey Kuenn, Det	SS	1972	Carlton Fisk, Bos	C	1990	Sandy Alomar Jr., Cle	C
1954	Bob Grim, NY	P	1973	Al Bumbry, Bal	OF	1991	Chuck Knoblauch, Min	2B
1955	Herb Score, Cle	P	1974	Mike Hargrove, Tex	1B	1992	Pat Listach, Mil	SS
1956	Luis Aparicio, Chi	SS	1975	**Fred Lynn**, Bos	OF	1993	Tim Salmon, Cal	OF
1957	Tony Kubek, NY	INF-OF	1976	Mark Fidrych, Det	P	1994	Bob Hamelin, KC	DH
1958	Albie Pearson, Wash	OF	1977	Eddie Murray, Bal	DH-1B	1995	Marty Cordova, Min	OF
1959	Bob Allison, Wash	OF	1978	Lou Whitaker, Det	2B	1996	Derek Jeter, NY	SS
1960	Ron Hansen, Bal	SS	1979	John Castino, Min	3B	1997	Nomar Garciaparra, Bos	SS
1961	Don Schwall, Bos	P		& Alfredo Griffin, Tor	SS	1998	Ben Grieve, Oak	OF
1962	Tom Tresh, NY	SS-OF	1980	Joe Charboneau, Cle	OF-DH	1999	Carlos Beltran, KC	OF
1963	Gary Peters, Chi	P	1981	Dave Righetti, NY	P	2000	Kazuhiro Sasaki, Sea	P
1964	Tony Oliva, Min	OF	1982	Cal Ripken Jr., Bal	SS-3B	2001	**Ichiro Suzuki**, Sea	OF
1965	Curt Blefary, Bal	OF	1983	Ron Kittle, Chi	OF	2002	Eric Hinske, Tor	3B
1966	Tommie Agee, Chi	OF	1984	Alvin Davis, Sea	1B	2003	Angel Berroa, KC	SS
1967	Rod Carew, Min	2B	1985	Ozzie Guillen, Chi	SS			

MANAGER OF THE YEAR

Voted on by the Baseball Writers Association of America. Two awards (one for each league) presented since 1983. Note that (*) indicates manager's team won division championship and (†) indicates unofficial division won in 1994.

Multiple winners: Tony La Russa (4); Dusty Baker (3); Sparky Anderson, Bobby Cox, Tommy Lasorda, Jim Leyland, Jack McKeon, Lou Piniella and Joe Torre (2).

National League

Year		Improvement		
1983	Tommy Lasorda, LA	88-74	to	91-71*
1984	Jim Frey, Chi	71-91	to	96-75*
1985	Whitey Herzog, St. L	84-78	to	101-61*
1986	Hal Lanier, Hou.	83-79	to	96-66*
1987	Buck Rodgers, Mon	78-83	to	91-71
1988	Tommy Lasorda, LA.	73-89	to	94-67*
1989	Don Zimmer, Chi	77-85	to	93-69*
1990	Jim Leyland, Pit	74-88	to	95-67*
1991	Bobby Cox, Atl	65-97	to	94-68*
1992	Jim Leyland, Pit	98-64*	to	96-66*
1993	Dusty Baker, SF	72-90	to	103-59
1994	Felipe Alou, Mon	94-68	to	74-40†
1995	Don Baylor, Col	53-64	to	77-67
1996	Bruce Bochy, SD.	70-74	to	91-71
1997	Dusty Baker, SF	68-94	to	90-72
1998	Larry Dierker, Hou	84-78	to	102-60*
1999	Jack McKeon, Cin	77-85	to	96-67
2000	Dusty Baker, SF	86-76	to	97-65*
2001	Larry Bowa, Phi	65-97	to	86-76
2002	Tony La Russa, St.L	93-69	to	97-65*
2003	Jack McKeon, Fla.	79-83	to	91-71

American League

Year		Improvement		
1983	Tony La Russa, Chi	87-75	to	99-63*
1984	Sparky Anderson, Det.	92-70	to	104-58*
1985	Bobby Cox, Tor	89-73	to	99-62*
1986	John McNamara, Bos	81-81	to	95-66*
1987	Sparky Anderson, Det.	87-75	to	98-64*
1988	Tony La Russa, Oak	81-81	to	104-58*
1989	Frank Robinson, Bal	54-107	to	87-75
1990	Jeff Torborg, Chi.	69-92	to	94-68
1991	Tom Kelly, Min.	74-88	to	95-67*
1992	Tony La Russa, Oak	84-78	to	96-66*
1993	Gene Lamont, Chi.	86-76	to	94-68†
1994	Buck Showalter, NY	88-74	to	70-43†
1995	Lou Piniella, Sea.	49-63	to	79-66*
1996	Joe Torre, NY.	79-65	to	92-70
	& Johnny Oates, Tex.	74-70	to	90-72
1997	Davey Johnson, Bal	88-74	to	98-64*
1998	Joe Torre, NY.	96-66	to	114-48*
1999	Jimy Williams, Bos	92-70	to	94-68
2000	Jerry Manuel, Chi.	75-86	to	95-67*
2001	Lou Piniella, Sea.	91-71	to	116-46*
2002	Mike Scioscia, Ana	75-87	to	99-63
2003	Tony Pena, KC.	62-100	to	83-79

COLLEGE BASEBALL

College World Series

The NCAA Division I College World Series has been held in Kalamazoo, Mich. (1947-48), Wichita, Kan. (1949) and Omaha, Neb. (since 1950). Beginning in 2003, the championship series has been best-of-three. Score listed is the deciding game.

Multiple winners: USC (12); Arizona St., LSU and Texas (5); CS-Fullerton and Miami-FL (4); Arizona and Minnesota (3); California, Michigan, Oklahoma and Stanford (2).

Year	Winner	Coach	Score	Runner-up	Year	Winner	Coach	Score	Runner-up
1947	California	Clint Evans	8-7	Yale	1976	Arizona	Jerry Kindall	7-1	E. Michigan
1948	USC	Sam Barry	9-2	Yale	1977	Arizona St.	Jim Brock	2-1	S. Carolina
1949	Texas	Bibb Falk	10-3	W. Forest	1978	USC	Rod Dedeaux	10-3	Ariz. St.
1950	Texas	Bibb Falk	3-0	Wash. St.	1979	CS-Fullerton	Augie Garrido	2-1	Arkansas
1951	Oklahoma	Jack Baer	3-2	Tennessee	1980	Arizona	Jerry Kindall	5-3	Hawaii
1952	Holy Cross	Jack Barry	8-4	Missouri	1981	Arizona St.	Jim Brock	7-4	Okla. St.
1953	Michigan	Ray Fisher	7-5	Texas	1982	Miami-FL	Ron Fraser	9-3	Wichita St.
1954	Missouri	Hi Simmons	4-1	Rollins	1983	Texas	Cliff Gustafson	4-3	Alabama
1955	Wake Forest	Taylor Sanford	7-6	W. Mich.	1984	CS-Fullerton	Augie Garrido	3-1	Texas
1956	Minnesota	Dick Siebert	12-1	Arizona	1985	Miami-FL	Ron Fraser	10-6	Texas
1957	California	Geo. Wolfman	1-0	Penn St.	1986	Arizona	Jerry Kindall	10-2	Fla. St.
1958	USC	Rod Dedeaux	8-7	Missouri	1987	Stanford	M. Marquess	9-5	Okla. St.
1959	Oklahoma St.	Toby Greene	5-3	Arizona	1988	Stanford	M. Marquess	9-4	Ariz. St.
1960	Minnesota	Dick Siebert	2-1	USC	1989	Wichita St.	G. Stephenson	5-3	Texas
1961	USC	Rod Dedeaux	1-0	Okla. St.	1990	Georgia	Steve Webber	2-1	Okla. St.
1962	Michigan	Don Lund	5-4	S. Clara	1991	LSU	Skip Bertman	6-3	Wichita St.
1963	USC	Rod Dedeaux	5-2	Arizona	1992	Pepperdine	Andy Lopez	3-2	CS-Fullerton
1964	Minnesota	Dick Siebert	5-1	Missouri	1993	LSU	Skip Bertman	8-0	Wichita St.
1965	Arizona St.	Bobby Winkles	2-1	Ohio St.	1994	Oklahoma	Larry Cochell	13-5	Ga. Tech
1966	Ohio St.	Marty Karow	8-2	Okla. St.	1995	CS-Fullerton	Augie Garrido	11-5	USC
1967	Arizona St.	Bobby Winkles	11-2	Houston	1996	LSU	Skip Bertman	9-8	Miami-FL
1968	USC	Rod Dedeaux	4-3	So. Ill.	1997	LSU	Skip Bertman	13-6	Alabama
1969	Arizona St.	Bobby Winkles	10-1	Tulsa	1998	USC	Mike Gillespie	21-14	Arizona St.
1970	USC	Rod Dedeaux	2-1	Fla. St.	1999	Miami-FL	Jim Morris	6-5	Fla. St.
1971	USC	Rod Dedeaux	7-2	So. Ill.	2000	LSU	Skip Bertman	6-5	Stanford
1972	USC	Rod Dedeaux	1-0	Ariz. St.	2001	Miami-FL	Jim Morris	12-1	Stanford
1973	USC	Rod Dedeaux	4-3	Ariz. St.	2002	Texas	Augie Garrido	12-6	S.Carolina
1974	USC	Rod Dedeaux	7-3	Miami-FL	2003	Rice	Wayne Graham	14-2	Stanford
1975	Texas	Cliff Gustafson	5-1	S. Carolina	2004	CS-Fullerton	George Horton	3-2	Texas

Most Outstanding Player

The Most Outstanding Player has been selected every year of the College World Series since 1949. Winners who did not play for the CWS champion are listed in **bold** type. No player has won the award more than once.

Year		Year		Year	
1949	**Charles Teague,** W. Forest, 2B	1968	Bill Seinsoth, USC, 1B	1987	Paul Carey, Stanford, RF
1950	**Ray VanCleef,** Rutgers, CF	1969	John Dolinsek, Ariz. St., LF	1988	Lee Plemel, Stanford, P
1951	**Sidney Hatfield,** Tenn., P-1B	1970	**Gene Ammann,** Fla. St., P	1989	Greg Brummett, Wich. St., P
1952	James O'Neill, Holy Cross, P	1971	**Jerry Tabb,** Tulsa, 1B	1990	Mike Rebhan, Georgia, P
1953	**J.L. Smith,** Texas, P	1972	Russ McQueen, USC, P	1991	Gary Hymel, LSU, C
1954	**Tom Yewcic,** Mich. St., C	1973	**Dave Winfield,** Minn., P-OF	1992	**Phil Nevin,** CS-Fullerton, 3B
1955	**Tom Borland,** Okla. St., P	1974	George Milke, USC, P	1993	Todd Walker, LSU, 2B
1956	Jerry Thomas, Minn., P	1975	Mickey Reichenbach, Texas, 1B	1994	Chip Glass, Oklahoma, OF
1957	**Cal Emery,** Penn St., P-1B	1976	Steve Powers, Arizona, P-DH	1995	Mark Kotsay, CS-Fullerton, OF
1958	Bill Thom, USC, P	1977	Bob Horner, Ariz. St., 3B	1996	**Pat Burrell,** Miami-FL, 3B
1959	Jim Dobson, Okla. St., 3B	1978	Rod Boxberger, USC, P	1997	Brandon Larson, LSU, SS
1960	John Erickson, Minn., 2B	1979	Tony Hudson, CS-Fullerton, P	1998	Wes Rachels, USC, 2B
1961	**Littleton Fowler,** Okla. St., P	1980	Terry Francona, Arizona, LF	1999	**Marshall McDougall,** Fla. St., 2B
1962	**Bob Garibaldi,** Santa Clara, P	1981	Stan Holmes, Ariz. St., LF	2000	Trey Hodges, LSU, P
1963	Bud Hollowell, USC, C	1982	Dan Smith, Miami-FL, P	2001	Charlton Jimerson, Miami-FL, CF
1964	**Joe Ferris,** Maine, P	1983	Calvin Schiraldi, Texas, P	2002	Huston Street, Texas, P
1965	Sal Bando, Ariz. St., 3B	1984	John Fishel, Miami-FL, OF	2003	**John Hudgins,** Stanford, P
1966	Steve Arlin, Ohio St., P	1985	Greg Ellena, Miami-FL, LF	2004	Jason Windsor, CS-Fullerton, P
1967	Ron Davini, Ariz. St., C	1986	Mike Senne, Arizona, DH		

Annual Awards

Golden Spikes Award

First presented in 1978 by USA Baseball, honoring the nation's best amateur player; sponsored by the Major League Baseball Players Association. Alex Fernandez, the 1990 winner, has been the only junior college player chosen.

Year		Year		Year	
1978	Bob Horner, Ariz. St, 2B	1987	Jim Abbott, Michigan, P	1996	Travis Lee, San Diego St., 1B
1979	Tim Wallach, CS-Fullerton, 1B	1988	Robin Ventura, Okla. St., 3B	1997	J.D. Drew, Florida St., OF
1980	Terry Francona, Arizona, OF	1989	Ben McDonald, LSU, P	1998	Pat Burrell, Miami-FL, 3B
1981	Mike Fuentes, Fla. St., OF	1990	Alex Fernandez, Miami-Dade, P	1999	Jason Jennings, Baylor, DH/P
1982	Augie Schmidt, N. Orleans, SS	1991	Mike Kelly, Ariz. St., OF	2000	Kip Bouknight, South Carolina, P
1983	Dave Magadan, Alabama, 1B	1992	Phil Nevin, CS-Fullerton, 3B	2001	Mark Prior, USC, P
1984	Oddibe McDowell, Ariz. St., OF	1993	Darren Dreifort, Wichita St., P	2002	Khalil Greene, Clemson, SS
1985	Will Clark, Miss. St., 1B	1994	Jason Varitek, Ga. Tech, C	2003	Rickie Weeks, Southern, 2B
1986	Mike Loynd, Fla. St., P	1995	Mark Kotsay, CS-Fullerton, OF	2004	Jered Weaver, Long Beach St., P

Baseball America Player of the Year

Presented to the College Player of the Year since 1981 by *Baseball America*.

Year		Year		Year	
1981	Mike Sodders, Ariz. St., 3B	1989	Ben McDonald, LSU, P	1997	J.D. Drew, Florida St., OF
1982	Jeff Ledbetter, Fla. St., OF/P	1990	Mike Kelly, Ariz. St., OF	1998	Jeff Austin, Stanford, P
1983	Dave Magadan, Alabama, 1B	1991	David McCarty, Stanford, 1B	1999	Jason Jennings, Baylor, DH/P
1984	Oddibe McDowell, Ariz. St., OF	1992	Phil Nevin, CS-Fullerton, 3B	2000	Mark Teixeira, Ga. Tech, 3B
1985	Pete Incaviglia, Okla. St., OF	1993	Brooks Kieschnick, Texas, DH/P	2001	Mark Prior, USC, P
1986	Casey Close, Michigan, OF	1994	Jason Varitek, Ga. Tech, C	2002	Khalil Greene, Clemson, SS
1987	Robin Ventura, Okla. St., 3B	1995	Todd Helton, Tenn., 1B/P	2003	Rickie Weeks, Southern, 2B
1988	John Olerud, Wash. St., 1B/P	1996	Kris Benson, Clemson, P	2004	Jered Weaver, Long Beach St., P

Dick Howser Trophy

Sponsored by Xanthus and presented to the College Player of the Year since 1987, by the American Baseball Coaches Association (ABCA) from 1987-98 and the National Collegiate Baseball Writers Association (NCBWA) beginning in 1999. Founded and college coach at Florida State. Howser was also a major league manager with Kansas City and the New York Yankees.
Multiple winner: Brooks Kieschnick (2).

Year		Year		Year	
1987	Mike Fiore, Miami-FL, OF	1993	Brooks Kieschnick, Texas, DH/P	1999	Jason Jennings, Baylor, DH/P
1988	Robin Ventura, Okla. St., 3B	1994	Jason Varitek, Ga. Tech, C	2000	Mark Teixeira, Ga. Tech, 3B
1989	Scott Bryant, Texas, DH	1995	Todd Helton, Tenn., 1B/P	2001	Mark Prior, USC, P
1990	Paul Ellis, UCLA, C	1996	Kris Benson, Clemson, P	2002	Khalil Greene, Clemson, SS
1991	Bobby Jones, Fresno St., P	1997	J.D. Drew, Florida St., OF	2003	Rickie Weeks, Southern, 2B
1992	Brooks Kieschnick, Texas, DH/P	1998	Eddie Furniss, LSU, 1B	2004	Jered Weaver, Long Beach St., P

Baseball America Coach of the Year

Presented to the College Coach of the Year since 1981 by *Baseball America*.
Multiple winners: Skip Bertman, Augie Garrido, Dave Snow and Gene Stephenson (2).

Year		Year		Year	
1981	Ron Fraser, Miami-FL	1989	Dave Snow, Long Beach St.	1998	Pat Murphy, Arizona St.
1982	Gene Stephenson, Wichita St.	1990	Steve Webber, Georgia	1999	Wayne Graham, Rice
1983	Barry Shollenberger, Alabama	1991	Jim Hendry, Creighton	2000	Ray Tanner, S. Carolina
1984	Augie Garrido, CS-Fullerton	1992	Andy Lopez, Pepperdine	2001	Dave Van Horn, Nebraska
1985	Ron Polk, Mississippi St.	1993	Gene Stephenson, Wichita St.	2002	Augie Garrido, Texas
1986	Skip Bertman, LSU	1994	Jim Morris, Miami-FL	2003	George Horton, CS-Fullerton
	& Dave Snow, Loyola-CA	1995	Rod Delmonico, Tennessee	2004	Dave Perno, Georgia
1987	Mark Marquess, Stanford	1996	Skip Bertman, LSU		
1988	Jim Brock, Arizona St.	1997	Jim Wells, Alabama		

All-Time Winningest Coaches

Coaches active in 2004 are in **bold** type. Records given are for four-year colleges only. For winning percentage, a minimum 10 years in Division I is required.

Top 25 Winning Percentage

		Yrs	W	L	T	Pct
1	John Barry	40	619	146	5	.807
2	Cliff Gustafson	29	1427	373	2	.792
3	Harry Carlson	17	143	41	0	.777
4	**Gene Stephenson**	27	1455	465	3	.757
5	Bobby Winkles	13	524	173	0	.752
6	**Mike Martin**	25	1338	452	4	.747
7	Frank Sancet	23	831	283	8	.744
8	Bob Wren	23	464	160	4	.742
9	George Jacobs	11	106	37	0	.741
10	Ron Fraser	30	1267	440	9	.741
11	Gary Ward	21	1022	361	1	.739
12	W.J. Disch	29	513	180	12	.736
13	Bibb Falk	25	444	160	9	.732
14	Sam Barry	18	342	126	4	.729
15	Skip Bertman	18	870	330	3	.724
16	Bud Middaugh	22	820	319	1	.720
17	J.F. "Pop" McKale	30	302	118	7	.715
18	Jim Brock	23	1099	441	1	.713
19	**Wayne Graham**	13	582	238	0	.710
20	**Jim Morris**	23	1026	422	2	.708
21	Toby Green	17	318	132	0	.707
22	Joe Arnold	18	750	313	2	.705
23	Lawrence Haskell	15	176	74	2	.702
24	**Ray Tanner**	17	767	325	3	.702
25	Joe Bedenk	32	380	159	3	.701

Top 25 Victories

		Yrs	W	L	T	Pct
1	**Augie Garrido**	36	**1488**	701	8	.679
2	**Gene Stephenson**	27	**1455**	465	3	.757
3	Cliff Gustafson	29	**1427**	373	2	.792
4	Chuck Hartman	45	**1401**	755	8	.649
5	**Larry Hays**	34	**1390**	752	2	.649
6	Rod Dedeaux	44	**1342**	597	16	.691
7	**Mike Martin**	25	**1338**	452	4	.747
8	**Larry Cochell**	38	**1307**	794	3	.622
9	Bob Bennett	34	**1300**	757	8	.631
10	Ron Fraser	30	**1267**	440	9	.741
11	Jack Stallings	39	**1257**	799	10	.611
12	Ron Polk	31	**1233**	602	2	.672
13	Jim Dietz	31	**1230**	751	12	.620
14	Al Ogletree	39	**1218**	711	1	.631
15	**Richard Jones**	38	**1209**	729	5	.624
16	**Mark Marquess**	28	**1190**	565	5	.678
17	**Gary Adams**	35	**1172**	892	12	.567
18	Bill Wilhelm	36	**1163**	536	10	.685
19	Chuck Brayton	33	**1162**	523	8	.689
20	Norm DeBriyn	33	**1161**	650	6	.641
21	Jim Brock	23	**1099**	441	1	.713
22	**Jay Bergman**	28	**1091**	605	3	.643
23	Les Murakami	30	**1077**	570	4	.654
24	John Scolinos	45	**1076**	954	13	.530
25	Bob Hannah	36	**1054**	463	6	.694

Other NCAA Champions

Division II

Multiple winners: Florida Southern (8); Cal Poly Pomona and Tampa (3); Central Missouri St., CS-Chico, CS-Northridge, Jacksonville St., Troy St., UC-Irvine and UC-Riverside (2).

Year		Year		Year		Year	
1968	Chapman, CA	1978	Florida Southern	1988	Florida Southern	1998	Tampa
1969	Illinois St.	1979	Valdosta St., GA	1989	Cal Poly SLO	1999	CS-Chico
1970	CS-Northridge	1980	Cal Poly Pomona	1990	Jacksonville St., AL	2000	Southeastern Okla.
1971	Florida Southern	1981	Florida Southern	1991	Jacksonville St., AL	2001	St. Mary's, TX
1972	Florida Southern	1982	UC-Riverside	1992	Tampa	2002	Columbus St., GA
1973	UC-Irvine	1983	Cal Poly Pomona	1993	Tampa	2003	Central Missouri St.
1974	UC-Irvine	1984	CS-Northridge	1994	Central Missouri St.	2004	Delta St., MS
1975	Florida Southern	1985	Florida Southern	1995	Florida Southern		
1976	Cal Poly Pomona	1986	Troy St., AL	1996	Kennesaw St., GA		
1977	UC-Riverside	1987	Troy St., AL	1997	CS-Chico		

Division III

Multiple winners: Eastern Conn. St. (4); Marietta and Montclair St. (3); CS-Stanislaus, Glassboro St., Ithaca, NC-Wesleyan, Southern Maine and Wm. Paterson, NJ (2).

Year		Year		Year		Year	
1976	CS-Stanislaus	1984	Ramapo, NJ	1992	Wm. Paterson, NJ	2000	Montclair St., NJ
1977	CS-Stanislaus	1985	Wisconsin-Oshkosh	1993	Montclair St., NJ	2001	St. Thomas, MN
1978	Glassboro St., NJ	1986	Marietta, OH	1994	Wisconsin-Oshkosh	2002	Eastern Conn. St.
1979	Glassboro St., NJ	1987	Monclair St., NJ	1995	La Verne, CA	2003	Chapman, CA
1980	Ithaca, NY	1988	Ithaca, NY	1996	Wm. Paterson, NJ	2004	George Fox, OR
1981	Marietta, OH	1989	NC-Wesleyan	1997	Southern Maine		
1982	Eastern Conn. St.	1990	Eastern Conn. St.	1998	Eastern Conn. St.		
1983	Marietta, OH	1991	Southern Maine	1999	NC-Wesleyan		

Major League Number One Draft Picks

The Major League First-Year Player Draft has been held every year since 1965. Clubs select in reverse order of their won-loss records from the previous regular season with National League and American League teams alternating. AL teams select first in odd-numbered years while NL teams go first in even-numbered years. The pool of draftees consists of graduated high school players, junior or senior college players, Junior college players and anyone over the age of 21. Listed are the top selections from each draft.

Year		Pos	Team	Year		Pos	Team
1965	Rick Monday	OF	Kansas City Athletics	1985	B.J. Surhoff	C	Milwaukee Brewers
1966	Steve Chilcott	C	New York Mets	1986	Jeff King	IF	Pittsburgh Pirates
1967	Rom Blomberg	1B	New York Yankees	1987	Ken Griffey Jr.	OF	Seattle Mariners
1968	Tim Foli	IF	New York Mets	1988	Andy Benes	P	San Diego Padres
1969	Jeff Burroughs	OF	Washington Senators	1989	Ben McDonald	P	Baltimore Orioles
1970	Mike Ivie	C	San Diego Padres	1990	Chipper Jones	SS	Atlanta Braves
1971	Danny Goodwin	C	Chicago White Sox	1991	Brien Taylor	P	New York Yankees
1972	Dave Roberts	IF	San Diego Padres	1992	Phil Nevin	3B	Houston Astros
1973	David Clyde	P	Texas Rangers	1993	Alex Rodriguez	SS	Seattle Mariners
1974	Bill Almon	IF	San Diego Padres	1994	Paul Wilson	P	New York Mets
1975	Danny Goodwin	C	California Angels	1995	Darin Erstad	OF/P	California Angels
1976	Floyd Bannister	P	Houston Astros	1996	Kris Benson	P	Pittsburgh Pirates
1977	Harold Baines	OF	Chicago White Sox	1997	Matt Anderson	P	Detroit Tigers
1978	Bob Horner	3B	Atlanta Braves	1998	Pat Burrell	3B	Philadelphia Phillies
1979	Al Chambers	OF	Seattle Mariners	1999	Josh Hamilton	OF	T.B. Devil Rays
1980	Darryl Strawberry	OF	New York Mets	2000	Adrian Gonzalez	1B	Florida Marlins
1981	Mike Moore	P	Seattle Mariners	2001	Joe Mauer	C	Minnesota Twins
1982	Shawon Dunston	SS	Chicago Cubs	2002	Bryan Bullington	P	Pittsburgh Pirates
1983	Tim Belcher	P	Minnesota Twins	2003	Delmon Young	OF	T.B. Devil Rays
1984	Shawn Abner	OF	New York Mets	2004	Matt Bush	SS	San Diego Padres

Straight to the Majors

Since Major League baseball began its First-Year Player Draft in 1965, 19 selections have advanced directly to the major leagues without first playing in the minors.

Draft		Pos	Team	Draft		Pos	Team
1967	Mike Adamson, USC	P	Baltimore	1978	Tim Conroy, Gateway HS (Pa.)	P	Oakland
1969	Steve Dunning, Stanford	P	Cleveland		Bob Horner, Arizona St.	3B	Atlanta
1971	Pete Broberg, Dartmouth	P	Washington		Brian Milner, Southwest HS (Tex.)	C	Toronto
	Rob Ellis, Michigan St.	OF	Milwaukee		Mike Morgan, Valley HS (Nev.)	P	Oakland
	Burt Hooton, Texas	P	Chicago-NL	1985	Pete Incaviglia, Oklahoma St.	OF	Montreal
1972	Dave Roberts, Oregon	3B	San Diego	1988	Jim Abbott, Michigan	P	California
1973	Dick Ruthven, Fresno St.	P	Philadelphia	1989	John Olerud, Washington St.	1B	Toronto
	David Clyde, Westchester HS (Tex.)	P	Texas	1995	Ariel Prieto, Fajardo U (Cuba)	P	Oakland
	Dave Winfield, Minnesota	OF	San Diego	2000	Xavier Nady, California	3B	San Diego
	Eddie Bane, Arizona St.	P	Minnesota				

College Football

USC head coach **Pete Carroll** took a cold shower after his Trojans beat Michigan in the Rose Bowl and won a share of the national title.

AP/Wide World Photos

Two Champs not Better than One

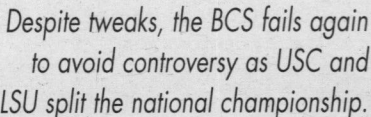

Despite tweaks, the BCS fails again to avoid controversy as USC and LSU split the national championship.

Chris Fowler
is the host of ESPN's College GameDay

There they were, in the late day California glow, smiling and raising their fingers in the air. The USC Trojans felt like national champions. They had certainly played like champs, dominating Michigan in a Rose Bowl more lopsided than the 28-14 final score might indicate.

Pete Carroll, architect of Troy's renaissance, was smiling ear to ear and hugging everyone in sight, including MVP Matt Leinart. USC's quarterback had just capped a stunning season as a first-year starter, outdoing the Heisman stats of last year's starter, Carson Palmer, by shredding Michigan with 327 passing yards.

Meanwhile, the Trojan defense was overwhelming the Maize and Blue pass protectors for an amazing nine sacks.

As USC celebrated, I was struck by what was missing. The unbridled joy that is universal after a championship game seemed muted. I've witnessed about 15 national championship games and never seen a winning side fail to let loose.

I hadn't been around the Trojans much. Were these guys just SoCal laid back? Or, was the reason for their muted reaction the muddy nature of the 2003 championship chase? That's the way it felt to me.

Three nights later, there was nothing muted about the scene in the Superdome. The Nokia Sugar Bowl may have been tarnished nationally by the controversial pairing of Oklahoma (a 35-7 loser to Kansas State in the Big 12 title game and ranked third in both polls) with LSU, but it made no difference to the loud and rowdy legions of Bayou Bengals fans.

As the dome filled with purple and gold, I flashed back to the collision of Alabama and Miami in the same building a dozen years earlier. That night, the feeling in the climate controlled air was thick with danger for the favored but outnumbered Hurricanes. Feeding off the frenzy, the Tide made it ugly early and rolled to the title.

This one had the same feeling. LSU's defense was smothering, as the Tigers hounded and pounded OU quarter-

AP/Wide World Photos

Nick Saban's LSU Tigers won the BCS Championship Game, beating Oklahoma in the Sugar Bowl, but had to split the national title glory with USC.

back Jason White. Coming in, the Heisman Trophy winner was banged up, clearly hampered by his various sore body parts. They only got sorer. The seven point margin understated LSU's dominance.

Still, LSU's backyard mugging of OU wasn't sufficient to sway nearly enough AP pollsters, including this one. The Trojans learned that a landslide had earned them a piece of the crown on *SportsCenter*, perhaps an hour after the Tigers had passed around the crystal football symbolic of the BCS crown. The coaches' poll voters were told to vote for the Sugar Bowl winner. Although coaches don't like to be told what to do, only a few rebelled.

So, college football had two national champions for the first time in the era of the BCS, the device created to supposedly avoid this. Computers were the culprit, viewing OU's four-touchdown loss in the Big 12 title game no differently than USC's triple OT loss at Cal in September or LSU's narrow loss to Florida.

The timing of a loss means nothing to a computer and margin of victory had been removed from the BCS formula the year before. It was a misguided move, pressured for by the coaches. The final BCS formula only reinforced that human judgement, however potentially biased, is still superior to the various power ratings at choosing the two most worthy teams.

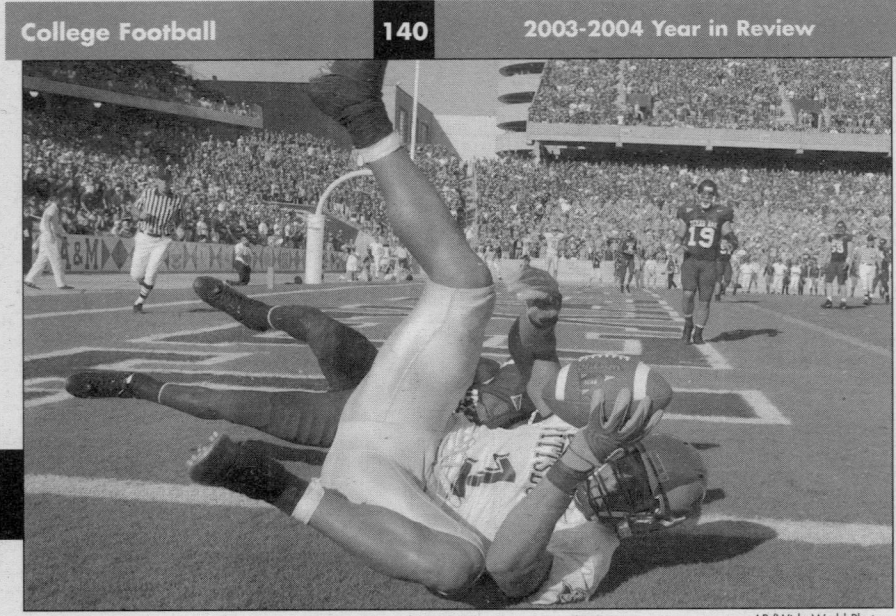

AP/Wide World Photos

*Pittsburgh wide receiver **Larry Fitzgerald** may have been the best player in college football in 2003. He caught a touchdown pass in every regular season game, but couldn't get his hands on the Heisman Trophy which went to Oklahoma quarterback Jason White.*

For the 2004 season, computers were stripped of much authority, with the two polls combining for two-thirds of the formula. Under the 2004 formula, LSU would have met USC for the undisputed title in New Orleans. It reminded me of the tweaking after the contoversial decimal point duel in 2000, when Florida State was rated ahead of Miami, despite losing to the 'Canes.

It still seems that the BCS chiefs are trying to fine tune an engine that really needs to be rebuilt. Fix one part, another just breaks down. It's been improved. More protection exists against the quirkiness of computer programs. But the BCS will never ensure a clean, decisive end to the season. To some that's OK. Very little else about the sport is tidy anyway. Personally, I don't mind attending two great bowls with national title atmospheres within four days.

It would have been nice if LSU could have just celebrated its title without being asked to apologize for the system. It would have nice if the Trojans could have walked off winners in Pasadena without having to wait for a poll to make it official 75 hours later.

The Pasadena-to-New Orleans caravan was a blast. However, the saying goes that when you crown two champions...you really don't have even one.

It won't be the last time.

Lee Corso's Ten Biggest Stories of the Year in College Football

10 Coach John Gagliardi of little St. John's College (Div. III) of Minnesota wins for the 409th time in his 55-year career, passing Grambling legend Eddie Robinson as the all-time winningest coach in college football history regardless of division. Gagliardi finishes the season with 414 wins.

9 Kansas State hands the Oklahoma Sooners their first loss of the season, 35-7, in the Big 12 Championship Game as Darren Sproles rushes for 235 yards and scores on a 60-yard reception.

8 Virginia Tech snaps the Miami Hurricanes' 39-game regular-season and 27-game Big East winning streaks with a 31-7 victory in Blacksburg.

7 Pittsburgh wide receiver Larry Fitzgerald, the Heisman runner-up, has his NCAA record string of 18 consecutive games with a touchdown catch snapped in a 23-16 Continental Tire Bowl loss to the Virginia Cavaliers.

6 Oklahoma quarterback Jason White wins the Heisman Trophy and is granted a sixth year of eligibility, giving him a shot at becoming the first two-time Heisman winner since Ohio State running back Archie Griffin (1974-75).

5 Miami, Virginia Tech and Boston College bolt the Big East Conference in favor of the Atlantic Coast Conference.

4 Nebraska fires coach Frank Solich after a 9-3 season and hires Bill Callahan, outsted coach of the NFL's Oakland Raiders, to succeed him. Callahan junks Nebraska's traditional ground-oriented option offense and says the Cornhuskers will throw the football.

3 Sylvester Croom, former player and assistant coach at Alabama and an assistant coach in the NFL since 1987 with five different teams, is named to succeed Jackie Sherrill as head coach at Mississippi State, becoming the first African-American head football coach in the Southeastern Conference.

2 Split national championship. LSU defeats Oklahoma, 21-14, in the Sugar Bowl to win the BCS national championship, while USC beats Michigan, 28-14, in the Rose Bowl and captures the Associated Press national title.

1 The BCS backs itself into a corner and looks foolish by naming LSU and Oklahoma to play in the championship game, while the Associated Press votes USC No. 1 in their poll.

Fading Down the Stretch

Oklahoma won the national title in 2000 but, despite some great starts, the Sooners have not been able to get back to the mountain top. Here's a look at how the Sooners have begun and ended the three seasons since their last championship.

Year	Started	Finished
2003	12-0*	0-2
2002	8-0*	4-2
2001	7-0	4-2

*ranked No. 1 in BCS Standings.

Touchdown Streak

Pittsburgh wide receiver Larry Fitzgerald shattered the NCAA Div. 1-A record for consecutive games with a touchdown catch with 18 before failing to score in Pitt's bowl game.

	Consecutive games with a TD catch
Larry Fitzgerald, Pitt.	18
Charles Rogers, Mich. St.	13
Desmond Howard, Mich.	12
Aaron Turner, Pacific	12
Randy Moss, Marshall	12

Splitsville USA

The 2003 season was the first under the Bowl Championship Series in which the national championship was split. Here's a look at the last three split national championships and the aftermath.

Year	AP/Coaches	Major Changes
2003	USC/LSU	BCS formula changes
1997	Michigan/Nebraska	BCS formed for 1998 season
1991	Miami-FL/Washington	Bowl Coalition formed for 1992 season

Note: The Bowl Coalition was an early attempt to avoid split national titles by bringing together four major bowl games (Orange, Sugar, Fiesta and Cotton) and five major conferences (ACC, Big East, Big Eight, SEC and SWC, plus independent Notre Dame) into a national championship game rotation. It did not include the Rose Bowl and therefore did not match the top two teams in 1994 when Big Ten champion and No. 2 Penn State was obligated to play in the Rose Bowl. The Bowl Alliance succeeded the Bowl Coalition in 1995 and that gave way to the BCS, which included the Rose Bowl and therefore the Big Ten and Pac-10 champs for the first time, in 1998.

2003-2004
Season in Review

ESPN SPORTS ALMANAC

Final AP Top 25 Poll

Voted on by panel of 65 sportswriters & broadcasters and released on Jan. 5, 2004, following the Fiesta Bowl: winning team receives the Bear Bryant Trophy, given since 1983; first place votes in parentheses, records, total points (based on 25 for 1st, 24 for 2nd, etc.) bowl game result, head coach and career record, preseason rank (released Aug. 16, 2003) and final regular season rank (released Dec. 7, 2003).

	Final Record	Points	Bowl Game	Head Coach	Aug. 16 Rank	Dec. 7 Rank
1 USC (48)	12-1	1,608	won Rose	Pete Carroll (3 yrs: 29-9)	8	1
2 LSU (17)	13-1	1,576	won Sugar	Nick Saban (10 yrs: 82-39-1)	14	2
3 Oklahoma	12-2	1,476	lost Sugar	Bob Stoops (6 yrs: 67-13)	1	3
4 Ohio St.	11-2	1,411	won Fiesta	Jim Tressel (18 yrs: 167-64-2)	2	7
5 Miami-FL	11-2	1,329	won Orange	Larry Coker (3 yrs: 35-3)	3	10
6 Michigan	10-3	1,281	lost Rose	Lloyd Carr (9 yrs: 86-24)	4	5
7 Georgia	11-3	1,255	won Capital One	Mark Richt (3 yrs: 32-8)	8	4
8 Iowa	10-3	1,107	won Outback	Kirk Ferentz (8 yrs: 44-50)	NR	13
9 Washington St.	10-3	1,060	won Holiday	Bill Doba (1 yr: 10-3)	NR	15
10 Miami-OH	13-1	932	won GMAC	Terry Hoeppner (5 yrs: 40-20)	NR	14
11 Florida St.	10-3	905	lost Orange	Bobby Bowden (38 yrs: 342-97-4)	13	9
12 Texas	10-3	887	lost Holiday	Mack Brown (20 yrs: 145-92-1)	5	5
13 Mississippi	10-3	845	won Cotton	David Cutcliffe (5 yrs: 40-22)	NR	16
14 Kansas St.	11-4	833	lost Fiesta	Bill Snyder (15 yrs: 127-55-1)	7	8
15 Tennessee	10-3	695	lost Peach	Philip Fullmer (12 yrs: 113-28)	12	6
16 Boise St.	13-1	645	won Fort Worth	Dan Hawkins (6 yrs: 72-17-1)	NR	18
17 Maryland	10-3	564	won Gator	Ralph Friedgen (3 yrs: 31-8)	15	23
18 Purdue	9-4	526	lost Capital One	Joe Tiller (13 yrs: 94-62-1)	19	12
19 Nebraska	10-3	520	won Alamo	Frank Solich (6 yrs: 58-19) & Bo Pelini (1 yr: 1-0)	NR	22
20 Minnesota	10-3	368	won Sun	Glen Mason (18 yrs: 103-104-1)	NR	24
21 Utah	10-2	308	won Liberty	Urban Meyer (3 yrs: 27-8)	NR	25
22 Clemson	9-4	230	won Peach	Tommy Bowden (7 yrs: 56-28)	NR	NR
23 Bowling Green	11-3	189	won Motor City	Gregg Brandon (1 yr: 11-3)	NR	NR
24 Florida	8-5	165	lost Outback	Ron Zook (2 yrs: 16-10)	NR	17
25 TCU	11-2	126	lost Fort Worth	Gary Patterson (3 yrs: 27-11)	25	19

Other teams receiving votes: 26. Oklahoma State (9-4, lost Cotton Bowl, 109 pts); **27. Arkansas** (9-4, won Independence Bowl, 73 pts); 28. **Virginia** (8-5, won Continental Tire Bowl, 36 pts); 29. **Northern Illinois** (10-2, no bowl, 30 pts); 30. **Auburn** (8-5, won Music City, 8 pts) and **Oregon State** (8-5, won Las Vegas Bowl, 8 pts); 32. **N.C. State** (8-5, won Tangerine Bowl, 7pts) and **Pittsburgh** (8-5, lost Continental Tire Bowl, 7 pts); 34. **West Virginia** (8-5, lost Gator Bowl, 4 pts); 35. **Connecticut** (9-3, no bowl, 2 pts).

AP Preseason and Final Regular Season Polls

First place votes in parentheses.

Top 25
(Aug. 16, 2003)

		Pts			Pts
1	Oklahoma (32)	1,573	14	LSU	736
2	Ohio St. (27)	1,532	15	Maryland	705
3	Miami-FL (2)	1,484	16	N.C. State	678
4	Michigan (2)	1,329	17	Washington	643
5	Texas	1,322	18	Virginia	557
6	Auburn (1)	1,300	19	Purdue	468
7	Kansas St. (1)	1,221	20	Notre Dame	439
8	USC	1,126	21	Wisconsin	350
9	Virginia Tech	1,046	22	Arizona St.	248
10	Pittsburgh	952	23	Colorado St.	205
11	Georgia	928	24	Oklahoma St.	156
12	Tennessee	766	25	TCU	95
13	Florida St.	737			

Top 25
(Dec. 7, 2003)

		Pts			Pts
1	USC (42)	1,595	14	Miami-OH	756
2	LSU (21)	1,580	15	Washington St.	638
3	Oklahoma (2)	1,491	16	Mississippi	637
4	Michigan	1,437	17	Florida	619
5	Texas	1,322	18	Boise St.	540
6	Tennessee	1,228	19	TCU	392
7	Ohio St.	1,208	20	West Virginia	320
8	Kansas St.	1,151	21	Oklahoma St.	299
9	Florida St.	1,128	22	Nebraska	278
10	Miami-FL	1,075	23	Maryland	221
11	Georgia	1,018	24	Minnesota	134
12	Purdue	849	25	Utah	106
13	Iowa	771			

2003-2004 Bowl Games

Listed by bowls matching highest-ranked teams as of final regular season AP poll (released Dec. 7, 2003). Attendance figures indicate tickets sold.

Bowl		Winner	Regular Season		Loser	Regular Season	Score	Date	Attendance
Rose	#1	USC	11-1	#4	Michigan	10-2	28-14	Jan. 1	93,849
Sugar	#2	LSU	12-1	#3	Oklahoma	12-1	21-14	Jan. 4	79,342
Holiday	#15	Washington St.	9-3	#5	Texas	10-2	28-20	Dec. 30	61,102
Peach		Clemson	8-4	#6	Tennessee	10-2	27-14	Jan. 2	75,125
Fiesta	#7	Ohio St.	10-2	#8	Kansas St.	11-3	35-28	Jan. 2	73,425
Orange	#10	Miami-FL	10-2	#9	Florida St.	10-2	16-14	Jan. 2	76,739
Capital One	#11	Georgia	10-3	#12	Purdue	9-3	34-27 (OT)	Jan. 1	64,565
Outback	#13	Iowa	9-3	#17	Florida	8-4	37-17	Jan. 1	65,372
GMAC	#14	Miami-OH	12-1		Louisville	9-3	49-28	Dec. 18	40,620
Cotton	#16	Mississippi	9-3	#21	Oklahoma St.	9-3	31-28	Jan. 2	73,928
Fort Worth	#18	Boise St.	12-1	#19	TCU	11-1	34-31	Dec. 23	38,028
Gator	#23	Maryland	9-3	#20	West Virginia	8-4	41-7	Jan. 1	78,892
Alamo	#22	Nebraska	9-3		Michigan St.	8-4	17-3	Dec. 29	56,226
Sun	#24	Minnesota	9-3		Oregon	8-4	31-30	Dec. 31	49,894
Liberty	#25	Utah	9-2		Southern Miss.	9-3	17-0	Dec. 31	55,989
Motor City		Bowling Green	10-3		Northwestern	6-6	28-24	Dec. 26	51,286
Continental Tire		Virginia	7-5		Pittsburgh	8-4	23-16	Dec. 27	51,236
Independence		Arkansas	8-4		Missouri	8-4	27-14	Dec. 31	49,625
Insight		California	7-6		Virginia Tech	8-4	52-49	Dec. 26	42,364
New Orleans		Memphis	8-4		North Texas	9-3	27-17	Dec. 16	25,184
Humanitarian		Georgia Tech	6-6		Tulsa	8-4	52-10	Jan. 3	23,118
San Francisco		Boston College	7-5		Colorado St.	7-5	35-21	Dec. 31	25,621
Music City		Auburn	7-5		Wisconsin	7-5	28-14	Dec. 31	55,109
Silicon Valley Classic		Fresno St.	8-5		UCLA	6-6	17-9	Dec. 30	20,126
Houston		Texas Tech	7-5		Navy	8-4	38-14	Dec. 30	51,068
Las Vegas		Oregon St.	7-5		New Mexico	8-4	55-14	Dec. 24	25,437
Hawaii		Hawaii	8-5		Houston	7-5	54-48 (3OT)	Dec. 25	29,005
Tangerine		N.C. State	7-5		Kansas	6-6	56-26	Dec. 22	26,482

2003 Final BCS Rankings

The Bowl Championship Series rankings were used for the first time during the 1998 season to determine BCS bowl match-ups and revised slightly for the 1999, 2001 and 2002 seasons. The final rankings were released Dec. 7, 2003. Note that S-rank refers to schedule rank and L refers to games lost.

	Polls		Computer Rankings								Sched.	S-rank	L	Sub Total	Quality wins	Total
	AP	ESPN	A&H	R.B.	C.M.	K.M.	NYT	J.S.	P.W.	Avg.						
1 Oklahoma	3	3	1	1	1	2	5	1	1	1.17	11	0.44	1	5.61	-0.5	5.11
2 LSU	2	2	2	2	2	1	2	2	2	1.83	29	1.16	1	5.99		5.99
3 USC	1	1	3	3	3	1	4	3	3	2.67	37	1.48	1	6.15		6.15
4 Michigan	4	4	7	4	6	5	3	5	5	4.67	14	0.56	2	11.23	-0.6	10.63
5 Ohio St.	7	6	6	6	4	4	8	6	7	5.50	7	0.28	2	14.28		14.28
6 Texas	5	5	5	9	8	7	4	10	6	6.83	20	0.80	2	14.63	-0.1	14.53
7 Florida St.	9	8	8	8	5	8	7	7	6	6.83	15	0.60	2	17.93		17.93
8 Tennessee	6	7	10	7	10	11	9	10	11	9.50	46	1.84	2	19.84	-0.2	19.64
9 Miami-FL	10	9	9	5	7	9	10	9	8	8.17	13	0.52	2	20.19	-0.4	19.79
10 Kansas St.	8	10	16	12	12	12	6	13	13	11.33	10	0.40	3	23.73	-1.0	22.73
11 Miami-OH	14	15	4	10	9	6	22	3	4	6.00	68	2.72	1	24.22		24.22
12 Georgia	11	11	11	11	11	10	12	9	8	10.17	18	0.72	3	24.89	-0.3	24.59
13 Iowa	13	12	14	16	15	13	15	12	12	13.50	16	0.64	3	29.64	-0.7	28.94
14 Purdue	12	13	13	15	17	17	14	18	15	15.83	40	1.60	3	32.93		32.93
15 Florida	17	17	17	24	14	23	15	13	16	16.50	5	0.20	4	37.70	-0.9	36.80
16 Washington St.	15	14	18	19	19	22	21	21	21	19.83	44	1.76	3	39.09		39.09
17 Boise St.	18	16	16	21	13	16	21	34	17	16.83	105	4.20	1	39.53		39.53
18 TCU	19	19	19	11	15	13	24	39	22	16.67	95	3.80	1	40.47		40.47
19 Mississippi	16	18	23	20	24	20	17	24	24	21.33	70	2.80	3	44.13		44.13
20 Nebraska	22	21	17	29	18	18	19.5	18	20	18.42	32	1.28	3	44.20		44.20
21 Oklahoma St.	21	22	19	25	21	16	16	20	22	19.00	58	2.32	3	45.82	-0.1	45.72
22 Utah	25	23	25	13	21	14	17	33	19	17.17	59	2.36	2	46.53		46.53
23 Maryland	23	24	24	25	31	20	23	11	23	20.83	56	2.24	3	49.57		49.57
24 Bowling Green	26	30	29	26	22	19	36	14	14	20.67	36	1.44	3	53.11		53.11
25 Minnesota	24	24	28	28	28	28	32	28	27	21.67	83	3.32	3	55.49		55.49

Explanation Key

Computer Rankings—A&H refers to Anderson & Hester, R.B. refers to Richard Billingsley, C.M. refers to Colley Matrix, K.M. refers to Kenneth Massey, NYT refers to *New York Times*, J.S. refers to Jeff Sagarin, P.W. refers to Peter Wolfe, Avg. refers to the teams average position in the computer rankings. *Schedule Rank*—Rank of schedule strength compared to other Division I-A teams divided by 25. This component is calculated by determining the cumulative won/loss records of the team's opponents (66.6 percent) and the cumulative won/loss record of the team's opponents' opponents (33.3 percent). *Quality Wins*—This component will reward teams that defeat opponents ranked among the top 10 in the weekly standings. The scale will range from 1.0 points for a win over the top ranked team to 0.1 for a win over the 10th-ranked BCS team. The final BCS Standings determine final quality win points. If a team beats a team more than once during the regular season, quality points will be awarded just once.

Co-National Champions

Despite holding the top two spots of both polls, LSU and USC finished second and third, respectively, in the final Bowl Championship Series rankings (see box on p. 144) and therefore did not meet in the BCS National Championship Game at the Sugar Bowl on Jan. 4. USC won the Rose Bowl and finished first in the final Associated Press poll while LSU beat Oklahoma (the top team in the final BCS rankings) in the Sugar Bowl and claimed the top spot in the ESPN/*USA Today* coaches poll. Opponents' records and AP rank listed below are day of game. Final statistics listed below include the bowl games.

LSU Tigers (13-1)

Date	AP Rank	Opponent	Result
Aug. 30	#13	Louisiana-Monroe (0-0)	W, 49-7
Sept. 6	#13	at Arizona (1-0)	W, 59-13
Sept. 13	#12	Western Illinois (2-0)	W, 35-7
Sept. 20	#11	#7 Georgia (3-0)	W, 17-10
Sept. 27	#7	at Mississippi St. (0-3)	W, 41-6
Oct. 11	#6	Florida (3-3)	L, 7-19
Oct. 18	#10	at South Carolina (4-2)	W, 33-7
Oct. 25	#4	#17 Auburn (5-2)	W, 31-7
Nov. 1	#3	Louisiana Tech (4-4)	W, 49-10
Nov. 15	#3	at Alabama (4-6)	W, 27-3
Nov. 22	#3	at #15 Mississippi (8-2)	W, 17-14
Nov. 28	#3	Arkansas (8-3)	W, 55-24
Dec. 6	#2	#5 Georgia (10-2)*	W, 34-13
Jan. 4	#2	#3 Oklahoma (12-1)†	W, 21-14

*SEC Championship Game at the Georgia Dome.
†Sugar Bowl

Final Statistics

Passing (5 Att)	Att	Cmp	Pct.	Yds	TD	Rate
Matt Mauck	.358	229	64.0	2825	28	148.2
Marcus Randall	.40	25	62.5	403	2	158.6

Interceptions: Mauck 14, Randall 1.

Top Receivers	No	Yds	Avg	Long	TD
Michael Clayton	.78	1079	13.8	66	10
Devery Henderson	.53	861	16.2	64	11
Skyler Green	.48	519	10.8	40	5
Eric Edwards	.16	155	9.7	23	2
Joseph Addai	.14	86	6.1	25	1
David Jones	.13	232	17.8	37	1
Dwayne Bowe	.9	106	11.8	24	0

Top Rushers	Car	Yds	Avg	Long	TD
Justin Vincent	.154	1001	6.5	87	10
Joseph Addai	.114	520	4.6	21	2
Alley Broussard	.85	408	4.6	33	4
Shyrone Carey	.78	338	4.3	35	6
Barrington Edwards	.41	169	4.1	32	0
Matt Mauck	.79	97	1.2	16	1
Skyler Green	.8	99	11.2	24	1

Most Touchdowns	TD	Run	Rec	Ret	Pts
Devery Henderson	.11	0	11	0	66
Michael Clayton	.10	0	10	0	60
Justin Vincent	.10	10	0	0	60
Skyler Green	.8	5	1	2	48
Shyrone Carey	.6	6	0	0	36
Alley Broussard	.4	4	0	0	24

2-Pt. Conversions: Matt Mauck (1-2).

Kicking	FG/Att	Lg	PAT/Att	Pts
Ryan Gaudet	.7/12	47	36/38	57
Chris Jackson	.5/8	47	21/23	36

Punting	No	Yds	Long	Blkd	Avg
Donnie Jones	.65	2757	67	1	42.4

Most Interceptions		Most Sacks	
Corey Webster	.7	Chad Lavais	.7.0
Jack Hunt	.4	Marcus Spears	.6.0
Three tied	.2	Marquise Hill	.6.0

USC Trojans (12-1)

Date	AP Rank	Opponent	Result
Aug. 30	#4	at #6 Auburn (0-0)	W, 23-0
Sept. 6	#4	BYU (1-0)	W, 35-18
Sept. 13	#4	Hawaii (1-0)	W, 61-32
Sept. 27	#3	at California (2-3)	L, 31-34 (3 OT)
Oct. 4	#10	at Arizona St. (2-2)	W, 37-17
Oct. 11	#9	Stanford (3-1)	W, 44-21
Oct. 18	#5	at Notre Dame (2-3)	W, 45-14
Oct. 25	#5	at Washington (4-3)	W, 43-23
Nov. 1	#3	#6 Washington St. (7-1)	W, 43-16
Nov. 15	#2	at Arizona (2-8)	W, 45-0
Nov. 22	#2	UCLA (6-4)	W, 47-22
Dec. 6	#2	Oregon St. (7-4)	W, 52-28
Jan. 1	#1	#4 Michigan (10-2)†	W, 28-14

†Rose Bowl

Final Statistics

Passing (5 Att)	Att	Cmp	Pct.	Yds	TD	Rate
Matt Leinart	.402	255	63.4	3556	38	164.5
J.D. Booty	.14	7	50.0	90	0	104.0
Matt Cassel	.13	6	46.2	63	0	86.9
Brandon Hance	.9	4	44.4	44	0	85.5

Interceptions: Leinart 9.

Top Receivers	No	Yds	Avg	Long	TD
Mike Williams	.13	1314	13.8	40	16
Keary Colbert	.13	1013	14.7	57	9
Steve Smith	.12	319	18.8	73	2
Gregg Guenther Jr.	.17	167	9.8	23	2
Reggie Bush	.15	314	20.9	60	4
Dominique Byrd	.14	268	19.1	55	1
Brandon Hancock	.13	160	12.3	52	2
Hershel Dennis	.10	62	6.2	20	1

Top Rushers	Car	Yds	Avg	Long	TD
LenDale White	.141	754	5.3	66	13
Hershel Dennis	.137	661	4.8	34	4
Reggie Bush	.90	521	5.8	58	3
Chauncey Washington	.19	65	3.4	10	0
Keary Colbert	.3	29	9.7	12	0
Mike Williams	.3	26	8.7	17	0
David Kirtman	.5	24	4.6	9	0

Most Touchdowns	TD	Run	Rec	Ret	Pts
Mike Williams	.16	0	16	0	96
LenDale White	.14	13	1	0	84
Keary Colbert	.9	0	9	0	54
Reggie Bush	.8	3	4	1	48
Hershel Dennis	.5	4	1	0	30

2-Pt. Conversions: none.

Kicking	FG/Att	Lg	PAT/Att	Pts
Ryan Killeen	.19/24	45	65/67	122

Punting	No	Yds	Long	Blkd	Avg
Tom Malone	.42	2060	70	2	49.0

Most Interceptions		Most Sacks	
Will Poole	.7	Kenechi Udeze	.16.5
Lofa Tatupu	.4	Mike Patterson	.7.0
		Shaun Cody	.6.0

Sugar Bowl

Sun., Jan. 4, 2004 at Louisiana Superdome, New Orleans

	1	2	3	4	F
#2 LSU (SEC)	7	7	7	0	21
#3 Oklahoma (Big 12)	0	7	0	7	14

1st: 11:38; **LSU**—Skyler Green 24-yd run (Ryan Gaudet kick), 3 plays, 32 yards, 1:09.
2nd: 7:31; **OU**—Kejuan Jones 1-yd run (Trey DiCarlo kick), 3 plays, 2 yards, 1:04.
2nd: 4:21; **LSU**—Justin Vincent 18-yd run (Gaudet kick), 9 plays, 80 yards, 3:10.
3rd: 14:13; **LSU**—Marcus Spears 20-yd interception return (Gaudet kick).
4th: 11:01; **OU**—Kejuan Jones 1-yd run (DiCarlo kick), 9 plays, 31 yards, 3:45.

Favorite: Oklahoma by 6½ **Attendance:** 79,342
Field: Turf **Weather:** Indoors
Time: 3:43 **TV Rating:** 14.8/23 (ABC)
MVP: Justin Vincent, LSU, RB

Team Statistics

	LSU	OU
First downs	13	12
Total Plays	64	70
Total Net Yards	312	154
Carries/yards (includ. sacks)	40/159	33/52
Passing yards	153	102
Completions/attempts	14/24	13/37
Had intercepted	2	2
Fumbles/lost	0/0	0/0
Penalties/yards	8/65	11/70
Punts/average	8/34.0	8/45.9
3rd down conversions	6/17	4/15
4th down conversions	0/1	1/3
Red-Zone scores/chances	1/3	2/3
Sacks by/yards	5/46	5/12
Time of possession	31:19	28:41

Individual Statistics

Rushing: LSU—Justin Vincent 16 carries for 117 yards, Matt Mauck 14 carries for 27 yards, Skyler Green 3 carries for 22 yards, Alley Broussard 2 carries for 6 yards, Joseph Addai 2 carries for -1 yards, Team 3 carries for -12 yards. **OU**—Kejuan Jones 20 carries for 59 yards, Mark Clayton 4 carries for 38 yards, Renaldo Works 1 carry for 2 yards, Team 1 carry for -1 yards, Jason White 7 carries for -46 yards.
Passing: LSU—Matt Mauck 13 for 22 for 124 yards and 2 interceptions, Blain Bech 1 for 1 for 29 yards, Michael Clayton 0 for 1. **OU**—Jason White 13 for 37 for 102 yards and 2 interceptions.
Receiving: LSU—Michael Clayton 4 catches for 38 yards, David Jones 3 catches for 54 yards, Devery Henderson 2 catches for 24 yards, Skyler Green 2 catches for 23 yards, Joseph Addai 2 catches for 12 yards, Eric Edwards 1 catch for 2 yards. **OU**—Mark Clayton 4 catches for 32 yards, Travis Wilson 3 catches for 31 yards, Kejuan Jones 2 catches for 6 yards, Mark Bradley 1 catch for 9 yards, Brandon Jones 1 catch for 5 yards.

Rose Bowl

Thur., Jan. 1, 2004 at Rose Bowl, Pasadena, Calif.

	1	2	3	4	F
#4 Michigan (Big Ten)	0	0	7	7	14
#1 USC (Pac 10)	7	7	14	0	28

1st: 8:08; **USC**—Keary Colbert 25-yd pass from Matt Leinart (Ryan Killeen kick), 4 plays, 54 yards, 0:37.
2nd: 4:50; **USC**—LenDale White 6-yd pass from Leinart (Killeen kick), 3 plays, 3 yards, 0:52.
3rd: 13:45; **USC**—Colbert 47-yd pass from Leinart (Killeen kick), 5 plays, 83 yards, 1:15.
3rd: 5:49; **MICH**—Tim Massaquoi 5-yd pass from John Navarre (Garrett Rivas kick), 16 plays, 76 yards, 7:56.
3rd: 3:44; **USC**—Leinart 15-yd pass from Mike Williams (Killeen kick), 8 plays, 72 yards, 2:05.
4th: 11:06; **MICH**—Chris Perry 2-yd run (Rivas kick), 11 plays, 85 yards, 2:56.

Favorite: USC by 7 **Attendance:** 93,849
Field: Grass **Weather:** Fair, 59 degrees
Time: 3:15 **TV Rating:** 14.3/25 (ABC)
MVP: Matt Leinart, USC, QB

Team Statistics

	USC	MICH
First downs	19	25
Total Plays	60	84
Total Net Yards	410	320
Carries/yards (includ. sacks)	25/68	38/49
Passing yards	342	271
Completions/attempts	24/35	27/46
Had intercepted	1	0
Fumbles/lost	2/1	3/0
Penalties/yards	3/22	2/10
Punts/average	3/46.7	4/44.0
3rd down conversions	6/11	9/19
4th down conversions	1/1	2/4
Red-Zone scores/chances	2/5	2/2
Sacks by/yards	9/69	1/11
Time of possession	25:34	34:26

Individual Statistics

Rushing: USC—Reggie Bush 8 carries for 41 yards, LenDale White 8 carries for 26 yards, Hershel Dennis 7 carries for 17 yards, Matt Leinart 2 carries for -16 yards. **MICH**—Chris Perry 23 carries for 85 yards, Steve Breaston 2 carries for 21 yards, Pierre Rembert 1 carry for 1 yard, John Navarre 12 carries for -58 yards.
Passing: USC—Matt Leinart 23 for 34 for 327 yards and 3 touchdowns and 1 interception, Mike Williams 1 for 1 for 15 yards. **MICH**—John Navarre 27 for 46 for 271 yards and 1 touchdown.
Receiving: USC—Mike Williams 8 catches for 88 yards, Keary Colbert 6 catches for 149 yards, Reggie Bush 2 catches for 42 yards, Brandon Hancock 2 catches for 8 yards, LenDale White 2 catches for 4 yards, Gregg Guenther Jr. 1 catch for 19 yards, Matt Leinart 1 catch for 15 yards, Steve Smith 1 catch for 9 yards, David Kirtman 1 catch for 8 yards. **MICH**—Barrington Edwards 10 catches for 107 yards, Steve Breaston 6 catches for 61 yards, Jason Avant 4 catches for 61 yards, Tyler Ecker 3 catches for 31 yards, Chris Perry 2 catches for 1 yard, Tim Massaquoi 1 catch for 5 yards, Brian Thompson 1 catch for 5 yards.

LSU became only the sixth team since the AP poll began in 1936 to finish No. 1 in either the AP or coaches' poll after losing a home game. The Tigers became the first such team to accomplish this since Oklahoma in 1985.

Other Final Division I-A Polls
USA Today/ESPN Coaches Poll

Voted on by panel of 61 Division I-A head coaches; winning team receives the Sears Trophy (originally the McDonald's Trophy, 1991-93); first place votes in parentheses with total points (based on 25 for 1st, 24 for 2nd, etc.).

	Pts			Pts			Pts			Pts
1 LSU (60)	1,572	8 Iowa	1,119	15 Boise St.	.74	22 Clemson	.219
2 USC (3)	1,514	9 Washington St.	.983	16 Tennessee	.684	23 Bowling Green	.170
3 Oklahoma	1,429	10 Florida St.	.929	17 Minnesota	.553	24 TCU	.145
4 Ohio St.	1,370	11 Texas	.894	18 Nebraska	.532	25 Florida	.124
5 Miami-FL	1,306	12 Miami-OH	.800	19 Purdue	.510		
6 Georgia	1,183	13 Kansas St.	.746	20 Maryland	.462		
7 Michigan	1,140	14 Mississippi	.730	21 Utah	.327		

Other teams receiving votes: 26. Northern Illinois (80 points), 27. Arkansas (74), 28. Oklahoma St. (63), 29. Auburn (20), 30. N.C. State (17), 31. Oregon St. (15), 32. West Virginia (14), 33. Southern Miss. (12), 34. Fresno St. and Hawaii (6), 36. Pittsburgh (5), 37. Texas Tech (4), 38. Virginia and Marshall (3), 40. Boston College (2), 41. California, Connecticut, Memphis, Michigan St., Missouri and North Texas (1).

AP Weekly Rankings

The Associated Press Top 25 college football polls on a weekly basis are listed below. The table starts with the preseason and progresses through the season.

		Sept				Oct				Nov				Dec	Jan
	Pre	7	14	21	28	5	12	19	26	2	9	16	23	30	7	5
Oklahoma	1	1	1	1	1	1	1	1	1	1	1	1	1.	1	3	3
Ohio St.	2	3	5	4	3	3	8	8	8	7	4	4	8	8	7	4
Miami-FL	3	2	2	2	2	2	2	2	2	6	14	13	10	10	10	5
USC	4	4	4	3	10	9	5	5	3	2	2	2	2	2	1	1
Michigan	5	5	3	11	9	20	17	13	11	8	5	5	4	4	4	6
Texas	6	6	13	14	13	11	20	19	16	11	6	7	6	6	5	12
Kansas St.	7	7	6	16	16	22	-	-	-	-	-	19	14	13	8	14
Georgia	8	8	7	12	11	8	4	4	4	9	7	6	5	5	11	7
Virginia Tech	9	9	8	5	4	4	3	3	10	5	12	12	21	-	-	-
Pittsburgh	10	11	9	17	15	15	-	-	25	25	16	21	20	-	-	-
Florida St.	11	10	10	6	5	5	7	6	5	3	13	11	9	9	9	11
Tennessee	12	13	12	8	7	13	21	22	19	18	9	9	7	7	6	15
LSU	13	12	11	7	6	6	10	9	7	4	3	3	3	3	2	2
N.C. State	14	24	-	-	-	-	-	-	-	-	-	-	-	-	-	-
Virginia	15	-	-	-	25	-	-	-	-	-	-	-	-	-	-	-
Purdue	16	-	25	22	22	18	13	10	18	16	11	16	12	11	12	18
Auburn	17	-	-	-	-	-	19	17	-	-	-	-	-	-	-	-
Wisconsin	18	14	-	-	-	23	14	20	-	-	-	-	-	-	-	-
Notre Dame	19	15	-	-	-	-	-	-	-	-	-	-	-	-	-	-
Arizona St.	20	16	16	-	-	-	-	-	-	-	-	-	-	-	-	-
Florida	21	19	17	25	24	-	-	25	23	17	15	13	11	16	17	24
Washington	22	21	19	18	18	-	-	-	-	-	-	-	-	-	-	-
Nebraska	23	18	15	15	12	10	18	14	12	19	18	23	25	23	22	19
Colorado	24	17	-	-	-	-	-	-	-	-	-	-	-	-	-	-
TCU	25	22	20	19	20	18	16	15	15	13	10	10	19	19	19	25
Wake Forest	-	20	-	-	-	-	-	-	-	-	-	-	-	-	-	-
Iowa	-	23	18	13	23	14	9	16	13	10	20	17	13	12	13	8
South Carolina	-	25	-	-	-	-	-	-	-	-	-	-	-	-	-	-
Arkansas	-	-	14	9	8	7	11	21	-	-	-	-	-	-	-	-
Alabama	-	-	21	-	-	-	-	-	-	-	-	-	-	-	-	-
Oregon	-	-	22	10	19	-	-	-	-	-	-	-	-	-	-	-
Missouri	-	-	23	23	-	-	24	-	21	22	-	-	-	-	-	-
Washington St.	-	-	24	21	14	12	6	6	6	12	8	8	16	15	15	9
Northern Illinois	-	-	-	20	17	16	12	12	21	23	21	-	-	-	-	-
Minnesota	-	-	-	24	21	17	25	-	24	24	19	-	-	25	24	20
Michigan St.	-	-	-	-	25	21	15	11	9	14	21	-	-	-	-	-
Oregon St.	-	-	-	-	-	24	22	-	-	-	-	-	-	-	-	-
Oklahoma St.	-	-	-	-	-	23	18	14	21	-	24	23	22	21	-	-
Bowling Green	-	-	-	-	-	-	23	17	15	25	22	22	20	-	-	23
Utah	-	-	-	-	-	-	24	-	-	-	-	-	-	25	21	-
Mississippi	-	-	-	-	-	-	-	20	20	17	15	17	17	16	13	13
Miami-Ohio	-	-	-	-	-	-	-	-	-	-	23	18	15	14	14	10
Boise St.	-	-	-	-	-	-	-	-	-	24	20	18	18	18	16
West Virginia	-	-	-	-	-	-	-	-	-	-	-	25	24	21	20	-
Maryland	-	-	-	-	-	-	-	-	-	-	-	-	-	24	23	17

NCAA Division I-A Final Standings

Standings based on conference games only; overall records include postseason games.

Atlantic Coast Conference

	Conference				Overall		
	W	L	PF	PA	W	L	PF	PA
*Florida St.	.7	1	269	138	10	3	419	219
*Maryland	.6	2	220	159	10	3	406	206
*Clemson	.5	3	212	168	9	4	367	250
*N.C. State	.4	4	256	250	8	5	489	385
*Virginia	.4	4	187	164	8	5	364	265
*Georgia Tech	.4	4	151	178	7	6	274	266
Wake Forest	.3	5	242	236	5	7	335	357
Duke	.2	6	139	265	4	8	210	343
North Carolina	.1	7	184	322	2	10	317	459

*__Bowls (5-1):__ Florida St. (lost Orange); Maryland (won Gator); Clemson (won Peach); N.C. State (won Tangerine); Virginia (won Continental Tire); Georgia Tech (won Humanitarian).

Big East Conference

	Conference				Overall		
	W	L	PF	PA	W	L	PF	PA
*Miami-FL	.6	1	193	113	11	2	361	196
*West Virginia	.6	1	248	158	8	5	376	297
*Pittsburgh	.5	2	206	183	8	5	389	311
*Virginia Tech	.4	3	216	152	8	5	460	299
*Boston College	.3	4	176	196	8	5	370	331
Syracuse	.2	5	141	191	6	6	330	301
Rutgers	.2	5	145	231	5	7	329	354
Temple	.0	7	125	260	1	11	235	393

*__Bowls (2-3):__ Miami-FL (won Orange); West Virginia (lost Gator); Pittsburgh (lost Continental Tire); Virginia Tech (lost Insight); Boston College (won San Francisco).

Big Ten Conference

	Conference				Overall		
	W	L	PF	PA	W	L	PF	PA
*Michigan	.7	1	286	150	10	3	460	219
*Ohio St.	.6	2	175	124	11	2	322	229
*Purdue	.6	2	198	138	9	4	349	226
*Iowa	.5	3	198	160	10	3	373	210
*Minnesota	.5	3	285	204	10	3	503	285
*Michigan St.	.5	3	249	191	8	5	363	293
*Wisconsin	.4	4	226	180	7	6	355	306
*Northwestern	.4	4	148	202	6	7	263	326
Penn St.	.1	7	154	190	3	9	233	255
Indiana	.1	7	104	279	2	10	177	388
Illinois	.0	8	112	317	1	11	203	398

*__Bowls (3-5):__ Michigan (lost Rose), Ohio St. (won Fiesta); Purdue (lost Capital One); Iowa (won Outback); Minnesota (won Sun); Michigan St. (lost Alamo); Wisconsin (lost Music City), Northwestern (lost Motor City).

I-A Independents

	W	L	PF	PA
Connecticut	.9	3	408	300
*Navy	.8	5	396	283
Troy State	.6	6	185	272
Notre Dame	.5	7	243	315

*__Bowls (0-1):__ Navy (lost Houston).

Big 12 Conference

North	Conference				Overall		
	W	L	PF	PA	W	L	PF	PA
*Kansas St.	.6	2	290	121	11	4	549	249
*Nebraska	.5	3	188	154	10	3	322	188
*Missouri	.4	4	250	198	8	5	399	287
*Kansas	.3	5	209	247	6	7	384	396
Colorado	.3	5	228	255	5	7	319	398
Iowa St.	.0	8	71	343	2	10	173	437

South	Conference				Overall		
	W	L	PF	PA	W	L	PF	PA
*Oklahoma	.8	0	412	90	12	2	601	214
*Texas	.7	1	308	182	10	3	533	280
*Oklahoma St.	.5	3	241	259	9	4	467	326
*Texas Tech	.4	4	344	296	8	5	552	442
Texas A&M	.2	6	205	356	4	8	304	465
Baylor	.1	7	121	366	3	9	191	455

Big 12 championship game: Kansas St. 35, Oklahoma 7 (Dec. 6, 2003).
*__Bowls (2-6):__ Oklahoma (lost Sugar); Kansas St. (lost Fiesta); Oklahoma St. (lost Cotton); Missouri (lost Independence); Texas (lost Holiday); Texas Tech (won Houston); Nebraska (won Alamo); Kansas (lost Tangerine).

Conference USA

	Conference				Overall		
	W	L	PF	PA	W	L	PF	PA
*Southern Miss	.8	0	226	117	9	4	291	226
*TCU	.7	1	269	202	11	2	380	276
*Louisville	.5	3	289	242	9	4	450	361
*Memphis	.5	3	217	138	9	4	393	250
South Florida	.5	3	177	160	7	4	276	224
*Houston	.4	4	286	301	7	6	448	468
UAB	.4	4	189	190	5	7	249	287
Tulane	.3	5	244	274	5	7	337	424
Cincinnati	.2	6	190	216	5	7	303	319
East Carolina	.1	7	174	280	1	11	217	428
Army	.0	8	127	268	0	13	206	476

*__Bowls (1-4):__ Southern Miss (lost Liberty); TCU (lost Fort Worth); Louisville (lost GMAC); Memphis (won New Orleans); Houston (lost Hawaii).

Mid-American Conference

East	Conference				Overall		
	W	L	PF	PA	W	L	PF	PA
*Miami-OH	.8	0	374	124	13	1	602	272
Marshall	.6	2	230	170	8	4	350	278
Akron	.5	3	257	246	7	5	435	353
Kent St.	.4	4	261	274	5	7	321	396
Central Florida	.2	6	131	221	3	9	224	373
Ohio	.1	7	191	244	2	10	263	372
Buffalo	.1	7	138	289	1	11	177	455

West	Conference				Overall		
	W	L	PF	PA	W	L	PF	PA
*Bowling Green	.7	1	246	165	11	3	470	304
Toledo	.6	2	280	189	8	4	389	285
Northern Illinois	.6	2	281	196	10	2	386	258
Western Michigan	4	4	211	220	5	7	331	370
Ball St.	.3	5	173	249	4	8	261	386
Eastern Michigan	.2	6	145	240	3	9	205	371
Central Michigan	.1	7	154	246	3	9	277	428

MAC championship game: Miami-OH 49, Bowling Green 27 (Dec. 4, 2003).
*__Bowls (2-0):__ Miami-OH (won GMAC); Bowling Green (won Motor City).

Mountain West Conference

	Conference				Overall			
	W	L	PF	PA	W	L	PF	PA
*Utah	6	1	213	144	10	2	344	229
*New Mexico	5	2	206	138	8	5	391	290
*Colorado State	4	3	216	162	7	6	381	318
Air Force	3	4	161	169	7	5	322	242
San Diego St.	3	4	111	145	6	6	224	207
BYU	3	4	114	161	4	8	196	310
UNLV	2	5	132	169	6	6	256	272
Wyoming	2	5	141	206	4	8	286	360

Bowls (1-2): Utah (won Liberty); New Mexico (lost Las Vegas); Colorado St. (lost San Francisco).

Pacific 10 Conference

	Conference				Overall			
	W	L	PF	PA	W	L	PF	PA
*USC	7	1	342	161	12	1	534	239
*Washington St.	6	2	245	169	10	3	394	258
*Oregon	5	3	209	216	8	5	356	348
*California	5	3	267	170	8	6	457	341
*Oregon St.	4	4	270	224	8	5	433	301
Washington	4	4	203	233	6	6	312	317
*UCLA	4	4	175	200	6	7	250	305
Arizona St.	2	6	203	246	5	7	298	328
Stanford	2	6	130	243	4	7	186	324
Arizona	1	7	182	267	2	10	181	429

Bowls (4-2): USC (won Rose); Washington St. (won Holiday); Oregon (lost Sun); California (won Insight); Oregon St. (won Las Vegas); UCLA (lost Silicon Valley Classic).

Sun Belt Conference

	Conference				Overall			
	W	L	PF	PA	W	L	PF	PA
*North Texas	7	0	237	142	9	4	358	285
LA-Lafayette	4	3	225	228	4	8	266	415
Middle Tenn. St.	4	3	213	204	4	8	332	375
Arkansas St.	3	4	131	273	5	7	242	401
Utah St.	3	4	193	136	3	9	264	315
Idaho	3	4	191	171	3	9	248	314
New Mexico St	2	5	154	172	3	9	262	341
LA-Monroe	1	6	180	249	1	11	239	467

Bowl (0-1): North Texas (lost New Orleans).

Southeastern Conference

	Conference				Overall			
Eastern	W	L	PF	PA	W	L	PF	PA
*Georgia	6	2	215	102	11	3	371	203
*Tennessee	6	2	260	170	10	3	365	239
*Florida	6	2	178	152	8	5	390	271
South Carolina	2	6	164	227	5	7	268	314
Vanderbilt	1	7	126	261	2	10	235	358
Kentucky	1	7	198	244	4	8	328	321

	Conference				Overall			
Western	W	L	PF	PA	W	L	PF	PA
*LSU	7	1	228	90	13	1	475	154
*Mississippi	7	1	218	150	10	3	442	285
*Auburn	5	3	190	148	8	5	342	212
*Arkansas	4	4	247	223	9	4	436	305
Mississippi St.	1	7	93	329	2	10	225	471
Alabama	2	6	216	237	4	9	331	333

SEC championship game: LSU 34, Georgia 13 (Dec. 6, 2003).

Bowls (5-2): Georgia (won Capital One); Tennessee (lost Peach); Florida (lost Outback); LSU (won Sugar); Mississippi (won Cotton); Auburn (won Music City); Arkansas (won Independence).

Note: Alabama was ineligible for SEC title.

Western Athletic Conference

	Conference				Overall			
	W	L	PF	PA	W	L	PF	PA
*Boise St.	8	0	375	143	13	1	602	239
*Tulsa	6	2	272	193	8	5	400	361
*Fresno St.	6	2	203	168	9	5	322	317
*Hawaii	5	3	242	211	9	5	486	427
Rice	5	3	292	217	5	7	343	378
Nevada	4	4	195	251	6	6	282	338
La. Tech	3	5	237	275	5	7	310	394
San Jose St.	2	6	217	290	3	8	259	386
UTEP	1	7	195	332	2	11	288	498
SMU	0	8	98	246	0	12	134	386

Bowls (3-1): Boise St. (won Fort Worth); Tulsa (lost Humanitarian); Fresno St. (won Silicon Valley Classic); Hawaii (won Hawaii).

NCAA Division I-A Individual Leaders

Total Offense

		Rushing				Passing		Total Offense			
	Cl	Car	Gain	Loss	Net	Att	Yds	Plays	Yds	YdsPP	YdsPG
B. J. Symons, Texas Tech	Sr.	79	340	197	143	719	5833	798	5976	7.49	459.7
Philip Rivers, N.C. State	Sr.	78	251	142	109	483	4491	561	4600	8.20	353.8
Josh Harris, Bowling Green	Sr.	215	972	142	830	494	3813	709	4643	6.55	331.6
Ben Roethlisberger, Miami-OH	Jr.	67	285	174	111	495	4486	562	4597	8.18	328.4
Charlie Frye, Akron	Jr.	111	510	222	288	421	3549	532	3837	7.21	319.8
Timmy Chang, Hawaii	Jr.	43	114	174	-60	601	4199	644	4139	6.43	318.4
Ryan Dinwiddie, Boise St.	Sr.	81	214	171	43	446	4356	527	4399	8.35	314.2
Bruce Gradkowski, Toledo	So.	91	576	72	504	389	3210	480	3714	7.74	309.5
Derek Anderson, Oregon St.	Jr.	57	100	225	-125	510	4058	567	3933	6.94	302.5
Rod Rutherford, Pittsburgh	Sr.	136	515	365	150	413	3679	549	3829	6.97	294.5

All-Purpose Yards

	Cl	Gm	Rush	Rec	PR	KOR	Total Yds	YdsPG
DeAngelo Williams, Memphis	So.	11	1430	384	0	299	2119	192.09
Darren Sproles, Kansas State	Jr.	15	1986	287	190	272	2735	182.33
Jerry Seymour, Central Michigan	Fr.	9	1117	103	0	330	1550	172.22
Howard Jackson, UTEP	Jr.	13	1146	391	0	609	2146	165.08
Michael Turner, Northern Illinois	Sr.	12	1648	230	0	58	1936	161.33
Patrick Cobbs, North Texas	Jr.	11	1680	43	8	40	1771	161.00
Lance Moore, Toledo	Jr.	12	26	1194	219	456	1895	157.92
Chris Perry, Michigan	Sr.	13	1674	367	0	0	2041	157.00
Steve Jackson, Oregon St.	Jr.	13	1545	470	0	0	2015	155.00
Anthony Sherrell, Eastern Michigan	Jr.	12	1531	304	0	0	1835	152.92

Texas Tech

B.J. Symons
Total Offense

N.C. State

Philip Rivers
Passing Efficiency

North Texas

Patrick Cobbs
Rushing

LSU

Skyler Green
Punt Returns

Passing Efficiency
(Minimum 15 attempts per game)

	Cl	Gm	Att	Cmp	Cmp Pct	Int	Int Pct	Yds	Yds/Att	TD	TD Pct	Rating Points
Philip Rivers, N.C. State	Sr.	13	483	348	72.05	7	1.45	4491	9.30	34	7.04	170.5
Ben Roethlisberger, Miami-OH	Jr.	14	495	342	69.09	10	2.02	4486	9.06	37	7.47	165.8
Matt Leinart, USC	So.	13	402	255	63.43	9	2.24	3556	8.85	38	9.45	164.5
Ryan Dinwiddie, Boise St. . . .	Sr.	14	446	276	61.88	7	1.57	4356	9.77	31	6.95	163.7
Asad Abdul-Khaliq, Minnesota	Sr.	13	250	158	63.20	5	2.00	2401	9.60	17	6.80	162.3
Bruce Gradkowski, Toledo . . .	So.	12	389	277	71.21	7	1.80	3210	8.25	29	7.46	161.5
Jason White, Oklahoma	Sr.	14	451	278	61.64	10	2.22	3846	8.53	40	8.87	158.1
Rod Rutherford, Pittsburgh . . .	Sr.	13	413	247	59.81	14	3.39	3679	8.91	37	8.96	157.4
Bill Whittemore, Kansas	Sr.	10	263	159	60.46	6	2.28	2385	9.07	18	6.84	154.7
Kevin Kolb, Houston	Fr.	13	360	220	61.11	6	1.67	3131	8.70	25	6.94	153.8
Bradlee Van Pelt, Colorado St.	Sr.	13	297	180	60.61	13	4.38	2845	9.58	19	6.40	153.4
Alex Smith, Utah	So.	11	266	173	65.04	3	1.13	2247	8.45	15	5.64	152.3
B.J. Symons, Texas Tech	Sr.	13	719	470	65.37	22	3.06	5833	8.11	52	7.23	151.3
Buck Pierce, New Mexico St. .	Jr.	11	170	118	69.41	6	3.53	1510	8.88	7	4.12	150.6
Charlie Frye, Akron	Jr.	12	421	273	64.85	9	2.14	3549	8.43	22	5.23	148.6

Rushing

	Cl	Car	Yds	TD	YdsPG
Patrick Cobbs, North Texas . .	Jr.	307	1680	19	152.73
Michael Turner, N. Illinois . . .	Sr.	310	1648	14	137.33
Darren Sproles, Kansas St. . . .	Jr.	306	1986	16	132.40
Derrick Knight, Boston College	Sr.	321	1721	11	132.38
DeAngelo Williams, Mempis . .	So.	243	1430	10	130.00
Chris Perry, Michigan	Sr.	338	1674	18	128.77
Anthony Sherrell, E. Michigan	Jr.	338	1531	12	127.58
Kevin Jones, Virginia Tech . . .	Jr.	281	1647	21	126.69
Jerry Seymour, C. Michigan . .	Fr.	205	1117	8	124.11
Steven Jackson, Oregon St. . .	Jr.	350	1545	19	118.85

Games: All played 13, except Sproles (15), Turner and Sherrell (12), Cobbs and Williams (11) and Seymour (9).

Receptions

	Cl	No	Yds	TD	P/Gm
Lance Moore, Toledo	Jr.	103	1194	9	8.58
Chad Owens, Hawaii	Jr.	85	1134	9	7.73
Wes Welker, Texas Tech	Sr.	97	1099	9	7.46
Dante Ridgeway, Ball St. . . .	So.	89	1075	10	7.42
Reggie Williams, Washington	Jr.	89	1109	8	7.42
Mike Williams, USC	So.	95	1314	16	7.31
Terrance Copper, E. Carolina	Sr.	87	897	2	7.25
Larry Fitzgerald, Pittsburgh . .	So.	92	1672	22	7.08
Cole Magner, Bowling Green	Jr.	99	1138	10	7.07
Paris Warren, Utah	Jr.	76	809	4	6.91

Games: All played 12, except Owens and Warren (11), Welker, Williams and Fitzgerald (13) and Magner (14).

Field Goals

	Cl	FG/Att	Pct	P/Gm
Bill Bennett, Georgia	Sr.	31/38	.816	2.21
Nick Browne, TCU	Sr.	28/33	.848	2.15
Drew Dunning, Washington St.	Sr.	27/31	.871	2.08
Ben Jones, Purdue	So.	25/30	.833	1.92
Jonathan Nichols, Mississippi	Jr.	25/29	.862	1.92
Nick Novak, Maryland	Jr.	24/32	.750	1.85
Connor Hughes, Virginia . . .	So.	23/25	.920	1.77
Steve Azar, N. Illinois	Sr.	21/26	.808	1.75
Josh Scobee, La. Tech	Sr.	21/31	.677	1.75
Jon Peattie, Miami-FL	Fr.	22/28	.786	1.69
David Rayner, Michigan St. . .	Jr.	22/29	.759	1.69

Games: All played 13, except Bennett (14), Azar and Scobee (12).

Interceptions

	Cl	No	Yds	TD	P/Gm
Sean Taylor, Miami-FL	Jr.	10	184	3	0.83
Josh Bullocks, Nebraska	So.	10	154	0	0.77
Derrick Ansley, Troy St.	Jr.	9	74	1	0.75
Jonathan Burke, Arkansas St. .	Sr.	9	120	0	0.75
Keiwan Ratliff, Florida	Sr.	9	182	2	0.69
J.R. Reed, S. Florida	Sr.	7	45	0	0.64
Gerald Jones, San Jose St. . .	Sr.	6	178	2	0.55
Jim Leonhard, Wisconsin . . .	Jr.	7	98	0	0.54
Erik Coleman, Washington St.	Sr.	7	22	0	0.54
Will Poole, USC	So.	7	70	1	0.54

Games: All played 13 except, Taylor, Ansley and Burke (12), Reed and Jones (11).

Scoring

Non-Kickers

	Cl	TD	Pts	P/Gm
Patrick Cobbs, North Texas . .	Jr.	21	126	11.45
Cedric Benson, Texas	Jr.	22	134	11.17
Walter Reyes, Syracuse	Jr.	21	128	10.67
Larry Fitzgerald, Pittsburgh . .	So.	22	132	10.15
Steve Jackson, Oregon St. . . .	Jr.	22	132	10.25
Jason Wright, Northwestern . .	Sr.	21	126	9.69
Kevin Jones, Virginia Tech . . .	Jr.	21	126	9.69
DonTrell Moore, New Mexico	So.	21	126	9.69
Chris Perry, Michigan	Sr.	20	120	9.23
Brad Smith, Missouri	So.	19	118	9.08

Games: All played 13, except Cobbs (11), Benson and Reyes (12).

Kickers

	FG/Att	PAT/Att	Pts	P/Gm
Nick Browne, TCU	.28/33	38/38	124	9.54
Jonathan Nichols, Miss. . . .	.25/29	49/49	124	9.54
Tyler Jones, Boise St.	.19/25	75/76	132	9.43
Ryan Killeen, USC	.19/24	65/67	122	9.38
Billy Bennett, Georgia	.31/38	38/39	131	9.36
Trey DiCarlo, Oklahoma . .	.19/22	74/76	131	9.36
Drew Dunning, Wash. St. . .	.27/31	35/40	116	8.92
Steve Azar, No. Illinois . . .	.21/26	41/43	104	8.67
Kirk Yliniemi, Oregon St. . .	.19/23	46/47	103	8.58
Ben Jones, Purdue	.25/30	36/37	111	8.54
Nick Novak, Maryland . .	.24/32	38/42	110	8.46

Games: All played 13, Jones, Bennett, DiCarlo (14), Azar and Yliniemi (12).

Punting

(Minimum of 3.6 per game)

	Cl	No	Yds	Avg
Matt Prater, UCF	So.	58	2781	47.95
Brandon Fields, Michigan St. .	So.	62	2878	46.42
Joel Stelly, LA-Monroe	So.	67	3099	46.25
Jared Scruggs, Rice	Fr.	51	2341	45.90
Ryan Plackemeier, Wake Forest	So.	57	2600	45.61
Dustin Colquitt, Tennessee . . .	Jr.	68	3081	45.31
Kyle Larson, Nebraska	Sr.	66	2978	45.12
Eric Wilbur, Florida	Fr.	66	2954	44.76
Ryan Dougherty, E. Carolina .	Fr.	64	2846	44.47

Punt Returns

(Minimum of 1.2 per game)

	Cl	No	Yds	TD	Avg
Skyler Green, LSU	So.	25	462	2	18.48
Ryne Robinson, Miami-OH . .	Fr.	38	654	3	17.21
Mark Jones, Tennessee	Sr.	20	303	1	15.15
Gabe Lindsay, Oklahoma St.	Sr.	26	393	1	15.12
DeAngelo Hall, Va. Tech . . .	Jr.	33	487	3	14.76
Marcus James, Missouri	Sr.	26	377	0	14.50
Marion Barber III, Minnesota	Jr.	28	405	0	14.46
Jim Leonhard, Wisconsin . . .	Jr.	34	470	2	13.82
Steve Breaston, Michigan . . .	So.	45	619	2	13.76

Kickoff Returns

(Minimum of 1.2 per game)

	Cl	No	Yds	TD	Avg
Michael Waddell, N. Carolina	Sr.	15	475	1	31.67
J.R. Reed, South Florida	Sr.	18	570	1	31.67
Mike Imoh, Va. Tech	So.	18	549	1	30.50
John Eubanks, So. Miss.	So.	17	499	1	29.35
Dexter Wynn, Colorado St. . .	Sr.	27	782	0	28.96
Devin Hester, Miami-FL	Fr.	18	517	1	28.72
Senterrio Landrum, Duke . . .	Jr.	25	709	0	28.36
Kendrick Starling, San Jose St.	Sr.	20	562	0	28.10
Charles Estes, LA-Monroe . . .	Jr.	36	988	1	27.44

NCAA Division I-A Team Leaders

Scoring Offense

	Gm	Record	Pts	Avg
Boise St.	14	13-1	602	43.00
Miami-OH	14	13-1	602	43.00
Oklahoma	14	12-2	601	42.93
Texas Tech	13	8-5	552	42.46
USC	13	12-1	534	41.08
Texas	13	10-3	533	41.00
Minnesota	13	10-3	503	38.69
N.C. State	13	8-5	489	37.62
Kansas St.	15	11-4	549	36.60
Akron	12	7-5	435	36.25

Scoring Defense

	Gm	Record	Pts	Avg
LSU	14	13-1	154	11.00
Nebraska	13	10-3	188	14.5
Georgia	13	11-3	196	14.5
Miami-FL	13	11-2	196	15.1
Oklahoma	14	12-2	214	15.3
Maryland	13	10-3	206	15.8
Iowa	13	10-3	210	16.2
Kansas St.	15	11-4	244	16.3
Auburn	13	8-5	212	16.3
Florida St.	13	10-3	217	16.7

Total Offense

	Gm	Plays	Yds	Avg	TD	YdsPG
Texas Tech	13	1088	7576	6.96	76	582.77
Miami-OH	14	1053	7016	6.66	82	501.14
Bowling Green	14	1111	6954	6.26	61	496.71
Minnesota	13	970	6430	6.63	66	494.62
Louisville	13	913	6355	6.96	58	488.85
Hawaii	14	1072	6834	6.38	63	488.14
Boise St.	14	1061	6809	6.42	77	486.36
Connecticut	12	946	5730	6.06	54	477.50
Akron	12	923	5643	6.11	55	470.25
Oregon St.	13	1060	6019	5.68	53	463.00

Note: Touchdowns scored by rushing and passing only.

Total Defense

	Gm	Plays	Yds	Avg	TD	YdsPG
LSU	14	877	3528	4.02	19	252.00
Miami-FL	13	786	3348	4.26	23	257.54
Oklahoma	14	881	3635	4.13	27	259.64
Georgia	14	880	3876	4.40	23	276.86
Auburn	13	802	3661	4.56	25	281.62
Kansas St.	15	996	4246	4.26	31	283.07
Oregon St.	13	914	3753	4.11	38	288.69
San Diego St.	12	813	3477	4.28	22	289.75
Memphis	13	879	3845	4.37	32	295.77
Ohio St.	13	930	3859	4.15	28	296.85

Note: Opponents' TDs scored by rushing and passing only.

Single Game Highs
INDIVIDUAL

Rushing Yards

Yds	
307	P.J. Daniels, Georgia Tech vs. Tulsa (Jan. 3)
291	Brad Smith, Missouri vs. Texas Tech(Oct. 25)
283	Cedric Benson, Texas vs. Texas A&M (Nov. 28)
273	Darren Sproles, Kansas St. vs. Missouri (Nov. 22)

Total Offense

Yds	
681	B.J. Symons, Texas Tech vs. Mississippi (Sept. 27)
618	B.J. Symons, Texas Tech vs. N.C. State (Sept. 20)
578	Kevin Kolb, Houston vs. TCU (Oct. 25)

Passing Yards

Yds	
661	B.J. Symons, Texas Tech vs. Mississippi (Sept. 27)
586	B.J. Symons, Texas Tech vs. N.C. State (Sept. 20)
552	B.J. Symons, Texas Techvs. Oklahoma St. (Oct. 18)

Passes Completed

No	
49	Bruce Gradkowski, Toledo vs. Pittsburgh (Sept. 20)
45	B.J. Symons, Texas Tech vs. Iowa St. (Oct. 11)

Receptions

No	
16	Five players tied (including Purdue's Taylor Stubblefield who did it twice).

Receiving Yards

Yds	
258	Lee Evans, Wisconsin vs. Michigan St. (Nov. 15)
255	Tim Gilligan, Boise St. vs. Louisiana Tech (Oct. 4)

Touchdowns

No	
7	Rashaun Woods, Oklahoma St. vs. SMU (Sept. 20)

TEAM

Total Offense Yards Gained

Yds	
782	TCU vs. Houston (Oct. 25)
779	Louisville vs. Houston (Nov. 22)

Total Defense Yards Allowed

Yds	
54	Oklahoma vs. Texas A&M (Nov. 8)
93	Vanderbilt vs. Chattanooga (Sept. 6)

Annual Awards

Players of the Year

Jason White, Oklahoma, QB . . . . .AP, Heisman
Eli Manning, Mississippi, QB . . . . .Maxwell
Larry Fitzgerald, Pittsburgh, WR . . . . .Camp

Payton Award (I-AA) . . . . . . .Jamaal Branch, Colgate, RB
Hill Trophy (Div. II) . . . . .Will Hall, N. Alabama, QB
Gagliardi Trophy (Div. III) . . . . .Blake Elliot, St. John's, WR

Position Players of the Year

O'Brien Award (Quarterback) . . . Jason White, Oklahoma
Walker Award (Running Back) . . . . .Chris Perry, Michigan
Biletnikoff Award (Receiver) . . . .Larry Fitzgerald, Pittsburgh
Outland Trophy (Int. Lineman) . . . .Robert Gallery, Iowa, OT
Lombardi Award (Lineman) . .Tommie Harris, Oklahoma, DT
Butkus Award (Linebacker) . . . . .Teddy Lehman, Oklahoma
Thorpe Award (Def. Back) . . . . . .Derrick Strait, Oklahoma
Nagurski Award (Def. Player) . . .Derrick Strait, Oklahoma
Bednarik Award (Def. Player) . . .Teddy Lehman, Oklahoma
Groza Award (Kicker) . . . . . .Jonathan Nichols, Mississippi
Ray Guy Award (Punter) . . . . .B.J. Sander, Ohio St.
Mackey Award (Tight End) . . . . .Kellen Winslow, Miami-FL

Coaches of the Year

Nick Saban, LSU .AP, FWAA
Bob Stoops, Oklahoma . . . . .Camp, Dodd
Peter Carroll, USC . . . . .AFCA

Heisman Trophy Vote

Presented since 1935 by the Downtown Athletic Club of New York City and named after former college coach and DAC athletic director John W. Heisman. Voting done by national media and former Heisman winners. Each ballot allows for three names (points based on 3 for 1st, 2 for 2nd and 1 for 3rd).

Top 10 Vote-Getters

	Pos	1st	2nd	3rd	Pts
Jason White, Oklahoma . . .	QB	319	204	116	1481
Larry Fitzgerald, Pittsburgh	WR	253	233	128	1353
Eli Manning, Mississippi . .	QB	95	132	161	710
Chris Perry, Michigan	RB	27	66	128	341
Darren Sproles, Kansas St. .	RB	15	30	29	134
Matt Leinart, USC	QB	5	27	58	127
Philip Rivers, N.C. State . .	QB	18	20	24	118
Mike Williams, USC	WR	12	12	18	78
Ben Roethlisberger, Mia-OH	QB	5	9	14	47
B.J. Symons, Texas Tech . .	QB	1	7	21	38

Consensus All-America Team

NCAA Division I-A players cited most frequently by the following selectors: AFCA, AP, and Walter Camp Foundation. (*) indicates unanimous selection. Holdovers from the 2002 team are in **bold** type.

Offense

	Player	Class	Ht	Wt
WR	Larry Fitzgerald*, Pittsburgh . . . .So.	6-3	225
WR	Mike Williams, USC . . . . .So.	6-5	230
TE	Kellen Winslow*, Miami-FL . . . . .Jr.	6-5	250
C	Jake Grove*, Virginia Tech . . . . . .Sr.	6-3	300
OL	Robert Gallery*, Iowa . . . . .Sr.	6-7	321
OL	Jacob Rogers*, USC . . . . .Sr.	6-6	305
OL	Alex Barron, Florida St. . . . . .Jr.	6-6	316
OL	**Shawn Andrews***, Arkansas . .Jr.	6-6	353
QB	Jason White*, Oklahoma . . . . . . .Sr.	6-3	221
RB	Chris Perry*, Michigan . . . . .Sr.	6-1	218
RB	Kevin Jones, Virginia Tech . . . . . .Jr.	6-0	221
K	Nate Kaeding, Iowa . . . . .Sr.	6-0	180

Defense

	Player	Class	Ht	Wt
DL	**Tommie Harris***, Oklahoma . . .Jr.	6-3	289
DL	Dave Ball*, UCLA . . . . .Sr.	6-6	269
DL	Will Smith, Ohio St. . . . . .Sr.	6-4	265
DL	Chad Lavalais, LSU . . . . .Sr.	6-1	293
LB	Jonathan Vilma, Miami-FL . . . . . .Sr.	6-2	223
LB	Karlos Dansby, Auburn . . . . .Sr.	6-5	234
LB	**Teddy Lehman***, Oklahoma . . .Jr.	6-3	243
DB	Sean Taylor*, Miami-FL . . . . .Jr.	6-3	230
DB	Derrick Strait*, Oklahoma . . . . . .Sr.	5-11	195
DB	Will Allen, Ohio St. . . . . .Sr.	6-2	190
DB	Keiwan Ratliff, Florida . . . . .Sr.	5-10	187
P	Dustin Colquitt, Tennessee . . . . . .Jr.	6-2	196

Underclassmen who declared for the 2004 draft

Forty-two players forfeited the remainder of their college eligibility and declared for the NFL draft in 2004. NFL teams drafted 33 underclassmen. Players listed in alphabetical order; first round selections in **bold** type.

	Pos	Drafted by	Overall Pick
Shawn Andrews, Arkansas	.OT	Philadelphia	16
Matthias Askew, Michigan St.	.DT	Cincinnati	114
Kelly Butler, Purdue	.OT	Detroit	172
Ahmad Carroll, Arkansas	.DB	Green Bay	25
Michael Clayton, LSU	.WR	Tampa Bay	15
Brooks Daniels, Alabama	.LB	not drafted	–
Devard Darling, Wash. St.	.WR	Baltimore	82
Nat Dorsey, Georgia Tech	.OT	Minnesota	115
Chris Gamble, Ohio St.	.DB	Carolina	28
Robert Geathers, Georgia	.DE	Cincinnati	117
Greg Golden, N.C. State	.DB	not drafted	–
Amon Gordon, Stanford	.DT	Cleveland	161
DeAngelo Hall, Va. Tech	.DB	Atlanta	8
Derrick Hamilton, Clemson	.WR	San Francisco	77
Tony Hargrove, Georgia Tech	.DE	St. Louis	91
Tommie Harris, Oklahoma	.DT	Chicago	14
Steven Jackson, Oregon St.	.RB	St. Louis	24
Kevin Jones, Virginia Tech	.RB	Detroit	30
Sean Jones, Georgia	.DB	Cleveland	59
Tyrone Jordan, Valdosta St.	.	not drafted	–

	Pos	Drafted by	Overall Pick
Omar Laurence, C. Florida	.DB	not drafted	–
Matt Mauck, LSU	.QB	Denver	225
Antwan Odom, Alabama	.DE	Tennessee	57
Igor Olshansky, Oregon	.DT	San Diego	35
Jason Peters, Arkansas	.TE	not drafted	–
Mark Pierce, Arkansas	.FB	not drafted	–
Ben Roethlisberger, Mia-OH	QB	Pittsburgh	11
P.K. Sam, Florida St.	.WR	New England	164
Jason Shivers, Arizona St.	.DB	St. Louis	158
Justin Smiley, Alabama	.G	San Francisco	46
Chris Snee, Boston College	.G	New York	34
Randy Starks, Maryland	.DT	Tennessee	71
Sean Taylor, Miami-FL	.DB	Washington	5
Kenechi Udeze, USC	.DE	Minnesota	20
Matt Ware, UCLA	.DB	Philadelphia	89
Donnell Washington, Clemson	.DT	Green Bay	72
Vince Wilfork, Miami-FL	.DT	New England	21
Reggie Williams, Washington	WR	Jacksonville	9
Kellen Winslow, Miami-FL	.TE	Cleveland	6
Chris Wright, Oklahoma St.	.WR	not drafted	–

Note: Sophmores Maurice Clarett (Ohio St.), Mike Williams (USC) and seven others challenged the NFL rule that players must wait 3 years after high school before they may enter the draft but the U.S. Supreme Court ultimately denied their bid.

NCAA Division I-AA Final Standings

Standings based on conference games only; overall records include postseason games.

Atlantic 10 Conference

	Conference				Overall			
	W	L	PF	PA	W	L	PF	PA
*Delaware	8	1	295	193	15	1	555	247
*Massachusetts	8	1	276	209	10	3	368	295
Northeastern	6	3	265	185	8	4	414	219
Maine	5	4	176	169	7	5	297	237
Villanova	5	4	250	152	7	4	314	178
William & Mary	4	4	229	219	5	5	287	299
James Madison	4	5	214	228	6	6	307	284
New Hampshire	3	6	261	303	5	7	406	380
Rhode Island	3	6	230	278	4	8	309	381
Hofstra	2	7	161	249	2	10	247	368
Richmond	1	8	137	314	2	9	189	370

Playoffs (4-1): Delaware (4-0), Massachusetts (0-1).
Note: The Sept. 27 game between Maine and Wm. & Mary was cancelled in the aftermath of Hurricane Isabel. It was declared a win for Maine and a no-contest for Wm. & Mary.

Big Sky Conference

	Conference				Overall			
	W	L	PF	PA	W	L	PF	PA
*Montana St.	5	2	197	118	7	6	330	215
*Montana	5	2	240	122	9	4	430	266
*Northern Arizona	5	2	233	192	9	4	409	305
Weber St.	4	3	183	165	8	4	325	241
Idaho St.	4	3	224	260	8	4	394	423
Eastern Wash.	3	4	230	247	6	5	344	321
Portland St.	1	6	105	214	4	7	220	327
Sacramento St.	1	6	117	211	2	9	237	332

Playoffs (1-3): Montana St. (0-1), Montana (0-1), Northern Arizona (1-1).

Big South Conference

	Conference				Overall			
	W	L	PF	PA	W	L	PF	PA
Gardner-Webb	4	0	148	59	8	4	335	254
Liberty	3	1	103	82	6	6	306	378
VMI	2	2	122	85	6	6	359	257
Coastal Carolina	1	3	96	109	6	5	309	253
Charleston So.	0	4	27	161	1	11	148	513

Playoffs: No teams invited.

Gateway Football Conference

	Conference				Overall			
	W	L	PF	PA	W	L	PF	PA
*Southern Ill.	6	1	231	153	10	2	437	229
*Northern Iowa	6	1	195	144	10	3	390	246
*Western Ill.	5	2	270	213	9	4	472	331
*Western Ky.	5	2	208	121	9	4	427	219
Illinois St.	3	4	189	183	6	6	318	293
Youngstown St.	2	5	148	228	5	7	281	283
SW Missouri St.	1	6	169	210	4	7	288	276
Indiana St.	0	7	107	265	3	9	170	356

Playoffs (3-4): Southern Ill. (0-1), Northern Iowa (1-1), Western Ill. (1-1), Western Ky. (1-1).

Ivy League

	Conference				Overall			
	W	L	PF	PA	W	L	PF	PA
Pennsylvania	7	0	250	171	10	0	346	164
Harvard	4	3	212	151	7	3	317	221
Yale	4	3	211	188	6	4	354	284
Brown	4	3	193	192	5	5	244	246
Dartmouth	4	3	161	168	5	5	211	261
Columbia	3	4	135	189	4	6	211	283
Princeton	2	5	175	181	2	8	204	267
Cornell	0	7	65	216	1	9	130	304

Playoffs: League does not play postseason games.

Metro Atlantic Athletic Conference

	Conference				Overall			
	W	L	PF	PA	W	L	PF	PA
Duquesne	5	0	210	70	8	3	345	202
Iona	4	1	135	104	6	5	267	275
La Salle	2	3	121	164	3	8	233	353
Marist	2	3	102	130	4	6	187	324
St. Peter's	2	3	86	114	2	8	144	304
Siena	0	5	65	137	0	11	109	345

Playoffs: No teams invited.

NCAA Division I-AA Final Standings (Cont.)

Mid-Eastern Athletic Conference

	Conference				Overall			
	W	L	PF	PA	W	L	PF	PA
*N. Carolina A&T	.6	1	182	133	10	3	294	236
*Bethune-Cookman	5	2	196	133	9	3	376	252
Hampton	.5	2	221	124	7	4	351	212
S. Carolina St.	.5	2	210	135	8	4	364	229
Morgan St.	.4	3	223	185	6	5	318	318
Howard	.2	5	117	156	4	7	208	265
Delaware St.	.1	6	120	236	1	10	182	348
Norfolk St.	.0	7	130	297	1	11	192	479
Florida A&M	.0	0	0	0	6	6	278	280

*Playoffs (0-2): N.C. A&T (0-1), Bethune-Cookman (0-1).
Note: Florida A&M was not eligible for the MEAC title because of their plans on moving up to Division 1-A.

Northeast Conference

	Conference				Overall			
	W	L	PF	PA.	W	L	PF	PA
Monmouth (N.J.)	.6	1	121	73	10	2	247	102
Albany	.6	1	216	69	7	4	299	185
Robert Morris	.4	3	154	139	6	4	246	219
Stony Brook	.4	3	201	165	6	4	284	237
Sacred Heart	.3	7	134	181	6	5	286	280
Wagner	.3	4	140	150	6	5	231	203
Central Conn St.	.2	5	147	195	3	8	231	359
St. Francis (Pa.)	.0	7	109	250	1	9	168	367

Playoffs: No teams invited.

Ohio Valley Conference

	Conference				Overall			
	W	L	PF	PA	W	L	PF	PA
*Jacksonville St.	.7	1	287	161	8	4	316	278
Eastern Ky.	.6	2	255	204	7	5	347	352
Samford	.5	3	258	188	7	4	350	276
Tennessee St.	.5	3	236	210	7	5	348	285
SE Missouri St.	.5	3	239	207	5	7	262	209
Murray St.	.3	5	168	252	4	8	225	338
Eastern Ill.	.3	5	162	187	4	8	210	268
Tennessee Tech	.1	7	183	248	2	9	245	340
Tenn.-Martin	.1	7	164	286	2	10	198	439

*Playoffs (0-1): Jacksonville St. (0-1).

Patriot League

	Conference				Overall			
	W	L	PF	PA	W	L	PF	PA
*Colgate	.7	0	219	115	15	1	480	303
Lehigh	.6	1	226	99	8	3	327	185
Fordham	.4	3	179	158	9	3	386	251
Bucknell	.4	3	175	197	6	6	284	299
Towson	.3	4	108	142	6	6	271	274
Lafayette	.2	5	170	175	5	6	315	248
Georgetown	.1	6	126	223	4	8	272	334
Holy Cross	.1	6	185	290	1	11	322	478

*Playoffs (3-1): Colgate (3-1).

NCAA I-AA Independents

	W	L	PF	PA
*Florida Atlantic	11	3	404	306
Northern Colorado	9	2	425	180
Cal Poly-SLO	7	4	316	241
SE Louisiana	5	7	369	382
Southern Utah	4	7	240	286
Florida International	2	10	270	341
St. Mary's (Ca.)	1	11	162	471
Savannah St.	0	12	109	488

*Playoffs: Florida Atlantic (2-1).

Pioneer Football League

North	Conference				Overall			
	W	L	PF	PA	W	L	PF	PA
Valparaiso	.3	1	146	132	8	4	406	333
San Diego	.3	1	169	113	8	2	399	215
Dayton	.2	2	129	89	9	2	400	183
Drake	.1	3	119	130	6	6	342	307
Butler	.1	3	39	138	2	9	119	418

South	Conference				Overall			
	W	L	PF	PA	W	L	PF	PA
Morehead St.	.3	0	104	26	8	3	327	185
Jacksonville	.1	2	75	57	5	6	268	307
Austin Peay	.1	2	31	100	4	7	194	276
Davidson	.1	2	68	95	3	8	246	364

PFL Championship Game: Valparaiso 54, M'head St. 42
Playoffs: No teams invited.

Southern Conference

	Conference				Overall			
	W	L	PF	PA	W	L	PF	PA
*Wofford	.8	0	246	91	12	2	383	207
Appalachian St.	.6	2	204	123	7	4	252	219
Ga. Southern	.5	3	224	163	7	4	311	232
Furman	.4	4	185	110	6	5	278	155
The Citadel	.4	4	163	176	6	6	261	311
W. Carolina	.3	5	144	197	5	7	251	301
Chattanooga	.3	5	143	281	3	9	195	421
East Tenn St.	.2	6	158	175	5	7	270	233
Elon	.1	7	70	221	2	10	119	314

*Playoffs (2-1): Wofford (2-1).

Southland Conference

	Conference				Overall			
	W	L	PF	PA	W	L	PF	PA
*McNeese St.	.5	0	190	119	10	2	405	284
Stephen F. Austin	.4	1	167	108	7	4	343	230
Nicholls St.	.3	2	152	146	5	6	389	280
Northwestern St.	.1	4	126	145	6	6	386	265
Texas St.	.1	4	136	190	4	8	315	417
Sam Houston St.	.1	4	137	200	2	9	239	406

*Playoffs (0-1): McNeese St. (0-1).

Southwestern Athletic Conference

Eastern	Conference				Overall			
	W	L	PF	PA	W	L	PF	PA
Alabama St.	.5	2	255	167	8	5	434	327
Alcorn St.	.5	2	213	163	7	5	361	318
Alabama A&M	.4	3	210	161	8	4	398	194
Jackson St.	.2	5	139	203	2	10	201	338
Miss. Valley St.	.1	6	108	211	2	9	181	331

Western	Conference				Overall			
	W	L	PF	PA	W	L	PF	PA
Southern	.6	1	307	143	12	1	520	195
Grambling St.	.6	1	309	119	9	3	439	258
Texas Southern	.3	4	151	167	5	6	213	331
Ark.-Pine Bluff	.3	4	125	166	4	7	211	291
Prairie View A&M	.0	7	44	361	1	9	99	522

SWAC Championship Game: Southern 20, Alabama St. 9.
Playoffs: No teams invited.

San Diego
Eric Rasmussen
Passing Efficiency

Brown
Nick Hartigan
Rushing

Colgate
Jamaal Branch
Touchdowns

Fordham
Javarus Dudley
Receptions

NCAA Division I-AA Leaders
INDIVIDUAL
Passing Efficiency
(Minimum 15 attempts per game)

	Cl	Gm	Att	Cmp	Cmp Pct	Int	Int Pct	Yds	Yds/ Att	TD	TD Pct	Rating Points
Eric Rasmussen, San Diego	Sr.	10	318	195	61.32	3	0.94	2982	9.38	35	11.01	174.5
Quincy Richards, Southern	Sr.	13	389	256	65.81	15	3.86	3427	8.81	33	8.48	160.1
David Macchi, Valparaiso	Sr.	12	412	238	57.77	10	2.43	3763	9.13	38	9.22	160.1
Jaren Allen, Florida Atlantic	Jr.	14	346	218	63.01	9	2.60	3003	8.68	24	6.94	153.6
Scott Pendarvis, McNeese St.	Jr.	12	244	142	58.20	6	2.46	2186	8.96	18	7.38	152.9
Erik Meyer, E. Washington	So.	11	281	176	62.63	3	1.07	2301	8.19	20	7.12	152.8
Lang Campbell, Wm. & Mary	Jr.	10	285	182	63.86	7	2.46	2296	8.06	22	7.72	152.1
Kyle Keating, Lehigh	Jr.	11	179	109	60.89	5	2.79	1419	7.93	16	8.94	151.4
Mike Mitchell, Pennsylvania	Jr.	9	319	200	62.70	7	2.19	2470	7.74	26	8.15	150.2
Chris Peterson, Cal Poly	Sr.	10	222	135	60.81	3	1.35	1798	8.10	15	6.76	148.4
Jason Murrietta, N. Arizona	Fr.	13	412	243	58.98	12	2.91	3472	8.43	29	7.04	147.2
Niel Loebig, Duquesne	So.	11	351	207	58.97	17	4.84	3086	8.79	25	7.12	146.6

Total Offense

	Cl	Rush	Pass	Yds	YdsPG
Bruce Eugene, Grambling	Jr.	412	3808	4220	351.7
Alvin Cowan, Yale	Sr.	451	2994	3445	344.5
David Macchi, Valparaiso	Jr.	316	3763	4079	339.9
Eric Rasmussen, San Diego	Sr.	29	2982	3011	301.1
Ben Dougherty, Florida A&M	Jr.	674	2502	3176	288.7
Ramon Nelson, Samford	Sr.	381	2759	3140	285.5
David Caudill, Morehead St.	Sr.	454	2660	3114	283.1
Martin Hankins, SE La.	Fr.	-147	3537	3390	282.5
Barrick Nealy, Texas St.	So.	261	3129	3390	282.5
Quincy Richard, Southern	Sr.	221	3427	3648	280.6
Connor Jostes, Drake	So.	149	2646	2795	279.5

Games: All played 12, except Cowan, Rasmussen, Jostes (10), Dougherty, Nelson, Caudill (11) and Richard (13).

Rushing

	Cl	Car	Yds	TD	YdsPG
Nick Hartigan, Brown	So.	275	1498	15	149.80
Evan Harney, San Diego	Fr.	285	1475	17	147.50
Jamaal Branch, Colgate	Jr.	450	2326	29	145.38
Charles Anthony, Tenn. St.	Jr.	322	1708	13	142.33
Mike Hilliard, Duquesne	Sr.	306	1544	15	140.36
Gary Jones, Albany	Sr.	211	1524	18	138.55
Nick Chournos, Weber St.	Jr.	297	1649	13	137.42
Emmett Hunter, Jacksonville	Sr.	304	1467	11	133.36
Jermaine Austin, Ga. Southern	So.	224	1461	6	132.82
Clifton Dawson, Harvard	Fr.	215	1187	12	131.89
Sam Matthews, Pennsylvania	So.	276	1266	10	126.60

Games: All played 11, except Hartigan, Harney, Matthews (10), Branch (16), Anthony, Chournos (12) and Dawson (9).

Receptions

	Cl	No	Yds	TD	P/Gm
Javarus Dudley, Fordham	Sr.	101	1439	14	8.42
Efrem Hill, Samford	Jr.	92	1387	15	8.36
Lorenza Hill, Brown	So.	76	869	5	7.60
Alonzo Nix, Chattanooga	Jr.	90	1060	7	7.50
Ari Confesor, Holy Cross	Sr.	90	1213	9	7.50
Adam Hannula, San Diego	So.	72	1161	13	7.20
Nate Lawrie, Yale	Sr.	72	810	3	7.20
Dan Castles, Pennsylvania	Jr.	71	1067	13	7.10
Jay Barnard, Dartmouth	Sr.	70	861	5	7.00
Tramon Douglas, Grambling	Sr.	77	917	10	7.00
Sean Simmons, Wagner	Sr.	74	894	7	6.73

Games: All played 10, except Dudley, Nix, Confesor (12), Hill, Douglas and Simmons (11).

Interceptions

	Cl	No	Yds	TD	Int/Gm
Brandon Martin, Butler	Sr.	8	76	0	0.73
James Niklos, Robert Morris	Fr.	6	53	2	0.67
Levy Brown, Florida A&M	Jr.	7	90	0	0.64
Corey Lynch, Appalachian St.	Fr.	6	61	0	0.60
Steve Costello, Massachusetts	Jr.	6	24	0	0.60
Joe Glenn, Bucknell	Jr.	7	126	1	0.58
Tyrone Parsons, Alcorn St.	Sr.	7	157	1	0.58
Emery Beckles, Idaho St.	Sr.	5	31	0	0.56
Nick Collins, Bethune-Cookman	Jr.	6	84	1	0.55
O'Keefe Henderson, Miss.Vly	So.	6	61	1	0.55
Terrell Hammonds, Ark-PB	Jr.	6	74	0	0.55
Tyrone Walker, Ark-PB	JR.	6	169	2	0.55

Games: All played 11, except Niklos, Beckles (9), Lynch, Costello (10), Glenn and Parsons (12).

NCAA Division I-AA Leaders (Cont.)

Scoring
(ranked by points per game)
Non-Kickers

	Cl	TD	XPt	Pts	P/Gm
Evan Harney, San Diego	.Fr.	20	0	122	12.20
Rob Giancola, Valparaiso	.Jr.	23	0	140	11.67
Jamaal Branch, Colgate	.Jr.	29	0	174	10.88
Kirwin Watson, Fordham	.Sr.	21	0	126	10.50
Gary Jones, Albany	.Sr.	19	0	114	10.36
Alonzo Coleman, Hampton	.Fr.	18	0	108	9.82
Travis Glasford, W. Illinois	.So.	21	0	126	9.69
Nick Hartigan, Brown	.So.	16	0	96	9.60
Joe McCourt, Lafayette	.Jr.	17	0	104	9.45

Games: All played 11, except Harney, Hartigan (10), Giancola, Watson (12), Branch (16) and Glasford (13).

Kickers

	FG/Att	PAT/Att	Pts	P/Gm
Chris Snyder, Montana	.25/30	47/48	124	9.54
Matt Lange, W. Kentucky	.23/28	48/50	117	9.00
John Troost, Yale	.15/19	39/44	84	8.40
Paul Ernster, N. Arizona	.18/30	47/49	101	7.77
John Marino, McNeese St.	16/21	45/48	93	7.75
Justin Langan, Western Ill.	.15/22	53/55	100	7.69
Jeremy Hershey, Idaho St.	.18/26	38/40	92	7.67
Peter Veldman, Penn	.13/17	37/39	76	7.60

Games: All played 13, except Troost, Veldman (10), Marino and Hershey (12).

Field Goals

	Cl	FG/Att	Pct	P/Gm
Chris Snyder, Montana	.Sr.	25/30	.833	1.92
Matt Lange, W. Kentucky	.Sr.	23/28	.821	1.77
Jeremy Hershey, Idaho St.	.Sr.	18/26	.692	1.50
John Troost, Yale	.Jr.	15/19	.789	1.50
Danny Marshall, Furman	.Sr.	16/20	.800	1.45
Matt Sharpe, VMI	.Jr.	17/24	.708	1.42
Paul Ernster, N. Arizona	.Sr.	18/30	.600	1.38
John Marino, McNeese St.	.Jr.	16/21	.762	1.33

Games: All played 12, except Snyder, Lange, Ernster (13), Troost (10) and Marshall (11).

Punt/Kickoff Leaders

Punting

	Cl	No	Yds	Avg
Graham Whitlock, Gardner-Webb	Jr.	57	2593	45.49
Mark Gould, N. Arizona	.Sr.	58	2610	45.00
Nate McKinney, Appalachian St.	.Sr.	74	3294	44.51

Punt Returns

	Cl	No	Yds	TD	Avg
James Norris, W. Illinois	.Jr.	15	287	1	19.13
Emery Beckles, Idaho St.	.Sr.	23	377	1	16.39
Donnie Rose, C. Conn. St.	.Jr.	17	267	1	15.71

Kickoff Returns

	Cl	No	Yds	TD	Avg
Corey Smith, Montana St.	.Jr.	20	664	2	33.20
Chris Crawford, Nicholls St.	.So.	20	646	2	32.30
Lewis Barr, Ga. Southern	.So.	20	598	0	29.90

TEAM

Scoring Offense

	Gm	Record	Pts	Avg
Southern	.13	12-1	520	40.00
San Diego	.10	8-2	399	39.90
Grambling	.12	9-3	439	36.58
Southern Ill.	.12	10-2	437	36.42
Dayton	.11	9-2	400	36.36
Western Illinois	.13	9-4	472	36.31
Yale	.10	6-4	354	35.40
Nicholls St.	.11	5-6	389	35.36
Delaware	.16	15-1	555	34.69
Pennsylvania	.10	10-0	346	34.60
Northeastern	.12	8-4	414	34.50
New Hampshire	.12	5-7	406	33.83
Valparaiso	.12	8-4	406	33.83
McNeese St.	.12	10-2	405	33.75
Alabama St.	.13	8-5	434	33.38
Alabama A&M	.12	8-4	398	33.17

Scoring Defense

	Gm	Record	Pts	Avg
Monmouth	.12	10-2	102	8.5
Furman	.11	6-5	155	14.1
Wofford	.14	12-2	207	14.8
Southern	.13	12-1	195	15.0
Delaware	.16	15-1	247	15.4
Alabama A&M	.12	8-4	194	16.2
Villanova	.11	7-4	178	16.2
Pennsylvania	.10	10-0	164	16.4
Montana St.	.13	7-6	215	16.5
Dayton	.11	9-2	183	16.6
Albany	.11	7-4	185	16.8
Lehigh	.11	8-3	185	16.8
Morehead St.	.11	8-3	185	16.8
Western Kentucky	.13	9-4	219	16.8
North Carolina A&T	.13	10-3	236	18.2
Northeastern	.12	8-4	219	18.3

Total Offense

	Record	Plays	Yds	Avg
San Diego	.8-2	741	4833	483.30
Yale	.6-4	795	4797	479.70
Grambling	.9-3	883	5585	465.42
Harvard	.7-3	769	4618	461.80
Duquesne	.8-3	789	5010	455.45
Valparaiso	.8-4	838	5370	447.50
Texas St.	.4-8	946	5321	443.42
Drake	.6-6	873	5281	440.08
Pennsylvania	.10-0	766	4382	438.20
Dayton	.9-2	789	4763	433.00
Northeastern	.8-4	802	5182	431.83
McNeese St.	.10-2	876	5098	424.83
Northern Arizona	.9-4	1007	5503	423.31
Southern	.12-1	855	5483	421.77
Illinois St.	.6-6	914	5040	420.00
Western Illinois	.9-4	929	5416	416.62

Total Defense

	Record	Plays	Yds	Avg
Monmouth	.10-2	783	2931	244.25
Alabama A&M	.8-4	790	3072	256.00
North Carolina A&T	.10-3	801	3486	268.15
Furman	.6-5	716	2998	272.55
Albany	.7-4	727	3070	279.09
Western Kentucky	.9-4	851	3688	283.69
Hampton	.7-4	763	3151	286.45
Bethune-Cookman	.9-3	792	3440	286.67
Northwestern St.	.6-6	773	3448	287.33
Dayton	.9-2	697	3161	287.36
Robert Morris	.6-4	617	2901	290.10
Montana St.	.7-6	878	3852	296.31
Southern	.12-1	837	3909	300.69
Villanova	.7-4	731	3322	302.00
Colgate	.15-1	1074	4835	302.19
Delaware	.15-1	1065	4848	303.00

NCAA Playoffs

Division I-AA

First Round (Nov. 29)

Northern Arizona 35 . . . . .at McNeese St. 3
Florida Atlantic 32 . . . . .at Bethune-Cookman 24
at Colgate 19 . . . . .Massachusetts 7
Western Illinois 43 . . . . . . .2OT . . . . . . .at Montana 40
at Wofford 31 . . . . .N.C. A&T 10
at Western Kentucky 45 . . . . .Jacksonville St. 7
at Delaware 48 . . . . .Southern Ill. 7
at Northern Iowa 35 . . . . .Montana St. 14

Quarterfinals (Dec. 6)

Florida Atlantic 48 . . . . .at McNeese St. 25
at Colgate 38 . . . . .Western Illinois 27
at Wofford 34 . . . . .Western Kentucky 17
at Delaware 37 . . . . .at Northern Iowa 7

Semifinals (Dec. 13)

Colgate 36 . . . . .at Florida Atlantic 24
at Delaware 24 . . . . .Wofford 9

Championship Game

Dec. 19 at Chattanooga, Tenn. (Att: 14,281)

Delaware 40 . . . . .Colgate 0
(15-1)   (15-1)

Division II

First Round (Nov. 22)

at North Dakota 24 . . . . .Pittsburgh St. 14
at Winona St. 10 . . . . .Emporia St. 3
at North Alabama 48 . . . . .Southern Arkansas 24
Carson-Newman 35 . . . . .at Valdosta St. 29
at Saginaw Valley St. 33 . . . . .Edinboro (Pa.) 9
Grand Valley St. 65 . . . . .at Bentley College 36
Central Oklahoma 20 . . . . .at Mesa St. 15
at Texas A&M-Kingsville 34 . . . . .Tarleton St. 10

Quarterfinals (Nov. 29)

at North Dakota 36 . . . . .Winona St. 29
Grand Valley St. 10 . . . . .at Saginaw Valley St. 3
at North Alabama 41 . . . . .Carson-Newman 9
at Texas A&M-Kingsville 49 . . . . . . .Central Oklahoma 6

Semifinals (Dec. 6)

at North Dakota 29 . . . . .North Alabama 22
Grand Valley St. 31 . . . . .at Texas A&M-Kingsville 3

Championship Game

Dec. 13 at Florence, Ala. (Att: 7,236)

Grand Valley St. 10 . . . . .North Dakota 3
(14-1)   (12-2)

Division I-AA, II and III Awards

AFCA Coaches of the Year

NCAA Div. I-AA . . . . .Dick Biddle, Colgate
College Div. II/NAIA . . . .Brian Kelly, Grand Valley St.
            & Mike Van Diest, Carroll (Mont.)
NCAA Div. III . . . . .John Gagliardi, St. John's (Minn.)

Players of the Year

NCAA I-AA . . . . .Jamaal Branch, Colgate, RB
NCAA II . . . . .Will Hall, N. Alabama, QB
NCAA III . . . . .Blake Elliot, St. John's, WR
NAIA . . . . .Tyler Emmert, Carroll (Mont.), QB

Division III

First Round (Nov. 22)

at Wisconsin-La Crosse . . . . .Concordia (Wisc.) 13
at Baldwin-Wallace 54 . . . . .Hanover 32
at Wheaton (Ill.) 55 .Hope 45
at East Texas Baptist 42 . . . . .OT . . . . . .Trinity (Tex.) 41
at Bridgewater (Va.) 28 . . . . .Waynesburg 24
at Christopher Newport 24 . . . . .Muhlenberg 20
at Rensselaer 34 . . . . .Curry 20
Ithaca 14 . . . . .at Brockport St. 13
at Montclair St. 20 . . . . .Allegheny 19
at St. Nortbert 27 . . . . .2 OT . . . . . . .Simpson 20
at Wartburg 21 . . . . .Bethel (Minn.) 7
at Linfield 31 .Redlands 23

Second Round (Nov. 29)

Bridgewater 26 . . . . .at Christopher Newport 3
Ithaca 33 . . . . .at Montclair St. 13
at Mount Union 39 . . . . .Wisconsin-La Crosse 14
at Lycoming 13 . . . . .OT . . .East Texas Baptist 7
at Wheaton 16 . . . . .Baldwin-Wallace 12
Rensselaer 40 . . . . .at Springfield 34
at St. John's (Minn.) 38 . . . . .St. Norbert 13
at Linfield 25 .Wartburg 20

Quarterfinals (Dec. 6-7)

Bridgewater 13 . . . . .at Lycoming 9
at Mount Union 56 . . . . .Wheaton 10
at Rensselaer 21 .Ithaca 16
at St. John's 31 .Linfield 25

Semifinals (Dec. 13)

at Mount Union 66 . . . . .Bridgewater 0
at St. John's 38 . . . . .Rensselaer 10

Amos Alonzo Stagg Bowl

Dec. 20 at Salem, Va. (Att: 5,073)

St. John's 24 . . . . .Mount Union 6
(14-0)   (13-1)

NAIA Playoffs

Division I

First Round (Nov. 22)

St. Francis (Ind.) 34 . . . . .Georgetown (Ky.) 23
St. Ambrose (Iowa) 32 . .Mid America Nazarene (Kan.) 31
Mary (N.D.) 20 . . . . .Azusa Pacific 2
Sioux Falls (S.D.) 24 . . . . .Benedictine (Kan.) 21
Northwestern (Iowa) 36 . . . . .Ottawa (Kan.) 33
NW Oklahoma St. 63 . . . . .Tabor (Kan.) 21
Dickinson St. (N.D.) 12 . . . . .Lambuth (Tenn.) 6
Carroll (Mont.) 40 . . . . .McKendree (Ill.) 7

Quarterfinals (Nov. 29)

St. Francis 41 . . . . .St. Ambrose 14
Carroll 49 . . . . .Mary 7
NW Oklahoma St. 24 . . . . .Dickinson St. 17
Sioux Falls 33 . . . . .Northwestern 7

Semifinals (Dec. 6)

Carroll 38 .St. Francis 14
NW Oklahoma St. 16 . . . . .Sioux Falls 13

Championship

Dec. 20 at Savannah, Tenn. (Att: 5,189)

Carroll 41 . . . . .NW Oklahoma St. 28
(15-0)   (11-2)

1869-2004
Through the Years

ESERI SPORTS ALMANAC

National Champions

Over the last 132 years, there have been 25 major selectors of national champions by way of polls (11), mathematical rating systems (10) and historical research (4). The best-known and most widely circulated of these surveys, the Associated Press poll of sportswriters and broadcasters, first appeared during the 1936 season. Champions prior to 1936 have been determined by retro polls, ratings and historical research.

The Early Years (1869-1935)

National champions based on the Dickinson mathematical system (DS) and three historical retro polls taken by the College Football Researchers Association (CFRA), the National Championship Foundation (NCF) and the Helms Athletic Foundation (HF). The CFRA and NCF polls start in 1869, college football's inaugural year, while the Helms poll begins in 1883, the first season the game adopted a point system for scoring. Frank Dickinson, an economics professor at Illinois, introduced his system in 1926 and retro-picked winners in 1924 and '25. Bowl game results were counted in the Helms selections, but not in the other three.

Multiple champions: Yale (18); Princeton (17); Harvard (9); Michigan (7); Notre Dame and Penn (4); Alabama, California, Cornell, Illinois, Pittsburgh and USC (3); Georgia Tech, Minnesota and Penn St. (2).

Year		Record	Year		Record	Year		Record
1869	**Princeton**	1-1-0	1880	**Yale** (CFRA)	4-0-1	1891	**Yale**	13-0-0
1870	**Princeton**	1-0-0		& **Princeton** (NCF)	4-0-1	1892	**Yale**	13-0-0
1871	No games played		1881	**Yale**	5-0-1	1893	**Princeton**	11-0-0
1872	**Princeton**	1-0-0	1882	**Yale**	8-0-0	1894	**Yale**	16-0-0
1873	**Princeton**	1-0-0	1883	**Yale**	8-0-0	1895	**Penn**	14-0-0
1874	**Yale**	3-0-0	1884	**Yale**	8-0-1	1896	**Princeton** (CFRA)	10-0-1
1875	**Princeton** (CFRA)	2-0-0	1885	**Princeton**	9-0-0		& **Lafayette** (NCF)	11-0-1
	& **Harvard** (NCF)	4-0-0	1886	**Yale**	9-0-1	1897	**Penn**	15-0-0
1876	**Yale**	3-0-0	1887	**Yale**	9-0-0	1898	**Harvard**	11-0-0
1877	**Yale**	3-0-1	1888	**Yale**	13-0-0	1899	**Princeton** (CFRA)	12-1-0
1878	**Princeton**	6-0-0	1889	**Princeton**	10-0-0		& **Harvard** (NCF, HF)	10-0-1
1879	**Princeton**	4-0-1	1890	**Harvard**	11-0-0			

Year		Record	Bowl Game	Head Coach	Outstanding Player
1900	**Yale**	12-0-0	No bowl	Malcolm McBride	Perry Hale, HB
1901	**Harvard** (CFRA)	12-0-0	No bowl	Bill Reid	Bob Kernan, HB
	& **Michigan** (NCF, HF)	11-0-0	Won Rose	Hurry Up Yost	Neil Snow, E
1902	**Michigan**	11-0-0	No bowl	Hurry Up Yost	Boss Weeks, QB
1903	**Princeton**	11-0-0	No bowl	Art Hillebrand	John DeWitt, G
1904	**Penn** (CFRA, HF)	12-0-0	No bowl	Carl Williams	Andy Smith, FB
	& **Michigan** (NCF)	10-0-0	No bowl	Hurry Up Yost	Willie Heston, HB
1905	**Chicago**	10-0-0	No bowl	Amos Alonzo Stagg	Walter Eckersall, QB
1906	**Princeton**	9-0-1	No bowl	Bill Roper	Cap Wister, E
1907	**Yale**	9-0-1	No bowl	Bill Knox	Tad Jones, HB
1908	**Penn** (CFRA, HF)	11-0-1	No bowl	Sol Metzger	Hunter Scarlett, E
	& **LSU** (NCF)	10-0-0	No bowl	Edgar Wingard	Doc Fenton, QB
1909	**Yale**	12-1-0	No bowl	Howard Jones	Ted Coy, FB
1910	**Harvard** (CFRA, HF)	8-0-1	No bowl	Percy Haughton	Percy Wendell, HB
	& **Pittsburgh** (NCF)	9-0-0	No bowl	Joe Thompson	Ralph Galvin, C
1911	**Princeton** (CFRA, HF)	8-0-2	No bowl	Bill Roper	Sam White, E
	& **Penn St.** (NCF)	8-0-1	No bowl	Bill Hollenback	Dexter Very, E
1912	**Harvard** (CFRA, HF)	9-0-0	No bowl	Percy Haughton	Charley Brickley, HB
	& **Penn St.** (NCF)	8-0-0	No bowl	Bill Hollenback	Dexter Very, E
1913	**Harvard**	9-0-0	No bowl	Percy Haughton	Eddie Mahan, FB
1914	**Army**	9-0-0	No bowl	Charley Daly	John McEwan, C
1915	**Cornell**	9-0-0	No bowl	Al Sharpe	Charley Barrett, QB
1916	**Pittsburgh**	8-0-0	No bowl	Pop Warner	Bob Peck, C
1917	**Georgia Tech**	9-0-0	No bowl	John Heisman	Ev Strupper, HB
1918	**Pittsburgh** (CFRA, HF)	4-1-0	No bowl	Pop Warner	Tom Davies, HB
	& **Michigan** (NCF)	5-0-0	No bowl	Hurry Up Yost	Frank Steketee, FB
1919	**Harvard** (CFRA-tie, HF)	9-0-1	Won Rose	Bob Fisher	Eddie Casey, HB
	Illinois (CFRA-tie)	6-1-0	No bowl	Bob Zuppke	Chuck Carney, E
	& **Notre Dame** (NCF)	9-0-0	No bowl	Knute Rockne	George Gipp, HB
1920	**California**	9-0-0	Won Rose	Andy Smith	Dan McMillan, T
1921	**California**	9-0-1	Tied Rose	Andy Smith	Brick Muller, E
	& **Cornell** (NCF, HF)	8-0-0	No bowl	Gil Dobie	Eddie Kaw, HB
1922	**Princeton** (CFRA)	8-0-0	No bowl	Bill Roper	Herb Treat, T
	California (NCF)	9-0-0	No bowl	Andy Smith	Brick Muller, E
	& **Cornell** (HF)	8-0-0	No bowl	Gil Dobie	Eddie Kaw, HB

Year		Record	Bowl Game	Head Coach	Outstanding Player
1923	**Illinois** (CFRA, HF)	.8-0-0	No bowl	Bob Zuppke	Red Grange, HB
	& Michigan (NCF)	.8-0-0	No bowl	Hurry Up Yost	Jack Blott, C
1924	**Notre Dame**	.10-0-0	Won Rose	Knute Rockne	"The Four Horsemen"*
1925	**Alabama** (CFRA, HF)	.10-0-0	Won Rose	Wallace Wade	Johnny Mack Brown, HB
	& Dartmouth (DS)	.8-0-0	No bowl	Jesse Hawley	Swede Oberlander, HB
1926	**Alabama** (CFRA, HF)	.9-0-1	Tied Rose	Wallace Wade	Hoyt Winslett, E
	& Stanford (DS)	.10-0-1	Tied Rose	Pop Warner	Ted Shipkey, E
1927	**Yale** (CFRA)	.7-1-0	No bowl	Tad Jones	Bill Webster, G
	& Illinois (NCF, HF, DS)	.7-0-1	No bowl	Bob Zuppke	Bob Reitsch, C
1928	**Georgia Tech** (CFRA, NCF, HF)	.10-0-0	Won Rose	Bill Alexander	Pete Pund, C
	& USC (DS)	.9-0-1	No bowl	Howard Jones	Jesse Hibbs, T
1929	**Notre Dame**	.9-0-0	No bowl	Knute Rockne	Frank Carideo, QB
1930	**Alabama** (CFRA)	.10-0-0	Won Rose	Wallace Wade	Fred Sington, T
	& Notre Dame (NCF, HF, DS)	.10-0-0	No bowl	Knute Rockne	Marchy Schwartz, HB
1931	**USC**	.10-1-0	Won Rose	Howard Jones	John Baker, G
1932	**USC** (CFRA, NCF, HF)	.10-0-0	Won Rose	Howard Jones	Ernie Smith, T
	& Michigan (DS)	.8-0-0	No bowl	Harry Kipke	Harry Newman, QB
1933	**Michigan**	.8-0-0	No bowl	Harry Kipke	Chuck Bernard, C
1934	**Minnesota**	.8-0-0	No bowl	Bernie Bierman	Pug Lund, HB
1935	**Minnesota** (CFRA, NCF, HF)	.8-0-0	No bowl	Bernie Bierman	Dick Smith, T
	& SMU (DS)	.12-1-0	Lost Rose	Matty Bell	Bobby Wilson, HB

*Notre Dame's Four Horsemen were Harry Stuhldreher (QB), Jim Crowley (HB), Don Miller (HB-P) and Elmer Layden (FB).

The Media Poll Years (since 1936)

National champions according to seven media and coaches' polls: Associated Press (since 1936), United Press (1950-57), International News Service (1952-57), United Press International (1958-92), Football Writers Association of America (since 1954), National Football Foundation and Hall of Fame (since 1959) and USA Today/CNN (since 1991). In 1991, the American Football Coaches Association switched outlets for its poll from UPI to USA Today/CNN and then to USA Today/ESPN in 1997.

After 29 years of releasing its final Top 20 poll in early December, AP named its 1965 national champion following that season's bowl games. AP returned to a pre-bowls final vote in 1966 and '67, but has polled its writers and broadcasters after the bowl games since the 1968 season. The FWAA has selected its champion after the bowl games since the 1955 season, the NFF-Hall of Fame since 1971, UPI after 1974, USA Today/CNN 1991-96, and USA Today/ESPN since 1997.

The Associated Press changed the name of its national championship award from the AP trophy to the Bear Bryant Trophy after the legendary Alabama coach's death in 1983. The FootballWriters' trophy is called the Grantland Rice Award (after the celebrated sportswriter) and the NFF-Hall of Fame trophy is called the MacArthur Bowl (in honor of Gen. Douglas MacArthur).

Multiple champions: Notre Dame (9); Alabama, Ohio St. and Oklahoma (7); USC (6); Miami-FL and Nebraska (5); Minnesota (4); Michigan St. and Texas (3); Army, Florida St., Georgia Tech, LSU, Michigan, Penn St., Pittsburgh and Tennessee (2).

Year		Record	Bowl Game	Head Coach	Outstanding Player
1936	**Minnesota**	.7-1-0	No bowl	Bernie Bierman	Ed Widseth, T
1937	**Pittsburgh**	.9-0-1	No bowl	Jock Sutherland	Marshall Goldberg, HB
1938	**TCU**	.11-0-0	Won Sugar	Dutch Meyer	Davey O'Brien, QB
1939	**Texas A&M**	.11-0-0	Won Sugar	Homer Norton	John Kimbrough, FB
1940	**Minnesota**	.8-0-0	No bowl	Bernie Bierman	George Franck, HB
1941	**Minnesota**	.8-0-0	No bowl	Bernie Bierman	Bruce Smith, HB
1942	**Ohio St.**	.9-1-0	No bowl	Paul Brown	Gene Fekete, FB
1943	**Notre Dame**	.9-1-0	No bowl	Frank Leahy	Angelo Bertelli, QB
1944	**Army**	.9-0-0	No bowl	Red Blaik	Glenn Davis, HB
1945	**Army**	.9-0-0	No bowl	Red Blaik	Doc Blanchard, FB
1946	**Notre Dame**	.8-0-1	No bowl	Frank Leahy	Johnny Lujack, QB
1947	**Notre Dame**	.9-0-0	No bowl	Frank Leahy	Johnny Lujack, QB
1948	**Michigan**	.9-0-0	No bowl	Bennie Oosterbaan	Dick Rifenburg, E
1949	**Notre Dame**	.10-0-0	No bowl	Frank Leahy	Leon Hart, E
1950	**Oklahoma**	.10-1-0	Lost Sugar	Bud Wilkinson	Leon Heath, FB
1951	**Tennessee**	.10-1-0	Lost Sugar	Bob Neyland	Hank Lauricella, TB
1952	**Michigan St.** (AP, UP)	.9-0-0	No bowl	Biggie Munn	Don McAuliffe, HB
	& Georgia Tech (INS)	.12-0-0	Won Sugar	Bobby Dodd	Hal Miller, T
1953	**Maryland**	.10-1-0	Lost Orange	Jim Tatum	Bernie Faloney, QB
1954	**Ohio St.** (AP, INS)	.10-0-0	Won Rose	Woody Hayes	Howard Cassady, HB
	& UCLA (UP, FW)	.9-0-0	No bowl	Red Sanders	Jack Ellena, T
1955	**Oklahoma**	.11-0-0	Won Orange	Bud Wilkinson	Jerry Tubbs, C
1956	**Oklahoma**	.10-0-0	No bowl	Bud Wilkinson	Tommy McDonald, HB
1957	**Auburn** (AP)	.10-0-0	No bowl	Shug Jordan	Jimmy Phillips, E
	& Ohio St. (UP, FW, INS)	.9-1-0	Won Rose	Woody Hayes	Bob White, FB
1958	**LSU** (AP, UPI)	.11-0-0	Won Sugar	Paul Dietzel	Billy Cannon, HB
	& Iowa (FW)	.8-1-1	Won Rose	Forest Evashevski	Randy Duncan, QB
1959	**Syracuse**	.11-0-0	Won Cotton	Ben Schwartzwalder	Ernie Davis, HB
1960	**Minnesota** (AP, UPI, NFF)	.8-2-0	Lost Rose	Murray Warmath	Tom Brown, G
	& Mississippi (FW)	.10-0-1	Won Sugar	Johnny Vaught	Jake Gibbs, QB
1961	**Alabama** (AP, UPI, NFF)	.11-0-0	Won Sugar	Bear Bryant	Billy Neighbors, T
	& Ohio St. (FW)	.8-0-1	No bowl	Woody Hayes	Bob Ferguson, HB
1962	**USC**	.11-0-0	Won Rose	John McKay	Hal Bedsole, E
1963	**Texas**	.11-0-0	Won Cotton	Darrell Royal	Scott Appleton, T

National Champions (Cont.)

Year		Record	Bowl Game	Head Coach	Outstanding Player
1964	**Alabama** (AP, UPI), ...10-1-0		Lost Orange	Bear Bryant	Joe Namath, QB
	Arkansas (FW) 11-0-0		Won Cotton	Frank Broyles	Ronnie Caveness, LB
	& **Notre Dame** (NFF) 9-1-0		No bowl	Ara Parseghian	John Huarte, QB
1965	**Alabama** (AP, FW-tie) 9-1-1		Won Orange	Bear Bryant	Paul Crane, C
	& **Michigan St.** (UPI, NFF, FW-tie) .10-1-0		Lost Rose	Duffy Daugherty	George Webster, LB
1966	**Notre Dame** (AP, UPI, FW, NFF-tie) .9-0-1		No bowl	Ara Parseghian	Jim Lynch, LB
	& **Michigan St.** (NFF-tie) 9-0-1		No bowl	Duffy Daugherty	Bubba Smith, DE
1967	**USC** 10-1-0		Won Rose	John McKay	O.J. Simpson, HB
1968	**Ohio St.** 10-0-0		Won Rose	Woody Hayes	Rex Kern, QB
1969	**Texas** 11-0-0		Won Cotton	Darrell Royal	James Street, QB
1970	**Nebraska** (AP, FW) 11-0-1		Won Orange	Bob Devaney	Jerry Tagge, QB
	Texas (UPI, NFF-tie), ...10-1-0		Lost Cotton	Darrell Royal	Steve Worster, RB
	& **Ohio St.** (NFF-tie) 9-1-0		Lost Rose	Woody Hayes	Jim Stillwagon, MG
1971	**Nebraska** 13-0-0		Won Orange	Bob Devaney	Johnny Rodgers, WR
1972	**USC** 12-0-0		Won Rose	John McKay	Charles Young, TE
1973	**Notre Dame** (AP, FW, NFF) 11-0-0		Won Sugar	Ara Parseghian	Mike Townsend, DB
	& **Alabama** (UPI) 11-1-0		Lost Sugar	Bear Bryant	Buddy Brown, OT
1974	**Oklahoma** (AP) 11-0-0		No bowl	Barry Switzer	Joe Washington, RB
	& **USC** (UPI, FW, NFF) 10-1-1		Won Rose	John McKay	Anthony Davis, RB
1975	**Oklahoma** 11-1-0		Won Orange	Barry Switzer	Lee Roy Selmon, DT
1976	**Pittsburgh** 12-0-0		Won Sugar	Johnny Majors	Tony Dorsett, RB
1977	**Notre Dame** 11-1-0		Won Cotton	Dan Devine	Ross Browner, DE
1978	**Alabama** (AP, FW, NFF) 11-1-0		Won Sugar	Bear Bryant	Marty Lyons, DT
	& **USC** (UPI) 12-1-0		Won Rose	John Robinson	Charles White, RB
1979	**Alabama** 12-0-0		Won Sugar	Bear Bryant	Jim Bunch, OT
1980	**Georgia** 12-0-0		Won Sugar	Vince Dooley	Herschel Walker, RB
1981	**Clemson** 12-0-0		Won Orange	Danny Ford	Jeff Davis, LB
1982	**Penn St.** 11-1-0		Won Sugar	Joe Paterno	Todd Blackledge, QB
1983	**Miami-FL** 11-1-0		Won Orange	H. Schnellenberger	Bernie Kosar, QB
1984	**BYU** 13-0-0		Won Holiday	LaVell Edwards	Robbie Bosco, QB
1985	**Oklahoma** 11-1-0		Won Orange	Barry Switzer	Brian Bosworth, LB
1986	**Penn St.** 12-0-0		Won Fiesta	Joe Paterno	D.J. Dozier, RB
1987	**Miami-FL** 12-0-0		Won Orange	Jimmy Johnson	Steve Walsh, QB
1988	**Notre Dame** 12-0-0		Won Fiesta	Lou Holtz	Tony Rice, QB
1989	**Miami-FL** 11-1-0		Won Sugar	Dennis Erickson	Craig Erickson, QB
1990	**Colorado** (AP, FW, NFF) 11-1-1		Won Orange	Bill McCartney	Eric Bieniemy, RB
	& **Georgia Tech** (UP) 11-0-1		Won Citrus	Bobby Ross	Shawn Jones, QB
1991	**Miami-FL** (AP) 12-0-0		Won Orange	Dennis Erickson	Gino Torretta, QB
	& **Washington** (USA, FW, NFF) . .12-0-0		Won Rose	Don James	Steve Emtman, DT
1992	**Alabama** 13-0-0		Won Sugar	Gene Stallings	Eric Curry, DE
1993	**Florida St.** 12-1-0		Won Orange	Bobby Bowden	Charlie Ward, QB
1994	**Nebraska** 13-0-0		Won Orange	Tom Osborne	Zach Wiegert, OT
1995	**Nebraska** 12-0-0		Won Fiesta	Tom Osborne	Tommie Frazier, QB
1996	**Florida** 12-1*		Won Sugar	Steve Spurrier	Danny Wuerffel, QB
1997	**Michigan** (AP, FW, NFF) 12-0		Won Rose	Lloyd Carr	Charles Woodson, DB
	& **Nebraska** (ESPN/USA) 13-0		Won Orange	Tom Osborne	Ahman Green, RB
1998	**Tennessee** 13-0		Won Fiesta	Phillip Fulmer	Peerless Price, WR
1999	**Florida St.** 12-0		Won Sugar	Bobby Bowden	Peter Warrick, WR
2000	**Oklahoma** 13-0		Won Orange	Bob Stoops	Josh Heupel, QB
2001	**Miami-FL** 12-0		Won Rose	Larry Coker	Ken Dorsey, QB
2002	**Ohio St.** 14-0		Won Fiesta	Jim Tressel	Craig Krenzler, QB
2003	**USC** (AP) 12-1		Won Rose	Pete Carroll	Matt Leinart, QB
	& **LSU** (ESPN/USA) 13-1		Won Sugar	Nick Saban	Matt Mauck, QB

*The NCAA instituted overtime for regular season games in 1996.

Number 1 vs. Number 2

Since the Associated Press writers poll started keeping track of such things in 1936, the No. 1 and No. 2 ranked teams in the country have met 33 times; 20 during the regular season and 13 in bowl games. Since the first showdown in 1943, the No. 1 team has beaten the No. 2 team 20 times, lost 10 and there have been two ties. Each showdown is listed below with the date, the match-up, each team's record going into the game, the final score, the stadium and site.

Date		Match-up	Stadium	Date		Match-up	Stadium
Oct. 9	#1	Notre Dame (2-0) . . .35	Michigan	Nov. 10	#1	Army (6-0) 48	Yankee
1943	#2	Michigan (3-0) 12	(Ann Arbor)	1945	#2	Notre Dame (5-0-1) . . .0	(New York)
Nov. 20	#1	Notre Dame (8-0) . . .14	Notre Dame	Dec. 1	#1	Army (8-0) 32	Municipal
1943	#2	Iowa Pre-Flight (8-0) .13	(South Bend)	1945	#2	Navy (7-0-1) 13	(Philadelphia)
Dec. 2	#1	Army (8-0) 23	Municipal	Nov. 9	#1	Army (7-0) 0	Yankee
1944	#2	Navy (6-2) 7	(Baltimore)	1946	#2	Notre Dame (5-0) 0	(New York)

Date		Match-up	Stadium	Date		Match-up	Stadium
Jan. 1	#1	USC (10-0) 42	ROSE BOWL	Jan. 2	#2	Penn St. (11-0) 14	FIESTA BOWL
1963	#2	Wisconsin (8-1) 37	(Pasadena)	1987	#1	Miami-FL (11-0) 10	(Tempe)
Oct. 12	#2	Texas (3-0) 28	Cotton Bowl	Nov. 21	#2	Oklahoma (10-0) 17	Memorial
1963	#1	Oklahoma (2-0) 7	(Dallas)	1987	#1	Nebraska (10-0) 7	(Lincoln)
Jan. 1	#1	Texas (10-0) 28	COTTON BOWL	Jan. 1	#2	Miami-FL (11-0) 20	ORANGE BOWL
1964	#2	Navy (9-1) 6	(Dallas)	1988	#1	Oklahoma (11-0) 14	(Miami)
Nov. 19	#1	Notre Dame (8-0) . . .10	Spartan	Nov. 26	#1	Notre Dame (10-0) . . .27	Coliseum
1966	#2	Michigan St. (9-0) . . .10	(East Lansing)	1988	#2	USC (10-0) 10	(Los Angeles)
Sept. 28	#1	Purdue (1-0) 37	Notre Dame	Sept. 16	#1	Notre Dame (1-0) 24	Michigan
1968	#2	Notre Dame (1-0) . . .22	(South Bend)	1989	#2	Michigan (0-0) 19	(Ann Arbor)
Jan. 1	#1	Ohio St. (9-0) 27	ROSE BOWL	Nov. 16	#2	Miami-FL (8-0) 17	Doak Campbell
1969	#2	USC (9-0-1) 16	(Pasadena)	1991	#1	Florida St. (10-0) 16	(Tallahassee)
Dec. 6	#1	Texas (9-0) 15	Razorback	Jan. 1	#2	Alabama (12-0) 34	SUGAR BOWL
1969	#2	Arkansas (9-0) 14	(Fayetteville)	1993	#1	Miami-FL (11-0) 13	(New Orleans)
Nov. 25	#1	Nebraska (10-0) 35	Owen·Field	Nov. 13	#2	Notre Dame (9-0) 31	Notre Dame
1971	#2	Oklahoma (9-0) 31	(Norman)	1993	#1	Florida St. (9-0) 24	(South Bend)
Jan. 1	#1	Nebraska (12-0) 38	ORANGE BOWL	Jan. 1	#1	Florida St. (11-1) 18	ORANGE BOWL
1972	#2	Alabama (11-0) 6	(Miami)	1994	#2	Nebraska (11-0) 16	(Miami)
Jan. 1	#2	Alabama (10-1) 14	SUGAR BOWL	Jan. 2	#2	Nebraska (11-0) 62	FIESTA BOWL
1979	#1	Penn St. (11-0) 7	(New Orleans)	1996	#2	Florida (12-0) 24	(Tempe)
Sept. 26	#1	USC (2-0) 28	Coliseum	Nov. 30	#2	Florida St. (10-0) 24	Doak Campbell
1981	#2	Oklahoma (1-0) 24	(Los Angeles)	1996	#1	Florida (10-1) 21	(Tallahassee)
Jan. 1	#2	Penn St. (10-1) 27	SUGAR BOWL	Jan. 4	#1	Tennessee (12-0) 23	FIESTA BOWL
1983	#1	Georgia (11-0) 23	(New Orleans)	1999	#2	Florida St. (11-1) 16	(Tempe)
Oct. 19	#1	Iowa (5-0) 12	Kinnick	Jan. 4	#1	Florida St. (11-0) 46	SUGAR BOWL
1985	#2	Michigan (5-0) 10	(Iowa City)	2000	#2	Virginia Tech (11-0) .29	(New Orleans)
Sept. 27	#2	Miami-FL (3-0) 28	Orange Bowl	Jan. 3	#2	Ohio St. (13-0) 31	FIESTA BOWL
1986	#1	Oklahoma (2-0) 16	(Miami)	2003	#1	Miami-FL (12-0) .2OT 24	(Tempe)

Note: Bowl games are listed in CAPITAL letters.

Top 50 Rivalries

Top Division I-A and I-AA series records, including games through the 2003 season. All rivalries listed below are renewed annually with the following exception. **Nebraska-Oklahoma** now play only when matched up as part of the rotating Big 12 schedule.

RECENTLY DISCONTINUED SERIES: **LSU vs Tulane** in 2002 after 94 games (LSU ahead 65-22-7)*; **Penn State vs Pitt** in 2001 after 96 games (Penn State ahead 50-42-4), **Baylor vs TCU** in 1995 after 102 games (Baylor ahead 48-47-7); **Florida vs Miami-FL** in 1991 after 49 games (Florida ahead, 25-24); **Miami-FL vs Notre Dame** in 1990 after 23 games (ND ahead, 15-7-1). Note that Miami beat Florida in the 2000 Sugar Bowl and Florida St. in the 2004 Orange Bowl.

	Gm	Series Leader		Gm	Series Leader
Air Force-Army	.38	Air Force (25-12-1)	**Michigan-Michigan St.**	.96	Michigan (63-28-5)
Air Force-Navy	.36	Air Force (25-11-0)	**Michigan-Notre Dame**	.31	Michigan (18-12-1)
Alabama-Auburn	.68	Alabama (38-29-1)	**Michigan-Ohio St.**	.100	Michigan (57-37-6)
Alabama-Tennessee	.86	Alabama (43-36-7)	**Minnesota-Wisconsin**	.112	Minnesota (57-37-6)
Arizona-Arizona.St.	.77	Arizona (43-33-1)	**Mississippi-Miss. St.**	.100	Ole Miss (57-37-6)
Army-Navy	.104	Army (49-48-7)	**Missouri-Kansas**	.112	Missouri (52-51-9)
Auburn-Georgia	.107	Auburn (51-48-8)	**Nebraska-Oklahoma**	.80	Oklahoma (40-37-3)
California-Stanford	.106	Stanford (54-41-11)	**N. Mexico-N. Mexico St.**	.93	New Mexico (60-28-5)
The Citadel-VMI	.63	The Citadel (31-30-2)	**N. Carolina-N.C. State**	.93	N. Carolina (60-27-6)
Clemson-S. Carolina	.101	Clemson (61-36-4)	**Notre Dame-Purdue**	.75	Notre Dame (49-24-2)
Colorado-Nebraska	.62	Nebraska (44-16-2)	**Notre Dame-USC**	.75	Notre Dame (42-28-5)
Colo. St.-Wyoming	.93	Colorado St. (49-39-5)	**Oklahoma-Okla. St.**	.98	Oklahoma (75-16-7)
Duke-N. Carolina	.89	N. Carolina (50-36-4)*	**Oregon-Oregon St.**	.107	Oregon (54-43-10)
Florida-Florida St.	.48	Florida (27-19-2)	**Penn-Cornell**	.110	Penn (64-41-5)
Florida-Georgia	.82	Georgia (46-34-2)	**Pittsburgh-West Va**	.96	Pitt (57-36-3)
Florida St.-Miami,FL	.48	Miami (28-20-0)	**Princeton-Yale**	.126	Yale (67-49-10)
Georgia-Georgia Tech	.98	Georgia (55-38-5)*	**Purdue-Indiana**	.106	Purdue (65-35-6)
Grambling-Southern	.52	Southern (28-24-0)	**Richmond-Wm. & Mary**	113	Wm. & Mary (58-50-5)
Harvard-Yale	.120	Yale (64-48-8)	**Tennessee-Vanderbilt**	.97	Tennessee (66-26-5)
Iowa-Iowa St.	.51	Iowa (34-17-0)	**Texas-Oklahoma**	.98	Texas (56-37-5)
Kansas-Kansas St.	.101	Kansas (61-35-5)	**Texas-Texas A&M**	.110	Texas (71-34-5)
Kentucky-Tennessee	.99	Tennessee (67-23-9)	**UCLA-USC**	.73	USC (38-28-7)
Lafayette-Lehigh	.139	Lafayette (72-62-5)	**Utah-BYU**	.79	Utah (47-28-4)*
LSU-Mississippi	.92	LSU (51-37-4)	**Utah-Utah St.**	.101	Utah (68-29-4)
Miami,OH-Cincinnati	.108	Miami (58-43-7)	**Washington-Wash. St.**	.96	Washington (64-26-6)

*Disputed series records: UNC claims lead of 51-35-4; Georgia claims lead of 55-36-5; Tulane claims LSU leads 62-23-7; Utah claims lead of 50-31-4

Associated Press Final Polls

The Associated Press introduced its weekly college football poll of sportswriters (later, sportswriters and broadcasters) in 1936. The final AP poll was released at the end of the regular season until 1965, when bowl results were included for one year. After a two-year return to regular season games only, the final poll has come out after the bowls since 1968. Starting in 1989, the AP Poll has ranked 25 teams.

1936

Final poll released Nov. 30. Top 20 regular season results after that: **Dec. 5**–#8 Notre Dame tied USC, 13-13; #17 Tennessee tied Ole Miss, 0-0; #18 Arkansas over Texas, 6-0. **Dec. 12**–#16 TCU over #6 Santa Clara, 9-0.

	As of Nov. 30	Head Coach	After Bowls
1 Minnesota	.7-1-0	Bernie Bierman	same
2 LSU	.9-0-1	Bernie Moore	9-1-1
3 Pittsburgh	.7-1-1	Jock Sutherland	8-1-1
4 Alabama	.8-0-1	Frank Thomas	same
5 Washington	.7-1-1	Jimmy Phelan	7-2-1
6 Santa Clara	.7-0-0	Buck Shaw	8-1-0
7 Northwestern	.7-1-0	Pappy Waldorf	same
8 Notre Dame	.6-2-0	Elmer Layden	6-2-1
9 Nebraska	.7-2-0	Dana X. Bible	same
10 Penn	.7-1-0	Harvey Harman	same
11 Duke	.9-1-0	Wallace Wade	same
12 Yale	.7-1-0	Ducky Pond	same
13 Dartmouth	.7-1-1	Red Blaik	same
14 Duquesne	.7-2-0	John Smith	8-2-0
15 Fordham	.5-1-2	Jim Crowley	same
16 TCU	.7-2-2	Dutch Meyer	9-2-2
17 Tennessee	.6-2-1	Bob Neyland	6-2-2
18 Arkansas	.6-3-0	Fred Thomsen	7-3-0
Navy	.6-3-0	Tom Hamilton	same
20 Marquette	.7-1-0	Frank Murray	7-2-0

Key Bowl Games

Sugar–#6 Santa Clara over #2 LSU, 21-14; **Rose**–#3 Pitt over #5 Washington, 21-0; **Orange**–#14 Duquesne over Mississippi St., 13-12; **Cotton**–#16 TCU over #20 Marquette, 16-6.

1937

Final poll released Nov. 29. Top 20 regular season results after that: **Dec. 4**–#18 Rice over SMU, 15-7.

	As of Nov. 29	Head Coach	After Bowls
1 Pittsburgh	.9-0-1	Jock Sutherland	same
2 California	.9-0-1	Stub Allison	10-0-1
3 Fordham	.7-0-1	Jim Crowley	same
4 Alabama	.9-0-0	Frank Thomas	9-1-0
5 Minnesota	.6-2-0	Bernie Bierman	same
6 Villanova	.8-0-1	Clipper Smith	same
7 Dartmouth	.7-0-2	Red Blaik	same
8 LSU	.9-1-0	Bernie Moore	9-2-0
9 Notre Dame	.6-2-1	Elmer Layden	same
Santa Clara	.8-0-0	Buck Shaw	9-0-0
11 Nebraska	.6-1-2	Biff Jones	same
12 Yale	.6-1-1	Ducky Pond	same
13 Ohio St.	.6-2-0	Francis Schmidt	same
14 Holy Cross	.8-0-2	Eddie Anderson	same
Arkansas	.6-2-2	Fred Thomsen	same
16 TCU	.4-2-2	Dutch Meyer	same
17 Colorado	.8-0-0	Bunnie Oakes	8-1-0
18 Rice	.4-3-2	Jimmy Kitts	6-3-2
19 North Carolina	.7-1-1	Ray Wolf	same
20 Duke	.7-2-1	Wallace Wade	same

Key Bowl Games

Rose–#2 Cal over #4 Alabama, 13-0; **Sugar**–#9 Santa Clara over #8 LSU, 6-0; **Cotton**–#18 Rice over #17 Colorado, 28-14; **Orange**–Auburn over Michigan St., 6-0.

1938

Final poll released Dec. 5. Top 20 regular season results after that: **Dec. 26**–#14 Cal over Georgia Tech, 13-7.

	As of Dec. 5	Head Coach	After Bowls
1 TCU	.10-0-0	Dutch Meyer	11-0-0
2 Tennessee	.10-0-0	Bob Neyland	11-0-0
3 Duke	.9-0-0	Wallace Wade	9-1-0
4 Oklahoma	.10-0-0	Tom Stidham	10-1-0
5 Notre Dame	.8-1-0	Elmer Layden	same
6 Carnegie Tech	.7-1-0	Bill Kern	7-2-0
7 USC	.8-2-0	Howard Jones	9-2-0
8 Pittsburgh	.8-2-0	Jock Sutherland	same
9 Holy Cross	.8-1-0	Eddie Anderson	same
10 Minnesota	.6-2-0	Bernie Bierman	same
11 Texas Tech	.10-0-0	Pete Cawthon	10-1-0
12 Cornell	.5-1-1	Carl Snavely	same
13 Alabama	.7-1-1	Frank Thomas	same
14 California	.9-1-0	Stub Allison	10-1-0
15 Fordham	.6-1-2	Jim Crowley	same
16 Michigan	.6-1-1	Fritz Crisler	same
17 Northwestern	.4-2-2	Pappy Waldorf	same
18 Villanova	.8-0-1	Clipper Smith	same
19 Tulane	.7-2-1	Red Dawson	same
20 Dartmouth	.7-2-0	Red Blaik	same

Key Bowl Games

Sugar–#1 TCU over #6 Carnegie Tech, 15-7; **Orange**–#2 Tennessee over #4 Oklahoma, 17-0; **Rose**–#7 USC over #3 Duke, 7-3; **Cotton**–St. Mary's over #11 Texas Tech 20-13.

1939

Final poll released Dec. 11. Top 20 regular season results after that: None.

	As of Dec. 11	Head Coach	After Bowls
1 Texas A&M	.10-0-0	Homer Norton	11-0-0
2 Tennessee	.10-0-0	Bob Neyland	10-1-0
3 USC	.7-0-2	Howard Jones	8-0-2
4 Cornell	.8-0-0	Carl Snavely	same
5 Tulane	.8-0-1	Red Dawson	8-1-1
6 Missouri	.8-1-0	Don Faurot	8-2-0
7 UCLA	.6-0-4	Babe Horrell	same
8 Duke	.8-1-0	Wallace Wade	same
9 Iowa	.6-1-1	Eddie Anderson	same
10 Duquesne	.8-0-1	Buff Donelli	same
11 Boston College	.9-1-0	Frank Leahy	9-2-0
12 Clemson	.8-1-0	Jess Neely	9-1-0
13 Notre Dame	.7-2-0	Elmer Layden	same
14 Santa Clara	.5-1-3	Buck Shaw	same
15 Ohio St.	.6-2-0	Francis Schmidt	same
16 Georgia Tech	.7-2-0	Bill Alexander	8-2-0
17 Fordham	.6-2-0	Jim Crowley	same
18 Nebraska	.7-1-1	Biff Jones	same
19 Oklahoma	.6-2-1	Tom Stidham	same
20 Michigan	.6-2-0	Fritz Crisler	same

Key Bowl Games

Sugar–#1 Texas A&M over #5 Tulane, 14-13; **Rose** –#3 USC over #2 Tennessee, 14-0; **Orange**–#16 Georgia Tech over #6 Missouri, 21-7; **Cotton**–#12 Clemson over #11 Boston College, 6-3.

1940

Final poll released Dec. 2. Top 20 regular season results after that: **Dec. 7**–#16 SMU over Rice, 7-6.

	As of Dec. 2	Head Coach	After Bowls
1 Minnesota	8-0-0	Bernie Bierman	same
2 Stanford	9-0-0	Clark Shaughnessy	10-0-0
3 Michigan	7-1-0	Fritz Crisler	same
4 Tennessee	10-0-0	Bob Neyland	10-1-0
5 Boston College	10-0-0	Frank Leahy	11-0-0
6 Texas A&M	8-1-0	Homer Norton	9-1-0
7 Nebraska	8-1-0	Biff Jones	8-2-0
8 Northwestern	6-2-0	Pappy Waldorf	same
9 Mississippi St.	9-0-1	Allyn McKeen	10-0-1
10 Washington	7-2-0	Jimmy Phelan	same
11 Santa Clara	6-1-1	Buck Shaw	same
12 Fordham	7-1-0	Jim Crowley	7-2-0
13 Georgetown	8-1-0	Jack Hagerty	8-2-0
14 Penn	6-1-1	George Munger	same
15 Cornell	6-2-0	Carl Snavely	same
16 SMU	7-1-1	Matty Bell	8-1-1
17 Hardin-Simmons	9-0-0	Warren Woodson	same
18 Duke	7-2-0	Wallace Wade	same
19 Lafayette	9-0-0	Hooks Mylin	same
20 –			

Note: Only 19 teams ranked.

Key Bowl Games

Rose–#2 Stanford over #7 Nebraska, 21-13; **Sugar**– #5 Boston College over #4 Tennessee, 19-13; **Cotton**–#6 Texas A&M over #12 Fordham, 13-12; **Orange**–#9 Mississippi St. over #13 Georgetown, 14-7.

1941

Final poll released Dec. 1. Top 20 regular season results after that: **Dec. 6**–#4 Texas over Oregon, 71-7; #9 Texas A&M over #19 Washington St., 7-0; #16 Mississippi St. over San Francisco, 26-13.

	As of Dec. 1	Head Coach	After Bowls
1 Minnesota	8-0-0	Bernie Bierman	same
2 Duke	9-0-0	Wallace Wade	9-1-0
3 Notre Dame	8-0-1	Frank Leahy	same
4 Texas	7-1-1	Dana X. Bible	8-1-1
5 Michigan	6-1-1	Fritz Crisler	same
6 Fordham	7-1-0	Jim Crowley	8-1-0
7 Missouri	8-1-0	Don Faurot	8-2-0
8 Duquesne	8-0-0	Buff Donelli	same
9 Texas A&M	8-1-0	Homer Norton	9-2-0
10 Navy	7-1-1	Swede Larson	same
11 Northwestern	5-3-0	Pappy Waldorf	same
12 Oregon St.	7-2-0	Lon Stiner	8-2-0
13 Ohio St.	6-1-1	Paul Brown	same
14 Georgia	8-1-1	Wally Butts	9-1-1
15 Penn	7-1-1	George Munger	same
16 Mississippi St.	7-1-1	Allyn McKeen	8-1-1
17 Mississippi	6-2-1	Harry Mehre	same
18 Tennessee	8-2-0	John Barnhill	same
19 Washington St.	6-3-0	Babe Hollingbery	6-4-0
20 Alabama	8-2-0	Frank Thomas	9-2-0

Note: 1942 Rose Bowl moved to Durham, N.C., for one year after outbreak of World War II.

Key Bowl Games

Rose–#12 Oregon St. over #2 Duke, 20-16; **Sugar**–#6 Fordham over #7 Missouri, 2-0; **Cotton**–#20 Alabama over #9 Texas A&M, 29-21; **Orange**–#14 Georgia over TCU, 40-26.

1942

Final poll released Nov. 30. Top 20 regular season results after that: **Dec. 5**–#6 Notre Dame tied Great Lakes Naval Station, 13-13; #13 UCLA over Idaho, 40-13; #14 William & Mary over Oklahoma, 14-7; #17 Washington St. lost to Texas A&M, 21-0; #18 Mississippi St. over San Francisco, 19-7. **Dec. 12**–#13 UCLA over USC, 14-7.

	As of Nov. 30	Head Coach	After Bowls
1 Ohio St.	9-1-0	Paul Brown	same
2 Georgia	10-1-0	Wally Butts	11-1-0
3 Wisconsin	8-1-1	Harry Stuhldreher	same
4 Tulsa	10-0-0	Henry Frnka	10-1-0
5 Georgia Tech	9-1-0	Bill Alexander	9-2-0
6 Notre Dame	7-2-1	Frank Leahy	7-2-2
7 Tennessee	8-1-1	John Barnhill	9-1-1
8 Boston College	8-1-0	Denny Myers	8-2-0
9 Michigan	7-3-0	Fritz Crisler	same
10 Alabama	7-3-0	Frank Thomas	8-3-0
11 Texas	8-2-0	Dana X. Bible	9-2-0
12 Stanford	6-4-0	Marchy Schwartz	same
13 UCLA	5-3-0	Babe Horrell	7-4-0
14 William & Mary	8-1-1	Carl Voyles	9-1-1
15 Santa Clara	7-2-0	Buck Shaw	same
16 Auburn	6-4-1	Jack Meagher	same
17 Washington St.	6-1-2	Babe Hollingbery	6-2-2
18 Mississippi St.	7-2-0	Allyn McKeen	8-2-0
19 Minnesota	5-4-0	George Hauser	same
Holy Cross	5-4-1	Ank Scanlon	same
Penn St.	6-1-1	Bob Higgins	same

Key Bowl Games

Rose–#2 Georgia over #13 UCLA, 9-0; **Sugar**–#7 Tennessee over #4 Tulsa, 14-7; **Cotton**–#11 Texas over #5 Georgia Tech, 14-7; **Orange**–#10 Alabama over #8 Boston College, 37-21.

1943

Final poll released Nov. 29. Top 20 regular season results after that: **Dec.11**–#10 March Field over #19 Pacific, 19-0.

	As of Nov. 29	Head Coach	After Bowls
1 Notre Dame	9-1-0	Frank Leahy	same
2 Iowa Pre-Flight	9-1-0	Don Faurot	same
3 Michigan	8-1-0	Fritz Crisler	same
4 Navy	8-1-0	Billick Whelchel	same
5 Purdue	9-0-0	Elmer Burnham	same
6 Great Lakes Naval Station	10-2-0	Tony Hinkle	same
7 Duke	8-1-0	Eddie Cameron	same
8 DelMonte Pre-Flight	7-1-0	Bill Kern	same
9 Northwestern	6-2-0	Pappy Waldorf	same
10 March Field	8-1-0	Paul Schissler	9-1-0
11 Army	7-2-1	Red Blaik	same
12 Washington	4-0-0	Ralph Welch	4-1-0
13 Georgia Tech	7-3-0	Bill Alexander	8-3-0
14 Texas	7-1-0	Dana X. Bible	7-1-1
15 Tulsa	6-0-1	Henry Frnka	6-1-1
16 Dartmouth	6-1-0	Earl Brown	same
17 Bainbridge Navy Training School	7-0-0	Joe Maniaci	same
18 Colorado College	7-0-0	Hal White	same
19 Pacific	7-1-0	Amos A. Stagg	7-2-0
20 Penn	6-2-1	George Munger	same

Key Bowl Games

Rose–USC over #12 Washington, 29-0; **Sugar**–#13 Georgia Tech over #15 Tulsa, 20-18; **Cotton**–#14 Texas tied Randolph Field, 7-7; **Orange**–LSU over Texas A&M, 19-14.

Associated Press Final Polls (Cont.)

1944

Final poll released Dec. 4. Top 20 regular season results after that: **Dec. 10**–#3 Randolph Field over #10 March Field, 20-7; #18 Fort Pierce over Kessler Field, 34-7; Morris Field over #20 Second Air Force, 14-7.

		As of Dec. 4	Head Coach	After Bowls
1	Army	9-0-0	Red Blaik	same
2	Ohio St.	9-0-0	Carroll Widdoes	same
3	Randolph Field	10-0-0	Frank Tritico	12-0-0
4	Navy	6-3-0	Oscar Hagberg	same
5	Bainbridge Navy Training School	10-0-0	Joe Maniaci	same
6	Iowa Pre-Flight	10-1-0	Jack Meagher	same
7	USC	7-0-2	Jeff Cravath	8-0-2
8	Michigan	8-2-0	Fritz Crisler	same
9	Notre Dame	8-2-0	Ed McKeever	same
10	March Field	7-0-2	Paul Schissler	7-1-2
11	Duke	5-4-0	Eddie Cameron	6-4-0
12	Tennessee	7-0-1	John Barnhill	7-1-1
13	Georgia Tech	8-2-0	Bill Alexander	8-3-0
14	Norman Pre-Flight	6-0-0	John Gregg	same
15	Illinois	5-4-1	Ray Eliot	same
16	El Toro Marines	8-1-0	Dick Hanley	same
17	Great Lakes Naval Station	9-2-1	Paul Brown	same
18	Fort Pierce	8-0-0	Hamp Pool	9-0-0
19	St. Mary's Pre-Flight	4-4-0	Jules Sikes	same
20	Second Air Force	10-2-1	Bill Reese	10-4-1

Key Bowl Games

Treasury–#3 Randolph Field over #20 Second Air Force, 13-6; **Rose**–#7 USC over #12 Tennessee, 25-0; **Sugar**–#11 Duke over Alabama, 29-26; **Orange**–Tulsa over #13 Georgia Tech, 26-12; **Cotton**–Oklahoma A&M over TCU, 34-0.

1945

Final poll released Dec. 3. Top 20 regular season results after that: None.

		As of Dec. 3	Head Coach	After Bowls
1	Army	9-0-0	Red Blaik	same
2	Alabama	9-0-0	Frank Thomas	10-0-0
3	Navy	7-1-1	Oscar Hagberg	same
4	Indiana	9-0-1	Bo McMillan	same
5	Oklahoma A&M	8-0-0	Jim Lookabaugh	9-0-0
6	Michigan	7-3-0	Fritz Crisler	same
7	St. Mary's-CA	7-1-0	Jimmy Phelan	7-2-0
8	Penn	6-2-0	George Munger	same
9	Notre Dame	7-2-1	Hugh Devore	same
10	Texas	9-1-0	Dana X. Bible	10-1-0
11	USC	7-3-0	Jeff Cravath	7-4-0
12	Ohio St.	7-2-0	Carroll Widdoes	same
13	Duke	6-2-0	Eddie Cameron	same
14	Tennessee	8-1-0	John Barnhill	same
15	LSU	7-2-0	Bernie Moore	same
16	Holy Cross	8-1-0	John DeGrosa	8-2-0
17	Tulsa	8-2-0	Henry Frnka	8-3-0
18	Georgia	8-2-0	Wally Butts	9-2-0
19	Wake Forest	4-3-1	Peahead Walker	5-3-1
20	Columbia	8-1-0	Lou Little	same

Key Bowl Games

Rose–#2 Alabama over #11 USC, 34-14; **Sugar**–#5 Oklahoma A&M over #7 St. Mary's, 33-13; **Cotton**–#10 Texas over Missouri, 40-27; **Orange**–Miami-FL over #16 Holy Cross, 13-6.

1946

Final poll released Dec. 2. Top 20 regular season results after that: None.

		As of Dec. 2	Head Coach	After Bowls
1	Notre Dame	8-0-1	Frank Leahy	same
2	Army	9-0-1	Red Blaik	same
3	Georgia	10-0-0	Wally Butts	11-0-0
4	UCLA	10-0-0	Bert LaBrucherie	10-1-0
5	Illinois	7-2-0	Ray Eliot	8-2-0
6	Michigan	6-2-1	Fritz Crisler	same
7	Tennessee	9-1-0	Bob Neyland	9-2-0
8	LSU	9-1-0	Bernie Moore	9-1-1
9	North Carolina	8-1-1	Carl Snavely	8-2-1
10	Rice	8-2-0	Jess Neely	9-2-0
11	Georgia Tech	8-2-0	Bobby Dodd	9-2-0
12	Yale	7-1-1	Howard Odell	same
13	Penn	6-2-0	George Munger	same
14	Oklahoma	7-3-0	Jim Tatum	8-3-0
15	Texas	8-2-0	Dana X. Bible	same
16	Arkansas	6-3-1	John Barnhill	6-3-2
17	Tulsa	9-1-0	J.O. Brothers	same
18	N.C. State	8-2-0	Beattie Feathers	8-3-0
19	Delaware	9-0-0	Bill Murray	10-0-0
20	Indiana	6-3-0	Bo McMillan	same

Key Bowl Games

Sugar–#3 Georgia over #9 N. Carolina, 20-10; **Rose**–#5 Illinois over #4 UCLA, 45-14; **Orange**–#10 Rice over #7 Tennessee, 8-0; **Cotton**–#8 LSU tied #16 Arkansas, 0-0.

1947

Final poll released Dec. 8. Top 20 regular season results after that: None.

		As of Dec. 8	Head Coach	After Bowls
1	Notre Dame	9-0-0	Frank Leahy	same
2	Michigan	9-0-0	Fritz Crisler	10-0-0
3	SMU	9-0-1	Matty Bell	9-0-2
4	Penn St.	9-0-0	Bob Higgins	9-0-1
5	Texas	9-1-0	Blair Cherry	10-1-0
6	Alabama	8-2-0	Red Drew	8-3-0
7	Penn	7-0-1	George Munger	same
8	USC	7-1-1	Jeff Cravath	7-2-1
9	North Carolina	8-2-0	Carl Snavely	same
10	Georgia Tech	9-1-0	Bobby Dodd	10-1-0
11	Army	5-2-2	Red Blaik	same
12	Kansas	8-0-2	George Sauer	8-1-2
13	Mississippi	8-2-0	Johnny Vaught	9-2-0
14	William & Mary	9-1-0	Rube McCray	9-2-0
15	California	9-1-0	Pappy Waldorf	same
16	Oklahoma	7-2-1	Bud Wilkinson	same
17	N.C. State	5-3-1	Beattie Feathers	same
18	Rice	6-3-1	Jess Neely	same
19	Duke	4-3-2	Wallace Wade	same
20	Columbia	7-2-0	Lou Little	same

Key Bowl Games

Rose–#2 Michigan over #8 USC, 49-0; **Cotton**–#3 SMU tied #4 Penn St., 13-13; **Sugar**–#5 Texas over #6 Alabama, 27-7; **Orange**–#10 Georgia Tech over #12 Kansas, 20-14.

Note: An unprecedented "Who's No. 1?" poll was conducted by AP after the Rose Bowl game, pitting Notre Dame against Michigan. The Wolverines won the vote, 226-119, but AP ruled that the Irish would be the No. 1 team of record.

1948

Final poll released Nov. 29. Top 20 regular season results after that: **Dec. 3**–#12 Vanderbilt over Miami-FL, 33-6. **Dec. 4**–#2 Notre Dame tied USC, 14-14; #11 Clemson over The Citadel, 20-0.

		As of Nov. 29	Head Coach	After Bowls
1	Michigan	9-0-0	Bennie Oosterbaan	same
2	Notre Dame	9-0-0	Frank Leahy	9-0-1
3	North Carolina	9-0-1	Carl Snavely	9-1-1
4	California	10-0-0	Pappy Waldorf	10-1-0
5	Oklahoma	9-1-0	Bud Wilkinson	10-1-0
6	Army	8-0-1	Red Blaik	same
7	Northwestern	7-2-0	Bob Voigts	8-2-0
8	Georgia	9-1-0	Wally Butts	9-2-0
9	Oregon	9-1-0	Jim Aiken	9-2-0
10	SMU	8-1-1	Matty Bell	9-1-1
11	Clemson	9-0-0	Frank Howard	11-0-0
12	Vanderbilt	7-2-1	Red Sanders	8-2-1
13	Tulane	9-1-0	Henry Frnka	same
14	Michigan St.	6-2-2	Biggie Munn	same
15	Mississippi	8-1-0	Johnny Vaught	same
16	Minnesota	7-2-0	Bernie Bierman	same
17	William & Mary	6-2-2	Rube McCray	7-2-2
18	Penn St.	7-1-1	Bob Higgins	same
19	Cornell	8-1-0	Lefty James	same
20	Wake Forest	6-3-0	Peahead Walker	6-4-0

Note: Big Nine "no-repeat" rule kept Michigan from Rose Bowl.

Key Bowl Games

Sugar–#5 California over #3 North Carolina, 14-6; **Rose**–#7 Northwestern over #4 Cal, 20-14; **Orange**–Texas over #8 Georgia, 41-28; **Cotton**–#10 SMU over #9 Oregon, 21-13.

1949

Final poll released Nov. 28. Top 20 regular season results after that: **Dec. 2**–#14 Maryland over Miami-FL, 13-0. **Dec. 3**–#1 Notre Dame over SMU, 27-20; #10 Pacific over Hawaii, 75-0.

		As of Nov. 28	Head Coach	After Bowls
1	Notre Dame	9-0-0	Frank Leahy	10-0-0
2	Oklahoma	10-0-0	Bud Wilkinson	11-0-0
3	California	10-0-0	Pappy Waldorf	10-1-0
4	Army	9-0-0	Red Blaik	same
5	Rice	9-1-0	Jess Neely	10-1-0
6	Ohio St.	6-1-2	Wes Fesler	7-1-2
7	Michigan	6-2-1	Bennie Oosterbaan	same
8	Minnesota	7-2-0	Bernie Bierman	same
9	LSU	8-2-0	Gaynell Tinsley	8-3-0
10	Pacific	10-0-0	Larry Siemering	11-0-0
11	Kentucky	9-2-0	Bear Bryant	9-3-0
12	Cornell	8-1-0	Lefty James	same
13	Villanova	8-1-0	Jim Leonard	same
14	Maryland	7-1-0	Jim Tatum	9-1-0
15	Santa Clara	7-2-1	Len Casanova	8-2-1
16	North Carolina	7-3-0	Carl Snavely	7-4-0
17	Tennessee	7-2-1	Bob Neyland	same
18	Princeton	6-3-0	Charlie Caldwell	same
19	Michigan St.	6-3-0	Biggie Munn	same
20	Missouri	7-3-0	Don Faurot	7-4-0
	Baylor	8-2-0	Bob Woodruff	same

Key Bowl Games

Sugar–#2 Oklahoma over #9 LSU, 35-0; **Rose**–#6 Ohio St. over #3 Cal, 17-14; **Cotton**–#5 Rice over #16 North Carolina, 27-13; **Orange**–#15 Santa Clara over #11 Kentucky, 21-13.

1950

Final poll released Nov. 27. Top 20 regular season results after that: **Nov. 30**–#3 Texas over Texas A&M, 17-0. **Dec. 1**–#15 Miami-FL over Missouri, 27–9. **Dec. 2**–#1 Oklahoma over Okla. A&M, 41-14; Navy over #2 Army, 14-2; #4 Tennessee over Vanderbilt, 43-0; #16 Alabama over Auburn, 34-0; #19 Tulsa over Houston, 28-21; #20 Tulane tied LSU, 14-14. **Dec. 9**–#3 Texas over LSU, 21-6.

		As of Nov. 27	Head Coach	After Bowls
1	Oklahoma	9-0-0	Bud Wilkinson	10-1-0
2	Army	8-0-0	Red Blaik	8-1-0
3	Texas	7-1-0	Blair Cherry	9-2-0
4	Tennessee	9-1-0	Bob Neyland	11-1-0
5	California	9-0-1	Pappy Waldorf	9-1-1
6	Princeton	9-0-0	Charlie Caldwell	same
7	Kentucky	10-1-0	Bear Bryant	11-1-0
8	Michigan St.	8-1-0	Biggie Munn	same
9	Michigan	5-3-1	Bennie Oosterbaan	6-3-1
10	Clemson	8-0-1	Frank Howard	9-0-1
11	Washington	8-2-0	Howard Odell	same
12	Wyoming	9-0-0	Bowden Wyatt	10-0-0
13	Illinois	7-2-0	Ray Eliot	same
14	Ohio St.	6-3-0	Wes Fesler	same
15	Miami-FL	8-0-1	Andy Gustafson	9-1-1
16	Alabama	8-2-0	Red Drew	9-2-0
17	Nebraska	6-2-1	Bill Glassford	same
18	Wash. & Lee	8-2-0	George Barclay	8-3-0
19	Tulsa	8-1-1	J.O. Brothers	9-1-1
20	Tulane	6-2-0	Henry Frnka	6-2-1

Key Bowl Games

Sugar–#7 Kentucky over #1 Oklahoma, 13-7; **Cotton**–#4 Tennessee over #3 Texas, 20-14; **Rose**–#9 Michigan over #5 Cal, 14-6; **Orange**–#10 Clemson over #15 Miami-FL, 15-14.

1951

Final poll released Dec. 3. Top 20 regular season results after that: None.

		As of Dec. 3	Head Coach	After Bowls
1	Tennessee	10-0-0	Bob Neyland	10-1-0
2	Michigan St.	9-0-0	Biggie Munn	same
3	Maryland	9-0-0	Jim Tatum	10-0-0
4	Illinois	8-0-1	Ray Eliot	9-0-1
5	Georgia Tech	10-0-1	Bobby Dodd	11-0-1
6	Princeton	9-0-0	Charlie Caldwell	same
7	Stanford	9-1-0	Chuck Taylor	9-2-0
8	Wisconsin	7-1-1	Ivy Williamson	same
9	Baylor	8-1-1	George Sauer	8-2-1
10	Oklahoma	8-2-0	Bud Wilkinson	same
11	TCU	6-4-0	Dutch Meyer	6-5-0
12	California	8-2-0	Pappy Waldorf	same
13	Virginia	8-1-0	Art Guepe	same
14	San Francisco	9-0-0	Joe Kuharich	same
15	Kentucky	7-4-0	Bear Bryant	8-4-0
16	Boston Univ.	6-4-0	Buff Donelli	same
17	UCLA	5-3-1	Red Sanders	same
18	Washington St.	7-3-0	Forest Evashevski	same
19	Holy Cross	8-2-0	Eddie Anderson	same
20	Clemson	7-2-0	Frank Howard	7-3-0

Key Bowl Games

Sugar–#3 Maryland over #1 Tennessee, 28-13; **Rose**–#4 Illinois over #7 Stanford, 40-7; **Orange**–#5 Georgia Tech over #9 Baylor, 17-14; **Cotton**–#15 Kentucky over #11 TCU, 20-7.

Associated Press Final Polls (Cont.)

1952

Final poll released Dec. 1. Top 20 regular season results after that: **Dec. 6**–#15 Florida over #20 Kentucky, 27-20.

		As of Dec. 1	Head Coach	After Bowls
1	Michigan St.	9-0-0	Biggie Munn	same
2	Georgia Tech	11-0-0	Bobby Dodd	12-0-0
3	Notre Dame	7-2-1	Frank Leahy	same
4	Oklahoma	8-1-1	Bud Wilkinson	same
5	USC	9-1-0	Jess Hill	10-1-0
6	UCLA	8-1-0	Red Sanders	same
7	Mississippi	8-0-2	Johnny Vaught	8-1-2
8	Tennessee	8-1-1	Bob Neyland	8-2-1
9	Alabama	9-2-0	Red Drew	10-2-0
10	Texas	8-2-0	Ed Price	9-2-0
11	Wisconsin	6-2-1	Ivy Williamson	6-3-1
12	Tulsa	8-1-1	J.O. Brothers	8-2-1
13	Maryland	7-2-0	Jim Tatum	same
14	Syracuse	7-2-0	Ben Schwartzwalder	7-3-0
15	Florida	6-3-0	Bob Woodruff	8-3-0
16	Duke	8-2-0	Bill Murray	same
17	Ohio St.	6-3-0	Woody Hayes	same
18	Purdue	4-3-2	Stu Holcomb	same
19	Princeton	8-1-0	Charlie Caldwell	same
20	Kentucky	5-3-2	Bear Bryant	5-4-2

Note: Michigan St. would officially join Big Ten in 1953.

Key Bowl Games

Sugar–#2 Georgia Tech over #7 Ole Miss, 24-7; **Rose**–#5 USC over #11 Wisconsin, 7-0; **Cotton**–#10 Texas over #8 Tennessee, 16-0; **Orange**–#9 Alabama over #14 Syracuse, 61-6.

1953

Final poll released Nov. 30. Top 20 regular season results after that: **Dec. 5**–#2 Notre Dame over SMU, 40-14.

		As of Nov. 30	Head Coach	After Bowls
1	Maryland	10-0-0	Jim Tatum	10-1-0
2	Notre Dame	8-0-1	Frank Leahy	9-0-1
3	Michigan St.	8-1-0	Biggie Munn	9-1-0
4	Oklahoma	8-1-1	Bud Wilkinson	9-1-1
5	UCLA	8-1-0	Red Sanders	8-2-0
6	Rice	8-2-0	Jess Neely	9-2-0
7	Illinois	7-1-1	Ray Eliot	same
8	Georgia Tech	8-2-1	Bobby Dodd	9-2-1
9	Iowa	5-3-1	Forest Evashevski	same
10	West Virginia	8-1-0	Art Lewis	8-2-0
11	Texas	7-3-0	Ed Price	same
12	Texas Tech	10-1-0	DeWitt Weaver	11-1-0
13	Alabama	6-2-3	Red Drew	6-3-3
14	Army	7-1-1	Red Blaik	same
15	Wisconsin	6-2-1	Ivy Williamson	same
16	Kentucky	7-2-1	Bear Bryant	same
17	Auburn	7-2-1	Shug Jordan	7-3-1
18	Duke	7-2-1	Bill Murray	same
19	Stanford	6-3-1	Chuck Taylor	same
20	Michigan	6-3-0	Bennie Oosterbaan	same

Key Bowl Games

Orange–#4 Oklahoma over #1 Maryland, 7-0; **Rose**–#3 Michigan St. over #5 UCLA, 28-20; **Cotton**–#6 Rice over #13 Alabama, 28-6; **Sugar**–#8 Georgia Tech over #10 West Virginia, 42-19.

1954

Final poll released Nov. 29. Top 20 regular season results after that: **Dec. 4**–#4 Notre Dame over SMU, 26-14.

		As of Nov. 29	Head Coach	After Bowls
1	Ohio St.	9-0-0	Woody Hayes	10-0-0
2	UCLA	9-0-0	Red Sanders	same
3	Oklahoma	10-0-0	Bud Wilkinson	same
4	Notre Dame	8-1-0	Terry Brennan	9-1-0
5	Navy	7-2-0	Eddie Erdelatz	8-2-0
6	Mississippi	9-1-0	Johnny Vaught	9-2-0
7	Army	7-2-0	Red Blaik	same
8	Maryland	7-2-1	Jim Tatum	same
9	Wisconsin	7-2-0	Ivy Williamson	same
10	Arkansas	8-2-0	Bowden Wyatt	8-3-0
11	Miami-FL	8-1-0	Andy Gustafson	same
12	West Virginia	8-1-0	Art Lewis	same
13	Auburn	7-3-0	Shug Jordan	8-3-0
14	Duke	7-2-1	Bill Murray	8-2-1
15	Michigan	6-3-0	Bennie Oosterbaan	same
16	Virginia Tech	8-0-1	Frank Moseley	same
17	USC	8-3-0	Jess Hill	8-4-0
18	Baylor	7-3-0	George Sauer	7-4-0
19	Rice	7-3-0	Jess Neely	same
20	Penn St.	7-2-0	Rip Engle	same

Note: PCC and Big Seven "no-repeat" rules kept UCLA and Oklahoma from Rose and Orange bowls, respectively.

Key Bowl Games

Rose–#1 Ohio St. over #17 USC, 20-7; **Sugar**–#5 Navy over #6 Ole Miss, 21-0; **Cotton**–Georgia Tech over #10 Arkansas, 14-6; **Orange**–#14 Duke over Nebraska, 34-7.

1955

Final poll released Nov. 28. Top 20 regular season results after that: None.

		As of Nov. 28	Head Coach	After Bowls
1	Oklahoma	10-0-0	Bud Wilkinson	11-0-0
2	Michigan St.	8-1-0	Duffy Daugherty	9-1-0
3	Maryland	10-0-0	Jim Tatum	10-1-0
4	UCLA	9-1-0	Red Sanders	9-2-0
5	Ohio St.	7-2-0	Woody Hayes	same
6	TCU	9-1-0	Abe Martin	9-2-0
7	Georgia Tech	8-1-1	Bobby Dodd	9-1-1
8	Auburn	8-1-1	Shug Jordan	8-2-1
9	Notre Dame	8-2-0	Terry Brennan	same
10	Mississippi	9-1-0	Johnny Vaught	10-1-0
11	Pittsburgh	7-3-0	John Michelosen	7-4-0
12	Michigan	7-2-0	Bennie Oosterbaan	same
13	USC	6-4-0	Jess Hill	same
14	Miami-FL	6-3-0	Andy Gustafson	same
15	Miami-OH	9-0-0	Ara Parseghian	same
16	Stanford	6-3-1	Chuck Taylor	same
17	Texas A&M	7-2-1	Bear Bryant	same
18	Navy	6-2-1	Eddie Erdelatz	same
19	West Virginia	8-2-0	Art Lewis	same
20	Army	6-3-0	Red Blaik	same

Note: Big Ten "no-repeat" rule kept Ohio St. from Rose Bowl.

Key Bowl Games

Orange–#1 Oklahoma over #3 Maryland, 20-6; **Rose**–#2 Michigan St. over #4 UCLA, 17-14; **Cotton**–#10 Ole Miss over #6 TCU, 14-13; **Sugar**–#7 Georgia Tech over #11 Pitt, 7-0; **Gator**–Vanderbilt over #8 Auburn, 25-13.

1956

Final poll released Dec. 3. Top 20 regular season results after that: **Dec. 8**—#13 Pitt over #6 Miami-FL, 14-7.

	As of Dec. 3	Head Coach	After Bowls
1	Oklahoma 10-0-0	Bud Wilkinson	same
2	Tennessee 10-0-0	Bowden Wyatt	10-1-0
3	Iowa 8-1-0	Forest Evashevski	9-1-0
4	Georgia Tech . .9-1-0	Bobby Dodd	10-1-0
5	Texas A&M 9-0-1	Bear Bryant	same
6	Miami-FL 8-0-1	Andy Gustafson	8-1-1
7	Michigan 7-2-0	Bennie Oosterbaan	same
8	Syracuse 7-1-0	Ben Schwartzwalder	7-2-0
9	Michigan St. 7-2-0	Duffy Daugherty	same
10	Oregon St. 7-2-1	Tommy Prothro	7-3-1
11	Baylor 8-2-0	Sam Boyd	9-2-0
12	Minnesota 6-1-2	Murray Warmath	same
13	Pittsburgh 6-2-1	John Michelosen	7-3-1
14	TCU 7-3-0	Abe Martin	8-3-0
15	Ohio St. 6-3-0	Woody Hayes	same
16	Navy 6-1-2	Eddie Erdelatz	same
17	G. Washington . .7-1-1	Gene Sherman	8-1-1
18	USC 8-2-0	Jess Hill	same
19	Clemson 7-1-2	Frank Howard	7-2-2
20	Colorado 7-2-1	Dallas Ward	8-2-1

Note: Big Seven "no-repeat" rule kept Oklahoma from Orange Bowl and Texas A&M was on probation.

Key Bowl Games

Sugar—#11 Baylor over #2 Tennessee, 13-7; **Rose**—#3 Iowa over #10 Oregon St., 35-19; **Gator**—#4 Georgia Tech over #13 Pitt, 21-14; **Cotton**—#14 TCU over #8 Syracuse, 28-27; **Orange**—#20 Colorado over #19 Clemson, 27-21.

1957

Final poll released Dec. 2. Top 20 regular season results after that: **Dec. 7**—#10 Notre Dame over SMU, 54-21.

	As of Dec. 2	Head Coach	After Bowls
1	Auburn 10-0-0	Shug Jordan	same
2	Ohio St. 8-1-0	Woody Hayes	9-1-0
3	Michigan St. 8-1-0	Duffy Daugherty	same
4	Oklahoma 9-1-0	Bud Wilkinson	10-1-0
5	Navy 8-1-1	Eddie Erdelatz	9-1-1
6	Iowa 7-1-1	Forest Evashevski	same
7	Mississippi 8-1-1	Johnny Vaught	9-1-1
8	Rice 7-3-0	Jess Neely	7-4-0
9	Texas A&M 8-2-0	Bear Bryant	8-3-0
10	Notre Dame . . .6-3-0	Terry Brennan	7-3-0
11	Texas 6-3-1	Darrell Royal	6-4-1
12	Arizona St. 10-0-0	Dan Devine	same
13	Tennessee 7-3-0	Bowden Wyatt	8-3-0
14	Mississippi St. . . .6-2-1	Wade Walker	same
15	N.C. State 7-1-2	Earle Edwards	same
16	Duke 6-2-2	Bill Murray	6-3-2
17	Florida 6-2-1	Bob Woodruff	same
18	Army 7-2-0	Red Blaik	same
19	Wisconsin 6-3-0	Milt Bruhn	same
20	VMI 9-0-1	John McKenna	same

Note: Auburn on probation, ineligible for bowl game.

Key Bowl Games

Rose—#2 Ohio St. over Oregon, 10-7; **Orange**—#4 Oklahoma over #16 Duke, 48-21; **Cotton**—#5 Navy over #8 Rice, 20-7; **Sugar**—#7 Ole Miss over #11 Texas, 39-7; **Gator**—#13 Tennessee over #9 Texas A&M, 3-0.

1958

Final poll released Dec. 1. Top 20 regular season results after that: None.

	As of Dec. 1	Head Coach	After Bowls
1	LSU 10-0-0	Paul Dietzel	11-0-0
2	Iowa 7-1-1	Forest Evashevski	8-1-1
3	Army 8-0-1	Red Blaik	same
4	Auburn 9-0-1	Shug Jordan	same
5	Oklahoma 9-1-0	Bud Wilkinson	10-1-0
6	Air Force 9-0-1	Ben Martin	9-0-2
7	Wisconsin 7-1-1	Milt Bruhn	same
8	Ohio St. 6-1-2	Woody Hayes	same
9	Syracuse 8-1-0	Ben Schwartzwalder	8-2-0
10	TCU 8-2-0	Abe Martin	8-2-1
11	Mississippi 8-2-0	Johnny Vaught	9-2-0
12	Clemson 8-2-0	Frank Howard	8-3-0
13	Purdue 6-1-2	Jack Mollenkopf	same
14	Florida 6-3-1	Bob Woodruff	6-4-1
15	South Carolina . .7-3-0	Warren Giese	same
16	California 7-3-0	Pete Elliott	7-4-0
17	Notre Dame 6-4-0	Terry Brennan	same
18	SMU 6-4-0	Bill Meek	same
19	Oklahoma St. . . .7-3-0	Cliff Speegle	8-3-0
20	Rutgers 8-1-0	John Stiegman	same

Key Bowl Games

Sugar—#1 LSU over #12 Clemson, 7-0; **Rose**—#2 Iowa over #16 Cal, 38-12; **Orange**—#5 Oklahoma over #9 Syracuse, 21-6; **Cotton**—#6 Air Force tied #10 TCU, 0-0.

1959

Final poll released Dec. 7. Top 20 regular season results after that: None.

	As of Dec. 7	Head Coach	After Bowls
1	Syracuse 10-0-0	Ben Schwartzwalder	11-0-0
2	Mississippi 9-1-0	Johnny Vaught	10-1-0
3	LSU 9-1-0	Paul Dietzel	9-2-0
4	Texas 9-1-0	Darrell Royal	9-2-0
5	Georgia 9-1-0	Wally Butts	10-1-0
6	Wisconsin 7-2-0	Milt Bruhn	7-3-0
7	TCU 8-2-0	Abe Martin	8-3-0
8	Washington 9-1-0	Jim Owens	10-1-0
9	Arkansas 8-2-0	Frank Broyles	9-2-0
10	Alabama 7-1-2	Bear Bryant	7-2-2
11	Clemson 8-2-0	Frank Howard	9-2-0
12	Penn St. 8-2-0	Rip Engle	9-2-0
13	Illinois 5-3-1	Ray Eliot	same
14	USC 8-2-0	Don Clark	same
15	Oklahoma 7-3-0	Bud Wilkinson	same
16	Wyoming 9-1-0	Bob Devaney	same
17	Notre Dame 5-5-0	Joe Kuharich	same
18	Missouri 6-4-0	Dan Devine	6-5-0
19	Florida 5-4-1	Bob Woodruff	same
20	Pittsburgh 6-4-0	John Michelosen	same

Note: Big Seven "no-repeat" rule kept Oklahoma from Orange Bowl.

Key Bowl Games

Cotton—#1 Syracuse over #4 Texas, 23-14; **Sugar**—#2 Ole Miss over #3 LSU, 21-0; **Orange**—#5 Georgia over #18 Missouri, 14-0; **Rose**—#8 Washington over #6 Wisconsin, 44-8; **Bluebonnet**—#11 Clemson over #7 TCU, 23-7; **Gator**—#9 Arkansas over Georgia Tech, 14-7; **Liberty**—#12 Penn St. over #10 Alabama, 7-0.

Associated Press Final Polls (Cont.)

1960

Final poll released Nov. 28. Top 20 regular season results after that: **Dec. 3**–UCLA over #10 Duke, 27-6.

	As of Nov. 28	Head Coach	After Bowls
1	Minnesota 8-1-0	Murray Warmath	8-2-0
2	Mississippi 9-0-1	Johnny Vaught	10-0-1
3	Iowa 8-1-0	Forest Evashevski	same
4	Navy 9-1-0	Wayne Hardin	9-2-0
5	Missouri 9-1-0	Dan Devine	10-1-0
6	Washington 9-1-0	Jim Owens	10-1-0
7	Arkansas 8-2-0	Frank Broyles	8-3-0
8	Ohio St. 7-2-0	Woody Hayes	same
9	Alabama 8-1-1	Bear Bryant	8-1-2
10	Duke 7-2-0	Bill Murray	8-3-0
11	Kansas 7-2-1	Jack Mitchell	same
12	Baylor 8-2-0	John Bridgers	8-3-0
13	Auburn 8-2-0	Shug Jordan	same
14	Yale 9-0-0	Jordan Olivar	same
15	Michigan St. 6-2-1	Duffy Daugherty	same
16	Penn St. 6-3-0	Rip Engle	7-3-0
17	New Mexico St. 10-0-0	Warren Woodson	11-0-0
18	Florida 8-2-0	Ray Graves	9-2-0
19	Syracuse 7-2-0	Ben Schwartzwalder	same
	Purdue 4-4-1	Jack Mollenkopf	same

Key Bowl Games
Rose–#6 Washington over #1 Minnesota, 17-7; **Sugar**–#2 Ole Miss over Rice, 14-6; **Orange**–#5 Missouri over #4 Navy, 21-14; **Cotton**–#10 Duke over #7 Arkansas, 7-6; **Bluebonnet**–#9 Alabama tied Texas, 3-3.

1961

Final poll released Dec. 4. Top 20 regular season results after that: None.

	As of Dec. 4	Head Coach	After Bowls
1	Alabama 10-0-0	Bear Bryant	11-0-0
2	Ohio St. 8-0-1	Woody Hayes	same
3	Texas 9-1-0	Darrell Royal	10-1-0
4	LSU 9-1-0	Paul Dietzel	10-1-0
5	Mississippi 9-1-0	Johnny Vaught	9-2-0
6	Minnesota 7-2-0	Murray Warmath	8-2-0
7	Colorado 9-1-0	Sonny Grandelius	9-2-0
8	Michigan St. 7-2-0	Duffy Daugherty	same
9	Arkansas 8-2-0	Frank Broyles	8-3-0
10	Utah St. 9-0-1	John Ralston	9-1-1
11	Missouri 7-2-1	Dan Devine	same
12	Purdue 6-3-0	Jack Mollenkopf	same
13	Georgia Tech . . .7-3-0	Bobby Dodd	7-4-0
14	Syracuse 7-3-0	Ben Schwartzwalder	8-3-0
15	Rutgers 9-0-0	John Bateman	same
16	UCLA 7-3-0	Bill Barnes	7-4-0
17	Rice 7-3-0	Jess Neely	7-4-0
	Penn St. 7-3-0	Rip Engle	8-3-0
	Arizona 8-1-1	Jim LaRue	same
20	Duke 7-3-0	Bill Murray	same

Note: Ohio St. faculty council turned down Rose Bowl invitation citing concern with OSU's overemphasis on sports.

Key Bowl Games
Sugar–#1 Alabama over #9 Arkansas, 10-3; **Cotton**–#3 Texas over #5 Ole Miss, 12-7; **Orange**–#4 LSU over #7 Colorado, 25-7; **Rose**–#6 Minnesota over #16 UCLA, 21-3; **Gotham**–Baylor over #10 Utah St., 24-9.

1962

Final poll released Dec. 3. Top 10 regular season results after that: None.

	As of Dec. 3	Head Coach	After Bowls
1	USC 10-0-0	John McKay	11-0-0
2	Wisconsin 8-1-0	Milt Bruhn	8-2-0
3	Mississippi 9-0-0	Johnny Vaught	10-0-0
4	Texas 9-0-1	Darrell Royal	9-1-1
5	Alabama 9-1-0	Bear Bryant	10-1-0
6	Arkansas 9-1-0	Frank Broyles	9-2-0
7	LSU 8-1-1	Charlie McClendon	9-1-1
8	Oklahoma 8-2-0	Bud Wilkinson	8-3-0
9	Penn St. 9-1-0	Rip Engle	9-2-0
10	Minnesota 6-2-1	Murray Warmath	same

Key Bowl Games
Rose–#1 USC over #2 Wisconsin, 42-37; **Sugar**–#3 Ole Miss over #6 Arkansas, 17-13; **Cotton**–#7 LSU over #4 Texas, 13-0; **Orange**–#5 Alabama over #8 Oklahoma, 17-0; **Gator**–Florida over #9 Penn St., 17-7.

1963

Final poll released Dec. 9. Top 10 regular season results after that: **Dec.14**–#8 Alabama over Miami-FL, 17-12.

	As of Dec. 9	Head Coach	After Bowls
1	Texas 10-0-0	Darrell Royal	11-0-0
2	Navy 9-1-0	Wayne Hardin	9-2-0
3	Illinois 7-1-1	Pete Elliott	8-1-1
4	Pittsburgh 9-1-0	John Michelosen	same
5	Auburn 9-1-0	Shug Jordan	9-2-0
6	Nebraska 9-1-0	Bob Devaney	10-1-0
7	Mississippi 7-0-2	Johnny Vaught	7-1-2
8	Alabama 7-2-0	Bear Bryant	9-2-0
9	Michigan St. 6-2-1	Duffy Daugherty	same
10	Oklahoma 8-2-0	Bud Wilkinson	same

Key Bowl Games
Cotton–#1 Texas over #2 Navy, 28-6; **Rose**–#3 Illinois over Washington, 17-7; **Orange**–#6 Nebraska over #5 Auburn, 13-7; **Sugar**–#8 Alabama over #7 Ole Miss, 12-7.

1964

Final poll released Nov. 30. Top 10 regular season results after that: **Dec.5**–Florida over #7 LSU, 20-6.

	As of Nov. 30	Head Coach	After Bowls
1	Alabama 10-0-0	Bear Bryant	10-1-0
2	Arkansas 10-0-0	Frank Broyles	11-0-0
3	Notre Dame 9-1-0	Ara Parseghian	same
4	Michigan 8-1-0	Bump Elliott	9-1-0
5	Texas 9-1-0	Darrell Royal	10-1-0
6	Nebraska 9-1-0	Bob Devaney	9-2-0
7	LSU 7-1-1	Charlie McClendon	8-2-1
8	Oregon St. 8-2-0	Tommy Prothro	8-3-0
9	Ohio St. 7-2-0	Woody Hayes	same
10	USC 7-3-0	John McKay	same

Key Bowl Games
Orange–#5 Texas over #1 Alabama, 21-17; **Cotton**–#2 Arkansas over #6 Nebraska, 10-7; **Rose**–#4 Michigan over #8 Oregon St., 34-7; **Sugar**–#7 LSU over Syracuse, 13-10.

1965

Final poll taken after bowl games for the first time.

		After Bowls	Head Coach	Regular Season
1	Alabama	9-1-1	Bear Bryant	8-1-1
2	Michigan St	10-1-0	Duffy Daugherty	10-0-0
3	Arkansas	10-1-0	Frank Broyles	10-0-0
4	UCLA	8-2-1	Tommy Prothro	7-1-1
5	Nebraska	10-1-0	Bob Devaney	10-0-0
6	Missouri	8-2-1	Dan Devine	7-2-1
7	Tennessee	8-1-2	Doug Dickey	6-1-2
8	LSU	8-3-0	Charlie McClendon	7-3-0
9	Notre Dame	7-2-1	Ara Parseghian	same
10	USC	7-2-1	John McKay	same

Key Bowl Games

Rankings below reflect final regular season poll, released Nov. 29. No bowls for then #8 USC or #9 Notre Dame. **Rose**–#5 UCLA over #1 Michigan St., 14-12; **Cotton**–LSU over #2 Arkansas, 14-7; **Orange**–#4 Alabama over #3 Nebraska, 39-28; **Sugar**–#6 Missouri over Florida, 20-18; **Bluebonnet**–#7 Tennessee over Tulsa, 27-6; **Gator**–Georgia Tech over #10 Texas Tech, 31-21.

1966

Final poll released Dec. 5, returning to pre-bowl status. Top 10 regular season results after that: None.

		As of Dec. 5	Head Coach	After Bowls
1	Notre Dame	9-0-1	Ara Parseghian	same
2	Michigan St	9-0-1	Duffy Daugherty	same
3	Alabama	10-0-0	Bear Bryant	11-0-0
4	Georgia	9-1-0	Vince Dooley	10-1-0
5	UCLA	9-1-0	Tommy Prothro	same
6	Nebraska	9-1-0	Bob Devaney	9-2-0
7	Purdue	8-2-0	Jack Mollenkopf	9-2-0
8	Georgia Tech	9-1-0	Bobby Dodd	9-2-0
9	Miami-FL	7-2-1	Charlie Tate	8-2-1
10	SMU	8-2-0	Hayden Fry	8-3-0

Key Bowl Games

Sugar–#3 Alabama over #6 Nebraska, 34-7; **Cotton**–#4 Georgia over #10 SMU, 24-9; **Rose**–#7 Purdue over USC, 14-13; **Orange**–Florida over #8 Georgia Tech, 27-12; **Liberty**–#9 Miami-FL over Virginia Tech, 14-7.

1967

Final poll released Nov. 27. Top 10 regular season results after that: **Dec. 2**–#2 Tennessee over Vanderbilt, 41-14; #3 Oklahoma over Oklahoma St., 38-14; #8 Alabama over Auburn, 7-3.

		As of Nov. 27	Head Coach	After Bowls
1	USC	9-1-0	John McKay	10-1-0
2	Tennessee	8-1-0	Doug Dickey	9-2-0
3	Oklahoma	8-1-0	Chuck Fairbanks	10-1-0
4	Indiana	9-1-0	John Pont	9-2-0
5	Notre Dame	8-2-0	Ara Parseghian	same
6	Wyoming	10-0-0	Lloyd Eaton	10-1-0
7	Oregon St.	7-2-1	Dee Andros	same
8	Alabama	7-1-1	Bear Bryant	8-2-1
9	Purdue	8-2-0	Jack Mollenkopf	same
10	Penn St.	8-2-0	Joe Paterno	8-2-1

Key Bowl Games

Rose–#1 USC over #4 Indiana, 14-3; **Orange**–#3 Oklahoma over #2 Tennessee, 26-24; **Sugar**–LSU over #6 Wyoming, 20-13; **Cotton**–Texas A&M over #8 Alabama, 20-16; **Gator**–#10 Penn St. tied Florida St. 17-17.

1968

Final poll taken after bowl games for first time since close of 1965 season.

		After Bowls	Head Coach	Regular Season
1	Ohio St.	10-0-0	Woody Hayes	9-0-0
2	Penn St.	11-0-0	Joe Paterno	10-0-0
3	Texas	9-1-1	Darrell Royal	8-1-1
4	USC	9-1-1	John McKay	9-0-1
5	Notre Dame	7-2-1	Ara Parseghian	same
6	Arkansas	10-1-0	Frank Broyles	9-1-0
7	Kansas	9-2-0	Pepper Rodgers	9-1-0
8	Georgia	8-1-2	Vince Dooley	8-0-2
9	Missouri	8-3-0	Dan Devine	7-3-0
10	Purdue	8-2-0	Jack Mollenkopf	same
11	Oklahoma	7-4-0	Chuck Fairbanks	7-3-0
12	Michigan	8-2-0	Bump Elliott	same
13	Tennessee	8-2-1	Doug Dickey	8-1-1
14	SMU	8-3-0	Hayden Fry	7-3-0
15	Oregon St.	7-3-0	Dee Andros	same
16	Auburn	7-4-0	Shug Jordan	6-4-0
17	Alabama	8-3-0	Bear Bryant	8-2-0
18	Houston	6-2-2	Bill Yeoman	same
19	LSU	8-3-0	Charlie McClendon	7-3-0
20	Ohio Univ	10-1-0	Bill Hess	10-0-0

Key Bowl Games

Rankings below reflect final regular season poll, released Dec. 2. No bowls for then #7 Notre Dame and #11 Pudue. **Rose**–#1 Ohio St. over #2 USC, 27-16; **Orange**–#3 Penn St. over #6 Kansas, 15-14; **Sugar**–#9 Arkansas over #4 Georgia, 16-2; **Cotton**–#5 Texas over #8 Tennessee, 36-13; **Bluebonnet**–#20 SMU over #10 Oklahoma, 28-27; **Gator**–#16 Missouri over #12 Alabama, 35-10.

1969

Final poll taken after bowl games.

		After Bowls	Head Coach	Regular Season
1	Texas	11-0-0	Darrell Royal	10-0-0
2	Penn St	11-0-0	Joe Paterno	10-0-0
3	USC	10-0-1	John McKay	9-0-1
4	Ohio St.	8-1-0	Woody Hayes	same
5	Notre Dame	8-2-1	Ara Parseghian	8-1-1
6	Missouri	9-2-0	Dan Devine	9-1-0
7	Arkansas	9-2-0	Frank Broyles	9-1-0
8	Mississippi	8-3-0	Johnny Vaught	7-3-0
9	Michigan	8-3-0	Bo Schembechler	8-2-0
10	LSU	9-1-0	Charlie McClendon	same
11	Nebraska	9-2-0	Bob Devaney	8-2-0
12	Houston	9-2-0	Bill Yeoman	8-2-0
13	UCLA	8-1-1	Tommy Prothro	same
14	Florida	9-1-1	Ray Graves	8-1-1
15	Tennessee	9-2-0	Doug Dickey	9-1-0
16	Colorado	8-3-0	Eddie Crowder	7-3-0
17	West Virginia	10-1-0	Jim Carlen	9-1-0
18	Purdue	8-2-0	Jack Mollenkopf	same
19	Stanford	7-2-1	John Ralston	same
20	Auburn	8-3-0	Shug Jordan	8-2-0

Key Bowl Games

Rankings below reflect final regular season poll, released Dec. 8. No bowls for then #4 Ohio St., #8 LSU and #10 UCLA. **Cotton**–#1 Texas over #9 Notre Dame, 21-17; **Orange**–#2 Penn St. over #6 Missouri, 10-3; **Sugar**–#13 Ole Miss over #3 Arkansas, 27-22; **Rose**–#5 USC over #7 Michigan, 10-3.

Associated Press Final Polls (Cont.)

1970

		After Bowls	Head Coach	Regular Season
1	Nebraska	11-0-1	Bob Devaney	10-0-1
2	Notre Dame	10-1-0	Ara Parseghian	9-0-1
3	Texas	10-1-0	Darrell Royal	10-0-0
4	Tennessee	11-1-0	Bill Battle	10-1-0
5	Ohio St.	9-1-0	Woody Hayes	9-0-0
6	Arizona St.	11-0-0	Frank Kush	10-0-0
7	LSU	9-3-0	Charlie McClendon	9-2-0
8	Stanford	9-3-0	John Ralston	8-3-0
9	Michigan	9-1-0	Bo Schembechler	same
10	Auburn	9-2-0	Shug Jordan	8-2-0
11	Arkansas	9-2-0	Frank Broyles	same
12	Toledo	12-0-0	Frank Lauterbur	11-0-0
13	Georgia Tech	9-3-0	Bud Carson	8-3-0
14	Dartmouth	9-0-0	Bob Blackman	same
15	USC	6-4-1	John McKay	same
16	Air Force	9-3-0	Ben Martin	9-2-0
17	Tulane	8-4-0	Jim Pittman	7-4-0
18	Penn St.	7-3-0	Joe Paterno	same
19	Houston	8-3-0	Bill Yeoman	same
20	Oklahoma	7-4-1	Chuck Fairbanks	7-4-0
	Mississippi	7-4-0	Johnny Vaught	7-3-0

Key Bowl Games

Rankings below reflect final regular season poll, released Dec. 7. No bowls for then #4 Arkansas and #7 Michigan.
Cotton–#6 Notre Dame over #1 Texas, 24-11; **Rose**–#12 Stanford over #2 Ohio St., 27-17; **Orange**–#3 Nebraska over #8 LSU, 17-12; **Sugar**–#5 Tennessee over #11 Air Force, 34-13; **Peach**–#9 Ariz. St. over N. Carolina, 48-26.

1971

		After Bowls	Head Coach	Regular Season
1	Nebraska	13-0-0	Bob Devaney	12-0-0
2	Oklahoma	11-1-0	Chuck Fairbanks	10-1-0
3	Colorado	10-2-0	Eddie Crowder	9-2-0
4	Alabama	11-1-0	Bear Bryant	11-0-0
5	Penn St.	11-1-0	Joe Paterno	10-1-0
6	Michigan	11-1-0	Bo Schembechler	11-0-0
7	Georgia	11-1-0	Vince Dooley	10-1-0
8	Arizona St.	11-1-0	Frank Kush	10-1-0
9	Tennessee	10-2-0	Bill Battle	9-2-0
10	Stanford	9-3-0	John Ralston	8-3-0
11	LSU	9-3-0	Charlie McClendon	8-3-0
12	Auburn	9-2-0	Shug Jordan	9-1-0
13	Notre Dame	8-2-0	Ara Parseghian	same
14	Toledo	12-0-0	John Murphy	11-0-0
15	Mississippi	10-2-0	Billy Kinard	9-2-0
16	Arkansas	8-3-1	Frank Broyles	8-2-1
17	Houston	9-3-0	Bill Yeoman	9-2-0
18	Texas	8-3-0	Darrell Royal	8-2-0
19	Washington	8-3-0	Jim Owens	same
20	USC	6-4-1	John McKay	same

Key Bowl Games

Rankings below reflect final regular season poll, released Dec. 6.
Orange–#1 Nebraska over #2 Alabama, 38-6; **Sugar**–#3 Oklahoma over #5 Auburn, 40-22; **Rose**–#16 Stanford over #4 Michigan, 13-12; **Gator**–#6 Georgia over N. Carolina, 7-3; **Bluebonnet**–#7 Colorado over #15 Houston, 29-17; **Fiesta**–#8 Ariz. St. over Florida St., 45-38; **Cotton**–#10 Penn St. over #12 Texas, 30-6.

1972

		After Bowls	Head Coach	Regular Season
1	USC	12-0-0	John McKay	11-0-0
2	Oklahoma	11-1-0	Chuck Fairbanks	10-1-0
3	Texas	10-1-0	Darrell Royal	9-1-0
4	Nebraska	9-2-1	Bob Devaney	8-2-1
5	Auburn	10-1-0	Shug Jordan	9-1-0
6	Michigan	10-1-0	Bo Schembechler	same
7	Alabama	10-2-0	Bear Bryant	10-1-0
8	Tennessee	10-2-0	Bill Battle	9-2-0
9	Ohio St.	9-2-0	Woody Hayes	9-1-0
10	Penn St.	10-2-0	Joe Paterno	10-1-0
11	LSU	9-2-1	Charlie McClendon	9-1-1
12	North Carolina	11-1-0	Bill Dooley	10-1-0
13	Arizona St.	10-2-0	Frank Kush	9-2-0
14	Notre Dame	8-3-0	Ara Parseghian	8-2-0
15	UCLA	8-3-0	Pepper Rodgers	same
16	Colorado	8-4-0	Eddie Crowder	8-3-0
17	N.C. State	8-3-1	Lou Holtz	7-3-1
18	Louisville	9-1-0	Lee Corso	same
19	Washington St.	7-4-0	Jim Sweeney	same
20	Georgia Tech	7-4-1	Bill Fulcher	6-4-1

Key Bowl Games

Rankings below reflect final regular season poll, released Dec. 4. No bowl for then #8 Michigan.
Rose–#1 USC over #3 Ohio St., 42-17; **Sugar**–#2 Oklahoma over #5 Penn St., 14-0; **Cotton**–#7 Texas over #4 Alabama, 17-13; **Orange**–#9 Nebraska over #12 Notre Dame, 40-6; **Gator**–#6 Auburn over #13 Colorado, 24-3; **Bluebonnet**–#11 Tennessee over #10 LSU, 24-17.

1973

		After Bowls	Head Coach	Regular Season
1	Notre Dame	11-0-0	Ara Parseghian	10-0-0
2	Ohio St.	10-0-1	Woody Hayes	9-0-1
3	Oklahoma	10-0-1	Barry Switzer	same
4	Alabama	11-1-0	Bear Bryant	11-0-0
5	Penn St.	12-0-0	Joe Paterno	11-0-0
6	Michigan	10-0-1	Bo Schembechler	same
7	Nebraska	9-2-1	Tom Osborne	8-2-1
8	USC	9-2-1	John McKay	9-1-1
9	Arizona St.	11-1-0	Frank Kush	10-1-0
	Houston	11-1-0	Bill Yeoman	10-1-0
11	Texas Tech	11-1-0	Jim Carlen	10-1-0
12	UCLA	9-2-0	Pepper Rodgers	same
13	LSU	9-3-0	Charlie McClendon	9-2-0
14	Texas	8-3-0	Darrell Royal	8-2-0
15	Miami-OH	11-0-0	Bill Mallory	10-0-0
16	N.C. State	9-3-0	Lou Holtz	8-3-0
17	Missouri	8-4-0	Al Onofrio	7-4-0
18	Kansas	7-4-1	Don Fambrough	7-3-1
19	Tennessee	8-4-0	Bill Battle	8-3-0
20	Maryland	8-4-0	Jerry Claiborne	8-3-0
	Tulane	9-3-0	Bennie Ellender	9-2-0

Key Bowl Games

Rankings below reflect final regular season poll, released Dec. 3. No bowls for then #2 Oklahoma (probation), #5 Michigan and #9 UCLA.
Sugar–#3 Notre Dame over #1 Alabama, 24-23; **Rose**–#4 Ohio St. over #7 USC, 42-21; **Orange**–#6 Penn St. over #13 LSU, 16-9; **Cotton**–#12 Nebraska over #8 Texas, 19-3; **Fiesta**–#10 Ariz. St. over Pitt, 28-7; **Bluebonnet**–#14 Houston over #17 Tulane, 47-7.

1974

		After Bowls	Head Coach	Regular Season
1	Oklahoma	11-0-0	Barry Switzer	same
2	USC	10-1-1	John McKay	9-1-1
3	Michigan	10-1-0	Bo Schembechler	same
4	Ohio St.	10-2-0	Woody Hayes	10-1-0
5	Alabama	11-1-0	Bear Bryant	11-0-0
6	Notre Dame	10-2-0	Ara Parseghian	9-2-0
7	Penn St.	10-2-0	Joe Paterno	9-2-0
8	Auburn	10-2-0	Shug Jordan	9-2-0
9	Nebraska	9-3-0	Tom Osborne	8-3-0
10	Miami-OH	10-0-1	Dick Crum	9-0-1
11	N.C. State	9-2-1	Lou Holtz	9-2-0
12	Michigan St.	7-3-1	Denny Stolz	same
13	Maryland	8-4-0	Jerry Claiborne	8-3-0
14	Baylor	8-4-0	Grant Teaff	8-3-0
15	Florida	8-4-0	Doug Dickey	8-3-0
16	Texas A&M	8-3-0	Emory Ballard	same
17	Mississippi St.	9-3-0	Bob Tyler	8-3-0
	Texas	8-4-0	Darrell Royal	8-3-0
19	Houston	8-3-1	Bill Yeoman	8-3-0
20	Tennessee	7-3-2	Bill Battle	6-3-2

Key Bowl Games

Rankings below reflect final regular season poll, released Dec. 2. No bowls for #1 Oklahoma (probation) and then #4 Michigan.

Orange–#9 Notre Dame over #2 Alabama, 13-11; **Rose**–#5 USC over #3 Ohio St., 18-17; **Gator**–#6 Auburn over #11 Texas, 27-3; **Cotton**–#7 Penn St. over #12 Baylor, 41-20; **Sugar**–#8 Nebraska over #18 Florida, 13-10; **Liberty**–Tennessee over #10 Maryland, 7-3.

1975

		After Bowls	Head Coach	Regular Season
1	Oklahoma	11-1-0	Barry Switzer	10-1-0
2	Arizona St.	12-0-0	Frank Kush	11-0-0
3	Alabama	11-1-0	Bear Bryant	10-1-0
4	Ohio St.	11-1-0	Woody Hayes	11-0-0
5	UCLA	9-2-1	Dick Vermeil	8-2-1
6	Texas	10-2-0	Darrell Royal	9-2-0
7	Arkansas	8-2-2	Frank Broyles	9-2-0
8	Michigan	8-2-2	Bo Schembechler	8-1-2
9	Nebraska	10-2-0	Tom Osborne	10-1-0
10	Penn St.	9-3-0	Joe Paterno	9-2-0
11	Texas A&M	10-2-0	Emory Bellard	10-1-0
12	Miami-OH	11-1-0	Dick Crum	10-1-0
13	Maryland	9-2-1	Jerry Claiborne	8-2-1
14	California	8-3-0	Mike White	same
15	Pittsburgh	8-4-0	Johnny Majors	7-4-0
16	Colorado	9-3-0	Bill Mallory	9-2-0
17	USC	8-4-0	John McKay	7-4-0
18	Arizona	9-2-0	Jim Young	same
19	Georgia	9-3-0	Vince Dooley	9-2-0
20	West Virginia	9-3-0	Bobby Bowden	8-3-0

Key Bowl Games

Rankings below reflect final regular season poll, released Dec. 1. Texas A&M was unbeaten and ranked 2nd in that poll, but lost to #18 Arkansas, 31-6, in its final regular season game on Dec.6.

Rose–#11 UCLA over #1 Ohio St., 23-10; **Liberty**–#17 USC over #2 Texas A&M, 20-0; **Orange**–#3 Oklahoma over #5 Michigan, 14-6; **Sugar**–#4 Alabama over #8 Penn St., 13-6; **Fiesta**–#7 Ariz. St. over #6 Nebraska, 17-14; **Bluebonnet**–#9 Texas over #10 Colorado, 38-21; **Cotton**–#18 Arkansas over #12 Georgia, 31-10.

1976

		After Bowls	Head Coach	Regular Season
1	Pittsburgh	12-0-0	Johnny Majors	11-0-0
2	USC	11-1-0	John Robinson	10-1-0
3	Michigan	10-2-0	Bo Schembechler	10-1-0
4	Houston	10-2-0	Bill Yeoman	9-2-0
5	Oklahoma	9-2-1	Barry Switzer	8-2-1
6	Ohio St.	9-2-1	Woody Hayes	8-2-1
7	Texas A&M	10-2-0	Emory Bellard	9-2-0
8	Maryland	11-1-0	Jerry Claiborne	11-0-0
9	Nebraska	9-3-1	Tom Osborne	8-3-1
10	Georgia	10-2-0	Vince Dooley	10-1-0
11	Alabama	9-3-0	Bear Bryant	8-3-0
12	Notre Dame	9-3-0	Dan Devine	8-3-0
13	Texas Tech	10-2-0	Steve Sloan	10-1-0
14	Oklahoma St.	9-3-0	Jim Stanley	8-3-0
15	UCLA	9-2-1	Terry Donahue	9-1-1
16	Colorado	8-4-0	Bill Mallory	8-3-0
17	Rutgers	11-0-0	Frank Burns	same
18	Kentucky	8-4-0	Fran Curci	7-4-0
19	Iowa St.	8-3-0	Earle Bruce	same
20	Mississippi St.	9-2-0	Bob Tyler	same

Key Bowl Games

Rankings below reflect final regular season poll, released Nov. 29. No bowl for then #20 Miss. St. (probation).

Sugar–#1 Pitt over #5 Georgia, 27-3; **Rose**–#3 USC over #2 Michigan, 14-6; **Cotton**–#6 Houston over #4 Maryland, 30-21; **Liberty**–#16 Alabama over #7 UCLA, 36-6; **Fiesta**–#8 Oklahoma over Wyoming, 41-7; **Bluebonnet**–#13 Nebraska over #9 Texas Tech, 27-24; **Sun**–#10 Texas A&M over Florida, 37-14; **Orange**–#11 Ohio St. over #12 Colorado, 27-10.

1977

		After Bowls	Head Coach	Regular Season
1	Notre Dame	11-1-0	Dan Devine	10-1-0
2	Alabama	11-1-0	Bear Bryant	10-1-0
3	Arkansas	11-1-0	Lou Holtz	10-1-0
4	Texas	11-1-0	Fred Akers	11-0-0
5	Penn St.	11-1-0	Joe Paterno	10-1-0
6	Kentucky	10-1-0	Fran Curci	same
7	Oklahoma	10-2-0	Barry Switzer	10-1-0
8	Pittsburgh	9-2-1	Jackie Sherrill	8-2-1
9	Michigan	10-2-0	Bo Schembechler	10-1-0
10	Washington	8-4-0	Don James	7-4-0
11	Ohio St.	9-3-0	Woody Hayes	9-2-0
12	Nebraska	9-3-0	Tom Osborne	8-3-0
13	USC	8-4-0	John Robinson	7-4-0
14	Florida St.	10-2-0	Bobby Bowden	9-2-0
15	Stanford	9-3-0	Bill Walsh	8-3-0
16	San Diego St.	10-1-0	Claude Gilbert	same
17	North Carolina	8-3-1	Bill Dooley	8-2-1
18	Arizona St.	9-3-0	Frank Kush	9-2-0
19	Clemson	8-3-1	Charley Pell	8-2-1
20	BYU	9-2-0	LaVell Edwards	same

Key Bowl Games

Rankings below reflect final regular season poll, released Nov. 28. No bowl for then #7 Kentucky (probation).

Cotton–#5 Notre Dame over #1 Texas, 38-10; **Orange**–#6 Arkansas over #2 Oklahoma, 31-6; **Sugar**–#3 Alabama over #9 Ohio St., 35-6; **Rose**–#13 Washington over #4 Michigan, 27-20; **Fiesta**–#8 Penn St. over #15 Ariz. St., 42-30; **Gator**–#10 Pitt over #11 Clemson, 34-3.

Associated Press Final Polls (Cont.)

1978

		After Bowls	Head Coach	Regular Season
1	Alabama	11-1-0	Bear Bryant	10-1-0
2	USC	12-1-0	John Robinson	11-1-0
3	Oklahoma	11-1-0	Barry Switzer	10-1-0
4	Penn St.	11-1-0	Joe Paterno	11-0-0
5	Michigan	10-2-0	Bo Schembechler	10-1-0
6	Clemson	11-1-0	Charley Pell	10-1-0
7	Notre Dame	9-3-0	Dan Devine	8-3-0
8	Nebraska	9-3-0	Tom Osborne	9-2-0
9	Texas	9-3-0	Fred Akers	8-3-0
10	Houston	9-3-0	Bill Yeoman	9-2-0
11	Arkansas	9-2-1	Lou Holtz	9-2-0
12	Michigan St.	8-3-0	Darryl Rogers	same
13	Purdue	9-2-1	Jim Young	8-2-1
14	UCLA	8-3-1	Terry Donahue	8-3-0
15	Missouri	8-4-0	Warren Powers	7-4-0
16	Georgia	9-2-1	Vince Dooley	9-1-1
17	Stanford	8-4-0	Bill Walsh	7-4-0
18	N.C. State	9-3-0	Bo Rein	8-3-0
19	Texas A&M	8-4-0	Emory Bellard (4-2) & Tom Wilson (4-2)	7-4-0
20	Maryland	9-3-0	Jerry Claiborne	9-2-0

Key Bowl Games

Rankings below reflect final regular season poll, released Dec. 4. No bowl for then #12 Michigan St. (probation).
Sugar–#2 Alabama over #1 Penn St., 14-7; **Rose**–#3 USC over #5 Michigan, 17-10; **Orange**–#4 Oklahoma over #6 Nebraska, 31-24; **Gator**–#7 Clemson over #20 Ohio St., 17-15; **Fiesta**–#8 Arkansas tied #15 UCLA, 10-10; **Cotton**–#10 Notre Dame over #9 Houston, 35-34.

1979

		After Bowls	Head Coach	Regular Season
1	Alabama	12-0-0	Bear Bryant	11-0-0
2	USC	11-0-1	John Robinson	10-0-1
3	Oklahoma	11-1-0	Barry Switzer	10-1-0
4	Ohio St.	11-1-0	Earle Bruce	11-0-0
5	Houston	11-1-0	Bill Yeoman	10-1-0
6	Florida St.	11-1-0	Bobby Bowden	11-0-0
7	Pittsburgh	11-1-0	Jackie Sherrill	10-1-0
8	Arkansas	10-2-0	Lou Holtz	10-1-0
9	Nebraska	10-2-0	Tom Osborne	10-1-0
10	Purdue	10-2-0	Jim Young	9-2-0
11	Washington	9-3-0	Don James	8-3-0
12	Texas	9-3-0	Fred Akers	9-2-0
13	BYU	11-1-0	LaVell Edwards	11-0-0
14	Baylor	8-4-0	Grant Teaff	7-4-0
15	North Carolina	8-3-1	Dick Crum	7-3-1
16	Auburn	8-3-0	Doug Barfield	same
17	Temple	10-2-0	Wayne Hardin	9-2-0
18	Michigan	8-4-0	Bo Schembechler	8-3-0
19	Indiana	8-4-0	Lee Corso	7-4-0
20	Penn St.	8-4-0	Joe Paterno	7-4-0

Key Bowl Games

Rankings below reflect final regular season poll, released Dec. 3. No bowl for then #17 Auburn (probation).
Sugar–#2 Alabama over #6 Arkansas, 24-9; **Rose**–#3 USC over #1 Ohio St., 17-16; **Orange**–#5 Oklahoma over #4 Florida St., 24-7; **Sun**–#13 Washington over #11 Texas, 14-7; **Cotton**–#8 Houston over #7 Nebraska, 17-14; **Fiesta**–#10 Pitt over Arizona, 16-10.

1980

		After Bowls	Head Coach	Regular Season
1	Georgia	12-0-0	Vince Dooley	11-0-0
2	Pittsburgh	11-1-0	Jackie Sherrill	10-1-0
3	Oklahoma	10-2-0	Barry Switzer	9-2-0
4	Michigan	10-2-0	Bo Schembechler	9-2-0
5	Florida St.	10-2-0	Bobby Bowden	10-1-0
6	Alabama	10-2-0	Bear Bryant	9-2-0
7	Nebraska	10-2-0	Tom Osborne	9-2-0
8	Penn St.	10-2-0	Joe Paterno	9-2-0
9	Notre Dame	9-2-1	Dan Devine	9-1-1
10	North Carolina	11-1-0	Dick Crum	10-1-0
11	USC	8-2-1	John Robinson	same
12	BYU	12-1-0	LaVell Edwards	11-1-0
13	UCLA	9-2-0	Terry Donahue	same
14	Baylor	10-2-0	Grant Teaff	10-1-0
15	Ohio St.	9-3-0	Earle Bruce	9-2-0
16	Washington	9-3-0	Don James	9-2-0
17	Purdue	9-3-0	Jim Young	8-3-0
18	Miami-FL	9-3-0	H. Schnellenberger	8-3-0
19	Mississippi St.	9-3-0	Emory Bellard	9-2-0
20	SMU	8-4-0	Ron Meyer	8-3-0

Key Bowl Games

Rankings below reflect final regular season poll, released Dec. 8.
Sugar–#1 Georgia over #7 Notre Dame, 17-10; **Orange**–#4 Oklahoma over #2 Florida St., 18-17; **Gator**–#3 Pitt over #18 S. Carolina, 37-9; **Rose**–#5 Michigan over #16 Washington, 23-6; **Cotton**–#9 Alabama over #6 Baylor, 30-2; **Sun**–#8 Nebraska over #17 Miss. St., 31-17; **Fiesta**–#10 Penn St. over #11 Ohio St., 31-19; **Bluebonnet**–#13 N. Carolina over Texas, 16-7.

1981

		After Bowls	Head Coach	Regular Season
1	Clemson	12-0-0	Danny Ford	11-0-0
2	Texas	10-1-1	Fred Akers	9-1-1
3	Penn St.	10-2-0	Joe Paterno	9-2-0
4	Pittsburgh	11-1-0	Jackie Sherrill	10-1-0
5	SMU	10-1-0	Ron Meyer	same
6	Georgia	10-2-0	Vince Dooley	10-1-0
7	Alabama	9-2-1	Bear Bryant	9-1-1
8	Miami-FL	9-2-0	H. Schnellenberger	same
9	North Carolina	10-2-0	Dick Crum	9-2-0
10	Washington	10-2-0	Don James	9-2-0
11	Nebraska	9-3-0	Tom Osborne	9-2-0
12	Michigan	9-3-0	Bo Schembechler	8-3-0
13	BYU	11-2-0	LaVell Edwards	10-2-0
14	USC	9-3-0	John Robinson	9-2-0
15	Ohio St.	9-3-0	Earle Bruce	8-3-0
16	Arizona St.	9-2-0	Darryl Rogers	same
17	West Virginia	9-3-0	Don Nehlen	8-3-0
18	Iowa	8-4-0	Hayden Fry	8-3-0
19	Missouri	8-4-0	Warren Powers	7-4-0
20	Oklahoma	7-4-1	Barry Switzer	6-4-1

Key Bowl Games

Rankings below reflect final regular season poll, released Nov. 30. No bowl for then #5 SMU (probation), #9 Miami-FL (probation), and #17 Ariz. St. (probation).
Orange–#1 Clemson over #4 Nebraska, 22-15; **Sugar**–#10 Pitt over #2 Georgia, 24-20; **Cotton**–#6 Texas over #3 Alabama, 14-12; **Fiesta**–#7 Penn St. over #8 USC, 26-10; **Gator**–#11 N. Carolina over Arkansas, 31-27; **Rose**–#12 Washington over #13 Iowa, 28-0.

1982

		After Bowls	Head Coach	Regular Season
1	Penn St.	11-1-0	Joe Paterno	10-1-0
2	SMU	11-0-1	Bobby Collins	10-0-1
3	Nebraska	12-1-0	Tom Osborne	11-1-0
4	Georgia	11-1-0	Vince Dooley	11-0-0
5	UCLA	10-1-1	Terry Donahue	9-1-1
6	Arizona St.	10-2-0	Darryl Rogers	9-2-0
7	Washington	10-2-0	Don James	9-2-0
8	Clemson	9-1-1	Danny Ford	same
9	Arkansas	9-2-1	Lou Holtz	8-2-1
10	Pittsburgh	9-3-0	Foge Fazio	9-2-0
11	LSU	8-3-1	Jerry Stovall	8-2-1
12	Ohio St.	9-3-0	Earle Bruce	8-3-0
13	Florida St.	9-3-0	Bobby Bowden	8-3-0
14	Auburn	9-3-0	Pat Dye	8-3-0
15	USC	8-3-0	John Robinson	same
16	Oklahoma	8-4-0	Barry Switzer	8-3-0
17	Texas	9-3-0	Fred Akers	9-2-0
18	North Carolina	8-4-0	Dick Crum	7-4-0
19	West Virginia	9-3-0	Don Nehlen	9-2-0
20	Maryland	8-4-0	Bobby Ross	8-3-0

Key Bowl Games

Rankings below reflect final regular season poll, released Dec. 6. No bowl for then #7 Clemson (probation) and #15 USC (probation).

Sugar–#2 Penn St. over #1 Georgia, 27-23; **Orange**–#3 Nebraska over #13 LSU, 21-20; **Cotton**–#4 SMU over #6 Pitt, 7-3; **Rose**–#5 UCLA over #19 Michigan, 24-14; **Aloha**–#9 Washington over #16 Maryland, 21-20; **Fiesta**–#11 Ariz. St. over #12 Oklahoma, 32-21; **Bluebonnet**–#14 Arkansas over Florida, 28-24.

1983

		After Bowls	Head Coach	Regular Season
1	Miami-FL	11-1-0	H. Schnellenberger	10-1-0
2	Nebraska	12-1-0	Tom Osborne	12-0-0
3	Auburn	11-1-0	Pat Dye	10-1-0
4	Georgia	10-1-1	Vince Dooley	9-1-1
5	Texas	11-1-0	Fred Akers	11-0-0
6	Florida	9-2-1	Charley Pell	8-2-1
7	BYU	11-1-0	LaVell Edwards	10-1-0
8	Michigan	9-3-0	Bo Schembechler	9-2-0
9	Ohio St.	9-3-0	Earle Bruce	8-3-0
10	Illinois	10-2-0	Mike White	10-1-0
11	Clemson	9-1-1	Danny Ford	same
12	SMU	10-2-0	Bobby Collins	10-1-0
13	Air Force	10-2-0	Ken Hatfield	9-2-0
14	Iowa	9-3-0	Hayden Fry	9-2-0
15	Alabama	8-4-0	Ray Perkins	7-4-0
16	West Virginia	9-3-0	Don Nehlen	8-3-0
17	UCLA	7-4-1	Terry Donahue	6-4-1
18	Pittsburgh	8-3-1	Foge Fazio	8-2-1
19	Boston College	9-3-0	Jack Bicknell	9-2-0
20	East Carolina	8-3-0	Ed Emory	same

Key Bowl Games

Rankings below reflect final regular season poll, released Dec. 5. No bowl for then #12 Clemson (probation).

Orange–#5 Miami-FL over #1 Nebraska, 31-30; **Cotton**–#7 Georgia over #2 Texas, 10-9; **Sugar**–#3 Auburn over #8 Michigan, 9-7; **Rose**–UCLA over #4 Illinois, 45-9; **Holiday**–#9 BYU over Missouri, 21-17; **Gator**–#11 Florida over #10 Iowa, 14-6; **Fiesta**–#14 Ohio St. over #15 Pitt, 28-23.

1984

		After Bowls	Head Coach	Regular Season
1	BYU	13-0-0	LaVell Edwards	12-0-0
2	Washington	11-1-0	Don James	10-1-0
3	Florida	9-1-1	Charley Pell (0-1-1) & Galen Hall (9-0)	same
4	Nebraska	10-2-0	Tom Osborne	9-2-0
5	Boston College	10-2-0	Jack Bicknell	9-2-0
6	Oklahoma	9-2-1	Barry Switzer	9-1-1
7	Oklahoma St.	10-2-0	Pat Jones	9-2-0
8	SMU	10-2-0	Bobby Collins	9-2-0
9	UCLA	9-3-0	Terry Donahue	8-3-0
10	USC	9-3-0	Ted Tollner	8-3-0
11	South Carolina	10-2-0	Joe Morrison	10-1-0
12	Maryland	9-3-0	Bobby Ross	8-3-0
13	Ohio St.	9-3-0	Earle Bruce	9-2-0
14	Auburn	9-4-0	Pat Dye	8-4-0
15	LSU	8-3-1	Bill Arnsparger	8-2-1
16	Iowa	8-4-1	Hayden Fry	7-4-1
17	Florida St.	7-3-2	Bobby Bowden	7-3-1
18	Miami-FL	8-5-0	Jimmy Johnson	8-4-0
19	Kentucky	9-3-0	Jerry Claiborne	8-3-0
20	Virginia	8-2-2	George Welsh	7-2-2

Key Bowl Games

Rankings below reflect final regular season poll, released Dec. 3. No bowl for then #3 Florida (probation).

Holiday–#1 BYU over Michigan, 24-17; **Orange**–#4 Washington over #2 Oklahoma, 28-17; **Sugar**–#5 Nebraska over #11 LSU, 28-10; **Rose**–#18 USC over #6 Ohio St., 20-17; **Gator**–#9 Okla. St. over #7 S. Carolina, 21-14; **Cotton**–#8 BC over Houston, 45-28; **Aloha**–#10 SMU over #17 Notre Dame, 27-20.

1985

		After Bowls	Head Coach	Regular Season
1	Oklahoma	11-1-0	Barry Switzer	10-1-0
2	Michigan	10-1-1	Bo Schembechler	9-1-1
3	Penn St.	11-1-0	Joe Paterno	11-0-0
4	Tennessee	9-1-2	Johnny Majors	8-1-2
5	Florida	9-1-1	Galen Hall	same
6	Texas A&M	10-2-0	Jackie Sherrill	9-2-0
7	UCLA	9-2-1	Terry Donahue	8-2-1
8	Air Force	12-1-0	Fisher DeBerry	11-1-0
9	Miami-FL	10-2-0	Jimmy Johnson	10-1-0
10	Iowa	10-2-0	Hayden Fry	10-1-0
11	Nebraska	9-3-0	Tom Osborne	9-2-0
12	Arkansas	10-2-0	Ken Hatfield	9-2-0
13	Alabama	9-2-1	Ray Perkins	8-2-1
14	Ohio St.	9-3-0	Earle Bruce	8-3-0
15	Florida St.	9-3-0	Bobby Bowden	8-3-0
16	BYU	11-3-0	LaVell Edwards	11-2-0
17	Baylor	9-3-0	Grant Teaff	8-3-0
18	Maryland	9-3-0	Bobby Ross	8-3-0
19	Georgia Tech	9-2-1	Bill Curry	8-2-1
20	LSU	9-2-1	Bill Arnsparger	9-1-1

Key Bowl Games

Rankings below reflect final regular season poll, released Dec. 9. No bowl for then #6 Florida (probation).

Orange–#3 Oklahoma over #1 Penn St., 25-10; **Sugar**–#8 Tennessee over #2 Miami-FL, 35-7; **Rose**–#13 UCLA over #4 Iowa, 45-28; **Fiesta**–#5 Michigan over #7 Nebraska, 27-23; **Bluebonnet**–#10 Air Force over Texas, 24-16; **Cotton**–#11 Texas A&M over #16 Auburn, 36-16.

Associated Press Final Polls (Cont.)

1986

		After Bowls	Head Coach	Regular Season
1	Penn St.	12-0-0	Joe Paterno	11-0-0
2	Miami-FL	11-1-0	Jimmy Johnson	11-0-0
3	Oklahoma	11-1-0	Barry Switzer	10-1-0
4	Arizona St.	10-1-1	John Cooper	9-1-1
5	Nebraska	10-2-0	Tom Osborne	9-2-0
6	Auburn	10-2-0	Pat Dye	9-2-0
7	Ohio St.	10-3-0	Earle Bruce	9-3-0
8	Michigan	11-2-0	Bo Schembechler	11-1-0
9	Alabama	10-3-0	Ray Perkins	9-3-0
10	LSU	9-3-0	Bill Arnsparger	9-2-0
11	Arizona	9-3-0	Larry Smith	8-3-0
12	Baylor	9-3-0	Grant Teaff	8-3-0
13	Texas A&M	9-3-0	Jackie Sherrill	9-2-0
14	UCLA	8-3-1	Terry Donahue	7-3-1
15	Arkansas	9-3-0	Ken Hatfield	9-2-0
16	Iowa	9-3-0	Hayden Fry	8-3-0
17	Clemson	8-2-2	Danny Ford	7-2-2
18	Washington	8-3-1	Don James	8-2-1
19	Boston College	9-3-0	Jack Bicknell	8-3-0
20	Virginia Tech	9-2-1	Bill Dooley	8-2-1

Key Bowl Games

Rankings below reflect final regular season poll, released Dec. 1.

Fiesta–#2 Penn St. over #1 Miami-FL, 14-10; **Orange**–#3 Oklahoma over #9 Arkansas, 42-8; **Rose**–#7 Ariz. St. over #4 Michigan, 22-15; **Sugar**–#6 Nebraska over #5 LSU, 30-15; **Cotton**–#11 Ohio St. over #8 Texas A&M, 28-12; **Citrus**–#10 Auburn over USC, 16-7; **Sun**–#13 Alabama over #12 Washington, 28-6.

1987

		After Bowls	Head Coach	Regular Season
1	Miami-FL	12-0-0	Jimmy Johnson	11-0-0
2	Florida St.	11-1-0	Bobby Bowden	10-1-0
3	Oklahoma	11-1-0	Barry Switzer	11-0-0
4	Syracuse	11-0-1	Dick MacPherson	11-0-0
5	LSU	10-1-1	Mike Archer	9-1-1
6	Nebraska	10-2-0	Tom Osborne	10-1-0
7	Auburn	9-1-2	Pat Dye	9-1-1
8	Michigan St.	9-2-1	George Perles	8-2-1
9	UCLA	10-2-0	Terry Donahue	9-2-0
10	Texas A&M	10-2-0	Jackie Sherrill	9-2-0
11	Oklahoma St.	10-2-0	Pat Jones	9-2-0
12	Clemson	10-2-0	Danny Ford	9-2-0
13	Georgia	9-3-0	Vince Dooley	8-3-0
14	Tennessee	10-2-1	Johnny Majors	9-2-1
15	South Carolina	8-4-0	Joe Morrison	8-3-0
16	Iowa	10-3-0	Hayden Fry	9-3-0
17	Notre Dame	8-4-0	Lou Holtz	8-3-0
18	USC	8-4-0	Larry Smith	8-3-0
19	Michigan	8-4-0	Bo Schembechler	7-4-0
20	Arizona St.	7-4-1	John Cooper	6-4-1

Key Bowl Games

Rankings below reflect final regular season poll, released Dec. 7.

Orange–#2 Miami-FL over #1 Oklahoma, 20-14; **Fiesta**–#3 Florida St. over #5 Nebraska, 31-28; **Sugar**–#4 Syracuse tied #6 Auburn, 16-16; **Gator**–#7 LSU over #9 S. Carolina, 30-13; **Rose**–#8 Mich. St. over #16 USC, 20-17; **Aloha**–#10 UCLA over Florida, 20-16; **Cotton**–#13 Texas A&M over #12 Notre Dame, 35-10.

1988

		After Bowls	Head Coach	Regular Season
1	Notre Dame	12-0-0	Lou Holtz	11-0-0
2	Miami-FL	11-1-0	Jimmy Johnson	10-1-0
3	Florida St.	11-1-0	Bobby Bowden	10-1-0
4	Michigan	9-2-1	Bo Schembechler	8-2-1
5	West Virginia	11-1-0	Don Nehlen	11-0-0
6	UCLA	10-2-0	Terry Donahue	9-2-0
7	USC	10-2-0	Larry Smith	10-1-0
8	Auburn	10-2-0	Pat Dye	10-1-0
9	Clemson	10-2-0	Danny Ford	9-2-0
10	Nebraska	11-2-0	Tom Osborne	11-1-0
11	Oklahoma St.	10-2-0	Pat Jones	9-2-0
12	Arkansas	10-2-0	Ken Hatfield	10-1-0
13	Syracuse	10-2-0	Dick MacPherson	9-2-0
14	Oklahoma	9-3-0	Barry Switzer	9-2-0
15	Georgia	9-3-0	Vince Dooley	8-3-0
16	Washington St.	9-3-0	Dennis Erickson	8-3-0
17	Alabama	9-3-0	Bill Curry	8-3-0
18	Houston	9-3-0	Jack Pardee	9-2-0
19	LSU	8-4-0	Mike Archer	8-3-0
20	Indiana	8-3-1	Bill Mallory	7-3-1

Key Bowl Games

Rankings below reflect final regular season poll, released Dec. 5.

Fiesta–#1 Notre Dame over #3 West Va., 34-21; **Orange**–#2 Miami-FL over #6 Nebraska, 23-3; **Sugar**–#4 Florida St. over #7 Auburn, 13-7; **Rose**–#11 Michigan over #5 USC, 22-14; **Cotton**–#9 UCLA over #8 Arkansas, 17-3; **Citrus**–#13 Clemson over #10 Oklahoma, 13-6.

1989

		After Bowls	Head Coach	Regular Season
1	Miami-FL	11-1-0	Dennis Erickson	10-1-0
2	Notre Dame	12-1-0	Lou Holtz	11-1-0
3	Florida St.	10-2-0	Bobby Bowden	9-2-0
4	Colorado	11-1-0	Bill McCartney	11-0-0
5	Tennessee	11-1-0	Johnny Majors	10-1-0
6	Auburn	10-2-0	Pat Dye	9-2-0
7	Michigan	10-2-0	Bo Schembechler	10-1-0
8	USC	9-2-1	Larry Smith	8-2-1
9	Alabama	10-2-0	Bill Curry	10-1-0
10	Illinois	10-2-0	John Mackovic	9-2-0
11	Nebraska	10-2-0	Tom Osborne	10-1-0
12	Clemson	10-2-0	Danny Ford	9-2-0
13	Arkansas	10-2-0	Ken Hatfield	10-1-0
14	Houston	9-2-0	Jack Pardee	same
15	Penn St.	8-3-1	Joe Paterno	7-3-1
16	Michigan St.	8-4-0	George Perles	7-3-1
17	Pittsburgh	8-3-1	Mike Gottfried (7-3-1) & Paul Hackett (1-0)	7-3-1
18	Virginia	10-3-0	George Welsh	10-2-0
19	Texas Tech	9-3-0	Spike Dykes	8-3-0
20	Texas A&M	8-4-0	R.C. Slocum	8-3-0
21	West Virginia	8-3-1	Don Nehlen	8-2-1
22	BYU	10-3-0	LaVell Edwards	10-2-0
23	Washington	8-4-0	Don James	7-4-0
24	Ohio St.	8-4-0	John Cooper	8-3-0
25	Arizona	8-4-0	Dick Tomey	7-4-0

Key Bowl Games

Rankings below reflect final regular season poll, released Dec. 11. No bowl for then #13 Houston (probation).

Orange–#4 Notre Dame over #1 Colorado, 21-6; **Sugar**–#2 Miami-FL over #7 Alabama, 33-25; **Rose**–#12 USC over #3 Michigan, 17-10; **Fiesta**–#5 Florida St. over #6 Nebraska, 41-17; **Hall of Fame**–#9 Auburn over #21 Ohio St., 31-14; **Citrus**–#11 Illinois over #15 Virginia, 31-21.

1990

		After Bowls	Head Coach	Regular Season
1	Colorado	11-1-1	Bill McCartney	10-1-1
2	Georgia Tech	11-0-1	Bobby Ross	10-0-1
3	Miami-FL	10-2-0	Dennis Erickson	9-2-0
4	Florida St.	10-2-0	Bobby Bowden	9-2-0
5	Washington	10-2-0	Don James	9-2-0
6	Notre Dame	9-3-0	Lou Holtz	9-2-0
7	Michigan	9-3-0	Gary Moeller	8-3-0
8	Tennessee	9-2-2	Johnny Majors	8-2-2
9	Clemson	10-2-0	Ken Hatfield	9-2-0
10	Houston	10-1-0	John Jenkins	same
11	Penn St.	9-3-0	Joe Paterno	9-2-0
12	Texas	10-2-0	David McWilliams	10-1-0
13	Florida	9-2-0	Steve Spurrier	same
14	Louisville	10-1-1	H. Schnellenberger	9-1-1
15	Texas A&M	9-3-1	R.C. Slocum	8-3-1
16	Michigan St.	8-3-1	George Perles	7-3-1
17	Oklahoma	8-3-0	Gary Gibbs	same
18	Iowa	8-4-0	Hayden Fry	8-3-0
19	Auburn	8-3-1	Pat Dye	7-3-1
20	USC	8-4-1	Larry Smith	8-3-1
21	Mississippi	9-3-0	Billy Brewer	9-2-0
22	BYU	10-3-0	LaVell Edwards	10-2-0
23	Virginia	8-4-0	George Welsh	8-3-0
24	Nebraska	9-3-0	Tom Osborne	9-2-0
25	Illinois	8-4-0	John Mackovic	8-3-0

Key Bowl Games

Rankings below reflect final regular season poll, released Dec. 3. No bowl for then #9 Houston (probation), #11 Florida (probation) and #20 Oklahoma (probation).

Orange—#1 Colorado over #5 Notre Dame, 10-9; **Citrus**—#2 Ga. Tech over #19 Nebraska, 45-21; **Cotton**—#4 Miami-FL over #3 Texas, 46-3; **Blockbuster**—#6 Florida St. over #7 Penn St., 24-17; **Rose**—#8 Washington over #17 Iowa, 46-34; **Sugar**—#10 Tennessee over Virginia, 23-22; **Gator**—#12 Michigan over #15 Ole Miss, 35-3.

1991

		After Bowls	Head Coach	Regular Season
1	Miami-FL	12-0-0	Dennis Erickson	11-0-0
2	Washington	12-0-0	Don James	11-0-0
3	Penn St.	11-2-0	Joe Paterno	10-2-0
4	Florida St.	11-2-0	Bobby Bowden	10-2-0
5	Alabama	11-1-0	Gene Stallings	10-1-0
6	Michigan	10-2-0	Gary Moeller	10-1-0
7	Florida	10-2-0	Steve Spurrier	10-1-0
8	California	10-2-0	Bruce Snyder	9-2-0
9	East Carolina	11-1-0	Bill Lewis	10-1-0
10	Iowa	10-1-1	Hayden Fry	10-1-1
11	Syracuse	10-2-0	Paul Pasqualoni	9-2-0
12	Texas A&M	10-2-0	R.C. Slocum	10-1-0
13	Notre Dame	10-3-0	Lou Holtz	9-3-0
14	Tennessee	9-3-0	Johnny Majors	9-2-0
15	Nebraska	9-2-1	Tom Osborne	9-1-1
16	Oklahoma	9-3-0	Gary Gibbs	8-3-0
17	Georgia	9-3-0	Ray Goff	8-3-0
18	Clemson	9-2-1	Ken Hatfield	9-1-1
19	UCLA	9-3-0	Terry Donahue	8-3-0
20	Colorado	8-3-1	Bill McCartney	8-2-1
21	Tulsa	10-2-0	David Rader	9-2-0
22	Stanford	8-4-0	Dennis Green	8-3-0
23	BYU	8-3-2	LaVell Edwards	8-3-1
24	N.C. State	9-3-0	Dick Sheridan	9-2-0
25	Air Force	10-3-0	Fisher DeBerry	9-3-0

Key Bowl Games

Rankings below reflect final regular season poll, taken Dec. 2.

Orange—#1 Miami-FL over #11 Nebraska, 22-0; **Rose**—#2 Washington over #4 Michigan, 34-14; **Sugar**—#18 Notre Dame over #3 Florida, 39-28; **Cotton**—#5 Florida St. over #9 Texas A&M, 10-2; **Fiesta**—#6 Penn St. over #10 Tennessee, 42-17; **Holiday**—#7 Iowa tied BYU, 13-13; **Blockbuster**—#8 Alabama over #15 Colorado, 30-25; **Citrus**—#14 California over #13 Clemson, 37-13; **Peach**—#12 East Carolina over #21 N.C. State, 37-34.

1992

		After Bowls	Head Coach	Regular Season
1	Alabama	13-0-0	Gene Stallings	12-0-0
2	Florida St.	11-1-0	Bobby Bowden	10-1-0
3	Miami-FL	11-1-0	Dennis Erickson	11-0-0
4	Notre Dame	10-1-1	Lou Holtz	9-1-1
5	Michigan	9-0-3	Gary Moeller	8-0-3
6	Syracuse	10-2-0	Paul Pasqualoni	9-2-0
7	Texas A&M	12-1-0	R.C. Slocum	12-0-0
8	Georgia	10-2-0	Ray Goff	9-2-0
9	Stanford	10-3-0	Bill Walsh	9-3-0
10	Florida	9-4-0	Steve Spurrier	8-4-0
11	Washington	9-3-0	Don James	9-2-0
12	Tennessee	9-3-0	Johnny Majors (5-3) & Phillip Fulmer (4-0)	8-3-0
13	Colorado	9-2-1	Bill McCartney	9-1-1
14	Nebraska	9-3-0	Tom Osborne	9-2-0
15	Washington St.	9-3-0	Mike Price	8-3-0
16	Mississippi	9-3-0	Billy Brewer	8-3-0
17	N.C. State	9-3-1	Dick Sheridan	9-2-1
18	Ohio St.	8-3-1	John Cooper	8-2-1
19	North Carolina	9-3-0	Mack Brown	8-3-0
20	Hawaii	11-2-0	Bob Wagner	10-2-0
21	Boston College	8-3-1	Tom Coughlin	8-2-1
22	Kansas	8-4-0	Glen Mason	7-4-0
23	Mississippi St.	7-5-0	Jackie Sherrill	7-4-0
24	Fresno St.	9-4-0	Jim Sweeney	9-3-0
25	Wake Forest	8-4-0	Bill Dooley	7-4-0

Key Bowl Games

Rankings below reflect final regular season poll, taken Dec. 5.
Sugar—#2 Alabama over #1 Miami-FL, 34-13; **Orange**—#3 Florida St. over #11 Nebraska, 27-14; **Cotton**—#5 Notre Dame over #4 Texas A&M, 28-3; **Fiesta**—#6 Syracuse over #10 Colorado, 26-22; **Rose**—#7 Michigan over #9 Washington, 38-31; **Citrus**—#8 Georgia over #15 Ohio St., 21-14.

All-Time AP Top 20

The composite AP Top 20 from the 1936 season through the 2003 season, based on the final rankings of each year. The final AP poll has been taken after the bowl games in 1965 and since 1968. Team point totals are based on 20 points for all 1st place finishes, 19 for each 2nd, etc. Also listed are the number of times each team has been named national champion by AP and times ranked in the final Top 10 and Top 20.

		Pts	No.1	Top 10	Top 20
1	Notre Dame	636	8	34	46
2	Michigan	629	2	36	51
3	Oklahoma	627	7	33	45
4	Alabama	574	6	31	43
5	Ohio St	555	4	26	43
6	Nebraska	548	4	29	42
7	Tennessee	456	2	22	38
8	Texas	455	2	21	36
9	USC	451	4	22	38
10	Penn St	408	2	21	36
11	Miami-FL	345	5	17	27
12	Florida St	330	2	16	22
13	UCLA	322	0	16	29
14	LSU	310	1	16	27
15	Georgia	294	1	16	26
16	Auburn	291	1	14	28
17	Arkansas	267	0	13	25
18	Florida	257	1	13	22
19	Michigan St	252	1	13	20
20	Washington	222	0	11	21

Associated Press Final Polls (Cont.)

1993

		After Bowls	Head Coach	Regular Season
1	Florida St	12-1-0	Bobby Bowden	11-1-0
2	Notre Dame	11-1-0	Lou Holtz	10-1-0
3	Nebraska	11-1-0	Tom Osborne	11-0-0
4	Auburn	11-0-0	Terry Bowden	11-0-0
5	Florida	11-2-0	Steve Spurrier	10-2-0
6	Wisconsin	10-1-1	Barry Alvarez	9-1-1
7	West Virginia	11-1-0	Don Nehlen	11-0-0
8	Penn St	10-2-0	Joe Paterno	9-2-0
9	Texas A&M	10-2-0	R.C. Slocum	10-1-0
10	Arizona	10-2-0	Dick Tomey	9-2-0
11	Ohio St	10-1-1	John Cooper	9-1-1
12	Tennessee	9-2-1	Phillip Fulmer	9-1-1
13	Boston College	9-3-0	Tom Coughlin	8-3-0
14	Alabama	9-3-1	Gene Stallings	8-3-1
15	Miami-FL	9-3-0	Dennis Erickson	9-2-0
16	Colorado	8-3-1	Bill McCartney	7-3-1
17	Oklahoma	9-3-0	Gary Gibbs	8-3-0
18	UCLA	8-4-0	Terry Donahue	8-3-0
19	North Carolina	10-3-0	Mack Brown	10-2-0
20	Kansas St	9-2-1	Bill Snyder	8-2-1
21	Michigan	8-4-0	Gary Moeller	7-4-0
22	Va. Tech	9-3-0	Frank Beamer	9-2-0
23	Clemson	9-3-0	Ken Hatfield (8-3) & Tommy West (1-0)	8-3-0
24	Louisville	9-3-0	H. Schnellenberger	8-3-0
25	California	9-4-0	Keith Gilbertson	8-4-0

Key Bowl Games

Rankings below reflect final regular season poll, taken Dec. 5. No bowl for then #5 Auburn (probation). **Orange**—#1 Florida St. over #2 Nebraska, 18-16; **Sugar**—#8 Florida over #3 West Virginia, 41-7; **Cotton**—#4 Notre Dame over #7 Texas A&M, 24-21; **Citrus**—#13 Penn St. over #6 Tennessee, 31-13; **Rose**—#9 Wisconsin over #14 UCLA, 21-16; **Fiesta**—#16 Arizona over #10 Miami- FL, 29-0;

1994

		After Bowls	Head Coach	Regular Season
1	Nebraska	13-0-0	Tom Osborne	12-0-0
2	Penn St	12-0-0	Joe Paterno	11-0-0
3	Colorado	11-1-0	Bill McCartney	10-1-0
4	Florida St	10-1-1	Bobby Bowden	9-1-1
5	Alabama	12-1-0	Gene Stallings	11-1-0
6	Miami-FL	10-2-0	Dennis Erickson	10-1-0
7	Florida	10-2-1	Steve Spurrier	10-1-1
8	Texas A&M	10-0-1	R.C. Slocum	same
9	Auburn	9-1-1	Terry Bowden	same
10	Utah	10-2-0	Ron McBride	9-2-0
11	Oregon	9-4-0	Rich Brooks	9-3-0
12	Michigan	8-4-0	Gary Moeller	7-4-0
13	USC	8-3-1	John Robinson	7-3-1
14	Ohio St	9-4-0	John Cooper	9-3-0
15	Virginia	9-3-0	George Welsh	8-3-0
16	Colorado St	10-2-0	Sonny Lubick	10-1-0
17	N.C. State	9-3-0	Mike O'Cain	8-3-0
18	BYU	10-3-0	LaVell Edwards	9-3-0
19	Kansas St	9-3-0	Bill Snyder	9-2-0
20	Arizona	8-4-0	Dick Tomey	8-3-0
21	Washington St	8-4-0	Mike Price	7-4-0
22	Tennessee	8-4-0	Phillip Fulmer	7-4-0
23	Boston College	7-4-1	Dan Henning	6-4-1
24	Mississippi St	8-4-0	Jackie Sherrill	8-3-0
25	Texas	8-4-0	John Mackovic	7-4-0

Key Bowl Games

Rankings below reflect final regular season poll, taken Dec. 4. No bowls for then #8 Texas A&M (probation) and #9 Auburn (probation). **Orange**—#1 Nebraska over #3 Miami-FL, 24-17; **Rose**—#2 Penn St. over #12 Oregon, 38-20; **Fiesta**—#4 Colorado over Notre Dame, 41-24; **Sugar**—#7 Florida St. over #5 Florida, 23-17; **Citrus**—#6 Alabama over #13 Ohio St., 24-17; **Freedom**—#14 Utah over #15 Arizona, 16-13.

1995

		After Bowls	Head Coach	Regular Season
1	Nebraska	12-0-0	Tom Osborne	11-0-0
2	Florida	12-1-0	Steve Spurrier	12-0-0
3	Tennessee	11-1-0	Phillip Fulmer	10-1-0
4	Florida St	10-2-0	Bobby Bowden	9-2-0
5	Colorado	10-2-0	Rick Neuheisel	9-2-0
6	Ohio St	11-2-0	John Cooper	11-1-0
7	Kansas St	10-2-0	Bill Snyder	9-2-0
8	Northwestern	10-2-0	Gary Barnett	10-1-0
9	Kansas	10-2-0	Glen Mason	9-2-0
10	Va. Tech	10-2-0	Frank Beamer	9-2-0
11	Notre Dame	9-3-0	Lou Holtz	9-2-0
12	USC	9-2-1	John Robinson	8-2-1
13	Penn St	9-3-0	Joe Paterno	8-3-0
14	Texas	10-2-1	John Mackovic	10-1-1
15	Texas A&M	9-3-0	R.C. Slocum	8-3-0
16	Virginia	9-4-0	George Welsh	8-4-0
17	Michigan	9-4-0	Lloyd Carr	9-3-0
18	Oregon	9-3-0	Mike Bellotti	9-2-0
19	Syracuse	9-3-0	Paul Pasqualoni	8-3-0
20	Miami-FL	8-3-0	Butch Davis	same
21	Alabama	8-3-0	Gene Stallings	same
22	Auburn	8-4-0	Terry Bowden	8-3-0
23	Texas Tech	9-3-0	Spike Dykes	8-3-0
24	Toledo	11-0-1	Gary Pinkel	10-0-1
25	Iowa	8-4-0	Hayden Fry	7-4-0

Key Bowl Games

Rankings below reflect final regular season poll, taken Dec. 3. No bowl for then #21 Ala. (probation) and #22 Miami-FL (probation). **Fiesta**—#1 Neb. over #2 Fla., 62-24; **Rose**—#17 USC over #3 Northwestern, 41-32; **Citrus**—#4t Tenn. over #4t Ohio St., 20-14; **Orange**—#8 Fla. St. over N. Dame, 31-26; **Cotton**—#7 Colo. over #12 Oregon, 38-6; **Sugar**—#13 Va. Tech over #9 Texas, 28-10.

1996

		After Bowls	Head Coach	Regular Season
1	Florida	12-1	Steve Spurrier	11-1
2	Ohio St.	11-1	John Cooper	10-1
3	Florida St.	11-1	Bobby Bowden	11-0
4	Arizona St	11-1	Bruce Snyder	11-0
5	BYU	14-1	LaVell Edwards	13-1
6	Nebraska	11-2	Tom Osborne	10-2
7	Penn St	11-2	Joe Paterno	10-2
8	Colorado	10-2	Rick Neuheisel	9-2
9	Tennessee	10-2	Phillip Fulmer	9-2
10	North Carolina	10-2	Mack Brown	9-2
11	Alabama	10-3	Gene Stallings	9-3
12	LSU	10-2	Gerry DiNardo	9-2
13	Virginia Tech	10-2	Frank Beamer	10-1
14	Miami-FL	9-3	Butch Davis	8-3
15	Northwestern	9-3	Gary Barnett	9-2
16	Washington	9-3	Jim Lambright	9-2
17	Kansas St.	9-3	Bill Snyder	9-2
18	Iowa	9-3	Hayden Fry	8-3
19	Notre Dame	8-3	Lou Holtz	same
20	Michigan	8-4	Lloyd Carr	8-3
21	Syracuse	9-3	Paul Pasqualoni	8-3
22	Wyoming	10-2	Joe Tiller	same
23	Texas	8-5	John Mackovic	8-4
24	Auburn	8-4	Terry Bowden	7-4
25	Army	10-2	Bob Sutton	10-1

Key Bowl Games

Rankings below reflect final regular season poll, taken Dec. 8. No bowl for then #18 N. Dame and #22 Wyoming. **Sugar**—#3 Fla. over #1 Fla. St., 52-20; **Rose**—#4 Ohio St. over #2 Ariz. St., 20-17; **Fiesta**—#7 Penn St. over #20 Texas, 38-15; **Cotton**—#5 BYU over #14 Kansas St., 19-15; **Citrus**—#9 Tenn. over #11 Northwestern, 48-28; **Orange**—#6 Neb. over #10 Va. Tech, 41-21.

1997

	After Bowls	Head Coach	Regular Season
1 Michigan	12-0	Lloyd Carr	11-0
2 Nebraska	13-0	Tom Osborne	12-0
3 Florida St	11-1	Bobby Bowden	10-1
4 Florida	10-2	Steve Spurrier	9-2
5 UCLA	10-2	Bob Toledo	9-2
6 North Carolina	11-1	Mack Brown (10-1) & Carl Torbush	10-1 (1-0)
7 Tennessee	11-2	Phillip Fulmer	11-1
8 Kansas St	11-1	Bill Snyder	10-1
9 Washington St.	10-2	Mike Price	10-1
10 Georgia	10-2	Jim Donnan	9-2
11 Auburn	10-3	Terry Bowden	9-3
12 Ohio St.	10-3	John Cooper	10-2
13 LSU	9-3	Gerry DiNardo	8-3
14 Arizona St.	8-3	Bruce Snyder	7-3
15 Purdue	9-3	Joe Tiller	8-3
16 Penn St.	9-3	Joe Paterno	9-2
17 Colorado St.	11-2	Sonny Lubick	10-2
18 Washington	8-4	Jim Lambright	7-4
19 So. Mississippi	9-3	Jeff Bower	8-3
20 Texas A&M	9-4	R.C. Slocum	9-3
21 Syracuse	9-4	Paul Pasqualoni	9-3
22 Mississippi	8-4	Tommy Tuberville	7-4
23 Missouri	7-5	Larry Smith	6-5
24 Oklahoma St.	8-4	Bobby Simmons	8-3
25 Georgia Tech	7-5	George O'Leary	6-5

Key Bowl Games

Rankings below reflect final regular season poll, taken Dec. 7. **Rose**–#1 Michigan over #7 Washington St., 21-16; **Orange**–#2 Nebraska over #3 Tennessee, 42-17; **Sugar**–#4 Florida St. over #10 Ohio St., 31-14; **Gator**–#5 North Carolina over Virginia Tech, 42-3; **Cotton**–#6 UCLA over #19 Texas A&M, 29-23; **Citrus**–#8 Florida over #12 Penn St., 21-6; **Fiesta**–#9 Kansas St. over #14 Syracuse, 35-18.

1998

	After Bowls	Head Coach	Regular Season
1 Tennessee	13-0	Phillip Fulmer	12-0
2 Ohio St.	11-1	John Cooper	10-1
3 Florida St.	11-2	Bobby Bowden	11-1
4 Arizona	12-1	Dick Tomey	11-1
5 Florida	10-2	Steve Spurrier	9-2
6 Wisconsin	11-1	Barry Alvarez	10-1
7 Tulane	12-0	Tommy Bowden	11-0
8 UCLA	10-2	Bob Toledo	10-1
9 Georgia Tech	10-2	George O'Leary	9-2
10 Kansas St.	11-2	Bill Snyder	11-1
11 Texas A&M	11-3	R.C. Slocum	11-2
12 Michigan	10-3	Lloyd Carr	9-3
13 Air Force	12-1	Fisher DeBerry	11-1
14 Georgia	9-3	Jim Donnan	8-3
15 Texas	9-3	Mack Brown	8-3
16 Arkansas	9-3	Houston Nutt	9-2
17 Penn St.	9-3	Joe Paterno	8-3
18 Virginia	9-3	George Welsh	9-2
19 Nebraska	9-4	Frank Solich	9-3
20 Miami-FL	9-3	Butch Davis	8-3
21 Missouri	8-4	Larry Smith	7-4
22 Notre Dame	9-3	Bob Davie	9-2
23 Va. Tech	9-3	Frank Beamer	8-3
24 Purdue	9-4	Joe Tiller	8-4
25 Syracuse	8-4	Paul Pasqualoni	8-3

Key Bowl Games

Rankings below reflect final regular season poll, taken Dec. 6. **Fiesta**– #1 Tennessee over #2 Florida St., 23-16; **Sugar**–#3 Ohio St. over #8 Texas A&M, 24-14; **Orange**–#7 Florida over #18 Syracuse, 31-10; **Rose**–#9 Wisconsin over #6 UCLA, 38-31; **Holiday**–#5 Arizona over #14 Nebraska, 23-20; **Alamo**–Purdue over #4 Kansas St., 37-34.

1999

	After Bowls	Head Coach	Regular Season
1 Florida St.	12-0	Bobby Bowden	11-0
2 Va. Tech	11-1	Frank Beamer	11-0
3 Nebraska	12-1	Frank Solich	11-1
4 Wisconsin	10-2	Barry Alvarez	9-2
5 Michigan	10-2	Lloyd Carr	9-2
6 Kansas St	11-1	Bill Snyder	10-1
7 Michigan St.	10-2	Nick Saban (9-2) & B. Williams	9-2 (1-0)
8 Alabama	10-3	Mike DuBose	10-2
9 Tennessee	9-3	Phillip Fulmer	8-3
10 Marshall	13-0	Bob Pruett	12-0
11 Penn St.	10-3	Joe Paterno	9-3
12 Florida	9-4	Steve Spurrier	9-3
13 Mississippi St.	10-2	Jackie Sherrill	9-2
14 Southern Miss.	9-3	Jeff Bower	8-3
15 Miami-FL	9-4	Butch Davis	8-4
16 Georgia	8-4	Jim Donnan	7-4
17 Arkansas	8-4	Houston Nutt	7-4
18 Minnesota	8-4	Glen Mason	8-3
19 Oregon	9-3	Mike Bellotti	8-3
20 Georgia Tech	8-4	George O'Leary	8-3
21 Texas	9-5	Mack Brown	9-4
22 Mississippi	8-4	David Cutcliffe	7-4
23 Texas A&M	8-4	R.C. Slocum	8-3
24 Illinois	8-4	Ron Turner	7-4
25 Purdue	7-5	Joe Tiller	7-4

Key Bowl Games

Rankings below reflect final regular season poll, taken Dec. 5. **Sugar**–#1 Florida St. over #2 Va. Tech, 46-29; **Fiesta**–#3 Nebraska over #6 Tennessee, 31-21; **Rose**–#4 Wisconsin over #22 Stanford, 17-9; **Orange**–#8 Michigan over #5 Alabama, 35-34; **Holiday**–#7 Kansas St. over Washington, 24-20; **Citrus**–#9 Michigan St. over #10 Florida, 37-34.

2000

	After Bowls	Head Coach	Regular Season
1 Oklahoma	13-0	Bob Stoops	12-0
2 Miami-FL	11-1	Butch Davis	10-1
3 Washington	11-1	Rick Neuheisel	10-1
4 Oregon St.	11-1	Dennis Erickson	10-1
5 Florida St.	11-2	Bobby Bowden	11-1
6 Va. Tech	11-1	Frank Beamer	10-1
7 Oregon	10-2	Mike Bellotti	9-2
8 Nebraska	10-2	Frank Solich	9-2
9 Kansas St.	11-3	Bill Snyder	10-3
10 Florida	10-3	Steve Spurrier	10-2
11 Michigan	9-3	Lloyd Carr	8-3
12 Texas	9-3	Mack Brown	9-2
13 Purdue	8-4	Joe Tiller	8-3
14 Colorado St.	10-2	Sonny Lubick	9-2
15 Notre Dame	9-3	Bob Davie	9-2
16 Clemson	9-3	Tommy Bowden	9-2
17 Georgia Tech	9-3	George O'Leary	9-2
18 Auburn	9-4	Tommy Tuberville	9-3
19 South Carolina	8-4	Lou Holtz	7-4
20 Georgia	8-4	Jim Donnan	7-4
21 TCU	10-2	D. Franchione (10-1) & G. Patterson	10-1 (0-1)
22 LSU	8-4	Nick Saban	7-4
23 Wisconsin	9-4	Barry Alvarez	8-4
24 Mississippi St.	8-4	Jackie Sherrill	7-4
25 Iowa St.	9-3	Dan McCarney	8-3

Key Bowl Games

Rankings below reflect final regular season poll, taken Dec. 4. **Orange**–#1 Oklahoma over #3 Florida St., 13-2; **Sugar**–#2 Miami-FL over #4 Purdue, 37-20; **Rose**–#4 Washington over #14 Purdue, 34-24; **Fiesta**–#5 Oregon St. over #10 Notre Dame, 41-9; **Gator**–#6 Virginia Tech over #16 Clemson, 41-20; **Holiday**–#8 Oregon over #12 Texas, 35-30; **Alamo**–#9 Nebraska over #18 Northwestern, 66-17.

Associated Press Final Polls (Cont.)

2001

		After Bowls	Head Coach	Regular Season
1	Miami-FL	12-0	Larry Coker	11-0
2	Oregon	11-1	Mike Bellotti	10-1
3	Florida	10-2	Steve Spurrier	9-2
4	Tennessee	11-2	Phillip Fulmer	10-2
5	Texas	11-2	Mack Brown	10-2
6	Oklahoma	11-2	Bob Stoops	10-2
7	LSU	10-3	Nick Saban	9-3
8	Nebraska	11-2	Frank Solich	11-1
9	Colorado	10-3	Gary Barnett	10-2
10	Washington St.	10-2	Mike Price	9-2
11	Maryland	10-2	Ralph Friedgen	10-1
12	Illinois	10-2	Ron Turner	10-1
13	South Carolina	9-3	Lou Holtz	8-3
14	Syracuse	10-3	Paul Pasqualoni	9-3
15	Florida St.	8-4	Bobby Bowden	7-4
16	Stanford	9-3	Tyrone Willingham	9-2
17	Louisville	11-2	John L. Smith	10-2
18	Va. Tech	8-4	Frank Beamer	8-3
19	Washington	8-4	Rick Neuheisel	8-3
20	Michigan	8-4	Lloyd Carr	8-3
21	Boston College	8-4	Tom O'Brien	7-4
22	Georgia	8-4	Mark Richt	8-3
23	Toledo	10-2	Tom Amstutz	9-2
24	Georgia Tech	8-5	George O'Leary (7-5) & Mac McWhorter (1-0)	7-5
25	BYU	12-2	Gary Crowton	12-1

Key Bowl Games

Rankings below reflect final regular season poll, taken Dec. 9. **Rose**–#1 Miami-FL over #4 Nebraska, 37-14; **Fiesta**–#2 Oregon over #3 Colorado, 38-16; **Orange**–#5 Florida over #6 Maryland, 56-23; **Sugar**–#12 LSU over #7 Illinois 47-34; **Citrus**–#8 Tennessee over #17 Michigan, 45-17; **Holiday**–#9 Texas over #21 Washington, 47-43; **Cotton**–#10 Oklahoma over Arkansas, 10-3;

2002

		After Bowls	Head Coach	Regular Season
1	Ohio St.	14-0	Jim Tressel	13-0
2	Miami-FL	12-1	Larry Coker	12-0
3	Georgia	13-1	Mark Richt	12-1
4	USC	11-2	Pete Carroll	10-2
5	Oklahoma	12-2	Bob Stoops	11-2
6	Texas	11-2	Mack Brown	10-2
7	Kansas St.	11-2	Bill Snyder	10-2
8	Iowa	11-2	Kirk Ferentz	11-1
9	Michigan	10-3	Lloyd Carr	9-3
10	Washington St.	10-3	Mike Price	10-2
11	Alabama	10-3	Dennis Franchione	10-3
12	N.C. State	11-3	Chuck Amato	10-3
13	Maryland	11-3	Ralph Friedgen	10-3
14	Auburn	9-4	Tommy Tuberville	8-4
15	Boise St.	12-1	Dan Hawkins	11-1
16	Penn St.	9-4	Joe Paterno	9-2
17	Notre Dame	10-3	Tyrone Willingham	10-2
18	Va. Tech	10-4	Frank Beamer	9-4
19	Pittsburgh	9-4	Walt Harris	8-4
20	Colorado	9-5	Gary Barnett	9-4
21	Florida St.	9-5	Bobby Bowden	9-4
22	Virginia	9-5	Al Groh	8-5
23	TCU	10-2	Gary Patterson	9-2
24	Marshall	11-2	Bob Pruett	10-2
25	West Virginia	9-4	Rich Rodriguez	9-3

Key Bowl Games

Rankings below reflect final regular season poll, taken Dec. 8. No bowl for then #13 Alabama (probation). **Fiesta**–#2 Ohio St. over #1 Miami-FL, 31-24 (2OT); **Orange**–#5 USC over #3 Iowa, 38-17; **Sugar**–#4 Georgia over #16 Florida St. 26-13; **Holiday**–#6 Kansas St. over Arizona St., 34-27; **Rose**–#8 Oklahoma over #7 Washington St., 34-14; **Cotton**–#9 Texas over LSU, 35-20; **Capital One**–#19 Auburn over #10 Penn St., 13-9;

2003

		After Bowls	Head Coach	Regular Season
1	USC	12-1	Pete Carroll	11-1
2	LSU	13-1	Nick Saban	12-1
3	Oklahoma	12-2	Bob Stoops	12-1
4	Ohio State	11-2	Jim Tressel	10-2
5	Miami-FL	11-2	Larry Coker	10-2
6	Michigan	10-3	Lloyd Carr	11-1
7	Georgia	11-3	Mark Richt	10-3
8	Iowa	10-3	Kirk Ferentz	9-3
9	Washington St.	10-3	Bill Doba	9-3
10	Miami-OH	13-1	Terry Hoeppner	12-1
11	Florida St.	10-3	Bobby Bowden	10-2
12	Texas	10-3	Mack Brown	10-2
13	Mississippi	10-3	David Cutcliffe	9-3
14	Kansas St.	11-4	Bill Snyder	11-3
15	Tennessee	10-3	Phillip Fulmer	10-2
16	Boise St.	13-1	Dan Hawkins	12-1
17	Maryland	10-3	Ralph Friedgen	9-3
18	Purdue	9-4	Joe Tiller	9-3
19	Nebraska	10-3	Frank Solich (9-3) & Bo Pelini (1-0)	9-3
20	Minnesota	10-3	Glen Mason	9-3
21	Utah	10-2	Urban Meyer	9-2
22	Clemson	9-4	Tommy Bowden	8-4
23	Bowling Green	11-3	Gregg Brandon	10-3
24	Florida	8-5	Ron Zook	8-4
25	TCU	11-2	Gary Patterson	11-1

Key Bowl Games

Rankings below reflect final regular season poll, taken Dec. 7. **Rose**–#1 USC over #4 Michigan, 28-14; **Sugar**–#2 LSU over #3 Oklahoma, 21-14; **Holiday**–#14 Washington St. over #5 Texas, 28-20; **Fiesta**–#6 Ohio St. over #10 Kansas St., 35-28; **Peach**–Clemson over #7 Tennessee, 27-14; **Orange**–#9 Miami-FL over #8 Florida St., 16-14.

The Special Election That Didn't Count

There was one No. 1 vs. No. 2 confrontation not noted in the Number 1 vs. Number 2 table on pages 156-157. It came in a special election or re-vote of Associated Press selectors following the 1948 Rose Bowl. Here's what happened: Unbeaten Notre Dame was declared 1947 national champion by the AP on Dec. 8, two days after closing out an undefeated season with a 38-7 rout of then third-ranked USC in Los Angeles. Twenty-four days later, however, unbeaten Michigan, AP's final No. 2 team, clobbered now eighth-ranked USC, 49-0, in the Rose Bowl. An immediate cry went up for an unprecedented two-team "Who's No. 1?" ballot and the AP gave in. Michigan won the election 226-119, with 12 voters calling it even. However, AP ruled that the Dec. 8 final poll vote won by Notre Dame would be the poll of record.

Bowl Games

From Jan. 1, 1902 through Jan. 4, 2004. Please note that the Bowl selection process is now dominated by the Bowl Championship Series (which includes the Fiesta, Orange, Rose and Sugar bowls) and the following non-BCS bowls' so called "automatic berths" are contingent upon several factors, including the leftovers from the BCS, Notre Dame's record and the record of their designated choices.

Rose Bowl

City: Pasadena, Calif. **Stadium:** Rose Bowl. **Capacity:** 102,083. **Playing surface:** Grass. **First game:** Jan. 1, 1902. **Playing sites:** Tournament Park (1902, 1916-22), Rose Bowl (1923-41 and since 1943) and Duke Stadium in Durham, N.C. (1942, due to wartime restrictions following Japan's attack on Pearl Harbor on Dec. 7, 1941). **Corporate sponsors:** AT&T (1998-2002), Sony Playstation 2 (2003) and Citi (2004).

Automatic berths: Pacific Coast Conference champion vs. opponent selected by PCC (1924-45 seasons); Big Ten champion vs. Pac-10 champion (1946-97); Bowl Championship Series: Big Ten champion vs. Pac-10 champion, if available (1998-2000, 2002-05 seasons) and #1 vs. #2 in Jan. 2002 and Jan. 2006.

Multiple wins: USC (21); Michigan (8); Washington (7); Ohio St. (6); Stanford and UCLA (5); Alabama (4); Illinois, Michigan St. and Wisconsin (3); California and Iowa (2).

Year		Year		Year	
1902*	Michigan 49, Stanford 0	1945	USC 25, Tennessee 0	1975	USC 18, Ohio St. 17
1916	Washington St. 14, Brown 0	1946	Alabama 34, USC 14	1976	UCLA 23, Ohio St. 10
1917	Oregon 14, Penn 0	1947	Illinois 45, UCLA 14	1977	USC 14, Michigan 6
1918	Mare Island 19, Camp Lewis 7	1948	Michigan 49, USC 0	1978	Washington 27, Michigan 20
1919	Great Lakes 17, Mare Island 0	1949	Northwestern 20, California 14	1979	USC 17, Michigan 10
1920	Harvard 7, Oregon 6	1950	Ohio St. 17, California 14	1980	USC 17, Ohio St. 16
1921	California 28, Ohio St. 0	1951	Michigan 14, California 6	1981	Michigan 23, Washington 6
1922	0-0, California vs Wash. & Jeff.	1952	Illinois 40, Stanford 7	1982	Washington 28, Iowa 0
1923	USC 14, Penn St. 0	1953	USC 7, Wisconsin 0	1983	UCLA 24, Michigan 14
1924	14-14, Navy vs Washington	1954	Michigan St. 28, UCLA 20	1984	UCLA 45, Illinois 9
1925	Notre Dame 27, Stanford 10	1955	Ohio St. 20, USC 7	1985	USC 20, Ohio St. 17
1926	Alabama 20, Washington 19	1956	Michigan St. 17, UCLA 14	1986	UCLA 45, Iowa 28
1927	7-7, Alabama vs Stanford	1957	Iowa 35, Oregon St. 19	1987	Arizona St. 22, Michigan 15
1928	Stanford 7, Pittsburgh 6	1958	Ohio St. 10, Oregon 7	1988	Michigan St. 20, USC 17
1929	Georgia Tech 8, California 7	1959	Iowa 38, California 12	1989	Michigan 22, USC 14
1930	USC 47, Pittsburgh 14	1960	Washington 44, Wisconsin 8	1990	USC 17, Michigan 10
1931	Alabama 24, Washington St. 0	1961	Washington 17, Minnesota 7	1991	Washington 46, Iowa 34
1932	USC 21, Tulane 12	1962	Minnesota 21, UCLA 3	1992	Washington 34, Michigan 14
1933	USC 35, Pittsburgh 0	1963	USC 42, Wisconsin 37	1993	Michigan 38, Washington 31
1934	Columbia 7, Stanford 0	1964	Illinois 17, Washington 7	1994	Wisconsin 21, UCLA 16
1935	Alabama 29, Stanford 13	1965	Michigan 34, Oregon St. 7	1995	Penn St. 38, Oregon 20
1936	Stanford 7, SMU 0	1966	UCLA 14, Michigan St. 12	1996	USC 41, Northwestern 32
1937	Pittsburgh 21, Washington 0	1967	Purdue 14, USC 13	1997	Ohio St. 20, Arizona St. 17
1938	California 13, Alabama 0	1968	USC 14, Indiana 3	1998	Michigan 21, Washington St. 16
1939	USC 7, Duke 3	1969	Ohio St. 27, USC 16	1999	Wisconsin 38, UCLA 31
1940	USC 14, Tennessee 0	1970	USC 10, Michigan 3	2000	Wisconsin 17, Stanford 9
1941	Stanford 21, Nebraska 13	1971	Stanford 27, Ohio St. 17	2001	Washington 34, Purdue 24
1942	Oregon St. 20, Duke 16	1972	Stanford 13, Michigan 12	2002	Miami-FL 37, Nebraska 14
1943	Georgia 9, UCLA 0	1973	USC 42, Ohio St. 17	2003	Oklahoma 34, Washington St. 14
1944	USC 29, Washington 0	1974	Ohio St. 42, USC 21	2004	USC 28, Michigan 14
					* January game since 1902.

Fiesta Bowl

City: Tempe, Ariz. **Stadium:** Sun Devil. **Capacity:** 73,656. **Playing surface:** Grass. **First game:** Dec. 27, 1971. **Playing sites:** Sun Devil Stadium (since 1971). **Corporate title sponsors:** Sunkist Citrus Growers (1986-91), IBM OS/2 (1993-95) and Frito-Lay Tostitos chips (since 1996).

Automatic berths: Western Athletic Conference champion vs. at-large opponent (1971-79 seasons); Two of first five picks from 8-team Bowl Coalition pool (1992-94). Bowl Alliance (#1 vs. #2 on Jan. 2, 1996; #3 vs. #5 on Jan. 1, 1997; and #4 vs. #6 on Dec. 31, 1997); Big 12 champion vs. next best team in pool (New Bowl Alliance 1995-1997 seasons); Bowl Championship Series: #1 vs. #2 on Jan. 4, 1999 and Jan., 2003 and Big 12 champion, if available (1999-2001 and 2003-05 seasons).

Multiple wins: Penn St. (6); Arizona St. (5); Ohio St. (3); Florida St. and Nebraska (2).

Year		Year		Year	
1971†	Arizona St. 45, Florida St. 38	1984	Ohio St. 28, Pittsburgh 23	1996	Nebraska 62, Florida 24
1972	Arizona St. 49, Missouri 35	1985	UCLA 39, Miami-FL 37	1997	Penn St. 38, Texas 15
1973	Arizona St. 28, Pittsburgh 7	1986	Michigan 27, Nebraska 23	1997†	Kansas St. 35, Syracuse 18
1974	Oklahoma 16, BYU 6	1987	Penn St. 14, Miami-FL 10	1999	Tennessee 23, Florida St. 16
1975	Arizona St. 17, Nebraska 14	1988	Florida St. 31, Nebraska 28		
1976	Oklahoma 41, Wyoming 7	1989	Notre Dame 34, West Va. 21	2000	Nebraska 31, Tennessee 21
1977	Penn St. 42, Arizona St. 30			2001	Oregon St. 41, Notre Dame 9
1978	10-10, Arkansas vs UCLA	1990	Florida St. 41, Nebraska 17	2002	Oregon 38, Colorado 16
1979	Pittsburgh 16, Arizona 10	1991	Louisville 34, Alabama 7	2003	Ohio St. 31, Miami-FL 24 (2OT)
		1992	Penn St. 42, Tennessee 17	2004	Ohio St. 35, Kansas St. 28
1980	Penn St. 31, Ohio St. 19	1993	Syracuse 26, Colorado 22	†December game from 1971-80 and
1982*	Penn St. 26, USC 10	1994	Arizona 29, Miami-FL 0	in '97.
1983	Arizona St. 32, Oklahoma 21	1995	Colorado 41, Notre Dame 24	*January game since 1982.

Bowl Games (Cont.)
Sugar Bowl

City: New Orleans, La. **Stadium:** Louisiana Superdome. **Capacity:** 77,446. **Playing surface:** Turf. **First game:** Jan. 1, 1935. **Playing sites:** Tulane Stadium (1935-74) and Superdome (since 1975). **Corporate title sponsors:** USF&G Financial Services (1987-95) and Nokia (starting in 1995).

Automatic berths: SEC champion vs. at-large opponent (1976-91 seasons); SEC champion vs. one of first five picks from 8-team Bowl Coalition pool (1992-94 seasons); #4 vs. #6 on Dec. 31, 1995; #1 vs. #2 on Jan. 2, 1997; and #3 vs. #5 on Jan. 1, 1998; Bowl Championship Series: SEC champion, if available, vs. at-large (1998-99, 2000-02, 2004-05 seasons) and #1 vs. #2 on Jan. 4, 2000 and Jan. 2004.

Multiple wins: Alabama (8); LSU and Mississippi (5); Florida St., Georgia Tech, Oklahoma and Tennessee (4); Georgia and Nebraska (3); Florida, LSU, Miami-FL, Notre Dame, Pittsburgh, Santa Clara and TCU (2).

Year		Year		Year	
1935*	Tulane 20, Temple 14	1960	Mississippi 21, LSU 0	1985	Nebraska 28, LSU 10
1936	TCU 3, LSU 2	1961	Mississippi 14, Rice 6	1986	Tennessee 35, Miami-FL 7
1937	Santa Clara 21, LSU 14	1962	Alabama 10, Arkansas 3	1987	Nebraska 30, LSU 15
1938	Santa Clara 6, LSU 0	1963	Mississippi 17, Arkansas 13	1988	16-16, Syracuse vs Auburn
1939	TCU 15, Carnegie Tech 7	1964	Alabama 12, Mississippi 7	1989	Florida St. 13, Auburn 7
1940	Texas A&M 14, Tulane 13	1965	LSU 13, Syracuse 10	1990	Miami-FL 33, Alabama 25
1941	Boston College 19, Tennessee 13	1966	Missouri 20, Florida 18	1991	Tennessee 23, Virginia 22
1942	Fordham 2, Missouri 0	1967	Alabama 34, Nebraska 7	1992	Notre Dame 39, Florida 28
1943	Tennessee 14, Tulsa 7	1968	LSU 20, Wyoming 13	1993	Alabama 34, Miami-FL 13
1944	Georgia Tech 20, Tulsa 18	1969	Arkansas 16, Georgia 2	1994	Florida 41, West Va. 7
1945	Duke 29, Alabama 26	1970	Mississippi 27, Arkansas 22	1995	Florida St. 23, Florida 17
1946	Okla. A&M 33, St.Mary's 13	1971	Tennessee 34, Air Force 13	1995†	Va. Tech 28, Texas 10
1947	Georgia 20, N. Carolina 10	1972	Oklahoma 40, Auburn 22	1997	Florida 52, Florida St. 20
1948	Texas 27, Alabama 7	1972†	Oklahoma 14, Penn St. 0	1998	Florida St. 31, Ohio St. 14
1949	Oklahoma 14, N. Carolina 6	1973	Notre Dame 24, Alabama 23	1999	Ohio St. 24, Texas A&M 14
1950	Oklahoma 35, LSU 0	1974	Nebraska 13, Florida 10	2000	Florida St. 46, Va. Tech 29
1951	Kentucky 13, Oklahoma 7	1975	Alabama 13, Penn St. 6	2001	Miami-FL 37, Florida 20
1952	Maryland 28, Tennessee 13	1977*	Pittsburgh 27, Georgia 3	2002	LSU 47, Illinois 34
1953	Georgia Tech 24, Mississippi 7	1978	Alabama 35, Ohio St. 6	2003	Georgia 26, Florida St. 13
1954	Georgia Tech 42, West Va. 19	1979	Alabama 14, Penn St. 7	2004	LSU 21, Oklahoma 14
1955	Navy 21, Mississippi 0	1980	Alabama 24, Arkansas 9		
1956	Georgia Tech 7, Pittsburgh 0	1981	Georgia 17, Notre Dame 10	* January game from 1935-72 and
1957	Baylor 13, Tennessee 7	1982	Pittsburgh 24, Georgia 20	since 1977 (except in 1995).
1958	Mississippi 39, Texas 7	1983	Penn St. 27, Georgia 23	† Game played on Dec. 31 from
1959	LSU 7, Clemson 0	1984	Auburn 9, Michigan 7	1972-75 and in 1995.

Orange Bowl

City: Miami, Fla. **Stadium:** Pro Player. **Capacity:** 74,916. **Playing surface:** Grass. **First game:** Jan. 1, 1935. **Playing sites:** Orange Bowl (1935-95); Pro Player Stadium (since 1996). **Corporate title sponsor:** Federal Express (since 1989).

Automatic berths: Big 8 champion vs. Atlantic Coast Conference champion (1953-57 seasons); Big 8 champion vs. at-large opponent (1958-63 seasons and 1975-91 seasons); #3 vs. #5 on Jan. 1, 1996; #4 vs. #6 on Dec. 31, 1996; and #1 vs. #2 on Jan. 2, 1998 (New Bowl Alliance 1995-97 seasons); Bowl Championship Series: Big East or ACC champion, if available, vs. at-large (1998-99, 2001-03, 2005 seasons) and #1 vs. #2 on Jan. 3, 2001 and Jan. 2005.

Multiple wins: Oklahoma (12); Nebraska (8); Miami-FL (6); Alabama (4); Florida, Florida State, Georgia Tech and Penn St. (3); Clemson, Colorado, Georgia, LSU, Notre Dame and Texas (2).

Year		Year		Year	
1935*	Bucknell 26, Miami-FL 0	1955	Duke 34, Nebraska 7	1975	Notre Dame 13, Alabama 11
1936	Catholic U. 20, Mississippi 19	1956	Oklahoma 20, Maryland 6	1976	Oklahoma 14, Michigan 6
1937	Duquesne 13, Mississippi St. 12	1957	Colorado 27, Clemson 21	1977	Ohio St. 27, Colorado 10
1938	Auburn 6, Michigan St. 0	1958	Oklahoma 48, Duke 21	1978	Arkansas 31, Oklahoma 6
1939	Tennessee 17, Oklahoma 0	1959	Oklahoma 21, Syracuse 6	1979	Oklahoma 31, Nebraska 24
1940	Georgia Tech 21, Missouri 7	1960	Georgia 14, Missouri 0	1980	Oklahoma 24, Florida St. 7
1941	Mississippi St. 14, Georgetown 7	1961	Missouri 21, Navy 14	1981	Oklahoma 18, Florida St. 17
1942	Georgia 40, TCU 26	1962	LSU 25, Colorado 7	1982	Clemson 22, Nebraska 15
1943	Alabama 37, Boston College 21	1963	Alabama 17, Oklahoma 0	1983	Nebraska 21, LSU 20
1944	LSU 19, Texas A&M 14	1964	Nebraska 13, Auburn 7	1984	Miami-FL 31, Nebraska 30
1945	Tulsa 26, Georgia Tech 12	1965†	Texas 21, Alabama 17	1985	Washington 28, Oklahoma 17
1946	Miami-FL 13, Holy Cross 6	1966	Alabama 39, Nebraska 28	1986	Oklahoma 25, Penn St. 10
1947	Rice 8, Tennessee 0	1967	Florida 27, Georgia Tech 12	1987	Oklahoma 42, Arkansas 8
1948	Georgia Tech 20, Kansas 14	1968	Oklahoma 26, Tennessee 24	1988	Miami-FL 20, Oklahoma 14
1949	Texas 41, Georgia 28	1969	Penn St. 15, Kansas 14	1989	Miami-FL 23, Nebraska 3
1950	Santa Clara 21, Kentucky 13	1970	Penn St. 10, Missouri 3	1990	Notre Dame, 21, Colorado 6
1951	Clemson 15, Miami-FL 14	1971	Nebraska 17, LSU 12	1991	Colorado 10, Notre Dame 9
1952	Georgia Tech 17, Baylor 14	1972	Nebraska 38, Alabama 6	1992	Miami-FL 22, Nebraska 0
1953	Alabama 61, Syracuse 6	1973	Nebraska 40, Notre Dame 6	1993	Florida St. 27, Nebraska 14
1954	Oklahoma 7, Maryland 0	1974	Penn St. 16, LSU 9	1994	Florida St. 18, Nebraska 16

Year		Year		Year	
1995	Nebraska 24, Miami-FL 17	2000	Michigan 35, Alabama 34	2004	Miami-FL 16, Florida St. 14
1996	Florida St. 31, Notre Dame 26	2001	Oklahoma 13, Florida St. 2	* January game 1935-1996 and since	
1996**	Nebraska 41, Virginia Tech 21	2002	Florida 56, Maryland 23	'98.	
1998*	Nebraska 42, Tennessee 17	2003	USC 38, Iowa 17	** December game in 1996	
1999	Florida 31, Syracuse 10			† Night game since 1965.	

Cotton Bowl

City: Dallas, Tex. **Stadium:** Cotton Bowl. **Capacity:** 68,252. **Playing surface:** Grass. **First game:** Jan 1, 1937. **Playing sites:** Fair Park Stadium (1937) and Cotton Bowl (since 1938). **Corporate title sponsor:** Mobil Corporation (1988-95), SBC Communications Inc., previously Southwestern Bell, (since 1997).

Automatic berths: SWC champion vs. at-large opponent (1941-91 seasons); SWC champion vs. one of first five picks from 8-team Bowl Coalition pool (1992-1994 seasons); second pick from Big 12 vs. first choice of WAC champion or second pick from Pac-10 (1995-97 seasons); Big 12 vs. SEC (since 1998).

Multiple wins: Texas (11); Notre Dame (9); Texas A&M (4); Arkansas and Rice (3); Alabama, Georgia, Houston, LSU, Mississippi, Penn St., SMU, Tennessee, TCU and UCLA (2).

Year		Year		Year	
1937*	TCU 16, Marquette 6	1961	Duke 7, Arkansas 6	1985	Boston College 45, Houston 28
1938	Rice 28, Colorado 14	1962	Texas 12, Mississippi 7	1986	Texas A&M 36, Auburn 16
1939	St. Mary's 20, Texas Tech 13	1963	LSU 13, Texas 0	1987	Ohio St. 28, Texas A&M 12
1940	Clemson 6, Boston College 3	1964	Texas 28, Navy 6	1988	Texas A&M 35, Notre Dame 10
1941	Texas A&M 13, Fordham 12	1965	Arkansas 10, Nebraska 7	1989	UCLA 17, Arkansas 3
1942	Alabama 29, Texas A&M 21	1966	LSU 14, Arkansas 7	1990	Tennessee 31, Arkansas 27
1943	Texas 14, Georgia Tech 7	1966†	Georgia 24, SMU 9	1991	Miami-FL 46, Texas 3
1944	7-7, Texas vs Randolph Field	1968*	Texas A&M 20, Alabama 16	1992	Florida St. 10, Texas A&M 2
1945	Oklahoma A&M 34, TCU 0	1969	Texas 36, Tennessee 13	1993	Notre Dame 28, Texas A&M 3
1946	Texas 40, Missouri 27	1970	Texas 21, Notre Dame 17	1994	Notre Dame 24, Texas A&M 21
1947	0-0, Arkansas vs LSU	1971	Notre Dame 24, Texas 11	1995	USC 55, Texas Tech 14
1948	13-13, SMU vs Penn St.	1972	Penn St. 30, Texas 6	1996	Colorado 38, Oregon 6
1949	SMU 21, Oregon 13	1973	Texas 17, Alabama 13	1997	BYU 19, Kansas St. 15
1950	Rice 27, N. Carolina 13	1974	Nebraska 19, Texas 3	1998	UCLA 29, Texas A&M 23
1951	Tennessee 20, Texas 14	1975	Penn St. 41, Baylor 20	1999	Texas 38, Mississippi St. 11
1952	Kentucky 20, TCU 7	1976	Arkansas 31, Georgia 10	2000	Arkansas 27, Texas 6
1953	Texas 16, Tennessee 0	1977	Houston 30, Maryland 21	2001	Kansas St. 35, Tennessee 21
1954	Rice 28, Alabama 6	1978	Notre Dame 38, Texas 10	2002	Oklahoma 10, Arkansas 3
1955	Georgia Tech 14, Arkansas 6	1979	Notre Dame 35, Houston 34	2003	Texas 35, LSU 20
1956	Mississippi 14, TCU 13	1980	Houston 17, Nebraska 14	2004	Mississippi 31, Oklahoma St. 28
1957	TCU 28, Syracuse 27	1981	Alabama 30, Baylor 2	* January game from 1937-66 and	
1958	Navy 20, Rice 7	1982	Texas 14, Alabama 12	since 1968.	
1959	0-0, TCU vs Air Force	1983	SMU 7, Pittsburgh 3	† Game played on Dec. 31, 1966.	
1960	Syracuse 23, Texas 14	1984	Georgia 10, Texas 9		

Capital One Bowl

City: Orlando, Fla. **Stadium:** Florida Citrus Bowl. **Capacity:** 70,188. **Playing surface:** Grass. **First game:** Jan. 1, 1947. **Name change:** Tangerine Bowl (1947-82), Florida Citrus Bowl (1983-2002) and Capital One Bowl (since 2003). **Playing sites:** Tangerine Bowl (1947-72, 1974-82), Florida Field in Gainesville (1973), Orlando Stadium (1983-85) and Florida Citrus Bowl (since 1986). The Tangerine Bowl, Orlando Stadium and Florida Citrus Bowl are all the same stadium. **Corporate title sponsors:** Florida Department of Citrus (1983-2002), CompUSA (1992-99), Ourhouse.com (2000) and Capital One (since 2001).

Automatic berths: Championship game of Atlantic Coast Regional Conference (1964-67 seasons); Mid-American Conference champion vs. Southern Conference champion (1968-71 seasons); ACC champion vs. at-large opponent (1988-91 seasons); second pick from SEC, if available, vs. second pick from Big 10, if available (since 1992 season).

Multiple wins: Tennessee (4); Auburn, East Texas St., Miami-OH and Toledo (3); Catawba, Clemson, East Carolina, Florida, Georgia and Michigan (2).

Year		Year		Year	
1947*	Catawba 31, Maryville 6	1967	Tenn-Martin 25, West Chester 8	1989	Clemson 13, Oklahoma 6
1948	Catawba 7, Marshall 0	1968	Richmond 49, Ohio U. 42	1990	Illinois 31, Virginia 21
1949	21-21, Murray St. vs Sul Ross St.	1969	Toledo 56, Davidson 33	1991	Georgia Tech 45, Nebraska 21
1950	St. Vincent 7, Emory & Henry 6	1970	Toledo 40, Wm. & Mary 12	1992	California 37, Clemson 13
1951	M. Harvey 35, Emory & Henry 14	1971	Toledo 28, Richmond 3	1993	Georgia 21, Ohio St. 14
1952	Stetson 35, Arkansas St. 20	1972	Tampa 21, Kent St. 18	1994	Penn St. 31, Tennessee 13
1953	E. Texas St. 33, Tenn. Tech 0	1973	Miami-OH 16, Florida 7	1995	Alabama 24, Ohio St. 17
1954	7-7, E. Texas St. vs Arkansas St.	1974	Miami-OH 21, Georgia 10	1996	Tennessee 20, Ohio St. 14
1955	Neb.-Omaha 7, Eastern Ky. 6	1975	Miami-OH 20, S. Carolina 7	1997	Tennessee 48, Northwestern 28
1956	6-6, Juniata vs Missouri Valley	1976	Oklahoma 49, BYU 21	1998	Florida 21, Penn St. 6
1957	W. Texas St. 20, So. Miss. 13	1977	Florida St. 40, Texas Tech 17	1999	Michigan 45, Arkansas 31
1958	E. Texas St. 10, So. Miss. 9	1978	N.C. State 30, Pittsburgh 17	2000	Michigan St. 37, Florida 34
1958†	E. Texas St. 26, Mo. Valley 7	1979	LSU 34, Wake Forest 10	2001	Michigan 31, Auburn 28
1960*	Mid. Tenn. 21, Presbyterian 12	1980	Florida 35, Maryland 20	2002	Tennessee 45, Michigan 17
1960†	Citadel 27, Tenn. Tech 0	1981	Missouri 19, Southern Miss. 17	2003	Auburn 13, Penn St. 9
1961	Lamar 21, Middle Tenn. 14	1982	Auburn 33, Boston College 26	2004	Georiga 34, Purdue 27 OT
1962	Houston 49, Miami-OH 21	1983	Tennessee 30, Maryland 23	*January game from 1947-58, in 1960	
1963	Western Ky. 27, Coast Guard 0	1984	17-17, Florida St. vs Georgia	and since 1987.	
1964	E. Carolina 14, Massachusetts 13	1985	Ohio St. 10, BYU 7	†December game in 1958, 1960-85.	
1965	E. Carolina 31, Maine 0	1987*	Auburn 16, USC 7		
1966	Morgan St. 14, West Chester 6	1988	Clemson 35, Penn St. 10		

Bowl Games (Cont.)
Gator Bowl

City: Jacksonville, Fla. **Stadium:** ALLTEL Stadium. **Capacity:** 73,000. **Playing surface:** Grass. **First game:** Jan. 1, 1946. **Playing sites:** Gator Bowl (1946-93), Florida Field in Gainesville (1994) and New Gator Bowl (since 1995). Name was changed to ALLTEL Stadium in 1997. **Corporate title sponsors:** Mazda Motors of America, Inc. (1986-91), Outback Steakhouse, Inc. (1992-94) and Toyota Motor Co. (since 1995).

Automatic berths: Third pick from SEC vs. sixth pick from 8-team Bowl Coalition pool (1992-94 seasons); second pick from ACC, if available, vs. second pick from Big East or Notre Dame, if available (since 1995 season).

Multiple wins: Florida (6); North Carolina (5); Auburn, Clemson and Florida St. (4); Georgia Tech, Maryland and Tennessee (3); Georgia, Miami-FL, Oklahoma, Pittsburgh, and Texas Tech (2).

Year		Year		Year	
1946*	Wake Forest 26, S. Carolina 14	1967	17-17, Florida St. vs Penn St.	1989†	Clemson 27, West Va. 7
1947	Oklahoma 34, N.C. State 13	1968	Missouri 35, Alabama 10	1991*	Michigan 35, Mississippi 3
1948	20-20, Maryland vs Georgia	1969	Florida 14, Tennessee 13	1991†	Oklahoma 48, Virginia 14
1949	Clemson 24, Missouri 23	1971*	Auburn 35, Mississippi 28	1992	Florida 27, N.C. State 10
1950	Maryland 20, Missouri 7	1971†	Georgia 7, N. Carolina 3	1993	Alabama 24, N. Carolina 10
1951	Wyoming 20, Wash. & Lee 7	1972	Auburn 24, Colorado 3	1994	Tennessee 45, Va. Tech 23
1952	Miami-FL 14, Clemson 0	1973	Texas Tech 28, Tennessee 19	1996*	Syracuse 41, Clemson 0
1953	Florida 14, Tulsa 13	1974	Auburn 27, Texas 3	1997	N. Carolina 20, West Va. 13
1954	Texas Tech 35, Auburn 13	1975	Maryland 13, Florida 0	1998	N. Carolina 42, Va. Tech 3
1954†	Auburn 33, Baylor 13	1976	Notre Dame 20, Penn St. 9	1999	Ga. Tech 35, Notre Dame 28
1955	Vanderbilt 25, Auburn 13	1977	Pittsburgh 34, Clemson 3	2000	Miami-FL 28, Ga. Tech 13
1956	Georgia Tech 21, Pittsburgh 14	1978	Clemson 17, Ohio St. 15	2001	Va. Tech 41, Clemson 20
1957	Tennessee 3, Texas A&M 0	1979	N. Carolina 17, Michigan 15	2002	Florida St. 30, Va. Tech 17
1958	Mississippi 7, Florida 3	1980	Pittsburgh 37, S. Carolina 9	2003	N.C. State 28, Notre Dame 6
1960*	Arkansas 14, Georgia Tech 7	1981	N. Carolina 31, Arkansas 27	2004	Maryland 41, West Va. 7
1960†	Florida 13, Baylor 12	1982	Florida St. 31, West Va. 12	* January game from 1946-54, 1960,
1961	Penn St. 30, Georgia Tech 15	1983	Florida 14, Iowa 6	1965, 1971, 1989, 1991 and since
1962	Florida 17, Penn St. 7	1984	Oklahoma St. 21, S. Carolina 14	1996.
1963	N. Carolina 35, Air Force 0	1985	Florida St. 34, Oklahoma St. 23	† December game from 1954-58, 1960-
1965*	Florida St. 36, Oklahoma 19	1986	Clemson 27, Stanford 21	63, 1965-69, 1971-87, 1989 and
1965†	Georgia Tech 31, Texas Tech 21	1987	LSU 30, S. Carolina 13	1991-94.
1966	Tennessee 18, Syracuse 12	1989*	Georgia 34, Michigan St. 27		

Holiday Bowl

City: San Diego, Calif. **Stadium:** Qualcomm. **Capacity:** 71,000. **Playing surface:** Grass. **First game:** Dec. 22, 1978. **Playing site:** San Diego/Jack Murphy Stadium (since 1978). Name changed to Qualcomm Stadium in 1997. **Corporate title sponsors:** SeaWorld (1986-90), Thrifty Car Rental (1991-94), Chrysler-Plymouth Division of Chrysler Corp. (1995-97), U.S. Filter/Culligan Water Tech. (1998-2001) and Pacific Life Insurance Co. (since 2002).

Automatic berths: WAC champion vs. at-large opponent (1978-84, 1986-90 seasons); WAC champ vs. second pick from Big 10 (1991 season); WAC champ vs. third pick from Big 10 (1992-94 seasons); choice of WAC champion, if available, or second pick from Pac-10, if available vs. third pick from Big 12, if available (1995-99); second pick from Pac-10 vs. third pick from Big 12 (since 2000).

Multiple wins: BYU (4); Kansas St. (3) Iowa and Ohio St. (2).

Year		Year		Year	
1978†	Navy 23, BYU 16	1987	Iowa 20, Wyoming 19	1996	Colorado 33, Washington 21
1979	Indiana 38, BYU 37	1988	Oklahoma St. 62, Wyoming 14	1997	Colorado St. 35, Missouri 24
1980	BYU 46, SMU 45	1989	Penn St. 50, BYU 39	1998	Arizona 23, Nebraska 20
1981	BYU 38, Washington St. 36	1990	Texas A&M 65, BYU 14	1999	Kansas St. 24, Washington 20
1982	Ohio St. 47, BYU 17	1991	13-13, Iowa vs BYU	2000	Oregon 35, Texas 30
1983	BYU 21, Missouri 17	1992	Hawaii 27, Illinois 17	2001	Texas 47, Washington 43
1984	BYU 24, Michigan 17	1993	Ohio St. 28, BYU 21	2002	Kansas St. 34, Arizona St. 27
1985	Arkansas 18, Arizona St. 17	1994	Michigan 24, Colo. St. 14	2003	Washington St. 28, Texas 20
1986	Iowa 39, San Diego St. 38	1995	Kansas St. 54, Colorado St. 21	†December game since 1978.	

Outback Bowl

City: Tampa, Fla. **Stadium:** Raymond James. **Capacity:** 66,005. **Playing surface:** Grass. **First game:** Dec. 23, 1986. **Name change:** Hall of Fame Bowl (1986-95) and Outback Bowl (since 1995). **Playing sites:** Tampa/Houlihan's Stadium (1986-98) and Raymond James Stadium (since 1999). **Corporate title sponsor:** Outback Steakhouse, Inc. (since 1995).

Automatic berths: Fourth pick from ACC vs. fourth pick from Big 10 (1993-94 seasons); third pick from Big 10, if available, vs. third pick from SEC, if available (1995-99); fourth pick from Big 10 vs. third pick from SEC (2000 season).

Multiple wins: Michigan (3); Georgia, Penn St., South Carolina and Syracuse (2).

Year		Year		Year	
1986†	Boston College 27, Georgia 24	1994	Michigan 42, N.C. State 7	2001	S. Carolina 24, Ohio St. 7
1988*	Michigan 28, Alabama 24	1995	Wisconsin 34, Duke 20	2002	S. Carolina 31, Ohio St. 28
1989	Syracuse 23, LSU 10	1996	Penn St. 43, Auburn 14	2003	Michigan 38, Florida 30
1990	Auburn 31, Ohio St. 14	1997	Alabama 17, Michigan 14	2004	Iowa 37, Florida 17
1991	Clemson 30, Illinois 0	1998	Georgia 33, Wisconsin 6		
1992	Syracuse 24, Ohio St. 17	1999	Penn St. 26, Kentucky 14	†December game in 1986.	
1993	Tennessee 38, Boston Col. 23	2000	Georgia 28, Purdue 25	*January game since 1988.	

Peach Bowl

City: Atlanta, Ga. **Stadium:** Georgia Dome. **Capacity:** 71,228. **Playing surface:** Turf. **First game:** Dec. 30, 1968. **Playing sites:** Grant Field (1968-70), Atlanta-Fulton County Stadium (1971-92) and Georgia Dome (since 1993). **Corporate title sponsor:** Chick-fil-A (since 1998).

Automatic berths: Third pick from ACC vs. at-large opponent (1992 season); third pick from ACC vs. fourth pick from SEC (1993-94 seasons); third pick from ACC, if available, vs. fourth pick from SEC, if available (since 1995 season).

Multiple wins: N.C. State (4); LSU and West Virginia (3); Auburn, Clemson, Georgia, North Carolina and Virginia (2).

Year		Year		Year	
1968†	LSU 31, Florida St. 27	1982	Iowa 28, Tennessee 22	1996	LSU 10, Clemson 7
1969	West Va. 14, S. Carolina 3	1983	Florida St. 28, N. Carolina 3	1998*	Auburn 21, Clemson 17
1970	Arizona St. 48, N. Carolina 26	1984	Virginia 27, Purdue 24	1998†	Georgia 35, Virginia 33
1971	Mississippi 41, Georgia Tech 18	1985	Army 31, Illinois 29	1999	Mississippi St. 17, Clemson 7
1972	N.C. State 49, West Va. 13	1986	Va. Tech 25, N.C. State 24	2000	LSU 28, Ga. Tech 14
1973	Georgia 17, Maryland 16	1988*	Tennessee 27, Indiana 22	2001	N. Carolina 16, Auburn 10
1974	6-6, Vanderbilt vs Texas Tech	1988†	N.C. State 28, Iowa 23	2002	Maryland 30, Tennessee 3
1975	West Va. 13, N.C. State 10	1989	Syracuse 19, Georgia 18	2004*	Clemson 27, Tennessee 14
1976	Kentucky 21, N. Carolina 0	1990	Auburn 27, Indiana 23		
1977	N.C. State 24, Iowa St. 14	1992*	E. Carolina 37, N.C. State 34	†December game from 1968-79,
1978	Purdue 41, Georgia Tech 21	1993	N. Carolina 21, Miss. St. 17	1981-86, 1988-90, 1993, 1995,
1979	Baylor 24, Clemson 18	1993†	Clemson 14, Kentucky 13	1996, 1998 and 1999-2002.
1981*	Miami-FL 20, Va. Tech 10	1995*	N.C. State 24, Miss. St. 24	*January game in 1981, 1988, 1992-
1981†	West Va. 26, Florida 6	1995†	Virginia 34, Georgia 27	93, 1995 and 1998 and 2004.

Alamo Bowl

City: San Antonio, Tex. **Stadium:** Alamodome. **Capacity:** 65,000. **Playing surface:** Turf. **First game:** Dec. 31, 1993. **Playing site:** Alamodome (since 1993). **Corporate title sponsor:** Builders Square (1993-98), Sylvania (1999-2001) and Mastercard (2004).

Automatic berths: third pick from SWC vs. fourth pick from Pac-10 (1993-94 seasons); fourth pick from Big 10, if available vs. fourth pick from Big 12, if available (1995-99 seasons); fourth pick from Big 12 vs. third pick from Big 10 (2000 season).

Multiple wins: Iowa, Nebraska and Purdue (2).

Year		Year		Year	
1993†	California 37, Iowa 3	1997	Purdue 33, Oklahoma St. 20	2001	Iowa 19, Texas Tech 16
1994	Washington 10, Baylor 3	1998	Purdue 37, Kansas St. 34	2002	Wisconsin 31, Colorado 28 (OT)
1995	Texas A&M 22, Michigan 20	1999	Penn St. 24, Texas A&M 0	2003	Nebraska 17, Michigan St. 3
1996	Iowa 27, Texas Tech 0	2000	Nebraska 66, Northwestern 17	†December game since 1993.

Sun Bowl

City: El Paso, Tex. **Stadium:** Sun Bowl. **Capacity:** 52,000. **Playing surface:** Turf. **First game:** Jan. 1, 1936. **Name changes:** Sun Bowl (1936-85), John Hancock Sun Bowl (1986-88), John Hancock Bowl (1989-93) and Sun Bowl (since 1994). **Playing sites:** Kidd Field (1936-62) and Sun Bowl (since 1963). **Corporate title sponsors:** John Hancock Financial Services (1986-93), Norwest Bank (1996-98), Wells Fargo (1999-2003) and Vitalis (since 2004).

Automatic berths: Eighth pick from 8-team Bowl Coalition pool vs. at-large opponent (1992); Seventh and eighth picks from 8-team Bowl Coalition pool (1993-94 seasons); third pick from Pac-10, if available, vs. fifth pick from Big 10, if available (since 1995 season).

Multiple wins: Texas Western/UTEP (5); Alabama and Wyoming (3); Nebraska, New Mexico St., North Carolina, Oklahoma, Oregon, Pittsburgh, Southwestern, Stanford, Texas, West Texas St. and West Virginia (2).

Year		Year		Year	
1936*	14-14, Hardin-Simmons vs New Mexico St.	1958†	Wyoming 14, Hardin-Simmons 6	1983	Alabama 28, SMU 7
1937	Hardin-Simmons 34, Texas Mines 6	1959	New Mexico St. 28, N. Texas 8	1984	Maryland 28, Tennessee 27
1938	West Va. 7, Texas Tech 6	1960	New Mexico St. 20, Utah St. 13	1985	13-13, Georgia vs Arizona
1939	Utah 26, New Mexico 0	1961	Villanova 17, Wichita 9	1986	Alabama 28, Washington 6
1940	0-0, Catholic U. vs Arizona St.	1962	West Texas 15, Ohio U. 14	1987	Oklahoma St. 35, West Va. 33
1941	W. Reserve 26, Arizona St. 13	1963	Oregon 21, SMU 14	1988	Alabama 29, Army 28
1942	Tulsa 6, Texas Tech 0	1964	Georgia 7, Texas Tech 0	1989	Pittsburgh 31, Texas A&M 28
1943	Second Air Force 13, Hardin-Simmons 7	1965	Texas Western 13, TCU 12	1990	Michigan St. 17, USC 16
1944	Southwestern 7, New Mexico 0	1966	Wyoming 28, Florida St. 20	1991	UCLA 6, Illinois 3
1945	Southwestern 35, U. of Mexico 0	1967	UTEP 14, Mississippi 7	1992	Baylor 20, Arizona 15
1946	New Mexico 34, Denver 24	1968	Auburn 34, Arizona 10	1993	Oklahoma 41, Texas Tech 10
1947	Cincinnati 18, Virginia 6	1969	Nebraska 45, Georgia 6	1994	Texas 35, N. Carolina 31
1948	Miami-OH 13, Texas Tech 12	1970	Georgia Tech 17, Texas Tech 9	1995	Iowa 38, Washington 18
1949	West Va. 21, Texas Mines 12	1971	LSU 33, Iowa St. 15	1996	Stanford 38, Michigan St. 0
1950	Tex. Western 33, Georgetown 20	1972	N. Carolina 32, Texas Tech 28	1997	Arizona St. 17, Iowa 7
1951	West Texas 14, Cincinnati 13	1973	Missouri 34, Auburn 17	1998	TCU 28, USC 19
1952	Texas Tech 25, Pacific 14	1974	Miss. St. 26, N. Carolina 24	1999	Oregon 24, Minnesota 20
1953	Pacific 26, Southern Miss. 7	1975	Pittsburgh 33, Kansas 19	2000	Wisconsin 21, UCLA 20
1954	Tex. Western 37, So. Miss. 14	1977*	Texas A&M 37, Florida 14	2001	Washington St. 33, Purdue 27
1955	Tex. Western 47, Florida St. 20	1977†	Stanford 24, LSU 14	2002	Purdue 34, Washington 24
1956	Wyoming 21, Texas Tech 14	1978	Texas 42, Maryland 0	2003	Minnesota 31, Oregon 30
1957	Geo. Wash. 13, Tex. Western 0	1979	Washington 14, Texas 7	*January game from 1936-58 and in 1977.
1958*	Louisville 34, Drake 20	1980	Nebraska 31, Miss. St. 17	†December game from 1958-75 and since 1977.
		1981	Oklahoma 40, Houston 14		
		1982	N. Carolina 26, Texas 10		

Bowl Games (Cont.)
Insight Bowl

City: Phoenix, Ariz. **Stadium:** Bank One Ballpark. **Capacity:** 42,915. **Playing surface:** Grass. **First game:** Dec. 31, 1989. **Name change:** Copper Bowl (1989-1996), Insight.com Bowl (1997-2001) and Insight Bowl (since 2002). **Playing sites:** Arizona Stadium (1989-2000) and Bank One Ballpark (since 2000). **Corporate title sponsors:** Domino's Pizza (1990-91), Weiser Lock (1992-1996) and Insight Enterprises (since 1997).

    Automatic berths: Third pick from WAC vs. at-large opponent (1992 season); third pick from WAC vs. fourth pick from Big Eight (1993-94 seasons); second pick from WAC vs. sixth pick from Big 12 (1995-97); third pick from Big East or Notre Dame, if available vs. fifth pick from Big 12, if available (since 1998 season).

    Multiple wins: Arizona and California (2).

Year		Year		Year	
1989†	Arizona 17, N.C. State 10	1995	Texas Tech 55, Air Force 41	2001	Syracuse 26, Kansas St. 3
1990	California 17, Wyoming 15	1996	Wisconsin 38, Utah 10	2002	Pittsburgh 38, Oregon St. 13
1991	Indiana 24, Baylor 0	1997	Arizona 20, New Mexico 14	2003	California 52, Virginia Tech 49
1992	Washington St. 31, Utah 28	1998	Missouri 34, W. Virginia 31	†December game since 1989.
1993	Kansas St. 52, Wyoming 17	1999	Colorado 62, Boston College 28		
1994	BYU 31, Oklahoma 6	2000	Iowa St. 37, Pittsburgh 29		

Liberty Bowl

City: Memphis, Tenn. **Stadium:** Liberty Bowl Memorial. **Capacity:** 62,380. **Playing surface:** Grass. **First game:** Dec. 19, 1959. **Playing sites:** Municipal Stadium in Philadelphia (1959-63), Convention Hall in Atlantic City, N.J. (1964), Memphis Memorial Stadium (1965-75) and Liberty Bowl Memorial Stadium (since 1976). Memphis Memorial Stadium renamed Liberty Bowl Memorial in 1976. **Corporate title sponsors:** St. Jude's Hospital (since 1993), AXA/Equitable (since 1997).

    Automatic berths: Commander-in-Chief's Trophy winner (Army, Navy or Air Force) vs. at-large opponent (1989-92 seasons); none (1993 season); first pick from independent group of Cincinnati, East Carolina, Memphis, Southern Miss. and Tulane vs. at-large opponent (for 1994 and '95 seasons); Conference USA champion vs. fourth pick from the Big East (1996-97 seasons); Conference USA champion, if available, vs. fifth, sixth or seventh pick or at-large from SEC (1998-99 seasons); Mountain West champion vs. Conference USA champion, if available (2000 season).

    Multiple wins: Mississippi (4); Penn St. and Tennessee (3); Air Force, Alabama, Louisville, N.C. State, Southern Miss., Syracuse and Tulane (2).

Year		Year		Year	
1959†	Penn St. 7, Alabama 0	1975	USC 20, Texas A&M 0	1991	Air Force 38, Mississippi St. 15
1960	Penn St. 41, Oregon 12	1976	Alabama 36, UCLA 6	1992	Mississippi 13, Air Force 0
1961	Syracuse 15, Miami-FL 14	1977	Nebraska 21, N. Carolina 17	1993	Louisville 18, Michigan St. 7
1962	Oregon St. 6, Villanova 0	1978	Missouri 20, LSU 15	1994	Illinois 30, E. Carolina 0
1963	Mississippi St. 16, N.C. State 12	1979	Penn St. 9, Tulane 6	1995	E. Carolina 19, Stanford 13
1964	Utah 32, West Virginia 6	1980	Purdue 28, Missouri 25	1996	Syracuse 30, Houston 17
1965	Mississippi 13, Auburn 7	1981	Ohio St. 31, Navy 28	1997	Southern Miss. 41, Pittsburgh 7
1966	Miami-FL 14, Virginia Tech 7	1982	Alabama 21, Illinois 15	1998	Tulane 41, BYU 27
1967	N.C. State 14, Georgia 7	1983	Notre Dame 19, Boston Col. 18	1999	Southern Miss. 23, Colorado St. 17
1968	Mississippi 34, Virginia Tech 17	1984	Auburn 21, Arkansas 15	2000	Colorado St. 22, Louisville 17
1969	Colorado 47, Alabama 33	1985	Baylor 21, LSU 7	2001	Louisville 28, BYU 10
1970	Tulane 17, Colorado 3	1986	Tennessee 21, Minnesota 14	2002	TCU 17, Colorado St. 3
1971	Tennessee 14, Arkansas 13	1987	Georgia 20, Arkansas 17	2003	Utah 17, Southern Miss. 0
1972	Georgia Tech 31, Iowa St. 30	1988	Indiana 34, S. Carolina 10		
1973	N.C. State 31, Kansas 18	1989	Mississippi 42, Air Force 29	† December game since 1959.
1974	Tennessee 7, Maryland 3	1990	Air Force 23, Ohio St. 11		

Tangerine Bowl

City: Orlando, Fla. **Stadium:** Florida Citrus. **Capacity:** 65,525. **Playing surface:** Grass. **First game:** Dec. 28, 1990. **Name change:** Blockbuster Bowl (1990-93), Carquest Bowl (1994-97), Micron PC Bowl (1998), MicronPC.com Bowl (1999-2000) and Tangerine Bowl (since 2001). The game was called the Sunshine Football Classic for a short time in the offseason after Carquest Auto Parts dropped its sponsorship and before Micron signed on. Also, this game should not be confused with the Tangerine Bowl that became the Citrus Bowl in 1982. **Playing sites:** Joe Robbie Stadium (1990-2000). Name changed to Pro Player Stadium in 1996. **Corporate title sponsors:** Blockbuster Video (1990-93), Carquest Auto Parts (1993-97), Micron Electronics (1998-2000) and Mazda (since 2002).

    Automatic berths: Penn St. vs. seventh pick from 8-team Bowl Coalition pool (1992 season); third pick from Big East vs. fifth pick from SEC (1993-94 seasons); third pick from Big East vs. fifth pick from SEC (1995 season); third pick from Big East vs. fourth pick from ACC (1996-97 seasons); sixth pick from Big Ten, if available, vs. fourth pick from ACC, if available (1998-2000 seasons); fifth pick from ACC vs. fifth pick from Big East (2001).

    Multiple wins: Miami-FL and N.C. State (2).

Year		Year		Year	
1990†	Florida St. 24, Penn St. 17	1996	Miami-FL 31, Virginia 21	2002	Texas Tech 55, Clemson 15
1991	Alabama 30, Colorado 25	1997	Ga. Tech 35, W. Virginia 30	2003	N.C. State 56, Kansas 26
1993*	Stanford 24, Penn St. 3	1998	Miami-FL 46, N.C. State 23	†December game from 1990-91 and
1994	Boston College 31, Virginia 13	1999	Illinois 63, Virginia 21	since 1995.
1995	S. Carolina 24, West Va. 21	2000	N.C. State 38, Minnesota 30	*January game 1993-95.
1995†	N. Carolina 20, Arkansas 10	2001	Pittsburgh 34, N.C. State 19		

Humanitarian Bowl

City: Boise, Idaho. **Stadium:** Bronco. **Capacity:** 30,000. **Playing surface:** Turf. **First game:** Dec. 29, 1997. **Playing sites:** Bronco Stadium (since 1997). **Corporate title sponsors:** World Sports Humanitarian Hall of Fame (since 1997) and Crucial.com (1999-2002), MPC Computers (starting in Dec. 2004).
    Automatic berths: Big West champion, if available, vs. at-large (1997-2002) WAC vs. ACC (since 2004).
    Multiple wins: Boise St. (3).

Year		Year		Year	
1997†	Cincinnati 35, Utah St. 19	2000	Boise St. 38, UTEP 23	2004*	Georgia Tech 52, Tulsa 10
1998	Idaho 42, Southern Miss. 35	2001	Clemson 49, La. Tech 24		†December game 1997-2002.
1999	Boise St. 34, Louisville 31	2002	Boise St. 34, Iowa St. 16		*January game in 2004

Las Vegas Bowl

City: Las Vegas, Nev. **Stadium:** Sam Boyd. **Capacity:** 40,000. **Playing surface:** Turf. **First game:** Dec. 18, 1992. **Playing site:** Sam Boyd Stadium (since 1992). **Corporate title sponsors:** EA Sports (1999-2000) Sega Sports (2001-02).
    Automatic berths: Mid-American champion vs. Big West champion (1992-96 season); none (1997 season); second or third pick from WAC, if available vs. at-large (1998-2000), second pick from Mountain West vs. fifth pick from Pac-10 (since 2001).
    Multiple wins: Fresno St. (4); UNLV (3); Bowling Green, San Jose St., Toledo and Utah (2).

Year		Year		Year	
1981†	Toledo 27, San Jose St. 25	1990	San Jose St. 48, C. Michigan 24	1999	Utah 17, Fresno St. 16
1982	Fresno St. 29, Bowling Green 8	1991	Bowling Green 28, Fresno St. 21	2000	UNLV 31, Arkansas 14
1983	Northern Ill. 20, CS-Fullerton 13	1992	Bowling Green 35, Nevada 34	2001	Utah 10, USC 6
1984*	UNLV 30, Toledo 13	1993	Utah St. 42, Ball St. 33	2002	UCLA 27, New Mexico 13
1985	Fresno St. 51, Bowling Green 7	1994	UNLV 52, C. Michigan 24	2003	Oregon St. 55, New Mexico 14
1986	San Jose St. 37, Miami-OH 7	1995	Toledo 40, Nevada 37 (OT)		†December game since 1981.
1987	E. Michigan 30, San Jose St. 27	1996	Nevada 18, Ball St. 15		*Toledo later ruled winner of 1984
1988	Fresno St. 35, W. Michigan 30	1997	Oregon 41, Air Force 13		game by forfeit because UNLV used
1989	Fresno St. 27, Ball St. 6	1998	N. Carolina 20, San Diego St. 13		ineligible players.

    Note: The MAC and Big West champs met in a bowl game from 1981 to 1996, originally in Fresno at the California Bowl (1981-88, 1992) and California Raisin Bowl (1989-91). The results from 1981-91 are included above.

Independence Bowl

City: Shreveport, La. **Stadium:** Independence. **Capacity:** 50,832. **Playing surface:** Grass. **First game:** Dec. 13, 1976. **Playing site:** Independence Stadium (since 1976). **Corporate title sponsors:** Poulan/Weed Eater (1990-97), Sanford (1998-2000) and MainStay (since 2001). **Automatic berths:** Southland Conference champion vs. at-large opponent (1976-81 seasons); none (1982-95 seasons); fifth pick from SEC, if available, vs. at-large (1995-97 season); fifth, sixth or seventh pick from SEC, if available, vs. at-large (1998-99 season); sixth pick from Big 12 vs. SEC (since 2000 season).
    Multiple wins: Mississippi (3); Air Force, LSU and Southern Miss (2).

Year		Year		Year	
1976†	McNeese St. 20, Tulsa 16	1986	Mississippi 20, Texas Tech 17	1996	Auburn 32, Army 29
1977	La. Tech 24, Louisville 14	1987	Washington 24, Tulane 12	1997	LSU 27, Notre Dame 9
1978	E. Carolina 35, La. Tech 13	1988	Southern Miss 38, UTEP 18	1998	Mississippi 35, Texas Tech 18
1979	Syracuse 31, McNeese St. 7	1989	Oregon 27, Tulsa 24	1999	Mississippi 27, Oklahoma 25
1980	Southern Miss 16, McNeese St. 14	1990	34-34, La. Tech vs Maryland	2000	Mississippi St. 43, Texas A&M 41
1981	Texas A&M 33, Oklahoma St. 16	1991	Georgia 24, Arkansas 15	2001	Alabama 14, Iowa St. 13
1982	Wisconsin 14, Kansas St. 3	1992	Wake Forest 39, Oregon 35	2002	Mississippi 27, Nebraska 23
1983	Air Force 9, Mississippi 3	1993	Va. Tech 45, Indiana 20	2003	Arkansas 27, Missouri 14
1984	Air Force 23, Va. Tech 7	1994	Virginia 20, TCU 10		†December game since 1976.
1985	Minnesota 20, Clemson 13	1995	LSU 45, Michigan St. 26		

Motor City Bowl

City: Detroit, Mich. **Stadium:** Ford Field. **Capacity:** 65,000. **Playing surface:** Turf. **First game:** Dec. 26, 1997. **Playing sites:** Pontiac Silverdome (1997-2001) and Ford Field (since 2002). **Corporate title sponsor:** Ford Division of Ford Motor Company (since 1997), Daimler Chrysler and General Motors (since 2002). **Automatic berths:** Mid-American champions vs at-large (1997-99 season); Mid-American champions vs. fourth pick from Conference USA (2000 season).
    Multiple wins: Marshall (3).

Year		Year		Year	
1997†	Mississippi 34, Marshall 31	2000	Marshall 25, Cincinnati 14	2003	Bowling Green 28, N'western 24
1998	Marshall 48, Louisville 29	2001	Toledo 23, Cincinnati 16		†December game since 1997.
1999	Marshall 21, BYU 3	2002	Boston College 51, Toledo 25		

Music City Bowl

City: Nashville, Tenn. **Stadium:** The Coliseum. **Capacity:** 67,000. **Playing surface:** Grass. **First game:** Dec. 29, 1998. **Playing sites:** Vanderbilt Stadium (1998) and Adelphia Coliseum (since 1999). **Corporate title sponsors:** American General (1998), HomePoint.com (1999-2000) and Gaylord Hotels (since 2002). **Automatic berths:** sixth choice from the SEC, if available, vs. at-large (1998-99 season); fourth pick from Big East, if available vs. SEC (2000 season).

Year		Year		Year	
1998†	Va. Tech 38, Alabama 7	2000	West Va. 49, Mississippi 38	2002	Minnesota 29, Arkansas 14
1999	Syracuse 20, Kentucky 13	2001	Boston College 20, Georgia 16	2003	Auburn 28, Wisconsin 14
					†December game since 1998.

Bowl Games (Cont.)

GMAC Bowl

City: Mobile, Ala. **Stadium:** Ladd-Peebles. **Capacity:** 40,646. **Playing surface:** Grass. **First game:** Dec. 22, 1999. **Name change:** Mobile Bowl (1999-2000), GMAC Bowl (since 2001). **Playing sites:** Ladd-Peebles Stadium (since 1999). **Corporate title sponsors:** GMAC Financial Services (since 2001). **Automatic berths:** WAC champions (if team is from the east) or second pick from WAC vs. second pick from Conference USA, if available (2000 season). **Multiple wins:** Marshall (2).

Year		Year		Year	
1999†	TCU 28, E. Carolina 14	2001	Marshall 64, East Carolina 61	2003	Miami-OH 49, Louisville 28
2000	So. Miss 28, TCU 21	2002	Marshall 38, Louisville 15	†December game since 1999.	

Houston Bowl

City: Houston, Tex. **Stadium:** Reliant. **Capacity:** 69,500. **Playing surface:** Turf. **First game:** Dec. 27, 2000. **Name change:** GalleryFurniture.com Bowl (2000-01), Houston Bowl (2002) and EV1.net Houston Bowl (since 2003). **Playing sites:** Astrodome (2000-2002), Reliant Stadium (since 2003). **Corporate title sponsors:** GalleryFurniture.com (2000-2002) and EV1 (since 2003). **Automatic berths:** Big 12 vs. Conference USA.

Year		Year		
2000†	E. Carolina 40, Tex. Tech 27	2002	Oklahoma St. 33, So. Miss. 23	†December game since 2000.
2001	Texas A&M 28, TCU 9	2003	Texas Tech 38, Navy 14	

Silicon Valley Classic

City: San Jose, Calif. **Stadium:** Spartan. **Capacity:** 30,578. **Playing surface:** Grass. **First game:** Dec. 31, 2000. **Playing sites:** Spartan Stadium (since 2000). **Corporate title sponsors:** none. **Automatic berths:** WAC vs. at-large. **Multiple wins:** Fresno St. (2).

Year		Year		
2000†	Air Force 37, Fresno St. 34	2002	Fresno St. 30, Ga. Tech 21	†December game since 2000.
2001	Michigan St. 44, Fresno St. 35	2003	Fresno St. 17, UCLA 9	

New Orleans Bowl

City: New Orleans, La. **Stadium:** Louisiana Superdome. **Capacity:** 70,200. **Playing surface:** Turf. **First game:** Dec. 18, 2001. **Playing sites:** Louisiana Superdome (since 2001). **Corporate title sponsors:** none. **Automatic berths:** Sun Belt champion vs. Conference USA (since 2002).

Year		Year		
2001†	Colorado St. 45, North Texas 20	2003	Memphis 27, North Texas 17	
2002	North Texas 24, Cincinnati 19			†December game since 2001.

San Francisco Bowl

City: San Francisco, Calif. **Stadium:** SBC Park. **Capacity:** 37,000. **Playing surface:** Grass. **First game:** Dec. 31, 2002. **Playing site:** SBC (formerly known as Pacific Bell) Park (since 2002). **Corporate title sponsors:** Diamond Walnut (since 2002). **Automatic berths:** Mountain West vs. Big East or Notre Dame (since 2002).

Year		
2002†	Virginia Tech 20, Air Force 13	
2003	Boston Col. 35, Colorado St. 21	†December game since 2002.

Continental Tire Bowl

City: Charlotte, N.C. **Stadium:** Bank of America. **Capacity:** 73,367. **Playing surface:** Grass. **First game:** Dec. 28, 2002. **Playing site:** Bank of America (formerly known as Ericsson) Stadium (since 2002). **Corporate title sponsors:** Continental Tire North America (since 2002). **Automatic berths:** ACC vs. Big East or Notre Dame (since 2002). **Multiple wins:** Virginia (2).

Year		
2002†	Virginia 48, West Va. 22	
2003	Virginia 23, Pittsburgh 16	†December game since 2002.

Hawaii Bowl

City: Honolulu, Hi. **Stadium:** Aloha Bowl. **Capacity:** 50,000. **Playing surface:** Turf. **First game:** Dec. 25, 2002. **Playing sites:** Aloha Bowl (since 2002). **Corporate title sponsors:** ConAgra Foods (2002) and Sheraton Hotels & Resorts (since 2003). **Automatic berths:** Hawaii (if bowl eligible) otherwise another WAC school vs. Conference USA (since 2002).

Year		
2002†	Tulane 36, Hawaii 28	
2003	Hawaii 54, Houston 48 3OT	†December game since 2002.

Forth Worth Bowl

City: Fort Worth, Tex. **Stadium:** Amon Carter. **Capacity:** 46,000. **Playing surface:** Grass **First game:** Dec. 23, 2003. **Playing sites:** Amon Carter Stadium (since 2003). **Corporate title sponsors:** PlainsCapital Corp. (since 2003). **Automatic berths:** Big 12 vs. Conference USA (since 2003).

Year		
2003†	Bosie St. 34, TCU 31	†December game since 2003.

Division I-A Teams

Schools classified as Division I-A for at least 10 years; through 2003 season (including bowl games).

Top 25 Winning Percentage

		Yrs	Gm	W	L	T	Pct	Bowls App	Record	2003 Season Bowl	Record
1	Notre Dame	115	1095	796	257	42	.746	25	13-12-0	none	5-7
2	Michigan	124	1141	833	272	36	.746	35	18-17-0	lost Rose	10-3
3	Alabama*	109	1094	758	293	43	.713	51	29-19-3	none	4-9
4	Oklahoma	109	1074	737	284	53	.711	37	23-13-1	lost Sugar	12-2
5	Ohio St.	114	1103	756	294	53	.709	35	16-19-0	won Fiesta	11-2
6	Texas	111	1118	776	309	33	.709	43	20-21-2	lost Holiday	10-3
7	Nebraska	114	1132	781	311	40	.708	42	21-21-0	won Alamo	10-3
8	Tennessee*	107	1090	736	302	52	.699	44	23-21-0	lost Peach	10-3
9	USC	111	1058	707	297	54	.694	42	27-15-0	won Rose	12-1
10	Penn St.	117	1128	756	331	41	.688	37	23-12-2	none	3-9
11	Florida St.*	57	633	419	197	17	.675	32	18-12-2	lost Orange	10-3
12	Miami-OH*	115	1011	624	343	44	.639	8	6-2-0	won GMAC	13-1
13	Georgia	110	1097	673	370	54	.638	39	21-15-3	won Capital One	11-3
14	Washington*	114	1041	638	353	50	.637	29	14-14-1	none	6-6
15	Miami-FL	77	811	507	285	19	.637	28	16-12-0	won Orange	11-2
16	LSU*	110	1065	649	369	47	.631	35	17-17-1	won Sugar	13-1
17	Auburn*	111	1060	634	379	47	.620	30	16-12-2	won Music City	8-5
18	Arizona St.	91	841	507	310	24	.617	20	10-9-1	none	5-7
19	Florida	97	989	590	359	40	.617	31	14-17-0	lost Outback	8-5
20	Colorado*	114	1062	635	391	36	.615	25	11-14-0	none	5-7
21	Central Michigan	103	884	522	326	36	.611	2	0-2-0	none	3-9
22	Texas A&M	109	1079	627	404	48	.603	27	13-14-0	none	4-8
23	Syracuse	114	1135	658	428	49	.601	21	12-8-1	none	6-6
24	UCLA	85	872	505	330	37	.600	25	12-12-1	lost Silicon Valley Classic	6-7
25	Army	114	1079	622	406	51	.600	4	2-2-0	none	0-13

*Includes games forfeited following rulings by the NCAA Executive Council and/or the Committee on Infractions.

Top 50 Victories

		Wins			Wins			Wins
1	Michigan	833	18	Miami-OH	624	35	Boston College	561
2	Notre Dame	796	19	Georgia Tech	623	36	Rutgers	558
3	Nebraska	781		West Virginia	623	37	Missouri	557
4	Texas	776	21	Army	622	38	Wisconsin	556
5	Alabama	758	22	Pittsburgh	620	39	Utah	547
6	Penn St	756	23	Arkansas	619	40	Illinois	542
	Ohio St	756	24	North Carolina	613	41	Purdue	538
8	Oklahoma	737	25	Minnesota	609	42	Stanford	533
9	Tennessee	736	26	Virginia Tech	605	43	Kentucky	532
10	USC	707	27	Clemson	594	44	Vanderbilt	531
11	Georgia	673	28	Florida	590	45	Iowa	529
12	Syracuse	658	29	Navy	589	46	Kansas	526
13	LSU	649	30	Mississippi	583	47	Central Michigan	522
14	Washington	638	31	Michigan St	580	48	Arizona	519
15	Colorado	635	32	Virginia	578	49	Oregon	517
16	Auburn	634	33	California	574	50	Louisiana Tech	510
17	Texas A&M	627	34	Maryland	566		TCU	510

Top 30 Bowl Appearances

		App	Record			App	Record			App	Record
1	Alabama	51	29-19-3	12	Arkansas	34	11-20-3	23	Notre Dame	25	13-12-0
2	Tennessee	44	23-21-0	13	Georgia Tech	32	21-11-0		Colorado	25	11-14-0
3	Texas	43	20-21-2		Florida St	32	18-12-2		UCLA	25	12-12-1
4	USC	42	27-15-0	15	Mississippi	31	19-12-0	26	North Carolina	24	12-12-0
	Nebraska	42	21-21-0		Florida	31	14-17-0	27	BYU	23	7-15-1
6	Georgia	39	21-15-3	17	Auburn	30	16-12-2	28	Pittsburgh	23	10-13-0
7	Penn St	37	23-12-2	18	Washington	29	14-14-1		West Virginia	23	9-14-0
	Oklahoma	37	23-13-1	19	Miami-FL	28	16-12-0	30	Missouri	22	9-13-0
9	LSU	35	17-17-1	20	Texas A&M	27	13-14-0				
	Ohio St	35	16-19-0		Texas Tech	27	7-19-1				
	Michigan	35	18-17-0		Clemson	27	14-13-0				

Major Conference Champions
Atlantic Coast Conference

Founded in 1953 when charter members all left Southern Conference to form ACC. **Charter members** (7): Clemson, Duke, Maryland, North Carolina, N.C. State, South Carolina and Wake Forest. **Admitted later** (6): Virginia in 1953 (began play in '54), Georgia Tech in 1979 (began play in '83), Florida St. in 1990 (began play in '92), Boston College, Virginia Tech and Miami-FL in 2003 (Virginia Tech and Miami began play in '04, Boston College in '05). **Withdrew later** (1): South Carolina in 1971 (became an independent after '70 season).
2004 playing membership (11): Clemson, Duke, Florida St., Georgia Tech, Maryland, Miami-FL, North Carolina, N.C. State, Virginia, Virginia Tech and Wake Forest.
　　Multiple titles: Clemson (13); Florida St. (11); Maryland (9); Duke and N.C. State (7); North Carolina (5); Georgia Tech & Virginia (2).

Year		Year		Year		Year	
1953	Duke (4-0)	1965	Clemson (5-2)	1980	North Carolina (6-0)	1994	Florida St. (8-0)
	& Maryland (3-0)		& N.C. State (5-2)	1981	Clemson (6-0)	1995	Virginia (7-1)
1954	Duke (4-0)	1966	Clemson (6-1)	1982	Clemson (6-0)		& Florida St. (7-1)
1955	Maryland (4-0)	1967	Clemson (6-0)	1983	Clemson (7-0) †	1996	Florida St. (8-0)
	& Duke (4-0)	1968	N.C. State (6-1)		& Maryland (5-0)	1997	Florida St. (8-0)
1956	Clemson (4-0-1)	1969	South Carolina (6-0)	1984	Maryland (5-0)	1998	Florida St. (7-1)
1957	N.C. State (5-0-1)	1970	Wake Forest (5-1)	1985	Maryland (6-0)		& Georgia Tech (7-1)
1958	Clemson (6-1)	·1971	North Carolina (6-0)	1986	Clemson (5-1-1)	1999	Florida St. (8-0)
1959	Clemson (6-1)	1972	North Carolina (6-0)	1987	Clemson (6-1)	2000	Florida St. (8-0)
1960	Duke (5-1)	1973	N.C. State (6-0)	1988	Clemson (6-1)	2001	Maryland (7-1)
1961	Duke (5-1)	1974	Maryland (6-0)	1989	Virginia (6-1)	2002	Florida St. (7-1)
1962	Duke (6-0)	1975	Maryland (5-0)		& Duke (6-1)	2003	Florida St. (7-1)
1963	North Carolina (6-1)	1976	Maryland (5-0)	1990	Georgia Tech (6-0-1)		
	& N.C. State (6-1)	1977	North Carolina (5-0-1)	1991	Clemson (6-0-1)	†On probation, ineligible	
1964	N.C. State (5-2)	1978	Clemson (6-0)	1992	Florida St. (8-0)	for championship.	
		1979	N.C. State (5-1)	1993	Florida St. (8-0)		

Big East Conference

Founded in 1991 when charter members gave up independent football status to form Big East. **Charter members** (8): Boston College, Miami-FL, Pittsburgh, Rutgers, Syracuse, Temple, Virginia Tech and West Virginia. **Admitted later** (4): Connecticut (a charter member in all other sports) in 2004; Cincinnati, Louisville and South Florida in 2003 (to begin play in '05). **Withdrew later** (4): Boston College, Miami-FL and Virginia Tech in 2003 (Miami and Va. Tech joined ACC for 2004 season, Boston College goes to ACC in 2005). Temple to become an independent following '04 season
2004 playing membership (7): Boston College, Connecticut, Pittsburgh, Rutgers, Syracuse, Temple, and West Virginia.
　　Conference champion: Member schools needed two years to adjust their regular season schedules in order to begin round-robin conference play in 1993. In the meantime, the 1991 and '92 Big East titles went to the highest-ranked member in the final regular season *USA Today*/CNN coaches' poll.
　　Multiple titles: Miami-FL (9); Syracuse (4); Virginia Tech (3); West Virginia (2).

Year		Year		Year		Year	
1991	Miami-FL (2-0, #1)	1995	Virginia Tech (6-1)	1997	Syracuse (6-1)	2002	Miami-FL (7-0)
	& Syracuse (5-0, #16)		& Miami-FL (6-1)	1998	Syracuse (6-1)	2003	Miami-FL (6-1)
1992	Miami-FL (4-0, #1)	1996	Virginia Tech (6-1),	1999	Virginia Tech (7-0)		& West Virginia (6-1)
1993	West Virginia (7-0)		Miami-FL (6-1)	2000	Miami-FL (7-0)		
1994	Miami-FL (7-0)		& Syracuse (6-1)	2001	Miami-FL (7-0)		

Big Ten Conference

Originally founded in 1895 as the Intercollegiate Conference of Faculty Representatives, better known as theWestern Conference. **Charter members** (7): Chicago, Illinois, Michigan, Minnesota, Northwestern, Purdue and Wisconsin. **Admitted later** (4): Indiana and Iowa in 1899; Ohio St. in 1912; Michigan St. in 1950 (began play in '53); Penn St. in 1990 (began play in '93). **Withdrew later** (2): Michigan in 1907 (rejoined in '17); Chicago in 1940 (dropped football after '39 season).
Note: Iowa belonged to both the Western and Missouri Valley conferences from 1907-10.
　　Unofficially called the **Big Ten** from 1912 until Chicago's withdrawal in 1939, then the **Big Nine** from 1940 until Michigan St. began conference play in 1953. Formally named the **Big Ten** in 1984 and has kept the name even after adding Penn St. as its 11th member in 1990.
2004 playing membership (11): Illinois, Indiana, Iowa, Michigan, Michigan St., Minnesota, Northwestern, Ohio St., Penn St., Purdue and Wisconsin.
　　Multiple titles: Michigan (41); Ohio St. (29); Minnesota (18); Illinois (15); Wisconsin (11); Iowa (10); Purdue and Northwestern (8); Chicago and Michigan St. (6); Indiana (2).

Year		Year		Year		Year	
1896	Wisconsin (2-0-1)	1906	Wisconsin (3-0),	1917	Ohio St. (4-0)	1927	Illinois (5-0)
1897	Wisconsin (3-0)		Minnesota (2-0)	1918	Illinois (4-0),		& Minnesota (3-0-1)
1898	Michigan (3-0)		& Michigan (1-0)		Michigan (2-0)	1928	Illinois (4-1)
1899	Chicago (4-0)	1907	Chicago (4-0)		& Purdue (1-0)	1929	Purdue (5-0)
1900	Iowa (3-0-1)	1908	Chicago (5-0)	1919	Illinois (6-1)	1930	Michigan (5-0)
	& Minnesota (3-0-1)	1909	Minnesota (3-0)	1920	Ohio St. (5-0)		& Northwestern (5-0)
1901	Michigan (4-0)	1910	Illinois (4-0)	1921	Iowa (5-0)	1931	Purdue (5-1),
	& Wisconsin (2-0)		& Minnesota (2-0)	1922	Iowa (5-0)		Michigan (5-1)
1902	Michigan (5-0)	1911	Minnesota (3-0-1)		& Michigan (4-0)		& Northwestern (5-1)
1903	Michigan (3-0-1),	1912	Wisconsin (6-0)	1923	Illinois (5-0)	1932	Michigan (6-0)
	Minnesota (3-0-1)	1913	Chicago (7-0)		& Michigan (4-0)		& Purdue (5-0-1)
	& Northwestern (1-0-2)	1914	Illinois (6-0)	1924	Chicago (3-0-3)	1933	Michigan (5-0-1)
1904	Minnesota (3-0)	1915	Minnesota (3-0-1)	1925	Michigan (5-1)		& Minnesota (2-0-4)
	& Michigan (2-0)		& Illinois (3-0-2)	1926	Michigan (5-0)	1934	Minnesota (5-0)
1905	Chicago (7-0)	1916	Ohio St. (4-0)		& Northwestern (5-0)	1935	Minnesota (5-0)
							& Ohio St. (5-0)

Year		Year		Year		Year	
1936	Northwestern (6-0)	1957	Ohio St. (7-0)	1975	Ohio St. (8-0)	1992	Michigan (6-0-2)
1937	Minnesota (5-0)	1958	Iowa (5-1)	1976	Michigan (7-1)	1993	Wisconsin (6-1-1)
1938	Minnesota (4-1)	1959	Wisconsin (5-2)		& Ohio St. (7-1)		& Ohio St. (6-1-1)
1939	Ohio St. (5-1)	1960	Minnesota (5-1)	1977	Michigan (7-1)	1994	Penn St. (8-0)
1940	Minnesota (6-0)		& Iowa (5-1)		& Ohio St. (7-1)	1995	Northwestern (8-0)
1941	Minnesota (5-0)	1961	Ohio St. (6-0)	1978	Michigan (7-1)	1996	Ohio St. (7-1)
1942	Ohio St. (5-1)	1962	Wisconsin (6-1)		& Michigan St. (7-1)		& Northwestern (7-1)
1943	Purdue (6-0)	1963	Illinois (5-1-1)	1979	Ohio St. (8-0)	1997	Michigan (8-0)
	& Michigan (6-0)	1964	Michigan (6-1)	1980	Michigan (8-0)	1998	Ohio St. (7-1),
1944	Ohio St. (6-0)	1965	Michigan St. (7-0)	1981	Iowa (6-2)		Wisconsin (7-1)
1945	Indiana (5-0-1)	1966	Michigan St. (7-0)		& Ohio St. (6-2)		& Michigan (7-1)
1946	Illinois (6-1)	1967	Indiana (6-1),	1982	Michigan (8-1)	1999	Wisconsin (7-1)
1947	Michigan (6-0)		Purdue (6-1)	1983	Illinois (9-0)	2000	Purdue (6-2),
1948	Michigan (6-0)		& Minnesota (6-1)	1984	Ohio St. (7-2)		Michigan (6-2)
1949	Ohio St. (4-1-1)	1968	Ohio St. (7-0)	1985	Iowa (7-1)		& Northwestern (6-2)
	& Michigan (4-1-1)	1969	Ohio St. (6-1)	1986	Michigan (7-1)	2001	Illinois (7-1)
1950	Michigan (4-1-1)		& Michigan (6-1)		& Ohio St. (7-1)	2002	Ohio St. (8-0)
1951	Illinois (5-0-1)	1970	Ohio St. (7-0)	1987	Michigan St. (7-0-1)		& Iowa (8-0)
1952	Wisconsin (4-1-1)	1971	Michigan (8-0)	1988	Michigan (7-0-1)	2003	Michigan (7-1)
	& Purdue (4-1-1)	1972	Ohio St. (7-1)	1989	Michigan (8-0)		
1953	Michigan St. (5-1)		& Michigan (7-1)	1990	Iowa (6-2),		
	& Illinois (5-1)	1973	Ohio St. (7-0-1)		Michigan (6-2),		
1954	Ohio St. (7-0)		& Michigan (7-0-1)		Michigan St. (6-2)		
1955	Ohio St. (6-0)	1974	Ohio St. (7-1)		& Illinois (6-2)		
1956	Iowa (5-1)		& Michigan (7-1)	1991	Michigan (8-.90)		

Big Eight Conference (1907-1996)

Originally founded in 1907 as the Missouri Valley Intercollegiate Athletic Assn. **Charter members** (5): Iowa, Kansas, Missouri, Nebraska and Washington University of St. Louis. **Admitted later** (11): Drake and Iowa St. (then Ames College) in 1908; Kansas St. (then Kansas College of Applied Science and Agriculture) in 1913; Grinnell (Iowa) College in 1919; Oklahoma in 1920; Oklahoma A&M (now Oklahoma St.) in 1925; Colorado in 1947 (began play in '48).

Withdrew later (9): Iowa in 1911 (left for Big Ten after 1910 season), Colorado, Iowa St., Kansas, Kansas St. Missouri, Nebraska, Oklahoma and Oklahoma St. in 1996 (left for Big 12 after 1995 season); **Excluded later** (4): Drake, Grinnell, Oklahoma A&M and Washington-MO (left out when MVIAA cut membership to six teams in 1928).

Streamlined MVIAA unofficially called **Big Six** from 1928-47 with surviving members Iowa St., Kansas, Kansas St., Missouri, Nebraska and Oklahoma. Became the **Big Seven** after 1947 season when Colorado came over from the Skyline Conference, and then the **Big Eight** with the return of Oklahoma A&M in 1957. A&M, which resumed conference play in '60, became Oklahoma St. on July 10, 1957. The MVIAA was officially renamed the Big Eight in 1964. The league folded in 1996 when the existing members formed the newly created Big 12 along with four schools from the Southwest Conference.

Multiple titles: Nebraska (43); Oklahoma (34); Missouri (12); Colorado and Kansas (5); Iowa St. and Oklahoma St. (2).

Year		Year		Year		Year	
1907	Iowa (1-0)	1928	Nebraska (4-0)	1952	Oklahoma (5-0-1)	1976	Colorado (5-2),
	& Nebraska (1-0)	1929	Nebraska (3-0-2)	1953	Oklahoma (6-0)		Oklahoma (5-2)
1908	Kansas (4-0)	1930	Kansas (4-1)	1954	Oklahoma (6-0)		& Oklahoma St.
1909	Missouri (4-0-1)	1931	Nebraska (5-0)	1955	Oklahoma (6-0)		(5-2)
1910	Nebraska (2-0)	1932	Nebraska (5-0)	1956	Oklahoma (6-0)	1977	Oklahoma (7-0)
1911	Iowa St. (2-0-1)	1933	Nebraska (5-0)	1957	Oklahoma (6-0)	1978	Nebraska (6-1)
	& Nebraska (2-0-1)	1934	Kansas St. (5-0)	1958	Oklahoma (6-0)		& Oklahoma (6-1)
1912	Iowa St. (2-0)	1935	Nebraska (4-0-1)	1959	Oklahoma (5-1)	1979	Oklahoma (7-0)
	& Nebraska (2-0)	1936	Nebraska (5-0)	1960	Missouri (7-0)	1980	Oklahoma (7-0)
1913	Missouri (4-0)	1937	Nebraska (3-0-2)	1961	Colorado (7-0)	1981	Nebraska (7-0)
	& Nebraska (3-0)	1938	Oklahoma (5-0)	1962	Oklahoma (7-0)	1982	Nebraska (7-0)
1914	Nebraska (3-0)	1939	Missouri (5-0)	1963	Nebraska (7-0)	1983	Nebraska (7-0)
1915	Nebraska (4-0)	1940	Nebraska (5-0)	1964	Nebraska (6-1)	1984	Oklahoma (6-1)
1916	Nebraska (3-0)	1941	Missouri (5-0)	1965	Nebraska (7-0)		& Nebraska (6-1)
1917	Nebraska (2-0)	1942	Missouri (4-0-1)	1966	Nebraska (6-1)	1985	Oklahoma (7-0)
1918	Vacant (WW I)	1943	Oklahoma (5-0)	1967	Oklahoma (7-0)	1986	Oklahoma (7-0)
1919	Missouri (4-0-1)	1944	Oklahoma (4-0-1)	1968	Kansas (6-1)	1987	Oklahoma (7-0)
1920	Oklahoma (4-0-1)	1945	Missouri (5-0)		& Oklahoma (6-1)	1988	Nebraska (7-0)
1921	Nebraska (3-0)	1946	Oklahoma (4-1)	1969	Missouri (6-1)	1989	Colorado (7-0)
1922	Nebraska (5-0)		& Kansas (4-1)		& Nebraska (6-1)	1990	Colorado (7-0)
1923	Nebraska (3-0-2)	1947	Kansas (4-0-1)	1970	Nebraska (7-0)	1991	Nebraska (6-0-1)
	& Kansas (3-0-3)		& Oklahoma (4-0-1)	1971	Nebraska (7-0)		& Colorado (6-0-1)
1924	Missouri (5-1)	1948	Oklahoma (5-0)	1972	Nebraska (5-1-1)*	1992	Nebraska (6-1)
1925	Missouri (5-1)	1949	Oklahoma (5-0)	1973	Oklahoma (7-0)	1993	Nebraska (7-0)
1926	Okla. A&M (3-0-1)	1950	Oklahoma (6-0)	1974	Oklahoma (7-0)	1994	Nebraska (7-0)
1927	Missouri (5-1)	1951	Oklahoma (6-0)	1975	Nebraska (6-1)	1995	Nebraska (7-0)
					& Oklahoma (6-1)		

*Oklahoma (6-1) forfeited title in 1972 after a player was ruled ineligible.

Major Conference Champions (Cont.)
Big 12 Conference

Originally founded in 1996 by the former teams of the Big Eight and four schools from the Southwest Conference. The league stages a conference championship game between the two division winners on the first Saturday in December. **Playing sites:** Trans World Dome in St. Louis (1996, 1998), the Alamodome in San Antonio (1997, 1999), Arrowhead Stadium in Kansas City, Mo. (2000, 2003, 2004), Texas Stadium in Irving, Texas (2001) and Reliant Stadium in Houston, Texas (2002.)
   2004 playing membership: (12) NORTH—Colorado, Iowa St., Kansas, Kansas St., Missouri and Nebraska; SOUTH—Baylor, Oklahoma, Oklahoma St., Texas, Texas A&M and Texas Tech.
   Multiple titles: Nebraska and Oklahoma (2).

Year		Year		Year	
1996	Texas 37, Nebraska 27	1999	Nebraska 22, Texas 6	2002	Oklahoma 29, Colorado 7
1997	Nebraska 54, Texas A&M 15	2000	Oklahoma 27, Kansas St. 24	2003	Kansas St. 35, Oklahoma 7
1998	Texas A&M 36, Kansas St. 33	2001	Colorado 39, Texas 37		

Big West Conference (1969-2000)

Originally founded in 1969 as Pacific Coast Athletic Assn. **Charter members** (7): CS-Los Angeles, Fresno St., Long Beach St., Pacific, San Diego St., San Jose St. and UC-Santa Barbara. **Admitted later** (12): CS-Fullerton in 1974; Utah St. in 1977 (began play in '78); UNLV in 1982; New Mexico St. in 1983 (began play in '84); Nevada in 1991 (began play in '92); Arkansas St., Louisiana Tech, Northern Illinois and SW Louisiana in 1992 (all four began play in football only in '93); Boise St., Idaho and North Texas in 1994 (all three began play in '96); Arkansas St. rejoined in 1999 (in football only). **Withdrew later** (14): CS-Los Angeles and UC-Santa Barbara in 1972 (both dropped football after '71 season); San Diego St. in 1975 (became an independent after '75 season); Fresno St. in 1991 (left for WAC after '91 season); Long Beach St. in 1991 (dropped football after '91 season); CS-Fullerton in 1992 (dropped football after '92 season); San Jose St. and UNLV in 1994 (left for WAC after '95 season); Pacific in 1995 (dropped football after '95 season); Arkansas St., Louisiana Tech, Northern Illinois and SW Louisiana in 1995 (all four returned to independent football status after '95 season); Nevada in 2000 (left for WAC after '99 season). **Conference renamed** Big West in 1988.
   Multiple titles: San Jose St. (8); Fresno St. (6); Nevada, San Diego St. and Utah St. (5); Long Beach St. (3); Boise St., CS-Fullerton and SW Louisiana (2).

Year		Year		Year	
1969	San Diego St. (6-0)	1982	Fresno St. (6-0)	1994	UNLV (5-1),
1970	Long Beach St. (5-1)	1983	CS-Fullerton (5-1)		Nevada (5-1),
	& San Diego St. (5-1)	1984	CS-Fullerton (6-1)†		& SW Louisiana (5-1)
1971	Long Beach St. (6-1)	1985	Fresno St. (7-0)	1995	Nevada (6-0)
1972	San Diego St. (4-0)	1986	San Jose St. (7-0)	1996	Nevada (4-1)
1973	San Diego St. (3-0-1)	1987	San Jose St. (7-0)		& Utah St. (4-1)
1974	San Diego St. (4-0)	1988	Fresno St. (7-0)	1997	Utah St. (4-1)
1975	San Jose St. (5-0)	1989	Fresno St. (7-0)		& Nevada (4-1)
1976	San Jose St. (4-0)	1990	San Jose St. (7-0)	1998	Idaho (4-1)
1977	Fresno St. (4-0)	1991	Fresno St. (6-1)	1999	Boise St. (5-1)
1978	San Jose St. (4-1)		& San Jose St. (6-1)	2000	Boise St. (5-0)
	& Utah St. (4-1)	1992	Nevada (5-1)	*San Jose St. (4-0-1) forfeited share of
1979	Utah St. (4-0-1)*	1993	Utah St. (5-1)	1979 title for using ineligible player.
1980	Long Beach St. (5-0)		& SW Louisiana (5-1)	†UNLV (7-0) forfeited title in 1984 for
1981	San Jose St. (5-0)			use of ineligible players.

Conference USA

Founded in 1994 by six independent football schools which began play as a conference in 1996. **Charter members** (6): Cincinnati, Houston, Louisville, Memphis, Southern Mississippi and Tulane. **Admitted later** (11): East Carolina in 1997, Army in 1998, Univ. of Alabama-Birmingham in 1999, Texas Christian Univ. in 2001, South Florida in 2003, Central Florida, Marshall, Rice, SMU, Tulsa and UTEP in 2005. **Withdrew later** (5): Cincinnati, Louisville and South Florida are set to leave for the Big East in 2005; Army is going back to independent and TCU is going to the Mountain West in 2005.
   2004 playing members (11): Alabama-Birmingham, Army, Cincinnati, East Carolina, Houston, Louisville, Memphis, South Florida, Southern Mississippi, TCU and Tulane.
   Multiple titles: Southern Mississippi (4), Louisville (2).

Year		Year		Year	
1996	Southern Mississippi (4-1)	1999	Southern Mississippi (6-0)	2002	TCU (6-2)
	& Houston (4-1)	2000	Louisville (6-1)		& Cincinnati (6-2)
1997	Southern Mississippi (6-0)	2001	Louisville (6-1)	2003	Southern Mississippi (8-0)
1998	Tulane (6-0)				

Mid-American Conference

Founded in 1946. **Charter members** (6): Butler, Cincinnati, Miami-OH, Ohio University, Western Michigan and Western Reserve (Miami and WMU began play in '48). **Admitted later** (12): Kent St. (now Kent) and Toledo in 1951 (Toledo began play in '52); Bowling Green in 1952; Marshall in 1954; Central Michigan and Eastern Michigan in 1972 (CMU began play in '75 and EMU in '76); Ball St. and Northern Illinois in 1973 (both began play in '75); Akron in 1991 (began play in '92); Marshall and Northern Illinois in 1995 (both resumed play in '97); Buffalo in 1995 (resumed play in '99); Central Florida in 2002. **Withdrew later** (5): Butler in 1950 (left for the Indiana Collegiate Conference); Cincinnati in 1953 (went independent); Western Reserve (now Case Western) in 1955 (left for President's Athletic Conference); Marshall in 1969 (went independent) and again in 2005 (leaving for Conference USA); Northern Illinois in 1986 (went independent).
   2004 playing membership (14): EAST—Akron, Buffalo, Central Florida, Kent St., Marshall, Miami-OH and Ohio University; WEST—Ball St., Bowling Green, Central Michigan, Eastern Michigan, Northern Illinois, Toledo and Western Michigan.
   Multiple titles: Miami-OH (14); Bowling Green (10); Toledo (8); Ball St., Marshall and Ohio University (5); Central Michigan, Cincinnati (4); Western Michigan (2).

Year		Year		Year		Year	
1947	Cincinnati (3-1)	1959	Bowling Green (6-0)	1970	Toledo (5-0)	1984	Toledo (7-1-1)
1948	Miami-OH (4-0)	1960	Ohio Univ. (6-0)	1971	Toledo (5-0)	1985	Bowling Green (9-0)
1949	Cincinnati (4-0)	1961	Bowling Green (5-1)	1972	Kent St. (4-1)	1986	Miami-OH (6-2)
1950	Miami-OH (4-0)	1962	Bowling Green (5-0-1)	1973	Miami-OH (5-0)	1987	Eastern Mich. (7-1)
1951	Cincinnati (3-0)	1963	Ohio Univ. (5-1)	1974	Miami-OH (5-0)	1988	Western Mich. (7-1)
1952	Cincinnati (3-0)	1964	Bowling Green (5-1)	1975	Miami-OH (6-0)	1989	Ball St. (6-1-1)
1953	Ohio Univ. (5-0-1)	1965	Bowling Green (5-1)	1976	Ball St. (4-1)	1990	Central Mich. (7-1)
	& Miami-OH (3-0-1)		& Miami-OH (5-1)	1977	Miami-OH (5-0)		& Toledo (7-1)
1954	Miami-OH (4-0)	1966	Miami-OH (5-1)	1978	Ball St. (8-0)	1991	Bowling Green (8-0)
1955	Miami-OH (5-0)		& Western Mich. (5-1)	1979	Central Mich. (8-0-1)	1992	Bowling Green (8-0)
1956	Bowling Green (5-0-1)	1967	Toledo (5-1)			1993	Ball St. (7-0-1)
	& Miami-OH (4-0-1)		& Ohio Univ. (5-1)	1980	Central Mich. (7-2)	1994	Central Mich. (8-1)
1957	Miami-OH (5-0)	1968	Ohio Univ. (6-0)	1981	Toledo (8-1)	1995	Toledo (7-0-1)
1958	Miami-OH (5-0)	1969	Toledo (5-0)	1982	Bowling Green (7-2)	1996	Ball St. (7-1)
				1983	Northern Ill. (8-1)		

MAC Championship Game

After expanding to 12 teams (and then 13 in 1999 with the addition of Buffalo) and splitting into two divisions in 1997, the MAC now stages a conference championship game between the two division winners on the first Saturday in December. The game was played at Marshall Stadium in Huntington, W.V. (1997-2000, 2002), Glass Bowl Stadium in Toledo, Ohio (2001) and Doyt Perry Stadium in Bowling Green, Ohio (2003).

Year		Year		Year	
1997	Marshall 34, Toledo 13	2000	Marshall 19, W. Michigan 14	2003	Miami-OH 49, Bowl. Green 27
1998	Marshall 23, Toledo 17	2001	Toledo 41, Marshall 36		
1999	Marshall 34, W. Michigan 30	2002	Marshall 49, Toledo 45		

Mountain West Conference

Founded in 1999. **Charter members** (8): Air Force, Brigham Young, Colorado St., New Mexico, Nevada-Las Vegas, San Diego St., Utah and Wyoming. **Admitted later** (1): TCU (from Conference USA) is set to join in 2005.

2004 playing membership (8): Air Force, Brigham Young, Colorado St., New Mexico, Nevada-Las Vegas, San Diego St., Utah and Wyoming.

Multiple titles: Colorado St. (3), BYU and Utah (2).

Year		Year		Year	
1999	BYU (5-2),	2000	Colorado St. (6-1)	2002	Colorado St. (6-1)
	Colorado St. (5-2)	2001	BYU (7-0)	2003	Utah (6-1)
	& Utah (5-2)				

Pacific-10 Conference

Originally founded in 1915 as Pacific Coast Conference. **Charter members** (4): California, Oregon, Oregon St. and Washington. **Admitted later** (6): Washington St. in 1917; Stanford in 1918; Idaho and USC (Southern Cal) in 1922; Montana in 1924; and UCLA in 1928. **Withdrew later** (1): Montana in 1950 (left for the Mountain States Conf.).

The **PCC** dissolved in 1959 and the **AAWU** (Athletic Assn. of Western Universities) was founded. **Charter members** (5): California, Stanford, UCLA, USC and Washington. **Admitted later** (5): Washington St. in 1962; Oregon and Oregon St. in 1964; Arizona and Arizona St. in 1978. **Conference renamed** Pacific-8 in 1968 and Pacific-10 in 1978.

2004 playing membership (10): Arizona, Arizona St., California, Oregon, Oregon St., Stanford, UCLA, USC, Washington and Washington St.

Multiple titles: USC (33); UCLA (17); Washington (15); California (13); Stanford (12); Oregon (7); Oregon St. (5); Washington St. (4); Arizona St. (2).

Year		Year		Year		Year	
1916	Washington (3-0-1)	1938	USC (6-1)	1960	Washington (4-0)	1986	Arizona St. (5-1-1)
1917	Washington St. (3-0)		& California (6-1)	1961	UCLA (3-1)	1987	USC (7-1)
1918	California (3-0)	1939	USC (5-0-2)	1962	USC (4-0)		& UCLA (7-1)
1919	Oregon (2-1)		& UCLA (5-0-3)	1963	Washington (4-1)	1988	USC (8-0)
	& Washington (2-1)	1940	Stanford (7-0)	1964	Oregon St. (3-1)	1989	USC (6-0-1)
1920	California (3-0)	1941	Oregon St. (7-2)		& USC (3-1)	1990	Washington (7-1)
1921	California (5-0)	1942	UCLA (6-1)	1965	UCLA (4-0)	1991	Washington (8-0)
1922	California (3-0)	1943	USC (4-0)	1966	USC (4-1)	1992	Washington (6-2)
1923	California (5-0)	1944	USC (3-0-2)	1967	USC (6-1)		& Stanford (6-2)
1924	Stanford (3-0-1)	1945	USC (5-1)	1968	USC (6-0)	1993	UCLA (6-2),
1925	Washington (5-0)	1946	UCLA (7-0)	1969	USC (6-0)		Arizona (6-2)
1926	Stanford (4-0)	1947	USC (6-0)	1970	Stanford (6-1)		& USC (6-2)
1927	USC (4-0-1)	1948	California (6-0)	1971	Stanford (6-1)	1994	Oregon (7-1)
	& Stanford (4-0-1)		& Oregon (6-0)	1972	USC (7-0)	1995	USC (6-1-1)
1928	USC (4-0-1)	1949	California (7-0)	1973	USC (7-0)		& Washington (6-1-1)
1929	USC (6-1)	1950	California (5-0-1)	1974	USC (6-0-1)	1996	Arizona St. (8-0)
1930	Washington St. (6-0)	1951	Stanford (6-1)	1975	UCLA (6-1)	1997	Washington St. (7-1)
1931	USC (7-0)	1952	USC (6-0)		& California (6-1)		& UCLA (7-1)
1932	USC (6-0)	1953	UCLA (6-1)	1976	USC (7-0)	1998	UCLA (8-0)
1933	Oregon (4-1)	1954	UCLA (6-0)	1977	Washington (6-1)	1999	Stanford (7-1)
	& Stanford (4-1)	1955	UCLA (6-0)	1978	USC (6-1)	2000	Washington (7-1),
1934	Stanford (5-0)	1956	Oregon St. (6-1-1)	1979	USC (6-0-1)		Oregon St. (7-1)
1935	California (4-1),	1957	Oregon (6-2)	1980	Washington (6-1)		& Oregon (7-1)
	Stanford (4-1)		& Oregon St. (6-2)	1981	Washington (6-2)	2001	Oregon (7-1)
	& UCLA (4-1)	1958	California (6-1)	1982	UCLA (5-1-1)	2002	Washington St. (7-1)
1936	Washington (6-0-1)	1959	Washington (3-1),	1983	UCLA (6-1-1)		& USC (7-1)
1937	California (6-0-1)		USC (3-1)	1984	USC (7-1)	2003	USC (7-1)
			& UCLA (3-1)	1985	UCLA (6-2)		

Major Conference Champions (Cont.)

Southwest Conference (1914-95)

Founded in 1914 as Southwest Intercollegiate Athletic Conference. **Charter members** (8): Arkansas, Baylor, Oklahoma, Oklahoma A&M (now Oklahoma St.), Rice, Southwestern, Texas and Texas A&M. **Admitted later** (5): SMU (Southern Methodist) in 1918; Phillips University in 1920; TCU (Texas Christian) in 1923; Texas Tech in 1956 (began play in '60; Houston in 1971 (began play in '76). **Withdrew later** (13): Southwestern in 1917 (went independent); Oklahoma in 1920 (left for Missouri Valley after '19 season); Phillips in 1921; Oklahoma A&M (now Oklahoma St.) in 1925 (left for Big Six); Arkansas in 1990 (left for SEC after '91 season); Baylor, Texas, Texas A&M and Texas Tech in 1994 (all four left for Big 12 after '95 season); Rice, SMU and TCU in 1994 (all three left for WAC after '95 season); Houston in 1994 (left for Conference USA after '95 season). Conference folded on June 30, 1996.

Multiple titles: Texas (25); Texas A&M (17); Arkansas (13); SMU (9); TCU (9); Rice (7); Baylor (5); Houston (4); Texas Tech (2).

Year		Year		Year		Year	
1914	No champion	1940	Texas A&M (5-1)	1961	Texas (6-1)	1981	SMU (7-1)
1915	Oklahoma (3-0)	1941	Texas A&M (5-1)		& Arkansas (6-1)	1982	SMU (7-0-1)
1916	No champion	1942	Texas (5-1)	1962	Texas (6-0-1)	1983	Texas (8-0)
1917	Texas A&M (2-0)	1943	Texas (5-0)	1963	Texas (7-0)	1984	SMU (6-2)
1918	No champion	1944	TCU (3-1-1)	1964	Arkansas (7-0)		& Houston (6-2)
1919	Texas A&M (4-0)	1945	Texas (5-1)	1965	Arkansas (7-0)	1985	Texas A&M (7-1)
1920	Texas (5-0)	1946	Rice (5-1)	1966	SMU (6-1)	1986	Texas A&M (7-1)
1921	Texas A&M (3-0-2)		& Arkansas (5-1)	1967	Texas A&M (6-1)	1987	Texas A&M (6-1)
1922	Baylor (5-0)	1947	SMU (5-0-1)	1968	Arkansas (6-1)	1988	Arkansas (7-0)
1923	SMU (5-0)	1948	SMU (5-0-1)		& Texas (6-1)	1989	Arkansas (7-0)
1924	Baylor (4-0-1)	1949	Rice (6-0)	1969	Texas (7-0)	1990	Texas (8-0)
1925	Texas A&M (4-1)	1950	Texas (6-0)	1970	Texas (7-0)	1991	Texas A&M (8-0)
1926	SMU (5-0)	1951	TCU (5-1)	1971	Texas (6-1)	1992	Texas A&M (7-0)
1927	Texas A&M (4-0-1)	1952	Texas (6-0)	1972	Texas (7-0)	1993	Texas A&M (7-0)
1928	Texas (5-1)	1953	Rice (5-1)	1973	Texas (7-0)	1994	Baylor, Rice, TCU,
1929	TCU (4-0-1)		& Texas (5-1)	1974	Baylor (6-1)		Texas and Texas Tech†
1930	Texas (4-1)	1954	Arkansas (5-1)	1975	Arkansas (6-1),		(4-3)
1931	SMU (5-0-1)	1955	TCU (5-1)		Texas (6-1)	1995	Texas (7-0)
1932	TCU (6-0)	1956	Texas A&M (6-0)		& Texas A&M (6-1)		
1933	Arkansas (4-1)*	1957	Rice (5-1)	1976	Houston (7-1)	*Arkansas (4-1) forced to vacate 1933 title for use of ineligible player.
1934	Rice (5-1)	1958	TCU (5-1)		& Texas Tech (7-1)	
1935	SMU (6-0)	1959	Texas (5-1),	1977	Texas (8-0)	
1936	Arkansas (5-1)		TCU (5-1)	1978	Houston (7-1)	†Texas A&M had the best record (6-0-1) in 1994 but was on probation and therefore ineligible for the Southwest championship.
1937	Rice (4-1-1)		& Arkansas (5-1)	1979	Houston (7-1)	
1938	TCU (6-0)	1960	Arkansas (6-1)		& Arkansas (7-1)	
1939	Texas A&M (6-0)			1980	Baylor (8-0)	

Southeastern Conference

Founded in 1933 when charter members all left Southern Conference to form SEC. **Charter members** (13): Alabama, Auburn, Florida, Georgia, Georgia Tech, Kentucky, LSU, Mississippi, Mississippi St., Sewanee, Tennessee, Tulane and Vanderbilt. **Admitted later** (2): Arkansas and South Carolina in 1990 (both began play in '92). **Withdrew later** (3): Sewanee in 1940; Georgia Tech in 1964; and Tulane in 1966.

2004 playing membership (12): Alabama, Arkansas, Auburn, Florida, Georgia, Kentucky, LSU, Mississippi, Mississippi St., South Carolina, Tennessee and Vanderbilt. **Note:** Conference title decided by championship game between Western and Eastern division winners since 1992.

Multiple titles: Alabama (21); Tennessee (13); Georgia (11); Florida and LSU (9); Mississippi (6); Auburn and Georgia Tech (5); Kentucky and Tulane (3).

Year		Year		Year		Year	
1933	Alabama (5-0-1)	1948	Georgia (6-0)	1965	Alabama (6-1-1)	1981	Georgia (6-0)
1934	Tulane (8-0)	1949	Tulane (5-1)	1966	Alabama (6-0)		& Alabama (6-0)
	& Alabama (7-0)	1950	Kentucky (5-1)		& Georgia (6-0)	1982	Georgia (6-0)
1935	LSU (5-0)	1951	Georgia Tech (7-0)	1967	Tennessee (6-0)	1983	Auburn (6-0)
1936	LSU (6-0)		& Tennessee (5-1)	1968	Georgia (5-0-1)	1984	Florida (5-0-1)*
1937	Alabama (6-0)	1952	Georgia Tech (6-0)	1969	Tennessee (5-1)	1985	Florida (5-1)†
1938	Tennessee (7-0)	1953	Alabama (4-0-3)	1970	LSU (5-0)		& Tennessee (5-1)
1939	Tennessee (6-0),	1954	Mississippi (5-1)	1971	Alabama (7-0)	1986	LSU (5-1)
	Georgia Tech (6-0)	1955	Mississippi (5-1)	1972	Alabama (7-1)	1987	Auburn (5-0-1)
	& Tulane (5-0)	1956	Tennessee (6-0)	1973	Alabama (8-0)	1988	Auburn (6-1)
1940	Tennessee (5-0)	1957	Auburn (7-0)	1974	Alabama (6-0)		& LSU (6-1)
1941	Mississippi St. (4-0-1)	1958	LSU (6-0)	1975	Alabama (6-0)	1989	Alabama (6-1),
1942	Georgia (6-1)	1959	Georgia (7-0)	1976	Georgia (5-1)		Tennessee (6-1)
1943	Georgia Tech (3-0)	1960	Mississippi (5-0-1)		& Kentucky (5-1)		& Auburn (6-1)
1944	Georgia Tech (4-0)	1961	Alabama (7-0)	1977	Alabama (7-0)	1990	Florida (6-1)†
1945	Alabama (6-0)		& LSU (6-0)		& Kentucky (5-1)		& Tennessee (5-1-1)
1946	Georgia (5-0)	1962	Mississippi (6-0)	1978	Alabama (6-0)	1991	Florida (7-0)
	& Tennessee (5-0)	1963	Mississippi (5-0-1)	1979	Alabama (6-0)	*Title vacated.
1947	Mississippi (6-1)	1964	Alabama (8-0)	1980	Georgia (6-0)	†On probation, ineligible for championship.

SEC Championship Game

Since expanding to 12 teams and splitting into two divisions in 1992, the SEC has staged a conference championship game between the two division winners on the first Saturday in December. The game has been played at Legion Field in Birmingham, Ala., (1992-93) and the Georgia Dome in Atlanta (since 1994). The divisions: EAST— Florida, Georgia, Kentucky, South Carolina, Tennessee and Vanderbilt; WEST— Alabama, Arkansas, Auburn, LSU, Mississippi and Mississippi St.

Year		Year		Year	
1992	Alabama 28, Florida 21	1996	Florida 45, Alabama 30	2000	Florida 28, Auburn 6
1993	Florida 28, Alabama 23	1997	Tennessee 30, Auburn 29	2001	LSU 31, Tennessee 20
1994	Florida 24, Alabama 23	1998	Tennessee 24, Miss. St. 14	2002	Georgia 30, Arkansas 3
1995	Florida 34, Arkansas 3	1999	Alabama 34, Florida 7	2003	LSU 34, Georgia 13

Sun Belt Conference

Founded in 2001 when the Sun Belt Conference sponsored football for the first time. **Charter members** (7): Arkansas State, Idaho, Louisiana-Lafayette, Louisiana-Monroe, Middle Tennessee State, New Mexico State and North Texas. **2004 playing members** (9): Arkansas State, Idaho, Louisiana-Lafayette, Louisiana-Monroe, Middle Tennessee State, New Mexico State and North Texas. **Admitted later** (4): Utah St. in 2003, Troy St. in 2004, Florida Atlantic and Florida International in 2005. **Withdrew later** (2): New Mexico St. and Utah St. in 2005 (left for WAC).
   Multiple titles: North Texas (3)

Year		Year		Year	
2001	North Texas (5-1) & Mid. Tenn. St. (5-1)	2002	North Texas (6-0)	2003	North Texas (7-0)

Western Athletic Conference

Founded in 1962 when charter members left the Skyline and Border conferences to form the WAC. **Charter members** (6): Arizona and Arizona St. from Border; BYU (Brigham Young), New Mexico, Utah and Wyoming from Skyline. **Admitted later** (17): Colorado St. and UTEP (Texas-El Paso) in 1967 (both began play in '68); San Diego St. in 1978; Hawaii in 1979; Air Force in 1980; Fresno St. in 1991 (began play in '92); Rice, San Jose St., SMU , TCU , Tulsa and UNLV in 1994 (all began play in '96); Nevada in 2000; Boise St. and Louisiana Tech in 2001; New Mexico St. and Utah St. in 2005. **Withdrew later** (13): Arizona and Arizona St. in 1978 (left for Pac-10 after '77 season); Air Force, BYU, Colorado St., New Mexico, San Diego St., UNLV, Utah and Wyoming (left to form Mountain West conference in '99); TCU in 2000 (left for Conference USA after 2000 season); Rice, SMU and Tulsa in 2005 (left for Conference USA).
   2004 playing membership (10): Boise St., Fresno St., Hawaii, Louisiana Tech, Nevada, Rice, San Jose St., SMU, Tulsa and UTEP.
   Multiple titles: BYU (19); Arizona St. and Wyoming (7); Air Force, Fresno St., New Mexico and Colorado St. (3); Arizona, Boise St., Hawaii, TCU and Utah (2).

Year		Year		Year		Year	
1962	New Mexico (2-1-1)	1974	BYU (6-0-1)	1986	San Diego St. (7-1)	1995	Colorado St. (6-2),
1963	New Mexico (3-1)	1975	Arizona St. (7-0)	1987	Wyoming (8-0)		Air Force (6-2),
1964	Utah (3-1),	1976	BYU (6-1)	1988	Wyoming (8-0)		BYU (6-2)
	New Mexico (3-1)		& Wyoming (6-1)	1989	BYU (7-1)		& Utah (6-2)
	& Arizona (3-1)	1977	Arizona St. (6-1)	1990	BYU (7-1)	1999	Fresno St. (5-2),
1965	BYU (4-1)		& BYU (6-1)	1991	BYU (7-0-1)		Hawaii (7-2)
1966	Wyoming (5-0)	1978	BYU (5-1)	1992	Hawaii (6-2),		& TCU (7-2)
1967	Wyoming (5-0)	1979	BYU (7-0)		BYU (6-2)	2000	TCU (7-1)
1968	Wyoming (6-1)	1980	BYU (7-0)		& Fresno St. (6-2)		& UTEP (7-1)
1969	Arizona St. (6-1)	1981	BYU (7-1)	1993	BYU (6-2),	2001	La. Tech (7-1)
1970	Arizona St. (7-0)	1982	BYU (7-1)		Fresno St. (6-2)	2002	Boise St. (8-0)
1971	Arizona St. (7-0)	1983	BYU (7-0)		& Wyoming (6-2)	2003	Boise St. (8-0)
1972	Arizona St. (5-1)	1984	BYU (8-0)	1994	Colorado St. (7-1)		
1973	Arizona St. (6-1) & Arizona (6-1)	1985	Air Force (7-1) & BYU (7-1)				

Longest Division I Streaks

Winning Streaks
(Including bowl games)

No		Seasons	Spoiler	Score
47	Oklahoma	1953-57	Notre Dame	7-0
39	Washington	1908-14	Oregon St.	0-0
37	Yale	1890-93	Princeton	6-0
37	Yale	1887-89	Princeton	10-0
35	Toledo	1969-71	Tampa	21-0
34	Miami-FL	2000-02	Ohio St.	31-24*
34	Penn	1894-96	Lafayette	6-4
31	Oklahoma	1948-50	Kentucky	13-7*
31	Pittsburgh	1914-18	Cleve. Naval	10-9
31	Penn	1896-98	Harvard	10-0
30	Texas	1968-70	Notre Dame	24-11*
29	Miami-FL	1990-93	Alabama	34-13
29	Michigan	1901-03	Minnesota	6-6

*Ohio St. beat Miami in 2003 Fiesta Bowl in double overtime. Kentucky beat Oklahoma in 1951 Sugar Bowl and Notre Dame beat Texas in 1971 Cotton Bowl.

Unbeaten Streaks
(Including bowl games)

No	W-T	Seasons	Spoiler	Score
63	59-4	Washington	1907-17	California	27-0
56	55-1	Michigan	1901-05	Chicago	2-0
50	46-4	California	1920-25	Olympic Club	15-0
48	47-1	Oklahoma	1953-57	N. Dame	7-0
48	47-1	Yale	1885-89	Princeton	10-0
47	42-5	Yale	1879-85	Princeton	6-5
44	42-2	Yale	1894-96	Princeton	24-6
42	39-3	Yale	1904-08	Harvard	4-0
39	37-2	N. Dame	1946-50	Purdue	28-14

Losing Streaks

No		Seasons	Victim	Score
80	Prairie View	1989-98	Langston	14-12
44	Columbia	1983-88	Princeton	16-14
34	Northwestern	1979-82	No. Illinois	31-6
28	Virginia	1958-60	Wm. & Mary	21-6
28	Kansas St	1944-48	Arkansas St.	37-6

Note: Virginia ended its losing streak in the opening game of the 1961 season.

Major Conference Champions (Cont.)

WAC Championship Game (1996-98)

In addition to expanding to 16 teams and splitting into two divisions in 1996, the WAC staged a conference championship game between the two division winners on the first Saturday in December at Sam Boyd Stadium in Las Vegas until eight teams split off and formed the Mountain West Conference in 1999. The divisions: PACIFIC—BYU, Fresno St., Hawaii, New Mexico, San Diego St., San Jose St., UTEP, Utah; MOUNTAIN—Air Force, Colorado St., Rice, SMU, TCU, Tulsa, UNLV, Wyoming.

Year		Year		Year	
1996	BYU 28, Wyoming 25 (OT)	1997	Colorado St. 41, New Mexico 13	1998	Air Force 20, BYU 13

Annual NCAA Division I-A Leaders

Note that Oklahoma A&M is now Oklahoma St. and Texas Mines is now UTEP.

Rushing

Individual championship decided on Rushing Yards (1937-69), and on Yards Per Game (since 1970).

Multiple winners: Troy Davis, Marshall Faulk, Art Luppino, Ed Marinaro, Rudy Mobley, Jim Pilot, O.J. Simpson, LaDainian Tomlinson and Ricky Williams (2).

Year		Car	Yards	Year		Car	Yards	P/Gm
1937	Byron (Whizzer) White, Colorado	181	1121	1970	Ed Marinaro, Cornell	285	1425	158.3
1938	Len Eshmont, Fordham	132	831	1971	Ed Marinaro, Cornell	356	1881	209.0
1939	John Polanski, Wake Forest	137	882	1972	Pete VanValkenburg, BYU	232	1386	138.6
1940	Al Ghesquiere, Detroit	146	957	1973	Mark Kellar, Northern Ill	291	1719	156.3
1941	Frank Sinkwich, Georgia	209	1103	1974	Louie Giammona, Utah St.	329	1534	153.4
1942	Rudy Mobley, Hardin-Simmons	187	1281	1975	Ricky Bell, USC	357	1875	170.5
1943	Creighton Miller, Notre Dame	151	911	1976	Tony Dorsett, Pittsburgh	338	1948	177.1
1944	Red Williams, Minnesota	136	911	1977	Earl Campbell, Texas	267	1744	158.5
1945	Bob Fenimore, Oklahoma A&M	142	1048	1978	Billy Sims, Oklahoma.	231	1762	160.2
1946	Rudy Mobley, Hardin-Simmons	227	1262	1979	Charles White, USC.	293	1803	180.3
1947	Wilton Davis, Hardin-Simmons.	193	1173	1980	George Rogers, S. Carolina	297	1781	161.9
1948	Fred Wendt, Texas Mines	184	1570	1981	Marcus Allen, USC.	403	2342	212.9
1949	John Dottley, Ole Miss	208	1312	1982	Ernest Anderson, Okla. St.	353	1877	170.6
1950	Wilford White, Arizona St	199	1502	1983	Mike Rozier, Nebraska	275	2148	179.0
1951	Ollie Matson, San Francisco	245	1566	1984	Keith Byars, Ohio St.	313	1655	150.5
1952	Howie Waugh, Tulsa	164	1372	1985	Lorenzo White, Mich. St.	386	1908	173.5
1953	J.C. Caroline, Illinois	194	1256	1986	Paul Palmer, Temple	346	1866	169.6
1954	Art Luppino, Arizona	179	1359	1987	Ickey Woods, UNLV	259	1658	150.7
1955	Art Luppino, Arizona	209	1313	1988	Barry Sanders, Okla. St.	344	2628	238.9
1956	Jim Crawford, Wyoming	200	1104	1989	Anthony Thompson, Ind	358	1793	163.0
1957	Leon Burton, Arizona St	117	1126	1990	Gerald Hudson, Okla. St	279	1642	149.3
1958	Dick Bass, Pacific	205	1361	1991	Marshall Faulk, S. Diego St.	201	1429	158.8
1959	Pervis Atkins, New Mexico St	130	971	1992	Marshall Faulk, S. Diego St.	265	1630	163.0
1960	Bob Gaiters, New Mexico St	197	1338	1993	LeShon Johnson, No. Ill.	327	1976	179.6
1961	Jim Pilot, New Mexico St	191	1278	1994	Rashaan Salaam, Colorado	298	2055	186.8
1962	Jim Pilot, New Mexico St	208	1247	1995	Troy Davis, Iowa St.	345	2010	182.7
1963	Dave Casinelli, Memphis St	219	1016	1996	Troy Davis, Iowa St.	402	2185	198.6
1964	Brian Piccolo, Wake Forest	252	1044	1997	Ricky Williams, Texas.	279	1893	172.1
1965	Mike Garrett, USC	267	1440	1998	Ricky Williams, Texas.	361	2124	193.1
1966	Ray McDonald, Idaho	259	1329	1999	LaDainian Tomlinson, TCU	268	1850	168.2
1967	O.J. Simpson, USC.	266	1415	2000	LaDainian Tomlinson, TCU	369	2158	196.2
1968	O.J. Simpson, USC.	355	1709	2001	Chance Kretschmer, Nevada	302	1732	157.5
1969	Steve Owens, Oklahoma	358	1523	2002	Larry Johnson, Penn St.	271	2087	160.5
				2003	Patrick Cobbs, No. Texas	307	1680	152.7

All-Purpose Yardage

Multiple winners: Marcus Allen, Pervis Atkins, Ryan Benjamin, Troy Davis, Troy Edwards, Louie Giammona, Tom Harmon, Art Luppino, Napolean McCallum, O.J. Simpson, Charles White and Gary Wood (2).

Year		Yards	P/Gm	Year		Yards	P/Gm
1937	Byron (Whizzer) White, Colorado	1970	246.3	1953	J.C. Caroline, Illinois	1470	163.3
1938	Parker Hall, Ole Miss	1420	129.1	1954	Art Luppino, Arizona	2193	219.3
1939	Tom Harmon, Michigan	1208	151.0	1955	Jim Swink, TCU	1702	170.2
1940	Tom Harmon, Michigan	1312	164.0		& Art Luppino, Arizona	1702	170.2
1941	Bill Dudley, Virginia	1674	186.0	1956	Jack Hill, Utah St	1691	169.1
1942	Complete records not available			1957	Overton Curtis, Utah St	1608	160.8
1943	Stan Koslowski, Holy Cross	1411	176.4	1958	Dick Bass, Pacific	1878	187.8
1944	Red Williams, Minnesota	1467	163.0	1959	Pervis Atkins, New Mexico St	1800	180.0
1945	Bob Fenimore, Oklahoma A&M	1577	197.1	1960	Pervis Atkins, New Mexico St	1613	161.3
1946	Rudy Mobley, Hardin-Simmons	1765	176.5	1961	Jim Pilot, New Mexico St	1606	160.6
1947	Wilton Davis, Hardin-Simmons	1798	179.8	1962	Gary Wood, Cornell	1395	155.0
1948	Lou Kusserow, Columbia	1737	193.0	1963	Gary Wood, Cornell	1508	167.6
1949	Johnny Papit, Virginia	1611	179.0	1964	Donny Anderson, Texas Tech	1710	171.0
1950	Wilford White, Arizona St.	2065	206.5	1965	Floyd Little, Syracuse	1990	199.0
1951	Ollie Matson, San Francisco	2037	226.3	1966	Frank Quayle, Virginia	1616	161.6
1952	Billy Vessels, Oklahoma	1512	151.2	1967	O.J. Simpson, USC	1700	188.9

Year		Yards	P/Gm
1968	O.J. Simpson, USC.	1966	196.6
1969	Lynn Moore, Army	1795	179.5
1970	Don McCauley, North Carolina	2021	183.7
1971	Ed Marinaro, Cornell	1932	214.7
1972	Howard Stevens, Louisville.	2132	213.2
1973	Willard Harrell, Pacific	1777	177.7
1974	Louie Giammona, Utah St	1984	198.4
1975	Louie Giammona, Utah St	2045	185.9
1976	Tony Dorsett, Pittsburgh	2021	183.7
1977	Earl Campbell, Texas	1855	168.6
1978	Charles White, USC.	2096	174.7
1979	Charles White, USC.	1941	194.1
1980	Marcus Allen, USC.	1794	179.4
1981	Marcus Allen, USC.	2559	232.6
1982	Carl Monroe, Utah	2036	185.1
1983	Napoleon McCallum, Navy	2385	216.8
1984	Keith Byars, Ohio St	2284	207.6
1985	Napoleon McCallum, Navy	2330	211.8

Year		Yards	P/Gm
1986	Paul Palmer, Temple	2633	239.4
1987	Eric Wilkerson, Kent St.	2074	188.6
1988	Barry Sanders, Oklahoma St.	3250	295.5
1989	Mike Pringle, CS-Fullerton	2690	244.6
1990	Glyn Milburn, Stanford	2222	202.0
1991	Ryan Benjamin, Pacific.	2995	249.6
1992	Ryan Benjamin, Pacific.	2597	236.1
1993	LeShon Johnson, Northern Ill.	2082	189.3
1994	Rashaan Salaam, Colorado	2349	213.5
1995	Troy Davis, Iowa St.	2466	224.2
1996	Troy Davis, Iowa St.	2364	214.9
1997	Troy Edwards, La. Tech	2144	194.9
1998	Troy Edwards, La. Tech	2784	232.0
1999	Trevor Insley, Nevada	2176	197.8
2000	Emmett White, Utah St.	2628	238.9
2001	Levron Williams, Indiana	2201	200.1
2002	Larry Johnson, Penn St.	2655	204.2
2003	DeAngelo Williams, Memphis	2113	192.1

Total Offense

Individual championship decided on Total Yards (1937-69) and on Yards Per Game (since 1970).

Multiple winners: Tim Rattay (3); Johnny Bright, Bob Fenimore, Mike Maxwell and Jim McMahon (2).

Year		Plays	Yards
1937	Byron (Whizzer) White, Colorado.	224	1596
1938	Davey O'Brien, TCU	291	1847
1939	Kenny Washington, UCLA	259	1370
1940	Johnny Knolla, Creighton	298	1420
1941	Bud Schwenk, Washington-MO	354	1928
1942	Frank Sinkwich, Georgia.	341	2187
1943	Bob Hoernschemeyer, Indiana	355	1648
1944	Bob Fenimore, Oklahoma A&M.	241	1758
1945	Bob Fenimore, Oklahoma A&M.	203	1641
1946	Travis Bidwell, Auburn	339	1715
1947	Fred Enke, Arizona	329	1941
1948	Stan Heath, Nevada-Reno	233	1992
1949	Johnny Bright, Drake	275	1950
1950	Johnny Bright, Drake	320	2400
1951	Dick Kazmaier, Princeton	272	1827
1952	Ted Marchibroda, Detroit	305	1813
1953	Paul Larson, California	262	1572
1954	George Shaw, Oregon	276	1536
1955	George Welsh, Navy	203	1348
1956	John Brodie, Stanford.	295	1642
1957	Bob Newman, Washington St	263	1444
1958	Dick Bass, Pacific	218	1440
1959	Dick Norman, Stanford	319	2018
1960	Billy Kilmer, UCLA.	292	1889
1961	Dave Hoppmann, Iowa St.	320	1638
1962	Terry Baker, Oregon St	318	2276
1963	George Mira, Miami-FL	394	2318
1964	Jerry Rhome, Tulsa	470	3128
1965	Bill Anderson, Tulsa	580	3343
1966	Virgil Carter, BYU.	388	2545
1967	Sal Olivas, New Mexico St.	368	2184
1968	Greg Cook Cincinnati	507	3210
1969	Dennis Shaw, San Diego St	388	3197

Year		Plays	Yards	P/Gm
1970	Pat Sullivan, Auburn.	333	2856	285.6
1971	Gary Huff, Florida St	386	2653	241.2
1972	Don Strock, Va. Tech	480	3170	288.2
1973	Jesse Freitas, San Diego St.	410	2901	263.7
1974	Steve Joachim, Temple	331	2227	222.7
1975	Gene Swick, Toledo	490	2706	246.0
1976	Tommy Kramer, Rice.	562	3272	297.5
1977	Doug Williams, Gambling	377	3229	293.5
1978	Mike Ford, SMU	459	2957	268.8
1979	Marc Wilson, BYU	488	3580	325.5
1980	Jim McMahon, BYU	540	4627	385.6
1981	Jim McMahon, BYU	487	3458	345.8
1982	Todd Dillon, Long Beach St	585	3587	326.1
1983	Steve Young, BYU.	531	4346	395.1
1984	Robbie Bosco, BYU	543	3932	327.7
1985	Jim Everett, Purdue	518	3589	326.3
1986	Mike Perez, San Jose St.	425	2969	329.9
1987	Todd Santos, San Diego St.	562	3688	307.3
1988	Scott Mitchell, Utah	589	4299	390.8
1989	Andre Ware, Houston	628	4661	423.7
1990	David Klingler, Houston.	704	5221	474.6
1991	Ty Detmer, BYU	478	4001	333.4
1992	Jimmy Klingler, Houston.	544	3768	342.6
1993	Chris Vargas, Nevada.	535	4332	393.8
1994	Mike Maxwell, Nevada.	477	3498	318.0
1996	Mike Maxwell, Nevada.	443	3623	402.6
1996	Josh Wallwork, Wyoming	525	4209	350.8
1997	Tim Rattay, La. Tech	541	3968	360.7
1998	Tim Rattay, La. Tech	602	4840	403.3
1999	Tim Rattay, La. Tech	535	3810	381.0
2000	Drew Brees, Purdue	564	3939	358.1
2001	Rex Grossman, Florida	429	3904	354.9
2002	Byron Leftwich, Marshall	528	4267	355.6
2003	B.J. Symons, Texas Tech	798	5976	459.7

Passing

Individual championship decided on Completions (1937-69), on Completions Per Game (1970-78) and on Passing Efficiency rating points (since 1979).

Multiple winners: Elvis Grbac, Don Heinrich, Jim McMahon, Davey O'Brien and Don Trull (2).

Year		Cmp	Pct	TD	Yds
1937	Davey O'Brien, TCU.	94	.402	–	969
1938	Davey O'Brien, TCU.	93	.557	–	1457
1939	Kay Eakin, Arkansas.	78	.404	–	962
1940	Billy Sewell, Wash. St	86	.494	–	1023
1941	Bud Schwenk, Wash.-MO	114	.487	–	1457
1942	Ray Evans, Kansas	101	.505	–	1117
1943	Johnny Cook, Georgia	73	.465	–	1007
1944	Paul Rickards, Pittsburgh	84	.472	–	997
1945	Al Dekdebrun, Cornell	90	.464	–	1227
1946	Travis Tidwell, Auburn	79	.500	5	943
1947	Charlie Conerly, Ole Miss	133	.571	18	1367
1948	Stan Heath, Nev-Reno	126	.568	22	2005

Year		Cmp	Pct	TD	Yds
1949	Adrian Burk, Baylor	110	.576	14	1428
1950	Don Heinrich, Washington	134	.606	14	1846
1951	Don Klosterman, Loyola-CA	159	.505	9	1843
1952	Don Heinrich, Washington	137	.507	13	1647
1953	Bob Garrett, Stanford	118	.576	17	1637
1954	Paul Larson, California	125	.641	10	1537
1955	George Welsh, Navy.	94	.627	8	1319
1956	John Brodie, Stanford	139	.579	12	1633
1957	Ken Ford, H-Simmons	115	.561	14	1254
1958	Buddy Humphrey, Baylor	112	.574	7	1316
1959	Dick Norman, Stanford	152	.578	11	1963
1960	Harold Stephens, H-Simm	145	.566	3	1254

Annual NCAA Division I-A Leaders (Cont.)

Year		Cmp	Pct	TD	Yds	Year		Cmp	TD	Yds	Rating
1961	Chon Gallegos, S. Jose St	.117	.594	14	1480	1979	Turk Schonert, Stanford	.148	19	1922	163.0
1962	Don Trull, Baylor	.125	.546	11	1627	1980	Jim McMahon, BYU	.284	47	4571	176.9
1963	Don Trull, Baylor	.174	.565	12	2157	1981	Jim McMahon, BYU	.272	30	3555	155.0
1964	Jerry Rhome, Tulsa	.224	.687	32	2870	1982	Tom Ramsey, UCLA	.191	21	2824	153.5
1965	Bill Anderson, Tulsa	.296	.582	30	3464	1983	Steve Young, BYU	.306	33	3902	168.5
1966	John Eckman, Wichita St	.195	.426	7	2339	1984	Doug Flutie, BC	.233	27	3454	152.9
1967	Terry Stone, N. Mexico	.160	.476	9	1946	1985	Jim Harbaugh, Michigan	.139	18	1913	163.7
1968	Chuck Hixson, SMU	.265	.566	21	3103	1986	Vinny Testaverde, Miami-FL	.175	26	2557	165.8
1969	John Reaves, Florida	.222	.561	24	2896	1987	Don McPherson, Syracuse	.129	22	2341	164.3
						1988	Timm Rosenbach, Wash. St.	.199	23	2791	162.0
						1989	Ty Detmer, BYU	.265	32	4560	175.6

Year		CmpP/Gm	TD	Yds	Year		Cmp	TD	Yds	Rating
1970	Sonny Sixkiller, Wash	.186	18.6	15	2303	1990	Shawn Moore, Virginia	.144	21	2262	160.7
1971	Brian Sipe, S. Diego St	.196	17.8	17	2532	1991	Elvis Grbac, Michigan	.152	24	1955	169.0
1972	Don Strock, Va. Tech	.228	20.7	16	3243	1992	Elvis Grbac, Michigan	.112	15	1465	154.2
1973	Jesse Freitas, S. Diego St.	.227	20.6	21	2993	1993	Trent Dilfer, Fresno St.	.217	28	3276	173.1
1974	Steve Bartkowski, Cal	.182	16.5	12	2580	1994	Kerry Collins, Penn St.	.176	21	2679	172.9
1975	Craig Penrose, S. Diego St.	.198	18.0	15	2660	1995	Danny Wuerffel, Florida	.210	35	3266	178.4
1976	Tommy Kramer, Rice	.269	24.5	21	3317	1996	Steve Sarkisian, BYU	.278	33	4027	173.6
1977	Guy Benjamin, Stanford	.208	20.8	19	2521	1997	Cade McNown, UCLA	.173	22	2877	168.6
1978	Steve Dils, Stanford	.247	22.5	22	2943	1998	Shaun King, Tulane	.223	36	3232	183.3
						1999	Michael Vick, Va. Tech	.90	12	1840	180.4
						2000	Bart Hendricks, Boise St.	.210	35	3364	170.6
						2001	Rex Grossman, Florida	.259	34	3896	170.8
						2002	Brad Banks, Iowa	.170	26	2573	157.1
						2003	Philip Rivers, N.C. State	.348	34	4491	170.5

Receptions

Championship decided on Passes Caught (1937-69) and on Catches Per Game (since 1970). Touchdown totals unavailable in 1939 and 1941-45.

Multiple winners: Neil Armstrong, Hugh Campell, Manny Hazard, Reid Moseley, Jason Phillips, Howard Twilley and Alex Van Dyke (2).

Year		No	TD	Yds	Year		No	P/Gm	TD	Yds
1937	Jim Benton, Arkansas	.47	7	754	1970	Mike Mikolayunas, Davidson	87	8.7	8	1128
1938	Sam Boyd, Baylor	.32	5	537	1971	Tom Reynolds, San Diego St	.67	6.7	7	1070
1939	Ken Kavanaugh, LSU	.30	–	467	1972	Tom Forzani, Utah St	.85	7.7	8	1169
1940	Eddie Bryant, Virginia	.30	2	222	1973	Jay Miller, BYU	.100	9.1	8	1181
1941	Hank Stanton, Arizona	.50	–	820	1974	D. McDonald, San Diego St	.86	7.8	7	1157
1942	Bill Rogers, Texas A&M	.39	–	432	1975	Bob Farnham, Brown	.56	6.2	2	701
1943	Neil Armstrong, Okla. A&M	.39	–	317	1976	Billy Ryckman, La. Tech	.77	7.0	10	1382
1944	Reid Moseley, Georgia	.32	–	506	1977	W. Tolleson, W. Carolina	.73	6.6	7	1101
1945	Reid Moseley, Georgia	.31	–	662	1978	Dave Petzke, Northern Ill	.91	8.3	11	1217
1946	Neil Armstrong, Okla. A&M	.32	1	479	1979	Rick Beasley, Appalach. St	.74	6.7	12	1205
1947	Barney Poole, Ole Miss	.52	8	513	1980	Dave Young, Purdue	.67	6.1	8	917
1948	Red O'Quinn, Wake Forest	.39	7	605	1981	Pete Harvey, N. Texas St	.57	6.3	3	743
1949	Art Weiner, N. Carolina	.52	7	762	1982	Vincent White, Stanford	.68	6.8	8	677
1950	Gordon Cooper, Denver	.46	8	569	1983	Keith Edwards, Vanderbilt	.97	8.8	8	909
1951	Dewey McConnell, Wyoming	.47	9	725	1984	David Williams, Illinois	.101	9.2	8	1278
1952	Ed Brown, Fordham	.57	6	774	1985	Rodney Carter, Purdue	.98	8.9	4	1099
1953	John Carson, Georgia	.45	4	663	1986	Mark Templeton, L. Beach St	.99	9.0	2	688
1954	Jim Hanifan, California	.44	7	569	1987	Jason Phillips, Houston	.99	9.0	3	875
1955	Hank Burnine, Missouri	.44	2	594	1988	Jason Phillips, Houston	.108	9.8	15	1444
1956	Art Powell, San Jose St	.40	5	583	1989	Manny Hazard, Houston	.142	12.9	22	1689
1957	Stuart Vaughan, Utah	.53	5	756	1990	Manny Hazard, Houston	.78	7.8	9	946
1958	Dave Hibbert, Arizona	.61	4	606	1991	Fred Gilbert, Houston	.106	9.6	7	957
1959	Chris Burford, Stanford	.61	6	756	1992	Sherman Smith, Houston	.103	9.4	6	923
1960	Hugh Campbell, Wash. St	.66	10	881	1993	Chris Penn, Tulsa	.105	9.6	12	1578
1961	Hugh Campbell, Wash. St	.53	5	723	1994	Alex Van Dyke, Nevada	.98	8.9	10	1246
1962	Vern Burke, Oregon St	.69	10	1007	1995	Alex Van Dyke, Nevada	.129	11.7	16	1854
1963	Lawrence Elkins, Baylor	.70	8	873	1996	Damond Wilkins, Nevada	.114	10.4	4	1121
1964	Howard Twilley, Tulsa	.95	13	1178	1997	Eugene Baker, Kent	.103	9.4	18	1549
1965	Howard Twilley, Tulsa	.134	16	1779	1998	Troy Edwards, La. Tech	.140	11.7	27	1996
1966	Glenn Meltzer, Wichita St	.91	4	1115	1999	Trevor Insley, Nevada	.134	12.2	13	2060
1967	Bob Goodridge, Vanderbilt	.79	6	1114	2000	James Jordan, La. Tech	.109	9.1	4	1003
1968	Ron Sellers, Florida St	.86	12	1496	2001	Kevin Curtis, Utah St.	.100	9.1	10	1531
1969	Jerry Hendren, Idaho	.95	12	1452	2002	Nate Burleson, Nevada	.138	11.5	12	1629
					2003	Lance Moore, Toledo	.103	8.6	9	1194

Scoring

Championship decided on Total Points (1937-69) and on Points Per Game (since 1970).

Multiple winners: Tom Harmon and Billy Sims (2).

Year		TD	XP	FG	Pts
1937	Byron (Whizzer) White, Colo	16	23	1	122
1938	Parker Hall, Ole Miss	11	7	0	73
1939	Tom Harmon, Michigan	14	15	1	102
1940	Tom Harmon, Michigan	16	18	1	117
1941	Bill Dudley, Virginia	18	23	1	134
1942	Bob Steuber, Missouri	18	13	0	121
1943	Steve Van Buren, LSU	14	14	0	98
1944	Glenn Davis, Army	20	0	0	120
1945	Doc Blanchard, Army	19	1	0	115
1946	Gene Thomas, Tenn-Chatt.	18	9	0	117
1947	Lou Gambino, Maryland	16	0	0	96
1948	Fred Wendt, Texas Mines	20	32	0	152
1949	George Thomas, Oklahoma	19	3	0	117
1950	Bobby Reynolds, Nebraska	22	25	0	157
1951	Ollie Matson, San Francisco	21	0	0	126
1952	Jackie Parker, Miss. St.	16	24	0	120
1953	Earl Lindley, Utah St.	13	3	0	81
1954	Art Luppino, Arizona	24	22	0	166
1955	Jim Swink, TCU	20	5	0	125
1956	Clendon Thomas, Oklahoma	18	0	0	108
1957	Leon Burton, Ariz. St.	16	0	0	96
1958	Dick Bass, Pacific	18	8	0	116
1959	Pervis Atkins, N. Mexico St.	17	5	0	107
1960	Bob Gaiters, N. Mexico St.	23	7	0	145
1961	Jim Pilot, N. Mexico St.	21	12	0	138
1962	Jerry Logan, W. Texas St.	13	32	0	110
1963	Cosmo Iacavazzi, Princeton	14	0	0	84
	& Dave Casinelli, Memphis St.	14	0	0	84
1964	Brian Piccolo, Wake Forest	17	9	0	111
1965	Howard Twilley, Tulsa	16	31	0	127
1966	Ken Hebert, Houston	11	41	0	113
1967	Leroy Keyes, Purdue	19	0	0	114
1968	Jim O'Brien, Cincinnati	12	31	13	142
1969	Steve Owens, Oklahoma	23	0	0	138

Year		TD	XP	FG	Pts	P/Gm
1970	Brian Bream, Air Force	20	0	0	120	12.0
	& Gary Kosins, Dayton	18	0	0	108	12.0
1971	Ed Marinaro, Cornell	24	4	0	148	16.4
1972	Harold Henson, Ohio St	20	0	0	120	12.0
1973	Jim Jennings, Rutgers	21	2	0	128	11.6
1974	Bill Marek, Wisconsin	19	0	0	114	12.7
1975	Pete Johnson, Ohio St	25	0	0	150	13.6
1976	Tony Dorsett, Pitt	22	2	0	134	12.2
1977	Earl Campbell, Texas	19	0	0	114	10.4
1978	Billy Sims, Oklahoma	20	0	0	120	10.9
1979	Billy Sims, Oklahoma	22	0	0	132	12.0
1980	Sammy Winder, So. Miss	20	0	0	120	10.9
1981	Marcus Allen, USC	23	0	0	138	12.5
1982	Greg Allen, Fla. St.	21	0	0	126	11.5
1983	Mike Rozier, Nebraska	29	0	0	174	14.5
1984	Keith Byars, Ohio St	24	0	0	144	13.1
1985	Bernard White, B. Green	19	0	0	114	10.4
1986	Steve Bartalo, Colo. St	19	0	0	114	10.4
1987	Paul Hewitt, S. Diego St.	24	0	0	144	12.0
1988	Barry Sanders, Okla.St.	39	0	0	234	21.3
1989	Anthony Thompson, Ind	25	4	0	154	14.0
1990	Stacey Robinson, No. Ill.	19	6	0	120	10.9
1991	Marshall Faulk, S.D. St.	23	2	0	140	15.6
1992	Garrison Hearst, Georgia	21	0	0	126	11.5
1993	Bam Morris, Texas Tech	22	2	0	134	12.2
1994	Rashaan Salaam, Colo	24	0	0	144	13.1
1995	Eddie George, Ohio St.	24	0	0	144	12.0
1996	Corey Dillon, Washington	23	0	0	138	12.6
1997	Ricky Williams, Texas	25	2	0	152	13.8
1998	Troy Edwards, La. Tech	31	2	0	188	15.7
1999	Shaun Alexander, Alabama	24	0	0	144	13.1
2000	Lee Suggs, Va. Tech	28	0	0	168	15.3
2001	Luke Staley, BYU	28	2	0	170	15.5
2002	Brock Forsey, Boise St.	32	0	0	192	14.8
2003	Patrick Cobbs, No. Texas	21	0	0	126	11.5

All-Time NCAA Division I-A Leaders

Through the 2003 regular season. The NCAA does not recognize active players among career Per Game leaders.

CAREER

Passing

(Minimum 500 Completions)

Passing Efficiency		Years	Rating
1	Ryan Dinwiddie, Boise St.	2000-03	168.4
2	Danny Wuerffel, Florida	1993-96	163.6
3	Ty Detmer, BYU	1988-91	162.7
4	Steve Sarkisian, BYU	1995-96	162.0
5	Billy Blanton, San Diego St.	1993-96	157.1

Yards Gained		Years	Yards
1	Ty Detmer, BYU	1988-91	15,031
2	Philip Rivers, N.C. State	2000-03	13,484
3	Timmy Chang, Hawaii	2000-03	12,814
4	Tim Rattay, La. Tech	1997-99	12,746
5	Luke McCown, La. Tech	2000-03	12,666

Completions		Years	No
1	Kliff Kingsbury, Texas Tech	1999-02	1231
2	Philip Rivers, N.C. State	2000-03	1147
3	Chris Redman, Louisville	1996-99	1031
4	Tim Rattay, La. Tech	1997-99	1015
5	Ty Detmer, BYU	1988-91	958

Receptions

Catches		Years	No
1	Arnold Jackson, Louisville	1997-00	300
2	Trevor Insley, Nevada	1996-99	298
3	Geoff Noisy, Nevada	1995-98	295
4	Rashaun Woods, Oklahoma St.	2000-03	293
5	Troy Edwards, La. Tech	1996-98	280

Catches Per Game		Years	No	P/Gm
1	Manny Hazard, Houston	1989-90	220	10.5
2	Alex Van Dyke, Nevada	1994-95	227	10.3
3	Howard Twilley, Tulsa	1963-65	261	9.0
4	Jason Phillips, Houston	1987-88	207	9.4
5	Troy Edwards, La. Tech	1996-98	280	8.2

Yards Gained		Years	No	Yards
1	Trevor Insley, Nevada	1996-99	298	5005
2	Marcus Harris, Wyoming	1993-96	259	4518
3	Rashaun Woods, Oklahoma St.	2000-03	293	4412
4	Ryan Yarborough, Wyoming	1990-93	229	4357
5	Troy Edwards, La. Tech	1996-98	280	4352

Rushing

Yards Gained		Years	Yards
1	Ron Dayne, Wisconsin	1996-99	6397
2	Ricky Williams, Texas	1995-98	6279
3	Tony Dorsett, Pittsburgh	1973-76	6082
4	Charles White, USC	1976-79	5598
5	Travis Prentice, Miami-OH	1996-99	5596

Yards Per Game		Years	Yards	P/Gm
1	Ed Marinaro, Cornell	1969-71	4715	174.6
2	O.J. Simpson, USC	1967-68	3124	164.4
3	Herschel Walker, Georgia	1980-82	5259	159.4
4	LeShon Johnson, No. Ill.	1992-93	3314	150.6
5	Ron Dayne, Wisconsin	1996-99	6397	148.8

All-Time NCAA Division I-A Leaders (Cont.)
Total Offense

Yards Gained	Years	Yards		Yards Per Game	Years	Yards	P/Gm
1 Ty Detmer, BYU.	1988-91	14,665		1 Tim Rattay, La. Tech	1997-99	12,689	382.4
2 Philip Rivers, N.C. State	2000-03	13,582		2 Chris Vargas, Nevada.	1992-93	6,417	320.9
3 Luke McCown, La. Tech	2000-03	12,731		3 Ty Detmer, BYU.	1988-91	14,665	318.8
4 Timmy Chang, Hawaii	2000-03	12,637		4 Daunte Culpepper*, C. Fla.	1996-98	10,344	313.5
5 Tim Rattay, La. Tech	1997-99	12,618		5 Mike Perez, San Jose St	1986-87	6,182	309.1

*Culpepper played I-AA with Central Florida in 1995.

All-Purpose Yardage

Yards Gained	Years	Yards		Yards Per Game	Years	Yards	P/Gm
1 Ricky Williams, Texas	1995-98	7206		1 Ryan Benjamin, Pacific	1990-92	5706	237.8
2 Napoleon McCallum, Navy	1981-85	7172		2 Sheldon Canley, S. Jose St..	1988-90	5146	205.8
3 Darrin Nelson, Stanford	1977-78, 80-81	6885		3 Howard Stevens, Louisville	1971-72	3873	193.7
4 Kevin Faulk, LSU	1995-98	6833		4 O.J. Simpson, USC	1967-68	3666	192.9
5 Ron Dayne, Wisconsin	1996-99	6701		5 Alex Van Dyke, Nevada	1994-95	4146	188.5

Miscellaneous

Interceptions	Years	No		Punt Return Average*	Years	Avg
1 Al Brosky, Illinois	1950-52	29		1 Jack Mitchell, Oklahoma.	1946-48	23.6
2 John Provost, Holy Cross	1972-74	27		2 Gene Gibson, Cincinnati	1949-50	20.5
Martin Bayless, Bowling Green	1980-83	27		3 Eddie Macon, Pacific.	1949-51	18.9
4 Tom Curtis, Michigan	1967-69	25		4 Jackie Robinson, UCLA	1939-40	18.8
Tony Thurman, Boston College	1981-84	25		5 Mike Fuller, Auburn	1972-74	17.7
Tracy Saul, Texas Tech.	1989-92	25		*Minimum 1.2 punt returns per game and 30 career returns.		

Punting Average*	Years	Avg		Kickoff Return Average*	Years	Avg
1 Shane Lechler, Texas A&M	1996-99	44.7		1 Anthony Davis, USC	1972-74	35.1
2 Bill Smith, Mississippi	1983-86	44.3		2 Eric Booth, So. Miss.	1994-97	32.4
3 Jim Arnold, Vanderbilt	1979-82	43.9		3 Overton Curtis, Utah St	1957-58	31.0
4 Ralf Mojsiejenko, Michigan St.	1981-84	43.6		4 Fred Montgomery, New Mexico St.	1991-92	30.5
5 Jim Miller, Mississippi.	1976-79	43.4		5 Altie Taylor, Utah St.	1966-68	29.3

*Minimum 250 punts.   *Minimum 1.2 kickoff returns per game and 30 career returns.

Scoring
Non-kickers

Points	Years	TD	Xpt	FG	Pts		Touchdown Catches	Years	No
1 Travis Prentice, Miami-OH	1996-99	78	0	0	468		1 Troy Edwards, La. Tech	1996-98	50
2 Ricky Williams, Texas	1995-98	75	2	0	452		2 Darius Watts, Marshall	2000-03	47
3 Brock Forsey, Boise St.	1999-02	68	0	0	408		3 Aaron Turner, Pacific	1989-92	43
4 Anthony Thompson, Ind.	1986-89	65	4	0	394		4 Ryan Yarborough, Wyoming	1990-93	42
5 Ron Dayne, Wisconsin	1996-99	63	0	0	378		Rashaun Woods, Oklahoma St.	2000-03	42

Points Per Game	Years	Pts	P/Gm
1 Marshall Faulk, S. Diego St.	1991-93	376	12.1
2 Ed Marinaro, Cornell.	1969-71	318	11.8
3 Bill Burnett, Arkansas	1968-70	294	11.3
4 Steve Owens, Oklahoma	1967-69	336	11.2
5 Eddie Talboom, Wyoming	1948-50	303	10.8

Touchdowns Rushing	Years	No
1 Travis Prentice, Miami-OH	1996-99	73
2 Ricky Williams, Texas	1995-98	72
3 Anthony Thompson, Indiana.	1986-89	64
4 Ron Dayne, Wisconsin	1996-99	63
5 Eric Crouch, Nebraska	1998-01	59

Touchdowns Passing	Years	No
1 Ty Detmer, BYU.	1988-91	121
2 Tim Rattay, La. Tech	1997-99	115
3 Danny Wuerffel, Florida	1993-96	114
4 Chad Pennington, Marshall	1997-99	100
5 Kliff Kingsbury, Texas Tech.	1999-02	95
Philip Rivers, N.C. State	2000-03	95

Kickers

Points	Years	FG	XP	Pts
1 Roman Anderson, Hou	1988-91	70	213	423
2 Carlos Huerta, Mia-FL	1988-91	73	178	397
3 Jason Elam, Hawaii	1988-89, 91-92	79	158	395
4 Derek Schmidt, Fla. St	1984-87	73	174	393
5 Kris Brown, Nebraska	1995-98	57	217	388

Field Goals	Years	No
1 Billy Bennett, Georgia	2000-03	87
2 Jeff Jaeger, Washington	1983-86	80
3 John Lee, UCLA	1982-85	79
Jason Elam, Hawaii.	1988-89, 91-92	79
5 Philip Doyle, Alabama	1987-90	78
Luis Zendejas, Arizona St	1981-84	78

SINGLE SEASON
Rushing

Note that starting with the 2002 season postseason and bowl games are included in single season records

Yards Gained	Year	Gm	Car	Yards		Yards Per Game	Year	Gm	Yards	P/Gm
Barry Sanders, Okla. St	1988	11	344	2628		Barry Sanders, Okla. St	1988	11	2628	238.9
Marcus Allen, USC	1981	11	403	2342		Marcus Allen, USC	1981	11	2342	212.9
Troy Davis, Iowa St.	1996	11	402	2185		Ed Marinaro, Cornell.	1971	9	1881	209.0
LaDainian Tomlinson, TCU	2000	11	369	2158		Troy Davis, Iowa St.	1996	11	2185	198.6
Mike Rozier, Nebraska	1983	12	275	2148		LaDainian Tomlinson, TCU	2000	11	2158	196.2

Passing
(Minimum 15 Attempts Per Game)

Passing Efficiency	Year	Rating
Shaun King, Tulane	1998	183.3
Michael Vick, Va. Tech	1999	180.4
Danny Wuerffel, Florida	1995	178.4
Jim McMahon, BYU	1980	176.9
Ty Detmer, BYU	1989	175.6

Yards Gained	Year	Yards
B.J. Symons, Texas Tech	2003	5833
Ty Detmer, BYU	1990	5188
David Klingler, Houston	1990	5140
Kliff Kingsbury, Texas Tech	2002	5017
Tim Rattay, La. Tech	1998	4943

Completions	Year	Att	No
Kliff Kingsbury, Texas Tech	2002	712	479
B.J. Symons, Texas Tech	2003	719	470
Tim Rattay, La. Tech	1998	559	380
David Klingler, Houston	1990	643	374
Andre Ware, Houston	1989	578	365

Receptions

Catches	Year	Gm	No
Manny Hazard, Houston	1989	11	142
Troy Edwards, La. Tech	1998	12	140
Nate Burleson, Nevada	2002	12	138
Howard Twilley, Tulsa	1965	10	134
Trevor Insley, Nevada	1999	11	134

Catches Per Game	Year	No	P/Gm
Howard Twilley, Tulsa	1965	134	13.4
Manny Hazard, Houston	1989	142	12.9
Trevor Insley, Nevada	1999	134	12.2
Alex Van Dyke, Nevada	1995	129	11.7
Troy Edwards, La. Tech	1998	140	11.7

Yards Gained	Year	No	Yards
Trevor Insley, Nevada	1999	134	2060
Troy Edwards, La. Tech	1998	140	1996
Alex Van Dyke, Nevada	1995	129	1854
J.R. Tolver, San Diego St.	2002	128	1785
Howard Twilley, Tulsa	1965	134	1779
Josh Reed, LSU	2001	94	1740

Total Offense

Yards Gained	Year	Gm	Plays	Yards
B.J. Symons, Texas Tech	2003	13	798	5976
David Klingler, Houston	1990	11	704	5221
Ty Detmer, BYU	1990	12	635	5022
Kliff Kingsbury, Texas Tech	2002	14	814	4903
Tim Rattay, La. Tech	1998	12	602	4840

Yards Per Game	Year	Gm	Yards	P/Gm
David Klingler, Houston	1990	11	5221	474.6
B.J. Symons, Texas Tech	2003	13	5976	459.7
Andre Ware, Houston	1989	11	4661	423.7
Ty Detmer, BYU	1990	12	5022	418.5
Tim Rattay, La. Tech	1998	12	4840	403.3

All-Purpose Yardage

Yards Gained	Year	Yards
Barry Sanders, Okla. St	1988	3250
Ryan Benjamin, Pacific	1991	2995
Troy Edwards, La. Tech	1998	2784
Darren Sproles, Kansas St.	2003	2735
Mike Pringle, CS-Fullerton	1989	2690

Yards Per Game	Year	Yards	P/Gm
Barry Sanders, Okla. St	1988	3250	295.5
Ryan Benjamin, Pacific	1991	2995	249.6
Byron (Whizzer) White, Colo	1937	1970	246.3
Mike Pringle, CS-Fullerton	1989	2690	244.6
Paul Palmer, Temple	1986	2633	239.4

Scoring

Points	Year	TD	Xpt	FG	Pts
Barry Sanders, Okla. St	1988	39	0	0	234
Brock Forsey, Boise St.	2002	32	0	0	192
Troy Edwards, La. Tech	1998	31	2	0	188
Mike Rozier, Nebraska	1983	29	0	0	174
Lydell Mitchell, Penn St	1971	29	0	0	174

Points Per Game	Year	Pts	P/Gm
Barry Sanders, Okla. St	1988	234	21.3
Bobby Reynolds, Nebraska	1950	157	17.4
Art Luppino, Arizona	1954	166	16.6
Ed Marinaro, Cornell	1971	148	16.4
Lydell Mitchell, Penn St	1971	174	15.8

Touchdowns Rushing	Year	No
Barry Sanders, Okla. St	1988	37
Mike Rozier, Nebraska	1983	29
Willis McGahee, Miami-FL	2002	28
Ricky Williams, Texas	1998	27
Lee Suggs, Va. Tech	2000	27
Brock Forsey, Boise St.	2002	26

Touchdowns Passing	Year	No
David Klingler, Houston	1990	54
B.J. Symons, Texas Tech	2003	52
Jim McMahon, BYU	1980	47
Andre Ware, Houston	1989	46
Tim Rattay, La. Tech	1998	46

Touchdown Catches	Year	No
Troy Edwards, La. Tech	1998	27
Randy Moss, Marshall	1997	25
Manny Hazard, Houston	1989	22
Larry Fitzgerald, Pittsburgh	2003	22
Desmond Howard, Michigan	1991	19
Ashley Lelie, Hawaii	2001	19

Field Goals	Year	No
Billy Bennett, Georgia	2003	31
John Lee, UCLA	1984	29
Paul Woodside, West Virginia	1982	28
Luis Zendejas, Arizona St	1983	28
Nick Browne, TCU	2003	28

Miscellaneous

Interceptions	Year	No
Al Worley, Washington	1968	14
George Shaw, Oregon	1951	13
Eight tied with 12 each.		

Punting Average*	Year	Avg
Chad Kessler, LSU	1997	50.3
Reggie Roby, Iowa	1981	49.8
Kirk Wilson, UCLA	1956	49.3
Todd Sauerbrun, West Virginia	1994	48.4
Travis Dorsch, Purdue	2001	48.4

*Qualifiers for championship.

Punt Return Average*	Year	Avg
Bill Blackstock, Tennessee	1951	25.9
George Sims, Baylor	1948	25.0
Gene Derricotte, Michigan	1947	24.8

*At least 1.2 returns per game.

Kickoff Return Average*	Year	Avg
Paul Allen, BYU	1961	40.1
Tremain Mack, Miami-FL	1996	39.5
Leeland McElroy, Texas A&M	1993	39.3
Forrest Hall, San Francisco	1946	38.2
Tony Ball, Tenn-Chattanooga	1977	36.4

*At least 1.2 kickoff returns per game.

All-Time NCAA Division I-A Leaders (Cont.)
SINGLE GAME

Rushing

Yards Gained	Opponent	Year	Yds
LaDainian Tomlinson, TCU	UTEP	1999	406
Tony Sands, Kansas	Missouri	1991	396
Marshall Faulk, San Diego St	Pacific	1991	386
Troy Davis, Iowa St.	Missouri	1996	378
Anthony Thompson, Indiana	Wisconsin	1989	377
Robbie Mixon, C. Michigan	E. Michigan	2002	377

Passing

Yards Gained	Opponent	Year	Yds
David Klingler, Houston	Arizona St.	1990	716
Matt Vogler, TCU	Houston	1990	690
B.J. Symons, Texas Tech	Mississippi	2003	661
Brian Lindgren, Idaho	Mid. Tenn. St.	2001	637
Scott Mitchell, Utah	Air Force	1988	631

Completions	Opponent	Year	No
Drew Brees, Purdue	Wisconsin	1998	55
Rusty LaRue, Wake Forest	Duke	1995	55
Rusty LaRue, Wake Forest	N.C. St.	1995	50

Four tied with 49 each (including twice by Kliff Kingsbury).

Scoring

Points	Opponent	Year	Pts
Howard Griffith, Illinois	So. Ill.	1990	48
Marshall Faulk, S. Diego St	Pacific	1991	44
Jim Brown, Syracuse	Colgate	1956	43
Showboat Boykin, Ole Miss	Miss. St.	1951	42
Fred Wendt, UTEP*	N. Mex. St.	1948	42
Rashaun Woods, Oklahoma St.	SMU	2003	42

*UTEP was Texas Mines in 1948.

Touchdowns Rushing	Opponent	Year	No
Howard Griffith, Illinois	So. Ill	1990	8
Showboat Boykin, Ole Miss	Miss. St.	1951	7

Note: Griffith's TD runs (5-51-7-41-5-18-5-3).

Touchdown Catches	Opponent	Year	No
Rashaun Woods, Oklahoma St.	SMU	2003	7
Tim Delaney, S. Diego St	N. Mex. St.	1969	6

Note: Woods's TD catches (2-10-34-32-25-5-11).

Total Offense

Yards Gained	Opponent	Year	Yds
David Klingler, Houston	Arizona St.	1990	732
Matt Vogler, TCU	Houston	1990	696
B.J. Symons, Texas Tech	Mississippi	2003	681
David Klingler, Houston	TCU	1990	625
Scott Mitchell, Utah	Air Force	1988	625

Receiving

Catches	Opponent	Year	No
Randy Gatewood, UNLV	Idaho	1994	23
Jay Miller, BYU	New Mexico	1973	22
Troy Edwards, La. Tech	Nebraska	1998	21
Chris Daniels, Purdue	Mich. St.	1999	21

Two tied with 20 each.

Yards Gained	Opponent	Year	Yds
Troy Edwards, La. Tech	Nebraska	1998	405
Randy Gatewood, UNLV	Idaho	1994	363
Chuck Hughes, UTEP*	N. Texas St.	1965	349
Nate Burleson, Nevada	San Jose St.	2001	326
Rick Eber, Tulsa	Idaho St.	1967	322

*UTEP was Texas Western in 1965.

Touchdowns Passing	Opponent	Year	No
David Klingler, Houston	E.Wash.	1990	11
Dennis Shaw, San Diego St	N. Mex. St.	1969	9

Note: Klingler's TD passes (5-48-29-7-3-7-40-8-7-8-51).

Field Goals	Opponent	Year	No
Dale Klein, Nebraska	Missouri	1985	7
Mike Prindle, W. Michigan	Marshall	1984	7

Note: Klein's FGs (32-22-43-44-29-43-43); Prindle's FGs (32-44-42-23-48-41-27).

Extra Points (Kick)	Opponent	Year	No
Terry Leiweke, Houston	Tulsa	1968	13
Derek Mahoney, Fresno St	New Mexico	1991	13

Longest Plays (since 1941)

Rushing	Opponent	Year	Yds
Gale Sayers, Kansas	Nebraska	1963	99
Max Anderson, Ariz. St	Wyoming	1967	99
Ralph Thompson, W. Texas St	Wich. St.	1970	99
Kelsey Finch, Tennessee	Florida	1977	99
Eric Vann, Kansas	Oklahoma	1997	99

Eleven tied at 98 each.

Passing	Opponent	Year	Yds
Fred Owens to Jack Ford, Portland	St. Mary's	1947	99
Bo Burris to Warren McVea, Houston Wash. St.		1966	99
Colin Clapton to Eddie Jenkins, Holy Cross	Boston U.	1970	99
Terry Peel to Robert Ford, Houston	Syracuse	1970	99
Terry Peel to Robert Ford, Houston	S. Diego St.	1972	99
Cris Collinsworth to Derrick Gaffney, Florida	Rice	1977	99
Scott Ankrom to James Maness, TCU	Rice	1984	99
Gino Torretta to Horace Copeland, Miami-FL	Ark.	1991	99

Passing	Opponent	Year	Yds
John Paci to Thomas Lewis, Indiana	Penn St.	1993	99
Troy DeGar to West Caswell, Tulsa	Oklahoma	1996	99
Drew Brees to Vinny Sutherland, Purdue	N'western	1999	99
Dan Urban to Justin McCariens, N. Ill	Ball St.	2000	99
Jason Johnson to Brandon Marshall, Ariz.	Idaho	2001	99
Jim Sorgi to Lee Evans, Wisconsin	Akron	2003	99
Dondrial Pinkins to Troy Williamson, South Carolina	Virginia	2003	99

Field Goals	Opponent	Year	Yds
Steve Little, Arkansas	Texas	1977	67
Russell Erxleben, Texas.	Rice	1977	67
Joe Williams, Wichita St	So. Ill.	1978	67
Tony Franklin, Tex. A&M	Baylor	1976	65
Martin Gramatica, Kan. St.	No. Ill.	1998	65

Note: Gramatica's FG is the only one listed above that was not off a tee and through the narrower (18'6") goal posts.

Annual Awards
Heisman Trophy

Originally presented in 1935 as the DAC Trophy by the Downtown Athletic Club of New York City to the best college football player east of the Mississippi. In 1936, players across the country were eligible and the award was renamed the Heisman Trophy following the death of former college coach and DAC athletic director John W. Heisman.

Multiple winner: Archie Griffin (2).

Winners in junior year (13): Doc Blanchard (1945), Ty Detmer (1990); Archie Griffin (1974), Desmond Howard (1991), Vic Janowicz (1950), Rashaan Salaam (1994), Barry Sanders (1988), Billy Sims (1978), Roger Staubach (1963), Doak Walker (1948), Herschel Walker (1982), Andre Ware (1989) and Charles Woodson (1997).

Winners on AP national champions (10): Angelo Bertelli (Notre Dame, 1943); Doc Blanchard (Army, 1945); Tony Dorsett (Pittsburgh, 1976); Leon Hart (Notre Dame, 1949); Johnny Lujack (Notre Dame, 1947); Davey O'Brien (TCU, 1938); Bruce Smith (Minnesota, 1941); CharlieWard (Florida St., 1993); DannyWuerffel (Florida, 1996); and CharlesWoodson (Michigan, 1997).

Year		Points
1935	**Jay Berwanger,** Chicago, HB	.84
	2nd—Monk Meyer, Army, HB	.29
	3rd—Bill Shakespeare, Notre Dame, HB	.23
	4th—Pepper Constable, Princeton, FB	.20
1936	**Larry Kelley,** Yale, E	.219
	2nd—Sam Francis, Nebraska, FB	.47
	3rd—Ray Buivid, Marquette, HB	.43
	4th—Sammy Baugh, TCU, HB	.39
1937	**Clint Frank,** Yale, HB	.524
	2nd—Byron (Whizzer) White, Colo., HB	.264
	3rd—Marshall Goldberg, Pitt, HB	.211
	4th—Alex Wojciechowicz, Fordham, C	.85
1938	**Davey O'Brien,** TCU, QB	.519
	2nd—Marshall Goldberg, Pitt, HB	.294
	3rd—Sid Luckman, Columbia, QB	.154
	4th—Bob MacLeod, Dartmouth, HB	.78
1939	**Nile Kinnick,** Iowa, HB	.651
	2nd—Tom Harmon, Michigan, HB	.405
	3rd—Paul Christman, Missouri, QB	.391
	4th—George Cafego, Tennessee, QB	.296
1940	**Tom Harmon,** Michigan, HB	.1303
	2nd—John Kimbrough, Texas A&M, FB	.841
	3rd—George Franck, Minnesota, HB	.102
	4th—Frankie Albert, Stanford, QB	.90
1941	**Bruce Smith,** Minnesota, HB	.554
	2nd—Angelo Bertelli, Notre Dame, QB	.345
	3rd—Frankie Albert, Stanford, QB	.336
	4th—Frank Sinkwich, Georgia, HB	.249
1942	**Frank Sinkwich,** Georgia, TB	.1059
	2nd—Paul Governali, Columbia, QB	.218
	3rd—Clint Castleberry, Ga. Tech, HB	.99
	4th—Mike Holovak, Boston College, FB	.95
1943	**Angelo Bertelli,** Notre Dame, QB	.648
	2nd—Bob Odell, Penn, HB	.177
	3rd—Otto Graham, Northwestern, QB	.140
	4th—Creighton Miller, Notre Dame, HB	.134
1944	**Les Horvath,** Ohio St., TB-QB	.412
	2nd—Glenn Davis, Army, HB	.287
	3rd—Doc Blanchard, Army, FB	.237
	4th—Don Whitmire, Navy, T	.115
1945	**Doc Blanchard,** Army, FB	.860
	2nd—Glenn Davis, Army, HB	.638
	3rd—Bob Fenimore, Oklahoma A&M, HB	.187
	4th—Herman Wedemeyer, St. Mary's, HB	.152
1946	**Glenn Davis,** Army, HB	.792
	2nd—Charlie Trippi, Georgia, HB	.435
	3rd—Johnny Lujack, Notre Dame, QB	.379
	4th—Doc Blanchard, Army, FB	.267
1947	**Johnny Lujack,** Notre Dame, QB	.742
	2nd—Bob Chappuis, Michigan, HB	.555
	3rd—Doak Walker, SMU, HB	.196
	4th—Charlie Conerly, Mississippi, QB	.186
1948	**Doak Walker,** SMU, HB	.778
	2nd—Charlie Justice, N. Carolina, HB	.443
	3rd—Chuck Bednarik, Penn, C	.336
	4th—Jackie Jensen, California, HB	.143
1949	**Leon Hart,** Notre Dame, E	.995
	2nd—Charlie Justice, N. Carolina, HB	.272
	3rd—Doak Walker, SMU, HB	.229
	4th—Arnold Galiffa, Army QB	.196
1950	**Vic Janowicz,** Ohio St., HB	.633
	2nd—Kyle Rote, SMU, HB	.280
	3rd—Reds Bagnell, Penn, HB	.231
	4th—Babe Parilli, Kentucky, QB	.214
1951	**Dick Kazmaier,** Princeton, TB	.1777
	2nd—Hank Lauricella, Tennessee, HB	.424
	3rd—Babe Parilli, Kentucky, QB	.344
	4th—Bill McColl, Stanford, E	.313
1952	**Billy Vessels,** Oklahoma, HB	.525
	2nd—Jack Scarbath, Maryland, QB	.367
	3rd—Paul Giel, Minnesota, HB	.329
	4th—Donn Moomaw, UCLA, C	.257
1953	**Johnny Lattner,** Notre Dame, HB	.1850
	2nd—Paul Giel, Minnesota, HB	.1794
	3rd—Paul Cameron, UCLA, HB	.444
	4th—Bernie Faloney, Maryland, QB	.258

Year		Points
1954	**Alan Ameche,** Wisconsin, FB	.1068
	2nd—Kurt Burris, Oklahoma, C	.838
	3rd—Howard Cassady, Ohio St., HB	.810
	4th—Ralph Guglielmi, Notre Dame, QB	.691
1955	**Howard Cassady,** Ohio St., HB	.2219
	2nd—Jim Swink, TCU, HB	.742
	3rd—George Welsh, Navy, QB	.383
	4th—Earl Morrall, Michigan St., QB	.323
1956	**Paul Hornung,** Notre Dame, QB	.1066
	2nd—Johnny Majors, Tennessee, HB	.994
	3rd—Tommy McDonald, Oklahoma, HB	.973
	4th—Jerry Tubbs, Oklahoma, C	.724
1957	**John David Crow,** Texas A&M, HB	.1183
	2nd—Alex Karras, Iowa, T	.693
	3rd—Walt Kowalczyk, Mich. St., HB	.630
	4th—Lou Michaels, Kentucky, T	.330
1958	**Pete Dawkins,** Army, HB	.1394
	2nd—Randy Duncan, Iowa, QB	.1021
	3rd—Billy Cannon, LSU, HB	.975
	4th—Bob White, Ohio St., FB	.365
1959	**Billy Cannon,** LSU, HB	.1929
	2nd—Richie Lucas, Penn St., QB	.613
	3rd—Don Meredith, SMU, QB	.286
	4th—Bill Burrell, Illinois, G	.196
1960	**Joe Bellino,** Navy, HB	.1793
	2nd—Tom Brown, Minnesota, G	.731
	3rd—Jake Gibbs, Mississippi, QB	.453
	4th—Ed Dyas, Auburn, HB	.319
1961	**Ernie Davis,** Syracuse, HB	.824
	2nd—Bob Ferguson, Ohio St., HB	.771
	3rd—Jimmy Saxton, Texas, HB	.551
	4th—Sandy Stephens, Minnesota, QB	.543
1962	**Terry Baker,** Oregon St., QB	.707
	2nd—Jerry Stovall, LSU, HB	.618
	3rd—Bobby Bell, Minnesota, T	.429
	4th—Lee Roy Jordan, Alabama, C	.321
1963	**Roger Staubach,** Navy, QB	.1860
	2nd—Billy Lothridge, Ga. Tech, QB	.504
	3rd—Sherman Lewis, Mich. St., HB	.369
	4th—Don Trull, Baylor, QB	.253
1964	**John Huarte,** Notre Dame, QB	.1026
	2nd—Jerry Rhome, Tulsa, QB	.952
	3rd—Dick Butkus, Illinois, C	.505
	4th—Bob Timberlake, Michigan, QB	.361
1965	**Mike Garrett,** USC, HB	.926
	2nd—Howard Twilley, Tulsa, E	.528
	3rd—Jim Grabowski, Illinois, FB	.481
	4th—Donny Anderson, Texas Tech, HB	.408
1966	**Steve Spurrier,** Florida, QB	.1679
	2nd—Bob Griese, Purdue, QB	.816
	3rd—Nick Eddy, Notre Dame, HB	.456
	4th—Gary Beban, UCLA, QB	.318
1967	**Gary Beban,** UCLA, QB	.1968
	2nd—O.J. Simpson, USC, HB	.1722
	3rd—Leroy Keyes, Purdue, HB	.1366
	4th—Larry Csonka, Syracuse, FB	.136
1968	**O.J. Simpson,** USC, HB	.2853
	2nd—Leroy Keyes, Purdue, HB	.1103
	3rd—Terry Hanratty, Notre Dame, QB	.387
	4th—Ted Kwalick, Penn St., TE	.254
1969	**Steve Owens,** Oklahoma, HB	.1488
	2nd—Mike Phipps, Purdue, QB	.1344
	3rd—Rex Kern, Ohio St., QB	.856
	4th—Archie Manning, Mississippi, QB	.582
1970	**Jim Plunkett,** Stanford, QB	.2229
	2nd—Joe Theismann, Notre Dame, QB	.1410
	3rd—Archie Manning, Mississippi, QB	.849
	4th—Steve Worster, Texas, RB	398
1971	**Pat Sullivan,** Auburn, QB	.1597
	2nd—Ed Marinaro, Cornell, RB	.1445
	3rd—Greg Pruitt, Oklahoma, RB	.586
	4th—Johnny Musso, Alabama, RB	.365
1972	**Johnny Rodgers,** Nebraska, FL	.1310
	2nd—Greg Pruitt, Oklahoma, RB	.966
	3rd—Rich Glover, Nebraska, MG	.652
	4th—Bert Jones, LSU, QB	.351

Annual Awards (Cont.)

Year		Points
1973	**John Cappelletti,** Penn St., RB	1057
	2nd–John Hicks, Ohio St., OT	.524
	3rd–Roosevelt Leaks, Texas, RB	.482
	4th–David Jaynes, Kansas, QB	.394
1974	**Archie Griffin,** Ohio St., RB	1920
	2nd–Anthony Davis, USC, RB	.819
	3rd–Joe Washington, Oklahoma, RB	.661
	4th–Tom Clements, Notre Dame, QB	.244
1975	**Archie Griffin,** Ohio St., RB	1800
	2nd–Chuck Muncie, California, RB	.730
	3rd–Ricky Bell, USC, RB	.708
	4th–Tony Dorsett, Pitt, RB	.616
1976	**Tony Dorsett,** Pittsburgh, RB	2357
	2nd–Ricky Bell, USC, RB	1346
	3rd–Rob Lytle, Michigan, RB	.413
	4th–Terry Miller, Oklahoma St., RB	.197
1977	**Earl Campbell,** Texas, RB	1547
	2nd–Terry Miller, Oklahoma St., RB	.812
	3rd–Ken MacAfee, Notre Dame, TE	.343
	4th–Doug Williams, Grambling, QB	.266
1978	**Billy Sims,** Oklahoma, RB	.827
	2nd–Chuck Fusina, Penn St., QB	.750
	3rd–Rick Leach, Michigan, QB	.435
	4th–Charles White, USC, RB	.354
1979	**Charles White,** USC, RB	1695
	2nd–Billy Sims, Oklahoma, RB	.773
	3rd–Marc Wilson, BYU, QB	.589
	4th–Art Schlichter, Ohio St., QB	.251
1980	**George Rogers,** South Carolina, RB	1128
	2nd–Hugh Green, Pittsburgh, DE	.861
	3rd–Herschel Walker, Georgia, RB	.683
	4th–Mark Herrmann, Purdue, QB	.405
1981	**Marcus Allen,** USC, RB	1797
	2nd–Herschel Walker, Georgia, RB	1199
	3rd–Jim McMahon, BYU, QB	.706
	4th–Dan Marino, Pitt, QB	.256
1982	**Herschel Walker,** Georgia, RB	1926
	2nd–John Elway, Stanford, QB	1231
	3rd–Eric Dickerson, SMU, RB	.465
	4th–Anthony Carter, Michigan, WR	.142
1983	**Mike Rozier,** Nebraska, RB	1801
	2nd–Steve Young, BYU, QB	1172
	3rd–Doug Flutie, Boston College, QB	.253
	4th–Turner Gill, Nebraska, QB	.190
1984	**Doug Flutie,** Boston College, QB	2240
	2nd–Keith Byars, Ohio St., RB	1251
	3rd–Robbie Bosco, BYU, QB	.443
	4th–Bernie Kosar, Miami-FL, QB	.320
1985	**Bo Jackson,** Auburn, RB	1509
	2nd–Chuck Long, Iowa, QB	1464
	3rd–Robbie Bosco, BYU, QB	.459
	4th–Lorenzo White, Michigan St., RB	.391
1986	**Vinny Testaverde,** Miami-FL, QB	2213
	2nd–Paul Palmer, Temple, RB	.672
	3rd–Jim Harbaugh, Michigan, QB	.458
	4th–Brian Bosworth, Oklahoma, LB	.395
1987	**Tim Brown,** Notre Dame, WR	1442
	2nd–Don McPherson, Syracuse, QB	.831
	3rd–Gordie Lockbaum, Holy Cross, WR-DB	.657
	4th–Lorenzo White, Michigan St., RB	.632
1988	**Barry Sanders,** Oklahoma St., RB	1878
	2nd–Rodney Peete, USC, QB	.912
	3rd–Troy Aikman, UCLA, QB	.582
	4th–Steve Walsh, Miami-FL, QB	.341

Year		Points
1989	**Andre Ware,** Houston, QB	1073
	2nd–Anthony Thompson, Ind., RB	1003
	3rd–Major Harris, West Va., QB	.709
	4th–Tony Rice, Notre Dame, QB	.523
1990	**Ty Detmer,** BYU, QB	1482
	2nd–Rocket Ismail, Notre Dame, FL	1177
	3rd–Eric Bieniemy, Colorado, RB	.798
	4th–Shawn Moore, Virginia, QB	.465
1991	**Desmond Howard,** Michigan, WR	2077
	2nd–Casey Weldon, Florida St., QB	.503
	3rd–Ty Detmer, BYU, QB	.445
	4th–Steve Emtman, Washington, DT	.357
1992	**Gino Torretta,** Miami-FL, QB	1400
	2nd–Marshall Faulk, San Diego St., RB	1080
	3rd–Garrison Hearst, Georgia, RB	.982
	4th–Marvin Jones, Florida St., LB	.392
1993	**Charlie Ward,** Florida St., QB	2310
	2nd–Heath Shuler, Tennessee, QB	.688
	3rd–David Palmer, Alabama, RB	.292
	4th–Marshall Faulk, S. Diego St., RB	.250
1994	**Rashaan Salaam,** Colorado, RB	1743
	2nd–Ki-Jana Carter, Penn St., RB	.901
	3rd–Steve McNair, Alcorn St., QB	.655
	4th–Kerry Collins, Penn St., QB	.639
1995	**Eddie George,** Ohio St., RB	1460
	2nd–Tommie Frazier, Nebraska, QB	1196
	3rd–Danny Wuerffel, Florida, QB	.987
	4th–Darnell Autry, Northwestern, RB	.535
1996	**Danny Wuerffel,** Florida, QB	1363
	2nd–Troy Davis, Iowa St., RB	1174
	3rd–Jake Plummer, Arizona St., QB	.685
	4th–Orlando Pace, Ohio St., OT	.599
1997	**Charles Woodson,** Michigan, DB-WR	1815
	2nd–Peyton Manning, Tennessee, QB	1543
	3rd–Ryan Leaf, Washington St., QB	.861
	4th–Randy Moss, Marshall, WR	.253
1998	**Ricky Williams,** Texas, RB	2355
	2nd–Michael Bishop, Kansas St., QB	.792
	3rd–Cade McNown, UCLA, QB	.696
	4th–Tim Couch, Kentucky, QB	.527
1999	**Ron Dayne,** Wisconsin, RB	2042
	2nd–Joe Hamilton, Ga. Tech, QB	.994
	3rd–Michael Vick, Va. Tech, QB	.319
	4th–Drew Brees, Purdue, QB	.308
2000	**Chris Weinke,** Florida St., QB	1628
	2nd–Josh Heupel, Oklahoma, QB	1552
	3rd–Drew Brees, Purdue, QB	.619
	4th–LaDainian Tomlinson, TCU, RB	.566
2001	**Eric Crouch,** Nebraska, QB	.770
	2nd–Rex Grossman, Florida, QB	.708
	3rd–Ken Dorsey, Miami-FL, QB	.638
	4th–Joey Harrington, Oregon, QB	.364
2002	**Carson Palmer,** USC, QB	1328
	2nd–Brad Banks, Iowa, QB	1095
	3rd–Larry Johnson, Penn St., RB	.726
	4th–Willis McGahee, Miami-FL, RB	.660
2003	**Jason White,** Oklahoma, QB	1481
	2nd–Larry Fitzgerald, Pittsburgh, WR	1353
	3rd–Eli Manning, Mississippi, QB	.710
	4th–Chris Perry, Michigan, RB	.341

Maxwell Award

First presented in 1937 by the Maxwell Memorial Football Club of Philadelphia, the award is named after Robert (Tiny) Maxwell, a Philadelphia native who was a standout lineman at the University of Chicago at the turn of the century. Like the Heisman, the Maxwell is given to the outstanding college player in the nation. Both awards have gone to the same player in the same season 34 times: Those players are preceded by (#). Glenn Davis of Army and Doak Walker of SMU won both but in different years.

Multiple winner: Johnny Lattner (2).

Year		Year		Year	
1937	#Clint Frank, Yale, HB	1960	#Joe Bellino, Navy, HB	1983	#Mike Rozier, Nebraska, RB
1938	#Davey O'Brien, TCU, QB	1961	Bob Ferguson, Ohio St., HB	1984	#Doug Flutie, Boston Col., QB
1939	#Nile Kinnick, Iowa, HB	1962	#Terry Baker, Oregon St., QB	1985	Chuck Long, Iowa, QB
1940	#Tom Harmon, Michigan, HB	1963	#Roger Staubach, Navy, QB	1986	#V. Testaverde, Miami-FL, QB
1941	Bill Dudley, Virginia, HB	1964	Glenn Ressler, Penn St., G	1987	Don McPherson, Syracuse, QB
1942	Paul Governali, Columbia, QB	1965	Tommy Nobis, Texas, LB	1988	#Barry Sanders, Okla. St., RB
1943	Bob Odell, Penn, HB	1966	Jim Lynch, Notre Dame, LB	1989	Anthony Thompson, Indiana, RB
1944	Glenn Davis, Army, HB	1967	#Gary Beban, UCLA, QB	1990	#Ty Detmer, BYU, QB
1945	#Doc Blanchard, Army, FB	1968	#O.J. Simpson, USC, HB	1991	#Desmond Howard, Mich., WR
1946	Charley Trippi, Georgia, HB	1969	Mike Reid, Penn St., DT	1992	#Gino Torretta, Miami-FL, QB
1947	Doak Walker, SMU, HB	1970	#Jim Plunkett, Stanford, QB	1993	#Charlie Ward, Florida St., QB
1948	Chuck Bednarik, Penn, C	1971	Ed Marinaro, Cornell, RB	1994	Kerry Collins, Penn St., QB
1949	#Leon Hart, Notre Dame, E	1972	Brad Van Pelt, Michigan St., DB	1995	#Eddie George, Ohio St., RB
1950	Reds Bagnell, Penn, HB	1973	#John Cappelletti, Penn St., RB	1996	#Danny Wuerffel, Florida, QB
1951	#Dick Kazmaier, Princeton, TB	1974	Steve Joachim, Temple, QB	1997	Peyton Manning, Tennessee, QB
1952	Johnny Lattner, Notre Dame, HB	1975	#Archie Griffin, Ohio St., RB	1998	#Ricky Williams, Texas, RB
1953	#Johnny Lattner, N. Dame, HB	1976	#Tony Dorsett, Pitt, RB	1999	#Ron Dayne, Wisconsin, RB
1954	Ron Beagle, Army, E	1977	Ross Browner, Notre Dame, DE	2000	Drew Brees, Purdue, QB
1955	#Howard Cassady, Ohio St., HB	1978	Chuck Fusina, Penn St., QB	2001	Ken Dorsey, Miami-FL, QB
1956	Tommy McDonald, Okla., HB	1979	#Charles White, USC, RB	2002	Larry Johnson, Penn St., RB
1957	Bob Reifsnyder, Navy, T	1980	Hugh Green, Pitt, DE	2003	Eli Manning, Mississippi, QB
1958	#Pete Dawkins, Army, HB	1981	#Marcus Allen, USC, RB		
1959	Rich Lucas, Penn St., QB	1982	#Herschel Walker, Georgia, RB		

Outland Trophy

First presented in 1946 by the Football Writers Association of America, honoring the nation's outstanding interior lineman. The award is named after its benefactor, Dr. John H. Outland (Kansas, Class of 1898). Players listed in **bold** type helped lead their team to a national championship (according to AP).

Multiple winner: Dave Rimington (2). **Winners in junior year:** Ross Browner (1976), Steve Emtman (1991), Rien Long (2002), Orlando Pace (1996) and Rimington (1981).

Year		Year		Year	
1946	**George Connor,** N. Dame, T	1966	Loyd Phillips, Arkansas, T	1986	Jason Buck, BYU, DT
1947	Joe Steffy, Army, G	1967	**Ron Yary,** USC, T	1987	Chad Hennings, Air Force, DT
1948	Bill Fischer, Notre Dame, G	1968	Bill Stanfill, Georgia, T	1988	Tracy Rocker, Auburn, DT
1949	Ed Bagdon, Michigan St., G	1969	Mike Reid, Penn St., DT	1989	Mohammed Elewonibi, BYU, G
1950	Bob Gain, Kentucky, T	1970	Jim Stillwagon, Ohio St., MG	1990	Russell Maryland, Miami-FL, NT
1951	Jim Weatherall, Oklahoma, T	1971	**Larry Jacobson,** Neb., T	1991	Steve Emtman, Washington, DT
1952	Dick Modzelewski, Maryland, T	1972	Rich Glover, Nebraska, MG	1992	Will Shields, Nebraska, G
1953	J.D. Roberts, Oklahoma, G	1973	John Hicks, Ohio St., OT	1993	Rob Waldrop, Arizona, NG
1954	Bill Brooks, Arkansas, T	1974	Randy White, Maryland, DT	1994	**Zach Wiegert,** Nebraska, OT
1955	Calvin Jones, Iowa, G	1975	**Lee Roy Selmon,** Okla., DT	1995	Jonathan Ogden, UCLA, OT
1956	Jim Parker, Ohio St., G	1976	Ross Browner, Notre Dame, DE	1996	Orlando Pace, Ohio St., OT
1957	Alex Karras, Iowa, T	1977	Brad Shearer, Texas, DT	1997	Aaron Taylor, Nebraska, G
1958	Zeke Smith, Auburn, G	1978	Greg Roberts, Oklahoma, G	1998	Kris Farris, UCLA, OT
1959	Mike McGee, Duke, T	1979	Jim Richter, N.C. State, C	1999	Chris Samuels, Alabama, OT
1960	**Tom Brown,** Minnesota, G	1980	Mark May, Pittsburgh, OT	2000	John Henderson, Tennessee, DT
1961	Merlin Olsen, Utah St., T	1981	Dave Rimington, Nebraska, C	2001	**Bryant McKinnie,** Miami-FL, OT
1962	Bobby Bell, Minnesota, T	1982	Dave Rimington, Nebraska, C	2002	Rien Long, Washington St., DT
1963	**Scott Appleton,** Texas, T	1983	Dean Steinkuhler, Nebraska, G	2003	Robert Gallery, Iowa, OT
1964	Steve DeLong, Tennessee, T	1984	Bruce Smith, Virginia Tech, DT		
1965	Tommy Nobis, Texas, G	1985	Mike Ruth, Boston College, NG		

Butkus Award

First presented in 1985 by the Downtown Athletic Club of Orlando, Fla., to honor the nation's outstanding linebacker. The award is named after Dick Butkus, two-time consensus All-America at Illinois and six-time All-Pro with the Chicago Bears.

Multiple winner: Brian Bosworth (2).

Year		Year		Year	
1985	Brian Bosworth, Oklahoma	1992	Marvin Jones, Florida St.	1999	LaVar Arrington, Penn St.
1986	Brian Bosworth, Oklahoma	1993	Trev Alberts, Nebraska	2000	Dan Morgan, Miami-FL
1987	Paul McGowan, Florida St.	1994	Dana Howard, Illinois	2001	Rocky Calmus, Oklahoma
1988	Derrick Thomas, Alabama	1995	Kevin Hardy, Illinois	2002	E.J. Henderson, Maryland
1989	Percy Snow, Michigan St.	1996	Matt Russell, Colorado	2003	Teddy Lehman, Oklahoma
1990	Alfred Williams, Colorado	1997	Andy Katzenmoyer, Ohio St.		
1991	Erick Anderson, Michigan	1998	Chris Claiborne, USC		

Lombardi Award

First presented in 1970 by the Rotary Club of Houston, honoring the nation's best lineman. The award is named after pro football coach Vince Lombardi, who, as a guard, was a member of the famous "Seven Blocks of Granite" at Fordham in the 1930s. The Lombardi and Outland awards have gone to the same player in the same year ten times. Those players are preceded by (#). Ross Browner of Notre Dame won both, but in different years.

Multiple winner: Orlando Pace (2).

Year		Year		Year	
1970	#Jim Stillwagon, Ohio St., MG	1972	#Rich Glover, Nebraska, MG	1974	#Randy White, Maryland, DT
1971	Walt Patulski, Notre Dame, DE	1973	#John Hicks, Ohio St., OT	1975	#Lee Roy Selmon, Okla., DT

Annual Awards (Cont.)
Lombardi Award (Cont.)

Year		Year		Year	
1976	Wilson Whitley, Houston, DT	1986	Cornelius Bennett, Alabama, LB	1996	#Orlando Pace, Ohio St., OT
1977	Ross Browner, Notre Dame, DE	1987	Chris Spielman, Ohio St., LB	1997	Grant Wistrom, Nebraska, DE
1978	Bruce Clark, Penn St., DT	1988	#Tracy Rocker, Auburn, DT	1998	Dat Nguyen, Tex. A&M, LB
1979	Brad Budde, USC, G	1989	Percy Snow, Michigan St., LB	1999	Corey Moore, Va. Tech, DE
1980	Hugh Green, Pitt, DE	1990	Chris Zorich, Notre Dame, NT	2000	Jamal Reynolds, Florida St., DE
1981	Kenneth Sims, Texas, DT	1991	#Steve Emtman, Wash., DT	2001	Julius Peppers, N. Carolina, DE
1982	#Dave Rimington, Neb., C	1992	Marvin Jones, Florida St., LB	2002	Terrell Suggs, Arizona St., DE
1983	#Dean Steinkuhler, Neb., G	1993	Aaron Taylor, Notre Dame, OT	2003	Tommie Harris, Oklahoma, DT
1984	Tony Degrate, Texas, DT	1994	Warren Sapp, Miami-FL, DT		
1985	Tony Casillas, Oklahoma, NG	1995	Orlando Pace, Ohio St., OT		

O'Brien Quarterback Award

First presented in 1977 as the O'Brien Memorial Trophy, the award went to the outstanding player in the Southwest. In 1981, however, the Davey O'Brien Educational and Charitable Trust of Ft. Worth renamed the prize the O'Brien National Quarterback Award and now honors the nation's best quarterback. The award is named after 1938 Heisman Trophy-winning QB Davey O'Brien of Texas Christian.

Multiple winners: Ty Detmer, Mike Singletary and Danny Wuerffel (2).

Memorial Trophy

Year		Year		Year	
1977	Earl Campbell, Texas, RB	1979	Mike Singletary, Baylor, LB	1980	Mike Singletary, Baylor, LB
1978	Billy Sims, Oklahoma, RB				

National QB Award

Year		Year		Year	
1981	Jim McMahon, BYU	1989	Andre Ware, Houston	1997	Peyton Manning, Tennessee
1982	Todd Blackledge, Penn St.	1990	Ty Detmer, BYU	1998	Michael Bishop, Kansas St.
1983	Steve Young, BYU	1991	Ty Detmer, BYU	1999	Joe Hamilton, Ga. Tech
1984	Doug Flutie, Boston College	1992	Gino Torretta, Miami-FL	2000	Chris Weinke, Florida St.
1985	Chuck Long, Iowa	1993	Charlie Ward, Florida St.	2001	Eric Crouch, Nebraska
1986	Vinny Testaverde, Miami, FL	1994	Kerry Collins, Penn St.	2002	Brad Banks, Iowa
1987	Don McPherson, Syracuse	1995	Danny Wuerffel, Florida	2003	Jason White, Oklahoma
1988	Troy Aikman, UCLA	1996	Danny Wuerffel, Florida		

Thorpe Award

First presented in 1986 by the Jim Thorpe Athletic Club of Oklahoma City to honor the nation's outstanding defensive back. The award is named after Jim Thorpe–Olympic champion and two-time consensus All-America halfback at Carlisle.

Year		Year		Year	
1986	Thomas Everett, Baylor	1992	Deon Figures, Colorado	1999	Tyrone Carter, Minnesota
1987	Bennie Blades, Miami-FL	1993	Antonio Langham, Alabama	2000	Jamar Fletcher, Wisconsin
	& Rickey Dixon, Oklahoma	1994	Chris Hudson, Colorado	2001	Roy Williams, Oklahoma
1988	Deion Sanders, Florida St.	1995	Greg Myers, Colorado St.	2002	Terence Newman, Kansas St.
1989	Mike Carrier, USC	1996	Lawrence Wright, Florida	2003	Derrick Strait, Oklahoma
1990	Darryl Lewis, Arizona	1997	Charles Woodson, Michigan		
1991	Terrell Buckley, Florida St.	1998	Antoine Winfield, Ohio St.		

Payton Award

First presented in 1987 by the Sports Network and Division I-AA sports information directors to honor the nation's outstanding Division I-AA player. The award is named after Walter Payton, the NFL's all-time leading rusher who was an All-America running back at Jackson St.

Year		Year		Year	
1987	Kenny Gamble, Colgate, RB	1993	Doug Nussmeier, Idaho, QB	1999	Adrian Peterson, Ga. Southern, RB
1988	Dave Meggett, Towson St., RB	1994	Steve McNair, Alcorn St., QB	2000	Louis Ivory, Furman, RB
1989	John Friesz, Idaho, QB	1995	Dave Dickenson, Montana, QB	2001	Brian Westbrook, Villanova, RB
1990	Walter Dean, Grambling, RB	1996	Archie Amerson, N. Arizona, RB	2002	Tony Romo, Eastern Illinois, QB
1991	Jamie Martin, Weber St., QB	1997	Brian Finneran, Villanova, WR	2003	Jamaal Branch, Colgate, RB
1992	Michael Payton, Marshall, QB	1998	Jerry Azumah, N. Hampshire, RB		

Hill Trophy

First presented in 1986 by the Harlon Hill Awards Committee in Florence, Ala., to honor the nation's outstanding Division II player. The award is named after three-time NFL All-Pro Harlon Hill, who played college ball at North Alabama.

Multiple winners: Johnny Bailey (3), Dusty Bonner (2).

Year		Year		Year	
1986	Jeff Bentrim, N. Dakota St., QB	1992	Ronald Moore, Pittsburg St., RB	1998	Brian Shay, Emporia St., RB
1987	Johnny Bailey, Texas A&I, RB	1993	Roger Graham, New Haven, RB	1999	Corte McGuffet, N. Colo., QB
1988	Johnny Bailey, Texas A&I, RB	1994	Chris Hatcher, Valdosta St., QB	2000	Dusty Bonner, Valdosta St., QB
1989	Johnny Bailey, Texas A&I, RB	1995	Ronald McKinnon, N. Alabama, LB	2001	Dusty Bonner, Valdosta St., QB
1990	Chris Simdorn, N. Dakota St., QB	1996	Jarrett Anderson, Truman St., RB	2002	Curt Anes, Grand Valley St., QB
1991	Ronnie West, Pittsburg St., WR	1997	Irv Sigler, Bloomsburg, RB	2003	Will Hall, N. Alabama, QB

All-Time Winningest Division I-A Coaches

Minimum of 10 years in Division I-A through 2003 season. Regular season and bowl games included. Coaches active in 2003 in **bold** type.

Top 25 Winning Percentage

		Yrs	W	L	T	Pct
1	Knute Rockne	13	105	12	5	.881
2	Frank Leahy	13	107	13	9	.864
3	George Woodruff	12	142	25	2	.846
4	Barry Switzer	16	157	29	4	.837
5	Tom Osborne	25	255	49	3	.836
6	Percy Haughton	13	96	17	6	.832
7	Bob Neyland	21	173	31	12	.829
8	Hurry Up Yost	29	196	36	12	.828
9	Bud Wilkinson	17	145	29	4	.826
10	Jock Sutherland	20	144	28	14	.812
11	Bob Devaney	16	136	30	7	.806
12	**Phillip Fulmer**	12	113	28	0	.801
13	Frank Thomas	19	141	33	9	.795
14	Henry Williams	23	141	34	12	.786
15	Gil Dobie	33	180	45	15	.781
16	Bear Bryant	38	323	85	17	.780
17	Fred Folsom	19	106	28	6	.779
18	Steve Spurrier	15	142	40	2	.777
19	**Bobby Bowden**	38	342	97	4	.777
20	Bo Schembechler	27	234	65	8	.775
21	Fritz Crisler	18	116	32	9	.768
22	Charley Moran	18	122	33	12	.766
23	Wallace Wade	24	171	49	10	.765
24	Frank Kush	22	176	54	11	.764
25	Dan McGugin	30	197	55	19	.762

Top 25 Victories

		Yrs	W	L	T	Pct
1	**Bobby Bowden**	38	**342**	97	4	.777
2	**Joe Paterno**	38	**339**	109	3	.755
3	Bear Bryant	38	**323**	85	17	.780
4	Pop Warner	44	**319**	106	32	.733
5	Amos Alonzo Stagg	57	**314**	199	35	.605
6	LaVell Edwards	29	**257**	101	3	.722
7	Tom Osborne	25	**255**	49	3	.836
8	**Lou Holtz**	32	**243**	127	7	.654
9	Woody Hayes	33	**238**	72	10	.759
10	Bo Schembechler	27	**234**	65	8	.775
11	Hayden Fry	37	**232**	178	10	.564
12	Jess Neely	40	**207**	176	19	.539
13	Warren Woodson	31	**203**	95	14	.673
14	Don Nehlen	30	**202**	128	8	.609
15	Vince Dooley	25	**201**	77	10	.715
	Eddie Anderson	39	**201**	128	15	.606
17	Jim Sweeney	32	**200**	154	4	.564
18	Dana X. Bible	33	**198**	72	23	.715
19	Dan McGugin	30	**197**	55	19	.762
20	Hurry Up Yost	29	**196**	36	12	.828
21	Howard Jones	29	**194**	64	21	.733
22	John Cooper	24	**192**	84	6	.691
23	Johnny Vaught	25	**190**	61	12	.745
24	George Welsh	28	**189**	132	4	.588
25	John Heisman	36	**185**	70	17	.711
	Johnny Majors	29	**185**	137	10	.572

Note: John Gagliardi of Division III St. John's (Minn.) became the all-time leader in college football coaching wins in 2003 (passing Grambling's Eddie Robinson at 408 wins), finishing the year with a career record of 414-114-11 over 52 seasons at St. John's and three seasons at Montana's Carroll College.

Where They Coached

Anderson–Loras (1922-24), DePaul (1925-31), Holy Cross (1933-38), Iowa (1939-42), Holy Cross (1950-64); **Bible**– Mississippi College (1913-15), LSU (1916), Texas A&M (1917,1919-28), Nebraska (1929-36), Texas (1937-46); **Bowden**– Samford (1959-62), West Virginia (1970-75), Florida St. (1976–); **Bryant**–Maryland (1945), Kentucky (1946-53), Texas A&M (1954-57), Alabama (1958-82); **Cooper**– Tulsa (1977-84), Arizona St. (1985-87), Ohio St. (1988-2000); **Crisler**–Minnesota (1930-31), Princeton (1932-37), Michigan (1938-47); **Devaney**–Wyoming (1957-61), Nebraska (1962-72); **Dobie**–North Dakota St. (1906-07), Washington (1908-16), Navy (1917-19), Cornell (1920-35), Boston College (1936- 38); **V. Dooley**–Georgia (1964-88); **Edwards**–BYU (1972-2000); **Folsom**–Colorado (1895-99, 1901-02), Dartmouth (1903-06), Colorado (1908-15); **Fry**–SMU (1962-72), North Texas St. (1973-78), Iowa (1979-98); **Fulmer**–Tennessee (1992–).

Haughton–Cornell (1899-1900), Harvard (1908-16), Columbia (1923-24); **Hayes**–Denison (1946-48), Miami-OH (1949-50), Ohio St. (1951-78); **Heisman**–Oberlin (1892), Akron (1893), Oberlin (1894), Auburn (1895-99), Clemson (1900-03), Georgia Tech (1904-19), Penn (1920-22), Washington & Jefferson (1923), Rice (1924-27); **Holtz**–William & Mary (1969-71), N.C. State (1972-75), Arkansas (1977-83), Minnesota (1984-85), Notre Dame (1986-96), South Carolina (1999–); **Jones**–Syracuse (1908), Yale (1909), Ohio St. (1910), Yale (1913), Iowa (1916-23), Duke (1924), USC (1925-40); **Kush**–Arizona St. (1958-79); **Leahy**–Boston College (1939-40), Notre Dame (1941-43, 1946-53); **Majors**–Iowa St. (1968-72), Pittsburgh (1973-76, 93-96), Tennessee (1977-92); **Moran**–Texas A&M (1909-14), Centre (1919-23), Bucknell (1924-26), Catawba (1930-33).

Neely–Rhodes (1924-27), Clemson (1931-39), Rice (1940-66); **Nehlen**–Bowling Green (1968-76), West Virginia (1980-2000); **Neyland**–Tennessee (1926-34, 1936-40, 1946-52); **Osborne**–Nebraska (1973-97); **Paterno**–Penn St. (1966–); Rockne–Notre Dame (1918-30); **Schembechler**–Miami-OH (1963-68), Michigan (1969-89); **Spurrier**–Duke (1987-89), Florida (1990-2001); **Stagg**–Springfield College (1890-91), Chicago (1892-1932), Pacific (1933-46); **Sutherland**–Lafayette (1919-23), Pittsburgh (1924-38); **Sweeney**–Montana St. (1963-67), Washington St. (1968-75), Fresno St. (1976-96); **Switzer**–Oklahoma (1973-88).

Thomas–Chattanooga (1925-28), Alabama (1931-42, 1944-46); **Vaught**–Mississippi (1947-70); **Wade**–Alabama (1923-30), Duke (1931-41, 1946-50); **Warner**–Georgia (1895-96), Cornell (1897-98), Carlisle (1899-1903), Cornell (1904-06), Carlisle (1907-13), Pittsburgh (1915-23), Stanford (1924-32), Temple (1933-38); **Welsh**–Navy (1973-81), Virginia (1982-2000); **Wilkinson**–Oklahoma (1947-63); **Williams**–Army (1891), Minnesota (1900-21); **Woodson**–Central Arkansas (1935-39), Hardin-Simmons (1941-42, 1946-51), Arizona (1952-56), New Mexico St. (1958-67), Trinity-TX (1972-73); **Woodruff**–Penn (1892-1901), Illinois (1903), Carlisle (1905); **Yost**–Ohio Wesleyan (1897), Nebraska (1898), Kansas (1899), Stanford (1900), Michigan (1901-23, 1925-26).

All-Time Winningest Division I-A Coaches (Cont.)

All-Time Bowl Appearances
Coaches active in 2003 in **bold** type.

		App	W	L	T
1	**Joe Paterno**	31	20	10	1
2	Bear Bryant	29	15	12	2
3	**Bobby Bowden**	27	18	8	1
4	Tom Osborne	25	12	13	0
5	LaVell Edwards	22	7	14	1
	Lou Holtz	22	12	8	2
7	Vince Dooley	20	8	10	2
8	Johnny Vaught	18	10	8	0
9	Hayden Fry	17	7	9	1
	Bo Schembechler	17	5	12	0
11	Johnny Majors	16	9	7	0
	Darrell Royal	16	8	7	1
13	Don James	15	10	5	0
	George Welsh	15	5	10	0
15	John Cooper	14	5	9	0
	Jackie Sherrill	14	8	6	0
17	Bobby Dodd	13	9	4	0
	Terry Donahue	13	8	4	1
	Barry Switzer	13	8	5	0
	Charlie McClendon	13	7	6	0
	Don Nehlen	13	4	9	0

Active Coaches' Victories
(Minimum 5 years in Division I-A.)

		Yrs	W	L	T	Pct
1	Bobby Bowden, Fla. St	38	342	97	4	.777
2	Joe Paterno, Penn St	38	339	109	3	.755
3	Lou Holtz, South Carolina	32	243	127	7	.654
4	Frank Beamer, Va. Tech	23	167	97	4	.631
5	Ken Hatfield, Rice	24	164	122	4	.572
6	Dennis Franchione, Tex. A&M	20	159	82	2	.658
7	Fisher DeBerry, Air Force	20	156	88	1	.639
8	Mack Brown, Texas	20	145	92	1	.611
9	Paul Pasqualoni, Syracuse	18	135	70	1	.658
10	John Robinson, UNLV	17	130	68	4	.653
11	Bill Snyder, Kansas St.	15	127	55	1	.697
12	John L. Smith, Michigan St.	15	118	65	0	.645
13	Phillip Fulmer, Tennessee	12	113	28	0	.801
14	Sonny Lubick, Colorado St.	15	112	63	0	.640
15	Glen Mason, Minnesota	18	103	104	1	.498
16	Barry Alvarez, Wisconsin	14	99	67	4	.584
	Bobby Wallace, Temple	16	99	87	1	.532
18	Mike Bellotti, Oregon	14	96	59	2	.618
19	Rich Brooks, Kentucky	19	95	117	0	.448
	Joe Tiller, Purdue	13	94	62	1	.602

AFCA Coach of the Year
First presented in 1935 by the American Football Coaches Association.

Multiple winners: Joe Paterno (4), Bear Bryant (3), John McKay and Darrell Royal (2).

Year		Year		Year	
1935	Pappy Waldorf, Northwestern	1960	Murray Warmath, Minnesota	1983	Ken Hatfield, Air Force
1936	Dick Harlow, Harvard	1961	Bear Bryant, Alabama	1984	LaVell Edwards, BYU
1937	Hooks Mylin, Lafayette	1962	John McKay, USC	1985	Fisher DeBerry, Air Force
1938	Bill Kern, Carnegie Tech	1963	Darrell Royal, Texas	1986	Joe Paterno, Penn St.
1939	Eddie Anderson, Iowa	1964	Frank Broyles, Arkansas	1987	Dick MacPherson, Syracuse
1940	Clark Shaughnessy, Stanford		& Ara Parseghian, Notre Dame	1988	Don Nehlen, West Virginia
1941	Frank Leahy, Notre Dame	1965	Tommy Prothro, UCLA	1989	Bill McCartney, Colorado
1942	Bill Alexander, Georgia Tech	1966	Tom Cahill, Army	1990	Bobby Ross, Georgia Tech
1943	Amos Alonzo Stagg, Pacific	1967	John Pont, Indiana	1991	Bill Lewis, East Carolina
1944	Carroll Widdoes, Ohio St.	1968	Joe Paterno, Penn St.	1992	Gene Stallings, Alabama
1945	Bo McMillin, Indiana	1969	Bo Schembechler, Michigan	1993	Barry Alvarez, Wisconsin
1946	Red Blaik, Army	1970	Charlie McClendon, LSU	1994	Tom Osborne, Nebraska
1947	Fritz Crisler, Michigan		& Darrell Royal, Texas	1995	Gary Barnett, Northwestern
1948	Bennie Oosterbaan, Michigan	1971	Bear Bryant, Alabama	1996	Bruce Snyder, Arizona St.
1949	Bud Wilkinson, Oklahoma	1972	John McKay, USC	1997	Lloyd Carr, Michigan
1950	Charlie Caldwell, Princeton	1973	Bear Bryant, Alabama	1998	Phillip Fulmer, Tennessee
1951	Chuck Taylor, Stanford	1974	Grant Teaff, Baylor	1999	Frank Beamer, Va. Tech
1952	Biggie Munn, Michigan St.	1975	Frank Kush, Arizona St.	2000	Bob Stoops, Oklahoma
1953	Jim Tatum, Maryland	1976	Johnny Majors, Pittsburgh	2001	Ralph Friedgen, Maryland
1954	Red Sanders, UCLA	1977	Don James, Washington		& Larry Coker, Miami-FL
1955	Duffy Daugherty, Michigan St.	1978	Joe Paterno, Penn St.	2002	Jim Tressel, Ohio St.
1956	Bowden Wyatt, Tennessee	1979	Earle Bruce, Ohio St.	2003	Pete Carroll, USC
1957	Woody Hayes, Ohio St.	1980	Vince Dooley, Georgia		
1958	Paul Dietzel, LSU	1981	Danny Ford, Clemson		
1959	Ben Schwartzwalder, Syracuse	1982	Joe Paterno, Penn St.		

FWAA Coach of the Year
First presented in 1957 by the Football Writers Association of America. The FWAA and AFCA awards have both gone to the same coach in the same season 32 times. Those double winners are preceded by (#).

Multiple winners: Woody Hayes and Joe Paterno (3); Lou Holtz, Johnny Majors and John McKay (2).

Year		Year		Year	
1957	#Woody Hayes, Ohio St.	1966	#Tom Cahill, Army	1975	Woody Hayes, Ohio St.
1958	#Paul Dietzel, LSU	1967	#John Pont, Indiana	1976	#Johnny Majors, Pitt
1959	#Ben Schwartzwalder, Syracuse	1968	Woody Hayes, Ohio St.	1977	Lou Holtz, Arkansas
1960	#Murray Warmath, Minnesota	1969	#Bo Schembechler, Michigan	1978	#Joe Paterno, Penn St.
1961	Darrell Royal, Texas	1970	Alex Agase, Northwestern	1979	#Earle Bruce, Ohio St.
1962	#John McKay, USC	1971	Bob Devaney, Nebraska	1980	#Vince Dooley, Georgia
1963	#Darrell Royal, Texas	1972	#John McKay, USC	1981	#Danny Ford, Clemson
1964	#Ara Parseghian, Notre Dame	1973	Johnny Majors, Pitt	1982	#Joe Paterno, Penn St.
1965	Duffy Daugherty, Michigan St.	1974	#Grant Teaff, Baylor	1983	Howard Schnellenberger, Miami-FL

Year		Year		Year	
1984	#LaVell Edwards, BYU	1992	#Gene Stallings, Alabama	2000	#Bob Stoops, Oklahoma
1985	#Fisher DeBerry, Air Force	1993	Terry Bowden, Auburn	2001	#Ralph Friedgen, Maryland
1986	#Joe Paterno, Penn St.	1994	Rich Brooks, Oregon	2002	#Jim Tressel, Ohio St.
1987	#Dick MacPherson, Syracuse	1995	#Gary Barnett, Northwestern	2003	Nick Saban, LSU
1988	Lou Holtz, Notre Dame	1996	#Bruce Snyder, Arizona St.		
1989	#Bill McCartney, Colorado	1997	Mike Price, Washington St.		
1990	#Bobby Ross, Georgia Tech	1998	#Phillip Fulmer, Tennessee		
1991	Don James, Washington	1999	#Frank Beamer, Va. Tech		

All-Time NCAA Division I-AA Leaders
CAREER

Total Offense

	Yards Gained	Years	Yards
1	Steve McNair, Alcorn St.	1991-94	16,823
2	Marcus Brady, CS-Northridge	1998-01	13,095
3	Willie Totten, Miss. Valley	1982-85	13,007
4	Robert Kent, Jackson St.	2000-03	12,538
5	Jamie Martin, Weber St.	1989-92	12,287

	Yards per Game	Years	Yards	P/Gm
1	Steve McNair, Alcorn St.	1991-94	16,823	400.5
2	Neil Lomax, Portland St.	1978-80	11,647	352.9
3	Aaron Flowers, CS-N'ridge	1996-97	6,754	337.7
4	David Macchi, Valparaiso	2002-03	7,628	331.7
5	Chris Sanders, Chatt.	1999-00	7,247	329.4

Passing
(Minimum 300 Completions)

	Passing Efficiency	Years	Rating
1	Shawn Knight, William & Mary	1991-94	170.8
2	Dave Dickenson, Montana	1992-95	166.3
3	Drew Miller, Montana	1999-00	160.5
4	Eric Rasmussen, San Diego	2001-03	160.1
5	Doug Nussmeier, Idaho	1990-93	154.4

	Yards Gained	Years	Yards
1	Steve McNair, Alcorn St.	1991-94	14,496
2	Willie Totten, Miss. Valley	1982-85	12,711
3	Marcus Brady, CS-Northridge	1998-01	12,479
4	Jamie Martin, Weber St.	1989-92	12,207
5	Robert Kent, Jackson St.	2000-03	11,784

Receiving

	Catches	Years	No
1	Jacquay Nunnally, Fla. A&M	1997-00	317
2	Stephen Campbell, Brown	1997-00	305
3	Jerry Rice, Miss. Valley	1981-84	301
4	Javarus Dudley, Fordham	2000-03	295
5	Chas Gessner, Brown	1999-02	292

	Yards Gained	Years	No	Yards
1	Jerry Rice, Miss. Valley	1981-84	301	4693
2	Jacquay Nunnally, Fla. A&M	1997-00	317	4239
3	Javarus Dudley, Fordham	2000-03	295	4197
4	Rich Musinski, Wm. & Mary	2000-03	219	4017
5	C.J. Johnson, Tennessee St.	2000-03	194	3903

All-Purpose Yardage

	Yards per Game	Years	Yards	P/Gm
1	B. Westbrook, Villanova	1997-98,00-01	9512	216.2
2	Jerry Azumah, N. Hampshire	1995-98	9376	204.3
3	Arnold Mickens, Butler	1994-95	3947	197.4
4	Tim Hall, Robert Morris	1994-95	3701	194.8
5	Reggie Greene, Siena	1994-97	6959	193.3

Rushing

	Yards Gained	Years	Yards
1	Adrian Peterson, Ga. So.	1998-01	6559
2	Charles Roberts, CS-Sac.	1997-00	6553
3	Jerry Azumah, N. Hampshire	1995-98	6193
4	Matt Cannon, S. Utah	1997-00	5489
5	Reggie Greene, Siena	1994-97	5415

	Yards per Game	Years	Yards	P/Gm
1	Arnold Mickens, Butler	1994-95	3813	190.7
2	Adrian Peterson, Ga. So.	1998-01	6559	156.2
3	Aaron Stecker, W. Ill.	1997-98	3081	154.1
4	Tim Hall, Robert Morris	1994-95	2908	153.1
5	Jerry Azumah, N. Hampshire	1995-98	6193	151.0

Miscellaneous

	Interceptions	Years	No
1	Rashean Mathis, Bethune-Cookman	1999-02	31
2	Dave Murphy, Holy Cross	1986-89	28
	Leigh Bodde, Duquesne	1999-02	28
4	Cedric Walker, S.F. Austin	1990-93	25
5	Issiac Holt, Alcorn St.	1981-84	24
	Bill McGovern, Holy Cross	1981-84	24
	Darren Sharper, Wm. & Mary	1993-96	24

	Punting Average (min. 150 punts)	Years	Avg
1	Mark Gould, Northern Ariz.	2000-03	44.8
2	Pumpy Tudors, Tenn.-Chatt.	1989-91	44.4
3	Case de Brujin, Idaho St.	1978-81	43.7
4	Mike Scifres, Western Illinois	1999-02	43.6
5	Terry Belden, Northern Ariz.	1990-93	43.4

Note: Northeastern's Tyler Grogan holds the 1-AA record for longest punt with a 93-yarder against Villanova in 2001.

	Punt Return Average*	Years	Avg
1	Willie Ware, Miss. Valley	1982-85	16.4
2	Buck Phillips, Western Ill.	1994-95	16.4
3	Tim Egerton, Delaware St.	1986-89	16.1
4	Mark Orlando, Towson St.	1991-94	15.7
5	Joseph Jefferson, Western Ky.	1998-01	15.3

	Kickoff Return Average*	Years	Avg
1	Lamont Brightful, E. Wash.	1998-01	30.0
2	Troy Brown, Marshall	1991-92	29.7
3	Charles Swann, Indiana St.	1989-91	29.3
4	Craig Richardson, Eastern Wash.	1983-86	28.5
5	Ramondo North, N.C. A&T	1998-00	28.3

*(Minimum 1.2 returns per game)

Scoring
Non-Kickers

	Points	Years	TD	XP	Pts
1	B. Westbrook, Villanova	1997-98,00-01	89	10	544
2	Adrian Peterson, Ga. Southern	1998-01	87	2	524
3	Matt Cannon, S. Utah	1997-00	69	6	420
4	Jerry Azumah, New Hampshire	1995-98	69	4	418
5	David Dinkins, Morehead St.	1997-00	63	6	384

	Touchdowns Passing	Years	No
1	Willie Totten, Miss. Valley	1982-85	139
2	Steve McNair, Alcorn St.	1991-94	119
3	Marcus Brady, CS-Northridge	1998-01	109
4	Robert Kent, Jackson St.	2000-03	104
5	Dave Dickenson, Montana	1992-95	96

	Touchdowns Rushing	Years	No
1	Adrian Peterson, Ga. Southern	1998-01	84
2	Matt Cannon, S. Utah	1997-00	69
3	David Dinkins, Morehead St.	1997-00	63
4	Jerry Azumah, New Hampshire	1995-98	60
5	Charles Roberts, CS-Sacramento	1997-00	56

	Touchdown Catches	Years	No
1	Jerry Rice, Miss. Valley	1981-84	50
2	Rennie Benn, Lehigh	1982-85	44
3	Dedric Ward, N. Iowa	1993-96	41
4	Sean Morey, Brown	1995-98	39
	Gharun Hester, Georgetown	1997-00	39

All-Time NCAA Division I-AA Leaders (Cont.)

Kickers

	Points	Years	FG	XP	Pts		Field Goals	Years	No
1	Chris Snyder, Montana	2000-03	70	182	394	1	Marty Zendejas, Nevada	1984-87	72
2	Marty Zendejas, Nevada	1984-87	72	169	385	2	Kirk Roach, Western Carolina	1984-87	71
3	Dave Ettinger, Hofstra	1994-97	62	140	326	3	Tony Zendejas, Nevada	1981-83	70
4	B. Mitchell, Marshall/N.Iowa	1987,89-91	64	130	322		Chris Snyder, Montana	2000-03	70
	Scott Shields, Weber St.	1995-98	67	109	322	5	Scott Shields, Weber St.	1995-98	67

Note: Chris Snyder's point total includes 1 2-point conversion. Scott Shields's point total includes 2 touchdowns.

Note: South Florida's Bill Gramatica, Arkansas State's Scott Roper and Georgia Southern's Tim Foley share the 1-AA record for longest field goal at 63 yards.

All-Time NCAA Division I-AA Winningest Programs

Includes record at a senior college only, minimum of 20 seasons of competition. Bowl and playoff games are included in the overall records but only 1-AA playoff games (since they began in 1978) are included in the W-L column under 1-AA playoffs.

Top 20 Winning Percentage

		Yrs	Gm	W	L	T	Pct.	1-AA Playoffs W-L	Titles
1	Georgia Southern	22	288	218	69	1	.759	38-8	6
2	Yale	131	1191	821	315	55	.712	0-0	0
3	Grambling St.	61	658	460	183	15	.710	9-7	0
4	Florida A&M	71	727	503	206	18	.704	5-6	1
5	Tennessee St.	76	718	478	210	30	.687	2-5	0
6	Princeton	134	1143	751	342	50	.679	0-0	0
7	Harvard	129	1172	757	365	50	.667	0-0	0
8	Jackson St.	58	600	378	209	13	.641	0-12	0
9	Southern	82	806	500	281	25	.636	0-0	0
10	Pennsylvania	127	1243	768	433	42	.635	0-0	0
11	Eastern Kentucky	80	801	493	281	27	.632	16-15	2
12	Fordham	105	1173	715	405	53	.632	1-1	0
13	Dayton	96	917	563	326	26	.628	0-0	0
14	McNeese St.	53	580	357	209	14	.628	11-10	0
15	Dartmouth	122	1059	635	378	46	.621	0-0	0
16	Appalachian St.	74	784	472	283	29	.621	8-12	0
17	Albany	31	311	192	119	0	.617	0-0	0
18	Hofstra	63	615	373	231	11	.615	2-5	0
19	S. Carolina St.	76	712	422	263	27	.612	2-2	0
20	Delaware	112	1022	598	380	44	.607	15-11	1

Top 50 Victories

		Wins			Wins			Wins
1	Yale	.821	18	Butler	.513		Western Ill.	.454
2	Pennsylvania	.768	19	Drake	.512	36	Maine	.453
3	Harvard	.757	20	Furman	.508	37	Georgetown	.450
4	Princeton	.751	21	Florida A&M	.503	38	Howard	.443
5	Fordham	.715	22	Southern	.500		VMI	.443
6	Dartmouth	.635	23	Massachusetts	.496	40	Richmond	.437
7	Lafayette	.604	24	William & Mary	.493		Texas St.-San Marcos	.437
8	Delaware	.598		E. Kentucky	.493	42	Elon	.435
9	Cornell	.593	26	W. Kentucky	.480	43	The Citadel	.428
10	Lehigh	.592	27	Tennessee St.	.478		Idaho St.	.428
11	Dayton	.563	28	Hampton	.475	45	Eastern Ill.	.425
12	Holy Cross	.553	29	Appalachian St.	.472	46	S. Carolina St.	.422
13	Colgate	.552	30	Northwestern St.	.464	47	Wofford	.421
14	N. Iowa	.546	31	Grambling St.	.460	48	Murray St.	.420
15	Bucknell	.537	32	Montana	.459	49	N.C. A&T	.415
16	Brown	.534	33	Chattanooga	.456	50	E. Washington	.414
17	Villanova	.514	34	New Hampshire	.454			

Top 10 Playoff Game Appearances

Ranked by NCAA Division 1-AA playoff games played from 1978-2003. CH refers to championships won.

		Years	Games	Record	CH			Years	Games	Record	CH
1	Georgia Southern	14	46	38-8	6	6	Delaware	12	26	15-11	1
2	Eastern Ky.	17	31	16-15	2	7	Furman	12	25	14-11	1
	Montana	14	31	19-12	2	8	Northern Iowa	11	23	12-11	0
4	Marshall*	8	29	23-6	2	9	McNeese St.	11	22	11-11	0
	Youngstown St.	10	29	23-6	4	10	Appalachian St.	12	20	8-12	0

*Marshall moved up to I-A in 1997.

Active Division I-AA Coaches
Minimum of 5 years as a Division I-A and/or Division I-AA through 2003 season.

Top 10 Winning Percentage

		Yrs	W	L	T	Pct
1	Mike Kelly, Dayton	.23	215	43	1	.832
2	Al Bagnoli, Pennsylvania	.22	173	51	0	.772
3	Greg Gattuso, Duquesne	.11	90	28	0	.763
4	Pete Richardson, Southern	.16	138	48	1	.741
5	Dick Biddle, Colgate	.8	69	27	0	.719
6	Joe Taylor, Hampton	.21	160	68	4	.698
7	Billy Joe, Florida A&M	.30	234	100	4	.698
8	Alvin Wyatt, Bet-Cookman	.7	54	25	0	.684
9	Walt Hameline, Wagner	.23	163	76	2	.680
10	Doug Williams, Grambling St.	7	55	26	0	.679

Top 10 Victories

		Yrs	W	L	T	Pct
1	Billy Joe, Florida A&M	.30	234	100	4	.698
2	Mike Kelly, Dayton	.23	215	43	1	.832
3	Ron Randleman, Sam Houston St.	35	207	164	6	.557
4	Al Bagnoli, Pennsylvania	.22	173	51	0	.772
5	Walt Hameline, Wagner	.23	163	76	2	.680
6	Joe Taylor, Hampton	.21	160	68	4	.698
7	Andy Talley, Villanova	.24	159	95	2	.625
	Jimmye Laycock, Wm. & Mary	.24	159	110	2	.590
9	Rob Ash, Drake	.24	151	91	5	.621
10	Jerry Moore, Appalachian St.	.22	149	107	2	.581

Note: Eddie Robinson of Grambling State (1941-42, 1945-97) retired following the 1997 season as the all-time NCAA leader in coaching wins with a 408-165-15 record and a .707 winning percentage over 55 seasons.

Division I-AA Coach of the Year
First presented in 1983 by the American Football Coaches Association.

Multiple winners: Mark Duffner, Paul Johnson and Erk Russell (2).

Year		Year		Year	
1983	Rey Dempsey, Southern Ill.	1990	Tim Stowers, Ga. Southern	1997	Andy Talley, Villanova
1984	Dave Arnold, Montana St.	1991	Mark Duffner, Holy Cross	1998	Mark Whipple, Massachusetts
1985	Dick Sheridan, Furman	1992	Charlie Taafe, Citadel	1999	Paul Johnson, Ga. Southern
1986	Erk Russell, Ga. Southern	1993	Dan Allen, Boston Univ.	2000	Paul Johnson, Ga. Southern
1987	Mark Duffner, Holy Cross	1994	Jim Tressel, Youngstown St.	2001	Bobby Johnson, Furman
1988	Jimmy Satterfield, Furman	1995	Don Read, Montana	2002	Jack Harbaugh, E. Kentucky
1989	Erk Russell, Ga. Southern	1996	Ray Tellier, Columbia	2003	Dick Biddle, Colgate

NCAA Playoffs

Division I-AA
Established in 1978 as a four-team playoff. Tournament field increased to eight teams in 1981, 12 teams in 1982 and 16 teams in 1986. Automatic berths are awarded to champions of the Big Sky, Gateway, Mid-Eastern Athletic, Ohio Valley, Patriot, Southern, Southland and Atlantic 10 (formerly Yankee) conferences.

Multiple winners: Georgia Southern (6); Youngstown St. (4); Eastern Kentucky, Marshall and Montana (2).

Year	Winner	Score	Loser	Year	Winner	Score	Loser
1978	Florida A&M	.35-28	Massachusetts	1991	Youngstown St., OH	.25-17	Marshall
1979	Eastern Kentucky	.30-7	Lehigh, PA	1992	Marshall	.31-28	Youngstown St.
1980	Boise St., ID	.31-29	Eastern Kentucky	1993	Youngstown St.	.17-5	Marshall
1981	Idaho St.	.34-23	Eastern Kentucky	1994	Youngstown St.	.28-14	Boise St.
1982	Eastern Kentucky	.17-14	Delaware	1995	Montana	.22-20	Marshall
1983	Southern Illinois	.43-7	Western Carolina	1996	Marshall	.49-29	Montana
1984	Montana St.	.19-6	Louisiana Tech	1997	Youngstown St.	.10-9	McNeese St.
1985	Georgia Southern	.44-42	Furman, SC	1998	Massachusetts	.55-43	Georgia Southern
1986	Georgia Southern	.48-21	Arkansas St.	1999	Georgia Southern	.59-24	Youngstown St.
1987	NE Louisiana	.43-42	Marshall, WV	2000	Georgia Southern	.27-25	Montana
1988	Furman, SC	.17-12	Georgia Southern	2001	Montana	.13-6	Furman
1989	Georgia Southern	.37-34	S.F. Austin St.	2002	Western Kentucky	.34-14	McNeese St.
1990	Georgia Southern	.36-13	Nevada-Reno	2003	Delaware	.40-0	Colgate

Division II
Established in 1973 as an eight-team playoff. Tournament field increased to 16 teams in 1988. From 1964-72, eight qualifying NCAA College Division member institutions competed in four regional bowl games, but there was no tournament and no national championship until 1973.

Multiple winners: North Dakota St. (5); North Alabama (3); Grand Valley St., Northern Colorado, Northwest Missouri St., Southwest Texas St. and Troy St. (2).

Year	Winner	Score	Loser	Year	Winner	Score	Loser
1973	Louisiana Tech	.34-0	Western Kentucky	1989	Mississippi Col.	.3-0	Jacksonville St., AL
1974	Central Michigan	.54-14	Delaware	1990	North Dakota St.	.51-11	Indiana, PA
1975	Northern Michigan	.16-14	Western Kentucky	1991	Pittsburg St., KS	.23-6	Jacksonville St., AL
1976	Montana St.	.24-13	Akron, OH	1992	Jacksonville St., AL	.17-13	Pittsburg St., KS
1977	Lehigh, PA	.33-0	Jacksonville St., AL	1993	North Alabama	.41-34	Indiana, PA
1978	Eastern Illinois	.10-9	Delaware	1994	North Alabama	.16-10	Tex. A&M (Kings.)
1979	Delaware	.38-21	Youngstown St., OH	1995	North Alabama	.22-7	Pittsburg St., KS
1980	Cal Poly-SLO	.21-13	Eastern Illinois	1996	Northern Colorado	.23-14	Carson-Newman
1981	SW Texas St.	.42-13	North Dakota St.	1997	Northern Colorado	.51-0	New Haven
1982	SW Texas St.	.34-9	UC-Davis	1998	NW Missouri St.	.24-6	Carson-Newman
1983	North Dakota St.	.41-21	Central St., OH	1999	NW Missouri St.	.58-52*	Carson-Newman
1984	Troy St., AL	.18-17	North Dakota St.	2000	Delta St., MS	.63-34	Bloomsburg, PA
1985	North Dakota St.	.35-7	North Alabama	2001	North Dakota	.17-14	Grand Valley St.
1986	North Dakota St.	.27-7	South Dakota	2002	Grand Valley St., OH	.31-24	Valdosta St., GA
1987	Troy St., AL	.31-17	Portland St., OR	2003	Grand Valley St., OH	.10-3	North Dakota
1988	North Dakota St.	.35-21	Portland St., OR		*Four overtimes		

Division III

Established in 1973 as a four-team playoff. Tournament field increased to eight teams in 1975, 16 teams in 1985 and 28 teams in 1999. From 1969-72, four qualifying NCAA College Division member institutions competed in two regional bowl games, but there was no tournament and no national championship until 1973. (*) denotes overtime.

Multiple winners: Mt. Union (7); Augustana (4); Ithaca (3); Dayton, St. John's, Widener, WI-La Crosse and Wittenberg (2).

Year	Winner	Score	Loser	Year	Winner	Score	Loser
1973	Wittenberg, OH	41-0	Juniata, PA	1989	Dayton, OH	17-7	Union, NY
1974	Central, IA	10-8	Ithaca, NY	1990	Allegheny, PA	21-14*	Lycoming, PA
1975	Wittenberg, OH	28-0	Ithaca, NY	1991	Ithaca, NY	34-20	Dayton, OH
1976	St. John's, MN	31-28	Towson St., MD	1992	WI-La Crosse	16-12	Wash. & Jeff., PA
1977	Widener, PA	39-36	Wabash, IN	1993	Mt. Union, OH	34-24	Rowan, NJ
1978	Baldwin-Wallace	24-10	Wittenberg, OH	1994	Albion, MI	38-15	Wash. & Jeff.
1979	Ithaca, NY	14-10	Wittenberg, OH	1995	WI-La Crosse	36-7	Rowan, NJ
1980	Dayton, OH	63-0	Ithaca, NY	1996	Mt. Union, OH	56-24	Rowan, NJ
1981	Widener, PA	17-10	Dayton, OH	1997	Mt. Union, OH	61-12	Lycoming
1982	West Georgia	14-0	Augustana, IL	1998	Mt. Union, OH	44-24	Rowan, NJ
1983	Augustana, IL	21-17	Union, NY	1999	Pacific Lutheran	42-13	Rowan, NJ
1984	Augustana, IL	21-12	Central, IA	2000	Mt. Union, OH	10-7	St. John's, MN
1985	Augustana, IL	20-7	Ithaca	2001	Mt. Union, OH	30-27	Bridgewater, VA
1986	Augustana, IL	31-3	Salisbury St., MD	2002	Mt. Union, OH	48-7	Trinity, TX
1987	Wagner, NY	19-3	Dayton, OH	2003	St. John's, MN	24-6	Mt. Union, OH
1988	Ithaca, NY	39-24	Central, IA				

NAIA Playoffs

Division I

Established in 1956 as two-team playoff. Tournament field increased to four teams in 1958, eight teams in 1978 and 16 teams in 1987 before cutting back to eight teams in 1989. NAIA went back to a single division 16-team playoff in 1997. The title game has ended in a tie four times (1956, '64, '84 and '85). Note that Northeastern St., OK was called NE Oklahoma in 1958.

Multiple winners: Texas A&I (7); Carson-Newman (5); Central Arkansas and Central St-OH (3); Abilene Christian, Carroll-MT, Central St-OK, Elon, Georgetown-KY, Northeastern St-OK, Pittsburg St. and St. John's-MN (2).

Year	Winner	Score	Loser	Year	Winner	Score	Loser
1956	Montana St.	0-0	St. Joseph's, IN	1980	Elon, NC	17-10	NE Oklahoma
1957	Pittsburg St., KS	27-26	Hillsdale, MI	1981	Elon, NC	3-0	Pittsburg St., KS
1958	NE Oklahoma	19-13	Northern Arizona	1982	Central St., OK	14-11	Mesa, CO
1959	Texas A&I	20-7	Lenoir-Rhyne, NC	1983	Car-Newman, TN	36-28	Mesa, CO
1960	Lenoir-Rhyne, NC	15-14	Humboldt St., CA	1984	Car-Newman, TN	19-19	Central Arkansas
1961	Pittsburg St., KS	12-7	Linfield, OR	1985	Hillsdale, MI	10-10	Central Arkansas
1962	Central St., OK	28-13	Lenoir-Rhyne, NC	1986	Car-Newman, TN	17-0	Cameron, OK
1963	St. John's, MN	33-27	Prairie View, TX	1987	Cameron, OK	30-2	Car-Newman, TN
1964	Concordia, MN	7-7	Sam Houston, TX	1988	Car-Newman, TN	56-21	Adams St., CO
1965	St. John's, MN	33-0	Linfield, OR	1989	Car-Newman, TN	34-20	Emporia St., KS
1966	Waynesburg, PA	42-21	WI-Whitewater	1990	Central St., OH	38-16	Mesa, CO
1967	Fairmont St., WV	28-21	Eastern Wash.	1991	Central Arkansas	19-16	Central St., OH
1968	Troy St., AL	43-35	Texas A&I	1992	Central St., OH	19-16	Gardner-Webb, NC
1969	Texas A&I	32-7	Concordia, MN	1993	E. Central, OK	49-35	Glenville St., WV
1970	Texas A&I	48-7	Wofford, SC	1994	N'eastern St., OK	13-12	Ark-Pine Bluff
1971	Livingston, AL	14-12	Arkansas Tech	1995	Central St., OH	37-7	N'eastern St., OK
1972	East Texas St.	21-18	Car-Newman, TN	1996	SW Oklahoma St.	33-31	Montana Tech
1973	Abilene Christian	42-14	Elon, NC	1997	Findlay, OH	14-7	Willamette, ORE
1974	Texas A&I	34-23	Henderson St., AR	1998	Azusa Pacific, CA	17-14	Olivet Nazarene, IL
1975	Texas A&I	37-0	Salem, WV	1999	NW Oklahoma St.	34-26	Georgetown, KY
1976	Texas A&I	26-0	Central Arkansas	2000	Georgetown, KY	20-0	NW Oklahoma St.
1977	Abilene Christian	24-7	SW Oklahoma	2001	Georgetown, KY	49-27	Sioux Falls, S.D.
1978	Angelo St., TX	34-14	Elon, NC	2002	Carroll, MT	28-7	Georgetown, KY
1979	Texas A&I	20-14	Central St., OK	2003	Carroll, MT	41-28	NW Oklahoma St.

Division II

Established in 1970 as four-team playoff. Tournament field increased to eight teams in 1978 and 16 teams in 1987. NAIA went back to a single division playoff in 1997. The title game has ended in a tie twice (1981 and '87).

Multiple winners: Westminster (6); Findlay, Linfield and Pacific Lutheran (3); Concordia-MN, Northwestern-IA and Texas Lutheran (2).

Year	Winner	Score	Loser	Year	Winner	Score	Loser
1970	Westminster, PA	21-16	Anderson, IN	1984	Linfield, OR	33-22	Northwestern, IA
1971	Calif. Lutheran	20-14	Westminster, PA	1985	WI-La Crosse	24-7	Pacific Lutheran
1972	Missouri Southern	21-14	Northwestern, IA	1986	Linfield, OR	17-0	Baker, KS
1973	Northwestern, IA	10-3	Glenville St., WV	1987	Pacific Lutheran	16-16	WI-Stevens Pt.*
1974	Texas Lutheran	42-0	Missouri Valley	1988	Westminster, PA	21-14	WI-La Crosse
1975	Texas Lutheran	34-8	Calif. Lutheran	1989	Westminster, PA	51-30	WI-La Crosse
1976	Westminster, PA	20-13	Redlands, CA	1990	Peru St., NE	17-7	Westminster, PA
1977	Westminster, PA	17-9	Calif. Lutheran	1991	Georgetown, KY	28-20	Pacific Lutheran
1978	Concordia, MN	7-0	Findlay, OH	1992	Findlay, OH	26-13	Linfield, OR
1979	Findlay, OH	51-6	Northwestern, IA	1993	Pacific Lutheran	50-20	Westminster, PA
1980	Pacific Lutheran	38-10	Wilmington, OH	1994	Westminster, PA	27-7	Pacific Lutheran
1981	Austin College, TX	24-24	Concordia, MN	1995	Findlay, OH	21-21	Central Wash.
1982	Linfield, OR	33-15	Wm. Jewell, MO	1996	Sioux Falls, SD	47-25	W. Washington
1983	Northwestern, IA	25-21	Pacific Lutheran				

*Wisconsin-Stevens Point forfeited its entire 1987 schedule due to its use of an ineligible player.

Pro Football

For the second time in three years, **Adam Vinatieri's** kick sailed through the uprights.

Patriot Games

Vinatieri is golden once again as the Pats win their final 15 en route to a Super Bowl victory over the Panthers.

Chris Berman
is the host of ESPN's NFL Prime Time.

Stop me if you've heard this one before. Ricky Proehl scores a game-tying touchdown with less than two minutes to play, Tom Brady drives his club into field goal range in the closing moments and Adam Vinatieri boots a game-winning field goal to win the Super Bowl.

Just two years removed from their 20-17 upset victory over the Rams at the Louisiana Superdome, Bill Belichick and his squad came up big again as Vinatieri's 41-yard field goal with :04 to play gave the New England Patriots a thrilling 32-29 victory over the very game Carolina Panthers in Super Bowl XXXVIII at Houston's Reliant Stadium.

While the victory was indeed sweet for Pats' fans, it also elevated Brady into elite status as he joined Joe Montana, Terry Bradshaw and Bart Starr (all members of the Pro Football Hall of Fame) as the only players to be named Super Bowl MVP more than once. But he

was far from a one-man band as no team used its roster more to its fullest than the Patriots. Forty-two different players started at least one game for the eventual champs. And it all worked. After a 2-2 start, the Pats rolled off an amazing 15 straight wins, including a stretch in which Belichick's team didn't even trail in a game from late November until late in the Super Bowl.

But the Patriots' Super opponent didn't exactly come from nowhere. Carolina finished the 2001 season with 15 straight losses after an opening day win. Now coach John Fox's team would make history in becoming the first team to ever rebound from a 1-15 season and reach the Super Bowl two years later. Including the playoffs, Fox's club won 14 games, seven of which were by three points or less and four of which were in overtime on the road. The catalysts were QB Jake Delhomme, RB Stephen Davis and WR Steve Smith, but the keys were arguably the best offensive and defensive line combination in the league.

AP/Wide World Photos

It's like deja-vu all over again. **Tom Brady** *was named MVP after driving his team downfield late in the game to set up the Super Bowl-winning field goal.*

But there were plenty of other stories during the NFL's 84th season. Tampa Bay and Oakland both fell on their faces in 2003 as the Super Bowl participants from the previous year failed to make the play-offs for the third time in five years.

For the first time, four players (Baltimore's Jamal Lewis, Green Bay's Ahman Green, San Diego's LaDainian Tomlinson and New Orleans' Deuce McAllister) ran for at least 1,600 yards. Lewis set an NFL single-game record with 295 yards rushing vs. the Browns in September and finished with 2,066 yards, second best ever, while Green ran for 1,883 yards, tied for the seventh-best total in league annals. And least we forget

Kansas City's RB Priest Holmes, who set an NFL mark with 27 touchdowns (all rushing, also a league record). It is so deep a corps of running backs that Tomlinson, arguably the best of the bunch, wasn't named to the Pro Bowl after becoming the first player to ever run for 1,000-plus yards and catch 100 passes in the same season.

Quarterbacks made their mark in 2003 as well. Indianapolis' Peyton Manning not only shared NFL MVP honors with Tennessee's Steve McNair, he finally shook off the stigma of not being able to win the big game as the Colts spent the year disposing of many of their albatrosses and getting within a game of the Super Bowl.

AP/Wide World Photos

*Indianapolis QB **Peyton Manning** shared season MVP honors with Tennessee's Steve McNair and led the Colts to the AFC Championship Game.*

Donovan McNabb and the Eagles opened 0-2, but he would shake off many distractions to get his team to the NFC title game for the third straight year. But there was no better story than the best. Green Bay's Brett Favre took a back seat to the running game in "Titletown" and still wound up leading the league in touchdown passes, his most inspiring performance coming on a Monday night at Oakland one day after the sudden death of his father.

And there were comebacks. Bill Parcells couldn't stay away from the game he loves, taking over a Cowboys' team that had gone 5-11 three straight years and leading them into the playoffs. He became the first coach ever to lead four different teams to the postseason. There was the ageless Dick Vermeil, who became only the third coach to win division titles with three different clubs as his Chiefs opened 9-0 en route to the AFC West title. And although their playoff drought was extended to 13 seasons, Marvin Lewis' debut in the Queen City was an enormous success as the Bengals went from 2-14 to 8-8 and were in the postseason hunt until the final weekend.

But most of all, there were the Patriots, who took that amazing 15-game winning streak into 2004. Of course, chances are by the time you read this that string of success will have come to an end.

Then again...

The Ten Biggest Stories of the Year in Pro Football

10 The New Orleans Saints pull off a stunning play in Week 16 against Jacksonville that brings back memories of the Cal-Stanford "band on the field" game. Down 20-13 at the Saints' 25 with six seconds remaining, QB Aaron Brooks completes a pass to Donte' Stallworth, who laterals to Michael Lewis, who flips to Deuce McAlister, who pitches to Jerome Pathon who runs into the endzone for the score. Perhaps even more amazingly, kicker John Carney misses the extra point to give the Jaguars the 20-19 win.

9 In "Saints Oddities Part Two," WR Joe Horn hauls in four TD passes in a 45-7 trouncing of the NY Giants, but his celebration after the second grabs all the headlines. Horn had hidden a cell phone in the padding of one of the goal posts before the game and pulls it out after the score to "make a call." He is later fined $30,000 for the stunt.

8 The Cincinnati Bengals' records from 1998-2002 were as follows: 3-13, 4-12, 4-12, 6-10 and 2-14. And then Marvin Lewis took over. While the Bengals miss out once again on the postseason in 2003, they gain immediate respectability and their 8-8 mark has them in the playoff hunt until the very end.

7 Just one day after the sudden death of his father, Packers QB Brett Favre leads his team to an emotional 41-7 win over Oakland on Monday Night Football. Favre throws for four TD and 399 yards, just three yards shy of his career high.

6 Ravens RB Jamal Lewis runs for 295 yards in the Ravens' 33-13 win over the Browns in Week 2, shattering the single game rushing mark previously held by Corey Dillon (278). He didn't stop there, becoming the fifth player to rush for over 2,000 yards in a season. Needing 153 yards in the final game against Pittsburgh to surpass Eric Dickerson's record of 2,105, Lewis settles for 114 for a season total of 2,066.

5 Offseason hip surgery had many wondering whether Chiefs RB Priest Holmes could duplicate his brilliant 24-TD season in 2002. As it turns out, he could...and then some. Holmes blasted into the endzone 27 times in 2003 (all by way of the rush), breaking the all-time record for touchdowns in a season and leading the Chiefs to a 13-3 mark.

4 Bill Parcells does it again. He returns to the NFL after a three-year hiatus and guides a Dallas Cowboys team that had gone 5-11 the past three years to a 10-6 record and their first playoff berth since 1999.

3 Faced with a looming drug suspension, free-spirited Miami RB Ricky Williams, 27, leaves his team in the lurch, announcing his retirement from the game just a week prior to training camp for the 2004 season. According to agent, Leigh Steinberg, Williams "simply didn't feel the passion and motivation that is a prerequisite for playing his position." Miami immediately searches for his replacement.

2   The Carolina Panthers and head coach John Fox go from 1-15 in 2001-02 to 11-5 in 2003-04 and take a well-deserved trip to the Super Bowl. Led by a stifling defense, the legs of Stephen Davis and the right arm of Jake Delhomme, the Panthers power through the Cowboys, Rams and Eagles in the NFC playoffs on their way to Super Bowl XXXVIII.

1   The New England Patriots begin the season with a 2-2 mark, then reel off 15 consecutive wins, culminating with a thrilling 32-29 victory over Carolina for their second Super Bowl win in the last three seasons. Tied, 29-29, with just over a minute left, MVP Tom Brady calmly leads the offense downfield to set up the game-winning 41-yd FG by Adam Vinatieri.

All for Not

Conventional wisdom tells you that success running the ball in the playoffs generally results in a win. Such was not the case on Jan. 11 as Priest Holmes and Ahman Green recorded two of the top rushing performances ever in a play-off loss.

	Date	Yards
Priest Holmes, KC	1/11/04	176
Barry Sanders, Det.	1/8/94	169
Paul Lowe, SD	1/1/61	165
Earnest Byner, Cle.	1/4/86	161
E. Dickerson, LA Rams	12/28/86	158
Ahman Green, GB	1/11/04	156

Steady Progress

The Carolina Panthers, under John Fox, achieved the greatest three-season turnaround in NFL history.

Year	Record	Result
2001	1-15	Worst record in NFL
2002	7-9	Last place, NFC South
2003	11-5	Loss in Super Bowl

Hail to the Chief

While he was certainly an accomplished running back with the Baltimore Ravens, Priest Holmes truly hit his stride when he joined the Chiefs in 2001.

	Games	Yards from Scrimmage	TDs
Chiefs (2001-03)	46	6,800	61
Ravens (1997-00)	40	2,687	11

Running on Empty

The Pittsburgh Steelers' reputation as a gritty, smashmouth rushing team dates back to Franco Harris and their Super Bowl teams of the 1970s. Surprisingly in 2003, the Steelers ranked 31st in rushing, behind only the Detroit Lions.

	Rushing Yds/Game	Rank
1970-2002	142.6	1st
2003	93.0	31st

2003-2004
Season in Review

Final NFL Standings

Division champions (*) and wild card playoff qualifiers (†) are noted; division champions with two best records received first round byes. Number of seasons listed after each head coach refers to latest tenure with club through 2003 season.

American Football Conference

East Division

	W	L	T	PF	PA	vs Div	vs AFC
*New England	14	2	0	348	238	5-1	11-1
Miami	10	6	0	311	261	4-2	7-5
Buffalo	6	10	0	243	279	2-4	4-8
NY Jets	6	10	0	283	299	1-5	6-6

2003 Head Coaches: NE—Bill Belichick (4th season); **Mia**—Dave Wannstedt (4th); **Buf**—Gregg Williams (3rd); **NY**—Herman Edwards (3rd).
2002 Standings: 1. NY Jets (9-7); 2. New England (9-7); 3. Miami (9-7); 4. Buffalo (8-8).

North Division

	W	L	T	PF	PA	vs Div	vs AFC
*Baltimore	10	6	0	391	281	4-2	7-5
Cincinnati	8	8	0	346	384	3-3	6-6
Pittsburgh	6	10	0	300	327	3-3	5-7
Cleveland	5	11	0	254	322	2-4	3-9

2003 Head Coaches: Bal—Brian Billick (5th season); **Cin**—Marvin Lewis (1st) **Pit**—Bill Cowher (12th); **Cle**—Butch Davis (3rd).
2002 Standings: 1. Pittsburgh (10-5-1); 2. Cleveland (9-7); 3. Baltimore (7-9); 4. Cincinnati (2-14).

South Division

	W	L	T	PF	PA	vs Div	vs AFC
*Indianapolis	12	4	0	447	336	5-1	9-3
†Tennessee	12	4	0	435	324	4-2	8-4
Jacksonville	5	11	0	276	331	2-4	3-9
Houston	5	11	0	255	380	1-5	2-10

2003 Head Coaches: Ind—Tony Dungy (2nd season); **Ten**—Jeff Fisher (10th); **Jax**—Jack Del Rio (1st); **Hou**—Dom Capers (2nd).
2002 Standings: 1. Tennessee (11-5); 2. Indianapolis (10-6); 3. Jacksonville (6-10); 4. Houston (4-12).
Note: Indianapolis (12-4) won the division over Tennessee (12-4) due to a 2-0 record in head-to-head games.

West Division

	W	L	T	PF	PA	vs Div	vs AFC
*Kansas City	13	3	0	484	332	5-1	10-2
†Denver	10	6	0	381	301	5-1	9-3
Oakland	4	12	0	270	379	1-5	3-9
San Diego	4	12	0	313	441	1-5	2-10

2003 Head Coaches: KC—Dick Vermeil (3rd season); **Den**—Mike Shanahan (9th); **Oak**—Bill Callahan (2nd); **SD**—Marty Schottenheimer (2nd).
2002 Standings: 1. Oakland (11-5); 2. Denver (9-7); 3. San Diego (8-8); 4. Kansas City (8-8).
Note: Denver (10-6) qualified for a wildcard berth over Miami (10-6) due to a better record within the AFC.

National Football Conference

East Division

	W	L	T	PF	PA	vs Div	vs NFC
*Philadelphia	12	4	0	374	287	5-1	9-3
†Dallas	10	6	0	289	260	5-1	8-4
Washington	5	11	0	287	372	1-5	3-9
NY Giants	4	12	0	243	387	1-5	3-9

2003 Head Coaches: Phi—Andy Reid (5th season); **Dal**—Bill Parcells (1st); **Wash**—Steve Spurrier (2nd); **NY**—Jim Fassel (7th).
2002 Standings: 1. Philadelphia (12-4); 2. NY Giants (10-6); 3. Washington (7-9); 4. Dallas (5-11).

North Division

	W	L	T	PF	PA	vs Div	vs NFC
*Green Bay	10	6	0	442	307	4-2	7-5
Minnesota	9	7	0	416	353	4-2	7-5
Chicago	7	9	0	283	346	2-4	4-8
Detroit	5	11	0	270	379	2-4	4-8

2003 Head Coaches: GB—Mike Sherman (4th season); **Min**—Mike Tice (3rd); **Chi**—Dick Jauron (5th); **Det**—Steve Mariucci (1st).
2002 Standings: 1. Green Bay (12-4); 2. Minnesota (6-10); 3. Chicago (4-12); 4. Detroit (3-13).

South Division

	W	L	T	PF	PA	vs Div	vs NFC
*Carolina	11	5	0	325	304	5-1	9-3
New Orleans	8	8	0	340	326	3-3	7-5
Tampa Bay	7	9	0	301	264	2-4	6-6
Atlanta	5	11	0	299	422	2-4	4-8

2003 Head Coaches: Car—John Fox (2nd season); **NO**—Jim Haslett (4th); **TB**—Jon Gruden (2nd); **Atl**—Dan Reeves (7th, 3-10) was fired on Dec. 10 and replaced by def. coordinator Wade Phillips (2-1).
2002 Standings: 1. Tampa Bay (12-4); 2. Atlanta (9-6-1); 3. New Orleans (9-7); 4. Carolina (7-9).

West Division

	W	L	T	PF	PA	vs Div	vs NFC
*St. Louis	12	4	0	447	328	4-2	8-4
†Seattle	10	6	0	404	327	5-1	8-4
San Francisco	7	9	0	384	337	2-4	6-6
Arizona	4	12	0	225	452	1-5	3-9

2003 Head Coaches: St.L—Mike Martz (4th season); **Sea**—Mike Holmgren (5th); **SF**—Dennis Erickson (1st); **Ariz**—Dave McGinnis (4th).
2002 Standings: 1. San Francisco (10-6); 2. St. Louis (7-9); 3. Seattle (7-9); 4. Arizona (5-11).

NFL Regular Season Individual Leaders
(* indicates rookies)

Passing Efficiency
(Minimum of 224 attempts)

AFC	Att	Cmp	Cmp Pct	Yds	Yds/ Att	TD	Long	Int	Sack/Lost	Rating Points
Steve McNair, Ten	400	250	62.5	3215	8.04	24	73	7	19/108	100.4
Peyton Manning, Ind	566	379	67.0	4267	7.54	29	79-td	10	18/107	99.0
Trent Green, KC	523	330	63.1	4039	7.72	24	67-td	12	20/130	92.6
Jake Plummer, Den	302	189	62.6	2182	7.23	15	60	7	14/73	91.2
Jon Kitna, Cin	520	324	62.3	3591	6.91	26	82-td	15	37/249	87.4
Tom Brady, NE	527	317	60.2	3620	6.87	23	82-td	12	32/219	85.9
Chad Pennington, NYJ	297	189	63.6	2139	7.20	13	65-td	12	25/160	82.9
Tommy Maddox, Pit	519	298	57.4	3414	6.58	18	53	17	41/242	75.3
Kelly Holcomb, Cle	302	193	63.9	1797	5.95	10	68-td	12	21/166	74.6
Rich Gannon, Oak	225	125	55.6	1274	5.66	6	46-td	4	17/90	73.5
Byron Leftwich*, Jax	418	239	57.2	2819	6.74	14	84-td	16	19/90	73.0
Drew Bledsoe, Buf	471	274	58.2	2860	6.07	11	54-td	12	49/371	73.0
Jay Fiedler, Mia	314	179	57.0	2138	6.81	11	59	13	19/126	72.4
David Carr, Hou	295	167	56.6	2013	6.82	9	78-td	13	15/90	69.5
Drew Brees, SD	356	205	57.6	2108	5.92	11	68-td	15	21/178	67.5

NFC	Att	Cmp	Cmp Pct	Yds	Yds/ Att	TD	Long	Int	Sack/Lost	Rating Points
Daunte Culpepper, Min	454	295	65.0	3479	7.66	25	59-td	11	37/196	96.4
Brett Favre, GB	471	308	65.4	3361	7.14	32	66-td	21	19/137	90.4
Aaron Brooks, NO	518	306	59.1	3546	6.85	24	76-td	8	34/195	88.8
Matt Hasselbeck, Sea	513	313	61.0	3841	7.49	26	80-td	15	42/246	88.8
Brad Johnson, TB	570	354	62.1	3811	6.69	26	76-td	21	20/111	81.5
Marc Bulger, St.L	532	336	63.2	3845	7.23	22	48	22	37/288	81.4
Jake Delhomme, Car	449	266	59.2	3219	7.17	19	67-td	16	23/168	80.6
Jeff Garcia, SF	392	225	57.4	2704	6.90	18	75-td	13	21/104	80.1
Donovan McNabb, Phi	478	275	57.5	3216	6.73	16	59	11	43/253	79.6
Patrick Ramsey, Wash	337	179	53.1	2166	6.43	14	64	9	30/206	75.8
Quincy Carter, Dal	505	292	57.8	3302	6.54	17	64	21	37/185	71.4
Kerry Collins, NYG	500	284	56.8	3110	6.22	13	77-td	16	28/164	70.7
Jeff Blake, Ari	367	208	56.7	2247	6.12	13	71-td	15	19/132	69.6
Doug Johnson, Atl	243	136	56.0	1655	6.81	8	86-td	12	19/121	67.5
Joey Harrington, Det	554	309	55.8	2880	5.20	17	72-td	22	9/55	63.9

Receptions

AFC	No	Yds	Avg	Long	TD
LaDainian Tomlinson, SD	100	725	7.3	73-td	4
Derrick Mason, Ten	95	1303	13.7	50-td	8
Hines Ward, Pit	95	1163	12.2	50	10
Marvin Harrison, Ind	94	1272	13.5	79-td	10
Chad Johnson, Cin	90	1355	15.1	82-td	10
Peter Warrick, Cin	79	819	10.4	77-td	7
Santana Moss, NYJ	74	1105	14.9	65-td	10
Rod Smith, Den	74	845	11.4	38	3
Priest Holmes, KC	74	690	9.3	36	0
Tony Gonzalez, KC	71	916	12.9	67	10
David Boston, SD	70	880	12.6	46-td	7
Reggie Wayne, Ind	68	838	12.3	57-td	7
Andre Johnson*, Hou	66	976	14.8	46-td	4
Two tied with 64 each.					

NFC	No	Yds	Avg	Long	TD
Torry Holt, St.L	117	1696	14.5	48	12
Randy Moss, Min	111	1632	14.7	72	17
Anquan Boldin*, Ari	101	1377	13.6	71-td	8
Steve Smith, Car	88	1110	12.6	67-td	7
Keenan McCardell, TB	84	1174	14.0	76-td	8
Laveranues Coles, Wash	82	1204	14.7	64	6
Terrell Owens, SF	80	1102	13.8	75-td	9
Joe Horn, NO	78	973	12.5	50-td	10
Michael Pittman, TB	75	597	8.0	68-td	2
Isaac Bruce, St.L	69	981	14.2	41	5
Deuce McAllister, NO	69	516	7.5	39	0
Richie Anderson, Dal	69	493	7.1	37	4
Tiki Barber, NYG	69	461	6.7	36	1
Darrell Jackson, Sea	68	1137	16.7	80-td	9

Rushing Yards

AFC	Att	Yds	Avg	Long	TD
Jamal Lewis, Bal	387	2066	5.3	82-td	14
LaDainian Tomlinson, SD	313	1645	5.3	73-td	13
Clinton Portis, Den	290	1591	5.5	65-td	14
Fred Taylor, Jax	345	1572	4.6	62	6
Priest Holmes, KC	320	1420	4.4	31-td	27
Ricky Williams, Mia	392	1372	3.5	45	9
Travis Henry, Buf	331	1356	4.1	64	10
Curtis Martin, NYJ	323	1308	4.0	56	2
Edgerrin James, Ind	310	1259	4.1	43	11
Domanick Davis*, Hou	238	1031	4.3	51	8
Eddie George, Ten	312	1031	3.3	27	5
Rudi Johnson, Cin	215	957	4.5	54	9
Jerome Bettis, Pit	246	811	3.3	21	7
Tyrone Wheatley, Oak	159	678	4.3	41	4

NFC	Att	Yds	Avg	Long	TD
Ahman Green, GB	355	1883	5.3	98-td	15
Deuce McAllister, NO	351	1641	4.7	76-td	8
Stephen Davis, Car	318	1444	4.5	40	8
Shaun Alexander, Sea	326	1435	4.4	55	14
Tiki Barber, NYG	278	1216	4.4	27	2
Kevan Barlow, SF	201	1024	5.1	78-td	6
Anthony Thomas, Chi	244	1024	4.2	67-td	6
Troy Hambrick, Dal	275	972	3.5	42	5
Marcel Shipp, Ari	228	830	3.6	36	0
Marshall Faulk, St.L	209	818	3.9	52	10
T.J. Duckett, Atl	197	779	4.0	55	11
Garrison Hearst, SF	178	768	4.3	36	3
Michael Pittman, TB	187	751	4.0	17	0
Moe Williams, Min	174	745	4.3	61	5

Tennessee Titans
Steve McNair
Passing Efficiency

St. Louis Rams
Torry Holt
Receptions

Kansas City Chiefs
Priest Holmes
Scoring

NY Giants
Michael Strahan
Sacks

All-Purpose Yardage

AFC	Rush	Rec	Ret	Total	NFC	Rush	Rec	Ret	Total
Dante Hall, KC 73		423	1950	2446	Ahman Green, GB 1883		367	0	2250
LaDainian Tomlinson, SD . . 1645		725	0	2370	Deuce McAllister, NO 1641		516	0	2157
Jamal Lewis, Bal 2066		205	0	2271	Steve Smith, Car 42		1110	748	1900
Priest Holmes, KC 1420		690	0	2110	Allen Rossum, Atl 0		0	1836	1836
Fred Taylor, Jax 1572		370	0	1942	Brian Westbrook, Phi 613		332	793	1738
Clinton Portis, Den 1591		314	0	1905	Shaun Alexander, Sea 1435		295	0	1730
Ricky Williams, Mia 1372		351	0	1723	Torry Holt, St.L 5		1696	0	1701
J.J. Moses, Hou 0		0	1599	1599	Josh Scobey, Ari 0		9	1684	1693
Curtis Martin, NYJ. 1308		262	0	1570	Tiki Barber, NYG. 1216		461	0	1677
Edgerrin James, Ind 1259		292	0	1551	Randy Moss, Min 18		1632	22	1672
Derrick Mason, Ten 11		1303	205	1519	Chad Morton, Wash 216		187	1217	1620
Travis Henry, Buf 1356		158	0	1514	Stephen Davis, Car 1444		159	0	1603
Santana Moss, NYJ 67		1105	332	1504	Michael Lewis, NO 2		226	1343	1571
Brandon Bennett, Cin. 173		176	1146	1495	Arlen Harris*, St.L. 255		102	1211	1568
Antwaan Randle El, Pit. 75		364	1008	1447	Anquan Boldin*, Ari 40		1377	130	1547

Ret column indicates all kickoff, punt, fumble and interception returns.

Scoring

Touchdowns

AFC	TD	Rush	Rec	Ret	Pts
Priest Holmes, KC 27		27	0	0	162
LaDainian Tomlinson, SD . . . 17		13	4	0	102
Clinton Portis, Den 14		14	0	0	86†
Jamal Lewis, Bal. 14		14	0	0	84
Chris Chambers, Mia 11		0	11	0	66
Travis Henry, Buf 11		10	1	0	66
Edgerrin James, Ind 11		11	0	0	66
Tony Gonzalez, KC 10		0	10	0	60
Marvin Harrison, Ind 10		0	10	0	60
Chad Johnson, Cin. 10		0	10	0	60
Santana Moss, NYJ 10		0	10	0	60
Hines Ward, Pit 10		0	10	0	60
Ricky Williams, Mia 10		9	1	0	60

† Two-point conversions: Portis (1).

NFC	TD	Rush	Rec	Ret	Pts
Ahman Green, GB 20		15	5	0	120
Randy Moss, Min 17		0	17	0	102
Shaun Alexander, Sea . . . 16		14	2	0	96
Brian Westbrook, Phi 13		7	4	2	78
Torry Holt, St.L 12		0	12	0	72
T.J. Duckett, Atl. 11		11	0	0	66
Marshall Faulk, St.L 11		10	1	0	66
Joe Horn, NO 10		0	10	0	60
Correll Buckhalter, Phi. 9		8	1	0	54
Darrell Jackson, Sea. 9		0	9	0	54
Keenan McCardell, TB 9		0	8	1	54
Terrell Owens, SF 9		0	9	0	54
Javon Walker, GB 9		0	9	0	54

Kickers

AFC	PAT	FG	Long	Pts
Mike Vanderjagt, Ind. 46/46	37/37	50	157
Matt Stover, Bal 35/35	33/38	49	134
Gary Anderson, Ten 42/42	27/31	43	123
Jason Elam, Den 39/39	27/31	51	120
Adam Vinatieri, NE. 37/38	25/34	48	112
Morten Anderen, KC 58/59	16/20	49	106
Shayne Graham, Cin 40/40	22/25	48	106
Doug Brien, NYJ 24/24	27/32	48	105
Jeff Reed, Pit. 31/32	23/32	51	100
Olindo Mare, Mia 33/34	22/29	52	99
Sebastian Janikowski, Oak. . 28/29	22/25	55	94
Seth Marler*, Jax 30/30	20/33	53	90
Kris Brown, Hou 27/27	18/22	50	81
Steve Christie, SD 36/36	15/20	51	81

NFC	PAT	FG	Long	Pts
Jeff Wilkins, St.L 46/46	39/42	53	163
John Kasay, Car 29/30	32/38	53	125
Ryan Longwell, GB 51/51	23/26	50	120
David Akers, Phi. 42/42	24/29	57	114
Josh Brown*, Sea 48/48	22/30	58	114
Paul Edinger, Chi 27/27	26/36	54	105
John Carney, NO 36/37	22/30	50	102
Aaron Elling, Min 48/48	18/25	51	102
John Hall, Wash 26/27	25/33	54	101
Billy Cundiff, Dal. 30/31	23/29	52	99
Jason Hanson, Det 26/27	22/23	54	92
Jay Feely, Atl 32/33	19/27	46	89
Martin Gramatica, TB 33/34	16/26	50	81

NFL Regular Season Individual Leaders (Cont.)

Sacks

AFC	No
Adewale Ogunleye, Mia	15.0
Jason Taylor, Mia	13.0
Shaun Ellis, NYJ	12.5
Terrell Suggs*, Bal	12.0
Bert Berry, Den	11.5
Aaron Schobel, Buf	11.5

NFC	No
Michael Strahan, NYG	18.5
Simeon Rice, TB	15.0
Leonard Little, St.L	12.5
Mike Rucker, Car	12.0
Kevin Williams*, Min	10.5

Interceptions

AFC	No	Yds	Long	TD
Ed Reed, Bal	7	132	54-td	1
Marcus Coleman, Hou	7	95	41	0
Patrick Surtain, Mia	7	59	32	0
Eight tied with 6 int's each.				

NFC	No	Yds	Long	TD
Tony Parrish, SF	9	202	49	0
Brian Russell, Min	9	185	50	0
Corey Chavous, Min	8	143	39	1
Dexter Jackson, Ari	6	122	30	0
Dre' Bly, Det	6	89	48-td	1

Punting

AFC	No	Yds	Lg	Avg	In20
Shane Lechler, Oak	96	4503	73	46.9	27
Brian Moorman, Buf	85	3788	71	44.6	20
Craig Hentrich, Ten	71	3117	58	43.9	26
Micah Knorr, Den	68	2937	62	43.2	14
Hunter Smith, Ind	62	2617	55	42.2	20

NFC	No	Yds	Lg	Avg	In20
Todd Sauerbrun, Car	77	3433	64	44.6	22
Mitch Berger, NO	71	3144	59	44.3	28
Tom Tupa, TB	83	3590	60	43.3	26
Scott Player, Ari	82	3511	64	42.8	19
Sean Landeta, St.L	59	2525	57	42.8	14

Punt Returns
(Minimum of 20 returns)

AFC	No	Yds	Avg	Long	TD
Dante Hall, KC	29	472	16.3	93-td	2
Phillip Buchanon, Oak	36	491	13.6	80-td	2
Antwaan Randle El, Pit	45	542	12.0	84-td	2
David Allen*, Jax	27	324	12.0	52	0
Justin McCareins, Ten	29	330	11.4	58-td	1

NFC	No	Yds	Avg	Long	TD
Brian Westbrook, Phi	20	306	15.3	84-td	2
Allen Rossum, Atl	39	545	14.0	72	1
Reggie Swinton, Dal-GB-Det.	24	318	13.3	89-td	1
R.W. McQuarters, Chi	37	452	12.2	60-td	1
Bobby Engram, Sea	31	320	10.3	83-td	1

Kickoff Returns
(Minimum of 20 returns)

AFC	No	Yds	Avg	Long	TD
Bethel Johnson*, NE	30	847	28.2	92-td	1
Dante Hall, KC	57	1478	25.9	100-td	2
Lamont Brightful, Bal	29	716	24.7	75	0
Chris Cole, Den	30	714	23.8	34	0
J.J. Moses, Hou	58	1355	23.4	70	0

NFC	No	Yds	Avg	Long	TD
Jerry Azumah, Chi	41	1191	29.0	89-td	2
Michael Bates, NYJ-Dal	26	686	26.4	48	0
James Thrash, Phi	34	815	24.0	54	0
Reggie Swinton, Dal-GB-Det.	43	1029	23.9	96-td	1
Michael Lewis, NO	45	1068	23.7	53	0

Single Game Highs

Passing Yards

AFC	Cmp/Att	Yds	TD
Steve McNair, Ten vs. Hou (10/12)	18/27	421	3
Peyton Manning, Ind vs. NYJ (11/16)	27/36	401	1
Trent Green, KC vs. GB (10/12, OT)	27/45	400	3
Trent Green, KC vs. Den (12/7)	34/47	397	1
Kelly Holcomb, Cle vs. Ari (11/16)	29/35	392	3

NFC	Cmp/Att	Yds	TD
Brett Favre, GB vs. Oak (12/22)	22/30	399	4
Daunte Culpepper, Min vs. Oak (11/16)	27/49	396	1
Marc Bulger, St.L vs. SF (11/2)	26/42	378	1
Marc Bulger, St.L vs. Pit (10/26)	22/37	375	1
Kerry Collins, NYG vs. Min (10/26)	23/39	375	2

Receiving Yards

AFC	Ct	Yds	TD
David Boston, SD vs. Jax (10/5)	14	181	2
Derrick Mason, Ten vs. Hou (10/12)	6	177	3
Marvin Harrison, Ind vs. TB (10/6, OT)	11	176	2
Jerry Rice, Oak vs. GB (12/22)	10	159	0
Marvin Harrison, Ind vs. NO (9/21)	6	158	3

NFC	Ct	Yds	TD
Anquan Boldin*, Ari vs. Det (9/7)	10	217	2
Torry Holt, St.L vs. SF (11/2)	11	200	1
Muhsin Muhammad, Car vs. Wash (11/16)	9	189	0
Laveranues Coles, Wash vs. Atl (9/14)	11	180	1
Torry Holt, St.L vs. Pit (10/26)	7	174	1

Rushing Yards

AFC	Car	Yds	TD
Jamal Lewis, Bal vs. Cle (9/14)	30	295	2
LaDainian Tomlinson, SD vs. Oak (12/28)	31	243	2
Clinton Portis, Den vs. KC (12/7)	22	218	5
Jamal Lewis, Bal vs. Cle (12/21)	22	205	2
LaDainian Tomlinson, SD vs. Cle (10/19)	26	200	1

NFC	Car	Yds	TD
Ahman Green, GB vs. Den (12/28)	20	218	2
Ahman Green, GB vs. Phi (11/10)	29	192	1
Troy Hambrick, Dal vs. Wash (12/14)	33	189	0
Deuce McAllister, NO vs. Phi (11/23)	19	184	2
Warrick Dunn, Atl vs. NYG (11/9)	25	178	1
Stephen Davis, Car vs. NO (10/26, OT)	31	178	2

NFL Bests

Longest Field Goal
58 yds . . . . Josh Brown*, Sea vs. GB (10/5)
Longest Run from Scrimmage
98 yds . . . . Ahman Green, GB vs. Den (12/28) TD
Longest Pass Play
86 yds . . . . D. Johnson to W. Dunn, Atl vs. Ten (11/23) TD
Longest Interception Return
95 yds . . . . Marlon McCree, Hou vs. Ten (12/21) TD
Longest Punt Return
93 yds . . . . Dante Hall, KC vs. Den (10/5) TD
Longest Kickoff Return
100 yds . . . . Accomplished by 3 players

NFL Regular Season Team Leaders

Offense

AFC	Points For	Avg	Rush	Pass	Yardage Total	Avg
Kansas City	484	30.3	1929	3981	5910	369.4
Indianapolis	447	27.9	1695	4179	5874	367.1
Denver	381	23.8	2629	2969	5598	349.9
Tennessee	435	27.2	1623	3878	5501	343.8
Jacksonville	276	17.3	2073	3285	5358	334.9
Cincinnati	346	21.6	1987	3342	5329	333.1
San Diego	313	19.6	2146	3021	5167	322.9
New England	348	21.8	1607	3432	5039	314.9
NY Jets	283	17.7	1635	3316	4951	309.4
Baltimore	391	24.4	2674	2255	4929	308.1
Pittsburgh	300	18.8	1488	3304	4792	299.5
Miami	311	19.4	1817	2792	4609	288.1
Oakland	270	16.9	1822	2751	4573	285.8
Cleveland	254	15.9	1670	2834	4504	281.5
Buffalo	243	15.2	1664	2684	4348	271.8
Houston	255	15.9	1651	2655	4306	269.1

Defense

AFC	Points Opp	Avg	Rush	Pass	Yardage Total	Avg
Buffalo	279	17.4	1606	2707	4313	269.6
Baltimore	281	17.6	1536	2805	4341	271.3
Denver	301	18.8	1605	2828	4433	277.1
Jacksonville	331	20.7	1406	3251	4657	291.1
New England	238	14.9	1434	3232	4666	291.6
Pittsburgh	327	20.4	1741	3042	4783	298.9
Miami	261	16.3	1452	3335	4787	299.2
Indianapolis	336	21.0	1980	2809	4789	299.3
Tennessee	324	20.3	1295	3606	4901	306.3
Cleveland	322	20.1	2113	2846	4959	309.9
NY Jets	299	18.7	2294	3025	5319	332.4
San Diego	441	27.6	2218	3375	5593	349.6
Cincinnati	384	24.0	2218	3402	5620	351.3
Kansas City	332	20.8	2344	3363	5707	356.7
Oakland	379	23.7	2510	3394	5904	369.0
Houston	380	23.8	2370	3712	6082	380.1

NFC	Points For	Avg	Rush	Pass	Yardage Total	Avg
Minnesota	416	26.0	2343	3951	6294	393.4
Green Bay	442	27.6	2558	3240	5798	362.4
San Francisco	384	24.0	2279	3408	5687	355.4
Seattle	404	25.3	2009	3618	5627	351.7
St. Louis	447	27.9	1496	3961	5457	341.1
Tampa Bay	301	18.8	1648	3805	5453	340.8
New Orleans	340	21.3	2000	3438	5438	339.9
Dallas	289	18.1	1999	3162	5161	322.6
Carolina	325	20.3	2091	3050	5141	321.3
Philadelphia	374	23.4	2015	3020	5035	314.7
NY Giants	243	15.2	1559	3383	4942	308.9
Washington	287	17.9	1653	3006	4659	291.2
Arizona	225	14.1	1531	2959	4490	280.6
Chicago	283	17.7	1763	2617	4380	273.8
Atlanta	299	18.7	1949	2408	4357	272.3
Detroit	270	16.9	1338	2924	4262	266.4

NFC	Points Opp	Avg	Rush	Pass	Yardage Total	Avg
Dallas	260	16.3	1425	2631	4056	253.5
Tampa Bay	264	16.5	1756	2710	4466	279.1
Carolina	304	19.0	1722	3003	4725	295.3
San Francisco	337	21.1	1690	3238	4928	308.0
Chicago	346	21.6	1865	3082	4947	309.2
St. Louis	328	20.5	1980	3072	5052	315.8
Green Bay	307	19.2	1701	3400	5101	318.8
New Orleans	326	20.4	2241	2993	5234	327.1
Seattle	327	20.4	1759	3480	5239	327.4
Philadelphia	287	17.9	2071	3236	5307	331.7
NY Giants	387	24.2	1908	3412	5320	332.5
Minnesota	353	22.1	1879	3477	5356	334.8
Detroit	379	23.7	1782	3578	5360	335.0
Washington	372	23.3	2217	3195	5412	338.3
Arizona	452	28.3	1915	3589	5504	344.0
Atlanta	422	26.4	2308	3800	6108	381.8

Overall Club Rankings

Combined AFC and NFC rankings by yards gained on offense and yards given up on defense. Teams are ranked by offense, with AFC teams in *italics*. (†) indicates tied for position.

Team	Offense Rush	Pass	Rank	Defense Rush	Pass	Rank
Minnesota	4	4	1	17	26	23
Kansas City	15	2	2	30	20	29
Indianapolis	19	1	3	20t	5	11
Green Bay	3	16	4	10	23	17
San Francisco	5	10	5	9	17	13
Seattle	10	7	6	14	27	19
Denver	2	22	7	7	6	4
Tennessee	26	5	8	1	30	12
St. Louis	30	3	9	20t	12	16
Tampa Bay	24	6	10	13	3	5
New Orleans	11	8	11	27	8	18
Jacksonville	8	15	12	2	18	6
Cincinnati	13	12	13	25t	24	28
San Diego	6	19	14	25t	21	27
Dallas	12	17	15	3	1	1
Carolina	7	18	16	11	9	8

Team	Offense Rush	Pass	Rank	Defense Rush	Pass	Rank
New England	27	9	17	4	15	7
Philadelphia	9	20	18	22	16	20
NY Jets	25	13	19	28	10	21
NY Giants	28	11	20	18	25	22
Baltimore	1	32	21	6	4	3
Pittsburgh	31	14	22	12	11	9
Washington	22	21	23	24	14	25
Miami	17	26	24	5	19	10
Oakland	16	27	25	32	22	30
Cleveland	20	25	26	23	7	15
Arizona	29	23	27	19	29	26
Chicago	18	30	28	16	13	14
Atlanta	14	31	29	29	32	32
Buffalo	21	28	30	8	2	2
Houston	23	29	31	31	31	31
Detroit	32	24	32	15	28	24

AFC Team by Team Results
(*) indicates overtime game.

Baltimore Ravens (10-6)

at Pittsburgh	L, 15-34
Cleveland	W, 33-13
at San Diego	W, 24-10
Kansas City	L, 10-17
OPEN	—
at Arizona	W, 26-18
at Cincinnati	L, 26-34
Denver	W, 26-6
Jacksonville	W, 24-17
at St. Louis	L, 22-33
at Miami	L, 6-9*
Seattle	W, 44-41*
San Francisco	W, 44-6
Cincinnati	W, 31-13
at Oakland	L, 12-20
at Cleveland	W, 35-0
Pittsburgh	W, 13-10*

Buffalo Bills (6-10)

New England	W, 31-0
at Jacksonville	W, 38-17
at Miami	L, 7-17
Philadelphia	L, 13-23
Cincinnati	W, 22-16*
at NY Jets	L, 3-30
Washington	W, 24-7
at Kansas City	L, 5-38
OPEN	—
at Dallas	L, 6-10
Houston	L, 10-12
Indianapolis	L, 14-17
at NY Giants	W, 24-7
NY Jets	W, 17-6
at Tennessee	L, 26-28
Miami	L, 3-20
at New England	L, 0-31

Cincinnati Bengals (8-8)

Denver	L, 10-30
at Oakland	L, 20-23
Pittsburgh	L, 10-17
at Cleveland	W, 21-14
at Buffalo	L, 16-22*
OPEN	—
Baltimore	W, 34-26
Seattle	W, 27-24
at Arizona	L, 14-17
Houston	W, 34-27
Kansas City	W, 24-19
at San Diego	W, 34-27
at Pittsburgh	W, 34-20
at Baltimore	L, 13-31
San Francisco	W, 41-38
at St. Louis	L, 10-27
Cleveland	L, 14-22

Cleveland Browns (5-11)

Indianapolis	L, 6-9
at Baltimore	L, 13-33
at San Fran.	W, 13-12
Cincinnati	L, 14-21
at Pittsburgh	W, 33-13
Oakland	W, 13-7
San Diego	L, 20-26
at New England	L, 3-9
OPEN	—
at Kansas City	L, 20-41
Arizona	W, 44-6
Pittsburgh	L, 6-13
at Seattle	L, 7-34
St. Louis	L, 20-26
at Denver	L, 20-23*
Baltimore	L, 0-35
at Cincinnati	W, 22-14

Denver Broncos (10-6)

at Cincinnati	W, 30-10
at San Diego	W, 37-13
Oakland	W, 31-10
Detroit	W, 20-16
at Kansas City	L, 23-24
Pittsburgh	W, 17-14
at Minnesota	L, 20-28
at Baltimore	L, 6-26
New England	L, 26-30
OPEN	—
San Diego	W, 37-8
Chicago	L, 10-19
at Oakland	W, 22-8
Kansas City	W, 45-27
Cleveland	W, 23-20*
at Indianapolis	W, 31-17
at Green Bay	L, 3-31

Houston Texans (5-11)

at Miami	W, 21-20
at New Orleans	L, 10-31
Kansas City	L, 14-42
Jacksonville	W, 24-20
OPEN	—
at Tennessee	L, 17-38
NY Jets	L, 14-19
at Indianapolis	L, 21-30
Carolina	W, 14-10
at Cincinnati	L, 27-34
at Buffalo	W, 12-10
New England	L, 20-23*
Atlanta	W, 17-13
at Jacksonville	L, 0-21
at Tampa Bay	L, 3-16
Tennessee	L, 24-27
Indianapolis	L, 17-20

Indianapolis Colts (12-4)

at Cleveland	W, 9-6
Tennessee	W, 33-7
Jacksonville	W, 23-13
at New Orleans	W, 55-21
at Tampa Bay	W, 38-35*
Carolina	L, 20-23*
OPEN	—
Houston	W, 30-21
at Miami	W, 23-17
at Jacksonville	L, 23-28
NY Jets	W, 38-31
at Buffalo	W, 17-14
New England	L, 34-38
at Tennessee	W, 29-27
Atlanta	W, 38-7
Denver	L, 17-31
at Houston	W, 20-17

Jacksonville Jaguars (5-11)

at Carolina	L, 23-24
Buffalo	L, 17-38
at Indianapolis	L, 13-23
at Houston	L, 20-24
San Diego	W, 27-21
Miami	L, 10-24
OPEN	—
Tennessee	L, 17-30
at Baltimore	L, 17-24
Indianapolis	W, 28-23
at Tennessee	L, 3-10
at NY Jets	L, 10-13
Tampa Bay	W, 17-10
Houston	W, 27-0
at New England	L, 13-27
New Orleans	W, 20-19
at Atlanta	L, 14-21

Kansas City Chiefs (13-3)

San Diego	W, 27-14
Pittsburgh	W, 41-20
at Houston	W, 42-14
at Baltimore	W, 17-10
Denver	W, 24-23
at Green Bay	W, 40-34*
at Oakland	W, 17-10
Buffalo	W, 38-5
OPEN	—
Cleveland	W, 41-20
at Cincinnati	L, 19-24
Oakland	W, 27-24
at San Diego	W, 28-24
at Denver	L, 27-45
Detroit	W, 45-17
at Minnesota	L, 20-45
Chicago	W, 31-3

Miami Dolphins (10-6)

Houston	L, 20-21
at NY Jets	W, 21-10
Buffalo	W, 17-7
OPEN	—
at NY Giants	W, 23-10
at Jacksonville	W, 24-10
New England	L, 13-19*
at San Diego	W, 26-10
Indianapolis	L, 17-23
at Tennessee	L, 7-31
Baltimore	W, 9-6*
Washington	W, 24-23
at Dallas	W, 40-21
at New England	L, 0-12
Philadelphia	L, 27-34
at Buffalo	W, 20-3
NY Jets	W, 23-21

New England Patriots (14-2)

at Buffalo	L, 0-31
at Philadelphia	W, 31-10
NY Jets	W, 23-16
at Washington	L, 17-20
Tennessee	W, 38-30
NY Giants	W, 17-6
at Miami	W, 19-13*
Cleveland	W, 9-3
at Denver	W, 30-26
OPEN	—
Dallas	W, 12-0
at Houston	W, 23-20*
at Indianapolis	W, 38-34
Miami	W, 12-0
Jacksonville	W, 27-13
at NY Jets	W, 21-16
Buffalo	W, 31-0

New York Jets (6-10)

at Washington	L, 13-16
Miami	L, 10-21
at New England	L, 16-23
Dallas	L, 6-17
OPEN	—
Buffalo	W, 30-3
at Houston	W, 19-14
at Philadelphia	L, 17-24
NY Giants	L, 28-31*
at Oakland	W, 27-24*
at Indianapolis	L, 31-38
Jacksonville	W, 13-10
Tennessee	W, 24-17
at Buffalo	L, 6-17
Pittsburgh	W, 6-0
New England	L, 16-21
at Miami	L, 21-23

Oakland Raiders (4-12)

at Tennessee	L,	20-25
Cincinnati	W,	23-20
at Denver	L,	10-31
San Diego	W,	34-31*
at Chicago	L,	21-24
at Cleveland	L,	7-13
Kansas City	L,	10-17
OPEN	—	
at Detroit	L,	13-23
NY Jets	L,	24-27*
Minnesota	W,	28-18
at Kansas City	L,	24-27
Denver	L,	8-22
at Pittsburgh	L,	7-27
Baltimore	W,	20-12
Green Bay	L,	7-41
at San Diego	L,	14-21

Pittsburgh Steelers (6-10)

Baltimore	W,	34-15
at Kansas City	L,	20-41
at Cincinnati	W,	17-10
Tennessee	L,	13-30
Cleveland	L,	13-33
at Denver	L,	14-17
OPEN	—	
St. Louis	L,	21-33
at Seattle	L,	16-23
Arizona	W,	28-15
at San Fran.	L,	14-30
at Cleveland	W,	13-6
Cincinnati	L,	20-24
Oakland	W,	27-7
at NY Jets	L,	0-6
San Diego	W,	40-24
at Baltimore	L,	10-13*

San Diego Chargers (4-12)

at Kansas City	L,	14-27
Denver	L,	13-37
Baltimore	L,	10-24
at Oakland	L,	31-34*
at Jacksonville	L,	21-27
OPEN	—	
at Cleveland	W,	26-20
Miami	L,	10-26
at Chicago	L,	7-20
Minnesota	W,	42-28
at Denver	L,	8-37
Cincinnati	L,	27-34
Kansas City	L,	24-28
at Detroit	W,	14-7
Green Bay	L,	21-38
at Pittsburgh	L,	24-40
Oakland	W,	21-14

Tennessee Titans (12-4)

Oakland	W,	25-20
at Indianapolis	L,	7-33
New Orleans	W,	27-12
at Pittsburgh	W,	30-13
at New England	L,	30-38
Houston	W,	38-17
at Carolina	W,	37-17
at Jacksonville	W,	30-17
OPEN	—	
Miami	W,	31-7
Jacksonville	W,	10-3
at Atlanta	W,	38-31
at NY Jets	L,	17-24
Indianapolis	L,	27-29
Buffalo	W,	28-26
at Houston	W,	27-24
Tampa Bay	W,	33-13

NFC Team by Team Results
(*) indicates overtime game

Arizona Cardinals (4-12)

at Detroit	L,	24-42
Seattle	L,	0-38
Green Bay	W,	20-13
at St. Louis	L,	13-37
at Dallas	L,	7-24
Baltimore	L,	18-26
OPEN	—	
San Francisco	W,	16-13*
Cincinnati	W,	17-14
at Pittsburgh	L,	15-28
at Cleveland	L,	6-44
St. Louis	L,	27-30*
at Chicago	L,	3-28
at San Francisco	L,	14-50
Carolina	L,	17-20
at Seattle	L,	10-28
Minnesota	W,	18-17

Atlanta Falcons (5-11)

at Dallas	W,	27-13
Washington	L,	31-33
Tampa Bay	L,	10-31
at Carolina	L,	3-23
Minnesota	L,	26-39
at St. Louis	L,	0-36
New Orleans	L,	17-45
OPEN	—	
Philadelphia	L,	16-23
at NY Giants	W,	27-7
at New Orleans	L,	20-23*
Tennessee	L,	31-38
at Houston	L,	13-17
Carolina	W,	20-14*
at Indianapolis	L,	7-38
at Tampa Bay	W,	30-28
Jacksonville	W,	21-14

Carolina Panthers (11-5)

Jacksonville	W,	24-23
at Tampa Bay	W,	12-9*
OPEN	—	
Atlanta	W,	23-3
New Orleans	W,	19-13
at Indianapolis	W,	23-20*
Tennessee	L,	17-37
at New Orleans	W,	23-20*
at Houston	L,	10-14
Tampa Bay	W,	27-24
Washington	L,	20-17
at Dallas	L,	20-24
Philadelphia	L,	16-25
at Atlanta	L,	14-20*
at Arizona	W,	20-17
Detroit	W,	20-14
at NY Giants	W,	37-24

Chicago Bears (7-9)

at San Francisco	L,	7-49
at Minnesota	L,	13-24
OPEN	—	
Green Bay	L,	23-38
Oakland	W,	24-21
at New Orleans	L,	13-20
at Seattle	L,	17-24
Detroit	W,	24-16
San Diego	W,	20-7
at Detroit	L,	10-12
St. Louis	L,	21-23
at Denver	L,	19-10
Arizona	W,	28-3
at Green Bay	L,	21-34
Minnesota	W,	13-10
Washington	W,	27-24
at Kansas City	L,	3-31

Dallas Cowboys (10-6)

Atlanta	L,	13-27
at NY Giants	W,	35-32*
OPEN	—	
at NY Jets	W,	17-6
Arizona	W,	24-7
Philadelphia	W,	23-21
at Detroit	W,	38-7
at Tampa Bay	L,	0-16
Washington	W,	21-14
Buffalo	W,	10-6
at New England	L,	0-12
Carolina	W,	24-20
Miami	L,	21-40
at Philadelphia	L,	10-36
at Washington	W,	27-0
NY Giants	W,	19-3
at New Orleans	L,	7-13

Detroit Lions (5-11)

Arizona	W,	42-24
at Green Bay	L,	6-31
Minnesota	L,	13-23
at Denver	L,	16-20
at San Francisco	L,	17-24
OPEN	—	
Dallas	L,	7-38
at Chicago	W,	16-24
Oakland	W,	23-13
Chicago	W,	12-10
at Seattle	L,	14-35
at Minnesota	L,	14-24
Green Bay	W,	22-14
San Diego	L,	7-14
at Kansas City	L,	17-45
at Carolina	L,	14-20
St. Louis	W,	30-20

Green Bay Packers (10-6)

Minnesota	L,	25-30
Detroit	W,	31-6
at Arizona	L,	13-20
at Chicago	W,	38-23
Seattle	W,	35-13
Kansas City	L,	34-40*
at St. Louis	L,	24-34
OPEN	—	
at Minnesota	W,	30-27
Philadelphia	L,	14-17
at Tampa Bay	W,	20-13
San Francisco	W,	20-10
at Detroit	L,	14-22
Chicago	W,	34-21
at San Diego	W,	38-21
at Oakland	W,	41-7
Denver	W,	31-3

Minnesota Vikings (9-7)

at Green Bay	W,	30-25
Chicago	W,	24-13
at Detroit	W,	23-13
San Francisco	W,	35-7
at Atlanta	W,	39-26
OPEN	—	
Denver	W,	28-20
NY Giants	L,	17-29
Green Bay	L,	27-30
at San Diego	L,	28-42
at Oakland	L,	18-28
Detroit	W,	24-14
at St. Louis	L,	17-48
Seattle	W,	34-7
at Chicago	L,	10-13
Kansas City	W,	45-20
at Arizona	L,	17-18

NFC Team by Team Results (Cont.)

New Orleans Saints (8-8)

at Seattle	L, 10-27
Houston	W, 31-10
at Tennessee	L, 12-27
Indianapolis	L, 21-55
at Carolina	L, 13-19
Chicago	W, 20-13
at Atlanta	W, 45-17
Carolina	L, 20-23*
at Tampa Bay	W, 17-14
OPEN	—
Atlanta	W, 23-20*
at Philadelphia	L, 20-33
at Washington	W, 24-20
Tampa Bay	L, 7-14
NY Giants	W, 45-7
at Jacksonville	L, 19-20
Dallas	W, 13-7

New York Giants (4-12)

St. Louis	W, 23-13
Dallas	L, 32-35*
at Washington	W, 24-21*
OPEN	—
Miami	L, 10-23
at New England	L, 6-17
Philadelphia	L, 10-14
at Minnesota	W, 29-17
at NY Jets	W, 31-28*
Atlanta	L, 7-27
at Philadelphia	L, 10-28
at Tampa Bay	L, 13-19
Buffalo	L, 7-24
Washington	L, 7-20
at New Orleans	L, 7-45
at Dallas	L, 3-19
Carolina	L, 24-37

Philadelphia Eagles (12-4)

Tampa Bay	L, 0-17
New England	L, 10-31
OPEN	—
at Buffalo	W, 23-13
Washington	W, 27-25
at Dallas	L, 21-23
at NY Giants	W, 14-10
NY Jets	W, 24-17
at Atlanta	W, 23-16
at Green Bay	W, 17-14
NY Giants	W, 28-10
New Orleans	W, 33-20
at Carolina	W, 25-16
Dallas	W, 36-10
at Miami	W, 34-27
San Francisco	L, 28-31*
at Washington	W, 31-7

St. Louis Rams (12-4)

at NY Giants	L, 13-23
San Francisco	W, 27-24*
at Seattle	L, 23-24
Arizona	W, 37-13
OPEN	—
Atlanta	W, 36-0
Green Bay	W, 34-24
at Pittsburgh	W, 33-21
at San Francisco	L, 10-30
Baltimore	W, 33-22
at Chicago	W, 23-21
at Arizona	W, 30-27*
Minnesota	W, 48-17
at Cleveland	W, 26-20
Seattle	W, 27-22
Cincinnati	W, 27-10
at Detroit	L, 20-30

San Francisco 49ers (7-9)

Chicago	W, 49-7
at St. Louis	L, 24-27*
Cleveland	L, 12-13
at Minnesota	L, 7-35
Detroit	W, 24-17
at Seattle	L, 19-20
Tampa Bay	W, 24-7
at Arizona	L, 13-16*
St. Louis	W, 30-10
OPEN	—
Pittsburgh	W, 30-14
at Green Bay	L, 10-20
at Baltimore	L, 6-44
Arizona	W, 50-14
at Cincinnati	L, 38-41
at Philadelphia	W, 31-28*
Seattle	L, 17-24

Seattle Seahawks (10-6)

New Orleans	W, 27-10
at Arizona	W, 38-0
St. Louis	W, 24-23
OPEN	—
at Green Bay	L, 13-35
San Francisco	W, 20-19
Chicago	W, 24-17
at Cincinnati	L, 24-27
Pittsburgh	W, 23-16
at Washington	L, 20-27
Detroit	W, 35-14
at Baltimore	L, 41-44*
Cleveland	W, 34-7
at Minnesota	L, 7-34
at St. Louis	L, 22-27
Arizona	W, 28-10
at San Fran.	W, 24-17

Tampa Bay Buccaneers (7-9)

at Philadelphia	W, 17-0
Carolina	L, 9-12*
at Atlanta	W, 31-10
OPEN	—
Indianapolis	L, 35-38*
at Washington	W, 35-13
at San Francisco	L, 7-24
Dallas	W, 16-0
New Orleans	L, 14-17
at Carolina	L, 24-27
Green Bay	L, 13-20
NY Giants	W, 19-13
at Jacksonville	L, 10-17
at New Orleans	W, 14-7
Houston	W, 16-3
Atlanta	L, 28-30
at Tennessee	L, 13-33

Washington Redskins (5-11)

NY Jets	W, 16-13
at Atlanta	W, 33-31
NY Giants	L, 21-24*
New England	W, 20-17
at Philadelphia	L, 25-27
Tampa Bay	L, 13-35
at Buffalo	L, 7-24
OPEN	—
at Dallas	L, 14-21
Seattle	W, 27-20
at Carolina	L, 17-20
at Miami	L, 23-24
New Orleans	L, 20-24
at NY Giants	W, 20-7
Dallas	L, 0-27
at Chicago	L, 24-27
Philadelphia	L, 7-31

Takeaways/Giveaways

	Takeaways			Giveaways			Net		Takeaways			Giveaways			Net
AFC	Int	Fum	Total	Int	Fum	Total	Diff	**NFC**	Int	Fum	Total	Int	Fum	Total	Diff
Kansas City	25	12	37	12	6	18	+19	San Francisco	23	14	37	15	10	25	+12
New England	29	12	41	13	11	24	+17	Minnesota	28	7	35	13	11	24	+11
Tennessee	21	13	34	9	12	21	+13	St. Louis	24	22	46	23	16	39	+7
Indianapolis	15	15	30	10	10	20	+10	Philadelphia	13	13	26	11	11	22	+4
Baltimore	24	17	41	19	19	38	+3	Tampa Bay	20	13	33	22	9	31	+2
Cincinnati	14	10	24	15	7	22	+2	Washington	17	13	30	16	12	28	+2
Miami	22	14	36	19	15	34	+2	Atlanta	15	16	31	21	10	31	0
NY Jets	11	9	20	14	6	20	0	Detroit	15	13	28	24	4	28	0
Oakland	14	11	25	14	12	26	-1	Green Bay	21	11	32	21	11	32	0
Pittsburgh	14	11	25	17	11	28	-3	New Orleans	14	13	27	8	20	28	-1
Denver	9	11	20	18	6	24	-4	Seattle	16	12	28	16	13	29	-1
Jacksonville	15	12	27	17	14	31	-4	Dallas	13	12	25	21	8	29	-4
Houston	14	8	22	18	9	27	-5	Carolina	16	10	26	16	15	31	-5
Cleveland	15	7	22	18	15	33	-11	Chicago	15	5	20	20	9	29	-9
San Diego	13	7	20	19	12	31	-11	Arizona	13	10	23	22	14	36	-13
Buffalo	10	8	18	17	17	34	-16	NY Giants	10	12	22	20	18	38	-16
TOTALS	265	177	442	249	182	431	+11	TOTALS	273	196	469	289	191	480	-11

AFC Team by Team Statistics

Players with more than one team during the regular season are listed with club they ended season with; (*) indicates rookies.

Baltimore Ravens

Passing (5 Att)	Att	Cmp	Pct	Yds	TD	Rate
Kyle Boller*	224	116	51.8	1260	7	62.4
Anthony Wright	178	94	52.8	1199	9	72.3
Chris Redman	13	7	53.8	58	0	26.0

Interceptions: Boller 9, Wright 8, Redman 2.

Top Receivers	No	Yds	Avg	Long	TD
Todd Heap	57	693	12.2	33-td	3
Travis Taylor	39	632	16.2	73-td	3
Marcus Robinson	31	451	14.5	50-td	6
Jamal Lewis	26	205	7.9	26	0
Chester Taylor	20	132	6.6	23	0
Terry Jones	19	159	8.4	25	3

Top Rushers	Car	Yds	Avg	Long	TD
Jamal Lewis	387	2066	5.3	82-td	14
Chester Taylor	63	276	4.4	32	2
Alan Ricard	19	79	4.2	30	0
Anthony Wright	28	73	2.6	17	0

Most Touchdowns	TD	Run	Rec	Ret	Pts
Jamal Lewis	14	14	0	0	84
Marcus Robinson	6	0	6	0	36
Todd Heap	3	0	3	0	26
Terry Jones	3	0	3	0	18
Ed Reed	3	0	0	3	18
Travis Taylor	3	0	3	0	18

2-Pt. Conversions: (4-6) Heap 4.

Kicking	PAT/Att	FG/Att	Lg	Pts
Matt Stover	35/35	33/38	49	134
Wade Richey	0/0	1/2	56	3

Punts (10 or more)	No	Yds	Long	Avg	In20
Dave Zastudil*	89	3649	67	41.0	21

Most Interceptions		Most Sacks	
Ed Reed	7	Terrell Suggs*	12

Buffalo Bills

Passing (5 Att)	Att	Cmp	Pct	Yds	TD	Rate
Drew Bledsoe	471	274	58.2	2860	11	73.0
Travis Brown	18	14	77.8	160	0	80.6
Alex Van Pelt	12	5	41.7	49	0	14.2

Interceptions: Bledsoe 12, Van Pelt 3, Brown 1.

Top Receivers	No	Yds	Avg	Long	TD
Eric Moulds	64	780	12.2	49	1
Josh Reed	58	588	10.1	26	2
Bobby Shaw	56	732	13.1	54-td	4
Mark Campbell	34	339	10.0	31	1
Travis Henry	28	158	5.6	18	1

Top Rushers	Car	Yds	Avg	Long	TD
Travis Henry	331	1356	4.1	64	10
Joe Burns	39	113	2.9	12	0
Sammy Morris	19	70	3.7	12	1
Josh Reed	3	38	12.7	16	0

Most Touchdowns	TD	Run	Rec	Ret	Pts
Travis Henry	11	10	1	0	66
Bobby Shaw	4	0	4	0	24
Drew Bledsoe	2	2	0	0	12
Dave Moore	2	0	2	0	12
Josh Reed	2	0	2	0	12

2-Pt. Conversions: (0-2).

Kicking	PAT/Att	FG/Att	Lg	Pts
Rian Lindell	24/24	17/24	44	75

Punts (10 or more)	No	Yds	Long	Avg	In20
Brian Moorman	85	3788	71	44.6	20

Most Interceptions		Most Sacks	
Nate Clements	3	Aaron Schobel	11.5

Cincinnati Bengals

Passing (5 Att)	Att	Cmp	Pct	Yds	TD	Rate
Jon Kitna	520	324	62.3	3591	26	87.4

Interceptions: Kitna 15.

Top Receivers	No	Yds	Avg	Long	TD
Chad Johnson	90	1355	15.1	82-td	10
Peter Warrick	79	819	10.4	77-td	7
Brandon Bennett	25	176	7.0	16	1
Matt Schobel	24	332	13.8	45-td	2
Kelley Washington*	22	299	13.6	51-td	4

Top Rushers	Car	Yds	Avg	Long	TD
Rudi Johnson	215	957	4.5	54	9
Corey Dillon	138	541	3.9	39	2
Brandon Bennett	56	173	3.1	19	0
Peter Warrick	18	157	8.7	50	0

Most Touchdowns	TD	Run	Rec	Ret	Pts
Chad Johnson	10	0	10	0	60
Rudi Johnson	9	9	0	0	54
Peter Warrick	8	0	7	1	48
Kelley Washington*	4	0	4	0	24

Three tied with 2 TD each.

2-Pt. Conversions: (0-0).

Kicking	PAT/Att	FG/Att	Lg	Pts
Shayne Graham	40/40	22/25	48	106

Punts (10 or more)	No	Yds	Long	Avg	In20
Kyle Richardson	49	1961	58	40.0	9

Waived: Nick Harris on Oct. 7 (see Det.). **Signed:** Richardson on Oct. 7.

Most Interceptions		Most Sacks	
Tory James	4	Duane Clemons	6.0
		John Thornton	6.0

Cleveland Browns

Passing (5 Att)	Att	Cmp	Pct	Yds	TD	Rate
Kelly Holcomb	302	193	63.9	1797	10	74.6
Tim Couch	203	120	59.1	1319	7	77.6

Interceptions: Holcomb 12, Couch 6.

Top Receivers	No	Yds	Avg	Long	TD
Dennis Northcutt	62	729	11.8	44	2
Jamel White	46	303	6.6	22	1
Andre Davis	40	576	14.4	49	5
Quincy Morgan	38	516	13.6	71-td	3

Waived: Kevin Johnson on Nov. 11 (see Jax.).

Top Rushers	Car	Yds	Avg	Long	TD
William Green	142	559	3.9	26	1
James Jackson	102	382	3.7	18	3
Lee Suggs*	56	289	5.2	78-td	2
Jamel White	70	266	3.8	23	1

Most Touchdowns	TD	Run	Rec	Ret	Pts
Andre Davis	5	0	5	0	30
James Jackson	3	3	0	0	18
Quincy Morgan	3	0	3	0	18

Five tied with 2 TD each.

2-Pt. Conversions: (0-3).

Kicking	PAT/Att	FG/Att	Lg	Pts
Phil Dawson	20/21	18/21	52	74
Brett Conway	9/9	14/19	48	51
NYG	6/6	9/12	44	33
CLE	3/3	5/7	48	18

Signed: Conway on Dec. 10.

Punts (10 or more)	No	Yds	Long	Avg	In20
Chris Gardocki	72	3019	60	41.9	18

Most Interceptions		Most Sacks	
Earl Little	6	Kenard Lang	8.0

Denver Broncos

Passing (5 Att)

	Att	Cmp	Pct	Yds	TD	Rate
Jake Plummer 302		189	62.6	2182	15	91.2
Danny Kannell 103		53	51.5	442	2	49.1
Steve Beuerlein 63		33	52.4	389	2	49.0
Jarious Jackson 9		4	44.4	41	0	18.5

Interceptions: Plummer 7, Kannell and Beuerlein 5, Jackson 1.

Top Receivers

	No	Yds	Avg	Long	TD
Rod Smith 74		845	11.4	38	3
Shannon Sharpe 62		770	12.4	28	8
Clinton Portis 38		314	8.3	72	0
Ashley Lelie 37		628	17.0	60	2
Ed McCaffrey 19		195	10.3	23	0
Mike Anderson 12		53	4.4	18	2

Top Rushers

	Car	Yds	Avg	Long	TD
Clinton Portis 290		1591	5.5	65-td	14
Quentin Griffin* 94		345	3.7	23	0
Mike Anderson 70		257	3.7	44	3
Jake Plummer 37		205	5.5	40	3

Most Touchdowns

	TD	Run	Rec	Ret	Pts
Clinton Portis 14		14	0	0	86
Shannon Sharpe 8		0	8	0	48
Mike Anderson 5		3	2	0	30
Rod Smith 4		0	3	1	24
Jake Plummer 3		3	0	0	18

2-Pt. Conversions: (1-1) Portis.

Kicking

	PAT/Att	FG/Att	Lg	Pts
Jason Elam 39/39		27/31	51	120
Micah Knorr 2/2		1/1	27	5

Punts (10 or more)

	No	Yds	Long	Avg	In20
Micah Knorr 68		2937	62	43.2	14

Most Interceptions
Kelly Herndon 3

Most Sacks
Bertrand Berry 11.5

Houston Texans

Passing (5 Att)

	Att	Cmp	Pct	Yds	TD	Rate
David Carr 295		167	56.6	2013	9	69.5
Tony Banks 102		61	59.8	693	5	84.3
Dave Ragone* 40		20	50.0	135	0	47.4

Interceptions: Carr 13, Banks 3, Ragone 1.

Top Receivers

	No	Yds	Avg	Long	TD
Andre Johnson* 66		976	14.8	46-td	4
Domanick Davis* 47		351	7.5	17	0
Billy Miller 40		355	8.9	25	3
Jabar Gaffney 34		402	11.8	33	2
Corey Bradford 24		460	19.2	78-td	4

Top Rushers

	Car	Yds	Avg	Long	TD
Domanick Davis* 238		1031	4.3	51	8
Stacey Mack 93		253	2.7	13	4
David Carr 27		151	5.6	36	2
Tony Hollings* 38		102	2.7	17	0

Most Touchdowns

	TD	Run	Rec	Ret	Pts
Domanick Davis* 8		8	0	0	48
Corey Bradford 4		0	4	0	24
Andre Johnson* 4		0	4	0	24
Stacey Mack 4		4	0	0	24
Billy Miller 3		0	3	0	18

2-Pt. Conversions: (0-2).

Kicking

	PAT/Att	FG/Att	Lg	Pts
Kris Brown 27/27		18/22	50	81

Punts (10 or more)

	No	Yds	Long	Avg	In20
Chad Stanley 97		4028	54	41.5	36

Most Interceptions
Marcus Coleman 7

Most Sacks
Jamie Sharper 4.0

Indianapolis Colts

Passing (5 Att)

	Att	Cmp	Pct	Yds	TD	Rate
Peyton Manning . . .566		379	67.0	4267	29	99.0

Interceptions: Manning 10.

Top Receivers

	No	Yds	Avg	Long	TD
Marvin Harrison 94		1272	13.5	79-td	10
Reggie Wayne 68		838	12.3	57-td	7
Edgerrin James 51		292	5.7	17	0
Marcus Pollard 40		541	13.5	70	3
Troy Walters 36		456	12.7	46-td	3
Dallas Clark* 29		340	11.7	42	1

Top Rushers

	Car	Yds	Avg	Long	TD
Edgerrin James 310		1259	4.1	43	11
Dominic Rhodes 37		157	4.2	25	0
Ricky Williams 48		155	3.2	19	2
James Mungro 24		60	2.5	9	2

Most Touchdowns

	TD	Run	Rec	Ret	Pts
Edgerrin James 11		11	0	0	66
Marvin Harrison 10		0	10	0	60
Reggie Wayne 7		0	7	0	42
Marcus Pollard 3		0	3	0	18
Brandon Stokley 3		0	3	0	18
Troy Walters 3		0	3	0	18
Ricky Williams 3		2	1	0	18

2-Pt. Conversions: (1-2) Mungro.

Kicking

	PAT/Att	FG/Att	Lg	Pts
Mike Vanderjagt 46/46		37/37	50	157

Punts (10 or more)

	No	Yds	Long	Avg	In20
Hunter Smith 62		2617	55	42.2	20

Most Interceptions
Nick Harper 4

Most Sacks
Dwight Freeney 11.0

Jacksonville Jaguars

Passing (15 Att)

	Att	Cmp	Pct	Yds	TD	Rate
Byron Leftwich* . . .418		239	57.2	2819	14	73.0
Mark Brunell 82		54	65.9	484	2	89.7

Interceptions: Leftwich 16.

Top Receivers

	No	Yds	Avg	Long	TD
Kevin Johnson 58		634	10.9	41	3
CLE 41		381	9.3	41	2
JAX 17		253	14.9	28	1
Jimmy Smith 54		805	14.9	67	4
Fred Taylor 48		370	7.7	60-td	1
Troy Edwards 35		487	13.9	84-td	3

Claimed: Johnson off waivers from Cle. (Nov. 12).

Top Rushers

	Car	Yds	Avg	Long	TD
Fred Taylor 345		1572	4.6	62	6
LaBrandon Toefield* . .53		212	4.0	30	2
C. Fuamatu-Ma'afala . .35		144	4.1	18	1
Byron Leftwich* 25		108	4.3	18	2

Most Touchdowns

	TD	Run	Rec	Ret	Pts
Fred Taylor 7		6	1	0	42
Jimmy Smith 4		0	4	0	24

Three tied with 3 TD each.

2-Pt. Conversions: (0-1).

Kicking

	PAT/Att	FG/Att	Lg	Pts
Seth Marler* 30/30		20/33	53	90

Punts (10 or more)

	No	Yds	Long	Avg	In20
Mark Royals 61		2495	51	40.9	14
MIA 16		643	50	40.2	5
JAX 45		1852	51	41.2	9
Chris Hanson 23		1001	58	43.5	4

Signed: Royals on Oct. 9.

Most Interceptions
Mike Peterson 3

Most Sacks
Tony Brackens 6.0

Kansas City Chiefs

Passing (5 Att)

	Att	Cmp	Pct	Yds	TD	Rate
Trent Green	.523	330	63.1	4039	24	92.6
Todd Collins	.12	9	75.0	74	0	90.3

Interceptions: Green 12.

Top Receivers

	No	Yds	Avg	Long	TD
Priest Holmes	.74	690	9.3	36	0
Tony Gonzalez	.71	916	12.9	67	10
Eddie Kennison	.56	853	15.2	51-td	5
Johnnie Morton	.50	740	14.8	50	4
Dante Hall	.40	423	10.6	67-td	1

Top Rushers

	Car	Yds	Avg	Long	TD
Priest Holmes	.320	1420	4.4	31-td	27
Derrick Blaylock	.22	112	5.1	25-td	2
Johnnie Morton	.8	94	11.8	39	0
Larry Johnson*	.20	85	4.3	15	1
Trent Green	.26	83	3.2	14	2

Most Touchdowns

	TD	Run	Rec	Ret	Pts
Priest Holmes	27	27	0	0	162
Tony Gonzalez	10	0	10	0	60
Dante Hall	5	0	1	4	30
Eddie Kennison	5	0	5	0	30
Johnnie Morton	4	0	4	0	24

2-Pt. Conversions: (0-3).

Kicking

	PAT/Att	FG/Att	Lg	Pts
Morten Andersen	58/59	16/20	49	106

Punts (10 or more)

	No	Yds	Long	Avg	In20
Jason Baker	.80	3156	68	39.5	21

Most Interceptions
Greg Wesley 6
Dexter McCleon 6

Most Sacks
Vonnie Holliday 5.5

Miami Dolphins

Passing (5 Att)

	Att	Cmp	Pct	Yds	TD	Rate
Jay Fiedler	.314	179	57.0	2138	11	72.4
Brian Griese	.130	74	56.9	813	5	69.2
Sage Rosenfels	.6	4	66.7	50	1	131.9

Interceptions: Fiedler 13, Griese 6.

Top Receivers

	No	Yds	Avg	Long	TD
Chris Chambers	.64	963	15.0	57-td	11
Ricky Williams	.50	351	7.0	59	1
Randy McMichael	.49	598	12.2	46	2
Derrius Thompson	.26	359	13.8	31	0
James McKnight	.23	285	12.4	80-td	2
Rob Konrad	.16	166	10.4	25	0

Top Rushers

	Car	Yds	Avg	Long	TD
Ricky Williams	.392	1372	3.5	45	9
Travis Minor	.41	193	4.7	26	1
Jay Fiedler	.34	88	2.6	14	3
James McKnight	.2	75	37.5	68-td	1

Most Touchdowns

	TD	Run	Rec	Ret	Pts
Chris Chambers	11	0	11	0	66
Ricky Williams	10	9	1	0	60
Jay Fiedler	3	3	0	0	18
James McKnight	3	1	2	0	18
Randy McMichael	3	0	2	1	18

2-Pt. Conversions: (0-1).

Kicking

	PAT/Att	FG/Att	Lg	Pts
Olindo Mare	.33/34	22/29	52	99

Punts (10 or more)

	No	Yds	Long	Avg	In20
Matt Turk	.68	2631	57	38.7	23

Signed: Turk on Sept. 29. **Released:** Mark Royals on Sept. 29 (see Jax.).

Most Interceptions
Patrick Surtain 7

Most Sacks
Adewale Ogunleye ..15.0

New England Patriots

Passing (5 Att)

	Att	Cmp	Pct	Yds	TD	Rate
Tom Brady	.527	317	60.2	3620	23	85.9
Rohan Davey	.7	3	42.9	31	0	56.3

Interceptions: Brady 12.

Top Receivers

	No	Yds	Avg	Long	TD
Deion Branch	.57	803	14.1	66-td	3
Kevin Faulk	.48	440	9.2	27	0
Troy Brown	.40	472	11.8	82-td	4
Daniel Graham	.38	409	10.8	38	4
David Givens	.34	510	15.0	57	6
Christian Fauria	.28	285	10.2	28	2

Top Rushers

	Car	Yds	Avg	Long	TD
Antowain Smith	.182	642	3.5	30	3
Kevin Faulk	.178	638	3.6	23	0
Mike Cloud	.27	118	4.4	42	5
Larry Centers	.21	82	3.9	13	0

Most Touchdowns

	TD	Run	Rec	Ret	Pts
David Givens	6	0	6	0	36
Mike Cloud	5	5	0	0	30
Troy Brown	4	0	4	0	24
Daniel Graham	4	0	4	0	24

Three tied with 3 TD each.
2-Pt. Conversions: (0-0).

Kicking

	PAT/Att	FG/Att	Lg	Pts
Adam Vinatieri	.37/38	25/34	48	112

Punts (10 or more)

	No	Yds	Long	Avg	In20
Ken Walter	.76	2865	52	37.7	25
Brooks Barnard*	.10	365	49	36.5	4

Released: Walter on Dec. 2; Barnard on Dec. 12. **Signed:** Barnard on Dec. 3; Walter on Dec. 12.

Most Interceptions
Ty Law 6
Tyrone Poole 6

Most Sacks
Mike Vrabel 9.5

New York Jets

Passing (5 Att)

	Att	Cmp	Pct	Yds	TD	Rate
Chad Pennington	.297	189	63.6	2139	13	82.9
Vinny Testaverde	.198	123	62.1	1385	7	90.6

Interceptions: Pennington 12, Testaverde 2.

Top Receivers

	No	Yds	Avg	Long	TD
Santana Moss	.74	1105	14.9	65-td	10
Jerald Sowell	.47	436	9.3	44	1
Curtis Conway	.46	640	13.9	45	2
Curtis Martin	.42	262	6.2	29	0
Anthony Becht	.40	356	8.9	29	4
Wayne Chrebet	.27	289	10.7	29-td	1
Chris Baker	.14	137	9.8	24	0

Top Rushers

	No	Yds	Avg	Long	TD
Curtis Martin	.323	1308	4.0	56	2
LaMont Jordan	.46	190	4.1	39	4
Santana Moss	.10	67	6.7	25	0
Chad Pennington	.21	42	2.0	10-td	2

Most Touchdowns

	TD	Run	Rec	Ret	Pts
Santana Moss	10	0	10	0	60
Anthony Becht	4	0	4	0	26
LaMont Jordan	4	4	0	0	24

Four tied with 2 each.
2-Pt. Conversions: (3-3) Martin, Becht, Coles.

Kicking

	PAT/Att	FG/Att	Lg	Pts
Doug Brien	.24/24	27/32	48	105

Punts (10 or more)

	No	Yds	Long	Avg	In20
Dan Stryzinski	.71	2655	55	37.4	22

Most Interceptions
Aaron Beasley 3

Most Sacks
Shaun Ellis 12.5

Oakland Raiders

Passing (5 Att)	Att	Cmp	Pct	Yds	TD	Rate
Rich Gannon	.225	125	55.6	1274	6	73.5
Rick Mirer	.221	116	52.5	1267	3	64.8
Marques Tuiasosopo	45	25	55.6	324	0	50.6
Rob Johnson	.20	11	55.0	93	0	46.5
WASH	.7	5	71.4	39	0	84.8
OAK	.13	6	46.2	54	0	25.8
Rob Johnson	.20	11	55.0	93	0	46.5
Tee Martin	.16	6	37.5	69	0	25.3

Signed: Johnson on Nov. 4.

Top Receivers	No	Yds	Avg	Long	TD
Jerry Rice	.63	869	13.8	47-td	2
Tim Brown	.52	567	10.9	36-td	2
Charlie Garner	.48	386	8.0	46-td	1
Doug Jolley	.31	250	8.1	26	1
Jerry Porter	.28	361	12.9	35	1

Top Rushers	Car	Yds	Avg	Long	TD
Tyrone Wheatley	.159	678	4.3	41	4
Charlie Garner	.120	553	4.6	33	3
Justin Fargas*	.40	203	5.1	53	0
Zack Crockett	.48	145	3.0	44	7

Most Touchdowns	TD	Run	Rec	Ret	Pts
Zack Crockett	.7	7	0	0	42
Phillip Buchanon	.4	0	0	4	24
Charlie Garner	.4	3	1	0	24
Tyrone Wheatley	.4	4	0	0	24

Two tied with 2 TD each.
2-Pt. Conversions: (0-0).

Kicking	PAT/Att	FG/Att	Lg	Pts
Sebastian Janikowski	.28/29	22/25	55	94

Punts (10 or more)	No	Yds	Long	Avg	In20
Shane Lechler	.96	4503	73	46.9	27

Most Interceptions		Most Sacks	
Phillip Buchanon	.6	Rod Coleman	.5.5

Pittsburgh Steelers

Passing (5 Att)	Att	Cmp	Pct	Yds	TD	Rate
Tommy Maddox	.519	298	57.4	3414	18	75.3
Charlie Batch	.8	4	50.0	47	0	68.2

Interceptions: Maddox 17.

Top Receivers	No	Yds	Avg	Long	TD
Hines Ward	.95	1163	12.2	50	10
Plaxico Burress	.60	860	14.3	47	4
Amos Zereoue	.40	310	7.8	29	0
Antwaan Randle El	.37	364	9.8	32-td	1
Chris Doering	.18	240	13.3	53	1

Top Rushers	Car	Yds	Avg	Long	TD
Jerome Bettis	.246	811	3.3	21	7
Amos Zereoue	.132	433	3.3	22	2
Antwaan Randle El	.15	75	5.0	32	0
Verron Haynes	.20	63	3.2	15	0

Most Touchdowns	TD	Run	Rec	Ret	Pts
Hines Ward	.10	0	10	0	60
Jerome Bettis	.7	7	0	0	44
Plaxico Burress	.4	0	4	0	24
Antwaan Randle El	.3	0	1	2	18
Amos Zereoue	.2	2	0	0	12

2-Pt. Conversions: (1-1) Bettis.

Kicking	PAT/Att	FG/Att	Lg	Pts
Jeff Reed	.31/32	23/32	51	100

Punts (10 or more)	No	Yds	Long	Avg	In20
Josh Miller	.84	3521	72	41.9	27

Most Interceptions		Most Sacks	
Brent Alexander	.4	Kimo von Oelhoffen	.8.0

San Diego Chargers

Passing (5 Att)	Att	Cmp	Pct	Yds	TD	Rate
Drew Brees	.356	205	57.6	2108	11	67.5
Doug Flutie	.167	91	54.5	1097	9	82.8

Interceptions: Brees 15, Flutie 4.

Top Receivers	No	Yds	Avg	Long	TD
LaDainian Tomlinson	.100	725	7.3	73-td	4
David Boston	.70	880	12.6	46-td	7
Antonio Gates*	.24	389	16.2	48	2
Eric Parker	.18	244	13.6	33-td	3
Justin Peelle	.16	133	8.3	24	1
Lorenzo Neal	.16	62	3.9	11	0
Tim Dwight	.14	193	13.8	32	0

Top Rushers	No	Yds	Avg	Long	TD
LaDainian Tomlinson	.313	1645	5.3	73-td	13
Doug Flutie	.33	168	5.1	17	2
Tim Dwight	.9	88	9.8	20	0
Drew Brees	.21	84	4.0	18	0

Most Touchdowns	TD	Run	Rec	Ret	Pts
LaDainian Tomlinson	.17	13	4	0	102
David Boston	.7	0	7	0	44
Eric Parker	.3	0	3	0	18

Three tied with 2 TD each.
2-Pt. Conversions: (2-2) Boston, Stephen Alexander.

Kicking	PAT/Att	FG/Att	Lg	Pts
Steve Christie	.36/36	15/20	51	81

Punts (10 or more)	No	Yds	Long	Avg	In20
Darren Bennett	.82	3436	56	41.9	28

Most Interceptions		Most Sacks	
Quentin Jammer	.4	Dequincy Scott	.6.5

Tennessee Titans

Passing (10 Att)	Att	Cmp	Pct	Yds	TD	Rate
Steve McNair	.400	250	62.5	3215	24	100.4
Billy Volek	.69	44	63.8	545	4	101.4
Neil O'Donnell	.27	18	66.7	232	2	102.7

Interceptions: McNair 7, Volek and O'Donnell 1.

Top Receivers	No	Yds	Avg	Long	TD
Derrick Mason	.95	1303	13.7	50-td	8
Justin McCareins	.47	813	17.3	73	7
Erron Kinney	.41	381	9.3	28	3
Drew Bennett	.32	504	15.8	48	4
Eddie George	.22	163	7.4	22	0
Robert Holcombe	.19	121	6.4	11	1
Tyrone Calico*	.18	297	16.5	45	4

Top Rushers	Car	Yds	Avg	Long	TD
Eddie George	.312	1031	3.3	27	5
Chris Brown*	.56	221	3.9	28	0
Robert Holcombe	.63	201	3.2	21	1
Steve McNair	.38	138	3.6	23	4

Most Touchdowns	TD	Run	Rec	Ret	Pts
Derrick Mason	.8	0	8	0	48
Justin McCareins	.8	0	7	1	48
Eddie George	.5	5	0	0	30

Four tied with 4 TD each.
2-Pt. Conversions: (3-4) Calico, Holcombe, McNair.

Kicking	PAT/Att	FG/Att	Lg	Pts
Gary Anderson	.42/42	27/31	43	123
Craig Hentrich	.1/1	4/5	49	13
Joe Nedney	.0/1	1/1	50	3

Signed: Anderson on Sept. 10.

Punts (10 or more)	No	Yds	Long	Avg	In20
Craig Hentrich	.71	3117	58	43.9	26

Most Interceptions		Most Sacks	
Samari Rolle	.5	Jevon Kearse	.9.5

NFC Team by Team Statistics

Players with more than one team during the regular season are listed with club they ended season with; (*) indicates rookies.

Arizona Cardinals

Passing (5 Att)	Att	Cmp	Pct	Yds	TD	Rate
Jeff Blake	.367	208	56.7	2247	13	69.6
Josh McCown	.166	95	57.2	1018	5	70.3

Interceptions: Blake 15, McCown 6.

Top Receivers	No	Yds	Avg	Long	TD
Anquan Boldin*	.101	1377	13.6	71-td	8
Freddie Jones	.55	517	9.4	34	3
Bryant Johnson*	.35	438	12.5	54-td	1
Marcel Shipp	.30	184	6.1	34	0
Bryan Gilmore	.17	208	12.2	32	2

Top Rushers	Car	Yds	Avg	Long	TD
Marcel Shipp	.228	830	3.6	36	0
Emmitt Smith	.90	256	2.8	22	2
Jeff Blake	.30	177	5.9	19	2
Josh McCown	.28	158	5.6	16-td	1

Most Touchdowns	TD	Run	Rec	Ret	Pts
Anquan Boldin*	.8	0	8	0	48
Freddie Jones	.3	0	3	0	18
Jeff Blake	.2	2	0	0	14
Bryan Gilmore	.2	0	2	0	12
James Hodgins	.2	2	0	0	12
Emmitt Smith	.2	2	0	0	12

2-Pt. Conversions: (1-5) Blake.

Kicking	PAT/Att	FG/Att	Lg	Pts
Neil Rackers	.8/8	9/12	49	35
Tim Duncan*	.5/6	6/10	53	18
Bill Gramatica	.6/6	3/4	38	15

Waived: Duncan on Nov. 10. **Signed:** Rackers on Nov. 11.

Punts (10 or more)	No	Yds	Long	Avg	In20
Scott Player	.82	3511	64	42.8	19

Most Interceptions | | **Most Sacks** |
---|---|---|---
Dexter Jackson | .6 | Dennis Johnson | .3.0
 | | Ray Thompson | .3.0

Atlanta Falcons

Passing (5 Att)	Att	Cmp	Pct	Yds	TD	Rate
Doug Johnson	.243	136	56.0	1655	8	67.5
Kurt Kittner	.114	44	38.6	391	2	32.5
Michael Vick	.100	50	50.0	585	4	69.0

Interceptions: Johnson 12, Kittner 6, Vick 3.

Top Receivers	No	Yds	Avg	Long	TD
Peerless Price	.64	838	13.1	49	3
Alge Crumpler	.44	552	12.5	63	3
Warrick Dunn	.37	336	9.1	86-td	2
Brian Finneran	.26	368	14.2	38	2
Justin Griffith*	.21	122	5.8	24	2

Top Rushers	Car	Yds	Avg	Long	TD
T.J. Duckett	.197	779	4.0	55	11
Warrick Dunn	.125	672	5.4	69-td	3
Michael Vick	.40	255	6.4	43	1
Justin Griffith*	.38	168	4.4	15	0

Most Touchdowns	TD	Run	Rec	Ret	Pts
T.J. Duckett	.11	11	0	0	66
Warrick Dunn	.5	3	2	0	30
Alge Crumpler	.3	0	3	0	18
Peerless Price	.3	0	3	0	18

2-Pt. Conversions: (0-1).

Kicking	PAT/Att	FG/Att	Lg	Pts
Jay Feely	.32/33	19/27	46	89

Punts (10 or more)	No	Yds	Long	Avg	In20
Chris Mohr	.87	3473	54	39.9	19

Most Interceptions	**Most Sacks**
Three tied with 3 each.	Ellis Johnson	.8.0

Carolina Panthers

Passing (5 Att)	Att	Cmp	Pct	Yds	TD	Rate
Jake Delhomme	.449	266	59.2	3219	19	80.6
Rodney Peete	.10	4	40.0	19	0	47.9

Interceptions: Delhomme 16.

Top Receivers	No	Yds	Avg	Long	TD
Steve Smith	.88	1110	12.6	67-td	7
Muhsin Muhammad	.54	837	15.5	60	3
Ricky Proehl	.27	389	14.4	66-td	4
DeShaun Foster	.26	207	8.0	47	2
Kris Mangum	.17	199	11.7	34	0

Top Rushers	Car	Yds	Avg	Long	TD
Stephen Davis	.318	1444	4.5	40	8
DeShaun Foster	.113	429	3.8	21	0
Nick Goings	.10	69	6.9	17	0
Rod Smart	.20	49	2.5	6	0

Most Touchdowns	TD	Run	Rec	Ret	Pts
Stephen Davis	.8	8	0	0	48
Steve Smith	.8	0	7	1	48
Ricky Proehl	.4	0	4	0	24
Muhsin Muhammad	.3	0	3	0	18

2-Pt. Conversions: (0-3).

Kicking	PAT/Att	FG/Att	Lg	Pts
John Kasay	.29/30	32/38	53	125

Punts (10 or more)	No	Yds	Long	Avg	In20
Todd Sauerbrun	.77	3433	64	44.6	22

Most Interceptions		**Most Sacks**
Mike Minter	.3	Mike Rucker	.12.0
Ricky Manning Jr.*	.3	
Deon Grant	.3	

Chicago Bears

Passing (5 Att)	Att	Cmp	Pct	Yds	TD	Rate
Kordell Stewart	.251	126	50.2	1418	7	56.8
Chris Chandler	.192	107	55.7	1050	3	61.3
Rex Grossman*	.72	38	52.8	437	2	74.8

Interceptions: Stewart 12, Chandler 7, Grossman 1.

Top Receivers	No	Yds	Avg	Long	TD
Marty Booker	.52	715	13.8	61-td	4
Dez White	.49	583	11.9	49	3
Desmond Clark	.44	433	9.8	31	2
David Terrell	.43	361	8.4	35	1
Stanley Pritchett	.18	83	4.6	20	0
Justin Gage*	.17	338	19.9	57	2

Top Rushers	Car	Yds	Avg	Long	TD
Anthony Thomas	.244	1024	4.2	67-td	6
Kordell Stewart	.59	290	4.9	25	3
Brock Forsey*	.50	191	3.8	17	2
Stanley Pritchett	.21	93	4.4	18	2
Adrian Peterson	.22	70	3.2	10	0

Most Touchdowns	TD	Run	Rec	Ret	Pts
Anthony Thomas	.6	6	0	0	36
Marty Booker	.4	0	4	0	24
Kordell Stewart	.3	3	0	0	20
Dez White	.3	0	3	0	18

2-Pt. Conversions: (2-2) Stewart, Chandler.

Kicking	PAT/Att	FG/Att	Lg	Pts
Paul Edinger	.27/27	26/36	54	105

Punts (10 or more)	No	Yds	Long	Avg	In20
Brad Maynard	.79	3258	53	41.2	23

Most Interceptions	**Most Sacks**
Jerry Azumah	.4	Alex Brown	.5.5
Charles Tillman*	.4	

Dallas Cowboys

Passing (5 Att)

	Att	Cmp	Pct	Yds	TD	Rate
Quincy Carter	.505	292	57.8	3302	17	71.4

Interceptions: Carter 21.

Top Receivers

	No	Yds	Avg	Long	TD
Richie Anderson	.69	493	7.1	37	4
Terry Glenn	.52	754	14.5	51-td	5
Antonio Bryant	.39	550	14.1	54	2
Jason Witten*	.35	347	9.9	36-td	1
Joey Galloway	.34	672	19.8	64	2
Dan Campbell	.20	195	9.8	23	1

Top Rushers

	Car	Yds	Avg	Long	TD
Troy Hambrick	.275	972	3.5	42	5
Richie Anderson	.70	306	4.4	19	1
Quincy Carter	.68	257	3.8	19	2
Aveion Cason	.40	220	5.5	63-td	2
Adrian Murrell	.28	107	3.8	17	0

Most Touchdowns

	TD	Run	Rec	Ret	Pts
Richie Anderson	.5	1	4	0	30
Terry Glenn	.5	0	5	0	30
Troy Hambrick	.5	5	0	0	30

Five tied with 2 TD each.

2-Pt. Conversions: (0-0).

Kicking

	PAT/Att	FG/Att	Lg	Pts
Billy Cundiff	.30/31	23/29	52	99

Punts (10 or more)

	No	Yds	Long	Avg	In20
Toby Gowin	.94	3665	59	39.0	25

Most Interceptions
Terence Newman* 4

Most Sacks
Greg Ellis 8.0

Detroit Lions

Passing (5 Att)

	Att	Cmp	Pct	Yds	TD	Rate
Joey Harrington	.554	309	55.8	2880	17	63.9
Mike McMahon	.31	9	29.0	87	0	12.7

Interceptions: Harrington 22, McMahon 2.

Top Receivers

	No	Yds	Avg	Long	TD
Shawn Bryson	.54	340	6.3	26	0
Az-Zahir Hakim	.49	449	9.2	28	4
Mikhael Ricks	.37	434	11.7	38	2
Bill Schroeder	.36	397	11.0	26	2
Cory Schlesinger	.34	247	7.3	33-td	2
Casey Fitzsimmons*	.23	160	7.0	22	2
Charles Rogers	.22	243	11.0	33-td	3
Scotty Anderson	.17	325	19.1	72-td	2

Top Rushers

	Car	Yds	Avg	Long	TD
Shawn Bryson	.158	606	3.8	39	3
Olandis Gary	.113	384	3.4	27	2
Artose Pinner*	.39	99	2.5	12	0
Joey Harrington	.30	86	2.9	26	0

Most Touchdowns

	TD	Run	Rec	Ret	Pts
Az-Zahir Hakim	.4	0	4	0	26
Shawn Bryson	.3	3	0	0	18
Charles Rogers*	.3	0	3	0	18

Eight tied with 2 TD each.

2-Pt. Conversions: (2-2) Anderson, Hakim.

Kicking

	PAT/Att	FG/Att	Lg	Pts
Jason Hanson	.26/27	22/23	54	92

Punts (10 or more)

	No	Yds	Long	Avg	In20
Nick Harris	.91	3615	53	39.7	16
CIN	.28	1084	53	38.7	5
DET	.63	2531	51	40.2	11
John Jett	.25	995	58	39.8	8

Signed: Harris on Oct. 15.

Most Interceptions
Dre' Bly 6

Most Sacks
James Hall 4.5
Robert Porcher 4.5

Green Bay Packers

Passing (5 Att)

	Att	Cmp	Pct	Yds	TD	Rate
Brett Favre	.471	308	65.4	3361	32	90.4

Interceptions: Favre 21.

Top Receivers

	No	Yds	Avg	Long	TD
Donald Driver	.52	621	11.9	41	2
Ahman Green	.50	367	7.3	27	5
Javon Walker	.41	716	17.5	66-td	9
Robert Ferguson	.38	520	13.7	47	4
Bubba Franks	.30	241	8.0	24	4
William Henderson	.24	214	8.9	22	3
Tony Fisher	.21	206	9.8	32	2

Top Rushers

	Car	Yds	Avg	Long	TD
Ahman Green	.355	1883	5.3	98-td	15
Najeh Davenport	.77	420	5.5	76-td	4
Tony Fisher	.40	200	5.0	19	1
Donald Driver	.5	51	10.2	45	0

Most Touchdowns

	TD	Run	Rec	Ret	Pts
Ahman Green	.20	15	5	0	120
Javon Walker	.9	0	9	0	54
Bubba Franks	.4	0	4	0	28
Robert Ferguson	.4	0	4	0	24
Tony Fisher	.3	1	2	0	18
William Henderson	.3	0	3	0	18

2-Pt. Conversions: (2-2) Franks 2.

Kicking

	PAT/Att	FG/Att	Lg	Pts
Ryan Longwell	.51/51	23/26	50	120

Punts (10 or more)

	No	Yds	Long	Avg	In20
Josh Bidwell	.69	2875	60	41.7	16

Most Interceptions
Darren Sharper 5

Most Sacks
Kabeer Gbaja-
Biamila 10.0

Minnesota Vikings

Passing (5 Att)

	Att	Cmp	Pct	Yds	TD	Rate
Daunte Culpepper	.454	295	65.0	3479	25	96.4
Gus Frerotte	.65	38	58.5	690	7	118.1

Interceptions: Culpepper 11, Frerotte 2.

Top Receivers

	No	Yds	Avg	Long	TD
Randy Moss	.111	1632	14.7	72	17
Moe Williams	.65	644	9.9	42	3
Jim Kleinsasser	.46	401	8.7	19	4
Nate Burleson*	.29	455	15.7	52	2
Kelly Campbell	.25	522	20.9	72-td	4
D'Wayne Bates	.15	151	10.1	18	1
Onterrio Smith*	.15	129	8.6	20	0

Top Rushers

	Car	Yds	Avg	Long	TD
Moe Williams	.174	745	4.3	61	5
Onterrio Smith*	.107	579	5.4	47	5
Michael Bennett	.90	447	5.0	28	1
Daunte Culpepper	.73	422	5.8	42	4
Kelly Campbell	.10	71	7.1	19	0

Most Touchdowns

	TD	Run	Rec	Ret	Pts
Randy Moss	.17	0	17	0	102
Moe Williams	.8	5	3	0	48
Onterrio Smith*	.5	5	0	0	32
Kelly Campbell	.4	0	4	0	24
Daunte Culpepper	.4	4	0	0	24
Jim Kleinsasser	.4	0	4	0	24

2-Pt. Conversions: (2-3) Smith and Hunter Goodwin.

Kicking

	PAT/Att	FG/Att	Lg	Pts
Aaron Elling*	.48/48	18/25	51	102

Punts (10 or more)

	No	Yds	Long	Avg	In20
Eddie Johnson*	.56	2191	55	39.1	12

Most Interceptions
Brian Russell 9

Most Sacks
Kevin Williams* 10.5

New Orleans Saints

Passing (5 Att)	Att	Cmp	Pct	Yds	TD	Rate
Aaron Brooks	.518	306	59.1	3546	24	88.8
Todd Bouman	.13	7	53.8	81	1	98.6

Interceptions: Brooks 8.

Top Receivers	No	Yds	Avg	Long	TD
Joe Horn	.78	973	12.5	50-td	10
Deuce McAllister	.69	516	7.5	39	0
Jerome Pathon	.44	578	13.1	40	4
Boo Williams	.41	436	10.6	31-td	5
Ernie Conwell	.26	290	11.2	32	2
Donte' Stallworth	.25	485	19.4	76-td	3
Michael Lewis	.12	226	18.8	39	1

Top Rushers	Car	Yds	Avg	Long	TD
Deuce McAllister	.351	1641	4.7	76-td	8
Aaron Brooks	.54	175	3.2	15	2
Ki-Jana Carter	.19	72	3.8	31	1
Lamar Smith	.11	61	5.5	17	0

Most Touchdowns	TD	Run	Rec	Ret	Pts
Joe Horn	10	0	10	0	60
Deuce McAllister	8	8	0	0	48
Boo Williams	5	0	5	0	30
Jerome Pathon	4	0	4	0	24
Donte' Stallworth	3	0	3	0	18

2-Pt. Conversions: (1-2) James Fenderson.

Kicking	PAT/Att	FG/Att	Lg	Pts
John Carney	.36/37	22/30	50	102

Punts (10 or more)	No	Yds	Long	Avg	In20
Mitch Berger	.71	3144	59	44.3	28

Most Interceptions		Most Sacks	
Fred Thomas	.4	Charles Grant	.10.0

New York Giants

Passing (5 Att)	Att	Cmp	Pct	Yds	TD	Rate
Kerry Collins	.500	284	56.8	3110	13	70.7
Jesse Palmer	.116	60	51.7	532	3	58.5

Interceptions: Collins 16, Palmer 6.

Top Receivers	No	Yds	Avg	Long	TD
Tiki Barber	.69	461	6.7	36	1
Amani Toomer	.63	1057	16.8	77-td	5
Ike Hilliard	.60	608	10.1	38	6
Jeremy Shockey	.48	535	11.1	46	2
Tim Carter	.26	309	11.9	30	0
Marcellus Rivers	.17	155	9.1	27	0
David Tyree*	.16	211	13.2	48	0

Top Rushers	Car	Yds	Avg	Long	TD
Tiki Barber	.278	1216	4.4	27	2
Dorsey Levens	.68	197	2.9	17	3
Kerry Collins	.17	49	2.9	22	0
Delvin Joyce	.11	39	3.5	8	0

Most Touchdowns	TD	Run	Rec	Ret	Pts
Ike Hilliard	6	0	6	0	36
Amani Toomer	5	0	5	0	30
Tiki Barber	3	2	1	0	20
Dorsey Levens	3	3	0	0	18

2-Pt. Conversions: (2-3) Barber, Collins.

Kicking	PAT/Att	FG/Att	Lg	Pts
Matt Bryant	17/17	11/14	47	50
Jeff Feagles	0/0	0/1	—	0

Signed: Brett Conway on Oct. 7. **Waived:** Conway on Nov. 15 (see Cle.).

Punts (10 or more)	No	Yds	Long	Avg	In20
Jeff Feagles	.90	3641	59	40.5	31

Most Interceptions	Most Sacks	
Four tied with 2 each.	Michael Strahan	.18.5

Philadelphia Eagles

Passing (5 Att)	Att	Cmp	Pct	Yds	TD	Rate
Donovan McNabb	478	275	57.5	3216	16	79.6
Koy Detmer	.5	3	60.0	32	0	78.8

Interceptions: McNabb 11.

Top Receivers	No	Yds	Avg	Long	TD
James Thrash	.49	558	11.4	51	1
Brian Westbrook	.37	332	9.0	38	4
Todd Pinkston	.36	575	16.0	59	2
Duce Staley	.36	382	10.6	52-td	2
Freddie Mitchell	.35	498	14.2	39	2
L.J. Smith*	.27	321	11.9	36	1
Chad Lewis	.23	293	12.7	29	1

Top Rushers	Car	Yds	Avg	Long	TD
Brian Westbrook	.117	613	5.2	62-td	7
Correll Buckhalter	.126	542	4.3	64-td	8
Duce Staley	.96	463	4.8	22	5
Donovan McNabb	.71	355	5.0	34	3

Most Touchdowns	TD	Run	Rec	Ret	Pts
Brian Westbrook	13	7	4	2	78
Correll Buckhalter	9	8	1	0	54
Duce Staley	7	5	2	0	42
Donovan McNabb	3	3	0	0	18
Jon Ritchie	3	0	3	0	18

2-Pt. Conversions: (0-1).

Kicking	PAT/Att	FG/Att	Lg	Pts
David Akers	.42/42	24/29	57	114

Punts (15 or more)	No	Yds	Long	Avg	In20
Dirk Johnson	.79	3207	60	40.6	27

Most Interceptions		Most Sacks	
Michael Lewis	.3	Corey Simon	.7.5
Troy Vincent	.3		

St. Louis Rams

Passing (5 Att)	Att	Cmp	Pct	Yds	TD	Rate
Marc Bulger	.532	336	63.2	3845	22	81.4
Kurt Warner	.65	38	58.5	365	1	72.9

Interceptions: Bulger 22, Warner 1.

Top Receivers	No	Yds	Avg	Long	TD
Torry Holt	.117	1696	14.5	48	12
Isaac Bruce	.69	981	14.2	41	5
Dane Looker	.47	495	10.5	41	3
Marshall Faulk	.45	290	6.4	30	1
Brandon Manumaleuna	29	238	8.2	39	2
Mike Furrey	.20	189	9.5	24	0
Arlen Harris*	.15	102	6.8	26	0

Top Rushers	Car	Yds	Avg	Long	TD
Marshall Faulk	.209	818	3.9	52	10
Lamar Gordon	.71	298	4.2	20	1
Arlen Harris*	.85	255	3.0	18	4
Marc Bulger	.29	75	2.6	28	4

Most Touchdowns	TD	Run	Rec	Ret	Pts
Torry Holt	12	0	12	0	72
Marshall Faulk	11	10	1	0	66
Isaac Bruce	5	0	5	0	30
Marc Bulger	4	4	0	0	24
Arlen Harris*	4	4	0	0	24
Dane Looker	3	0	3	0	18

2-Pt. Conversions: (0-1).

Kicking	PAT/Att	FG/Att	Lg	Pts
Jeff Wilkins	.46/46	39/42	53	163

Punts (10 or more)	No	Yds	Long	Avg	In20
Sean Landeta	.59	2525	57	42.8	14

Most Interceptions	Most Sacks	
Four tied with 4 each.	Leonard Little	.12.5

San Francisco 49ers

Passing (5 Att)	Att	Cmp	Pct	Yds	TD	Rate
Jeff Garcia	.392	225	57.4	2704	18	80.1
Tim Rattay	.118	73	61.9	856	7	96.6

Interceptions: Garcia 13, Rattay 2.

Top Receivers	No	Yds	Avg	Long	TD
Terrell Owens	.80	1102	13.8	75-td	9
Tai Streets	.47	595	12.7	41-td	7
Jed Weaver	.35	437	12.5	30	1
Cedrick Wilson	.35	396	11.3	29	2
Kevan Barlow	.35	307	8.8	48	1
Garrison Hearst	.25	211	8.4	26	1

Top Rushers	Car	Yds	Avg	Long	TD
Kevan Barlow	.201	1024	5.1	78-td	6
Garrison Hearst . . .	.178	768	4.3	36	3
Jeff Garcia	.56	319	5.7	21-td	7
Jamal Robertson . . .	.32	136	4.3	23	0

Most Touchdowns	TD	Run	Rec	Ret	Pts
Terrell Owens	.9	0	9	0	54
Kevan Barlow	.7	6	1	0	42
Jeff Garcia	.7	7	0	0	42
Tai Streets	.7	0	7	0	42
Garrison Hearst	.4	3	1	0	24

2-Pt. Conversions: (1-3) Brandon Lloyd.

Kicking	PAT/Att	FG/Att	Lg	Pts
Todd Peterson	.22/23	12/15	48	58
Owen Pochman	.9/10	8/15	48	33
Jeff Chandler	.7/8	6/7	35	25

Waived: Chandler on Sept. 16; Pochman on Oct. 28.
Signed: Pochman on Sept. 16; Peterson on Oct. 28.

Punts (10 or more)	No	Yds	Long	Avg	In20
Bill LaFleur	.68	2629	56	38.7	17

Most Interceptions		Most Sacks	
Tony Parrish	.9	Julian Peterson	.7.0

Seattle Seahawks

Passing (5 Att)	Att	Cmp	Pct	Yds	TD	Rate
Matt Hasselbeck . .	.513	313	61.0	3841	26	88.8
Trent Dilfer	.8	4	50.0	31	1	59.9

Interceptions: Hasselbeck 15, Dilfer 1.

Top Receivers	No	Yds	Avg	Long	TD
Darrell Jackson	.68	1137	16.7	80-td	9
Koren Robinson	.65	896	13.8	38-td	4
Bobby Engram	.52	637	12.3	34-td	6
Itula Mili	.46	492	10.7	46-td	4
Shaun Alexander . . .	.42	295	7.0	22	2
Mack Strong	.29	216	7.4	32	0

Top Rushers	Car	Yds	Avg	Long	TD
Shaun Alexander . . .	.326	1435	4.4	55	14
Maurice Morris	.38	239	6.3	43	0
Mack Strong	.37	174	4.7	21-td	1
Matt Hasselbeck . . .	.36	125	3.5	18	2

Most Touchdowns	TD	Run	Rec	Ret	Pts
Shaun Alexander	.16	14	2	0	96
Darrell Jackson	.9	0	9	0	54
Bobby Engram	.7	0	6	1	42
Koren Robinson	.5	0	4	1	30
Itula Mili	.4	0	4	0	24
Matt Hasselbeck	.2	2	0	0	12

2-Pt. Conversions: (0-0).

Kicking	PAT/Att	FG/Att	Lg	Pts
Josh Brown*	.48/48	22/30	58	114

Punts (10 or more)	No	Yds	Long	Avg	In20
Tom Rouen	.67	2762	61	41.2	29

Most Interceptions		Most Sacks	
Reggie Tongue	.4	Chike Okeafor	.8.0

Tampa Bay Buccaneers

Passing (5 Att)	Att	Cmp	Pct	Yds	TD	Rate
Brad Johnson	.570	354	62.1	3811	26	81.5
Shaun King	.22	15	68.2	130	1	79.7

Interceptions: B. Johnson 21, King 1.

Top Receivers	No	Yds	Avg	Long	TD
Keenan McCardell . .	.84	1174	14.0	76-td	8
Michael Pittman	.75	597	8.0	68-td	2
Keyshawn Johnson . .	.45	600	13.3	39-td	3
Charles Lee	.33	432	13.1	72	2
Thomas Jones	.24	180	7.5	29	0
Ken Dilger	.22	244	11.1	48	1
Jameel Cook	.20	120	6.0	19	1
Joe Jurevicius	.12	118	9.8	22	2

Top Rushers	Car	Yds	Avg	Long	TD
Michael Pittman	.187	751	4.0	17	0
Thomas Jones	.137	627	4.6	61	3
Aaron Stecker	.37	125	3.4	15	0
Mike Alstott	.27	77	2.9	29	2
Brad Johnson	.25	33	1.3	13	0

Most Touchdowns	TD	Run	Rec	Ret	Pts
Keenan McCardell	.9	0	8	1	54
Keyshawn Johnson	.3	0	3	0	18
Thomas Jones	.3	3	0	0	18

Six tied with 2 TD each.
2-Pt. Conversions: (1-2) Karl Williams.

Kicking	PAT/Att	FG/Att	Lg	Pts
Martin Gramatica	.33/34	16/26	50	81

Punts (10 or more)	No	Yds	Long	Avg	In20
Tom Tupa	.83	3590	60	43.3	26

Most Interceptions		Most Sacks	
Dwight Smith	.5	Simeon Rice	.15.0

Washington Redskins

Passing (5 Att)	Att	Cmp	Pct	Yds	TD	Rate
Patrick Ramsey	.337	179	53.1	2166	14	75.8
Tim Hasselbeck . . .	.177	95	53.7	1012	5	63.6

Interceptions: Ramsey 9, Hasselbeck 7.
Cut: Rob Johnson on Oct. 22 (see Oak.).

Top Receivers	No	Yds	Avg	Long	TD
Laveranues Coles . . .	.68	1137	16.7	80-td	9
Rod Gardner	.59	600	10.2	35	5
Darnerien McCants . .	.27	360	13.3	32-td	6
Rock Cartwright	.18	176	9.8	40	0
Chad Morton	.15	187	12.5	36-td	1
Patrick Johnson	.15	170	11.3	31	1
Ladell Betts	.15	167	11.1	34	0

Top Rushers	Car	Yds	Avg	Long	TD
Trung Canidate	.142	600	4.2	38	1
Rock Cartwright	.107	411	3.8	22	4
Ladell Betts	.77	255	3.3	13-td	2
Chad Morton	.48	216	4.5	27	0
Patrick Ramsey	.15	62	4.1	24	1

Most Touchdowns	TD	Run	Rec	Ret	Pts
Darnerien McCants	.6	0	6	0	40
Laveranues Coles	.6	0	6	0	36
Rod Gardner	.5	0	5	0	30
Rock Cartwright	.4	4	0	0	24

Three tied with 2 TD each.
2-Pt. Conversions: (2-3) McCants.

Top Kickers	PAT/Att	FG/Att	Lg	Pts
John Hall	.26/27	25/33	54	101

Punts (10 or more)	No	Yds	Long	Avg	In20
Bryan Barker	.84	3377	69	40.2	24

Most Interceptions		Most Sacks	
Fred Smoot	.4	Jessie Armstead	.6.5

NFL Playoffs

| 1ST ROUND | SEMIFINALS | FINAL | | FINAL | SEMIFINALS | 1ST ROUND |

†Denver   10
Indianapolis 41

Indianapolis 38

Indianapolis 14

Kansas City 31

AFC

Carolina 14

Carolina   29
New England 32

NFC

Carolina   29
(2OT)

Carolina 29

St. Louis 23

†Dallas   10
Carolina 29

†Tennessee 20
Baltimore 17

Tennessee 14

New England 24

New England 17

Carolina 29
New England 32

Philadelphia 3

Green Bay 17
(OT)

Philadelphia 20

Green Bay 33
(OT)

†Seattle   27
Green Bay 33

SUPER XXXVIII BOWL

Feb. 1, 2004
Reliant Stadium, Houston

†Wild Card Team

†Wild Card Team

Playoff Game Summaries
Team records listed in parentheses indicate records before game.
WILD CARD ROUND

AFC

Titans, 20-17

Tennessee (12-4)	.7	0	7	6—	**20**
Baltimore (10-6)	.7	3	0	7—	**17**

Date—Jan. 3. **Att**—69,452. **Time**—2:59.
1st Quarter: TEN—Chris Brown 6-yd run (Gary Anderson kick), 8:54; BAL—Will Demps 56-yd int. return (Matt Stover kick), 6:12.
2nd Quarter: BAL—Stover 43-yd FG, 1:55.
3rd Quarter: TEN—Justin McCareins 49-yd pass from Steve McNair (Anderson kick), 7:59.
4th Quarter: TEN—Anderson 45-yd FG, 9:13; BAL—Todd Heap 35-yd pass from Anthony Wright (Stover kick), 4:30; TEN—Anderson 46-yd FG, 0:29.

Colts, 41-10

Denver (10-6)	.3	0	0	7—	**10**
Indianapolis (12-4)	.14	17	10	0—	**41**

Date—Jan. 4. **Att**—56,586. **Time**—2:39.
1st Quarter: IND—Brandon Stokley 31-yd pass from Peyton Manning (Mike Vanderjagt kick), 11:55; DEN—Jason Elam 49-yd FG, 3:41; IND—Marvin Harrison 46-yd pass from Manning (Vanderjagt kick), 0:24.
2nd Quarter: IND—Harrison 23-yd pass from Manning (Vanderjagt kick), 7:28; IND—Stokley 87-yd pass from Manning (Vanderjagt kick), 1:51; IND—Vanderjagt 27-yd FG, 0:00.
3rd Quarter: IND—Reggie Wayne 7-yd pass from Manning (Vanderjagt kick), 5:19; IND—Vanderjagt 20-yd FG, 0:55.
4th Quarter: DEN—Rod Smith 7-yd pass from Jake Plummer (Elam kick), 7:04.

NFC

Panthers, 29-10

Dallas (10-6)	.0	3	0	7—	**10**
Carolina (11-5)	.6	10	7	6—	**29**

Date—Jan. 3. **Att**—73,014. **Time**—2:56.
1st Quarter: CAR—John Kasay 18-yd FG, 8:40; CAR—Kasay 38-yd FG, 1:02.
2nd Quarter: CAR—Stephen Davis 23-yd run (Kasay kick), 6:10; DAL—Billy Cundiff 37-yd FG, 1:12; CAR—Kasay 19-yd FG, 0:01.
3rd Quarter: CAR—Steve Smith 32-yd pass from Jake Delhomme (Kasay kick), 9:44.
4th Quarter: CAR—Kasay 32-yd FG, 12:45; DAL—Quincy Carter 9-yd run (Cundiff kick), 7:36; CAR—Kasay 34-yd FG, 3:12.

Packers, 33-27 (OT)

Seattle (10-6)	.3	3	14	7—	**27**
Green Bay (10-6)	.0	13	0	14	6—	**33**

Date—Jan. 4. **Att**—71,457. **Time**—3:27.
1st Quarter: SEA—Josh Brown 30-yd FG, 7:01.
2nd Quarter: GB—Ryan Longwell 31-yd FG, 9:13; SEA—Brown 35-yd FG, 6:50; GB—Bubba Franks 23-yd pass from Brett Favre (Longwell kick), 4:37; GB—Longwell 27-yd FG, 0:46.
3rd Quarter: SEA—Shaun Alexander 1-yd run (Brown kick), 9:28; SEA—Alexander 1-yd run (Brown kick), 1:57.
4th Quarter: SEA—Alexander 1-yd run (Brown kick), 10:01; GB—Green 1-yd run (Longwell kick), 2:44; SEA—Alexander 1-yd run (Brown kick), 0:51.
Overtime: GB—Al Harris 52-yd int. return, 10:35.

NFL Playoffs (Cont.)
DIVISIONAL PLAYOFFS

Patriots, 17-14

Tennessee (13-4)	7	0	7	0—	**14**
New England (14-2)	7	7	0	3—	**17**

Date—Jan. 10. **Att**—68,436. **Time**—3:13.

1st Quarter: NE—Bethel Johnson 41-yd pass from Tom Brady (Adam Vinatieri kick), 10:59; TEN—Chris Brown 5-yd run (Gary Anderson kick), 7:31.

2nd Quarter: NE—Antowain Smith 1-yd run (Vinatieri kick), 13:46.

3rd Quarter: TEN—Derrick Mason 11-yd pass from Steve McNair (Anderson kick), 4:14.

4th Quarter: NE—Vinatieri 46-yd FG, 4:06.

Colts, 38-31

Indianapolis (13-4)	14	7	10	7—	**38**
Kansas City (13-3)	3	7	14	7—	**31**

Date—Jan. 11. **Att**—79,159. **Time**—2:56.

1st Quarter: IND—Brandon Stokley 29-yd pass from Peyton Manning (Mike Vanderjagt kick), 9:20; KC—Morten Andersen 22-yd FG, 3:38; IND—Edgerrin James 11-yd run (Vanderjagt kick), 0:37.

2nd Quarter: KC—Dante Hall 9-yd pass from Trent Green (Andersen kick), 8:35; IND—Tom Lopienski 2-yd pass from Manning (Vanderjagt kick), 4:29.

3rd Quarter: IND—Vanderjagt 45-yd FG, 9:24; KC—Priest Holmes 1-yd run (Andersen kick), 5:26; IND—Reggie Wayne 19-yd pass from Manning (Vanderjagt kick), 1:48; KC—Hall 92-yd kickoff return (Andersen kick), 1:35.

4th Quarter: IND—James 1-yd run (Vanderjagt kick), 11:14; KC—Holmes 1-yd run (Andersen kick), 4:22.

Panthers, 29-23 (2OT)

Carolina (12-5)	0	10	6	7	0	6—	**29**
St. Louis (12-4)	3	6	3	11	0	0—	**23**

Date—Jan. 10. **Att**—66,165. **Time**—4:06.

1st Quarter: ST.L—Jeff Wilkins 20-yd FG, 5:34.

2nd Quarter: ST.L—Wilkins 26-yd FG, 13:26; CAR—Muhsin Muhammad fumble recovery in end zone (John Kasay kick), 11:22; ST.L—Wilkins 24-yd FG, 6:58; CAR—Kasay 45-yd FG, 1:07.

3rd Quarter: ST.L—Wilkins 51-yd FG, 11:25; CAR—Kasay 52-yd FG, 7:45; CAR—Kasay 34-yd FG, 0:43.

4th Quarter: CAR—Brad Hoover 7-yd run (Kasay kick), 8:50; ST.L—Marshall Faulk 1-yd run (Dane Looker pass from Marc Bulger), 2:39; ST.L—Wilkins 33-yd FG, 0:00.

2nd Overtime: CAR—Steve Smith 69-yd pass from Jake Delhomme, 14:50.

Eagles, 20-17 (OT)

Green Bay (11-6)	14	0	0	3	0—	**17**
Philadelphia (12-4)	0	7	0	10	3—	**20**

Date—Jan. 11. **Att**—67,707. **Time**—3:28.

1st Quarter: GB—Robert Ferguson 40-yd pass from Brett Favre (Ryan Longwell kick), 7:37; GB—Ferguson 17-yd pass from Favre (Longwell kick), 1:22.

2nd Quarter: PHI—Duce Staley 7-yd pass from Donovan McNabb (David Akers kick), 6:29.

4th Quarter: PHI—Todd Pinkston 12-yd pass from McNabb (Akers kick), 14:48; GB—Longwell 21-yd FG, 10:22; PHI—Akers 37-yd FG, 0:05.

Overtime: PHI—Akers 31-yd FG, 10:12.

CONFERENCE CHAMPIONSHIPS

Patriots, 24-14

Indianapolis (14-4)	0	0	7	7—	**14**
New England (15-2)	7	8	6	3—	**24**

Date—Jan. 18. **Att**—68,436. **Time**—3:05.

1st Quarter: NE—David Givens 7-yd pass from Tom Brady (Adam Vinatieri kick), 8:16.

2nd Quarter: NE—Vinatieri 31-yd FG, 12:44; NE—Vinatieri 25-yd FG, 8:06; NE—Ball through IND end zone for safety, 4:08.

3rd Quarter: IND—Edgerrin James 2-yd run (Mike Vanderjagt kick), 9:44; NE—Vinatieri 27-yd FG, 7:20; NE—Vinatieri 21-yd FG, 1:32.

4th Quarter: IND—Marcus Pollard 7-yd pass from Peyton Manning (Vanderjagt kick), 2:27; NE—Vinatieri 34-yd FG, 0:50.

Panthers, 14-3

Carolina (13-5)	0	7	7	0—	**14**
Philadelphia (13-4)	0	3	0	0—	**3**

Date—Jan. 18. **Att**—65,158. **Time**—2:58.

2nd Quarter: CAR—Muhsin Muhammad 24-yd pass from Jake Delhomme (John Kasay kick), 10:12; PHI—David Akers 41-yd FG, 2:56.

3rd Quarter: CAR—DeShaun Foster 1-yd run (Kasay kick), 4:11.

Super Bowl XXXVIII
Sunday, Feb. 1, 2004 at Reliant Stadium in Houston, Texas

Carolina (14-5)	0	10	0	19—	**29**
New England (16-2)	0	14	0	18—	**32**

2nd Quarter: NE—Deion Branch 5-yd pass from Tom Brady (Adam Vinatieri kick), 3:05. Drive: 20 yards in 4 plays. Key play: Richard Seymour recovery of Jake Delhomme fumble at CAR 20. **CAR**—Steve Smith 39-yd pass from Delhomme (John Kasay kick), 1:07. Drive: 95 yards in 8 plays. Key play: Muhsin Muhammad 23-yd pass from Delhomme to CAR 46. **NE**—David Givens 5-yd pass from Brady (Vinatieri kick), 0:18. Drive: 78 yards in 6 plays. Key play: Branch 52-yd pass from Brady to CAR 14. **CAR**—Kasay 50-yd FG, 0:00. Drive: 21 yards in 2 plays. Key play: Stephen Davis 21-yd run to NE 32.

4th Quarter: NE—Antowain Smith 2-yd run (Vinatieri kick), 14:49. Drive: 71 yards in 8 plays. Key play: Daniel Graham 33-yd pass from Brady to CAR 9. **CAR**—DeShaun Foster 33-yd run (2-pt. pass conversion failed), 12:39. Drive: 81 yards in 6 plays. Key play: Smith 22-yd pass from Delhomme to NE 33. **CAR**—Muhammad 85-yd pass from Delhomme (2-pt. pass conversion failed), 6:53. Drive: 90 yards in 3 plays. Key play: Reggie Howard 12-yd int. return to CAR 10. **NE**—Mike Vrabel 1-yd pass from Brady (Kevin Faulk run), 2:51. Drive: 68 yards in 11 plays. Key play: Givens 25-yd pass from Brady to CAR 22. **CAR**—Ricky Proehl 12-yd pass from Delhomme (Kasay kick), 1:08. Drive: 80 yards in 7 plays. Key play: Proehl 31-yd pass from Delhomme to NE 14. **NE**—Vinatieri 41-yd FG, 0:04. Drive: 37 yards in 6 plays. Key play: Kasay kickoff out of bounds.

Favorite: Patriots by 7 **Attendance:** 71,525
Time: 4:05 **TV Rating:** 41.4/63 share (CBS)
MVP—Tom Brady, New England, QB

Team Statistics

	Panthers	Patriots
First downs	17	29
Rushing	3	7
Passing	12	19
Penalty	2	3
3rd down efficiency	4/12	8/17
4th down efficiency	0/0	1/1
Total offense (net yards)	387	481
Plays	53	83
Average gain	7.3	5.8
Rushes/yards	16/92	35/127
Yards per rush	5.8	3.6
Passing yards (net)	295	354
Times sacked/yards lost	4/28	0/0
Passing yards (gross)	323	354
Completions/attempts	16/33	32/48
Yards per pass	8.0	7.4
Times intercepted	0	1
Return yardage	130	120
Punt returns/yards	1/2	5/42
Kickoff returns/yards	6/116	4/78
Interceptions/yards	1/12	0/0
Fumbles/lost	1/1	1/0
Penalties/yards	12/73	8/60
Punts/average	7/44.3	5/34.6
Punts blocked	0	0
Field Goals made/attempted	1/1	1/3
Time of possession	21:02	38:58

Individual Statistics

Carolina Panthers

Passing

	Att	Cmp	Pct.	Yds	TD	Int
Jake Delhomme	33	16	48.5	323	3	0

Receiving

	No	Yds	Avg	Long	TD
Muhsin Muhammad	4	140	35.0	85-td	1
Steve Smith	4	80	20.0	39-td	1
Ricky Proehl	4	71	17.8	31	1
Jermaine Wiggins	2	21	10.5	15	0
DeShaun Foster	1	9	9.0	9	0
Kris Mangum	1	2	2.0	2	0
TOTAL	16	323	20.2	85-td	3

Rushing

	Car	Yds	Avg	Long	TD
Stephen Davis	13	49	3.8	21	0
DeShaun Foster	3	43	14.3	33-td	1
TOTAL	16	92	5.8	33-td	1

Field Goals

	20-29	30-39	40-49	50-59	Total
John Kasay	0-0	0-0	0-0	1-1	1-1

Punting

	No	Yds	Avg	Long	In20	Blk
Todd Sauerbrun	7	310	44.3	51	1	0

Punt Returns

	Ret	Yds	Avg	Long	FC	TD
Steve Smith	1	2	2.0	2	1	0

Kickoff Returns

	Ret	Yds	Avg	Long	FC	TD
Rod Smart	4	74	18.5	22	0	0
Steve Smith	1	30	30.0	30	0	0
Kris Mangum	1	12	12.0	12	0	0
TOTAL	6	116	19.3	30	0	0

Interceptions

	No	Yds	Avg	Long	TD
Reggie Howard	1	12	12.0	12	0

Sacks
none

Most Tackles (solo)
Dan Morgan 11
Mike Minter 9
Will Witherspoon 7

New England Patriots

Passing

	Att	Cmp	Pct.	Yds	TD	Int
Tom Brady	48	32	66.7	354	3	1

Receiving

	No	Yds	Avg	Long	TD
Deion Branch	10	143	14.3	52	1
Troy Brown	8	76	9.5	13	0
David Givens	5	69	13.8	25	1
Daniel Graham	4	46	11.5	33	0
Kevin Faulk	4	19	4.8	7	0
Mike Vrabel	1	1	1.0	1-td	1
TOTAL	32	354	11.1	52	3

Rushing

	Car	Yds	Avg	Long	TD
Antowain Smith	26	83	3.2	9	1
Kevin Faulk	6	42	7.0	23	0
Tom Brady	2	12	6.0	12	0
Troy Brown	1	-10	-10.0	-10	0
TOTAL	35	127	3.6	23	1

Field Goals

	20-29	30-39	40-49	50-59	Total
Adam Vinatieri	0-0	0-2	1-1	0-0	1-3

Punting

	No	Yds	Avg	Long	In20	Blk
Ken Walter	5	173	34.6	51	2	0

Punt Returns

	Ret	Yds	Avg	Long	FC	TD
Troy Brown	4	40	10.0	28	1	0
Deion Branch	1	2	2.0	2	1	0
TOTAL	5	42	8.4	28	2	0

Kickoff Returns

	Ret	Yds	Avg	Long	FC	TD
Bethel Johnson	4	78	19.5	29	0	0

Interceptions
none

Sacks
Mike Vrabel 2.0
Rodney Harrison 1.0
Willie McGinest 1.0

Most Tackles (solo)
Rodney Harrison 8
Ty Law 5
Two tied with 4 each.

Super Bowl Finalists' Playoff Statistics

Carolina Panthers (3-1)

Passing (5 att)   **Att**   **Cmp**   **Pct.**   **Yds**   **TD**   **Rating**
Jake Delhomme . . .102   59   57.8   987   6   106.1
Interceptions: Delhomme 1.

Top Receivers	No	Yds	Avg	Long	TD
Steve Smith	18	404	22.4	70	3
Muhsin Muhammad	15	352	23.5	85-td	2
Ricky Proehl	5	78	15.6	31	1
Jermaine Wiggins	5	43	8.6	21	0
Brad Hoover	5	35	7.0	11	0
DeShaun Foster	5	35	7.0	12	0

Top Rushers	Car	Yds	Avg	Long	TD
Stephen Davis	64	315	4.9	64	1
DeShaun Foster	42	196	4.7	33-td	2

Touchdowns	TD	Run	Rec	Ret	Pts
Steve Smith	3	0	0	0	18
Muhsin Muhammad	3	0	2*	0	18
DeShaun Foster	2	2	0	0	12

Three tied with 1 TD each.
*Muhammad recovered a fumble in the endzone for a TD.
2-Pt. Conversions: (0-2).

Kicking	PAT/Att	FG/Att	Lg	Pts
John Kasay	8/8	9/11	52	35

Punts	No	Yds	Avg	Long	In20
Todd Sauerbrun	21	910	43.3	59	5
John Kasay	1	21	21.0	21	1

Most Interceptions
Ricky Manning Jr. 4

Most Sacks
Brentson Buckner 1.5

New England Patriots (3-0)

Passing (5 att)   **Att**   **Cmp**   **Pct.**   **Yds**   **TD**   **Rating**
Tom Brady 126   75   59.5   792   5   84.5
Interceptions: Brady 2.

Top Receivers	No	Yds	Avg	Long	TD
Troy Brown	17	175	10.3	18	0
David Givens	17	163	9.6	25	2
Deion Branch	15	176	11.7	52	1
Kevin Faulk	8	58	7.3	19	0
Daniel Graham	5	45	9.0	33	0

Top Rushers	Car	Yds	Avg	Long	TD
Antowain Smith	64	252	3.9	35	2
Kevin Faulk	14	72	5.1	23	0
Tom Brady	12	18	1.5	12	0

Touchdowns	TD	Run	Rec	Ret	Pts
Antowain Smith	2	2	0	0	12
David Givens	2	0	2	0	12
Bethel Johnson	1	0	1	0	6
Deion Branch	1	0	1	0	6
Mike Vrabel	1	0	1	0	6

2-Pt. Conversions: (1-1) Faulk.

Kicking	PAT/Att	FG/Att	Lg	Pts
Adam Vinatieri	6/6	7/10	46	27

Punts	No	Yds	Avg	Long	In20
Ken Walter	11	355	32.3	51	3

Most Interceptions
Ty Law 3
Rodney Harrison 2

Most Sacks
Willie McGinest 5.0
Mike Vrabel 3.0

NFL Playoff Leaders

Passing Efficiency

(Minimum of 25 attempts)

	Gm	Att	Cmp	Cmp%	Yards	Avg Gain	TD	TD%	Int	Int%	Rating
Peyton Manning, Ind	3	103	67	65.0	918	8.9	9	8.7	4	3.9	106.4
Jake Delhomme, Car	4	102	59	57.8	987	9.7	6	5.9	1	1.0	106.1
Brett Favre, GB	2	66	41	62.1	499	7.6	3	4.5	1	1.5	94.2
Trent Green, KC	1	30	18	60.0	212	7.1	1	3.3	0	0.0	92.6
Tom Brady, NE	3	126	75	59.5	792	6.3	5	4.0	2	1.6	84.5

Receptions

	No	Yds	Avg	Long	TD
Steve Smith, Car.	18	404	22.4	70	3
Troy Brown, NE	17	175	10.3	18	0
David Givens, NE.	17	163	9.6	25	2
Marvin Harrison, Ind	16	250	15.6	46-td	2

Three tied with 15 each.

Kicking

	PAT	FG	Long	Pts
John Kasay, Car	8/8	9/11	52	35
Adam Vinatieri, NE	6/6	7/10	46	27
Mike Vanderjagt, Ind	12/12	3/3	45	21
Jeff Wilkins, St.L	0/0	5/6	51	15
Ryan Longwell, GB	5/5	3/4	31	14

Rushing

	No	Yds	Avg	Long	TD
Stephen Davis, Car.	64	315	4.9	64	1
Edgerrin James, Ind	62	281	4.5	18	3
Antowain Smith, NE	64	252	3.9	35	2
Ahman Green, GB	48	222	4.6	33	2
DeShaun Foster, Car.	42	196	4.7	33-td	2

Interceptions

	No	Yds	Long	TD
Ricky Manning Jr., Car.	4	15	13	0
Ty Law, NE	3	26	20	0
David Macklin, Ind	2	52	31	0
Rodney Harrison, NE	2	7	7	0

Fourteen tied with 1 each.

Touchdowns

	TD	Rush	Rec	Ret	Pts
Edgerrin James, Ind	3	3	0	0	18
Brandon Stokley, Ind	3	0	3	0	18
Shaun Alexander, Sea	3	3	0	0	18
Muhsin Muhammad, Car.	3	0	2*	0	18
Steve Smith, Car.	3	0	3	0	18

*Muhammad recovered a fumble in the endzone for a TD.

Sacks

	No
Willie McGinest, NE	5.0
Aaron Kampman, GB	3.0
Mike Vrabel, NE	3.0
Jarvis Green, NE	2.5
Brian Young, St.L	2.0

NFL Pro Bowl

54th NFL Pro Bowl Game and 34th AFC-NFC contest (Series is tied,17-17). **Date:** Feb. 8, 2004 at Aloha Stadium in Honolulu. **Coaches:** Tony Dungy, Ind. (AFC) and Andy Reid, Phi. (NFC). **Most Valuable Player:** QB Marc Bulger, St.L (12 for 21 for 152 yards and a Pro Bowl record four TD passes). **Attendance:** 50,127. **TV Rating:** 3.9 (ESPN). **Time:** 3:51.

AFC	....	17	14	7	14— **52**
NFC	....	10	3	14	28— **55**

1st: AFC—Chad Johnson 90-yd pass from Steve McNair (Mike Vanderjagt kick), 12:25; AFC—Ed Reed 23-yd return of a blocked punt (Vanderjagt kick), 11:02; NFC—Shaun Alexander 12-yd run (Jeff Wilkins kick), 7:29; NFC—Wilkins 28-yd FG, 2:52; AFC—Vanderjagt 27-yd FG, 0:11.

2nd: NFC—Wilkins 38-yd FG, 10:07; AFC—Marvin Harrison 50-yd pass from Peyton Manning (Vanderjagt kick), 6:44; AFC—Tony Gonzalez 9-yd pass from Manning (Vanderjagt kick).

3rd: AFC—Jamal Lewis 22-yd run (Vanderjagt kick), 11:08; NFC—Torry Holt 12-yd pass from Marc Bulger (Wilkins kick), 8:08; NFC—Keenan McCardell 2-yd pass from Bulger (Wilkins kick), 5:47.

4th: AFC—Clinton Portis 23-yd pass from Trent Green (Vanderjagt kick), 13:14; NFC—Alge Crumpler 33-yd pass from Bulger (Wilkins kick), 12:54; NFC—Alexander 5-yd pass from Bulger (pass failed), 5:43; NFC—Dre' Bly 32-yd int. return (Ahman Green run), 4:50; NFC—Alexander 2-yd run (Wilkins kick), 3:32; AFC—Hines Ward 10-yd pass from Manning (Vanderjagt kick), 1:54.

STARTING LINEUPS

As voted on by NFL players, coaches, and fans. (*) denotes injured and unable to play. Note that Simeon Rice was removed from the NFC lineup for disciplinary reasons and Derrick Brooks missed the game due to a family illness.

American Conference

Pos	Offense	Pos	Defense
WR	Marvin Harrison, Ind.	E	Dwight Freeney, Ind.
WR	Chad Johnson, Cin.	E	Adewale Ogunleye, Mia.
TE	Tony Gonzalez, KC	T	Richard Seymour, NE
T	Willie Roaf*, KC	T	Marcus Stroud, Jax
T	Jonathan Ogden, Bal.	LB	Keith Bulluck, Ten.
G	Alan Faneca, Pit.	LB	Takeo Spikes, Buf.
G	Will Shields, KC	LB	Ray Lewis, Bal.
C	Kevin Mawae, NYJ	CB	Patrick Surtain, Mia.
QB	Steve McNair, Ten.	CB	Ty Law, NE
RB	Jamal Lewis, Bal.	SS	Ed Reed, Bal.
FB	Tony Richardson, KC	FS	Brock Marion, Mia.
K	Mike Vanderjagt, Ind.	P	Craig Hentrich, Ten.
KR	Dante Hall, KC	ST	Adalius Thomas*, Bal.

National Conference

Pos	Offense	Pos	Defense
WR	Torry Holt, St.L	E	Leonard Little, St.L
WR	Anquan Boldin, Ari.	E	Michael Strahan, NYG
TE	Alge Crumpler, Atl.	T	La'Roi Glover, Dal.
T	Flozell Adams, Dal.	T	Kris Jenkins, Car.
T	Orlando Pace, St.L	LB	LaVar Arrington, Wash.
G	Larry Allen, Dal.	LB	Julian Peterson, SF
G	Marco Rivera, GB	LB	Brian Urlacher, Chi.
C	Matt Birk, Min.	CB	Champ Bailey, Wash.
QB	Daunte Culpepper, Min.	CB	Dre' Bly, Det.
RB	Ahman Green, GB	SS	Corey Chavous, Min.
FB	Fred Beasley, SF	FS	Roy Williams, Dal.
K	Jeff Wilkins, St.L	P	Todd Sauerbrun, Car.
KR	Jerry Azumah, Chi.	ST	Alex Bannister, Sea.

Reserves

Offense: WR—Derrick Mason, Ten. and Hines Ward, Pit.; **TE**—Todd Heap, Bal.; **T**—Willie Anderson, Cin.; **G**—Ruben Brown, Buf.; **C**—Tom Nalen, Den.; **QB**—Trent Green, KC and Peyton Manning, Ind.; **RB**—Clinton Portis, Den. and Priest Holmes, KC.

Defense: E—Shaun Ellis, NYJ; **T**—Casey Hampton, Pit.; **LB**—Peter Boulware*, Bal., Zach Thomas, Mia. and Al Wilson, Den.; **CB**—Chris McAlister, Bal.; **FS**—Jerome Woods, KC.

Replacements: OFFENSE—T Brad Hopkins, Ten. for Roaf. DEFENSE—ST Gary Stills, KC for Thomas; LB Willie McGinest, NE for Boulware.

Reserves

Offense: WR—Randy Moss*, Min. and Terrell Owens*, SF; **TE**—Jeremy Shockey*, NYG; **T**— Walter Jones, Sea.; **G**—LeCharles Bentley*, NO; **C**—Olin Kreutz*, Chi.; **QB**—Brett Favre*, GB and Donovan McNabb*, Phi.; **RB**—Stephen Davis, Car. and Deuce McAllister*, NO.

Defense: E—Simeon Rice*, TB; **T**—Warren Sapp*, TB; **LB**—Derrick Brooks*, TB and Keith Brooking*, Atl.; **CB**—Troy Vincent, Phi.; **FS**—Aeneas Williams, St.L.

Replacements: OFFENSE—WR Laveranues Coles, Wash. for Moss; WR Keenan McCardell for Owens; G Steve Hutchinson, Sea. for Bentley; C Mike Flanagan, GB for Kreutz; TE Bubba Franks, GB for Shockey; QB Matt Hasselbeck, Sea. for Favre; QB Marc Bulger, St.L for McNabb; RB Shaun Alexander, Sea. for McAllister. DEFENSE—E Kabeer Gbaja-Biamila, GB for Rice; T Corey Simon, Phi. for Sapp; LB Dexter Coakley, Dal. for Brooks.

Annual Awards

The NFL does not sanction any of the major postseason awards for players and coaches, but many are given out. Among the presenters for the 2003 regular season were AP, The Maxwell Football Club of Philadelphia (Bert Bell Award for player; Greasy Neale Award for coach), The Sporting News and the Pro Football Writers of America/Pro Football Weekly.

Most Valuable Player

Peyton Manning, Indianapolis, QB ..... AP (tie), TSN, Bell
Steve McNair, Tennessee, QB .... AP (tie)
Jamal Lewis, Baltimore, RB .... PFWA

Offensive Player of the Year

Jamal Lewis, Baltimore, RB .... AP, PFWA

Defensive Player of the Year

Ray Lewis, Baltimore, LB .... AP, PFWA

Rookie of the Year

NFL	Anquan Boldin, Arizona, WR	.... TSN
Offense	Anquan Boldin, Arizona, WR	...AP, PFWA
Defense	Terrell Suggs, Baltimore, LB	.... AP, PFWA

Coach of the Year

Bill Belichick, New England .... AP, TSN, PFWA
Dick Vermeil, Kansas City .... Neale

2003 All-NFL Team

The 2003 All-NFL team combining the All-Pro selections of the Associated Press, *The Sporting News (TSN)* and the Pro Football Writers of America/*Pro Football Weekly* (PFWA). Holdovers from the 2002 All-NFL Team in **bold** type.

Offense

Pos		Selectors
WR—	Torry Holt, St. Louis	AP, *TSN*, PFWA
WR—	Randy Moss, Minnesota	AP, PFWA
WR—	**Marvin Harrison**, Indianapolis	*TSN*
TE—	**Tony Gonzalez**, Kansas City	AP, *TSN*, PFWA
T—	**Jonathan Ogden**, Baltimore	AP, *TSN*, PFWA
T—	Willie Roaf, Kansas City	AP, PFWA
T—	Orlando Pace, St. Louis	AP, *TSN*
G—	**Will Shields**, Kansas City	AP, *TSN*, PFWA
G—	Steve Hutchinson, Seattle	AP, *TSN*, PFWA
C—	Tom Nalen, Denver	AP, PFWA
C—	Matt Birk, Minnesota	*TSN*
QB—	Peyton Manning, Indianapolis	AP, *TSN*, PFWA
RB—	Jamal Lewis, Baltimore	AP, *TSN*, PFWA
RB—	**Priest Holmes**, Kansas City	AP, *TSN*, PFWA

Defense

Pos		Selectors
DE—	Michael Strahan, NY Giants	AP, *TSN*, PFWA
DE—	Leonard Little, St. Louis	AP, PFWA
DE—	**Simeon Rice**, Tampa Bay	*TSN*
DT—	Kris Jenkins, Carolina	AP, *TSN*, PFWA
DT—	Richard Seymour, New England	AP, *TSN*, PFWA
LB—	Ray Lewis, Baltimore	AP, *TSN*, PFWA
LB—	**Zach Thomas**, Miami	AP
LB—	Keith Bulluck, Tennessee	AP, PFWA
LB—	Julian Peterson, San Francisco	AP, PFWA
LB—	**Derrick Brooks**, Tampa Bay	*TSN*
CB—	Ty Law, New England	AP, PFWA
CB—	Chris McAlister, Baltimore	AP, PFWA
CB—	Champ Bailey, Washington	*TSN*
CB—	**Patrick Surtain**, Miami	*TSN*
S—	Roy Williams, Dallas	AP, *TSN*, PFWA
S—	Rodney Harrison, New England	AP
S—	Ed Reed, Baltimore	*TSN*, PFWA

Specialists

Pos		Selectors
K—	Mike Vanderjagt, Indianapolis	AP, *TSN*, PFWA
P—	Shane Lechler, Oakland	AP, PFWA
P—	**Todd Sauerbrun**, Carolina	*TSN*

Pos		Selectors
KR/PR—	Dante Hall, Kansas City	AP, *TSN*, PFWA
KR—	Jerry Azumah, Chicago	*TSN*
ST—	Alex Bannister, Seattle	PFWA

2004 College Draft

First and second round selections at the 69th annual NFL College Draft held April 24-25, 2004, at Madison Square Garden in New York City. Twenty underclassmen were among the first 63 players chosen and are listed in capital LETTERS.

First Round

No	Team		Pos
1	San Diego	Eli Manning*, Mississippi	QB
2	Oakland	Robert Gallery, Iowa	OT
3	Arizona	LARRY FITZGERALD, Pittsburgh	WR
4	NY Giants	Philip Rivers*, N.C. State	QB
5	Washington	SEAN TAYLOR, Miami-FL	FS
6	Cleveland	KELLEN WINSLOW, Miami-FL	TE
7	Detroit	Roy Williams, Texas	WR
8	Atlanta	DeANGELO HALL, Virginia Tech	CB
9	Jacksonville	REGGIE WILLIAMS, Washington	WR
10	Houston	Dunta Robinson, South Carolina	CB
11	Pittsburgh	BEN ROETHLISBERGER, Miami-OH	QB
12	NY Jets	Jonathan Vilma, Miami-FL	LB
13	Buffalo	Lee Evans, Wisconsin	WR
14	Chicago	TOMMIE HARRIS, Oklahoma	DT
15	Tampa Bay	MICHAEL CLAYTON, LSU	WR
16	Philadelphia	SHAWN ANDREWS, Arkansas	OT
17	Denver	D.J. Williams, Miami-FL	LB
18	New Orleans	Will Smith, Ohio St.	DE
19	Miami	Vernon Carey, Miami-FL	G
20	Minnesota	KENECHI UDEZE, USC	DE
21	New England	VINCE WILFORK, Miami-FL	DT
22	Buffalo	J.P. Losman, Tulane	QB
23	Seattle	Marcus Tubbs, Texas	DT
24	St. Louis	STEVEN JACKSON, Oregon St.	RB
25	Green Bay	AHMAD CARROLL, Arkansas	CB
26	Cincinnati	Chris Perry, Michigan	RB
27	Houston	Jason Babin, Western Mich.	DE
28	Carolina	CHRIS GAMBLE, Ohio St.	CB
29	Atlanta	Michael Jenkins, Ohio St.	WR
30	Detroit	KEVIN JONES, Virginia Tech	RB
31	San Francisco	Rashaun Woods, Oklahoma St.	WR
32	New England	Ben Watson, Georgia	TE

Second Round

No	Team		Pos
33	Arizona	Karlos Dansby, Auburn	LB
34	NY Giants	CHRIS SNEE, Boston College	G
35	San Diego	IGOR OLSHANSKY, Oregon	DT
36	Kansas City	Junior Siavii, Oregon	DT
37	Detroit	Teddy Lehman, Oklahoma	LB
38	Pittsburgh	Ricardo Colclough, Tusculum	CB
39	Jacksonville	Daryl Smith, Georgia Tech	LB
40	Tennessee	Ben Troupe, Florida	TE
41	Denver	Tatum Bell, Oklahoma St.	RB
42	Tennessee	Travis LaBoy, Hawaii	DE
43	Dallas	Julius Jones, Notre Dame	RB
44	Indianapolis	Bob Sanders, Iowa	SS
45	Oakland	Jake Grove, Virginia Tech	C
46	San Francisco	JUSTIN SMILEY, Alabama	G
47	Chicago	Terry Johnson, Washington	DT
48	Minnesota	Dontarrious Thomas, Auburn	LB
49	Cincinnati	Keiwan Ratliff, Florida	CB
50	New Orleans	Devery Henderson, LSU	WR
51	Baltimore	Dwan Edwards, Oregon St.	DT
52	Dallas	Jacob Rogers, USC	OT
53	Seattle	Michael Boulware, Florida St.	LB
54	Denver	Darius Watts, Marshall	WR
55	Jacksonville	Greg Jones, Florida St.	RB
56	Cincinnati	Madieu Williams, Maryland	FS
57	Tennessee	ANTWAN ODOM, Alabama	DE
58	San Francisco	Shawntae Spencer, Pittsburgh	CB
59	Cleveland	SEAN JONES, Georgia	FS
60	New Orleans	Courtney Watson, Notre Dame	LB
61	Kansas City	Kris Wilson, Pittsburgh	TE
62	Carolina	Keary Colbert, USC	WR
63	New England	Marquise Hill, LSU	DE

*San Diego later traded top selection Eli Manning to the NY Giants for #4 selection Philip Rivers, the Giants' 3rd round pick, plus their 2005 1st and 5th round picks.

NFL Europe

Final 2004 Standings

	W	L	T	Pct.	PF	PA
*Berlin	9	1	0	.900	289	195
*Frankfurt	7	3	0	.700	212	192
Amsterdam	5	5	0	.500	173	191
Cologne	4	6	0	.400	191	201
Rhein	3	7	0	.300	161	178
Scotland	2	8	0	.200	128	197

*The teams with the top two records after the regular season advance directly to the World Bowl.

World Bowl XII

June 12, 2004 at Arena AufSchalke,
Gelsenkirchen, Germany (Att: 35,413)

Frankfurt (7-3)	3	7	0	14—	24
Berlin (9-1)	7	3	13	7—	30

MVP: Eric McCoo, Berlin, RB (28 carries for a World Bowl record 167 yards and 1 TD)

Regular Season Individual Leaders

Team listed in parentheses indicates NFL affiliation, if any.

Passing Efficiency
(Min. 140 pass attempts)

	Att	Cmp	Cmp Pct	Yds	Yds/ Att	TD	TDPct	Long	Int	IntPct	Rating
Rohan Davey, Ber (NE)	206	126	61.2	1676	8.14	19	9.2	52-td	6	2.9	105.6
J.T. O'Sullivan, Fra (NO)	196	120	61.2	1527	7.79	10	5.1	72-td	5	2.6	91.9
Ryan Van Dyke, Col (NYG)	280	174	62.1	2003	7.15	16	5.7	81	14	5.0	81.9
Chad Hutchinson, Rhe (Dal)	207	126	60.9	1356	6.55	5	2.4	54-td	4	1.9	80.1
Clint Stoerner, Ams (Mia)	259	147	56.8	1788	6.90	11	4.2	57	10	3.9	76.2

Scoring

Touchdowns

	TD	Rus	Rec	Ret	Pts
Skip Hicks, Fra (Cin)	12	10	2	0	72
Chas Gessner, Ber (NE)	6	0	6	0	36
Richard Alston, Ber (Cle)	6	0	6	0	36
Todd Devoe, Col (Bal)	5	0	5	0	30
Chris Taylor, Ams (Hou)	5	0	5	0	30
Eric McCoo, Ber (Phi)	5	4	1	0	30

Kicking

	PAT	FG/FGA	Lg	Pts
Heinz Quast, Ber	34/37	7/7	32	55
Rob Hart, Sco	11/12	11/14	43	44
Ralf Kleinmann, Fra	23/25	5/8	42	38
Ola Kimrin, Col	21/21	4/4	27	33
Ingo Anderbrugge, Rhe	15/17	6/8	32	33

Rushing

	Car	Yards	Avg	Long	TD
Eric McCoo, Ber (Phi)	148	669	4.5	46-td	4
Skip Hicks, Fra (Cin)	183	661	3.6	59	10
Avon Cobourne, Col (Det)	134	570	4.3	33	0
Chris Downs, Ams (Oak)	118	511	4.3	34	3
Joffrey Reynolds, Rhe (Cle)	120	405	3.4	21	4

Receptions

	No	Yards	Avg	Long	TD
Scott McCready, Sco	59	472	8.0	32	1
Adam Herzing, Rhe (SF)	49	656	13.4	54-td	1
Willie Quinnie, Rhe (Atl)	46	408	8.9	22-td	3
Chris Taylor, Ams (Hou)	42	573	13.6	39	5
Reggie Newhouse, Col (Ari)	39	447	11.5	57	3

Punting

	No	Yards	Avg	Long	In20
Nick Murphy, Sco (Phi)	49	2007	41.0	56	13
Hayden Epstein, Ber (Den)	35	1416	40.5	51	7
Mike Barr, Fra (Pit)	48	1869	38.9	51	18
Steve Cheek, Col (Hou)	35	1358	38.8	57	14
Brooks Barnard, Rhe (Chi)	47	1777	37.8	55	14

Sacks

	No
Felipe Claybrooks, Col (Cle)	10.0
Corey Jackson, Fra (Cle)	9.5
Bobby Setzer, Fra (Oak)	8.0
Corey Smith, Ber (TB)	7.5
David Nugent, Rhe (Oak)	6.0
T.J. Bingham, Ber	5.0
Charles Alston, Ams (Atl)	5.0

Interceptions

	No	Yds	Long	TD
Abdual Howard, Rhe	5	107	77-td	1
Keith Davis, Ber (Dal)	4	56	29	0
James Thornton, Ber	4	39	31	0
Willie Ford, Ber (KC)	3	1	1	0
Mason Unck, Fra (Cle)	3	12	8	0

Eight tied with 2 each.

All-NFL Europe League Team

The All-NFL Europe League Team as selected by NFL Europe coaches, media and fans.

Offense

QB	Rohan Davey, Ber.
RB	Skip Hicks, Fra.
WR	Chas Gessner, Ber.
WR	Adam Herzing, Rhe.
WR	Scott McCready, Sco.
TE	Tony Donald, Ams.
T	Dave Kadela, Ber.
G	Dave Volk, Ams.
C	Ben Claxton, Ber.
G	Troy Andrew, Ber.
T	David Pruce, Fra.

Defense

DE	Bobby Setzer, Fra.
DT	David Nugent, Rhe.
DT	Alan Harper, Sco.
DE	Corey Jackson, Fra.
LB	Jimmy McClain, Sco.
LB	Mason Unck, Fra.
LB	Bobby Brooks, Col.
CB	Alphonso Roundtree, Sco.
S	Keith Davis, Ber.
S	Abdual Howard, Rhe.
CB	Will Hunter, Col.

Special Teams

K	Rob Hart, Sco.
P	Nick Murphy, Sco.
Spec.	Shockmain Davis, Rhe.

Annual Awards

Offensive MVP	Rohan Davey, Berlin (NE), QB
Defensive MVP	Corey Jackson, Frankfurt (Cle), DE
Coach of the Year	Rick Lantz, Berlin

Canadian Football League
Final 2003 Standings

Division champions (*) and playoff qualifiers (†) are noted. Wins are worth two points in the standings, ties are worth one point.

East Division

	W	L	T	Pts	PF	PA
*Montreal	13	5	0	26	562	409
†Toronto	9	9	0	18	473	433
Ottawa	7	11	0	14	467	581
Hamilton	1	17	0	2	293	583

West Division

	W	L	T	Pts	PF	PA
*Edmonton	13	5	0	26	569	414
†Winnipeg	11	7	0	22	514	487
†Saskatchewan	11	7	0	22	535	430
†British Columbia	11	7	0	22	531	430
Calgary	5	13	0	10	323	502

Playoffs
Division Semifinals (Nov. 2)
East: at Toronto 28 . . . . British Columbia 7
West: Saskatchewan 37 . . . . at Winnipeg 21

Division Finals (Nov. 9)
East: at Montreal 30 . . . . Toronto 26
West: at Edmonton 30 . . . . Saskatchewan 23

91st Grey Cup Championship
November 16, 2003
at Taylor Field in Regina, Saskatchewan
(Att: 50,909)

Montreal	. . . .	0	21	1	0— 22
Edmonton	. . . .	7	17	0	10— 34

MVP: Jason Tucker, Edmonton, WR (7 catches for 132 yards and 2 TD)

Regular Season Individual Leaders
Passing Yards

	Att	Cmp	Cmp Pct	Yds	Yds/ Att	TD	TD Pct	Int	IntPct	Rating
Anthony Calvillo, Mon	675	408	60.4	5891	8.7	37	5.5	14	2.1	98.4
Dave Dickenson, B.C.	549	370	67.4	5496	10.0	36	6.6	12	2.2	112.7
Ricky Ray, Edm	515	348	67.6	4640	9.0	35	6.8	13	2.5	108.1
Khari Jones, Win	502	274	54.6	4016	8.0	25	5.0	15	3.0	85.1
Kerry Joseph, Ott	475	269	56.6	3694	7.8	19	4.0	20	4.2	77.5

Scoring

Touchdowns	TD	Rus	Rec	Ret	Pts
Mike Pringle, Edm	15	13	2	0	90
Milt Stegall, Win	15	0	15	0	90
Ben Cahoon, Mon	15	1	13	1	90
Geroy Simon, B.C.	14	1	13	0	84
Jermaine Copeland, Mon	14	0	14	0	84

Kicking	PAT	FG	S*	Pts
Lawrence Tynes, Ott	36/36	51/62	9	198
Troy Westwood, Win	48/48	47/61	9	198
Matt Kellett, Mon	56/56	43/55	6	191
Curtis Head, B.C.	51/52	44/56	5	188
Paul McCallum, Sask	53/53	41/48	5	181

*Singles (or Rouges)

Rushing

	Car	Yards	Avg	TD
Charles Roberts, Win	264	1554	5.9	8
Mike Pringle, Edm	273	1376	5.0	13
Troy Davis, Ham	227	1206	5.3	5
Josh Ranek, Ott	176	1122	6.4	7
Kelvin Anderson, B.C.	188	1048	5.6	6

Receptions

	No	Yards	Avg	TD
Ben Cahoon, Mon	112	1561	13.9	13
Terry Vaughn, Edm	106	1558	14.7	7
Jermaine Copeland, Mon	99	1757	17.7	14
Geroy Simon, B.C.	94	1687	17.9	13
Matt Dominguez, Sask	75	1071	14.3	3
Archie Amerson, Ham	75	960	12.8	4

All-CFL Team

	Offense			Defense
WR	Ed Hervey, Edm.		E	Daved Benefield, Win.
WR	Tony Miles, Tor.		E	Ray Jacobs, B.C.
T	Bruce Beaton, Edm.		T	Joe Fleming, Calg.
T	Uzooma Okeke, Mon.		T	Eric England, Tor.
G	Andrew Greene, Sask.		LB	Barrin Simpson, B.C.
G	Scott Flory, Mon.		LB	Reggie Hunt, Sask.
C	Bryan Chiu, Mon.		LB	Jackie Mitchell, Sask.
QB	Anthony Calvillo, Mon.		CB	Adrion Smith, Tor.
RB	Mike Pringle, Edm.		CB	Omarr Morgan, Sask.
RB	Charles Roberts, Win.		DB	Donny Brady, Edm.
SB	Jermaine Copeland, Mon.		DB	Clifford Ivory, Tor.
SB	Geroy Simon, B.C.		S	Orlondo Steinauer, Tor.

Specialists

PK	Lawrence Tynes, Ott.		P	Noel Prefontaine, Tor.

Special Teams Bashir Levingston, Toronto

Most Outstanding Awards

Player	. . . . Anthony Calvillo, Montreal, QB	Rookie . . . . Frank Cutolo, B.C., WR
Canadian	. . . . Ben Cahoon, Montreal, SB	Special Teams . . . . Bashir Levingston, Toronto, WR
Offensive Lineman	. . . Andrew Greene, Saskatchewan, G	Coach (Annis Stukus award) . . . . Tom Higgins, Edmonton
Defensive Player	. . . . Joe Fleming, Calgary, DT	Tom Pate Award (Sportsmanship) . Steve Hardin, B.C., OT

Arena Football
Final 2004 Standings

Division champions (*) and playoff qualifiers (†) are noted; top eight teams advance to the playoffs.

American Conference
Central Division

	W	L	T	Pct.	PF	PA
*Chicago	11	5	0	.688	847	727
†Colorado	11	5	0	.688	793	744
Indiana	8	8	0	.500	801	743
Detroit	5	11	0	.313	761	854
Grand Rapids	1	15	0	.063	581	871

Western Division

	W	L	T	Pct.	PF	PA
*Arizona	11	5	0	.688	836	738
†San Jose	11	5	0	.688	885	754
†Los Angeles	9	7	0	.563	904	811
Las Vegas	8	8	0	.500	868	791

National Conference
Eastern Division

	W	L	T	Pct.	PF	PA
New York	9	7	0	.563	849	770
Carolina	6	10	0	.375	735	868
Columbus	6	10	0	.375	791	862
Dallas	6	10	0	.375	782	855
Philadelphia	5	11	0	.313	737	796

Southern Division

	W	L	T	Pct.	PF	PA
*New Orleans	11	5	0	.688	723	721
†Orlando	10	6	0	.625	777	690
†Tampa Bay	9	7	0	.563	815	799
Austin	8	8	0	.500	764	793
Georgia	7	9	0	.438	710	772

Annual Awards

Ironman of the Year . . . . . Cory Fleming, Orlando, WR/LB
Offensive Player of the Year . . Marcus Nash, Las Vegas, OS
Defensive Player of the Year . . Kenny McEntyre, Orlando, DS
Lineman of the Year . . . . . . John Moyer, Chicago, OL/DL
Rookie of the Year . . . . . . Adrian McPherson, Indiana, QB
Coach of the Year . . . . Mike Neu, New Orleans

ArenaBowl XVIII

June 27, 2004 at America West Arena in Phoenix, Ariz.
(Att: 17,391)

San Jose	14	21	7	27—	**69**
Arizona	14	14	14	20—	**62**

MVP: Off—Mark Grieb, SJ, QB (27-36 for 328 yds, 8TD)

Def—Ricky Parker, Ari., DS (6 tackles)

---

arenafootball2
Final 2004 Standings

Division champions (*) and playoff qualifiers (†) are noted; division champions with four best records received first round byes.

American Conference
Northeast Division

	W	L	T	Pct.	PF	PA
*Wilkes-Barre/Scranton	13	3	0	.813	819	657
†Cape Fear	12	4	0	.750	848	694
Albany	6	10	0	.375	759	834
Manchester	5	11	0	.313	707	788

South Division

	W	L	T	Pct.	PF	PA
*Florida	10	6	0	.625	785	611
†Birmingham	10	6	0	.625	779	726
Columbus	6	10	0	.375	714	861
Macon	3	13	0	.188	599	779

Mid-South Division

	W	L	T	Pct.	PF	PA
*Tennessee Valley	12	4	0	.750	797	642
†Memphis	10	6	0	.625	774	732
Bossier-Shreveport	5	11	0	.313	789	868
Arkansas	4	12	0	.250	668	786

National Conference
Midwest Division

	W	L	T	Pct.	PF	PA
*Quad City	10	6	0	.625	801	617
†Peoria	9	7	0	.563	560	600
†Louisville	9	7	0	.563	844	848
Green Bay	6	10	0	.375	774	834

Southwest Division

	W	L	T	Pct.	PF	PA
*Tulsa	13	3	0	.813	922	737
†Oklahoma City	10	6	0	.625	908	769
Wichita	8	8	0	.500	711	694
Rio Grande Valley	6	10	0	.375	680	709
Laredo	3	13	0	.188	602	939

West Division

	W	L	T	Pct.	PF	PA
*Bakersfield	11	5	0	.688	726	677
San Diego	8	8	0	.500	823	770
Hawaii	8	8	0	.500	856	845
Central Valley	3	13	0	.188	604	824

Annual Awards

Ironman of the Year . . . . . Tim Dodge, Quad City, WR/DB
Offensive Player of the Year . Matt Burstein, Cape Fear, OS
Defensive Player of the Year . . . . Traco Rachal, Laredo, DS
Lineman of the Year . . . James Landers, Okla. City, OL/DL
Rookie of the Year . . . . . J.R. Thomas, W.B./Scranton, OS
Coach of the Year . . . . . Les Moss, Wilkes-Barre/Scranton

ArenaCup 2004

August 27, 2004 at Germain Arena in Estero, Fla.
(Att: 6,491)

Peoria	0	13	0	13—	**26**
Florida	6	13	17	3—	**39**

MVP: Off—Magic Benton, Fla., OS (7 rec., 74 yds, 2 TD)

Def—Comone Fisher, Fla., DL (1 interception)

1920-2004
Through the Years

ESPN SPORTS ALMANAC

The Super Bowl

The first AFL-NFL World Championship Game, as it was originally called, was played seven months after the two leagues agreed to merge in June of 1966. It became the Super Bowl (complete with roman numerals) by the third game in 1969. The Super Bowl winner has been presented the Vince Lombardi Trophy since 1971. Lombardi, whose Green Bay teams won the first two title games, died in 1970. NFL champions (1966-69) and NFC champions (since 1970) are listed in CAPITAL letters.

Multiple winners: Dallas and San Francisco (5); Pittsburgh (4); Green Bay, Oakland-LA Raiders and Washington (3); Denver, Miami, New England and NY Giants (2).

Bowl	Date	Winner	Head Coach	Score	Loser	Head Coach	Site
I	1/15/67	GREEN BAY	Vince Lombardi	35-10	Kansas City	Hank Stram	Los Angeles
II	1/14/68	GREEN BAY	Vince Lombardi	33-14	Oakland	John Rauch	Miami
III	1/12/69	NY Jets	Weeb Ewbank	16-7	BALT. COLTS	Don Shula	Miami
IV	1/11/70	Kansas City	Hank Stram	23-7	MINNESOTA	Bud Grant	New Orleans
V	1/17/71	Balt. Colts	Don McCafferty	16-13	DALLAS	Tom Landry	Miami
VI	1/16/72	DALLAS	Tom Landry	24-3	Miami	Don Shula	New Orleans
VII	1/14/73	Miami	Don Shula	14-7	WASHINGTON	George Allen	Los Angeles
VIII	1/13/74	Miami	Don Shula	24-7	MINNESOTA	Bud Grant	Houston
IX	1/12/75	Pittsburgh	Chuck Noll	16-6	MINNESOTA	Bud Grant	New Orleans
X	1/18/76	Pittsburgh	Chuck Noll	21-17	DALLAS	Tom Landry	Miami
XI	1/9/77	Oakland	John Madden	32-14	MINNESOTA	Bud Grant	Pasadena
XII	1/15/78	DALLAS	Tom Landry	27-10	Denver	Red Miller	New Orleans
XIII	1/21/79	Pittsburgh	Chuck Noll	35-31	DALLAS	Tom Landry	Miami
XIV	1/20/80	Pittsburgh	Chuck Noll	31-19	LA RAMS	Ray Malavasi	Pasadena
XV	1/25/81	Oakland	Tom Flores	27-10	PHILADELPHIA	Dick Vermeil	New Orleans
XVI	1/24/82	SAN FRANCISCO	Bill Walsh	26-21	Cincinnati	Forrest Gregg	Pontiac, MI
XVII	1/30/83	WASHINGTON	Joe Gibbs	27-17	Miami	Don Shula	Pasadena
XVIII	1/22/84	LA Raiders	Tom Flores	38-9	WASHINGTON	Joe Gibbs	Tampa
XIX	1/20/85	SAN FRANCISCO	Bill Walsh	38-16	Miami	Don Shula	Stanford
XX	1/26/86	CHICAGO	Mike Ditka	46-10	New England	Raymond Berry	New Orleans
XXI	1/25/87	NY GIANTS	Bill Parcells	39-20	Denver	Dan Reeves	Pasadena
XXII	1/31/88	WASHINGTON	Joe Gibbs	42-10	Denver	Dan Reeves	San Diego
XXIII	1/22/89	SAN FRANCISCO	Bill Walsh	20-16	Cincinnati	Sam Wyche	Miami
XXIV	1/28/90	SAN FRANCISCO	George Seifert	55-10	Denver	Dan Reeves	New Orleans
XXV	1/27/91	NY GIANTS	Bill Parcells	20-19	Buffalo	Marv Levy	Tampa
XXVI	1/26/92	WASHINGTON	Joe Gibbs	37-24	Buffalo	Marv Levy	Minneapolis
XXVII	1/31/93	DALLAS	Jimmy Johnson	52-17	Buffalo	Marv Levy	Pasadena
XXVIII	1/30/94	DALLAS	Jimmy Johnson	30-13	Buffalo	Marv Levy	Atlanta
XXIX	1/29/95	SAN FRANCISCO	George Seifert	49-26	San Diego	Bobby Ross	Miami
XXX	1/28/96	DALLAS	Barry Switzer	27-17	Pittsburgh	Bill Cowher	Tempe, AZ
XXXI	1/26/97	GREEN BAY	Mike Holmgren	35-21	New England	Bill Parcells	New Orleans
XXXII	1/25/98	Denver	Mike Shanahan	31-24	GREEN BAY	Mike Holmgren	San Diego
XXXIII	1/31/99	Denver	Mike Shanahan	34-19	ATLANTA	Dan Reeves	Miami
XXXIV	1/30/00	ST.L RAMS	Dick Vermeil	23-16	Tennessee	Jeff Fisher	Atlanta
XXXV	1/28/01	Balt. Ravens	Brian Billick	34-7	NY GIANTS	Jim Fassel	Tampa
XXXVI	2/3/02	New England	Bill Belichick	20-17	ST.L RAMS	Mike Martz	New Orleans
XXXVII	1/26/03	TAMPA BAY	Jon Gruden	48-21	Oakland	Bill Callahan	San Diego
XXXVIII	2/1/04	New England	Bill Belichick	32-29	CAROLINA	John Fox	Houston

DID YOU KNOW?

Tampa Bay and Oakland both missed the playoffs in 2003, the third time in the past five years that both Super Bowl participants from the previous season failed to reach the post-season. In the previous 32 years, it happened just once (Washington and Denver both missed the playoffs following their meeting in Super Bowl XXII in 1988).

Super Bowl Appearances

App		W	L	Pct	PF	PA	App		W	L	Pct	PF	PA
8	Dallas	5	3	.625	221	132	2	Baltimore Colts	1	1	.500	23	29
6	Denver	2	4	.333	115	206	2	Kansas City	1	1	.500	33	42
5	San Francisco	5	0	1.000	188	89	2	Cincinnati	0	2	.000	37	46
5	Pittsburgh	4	1	.800	120	100	1	Baltimore Ravens	1	0	1.000	34	7
5	Oak/LA Raiders	3	2	.600	132	114	1	Chicago	1	0	1.000	46	10
5	Washington	3	2	.600	122	103	1	NY Jets	1	0	1.000	16	7
5	Miami	2	3	.400	74	103	1	Tampa Bay	1	0	1.000	48	21
4	Green Bay	3	1	.750	127	76	1	Atlanta	0	1	.000	19	34
4	New England	2	2	.500	83	127	1	Carolina	0	1	.000	29	32
4	Buffalo	0	4	.000	73	139	1	Philadelphia	0	1	.000	10	27
4	Minnesota	0	4	.000	34	95	1	San Diego	0	1	.000	26	49
3	NY Giants	2	1	.667	66	73	1	Tennessee	0	1	.000	16	23
3	LA/St.L Rams	1	2	.333	59	67							

Pete Rozelle Award (MVP)

The Most Valuable Player in the Super Bowl. Currently selected by a 16-member panel made up of national pro football writers and broadcasters chosen by the NFL (80 percent) and fans voting via the internet and text message (20 percent). Presented by *Sport* magazine from 1967-89 and by the NFL since 1990. Named after former NFL commissioner Pete Rozelle in 1990. Winner who did not play for Super Bowl champion is in **bold** type.

Multiple winners: Joe Montana (3); Terry Bradshaw, Tom Brady and Bart Starr (2).

Bowl		Bowl		Bowl	
I	Bart Starr, Green Bay, QB	XIII	Terry Bradshaw, Pittsburgh, QB	XXVI	Mark Rypien, Washington, QB
II	Bart Starr, Green Bay, QB	XIV	Terry Bradshaw, Pittsburgh, QB	XXVII	Troy Aikman, Dallas, QB
III	Joe Namath, NY Jets, QB	XV	Jim Plunkett, Oakland, QB	XXVIII	Emmitt Smith, Dallas, RB
IV	Len Dawson, Kansas City, QB	XVI	Joe Montana, San Francisco, QB	XXIX	Steve Young, San Fran., QB
V	Chuck Howley, Dallas, LB	XVII	John Riggins, Washington, RB	XXX	Larry Brown, Dallas, CB
VI	Roger Staubach, Dallas, QB	XVIII	Marcus Allen, LA Raiders, RB	XXXI	Desmond Howard, Gr. Bay, KR
VII	Jake Scott, Miami, S	XIX	Joe Montana, San Francisco, QB	XXXII	Terrell Davis, Denver, RB
VIII	Larry Csonka, Miami, RB	XX	Richard Dent, Chicago, DE	XXXIII	John Elway, Denver, QB
IX	Franco Harris, Pittsburgh, RB	XXI	Phil Simms, NY Giants, QB	XXXIV	Kurt Warner, St. Louis, QB
X	Lynn Swann, Pittsburgh, WR	XXII	Doug Williams, Washington, QB	XXXV	Ray Lewis, Baltimore, LB
XI	Fred Biletnikoff, Oakland, WR	XXIII	Jerry Rice, San Francisco, WR	XXXVI	Tom Brady, New England, QB
XII	Harvey Martin, Dallas, DE	XXIV	Joe Montana, San Francisco, QB	XXXVII	Dexter Jackson, Tampa Bay, S
	& Randy White, Dallas, DT	XXV	Ottis Anderson, NY Giants, RB	XXXVIII	Tom Brady, New England, QB

All-Time Super Bowl Leaders

Through 2004; participants in Super Bowl XXXVIII in **bold** type.

CAREER

Passing Efficiency

		Gm	Att	Cmp	Cmp%	Yards	Avg Gain	TD	TD%	Int	Int%	Rating
1	Phil Simms, NYG	1	25	22	88.0	268	10.72	3	12.0	0	0.0	150.9
2	Steve Young, SF	2	39	26	66.7	345	8.85	6	15.4	0	0.0	134.1
3	Doug Williams, Wash	1	29	18	62.1	340	11.72	4	13.8	1	3.4	128.1
4	Joe Montana, SF	4	122	83	68.0	1142	9.36	11	9.0	0	0.0	127.8
5	Jim Plunkett, Raiders	2	46	29	63.0	433	9.41	4	8.7	0	0.0	122.8
6	**Jake Delhomme**, Car	1	33	16	48.5	323	9.79	3	9.1	0	0.0	113.6
7	Terry Bradshaw, Pit	4	84	49	58.3	932	11.10	9	10.7	4	4.8	112.8
8	Troy Aikman, Dal	3	80	56	70.0	689	8.61	5	6.3	1	1.3	111.9
9	Bart Starr, GB	2	47	29	61.7	452	9.62	3	6.4	1	2.1	106.0
10	Brett Favre, GB	2	69	39	56.5	502	7.28	5	7.2	1	1.4	97.6

Ratings based on performance standards established for completion percentage, average gain, touchdown percentage and interception percentage. Quarterbacks are allocated points according to how their statistics measure up to those standards. Minimum 25 passing attempts.

Passing Yards

		Gm	Att	Cmp	Pct	Yds
1	Joe Montana, SF	4	122	83	68.0	1142
2	John Elway, Den	5	152	76	50.0	1128
3	Terry Bradshaw, Pit	4	84	49	58.3	932
4	Jim Kelly, Buf	4	145	81	55.9	829
5	Kurt Warner, St.L	2	89	52	58.4	779
6	Roger Staubach, Dal	4	98	61	62.2	734
7	Troy Aikman, Dal	3	80	56	70.0	689
8	Brett Favre, GB	2	69	39	56.5	502
9	**Tom Brady**, NE	2	75	48	64.0	499
10	Fran Tarkenton, Min	3	89	46	51.7	489

Receptions

		Gm	No	Yds	Avg	TD
1	Jerry Rice, SF-Oak	4	33	589	17.8	8
2	Andre Reed, Buf	4	27	323	12.0	0
3	Roger Craig, SF	3	20	212	10.6	2
	Thurman Thomas, Buf	4	20	144	7.2	0
5	Jay Novacek, Dal	3	17	148	8.7	2
6	Lynn Swann, Pit	4	16	364	22.8	3
	Michael Irvin, Dal	3	16	256	16.0	2
8	Chuck Foreman, Min	3	15	139	9.3	0
9	Cliff Branch, Raiders	3	14	181	12.9	3
	Troy Brown, NE	2	14	165	11.8	0

All-Time Super Bowl Leaders (Cont.)

Rushing

	Gm	Car	Yds	Avg	TD
1 Franco Harris, Pit	4	101	354	3.5	4
2 Larry Csonka, Mia	3	57	297	5.2	2
3 Emmitt Smith, Dal	3	70	289	4.1	5
4 Terrell Davis, Den	2	55	259	4.7	3
5 John Riggins, Wash	2	64	230	3.6	2
6 Timmy Smith, Wash	1	22	204	9.3	2
Thurman Thomas, Buf	4	52	204	3.9	4
8 Roger Craig, SF	3	52	201	3.9	2
9 Marcus Allen, Raiders	1	20	191	9.5	2
10 **Antowain Smith**, NE	2	44	175	4.0	1

All-Purpose Yards

	Gm	Rush	Rec	Ret	Total
1 Jerry Rice, SF-Oak	4	15	589	0	604
2 Franco Harris, Pit	4	354	114	0	468
3 Roger Craig, SF	3	201	212	0	413
4 Lynn Swann, Pit	4	-7	364	34	391
5 Thurman Thomas, Buf	4	204	144	0	348
6 Emmitt Smith, Dal	3	289	56	0	345
7 Antonio Freeman, GB	2	0	231	104	335
8 Andre Reed, Buf	4	0	323	0	323
9 Terrell Davis, Den.	2	259	58	0	317
10 Larry Csonka, Mia	3	297	17	0	314

Scoring

Points

	Gm	TD	FG	PAT	Pts
1 Jerry Rice, SF-Oak	4	8	0	0	48
2 Emmitt Smith, Dal	3	5	0	0	30
3 Roger Craig, SF	3	4	0	0	24
Franco Harris, Pit	4	4	0	0	24
Thurman Thomas, Buf	4	4	0	0	24
John Elway, Den	5	4	0	0	24
7 Ray Wersching, SF	2	0	5	7	22
8 Don Chandler, GB	2	0	4	8	20
9 Six tied with 18 pts. each.					

Touchdowns

	Gm	Rush	Rec	Ret	TD
1 Jerry Rice, SF-Oak	4	0	8	0	8
2 Emmitt Smith, Dal	3	5	0	0	5
3 Roger Craig, SF	3	2	2	0	4
Franco Harris, Pit	4	4	0	0	4
John Elway, Den	5	4	0	0	4
Thurman Thomas, Buf	4	4	0	0	4
7 Cliff Branch, Raiders	3	0	3	0	3
John Stallworth, Pit	4	0	3	0	3
Lynn Swann, Pit	4	0	3	0	3
Ricky Watters, SF	1	1	2	0	3
Terrell Davis, Den	2	3	0	0	3
Antonio Freeman, GB	2	0	3	0	3

Punting

(Minimum 10 Punts)	Gm	No	Yds	Avg.
1 Jerrel Wilson, KC	2	11	511	46.5
2 Tom Tupa, NE-TB	2	12	516	43.0
Kyle Richardson, Bal	1	10	430	43.0
4 Ray Guy, Raiders	3	14	587	41.9
5 Larry Seiple, Mia	3	15	620	41.3

Punt Returns

(Minimum 4 Returns)	Gm	No	Yds	Avg.	TD
1 John Taylor, SF	3	6	94	15.7	0
2 Desmond Howard, GB	1	6	90	15.0	0
3 Neal Colzie, Raiders	1	4	43	10.8	0
4 Dana McLemore, SF	1	5	51	10.2	0
5 **Troy Brown**, NE	2	5	44	8.8	0

Interceptions

	Gm	No	Yds	TD
1 Larry Brown, Dal	3	3	77	0
Chuck Howley, Dal	2	3	63	0
Rod Martin, Raiders	1	3	44	0
4 Randy Beverly, NYJ	1	2	0	0
Mel Blount, Pit	4	2	23	0
Brad Edwards, Wash	1	2	56	0
Thomas Everett, Dal	2	2	22	0
Darrien Gordon, SD-Den-Oak ...	4	2	108	0
Dexter Jackson, TB	1	2	34	0
Jake Scott, Mia	3	2	63	0
Dwight Smith, TB	1	2	94	2
Mike Wagner, Pit	3	2	45	0
James Washington, Dal	2	2	25	0
Barry Wilburn, Wash	1	2	11	0
Eric Wright, SF	4	2	25	0

Kickoff Returns

(Minimum 4 Returns)	Gm	No	Yds	Avg.	TD
1 Tim Dwight, Atl	1	5	210	42.0	1
2 Desmond Howard, GB	1	4	154	38.5	1
3 Fulton Walker, Mia	2	8	283	35.4	1
4 Andre Coleman, SD	1	8	242	30.3	1
5 Larry Anderson, Pit	2	8	207	25.9	0

Sacks

	Gm	No
1 Charles Haley, SF-Dal	5	4.5
2 Reggie White, GB	2	3.0
Leonard Marshall, NYG	2	3.0
Danny Stubbs, SF	2	3.0
Jeff Wright, Buf	4	3.0

SINGLE GAME

Passing

Yards Gained	Year	Att/Cmp	Yds
1 Kurt Warner, St.L vs Ten ..2000		45/24	414
2 Kurt Warner, St.L vs NE ..2002		44/28	365
3 Joe Montana, SF vs Cin ..1989		36/23	357
4 **Tom Brady**, NE vs Car ..2004		48/32	354
5 Doug Williams, Wash vs Den ..1988		29/18	340
6 John Elway, Den vs Atl 1999		29/18	336
7 Joe Montana, SF vs Mia ..1985		35/24	331
8 Steve Young, SF vs SD 1995		36/24	325
9 **Jake Delhomme**, Car vs NE 2004		33/16	323
10 Terry Bradshaw, Pit vs Dal ..1979		30/17	318
Dan Marino, Mia vs SF 1985		50/29	318

Touchdown Passes	Year	TD	Int
1 Steve Young, SF vs SD 1995		6	0
2 Joe Montana, SF vs Den 1990		5	0
3 Terry Bradshaw, Pit vs Dal 1979		4	1
Doug Williams, Wash vs Den ..1988		4	1
Troy Aikman, Dal vs Buf 1993		4	0
6 Roger Staubach, Dal vs Pit 1979		3	1
Jim Plunkett, Raiders vs Phi ...1981		3	0
Joe Montana, SF vs Mia 1985		3	0
Phil Simms, NYG vs Den 1987		3	0
Brett Favre, GB vs Den 1998		3	1
Jake Delhomme, Car vs NE ...2004		3	0
Tom Brady, NE vs Car 2004		3	1

Receiving

Catches

		Year	No	Yds	TD
1	Dan Ross, Cin vs SF 1982	11	104	2
	Jerry Rice, SF vs Cin 1989	11	215	1
3	Tony Nathan, Mia vs SF 1985	10	83	0
	Jerry Rice, SF vs SD 1995	10	149	3
	Andre Hastings, Pit vs Dal 1996	10	98	0
	Deion Branch, NE vs Car 2004	10	143	1
7	Ricky Sanders, Wash vs Den . . .1988	9	193	2
	Antonio Freeman, GB vs Den . . .1998	9	126	2
9	Six tied with 8 each, including twice by Andre Reed.			

Yards Gained

		Year	No	Yds	TD
1	Jerry Rice, SF vs Cin 1989	11	215	1
2	Ricky Sanders, Wash vs Den . . .1988	9	193	2
3	Isaac Bruce, St.L vs Ten 2000	6	162	1
4	Lynn Swann, Pit vs Dal 1976	4	161	1
5	Andre Reed, Buf vs Dal 1993	8	152	0
	Rod Smith, Den vs Atl 1999	5	152	1
7	Jerry Rice, SF vs SD 1995	10	149	3
8	Jerry Rice, SF vs Den 1990	7	148	3
9	**Deion Branch**, NE vs Car 2004	10	143	1
10	**M. Muhammad**, Car vs NE . . .2004	4	140	1

Rushing

Yards Gained

		Year	Car	Yds	TD
1	Timmy Smith, Wash vs Den 1988	22	204	2
2	Marcus Allen, Raiders vs Wash .1984	20	191	2
3	John Riggins, Wash vs Mia 1983	38	166	1
4	Franco Harris, Pit vs Min 1975	34	158	1
5	Terrell Davis, Den vs GB 1998	30	157	3
6	Larry Csonka, Mia vs Min 1974	33	145	2
7	Clarence Davis, Raiders vs Min. .1977	16	137	0
8	Thurman Thomas, Buf vs NYG . .1991	15	135	1
9	Emmitt Smith, Dal vs Buf 1994	30	132	2
10	Michael Pittman, TB vs Oak 2003	29	124	0

Scoring

Points

		Year	TD	FG	PAT	Pts
1	Roger Craig, SF vs Mia 1985	3	0	0	18
	Jerry Rice, SF vs Den 1990	3	0	0	18
	Jerry Rice, SF vs SD 1995	3	0	0	18
	Ricky Watters, SF vs SD 1995	3	0	0	18
	Terrell Davis, Den vs GB 1998	3	0	0	18

Touchdowns

		Year	TD	Rush	Rec
1	Roger Craig, SF vs Mia 1985	3	1	2
	Jerry Rice, SF vs Den 1990	3	0	3
	Jerry Rice, SF vs SD 1995	3	0	3
	Ricky Watters, SF vs SD 1995	3	1	2
	Terrell Davis, Den vs GB 1998	3	3	0

All-Purpose Yards

Yards Gained

		Year	Run	Rec	Tot
1	Desmond Howard, GB vs NE .1997	0	0	244
2	Andre Coleman, SD vs SF 1995	0	0	242
3	Ricky Sanders, Wash vs Den . .1988	193	-4	235
4	Antonio Freeman, GB vs Den . .1998	0	126	230
5	Jerry Rice, SF vs Cin 1989	5	215	220
6	Tim Dwight, Atl vs Den 1999	5	0	215
7	Timmy Smith, Wash vs Den . . .1988	204	9	213
8	Marcus Allen, Raiders vs Wash .1984	191	18	209
9	Stephen Starring, NE vs Chi . . .1986	0	39	192
10	Fulton Walker, Mia vs Wash . . .1983	0	0	190
	Thurman Thomas, Buf vs NYG .1991	135	55	190

Return Yardage: Howard 244, Coleman 242, Sanders 46, Freeman 104, Dwight 210, Starring 153, Walker 190.

Interceptions

		Year	No	Yds	TD
1	Rod Martin, Raiders vs Phi 1981	3	44	0
	Ten tied with 2 each.			

Punting
(Minimum 4 punts)

		Year	No	Yds	Avg
1	Bryan Wagner, SD vs SF 1995	4	195	48.8
2	Jerrel Wilson, KC vs Min 1970	4	194	48.5
3	Jim Miller, SF vs Cin 1982	4	185	46.3
4	Jerrel Wilson, KC vs GB 1967	7	317	45.3
5	Tom Tupa, NE vs GB 1997	8	361	45.1

Punt Returns
(Minimum 3 returns)

		Year	No	Yds	Avg
1	John Taylor, SF vs Cin 1989	3	56	18.7
2	Desmond Howard, GB vs NE .1997	6	90	15.0
3	John Taylor, SF vs Den 1990	3	38	12.7
4	Kelvin Martin, Dal vs Buf 1993	3	35	11.7
5	Lynn Swann, Pit vs Min 1975	3	34	11.3
	Jermaine Lewis, Bal vs NYG . . .2001	3	34	11.3

Kickoff Returns
(Minimum 3 returns)

		Year	No	Yds	Avg
1	Fulton Walker, Mia vs Wash . . .1983	4	190	47.5
2	Tim Dwight, Atl vs Den 1999	5	210	42.0
3	Desmond Howard, GB vs NE . .1997	4	154	38.5
4	Larry Anderson, Pit vs Rams . . .1980	5	162	32.4
5	Rick Upchurch, Den vs Dal 1978	3	94	31.3

Super Bowl Playoffs

The Super Bowl forced the NFL to set up pro football's first guaranteed multiple-game playoff format. Over the years, the NFL-AFL merger, the creation of two conferences comprised of four divisions each and the proliferation of wild card entries has seen the postseason field grow from four teams (1966), to six (1967-68), to eight (1969-77), to 10 (1978-81, 1983-89), to the present 12 (since1990). In 1968, there was a special playoff between Oakland and Kansas City which were both 12-2 and tied for first in the AFL's Western Division. In 1982, when a 57-day players' strike shortened the regular season to just nine games, playoff berths were extended to 16 teams (eight from each conference) and a 15-game tournament was played.

Note that in the following year-by-year summary, records of finalists include all games leading up to the Super Bowl; (*) indicates non-division winners or wild card teams.

1966 SEASON

AFL Playoffs

Championship . . . . .Kansas City 31, at Buffalo 7

NFL Playoffs

Championship . . . . .Green Bay 34, at Dallas 27

Super Bowl I

Jan. 15, 1967
Memorial Coliseum, Los Angeles
Favorite: Packers by 14—Attendance: 61,946

Kansas City (12-2-1) . . . . .0 10 0 0 —**10**
Green Bay (13-2) . . . . .7 7 14 7 —**35**
MVP: Green Bay QB Bart Starr (16 for 23, 250 yds, 2 TD)

Super Bowl Playoffs (Cont.)

1967 SEASON

AFL Playoffs
Championship . . . . .at Oakland 40, Houston 7

NFL Playoffs
Eastern Conference . . . . .at Dallas 52, Cleveland 14
Western Conference . . . . . .at Green Bay 28, LA Rams 7
Championship . . . . .at Green Bay 21, Dallas 17

Super Bowl II
Jan. 14, 1968
Orange Bowl, Miami
Favorite: Packers by 13½—Attendance: 75,546

Green Bay (11-4-1) . . . . .3 13 10   7 **—33**
Oakland (14-1) 0   7   0   7 **—14**
MVP: Green Bay QB Bart Starr (13 for 24, 202 yds,1 TD)

1968 SEASON

AFL Playoffs
Western Div. Playoff . . . . . .at Oakland 41, Kansas City 6
AFL Championship . . . . .at NY Jets 27, Oakland 23

NFL Playoffs
Eastern Conference . . . . .at Cleveland 31, Dallas 20
Western Conference . . . . . .at Baltimore 24, Minnesota 14
NFL Championship . . . . .Baltimore 34, Cleveland 0

Super Bowl III
Jan. 12, 1969
Orange Bowl, Miami
Favorite: Colts by 18—Attendance: 75,389

NY Jets (12-3) 0   7   6   3 **— 16**
Baltimore (15-1) 0   0   0   7 **— 7**
MVP: NY Jets QB Joe Namath (17 for 28, 206 yds)

1969 SEASON

AFL Playoffs
Inter-Division . . . .*Kansas City 13, at NY Jets 6
at Oakland 56, *Houston 7
AFL Championship . . . . . . .Kansas City 17, at Oakland 7

NFL Playoffs
Eastern Conference . . . . .Cleveland 38, at Dallas 14
Western Conference . . . . . .at Minnesota 23, LA Rams 20
NFL Championship . . . . . .at Minnesota 27, Cleveland 7

Super Bowl IV
Jan. 11, 1970
Tulane Stadium, New Orleans
Favorite: Vikings by 12—Attendance: 80,562

Minnesota (14-2) 0   0   7   0 **— 7**
Kansas City (13-3) . . . . .3 13   7   0 **— 23**
MVP: KC QB Len Dawson (12 for 17, 142 yds, 1 TD, 1Int)

1970 SEASON

AFC Playoffs
First Round . . . . .at Baltimore 17, Cincinnati 0
at Oakland 21,*Miami 14
Championship . . . . .at Baltimore 27, Oakland 17

NFC Playoffs
First Round. . . . . .at Dallas 5, *Detroit 0
San Francisco 17, at Minnesota 14
Championship . . . . .Dallas 17, at San Francisco 10

Super Bowl V
Jan. 17, 1971
Orange Bowl, Miami
Favorite: Cowboys by 2½—Attendance: 79,204

Baltimore (13-2-1) 0   6   0 10 **— 16**
Dallas (12-4) . . . . .3 10   0   0 **— 13**
MVP: Dallas LB Chuck Howley (2 interceptions for 22 yds)

1971 SEASON

AFC Playoffs
First Round . . . . .Miami 27, at Kansas City 24 (OT)
*Baltimore 20, at Cleveland 3
Championship . . . . .at Miami 21, Baltimore 0

NFC Playoffs
First Round . . . . .Dallas 20, at Minnesota 12
at San Francisco 24,*Washington 20
Championship . . . . .at Dallas 14, San Francisco 3

Super Bowl VI
Jan. 16, 1972
Tulane Stadium, New Orleans
Favorite: Cowboys by 6—Attendance: 81,023

Dallas (13-3) 3   7   7   7 **— 24**
Miami (12-3-1) 0   3   0   0 **— 3**
MVP: Dallas QB Roger Staubach (12 for 19, 119 yds, 2 TD)

1972 SEASON

AFC Playoffs
First Round . . . . .at Pittsburgh 13, Oakland 7
at Miami 20, *Cleveland 14
Championship . . . . .Miami 21, at Pittsburgh 17

NFC Playoffs
First Round . . . .*Dallas 30, at San Francisco 28
at Washington 16, Green Bay 3
Championship . . . . .at Washington 26, Dallas 3

Super Bowl VII
Jan. 14, 1973
Memorial Coliseum, Los Angeles
Favorite: Redskins by 1½—Attendance: 90,182

Miami (16-0) 7   7   0   0 **— 14**
Washington (13-3) 0   0   0   7 **— 7**
MVP: Miami safety Jake Scott (2 Interceptions for 63 yds)

1973 SEASON

AFC Playoffs
First Round . . . . .at Oakland 33, *Pittsburgh 14
at Miami 34, Cincinnati 16
Championship . . . . .at Miami 27, Oakland 10

NFC Playoffs
First Round . . . . .at Minnesota 27, *Washington 20
at Dallas 27, LA Rams 16
Championship . . . . .Minnesota 27, at Dallas 10

Super Bowl VIII
Jan. 13, 1974
Rice Stadium, Houston
Favorite: Dolphins by 6½—Attendance: 71,882

Minnesota (14-2) 0   0   0   7 **— 7**
Miami (12-4) 14   3   7   0 **— 24**
MVP: Miami FB Larry Csonka (33 carries, 145 yds, 2 TD)

1974 SEASON

AFC Playoffs

First Round . . . . .at Oakland 28, Miami 26
at Pittsburgh 32, *Buffalo 14
Championship . . . . .Pittsburgh 24, at Oakland 13

NFC Playoffs

First Round . . . . .at Minnesota 30, St. Louis 14
at LA Rams 19, *Washington 14
Championship . . . . .at Minnesota 14, LA Rams 10

Super Bowl IX
Jan. 12, 1975
Tulane Stadium, New Orleans
Favorite: Steelers by 3—Attendance: 80,997

Pittsburgh (12-3-1) . . .: 0   2   7   7 — **16**
Minnesota (12-4) 0   0   0   6 — **6**
MVP: Pittsburgh RB Franco Harris (34 carries, 158 yds, 1 TD)

1975 SEASON

AFC Playoffs

First Round . . . . .at Pittsburgh 28, Baltimore 10
at Oakland 31, *Cincinnati 28
Championship . . . . .at Pittsburgh 16, Oakland 10

NFC Playoffs

First Round . . . . .at LA Rams 35, St. Louis 23
*Dallas 17, at Minnesota 14
Championship . . . . .Dallas 37, at LA Rams 7

Super Bowl X
Jan. 18, 1976
Orange Bowl, Miami
Favorite: Steelers by 6½—Attendance: 80,187

Dallas (12-4) 7   3   0   7 — **17**
Pittsburgh (14-2) 7   0   0   14 — **21**
MVP: Pittsburgh WR Lynn Swann (4 catches, 161 yds, 1 TD)

1976 SEASON

AFC Playoffs

First Round . . . . .at Oakland 24, *New England 21
Pittsburgh 40, at Baltimore 14
Championship . . . . .at Oakland 24, Pittsburgh 7

NFC Playoffs

First Round . . . . . . .at Minnesota 35, *Washington 20
LA Rams 14, at Dallas 12
Championship . . . . .at Minnesota 24, LA Rams 13

Super Bowl XI
Jan. 9, 1977
Rose Bowl, Pasadena
Favorite: Raiders by 4½—Attendance: 103,438

Oakland (15-1) 0   16   3   13 —**32**
Minnesota (13-2-1) 0   0   7   7 —**14**
MVP: Oakland WR Fred Biletnikoff (4 catches, 79 yds)

1977 SEASON

AFC Playoffs

First Round . . . . .at Denver 34, Pittsburgh 21
*Oakland 37, at Baltimore 31 (OT)
Championship . . . . .at Denver 20, Oakland 17

NFC Playoffs

First Round . . . . .at Dallas 37, *Chicago 7
Minnesota 14, at LA Rams 7
Championship . . . . .at Dallas 23, Minnesota 6

Super Bowl XII
Jan. 15, 1978
Louisiana Superdome, New Orleans
Favorite: Cowboys by 6—Attendance: 75,583

Dallas (14-2) 10   3   7   7 — **27**
Denver (14-2) 0   0   10   0 — **10**
MVPs: Dallas DE Harvey Martin and DT Randy White (Cowboys' defense forced 8 turnovers)

1978 SEASON

AFC Playoffs

First Round . . . .*Houston 17, at *Miami 9
Second Round . . . . .Houston 31, at New England 14
at Pittsburgh 33, Denver 10
Championship . . . . .at Pittsburgh 34, Houston 5

NFC Playoffs

First Round . . . . .at *Atlanta 14, *Philadelphia 13
Second Round . . . . .at Dallas 27, Atlanta 20
at LA Rams 34, Minnesota 10
Championship . . . . .Dallas 28, at LA Rams 0

Super Bowl XIII
Jan. 21, 1979
Orange Bowl, Miami
Favorite: Steelers by 4—Attendance: 79,484

Pittsburgh (16-2) 7   14   0   14 — **35**
Dallas (14-4) 7   7   3   14 — **31**
MVP: Pit. QB Terry Bradshaw (17 for 30, 318 yds, 4 TD)

1979 SEASON

AFC Playoffs

First Round . . . . .at *Houston 13, *Denver 7
Second Round . . . . .Houston 17, at San Diego 14
at Pittsburgh 34, Miami 14
Championship . . . . .at Pittsburgh 27, Houston 13

NFC Playoffs

First Round . . . . .at *Philadelphia 27, *Chicago 17
Second Round . . . . . . .at Tampa Bay 24, Philadelphia 17
LA Rams 21, at Dallas 19
Championship . . . . .LA Rams 9, at Tampa Bay 0

Super Bowl XIV
Jan. 20, 1980
Rose Bowl, Pasadena
Favorite: Steelers by 10½—Attendance: 103,985

LA Rams (11-7) 7   6   6   0 — **19**
Pittsburgh (14-4) 3   7   7   14 — **31**
MVP: Pit. QB Terry Bradshaw (14 for 21, 309 yds, 2 TD)

1980 SEASON

AFC Playoffs

First Round . . . . .at *Oakland 27, *Houston 7
Second Round . . . . .at San Diego 20, Buffalo 14
Oakland 14, at Cleveland 12
Championship . . . . .Oakland 34, at San Diego 27

NFC Playoffs

First Round . . . . .at *Dallas 34, *LA Rams 13
Second Round . . . . . . .at Philadelphia 31, Minnesota 16
Dallas 30, at Atlanta 27
Championship . . . . .at Philadelphia 20, Dallas 7

Super Bowl XV
Jan. 25, 1981
Louisiana Superdome, New Orleans
Favorite: Eagles by 3—Attendance: 76,135

Oakland (14-5) 14   0   10   3 — **27**
Philadelphia (14-4) 0   3   0   7 — **10**
MVP: Oakland QB Jim Plunkett (13 for 21, 261 yds, 3 TD)

Super Bowl Playoffs (Cont.)

1981 SEASON

AFC Playoffs

First Round	.*Buffalo 31, at *NY Jets 27
Second Round	.San Diego 41, at Miami 38 (OT)
	at Cincinnati 28, Buffalo 21
Championship	.at Cincinnati 27, San Diego 7

NFC Playoffs

First Round	.*NY Giants 27, at *Philadelphia 21
Second Round	.at Dallas 38, Tampa Bay 0
	at San Francisco 38, NY Giants 24
Championship	.at San Francisco 28, Dallas 27

Super Bowl XVI

Jan. 24, 1982
Pontiac Silverdome, Pontiac, Mich.
Favorite: Pick'em—Attendance: 81,270

San Francisco (15-3) . . . . .7 13   0   6 — **26**
Cincinnati (14-4) 0   0   7 14 — **21**
MVP: San Francisco QB Joe Montana (14 for 22, 157 yds, 1 TD; 6 carries, 18 yds, 1 TD)

1982 SEASON

A 57-day players' strike shortened the regular season from 16 games to nine. The playoff format was changed to a 16-team tournament open to the top eight teams in each conference.

AFC Playoffs

First Round	.at LA Raiders 27, Cleveland 10
	at Miami 28, New England 3
	NY Jets 44, at Cincinnati 17
	San Diego 31, at Pittsburgh 28
Second Round	.NY Jets 17, at LA Raiders 14
	at Miami 34, San Diego 13
Championship	.at Miami 14, NY Jets 0

NFC Playoffs

First Round	.at Washington 31, Detroit 7
	at Dallas 30, Tampa Bay 17
	at Green Bay 41, St. Louis 16
	at Minnesota 30, Atlanta 24
Second Round	.at Washington 21, Minnesota 7
	at Dallas 37, Green Bay 26
Championship	.at Washington 31, Dallas 17

Super Bowl XVII

Jan. 30, 1983
Rose Bowl, Pasadena
Favorite: Dolphins by 3—Attendance: 103,667

Miami (10-2) 7   10   0   0 — **17**
Washington (11-1) 0   10   3 14 — **27**
MVP: Washington RB John Riggins (38 carries, 166 yds, 1 TD; 1 catch, 15 yds)

Most Popular Playing Sites
Stadiums hosting more than one Super Bowl.

No		Years
6	Superdome (N. Orleans)	1978, 81, 86, 90, 97, 2002
5	Orange Bowl (Miami)	1968-69, 71, 76, 79
5	Rose Bowl (Pasadena)	1977, 80, 83, 87, 93
3	Tulane Stadium (N. Orleans)	1970, 72, 75
3	Joe Robbie/Pro Player Stadium (Miami)	1989, 95, 99
3	Jack Murphy/Qualcomm Stadium (San Diego)	1988, 98, 2003
2	LA Memorial Coliseum	1967, 73
2	Tampa Stadium	1984, 91
2	Georgia Dome (Atlanta)	1994, 2000

1983 SEASON

AFC Playoffs

First Round	.at *Seattle 31, *Denver 7
Second Round	.Seattle 27, at Miami 20
	at LA Raiders 38, Pittsburgh 10
Championship	.at LA Raiders 30, Seattle 14

NFC Playoffs

First Round	.*LA Rams 24, at *Dallas 17
Second Round	.at San Francisco 24, Detroit 23
	at Washington 51, LA Rams 7
Championship	.at Washington 24, San Francisco 21

Super Bowl XVIII

Jan. 22, 1984
Tampa Stadium, Tampa
Favorite: Redskins by 3—Attendance: 72,920

Washington (16-2) 0   3   6   0 — **9**
LA Raiders (14-4) 7   14 14   3 — **38**
MVP: LA Raiders RB Marcus Allen (20 carries, 191 yds, 2 TD; 2 catches, 18 yds)

1984 SEASON

AFC Playoffs

First Round	.at *Seattle 13, *LA Raiders 7
Second Round	.at Miami 31, Seattle 10
	Pittsburgh 24, at Denver 17
Championship	.at Miami 45, Pittsburgh 28

NFC Playoffs

First Round	.*NY Giants 16, at *LA Rams 13
Second Round	.at San Francisco 21, NY Giants 10
	Chicago 23, at Washington 19
Championship	.at San Francisco 23, Chicago 0

Super Bowl XIX

Jan. 20, 1985
Stanford Stadium, Stanford, Calif.
Favorite: 49ers by 3—Attendance: 84,059

Miami (16-2) 10   6   0   0 — **16**
San Francisco (17-1) 7   21 10   0 — **38**
MVP: San Francisco QB Joe Montana (24 for 35, 331 yds, 2 TD; 5 carries, 59 yards, 1 TD)

1985 SEASON

AFC Playoffs

First Round	.*New England 26, at *NY Jets 14
Second Round	.at Miami 24, Cleveland 21
	New England 27, at LA Raiders 20
Championship	.New England 31, at Miami 14

NFC Playoffs

First Round	.at *NY Giants 17, *San Francisco 3
Second Round	.at LA Rams 20, Dallas 0
	at Chicago 21, NY Giants 0
Championship	.at Chicago 24, LA Rams 0

Super Bowl XX

Jan. 26, 1986
Louisiana Superdome, New Orleans
Favorite: Bears by 10—Attendance: 73,818

Chicago Bears (17-1) 13   10 21   2 — **46**
New England (14-5) 3   0   0   7 — **10**
MVP: Chicago DE Richard Dent (Bears defense: 7 sacks, 6 turnovers, 1 safety and gave up just 123 total yards)

1986 SEASON

AFC Playoffs

First Round . . . . .at *NY Jets 35, *Kansas City 15
Second Round . . . . . . .at Cleveland 23, NY Jets 20 (OT)
at Denver 22, New England 17
Championship . . . . . . .Denver 23, at Cleveland 20 (OT)

NFC Playoffs

First Round . . . . .at *Washington 19, *LA Rams 7
Second Round . . . . .Washington 27, at Chicago 13
at NY Giants 49, San Francisco 3
Championship . . . . .at NY Giants 17, Washington 0

Super Bowl XXI
Jan. 25, 1987
Rose Bowl, Pasadena
Favorite: Giants by 9½—Attendance: 101,063

Denver (13-5) 10   0   0 10 — **20**
NY Giants (16-2) 7   2 17 13 — **39**
MVP: NY Giants QB Phil Simms (22 for 25, 268 yds, 3 TD; 3 carries, 25 yds)

1987 SEASON

A 24-day players' strike shortened the regular season to 15 games with replacement teams playing for three weeks.

AFC Playoffs

First Round . . . . .at *Houston 23, *Seattle 20 (OT)
Second Round . . . . . . .at Cleveland 38, Indianapolis 21
at Denver 34, Houston 10
Championship . . . . .at Denver 38, Cleveland 33

NFC Playoffs

First Round . . . .*Minnesota 44, at *New Orleans 10
Second Round . . . . . .Minnesota 36, at San Francisco 24
Washington 21, at Chicago 17
Championship . . . . . . .at Washington 17, Minnesota 10

Super Bowl XXII
Jan. 31, 1988
San Diego/Jack Murphy Stadium
Favorite: Broncos by 3½—Attendance: 73,302

Washington (13-4) . . . . .0 35   0   7 — **42**
Denver (12-4-1) 10   0   0   0 — **10**
MVP: Washington QB Doug Williams (18 for 29, 340 yds, 4 TD, 1 Int)

1988 SEASON

AFC Playoffs

First Round . . . .*Houston 24, at *Cleveland 23
Second Round . . . . .at Buffalo 17, Houston 10
at Cincinnati 21, Seattle 13
Championship . . . . .at Cincinnati 21, Buffalo 10

NFC Playoffs

First Round . . . . .at *Minnesota 28, *LA Rams 17
Second Round . . . . . . .at San Francisco 34, Minnesota 9
at Chicago 20, Philadelphia 12
Championship . . . . . . .San Francisco 28, at Chicago 3

Super Bowl XXIII
Jan. 22, 1989
Joe Robbie Stadium, Miami
Favorite: 49ers by 7—Attendance: 75,129

Cincinnati (14-4) 0   3 10   3 — **16**
San Francisco (12-6) 3   0   3 14 — **20**
MVP: San Francisco WR Jerry Rice (11 catches, 215 yds, 1 TD; 1 carry, 5 yds)

1989 SEASON

AFC Playoffs

First Round . . . .*Pittsburgh 26, at *Houston 23
Second Round . . . . .at Cleveland 34, Buffalo 30
at Denver 24, Pittsburgh 23
Championship . . . . .at Denver 37, Cleveland 21

NFC Playoffs

First Round . . . .*LA Rams 21, at *Philadelphia 7
Second Round . . . . .LA Rams 19, NY Giants 13 (OT)
at San Francisco 41, Minnesota 13
Championship . . . . .at San Francisco 30, LA Rams 3

Super Bowl XXIV
Jan. 28, 1990
Louisiana Superdome, New Orleans
Favorite: 49ers by 12½—Attendance: 72,919

San Francisco (17-2) . . . . .13 14 14 14 — **55**
Denver (13-6) 3   0   7   0 — **10**
MVP: San Francisco QB Joe Montana (22 for 29, 297 yds, 5 TD)

1990 SEASON

AFC Playoffs

First Round . . . . .at *Miami 17, *Kansas City 16
at Cincinnati 41, *Houston 14
Second Round . . . . .at Buffalo 44, Miami 34
at LA Raiders 20, Cincinnati 10
Championship . . . . .at Buffalo 51, LA Raiders 3

NFC Playoffs

First Round . . . .*Washington 20, at *Philadelphia 6
at Chicago 16, *New Orleans 6
Second Round . . . . . .at San Francisco 28, Washington 10
at NY Giants 31, Chicago 3
Championship . . . . . . .NY Giants 15, at San Francisco 13

Super Bowl XXV
Jan. 27, 1991
Tampa Stadium, Tampa
Favorite: Bills by 7—Attendance: 73,813

Buffalo (15-4) 3   9   0   7 — **19**
NY Giants (16-3) 3   7   7   3 — **20**
MVP: NY Giants RB Ottis Anderson (21 carries, 102 yds, 1 TD; 1 catch, 7 yds)

1991 SEASON

AFC Playoffs

First Round . . . . .at *Kansas City 10, *LA Raiders 6
at Houston 17, *NY Jets 10
Second Round . . . . .at Denver 26, Houston 24
at Buffalo 37, Kansas City 14
Championship . . . . .at Buffalo 10, Denver 7

NFC Playoffs

First Round . . . .*Atlanta 27, at New Orleans 20
*Dallas 17, at *Chicago 13
Second Round . . . . .at Washington 24, Atlanta 7
at Detroit 38, Dallas 6
Championship . . . . .at Washington 41, Detroit 10

Super Bowl XXVI
Jan. 26, 1992
Hubert Humphrey Metrodome, Minneapolis
Favorite: Redskins by 7—Attendance: 63,130

Washington (16-2) . . . . .0 17 14   6 — **37**
Buffalo (15-3) 0   0 10 14 — **24**
MVP: Washington QB Mark Rypien (18 for 33, 292 yds, 2 TD, 1 Int)

Super Bowl Playoffs (Cont.)

1992 SEASON

AFC Playoffs

First Round	at *Buffalo 41, *Houston 38 (OT)
	at San Diego 17, *Kansas City 0
Second Round	Buffalo 24, at Pittsburgh 3
	at Miami 31, San Diego 0
Championship	Buffalo 29, at Miami 10

NFC Playoffs

First Round	*Washington 24, at Minnesota 7
	*Philadelphia 36, at *New Orleans 20
Second Round	at San Francisco 20, Washington 13
	at Dallas 34, Philadelphia 10
Championship	Dallas 30, at San Francisco 20

Super Bowl XXVII
Jan. 31, 1993
Rose Bowl, Pasadena
Favorite: Cowboys by 7—Attendance: 98,374

Buffalo (14-5) 7   3   7   0 — **17**
Dallas (15-3) ....14 14   3 21 — **52**
MVP: Dallas QB Troy Aikman (22 for 30, 273 yds, 4 TD)

1993 SEASON

AFC Playoffs

First Round	at Kansas City 27, *Pittsburgh 24 (OT)
	at *LA Raiders 42, *Denver 24
Second Round	at Buffalo 29, LA Raiders 23
	Kansas City 28, at Houston 20
Championship	at Buffalo 30, Kansas City 13

NFC Playoffs

First Round	*Green Bay 28, at Detroit 24
	at *NY Giants 17, *Minnesota 10
Second Round	at San Francisco 44, NY Giants 3
	at Dallas 27, Green Bay 17
Championship	at Dallas 38, San Francisco 21

Super Bowl XXVIII
Jan. 30, 1994
Georgia Dome, Atlanta
Favorite: Cowboys by 10½—Attendance: 72,817

Dallas (15-4) 6   0 14 10 — **30**
Buffalo (14-5) .... 3 10   0   0 — **13**
MVP: Dallas RB Emmitt Smith (30 carries, 132 yds, 2 TDs;
4 catches, 26 yds)

1994 SEASON

AFC Playoffs

First Round	at Miami 27, *Kansas City 17
	at *Cleveland 20, *New England 13
Second Round	at Pittsburgh 29, Cleveland 9
	at San Diego 22, Miami 21
Championship	San Diego 17, at Pittsburgh 13

NFC Playoffs

First Round	at *Green Bay 16, *Detroit 12
	*Chicago 25, at Minnesota 18
Second Round	at San Francisco 44, Chicago 15
	at Dallas 35, Green Bay 9
Championship	at San Francisco 38, Dallas 28

Super Bowl XXIX
Jan. 29, 1995
Joe Robbie Stadium, Miami
Favorite: 49ers by 18 —Attendance: 74,107

San Diego (13-5) 7   3   8   8 — **26**
San Francisco (15-3) ......14 14 14   7 — **49**
MVP: San Francisco QB Steve Young (24 for 36, 325 yds,
6 TD)

1995 SEASON

AFC Playoffs

First Round	at Buffalo 37, *Miami 22
	*Indianapolis 35, at *San Diego 20
Second Round	at Pittsburgh 40, Buffalo 21
	Indianapolis 10, at Kansas City 7
Championship	at Pittsburgh 20, Indianapolis 16

NFC Playoffs

First Round	at *Philadelphia 58, *Detroit 37
	at Green Bay 37, *Atlanta 20
Second Round	Green Bay 27, at San Francisco 17
	at Dallas 38, Philadelphia 11
Championship	at Dallas 38, Green Bay 27

Super Bowl XXX
Jan. 28, 1996
Sun Devil Stadium, Tempe, Ariz.
Favorite: Cowboys by 13½—Attendance: 76,347

Dallas (14-4) 10   3   7   7 — **27**
Pittsburgh (13-5) 0   7   0 10 — **17**
MVP: Dallas CB Larry Brown (2 interceptions for 77 yds)

1996 SEASON

AFC Playoffs

First Round	*Jacksonville 30, at *Buffalo 27
	at Pittsburgh 42, *Indianapolis 14
Second Round	Jacksonville 30, at Denver 27
	at New England 28, Pittsburgh 3
Championship	at New England 20, Jacksonville 6

NFC Playoffs

First Round	at Dallas 40, *Minnesota 15
	at *San Francisco 14, *Philadelphia 0
Second Round	at Green Bay 35, San Francisco 14
	at Carolina 26, Dallas 17
Championship	at Green Bay 30, Carolina 13

Super Bowl XXXI
Jan. 26, 1997
Louisiana Superdome, New Orleans
Favorite: Packers by 14—Attendance: 72,301

New England (13-5) 14   0   7   0 — **21**
Green Bay (15-3) ....10 17   8   0 — **35**
MVP: Green Bay KR Desmond Howard (4 kickoff returns for
154 yds and 1 TD, also 6 punt returns for 90 yds)

1997 SEASON

AFC Playoffs

First Round	at *Denver 42, *Jacksonville 17
	at New England 17, *Miami 3
Second Round	at Pittsburgh 7, New England 6
	Denver 14, at Kansas City 10
Championship	Denver 24, at Pittsburgh 21

NFC Playoffs

First Round	*Minnesota 23, at NY Giants 22
	at *Tampa Bay 20, *Detroit 10
Second Round	at San Francisco 38, Minnesota 22
	at Green Bay 21, Tampa Bay 7
Championship	Green Bay 23, at San Francisco 10

Super Bowl XXXII
Jan. 25, 1998
Qualcomm Stadium, San Diego
Favorite: Packers by 11½—Attendance: 68,912

Green Bay (15-3) 7   7   3   7 — **24**
Denver (15-4) .... 7 10   7   7 — **31**
MVP: Denver RB Terrell Davis (30 carries, 157 yds, 3 TDs; 2
catches, 8 yds)

1998 SEASON

AFC Playoffs

First Round . . . . .at *Miami 24, *Buffalo 17
at Jacksonville 25, *New England 10
Second Round . . . . .at NY Jets 34, Jacksonville 24
at Denver 38, Miami 3
Championship . . . . at Denver 23, NY Jets 10

NFC Playoffs

First Round . . . . . . .at *San Francisco 30, *Green Bay 27
*Arizona 20, at Dallas 7
Second Round . . . . .at Atlanta 20, San Francisco 18
at Minnesota 41, Arizona 21
Championship . . . . . . .Atlanta 30, at Minnesota 27 (OT)

Super Bowl XXXIII
Jan. 31, 1999
Pro Player Stadium, Miami
Favorite: Broncos by 7½—Attendance: 74,803

Denver (16-2)	7	10	0	17	**34**
Atlanta (16-2)	3	3	0	13	**19**

MVP: Denver QB John Elway (18 for 29, 336 yds, 1 TD, 1 Int and 1 rushing TD)

1999 SEASON

AFC Playoffs

First Round . . . . .at *Tennessee 22, *Buffalo 16
*Miami 20, at Seattle 17
Second Round . . . . .at Jacksonville 62, Miami 7
Tennessee 19, at Indianapolis 16
Championship . . . . . . .Tennessee 33, at Jacksonville 14

NFC Playoffs

First Round . . . . .at Washington 27, *Detroit 13
*Minnesota 27, *Dallas 10
Second Round . . . . . .at Tampa Bay 14, Washington 13
at St. Louis 49, Minnesota 37
Championship . . . . . . .at St. Louis 11, Tampa Bay 6

Super Bowl XXXIV
Jan. 30, 2000
Georgia Dome, Atlanta
Favorite: Rams by 7—Attendance: 72,625

St. Louis (15-3)	3	6	7	7	**23**
Tennessee (16-3)	0	0	6	10	**16**

MVP: St. Louis QB Kurt Warner (24 for 45, 414 yds, 2 TDs)

2000 SEASON

AFC Playoffs

First Round . . . . .at Miami 23, *Indianapolis 17 (OT)
at *Baltimore 21, *Denver 3
Second Round . . . . .at Oakland 27, Miami 0
Baltimore 24, at Tennessee 10
Championship . . . . .Baltimore 16, at Oakland 3

NFC Playoffs

First Round . . . . .at New Orleans 31, *St. Louis 28
at *Philadelphia 21, *Tampa Bay 3
Second Round . . . . . .at Minnesota 34, New Orleans 16
at NY Giants 20, Philadelphia 10
Championship . . . . .at NY Giants 41, Minnesota 0

Super Bowl XXXV
Jan. 28, 2001
Raymond James Stadium, Tampa
Favorite: Ravens by 3—Attendance: 71,921

Baltimore (15-4)	7	3	14	10	**34**
NY Giants (14-4)	0	0	7	0	**7**

MVP: Baltimore LB Ray Lewis (5 tackles, 4 passes defended)

2001 SEASON

AFC Playoffs

First Round . . . . .at Oakland 38, *NY Jets 24
*Baltimore 20, at *Miami 3
Second Round . . . .at New England 16, Oakland 13 (OT)
at Pittsburgh 27, Baltimore 10
Championship . . . . New England 24, at Pittsburgh 17

NFC Playoffs

First Round . . . . .at Philadelphia 31, *Tampa Bay 9
at *Green Bay 25, *San Francisco 15
Second Round . . . . .Philadelphia 33, at Chicago 19
at St. Louis 45, Green Bay 17
Championship . . . . . . .at St. Louis 29, Philadelphia 24

Super Bowl XXXVI
Feb. 3, 2002
Louisiana Superdome, New Orleans
Favorite: Rams by 14—Attendance: 72,922

St. Louis (16-2)	3	0	0	14	**17**
New England (13-5)	0	14	3	3	**20**

MVP: New England QB Tom Brady (16 for 27, 145 yds, 1 TD)

2002 SEASON

AFC Playoffs

First Round . . . . .at NY Jets 41, *Indianapolis 0
at Pittsburgh 36, *Cleveland 33
Second Round . . . . .at Tennessee 34, Pittsburgh 31 (OT)
at Oakland 30, NY Jets 10
Championship . . . . .at Oakland 41, Tennessee 24

NFC Playoffs

First Round . . . .*Atlanta 27, at Green Bay 7
at San Francisco 39, *NY Giants 38
Second Round . . . . .at Philadelphia 20, Atlanta 6
at Tampa Bay 31, San Francisco 6
Championship . . . . . . Tampa Bay 27, at Philadelphia 10

Super Bowl XXXVII
Jan. 26, 2003
Qualcomm Stadium, San Diego
Favorite: Raiders by 3½—Attendance: 67,603

Oakland (13-5)	3	0	6	12	**21**
Tampa Bay (14-4)	3	17	14	14	**48**

MVP: Tampa Bay S Dexter Jackson (2 interceptions for 34 yards)

2003 SEASON

AFC Playoffs

First Round . . . .*Tennessee 20, at Baltimore 17
at Indianapolis 41, *Denver 10
Second Round . . . . . .at New England 17, Tennessee 14
Indianapolis 38, at Kansas City 31
Championship . . . . at New England 24, Indianapolis 14

NFC Playoffs

First Round . . . . .at Carolina 29, *Dallas 10
at Green Bay 33, Seattle 27 (OT)
Second Round . . . . . .Carolina 29, at St. Louis 23 (2OT)
at Philadelphia 20, Green Bay 17 (OT)
Championship . . . . Carolina 14, at Philadelphia 3

Super Bowl XXXVIII
Feb. 1, 2004
Reliant Stadium, Houston
Favorite: Patriots by 7—Attendance: 71,525

Carolina (14-5)	0	10	0	19	**29**
New England (16-2)	0	14	0	18	**32**

MVP: New England QB Tom Brady (32 for 48, 354 yds, 3 TD, 1 Int)

Before the Super Bowl

The first NFL champion was the Akron Pros in 1920, when the league was called the American Professional Football Association (APFA) and the title went to the team with the best regular season record. The APFA changed its name to the National Football League in 1922.

The first playoff game with the championship at stake came in 1932, when the Chicago Bears (6-1-6) and Portsmouth (Ohio) Spartans (6-1-4) ended the regular season tied for first place. The Bears won the subsequent playoff, 9-0. Due to a snowstorm and cold weather, the game was moved from Wrigley Field to an improvised 80-yard dirt field at Chicago Stadium, making it the first indoor title game as well.

The NFL Championship Game decided the league title until the NFL merged with the AFL and the first Super Bowl was played following the 1966 season.

NFL Champions, 1920-32

Winning player-coaches noted by position.
Multiple winners: Canton-Cleveland Bulldogs and Green Bay (3); Chicago Staleys/Bears (2).

Year	Champion	Head Coach	Year	Champion	Head Coach
1920	Akron Pros	Fritz Pollard, HB & Elgie Tobin, QB	1927	New York Giants	Earl Potteiger, QB
1921	Chicago Staleys	George Halas, E	1928	Providence Steam Roller	Jimmy Conzelman, HB
1922	Canton Bulldogs	Guy Chamberlin, E	1929	Green Bay Packers	Curly Lambeau, QB
1923	Canton Bulldogs	Guy Chamberlin, E	1930	Green Bay Packers	Curly Lambeau
1924	Cleveland Bulldogs	Guy Chamberlin, E	1931	Green Bay Packers	Curly Lambeau
1925	Chicago Cardinals	Norm Barry	1932	Chicago Bears	Ralph Jones
1926	Frankford Yellow Jackets	Guy Chamberlin, E		(Bears beat Portsmouth-OH in playoff, 9-0)	

NFL-NFC Championship Game

NFL Championship games from 1933-69 and NFC Championship games since the completion of the NFL-AFL merger following the 1969 season.
Multiple winners: Green Bay (10); Dallas (8); Chicago Bears and Washington (7); NY Giants (6); San Francisco and Cle-LA-St.L Rams (5); Cleveland Browns, Detroit, Minnesota, and Philadelphia (4); Baltimore Colts (3).

Season	Winner	Head Coach	Score	Loser	Head Coach	Site
1933	Chicago Bears	George Halas	23-21	New York	Steve Owen	Chicago
1934	New York	Steve Owen	30-13	Chicago Bears	George Halas	New York
1935	Detroit	Potsy Clark	26-7	New York	Steve Owen	Detroit
1936	Green Bay	Curly Lambeau	21-6	Boston Redskins	Ray Flaherty	New York
1937	Washington Redskins	Ray Flaherty	28-21	Chicago Bears	George Halas	Chicago
1938	New York	Steve Owen	23-17	Green Bay	Curly Lambeau	New York
1939	Green Bay	Curly Lambeau	27-0	New York	Steve Owen	Milwaukee
1940	Chicago Bears	George Halas	73-0	Washington	Ray Flaherty	Washington
1941	Chicago Bears	George Halas	37-9	New York	Steve Owen	Chicago
1942	Washington	Ray Flaherty	14-6	Chicago Bears	Hunk Anderson & Luke Johnsos	Washington
1943	Chicago Bears	Hunk Anderson & Luke Johnsos	41-21	Washington	Arthur Bergman	Chicago
1944	Green Bay	Curly Lambeau	14-7	New York	Steve Owen	New York
1945	Cleveland Rams	Adam Walsh	15-14	Washington	Dudley DeGroot	Cleveland
1946	Chicago Bears	George Halas	24-14	New York	Steve Owen	New York
1947	Chicago Cardinals	Jimmy Conzelman	28-21	Philadelphia	Greasy Neale	Chicago
1948	Philadelphia	Greasy Neale	7-0	Chicago Cardinals	Jimmy Conzelman	Philadelphia
1949	Philadelphia	Greasy Neale	14-0	Los Angeles Rams	Clark Shaughnessy	Los Angeles
1950	Cleveland Browns	Paul Brown	30-28	Los Angeles	Joe Stydahar	Cleveland
1951	Los Angeles	Joe Stydahar	24-17	Cleveland	Paul Brown	Los Angeles
1952	Detroit	Buddy Parker	17-7	Cleveland	Paul Brown	Cleveland
1953	Detroit	Buddy Parker	17-16	Cleveland	Paul Brown	Detroit
1954	Cleveland	Paul Brown	56-10	Detroit	Buddy Parker	Cleveland
1955	Cleveland	Paul Brown	38-14	Los Angeles	Sid Gillman	Los Angeles
1956	New York	Jim Lee Howell	47-7	Chicago Bears	Paddy Driscoll	New York
1957	Detroit	George Wilson	59-14	Cleveland	Paul Brown	Detroit
1958	Balt. Colts	Weeb Ewbank	23-17*	New York	Jim Lee Howell	New York
1959	Balt. Colts	Weeb Ewbank	31-16	New York	Jim Lee Howell	Baltimore
1960	Philadelphia	Buck Shaw	17-13	Green Bay	Vince Lombardi	Philadelphia
1961	Green Bay	Vince Lombardi	37-0	New York	Allie Sherman	Green Bay
1962	Green Bay	Vince Lombardi	16-7	New York	Allie Sherman	New York
1963	Chicago	George Halas	14-10	New York	Allie Sherman	Chicago
1964	Cleveland	Blanton Collier	27-0	Balt. Colts	Don Shula	Cleveland
1965	Green Bay	Vince Lombardi	23-12	Cleveland	Blanton Collier	Green Bay
1966	Green Bay	Vince Lombardi	34-27	Dallas	Tom Landry	Dallas
1967	Green Bay	Vince Lombardi	21-17	Dallas	Tom Landry	Green Bay

Season	Winner	Head Coach	Score	Loser	Head Coach	Site
1968	Balt. Colts	Don Shula	34-0	Cleveland	Blanton Collier	Cleveland
1969	Minnesota	Bud Grant	27-7	Cleveland	Blanton Collier	Minnesota
1970	Dallas	Tom Landry	17-10	San Francisco	Dick Nolan	San Francisco
1971	Dallas	Tom Landry	14-3	SanFrancisco	Dick Nolan	Dallas
1972	Washington	George Allen	26-3	Dallas	Tom Landry	Washington
1973	Minnesota	Bud Grant	27-10	Dallas	Tom Landry	Dallas
1974	Minnesota	Bud Grant	14-10	Los Angeles	Chuck Knox	Minnesota
1975	Dallas	Tom Landry	37-7	Los Angeles	Chuck Knox	Los Angeles
1976	Minnesota	Bud Grant	24-13	Los Angeles	Chuck Knox	Minnesota
1977	Dallas	Tom Landry	23-6	Minnesota	Bud Grant	Dallas
1978	Dallas	Tom Landry	28-0	Los Angeles	Ray Malavasi	Los Angele
1979	Los Angeles	Ray Malavasi	9-0	Tampa Bay	John McKay	Tampa Bay
1980	Philadelphia	Dick Vermeil	20-7	Dallas	Tom Landry	Philadelphia
1981	San Francisco	Bill Walsh	28-27	Dallas	Tom Landry	San Francisco
1982	Washington	Joe Gibbs	31-17	Dallas	Tom Landry	Washington
1983	Washington	Joe Gibbs	24-21	San Francisco	Bill Walsh	Washington
1984	San Francisco	Bill Walsh	23-0	Chicago	Mike Ditka	San Francisco
1985	Chicago	Mike Ditka	24-0	Los Angeles	John Robinson	Chicago
1986	New York	Bill Parcells	17-0	Washington	Joe Gibbs	New York
1987	Washington	Joe Gibbs	17-10	Minnesota	Jerry Burns	Washington
1988	San Francisco	Bill Walsh	28-3	Chicago	Mike Ditka	Chicago
1989	San Francisco	George Seifert	30-3	Los Angeles	John Robinson	San Francisco
1990	New York	Bill Parcells	15-13	San Francisco	George Seifert	San Francisco
1991	Washington	Joe Gibbs	41-10	Detroit	Wayne Fontes	Washington
1992	Dallas	Jimmy Johnson	30-20	San Francisco	George Seifert	San Francisco
1993	Dallas	Jimmy Johnson	38-21	San Francisco	George Seifert	Dallas
1994	San Francisco	George Seifert	38-28	Dallas	Barry Switzer	San Francisco
1995	Dallas	Barry Switzer	38-27	Green Bay	Mike Holmgren	Dallas
1996	Green Bay	Mike Holmgren	30-13	Carolina	Dom Capers	Green Bay
1997	Green Bay	Mike Holmgren	23-10	San Francisco	Steve Mariucci	San Francisco
1998	Atlanta	Dan Reeves	30-27*	Minnesota	Dennis Green	Minnesota
1999	St. Louis	Dick Vermeil	11-6	Tampa Bay	Tony Dungy	St. Louis
2000	New York	Jim Fassel	41-0	Minnesota	Dennis Green	New York
2001	St. Louis	Mike Martz	29-24	Philadelphia	Andy Reid	St. Louis
2002	Tampa Bay	Jon Gruden	27-10	Philadelphia	Andy Reid	Philadelphia
2003	Carolina	John Fox	14-3	Philadelphia	Andy Reid	Philadelphia

*Sudden death overtime

NFL-NFC Championship Game Appearances

App		W	L	Pct	PF	PA	App		W	L	Pct	PF	PA
17	NY Giants	6	11	.353	281	322	8	Minnesota	4	4	.500	135	151
16	Dallas Cowboys	8	8	.500	361	319	8	Philadelphia	4	4	.500	116	118
14	Cle-LA-St.L Rams	5	9	.357	163	300	6	Detroit	4	2	.667	139	141
13	Green Bay Packers	10	3	.769	303	177	4	Baltimore Colts	3	1	.750	88	60
13	Chicago Bears	7	6	.538	286	245	3	Tampa Bay	1	2	.333	33	30
12	Boston-Wash. Redskins	7	5	.583	222	255	2	Chicago Cardinals	1	1	.500	28	28
12	San Francisco	5	7	.417	245	222	2	Carolina	1	1	.500	27	33
11	Cleveland Browns	4	7	.364	224	253	1	Atlanta	1	0	1.000	30	27

AFL-AFC Championship Game

AFL Championship games from 1960-69 and AFC Championship games since the completion of the NFL-AFL merger following the 1969 season.

Multiple winners: Buffalo and Denver (6); Miami, Oakland-LA Raiders and Pittsburgh (5); New England (4); Dallas Texans-KC Chiefs and Houston Oilers-Tennessee Titans (3); Cincinnati and San Diego (2).

Season	Winner	Head Coach	Score	Loser	Head Coach	Site
1960	Houston	Lou Rymkus	24-16	LA Chargers	Sid Gillman	Houston
1961	Houston	Wally Lemm	10-3	SD Chargers	Sid Gillman	San Diego
1962	Dallas	Hank Stram	20-17*	Houston	Pop Ivy	Houston
1963	San Diego	Sid Gillman	51-10	Boston Patriots	Mike Holovak	San Diego
1964	Buffalo	Lou Saban	20-7	SanDiego	Sid Gillman	Buffalo
1965	Buffalo	Lou Saban	23-0	San Diego	Sid Gillman	San Diego
1966	Kansas City	Hank Stram	31-7	Buffalo	Joel Collier	Buffalo
1967	Oakland	John Rauch	40-7	Houston	Wally Lemm	Oakland
1968	NY Jets	Weeb Ewbank	27-23	Oakland	John Rauch	New York
1969	Kansas City	Hank Stram	17-7	Oakland	John Madden	Oakland
1970	Balt. Colts	Don McCafferty	27-17	Oakland	John Madden	Baltimore
1971	Miami	Don Shula	21-0	Balt. Colts	Don McCafferty	Miami
1972	Miami	Don Shula	21-17	Pittsburgh	Chuck Noll	Pittsburgh

AFL-AFC Championship Game (Cont.)

Season	Winner	Head Coach	Score	Loser	Head Coach	Site
1973	Miami	Don Shula	27-10	Oakland	John Madden	Miami
1974	Pittsburgh	Chuck Noll	24-13	Oakland	John Madden	Oakland
1975	Pittsburgh	Chuck Noll	16-10	Oakland	John Madden	Pittsburgh
1976	Oakland	John Madden	24-7	Pittsburgh	Chuck Noll	Oakland
1977	Denver	Red Miller	20-17	Oakland	John Madden	Denver
1978	Pittsburgh	Chuck Noll	34-5	Houston	Bum Phillips	Pittsburgh
1979	Pittsburgh	Chuck Noll	27-13	Houston	Bum Phillips	Pittsburgh
1980	Oakland	Tom Flores	34-27	San Diego	Don Coryell	San Diego
1981	Cincinnati	Forrest Gregg	27-7	San Diego	Don Coryell	Cincinnati
1982	Miami	Don Shula	14-0	NYJets	Walt Michaels	Miami
1983	LA Raiders	Tom Flores	30-14	Seattle	Chuck Knox	Los Angeles
1984	Miami	Don Shula	45-28	Pittsburgh	Chuck Noll	Miami
1985	New England	Raymond Berry	31-14	Miami	Don Shula	Miami
1986	Denver	Dan Reeves	23-20*	Cleveland	Marty Schottenheimer	Cleveland
1987	Denver	Dan Reeves	38-33	Cleveland	Marty Schottenheimer	Denver
1988	Cincinnati	Sam Wyche	21-10	Buffalo	Marv Levy	Cincinnati
1989	Denver	Dan Reeves	37-21	Cleveland	Bud Carson	Denver
1990	Buffalo	Marv Levy	51-3	LA Raiders	Art Shell	Buffalo
1991	Buffalo	Marv Levy	10-7	Denver	Dan Reeves	Buffalo
1992	Buffalo	Marv Levy	29-10	Miami	Don Shula	Miami
1993	Buffalo	Marv Levy	30-13	Kansas City	Marty Schottenheimer	Buffalo
1994	San Diego	Bobby Ross	17-13	Pittsburgh	Bill Cowher	Pittsburgh
1995	Pittsburgh	Bill Cowher	20-16	Indianapolis	Ted Marchibroda	Pittsburgh
1996	New England	Bill Parcells	20-6	Jacksonville	Tom Coughlin	New England
1997	Denver	Mike Shanahan	24-21	Pittsburgh	Bill Cowher	Pittsburgh
1998	Denver	Mike Shanahan	23-10	NY Jets	Bill Parcells	Denver
1999	Tennessee	Jeff Fisher	33-14	Jacksonville	Tom Coughlin	Jacksonville
2000	Balt. Ravens	Brian Billick	16-3	Oakland	Jon Gruden	Oakland
2001	New England	Bill Belichick	24-17	Pittsburgh	Bill Cowher	Pittsburgh
2002	Oakland	Bill Callahan	41-24	Tennessee	Jeff Fisher	Oakland
2003	New England	Bill Belichick	24-14	Indianapolis	Tony Dungy	New England

*Sudden death overtime

AFL-AFC Championship Game Appearances

App		W	L	Pct	PF	PA	App		W	L	Pct	PF	PA
14	Oakland-LA Raiders	9	5	.357	272	304	4	Dallas Texans/KC Chiefs	1	3	.750	81	61
11	Pittsburgh	5	6	.455	224	212	4	Baltimore-Indy Colts	1	3	.250	57	82
8	Buffalo	6	2	.750	180	92	3	NY Jets	1	2	.333	37	60
8	Houston Oilers/Ten. Titans	3	5	.375	133	195	3	Cleveland	0	3	.000	74	98
8	LA-San Diego Chargers	2	6	.250	128	161	2	Cincinnati	2	0	1.000	48	17
7	Denver	6	1	.857	172	132	2	Jacksonville	0	2	.000	20	53
7	Miami	5	2	.714	152	115	1	Baltimore Ravens	1	0	1.000	16	3
5	Boston-NE Patriots	4	1	.800	109	102	1	Seattle	0	1	.000	14	30

NFL Divisional Champions

The NFL adopted divisional play for the first time in 1967, splitting both conferences into two four-team divisions—the Capitol and Century divisions in the East and the Central and Coastal divisions in the West. A merger with the AFL in 1970 increased NFL membership to 26 teams and made it necessary for realignment. Two 13-team conferences—the AFC and NFC—were formed by moving established NFL clubs in Baltimore, Cleveland and Pittsburgh to the AFC and rearranging both conferences into Eastern, Central and Western divisions. Expansion has since increased the league to 32 teams (beginning in 2002) with four NFC divisions and four AFC divisions, all with four teams each.

Division champions are listed below; teams that went on to win the Super Bowl are in **bold** type. Note that in the 1980 season, Oakland won the Super Bowl as a wild card team, as did Denver in 1997 and Baltimore in 2000; and in 1982, the players' strike shortened the regular season to nine games and eliminated divisional play for one season.

Multiple champions (since 1970): **AFC**—Pittsburgh (16); Miami and Oakland-LA Raiders (12); Denver (9); Baltimore-Indianapolis Colts and Buffalo (7); Cleveland and New England (6); Cincinnati, Kansas City and San Diego (5); Houston Oilers-Tennessee Titans (4); Jacksonville, NY Jets and Seattle (2). **NFC**—San Francisco (17); Dallas (15); Minnesota (14); LA-St. Louis Rams (11); Chicago (7); Green Bay and Washington (6); NY Giants and Philadelphia (5); Tampa Bay (4); Detroit (3); Atlanta, Carolina, New Orleans and St. Louis Cardinals (2).

	American Football League			National Football League			
Season	East	West		Season	East	West	
1966	Buffalo	Kansas City		1966	Dallas	**Green Bay**	

Season	East	West		Season	Capitol	Century	Central	Coastal
1967	Houston	Oakland		1967	Dallas	Cleveland	**Green Bay**	LA Rams
1968	**NY Jets**	Oakland		1968	Dallas	Cleveland	Minnesota	Baltimore
1969	NY Jets	Oakland		1969	Dallas	Cleveland	Minnesota	LA Rams

Note: Kansas City, an AFL second-place team, won the Super Bowl in the 1969 season.

American Football Conference

Season	East	Central	West
1970	**Balt. Colts**	Cincinnati	Oakland
1971	Miami	Cleveland	Kansas City
1972	**Miami**	Pittsburgh	Oakland
1973	**Miami**	Cincinnati	Oakland
1974	Miami	**Pittsburgh**	Oakland
1975	Balt.Colts	**Pittsburgh**	Oakland
1976	Balt.Colts	Pittsburgh	**Oakland**
1977	Balt.Colts	Pittsburgh	Denver
1978	New England	**Pittsburgh**	Denver
1979	Miami	**Pittsburgh**	San Diego
1980	Buffalo	Cleveland	San Diego
1981	Miami	Cincinnati	San Diego
1982	—	—	—
1983	Miami	Pittsburgh	**LA Raiders**
1984	Miami	Pittsburgh	Denver
1985	Miami	Cleveland	LA Raiders
1986	New England	Cleveland	Denver
1987	Indianapolis	Cleveland	Denver
1988	Buffalo	Cincinnati	Seattle
1989	Buffalo	Cleveland	Denver
1990	Buffalo	Cincinnati	LA Raiders
1991	Buffalo	Houston	Denver
1992	Miami	Pittsburgh	San Diego
1993	Buffalo	Houston	Kansas City
1994	Miami	Pittsburgh	San Diego
1995	Buffalo	Pittsburgh	Kansas City
1996	New England	Pittsburgh	Denver
1997	New England	Pittsburgh	Kansas City
1998	NY Jets	Jacksonville	**Denver**
1999	Indianapolis	Jacksonville	Seattle
2000	Miami	Tennessee	Oakland
2001	**New England**	Pittsburgh	Oakland

Season	East	North	South	West
2002	NY Jets	Pittsburgh	Tennessee	Oakland
2003	**New Eng.**	Baltimore	Indianapolis	Kansas City

National Football Conference

Season	East	Central	West
1970	Dallas	Minnesota	San Francisco
1971	**Dallas**	Minnesota	San Francisco
1972	Washington	Green Bay	San Francisco
1973	Dallas	Minnesota	LA Rams
1974	St. Louis	Minnesota	LA Rams
1975	St. Louis	Minnesota	LA Rams
1976	Dallas	Minnesota	LA Rams
1977	**Dallas**	Minnesota	LA Rams
1978	Dallas	Minnesota	LA Rams
1979	Dallas	Tampa Bay	LA Rams
1980	Philadelphia	Minnesota	Atlanta
1981	Dallas	Tampa Bay	**San Francisco**
1982	—	—	—
1983	Washington	Detroit	San Francisco
1984	Washington	Chicago	**San Francisco**
1985	Dallas	**Chicago**	LA Rams
1986	**NY Giants**	Chicago	San Francisco
1987	**Washington**	Chicago	San Francisco
1988	Philadelphia	Chicago	**San Francisco**
1989	NY Giants	Minnesota	**San Francisco**
1990	**NY Giants**	Chicago	San Francisco
1991	**Washington**	Detroit	New Orleans
1992	**Dallas**	Minnesota	San Francisco
1993	**Dallas**	Detroit	San Francisco
1994	Dallas	Minnesota	**San Francisco**
1995	**Dallas**	Green Bay	San Francisco
1996	Dallas	**Green Bay**	Carolina
1997	NY Giants	Green Bay	San Francisco
1998	Dallas	Minnesota	Atlanta
1999	Washington	Tampa Bay	**St. Louis**
2000	NY Giants	Minnesota	New Orleans
2001	Philadelphia	Chicago	St. Louis

Season	East	North	South	West
2002	Philadelphia	Green Bay	**Tampa Bay**	San Fran.
2003	Philadelphia	Green Bay	Carolina	St. Louis

Overall Postseason Games

The postseason records of all NFL teams, ranked by number of playoff games participated in from 1933-2003.

Gm		W	L	Pct	PF	PA
54	Dallas Cowboys	.32	22	.593	1281	1008
43	Oakland-LA Raiders	.25	18	.581	1028	797
42	San Francisco 49ers	.25	17	.595	1044	853
41	Cle-LA-St.L Rams	.18	23	.439	726	877
40	Pittsburgh Steelers	.23	17	.575	912	808
40	Minnesota Vikings	.17	23	.425	779	913
39	Miami Dolphins	.20	19	.513	780	848
37	Green Bay Packers	.24	13	.649	871	692
37	Boston-Wash. Redskins	.22	15	.595	778	642
37	New York Giants	.16	21	.432	647	699
31	Houston Oilers/Ten. Titans	14	17	.452	563	732
31	Cleveland Browns	.11	20	.355	629	728
29	Denver Broncos	.16	13	.552	626	698
29	Buffalo Bills	.14	15	.483	681	658
29	Chicago Bears	.14	15	.483	598	585
29	Philadelphia Eagles	.14	15	.483	531	513

Gm		W	L	Pct	PF	PA
26	Balt-Indianapolis Colts	.12	14	.462	486	537
23	Boston-NE Patriots	.13	10	.565	443	461
20	Dallas Texans/KC Chiefs	.8	12	.400	332	422
18	LA-San Diego Chargers	.7	11	.389	332	428
17	Detroit Lions	.7	10	.412	365	404
16	New York Jets	.7	9	.438	335	315
13	Tampa Bay Buccaneers	.6	7	.462	206	238
12	Cincinnati Bengals	.5	7	.417	246	257
12	Atlanta Falcons	.5	7	.417	241	287
9	Seattle Seahawks	.3	6	.333	172	192
8	Jacksonville Jaguars	.4	4	.500	208	200
7	Baltimore Ravens	.5	2	.714	142	73
7	Chi-St.L.-Ari. Cardinals	.2	5	.286	122	182
6	Carolina Panthers	.4	2	.667	140	115
6	New Orleans Saints	.1	5	.167	103	185

Champions of Leagues That No Longer Exist

No professional league in American sports has had to contend with more pretenders to the throne than the NFL. Eight times in nine decades, a rival league has risen up to challenge the NFL and seven of them (including the XFL) went under in less than five seasons. Only the fourth American Football League (1960-69) succeeded, forcing the older league to sue for peace and a full partnership in 1966.

Of the seven leagues that didn't make it, only the All-America Football Conference (1946-49) lives on—the Cleveland Browns and San Francisco 49ers joined the NFL after the AAFC folded in 1949. The champions of leagues past are listed below.

American Football League I

Year		Head Coach
1926	Philadelphia Quakers (8-2)	Bob Folwell

Note: Philadelphia was challenged to a postseason game by the 7th place New York Giants (8-4-1) of the NFL. The Giants won, 31-0, in a snowstorm.

American Football League II

Year		Head Coach
1936	Boston Shamrocks (8-3)	George Kenneally
1937	Los Angeles Bulldogs (9-0)	Gus Henderson

Note: Boston was scheduled to play 2nd place Cleveland (5-2-2) in the '36 championship game, but the Shamrock players refused to participate because they were owed pay for past games.

American Football League III

Year		Head Coach
1940	Columbus Bullies (8-1-1)	Phil Bucklew
1941	Columbus Bullies (5-1-2)	Phil Bucklew

All-America Football Conference

Year	Winner	Head Coach	Score	Loser	Head Coach	Site
1946	Cleveland Browns	Paul Brown	14-9	NY Yankees	Ray Flaherty	Cleveland
1947	Cleveland Browns	Paul Brown	14-3	NY Yankees	Ray Flaherty	New York
1948	Cleveland Browns	Paul Brown	49-7	Buffalo Bills	Red Dawson	Cleveland
1949	Cleveland Browns	Paul Brown	21-7	S.F. 49ers	Buck Shaw	Cleveland

World Football League

Year	Winner	Head Coach	Score	Loser	Head Coach	Site
1974	Birmingham Americans	Jack Gotta	22-21	Florida Blazers	Jack Pardee	Birmingham

United States Football League

Year	Winner	Head Coach	Score	Loser	Head Coach	Site
1983	Michigan Panthers	Jim Stanley	24-22	Philadelphia Stars	Jim Mora	Denver
1984	Philadelphia Stars	Jim Mora	23-3	Arizona Wranglers	George Allen	Tampa
1985	Baltimore Stars	Jim Mora	28-24	Oakland Invaders	Charlie Sumner	E. Rutherford

XFL

Year	Winner	Head Coach	Score	Loser	Head Coach	Site
2001	Los Angeles Xtreme	Al Luginbill	38-6	San Fran. Demons	Jim Skipper	Los Angeles

Defunct Leagues

AFL I (1926): Boston Bulldogs, Brooklyn Horseman, Chicago Bulls, Cleveland Panthers, Los Angeles Wildcats, New York Yankees, Newark Bears, Philadelphia Quakers, Rock Island Independents.

AFL II (1936-37): Boston Shamrocks (1936-37); Brooklyn Tigers (1936); Cincinnati Bengals (1937); Cleveland Rams (1936); Los Angeles Bulldogs (1937); New York Yankees (1936-37); Pittsburgh Americans (1936-37); Rochester Tigers (1936-37).

AFL III (1940-41): Boston Bears (1940); Buffalo Indians (1940-41); Cincinnati Bengals (1940-41); Columbus Bullies (1940-41); Milwaukee Chiefs (1940-41); New York Yankees (1940) renamed Americans (1941).

AAFC (1946-49): Brooklyn Dodgers (1946-48) merged to become Brooklyn-New York Yankees (1949); Buffalo Bisons (1946) renamed Bills (1947-49); Chicago Rockets (1946-48) renamed Hornets (1949); Cleveland Browns (1946-49); Los Angeles Dons (1946-49); Miami Seahawks (1946) became Baltimore Colts (1947-49); New York Yankees (1946-48) merged to become Brooklyn-New York Yankees (1949); San Francisco 49ers (1946-49).

WFL (1974-75): Birmingham Americans (1974) renamed Vulcans (1975); Chicago Fire (1974) renamed Winds (1975); Detroit Wheels (1974); Florida Blazers (1974) became San Antonio Wings (1975); The Hawaiians (1974-75); Houston Texans (1974) became Shreveport (La.) Steamer (1974-75); Jacksonville Sharks (1974) renamed Express (1975); Memphis Southmen (1974) also known as Grizzlies (1975); New York Stars (1974) became Charlotte Hornets (1974-75); Philadelphia Bell (1974-75); Portland Storm (1974) renamed Thunder (1975); Southern California Sun (1974-75).

USFL (1983-85): Arizona Wranglers (1983-84) merged with Oklahoma to become Arizona Outlaws (1985); Birmingham Stallions (1983-85); Boston Breakers (1983) became New Orleans Breakers (1984) and then Portland Breakers (1985); Chicago Blitz (1983-84); Denver Gold (1983-85); Houston Gamblers (1984-85); Jacksonville Bulls (1984-85); Los Angeles Express (1983-85); Memphis Showboats (1984-85).

Michigan Panthers (1983-84) merged with Oakland (1985); New Jersey Generals (1983-85); Oakland Invaders (1983-85); Oklahoma Outlaws (1984) merged with Arizona to become Arizona Outlaws (1985); Philadelphia Stars (1983-84) became Baltimore Stars (1985); Pittsburgh Maulers (1984); San Antonio Gunslingers (1984-85); Tampa Bay Bandits (1983-85); Washington Federals (1983-84) became Orlando Renegades (1985).

XFL (2001): Birmingham Thunderbolts, Chicago Enforcers, Las Vegas Outlaws, Los Angeles Xtreme, Memphis Maniax, New York New Jersey Hitmen, Orlando Rage, San Francisco Demons.

NFL Pro Bowl

A postseason All-Star game between the new league champion and a team of professional all-stars was added to the NFL schedule in 1939. In the first game at Wrigley Field in Los Angeles, the NY Giants beat a team made up of players from NFL teams and two independent clubs in Los Angeles (the LA Bulldogs and Hollywood Stars). An all-NFL All-Star team provided the opposition over the next four seasons, but the game was cancelled in 1943.

The Pro Bowl was revived in 1951 as a contest between conference all-star teams: American vs National (1951-53), Eastern vs Western (1954-70), and AFC vs NFC (since 1971). The current AFC-NFC series is tied, 17-17.

The MVP trophy was named the Dan McGuire Award in 1984 after the late SF 49ers publicist and *Honolulu Advertiser* sports columnist.

Year	Winner	Score	Loser	Year	Winner	MVP
1939	NY Giants	13-10	All-Stars	1971	NFC, 27-6	Back—Mel Renfro, Dal.
1940	Green Bay	16-7	All-Stars			Line—Fred Carr, GB
1940	Chicago Bears	28-14	All-Stars	1972	AFC, 26-13	Off—Jan Stenerud, KC
1942	Chicago Bears	35-24	All-Stars			Def—Willie Lanier, KC
1942	All-Stars	17-14	Washington	1973	AFC, 33-28	O.J. Simpson, Buf., RB
1943-50		No game		1974	AFC, 15-13	Garo Yepremian, Mia., PK
				1975	NFC, 17-10	James Harris, LA Rams, QB

Year	Winner	MVP		Year	Winner	MVP
				1976	NFC, 23-20	Billy Johnson, Hou., KR
1951	American, 28-27	Otto Graham, Cle., QB		1977	AFC, 24-14	Mel Blount, Pit., CB
1952	National, 30-13	Dan Towler, LA Rams, HB		1978	NFC, 14-13	Walter Payton, Chi., RB
1953	National, 27-7	Don Doll, Det., DB		1979	NFC, 13-7	Ahmad Rashad, Min., WR
1954	East, 20-9	Chuck Bednarik, Phi., LB				
1955	West, 26-19	Billy Wilson, SF, E		1980	NFC, 37-27	Chuck Muncie, NO, RB
1956	East, 31-30	Ollie Matson, Cards, HB		1981	NFC, 21-7	Eddie Murray, Det., PK
1957	West, 19-10	Back—Bert Rechichar, Bal.		1982	AFC, 16-13	Kellen Winslow, SD, WR
		Line—Ernie Stautner, Pit.				& Lee Roy Selmon, TB, DE
1958	West, 26-7	Back—Hugh McElhenny, SF		1983	NFC, 20-19	Dan Fouts, SD, QB
		Line—Gene Brito, Wash.				& John Jefferson, GB, WR
1959	East, 28-21	Back—Frank Gifford, NY		1984	NFC, 45-3	Joe Theismann, Wash., QB
		Line—Doug Atkins, Chi.		1985	AFC, 22-14	Mark Gastineau, NYJ, DE
1960	West, 38-21	Back—Johnny Unitas, Bal.		1986	NFC, 28-24	Phil Simms, NYG, QB
		Line—Big Daddy Lipscomb, Pit.		1987	AFC, 10-6	Reggie White, Phi., DE
1961	West, 35-31	Back—Johnny Unitas, Bal.		1988	AFC, 15-6	Bruce Smith, Buf., DE
		Line—Sam Huff, NY		1989	NFC, 34-3	Randall Cunningham, Phi., QB
1962	West, 31-30	Back—Jim Brown, Cle.		1990	NFC, 27-21	Jerry Gray, LA Rams, CB
		Line—Henry Jordan, GB		1991	AFC, 23-21	Jim Kelly, Buf., QB
1963	East, 30-20	Back—Jim Brown, Cle.		1992	NFC, 21-15	Michael Irvin, Dal., WR
		Line—Big Daddy Lipscomb, Pit.		1993	AFC, 23-20 (OT)	Steve Tasker, Buf., Sp. Teams
1964	West, 31-17	Back—Johnny Unitas, Bal.		1994	NFC, 17-3	Andre Rison, Atl., WR
		Line—Gino Marchetti, Bal.		1995	AFC, 41-13	Marshall Faulk, Ind., RB
1965	West, 34-14	Back—Fran Tarkenton, Min.		1996	NFC, 20-13	Jerry Rice, SF, WR
		Line—Terry Barr, Det.		1997	AFC, 26-23 (OT)	Mark Brunell, Jax, QB
1966	East, 36-7	Back—Jim Brown, Cle.		1998	AFC, 29-24	Warren Moon, Sea., QB
		Line—Dale Meinhart, St. L.		1999	AFC, 23-10	Ty Law, NE, CB
1967	East, 20-10	Back—Gale Sayers, Chi.				& Keyshawn Johnson, NYJ, WR
		Line—Floyd Peters, Phi.				
1968	West, 38-20	Back—Gale Sayers, Chi.		2000	NFC, 51-31	Randy Moss, Min., WR
		Line—Dave Robinson, GB		2001	AFC, 38-17	Rich Gannon, Oak., QB
1969	West, 10-7	Back—Roman Gabriel, LA Rams		2002	AFC, 38-30	Rich Gannon, Oak., QB
		Line—Merlin Olsen, LA Rams		2003	AFC, 45-20	Ricky Williams, Mia., RB
1970	West, 16-13	Back—Gale Sayers, Chi.		2004	NFC, 55-52	Marc Bulger, St.L, QB
		Line—George Andrie, Dal.				

Playing sites: Wrigley Field in Los Angeles (1939); Gilmore Stadium in Los Angeles (1940–both games); Polo Grounds in New York (Jan., 1942); Shibe Park in Philadelphia (Dec., 1942); Memorial Coliseum in Los Angeles (1951-72 and 1979); Texas Stadium in Irving, TX (1973); Arrowhead Stadium in Kansas City (1974); Orange Bowl in Miami (1975); Superdome in New Orleans (1976); Kingdome in Seattle (1977); Tampa Stadium in Tampa (1978) and Aloha Stadium in Honolulu (since 1980).

AFL All-Star Game

The AFL did not play an All-Star game after its first season in 1960 but did stage All-Star games from 1962-70. All-Star teams from the Eastern and Western divisions played each other every year except 1966 with the West winning the series, 6-2. In 1966, the league champion Buffalo Bills met an elite squad made up of the best players from the league's other eight clubs and lost, 30-19.

Year	Winner	MVP	Year	Winner	MVP
1962	West, 47-27	Cotton Davidson, Oak., QB	1967	East, 30-23	Off—Babe Parilli, Bos.
1963	West, 21-14	Off—Curtis McClinton, Dal.			Def—Verlon Biggs, NY
		Def—Earl Faison, SD	1968	East, 25-24	Off—Joe Namath, NY
1964	West, 27-24	Off—Keith Lincoln, SD			& Don Maynard, NY
		Def—Archie Matsos, Oak.			Def—Speedy Duncan, SD
1965	West, 38-14	Off—Keith Lincoln, SD	1969	West, 38-25	Off—Len Dawson, KC
		Def—Willie Brown, Den.			Def—George Webster, Hou.
1966	All-Stars 30	Off—Joe Namath, NY	1970	West, 26-3	John Hadl, SD, QB
	Buffalo 19	Def—Frank Buncom, SD			

Playing sites: Balboa Stadium in San Diego (1962-64); Jeppesen Stadium in Houston (1965); Rice Stadium in Houston (1966); Oakland Coliseum (1967); Gator Bowl in Jacksonville (1968-69) and Astrodome in Houston (1970).

NFL Franchise Origins

Here is what the current 32 teams in the National Football League have to show for the years they have put in as members of the American Professional Football Association (APFA), the NFL, the All-America Football Conference (AAFC) and the American Football League (AFL). Years given for league titles indicate seasons championships were won.

American Football Conference

	First Season	League Titles	Franchise Stops
Baltimore Ravens	1996 (NFL)	1 Super Bowl (2000)	• Baltimore (1996–)
Buffalo Bills	1960 (AFL)	2 AFL (1964-65)	• Buffalo (1960-72) Orchard Park, NY (1973–)
Cincinnati Bengals	1968 (AFL)	None	• Cincinnati (1968–)
Cleveland Browns	1946 (AAFC)	4 AAFC (1946-49) 4 NFL (1950,54-55,64)	• Cleveland (1946-95, 99–)
Denver Broncos	1960 (AFL)	2 Super Bowls (1997-98)	• Denver (1960–)
Houston Texans	2002 (NFL)	None	• Houston (2002–)
Indianapolis Colts	1953 (NFL)	3 NFL (1958-59,68) 1 Super Bowl (1970)	• Baltimore (1953-83) • Indianapolis (1984–)
Jacksonville Jaguars	1995 (NFL)	None	• Jacksonville, FL (1995–)
Kansas City Chiefs	1960 (AFL)	3 AFL (1962,66,69) 1 Super Bowl (1969)	• Dallas (1960-62) Kansas City (1963–)
Miami Dolphins	1966 (AFL)	2 Super Bowls (1972-73)	• Miami (1966–)
New England Patriots	1960 (AFL)	2 Super Bowls (2001,03)	• Boston (1960-70) Foxboro, MA (1971–)
New York Jets	1960 (AFL)	1 AFL (1968) 1 Super Bowl (1968)	• New York (1960-83) E. Rutherford, NJ (1984–)
Oakland Raiders	1960 (AFL)	1 AFL (1967) 3 Super Bowls (1976,80,83)	• Oakland (1960-81, 1995–) Los Angeles (1982-94)
Pittsburgh Steelers	1933 (NFL)	4 Super Bowls (1974-75,78-79)	• Pittsburgh (1933–)
San Diego Chargers	1960 (AFL)	1 AFL (1963)	• Los Angeles (1960) San Diego (1961–)
Tennessee Titans	1960 (AFL)	2 AFL (1960-61)	• Houston (1960-96) Memphis (1997) Nashville (1998–)

National Football Conference

	First Season	League Titles	Franchise Stops
Arizona Cardinals	1920 (APFA)	2 NFL (1925,47)	• Chicago (1920-59) St. Louis (1960-87) Tempe, AZ (1988–)
Atlanta Falcons	1966 (NFL)	None	• Atlanta (1966–)
Carolina Panthers	1995 (NFL)	None	• Clemson, SC (1995) Charlotte, NC (1996–)
Chicago Bears	1920 (APFA)	8 NFL (1921, 32-33,40-41,43,46,63) 1 Super Bowl (1985)	• Decatur, IL (1920) Chicago (1921–)
Dallas Cowboys	1960 (NFL)	5 Super Bowls (1971,77,92-93,95)	• Dallas (1960-70) Irving, TX (1971–)
Detroit Lions	1930 (NFL)	4 NFL (1935,52-53,57)	• Portsmouth, OH (1930-33) Detroit (1934-74, 2002–) Pontiac, MI (1975-2001)
Green Bay Packers	1921 (APFA)	11 NFL (1929-31,36,39,44,61-62,65-67) 3 Super Bowls (1966-67,96)	• Green Bay (1921–)
Minnesota Vikings	1961 (NFL)	1 NFL (1969)	• Bloomington, MN (1961-81) Minneapolis, MN (1982–)
New Orleans Saints	1967 (NFL)	None	• New Orleans (1967–)
New York Giants	1925 (NFL)	4 NFL (1927,34,38,56) 2 Super Bowls (1986,90)	• New York (1925-73,75) New Haven, CT (1973-74) E. Rutherford, NJ (1976–)
Philadelphia Eagles	1933 (NFL)	3 NFL (1948-49,60)	• Philadelphia (1933–)
St. Louis Rams	1937 (NFL)	2 NFL (1945,51) 1 Super Bowl (1999)	• Cleveland (1937-45) Los Angeles (1946-79) Anaheim (1980-94) St. Louis (1995–)
San Francisco 49ers	1946 (AAFC)	5 Super Bowls (1981,84,88-89,94)	• San Francisco (1946–)
Seattle Seahawks	1976 (NFL)	None	• Seattle (1976–)
Tampa Bay Buccaneers	1976 (NFL)	1 Super Bowl (2002)	• Tampa, FL (1976–)
Washington Redskins	1932 (NFL)	2 NFL (1937,42) 3 Super Bowls (1982,87,91)	• Boston (1932-36) Washington, DC (1937-96) Raljon, MD (1997–)

The Growth of the NFL

Of the 14 franchises that comprised the American Professional Football Association in 1920, only two remain—the Arizona Cardinals (then the Chicago Cardinals) and the Chicago Bears (originally the Decatur-IL Staleys). Green Bay joined the APFC in 1921 and the league changed its name to the NFL in 1922. Since then, 54 NFL clubs have come and gone, six rival leagues have expired and two other leagues have been swallowed up.

The NFL merged with the **All-America Football Conference** (1946-49) following the 1949 season and adopted three of its seven clubs—the Baltimore Colts, Cleveland Browns and San Francisco 49ers. The four remaining AAFC teams—the Brooklyn/NY Yankees, Buffalo Bills, Chicago Hornets and Los Angeles Dons—did not survive. After the 1950 season, the financially troubled Colts were sold back to the NFL. The league folded the team and added its players to the 1951 college draft pool. A new Baltimore franchise, also named the Colts, joined the NFL in 1953.

The formation of the **American Football League** (1960-69) was announced in 1959 with ownership lined up in eight cities—Boston, Buffalo, Dallas, Denver, Houston, Los Angeles, Minneapolis and New York. Set to begin play in the autumn of 1960, the AFL was stunned early that year when Minneapolis withdrew to accept an offer to join the NFL as an expansion team in 1961. The new league responded by choosing Oakland to replace Minneapolis and inherit the departed team's draft picks. Since no AFL team actually played in Minneapolis, it is not considered the original home of the Oakland Raiders.

In 1966, the NFL and AFL agreed to a merger that resulted in the first Super Bowl (originally called the AFL-NFL World Championship Game) following the '66 league playoffs. In 1970, the now 10-member AFL officially joined the NFL, forming a 26-team league made up of two conferences of three divisions each. In 2002, the 32-team league was realigned into two conferences of four divisions each.

Expansion/Merger Timetable

For teams currently in NFL.

1921–Green Bay Packers; **1925**–New York Giants; **1930**–Portsmouth-OH Spartans (now Detroit Lions); **1932**–Boston Braves (now Washington Redskins); **1933**–Philadelphia Eagles and Pittsburgh Pirates (now Steelers); **1937**–Cleveland Rams (now St. Louis); **1950**–added AAFC's Cleveland Browns and San Francisco 49ers; **1953**–Baltimore Colts (now Indianapolis). **1960**–Dallas Cowboys; **1961**–Minnesota Vikings; **1966**–Atlanta Falcons; **1967**–New Orleans Saints; **1970**–added AFL's Boston Patriots (now New England), Buffalo Bills, Cincinnati Bengals (1968 expansion team), Denver Broncos, Houston Oilers (now Tennessee Titans), Kansas City Chiefs, Miami Dolphins (1966 expansion team), New York Jets, Oakland Raiders and San Diego Chargers (the AFL-NFL merger divided the league into two 13-team conferences with old-line NFL clubs Baltimore, Cleveland and Pittsburgh moving to the AFC); **1976**–Seattle Seahawks and Tampa Bay Buccaneers (Seattle was originally in the NFC West and Tampa Bay in the AFC West, but were switched to AFC West and NFC Central, respectively, in 1977); **1995**–Carolina Panthers and Jacksonville Jaguars; **1996**–Cleveland Browns move to Baltimore and become Ravens. City of Cleveland retains rights to team name, colors and all memorabilia; **1999**–Cleveland Browns return to the NFL. **2002**–Houston Texans. Seattle moves back to the NFC West.

City and Nickname Changes

1921—Decatur Staleys move to Chicago; **1922**—Chicago Staleys renamed Bears; **1933**—Boston Braves renamed Redskins; **1937**—Boston Redskins move to Washington; **1934**—Portsmouth (Ohio) Spartans move to Detroit and become Lions; **1941**—Pittsburgh Pirates renamed Steelers; **1943**—Philadelphia and Pittsburgh merge for one season and become Phil-Pitt, or the "Steagles"; **1944**—Chicago Cardinals and Pittsburgh merge for one season and become Card-Pitt; **1946**—Cleveland Rams move to Los Angeles.

1960—Chicago Cardinals move to St. Louis; **1961**—Los Angeles Chargers (AFL) move to San Diego; **1963**—New York Titans (AFL) renamed Jets and Dallas Texans (AFL) move to Kansas City and become Chiefs; **1971**—Boston Patriots become New England Patriots; **1982**—Oakland Raiders move to Los Angeles; **1984**—Baltimore Colts move to Indianapolis; **1988**—St. Louis Cardinals move to Phoenix; **1994**—Phoenix Cardinals become Arizona Cardinals; **1995**—L.A. Rams move to St. Louis and L.A. Raiders move back to Oakland; **1996**—Cleveland Browns move to Baltimore and become Ravens. City of Cleveland retains rights to team name, colors and all memorabilia; **1997**—Houston Oilers move to Memphis and become Tennessee Oilers; **1998**—Tennessee Oilers move to Nashville; **1999**—Tennessee Oilers renamed Titans.

Defunct NFL Teams

Teams that once played in the APFA and NFL, but no longer exist.

Akron-OH–Pros (1920-25) and Indians (1926); **Baltimore**–Colts (1950); **Boston**–Bulldogs (1926) and Yanks (1944-48); **Brooklyn**–Lions (1926), Dodgers (1930-43) and Tigers (1944); **Buffalo**–All-Americans (1920-23), Bisons (1924-25), Rangers (1926), Bisons (1927,1929); **Canton-OH**–Bulldogs (1920-23,1925-26); **Chicago**–Tigers (1920); **Cincinnati**–Celts (1921) and Reds (1933-34); **Cleveland**–Tigers (1920), Indians (1921), Indians (1923), Bulldogs (1924-25,1927) and Indians (1931); **Columbus-OH**–Panhandles (1920-22) and Tigers (1923-26); **Dallas**–Texans (1952); **Dayton-OH**–Triangles (1920-29).

Detroit–Heralds (1920-21), Panthers (1925-26) and Wolverines (1928); **Duluth-MN**–Kelleys (1923-25) and Eskimos (1926-27); **Evansville-IN**–Crimson Giants (1921-22); **Frankford-PA**–Yellow Jackets (1924-31); **Hammond-IN**–Pros (1920-26); **Hartford**–Blues (1926); **Kansas City**–Blues (1924) and Cowboys (1925-26); **Kenosha-WI**–Maroons (1924); **Los Angeles**–Buccaneers (1926); **Louisville**–Brecks (1921-23) and Colonels (1926); **Marion-OH**–Oorang Indians (1922-23); **Milwaukee**–Badgers (1922-26); **Minneapolis**–Marines (1922-24) and Red Jackets (1929-30); **Muncie-IN**–Flyers (1920-21).

New York–Giants (1921), Yankees (1927-28), Bulldogs (1949) and Yankees (1950-51); **Newark-NJ**–Tornadoes (1930); **Orange-NJ**–Tornadoes (1929); **Pottsville-PA**–Maroons (1925-28); **Providence-RI**–Steam Roller (1925-31); **Racine-WI**–Legion (1922-24) and Tornadoes (1926); **Rochester-NY**–Jeffersons (1920-25); **Rock Island-IL**– Independents (1920-26); **Staten Island-NY**–Stapletons (1929-32); **St. Louis**–All-Stars (1923) and Gunners (1934); **Toledo-OH**–Maroons (1922-23); **Tonawanda-NY**–Kardex (1921), also called Lumbermen; **Washington**–Senators (1921).

Annual NFL Leaders

Individual leaders in NFL (1932-69), NFC (since 1970), AFL (1960-69) and AFC (since 1970).

Passing

Since 1932, the NFL has used several formulas to determine passing leadership, from Total Yards alone (1932-37), to the current rating system—adopted in 1973—that takes Completions, Completion Percentage, Yards Gained, TD Passes, Interceptions, Interception Percentage and other factors into account. The quarterbacks listed below all led the league according to the system in use at the time.

NFL-NFC

Multiple winners: Sammy Baugh and Steve Young (6); Joe Montana and Roger Staubach (5); Arnie Herber, Sonny Jurgensen, Bart Starr and Norm Van Brocklin (3); Ed Danowski, Otto Graham, Cecil Isbell, Milt Plum, Kurt Warner and Bob Waterfield (2).

Year		Att	Cmp	Yds	TD	Year		Att	Cmp	Yds	TD
1932	Arnie Herber, GB	101	37	639	9	1968	Earl Morrall, Bal	317	182	2909	26
1933	Harry Newman, NY	136	53	973	11	1969	Sonny Jurgensen, Wash	442	274	3102	22
1934	Arnie Herber, GB	115	42	799	8	1970	John Brodie, SF	378	223	2941	24
1935	Ed Danowski, NY	113	57	794	10	1971	Roger Staubach, Dal	211	126	1882	15
1936	Arnie Herber, GB	173	77	1239	11	1972	Norm Snead, NY	325	196	2307	17
1937	Sammy Baugh, Wash	171	81	1127	8	1973	Roger Staubach, Dal	286	179	2428	23
1938	Ed Danowski, NY	129	70	848	7	1974	Sonny Jurgensen, Wash	167	107	1185	11
1939	Parker Hall, Cle. Rams	208	106	1227	9	1975	Fran Tarkenton, Min	425	273	2994	25
1940	Sammy Baugh, Wash	177	111	1367	12	1976	James Harris, LA	158	91	1460	8
1941	Cecil Isbell, GB	206	117	1479	15	1977	Roger Staubach, Dal	361	210	2620	18
1942	Cecil Isbell, GB	268	146	2021	24	1978	Roger Staubach, Dal	413	231	3190	25
1943	Sammy Baugh, Wash	239	133	1754	23	1979	Roger Staubach, Dal	461	267	3586	27
1944	Frank Filchock, Wash	147	84	1139	13	1980	Ron Jaworski, Phi	451	257	3529	27
1945	Sammy Baugh, Wash	182	128	1669	11	1981	Joe Montana, SF	488	311	3565	19
	& Sid Luckman, Chi. Bears	217	117	1725	14	1982	Joe Theismann, Wash	252	161	2033	13
1946	Bob Waterfield, LA	251	127	1747	18	1983	Steve Bartkowski, Atl	432	274	3167	22
1947	Sammy Baugh, Wash	354	210	2938	25	1984	Joe Montana, SF	432	279	3630	28
1948	Tommy Thompson, Phi	246	141	1965	25	1985	Joe Montana, SF	494	303	3653	27
1949	Sammy Baugh, Wash	255	145	1903	18	1986	Tommy Kramer, Min	372	208	3000	24
1950	Norm Van Brocklin, LA	233	127	2061	18	1987	Joe Montana, SF	398	266	3054	31
1951	Bob Waterfield, LA	176	88	1566	13	1988	Wade Wilson, Min	332	204	2746	15
1952	Norm Van Brocklin, LA	205	113	1736	14	1989	Don Majkowski, GB	599	353	4318	27
1953	Otto Graham, Cle	258	167	2722	11	1990	Joe Montana, SF	520	321	3944	26
1954	Norm Van Brocklin, LA	260	139	2637	13	1991	Steve Young, SF	279	180	2517	17
1955	Otto Graham, Cle	185	98	1721	15	1992	Steve Young, SF	402	268	3465	25
1956	Ed Brown, Chi. Bears	168	96	1667	11	1993	Steve Young, SF	462	314	4023	29
1957	Tommy O'Connell, Cle	110	63	1229	9	1994	Steve Young, SF	461	324	3969	35
1958	Eddie LeBaron, Wash	145	79	1365	11	1995	Brett Favre, GB	570	359	4413	38
1959	Charlie Conerly, NY	194	113	1706	14	1996	Steve Young, SF	316	214	2410	14
1960	Milt Plum, Cle	250	151	2297	21	1997	Steve Young, SF	356	241	3029	19
1961	Milt Plum, Cle	302	177	2416	16	1998	Randall Cunningham, Min	425	259	3704	34
1962	Bart Starr, GB	285	178	2438	12	1999	Kurt Warner, St.L	499	325	4353	41
1963	Y.A. Tittle, NY	367	221	3145	36	2000	Trent Green, St.L	240	145	2063	16
1964	Bart Starr, GB	272	163	2144	15	2001	Kurt Warner, St.L	546	375	4830	36
1965	Rudy Bukich, Chi	312	176	2641	20	2002	Brad Johnson, TB	451	281	3049	22
1966	Bart Starr, GB	251	156	2257	14	2003	Daunte Culpepper, Min	454	295	3479	25
1967	Sonny Jurgensen, Wash	508	288	3747	31						

Note: In 1945, Sammy Baugh and Sid Luckman tied with 8 points on an inverse rating system.

AFL-AFC

Multiple winners: Dan Marino (5); Ken Anderson and Len Dawson (4); Bob Griese, Daryle Lamonica, Warren Moon and Ken Stabler (2).

Year		Att	Cmp	Yds	TD	Year		Att	Cmp	Yds	TD
1960	Jack Kemp, LA	406	211	3018	20	1982	Ken Anderson, Cin	309	218	2495	12
1961	George Blanda, Hou	362	187	3330	36	1983	Dan Marino, Mia	296	173	2210	20
1962	Len Dawson, Dal	310	189	2759	29	1984	Dan Marino, Mia	564	362	5084	48
1963	Tobin Rote, SD	286	170	2510	20	1985	Ken O'Brien, NY	488	297	3888	25
1964	Len Dawson, KC	354	199	2879	30	1986	Dan Marino, Mia	623	378	4746	44
1965	John Hadl, SD	348	174	2798	20	1987	Bernie Kosar, Cle	389	241	3033	22
1966	Len Dawson, KC	284	159	2527	26	1988	Boomer Esiason, Cin	388	223	3572	28
1967	Daryle Lamonica, Oak	425	220	3228	30	1989	Dan Marino, Mia	550	308	3997	24
1968	Len Dawson, KC	224	131	2109	17	1990	Warren Moon, Hou	584	362	4689	33
1969	Greg Cook, Cin	197	106	1854	15	1991	Jim Kelly, Buf	474	304	3844	33
1970	Daryle Lamonica, Oak	356	179	2516	22	1992	Warren Moon, Hou	346	224	2521	18
1971	Bob Griese, Mia	263	145	2089	19	1993	John Elway, Den	551	348	4030	25
1972	Earl Morrall, Mia	150	83	1360	11	1994	Dan Marino, Mia	615	385	4453	30
1973	Ken Stabler, Oak	260	163	1997	14	1995	Jim Harbaugh, Ind	314	200	2575	17
1974	Ken Anderson, Cin	328	213	2667	18	1996	John Elway, Den	466	287	3328	26
1975	Ken Anderson, Cin	377	228	3169	21	1997	Mark Brunell, Jax	435	264	3281	18
1976	Ken Stabler, Oak	291	194	2737	27	1998	Vinny Testaverde, NYJ	421	259	3256	29
1977	Bob Griese, Mia	307	180	2252	22	1999	Peyton Manning, Ind	533	331	4135	26
1978	Terry Bradshaw, Pit	368	207	2915	28	2000	Brian Griese, Den	336	216	2688	19
1979	Dan Fouts, SD	530	332	4082	24	2001	Rich Gannon, Oak	549	361	3828	27
1980	Brian Sipe, Cle	554	337	4132	30	2002	Chad Pennington, NYJ	399	275	3120	22
1981	Ken Anderson, Cin	479	300	3753	29	2003	Steve McNair, Ten	400	250	3215	24

Receptions
NFL-NFC

Multiple winners: Don Hutson (8); Raymond Berry, Tom Fears, Pete Pihos, Jerry Rice, Sterling Sharpe and Billy Wilson (3); Dwight Clark, Herman Moore, Muhsin Muhammad, Ahmad Rashad and Charley Taylor (2).

Year	Player	No	Yds	Avg	TD
1932	Ray Flaherty, NY	21	350	16.7	3
1933	Shipwreck Kelly, Bklyn	22	246	11.2	3
1934	Joe Carter, Phi	16	238	14.9	4
	& Red Badgro, NY	16	206	12.9	1
1935	Tod Goodwin, NY	26	432	16.6	4
1936	Don Hutson, GB	34	536	15.8	8
1937	Don Hutson, GB	41	552	13.5	7
1938	Gaynell Tinsley, Chi. Cards	41	516	12.6	1
1939	Don Hutson, GB	34	846	24.9	6
1940	Don Looney, Phi	58	707	12.2	4
1941	Don Hutson, GB	58	739	12.7	10
1942	Don Hutson, GB	74	1211	16.4	17
1943	Don Hutson, GB	47	776	16.5	11
1944	Don Hutson, GB	58	866	14.9	9
1945	Don Hutson, GB	47	834	17.7	9
1946	Jim Benton, LA	63	981	15.6	6
1947	Jim Keane, Chi. Bears	64	910	14.2	10
1948	Tom Fears, LA	51	698	13.7	4
1949	Tom Fears, LA	77	1013	13.2	9
1950	Tom Fears, LA	84	1116	13.3	7
1951	Elroy Hirsch, LA	66	1495	22.7	17
1952	Mac Speedie, Cle	62	911	14.7	5
1953	Pete Pihos, Phi	63	1049	16.7	10
1954	Pete Pihos, Phi	60	872	14.5	10
	& Billy Wilson, SF	60	830	13.8	5
1955	Pete Pihos, Phi	62	864	13.9	7
1956	Billy Wilson, SF	60	889	14.8	5
1957	Billy Wilson, SF	52	757	14.6	6
1958	Raymond Berry, Bal	56	794	14.2	9
	& Pete Retzlaff, Phi	56	766	13.7	2
1959	Raymond Berry, Bal	66	959	14.5	14
1960	Raymond Berry, Bal	74	1298	17.5	10
1961	Red Phillips, LA	78	1092	14.0	5
1962	Bobby Mitchell, Wash	72	1384	19.2	11
1963	Bobby Joe Conrad, St.L	73	967	13.2	10
1964	Johnny Morris, Chi. Bears	93	1200	12.9	10
1965	Dave Parks, SF	80	1344	16.8	12
1966	Charley Taylor, Wash	72	1119	15.5	12
1967	Charley Taylor, Wash	70	990	14.1	9
1968	Clifton McNeil, SF	71	994	14.0	7
1969	Dan Abramowicz, NO	73	1015	13.9	7
1970	Dick Gordon, Chi	71	1026	14.5	13
1971	Bob Tucker, NY	59	791	13.4	4
1972	Harold Jackson, Phi	62	1048	16.9	4
1973	Harold Carmichael, Phi	67	1116	16.7	9
1974	Charles Young, Phi	63	696	11.0	3
1975	Chuck Foreman, Min	73	691	9.5	9
1976	Drew Pearson, Dal	58	806	13.9	6
1977	Ahmad Rashad, Min	51	681	13.4	2
1978	Rickey Young, Min	88	704	8.0	5
1979	Ahmad Rashad, Min	80	1156	14.5	9
1980	Earl Cooper, SF	83	567	6.8	4
1981	Dwight Clark, SF	85	1105	13.0	4
1982	Dwight Clark, SF	60	913	12.2	5
1983	Roy Green, St.L	78	1227	15.7	14
	Charlie Brown, Wash	78	1225	15.7	8
	& Earnest Gray, NY	78	1139	14.6	5
1984	Art Monk, Wash	106	1372	12.9	7
1985	Roger Craig, SF	92	1016	11.0	6
1986	Jerry Rice, SF	86	1570	18.3	15
1987	J.T. Smith, St.L	91	1117	12.3	8
1988	Henry Ellard, LA	86	1414	16.4	10
1989	Sterling Sharpe, GB	90	1423	15.8	12
1990	Jerry Rice, SF	100	1502	15.0	13
1991	Michael Irvin, Dal	93	1523	16.4	8
1992	Sterling Sharpe, GB	108	1461	13.5	13
1993	Sterling Sharpe, GB	112	1274	11.4	11
1994	Cris Carter, Min	122	1256	10.3	7
1995	Herman Moore, Det	123	1686	13.7	14
1996	Jerry Rice, SF	108	1254	11.6	8
1997	Herman Moore, Det	104	1293	12.4	8
1998	Frank Sanders, Ari	89	1145	12.9	3
1999	Muhsin Muhammad, Car	96	1253	13.1	8
2000	Muhsin Muhammad, Car	102	1183	11.6	6
2001	Keyshawn Johnson, TB	106	1266	11.9	1
2002	Randy Moss, Min	106	1347	12.7	7
2003	Torry Holt, St.L	117	1696	14.5	12

AFL-AFC

Multiple winners: Lionel Taylor (5); Lance Alworth, Haywood Jeffires, Lydell Mitchell and Kellen Winslow (3); Fred Biletnikoff, Todd Christensen, Marvin Harrison, Carl Pickens and Al Toon (2).

Year	Player	No	Yds	Avg	TD
1960	Lionel Taylor, Den	92	1235	13.4	12
1961	Lionel Taylor, Den	100	1176	11.8	4
1962	Lionel Taylor, Den	77	908	11.8	4
1963	Lionel Taylor, Den	78	1101	14.1	10
1964	Charley Hennigan, Hou	101	1546	15.3	8
1965	Lionel Taylor, Den	85	1131	13.3	6
1966	Lance Alworth, SD	73	1383	18.9	13
1967	George Sauer, NY	75	1189	15.9	6
1968	Lance Alworth, SD	68	1312	19.3	10
1969	Lance Alworth, SD	64	1003	15.7	4
1970	Marlin Briscoe, Buf	57	1036	18.2	8
1971	Fred Biletnikoff, Oak	61	929	15.2	9
1972	Fred Biletnikoff, Oak	58	802	13.8	7
1973	Fred Willis, Hou	57	371	6.5	1
1974	Lydell Mitchell, Bal	72	544	7.6	2
1975	Reggie Rucker, Cle	60	770	12.8	3
	& Lydell Mitchell, Bal	60	544	9.1	4
1976	MacArthur Lane, KC	66	686	10.4	1
1977	Lydell Mitchell, Bal	71	620	8.7	4
1978	Steve Largent, Sea	71	1168	16.5	8
1979	Joe Washington, Bal	82	750	9.1	3
1980	Kellen Winslow, SD	89	1290	14.5	9
1981	Kellen Winslow, SD	88	1075	12.2	10
1982	Kellen Winslow, SD	54	721	13.4	6
1983	Todd Christensen, LA	92	1247	13.6	12
1984	Ozzie Newsome, Cle	89	1001	11.2	5
1985	Lionel James, SD	86	1027	11.9	6
1986	Todd Christensen, LA	95	1153	12.1	8
1987	Al Toon, NY	68	976	14.4	5
1988	Al Toon, NY	93	1067	11.5	5
1989	Andre Reed, Buf	88	1312	14.9	9
1990	Haywood Jeffires, Hou	74	1048	14.2	8
	& Drew Hill, Hou	74	1019	13.8	5
1991	Haywood Jeffires, Hou	100	1181	11.8	7
1992	Haywood Jeffires, Hou	90	913	10.1	9
1993	Reggie Langhorne, Ind	85	1038	12.2	3
1994	Ben Coates, NE	96	1174	12.2	7
1995	Carl Pickens, Cin	99	1234	12.5	17
1996	Carl Pickens, Cin	100	1180	11.8	12
1997	Tim Brown, Oak	104	1408	13.5	5
1998	O.J. McDuffie, Mia	90	1050	11.7	7
1999	Jimmy Smith, Jax	116	1636	14.1	6
2000	Marvin Harrison, Ind	102	1413	13.9	14
2001	Rod Smith, Den	113	1343	11.9	11
2002	Marvin Harrison, Ind	143	1722	12.0	11
2003	LaDainian Tomlinson, SD	100	725	7.3	4

Annual NFL Leaders (Cont.)
Rushing
NFL-NFC

Multiple winners: Jim Brown (8); Walter Payton and Barry Sanders (5); Emmitt Smith and Steve Van Buren (4); Eric Dickerson (3); Cliff Battles, John Brockington, Larry Brown, Bill Dudley, Leroy Kelly, Bill Paschal, Joe Perry, Gale Sayers, Stephen Davis and Whizzer White (2).

Year		Car	Yds	Avg	TD	Year		Car	Yds	Avg	TD
1932	Cliff Battles, Bos	148	576	3.9	3	1968	Leroy Kelly, Cle	248	1239	5.0	16
1933	Jim Musick, Bos	173	809	4.7	5	1969	Gale Sayers, Chi	236	1032	4.4	8
1934	Beattie Feathers, Chi. Bears	119	1004	8.4	8	1970	Larry Brown, Wash	237	1125	4.7	5
1935	Doug Russell, Chi. Cards	140	499	3.6	0	1971	John Brockington, GB	216	1105	5.1	4
1936	Tuffy Leemans, NY	206	830	4.0	2	1972	Larry Brown, Wash	285	1216	4.3	8
1937	Cliff Battles, Wash	216	874	4.0	5	1973	John Brockington, GB	265	1144	4.3	3
1938	Whizzer White, Pit	152	567	3.7	4	1974	Lawrence McCutcheon, LA	236	1109	4.7	3
1939	Bill Osmanski, Chi. Bears	121	699	5.8	7	1975	Jim Otis, St.L	269	1076	4.0	5
1940	Whizzer White, Det	146	514	3.5	5	1976	Walter Payton, Chi	311	1390	4.5	13
1941	Pug Manders, Bklyn	111	486	4.4	5	1977	Walter Payton, Chi	339	1852	5.5	14
1942	Bill Dudley, Pit	162	696	4.3	5	1978	Walter Payton, Chi	333	1395	4.2	11
1943	Bill Paschal, NY	147	572	3.9	10	1979	Walter Payton, Chi	369	1610	4.4	14
1944	Bill Paschal, NY	196	737	3.8	9	1980	Walter Payton, Chi	317	1460	4.6	6
1945	Steve Van Buren, Phi	143	832	5.8	15	1981	George Rogers, NO	378	1674	4.4	13
1946	Bill Dudley, Pit	146	604	4.1	3	1982	Tony Dorsett, Dal	177	745	4.2	5
1947	Steve Van Buren, Phi	217	1008	4.6	13	1983	Eric Dickerson, LA	390	1808	4.6	18
1948	Steve Van Buren, Phi	201	945	4.7	10	1984	Eric Dickerson, LA	379	2105	5.6	14
1949	Steve Van Buren, Phi	263	1146	4.4	11	1985	Gerald Riggs, Atl	397	1719	4.3	10
1950	Marion Motley, Cle	140	810	5.8	3	1986	Eric Dickerson, LA	404	1821	4.5	11
1951	Eddie Price, NY Giants	271	971	3.6	7	1987	Charles White, LA	324	1374	4.2	11
1952	Dan Towler, LA	156	894	5.7	10	1988	Herschel Walker, Dal	361	1514	4.2	5
1953	Joe Perry, SF	192	1018	5.3	10	1989	Barry Sanders, Det	280	1470	5.3	14
1954	Joe Perry, SF	173	1049	6.1	8	1990	Barry Sanders, Det	255	1304	5.1	13
1955	Alan Ameche, Bal	213	961	4.5	9	1991	Emmitt Smith, Dal	365	1563	4.3	12
1956	Rick Casares, Chi. Bears	234	1126	4.8	12	1992	Emmitt Smith, Dal	373	1713	4.6	18
1957	Jim Brown, Cle	202	942	4.7	9	1993	Emmitt Smith, Dal	283	1486	5.3	9
1958	Jim Brown, Cle	257	1527	5.9	17	1994	Barry Sanders, Det	331	1883	5.7	7
1959	Jim Brown, Cle	290	1329	4.6	14	1995	Emmitt Smith, Dal	377	1773	4.7	25
1960	Jim Brown, Cle	215	1257	5.8	9	1996	Barry Sanders, Det	307	1553	5.1	11
1961	Jim Brown, Cle	305	1408	4.6	8	1997	Barry Sanders, Det	335	2053	6.1	11
1962	Jim Taylor, GB	272	1474	5.4	19	1998	Jamal Anderson, Atl	410	1846	4.5	14
1963	Jim Brown, Cle	291	1863	6.4	12	1999	Stephen Davis, Wash	290	1405	4.8	17
1964	Jim Brown, Cle	280	1446	5.2	7	2000	Robert Smith, Min	295	1521	5.2	7
1965	Jim Brown, Cle	289	1544	5.3	17	2001	Stephen Davis, Wash	356	1432	4.0	5
1966	Gale Sayers, Chi	229	1231	5.4	8	2002	Deuce McAllister, NO	325	1388	4.3	13
1967	Leroy Kelly, Cle	235	1205	5.1	11	2003	Ahman Green, GB	355	1883	5.3	15

Note: Jim Brown led the NFL in rushing eight of his nine years in the league. The one season he didn't win (1962) he finished fourth (996 yds) behind Jim Taylor, John Henry Johnson of Pittsburgh (1,141 yds) and Dick Bass of the LA Rams (1,033 yds).

AFL-AFC

Multiple winners: Earl Campbell and O.J. Simpson (4); Terrell Davis and Thurman Thomas (3); Eric Dickerson, Cookie Gilchrist, Edgerrin James, Floyd Little, Jim Nance and Curt Warner (2).

Year		Car	Yds	Avg	TD	Year		Car	Yds	Avg	TD
1960	Abner Haynes, Dal	157	875	5.6	9	1982	Freeman McNeil, NY	151	786	5.2	6
1961	Billy Cannon, Hou	200	948	4.7	6	1983	Curt Warner, Sea	335	1449	4.3	13
1962	Cookie Gilchrist, Buf	214	1096	5.1	13	1984	Earnest Jackson, SD	296	1179	4.0	8
1963	Clem Daniels, Oak	215	1099	5.1	3	1985	Marcus Allen, LA	380	1759	4.6	11
1964	Cookie Gilchrist, Buf	230	981	4.3	6	1986	Curt Warner, Sea	319	1481	4.6	13
1965	Paul Lowe, SD	222	1121	5.0	7	1987	Eric Dickerson, Ind	223	1011	4.5	5
1966	Jim Nance, Bos	299	1458	4.9	11	1988	Eric Dickerson, Ind	388	1659	4.3	14
1967	Jim Nance, Bos	269	1216	4.5	7	1989	Christian Okoye, KC	370	1480	4.0	12
1968	Paul Robinson, Cin	238	1023	4.3	8	1990	Thurman Thomas, Buf	271	1297	4.8	11
1969	Dickie Post, SD	182	873	4.8	6	1991	Thurman Thomas, Buf	288	1407	4.9	7
1970	Floyd Little, Den	209	901	4.3	3	1992	Barry Foster, Pit	390	1690	4.3	11
1971	Floyd Little, Den	284	1133	4.0	6	1993	Thurman Thomas, Buf	355	1315	3.7	6
1972	O.J. Simpson, Buf	292	1251	4.3	6	1994	Chris Warren, Sea	333	1545	4.6	9
1973	O.J. Simpson, Buf	332	2003	6.0	12	1995	Curtis Martin, NE	368	1487	4.0	14
1974	Otis Armstrong, Den	263	1407	5.3	9	1996	Terrell Davis, Den	345	1538	4.5	13
1975	O.J. Simpson, Buf	329	1817	5.5	16	1997	Terrell Davis, Den	369	1750	4.7	15
1976	O.J. Simpson, Buf	290	1503	5.2	8	1998	Terrell Davis, Den	392	2008	5.1	21
1977	Mark van Eeghen, Oak	324	1273	3.9	7	1999	Edgerrin James, Ind	369	1553	4.2	13
1978	Earl Campbell, Hou	302	1450	4.8	13	2000	Edgerrin James, Ind	387	1709	4.4	13
1979	Earl Campbell, Hou	368	1697	4.6	19	2001	Priest Holmes, KC	327	1555	4.8	8
1980	Earl Campbell, Hou	373	1934	5.2	13	2002	Ricky Williams, Mia	383	1853	4.8	16
1981	Earl Campbell, Hou	361	1376	3.8	10	2003	Jamal Lewis, Bal	387	2066	5.3	14

Note: Eric Dickerson was traded to Indianapolis from the NFC's LA Rams during the 1987 season. In three games with the Rams, he carried the ball 60 times for 277 yds, a 4.6 avg and 1 TD. His official AFC statistics above came in nine games with the Colts.

Scoring
NFL-NFC

Multiple winners: Don Hutson (5); Dutch Clark, Pat Harder, Paul Hornung, Chip Lohmiller and Mark Moseley (3); Kevin Butler, Mike Cofer, Fred Cox, Marshall Faulk, Jack Manders, Chester Marcol, Eddie Murray, Emmitt Smith, Gordy Soltau, Jeff Wilkins and Doak Walker (2).

Year		TD	FG	PAT	Pts
1932	Dutch Clark, Portsmouth	6	3	10	55
1933	Glenn Presnell, Portsmouth	6	6	10	64
	& Ken Strong, NY	6	5	13	64
1934	Jack Manders, Chi. Bears	3	10	31	79
1935	Dutch Clark, Det	6	1	16	55
1936	Dutch Clark, Det	7	4	19	73
1937	Jack Manders, Chi. Bears	5	8	15	69
1938	Clarke Hinkle, GB	7	3	7	58
1939	Andy Farkas, Wash	11	0	2	68
1940	Don Hutson, GB	7	0	15	57
1941	Don Hutson, GB	12	1	20	95
1942	Don Hutson, GB	17	1	33	138
1943	Don Hutson, GB	12	3	26	117
1944	Don Hutson, GB	9	0	31	85
1945	Steve Van Buren, Phi	18	0	2	110
1946	Ted Fritsch, GB	10	9	13	100
1947	Pat Harder, Chi. Cards	7	7	39	102
1948	Pat Harder, Chi. Cards	6	7	53	110
1949	Gene Roberts, NY Giants	17	0	0	102
	& Pat Harder, Chi. Cards	8	3	45	102
1950	Doak Walker, Det	11	8	38	128
1951	Elroy Hirsch, LA	17	0	0	102
1952	Gordy Soltau, SF	7	6	34	94
1953	Gordy Soltau, SF	6	10	48	114
1954	Bobby Walston, Phi	11	4	36	114
1955	Doak Walker, Det	7	9	27	96
1956	Bobby Layne, Det	5	12	33	99
1957	Sam Baker, Wash	1	14	29	77
	& Lou Groza, Cle	0	15	32	77
1958	Jim Brown, Cle	18	0	0	108
1959	Paul Hornung, GB	7	7	31	94
1960	Paul Hornung, GB	15	15	41	176
1961	Paul Hornung, GB	10	15	41	146
1962	Jim Taylor, GB	19	0	0	114
1963	Don Chandler, NY	0	18	52	106
1964	Lenny Moore, Bal	20	0	0	120
1965	Gale Sayers, Chi	22	0	0	132
1966	Bruce Gossett, LA	0	28	29	113
1967	Jim Bakken, St.L	0	27	36	117
1968	Leroy Kelly, Cle	20	0	0	120
1969	Fred Cox, Min	0	26	43	121
1970	Fred Cox, Min	0	30	35	125
1971	Curt Knight, Wash	0	29	27	114
1972	Chester Marcol, GB	0	33	29	128
1973	David Ray, LA	0	30	40	130
1974	Chester Marcol, GB	0	25	19	94
1975	Chuck Foreman, Min	22	0	0	132
1976	Mark Moseley, Wash	0	22	31	97
1977	Walter Payton, Chi	16	0	0	96
1978	Frank Corral, LA	0	29	31	118
1979	Mark Moseley, Wash	0	25	39	114
1980	Eddie Murray, Det	0	27	35	116
1981	Rafael Septien, Dal	0	27	40	121
	& Eddie Murray, Det	0	25	46	121
1982	Wendell Tyler, LA	13	0	0	78
1983	Mark Moseley, Wash	0	33	62	161
1984	Ray Wersching, SF	0	25	56	131
1985	Kevin Butler, Chi	0	31	51	144
1986	Kevin Butler, Chi	0	28	36	120
1987	Jerry Rice, SF	23	0	0	138
1988	Mike Cofer, SF	0	27	40	121
1989	Mike Cofer, SF	0	29	49	136
1990	Chip Lohmiller, Wash	0	30	41	131
1991	Chip Lohmiller, Wash	0	31	56	149
1992	Chip Lohmiller, Wash	0	30	30	120
	& Morten Andersen, NO	0	29	33	120
1993	Jason Hanson, Det	0	34	28	130
1994	Emmitt Smith, Dal	22	0	0	132
	& Fuad Reveiz, Min	0	34	30	132
1995	Emmitt Smith, Dal	25	0	0	150
1996	John Kasay, Car.	0	37	34	145
1997	Richie Cunningham, Dal	0	34	24	126
1998	Gary Anderson, Min	0	35	59	164
1999	Jeff Wilkins, St.L	0	20	64	124
2000	Marshall Faulk, St.L	26	0	4	160
2001	Marshall Faulk, St.L	21	0	2	128
2002	Jay Feely, Atl	0	32	42	138
2003	Jeff Wilkins, St.L	0	39	46	163

AFL-AFC

Multiple winners: Gino Cappelletti (5); Gary Anderson (3); Jim Breech, Roy Gerela, Priest Holmes, Gene Mingo, Nick Lowery, John Smith, Pete Stoyanovich, Jim Turner and Mike Vanderjagt (2).

Year		TD	FG	PAT	Pts
1960	Gene Mingo, Den	6	18	33	123
1961	Gino Cappelletti, Bos	8	17	48	147
1962	Gene Mingo, Den	4	27	32	137
1963	Gino Cappelletti, Bos	2	22	35	113
1964	Gino Cappelletti, Bos	7	25	36	155
1965	Gino Cappelletti, Bos	9	17	27	132
1966	Gino Cappelletti, Bos	6	16	35	119
1967	George Blanda, Oak	0	20	56	116
1968	Jim Turner, NY	0	34	43	145
1969	Jim Turner, NY	0	32	33	129
1970	Jan Stenerud, KC	0	30	26	116
1971	Garo Yepremian, Mia	0	28	33	117
1972	Bobby Howfield, NY	0	27	40	121
1973	Roy Gerela, Pit	0	29	36	123
1974	Roy Gerela, Pit	0	20	33	93
1975	O.J. Simpson, Buf	23	0	0	138
1976	Toni Linhart, Bal	0	20	49	109
1977	Errol Mann, Oak	0	20	39	99
1978	Pat Leahy, NY	0	22	41	107
1979	John Smith, NE	0	23	46	115
1980	John Smith, NE	0	26	51	129
1981	Nick Lowery, KC	0	26	37	115
	& Jim Breech, Cin	0	22	49	115
1982	Marcus Allen, LA	14	0	0	84
1983	Gary Anderson, Pit	0	27	38	119
1984	Gary Anderson, Pit	0	24	45	117
1985	Gary Anderson, Pit	0	33	40	139
1986	Tony Franklin, NE	0	32	44	140
1987	Jim Breech, Cin	0	24	25	97
1988	Scott Norwood, Buf	0	32	33	129
1989	David Treadwell, Den	0	27	39	120
1990	Nick Lowery, KC	0	34	37	139
1991	Pete Stoyanovich, Mia	0	31	28	115
1992	Pete Stoyanovich, Mia	0	30	34	124
1993	Jeff Jaeger, LA	0	35	27	132
1994	John Carney, SD	0	34	33	135
1995	Norm Johnson, Pit	0	34	39	141
1996	Cary Blanchard, Ind	0	36	27	135
1997	Mike Hollis, Jax	0	31	41	134
1998	Steve Christie, Buf	0	33	41	140
1999	Mike Vanderjagt, Ind	0	34	43	145
2000	Matt Stover, Bal	0	35	30	135
2001	Mike Vanderjagt, Ind	0	28	41	125
2002	Priest Holmes, KC	24	0	0	144
2003	Priest Holmes, KC	27	0	0	162

All-Time NFL Leaders
Through 2003 regular season.

CAREER
Players active in 2003 in **bold** type.

Passing Efficiency

Ratings based on performance standards established for completion percentage, average gain, touchdown percentage and interception percentage. Quarterbacks are allocated points according to how their statistics measure up to those standards. Minimum 1500 passing attempts.

		Yrs	Att	Cmp	Cmp%	Yards	Avg Gain	TD	TD%	Int	Int%	Rating
1	**Kurt Warner**	6	1688	1121	66.4	14,447	8.56	102	6.0	65	3.9	97.2
2	Steve Young	15	4149	2667	64.3	33,124	7.98	232	5.6	107	2.6	96.8
3	Joe Montana	15	5391	3409	63.2	40,551	7.52	273	5.1	139	2.6	92.3
4	**Jeff Garcia**	5	2360	1449	61.4	16,408	6.95	113	4.8	56	2.4	88.3
5	**Peyton Manning**	6	3383	2128	62.9	24,885	7.36	167	4.9	110	3.3	88.1
6	**Daunte Culpepper**	5	1843	1160	62.9	13,881	7.53	90	4.9	63	3.4	88.0
7	**Brett Favre**	13	6464	3960	61.3	45,646	7.06	346	5.4	209	3.2	86.9
8	Dan Marino	17	8358	4967	59.4	61,361	7.34	420	5.0	252	3.0	86.4
9	**Trent Green**	6	2266	1336	59.0	17,016	7.51	106	4.7	65	2.9	86.1
10	**Tom Brady**	4	1544	955	61.9	10,233	6.63	69	4.5	38	2.5	85.9
11	**Mark Brunell**	10	3643	2196	60.3	25,793	7.08	144	4.0	86	2.4	85.2
12	**Rich Gannon**	15	4138	2492	60.2	28,219	6.82	177	4.3	102	2.5	84.7
13	Jim Kelly	11	4779	2874	60.1	35,467	7.42	237	5.0	175	3.7	84.4
14	**Brad Johnson**	12	3401	2101	61.8	23,239	6.83	140	4.1	95	2.8	84.1
15	**Steve McNair**	9	3180	1884	59.2	22,637	7.12	132	4.2	83	2.6	84.1
16	Roger Staubach	11	2958	1685	57.0	22,700	7.67	153	5.2	109	3.7	83.4
17	**Brian Griese**	6	1808	1118	61.8	12,576	6.96	76	4.2	59	3.3	83.0
18	Neil Lomax	8	3153	1817	57.6	22,771	7.22	136	4.3	90	2.9	82.7
19	Sonny Jurgensen	18	4262	2433	57.1	32,224	7.56	255	6.0	189	4.4	82.6
20	Len Dawson	19	3741	2136	57.1	28,711	7.67	239	6.4	183	4.9	82.6
21	**Aaron Brooks**	4	1798	1014	56.4	12,464	6.93	86	4.8	51	2.8	82.1
22	Ken Anderson	16	4475	2654	59.3	32,838	7.34	197	4.4	160	3.6	81.9
23	Bernie Kosar	12	3365	1994	59.3	23,301	6.92	124	3.7	87	2.6	81.8
24	**Neil O'Donnell**	14	3229	1865	57.8	21,690	6.72	120	3.7	68	2.1	81.8
25	Danny White	13	2950	1761	59.7	21,959	7.44	155	5.3	132	4.5	81.7

Note: The NFL does not recognize records from the All-American Football Conference (1946-49). If it did, **Otto Graham** would rank 8th (after Favre) with the following stats: 10 Yrs; 2,626 Att; 1,464 Comp; 55.8 Comp Pct; 23,584 Yards; 8.98 Avg Gain; 174 TD; 6.6 TD Pct; 135 Int; 5.1 Int Pct; and 86.6 Rating Pts.

Touchdown Passes

		No
1	Dan Marino	420
2	**Brett Favre**	346
3	Fran Tarkenton	342
4	John Elway	300
5	Warren Moon	291
6	Johnny Unitas	290
7	Joe Montana	273
8	Dave Krieg	261
9	Sonny Jurgensen	255
10	Dan Fouts	254
11	**Vinny Testaverde**	251
12	Boomer Esiason	247
13	John Hadl	244
14	Len Dawson	239
15	Jim Kelly	237

		No
16	George Blanda	236
17	Steve Young	232
18	John Brodie	214
19	Terry Bradshaw	212
	Y.A. Tittle	212
21	Jim Hart	209
22	Randall Cunningham	207
23	Jim Everett	203
24	Roman Gabriel	201
	Drew Bledsoe	201
26	Phil Simms	199
27	Ken Anderson	197
28	Joe Ferguson	196
	Bobby Layne	196
	Steve DeBerg	196
	Norm Snead	196

		No
32	Ken Stabler	194
33	Bob Griese	192
34	Sammy Baugh	187
35	Craig Morton	183
36	Steve Grogan	182
37	Ron Jaworski	179
38	Babe Parilli	178
39	**Rich Gannon**	177
40	Charlie Conerly	173
	Joe Namath	173
	Norm Van Brocklin	173
43	Charley Johnson	170
44	**Chris Chandler**	168
45	**Peyton Manning**	167

Note: The NFL does not recognize records from the All-American Football Conference (1946-49). If it did, **Y.A. Tittle** would move up from 19th to 14th (after Hadl) with 242 TDs and **Otto Graham** would rank 40th (after Gannon) with 174 TDs.

Passes Intercepted

		No
1	George Blanda	277
2	John Hadl	268
3	Fran Tarkenton	266
4	Norm Snead	257
5	Johnny Unitas	253
6	Dan Marino	252
7	Jim Hart	247
8	Bobby Layne	245
9	Dan Fouts	242

		No
10	**Vinny Testaverde**	235
11	Warren Moon	233
12	John Elway	226
13	John Brodie	224
14	Ken Stabler	222
15	Y.A. Tittle	221
16	Joe Namath	220
	Babe Parilli	220
18	Terry Bradshaw	210

		No
19	Joe Ferguson	209
	Brett Favre	209
21	Steve Grogan	208
22	Steve DeBerg	204
23	Sammy Baugh	203
24	Dave Krieg	199
25	Jim Plunkett	198

Passing Yards

		Yrs	Att	Comp	Pct	Yards
1	Dan Marino	17	8358	4967	59.4	61,361
2	John Elway	16	7250	4123	56.9	51,475
3	Warren Moon	17	6823	3988	58.5	49,325
4	Fran Tarkenton	18	6467	3686	57.0	47,003
5	**Brett Favre**	13	6464	3960	61.3	45,646
6	Dan Fouts	15	5604	3297	58.8	43,040
7	**Vinny Testaverde**	17	5925	3334	56.3	40,943
8	Joe Montana	15	5391	3409	63.2	40,551
9	Johnny Unitas	18	5186	2830	54.6	40,239
10	Dave Krieg	19	5311	3105	58.5	38,147
11	Boomer Esiason	14	5205	2969	57.0	37,920
12	**Drew Bledsoe**	11	5599	3193	57.0	36,876
13	Jim Kelly	11	4779	2874	60.1	35,467
14	Jim Everett	12	4923	2841	57.7	34,837
15	Jim Hart	19	5076	2593	51.1	34,665
16	Steve DeBerg	17	5024	2874	57.2	34,241
17	John Hadl	16	4687	2363	50.4	33,503
18	Phil Simms	14	4647	2576	55.4	33,462
19	Steve Young	15	4149	2667	64.3	33,124
20	Troy Aikman	12	4715	2898	61.5	32,942
21	Ken Anderson	16	4475	2654	59.3	32,838
22	Sonny Jurgensen	18	4262	2433	57.1	32,224
23	John Brodie	17	4491	2469	55.0	31,548
24	Norm Snead	15	4353	2276	52.3	30,797
25	Randall Cunningham	17	4289	2429	56.6	29,979

Note: The NFL does not recognize records from the All-American Football Conference (1946-49). If it did, **Y.A. Tittle** would rank 20th (after Young) with the following stats: 17 Yrs; 4,395 Att; 2,427 Comp; 55.2 Pct; and 33,070 Yards.

Receptions

		Yrs	No	Yards	Avg	TD
1	**Jerry Rice**	19	1519	22,466	14.8	194
2	Cris Carter	16	1101	13,899	12.6	130
3	**Tim Brown**	16	1070	14,734	13.8	99
4	Andre Reed	16	951	13,198	13.9	87
5	Art Monk	16	940	12,721	13.5	68
6	Irving Fryar	17	851	12,785	15.0	84
7	**Larry Centers**	14	827	6,797	8.2	28
8	Steve Largent	14	819	13,089	16.0	100
9	**Shannon Sharpe**	14	815	10,060	12.3	62
10	Henry Ellard	16	814	13,777	16.9	65
11	James Lofton	16	764	14,004	18.3	75
12	**Marvin Harrison**	8	759	10,072	13.3	83
13	Charlie Joiner	18	750	12,146	16.2	65
	Michael Irvin	12	750	11,904	15.9	65
15	Andre Rison	12	743	10,205	13.7	84
16	**Keenan McCardell**	12	724	9,370	12.9	52
17	**Jimmy Smith**	10	718	10,092	14.1	55
18	Gary Clark	11	699	10,856	15.5	65
19	Terance Mathis	13	689	8,809	12.8	63
20	**Isaac Bruce**	10	688	10,461	15.2	68
21	**Marshall Faulk**	10	673	6,274	9.3	34
22	Herman Moore	12	670	9,174	13.7	62
23	Ozzie Newsome	13	662	7,980	12.1	47
24	Charley Taylor	13	649	9,110	14.0	79
25	Drew Hill	15	634	9,831	15.5	60

Rushing

		Yrs	Car	Yards	Avg	TD
1	**Emmitt Smith**	14	4142	17,418	4.2	155
2	Walter Payton	13	3838	16,726	4.4	110
3	Barry Sanders	10	3062	15,269	5.0	99
4	Eric Dickerson	11	2996	13,259	4.4	90
5	Tony Dorsett	12	2936	12,739	4.3	77
6	**Jerome Bettis**	11	3119	12,353	4.0	69
7	Jim Brown	9	2359	12,312	5.2	106
8	Marcus Allen	16	3022	12,243	4.1	123
9	Franco Harris	13	2949	12,120	4.1	91
10	Thurman Thomas	13	2877	12,074	4.2	65
11	**Curtis Martin**	9	2927	11,669	4.0	73
12	John Riggins	14	2916	11,352	3.9	104
13	O.J. Simpson	11	2404	11,236	4.7	61
14	**Marshall Faulk**	11	2576	11,213	4.4	97
15	Ricky Watters	10	2622	10,643	4.1	78
16	Ottis Anderson	14	2562	10,273	4.0	81
17	**Eddie George**	8	2733	10,009	3.7	64
18	Earl Campbell	8	2187	9,407	4.3	74
19	Terry Allen	10	2152	8,614	4.0	73
20	Jim Taylor	10	1941	8,597	4.4	83
21	Joe Perry	14	1737	8,378	4.8	53
22	Ernest Byner	14	2095	8,261	3.9	56
23	Herschel Walker	12	1954	8,225	4.2	61
24	Roger Craig	11	1991	8,189	4.1	56
25	Gerald Riggs	10	1989	8,188	4.1	69

Note: The NFL does not recognize records from the All-American Football Conference (1946-49). If it did, **Joe Perry** would move up from 21st to 18th (after George) with the following stats: 16 Yrs; 1,929 Att; 9,723 Yards; 5.0 Avg; and 71 TD.

All-Purpose Yards

		Rush	Rec	Ret	Total
1	**Brian Mitchell**	1,967	2,336	19,027	23,330
2	Jerry Rice	645	22,466	6	23,117
3	Walter Payton	16,726	4,538	539	21,803
4	**Emmitt Smith**	17,418	3,119	0	20,537
5	**Tim Brown**	190	14,734	4,510	19,434
6	Barry Sanders	15,269	2,921	118	18,308
7	Herschel Walker	8,225	4,859	5,084	18,168
8	Marcus Allen	12,243	5,411	-6	17,648
9	**Marshall Faulk**	11,213	6,274	36	17,523
10	Eric Metcalf	2,392	5,572	9,266	17,230
11	Thurman Thomas	12,074	4,458	0	16,532
12	Tony Dorsett	12,739	3,554	33	16,326
13	Henry Ellard	50	13,777	1,891	15,718
14	Irving Fryar	242	12,785	2,567	15,594
15	Jim Brown	12,312	2,499	648	15,459
16	Eric Dickerson	13,259	2,137	15	15,411
17	Glyn Milburn	817	1,322	12,772	14,911
18	James Brooks	7,962	3,621	3,327	14,910
19	Ricky Watters	10,643	4,248	0	14,891
20	**Curtis Martin**	11,669	2,966	0	14,635
21	Franco Harris	12,120	2,287	215	14,622
22	O.J. Simpson	11,236	2,142	990	14,368
23	James Lofton	246	14,004	27	14,277
24	Cris Carter	41	13,899	244	14,184
25	Bobby Mitchell	2,735	7,954	3,389	14,078

Years played: Allen (16), Brooks (12), J. Brown (9), T. Brown (16), Carter (16), Dickerson (11), Dorsett (12), Ellard (16), Faulk (12), Fryar (16), Harris (13), Lofton (16), Martin (9), Metcalf (13), Milburn (9), Bri. Mitchell (14), Bo. Mitchell (11), Payton (13), Rice (19), Sanders (10), Simpson (11), Smith (14), Thomas (13), Walker (12) and Watters (10).

All-Time NFL Leaders (Cont.)
Scoring

Points

		Yrs	TD	FG	PAT	Total
1	**Gary Anderson**	22	0	521	783	2346
2	**Morten Andersen**	22	0	502	753	2259
3	George Blanda	26	9	335	943	2002
4	Norm Johnson	18	0	366	638	1736
5	Nick Lowery	18	0	383	562	1711
6	Jan Stenerud	19	0	373	580	1699
7	Eddie Murray	19	0	352	538	1594
8	Al Del Greco	17	0	347	543	1584
9	Pat Leahy	18	0	304	558	1470
10	Jim Turner	16	1	304	521	1439
11	**John Carney**	16	0	343	404	1433
12	Matt Bahr	17	0	300	522	1422
13	Mark Moseley	16	0	300	482	1382
14	Jim Bakken	17	0	282	534	1380
15	**Steve Christie**	14	0	314	435	1377
16	Fred Cox	15	0	282	519	1365
17	**Matt Stover**	13	0	321	401	1364
18	Lou Groza	17	1	234	641	1349
19	**Jason Elam**	11	0	288	449	1313
20	Jim Breech	14	0	243	517	1246
21	Jerry Rice	19	205	0	0	1238†
22	**Jason Hanson**	12	0	284	384	1236
	Pete Stoyanovich	12	0	272	420	1236
24	Chris Bahr	14	0	241	490	1213
25	Kevin Butler	13	0	265	413	1208

†Rice's total includes four 2-point conversions.
Note: The NFL does not recognize records from the All-American Football Conference (1946-49). If it did, **Lou Groza** would move up from 18th to 7th (after Stenerud) with the following stats: 21 Yrs; 1 TD; 264 FG, 810 PAT; 1,608 Pts.

Interceptions

		Yrs	No	Yards	TD
1	Paul Krause	16	81	1185	3
2	Emlen Tunnell	14	79	1282	4
3	**Rod Woodson**	17	71	1483	12
4	Dick (Night Train) Lane	14	68	1207	5
5	Ken Riley	15	65	596	5

Sacks

		Yrs	No
1	**Bruce Smith**	19	200.0
2	Reggie White	15	198.0
3	Kevin Greene	15	160.0
4	Chris Doleman	15	150.5
5	Richard Dent	15	137.5
	John Randle	14	137.5

Note: The NFL did not begin officially compiling sacks until 1982. Deacon Jones, who played with the Rams, Chargers and Redskins from 1961-74, is often credited with 173.5 sacks. Jack Youngblood and Alan Page are unofficially credited with 150.5 and 148, respectively. Also, Lawrence Taylor has 142 career sacks if you count his rookie year of 1981, the year before sacks became an official stat.

Safeties

		Yrs	No
1	Ted Hendricks	15	4
	Doug English	10	4
3	Seventeen players tied with 3 each.		

Touchdowns

		Yrs	Rush	Rec	Ret	Total
1	Jerry Rice	19	10	194	1	205
2	Emmitt Smith	14	155	11	0	166
3	Marcus Allen	16	123	21	1	145
4	Cris Carter	16	0	130	1	131
	Marshall Faulk	10	97	34	0	131
6	Jim Brown	9	106	20	0	126
7	Walter Payton	13	110	15	0	125
8	John Riggins	14	104	12	0	116
9	Lenny Moore	12	63	48	2	113
10	Barry Sanders	10	99	10	0	109
11	Don Hutson	11	3	99	3	105
12	**Tim Brown**	16	1	99	4	104
13	Steve Largent	14	1	100	0	101
14	Franco Harris	13	91	9	0	100
15	Eric Dickerson	11	90	6	0	96
16	Jim Taylor	10	83	10	0	93
17	Tony Dorsett	12	77	13	1	91
	Bobby Mitchell	11	18	65	8	91
	Ricky Watters	10	78	13	0	91
20	Leroy Kelly	10	74	13	3	90
	Charley Taylor	13	11	79	0	90
22	Irving Fryar	17	1	84	3	88
	Don Maynard	15	0	88	0	88
	Andre Reed	16	1	87	0	88
	Thurman Thomas	13	65	23	0	88

Kickoff Returns
Minimum 75 returns.

		Yrs	No	Yards	Avg	TD
1	Gale Sayers	7	91	2781	30.6	6
2	Lynn Chandnois	7	92	2720	29.6	3
3	Abe Woodson	9	193	5538	28.7	5
4	Buddy Young	6	90	2514	27.9	2
5	Travis Williams	5	102	2801	27.5	6

Punting
Minimum 300 punts.

		Yrs	No	Yards	Avg
1	Sammy Baugh	16	338	15,245	45.1
2	Tommy Davis	11	511	22,833	44.7
3	Yale Lary	11	503	22,279	44.3
4	**Todd Sauerbrun**	9	684	30,092	44.0
5	Horace Gillom	7	385	16,872	43.8

Punt Returns
Minimum 75 returns.

		Yrs	No	Yards	Avg	TD
1	George McAfee	8	112	1431	12.8	2
2	Jack Christiansen	8	85	1084	12.8	3
3	Claude Gibson	5	110	1381	12.6	3
4	Bill Dudley	9	124	1515	12.2	3
5	Rick Upchurch	9	248	3008	12.1	8

Long-Playing Records

Seasons

		No
1	George Blanda, QB-K	26
2	**Gary Anderson**, K	22
	Morten Andersen, K	22
4	Earl Morrall, QB	21
5	Three tied with 20 each.	

Games

		No
1	George Blanda, QB-K	340
2	**Gary Anderson**, K	338
	Morten Andersen, K	338
4	Bruce Matthews, OL	296
5	Darrell Green, DB	295

Consecutive Games

		No
1	Jim Marshall, DE	282
2	**Jeff Feagles**, P	256
3	**Morten Andersen**, K	248
4	**Bill Romanowski**, LB	243
5	Mick Tingelhoff, C	240

SINGLE SEASON
Passing

Yards Gained	Year	Att	Cmp	Pct	Yds
Dan Marino, Mia	1984	564	362	64.2	5084
Kurt Warner, St.L	2001	546	375	68.7	4830
Dan Fouts, SD	1981	609	360	59.1	4802
Dan Marino, Mia	1986	623	378	60.7	4746
Dan Fouts, SD	1980	589	348	59.1	4715
Warren Moon, Hou	1991	655	404	61.7	4690
Rich Gannon, Oak	2002	618	418	67.6	4689
Warren Moon, Hou	1990	584	362	62.0	4689
Neil Lomax, St.L	1984	560	345	61.6	4614
Drew Bledsoe, NE	1994	691	400	57.9	4555

Efficiency	Year	Att/Cmp	TD	Rtg
Steve Young, SF	1994	461/324	35	112.8
Joe Montana, SF	1989	386/271	26	112.4
Milt Plum, Cle	1960	250/151	21	110.4
Sammy Baugh, Wash	1945	182/128	11	109.9
Kurt Warner, St.L	1999	499/325	41	109.2
Dan Marino, Mia	1984	564/362	48	108.9
Sid Luckman, Chi. Bears	1943	202/110	28	107.5
Steve Young, SF	1992	402/268	25	107.0
Randall Cunningham, Min	1998	425/259	34	106.0
Bart Starr, GB	1966	251/156	14	105.0

Receptions

Catches	Year	No	Yds
Marvin Harrison, Ind	2002	143	1722
Herman Moore, Det	1995	123	1686
Jerry Rice, SF	1995	122	1848
Cris Carter, Min	1995	122	1371
Cris Carter, Min	1994	122	1256
Isaac Bruce, St.L	1995	119	1781
Torry Holt, St.L	2003	117	1696
Jimmy Smith, Jax	1999	116	1636
Marvin Harrison, Ind	1999	115	1663
Rod Smith, Den	2001	113	1343
Hines Ward, Pit	2002	112	1329
Jimmy Smith, Jax	2001	112	1373
Jerry Rice, SF	1994	112	1499
Sterling Sharpe, GB	1993	112	1274

Rushing

Yards Gained	Year	Car	Yds	Avg
Eric Dickerson, LA Rams	1984	379	2105	5.6
Jamal Lewis, Bal.	2003	387	2066	5.3
Barry Sanders, Det	1997	335	2053	6.1
Terrell Davis, Den	1998	392	2008	5.1
O.J. Simpson, Buf	1973	332	2003	6.0
Earl Campbell, Hou	1980	373	1934	5.2
Barry Sanders, Det	1994	331	1883	5.7
Ahman Green, GB	2003	355	1883	5.3
Jim Brown, Cle	1963	291	1863	6.4
Ricky Williams, Mia	2002	383	1853	4.8
Walter Payton, Chi	1977	339	1852	5.5
Jamal Anderson, Atl	1998	410	1846	4.5
Eric Dickerson, LA Rams	1986	404	1821	4.5
O.J. Simpson, Buf	1975	329	1817	5.5

Scoring

Points

	Year	TD	PAT	FG	Pts
Paul Hornung, GB	1960	15	41	15	176
Gary Anderson, Min	1998	0	59	35	164
Jeff Wilkins, St.L	2003	0	46	39	163
Priest Holmes, KC	2003	27	0	0	162
Mark Moseley, Wash	1983	0	62	33	161
Marshall Faulk, St.L	2000	26	4	0	160
Mike Vanderjagt, Ind	2003	0	46	37	157
Gino Cappelletti, Bos	1964	7	38	25	155
Emmitt Smith, Dal	1995	25	0	0	150
Chip Lohmiller, Wash	1991	0	56	31	149
Gino Cappelletti, Bos	1961	8	48	17	147
Paul Hornung, GB	1961	10	41	15	146
Jim Turner, Jets	1968	0	43	34	145
John Kasay, Car.	1996	0	34	37	145
Mike Vanderjagt, Ind	1999	0	43	34	145

Touchdowns

	Year	Rush	Rec	Ret	Total
Priest Holmes, KC	2003	27	0	0	27
Marshall Faulk, St.L	2000	18	8	0	26
Emmitt Smith, Dal	1995	25	0	0	25
John Riggins, Wash	1983	24	0	0	24
Priest Holmes, KC	2002	21	3	0	24
Terrell Davis, Den	1998	21	2	0	23
O.J. Simpson, Buf	1975	16	7	0	23
Jerry Rice, SF	1987	1	22	0	23
Gale Sayers, Chi	1966	14	6	2	22
Chuck Foreman, Min	1975	13	9	0	22
Emmitt Smith, Dal	1994	21	1	0	22
Jim Brown, Cle	1965	17	4	0	21
Joe Morris, NY Giants	1985	21	0	0	21
Terry Allen, Wash	1996	21	0	0	21
Marshall Faulk, St.L	2001	12	9	0	21

Note: The NFL regular season schedule grew from 12 games (1947-60) to 14 (1961-77) to 16 (1978-present). The AFL regular season schedule was always 14 games (1960-69).

Touchdowns Passing

	Year	No
Dan Marino, Miami	1984	48
Dan Marino, Miami	1986	44
Kurt Warner, St. Louis	1999	41
Brett Favre, Green Bay	1996	39
Brett Favre, Green Bay	1995	38
George Blanda, Houston	1961	36
Y.A. Tittle, NY Giants	1963	36
Steve Young, San Francisco	1998	36
Steve Beuerlein, Carolina	1999	36
Kurt Warner, St. Louis	2001	36
Brett Favre, Green Bay	1997	35
Steve Young, San Francisco	1994	35
Randall Cunningham, Minnesota	1998	34

Nine tied with 33 each, incl. Warren Moon twice.

Touchdowns Receiving

	Year	No
Jerry Rice, San Francisco	1987	22
Mark Clayton, Miami	1984	18
Sterling Sharpe, Green Bay	1994	18
Don Hutson, Green Bay	1942	17
Elroy (Crazylegs) Hirsch, LA Rams	1951	17
Bill Groman, Houston	1961	17
Jerry Rice, San Francisco	1989	17
Cris Carter, Minnesota	1995	17
Carl Pickens, Cincinnati	1995	17
Randy Moss, Minnesota	1998	17
Randy Moss, Minnesota	2003	17
Art Powell, Oakland	1963	16
Terrell Owens, SF	2001	16

Eight tied with 15 each, incl. Rice three times.

All-Time NFL Leaders (Cont.)

Touchdowns Rushing

	Year	No
Priest Holmes, Kansas City	2003	27
Emmitt Smith, Dallas	1995	25
John Riggins, Washington	1983	24
Joe Morris, NY Giants	1985	21
Emmitt Smith, Dallas	1994	21
Terry Allen, Washington	1996	21
Terrell Davis, Denver	1998	21
Priest Holmes, Kansas City	2002	21
Jim Taylor, Green Bay	1962	19
Earl Campbell, Houston	1979	19
Chuck Muncie, San Diego	1981	19

Field Goals

	Year	Att	No
Jeff Wilkins, St. Louis	2003	42	39
Olindo Mare, Miami	1999	46	39
Mike Vanderjagt, Indianapolis	2003	37	37
John Kasay, Carolina	1996	45	37
Cary Blanchard, Indianapolis	1996	40	36
Al Del Greco, Tennessee	1998	39	36
Ali Haji-Sheikh, NY Giants	1983	42	35
Jeff Jaeger, LA Raiders	1993	44	35
Gary Anderson, Minnesota	1998	35	35
Matt Stover, Baltimore	2000	39	35
Ten tied with 34 FG each.			

Interceptions

	Year	No
Dick (Night Train) Lane, Detroit	1952	14
Dan Sandifer, Washington	1948	13
Spec Sanders, NY Yanks	1950	13
Lester Hayes, Oakland	1980	13
Nine tied with 12 each.		

Punting

Qualifiers	Year	Avg
Sammy Baugh, Washington	1940	51.4
Yale Lary, Detroit	1963	48.9
Sammy Baugh, Washington	1941	48.7
Yale Lary, Detroit	1961	48.4
Sammy Baugh, Washington	1942	48.2

Kickoff Returns

	Year	Avg
Travis Williams, Green Bay	1967	41.1
Gale Sayers, Chicago Bears	1967	37.7
Ollie Matson, Chicago Cards	1958	35.5
Jim Duncan, Baltimore Colts	1970	35.4
Lynn Chandnois, Pittsburgh	1952	35.2

Punt Returns

	Year	Avg
Herb Rich, Baltimore	1950	23.0
Jack Christiansen, Detroit	1952	21.5
Dick Christy, NY Titans	1961	21.3
Bob Hayes, Dallas	1968	20.8
Claude Young, NY Yanks	1951	19.3

Sacks

	Year	No		Year	No
Michael Strahan, NY Giants	2001	22.5	Chris Doleman, Minnesota	1989	21
Mark Gastineau, NY Jets	1984	22	Lawrence Taylor, NY Giants	1986	20.5
Reggie White, Philadelphia	1987	21	Derrick Thomas, Kansas City	1990	20

Note: The NFL did not begin officially compiling sacks until 1982. Cincinnati's Coy Bacon is widely, although not officially, credited with 26 sacks during the 1976 season.

SINGLE GAME

Passing

Yards Gained

	Date	Yds
Norm Van Brocklin, LA vs NY Yanks	9/28/51	554
Warren Moon, Hou vs KC	12/16/90	527
Boomer Esiason, Ariz vs Wash.	11/10/96	522
Dan Marino, Mia vs NYJ	10/23/88	521
Phil Simms, NYG vs Cin	10/13/85	513

Completions

	Date	No
Drew Bledsoe, NE vs Min	11/13/94	45
Rich Gannon, Oak vs Pit	9/15/02	43
Richard Todd, NYJ vs SF	9/21/80	42
Vinny Testaverde, NYJ vs Sea	12/6/98	42
Warren Moon, Hou vs Dal	11/10/91	41
Three tied with 40 each.		

Receiving

Catches

	Date	No
Terrell Owens, SF vs Chi	12/17/00	20
Tom Fears, LA vs GB	12/3/50	18
Clark Gaines, NYJ vs SF	9/21/80	17
Four tied with 16 each.		

Yards Gained

	Date	Yds
Flipper Anderson, LA Rams vs NO	11/26/89	336
Stephone Paige, KC vs SD	12/22/85	309
Jim Benton, Cle vs Det	11/22/45	303
Cloyce Box, Det vs Bal	12/3/50	302
Jimmy Smith, Jax vs Bal	9/10/00	291
Jerry Rice, SF vs Det	9/25/95	289

Rushing

Yards Gained

	Date	Yds
Jamal Lewis, Bal vs Cle	9/14/03	295
Corey Dillon, Cin vs Den	10/22/00	278
Walter Payton, Chi vs Min	11/20/77	275
O.J. Simpson, Buf vs Det	11/25/76	273
Shaun Alexander, Sea vs Oak	11/11/01	266
Mike Anderson, Den vs NO	12/3/00	251
O.J. Simpson, Buf vs NE	9/16/73	250
Willie Ellison, LA Rams vs NO	12/5/71	247

All-Purpose Yards

	Date	Yds
Glyn Milburn, Den vs Sea	12/10/95	404
Billy Cannon, Hou vs NY Titans	12/10/61	373
Michael Lewis, NO vs Wash	10/13/02	356
Tyrone Hughes, NO vs LA Rams	10/23/94	347
Lionel James, SD vs Raiders	11/10/85	345
Timmy Brown, Phi vs St.L	12/16/62	341
Gale Sayers, Chi vs Min	12/18/66	339
Gale Sayers, Chi vs SF	12/12/65	336
Flipper Anderson, LA Rams vs NO	11/26/89	336

Scoring

Points

	Date	Pts
Ernie Nevers, Chi. Cards vs Chi. Bears	11/28/29	40
Dub Jones, Cle vs Chi. Bears	11/25/51	36
Gale Sayers, Chi vs SF	12/12/65	36
Paul Hornung, GB vs Bal	10/8/61	33
Bob Shaw, Chi. Cards vs Bal	10/2/50	30
Jim Brown, Cle vs Bal	11/1/59	30
Abner Haynes, Dal. Texans vs Oak	11/26/61	30
Billy Cannon, Hou vs NY Titans	12/10/61	30
Cookie Gilchrist, Buf vs NY Jets	12/8/63	30
Kellen Winslow, SD vs Oak	11/22/81	30
Jerry Rice, SF vs Atl	10/14/90	30
James Stewart, Jax vs Phi.	10/12/97	30
Shaun Alexander, Sea vs Min.	9/29/02	30
Clinton Portis, Den vs KC	12/7/03	30

Note: Nevers celebrated Thanksgiving, 1929, by scoring all of the Chicago Cardinals' points on six rushing TDs and four PATs. The Cards beat Red Grange and the Chicago Bears, 40-6.

Touchdowns Passing

	Date	No
Sid Luckman, Chi. Bears vs NYG	11/14/43	7
Adrian Burk, Phi vs Wash	10/17/54	7
George Blanda, Hou vs NY Titans	11/19/61	7
Y.A. Tittle, NYG vs Wash	10/28/62	7
Joe Kapp, Min vs Bal	9/28/69	7

Touchdowns Receiving

	Date	No
Bob Shaw, Chi. Cards vs Bal	10/2/50	5
Kellen Winslow, SD vs Oak	11/22/81	5
Jerry Rice, SF vs Atl	10/14/90	5

Touchdowns Rushing

	Date	No
Ernie Nevers, Chi. Cards vs Chi. Bears	11/28/29	6
Jim Brown, Cle vs Bal	11/1/59	5
Cookie Gilchrist, Buf vs NY Jets	12/8/63	5
James Stewart, Jax vs Phi.	10/12/97	5
Clinton Portis, Den vs KC	12/7/03	5

Field Goals

	Date	No
Jim Bakken, St.L vs Pit	9/24/67	7
Rich Karlis, Min vs LA Rams	11/5/89	7
Chris Boniol, Dal vs GB	11/18/96	7
Billy Cundiff, Dal vs NYG	9/15/03	7

Note: Bakken was 7-for-9, Cundiff was 7-for-8, Boniol and Karlis were 7-for-7.

Extra Point Kicks

	Date	No
Pat Harder, Cards vs NYG	10/17/48	9
Bob Waterfield, Rams vs Bal	10/22/50	9
Charlie Gogolak, Wash vs NYG	11/27/66	9

Interceptions

	No
By 18 players	4

Sacks

	Date	No
Derrick Thomas, KC vs Sea	11/11/90	7.0
Fred Dean, SF vs NO	11/13/83	6.0
Derrick Thomas, KC vs Oak	9/6/98	6.0
William Gay, Det vs TB	9/4/83	5.5

Longest Plays

Passing (all for TDs)

	Date	Yds
Frank Filchock to Andy Farkas, Wash vs Pit	10/15/39	99
George Izo to Bobby Mitchell, Wash vs Cle	9/15/63	99
Karl Sweetan to Pat Studstill, Det vs Bal	10/16/66	99
Sonny Jurgensen to Gerry Allen, Wash vs Chi	9/15/68	99
Jim Plunkett to Cliff Branch, LA Raiders vs Wash	10/2/83	99
Ron Jaworski to Mike Quick, Phi vs Atl	11/10/85	99
Stan Humphries to Tony Martin, SD vs Sea	9/18/94	99
Brett Favre to Robert Brooks, GB vs Chi	9/11/95	99
Trent Green to Marc Boerigter, KC vs SD	12/22/02	99

Runs from Scrimmage (all for TDs)

	Date	Yds
Tony Dorsett, Dal vs Min	1/3/83	99
Ahman Green, GB vs Den	12/28/03	98
Andy Uram, GB vs Chi. Cards	10/8/39	97
Bob Gage, Pit vs Bears	12/4/49	97
Jim Spavital, Balt. Colts vs GB	11/5/50	96
Bob Hoernschemeyer, Det vs NY Yanks	11/23/50	96
Garrison Hearst, SF vs NYJ	9/6/98	96
Corey Dillon, Cin vs Det	10/28/01	96

Punts

	Date	Yds
Steve O'Neal, NYJ vs Den	9/21/69	98
Joe Lintzenich, Chi. Bears vs NYG	11/15/31	94
Shawn McCarthy, NE vs Buf	11/3/91	93

Field Goals

	Date	Yds
Tom Dempsey, NO vs Det	11/8/70	63
Jason Elam, Den vs Jax	10/25/98	63
Steve Cox, Cle vs Cin	10/21/84	60
Morten Andersen, NO vs Chi	10/27/91	60
Tony Franklin, Phi vs Dal	11/12/79	59
Pete Stoyanovich, Mia vs NYJ	11/12/89	59
Steve Christie, Buf vs Mia	9/26/93	59
Morten Andersen, Atl vs SF	12/24/95	59

Punt Returns (all for TDs)

	Date	Yds
Robert Bailey, Rams vs NO	10/23/94	103
Gil LeFebvre, Cin vs Bklyn	12/3/33	98
Charlie West, Min vs Wash	11/3/68	98
Dennis Morgan, Dal vs St.L	10/13/74	98
Terance Mathis, NYJ vs Dal	11/4/90	98
Greg Pruitt, LA Raiders vs Wash.	10/2/83	97

Kickoff Returns (all for TDs)

	Date	Yds
Al Carmichael, GB vs Chi. Bears	10/7/56	106
Noland Smith, KC vs Den	12/17/67	106
Roy Green, St.L vs Dal	10/21/79	106

Interception Returns (all for TDs)

	Date	Yds
James Willis (14 yds) lateral to Troy Vincent (90 yds), Phi vs Dal	11/3/96	104
Vencie Glenn, SD vs Den	11/29/87	103
Louis Oliver, Mia vs Buf	10/4/92	103

Seven players tied with 102-yd returns.

Note: On 9/30/02 Baltimore's Chris McAlister returned a missed FG 107 yards, the longest play in NFL history.

Chicago College All-Star Game

On Aug. 31, 1934, a year after sponsoring Major League Baseball's first All-Star Game, *Chicago Tribune* sports editor Arch Ward presented the first Chicago College All-Star Game at Soldier Field. A crowd of 79,432 turned out to see an all-star team of graduated college seniors battle the 1933 NFL champion Chicago Bears to a scoreless tie. The preseason game was played at Soldier Field and pitted the College All-Stars against the defending NFL champions (1933-1966) or Super Bowl champions (1967-75) every year except 1935 until it was cancelled in 1977. The NFL champs won the series, 31-9-1.

Year		Year		Year	
1934	Chi. Bears 0, All-Stars 0	1949	Philadelphia 38, All-Stars 0	1964	Chi. Bears 28, All-Stars 17
1935	Chi. Bears 5, All-Stars 0			1965	Cleveland 24, All-Stars 16
1936	Detroit 7, All-Stars 0	1950	All-Stars 17, Philadelphia 7	1966	Green Bay 38, All-Stars 0
1937	All-Stars 6, Green Bay 0	1951	Cleveland 33, All-Stars 0	1967	Green Bay 27, All-Stars 0
1938	All-Stars 28, Washington 16	1952	LA Rams 10, All-Stars 7	1968	Green Bay 34, All-Stars 17
1939	NY Giants 9, All-Stars 0	1953	Detroit 24, All-Stars 10	1969	NY Jets 26, All-Stars 24
		1954	Detroit 31, All-Stars 6		
1940	Green Bay 45, All-Stars 28	1955	All-Stars 30, Cleveland 27	1970	Kansas City 24, All-Stars 3
1941	Chi. Bears 37, All-Stars 13	1956	Cleveland 26, All-Stars 0	1971	Baltimore 24, All-Stars 17
1942	Chi. Bears 21, All-Stars 0	1957	NY Giants 22, All-Stars 12	1972	Dallas 20, All-Stars 7
1943	All-Stars 27, Washington 7	1958	All-Stars 35, Detroit 19	1973	Miami 14, All-Stars 3
1944	Chi. Bears 24, All-Stars 21	1959	Baltimore 29, All-Stars 0	1974	No Game (NFLPA Strike)
1945	Green Bay 19, All-Stars 7			1975	Pittsburgh 21, All-Stars 14
1946	All-Stars 16, LA Rams 0	1960	Baltimore 32, All-Stars 7	1976	Pittsburgh 24, All-Stars 0*
1947	All-Stars 16, Chi. Bears 0	1961	Philadelphia 28, All-Stars 14		
1948	Chi. Cards 28, All-Stars 0	1962	Green Bay 42, All-Stars 20	*Downpour flooded field, game called
		1963	All-Stars 20, Green Bay 17	with 1:22 left in 3rd quarter.

Number One Draft Choices

In an effort to blunt the dominance of the Chicago Bears and New York Giants in the 1930s and distribute talent more evenly throughout the league, the NFL established the college draft in 1936. The first player chosen in the first draft was Jay Berwanger, who was also college football's first Heisman Trophy winner. In all, 17 Heisman winners have also been the NFL's No. 1 draft choice. They are noted in **bold** type. The American Football League (formed in 1960) held its own draft for six years before agreeing to merge with the NFL and select players in a common draft starting in 1967.

Year	Team		Year	Team	
1936	Philadelphia	**Jay Berwanger**, HB, Chicago	1967	Baltimore	Bubba Smith, DT, Michigan St.
1937	Philadelphia	Sam Francis, FB, Nebraska	1968	Minnesota	Ron Yary, T, USC
1938	Cleveland Rams	Corbett Davis, FB, Indiana	1969	Buffalo	**O.J. Simpson**, RB, USC
1939	Chicago Cards	Ki Aldrich, C, TCU			
			1970	Pittsburgh	Terry Bradshaw, QB, La.Tech
1940	Chicago Cards	George Cafego, HB, Tennessee	1971	New England	**Jim Plunkett**, QB, Stanford
1941	Chicago Bears	**Tom Harmon**, HB, Michigan	1972	Buffalo	Walt Patulski, DE, Notre Dame
1942	Pittsburgh	Bill Dudley, HB, Virginia	1973	Houston	John Matuszak, DE, Tampa
1943	Detroit	**Frank Sinkwich**, HB, Georgia	1974	Dallas	Ed (Too Tall) Jones, DE, Tenn. St.
1944	Boston Yanks	**Angelo Bertelli**, QB, N. Dame	1975	Atlanta	Steve Bartkowski, QB, Calif.
1945	Chicago Cards	Charley Trippi, HB,Georgia	1976	Tampa Bay	Lee Roy Selmon, DE, Oklahoma
1946	Boston Yanks	Frank Dancewicz, QB, N. Dame	1977	Tampa Bay	Ricky Bell, RB, USC
1947	Chicago Bears	Bob Fenimore, HB, Okla. A&M	1978	Houston	**Earl Campbell**, RB, Texas
1948	Washington	Harry Gilmer, QB, Alabama	1979	Buffalo	Tom Cousineau, LB, Ohio St.
1949	Philadelphia	Chuck Bednarik, C, Penn			
			1980	Detroit	**Billy Sims**, RB, Oklahoma
1950	Detroit	**Leon Hart**, E, Notre Dame	1981	New Orleans	**George Rogers**, RB, S. Carolina
1951	NY Giants	Kyle Rote, HB, SMU	1982	New England	Kenneth Sims, DT, Texas
1952	LA Rams	Bill Wade, QB, Vanderbilt	1983	Baltimore	John Elway, QB, Stanford
1953	San Francisco	Harry Babcock, E, Georgia	1984	New England	Irving Fryar, WR, Nebraska
1954	Cleveland	Bobby Garrett, QB, Stanford	1985	Buffalo	Bruce Smith, DE, Va. Tech
1955	Baltimore	George Shaw, QB, Oregon	1986	Tampa Bay	**Bo Jackson**, RB, Auburn
1956	Pittsburgh	Gary Glick, DB, Colo. A&M	1987	Tampa Bay	**V. Testaverde**, QB, Miami-FL
1957	Green Bay	**Paul Hornung**, QB, N. Dame	1988	Atlanta	Aundray Bruce, LB, Auburn
1958	Chicago Cards	King Hill, QB, Rice	1989	Dallas	Troy Aikman, QB, UCLA
1959	Green Bay	Randy Duncan, QB, Iowa			
			1990	Indianapolis	Jeff George, QB, Illinois
1960	NFL–LA Rams	**Billy Cannon**, HB, LSU	1991	Dallas	Russell Maryland, DT, Miami-FL
	AFL–No choice		1992	Indianapolis	Steve Emtman, DT, Washington
1961	NFL–Minnesota	Tommy Mason, HB, Tulane	1993	New England	Drew Bledsoe, QB, Washington St.
	AFL–Buffalo	Ken Rice, G, Auburn	1994	Cincinnati	Dan Wilkinson, DT, Ohio St.
1962	NFL–Washington	**Ernie Davis**, HB, Syracuse	1995	Cincinnati	Ki-Jana Carter, RB, Penn St.
	AFL–Oakland	Roman Gabriel, QB, N.C. State	1996	NY Jets	Keyshawn Johnson, WR, USC
1963	NFL–LA Rams	**Terry Baker**, QB, Oregon St.	1997	St. Louis	Orlando Pace, OT, Ohio St.
	AFL–Kan.City	Buck Buchanan, DT, Grambling	1998	Indianapolis	Peyton Manning, QB, Tennessee
1964	NFL–San Fran	Dave Parks, E, Texas Tech	1999	Cleveland	Tim Couch, QB, Kentucky
	AFL–Boston	Jack Concannon, QB, Boston Col.			
1965	NFL–NY Giants	Tucker Frederickson, FB, Auburn	2000	Cleveland	Courtney Brown, DE, Penn St.
	AFL–Houston	Lawrence Elkins, E, Baylor	2001	Atlanta	Michael Vick, QB, Va. Tech
1966	NFL–Atlanta	Tommy Nobis, LB, Texas	2002	Houston	David Carr, QB, Fresno St.
	AFL–Miami	Jim Grabowski, FB, Illinois	2003	Cincinnati	**Carson Palmer**, QB, USC
			2004	San Diego	Eli Manning, QB, Mississippi

AP/Wide World Photos
Don Shula

NFL Media
Marty Schottenheimer

NFL Media
Bill Parcells

NFL Media
Mike Holmgren

All-Time Winningest NFL Coaches

NFL career victories through the 2003 season. Career, regular season and playoff records are noted along with NFL, AFL and Super Bowl titles won. Coaches active during 2003 season in **bold** type.

			Career				Regular Season				Playoffs			
		Yrs	W	L	T	Pct	W	L	T	Pct	W	L	Pct.	League Titles
1	Don Shula	.33	**347**	173	6	.665	328	156	6	.676	19	17	.528	2 Super Bowls and 1 NFL
2	George Halas	.40	**324**	151	31	.671	318	148	31	.671	6	3	.667	5 NFL
3	Tom Landry	.29	**270**	178	6	.601	250	162	6	.605	20	16	.556	2 Super Bowls
4	Curly Lambeau	.33	**229**	134	22	.623	226	132	22	.624	3	2	.600	6 NFL
5	Chuck Noll	.23	**209**	156	1	.572	193	148	1	.566	16	8	.667	4 Super Bowls
6	**Dan Reeves**	.23	**201**	174	2	.536	190	165	2	.535	11	9	.550	—None—
7	Chuck Knox	.22	**193**	158	1	.550	186	147	1	.558	7	11	.389	—None—
8	Paul Brown	.21	**170**	108	6	.609	166	100	6	.621	4	8	.333	3 NFL
	M. Schottenheimer	.18	**170**	124	1	.579	165	113	1	.593	5	11	.313	—None—
10	Bud Grant	.18	**168**	108	5	.607	158	96	5	.620	10	12	.455	1 NFL
11	**Bill Parcells**	.16	**159**	113	1	.584	148	106	1	.582	11	7	.611	2 Super Bowls
12	Marv Levy	.17	**154**	120	0	.562	143	112	0	.561	11	8	.579	—None—
13	Steve Owen	.23	**153**	108	17	.581	151	100	17	.595	2	8	.200	2 NFL
14	Joe Gibbs	.12	**140**	65	0	.683	124	60	0	.674	16	5	.762	3 Super Bowls
15	Hank Stram	.17	**136**	100	10	.573	131	97	10	.571	5	3	.625	1 Super Bowl and 3 AFL
16	Weeb Ewbank	.20	**134**	130	7	.507	130	129	7	.502	4	1	.800	1 Super Bowl, 2 NFL, and 1 AFL
17	Mike Ditka	.14	**127**	101	0	.557	121	95	0	.560	6	6	.500	1 Super Bowl
18	**Mike Holmgren**	.12	**125**	83	0	.601	116	76	0	.604	9	7	.563	1 Super Bowl
	Jim Mora	.15	**125**	112	0	.527	125	106	0	.541	0	6	.000	—None—
20	George Seifert	.11	**124**	67	0	.649	114	62	0	.648	10	5	.667	2 Super Bowls
21	Sid Gillman	.18	**123**	104	7	.541	122	99	7	.550	1	5	.167	1 AFL
22	**Bill Cowher**	.12	**122**	84	1	.592	115	76	1	.602	7	8	.467	—None—
23	George Allen	.12	**118**	54	5	.681	116	47	5	.705	2	7	.222	—None—
24	Don Coryell	.14	**114**	89	1	.561	111	83	1	.572	3	6	.333	—None—
25	John Madden	.10	**112**	39	7	.731	103	32	7	.750	9	7	.563	1 Super Bowl

Notes: The NFL does not recognize records from the All-American Football Conference (1946-49). If it did, **Paul Brown** (52-4-3 in four AAFC seasons) would move up from 8th to 5th on the all-time list with the following career stats— 25 Yrs; 222 Wins; 112 Losses; 9 Ties; .660 Pct; 9-8 playoff record; and 4 AAFC titles.

The NFL also considers the Playoff Bowl or "Runner-up Bowl" (officially: the Bert Bell Benefit Bowl) as a postseason exhibition game. The Playoff Bowl was contested every year from 1960-69 in Miami between Eastern and Western Conference second place teams. While the games did not count, six of the coaches above went to the Playoff Bowl at least once and came away with the following records— Allen (2-0), Brown (0-1), Grant (0-1), Landry (1-2) and Shula (2-0).

Where They Coached

Allen—LA Rams (1966-70), Washington (1971-77); **Brown**—Cleveland (1950-62), Cincinnati (1968-75); **Coryell**—St. Louis (1973-77), San Diego (1978-86); **Cowher**—Pittsburgh (1992–); **Ditka**— Chicago (1982-92), New Orleans (1997-99); **Ewbank**— Baltimore (1954-62), NY Jets (1963-73); **Gibbs**—Washington (1981-92, 2004–); **Gillman**—LA Rams (1955-59), LA-San Diego Chargers (1960-69), Houston (1973-74).

Grant—Minnesota (1967-83,1985); **Halas**—Chicago Bears (1920-29,33-42,46-55,58-67); **Holmgren**—Green Bay (1992-98), Seattle (1999–); **Knox**— LA Rams (1973-77, 1992-94), Buffalo (1978-82), Seattle (1983-91); **Lambeau**—Green Bay (1921-49), Chicago Cards (1950-51), Washington (1952-53); **Landry**—Dallas (1960-88); **Levy**— Kansas City (1978-82), Buffalo (1986-97); **Madden**—Oakland (1969-78); **Mora**—New Orleans (1986-1995), Indianapolis (1998-2001).

Noll—Pittsburgh (1969-91); **Owen**—NY Giants (1931-53); **Parcells**— NY Giants (1983-90), New England (1993-97), NY Jets (1997-99), Dallas (2003–); **Reeves**— Denver (1981-92), NY Giants (1993-96), Atlanta (1997-2003); **Schottenheimer**—Cleveland (1984-88), Kansas City (1989-98), Washington (2001), San Diego (2002–); **Seifert**—San Francisco (1989-96), Carolina (1999-2001); **Shula**—Baltimore (1963-69), Miami (1970-95); **Stram**—Dallas-Kansas City (1960-74), New Orleans (1976-77).

Top Winning Percentages

Minimum of 85 NFL victories, including playoffs.

		Yrs	W	L	T	Pct
1	Vince Lombardi	10	105	35	6	**.740**
2	John Madden	10	112	39	7	**.731**
3	Joe Gibbs	12	140	65	0	**.683**
4	George Allen	12	118	54	5	**.681**
5	George Halas	40	324	151	31	**.671**
6	Don Shula	33	347	173	6	**.665**
7	George Seifert	11	124	67	0	**.649**
8	Curly Lambeau	33	229	134	22	**.623**
9	Bill Walsh	10	102	63	1	**.617**
10	**Mike Shanahan**	11	106	68	0	**.609**
11	Paul Brown	21	170	108	6	**.609**
12	Bud Grant	18	168	108	5	**.607**
13	Tom Landry	29	270	178	6	**.601**
14	**Mike Holmgren**	12	125	83	0	**.601**
15	**Bill Cowher**	12	122	84	1	**.592**
16	Dennis Green	10	101	70	0	**.591**
17	**Jeff Fisher**	10	93	66	0	**.585**
18	**Bill Parcells**	16	159	113	1	**.584**
19	Steve Owen	23	153	108	17	**.581**
20	Buddy Parker	15	107	76	9	**.581**
21	**Marty Schottenheimer**	18	170	124	1	**.578**
22	Hank Stram	17	136	100	10	**.573**
23	Chuck Noll	23	209	156	1	**.572**
24	Jimmy Johnson	9	89	68	0	**.567**
25	Marv Levy	17	154	120	0	**.562**

Note: If AAFC records are included, **Paul Brown** moves from 12th to 7th with a percentage of .660 (25 yrs, 222-112-9) and **Buck Shaw** would be 11th at .619 (8 yrs, 91-55-5).

Active Coaches' Victories

Through 2003 season, including playoffs.

		Yrs	W	L	T	Pct
1	Marty Schottenheimer, SD	18	**170**	124	1	.578
2	Bill Parcells, Dallas	16	**159**	113	1	.584
3	Joe Gibbs, Washington	12	**140**	65	0	.683
4	Mike Holmgren, Seattle	12	**125**	83	0	.601
5	Bill Cowher, Pittsburgh	12	**122**	84	1	.592
6	Dick Vermeil, KC	13	**109**	99	0	.524
7	Mike Shanahan, Denver	11	**106**	68	0	.609
8	Dennis Green, Arizona	10	**101**	70	0	.591
9	Jeff Fisher, Tennessee	10	**93**	66	0	.585
10	Dave Wannstedt, Miami	10	**83**	82	0	.503
11	Bill Belichick, New England	9	**82**	70	0	.539
12	Tony Dungy, Indianapolis	8	**80**	58	0	.580
13	Tom Coughlin, NY Giants	8	**72**	64	0	.529
14	Steve Mariucci, Detroit	7	**65**	54	0	.546
15	Jon Gruden, Tampa Bay	6	**62**	41	0	.602
16	Andy Reid, Philadelphia	5	**56**	33	0	.629
17	Brian Billick, Baltimore	5	**52**	35	0	.598
18	Norv Turner, Oakland	7	**50**	60	1	.455
19	Mike Sherman, Green Bay	4	**45**	24	0	.652
	Mike Martz, St. Louis	4	**45**	24	0	.652
21	Dom Capers, Houston	6	**40**	58	0	.408
22	Dennis Erickson, San Fran.	5	**38**	42	0	.475
23	Jim Haslett, New Orleans	4	**35**	31	0	.530
24	Herman Edwards, NY Jets	3	**26**	25	0	.510
25	John Fox, Carolina	2	**21**	15	0	.583
	Butch Davis, Cleveland	3	**21**	28	0	.429
27	Mike Tice, Minnesota	3	**15**	18	0	.455
28	Marvin Lewis, Cincinnati	1	**8**	8	0	.500
29	Jack Del Rio, Jacksonville	1	**5**	11	0	.313
30	Jim Mora Jr., Atlanta	0	**0**	0	0	.000
	Mike Mularkey, Buffalo	0	**0**	0	0	.000
	Lovie Smith, Chicago	0	**0**	0	0	.000

Annual Awards
Most Valuable Player

Currently, the NFL does not sanction an official MVP award. It awarded the Joe F. Carr Trophy (Carr was NFL president from 1921-39) to the league MVP from 1938 to 1946. Since then, four principal MVP awards have been given out throughout the years and are noted below: UPI (1953-69), AP (since 1957), the Maxwell Club of Philadelphia's Bert Bell Trophy (since 1959) and the Pro Football Writers Assn. (since 1976). UPI switched to AFC and NFC Player of the Year awards in 1970 and then discontinued its awards in 1997.

Multiple winners (more than one season): Jim Brown (4); Randall Cunningham, Brett Favre, Johnny Unitas and Y.A. Tittle (3); Earl Campbell, Marshall Faulk, Rich Gannon, Otto Graham, Don Hutson, Joe Montana, Walter Payton, Barry Sanders, Ken Stabler, Joe Theismann, Kurt Warner and Steve Young (2).

Year	Awards
1938 Mel Hein, NY Giants, C	Carr
1939 Parker Hall, Cleveland Rams, HB	Carr
1940 Ace Parker, Brooklyn, HB	Carr
1941 Don Hutson, Green Bay, E	Carr
1942 Don Hutson, Green Bay, E	Carr
1943 Sid Luckman, Chicago Bears, QB	Carr
1944 Frank Sinkwich, Detroit, HB	Carr
1945 Bob Waterfield, Cleveland Rams, QB	Carr
1946 Bill Dudley, Pittsburgh, HB	Carr
1947-52 No award	
1953 Otto Graham, Cleveland Browns, QB	UPI
1954 Joe Perry, San Francisco, FB	UPI
1955 Otto Graham, Cleveland, QB	UPI
1956 Frank Gifford, NY Giants, HB	UPI
1957 Y.A. Tittle, San Francisco, QB	UPI
& Jim Brown, Cleveland, FB	AP
1958 Jim Brown, Cleveland, FB	UPI
& Gino Marchetti, Baltimore, DE	AP
1959 Johnny Unitas, Baltimore, QB	UPI, Bell
& Charley Conerly, NY Giants, QB	AP
1960 Norm Van Brocklin, Phi., QB	UPI, AP (tie), Bell
& Joe Schmidt, Detroit, LB	AP (tie)
1961 Paul Hornung, Green Bay, HB	UPI, AP, Bell
1962 Y.A. Tittle, NY Giants, QB	UPI
Jim Taylor, Green Bay, FB	AP
& Andy Robustelli, NY Giants, DE	Bell
1963 Jim Brown, Cleveland, FB	UPI, Bell
& Y.A. Tittle, NY Giants, QB	AP

Year	Awards
1964 Johnny Unitas, Baltimore, QB	UPI, AP, Bell
1965 Jim Brown, Cleveland, FB	UPI, AP
& Pete Retzlaff, Philadelphia, TE	Bell
1966 Bart Starr, Green Bay, QB	UPI, AP
& Don Meredith, Dallas, QB	Bell
1967 Johnny Unitas, Baltimore, QB	UPI, AP, Bell
1968 Earl Morrall, Baltimore, QB	UPI, AP
& Leroy Kelly, Cleveland, RB	Bell
1969 Roman Gabriel, LA Rams, QB	UPI, AP, Bell
1970 John Brodie, San Francisco, QB	AP
& George Blanda, Oakland, QB-PK	Bell
1971 Alan Page, Minnesota, DT	AP
& Roger Staubach, Dallas, QB	Bell
1972 Larry Brown, Washington, RB	AP, Bell
1973 O.J. Simpson, Buffalo, RB	AP, Bell
1974 Ken Stabler, Oakland, QB	AP
& Merlin Olsen, LA Rams, DT	Bell
1975 Fran Tarkenton, Minnesota, QB	AP, Bell
1976 Bert Jones, Baltimore, QB	AP, PFWA
& Ken Stabler, Oakland, QB	Bell
1977 Walter Payton, Chicago, RB	AP, PFWA
& Bob Griese, Miami, QB	Bell
1978 Terry Bradshaw, Pittsburgh, QB	AP, Bell
& Earl Campbell, Houston, RB	PFWA
1979 Earl Campbell, Houston, RB	AP, Bell, PFWA
1980 Brian Sipe, Cleveland, QB	AP, PFWA
& Ron Jaworski, Philadelphia, QB	Bell
1981 Ken Anderson, Cincinnati, QB	AP, Bell, PFWA

Year	Awards	Year	Awards
1982 Mark Moseley, Washington, PK ....AP		1992 Steve Young, San Francisco, QB ....AP, Bell, PFWA	
Joe Theismann, Washington, QB ....Bell		1993 Emmitt Smith, Dallas, RB ....AP, Bell, PFWA	
& Dan Fouts, San Diego, QB ....PFWA		1994 Steve Young, San Francisco, QB ...AP, Bell, PFWA	
1983 Joe Theismann, Washington, QB .....AP, PFWA		1995 Brett Favre, Green Bay, QB ....AP, Bell, PFWA	
& John Riggins, Washington, RB ....Bell		1996 Brett Favre, Green Bay, QB ....AP, Bell, PFWA	
1984 Dan Marino, Miami, QB ....AP, Bell, PFWA		1997 Barry Sanders, Detroit, RB .....AP (tie), Bell, PFWA	
1985 Marcus Allen, LA Raiders, RB ......AP, PFWA		& Brett Favre, Green Bay, QB ....AP (tie)	
& Walter Payton, Chicago, RB ....Bell		1998 Terrell Davis, Denver, RB ....AP, PFWA	
1986 Lawrence Taylor, NY Giants, LB ....AP, Bell, PFWA		& Randall Cunningham, Minnesota, QB ....Bell	
1987 Jerry Rice, San Francisco, WR ....Bell, PFWA		1999 Kurt Warner, St. Louis, QB ......AP, Bell, PFWA	
& John Elway, Denver, QB ....AP		2000 Marshall Faulk, St. Louis, RB ....AP, PFWA	
1988 Boomer Esiason, Cincinnati, QB ......AP, PFWA &		& Rich Gannon, Oakland, QB ....Bell	
Randall Cunningham, Phila., QB ....Bell		2001 Kurt Warner, St. Louis, QB ....AP	
1989 Joe Montana, San Francisco, QB ...AP, Bell, PFWA		& Marshall Faulk, St. Louis, RB ......Bell, PFWA	
1990 Randall Cunningham, Phila., QB ....Bell, PFWA		2002 Rich Gannon, Oakland, QB ....AP, Bell, PFWA	
& Joe Montana, San Francisco, QB ....AP		2003 Peyton Manning, Indianapolis, QB ...AP (tie), Bell	
1991 Thurman Thomas, Buffalo, RB ......AP, PFWA		Steve McNair, Tennessee, QB ....AP (tie)	
& Barry Sanders, Detroit, RB ....Bell		& Jamal Lewis, Baltimore, RB ....PFWA	

AP Offensive Player of the Year

Selected by The Associated Press in balloting by a nationwide media panel. Given out since 1972. Rookie winners are in **bold** type.
Multiple winners: Earl Campbell and Marshall Faulk (3); Terrell Davis, Jerry Rice and Barry Sanders (2).

Year	Pos	Year	Pos	Year	Pos
1972 Larry Brown, Was ......RB		1983 Joe Theismann, Was ......QB		1994 Barry Sanders, Det ......RB	
1973 O.J. Simpson, Buf ......RB		1984 Dan Marino, Mia ......QB		1995 Brett Favre, GB ......QB	
1974 Ken Stabler, Oak .....QB		1985 Marcus Allen, Raiders ....RB		1996 Terrell Davis, Den ......RB	
1975 Fran Tarkenton, Min ....QB		1986 Eric Dickerson, Rams ....RB		1997 Barry Sanders, Det ......RB	
1976 Bert Jones, Bal ......QB		1987 Jerry Rice, SF ......WR		1998 Terrell Davis, Den ......RB	
1977 Walter Payton, Chi ....RB		1988 Roger Craig, SF ......RB		1999 Marshall Faulk, St.L ......RB	
1978 **Earl Campbell**, Hou ....RB		1989 Joe Montana, SF ......QB		2000 Marshall Faulk, St.L ......RB	
1979 Earl Campbell, Hou .....RB		1990 Warren Moon, Hou ......QB		2001 Marshall Faulk, St.L ......RB	
1980 Earl Campbell, Hou .....RB		1991 Thurman Thomas, Buf ....RB		2002 Priest Holmes, KC ......RB	
1981 Ken Anderson, Cin ......QB		1992 Steve Young, SF ....QB		2003 Jamal Lewis, Bal ....RB	
1982 Dan Fouts, SD ....QB		1993 Jerry Rice, SF ....WR			

AP Defensive Player of the Year

Selected by The Associated Press in balloting by a nationwide media panel. Given out since 1971. Rookie winners are in **bold** type.
Multiple winners: Lawrence Taylor (3); Joe Greene, Ray Lewis, Mike Singletary, Bruce Smith and Reggie White (2).

Year	Pos	Year	Pos	Year	Pos
1971 Alan Page, Min ....DT		1982 Lawrence Taylor, NYG ....LB		1993 Rod Woodson, Pit ....CB	
1972 Joe Greene, Pit ....DT		1983 Doug Betters, Mia ....DE		1994 Deion Sanders, SF ....CB	
1973 Dick Anderson, Mia ......S		1984 Kenny Easley, Sea ....S		1995 Bryce Paup, Buf ....LB	
1974 Joe Greene, Pit ....DT		1985 Mike Singletary, Chi ......LB		1996 Bruce Smith, Buf ....DE	
1975 Mel Blount, Pit ....CB		1986 Lawrence Taylor, NYG ....LB		1997 Dana Stubblefield, SF ....DT	
1976 Jack Lambert, Pit ....LB		1987 Reggie White, Phi ....DE		1998 Reggie White, GB ......DE	
1977 Harvey Martin, Dal ......DE		1988 Mike Singletary, Chi ......LB		1999 Warren Sapp, TB ......DT	
1978 Randy Gradishar, Den ....LB		1989 Keith Millard, Min ....DT		2000 Ray Lewis, Bal ....LB	
1979 Lee Roy Selmon, TB .....DE		1990 Bruce Smith, Buf ....DE		2001 Michael Strahan, NYG ...DE	
1980 Lester Hayes, Oak ......CB		1991 Pat Swilling, NO ....LB		2002 Derrick Brooks, TB ....LB	
1981 **Lawrence Taylor**, NYG ..LB		1992 Cortez Kennedy, Sea .....DT		2003 Ray Lewis, Bal ....LB	

UPI NFC Player of the Year

Given out by UPI from 1970-96. Offensive and defensive players honored since 1983. Rookie winners are in **bold** type.
Multiple winners: Eric Dickerson, Reggie White and Mike Singletary (3); Brett Favre, Charles Haley, Walter Payton, Lawrence Taylor and Steve Young (2).

Year	Pos	Year	Pos	Year	Pos
1970 John Brodie, SF ......QB		1984 Off–Eric Dickerson, Rams RB		1991 Off–Mark Rypien, Was ...QB	
1971 Alan Page, Min ....DT		Def–Mike Singletary, Chi ..LB		Def–Reggie White, Phi ...DE	
1972 Larry Brown, Was ......RB		1985 Off–Walter Payton, Chi ....RB		1992 Off–Steve Young, SF ......QB	
1973 John Hadl, Rams ......QB		Def–Mike Singletary, Chi ...LB		Def–Chris Doleman, Min ...DE	
1974 Jim Hart, St.L ....QB		1986 Off–Eric Dickerson, Rams ...RB		1993 Off–Emmitt Smith, Dal ....RB	
1975 Fran Tarkenton, Min ....QB		Def–Lawrence Taylor, NYG ..LB		Def–Eric Allen, Phi ....CB	
1976 Chuck Foreman, Min ....RB		1987 Off–Jerry Rice, SF ......WR		1994 Off–Steve Young, SF ......QB	
1977 Walter Payton, Chi ......RB		Def–Reggie White, Phi ....DE		Def–Charles Haley, Dal ....DE	
1978 Archie Manning, NO .....QB		1988 Off–Roger Craig, SF ......RB		1995 Off–Brett Favre, GB ......QB	
1979 Ottis Anderson, St.L .....RB		Def–Mike Singletary, Chi ..LB		Def–Reggie White, GB ....DE	
1980 Ron Jaworski, Phi ......QB		1989 Off–Joe Montana, SF ....QB		1996 Off–Brett Favre, GB ......QB	
1981 Tony Dorsett, Dal ......RB		Def–Keith Millard, Min ....DT		Def–Kevin Greene, Car ....LB	
1982 Mark Moseley, Was .....PK		1990 Off–Randall Cunningham, Phi.QB		1997 Award discontinued.	
1983 Off–Eric Dickerson, Rams ...RB		Def–Charles Haley, SF .....LB			
Def–Lawrence Taylor, NYG .LB					

Annual Awards (Cont.)
UPI AFL-AFC Player of the Year

Presented by UPI to the top player in the AFL (1960-69) and AFC (1970-96). Offensive and defensive players have been honored since 1983. Rookie winners are in **bold** type.

Multiple winners: Bruce Smith (4); O.J. Simpson (3); Cornelius Bennett, George Blanda, John Elway, Dan Fouts, Daryle Lamonica, Dan Marino and Curt Warner (2).

Year	Pos	Year	Pos	Year	Pos
1960 **Abner Haynes**, Dal	HB	1978 **Earl Campbell**, Hou	RB	1989 Off—Christian Okoye, KC	RB
1961 George Blanda, Hou	QB	1979 Dan Fouts, SD	QB	Def—Michael Dean Perry,Cle	NT
1962 Cookie Gilchrist, Buf	FB	1980 Brian Sipe, Cle	QB	1990 Off—Warren Moon, Hou	QB
1963 Lance Alworth, SD	FL	1981 Ken Anderson, Cin	QB	Def—Bruce Smith,Buf	DE
1964 Gino Cappelletti, Bos	FL-PK	1982 Dan Fouts, SD	QB	1991 Off—Thurman Thomas, Buf	RB
1965 Paul Lowe, SD	HB	1983 Off—**Curt Warner**, Sea	RB	Def—Cornelius Bennett, Buf	LB
1966 Jim Nance, Bos	FB	Def—Rod Martin, Raiders	LB	1992 Off—Barry Foster, Pit	RB
1967 Daryle Lamonica, Raiders	QB	1984 Off—Dan Marino, Mia	QB	Def—Junior Seau, SD	LB
1968 Joe Namath, NYJ	QB	Def—Mark Gastineau, NYJ	DE	1993 Off—John Elway, Den	QB
1969 Daryle Lamonica, Raiders	QB	1985 Off—Marcus Allen, Raiders	RB	Def—Rod Woodson, Pit	CB
1970 George Blanda, Raiders	QB-PK	Def—Andre Tippett, NE	LB	1994 Off—Dan Marino, Mia	QB
1971 Otis Taylor, KC	WR	1986 Off—Curt Warner, Sea	RB	Def—Greg Lloyd, Pit	LB
1972 O.J. Simpson, Buf	RB	Def—Rulon Jones, Den	DE	1995 Off—Jim Harbaugh, Ind	QB
1973 O.J. Simpson, Buf	RB	1987 Off—John Elway, Den	QB	Def—Bryce Paup, Buf	LB
1974 Ken Stabler, Raiders	QB	Def—Bruce Smith, Buf	DE	1996 Off—Terrell Davis, Den	RB
1975 O.J. Simpson, Buf	RB	1988 Off—Boomer Esiason, Cin	QB	Def—Bruce Smith, Buf	DE
1976 Bert Jones, Bal	QB	Def—Bruce Smith, Buf	DE	1997 Award discontinued.	
1977 Craig Morton, Den	QB	& Cornelius Bennett, Buf	LB		

UPI NFL-NFC Rookie of the Year

Presented by UPI to the top rookie in the NFL (1955-69) and NFC (1970-96). Players who were the overall first pick in the NFL draft are in **bold** type.

Year	Pos	Year	Pos	Year	Pos
1955 Alan Ameche, Bal	FB	1970 Bruce Taylor, SF	DB	1985 Jerry Rice, SF	WR
1956 Lenny Moore, Bal	HB	1971 John Brockington, GB	RB	1986 Reuben Mayes, NO	RB
1957 Jim Brown, Cle	FB	1972 Chester Marcol, GB	PK	1987 Robert Awalt, St.L	TE
1958 Jimmy Orr, Pit	FL	1973 Charle Young, Phi	TE	1988 Keith Jackson, Phi	TE
1959 Boyd Dowler, GB	FL	1974 John Hicks, NY	G	1989 Barry Sanders, Det	RB
1960 Gail Cogdill, Det	FL	1975 Mike Thomas, Wash	RB	1990 Mark Carrier, Chi	S
1961 Mike Ditka, Chi	TE	1976 Sammy White, Min	WR	1991 Lawrence Dawsey, TB	WR
1962 Ronnie Bull, Chi	FB	1977 Tony Dorsett, Dal	RB	1992 Robert Jones, Dal	LB
1963 Paul Flatley, Min	FL	1978 Bubba Baker, Det	DE	1993 Jerome Bettis, LA	RB
1964 Charley Taylor, Wash	HB	1979 Ottis Anderson, St.L	RB	1994 Bryant Young, SF	DT
1965 Gale Sayers, Chi	HB	1980 **Billy Sims**, Det	RB	1995 Rashaan Salaam, Chi	RB
1966 Johnny Roland, St.L	HB	1981 **George Rogers**, NO	RB	1996 Simeon Rice, Ari.	DE
1967 Mel Farr, Det	RB	1982 Jim McMahon, Chi	QB	1997 Award discontinued.	
1968 Earl McCullough, Det	FL	1983 Eric Dickerson, LA	RB		
1969 Calvin Hill, Dal	RB	1984 Paul McFadden, Phi	PK		

UPI AFL-AFC Rookie of the Year

Presented by UPI to the top rookie in the AFL (1960-69) and AFC (1970-96). Players who were the overall first pick in the AFL or NFL draft are in **bold** type.

Year	Pos	Year	Pos	Year	Pos
1960 Abner Haynes, Dal	HB	1973 Bobbie Clark, Cin	RB	1986 Leslie O'Neal, SD	DE
1961 Earl Faison, SD	DE	1974 Don Woods, SD	RB	1987 Shane Conlan, Buf	LB
1962 Curtis McClinton, Dal	FB	1975 Robert Brazile, Hou	LB	1988 John Stephens, NE	RB
1963 Billy Joe, Den	FB	1976 Mike Haynes, NE	DB	1989 Derrick Thomas, KC	LB
1964 Matt Snell, NY	FB	1977 A.J. Duhe, Mia	DE	1990 Richmond Webb, Mia	OT
1965 Joe Namath, NY	QB	1978 **Earl Campbell**, Hou	RB	1991 Mike Croel, Den	LB
1966 Bobby Burnett, Buf	RB	1979 Jerry Butler, Buf	WR	1992 Dale Carter, KC	CB
1967 George Webster, Hou	LB	1980 Joe Cribbs, Buf	RB	1993 Rick Mirer, Sea	QB
1968 Paul Robinson, Cin	RB	1981 Joe Delaney, KC	RB	1994 Marshall Faulk, Ind	RB
1969 Greg Cook, Cin	QB	1982 Marcus Allen, LA	RB	1995 Curtis Martin, NE	RB
1970 Dennis Shaw, Buf	QB	1983 Curt Warner, Sea	RB	1996 Terry Glenn, NE	WR
1971 **Jim Plunkett**, NE	QB	1984 Louis Lipps, Pit	WR	1997 Award discontinued.	
1972 Franco Harris, Pit	RB	1985 Kevin Mack, Cle	RB		

AP Offensive Rookie of the Year

Selected by The Associated Press in balloting by a nationwide media panel. Given out since 1967.

Year	Pos	Year	Pos	Year	Pos
1967 Mel Farr, Det	.RB	1980 Billy Sims, Det	.RB	1993 Jerome Bettis, Rams	.RB
1968 Earl McCullouch, Det	.OE	1981 George Rogers, NO	.RB	1994 Marshall Faulk, Ind	.RB
1969 Calvin Hill, Dal	.RB	1982 Marcus Allen, Raiders	.RB	1995 Curtis Martin, NE	.RB
1970 Dennis Shaw, Buf	.QB	1983 Eric Dickerson, Rams	.RB	1996 Eddie George, Hou	.RB
1971 John Brockington, GB	.RB	1984 Louis Lipps, Pit	.WR	1997 Warrick Dunn, TB	.RB
1972 Franco Harris, Pit	.RB	1985 Eddie Brown, Cin	.WR	1998 Randy Moss, Min	.WR
1973 Chuck Foreman, Min	.RB	1986 Reuben Mayes, NO	.RB	1999 Edgerrin James, Ind	.RB
1974 Don Woods, SD	.RB	1987 Troy Stradford, Mia	.RB	2000 Mike Anderson, Den	.RB
1975 Mike Thomas, Was	.RB	1988 John Stephens, NE	.RB	2001 Anthony Thomas, Chi	.RB
1976 Sammy White, Min	.WR	1989 Barry Sanders, Det	.RB	2002 Clinton Portis, Den	.RB
1977 Tony Dorsett, Dal	.RB	1990 Emmitt Smith, Dal	.RB	2003 Anquan Boldin, Ari	.WR
1978 Earl Campbell, Hou	.RB	1991 Leonard Russell, NE	.RB		
1979 Ottis Anderson, St.L	.RB	1992 Carl Pickens, Cin	.WR		

AP Defensive Rookie of the Year

Selected by The Associated Press in balloting by a nationwide media panel. Given out since 1967.

Year	Pos	Year	Pos	Year	Pos
1967 Lem Barney, Det	.CB	1980 Buddy Curry, Atl	.LB	1992 Dale Carter, KC	.CB
1968 Claude Humphrey, Atl	.DE	& Al Richardson, Atl	.LB	1993 Dana Stubblefield, SF	.DT
1969 Joe Greene, Pit	.DT	1981 Lawrence Taylor, NYG	.LB	1994 Tim Bowens, Mia	.DT
1970 Bruce Taylor, SF	.CB	1982 Chip Banks, Cle	.LB	1995 Hugh Douglas, NYJ	.DE
1971 Isiah Robertson, Rams	.LB	1983 Vernon Maxwell, Bal	.LB	1996 Simeon Rice, Ari	.DE
1972 Willie Buchanon, GB	.CB	1984 Bill Maas, KC	.DT	1997 Peter Boulware, Bal	.LB
1973 Wally Chambers, Chi	.DT	1985 Duane Bickett, Ind	.LB	1998 Charles Woodson, Raiders	.CB
1974 Jack Lambert, Pit	.LB	1986 Leslie O'Neal, SD	.DE	1999 Jevon Kearse, Ten	.DE
1975 Robert Brazile, Hou	.LB	1987 Shane Conlan, Buf	.LB	2000 Brian Urlacher, Chi	.LB
1976 Mike Haynes, NE	.CB	1988 Erik McMillan, NYJ	.S	2001 Kendrell Bell, Pit	.LB
1977 A.J. Duhe, Mia	.DE	1989 Derrick Thomas, KC	.LB	2002 Julius Peppers, Car	.DE
1978 Al Baker, Det	.DE	1990 Mark Carrier, Chi	.S	2003 Terrell Suggs, Bal	.LB
1979 Jim Haslett, Buf	.LB	1991 Mike Croel, Den	.LB		

Coach of the Year

Presented by UPI to the top coach in the AFL-NFL (1955-69) and AFC-NFC (1970-96). In 1997, the UPI awards were discontinued. Awards beginning in 1997 are the consensus selections from presenters such as AP, The Maxwell Football Club of Philadelphia, *The Sporting News* and the Pro Football Writers Association. Records indicate the team's change in record from the previous season.

Multiple winners: Dan Reeves (4); Paul Brown, Chuck Knox and Don Shula (3); George Allen, Leeman Bennett, Mike Ditka, George Halas, Tom Landry, Marv Levy, Bill Parcells, Jack Pardee, Sam Rutigliano, Lou Saban, Allie Sherman, Marty Schottenheimer, Dick Vermeil and Bill Walsh (2).

Year	Improvement	Year	Improvement
1955 NFL–Joe Kuharich, Washington	.3-9 to 8-4	1970 NFC–Alex Webster, New York	.6-8 to 9-5
1956 NFL–Buddy Parker, Detroit	.3-9 to 9-3	AFC–Paul Brown, Cincinnati	.4-9-1 to 8-6
1957 NFL–Paul Brown, Cleveland	.5-7 to 9-2-1	1971 NFC–George Allen, Washington	.6-8 to 9-4-1
1958 NFL–Weeb Ewbank, Baltimore	.7-5 to 9-3	AFC–Don Shula, Miami	.10-4 to 10-3-1
1959 NFL–Vince Lombardi, Green Bay	.1-10-1 to 7-5	1972 NFC–Dan Devine, Green Bay	.4-8-2 to 10-4
1960 NFL–Buck Shaw, Philadelphia	.7-5 to 10-2	AFC–Chuck Noll, Pittsburgh	.6-8 to 11-3
AFL–Lou Rymkus, Houston	.10-4	1973 NFC–Chuck Knox, Los Angeles	.6-7-1 to 12-2
1961 NFL–Allie Sherman, New York	.6-4-2 to 10-3-1	AFC–John Ralston, Denver	.5-9 to 7-5-2
AFL–Wally Lemm, Houston	.10-4 to 10-3-1	1974 NFC–Don Coryell, St. Louis	.4-9-1 to 10-4
1962 NFL–Allie Sherman, New York	.10-3-1 to 12-2	AFC–Sid Gillman, Houston	.1-13 to 7-7
AFL–Jack Faulkner, Denver	.3-11 to 7-7	1975 NFC–Tom Landry, Dallas	.8-6 to 10-4
1963 NFL–George Halas, Chicago	.9-5 to 11-1-2	AFC–Ted Marchibroda, Baltimore	.2-12 to 10-4
AFL–Al Davis, Oakland	.1-13 to 10-4	1976 NFC–Jack Pardee, Chicago	.4-10 to 7-7
1964 NFL–Don Shula, Baltimore	.8-6 to 12-2	AFC–Chuck Fairbanks, New England	.3-11 to 11-3
AFL–Lou Saban, Buffalo	.7-6-1 to 12-2	1977 NFC–Leeman Bennett, Atlanta	.4-10 to 7-7
1965 NFL–George Halas, Chicago	.5-9 to 9-5	AFC–Red Miller, Denver	.9-5 to 12-2
AFL–Lou Saban, Buffalo	.12-2 to 10-3-1	1978 NFC–Dick Vermeil, Philadelphia	.5-9 to 9-7
1966 NFL–Tom Landry, Dallas	.7-7 to 10-3-1	AFC–Walt Michaels, New York	.3-11 to 8-8
AFL–Mike Holovak, Boston	.4-8-2 to 8-4-2	1979 NFC–Jack Pardee, Washington	.8-8 to 10-6
1967 NFC–George Allen, Los Angeles	.8-6 to 11-1-2	AFC–Sam Rutigliano, Cleveland	.8-8 to 9-7
AFL–John Rauch, Oakland	.8-5-1 to 13-1	1980 NFC–Leeman Bennett, Atlanta	.6-10 to 12-4
1968 NFL–Don Shula, Baltimore	.11-1-2 to 13-1	AFC–Sam Rutigliano, Cleveland	.9-7 to 11-5
AFL–Hank Stram, Kansas City	.9-5 to 12-2	1981 NFC–Bill Walsh, San Francisco	.6-10 to 13-3
1969 NFL–Bud Grant, Minnesota	.8-6 to 12-2	AFC–Forrest Gregg, Cincinnati	.6-10 to 12-4
AFL–Paul Brown, Cincinnati	.3-11 to 4-9-1	1982 NFC–Joe Gibbs, Washington	.8-8 to 8-1
		AFC–Tom Flores, Los Angeles	.7-9 to 8-1

Annual Awards (Cont.)

Year	Improvement
1983 NFC–John Robinson, Los Angeles	2-7 to 9-7
AFC–Chuck Knox, Seattle	4-5 to 9-7
1984 NFC–Bill Walsh, San Francisco	10-6 to 15-1
AFC–Chuck Knox, Seattle	9-7 to 12-4
1985 NFC–Mike Ditka, Chicago	10-6 to 15-1
AFC–Raymond Berry, New England	9-7 to 11-5
1986 NFC–Bill Parcells, New York	10-6 to 14-2
AFC–Marty Schottenheimer, Cleveland	8-8 to 12-4
1987 NFC–Jim Mora, New Orleans	7-9 to 12-3
AFC–Ron Meyer, Indianapolis	3-13 to 9-6
1988 NFC–Mike Ditka, Chicago	11-4 to 12-4
AFC–Marv Levy, Buffalo	7-8 to 12-4
1989 NFC–Lindy Infante, Green Bay	4-12 to 10-6
AFC–Dan Reeves, Denver	8-8 to 11-5
1990 NFC–Jimmy Johnson, Dallas	1-15 to 7-9
AFC–Art Shell, Los Angeles	8-8 to 12-4
1991 NFC–Wayne Fontes, Detroit	6-10 to 12-4
AFC–Dan Reeves, Denver	5-11 to 12-4

Year	Improvement
1992 NFC–Dennis Green, Minnesota	8-8 to 11-5
AFC–Bobby Ross, San Diego	4-12 to 11-5
1993 NFC–Dan Reeves, New York	6-10 to 11-5
AFC–Marv Levy, Buffalo	11-5 to 12-4
1994 NFC–Dave Wannstedt, Chicago	7-9 to 9-7
AFC–Bill Parcells, New England	5-11 to 10-6
1995 NFC–Ray Rhodes, Philadelphia	7-9 to 10-6
AFC–Marty Schottenheimer, Kansas City	9-7 to 13-3
1996 NFC–Dom Capers, Carolina	7-9 to 12-4
AFC–Tom Coughlin, Jacksonville	4-12 to 9-7
1997 NFL–Jim Fassel, NY Giants	6-10 to 10-5-1
1998 NFL–Dan Reeves, Atlanta	7-9 to 14-2
1999 NFL–Dick Vermeil, St. Louis	4-12 to 13-3
2000 NFL–Jim Haslett, New Orleans	3-13 to 10-6
2001 NFL–Dick Jauron, Chicago	5-11 to 13-3
2002 NFL–Andy Reid, Philadelphia	11-5 to 12-4
2003 NFL–Bill Belichick, New England	9-7 to 14-2

CANADIAN FOOTBALL

The Grey Cup

Earl Grey, the Governor-General of Canada (1904-11), donated a trophy in 1909 for the Rugby Football Championship of Canada. The trophy, which later became known as the Grey Cup, was originally open to competition for teams registered with the Canada Rugby Union. Since 1954, the Cup has gone to the champion of the Canadian Football League (CFL).

Overall multiple winners: Toronto Argonauts (14); Edmonton Eskimos (12); Winnipeg Blue Bombers (9); Hamilton Tiger-Cats (8); Ottawa Rough Riders (7); Calgary Stampeders, Hamilton Tigers and Montreal Alouettes (5); B.C. Lions and University of Toronto (4); Queen's University (3); Ottawa Senators, Sarnia Imperials, Saskatchewan Roughriders and Toronto Balmy Beach (2).

CFL multiple winners (since 1954): Edmonton (12); Hamilton and Winnipeg (7); Ottawa (5); B.C. Lions, Calgary, Montreal and Toronto (4); Saskatchewan (2).

Year	Cup Final
1909	Univ. of Toronto 26, Toronto Parkdale 6
1910	Univ. of Toronto 16, Hamilton Tigers 7
1911	Univ. of Toronto 14, Toronto Argonauts 7
1912	Hamilton Alerts 11, Toronto Argonauts 4
1913	Hamilton Tigers 44, Toronto Parkdale 2
1914	Toronto Argonauts 14, Univ. of Toronto 2
1915	Hamilton Tigers 13, Toronto Rowing 7
1916-19	Not held (WWI)
1920	Univ. of Toronto 16, Toronto Argonauts 3
1921	Toronto Argonauts 23, Edmonton Eskimos 0
1922	Queens Univ. 13, Edmonton Elks 1
1923	Queens Univ. 54, Regina Roughriders 0
1924	Queens Univ. 11, Toronto Balmy Beach 3
1925	Ottawa Senators 24, Winnipeg Tigers 1
1926	Ottawa Senators 10, Univ. of Toronto 7
1927	Toronto Balmy Beach 9, Hamilton Tigers 6
1928	Hamilton Tigers 30, Regina Roughriders 0
1929	Hamilton Tigers 14, Regina Roughriders 3
1930	Toronto Balmy Beach 11, Regina Roughriders 6
1931	Montreal AAA 22, Regina Roughriders 0
1932	Hamilton Tigers 25, Regina Roughriders 6
1933	Toronto Argonauts 4, Sarnia Imperials 3

Year	Cup Final
1934	Sarnia Imperials 20, Regina Roughriders 12
1935	Winnipeg 'Pegs 18, Hamilton Tigers 12
1936	Sarnia Imperials 26, Ottawa Rough Riders 20
1937	Toronto Argonauts 4, Winnipeg Blue Bombers 3
1938	Toronto Argonauts 30, Winnipeg Blue Bombers 7
1939	Winnipeg Blue Bombers 8, Ottawa Rough Riders 7
1940	Gm 1: Ottawa Rough Riders 8, Toronto B-Beach 2
	Gm 2: Ottawa Rough Riders 12, Toronto B-Beach 5
1941	Winnipeg Blue Bombers 18, Ottawa Rough Riders 16
1942	Toronto RACF 8, Winnipeg RACF 5
1943	Hamilton Wildcats 23, Winnipeg RACF 14
1944	Montreal HMCS 7, Hamilton Wildcats 6
1945	Toronto Argonauts 35, Winnipeg Blue Bombers 0
1946	Toronto Argonauts 28, Winnipeg Blue Bombers 6
1947	Toronto Argonauts 10, Winnipeg Blue Bombers 9
1948	Calgary Stampeders 12, Ottawa Rough Riders 7
1949	Montreal Alouettes 28, Calgary Stampeders 15
1950	Toronto Argonauts 13, Winnipeg Blue Bombers 0
1951	Ottawa Rough Riders 21, Saskatch. Roughriders 14
1952	Toronto Argonauts 21, Edmonton Eskimos 11
1953	Hamilton Tiger-Cats 12, Winnipeg Blue Bombers 6

Year	Winner	Head Coach	Score	Loser	Head Coach	Site
1954	Edmonton	Frank (Pop) Ivy	26-25	Montreal	Doug Walker	Toronto
1955	Edmonton	Frank (Pop) Ivy	34-19	Montreal	Doug Walker	Vancouver
1956	Edmonton	Frank (Pop) Ivy	50-27	Montreal	Doug Walker	Toronto
1957	Hamilton	Jim Trimble	32-7	Winnipeg	Bud Grant	Toronto
1958	Winnipeg	Bud Grant	35-28	Hamilton	Jim Trimble	Vancouver
1959	Winnipeg	Bud Grant	21-7	Hamilton	Jim Trimble	Toronto
1960	Ottawa	Frank Clair	16-6	Edmonton	Eagle Keys	Vancouver
1961	Winnipeg	Bud Grant	21-14 (OT)	Hamilton	Jim Trimble	Toronto
1962	Winnipeg	Bud Grant	28-27 *	Hamilton	Jim Trimble	Toronto

Year	Winner	Head Coach	Score	Loser	Head Coach	Site
1963	Hamilton	Ralph Sazio	21-10	B.C. Lions	Dave Skrien	Vancouver
1964	B.C. Lions	Dave Skrien	34-24	Hamilton	Ralph Sazio	Toronto
1965	Hamilton	Ralph Sazio	22-16	Winnipeg	Bud Grant	Toronto
1966	Saskatchewan	Eagle Keys	29-14	Ottawa	Frank Clair	Vancouver
1967	Hamilton	Ralph Sazio	24-1	Saskatchewan	Eagle Keys	Ottawa
1968	Ottawa	Frank Clair	24-21	Calgary	Jerry Williams	Toronto
1969	Ottawa	Frank Clair	29-11	Saskatchewan	Eagle Keys	Montreal
1970	Montreal	Sam Etcheverry	23-10	Calgary	Jim Duncan	Toronto
1971	Calgary	Jim Duncan	14-11	Toronto	Leo Cahill	Vancouver
1972	Hamilton	Jerry Williams	13-10	Saskatchewan	Dave Skrien	Hamilton
1973	Ottawa	Jack Gotta	22-18	Edmonton	Ray Jauch	Toronto
1974	Montreal	Marv Levy	20-7	Edmonton	Ray Jauch	Vancouver
1975	Edmonton	Ray Jauch	9-8	Montreal	Marv Levy	Calgary
1976	Ottawa	George Brancato	23-20	Saskatchewan	John Payne	Toronto
1977	Montreal	Marv Levy	41-6	Edmonton	Hugh Campbell	Montreal
1978	Edmonton	Hugh Campbell	20-13	Montreal	Joe Scannella	Toronto
1979	Edmonton	Hugh Campbell	17-9	Montreal	Joe Scannella	Montreal
1980	Edmonton	Hugh Campbell	48-10	Hamilton	John Payne	Toronto
1981	Edmonton	Hugh Campbell	26-23	Ottawa	George Brancato	Montreal
1982	Edmonton	Hugh Campbell	32-16	Toronto	Bob O'Billovich	Toronto
1983	Toronto	Bob O'Billovich	18-17	B.C. Lions	Don Matthews	Vancouver
1984	Winnipeg	Cal Murphy	47-17	Hamilton	Al Bruno	Edmonton
1985	B.C. Lions	Don Matthews	37-24	Hamilton	Al Bruno	Montreal
1986	Hamilton	Al Bruno	39-15	Edmonton	Jack Parker	Vancouver
1987	Edmonton	Joe Faragalli	38-36	Toronto	Bob O'Billovich	Vancouver
1988	Winnipeg	Mike Riley	22-21	B.C. Lions	Larry Donovan	Ottawa
1989	Saskatchewan	John Gregory	43-40	Hamilton	Al Bruno	Toronto
1990	Winnipeg	Mike Riley	50-11	Edmonton	Joe Faragalli	Vancouver
1991	Toronto	Adam Rita	36-21	Calgary	Wally Buono	Winnipeg
1992	Calgary	Wally Buono	24-10	Winnipeg	Urban Bowman	Toronto
1993	Edmonton	Ron Lancaster	33-23	Winnipeg	Cal Murphy	Calgary
1994	B.C. Lions	Dave Ritchie	26-23	Baltimore	Don Matthews	Vancouver
1995	Baltimore	Don Matthews	37-20	Calgary	Wally Buono	Regina
1996	Toronto	Don Matthews	43-37	Edmonton	Ron Lancaster	Hamilton
1997	Toronto	Don Matthews	47-23	Saskatchewan	Jim Daley	Edmonton
1998	Calgary	Wally Buono	26-24	Hamilton	Ron Lancaster	Winnipeg
1999	Hamilton	Ron Lancaster	32-21	Calgary	Wally Buono	Vancouver
2000	B.C. Lions	Steve Buratto	28-26	Montreal	Charlie Taaffe	Calgary
2001	Calgary	Wally Buono	27-19	Winnipeg	Dave Ritchie	Montreal
2002	Montreal	Don Matthews	25-16	Edmonton	Tom Higgins	Edmonton
2003	Edmonton	Tom Higgins	34-22	Montreal	Don Matthews	Regina

*Halted by fog in 4th quarter, final 9:29 played the following day.

CFL Most Outstanding Player

Regular season Player of the Year as selected by The Football Reporters of Canada since 1953.

Multiple winners: Doug Flutie (6); Russ Jackson and Jackie Parker (3); Dieter Brock, Ron Lancaster and Mike Pringle (2).

Year		
1953 Billy Vessels, Edmonton, RB	1970 Ron Lancaster, Saskatch., QB	1987 Tom Clements, Winnipeg, QB
1954 Sam Etcheverry, Montreal, QB	1971 Don Jonas, Winnipeg, QB	1988 David Williams, B.C. Lions, WR
1955 Pat Abbruzzi, Montreal, RB	1972 Garney Henley, Hamilton, WR	1989 Tracy Ham, Edmonton, QB
1956 Hal Patterson, Montreal, E-DB	1973 Geo. McGowan, Edmonton, WR	1990 Mike Clemons, Toronto, RB
1957 Jackie Parker, Edmonton, RB	1974 Tom Wilkinson, Edmonton, QB	1991 Doug Flutie, B.C. Lions, QB
1958 Jackie Parker, Edmonton, QB	1975 Willie Burden, Calgary, RB	1992 Doug Flutie, Calgary, QB
1959 Johnny Bright, Edmonton, RB	1976 Ron Lancaster, Saskatch., QB	1993 Doug Flutie, Calgary, QB
1960 Jackie Parker, Edmonton, QB	1977 Jimmy Edwards, Hamilton, RB	1994 Doug Flutie, Calgary, QB
1961 Bernie Faloney, Hamilton, QB	1978 Tony Gabriel, Ottawa, TE	1995 Mike Pringle, Baltimore, RB
1962 George Dixon, Montreal, RB	1979 David Green, Montreal, RB	1996 Doug Flutie, Toronto, QB
1963 Russ Jackson, Ottawa, QB	1980 Dieter Brock, Winnipeg, QB	1997 Doug Flutie, Toronto, QB
1964 Lovell Coleman, Calgary, RB	1981 Dieter Brock, Winnipeg, QB	1998 Mike Pringle, Montreal, RB
1965 George Reed, Saskatchewan, RB	1982 Condredge Holloway, Tor., QB	1999 Danny McManus, Hamilton, QB
1966 Russ Jackson, Ottawa, QB	1983 Warren Moon, Edmonton, QB	2000 Dave Dickenson, Calgary, QB
1967 Peter Liske, Calgary, QB	1984 Willard Reaves, Winnipeg, RB	2001 Khari Jones, Winnipeg, QB
1968 Bill Symons, Toronto, RB	1985 Merv Fernandez, B.C. Lions, WR	2002 Milt Stegall, Winnipeg, SB
1969 Russ Jackson, Ottawa, QB	1986 James Murphy, Winnipeg, WR	2003 Anthony Calvillo, Montreal, QB

NFL EUROPE

The World League of American Football was formed in 1991 with hopes of expanding the popularity of the NFL to overseas markets. Funded by the NFL, the inaugural league in 1991 consisted of three European teams (London, Barcelona and Frankfurt), and seven North American teams (New York/New Jersey, Orlando, Montreal, Raleigh-Durham, Birmingham, Sacramento and San Antonio). The second season used the same format with Columbus, Ohio, replacing Raleigh-Durham.

In the fall of 1992, the NFL and WLAF Board of Directors voted to restructure the league to include more European teams. Play was subsequently suspended. In 1993, NFL clubs approved a six-team European-only league to resume play in 1995 with teams in Amsterdam, Barcelona, Frankfurt, London, Rhein and Scotland. In January 1998, the name of the league was changed to NFL Europe. In 1999, Berlin was added and London was disbanded. In 2004, Cologne was added and Barcelona was disbanded.

The World Bowl

In 1991 and 1992, when the league consisted of three divisions, the top team from each division and one wild-card team advanced to the playoffs, with the winners of each game advancing to the World Bowl. There was no game played in 1993 or 1994. Since 1995, the top two regular season teams advance directly to the World Bowl.

Multiple Winners: Frankfurt (3); Berlin and Rhein (2).

Bowl	Year	Winner	Head Coach	Score	Loser	Head Coach	Site
I	1991	London	Larry Kennan	21-0	Barcelona	Jack Bicknell	London
II	1992	Sacramento	Kay Stephenson	21-17	Orlando	Galen Hall	Montreal
III	1995	Frankfurt	Ernie Stautner	26-22	Amsterdam	Al Luginbill	Amsterdam
IV	1996	Scotland	Jim Criner	32-27	Frankfurt	Ernie Stautner	Edinburgh, Scot.
V	1997	Barcelona	Jack Bicknell	38-24	Rhein	Galen Hall	Barcelona
VI	1998	Rhein	Galen Hall	34-10	Frankfurt	Dick Curl	Frankfurt
VII	1999	Frankfurt	Dick Curl	38-24	Barcelona	Jack Bicknell	Dusseldorf
VIII	2000	Rhein	Galen Hall	13-10	Scotland	Jim Criner	Frankfurt
IX	2001	Berlin	Peter Vaas	24-17	Barcelona	Jack Bicknell	Amsterdam
X	2002	Berlin	Peter Vaas	26-20	Rhein	Pete Kuharchek	Dusseldorf
XI	2003	Frankfurt	Doug Graber	35-16	Rhein	Pete Kuharchek	Glasgow
XII	2004	Berlin	Rick Lantz	30-24	Frankfurt	Mike Jones	Gelsenkirchen, Ger.

World Bowl MVP

Year	Year	Year
1991 Dan Crossman, London, S	1997 Jon Kitna, Barcelona, QB	2001 Jonathan Quinn, Berlin, QB
1992 Davis Archer, Sacramento, QB	1998 Jim Arellanes, Rhein, QB	2002 Dane Looker, Berlin, WR
1995 Paul Justin, Frankfurt, QB	1999 Andy McCullough, Frankfurt, WR	2003 Jonas Lewis, Frankfurt, RB
1996 Yo Murphy, Scotland, WR	2000 Aaron Stecker, Scotland, RB	2004 Eric McCoo, Berlin, RB

ARENA FOOTBALL

The Arena Football League debuted in June of 1987 with four teams in Chicago, Denver, Pittsburgh and Washington D.C. Currently there are 19 teams in the league, divided into two conferences and four divisions.

ArenaBowl

Multiple Winners: Tampa Bay (5); Detroit (4); Arizona, Orlando and San Jose (2).

Bowl	Year	Winner	Head Coach	Score	Loser	Head Coach	Site
I	1987	Denver	Tim Marcum	45-16	Pittsburgh	Joe Haering	Pittsburgh
II	1988	Detroit	Tim Marcum	24-13	Chicago	Perry Moss	Chicago
III	1989	Detroit	Tim Marcum	39-26	Pittsburgh	Joe Haering	Detroit
IV	1990	Detroit	Perry Moss	51-27	Dallas	Ernie Stautner	Detroit
V	1991	Tampa Bay	Fran Curci	48-42	Detroit	Tim Marcum	Detroit
VI	1992	Detroit	Tim Marcum	56-38	Orlando	Perry Moss	Orlando
VII	1993	Tampa Bay	Lary Kuharich	51-31	Detroit	Tim Marcum	Detroit
VIII	1994	Arizona	Danny White	36-31	Orlando	Perry Moss	Orlando
IX	1995	Tampa Bay	Tim Marcum	48-35	Orlando	Perry Moss	St. Petersburg
X	1996	Tampa Bay	Tim Marcum	42-38	Iowa	John Gregory	Des Moines
XI	1997	Arizona	Danny White	55-33	Iowa	John Gregory	Phoenix
XII	1998	Orlando	Jay Gruden	62-31	Tampa Bay	Tim Marcum	Tampa
XIII	1999	Albany	Mike Dailey	59-48	Orlando	Jay Gruden	Albany
XIV	2000	Orlando	Jay Gruden	41-38	Nashville	Pat Sperduto	Orlando
XV	2001	Grand Rapids	Michael Trigg	64-42	Nashville	Pat Sperduto	Grand Rapids
XVI	2002	San Jose	Darren Arbet	52-14	Arizona	Danny White	San Jose
XVII	2003	Tampa Bay	Tim Marcum	43-29	Arizona	Danny White	Tampa
XVIII	2004	San Jose	Darren Arbet	69-62	Arizona	Danny White	Phoenix

ArenaBowl MVP

Multiple Winners: George LaFrance (3); Stevie Thomas (2).

Year	Year	Year
1987 Gary Mullen, Denver, WR	1994 Sherdrick Bonner, Arizona, QB	2001 Terrill Shaw, Grand Rapids, OS
1988 Steve Griffin, Detroit, WR/DB	1995 George LaFrance, Tampa Bay, OS	2002 John Dutton, San Jose, QB
1989 George LaFrance, Det., WR/DB	1996 Stevie Thomas, TB, WR/LB	2003 Lawrence Samuels, TB, WR/LB
1990 Art Schlichter, Detroit, QB	1997 Donnie Davis, Arizona, WR	2004 Off–Mark Grieb, San Jose, QB
1991 Stevie Thomas, TB, WR/LB	1998 Rick Hamilton, Orlando, FB/LB	Def–Ricky Parker, Arizona, DS
1992 George LaFrance, Detroit, OS	1999 Eddie Brown, Albany, OS	
1993 Jay Gruden, Tampa Bay, QB	2000 Connell Maynor, Orlando, QB	

College Basketball

Connecticut was the center of the college basketball world in 2004, winning both the men's and women's NCAA championships.

Huskies Make History

Connecticut basketball rose to a new level in 2004, sweeping both the men's and women's national titles.

Andy Katz
covers college basketball for ESPN.com

Jim Calhoun didn't let Connecticut leave the Alamodome after a Sweet 16 loss to Texas in 2003 without letting the players know the destination of the 2004 Final Four.

Right here.

San Antonio.

Who knows, maybe the Huskies would even get the same locker room? Calhoun was drilling home to his players that they better feel comfortable in San Antonio since they would be coming back in a year.

He had every reason to be prophetic. Calhoun had an inkling that Emeka Okafor and Ben Gordon weren't going to pass on their junior seasons and leave early for the NBA. He had no idea at the time that he would pick up a *McDonald's All-American* role player in Charlie Villanueva in June once he withdrew from the draft.

But he had the foresight to tell his players that they better start thinking national title—now.

He even took back with him a team photo taken on a riverboat, putting the snapshot in a small frame on his desk. He said his plan was to have another one put in the same spot once they were in the Final Four.

True to his word, the Huskies took that shot in April 2004, drifting down the San Antonio River two days before the national semifinal game against Duke.

Getting back to San Antonio was hardly an easy chore. The Huskies had to weather Okafor's season-long back injury. Villanueva started the season dealing with NCAA issues, forcing him to sit six games.

The Huskies dealt with a humbling loss to Georgia Tech in the Preseason NIT semifinals (a foreshadowing game), losing to North Carolina on the road and still finding it tough to win at Pittsburgh, Notre Dame and Providence at home. The Huskies looked extremely vulnerable when they lost at Syracuse without Okafor, who had been diagnosed with a stress fracture in his back.

But that was just a tease. Connecticut didn't get a No. 1 seed in the NCAAs, but the top seed in the Phoenix Region, Stanford, was upset by Alabama, setting up a cruise for the Huskies to the Final Four. Playing Duke in the semifinal was perfect fodder for

AP/Wide World Photos

*UConn's **Hilton Armstrong** and **Ben Gordon** show off the headlines and the hardware after beating Georgia Tech for the 2004 national championship.*

the Huskies. Calhoun has always measured his program against the Blue Devils. He beat Duke for the 1999 national title. He wanted a shot at them to win the 2004 championship.

And to beat the Blue Devils he had to rely on his star. Okafor took the game over with two minutes remaining, scoring five of the next seven points to take a three-point deficit and turn it into a one-point lead with 25 seconds remaining. In the anti-climactic final, Georgia Tech couldn't hang with Connecticut as Okafor and Gordon dominated.

Winning two national titles cemented Calhoun as one of the greatest coaches of his era. Winning a pair of national titles in the past six years put the Huskies' program in the class of Duke, North Carolina and Kentucky.

Earning that kind of respect was a hard climb for the men. It became commonplace for the women, who won their third straight national title. Geno Auriemma's Huskies weren't a lock to win the national title, but they had the game's best player in Diana Taurasi. Their run had a few bumps, like a loss to Boston College in the Big East tournament in Hartford. But the NCAA Tournament women's basketball committee gave the Huskies a huge advantage when they played in Hartford as a two-seed to the top-seeded Penn State.

The Connecticut sweep, the first in NCAA Division I history, was the story in early April.

But the men's game had plenty of other storylines that made the 2003-04 season one of the more memorable in recent history.

*Coach Phil Martelli's **St. Joseph's Hawks** had a great year, thanks to his sensational backcourt of Delonte West (second from left) and consensus Player of the Year Jameer Nelson (far right) .*

Okafor was the most outstanding player in the NCAA Tournament, but Saint Joseph's senior point guard Jameer Nelson was the national player of the year. He led the Hawks to an improbable 27-0 regular-season record before Xavier upended the Hawks in the Atlantic 10 tournament quarterfinals.

The Hawks earned a No. 1 seed and ended up playing in the best game of the tournament, losing to Oklahoma State in the Elite Eight on a 3-pointer by John Lucas with 6.9 seconds remaining.

Stanford wasn't too far behind the Hawks. The Cardinal ripped off 26 straight wins before losing in the regular-season finale at Washington. The Cardinal had the most memorable finish, beating Arizona at Maples Pavilion on a last-second 3-pointer by Nick Robinson.

The Cardinal, Hawks and Huskies saved the sport last season after a downright brutal offseason that included the murder of a Baylor player, allegedly by his teammate, a coverup of rules violations with the Bears, the NCAA investigation at Missouri, the firing of Iowa State coach Larry Eustachy for his questionable behavior and all the carryover from NCAA issues at St. Bonaventure and Georgia.

The National Association of Basketball Coaches held a summit in Chicago in October because of many of these issues. What the NABC, and the rest of college basketball, really needed was a scandal-free season filled with great storylines. They got that for the most part in 2003-04, culminating by Connecticut's historic sweep.

Dick Vitale's Ten Biggest Stories of the Year in College Basketball

10 Georgia Tech, picked to finish seventh in the ACC preseason poll, has a great season, culminating in a run to the Final Four before eventually losing to Connecticut in the national title game. Head coach Paul Hewitt does an amazing job for the Yellow Jackets.

9 St. John's program has a troubling year to say the least. Head coach Mike Jarvis is fired after a 2-4 start and the woes increase for the Red Storm when the team is hit with controversy after several players break curfew and are caught up in a sex scandal while the team is on a road trip to Pittsburgh.

8 The Indiana Hoosiers finish the season with a losing (14-15) record, missing out on the NCAA tourney for the first time since 1985. Indiana does not even get a call from the NIT.

7 Diaper Dandy coaches make some noise in their first seasons. Jamie Dixon at Pittsburgh, Matt Painter at Southern Illinois and Steve Hawkins at Western Michigan all have big years. Painter takes the associate head coaching job at Purdue following the season reportedly with the expectation that he will replace Gene Keady when he retires in 2005.

6 New North Carolina head coach Roy Williams brings back the buzz at his alma mater and guides the Tar Heels back into the big dance. Williams made his 15th consecutive NCAA Tournament appearance in 2004, tying the third-longest streak in NCAA Tournament history.

5 Stanford dominates the West, starting the season with 26 straight wins before finally losing at Washington in their final regular-season game. The team bounced back to win the Pac-10 tournament but lost to Alabama in the second round of the NCAAs. Nonetheless, it was a magical season for Mike Montgomery and the Cardinal.

4 Coach K and Duke University still reign supreme as the Blue Devils make the Final Four yet again. Mike Krzyzewski now has made 10 Final Four appearances and is starting to close the gap on John Wooden, the Wizard of Westwood. Wooden still leads with 12 Final Fours.

3 Missouri is a big disappointment. Picked in the top 10 in most preseason magazine polls, the Tigers don't make the tourney and the entire season is overshadowed by the claims made by disgruntled former point guard Ricky Clemons that he was paid by former Missouri coaches.

2   St. Joseph's goes undefeated (27-0) in the regular season — an incredible achievement. Then the competitive Atlantic 10 conference finally gets some well-earned respect in the postseason thanks to St. Joe's and Xavier's deep runs in the NCAA tournament. Hawks' head coach Phil Martelli and senior point guard Jameer Nelson clean up in the coach of the year and player of the year honors, respectively.

1   Storrs, Conn. is home to the kings and queens of college basketball. UConn becomes the toast of the basketball world when both the men's and women's programs win the national title in 2004. Men's head coach Jim Calhoun and women's head coach Geno Auriemma each wield a special velvet touch in guiding their teams to victory. The matching championships are a first in the history of NCAA division 1 basketball.

Different Era

The last decade and a half has been special for basketball in Connecticut. Both the men's and women's programs have been on an amazing tear. Here's a look at their combined numbers from the last 15 seasons and from the previous 15-year interval.

	1974-75 to 1988-89	1989-90 to 2003-04
Win Pct.	.501	.827
NCAA Tourn.	3	27
NCAA W-L	1-3	87-20*
All-Americans	0	15

*seven combined national championships.

Two for Two

UConn's Jim Calhoun has been to the Final Four twice—and has won the national championship both times. Here's a look at the list of coaches to win national titles in their first two trips to the Final Four.

Coach	NCAA Titles
Jim Calhoun, Connecticut	1999, 2004
Ed Jucker, Cincinnati	1961, 1962
Phil Woolpert, San Francisco	1955, 1956
Henry Iba, Oklahoma St.	1945, 1946
Branch McCracken, Indiana	1940, 1943

Note: Jim Calhoun is the 11th coach to win two national titles.

2003-2004
Season in Review

SPORTS ALMANAC

Final Regular Season AP Men's Top 25 Poll
Taken **before** start of NCAA tournament.

The sportswriters & broadcasters poll: first place votes in parentheses; records through Monday, March 15, 2004; total points (based on 25 for 1st, 24 for 2nd, etc.); record in NCAA tourney and team lost to; head coach (career years and record including 2004 postseason), and preseason ranking. Teams in **bold** type went on to reach NCAA Final Four. Indiana, which did not make the final regular-season Top 25, was the other Final Four team.

		Mar. 15 Record	Points	NCAA Recap	Head Coach	Preseason Rank
1	Stanford (55)	29-1	1771	1-1 (Alabama)	Mike Montgomery (26 yrs: 547-244)	19
2	Kentucky (9)	26-4	1621	1-1 (UAB)	Tubby Smith (13 yrs: 315-114)	11
3	Gonzaga (2)	27-2	1620	1-1 (Nevada)	Mark Few (5 yrs: 133-32)	10
4	**Oklahoma St.** (4)	27-3	1569	4-1 (Georgia Tech)	Eddie Sutton (34 yrs: 755-292)	25
5	St. Joseph's (1)	27-1	1535	3-1 (Oklahoma St.)	Phil Martelli (9 yrs: 179-99)	17
6	**Duke**	27-5	1472	4-1 (Connecticut)	Mike Krzyzewski (29 yrs: 694-240)	2
7	**Connecticut** (1)	27-6	1397	6-0	Jim Calhoun (32 yrs: 680-302)	1
8	Mississippi St.	25-3	1292	1-1 (Xavier)	Rick Stansbury (5 yrs: 126-64)	NR
9	Pittsburgh	29-4	1261	2-1 (Oklahoma St.)	Jamie Dixon (1 yr: 31-5)	22
10	Wisconsin	24-6	1147	1-1 (Pittsburgh)	Bo Ryan (20 yrs: 451-131)	15
11	Cincinnati	24-6	1018	1-1 (Illinois)	Bob Huggins (23 yrs: 542-191)	18
12	Texas	23-7	985	2-1 (Xavier)	Rick Barnes (16 yrs: 318-184)	12
13	Illinois	24-6	863	2-1 (Duke)	Bruce Weber (6 yrs: 129-61)	13
14	**Georgia Tech**	23-9	845	5-1 (Connecticut)	Paul Hewitt (6 yrs: 142-81)	NR
15	N.C. State	20-9	680	1-1 (Vanderbilt)	Herb Sendek (11 yrs: 211-134)	24
16	Kansas	21-8	629	3-1 (Georgia Tech)	Bill Self (11 yrs: 231-114)	6
17	Wake Forest	19-9	552	2-1 (St. Joseph's)	Skip Prosser (11 yrs: 232-107)	20
18	North Carolina	18-10	518	1-1 (Texas)	Roy Williams (16 yrs: 437-112)	9
19	Maryland	19-11	421	1-1 (Syracuse)	Gary Williams (26 yrs: 522-293)	NR
20	Syracuse	21-7	414	2-1 (Alabama)	Jim Boeheim (28 yrs: 676-234)	7
21	Providence	20-8	324	0-1 (Pacific)	Tim Welsh (9 yrs: 171-104)	NR
22	Arizona	20-9	233	0-1 (Seton Hall)	Lute Olson (31 yrs: 710-250)	4
23	So. Illinois	25-4	183	0-1 (Alabama)	Matt Painter (1 yr: 25-5)	NR
24	Memphis	21-7	143	1-1 (Oklahoma St.)	John Calipari (12 yrs: 282-109)	NR
25	Boston College	23-9	106	1-1 (Georgia Tech)	Al Skinner (16 yrs: 260-221)	NR
	Utah St.	25-3	106	did not play	Stew Morrill (18 yrs: 361-184)	NR

Others receiving votes: 26. **Florida** (20-10) 96 points; 27. **Washington** (19-11) and **Xavier** (23-10) 87; 29. **DePaul** (21-9) 86; 30. **Michigan St.** (18-11) 72; 31. **Western Michigan** (26-4) 51; 32. **Air Force** (22-6) 29; 33. **Nevada** (23-8) and **Texas Tech** (22-10) 28; 35. **Vanderbilt** (21-9) 22; 36. **Utah** (24-8) 19; 37. **Dayton** (24-8) 18; 38. **East Tennessee St.** (27-4) and **Louisville** (20-9) 17; 40. **Charlotte** (21-8) 16; 41. **Manhattan** (24-5) and **UTEP** (23-7) 6; 43. **UAB** (20-9) 3; 44. **Pacific** (23-7), **Seton Hall** (20-9) and **Va. Commonwealth** (23-7) 2; 47. **Vermont** (22-8) 1.

NCAA Men's Division I Tournament Seeds

	PHOENIX		ST. LOUIS		ATLANTA		EAST RUTHERFORD
1	Stanford (29-1)	1	Kentucky (26-4)	1	Duke (27-5)	1	St. Joseph's (27-1)
2	Connecticut (27-6)	2	Gonzaga (27-2)	2	Mississippi St. (25-3)	2	Oklahoma St. (27-3)
3	N.C. State (20-9)	3	Georgia Tech (23-9)	3	Texas (23-7)	3	Pittsburgh (29-4)
4	Maryland (19-11)	4	Kansas (21-8)	4	Cincinnati (24-6)	4	Wake Forest (19-9)
5	Syracuse (21-7)	5	Providence (20-8)	5	Illinois (24-6)	5	Florida (20-10)
6	Vanderbilt (21-9)	6	Boston College (23-9)	6	North Carolina (18-10)	6	Wisconsin (24-6)
7	DePaul (21-9)	7	Michigan St. (18-11)	7	Xavier (23-10)	7	Memphis (21-7)
8	Alabama (17-12)	8	Washington (19-11)	8	Seton Hall (20-9)	8	Texas Tech (22-10)
9	So. Illinois (25-4)	9	UAB (20-9)	9	Arizona (20-9)	9	Charlotte (21-8)
10	Dayton (24-8)	10	Nevada (23-8)	10	Louisville (20-9)	10	South Carolina (23-10)
11	W. Michigan (26-4)	11	Utah (24-8)	11	Air Force (22-6)	11	Richmond (20-12)
12	BYU (21-8)	12	Pacific (24-7)	12	Murray St. (28-5)	12	Manhattan (24-5)
13	UTEP (24-7)	13	Illinois-Chicago (24-7)	13	E. Tenn. St. (27-5)	13	VCU (23-7)
14	LA-Lafayette (20-8)	14	Northern Iowa (21-9)	14	Princeton (20-7)	14	C. Florida (25-5)
15	Vermont (22-8)	15	Valparaiso (18-12)	15	Monmouth (21-11)	15	E. Washington (17-12)
16	Texas-San Antonio (19-13)	16	Florida A&M* (15-16)	16	Alabama St. (16-14)	16	Liberty (18-14)

*Florida A&M defeated Lehigh, 72-57, in the NCAA Tournament "opening-round" play-in game for a berth in the field of 64.

2004 NCAA Tournament Men's Division

NCAA Men's Championship Game

66th NCAA Division I Championship Game. **Date:** Monday, April 5, at the Alamodome in San Antonio. **Coaches:** Jim Calhoun of Connecticut and Paul Hewitt of Georgia Tech. **Favorite:** Connecticut by 5.
Attendance: 44,468; **Officials:** Dick Cartmell, Verne Harris, Randy McCall; **TV Rating:** 11.0/18 share (CBS).

Georgia Tech 73

	Min	FG M-A	FT M-A	Pts	Reb O-T	A	PF
Marvin Lewis	23	3-9	0-0	6	0-1	1	3
Anthony McHenry	20	1-3	0-0	3	2-4	0	4
Luke Schenscher	28	4-7	1-2	9	7-11	0	2
B.J. Elder	28	4-15	3-4	14	2-4	0	4
Jarrett Jack	26	1-8	5-6	7	0-4	3	3
Isma'il Muhammad	16	5-12	0-0	10	4-5	0	3
Will Bynum	23	6-11	2-6	17	0-2	5	4
Robert Brooks	1	0-0	0-0	0	0-0	0	0
Clarence Moore	24	3-5	1-3	7	2-10	0	2
Theodis Tarver	11	0-1	0-0	0	1-2	0	1
TOTALS	200	27-71	12-21	73	18-43	9	26

Three-point FG: 7-22 (Elder 3-8, Bynum 3-6, McHenry 1-1, Lewis 0-5, Jack 0-1, Moore 0-1); **Team Rebounds:** 0; **Blocked Shots:** 1 (McHenry); **Turnovers:** 14 (Jack 5, Lewis 2, McHenry 2, Schenscher 2, Elder, Muhammad, Bynum); **Steals:** 10 (Jack 4, Muhammad 2, Tarver 2, Lewis and Bynum); **Percentages:** 2-Pt FG (.408), 3-Pt FG (.318), Total FG (.380), Free Throws (.571).

Connecticut 82

	Min	FG M-A	FT M-A	Pts	Reb O-T	A	PF
Josh Boone	29	4-6	1-4	9	5-6	1	2
Rashad Anderson	31	5-10	6-8	18	2-6	1	1
Emeka Okafor	38	10-17	4-8	24	7-15	1	3
Ben Gordon	30	5-17	8-9	21	0-2	4	1
Taliek Brown	37	2-6	5-8	9	0-6	4	3
Charlie Villanueva	7	0-0	0-0	0	0-1	1	1
Hilton Armstrong	7	0-1	1-2	1	0-6	0	1
Shamon Tooles	2	0-0	0-0	0	0-0	0	0
Denham Brown	19	0-4	0-0	0	3-6	0	3
TOTALS	200	26-61	25-39	82	17-48	10	18

Three-point FGs: 5-17 (Gordon 3-8, Anderson 2-7, Brown 0-2); **Team Rebounds:** 2; **Blocked Shots:** 2 (Okafor 2); **Turnovers:** 16 (Okafor 6, Gordon 4, T. Brown 2, D. Brown 2, Anderson, Villanueva); **Steals:** 5 (Anderson 2, Gordon 2, Okafor). **Percentages:** 2-Pt FG (.478), 3-Pt FG (.294), Total FG (.426), Free Throws (.641).

Georgia Tech (ACC)	26	47 —	73
Connecticut (Big East)	41	41 —	82

Final ESPN/USA Today Coaches' Poll

Taken **after** NCAA Tournament.
Voted on by a panel of 31 Division I head coaches following the NCAA tournament; first place votes in parentheses with total points (based on 25 for 1st, 24 for 2nd, etc.). Schools on major probation are ineligible to be ranked.

		W-L	Pts	Before NCAAs W-L	Rank
1	Connecticut (31)	33-6	775	25-6	7
2	Duke	31-6	722	27-4	6
3	Georgia Tech	28-10	721	22-8	15
4	Oklahoma St.	31-4	688	27-2	3
5	St. Joseph's	30-2	644	27-1	5
6	Stanford	30-2	553	29-1	1
7	Pittsburgh	31-5	544	29-4	8
8	Kentucky	27-5	522	26-4	4
9	Kansas	24-9	465	21-8	14
10	Texas	25-8	437	23-7	11
11	Illinois	26-7	419	24-6	13
12	Gonzaga	28-3	415	27-2	2
13	Mississippi St.	26-4	373	25-3	9
14	Xavier	26-11	361	23-10	NR
15	Wake Forest	21-10	357	19-9	16
16	Wisconsin	25-7	334	24-6	10
17	Alabama	20-13	248	17-12	NR
18	Cincinnati	25-7	239	24-6	12
19	Syracuse	23-8	218	21-7	24
20	N.C. State	21-10	157	20-9	17
21	Nevada	25-9	156	23-8	NR
22	North Carolina	19-11	135	18-10	20
23	UAB	22-10	124	20-9	NR
24	Maryland	20-12	119	19-11	21
25	Vanderbilt	23-10	102	21-9	NR

Others receiving votes: 26. **Southern Illinois** (37 pts); 27. **Memphis** (34); 28. **Providence** (29); 29. **Arizona** (28); 30. **Boston College** (24); 31.**Texas Tech** (23); 32. **Michigan** (13); 33. **Utah St.** (12); 34. **DePaul** (10); 35. **Pacific** (7); 36. **Western Michigan** and **Manhattan** (6); 38. **Seton Hall** (5); 39. **Air Force** and **Central Florida** (4); 41. **Michigan St.** and **South Carolina** (2); 43. **Louisiana-Lafayette** (1).

THE FINAL FOUR

at the Alamodome in San Antonio.
(April 3-5, 2004).

Semifinal — Game One

St. Louis Regional champ Georgia Tech vs. East Rutherford Regional champ Oklahoma St.; Saturday, Apr. 3 (5:07 p.m. tipoff). **Coaches:** Paul Hewitt, Georgia Tech and Eddie Sutton, Oklahoma St. **Favorite:** Oklahoma State by 5.

Georgia Tech (ACC)	37	30—	67
Oklahoma St. (Big 12)	30	35—	65

High scorers— Luke Schenscher, Ga. Tech (19) and Joey Graham, Oklahoma St. (17); **Att—** 44,417; **TV rating**—8.3/16 share (CBS).

Semifinal — Game Two

Atlanta Regional champion Duke vs. Phoenix Regional champ Connecticut; Saturday, Apr. 3 (7:47 p.m. tipoff). **Coaches:** Mike Krzyzewski, Duke and Jim Calhoun, Connecticut. **Favorite:** Connecticut by 2.

Connecticut (Big East)	34	45—	79
Duke (ACC)	41	37—	78

High scorers— Emeka Okafor and Ben Gordon, Connecticut (18) and Luol Deng, Duke (16); **Att—** 44,417; **TV rating**—10.5/20 share (CBS).

Most Outstanding Player

Emeka Okafor, Connecticut junior center. SEMIFINAL—22 minutes, 18 points, 7 rebounds, 1 assist, 2 blocks; FINAL—38 minutes, 24 points, 15 rebounds, 1 assist, 2 blocks.

All-Final Four Team

Emeka Okafor, junior guard Ben Gordon and sophomore guard Rashad Anderson of Connecticut, Georgia Tech junior center Luke Schenscher and junior guard Will Bynum.

NCAA Finalists' Tournament and Season Statistics
At least 10 games played during the overall season.

Georgia Tech (28-10)

| | NCAA Tournament | | | | | | Overall Season | | | | | |
| | | | —Per Game— | | | | | | —Per Game— | | |
	Gm	FG %	TPts	Pts	Reb	Ast	Gm	FG %	TPts	Pts	Reb	Ast
Jarrett Jack	6	.383	68	11.3	5.0	4.3	38	.456	474	12.5	4.9	5.6
Luke Schenscher	6	.605	64	10.8	7.0	0.7	38	.565	348	9.2	6.6	0.8
Will Bynum	6	.500	56	9.3	1.7	1.8	30	.413	287	9.6	2.2	2.5
Marvin Lewis	6	.388	54	9.0	3.3	1.5	38	.440	418	11.0	2.8	1.4
B.J. Elder	6	.347	46	7.7	1.8	0.7	38	.415	568	14.9	2.8	1.4
Clarence Moore	6	.412	40	6.7	5.7	1.0	37	.429	220	5.9	4.7	1.1
Anthony McHenry	6	.600	39	6.5	4.0	1.3	38	.481	128	3.4	3.2	1.2
Isma'il Muhammad	6	.390	39	6.5	5.0	1.0	38	.570	354	9.3	4.7	1.4
Theodis Tarver	6	.250	6	1.0	2.5	0.0	24	.364	33	1.4	1.8	0.7
Robert Brooks	2	-	0	0.0	0.0	0.0	28	.455	38	1.4	1.5	0.1
Mario West	1	-	0	0.0	0.0	0.0	19	.250	7	0.4	1.2	0.1
Jim Nystrom	0	-	-	-	-	-	12	.800	31	2.6	0.3	0.2
David Nelson	0	-	-	-	-	-	12	.400	5	0.4	0.1	0.2
GEORGIA TECH	6	.438	413	68.8	37.2	12.3	38	.465	2911	76.6	37.4	15.2
OPPONENTS	6	.399	399	66.5	37.3	11.5	38	.388	2552	67.2	37.3	12.3

Three-pointers: NCAA TOURNAMENT—Lewis (10-34), Bynum (9-19), Elder (9-25), Moore (4-15), McHenry (2-4), Jack (1-10), Muhammad (0-2), Team (35-109 for .321 pct.); OVERALL—Lewis (82-206), Elder (77-206), Bynum (34-97), Jack (30-95), Moore (32-83), McHenry (7-26), Nystrom (5-8), Nelson (0-2), West (0-2), Muhammad (0-4), Team 267-729 for .366 pct.).

Connecticut (33-6)

| | NCAA Tournament | | | | | | Overall Season | | | | | |
| | | | —Per Game— | | | | | | —Per Game— | | |
	Gm	FG %	TPts	Pts	Reb	Ast	Gm	FG %	TPts	Pts	Reb	Ast
Ben Gordon	6	.394	127	21.2	4.3	3.2	39	.434	723	18.5	4.7	4.5
Rashad Anderson	6	.492	104	17.3	4.5	1.5	39	.437	438	11.2	2.9	0.8
Emeka Okafor	6	.571	81	13.5	11.3	1.5	36	.599	635	17.6	11.5	1.0
Taliek Brown	6	.465	53	8.8	5.2	5.5	39	.417	244	6.3	3.8	6.5
Josh Boone	6	.571	38	6.3	6.5	0.5	38	.554	226	5.9	5.8	0.7
Charlie Villanueva	6	.500	26	4.3	4.0	0.3	32	.514	286	8.9	5.3	0.7
Denham Brown	6	.368	22	3.7	2.3	0.2	39	.438	347	8.9	3.9	1.2
Hilton Armstrong	6	.556	12	2.0	3.2	0.5	35	.500	83	2.4	2.8	0.3
Ryan Swaller	1	-	0	0.0	0.0	0.0	14	.429	6	0.4	0.3	0.1
Shamon Tooles	5	-	0	0.0	0.4	0.0	37	.643	24	0.6	1.2	0.1
Marcus Williams	0	-	0	0.0	0.0	0.0	16	.370	1	0.1	1.3	4.3
Justin Evanovich	0	-	0	0.0	0.0	0.0	12	.333	4	0.3	0.3	0.3
Jason Baisch	0	-	0	0.0	0.0	0.0	11	.143	3	0.3	0.5	0.0
CONNECTICUT	6	.476	463	77.2	44.0	13.2	39	.480	3073	78.8	44.7	17.5
OPPONENTS	6	.370	383	63.8	33.0	11.2	39	.369	2493	63.9	34.9	12.0

Three-pointers: NCAA TOURNAMENT— Anderson (21-43), Gordon (14-38), Villanueva (2-5), D. Brown (1-5), Armstrong (0-1), Team (160-336 for .476 pct.); OVERALL— Gordon (104-240), Anderson (87-212), D. Brown (36-92), Villanueva (18-49), Williams (3-17), T. Brown (1-5), Swaller (0-3), Armstrong (0-1), Team (249-619 for .402 pct.).

Georgia Tech's Schedule

Reg. Season
(22-8)

W	LA-Lafayette	79-45
W	Hofstra	75-56
W	Cornell	90-69
W	Connecticut	77-61
W	Texas Tech	85-65
W	Ohio St.	73-53
W	Tennessee St.	94-43
W	St. Louis	75-62
W	Alabama A&M	74-41
W	St. John's	79-66
W	Marist	90-40
W	VCU	86-65
L	Georgia (2ot)	80-83
L	No. Carolina	88-103
W	Virginia	75-57
W	Maryland	81-71
W	Wake Forest	73-66
L	N.C. State	72-76
W	Clemson	76-69
L	Duke	74-82
L	Florida St.	65-81
W	Tennessee	77-62
W	No. Carolina	88-77
L	Virginia	80-82
W	Maryland	75-64
L	Wake Forest	76-80
W	N.C. State	69-79
W	Clemson	79-60
W	Duke	76-68
W	Florida St.	63-60

ACC Tourney
(1-1)

| W | No. Carolina | 83-82 |
| L | Duke | 71-85 |

NCAA Tourney
(5-1)

W	Northern Iowa	65-60
W	Boston College	57-54
W	Nevada	72-67
W	Kansas	79-71
W	Oklahoma St.	67-65
L	Connecticut	73-82

Connecticut's Schedule

Reg. Season
(24-6)

W	Yale	70-60
W	Nevada	93-79
W	Sacred Heart	111-64
L	Georgia Tech	61-77
W	Utah	76-44
W	Lehigh	75-55
W	Army	74-46
W	Quinnipiac	88-55
W	Iona	104-54
W	Ball State	101-62
W	Massachusetts	91-67
W	at Rice	92-83
W	at Rutgers	75-74
W	Oklahoma	86-59
W	Georgetown	94-70
L	at No. Carolina	83-86
W	Pittsburgh	68-65
L	Providence	56-66
W	at Virginia Tech	96-60
W	at Boson College	63-58
W	Syracuse	84-56
W	West Virginia	88-58
L	at Notre Dame	74-80
L	at Pittsburgh	68-75
W	Miami	76-63
W	Notre Dame	61-50
W	at St. John's	71-53
W	at Villanova (ot)	75-74
W	Seton Hall	89-67
L	at Syracuse	56-67

Big East Tourney
(3-0)

W	Notre Dame	66-58
W	Villanova	84-67
W	Pittsburgh	61-58

NCAA Tourney
(6-0)

W	Vermont	70-53
W	DePaul	72-55
W	Vanderbilt	73-53
W	Alabama	87-71
W	Duke	79-78
W	Georgia Tech	82-73

Final NCAA Men's Division I Standings

Conference records include regular season games only. Overall records include all postseason tournament games.

America East Conference

Team	Conference			Overall		
	W	L	Pct	W	L	Pct
†Boston University	17	1	.944	23	6	.793
*Vermont	15	·3	.833	22	9	.710
Northeastern	13	5	.722	19	11	.633
Maine	12	6	.667	20	10	.667
Binghamton	10	8	.556	14	16	.467
Hartford	6	12	.333	12	17	.414
New Hampshire	5	13	.278	10	20	.333
Stony Brook	5	13	.278	10	20	.333
UMBC	4	14	.222	7	21	.250
Albany	3	15	.167	5	23	.179

Conf. Tourney Final: Vermont 72, Maine 53.
*NCAA Tourney (0-1): Vermont (0-1).
†NIT (0-1): Boston University (0-1).

Atlantic Coast Conference

Team	Conference			Overall		
	W	L	Pct	W	L	Pct
*Duke	13	3	.812	31	6	.838
*N.C. State	11	5	.688	21	10	.677
*Georgia Tech	9	7	.562	28	10	.737
*Wake Forest	9	7	.562	21	10	.677
*North Carolina	8	8	.500	19	11	.633
*Maryland	7	9	.438	20	12	.625
†Virginia	6	10	.375	18	13	.581
†Florida St	6	10	.375	19	14	.576
Clemson	3	13	.188	10	18	.357

Conf. Tourney Final: Maryland 95, Duke 87 OT.
*NCAA Tourney (14-6): Duke (4-1), N.C. State (1-1), Georgia Tech (5-1), Wake Forest (2-1), North Carolina (1-1), Maryland (1-1).
†NIT (2-2): Virginia (1-1), Florida St. (1-1).

Atlantic Sun Conference

Team	Conference			Overall		
	W	L	Pct	W	L	Pct
†Troy St.	18	2	.900	24	7	.774
*Central Florida	17	3	.850	25	6	.806
†Belmont	15	5	.750	21	9	.700
Georgia St.	14	6	.700	20	9	.690
Stetson	10	10	.500	12	15	.444
Mercer	9	11	.450	12	18	.400
Jacksonville	8	12	.400	13	15	.464
Florida Atlantic	6	14	.300	9	19	.321
Gardner-Webb	6	14	.300	9	20	.310
Lipscomb	4	16	.200	7	21	.250
Campbell	3	17	.150	3	24	.111

Conf. Tourney Final: Central Florida 60, Troy St. 55
*NCAA Tourney (0-1): Central Florida (0-1).
†NIT (0-2): Troy St. (0-1), Belmont (0-1).

Atlantic 10 Conference

East	Conference			Overall		
	W	L	Pct	W	L	Pct
*St. Joseph's	16	0	1.000	30	2	.938
†Temple	9	7	.562	15	14	.517
†Rhode Island	7	9	.438	20	14	.588
Massachusetts	4	12	.250	10	19	.345
St. Bonaventure	3	13	.188	7	21	.250
Fordham	3	13	.188	6	22	.214

West						
	W	L	Pct	W	L	Pct
*Dayton	12	4	.750	24	9	.727
†Geo. Washington	11	5	.688	18	12	.600
Richmond	10	6	.625	20	13	.606
*Xavier	10	6	.625	26	11	.703
Duquesne	6	10	.375	12	17	.414
La Salle	5	11	.313	10	20	.333

Conf. Tourney Final: Xavier 58, Dayton 49.
*NCAA Tourney (6-3): Xavier (3-1), St. Joseph's (3-1), Dayton (0-1).
†NIT (1-3): Temple (0-1), Rhode Island (1-1), G. Wash. (0-1).

Big East Conference

East	Conference			Overall		
	W	L	Pct	W	L	Pct
*Pittsburgh	13	3	.813	31	5	.861
*Connecticut	12	4	.750	33	6	.846
*Providence	11	5	.688	20	9	.690
*Syracuse	11	5	.688	23	8	.742
*Boston College	10	6	.625	24	10	.706
*Seton Hall	10	6	.625	21	10	.677
†Notre Dame	9	7	.563	19	13	.594
Virginia Tech	7	9	.438	15	14	.517
†Rutgers	7	9	.438	20	13	.606
†West Virginia	7	9	.438	17	14	.548
†Villanova	6	10	.375	18	17	.514
Georgetown	4	12	.250	13	15	.464
Miami-FL	4	12	.250	14	16	.467
St. John's	1	15	.063	6	21	.222

Conf. Tourney Final: Connecticut 61, Pittsburgh 58.
*NCAA Tourney (12-5): Pittsburgh (2-1), Connecticut (6-0), Providence (0-1), Syracuse (2-1), Boston College (1-1), Seton Hall (1-1).
†NIT (10-4): West Virginia (2-1), Rutgers (4-1), Villanova (2-1), Notre Dame (2-1).

Big Sky Conference

Team	Conference			Overall		
	W	L	Pct	W	L	Pct
*Eastern Washington	11	3	.786	17	13	.567
Northern Arizona	7	7	.500	15	14	.517
Idaho St	7	7	.500	13	18	.419
Sacramento St.	7	7	.500	13	15	.464
Weber St	7	7	.500	15	14	.517
Montana	6	8	.429	10	18	.357
Montana St	6	8	.429	14	13	.519
Portland St.	5	9	.357	11	16	.407

Conf. Tourney Final: E. Washington 71, N. Arizona 59.
*NCAA Tourney (0-1): E. Washington (0-1).

Big South Conference

Team	Conference			Overall		
	W	L	Pct	W	L	Pct
Birmingham-Southern	12	4	.750	20	7	.741
*Liberty	12	4	.563	18	15	.545
High Point	10	6	.625	19	11	.633
Winthrop	10	6	.625	16	12	.571
Coastal Carolina	8	8	.500	14	15	.483
Radford	7	9	.438	12	16	.429
NC-Asheville	6	10	.375	9	20	.310
VMI	4	12	.250	6	22	.214
Charleston Southern	3	13	.200	6	22	.214

Conf. Tourney Final: Liberty 89, High Point 44.
*NCAA Tourney (0-1): Liberty (0-1).

Big Ten Conference

Team	Conference			Overall		
	W	L	Pct	W	L	Pct
*Illinois	13	3	.812	26	7	.788
*Wisconsin	12	4	.750	25	7	.781
*Michigan St	12	4	.750	18	12	.600
†Iowa	9	7	.562	16	13	.552
†Michigan	8	8	.500	23	11	.676
Northwestern	8	8	.500	14	15	.483
†Purdue	7	9	.438	17	14	.548
Indiana	7	9	.438	14	15	.483
Ohio St	6	10	.375	14	16	.467
Minnesota	3	13	.188	12	18	.400
Penn St	3	13	.188	9	19	.321

Conf. Tourney Final: Wisconsin 70, Illinois 53.
*NCAA Tourney (3-3): Illinois (2-1), Wisconsin (1-1), Michigan State (0-1).
†NIT (4-2): Michigan (4-0), Purdue (0-1), Iowa (0-1).

Final NCAA Men's Division I Standings (Cont.)

Big 12 Conference

Team	Conference			Overall		
	W	L	Pct	W	L	Pct
*Oklahoma St.	14	2	.875	31	4	.886
*Texas	12	4	.750	25	8	.758
*Kansas	12	4	.750	24	9	.727
†Colorado	10	6	.625	18	11	.621
*Texas Tech	9	7	.563	23	11	.676
†Missouri	9	7	.563	16	14	.533
†Oklahoma	8	8	.500	20	11	.645
†Iowa St.	7	9	.438	20	13	.606
Kansas St	6	10	.375	14	14	.500
†Nebraska	6	10	.375	18	13	.580
Baylor	3	13	.188	8	21	.276
Texas A&M	0	16	.000	7	21	.250

Conf. Tourney Final: Oklahoma St. 65, Texas 49.
***NCAA Tourney (10-4):** Oklahoma St. (4-1), Texas (2-1), Kansas (3-1), Texas Tech (1-1).
†NIT (6-5): Colorado (0-1), Missouri (0-1), Nebraska (2-1), Oklahoma (1-1), Iowa St. (3-1)

Big West Conference

Team	Conference			Overall		
	W	L	Pct	W	L	Pct
†Utah St	17	1	.944	25	4	.862
*Pacific	17	1	.944	25	8	.758
UC-Santa Barbara	10	8	.556	16	12	.571
Idaho	9	9	.500	14	16	.467
UC-Riverside	7	11	.389	11	17	.393
Cal St.-Northridge	7	11	.389	14	16	.467
Cal St.-Fullerton	7	11	.389	11	17	.393
Cal Poly	6	12	.333	11	16	.407
UC-Irvine	6	12	.333	11	17	.393
Long Beach St	4	14	.222	6	21	.222

Conf. Tourney Final: Pacific 75, CS-Northridge 73.
***NCAA Tourney (1-1):** Pacific (1-1).
†NIT (0-1): Utah St. (0-1).

Colonial Athletic Association

Team	Conference			Overall		
	W	L	Pct	W	L	Pct
*Va. Commonwealth	14	4	.778	23	8	.742
†Drexel	13	5	.722	18	11	.621
†George Mason	12	6	.667	23	10	.697
Old Dominion	11	7	.611	17	12	.586
Delaware	10	8	.556	16	12	.571
Hofstra	10	8	.556	14	15	.483
NC-Wilmington	9	9	.500	15	15	.500
Towson	4	14	.222	8	21	.276
William & Mary	4	14	.222	7	21	.250
James Madison	3	15	.167	7	21	.250

Conf. Tourney Final: VCU 55, George Mason 54.
***NCAA Tourney (0-1):** VCU (0-1).
†NIT (2-2): George Mason (2-1), Drexel (0-1).

Division I Independents

Team	Overall		
	W	L	Pct
Texas A&M-Corpus Christi	14	11	.560
Texas-Pan American	14	14	.500
Savannah St.	4	24	.143
IPFW	4	25	.138

Conference USA

Team	Conference			Overall		
	W	L	Pct	W	L	Pct
*DePaul	12	4	.750	22	10	.688
*Memphis	12	4	.750	22	8	.733
*Cincinnati	12	4	.750	25	7	.781
*Ala-Birmingham	12	4	.750	22	10	.688
*Charlotte	12	4	.750	21	9	.700
*Louisville	9	7	.563	20	10	.667
†Saint Louis	9	7	.563	19	13	.594
†Marquette	8	8	.500	19	12	.613
Texas Christian	7	9	.438	12	17	.414
So. Mississippi	6	10	.375	13	15	.464
East Carolina	5	11	.313	13	14	.481
Tulane	4	12	.250	11	17	.393
Houston	3	13	.188	9	18	.333
So. Florida	1	15	.063	7	20	.259

Conf. Tourney Final: Cincinnati 55, DePaul 50.
***NCAA Tourney (5-6):** DePaul (1-1), Memphis (1-1), Cincinnati (1-1), UAB (2-1), Charlotte (0-1), Louisville (0-1).
†NIT (3-2): Saint Louis (1-1), Marquette (2-1).

Horizon League

Team	Conference			Overall		
	W	L	Pct	W	L	Pct
†WI-Milwaukee	13	3	.812	20	11	.645
*Illinois-Chicago	12	4	.750	24	8	.750
WI-Green Bay	11	5	.688	17	11	.607
Detroit	10	6	.625	19	11	.633
Wright St	10	6	.625	14	14	.500
Butler	8	8	.500	16	14	.533
Loyola-IL	4	12	.250	9	20	.310
Youngstown St.	4	12	.250	8	20	.286
Cleveland St.	0	16	.000	4	25	.138

Conf. Tourney Final: Illinois-Chicago 65, WI-Milw. 62.
***NCAA Tourney (0-1):** Illinois-Chicago (0-1).
†NIT Tourney (1-1): WI-Milwaukee (1-1).

Ivy League

Team	Conference			Overall		
	W	L	Pct	W	L	Pct
*Princeton	13	1	.927	20	8	.714
Pennsylvania	10	4	.714	17	10	.630
Brown	10	4	.714	14	13	.519
Yale	7	7	.500	12	15	.444
Cornell	6	8	.429	11	16	.407
Columbia	6	8	.429	10	17	.370
Harvard	3	11	.214	4	23	.148
Dartmouth	1	13	.071	3	25	.107

Conf. Tourney Final: Ivy League has no tournament.
***NCAA Tourney (0-1):** Princeton (0-1).

Metro Atlantic Athletic Conference

Team	Conference			Overall		
	W	L	Pct	W	L	Pct
*Manhattan	16	2	.889	25	6	.806
†Niagara	13	5	.722	22	10	.688
Fairfield	12	6	.667	19	11	.633
Saint Peter's	12	6	.667	17	12	.586
Rider	10	8	.556	17	14	.548
Siena	9	9	.500	14	16	.467
Iona	8	10	.444	11	18	.379
Canisius	5	13	.278	10	20	.333
Marist	4	14	.222	6	22	.214
Loyola	1	17	.056	1	27	.036

Conf. Tourney Final: Manhattan 62, Niagara 61.
***NCAA Tourney (1-1):** Manhattan (1-1).
†NIT (1-2): Niagara (1-1), Fairfield (0-1).

Mid-American Conference

	Conference			Overall		
East	**W**	**L**	**Pct**	**W**	**L**	**Pct**
†Kent St.	13	5	.722	22	9	.710
Miami-OH	12	6	.667	18	11	.621
Buffalo	11	7	.611	17	12	.586
Marshall	8	10	.444	12	17	.414
Akron	7	11	.389	13	15	.464
Ohio	7	11	.389	10	20	.333
West	**W**	**L**	**Pct**	**W**	**L**	**Pct**
*Western Mich	15	3	.833	26	5	.839
†Toledo	12	6	.667	20	11	.645
Ball St.	10	8	.556	14	15	.483
Bowling Green	8	10	.444	14	17	.452
Eastern Mich	7	11	.389	13	15	.464
N. Illinois	5	13	.278	10	20	.333
Central Mich	2	16	.111	6	24	.200

Conf. Tourney Final: Western Michigan 77, Kent St. 66.
***NCAA Tourney (1-1):** Western Michigan (0-1).
†**NIT (0-2):** Kent St. (0-1), Toledo (0-1).

Mid-Continent Conference

	Conference			Overall		
Team	**W**	**L**	**Pct**	**W**	**L**	**Pct**
*Valparaiso	11	5	.688	18	13	.581
IUPUI	10	6	.625	21	11	.656
Centenary	10	6	.625	16	12	.571
Oral Roberts	10	6	.625	17	11	.607
Missouri-KC	9	7	.563	15	14	.517
Chicago St.	9	7	.563	12	20	.375
Southern Utah	6	10	.375	10	18	.357
Oakland	6	10	.375	13	17	.433
Western Illinois	1	15	.063	3	25	.107

Conf. Tourney Final: Valparaiso 75, Indiana-Purdue 70.
***NCAA Tourney (0-1):** Valparaiso (0-1).

Mid-Eastern Athletic Conference

	Conference			Overall		
Team	**W**	**L**	**Pct**	**W**	**L**	**Pct**
S.C. State	14	4	.778	18	11	.621
Coppin St.	14	4	.778	18	14	.562
Delaware St.	11	7	.611	13	15	.464
Hampton	11	7	.611	13	17	.433
*Florida A&M	10	8	.555	15	17	.469
Norfolk St.	10	8	.555	12	17	.414
Morgan St.	9	9	.500	11	16	.407
Bethune-Cookman	7	11	.389	8	21	.276
MD-Eastern Shore	6	12	.333	8	21	.276
Howard	4	14	.222	6	22	.214
N. Carolina A&T	3	15	.167	3	25	.107

Conf. Tourney Final: Florida A&M 58, Coppin St. 51.
***NCAA Tourney (1-1):** Florida A&M (1-1).

Missouri Valley Conference

	Conference			Overall		
Team	**W**	**L**	**Pct**	**W**	**L**	**Pct**
*Southern Illinois	17	1	.944	25	5	.833
†Creighton	12	6	.667	20	9	.690
*Northern Iowa	12	6	.667	21	10	.677
†Wichita St.	12	6	.667	21	11	.656
SW Missouri St.	9	9	.500	19	14	.576
Bradley	7	11	.389	15	16	.484
Drake	7	11	.389	12	16	.429
Indiana St.	5	13	.278	9	19	.321
Evansville	5	13	.278	7	22	.241
Illinois St.	4	14	.222	10	19	.345

Conf. Tourney Final: Northern Iowa 79, SW Mo. St. 74 (2OT).
***NCAA Tourney (0-2):** Southern Illinois (0-1), Northern Iowa (0-1).
†**NIT (0-2):** Creighton (0-1), Wichita St. (0-1).

Mountain West Conference

	Conference			Overall		
Team	**W**	**L**	**Pct**	**W**	**L**	**Pct**
*Air Force	12	2	.857	22	7	.759
*BYU	10	4	.714	21	9	.700
*Utah	9	5	.643	24	9	.727
†UNLV	7	7	.500	18	13	.581
New Mexico	5	9	.357	14	14	.500
San Diego St.	5	9	.357	14	16	.467
Colorado St.	4	10	.286	13	16	.448
Wyoming	4	10	.286	11	17	.393

Conf. Tourney Final: Utah 73, UNLV 70.
***NCAA Tourney (0-3):** Air Force (0-1), Utah (0-1), BYU (0-1).
†**NIT (0-1):** UNLV (0-1).

Northeast Conference

	Conference			Overall		
Team	**W**	**L**	**Pct**	**W**	**L**	**Pct**
*Monmouth	12	6	.667	21	12	.636
St. Francis-NY	12	6	.667	15	13	.536
Fairleigh Dickinson	11	7	.611	17	12	.586
Robert Morris	10	8	.556	14	15	.483
St. Francis-PA	10	8	.556	13	15	.464
Wagner	10	8	.556	13	16	.448
Central Connecticut St.	9	9	.500	14	14	.500
Sacred Heart	8	10	.444	12	15	.444
Mt. St. Mary's	8	10	.444	10	19	.345
Quinnipiac	5	13	.278	9	20	.310
LIU Brooklyn	4	14	.222	8	19	.296

Conf. Tourney Final: Monmouth 67, C. Conn. St. 55.
***NCAA Tourney (0-1):** Monmouth (0-1).

Ohio Valley Conference

	Conference			Overall		
Team	**W**	**L**	**Pct**	**W**	**L**	**Pct**
†Austin Peay	16	0	1.000	22	10	.710
*Murray St.	14	2	.875	28	6	.824
Morehead St.	10	6	.625	16	13	.552
Eastern Kentucky	8	8	.500	14	15	.483
Jacksonville St.	7	9	.438	14	14	.500
Tennessee Tech	7	9	.438	13	15	.464
Samford	7	9	.438	12	16	.429
Tennessee St.	6	10	.375	7	21	.250
Tennessee-Martin	5	11	.313	10	18	.357
SE Missouri St	4	12	.250	11	16	.407
Eastern Illinois	4	12	.250	6	21	.222

Conf. Tourney Final: Murray St. 66, Austin Peay 60.
***NCAA Tourney (0-1):** Murray St. (0-1).
†**NIT (1-1):** Austin Peay (1-1).

Pacific-10 Conference

	Conference			Overall		
Team	**W**	**L**	**Pct**	**W**	**L**	**Pct**
*Stanford	17	1	.944	30	2	.938
*Washington	12	6	.667	19	12	.613
*Arizona	11	7	.611	20	10	.667
†Oregon	9	9	.500	18	13	.581
California	9	9	.500	13	15	.464
USC	8	10	.444	13	15	.464
Washington St	7	11	.389	13	16	.448
UCLA	7	11	.389	11	17	.393
Oregon St	6	12	.333	12	16	.429
Arizona St	4	14	.222	10	17	.370

Conf. Tourney Final: Stanford 77, Washington 66.
***NCAA Tourney (1-3):** Stanford (1-1), Washington (0-1), Arizona (0-1).
†**NIT (3-1):** Oregon (3-1).

Final NCAA Men's Division I Standings (Cont.)

Patriot League

Team	Conference			Overall		
	W	L	Pct	W	L	Pct
*Lehigh	10	4	.714	20	11	.645
American	10	4	.714	18	13	.581
Lafayette	9	5	.643	18	10	.643
Bucknell	9	5	.643	14	15	.483
Holy Cross	7	7	.500	13	15	.464
Colgate	6	8	.429	15	14	.517
Army	3	11	.214	6	21	.222
Navy	2	12	.143	5	23	.179

Conf. Tourney Final: Lehigh 59, American 57.
*NCAA Tourney (0-1): Lehigh (0-1).

Southeastern Conference

Eastern Div.	Conference			Overall		
	W	L	Pct	W	L	Pct
*Kentucky	13	3	.813	27	5	.844
*Florida	9	7	.563	20	11	.645
*South Carolina	8	8	.500	23	11	.676
*Vanderbilt	8	8	.500	23	10	.697
†Georgia	7	9	.438	16	14	.533
†Tennessee	7	9	.438	15	14	.517

Western Div.	Conference			Overall		
	W	L	Pct	W	L	Pct
*Mississippi St	14	2	.875	26	4	.867
*Alabama	8	8	.500	20	13	.606
†LSU	8	8	.500	18	11	.620
Auburn	5	11	.313	14	14	.500
Mississippi	5	11	.313	13	15	.500
Arkansas	4	12	.250	12	16	.429

Conf. Tourney Final: Kentucky 89, Florida 73.
*NCAA Tourney (7-6): Kentucky (1-1), Florida (0-1), Alabama (3-1), South Carolina (0-1), Vanderbilt (2-1), Mississippi St. (1-1).
†NIT (0-3): Georgia (0-1), Tennessee (0-1), LSU (0-1).

Southern Conference

North Div.	Conference			Overall		
	W	L	Pct	W	L	Pct
*East Tennessee St	15	1	.983	27	6	.818
Chattanooga	10	6	.625	19	11	.633
Elon	7	9	.438	12	18	.400
NC-Greensboro	7	9	.438	11	17	.393
W. Carolina	6	10	.375	13	15	.464
Appalachian St	4	12	.250	9	21	.300

South Div.	Conference			Overall		
	W	L	Pct	W	L	Pct
Georgia Southern	11	5	.688	21	8	.724
College of Charleston	11	5	.688	20	9	.690
Davidson	11	5	.688	17	12	.586
Furman	8	8	.500	17	12	.586
Wofford	4	12	.250	9	20	.310
The Citadel	2	14	.125	6	22	.214

Conf. Tourney Final: East Tenn. St. 78, Chattanooga 62.
*NCAA Tourney (0-1): East Tennessee St. (0-1).

Best in Show

Conferences with the most wins in the 2004 NCAA tournament. Number of tourney teams in parentheses.

Conference	W-L	Pct.
ACC (6)	14-6	.700
Big East (6)	12-5	.706
Big 12 (4)	10-4	.714
SEC (6)	7-6	.538
Atlantic 10 (3)	6-3	.667

Southland Conference

Team	Conference			Overall		
	W	L	Pct	W	L	Pct
SE Louisiana	11	5	.688	20	9	.690
Texas-Arlington	11	5	.688	17	12	.586
*Texas-San Antonio	11	5	.688	19	14	.576
Stephen F. Austin	10	6	.625	21	9	.700
Sam Houston St	8	8	.500	13	15	.464
Texas St.	8	8	.500	13	15	.464
Northwestern St.	8	8	.500	11	17	.393
Louisiana-Monroe	8	8	.500	12	19	.387
McNeese St	7	9	.438	11	16	.407
Lamar	5	11	.313	11	18	.379
Nicholls St	1	15	.063	6	21	.222

Conf. Tourney Final: Texas-San Antonio 74, S.F. Austin 70
*NCAA Tourney (0-1): Texas-San Antonio (0-1).

Southwestern Athletic Conference

Team	Conference			Overall		
	W	L	Pct	W	L	Pct
Miss. Valley St	16	2	.889	22	7	.759
*Alabama St	11	7	.611	16	15	.516
Texas Southern	10	8	.556	14	15	.483
Alabama A&M	9	9	.500	13	17	.433
Southern	9	9	.500	12	16	.429
Jackson St	9	9	.500	12	17	.414
Grambling	9	9	.500	11	18	.379
Alcorn St.	9	9	.500	11	18	.379
Prairie View A&M	7	11	.389	7	20	.259
Ark-Pine Bluff	1	17	.056	1	26	.037

Conf. Tourney Final: Alabama St. 63, Alabama A&M 58.
*NCAA Tourney (0-1): Alabama St. (0-1).

Sun Belt Conference

East Div.	Conference			Overall		
	W	L	Pct	W	L	Pct
Arkansas-Little Rock	9	5	.643	17	12	.586
Western Kentucky	8	6	.571	15	13	.536
Middle Tennessee	8	6	.571	17	12	.586
Arkansas St	7	7	.500	17	11	.607
Florida International	1	13	.071	5	22	.185

West Div.	Conference			Overall		
	W	L	Pct	W	L	Pct
*Louisiana-Lafayette	12	3	.800	20	9	.690
New Orleans	9	6	.600	17	14	.548
North Texas	8	7	.533	13	15	.464
South Alabama	6	9	.400	12	16	.429
Denver	6	9	.400	14	13	.519
New Mexico St.	6	9	.400	13	14	.481

Conf. Tourney Final: LA-Lafayette 67, New Orleans 58.
*NCAA Tourney (0-1): Louisiana-Lafayette (0-1).

West Coast Conference

Team	Conference			Overall		
	W	L	Pct	W	L	Pct
*Gonzaga	14	0	1.000	28	3	.903
St. Mary's-CA	9	5	.683	19	12	.613
Pepperdine	9	5	.683	15	16	.484
San Francisco	7	7	.500	17	14	.548
Santa Clara	6	8	.429	16	16	.500
Loyola Marymount	5	9	.357	15	14	.517
Portland	5	9	.357	11	17	.393
San Diego	1	13	.071	4	26	.133

Conf. Tourney Final: Gonzaga 84, St. Mary's 71.
*NCAA Tourney (1-1): Gonzaga (1-1).

Western Athletic Conference

Team	Conference			Overall		
	W	L	Pct	W	L	Pct
*Nevada	13	5	.722	25	9	.735
*UTEP	13	5	.722	24	8	.750
†Boise St.	12	6	.667	23	10	.697
†Rice	12	6	.667	22	11	.667
†Hawaii	11	7	.611	21	12	.636
Fresno St.	10	8	.556	14	15	.483
Louisiana Tech	8	10	.444	15	15	.500
SMU	5	13	.278	12	19	.400
Tulsa	5	13	.278	9	20	.310
San Jose St	1	17	.056	6	23	.207

Conf. Tourney Final: Nevada 66, UTEP 60.
***NCAA Tourney (2-2):** Nevada (2-1), UTEP (0-1).
†NIT (4-3): Boise St. (2-1), Rice (0-1), Hawaii (2-1).

DID YOU KNOW?

In 2003-04, Stanford & St. Joseph's became only the fourth and fifth teams since 1979 to be undefeated on March 1st, joining 1991 UNLV, 1981 Oregon St. and 1979 Indiana St. **Did you know**, none of those five teams went on to win the National Championship?

Annual Awards

Players of the Year

Jameer Nelson, St. Joseph's, G . . . . AP, Naismith, Wooden, USBWA, co-NABC
Emeka Okafor, Connecticut, F/C . . . . co-NABC

Wooden Award Voting

Presented since 1977 by the Los Angeles Athletic Club and named after the former Purdue All-America and UCLA coach John Wooden. Voting done by 1,047-member panel of national media; candidates must have a cumulative college grade point average of 2.0 (out of 4.0) and be making progress toward graduation.

		Cl	Pos	Pts
1	Jameer Nelson, St. Joseph's	Sr.	G	5408
2	Emeka Okafor, Connecticut	Jr.	F/C	5215
3	Josh Childress, Stanford	Jr.	F	3052
4	Chris Duhon, Duke	Jr.	G	2571
5	Lawrence Roberts, Mississippi St.	Jr.	F	2296

Defensive Player of the Year

Formerly the Henry Iba Award, for defensive skills, sportsmanship and dedication; first presented by the Rotary Club of River Oaks in Houston in 1987 and named after the late Oklahoma State and U.S. Olympic team coach. Voting done by the National Association of Basketball Coaches.

Emeka Okafor, Connecticut, F/C

Div. II and III Annual Awards

Awarded by the National Association of Basketball Coaches.

Players of the Year
Div. II . . . . .Elad Inbar, MA-Lowell
Div. III . . . . .Richard Melzer, WI-River Falls
Coaches of the Year
Div. II . . . . .Tony Ingle, Kennesaw St.
Div. III . . . . .David Paulsen, Williams

Coaches of the Year

Phil Martelli, St. Joseph's . . . . .AP, Naismith, USBWA, co-NABC
Mike Montgomery, Stanford . . . . .co-NABC

Consensus All-America Teams

The NCAA Division I players cited most frequently by the following All-America selectors: Associated Press, U.S. Basketball Writers, National Association of Basketball Coaches and Wooden Award Committee. (*) indicates unanimous first team selection. There were no holdovers from the 2002-03 first team.

First Team

	Class	Hgt	Pos
Jameer Nelson*, St. Joseph's	Sr.	5-11	G
Emeka Okafor*, Connecticut	Jr.	6-9	F/C
Lawrence Roberts*, Mississippi St.	Jr.	6-9	F
Ryan Gomes, Providence	Jr.	6-7	F/C
Josh Childress, Stanford	Jr.	6-8	G/F

Second Team

	Class	Hgt	Pos
Andre Emmett, Texas Tech	Sr.	6-5	G/F
Devin Harris, Wisconsin	Jr.	6-3	G
John Lucas, Oklahoma St.	Jr.	5-11	G
Blake Stepp, Gonzaga	Sr.	6-4	G
Julius Hodge, N.C. State	Jr.	6-7	G/F

Third Team

	Class	Hgt	Pos
Chris Duhon, Duke	Sr.	6-1	G
Luke Jackson, Oregon	Sr.	6-7	F
Rashad McCants, North Carolina	So.	6-4	F/G
Wayne Simien, Kansas	So.	6-9	F
Hakim Warrick, Syracuse	Jr.	6-8	F

NCAA Men's Division I Leaders

Includes games through NCAA and NIT tourneys.

INDIVIDUAL

Scoring

	Cl	Gm	FG%	3FG/Att	FT%	Reb	Ast	Stl	Blk	Pts	Avg	Hi
Keydren Clark, St. Peter's	So.	29	.415	112/295	.845	124	125	51	4	775	**26.7**	38
Kevin Martin, W. Carolina	Jr.	27	.474	51/152	.817	130	47	50	8	673	**24.9**	44
David Hawkins, Temple	Sr.	29	.392	84/276	.756	149	51	78	9	709	**24.4**	41
Taylor Coppenrath, Vermont	Jr.	24	.510	14/47	.750	173	34	30	15	579	**24.1**	43
Luis Flores, Manhattan	Sr.	31	.442	68/182	.863	122	50	60	4	744	**24.0**	32
Michael Watson, UMKC	Sr.	29	.403	96/257	.374	99	104	42	5	680	**23.4**	40
Michael Helms, Oakland	Sr.	30	.403	79/228	.346	109	71	45	16	695	**23.2**	39
Odell Bradley, IUPUI	Sr.	29	.483	31/99	.313	247	68	24	6	671	**23.1**	41
Ike Diogu, Arizona St.	So.	27	.530	14/37	.378	241	44	13	47	615	**22.8**	38
Derrick Tarver, Akron	Sr.	27	.490	47/151	.752	77	43	23	0	612	**22.7**	44
Bryant Matthews, Va. Tech	Sr.	29	.473	31/86	.360	259	43	72	24	641	**22.1**	37
Andrew Wisniewski, Centenary	Sr.	28	.512	66/158	.786	98	121	45	1	612	**21.9**	34
Ricky Minard, Morehead St.	Sr.	29	.451	45/138	.776	213	147	60	15	631	**21.8**	37
Kris Humphries, Minnesota	Fr.	29	.444	17/50	.742	293	20	27	33	629	**21.7**	36
Luke Jackson, Oregon	Sr.	31	.488	73/166	.862	223	139	39	5	656	**21.2**	42
Dylan Page, WI-Milwaukee	Sr.	31	.507	59/146	.775	204	38	14	37	647	**20.9**	38
Jose Juan Barea, Northeastern	So.	26	.385	73/204	.719	94	150	44	0	538	**20.7**	33
Ken Tutt, Oral Roberts	Fr.	28	.447	101/225	.844	66	57	25	1	579	**20.7**	30
Andre Emmett, Texas Tech	Sr.	34	.524	16/45	.730	225	62	44	10	701	**20.6**	38
Jameer Nelson, St. Josephs	Sr.	32	.475	73/187	.792	150	168	89	1	659	**20.6**	33

Rebounding

	Cl	Gm	No	Avg
Paul Millsap, Louisiana Tech	Fr.	30	374	12.5
Jaime Lloreda, LSU	Sr.	22	256	11.6
Emeka Okafor, Connecticut	Jr.	36	415	11.5
Nate Lofton, SE Louisiana	Jr.	29	315	10.9
Nigel Wyatte, Wagner	Sr.	28	292	10.4
Charles Gaines, So. Miss.	Sr.	28	290	10.4
Nigel Dixon, Western Ky.	Sr.	28	287	10.3
Cuthbert Victor, Murray St.	Sr.	34	347	10.2
Odartey Blankson, UNLV	Jr.	31	315	10.2
Kris Humphries, Minnesota	Fr.	29	293	10.1
Rafael Araujo, BYU	Sr.	30	303	10.1
Lawrence Roberts, Mississippi St.	Jr.	30	303	10.1
Caleb Green, Oral Roberts	Fr.	28	278	9.9
Keith Waleskowski, Dayton	Sr.	33	327	9.9
Andrew Bogut, Utah	Fr.	33	326	9.9
Aerick Sanders, San Diego St.	Sr.	30	295	9.8
Sean May, North Carolina	So.	29	285	9.8
David Simon, IPFW	Jr.	28	275	9.8
Kim Adams, Arkansas St.	Sr.	28	273	9.8
Ron Robinson, C. Conn. St.	Sr.	27	263	9.7

Assists

	Cl	Gm	No	Avg
Greg Davis, Troy St.	Sr.	31	256	8.3
Martell Bailey, Illinois-Chicago	Sr.	32	250	7.8
Aaron Miles, Kansas	Jr.	33	242	7.3
Andres Rodriguez, American	Jr.	31	225	7.3
Raymond Felton, North Carolina	So.	30	212	7.1
Maurice Searight, Grambling	So.	28	195	7.0
Blake Stepp, Gonzaga	Sr.	31	207	6.7
Jerel Blassingame, UNLV	Jr.	31	205	6.6
Walker Russell, Jacksonville St.	So.	28	182	6.5
Mike McGrain, San Diego	Jr.	26	169	6.5
Taliek Brown, Connecticut	Sr.	39	253	6.5
Deron Williams, Illinois	So.	30	185	6.2
Jonathan Bluitt, Oral Roberts	So.	27	165	6.1
Chris Duhon, Duke	Sr.	37	225	6.1
Travis Diener, Marquette	Jr.	31	187	6.0
Alvin Cruz, Niagara	Jr.	32	191	6.0
Ali Berdiel, Valparaiso	Jr.	31	185	6.0
Eric Dobson, Maine	Sr.	30	179	6.0
Marquis Poole, Idaho St.	Sr.	28	167	6.0
Martin Osimani, Duquesne	Jr.	29	172	5.9

Field Goal Percentage

Minimum 5 Field Goals made per game.

	Cl	Gm	FG	FGA	Pct
Nigel Dixon, Western Ky.	Sr.	28	179	264	67.8
Sean Finn, Dayton	Sr.	33	175	264	66.3
Adam Mark, Belmont	Sr.	30	233	352	66.2
David Harrison, Colorado	Jr.	29	186	294	63.1
Cuthbert Victor, Murray St.	Sr.	34	190	302	62.9
Jon Bentley, Eastern Ky.	Sr.	29	154	245	62.9
Michael Harris, Rice	Jr.	33	217	360	60.3
Dominick Martin, Yale	Jr.	27	138	229	60.3
Emeka Okafor, Connecticut	Jr.	36	261	436	59.9
Jai Lewis, George Mason	So.	33	187	313	59.7
Sean Brooks, Drexel	Jr.	29	154	258	59.7
Matt Nelson, Colorado St.	Jr.	24	133	225	59.1
Frank Bennett, Ga. Southern	Sr.	29	163	276	59.1
Caleb Green, Oral Roberts	Fr.	28	177	300	59.0
Paul Millsap, Louisiana Tech	Fr.	30	175	298	58.7

Free Throw Percentage

Minimum 2.5 Free Throws made per game.

	Cl	Gm	FT	FTA	Pct
Blake Ahearn, SW Mo. St.	Fr.	33	117	120	97.5
J.J. Reddick, Duke	So.	37	143	150	95.3
Jake Sullivan, Iowa St.	Sr.	33	83	89	93.3
Steve Drabyn, Belmont	Sr.	30	96	105	91.4
Chris Hernandez, Stanford	So.	30	96	105	91.4
Scotter McFadgon, Tennessee	Jr.	28	134	147	91.2
Terry Williams, Ga. Southern	Jr.	29	81	90	90.0
Delonte West, St. Joseph's	Jr.	32	124	139	89.2
Antoine Jordan, Siena	Sr.	25	63	71	88.7
Leon Pattman, Dartmouth	Fr.	26	70	79	88.6
Travis Diener, Marquette	Jr.	31	136	154	88.3
Anthony Winchester, W. Ky.	So.	28	72	82	87.8
Jason Grachowalski, Boston U.	Sr.	24	64	73	87.7
Ilian Evtimov, N.C. State	So.	31	78	89	87.6
Gerry McNamara, Syracuse	So.	31	123	141	87.2

St. Peter's	Louisiana Tech	Troy St.	St. Bonaventure
Keydren Clark	**Paul Millsap**	**Greg Davis**	**Marques Green**
Scoring	Rebounds	Assists	Steals

3-Pt Field Goal Percentage

Minimum 2.5 Three-Point FGs made per game.

	Cl	Gm	FG	FGA	Pct
Brad Lechtenberg, San Diego . . .Sr.	Sr.	23	71	139	51.1
James Odoms, Mercer . . . . .Jr.	Jr.	23	59	121	48.8
Tyson Dorsey, Samford . . . . . . .Sr.	Sr.	28	74	152	48.7
Antonio Burks, S.F. Austin . . . . . .Sr.	Sr.	30	78	164	47.6
Trey Guidry, Illinois St. . . . . . . .Jr.	Jr.	29	86	187	46.0
Pat Carroll, St. Joseph's . . . . . .Jr.	Jr.	32	81	177	45.8
Dewarick Spencer, Arkansas St. Jr.	Jr.	28	86	188	45.7
Aaron Thomas, Robert Morris . . .Sr.	Sr.	29	78	171	45.6
Tim Begley, Pennsylvania . . . . . .Jr.	Jr.	27	83	182	45.6
Chris Hill, Michigan St. . . . . . .Jr.	Jr.	30	84	185	45.4
Travis Diener, Marquette . . . . . .Jr.	Jr.	31	90	200	45.0

3-Pt Field Goals Per Game

	Cl	Gm	No	Avg
Terrence Woods, Florida A&M . . . . .S.	S.	31	140	4.5
Keydren Clark, St. Peter's . . . . . . .So.	So.	29	112	3.9
Marques Green, St. Bonaventure . .Sr.	Sr.	27	98	3.6
Ken Tutt, Oral Roberts . . . . .Sr.	Sr.	28	101	3.6
Erik Benzel, Denver . . . . .Jr.	Jr.	27	97	3.6
Akeem Clark, IUPUI . . . . .Jr.	Jr.	32	109	3.4
Gerry McNamara, Syracuse . . . . .So.	So.	31	105	3.4
Ed McCants, WI-Milwaukee . . . . . .Jr.	Jr.	31	104	3.4
Brendan Plavich, Charlotte . . . . . .Sr.	Sr.	29	97	3.3
Tim Pickett, Florida St. . . . . .Sr.	Sr.	33	110	3.3
Michael Watson, UMKC . . . . .Sr.	Sr.	29	96	3.3

Blocked Shots

	Cl	Gm	No	Avg
Anwar Ferguson, Houston . . . . .Sr.	Sr.	27	111	4.1
Emeka Okafor, Connecticut . . . . . .Jr.	Jr.	36	147	4.1
D'or Fischer, West Virginia . . . . . . .Jr.	Jr.	31	124	4.0
Gerrick Morris, South Florida . . . . .Sr.	Sr.	27	108	4.0
Nick Billings, Binghamton . . . . .Jr.	Jr.	30	105	3.5
Moussa Badiane, E. Carolina . . . . .Jr.	Jr.	27	90	3.3
Marcus Douthit, Providence . . . . . .Sr.	Sr.	29	92	3.2
Herve Lamizana, Rutgers . . . . .Sr.	Sr.	33	102	3.1
Shelden Williams, Duke . . . . .So.	So.	37	111	3.0
Haminn Quaintance, Jacksonville . .Fr.	Fr.	28	84	3.0
Shawnson Johnson, N. Texas . . . . .Sr.	Sr.	23	69	3.0
David Harrison, Colorado . . . . .Jr.	Jr.	29	85	2.9
C.J. Walker, NC-Asheville . . . . . . .Fr.	Fr.	29	85	2.9

Steals

	Cl	Gm	No	Avg
Marques Green, St. Bonaventure . . .Sr.	Sr.	27	107	4.0
Obie Trotter, Alabama A&M . . . . . .So.	So.	29	88	3.0
Chakowby Hicks, Norfolk St. . . . . . .Jr.	Jr.	29	86	3.0
Zakeed Wadood, E. Tenn. St. . . . . .Sr.	Sr.	33	92	2.8
Jameer Nelson, St. Joseph's . . . . . .Sr.	Sr.	32	89	2.8
Louis Ford, Howard . . . . .So.	So.	28	77	2.8
Jamon Gordon, Va. Tech . . . . .Fr.	Fr.	24	66	2.8
Chris Paul, Wake Forest . . . . .Fr.	Fr.	31	84	2.7
David Hawkins, Temple . . . . .Sr.	Sr.	29	78	2.7
Tory Cavalieri, St. Francis-NY . . . . .Jr.	Jr.	28	75	2.7
Andres Rodriguez, American . . . . . .Sr.	Sr.	31	82	2.6

Single Game Highs

Points

No		Opponent	Date
45	Alex Loughton, Old Dominion .Charlotte	Charlotte	Dec. 6
44	Derrick Tarver, Akron . . . . . . .Wright St.	Wright St.	Dec. 30
44	Derrick Tarver, Akron . . . . . .Hampton	Hampton	Dec. 1
44	Kevin Martin, W. Carolina . . . .Georgia	Georgia	Nov. 21
43	Taylor Coppenrath, Vermont . . . .Maine	Maine	Mar. 13
43	Marques Green, St. Bonav. . . . .Niagara	Niagara	Dec. 17

Rebounds

No		Opponent	Date
22	Nate Lofton, SE La. . . . .TX-San Antonio	TX-San Antonio	Mar. 10
22	Caleb Green, Oral Roberts . . . .S. Utah	S. Utah	Feb. 28
22	Emeka Okafor, Connecticut .Notre Dame	Notre Dame	Feb. 21

Assists

No		Opponent	Date
19	Andres Rodriguez, American . . . .Navy	Navy	Jan. 14
18	Raymond Felton, N. Carolina .G. Mason	G. Mason	Dec. 7
15	Four tied.		

Blocks

No		Opponent	Date
10	Gerrick Morris, S. Florida . . . . .Houston	Houston	Feb. 21
10	Nick Billings, Binghamton . . . . .Hartford	Hartford	Jan. 31
10	Emeka Okafor, Connecticut . . . . .Army	Army	Dec. 6
10	Gerrick Morris, S. Florida . . .Wright St.	Wright St.	Nov. 29

Steals

No		Opponent	Date
9	Linas Lekavicius, American . . . .Bucknell	Bucknell	Feb. 7
9	James Denson, J'ville St. . . . .Morehead St.	Morehead St.	Jan. 24
9	Edward O'Neil, Charls. So. . . .C. Carolina	C. Carolina	Jan. 13
9	Derrick Obasohan, UTA . . . .Wichita St.	Wichita St.	Dec. 22
9	Ryan Price, McNeese St. . . . .G. Mason	G. Mason	Dec. 18
9	Michael Ross, E. Michigan . .Concordia	Concordia	Nov. 25

3-point FGs

No		Opponent	Date
11	Earnest Crumbley, Fla. Atlantic Campbell	Campbell	Feb. 26
11	Kevin Bettencourt, Bucknell St. Francis-PA	St. Francis-PA	Dec. 6
10	Four tied.		

NCAA Men's Division I Leaders (Cont.)
TEAM

Scoring Offense

	Gm	W-L	Pts	Avg
Arizona	.30	20-10	2614	87.1
Troy St.	.31	24-7	2624	84.6
Wake Forest	.31	21-10	2590	83.5
North Carolina	.30	19-11	2464	82.1
Chattanooga	.30	19-11	2463	82.1
Washington	.31	19-12	2543	82.0
Gonzaga	.31	28-3	2536	81.8
Niagara	.32	22-10	2611	81.6
Oral Roberts	.28	17-11	2265	80.9
Georgia Southern	.29	21-8	2337	80.6
Murray St.	.34	28-6	2730	80.3
Duke	.37	31-6	2954	79.8
East Tennessee St.	.33	27-6	2618	79.3
Charlotte	.30	21-9	2374	79.1
Lamar	.29	11-18	2294	79.1
Pepperdine	.31	15-16	2446	78.9
Connecticut	.39	33-6	3073	78.8
Western Michigan	.31	26-5	2434	78.5
IUPUI	.32	21-11	2504	78.3
UTEP	.32	24-8	2479	77.5

Won-Lost Percentage

	W	L	Pct
St. Joseph's	.30	2	93.8
Stanford	.30	2	93.8
Gonzaga	.28	3	90.3
Oklahoma St.	.31	4	88.6
Mississippi St.	.26	4	86.7
Utah St.	.25	4	86.2
Pittsburgh	.31	5	86.1
Connecticut	.33	6	84.6
Kentucky	.27	5	84.4
Western Michigan	.26	5	83.9
Duke	.31	6	83.8
Southern Illinois	.25	5	83.3
Murray St.	.28	6	82.4
East Tennessee St.	.27	6	81.8
Central Florida	.25	6	80.6
Manhattan	.25	6	80.6
Boston University	.23	6	79.3
Illinois	.26	7	78.8
Cincinnati	.25	7	78.1
Wisconsin	.25	7	78.1

Scoring Defense

	Gm	W-L	Pts	Avg
Air Force	.29	22-7	1475	50.9
Pittsburgh	.36	31-5	2031	56.4
Princeton	.28	20-8	1591	56.8
Wisconsin	.32	25-7	1823	57.0
Utah	.33	24-9	1893	57.4
Utah St.	.29	25-4	1684	58.1
Holy Cross	.28	13-15	1641	58.6
Richmond	.33	20-13	1964	59.5
Boston University	.29	23-6	1726	59.5
Detroit	.30	19-11	1787	59.6
NC-Wilmington	.30	15-15	1787	59.6
Washington St.	.29	13-16	1730	59.7
St. Louis	.32	19-13	1918	59.9
Butler	.30	16-14	1805	60.2
Mississippi Valley St.	.29	22-7	1750	60.3
Austin Peay	.32	22-10	1935	60.5
Stanford	.32	30-2	1936	60.5
Purdue	.31	17-14	1880	60.6
Bucknell	.29	14-15	1759	60.7
S.F. Austin	.30	21-9	1821	60.7

Field Goal Percentage

	FG	FGA	Pct
Oklahoma St.	.1002	1953	51.3
Gonzaga	.899	1765	50.9
Utah St.	.711	1397	50.9
Murray St.	.994	2009	49.5
Michigan St.	.748	1519	49.2
Chattanooga	.261	1751	49.2
Samford	.644	1318	48.9
Brigham Young	.764	1571	48.6
Arizona	.942	1938	48.6
Lafayette	.731	1513	48.3
Florida	.829	1719	48.2
Birmingham-Southern	.680	1412	48.2
Air Force	.585	1216	48.1
Princeton	.634	1319	48.1
Southern Utah	.636	1324	48.0
Connecticut	.1154	2403	48.0
Stanford	.849	1771	47.9
UTEP	.834	1748	47.7
WI-Milwaukee	.838	1757	47.7
Oral Roberts	.776	1630	47.6

Scoring Margin

	Off	Def	Mar
Gonzaga	.81.8	66.2	15.6
St. Joseph's	.77.4	62.3	15.1
Connecticut	.78.8	63.9	14.9
Duke	.79.8	65.0	14.8
Oklahoma St.	.77.1	62.5	14.6
Stanford	.73.6	60.5	13.1
Cincinnati	.76.7	64.3	12.5
Western Michigan	.78.5	66.1	12.4
Troy St.	.84.6	72.7	12.0
Louisville	.73.2	61.5	11.6
Pittsburgh	.67.9	56.4	11.5
Wisconsin	.68.4	57.0	11.5
Murray St.	.80.3	68.9	11.4
Utah St.	.69.3	58.1	11.2
Mississippi St.	.77.3	66.6	10.7
Stephen F. Austin	.71.3	60.7	10.6
Manhattan	.74.5	64.0	10.5
Kentucky	.73.9	63.6	10.3
Texas	.76.6	66.5	10.1
UTEP	.77.5	67.5	9.9

Field Goal Percentage Defense

	FG	FGA	Pct
Connecticut	.924	2502	36.9
Louisville	.638	1672	38.2
Gonzaga	.725	1890	38.4
Stanford	.671	1745	38.5
Pittsburgh	.765	1984	38.6
Georgia Tech	.865	2228	38.8
Mississippi Valley St.	.588	1509	39.0
Kansas	.766	1959	39.1
Maine	.680	1730	39.3
East Carolina	.601	1526	39.4
Cincinnati	.674	1710	39.4
Wichita St.	.717	1819	39.4
South Carolina	.752	1907	39.4
Texas Southern	.666	1688	39.5
Texas	.740	1867	39.6
Richmond	.684	1724	39.7
Central Florida	.655	1648	39.7
Houston	.578	1446	40.0
Kansas St.	.652	1629	40.0
Nebraska	.685	1711	40.1

Rebound Margin

	Off	Def	Mar
Connecticut	44.7	31.9	9.7
Gonzaga	39.7	31.5	8.2
Mississippi St.	41.0	33.1	8.0
Rhode Island	40.6	33.1	7.5
Utah	34.5	27.2	7.4
Western Kentucky	38.8	31.6	7.2
Louisiana Tech	39.3	32.3	7.0
Dayton	38.4	31.4	6.9
Texas-Corpus Christi	37.3	30.4	6.9
Stanford	36.8	30.1	6.8
Texas	32.8	26.3	6.7
Utah St.	32.8	26.3	6.5
Wagner	41.0	34.8	6.2
Siena	40.9	34.8	6.1
Fresno St.	35.4	29.5	5.9

Free Throw Percentage

	FT	FTA	Pct
N.C. State	481	602	79.9
Arizona	511	650	78.6
Bowling Green	551	711	77.5
Michigan St.	452	586	77.1
Butler	335	439	76.3
Manhattan	607	798	76.1
Oral Roberts	492	647	76.0
Robert Morris	384	509	75.4
UTEP	614	817	75.2
Stanford	489	651	75.1
Gonzaga	543	724	75.0
Florida	462	616	75.0
Washington St.	325	434	74.9
Louisville	480	641	74.9
Marquette	510	683	74.7

3-point FG Percentage

	3PT	3PTA	Pct
Birmingham-Southern	243	565	43.0
Southern Utah	178	420	42.4
San Diego	209	514	40.7
St. Joseph's	313	775	40.4
Connecticut	249	619	40.2
Marquette	231	575	40.2
Utah St.	168	419	40.1
Michigan St.	190	474	40.1
Lafayette	221	553	40.0
Pennsylvania	236	594	39.7
Gonzaga	195	491	39.7
Oregon	280	708	39.5
Va. Commonwealth	208	530	39.2
Samford	264	673	39.2
Portland	207	529	39.1

3-point FG Made Per Game

	Gm	No	Avg
Troy St.	31	364	11.7
St. Joseph's	32	313	9.8
Belmont	30	293	9.8
Samford	28	264	9.4
St. Francis-NY	28	258	9.2
Oregon	31	280	9.0
Birmingham-Southern	27	243	9.0
Florida St.	33	296	9.0
St. Peter's	29	259	8.9
Pennsylvania	27	236	8.7
UMKC	29	253	8.7
Memphis	30	259	8.6
Northeastern	30	256	8.5
Kent St.	31	264	8.5
Florida A&M	32	271	8.5

Underclassmen in NBA Draft

Thirty-one collegiate and high school players (not included below) forfeited their college eligibility and declared for the 2004 NBA Draft which took place at Madison Square Garden in New York City on June 24. First round selections in **bold** type, high school players in *italics*.

	Cl	Drafted by	Overall Pick
Chris Acker, Chaminade	Jr.	not drafted	–
Trevor Ariza, UCLA	Fr.	not drafted	–
Brandon Bender, Robert Morris	Jr.	not drafted	–
Evan Burns, San Diego St.	Fr.	not drafted	–
Jackie Butler, Co. Christian Acad.	HS	not drafted	–
Josh Childress, Stanford	Jr.	Atlanta	6
Cortez Davis, Rutgers (2003)	Jr.	not drafted	–
Luol Deng, Duke	Fr.	Phoenix	7
Ben Gordon, Connecticut	Jr.	Chicago	3
Devin Harris, Wisconsin	Jr.	Washington	5
David Harrison, Colorado	Jr.	Indiana	29
JaQuan Hart, E. Michigan	Jr.	not drafted	–
Dwight Howard, SW Atlanta Christian Academy	HS	Orlando	1
Kris Humphries, Minnesota	Fr.	Utah	14
Sani Ibrahim, Gulf Coast CC	So.	not drafted	–
Andre Iguodala, Arizona	So.	Philadelphia	9
Al Jefferson, Prentiss (Miss.)	HS	Boston	15
Shaun Livingston, Peoria Cen.	HS	L.A. Clippers	4
Kevin Martin, W. Carolina	Jr.	Sacramento	26
Emeka Okafor, Connecticut	Jr.	Charlotte	2
Randall Orr, Ga. Perimeter Coll.	So.	not drafted	–
Jason Parker, Kentucky (2001)	Jr.	not drafted	–
Donta Smith, SE Illinois JC	So.	Atlanta	34
Josh Smith, Oak Hill Acad.	HS	Atlanta	17
J.R. Smith, St. Benedict's (N.J.)	HS	New Orleans	18
Kirk Snyder, Nevada	Jr.	Utah	16
Robert Swift, Bakersfield (Calif.)	HS	Seattle	12
Sebastian Telfair, Lincoln (N.Y.)	HS	Portland	13
Harvey Thomas, Baylor	Jr.	not drafted	–
Delonte West, St. Joseph's	Jr.	Boston	24
Dorell Wright, S. Kent Prep (Ct.)	HS	not drafted	–

Note: Fifty-three American and international players (including Providence's All-American Ryan Gomes), who initially declared themselves eligible for the 2004 NBA Draft withdrew their names before the June 17 deadline.

DID YOU KNOW?

Connecticut teammates Emeka Okafor (picked second) and Ben Gordon (third) were the first two collegiate players taken after Orlando selected high schooler Dwight Howard first overall in the 2004 NBA Draft.

Did you know they are tied for the second-highest drafted teammates with Duke's Jay Williams (2) and Mike Dunleavy (3), who went in the 2002 draft? UCLA's Lew Alcindor (who later became Kareem Abdul-Jabbar) and Lucius Allen went first and second, respectively, in 1969.

Other 2004 Men's Tournaments

NIT Tournament

The 67th annual National Invitation Tournament had a 40-team field. First three rounds played on home courts of higher seeded teams. Semifinal, Third Place and Championship games played Mar 30-April 1 at Madison Square Garden in New York City.

Opening Round

at Rhode Island 80	Boston University 52
West Virginia 65	at Kent St. 54
at Bosie St. 84	UNLV 69
at WI-Milwaukee 91	Rice 63
at George Mason 58	Tennessee 55
at Austin Peay 65	Belmont 59
Nebraska 71	at Creighton 70
at Niagara 87	Troy St. 83

1st Round

at Notre Dame 71	Purdue 59
at St. Louis 70	Iowa 69
at Oregon 77 OT	Colorado 72
at George Mason 66	Austin Peay 60
at Nebraska 78	Niagara 70
Hawaii 85	at Utah St.
at Oklahoma 70	LSU 61
at Michigan 65	Missouri 64
at Villanova 85	Drexel 70
at Virginia 9	George Washington 66
at Rutgers 76	Temple 71
at West Virginia 79	Rhode Island 72
at Boise St. 73	WI-Milwaukee 70
at Marquette 87	Toledo 72
Florida St. 91 2 OT	at Wichita St. 84
Iowa St. 82	Georgia 74

2nd Round

at Villanova	Virginia 63
at Rutgers 67	West Virginia 64
at Marquette 66	Boise St. 53
Iowa St. 62	at Florida St. 59
at Notre Dame 77	St. Louis 66
at Oregon 68	George Mason 54
at Hawaii 84	Nebraska 83
at Michigan 63	Oklahoma 52

Quarterfinals

Oregon 65	at Notre Dame 61
at Michigan 88	Hawaii 73
at Rutgers 72	Villanova 69
at Iowa St. 77	Marquette 69

Semifinals

Rutgers 84 OT	Iowa St. 81
Michigan 78	Oregon 53

Championship

Michigan 62	Rutgers 55

NCAA Division II

The eight regional winners of the 48-team field: NORTHEAST—UMass-Lowell (28-5); EAST—Pfeiffer (31-2); SOUTH ATLANTIC—Kennesaw St. (32-4); SOUTH—Rollins (27-5); SOUTH CENTRAL—Northwest Missouri St. (29-4); GREAT LAKES—Southern Indiana (26-6); NORTH CENTRAL—Metro St. (31-2); WEST—Humbolt St. (27-5).

The Elite Eight was played March 24-27, at Bakersfield, Calif. There was no Third Place game.

Quarterfinals

Southern Indiana 88	Northwest Missouri St. 81
Metro St. 88	Rollins 54
Kennesaw St. 86	Pfeiffer 79
Humbolt St. 89	UMass-Lowell 82

Semifinals

Southern Indiana 83	Metro St. 81
Kennesaw St. 81	Humbolt St. 67

Championship

Kennesaw St. 84	Southern Indiana 59

NCAA Division III

The four regional winners of the 48-team field: WI-Stevens Point (27-5), John Carroll (26-5), Williams (29-1), Amherst (27-3).

The Final Four was played March 19-20, at Salem Civic Center in Salem, Va.

Semifinals

WI-Stevens Point 87	John Carroll 62
Williams 86	Amherst 81

Third Place

John Carroll 96	Amherst 85

Championship

WI-Stevens Point 84	Williams 82

NAIA Division I

The quarterfinalists, in alphabetical order, after two rounds of the 32-team NAIA tournament: Barber-Scotia, NC (24-11), Concordia, CA (32-4), Georgetown, KY. (32-7); Lindsey Wilson (33-4); Mobile (29-9); Mountain St., WV (35-1); Oklahoma Baptist (31-6); Oklahoma City (20-12).

All tournament games played, March 27-30, at the Municipal Auditorium, Kansas City, Mo. There was no Third Place game.

Quarterfinals: Mountain St. def. Oklahoma Baptist, 87-84; Georgetown def. Barber-Scotia, 64-60; Concordia def. Lindsey Wilson, 61-58; Mobile def. Oklahoma City, 75-62.

Semifinals: Mountain St. def. Georgetown 96-77; Concordia def. Mobile 72-57.

Championship: Mountain St. def. Concordia, 74-70.

NAIA Division II

The quarterfinalists, in alphabetical order, after two rounds of the 32-team NAIA tournament: Bellevue, Neb. (32-5), Cedarville, Ohio (27-9), Daemen, N.Y. (24-10); MidAmerica Nazarene, Kan. (25-11); Oregon Tech. (28-9); St. Ambrose, Iowa (32-5), William Jewell, Mo. (33-6).

All tournament games played, March 13-16, at Point Lookout, Missouri. There was no Third Place game.

Quarterfinals: Oregon Tech def. Cedarville, 83-78; St. Ambrose def. William Jewell, 88-84 OT; Sioux Falls def. Daemen, 74-62; Bellevue def. MidAmerica Nazarene, 74-50.

Semifinals: Oregon Tech def. St. Ambrose 80-67; Bellevue def. Sioux Falls, 70-62.

Championship: Oregon Tech def. Bellevue, 81-72.

Final Regular Season AP Women's Top 25 Poll

Taken **before** start of NCAA tournament.

The sportswriters & broadcasters poll: first place votes in parentheses; records through Sunday, March 14, 2004; total points (based on 25 for 1st, 24 for 2nd, etc.); record in NCAA tourney and team lost to; head coach (career years and career record including 2004 postseason), and preseason ranking. Teams in **bold** type went on to reach the NCAA Final Four.

		Mar. 14 Record	Points	NCAA Recap	Head Coach	Preseason Rank
1	**Duke** (43)	27-3	1168	3-1 (Minnesota)	Gail Goestenkors (12 yrs: 302-88)	2
2	**Tennessee** (1)	26-3	1078	5-1 (Connecticut)	Pat Summitt (30 yrs: 852-167)	4
3	Purdue	27-3	1052	2-1 (Georgia)	Kristy Curry (5 yrs: 136-31)	7
4	**Texas**	28-4	1010	2-1 (LSU)	Jody Conradt (35 yrs: 847-269)	3
5	Penn St. (1)	25-5	1001	3-1 (Connecticut)	Rene Portland (28 yrs: 649-222)	8
6	**Connecticut**	25-4	989	6-0	Geno Auriemma (19 yrs: 532-103)	1
7	Louisiana Tech (2)	27-2	878	2-1 (Duke)	Kurt Budke (2 yrs: 60-6)	12
8	Kansas St.	24-5	769	1-1 (Minnesota)	Deb Patterson (8 yrs: 151-95)	5
9	Houston	27-3	737	1-1 (UC-Santa Barb.)	Joe Curl (5 yrs: 108-75)	NR
10	Stanford	24-6	681	3-1 (Tennessee)	Tara VanDerveer (25 yrs: 602-168)	6
11	Oklahoma	23-8	649	1-1 (Stanford)	Sherri Coale (8 yrs: 156-95)	21
12	North Carolina	24-6	629	0-1 (Mid. Tenn. St.)	Sylvia Hatchell (29 yrs: 654-262)	14
13	Vanderbilt	24-7	584	2-1 (Stanford)	Melanie Balcomb (11 yrs: 211-122)	NR
14	Texas Tech	24-7	554	1-1 (La. Tech)	Marsha Sharp (22 yrs: 532-167)	10
15	Baylor	24-8	502	2-1 (Tennessee)	Kim Mulkey-Robertson (4 yrs: 98-35)	NR
16	Georgia	22-9	447	3-1 (LSU)	Andy Landers (25 yrs: 610-189)	11
17	Colorado	22-7	422	0-1 (UC-Santa Barb.)	Ceal Barry (25 yrs: 501-265)	20
18	Boston College	25-6	415	2-1 (Minnesota)	Cathy Inglese (18 yrs: 318-203)	NR
19	LSU	23-7	380	4-1 (Tennessee)	Sue Gunter (34 yrs: 708-308)	9
20	TCU	24-6	311	1-1 (Georgia)	Jeff Mittie (12 yrs: 261-109)	24
21	Ohio St.	20-9	233	1-1 (Boston College)	Jim Foster (26 yrs: 547-245)	17
22	Auburn	21-8	154	1-1 (Connecticut)	Joe Ciampi (27 yrs: 602-168)	22
23	Michigan St.	21-8	114	1-1 (Texas)	Joanne P. McCallie (12 yrs: 235-125)	NR
24	Minnesota	21-8	110	4-1 (Connecticut)	Pam Borton (6 yrs: 119-45)	13
25	Villanova	22-6	74	1-1 (Purdue)	Harry Perretta (25 yrs: 468-258)	NR

Others receiving votes: 26. **Arizona** (24-8, 72 points); 27. **Miami-FL** (22-6, 39); 28. **DePaul** (22-6, 32); 29. **Florida** (18-10, 32); 30. **Old Dominion** (25-6, 26); 31. **Rutgers** (21-11) and **SW Missouri St.** (28-3, 22); 33. **Chattanooga** (28-2, 20); 34. **Montana** (27-4, 19); 35. **UC-Santa Barbara** (25-6, 18); 36. **New Mexico** (23-7, 11), 37. **West Virginia** (21-10, 5); 38. **George Washington** (22-7) and **Loyola Marymount** (24-5), **Utah** (24-7, 4); 41. **Temple** (21-9, 2); 42. **Marquette** (21-9, 1).

NCAA Women's Division I Tournament Seeds

	WEST		MIDWEST		MIDEAST		EAST
1	Texas (28-4)	1	Tennessee (26-3)	1	Duke (27-3)	1	Penn St. (25-5)
2	Purdue (27-3)	2	Vanderbilt (24-7)	2	Kansas St. (24-5)	2	Connecticut (25-4)
3	Georgia (22-9)	3	Oklahoma (23-8)	3	Boston College (25-6)	3	Houston (27-3)
4	LSU (23-7)	4	Baylor (24-8)	4	Texas Tech (24-7)	4	North Carolina (24-6)
5	Miami-FL (22-6)	5	Florida (18-10)	5	Louisiana Tech (27-2)	5	Notre Dame (19-10)
6	TCU (24-6)	6	Stanford (24-6)	6	Ohio St. (20-9)	6	Colorado (22-7)
7	Vllianova (22-6)	7	Rutgers (21-11)	7	Minnesota (21-8)	7	Auburn (21-8)
8	Michigan St. (21-8)	8	G. Washington (22-7)	8	Old Dominion (25-6)	8	Virginia Tech (22-7)
9	Arizona (24-8)	9	DePaul (22-6)	9	Marquette (21-9)	9	Iowa (16-12)
10	Mississippi (17-13)	10	Chattanooga (28-2)	10	UCLA (17-12)	10	N.C. State (17-14)
11	Temple (21-9)	11	Missouri (17-12)	11	West Virginia (21-10)	11	UC-Santa Barbara (25-6)
12	Maryland (17-12)	12	New Mexico (23-7)	12	Montana (27-4)	12	SW Missouri St. (28-3)
13	Austin Peay (23-7)	13	Loyola Marymount (24-5)	13	Maine (25-6)	13	Mid. Tennessee St. (23-7)
14	Liberty (25-6)	14	Marist (20-10)	14	E. Michigan (22-7)	14	WI-Green Bay (23-7)
15	St. Francis-PA (25-5)	15	Lipscomb (21-10)	15	Valparaiso (20-11)	15	Pennsylvania (17-10)
16	Southern U. (17-12)	16	Colgate (21-9)	16	Northwestern St. (24-6)	16	Hampton (17-12)

2004 NCAA Tournament Women's Division

EAST

1st ROUND March 20-21	2nd ROUND March 22-23	SWEET 16 March 27	ELITE EIGHT March 29
(1) Penn St. 79	Penn St. 61		
(16) Hampton 42		Penn St. 55	
(8) Va. Tech 89	Va. Tech 48		Penn St. 49
(9) Iowa 76			
(5) Notre Dame 69	Notre Dame 59		
(12) SW Mo. St. 65		Notre Dame 49	
(13) Mid. Tenn. 67	Mid. Tenn. 46		
(4) N. Carolina 62			Connecticut 66
(6) Colorado 49	UCSB 56		
(11) UCSB 76		UCSB 55	
(3) WI-Green Bay 47	Houston 52		
(14) Houston 62			Connecticut 63
(7) Auburn 79	Auburn 53		
(10) N.C. State 59		Connecticut 79	
(2) Connecticut 91	Connecticut 79		
(15) Penn 55			

MIDEAST

1st ROUND	2nd ROUND	SWEET 16	ELITE EIGHT
(1) Duke 103	Duke 76		
(16) N'western St. 51		Duke 63	
(8) ODU 64	Marquette 67		
(9) Marquette 67			Duke 75
(5) La. Tech 81	La. Tech 81		
(12) Montana 77		La. Tech 49	
(4) Texas Tech 60	Texas Tech 64		
(13) Maine 50			Minnesota 58
(6) Ohio St. 73	Ohio St. 48		
(11) West Virginia 67		Boston Coll. 63	
(3) Boston Coll. 58	Boston Coll. 63		
(14) E. Michigan 56			Minnesota 82
(7) Minnesota 92	Minnesota 80		
(10) UCLA 81		Minnesota 76	
(2) Kansas St. 71	Kansas St. 61		
(15) Valparaiso 63			

FINAL FOUR April 4

Connecticut 67

Minnesota 58

Connecticut 70 / Tennessee 61

NATIONAL CHAMPIONSHIP

Connecticut 70 / Tennessee 61

FINAL FOUR April 4

Tennessee 52

LSU 50

MIDWEST

SWEET 16 March 28	2nd ROUND March 22-23	1st ROUND March 20-21
Tennessee 71	Tennessee 79	(1) Tennessee 77
	DePaul 59	(16) Colgate 54
		(8) G. Wash. 46
		(9) DePaul 83
Baylor 69	Florida 76	(5) Florida 68
		(12) New Mexico 56
	Baylor 91	(4) Baylor 71
		(13) LMU 60
Stanford 57	Stanford 68	(6) Stanford 68
		(11) Missouri 44
	Oklahoma 43	(3) Oklahoma 58
		(14) Marist 45
Vanderbilt 55	Chattanooga 44	(7) Rutgers 69
		(10) Chattanooga 74
	Vanderbilt 60	(2) Vanderbilt 76
		(15) Lipscomb 45

Tennessee 62

Stanford 60

WEST

ELITE EIGHT March 30	SWEET 16	2nd ROUND	1st ROUND
Texas 55	Texas 80	(1) Texas 92	
		(16) Southern U. 57	
	Michigan St. 61	(8) Michigan St. 72	
		(9) Arizona 60	
LSU 71	Maryland 61	(5) Miami-FL 85	
		(12) Maryland 86	
	LSU 76	(4) LSU 83	
		(13) Austin Peay 66	
Georgia 66	TCU 71	(1) TCU 70	
		(11) Temple 57	
	Georgia 85	(3) Georgia 78	
		(14) Liberty 53	
Purdue 64	Villanova 42	(7) Villanova 66	
		(10) Mississippi 63	
	Purdue 60	(2) Purdue 78	
		(15) St. Francis-PA 59	

Texas 62

Georgia 60

New Orleans Arena
New Orleans, Louisiana
Tuesday, April 6, 2004

NCAA Championship Game

Connecticut 70

	Min	FG M-A	FT M-A	Pts	Reb O-T	A	PF
Barbara Turner	.33	4-12	3-6	12	1-9	4	2
Jessica Moore	.30	6-9	2-2	14	6-9	1	3
Diana Taurasi	.37	6-11	2-4	17	0-3	2	1
Maria Conlon	.33	1-4	4-4	7	0-2	5	0
Ann Strother	.37	5-8	3-3	14	0-2	2	1
Ashley Battle	.15	1-4	0-0	3	0-1	0	1
Willnett Crockett	.15	1-3	1-1	3	0-2	1	2
TOTALS	.200	24-51	15-20	70	7-28	15	10

Three-point FG: 7-14 (Turner 1-2, Taurasi 3-7, Conlon 1-2, Strother 1-2, Battle 1-1); **Team Rebounds:** 3; **Blocked Shots:** 2 (Turner 2); **Turnovers:** 10 (Taurasi 3, Moore 2, Crockett 2, Battle, Conlon, Strother); **Steals:** 7 (Conlon 2, Moore 2, Turner 2, Battle); **Percentages:** 2-Pt FG (.459); 3-Pt FG (.500); Total FG (.471); Free Throws (.750).

Tennessee 61

	Min	FG M-A	FT M-A	Pts	Reb O-T	A	PF
LaToya Davis	.30	3-8	0-0	6	1-1	7	5
Shyra Ely	.26	4-10	2-4	10	2-7	0	2
Ashley Robinson	.39	6-10	1-4	13	4-7	1	1
Tasha Butts	.32	1-10	6-6	8	3-6	2	2
Shanna Zolman	.37	6-11	4-4	19	2-9	1	2
Sidney Spencer	.14	0-1	0-0	0	0-1	0	4
Dominique Redding	.3	0-1	0-0	0	0-0	1	0
Brittany Jackson	.11	1-7	0-0	3	0-1	1	2
Tye'sha Fluker	.8	1-3	0-0	2	1-1	0	0
TOTALS	.200	22-61	13-18	61	13-33	13	18

Three-point FG: 4-16 (Butts 0-6, Zolman 3-6, Jackson 1-4); **Team Rebounds:** 6; **Blocked Shots:** 2 (Robinson 2); **Turnovers:** 11 (Davis 3, Ely 3, Jackson 2, Butts, Robinson, Zolman); **Steals:** 8 (Davis 4, Butts 3, Zolman); **Percentages:** 2-Pt FG (.400); 3-Pt FG (.250); Total FG (.361); Free Throws (.722).

Connecticut (Big East)	.30	40—	**70**
Tennessee (SEC)	.24	37—	**61**

Technical Fouls: None. **Officials:** Lisa Mattingly, Denise Kantner, Bryan Enterline. **Attendance:** 18,211. **TV Rating:** 4.3 (ESPN).

Final *ESPN/USA Today* Coaches' Poll

Taken **after** NCAA tournament.

Voted on by panel of 40 women's coaches and media following the NCAA tournament: first place votes in parentheses.

		Pts			Pts
1	Connecticut (40)	.1,000	14	Boston College	..464
2	Tennessee	..959	15	Kansas St.	..377
3	LSU	..895	16	Houston	..342
4	Minnesota	..883	17	Texas Tech	..314
5	Duke	..787	18	Oklahoma	..281
6	Penn St.	..769	19	Santa Barbara	..266
7	Stanford	..759	20	Notre Dame	..173
8	Georgia	..678	21	North Carolina	..167
9	Purdue	..644	22	TCU	..157
10	Texas	..630	23	Auburn	..138
11	Baylor	..584	24	Colorado	..119
12	Louisiana Tech	...580	25	DePaul	..100
13	Vanderbilt	..521			

WOMEN'S FINAL FOUR

at New Orleans, La. (April 4-6).

Semifinals

Connecticut 67 . . . . .Minnesota 58
Tennessee 52 . . . . .LSU 50

Championship

Connecticut 70 . . . . .Tennessee 61

Final Records: Connecticut (31-4), Tennessee (31-4), Minnesota (25-9), LSU (27-8).

Most Outstanding Player: Diana Taurasi, Connecticut forward. SEMIFINAL—37 minutes, 18 points, 6 rebounds, 3 assists, 3 blocks; FINAL—37 minutes, 17 points, 3 rebounds, 2 assists.

All-Tournament Team: Taurasi, guard Ann Strother and center Jessica Moore of Connecticut; center Janel McCarville of Minnesota and guard Shanna Zolman of Tennessee.

Annual Awards

Players of the Year

Alana Beard, Duke . . . . .AP, USBWA, Wade, Wooden
Diana Taurasi, Connecticut . . . . .Broderick, Naismith

Coaches of the Year

Joe Curl, Houston . . . . .AP, USBWA
Rene Portland, Penn St. . . . . .WBCA
Pat Summitt, Tennessee . . . . .Naismith

Consensus All-America Team

The NCAA Division I players cited most frequently by the Associated Press, US Basketball Writers Association and the Women's Basketball Coaches Association. Holdovers from 2002-03 All-America first team in **bold** type; (*) indicates unanimous first team selection.

First Team

		Class	Hgt	Pos
Diana Taurasi*, Connecticut		Sr.	6-0	G/F
Alana Beard*, Duke		Sr.	5-11	G/F
Kelly Mazzante*, Penn St.		Sr.	6-0	G
Nicole Ohlde*, Kansas St.		Sr.	6-5	C
Nicole Powell*, Stanford		Sr.	6-2	F

Second Team

		Class	Hgt	Pos
Lindsay Whalen, Minnesota		Sr.	5-9	G
Shyra Ely, Tennessee		Jr.	6-2	F
Chandi Jones, Houston		Sr.	5-10	F/G
Stacy Stephens, Texas		Sr.	6-1	F/C
Shereka Wright, Purdue		Sr.	5-10	F

Players also named: Vanessa Hayden, Florida; Seimone Augustus, LSU; Janel McCarville, Minnesota.

Other Women's Tournaments

WNIT (Mar. 30 at Omaha, Nebraska): Final— Creighton def. UNLV, 72-53.

NCAA Division II (Mar. 27 at St. Joseph, Missouri): California (Pa.) def. Drury, 75-72.

NCAA Division III (Mar. 20 at Norfolk, Va.): Final— Wilmington (Ohio) def. Bowdoin, 59-53.

NAIA Division I (Mar. 23 at Jackson, Tenn.): Final— Southern Nazarene (Okla.) def. Oklahoma City, 77-61.

NAIA Division II (Mar. 16 at Sioux City, Iowa): Final— Morningside (Iowa) def. Cedarville (Ohio), 87-74.

NCAA Women's Division I Leaders

Includes games through NCAA and NIT tourneys.

INDIVIDUAL

Scoring

	Cl	Gm	Pts	Avg
Emily Faurholt, Idaho	So.	29	737	25.4
Hana Peljito, Harvard	Sr.	27	641	23.7
Chandi Jones, Houston	Sr.	32	727	22.7
Cyndy Wilks, Va. Commonwealth	Sr.	28	618	22.1
Shameka Christon, Arkansas	Sr.	28	611	21.8
Candace Futrell, Duquesne	Sr.	29	621	21.4
Giuliana Mendiola, Washington	Jr.	31	661	21.3
Jennifer Smith, Michigan	Sr.	31	659	21.3
Beth Swink, St. Francis-PA	Jr.	31	659	21.3
Katie Feenstra, Liberty	Jr.	32	674	21.1
Lindsay Whalen, Minnesota	Sr.	27	554	20.5
Crystal Kitt, Alabama St.	Jr.	28	573	20.5
Emily Christian, Tenn. Tech	So.	27	552	20.4
Khara Smith, DePaul	So.	30	611	20.4
Nicole Powell, Stanford	Sr.	31	627	20.2
Tan White, Mississippi St.	Jr.	29	585	20.2
Shereka Wright, Purdue	Sr.	33	662	20.1
Kelly Mazzante, Penn St.	Sr.	34	681	20.0
Katie Donovan, Illinois St.	Jr.	29	578	19.9
Casey Rost, Western Michigan	Jr.	24	475	19.8

Assists

	Cl	Gm	No	Avg
La'Terrica Dobin, Northwestern St.	Sr.	26	249	9.6
Temeka Johnson, LSU	Sr.	35	289	8.3
Leah Cannon, Oral Roberts	Sr.	28	231	8.3
Yolanda Paige, West Virginia	Jr.	32	253	7.9
Brooklynn Lorenzen, Montana	Sr.	32	251	7.8
Toccara Williams, Texas A&M	Sr.	27	192	7.1
Tanara Golston, Brown	Sr.	27	188	7.0
Latesha Lee, Jackson St.	Sr.	30	202	6.7
Malika Willoughby, Kent St.	So.	29	194	6.7
Nancy Bowden, Butler	Sr.	29	193	6.7
Cricket Williams, San Jose St.	Sr.	28	185	6.6
Sara Nord, Louisville	Sr.	30	196	6.5
Karen Hewitt, St. Francis-PA	Jr.	31	202	6.5
Erin Grant, Texas Tech	So.	33	215	6.5
Kerri Fiehrer, Troy St.	Jr.	28	179	6.4

Rebounding

	Cl	Gm	No	Avg
Ashlee Kelly, Quinnipiac	Sr.	29	392	13.5
Desire Almind, Bucknell	Sr.	29	390	13.4
Sandora Irvin, TCU	Jr.	30	366	12.2
Rebekkah Brunson, Georgetown	Jr.	28	336	12.0
Khara Smith, DePaul	So.	30	351	11.7
Rosalee Mason, Manhattan	Sr.	28	325	11.6
Crystal Kitt, Alabama St.	Jr.	28	323	11.5
Angela Buckner, Wichita St.	Sr.	28	318	11.4
Nicole Powell, Stanford	Sr.	31	346	11.2
Katie Feenstra, Liberty	Jr.	32	353	11.0
Tiffany Winkfield, MD-Eastern Shore	Sr.	27	294	10.9
Maria Viall, WI-Milwaukee	Sr.	29	315	10.9
Janel McCarville, Minnesota	Sr.	34	368	10.8
Amisha Carter, La. Tech	Sr.	32	344	10.8
Vanessa Hayden, Florida	Sr.	30	317	10.6
Leisel Harry, Coppin St.	Sr.	29	306	10.6

Blocked Shots

	Cl	Gm	No	Avg
Brooke McAfee, IUPUI	So.	27	130	4.8
Arnie Williams, Jackson St.	Sr.	30	127	4.2
Sandora Irvin, TCU	Jr.	30	117	3.9
Zane Teilane, W. Illinois	So.	29	112	3.9
Katie Beth Pate, Lipscomb	So.	31	113	3.6
Ashley Sparkman, Northwestern Sr.	Jr.	31	110	3.5

Steals

	Cl	Gm	No	Avg
Toccara Williams, Texas A&M	Sr.	27	111	4.1
Chanel Spriggs, American	Sr.	30	117	3.9
Nancy Bowden, Butler	Sr.	29	106	3.7
Keisha McClinic, Mid. Tenn. St.	Sr.	32	112	3.5
Maria Jilian, Western Michigan	Sr.	32	110	3.4

High-Point Games

Pts		Opponent	Date
46 Valerie King, Cincinnati		Charleston So.	Nov. 25
40 Seven players tied.			

TEAM

Scoring Offense

	Gm	W-L	Pts	Avg
DePaul	30	23-7	2531	84.4
Louisiana Tech	32	29-3	2639	82.5
Duke	34	30-4	2785	81.9
TCU	32	25-7	2498	78.1
SW Missouri St.	32	28-4	2486	77.7
Miami-OH	31	22-9	2391	77.1
Baylor	35	26-9	2696	77.0
Connecticut	35	31-4	2642	75.5
Kansas St.	31	25.6	2340	75.5
Harvard	27	16-11	2015	74.6

High-Point Games

Pts	Opponent	Date
127 Winthrop	So. Virginia	Nov. 24
126 Eastern Illinois	Indiana-Northwest	Nov. 21
125 TCU	East Carolina	Feb. 13
119 East Carolina	TCU	Feb. 13
119 Oral Roberts	Bacone	Nov. 29
119 Duke	Stephen F. Austin	Nov. 29
117 Western Michigan	UMKC	Nov. 26

Scoring Defense

	Gm	W-L	Pts	Avg
New Mexico	31	23-8	1584	51.1
Villanova	30	23-7	1587	52.9
Delaware St.	30	21-9	1601	53.4
Jackson St.	30	23-7	1611	53.7
Connecticut	35	31-4	1884	53.8
Utah	31	24-7	1689	54.5
NC-Asheville	28	19-9	1534	54.8
South Alabama	29	22-7	1595	55.0
Auburn	31	22-9	1715	55.3
Montana	32	27-5	1779	55.6

Scoring Margin

	Off	Def	Mar
Duke	81.9	57.4	24.5
Louisiana Tech	82.5	59.3	23.2
Connecticut	75.5	53.8	21.7
SW Missouri St.	77.7	58.5	19.2
Auburn	72.6	55.3	17.3
Kansas St.	75.5	59.0	16.5
DePaul	84.4	67.9	16.4
Texas	72.8	56.7	16.1
Baylor	77.0	61.2	15.8
Texas Tech	72.3	57.3	15.0

1901-2004
Through the Years

SPORTS ALMANAC

National Champions and NCAA Final Four

The Helms Foundation of Los Angeles, under the direction of founder Bill Schroeder, selected national college basketball champions from 1942-82 and researched retroactive picks from 1901-41. The first NIT tournament and then the NCAA tournament have settled the national championship since 1938, but there are four years (1939, '40, '44 and '54) where the Helms selections differ. In 1939, Helms picked undefeated LIU-Brooklyn (24-0), winners of the NIT. In 1940, Helms picked USC (20-3) although they were beaten by Kansas in the West Regionals of the NCAA tourney. In 1944, Helms picked unbeaten Army (15-0). Army did not lift its policy barring postseason play until the 1961 NIT. In 1954, Helms chose unbeaten Kentucky (25-0), even though Kentucky refused its NCAA bid after seniors Cliff Hagan, Frank Ramsey and Lou Tsioropoulos were declared ineligible.

Multiple champions (1901-37): Chicago, Columbia and Wisconsin (3); Kansas, Minnesota, Notre Dame, Penn, Pittsburgh, Syracuse and Yale (2).

Multiple champions (since 1938): UCLA (11); Kentucky (7); Indiana (5); Duke and North Carolina (3); Cincinnati, Connecticut, Kansas, Louisville, Michigan St., N.C. State, Oklahoma A&M (now Oklahoma St.) and San Francisco (2).

Year	Champion	Record		Head Coach	Outstanding Player
1901	**Yale**	10-4		No coach	G.M. Clark, F
1902	**Minnesota**	11-0		Louis Cooke	W.C. Deering, F
1903	**Yale**	15-1		W.H. Murphy	R.B. Hyatt, F
1904	**Columbia**	17-1		No coach	Harry Fisher, F
1905	**Columbia**	19-1		No coach	Harry Fisher, F
1906	**Dartmouth**	16-2		No coach	George Grebenstein, F
1907	**Chicago**	22-2		Joseph Raycroft	John Schommer, C
1908	**Chicago**	21-2		Joseph Raycroft	John Schommer, C
1909	**Chicago**	12-0		Joseph Raycroft	John Schommer, C
1910	**Columbia**	11-1		Harry Fisher	Ted Kiendl, F
1911	**St. John's-NY**	14-0		Claude Allen	John Keenan, F/C
1912	**Wisconsin**	15-0		Doc Meanwell	Otto Stangel, F
1913	**Navy**	9-0		Louis Wenzell	Laurence Wild, F
1914	**Wisconsin**	15-0		Doc Meanwell	Gene Van Gent, C
1915	**Illinois**	16-0		Ralph Jones	Ray Woods, G
1916	**Wisconsin**	20-1		Doc Meanwell	George Levis, F
1917	**Washington St**	25-1		Doc Bohler	Roy Bohler, G
1918	**Syracuse**	16-1		Edmund Dollard	Joe Schwarzer, G
1919	**Minnesota**	13-0		Louis Cooke	Arnold Oss, F
1920	**Penn**	22-1		Lon Jourdet	George Sweeney, F
1921	**Penn**	21-2		Edward McNichol	Danny McNichol, G
1922	**Kansas**	16-2		Phog Allen	Paul Endacott, G
1923	**Kansas**	17-1		Phog Allen	Paul Endacott, G
1924	**North Carolina**	25-0		Bo Shepard	Jack Cobb, F
1925	**Princeton**	21-2		Al Wittmer	Art Loeb, G
1926	**Syracuse**	19-1		Lew Andreas	Vic Hanson, F
1927	**Notre Dame**	19-1		George Keogan	John Nyikos, C
1928	**Pittsburgh**	21-0		Doc Carlson	Chuck Hyatt, F
1929	**Montana St.**	36-2		Schubert Dyche	John (Cat) Thompson, F
1930	**Pittsburgh**	23-2		Doc Carlson	Chuck Hyatt, F
1931	**Northwestern**	16-1		Dutch Lonborg	Joe Reiff, C
1932	**Purdue**	17-1		Piggy Lambert	John Wooden, G
1933	**Kentucky**	20-3		Adolph Rupp	Forest Sale, F
1934	**Wyoming**	26-3		Willard Witte	Les Witte, G
1935	**NYU**	19-1		Howard Cann	Sid Gross, F
1936	**Notre Dame**	22-2-1		George Keogan	John Moir, F
1937	**Stanford**	25-2		John Bunn	Hank Luisetti, F

Year			Record	Winner	Head Coach	Outstanding Player
1938	**Temple**		23-2	NIT	James Usilton	Meyer Bloom, G

Year	Champion	Runner-up	Score	Final Two	Head Coach	Third Place
1939	Oregon	Ohio St.	46-33	@ Evanston, IL	Oklahoma	Villanova
1940	Indiana	Kansas	60-42	@ Kansas City	Duquesne	USC
1941	Wisconsin	Washington St.	39-34	@ Kansas City	Arkansas	Pittsburgh
1942	Stanford	Dartmouth	53-38	@ Kansas City	Colorado	Kentucky
1943	Wyoming	Georgetown	46-34	@ New York	DePaul	Texas
1944	Utah	Dartmouth	42-40 (OT)	@ New York	Iowa St.	Ohio St.
1945	Oklahoma A&M	NYU	49-45	@ New York	Arkansas	Ohio St.

Year	Champion	Runner-up	Score	Final Two	Third Place	Fourth Place
1946	Oklahoma A&M	North Carolina	43-40	@ New York	Ohio St.	California
1947	Holy Cross	Oklahoma	58-47	@ New York	Texas	CCNY
1948	Kentucky	Baylor	58-42	@ New York	Holy Cross	Kansas St.
1949	Kentucky	Oklahoma A&M	46-36	@ Seattle	Illinois	Oregon St.
1950	CCNY	Bradley	71-68	@ New York	N.C. State	Baylor
1951	Kentucky	Kansas St.	68-58	@ Minneapolis	Illinois	Oklahoma A&M

Year	Champion	Runner-up	Score	Third Place	Fourth Place	Final Four
1952	Kansas	St. John's	80-63	Illinois	Santa Clara	@ Seattle
1953	Indiana	Kansas	69-68	Washington	LSU	@ Kansas City
1954	La Salle	Bradley	92-76	Penn St.	USC	@ Kansas City
1955	San Francisco	La Salle	77-63	Colorado	Iowa	@ Kansas City
1956	San Francisco	Iowa	83-71	Temple	SMU	@ Evanston, IL
1957	North Carolina	Kansas	54-53 (3OT)	San Francisco	Michigan St.	@ Kansas City
1958	Kentucky	Seattle	84-72	Temple	Kansas St.	@ Louisville
1959	California	West Virginia	71-70	Cincinnati	Louisville	@ Louisville
1960	Ohio St.	California	75-55	Cincinnati	NYU	@ San Francisco
1961	Cincinnati	Ohio St.	70-65 (OT)	St. Joseph's-PA	Utah	@ Kansas City
1962	Cincinnati	Ohio St.	71-59	Wake Forest	UCLA	@ Louisville
1963	Loyola-IL	Cincinnati	60-58 (OT)	Duke	Oregon St.	@ Louisville
1964	UCLA	Duke	98-83	Michigan	Kansas St.	@ Kansas City
1965	UCLA	Michigan	91-80	Princeton	Wichita St.	@ Portland, OR
1966	Texas Western	Kentucky	72-65	Duke	Utah	@ College Park, MD
1967	UCLA	Dayton	79-64	Houston	North Carolina	@ Louisville
1968	UCLA	North Carolina	78-55	Ohio St.	Houston	@ Los Angeles
1969	UCLA	Purdue	92-72	Drake	North Carolina	@ Louisville
1970	UCLA	Jacksonville	80-69	New Mexico St.	St. Bonaventure	@ College Park, MD
1971	UCLA	Villanova	68-62	Western Ky.	Kansas	@ Houston
1972	UCLA	Florida St.	81-76	North Carolina	Louisville	@ Los Angeles
1973	UCLA	Memphis St.	87-66	Indiana	Providence	@ St. Louis
1974	N.C. State	Marquette	76-64	UCLA	Kansas	@ Greensboro, NC
1975	UCLA	Kentucky	92-85	Louisville	Syracuse	@ San Diego
1976	Indiana	Michigan	86-68	UCLA	Rutgers	@ Philadelphia
1977	Marquette	North Carolina	67-59	UNLV	NC-Charlotte	@ Atlanta
1978	Kentucky	Duke	94-88	Arkansas	Notre Dame	@ St. Louis
1979	Michigan St.	Indiana St.	75-64	DePaul	Penn	@ Salt Lake City
1980	Louisville	UCLA	59-54	Purdue	Iowa	@ Indianapolis
1981	Indiana	North Carolina	63-50	Virginia	LSU	@ Philadelphia

Year	Champion	Runner-up	Score	Third Place		Final Four
1982	North Carolina	Georgetown	63-62	Houston	Louisville	@ New Orleans
1983	N.C. State	Houston	54-52	Georgia	Louisville	@ Albuquerque
1984	Georgetown	Houston	84-75	Kentucky	Virginia	@ Seattle
1985	Villanova	Georgetown	66-64	Memphis St.	St. John's	@ Lexington
1986	Louisville	Duke	72-69	Kansas	LSU	@ Dallas
1987	Indiana	Syracuse	74-73	Providence	UNLV	@ New Orleans
1988	Kansas	Oklahoma	83-79	Arizona	Duke	@ Kansas City
1989	Michigan	Seton Hall	80-79 (OT)	Duke	Illinois	@ Seattle
1990	UNLV	Duke	103-73	Arkansas	Georgia Tech	@ Denver
1991	Duke	Kansas	72-65	North Carolina	UNLV	@ Indianapolis
1992	Duke	Michigan	71-51	Cincinnati	Indiana	@ Minneapolis
1993	North Carolina	Michigan	77-71	Kansas	Kentucky	@ New Orleans
1994	Arkansas	Duke	76-72	Arizona	Florida	@ Charlotte
1995	UCLA	Arkansas	89-78	North Carolina	Oklahoma St.	@ Seattle
1996	Kentucky	Syracuse	76-67	UMass	Mississippi St.	@ E. Rutherford, NJ
1997	Arizona	Kentucky	84-79 (OT)	Minnesota	North Carolina	@ Indianapolis
1998	Kentucky	Utah	78-69	Stanford	North Carolina	@ San Antonio
1999	Connecticut	Duke	77-74	Michigan St.	Ohio St.	@ St. Petersburg, FL
2000	Michigan St.	Florida	89-76	Wisconsin	North Carolina	@ Indianapolis
2001	Duke	Arizona	82-72	Michigan St.	Maryland	@ Minneapolis
2002	Maryland	Indiana	64-52	Oklahoma	Kansas	@ Atlanta
2003	Syracuse	Kansas	81-78	Marquette	Texas	@ New Orleans
2004	Connecticut	Georgia Tech	82-73	Duke	Oklahoma St.	@ San Antonio

Note: Six teams have had their standing in the Final Four vacated for using ineligible players: 1961–St. Joseph's-PA (3rd place); 1971–Villanova (Runner-up) and Western Kentucky (3rd); 1980–UCLA (Runner-up); 1985–Memphis St. (3rd); 1996–UMass (3rd).

The Red Cross Benefit Games, 1943-45

For three seasons during World War II, the NCAA and NIT champions met in a benefit game at Madison Square Garden in New York to raise money for the Red Cross. The NCAA champs won all three games.

Year	Winner	Score	Loser
1943	Wyoming (NCAA)	52-47	St. John's (NIT)
1944	Utah (NCAA)	43-36	St. John's (NIT)
1945	Oklahoma A&M (NCAA)	52-44	DePaul (NIT)

Most Outstanding Player

A Most Outstanding Player has been selected every year of the NCAA tournament. Winners who did not play for the tournament champion are listed in **bold** type. The 1939 and 1951 winners are unofficial and not recognized by the NCAA. Statistics listed are for Final Four games only.

Multiple winners: Lew Alcindor (3); Alex Groza, Bob Kurland, Jerry Lucas and Bill Walton (2).

Year		Gm	FGM	Pct	3PTM	3PTA	FTM	Pct	Reb	Ast	Blk	Stl	PPG
1939	**Jimmy Hull**, Ohio St.	2	15	—	—	—	10	.833	—	—	—	—	20.0
1940	Marv Huffman, Indiana	2	7	—	—	—	4	—	—	—	—	—	9.0
1941	John Kotz, Wisconsin	2	8	—	—	—	6	—	—	—	—	—	11.0
1942	Howie Dallmar, Stanford	2	8	—	—	—	4	.667	—	—	—	—	10.0
1943	Kenny Sailors, Wyoming	2	10	—	—	—	8	.727	—	—	—	—	14.0
1944	Arnie Ferrin, Utah	2	11	—	—	—	6	—	—	—	—	—	14.0
1945	Bob Kurland, Okla. A&M	2	16	—	—	—	5	—	—	—	—	—	18.5
1946	Bob Kurland, Okla. A&M	2	21	—	—	—	10	.667	—	—	—	—	26.0
1947	George Kaftan, Holy Cross	2	18	—	—	—	12	.706	—	—	—	—	24.0
1948	Alex Groza, Kentucky	2	16	—	—	—	5	—	—	—	—	—	18.5
1949	Alex Groza, Kentucky	2	19	—	—	—	14	—	—	—	—	—	26.0
1950	Irwin Dambrot, CCNY	2	12	.429	—	—	4	.500	—	—	—	—	14.0
1951	**Bill Spivey**, Kentucky	2	20	.400	—	—	10	.625	37	—	—	—	25.0
1952	Clyde Lovellette, Kansas	2	24	—	—	—	18	—	—	—	—	—	33.0
1953	**B.H. Born**, Kansas	2	17	—	—	—	17	—	—	—	—	—	25.5
1954	Tom Gola, La Salle	2	12	—	—	—	14	—	—	—	—	—	19.0
1955	Bill Russell, San Francisco	2	19	—	—	—	9	—	—	—	—	—	23.5
1956	**Hal Lear**, Temple	2	32	—	—	—	16	—	—	—	—	—	40.0
1957	Wilt Chamberlain, Kansas	2	18	.514	—	—	19	.704	25	—	—	—	32.5
1958	**Elgin Baylor**, Seattle	2	18	.340	—	—	12	.750	41	—	—	—	24.0
1959	**Jerry West**, West Virginia	2	22	.667	—	—	22	.688	25	—	—	—	33.0
1960	Jerry Lucas, Ohio St.	2	16	.667	—	—	3	1.000	23	—	—	—	17.5
1961	**Jerry Lucas**, Ohio St.	2	20	.714	—	—	16	.941	25	—	—	—	28.0
1962	Paul Hogue, Cincinnati	2	23	.639	—	—	12	.632	38	—	—	—	29.0
1963	**Art Heyman**, Duke	2	18	.409	—	—	15	.682	19	—	—	—	25.5
1964	Walt Hazzard, UCLA	2	11	.550	—	—	8	.667	10	—	—	—	15.0
1965	**Bill Bradley**, Princeton	2	34	.630	—	—	19	.950	24	—	—	—	43.5
1966	**Jerry Chambers**, Utah	2	25	.532	—	—	20	.833	35	—	—	—	35.0
1967	Lew Alcindor, UCLA	2	14	.609	—	—	11	.458	38	—	—	—	19.5
1968	Lew Alcindor, UCLA	2	22	.629	—	—	9	.900	34	—	—	—	26.5
1969	Lew Alcindor, UCLA	2	23	.676	—	—	16	.640	41	—	—	—	31.0
1970	Sidney Wicks, UCLA	2	15	.714	—	—	9	.600	34	—	—	—	19.5
1971	**Howard Porter**, Villanova	2	20	.488	—	—	7	.778	24	—	—	—	23.5
1972	Bill Walton, UCLA	2	20	.690	—	—	17	.739	41	—	—	—	28.5
1973	Bill Walton, UCLA	2	28	.824	—	—	2	.400	30	—	—	—	29.0
1974	David Thompson, N.C. State	2	19	.514	—	—	11	.786	17	—	—	—	24.5
1975	Richard Washington, UCLA	2	23	.548	—	—	8	.727	20	—	—	—	27.0
1976	Kent Benson, Indiana	2	17	.500	—	—	7	.636	18	—	—	—	20.5
1977	Butch Lee, Marquette	2	11	.344	—	—	8	1.000	6	2	1	1	15.0
1978	Jack Givens, Kentucky	2	28	.651	—	—	8	.667	17	4	1	3	32.0
1979	Magic Johnson, Michigan St.	2	17	.680	—	—	19	.864	17	3	0	2	26.5
1980	Darrell Griffith, Louisville	2	23	.622	—	—	11	.688	7	15	0	2	28.5
1981	Isiah Thomas, Indiana	2	14	.560	—	—	9	.818	4	9	3	4	18.5
1982	James Worthy, N. Carolina	2	20	.741	—	—	2	.286	8	9	0	4	21.0
1983	**Akeem Olajuwon**, Houston	2	16	.552	—	—	9	.643	40	3	2	5	20.5
1984	Patrick Ewing, Georgetown	2	8	.571	—	—	2	1.000	18	1	15	1	9.0
1985	Ed Pinckney, Villanova	2	8	.571	—	—	12	.750	15	6	3	0	14.0
1986	Pervis Ellison, Louisville	2	15	.600	—	—	6	.750	24	2	3	1	18.0
1987	Keith Smart, Indiana	2	14	.636	0	1	7	.778	7	7	0	2	17.5
1988	Danny Manning, Kansas	2	25	.556	0	1	6	.667	17	4	8	9	28.0
1989	Glen Rice, Michigan	2	24	.490	7	16	4	1.000	16	1	0	3	29.5
1990	Anderson Hunt, UNLV	2	19	.613	9	16	2	.500	4	9	1	1	24.5
1991	Christian Laettner, Duke	2	12	.545	1	1	21	.913	17	2	1	2	23.0
1992	Bobby Hurley, Duke	2	10	.417	7	12	8	.800	3	11	0	3	17.5
1993	Donald Williams, N. Carolina	2	15	.652	10	14	10	1.000	4	1	0	2	25.0
1994	Corliss Williamson, Arkansas	2	21	.500	0	0	10	.714	21	8	3	4	26.0
1995	Ed O'Bannon, UCLA	2	16	.457	3	8	13	.769	25	3	1	7	22.5
1996	Tony Delk, Kentucky	2	15	.417	8	16	6	.546	9	2	3	2	22.0
1997	Miles Simon, Arizona	2	17	.459	3	10	17	.773	8	6	0	1	27.0
1998	Jeff Sheppard, Kentucky	2	16	.552	4	10	7	.778	10	7	0	4	21.5
1999	Richard Hamilton, Connecticut	2	20	.513	3	7	8	.727	12	4	1	2	25.5
2000	Mateen Cleaves, Michigan St.	2	8	.444	3	4	10	.833	6	5	0	2	14.5
2001	Shane Battier, Duke	2	13	.464	5	12	12	.706	19	8	6	2	21.5
2002	Juan Dixon, Maryland	2	16	.593	7	15	12	.800	8	5	0	7	25.5
2003	Carmelo Anthony, Syracuse	2	19	.543	6	9	9	.818	24	8	0	4	26.5
2004	Emeka Okafor, Connecticut	2	17	.654	0	0	8	.533	22	2	4	1	21.0

Final Four All-Decade Teams

To celebrate the 50th anniversary of the NCAA tournament in 1989, five All-Decade teams were selected by a blue ribbon panel of coaches and administrators. An All-Time Final Four team was also chosen. Selections were actually made prior to the 1988 tournament.

Selection panel: Vic Bubas, Denny Crum, Wayne Duke, Dave Gavitt, Joe B. Hall, Jud Heathcote, Hank Iba, Pete Newell, Dean Smith, John Thompson and John Wooden.

All-Time Team

	Years
Lew Alcindor, UCLA	1967-69
Larry Bird, Indiana St.	1979
Wilt Chamberlain, Kansas	1957
Magic Johnson, Mich. St	1979
Michael Jordan, N. Carolina	1982

All-1950s

	Years
Elgin Baylor, Seattle	1958
Wilt Chamberlain, Kansas	1957
Tom Gola, La Salle	1954
K.C. Jones, San Francisco	1955
Clyde Lovellette, Kansas	1952
Oscar Robertson, Cinn.	1959-60
Guy Rodgers, Temple	1958
Lennie Rosenbluth, N. Carolina	1957
Bill Russell, San Francisco	1955-56
Jerry West, West Virginia	1959

All-1970s

	Years
Kent Benson, Indiana	1976
Larry Bird, Indiana St	1979
Jack Givens, Kentucky	1978
Magic Johnson, Mich. St	1979
Marques Johnson, UCLA	1975-76
Scott May, Indiana	1976
David Thompson, N.C. State	1974
Bill Walton, UCLA	1972-74
Sidney Wicks, UCLA	1969-71
Keith Wilkes, UCLA	1972-74

All-1940s

	Years
Ralph Beard, Kentucky	1948-49
Howie Dallmar, Stanford	1942
Dwight Eddleman, Illinois	1949
Arnie Ferrin, Utah	1944
Alex Groza, Kentucky	1948-49
George Kaftan, Holy Cross	1947
Bob Kurland, Okla. A&M	1945-46
Jim Pollard, Stanford	1942
Kenny Sailors, Wyoming	1943
Gerry Tucker, Oklahoma	1947

All-1960s

	Years
Lew Alcindor, UCLA	1967-69
Bill Bradley, Princeton	1965
Gail Goodrich, UCLA	1964-65
John Havlicek, Ohio St	1961-62
Elvin Hayes, Houston	1967
Walt Hazzard, UCLA	1964
Jerry Lucas, Ohio St	1960-61
Jeff Mullins, Duke	1964
Cazzie Russell, Michigan	1965
Charlie Scott, N. Carolina	1968-69

All-1980s

	Years
Steve Alford, Indiana	1987
Johnny Dawkins, Duke	1986
Patrick Ewing, Georgetown	1982-84
Darrell Griffith, Louisville	1980
Michael Jordan, N. Carolina	1982
Rodney McCray, Louisville	1980
Akeem Olajuwon, Houston	1983-84
Ed Pinckney, Villanova	1985
Isiah Thomas, Indiana	1981
James Worthy, N. Carolina	1982

Note: Lew Alcindor later changed his name to Kareem Abdul-Jabbar; Keith Wilkes later changed his first name to Jamaal; and Akeem Olajuwon later changed the spelling of his first name to Hakeem.

Seeds at the Final Four

NCAA champions in **bold** type.

Year	Seeds (Total)	Teams
1979	1,2,2,9 (14)	Indiana St., **Mich. St.**, DePaul, Penn.
1980	2,5,6,8 (21)	**Louisville**, Iowa, Purdue, UCLA
1981	1,1,2,3 (7)	Virginia, LSU, N. Carolina, **Indiana**
1982	1,1,3,6 (11)	**N. Carolina**, Georgetown, Louisville, Houston
1983	1,1,4,6 (12)	Houston, Louisville, Georgia, **N.C. State**
1984	1,1,2,7 (11)	Kentucky, **Georgetown**, Houston, Virginia
1985	1,1,2,8 (12)	St. John's, Georgetown, Memphis, **Villanova**
1986	1,1,2,11 (15)	Duke, Kansas, **Louisville**, LSU
1987	1,1,2,6 (10)	UNLV, **Indiana**, Syracuse, Providence
1988	1,1,2,6 (10)	Arizona, Oklahoma, Duke, **Kansas**
1989	1,2,3,3 (9)	Illinois, Duke, Seton Hall, **Michigan**
1990	1,3,4,4 (12)	**UNLV**, Duke, Ga. Tech, Arkansas
1991	1,1,2,3 (7)	UNLV, N. Carolina, **Duke**, Kansas
1992	1,2,4,6 (13)	**Duke**, Indiana, Cincinnati, Michigan
1993	1,1,1,2 (5)	**N. Carolina**, Kentucky, Michigan, Kansas
1994	1,2,2,3 (8)	**Arkansas**, Arizona, Duke, Florida
1995	1,2,2,4 (9)	**UCLA**, Arkansas, N. Carolina, Okla. St.
1996	1,1,4,5 (11)	**Kentucky**, UMass, Syracuse, Miss. St.
1997	1,1,1,4 (7)	Kentucky, N. Carolina, Minnesota, **Arizona**
1998	1,2,3,3 (9)	N. Carolina, **Kentucky**, Stanford, Utah
1999	1,1,1,4 (7)	**Connecticut**, Duke, Michigan St., Ohio St.
2000	1,5,8,8 (22)	**Michigan St.**, Florida, Wisconsin, N. Carolina
2001	1,1,2,3 (7)	**Duke**, Michigan St., Arizona, Maryland
2002	1,1,2,5 (9)	**Maryland**, Kansas, Oklahoma, Indiana
2003	1,2,3,3 (9)	Texas, Kansas, **Syracuse**, Marquette
2004	1,2,2,3 (8)	Duke, **Connecticut**, Oklahoma St., Georgia Tech

Note: teams were not seeded before 1979.

All-Time Seeds Records

All-time records of NCAA tournament seeds since tourney began seeding teams in 1979. Records are through the 2004 NCAA Tournament. Note that 1st refers to championships. 2nd refers to runners-up and FF refers to Final Four appearances not including 1st and 2nd place finishes.

Seed	W	L	Pct.	1st	2nd	FF
1	315	92	.774	13	9	21
2	232	98	.703	6	6	11
3	167	101	.623	3	5	5
4	143	103	.581	1	1	6
5	121	105	.535	0	2	2
6	139	102	.577	2	1	3
7	86	104	.453	0	0	1
8	81	103	.440	1	1	2
9	60	105	.364	0	0	1
10	72	104	.409	0	0	0
11	43	100	.301	0	0	1
12	43	100	.301	0	0	0
13	19	80	.192	0	0	0
14	15	80	.158	0	0	0
15	4	80	.048	0	0	0
16	0	80	.000	0	0	0

Collegiate Commissioners Association Tournament

The Collegiate Commissioners Association staged an eight-team tournament for teams that didn't make the NCAA tournament in 1974 and '75.

Most Valuable Players: 1974–Kent Benson, Indiana; 1975–Bob Elliot, Arizona.

Year	Winner	Score	Loser	Site
1974	Indiana	85-60	USC	St. Louis
1975	Drake	83-76	Arizona	Louisville

NCAA Tournament Appearances

App		W-L	F4	Championships	App		W-L	F4	Championships
46	Kentucky	95-41	13	7 (1948-49, 51, 58, 78, 96, 98)	22	Georgetown	38-21	4	1 (1984)
38	UCLA	85-31	15	11 (1964-65,67-73,75,95)	22	Ohio St.	37-21	9	1 (1960)
36	N. Carolina	82-35	15	3 (1957,82,93)	22	Oklahoma	30-22	4	None
32	Indiana	58-27	8	5 (1940,53,76,81,87)	22	Texas	25-25	3	None
32	Kansas	68-32	11	2 (1952,88)	22	DePaul	21-25	2	None
31	Louisville	49-33	7	2 (1980,86)	21	Oklahoma St.	35-20	6	2 (1945-46)
29	Syracuse	48-29	4	1 (2003)	21	Missouri	18-21	0	None
28	Duke	81-25	14	3 (1991-92, 2001)	21	BYU	11-24	0	None
27	St. John's	27-29	2	None	21	Maryland	35-20	2	1 (2002)
27	Notre Dame	29-31	1	None	20	Michigan	41-19	6	1 (1989)
26	Arkansas	39-26	6	1 (1994)	20	Iowa	27-22	3	None
25	Connecticut	38-24	2	1 (1999, 2004)	20	Purdue	27-20	2	None
25	Villanova	37-25	3	1 (1985)	20	Pennsylvania	13-22	1	None
25	Temple	31-25	2	None	20	N.C. State	29-19	3	2 (1974,83)
25	Utah	33-28	4	1 (1944)	19	Wake Forest	26-19	1	None
24	Illinois	32-24	4	None	19	Western Ky.	15-20	1	None
23	Marquette	32-24	3	1 (1977)	18	Houston	26-23	5	None
23	Arizona	37-22	3	1 (1997)	18	West Virginia	13-18	1	None
23	Cincinnati	39-22	6	2 (1961-62)	18	Michigan St.	36-17	6	1 (1989)
23	Princeton	13-27	1	None	18	Memphis	19-18	2	None
22	Kansas St.	27-26	4	None	18	St. Joseph's	18-22	1	None

Note: Although all NCAA tournament appearances are included above, the NCAA has officially voided the records of Villanova (4-1) and Western Ky. (4-1) in 1971; UCLA (5-1) in 1980 and again (0-1) in 1999; Oregon St. (2-3) from 1980-82; Memphis (9-5) from 1982-86; DePaul (6-4) from 1986-89; N.C. State (0-2) from 1987-88; Kentucky (2-1) and Maryland (1-1) in 1988; Missouri (3-1) in 1994; Connecticut (2-1) and Purdue (1-1) in 1996; Arizona (0-1) in 1999.

All-Time NCAA Division I Tournament Leaders

Through 2004; minimum of six games; **Last** column indicates final year played.

CAREER

Scoring

Points

		Yrs	Last	Gm	Pts
1	Christian Laettner, Duke	4	1992	23	407
2	Elvin Hayes, Houston	3	1968	13	358
3	Danny Manning, Kansas	4	1988	16	328
4	Oscar Robertson, Cincinnati	3	1960	10	324
5	Glen Rice, Michigan	4	1989	13	308
6	Lew Alcindor, UCLA	3	1969	12	304
7	Bill Bradley, Princeton	3	1965	9	303
	Corliss Williamson, Arkansas	3	1995	15	303
9	Juan Dixon, Maryland	4	2002	16	294
10	Austin Carr, Notre Dame	3	1971	7	289

Average

		Yrs	Last	Pts	Avg
1	Austin Carr, Notre Dame	3	1971	289	41.3
2	Bill Bradley, Princeton	3	1965	303	33.7
3	Oscar Robertson, Cincinnati	3	1960	324	32.4
4	Jerry West, West Virginia	3	1960	275	30.6
5	Bob Pettit, LSU	2	1954	183	30.5
6	Dan Issel, Kentucky	3	1970	176	29.3
	Jim McDaniels, Western Ky	2	1971	176	29.3
8	Dwight Lamar, SW Louisiana	2	1973	175	29.2
9	Bo Kimble, Loyola-CA	3	1990	204	29.1
10	David Robinson, Navy	3	1987	200	28.6

Rebounds

Total

		Yrs	Last	Gm	No
1	Elvin Hayes, Houston	3	1968	13	222
2	Lew Alcindor, UCLA	3	1969	12	201
3	Jerry Lucas, Ohio St.	3	1962	12	197
4	Bill Walton, UCLA	3	1974	12	176
5	Christian Laettner, Duke	4	1992	23	169
6	Tim Duncan, Wake Forest	4	1997	11	165
7	Paul Hogue, Cincinnati	3	1962	12	160
8	Sam Lacey, New Mexico St.	3	1970	11	157
9	Derrick Coleman, Syracuse	4	1990	14	155
10	Akeem Olajuwon, Houston	3	1984	15	153

Average

		Yrs	Last	Reb	Avg
1	Johnny Green, Michigan St.	2	1959	118	19.7
2	Artis Gilmore, Jacksonville	2	1971	115	19.2
3	Paul Silas, Creighton	3	1964	111	18.5
4	Len Chappell, Wake Forest	2	1962	137	17.1
5	Elvin Hayes, Houston	3	1968	222	17.1
6	Lew Alcindor, UCLA	3	1969	201	16.8
7	Jerry Lucas, Ohio St.	3	1962	197	16.4
8	Tim Duncan, Wake Forest	4	1997	165	15.0
9	Bill Walton, UCLA	3	1974	176	14.7
10	Sam Lacey, New Mexico St.	3	1970	157	14.3

3-Pt Field Goals

Total

		Yrs	Last	Gm	No
1	Bobby Hurley, Duke	4	1993	20	42
2	Tony Delk, Kentucky	4	1996	17	40
3	Jeff Fryer, Loyola-CA	3	1990	7	38
	Donald Williams, North Carolina	4	1995	15	38
	Juan Dixon, Maryland	4	2002	16	38

Assists

Total

		Yrs	Last	Gm	No
1	Bobby Hurley, Duke	4	1993	20	145
2	Sherman Douglas, Syracuse	4	1989	14	106
3	Greg Anthony, UNLV	3	1991	15	100
4	Mark Wade, UNLV	2	1987	8	93
	Rumeal Robinson, Michigan	3	1990	11	93
	Jacque Vaughn, Kansas	4	1997	13	93
	Anthony Epps, Kentucky	4	1997	18	93

SINGLE TOURNAMENT

Scoring

Points

		Year	Gm	Pts
1	Glen Rice, Michigan	1989	6	184
2	Bill Bradley, Princeton	1965	5	177
3	Elvin Hayes, Houston	1968	5	167
4	Danny Manning, Kansas	1988	6	163
5	Hal Lear, Temple	1956	5	160
	Jerry West, West Virginia	1959	5	160

Average

		Year	Gm	Pts	Avg
1	Austin Carr, Notre Dame	1970	3	158	52.7
2	Austin Carr, Notre Dame	1971	3	125	41.7
3	Jerry Chambers, Utah	1966	4	143	35.8
	Bo Kimble, Loyola-CA	1990	4	143	35.8
5	Bill Bradley, Princeton	1965	5	177	35.4
6	Clyde Lovellette, Kansas	1952	4	141	35.3

Rebounds

	Total	Year	Gm	No	Avg
1	Elvin Hayes, Houston	1968	5	**97**	19.4
2	Artis Gilmore, Jacksonville	1970	5	**93**	18.6
3	Elgin Baylor, Seattle	1958	5	**91**	18.2
4	Sam Lacey, New Mexico St.	1970	5	**90**	18.0
5	Clarence Glover, Western Ky	1971	5	**89**	17.8
6	Len Chappell, Wake Forest	1962	5	**86**	17.2

Assists

	Total	Year	Gm	No	Avg
1	Mark Wade, UNLV	1987	5	**61**	12.2
2	Rumeal Robinson, Michigan	1989	6	**56**	9.3
3	T.J. Ford, Texas	2003	5	**51**	10.2
4	Sherman Douglas, Syracuse	1987	6	**49**	8.2
5	Bobby Hurley, Duke	1992	6	**47**	7.8
6	Lazarus Sims, Syracuse	1996	6	**46**	7.7

SINGLE GAME

Scoring

	Points	Year	Pts
1	Austin Carr, Notre Dame vs Ohio Univ	1970	61
2	Bill Bradley, Princeton vs Wichita St.	1965	58
3	Oscar Robertson, Cincinnati vs Arkansas	1958	56
4	Austin Carr, Notre Dame vs Kentucky	1970	52
	Austin Carr, Notre Dame vs TCU	1971	52
6	David Robinson, Navy vs Michigan	1987	50
7	Elvin Hayes, Houston vs Loyola-IL	1968	49
8	Hal Lear, Temple vs SMU	1956	48
9	Austin Carr, Notre Dame vs Houston	1971	47
10	Dave Corzine, DePaul vs Louisville	1978	46
11	Bob Houbregs, Washington vs Seattle	1953	45
	Austin Carr, Notre Dame vs Iowa	1970	45
	Bo Kimble, Loyola-CA vs New Mexico St.	1990	45
14	Seven players tied with 44 each.		

Rebounds

	Total	Year	No
1	Fred Cohen, Temple vs UConn	1956	34
2	Nate Thurmond, Bowl. Green vs Miss. St.	1963	31
3	Jerry Lucas, Ohio St. vs Kentucky	1961	30
4	Toby Kimball, UConn vs St. Joseph's-PA	1965	29
5	Elvin Hayes, Houston vs Pacific	1966	28
6	Four players tied with 27 each.		

Assists

	Total	Year	No
1	Mark Wade, UNLV vs Indiana	1987	18
2	Sam Crawford, N. Mexico St. vs Nebraska	1993	16
3	Kenny Patterson, DePaul vs Syracuse	1985	15
	Keith Smart, Indiana vs Auburn	1987	15
5	Six players tied with 14 each.		

SINGLE FINAL FOUR GAME

Letters in the **Year** column indicate the following: C for Consolation Game, F for Final and S for Semifinal.

Scoring

	Points	Year	Pts
1	Bill Bradley, Princeton vs Wichita St	1965-C	58
2	Hal Lear, Temple vs SMU	1956-C	48
3	Bill Walton, UCLA vs Memphis St	1973-F	44
4	Bob Houbregs, Washington vs LSU	1953-C	42
	Jack Egan, St. Joseph's-PA vs Utah	1961-C	42*
	Gail Goodrich, UCLA vs Michigan	1965-C	42
7	Jack Givens, Kentucky vs Duke	1978-F	41
8	Oscar Robertson, Cincinnati vs L'ville	1959-C	39
	Al Wood, N. Carolina vs Virginia	1981-S	39
10	Jerry West, West Va. vs Louisville	1959-S	38
	Jerry Chambers, Utah vs Texas Western	1966-S	38
	Freddie Banks, UNLV vs Indiana	1987-S	38

*Four overtimes.

Rebounds

	Total	Year	No
1	Bill Russell, San Francisco vs Iowa	1956-F	27
2	Elvin Hayes, Houston vs UCLA	1967-S	24
3	Bill Russell, San Francisco vs SMU	1956-S	23
4	Elgin Baylor, Seattle vs Kansas St.	1958-S	22
	Tom Sanders, NYU vs Ohio St.	1960-S	22
	Larry Kenon, Memphis vs Providence	1973-S	22
	Akeem Olajuwon, Houston vs Louisville	1983-S	22
8	Bill Spivey, Kentucky vs Kansas St.	1951-C	21
	Lew Alcindor, UCLA vs Drake	1969-C	21
	Artis Gilmore, Jacksonville vs St. Bonaventure	1970-S	21
	Bill Walton, UCLA vs Louisville	1972-S	21
	Nick Collison, Kansas vs Syracuse	2003-C	21

Assists

	Total	Year	No
1	Mark Wade, UNLV vs Indiana	1987-S	18
2	T.J. Ford, Texas vs. Syracuse	2003-C	13
3	Rumeal Robinson, Michigan vs Illinois	1989-S	12
	Edgar Padilla, UMass vs. Ky.	1996-S	12
5	Michael Jackson, G'town vs St. John's	1985-S	11
	Milt Wagner, Louisville vs LSU	1986-S	11
	Rumeal Robinson, Mich. vs Seton Hall	1989-F	11*
	Steve Blake, Maryland vs. Kansas	2002-S	11

*Overtime.

Blocked Shots

	Total	Year	No
1	Danny Manning, Kansas vs Duke	1988-S	6
	Marcus Camby, UMass vs Kentucky	1996-S	6
3	Six players tied with 4 each.		

Steals

	Total	Year	No
1	Tommy Amaker, Duke vs. Louisville	1986-C	7
	Mookie Blaylock, Oklahoma vs. Kansas	1988-C	7
3	Gilbert Arenas, Arizona vs. Michigan St.	2001-S	6
4	Five players tied with 5 each.		

Teams in Both NCAA and NIT

Fourteen teams played in both the NCAA and NIT tournaments from 1940-52. Colorado (1940), Utah (1944), Kentucky (1949) and BYU (1951) won one of the titles, while CCNY won two in 1950, beating Bradley in both championship games.

Year	NIT	NCAA
1940	Colorado . . . . . . **Won Final**	Lost 1st Rd
	Duquesne . . . . . Lost Final	Lost 2nd Rd
1944	Utah . . . . Lost 1st Rd	**Won Final**
1949	Kentucky . . . . . Lost Final	**Won Final**
1950	CCNY . . . . **Won Final**	**Won Final**
	Bradley . . . . . . Lost Final	Lost Final
1951	BYU . . . . **Won Final**	Lost 2nd Rd
	St. John's . . . . . Lost 3rd Rd	Lost 2nd Rd
	N.C. State . . . . Lost 2nd Rd	Lost 2nd Rd
	Arizona . . . . . . Lost 2nd Rd	Lost 1st Rd
1952	St. John's . . . . . Lost Final	Lost Final
	Dayton . . . . . . Lost Final	Lost 1st Rd
	Duquesne . . . . . Lost 3rd Rd	Lost 2nd Rd
	Saint Louis . . . . Lost 2nd Rd	Lost 2nd Rd

NIT Championship

The National Invitation Tournament began under the sponsorship of the Metropolitan New York Basketball Writers Association in 1938. The NIT is now administered by the Metropolitan Intercollegiate Basketball Association. All championship games have been played at Madison Square Garden.

Multiple winners: St. John's (6); Bradley (4); Michigan (3); BYU, Dayton, Kentucky, LIU-Brooklyn, Minnesota, Providence, Temple, Tulsa, Virginia and Virginia Tech (2).

Year	Winner	Score	Loser	Year	Winner	Score	Loser
1938	Temple	60-36	Colorado	1972	Maryland	100-69	Niagara
1939	LIU-Brooklyn	44-32	Loyola-IL	1973	Virginia Tech	92-91 (OT)	Notre Dame
1940	Colorado	51-40	Duquesne	1974	Purdue	97-81	Utah
1941	LIU-Brooklyn	56-42	Ohio Univ.	1975	Princeton	80-69	Providence
1942	West Virginia	47-45	Western Ky.	1976	Kentucky	71-67	NC-Charlotte
1943	St. John's	48-27	Toledo	1977	St. Bonaventure	94-91	Houston
1944	St. John's	47-39	DePaul	1978	Texas	101-93	N.C. State
1945	DePaul	71-54	Bowling Green	1979	Indiana	53-52	Purdue
1946	Kentucky	46-45	Rhode Island	1980	Virginia	58-55	Minnesota
1947	Utah	49-45	Kentucky	1981	Tulsa	86-84 (OT)	Syracuse
1948	Saint Louis	65-52	NYU	1982	Bradley	67-58*	Purdue
1949	San Francisco	48-47	Loyola-IL	1983	Fresno St.	69-60	DePaul
1950	CCNY	69-61	Bradley	1984	Michigan	83-63	Notre Dame
1951	BYU	62-43	Dayton	1985	UCLA	65-62	Indiana
1952	La Salle	75-64	Dayton	1986	Ohio St.	73-63	Wyoming
1953	Seton Hall	58-46	St. John's	1987	Southern Miss.	84-80	La Salle
1954	Holy Cross	71-62	Duquesne	1988	Connecticut	72-67	Ohio St.
1955	Duquesne	70-58	Dayton	1989	St. John's	73-65	Saint Louis
1956	Louisville	93-80	Dayton	1990	Vanderbilt	74-72	Saint Louis
1957	Bradley	84-83	Memphis St.	1991	Stanford	78-72	Oklahoma
1958	Xavier-OH	78-74 (OT)	Dayton	1992	Virginia	81-76 (OT)	Notre Dame
1959	St. John's	76-71 (OT)	Bradley	1993	Minnesota	62-61	Georgetown
1960	Bradley	88-72	Providence	1994	Villanova	80-73	Vanderbilt
1961	Providence	62-59	Saint Louis	1995	Virginia Tech	65-64 (OT)	Marquette
1962	Dayton	73-67	St. John's	1996	Nebraska	60-56	St. Joseph's
1963	Providence	81-66	Canisius	1997	Michigan	82-72	Florida St.
1964	Bradley	86-54	New Mexico	1998	Minnesota	79-72	Penn St.
1965	St. John's	55-51	Villanova	1999	California	61-60	Clemson
1966	BYU	97-84	NYU	2000	Wake Forest	71-61	Notre Dame
1967	Southern Illinois	71-56	Marquette	2001	Tulsa	79-60	Alabama
1968	Dayton	61-48	Kansas	2002	Memphis	72-62	South Carolina
1969	Temple	89-76	Boston Coll.	2003	St. John's	70-67	Georgetown
1970	Marquette	65-53	St. John's	2004	Michigan	62-55	Rutgers
1971	North Carolina	84-66	Georgia Tech				

Most Valuable Player

A Most Valuable Player has been selected every year of the NIT tournament. Winners who did not play for the tournament champion are listed in **bold** type.

Multiple winners: None. However, Tom Gola of La Salle is the only player to be named MVP in the NIT (1952) and Most Outstanding Player of the NCAA tournament (1954).

Year
1938 Don Shields, Temple
1939 **Bill Lloyd**, St. John's
1940 Bob Doll, Colorado
1941 **Frank Baumholtz**, Ohio U.
1942 Rudy Baric, West Virginia
1943 Harry Boykoff, St. John's
1944 Bill Kotsores, St. John's
1945 George Mikan, DePaul
1946 **Ernie Calverley**, Rhode Island
1947 Vern Gardner, Utah
1948 Ed Macauley, Saint Louis
1949 Don Lofgan, San Francisco
1950 Ed Warner, CCNY
1951 Roland Minson, BYU
1952 Tom Gola, La Salle
  & Norm Grekin, La Salle
1953 Walter Dukes, Seton Hall
1954 Togo Palazzi, Holy Cross
1955 **Maurice Stokes**, St. Francis-PA
1956 Charlie Tyra, Louisville
1957 **Win Wilfong**, Memphis St.
1958 Hank Stein, Xavier-OH
1959 Tony Jackson, St. John's
1960 **Lenny Wilkens**, Providence
1961 Vinny Ernst, Providence
1962 Bill Chmielewski, Dayton
1963 Ray Flynn, Providence

Year
1964 Lavern Tart, Bradley
1965 Ken McIntyre, St. John's
1966 **Bill Melchionni**, Villanova
1967 Walt Frazier, So. Illinois
1968 Don May, Dayton
1969 **Terry Driscoll**, Boston College
1970 Dean Meminger, Marquette
1971 Bill Chamberlain, N. Carolina
1972 Tom McMillen, Maryland
1973 **John Shumate**, Notre Dame
1974 **Mike Sojourner**, Utah
1975 **Ron Lee**, Oregon
1976 **Cedric Maxwell**, NC-Charlotte
1977 Greg Sanders, St. Bonaventure
1978 Ron Baxter, Texas
  & Jim Krivacs, Texas
1979 Clarence Carter, Indiana
  & Ray Tolbert, Indiana
1980 Ralph Sampson, Virginia
1981 Greg Stewart, Tulsa
1982 Mitchell Anderson, Bradley
1983 Ron Anderson, Fresno St.
1984 Tim McCormick, Michigan
1985 Reggie Miller, UCLA
1986 Brad Sellers, Ohio St.
1987 Randolph Keys, So. Miss.
1988 Phil Gamble, Connecticut

Year
1989 Jayson Williams, St. John's
1990 Scott Draud, Vanderbilt
1991 Adam Keefe, Stanford
1992 Bryant Stith, Virginia
1993 Voshon Lenard, Minnesota
1994 **Doremus Bennerman**, Siena
1995 Shawn Smith, Va. Tech
1996 Erick Strickland, Nebraska
1997 Robert Traylor, Michigan
1998 Kevin Clark, Minnesota
1999 Sean Lampley, California
2000 Robert O'Kelley, Wake Forest
2001 Marcus Hill, Tulsa
2002 Dajuan Wagner, Memphis
2003 Marcus Hatten, St. John's
2004 Daniel Horton, Michigan

All-Time NIT Team

As selected by a media panel
(Mar. 15, 1997).

Walt Frazier, S. Illinois
George Mikan, DePaul
Tom Gola, La Salle
Maurice Stokes, St. Francis-PA
Ralph Beard, Kentucky

All-Time Winningest Division I Teams
Top 25 Winning Percentage

Division I schools with best winning percentages through 2003-04 season (including tournament games). Years in Division I only; minimum 20 years. NCAA tournament columns indicate years in tournament, record and number of championships.

		First Year	Yrs	Games	Won	Lost	Tied	Pct	NCAA Tourney Yrs	W-L	Titles
1	Kentucky	1903	101	2454	1876	577	1	.765	46	95-41	7
2	North Carolina	1911	94	2504	1827	677	0	.730	36	82-36	3
3	UNLV	1959	46	1322	946	376	0	.716	14	30-13	1
4	Kansas	1899	106	2587	1825	762	0	.705	33	73-33	2
5	Duke	1906	99	2518	1737	781	0	.690	27	79-24	3
6	UCLA	1920	85	2220	1531	689	0	.690	38	85-31	11
7	Syracuse	1901	103	2370	1625	745	0	.686	29	48-29	1
8	St. John's	1908	97	2452	1668	784	0	.680	27	27-29	0
9	Western Kentucky	1915	85	2217	1481	736	0	.668	19	15-20	0
10	Utah	1909	96	2300	1516	784	0	.659	25	33-28	1
11	Indiana	1901	104	2394	1554	840	0	.649	32	58-27	5
12	Illinois	1906	99	2289	1484	805	0	.648	24	32-25	0
13	Louisville	1912	90	2239	1451	788	0	.648	31	49-33	2
14	Arkansas	1924	81	2147	1389	758	0	.647	26	39-26	1
15	Temple	1895	108	2511	1623	888	0	.646	25	31-25	0
16	Arizona	1905	99	2256	1458	798	0	.646	23	37-22	1
17	Chattanooga	1978	27	805	520	285	0	.646	8	3-8	0
18	Notre Dame	1898	99	2400	1548	851	1	.645	27	29-31	0
19	Weber St.	1963	42	1198	771	427	0	.644	13	6-14	0
20	Pennsylvania	1897	104	2460	1572	886	2	.639	20	13-22	0
21	DePaul	1924	81	2006	1280	726	0	.638	22	21-25	0
22	Cincinnati	1902	103	2307	1465	842	0	.635	23	39-22	2
23	Murray St.	1926	79	2051	1302	750	0	.635	12	1-12	0
24	Villanova	1921	84	2174	1379	805	0	.634	25	37-25	1
25	Connecticut	1901	101	2173	1374	799	0	.632	25	38-24	2

Top 35 All-Time Victories

Division I schools with most victories through 2003-04 (including postseason tournaments). Minimum 20 years in Division I.

	Wins		Wins		Wins		Wins
1 Kentucky	1876	10 Notre Dame	1548	19 Washington	1463	28 Alabama	1385
2 North Carolina	1827	11 UCLA	1531	20 Arizona	1458	29 Oklahoma	1384
3 Kansas	1825	12 Oregon St.	1529	21 Louisville	1451	30 St. Joseph's	1383
4 Duke	1737	13 Utah	1516	22 N.C. State	1440	31 Villanova	1379
5 St. John's	1668	14 Princeton	1495	23 Texas	1437	32 Montana St.	1374
6 Syracuse	1625	15 Illinois	1484	24 West Virginia	1429	Iowa	1374
7 Temple	1623	16 Western Ky.	1481	25 Bradley	1424	Connecticut	1374
8 Penn	1572	17 Purdue	1470	26 Arkansas	1389	35 Fordham	1373
9 Indiana	1554	18 Cincinnati	1465	Ohio St	1389		

Top 25 Single-Season Victories

Division I schools with most victories in a season through 2003-04 (including postseason tournaments). NCAA champions in **bold** type.

		Year	W-L			Year	W-L
1	UNLV	1987	37-2		**Connecticut**	1999	34-2
	Duke	1999	37-2		Duke	1992	34-2
	Duke	1986	37-3		**Kentucky**	1996	34-2
4	**Kentucky**	1948	36-3		Kansas	1997	34-2
5	Massachusetts	1996	35-2		Kentucky	1947	34-3
	Georgetown	1985	35-3		**Georgetown**	1984	34-3
	Arizona	1988	35-3		Arkansas	1991	34-4
	Duke	2001	35-4		**N. Carolina**	1993	34-4
	Kansas	1986	35-4		N. Carolina	1998	34-4
	Kansas	1998	35-4	25	Indiana St	1979	33-1
	Kentucky	1998	35-4		**Louisville**	1980	33-3
	Oklahoma	1988	35-4		Kansas	2002	33-4
	UNLV	1990	35-5		Michigan St.	1999	33-5
	Kentucky	1997	35-5		UNLV	1986	33-5
15	UNLV	1991	34-1		**Connecticut**	2004	33-6

*NCAA later stripped UMass of its four 1996 tournament victories after learning that center Marcus Camby accepted gifts from an agent.

Division I Winning Streaks
Full Season
(including tournaments)

No		Seasons	Broken by	Score
88	UCLA	1971-74	Notre Dame	71-70
60	San Francisco	1955-57	Illinois	62-33
47	UCLA	1966-68	Houston	71-69
45	UNLV	1990-91	Duke	79-77
44	Texas	1913-17	Rice	24-18
43	Seton Hall	1939-41	LIU-Bklyn	49-26
43	LIU-Brooklyn	1935-37	Stanford	45-31
41	UCLA	1968-69	USC	46-44
39	Marquette	1970-71	Ohio St.	60-59
37	Cincinnati	1962-63	Wichita St.	65-64
37	North Carolina	1957-58	West Virginia	75-64

Home Court

No		Seasons	Broken By	Score
129	Kentucky	1943-55	Georgia Tech	59-58
99	St. Bonaventure	1948-61	Detroit	77-70
98	UCLA	1970-76	Oregon	65-45
86	Cincinnati	1957-64	Kansas	51-47
81	Arizona	1945-51	Kansas St.	76-57
81	Marquette	1967-73	Notre Dame	71-69
80	Lamar	1978-84	Louisiana Tech	68-65

Associated Press Final Polls
Taken before NCAA, NIT and Collegiate Commissioner's Association (1974-75) tournaments.

The Associated Press introduced its weekly college basketball poll of sportswriters (later, sportswriters and broadcasters) during the 1948-49 season.

Since the NCAA Division I tournament has determined the national champion since 1939, the final AP poll ranks the nation's best teams through the regular season and conference tournaments.

Except for four seasons (see AP Post-Tournament Final Polls), the final AP poll has been released prior to the NCAA and NIT tournaments and has gone from a Top 10 (1949 and 1963-67) to a Top 20 (1950-62 and 1968-89) to a Top 25 (since 1990). Tournament champions are in **bold** type.

1949

		Before Tourns	Head Coach	Final Record
1	**Kentucky**	.29-1	Adolph Rupp	32-2
2	Oklahoma A&M	.21-4	Hank Iba	23-5
3	Saint Louis	.22-3	Eddie Hickey	22-4
4	Illinois	.19-3	Harry Combes	21-4
5	Western Ky.	.25-3	Ed Diddle	25-4
6	Minnesota	.18-3	Ozzie Cowles	same
7	Bradley	.25-6	Forddy Anderson	27-8
8	**San Francisco**	.21-5	Pete Newell	25-5
9	Tulane	.24-4	Cliff Wells	same
10	Bowling Green	.21-6	Harold Anderson	24-7

NCAA Final Four (at Edmundson Pavilion, Seattle): **Third Place**—Illinois 57, Oregon St. 53. **Championship**—Kentucky 46, Oklahoma A&M 36.

NIT Final Four (at Madison Square Garden): **Semifinals**—San Francisco 49, Bowling Green 39; Loyola-IL 55, Bradley 50. **Third Place**—Bowling Green 82, Bradley 77. **Championship**—San Francisco 48, Loyola-IL 47.

1950

		Before Tourns	Head Coach	Final Record
1	Bradley	.28-3	Forddy Anderson	32-5
2	Ohio St.	.21-3	Tippy Dye	22-4
3	Kentucky	.25-4	Adolph Rupp	25-5
4	Holy Cross	.27-2	Buster Sheary	27-4
5	N.C. State	.25-5	Everett Case	27-6
6	Duquesne	.22-5	Dudey Moore	23-6
7	UCLA	.24-5	John Wooden	24-7
8	Western Ky.	.24-5	Ed Diddle	25-6
9	St. John's	.23-4	Frank McGuire	24-5
10	La Salle	.20-3	Ken Loeffler	21-4
11	Villanova	.25-4	Al Severance	same
12	San Francisco	.19-6	Pete Newell	19-7
13	LIU-Brooklyn	.20-4	Clair Bee	20-5
14	Kansas St.	.17-7	Jack Gardner	same
15	Arizona	.26-4	Fred Enke	26-5
16	Wisconsin	.17-5	Bud Foster	same
17	San Jose St.	.21-7	Walter McPherson	same
18	Washington St.	.19-13	Jack Friel	same
19	Kansas	.14-11	Phog Allen	same
20	Indiana	.17-5	Branch McCracken	same

Note: Unranked **CCNY**, coached by Nat Holman, won both the NCAAs and NIT. The Beavers entered the postseason at 17-5 and had a final record of 24-5.

NCAA Final Four (at Madison Square Garden): **Third Place**—N. Carolina St. 53, Baylor 41. **Championship**—CCNY 71, Bradley 68.

NIT Final Four (at Madison Square Garden): **Semifinals**—Bradley 83, St. John's 72; CCNY 62, Duquesne 52. **Third Place**—St. John's 69, Duquesne 67 (OT). **Championship**—CCNY 69, Bradley 61.

1951

		Before Tourns	Head Coach	Final Record
1	**Kentucky**	.28-2	Adolph Rupp	32-2
2	Oklahoma A&M	.27-4	Hank Iba	29-6
3	Columbia	.22-0	Lou Rossini	22-1
4	Kansas St.	.22-3	Jack Gardner	25-4
5	Illinois	.19-4	Harry Combes	22-5
6	Bradley	.32-6	Forddy Anderson	same
7	Indiana	.19-3	Branch McCracken	same
8	N.C. State	.29-4	Everett Case	30-7
9	St. John's	.22-3	Frank McGuire	26-5
10	Saint Louis	.21-7	Eddie Hickey	22-8
11	**BYU**	.22-8	Stan Watts	26-10
12	Arizona	.24-4	Fred Enke	24-6
13	Dayton	.24-4	Tom Blackburn	27-5
14	Toledo	.23-8	Jerry Bush	same
15	Washington	.22-5	Tippy Dye	24-6
16	Murray St.	.21-6	Harlan Hodges	same
17	Cincinnati	.18-3	John Wiethe	18-4
18	Siena	.19-8	Dan Cunha	same
19	USC	.21-6	Forrest Twogood	same
20	Villanova	.25-6	Al Severance	25-7

NCAA Final Four (at Williams Arena, Minneapolis): **Third Place**—Illinois 61, Oklahoma St. 46. **Championship**—Kentucky 68, Kansas St. 58.

NIT Final Four (at Madison Sq. Garden): **Semifinals**—Dayton 69, St. John's 62 (OT); BYU 69, Seton Hall 59. **Third Place**—St. John's 70, Seton Hall 68 (2 OT). **Championship**—BYU 62, Dayton 43.

1952

		Before Tourns	Head Coach	Final Record
1	Kentucky	.28-2	Adolph Rupp	29-3
2	Illinois	.19-3	Harry Combes	22-4
3	Kansas St.	.19-5	Jack Gardner	same
4	Duquesne	.21-1	Dudey Moore	23-4
5	Saint Louis	.22-6	Eddie Hickey	23-8
6	Washington	.25-6	Tippy Dye	same
7	Iowa	.19-3	Bucky O'Connor	same
8	**Kansas**	.24-3	Phog Allen	28-3
9	West Virginia	.23-4	Red Brown	same
10	St. John's	.22-3	Frank McGuire	25-5
11	Dayton	.24-3	Tom Blackburn	28-5
12	Duke	.24-6	Harold Bradley	same
13	Holy Cross	.23-3	Buster Sheary	24-4
14	Seton Hall	.25-2	Honey Russell	25-3
15	St. Bonaventure	.19-5	Ed Melvin	21-6
16	Wyoming	.27-6	Everett Shelton	28-7
17	Louisville	.20-5	Peck Hickman	20-6
18	Seattle	.29-7	Al Brightman	29-8
19	UCLA	.19-10	John Wooden	19-12
20	SW Texas St.	.30-1	Milton Jowers	same

Note: Unranked La Salle, coached by Ken Loeffler, won the NIT. The Explorers entered the postseason at 21-7 and had a final record of 25-7.

NCAA Final Four (at Edmundson Pavillion, Seattle): **Semifinals**—St. John's 61, Illinois 59; Kansas 74, Santa Clara 59. **Third Place**—Illinois 67, Santa Clara 64. **Championship**—Kansas 80, St. John's 63.

NIT Final Four (at Madison Sq. Garden): **Semifinals**—La Salle 59, Duquesne 46; Dayton 69, St. Bonaventure 62. **Third Place**—St. Bonaventure 48, Duquesne 34. **Championship**—La Salle 75, Dayton 64.

Associated Press Final Polls (Cont.)

1953

		Before Tours	Head Coach	Final Record
1	**Indiana**	.18-3	Branch McCracken	23-3
2	La Salle	.25-2	Ken Loeffler	25-3
3	**Seton Hall**	.28-2	Honey Russell	31-2
4	Washington	.27-2	Tippy Dye	30-3
5	LSU	.22-1	Harry Rabenhorst	24-3
6	Kansas	.16-5	Phog Allen	19-6
7	Oklahoma A&M	.22-6	Hank Iba	23-7
	Kansas St.	.17-4	Jack Gardner	same
9	Western Ky.	.25-5	Ed Diddle	25-6
10	Illinois	.18-4	Harry Combes	same
11	Oklahoma City	.18-4	Doyle Parrick	18-6
12	N.C. State	.26-6	Everett Case	same
13	Notre Dame	.17-4	John Jordan	19-5
14	Louisville	.21-5	Peck Hickman	22-6
	Seattle	.27-3	Al Brightman	29-4
16	Miami-OH	.17-5	Bill Rohr	17-6
17	Eastern Ky.	.16-8	Paul McBrayer	16-9
18	Duquesne	.18-7	Dudey Moore	21-8
	Navy	.16-4	Ben Carnevale	16-5
20	Holy Cross	.18-5	Buster Sheary	20-6

NCAA Final Four (at Municipal Auditorium, Kansas City): **Semifinals**–Indiana 80, LSU 67; Kansas 79, Washington 53. **Third Place**–Washington 88, LSU 69. **Championship**–Indiana 69, Kansas 68.

NIT Final Four (at Madison Sq. Garden): **Semifinals**–Seton Hall 74, Manhattan 56; St. John's 64, Duquesne 55. **Third Place**–Duquesne 81, Manhattan 67. **Championship**–Seton Hall 58, St. John's 46.

1955

		Before Tours	Head Coach	Final Record
1	**San Francisco**	.23-1	Phil Woolpert	28-1
2	Kentucky	.22-2	Adolph Rupp	23-3
3	La Salle	.22-4	Ken Loeffler	26-5
4	N.C. State	.28-4	Everett Case	same
5	Iowa	.17-5	Bucky O'Connor	19-7
6	**Duquesne**	.19-4	Dudey Moore	22-4
7	Utah	.23-3	Jack Gardner	24-4
8	Marquette	.22-2	Jack Nagle	24-3
9	Dayton	.23-3	Tom Blackburn	25-4
10	Oregon St.	.21-7	Slats Gill	22-8
11	Minnesota	.15-7	Ozzie Cowles	same
12	Alabama	.19-5	Johnny Dee	same
13	UCLA	.21-5	John Wooden	same
14	G. Washington	.24-6	Bill Reinhart	same
15	Colorado	.16-5	Bebe Lee	19-6
16	Tulsa	.20-6	Clarence Iba	21-7
17	Vanderbilt	.16-6	Bob Polk	same
18	Illinois	.17-5	Harry Combes	same
19	West Virginia	.19-10	Fred Schaus	19-11
20	Saint Louis	.19-7	Eddie Hickey	20-8

NCAA Final Four (at Municipal Auditorium, Kansas City): **Semifinals**–La Salle 76, Iowa 73; San Francisco 62, Colorado 50. **Third Place**–Colorado 75, Iowa 74. **Championship**–San Francisco 77, La Salle 63.

NIT Final Four (at Madison Square Garden): **Semifinals**–Dayton 79, St. Francis-PA 73 (OT); Duquesne 65, Cincinnati 51. **Third Place**–Cincinnati 96, St. Francis-PA 91 (OT). **Championship**–Duquesne 70, Dayton 58.

1954

		Before Tours	Head Coach	Final Record
1	Kentucky	.25-0	Adolph Rupp	same*
2	Indiana	.19-3	Branch McCracken	20-4
3	Duquesne	.24-2	Dudey Moore	26-3
4	Western Ky.	.28-1	Ed Diddle	29-3
5	Oklahoma A&M	.23-4	Hank Iba	24-5
6	Notre Dame	.20-2	John Jordan	22-3
7	Kansas	.16-5	Phog Allen	same
8	**Holy Cross**	.23-2	Buster Sheary	26-2
9	LSU	.21-3	Harry Rabenhorst	21-5
10	**La Salle**	.21-4	Ken Loeffler	26-4
11	Iowa	.17-5	Bucky O'Connor	same
12	Duke	.22-6	Harold Bradley	same
13	Colorado A&M	.22-5	Bill Strannigan	22-7
14	Illinois	.17-5	Harry Combes	same
15	Wichita	.27-3	Ralph Miller	27-4
16	Seattle	.26-1	Al Brightman	26-2
17	N.C. State	.26-6	Everett Case	28-7
18	Dayton	.24-6	Tom Blackburn	25-7
	Minnesota	.17-5	Ozzie Cowles	same
20	Oregon St.	.19-10	Slats Gill	same
	UCLA	.18-7	John Wooden	same
	USC	.17-12	Forrest Twogood	19-14

*Kentucky turned down invitation to NCAA tournament after NCAA declared seniors Cliff Hagan, Frank Ramsey and Lou Tsioropoulos ineligible for postseason play.

NCAA Final Four (at Municipal Auditorium, Kansas City): **Semifinals**–La Salle 69, Penn St. 54; Bradley 74, USC 72. **Third Place**–Penn St. 70, USC 61. **Championship**–La Salle 92, Bradley 76.

NIT Final Four (at Madison Square Garden): **Semifinals**–Duquesne 66, Niagara 51; Holy Cross 75, Western Ky. 69. **Third Place**–Niagara 71, Western Ky. 65. **Championship**–Holy Cross 71, Duquesne 62.

1956

		Before Tours	Head Coach	Final Record
1	**San Francisco**	.25-0	Phil Woolpert	29-0
2	N.C. State	.24-3	Everett Case	24-4
3	Dayton	.24-3	Tom Blackburn	25-4
4	Iowa	.17-5	Bucky O'Connor	20-6
5	Alabama	.21-3	Johnny Dee	same
6	**Louisville**	.23-3	Peck Hickman	26-3
7	SMU	.22-2	Doc Hayes	25-4
8	UCLA	.21-5	John Wooden	22-6
9	Kentucky	.19-5	Adolph Rupp	20-6
10	Illinois	.18-4	Harry Combes	same
11	Oklahoma City	.18-6	Abe Lemons	20-7
12	Vanderbilt	.19-4	Bob Polk	same
13	North Carolina	.18-5	Frank McGuire	same
14	Holy Cross	.22-4	Roy Leenig	22-5
15	Temple	.23-3	Harry Litwack	27-4
16	Wake Forest	.19-9	Murray Greason	same
17	Duke	.19-7	Harold Bradley	same
18	Utah	.21-5	Jack Gardner	22-6
19	Oklahoma A&M	.18-8	Hank Iba	18-9
20	West Virginia	.21-8	Fred Schaus	21-9

NCAA Final Four (at McGaw Hall, Evanston, IL): **Semifinals**–Iowa 83, Temple 76; San Francisco 86, SMU 68. **Third Place**–Temple 90, SMU 81. **Championship**–San Francisco 83, Iowa 71.

NIT Final Four (at Madison Square Garden): **Semifinals**–Dayton 89, St. Francis-NY 58; Louisville 89, St. Joseph's-PA 79. **Third Place**–St. Joseph's-PA 93, St. Francis-NY 82. **Championship**–Louisville 93, Dayton 80.

1957

		Before Tourns	Head Coach	Final Record
1	**N. Carolina**	.27-0	Frank McGuire	32-0
2	Kansas	.21-2	Dick Harp	24-3
3	Kentucky	.22-4	Adolph Rupp	23-5
4	SMU	.21-3	Doc Hayes	22-4
5	Seattle	.24-2	John Castellani	24-3
6	Louisville	.21-5	Peck Hickman	same
7	West Va.	.25-4	Fred Schaus	25-5
8	Vanderbilt	.17-5	Bob Polk	same
9	Oklahoma City	.17-8	Abe Lemons	19-9
10	Saint Louis	.19-7	Eddie Hickey	19-9
11	Michigan St.	.14-8	Forddy Anderson	16-10
12	Memphis St.	.21-5	Bob Vanatta	24-6
13	California	.20-4	Pete Newell	21-5
14	UCLA	.22-4	John Wooden	same
15	Mississippi St.	.17-8	Babe McCarthy	same
16	Idaho St.	.24-2	John Grayson	25-4
17	Notre Dame	.18-7	John Jordan	20-8
18	Wake Forest	.19-9	Murray Greason	same
19	Canisius	.20-5	Joe Curran	22-6
20	Oklahoma A&M	.17-9	Hank Iba	same

Note: Unranked **Bradley**, coached by Chuck Orsborn, won the NIT. The Braves entered the tourney at 19-7 and had a final record of 22-7.
NCAA Final Four (at Municipal Auditorium, Kansas City): **Semifinals**—North Carolina 74, Michigan St. 70 (3 OT); Kansas 80, San Francisco 56. **Third Place**—San Francisco 67, Michigan St. 60. **Championship**—North Carolina 54, Kansas 53 (3 OT).
NIT Final Four (at Madison Square Garden): **Semifinals**—Memphis St. 80, St. Bonaventure 78; Bradley 78, Temple 66. **Third Place**—Temple 67, St. Bonaventure 50. **Championship**—Bradley 84, Memphis St. 83.

1958

		Before Tourns	Head Coach	Final Record
1	West Virginia	.26-1	Fred Schaus	26-2
2	Cincinnati	.24-2	George Smith	25-3
3	Kansas St.	.20-3	Tex Winter	22-5
4	San Francisco	.24-1	Phil Woolpert	25-2
5	Temple	.24-2	Harry Litwack	27-3
6	Maryland	.20-6	Bud Millikan	22-7
7	Kansas	.18-5	Dick Harp	same
8	Notre Dame	.22-4	John Jordan	24-5
9	**Kentucky**	.19-6	Adolph Rupp	23-6
10	Duke	.18-7	Harold Bradley	same
11	Dayton	.23-3	Tom Blackburn	25-4
12	Indiana	.12-10	Branch McCracken	13-11
13	North Carolina	.19-7	Frank McGuire	same
14	Bradley	.20-6	Chuck Orsborn	20-7
15	Mississippi St.	.20-5	Babe McCarthy	same
16	Auburn	.16-6	Joel Eaves	same
17	Michigan St.	.16-6	Forddy Anderson	same
18	Seattle	.20-6	John Castellani	24-7
19	Oklahoma St.	.19-7	Hank Iba	21-8
20	N.C. State	.18-6	Everett Case	same

Note: Unranked **Xavier-OH**, coached by Jim McCafferty, won the NIT. The Musketeers entered the tourney at 15-11 and had a final record of 19-11.
NCAA Final Four (at Freedom Hall, Louisville): **Semifinals**—Kentucky 61, Temple 60; Seattle 73, Kansas St. 51. **Third Place**—Temple 67, Kansas St. 57. **Championship**—Kentucky 84, Seattle 72.
NIT Final Four (at Madison Square Garden): **Semifinals**—Dayton 80, St. John's 56; Xavier-OH 72, St. Bonaventure 53. **Third Place**—St. Bonaventure 84, St. John's 69. **Championship**—Xavier-OH 78, Dayton 74 (OT).

1959

		Before Tourns	Head Coach	Final Record
1	Kansas St.	.24-1	Tex Winter	25-2
2	Kentucky	.23-2	Adolph Rupp	24-3
3	Mississippi St.	.24-1	Babe McCarthy	same*
4	Bradley	.23-3	Chuck Orsborn	25-4
5	Cincinnati	.23-3	George Smith	26-4
6	N.C. State	.22-4	Everett Case	same
7	Michigan St.	.18-3	Forddy Anderson	19-4
8	Auburn	.20-2	Joel Eaves	same
9	North Carolina	.20-4	Frank McGuire	20-5
10	West Virginia	.25-4	Fred Schaus	29-5
11	**California**	.21-4	Pete Newell	25-4
12	Saint Louis	.20-5	John Benington	20-6
13	Seattle	.23-6	Vince Cazzetta	same
14	St. Joseph's-PA	.22-3	Jack Ramsay	22-5
15	St. Mary's-CA	.13-8	Jim Weaver	19-6
16	TCU	.19-5	Buster Brannon	20-6
17	Oklahoma City	.20-6	Abe Lemons	20-7
18	Utah	.21-5	Jack Gardner	21-7
19	St. Bonaventure	.20-2	Eddie Donovan	20-3
20	Marquette	.22-4	Eddie Hickey	23-6

*Mississippi St. turned down invitation to NCAA tournament because it was an integrated event.
Note: Unranked **St. John's**, coached by Joe Lapchick, won the NIT. The Redmen entered the tourney at 16-6 and had a final record of 20-6.
NCAA Final Four (at Freedom Hall, Louisville): **Semifinals**—West Virginia 94, Louisville 79; California 64, Cincinnati 58. **Third Place**—Cincinnati 98, Louisville 85. **Championship**—California 71, West Virginia 70.
NIT Final Four (at Madison Square Garden): **Semifinals**—Bradley 59, NYU 57; St. John's 76, Providence 55. **Third Place**—NYU 71, Providence 57. **Championship**—St. John's 76, Bradley 71 (OT).

1960

		Before Tourns	Head Coach	Final Record
1	Cincinnati	.25-1	George Smith	28-2
2	California	.24-1	Pete Newell	28-2
3	**Ohio St.**	.21-3	Fred Taylor	25-3
4	**Bradley**	.24-2	Chuck Orsborn	27-2
5	West Virginia	.24-4	Fred Schaus	26-5
6	Utah	.24-2	Jack Gardner	26-3
7	Indiana	.20-4	Branch McCracken	same
8	Utah St.	.22-4	Cecil Baker	24-5
9	St. Bonaventure	.19-3	Eddie Donovan	21-5
10	Miami-FL	.23-3	Bruce Hale	23-4
11	Auburn	.19-3	Joel Eaves	same
12	NYU	.19-4	Lou Rossini	22-5
13	Georgia Tech	.21-5	Whack Hyder	22-6
14	Providence	.21-4	Joe Mullaney	24-5
15	Saint Louis	.19-7	John Benington	19-8
16	Holy Cross	.20-5	Roy Leenig	20-6
17	Villanova	.19-5	Al Severance	20-6
18	Duke	.15-10	Vic Bubas	17-11
19	Wake Forest	.21-7	Bones McKinney	same
20	St. John's	.17-7	Joe Lapchick	17-8

NCAA Final Four (at the Cow Palace, San Fran.): **Semifinals**—Ohio St. 76, NYU 54; California 77, Cincinnati 69. **Third Place**—Cincinnati 95, NYU 71. **Championship**—Ohio St. 75, California 55.
NIT Final Four (at Madison Square Garden): **Semifinals**—Bradley 82, St. Bonaventure 71; Providence 68, Utah St. 62. **Third Place**—Utah St. 99, St. Bonaventure 93. **Championship**—Bradley 88, Providence 72.

Associated Press Final Polls (Cont.)

1961

		Before Tourns	Head Coach	Final Record
1	Ohio St.	.24-0	Fred Taylor	27-1
2	**Cincinnati**	.23-3	Ed Jucker	27-3
3	St. Bonaventure	.22-3	Eddie Donovan	24-4
4	Kansas St.	.22-3	Tex Winter	23-4
5	North Carolina	.19-4	Frank McGuire	same
6	Bradley	.21-5	Chuck Orsborn	same
7	USC	.20-6	Forrest Twogood	21-8
8	Iowa	.18-6	S. Scheuerman	same
9	West Virginia	.23-4	George King	same
10	Duke	.22-6	Vic Bubas	same
11	Utah	.21-6	Jack Gardner	23-8
12	Texas Tech	.14-9	Polk Robison	15-10
13	Niagara	.16-4	Taps Gallagher	16-5
14	Memphis St.	.20-2	Bob Vanatta	20-3
15	Wake Forest	.17-10	Bones McKinney	19-11
16	St. John's	.20-4	Joe Lapchick	20-5
17	St. Joseph's-PA	.22-4	Jack Ramsay	25-5
18	Drake	.19-7	Maury John	same
19	Holy Cross	.19-4	Roy Leenig	22-5
20	Kentucky	.18-8	Adolph Rupp	19-9

Note: Unranked **Providence**, coached by Joe Mullaney, won the NIT. The Friars entered the tourney at 20-5 and had a final record of 24-5.

NCAA Final Four (at Municipal Auditorium, Kansas City): **Semifinals**–Ohio St. 95, St. Joseph's-PA 69; Cincinnati 82, Utah 67. **Third Place**–St. Joseph's-PA 127, Utah 120 (4 OT). **Championship**–Cincinnati 70, Ohio St. 65 (OT).
NIT Final Four (at Madison Square Garden) **Semifinals**–St. Louis 67, Dayton 60; Providence 90, Holy Cross 83 (OT). **Third Place**–Holy Cross 85, Dayton 67. **Championship**–Providence 62, St. Louis 59.

1962

		Before Tourns	Head Coach	Final Record
1	Ohio St.	.23-1	Fred Taylor	26-2
2	**Cincinnati**	.25-2	Ed Jucker	29-2
3	Kentucky	.22-2	Adolph Rupp	23-3
4	Mississippi St.	.19-6	Babe McCarthy	same
5	Bradley	.21-6	Chuck Orsborn	21-7
6	Kansas St.	.22-3	Tex Winter	same
7	Utah	.23-3	Jack Gardner	same
8	Bowling Green	.21-3	Harold Anderson	same
9	Colorado	.18-6	Sox Walseth	19-7
10	Duke	.20-5	Vic Bubas	same
11	Loyola-IL	.21-3	George Ireland	23-4
12	St. John's	.19-4	Joe Lapchick	21-5
13	Wake Forest	.18-8	Bones McKinney	22-9
14	Oregon St.	.22-4	Slats Gill	24-5
15	West Virginia	.24-5	George King	24-6
16	Arizona St.	.23-3	Ned Wulk	23-4
17	Duquesne	.20-5	Red Manning	22-7
18	Utah St.	.21-5	Ladell Andersen	22-7
19	UCLA	.16-9	John Wooden	18-11
20	Villanova	.19-6	Jack Kraft	21-7

Note: Unranked **Dayton**, coached by Tom Blackburn, won the NIT. The Flyers entered the tourney at 20-6 and had a final record of 24-6.

NCAA Final Four (at Freedom Hall, Louisville): **Semifinals**–Ohio St. 84, Wake Forest 68; Cincinnati 72, UCLA 70. **Third Place**–Wake Forest 82, UCLA 80. **Championship**–Cincinnati 71, Ohio St. 59.
NIT Final Four (at Madison Square Garden): **Semifinals**–Dayton 98, Loyola-IL 82; St. John's 76, Duquesne 65. **Third Place**–Loyola-IL 95, Duquesne 84. **Championship**–Dayton 73, St. John's 67.

1963

AP ranked only 10 teams from the 1962-63 season through 1967-68.

		Before Tourns	Head Coach	Final Record
1	Cincinnati	.23-1	Ed Jucker	26-2
2	Duke	.24-2	Vic Bubas	27-3
3	**Loyola-IL**	.24-2	George Ireland	29-2
4	Arizona St.	.24-2	Ned Wulk	26-3
5	Wichita	.19-7	Ralph Miller	19-8
6	Mississippi St.	.21-5	Babe McCarthy	22-6
7	Ohio St.	.20-4	Fred Taylor	same
8	Illinois	.19-5	Harry Combes	20-6
9	NYU	.17-3	Lou Rossini	18-5
10	Colorado	.19-5	Sox Walseth	19-7

Note: Unranked **Providence**, coached by Joe Mullaney, won the NIT. The Friars entered the tourney at 21-4 and had a final record of 24-4.

NCAA Final Four (at Freedom Hall, Louisville): **Semifinals**–Loyola-IL 94, Duke 75; Cincinnati 80, Oregon St. 46. **Third Place**–Duke 85, Oregon St. 63. **Championship**–Loyola-IL 60, Cincinnati 58 (OT).
NIT Final Four (at Madison Square Garden): **Semifinals**–Providence 70, Marquette 64; Canisius 61, Villanova 46. **Third Place**–Marquette 66, Villanova 58. **Championship**–Providence 81, Canisius 66.

1964

AP ranked only 10 teams from the 1962-63 season through 1967-68.

		Before Tourns	Head Coach	Final Record
1	**UCLA**	.26-0	John Wooden	30-0
2	Michigan	.20-4	Dave Strack	23-5
3	Duke	.23-4	Vic Bubas	26-5
4	Kentucky	.21-4	Adolph Rupp	21-6
5	Wichita St.	.22-5	Ralph Miller	23-6
6	Oregon St.	.25-3	Slats Gill	25-4
7	Villanova	.22-3	Jack Kraft	24-4
8	Loyola-IL	.20-5	George Ireland	22-6
9	DePaul	.21-3	Ray Meyer	21-4
10	Davidson	.22-4	Lefty Driesell	same

Note: Unranked **Bradley**, coached by Chuck Orsborn, won the NIT. The Braves entered the tourney at 20-6 and finished with a record of 23-6.

NCAA Final Four (at Municipal Auditorium, Kansas City): **Semifinals**–Duke 91, Michigan 80; UCLA 90, Kansas St. 84. **Third Place**–Michigan 100, Kansas St. 90. **Championship**–UCLA 98, Duke 83.
NIT Final Four (at Madison Square Garden): **Semifinals**–New Mexico 72, NYU 65; Bradley 67, Army 52. **Third Place**–Army 60, NYU 59. **Championship**–Bradley 86, New Mexico 54.

Undefeated National Champions

Seven NCAA seasons have ended with an undefeated national champion. UCLA has accomplished the feat four times.

Year		W-L
1956	San Francisco	29-0
1957	North Carolina	32-0
1964	UCLA	30-0
1967	UCLA	30-0
1972	UCLA	30-0
1973	UCLA	30-0
1976	Indiana	32-0

1965

AP ranked only 10 teams from the 1962-63 season through 1967-68.

		Before Tours	Head Coach	Final Record
1	Michigan	21-3	Dave Strack	24-4
2	UCLA	24-2	John Wooden	28-2
3	St. Joseph's-PA	25-1	Jack Ramsay	26-3
4	Providence	22-1	Joe Mullaney	24-2
5	Vanderbilt	23-3	Roy Skinner	24-4
6	Davidson	24-2	Lefty Driesell	same
7	Minnesota	19-5	John Kundla	same
8	Villanova	21-4	Jack Kraft	23-5
9	BYU	21-5	Stan Watts	21-7
10	Duke	20-5	Vic Bubas	same

Note: Unranked **St. John's,** coached by Joe Lapchick, won the NIT. The Redmen entered the tourney at 17-8 and finished with a record of 21-8.
NCAA Final Four (at Memorial Coliseum, Portland, OR): **Semifinals**–Michigan 93, Princeton 76; UCLA 108, Wichita St. 89. **Third Place**–Princeton 118, Wichita St. 82. **Championship**–UCLA 91, Michigan 80.
NIT Final Four (at Madison Square Garden): **Semifinals**–Villanova 91, NYU 69; St. John's 67, Army 60. **Third Place**–Army 75, NYU 74. **Championship**– St. John's 55, Villanova 51.

1966

AP ranked only 10 teams from the 1962-63 season through 1967-68.

		Before Tours	Head Coach	Final Record
1	Kentucky	24-1	Adolph Rupp	27-2
2	Duke	23-3	Vic Bubas	26-4
3	**Texas Western**	23-1	Don Haskins	28-1
4	Kansas	22-3	Ted Owens	23-4
5	St. Joseph's-PA	22-4	Jack Ramsay	24-5
6	Loyola-IL	22-2	George Ireland	22-3
7	Cincinnati	21-5	Tay Baker	21-7
8	Vanderbilt	22-4	Roy Skinner	same
9	Michigan	17-7	Dave Strack	18-8
10	Western Ky.	23-2	Johnny Oldham	25-3

Note: Unranked **BYU,** coached by Stan Watts, won the NIT. The Cougars entered the tourney at 17-5 and had a final record of 20-5.
NCAA Final Four (at Cole Fieldhouse, College Park, MD): **Semifinals**–Kentucky 83, Duke 79; Texas Western 85, Utah 78. **Third Place**–Duke 79, Utah 77. **Championship**–Texas Western 72, Kentucky 65.
NIT Final Four (at Madison Square Garden): **Semifinals**–BYU 66, Army 60; NYU 69, Villanova 63. **Third Place**–Villanova 76, Army 65. **Championship**–BYU 97, NYU 84.

1967

AP ranked only 10 teams from the 1962-63 season through 1967-68.

		Before Tours	Head Coach	Final Record
1	UCLA	26-0	John Wooden	30-0
2	Louisville	23-3	Peck Hickman	23-5
3	Kansas	22-3	Ted Owens	23-4
4	North Carolina	24-4	Dean Smith	26-6
5	Princeton	23-2	B. van Breda Kolff	25-3
6	Western Ky.	23-2	Johnny Oldham	23-3
7	Houston	23-3	Guy Lewis	27-4
8	Tennessee	21-5	Ray Mears	21-7
9	Boston College	19-2	Bob Cousy	21-3
10	Texas Western	20-5	Don Haskins	22-6

Note: Unranked **Southern Illinois,** coached by Jack Hartman, won the NIT. The Salukis entered the tourney at 20-2 and had a final record of 24-2.
NCAA Final Four (at Freedom Hall, Louisville): **Semifinals**–Dayton 76, N. Carolina 62; UCLA 73, Houston 58. **Third Place**–Houston 84, N. Carolina 62. **Championship**–UCLA 79, Dayton 64.
NIT Final Four (at Madison Square Garden): **Semifinals**–Marquette 83, Marshall 78; Southern Ill. 79, Rutgers 70. **Third Place**–Rutgers 93, Marshall 76. **Championship**–Southern Ill. 71, Marquette 56.

1968

AP ranked only 10 teams from the 1962-63 season through 1967-68.

		Before Tours	Head Coach	Final Record
1	Houston	28-0	Guy Lewis	31-2
2	UCLA	25-1	John Wooden	29-1
3	St. Bonaventure	22-0	Larry Weise	23-2
4	North Carolina	25-3	Dean Smith	28-4
5	Kentucky	21-4	Adolph Rupp	22-5
6	New Mexico	23-3	Bob King	23-5
7	Columbia	21-4	Jack Rohan	23-5
8	Davidson	22-4	Lefty Driesell	24-5
9	Louisville	20-6	John Dromo	21-7
10	Duke	21-5	Vic Bubas	22-6

Note: Unranked **Dayton,** coached by Don Donoher, won the NIT. The Flyers entered the tourney at 17-9 and had a final record of 21-9.
NCAA Final Four (at the Sports Arena, Los Angeles): **Semifinals**–N. Carolina 80, Ohio St. 66; UCLA 101, Houston 69. **Third Place**–Ohio St. 89, Houston 85. **Championship**–UCLA 78, N. Carolina 55.
NIT Final Four (at Madison Square Garden): **Semifinals**–Dayton 76, Notre Dame 74 (OT); Kansas 58, St. Peter's 46. **Third Place**–Notre Dame 81, St.Peter's 78. **Championship**–Dayton 61, Kansas 48.

All-Time AP Top 20

The composite AP Top 20 from the 1948-49 season through 2003-04, based on the final regular season rankings of each year. The final AP poll has been taken before the NCAA and NIT tournaments each season since 1949 except in 1953 and '54 and again in 1974 and '75 when the final poll came out after the postseason. Team point totals are based on 20 points for all 1st place finishes, 19 for each 2nd, etc. Also listed are the number of times ranked No.1 by AP going into the tournaments, and times ranked in the pre-tournament Top 10 and Top 20.

		Pts	No.1	Top10	Top20			Pts	No.1	Top10	Top20
1	Kentucky	658	8	37	44	11	Michigan	200	2	10	15
2	North Carolina	513	5	28	37	12	Notre Dame	190	0	12	18
3	UCLA	449	7	22	35	13	Marquette	187	0	12	17
4	Duke	444	6	25	34	14	N.C. State	182	1	9	17
5	Kansas	360	1	19	28	15	Ohio St	176	2	10	13
6	Indiana	293	4	16	24	16	UNLV	173	2	8	13
7	Cincinnati	259	2	13	19	17	Syracuse	169	0	9	19
8	Louisville	240	0	11	23	18	Arkansas	166	0	9	15
9	Arizona	233	1	11	19	19	Maryland	160	0	8	17
10	Illinois	207	0	9	22	20	Oklahoma	153	1	7	12

Associated Press Final Polls (Cont.)

1969

		Before Tourns	Head Coach	Final Record
1	UCLA	.25-1	John Wooden	29-1
2	La Salle	.23-1	Tom Gola	same*
3	Santa Clara	.26-1	Dick Garibaldi	27-2
4	North Carolina	.25-3	Dean Smith	27-5
5	Davidson	.24-2	Lefty Driesell	26-3
6	Purdue	.20-4	George King	23-5
7	Kentucky	.22-4	Adolph Rupp	23-5
8	St. John's	.22-4	Lou Carnesecca	23-6
9	Duquesne	.19-4	Red Manning	21-5
10	Villanova	.21-4	Jack Kraft	21-5
11	Drake	.23-4	Maury John	26-5
12	New Mexico St.	.23-3	Lou Henson	24-5
13	South Carolina	.20-6	Frank McGuire	21-7
14	Marquette	.22-4	Al McGuire	24-5
15	Louisville	.20-5	John Dromo	21-6
16	Boston College	.21-3	Bob Cousy	24-4
17	Notre Dame	.20-6	Johnny Dee	20-7
18	Colorado	.20-6	Sox Walseth	21-7
19	Kansas	.20-6	Ted Owens	20-7
20	Illinois	.19-5	Harvey Schmidt	same

*On probation

Note: Unranked **Temple,** coached by Harry Litwack, won the NIT. The Owls entered the tourney at 18-8 and finished with a record of 22-8.

NCAA Final Four (at Freedom Hall, Louisville): **Semifinals**—Purdue 92, N. Carolina 65; UCLA 85, Drake 82. **Third Place**—Drake 104, N. Carolina 84. **Championship**—UCLA 92, Purdue 72.

NIT Final Four (at Madison Square Garden): **Semifinals**—Temple 63, Tennessee 58; Boston College 73, Army 61. **Third Place**—Tennessee 64, Army 52. **Championship**—Temple 89, Boston College 76.

1970

		Before Tourns	Head Coach	Final Record
1	Kentucky	.25-1	Adolph Rupp	26-2
2	UCLA	.24-2	John Wooden	28-2
3	St. Bonaventure	.22-1	Larry Weise	25-3
4	Jacksonville	.23-1	Joe Williams	27-2
5	New Mexico St.	.23-2	Lou Henson	27-3
6	South Carolina	.25-3	Frank McGuire	25-3
7	Iowa	.19-4	Ralph Miller	20-5
8	Marquette	.22-3	Al McGuire	26-3
9	Notre Dame	.20-6	Johnny Dee	21-8
10	N.C. State	.22-6	Norm Sloan	23-7
11	Florida St.	.23-3	Hugh Durham	23-3
12	Houston	.24-3	Guy Lewis	25-5
13	Penn	.25-1	Dick Harter	25-2
14	Drake	.21-6	Maury John	22-7
15	Davidson	.22-4	Terry Holland	22-5
16	Utah St.	.20-6	Ladell Andersen	22-7
17	Niagara	.21-5	Frank Layden	22-7
18	Western Ky.	.22-2	John Oldham	22-3
19	Long Beach St.	.23-3	Jerry Tarkanian	24-5
20	USC	.18-8	Bob Boyd	18-8

NCAA Final Four (at Cole Fieldhouse, College Park, MD): **Semifinals**—Jacksonville 91, St. Bonaventure 83; UCLA 93, New Mexico St. 77. **Third Place**—N. Mexico St. 79, St. Bonaventure 73. **Championship**—UCLA 80, Jacksonville 69.

NIT Final Four (at Madison Square Garden): **Semifinals**—St. John's 60, Army 59; Marquette 101, LSU 79. **Third Place**—Army 75, LSU 68. **Championship**—Marquette 65, St. John's 53.

1971

		Before Tourns	Head Coach	Final Record
1	UCLA	.25-1	John Wooden	29-1
2	Marquette	.26-0	Al McGuire	28-1
3	Penn	.26-0	Dick Harter	28-1
4	Kansas	.25-1	Ted Owens	27-3
5	USC	.24-2	Bob Boyd	24-2
6	South Carolina	.23-4	Frank McGuire	23-6
7	Western Ky.	.20-5	John Oldham	24-6
8	Kentucky	.22-4	Adolph Rupp	22-6
9	Fordham	.25-1	Digger Phelps	26-3
10	Ohio St.	.19-5	Fred Taylor	20-6
11	Jacksonville	.22-3	Tom Wasdin	22-4
12	Notre Dame	.19-7	Johnny Dee	20-9
13	N. Carolina	.22-6	Dean Smith	26-6
14	Houston	.20-6	Guy Lewis	22-7
15	Duquesne	.21-3	Red Manning	21-4
16	Long Beach St.	.21-4	Jerry Tarkanian	23-5
17	Tennessee	.20-6	Ray Mears	21-7
18	Villanova	.19-5	Jack Kraft	23-6
19	Drake	.20-7	Maury John	21-8
20	BYU	.18-9	Stan Watts	18-11

NCAA Final Four (at the Astrodome, Houston): **Semifinals**—Villanova 92, Western Ky. 89 (2 OT); UCLA 68, Kansas 60. **Third Place**—Western Ky. 77, Kansas 75. **Championship**—UCLA 68, Villanova 62.

NIT Final Four (at Madison Square Garden): **Semifinals**—N. Carolina 73, Duke 69; Ga.Tech 76, St. Bonaventure 71 (2 OT). **Third Place**—St. Bonaventure 92, Duke 88 (OT). **Championship**—N. Carolina 84, Ga. Tech 66.

1972

		Before Tourns	Head Coach	Final Record
1	UCLA	.26-0	John Wooden	30-0
2	North Carolina	.23-4	Dean Smith	26-5
3	Penn	.23-2	Chuck Daly	25-3
4	Louisville	.23-4	Denny Crum	26-5
5	Long Beach St.	.23-3	Jerry Tarkanian	25-4
6	South Carolina	.22-4	Frank McGuire	24-5
7	Marquette	.24-2	Al McGuire	25-4
8	SW Louisiana	.23-3	Beryl Shipley	25-4
9	BYU	.21-4	Stan Watts	21-5
10	Florida St.	.23-5	Hugh Durham	27-6
11	Minnesota	.17-6	Bill Musselman	18-7
12	Marshall	.23-3	Carl Tacy	23-4
13	Memphis St.	.21-6	Gene Bartow	21-7
14	Maryland	.23-5	Lefty Driesell	27-5
15	Villanova	.19-6	Jack Kraft	20-8
16	Oral Roberts	.25-1	Ken Trickey	26-2
17	Indiana	.17-7	Bob Knight	17-8
18	Kentucky	.20-6	Adolph Rupp	21-7
19	Ohio St.	.18-6	Fred Taylor	same
20	Virginia	.20-6	Bill Gibson	21-7

NCAA Final Four (at the Sports Arena, Los Angeles): **Semifinals**—Florida St. 79, N. Carolina 75; UCLA 96, Louisville 77. **Third Place**—N. Carolina 105, Louisville 91. **Championship**—UCLA 81, Florida St. 76.

NIT Final Four (at Madison Square Garden): **Semifinals**—Maryland 91, Jacksonville 77; Niagara 69, St. John's 67. **Third Place**—Jacksonville 83, St. John's 80. **Championship**—Maryland 100, Niagara 69.

1973

		Before Tourns	Head Coach	Final Record
1	UCLA	.26-0	John Wooden	30-0
2	N.C. State	.27-0	Norm Sloan	same*
3	Long Beach St.	.24-2	Jerry Tarkanian	26-3
4	Providence	.24-2	Dave Gavitt	27-4
5	Marquette	.23-3	Al McGuire	25-4
6	Indiana	.19-5	Bob Knight	22-6
7	SW Louisiana	.23-2	Beryl Shipley	24-5
8	Maryland	.22-6	Lefty Driesell	23-7
9	Kansas St.	.22-4	Jack Hartman	23-5
10	Minnesota	.20-4	Bill Musselman	21-5
11	North Carolina	.22-7	Dean Smith	25-8
12	Memphis St.	.21-5	Gene Bartow	24-6
13	Houston	.23-3	Guy Lewis	23-4
14	Syracuse	.22-4	Roy Danforth	24-5
15	Missouri	.21-5	Norm Stewart	21-6
16	Arizona St.	.18-7	Ned Wulk	19-9
17	Kentucky	.19-7	Joe B. Hall	20-8
18	Penn	.20-5	Chuck Daly	21-7
19	Austin Peay	.21-5	Lake Kelly	22-7
20	San Francisco	.22-4	Bob Gaillard	23-5

*N.C. State was ineligible for NCAA tournament for using improper methods to recruit David Thompson.

Note: Unranked **Virginia Tech**, coached by Don DeVoe, won the NIT. The Hokies entered the tourney at 18-5 and finished with a record of 22-5.

NCAA Final Four (at The Arena, St. Louis): **Semifinals**—Memphis St. 98, Providence 85; UCLA 70, Indiana 59. **Third Place**—Indiana 97, Providence 79. **Championship**—UCLA 87, Memphis St. 66.

NIT Final Four (at Madison Square Garden): **Semifinals**—Va. Tech 74, Alabama 73; Notre Dame 78, N. Carolina 71. **Third Place**—N. Carolina 88, Alabama 69. **Championship**—Va. Tech 92, Notre Dame 91 (OT).

1975

		Before Tourns	Head Coach	Final Record
1	Indiana	.29-0	Bob Knight	31-1
2	UCLA	.23-3	John Wooden	28-3
3	Louisville	.24-2	Denny Crum	28-3
4	Maryland	.22-4	Lefty Driesell	24-5
5	Kentucky	.22-4	Joe B. Hall	26-5
6	North Carolina	.21-7	Dean Smith	23-8
7	Arizona St.	.23-3	Ned Wulk	25-4
8	N.C.State	.22-6	Norm Sloan	22-6
9	Notre Dame	.18-8	Digger Phelps	19-10
10	Marquette	.23-3	Al McGuire	23-4
11	Alabama	.22-4	C.M. Newton	22-5
12	Cincinnati	.21-5	Gale Catlett	23-6
13	Oregon St.	.18-10	Ralph Miller	19-12
14	Drake	.16-10	Bob Ortegel	19-10
15	Penn	.23-4	Chuck Daly	23-5
16	UNLV	.22-4	Jerry Tarkanian	24-5
17	Kansas St.	.18-8	Jack Hartman	20-9
18	USC	.18-7	Bob Boyd	18-8
19	Centenary	.25-4	Larry Little	same
20	Syracuse	.20-7	Roy Danforth	23-9

NCAA Final Four (at San Diego Sports Arena): **Semifinals**—Kentucky 95, Syracuse 79; UCLA 75, Louisville 74 (OT). **Third Place**—Louisville 96, Syracuse 88 (OT). **Championship**—UCLA 92, Kentucky 85.

NIT Championship (at Madison Sq. Garden): Princeton 80, Providence 69. No Top 20 teams played in NIT.

CCA Championship (at Freedom Hall, Louisville): Drake 83, Arizona 76. No.14 Drake and No.18 USC were only Top 20 teams in CCA.

1974

		Before Tourns	Head Coach	Final Record
1	N.C. State	.26-1	Norm Sloan	30-1
2	UCLA	.23-3	John Wooden	26-4
3	Notre Dame	.24-2	Digger Phelps	26-3
4	Maryland	.23-5	Lefty Driesell	same
5	Providence	.26-3	Dave Gavitt	28-4
6	Vanderbilt	.23-3	Roy Skinner	23-5
7	Marquette	.22-4	Al McGuire	26-5
8	North Carolina	.22-5	Dean Smith	22-6
9	Long Beach St.	.24-2	Lute Olson	same
10	Indiana	.20-5	Bob Knight	23-5
11	Alabama	.22-4	C.M. Newton	same
12	Michigan	.21-4	Johnny Orr	22-5
13	Pittsburgh	.23-3	Buzz Ridl	25-4
14	Kansas	.21-5	Ted Owens	23-7
15	USC	.22-4	Bob Boyd	24-5
16	Louisville	.21-6	Denny Crum	21-7
17	New Mexico	.21-6	Norm Ellenberger	22-7
18	South Carolina	.22-4	Frank McGuire	22-5
19	Creighton	.22-6	Eddie Sutton	23-7
20	Dayton	.19-7	Don Donoher	20-9

NCAA Final Four (at Greensboro, NC, Coliseum): **Semifinals**—N.C. State 80, UCLA 77 (2 OT); Marquette 64, Kansas 51. **Third Place**—UCLA 78, Kansas 61. **Championship**—N.C. State 76, Marquette 64.

NIT Final Four (at Madison Square Garden): **Semifinals**—Purdue 78, Jacksonville 63; Utah 117, Boston Col. 93. **Third Place**—Boston Col. 87, Jacksonville 77. **Championship**—Purdue 87, Utah 81.

CCA Final Four (at The Arena, St. Louis): **Semifinals**—Indiana 73, Toledo 72; USC 74, Bradley 73. **Championship**—Indiana 85, USC 60.

1976

		Before Tourns	Head Coach	Final Record
1	Indiana	.27-0	Bob Knight	32-0
2	Marquette	.25-1	Al McGuire	27-2
3	UNLV	.28-1	Jerry Tarkanian	29-2
4	Rutgers	.28-0	Tom Young	31-2
5	UCLA	.24-3	Gene Bartow	28-4
6	Alabama	.22-4	C.M. Newton	23-5
7	Notre Dame	.22-5	Digger Phelps	23-6
8	North Carolina	.25-3	Dean Smith	25-4
9	Michigan	.21-6	Johnny Orr	25-7
10	Western Mich.	.24-2	Eldon Miller	25-3
11	Maryland	.22-6	Lefty Driesell	same
12	Cincinnati	.25-5	Gale Catlett	25-6
13	Tennessee	.21-5	Ray Mears	21-6
14	Missouri	.24-4	Norm Stewart	26-5
15	Arizona	.22-8	Fred Snowden	24-9
16	Texas Tech	.24-5	Gerald Myers	25-6
17	DePaul	.19-8	Ray Meyer	20-9
18	Virginia	.18-11	Terry Holland	18-12
19	Centenary	.22-5	Larry Little	same
20	Pepperdine	.21-5	Gary Colson	22-6

NCAA Final Four (at the Spectrum, Phila.); **Semifinals**—Michigan 86, Rutgers 70; Indiana 65, UCLA 51. **Third Place**—UCLA 106, Rutgers 92. **Championship**—Indiana 86, Michigan 68.

NIT Championship (at Madison Square Garden): Kentucky 71, NC-Charlotte 67. No Top 20 teams played in NIT.

Associated Press Final Polls (Cont.)

1977

		Before Tourns	Head Coach	Final Record
1	Michigan	24-3	Johnny Orr	26-4
2	UCLA	24-3	Gene Bartow	25-4
3	Kentucky	24-3	Joe B. Hall	26-4
4	UNLV	25-2	Jerry Tarkanian	29-3
5	North Carolina	24-4	Dean Smith	28-5
6	Syracuse	25-3	Jim Boeheim	26-4
7	**Marquette**	20-7	Al McGuire	25-7
8	San Francisco	29-1	Bob Gaillard	29-2
9	Wake Forest	20-7	Carl Tacy	22-8
10	Notre Dame	21-6	Digger Phelps	22-7
11	Alabama	23-4	C.M. Newton	25-6
12	Detroit	24-3	Dick Vitale	25-4
13	Minnesota	24-3	Jim Dutcher	same*
14	Utah	22-6	Jerry Pimm	23-7
15	Tennessee	22-5	Ray Mears	22-6
16	Kansas St.	23-6	Jack Hartman	24-7
17	NC-Charlotte	25-3	Lee Rose	28-5
18	Arkansas	26-1	Eddie Sutton	26-2
19	Louisville	21-6	Denny Crum	21-7
20	VMI	25-3	Charlie Schmaus	26-4

*On probation

NCAA Final Four (at the Omni, Atlanta): **Semifinals**—Marquette 51, NC-Charlotte, 49; N. Carolina 84, UNLV 83. **Third Place**—UNLV 106, NC-Charlotte 94. **Championship**—Marquette 67, N. Carolina 59.
NIT Championship (at Madison Square Garden): St. Bonaventure 94, Houston 91. No.11 Alabama was only Top 20 team in NIT.

1978

		Before Tourns	Head Coach	Final Record
1	**Kentucky**	25-2	Joe B. Hall	30-2
2	UCLA	24-2	Gary Cunningham	25-3
3	DePaul	25-2	Ray Meyer	27-3
4	Michigan St.	23-4	Jud Heathcote	25-5
5	Arkansas	28-3	Eddie Sutton	32-3
6	Notre Dame	20-6	Digger Phelps	23-8
7	Duke	23-6	Bill Foster	27-7
8	Marquette	24-3	Hank Raymonds	24-4
9	Louisville	22-6	Denny Crum	23-7
10	Kansas	24-4	Ted Owens	24-5
11	San Francisco	22-5	Bob Gaillard	23-6
12	New Mexico	24-3	Norm Ellenberger	24-4
13	Indiana	20-7	Bob Knight	21-8
14	Utah	22-5	Jerry Pimm	23-6
15	Florida St.	23-5	Hugh Durham	23-6
16	North Carolina	23-7	Dean Smith	23-8
17	**Texas**	22-5	Abe Lemons	26-5
18	Detroit	24-3	Dave Gaines	25-4
19	Miami-OH	18-8	Darrell Hedric	19-9
20	Penn	19-7	Bob Weinhauer	20-8

NCAA Final Four (at the Checkerdome, St. Louis): **Semifinals**—Kentucky 64, Arkansas 59; Duke 90, Notre Dame 86. **Third Place**—Arkansas 71, Notre Dame 69. **Championship**—Kentucky 94, Duke 88.
NIT Championship (at Madison Square Garden): Texas 101, N.C. State 93. No. 17 Texas and No. 18 Detroit were only Top 20 teams in NIT.

1979

		Before Tourns	Head Coach	Final Record
1	Indiana St.	29-0	Bill Hodges	33-1
2	UCLA	23-4	Gary Cunningham	25-5
3	**Michigan St.**	21-6	Jud Heathcote	26-6
4	Notre Dame	22-5	Digger Phelps	24-6
5	Arkansas	23-4	Eddie Sutton	25-5
6	DePaul	22-5	Ray Meyer	26-6
7	LSU	22-5	Dale Brown	23-6
8	Syracuse	25-3	Jim Boeheim	26-4
9	North Carolina	23-5	Dean Smith	23-6
10	Marquette	21-6	Hank Raymonds	22-7
11	Duke	22-7	Bill Foster	22-8
12	San Francisco	21-6	Dan Belluomini	22-7
13	Louisville	23-7	Denny Crum	24-8
14	Penn	21-5	Bob Weinhauer	25-7
15	Purdue	23-7	Lee Rose	27-8
16	Oklahoma	20-9	Dave Bliss	21-10
17	St. John's	18-10	Lou Carnesecca	21-11
18	Rutgers	21-8	Tom Young	22-9
19	Toledo	21-6	Bob Nichols	22-7
20	Iowa	20-7	Lute Olson	20-8

NCAA Final Four (at Special Events Center, Salt Lake City): **Semifinals**—Michigan St. 101, Penn 67; Indiana St. 76, DePaul 74; **Third Place**—DePaul 96, Penn 93; **Championship**—Michigan St. 75, Indiana St. 64.
NIT Championship (at Madison Square Garden): Indiana 53, Purdue 52. No. 15 Purdue was the only Top 20 team in NIT.

1980

		Before Tourns	Head Coach	Final Record
1	DePaul	26-1	Ray Meyer	26-2
2	**Louisville**	28-3	Denny Crum	33-3
3	LSU	24-5	Dale Brown	26-6
4	Kentucky	28-5	Joe B. Hall	29-6
5	Oregon St.	26-3	Ralph Miller	26-4
6	Syracuse	25-3	Jim Boeheim	26-4
7	Indiana	20-7	Bob Knight	21-8
8	Maryland	23-6	Lefty Driesell	24-7
9	Notre Dame	20-7	Digger Phelps	20-8
10	Ohio St.	24-5	Eldon Miller	21-8
11	Georgetown	24-5	John Thompson	26-6
12	BYU	24-4	Frank Arnold	24-5
13	St. John's	24-4	Lou Carnesecca	24-5
14	Duke	22-8	Bill Foster	24-9
15	North Carolina	21-7	Dean Smith	21-8
16	Missouri	23-5	Norm Stewart	25-6
17	Weber St.	26-2	Neil McCarthy	26-3
18	Arizona St.	21-6	Ned Wulk	22-7
19	Iona	28-4	Jim Valvano	29-5
20	Purdue	19-9	Lee Rose	23-10

NCAA Final Four (at Market Square Arena, Indianapolis): **Semifinals**—Louisville 80, Iowa 72; UCLA 67, Purdue 62; **Championship**—Louisville 59, UCLA 54.
NIT Championship (at Madison Square Garden): Virginia 58, Minnesota 55. No Top 20 teams played in NIT.

1981

		Before Tourns	Head Coach	Final Record
1	DePaul	27-1	Ray Meyer	27-2
2	Oregon St.	26-1	Ralph Miller	26-2
3	Arizona St.	24-3	Ned Wulk	24-4
4	LSU	28-3	Dale Brown	31-5
5	Virginia	25-3	Terry Holland	29-4
6	North Carolina	25-7	Dean Smith	29-8
7	Notre Dame	22-5	Digger Phelps	23-6
8	Kentucky	22-5	Joe B. Hall	22-6
9	**Indiana**	21-9	Bob Knight	26-9
10	UCLA	20-6	Larry Brown	20-7
11	Wake Forest	22-6	Carl Tacy	22-7
12	Louisville	21-8	Denny Crum	21-9
13	Iowa	21-6	Lute Olson	21-7
14	Utah	24-4	Jerry Pimm	25-5
15	Tennessee	20-7	Don DeVoe	21-8
16	BYU	22-6	Frank Arnold	25-7
17	Wyoming	23-5	Jim Brandenburg	24-6
18	Maryland	20-9	Lefty Driesell	21-10
19	Illinois	20-7	Lou Henson	21-8
20	Arkansas	22-7	Eddie Sutton	24-8

NCAA Final Four (at the Spectrum, Phila.): **Semifinals**–N. Carolina 78, Virginia 65; Indiana 67, LSU 49. **Third Place**–Virginia 78, LSU 74. **Championship**–Indiana 63, N. Carolina 50.

NIT Championship (at Madison Square Garden): Tulsa 86, Syracuse 84. No Top 20 teams played in NIT.

1982

		Before Tourns	Head Coach	Final Record
1	**N. Carolina**	27-2	Dean Smith	32-2
2	DePaul	26-1	Ray Meyer	26-2
3	Virginia	29-3	Terry Holland	30-4
4	Oregon St.	23-4	Ralph Miller	25-5
5	Missouri	26-3	Norm Stewart	27-4
6	Georgetown	26-6	John Thompson	30-7
7	Minnesota	22-5	Jim Dutcher	23-6
8	Idaho	26-2	Don Monson	27-3
9	Memphis St.	23-4	Dana Kirk	24-5
10	Tulsa	24-5	Nolan Richardson	24-6
11	Fresno St.	26-2	Boyd Grant	27-3
12	Arkansas	23-5	Eddie Sutton	23-6
13	Alabama	23-6	Wimp Sanderson	24-7
14	West Virginia	26-3	Gale Catlett	27-4
15	Kentucky	22-7	Joe B. Hall	22-8
16	Iowa	20-7	Lute Olson	21-8
17	Ala-Birmingham	23-5	Gene Bartow	25-6
18	Wake Forest	20-8	Carl Tacy	21-9
19	UCLA	21-6	Larry Farmer	21-6
20	Louisville	20-9	Denny Crum	23-10

NCAA Final Four (at the Superdome, New Orleans): **Semifinals**–N. Carolina 68, Houston 63; Georgetown 50, Louisville 46. **Championship**–N. Carolina 63, Georgetown 62.

NIT Championship (at Madison Square Garden): Bradley 67, Purdue 58. No Top 20 teams played in NIT.

1983

		Before Tourns	Head Coach	Final Record
1	Houston	27-2	Guy Lewis	31-3
2	Louisville	29-3	Denny Crum	32-4
3	St. John's	27-4	Lou Carnesecca	28-5
4	Virginia	27-4	Terry Holland	29-5
5	Indiana	23-5	Bob Knight	24-6
6	UNLV	28-2	Jerry Tarkanian	28-3
7	UCLA	23-5	Larry Farmer	23-6
8	North Carolina	26-7	Dean Smith	28-8
9	Arkansas	25-3	Eddie Sutton	26-4
10	Missouri	26-7	Norm Stewart	26-8
11*	Boston College	24-6	Gary Williams	25-7
12	Kentucky	22-7	Joe B. Hall	23-8
13	Villanova	22-7	Rollie Massimino	24-8
14	Wichita St.	25-3	Gene Smithson	same*
15	Tenn-Chatt.	26-3	Murray Arnold	26-4
16	**N.C. State**	20-10	Jim Valvano	26-10
17	Memphis St.	22-7	Dana Kirk	23-8
18	Georgia	21-9	Hugh Durham	24-10
19	Oklahoma St.	24-6	Paul Hansen	24-7
20	Georgetown	21-9	John Thompson	22-10

*On probation

NCAA Final Four (at The Pit, Albuquerque, NM): **Semifinals**–N.C. State 67, Georgia 60; Houston 94, Louisville 81. **Championship**–N.C. State 54, Houston 52.

NIT Championship (at Madison Square Garden): Fresno St. 69, DePaul 60. No Top 20 teams played in NIT.

1984

		Before Tourns	Head Coach	Final Record
1	North Carolina	27-2	Dean Smith	28-3
2	**Georgetown**	29-3	John Thompson	34-3
3	Kentucky	26-4	Joe B. Hall	29-5
4	DePaul	26-2	Ray Meyer	27-3
5	Houston	28-4	Guy Lewis	32-5
6	Illinois	24-4	Lou Henson	26-5
7	Oklahoma	29-4	Billy Tubbs	29-5
8	Arkansas	25-6	Eddie Sutton	25-7
9	UTEP	27-3	Don Haskins	27-4
10	Purdue	22-6	Gene Keady	22-7
11	Maryland	23-7	Lefty Driesell	24-8
12	Tulsa	27-3	Nolan Richardson	27-4
13	UNLV	27-5	Jerry Tarkanian	29-6
14	Duke	24-9	Mike Krzyzewski	24-10
15	Washington	22-6	Marv Harshman	24-7
16	Memphis St.	24-6	Dana Kirk	26-7
17	Oregon St.	22-6	Ralph Miller	22-7
18	Syracuse	22-8	Jim Boeheim	23-9
19	Wake Forest	21-8	Carl Tacy	23-9
20	Temple	25-4	John Chaney	26-5

NCAA Final Four (at the Kingdome, Seattle): **Semifinals**–Houston 49, Virginia 47 (OT); Georgetown 53, Kentucky 40. **Championship**–Georgetown 84, Houston 75.

NIT Championship (at Madison Square Garden): Michigan 83, Notre Dame 63. No Top 20 teams played in NIT.

Highest-Rated College Games on TV

The dozen highest-rated college basketball games seen on U.S. television have been NCAA tournament championship games, led by the 1979 Michigan State-Indiana State final that featured Magic Johnson and Larry Bird.

Listed below are the finalists (winning team first), date of game, TV network, and TV rating and audience share (according to Nielson Media Research).

		Date	Net	Rtg/Sh			Date	Net	Rtg/Sh
1	Michigan St.-Indiana St.	3/26/79	NBC	24.1/38	7	N. Carolina-Georgetown	3/29/82	CBS	21.6/31
2	Villanova-Georgetown	4/1/85	CBS	23.3/33	8	UCLA-Kentucky	3/31/75	NBC	21.3/33
3	Duke-Michigan	4/6/92	CBS	22.7/35	9	Michigan-Seton Hall	4/3/89	CBS	21.3/33
4	N.C. State-Houston	4/4/83	CBS	22.3/32	10	Louisville-Duke	3/31/86	CBS	20.7/31
5	N. Carolina-Michigan	4/5/93	CBS	22.2/34	11	Indiana-N. Carolina	3/30/81	NBC	20.7/29
6	Arkansas-Duke	4/4/94	CBS	21.6/33	12	UCLA-Memphis St.	3/26/73	NBC	20.5/32

Associated Press Final Polls (Cont.)

1985

		Before Tourns	Head Coach	Final Record
1	Georgetown	.30-2	John Thompson	35-3
2	Michigan	.25-3	Bill Frieder	26-4
3	St. John's	.27-3	Lou Carnesecca	31-4
4	Oklahoma	.28-5	Billy Tubbs	31-6
5	Memphis St.	.27-3	Dana Kirk	31-4
6	Georgia Tech	.24-7	Bobby Cremins	27-8
7	North Carolina	.24-8	Dean Smith	27-9
8	Louisiana Tech	.27-2	Andy Russo	29-3
9	UNLV	.27-3	Jerry Tarkanian	28-4
10	Duke	.22-7	Mike Krzyzewski	23-8
11	VCU	.25-5	J.D. Barnett	26-6
12	Illinois	.24-8	Lou Henson	26-9
13	Kansas	.25-7	Larry Brown	26-8
14	Loyola-IL	.25-5	Gene Sullivan	27-6
15	Syracuse	.21-8	Jim Boeheim	22-9
16	N.C. State	.20-9	Jim Valvano	23-10
17	Texas Tech	.23-7	Gerald Myers	23-8
18	Tulsa	.23-7	Nolan Richardson	23-8
19	Georgia	.21-8	Hugh Durham	22-9
20	LSU	.19-9	Dale Brown	19-10

Note: Unranked **Villanova**, coached by Rollie Massimino, won the NCAAs. The Wildcats entered the tourney at 19-10 and had a final record of 25-10.

NCAA Final Four (at Rupp Arena, Lexington, KY): **Semifinals**— Georgetown 77, St. John's 59; Villanova 52, Memphis St. 45. **Championship**—Villanova 66, Georgetown 64.

NIT Championship (at Madison Square Garden): UCLA 65, Indiana 62. No Top 20 teams played in NIT.

1987

		Before Tourns	Head Coach	Final Record
1	UNLV	.33-1	Jerry Tarkanian	37-2
2	North Carolina	.29-3	Dean Smith	32-4
3	**Indiana**	.24-4	Bob Knight	30-4
4	Georgetown	.26-4	John Thompson	29-5
5	DePaul	.26-2	Joey Meyer	28-3
6	Iowa	.27-4	Tom Davis	30-5
7	Purdue	.24-4	Gene Keady	25-5
8	Temple	.31-3	John Chaney	32-4
9	Alabama	.26-4	Wimp Sanderson	28-5
10	Syracuse	.26-6	Jim Boeheim	31-7
11	Illinois	.23-7	Lou Henson	23-8
12	Pittsburgh	.24-7	Paul Evans	25-8
13	Clemson	.25-5	Cliff Ellis	25-6
14	Missouri	.24-9	Norm Stewart	24-10
15	UCLA	.24-6	Walt Hazzard	25-7
16	New Orleans	.25-3	Benny Dees	26-4
17	Duke	.22-8	Mike Krzyzewski	24-9
18	Notre Dame	.22-7	Digger Phelps	24-8
19	TCU	.23-6	Jim Killingsworth	24-7
20	Kansas	.23-10	Larry Brown	25-11

NCAA Final Four (at the Superdome, New Orleans): **Semifinals**—Syracuse 77, Providence 63; Indiana 97, UNLV 93. **Championship**—Indiana 74, Syracuse 73.

NIT Championship (at Madison Square Garden): Southern Miss. 84, La Salle 80. No Top 20 teams played in NIT.

1986

		Before Tourns	Head Coach	Final Record
1	Duke	.32-2	Mike Krzyzewski	37-3
2	Kansas	.31-3	Larry Brown	35-4
3	Kentucky	.29-3	Eddie Sutton	32-4
4	St. John's	.30-4	Lou Carnesecca	31-5
5	Michigan	.27-4	Bill Frieder	28-5
6	Georgia Tech	.25-6	Bobby Cremins	27-7
7	**Louisville**	.26-7	Denny Crum	32-7
8	North Carolina	.26-5	Dean Smith	28-6
9	Syracuse	.25-5	Jim Boeheim	26-6
10	Notre Dame	.23-5	Digger Phelps	23-6
11	UNLV	.31-4	Jerry Tarkanian	33-5
12	Memphis St.	.27-5	Dana Kirk	28-6
13	Georgetown	.23-7	John Thompson	24-8
14	Bradley	.31-2	Dick Versace	32-3
15	Oklahoma	.25-8	Billy Tubbs	26-9
16	Indiana	.21-7	Bob Knight	21-8
17	Navy	.27-4	Paul Evans	30-5
18	Michigan St.	.21-7	Jud Heathcote	23-8
19	Illinois	.21-9	Lou Henson	22-10
20	UTEP	.27-5	Don Haskins	27-6

NCAA Final Four (at Reunion Arena, Dallas): **Semifinals**—Duke 71, Kansas 67; Louisville 88, LSU 77. **Championship**—Louisville 72, Duke 69.

NIT Championship (at Madison Square Garden): Ohio St. 73, Wyoming 63. No Top 20 teams played in NIT.

1988

		Before Tourns	Head Coach	Final Record
1	Temple	.29-1	John Chaney	32-2
2	Arizona	.31-2	Lute Olson	35-3
3	Purdue	.27-3	Gene Keady	29-4
4	Oklahoma	.30-3	Billy Tubbs	35-4
5	Duke	.24-6	Mike Krzyzewski	28-7
6	Kentucky	.25-5	Eddie Sutton	27-6
7	North Carolina	.24-6	Dean Smith	27-7
8	Pittsburgh	.23-6	Paul Evans	24-7
9	Syracuse	.25-8	Jim Boeheim	26-9
10	Michigan	.24-7	Bill Frieder	26-8
11	Bradley	.26-4	Stan Albeck	26-5
12	UNLV	.27-5	Jerry Tarkanian	28-6
13	Wyoming	.26-5	Benny Dees	26-6
14	N.C. State	.24-7	Jim Valvano	24-8
15	Loyola-CA	.27-3	Paul Westhead	28-4
16	Illinois	.22-9	Lou Henson	23-10
17	Iowa	.22-9	Tom Davis	24-10
18	Xavier-OH	.26-3	Pete Gillen	26-4
19	BYU	.25-5	Ladell Andersen	26-6
20	Kansas St.	.22-8	Lon Kruger	25-9

Note: Unranked **Kansas**, coached by Larry Brown, won the NCAAs. The Jayhawks entered the tourney at 21-11 and had a final record of 27-11.

NCAA Final Four (at Kemper Arena, Kansas City): **Semifinals**—Kansas 66, Duke 59; Oklahoma 86, Arizona 78. **Championship**—Kansas 83, Oklahoma 79.

NIT Championship (at Madison Square Garden): Connecticut 72, Ohio St. 67. No Top 20 teams played in NIT.

1989

		Before Tourns	Head Coach	Final Record
1	Arizona	27-3	Lute Olson	29-4
2	Georgetown	26-4	John Thompson	29-5
3	Illinois	27-4	Lou Henson	31-5
4	Oklahoma	28-5	Billy Tubbs	30-6
5	North Carolina	27-7	Dean Smith	29-8
6	Missouri	27-7	Norm Stewart & Rich Daly*	29-8
7	Syracuse	27-7	Jim Boeheim	30-8
8	Indiana	25-7	Bob Knight	27-8
9	Duke	24-7	Mike Krzyzewski	28-8
10	**Michigan**	24-7	Bill Frieder (24-7) & Steve Fisher (6-0)	30-7
11	Seton Hall	26-6	P.J. Carlesimo	31-7
12	Louisville	22-8	Denny Crum	24-9
13	Stanford	26-6	Mike Montgomery	26-7
14	Iowa	22-9	Tom Davis	23-10
15	UNLV	26-7	Jerry Tarkanian	29-8
16	Florida St.	22-7	Pat Kennedy	22-8
17	West Virginia	25-4	Gale Catlett	26-5
18	Ball State	28-2	Rick Majerus	29-3
19	N.C. State	20-8	Jim Valvano	22-9
20	Alabama	23-7	Wimp Sanderson	23-8

NCAA Final Four (at The Kingdome, Seattle): **Semifinals**–Seton Hall 95, Duke 78; Illinois 81. **Championship**–Michigan 80, Seton Hall 79 (OT).
NIT Championship (at Madison Square Garden): St. John's 73, St. Louis 65. No Top 20 teams played in NIT.
*Norm Stewart's assistant Rich Daly temporarily took over for his ailing boss (Daly coached the final 14 games of the season) but returned to his role as an assistant when Stewart recovered before the start of the following season.

1991

		Before Tourns	Head Coach	Final Record
1	UNLV	30-0	Jerry Tarkanian	34-1
2	Arkansas	31-3	Nolan Richardson	34-4
3	Indiana	27-4	Bob Knight	29-5
4	North Carolina	25-5	Dean Smith	29-6
5	Ohio St.	25-3	Randy Ayers	27-4
6	**Duke**	26-7	Mike Krzyzewski	32-7
7	Syracuse	26-5	Jim Boeheim	26-6
8	Arizona	26-6	Lute Olson	28-7
9	Kentucky	22-6	Rick Pitino	same*
10	Utah	28-3	Rick Majerus	30-4
11	Nebraska	26-7	Danny Nee	26-8
12	Kansas	22-7	Roy Williams	27-8
13	Seton Hall	22-8	P.J. Carlesimo	25-9
14	Oklahoma St.	22-7	Eddie Sutton	24-8
15	New Mexico St.	23-5	Neil McCarthy	23-6
16	UCLA	23-8	Jim Harrick	23-9
17	E.Tennessee St.	28-4	Alan LaForce	28-5
18	Princeton	24-2	Pete Carril	24-3
19	Alabama	21-9	Wimp Sanderson	23-10
20	St. John's	20-8	Lou Carnesecca	23-9
21	Mississippi St.	20-8	Richard Williams	20-9
22	LSU	20-9	Dale Brown	20-10
23	Texas	22-8	Tom Penders	23-9
24	DePaul	20-8	Joey Meyer	20-9
25	Southern Miss.	21-7	M.K. Turk	21-8

*On probation
NCAA Final Four (at the Hoosier Dome, Indianapolis): **Semifinals**–Kansas 79, North Carolina 73; Duke 79, UNLV 77. **Championship**–Duke 72, Kansas 65.
NIT Championship (at Madison Square Garden): Stanford 78, Oklahoma 72. No Top 25 teams played in NIT.

1990

		Before Tourns	Head Coach	Final Record
1	Oklahoma	26-4	Billy Tubbs	27-5
2	**UNLV**	29-5	Jerry Tarkanian	35-5
3	Connecticut	28-5	Jim Calhoun	31-6
4	Michigan St.	26-5	Jud Heathcote	28-6
5	Kansas	29-4	Roy Williams	30-5
6	Syracuse	24-6	Jim Boeheim	26-7
7	Arkansas	26-4	Nolan Richardson	30-5
8	Georgetown	23-6	John Thompson	24-7
9	Georgia Tech	24-6	Bobby Cremins	28-7
10	Purdue	21-7	Gene Keady	22-8
11	Missouri	26-5	Norm Stewart	26-6
12	La Salle	29-1	Speedy Morris	30-2
13	Michigan	22-7	Steve Fisher	23-8
14	Arizona	24-6	Lute Olson	25-7
15	Duke	24-8	Mike Krzyzewski	29-9
16	Louisville	26-7	Denny Crum	27-8
17	Clemson	24-8	Cliff Ellis	26-9
18	Illinois	21-7	Lou Henson	21-8
19	LSU	22-8	Dale Brown	23-9
20	Minnesota	20-8	Clem Haskins	23-9
21	Loyola-CA	23-5	Paul Westhead	26-6
22	Oregon St.	22-6	Jim Anderson	22-7
23	Alabama	24-8	Wimp Sanderson	26-9
24	New Mexico St.	26-4	Neil McCarthy	26-5
25	Xavier-OH	26-4	Pete Gillen	28-5

NCAA Final Four (at McNichols Sports Arena, Denver): **Semifinals**–Duke 97, Arkansas 83; UNLV 90, Georgia Tech 81. **Championship**–UNLV 103, Duke 73.
NIT Championship (at Madison Square Garden): Vanderbilt 74, St. Louis 72. No Top 25 teams played in NIT.

1992

		Before Tourns	Head Coach	Final Record
1	**Duke**	28-2	Mike Krzyzewski	34-2
2	Kansas	26-4	Roy Williams	27-5
3	Ohio St.	23-5	Randy Ayers	26-6
4	UCLA	25-4	Jim Harrick	28-5
5	Indiana	23-6	Bob Knight	27-7
6	Kentucky	26-6	Rick Pitino	29-7
7	UNLV	26-2	Jerry Tarkanian	same*
8	USC	23-5	George Raveling	24-6
9	Arkansas	25-7	Nolan Richardson	26-8
10	Arizona	24-6	Lute Olson	24-7
11	Oklahoma St.	26-7	Eddie Sutton	28-8
12	Cincinnati	25-4	Bob Huggins	29-5
13	Alabama	25-8	Wimp Sanderson	26-9
14	Michigan St.	21-7	Jud Heathcote	22-8
15	Michigan	20-8	Steve Fisher	25-9
16	Missouri	20-8	Norm Stewart	21-9
17	Massachusetts	28-4	John Calipari	30-5
18	North Carolina	21-9	Dean Smith	23-10
19	Seton Hall	21-8	P.J. Carlesimo	23-9
20	Florida St.	20-9	Pat Kennedy	22-10
21	Syracuse	21-9	Jim Boeheim	22-10
22	Georgetown	21-9	John Thompson	22-10
23	Oklahoma	21-8	Billy Tubbs	21-9
24	DePaul	20-8	Joey Meyer	20-9
25	LSU	20-9	Dale Brown	21-10

*On probation
NCAA Final Four (at the Metrodome, Minneapolis): **Semifinals**–Michigan 76, Cincinnati 72; Duke 81, Indiana 78. **Championship**–Duke 71, Michigan 51.
NIT Championship (at Madison Square Garden): Virginia 81, Notre Dame 76 (OT). No Top 25 teams played in NIT.

Associated Press Final Polls (Cont.)

1993

		Before Tourns	Head Coach	Final Record
1	Indiana	28-3	Bob Knight	31-4
2	Kentucky	26-3	Rick Pitino	30-4
3	Michigan	26-4	Steve Fisher	31-5
4	**N. Carolina**	28-4	Dean Smith	34-4
5	Arizona	24-3	Lute Olson	24-4
6	Seton Hall	27-6	P.J. Carlesimo	28-7
7	Cincinnati	24-4	Bob Huggins	27-5
8	Vanderbilt	26-5	Eddie Fogler	28-6
9	Kansas	25-6	Roy Williams	29-7
10	Duke	23-7	Mike Krzyzewski	24-8
11	Florida St.	22-9	Pat Kennedy	25-10
12	Arkansas	20-8	Nolan Richardson	22-9
13	Iowa	22-8	Tom Davis	23-9
14	Massachusetts	23-6	John Calipari	24-7
15	Louisville	20-8	Denny Crum	22-9
16	Wake Forest	19-8	Dave Odom	21-9
17	New Orleans	26-3	Tim Floyd	26-4
18	Georgia Tech	19-10	Bobby Cremins	19-11
19	Utah	23-6	Rick Majerus	24-7
20	Western Ky.	24-5	Ralph Willard	26-6
21	New Mexico	24-6	Dave Bliss	24-7
22	Purdue	18-9	Gene Keady	18-10
23	Oklahoma St.	19-8	Eddie Sutton	20-9
24	New Mexico St.	25-7	Neil McCarthy	26-8
25	UNLV	21-7	Rollie Massimino	21-8

NCAA Final Four (at the Superdome, New Orleans): **Semifinals**–North Carolina 78, Kansas 68; Michigan 81, Kentucky 78 (OT). **Championship**–North Carolina 77, Michigan 71.

NIT Championship (at Madison Square Garden): Minnesota 62, Georgetown 61. No. 25 UNLV was the only Top 25 team that played in the NIT.

1994

		Before Tourns	Head Coach	Final Record
1	North Carolina	27-6	Dean Smith	28-7
2	**Arkansas**	25-3	Nolan Richardson	31-3
3	Purdue	26-4	Gene Keady	29-5
4	Connecticut	27-4	Jim Calhoun	29-5
5	Missouri	25-3	Norm Stewart	28-4
6	Duke	23-5	Mike Krzyzewski	28-6
7	Kentucky	26-6	Rick Pitino	27-7
8	Massachusetts	27-6	John Calipari	28-7
9	Arizona	25-5	Lute Olson	29-6
10	Louisville	26-5	Denny Crum	28-6
11	Michigan	21-7	Steve Fisher	24-8
12	Temple	22-7	John Chaney	23-8
13	Kansas	25-7	Roy Williams	27-8
14	Florida	25-7	Lon Kruger	29-8
15	Syracuse	21-6	Jim Boeheim	23-7
16	California	22-7	Todd Bozeman	22-8
17	UCLA	21-6	Jim Harrick	21-7
18	Indiana	19-8	Bob Knight	21-9
19	Oklahoma St.	23-9	Eddie Sutton	24-10
20	Texas	25-7	Tom Penders	26-8
21	Marquette	22-8	Kevin O'Neill	24-9
22	Nebraska	20-9	Danny Nee	20-10
23	Minnesota	20-11	Clem Haskins	21-12
24	Saint Louis	23-5	Charlie Spoonhour	23-6
25	Cincinnati	22-9	Bob Huggins	22-10

NCAA Final Four (at the Charlotte Coliseum): **Semifinals**– Arkansas 91, Arizona 82; Duke 70, Florida 65. **Championship**– Arkansas 76, Duke 72.

NIT Championship (at Madison Square Garden): Villanova 80, Vanderbilt 73. No top 25 teams played in NIT.

1995

		Before Tourns	Head Coach	Final Record
1	**UCLA**	25-2	Jim Harrick	31-2
2	Kentucky	25-4	Rick Pitino	28-5
3	Wake Forest	24-5	Dave Odom	26-6
4	North Carolina	24-5	Dean Smith	28-6
5	Kansas	23-5	Roy Williams	25-6
6	Arkansas	27-6	Nolan Richardson	32-7
7	Massachusetts	26-4	John Calipari	26-5
8	Connecticut	25-4	Jim Calhoun	28-5
9	Villanova	25-7	Steve Lappas	25-8
10	Maryland	24-7	Gary Williams	26-8
11	Michigan St.	22-5	Jud Heathcote	22-6
12	Purdue	24-6	Gene Keady	25-7
13	Virginia	22-8	Jeff Jones	25-9
14	Oklahoma St.	23-9	Eddie Sutton	27-10
15	Arizona	23-7	Lute Olson	23-8
16	Arizona St.	22-8	Bill Frieder	24-9
17	Oklahoma	23-8	Kelvin Sampson	23-9
18	Mississippi St.	20-7	Richard Williams	22-8
19	Utah	27-5	Rick Majerus	28-6
20	Alabama	22-9	David Hobbs	23-10
21	Western Ky.	26-3	Matt Kilcullen	27-4
22	Georgetown	19-9	John Thompson	21-10
23	Missouri	19-8	Norm Stewart	20-9
24	Iowa St.	22-10	Tim Floyd	23-11
25	Syracuse	19-9	Jim Boeheim	20-10

NCAA Final Four (at the Kingdome, Seattle): **Semifinals**– UCLA 74, Oklahoma St. 61; Arkansas 75, North Carolina 68. **Championship**– UCLA 89, Arkansas 78.

NIT Championship (at Madison Square Garden):Virginia Tech 65, Marquette 64 (OT). No top 25 teams played in NIT.

1996

		Before Tourns	Head Coach	Final Record
1	Massachusetts	31-1	John Calipari	35-2
2	**Kentucky**	28-2	Rick Pitino	34-2
3	Connecticut	30-2	Jim Calhoun	32-3
4	Georgetown	26-7	John Thompson	29-8
5	Kansas	26-4	Roy Williams	29-5
6	Purdue	25-5	Gene Keady	26-6
7	Cincinnati	25-4	Bob Huggins	28-5
8	Texas Tech	28-1	James Dickey	30-2
9	Wake Forest	23-5	Dave Odom	26-6
10	Villanova	25-6	Steve Lappas	26-7
11	Arizona	24-6	Lute Olson	26-7
12	Utah	25-6	Rick Majerus	27-7
13	Georgia Tech	22-11	Bobby Cremins	24-12
14	UCLA	23-7	Jim Harrick	23-8
15	Syracuse	24-8	Jim Boeheim	29-9
16	Memphis	22-7	Larry Finch	22-8
17	Iowa St.	23-8	Tim Floyd	24-9
18	Penn St.	21-6	Jerry Dunn	21-7
19	Mississippi St.	22-7	Richard Williams	26-8
20	Marquette	22-7	Mike Deane	23-8
21	Iowa	22-8	Tom Davis	23-9
22	Virginia Tech	22-5	Bill Foster	23-6
23	New Mexico	27-4	Dave Bliss	28-5
24	Louisville	20-11	Denny Crum	22-12
25	North Carolina	20-10	Dean Smith	21-11

NCAA Final Four (at the Meadowlands, E. Rutherford, N.J.): **Semifinals**– Kentucky 81, Massachusetts 74; Syracuse 77, Mississippi St. 69. **Championship**– Kentucky 76, Syracuse 67.

NIT Championship (at Madison Square Garden): Nebraska 60, St. Joseph's 56. No top 25 teams played in NIT.

1997

		Before Tourns	Head Coach	Final Record
1	Kansas	32-1	Roy Williams	34-2
2	Utah	26-3	Rick Majerus	29-4
3	Minnesota	27-3	Clem Haskins	31-4
4	North Carolina	24-6	Dean Smith	28-7
5	Kentucky	30-4	Rick Pitino	35-5
6	South Carolina	24-7	Eddie Fogler	24-8
7	UCLA	21-7	Steve Lavin	24-8
8	Duke	23-8	Mike Krzyzewski	24-9
9	Wake Forest	23-6	Dave Odom	24-7
10	Cincinnati	25-7	Bob Huggins	26-8
11	New Mexico	24-7	Dave Bliss	25-8
12	St. Joseph's	24-6	Phil Martelli	26-7
13	Xavier	22-5	Skip Prosser	23-6
14	Clemson	21-9	Rick Barnes	23-10
15	**Arizona**	19-9	Lute Olson	25-9
16	Charleston	28-2	John Kresse	29-3
17	Georgia	24-8	Tubby Smith	24-9
18	Iowa St.	20-8	Tim Floyd	22-9
19	Illinois	21-9	Lon Kruger	22-10
20	Villanova	23-9	Steve Lappas	24-10
21	Stanford	20-7	Mike Montgomery	22-8
22	Maryland	21-10	Gary Williams	21-11
23	Boston College	21-8	Jim O'Brien	22-9
24	Colorado	21-9	Ricardo Patton	22-10
25	Louisville	23-8	Denny Crum	26-9

NCAA Final Four (at the RCA Dome, Indianapolis): **Semifinals**– Kentucky 78, Minnesota 69; Arizona 66, North Carolina 58. **Championship**– Arizona 84, Kentucky 79 (OT).

NIT Championship (at Madison Square Garden): Michigan 82, Florida St. 72. No top 25 teams played in NIT.

1998

		Before Tourns	Head Coach	Final Record
1	North Carolina	30-3	Bill Guthridge	34-4
2	Kansas	34-3	Roy Williams	35-4
3	Duke	29-3	Mike Krzyzewski	32-4
4	Arizona	27-4	Lute Olson	30-5
5	**Kentucky**	29-4	Tubby Smith	35-4
6	Connecticut	29-4	Jim Calhoun	32-5
7	Utah	25-3	Rick Majerus	30-4
8	Princeton	26-1	Bill Carmody	27-2
9	Cincinnati	26-5	Bob Huggins	27-6
10	Stanford	26-4	Mike Montgomery	30-5
11	Purdue	26-7	Gene Keady	28-8
12	Michigan	24-8	Brian Ellerbe	25-9
13	Mississippi	22-6	Rob Evans	22-7
14	South Carolina	23-7	Eddie Fogler	23-8
15	TCU	27-5	Billy Tubbs	27-6
16	Michigan St.	20-7	Tom Izzo	22-8
17	Arkansas	23-8	Nolan Richardson	24-9
18	New Mexico	23-7	Dave Bliss	24-8
19	UCLA	22-8	Steve Lavin	24-9
20	Maryland	19-10	Gary Williams	21-11
21	Syracuse	24-8	Jim Boeheim	26-9
22	Illinois	22-9	Lon Kruger	23-10
23	Xavier	22-7	Skip Prosser	22-8
24	Temple	21-8	John Chaney	21-9
25	Murray St.	29-3	Mark Gottfried	29-4

NCAA Final Four (at the Alamodome, San Antonio): **Semifinals**– Kentucky 86, Stanford 85 (OT); Utah 65, North Carolina 59. **Championship**– Kentucky 78, Utah 69.

NIT Championship (at Madison Square Garden): Minnesota 79, Penn St. 72. No top 25 teams played in NIT.

AP Post-Tournament Final Polls

The final AP Top 20 poll has been released after the NCAA tournament and NIT four times– in 1953 and '54 and again in 1974 and '75. Those four polls are listed below; teams that were not included in the last regular season polls are in CAPITAL italic letters.

1953

		Final Record
1	Indiana	23-3
2	Seton Hall	31-2
3	Kansas	19-6
4	Washington	30-3
5	LSU	24-3
6	La Salle	25-3
7	*ST. JOHN'S*	17-6
8	Okla. A&M	23-7
9	Duquesne	21-8
10	Notre Dame	19-5
11	Illinois	18-4
12	Kansas St.	17-4
13	Holy Cross	20-6
14	Seattle	29-4
15	*WAKE FOREST*	22-7
16	*SANTA CLARA*	20-7
17	Western Ky.	25-6
18	N.C. State	26-6
19	*DEPAUL*	19-9
20	*SW MISSOURI*	24-4

1954

		Final Record
1	Kentucky	25-0
2	La Salle	26-4
3	Holy Cross	26-2
4	Indiana	20-4
5	Duquesne	26-3
6	Notre Dame	22-3
7	*BRADLEY*	19-13
8	Western Ky.	29-3
9	*PENN ST.*	18-6
10	Okla. A&M	24-5
11	USC	19-14
12	*GEO. WASH.*	23-3
13	Iowa	17-5
14	LSU	21-5
15	Duke	22-6
16	*NIAGARA*	24-6
17	Seattle	26-2
18	Kansas	16-5
19	Illinois	17-5
20	*MARYLAND*	23-7

1974

		Final Record
1	N.C. State	30-1
2	UCLA	26-4
3	Marquette	26-5
4	Maryland	23-5
5	Notre Dame	26-3
6	Michigan	22-5
7	Kansas	23-7
8	Providence	28-4
9	Indiana	23-5
10	Long Beach St.	24-2
11	*PURDUE*	22-8
12	North Carolina	22-6
13	Vanderbilt	23-5
14	Alabama	22-4
15	*UTAH*	22-8
16	Pittsburgh	25-4
17	USC	24-5
18	*ORAL ROBERTS*	23-6
19	South Carolina	22-5
20	Dayton	20-9

1975

		Final Record
1	UCLA	28-3
2	Kentucky	26-5
3	Indiana	31-1
4	Louisville	28-3
5	Maryland	24-5
6	Syracuse	23-9
7	N.C. State	22-6
8	Arizona St.	25-4
9	North Carolina	23-8
10	Alabama	22-5
11	Marquette	23-4
12	*PRINCETON*	22-8
13	Cincinnati	23-6
14	Notre Dame	19-10
15	Kansas St.	20-9
16	Drake	19-10
17	UNLV	24-5
18	Oregon St.	19-12
19	*MICHIGAN*	19-8
20	Penn	23-5

Pre-Tournament Records

1953– St. John's (Al DeStefano, 14-5); Wake Forest (Murray Greason, 21-6); Santa Clara (Bob Feerick, 18-6); DePaul (Ray Meyer, 18-7); SW Missouri St. (Bob Vanatta, 19-4 before NAIA tourney). **1954**– Bradley (Forddy Anderson, 15-12); Penn St. (Elmer Gross, 14-5); George Washington (Bill Reinhart, 23-2); Niagara (Taps Gallagher, 22-5); Maryland (Bud Millikan, 23-7). **1974**– Purdue (Fred Schaus, 18-8); Utah (Bill Foster, 19-7); Oral Roberts (Ken Trickey, 21-5). **1975**– Princeton (Pete Carril, 18-8); Michigan (Johnny Orr, 19-7).

Associated Press Final Polls (Cont.)

1999

		Before Tourns	Head Coach	Final Record
1	Duke	32-1	Mike Krzyzewski	37-2
2	Michigan St.	29-4	Tom Izzo	33-5
3	**Connecticut**	28-2	Jim Calhoun	34-2
4	Auburn	27-3	Cliff Ellis	29-4
5	Maryland	26-5	Gary Williams	28-6
6	Utah	27-4	Rick Majerus	28-5
7	Stanford	25-6	Mike Montgomery	26-7
8	Kentucky	25-8	Tubby Smith	28-9
9	St. John's	25-8	Mike Jarvis	28-9
10	Miami-FL	22-6	Leonard Hamilton	23-7
11	Cincinnati	26-5	Bob Huggins	27-6
12	Arizona	22-6	Lute Olson	22-7
13	North Carolina	24-9	Bill Guthridge	24-10
14	Ohio St.	23-8	Jim O'Brien	27-9
15	UCLA	22-8	Steve Lavin	22-9
16	College of Charleston	28-2	John Kresse	28-3
17	Arkansas	22-10	Nolan Richardson	23-11
18	Wisconsin	22-9	Dick Bennett	22-10
19	Indiana	22-10	Bobby Knight	23-11
20	Tennessee	20-8	Jerry Green	21-9
21	Iowa	18-9	Tom Davis	20-10
22	Kansas	22-9	Roy Williams	23-10
23	Florida	20-8	Billy Donovan	22-9
24	NC-Charlotte	22-10	Bob Lutz	23-11
25	New Mexico	24-8	Dave Bliss	25-9

NCAA Final Four (at the Tropicana Field, St. Petersburg): **Semifinals**– Duke 68, Michigan St. 62; Connecticut 64, Ohio St. 58. **Championship**– Connecticut 77, Duke 74.
NIT Championship (at Madison Square Garden): California 61, Clemson 60. No top 25 teams played in NIT.

2001

		Before Tourns	Head Coach	Final Record
1	**Duke**	29-4	Mike Krzyzewski	35-4
2	Stanford	28-2	Mike Montgomery	31-3
3	Michigan St.	24-4	Tom Izzo	28-5
4	Illinois	24-7	Bill Self	27-8
5	Arizona	23-7	Lute Olson	28-8
6	North Carolina	25-6	Matt Doherty	26-7
7	Boston College	26-4	Al Skinner	27-5
8	Florida	23-6	Billy Donovan	24-7
9	Kentucky	22-9	Tubby Smith	24-10
10	Iowa St.	25-5	Larry Eustachy	25-6
11	Maryland	21-10	Gary Williams	25-11
12	Kansas	24-6	Roy Williams	26-7
13	Oklahoma	26-6	Kelvin Sampson	26-7
14	Mississippi	25-7	Rod Barnes	27-8
15	UCLA	21-8	Steve Lavin	23-9
16	Virginia	20-8	Pete Gillen	20-9
17	Syracuse	24-8	Jim Boeheim	25-9
18	Texas	25-8	Rick Barnes	25-9
19	Notre Dame	19-9	Mike Brey	20-10
20	Indiana	21-12	Mike Davis	21-13
21	Georgetown	23-7	Craig Esherick	25-8
22	St. Joseph's	25-6	Phil Martelli	26-7
23	Wake Forest	19-10	Dave Odom	19-11
24	Iowa	22-11	Steve Alford	23-12
25	Wisconsin	18-10	Dick Bennett (2-1) & Brad Soderberg (16-10)	18-11

NCAA Final Four (at the HHH Metrodome, Minneapolis): **Semifinals**–Duke 95, Maryland 84; Arizona 80, Michigan St. 61. **Championship**–Duke 82, Arizona 72.
NIT Championship (at Madison Square Garden): Tulsa 79, Alabama 60. No top 25 teams played in NIT.

2000

		Before Tourns	Head Coach	Final Record
1	Duke	27-4	Mike Krzyzewski	29-5
2	**Michigan St.**	26-7	Tom Izzo	32-7
3	Stanford	26-3	Mike Montgomery	27-4
4	Arizona	26-6	Lute Olson	27-7
5	Temple	26-5	John Chaney	27-6
6	Iowa St.	29-4	Larry Eustachy	32-5
7	Cincinnati	28-3	Bob Huggins	29-4
8	Ohio St.	22-6	Jim O'Brien	23-7
9	St. John's	24-7	Mike Jarvis	25-8
10	LSU	26-5	John Brady	28-6
11	Tennessee	24-6	Jerry Green	26-7
12	Oklahoma	26-6	Kelvin Sampson	27-7
13	Florida	24-7	Billy Donovan	29-8
14	Oklahoma St.	24-6	Eddie Sutton	27-7
15	Texas	23-8	Rick Barnes	24-9
16	Syracuse	26-6	Jim Boeheim	26-6
17	Maryland	24-9	Gary Williams	25-10
18	Tulsa	29-4	Bill Self	32-5
19	Kentucky	22-9	Tubby Smith	23-10
20	Connecticut	24-9	Jim Calhoun	25-10
21	Illinois	21-9	Lon Kruger	22-10
22	Indiana	20-8	Bobby Knight	20-9
23	Miami-FL	21-10	Leonard Hamilton	23-11
24	Auburn	23-9	Cliff Ellis	24-10
25	Purdue	21-9	Gene Keady	24-10

NCAA Final Four (at the RCA Dome, Indianapolis): **Semifinals**– Michigan St. 53, Wisconsin 41; Florida 71, North Carolina 59. **Championship**– Michigan St. 89, Florida 76.
NIT Championship (at Madison Square Garden): Wake Forest 71, Notre Dame 61. No top 25 teams played in NIT.

2002

		Before Tourns	Head Coach	Final Record
1	Duke	29-3	Mike Krzyzewski	32-4
2	Kansas	29-3	Roy Williams	33-4
3	Oklahoma	27-4	Kelvin Sampson	31-5
4	**Maryland**	26-4	Gary Williams	32-4
5	Cincinnati	30-3	Bob Huggins	31-4
6	Gonzaga	29-3	Mark Few	29-4
7	Arizona	22-9	Lute Olson	24-10
8	Alabama	26-7	Mark Gottfried	27-8
9	Pittsburgh	27-5	Ben Howland	29-6
10	Connecticut	24-6	Jim Calhoun	27-7
11	Oregon	23-8	Ernie Kent	26-9
12	Marquette	26-6	Tom Crean	26-7
13	Illinois	24-8	Bill Self	26-9
14	Ohio St.	23-7	Jim O'Brien	24-8
15	Florida	22-8	Billy Donovan	22-9
16	Kentucky	20-9	Tubby Smith	22-10
17	Mississippi St.	26-7	Rick Stansbury	27-8
18	USC	22-9	Henry Bibby	22-10
19	Western Ky.	28-3	Dennis Felton	28-4
20	Oklahoma St.	23-8	Eddie Sutton	23-9
21	Miami-FL	24-7	Perry Clark	24-8
22	Xavier	25-5	Thad Matta	26-6
23	Georgia	21-9	Jim Harrick	22-10
24	Stanford	19-9	Mike Montgomery	20-10
25	Hawaii	27-5	Riley Wallace	27-6

NCAA Final Four (at the Georgia Dome, Atlanta): **Semifinals**–Maryland 97, Kansas 88; Indiana 73, Oklahoma 64. **Championship**–Maryland 64, Indiana 52.
NIT Championship (at Madison Square Garden): Memphis 72, South Carolina 62. No top 25 teams played in NIT.

2003

		Before Tourns	Head Coach	Final Record
1	Kentucky	29-3	Tubby Smith	32-4
2	Arizona	25-3	Lute Olson	28-4
3	Oklahoma	24-6	Kelvin Sampson	27-7
4	Pittsburgh	26-4	Ben Howland	28-5
5	Texas	22-6	Rick Barnes	26-7
6	Kansas	25-7	Roy Williams	30-8
7	Duke	24-6	Mike Krzyzewski	26-7
8	Wake Forest	24-5	Skip Prosser	25-6
9	Marquette	23-5	Tom Crean	27-6
10	Florida	24-7	Billy Donovan	25-8
11	Illinois	24-6	Bill Self	25-7
12	Xavier	25-5	Thad Matta	26-6
13	**Syracuse**	24-5	Jim Boeheim	30-5
14	Louisville	24-6	Rick Pitino	25-7
15	Creighton	29-4	Dana Altman	29-5
16	Dayton	25-5	Oliver Purnell	25-6
17	Maryland	19-9	Gary Williams	21-10
18	Stanford	23-8	Mike Montgomery	23-9
19	Memphis	23-6	John Calipari	23-7
20	Mississippi St.	21-9	Rick Stansbury	21-10
21	Wisconsin	22-7	Bo Ryan	24-8
22	Notre Dame	22-9	Mike Brey	24-10
23	Connecticut	21-9	Jim Calhoun	23-10
24	Missouri	21-10	Quin Snyder	22-11
25	Georgia	19-8	Jim Harrick	same*

*Georgia chose not to participate in any postseason tournaments due to an investigation into academic fraud.
NCAA Final Four (at the Superdome, New Orleans):
Semifinals–Syracuse 95, Texas 84; Kansas 94, Marquette 61. **Championship**–Syracuse 81, Kansas 78.
NIT Championship (at Madison Square Garden): St. John's 70, Georgetown 67. No top 25 teams played in NIT.

2004

		Before Tourns	Head Coach	Final Record
1	Stanford	29-1	Mike Montgomery	30-2
2	Kentucky	26-4	Tubby Smith	27-5
3	Gonzaga	27-2	Mark Few	28-3
4	Oklahoma St.	27-3	Eddie Sutton	31-4
5	St. Joseph's	27-1	Phil Martelli	30-2
6	Duke	27-5	Mike Krzyzewski	31-6
7	Connecticut	27-6	Jim Calhoun	33-6
8	Mississippi St.	25-3	Rick Stansbury	26-4
9	Pittsburgh	29-4	Jamie Dixon	31-5
10	Wisconsin	24-6	Bo Ryan	25-7
11	Cincinnati	24-6	Bob Huggins	25-7
12	Texas	23-7	Rick Barnes	25-8
13	Illinois	24-6	Bruce Weber	26-7
14	Georgia Tech	23-9	Paul Hewitt	28-10
15	N.C. State	20-9	Herb Sendek	21-10
16	Kansas	21-8	Bill Self	24-9
17	Wake Forest	19-9	Skip Prosser	21-10
18	North Carolina	18-10	Roy Williams	19-11
19	Maryland	19-11	Gary Williams	20-12
20	Syracuse	21-7	Jim Boeheim	23-8
21	Providence	20-8	Tim Welsh	20-9
22	Arizona	20-9	Lute Olson	20-10
23	So. Illinois	25-4	Matt Painter	25-5
24	Memphis	21-7	John Calipari	22-8
25	Boston College	23-9	Al Skinner	24-10
	Utah St.	25-3	Stew Morrill	25-4

NCAA Final Four (at the Alamodome, San Antonio):
Semifinals–Georgia Tech 67, Oklahoma St. 65; Connecticut 79, Duke 78. **Championship**–Connecticut 82, Georgia Tech 73.
NIT Championship (at Madison Square Garden): Michigan 62, Rutgers 55. No. 25 Utah St. was the only Top 25 team that played in the NIT.

Annual NCAA Division I Leaders
Scoring

The NCAA did not begin keeping individual scoring records until the 1947-48 season. All averages include postseason games where applicable.

Multiple winners: Pete Maravich and Oscar Robertson (3); Darrell Floyd, Charles Jones, Harry Kelly, Frank Selvy and Freeman Williams (2).

Year		Gm	Pts	Avg	Year		Gm	Pts	Avg
1948	Murray Wier, Iowa	19	399	21.0	1977	Freeman Williams, Portland St.	26	1010	38.8
1949	Tony Lavelli, Yale	30	671	22.4	1978	Freeman Williams, Portland St.	27	969	35.9
1950	Paul Arizin, Villanova	29	735	25.3	1979	Lawrence Butler, Idaho St.	27	812	30.1
1951	Bill Mlkvy, Temple	25	731	29.2	1980	Tony Murphy, Southern-BR	29	932	32.1
1952	Clyde Lovellette, Kansas	28	795	28.4	1981	Zam Fredrick, S. Carolina	27	781	28.9
1953	Frank Selvy, Furman	25	738	29.5	1982	Harry Kelly, Texas Southern	29	862	29.7
1954	Frank Selvy, Furman	29	1209	41.7	1983	Harry Kelly, Texas Southern	29	835	28.8
1955	Darrell Floyd, Furman	25	897	35.9	1984	Joe Jakubick, Akron	27	814	30.1
1956	Darrell Floyd, Furman	28	946	33.8	1985	Xavier McDaniel, Wichita St	31	844	27.2
1957	Grady Wallace, S. Carolina	29	906	31.2	1986	Terrance Bailey, Wagner	29	854	29.4
1958	Oscar Robertson, Cincinnati	28	984	35.1	1987	Kevin Houston, Army	29	953	32.9
1959	Oscar Robertson, Cincinnati	30	978	32.6	1988	Hersey Hawkins, Bradley	31	1125	36.3
1960	Oscar Robertson, Cincinnati	30	1011	33.7	1989	Hank Gathers, Loyola-CA	31	1015	32.7
1961	Frank Burgess, Gonzaga	26	842	32.4	1990	Bo Kimble, Loyola-CA	32	1131	35.3
1962	Billy McGill, Utah	26	1009	38.8	1991	Kevin Bradshaw, US Int'l	28	1054	37.6
1963	Nick Werkman, Seton Hall	22	650	29.5	1992	Brett Roberts, Morehead St	29	815	28.1
1964	Howie Komives, Bowling Green	23	844	36.7	1993	Greg Guy, Texas-Pan Am	19	556	29.3
1965	Rick Barry, Miami-FL	26	973	37.4	1994	Glenn Robinson, Purdue	34	1030	30.3
1966	Dave Schellhase, Purdue	24	781	32.5	1995	Kurt Thomas, TCU	27	781	28.9
1967	Jimmy Walker, Providence	28	851	30.4	1996	Kevin Granger, Texas Southern	24	648	27.0
1968	Pete Maravich, LSU	26	1138	43.8	1997	Charles Jones, LIU-Brooklyn	30	903	30.1
1969	Pete Maravich, LSU	26	1148	44.2	1998	Charles Jones, LIU-Brooklyn	30	869	29.0
1970	Pete Maravich, LSU	31	1381	44.5	1999	Alvin Young, Niagara	29	728	25.1
1971	Johnny Neumann, Ole Miss	23	923	40.1	2000	Courtney Alexander, Fresno St.	27	669	24.8
1972	Dwight Lamar, SW La	29	1054	36.3	2001	Ronnie McCollum, Centenary	27	787	29.1
1973	Bird Averitt, Pepperdine	25	848	33.9	2002	Jason Conley, VMI	28	820	29.3
1974	Larry Fogle, Canisius	25	835	33.4	2003	Ruben Douglas, New Mexico	28	783	28.0
1975	Bob McCurdy, Richmond	26	855	32.9	2004	Keydren Clark, St. Peter's	29	775	26.7
1976	Marshall Rodgers, Texas-Pan Am	25	919	36.8					

Rebounds

The NCAA did not begin keeping individual rebounding records until the 1950-51 season. From 1956-62, the championship was decided on highest percentage of recoveries out of all rebounds made by both teams in all games. All averages include postseason games where applicable.

Multiple winners: Artis Gilmore, Jerry Lucas, Xavier McDaniel, Kermit Washington and Leroy Wright (2).

Year		Gm	No	Avg	Year		Gm	No	Avg
1951	Ernie Beck, Penn	27	556	20.6	1978	Ken Williams, N. Texas	28	411	14.7
1952	Bill Hannon, Army	17	355	20.9	1979	Monti Davis, Tennessee St.	26	421	16.2
1953	Ed Conlin, Fordham	26	612	23.5	1980	Larry Smith, Alcorn State	26	392	15.1
1954	Art Quimby, Connecticut	26	588	22.6	1981	Darryl Watson, Miss. Valley St.	27	379	14.0
1955	Charlie Slack, Marshall	21	538	25.6	1982	LaSalle Thompson, Texas	27	365	13.5
1956	Joe Holup, G. Washington	26	604	25.6	1983	Xavier McDaniel, Wichita St.	28	403	14.4
1957	Elgin Baylor, Seattle	25	508	23.5	1984	Akeem Olajuwon, Houston	37	500	13.5
1958	Alex Ellis, Niagara	25	536	26.2	1985	Xavier McDaniel, Wichita St.	31	460	14.8
1959	Leroy Wright, Pacific	26	652	23.8	1986	David Robinson, Navy	35	455	13.0
1960	Leroy Wright, Pacific	17	380	23.4	1987	Jerome Lane, Pittsburgh	33	444	13.5
1961	Jerry Lucas, Ohio St.	27	470	19.8	1988	Kenny Miller, Loyola-IL	29	395	13.6
1962	Jerry Lucas, Ohio St.	28	499	21.1	1989	Hank Gathers, Loyola-CA	31	426	13.7
1963	Paul Silas, Creighton	27	557	20.6	1990	Anthony Bonner, St. Louis	33	456	13.8
1964	Bob Pelkington, Xavier-OH	26	567	21.8	1991	Shaquille O'Neal, LSU	28	411	14.7
1965	Toby Kimball, Connecticut	23	483	21.0	1992	Popeye Jones, Murray St.	30	431	14.4
1966	Jim Ware, Oklahoma City	29	607	20.9	1993	Warren Kidd, Mid. Tenn. St.	26	386	14.8
1967	Dick Cunningham, Murray St.	22	479	21.8	1994	Jerome Lambert, Baylor	24	355	14.8
1968	Neal Walk, Florida	25	494	19.8	1995	Kurt Thomas, TCU	27	393	14.6
1969	Spencer Haywood, Detroit	22	472	21.5	1996	Marcus Mann, Miss. Valley St.	29	394	13.6
1970	Artis Gilmore, Jacksonville	28	621	22.2	1997	Tim Duncan, Wake Forest	31	457	14.7
1971	Artis Gilmore, Jacksonville	26	603	23.2	1998	Ryan Perryman, Dayton	33	412	12.5
1972	Kermit Washington, American	23	455	19.8	1999	Ian McGinnis, Dartmouth	26	317	12.2
1973	Kermit Washington, American	22	439	20.0	2000	Darren Phillip, Fairfield	29	405	14.0
1974	Marvin Barnes, Providence	32	597	18.7	2001	Chris Marcus, Western Ky.	31	374	12.1
1975	John Irving, Hofstra	21	323	15.4	2002	Jeremy Bishop, Quinnipiac	29	347	12.0
1976	Sam Pellom, Buffalo	26	420	16.2	2003	Brandon Hunter, Ohio	30	378	12.6
1977	Glenn Mosley, Seton Hall	29	473	16.3	2004	Paul Millsap, Louisiana Tech	30	374	12.5

Note: Only three players have ever led the NCAA in scoring and rebounding in the same season: Xavier McDaniel of Wichita St. (1985), Hank Gathers of Loyola-Marymount (1989) and Kurt Thomas of TCU (1995).

Assists

The NCAA did not begin keeping individual assist records until the 1983-84 season. All averages include postseason games where applicable.

Multiple winner: Avery Johnson (2).

Year		Gm	No	Avg
1984	Craig Lathen, IL-Chicago	29	274	9.45
1985	Rob Weingard, Hofstra	24	228	9.50
1986	Mark Jackson, St. John's	36	328	9.11
1987	Avery Johnson, Southern-BR	31	333	10.74
1988	Avery Johnson, Southern-BR	30	399	13.30
1989	Glenn Williams, Holy Cross	28	278	9.93
1990	Todd Lehmann, Drexel	28	260	9.29
1991	Chris Corchiani, N.C. State	31	299	9.65
1992	Van Usher, Tennessee Tech	29	254	8.76
1993	Sam Crawford, N. Mexico St	34	310	9.12
1994	Jason Kidd, California	30	272	9.06
1995	Nelson Haggerty, Baylor	28	284	10.14
1996	Raimonds Miglinieks, UC-Irvine	27	230	8.52
1997	Kenny Mitchell, Dartmouth	26	203	7.81
1998	Ahlon Lewis, Arizona St.	32	294	9.19
1999	Doug Gottlieb, Oklahoma St.	34	299	8.79
2000	Mark Dickel, UNLV	31	280	9.03
2001	Markus Carr, CS-Northridge	32	286	8.94
2002	T.J. Ford, Texas	33	273	8.27
2003	Martell Bailey, Illinois-Chicago	30	244	8.13
2004	Greg Davis, Troy St.	31	256	8.26

Blocked Shots

The NCAA did not begin keeping individual blocked shots records until the 1985-86 season. All averages include post-season games where applicable.

Multiple winners: Keith Closs, David Robinson and Tarvis Williams (2).

Year		Gm	No	Avg
1986	David Robinson, Navy	35	207	5.91
1987	David Robinson, Navy	32	144	4.50
1988	Rodney Blake, St. Joe's-PA	29	116	4.00
1989	Alonzo Mourning, G'town	34	169	4.97
1990	Kenny Green, Rhode Island	26	124	4.77
1991	Shawn Bradley, BYU	34	177	5.21
1992	Shaquille O'Neal, LSU	30	157	5.23
1993	Theo Ratliff, Wyoming	28	124	4.43
1994	Grady Livingston, Howard	26	115	4.42
1995	Keith Closs, Cen. Conn. St.	26	139	5.35
1996	Keith Closs, Cen. Conn. St.	28	178	6.36
1997	Adonal Foyle, Colgate	28	180	6.43
1998	Jerome James, Florida A&M	27	125	4.63
1999	Tarvis Williams, Hampton	27	135	5.00
2000	Ken Johnson, Ohio St.	30	161	5.37
2001	Tarvis Williams, Hampton	32	147	4.59
2002	Wojciech Myrda, La-Monroe	32	172	5.38
2003	Emeka Okafor, Connecticut	33	156	4.73
2004	Anwar Ferguson, Houston	27	111	4.11

All-Time NCAA Division I Individual Leaders

Through 2003-04; includes regular season and tournament games; **Last** column indicates final year played.

CAREER
Scoring

	Points	Yrs	Last	Gm	Pts
1	Pete Maravich, LSU	3	1970	83	3667
2	Freeman Williams, Port. St.	4	1978	106	3249
3	Lionel Simmons, La Salle	4	1990	131	3217
4	Alphonso Ford, Miss. Val. St.	4	1993	109	3165
5	Harry Kelly, Texas Southern	4	1983	110	3066
6	Hersey Hawkins, Bradley	4	1988	125	3008
7	Oscar Robertson, Cincinnati	3	1960	88	2973
8	Danny Manning, Kansas	4	1988	147	2951
9	Alfredrick Hughes, Loyola-IL	4	1985	120	2914
10	Elvin Hayes, Houston	3	1968	93	2884
11	Larry Bird, Indiana St.	3	1979	94	2850
12	Otis Birdsong, Houston	4	1977	116	2832
13	Kevin Bradshaw, Beth-Cook/US Int'l	4	1991	111	2804
14	Allan Houston, Tennessee	4	1993	128	2801
15	Hank Gathers, USC/Loyola-CA	4	1990	117	2723
16	Reggie Lewis, Northeastern	4	1987	122	2708
17	Daren Queenan, Lehigh	4	1988	118	2703
18	Byron Larkin, Xavier-OH	4	1988	121	2696
19	David Robinson, Navy	4	1987	127	2669
20	Wayman Tisdale, Oklahoma	3	1985	104	2661

	Average	Yrs	Last	Pts	Avg
1	Pete Maravich, LSU	3	1970	3667	44.2
2	Austin Carr, Notre Dame	3	1971	2560	34.6
3	Oscar Robertson, Cinn	3	1960	2973	33.8
4	Calvin Murphy, Niagara	3	1970	2548	33.1
5	Dwight Lamar, SW La	2	1973	1862	32.7
6	Frank Selvy, Furman	3	1954	2538	32.5
7	Rick Mount, Purdue	3	1970	2323	32.3
8	Darrell Floyd, Furman	3	1956	2281	32.1
9	Nick Werkman, Seton Hall	3	1964	2273	32.0
10	Willie Humes, Idaho St.	2	1971	1510	31.5
11	William Averitt, Pepperdine	2	1973	1541	31.4
12	Elgin Baylor, Idaho/Seattle	3	1958	2500	31.3
13	Elvin Hayes, Houston	3	1968	2884	31.0
14	Freeman Williams, Port. St.	4	1978	3249	30.7
15	Larry Bird, Indiana St.	3	1979	2850	30.3
16	Bill Bradley, Princeton	3	1965	2503	30.2
17	Rich Fuqua, Oral Roberts	2	1973	1617	29.9
18	Wilt Chamberlain, Kansas	2	1958	1433	29.9
19	Rick Barry, Miami-FL	3	1965	2298	29.8
20	Doug Collins, Illinois St.	3	1973	2240	29.1

	Field Goal Pct.	Yrs	Last	FG	FGA	Pct
1	Steve Johnson, Ore. St.	4	1981	828	1222	.678
2	Michael Bradley, Kentucky/ Villanova	3	2001	441	651	.677
3	Murray Brown, Fla. St.	4	1980	566	847	.668
4	Lee Campbell, M.Tenn St./ SW Mo.St.	3	1990	411	618	.665
5	Warren Kidd, M.Tenn.St.	3	1993	496	747	.664
6	Todd MacCulloch, Wash.	4	1999	702	1058	.664
7	Joe Senser, West Chester	4	1979	476	719	.662
8	Kevin Magee, UC-Irvine	2	1982	552	841	.656
9	Orlando Phillips, Pepperdine	2	1983	404	618	.654
10	Bill Walton, UCLA	3	1974	747	1147	.651

Note: minimum 400 FGs made and an average of four per game.

	Free Throw Pct.	Yrs	Last	FT	FTA	Pct
1	Gary Buchanan, Villanova	4	2003	324	355	.913
2	Greg Starrick, Ky/So.Ill	4	1972	341	375	.909
3	Jack Moore, Nebraska	4	1982	446	495	.901
4	Steve Henson, Kansas St.	4	1990	361	401	.900
5	Steve Alford, Indiana	4	1987	535	596	.898
6	Bob Lloyd, Rutgers	3	1967	543	605	.898
7	Jack Sullivan, Iowa St.	4	2004	354	395	.896
8	Jim Barton, Dartmouth	4	1989	394	440	.895
9	Tommy Boyer, Arkansas	3	1963	315	353	.892
10	Kyle Korver, Creighton	4	2003	312	350	.891

Note: minimum 300 FTs made and an average of 2.5 per game.

	3-Pt Field Goals	Yrs	Last	Gm	3FG
1	Curtis Staples, Virginia	4	1998	122	413
2	Keith Veney, Lamar/Marshall	4	1997	111	409
3	Doug Day, Radford	4	1993	117	401
4	Michael Watson, UMKC	4	2004	117	391
5	Ronnie Schmitz, Missouri-KC	4	1993	112	378

	3-Pt Field Goals/Game	Yrs	Last	3FG	Avg
1	Timothy Pollard, Miss. Vall	2	1989	256	4.57
2	Sydney Grider, LA-Lafayette	2	1990	253	4.36
3	Brian Merriweather, TX-Pan Am	3	2001	332	3.95
4	Josh Heard, Tenn. Tech	2	2000	210	3.82
5	Kareem Townes, La Salle	3	1995	300	3.70

	3-Pt Field Goal Pct.	Yrs	Last	3FG	Att	Pct
1	Tony Bennett, Wisc-GB	4	1992	290	584	.497
2	David Olson, Eastern Ill.	4	1992	262	562	.466
3	Ross Land, N. Arizona	4	2000	308	664	.464
4	Dan Dickau, Washington/ Gonzaga	4	2002	215	465	.462
5	Sean Jackson, Ohio/ Princeton	4	1992	243	528	.460

Note: minimum 200 3FGs made and an average of two per game.

	Games Played	Yrs	Last	Gms
1	Wayne Turner, Kentucky	4	1999	151
2	Christian Laettner, Duke	4	1992	148
3	Danny Manning, Kansas	4	1988	147
4	Shane Battier, Duke	4	2001	146
5	Stacey Augmon, UNLV	4	1991	145
	Jamaal Magloire, Kentucky	4	2000	145

All-Time Highest Scoring Teams
SINGLE SEASON
Scoring Offense

Team	Season	Gm	Pts	Avg
Loyola-CA	1990	32	3918	122.4
Loyola-CA	1989	31	3486	112.5
UNLV	1976	31	3426	110.5
Loyola-CA	1988	32	3528	110.3
UNLV	1977	32	3426	107.1
Oral Roberts	1972	28	2943	105.1
Southern-BR	1991	28	2924	104.4
Loyola-CA	1991	31	3211	103.6
Oklahoma	1988	39	4012	102.9
Oklahoma	1989	36	3680	102.2

All-Time NCAA Division I Individual Leaders (Cont.)
Rebounds

	Total (before 1973)	Yrs	Last	Gm	No
1	Tom Gola, La Salle	.4	1955	118	2201
2	Joe Holup, G. Washington	.4	1956	104	2030
3	Charlie Slack, Marshall	.4	1956	88	1916
4	Ed Conlin, Fordham	.4	1955	102	1884
5	Dickie Hemric, Wake Forest	.4	1955	104	1802
6	Paul Silas, Creighton	.3	1964	81	1751
7	Art Quimby, Connecticut	.4	1955	80	1716
8	Jerry Harper, Alabama	.4	1956	93	1688
9	Jeff Cohen, Wm. & Mary	.4	1961	103	1679
10	Steve Hamilton, Morehead St.	.4	1958	102	1675

	Total (since 1973)	Yrs	Last	Gm	No
1	Tim Duncan, Wake Forest	.4	1997	128	1570
2	Derrick Coleman, Syracuse	.4	1990	143	1537
3	Malik Rose, Drexel	.4	1996	120	1514
4	Ralph Sampson, Virginia	.4	1983	132	1511
5	Pete Padgett, Nevada-Reno	.4	1976	104	1464
6	Lionel Simmons, La Salle	.4	1990	131	1429
7	Anthony Bonner, St. Louis	.4	1990	133	1424
8	Tyrone Hill, Xavier-OH	.4	1990	126	1380
9	Popeye Jones, Murray St.	.4	1992	123	1374
10	Michael Brooks, La Salle	.4	1980	114	1372

	Average (before 1973)	Yrs	Last	No	Avg
1	Artis Gilmore, Jacksonville	.2	1971	1224	22.7
2	Charlie Slack, Marshall	.4	1956	1916	21.8
3	Paul Silas, Creighton	.3	1964	1751	21.6
4	Leroy Wright, Pacific	.3	1960	1442	21.5
5	Art Quimby, Connecticut	.4	1955	1716	21.5

Note: minimum 800 rebounds.

	Average (since 1973)	Yrs	Last	No	Avg
1	Glenn Mosley, Seton Hall	.4	1977	1263	15.2
2	Bill Campion, Manhattan	.3	1975	1070	14.2
3	Pete Padgett, Nevada-Reno	.4	1976	1464	14.1
4	Bob Warner, Maine	.4	1976	1304	13.6
5	Shaquille O'Neal, LSU	.3	1992	1217	13.5

Note: minimum 650 rebounds.

Assists

	Total	Yrs	Last	Gm	No
1	Bobby Hurley, Duke	.4	1993	140	1076
2	Chris Corchiani, N.C. State	.4	1991	124	1038
3	Ed Cota, N. Carolina	.4	2000	138	1030
4	Keith Jennings, E. Tenn. St.	.4	1991	127	983
5	Steve Blake, Maryland	.4	2003	138	972
6	Sherman Douglas, Syracuse	.4	1989	138	960
7	Tony Miller, Marquette	.4	1995	123	956
8	Greg Anthony, Portland/UNLV	.4	1991	138	950
9	Doug Gottlieb, ND/Okla St.	.4	2000	124	947
10	Gary Payton, Oregon St.	.4	1990	120	938

	Average	Yrs	Last	No	Avg
1	Avery Johnson, Southern	.2	1988	732	12.00
2	Sam Crawford, N. Mexico St.	.2	1993	592	8.84
3	Mark Wade, Okla/UNLV	.3	1987	693	8.77
4	Chris Corchiani, N.C. State	.4	1991	1038	8.37
5	Taurence Chisholm, Delaware	.4	1988	877	7.97
6	Van Usher, Tennessee Tech	.3	1992	676	7.95
7	Anthony Manuel, Bradley	.3	1989	855	7.92
8	Chico Fletcher, Ark. St.	.4	2000	893	7.83
9	Gary Payton, Oregon St.	.4	1990	938	7.82
10	Orlando Smart, San Francisco	.4	1994	902	7.78

Note: minimum 550 assists.

Blocked Shots

	Average	Yrs	Last	No	Avg
1	Keith Closs, Cen. Conn. St.	.2	1996	317	5.87
2	Adonal Foyle, Colgate	.3	1997	492	5.66
3	David Robinson, Navy	.2	1987	351	5.24
4	Wojciech Mydra, LA-Monroe	.4	2002	535	4.65
5	Shaquille O'Neal, LSU	.3	1992	412	4.58

Note: minimum 225 blocked shots.

Steals

	Average	Yrs	Last	No	Avg
1	Desmond Cambridge, Ala. A&M	.3	2002	330	3.93
2	Mookie Blaylock, Oklahoma	.2	1989	281	3.80
3	Ronn McMahon, Eastern Wash.	.3	1990	225	3.52
4	Eric Murdock, Providence	.4	1991	376	3.21
5	Van Usher, Tennessee Tech	.3	1992	270	3.18

Note: minimum 225 steals.

2000 Points/1000 Rebounds
For a combined total of 4000 or more.

		Gm	Pts	Reb	Total
1	Tom Gola, La Salle	.118	2462	2201	4663
2	Lionel Simmons, La Salle	.131	3217	1429	4646
3	Elvin Hayes, Houston	.93	2884	1602	4486
4	Dickie Hemric, W. Forest	.104	2587	1802	4389
5	Oscar Robertson, Cinn	.88	2973	1338	4311
6	Joe Holup, G. Wash	.104	2226	2030	4256
7	Harry Kelly, TX-Southern	.110	3066	1085	4151
8	Danny Manning, Kansas	.147	2951	1187	4138
9	Larry Bird, Indiana St.	.94	2850	1247	4097
10	Elgin Baylor, Col. Idaho/ Seattle	.80	2500	1559	4059
11	Michael Brooks, La Salle	.114	2628	1372	4000

Years Played–Baylor (1956-58); **Bird** (1977-79); **Brooks** (1977-80); **Gola** (1952-55); **Hayes** (1966-68); **Hemric** (1952-55); **Holup** (1953-56); **Kelly** (1980-83); **Manning** (1985-88); **Robertson** (1958-60); **Simmons** (1987-90).

SINGLE SEASON
Scoring

	Points	Year	Gm	Pts
1	Pete Maravich, LSU	1970	31	1381
2	Elvin Hayes, Houston	1968	33	1214
3	Frank Selvy, Furman	1954	29	1209
4	Pete Maravich, LSU	1969	26	1148
5	Pete Maravich, LSU	1968	26	1138
6	Bo Kimble, Loyola-CA	1990	32	1131
7	Hersey Hawkins, Bradley	1988	31	1125
8	Austin Carr, Notre Dame	1970	29	1106
9	Austin Carr, Notre Dame	1971	29	1101
10	Otis Birdsong, Houston	1977	36	1090

	Average	Year	Gm	Pts	Avg
1	Pete Maravich, LSU	1970	31	1381	44.5
2	Pete Maravich, LSU	1969	26	1148	44.2
3	Pete Maravich, LSU	1968	26	1138	43.8
4	Frank Selvy, Furman	1954	29	1209	41.7
5	Johnny Neumann, Ole Miss	1971	23	923	40.1
6	Freeman Williams, Port. St.	1977	26	1010	38.8
7	Billy McGill, Utah	1962	26	1009	38.8
8	Calvin Murphy, Niagara	1968	24	916	38.2
9	Austin Carr, Notre Dame	1970	29	1106	38.1
10	Austin Carr, Notre Dame	1971	29	1101	38.0

Field Goal Pct.

		Year	FG	FGA	Pct
1	Steve Johnson, Oregon St.	1981	235	315	.746
2	Dwayne Davis, Florida	1989	179	248	.722
3	Keith Walker, Utica	1985	154	216	.713
4	Steve Johnson, Oregon St.	1980	211	297	.710
5	Adam Mark, Belmont	2002	150	212	.708

Free Throw Pct.

		Year	FT	FTA	Pct
1	Blake Ahearn, SW Mo. St.	2004	117	120	.975
2	Craig Collins, Penn St.	1985	94	98	.959
3	J.J. Redick, Duke	2004	143	150	.953
4	Rod Foster, UCLA	1982	95	100	.950
5	Clay McKnight, Pacific	2000	74	78	.949

3-Pt Field Goal Pct.

		Year	3FG	Att	Pct
1	Glenn Tropf, Holy Cross	1988	52	82	.634
2	Sean Wightman, W. Mich	1992	48	76	.632
3	Keith Jennings, E. Tenn. St.	1991	84	142	.592
4	Dave Calloway, Monmouth	1989	48	82	.585
5	Steve Kerr, Arizona	1988	114	199	.573

Assists

		Year	Gm	No	Avg
	Average				
1	Avery Johnson, Southern-BR	1988	30	399	13.3
2	Anthony Manuel, Bradley	1988	31	373	12.0
3	Avery Johnson, Southern-BR	1987	31	333	10.7
4	Mark Wade, UNLV	1987	38	406	10.7
5	Nelson Haggerty, Baylor	1995	28	284	10.1
6	Glenn Williams, Holy Cross	1989	28	278	9.9
7	Chris Corchiani, N.C. State	1991	31	299	9.7
8	Tony Fairley, Charleston-So.	1987	28	270	9.6
9	Tyrone Bogues, Wake Forest	1987	29	276	9.5
10	Ron Weingard, Hofstra	1985	24	228	9.5

Rebounds

		Year	Gm	No	Avg
	Average (before 1973)				
1	Charlie Slack, Marshall	1955	21	538	25.6
2	Leroy Wright, Pacific	1959	26	652	25.1
3	Art Quimby, Connecticut	1955	25	611	24.4
4	Charlie Slack, Marshall	1956	22	520	23.6
5	Ed Conlin, Fordham	1953	26	612	23.5
	Average (since 1973)				
1	Kermit Washington, American	1973	25	511	20.4
2	Marvin Barnes, Providence	1973	30	571	19.0
3	Marvin Barnes, Providence	1974	32	597	18.7
4	Pete Padgett, Nevada	1973	26	462	17.8
5	Jim Bradley, Northern Ill	1973	24	426	17.8

Blocked Shots

		Year	Gm	No	Avg
	Average				
1	Adonal Foyle, Colgate	1997	28	180	6.42
2	Keith Closs, Cen. Conn. St.	1996	28	178	6.36
3	David Robinson, Navy	1986	35	207	5.91
4	Wojciech Myrda, La-Monroe	2002	32	172	5.38
5	Ken Johnson, Ohio St.	2000	30	161	5.37

Steals

		Year	Gm	No	Avg
	Average				
1	Desmond Cambridge, Ala. A&M	2002	29	160	5.52
2	Darron Brittman, Chicago St.	1986	28	139	4.96
3	Aldwin Ware, Florida A&M	1988	29	142	4.90
4	John Linehan, Providence	2002	31	139	4.48
5	Ronn McMahon, East Wash.	1990	29	130	4.48

SINGLE GAME

Scoring

	Points vs Div. I Team	Year	Pts
1	Kevin Bradshaw, US Int'l vs Loyola-CA	1991	72
2	Pete Maravich, LSU vs Alabama	1970	69
3	Calvin Murphy, Niagara vs Syracuse	1969	68
4	Jay Handlan, Wash. & Lee vs Furman	1951	66
	Pete Maravich, LSU vs Tulane	1969	66
	Anthony Roberts, Oral Rbts vs N.C. A&T	1977	66
7	Anthony Roberts, Oral Rbts vs Ore	1977	65
	Scott Haffner, Evansville vs Dayton	1989	65
9	Pete Maravich, LSU vs Kentucky	1970	64
10	Johnny Neumann, Ole Miss vs LSU	1971	63
	Hersey Hawkins, Bradley vs Detroit	1988	63

	Points vs Non-Div. I Team	Year	Pts
1	Frank Selvy, Furman vs Newberry	1954	100
2	Paul Arizin, Villanova vs Phi. NAMC	1949	85
3	Freeman Williams, Port. St. vs Rocky Mt	1978	81
4	Bill Mlkvy, Temple vs Wilkes	1951	73
5	Freeman Williams, Port. St. vs So. Ore	1977	71
6	Darrell Floyd, Furman vs Morehead St.	1955	67

Note: Bevo Francis of Division II Rio Grande (Ohio) scored an overall collegiate record 113 points against Hillsdale in 1954. He also scored 84 against Alliance and 82 against Bluffton that same season.

3-Pt Field Goals

		Year	No
1	Keith Veney, Marshall vs Morehead St.	1996	15
2	Dave Jamerson, Ohio U. vs Charleston	1989	14
	Askia Jones, Kansas St. vs Fresno St.	1994	14
	Ronald Blackshear, Marshall vs. Akron	2002	14
5	Gary Bossert, Niagara vs Siena	1987	12
	Darrin Fitzgerald, Butler vs Detroit	1987	12
	Al Dillard, Arkansas vs Delaware St.	1993	12
	Mitch Taylor, South-BR vs La. Christian	1995	12
	David McMahan, Winthrop vs C. Carolina	1996	12
	Clarence Gilbert, Missouri vs Colorado	2002	12
	Terrence Woods, Fla. A&M vs Coppin St.	2003	12

Assists

		Year	No
1	Tony Fairley, Baptist vs Armstrong St.	1987	22
	Avery Johnson, Southern-BR vs TX-South	1988	22
	Sherman Douglas, Syracuse vs Providence	1989	22
4	Mark Wade, UNLV vs Navy	1986	21
	Kelvin Scarborough, N. Mexico vs Hawaii	1987	21
	Anthony Manuel, Bradley vs UC-Irvine	1987	21
	Avery Johnson, Southern-BR vs Ala. St.	1988	21

Rebounds

	Total (before 1973)	Year	No
1	Bill Chambers, Wm. & Mary vs Virginia	1953	51
2	Charlie Slack, Marshall vs M. Harvey	1954	43
3	Tom Heinsohn, Holy Cross vs BC	1955	42
4	Art Quimby, UConn vs BU	1955	40
5	Three players tied with 39 each.		

	Total (since 1973)	Year	No
1	Larry Abney, Fresno St. vs SMU	2000	35
2	David Vaughn, Oral Roberts vs Brandeis	1973	34
3	Robert Parish, Centenary vs So. Miss	1973	33
4	Durand Macklin, LSU vs Tulane	1976	32
	Jervaughn Scales, South-BR vs Grambling	1994	32

Blocked Shots

		Year	No
1	David Robinson, Navy vs NC-Wilmington	1986	14
	Shawn Bradley, BYU vs Eastern Ky	1990	14
	Roy Rogers, Alabama vs Georgia	1996	14
	Loren Woods, Arizona vs Oregon	2000	14
5	Five players tied with 13 each.		

Steals

		Year	No
1	Mookie Blaylock, Oklahoma vs Centenary	1987	13
	Mookie Blaylock, Oklahoma vs Loyola-CA	1988	13
3	Kenny Robertson, Cleve. St. vs Wagner	1988	12
	Terry Evans, Oklahoma vs Florida A&M	1993	12
	Richard Duncan, Mid. Tenn St. vs E. Ky.	1999	12
	Greedy Daniels, TCU vs Ark-Pine Bluff	2001	12
	Jehiel Lewis, Navy vs Bucknell	2002	12

Players of the Year and Top Draft Picks

Consensus College Players of the Year and first overall selections in NBA draft since the abolition of the NBA's territorial draft in 1966. Top draft picks who became Rookie of the Year are in **bold** type; (*) indicates top draft pick chosen as junior, (**) indicates top draft pick chosen as sophomore, (†) indicates top draft pick chosen as a high school senior. Only five players have been the unanimous college player of the year, the first overall pick in the NBA draft and then the NBA Rookie of the year.

Year	Player of the Year	Top Draft Pick	Year	Player of the Year	Top Draft Pick
1966	Cazzie Russell, Mich.	Cazzie Russell, NY	1988	Hersey Hawkins, Bradley	
1967	Lew Alcindor, UCLA	Jimmy Walker, Det.		& Danny Manning, Kan.	Danny Manning, LAC
1968	Elvin Hayes, Houston	Elvin Hayes, SD	1989	Sean Elliott, Arizona	
1969	Lew Alcindor, UCLA	**Lew Alcindor**, Mil.		& Danny Ferry, Duke	Pervis Ellison, Sac.
1970	Pete Maravich, LSU	Bob Lanier, Det.	1990	Lionel Simmons, La Salle	**Derrick Coleman**, NJ
1971	Sidney Wicks, UCLA	Austin Carr, Cle.	1991	Larry Johnson, UNLV	
1972	Bill Walton, UCLA	LaRue Martin, Por.		& Shaquille O'Neal, LSU	**Larry Johnson**, Cha.
1973	Bill Walton, UCLA	Doug Collins, Phi.	1992	Christian Laettner, Duke	**Shaquille O'Neal**, Orl.*
1974	Bill Walton, UCLA	Bill Walton, Por.	1993	Calbert Cheaney, Ind.	**Chris Webber**, Orl.**
1975	David Thompson, N.C. St.	David Thompson, Atl.	1994	Glenn Robinson, Purdue	Glenn Robinson, Mil.*
1976	Scott May, Indiana	John Lucas, Hou.	1995	Ed O'Bannon, UCLA	
1977	Marques Johnson, UCLA	Kent Benson, Ind.		& Joe Smith, Maryland	Joe Smith, G. St.**
1978	Butch Lee, Marquette		1996	Marcus Camby, UMass	**Allen Iverson**, Phi.**
	& Phil Ford, N. Caro.	Mychal Thompson, Por.	1997	Tim Duncan, Wake Forest	**Tim Duncan**, SA
1979	Larry Bird, Indiana St.	Magic Johnson, LAL**	1998	Antawn Jamison, N. Caro.	M. Olowokandi, LAC
1980	Mark Aguirre, DePaul	Joe Barry Carroll, G. St.	1999	Elton Brand, Duke	**Elton Brand**, Chi.**
1981	Ralph Sampson, Va.		2000	Kenyon Martin, Cincinnati	Kenyon Martin, NJ
	& Danny Ainge, BYU	Mark Aguirre, Dal.	2001	Shane Battier, Duke	
1982	Ralph Sampson, Va.	James Worthy, LAL*		& Jason Williams, Duke	Kwame Brown, Wash.†
1983	Ralph Sampson, Va.	**Ralph Sampson**, Hou.	2002	Jason Williams, Duke	
1984	Michael Jordan, N. Caro.	Akeem Olajuwon, Hou.		& Drew Gooden, Kansas	Yao Ming, Hou.
1985	Patrick Ewing, Georgetown		2003	T.J. Ford, Texas	
	& Chris Mullin, St. John's	**Patrick Ewing**, NY		& David West, Xavier	**LeBron James**, Cle.†
1986	Walter Berry, St. John's	Brad Daugherty, Cle.	2004	Jameer Nelson, St. Joseph's	
1987	David Robinson, Navy	**David Robinson**, SA		& Emeka Okafor, UConn	Dwight Howard, Orl.†

Annual Awards

UPI picked the first national Division I Player of the Year in 1955. Since then, the U.S. Basketball Writers Assn. (1959), the Commonwealth Athletic Club of Kentucky's Adolph Rupp Trophy (1961), the Atlanta Tip-Off Club (1969), the National Assn. of Basketball Coaches (1975), and the LA Athletic Club's John Wooden Award (1977) have joined in. UPI discontinued its award in 1997. Since 1977, the first year all the following awards were given out, the same player has won all of them in the same season 14 times: Marques Johnson in 1977, Larry Bird in 1979, Ralph Sampson in both 1982 and '83, Michael Jordan in 1984, David Robinson in 1987, Lionel Simmons in 1990, Calbert Cheaney in 1993, Glenn Robinson in 1994, Tim Duncan in 1997, Antawn Jamison in 1998, Elton Brand in 1999, Kenyon Martin in 2000 and Jameer Nelson in 2004.

Wooden Award

Voted on by a panel of coaches, sportswriters and broadcasters and first presented in 1977 by the Los Angeles Athletic Club in the name of former Purdue All-American and UCLA coach John Wooden. Unlike the other five player of the year awards, candidates for the Wooden must have a minimum grade point average of 2.00 (out of 4.00).

Multiple winner: Ralph Sampson (2).

Year		Year		Year	
1977	Marques Johnson, UCLA	1987	David Robinson, Navy	1997	Tim Duncan, Wake Forest
1978	Phil Ford, North Carolina	1988	Danny Manning, Kansas	1998	Antawn Jamison, N. Carolina
1979	Larry Bird, Indiana St.	1989	Sean Elliott, Arizona	1999	Elton Brand, Duke
1980	Darrell Griffith, Louisville	1990	Lionel Simmons, La Salle	2000	Kenyon Martin, Cincinnati
1981	Danny Ainge, BYU	1991	Larry Johnson, UNLV	2001	Shane Battier, Duke
1982	Ralph Sampson, Virginia	1992	Christian Laettner, Duke	2002	Jason Williams, Duke
1983	Ralph Sampson, Virginia	1993	Calbert Cheaney, Indiana	2003	T.J. Ford, Texas
1984	Michael Jordan, N. Carolina	1994	Glenn Robinson, Purdue	2004	Jameer Nelson, St. Joseph's
1985	Chris Mullin, St. John's	1995	Ed O'Bannon, UCLA		
1986	Walter Berry St. John's	1996	Marcus Camby, UMass		

United Press International

Voted on by a panel of UPI college basketball writers and first presented in 1955.
Multiple winners: Oscar Robertson, Ralph Sampson and Bill Walton (3); Lew Alcindor and Jerry Lucas (2).

Year		Year		Year	
1955	Tom Gola, La Salle	1963	Art Heyman, Duke	1971	Austin Carr, Notre Dame
1956	Bill Russell, San Francisco	1964	Gary Bradds, Ohio St.	1972	Bill Walton, UCLA
1957	Chet Forte, Columbia	1965	Bill Bradley, Princeton	1973	Bill Walton, UCLA
1958	Oscar Robertson, Cincinnati	1966	Cazzie Russell, Michigan	1974	Bill Walton, UCLA
1959	Oscar Robertson, Cincinnati	1967	Lew Alcindor, UCLA	1975	David Thompson, N.C. State
1960	Oscar Robertson, Cincinnati	1968	Elvin Hayes, Houston	1976	Scott May, Indiana
1961	Jerry Lucas, Ohio St.	1969	Lew Alcindor, UCLA	1977	Marques Johnson, UCLA
1962	Jerry Lucas, Ohio St.	1970	Pete Maravich, LSU	1978	Butch Lee, Marquette

Year		Year		Year	
1979	Larry Bird, Indiana St.	1986	Walter Berry, St. John's	1993	Calbert Cheaney, Indiana
1980	Mark Aguirre, DePaul	1987	David Robinson, Navy	1994	Glenn Robinson, Purdue
1981	Ralph Sampson, Virginia	1988	Hersey Hawkins, Bradley	1995	Joe Smith, Maryland
1982	Ralph Sampson, Virginia	1989	Danny Ferry, Duke	1996	Ray Allen, UConn
1983	Ralph Sampson, Virginia	1990	Lionel Simmons, La Salle	1997	award discontinued
1984	Michael Jordan, N. Carolina	1991	Shaquille O'Neal, LSU		
1985	Chris Mullin, St. John's	1992	Jim Jackson, Ohio St.		

U.S. Basketball Writers Association

Voted on by the USBWA and first presented in 1959.
Multiple winners: Ralph Sampson and Bill Walton (3); Lew Alcindor, Jerry Lucas and Oscar Robertson (2).

Year		Year		Year	
1959	Oscar Robertson, Cincinnati	1975	David Thompson, N.C. State	1991	Larry Johnson, UNLV
1960	Oscar Robertson, Cincinnati	1976	Adrian Dantley, Notre Dame	1992	Christian Laettner, Duke
1961	Jerry Lucas, Ohio St.	1977	Marques Johnson, UCLA	1993	Calbert Cheaney, Indiana
1962	Jerry Lucas, Ohio St.	1978	Phil Ford, North Carolina	1994	Glenn Robinson, Purdue
1963	Art Heyman, Duke	1979	Larry Bird, Indiana St.	1995	Ed O'Bannon, UCLA
1964	Walt Hazzard, UCLA	1980	Mark Aguirre, DePaul	1996	Marcus Camby, UMass
1965	Bill Bradley, Princeton	1981	Ralph Sampson, Virginia	1997	Tim Duncan, Wake Forest
1966	Cazzie Russell, Michigan	1982	Ralph Sampson, Virginia	1998	Antawn Jamison, N. Carolina
1967	Lew Alcindor, UCLA	1983	Ralph Sampson, Virginia	1999	Elton Brand, Duke
1968	Elvin Hayes, Houston	1984	Michael Jordan, N. Carolina	2000	Kenyon Martin, Cincinnati
1969	Lew Alcindor, UCLA	1985	Chris Mullin, St. John's	2001	Shane Battier, Duke
1970	Pete Maravich, LSU	1986	Walter Berry, St. John's	2002	Jason Williams, Duke
1971	Sidney Wicks, UCLA	1987	David Robinson, Navy	2003	David West, Xavier
1972	Bill Walton, UCLA	1988	Hersey Hawkins, Bradley	2004	Jameer Nelson, St. Joseph's
1973	Bill Walton, UCLA	1989	Danny Ferry, Duke		
1974	Bill Walton, UCLA	1990	Lionel Simmons, La Salle		

Rupp Trophy

Voted on by AP sportswriters and broadcasters and first presented in 1961 by the Commonwealth Athletic Club of Kentucky in the name of former University of Kentucky coach Adolph Rupp.
Multiple winners: Ralph Sampson (3); Lew Alcindor, Jerry Lucas, David Thompson and Bill Walton (2).

Year		Year		Year	
1961	Jerry Lucas, Ohio St.	1976	Scott May, Indiana	1991	Shaquille O'Neal, LSU
1962	Jerry Lucas, Ohio St.	1977	Marques Johnson, UCLA	1992	Christian Laettner, Duke
1963	Art Heyman, Duke	1978	Butch Lee, Marquette	1993	Calbert Cheaney, Indiana
1964	Gary Bradds, Ohio St.	1979	Larry Bird, Indiana St.	1994	Glenn Robinson, Purdue
1965	Bill Bradley, Princeton	1980	Mark Aguirre, DePaul	1995	Joe Smith, Maryland
1966	Cazzie Russell, Michigan	1981	Ralph Sampson, Virginia	1996	Marcus Camby, UMass
1967	Lew Alcindor, UCLA	1982	Ralph Sampson, Virginia	1997	Tim Duncan, Wake Forest
1968	Elvin Hayes, Houston	1983	Ralph Sampson, Virginia	1998	Antawn Jamison, N. Carolina
1969	Lew Alcindor, UCLA	1984	Michael Jordan, N. Carolina	1999	Elton Brand, Duke
1970	Pete Maravich, LSU	1985	Patrick Ewing, Georgetown	2000	Kenyon Martin, Cincinnati
1971	Austin Carr, Notre Dame	1986	Walter Berry, St. John's	2001	Shane Battier, Duke
1972	Bill Walton, UCLA	1987	David Robinson, Navy	2002	Jason Williams, Duke
1973	Bill Walton, UCLA	1988	Hersey Hawkins, Bradley	2003	David West, Xavier
1974	David Thompson, N.C. State	1989	Sean Elliott, Arizona	2004	Jameer Nelson, St. Joseph's
1975	David Thompson, N.C. State	1990	Lionel Simmons, La Salle		

Naismith Award

Voted on by a panel of coaches, sportswriters and broadcasters and first presented in 1969 by the Atlanta Tip-Off Club in 1969 in the name of the inventor of basketball, Dr. James Naismith.
Multiple winners: Ralph Sampson and Bill Walton (3).

Year		Year		Year	
1969	Lew Alcindor, UCLA	1981	Ralph Sampson, Virginia	1993	Calbert Cheaney, Indiana
1970	Pete Maravich, LSU	1982	Ralph Sampson, Virginia	1994	Glenn Robinson, Purdue
1971	Austin Carr, Notre Dame	1983	Ralph Sampson, Virginia	1995	Joe Smith, Maryland
1972	Bill Walton, UCLA	1984	Michael Jordan, N. Carolina	1996	Marcus Camby, UMass
1973	Bill Walton, UCLA	1985	Patrick Ewing, Georgetown	1997	Tim Duncan, Wake Forest
1974	Bill Walton, UCLA	1986	Johnny Dawkins, Duke	1998	Antawn Jamison, N. Carolina
1975	David Thompson, N.C. State	1987	David Robinson, Navy	1999	Elton Brand, Duke
1976	Scott May, Indiana	1988	Danny Manning, Kansas	2000	Kenyon Martin, Cincinnati
1977	Marques Johnson, UCLA	1989	Danny Ferry, Duke	2001	Shane Battier, Duke
1978	Butch Lee, Marquette	1990	Lionel Simmons, La Salle	2002	Jason Williams, Duke
1979	Larry Bird, Indiana St.	1991	Larry Johnson, UNLV	2003	T.J. Ford, Texas
1980	Mark Aguirre, DePaul	1992	Christian Laettner, Duke	2004	Jameer Nelson, St. Joseph's

National Association of Basketball Coaches

Voted on by the National Assn. of Basketball Coaches and presented by the Eastman Kodak Co. from 1975-94.
Multiple winners: Ralph Sampson and Jason Williams (2).

Year		Year		Year	
1975	David Thompson, N.C. State	1986	Walter Berry, St. John's	1997	Tim Duncan, Wake Forest
1976	Scott May, Indiana	1987	David Robinson, Navy	1998	Antawn Jamison, N. Carolina
1977	Marques Johnson, UCLA	1988	Danny Manning, Kansas	1999	Elton Brand, Duke
1978	Phil Ford, North Carolina	1989	Sean Elliott, Arizona	2000	Kenyon Martin, Cincinnati
1979	Larry Bird, Indiana St.	1990	Lionel Simmons, La Salle	2001	Jason Williams, Duke
1980	Michael Brooks, La Salle	1991	Larry Johnson, UNLV	2002	Jason Williams, Duke
1981	Danny Ainge, BYU	1992	Christian Laettner, Duke		& Drew Gooden, Kansas
1982	Ralph Sampson, Virginia	1993	Calbert Cheaney, Indiana	2003	Nick Collison, Kansas
1983	Ralph Sampson, Virginia	1994	Glenn Robinson, Purdue	2004	Jameer Nelson, St. Joseph's
1984	Michael Jordan, N. Carolina	1995	Shawn Respert, Mich. St.		& Emeka Okafor, Connecticut
1985	Patrick Ewing, Georgetown	1996	Marcus Camby, UMass		

All-Time Winningest Division I Coaches

Minimum of 10 seasons as Division I head coach; regular season and tournament games included; coaches active during 2003-04 in **bold** type.

Top 30 Winning Percentage

		Yrs	W	L	Pct
1	Clair Bee	.21	412	87	**.826**
2	Adolph Rupp	.41	876	190	**.822**
3	John Wooden	.29	664	162	**.804**
4	John Kresse	.23	560	143	**.797**
5	**Roy Williams**	.16	437	112	**.796**
6	Jerry Tarkanian	.31	778	202	**.794**
7	Dean Smith	.36	879	254	**.776**
8	Harry Fisher	.13	147	44	**.770**
9	Frank Keaney	.27	387	117	**.768**
10	George Keogan	.24	385	117	**.767**
11	Jack Ramsay	.11	231	71	**.765**
12	Vic Bubas	.10	213	67	**.761**
13	Chick Davies	.21	314	106	**.748**
14	Ray Mears	.21	399	135	**.747**
15	**Mike Krzyzewski**	.29	694	240	**.743**
16	**Jim Boeheim**	.28	676	234	**.743**
17	**Rick Majerus**	.20	431	151	**.741**
18	**Lute Olson**	.31	710	250	**.740**
19	**Bob Huggins**	.23	542	191	**.739**
20	Al McGuire	.20	405	143	**.739**
21	Everett Case	.18	376	133	**.739**
22	Phog Allen	.48	746	264	**.739**
23	Walter Meanwell	.22	280	101	**.735**
24	**Tubby Smith**	.13	315	114	**.734**
25	**Rick Pitino**	.18	416	154	**.730**
26	Lew Andreas	.26	355	134	**.726**
27	Lou Carnesecca	.24	526	200	**.725**
28	Fred Schaus	.12	251	96	**.723**
29	Cam Henderson	.35	630	243	**.722**
30	**John Calipari**	.12	282	109	**.721**

Top 30 Victories

		Yrs	W	L	Pct
1	Dean Smith	.36	**879**	254	.776
2	Adolph Rupp	.41	**876**	190	.822
3	**Bob Knight**	.38	**832**	322	.721
4	Jim Phelan	.49	**830**	524	.613
5	**Lou Henson**	.41	**792**	412	.658
6	Lefty Driesell	.41	**786**	394	.666
7	Jerry Tarkanian	.31	**778**	202	.794
8	Hank Iba	.41	**767**	338	.694
9	Ed Diddle	.42	**759**	302	.715
10	**Eddie Sutton**	.34	**755**	292	.721
11	Phog Allen	.48	**746**	264	.739
12	Norm Stewart	.38	**731**	375	.661
13	Ray Meyer	.42	**724**	354	.672
14	Don Haskins	.38	**719**	353	.671
15	Lute Olson	.31	**710**	250	.740
16	**John Chaney**	.32	**708**	283	.714
17	**Mike Krzyzewski**	.29	**694**	240	.743
18	**Jim Calhoun**	.32	**680**	302	.692
19	**Jim Boeheim**	.28	**676**	234	.743
20	Denny Crum	.30	**675**	295	.696
21	John Wooden	.29	**664**	162	.804
22	Ralph Miller	.38	**657**	382	.632
23	Marv Harshman	.38	**654**	449	.593
24	Gene Bartow	.34	**647**	353	.647
25	Cam Henderson	.35	**630**	243	.722
26	Norm Sloan	.37	**624**	393	.614
27	**Hugh Durham**	.36	**617**	416	.597
28	**Billy Tubbs**	.29	**606**	315	.658
29	Slats Gill	.36	**599**	392	.604
30	Abe Lemons	.34	**597**	344	.634

Note: Clarence (Bighouse) Gaines of Division II Winston-Salem St. (1947-93) retired after the 1992-93 season to finish his 47-year career ranked No. 3 on the all-time NCAA list of all coaches regardless of division. His record is 828-446 with a .650 winning percentage.

Where They Coached

Allen–Baker (1906-08), Kansas (1908-09), Haskell (1909), Central Mo. St. (1913-19), Kansas (1920-56); **Andreas**–Syracuse (1925-43; 45-50); **Bartow**–Central Mo. St. (1962-64), Valparaiso (1965-70), Memphis St. (1971-74), Illinois (1975), UCLA (1976-77), UAB (1979-96); **Bee**–Rider (1929-31), LIU-Brooklyn (1932-45, 46-51); **Boeheim**–Syracuse (1977–); **Bubas**–Duke (1960-69); **Calhoun**–Northeastern (1973-86), Connecticut (1987–); **Calipari** (Massachusetts 1989-96), Memphis (2001–); **Carnesecca**–St. John's (1966-70, 74-92); **Case**–N.C. State (1947-64); **Chaney**–Cheyney St. (1973-82), Temple (1983–); **Crum**–Louisville (1972-01); **Davies**–Duquesne (1925-43, 47-48); **Diddle**–Western Ky. (1923-64); **Driesell**–Davidson (1961-69), Maryland (1970-86), J. Madison (1989-97), Georgia St. (1997-2003); **Durham**–Florida St. (1967-78), Georgia (1979-95), Jacksonville (1999–); **Fisher**–Columbia (1907-16), Army (1922-23, 25).

   Gill–Oregon St. (1929-64); **Harshman**–Pacific Lutheran (1946-58), Wash. St. (1959-71), Washington (1972-85); **Haskins**–UTEP (1962-99); **Henderson**–Muskingum (1920-22), Davis & Elkins (1923-35), Marshall (1936-55); **Henson**–Hardin-Simmons (1963-66), N. Mexico St. (1967-75), Illinois (1976-96), N. Mexico St. (1997–); **Huggins**–Walsh (1981-83), Akron (1985-89), Cincinnati (1990–); **Iba**–NW Missouri St. (1930-33), Colorado (1934), Oklahoma St. (1935-70); **Keaney**–Rhode Island (1921-48); **Keogan**–St. Louis (1916), Allegheny (1919), Valparaiso (1920-21), Notre Dame (1924-43); **Knight**–Army (1966-71), Indiana (1972-00), Texas Tech (2001–); **Kresse**–Charleston (1979-2002); **Krzyzewski**–Army (1976-80), Duke (1981–).

   Lemons–Okla. City (1956-73), Pan American (1974-76), Texas (1977-82), Okla. City (1984-90); **Majerus**–Marquette

(1984-86), Ball St. (1988-89), Utah (1991-2004); **McGuire**–Belmont Abbey (1958-64), Marquette (1965-77); **Meanwell**–Wisconsin (1912-17, 21-34), Missouri (1918-20); **Mears**–Wittenberg (1957-62), Tennessee (1963-77); **Meyer**–DePaul (1943-84); **Miller**–Wichita St. (1952-64), Iowa (1965-70), Oregon St. (1971-89); **Olson**–Long Beach St. (1974), Iowa (1975-83), Arizona (1984–); **Phelan**– Mount St. Mary's (1955-2003); **Pitino**–Boston Univ. (1979-83), Providence (1986-87), Kentucky (1989-97), Louisville (2001–).
Ramsay–St. Joseph's-PA (1956-66); **Rupp**–Kentucky (1931-72); **Schaus**–West Va. (1955-60), Purdue (1973-78); **Sloan**–Presbyterian (1952-55), Citadel (1957-60), Florida (1961-66), N.C. State (1967-80), Florida (1981-89); **D. Smith**–North Carolina (1962-97); **T. Smith**–Tulsa (1992-95), Georgia (1996-97), Kentucky (1998–); **Stewart**–No. Iowa (1962-67), Missouri (1968-99); **Sutton**–Creighton (1970-74), Arkansas (1975-85), Kentucky (1986-89), Oklahoma St. (1991–); **Tarkanian**–Long Beach St. (1969-73), UNLV (1974-92), Fresno St. (1995-2002); **Tubbs**–Southwestern (1971-73), Lamar (1976-80, 2003–), Oklahoma (1981-94), TCU (1995-2002); **Williams**–Kansas (1989-2003), North Carolina (2003–); **Wooden**–Indiana St. (1947-48), UCLA (1949-75).

Most NCAA Tournaments

Through 2004; listed are number of appearances, overall tournament record, times reaching Final Four, and number of NCAA championships. (*) denotes that actual records are different from official NCAA records.

App		W-L	F4	Championships
27	Dean Smith	65-27	11	2 (1982, 93)
25	**Bob Knight**	42-21	5	3 (1976, 81, 87)
25	**Lute Olson***	42-25	5	1 (1997)
25	**Eddie Sutton***	37-25	2	None
23	Denny Crum	42-23	6	2 (1980, 86)
23	**Jim Boeheim**	40-22	3	1 (2003)
20	Adolph Rupp	30-18	6	4 (1948-49, 51, 58)
20	John Thompson	34-19	3	1 (1984)
20	**Mike Krzyzewski**	64-17	10	3 (1991-92, 2001)
19	**Lou Henson**	19-20	2	None
18	Lou Carnesecca	17-20	1	None
18	Jerry Tarkanian	38-18	4	1 (1990)
18	**Gene Keady***	19-18	0	None
17	**Jim Calhoun***	37-15	2	2 (1999, 2004)
17	**John Chaney**	23-17	0	None
16	John Wooden	47-10	12	10 (1964-65, 67-73, 75)
16	Norm Stewart*	12-16	0	None
16	Nolan Richardson	26-15	3	1 (1994)
16	Jim Harrick	18-15	1	1 (1995)
15	**Roy Williams**	35-15	4	None
15	Digger Phelps	17-17	1	None
14	Don Haskins	14-13	1	1 (1966)
14	Guy Lewis	26-18	5	None
14	**Gary Williams**	26-13	2	1 (2002)
14	**Bob Huggins**	19-14	1	None

Active Coaches' Victories

Minimum five seasons in Division I.

		Yrs	W	L	Pct
1	Bob Knight, Texas Tech	38	832	322	.721
2	Lou Henson, N. Mexico St.	41	792	412	.658
3	Eddie Sutton, Okla. St.	34	755	292	.721
4	Lute Olson, Arizona	31	710	250	.740
5	John Chaney, Temple	32	708	283	.714
6	Mike Krzyzewski, Duke	29	694	240	.743
7	Jim Calhoun, UConn	32	680	302	.692
8	Jim Boeheim, Syracuse	28	676	234	.743
9	Hugh Durham, Jacksonville	36	617	416	.597
10	Billy Tubbs, Lamar	29	606	315	.658
11	Tom Davis, Drake	29	555	306	.645
12	Gene Keady, Purdue	26	543	268	.670
13	Bob Huggins, Cincinnati	23	542	191	.739
14	Cliff Ellis, Auburn	29	534	337	.613
15	Gary Williams, Maryland	26	522	293	.640
16	Ben Braun, California	27	490	337	.593
17	Pat Douglass, UC-Irvine	23	482	213	.694
18	Rick Byrd, Belmont	24	462	280	.623
19	Bo Ryan, Wisconsin	20	451	131	.776
20	Roy Williams, North Carolina	16	437	112	.796
21	Pat Kennedy, Towson	24	416	311	.572
	Rick Pitino, Louisville	18	416	154	.730
23	Dick Bennett, Washington St.	22	414	219	.654
24	Kelvin Sampson, Oklahoma	21	411	239	.632
25	John Beilein, West Virginia	22	403	244	.623
26	Danny Nee, Duquesne	24	398	336	.542
27	Mike Vining, Louisiana-Monroe	23	393	284	.581
28	Don Maestri, Troy	22	382	247	.607
29	Nick Macarchuk, Stony Brook	27	362	411	.468
30	Stew Morrill, Utah St.	18	361	184	.662

Annual Awards

UPI picked the first national Division I Coach of the Year in 1955. Since then, the U.S. Basketball Writers Assn. (1959), AP (1967), the National Assn. of Basketball Coaches (1969), and the Atlanta Tip-Off Club (1987) have joined in.

United Press International

Voted on by a panel of UPI college basketball writers and first presented in 1955.
Multiple winners: John Wooden (6); Bob Knight, Ray Meyer, Adolph Rupp, Norm Stewart, Fred Taylor and Phil Woolpert (2).

Year	Year	Year
1955 Phil Woolpert, San Francisco	1970 John Wooden, UCLA	1985 Lou Carnesecca, St. John's
1956 Phil Woolpert, San Francisco	1971 Al McGuire, Marquette	1986 Mike Krzyzewski, Duke
1957 Frank McGuire, North Carolina	1972 John Wooden, UCLA	1987 John Thompson, Georgetown
1958 Tex Winter, Kansas St.	1973 John Wooden, UCLA	1988 John Chaney, Temple
1959 Adolph Rupp, Kentucky	1974 Digger Phelps, Notre Dame	1989 Bob Knight, Indiana
1960 Pete Newell, California	1975 Bob Knight, Indiana	1990 Jim Calhoun, Connecticut
1961 Fred Taylor, Ohio St.	1976 Tom Young, Rutgers	1991 Rick Majerus, Utah
1962 Fred Taylor, Ohio St.	1977 Bob Gaillard, San Francisco	1992 Perry Clark, Tulane
1963 Ed Jucker, Cincinnati	1978 Eddie Sutton, Arkansas	1993 Eddie Fogler, Vanderbilt
1964 John Wooden, UCLA	1979 Bill Hodges, Indiana St.	1994 Norm Stewart, Missouri
1965 Dave Strack, Michigan	1980 Ray Meyer, DePaul	1995 Leonard Hamilton, Miami-FL
1966 Adolph Rupp, Kentucky	1981 Ralph Miller, Oregon St.	1996 Gene Keady, Purdue
1967 John Wooden, UCLA	1982 Norm Stewart, Missouri	1997 award discontinued
1968 Guy Lewis, Houston	1983 Jerry Tarkanian, UNLV	
1969 John Wooden, UCLA	1984 Ray Meyer, DePaul	

Annual Awards (Cont.)
U.S. Basketball Writers Association
Voted on by the USBWA and first presented in 1959.
Multiple winners: John Wooden (5); Bob Knight (3); Lou Carnesecca, John Chaney, Ray Meyer and Fred Taylor (2).

Year	Year	Year
1959 Eddie Hickey, Marquette	1975 Bob Knight, Indiana	1991 Randy Ayers, Ohio St.
1960 Pete Newell, California	1976 Bob Knight, Indiana	1992 Perry Clark, Tulane
1961 Fred Taylor, Ohio St.	1977 Eddie Sutton, Arkansas	1993 Eddie Fogler, Vanderbilt
1962 Fred Taylor, Ohio St.	1978 Ray Meyer, DePaul	1994 Charlie Spoonhour, St. Louis
1963 Ed Jucker, Cincinnati	1979 Dean Smith, North Carolina	1995 Kelvin Sampson, Oklahoma
1964 John Wooden, UCLA	1980 Ray Meyer, DePaul	1996 Gene Keady, Purdue
1965 Butch van Breda Kolff, Princeton	1981 Ralph Miller, Oregon St.	1997 Clem Haskins, Minnesota
1966 Adolph Rupp, Kentucky	1982 John Thompson, Georgetown	1998 Tom Izzo, Michigan St.
1967 John Wooden, UCLA	1983 Lou Carnesecca, St. John's	1999 Cliff Ellis, Auburn
1968 Guy Lewis, Houston	1984 Gene Keady, Purdue	2000 Larry Eustachy, Iowa St.
1969 Maury John, Drake	1985 Lou Carnesecca, St. John's	2001 Al Skinner, Boston College
1970 John Wooden, UCLA	1986 Dick Versace, Bradley	2002 Ben Howland, Pittsburgh
1971 Al McGuire, Marquette	1987 John Chaney, Temple	2003 Tubby Smith, Kentucky
1972 John Wooden, UCLA	1988 John Chaney, Temple	2004 Phil Martelli, St. Joseph's
1973 John Wooden, UCLA	1989 Bob Knight, Indiana	
1974 Norm Sloan, N.C. State	1990 Roy Williams, Kansas	

Associated Press
Voted on by AP sportswriters and broadcasters and first presented in 1967.
Multiple winners: John Wooden (5); Bob Knight (3); Guy Lewis, Ray Meyer, Ralph Miller and Eddie Sutton (2).

Year	Year	Year
1967 John Wooden, UCLA	1980 Ray Meyer, DePaul	1993 Eddie Fogler, Vanderbilt
1968 Guy Lewis, Houston	1981 Ralph Miller, Oregon St.	1994 Norm Stewart, Missouri
1969 John Wooden, UCLA	1982 Ralph Miller, Oregon St.	1995 Kelvin Sampson, Oklahoma
1970 John Wooden, UCLA	1983 Guy Lewis, Houston	1996 Gene Keady, Purdue
1971 Al McGuire, Marquette	1984 Ray Meyer, DePaul	1997 Clem Haskins, Minnesota
1972 John Wooden, UCLA	1985 Bill Frieder, Michigan	1998 Tom Izzo, Michigan St.
1973 John Wooden, UCLA	1986 Eddie Sutton, Kentucky	1999 Cliff Ellis, Auburn
1974 Norm Sloan, N.C. State	1987 Tom Davis, Iowa	2000 Larry Eustachy, Iowa St.
1975 Bob Knight, Indiana	1988 John Chaney, Temple	2001 Matt Doherty, North Carolina
1976 Bob Knight, Indiana	1989 Bob Knight, Indiana	2002 Ben Howland, Pittsburgh
1977 Bob Gaillard, San Francisco	1990 Jim Calhoun, Connecticut	2003 Tubby Smith, Kentucky
1978 Eddie Sutton, Arkansas	1991 Randy Ayers, Ohio St.	2004 Phil Martelli, St. Joseph's
1979 Bill Hodges, Indiana St.	1992 Roy Williams, Kansas	

National Association of Basketball Coaches
Voted on by NABC membership and first presented in 1969.
Multiple winners: John Wooden (3); Gene Keady and Mike Krzyzewski (2).

Year	Year	Year
1969 John Wooden, UCLA	1982 Don Monson, Idaho	1996 John Calipari, UMass
1970 John Wooden, UCLA	1983 Lou Carnesecca, St. John's	1997 Clem Haskins, Minnesota
1971 Jack Kraft, Villanova	1984 Marv Harshman, Washington	1998 Bill Guthridge, N. Carolina
1972 John Wooden, UCLA	1985 John Thompson, Georgetown	1999 Mike Krzyzewski, Duke
1973 Gene Bartow, Memphis St.	1986 Eddie Sutton, Kentucky	& Jim O'Brien, Ohio St.
1974 Al McGuire, Marquette	1987 Rick Pitino, Providence	2000 Gene Keady, Purdue
1975 Bob Knight, Indiana	1988 John Chaney, Temple	2001 Tom Izzo, Michigan St.
1976 Johnny Orr, Michigan	1989 P.J. Carlesimo, Seton Hall	2002 Kelvin Sampson, Oklahoma
1977 Dean Smith, North Carolina	1990 Jud Heathcote, Michigan St.	2003 Tubby Smith, Kentucky
1978 Bill Foster, Duke	1991 Mike Krzyzewski, Duke	2004 Phil Martelli, St. Joseph's
& Abe Lemons, Texas	1992 George Raveling, USC	& Mike Montgomery, Stanford
1979 Ray Meyer, DePaul	1993 Eddie Fogler, Vanderbilt	
1980 Lute Olson, Iowa	1994 Nolan Richardson, Arkansas	
1981 Ralph Miller, Oregon St.	& Gene Keady, Purdue	
& Jack Hartman, Kansas St.	1995 Jim Harrick, UCLA	

Naismith Award
Voted on by a panel of coaches, sportswriters and broadcasters and first presented by the Atlanta Tip-Off Club in 1987 in the name of the inventor of basketball, Dr. James Naismith.
Multiple winner: Mike Krzyzewski (3).

Year	Year	Year
1987 Bob Knight, Indiana	1993 Dean Smith, North Carolina	1999 Mike Krzyzewski, Duke
1988 Larry Brown, Kansas	1994 Nolan Richardson, Arkansas	2000 Mike Montgomery, Stanford
1989 Mike Krzyzewski, Duke	1995 Jim Harrick, UCLA	2001 Rod Barnes, Mississippi
1990 Bobby Cremins, Georgia Tech	1996 John Calipari, UMass	2002 Ben Howland, Pittsburgh
1991 Randy Ayers, Ohio St.	1997 Roy Williams, Kansas	2003 Tubby Smith, Kentucky
1992 Mike Krzyzewski, Duke	1998 Bill Guthridge, N. Carolina	2004 Phil Martelli, St. Joseph's

Player of the Year and NBA MVP

College Players of the Year who have gone on to win the NBA's Most Valuable Player award:

Bill Russell COLLEGE–San Francisco (1956); PROS–Boston Celtics (1958, 1961, 1962, 1963 and 1965).

Oscar Robertson COLLEGE–Cincinnati (1958, 1959 and 1960); PROS–Cincinnati Royals (1964).

Kareem Abdul-Jabbar COLLEGE–UCLA (1967 and 1969); PROS–Milwaukee Bucks (1971, 1972 and 1974) and LA Lakers (1976, 1977 and 1980).

Bill Walton COLLEGE–UCLA (1972, 1973 and 1974); PROS–Portland Trail Blazers (1978).

Larry Bird COLLEGE–Indiana St. (1979); PROS–Boston Celtics (1984, 1985, and 1986).

Michael Jordan COLLEGE–North Carolina (1984); PROS–Chicago Bulls (1988, 1991, 1992, 1996 and 1998).

David Robinson COLLEGE–Navy (1987); PROS–San Antonio Spurs (1995).

Shaquille O'Neal COLLEGE–LSU (1991); PROS–LA Lakers (2000).

Tim Duncan COLLEGE–Wake Forest (1997); PROS–San Antonio Spurs (2002, 2003).

Other Men's Champions

The NCAA has sanctioned national championship tournaments for Division II since 1957 and Division III since 1975. The NAIA sanctioned a single tournament from 1937-91, then split into two divisions in 1992.

NCAA Div. II Finals

Multiple winners: Kentucky Wesleyan (8); Evansville (5); CS-Bakersfield (3); Metropolitan State, North Alabama and Virginia Union (2).

Year	Winner	Score	Loser	Year	Winner	Score	Loser
1957	Wheaton, IL	89-65	Ky. Wesleyan	1982	Dist. of Columbia	73-63	Florida Southern
1958	South Dakota	75-53	St. Michael's, VT	1983	Wright St., OH	92-73	Dist. of Columbia
1959	Evansville, IN	83-67	SW Missouri St.	1984	Central Mo. St.	81-77	St. Augustine's, NC
1960	Evansville	90-69	Chapman, CA	1985	Jacksonville St.	74-73	South Dakota St.
1961	Wittenberg, OH	42-38	SE Missouri St.	1986	Sacred Heart, CT	93-87	SE Missouri St.
1962	Mt. St. Mary's, MD	58-57*	CS-Sacramento	1987	Ky. Wesleyan	92-74	Gannon, PA
1963	South Dakota St.	42-40	Wittenberg, OH	1988	Lowell, MA	75-72	AK-Anchorage
1964	Evansville	72-59	Akron, OH	1989	N.C. Central	73-46	SE Missouri St.
1965	Evansville	85-82*	Southern Illinois	1990	Ky. Wesleyan	93-79	CS-Bakersfield
1966	Ky. Wesleyan	54-51	Southern Illinois	1991	North Alabama	79-72	Bridgeport, CT
1967	Winston-Salem, NC	77-74	SW Missouri St.	1992	Virginia Union	100-75	Bridgeport
1968	Ky. Wesleyan	63-52	Indiana St.	1993	CS-Bakersfield	85-72	Troy St., AL
1969	Ky. Wesleyan	75-71	SW Missouri St.	1994	CS-Bakersfield	92-86	Southern Ind.
1970	Phila. Textile	76-65	Tennessee St.	1995	Southern Indiana	71-63	UC-Riverside
1971	Evansville	97-82	Old Dominion, VA	1996	Fort Hays St.	70-63	N. Kentucky
1972	Roanoke, VA	84-72	Akron, OH	1997	CS-Bakersfield	57-56	N. Kentucky
1973	Ky. Wesleyan	78-76*	Tennessee St.	1998	UC-Davis	83-77	Ky. Wesleyan
1974	Morgan St., MD	67-52	SW Missouri St.	1999	Ky. Wesleyan	75-60	Metropolitan St.
1975	Old Dominion	76-74	New Orleans	2000	Metropolitan St.	97-79	Ky. Wesleyan
1976	Puget Sound, WA	83-74	Tennessee-Chatt.	2001	Ky. Wesleyan	72-63	Washburn, KS
1977	Tennessee-Chatt.	71-62	Randolph-Macon	2002	Metropolitan St.	80-72	Ky. Wesleyan
1978	Cheyney, PA	47-40	WI-Green Bay	2003	Northeastern St., OK	75-64	Ky. Wesleyan
1979	North Alabama	64-50	WI-Green Bay	2004	Kennesaw St., GA	84-59	Southern Indiana
1980	Virginia Union	80-74	New York Tech	*Overtime			
1981	Florida Southern	73-68	Mt. St. Mary's, MD				

NCAA Div. III Finals

Multiple winners: North Park (5); WI-Platteville (4); Calvin, Potsdam St., Scranton and WI-Whitewater (2).

Year	Winner	Score	Loser	Year	Winner	Score	Loser
1975	LeMoyne-Owen, TN	57-54	Glassboro St., NJ	1991	WI-Platteville	81-74	Franklin Marshall
1976	Scranton, PA	60-57	Wittenberg, OH	1992	Calvin, MI	62-49	Rochester, NY
1977	Wittenberg, OH	79-66	Oneonta St., NY	1993	Ohio Northern	71-68	Augustana, IL
1978	North Park, IL	69-57	Widener, PA	1994	Lebanon Valley, PA	66-59*	NYU
1979	North Park, IL	66-62	Potsdam St., NY	1995	WI-Platteville	69-55	Manchester, IN
1980	North Park, IL	83-76	Upsala, NJ	1996	Rowan, NJ	100-93	Hope, MI
1981	Potsdam St., NY	67-65*	Augustana, IL	1997	Illinois Wesleyan	89-86	Neb-Wesleyan
1982	Wabash, IN	83-62	Potsdam St., NY	1998	WI-Platteville	69-56	Hope, MI
1983	Scranton, PA	64-63	Wittenberg, OH	1999	WI-Platteville	76-75**	Hampden-Sydney
1984	WI-Whitewater	103-86	Clark, MA	2000	Calvin, MI	79-74	WI-Eau Claire
1985	North Park, IL	72-71	Potsdam St., NY	2001	Catholic, DC	76-62	Wm. Paterson
1986	Potsdam St., NY	76-73	LeMoyne-Owen, TN	2002	Otterbein	102-83	Elizabethtown
1987	North Park, IL	106-100	Clark, MA	2003	Williams, MA	67-65	Gustavus Adolphus
1988	Ohio Wesleyan	92-70	Scranton, PA	2004	WI-Stevens Point	84-82	Williams
1989	WI-Whitewater	94-86	Trenton St., NJ	*Overtime			
1990	Rochester, NY	43-42	DePauw, IN	**Double overtime			

NAIA Finals, 1937-91

Multiple winners: Grand Canyon, Hamline, Kentucky St. and Tennessee St. (3); Central Missouri, Central St., Fort Hays St. and SW Missouri St. (2).

Year	Winner	Score	Loser	Year	Winner	Score	Loser
1937	Central Missouri	35-24	Morningside, IA	1975	Grand Canyon, AZ	65-54	M'western St., TX
1938	Central Missouri	45-30	Roanoke, VA	1976	Coppin St., MD	96-91	Henderson St., AR
1939	Southwestern, KS	32-31	San Diego St.	1977	Texas Southern	71-44	Campbell, NC
1940	Tarkio, MO	52-31	San Diego St.	1978	Grand Canyon	79-75	Kearney St., NE
1941	San Diego St.	36-32	Murray St., KY	1979	Drury, MO	60-54	Henderson St., AR
1942	Hamline, MN	33-31	SE Oklahoma	1980	Cameron, OK	84-77	Alabama St.
1943	SE Missouri St.	34-32	NW Missouri St.	1981	Beth. Nazarene, OK	86-85*	Al-Huntsville
1944	Not held			1982	SC-Spartanburg	51-38	Biola, CA
1945	Loyola-LA	49-36	Pepperdine, CA	1983	Charleston, SC	57-53	WV-Wesleyan
1946	Southern Illinois	49-40	Indiana St.	1984	Fort Hays St., KS	48-46*	WI-Stevens Pt.
1947	Marshall, WV	73-59	Mankato St., MN	1985	Fort Hays St.	82-80*	Wayland Bapt., TX
1948	Louisville, KY	82-70	Indiana St.	1986	David Lipscomb, TN	67-54	AR-Monticello
1949	Hamline, MN	57-46	Regis, CO	1987	Washburn, KS	79-77	West Virginia St.
1950	Indiana St.	61-47	East Central, OK	1988	Grand Canyon	88-86*	Auburn-Montg, AL
1951	Hamline, MN	69-61	Millikin, IL	1989	St. Mary's, TX	61-58	East Central, OK
1952	SW Missouri St.	73-64	Murray St., KY	1990	Birm-Southern, AL	88-80	WI-Eau Claire
1953	SW Missouri St.	79-71	Hamline, MN	1991	Oklahoma City	77-74	Central Arkansas
1954	St. Benedict's, KS	62-56	Western Illinois		*Overtime		
1955	East Texas St.	71-54	SE Oklahoma				
1956	McNeese St., LA	60-55	Texas Southern				
1957	Tennessee St.	92-73	SE Oklahoma				
1958	Tennessee St.	85-73	Western Illinois				
1959	Tennessee St.	97-87	Pacific-Luth., WA				
1960	SW Texas St.	66-44	Westminster, PA				
1961	Grambling, LA	95-75	Georgetown, KY				
1962	Prairie View, TX	62-53	Westminster, PA				
1963	Pan American, TX	73-62	Western Carolina				
1964	Rockhurst, MO	66-56	Pan American, TX				
1965	Central St., OH	85-51	Oklahoma Baptist				
1966	Oklahoma Baptist	88-59	Georgia Southern				
1967	St. Benedict's, KS	71-65	Oklahoma Baptist				
1968	Central St., OH	51-48	Fairmont St., WV				
1969	Eastern N. Mex	99-76	MD-Eastern Shore				
1970	Kentucky St.	79-71	Central Wash.				
1971	Kentucky St.	102-82	Eastern Michigan				
1972	Kentucky St.	71-62	WI-Eau Claire				
1973	Guilford, NC	99-96	MD-Eastern Shore				
1974	West Georgia	97-79	Alcorn St., MS				

NAIA Div. I Finals

NAIA split tournament into two divisions in 1992.

Multiple winners: Life, GA and Oklahoma City (3).

Year	Winner	Score	Loser
1992	Oklahoma City	82-73*	Central Arkansas
1993	Hawaii Pacific	88-83	Okla. Baptist
1994	Oklahoma City	99-81	Life, GA
1995	Birm-Southern	92-76	Pfeiffer, NC
1996	Oklahoma City	86-80	Georgetown, KY
1997	Life, GA	73-64	Okla. Baptist
1998	Georgetown, KY	83-69	So. Nazarene
1999	Life, GA	63-60	Mobile, AL
2000	Life, GA	61-59	Georgetown, KY
2001	Faulkner, AL	63-59	Science & Arts, OK
2002	Science & Arts, OK	96-79	Okla. Baptist
2003	Concordia, CA	88-84*	Mountain St., WV
2004	Mountain St., WV	74-70	Concordia, CA
	*Overtime		

NAIA Div. II Finals

NAIA split tournament into two divisions in 1992.

Multiple winners: Bethel, IN (3), Northwestern, IA (2).

Year	Winner	Score	Loser	Year	Winner	Score	Loser
1992	Grace, IN	85-79*	Northwestern, IA	2000	Embry-Riddle, FL	75-63	Ozarks, MO
1993	Williamette, OR	63-56	Northern St., SD	2001	Northwestern, IA	82-78	Mid. Am. Nazarene, KS
1994	Eureka, IL	98-95*	Northern St.				
1995	Bethel, IN	103-95*	NW Nazarene, ID	2002	Evangel, MO	84-61	Robert Morris, IL
1996	Albertson, ID	81-72*	Whitworth, WA	2003	Northwestern, IA	77-57	Bethany, KS
1997	Bethel, IN	95-94	Siena Heights, MI	2004	Oregon Tech	81-72	Bellevue, NE
1998	Bethel, IN	89-87	Oregon Tech		*Overtime		
1999	Cornerstone, MI	113-109	Bethel				

WOMEN

NCAA Final Four

Replaced the Association of Intercollegiate Athletics for Women (AIAW) tournament in 1982 as the official playoff for the national championship.

Multiple winners: Tennessee (6); Connecticut (5); Louisiana Tech, Stanford and USC (2)

Year	Champion	Head Coach	Score	Runner-up		Third Place
1982	Louisiana Tech	Sonya Hogg	76-62	Cheyney	Maryland	Tennessee
1983	USC	Linda Sharp	69-67	Louisiana Tech	Georgia	Old Dominion
1984	USC	Linda Sharp	72-61	Tennessee	Cheyney	Louisiana Tech
1985	Old Dominion	Marianne Stanley	70-65	Georgia	NE Louisiana	Western Ky.
1986	Texas	Jody Conradt	97-81	USC	Tennessee	Western Ky.
1987	Tennessee	Pat Summitt	67-44	Louisiana Tech	Long Beach St.	Texas
1988	Louisiana Tech	Leon Barmore	56-54	Auburn	Long Beach St.	Tennessee
1989	Tennessee	Pat Summitt	76-60	Auburn	Louisiana Tech	Maryland
1990	Stanford	Tara VanDerveer	88-81	Auburn	Louisiana Tech	Virginia
1991	Tennessee	Pat Summitt	70-67 (OT)	Virginia	Connecticut	Stanford

Year	Champion	Head Coach	Score	Runner-up		—Third Place—
1992	Stanford	Tara VanDerveer	78-62	Western Kentucky	SW Missouri St.	Virginia
1993	Texas Tech	Marsha Sharp	84-82	Ohio St.	Iowa	Vanderbilt
1994	N. Carolina	Sylvia Hatchell	60-59	Louisiana Tech	Alabama	Purdue
1995	Connecticut	Geno Auriemma	70-64	Tennessee	Georgia	Stanford
1996	Tennessee	Pat Summitt	83-65	Georgia	Connecticut	Stanford
1997	Tennessee	Pat Summitt	68-59	Old Dominion	Stanford	Notre Dame
1998	Tennessee	Pat Summitt	93-75	Louisiana Tech	Arkansas	N.C. State
1999	Purdue	Carolyn Peck	62-45	Duke	Louisiana Tech	Georgia
2000	Connecticut	Geno Auriemma	71-52	Tennessee	Penn St.	Rutgers
2001	Notre Dame	Muffet McGraw	68-66	Purdue	Connecticut	SW Missouri St.
2002	Connecticut	Geno Auriemma	82-70	Oklahoma	Tennessee	Duke
2003	Connecticut	Geno Auriemma	73-68	Tennessee	Texas	Duke
2004	Connecticut	Geno Auriemma	70-61	Tennessee	LSU	Minnesota

Final Four sites: 1982 (Norfolk, Va.), **1983** (Norfolk, Va.), **1984** (Los Angeles), **1985** (Austin), **1986** (Lexington), **1987** (Austin), **1988** (Tacoma), **1989** (Tacoma), **1990** (Knoxville), **1991** (New Orleans), **1992** (Los Angeles), **1993** (Atlanta), **1994** (Richmond), **1995** (Minneapolis), **1996** (Charlotte), **1997** (Cincinnati), **1998** (Kansas City), **1999** (San Jose), **2000** (Philadelphia), **2001** (St. Louis), **2002** (San Antonio), **2003** (Atlanta), **2004** (New Orleans), **2005** (Indianapolis).

Most Outstanding Player

A Most Outstanding Player has been selected every year of the NCAA tournament. Winner who did not play for the tournament champion is listed in **bold,** type.

  Multiple winners: Chamique Holdsclaw, Cheryl Miller and Diana Taurasi (2).

Year	Year	Year
1982 Janice Lawrence, La. Tech	1990 Jennifer Azzi, Stanford	1998 Chamique Holdsclaw, Tenn.
1983 Cheryl Miller, USC	1991 **Dawn Staley**, Virginia	1999 Ukari Figgs, Purdue
1984 Cheryl Miller, USC	1992 Molly Goodenbour, Stanford	2000 Shea Ralph, Connecticut
1985 Tracy Claxton, Old Dominion	1993 Sheryl Swoopes, Texas Tech	2001 Ruth Riley, Notre Dame
1986 Clarissa Davis, Texas	1994 Charlotte Smith, N. Carolina	2002 Swin Cash, Connecticut
1987 Tonya Edwards, Tennessee	1995 Rebecca Lobo, Connecticut	2003 Diana Taurasi, Connecticut
1988 Erica Westbrooks, La. Tech	1996 Michelle Marciniak, Tennessee	2004 Diana Taurasi, Connecticut
1989 Bridgette Gordon, Tennessee	1997 Chamique Holdsclaw, Tenn.	

All-Time NCAA Division I Tournament Leaders

Through 2003-04; minimum of six games; **Last** column indicates final year played.

CAREER

Scoring

	Total Points	Yrs	Last	Pts	Avg
1	Chamique Holdsclaw, Tennessee	4	1999	**479**	21.8
2	Diana Taurasi, Connecticut	4	2004	**428**	18.6
3	Bridgette Gordon, Tenn	4	1989	**388**	21.6
4	Alana Beard, Duke	4	2004	**352**	20.1
5	Cheryl Miller, USC	4	1986	**333**	20.8
6	Janice Lawrence, La. Tech	3	1984	**312**	22.3
7	Penny Toler, Long Beach St	4	1989	**291**	22.4
8	Ruth Riley, Notre Dame	4	2001	**274**	19.7
9	Dawn Staley, Virginia	4	1992	**274**	18.3
10	Tamika Cathcings, Tennessee	4	2000	**269**	16.8
11	Cindy Brown, Long Beach St	3	1987	**263**	21.9
	Venus Lacy, La. Tech	3	1990	**263**	18.8
13	Clarissa Davis, Texas	3	1989	**261**	21.8
14	Sue Bird, Connecticut	3	2002	**260**	15.3
15	Janet Harris, Georgia	4	1985	**254**	19.5

Rebounds

	Total Rebounds	Yrs	Last	No	Avg
1	Chamique Holdsclaw, Tennessee	4	1999	**197**	9.0
2	Cheryl Miller, USC	4	1986	**170**	10.6
3	Sheila Frost, Tennessee	4	1989	**162**	9.0
4	Val Whiting, Stanford	4	1993	**161**	10.1
5	Venus Lacy, La. Tech	3	1990	**148**	10.6
6	Bridgette Gordon, Tennessee	4	1989	**142**	7.9
	Tamika Catchings, Tennessee	3	2000	**142**	8.9
8	Kirsten Cummings, Long Beach St.	4	1985	**136**	10.5
9	Swin Cash, Connecticut	4	2002	**133**	6.7
10	Nora Lewis, La. Tech	3	1990	**130**	9.3
11	Pam McGee, USC	3	1984	**127**	9.8
12	Daedra Charles, Tennessee	3	1991	**125**	9.6
13	Paula McGee, USC	3	1984	**125**	9.6
14	Charlotte Smith, UNC	4	1995	**125**	10.4

SINGLE GAME

Scoring

		Year	Pts
1	Lorri Bauman, Drake vs Maryland	1982	50
2	Sheryl Swoopes, Texas Tech vs Ohio St	1993	47
3	Barbara Kennedy, Clemson vs Penn St	1982	43
4	Jackie Stiles, SW Mo. St. vs Duke	2001	41
5	LaTaunya Pollard, L. Beach St. vs Howard	1982	40
	Cindy Brown, L. Beach St. vs Ohio St	1987	40
	Tamika Whitmore, Memphis vs. YSU	1998	40
	Tara Mitchem, SW Mo. St. vs. Toledo	2001	40

Rebounds

		Year	No
1	Cheryl Taylor, Tenn. Tech vs Georgia	1985	23
	Charlotte Smith, N. Car. vs La. Tech	1994	23
3	Daedra Charles, Tenn. vs SW Missouri	1991	22
4	Cherie Nelson, USC vs Western Ky	1987	21
5	Alison Lang, Oregon vs Missouri	1982	20
	Shelda Arceneaux, S.D. St. vs L. Beach St.	1984	20
	Tracy Claxton, ODU vs Georgia	1985	20
	Brigette Combs, West. Ky. vs West Va	1989	20
	Tandreia Green, West. Ky. vs West Va	1989	20

Associated Press Final Top 10 Polls

The Associated Press weekly women's college basketball poll was begun by Mel Greenberg of *The Philadelphia Inquirer* during the 1976-77 season. Although the poll was started as a Top 20 in 1977 and was expanded to a Top 25 in 1990, only the Top 10 from each poll are listed below due to space constraints. The Association of Intercollegiate Athletics for Women (AIAW) Tournament determined the Division I national champion from 1972-81. The NCAA began its women's Division I tournament in 1982. The final AP Polls were taken before the NCAA tournament. Eventual national champions are in **bold** type.

1977
1 **Delta St.**
2 Immaculata
3 St. Joseph's-PA
4 CS-Fullerton
5 Tennessee
6 Tennessee Tech
7 Wayland Baptist
8 Montclair St.
9 S.F. Austin St.
10 N.C. State

1978
1 Tennessee
2 Wayland Baptist
3 N.C. State
4 Montclair St.
5 **UCLA**
6 Maryland
7 Queens-NY
8 Valdosta St.
9 Delta St.
10 LSU

1979
1 **Old Dominion**
2 Louisiana Tech
3 Tennessee
4 Texas
5 S.F. Austin St.
6 UCLA
7 Rutgers
8 Maryland
9 Cheyney
10 Wayland Baptist

1980
1 **Old Dominion**
2 Tennessee
3 Louisiana Tech
4 South Carolina
5 S.F. Austin St.
6 Maryland
7 Texas
8 Rutgers
9 Long Beach St.
10 N.C. State

1981
1 **Louisiana Tech**
2 Tennessee
3 Old Dominion
4 USC
5 Cheyney
6 Long Beach St.
7 UCLA
8 Maryland
9 Rutgers
10 Kansas

1982
1 **Louisiana Tech**
2 Cheyney
3 Maryland
4 Tennessee
5 Texas
6 USC
7 Old Dominion
8 Rutgers
9 Long Beach St.
10 Penn St.

1983
1 **USC**
2 Louisiana Tech
3 Texas
4 Old Dominion
5 Cheyney
6 Long Beach St.
7 Maryland
8 Penn St.
9 Georgia
10 Tennessee

1984
1 Texas
2 Louisiana Tech
3 Georgia
4 Old Dominion
5 **USC**
6 Long Beach St.
7 Kansas St.
8 LSU
9 Cheyney
10 Mississippi

1985
1 Texas
2 NE Louisiana
3 Long Beach St.
4 Louisiana Tech
5 **Old Dominion**
6 Mississippi
7 Ohio St.
8 Georgia
9 Penn St.
10 Auburn

1986
1 **Texas**
2 Georgia
3 USC
4 Louisiana Tech
5 Western Ky.
6 Virginia
7 Auburn
8 Long Beach St.
9 LSU
10 Rutgers

1987
1 Texas
2 Auburn
3 Louisiana Tech
4 Long Beach St.
5 Rutgers
6 Georgia
7 **Tennessee**
8 Mississippi
9 Iowa
10 Ohio St.

1988
1 Tennessee
2 Iowa
3 Auburn
4 Texas
5 **Louisiana Tech**
6 Ohio St.
7 Long Beach St.
8 Rutgers
9 Maryland
10 Virginia

1989
1 **Tennessee**
2 Auburn
3 Louisiana Tech
4 Stanford
5 Maryland
6 Texas
7 Long Beach St.
8 Iowa
9 Colorado
10 Georgia

1990
1 Louisiana Tech
2 **Stanford**
3 Washington
4 Tennessee
5 UNLV
6 S.F. Austin St.
7 Georgia
8 Texas
9 Auburn
10 Iowa

1991
1 Penn St.
2 Virginia
3 Georgia
4 **Tennessee**
5 Purdue
6 Auburn
7 N.C. State
8 LSU
9 Arkansas
10 Western Ky.

1992
1 Virginia
2 Tennessee
3 **Stanford**
4 S.F. Austin St.
5 Mississippi
6 Miami-FL
7 Iowa
8 Maryland
9 Penn St.
10 SW Missouri St.

1993
1 Vanderbilt
2 Tennessee
3 Ohio St.
4 Iowa
5 **Texas Tech**
6 Stanford
7 Auburn
8 Penn St.
9 Virginia
10 Colorado

1994
1 Tennessee
2 Penn St.
3 Connecticut
4 **North Carolina**
5 Colorado
6 Louisiana Tech
7 USC
8 Purdue
9 Texas Tech
10 Virginia

1995
1 **Connecticut**
2 Colorado
3 Tennessee
4 Stanford
5 Texas Tech
6 Vanderbilt
7 Penn St.
8 Louisiana Tech
9 Western Ky.
10 Virginia

1996
1 Louisiana Tech
2 Connecticut
3 Stanford
4 **Tennessee**
5 Georgia
6 Old Dominion
7 Iowa
8 Penn St.
9 Texas Tech
10 Alabama

1997
1 Connecticut
2 Old Dominion
3 Stanford
4 North Carolina
5 Louisiana Tech
6 Georgia
7 Florida
8 Alabama
9 LSU
10 **Tennessee**

1998
1 **Tennessee**
2 Old Dominion
3 Connecticut
4 Louisiana Tech
5 Stanford
6 Texas Tech
7 North Carolina
8 Duke
9 Arizona
10 N.C. State

1999
1 **Purdue**
2 Tennessee
3 Louisiana Tech
4 Colorado St.
5 Old Dominion
6 Connecticut
7 Rutgers
8 Notre Dame
9 Texas Tech
10 Duke

2000
1 **Connecticut**
2 Tennessee
3 Louisiana Tech
4 Georgia
5 Notre Dame
6 Penn St.
7 Iowa St.
8 Rutgers
9 UC-Santa Barbara
10 Duke

2001
1 Connecticut
2 **Notre Dame**
3 Tennessee
4 Georgia
5 Duke
6 Louisiana Tech
7 Oklahoma
8 Iowa St.
9 Purdue
10 Vanderbilt

2002
1 **Connecticut**
2 Oklahoma
3 Duke
4 Vanderbilt
5 Stanford
6 Tennessee
7 Baylor
8 Louisiana Tech
9 Purdue
10 Iowa St.

2003
1 **Connecticut**
2 Duke
3 LSU
4 Tennessee
5 Texas
6 Louisiana Tech
7 Texas Tech
8 Kansas St.
9 Stanford
10 Purdue

2004
1 Duke
2 Tennessee
3 Purdue
4 Texas
5 Penn St.
6 **Connecticut**
7 Louisiana Tech
8 Kansas St.
9 Houston
10 Stanford

All-Time AP Top 10

The composite AP Top 10 from the 1976-77 season through 2003-04, based on the final regular season rankings of each year. Team points are based on 10 points for all 1st place finishes, 9 for each 2nd, etc. Also listed are the number of times ranked No. 1 by AP going into the tournaments, and times ranked in the pre-tournament Top 10.

		Pts	No.1	Top 10			Pts	No.1	Top 10
1	Tennessee	198	5	26	6	Georgia	72	0	13
2	Louisiana Tech	173	4	24	7	Stanford	67	0	11
3	Connecticut	95	6	11	8	Penn St.	52	1	11
4	Texas	93	4	18	9	Long Beach St.	45	0	10
5	Old Dominion	81	2	11	10	Auburn	42	0	8

All-Time Winningest Division I Teams

Division I schools with best winning percentages (with a minimum of 350 victories) and most victories through 2003-04 (including postseason tournaments). Although official NCAA women's basketball records didn't begin until the 1981-82 season, results from previous seasons are included below.

Top 15 Winning Percentage

		Yrs	W	L	Pct
1	Louisiana Tech	30	853	139	.860
2	Tennessee	59	945	224	.808
3	Texas	30	768	224	.774
4	Old Dominion	35	773	255	.752
5	Montana	30	634	221	.742
6	Stephen F. Austin St.	32	738	260	.739
7	Utah	30	622	241	.721
8	Penn St.	40	692	270	.719
9	Stanford	30	626	255	.711
10	Auburn	33	659	272	.708
11	Texas Tech	29	665	277	.706
12	Virginia	31	648	272	.704
13	Maine	29	551	232	.704
14	St. Peter's	37	641	271	.703
15	Georgia	31	647	274	.702

Top 15 Victories

		Yrs	W	L	Pct
1	Tennessee	59	945	224	.808
2	Louisiana Tech	30	853	139	.860
3	Old Dominion	35	773	255	.752
4	Texas	30	768	224	.774
5	Stephen F. Austin St.	32	738	260	.739
6	James Madison	82	734	428	.632
7	Tennessee Tech	34	727	311	.700
8	Long Beach St.	42	720	327	.688
9	Penn St.	40	692	270	.719
10	Richmond	84	686	468	.594
11	Western Kentucky	42	673	334	.668
12	Ohio St.	39	666	320	.675
13	Texas Tech	29	665	277	.706
14	Auburn	33	659	272	.708
15	Kansas St.	36	654	398	.622

Annual NCAA Division I Leaders

All averages include postseason games

Scoring

Multiple winners: Cindy Blodgett, Andrea Congreaves and Jackie Stiles (2).

Year		Gm	Pts	Avg
1982	Barbara Kennedy, Clemson	31	908	29.3
1983	LaTaunya Pollard, L. Beach St	31	907	29.3
1984	Deborah Temple, Delta St	28	873	31.2
1985	Anucha Browne, Northwestern	28	855	30.5
1986	Wanda Ford, Drake	30	919	30.6
1987	Tresa Spaulding, BYU	28	810	28.9
1988	LeChandra LeDay, Grambling	28	850	30.4
1989	Patricia Hoskins, Miss. Valley	27	908	33.6
1990	Kim Perrot, SW Louisiana	28	839	30.0
1991	Jan Jensen, Drake	30	888	29.6
1992	Andrea Congreaves, Mercer	28	925	33.0
1993	Andrea Congreaves, Mercer	26	805	31.0
1994	Kristy Ryan, CS-Sacramento	26	727	28.0
1995	Koko Lahanas, CS-Fullerton	29	778	26.8
1996	Cindy Blodgett, Maine	32	889	27.8
1997	Cindy Blodgett, Maine	30	810	27.0
1998	Allison Feaster, Harvard	28	797	28.5
1999	Tamika Whitmore, Memphis	32	843	26.3
2000	Jackie Stiles, SW Missouri St.	32	890	27.8
2001	Jackie Stiles, SW Missouri St.	35	1062	30.3
2002	Kelly Mazzante, Penn St.	35	872	24.9
2003	Chandi Jones, Houston	28	770	27.5
2004	Emily Faurholt, Idaho	29	737	25.4

Rebounds

Multiple winner: Patricia Hoskins (2).

Year		Gm	No	Avg
1982	Anne Donovan, Old Dominion	28	412	14.7
1983	Deborah Mitchell, Miss. Col	28	447	16.0
1984	Joy Kellog, Oklahoma City	23	373	16.2
1985	Rosina Pearson, Beth-Cookman	26	480	18.5
1986	Wanda Ford, Drake	30	506	16.9
1987	Patricia Hoskins, Miss. Valley St.	28	476	17.0
1988	Katie Beck, East Tenn. St.	25	441	17.6
1989	Patricia Hoskins, Miss. Valley St.	27	440	16.3
1990	Pam Hudson, Northwestern St	29	438	15.1
1991	Tarcha Hollis, Grambling	29	443	15.3
1992	Christy Greis, Evansville	28	383	13.7
1993	Ann Barry, Nevada	25	355	14.2
1994	DeShawne Blocker, E. Tenn. St.	26	450	17.3
1995	Tera Sheriff, Jackson St.	29	401	13.8
1996	Dana Wynne, Seton Hall	29	372	12.8
1997	Etolia Mitchell, Georgia St.	25	330	13.2
1998	Alisha Hill, Howard	30	397	13.2
1999	Monica Logan, UMBC	27	364	13.5
2000	Malveata Johnson, N.C. A&T	27	363	13.4
2001	Andrea Gardner, Howard	31	439	14.2
2002	Mandi Carver, Idaho St.	27	336	12.4
2003	Jennifer Butler, Massachusetts	28	412	14.7
2004	Ashlee Kelly, Quinnipiac	29	392	13.5

Note: Wanda Ford (1986) and Patricia Hoskins (1989) each led the country in scoring and rebounds in the same year.

All-Time NCAA Division I Individual Leaders

Through 2003-04; includes regular season and tournament games; Official NCAA women's basketball records began with 1981-82 season. Players who competed earlier than that are not included below; **Last** column indicates final year played.

CAREER

Scoring

Average

		Yrs	Last	Pts	Avg
1	Patricia Hoskins, Miss. Valley St.	.4	1989	3122	28.4
2	Sandra Hodge, New Orleans	.4	1984	2860	26.7
3	Jackie Stiles, SW Mo. St.	.4	2001	3206	26.1
4	Lorri Bauman, Drake	.4	1984	3115	26.0
5	Andrea Congreaves, Mercer	.4	1993	2796	25.9
6	Cindy Blodgett, Maine	.4	1998	3005	25.5
7	Valorie Whiteside, Aplach St.	.4	1988	2944	25.4
8	Joyce Walker, LSU	.4	1984	2906	24.8
9	Tarcha Hollis, Grambling	.4	1991	2058	24.2
10	Korie Hlede, Duquesne	.4	1998	2631	24.1

Rebounds

Average

		Yrs	Last	Reb	Avg
1	Wanda Ford, Drake	.4	1986	1887	16.1
2	Patricia Hoskins, Miss. Valley St.	.4	1989	1662	15.1
3	Tarcha Hollis, Grambling	.4	1991	1185	13.9
4	Katie Beck, East Tenn. St.	.4	1988	1404	13.4
5	Marilyn Stephens, Temple	.4	1984	1519	13.0
6	Natalie Williams, UCLA	.4	1994	1137	12.8
7	Cheryl Taylor, Tenn. Tech	.4	1987	1532	12.8
8	DeShawne Blocker, E. Tenn. St.	.4	1995	1361	12.7
9	Olivia Bradley, West Virginia	.4	1985	1484	12.7
10	Judy Mosley, Hawaii	.4	1990	1441	12.6

SINGLE SEASON

Scoring

Average

		Year	Gm	Pts	Avg
1	Patricia Hoskins, Miss.Valley St.	1989	27	908	33.6
2	Andrea Congreaves, Mercer	1992	28	925	33.0
3	Deborah Temple, Delta St.	1984	28	873	31.2
4	Andrea Congreaves, Mercer	1993	26	810	31.0
5	Wanda Ford, Drake	1986	30	919	30.6
6	Anucha Browne, Northwestern	1985	28	855	30.5
7	LeChandra LeDay, Grambling	1988	28	850	30.4
8	Jackie Stiles, SW Mo. St.	2001	35	1062	30.3
9	Kim Perrot, SW Louisiana	1990	28	841	30.0
10	Tina Hutchinson, San Diego St.	1984	30	898	29.9

SINGLE GAME

Scoring

		Year	Pts
1	Cindy Brown, Long Beach St. vs San Jose St.	1987	60
2	Lorri Bauman, Drake vs SW Missouri St.	1984	58
	Kim Perrot, SW La. vs SE La	1990	58
4	Jackie Stiles, SW Mo. St. vs Evansville	2000	56
5	Patricia Hoskins, Miss.Valley St. vs South-BR	1989	55
	Patricia Hoskins, Miss.Valley St. vs Ala. St.	1989	55
7	Wanda Ford, Drake vs SW Missouri St.	1986	54
	Anjinea Hopson, Grambling vs Jackson St.	1994	54
	Mary Lowry, Baylor vs Texas	1994	54
10	Chris Starr, Nevada vs CS-Sacramento	1983	53
	Felisha Edwards, NE La. vs Southern Miss	1991	53
	Sheryl Swoopes, Texas Tech vs Texas	1993	53

Winningest Active Division I Coaches

Minimum of five seasons as Division I head coach; regular season and tournament games included.

Top 10 Winning Percentage

		Yrs	W	L	Pct
1	Geno Auriemma, Connecticut	.19	532	103	.840
2	Pat Summitt, Tennessee	.30	852	167	.836
3	Tara VanDerveer, Stanford	.25	602	168	.782
4	Robin Selvig, Montana	.26	602	172	.778
5	Tom Collen, Louisville	.6	149	43	.776
6	Gail Goestenkors, Duke	.12	302	88	.774
7	Wes Moore, Tenn-Chattanooga	.15	337	100	.771
8	Andy Landers, Georgia	.25	610	189	.763
9	Marsha Sharp, Texas Tech	.22	532	167	.761
10	Jody Conradt, Texas	.35	847	269	.759

Top 10 Victories

		Yrs	W	L	Pct
1	Pat Summitt, Tennessee	.30	852	167	.836
2	Jody Conradt, Texas	.35	847	269	.759
3	Vivian Stringer, Rutgers	.32	695	239	.744
4	Sylvia Hatchell, N. Carolina	.29	654	262	.714
5	Kay Yow, N.C. State	.33	653	300	.685
6	Rene Portland, Penn St.	.28	649	222	.745
7	Theresa Grentz, Illinois	.30	618	270	.696
8	Andy Landers, Georgia	.25	610	189	.763
9	Mike Granelli, St. Peter's	.32	607	249	.709
10	Tara VanDerveer, Stanford	.25	602	168	.782
	Robin Selvig, Montana	.26	602	172	.778

Annual Awards

The Broderick Award was first given out to the Women's Division I or Large School Player of the Year in 1977. Since then, the National Assn. for Girls and Women in Sports (1978), the Women's Basketball Coaches Assn. (1983), the Atlanta Tip-Off Club (1983) and the Associated Press (1995) have joined in.

Since 1983, the first year as many as four awards were given out, the same player has won all of them in the same season twice: Cheryl Miller of USC in 1985 and Rebecca Lobo of Connecticut in 1995.

Associated Press

Voted on by AP sportswriters and broadcasters and first presented in 1995.

Multiple winner: Chamique Holdsclaw (2).

Year	Year	Year
1995 Rebecca Lobo, Connecticut	1999 Chamique Holdsclaw, Tennessee	2003 Diana Taurasi, Connecticut
1996 Jennifer Rizzotti, Connecticut	2000 Tamika Catchings, Tennessee	2004 Alana Beard, Duke
1997 Kara Wolters, Connecticut	2001 Ruth Riley, Notre Dame	
1998 Chamique Holdsclaw, Tennessee	2002 Sue Bird, Connecticut	

Broderick Award

Voted on by a national panel of women's collegiate athletic directors and first presented by the late Thomas Broderick, an athletic outfitter, in 1977. Honda has presented the award since 1987. Basketball Player of the Year is one of 10 nominated for Collegiate Woman Athlete of the Year; (*) indicates player also won Athlete of the Year.

Multiple winners: Chamique Holdsclaw, Nancy Lieberman, Cheryl Miller, Dawn Staley and Diana Taurasi (2).

Year	Year	Year
1977 Lucy Harris, Delta St.*	1979 Nancy Lieberman, Old Dominion*	1981 Lynette Woodard, Kansas
1978 Ann Meyers, UCLA*	1980 Nancy Lieberman, Old Dominion*	1982 Pam Kelly, La. Tech

Year		Year		Year	
1983	Anne Donovan, Old Dominion	1991	Dawn Staley, Virginia	1999	Stephanie White-McCarty, Purdue
1984	Cheryl Miller, USC*	1992	Dawn Staley, Virginia	2000	Shea Ralph, Connecticut
1985	Cheryl Miller, USC	1993	Sheryl Swoopes, Texas Tech	2001	Jackie Stiles, SW Missouri St.*
1986	Kamie Ethridge, Texas*	1994	Lisa Leslie, USC	2002	Sue Bird, Connecticut
1987	Katrina McClain, Georgia	1995	Rebecca Lobo, Connecticut	2003	Diana Taurasi, Connecticut
1988	Teresa Weatherspoon, La. Tech*	1996	Jennifer Rizzotti, Connecticut	2004	Diana Taurasi, Connecticut
1989	Bridgette Gordon, Tennessee	1997	Chamique Holdsclaw, Tennessee		
1990	Jennifer Azzi, Stanford	1998	Chamique Holdsclaw, Tennessee*		

Wade Trophy

Originally voted on by the National Assn. for Girls and Women in Sports (NAGWS) and awarded for academics and community service as well as player performance. First presented in 1978 in the name of former Delta St. coach Lily Margaret Wade. Since 2002, the trophy has been awarded to the Women's Basketball Coaches Association player of the year.

Multiple winner: Nancy Lieberman (2).

Year		Year		Year	
1978	Carol Blazejowski, Montclair St.	1987	Shelly Pennefather, Villanova	1996	Jennifer Rizzotti, Connecticut
1979	Nancy Lieberman, Old Dominion	1988	Teresa Weatherspoon, La. Tech	1997	DeLisha Milton, Florida
1980	Nancy Lieberman, Old Dominion	1989	Clarissa Davis, Texas	1998	Ticha Penicheiro, Old Dominion
1981	Lynette Woodard, Kansas	1990	Jennifer Azzi, Stanford	1999	Stephanie White-McCarty, Purdue
1982	Pam Kelly, La. Tech	1991	Daedra Charles, Tennessee	2000	Edwina Brown, Texas
1983	LaTaunya Pollard, L. Beach St.	1992	Susan Robinson, Penn St.	2001	Jackie Stiles, SW Missouri St.
1984	Janice Lawrence, La. Tech	1993	Karen Jennings, Nebraska	2002	Sue Bird, Connecticut
1985	Cheryl Miller, USC	1994	Carol Ann Shudlick, Minnesota	2003	Diana Taurasi, Connecticut
1986	Kamie Ethridge, Texas	1995	Rebecca Lobo, Connecticut	2004	Alana Beard, Duke

Naismith Trophy

Voted on by a panel of coaches, sportswriters and broadcasters and first presented in 1983 by the Atlanta Tip-Off Club in the name of the inventor of basketball, Dr. James Naismith.

Multiple winners: Cheryl Miller (3); Clarissa Davis, Chamique Holdsclaw, Dawn Staley and Diana Taurasi (2).

Year		Year		Year	
1983	Anne Donovan, Old Dominion	1991	Dawn Staley, Virgina	1999	Chamique Holdsclaw, Tennessee
1984	Cheryl Miller, USC	1992	Dawn Staley, Virginia	2000	Tamika Catchings, Tennessee
1985	Cheryl Miller, USC	1993	Sheryl Swoopes, Texas Tech	2001	Ruth Riley, Notre Dame
1986	Cheryl Miller, USC	1994	Lisa Leslie, USC	2002	Sue Bird, Connecticut
1987	Clarissa Davis, Texas	1995	Rebecca Lobo, Connecticut	2003	Diana Taurasi, Connecticut
1988	Sue Wicks, Rutgers	1996	Saudia Roundtree, Georgia	2004	Diana Taurasi, Connecticut
1989	Clarissa Davis, Texas	1997	Kate Starbird, Stanford		
1990	Jennifer Azzi, Stanford	1998	Chamique Holdsclaw, Tennessee		

Women's Basketball Coaches Association

Voted on by the WBCA and first presented by Champion athletic outfitters in 1983.

Multiple winners: Chamique Holdsclaw, Cheryl Miller and Dawn Staley (2).

Year		Year		Year	
1983	Anne Donovan, Old Dominion	1990	Venus Lacy, La. Tech	1997	Kate Starbird, Stanford
1984	Janice Lawrence, La. Tech	1991	Dawn Staley, Virgina	1998	Chamique Holdsclaw, Tennessee
1985	Cheryl Miller, USC	1992	Dawn Staley, Virginia	1999	Chamique Holdsclaw, Tennessee
1986	Cheryl Miller, USC	1993	Sheryl Swoopes, Texas Tech	2000	Tamika Catchings, Tennessee
1987	Katrina McClain, Georgia	1994	Lisa Leslie, USC	2001	Ruth Riley, Notre Dame
1988	Michelle Edwards, Iowa	1995	Rebecca Lobo, Connecticut	2002	merged with Wade Trophy
1989	Clarissa Davis, Texas	1996	Saudia Roundtree, Georgia		

Wooden Award

Voted on by a panel of coaches, sportswriters and broadcasters and first presented in 2004 by the Los Angeles Athletic Club in the name of former Purdue All-American and UCLA coach John Wooden. Unlike the other player of the year awards, candidates for the Wooden must have a minimum grade point average of 2.00 (out of 4.00).

Year	
2004	Alana Beard, Duke

Coach of the Year Award

Voted on by the Women's Basketball Coaches Assn. and first presented by Converse athletic outfitters in 1983.

Multiple winners: Geno Auriemma and Pat Summitt (3), Jody Conradt, Rene Portland and Vivian Stringer (2).

Year		Year		Year	
1983	Pat Summitt, Tennessee	1991	Rene Portland, Penn St.	1999	Carolyn Peck, Purdue
1984	Jody Conradt, Texas	1992	Ferne Labati, Miami-FL	2000	Geno Auriemma, Connecticut
1985	Jim Foster, St. Joseph's-PA	1993	Vivian Stringer, Iowa	2001	Muffet McGraw, Notre Dame
1986	Jody Conradt, Texas	1994	Marsha Sharp, Texas Tech	2002	Geno Auriemma, Connecticut
1987	Theresa Grentz, Rutgers	1995	Pat Summitt, Tennessee	2003	Gail Goestenkors, Duke
1988	Vivian Stringer, Iowa	1996	Leon Barmore, La. Tech	2004	Rene Portland, Penn St.
1989	Tara VanDerveer, Stanford	1997	Geno Auriemma, Connecticut		
1990	Kay Yow, N.C. State	1998	Pat Summitt, Tennessee		

Other Women's Champions

The NCAA has sanctioned national championship tournaments for Division II and Division III since 1982. The NAIA sanctioned a single tournament from 1981-91, then split in to two divisions in 1992.

NCAA Div. II Finals

Multiple winners: North Dakota St. and Cal Poly Pomona (5); Delta St. and North Dakota (3).

Year	Winner	Score	Loser
1982	Cal Poly Pomona	93-74	Tuskegee, AL
1983	Virginia Union	73-60	Cal Poly Pomona
1984	Central Mo.St.	80-73	Virginia Union
1985	Cal Poly Pomona	80-69	Central Mo.St.
1986	Cal Poly Pomona	70-63	North Dakota St.
1987	New Haven, CT	77-75	Cal Poly Pomona
1988	Hampton, VA	65-48	West Texas St.
1989	Delta St., MS	88-58	Cal Poly Pomona
1990	Delta St., MS	77-43	Bentley, MA
1991	North Dakota St.	81-74	SE Missouri St.
1992	Delta St., MS	65-63	North Dakota St.
1993	North Dakota St.	95-63	Delta St.
1994	North Dakota St.	89-56	CS-San Bernadino
1995	North Dakota St.	98-85	Portland St.
1996	North Dakota St.	104-78	Shippensburg, PA
1997	North Dakota	94-78	S. Indiana
1998	North Dakota	92-76	Emporia St.
1999	North Dakota	80-63	Arkansas Tech
2000	Northern Kentucky	71-62	North Dakota St.
2001	Cal Poly Pomona	87-80*	North Dakota
2002	Cal Poly Pomona	74-62	SE Oklahoma St.
2003	South Dakota St.	65-60	Northern Kentucky
2004	California, PA	75-72	Drury, MO

*Overtime

NCAA Div. III Finals

Multiple winners: Washington (4); Capital, Elizabethtown and WI-Stevens Point (2).

Year	Winner	Score	Loser
1982	Elizabethtown, PA	67-66*	NC-Greensboro
1983	North Central, IL	83-71	Elizabethtown, PA
1984	Rust College, MS	51-49	Elizabethtown, PA
1985	Scranton, PA	68-59	New Rochelle, NY
1986	Salem St., MA	89-85	Bishop, TX
1987	WI-Stevens Pt.	81-74	Concordia, MN
1988	Concordia, MN	65-57	St. John Fisher, NY
1989	Elizabethtown, PA	66-65	CS-Stanislaus
1990	Hope, MI	65-63	St. John Fisher
1991	St. Thomas, MN	73-55	Muskingum, OH
1992	Alma, MI	79-75	Moravian, PA
1993	Central Iowa	71-63	Capital, OH
1994	Capital, OH	82-63	Washington, MO
1995	Capital, OH	59-55	WI-Oshkosh
1996	WI-Oshkosh	66-50	Mt. Union, OH
1997	NYU	72-70	WI-Eau Claire
1998	Washington, MO	77-69	So. Maine
1999	Washington, MO	74-65	Col.of St. Benedict, MN
2000	Washington, MO	79-33	So. Maine
2001	Washington, MO	67-45	Messiah, PA
2002	WI-Stevens Pt.	67-65	St. Lawrence, NY
2003	Trinity, TX	60-58	E. Connecticut St.
2004	Wilmington, OH	59-53	Bowdoin, ME

*Overtime

NAIA Finals

Multiple winners: One tournament–SW Oklahoma (4); Div. I tourney–Southern Nazarene (6), Oklahoma City (4); Arkansas Tech (2); Div. II tourney–Hastings, Northern St. and Western Oregon (2).

Year	Winner	Score	Loser
1981	Kentucky St.	73-67	Texas Southern
1982	SW Oklahoma	80-45	Mo. Southern
1983	SW Oklahoma	80-68	AL-Huntsville
1984	NC-Asheville	72-70*	Portland, OR
1985	SW Oklahoma	55-54	Saginaw Val., MI
1986	Francis Marion, SC	75-65	Wayland Baptist, TX
1987	SW Oklahoma	60-58	North Georgia
1988	Oklahoma City	113-95	Claflin, SC
1989	So. Nazarene, OK	98-96	Claflin, SC
1990	SW Oklahoma	82-75	AR-Monticello
1991	Ft. Hays St., KS	57-53	SW Oklahoma
1992	I– Arkansas Tech	84-68	Wayland Baptist, TX
	II– Northern St., SD	73-56	Tarleton St., TX
1993	I– Arkansas Tech	76-75	Union, TN
	II– No. Montana	71-68	Northern St., SD
1994	I– So. Nazarene	97-74	David Lipscomb, TN
	II– Northern St., SD	48-45	Western Oregon
1995	I– So. Nazarene	78-77	SE Oklahoma
	II– Western Oregon	75-67	NW Nazarene, ID
1996	I– So. Nazarene	80-79	SE Oklahoma
	II– Western Oregon	80-77	Huron, SD

Year	Winner	Score	Loser
1997	I– So. Nazarene	78-73	Union, TN
	II– NW Nazarene	64-46	Black Hills St., SD
1998	I– Union, TN	73-70	So. Nazarene
	II– Walsh, OH	73-66	Mary Hardin-Baylor
1999	I– Oklahoma City	72-55	Simon Fraser, B.C.
	II– Shawnee St., OH	80-65	St. Francis, IN
2000	I– Oklahoma City	64-55	Simon Fraser, B.C.
	II– Mary, N.D.	59-49	Northwestern, IA
2001	I– Oklahoma City	69-52	Auburn Montgomery, AL
	II– Northwestern, IA	77-50	Albertson, ID
2002	I– Oklahoma City	82-73	So. Nazarene
	II– Hastings, NE	73-69	Cornerstone, MI
2003	I–So. Nazarene	71-70	Oklahoma City
	II–Hastings, NE	59-53	Dakota Wesleyan
2004	I–So. Nazarene	77-61	Oklahoma City
	II–Morningside	70-62	Mary, N.D.

*Overtime

AIAW Finals

The Association of Intercollegiate Athletics for Women Large College tournament determined the women's national champion for 10 years until supplanted by the NCAA.

In 1982, most Division I teams entered the first NCAA tournament rather than the last one staged by the AIAW.

Year	Winner	Score	Loser	Year	Winner	Score	Loser
1972	Immaculata, PA	52-48	West Chester, PA	1978	UCLA	90-74	Maryland
1973	Immaculata, PA	59-52	Queens College, NY	1979	Old Dominion	75-65	Louisiana Tech
1974	Immaculata, PA	68-53	Mississippi College	1980	Old Dominion	68-53	Tennessee
1975	Delta St., MS	90-81	Immaculata, PA	1981	Louisiana Tech	79-59	Tennessee
1976	Delta St., MS	69-64	Immaculata, PA	1982	Rutgers	83-77	Texas
1977	Delta St., MS	68-55	LSU				

Professional Basketball

Chauncey Billups and the Detroit Pistons beat
the odds and Lakers, winning the 2004 NBA title.

AP/Wide World Photos

Surprise Endings

Larry Brown coached two teams in 2004. One was a pleasant surprise. The other? Not so much.

Jerry Bembry
is the NBA Editor for ESPN The Magazine.

It was at a late regular season game in March when NBA commissioner David Stern, in Minneapolis for a Timberwolves/Spurs game, was asked about the number of players who were either pulling out of their Olympic commitments or declining invites altogether. "My view," Stern said that night, "is that if we can't, out of the top 50 players in the NBA, send a team that competes with the best in the world, we've taken a big step back. I'm not worried about it."

Commish, there's a lot to worry about. The biggest basketball story of 2004 was not who won the NBA championship, or who stood out in a stellar rookie class, or who got traded. The biggest story turned out to be NBA players losing for the first time since they started representing Olympic competition and then having to fight and claw so they could step up to the medal stand to accept bronze (Argentina won gold, and Italy won silver).

And a summer that Allen Iverson, Tim Duncan and company assumed would be an extended Greek vacation where not a lot of ener-

gy would be exerted became one of the biggest stories of the year. The signs of what was to come were visible: Team USA failed miserably during the 2002 World Championships. The fallout will likely be the assembly of not the best team to market, but the best team (a couple of guys who can shoot won't be a bad thing).

Everyone assumed the best team, period, in 2004 would have been the Los Angeles Lakers. Gary Payton and Karl Malone joined forces with Kobe Bryant and Shaquille O'Neal, giving the Lakers four hall of famers in the starting lineup. But Payton's glove proved to be—based on the way guys blew by him—worn. And Mailman's knees, by playoff time, proved to be worn out. With Shaq feuding with Kobe, Kobe feuding with Phil and Phil feuding with management, it's miraculous that the Lakers even got to the Finals.

Just as in the Olympics, the best "team" came out victorious in the Finals. Let's be honest, after watching the Pistons score more than 75 points just twice in their Eastern Conference finals series with Indiana, it was hard to imagine Detroit even being competitive.

AP/Wide World Photos

*The **United States men's basketball team** took home an unfamiliar and unwelcome Olympic souvenir from its visit to Athens in 2004, the bronze medal.*

But heeding head coach Larry Brown's urging to do things "the right way" the Pistons, with no true superstar (eventual Finals MVP Chauncey Billups played for four teams in his first four seasons before finding a home in Detroit), crushed the Lakers in an outcome that was nearly as shocking as Team USA's Olympic shortcomings. "They had better individual talent," said Billups, the first MVP without an All-Star appearance since Joe Dumars in 1990. "We just felt like we had the better team."

And which team had the season's best rookie? Cleveland's LeBron James came away with the Rookie of the Year Award and demonstrated unbelievable ability and poise for a teenager who came into the league with a giant bulls-eye on his back. But when you put accomplishments over style you can argue that Denver's Carmelo Anthony and Miami's Dwyane Wade had better years because they both helped lead their teams into the playoffs.

Speaking of the playoffs, a couple of postseason mainstays—the Blazers and the Jazz—were noticeably absent this year. Portland's streak of 21 straight playoff appearances ended with their first non-winning (41-41) record since the 1988-89 season. Utah's own streak of 21 straight playoff appearances ended as well, but not without Jerry Sloan pulling off perhaps the finest coaching job of his long career in getting a 42-40 record out of a team playing in the wake of the departure of future hall of famers Karl Malone and John Stockton.

Kobe Bryant and *Shaquille O'Neal* are left wondering what may have been if they could have both stayed in Los Angeles. The duo won three titles in eight seasons together with the Lakers.

For a lot of NBA players—like K-Mart—it was a summer of change. The breakup of the Lakers resulted in Shaq being banished to South Beach, placing Lamar Odom—after resurrecting his career with Miami—back in Los Angeles. Steve Francis got a taste of the playoffs for the first time in his career with the Rockets, but got dealt for Tracy McGrady, who couldn't keep the Magic from the league's worst record. Other guys who took on new addresses over the summer: Steve Nash (Dallas to Phoenix), Antoine Walker (Dallas to Atlanta) and Carlos Boozer (Cleveland to Utah).

A guy lucky enough to maintain his current address is Kobe Bryant, who last season bounced—sometimes on the same day—from the court of law to the court of ball as allegations of a sexual assault threatened to send him to jail. By the end of the summer all of the criminal charges against Kobe were dropped, allowing him to shift his focus to reviving a Lakers' team that once dominated the NBA's top spot.

There was a time when Team USA, with its players from the NBA, dominated the world's top spot. But that air of superiority was shattered in Athens (the cracks had materialized during a fifth place finish in the 2002 World Championships).

It'll be a long four years for Team USA to lick those wounds from their 2004 Olympic Bronze. Let's just hope by 2008 we'll assemble a team based on the ability to hit a jump shot, as opposed to a team based on the ability of its players to sell a Wheaties box.

Jerry Bembry's Ten Biggest
Stories of the Year in Pro Basketball

10 **Comeback's a no 'Zo.** Alonzo Mourning's attempt was valiant, having missed the previous season with a life-threatening kidney ailment. But barely into his comeback, Mourning's concerns went from points and rebounds to finding a kidney that would keep him alive. After a successful kidney transplant, could Zo play again? Don't count this guy out.

9 **Beware the Grizzlies.** The Grizzlies, in eight seasons, had never won more than 28 games and were so bad Vancouver bailed on the team. Give Jerry West credit for hiring Hubie Brown. Give Brown praise for trusting Jason Williams. And give the players props for having faith in a system where 10 guys played big minutes with only one (Pau Gasol) averaging more than 30. The result: 50 wins and a playoff berth for the first time in history.

8 **KG's MVP season.** We all knew Kevin Garnett could ball. But with new sidekicks Sam Cassell and Latrell Sprewell, KG played at an another level in finishing third in the NBA in scoring (24.2), first in rebounding (13.9) and first in the league's MVP voting. More importantly, KG helped the Wolves to the best record in the West, and carried a team that had never won a playoff series to the conference finals.

7 **Who's the Coach?** Phil Jackson wins a record-tying nine rings as coach and gets ousted. Byron Scott takes the Nets to two straight Finals and gets canned. Rick Carlisle, after getting axed by the Pistons, takes the Pacers to an NBA-best 61 wins. Oh, yeah, the guy who replaced Carlisle in Detroit, Larry Brown, took the Pistons to the 2004 NBA crown. From the end of the 2002-03 season to the summer of 2004 every Eastern Conference team got a new coach. Bernie Bickerstaff had the sixth longest tenure in the East before coaching his first game with the expansion Charlotte Bobcats.

6 **Summer of change.** Coming to a discount rack near you: Shaq's Laker jersey, T-Mac's Magic jersey, and K-Mart's Nets jersey. It's hard to remember a summer where so many big names switched teams. Suddenly, the Heat (Shaq) and Magic (Steve Francis and Cuttino Mobley) are major players in the East, while out West, the Jazz (Carlos Boozer and Mehmet Okur) could return to the playoffs after a one-year absence.

5 **Youth is served.** Again. The Magic take Dwight Howard with the first pick of the draft and now in three of the last four drafts high school kids were the top selection. In all, four school kids were lottery picks and eight of the nine high schoolers in the draft were among the first 19 players taken. And the reason why expectations of these kids is so high is due to...

4 **LeBron mania.** From opening night when he dropped 25 points, nine assists and six boards on Sacramento, James demonstrated why Nike and Sprite gave him millions before he took his first shot. His prep-to-pros transition was the most successful in history, better than KG's, Kobe's and T-Mac's. But until he takes the Cavs through a couple of deep playoff runs, we'll refrain from anointing him king.

3 **Return of the Bad Boys.** We all gave the Pistons a chance to *reach* the Finals when they acquired Rasheed Wallace but who gave this team a shot against the Lakers in the Finals? Well, the Pistons crushed the Lakers, completing the first five-game sweep in playoff history (Detroit outplayed the Lakers in a Game 2 loss). Give Joe Dumars credit for assembling the coaching and talent, and Larry Brown credit for getting a team void of a true superstar to play an unselfish brand of basketball that led to the...

2 **Break up of the Lakers.** The feuding began in training camp, an ever-escalating spat that was ugly even by Shaq and Kobe's standards. And, still, they entered the playoffs as the NBA's most feared team. The fallout from losing in the Finals, 4-1, to Detroit was immediate. Phil Jackson was the first to go, despite taking the Lakers to four of the last five Finals. And in an era where you just don't trade a dominant big man, perhaps the most dominant center in NBA history, Shaq, was dealt to Miami. Now, the Lakers are shaped in Kobe's image. And we'll get to see just how good this kid really is.

1 **Gold crush.** The Olympics were supposed to be a breeze. Lodging on a luxury cruise ship, with occasional on-shore visits to the basketball venue to crush the competition and win gold. But an exhibition loss to Italy proved Team USA vulnerable. And a blowout loss to Puerto Rico in the opening game proved Athens was not going to be a vacation. The bronze medal proved that we are no longer, in basketball, the dominant nation and that much needs to be addressed before we assemble a team for China in 2008.

INSIDE the numbers

Sweet Dream to Nightmare

The rest of the basketball world appears to be gaining on the United States. The Dream Team's numbers had declined steadily and now precipitously since NBA players first played in the Olympics in 1992 at Barcelona.

Year	W-L	PPG	3pt. Pct.
2004	5-3	88.1	31.4
2000	8-0	95.0	42.2
1996	8-0	102.0	39.3
1992	8-0	117.3	40.0

Mail Still on Hold

Karl Malone left his longtime home with the Utah Jazz and signed with the LA Lakers with hopes of finally winning an NBA title. But "The Mailman" is still waiting on delivery. Here is a look at the players with the most playoff games without winning an NBA title.

	Gms
Karl Malone	193
John Stockton	182
Sam Perkins	167
Charles Oakley	144
Derrick McKey	142

2003-2004
Season in Review

ESPN
SPORTS ALMANAC

Final NBA Standings

Division champions (*) and playoff qualifiers (†) are noted. Number of seasons listed after each head coach refers to current tenure with club.

Western Conference
Midwest Division

	W	L	Pct	GB	For	Opp
*Minnesota	.58	24	.707	—	94.6	89.1
†San Antonio	.57	25	.695	1	91.5	84.3
†Dallas	.52	30	.634	6	105.2	100.8
†Memphis	.50	32	.610	8	96.7	94.3
†Houston	.45	37	.549	13	89.8	88.1
†Denver	.43	39	.524	15	97.2	96.2
Utah	.42	40	.512	16	88.7	89.9

Head Coaches: Min—Phil Saunders (9th season); **SA**—Gregg Popovich (8th); **Dal**—Don Nelson (7th); **Mem**—Hubie Brown (2nd); **Hou**—Jeff Van Gundy (1st); **Den**—Jeff Bzdelik (2nd); **Utah**—Jerry Sloan (16th).

2002-03 Standings: 1. San Antonio (60-22); 2. Dallas (60-22); 3. Minnesota (51-31); Utah (47-35); 5. Houston (43-39); 6. Memphis (28-54); 7. Denver (17-65).

Pacific Division

	W	L	Pct	GB	For	Opp
*LA Lakers	.56	26	.683	—	98.2	94.3
†Sacramento	.55	27	.671	1	102.8	97.8
†Portland	.41	41	.500	15	90.7	92.0
Golden St.	.37	45	.451	19	93.3	94.0
Seattle	.37	45	.451	19	97.1	97.8
Phoenix	.29	53	.354	27	94.2	97.9
LA Clippers	.28	54	.341	28	94.8	99.4

Head Coaches: LAL—Phil Jackson (5th season); **Sac**—Rick Adelman (6th); **Port**—Maurice Cheeks (3rd); **G.St.**—Eric Musselman (2nd); **Sea**—Nate McMillan (4th); **Pho**—Frank Johnson (3rd, 8-13) was fired on Dec. 10 and replaced by assistant Mike D'Antoni (21-40); **LAC**—Mike Dunleavy (1st).

2002-03 Standings: 1. Sacramento (59-23); 2. LA Lakers (50-32); 3. Portland (50-32); 4. Phoenix (44-38); 5. Seattle (40-42); 6. Golden St. (38-44); 7. LA Clippers (27-55).

Eastern Conference
Atlantic Division

	W	L	Pct	GB	For	Opp
*New Jersey	.47	35	.566	—	90.3	87.8
†Miami	.42	40	.512	5	90.3	89.7
†New York	.39	43	.476	8	92.0	93.5
†Boston	.36	46	.439	11	95.3	96.7
Philadelphia	.33	49	.402	14	88.0	90.5
Washington	.25	57	.305	22	91.8	97.4
Orlando	.21	61	.256	26	94.0	101.1

Head Coaches: NJ—Byron Scott (4th season, 22-20) was fired on Jan. 26 and replaced by asst. Lawrence Frank (25-15); **Mia**—Stan Van Gundy (1st); **NY**—Don Chaney (3rd, 15-24) was fired on Jan. 14 and replaced by Lenny Wilkens (23-19); **Bos**—Jim O'Brien (4th, 22-24) resigned on Jan. 27 and was replaced by asst. John Carroll (14-22) on an interim basis; **Phi**—Randy Ayers (1st, 21-31) was fired on Feb. 10 and replaced by asst. Chris Ford (12-18) on an interim basis; **Wash**—Eddie Jordan (1st) was fired on Nov. 18 and replaced by asst. Johnny Davis (20-51).

2002-03 Standings: 1. New Jersey (49-33); 2. Philadelphia (48-34); 3. Boston (44-38); 4. Orlando (42-40); 5. Washington (37-45); 6. New York (37-45); 7. Miami (25-57).

Central Division

	W	L	Pct	GB	For	Opp
*Indiana	.61	21	.744	—	91.4	85.6
†Detroit	.54	28	.659	7	90.1	84.3
†New Orleans	.41	41	.500	20	91.8	91.9
†Milwaukee	.41	41	.500	20	98.0	97.0
Cleveland	.35	47	.427	26	92.3	95.5
Toronto	.33	49	.402	28	85.4	88.5
Atlanta	.28	54	.349	33	92.8	97.5
Chicago	.23	59	.280	38	89.7	96.1

Head Coaches: Ind—Rick Carlisle (1st season); **Det**—Larry Brown (1st); **NO**—Tim Floyd (1st); **Mil**—Terry Porter (1st); **Cle**—Paul Silas (2nd); **Tor**—Kevin O'Neill (1st); **Atl**—Terry Stotts (35-47); **Chi**—Bill Cartwright (3rd, 4-10) was fired on Nov. 24 and replaced by asst. Pete Myers (0-2) for two games, then Scott Skiles (19-47).

2002-03 Standings: 1. Detroit (50-32); 2. Indiana (48-34); 3. N. Orleans (47-35); 4. Milwaukee (42-40); 5. Atlanta (35-47); 6. Chicago (30-52); 7. Toronto (24-58); 8. Cleveland (17-65).

Overall Conference Standings

Sixteen teams—eight from each conference—qualify for the NBA Playoffs; (*) indicates division champions.

Western Conference

		W	L	Home	Away	Conf	Div
1	Minnesota*	.58	24	31-10	27-14	34-18	14-10
2	LA Lakers*	.56	26	34-7	22-19	31-21	15-9
3	San Antonio	.57	25	33-8	24-17	35-17	15-9
4	Sacramento	.55	27	34-7	21-20	31-21	16-8
5	Dallas	.52	30	36-5	16-25	33-19	14-10
6	Memphis	.50	32	31-10	19-22	38-24	12-12
7	Houston	.45	37	27-14	18-23	21-31	8-16
8	Denver	.43	39	29-12	14-27	29-23	11-13
	Utah	.42	40	28-13	14-27	25-27	10-14
	Portland	.41	41	25-16	16-25	22-30	13-11
	Golden St.	.37	45	27-14	10-31	23-29	12-12
	Seattle	.37	45	21-20	16-25	22-30	11-13
	Phoenix	.29	53	18-23	11-30	16-36	9-15
	LA Clippers	.28	54	18-23	10-31	14-38	8-16

Eastern Conference

		W	L	Home	Away	Conf	Div
1	Indiana*	.61	21	34-7	27-14	41-13	20-8
2	New Jersey*	.47	35	28-13	19-23	34-21	18-7
3	Detroit	.54	28	31-10	23-18	37-17	17-11
4	Miami	.42	40	29-12	13-28	30-24	15-10
5	New Orleans	.41	41	25-16	16-25	30-24	14-14
6	Milwaukee	.41	41	27-14	14-27	33-21	15-13
7	New York	.39	43	23-18	16-25	31-23	17-7
8	Boston	.36	46	19-22	17-24	24-30	14-10
	Cleveland	.35	47	23-18	12-29	29-25	14-14
	Toronto	.33	49	18-23	15-26	22-32	11-17
	Philadelphia	.33	49	21-20	12-29	23-31	10-14
	Atlanta	.28	54	19-23	10-31	20-35	10-18
	Washington	.25	57	17-24	8-33	16-38	3-21
	Chicago	.23	59	14-27	9-32	19-35	11-17
	Orlando	.21	61	11-30	10-31	17-37	8-16

2004 NBA All-Star Game

West, 136-132

53rd NBA All-Star Game. **Date:** Feb. 15, at the Staples Center in Los Angeles; **Coaches:** Rick Carlisle, Indiana (East) and Flip Saunders, Minnesota (West); **MVP:** Shaquille O'Neal (24 points, 11 rebounds, 2 blocks); Starters chosen by fan vote, (Toronto's Vince Carter was the leading vote-getter for the fourth time, receiving 2,127,183); bench chosen by conference coaches' vote.

Western Conference

Pos	Starters	Min	FG M-A	Pts	Reb	A
G	Kobe Bryant, LAL	36	9-12	20	4	4
G	Steve Francis, Hou . .	23	6-9	13	4	4
F	Kevin Garnett, Min . . .	29	6-14	12	7	6
F	Tim Duncan, SA	26	6-11	14	13	5
C	Yao Ming, Hou	18	8-14	16	4	1
	Bench					
C	Shaquille O'Neal, LAL .	24	12-19	24	11	1
G	Ray Allen, Sea	23	6-13	16	3	4
G	Sam Cassell, Min	13	2-3	4	1	7
F	Dirk Nowitzki, Dal . . .	13	1-3	2	0	1
G	Peja Stojakovic, Sac . .	13	2-5	5	1	1
F	Andrei Kirilenko, Utah .	12	1-3	2	1	0
C	Brad Miller, Sac	10	4-5	8	3	0
	TOTALS	240	63-111	136	52	34

Three-Point FG: 5-18 (Bryant 2-3, Francis 1-2, Allen 1-4, Stojakovic 1-4, Garnett 0-1, Ming 0-2, Kirilenko 0-1); **Free Throws:** 5-10 (Allen 3-4, Duncan 2-4, Bryant 0-1, O'Neal 0-1); **Percentages:** FG (.568), Three-Pt. FG (.278), Free Throws (.500); **Turnovers:** 24 (Bryant 6, O'Neal 4, Allen 3, Duncan 2, Nowitzki 2, Stojakovic 2, Miller 2, Francis, Garnett, Cassell); **Steals:** 14 (Bryant 5, Garnett 2, O'Neal 2, Nowitzki 2, Duncan, Allen, Cassell); **Blocked Shots:** 5 (O'Neal 2, Bryant, Garnett, Kirilenko); **Fouls:** 13 (Bryant 3, O'Neal 3, Duncan 2, Ming 2, Allen 2, Francis); **Team Rebounds:** 4.

	1	2	3	4	F
East	33	31	37	31	**132**
West	31	27	45	33	**136**

NBA 3-point Shootout

Six players are invited to compete in the annual three-point shooting contest held during All-Star Weekend, since 1986. Each shooter has 60 seconds to shoot the 25 balls in five racks outside the three-point line. Each ball is worth one point, except the last ball in each rack, which is worth two points. Highest scores advance. First prize: $25,000.

First Round	Pts
Peja Stojakovic, Sacramento	.21
Kyle Korver, Philadelphia	.19
Voshon Lenard, Denver	.18

Failed to advance	Pts
Rashard Lewis, Seattle	.16
Cuttino Mobley, Houston	.13
Chauncey Billups, Detroit	.12

Finals	Pts
Voshon Lenard	.18
Peja Stojakovic	.16
Kyle Korver	.15

Eastern Conference

Pos	Starters	Min	FG M-A	Pts	Reb	A
G	Allen Iverson, Phi	23	1-6	3	1	11
G	Tracy McGrady, Orl . .	23	5-11	13	4	3
F	Jermaine O'Neal, Ind . .	28	7-13	16	9	2
F	Vince Carter, Tor	16	5-7	11	2	0
C	Ben Wallace, Det	23	2-5	4	7	0
	Bench					
F	Kenyon Martin, NJ . . .	23	8-10	17	7	3
G	Jason Kidd, NJ	22	4-6	14	3	10
C	Jamaal Magloire, NO .	21	9-16	19	8	0
F	Ron Artest, Ind	17	3-5	7	3	3
G	Baron Davis, NO	16	3-9	7	0	7
G	Michael Redd, Mil . . .	15	5-12	13	3	2
G	Paul Pierce, Bos	13	4-8	8	1	2
	TOTALS	240	56-108	132	48	43

Three-Point FG: 9-28 (Kidd 3-4, Redd 3-5, Carter 1-3, McGrady 1-6, Davis 1-6, Wallace 0-1, Pierce 0-1); **Free Throws:** 11-22 (Kidd 3-4, McGrady 2-4, O'Neal 2-4, Iverson 1-4, Magliore 1-2, Artest 1-2, Martin 1-2); **Percentages:** FG (.519), Three-Pt. FG (.321), Free Throws (.500); **Turnovers:** 20 (Iverson 4, Martin 3, Kidd 3, O'Neal 2, Carter 2, McGrady, Magloire, Artest, Davis, Redd, Pierce); **Steals:** 15 (Wallace 3, Redd 3, Carter 3, Kidd 2, O'Neal, Magloire, Artest, Davis, Pierce); **Blocked Shots:** 2 (Wallace, Magloire); **Fouls:** 12 (Iverson 3, Magloire 2, Artest 2, Pierce 2, Carter, Martine, Kidd); **Team Rebounds:** 12.

Halftime— East, 64-58; **Third Quarter—**West, 103-101; **Technical Fouls—** none; **Officials—** #29 Steve Javie; #37 Blane Reichelt, #49 Tom Washington; **Attendance—** 19,662; **TV Rating—** 5.1 (TNT).

Slam Dunk Contest

Four players competed at the 2004 NBA Slam Dunk contest. The Dunk contest was held annually from 1984-97 before being replaced by the 2Ball competition. It made its return in 2000. The competitors are selected based on "the creativity and artistry they have displayed in dunking" over the course of the season. The first round consists of three dunks. The dunks are judged by five judges on a scale from six to ten. The top two scorers from the first round advance to the final round and attempt two dunks. The combined score of the two dunks determines the winner. First prize: $25,000.

First Round	Pts
Jason Richardson, Golden State	.95
Fred Jones, Indiana	.92

Failed to advance	Pts
Chris Anderson, Denver	.88
Ricky Davis, Boston	.76

Finals	Score
Fred Jones def. Jason Richardson	.86-78

2004-05 NBA Realignment

With the addition of the expansion Charlotte Bobcats the NBA has announced a realignment plan that will take effect at the start of the 2004-05 season. Charlotte will enter the Eastern Conference with New Orleans moving to the West.

Western Conference

Southwest Division: Dallas Mavericks, Houston Rockets, Memphis Grizzlies, New Orleans Hornets, San Antonio Spurs. **Northwest Division:** Denver Nuggets, Minnesota Timberwolves, Portland Trail Blazers, Seattle SuperSonics, Utah Jazz. **Pacific Division:** Golden State Warriors, L.A. Clippers, L.A. Lakers, Phoenix Suns, Sacramento Kings.

Eastern Conference

Atlantic Division: Boston Celtics, New Jersey Nets, New York Knicks, Philadelphia 76ers, Toronto Raptors. **Central Division:** Chicago Bulls, Cleveland Cavaliers, Detroit Pistons, Indiana Pacers, Milwaukee Bucks. **Southeast Division:** Atlanta Hawks, Charlotte Bobcats, Miami Heat, Orlando Magic, Washington Wizards.

Orlando
Tracy McGrady
Scoring

Minnesota
Kevin Garnett
Rebounding

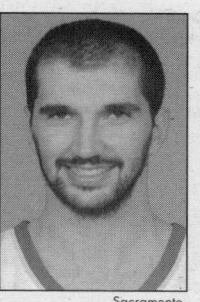
Sacramento
Peja Stojakovic
Free Throw Pct.

New Jersey
Jason Kidd
Assists

NBA Regular Season Individual Leaders
Scoring
(*indicates rookie)

	Gm	Min	FG	FG%	3pt/Att	FT	FT%	Reb	Ast	Stl	Blk	Pts	Avg	Hi
Tracy McGrady, Orl	.67	2675	653	.417	174/513	398	.796	402	370	93	42	1878	**28.0**	62
Predrag Stojakovic, Sac	.81	3264	665	.480	240/554	394	.927	508	173	108	14	1964	**24.2**	41
Kevin Garnett, Min	.82	3231	804	.499	11/43	368	.791	1139	409	120	178	1987	**24.2**	35
Kobe Bryant, LAL	.65	2447	516	.438	71/217	454	.852	359	330	112	28	1557	**24.0**	45
Paul Pierce, Bos	.80	3099	602	.402	115/384	517	.819	522	410	131	52	1836	**23.0**	41
Baron Davis, NO	.67	2686	554	.395	187/582	237	.673	287	501	158	27	1532	**22.9**	37
Vince Carter, Tor	.73	2785	608	.417	93/243	336	.806	349	348	88	65	1645	**22.5**	43
Tim Duncan, SA	.69	2527	592	.501	2/12	352	.599	859	213	62	185	1538	**22.3**	47
Dirk Nowitzki, Dal	.77	2915	605	.462	99/290	371	.877	670	207	92	104	1680	**21.8**	43
Michael Redd, Milw	.82	3021	633	.440	127/363	383	.868	407	185	81	6	1776	**21.7**	40
Shaquille O'Neal, LAL	.67	2464	554	.584	0/0	331	.490	769	196	34	166	1439	**21.5**	37
Carmelo Anthony*, Den	.82	2995	624	.426	69/214	408	.777	498	227	97	41	1725	**21.0**	41
LeBron James*, Cle	.79	3122	622	.417	63/217	347	.754	432	465	130	58	1654	**20.9**	41
Corey Maggette, LAC	.73	2628	453	.447	76/231	526	.848	430	224	65	16	1508	**20.7**	34
Stephon Marbury, Pho-NY	81	3254	598	.431	87/274	356	.817	263	719	129	9	1639	**20.2**	42
Jermaine O'Neal, Ind	.78	2788	608	.434	2/18	348	.757	778	164	59	199	1566	**20.1**	34
Zach Randolph, Port	.81	3067	663	.485	1/5	299	.761	851	163	68	41	1626	**20.1**	34
Elton Brand, LAC	.69	2670	484	.493	0/1	411	.773	714	227	64	154	1379	**20.0**	39
Sam Cassell, Min	.81	2838	620	.488	74/186	289	.873	271	592	102	18	1603	**19.8**	36
Shawn Marion, Pho	.79	3217	590	.440	90/265	228	.851	737	214	167	104	1498	**19.0**	32
Jason Richardson, GS	.78	2936	563	.438	77/273	258	.684	524	226	86	41	1461	**18.7**	35
Michael Finley, Dal	.72	2778	514	.443	150/370	164	.850	325	212	84	39	1342	**18.6**	38
Richard Jefferson, NJ	.82	3133	555	.498	48/132	357	.763	464	315	92	28	1515	**18.5**	35
Mike Bibby, Sac	.82	2980	527	.450	148/378	304	.815	277	444	112	18	1506	**18.4**	31
Ron Artest, Ind	.73	2714	468	.421	75/242	233	.733	385	272	152	50	1333	**18.3**	35
Stephen Jackson, Atl	.80	2940	536	.425	145/427	233	.785	370	244	142	20	1450	**18.1**	42
Rashard Lewis, Sea	.80	2931	535	.435	145/386	206	.763	518	175	99	54	1421	**17.8**	50
Pau Gasol, Mem	.78	2458	506	.482	4/15	365	.714	600	198	44	132	1381	**17.7**	37
Richard Hamilton, Det	.78	2772	530	.455	18/68	297	.868	279	310	103	17	1375	**17.6**	44
Yao Ming, Hou	.82	2692	535	.522	0/2	361	.809	735	122	22	156	1431	**17.5**	41

Rebounds

	Gm	Off	Def	Tot	Avg
Kevin Garnett, Min	.82	245	894	1139	13.9
Tim Duncan, SA	.69	227	632	859	12.4
Ben Wallace, Det	.81	324	682	1006	12.4
Erick Dampier, GS	.74	344	543	887	12.0
Carlos Boozer, Cle	.75	230	627	857	11.4
Zach Randolph, Port	.81	242	609	851	10.5
Jamaal Magloire, NO	.82	268	579	847	10.3
Brad Miller, Sac	.72	191	552	743	10.3
Kenny Thomas, Phi	.74	261	489	750	10.1
Marcus Camby, Den	.72	211	516	727	10.1
Jermaine O'Neal, Ind	.78	193	585	778	10.0
Donyell Marshall, Tor	.82	210	598	808	9.9
Lamar Odom, Mia	.80	160	616	776	9.7
Shawn Marion, Pho	.79	212	525	737	9.3
Yao Ming, Hou	.82	197	538	735	9.0

Assists

	Gm	Ast	Avg
Jason Kidd, NJ	.67	618	9.2
Stephon Marbury, Pho-NY	.81	719	8.9
Steve Nash, Dal	.78	687	8.8
Baron Davis, NO	.67	501	7.5
Sam Cassell, Min	.81	592	7.3
Eric Snow, Phi	.82	563	6.9
Jason Williams, Mem	.72	492	6.8
Kirk Hinrich*, Chi	.76	517	6.8
Steve Francis, Hou	.79	493	6.2
Jeff McInnis, Cle	.70	430	6.1
Andre Miller, Den	.82	501	6.1
Damon Stoudamire, Port	.82	500	6.1
LeBron James*, Cle	.79	465	5.9
Damon Jones, Milw	.82	478	5.8
Chauncey Billups, Det	.78	446	5.7

Field Goal Pct.

	Gm	FG	Att	Pct
Shaquille O'Neal, LAL	.67	554	948	.584
Mark Blount, Bos	.82	342	604	.566
Erick Dampier, GS	.74	348	650	.535
Antawn Jamison, Dal	.82	488	913	.535
Nene, Den	.77	334	630	.530
Carlos Boozer, Cle	.75	471	900	.523
Yao Ming, Hou	.82	535	1025	.522
Brad Miller, Sac	.72	373	731	.510
Corliss Williamson, Det	.79	304	602	.505
Tim Duncan, SA	.69	592	1181	.501
Kevin Garnett, Minn	.82	804	1611	.499

Free Throw Pct.

	Gm	FT	Att	Pct
Predrag Stojakovic, Sac	.81	394	425	.927
Steve Nash, Dal	.78	230	251	.916
Allan Houston, NY	.50	157	172	.913
Ray Allen, Sea	.56	245	271	.904
Reggie Miller, Ind	.80	146	165	.885
Chauncey Billups, Det	.78	404	460	.878
Brian Cardinal, GS	.76	238	271	.878
Dirk Nowitzki, Dal	.77	371	423	.877
Earl Boykins, Den	.82	142	162	.877
Damon Stoudamire, Port	.82	127	145	.876
Sam Cassell, Minn	.81	289	331	.873

3-Point Field Goal Pct.

	Gm	3FG	Att	Pct
Anthony Peeler, Sac	.75	68	141	.482
Brent Barry, Sea	.59	114	252	.452
Brian Cardinal, GS	.76	55	124	.444
Fred Hoiberg, Min	.79	76	172	.442
Aaron McKie, Phi	.75	75	172	.436
Predrag Stojakovic, Sac	.81	240	554	.433
Allan Houston, NY	.50	87	202	.431
Hedo Turkoglu, SA	.80	101	241	.419

High-Point Games

	Opp	Date	FG-FT–Pts
Tracy McGrady, Orl	.vs Wash.	3/10/04	20-17–62
Tracy McGrady, Orl	.at Den.	11/14/03	20-3–51
Rashard Lewis, Sea	.at LAC	10/31/03	18-10–50
Allen Iverson, Phi	.vs. Atl.	11/29/03	20-6–50
Jamal Crawford, Chi	.at Tor.	4/11/04	18-8–50
Tim Duncan, SA	.at Orl.	12/5/03	19-9–47
Kobe Bryant, LAL	.vs. GS	4/`3/04	14-17–45
Richard Hamilton, Det	.vs Cle	11/28/03	15-13–44
Quentin Richardson, LAC	vs. Den	12/31/03	17-5–44
Kobe Bryant, LAL	.at LAC	1/4/04	14-12–44
Tracy McGrady, Orl	.vs. Bos	1/16/04	16-7–44

Blocked Shots

	Gm	Blk	Avg
Theo Ratliff, Atl-Port	.85	307	3.61
Ben Wallace, Det	.81	246	3.04
Andrei Kirilenko, Utah	.78	215	2.76
Tim Duncan, SA	.69	185	2.68
Marcus Camby, Den	.72	187	2.60
Jermaine O'Neal, Ind	.78	199	2.55
Zydrunas Ilgauskas, Cle	.81	201	2.48
Shaquille O'Neal, LAL	.67	166	2.48
Samuel Dalembert, Phi	.82	189	2.30
Elton Brand, LAC	.69	154	2.23

Steals

	Gm	Stl	Avg
Baron Davis, NO	.67	158⁻	2.36
Shawn Marion, Pho	.79	167	2.11
Ron Artest, Ind	.73	152	2.08
Andrei Kirilenko, Utah	.78	150	1.92
Doug Christie, Sac	.82	151	1.84
Stephen Jackson, Atl	.80	142	1.78
Manu Ginobli, SA	.77	136	1.77
Ben Wallace, Det	.81	143	1.77
Steve Francis, Hou	.79	139	1.76
Andre Miller, Den	.82	142	1.73

Rookie Leaders

Scoring

	Gm	FG	FT	Pts	Avg
Carmelo Anthony, Den	.82	624	408	1725	21.0
LeBron James, Cle	.79	622	347	1654	20.9
Dwyane Wade, Mia	.61	371	233	991	16.2
Kirk Hinrich, Chi	.76	318	135	915	12.0
Chris Bosh, Tor	.75	327	202	861	11.5

Field Goal Pct.

	Gm	FG	Att	Pct
Marquis Daniels, Dal	.56	203	411	.494
Dwyane Wade, Mia	.61	371	798	.465
Chris Kaman, LAC	.82	200	435	.460
Chris Bosh, Tor	.75	327	712	.459
Udonis Haslem, Mia	.75	205	447	.459

Rebounds

	Gm	Off	Def	Tot	Avg
Chris Bosh, Tor	.75	191	366	557	7.4
Udonis Haslem, Mia	.75	189	284	473	6.3
Carmelo Anthony, Den	.82	183	315	498	6.1
Chris Kaman, LAC	.82	126	335	461	5.6
Josh Howard, Dal	.67	149	219	368	5.5

Assists

	Gm	No	Avg
Kirk Hinrich, Chi	.76	517	6.8
T.J. Ford, Mil	.55	356	6.5
LeBron James, Cle	.79	465	5.9
Dwyane Wade, Mia	.61	275	4.5
Raul Lopez, Utah	.82	305	3.7

Personal Fouls

Theo Ratliff, Atl-Port	.300
Kurt Thomas, NY	.298
Juwan Howard, Orl	.284
Nene, Den	.280
Jamaal Magloire, NO	.278
Zydrunas Ilgauskas, Cle	.277
Kirk Hinrich*, Chi	.276

Disqualifications

Eddy Curry, Chi	.11
Kirk Hinrich*, Chi	.9
Jake Voskuhl, Pho	.8
Andrew DeClerq, Orl	.7
Brad Miller, Sac	.7
Five players tied	.6

Turnovers

Paul Pierce, Bos	.303
Steve Francis, Hou	.294
LeBron James*, Cle	.273
Stephon Marbury, Pho-NY	.249
Carmelo Anthony*, Den	.247
Zach Randolph, Port	.247
Lamar Odom, Mia	.236

Triple Doubles

Jason Kidd, NJ	.9
Bob Sura, Det-Atl	.2
Gilbert Arenas, Wash	.2
Antoine Walker, Dal	.2
Brad Miller, Sac	.2
Kevin Garnett, Min	.2
Twelve players tied	.1

Minutes Played

Joe Johnson, Pho	.3331
Predrag Stojakovic, Sac	.3264
Stephon Marbury, Pho-NY	.3254
Kevin Garnett, Min	.3231
Cuttino Mobley, Hou	.3229
Shawn Marion, Pho	.3217
Steve Francis, Hou	.3194

Technical Fouls

Steve Francis, Hou	.19
Rasheed Wallace, Det	.18
Baron Davis, NO	.16
Kevin Garnett, Min	.16
Jermaine O'Neal, Ind	.16
Raja Bell, Utah	.15
Ben Wallace, Det	.13

Team by Team Statistics

Players who competed for more than one team during the regular season are listed with their final club; (*) indicates rookies.

Atlanta Hawks

	Gm	FG%	Tpts	PPG	RPG	APG
Stephen Jackson	.80	.425	1450	18.1	4.6	3.1
Jason Terry	.81	.417	1359	16.8	4.1	5.4
Jason Collier	.20	.479	226	11.6	5.6	0.9
Chris Crawford	.56	.448	569	10.2	3.1	0.8
Bob Sura	.80	.416	596	7.5	4.1	2.9
Wesley Person	.58	.401	40	5.8	2.0	1.1
Boris Diaw*	.76	.447	342	4.5	4.5	2.4
Alan Henderson	.6	.476	25	4.0	3.5	0.3
Zeljko Rebraca	.24	.442	91	3.8	2.4	0.3
Jacque Vaughn	.71	.386	270	3.8	1.6	2.7
Mamadou N'diaye	.28	.391	98	3.5	4.0	0.0
Travis Hansen*	.41	.354	123	3.0	1.7	0.5
Joel Przybilla	.17	.360	48	2.9	6.5	0.4
Hiram Fuller	.4	.375	8	2.0	2.8	0.5
Josh Davis	.4	.400	5	1.3	1.3	0.0
Michael Bradley	.16	.467	12	0.9	1.4	0.1

Triple Doubles: Sura (2). **3-pt FG leader:** Terry (146).
Steals leader: Jackson (142). **Blocks leader:** Diaw (37).
Signed: C N'diaye (Feb. 19); F Fuller (Feb. 27); F Collier (Mar. 9); F Davis (Mar. 10); F Bradley (Mar. 19).
Acquired: F/C Rasheed Wallace and G Person from Portland for Theo Ratliff, Dan Dickau and Shareef Abdur-Rahim (Feb.9); Michael Doleac and a 2005 2nd rd. pick from New York and Pryzbilla from Milwaukee in exchange for sending Nazr Mohammed to New York (Feb.15); G Sura, F Rebraca and a 2004 1st rd. pick from Detroit and Chris Mills from Boston in exchange for sending Rasheed Wallace to Detroit (Feb. 19).

Boston Celtics

	Gm	FG%	Tpts	PPG	RPG	APG
Paul Pierce	.80	.402	1836	23.0	6.5	5.1
Ricky Davis	.79	.469	1140	14.4	4.5	3.3
Mark Blount	.82	.566	843	10.3	7.2	0.9
Jiri Welsch	.81	.428	746	9.2	3.7	2.3
Chucky Atkins	.64	.397	538	8.4	1.5	3.5
Walter McCarty	.77	.388	605	7.9	3.1	1.6
Raef LaFrentz	.17	.460	132	7.8	4.6	1.4
Chris Mihm	.76	.488	330	6.3	5.4	0.3
Dana Barros	.1	.667	6	6.0	0.0	0.0
Marcus Banks*	.81	.400	480	5.9	1.6	2.2
Brandon Hunter*	.36	.457	125	3.5	3.3	0.5
Jumaine Jones	.42	.344	93	2.2	1.6	0.3
Kendrick Perkins*	.10	.533	22	2.2	1.4	0.3
Michael Stewart	.25	.417	5	0.5	1.2	0.0

Triple Doubles: Pierce (1). **3-pt FG leader:** McCarty (137). **Steals leaders:** Pierce (131). **Blocks leader:** Blount (106).
Signed: G Barros (Apr. 15). **Acquired:** G Davis, F/C Mihm and F/C Stewart and a 2nd rd. pick from Cleveland for Tony Battie, Kedrick Brown and Eric Williams (Dec. 15); G Lindsey Hunter, G Atkins, a 2004 first rd. pick and cash from Detroit in exchange for sending Mike James to Detroit and Chris Mills to Atlanta (Feb. 19).

Chicago Bulls

	Gm	FG%	Tpts	PPG	RPG	APG
Jamal Crawford	.80	.386	1383	17.3	3.5	5.1
Eddy Curry	.73	.496	1070	14.7	6.2	0.9
Kirk Hinrich*	.76	.386	915	12.0	3.4	6.8
Kendall Gill	.56	.392	539	9.6	3.4	1.6
Antonio Davis	.80	.403	579	8.9	8.4	1.7
Marcus Fizer	.46	.383	360	7.8	4.4	0.9
Jannero Pargo	.31	.407	207	6.7	1.2	2.3
Eddie Robinson	.51	.482	343	6.7	2.0	1.1
Jerome Williams	.68	.470	422	6.2	7.0	1.1
Ronald Dupree*	.47	.394	292	6.2	3.6	1.2
Tyson Chandler	.35	.424	213	6.1	7.7	0.7
Scottie Pippen	.23	.379	136	5.9	3.0	2.2
Linton Johnson III*	.41	.355	173	4.2	4.5	0.7
Chris Jeffries	.21	.375	84	4.0	1.4	0.3
Rick Brunson	.40	.381	118	3.0	0.9	2.1
Paul Shirley	.7	.435	21	3.0	2.3	0.6

Triple Doubles: Hinrich (1). **3-pt FG leader:** Crawford (165). **Steals leader:** Crawford (101). **Blocks leader:** Curry (83).
Signed: F Dupree (Jan. 7); F Shirley (Mar. 5); F Johnson III (Mar. 10); G Pargo (Mar. 26). **Acquired:** G Brunson from Toronto for Roger Mason Jr. (Dec. 16). F/C Davis, F Williams and F Jeffries from Toronto for G/F Jalen Rose, F Donyell Marshall and F Lonny Baxter (Dec. 1).

Cleveland Cavaliers

	Gm	FG%	Tpts	PPG	RPG	APG
LeBron James*	.79	.417	1654	20.9	5.5	5.9
Carlos Boozer	.75	.523	1162	15.5	11.4	2.0
Zydrunas Ilgauskas	.81	.483	1237	15.3	8.1	1.3
Jeff McInis	.70	.447	828	11.8	2.5	6.1
Eric Williams	.71	.386	712	10.0	4.0	1.7
Dajuan Wagner	.44	.366	287	6.5	1.3	1.2
Lee Nailon	.57	.450	341	6.0	2.5	0.7
Tony Battie	.73	.443	408	5.6	4.9	0.8
Kedrick Brown	.55	.461	289	5.3	2.7	1.2
Kevin Ollie	.82	.370	341	4.2	2.1	2.9
Ira Newble	.64	.391	254	4.0	2.4	1.1
Mateen Cleaves	.4	.304	15	3.8	1.8	4.8
Jason Kapono*	.41	.403	145	3.5	1.3	0.3
DeSagana Diop	.56	.388	126	2.3	3.6	0.6
Jelani McCoy	.2	.000	0	0.0	2.0	0.0

Triple Doubles: none. **3-pt FG leader:** James (63).
Steals leader: James (130). **Blocks leader:** Ilgauskas (201).
Signed: F Nailon (Mar. 4); G Cleaves (Mar. 30).
Acquired: C Battie, G Brown, and F Williams from Boston for Ricky Davis, Chris Mihm, Michael Stewart and a 2nd rd. pick (Dec. 15); G McInnis and C Ruben Boumtje Boumtje from Portland for F Darius Miles (Jan. 21).

Dallas Mavericks

	Gm	FG%	Tpts	PPG	RPG	APG
Dirk Nowitzki	.77	.462	2161	21.8	8.7	2.7
Michael Finley	.72	.443	1181	18.6	4.5	2.9
Antawn Jamison	.82	.535	1212	14.8	6.3	0.9
Steve Nash	.78	.470	1128	14.5	3.0	8.8
Antoine Walker	.82	.428	1151	14.0	8.3	4.5
Josh Howard*	.67	.430	575	8.6	5.5	1.4
Marquis Daniels*	.56	.494	477	8.5	2.6	2.1
Tony Delk	.33	.380	197	6.0	1.8	0.8
Scott Williams	.43	.484	198	4.6	3.1	0.4
Danny Fortson	.56	.511	217	3.9	4.5	0.2
Shawn Bradley	.66	.473	219	3.3	2.6	0.3
Eduardo Najera	.58	.444	176	3.0	2.7	0.4
Travis Best	.61	.372	171	2.8	1.1	1.8

Triple Doubles: Walker (2), Nash (1). **3-pt FG leader:** Finley (150). **Steals leader:** Nowitzki (92). **Blocks leader:** Nowitzki (104).
Claimed: C Williams off waivers (Jan. 30).

Individual Single Game Highs

Most Assists

19   Steve Nash, Dal. vs Sac. (4/1)

Most Rebounds

26   Shaquille O'Neal, LAL vs. Milw. (3/21)

Most Blocks

10   Dikembe Mutombo, NY vs. NJ (1/4)
10   Calvin Booth, Sea. vs. Cle (1/13)
10   Amare Stoudemire, Pho. vs. Utah (2/7)

Denver Nuggets

	Gm	FG%	Tpts	PPG	RPG	APG
Carmelo Anthony*	.82	.426	1725	21.0	6.1	2.8
Andre Miller	.82	.457	1214	14.8	4.5	6.1
Voshon Lenard	.73	.422	1038	14.2	2.7	2.1
Nene	.77	.530	908	11.8	6.5	2.2
Earl Boykins	.82	.419	839	10.2	1.7	3.6
Marcus Camby	.72	.477	622	8.6	10.1	1.8
Rodney White	.72	.459	541	7.5	2.3	0.8
Jon Barry	.57	.404	351	6.2	2.2	2.6
Michael Doleac	.72	.435	325	4.5	3.7	0.6
Francisco Elson*	.62	.472	218	3.5	3.3	0.5
Chris Andersen	.71	.443	243	3.4	4.2	0.5
Nikoloz Tskitishvili	.39	.328	106	2.7	1.6	0.3
Jeff Trepagnier	.11	.263	25	2.3	1.4	0.4
Ryan Bowen	.52	.340	46	0.9	1.7	0.3
Mark Pope	.4	.500	2	0.5	0.8	0.0

Triple Doubles: Miller (1). **3-pt FG leader:** Lenard (106).
Steals leader: Miller (142). **Blocks leader:** Camby (187).
Claimed: F/C Doleac off waivers (Feb. 20).

Detroit Pistons

	Gm	FG%	Tpts	PPG	RPG	APG
Richard Hamilton	.78	.455	1375	17.6	3.6	4.0
Chauncey Billups	.78	.394	1318	16.9	3.5	5.7
Rasheed Wallace	.68	.436	1088	16.0	6.8	2.3
Tayshaun Prince	.82	.467	841	10.3	4.8	2.3
Mehmet Okur	.71	.463	682	9.6	5.9	1.0
Ben Wallace	.81	.421	773	9.5	12.4	1.7
Corliss Williamson	.79	.505	752	9.5	3.2	0.7
Mike James	.81	.414	165	9.3	2.9	4.2
Elden Campbell	.65	.439	361	5.6	3.2	0.7
Lindsey Hunter	.33	.343	117	3.5	2.0	2.6
Darvin Ham	.54	.493	96	1.8	1.7	0.3
Darko Milicic*	.34	.262	48	1.4	1.3	0.2
Tremaine Fowlkes	.36	.313	44	1.2	1.5	0.4

Triple Doubles: Billups (1). **3-pt FG leader:** Billups (130). **Steals leader:** Wallace (143). **Blocks leader:** Wallace (246).
Signed: G Hunter (Feb. 27).
Acquired: F/C R. Wallace from Atlanta and G James from Boston in exchange for sending Chucky Atkins and Lindsey Hunter to Boston and Bob Sura and Zeljko Rebraca to Atlanta (Feb. 19).

Golden St. Warriors

	Gm	FG%	Tpts	PPG	RPG	APG
Jason Richardson	.78	.438	1461	18.7	6.7	2.9
Nick Van Exel	.39	.390	490	12.6	2.7	5.3
Erick Dampier	.74	.535	913	12.3	12.0	0.8
Clifford Robinson	.82	.387	967	11.8	3.9	3.3
Mike Dunleavy	.75	.449	877	11.7	5.9	2.9
Speedy Claxton	.60	.427	634	10.6	2.6	4.5
Troy Murphy	.28	.400	279	10.0	6.2	0.7
Brian Cardinal*	.76	.472	733	9.6	4.2	1.4
Calbert Cheaney	.79	.481	603	7.6	3.3	1.7
Mickael Pietrus*	.53	.416	279	5.3	2.2	0.5
Avery Johnson	.46	.402	212	4.6	0.7	2.4
Sean Lampley	.10	.650	34	3.4	1.1	0.2
J.R. Bremer	.36	.272	118	3.3	1.0	1.4
Adonal Foyle	.44	.454	137	3.1	3.8	0.4
Cherokee Parks	.12	.400	12	1.0	0.8	0.1
Rusty LaRue	.4	.333	4	1.0	0.8	0.5
Popeye Jones	.5	.000	0	0.0	0.2	0.0

Triple Doubles: none. **3-pt FG leader:** Robinson (112).
Steals leader: Claxton (97). **Blocks leader:** Dampier (137).
Signed: F/C Parks (Nov. 9); G Larue (Mar. 2); G Bremer (Mar. 12).

Houston Rockets

	Gm	FG%	Tpts	PPG	RPG	APG
Yao Ming	.82	.522	1431	17.5	9.0	1.5
Steve Francis	.79	.403	1310	16.6	5.5	6.2
Cuttino Mobley	.80	.426	1260	15.8	4.5	3.2
Jim Jackson	.80	.424	1033	12.9	6.1	2.8
Maurice Taylor	.75	.480	862	11.5	5.1	1.4
Kelvin Cato	.69	.447	418	6.1	6.8	1.0
Clarence Weatherspoon	.52	.493	261	5.0	3.9	0.6
Eric Piatkowski	.49	.377	201	4.1	1.5	0.5
Scott Padgett	.58	.443	200	3.4	2.4	0.4
Bostjan Nachbar	.45	.356	138	3.1	1.6	0.7
Mark Jackson	.42	.340	103	2.5	1.7	2.8
Mike Wilks	.26	.472	50	1.9	0.6	0.7
Alton Ford	.9	.545	15	1.7	1.2	0.3
Charles Oakley	.7	.333	9	1.3	0.7	0.3
Adrian Griffin	.19	.278	11	0.6	1.0	0.5

Triple Doubles: none. **3-pt FG leader:** Mobley (164).
Steals leader: Francis (132). **Blocks leader:** Ming (156).
Signed: F Ford (Nov. 9); F Oakley (Mar. 18).
Acquired: F Weatherspoon from New York for F/C John Amaechi and G Moochie Norris (Dec. 30).

Indiana Pacers

	Gm	FG%	Tpts	PPG	RPG	APG
Jermaine O'Neal	.78	.434	1566	20.1	10.0	2.1
Ron Artest	.73	.421	1333	18.3	5.3	3.7
Al Harrington	.79	.463	1048	13.3	6.4	1.7
Reggie Miller	.80	.438	800	10.0	2.4	3.1
Jamaal Tinsley	.52	.414	432	8.3	2.6	5.8
Jonathan Bender	.21	.472	148	7.0	1.9	0.4
Anthony Johnson	.73	.406	450	6.2	1.8	2.8
Jeff Foster	.82	.544	497	6.1	7.4	0.8
Kenny Anderson	.44	.441	262	6.0	1.8	2.8
Austin Croshere	.77	.388	387	5.0	3.2	0.7
Fred Jones	.81	.395	397	4.9	1.6	2.1
Jamison Brewer	.13	.371	32	2.5	0.8	1.3
Scot Pollard	.61	.412	106	1.7	2.7	0.2
Primoz Brezec	.18	.462	28	1.6	0.8	0.2
James Jones*	.6	.222	7	1.2	0.3	0.0

Triple Doubles: none. **3-pt FG leader:** Miller (134).
Steals leader: Artest (152). **Blocks leader:** O'Neal (199).

Los Angeles Clippers

	Gm	FG%	Tpts	PPG	RPG	APG
Corey Maggette	.73	.447	1508	20.7	5.9	3.1
Elton Brand	.69	.493	1379	20.0	10.3	3.3
Quentin Richardson	.65	.398	1121	17.2	6.4	2.1
Chris Wilcox	.65	.521	559	8.6	4.7	0.8
Marko Jaric	.58	.388	495	8.5	3.0	4.8
Bobby Simmons	.56	.394	437	7.8	4.7	1.7
Eddie House	.60	.359	409	6.8	2.3	2.5
Predrag Drobnjak	.61	.393	382	6.3	3.2	0.6
Keyon Dooling	.58	.389	360	6.2	1.4	2.2
Chris Kaman*	.82	.460	499	6.1	5.6	1.0
Matt Barnes*	.38	.457	171	4.5	4.0	1.3
Doug Overton	.61	.404	224	3.7	1.4	2.3
Melvin Ely	.42	.431	157	3.7	2.4	0.5
Glen Rice	.18	.289	66	3.7	2.3	1.3
Randy Livingston	.4	.200	8	2.0	1.8	1.0
Olden Polynice	.2	.000	0	0.0	1.0	0.5

Triple Doubles: none. **3-pt FG leader:** Richardson (120). **Steals leader:** Jaric (93). **Blocks leader:** Brand (154).
Signed: G Overton (Nov. 21); G Livingston (Mar. 29).

Los Angeles Lakers

	Gm	FG%	Tpts	PPG	RPG	APG
Kobe Bryant	.65	.438	1557	24.0	5.5	5.1
Shaquille O'Neal	.67	.584	1439	21.5	11.5	2.9
Gary Payton	.82	.471	1199	14.6	4.2	5.5
Karl Malone	.42	.483	554	13.2	8.7	3.9
Stanislav Medvedenko	.68	.441	563	8.3	5.0	0.8
Devean George	.82	.408	604	7.4	4.0	1.4
Derek Fisher	.82	.352	580	7.1	1.9	2.3
Kareem Rush	.72	.440	459	6.4	1.3	0.8
Rick Fox	.38	.392	183	4.8	2.7	2.6
Brian Cook*	.35	.475	155	4.4	2.9	0.6
Horace Grant	.55	.411	223	4.1	4.2	1.3
Bryon Russell	.72	.402	289	4.0	2.0	1.0
Jamal Sampson	.10	.478	29	2.9	5.2	0.7
Luke Walton*	.72	.425	174	2.4	1.8	1.6
Ime Udoka	.4	.333	8	2.0	1.3	0.5

Triple Doubles: Bryant, Malone and Payton (1). **3-pt FG leader:** Bryant (71). **Steals leader:** Bryant (112). **Blocks leader:** O'Neal (166).

Memphis Grizzlies

	Gm	FG%	Tpts	PPG	RPG	APG
Pau Gasol	.78	.482	1381	17.7	7.7	2.5
James Posey	.82	.478	1126	13.7	4.9	1.5
Bonzi Wells	.72	.427	886	12.3	3.6	1.9
Mike Miller	.65	.438	722	11.1	3.3	3.6
Jason Williams	.72	.407	782	10.9	2.0	6.8
Stromile Swift	.77	.469	727	9.4	4.9	0.5
Lorenzen Wright	.65	.439	610	9.4	6.8	1.1
Shane Battier	.79	.446	669	8.5	3.8	1.3
Earl Watson	.81	.371	460	5.7	2.2	5.0
Bo Outlaw	.82	.510	379	4.6	4.2	1.1
Jake Tsakalidis	.40	.504	170	4.3	3.2	0.5
Theron Smith	.20	.372	44	2.2	2.1	0.4
Dahntay Jones*	.20	.283	36	1.8	1.2	0.6
Troy Bell*	.6	.222	11	1.8	0.7	0.7
Ryan Humphrey	.2	.250	2	1.0	1.5	0.5

Triple Doubles: none. **3-pt FG leader:** Williams (120). **Steals leader:** Posey (137). **Blocks leader:** Gasol (132). **Acquired:** G/F Wells from Portland for Wesley Person, a conditional 1st rd. pick and cash (Dec. 3).

Miami Heat

	Gm	FG%	Tpts	PPG	RPG	APG
Eddie Jones	.81	.409	1401	17.3	3.8	3.2
Lamar Odom	.80	.430	1371	17.1	9.7	4.1
Dwyane Wade*	.61	.465	991	16.2	4.0	4.5
Rafer Alston	.82	.376	838	10.2	2.8	4.5
Caron Butler	.68	.380	623	9.2	4.8	1.9
Brian Grant	.76	.471	664	8.7	6.9	0.9
Udonis Haslem*	.75	.459	550	7.3	6.3	0.7
Rasual Butler	.45	.476	304	6.8	1.4	0.5
John Walllace	.37	.421	38	4.3	1.6	0.4
Malik Allen	.45	.419	191	4.2	2.6	0.4
Samaki Walker	.33	.384	105	3.2	3.4	0.2
Loren Woods	.38	.458	121	3.2	3.5	0.3
Wang Zhizhhi	.16	.370	47	2.9	1.1	0.1
Tyrone Hill	.5	.600	9	1.8	1.6	0.0
Kirk Penney	.2	.167	3	1.5	0.5	0.5
Bimbo Coles	.22	.353	28	1.3	0.5	0.7
Jerome Beasley*	.2	.333	2	1.0	0.5	0.0

Triple Doubles: Odom (1). **3-pt FG leader:** Jones (177). **Steals leader:** Alston (114). **Blocks leader:** Odom (71). **Signed:** G Penney (Nov. 3); F Hill (Nov. 7); C Zhizhi (Dec. 1).

Milwaukee Bucks

	Gm	FG%	Tpts	PPG	RPG	APG
Michael Redd	.82	.440	1776	21.7	5.0	2.3
Keith Van Horn	.72	.454	1162	16.1	7.0	1.7
Desmond Mason	.82	.472	1183	14.4	4.4	1.9
Joe Smith	.76	.439	830	10.9	8.5	1.0
Brian Skinner	.56	.497	589	10.5	7.3	0.9
Toni Kukoc	.73	.417	616	8.4	3.7	2.7
T.J. Ford*	.55	.384	391	7.1	3.2	6.5
Damon Jones	.82	.401	573	7.0	2.1	5.8
Dan Gadzuric	.75	.524	424	5.7	4.6	0.4
Erick Strickland	.43	.403	231	5.4	1.7	2.1
Brevin Knight	.56	.427	261	4.7	2.0	3.6
Daniel Santiago	.54	.479	217	4.0	2.4	0.4
Marcus Haislip	.31	.486	93	3.0	1.7	0.1
Dan Langhi	.9	.357	7	2.2	0.7	0.0

Triple Doubles: none. **3-pt FG leader:** Redd (127). **Steals leader:** Redd (81). **Blocks leader:** Gadzuric (105). **Signed:** G Knight (Mar. 5); F Langhi (Dec. 5). **Acquired:** F Van Horn from New York in exchange for sending Joel Przybilla to Atlanta in a three-team deal. (Feb. 15).

Minnesota Timberwolves

	Gm	FG%	Tpts	PPG	RPG	APG
Kevin Garnett	.82	.499	1987	24.2	13.9	5.0
Sam Cassell	.81	.488	1603	19.8	3.3	7.3
Latrell Sprewell	.82	.409	1375	16.8	3.8	3.5
Wally Szczerbiak	.28	.449	285	10.2	3.1	1.2
Troy Hudson	.29	.386	218	7.5	1.2	2.4
Fred Hoiberg	.79	.465	530	6.7	3.4	1.4
Michael Olowokandi	.43	.425	278	6.5	5.7	0.6
Gary Trent	.68	.473	379	5.6	3.2	0.7
Trenton Hassell	.81	.465	406	5.0	3.2	1.6
Mark Madsen	.72	.495	259	3.6	3.8	0.4
Darrick Martin	.16	.299	55	3.4	0.4	1.4
Keith McLeod	.33	.329	88	2.7	1.0	1.8
Oliver Miller	.48	.530	121	2.5	2.7	0.8
Ervin Johnson	.66	.534	127	1.9	3.5	0.4
Quincy Lewis	.14	.350	16	1.1	0.5	0.1
Ndubi Ebi*	.17	.429	13	0.8	0.2	0.2

Triple Doubles: Garnett (2) and Cassell (1). **3-pt FG leader:** Sprewell (99). **Steals leader:** Garnett (120). **Blocks leader:** Garnett (178). **Signed:** G Martin (Apr. 1).

New Jersey Nets

	Gm	FG%	Tpts	PPG	RPG	APG
Richard Jefferson	.82	.498	1515	18.5	5.7	3.8
Kenyon Martin	.65	.488	1086	16.7	9.5	2.5
Jason Kidd	.67	.384	1036	15.5	6.4	9.2
Kerry Kittles	.82	.453	1072	13.1	4.0	2.5
Alonzo Mourning	.12	.465	96	8.0	2.3	0.7
Rodney Rogers	.69	.410	539	7.8	4.4	2.0
Lucious Harris	.69	.404	478	6.9	2.0	2.0
Aaron Williams	.72	.503	450	6.3	4.1	1.1
Jason Collins	.78	.424	462	5.9	5.1	2.0
Brian Scalabrine	.69	.394	240	3.5	2.5	0.9
Zoran Planinic*	.49	.411	153	3.1	1.1	1.4
Brandon Armstrong	.56	.371	151	2.7	0.8	0.3
Tamar Slay	.22	.350	53	2.4	1.1	0.6
Robert Pack	.23	.423	49	1.9	0.7	1.0
Anthony Goldwire	.11	.318	17	1.5	0.6	1.0
Damone Brown	.3	.100	3	1.0	1.7	0.0
Hubert Davis	.17	.091	12	0.2	0.5	0.2

Triple Doubles: Kidd (9). **3-pt FG leader:** Kittles (97). **Steals leader:** Kittles (125). **Blocks leaders:** Martin (82). **Signed:** G Davis (Jan. 26); G Goldwire (Mar. 23).

New Orleans Hornets

	Gm	FG%	Tpts	PPG	RPG	APG
Baron Davis	.67	.395	1532	22.9	4.3	7.5
Jamal Mashburn	.19	.392	396	20.8	6.2	2.5
David Wesley	.61	.389	851	14.0	2.2	2.9
Jamaal Magloire	.82	.473	840	13.6	10.3	1.0
Darrell Armstrong	.79	.395	840	10.6	2.9	3.9
P.J. Brown	.80	.476	836	10.5	8.6	1.9
Stacey Augmon	.69	.412	397	5.8	2.5	1.2
Robert Traylor	.71	.505	362	5.1	3.7	0.6
Steve Smith	.71	.406	358	5.0	1.1	0.8
George Lynch	.78	.397	375	4.8	4.0	1.5
Shammond Williams	.53	.375	255	4.8	1.1	2.2
Maurice Carter	.10	.314	42	4.2	1.1	0.4
David West*	.71	.474	278	3.8	4.2	0.8
Tierre Brown	.3	.500	6	2.0	0.3	0.7
Bryce Drew	.15	.222	12	0.8	0.4	0.9

Triple Doubles: none. **3-pt FG leader:** Davis (187). **Steals leader:** Davis (158). **Blocks leader:** Magloire (101).
Signed: G Carter (Mar. 26). **Acquired:** G Williams from Orlando for C Sean Rooks (Feb. 19).

New York Knicks

	Gm	FG%	Tpts	PPG	RPG	APG
Stephon Marbury	.81	.431	1639	20.2	3.2	8.9
Allan Houston	.50	.435	924	18.5	2.4	2.0
Tim Thomas	.66	.446	970	14.7	4.8	1.9
Kurt Thomas	.80	.473	890	11.1	8.3	1.9
Vin Baker	.54	.481	531	9.8	5.2	1.2
Anfernee Hardaway	.76	.411	699	9.2	3.8	2.3
Shandon Anderson	.80	.422	635	7.9	2.8	1.5
Nazr Mohammed	.80	.521	592	7.4	5.9	0.5
Dikembe Mutombo	.65	.478	363	5.6	6.7	0.4
DerMarr Johnson	.21	.371	113	5.4	1.9	0.5
Othella Harrington	.56	.495	258	4.6	3.2	0.5
Mike Sweetney*	.42	.493	180	4.3	3.7	0.3
Frank Williams	.56	.385	219	3.9	0.9	2.2
Moochie Norris	.66	.369	154	3.5	1.0	1.8
Bruno Sundov	.5	.400	11	2.2	2.0	0.2
Cezary Trybanski	.7	.000	1	0.1	0.1	0.0

Triple Doubles: none. **3-pt FG leader:** Houston and Marbury (87). **Steals leader:** Marbury (129). **Blocks leader:** Mutombo (123).
Signed: G Sundov (Jan. 21); G Johnson (Feb. 3); F Baker (Mar. 13). **Acquired:** G Marbury, G Hardaway and C Trybanski from Phoenix (Jan. 5); F T. Thomas and C Mohammed in a three-team deal involving Milwaukee and Atlanta (Feb. 15); F/C John Amaechi and G Norris from Houston for F Clarence Weatherspoon (Dec. 30).

Orlando Magic

	Gm	FG%	Tpts	PPG	RPG	APG
Tracy McGrady	.67	.417	1878	28.0	6.0	5.5
Juwan Howard	.81	.453	1376	17.0	7.0	2.0
Drew Gooden	.79	.445	914	11.6	6.5	1.1
DeShawn Stevenson	.80	.432	291	11.4	3.7	2.0
Tyronn Lue	.76	.433	799	10.5	2.5	4.2
Keith Bogans*	.73	.403	498	6.8	4.3	1.3
Zaza Pachulia*	.55	.389	194	3.3	2.9	0.2
Andrew DeClercq	.71	.477	230	3.2	4.5	0.6
Desmond Penigar	.10	.500	32	3.2	2.4	0.3
Steven Hunter	.59	.529	187	3.2	2.9	0.2
Derrick Dial	.9	.321	26	2.9	1.4	0.2
Sean Rooks	.55	.358	141	2.6	1.8	0.5
Britton Johnsen*	.20	.288	42	2.1	2.3	0.6
Reece Gaines*	.38	.291	69	1.8	1.0	1.1
Pat Garrity	.2	.333	2	1.0	0.0	0.5

Triple Doubles: none. **3-pt FG leader:** McGrady (174). **Steals leader:** McGrady (93). **Blocks leader:** Hunter (73).
Acquired: G Stevenson from Utah for Gordon Giricek (Feb. 19); C Rooks from New Orleans for G Shammond Williams (Feb. 19).

Philadelphia 76ers

	Gm	FG%	Tpts	PPG	RPG	APG
Allen Iverson	.48	.387	1266	26.4	3.7	6.8
Glenn Robinson	.42	.448	698	16.6	4.5	1.4
Kenny Thomas	.74	.469	1006	13.6	10.1	1.5
Eric Snow	.82	.413	844	10.3	3.4	6.9
Marc Jackson	.22	.415	207	9.4	5.7	0.8
Aaron McKie	.75	.459	689	9.2	3.4	2.6
Derrick Coleman	.34	.413	271	8.0	5.6	1.4
Samuel Dalembert	.82	.541	652	8.0	7.6	0.3
Willie Green*	.53	.401	364	6.9	1.2	1.0
John Salmons	.77	.387	443	5.8	2.5	1.7
Kyle Korver*	.74	.352	330	4.5	1.5	0.5
Zendon Hamilton	.45	.537	169	3.8	3.2	0.3
Greg Buckner	.53	.377	164	3.1	1.9	0.8
Amal McCaskill	.59	.402	113	1.9	2.3	0.3

Triple Doubles: none. **3-pt FG leader:** Korver (81).
Steals leader: Iverson (115). **Blocks leader:** Dalembert (189).
Signed: F Hamilton (Dec. 10).

Phoenix Suns

	Gm	FG%	Tpts	PPG	RPG	APG
Amare Stoudemire	.55	.475	1498	20.6	9.0	1.4
Shawn Marion	.79	.440	1133	19.0	9.3	2.7
Joe Johnson	.82	.430	1367	16.7	4.7	4.4
Leandro Barbosa*	.70	.447	550	7.9	1.8	2.4
Antonio McDyess	.42	.470	290	6.9	6.1	0.9
Howard Eisley	.67	.368	240	6.9	1.9	4.1
Jake Voskuhl	.66	.507	438	6.6	5.2	0.9
Casey Jacobsen	.78	.417	466	6.0	2.6	1.3
Maciej Lampe*	.21	.489	96	4.6	2.1	0.4
Jahidi White	.62	.521	261	4.2	4.2	0.1
Zarko Cabarkapa*	.49	.411	203	4.1	2.0	0.8
Donnell Harvey	.60	.443	141	4.0	2.7	0.4

Triple Doubles: none. **3-pt FG leader:** Marion (90).
Steals leader: Marion (167). **Blocks leader:** Marion (104).
Acquired: C White from Washington for G Brevin Knight (Nov. 5); F Harvey from Orlando for a 2nd rd. pick. (Dec. 23); F McDyess, G Eisley, G Charlie Ward, F/C Lampe, two 1st rd. picks and cash from New York for G Stephon Marbury, G Anfernee Hardaway and C Cezary Trybanski.

Portland Trail Blazers

	Gm	FG%	Tpts	PPG	RPG	APG
Zach Randolph	.81	.485	1626	20.1	10.5	2.0
Shareef Abdur-Rahim	.85	.475	1384	16.3	7.5	2.0
Derek Anderson	.51	.459	694	13.6	3.6	4.5
Damon Stoudamire	.82	.401	1099	13.4	3.8	6.1
Darius Miles	.79	.485	861	10.9	4.5	2.1
Theo Ratliff	.85	.485	672	7.9	7.2	0.8
Ruben Patterson	.73	.506	507	6.9	3.7	1.9
Dale Davis	.76	.473	331	4.4	5.2	0.9
Qyntel Woods	.62	.371	224	3.6	2.2	0.7
Vladimir Stepania	.42	.417	108	2.6	3.0	0.5
Eddie Gill	.22	.417	50	2.3	0.8	0.7
Kaniel Dickens	.3	1.000	7	2.3	0.7	0.0
Dan Dickau	.43	.378	46	2.2	0.6	0.9
Desmond Ferguson	.7	.417	13	1.9	0.6	0.1
Tracy Murray	.8	.250	9	1.1	0.7	0.1
Travis Outlaw*	.8	.429	8	1.0	0.5	0.1
Omar Cook*	.17	.259	14	0.8	0.4	1.4
Slavko Vranes*	.1	.000	0	0.0	0.0	0.0

Triple Doubles: none. **3-pt FG leader:** Stoudamire (156). **Steals leader:** Stoudamire (99). **Blocks leader:** Ratliff (307).
Signed: C Vranes (Jan. 5); G Cook (Feb. 3).
Acquired: G/F Wesley Person and a 1st rd. pick from Memphis for G Bonzi Wells (Dec. 3); G/F Miles from Cleveland for G Jeff McInnis and C Ruben Boumtje Boumtje (Jan. 21); F Abdur-Rahim, C Ratliff and G Dickau from Atlanta for F/C Rasheed Wallace and G/F Welsey Person (Feb. 9).

Sacramento Kings

	Gm	FG%	Tpts	PPG	RPG	APG
Predrag Stojakovic	.81	.480	1964	24.2	6.3	2.1
Chris Webber	.23	.413	430	18.7	8.7	4.6
Mike Bibby	.82	.450	1506	18.4	3.4	5.4
Brad Miller	.72	.510	1014	14.1	10.3	4.3
Bobby Jackson	.50	.444	689	13.8	3.5	2.1
Doug Christie	.82	.461	831	10.1	4.0	4.2
Vlade Divac	.81	.470	800	9.9	5.7	5.3
Anthony Peeler	.75	.448	431	5.7	2.0	1.6
Darius Songaila*	.73	.487	337	4.6	3.1	0.7
Tony Massenburg	.59	.475	251	4.3	3.2	0.5
Jabari Smith	.31	.371	64	2.1	1.0	0.4
Gerald Wallace	.37	.360	75	2.0	2.0	0.5
Rodney Buford	.22	.339	41	1.9	0.7	0.3

Triple Doubles: Miller (2) and Divac (1). **3-pt FG leader:** Stojakovic (240).
Steals leader: Christie (151). **Blocks leader:** Miller (86).

San Antonio Spurs

	Gm	FG%	Tpts	PPG	RPG	APG
Tim Duncan	.69	.501	1538	22.3	12.4	3.1
Tony Parker	.75	.447	1099	14.7	3.2	5.5
Emanuel Ginobili	.77	.418	987	12.8	4.2	3.8
Hidayet Turkoglu	.80	.406	739	9.2	4.5	1.9
Radoslav Nesterovic	.82	.469	710	8.7	7.7	1.4
Malik Rose	.67	.428	529	7.9	4.8	1.0
Bruce Bowen	.82	.420	565	6.9	3.1	1.4
Charlie Ward	.71	.410	119	6.0	2.0	3.0
Ron Mercer	.39	.427	195	5.0	1.3	0.6
Robert Horry	.81	.405	392	4.8	3.4	1.2
Anthony Carter	.5	.297	22	4.4	2.2	2.4
Devin Brown	.58	.434	234	4.0	2.2	0.6
Shane Heal	.6	.292	22	3.7	0.7	0.8
Kevin Willis	.48	.467	164	3.4	2.0	0.2
Jason Hart	.53	.447	177	3.3	1.5	1.5
Alex Garcia*	.2	.143	3	1.5	0.0	0.0
Matt Carroll*	.16	.438	19	1.2	0.4	0.1

Triple Doubles: none. **3-pt FG leader:** Turkoglu (101).
Steals leader: Ginobili (136). **Blocks leader:** Duncan (185).
Signed: G Ward (Jan. 10); G Carroll (Mar. 8).

Seattle Supersonics

	Gm	FG%	Tpts	PPG	RPG	APG
Ray Allen	.56	.440	1287	23.0	5.1	4.8
Rashard Lewis	.80	.435	1421	17.8	6.5	2.2
Ronald Murray	.82	.425	1013	12.4	2.5	2.5
Vladimir Radmanovic	.77	.425	925	12.0	5.3	1.8
Brent Barry	.59	.504	635	10.8	3.5	5.8
Antonio Daniels	.71	.470	571	8.0	2.0	4.2
Vitaly Potapenko	.65	.489	459	7.1	4.4	0.8
Luke Ridnour*	.69	.414	382	5.5	1.6	2.4
Jerome James	.65	.498	324	5.0	3.5	0.5
Calvin Booth	.71	.466	345	4.9	3.9	0.4
Ansu Sesay	.57	.455	200	3.5	1.6	0.3
Richie Frahm	.54	.453	183	2.9	5.4	0.4
Reggie Evans	.75	.406	217	2.9	5.4	0.4
Leon Smith	.1	.500	2	2.0	2.0	0.0

Triple Doubles: Allen (1). **3-pt FG leader:** Allen (148).
Steals leader: Lewis (99). **Blocks leader:** Booth (101).

Toronto Raptors

	Gm	FG%	Tpts	PPG	RPG	APG
Vince Carter	.73	.417	1645	22.5	4.8	4.8
Jalen Rose	.66	.402	1022	15.5	4.0	5.0
Donyell Marshall	.82	.461	1205	14.7	9.9	1.5
Chris Bosh*	.75	.459	861	11.5	7.4	1.0
Dion Glover	.69	.390	620	9.0	3.9	1.9
Alvin Williams	.56	.405	494	8.8	2.7	4.0
Morris Peterson	.82	.405	678	8.3	3.2	1.4
Rod Strickland	.61	.425	382	6.3	2.5	4.0
Lamond Murray	.33	.353	197	6.0	2.7	0.8
Milt Palacio	.59	.349	257	4.4	1.7	3.1
Corie Blount	.62	.455	245	4.0	4.4	0.9
Roger Mason Jr.	.26	.327	93	3.7	1.2	1.0
Michael Curry	.70	.388	204	2.9	1.2	0.8
Jerome Moiso	.35	.476	102	2.9	3.2	0.2
Robert Archibald	.32	.273	32	1.0	1.6	0.4

Triple Doubles: none. **3-pt FG leader:** Marshall (131).
Steals leader: Marshall (93). **Blocks leader:** Marshall (124).
Signed: G Glover (Feb. 28); G Strickland (Mar. 5); F Blount (Mar. 12). **Acquired:** F/G Rose, F Marshall and F Lonny Baxter from Chicago for F/C Antonio Davis, F Jerome Williams and F Chris Jeffries. (Dec. 1); G Mason Jr. from Chicago for G Rick Brunson (Dec. 16); F Archibald from Orlando for C Mengke Bateer and Remon Van de Hare. (Jan. 2).

Utah Jazz

	Gm	FG%	Tpts	PPG	RPG	APG
Andrei Kirilenko	.78	.443	1284	16.5	8.1	3.1
Matt Harpring	.31	.471	502	16.2	8.0	2.0
Carlos Arroyo	.71	.441	897	12.6	2.6	5.0
Gordan Giricek	.73	.436	827	11.3	3.1	1.7
Raja Bell	.82	.409	915	11.2	2.9	1.3
Raul Lopez*	.82	.431	572	7.0	1.9	3.7
Greg Ostertag	.78	.476	529	6.8	7.4	1.6
Jarron Collins	.81	.498	482	6.0	3.9	1.0
Maurice Williams*	.57	.380	284	5.0	1.3	1.3
Aleksandr Pavlovic*	.79	.396	382	4.8	2.0	0.8
Mikki Moore	.32	.505	130	4.1	2.6	0.6
Ben Handlogten	.17	.532	68	4.0	3.2	0.4
Curtis Borchardt*	.16	.393	58	3.6	3.4	0.9
Tom Gugliotta	.55	.345	161	2.9	3.4	1.1
Paul Grant	.10	.478	25	2.5	1.7	0.3
Michael Ruffin	.41	.325	92	2.2	5.0	1.0

Triple Doubles: none. **3-pt FG leader:** Kirilenko (68).
Steals leader: Kirilenko (150). **Blocks leader:** Kirilenko (215).
Signed: C Grant (Jan. 1); C Moore (Jan. 28). **Acquired:** G Giricek from Orlando for DeShawn Stevenson and a conditional 2nd. rd. pick. (Feb. 19); F Gugliotta, two conditional 1st rd. picks, a 2005 2nd rd. pick and cash from Phoenix for F Keon Clark and F Handlogten (Jan. 28).

Washington Wizards

	Gm	FG%	Tpts	PPG	RPG	APG
Gilbert Arenas	.55	.392	1078	19.6	4.6	5.0
Larry Hughes	.61	.397	1148	18.8	5.3	2.4
Jerry Stackhouse	.26	.399	362	13.9	3.6	4.0
Kwame Brown	.74	.489	805	10.9	7.4	1.5
Jarvis Hayes*	.70	.400	673	9.6	3.8	1.5
Juan Dixon	.71	.388	664	9.4	2.1	1.9
Etan Thomas	.79	.489	705	8.9	6.7	0.9
Brendan Haywood	.77	.515	537	7.0	5.0	0.6
Steve Blake*	.75	.386	444	5.9	1.6	2.8
Christian Laettner	.48	.465	284	5.9	4.8	1.9
Jared Jeffries	.82	.377	464	5.7	5.2	1.1
Lonny Baxter	.62	.493	251	4.0	3.0	0.3
Mitchell Butler	.41	.435	134	3.3	1.7	0.8
Chris Whitney	.16	.378	47	2.9	0.9	0.9
Torraye Braggs	.15	.485	40	2.7	2.6	0.5

Triple Doubles: Arenas (3) **3-pt FG leader:** Arenas (125). **Steals leader:** Arenas (103). **Blocks leader:** Thomas (123).
Signed: F Braggs (Jan. 16). **Claimed:** F Baxter off waivers (Mar. 3).

NBA Regular Season Team Leaders

OFFENSE

WEST	Pts	Reb	Ast	FG%	3Pt%	FT%
Dallas	105.2	45.3	23.9	.459	.348	.796
Sacramento	102.8	41.2	26.2	.462	.401	.795
LA Lakers	98.2	43.1	23.7	.454	.327	.693
Denver	97.2	42.3	21.9	.443	.336	.767
Seattle	97.1	39.3	21.7	.446	.373	.765
Memphis	96.7	41.8	23.4	.445	.340	.727
LA Clippers	94.8	43.5	20.2	.428	.321	.785
Minnesota	94.6	42.9	23.1	.462	.363	.781
Phoenix	94.2	40.6	19.3	.443	.345	.746
Golden State	93.3	43.1	20.5	.442	.334	.725
San Antonio	91.5	45.1	20.4	.442	.358	.681
Portland	90.7	41.7	21.6	.448	.346	.731
Houston	89.8	42.6	19.3	.442	.366	.773
Utah	88.7	41.2	20.4	.436	.321	.746

EAST	Pts	Reb	Ast	FG%	3Pt%	FT%
Milwaukee	98.0	42.2	22.8	.447	.350	.775
Boston	95.3	40.1	20.5	.443	.346	.750
Orlando	94.0	40.9	19.3	.429	.344	.737
Cleveland	92.9	45.6	22.1	.433	.314	.753
Atlanta	92.8	42.7	20.1	.433	.335	.776
New York	92.0	42.6	20.7	.442	.364	.793
New Orleans	91.8	42.8	20.9	.420	.319	.751
Washington	91.8	42.8	18.7	.421	.341	.714
Indiana	92.4	41.7	21.6	.435	.351	.764
Miami	90.3	41.5	19.1	.425	.357	.762
New Jersey	90.3	40.7	24.5	.441	.336	.753
Detroit	90.1	42.8	20.8	.435	.344	.753
Chicago	89.7	43.5	21.9	.414	.342	.725
Philadelphia	88.0	40.8	20.0	.428	.342	.753
Toronto	85.4	39.6	18.5	.418	.356	.750

DEFENSE

WEST	Pts	Reb	Ast	FG%	3Pt%	FT%
San Antonio	84.3	41.1	17.3	.403	.327	.744
Houston	88.1	39.7	20.6	.412	.372	.737
Minnesota	89.1	41.5	20.7	.414	.334	.753
Utah	89.9	36.6	18.6	.432	.343	.771
Portland	92.0	40.3	23.3	.450	.341	.753
Golden State	94.0	42.8	21.5	.445	.374	.746
Memphis	94.3	44.0	20.4	.436	.338	.764
LA Lakers	94.3	42.4	20.8	.440	.337	.749
Denver	96.2	42.9	23.6	.453	.356	.728
Seattle	97.8	42.7	21.1	.450	.349	.774
Sacramento	97.8	43.9	21.3	.454	.339	.749
Phoenix	98.0	43.8	21.5	.446	.349	.765
LA Clippers	99.4	41.4	22.9	.460	.360	.741
Dallas	100.8	43.6	23.6	.459	.363	.746

EAST	Pts	Reb	Ast	FG%	3Pt%	FT%
Detroit	84.3	40.7	19.0	.413	.302	.744
Indiana	85.6	40.1	20.1	.432	.324	.750
New Jersey	87.8	40.8	19.8	.427	.350	.761
Toronto	88.5	45.1	18.5	.428	.343	.768
Miami	89.7	41.2	18.6	.428	.343	.744
Philadelphia	90.5	41.4	21.3	.432	.333	.744
New Orleans	91.9	42.1	21.8	.441	.341	.750
New York	93.5	41.4	20.4	.429	.338	.763
Cleveland	95.5	42.0	21.7	.437	.371	.749
Chicago	96.1	45.0	23.1	.436	.355	.748
Boston	96.7	43.8	23.0	.437	.362	.736
Milwaukee	97.0	42.7	22.8	.452	.352	.739
Washington	97.4	43.5	24.0	.454	.342	.771
Atlanta	97.5	43.1	22.0	.440	.358	.760
Orlando	101.1	44.4	24.4	.466	.377	.737

Playoff Series Summaries

WESTERN CONFERENCE

FIRST ROUND (Best of 7)

Sacramento Kings 4, Dallas Mavericks 1

Date	Winner	Home Court
Apr. 18	Kings, 116-105	at Sacramento
Apr. 20	Kings, 83-79	at Sacramento
Apr. 24	Mavericks, 104-79	at Dallas
Apr. 26	Kings, 94-92	at Dallas
Apr. 29	Kings, 119-118	at Sacramento

San Antonio Spurs 4, Memphis Grizzlies 0

Date	Winner	Home Court
Apr. 17	Spurs, 98-74	at San Antonio
Apr. 19	Spurs, 87-70	at San Antonio
Apr. 22	Spurs, 95-93	at Memphis
Apr. 26	Spurs, 110-97	at Memphis

Los Angeles Lakers 4, Houston Rockets 1

Date	Winner	Home Court
Apr. 17	Lakers, 72-71	at Los Angeles
Apr. 19	Lakers, 98-84	at Los Angeles
Apr. 23	Rockets, 102-91	at Houston
Apr. 25	Lakers, 92-88 OT	at Houston
Apr. 28	Lakers, 97-78	at Los Angeles

Minnesota Timberwolves 4, Denver Nuggets 1

Date	Winner	Home Court
Apr. 18	Timberwolves, 106-92	at Minnesota
Apr. 21	Timberwolves, 95-81	at Minnesota
Apr. 24	Nuggets, 107-86	at Denver
Apr. 27	Timberwolves, 84-82	at Denver
Apr. 30	Timberwolves, 102-91	at Minnesota

SEMIFINALS (Best of 7)

Los Angeles Lakers 4, San Antonio Spurs 2

Date	Winner	Home Court
May 2	Spurs, 88-78	at San Antonio
May 5	Spurs, 95-85	at San Antonio
May 9	Lakers, 105-81	at Los Angeles
May 11	Lakers, 98-90	at Los Angeles
May 13	Lakers, 74-73	at San Antonio
May 15	Lakers, 88-76	at Los Angeles

Minnesota Timberwolves 4, Sacramento Kings 3

Date	Winner	Home Court
May 4	Kings, 104-98	at Minnesota
May 8	Timberwolves, 94-89	at Minnesota
May 10	Timberwolves, 114-113 OT	at Sacramento
May 12	Kings, 87-81	at Sacramento
May 14	Timberwolves, 86-74	at Minnesota
May 16	Kings, 104-87	at Sacramento
May 19	Timberwolves, 83-80	at Minnesota

CHAMPIONSHIP (Best of 7)

Los Angeles Lakers 4, Minnesota Timberwolves 2

Date	Winner	Home Court
May 21	Lakers, 97-88	at Minnesota
May 23	Timberwolves, 89-71	at Minnesota
May 25	Lakers, 100-89	at Los Angeles
May 27	Lakers, 92-85	at Los Angeles
May 29	Timberwolves, 98-96	at Minnesota
May 31	Lakers, 96-90	at Los Angeles

2004 NBA PLAYOFFS

| | 1ST ROUND | SEMIFINALS | FINAL | | FINAL | SEMIFINALS | 1ST ROUND | |

PLAYOFFS 2004

(1) Indiana 4
(8) Boston 0
    Indiana 4

Indiana 2

(4) Miami 4
(5) New Orleans 3
    Miami 2

EASTERN CONFERENCE

Detroit 4
LA Lakers 1

(3) Detroit 4
(6) Milwaukee 1
    Detroit 4

Detroit 4

(2) New Jersey 4
(7) New York 0
    New Jersey 3

Minnesota 4
    (1) Minnesota 4
    (8) Denver 1

Minnesota 2

Sacramento 3
    (4) Sacramento 4
    (5) Dallas 1

WESTERN CONFERENCE

LA Lakers 4

San Antonio 2
    (3) San Antonio 4
    (6) Memphis 0

LA Lakers 4
    (2) LA Lakers 4
    (7) Houston 1

EASTERN CONFERENCE

FIRST ROUND (Best of 7)

New Jersey Nets 4, New York Knicks 0

Date	Winner	Home Court
Apr. 17	Nets, 107-83	at New Jersey
Apr. 20	Nets, 99-81	at New Jersey
Apr. 22	Nets, 81-78	at New York
Apr. 25	Nets, 100-94	at New York

Miami Heat 4, New Orleans Hornets 3

Date	Winner	Home Court
Apr. 18	Heat, 81-79	at Miami
Apr. 21	Heat, 93-63	at Miami
Apr. 24	Hornets, 77-71	at New Orleans
Apr. 27	Hornets, 96-85	at New Orleans
Apr. 30	Heat, 87-83	at Miami
May 2	Hornets, 89-83	at New Orleans
May 4	Heat, 85-77	at Miami

Detroit Pistons 4, Milwaukee Bucks 1

Date	Winner	Home Court
Apr. 18	Pistons, 108-82	at Detroit
Apr. 21	Bucks, 92-88	at Detroit
Apr. 24	Pistons, 95-85	at Milwaukee
Apr. 26	Pistons, 109-92	at Milwaukee
Apr. 29	Pistons, 91-77	at Detroit

Indiana Pacers 4, Boston Celtics 0

Date	Winner	Home Court
Apr. 17	Pacers, 104-88	at Indiana
Apr. 20	Pacers, 103-90	at Indiana
Apr. 23	Pacers, 108-85	at Boston
Apr. 25	Pacers, 90-75	at Boston

SEMIFINALS (Best of 7)

Indiana Pacers 4, Miami Heat 2

Date	Winner	Home Court
May 6	Pacers, 94-81	at Indiana
May 8	Pacers, 91-80	at Indiana
May 10	Heat, 94-87	at Miami
May 12	Heat, 100-88	at Miami
May 15	Pacers, 94-83	at Indiana
May 18	Pacers, 73-70	at Miami

Detroit Pistons 4, New Jersey Nets 3

Date	Winner	Home Court
May 3	Pistons, 78-56	at Detroit
May 7	Pistons, 95-80	at Detroit
May 9	Nets, 82-64	at New Jersey
May 11	Nets, 94-79	at New Jersey
May 14	Nets, 127-120 3OT	at Detroit
May 16	Pistons, 81-75	at New Jersey
May 20	Pistons, 90-69	at Detroit

CHAMPIONSHIP (Best of 7)

Detroit Pistons 4, Indiana Pacers 2

Date	Winner	Home Court
May 22	Pacers, 78-74	at Indiana
May 24	Pistons, 72-67	at Indiana
May 26	Pistons, 85-78	at Detroit
May 28	Pacers, 83-68	at Detroit
May 30	Pistons, 83-65	at Indiana
June 1	Pistons, 69-65	at Detroit

NBA FINALS (Best of 7)

	W-L	Avg.	Leading Scorer
Detroit	4-1	90.8	Hamilton (21.4)
LA Lakers	1-4	81.8	O'Neal (26.6)

Date	Winner	Home Court
June 6	Pistons, 87-75	at Los Angeles
June 8	Lakers, 99-91 OT	at Los Angeles
June 10	Pistons, 88-68	at Detroit
June 13	Pistons, 88-80	at Detroit
June 15	Pistons, 100-87	at Detroit

Finals MVP
Chauncey Billups, Detroit, G
21.0 ppg, 3.2 rpg, 5.2 apg, 1.2 spg

NBA Finals Box Scores

Game 1

Detroit 87, at LA Lakers 75

Pistons	Min	FG M-A	3PT M-A	FT M-A	Pts	Reb O-T	A	S	PF
R. Hamilton	43	5-16	0-0	2-4	12	3-7	5	1	0
C. Billups	39	8-14	2-4	4-4	22	1-3	4	3	1
T. Prince	35	5-10	1-4	0-0	11	1-6	4	2	3
R. Wallace	29	3-4	2-2	6-6	14	1-8	1	0	3
B. Wallace	41	4-8	0-0	1-2	9	1-8	0	1	1
E. Campbell	18	2-5	0-0	2-6	6	1-1	4	2	1
L. Hunter	13	1-5	1-2	2-2	5	0-1	0	0	2
C. Williamson	11	2-3	0-0	3-4	7	1-2	1	0	3
M. Okur	6	0-0	0-0	1-2	1	0-0	0	0	1
D. Ham	4	0-0	0-0	0-0	0	0-0	0	0	2
M. James	1	0-0	0-0	0-0	0	0-0	0	0	0
TOTALS	240	30-65	6-12	21-30	87	9-36	19	9	17

Team Rebs: 11; **Blocks:** 4 (Campbell 2, B. Wallace, R. Wallace); **Turnovers:** 14 (Hamilton 6, Billups 2, B. Wallace 2, R. Wallace, Campbell, Hunter, Okur); **Pcts:** FG (.462), 3-Pt FG (.500), FT (.700).

Lakers	Min	FG M-A	3PT M-A	FT M-A	Pts	Reb O-T	A	S	PF
K. Bryant	47	10-27	1-6	4-4	25	1-4	4	4	2
G. Payton	31	1-4	1-1	0-0	3	1-2	3	2	5
K. Malone	44	2-9	0-0	0-0	4	3-11	3	0	1
D. George	27	2-5	1-2	0-0	5	0-3	0	1	2
S. O'Neal	45	13-16	0-0	8-12	34	5-11	1	0	4
D. Fisher	20	1-9	0-2	0-0	2	3-3	3	1	2
K. Rush	16	0-3	0-0	0-0	0	0-2	0	1	4
S. Medvedenko	6	0-0	0-0	2-2	2	0-1	0	0	3
R. Fox	4	0-0	0-0	0-0	0	0-0	1	0	2
TOTALS	240	29-73	3-13	14-18	75	13-37	15	8	25

Team Rebs: 8; **Blocks:** 2 (Payton 2, O'Neal, Malone); **Turnovers:** 15 (O'Neal 6, Bryant 3, Payton 3, Rush 2, George, Fisher); **Pcts:** FG (.397), 3-Pt FG (.231), FT (.778).
Halftime: Lakers, 41-40; **Attendance:** 18,997; **Time:** 2:30.

Game 2

at LA Lakers 99, Detroit 91 OT

Pistons	Min	FG M-A	3PT M-A	FT M-A	Pts	Reb O-T	A	S	PF
T. Prince	47	2-6	1-2	0-0	5	4-5	0	3	2
R. Wallace	34	5-14	0-3	1-2	11	1-7	3	0	4
B. Wallace	43	5-11	0-0	2-8	12	4-14	1	2	5
R. Hamilton	47	10-25	2-4	4-5	26	5-8	2	0	2
C. Billups	47	6-15	2-2	13-14	27	2-4	9	0	1
E. Campbell	9	1-2	0-0	0-0	2	2-4	1	0	4
L. Hunter	12	2-4	1-3	0-0	5	0-0	2	1	1
C. Williamson	7	1-2	0-0	0-0	2	0-0	0	0	0
M. James	1	0-0	0-0	0-0	0	0-0	0	0	0
M. Okur	18	0-2	0-0	1-2	1	0-2	1	0	2
TOTALS	265	32-81	6-12	21-31	91	19-46	19	6	23

Team Rebs: 12; **Blocks:** 6 (Prince 2, R. Wallace 2, B. Wallace 2); **Turnovers:** 14 (Hamilton 5, Billups 3, Okur 3, Williamson 2, Campbell); **Pcts:** FG (.395), 3-Pt FG (.500), FT (.677).

Lakers	Min	FG M-A	3PT M-A	FT M-A	Pts	Reb O-T	A	S	PF
D. George	21	3-7	1-3	0-0	7	0-2	1	1	2
K. Malone	39	3-9	0-1	3-4	9	3-9	2	1	3
S. O'Neal	48	10-20	0-0	9-14	29	3-7	3	0	5
K. Bryant	49	14-27	1-5	4-5	33	0-4	7	2	5
G. Payton	28	1-3	0-1	0-0	2	1-3	3	1	4
L. Walton	27	3-3	1-1	0-0	7	1-5	6	2	1
D. Fisher	25	2-6	2-4	1-2	7	2-2	2	2	4
K. Rush	18	2-4	1-2	0-0	5	0-2	1	0	4
S. Medvedenko	9	0-1	0-0	0-0	0	0-0	1	0	0
B. Cook	1	0-0	0-0	0-0	0	0-0	0	0	0
TOTALS	265	38-80	6-17	17-25	99	9-38	28	7	27

Team Rebs: 13; **Blocks:** 3 (Walton 2, O'Neal); **Turnovers:** 14 (George 5, Payton 3, O'Neal 3, Rush, Cook, Malone); **Pcts:** FG (.475), 3-Pt FG (.353), FT (.680).
Halftime: Lakers, 44-36; **Attendance:** 18,997; **Time:** 3:05.

Game 3

at Detroit 88, LA Lakers 68

Lakers	Min	FG M-A	3PT M-A	FT M-A	Pts	Reb O-T	A	S	PF
D. George	21	3-8	2-6	0-0	8	0-3	0	2	3
K. Malone	18	2-4	0-0	1-2	5	0-4	2	0	2
S. O'Neal	38	7-14	0-0	0-2	14	2-8	1	1	5
K. Bryant	45	4-13	0-4	3-3	11	0-3	5	1	3
G. Payton	35	2-7	1-5	1-2	6	1-4	7	1	2
L. Walton	19	1-5	0-2	2-2	4	1-3	2	1	4
D. Fisher	16	4-9	1-3	0-0	9	1-2	1	0	1
K. Rush	18	3-8	2-7	0-0	8	0-1	0	1	2
S. Medvedenko	21	1-3	0-0	1-2	3	2-8	1	0	4
B. Cook	8	0-3	0-0	0-0	0	0-3	0	0	2
B. Russell	1	0-0	0-0	0-0	0	0-0	0	0	0
TOTALS	240	27-74	6-27	8-13	68	7-39	19	7	28

Team Rebs: 8; **Blocks:** 4 (George, Bryant, Payton, Medvedenko); **Turnovers:** 16 (Bryant 4, Fisher 3, Walton 2, O'Neal 2, Rush 2, George, Malone, Medvedenko); **Pcts:** FG (.365), 3-Pt FG (.222), FT (.615).

Pistons	Min	FG M-A	3PT M-A	FT M-A	Pts	Reb O-T	A	S	PF
T. Prince	36	5-13	1-5	0-2	11	3-6	2	3	1
R. Wallace	26	1-4	0-0	1-4	3	2-10	1	0	3
B. Wallace	38	3-9	0-1	1-4	7	2-11	3	2	3
R. Hamilton	43	11-22	2-4	7-7	31	3-6	3	2	1
C. Billups	36	5-11	2-5	7-7	19	0-2	3	1	1
E. Campbell	13	1-4	0-0	3-4	5	2-2	1	3	3
C. Williamson	15	2-4	0-0	2-2	6	0-3	0	0	0
L. Hunter	16	1-3	0-0	0-0	2	0-1	2	0	4
M. James	4	0-0	0-0	0-0	0	0-0	1	1	0
D. Ham	3	1-1	0-0	0-0	2	0-0	0	0	1
M. Okur	8	1-4	0-0	0-0	2	1-4	1	0	0
D. Milicic	1	0-0	0-0	0-0	0	0-0	0	0	0
TOTALS	240	31-76	5-15	21-30	88	15-51	17	11	16

Team Rebs: 8; **Blocks:** 4 (R. Wallace 2, Hunter 2); **Turnovers:** 11 (B. Wallace 3, Hamilton 3, Billups 2, Prince, R. Wallace, Williamson); **Pcts:** FG (.408), 3-Pt FG (.333), FT (.700).
Halftime: Pistons, 39-32; **Attendance:** 22,076; **Time:** 2:31.

Game 4

at Detroit 88, LA Lakers 80

Lakers	Min	FG M-A	3PT M-A	FT M-A	Pts	Reb O-T	A	S	PF
D. George	15	1-2	1-2	2-4	5	1-3	0	1	5
K. Malone	21	1-2	0-0	0-0	2	2-5	2	0	2
S. O'Neal	47	16-21	0-0	4-11	36	3-20	2	0	4
K. Bryant	45	8-25	2-6	2-2	20	0-0	2	1	3
G. Payton	43	4-11	0-0	0-0	8	1-2	5	0	4
R. Fox	16	1-4	0-1	0-0	2	0-1	6	0	3
D. Fisher	21	1-6	0-3	2-3	4	1-5	2	0	4
K. Rush	0	0-1	0-1	0-0	0	0-0	0	0	1
S. Medvedenko	13	1-5	0-0	1-2	3	1-1	1	0	3
L. Walton	12	0-1	0-0	0-1	0	0-1	3	2	6
B. Russell	1	0-0	0-0	0-0	0	0-0	0	0	0
TOTALS	240	33-78	3-16	11-22	80	9-38	23	4	35

Team Rebs: 8; **Blocks:** 1 (O'Neal); **Turnovers:** 10 (Bryant 3, Malone 2, O'Neal 2, Walton 2, Payton); **Pcts:** FG (.423), FT (.188), FT (.500).

Pistons	Min	FG M-A	3PT M-A	FT M-A	Pts	Reb O-T	A	S	PF
T. Prince	40	3-10	0-1	0-0	6	4-7	2	0	1
R. Wallace	41	10-23	0-5	6-6	26	2-13	2	2	4
B. Wallace	39	2-5	0-0	4-14	8	2-13	2	1	3
R. Hamilton	44	5-11	0-0	7-7	17	1-2	6	0	5
C. Billups	37	7-12	2-5	7-9	23	0-4	4	2	3
L. Hunter	10	0-1	0-0	4-4	4	0-2	0	0	1
E. Campbell	14	0-3	0-0	0-0	0	2-6	0	0	0
M. James	6	2-2	0-0	0-0	4	0-2	0	0	0
D. Ham	3	0-0	0-0	0-0	0	0-0	0	0	0
C. Williamson	5	0-1	0-0	0-0	0	0-0	0	0	0
D. Milicic	1	0-0	0-0	0-0	0	0-0	0	0	0
TOTALS	240	29-68	2-13	28-41	88	9-45	16	5	20

Team Rebs: 15; **Blocks:** 4 (R. Wallace 2, B. Wallace, Campbell); **Turnovers:** 12 (Hamilton 5, Billups 3, R. Wallace 2, B. Wallace, James); **Pcts:** FG (.426), 3-Pt FG (.154), FT (.683).
Halftime: Pistons, 41-38; **Attendance:** 22,076; **Time:** 2:49.

Game 5

at Detroit 100, LA Lakers 87

Lakers	Min	FG M-A	3PT M-A	FT M-A	Pts	Reb O-T	A	S	PF
D. George	.20	2-6	0-2	0-0	4	2-3	2	0	4
S. Medvedenko	23	4-8	0-0	2-2	10	2-5	1	0	1
S. O'Neal	..35	7-13	0-0	6-16	20	2-8	1	1	4
K. Bryant	.45	7-21	0-2	10-11	24	1-3	4	1	2
G. Payton	.31	1-3	0-1	0-0	2	2-4	4	2	2
B. Cook	.12	1-3	0-0	2-2	4	3-5	0	1	2
L. Walton	.19	1-4	0-2	0-0	2	1-3	5	3	2
D. Fisher	19	3-6	3-4	1-2	10	0-2	1	2	5
K. Rush	20	2-6	1-4	0-0	5	0-0	0	0	3
R. Fox	10	3-3	0-0	0-0	6	0-2	0	0	1
B. Russell	...6	0-2	0-0	0-0	0	1-1	0	0	1
TOTALS	...240	31-75	4-16	21-33	87	14-36	18	10	27

Team Rebs: 12; **Blocks:** 2 (George, Payton); **Turnovers:** 11 (Bryant 3, Walton 3, Medvedenko, O'Neal, Payton, Cook, Fox); **Pcts:** FG (.413), 3-Pt FG (.250), FT (.636)

Pistons	Min	FG M-A	3PT M-A	FT M-A	Pts	Reb O-T	A	S	PF
T. Prince	38	6-15	0-2	5-8	17	3-10	2	1	2
R. Wallace	..21	5-8	1-2	0-0	11	1-1	0	0	5
B. Wallace	..42	8-13	0-1	2-6	18	10-22	1	3	3
R. Hamilton	..45	6-18	0-4	9-11	21	0-3	4	1	1
C. Billups	..33	3-5	0-1	8-8	14	0-3	6	0	2
C. Williamson	14	1-5	0-0	4-4	6	2-3	0	0	2
E. Campbell	.14	2-2	0-0	0-0	4	1-4	2	0	3
L. Hunter	13	1-4	0-3	0-0	2	0-1	0	2	3
M. James	...10	0-2	0-0	0-0	0	1-1	3	0	2
M. Okur	7	3-3	1-1	0-0	7	0-0	0	0	4
D. Milicic	2	0-1	0-0	0-2	0	1-1	0	1	0
D. Ham	...1	0-0	0-0	0-0	0	1-1	0	0	0
TOTALS	...240	35-76	2-14	28-39	100	20-50	18	8	27

Team Rebs: 10; **Blocks:** 2 (R. Wallace, B. Wallace); **Turnovers:** 12 (Hamilton 4, Billups 3, Prince, Williamson, Campbell, Milicic, Ham); **Pcts:** FG (.461), 3-Pt FG (.143), FT (.718).
Halftime: Pistons, 55-45; **Attendance:** 22,076; **Time:** 2:32.

NBA Playoff Leaders

Scoring

	Gm	FG	FT	Pts	Avg
Dirk Nowitzki, Dal	.5	45	36	133	26.6
Kobe Bryant, LAL	.22	190	135	539	24.5
Kevin Garnett, Min	.18	168	97	438	24.3
Tim Duncan, SA	.10	83	55	221	22.1
Shaquille O'Neal, LAL	.22	182	109	473	21.5
Richard Hamilton, Det	.23	181	117	494	21.5
Stephon Marbury, NY	.4	31	17	85	21.3
Paul Pierce, Bos	.4	26	26	83	20.8
Mike Bibby, Sac	.12	85	48	240	20.0
Latrell Sprewell, Min	.18	130	60	357	19.8
Richard Jefferson, NJ	.11	66	77	218	19.8

Rebounds

	Gm	Off	Def	Tot	Avg
Kevin Garnett, Min	.18	38	224	263	14.6
Ben Wallace, Det	.23	95	233	328	14.3
Shaquille O'Neal, LAL	.22	91	200	291	13.2
Dirk Nowitzki, Dal	.5	13	46	59	11.8
Kurt Thomas, NY	.4	9	37	46	11.5

Assists

	Gm	No	Avg
Jason Kidd, NJ	.11	99	9.0
Steve Nash, Dal	.5	45	9.0
Steve Francis, Hou	.5	38	7.6
Damon Jones, Miw	.5	37	7.4
Mike Bibby, Sac	.12	84	7.0
Baron Davis, NO	.7	49	7.0
Tony Parker, SA	.10	70	7.0

NBA Finalists' Composite Box Scores

Los Angeles Lakers (13-9)

		Overall Playoffs			—Per Game—				Finals vs. Detroit			—Per Game—		
	Gm	FG%	3PT-A	TPts	Pts	Reb	Ast	Gm	FG%	3PT-A	TPts	Pts	Reb	Ast
Kobe Bryant	.22	.413	24-97	539	24.5	4.7	5.5	5	.381	4-23	113	22.6	2.8	4.4
Shaquille O'Neal	.22	.593	0-0	473	21.5	13.2	2.5	5	.631	0-0	133	26.6	10.8	1.6
Karl Malone	.21	.450	0-2	242	11.5	8.8	3.4	4	.333	0-1	20	5.0	7.3	2.3
Gary Payton	.22	.366	14-56	171	7.8	3.3	5.3	5	.321	2-10	21	4.2	3.0	4.4
Derek Fisher	.22	.405	23-55	166	7.5	2.5	2.2	5	.306	6-16	32	6.4	3.0	1.8
Devean George	.22	.430	22-59	121	5.5	2.3	0.5	5	.393	5-15	29	5.8	2.8	0.6
Stanislav Medvedenko	..21	.440	0-0	83	4.0	2.5	0.5	5	.353	0-0	18	3.6	3.6	0.6
Kareem Rush	.22	.318	20-50	82	3.7	0.7	0.8	5	.318	4-16	18	3.6	1.0	0.4
Luke Walton	.17	.345	5-13	32	1.9	1.3	1.5	4	.385	1-6	13	3.3	3.0	4.5
Rick Fox	.16	.400	1-7	18	1.1	1.4	1.1	3	.571	0-1	8	2.7	1.0	2.3
Brian Cook	.13	.333	5-15	12	0.9	0.9	0.1	3	.167	0-0	4	1.3	2.7	0.0
Byron Russell	..6	.000	0-3	0	0.0	0.2	0.3	3	.000	0-1	0	0.0	0.3	0.0
LAKERS	.22	.444	109-340	1939	88.1	40.2	22.6	5	.416	22-89	409	81.8	37.6	20.6
OPPONENTS	.22	.422	113-363	1919	87.2	43.0	17.9	5	.429	21-66	454	90.8	45.6	17.8

Detroit Pistons (16-7)

		Overall Playoffs			—Per Game—				Finals vs. LA Lakers			—Per Game—		
	Gm	FG%	3PT-A	TPts	Pts	Reb	Ast	Gm	FG%	3PT-A	TPts	Pts	Reb	Ast
Richard Hamilton	..23	.447	181-405	494	21.5	4.6	4.2	5	.402	4-10	107	21.4	5.2	4.0
Chauncey Billups	.23	.385	37-107	378	16.4	3.0	5.9	5	.509	8-17	105	21.0	3.2	5.2
Rasheed Wallace	.23	.413	17-70	299	13.0	7.8	1.6	5	.453	3-12	65	13.0	7.8	1.4
Ben Wallace	.23	.454	0-3	236	10.3	14.3	1.9	5	.478	0-2	54	10.8	13.6	1.4
Tayshaun Prince	.23	.410	13-49	228	9.9	6.0	2.3	5	.389	3-16	50	10.0	6.8	2.0
Corliss Williamson	.22	.364	0-1	126	5.7	2.2	0.7	5	.400	3-16	21	4.2	2.4	0.2
Mehmet Okur	.22	.470	2-5	82	3.7	2.8	0.4	4	.444	1-1	11	2.8	1.5	0.5
Mike James	.22	.396	6-14	57	2.6	1.2	1.1	5	.500	0-0	4	0.8	0.8	0.8
Lindsey Hunter	.23	.292	7-30	56	2.4	1.4	0.9	5	.294	2-8	18	3.6	1.4	0.8
Elden Campbell	.14	.286	0-0	30	2.1	1.8	0.7	5	.375	0-0	17	3.4	2.6	1.6
Darvin Ham	.21	.500	0-1	16	0.8	0.7	0.4	4	1.000	0-0	2	0.5	0.3	0.0
Darko Milicic	..8	.000	0-0	1	0.1	0.4	0.1	3	.000	0-0	0	0.0	0.7	0.0
PISTONS	.23	.412	97-319	2003	87.1	44.8	19.4	5	.429	21-66	454	90.8	45.6	17.8
OPPONENTS	.23	.392	108-390	1856	80.7	40.6	18.6	5	.416	22-89	409	81.8	37.6	20.6

Annual Awards

Most Valuable Player

The Maurice Podoloff Trophy; voting by 123-member panel of local and national pro basketball writers and broadcasters. Each ballot has five entries; points awarded on 10-7-5-3-1 basis.

	1st	2nd	3rd	4th	5th	Pts
Kevin Garnett, Minnesota	120	2	1	0	0	1219
Tim Duncan, San Antonio	0	72	34	13	3	716
Jermaine O'Neal, Indiana	2	29	46	17	19	523
Peja Stojakovic, Sacramento	1	8	16	34	33	281
Kobe Bryant, LA Lakers	0	7	14	22	27	212
Shaquille O'Neal, LA Lakers	0	5	11	23	19	178
Ben Wallace, Detroit	0	0	0	5	9	24
Jason Kidd, New Jersey	0	0	0	5	2	17
LeBron James, Cleveland	0	0	1	1	3	11
Baron Davis, New Orleans	0	0	0	1	1	4
Sam Cassell, Minnesota	0	0	0	1	1	4
Dirk Nowitzki, Dallas	0	0	0	1	1	4
Andrei Kirilenko, Utah	0	0	0	0	2	2
Yao Ming, Houston	0	0	0	0	1	1
Michael Redd, Milwaukee	0	0	0	0	1	1
Carmelo Anthony, Denver	0	0	0	0	1	1

All-NBA Teams

Voting by a 123-member panel of local and national pro basketball writers and broadcasters. Each ballot has entries for three teams; points awarded on 5-3-1 basis. First Team repeaters from 2002-03 are in **bold** type.

Pos	First Team	1st	Pts
F	**Tim Duncan**, San Antonio	114	597
F	**Kevin Garnett**, Minnesota	123	615
C	**Shaquille O'Neal**, LA Lakers	95	556
G	**Kobe Bryant**, LA Lakers	111	582
G	Jason Kidd, New Jersey	55	421

Pos	Second Team	1st	Pts
F	Jermaine O'Neal, Indiana	31	423
F	Peja Stojakovic, Sacramento	14	378
C	Ben Wallace, Detroit	2	195
G	Sam Cassell, Minnesota	34	322
G	Tracy McGrady, Orlando	16	274

Pos	Third Team	1st	Pts
F	Ron Artest, Indiana	0	90
F	Dirk Nowitzki, Dallas	0	145
C	Yao Ming, Houston	0	189
G	Baron Davis, New Orleans	10	176
G	Michael Redd, Milwaukee	4	95

All-Defensive Teams

Voting by NBA head coaches. Each ballot has entries for two teams; two points given for 1st team, one for 2nd. Coaches cannot vote for own players. First Team repeaters from 2002-03 are in **bold** type.

Pos	First Team	1st	Pts
F	Ron Artest, Indiana	26	54
F	**Kevin Garnett**, Minnesota	16	40
C	**Ben Wallace**, Detroit	21	48
G	Bruce Bowen, San Antonio	18	41
G	**Kobe Bryant**, LA Lakers	13	31

Pos	Second Team	1st	Pts
F	Andrei Kirilenko, Utah	11	36
F	Tim Duncan, San Antonio	10	33
C	Theo Ratliff, Portland	7	28
G	Doug Christie, Sacramento	5	25
G	Jason Kidd, New Jersey	3	15

Coach of the Year

The Red Auerbach Trophy; voting by a 122-member panel of local and national pro basketball writers and broadcasters.

	1st	2nd	3rd	Pts
Hubie Brown, Memphis	62	50	6	466
Jerry Sloan, Utah	56	44	12	424
Terry Porter, Milwaukee	1	5	34	54
Stan Van Gundy, Miami	1	10	19	54
Rick Carlisle, Indiana	2	3	22	41
Jeff Bzdelik, Denver	0	4	13	25
Flip Saunders, Minnesota	0	3	10	19
Phil Jackson, LA Lakers	0	2	2	8
Rick Adelman, Sacramento	0	1	0	3
Gregg Popovich, San Antonio	0	0	3	3
Paul Silas, Cleveland	0	0	1	1

Rookie of the Year

The Eddie Gottlieb Trophy; voting by 118-member panel of local and national pro basketball writers and broadcasters. Each ballot has entries for three players; points awarded on 5-3-1 basis.

	1st	2nd	3rd	Pts
LeBron James, Cleveland	78	39	1	508
Carmelo Anthony, Denver	40	76	2	430
Dwyane Wade, Miami	0	3	108	117
Kirk Hinrich, Chicago	0	0	4	4
Chris Bosh, Toronto	0	0	2	2
Marquis Daniels, Dallas	0	0	1	1

All-Rookie Team

Voting by NBA's 29 head coaches, who cannot vote for players on their own team. Each ballot has entries for two five-man teams, regardless of position; Coaches are not permitted to vote for players on their own team. two points given for 1st team, one for 2nd. First team votes in parentheses.

First Team	College	Pts
Carmelo Anthony, Denver (28)	Syracuse	56
LeBron James, Cleveland (28)	—	56
Dwyane Wade, Miami (28)	Marquette	56
Chris Bosh, Toronto (25)	Georgia Tech	53
Kirk Hinrich, Chicago (24)	Kansas	52

Second Team	College	Pts
Josh Howard, Dallas (3)	Wake Forest	29
T.J. Ford, Milwaukee (5)	Texas	27
Udonis Haslem, Miami (1)	Florida	21
Jarvis Hayes, Washington (1)	Georgia	20
Marquis Daniels, Dallas (1)	Auburn	20

J. Walter Kennedy Citizenship Award

The award, named for the NBA's second commissioner, is presented annually by the Professional Basketball Writers Association to honor an NBA player or coach "for outstanding community service and commitment to serve and give of his time outside the arena." The other nominees for this season's award were Golden State's Adonal Foyle and Nick Van Exel, Milwaukee's Desmond Mason and Philadelphia's Eric Snow.

Reggie Miller, Indiana

Sixth-Man Award

Voted on by a 120-member panel of local and national pro basketball writers and broadcasters. Each ballot has entries for three players; points awarded on 5-3-1 basis.

	1st	2nd	3rd	Pts
Antawn Jamison, Dallas	.43	33	24	338
Al Harrington, Indiana	.27	39	23	275
Emanuel Ginobili, San Antonio	.33	21	16	244
Bobby Jackson, Sacramento	.5	12	9	70
Earl Boykins, Denver	.3	5	16	46
Desmond Mason, Milwaukee	.4	6	7	45
Rafer Alston, Miami	.1	.1	6	14
Shane Battier, Memphis	.2	0	0	10
Raja Bell, Memphis	.1	0	4	9
Maurice Taylor, Houston	.1	0	3	8
Corliss Williamson, Detroit	.0	1	5	8
Bonzi Wells, Memphis	.0	1	2	5

Most Improved Player Award

Voted on by a 121-member panel of local and national pro basketball writers and broadcasters. Each ballot has entries for three players; points awarded on 5-3-1 basis.

	1st	2nd	3rd	Pts
Zach Randolph, Portland	.59	21	21	379
Carlos Boozer, Cleveland	.12	30	16	166
James Posey, Memphis	.17	14	10	137
Andrei Kirilenko, Utah	.11	12	10	101
Michael Redd, Milwaukee	.9	12	14	95
Lamar Odom, Miami	.1	8	2	31
Jamaal Magloire, New Orleans	.3	3	2	26
Samuel Dalembert, Philadelphia	.3	2	4	25
Joe Johnson, Phoenix	.1	4	3	20

Defensive Player of the Year Award

Voted on by a 121-member panel of local and national pro basketball writers and broadcasters.

	1st	2nd	3rd	Pts
Ron Artest, Indiana	.80	20	16	476
Ben Wallace, Detroit	.26	61	12	325
Theo Ratliff, Atlanta-Portland	.8	10	20	90
Bruce Bowen, San Antonio	.4	10	26	76
Andrei Kirilenko, Utah	.2	12	21	67
Kevin Garnett, Minnesota	.0	7	15	36
Tim Duncan, San Antonio	.0	1	5	8
Clifford Robinson, Golden St.	.1	0	0	5

Sportsmanship Award

Each of the 29 NBA teams nominated one player from their roster "who best represents the ideals of sportsmanship on the court," then a panel made up of former NBA players Walt Frazier, Mike Glenn, Tommy Heinsohn, Eddie Johnson, and Gil McGregor selected the four divisional winners from the pool of nominees. The award winner is chosen from the four divisional winners in vote by a panel of local and national pro basketball writers and broadcasters. The winner receives the Joe Dumars Trophy, named for the Detroit Pistons guard who won the inaugural sportsmanship award in 1996.

	1st	2nd	3rd	4th	Pts
P.J. Brown, New Orleans	.95	72	49	48	1220
Elton Brand, LA Clippers	.75	66	77	53	1139
Shane Battier, Memphis	.59	64	59	75	985
Kerry Kittles, New Jersey	.35	62	78	88	880

2004 College Draft

First and second round picks at the 58th annual NBA Draft held June 24, 2004 held in New York City at the Theatre at Madison Square Garden. The order of the first 14 positions were determined by a Draft Lottery held May 26, in Secaucus, N.J. Positions 15 through 29 reflect regular season records in reverse order. Note that Minnesota forfeited its first round pick as part of their illegal signing of Joe Smith in 1999. College seniors selected are noted in CAPITAL letters.

First Round

	Team		Pos
1	Orlando	Dwight Howard, SW Atl. Christ. Acad.	F
2	Charlotte	Emeka Okafor, Connecticut	F/C
3	Chicago	Ben Gordon, Connecticut	G
4	L.A. Clippers	Shaun Livingston, Peoria Central	G
5	Washington	Devin Harris, Wisconsin	G
6	Atlanta	Josh Childress, Stanford	F
7	Phoenix	Luol Deng, Duke	F
8	Toronto	RAFAEL ARAUJO, BYU	C
9	Philadelphia	Andre Iguodala, Arizona	G
10	Cleveland	Luke Jackson, Oregon	F
11	Golden State	Andris Biedrins, Latvia	F
12	Seattle	Robert Swift, Bakersfield HS	C
13	Portland	Sebastian Telfair, Abe Lincoln HS	G
14	Utah	Kris Humphries, Minnesota	F
15	Boston	Al Jefferson, Prentiss HS	F
16	Utah	Kirk Snyder, Nevada	G
17	Atlanta	Josh Smith, Oak Hill Acad.	F
18	New Orleans	J.R. Smith, St. Benedict's Prep	G
19	Miami	Dorell Wright, Leuzinger HS	F
20	Denver	JAMEER NELSON, St. Joseph's	G
21	Utah	Pavel Podkolzin, Russia	C
22	New Jersey	Viktor Khryapa, Russia	F
23	Portland	Sergei Monia, Russia	F
24	Boston	Delonte West, St. Joseph's	G
25	Boston	TONY ALLEN, Oklahoma St.	G
26	Sacramento	Kevin Martin, W. Carolina	G
27	L.A. Lakers	Sasha Vujacic, Slovenia	G
28	San Antonio	Beno Udrih, Slovenia	G
29	Indiana	David Harrison, Colorado	C

Second Round

	Team		Pos
30	Orlando	Anderson Varejao, Brazil	F
31	Chicago	JACKSON VROMAN, Iowa St.	F
32	Washington	Peter John Ramos, Puerto Rico	C
33	L.A. Clippers	LIONEL CHALMERS, Xavier	G
34	Atlanta	Donta Smith, SE Illinois College	G
35	Seattle	ANDRE EMMETT, Texas Tech	G
36	Orlando	ANTONIO BURKS, Memphis	G
37	Atlanta	ROYAL IVEY, Texas	G
38	Chicago	CHRIS DUHON, Duke	G
39	Toronto	Albert Miralles, Spain	F
40	Boston	JUSTIN REED, Mississippi	F
41	Seattle	DAVID YOUNG, N. Carolina Central	G
42	Atlanta	Viktor Sanikidze, Rep. of Georgia	F
43	New York	Trevor Ariza, UCLA	F
44	New Orleans	TIM PICKETT, Florida St.	G
45	Charlotte	BERNARD ROBINSON, Michigan	F
46	Portland	Ha Seung-Jin, South Korea	C
47	Miami	PAPE SOW, Cal St. Fullerton	F
48	Sacramento	RICKY MINARD, Morehead St.	F
49	Memphis	Sergei Lishouk, Ukraine	F
50	Dallas	Vassillis Spanoulis, Greece	G
51	New Jersey	Christian Drejer, Denmark	F
52	San Antonio	ROMAIN SATO, Xavier	G
53	Miami	MATT FREIJE, Vanderbilt	F
54	Detroit	RICKEY PAULDING, Missouri	G
55	Houston	LUIS FLORES, Manhattan	G
56	L.A. Lakers	MARCUS DOUTHIT, Providence	F/C
57	San Antonio	Sergei Karaulov, Russia	C
58	Minnesota	Blake Stepp, Gonzaga	G
59	Indiana	Rashad Wright, Georgia	G

Continental Basketball Association.
Final Standings

QW refers to quarters won. Teams get 3 points for a win, 1 point for each quarter won and $1/2$ point for any quarters tied. (*) denotes playoff qualifiers.

	W	L	Home	Away	QW	Pts	Avg
*Dakota Wizards	.34	14	21-3	13-11	114.0	**216.0**	4.5
*Idaho Stampede	.34	14	21-3	13-11	103.5	**205.5**	4.3
*Gary Steelheads	.27	21	16-8	11-13	96.0	**177.0**	3.7
*Rockford Lightning	.25	23	17-7	8-16	95.6	**171.5**	3.6
Sioux Falls Skyforce	.23	25	14-10	9-15	100.5	**169.5**	3.5
Great Lakes Storm	.15	33	11-13	4-20	83.0	**128.0**	2.7
Yakima Sun Kings	.10	38	7-17	3-21	78.5	**108.5**	2.3

Playoffs
Semifinals

Idaho vs. Gary

Mar. 9	at Idaho 107	Gary 98
Mar. 10	at Idaho	Gary 90
Mar. 12	at Gary 100	Idaho 97
Mar. 13	Idaho 111	at Gary 108

Idaho wins series, 3 games to 1

Dakota vs. Rockford

Mar. 9	at Dakota 111	Rockford 105
Mar. 10	Rockford 117	at Dakota 111
Mar. 14	at Dakota 120	Rockford 101
Mar. 17	Dakota 108	at Rockford 107

Dakota wins series, 3 games to 1

Final

Mon., Mar. 22 at Bismarck Civic Center, Bismarck, N.D.
Attendance: 5,130.

	1	2	3	4	F
Idaho Stampede	34	35	28	32	**—129**
Dakota Wizards	35	30	32	35	**—132**

Playoff MVP: Maurice Carter, Dakota, G (36 points, 14-14 FTs)

CBA Annual Awards

Most Valuable Player	Josh Davis, Idaho
Newcomer of the Year	Josh Davis, Idaho
Rookie of the Year	David Bailey, Idaho
Def. Player of the Year	DeSean Hadley, Idaho
Coach of the Year	Dave Joerger, Dakota

CBA Regular Season Individual Leaders

Scoring

	Gm	Pts	Avg
Ronnie Fields, Rockford	.43	1072	24.9
Anthony Goldwire, Yakima	.37	861	23.3
Ray Weathers, Great Lakers	.33	710	21.5
Jimmie Hunter, Rockford	.48	976	20.3
Leonard White, Sious Falls	.46	927	20.2
David Jackson, Sioux Falls	.48	938	19.5
Maurice Carter, Dakota	.35	666	19.0
Kaniel Dickens, Dakota	.29	550	19.0

Rebounding

	Gm	Reb	Avg
Leon Smith, Great Lakes	.30	367	12.2
Leonard White, Sioux Falls	.46	470	10.2
Shelly Clark, Gary	.37	361	9.8
Josh Davis, Idaho	.40	385	9.6
Ben Ebong, Dakota	.43	386	9.0
Sam Clancy, Yakima	.28	242	8.6
Marcus Hicks, Yakima	.28	188	6.7
DeSean Hadley, Idaho	.47	287	6.1

Field Goal Pct.

	FGM	FGA	Pct
Mario Woodson, Idaho	.78	120	.650
Immanuel McElroy, Gary	.325	503	.646
Paul McPherson, Idaho	.251	400	.628
Lawrence Nelson, Rockford	.179	289	.619
Noel Felix, Idaho	.123	204	.603
Marcus Hicks, Yakima	.177	299	.592
Josh Davis, Idaho	.299	507	.590
Casey Calvary, Idaho	.156	268	.582

Assists

	Gm	Ast	Avg
Jemeil Rich, Gary	.47	498	10.6
Randy Livingston, Idaho	.32	303	9.5
David Bailey, Idaho	.48	358	7.5
Darrick Martin, Sioux Falls	.27	199	7.4
Anthony Goldwire, Yakima	.24	140	5.8
Greg Grays, Yakima	.24	140	5.8
Ray Weathers, Great Lakes	.33	185	5.6
David Jackson, Sioux Falls	.48	205	4.3

Steals

	Gm	Stl	Avg
Ronnie Fields, Rockford	.43	137	3.2
Jemeil Rich, Gary	.47	127	2.7
Leonard White, Sioux Falls	.46	97	2.1
Randy Livingston, Idaho	.32	63	2.0
Jimmie Hunter, Rockford	.48	94	2.0
Darrick Martin, Sioux Falls	.27	48	1.8
Darrin Hancock, Sious Falls	.45	79	1.8
Paul McPherson, Idaho	.40	65	1.6

Free Throw Pct.

	FTM	FTA	Pct
Darrick Martin, Sioux Falls	.109	121	.901
David Jackson, Sioux Falls	.95	106	.896
David Graves, Gary	.127	142	.894
Randy Livingston, Idaho	.96	109	.881
Roberto Bergersen, Idaho	.89	101	.881
Anthony Goldwire, Yakima	.219	252	.869
Greg Grays, Yakima	.44	52	.846
Kaniel Dickens, Dakota	.115	137	.839

National Basketball Development League

The NBDL is a feeder league founded by the NBA in 2001. The individual teams do not have direct relationships with NBA clubs but players (and coaches) are called-up to the NBA occasionally. (*) denotes playoff qualifiers.

2004 Final Standings

	W	L	Pct	GB
*Asheville Altitude	28	18	.609	—
*Charleston Lowgators	27	19	.587	1
*Huntsville Flight	24	22	.522	4
*Fayetteville Patriots	21	25	.457	7
Roanoke Dazzle	20	26	.435	8
Columbus Riverdragons	18	28	.391	10

Head Coaches: Asheville—Joey Meyer (3rd season); Charleston—Doug Marty (2nd); Huntsville—Ralph Lewis (2nd); Fayetteville—Jeff Capel (3rd); Roanoke—Kent Davison (3rd); Columbus—Jeff Malone (2nd).

Note: Prior to the 2004 season the NBDL contracted two teams, the Greenville Grove and the Mobile Revelers.

Regular Season Individual Leaders

Scoring

	Gm	Pts	Avg
Desmond Penigar, Asheville	38	746	19.6
Tierre Brown, Charleston	41	763	18.6
Ime Udoke, Charleston	41	694	16.9
Junie Sanders, Fayetteville	44	743	16.9
Marque Perry, Roanoke	44	678	15.4
Jason Collier, Fayetteville	30	462	15.4
Alpha Bangura, Charleston	45	676	15.0
Britton Johnsen, Fayetteville	34	495	14.6
Josh Asselin, Roanoke	46	664	14.4
Philip Ricci, Hunstville	45	632	14.0
Rod Grizzard, Huntsville	44	615	14.0

Rebounds

	Gm	Reb	Avg
Rodney Bias, Huntsville	36	364	10.1
Coutney James, Columbus	46	377	8.2
Bryan Lucas, Fayetteville	45	367	8.2
Karim Shabazz, Charleston	46	348	7.6
Terence Morris, Columbus	46	340	7.4

Assists

	Gm	Ast	Avg
Omar Cook, Fayetteville	24	215	9.0
Kareem Reid, Asheville	43	290	6.7
Marque Perry, Roanoke	44	295	6.7
Tierre Brown, Charleston	41	265	6.5
Mateen Cleaves, Huntsville	42	248	5.9

Steals

	Gm	Stl	Avg
Omar Cook, Fayetteville	24	63	2.6
Tierre Brown, Charleston	41	74	1.8
Brandin Knight, Asheville	38	68	1.8
Ime Udoke, Charleston	41	64	1.6
Erick Barkley, Huntsville	42	64	1.5

Field Goal Pct.

	FG	FGA	Pct
Kris Lang, Asheville	206	336	.613
Greg Stevenson, Asheville	189	332	.569
Karim Shabazz, Charleston	113	206	.549
Rodney Bias, Huntsville	81	153	.529
Josh Asselin, Roanoke	238	452	.527
Darrell Jones, Roanoke	145	275	.527

Playoffs

Semifinals

Apr. 17 at Asheville

	1	2	3	4	F
Fayetteville Patriots	31	25	29	26	111
Asheville Altitude	31	33	24	28	116

Apr. 17 at Charleston

	1	2	3	4	F
Huntsville Flight	25	34	20	29	108
Charleston Lowgators	26	23	28	23	100

Final

Apr. 24 at Asheville. Attendance: 3891

	1	2	3	4	OT	F
Huntsville Flight	37	19	18	23	9	106
Asheville Altitude	21	27	21	28	11	108

Annual Awards

Most Valuable Player . . . . . .Tierre Brown, Charleston
Rookie of the Year . . . . .Desmond Penigar, Asheville
Def. Player of the Year . . . .Karim Shabazz, Charleston

All-NBDL First Team

Holdover from 2002-03 team is in **bold** type.

Pos		Team
F	Josh Asselin	Roanoke
F	Desmond Penigar	Asheville
C	Jason collier	Fayetteville
G	**Tierre Brown**	Charleston
G	Marque Perry	Roanoke

All-NBDL Second Team

Pos		Team
F	Britton Johnsen	Fayetteville
F	Phil Ricci	Huntsville
F	Ime Udoka	Charleston
C	Brandon Kurtz	Asheville
G	Omar Cook	Fayetteville
G	Junie Sanders	Fayetteville

Lowgators move to Florida

The Charleston Lowgators, one of the NBDL's inaugural franchises (known then as the *North* Charleston Lowgators) moved to Ft. Myers, Fla. following the 2003-04 season. The team was renamed the **Florida Flame** and became the first locally owned team in the D-League. All the other teams thus far have been owned and operated by the NBA.

The Lowgators was the league's winningest team over its three seasons in North Charleston (with a record of 89-63), but were unable to bring in enough fans to the 8,451-seat North Charleston Coliseum despite appearing in the postseason every year. They averaged fewer than 1,300 fans per game in 2003-04.

The Florida Flame can protect up to four players from the Lowgators 10-man roster which included 2004 NBDL MVP Tierre Brown, Defensive Player of the Year Karim Shabazz and the league's third-leading scorer Ime Udoke.

Women's National Basketball Association
2004 WNBA Final Standings

Conference champions (*) and playoff qualifiers (†) are noted. GB refers to Games Behind leader. Number of seasons listed after each head coach refers to current tenure with club.

Eastern Conference

	W	L	Pct	GB	Home	Road
*Connecticut	18	16	.529	—	10-7	8-9
†New York	18	16	.529	—	11-16	7-10
†Detroit	17	17	.500	1	8-9	9-8
†Washington ...	17	17	.500	1	11-6	6-11
Charlotte	16	18	.471	2	10-7	6-11
Indiana	15	19	.441	3	10-7	5-12

Head Coaches: Conn– Mike Thibault (2nd season); **NY–**Richie Adubato (6th, 7-9) was fired on July 3 and replaced on an interim basis by assistant Pat Coyle (11-7); **Det–**Bill Laimbeer (3rd); **Wash–**Michael Adams (1st); **Cha–**Trudi Lacey (2nd); **Ind–**Brian Winters (1st).

2003 Standings: 1. Detroit (25-9); 2. Connecticut (18-16); 3. Charlotte (18-16); 4. Cleveland (17-17); 5. New York (16-18); 6. Indiana (16-18); 7. Washington (9-25).

Note: Following the 2003 season, the Cleveland Rockers, one of the WNBA's original franchises folded and a dispersal draft was held for the team's players.

Western Conference

	W	L	Pct	GB	Home	Road
*Los Angeles ...	25	9	.735	—	15-2	10-7
†Seattle	20	14	.588	5	13.4	7-10
†Sacramento ...	18	16	.529	7	10-7	8-9
†Minnesota	18	16	.529	7	11-6	7-10
Phoenix	17	17	.500	8	10-7	7-10
Houston	13	21	.382	12	9-8	4-13
San Antonio ...	9	25	.265	16	6-11	3-14

Head Coaches: LA–Michael Cooper (4th season, 14-6) resigned and was replaced by assistant Karleen Thompson (11-3); **Sea–**Anne Donovan (2nd); **Sac–**John Whisenant (2nd); **Minn–**Suzie McConnell Serio (2nd); **Pho–**Carrie Graf (1st); **Hou–**Van Chancellor (8th); **SA–**Dee Brown (1st, 6-18) resigned and was replaced on an interim basis by assistant Shell Dailey (3-7); .

2003 Standings: 1. Los Angeles (24-10); 2. Houston (20-14); 3. Sacramento (19-15); 4. Minnesota (18-16); 5. Seattle (18-16); 6. San Antonio (12-22); 7. Phoenix (8-26).

WNBA Regular Season Individual Leaders

Scoring

	Gm	Pts	Avg
Lauren Jackson, Seattle	31	634	20.5
Tina Thompson, Houston	26	520	20.0
Lisa Leslie, Los Angeles	34	598	17.6
Diana Taurasi, Phoenix	34	578	17.0
Tamika Catchings, Indiana	34	568	16.7
Swin Cash, Detroit	32	526	16.4
Nykesha Sales, Connecticut	34	517	15.2
Sheryl Swoopes, Houston	31	459	14.8
Yolanda Griffith, Sacramento	34	494	14.5
Mwadi Mabika, Los Angeles	31	445	14.4
Anna DeForge, Phoenix	34	488	14.4
LaToya Thomas, San Antonio	31	440	14.2
Deanna Nolan, Detroit	34	464	13.6
Becky Hammon, New York	34	460	13.5
Penny Taylor, Phoenix	33	434	13.2

Rebounds

	Gm	Reb	Avg
Lisa Leslie, Los Angeles	34	336	9.9
Cheryl Ford, Detroit	31	297	9.6
Michelle Snow, Houston	31	239	7.7
Tamika Catchings, Indiana	34	249	7.3
Elena Baranova, New York	34	246	7.2
Yolanda Griffith, Sacramento ...	34	246	7.2
Taj McWilliams-Franklin, Connecticut	34	244	7.2
Adrienne Goodson, San Antonio ...	34	235	6.9
Natalie Williams, Indiana	34	235	6.9
Lauren Jackson, Seattle	31	207	6.7
Swin Cash, Detroit	32	208	6.5
Tammy Sutton-Brown, Charlotte ...	34	211	6.2
Tina Thompson, Houston	26	157	6.0
Tamika Williams, Minnesota	34	205	6.0
Ruth Riley, Detroit	34	199	5.9

Field Goal Pct.

	FGM	FGA	Pct
Tamika Williams, Minnesota	102	189	.540
Yolanda Griffith, Sacramento	177	341	.519
Lisa Leslie, Los Angeles	223	451	.494
LaToya Thomas, San Antonio	171	350	.489
Penny Taylor, Phoenix	150	310	.484
Lauren Jackson, Seattle	220	460	.478
Taj McWilliams-Franklin, Connecticut	168	352	.477
Tammy Sutton-Brown, Charlotte ...	106	224	.473
Swin Cash, Detroit	180	384	.469
Elena Baranova, New York	146	315	.463
Sue Bird, Seattle	151	326	.463

Assists

	Gm	Ast	Avg
Nikki Teasley, Los Angeles	34	207	6.1
Sue Bird, Seattle	34	184	5.4
Dawn Staley, Charlotte	34	171	5.0
Ticha Penicheiro, Sacramento	33	163	4.9
Lindsay Whalen, Connecticut	31	148	4.8
Elaine Powell, Detroit	30	134	4.5
Becky Hammon, New York	34	150	4.4
Shannon Johnson, San Antonio ...	31	136	4.4
Swin Cash, Detroit	32	135	4.2
Diana Taurasi, Phoenix	34	132	3.9
Vickie Johnson, New York	34	124	3.6

Steals

	Gm	Stl	Avg
Yolanda Griffith, Sacramento	34	75	2.21
Nykesha Sales, Connecticut	34	75	2.21
Alana Beard, Washington	34	69	2.03
Tamika Catchings, Indiana	34	67	1.97
Deanna Nolan, Detroit	34	66	1.94
Ticha Penicheiro, Sacramento	33	64	1.94

Blocks

	Gm	Blk	Avg
Lisa Leslie, Los Angeles	34	98	2.88
Tammy Sutton-Brown, Charlotte ...	34	71	2.09
Lauren Jackson, Seattle	31	62	2.00
Elena Baranova, New York	34	58	-1.71
Ruth Riley, Detroit	34	53	1.56
Margo Dydek, San Antonio	34	48	1.41

WNBA Playoffs
First Round (Best of 3)

East

Connecticut vs. Washington

Sept. 25 at Washington 67 . . . . .Connecticut 59
Sept. 28 at Connecticut 80 . . . . .Washington 70
Sept. 29 at Connecticut 76 . . . . .Washington 56

Connecticut Sun win series, 2-1

New York vs. Detroit

Sept. 24 New York 75 . . . . .at Detroit 62
Sept. 26 Detroit 76 . . . . .at New York 66
Sept. 28 at New York 66 . . . . .Detroit 64

New York Liberty win series, 2-1

West

Sacramento vs. Los Angeles

Sept. 24 at Sacramento 72 . . . . .Los Angeles 52
Sept. 26 at Los Angeles 71 . . . . .Sacramento 57
Sept. 28 Sacramento 73 . . . . .at Los Angeles 58

Sacramento Monarchs win series, 2-1

Seattle vs. Minnesota

Sept. 25 Seattle 70 . . . . .at Minnesota 58
Sept. 27 at Seattle 64 . . . . .Minnesota 54

Seattle Storm win series, 2-0

Conference Finals (Best of 3)
East

Connecticut vs. New York

Oct. 1 Connecticut 61 . . . . .at New York 51
Oct. 3 at Connecticut 60 . . . . .New York 57

Connecticut Sun win series, 2-0

West

Sacramento vs. Seattle

Oct. 1 at Sacramento 74 . . .OT . . . . .Seattle 72
Oct. 3 at Seattle 66 . . . . .Sacramento 54
Oct. 5 at Seattle 82 . . . . .Sacramento 62

Seattle Storm win series, 2-1

Championship Series (Best of 3)
Connecticut vs. Seattle

Seattle wins series, 2 games to 1

	W-L	Avg	Leading Scorer
Connecticut Sun	.1-2	64.3	Sales (22.7 ppg)
Seattle Storm	.2-1	68.3	Lennox (22.3 ppg)

Date	Winner	Home Court
Oct. 8 . . . . .Sun, 68-64		at Connecticut
Oct. 10. . . . . .Storm, 67-65		at Seattle
Oct. 12 . . . . .Storm, 74-60		at Seattle

Finals MVP: Betty Lennox, Seattle, G (22.3 ppg, 4.3 rpg, 2.0 apg)

Annual Awards

Most Valuable Player . . . .Lisa Leslie, Los Angeles
Rookie of the Year . . . . . .Diana Taurasi, Phoenix
Most Improved . . . . . . .Wendy Palmer, Connecticut
                                        & Kelly Miller, Indiana
Def. Player of the Year . . .Lisa Leslie, Los Angeles
Coach of the Year . . .Suzie McConnell Serio, Minn.
Sportsmanship Award . . . .Teresa Edwards, Minn.

All-WNBA First Team

Holdovers from 2002-03 team are in **bold** type.

Pos	Team
F	**Lauren Jackson**, Seattle
F	Tina Thompson, Houston
C	**Lisa Leslie**, Los Angeles
G	Diana Taurasi, Phoenix
G	**Sue Bird**, Seattle

2004 WNBA Draft
First Round

Pick	Team	Player, College, Pos
1	Phoenix	Diana Taurasi, Connecticut, G
2	Washington	Alana Beard, Duke, G
3	Charlotte	Nicole Powell, Stanford, G/F
4	Connecticut	Lindsay Whalen, Minnesota, G
5	New York	Shameka Christon, Arkansas, G/F
6	Minnesota	Nicole Ohlde, Kansas St., C
7	Minnesota	Vanessa Hayden, Florida, C
8	Phoenix	Chandi Jones, Houston, G/F
9	Indiana	Ebony Hoffman, USC, C
10	Sacramento	Rebekkah Brunson, Georgetown, F
11	Detroit	Iciss Tillis, Duke, C/F
12	Los Angeles	Christi Thomas, Georgia, F
13	Detroit	Shereka Wright, Purdue, F

All-WNBA First Team

Lauren Jackson *Tina Thompson* *Lisa Leslie* *Diana Taurasi* *Sue Bird*
Seattle **Houston** **Los Angeles** **Phoenix** **Seattle**

1938-2004
Through the Years

SPORTS ALMANAC

The NBA Finals

Although the National Basketball Association traces its first championship back to the 1946-47 season, the league was then called the Basketball Association of America (BAA). It did not become the NBA until after the 1948-49 season when the BAA and the National Basketball League (NBL) agreed to merge.

In the chart below, the Eastern finalists (representing the NBA Eastern Division from 1947-70, and the NBA Eastern Conference since 1971) are listed in CAPITAL letters. Also, each NBA champion's wins and losses are noted in parentheses after the series score.

Multiple winners: Boston (16); Minneapolis-LA Lakers (14); Chicago Bulls (6); Detroit, Phi-SF-Golden St. Warriors and Syracuse Nationals-Phi. 76ers (3); Houston, New York and San Antonio (2).

Year	Winner	Head Coach	Series	Loser	Head Coach
1947	PHILADELPHIA WARRIORS	Eddie Gottlieb	4-1 (WWWLW)	Chicago Stags	Harold Olsen
1948	Baltimore Bullets	Buddy Jeannette	4-2 (LWWWLW)	PHILA. WARRIORS	Eddie Gottlieb
1949	Minneapolis Lakers	John Kundla	4-2 (WWWLLW)	WASH. CAPITOLS	Red Auerbach
1950	Minneapolis Lakers	John Kundla	4-2 (WLWWLW)	SYRACUSE	Al Cervi
1951	Rochester	Les Harrison	4-3 (WWWWLLLW)	NEW YORK	Joe Lapchick
1952	Minneapolis Lakers	John Kundla	4-3 (WLWLWLW)	NEW YORK	Joe Lapchick
1953	Minneapolis Lakers	John Kundla	4-1 (LWWWW)	NEW YORK	Joe Lapchick
1954	Minneapolis Lakers	John Kundla	4-3 (WLWLWLW)	SYRACUSE	Al Cervi
1955	SYRACUSE	Al Cervi	4-3 (WWLLLWW)	Ft. Wayne Pistons	Charley Eckman
1956	PHILADELPHIA WARRIORS	George Senesky	4-1 (WLWW)	Ft. Wayne Pistons	Charley Eckman
1957	BOSTON	Red Auerbach	4-3 (LWLWLWW)	St. Louis Hawks	Alex Hannum
1958	St. Louis Hawks	Alex Hannum	4-2 (WLWLWW)	BOSTON	Red Auerbach
1959	BOSTON	Red Auerbach	4-0	Mpls. Lakers	John Kundla
1960	BOSTON	Red Auerbach	4-3 (WLWLWLW)	St. Louis Hawks	Ed Macauley
1961	BOSTON	Red Auerbach	4-1 (WWLWW)	St. Louis Hawks	Paul Seymour
1962	BOSTON	Red Auerbach	4-3 (WLLWLWW)	LA Lakers	Fred Schaus
1963	BOSTON	Red Auerbach	4-2 (WWWLW)	LA Lakers	Fred Schaus
1964	BOSTON	Red Auerbach	4-1 (WWLWW)	SF Warriors	Alex Hannum
1965	BOSTON	Red Auerbach	4-1 (WWWLW)	LA Lakers	Fred Schaus
1966	BOSTON	Red Auerbach	4-3 (LWWWLLW)	LA Lakers	Fred Schaus
1967	PHILADELPHIA 76ERS	Alex Hannum	4-2 (WLWWLW)	SF Warriors	Bill Sharman
1968	BOSTON	Bill Russell	4-2 (WLWLWW)	LA Lakers	B.van Breda Kolff
1969	BOSTON	Bill Russell	4-3 (LLWWLWW)	LA Lakers	B.van Breda Kolff
1970	NEW YORK	Red Holzman	4-3 (WLWLWLW)	LA Lakers	Joe Mullaney
1971	Milwaukee	Larry Costello	4-0	BALT. BULLETS	Gene Shue
1972	LA Lakers	Bill Sharman	4-1 (LWWWW)	NEW YORK	Red Holzman
1973	NEW YORK	Red Holzman	4-1 (LWWWW)	LA Lakers	Bill Sharman
1974	BOSTON	Tommy Heinsohn	4-3 (WLWLWLW)	Milwaukee	Larry Costello
1975	Golden St. Warriors	Al Attles	4-0	WASH. BULLETS	K.C. Jones
1976	BOSTON	Tommy Heinsohn	4-2 (WWLLWW)	Phoenix	John MacLeod
1977	Portland	Jack Ramsay	4-2 (LLWWWW)	PHILA. 76ERS	Gene Shue
1978	WASHINGTON BULLETS	Dick Motta	4-3 (LWLWLWW)	Seattle	Lenny Wilkens
1979	Seattle	Lenny Wilkens	4-1 (LWWWW)	WASH. BULLETS	Dick Motta
1980	LA Lakers	Paul Westhead	4-2 (WLWLWW)	PHILA. 76ERS	Billy Cunningham
1981	BOSTON	Bill Fitch	4-2 (WLWLWW)	Houston	Del Harris
1982	LA Lakers	Pat Riley	4-2 (WLWWLW)	PHILA. 76ERS	Billy Cunningham
1983	PHILADELPHIA 76ERS	Billy Cunningham	4-0	LA Lakers	Pat Riley
1984	BOSTON	K.C. Jones	4-3 (LWWLWLW)	LA Lakers	Pat Riley
1985	LA Lakers	Pat Riley	4-2 (LWWWLW)	BOSTON	K.C. Jones
1986	BOSTON	K.C. Jones	4-2 (WWLWLW)	Houston	Bill Fitch
1987	LA Lakers	Pat Riley	4-2 (WWLWLW)	BOSTON	K.C. Jones
1988	LA Lakers	Pat Riley	4-3 (LWWLLWW)	DETROIT PISTONS	Chuck Daly
1989	DETROIT PISTONS	Chuck Daly	4-0	LA Lakers	Pat Riley
1990	DETROIT	Chuck Daly	4-1 (WLWWW)	Portland	Rick Adelman
1991	CHICAGO	Phil Jackson	4-1 (LWWWW)	LA Lakers	Mike Dunleavy
1992	CHICAGO	Phil Jackson	4-2 (WWLLWW)	Portland	Rick Adelman
1993	CHICAGO	Phil Jackson	4-2 (WWLWLW)	Phoenix	Paul Westphal
1994	Houston	Rudy Tomjanovich	4-3 (WLWLLWW)	NEW YORK	Pat Riley
1995	Houston	Rudy Tomjanovich	4-0	ORLANDO	Brian Hill

Year	Winner	Head Coach	Series		Loser	Head Coach
1996	CHICAGO	Phil Jackson	4-2	(WWWLLW)	Seattle	George Karl
1997	CHICAGO	Phil Jackson	4-2	(WWLLWW)	Utah	Jerry Sloan
1998	CHICAGO	Phil Jackson	4-2	(WWLLWW)	Utah	Jerry Sloan
1999	San Antonio	Gregg Popovich	4-1	(WWLWW)	NEW YORK	Jeff Van Gundy
2000	LA Lakers	Phil Jackson	4-2	(WWLWLW)	INDIANA	Larry Bird
2001	LA Lakers	Phil Jackson	4-1	(LWWWW)	PHILA. 76ERS	Larry Brown
2002	LA Lakers	Phil Jackson	4-0		NEW JERSEY	Byron Scott
2003	San Antonio	Gregg Popovich	4-2	(WLWLWW)	NEW JERSEY	Byron Scott
2004	DETROIT	Larry Brown	4-1	(WLWWW)	LA Lakers	Phil Jackson

Note: Four finalists were led by player-coaches: **1948**—Buddy Jeannette (guard) of Baltimore; **1950**—Al Cervi (guard) of Syracuse; **1968**—Bill Russell (center) of Boston; **1969**—Bill Russell (center) of Boston.

Most Valuable Player

Selected by an 11-member media panel. Winner who did not play for the NBA champion is in **bold** type.

Multiple winners: Michael Jordan (6); Magic Johnson and Shaquille O'Neal (3); Kareem Abdul-Jabbar, Larry Bird, Tim Duncan, Hakeem Olajuwon and Willis Reed (2).

Year		Year		Year	
1969	**Jerry West**, LA Lakers, G	1981	Cedric Maxwell, Boston, F	1993	Michael Jordan, Chicago, G
1970	Willis Reed, New York, C	1982	Magic Johnson, LA Lakers, G	1994	Hakeem Olajuwon, Houston, C
1971	Lew Alcindor, Milwaukee, C	1983	Moses Malone, Philadelphia, C	1995	Hakeem Olajuwon, Houston, C
1972	Wilt Chamberlain, LA Lakers, C	1984	Larry Bird, Boston, F	1996	Michael Jordan, Chicago, G
1973	Willis Reed, New York, C	1985	K. Abdul-Jabbar, LA Lakers, C	1997	Michael Jordan, Chicago, G
1974	John Havlicek, Boston, F	1986	Larry Bird, Boston, F	1998	Michael Jordan, Chicago, G
1975	Rick Barry, Golden State, F	1987	Magic Johnson, LA Lakers, G	1999	Tim Duncan, San Antonio, F/C
1976	Jo Jo White, Boston, G	1988	James Worthy, LA Lakers, F	2000	Shaquille O'Neal, LA Lakers, C
1977	Bill Walton, Portland, C	1989	Joe Dumars, Detroit, G	2001	Shaquille O'Neal, LA Lakers, C
1978	Wes Unseld, Washington, C	1990	Isiah Thomas, Detroit, G	2002	Shaquille O'Neal, LA Lakers, C
1979	Dennis Johnson, Seattle, G	1991	Michael Jordan, Chicago, G	2003	Tim Duncan, San Antonio, F/C
1980	Magic Johnson, LA Lakers, G/C	1992	Michael Jordan, Chicago, G	2004	Chauncey Billups, Detroit, G

Note: Lew Alcindor changed his name to Kareem Abdul-Jabbar after the 1970-71 season.

All-Time NBA Playoff Leaders

Through the 2004 playoffs.

CAREER

Years listed indicate number of playoff appearances. Players active in 2004 in **bold** type. DNP indicates player that was active in 2004 but did not participate in playoffs.

Points

	Yrs	Gm	Pts	Avg
1 Michael Jordan	13	179	5987	33.4
2 Kareem Abdul-Jabbar	18	237	5762	24.3
3 **Karl Malone**	19	193	4761	24.7
4 Jerry West	13	153	4457	29.1
5 **Shaquille O'Neal**	11	158	4294	27.2
6 Larry Bird	12	164	3897	23.8
7 John Havlicek	13	172	3776	22.0
8 Hakeem Olajuwon	15	145	3755	25.9
9 Magic Johnson	13	190	3701	19.5
10 Elgin Baylor	12	134	3623	27.0
11 **Scottie Pippen** (DNP)	16	208	3642	17.5
12 Wilt Chamberlain	13	160	3607	22.5
13 Kevin McHale	13	169	3182	18.8
14 Dennis Johnson	13	180	3116	17.3
15 Julius Erving	11	141	3088	21.9
16 James Worthy	9	143	3022	21.1
17 Clyde Drexler	15	145	2963	20.4
18 Sam Jones	12	154	2909	18.9
19 Charles Barkley	13	123	2833	23.0
20 Robert Parish	16	184	2820	15.3

Scoring Average

Minimum of 25 games or 700 points.

	Yrs	Gm	Pts	Avg
1 Michael Jordan	13	179	5987	33.4
2 **Allen Iverson** (DNP)	5	57	1743	30.6
3 Jerry West	13	153	4457	29.1
4 **Shaquille O'Neal**	11	158	4294	27.2
5 Elgin Baylor	12	134	3623	27.0
6 George Gervin	9	59	1592	27.0
7 Hakeem Olajuwon	15	145	3755	25.9
8 Dominique Wilkins	9	55	1421	25.8
9 **Dirk Nowitzki**	6	40	1024	25.6
10 Bob Pettit	9	88	2240	25.5
11 **Paul Pierce**	3	30	748	24.9
12 Rick Barry	7	74	1833	24.8
13 **Karl Malone**	19	193	4761	24.7
14 Bernard King	5	28	687	24.5
15 Alex English	10	68	1661	24.4
16 Kareem Abdul-Jabbar	18	237	5762	24.3
17 Paul Arizin	8	49	1186	24.2
18 **Tim Duncan**	6	82	1960	23.9
19 Larry Bird	12	164	3897	23.8
20 George Mikan	9	91	2141	23.5

Field Goals

	Yrs	FG	Att	Pct
1 Kareem Abdul-Jabbar	18	2356	4422	.533
2 Michael Jordan	13	2188	4497	.487
3 **Karl Malone**	19	1743	3768	.463
4 **Shaquille O'Neal**	11	1658	2951	.562
5 Jerry West	13	1622	3460	.469
6 Hakeem Olajuwon	15	1504	2847	.528
7 Larry Bird	12	1458	3090	.472
8 John Havlicek	13	1451	3329	.436
9 Wilt Chamberlain	13	1425	2728	.522
10 Elgin Baylor	12	1388	3161	.439

Free Throws

	Yrs	FT	Att	Pct
1 Michael Jordan	13	1463	1766	.828
2 **Karl Malone**	19	1269	1725	.736
3 Jerry West	13	1213	1507	.805
4 Kareem Abdul-Jabbar	18	1050	1419	.740
5 Magic Johnson	13	1040	1241	.838
6 **Shaquille O'Neal**	11	978	1889	.518
7 Larry Bird	12	901	1012	.891
8 John Havlicek	13	874	1046	.836
9 Elgin Baylor	12	847	1101	.769
10 **Scottie Pippen** (DNP)	16	772	1067	.724

All-Time NBA Playoff Leaders (Cont.)

Assists

		Yrs	Gm	No	Avg
1	Magic Johnson	13	190	2346	12.3
2	John Stockton	19	182	1839	10.1
3	Larry Bird	12	164	1062	6.5
4	**Scottie Pippen** (DNP)	16	208	1048	5.0
5	Michael Jordan	13	179	1022	5.7

Rebounds

		Yrs	Gm	No	Avg
1	Bill Russell	13	165	4104	24.9
2	Wilt Chamberlain	13	160	3913	24.5
3	Kareem Abdul-Jabbar	18	237	2481	10.5
4	**Karl Malone**	19	193	2062	10.7
5	Wes Unseld	12	119	1777	14.9

Appearances

	No		No
Karl Malone	19	Sam Perkins	15
John Stockton	19	Jerome Kersey	15
Kareem Abdul-Jabbar	18	Tree Rollins	15
Robert Parish	16	Charles Oakley	15
Scottie Pippen (DNP)	16	Dolph Schayes	15
Terry Porter	16	Clyde Drexler	15

Games Played

	No		No
K. Abdul-Jabbar	237	Dennis Johnson	180
Scottie Pippen (DNP)	208	Michael Jordan	179
Danny Ainge	193	John Havlicek	172
Karl Malone	193	Kevin McHale	169
Magic Johnson	190	Michael Cooper	168
Robert Parish	184	Bill Russell	165
Byron Scott	183	Larry Bird	164
John Stockton	182	Paul Silas	163

SINGLE GAME

Points

	Date	FG-FT-Pts
Michael Jordan, Chi at Bos*	4/20/86	22-19-63
Elgin Baylor, LA at Bos	4/14/62	22-17-61
Wilt Chamberlain, Phi vs Syr	3/22/62	22-12-56
Michael Jordan, Chi at Mia	4/29/92	20-16-56
Charles Barkley, Pho vs G.St.	5/4/94	23-7-56
Rick Barry, SF vs Phi	4/18/67	22-11-55
Michael Jordan, Chi vs Cle	5/1/88	24-7-55
Michael Jordan, Chi vs Pho	4/16/93	21-13-55
Michael Jordan, Chi vs. Wash	4/27/97	22-10-55

*Double overtime.

Field Goals

	Date	FG	Att
Wilt Chamberlain, Phi vs Syr	3/14/60	24	42
John Havlicek, Bos vs Atl	4/1/73	24	36
Michael Jordan, Chi vs Cle	5/1/88	24	45

Eight tied with 22 each.

Miscellaneous

3-Pt Field Goals

	Date	No
Rex Chapman, Pho at Sea	4/25/97	9
Dan Majerle, Pho vs Sea	6/1/93	8
Allen Iverson, Phi vs Tor	5/16/01	8

Eight tied with 7 each.

Assists

	Date	No
Magic Johnson, LA vs Pho	5/15/84	24
John Stockton, Utah at LA Lakers	5/17/88	24
Magic Johnson, LA Lakers at Port	5/3/85	23
John Stockton, Utah vs Port	4/25/96	23
Doc Rivers, Atl vs Bos	5/16/88	22

Four tied with 21 each.

Rebounds

	Date	No
Wilt Chamberlain, Phi vs Bos	4/5/67	41
Bill Russell, Bos vs Phi	3/23/58	40
Bill Russell, Bos vs St.L	3/29/60	40
Bill Russell, Bos vs LA*	4/18/62	40

Three tied with 39 each.
*Overtime.

Appearances in NBA Finals

Standings of all NBA teams that have reached the NBA Finals since 1947.

App		Titles	Last Won
28	Minneapolis-LA Lakers	14	2002
19	Boston Celtics	16	1986
9	Syracuse Nats-Phila. 76ers	3	1983
8	New York Knicks	2	1973
6	Chicago Bulls	6	1998
6	Phila-SF-Golden St. Warriors	3	1975
6	Ft. Wayne-Detroit Pistons	3	2004
4	Houston Rockets	2	1995
4	St. Louis Hawks	1	1958
4	Baltimore-Washington Bullets	1	1978
3	Portland Trail Blazers	1	1977
3	Seattle SuperSonics	1	1979
2	San Antonio Spurs	2	2003
2	Milwaukee Bucks	1	1971
2	New Jersey Nets	0	—
2	Phoenix Suns	0	—
2	Utah Jazz	0	—
1	Baltimore Bullets	1	1948
1	Rochester Royals	1	1951
1	Chicago Stags	0	—
1	Orlando Magic	0	—
1	Washington Capitols	0	—
1	Indiana Pacers	0	—

Change of address: The St. Louis Hawks now play in Atlanta and the Rochester Royals are now the Sacramento Kings.
Teams now defunct: Baltimore Bullets (1947-55), Chicago Stags (1946-50) and Washington Capitols (1946-51).

NBA FINALS
Points

Series		Year	Pts
4-Gm	Shaquille O'Neal, LAL vs NJ	2002	145
5-Gm	Allen Iverson, Phi vs LAL	2001	178
6-Gm	Michael Jordan, Chi vs Pho	1993	246
7-Gm	Elgin Baylor, LA vs Bos	1962	284

Field Goals

Series		Year	No
4-Gm	Hakeem Olajuwon, Hou vs Orl	1995	56
5-Gm	Allen Iverson, Phi vs LAL	2001	66
6-Gm	Michael Jordan, Chi vs Pho	1993	101
7-Gm	Elgin Baylor, LA vs Bos	1962	101

Assists

Series		Year	No
4-Gm	Bob Cousy, Bos vs Mpls	1959	51
5-Gm	Magic Johnson, LAL vs Chi	1991	62
6-Gm	Magic Johnson, LAL vs Bos	1985	84
7-Gm	Magic Johnson, LA vs Bos	1984	95

Rebounds

Series		Year	No
4-Gm	Bill Russell, Bos vs Mpls	1959	118
5-Gm	Bill Russell, Bos vs St.L	1961	144
6-Gm	Wilt Chamberlain, Phi vs SF	1967	171
7-Gm	Bill Russell, Bos vs LA	1962	189

The National Basketball League

The NBL started with 13 previously independent teams in 1937-38 and although GE, Firestone and Goodyear were gone by late 1942, ran 12 years before merging with the three-year-old Basketball Association of America in 1949 to form the NBA.
Multiple champions: Akron Firestone Non-Skids, Fort Wayne Zollner Pistons, Oshkosh All-Stars (2).

Year	Winner		Series Loser	Year	Winner		Series Loser
1938	Goodyear Wingfoots	2-1	Oshkosh All-Stars	1944	Ft. Wayne Pistons	3-0	Sheboygan Redskins
1939	Firestone Non-Skids	3-2	Oshkosh All-Stars	1945	Ft. Wayne Pistons	3-2	Sheboygan Redskins
1940	Firestone Non-Skids	3-2	Oshkosh All-Stars	1946	Rochester Royals	3-0	Sheboygan Redskins
1941	Oshkosh All-Stars	3-0	Sheboygan Redskins	1947	Chicago Gears	3-2	Rochester Royals
1942	Oshkosh All-Stars	2-1	Ft. Wayne Pistons	1948	Minneapolis Lakers	3-1	Rochester Royals
1943	Sheboygan Redskins	2-1	Ft. Wayne Pistons	1949	Anderson Packers	3-0	Oshkosh All-Stars

NBA All-Star Game

The NBA staged its first All-Star Game before 10,094 at Boston Garden on March 2, 1951. From that year on, the game has matched the best players in the East against the best in the West. Winning coaches are listed first. East leads series, 32-19.

Multiple MVP winners: Bob Pettit (4); Michael Jordan and Oscar Robertson (3); Bob Cousy, Julius Erving, Magic Johnson, Karl Malone, Shaquille O'Neal and Isiah Thomas (2).

Year		Host	Coaches	Most Valuable Player
1951	East 111, West 94	Boston	Joe Lapchick, John Kundla	Ed Macauley, Boston
1952	East 108, West 91	Boston	Al Cervi, John Kundla	Paul Arizin, Philadelphia
1953	West 79, East 75	Ft. Wayne	John Kundla, Joe Lapchick	George Mikan, Minneapolis
1954	East 98, West 93 (OT)	New York	Joe Lapchick, John Kundla	Bob Cousy, Boston
1955	East 100, West 91	New York	Al Cervi, Charley Eckman	Bill Sharman, Boston
1956	West 108, East 94	Rochester	Charley Eckman, George Senesky	Bob Pettit, St. Louis
1957	East 109, West 97	Boston	Red Auerbach, Bobby Wanzer	Bob Cousy, Boston
1958	East 130, West 118	St. Louis	Red Auerbach, Alex Hannum	Bob Pettit, St. Louis
1959	West 124, East 108	Detroit	Ed Macauley, Red Auerbach	Bob Pettit, St. Louis & Elgin Baylor, Minneapolis
1960	East 125, West 115	Philadelphia	Red Auerbach, Ed Macauley	Wilt Chamberlain, Philadelphia
1961	West 153, East 131	Syracuse	Paul Seymour, Red Auerbach	Oscar Robertson, Cincinnati
1962	West 150, East 130	St. Louis	Fred Schaus, Red Auerbach	Bob Pettit, St. Louis
1963	East 115, West 108	Los Angeles	Red Auerbach, Fred Schaus	Bill Russell, Boston
1964	East 111, West 107	Boston	Red Auerbach, Fred Schaus	Oscar Robertson, Cincinnati
1965	East 124, West 123	St. Louis	Red Auerbach, Alex Hannum	Jerry Lucas, Cincinnati
1966	East 137, West 94	Cincinnati	Red Auerbach, Fred Schaus	Adrian Smith, Cincinnati
1967	West 135, East 120	San Francisco	Fred Schaus, Red Auerbach	Rick Barry, San Francisco
1968	East 144, West 124	New York	Alex Hannum, Bill Sharman	Hal Greer, Philadelphia
1969	East 123, West 112	Baltimore	Gene Shue, Richie Guerin	Oscar Robertson, Cincinnati
1970	East 142, West 135	Philadelphia	Red Holzman, Richie Guerin	Willis Reed, New York
1971	West 108, East 107	San Diego	Larry Costello, Red Holzman	Lenny Wilkens, Seattle
1972	West 112, East 110	Los Angeles	Bill Sharman, Tom Heinsohn	Jerry West, Los Angeles
1973	East 104, West 84	Chicago	Tom Heinsohn, Bill Sharman	Dave Cowens, Boston
1974	West 134, East 123	Seattle	Larry Costello, Tom Heinsohn	Bob Lanier, Detroit
1975	East 108, West 102	Phoenix	K.C. Jones, Al Attles	Walt Frazier, New York
1976	East 123, West 109	Philadelphia	Tom Heinsohn, Al Attles	Dave Bing, Washington
1977	West 125, East 124	Milwaukee	Larry Brown, Gene Shue	Julius Erving, Philadelphia
1978	East 133, West 125	Atlanta	Billy Cunningham, Jack Ramsay	Randy Smith, Buffalo
1979	West 134, East 129	Detroit	Lenny Wilkens, Dick Motta	David Thompson, Denver
1980	East 144, West 136 (OT)	Washington	Billy Cunningham, Lenny Wilkens	George Gervin, San Antonio
1981	East 123, West 120	Cleveland	Billy Cunningham, John MacLeod	Nate Archibald, Boston
1982	East 120, West 118	New Jersey	Bill Fitch, Pat Riley	Larry Bird, Boston
1983	East 132, West 123	Los Angeles	Billy Cunningham, Pat Riley	Julius Erving, Philadelphia
1984	East 154, West 145 (OT)	Denver	K.C. Jones, Frank Layden	Isiah Thomas, Detroit
1985	West 140, East 129	Indiana	Pat Riley, K.C. Jones	Ralph Sampson, Houston
1986	East 139, West 132	Dallas	K.C. Jones, Pat Riley	Isiah Thomas, Detroit
1987	West 154, East 149 (OT)	Seattle	Pat Riley, K.C. Jones	Tom Chambers, Seattle
1988	East 138, West 133	Chicago	Mike Fratello, Pat Riley	Michael Jordan, Chicago
1989	West 143, East 134	Houston	Pat Riley, Lenny Wilkens	Karl Malone, Utah
1990	East 130, West 113	Miami	Chuck Daly, Pat Riley	Magic Johnson, LA Lakers
1991	East 116, West 114	Charlotte	Chris Ford, Rick Adelman	Charles Barkley, Philadelphia
1992	West 153, East 113	Orlando	Don Nelson, Phil Jackson	Magic Johnson, LA Lakers
1993	West 135, East 132 (OT)	Salt Lake City	Paul Westphal, Pat Riley	Karl Malone, Utah & John Stockton, Utah
1994	East 127, West 118	Minneapolis	Lenny Wilkens, George Karl	Scottie Pippen, Chicago
1995	West 139, East 112	Phoenix	Paul Westphal, Brian Hill	Mitch Richmond, Sacramento
1996	East 129, West 118	San Antonio	Phil Jackson, George Karl	Michael Jordan, Chicago
1997	East 132, West 120	Cleveland	Doug Collins, Rudy Tomjanovich	Glen Rice, Charlotte
1998	East 135, West 114	New York	Larry Bird, George Karl	Michael Jordan, Chicago
1999	Not held--due to lockout			
2000	West 137, East 126	Oakland	Phil Jackson, Jeff Van Gundy	Tim Duncan, San Antonio & Shaquille O'Neal, LA Lakers
2001	East 111, West 110	Washington	Larry Brown, Rick Adelman	Allen Iverson, Philadelphia
2002	West 135, East 120	Philadelphia	Don Nelson, Byron Scott	Kobe Bryant, LA Lakers
2003	West 155, East 145 (2 OT)	Atlanta	Rick Adelman, Isiah Thomas	Kevin Garnett, Minnesota
2004	West 136, East 132	Los Angeles	Flip Saunders, Rick Carlisle	Shaquille O'Neal, LA Lakers

NBA Franchise Origins

Here is what the current 30 teams in the National Basketball Association have to show for the years they have put in as members of the National Basketball League (NBL), Basketball Association of America (BAA), the NBA, and the American Basketball Association (ABA). League titles are noted by year won.

Western Conference

	First Season	League Titles	Franchise Stops
Dallas Mavericks	1980-81 (NBA)	None	•Dallas (1980–)
Denver Nuggets	1967-68 (ABA)	None	•Denver (1967–)
Golden St. Warriors	1946-47 (BAA)	1 BAA (1947)	•Philadelphia (1946-62)
		2 NBA (1956, 75)	San Francisco (1962-71)
			Oakland (1971–)
Houston Rockets	1967-68 (NBA)	2 NBA (1994-95)	•San Diego (1967-71)
			Houston (1971–)
Los Angeles Clippers	1970-71 (NBA)	None	•Buffalo (1970-78)
			San Diego (1978-84)
			Los Angeles (1984–)
Los Angeles Lakers	1947-48 (NBL)	1 NBL (1948)	•Minneapolis (1947-60)
		1 BAA (1949)	Los Angeles (1960-67)
		14 NBA (1950,52-54,72,	Inglewood, CA (1967-99)
		80,82,85,87-88,00-02)	Los Angeles (1999–)
Memphis Grizzlies	1995-96 (NBA)	None	•Vancouver (1995-01)
			Memphis, TN (2001–)
Minnesota Timberwolves	1989-90 (NBA)	None	•Minneapolis (1989–)
New Orleans Hornets	1988-89 (NBA)	None	•Charlotte (1988-2002)
			New Orleans (2002–)
Phoenix Suns	1968-69 (NBA)	None	•Phoenix (1968–)
Portland Trail Blazers	1970-71 (NBA)	1 NBA (1977)	•Portland (1970–)
Sacramento Kings	1945-46 (NBL)	1 NBL (1946)	•Rochester, NY (1945-58)
		1 NBA (1951)	Cincinnati (1958-72)
			KC-Omaha (1972-75)
			Kansas City (1975-85)
			Sacramento (1985–)
San Antonio Spurs	1967-68 (ABA)	2 NBA (1999, 2003)	•Dallas (1967-73)
			San Antonio (1973–)
Seattle SuperSonics	1967-68 (NBA)	1 NBA (1979)	•Seattle (1967–)
Utah Jazz	1974-75 (NBA)	None	•New Orleans (1974-79)
			Salt Lake City (1979–)

Eastern Conference

	First Season	League Titles	Franchise Stops
Atlanta Hawks	1946-47 (NBL)	1 NBA (1958)	•Tri-Cities (1946-51)
			Milwaukee (1951-55)
			St. Louis (1955-68)
			Atlanta (1968–)
Boston Celtics	1946-47 (BAA)	16 NBA (1957,59-66,68-69	•Boston (1946–)
		74,76,81,84,86)	
Charlotte Bobcats	2004-05 (NBA)	None	•Charlotte (2004–)
Chicago Bulls	1966-67 (NBA)	6 NBA (1991-93,96-98)	•Chicago (1966–)
Cleveland Cavaliers	1970-71 (NBA)	None	•Cleveland (1970-74)
			Richfield, OH (1974-94)
			Cleveland (1994–)
Detroit Pistons	1941-42 (NBL)	2 NBL (1944-45)	•Ft. Wayne, IN (1941-57)
		3 NBA (1989-90, 2004)	Detroit (1957-78)
			Pontiac, MI (1978-88)
			Auburn Hills, MI (1988–)
Indiana Pacers	1967-68 (ABA)	3 ABA (1970,72-73)	•Indianapolis (1967–)
Miami Heat	1988-89 (NBA)	None	•Miami (1988–)
Milwaukee Bucks	1968-69 (NBA)	1 NBA (1971)	•Milwaukee (1968–)
New Jersey Nets	1967-68 (ABA)	2 ABA (1974,76)	•Teaneck, NJ (1967-68)
			Commack, NY (1968-69)
			W. Hempstead, NY (1969-71)
			Uniondale, NY (1971-77)
			Piscataway, NJ (1977-81)
			E. Rutherford, NJ (1981–)
New York Knicks	1946-47 (BAA)	2 NBA (1970,73)	•New York (1946–)
Orlando Magic	1989-90 (NBA)	None	•Orlando, FL (1989–)
Philadelphia 76ers	1949-50 (NBA)	3 NBA (1955,67,83)	•Syracuse, NY (1949-63)
			Philadelphia (1963–)
Toronto Raptors	1995-96 (NBA)	None	•Toronto (1995–)
Washington Wizards	1961-62 (NBA)	1 NBA (1978)	•Chicago (1961-63)
			Baltimore (1963-73)
			Landover, MD (1973–)

Note: The Tri-Cities Blackhawks represented Moline and Rock Island, Ill., and Davenport, Iowa.

The Growth of the NBA

Of the 11 franchises that comprised the Basketball Association of America (BAA) at the start of the 1946-47 season, only three remain—the Boston Celtics, New York Knickerbockers and Golden State Warriors (originally Philadelphia Warriors).

Just before the start of the 1948-49 season, four teams from the more established **National Basketball League** (NBL)—the Ft. Wayne Pistons (now Detroit), Indianapolis Jets, Minneapolis Lakers (now Los Angeles) and Rochester Royals (now Sacramento Kings)—joined the BAA.

A year later, the six remaining NBL franchises—Anderson (Ind.), Denver, Sheboygan (Wisc.), the Syracuse Nationals (now Philadelphia 76ers), Tri-Cities Blackhawks (now Atlanta Hawks) and Waterloo (Iowa)—joined along with the new Indianapolis Olympians and the BAA became the 17-team **National Basketball Association**.

The NBA was down to 10 teams by the 1950-51 season and slipped to eight by 1954-55 with Boston, New York, Philadelphia and Syracuse in the Eastern Division, and Ft. Wayne, Milwaukee (formerly Tri-Cities), Minneapolis and Rochester in the West.

By 1960, five of those surviving eight teams had moved to other cities but by the end of the decade the NBA was a 14-team league. It also had a rival, the **American Basketball Association**, which began play in 1967 with a red, white and blue ball, a three-point line and 11 teams. After a nine-year run, the ABA merged four clubs—the Denver Nuggets, Indiana Pacers, New York Nets and San Antonio Spurs—with the NBA following the 1975-76 season. The NBA adopted the three-point shot in 1979-80.

Expansion/Merger Timetable

For teams currently in NBA.

1948—Added NBL's Ft. Wayne Pistons (now Detroit), Minneapolis Lakers (now Los Angeles) and Rochester Royals (now Sacramento Kings); **1949**—Syracuse Nationals (now Philadelphia 76ers) and Tri-Cities Blackhawks (now Atlanta Hawks).

1961—Chicago Packers (now Washington Wizards); **1966**—Chicago Bulls; **1967**—San Diego Rockets (now Houston) and Seattle SuperSonics; **1968**—Milwaukee Bucks and Phoenix Suns.

1970—Buffalo Braves (now Los Angeles Clippers), Cleveland Cavaliers and Portland Trail Blazers; **1974**—New Orleans Jazz (now Utah); **1976**—added ABA's Denver Nuggets, Indiana Pacers, New York Nets (now New Jersey) and San Antonio Spurs.

1980—Dallas Mavericks; **1988**—Charlotte Hornets and Miami Heat; **1989**—Minnesota Timberwolves and Orlando Magic.

1995—Toronto Raptors and Vancouver Grizzlies (Now Memphis).

2004—Charlotte Bobcats.

City and Nickname Changes

1951—Tri-Cities Blackhawks, who divided home games between Moline and Rock Island, Ill., and Davenport, Iowa, move to Milwaukee and become the Hawks; **1955**—Milwaukee Hawks move to St. Louis; **1957**—Ft. Wayne Pistons move to Detroit, while Rochester Royals move to Cincinnati.

1960—Minneapolis Lakers move to Los Angeles; **1962**—Chicago Packers renamed Zephyrs, while Philadelphia Warriors move to San Francisco; **1963**—Chicago Zephyrs move to Baltimore and become Bullets, while Syracuse Nationals move to Philadelphia and become 76ers; **1968**—St. Louis Hawks move to Atlanta.

1971—San Diego Rockets move to Houston, while San Francisco Warriors move to Oakland and become Golden State Warriors; **1972**—Cincinnati Royals move to Midwest, divide home games between Kansas City, Mo., and Omaha, Neb., and become Kings; **1973**—Baltimore Bullets move to Landover, Md., outside Washington and become Capital Bullets; **1974**—Capital Bullets renamed Washington Bullets; **1975**—KC-Omaha Kings settle in Kansas City; **1977**—New York Nets move from Uniondale, N.Y., to Piscataway, N.J. (later East Rutherford) and become New Jersey Nets; **1978**—Buffalo Braves move to San Diego and become Clippers; **1979**—New Orleans Jazz move to Salt Lake City and become Utah Jazz.

1984—San Diego Clippers move to Los Angeles; **1985**—Kansas City Kings move to Sacramento.

1997—Washington Bullets become Washington Wizards.

2001—Vancouver Grizzlies move to Memphis, Tenn.; **2002**—Charlotte Hornets move to New Orleans.

Defunct NBA Teams

Teams that once played in the BAA and NBA, but no longer exist.

Anderson (Ind.)—Packers (1949-50); **Baltimore**—Bullets (1947-55); **Chicago**—Stags (1946-50); **Cleveland**—Rebels (1946-47); **Denver**—Nuggets (1949-50); **Detroit**—Falcons (1946-47); **Indianapolis**—Jets (1948-49) and Olympians (1949-53); **Pittsburgh**—Ironmen (1946-47); **Providence**—Steamrollers (1946-49); **St. Louis**—Bombers (1946-50); **Sheboygan (Wisc.)**—Redskins (1949-50); **Toronto**—Huskies (1946-47); **Washington**—Capitols (1946-51); **Waterloo (Iowa)**—Hawks (1949-50).

ABA Teams (1967-76)

Anaheim—Amigos (1967-68, moved to LA); **Baltimore**—Claws (1975, never played); **Carolina**—Cougars (1969-74, moved to St. Louis); **Dallas**—Chaparrals (1967-73, called Texas Chaparrals in 1970-71, moved to San Antonio); **Denver**—Rockets (1967-76, renamed Nuggets in 1974-76); **Miami**—Floridians (1968-72, called simply Floridians from 1970-72).

Houston—Mavericks (1967-69, moved to North Carolina); **Indiana**—Pacers (1967-76); **Kentucky**—Colonels (1967-76); **Los Angeles**—Stars (1968-70, moved to Utah); **Memphis**—Pros (1970-75, renamed Tams in 1972 and Sounds in 1974, moved to Baltimore); **Minnesota**—Muskies (1967-68, moved to Miami) and Pipers (1968-69, moved back to Pittsburgh); **New Jersey**—Americans (1967-68, moved to New York).

New Orleans—Buccaneers (1967-70, moved to Memphis); **New York**—Nets (1968-76); **Oakland**—Oaks (1967-69, moved to Washington); **Pittsburgh**—Pipers (1967-68, moved to Minnesota), Pipers (1969-72, renamed Condors in 1970); **St. Louis**—Spirits of St. Louis (1974-76); **San Antonio**—Spurs (1973-76); **San Diego**—Conquistadors (1972-75, renamed Sails in 1975); **Utah**—Stars (1970-75); **Virginia**—Squires (1970-76); **Washington**—Caps (1969-70, moved to Virginia).

Annual NBA Leaders
Scoring

Decided by total points from 1947-69, and per game average since 1970. A lockout in 1999 shortened the regular season to 50 games.

Multiple winners: Michael Jordan (10); Wilt Chamberlain (7); George Gervin (4); Allen Iverson, Neil Johnston, Bob McAdoo and George Mikan (3); Kareem Abdul-Jabbar, Paul Arizin, Adrian Dantley, Tracy McGrady, Shaquille O'Neal and Bob Pettit (2).

Year		Gm	Pts	Avg	Year		Gm	Pts	Avg
1947	Joe Fulks, Phi	60	1389	23.2	1976	Bob McAdoo, Buf	78	2427	31.1
1948	Max Zaslofsky, Chi	48	1007	21.0	1977	Pete Maravich, NO	73	2273	31.1
1949	George Mikan, Mpls	60	1698	28.3	1978	George Gervin, SA	82	2232	27.2
1950	George Mikan, Mpls	68	1865	27.4	1979	George Gervin, SA	80	2365	29.6
1951	George Mikan, Mpls	68	1932	28.4	1980	George Gervin, SA	78	2585	33.1
1952	Paul Arizin, Phi	66	1674	25.4	1981	Adrian Dantley, Utah	80	2452	30.7
1953	Neil Johnston, Phi	70	1564	22.3	1982	George Gervin, SA	79	2551	32.3
1954	Neil Johnston, Phi	72	1759	24.4	1983	Alex English, Den	82	2326	28.4
1955	Neil Johnston, Phi	72	1631	22.7	1984	Adrian Dantley, Utah	79	2418	30.6
1956	Bob Pettit, St.L	72	1849	25.7	1985	Bernard King, NY	55	1809	32.9
1957	Paul Arizin, Phi	71	1817	25.6	1986	Dominique Wilkins, Atl	78	2366	30.3
1958	George Yardley, Det	72	2001	27.8	1987	Michael Jordan, Chi	82	3041	37.1
1959	Bob Pettit, St.L	72	2105	29.2	1988	Michael Jordan, Chi	82	2868	35.0
1960	Wilt Chamberlain, Phi	72	2707	37.6	1989	Michael Jordan, Chi	81	2633	32.5
1961	Wilt Chamberlain, Phi	79	3033	38.4	1990	Michael Jordan, Chi	82	2753	33.6
1962	Wilt Chamberlain, Phi	80	4029	50.4	1991	Michael Jordan, Chi	82	2580	31.5
1963	Wilt Chamberlain, SF	80	3586	44.8	1992	Michael Jordan, Chi	80	2404	30.1
1964	Wilt Chamberlain, SF	80	2948	36.9	1993	Michael Jordan, Chi	78	2541	32.6
1965	Wilt Chamberlain, SF-Phi	73	2534	34.7	1994	David Robinson, SA	80	2383	29.8
1966	Wilt Chamberlain, Phi	79	2649	33.5	1995	Shaquille O'Neal, Orl	79	2315	29.3
1967	Rick Barry, SF	78	2775	35.6	1996	Michael Jordan, Chi	82	2491	30.4
1968	Dave Bing, Det	79	2142	27.1	1997	Michael Jordan, Chi	82	2431	29.7
1969	Elvin Hayes, SD	82	2327	28.4	1998	Michael Jordan, Chi	82	2357	28.7
1970	Jerry West, LA	74	2309	31.2	1999	Allen Iverson, Phi	48	1284	26.8
1971	Lew Alcindor, Mil	82	2596	31.7	2000	Shaquille O'Neal, LAL	79	2344	29.7
1972	Kareem Abdul-Jabbar, Mil	81	2822	34.8	2001	Allen Iverson, Phi	71	2207	31.1
1973	Nate Archibald, KC-Omaha	80	2719	34.0	2002	Allen Iverson, Phi	60	1883	31.4
1974	Bob McAdoo, Buf	74	2261	30.6	2003	Tracy McGrady, Orl	75	2407	32.1
1975	Bob McAdoo, Buf	82	2831	34.5	2004	Tracy McGrady, Orl	67	1878	28.0

Note: Lew Alcindor changed his name to Kareem Abdul-Jabbar after the 1970-71 season.

Rebounds

Decided by total rebounds from 1951-69 and per game average since 1970.

Multiple winners: Wilt Chamberlain (11); Dennis Rodman (7); Moses Malone (6); Bill Russell (4); Elvin Hayes, Dikembe Mutombo, Hakeem Olajuwon and Ben Wallace (2).

Year		Gm	No	Avg	Year		Gm	No	Avg
1951	Dolph Schayes, Syr	66	1080	16.4	1978	Len Robinson, NO	82	1288	15.7
1952	Larry Foust, Ft. Wayne	66	880	13.3	1979	Moses Malone, Hou	82	1444	17.6
	& Mel Hutchins, Mil	66	880	13.3	1980	Swen Nater, SD	81	1216	15.0
1953	George Mikan, Mpls	70	1007	14.4	1981	Moses Malone, Hou	80	1180	14.8
1954	Harry Gallatin, NY	72	1098	15.3	1982	Moses Malone, Hou	81	1188	14.7
1955	Neil Johnston, Phi	72	1085	15.1	1983	Moses Malone, Phi	78	1194	15.3
1956	Bob Pettit, St.L	72	1164	16.2	1984	Moses Malone, Phi	71	950	13.4
1957	Maurice Stokes, Roch	72	1256	17.4	1985	Moses Malone, Phi	79	1031	13.1
1958	Bill Russell, Bos	69	1564	22.7	1986	Bill Laimbeer, Det	82	1075	13.1
1959	Bill Russell, Bos	70	1612	23.0	1987	Charles Barkley, Phi	68	994	14.6
1960	Wilt Chamberlain, Phi	72	1941	27.0	1988	Michael Cage, LAC	72	938	13.0
1961	Wilt Chamberlain, Phi	79	2149	27.2	1989	Hakeem Olajuwon, Hou	82	1105	13.5
1962	Wilt Chamberlain, Phi	80	2052	25.7	1990	Hakeem Olajuwon, Hou	82	1149	14.0
1963	Wilt Chamberlain, SF	80	1946	24.3	1991	David Robinson, SA	82	1063	13.0
1964	Bill Russell, Bos	78	1930	24.7	1992	Dennis Rodman, Det	82	1530	18.7
1965	Bill Russell, Bos	78	1878	24.1	1993	Dennis Rodman, Det	62	1232	18.3
1966	Wilt Chamberlain, Phi	79	1943	24.6	1994	Dennis Rodman, SA	79	1132	17.3
1967	Wilt Chamberlain, Phi	81	1957	24.2	1995	Dennis Rodman, SA	49	823	16.8
1968	Wilt Chamberlain, Phi	82	1952	23.8	1996	Dennis Rodman, Chi	64	952	14.9
1969	Wilt Chamberlain, LA	81	1712	21.1	1997	Dennis Rodman, Chi	55	883	16.1
1970	Elvin Hayes, SD	82	1386	16.9	1998	Dennis Rodman, Chi	80	1201	15.0
1971	Wilt Chamberlain, LA	82	1493	18.2	1999	Chris Webber, Sac	42	545	13.0
1972	Wilt Chamberlain, LA	82	1572	19.2	2000	Dikembe Mutombo, Atl	82	1157	14.1
1973	Wilt Chamberlain, LA	82	1526	18.6	2001	Dikembe Mutombo, Atl-Phi	75	1015	13.5
1974	Elvin Hayes, Cap*	81	1463	18.1	2002	Ben Wallace, Det	80	1039	13.0
1975	Wes Unseld, Wash	73	1077	14.8	2003	Ben Wallace, Det	73	1126	15.4
1976	Kareem Abdul-Jabbar, LA	82	1383	16.9	2004	Kevin Garnett, Min	82	1139	13.9
1977	Bill Walton, Port	65	934	14.4					

*The Baltimore Bullets moved to Landover, Md. in 1973-74 and became first the Capital Bullets, then the Washington Bullets in 1974-75.

Assists

Decided by total assists from 1952-69 and per game average since 1970.

Multiple winners: John Stockton (9); Bob Cousy (8); Oscar Robertson (6); Jason Kidd (5); Magic Johnson and Kevin Porter (4); Andy Phillip and Guy Rodgers (2).

Year		No	Year		No	Year		APG
1947	Ernie Calverley, Prov	202	1967	Guy Rodgers, Chi	908	1987	Magic Johnson, LAL	12.2
1948	Howie Dallmar, Phi	120	1968	Wilt Chamberlain, Phi	702	1988	John Stockton, Utah	13.8
1949	Bob Davies, Roch	321	1969	Oscar Robertson, Cin	772	1989	John Stockton, Utah	13.6
1950	Dick McGuire, NY	386	1970	Lenny Wilkens, Sea	9.1	1990	John Stockton, Utah	14.5
1951	Andy Phillip, Phi	414	1971	Norm Van Lier, Chi	10.1	1991	John Stockton, Utah	14.2
1952	Andy Phillip, Phi	539	1972	Jerry West, LA	9.7	1992	John Stockton, Utah	13.7
1953	Bob Cousy, Bos	547	1973	Nate Archibald, KC-O	11.4	1993	John Stockton, Utah	12.0
1954	Bob Cousy, Bos	518	1974	Ernie DiGregorio, Buf	8.2	1994	John Stockton, Utah	12.6
1955	Bob Cousy, Bos	557	1975	Kevin Porter, Wash	8.0	1995	John Stockton, Utah	12.3
1956	Bob Cousy, Bos	642	1976	Slick Watts, Sea	8.1	1996	John Stockton, Utah	11.2
1957	Bob Cousy, Bos	478	1977	Don Buse, Ind	8.5	1997	Mark Jackson, Den-Ind	11.4
1958	Bob Cousy, Bos	463	1978	Kevin Porter, Det-NJ	10.2	1998	Rod Strickland, Wash	10.5
1959	Bob Cousy, Bos	557	1979	Kevin Porter, Det	13.4	1999	Jason Kidd, Pho	10.8
1960	Bob Cousy, Bos	715	1980	M.R. Richardson, NY	10.1	2000	Jason Kidd, Pho	10.1
1961	Oscar Robertson, Cin	690	1981	Kevin Porter, Wash	9.1	2001	Jason Kidd, Pho	9.8
1962	Oscar Robertson, Cin	899	1982	Johnny Moore, SA	9.6	2002	Andre Miller, Cle	10.9
1963	Guy Rodgers, SF	825	1983	Magic Johnson, LA	10.5	2003	Jason Kidd, NJ	8.9
1964	Oscar Robertson, Cin	868	1984	Magic Johnson, LA	13.1	2004	Jason Kidd, NJ	9.2
1965	Oscar Robertson, Cin	861	1985	Isiah Thomas, Det	13.9			
1966	Oscar Robertson, Cin	847	1986	Magic Johnson, LAL	12.6			

Field Goal Percentage

Multiple winners: Wilt Chamberlain (9); Shaquille O'Neal (7); Artis Gilmore (4); Neil Johnston (3); Bob Feerick, Johnny Green, Alex Groza, Cedric Maxwell, Kevin McHale, Gheorghe Muresan, Kenny Sears and Buck Williams (2).

Year		Pct	Year		Pct	Year		Pct
1947	Bob Feerick, Wash	.401	1967	Wilt Chamberlain, Phi	.683	1986	Steve Johnson, SA	.632
1948	Bob Feerick, Wash	.340	1968	Wilt Chamberlain, Phi	.595	1987	Kevin McHale, Bos	.604
1949	Arnie Risen, Roch	.423	1969	Wilt Chamberlain, LA	.583	1988	Kevin McHale, Bos	.604
1950	Alex Groza, Indpls	.478	1970	Johnny Green, Cin	.559	1989	Dennis Rodman, Det	.595
1951	Alex Groza, Indpls	.470	1971	Johnny Green, Cin	.587	1990	Mark West, Pho	.625
1952	Paul Arizin, Phi	.448	1972	Wilt Chamberlain, LA	.649	1991	Buck Williams, Port	.602
1953	Neil Johnston, Phi	.452	1973	Wilt Chamberlain, LA	.727	1992	Buck Williams, Port	.604
1954	Ed Macauley, Bos	.486	1974	Bob McAdoo, Buf	.547	1993	Cedric Ceballos, Pho	.576
1955	Larry Foust, Ft.W	.487	1975	Don Nelson, Bos	.539	1994	Shaquille O'Neal, Orl	.599
1956	Neil Johnston, Phi	.457	1976	Wes Unseld, Wash	.561	1995	Chris Gatling, G.St	.633
1957	Neil Johnston, Phi	.447	1977	K. Abdul-Jabbar, LA	.579	1996	Gheorghe Muresan, Wash	.584
1958	Jack Twyman, Cin	.452	1978	Bobby Jones, Den	.578	1997	Gheorghe Muresan, Wash	.604
1959	Kenny Sears, NY	.490	1979	Cedric Maxwell, Bos	.584	1998	Shaquille O'Neal, LAL	.584
1960	Kenny Sears, NY	.477	1980	Cedric Maxwell, Bos	.609	1999	Shaquille O'Neal, LAL	.576
1961	Wilt Chamberlain, Phi	.509	1981	Artis Gilmore, Chi	.670	2000	Shaquille O'Neal, LAL	.574
1962	Walt Bellamy, Chi	.519	1982	Artis Gilmore, Chi	.652	2001	Shaquille O'Neal, LAL	.572
1963	Wilt Chamberlain, SF	.528	1983	Artis Gilmore, SA	.626	2002	Shaquille O'Neal, LAL	.579
1964	Jerry Lucas, Cin	.527	1984	Artis Gilmore, SA	.631	2003	Eddy Curry, Chi	.585
1965	W. Chamberlain, SF-Phi	.510	1985	James Donaldson, LAC	.637	2004	Shaquille O'Neal, LAL	.584
1966	Wilt Chamberlain, Phi	.540						

Free Throw Percentage

Multiple winners: Bill Sharman (7); Rick Barry (6); Larry Bird and Reggie Miller (4); Mark Price and Dolph Schayes (3); Mahmoud Abdul-Rauf, Larry Costello, Ernie DiGregorio, Bob Feerick, Kyle Macy, Calvin Murphy, Oscar Robertson and Larry Siegfried (2).

Year		Pct	Year		Pct	Year		Pct
1947	Fred Scolari, Wash	.811	1967	Adrian Smith, Cin	.903	1987	Larry Bird, Bos	.910
1948	Bob Feerick, Wash	.788	1968	Oscar Robertson, Cin	.873	1988	Jack Sikma, Mil	.922
1949	Bob Feerick, Wash	.859	1969	Larry Siegfried, NY	.864	1989	Magic Johnson, LAL	.911
1950	Max Zaslofsky, Chi	.843	1970	Flynn Robinson, Mil	.898	1990	Larry Bird, Bos	.930
1951	Joe Fulks, Phi	.855	1971	Chet Walker, Chi	.859	1991	Reggie Miller, Ind	.918
1952	Bob Wanzer, Roch	.904	1972	Jack Marin, Bal	.894	1992	Mark Price, Cle	.947
1953	Bill Sharman, Bos	.850	1973	Rick Barry, G.St	.902	1993	Mark Price, Cle	.948
1954	Bill Sharman, Bos	.844	1974	Ernie DiGregorio, Buf	.902	1994	M. Abdul-Rauf, Den	.956
1955	Bill Sharman, Bos	.897	1975	Rick Barry, G.St	.904	1995	Spud Webb, Sac	.934
1956	Bill Sharman, Bos	.867	1976	Rick Barry, G.St	.923	1996	M. Abdul-Rauf, Den	.930
1957	Bill Sharman, Bos	.905	1977	Ernie DiGregorio, Buf	.945	1997	Mark Price, G.St	.906
1958	Dolph Schayes, Syr	.904	1978	Rick Barry, G.St	.924	1998	Chris Mullin, Ind	.939
1959	Bill Sharman, Bos	.932	1979	Rick Barry, Hou	.947	1999	Reggie Miller, Ind	.915
1960	Dolph Schayes, Syr	.892	1980	Rick Barry, Hou	.935	2000	Jeff Hornacek, Utah	.950
1961	Bill Sharman, Bos	.921	1981	Calvin Murphy, Hou	.958	2001	Reggie Miller, Ind	.928
1962	Dolph Schayes, Syr	.896	1982	Kyle Macy, Pho	.899	2002	Reggie Miller, Ind	.911
1963	Larry Costello, Syr	.881	1983	Calvin Murphy, Hou	.920	2003	Allan Houston, NY	.919
1964	Oscar Robertson, Cin	.853	1984	Larry Bird, Bos	.888	2004	Predrag Stojakovic, Sac	.927
1965	Larry Costello, Phi	.877	1985	Kyle Macy, Pho	.907			
1966	Larry Siegfried, Bos	.881	1986	Larry Bird, Bos	.896			

Blocked Shots

Multiple winners: Kareem Abdul-Jabbar and Mark Eaton (4); George Johnson, Dikembe Mutombo, Hakeem Olajuwon and Theo Ratliff (3); Manute Bol and Alonzo Mourning(2).

Year		Gm	No	Avg
1974	Elmore Smith, LA	.81	393	4.85
1975	Kareem Abdul-Jabbar, Mil	.65	212	3.26
1976	Kareem Abdul-Jabbar, LA	.82	338	4.12
1977	Bill Walton, Port	.65	211	3.25
1978	George Johnson, NJ	.81	274	3.38
1979	Kareem Abdul-Jabbar, LA	.80	316	3.95
1980	Kareem Abdul-Jabbar, LA	.82	280	3.41
1981	George Johnson, SA	.82	278	3.39
1982	George Johnson, SA	.75	234	3.12
1983	Tree Rollins, Atl	.80	343	4.29
1984	Mark Eaton, Utah	.82	351	4.28
1985	Mark Eaton, Utah	.82	456	5.56
1986	Manute Bol, Wash	.80	397	4.96
1987	Mark Eaton, Utah	.79	321	4.06
1988	Mark Eaton, Utah	.82	304	3.71
1989	Manute Bol, G.St.	.80	345	4.31
1990	Akeem Olajuwon, Hou	.82	376	4.59
1991	Hakeem Olajuwon, Hou	.56	221	3.95
1992	David Robinson, SA	.68	305	4.49
1993	Hakeem Olajuwon, Hou	.82	342	4.17
1994	Dikembe Mutombo, Den	.82	336	4.10
1995	Dikembe Mutombo, Den	.82	321	3.91
1996	Dikembe Mutombo, Den	.74	332	4.49
1997	Shawn Bradley, Dal-NJ	.73	248	3.40
1998	Marcus Camby, Tor.	.63	230	3.65
1999	Alonzo Mourning, Mia	.46	180	3.91
2000	Alonzo Mourning, Mia	.79	294	3.72
2001	Theo Ratliff, Phi-Atl	.50	187	3.74
2002	Ben Wallace, Det	.80	278	3.48
2003	Theo Ratliff, Atl	.81	262	3.23
2004	Theo Ratliff, Atl-Port	.85	307	3.61

Note: Akeem Olajuwon changed the spelling of his first name to Hakeem during the 1990-91 season.

Steals

Multiple winners: Allen Iverson, Michael Jordan, Micheal Ray Richardson and Alvin Robertson (3); Mookie Blaylock, Magic Johnson and John Stockton (2).

Year		Gm	No	Avg
1974	Larry Steele, Port	.81	217	2.68
1975	Rick Barry, G.St.	.80	228	2.85
1976	Slick Watts, Sea	.82	261	3.18
1977	Don Buse, Ind	.81	281	3.47
1978	Ron Lee, Pho	.82	225	2.74
1979	M.L. Carr, Det	.80	197	2.46
1980	Micheal Ray Richardson, NY	.82	265	3.23
1981	Magic Johnson, LA	.37	127	3.43
1982	Magic Johnson, LA	.78	208	2.67
1983	Micheal Ray Richardson, G. ST-NJ	.64	182	2.84
1984	Rickey Green, Utah	.81	215	2.65
1985	Micheal Ray Richardson, NJ	.82	243	2.96
1986	Alvin Robertson, SA	.82	301	3.67
1987	Alvin Robertson, SA	.81	260	3.21
1988	Michael Jordan, Chi	.82	259	3.16
1989	John Stockton, Utah	.82	263	3.21
1990	Michael Jordan, Chi	.82	227	2.77
1991	Alvin Robertson, SA	.81	246	3.04
1992	John Stockton, Utah	.82	244	2.98
1993	Michael Jordan, Chi	.78	221	2.83
1994	Nate McMillan, Sea	.73	216	2.96
1995	Scottie Pippen, Chi	.79	232	2.94
1996	Gary Payton, Sea	.81	231	2.85
1997	Mookie Blaylock, Atl	.78	212	2.72
1998	Mookie Blaylock, Atl.	.70	183	2.61
1999	Kendall Gill, NJ	.50	134	2.68
2000	Eddie Jones, Cha	.72	192	2.67
2001	Allen Iverson, Phi.	.71	178	2.51
2002	Allen Iverson, Phi.	.60	168	2.80
2003	Allen Iverson, Phi	.82	225	2.74
2004	Baron Davis, NO	.67	158	2.36

All-Time NBA Regular Season Leaders

Through the 2003-04 regular season.

CAREER

Players active in 2003-04 in **bold** type.

Points

		Yrs	Gm	Pts	Avg
1	Kareem Abdul-Jabbar	20	1560	38,387	24.6
2	**Karl Malone**	19	1476	36,928	25.0
3	Michael Jordan	15	1072	32,292	30.1
4	Wilt Chamberlain	14	1045	31,419	30.1
5	Moses Malone	19	1329	27,409	20.6
6	Elvin Hayes	16	1303	27,313	21.0
7	Hakeem Olajuwon	18	1238	26,946	21.8
8	Oscar Robertson	14	1040	26,710	25.7
9	Dominique Wilkins	15	1074	26,668	24.8
10	John Havlicek	16	1270	26,395	20.8
11	Alex English	15	1193	25,613	21.5
12	Jerry West	14	932	25,192	27.0
13	Patrick Ewing	17	1183	24,815	21.0
14	**Reggie Miller**	17	1323	24,305	18.4
15	Charles Barkley	16	1073	23,757	22.1
16	Robert Parish	21	1611	23,334	14.5
17	Adrian Dantley	15	955	23,177	24.3
18	Elgin Baylor	14	846	23,149	27.4
19	Clyde Drexler	15	1086	22,195	20.4
20	**Shaquille O'Neal**	12	809	21,914	27.1
21	Larry Bird	13	897	21,791	24.3
22	Hal Greer	15	1122	21,586	19.2
23	Walt Bellamy	14	1043	20,941	20.1
24	Bob Pettit	11	792	20,880	26.4
25	David Robinson	14	987	20,790	21.1
26	George Gervin	10	791	20,708	26.2
27	Mitch Richmond	14	976	20,497	21.0
28	Tom Chambers	16	1107	20,049	18.1
29	**Gary Payton**	15	1109	19,956	18.0
30	John Stockton	19	1504	19,711	13.1

Scoring Average

Minimum of 400 games or 10,000 points.

		Yrs	Gm	Pts	Avg
1	Michael Jordan	15	1072	32,292	30.1
2	Wilt Chamberlain	14	1045	31,419	30.1
3	Elgin Baylor	14	846	23,149	27.4
4	**Shaquille O'Neal**	12	809	21,914	27.1
5	Jerry West	14	932	25,192	27.0
6	**Allen Iverson**	8	535	14,436	27.0
7	Bob Pettit	11	792	20,880	26.4
8	George Gervin	10	791	20,708	26.2
9	Oscar Robertson	14	1040	26,710	25.7
10	**Karl Malone**	19	1476	36,928	25.0
11	Dominique Wilkins	15	1074	26,668	24.8
12	Kareem Abdul-Jabbar	20	1560	38,387	24.6
13	Larry Bird	13	897	21,791	24.3
14	Adrian Dantley	15	955	23,177	24.3
15	Pete Maravich	10	658	15,948	24.2
16	**Paul Pierce**	6	444	10,317	23.2
17	Rick Barry	10	794	18,395	23.2
18	Paul Arizin	10	713	16,266	22.8
19	**Tim Duncan**	7	520	11,862	22.8
20	George Mikan	9	520	11,764	22.6
21	Bernard King	14	874	19,655	22.5
22	David Thompson	8	509	11,264	22.1
23	Charles Barkley	16	1073	23,757	22.1
24	Bob McAdoo	14	852	18,787	22.1
25	**Chris Webber**	11	619	13,639	22.0
26	Julius Erving	11	836	18,364	22.0
27	Geoff Petrie	6	446	9,732	21.8
28	**Kobe Bryant**	8	561	12,215	21.8
29	Hakeem Olajuwon	18	1238	26,946	21.8
30	Alex English	15	1193	25,613	21.5

NBA-ABA Top 20

Points

All-Time combined regular season scoring leaders, including ABA service (1968-76). NBA players with ABA experience are listed in CAPITAL letters. Players active during 2003-04 are in **bold** type.

		Yrs	Pts	Avg
1	Kareem Abdul-Jabbar	.20	38,387	24.6
2	**Karl Malone**	.19	36,928	25.0
3	Wilt Chamberlain	.14	31,419	30.1
4	Michael Jordan	.15	32,292	30.1
5	JULIUS ERVING	.16	30,026	24.2
6	MOSES MALONE	.21	29,580	20.3
7	DAN ISSEL	.15	27,482	22.6
8	Elvin Hayes	.16	27,313	21.0
9	Hakeem Olajuwon	.18	26,946	21.8
10	Oscar Robertson	.14	26,710	25.7
11	Dominique Wilkins	.15	26,668	24.8
12	GEORGE GERVIN	.14	26,595	25.1
13	John Havlicek	.16	26,395	20.8
14	Alex English	.15	25,613	21.5
15	RICK BARRY	.14	25,279	24.8
16	Jerry West	.14	25,192	27.0
17	ARTIS GILMORE	.17	24,941	18.8
18	Patrick Ewing	.17	24,815	21.0
19	**Reggie Miller**	.17	24,305	18.4
20	Charles Barkley	.16	23,757	22.1

ABA Totals: BARRY (4 yrs, 226 gm, 6884 pts, 30.5 avg); ERVING (5 yrs, 407 gm, 11,662 pts, 28.7 avg); GERVIN (4 yrs, 269 gm, 5887 pts, 21.9 avg); GILMORE (5 yrs, 420 gm, 9362 pts, 22.3 avg); ISSEL (6 yrs, 500 gm, 12,823 pts, 25.6 avg); MALONE (2 yrs, 126 gm, 2171 pts, 17.2 avg).

Field Goals

		Yrs	FG	Att	Pct
1	Kareem Abdul-Jabbar	.20	15,837	28,307	.559
2	**Karl Malone**	.19	13,528	26,210	.516
3	Wilt Chamberlain	.14	12,681	23,497	.540
4	Michael Jordan	.15	12,681	24,537	.497
5	Elvin Hayes	.16	10,976	24,272	.452
6	Hakeem Olajuwon	.18	10,749	20,991	.512
7	Alex English	.15	10,659	21,036	.507
8	John Havlicek	.16	10,513	23,930	.439
9	Dominique Wilkins	.15	9,963	21,589	.461
10	Patrick Ewing	.17	9,702	19,241	.504
11	Robert Parish	.21	9,508	17,914	.537
12	Oscar Robertson	.14	9,508	19,620	.485

Note: If field goals made in the ABA are included, consider these NBA-ABA totals: Julius Erving (11,818), Dan Issel (10,431), George Gervin (10,368), Moses Malone (10,277) and Rick Barry (9,695).

Free Throws

		Yrs	FT	Att	Pct
1	**Karl Malone**	.19	9787	13,188	.742
2	Moses Malone	.19	8531	11,090	.769
3	Oscar Robertson	.14	7694	9,185	.838
4	Michael Jordan	.15	7327	8,772	.835
5	Jerry West	.14	7160	8,801	.814
6	Dolph Schayes	.16	6979	8,273	.844
7	Adrian Dantley	.15	6832	8,351	.818
8	Kareem Abdul-Jabbar	.20	6712	9,304	.721
9	Charles Barkley	.16	6349	8,643	.734
10	Bob Pettit	.11	6182	8,119	.761
11	Wilt Chamberlain	.14	6057	11,862	.511
12	David Robinson	.14	6035	8,201	.736

Note: If free throws made in the ABA are included, consider these totals: Moses Malone (9,018), Dan Issel (6,591), and Julius Erving (6,256).

Assists

		Yrs	Gm	No	Avg
1	John Stockton	.19	1504	15,806	10.5
2	**Mark Jackson**	.17	1296	10,334	8.0
3	Magic Johnson	.13	906	10,141	11.2
4	Oscar Robertson	.14	1040	9,887	9.5
5	Isiah Thomas	.13	979	9,061	9.3
6	**Gary Payton**	.14	1109	8,039	7.2
7	**Rod Strickland**	.16	1078	7,948	7.4
8	Maurice Cheeks	.15	1101	7,392	6.7
9	Lenny Wilkens	.15	1077	7,211	6.7
10	Terry Porter	.17	1274	7,160	5.6

Rebounds

		Yrs	Gm	No	Avg
1	Wilt Chamberlain	.14	1045	23,924	22.9
2	Bill Russell	.13	963	21,620	22.5
3	Kareem Abdul-Jabbar	.20	1560	17,440	11.2
4	Elvin Hayes	.16	1303	16,279	12.5
5	Moses Malone	.19	1329	16,212	12.2
6	**Karl Malone**	.19	1476	14,968	10.1
7	Robert Parish	.21	1611	14,715	9.1
8	Nate Thurmond	.14	964	14,464	15.0
9	Walt Bellamy	.14	1043	14,241	13.7
10	Wes Unseld	.13	984	13,769	14.0

Note: If rebounds accumulated in the ABA are included, consider the following totals: Moses Malone (17,834) and Artis Gilmore (16,330).

Steals

		Yrs	Gm	No
1	John Stockton	.19	1504	3265
2	Michael Jordan	.15	1072	2514
3	Maurice Cheeks	.15	1101	2310
4	**Scottie Pippen**	.17	1178	2307
5	**Gary Payton**	.14	1109	2243

Note: Steals have only been an official stat since the 1973-74 season.

Blocked Shots

		Yrs	Gm	No
1	Hakeem Olajuwon	.18	1238	3830
2	Kareem Abdul-Jabbar	.20	1560	3189
3	Mark Eaton	.11	875	3064
4	**Dikembe Mutombo**	.13	929	2996
5	David Robinson	.14	987	2954

Note: Blocked shots have only been an official stat since the 1973-74 season. Also, note that if ABA records are included, consider the following block totals: Artis Gilmore (3,178).

Games Played

		Yrs	Career	Gm
1	Robert Parish	.21	1976-97	1611
2	Kareem Abdul-Jabbar	.20	1970-89	1560
3	John Stockton	.19	1984-03	1504
4	**Karl Malone**	.19	1985–	1476
5	**Kevin Willis**	.19	1985–	1390

Note: If ABA records are included, consider the following game totals: Moses Malone (1,455).

Personal Fouls

		Yrs	Gm	Fouls	DQ
1	Kareem Abdul-Jabbar	.20	1560	4657	48
2	**Karl Malone**	.19	1476	4578	28
3	Robert Parish	.21	1611	4443	86
4	**Charles Oakley**	.19	1282	4421	63
5	Hakeem Olajuwon	.18	1238	4383	80

Note: If ABA records are included, consider the following personal foul totals: Artis Gilmore (4,529) and Caldwell Jones (4,436).

All-Time NBA Regular Season Leaders (Cont.)

SINGLE SEASON

Scoring Average

		Season	Avg
1	Wilt Chamberlain, Phi	1961-62	50.4
2	Wilt Chamberlain, SF	1962-63	44.8
3	Wilt Chamberlain, Phi	1960-61	38.4
4	Elgin Baylor, LA	1961-62	38.3
5	Wilt Chamberlain, Phi	1959-60	37.6
6	Michael Jordan, Chi	1986-87	37.1
7	Wilt Chamberlain, SF	1963-64	36.9
8	Rick Barry, SF	1966-67	35.6
9	Michael Jordan, Chi	1987-88	35.0
10	Elgin Baylor, LA	1960-61	34.8
	Kareem Abdul-Jabbar, Mil	1971-72	34.8

Field Goal Pct.

		Season	Pct
1	Wilt Chamberlain, LA	1972-73	.727
2	Wilt Chamberlain, SF	1966-67	.683
3	Artis Gilmore, Chi	1980-81	.670
4	Artis Gilmore, Chi	1981-82	.652
5	Wilt Chamberlain, LA	1971-72	.649

Free Throw Pct.

		Season	Pct
1	Calvin Murphy, Hou	1980-81	.958
2	Mahmoud Abdul-Rauf, Den.	1993-94	.956
3	Mark Price, Cle	1992-93	.948
4	Mark Price, Cle	1991-92	.947
	Rick Barry, Hou	1978-79	.947

3-Pt Field Goal Pct.

		Season	Pct
1	Steve Kerr, Chi	1994-95	.524
2	Jon Sundvold, Mia	1988-89	.522
3	Tim Legler, Wash	1995-96	.522
4	Steve Kerr, Chi	1995-96	.515
5	Detlef Schrempf, Sea	1994-95	.514

Assists

		Season	Avg
1	John Stockton, Utah	1989-90	14.5
2	John Stockton, Utah	1990-91	14.2
3	Isiah Thomas, Det	1984-85	13.9
4	John Stockton, Utah	1987-88	13.8
5	John Stockton, Utah	1991-92	13.7
6	John Stockton, Utah	1988-89	13.6
7	Kevin Porter, Det	1978-79	13.4
8	Magic Johnson, LAL	1983-84	13.1
9	Magic Johnson, LAL	1988-89	12.8
10	Magic Johnson, LAL	1984-85	12.6
	John Stockton, Utah	1993-94	12.6

Rebounds

		Season	Avg
1	Wilt Chamberlain, Phi	1960-61	27.2
2	Wilt Chamberlain, Phi	1959-60	27.0
3	Wilt Chamberlain, Phi	1961-62	25.7
4	Bill Russell, Bos	1963-64	24.7
5	Wilt Chamberlain, Phi	1965-66	24.6

Blocked Shots

		Season	Avg
1	Mark Eaton, Utah	1984-85	5.56
2	Manute Bol, Wash	1985-86	4.96
3	Elmore Smith, LA	1973-74	4.85
4	Mark Eaton, Utah	1985-86	4.61
5	Hakeem Olajuwon, Hou	1989-90	4.59

Steals

		Season	Avg
1	Alvin Robertson, SA	1985-86	3.67
2	Don Buse, Ind	1976-77	3.47
3	Magic Johnson, LAL	1980-81	3.43
4	Micheal Ray Richardson, NY	1979-80	3.23
5	Alvin Robertson, SA	1986-87	3.21

SINGLE GAME

Points

	Date	FG-FT	Pts
Wilt Chamberlain, Phi vs NY	3/2/62	36-28-	100
Wilt Chamberlain, Phi vs LA***	12/8/61	31-16-	78
Wilt Chamberlain, Phi vs Chi	1/13/62	29-15-	73
Wilt Chamberlain, SF at NY	11/16/62	29-15-	73
David Thompson, Den at Det	4/9/78	28-17-	73
Wilt Chamberlain, SF at LA	11/3/62	29-14-	72
Elgin Baylor, LA at NY	11/15/60	28-15-	71
David Robinson, SA at LAC	4/24/94	26-18-	71
Wilt Chamberlain, Phi at Syr	3/10/63	27-16-	70
Michael Jordan, Chi at Cle*	3/28/90	23-21-	69
Wilt Chamberlain, Phi at Chi	12/16/67	30- 8-	68
Pete Maravich, NO vs NYK	2/25/77	26-16-	68
Wilt Chamberlain, Phi vs NY	3/9/61	27-13-	67
Wilt Chamberlain, Phi at St. L	2/17/62	26-15-	67
Wilt Chamberlain, Phi vs NY	2/25/62	25-17-	67
Wilt Chamberlain, SF vs LA	1/11/63	28-11-	67
Wilt Chamberlain, LA vs Pho	2/9/69	29- 8-	66
Wilt Chamberlain, Phi at Cin	2/13/62	24-17-	65
Wilt Chamberlain, Phi at St. L	2/27/62	25-15-	65
Wilt Chamberlain, Phi vs LA	2/7/66	28- 9-	65
Elgin Baylor, Mpls vs Bos	11/8/59	25-14-	64
Rick Barry, G.St. vs Port	3/26/74	30- 4-	64
Michael Jordan, Chi vs Orl	1/16/93	27- 9-	64

*Overtime
***Triple overtime.
Note: Wilt Chamberlain's 100-point game vs New York was played at Hershey, Penn.

Field Goals

	Date	FG	Att
Wilt Chamberlain, Phi vs NY	3/2/62	36	63
Wilt Chamberlain, Phi vs LA***	12/8/61	31	62
Wilt Chamberlain, Phi at Chi	12/16/67	30	40
Rick Barry, G.St. vs Port	2/26/74	30	45

Wilt Chamberlain made 29 four times.
***Triple overtime.

Free Throws

	Date	FT	Att
Wilt Chamberlain, Phi vs NY	3/2/62	28	32
Adrian Dantley, Utah vs Hou	1/4/84	28	29
Adrian Dantley, Utah vs Den	11/25/83	27	31
Adrian Dantley, Utah vs Dal	10/31/80	26	29
Michael Jordan, Chi vs NJ	2/26/87	26	27

3-Pt Field Goals

	Date	No
Kobe Bryant, LAL vs Sea	1/7/03	12
Dennis Scott, Orl vs Atl	4/18/96	11
Ray Allen, Milw vs Char	4/14/02	10
Brian Shaw, Mia at Mil	4/8/93	10
Joe Dumars, Det vs Min	11/8/94	10
George McCloud, Dal vs Pho	12/16/95	10*

Many tied with 9 each
* Overtime

Assists

	Date	No
Scott Skiles, Orl vs Den	12/30/90	30
Kevin Porter, NJ vs Hou	2/24/78	29
Bob Cousy, Bos vs Mpls	2/27/59	28
Guy Rodgers, SF vs St.L	3/14/63	28
John Stockton, Utah vs SA	1/15/91	28

Rebounds

	Date	No
Wilt Chamberlain, Phi vs Bos	11/24/60	55
Bill Russell, Bos vs Syr	2/5/60	51
Bill Russell, Bos vs Phi	11/16/57	49
Bill Russell, Bos vs Det	3/11/65	49
Wilt Chamberlain, Phi vs Syr	2/6/60	45
Wilt Chamberlain, Phi vs LA	1/21/61	45

Blocked Shots

	Date	No
Elmore Smith, LA vs Port	10/28/73	17
Manute Bol, Wash vs Atl	1/25/86	15
Manute Bol, Wash vs Ind	2/26/87	15
Shaquille O'Neal, Orl at NJ	11/20/93	15

Steals

	Date	No
Larry Kenon, San Antonio at KC	12/26/76	11
Kendall Gill, NY vs Mia.	4/3/99	11

14 different players tied with 10 each, including Alvin Robertson, who had 10 steals in a game four times.

All-Time Winningest NBA Coaches

Top 25 NBA career victories through the 2003-04 season. Career, regular season and playoff records are noted along with NBA titles won. Coaches active during 2003-04 season in **bold** type.

		Career			Regular Season			Playoffs			
		Yrs	W	L	Pct	W	L	Pct	W	L	Pct	NBA Titles
1	**Lenny Wilkens**	31	**1395**	1231	.531	1315	1133	.537	80	98	.449	1 (1979)
2	Pat Riley	21	**1265**	669	.654	1110	569	.661	155	100	.608	4 (1982,85,87-88)
3	**Don Nelson**	26	**1218**	943	.564	1148	858	.572	70	85	.452	None
4	Red Auerbach	20	**1037**	548	.654	938	479	.662	99	69	.589	9 (1957, 59-66)
5	**Larry Brown**	21	**1018**	792	.562	933	713	.567	85	79	.518	1 (2004)
6	**Phil Jackson**	14	**1007**	385	.723	832	316	.725	175	69	.717	9 (1991-93,96-98,00-02)
7	Bill Fitch	25	**999**	1160	.463	944	1106	.460	55	54	.505	1 (1981)
8	**Jerry Sloan**	19	**995**	641	.608	917	561	.620	78	80	.494	None
9	Dick Motta	25	**991**	1087	.477	935	1017	.479	56	70	.444	1 (1978)
10	Jack Ramsay	21	**908**	841	.519	864	783	.525	44	58	.431	1 (1977)
11	Cotton Fitzsimmons	21	**867**	824	.513	832	775	.518	35	49	.417	None
12	Gene Shue	22	**814**	908	.473	784	861	.477	30	47	.390	None
13	George Karl	16	**767**	56	.575	708	499	.587	59	67	.468	None
14	Red Holzman	18	**754**	652	.536	696	604	.535	58	48	.547	2 (1970, 73)
	John MacLeod	18	**754**	711	.515	707	657	.518	47	54	.465	None
16	**Rick Adelman**	14	**725**	471	.606	658	411	.616	67	60	.583	None
17	Chuck Daly	14	**713**	488	.594	638	437	.593	75	51	.595	2 (1989-90)
18	Doug Moe	15	**661**	579	.533	628	529	.543	33	50	.398	None
19	K.C. Jones	10	**603**	309	.661	522	252	.674	81	57	.587	2 (1984,86)
20	Del Harris	14	**594**	507	.540	556	457	.549	38	50	.432	None
21	Mike Fratello	14	**592**	499	.543	572	465	.552	20	34	.370	None
22	Al Attles	14	**588**	548	.518	557	518	.518	31	30	.508	1 (1975)
23	Rudy Tomjanovich	12	**554**	436	.559	503	397	.559	51	39	.567	2 (1994-95)
24	Billy Cunningham	8	**520**	235	.689	454	196	.698	66	39	.629	1 (1983)
25	Alex Hannum	12	**518**	446	.537	471	412	.533	47	34	.580	2 (1958, 67)

Note: The NBA does not recognize records from the National Basketball League (1937-49), the American Basketball League (1961-62) or the American Basketball Assn. (1968-76), so the following NBL, ABL and ABA overall coaching records are not included above: NBL-**John Kundla** (51-19 and a title in 1 year). ABA-**Larry Brown** (249-129 in 4 yrs), **Alex Hannum** (194-164 and one title in 4 yrs), **K.C. Jones** (30-58 in 1 yr); **Kevin Loughery** (189-95 and one title in 3 yrs).

Where They Coached

Adelman—Portland (1988-94), Golden State (1995-97), Sacramento (1998–); **Attles**—Golden St. (1970-80,80-83); **Auerbach**—Washington (1946-49), Tri-Cities (1949-50), Boston (1950-66); **Brown**—Denver (1976-79), New Jersey (1981-83), San Antonio (1988-92), LA Clippers (1992-93), Indiana (1993-97), Philadelphia (1997-2003), Detroit (2003–); **Cunningham**—Philadelphia (1977-85); **Daly**—Cleveland (1981-82), Detroit (1983-92), New Jersey (1992-94), Orlando (1997-99); **Fitch**—Cleveland (1970-79), Boston (1979-83), Houston (1983-88), New Jersey (1989-92), LA Clippers (1994-98); **Fitzsimmons**—Phoenix (1970-72), Atlanta (1972-76), Buffalo (1977-78), Kansas City (1978-84), San Antonio (1984-86), Phoenix (1988-92, 95-96); **Fratello**—Atlanta (1980-90), Cleveland (1993-99).

Hannum—St. Louis (1957-58), Syracuse (1960-63), San Francisco (1963-66), Phila. 76ers (1966-68), Houston (1970-71); **Harris**—Houston (1979-83), Milwaukee (1987-92), LA Lakers (1994-99); **Holzman**—Milwaukee-St. Louis Hawks (1954-57), NY Knicks (1968-77,78-82); **Jackson**—Chicago (1989-98), LA Lakers (1999-2004); **Jones**—Washington (1973-76), Boston (1983-88), Seattle (1990-92); **Karl**—Cleveland (1984-86); Golden St. (1986-88), Seattle (1991-98), Milwaukee (1999-2003); **MacLeod**—Phoenix (1973-87), Dallas (1987-89), NY Knicks (1990-91); **Moe**—San Antonio (1976-80), Denver (1981-90), Philadelphia (1992-93).

Motta—Chicago (1968-76), Washington (1976-80), Dallas (1980-87), Sacramento (1990-91), Dallas (1994-96), Denver (1997); **Nelson**—Milwaukee (1976-87), Golden St. (1988-95), New York (1996), Dallas (1997-); **Ramsay**—Philadelphia (1968-72), Buffalo (1972-76), Portland (1976-86), Indiana (1986-89); **Riley**—LA Lakers (1981-90), New York (1991-95), Miami (1995-2003); **Shue**—Baltimore (1967-73), Philadelphia (1973-77), San Diego Clippers (1978-80), Washington (1980-86), LA Clippers (1987-89); **Sloan**—Chicago (1979-82), Utah (1988–); **Tomjanovich**—Houston (1991-2003), LA Lakers (2004–); **Wilkens**—Seattle (1969-72), Portland (1974-76), Seattle (1977-85), Cleveland (1986-93), Atlanta (1993-2000), Toronto (2000-03), New York (2004–).

All-Time Winningest NBA Coaches (Cont.)
Top Winning Percentages

Minimum of 350 victories, including playoffs; coaches active during 2003-04 season in **bold** type.

		Yrs	W	L	Pct
1	**Phil Jackson**	14	1007	385	**.723**
2	Billy Cunningham	8	520	235	**.689**
3	K.C. Jones	10	603	309	**.661**
4	Red Auerbach	20	1037	548	**.654**
5	Pat Riley	21	1265	669	**.654**
6	**Gregg Popovich**	8	449	244	**.648**
7	Tommy Heinsohn	9	474	296	**.616**
8	**Jerry Sloan**	19	995	641	**.608**
9	**Rick Adelman**	14	725	471	**.606**
10	Chuck Daly	14	713	488	**.594**
11	Larry Costello	10	467	323	**.591**
12	John Kundla	11	485	338	**.589**
13	Bill Sharman	7	368	267	**.580**
14	George Karl	16	767	566	**.575**
15	Al Cervi	9	359	267	**.573**
16	**Don Nelson**	26	1218	943	**.564**
17	**Larry Brown**	21	1018	792	**.562**
18	Joe Lapchick	9	356	277	**.562**
19	Rudy Tomjanovich	12	554	436	**.559**
20	Mike Fratello	14	592	499	**.543**
21	Bill Russell	8	375	317	**.542**
22	Del Harris	14	594	507	**.540**
23	Alex Hannum	12	518	446	**.537**
24	Red Holzman	18	754	652	**.536**
25	Doug Moe	15	661	579	**.533**
26	**Lenny Wilkens**	31	1395	1231	**.531**
27	Richie Guerin	8	353	325	**.521**
28	Jack Ramsay	21	908	841	**.519**
29	Al Attles	14	588	548	**.518**
30	John MacLeod	18	754	711	**.515**

Active Coaches' Victories

Through 2003-04 season, including playoffs.

		Yrs	W	L	Pct
1	Lenny Wilkens, New York	31	1395	1231	.531
2	Don Nelson, Dallas	26	1218	943	.564
3	Larry Brown, Detroit	21	1018	792	.562
4	Jerry Sloan, Utah	19	995	641	.608
5	Rick Adelman, Sacramento	14	725	471	.606
6	Rudy Tomjanovich, LA Lakers	12	554	436	.559
7	Mike Dunleavy, LA Clippers	11	457	472	.492
8	Gregg Popovich, San Antonio	8	449	244	.648
9	Hubie Brown, Memphis	12	433	512	.458
10	Phil Saunders, Minnesota	9	403	330	.550
11	Bernie Bickerstaff, Charlotte	10	338	348	.493
12	Paul Silas, Cleveland	10	334	386	.464
13	Jeff Van Gundy, Houston	8	331	245	.575
14	Rick Carlisle, Indiana	3	183	106	.633
15	Doc Rivers, Boston	5	176	178	.497
16	Byron Scott, New Orleans	5	174	154	.530
17	Jim O'Brien, Philadelphia	4	152	132	.535
18	Nate McMillan, Seattle	4	162	156	.509
19	Maurice Cheeks, Portland	3	143	113	.559
20	Scott Skiles, Chicago	4	140	134	.511
21	Jeff Bzdelik, Denver	2	61	144	.298
22	Eddie Jordan, Washington	3	58	121	.324
23	Stan Van Gundy, Miami	1	48	47	.505
24	Terry Porter, Milwaukee	1	42	45	.483
	Johnny Davis, Orlando	2	42	111	.275
26	Mike D'Antoni, Phoenix	2	35	76	.315
27	Lawrence Frank, New Jersey	1	32	19	.627
28	Sam Mitchell, Toronto	0	0	0	—
	Mike Woodson, Atlanta	0	0	0	—
	Mike Montgomery, Golden St.	0	0	0	—

Annual Awards
Most Valuable Player

The Maurice Podoloff Trophy for regular season MVP. Named after the first commissioner (then president) of the NBA. Winners first selected by the NBA players (1956-80) then a national panel of pro basketball writers and broadcasters (since 1981). Winners' scoring averages are provided; (*) indicates led league.

Multiple winners: Kareem Abdul-Jabbar (6); Michael Jordan and Bill Russell (5); Wilt Chamberlain (4); Larry Bird, Magic Johnson and Moses Malone (3); Tim Duncan, Karl Malone and Bob Pettit (2).

Year		Avg	Year		Avg
1956	Bob Pettit, St. Louis, F	25.7*	1982	Moses Malone, Houston, C	31.1
1957	Bob Cousy, Boston, G	20.6	1983	Moses Malone, Philadelphia, C	24.5
1958	Bill Russell, Boston, C	16.6	1984	Larry Bird, Boston, F	24.2
1959	Bob Pettit, St. Louis, F	29.2*	1985	Larry Bird, Boston, F	28.7
1960	Wilt Chamberlain, Philadelphia, C	37.6*	1986	Larry Bird, Boston, F	25.8
1961	Bill Russell, Boston, C	16.9	1987	Magic Johnson, LAL, G	23.9
1962	Bill Russell, Boston, C	18.9	1988	Michael Jordan, Chicago, G	35.0*
1963	Bill Russell, Boston, C	16.8	1989	Magic Johnson, LAL, G	22.5
1964	Oscar Robertson, Cincinnati, G	31.4	1990	Magic Johnson, LAL, G	22.3
1965	Bill Russell, Boston, C	14.1	1991	Michael Jordan, Chicago, G	31.5*
1966	Wilt Chamberlain, Philadelphia, C	33.5*	1992	Michael Jordan, Chicago, G	30.1*
1967	Wilt Chamberlain, Philadelphia, C	24.1	1993	Charles Barkley, Phoenix, F	25.6
1968	Wilt Chamberlain, Philadelphia, C	24.3	1994	Hakeem Olajuwon, Houston, C	27.3
1969	Wes Unseld, Baltimore, C	13.8	1995	David Robinson, San Antonio, C	27.6
1970	Willis Reed, New York, C	21.7	1996	Michael Jordan, Chicago, G	30.4*
1971	Lew Alcindor, Milwaukee, C	31.7*	1997	Karl Malone, Utah, F	27.4
1972	Kareem Abdul-Jabbar, Milwaukee, C	34.8*	1998	Michael Jordan, Chicago, G	28.7*
1973	Dave Cowens, Boston, C	20.5	1999	Karl Malone, Utah, F	23.8
1974	Kareem Abdul-Jabbar, Milwaukee, C	27.0	2000	Shaquille O'Neal, LA, C	29.7*
1975	Bob McAdoo, Buffalo, F	34.5*	2001	Allen Iverson, Philadelphia, G	31.1*
1976	Kareem Abdul-Jabbar, LA, C	27.7	2002	Tim Duncan, San Antonio, F/C	25.5
1977	Kareem Abdul-Jabbar, LA, C	26.2	2003	Tim Duncan, San Antonio, F/C	23.3
1978	Bill Walton, Portland, C	18.9	2004	Kevin Garnett, Minnesota, F	24.2
1979	Moses Malone, Houston, C	24.8			
1980	Kareem Abdul-Jabbar, LA, C	24.8			
1981	Julius Erving, Philadelphia, F	24.6			

Note: Lew Alcindor changed his name to Kareem Abdul-Jabbar after the 1970-71 season.

Rookie of the Year

The Eddie Gottlieb Trophy for outstanding rookie of the regular season. Named after the pro basketball pioneer and owner-coach of the first NBA champion Philadelphia Warriors. Winners selected by a national panel of pro basketball writers and broadcasters. Winners' scoring averages provided; (*) indicates led league; winners who were also named MVP are in **bold** type.

Year		Avg	Year		Avg
1953	Don Meineke, Ft. Wayne, F	10.8	1980	Larry Bird, Boston, F	21.3
1954	Ray Felix, Baltimore, C	17.6	1981	Darrell Griffith, Utah, G	20.6
1955	Bob Pettit, Milwaukee Hawks, F	20.4	1982	Buck Williams, New Jersey, F	15.5
1956	Maurice Stokes, Rochester, F/C	16.8	1983	Terry Cummings, San Diego, F	23.7
1957	Tommy Heinsohn, Boston, F	16.2	1984	Ralph Sampson, Houston, C	21.0
1958	Woody Sauldsberry, Philadelphia, F/C	12.8	1985	Michael Jordan, Chicago, G	28.2
1959	Elgin Baylor, Minneapolis, F	24.9	1986	Patrick Ewing, New York, C	20.0
1960	**Wilt Chamberlain**, Philadelphia, C	37.6*	1987	Chuck Person, Indiana, F	18.8
1961	Oscar Robertson, Cincinnati, G	30.5	1988	Mark Jackson, New York, G	13.6
1962	Walt Bellamy, Chicago Packers, C	31.6	1989	Mitch Richmond, Golden St., G	22.0
1963	Terry Dischinger, Chicago Zephyrs, F	25.5	1990	David Robinson, San Antonio, C	24.3
1964	Jerry Lucas, Cincinnati, F/C	17.7	1991	Derrick Coleman, New Jersey, F	18.4
1965	Willis Reed, New York, C	19.5	1992	Larry Johnson, Charlotte, F	19.2
1966	Rick Barry, San Francisco, F	25.7	1993	Shaquille O'Neal, Orlando, C	23.4
1967	Dave Bing, Detroit, G	20.0	1994	Chris Webber, Golden St., F	17.5
1968	Earl Monroe, Baltimore, G	24.3	1995	Grant Hill, Detroit, F	19.9
1969	**Wes Unseld**, Baltimore, C	13.8		& Jason Kidd, Dallas, G	11.7
1970	Lew Alcindor, Milwaukee Bucks, C	28.8	1996	Damon Stoudamire, Toronto, G	19.0
1971	Dave Cowens, Boston, C	17.0	1997	Allen Iverson, Philadelphia, G	23.5
	& Geoff Petrie, Portland, G	24.8	1998	Tim Duncan, San Antonio, F/C	21.6
1972	Sidney Wicks, Portland, F	24.5	1999	Vince Carter, Toronto, F	18.3
1973	Bob McAdoo, Buffalo, C/F	18.0	2000	Elton Brand, Chicago, F	20.1
1974	Ernie DiGregorio, Buffalo, G	15.2		& Steve Francis, Houston, G	18.0
1975	Keith Wilkes, Golden St., F	14.2	2001	Mike Miller, Orlando, G/F	11.9
1976	Alvan Adams, Phoenix, C	19.0	2002	Pau Gasol, Memphis, F	17.6
1977	Adrian Dantley, Buffalo, F	20.3	2003	Amare Stoudemire, Phoenix, F	13.5
1978	Walter Davis, Phoenix, G	24.2	2004	LeBron James, Cleveland, F	20.9
1979	Phil Ford, Kansas City, G	15.9			

Note: The Chicago Packers changed their name to the Zephyrs after 1961-62 season. Also, Lew Alcindor changed his name to Kareem Abdul-Jabbar after the 1970-71 season.

Number One Draft Choices

Overall first choices in the NBA draft since the abolition of the territorial draft in 1966. Players who became Rookie of the Year are in **bold** type. The draft lottery began in 1985.

Year		Overall 1st Pick	Year		Overall 1st Pick
1966	New York	Cazzie Russell, Michigan	1986	Cleveland	Brad Daugherty, N. Carolina
1967	Detroit	Jimmy Walker, Providence	1987	San Antonio	**David Robinson**, Navy
1968	San Diego	Elvin Hayes, Houston	1988	LA Clippers	Danny Manning, Kansas
1969	Milwaukee	**Lew Alcindor**, UCLA	1989	Sacramento	Pervis Ellison, Louisville
1970	Detroit	Bob Lanier, St. Bonaventure	1990	New Jersey	**Derrick Coleman**, Syracuse
1971	Cleveland	Austin Carr, Notre Dame	1991	Charlotte	**Larry Johnson**, UNLV
1972	Portland	LaRue Martin, Loyola-Chicago	1992	Orlando	**Shaquille O'Neal**, LSU
1973	Philadelphia	Doug Collins, Illinois St.	1993	Orlando	**Chris Webber**, Michigan
1974	Portland	Bill Walton, UCLA	1994	Milwaukee	Glenn Robinson, Purdue
1975	Atlanta	David Thompson, N.C. State	1995	Golden St.	Joe Smith, Maryland
1976	Houston	John Lucas, Maryland	1996	Philadelphia	**Allen Iverson**, Georgetown
1977	Milwaukee	Kent Benson, Indiana	1997	San Antonio	**Tim Duncan**, Wake Forest
1978	Portland	Mychal Thompson, Minnesota	1998	LA Clippers	Michael Olowokandi, Pacific
1979	LA Lakers	Magic Johnson, Michigan St.	1999	Chicago	**Elton Brand**, Duke
1980	Golden St	Joe Barry Carroll, Purdue	2000	New Jersey	Kenyon Martin, Cincinnati
1981	Dallas	Mark Aguirre, DePaul	2001	Washington	Kwame Brown, Glynn Acad.
1982	LA Lakers	James Worthy, N. Carolina	2002	Houston	Yao Ming, China
1983	Houston	**Ralph Sampson**, Virginia	2003	Cleveland	**LeBron James**, St. Vincent/St. Mary
1984	Houston	Akeem Olajuwon, Houston	2004	Orlando	Dwight Howard, SW Atlanta Christ.
1985	New York	**Patrick Ewing**, Georgetown			

Note: Lew Alcindor changed his name to Kareem Abdul-Jabbar after the 1970-71 season; Akeem Olajuwon changed his first name to Hakeem in 1991; in 1975 David Thompson signed with Denver of the ABA and did not play for Atlanta; David Robinson joined NBA for 1989-90 season after fulfilling military obligation.

Sixth Man Award

Awarded to the Best Player Off the Bench for the regular season. Winners selected by a national panel of pro basketball writers and broadcasters.

Multiple winners: Kevin McHale, Ricky Pierce and Detlef Schrempf (2).

Year		Year		Year	
1983	Bobby Jones, Phi., F	1991	Detlef Schrempf, Ind., F	1999	Darrell Armstrong, Orl., G
1984	Kevin McHale, Bos., F	1992	Detlef Schrempf, Ind., F	2000	Rodney Rogers, Pho., F
1985	Kevin McHale, Bos., F	1993	Cliff Robinson, Port., F	2001	Aaron McKie, Phi., G
1986	Bill Walton, Bos., F/C	1994	Dell Curry, Char., G	2002	Corliss Williamson, Det., F
1987	Ricky Pierce, Mil., G/F	1995	Anthony Mason, NY, F	2003	Bobby Jackson, Sac., G
1988	Roy Tarpley, Dal., F	1996	Toni Kukoc, Chi., F	2004	Antawn Jamison, Dal., F
1989	Eddie Johnson, Pho., F	1997	John Starks, NY, G		
1990	Ricky Pierce, Mil., G/F	1998	Danny Manning, Pho., F		

Defensive Player of the Year

Awarded to the Best Defensive Player for the regular season. Winners selected by a national panel of pro basketball writers and broadcasters.

Multiple winners: Dikembe Mutombo (4); Mark Eaton, Sidney Moncrief, Alonzo Mourning, Hakeem Olajuwon, Dennis Rodman and Ben Wallace (2).

Year		Year		Year	
1983	Sidney Moncrief, Mil., G	1991	Dennis Rodman, Det., F	1999	Alonzo Mourning, Mia., C
1984	Sidney Moncrief, Mil., G	1992	David Robinson, SA, C	2000	Alonzo Mourning, Mia., C
1985	Mark Eaton, Utah, C	1993	Hakeem Olajuwon, Hou., C	2001	Dikembe Mutombo, Atl.-Phi., C
1986	Alvin Robertson, SA, G	1994	Hakeem Olajuwon, Hou., C	2002	Ben Wallace, Det., C/F
1987	Michael Cooper, LAL, F	1995	Dikembe Mutombo, Den., C	2003	Ben Wallace, Det., C/F
1988	Michael Jordan, Chi., G	1996	Gary Payton, Sea., G	2004	Ron Artest, Ind., F
1989	Mark Eaton, Utah, C	1997	Dikembe Mutombo, Atl., C		
1990	Dennis Rodman, Det., F	1998	Dikembe Mutombo, Atl., C		

Most Improved Player

Awarded to the Most Improved Player for the regular season. Winners selected by a national panel of pro basketball writers and broadcasters.

Year		Year		Year	
1986	Alvin Robertson, SA, G	1993	Mahmoud Abdul-Rauf, Den., G	2000	Jalen Rose, Ind., G
1987	Dale Ellis, Sea., G	1994	Don MacLean, Wash., F	2001	Tracy McGrady, Orl., F
1988	Kevin Duckworth, Port., C	1995	Dana Barros, Phi., G	2002	Jermaine O'Neal, Ind., F
1989	Kevin Johnson, Pho., G	1996	Gheorghe Muresan, Wash., C	2003	Gilbert Arenas, G.St., G
1990	Rony Seikaly, Mia., C	1997	Isaac Austin, Miami, C	2004	Zach Randolph, Port., F
1991	Scott Skiles, Orl., G	1998	Alan Henderson, Atl., F		
1992	Pervis Ellison, Wash., C	1999	Darrell Armstrong, Orl., G		

Coach of the Year

The Red Auerbach Trophy for outstanding coach of the year. Renamed in 1967 for the former Boston coach who led the Celtics to nine NBA titles. Winners selected by a national panel of pro basketball writers and broadcasters. Previous season and winning season records are provided; (*) indicates division title.

Multiple winners: Don Nelson and Pat Riley (3); Hubie Brown, Bill Fitch, Cotton Fitzsimmons and Gene Shue (2).

Year		Improvement			Year		Improvement		
1963	Harry Gallatin, St. L	29-51	to	48-32	1984	Frank Layden, Utah	30-52	to	45-37*
1964	Alex Hannum, SF	31-49	to	48-32*	1985	Don Nelson, Mil	50-32*	to	59-23*
1965	Red Auerbach, Bos	59-21*	to	61-18*	1986	Mike Fratello, Atl	34-48	to	50-32
1966	Dolph Schayes, Phi	40-40	to	55-25*	1987	Mike Schuler, Port	40-42	to	49-33
1967	Johnny Kerr, Chi	Expan.	to	33-48	1988	Doug Moe, Den	37-45	to	54-28*
1968	Richie Guerin, St. L	39-42	to	56-26*	1989	Cotton Fitzsimmons, Pho	28-54	to	55-27
1969	Gene Shue, Balt	36-46	to	57-25*	1990	Pat Riley, LA Lakers	57-25*	to	63-19*
1970	Red Holzman, NY	54-28	to	60-22*	1991	Don Chaney, Hou	41-41	to	52-30
1971	Dick Motta, Chi	39-43	to	51-31	1992	Don Nelson, GS	44-38	to	55-27
1972	Bill Sharman, LA	48-34*	to	69-13*	1993	Pat Riley, NY	51-31	to	60-22
1973	Tommy Heinsohn, Bos	56-26*	to	68-14*	1994	Lenny Wilkens, Atl	43-39	to	57-25*
1974	Ray Scott, Det	40-42	to	52-30	1995	Del Harris, LA Lakers	33-49	to	48-34
1975	Phil Johnson, KC-Omaha	33-49	to	44-38	1996	Phil Jackson, Chi	47-35	to	72-10*
1976	Bill Fitch, Cle	40-42	to	49-33*	1997	Pat Riley, Mia	42-40	to	61-21
1977	Tom Nissalke, Hou	40-42	to	49-33*	1998	Larry Bird, Ind	39-43	to	58-24
1978	Hubie Brown, Atl	31-51	to	41-41	1999	Mike Dunleavy, Port.	46-36	to	35-15*
1979	Cotton Fitzsimmons, KC	31-51	to	48-34*	2000	Doc Rivers, Orlando	33-17	to	41-41
1980	Bill Fitch, Bos	29-53	to	61-21*	2001	Larry Brown, Phila.	49-33	to	56-26*
1981	Jack McKinney, Ind	37-45	to	44-38	2002	Rick Carlisle, Det	32-50	to	50-32*
1982	Gene Shue, Wash	39-43	to	43-39	2003	Gregg Popovich, SA	58-24*	to	60-22*
1983	Don Nelson, Mil	55-27*	to	51-31*	2004	Hubie Brown, Mem.	28-54	to	50-32

NBA's 50 Greatest Players

In October 1996, as part of its 50th anniversary celebration, the NBA named the 50 greatest players in league history. The voting was done by a league-approved panel of media, former players and coaches, current and former general managers and team executives. The players are listed alphabetically along with the dates of their professional careers and positions. Players active in 2003-04 are in **bold** type.

Player	Pos	Player	Pos	Player	Pos
Kareem Abdul-Jabbar, 1969-89	C	George Gervin, 1972-86	G	Robert Parish, 1976-97	C
Nate Archibald, 1970-84	G	Hal Greer, 1958-73	G	Bob Pettit, 1954-65	F/C
Paul Arizin, 1950-61	F/G	John Havlicek, 1962-78	F/G	**Scottie Pippen**, 1987–	F
Charles Barkley, 1984-00	F	Elvin Hayes, 1968-84	F/C	Willis Reed, 1964-74	C
Rick Barry, 1965-80	F	Magic Johnson, 1979-91, 96	G	Oscar Robertson, 1960-74	G
Elgin Baylor, 1958-72	F	Sam Jones, 1957-69	G	David Robinson, 1989-2003	C
Dave Bing, 1966-78	G	Michael Jordan, 1984-93,	G	Bill Russell, 1956-69	C
Larry Bird, 1979-92	F	95-98, 01-03		Dolph Schayes, 1948-64	F/C
Wilt Chamberlain, 1959-73	C	Jerry Lucas, 1963-74	F/C	Bill Sharman, 1950-61	G
Bob Cousy, 1950-63, 69-70	G	**Karl Malone**, 1985–	F	John Stockton, 1984-2003	G
Dave Cowens, 1970-80, 1982-83	C	Moses Malone, 1974-95	C	Isiah Thomas, 1981-94	G
Billy Cunningham, 1965-76	G	Pete Maravich, 1970-80	G	Nate Thurmond, 1963-77	C/F
Dave DeBusschere, 1962-74	F	Kevin McHale, 1980-93	F	Wes Unseld, 1968-81	C/F
Clyde Drexler, 1983-98	G	George Mikan, 1946-54, 55-56	C	Bill Walton, 1974-88	C
Julius Erving, 1971-87	F	Earl Monroe, 1967-80	G	Jerry West, 1960-74	G
Patrick Ewing, 1985-2002	C	Hakeem Olajuwon, 1984-2002	C	Lenny Wilkens, 1960-75	G
Walt Frazier, 1967-80	G	**Shaquille O'Neal**, 1992–	C	James Worthy, 1982-94	F

Note: Rick Barry, Billy Cunningham, Julius Erving, George Gervin and Moses Malone all played part of their pro careers in the ABA.

NBA's 10 Greatest Coaches

In December 1996, as part of its 50th anniversary celebration, the NBA named the 10 greatest coaches in league history. The voting was done by a league-approved panel of media. The coaches are listed alphabetically along with the dates of their professional coaching careers and overall records, including playoff games, and number of NBA titles won. Active coaches are in **bold** type.

Coach	W	L	Pct.	Titles	Coach	W	L	Pct.	Titles
Red Auerbach, 1946-66	1037	548	.654	9	**Don Nelson**, 1976-96, 97–	1218	943	.564	0
Chuck Daly, 1981-94, 97-99	713	488	.594	2	Jack Ramsay, 1968-89	908	841	.519	1
Bill Fitch, 1970-98	999	1160	.463	1	Pat Riley, 1981-2003	1265	669	.654	4
Red Holzman, 1953-82	754	652	.536	2	**Lenny Wilkens**, 1969–	1395	1231	.531	1
Phil Jackson, 1989-98, 99-04	1007	385	.723	9	TOTALS	9781	7255	.574	34
John Kundla, 1947-59	485	338	.589	5					

World Championships

The World Basketball Championships for men and women have been played regularly at four-year intervals (give or take a year) since 1970. The men's tournament began in 1950 and the women's in 1953. The Federation Internationale de Basketball Amateur (FIBA), which governs the World and Olympic tournaments, was founded in 1932. FIBA first allowed professional players from the NBA to participate in 1994. A team of collegians represented the USA in 1998.

Men

Multiple wins: Yugoslavia (5); Soviet Union and USA (3); Brazil (2).

Year

1950	**Argentina**, United States, Chile
1954	**United States**, Brazil, Philippines
1959	**Brazil**, United States, Chile
1963	**Brazil**, Yugoslavia, Soviet Union
1967	**Soviet Union**, Yugoslavia, Brazil
1970	**Yugoslavia**, Brazil, Soviet Union
1974	**Soviet Union**, Yugoslavia, United States
1978	**Yugoslavia**, Soviet Union, Brazil
1982	**Soviet Union**, United States, Yugoslavia
1986	**United States**, Soviet Union, Yugoslavia
1990	**Yugoslavia**, Soviet Union, United States
1994	**United States**, Russia, Croatia
1998	**Yugoslavia**, Russia, United States
2002	**Yugoslavia**, Argentina, Germany
2006	at Japan

Women

Multiple wins: USA (7); Soviet Union (6).

Year

1953	**United States**, Chile, France
1957	**United States**, Soviet Union, Czechoslovakia
1959	**Soviet Union**, Bulgaria, Czechoslovakia
1964	**Soviet Union**, Czechoslovakia, Bulgaria
1967	**Soviet Union**, South Korea, Czechoslovakia
1971	**Soviet Union**, Czechoslovakia, Brazil
1975	**Soviet Union**, Japan, Czechoslovakia
1979	**United States**, South Korea, Canada
1983	**Soviet Union**, United States, China
1986	**United States**, Soviet Union, Canada
1990	**United States**, Yugoslavia, Cuba
1994	**Brazil**, China, United States
1998	**United States**, Russia, Australia
2002	**United States**, Russia, Australia
2006	at Brazil

American Basketball Association
ABA Finals

The American Basketball Assn. began play in 1967-68 as a 10-team rival of the 21-year-old NBA. The ABA, which introduced the three-point basket, a multi-colored ball and the All-Star Game Slam Dunk Contest, lasted nine seasons before folding following the 1975-76 season. Four ABA teams–Denver, Indiana, New York and San Antonio–survived to enter the NBA in 1976-77. The NBA also adopted the three-point basket (in 1979-80) and the All-Star Game Slam Dunk Contest. The older league, however, refused to take in the ABA ball.

Multiple winners: Indiana (3); New York (2).

Year	Winner	Head Coach	Series		Loser	Head Coach
1968	Pittsburgh Pipers	Vince Cazzetta	4-3	(WLLLWWW)	New Orleans Bucs	Babe McCarthy
1969	Oakland Oaks	Alex Hannum	4-1	(WLWWW)	Indiana Pacers	Bob Leonard
1970	Indiana Pacers	Bob Leonard	4-2	(WWLLWLW)	Los Angeles Stars	Bill Sharman
1971	Utah Stars	Bill Sharman	4-3	(WWLLWLW)	Kentucky Colonels	Frank Ramsey
1972	Indiana Pacers	Bob Leonard	4-2	(WLWLWW)	New York Nets	Lou Carnesecca
1973	Indiana Pacers	Bob Leonard	4-3	(WLLWWLW)	Kentucky Colonels	Joe Mullaney
1974	New York Nets	Kevin Loughery	4-1	(WWWLW)	Utah Stars	Joe Mullaney
1975	Kentucky Colonels	Hubie Brown	4-1	(WWLWW)	Indiana Pacers	Bob Leonard
1976	New York Nets	Kevin Loughery	4-2	(WLWWLW)	Denver Nuggets	Larry Brown

Most Valuable Player

Winners' scoring averages provided; (*) indicates led league.

Multiple winners: Julius Erving (3); Mel Daniels (2).

Year		Avg
1968	Connie Hawkins, Pittsburgh, C	26.8*
1969	Mel Daniels, Indiana, C	24.0
1970	Spencer Haywood, Denver, C	30.0*
1971	Mel Daniels, Indiana, C	21.0
1972	Artis Gilmore, Kentucky, C	23.8
1973	Billy Cunningham, Carolina, F	24.1
1974	Julius Erving, New York, F	27.4*
1975	George McGinnis, Indiana, F	29.8*
	& Julius Erving, New York, F	27.9
1976	Julius Erving, New York, F	29.3*

Rookie of the Year

Winners' scoring averages provided; (*) indicates led league. Rookies who were also named Most Valuable Player are in **bold** type.

Year		Avg
1968	Mel Daniels, Minnesota, C	22.2
1969	Warren Armstrong, Oakland, G	21.5
1970	**Spencer Haywood**, Denver, C	30.0*
1971	Dan Issel, Kentucky, C	29.8*
	& Charlie Scott, Virginia, G	27.1
1972	**Artis Gilmore**, Kentucky, C	23.8
1973	Brian Taylor, New York, G	15.3
1974	Swen Nater, Virginia-SA, C	14.1
1975	Marvin Barnes, St. Louis, C	24.0
1976	David Thompson, Denver, F	26.0

Note: Warren Armstrong changed his name to Warren Jabali after the 1970-71 season.

Coach of the Year

Previous season and winning season records are provided; (*) indicates division title.

Multiple winner: Larry Brown (3).

Year			Improvement
1968	Vince Cazzetta, Pittsburgh		54-24*
1969	Alex Hannum, Oakland	22-56 to	60-18*
1970	Joe Belmont, Denver	44-34 to	51-33*
	& Bill Sharman, LA Stars	33-45 to	43-41
1971	Al Bianchi, Virginia	44-40 to	55-29*
1972	Tom Nissalke, Dallas	30-54 to	42-42
1973	Larry Brown, Carolina	35-49 to	57-27*
1974	Babe McCarthy, Kentucky	56-28 to	53-31
	& Joe Mullaney, Utah	55-29* to	51-33*
1975	Larry Brown, Denver	37-47 to	65-19*
1976	Larry Brown, Denver	65-19* to	60-24*

Scoring Leaders

Scoring championship decided by per game point average every season.

Multiple winner: Julius Erving (3).

Year		Gm	Avg	Pts
1968	Connie Hawkins, Pittsburgh	.70	1875	26.8
1969	Rick Barry, Oakland	.35	1190	34.0
1970	Spencer Haywood, Denver	.84	2519	30.0
1971	Dan Issel, Kentucky	.83	2480	29.8
1972	Charlie Scott, Virginia	.73	2524	34.6
1973	Julius Erving, Virginia	.71	2268	31.9
1974	Julius Erving, New York	.84	2299	27.4
1975	George McGinnis, Indiana	.79	2353	29.8
1976	Julius Erving, New York	.84	2462	29.3

ABA All-Star Game

The ABA All-Star Game was an Eastern Division vs. Western Division contest from 1968-75. League membership had dropped to seven teams by 1976, the ABA's last season, so the team in first place at the break (Denver) played an All-Star team made up from the other six clubs.

Series: East won 5, West 3 and Denver 1.

Year	Result	Host	Coaches	Most Valuable Player
1968	East 126, West 120	Indiana	Jim Pollard, Babe McCarthy	Larry Brown, New Orleans
1969	West 133, East 127	Louisville	Alex Hannum, Gene Rhodes	John Beasley, Dallas
1970	West 128, East 98	Indiana	Babe McCarthy, Bob Leonard	Spencer Haywood, Denver
1971	East 126, West 122	Carolina	Al Bianchi, Bill Sharman	Mel Daniels, Indiana
1972	East 142, West 115	Louisville	Joe Mullaney, Ladell Andersen	Dan Issel, Kentucky
1973	West 123, East 111	Utah	Ladell Andersen, Larry Brown	Warren Jabali, Denver
1974	East 128, West 112	Virginia	Babe McCarthy, Joe Mullaney	Artis Gilmore, Kentucky
1975	East 151, West 124	San Antonio	Kevin Loughery, Larry Brown	Freddie Lewis, St. Louis
1976	Denver 144, ABA 138	Denver	Larry Brown, Kevin Loughery	David Thompson, Denver

Continental Basketball Association

Originally named the Eastern Pennsylvania Basketball League when it formed on April 23, 1946, the league changed names several times before becoming known as the Eastern Basketball Association. In 1978, the EBA was redubbed the CBA. The CBA suspended operations following the 2000 season but reorganized for the 2001-02 season.

Multiple champions: Allentown and Wilkes-Barre (8); Scranton, Tampa Bay, Williamsport and Yakima (3); Albany, Dakota, La Crosse, Pottsville, Rochester and Wilmington (2).

League Champions

Year		Year		Year		Year	
1947	Wilkes-Barre Barons	1963	Allentown Jets	1977	Scranton Apollos	1992	La Crosse Catbirds
1948	Reading Keys	1964	Camden Bullets	1978	Wilkes-Barre Barons	1993	Omaha Racers
1949	Pottsville Packers	1965	Allentown Jets	1979	Rochester Zeniths	1994	Quad City Thunder
1950	Williamsport Billies	1966	Wilmington Blue	1980	Anchorage Northern	1995	Yakima Sun Kings
1951	Sunbury Mercuries		Bombers		Knights	1996	Sioux Falls Skyforce
1952	Pottsville Packers	1967	Wilmington Blue	1981	Rochester Zeniths	1997	Oklahoma City
1953	Williamsport Billies		Bombers	1982	Lancaster Lightning		Calvary
1954	Williamsport Billies	1968	Allentown Jets	1983	Detroit Spirits	1998	Quad City Thunder
1955	Wilkes-Barre Barons	1969	Wilkes-Barre Barons	1984	Albany Patroons	1999	Connecticut Pride
1956	Wilkes-Barre Barons	1970	Allentown Jets	1985	Tampa Bay Thrillers	2000	Yakima Sun Kings
1957	Scranton Miners	1971	Scranton Apollos	1986	Tampa Bay Thrillers	2001	suspended play
1958	Wilkes-Barre Barons	1972	Allentown Jets	1987	Rapid City Thrillers*	2002	Dakota Wizards
1959	Wilkes-Barre Barons	1973	Wilkes-Barre Barons	1988	Albany Patroons	2003	Yakima Sun Kings
1960	Easton Madisons	1974	Hartford Capitols	1989	Tulsa Fast Breakers	2004	Dakota Wizards
1961	Baltimore Bullets	1975	Allentown Jets	1990	La Crosse Catbirds		
1962	Allentown Jets	1976	Allentown Jets	1991	Wichita Falls Texans		

*The Tampa Bay Thrillers moved to Rapid City, S.D. at the end of the 1987 regular season.

National Basketball Development League

The NBDL, a.k.a. "The D League" was founded in 2001 as an eight-team player and coach development league owned and operated by the NBA. The individual teams do not have a direct relationship with NBA clubs but occasionally players and coaches are called up to the NBA. The NBDL champion was determined in a best-of-three championship series for the first two seasons of the league before changing the format to a single-game playoff in 2004.

The North Charleston Lowgators dropped the North from their name following the 2003 season and the franchise moved to Fort Myers, Florida following the 2004 season and became the first privately-owned team in the league. The league contracted to six teams for the 2004 season when the Greenville Groove and Mobile Revelers each ceased operations.

League Champions

Year	Champions	Head Coach	Score	Runners-up	Head Coach
2002	Greenville Groove	Milton Barnes	2-0	No. Charleston Lowgators	Alex English
2003	Mobile Revelers	Sam Vincent	2-1 (WLW)	Fayetteville Patriots	Jeff Capel
2004	Asheville Altitude	Joey Meyer	108-106 OT	Huntsville Flight	Ralph Lewis

Annual Awards

Most Valuable Player

Winner's scoring averages provided; (*) indicates led league.

Year		PPG
2002	Ansu Sesay, Greenville, F	16.5
2003	Devin Brown, Fayetteville, G	16.9
2004	Tierre Brown, Charleston, G	18.6

Scoring Champion

Scoring championship decided by per game point average every season.

Year		PPG
2002	Isaac Fontaine, Mobile	17.4
2003	Nate Johnson, Columbus	19.5
2004	Desmond Penigar, Asheville	19.6

Defensive Player of the Year

Year	
2002	Jeff Myers, Greenville
2003	Mikki Moore, Roanoke
2004	Karim Shabazz, Charleston

Rookie of the Year

Year	
2002	Fred House, N. Charleston
2003	Devin Brown, Fayetteville
2004	Desmond Penigar, Asheville

WOMEN
Women's National Basketball Association

The WNBA, owned and operated by the NBA, began play in 1997 as an eight-team summer league. The league added two teams prior to its second season (1998), then added two more teams before its third season in 1999. Four additional teams were added before the 2000 season, bringing the total number of teams to 16. Prior to the 2003 season two franchises were relocated and two were contracted and one franchise folded before the 2004 season. The WNBA champion was determined by a single-game playoff between the winners of the semifinals in the league's 1997 inaugural season, before going to a best-of-three championship series in 1998 and a best-of-five championship series starting in 2005.

Multiple winners: Houston (4); Los Angeles (2).

Year	Champions	Head Coach	Series		Runners-up	Head Coach
1997	Houston Comets	Van Chancellor	65-51		New York Liberty	Nancy Darsch
1998	Houston Comets	Van Chancellor	2-1	(LWW)	Phoenix Mercury	Cheryl Miller
1999	Houston Comets	Van Chancellor	2-1	(WLW)	New York Liberty	Richie Adubato
2000	Houston Comets	Van Chancellor	2-0		New York Liberty	Richie Adubato
2001	Los Angeles Sparks	Michael Cooper	2-0		Charlotte Sting	Anne Donovan
2002	Los Angeles Sparks	Michael Cooper	2-0		New York Liberty	Richie Adubato
2003	Detroit Shock	Bill Laimbeer	2-1	(LWW)	Los Angeles Sparks	Michael Cooper
2004	Seattle Storm	Anne Donovan	2-1	(LWW)	Connecticut Sun	Mike Thibault

Championship MVPs: 1997-Cynthia Cooper, Houston; 1998-Cynthia Cooper, Houston; 1999-Cynthia Cooper, Houston; 2000-Cynthia Cooper, Houston; 2001-Lisa Leslie, Los Angeles; 2002-Lisa Leslie, Los Angeles; 2003-Ruth Riley, Detroit; 2004-Betty Lennox, Seattle

Annual Awards

Most Valuable Player

Winner's scoring averages provided; (*) indicates led league.

Multiple winners: Cynthia Cooper, Lisa Leslie and Sheryl Swoopes (2).

Year		Avg
1997	Cynthia Cooper, Houston	22.2*
1998	Cynthia Cooper, Houston	22.7*
1999	Yolanda Griffith, Sacramento	18.8
2000	Sheryl Swoopes, Houston	20.7*
2001	Lisa Leslie, Los Angeles	19.5
2002	Sheryl Swoopes, Houston	18.5
2003	Lauren Jackson, Seattle	21.2*
2004	Lisa Leslie, Los Angeles	17.6

Coach of the Year

Previous season and winning season's record are provided; (*) indicates division title.

Multiple winner: Van Chancellor (3).

Year		Improvement
1997	Van Chancellor, Houston	18-10*
1998	Van Chancellor, Houston	18-10 to 27-3*
1999	Van Chancellor, Houston	27-3 to 26-6*
2000	Michael Cooper, Los Angeles	20-12 to 28-4*
2001	Dan Hughes, Cleveland	17-15 to 22-10*
2002	Marianne Stanley, Washington	10-22 to 17-15
2003	Bill Laimbeer, Detroit	9-23 to 25-9*
2004	Suzie McConnell Serio, Minnesota	18-16 to 18-16

Rookie of the Year

Year	
1998	Tracy Reid, Charlotte
1999	Chamique Holdsclaw, Washington
2000	Betty Lennox, Minnesota
2001	Jackie Stiles, Portland
2002	Tamika Catchings, Indiana
2003	Cheryl Ford, Detroit
2004	Diana Taurasi, Phoenix

Defensive Player of the Year

Multiple winners: Sheryl Swoopes (3); Teresa Weatherspoon (2).

Year	
1997	Teresa Weatherspoon, New York
1998	Teresa Weatherspoon, New York
1999	Yolanda Griffith, Sacramento
2000	Sheryl Swoopes, Houston
2001	Debbie Black, Miami
2002	Sheryl Swoopes, Houston
2003	Sheryl Swoopes, Houston
2004	Lisa Leslie, Los Angeles

WNBA Number One Draft Picks

Year		Overall First Pick
1997	Utah Starzz	Dena Head
1998	Utah Starzz	Margo Dydek
1999	Washington Mystics	Chamique Holdsclaw
2000	Cleveland Rockers	Ann Wauters
2001	Seattle Storm	Lauren Jackson
2002	Seattle Storm	Sue Bird
2003	Cleveland Rockers	LaToya Thomas
2004	Phoenix Mercury	Diana Taurasi

American Basketball League (1997-98)
League Champions

The American Basketball League began play in 1996 as an eight-team league. Before the 1997-98 season the league added an expansion franchise in Long Beach, Calif. while the Richmond Rage was relocated to Philadelphia. In the spring of 1998, the league announced plans to dissolve an original franchise, the Atlanta Glory, and expand to Chicago and Nashville before the 1998-99 season, increasing the league's size to 10 teams. The ABL finals was a best of five series. Each ABL champion's wins and losses are noted in parentheses after the series score. The ABL folded before the 1999 season.

Multiple winner: Columbus (2).

Year	Champions	Head Coach	Series		Runners-up	Head Coach
1997	Columbus Quest	Brian Agler	3-2	(WLLWW)	Richmond Rage	Lisa Boyer
1998	Columbus Quest	Brian Agler	3-2	(LLWWW)	Long Beach StingRays	Maura McHugh

Most Valuable Player

Winner's scoring averages provided; (*) indicates led league.

Year		Avg
1997	Nikki McCray, Columbus	19.9
1998	Natalie Williams, Portland	21.9*

Coach of the Year

Previous season and winning season's record are provided; (*) indicates division title.

Year		Improvement
1997	Brian Agler, Columbus	31-9*
1998	Lin Dunn, Portland	14-26 to 27-17

Hockey

After 22 seasons and 1,759 games, Lightning RW
Dave Andreychuk finally hoisted the Cup.

AP/Wide World Photos

Lightning Strike

Former league doormat Tampa Bay wins its first Stanley Cup in an emotional finals with Calgary.

Steve Levy *is a hockey play-by-play announcer and host of ESPN's National Hockey Night.*

In recent years we've seen such unlikely teams as Buffalo, Washington, Carolina and Anaheim reach the Stanley Cup finals. In 2003-04, one of those unlikely types was actually able to skate around the ice with the Cup.

The Tampa Bay Lightning are Stanley Cup champions. Wow. It still seems strange. The team with only 19 wins four seasons ago is now the NHL's best. It should give the Los Angeles Clippers hope for the future.

In fairness to the current "Bolts," maybe we shouldn't have been that surprised. After all, the team has steadily improved in each of the last four seasons and was the top seed in the Eastern Conference heading into the playoffs. So for those that say the NHL regular season doesn't mean anything, this year it clearly did. The finals couldn't have been any closer, with the Lightning edging the Calgary Flames,

2-1, in Game 7 at the St. Pete Times Forum, and many believe if the deciding game were in Calgary the outcome would have been different.

During my time at ESPN I have had the privilege of covering ten Stanley Cup finals and can honestly say that Madison Square Garden in 1994 and the Saddledome in Calgary in 2004 provided the best atmospheres.

The stories coming out of this Alberta city were priceless...and pricey, as area bars raked in the money during every game. Hordes of red-clad Flames fans filled Calgary streets after every win. During the games, however, it was another story. Statistics show crime went way down in Calgary during the three-plus hours the home team was on the ice. The city was clearly smitten with the Flames as evidenced by the 42 page pull-out preview in the *Calgary Herald*. Forty-two pages! And that was for the first round of the playoffs!

AP/Wide World Photos

*With a combined 50 playoff points, Conn Smythe winner **Brad Richards**, left, and Hart Trophy winner **Martin St. Louis** willed the Lightning to its first Cup.*

It was a team most hockey purists had to root for. Even in Edmonton, where some locals have coined the phrase "ABC," meaning "Anything But Calgary," Oilers fans were pulling for the Flames. The team was gritty, "small market" and Canadian, just like its leader. Fan-favorite Darryl Sutter succeeded at the two jobs many believed couldn't be done at the same time — coach and general manager.

While he couldn't compare to Tampa Bay coach John Tortorella when it came to a sound bite, Sutter was nonetheless entertaining during the entire ride. He played the underdog role to perfection, even proclaiming it was "Calgary against the world."

Sutter's greatest move as general manager was re-signing right wing Jarome Iginla to a two-year deal back in 2002. That move proved invaluable to Sutter *the coach* as well, since it gave him the ability to send the league's greatest player over the boards every game.

What sets Iginla apart from the greatest players of each and every era since Gordie Howe skated in the 1950's and 60's, is that he does everything. And yes, by "everything," I'm including fighting as well. Sure, fighting is against the rules, but its only five minutes against the

AP/Wide World Photos

*In September 2004, NHL Commissioner **Gary Bettman**, left with Chief Legal Officer **Bill Daly**, spoke of a "Grand Canyon-sized gap" between the owners and the players' association.*

rules. I've always believed that fighting plays a role in the game that goes beyond the actual fisticuffs. When Iginla took on mammoth Red Wings defenseman Derian Hatcher in the conference semifinals against Detroit, teammates stood up and took notice, much the same way the Lightning did when their star Vincent Lecavalier dropped the mitts against Iginla in the finals. Players don't necessarily have to win the fight to earn the respect of their peers. They just have to be willing.

Tampa Bay forwards Martin St. Louis and Brad Richards had been playing in Lecavalier's shadow for the past few years. After all, Lecavalier was the highly touted top overall pick in 1998, while Richards was a second round pick and St. Louis wasn't even drafted. It's safe to say that their time in the shadows has passed.

Richards was cool and clutch when the pressure was the highest. His 26 playoff points and amazing seven game-winning goals earned him the Conn Smythe Award as playoff MVP. While St. Louis, the NHL's regular season MVP, seemed to lose his focus for a

continued on page 392 ▶

Steve Levy's Top Ten Stories of the Year in Hockey

10 Todd Bertuzzi's premeditated attack on Colorado's Steve Moore is by no means a top story. It'd be more accurate to call it a bottom story, but no list of events from the past NHL season can be drawn up without at least mentioning it. Moore has already felt the pain. Bertuzzi and the Canucks will be feeling the effects for a long time.

9 Pat LaFontaine is inducted into the Hockey Hall of Fame. He represented America and the game in the best of ways. He was, simply put, everything that is great about hockey.

8 Unlike the NBA draft, the knock on the NHL draft is that no one can even pronounce the names, much less know who the players are. Everyone will remember at least one name next year. We've been waiting for 17-year-old Canadian Sidney Crosby for what seems like years already. Even Wayne Gretzky said if anyone can break his records, Crosby's the guy.

7 During a ho-hum January, goalie Brian Boucher makes everyone pay attention to the Coyotes when he breaks a 55-year-old league record by recording five consecutive shutouts.

6 Canada wins the World Cup of hockey and we're all treated to watching Mario Lemieux play in games that really count for maybe the last time. Defending his goalie by going after Steve Konowalchuk in the first game gets the tournament buzzing early.

5 We knew All-Star weekend in St. Paul, Minn. would be great and it didn't disappoint. The host city put on a tremendous show and its pure love of the game shined through. Tickets were as tough to come by as Super Bowl tickets.

4 Speaking of atmosphere, it's tough to top the Heritage Classic. More than 57,000 fans braved the elements in Edmonton as the NHL played its first outdoor game to count in the standings. They could've sold 80,000 tickets.

3 The Tampa Bay Lightning win the Stanley Cup. The former league laughingstocks can laugh at everyone else now. Dave Andreychuk finally gets his, while Brad Richards and Martin St. Louis join Vincent Lecavalier in the star department.

2 The Calgary Flames are one game short of winning it all but still show the world what the game can offer. Having the league's best player sure doesn't hurt. Fans turn the city into a sea of red.

1 There's no getting around it. I'll never experience labor pains, but I doubt it could be as painful as listening to the NHL's constant labor woes. As I write this, I'm afraid memories of the 2003-04 season will have to keep us company throughout what should be the 2004-05 campaign.

short time during the finals, he still found the net when he had to, scoring the game winner in double OT of Game 6.

With a cloud hovering that this might be the last NHL action we would see for some time, we were treated to a passionate seven-game Stanley Cup finals that had it all – drama, star quality, controversy and emotion. It was nice to see veteran Dave Andreychuk finally hoist the cup after 22 seasons.

For all that say the NHL needs big market, big spending teams in the finals to be successful, I say the Lightning and the Flames proved that theory wrong. Smart drafting, smart spending and solid checking (not to mention the always important checking of egos) proved to be just the right formula. The rest of the teams should take notice. In fact, they have no other choice.

Working Overtime

Martin St. Louis' goal in Game 6 was just the seventh time in Stanley Cup finals history that an overtime goal staved off elimination.

		Team	Opp.
2004	Martin St. Louis	TB*	Calg.
2000	Mike Modano	Dal.	NJ*
1964	Bob Baun	Tor.*	Det.
1954	Kenny Mosdell	Mon.	Det.*
1946	Terry Reardon	Bos.	Mon.*
1945	Eddie Bruneteau	Det.	Tor.*
1936	Buzz Boll	Tor.	Det.*

* Team won Stanley Cup.

Seventh Heaven

Since 1939 only five teams have won the final two rounds of the Stanley Cup playoffs in seven games each. Oddly it's happened in each of the last two seasons.

		Teams Beat
2004	Tampa Bay	Phi., Calg.
2003	New Jersey	Ott., Ana.
1994	NY Rangers	NJ, Van.
1964	Toronto	Mon., Det.
1950	Detroit	Tor., NYR

Note: The second team listed under "Teams Beat" is the finals opponent.

Tampa Bay's Dave Andreychuk won his first Stanley Cup after 1,759 career games (regular season and playoffs), the most in NHL history before winning a title. That dubious distinction among active players now belongs to Scott Mellanby with 1,423.

2003-2004
Season in Review

SPORTS ALMANAC

Final NHL Standings

Division champions (*) and playoff qualifiers (†) are noted. OL signifies any game that was tied after regulation play but lost in overtime. Number of seasons listed after each head coach refers to current tenure with club through 2003-04 season.

Western Conference

Central Division

	W	L	T	OL	Pts	GF	GA
*Detroit	48	21	11	2	109	255	189
†St. Louis	39	30	11	2	91	191	198
†Nashville	38	29	11	4	91	216	217
Columbus	25	45	8	4	62	177	238
Chicago	20	43	11	8	59	188	259

Head Coaches: Det—Dave Lewis (2nd season); **St.L**—Joel Quenneville (8th, 29-23-7-2) was fired on Feb. 24 and replaced by asst. Mike Kitchen (10-7-4-0); **Nash**—Barry Trotz (6th); **Clb**—Pres./GM/coach Doug MacLean (2nd, 9-21-4-3) relinquished coaching duties on Jan. 1 and replaced by asst. Gerard Gallant (16-24-4-1); **Chi**—Brian Sutter (3rd).

Northwest Division

	W	L	T	OL	Pts	GF	GA
*Vancouver	43	24	10	5	101	235	194
†Colorado	40	22	13	7	100	236	198
†Calgary	42	30	7	3	94	200	176
Edmonton	36	29	12	5	89	221	208
Minnesota	30	29	20	3	83	188	183

Head Coaches: Van—Marc Crawford (6th season); **Col**—Tony Granato (2nd); **Calg**—Darryl Sutter (2nd); **Edm**—Craig MacTavish (4th); **Min**—Jacques Lemaire (4th).

Pacific Division

	W	L	T	OL	Pts	GF	GA
*San Jose	43	21	12	6	104	219	183
†Dallas	41	26	13	2	97	194	175
Los Angeles	28	29	16	9	81	205	217
Anaheim	29	35	10	8	76	184	213
Phoenix	22	36	18	6	68	188	245

Head Coaches: SJ—Ron Wilson (2nd season); **Dal**—Dave Tippett (2nd); **LA**—Andy Murray (5th); **Ana**—Mike Babcock (2nd); **Pho**—Bob Francis (5th, 20-24-15-3) was fired on Feb. 24 and replaced by asst. Rick Bowness (2-12-3-3).

Eastern Conference

Northeast Division

	W	L	T	OL	Pts	GF	GA
*Boston	41	19	15	7	104	209	188
†Toronto	45	24	10	3	103	242	204
†Ottawa	43	23	10	6	102	262	189
†Montreal	41	30	7	4	93	208	192
Buffalo	37	34	7	4	85	220	221

Head Coaches: Bos—Mike Sullivan (1st season); **Tor**—Pat Quinn (6th); **Ott**—Jacques Martin (9th); **Mon**—Claude Julien (2nd); **Buf**—Lindy Ruff (7th).

Atlantic Division

	W	L	T	OL	Pts	GF	GA
*Philadelphia	40	21	15	6	101	229	186
†New Jersey	43	25	12	2	100	213	164
†NY Islanders	38	29	11	4	91	237	210
NY Rangers	27	40	7	8	69	206	250
Pittsburgh	23	47	8	4	58	190	303

Head Coaches: Phi—Ken Hitchcock (2nd season); **NJ**—Pat Burns (2nd); **NYI**—Steve Stirling (1st); **NYR**—Pres./GM/coach Glen Sather (2nd, 22-29-7-4) relinquished coaching duties on Feb. 25 and was replaced by asst. Tom Renney (5-11-0-4); **Pit**—Ed Olczyk (1st).

Southeast Division

	W	L	T	OL	Pts	GF	GA
*Tampa Bay	46	22	8	6	106	245	192
Atlanta	33	37	8	4	78	214	243
Carolina	28	34	14	6	76	172	209
Florida	28	35	15	4	75	188	221
Washington	23	46	10	3	59	186	253

Head Coaches: TB—John Tortorella (4th season); **Atl**—Bob Hartley (9th, 8-12-8-2) was fired on Dec. 15 and replaced by Peter Laviolette (20-22-6-4); **Car**—Paul Maurice (9th, 8-12-8-2) was fired on Dec. 15 and replaced by GM Rick Dudley (13-15-9-3) and then asst. John Torchetti (10-12-4-1) on Feb. 9; **Fla**—Mike Keenan (3rd, 5-8-2-0) was fired on Nov. 9 and replaced by GM Rick Dudley (13-15-9-3) and then asst. John Torchetti (10-12-4-1) on Feb. 9; **Wash**—Bruce Cassidy (2nd, 8-18-1-1) was fired on Dec. 10 and replaced by asst. Glen Hanlon (15-28-9-2).

Home & Away, Division, Conference Records

Sixteen teams—eight from each conference—qualify for the Stanley Cup Playoffs; (*) indicates division champions.

Western Conference

		Pts	Home	Away	Div
1	Detroit*	109	30-7-4-0	18-14-7-2	15-7-1-1
2	San Jose*	104	24-8-7-2	19-13-5-4	15-6-3-0
3	Vancouver*	101	21-13-7-0	22-11-3-5	10-7-6-1
4	Colorado	100	19-14-6-2	21-8-7-5	12-7-4-1
5	Dallas	97	26-7-8-0	15-19-5-2	9-8-6-1
6	Calgary	94	21-14-5-1	21-16-2-2	11-7-4-2
7	St. Louis	91	23-11-7-0	16-19-4-2	12-9-2-1
8	Nashville	91	23-12-5-0	15-17-6-4	11-9-2-2
	Edmonton	89	22-12-4-3	14-17-8-2	7-12-3-2
	Minnesota	83	19-13-7-2	11-16-13-1	8-9-7-0
	Los Angeles	81	15-16-9-1	13-13-7-8	9-9-5-1
	Anaheim	76	19-11-7-4	10-24-3-4	8-10-4-2
	Phoenix	68	11-19-7-4	11-17-11-2	8-10-4-2
	Columbus	62	17-18-4-2	8-27-4-2	9-13-0-2
	Chicago	59	13-17-6-5	7-26-5-3	10-11-1-2

Eastern Conference

		Pts	Home	Away	Div
1	Tampa Bay*	106	24-10-4-3	22-12-4-3	13-8-3-0
2	Boston*	104	18-12-9-2	23-7-6-5	13-6-2-3
3	Philadelphia*	101	24-11-3-3	16-10-12-3	13-6-5-0
4	Toronto	103	22-14-3-2	23-10-7-1	13-9-2-0
5	Ottawa	102	23-8-5-5	20-15-5-1	9-10-4-1
6	New Jersey	100	22-13-5-1	21-12-7-1	14-7-2-1
7	Montreal	93	23-13-4-1	18-17-3-3	9-13-1-1
8	NY Islanders	91	25-11-4-1	13-18-7-3	8-11-3-2
	Buffalo	85	21-13-4-3	16-21-3-1	10-8-3-3
	Atlanta	78	18-17-4-2	15-20-4-2	13-8-1-2
	Carolina	76	13-18-8-2	15-16-6-4	8-10-5-1
	Florida	75	16-15-7-3	12-20-8-1	8-10-5-1
	NY Rangers	69	13-21-3-4	14-19-4-4	11-10-1-2
	Washington	59	13-20-6-2	10-26-4-1	9-10-4-1
	Pittsburgh	58	13-22-6-0	10-25-2-4	6-12-5-1

2004 NHL All-Star Game
Eastern 6, Western 4

54th NHL All-Star Game. **Date:** Feb. 8 at XCel Energy Center in St. Paul, Minn.; **Coaches:** Pat Quinn, Toronto (Eastern) and Dave Lewis, Detroit (Western); **MVP:** Joe Sakic, Colorado center (Western)—three goals.

Starters were chosen by fan vote while reserves were selected by the NHL's Hockey Operations Department, after consultation with NHL general managers. Head coaches whose team had the best winning percentage in each conference on Jan. 8 (the half-way point of the season) were named all-star head coaches.

Defensemen Brian Rafalski and Pavel Kubina and right wing Glen Murray were added to the **Eastern Conference** team as injury replacements for Scott Stevens, Wade Redden and Marian Hossa, respectively.

Eastern Conference

Pos	Starters	G	A	Pts	PM
W	Ilya Kovalchuk, Atlanta	1	0	1	0
D	Scott Niedermayer, New Jersey	0	1	1	0
D	Brian Rafalski, New Jersey	0	0	0	0
C	Joe Thornton, Boston	0	0	0	0
W	Martin St. Louis, Tampa Bay	0	0	0	0
	Reserves				
W	Daniel Alfredsson, Ottawa	2	1	3	0
C	Mark Messier, NY Rangers	1	1	2	0
W	Gary Roberts, Toronto	1	1	2	0
C	Mats Sundin, Toronto	0	2	2	0
D	Adrian Aucoin, NY Islanders	1	0	1	0
W	Jaromir Jagr, NY Rangers	0	1	1	0
C	Robert Lang, Washington	0	1	1	0
D	Sheldon Souray, Montreal	0	1	1	0
D	Nick Boynton, Boston	0	0	0	0
D	Pavel Kubina, Tampa Bay	0	0	0	0
W	Glen Murray, Boston	0	0	0	0
C	Keith Primeau, Philadelphia	0	0	0	0
C	Jeremy Roenick, Philadelphia	0	0	0	0
	TOTALS	6	9	15	0

Goaltenders	Mins	Shots	Saves	GA
Martin Brodeur, NJ	20:00	11	10	1
Jose Theodore, Mon. (W)	20:00	12	10	2
Roberto Luongo, Fla.	20:00	9	8	1
TOTALS	60:00	32	28	4

Western Conference

Pos	Starters	G	A	Pts	PM
W	Todd Bertuzzi, Vancouver	0	2	2	0
D	Nicklas Lidstrom, Detroit	0	1	1	0
D	Rob Blake, Colorado	0	0	0	0
W	Bill Guerin, Dallas	0	0	0	0
C	Mike Modano, Dallas	0	0	0	0
	Reserves				
C	Joe Sakic, Colorado	3	0	3	0
W	Marcus Naslund, Vancouver	0	3	3	0
W	Shane Doan, Phoenix	1	0	1	0
W	Keith Tkachuk, St. Louis	0	1	1	0
C	Pavel Datsyuk, Detroit	0	0	0	0
W	Jarome Iginla, Calgary	0	0	0	0
D	Filip Kuba, Minnesota	0	0	0	0
C	Patrick Marleau, San Jose	0	0	0	0
W	Rick Nash, Columbus	0	0	0	0
D	Mattias Norstrom, Los Angeles	0	0	0	0
D	Chris Pronger, St. Louis	0	0	0	0
W	Alex Tanguay, Colorado	0	0	0	0
D	Kimmo Timonen, Nashville	0	0	0	0
	TOTALS	4	7	11	0

Goaltenders	Mins	Shots	Saves	GA
Marty Turco, Dal.	20:00	10	9	1
Tomas Vokoun, Nash. (L)	20:00	12	8	4
Dwayne Roloson, Min.	18:51	7	6	1
TOTALS	58:51	29	23	6

Score by Periods

	1	2	3	Final
Eastern	1	4	1	— 6
Western	1	2	1	— 4

Power plays: Eastern—0/0; Western—0/0.
Officials: Blaine Angus and Stephen Walkom (referees), Scott Driscoll and Thor Nelson (linesmen).
Attendance: 19,434.
TV Rating: 2.5/5 share (ABC).

2004 NHL Skills Competition
Eastern Conference, 13-6

Puck Control Relay
Team: Western (Datsyuk, Timonen, Doan)
Individual: Rick Nash (Western)

Fastest Skater
Team: Eastern (Avg.13.922 sec.: Kovalchuk, St. Louis, Niedermayer)
Individual: Scott Niedermayer, Eastern (13.783 sec.)

Hardest Shot
Team: Eastern (Avg. 99.9 mph: Thornton, Souray, Kubina, Aucoin)
Individual: Sheldon Souray, Eastern and Adrian Aucoin, Eastern (tie, 102.2 mph)

Shooting Accuracy (targets/shots)
Team: Eastern (13/28: Sundin, Murray, Messier, Roenick)
Individual: Jeremy Roenick, Eastern (4/4)

In the Zone
Team: Eastern Conference wins, 5-4

Breakaway Relay
Team: Eastern Conference wins, 9-6

Goaltender Competition
(combined In the Zone + Breakaway Relay)
Individual: Roberto Luongo, Eastern

Tampa Bay Lightning
Martin St. Louis
Scoring, Assists, +/-, ShG

Columbus Blue Jackets
Rick Nash
Goals, PP Goals

Calgary Flames
Miikka Kiprusoff
Goals Against Average

New Jersey Devils
Martin Brodeur
Wins, Shutouts

NHL Regular Season Individual Leaders

(*) indicates rookie eligible for Calder Trophy.

Scoring

	Pos	Gm	G	A	Pts	+/-	PM	PP	SH	GW	GT	Shots	Pct
Martin St. Louis, Tampa Bay	R	82	38	56	**94**	35	24	8	8	7	0	212	17.9
Ilya Kovalchuk, Atlanta	L	81	41	46	**87**	-10	63	16	1	6	0	341	12.0
Joe Sakic, Colorado	C	81	33	54	**87**	11	42	13	1	3	1	253	13.0
Markus Naslund, Vancouver	L	78	35	49	**84**	24	58	5	0	6	0	296	11.8
Marian Hossa, Ottawa	R	81	36	46	**82**	4	46	14	1	5	1	233	15.5
Patrik Elias, New Jersey	L	82	38	43	**81**	26	44	9	3	9	0	300	12.7
Daniel Alfredsson, Ottawa	R	77	32	48	**80**	12	24	9	0	5	1	230	13.9
Cory Stillman, Tampa Bay	L	81	25	55	**80**	18	36	11	1	6	0	178	14.0
Robert Lang, Wash.-Det.	C	69	30	49	**79**	4	24	10	0	3	1	163	18.4
Brad Richards, Tampa Bay	C	82	26	53	**79**	14	12	5	1	6	0	244	10.7
Alex Tanguay, Colorado	L	69	25	54	**79**	30	42	7	0	5	0	117	21.4
Milan Hejduk, Colorado	R	82	35	40	**75**	19	20	16	0	6	0	237	14.8
Mats Sundin, Toronto	C	81	31	44	**75**	11	52	11	1	10	0	226	13.7
Mark Recchi, Philadelphia	L	82	26	49	**75**	18	47	14	1	5	2	167	15.6
Jaromir Jagr, Wash.-NYR	R	77	31	43	**74**	-5	38	10	0	3	1	257	12.1
Jarome Iginla, Calgary	R	81	41	32	**73**	21	84	8	4	10	1	265	15.5
Steve Sullivan, Chi.-Nash.	R	80	24	49	**73**	1	48	11	2	4	0	218	11.0
Joe Thornton, Boston	C	77	23	50	**73**	18	98	4	0	6	0	187	12.3
Keith Tkachuk, St. Louis	L	75	33	38	**71**	8	83	18	0	8	2	233	14.2
Scott Gomez, New Jersey	C	80	14	56	**70**	18	70	3	0	1	0	189	7.4

Goals

Nash, Clb.	41
Iginla, Calg.	41
Kovalchuk, Atl.	41
Elias, NJ	38
St. Louis, TB	38
Hossa, Ott.	36
Naslund, Van.	35
Hejduk, Col.	35
Guerin, Dal.	34
Tkachuk, St.L	33
Sakic, Col.	33
Three tied with 32 each.	

Assists

Gomez, NJ	56
St. Louis, TB	56
Stillman, TB	55
Tanguay, Col	54
Sakic, Col	54
Richards, TB	53
Weight, St.L	51
Thornton, Bos	50
Lang, Wash.-Det.	49
Naslund, Van.	49
Sullivan, Chi.-Nash.	49
Recchi, Phi.	49
Alfredsson, Ott.	48

Defensemen Points

Gonchar, Wash.-Bos.	58
Pronger, St.L	54
Niedermayer, NJ	54
McCabe, Tor.	53
Zidlicky, Nash.	53
Tarnstrom, Pit.	52
Leetch, NYR-Tor.	51
Berard, Chi.	47
Schneider, Det.	46
Blake, Col.	46
Aucoin, NYI	44
Timonen, Nash.	44

Rookie Points

Ryder, Mon.	63
Hunter, NYI	51
Ruutu, Chi.	44
Malone, Pit.	43
Bergeron, Bos.	39
Zherdev, Clb.	34
Lupul, Ana.	34
Liles, Col.	34
McLean, Chi.	31
Staal, Car.	31
Lombardi, Calg.	29
Koltsov, Pit.	29

Plus/Minus

Malik, Van.	+35
St. Louis, TB	+35
Chara, Ott.	+33
Modin, TB	+31
Tanguay, Col.	+30
Ekman, SJ	+30
Lukowich, TB	+29
Aucoin, NYI	+29
Elias, NJ	+26
Jonsson, NYI	+25

Game Winning Goals

Sundin, Tor.	10
Iginla, Calg.	10
Guerin, Dal.	10
Murray, Bos.	9
Zednik, Mon.	9
Cheechoo, SJ	9
Elias, NJ	9
Four tied with 8 each.	

Power Play Goals

Nash, Clb.	19
Tkachuk, St.L	18
Kovalchuk, Atl.	16
Hejduk, Col.	16
Bondra, Wash.-Ott.	14
Hossa, Ott.	14
Recchi, Phi.	14
Havlat, Ott.	13
Sakic, Col.	13

Short-Handed Goals

St. Louis, TB	8
Draper, Det.	5
Adams, Car.	5
Blake, NYI	4
Maltby, Det.	4
Iginla, Calg.	4
Johnson, Nash.	4
Vyborny, Clb.	4
Ekman, SJ	4

Shots

Kovalchuk, Atl.	.341
Elias, NJ	.300
Naslund, Van	.296
Shanahan, Det.	.280
Jokinen, Fla.	.280
Sykora, Ana.	.277
Nash, Clb.	.269
Fedorov, Ana.	.268
Iginla, Calg.	.265
Guerin, Dal.	.263
Murray, Bos	.260

Shooting Pct.
(Min. 82 shots)

Parrish, NYI	.22.9
Roberts, Tor.	.22.6
Datsyuk, Det.	.22.1
Tanguay, Col.	.21.4
Forsberg, Col.	.21.2
Ribeiro, Mon.	.19.4
Morrow, Dal.	.18.9
Lang, Wash.-Det.	.18.4
St. Louis, TB	.17.9
Havlat, Ott.	.17.7

Penalty Minutes

Avery, LA	.261
Simon, NYR-Calg.	.250
Oliwa, Calg.	.247
Shelley, Clb.	.228
Brashear, Phi.	.212
Domi, Tor.	.208
Neil, Ott.	.194
Cairns, NYI	.189
Burnett, Ana.	.184
Lessard*, Atl.	.181
Worrell, Col.	.179

Minutes/Game
(Min. 50 Games)

Lidstrom, Det.	.27:39
Pronger, St.L	.27:27
Gonchar, Wash.-Bos.	27:26
Aucoin, NYI	.26:37
Leetch, NYR-Tor.	.26:17
Niedermayer, NJ	.25:53
Zubov, Dal.	.25:50
Ohlund, Van.	.25:47
McCabe, Tor.	.25:43
Hill, Car.	.25:24

Goaltending
(Minimum 24 games)

	Gm	Min	GAA	GA	Shots	Sv%	EN	ShO	Record	G	A	Pts	PM
Miikka Kiprusoff, SJ-Calg.	.38	2301	**1.69**	65	966	.933	4	4	24-10-4	0	1	1	15
Dwayne Roloson, Minnesota	.48	2847	**1.88**	89	1323	.933	2	5	19-18-11	0	1	1	8
Marty Turco, Dallas	.73	4359	**1.98**	144	1648	.913	6	9	37-21-13	0	1	1	32
Martin Brodeur, New Jersey	.75	4555	**2.03**	154	1845	.917	4	11	38-26-11	0	0	0	4
Robert Esche, Philadelphia	.40	2322	**2.04**	79	932	.915	1	3	21-11-7	0	0	0	31
Andrew Raycroft*, Boston	.57	3420	**2.05**	117	1586	.926	4	3	29-18-9	0	2	2	0
John Grahame, Tampa Bay	.29	1688	**2.06**	58	664	.913	2	1	18-9-1	0	0	0	4
Vesa Toskala, San Jose	.28	1541	**2.06**	53	760	.930	3	1	12-8-4	0	1	1	2
David Aebischer, Colorado	.62	3703	**2.09**	129	1703	.924	5	4	32-19-9	0	1	1	4
Manny Legace, Detroit	.41	2325	**2.12**	82	1019	.920	3	3	23-10-5	0	0	0	0
Martin Prusek, Ottawa	.29	1528	**2.12**	54	651	.917	0	1	16-6-3	0	1	1	0
Ed Belfour, Toronto	.59	3444	**2.13**	122	1483	.918	2	10	34-19-6	0	2	2	16
Evgeni Nabokov, San Jose	.59	3456	**2.20**	127	1610	.921	0	9	31-19-8	0	0	0	14
Chris Osgood. St. Louis	.67	3861	**2.24**	144	1604	.910	3	3	31-25-8	0	0	0	10
Martin Gerber, Anaheim	.32	1698	**2.26**	64	785	.918	3	2	11-12-4	0	0	0	4

Wins

Brodeur, NJ	.38
Turco, Dal.	.37
Belfour, Tor.	.34
Vokoun, Nash.	.34
Cloutier, Van.	.33
Theodore, Mon.	.33
Aebischer, Col.	.32
Nabokov, SJ	.31
Osgood, St.L	.31
Raycroft*, Bos.	.29
Khabibulin, TB	.28

Shutouts

Brodeur, NJ	.11
Belfour, Tor.	.10
Nabokov, SJ	.9
Turco, Dal.	.9
Luongo, Fla.	.7
Weekes, Car.	.6
Theodore, Mon.	.6
Seven tied with 5 each.	

Save Pct.

Roloson, Min.	.933
Kiprusoff, SJ-Calg.	.933
Luongo, Fla.	.931
Toskala, SJ	.930
Raycroft*, Bos.	.926
Aebischer, Col.	.924
Nabokov, SJ	.921
Legace, Det.	.920
Theodore, Mon.	.919
Gerber, Ana.	.918
Markkanen, NYR-Edm.	.918

Losses

Denis, Clb.	.36
Kolzig, Wash.	.35
Luongo, Fla.	.33
Giguere, Ana.	.31
Dunham, NYR	.30
Nurminen, Atl.	.30
Weekes, Car.	.30
Vokoun, Nash.	.29
Theodore, Mon.	.28
Brodeur, NJ	.26
Osgood, St.L	.25

Team Goaltending

WESTERN	GAA	Mins	GA	Shots	Sv%	EN	SO	EASTERN	GAA	Mins	GA	Shots	Sv%	EN	SO
Dallas	.2.10	4993	175	1902	.908	6	10	New Jersey	.1.97	5002	164	2001	.918	4	14
Calgary	.2.13	4968	176	2090	.916	8	11	Philadelphia	.2.23	5011	186	2092	.911	2	7
Minnesota	.2.18	5033	183	2383	.923	4	7	Boston	.2.24	5042	188	2280	.918	4	7
San Jose	.2.19	5016	183	2373	.923	3	11	Ottawa	.2.27	4996	189	2040	.907	3	8
Detroit	.2.27	4991	189	2151	.912	6	7	Tampa Bay	.2.31	4988	192	2085	.908	7	4
Vancouver	.2.32	5015	194	2183	.911	2	8	Montreal	.2.31	4979	192	2344	.918	4	6
Colorado	.2.37	5018	198	2325	.915	7	4	Toronto	.2.45	4991	204	2167	.906	3	11
St. Louis	.2.37	5014	198	2103	.906	5	4	Carolina	.2.50	5021	209	2150	.903	8	6
Edmonton	.2.49	5007	208	2175	.904	3	4	NY Islanders	2.53	4985	210	2244	.906	1	6
Anaheim	.2.56	5000	213	2443	.913	7	5	Florida	.2.64	5017	221	2828	.922	7	7
Nashville	.2.60	4999	217	2335	.907	12	4	Buffalo	.2.67	4971	221	2340	.906	4	4
Los Angeles	2.59	5029	217	2213	.902	10	8	Atlanta	.2.92	4989	243	2411	.899	14	4
Columbus	.2.86	4995	238	2623	.909	10	5	NY Rangers	3.01	4979	250	2396	.896	4	4
Phoenix	.2.92	5038	245	2506	.902	8	6	Washington	3.05	4976	253	2586	.902	9	3
Chicago	.3.10	5008	259	2521	.897	11	4	Pittsburgh	.3.65	4984	303	2720	.889	13	3

Power Play/Penalty Killing

Power play and penalty killing conversions. Power play: No—number of opportunities; GF—goals for; Pct—percentage. Penalty killing: No—number of times shorthanded; GA—goals against; Pct—percentage of penalties killed; SH—shorthanded goals for.

WESTERN	—Power Play—			—Penalty Killing—				EASTERN	—Power Play—			—Penalty Killing—		
	No	GF	Pct	No	GA	Pct	SH		No	GF	Pct	No	GA	Pct	SH
Colorado	.363	74	**20.4**	357	58	83.8	7	Ottawa	.371	80	**21.6**	347	57	83.6	6
Detroit	.314	63	**20.1**	317	42	86.8	15	Philadelphia	.314	65	**20.7**	348	58	83.3	7
Anaheim	.310	56	**18.1**	353	54	84.7	5	Toronto	.373	75	**20.1**	386	64	83.4	8
St. Louis	.341	61	**17.9**	369	57	84.6	7	Washington	.334	64	**19.2**	401	75	81.3	4
Nashville	.426	72	**16.9**	351	64	81.8	14	Pittsburgh	.360	65	**18.1**	369	84	77.2	7
San Jose	.337	56	**16.6**	319	47	85.3	9	Montreal	.319	55	**17.2**	314	55	82.5	5
Dallas	.328	52	**15.9**	311	44	85.9	5	Florida	.310	52	**16.8**	374	51	86.4	7
Chicago	.349	55	**15.8**	381	63	83.5	5	NY Islanders	.323	54	**16.7**	359	52	85.5	11
Calgary	.357	54	**15.1**	346	53	84.7	11	New Jersey	.312	51	**16.3**	266	39	85.3	8
Vancouver	.374	56	**15.0**	357	50	86.0	5	Tampa Bay	.339	55	**16.2**	278	42	84.9	15
Columbus	.401	58	**14.5**	337	50	85.2	5	Boston	.300	48	**16.0**	335	55	83.6	7
Phoenix	.358	51	**14.2**	398	71	82.2	9	Buffalo	.367	58	**15.8**	348	53	84.8	7
Los Angeles	.356	50	**14.0**	336	65	80.7	9	Atlanta	.409	60	**14.7**	391	58	85.2	11
Minnesota	.338	46	**13.6**	283	44	84.5	7	NY Rangers	.322	46	**14.3**	388	80	79.4	6
Edmonton	.338	44	**13.0**	349	66	81.1	13	Carolina	.384	41	**10.7**	359	66	81.6	9

Team by Team Statistics

High scorers and goaltenders with at least ten games played. Players who competed for more than one team during the regular season are listed with their final club; (*) indicates rookies eligible for Calder Trophy. Player positions are noted as follows: C—Center, L—Left wing, R—Right wing, D—Defenseman.

Mighty Ducks of Anaheim

Top Scorers	Gm	G	A	Pts	+/-	PM	PP
Sergei Fedorov, C	.80	31	34	65	-5	42	9
Vaclav Prospal, L	.82	19	35	54	-9	54	7
Petr Sykora, R	.81	23	29	52	-9	34	6
Steve Rucchin, C	.82	20	23	43	-14	12	9
Joffrey Lupul*, R	.75	13	21	34	-6	28	4
Andy McDonald, L	.79	9	21	30	-13	24	2
Rob Niedermayer, L	.55	12	16	28	-6	34	6
Niclas Havelid, D	.79	6	20	26	-28	35	5
Martin Skoula, D	.79	4	21	25	5	32	1
COL	.58	2	14	16	2	30	0
ANA	.21	2	7	9	3	2	1
Samuel Pahlsson, C	.82	8	14	22	-2	52	1
Jason Krog, R	.80	6	12	18	-4	16	1
Stanislav Chistov, R	.56	2	16	18	-16	26	2
Vitaly Vishnevski, D	.73	6	10	16	0	51	0
Sandis Ozolinsh, D	.36	5	11	16	-7	24	1
Ruslan Salei, D	.82	4	11	15	-1	110	1
Petr Schastlivy, L	.65	4	4	8	-4	18	1
OTT	.43	2	4	6	-1	14	1
ANA	.22	2	0	2	-3	4	0
Keith Carney, D	.69	2	5	7	-5	42	1
Chris Kunitz, L	.21	0	6	6	-1	12	0
Mike Leclerc, L	.10	1	3	4	-1	4	0
Lance Ward, D	.46	0	4	4	-1	94	0
Cam Severson*, L	.31	3	0	3	-3	50	1
Garrett Burnett, L	.39	1	2	3	0	184	0

Acquired: Schastlivy from Ott. for D Todd Simpson (Feb. 4); Skoula from Col. for D Kurt Sauer and a '05 4th-round pick (Feb. 21).

Goalies (10 Gm)	Gm	Min	GAA	Record	SV%
Martin Gerber	.32	1896	2.26	11-12-4	.918
Jean Sebastien Giguere	55	3210	2.62	17-31-6	.914
ANAHEIM	.82	5000	2.56	29-43-10	.913

Shutouts: Giguere (3), Gerber (2). **Assists:** Giguere (2). **PM:** Gerber and Giguere (4).

Atlanta Thrashers

Top Scorers	Gm	G	A	Pts	+/-	PM	PP
Ilya Kovalchuk, L	.81	41	46	87	-10	63	16
Shawn McEachern, R	.82	17	38	55	5	76	5
Slava Kozlov, C	.76	20	32	52	-12	74	6
Marc Savard, C	.45	19	33	52	-8	85	6
Patrik Stefan, C	.82	14	26	40	-7	26	3
Randy Robitaille, C	.69	11	26	37	-12	20	5
Ronald Petrovicky, R	.78	16	15	31	-9	123	0
Frantisek Kaberle, D	.67	3	26	29	2	30	2
Dany Heatley, R	.31	13	12	25	-8	18	5
Serge Aubin, L	.66	10	15	25	0	73	1
Andy Sutton, D	.65	8	13	21	0	94	7
Daniel Tjarnqvist, D	.68	5	15	20	-4	20	0
J.P. Vigier, R	.70	10	8	18	-18	22	2
Ivan Majesky, D	.63	3	7	10	-7	76	0
Yannick Tremblay, D	.38	2	8	10	-13	13	1
Garnet Exelby*, D	.71	1	9	10	-10	134	0
Chris Tamer, D	.38	2	5	7	-9	55	0
Brad Larsen, L	.32	2	2	4	0	13	0
COL	.26	2	2	4	2	11	0
ATL	.6	0	0	0	-2	2	0
Shawn Heins, D	.17	0	4	4	-1	16	0
Zdenek Blatny*, L	.16	3	0	3	0	6	0
Ben Simon, L	.52	3	0	3	-10	28	0
Tommi Santala*, C	.33	1	2	3	-7	22	0
Francis Lessard, R	.62	1	1	2	-5	181	0

Claimed: Larsen off waivers from Col. (Feb. 25).

Goalies (10 Gm)	Gm	Min	GAA	Record	SV%
Pasi Nurminen	.64	3738	2.78	25-30-7	.903
Byron Dafoe	.18	973	3.14	4-11-1	.898
ATLANTA	.82	4989	2.92	33-41-8	.899

Shutouts: Nurminen (3), Kari Lehtonen (1). **Assists:** Nurminen (2). **PM:** Nurminen (35), Dafoe (2).

Boston Bruins

Top Scorers	Gm	G	A	Pts	+/-	PM	PP
Joe Thornton, C 77	23	50	73	18	98	4
Glen Murray, R 81	32	28	60	17	56	11
Sergei Gonchar, D ...71	11	47	58	-14	56	6
WASH 56	7	42	49	-20	44	4
BOS 15	4	5	9	6	12	2
Brian Rolston, C 82	19	29	48	9	40	3
Mike Knuble, L 82	21	25	46	19	32	4
Sergei Samsonov, L ..58	17	23	40	12	4	3
Patrice Bergeron*, C ..71	16	23	39	5	22	7
Nick Boynton, D 81	6	24	30	17	98	1
Dan McGillis, D 80	5	23	28	-1	65	1
Jiri Slegr, D 52	6	20	26	11	35	1
VAN 16	2	5	7	6	8	1
BOS 36	4	15	19	5	27	0
Martin Lapointe, R ...78	15	10	25	-5	67	9
P.J. Axelsson, L 68	6	14	20	2	42	0
Travis Green, R 64	11	5	16	-6	67	2
Michael Nylander, C ...18	1	13	14	4	22	0
WASH 3	0	2	2	1	8	0
BOS 15	1	11	12	3	14	0
Ted Donato, C 63	6	5	11	2	18	0
Sean O'Donnell, D ...82	1	10	11	10	110	0
Rob Zamuner, L 57	4	5	9	3	16	0
Hal Gill, D 82	2	7	9	16	99	0

Acquired: Slegr from Van. for future consid. (Jan. 17); Gonchar from Wash. for D Shaone Morrisonn, a '04 1st-round pick and a '04 2nd-round pick (Mar. 3); Nylander from Wash. for a '06 2nd-round pick and future consid. (Mar. 4).

Goalies (10 Gm)	Gm	Min	GAA	Record	SV%
Andrew Raycroft* 57	3420	2.05	29-18-9	.926
Felix Potvin 28	1605	2.50	12-8-6	.903
BOSTON 82	5042	2.24	41-26-15	.918

Shutouts: Potvin (4), Raycroft (3). **Assists:** Raycroft (2). **PM:** Potvin (8).

Buffalo Sabres

Top Scorers	Gm	G	A	Pts	+/-	PM	PP
Daniel Briere, C 82	28	37	65	-7	70	11
Miroslav Satan, R 82	29	28	57	-15	30	11
J.P. Dumont, R 77	22	31	53	-9	40	10
Chris Drury, C 76	18	35	53	8	68	5
Jochen Hecht, L 64	15	37	52	17	49	2
Dmitri Kalinin, D 70	10	24	34	0	42	2
Maxim Afinogenov, R ..73	17	14	31	-4	57	3
Mike Grier, R 82	9	20	29	-9	36	1
WASH 68	8	12	20	-19	32	1
BUF 14	1	8	9	10	4	0
Alexei Zhitnik, D 68	4	24	28	-13	102	2
Ales Kotalik, L 62	15	11	26	-1	41	2
Taylor Pyatt, L 63	8	12	20	-7	25	1
Adam Mair, R 81	6	14	20	-3	146	1
Derek Roy*, C 49	9	10	19	-8	12	1
BOS 50	4	10	14	-1	35	1
BUF 14	0	3	3	-3	19	0
Chris Taylor, C 54	6	6	12	-2	22	0
James Patrick, D 55	4	7	11	11	12	0
Rory Fitzpatrick, D ...60	4	7	11	-5	44	2
Brian Campbell, D ...53	3	8	11	-8	12	0
Henrik Tallinder, D ...72	1	9	10	5	26	0

Acquired: Grier from Wash. for C Jakub Klepis (Mar. 9); Jillson and a '05 9th-round pick in a 3-team trade that sent C Curtis Brown to SJ and C Brad Boyes and D Andy Delmore to Bos. (Mar. 9).

Goalies (10 Gm)	Gm	Min	GAA	Record	Sv%
Martin Biron 52	2972	2.52	26-18-5	.913
Mika Noronen 35	1796	2.57	11-17-2	.906
BUFFALO 82	4971	2.67	37-38-7	.906

Shutouts: Biron and Noronen (2). **Goals:** Noronen (1). **Assists:** Biron (2). **PM:** Biron (10).

Calgary Flames

Top Scorers	Gm	G	A	Pts	+/-	PM	PP
Jarome Iginla, R 81	41	32	73	21	84	8
Craig Conroy, C 63	8	39	47	13	44	2
Shean Donovan, R 82	18	24	42	14	72	3
Martin Gelinas, L 76	17	18	35	10	70	5
Jordan Leopold, D 82	9	24	33	8	24	6
Dean McAmmond, L ...64	17	13	30	9	18	4
Matthew Lombardi*, C 79	16	13	29	4	32	3
Oleg Saprykin, L 69	12	17	29	1	41	4
Steve Reinprecht, C ...44	7	22	29	1	4	3
Chris Simon, L 78	17	11	28	15	250	4
NYR 65	14	9	23	14	225	3
CALG 13	3	2	5	1	25	1
Chris Clark, R 82	10	15	25	-3	106	4
Marcus Nilson, L 83	11	13	24	-6	40	2
FLA 69	6	13	19	-9	26	1
CALG 14	5	0	5	3	14	1
Ville Nieminen, R 79	5	16	21	-9	58	1
CHI 60	2	11	13	-15	40	1
CALG 19	3	5	8	6	18	0
Toni Lydman, D 67	4	16	20	6	30	2
Robyn Regehr, D 82	4	14	18	14	74	2
Chuck Kobasew*, R ..70	6	11	17	-12	51	3
Stephane Yelle, C 53	4	13	17	1	24	1
Rhett Warrener, D ...77	3	14	17	8	97	0
Andrew Ferrence, D ...72	4	12	16	5	53	1
Denis Gauthier, D 80	1	13	14	4	113	0

Acquired: Nieminen from Chi. for C Jason Morgan and a conditional pick (Feb. 24); Simon and a '04 7th-round pick from NYR for G Jamie McLennan, C Blair Betts and RW Greg Moore (Mar. 6); Nilson from Fla. for a '04 2nd-round pick (Mar. 8).

Goalies (10 Gm)	Gm	Min	GAA	Record	SV%
Miikka Kiprusoff 38	2301	1.69	24-10-4	.933
Roman Turek 18	1031	2.33	6-11-0	.914
CALGARY 82	4968	2.13	42-33-7	.916

Shutouts: Kiprusoff (4), Turek (3). **Assists:** Kiprusoff, Turek and Dany Sabourin (4). **PM:** Kiprusoff (15).

Carolina Hurricanes

Top Scorers	Gm	G	A	Pts	+/-	PM	PP
Josef Vasicek, L 82	19	26	45	-3	60	6
Justin Williams, R 79	11	33	44	12	64	4
PHI 47	6	20	26	10	32	3
CAR 32	5	13	18	2	32	1
Erik Cole, R 80	18	24	42	4	93	2
Sean Hill, D 80	13	26	39	-2	84	6
Rod Brind'Amour, C ..78	12	26	38	0	28	1
Jeff O'Neill, R 67	14	20	34	-12	60	7
Eric Staal*, C 81	11	20	31	-6	40	2
Radim Vrbata, D 80	12	13	25	-10	24	4
Bret Hedican, D 81	7	17	24	-10	64	2
Kevyn Adams, C 73	10	12	22	6	43	0
Craig Adams, L 80	7	10	17	-5	69	0
Marty Murray, C 66	5	7	12	6	8	0
Niclas Wallin, D 57	3	7	10	-8	51	0
Pavel Brendl, R 18	5	3	8	0	8	1
Aaron Ward, D 49	3	5	8	1	37	2
Jesse Boulerice, R 76	6	1	7	-5	127	0
Ryan Bayda*, L 44	3	3	6	-14	22	0
Glen Wesley, D 74	0	6	6	18	32	0
Jaroslav Svoboda, L ...33	3	1	4	3	6	0

Acquired: Williams from Phi. for D Danny Markov (Jan. 20).

Goalies (10 Gm)	Gm	Min	GAA	Record	Sv%
Kevin Weekes 66	3765	2.33	23-30-11	.912
Arturs Irbe 10	564	2.45	5-2-1	.899
Jamie Storr 14	660	2.91	0-8-2	.878
CAROLINA 82	5021	2.50	28-40-14	.903

Shutouts: Weekes (6). **Assists:** none. **PM:** Weekes (6), Irbe (2).

Chicago Blackhawks

Top Scorers

Top Scorers	Gm	G	A	Pts	+/-	PM	PP
Tyler Arnason, C	82	22	33	55	-13	16	6
Bryan Berard, D	58	13	34	47	-24	53	6
Mark Bell, L	82	21	24	45	-14	106	2
Tuomo Ruutu*, L	82	23	21	44	-31	58	10
Kyle Calder, L	66	21	18	39	-18	29	10
Brett McLean*, C	76	11	20	31	-11	54	5
Eric Nickulas, L	65	8	12	20	-8	52	1
ST.L	44	7	11	18	-2	44	1
CHI	21	1	1	2	-6	8	0
Scott Nichol, C	75	7	11	18	-16	145	0
Jim Vandermeer*, D	46	5	12	17	-11	83	1
PHI	23	3	2	5	-5	25	0
CHI	23	2	10	12	-6	58	1
Stephane Robidas, D	59	3	10	13	4	41	1
DAL	14	1	0	1	-2	8	1
CHI	45	2	10	12	6	33	0
Igor Korolev, C	62	3	10	13	-15	22	0
Eric Daze, R	19	4	7	11	-7	0	1
Igor Radulov*, R	36	4	7	11	-2	18	0
Deron Quint, D	51	4	7	11	-26	18	2

Acquired: Robidas and a '04 2nd-round pick from Dal. for D Jon Klemm and a '04 4th-round pick (Nov. 17); Vandermeer, C Colin Fraser and a '04 2nd-round pick from Phi. for C Alex Zhamnov and a '04 4th-round pick (Feb. 19). **Claimed:** L Nickulas off waivers from St.L (Feb. 24).

Goalies (10 Gm)

Goalies (10 Gm)	Gm	Min	GAA	Record	SV%
Craig Anderson*	21	1205	2.84	6-14-0	.905
Jocelyn Thibault	14	821	2.85	5-7-2	.913
Michael Leighton*	34	1988	2.99	6-18-8	.900
CHICAGO	82	5008	3.10	20-51-11	.897

Shutouts: Leighton (2), Anderson and Thibault (1). **Assists:** Leighton (2), Anderson and Thibault (1). **PM:** Anderson (4), Leighton and Adam Munro (2).

Colorado Avalanche

Top Scorers

Top Scorers	Gm	G	A	Pts	+/-	PM	PP
Joe Sakic, C	81	33	54	87	11	42	13
Alex Tanguay, L	69	25	54	79	30	42	7
Milan Hejduk, R	82	35	40	75	19	20	16
Peter Forsberg, C	39	18	37	55	16	30	3
Rob Blake, D	74	13	33	46	6	61	8
Matthew Barnaby, R	82	16	25	41	18	157	1
NYR	69	12	20	32	15	120	0
COL	13	4	5	9	3	37	1
Steve Konowalchuk, L	82	19	21	40	-3	70	3
WASH	6	0	1	1	-5	0	0
COL	76	19	20	39	2	70	3
Paul Kariya, L	51	11	25	36	-5	22	5
John-Michael Liles*, D	79	10	24	34	7	28	2
Teemu Selanne, R	79	16	16	32	2	32	6
Chris Gratton, C	81	13	19	32	-18	111	3
PHO	68	11	18	29	-19	93	3
COL	13	2	1	3	1	18	0
Adam Foote, D	73	8	22	30	13	87	5
Karlis Skrastins, D	82	5	8	13	18	26	0
Andrei Nikolishin, C	49	5	7	12	3	24	1
Steve Moore*, C	57	5	7	12	-5	37	0

Acquired: Konowalchuk and a '04 3rd-round pick from Wash. for L Bates Battaglia and R Jonas Johansson (Oct. 22); Barnaby and a '04 3rd-round pick from NYR for D Chris McAllister and D David Liffiton (Mar. 8); Gratton, D Ossi Vaananen and a '05 2nd-round pick from Pho. for D Derek Morris and D Keith Ballard (Mar. 9); Salo and a '05 6th-round pick from Edm. for D Tom Gilbert (Mar. 9).

Goalies (10 Gm)

Goalies (10 Gm)	Gm	Min	GAA	Record	SV%
David Aebischer	62	3703	2.09	32-19-9	.924
Tommy Salo	49	2791	2.56	18-21-7	.897
EDM	44	2487	2.58	17-18-6	.896
COL	5	304	2.37	1-3-1	.912
Philippe Sauve*	17	986	3.04	7-7-3	.896
COLORADO	82	5018	2.37	40-29-13	.915

Shutouts: Aebischer (4), Salo (3). **Assists:** Aebischer and Salo (1). **PM:** Aebischer (4), Salo and Sauve (2).

Columbus Blue Jackets

Top Scorers

Top Scorers	Gm	G	A	Pts	+/-	PM	PP
Rick Nash, L	80	41	16	57	-35	87	19
David Vyborny, R	82	22	31	53	-26	40	8
Nikolai Zherdev*, R	57	13	21	34	-11	54	5
Todd Marchant, C	77	9	25	34	-17	34	4
Trevor Letowski, R	73	15	17	32	-12	16	4
Anders Eriksson, D	66	7	20	27	-6	18	2
Andrew Cassels, C	58	6	20	26	-24	26	2
Manny Malhotra, C	65	12	13	25	-7	28	1
DAL	9	0	0	0	-2	4	0
CLB	56	12	13	25	-5	24	1
Brian Holzinger, C	74	7	15	22	-31	40	1
PIT	61	6	15	21	-27	38	1
CLB	13	1	0	1	-4	2	0
Jaroslav Spacek, D	58	5	17	22	-13	45	2
Tyler Wright, C	68	9	9	18	-19	63	2
Rostislav Klesla, D	47	2	11	13	-16	27	0
Alexander Svitov, C	40	2	9	11	-8	20	0
TB	11	0	3	3	0	4	0
CLB	29	2	6	8	-8	16	0
Derrick Walser, D	27	1	8	9	-6	22	1
Aaron Johnson*, D	29	2	6	8	-2	32	0
Duvie Westcott, D	34	0	7	7	-15	39	0

Acquired: Svitov and a '04 3rd-round pick from TB for D Darryl Sydor and a '04 4th-round pick (Jan. 27); Holzinger from Pit. for C Lasse Pirjeta (Mar. 9). **Claimed:** Malhotra off waivers from Dal. (Nov. 21).

Goalies (10 Gm)

Goalies (10 Gm)	Gm	Min	GAA	Record	SV%
Marc Denis	66	3796	2.56	21-36-7	.918
Fred Brathwaite	21	1050	3.37	4-11-1	.897
COLUMBUS	82	4995	2.86	25-49-8	.909

Shutouts: Denis (5). **Assists:** Denis (2). **PM:** Denis (10), Brathwaite (2).

Dallas Stars

Top Scorers

Top Scorers	Gm	G	A	Pts	+/-	PM	PP
Bill Guerin, R	82	34	35	69	14	109	9
Jason Arnott, C	73	21	36	57	23	66	5
Valeri Bure, R	68	22	30	52	3	26	8
FLA	55	20	25	45	0	20	8
DAL	13	2	5	7	3	6	0
Brenden Morrow, L	81	25	24	49	10	121	9
Mike Modano, C	76	14	30	44	-21	46	6
Sergei Zubov, D	77	7	35	42	0	20	4
Pierre Turgeon, C	75	15	25	40	17	20	6
Stu Barnes, C	77	11	18	29	7	18	0
Jere Lehtinen, R	58	13	13	26	0	20	4
Rob DiMaio, R	69	9	15	24	2	50	0
Philippe Boucher, D	70	8	16	24	15	64	2
Richard Matvichuk, D	75	1	20	21	0	36	0
Teppo Numminen, D	62	3	14	17	-5	18	0
Scott Young, R	53	8	8	16	-15	14	2
David Oliver, R	36	7	5	12	6	12	3
Steve Ott, L	73	2	10	12	-2	152	0
Don Sweeney, D	63	0	11	11	22	18	0
Shayne Corson, L	17	5	5	10	12	29	0
Chris Therien, D	67	1	9	10	6	52	0
PHI	56	1	9	10	2	50	0
DAL	11	0	0	0	4	2	0
Jon Klemm, D	77	2	5	7	16	44	0
CHI	19	0	1	1	6	20	0
DAL	58	2	4	6	10	24	0

Acquired: Klemm and a '04 4th-round pick from Chi. for D Stephane Robidas and a '04 2nd-round pick (Nov. 17); Bure from Fla. for D Drew Bagnall and a '04 compensatory pick (Mar. 8); Therien from PHI for a '04 8th-round pick and a '05 3rd-round pick (Mar. 8).

Goalies (10 Gm)

Goalies (10 Gm)	Gm	Min	GAA	Record	SV%
Marty Turco	73	4359	1.98	37-21-13	.913
Ron Tugnutt	11	548	2.41	3-7-0	.900
DALLAS	82	4993	2.10	41-28-13	.908

Shutouts: Turco (9), Tugnutt (1). **Assists:** Turco (1). **PM:** Turco (32).

Detroit Red Wings

Top Scorers	Gm	G	A	Pts	+/-	PM	PP
Robert Lang, C	.69	30	49	79	4	24	10
WASH	.63	29	45	74	2	24	10
DET	.6	1	4	5	2	0	0
Pavel Datsyuk, C	.75	30	38	68	-2	35	8
Brett Hull, R	.81	25	43	68	-4	12	10
Brendan Shanahan, L	.82	25	28	53	15	117	8
Steve Yzerman, C	.75	18	33	51	10	46	7
Mathieu Schneider, D	.78	14	32	46	22	56	4
Henrik Zetterberg, L	.61	15	28	43	15	14	7
Ray Whitney, L	.67	14	29	43	7	22	3
Kris Draper, C	.67	24	16	40	22	31	2
Nicklas Lidstrom, D	.81	10	28	38	19	18	3
Kirk Maltby, L	.79	14	19	33	24	80	1
Tomas Holmstrom, R	.67	15	15	30	8	38	6
Steve Thomas, L	.44	10	12	22	8	25	0
Chris Chelios, D	.69	2	19	21	12	61	0
Jason Woolley, D	.55	4	15	19	19	28	0
Jiri Fischer, D	.81	4	15	19	0	75	1
Boyd Devereaux, R	.61	6	9	15	-1	20	0
Jason Williams, C	.49	6	7	13	1	15	0
Mathieu Dandenault, D	65	3	9	12	9	40	0
Darren McCarty, R	.43	6	5	11	2	50	1
Mark Mowers, L	.52	3	8	11	3	6	0

Acquired: Lang from Wash. for L Tomas Fleischmann, a '04 1st-round pick and a '06 4th-round pick (Feb. 27).

Goalies (10 Gm)	Gm	Min	GAA	Record	Sv%
Manny Legace	.41	2325	2.12	23-10-5	.920
Dominik Hasek	.14	817	2.20	8-3-2	.907
Curtis Joseph	.31	1708	2.39	16-10-3	.909
DETROIT	.82	4991	2.27	48-23-11	.912

Shutouts: Legace (3), Hasek and Joseph (2). **Assists:** Hasek (2). **PM:** Hasek and Joseph (2).

Edmonton Oilers

Top Scorers	Gm	G	A	Pts	+/-	PM	PP
Ryan Smyth, L	.82	23	36	59	11	70	8
Radek Dvorak, R	.78	15	35	50	18	26	6
Petr Nedved, C	.81	19	27	46	-8	46	7
NYR	.65	14	17	31	-9	42	5
EDM	.16	5	10	15	1	4	2
Mike York, C	.61	16	26	42	18	15	1
Shawn Horcoff, C	.80	15	25	40	0	73	0
Raffi Torres, L	.80	20	14	34	12	65	5
Ales Hemsky, R	.71	12	22	34	-7	14	4
Ethan Moreau, L	.81	20	12	32	7	96	0
Fernando Pisani, R	.76	16	14	30	14	46	4
Steve Staios, D	.82	6	22	28	17	86	1
Marc-Andre Bergeron*,D	.77	17	26	13	26	3	
Eric Brewer, D	.77	7	18	25	-6	67	3
Jarret Stoll*, C	.68	10	11	21	8	42	1
Cory Cross, D	.68	7	14	21	9	56	1
Jason Smith, D	.68	7	12	19	13	98	0
Brad Isbister, L	.51	10	8	18	-2	54	1
Igor Ulanov, D	.42	5	13	18	19	28	1
Adam Oates, C	.60	2	16	18	0	8	1
Georges Laraque, R	.66	6	11	17	7	99	1
Jason Chimera, C	.60	4	8	12	-1	57	0
Marty Reasoner, C	.17	2	6	8	5	10	0

Acquired: Nedved and Markkanen from NYR for C Dwight Helminen, G Stephen Valiquette and a '04 2nd-round pick (Mar. 3).

Goalies (10 Gm)	Gm	Min	GAA	Record	Sv%
Jussi Markkanen	.33	1638	2.38	10-14-3	.918
NYR	.26	1244	2.56	8-12-1	.913
EDM	.7	394	1.83	2-2-2	.934
Ty Conklin	.38	2086	2.42	17-14-4	.912
EDMONTON	.82	5007	2.49	36-34-12	.904

Shutouts: Markkanen (2), Conklin (1). **Assists:** none. **PM:** Conklin (17), Markkanen (2).

Florida Panthers

Top Scorers	Gm	G	A	Pts	+/-	PM	PP
Olli Jokinen, C	.82	26	32	58	-16	81	8
Mike Van Ryn, D	.79	13	24	37	-16	52	6
Kristian Huselius, L	.76	10	21	31	-6	24	2
Stephen Weiss, C	.50	12	17	29	-10	10	3
Juraj Kolnik, R	.53	14	11	25	-7	14	2
Niklas Hagman, L	.75	10	13	23	-5	22	0
Nathan Horton*	.55	14	8	22	-5	57	6
Donald Audette, R	.51	9	12	21	-13	38	5
MON	.23	3	5	8	-4	16	0
FLA	.28	6	7	13	-9	22	5
Jay Bouwmeester, D	.61	2	18	20	-15	30	0
Matt Cullen, C	.56	6	13	19	-2	24	1
Lyle Odelein, D	.82	4	12	16	-7	88	2
Pavel Trnka, D	.67	3	13	16	2	51	1
Mathieu Baron, D	.57	3	10	13	-13	51	0
Byron Ritchie, C	.50	5	6	11	-10	84	0
Christian Berglund, R	.33	5	4	9	-6	14	0
NJ	.23	2	3	5	-4	4	0
FLA	.10	3	1	4	-2	10	0
Mikael Samuelsson, C	37	3	6	9	0	35	0
Vaclav Nedorost, C	.32	4	3	7	-6	12	2
Andreas Lilja, D	.79	3	4	7	-8	90	0
Lukas Krajicek*, D	.18	1	6	7	-2	12	1
Branislav Mezei, D	.45	0	7	7	-4	80	0

Acquired: Berglund and D Victor Uchevatov from NJ for C Viktor Kozlov (Mar. 1). **Signed:** free agent Audette (Jan. 15).

Goalies (10 Gm)	Gm	Min	GAA	Record	Sv%
Roberto Luongo	.72	4252	2.43	25-33-14	.931
Steve Shields	.16	732	3.44	3-6-1	.879
FLORIDA	.82	5017	2.64	28-39-15	.922

Shutouts: Luongo (7). **Assists:** Luongo (3). **PM:** Shields (6), Luongo (2).

Los Angeles Kings

Top Scorers	Gm	G	A	Pts	+/-	PM	PP
Luc Robitaille, L	.80	22	29	51	4	56	12
Alexander Frolov, L	.77	24	24	48	8	24	5
Trent Klatt, R	.82	17	26	43	2	46	6
Zigmund Palffy, R	.35	16	25	41	18	12	3
Jozef Stumpel, C	.64	8	29	37	5	16	4
Derek Armstrong, C	.57	14	21	35	4	33	5
Eric Belanger, C	.81	13	20	33	-16	44	3
Nathan Dempsey, D	.75	12	20	32	-12	32	3
CHI	.58	8	17	25	-5	30	2
LA	.17	4	3	7	-7	2	1
Jaroslav Modry, D	.79	5	27	32	11	44	1
Lubomir Visnovsky, D	.58	8	21	29	8	26	5
Anson Carter, R	.77	15	13	28	-15	20	6
NYR	.43	10	7	17	-12	14	4
WASH	.19	5	4	9	2	6	2
LA	.15	0	1	1	-5	0	0
Sean Avery, L	.76	9	19	28	2	261	6
Jeff Cowan, L	.71	11	16	27	1	92	2
ATL	.58	9	15	24	2	68	1
LA	.13	2	1	3	-1	24	1
Martin Straka, L	.54	10	16	26	-25	20	2
PIT	.22	4	8	12	-16	16	1
LA	.32	6	8	14	-9	4	1
Joe Corvo, D	.72	8	17	25	7	36	0

Acquired: Straka from Pit. for D Martin Strbak and L Sergei Anshakov (Nov. 30); Dempsey from Chi. for a '05 4th-round pick and future consid. (Mar. 2); Carter from Wash. for C Jared Aulin (Mar. 8); Cowan from Atl. for L Kip Brennan (Mar. 9).

Goalies (10 Gm)	Gm	Min	GAA	Record	Sv%
Cristobal Huet	.41	2199	2.43	10-16-10	.907
Roman Cechmanek	.49	2701	2.51	18-21-6	.906
LOS ANGELES	.82	5029	2.59	28-38-16	.902

Shutouts: Cechmanek (5), Huet (3). **Assists:** none. **PM:** Huet (4), Cechmanek (2).

Minnesota Wild

Top Scorers	Gm	G	A	Pts	+/-	PM	PP
Alexandre Daigle, L	.78	20	31	51	-4	14	6
Andrew Brunette, R	.82	15	34	49	3	12	7
Marian Gaborik, R	.65	18	22	40	10	20	3
Antti Laaksonen, L	.77	12	14	26	0	20	0
Pascal Dupuis, R	.59	11	15	26	5	20	2
Richard Park, R	.73	13	12	25	0	28	4
Wes Walz, C	.57	12	13	25	5	32	0
Filip Kuba, D	.77	5	19	24	-7	28	2
Jason Wiemer, C	.75	8	14	22	-7	130	1
NYI	.13	1	3	4	-1	24	0
MIN	.62	7	11	18	-6	106	1
Pierre-Marc Bouchard, L	61	4	18	22	-7	22	2
Marc Chouinard, C	.45	11	10	21	4	17	3
Andrei Zyuzin, D	.65	8	13	21	4	48	4
Nick Schultz, D	.79	6	10	16	12	16	1
Willie Mitchell, D	.70	1	13	14	12	83	0
Eric Chouinard, R	.48	6	4	10	-10	6	0
PHI	.17	3	0	3	-3	0	0
MIN	.31	3	4	7	-7	6	0
Stephane Veilleux, L	.19	2	1	10	0	20	1
Rickard Wallin*, C	.15	5	4	9	1	14	3
Christoph Brandner, R	.35	4	5	9	-2	8	1
Matt Johnson, L	.57	7	1	8	4	177	0
Alex Henry, L	.71	2	4	6	4	106	0
Brent Burns*, R	.36	1	5	6	-10	12	0

Acquired: Chouinard from Phi. for a '04 5th-round pick (Dec. 17). **Claimed:** Wiemer off waivers from NYI (Nov. 13).

Goalies (10 Gm)	Gm	Min	GAA	Record	Sv%
Dwayne Roloson	.48	2847	1.88	19-18-11	.933
Manny Fernandez	.37	2166	2.49	11-14-9	.915
MINNESOTA	.82	5033	2.18	30-32-20	.923

Shutouts: Roloson (5), Fernandez (2). **Assists:** Roloson (1). **PM:** Roloson (8), Fernandez (2).

Montreal Canadiens

Top Scorers	Gm	G	A	Pts	+/-	PM	PP
Mike Ribeiro, C	.81	20	45	65	15	34	7
Michael Ryder*, R	.81	25	38	63	10	26	10
Saku Koivu, C	.68	14	41	55	-5	52	5
Richard Zednik, L	.81	26	24	50	5	63	7
Alexei Kovalev, R	.78	14	31	45	-9	66	3
NYR	.66	13	29	42	-5	54	3
MON	.12	1	2	3	-4	12	0
Sheldon Souray, D	.63	15	20	35	4	104	6
Yanic Perreault, C	.69	16	15	31	-10	40	5
Patrice Brisebois, D	.71	4	27	31	17	22	2
Jan Bulis, L	.72	13	17	30	-8	30	1
Jim Dowd, C	.69	7	22	29	12	44	2
MIN	.55	4	20	24	6	38	2
MON	.14	3	2	5	6	6	0
Andrei Markov, D	.69	6	22	28	-2	20	2
Pierre Dagenais, R	.50	17	10	27	15	24	4
Niklas Sundstrom, R	.66	8	12	20	3	18	0
Francis Bouillon, D	.73	2	16	18	1	70	0
Steve Begin, C	.52	10	5	15	6	41	0
Joe Juneau, C	.70	5	10	15	-4	20	2
Jason Ward, R	.53	5	7	12	3	21	2
Andreas Dackell, R	.60	4	8	12	8	10	0
Craig Rivet, D	.80	4	8	12	-1	98	2
Stephane Quintal, D	.73	3	5	8	10	82	0
Mike Komisarek*, D	.46	0	4	4	4	34	0

Acquired: Kovalev from NYR for R Josef Balej and a '04 2nd-round pick (Mar. 2); Dowd from Min. for a '04 4th-round pick (Mar. 4).

Goalies (10 Gm)	Gm	Min	GAA	Record	Sv%
Jose Theodore	.67	3961	2.27	33-28-5	.919
Mathieu Garon	.19	1003	2.27	8-6-2	.921
MONTREAL	.82	4979	2.31	41-34-7	.918

Shutouts: Theodore (6). **Assists:** Theodore (3). **PM:** Theodore (4), Garon (2).

Nashville Predators

Top Scorers	Gm	G	A	Pts	+/-	PM	PP
Steve Sullivan, R	.80	24	49	73	1	48	11
CHI	.56	15	28	43	-7	36	4
NASH	.24	9	21	30	8	12	7
Scott Walker, R	.75	25	42	67	4	94	9
Marek Zidlicky, D	.82	14	39	53	-16	82	9
Martin Erat, L	.76	16	33	49	10	38	4
David Legwand, C	.82	18	29	47	9	46	5
Kimmo Timonen, D	.77	12	32	44	-7	52	8
Vladimir Orszagh, R	.82	16	21	37	-4	74	2
Scott Hartnell, L	.59	18	15	33	-5	87	5
Greg Johnson, C	.82	14	18	32	-21	33	1
Sergei Zholtok, C	.70	14	17	31	2	19	3
MIN	.59	13	16	29	4	19	3
NASH	.11	1	1	2	-2	0	0
Adam Hall, R	.79	13	14	27	-8	37	6
Andreas Johansson, L	.47	12	15	27	-2	26	3
Dan Hamhuis, D	.80	7	19	26	-12	57	2
Denis Arkhipov, C	.72	9	12	21	-2	22	3
Rem Murray, R	.39	8	9	17	-1	12	0
Jason York, D	.67	2	13	15	-4	64	0
Mark Eaton, D	.75	4	9	13	16	26	0
Jeremy Stevenson, R	.56	5	4	9	-3	105	3
MIN	.3	0	0	0	-1	2	0
NASH	.53	5	4	9	-2	103	3

Acquired: Sullivan from Chi. for a '04 2nd-round pick and a '05 2nd-round pick (Feb. 16); Zholtok and D Brad Bombardir from Min. for '04 3rd- and 4th-round picks (Mar. 5). **Claimed:** Stevenson off waivers from Min. (Oct. 23).

Goalies (10 Gm)	Gm	Min	GAA	Record	Sv%
Chris Mason	.17	744	2.18	4-4-1	.926
Tomas Vokoun	.73	4221	2.53	34-29-10	.909
NASHVILLE	.82	4999	2.60	38-33-11	.907

Shutouts: Vokoun (3), Mason (1). **Assists:** Vokoun (2). **PM:** Vokoun (35), Mason (4).

New Jersey Devils

Top Scorers	Gm	G	A	Pts	+/-	PM	PP
Patrik Elias, L	.82	38	43	81	26	44	9
Scott Gomez, C	.80	14	56	70	18	70	3
Scott Niedermayer, D	.81	14	40	54	20	44	9
Jeff Friesen, L	.81	17	20	37	8	26	5
Brian Rafalski, D	.69	6	30	36	6	24	2
John Madden, C	.80	12	23	35	7	22	1
Sergei Brylin, L	.82	14	19	33	10	20	7
Viktor Kozlov, R	.59	13	20	33	-4	18	3
FLA	.48	11	16	27	-4	16	3
NJ	.11	2	4	6	0	2	0
Jan Hrdina, C	.68	12	21	33	-6	40	5
PHO	.55	11	15	26	-10	30	5
NJ	.13	1	6	7	4	10	0
Brian Gionta, R	.75	21	8	29	19	36	0
Turner Stevenson, R	.61	14	13	27	0	76	4
Jay Pandolfo, L	.82	13	13	26	5	14	1
Jamie Langenbrunner, R	53	10	16	26	9	43	1
Paul Martin*, D	.70	6	18	24	12	4	2
Grant Marshall, R	.65	8	7	15	-9	67	5
Erik Rasmussen, L	.69	7	6	13	5	41	0
Colin White, D	.75	2	11	13	10	96	0
Scott Stevens, D	.38	3	9	12	3	22	1
Igor Larionov, C	.49	1	10	11	3	20	0

Acquired: Kozlov from Fla. for R Christian Berglund and D Victor Uchevatov (Mar. 1); Hrdina from Pho. for C Michael Rupp and a '04 2nd-round pick (Mar. 5).

Goalies (10 Gm)	Gm	Min	GAA	Record	Sv%
Martin Brodeur	.75	4555	2.03	38-26-11	.917
NEW JERSEY	.82	5002	1.97	43-27-12	.918

Shutouts: Brodeur (11), Scott Clemmensen (2), Corey Schwab (1). **Assists:** Schwab (1). **PM:** Brodeur (4), Schwab (2).

New York Islanders

Top Scorers	Gm	G	A	Pts	+/-	PM	PP
Trent Hunter*, R	.77	25	26	51	23	16	4
Oleg Kvasha, L	.81	15	36	51	4	48	5
Mariusz Czerkawski, R	81	25	24	49	8	16	9
Jason Blake, L	.75	22	25	47	11	56	1
Adrian Aucoin, D	.81	13	31	44	29	54	4
Michael Peca, C	.76	11	29	40	17	71	0
Mark Parrish, R	.59	24	11	35	8	18	6
Alexei Yashin, C	.47	15	19	34	-1	10	3
Shawn Bates, C	.69	9	12	32	-8	46	0
Roman Hamrlik, D	.81	7	22	29	2	68	2
Kenny Jonsson, D	.79	5	24	29	25	22	3
Janne Niinimaa, D	.82	9	19	28	12	64	4
Dave Scatchard, C	.61	9	16	25	12	78	1
Arron Asham, L	.79	12	12	24	-12	92	1
Cliff Ronning, C	.40	9	15	24	3	2	2
Mattias Weinhandl, R	.55	8	12	20	9	26	4
Justin Papineau*, C	.64	8	5	13	4	8	5
Eric Cairns, D	.72	2	6	8	-5	189	0
Alexander Karpovtsev, D	27	0	8	8	-16	18	0
CHI	.24	0	7	7	-17	14	0
NYI	.3	0	1	1	1	4	0
Radek Martinek, D	.47	4	3	7	-9	43	0
Sven Butenschon, D	.41	1	6	7	-3	30	0

Acquired: Karpovtsev from Chi. for a '05 4th-round pick (Mar. 9).

Goalies (10 Gm)	Gm	Min	GAA	Record	Sv%
Rick DiPietro	.50	2844	2.36	23-18-5	.911
Garth Snow	.39	2015	2.80	14-15-5	.899
NY ISLANDERS	.82	4985	2.53	38-33-11	.906

Shutouts: DiPietro (5), Snow (1). **Assists:** DiPietro (2), Snow (1). **PM:** Snow (28), DiPietro (22).

New York Rangers

Top Scorers	Gm	G	A	Pts	+/-	PM	PP
Jaromir Jagr, R	.77	31	43	74	-5	38	10
WASH	.46	16	29	45	-4	26	6
NYR	.31	15	14	29	-1	12	4
Bobby Holik, C	.82	25	31	56	4	96	8
Mark Messier, C	.76	18	25	43	3	42	1
Eric Lindros, C	.39	10	22	32	7	60	3
Jan Hlavac, L	.72	5	21	26	-8	16	2
Tom Poti, D	.67	10	14	24	-1	47	4
Karel Rachunek, D	.72	2	19	21	8	33	1
OTT	.60	1	16	17	17	29	0
NYR	.12	1	3	4	-9	4	1
Boris Mironov, D	.75	3	13	16	1	86	1
Josh Green, L	.50	5	6	11	-3	32	0
CALG	.36	2	4	6	-3	24	0
NYR	.14	3	2	5	0	8	0
Jamie Lundmark, C	.56	4	6	10	-8	33	0
Darius Kasparaitis, D	.44	1	9	10	11	48	0
Joel Bouchard, D	.28	1	7	8	2	10	0
Dan LaCouture, L	.59	5	2	7	-13	82	1
Fedor Tyutin*, D	.25	2	5	7	-4	14	0
Jed Ortmeyer*, R	.58	2	4	6	-10	16	0

Acquired: Jagr from Wash. for R Anson Carter (Jan. 23); McLennan, C Blair Betts and RW Greg Moore from Calg. for L Chris Simon and a '04 7th-round pick (Mar. 6); D Rachunek and C Alexandre Giroux from Ott. for D Greg de Vries (Mar. 9). **Claimed:** Green off waivers from Calg. (Mar. 6).

Goalies (10 Gm)	Gm	Min	GAA	Record	SV%
Jamie McLennan	.30	1690	2.31	13-12-3	.905
CALG	.26	1446	2.20	12-9-3	.910
NYR	.4	244	2.95	1-3-0	.876
Mike Dunham	.57	3148	3.03	16-30-6	.896
NY RANGERS	.82	4979	3.01	27-48-7	.896

Shutouts: McClennan (4), Dunham (2). **Assists:** McLennan and Jason LaBarbera (1). **PM:** McLennan (4), LaBarbera (2).

Ottawa Senators

Top Scorers	Gm	G	A	Pts	+/-	PM	PP
Marian Hossa, R	.81	36	46	82	4	46	14
Daniel Alfredsson, R	.77	32	48	80	12	24	9
Martin Havlat, R	.68	31	37	68	12	46	13
Jason Spezza, C	.78	22	33	55	22	71	5
Peter Bondra, R	.77	26	23	49	-16	38	14
WASH	.54	21	14	35	-17	22	12
OTT	.23	5	9	14	1	16	2
Bryan Smolinski, C	.80	19	27	46	22	49	4
Radek Bonk, C	.66	12	32	44	2	66	6
Wade Redden, D	.81	17	26	43	21	65	12
Zdeno Chara, D	.79	16	25	41	33	147	7
Peter Schaefer, L	.81	15	24	39	22	26	2
Todd White, C	.53	9	20	29	12	22	1
Chris Phillips, D	.82	7	16	23	15	46	0
Josh Langfeld, R	.38	7	10	17	6	16	2
Chris Neil, R	.82	8	8	16	13	194	0
Greg de Vries, D	.66	3	13	16	12	43	0
NYR	.53	3	12	15	12	37	0
OTT	.13	0	1	1	0	6	0
Antoine Vermette*, L	.57	7	7	14	5	16	0
Shaun Van Allen, C	.73	2	10	12	6	80	0
Vaclav Varada, L	.30	5	5	10	2	24	0
Mike Fisher, C	.24	4	6	10	-3	39	1

Acquired: Bondra from Wash. for C Brooks Laich and a '05 2nd-round pick (Feb. 18); de Vries from NYR for D Karel Rachunek & C Alexandre Giroux (Mar. 9).

Goalies (10 Gm)	Gm	Min	GAA	Record	Sv%
Martin Prusek	.29	1528	2.12	16-6-3	.917
Patrick Lalime	.57	3324	2.29	25-23-7	.905
OTTAWA	.82	4996	2.27	43-29-10	.907

Shutouts: Lalime (5), Prusek (3). **Assists:** Lalime (2), Prusek (1). **PM:** Lalime (17), Emery (2).

Philadelphia Flyers

Top Scorers	Gm	G	A	Pts	+/-	PM	PP
Mark Recchi, L	.82	26	49	75	18	47	14
Michal Handzus, C	.82	20	38	58	18	82	7
John LeClair, L	.75	23	32	55	20	51	8
Tony Amonte, R	.80	20	33	53	13	38	4
Jeremy Roenick, C	.62	19	28	47	1	62	10
Simon Gagne, L	.80	24	21	45	12	29	6
Kim Johnsson, D	.80	13	29	42	16	26	4
Alex Zhamnov, C	.43	11	25	36	-1	28	1
CHI	.23	6	12	18	-8	14	1
PHI	.20	5	13	18	7	14	0
Branko Radivojevic, R	.77	10	22	32	-5	72	2
PHO	.53	9	14	23	-5	36	2
PHI	.24	1	8	9	0	36	0
Sami Kapanen, R	.74	12	18	30	9	14	0
Joni Pitkanen*, D	.71	8	19	27	15	44	5
Keith Primeau, C	.54	7	15	22	11	80	0
Danny Markov, D	.78	6	13	19	-6	95	3
CAR	.44	4	10	14	-6	37	2
PHI	.34	2	3	5	0	58	1
Vladimir Malakhov, D	.62	3	16	19	-6	55	1
NYR	.56	3	15	18	-5	53	1
PHI	.6	0	1	1	-1	2	0
Marcus Ragnarsson, D	70	7	9	16	12	58	2

Acquired: Markov from Car. for R Justin Williams (Jan. 20); Radivojevic, Burke and L Ben Eager from Pho. for C Mike Comrie (Feb. 9); Zhamnov and a '04 4th-round pick from Chi. for D Jim Vandermeer, C Colin Fraser and a '04 2nd-round pick (Feb. 19); Malakhov from NYR for R Rick Kozak and a '05 2nd-round pick (Mar. 8).

Goalies (10 Gm)	Gm	Min	GAA	Record	Sv%
Robert Esche	.40	2322	2.04	21-11-7	.915
Jeff Hackett	.27	1630	2.39	10-10-6	.905
Sean Burke	.47	2620	2.73	16-20-7	.909
PHO	.32	1795	2.81	10-15-5	.908
PHI	.15	825	2.55	6-5-2	.910
PHILADELPHIA	.82	5011	2.23	40-27-15	.911

Shutouts: Esche and Hackett (3), Burke (2). **Assists:** Burke (2). **PM:** Esche (31), Burke (8).

Phoenix Coyotes

Top Scorers	Gm	G	A	Pts	+/-	PM	PP
Shane Doan, R	.79	27	41	68	-11	47	9
Ladislav Nagy, L	.55	24	28	52	11	46	11
Daymond Langkow, C	81	21	31	52	4	40	4
Paul Mara, D	.81	6	36	42	-11	48	1
Derek Morris, D	.83	6	26	32	-1	49	2
COL	.69	6	22	28	4	47	2
PHO	.14	0	4	4	-5	2	0
Mike Comrie, C	.49	12	12	24	-6	28	1
PHI	.21	4	5	9	2	12	0
PHO	.28	8	7	15	-8	16	1
Radoslav Suchy, D	.82	7	14	21	1	8	2
Cale Hulse, D	.82	3	17	20	-4	123	1
Jeff Taffe*, R	.59	8	10	18	-8	20	5
Daniel Cleary, L	.68	6	11	17	-8	42	0
Fredrik Sjostrom*, R	.57	7	6	13	-7	22	0
Michael Rupp, C	.57	6	6	12	-4	47	1
NJ	.51	6	5	11	-1	41	1
PHO	.6	0	1	1	-3	6	0
David Tanabe, D	.45	5	7	12	4	22	2
Krystofer Kolanos, C	.41	4	6	10	-9	24	1
Mike Johnson, R	.11	1	9	10	-1	10	1

Acquired: Comrie from Phi. for R Branko Radivojevic, G Sean Burke and L Ben Eager (Feb. 9); Johnson from St.L for C Mike Sillinger (Mar. 4); Rupp and a '04 2nd-round pick from NJ for C Jan Hrdina (Mar. 5); Morris and D Keith Ballard from Col. for C Chris Gratton, D Ossi Vaananen and a '05 2nd-round pick (Mar. 9).

Goalies (10 Gm)	Gm	Min	GAA	Record	Sv%
Brent Johnson	18	979	2.51	5-9-2	.908
ST.L	.10	493	2.43	4-3-1	.901
PHO	.8	486	2.59	1-6-1	.914
Brian Boucher	.40	2364	2.74	10-19-10	.906
PHOENIX	.82	5038	2.92	22-42-18	.902

Shutouts: Boucher (5), Johnson (1). **Assists:** none. **PM:** Boucher and Zac Bierk (2).

Pittsburgh Penguins

Top Scorers	Gm	G	A	Pts	+/-	PM	PP
Dick Tarnstrom, D	.80	16	36	52	-37	38	12
Aleksey Morozov, R	.75	16	34	50	-24	24	8
Ryan Malone*, L	.81	22	21	43	-23	64	5
Milan Kraft, C	.66	19	21	40	-22	18	6
Rico Fata, C	.73	16	18	34	-46	54	6
Ric Jackman, D	.54	9	21	30	-16	27	7
TOR	.29	2	4	6	-11	13	1
PIT	.25	7	17	24	-5	14	6
Konstantin Koltsov*, R	82	9	20	29	-30	30	2
Tomas Surovy, D	.47	11	12	23	-8	16	3
Tom Kostopoulos, R	.60	9	13	22	-14	67	2
Lasse Pirjeta, C	.70	8	14	22	-3	20	1
CLB	.57	2	8	10	-6	20	0
PIT	.13	6	6	12	3	0	1
Mike Eastwood, C	.82	4	15	19	-18	40	0
Jon Sim, L	.63	8	10	18	-4	33	0
LA	.48	6	7	13	0	27	0
PIT	.15	2	3	5	-4	6	0
Matt Bradley, R	.82	7	9	16	-27	65	0
Martin Strbak, D	.49	5	11	16	-10	46	0
LA	.5	2	0	2	1	8	0
PIT	.44	3	11	14	-11	38	0

Acquired: Strbak and L Sergei Anshakov from LA for L Martin Straka (Nov. 30); Jackman from Tor. for D Drake Berehowsky (Feb. 11); Pirjeta from Clb. for C Brian Holzinger (Mar. 9). **Claimed:** Sim off waivers from LA (Mar. 4).

Goalies (10 Gm)	Gm	Min	GAA	Record	Sv%
Jean-Sebastien Aubin	.22	1067	2.98	7-9-0	.908
Marc-Andre Fleury*	.21	1154	3.64	4-14-2	.896
Sebastien Caron	.40	2213	3.74	9-24-5	.883
PITTSBURGH	.82	4984	3.65	23-51-8	.889

Shutouts: Aubin, Fleury and Caron (1). **Assists:** none. **PM:** Caron (6), Aubin (2).

St. Louis Blues

Top Scorers	Gm	G	A	Pts	+/-	PM	PP
Keith Tkachuk, L	.75	33	38	71	8	83	18
Doug Weight, C	.75	14	51	65	-3	37	6
Pavol Demitra, C	.68	23	35	58	1	18	8
Chris Pronger, D	.80	14	40	54	-1	88	7
Dallas Drake, L	.79	13	22	35	10	65	3
Brian Savage, L	.74	16	16	32	-8	38	4
PHO	.61	12	13	25	-5	36	3
ST.L	.13	4	3	7	-3	2	1
Scott Mellanby, R	.68	14	17	31	-7	76	6
Petr Cajanek, C	.70	12	14	26	12	16	3
Mike Sillinger, C	.76	13	11	24	-10	68	0
PHO	.60	8	6	14	-14	54	0
ST.L	.16	5	5	10	4	14	0
Mark Rycroft*, R	.71	9	12	21	2	32	0
Eric Weinrich, D	.80	4	15	19	12	46	2
PHI	.54	2	7	9	11	32	1
ST.L	.26	2	8	10	1	14	1
Christian Backman*, D	66	5	13	18	3	16	1
Mike Danton*, L	.68	7	5	12	-8	141	0
Jamal Mayers, R	.80	6	5	11	-19	91	0
Ryan Johnson, C	.69	4	7	11	-2	8	0
Eric Boguniecki, R	.27	4	6	10	-1	20	2
Alexander Khavanov, D	48	3	7	10	2	18	2
Bryce Salvador, D	.69	3	5	8	-4	47	0

Acquired: Weinrich from Phi. for a '04 5th-round pick (Feb. 9); Sillinger from Pho. for G Brent Johnson (Mar. 4); Savage from Pho. for future considerations. (Mar. 9).

Goalies (10 Gm)	Gm	Min	GAA	Record	Sv%
Chris Osgood	.67	3861	2.24	31-25-8	.910
Reinhard Divis	.13	629	2.77	4-4-2	.900
ST. LOUIS	.82	5014	2.37	39-32-11	.906

Shutouts: Osgood (3). **Assists:** none. **PM:** Osgood (10), Divis (2).

San Jose Sharks

Top Scorers	Gm	G	A	Pts	+/-	PM	PP
Patrick Marleau, C	.80	28	29	57	-5	24	9
Nils Ekman, R	.82	22	33	55	30	34	1
Jonathan Cheechoo, R	81	28	19	47	5	33	8
Alyn McCauley, C	.82	20	27	47	23	28	5
Marco Sturm, R	.64	21	20	41	0	36	10
Vincent Damphousse, L	82	12	29	41	-5	66	7
Brad Stuart, D	.77	9	30	39	9	34	5
Alex Korolyuk, L	.63	19	18	37	20	18	4
Wayne Primeau, L	.72	9	20	29	4	90	0
Scott Thornton, L	.80	13	14	27	-6	84	1
Mike Ricci, C	.71	7	19	26	8	40	2
Curtis Brown, C	.80	11	14	25	3	36	2
BUF	.68	9	12	21	-2	30	2
SJ	.12	2	2	4	1	6	0
Niko Dimitrakos*, R	.68	9	15	24	6	49	2
Kyle McLaren, D	.64	2	24	10	10	60	0
Scott Hannan, D	.82	6	15	21	10	48	0
Tom Preissing, D	.69	2	17	19	8	12	2
Mike Rathje, D	.80	2	17	19	17	46	0
Christian Ehrhoff*, D	.41	1	12	14	4	14	0
Todd Harvey, C	.47	4	5	9	3	38	0
Jason Marshall, D	.24	1	6	7	-2	26	1
MIN	.12	1	4	5	-1	18	1
SJ	.12	0	2	2	-1	8	0

Acquired: Marshall from Min. for a '04 5th-round pick (Mar. 3); Brown in a 3-team trade that sent C Brad Boyes and D Andy Delmore to Bos. and D Jeff Jillson and a '05 9th-round pick to Buf. (Mar. 9).

Goalies (10 Gm)	Gm	Min	GAA	Record	Sv%
Vesa Toskala	.28	1541	2.06	12-8-4	.930
Evgeni Nabokov	.59	3456	2.20	31-19-8	.921
SAN JOSE	.82	5016	2.19	43-27-12	.923

Shutouts: Nabokov (9), Toskala (1). Nabokov and Toskala also shared a shutout. **Assists:** Toskala (1). **PM:** Nabokov (14), Toskala (2).

Tampa Bay Lightning

Top Scorers	Gm	G	A	Pts	+/-	PM	PP
Martin St. Louis, R	.82	38	56	94	35	24	8
Cory Stillman, L	.81	25	55	80	18	36	11
Brad Richards, C	.82	26	53	79	14	12	5
Vincent Lecavalier, C	.81	32	34	66	23	52	5
Fredrik Modin, L	.82	29	28	57	31	32	5
Dave Andreychuk, R	.82	21	18	39	-9	42	10
Ruslan Fedotenko, L	.77	17	22	39	14	30	0
Dan Boyle, D	.78	9	30	39	23	60	3
Pavel Kubina, D	.81	17	18	35	9	85	8
Tim Taylor, D	.82	7	15	22	-5	25	0
Darryl Sydor, D	.80	3	19	22	-16	32	1
CLB	.49	2	13	15	-19	26	1
TB	.31	1	6	7	3	6	0
Brad Lukowich, D	.79	5	14	19	29	24	0
Cory Sarich, D	.82	3	16	19	5	89	0
Dmitry Afanasenkov*, R	71	6	10	16	-4	12	0
Ben Clymer, R	.66	2	8	10	5	50	0
Martin Cibak, C	.63	2	7	9	-1	30	0
Jassen Cullimore, D	.79	2	5	7	8	58	0
Chris Dingman, L	.74	1	5	6	-9	140	0
Shane Willis, R	.12	0	6	6	1	2	0
Nolan Pratt, D	.58	1	3	4	11	42	0

Acquired: Sydor and a '04 4th-round pick from Clb. for C Alexander Svitov and a '04 3rd-round pick (Jan. 27)

Goalies (10 Gm)	Gm	Min	GAA	Record	SV%
John Grahame	.29	1648	2.06	18-9-1	.913
Nikolai Khabibulin	.55	3274	2.33	28-19-7	.910
TAMPA BAY	.82	4988	2.31	46-28-8	.908

Shutouts: Khabibulin (3), Grahame (1). **Assists:** Khabibulin (2). **PM:** Khabibulin (12), Grahame (4).

Toronto Maple Leafs

Top Scorers	Gm	G	A	Pts	+/-	PM	PP
Mats Sundin, C	.81	31	44	75	11	52	11
Bryan McCabe, D	.75	16	37	52	22	86	8
Brian Leetch, D	.72	15	36	51	6	34	5
NYR	.57	13	23	36	-5	24	4
TOR	.15	2	13	15	11	10	1
Joe Nieuwendyk, C	.64	22	28	50	7	26	10
Gary Roberts, L	.72	28	20	48	9	84	11
Owen Nolan, R	.65	19	29	48	4	110	7
Ron Francis, C	.80	13	27	40	-9	14	7
CAR	.68	10	20	30	-12	14	5
TOR	.12	3	7	10	3	0	2
Darcy Tucker, L	.64	21	11	32	4	68	8
Nik Antropov, C	.62	13	18	31	7	62	1
Tomas Kaberle, D	.71	3	28	31	16	18	0
Robert Reichel, C	.69	11	19	30	2	30	2
Alexander Mogilny, R	.37	8	22	30	9	12	4
Ken Klee, D	.66	4	25	29	-1	36	3
Alexei Ponikarovsky, L	.73	9	19	28	14	44	1
Matt Stajan*, C	.69	14	13	27	7	22	0
Mikael Renberg, L	.59	12	13	25	-1	50	2
Drake Berehowsky, D	.56	6	18	24	-11	67	3
PIT	.47	5	16	21	-16	50	3
TOR	.9	1	2	3	5	17	0
Tie Domi, R	.80	7	13	20	-2	208	1
Karel Pilar, D	.50	2	17	19	2	22	1

Acquired: Berehowsky from Pit. for D Ric Jackman (Feb. 11); Leetch and a conditional pick from NYR for D Maxim Kondratiev, C Jarkko Immonen, a '04 1st-round pick and a '05 2nd-round pick (Mar. 3); Francis from Car. for a '05 4th-round pick (Mar. 9).

Goalies (10 Gm)	Gm	Min	GAA	Record	Sv%
Ed Belfour	.59	3444	2.13	34-19-6	.918
Mikael Tellqvist*	.11	647	2.87	5-3-2	.894
Trevor Kidd	.15	883	3.26	6-5-2	.876
TORONTO	.82	4991	2.45	45-27-10	.906

Shutouts: Belfour (10), Kidd (1). **Assists:** Belfour and Kidd (2). **PM:** Belfour (16), Kidd (2).

Vancouver Canucks

Top Scorers	Gm	G	A	Pts	+/-	PM	PP
Markus Naslund, L	.78	35	49	84	24	58	5
Brendan Morrison, C	.82	22	38	60	16	50	5
Todd Bertuzzi, R	.69	17	43	60	21	122	8
Daniel Sedin, L	.82	18	36	54	18	18	1
Martin Rucinsky, L	.82	14	31	45	15	72	0
NYR	.69	13	29	42	13	62	0
VAN	.13	1	2	3	2	10	0
Henrik Sedin, C	.76	11	31	42	23	32	2
Brent Sopel, D	.80	10	32	42	11	36	6
Geoff Sanderson, L	.80	16	20	36	-10	38	6
CLB	.67	13	16	29	-9	34	5
VAN	.13	3	4	7	-1	4	1
Trevor Linden, C	.82	14	22	36	-6	26	4
Mattias Ohlund, D	.82	14	20	34	14	73	5
Sami Salo, D	.74	7	19	26	8	22	5
Matt Cooke, L	.53	11	12	23	5	73	1
Ed Jovanovski, D	.56	7	16	23	2	64	2
Jason King*, R	.47	12	9	21	0	8	6
Artem Chubarov, C	.65	12	7	19	1	14	1
Marek Malik, D	.78	3	16	19	35	45	0
Mike Keane, R	.64	8	9	17	7	20	0
Magnus Arvedson, C	.41	8	7	15	7	12	2
Jarkko Ruutu, R	.71	6	8	14	-13	133	1
Brad May, L	.70	5	6	11	-2	137	0

Acquired: Rucinsky from NYR for D Martin Grenier and C R.J. Umberger (Mar. 9); Sanderson from Clb. for a '04 3rd-round pick (Mar. 9).

Goalies (10 Gm)	Gm	Min	GAA	Record	SV%
Dan Cloutier	.60	3539	2.27	33-21-6	.914
Johan Hedberg	.21	1098	2.51	8-6-2	.900
VANCOUVER	.82	5015	2.32	43-29-10	.911

Shutouts: Cloutier (5), Hedberg (3). **Assists:** Cloutier (1). **PM:** Cloutier (22), Hedberg (10).

Washington Capitals

Top Scorers	Gm	G	A	Pts	+/-	PM	PP
Jeff Halpern, C	.79	19	27	46	-21	56	7
Kip Miller, L	.66	9	22	31	-10	8	6
Dainius Zubrus, C	.54	12	15	27	-16	38	6
Alexander Semin*, L	.52	10	12	22	-2	36	4
Brian Wilson, L	.49	10	5	15	-7	18	1
Josef Boumedienne*, R	37	2	12	14	-10	30	2
Matt Pettinger, L	.71	7	5	12	-9	37	1
Joel Kwiatkowski, D	.80	6	6	12	-28	89	2
Brendan Witt, D	.72	2	10	12	-22	123	0
Trent Whitfield, C	.44	6	5	11	-2	14	0
Bates Battaglia, L	.70	4	7	11	-24	42	0
COL	.4	0	1	1	-1	4	0
WASH	.66	4	6	10	-23	38	0
Craig Johnson, C	.64	2	9	11	-10	28	0
ANA	.39	1	2	3	-4	14	0
TOR	.10	1	1	2	0	0	0
WASH	.15	0	6	6	-6	8	0
Jason Doig, D	.65	2	9	11	-12	105	0
Shaone Morrisonn*, D	33	1	7	8	10	10	0
BOS	.30	1	7	8	10	10	0
WASH	.3	0	0	0	0	0	0
Boyd Gordon*, C	.41	1	5	6	-9	8	0
Rick Berry, D	.65	0	6	6	-5	108	0

Acquired: Battaglia and R Jonas Johansson from Col. for L Steve Konowalchuk and a '04 3rd-round pick (Oct. 22); Morrisonn, a '04 1st-round pick and a '04 2nd-round pick from Bos. for D Sergei Gonchar (Mar. 3). **Claimed:** Johnson off waivers from Tor. (Mar. 5).

Goalies (10 Gm)	Gm	Min	GAA	Record	Sv%
Olaf Kolzig	.63	3738	2.89	19-35-9	.908
WASHINGTON	.82	4976	3.05	23-49-10	.902

Shutouts: Kolzig (2), Maxime Ouellet (1). **Assists:** Kolzig and Ouellet (1). **PM:** Kolzig (6), Matthew Yeats (2).

Stanley Cup Playoffs

(1) Detroit 4		
(8) Nashville 2	Detroit 2	
(3) Vancouver 3		Calgary 4
(6) Calgary 4	Calgary 4	
		WESTERN CONFERENCE
(2) San Jose 4		
(7) St. Louis 1	San Jose 4	
(4) Colorado 4		San Jose 2
(5) Dallas 1	Colorado 2	

Tampa Bay 4 — Calgary 3

Tampa Bay 4		(1) Tampa Bay 4
	Tampa Bay 4	(8) NY Islanders 1
EASTERN CONFERENCE	Montreal 0	(2) Boston 3
		(7) Montreal 4
Philadelphia 3	Philadelphia 4	(3) Philadelphia 4
		(6) New Jersey 1
	Toronto 2	(4) Toronto 4
		(5) Ottawa 3

Stanley Cup Playoffs
Series Summaries

WESTERN CONFERENCE

FIRST ROUND (Best of 7)

	W-L	GF	Leading Scorers
Detroit	4-2	12	Lang (2-4-6)
Nashville	2-4	9	Four tied with 3 pts.

Date	Winner	Home Ice
April 7	Red Wings, 3-1	at Detroit
April 10	Red Wings, 2-1	at Detroit
April 11	Predators, 3-1	at Nashville
April 13	Predators, 3-0	at Nashville
April 15	Red Wings, 4-1	at Detroit
April 17	Red Wings, 2-0	at Nashville

Shutouts: Vokoun, Nashville; Joseph, Detroit.

	W-L	GF	Leading Scorers
San Jose	4-1	12	Damphousse (0-4-4) & Marleau (3-1-4)
St. Louis	1-4	9	Sillinger (3-1-4)

Date	Winner	Home Ice
April 8	Sharks, 1-0 (OT)	at San Jose
April 10	Sharks, 3-1	at San Jose
April 12	Blues, 4-1	at St. Louis
April 13	Sharks, 4-3	at St. Louis
April 15	Sharks, 3-1	at San Jose

Shutout: Nabokov, San Jose.

	W-L	GF	Leading Scorers
Calgary	4-3	19	Iginla (5-3-8)
Vancouver	3-4	16	Naslund (2-7-9)

Date	Winner	Home Ice
April 7	Canucks, 5-3	at Vancouver
April 9	Flames, 2-1	at Vancouver
April 11	Canucks, 2-1	at Calgary
April 13	Flames, 4-0	at Calgary
April 13	Flames, 2-1	at Vancouver
April 13	Canucks, 5-4 (3OT)	at Calgary
April 13	Flames, 3-2 (OT)	at Vancouver

Shutout: Kiprusoff, Calgary.

	W-L	GF	Leading Scorers
Colorado	4-1	19	Forsberg (3-5-8)
Dallas	1-4	10	Turgeon (1-3-4)

Date	Winner	Home Ice
April 7	Avalanche, 3-1	at Colorado
April 9	Avalanche, 5-2	at Colorado
April 12	Stars, 4-3 (OT)	at Dallas
April 14	Avalanche, 3-2 (2OT)	at Dallas
April 17	Avalanche, 5-1	at Colorado

SEMIFINALS (Best of 7)

	W-L	GF	Leading Scorers
Calgary	4-2	11	Gelinas (3-3-6)
Detroit	2-4	12	Lidstrom (1-4-5)

Date	Winner	Home Ice
April 22	Flames, 2-1 (OT)	at Detroit
April 24	Red Wings, 5-2	at Detroit
April 27	Flames, 3-2	at Calgary
April 29	Red Wings, 4-2	at Calgary
May 1	Flames, 1-0	at Detroit
May 3	Flames, 1-0 (OT)	at Calgary

Shutouts: Kiprusoff, Calgary (2).

	W-L	GF	Leading Scorers
San Jose	4-2	14	Damphousse (5-2-7)
Colorado	2-4	7	Sakic (3-3-6)

Date	Winner	Home Ice
April 22	Sharks, 5-2	at San Jose
April 24	Sharks, 4-1	at San Jose
April 26	Sharks, 1-0	at Colorado
April 28	Avalanche, 1-0 (OT)	at Colorado
May 1	Avalanche, 2-1 (OT)	at San Jose
May 4	Sharks, 3-1	at Colorado

Shutouts: Nabokov, San Jose; Aebischer, Colorado.

CHAMPIONSHIP (Best of 7)

	W-L	GF	Leading Scorers
Calgary	4-2	16	Conroy (3-3–6)
San Jose	2-4	12	Korolyuk (3-1–4)
			& Rathje (1-3–4)

Date	Winner	Home Ice
May 9	Flames, 4-3 (OT)	at San Jose
May 11	Flames, 4-1	at San Jose
May 13	Sharks, 3-0	at Calgary
May 16	Sharks, 4-2	at Calgary
May 17	Flames, 3-0	at San Jose
May 19	Flames, 3-1	at Calgary

Shutouts: Nabokov, SJ; Kiprusoff, Calgary.

EASTERN CONFERENCE

FIRST ROUND (Best of 7)

	W-L	GF	Leading Scorers
Tampa Bay	4-1	12	Modin (3-4–7)
NY Islanders	1-4	5	Niinimaa (1-2–3)
			& Parrish (1-2–3)

Date	Winner	Home Ice
April 8	Lightning, 3-0	at Tampa Bay
April 10	Islanders, 3-0	at Tampa Bay
April 12	Lightning, 3-0	at New York
April 14	Lightning, 3-0	at New York
April 16	Lightning, 3-2 (OT)	at Tampa Bay

Shutouts: Khabibulin, Tampa Bay (3); DiPietro, NY Islanders.

	W-L	GF	Leading Scorers
Montreal	4-3	19	Koivu (2-8–10)
Boston	3-4	14	Samsonov (2-5–7)

Date	Winner	Home Ice
April 7	Bruins, 3-0	at Boston
April 9	Bruins, 2-1 (OT)	at Boston
April 11	Canadiens, 3-2	at Montreal
April 13	Bruins, 4-3 (2OT)	at Montreal
April 15	Canadiens, 5-1	at Boston
April 17	Canadiens, 3-2	at Montreal
April 19	Canadiens, 2-0	at Boston

Shutout: Raycroft, Boston; Theodore, Montreal.

	W-L	GF	Leading Scorers
Philadelphia	4-1	14	Zhamnov (3-5–8)
New Jersey	1-4	9	Gomez (0-6–6)

Date	Winner	Home Ice
April 8	Flyers, 3-2	at Philadelphia
April 10	Flyers, 3-2	at Philadelphia
April 12	Devils, 4-2	at New Jersey
April 14	Flyers, 3-0	at New Jersey
April 17	Flyers, 3-1	at Philadelphia

Shutouts: Esche, Philadelphia.

	W-L	GF	Leading Scorers
Toronto	4-3	14	Nieuwendyk (5-0–5)
Ottawa	3-4	11	Hossa (3-1–4)

Date	Winner	Home Ice
April 8	Senators, 4-2	at Toronto
April 10	Maple Leafs, 2-0	at Toronto
April 12	Maple Leafs, 2-0	at Ottawa
April 14	Senators, 4-1	at Ottawa
April 16	Maple Leafs, 2-0	at Toronto
April 18	Senators, 2-1 (2OT)	at Ottawa
April 20	Maple Leafs, 4-1	at Toronto

Shutouts: Belfour, Toronto (3).

SEMIFINALS (Best of 7)

	W-L	GF	Leading Scorers
Tampa Bay	4-0	14	Lecavalier (5-2–7)
Montreal	0-4	5	Three tied with 2 pts.

Date	Winner	Home Ice
April 23	Lightning, 4-0	at Tampa Bay
April 25	Lightning, 3-1	at Tampa Bay
April 27	Lightning, 4-3 (OT)	at Montreal
April 29	Lightning, 3-1	at Montreal

Shutouts: Khabibulin, Tampa Bay.

	W-L	GF	Leading Scorers
Philadelphia	4-2	17	Primeau (3-2–5)
			& Gagne (2-3–5)
Toronto	2-4	13	Sundin (3-2–5)
			& Mogilny (2-3–5)

Date	Winner	Home Ice
April 22	Flyers, 3-1	at Philadelphia
April 25	Flyers, 2-1	at Philadelphia
April 28	Maple Leafs, 4-1	at Toronto
April 30	Maple Leafs, 3-1	at Toronto
May 2	Flyers, 7-2	at Philadelphia
May 4	Flyers, 3-2 (OT)	at Toronto

CHAMPIONSHIP (Best of 7)

	W-L	GF	Leading Scorers
Tampa Bay	4-3	21	Richards (4-4–8)
Philadelphia	3-4	19	Primeau (4-4–8)

Date	Winner	Home Ice
May 8	Lightning, 3-1	at Tampa Bay
May 10	Flyers, 6-2	at Tampa Bay
May 13	Lightning, 4-1	at Philadelphia
May 15	Flyers, 3-2	at Philadelphia
May 18	Lightning, 4-2	at Tampa Bay
May 20	Flyers, 5-4 (OT)	at Philadelphia
May 22	Lightning, 2-1	at Tampa Bay

Conn Smythe Trophy (Playoff MVP)
Brad Richards, Tampa Bay, C
23 games, 12 goals, 14 assists, 26 points, 7 GWG

STANLEY CUP FINALS (Best of 7)

	W-L	GF	Leading Scorers
Tampa Bay	4-3	13	Richards (4-4–8)
Calgary	3-4	14	Iginla (3-2–5)

Date	Winner	Home Ice
May 25	Flames, 4-1	at Tampa Bay
May 27	Lightning, 4-1	at Tampa Bay
May 29	Flames, 3-0	at Calgary
May 31	Lightning, 1-0	at Calgary
June 3	Flames, 3-2 (OT)	at Tampa Bay
June 5	Lightning, 3-2 (2OT)	at Calgary
June 7	Lightning, 2-1	at Tampa Bay

Shutouts: Kiprusoff, Calgary; Khabibulin, Tampa Bay.

Stanley Cup Finals Box Scores

Game 1

Tuesday, May 25, at Tampa Bay

Calgary	.1	2	1	**— 4**
Tampa Bay	.0	0	1	**— 1**

1st Period: CALG—Gelinas 7 (Conroy, Ference), 3:02. **2nd Period:** CALG—Iginla 11 (unassisted), 15:21 (sh); CALG—Yelle 3 (unassisted), 18:08. **3rd Period:** TB—St. Louis 6 (Richards, Boyle), 4:13 (pp); CALG—Simon 4 (Saprykin, Regehr), 19:40 (pp). **Shots on Goal:** Calgary—5-10-4-19; Tampa Bay—10-8-6-24. **Power plays:** Calgary 1-4; Tampa Bay 1-5. **Goalies:** Calgary, Kiprusoff (24 shots, 23 saves); Tampa Bay, Khabibulin (19 shots, 15 saves). **Attendance:** 21,674.

Game 2

Thursday, May 27, at Tampa Bay

Calgary	.0	0	1	**— 1**
Tampa Bay	.1	0	3	**— 4**

1st Period: TB—Fedotenko 10 (Cullimore, Lecavalier), 7:10. **3rd Period:** TB—Richards 9 (Andreychuk, St. Louis), 2:51; TB—Boyle 2 (Richards, Modin), 4:00; TB—St. Louis 7 (Lecavalier, Andreychuk), 5:58 (pp); CALG—Nieminen 4 (Donovan, Regehr), 12:21 (pp). **Shots on Goal:** Calgary—6-9-4-19; Tampa Bay—8-10-13-31. **Power plays:** Calgary 1-7; Tampa Bay 1-9. **Goalies:** Calgary, Kiprusoff (31 shots, 27 saves); Tampa Bay, Khabibulin (19 shots, 18 saves). **Attendance:** 22,222.

Game 3

Saturday, May 29, at Calgary

Tampa Bay	.0	0	0	**— 0**
Calgary	.0	2	1	**— 3**

2nd Period: CALG—Simon 5 (Iginla, Leopold), 13:53 (pp); CALG—Donovan 5 (unassisted), 17:09. **3rd Period:** CALG—Iginla 12 (Regehr, Simon), 18:28 (pp). **Shots on Goal:** Tampa Bay—5-6-10-21; Calgary—2-12-4-18. **Power plays:** Tampa Bay 0-4; Calgary 2-4. **Goalies:** Tampa Bay, Khabibulin (18 shots, 15 saves); Calgary, Kiprusoff (21 shots, 21 saves). **Attendance:** 19,221.

Game 4

Monday, May 31, at Calgary

Tampa Bay	.1	0	0	**— 1**
Calgary	.0	0	0	**— 0**

1st period: TB—Richards 10 (Andreychuk, Boyle), 2:48 (pp). **Shots on Goal:** Tampa Bay—12-7-5-24; Calgary—12-5-12-29. **Power plays:** Tampa Bay 1-5; Calgary 0-2. **Goalies:** Tampa Bay, Khabibulin (29 shots, 29 saves); Calgary, Kiprusoff (24 shots, 23 saves). **Attendance:** 19,221.

Game 5

Thursday, June 3, at Tampa Bay

Calgary	.1	1	0	1	**— 3**
Tampa Bay	.1	0	1	0	**— 2**

1st Period: CALG—Gelinas 8 (Lydman, Montador), 2:13 (pp); TB—St. Louis 8 (Cibak, Dingman), 19:26. **2nd Period:** CALG—Iginla 13 (unassisted), 15:10. **3rd Period:** TB—Modin 8 (Richards, Andreychuk), 0:37 (pp). **Overtime:** CALG—Saprykin 3 (Iginla, Nilson), 14:40. **Shots on Goal:** Calgary—11-14-4-7-36; Tampa Bay—9-3-8-8-28. **Power plays:** Calgary 1-2; Tampa Bay 1-2. **Goalies:** Calgary, Kiprusoff (28 shots, 26 saves); Tampa Bay, Khabibulin (36 shots, 33 saves). **Attendance:** 22,426.

Game 6

Saturday, June 5, at Calgary

Tampa Bay	.0	2	0	0	1	**— 3**
Calgary	.0	2	0	0	0	**— 2**

2nd Period: TB—Richards 11 (St. Louis, Fedotenko), 4:17 (pp); CALG—Clark 3 (Yelle, Nieminen), 9:05; TB—Richards 12 (unassisted), 10:52 (pp); CALG—Nilson 4 (Saprykin, Ference), 14:49. **2nd overtime:** TB—St. Louis 9 (Taylor, Cullimore), 0:33. **Shots on Goal:** Tampa Bay—6-5-7-7-2-27; Calgary—6-13-7-7-0-33. **Power plays:** Tampa Bay 2-4; Calgary 0-3. **Goalies:** Tampa Bay, Khabibulin (33 shots, 31 saves); Calgary, Kiprusoff (27 shots, 24 saves). **Attendance:** 19,221.

Game 7

Monday, June 7, at Tampa Bay

Calgary	.0	0	1	**— 1**
Tampa Bay	.1	1	0	**— 2**

1st Period: TB—Fedotenko 11 (Richards, Modin), 13:31 (pp). **2nd Period:** TB—Fedotenko 12 (Lecavalier, Stillman), 14:38. **3rd Period:** CALG—Conroy 6 (Leopold), 9:21 (pp). **Shots on Goal:** Calgary—3-4-10-17; Tampa Bay—6-4-5-15. **Power plays:** Calgary 1-2; Tampa Bay 1-5. **Goalies:** Calgary, Kiprusoff (15 shots, 13 saves); Tampa Bay, Khabibulin (17 shots, 16 saves). **Attendance:** 22,717.

Stanley Cup Leaders

Scoring

	Gm	G	A	Pts	+/-	PM	PP
Brad Richards, TB	.23	12	14	**26**	5	4	7
Martin St. Louis, TB	.23	9	15	**24**	6	14	3
Jarome Iginla, Calg.	.26	13	9	**22**	13	45	4
Fredrik Modin, TB	.23	8	11	**19**	7	10	3
Craig Conroy, Calg.	.26	6	11	**17**	12	12	2
Keith Primeau, Phi.	.18	9	7	**16**	11	22	0
Vincent Lecavalier, TB	.23	9	7	**16**	-2	25	2
Martin Gelinas, Calg.	.26	8	7	**15**	10	35	2

Four tied with 14 pts. each.

Goaltending

(Minimum 390 minutes)

	Gm	Min	W-L	ShO	GAA
Curtis Joseph, Det.	.9	518	4-4	1	1.39
Nikolai Khabibulin, TB	.23	1401	16-7	5	1.71
Evgeni Nabokov, SJ	.17	1052	10-7	3	1.71
Miikka Kiprusoff, Calg.	.26	1655	15-11	5	1.85
Patrick Lalime, Ott.	.7	398	3-4	0	1.96

Final Stanley Cup Standings

				—Goals—		
	Gm	W	L	For	Opp	Dif
Tampa Bay	.23	16	7	60	43	+17
Calgary	.26	15	11	60	53	+7
Philadelphia	.18	11	7	50	43	+7
San Jose	.17	10	7	38	32	+6
Colorado	.11	6	5	26	24	+2
Detroit	.12	6	6	24	20	+4
Toronto	.13	6	7	27	28	-1
Montreal	.11	4	7	24	28	-4
Vancouver	.7	3	4	16	19	-3
Ottawa	.7	3	4	11	14	-3
Boston	.7	3	4	14	19	-5
Nashville	.6	2	4	9	12	-3
St. Louis	.5	1	4	9	12	-3
New Jersey	.5	1	4	9	14	-5
NY Islanders	.5	1	4	5	12	-7
Dallas	.5	1	4	10	19	-9

Finalists' Composite Box Scores
Tampa Bay Lightning (16-7)

Top Scorers	Pos	Overall Playoffs								Finals vs Calgary							
		Gm	G	A	Pts	+/-	PM	PP	S	Gm	G	A	Pts	+/-	PM	PP	S
Brad Richards	C	23	12	14	26	5	4	7	88	7	4	4	8	-3	2	3	27
Martin St. Louis	R	23	9	15	24	6	14	3	58	7	4	2	6	0	2	2	15
Fredrik Modin	L	23	8	11	19	7	10	3	50	7	1	2	3	-3	4	1	14
Vincent Lecavalier	C	23	9	7	16	-2	25	-2	76	7	0	3	3	-1	9	0	18
Ruslan Fedotenko	L	22	12	2	14	0	14	5	43	6	3	1	4	0	4	1	11
Dave Andreychuk	R	23	1	13	14	-2	14	0	30	7	0	4	4	-1	4	0	12
Dan Boyle	D	23	2	8	10	7	16	1	25	7	1	2	3	-1	4	0	10
Cory Stillman	L	21	2	5	7	2	15	0	35	6	0	0	0	1	7	0	4
Darryl Sydor	D	23	0	6	6	-4	9	0	25	7	0	1	1	-3	0	0	7
Tim Taylor	C	23	2	3	5	-2	31	0	21	7	0	1	1	0	2	0	6
Pavel Kubina	D	22	0	4	4	0	50	0	29	6	0	0	0	-3	12	0	5
Andre Roy	R	21	1	2	3	3	61	0	11	5	0	0	0	0	21	0	2
Dmitry Afanasenkov*	R	23	1	2	3	-3	6	0	27	7	0	0	0	-1	4	0	9
Chris Dingman	L	23	1	1	2	1	63	0	13	7	0	1	1	0	24	0	4
Jassen Cullimore	D	11	0	2	2	7	6	0	7	2	0	2	2	5	4	0	5
Brad Lukowich	D	18	0	2	2	4	6	0	7	4	0	0	0	-1	4	0	2
Cory Sarich	D	23	0	2	2	1	25	0	32	7	0	0	0	2	14	0	11
Martin Cibak	C	6	0	1	1	0	0	0	3	4	0	1	1	1	0	0	3
Eric Perrin	C	12	0	1	1	0	6	0	0	0	0	0	0	0	0	0	0

Overtime goals—OVERALL (St. Louis 2, Richards); FINALS (St. Louis). **Shorthanded goals**—OVERALL (St. Louis, Stillman); FINALS (none). **Power Play conversions**—OVERALL (21 for 100, 21.0%); FINALS (7 for 34, 20.6%).

Goaltending	Gm	Min	GAA	GA	SA	Sv%	W-L	Gm	Min	GAA	GA	SA	Sv%	W-L
Nikolai Khabibulin	23	1401	1.71	40	598	.933	16-7	7	454	1.85	14	171	.918	4-3
John Grahame	1	34	3.53	2	17	.882	0-0	0	0	0.00	0	0	—	0-0
TOTAL	23	1439	1.79	43	616	.930	16-7	7	455	1.85	14	171	.918	4-3

Empty Net Goals—OVERALL (1), FINALS (none). **Shutouts**—OVERALL (Khabibulin 5), FINALS (Khabibulin). **Assists**—OVERALL (none), FINALS (none). **Penalty Minutes**—OVERALL (none), FINALS (none).

Calgary Flames (15-11)

Top Scorers	Pos	Overall Playoffs								Finals vs Tampa Bay							
		Gm	G	A	Pts	+/-	PM	PP	S	Gm	G	A	Pts	+/-	PM	PP	S
Jarome Iginla	R	26	13	9	22	13	45	4	93	7	3	2	5	3	5	1	20
Craig Conroy	C	26	6	11	17	12	12	2	49	7	1	1	2	2	4	1	10
Martin Gelinas	L	26	8	7	15	10	35	2	51	7	2	0	2	1	21	0	14
Marcus Nilson	L	26	4	7	11	0	12	0	37	7	1	1	2	-1	2	0	11
Shean Donovan	R	24	5	5	10	0	23	0	43	5	1	1	2	-1	6	0	5
Jordan Leopold	D	26	0	10	10	5	6	0	34	7	0	2	2	-1	2	0	7
Robyn Regehr	D	26	2	7	9	7	20	0	29	7	0	3	3	0	4	0	4
Ville Nieminen	R	24	4	4	8	0	55	1	41	6	1	1	2	-1	17	1	10
Chris Simon	L	16	5	2	7	0	74	4	34	7	2	1	3	-1	16	2	16
Stephane Yelle	C	23	3	3	6	-1	16	0	27	7	1	1	2	0	4	0	7
Oleg Saprykin	L	26	3	3	6	1	14	1	53	7	1	2	3	1	6	0	18
Chris Clark	R	26	3	3	6	0	30	1	29	7	0	1	1	1	8	0	12
Matthew Lombardi*	C	13	5	1	6	1	4	0	15	0	0	0	0	0	0	0	0
Steve Montador	D	20	1	2	3	4	6	0	44	7	0	1	1	0	0	0	8
Andrew Ference	D	26	0	3	3	5	25	0	37	7	0	2	2	4	13	0	13
Krzysztof Oliwa	L	20	2	0	2	-1	6	0	16	7	0	0	0	0	2	0	4
Mike Commodore	D	20	0	2	2	1	19	0	13	4	0	0	0	0	2	0	3
Toni Lydman	D	6	0	1	1	1	2	0	4	3	0	1	1	-1	0	0	1
Denis Gauthier	D	6	0	1	1	2	4	0	3	7	0	0	0	0	0	0	0
Rhett Warrener	D	24	0	1	1	1	6	0	27	7	0	0	0	0	2	0	7
Chuck Kobasew*	R	26	0	2	2	0	15	0	16	7	0	0	0	0	0	0	0

Overtime goals—OVERALL (Gelinas 2, Nilson, Saprykin, Montador); FINALS (Saprykin). **Shorthanded goals**—OVERALL (Iginla 2, Yelle); FINALS (Iginla). **Power Play conversions**—OVERALL (15 for 108, 13.9%); FINALS (6 for 24, 25.0%).

Goaltending	Gm	Min	GAA	GA	SA	Sv%	W-L	Gm	Min	GAA	GA	SA	Sv%	W-L
Roman Turek	1	19	0.00	0	3	100.0	0-0	0	0	0.00	0	0	—	0-0
Miikka Kiprusoff	26	1655	1.85	51	710	.928	15-11	7	454	1.72	13	170	.924	3-4
TOTAL	26	1680	1.89	53	715	.926	15-11	7	455	1.71	13	170	.924	3-4

Empty Net Goals—OVERALL (2), FINALS (none). **Shutouts**—OVERALL (Kiprusoff 5), FINALS (Kiprusoff). **Assists**—OVERALL (Kiprusoff), FINALS (none). **Penalty Minutes**—OVERALL (none), FINALS (none).

Annual Awards

Voting for the Hart, Calder, Norris, Lady Byng, Selke, and Masterton Trophies is conducted after the regular season by the Professional Hockey Writers' Association. The Vezina Trophy is selected by the NHL general managers, while the Jack Adams Award is selected by NHL broadcasters. Points are awarded on 10–7–5–3–1 basis except for the Vezina Trophy and the Adams Award which are awarded 5–3–1.

Hart Trophy
For Most Valuable Player

	Pos	1st	2nd	3rd	4th	5th	Pts
Martin St. Louis, TB	R	97	5	1	2	0—	1016
Jarome Iginla, Calg	R	2	20	15	3	9—	253
Martin Brodeur, NJ	G	2	14	11	11	7—	213
Miikka Kiprusoff, Calg	G	0	19	7	7	4—	193
Markus Naslund, Van	R	0	11	10	13	10—	176

Calder Trophy
For Rookie of the Year

	Pos	1st	2nd	3rd	4th	5th	Pts
Andrew Raycroft, Bos	G	93	8	3	0	1—	1002
Michael Ryder, Mon	R	11	77	13	3	0—	723
Trent Hunter, NYI	R	1	11	64	18	9—	470
John-Michael Liles, Col	D	0	2	4	15	16—	95
Ryan Malone, Pit	L	0	3	1	15	21—	92

Norris Trophy
For Best Defenseman

	1st	2nd	3rd	4th	5th	Pts
Scott Niedermayer, NJ	72	13	10	3	2—	872
Zdeno Chara, Ott	19	36	16	11	8—	563
Chris Pronger, St.L	7	19	16	17	11—	345
Bryan McCabe, Tor	1	12	10	10	15—	189
Adrian Aucoin, NYI	2	3	12	16	17—	166

Vezina Trophy
For Outstanding Goaltender

	1st	2nd	3rd	Pts
Martin Brodeur, NJ	15	4	2—	89
Miikka Kiprusoff, Calg	5	9	3—	55
Roberto Luongo, Fla	6	3	6—	45
Marty Turco, Dal	2	10	3—	43
Andrew Raycroft, Bos	1	1	6—	14

Lady Byng Trophy
For Sportsmanship and Gentlemanly Play

	Pos	1st	2nd	3rd	4th	5th	Pts
Brad Richards, TB	C	25	12	12	7	10—	425
Daniel Alfredsson, Ott	R	14	16	7	7	8—	316
Martin St. Louis, TB	R	19	8	7	10	3—	314
Nicklas Lidstrom, Det	D	9	7	9	9	10—	221
Brett Hull, Det	R	6	11	11	4	7—	211

Selke Trophy
For Best Defensive Forward

	Pos	1st	2nd	3rd	4th	5th	Pts
Kris Draper, Det	C	66	22	4	1	2—	839
John Madden, NJ	C	6	24	18	13	11—	368
Alyn McCauley, SJ	C	9	15	9	8	7—	271
Martin St. Louis, TB	R	15	9	8	3	5—	267
Michael Peca, NYI	C	0	13	8	11	14—	178

Adams Award
For Coach of the Year

	1st	2nd	3rd	Pts
John Tortorella, TB	35	16	8—	231
Ron Wilson, SJ	16	25	12—	167
Darryl Sutter, Calg	9	8	18—	87
Dave Lewis, Det	3	5	3—	33
Mike Sullivan, Bos	2	5	8—	33

AP/Wide World Photos

Tampa Bay's **Martin St. Louis** took home the Art Ross and Hart Trophies at the NHL awards ceremony on June 10.

Other Awards

Lester B. Pearson Award (NHL Players Assn. MVP)—Martin St. Louis, TB

Jennings Trophy (goaltenders with a minimum of 25 games played for team with fewest goals against)—Martin Brodeur, NJ

Maurice "Rocket" Richard Trophy (regular season goal-scoring leader)—(tie) Jarome Iginla, Calg., Ilya Kovalchuk, Atl. and Rick Nash, Clb.

Art Ross Trophy (regular season points leader)—Martin St. Louis, TB

Masterton Trophy (perseverance, sportsmanship, and dedication to hockey)—Bryan Berard, Chi.

King Clancy Trophy (leadership and humanitarian contributions to community)—Jarome Iginla, Calg.

Lester Patrick Trophy (outstanding service to hockey in the U.S.)—Mike Emrick, John Davidson and Ray Miron.

All-NHL Team

Voting by PHWA. Holdovers from 2002-03 first team in **bold**.

	First Team		Second Team
G	**Martin Brodeur**, NJ	G	Roberto Luongo, Fla
D	Scott Niedermayer, NJ	D	Chris Pronger, St.L
D	Zdeno Chara, Ott	D	Bryan McCabe, Tor
C	Joe Sakic, Col	C	Mats Sundin, Tor
R	Martin St. Louis, TB	R	Jarome Iginla, Calg
L	**Markus Naslund**, Van	L	Ilya Kovalchuk, Atl

All-Rookie Team

Voting by PHWA.

Pos		Pos	
G	Andrew Raycroft, Bos	F	Trent Hunter, NYI
D	John-Michael Liles, Col	F	Ryan Malone, Pit
D	Joni Pitkanen, Phi	F	Michael Ryder, Mon

2004 NHL Draft

First and second round selections at the 42nd annual NHL Entry Draft held June 26-27, 2004, at the RBC Center in Raleigh. The order of the first 14 positions were determined by a draft lottery of non-playoff teams held April 6 in New York City. Only the worst five teams from the 2003-04 regular season had the chance to win the first overall pick. No team could move up more than four spots in the draft order or drop more than one position. Positions 15 through 30 reflect regular season records in reverse order.

First Round

	Team	Player, Last Team	Pos
1	Washington	Alexander Ovechkin, Dynamo (Rus)	L
2	Pittsburgh	Evgeni Malkin, Magnitogorsk (Rus)	C
3	Chicago	Cameron Barker, Medicine Hat (WHL)	D
4	a-Carolina	Andrew Ladd, Calgary (WHL)	L
5	Phoenix	Blake Wheeler, Breck School, Minn. (HS)	R
6	NY Rangers	Al Montoya, Michigan (CCHA)	G
7	Florida	Rostislav Olesz, Vitkovice (Cze)	C
8	b-Columbus	Alexandre Picard, Lewiston (QMJHL)	L
9	Anaheim	Ladislav Smid, Liberec (Cze)	D
10	Atlanta	Boris Valabik, Kitchener (OHL)	D
11	Los Angeles	Lauri Tukonen, Blues (Fin)	R
12	Minnesota	A.J. Thelen, Michigan St. (CCHA)	D
13	Buffalo	Drew Stafford, North Dakota (WCHA)	R
14	Edmonton	Devan Dubnyk, Kamloops (WHL)	G
15	Nashville	Alexander Radulov, Dynamo (Rus)	R
16	NY Islanders	Petteri Nokelainen, Saipa (Fin)	R
17	St. Louis	Marek Schwarz, Sparta (Cze)	G
18	Montreal	Kyle Chipchura, Prince Albert (WHL)	C
19	c-NY Rangers	Lauri Korpikoski, TPS Jr. (Fin)	L
20	d-New Jersey	Travis Zajac, Salmon Arm (BCHL)	C
21	Colorado	Wojtek Wolski, Brampton (OHL)	L
22	e-San Jose	Lukas Kaspar, Litvinov (Cze)	R
23	Ottawa	Andrej Meszaros, Trencin (Svk)	D
24	f-Calgary	Kris Chucko, Salmon Arm (BCHL)	L
25	g-Edmonton	Rob Schremp, London (OHL)	C
26	Vancouver	Cory Schneider, Phillips-Andover, Mass. (HS)	G
27	h-Washington	Jeff Schultz, Calgary (WHL)	D
28	i-Dallas	Mark Fistric, Vancouver (WHL)	D
29	j-Washington	Mike Green, Saskatoon (WHL)	D
30	Tampa Bay	Andy Rogers, Calgary (WHL)	D

Second Round

	Team	Player, Last Team	Pos
31	Pittsburgh	Johannes Salmonsson, Djurgarden (Swe)	L
32	Chicago	Dave Bolland, London (OHL)	C
33	Washington	Christopher Bourque, Cushing Academy, Mass (HS)	C
34	k-Dallas	Johan Fransson, Lulea (Swe)	D
35	Phoenix	Logan Stephenson, Tri-City (WHL)	D
36	NY Rangers	Darin Oliver, N. Michigan (CCHA)	C
37	l-Florida	David Shantz, Mississauga (OHL)	G
38	Carolina	Justin Peters, Toronto St. Michaels (OHL)	G
39	Anaheim	Jordan Smith, Sault-Ste.-Marie (OHL)	D
40	Atlanta	Grant Lewis, Dartmouth (ECAC)	D
41	m-Chicago	Bryan Bickell, Ottawa (OHL)	L
42	Minnesota	Roman Voloshenko, Krylja (Rus)	L
43	Buffalo	Michael Funk, Portland (WHL)	D
44	Edmonton	Roman Teslyuk, Kamloops (WHL)	D
45	n-Chicago	Ryan Garlock, Windsor (OHL)	C
46	o-Columbus	Adam Pineault, Boston College (HE)	R
47	NY Islanders	Blake Comeau, Kelowna (WHL)	R
48	p-NY Rangers	Dane Byers, Prince Albert (WHL)	L
49	St. Louis	Carl Soderberg, Malmo (Swe)	C
50	q-Phoenix	Enver Lisin, Saratov (Rus)	R
51	r-NY Rangers	Bruce Graham, Moncton (QMJHL)	C
52	s-Dallas	Raymond Sawada, Nanaimo (BCHL)	R
53	t-Florida	David Booth, Michigan St. (CCHA)	L
54	u-Chicago	Jakub Sindel, Sparta (Cze)	C
55	Colorado	Victor Oreskovich, Green Bay (USHL)	R
56	Dallas	Niklas Grossman, Sodertalje Jr. (Swe)	D
57	v-Edmonton	Geoff Paukovich, U.S. National U-18	L
58	Ottawa	Kirill Lyamin, HC CSKA (Rus)	D
59	w-Columbus	Kyle Wharton, Ottawa (OHL)	D
60	x-NY Rangers	Brandon Dubinsky, Portland (WHL)	C
61	y-Pittsburgh	Alex Goligoski, Grand Rapids, Minn. (HS)	D
62	z-Washington	Michail Yunkov, Krylja (Rus)	C
63	aa-Boston	David Krejci, Kladno Jr. (Cze)	C
64	bb-Boston	Martins Karsums, Moncton (QMJHL)	R
65	Tampa Bay	Mark Tobin, Rimouski (QMJHL)	L

Acquired picks: a—from Clb; **b**—from Car; **c**—from Calg; **d**—from Dallas; **e**—from NJ via Dal; **f**—from Tor via NYR; **g**—from Phi; **h**—from Bos; **i**—from SJ; **j**—from Det; **k**—from Clb; **l**—from NYR via Col; **m**—from LA via Phi; **n**—from Nash; **o**—from NYR via Calg; **p**—from Edm; **q**—from Dal via Fla and NYR; **r**—from Mon; **s**—from SJ; **t**—from Calg; **u**—from Dal; **v**—from NJ via Pho; **w**—from Tor via Car; **x**—from Phi via Pho; **y**—from Van; **z**—from Bos; **aa**—from SJ; **bb**—from Det via LA.

U.S. Division I College Hockey

Final regular season standings; overall records, including all postseason tournament games, in parentheses.

Atlantic Hockey

	W	L	T	Pts	GF	GA
*Holy Cross (22-10-4)	17	4	3	37	83	54
Mercyhurst (20-14-2)	16	7	1	33	105	71
Quinnipiac (15-14-6)	12	6	6	30	67	53
Sacred Heart (14-17-5)	12	8	4	28	87	68
Connecticut (12-16-7)	9	10	5	23	89	86
Canisius (10-16-8)	9	11	4	22	67	73
Bentley (9-19-4)	7	13	4	18	55	71
Army (8-18-3)	6	15	3	15	55	84
American Int'l (5-25-4)	3	17	4	10	49	97

Conf. Tourney Final: Holy Cross 4, Sacred Heart 0.
***NCAA Tourney (0-1):** Holy Cross (0-1).

Central Collegiate Hockey Assn.

	W	L	T	Pts	GF	GA
*Michigan (27-14-2)	18	8	2	38	101	66
*Miami-OH (23-14-4)	17	8	3	37	99	74
*Michigan St. (24-16-2)	17	9	2	36	91	62
*Ohio St. (26-16-0)	16	12	0	32	89	70
*Notre Dame (20-15-4)	14	11	3	31	84	71
Alaska-Fairbanks (16-19-1)	14	13	1	29	92	92
N. Michigan (21-16-4)	13	13	2	28	66	79
W. Michigan (17-18-4)	12	13	3	27	87	101
Bowling Green (11-18-9)	9	13	6	24	69	83
Ferris St. (15-20-3)	10	17	1	21	71	97
Lake Superior (9-20-7)	7	16	5	19	60	83
Nebraska-Omaha (8-26-5)	5	19	4	14	60	91

Conf. Tourney Final: Ohio St. 4, Michigan 2.
***NCAA Tourney (1-5):** Michigan (1-1), Miami-OH (0-1), Michigan St. (0-1), Ohio St. (0-1), Notre Dame (0-1).

College Hockey America

	W	L	T	Pts	GF	GA
Bemidji State (20-13-3) . . .16	3	1	33	90	48
*Niagara (21-15-3) 14	6	0	28	72	52
Alab.-Huntsville (11-16-4) . .10	9	1	21	65	60
Findlay (11-22-5) 7	11	2	16	58	60
Air Force (14-21-2) 6	13	1	13	49	78
Wayne State (9-24-3) 4	15	1	9	44	80

Conf. Tourney Final: Niagara 4, Bemidji St. 3 (OT).
***NCAA Tourney (0-1):** Niagara (0-1).

Eastern Collegiate Athletic Conference

	W	L	T	Pts	GF	GA
Colgate (22-12-5) 14	6	2	30	65	44
Cornell (16-10-6) 13	6	3	29	53	32
Brown (15-11-5) 13	7	2	28	62	40
Rensselaer (22-15-2) 13	8	1	27	70	44
Dartmouth (14-11-9). 10	5	7	27	66	60
*Harvard (18-15-3) 10	10	2	22	58	55
Yale (12-19-0) 10	12	0	20	65	88
Union (15-16-5). 8	11	3	19	46	52
Clarkson (18-18-5). 8	12	2	18	51	61
St. Lawrence (14-21-6) 7	12	3	17	62	67
Vermont (9-22-4) 7	14	1	15	57	79
Princeton (5-24-2) 5	15	2	12	50	83

Conf. Tourney Final: Harvard 4, Clarkson 2.
***NCAA Tourney (0-1):** Harvard (0-1).

Hockey East Association

	W	L	T	Pts	GF	GA
*Boston College (29-9-4) . .17	4	3	37	88	45
*Maine (33-8-3) 17	5	2	36	77	42
UMass-Amherst (19-12-6) . .12	9	3	27	47	63
*New Hampshire (20-15-6) 10	8	6	26	82	76
Providence (16-14-7) 7	11	6	20	63	66
UMass-Lowell (10-23-7) . . .7	12	5	19	56	65
Merrimack (11-19-6) 6	12	6	18	53	79
Boston University (12-17-9) . .6	13	5	17	57	71
Northeastern (11-16-7) 5	13	6	16	56	72

Conf. Tourney Final: Maine 2, UMass-Amherst 1 (3OT).
***NCAA Tourney (5-3):** Boston College (2-1), Maine (3-1),
New Hampshire (0-1).

Western Collegiate Hockey Assn.

	W	L	T	Pts	GF	GA
*North Dakota (30-8-3) 20	5	3	43	122	62
*Minnesota Duluth (28-13-4) .19	7	2	40	119	71
*Wisconsin (22-13-8) 14	7	7	35	85	62
*Minnesota (27-14-3) 15	12	1	31	101	86
*Denver (27-12-5) 13	10	5	31	93	90
St. Cloud St. (18-16-4) 12	12	4	28	81	89
Colorado College (20-16-3) 11	15	2	24	77	75
Alaska-Anchorage (14-23-3) . .7	18	3	17	68	103
Minnesota St. (10-24-5) 6	18	4	16	83	139
Michigan Tech (8-25-5) 6	19	3	15	66	118

Conf. Tourney Final: Minnesota 5, North Dakota 4.
***NCAA Tourney (9-4):** North Dakota (1-1), Minnesota
Duluth (2-1), Wisconsin (1-1), Minnesota (1-1), Denver (4-0).

Hobey Baker Award

For College Hockey Player of the Year. Voting is done by
a 25-member panel of college hockey personnel, national media, and pro scouts, plus a one percent fan vote.

	Cl	Pos
Winner: Junior Lessard, Minnesota Duluth . . . .Sr.	F

NCAA Division I Tournament

Regional seeds in parentheses

East Regional

Held in Albany, N.Y., March 26-27.

First Round

(1) Maine 5 . . . .(4) Harvard 4
(3) Wisconsin 1 . . . . .OT . . . .(2) Ohio St. 0

Second Round

Maine 2 . . . . .OT . . . . .Wisconsin 1

Northeast Regional

Held in Manchester, N.H., March 27-28.

First Round

(1) Boston College 5 . . . .(4) Niagara 2
(2) Michigan 4 . . . .(3) New Hampshire 1

Second Round

Boston College 3 . . . . .OT . . . . .Michigan 2

West Regional

Held in Colorado Springs, Colo., March 26-27.

First Round

(1) North Dakota 3 . . . .(4) Holy Cross 0
(2) Denver 3 . . . .(3) Miami-OH 2

Second Round

Denver 1 . . . . .North Dakota 0

Midwest Regional

Held in Grand Rapids, Mich., March 27-28.

First Round

(1) Minnesota 5 . . . . (4) Notre Dame 2
(2) Minnesota Duluth 5 . . . .(3) Michigan St. 1

Second Round

Minnesota Duluth 3 . . . . .Minnesota 1

THE FROZEN FOUR

Held at the FleetCenter in Boston, Mass., April 8 and
April 10. Single elimination; no consolation game.

Semifinals

Denver 5 .Minnesota Duluth 3
Maine 2 .Boston College 1

Championship Game

Denver, 1-0

Denver (WCHA) 1	0	0	**—1**
Maine (HEA) 0	0	0	**—0**

1st Period: DEN—Gabe Gauthier 18 (Connor James),
12:26 (pp).

Shots on Goal: Denver—4-6-10—20; Maine—6-9-
9—24. **Power plays:** Denver 1-4; Maine 0-6.

Goalies: Denver—Adam Berkhoel (24 shots, 24 saves);
Maine—Jimmy Howard (20 shots, 19 saves).

Attendance: 18,597. **Time:** 2:38.

Most Outstanding Player: Adam Berkhoel, Denver
senior goalie: SEMIFINAL—29 shots, 26 saves; FINAL—
24 shots, 24 saves.

All-Tournament Team: Berkhoel, forward Connor
James and defenseman Ryan Caldwell of Denver; for-
ward Dustin Penner and defenseman Prestin Ryan of
Maine; forward Junior Lessard of Minnesota Duluth.

USA Today/American Hockey Magazine Coaches Poll

Taken after the NCAA Tournament. First place votes are in parentheses.

		League	W	L	T	Pts
1	Denver (34)	WCHA	27	12	5	510
2	Maine	HEA	33	8	3	476
3	Boston College	HEA	29	9	4	431
4	Minnesota Duluth	WCHA	28	13	4	411
5	North Dakota	WCHA	30	8	3	379
6	Minnesota	WCHA	27	14	3	322
7	Michigan	CCHA	27	14	2	310
8	Wisconsin	WCHA	22	13	8	252
9	Ohio St.	CCHA	26	16	0	201
10	Miami-OH	CCHA	23	14	4	199

Scoring Leaders

Including postseason games; minimum 20 games.

	Cl	Gm	G	A	Pts	Avg
Jared Ross, Ala.-Huntsville	Jr.	31	19	31	50	1.61
Zach Parise, North Dakota	So.	37	23	32	55	1.49
Brandon Bochenski, N. Dak.	Jr.	41	27	33	60	1.46
Junior Lessard, Minn. Duluth	Sr.	45	32	31	63	1.40
Thomas Vanek, Minnesota	So.	38	26	25	51	1.34

Goaltending Leaders

Including postseason games; minimum 15 games.

	Cl	Record	Sv%	GAA
Jimmy Howard, Maine	So.	14-4-3	.956	1.19
Matti Kaltiainen, BC	Jr.	27-7-4	.907	1.76
Frank Doyle, Maine	Sr.	19-4-0	.923	1.81
Yann Danis, Brown	Sr.	15-11-4	.942	1.81
Steve Silverthorn, Colgate	Jr.	18-9-4	.927	1.84

Division I All-America

First team JOFA Division I All-Americans as chosen by the American Hockey Coaches Association.

West Team

Pos		Yr	Hgt	Wgt
G	Bernd Bruckler, Wisconsin	Jr	6-1	192
D	Keith Ballard, Minnesota	Jr	5-11	208
D	Ryan Caldwell, Denver	Sr	6-3	195
F	Brandon Bochenski, North Dakota	Jr	6-2	195
F	Junior Lessard, Minnesota Duluth	Sr	6-0	195
F	Zach Parise, North Dakota	So	5-11	180

East Team

Pos		Yr	Hgt	Wgt
G	Yann Danis, Brown	Sr	6-0	190
D	Andrew Alberts, Boston College	Jr	6-4	215
D	Thomas Pock, UMass-Amherst	Sr	6-1	208
F	Steve Saviano, New Hampshire	Sr	5-7	167
F	Lee Stempniak, Dartmouth	Jr	6-0	195
F	Tony Voce, Boston College	Sr	5-8	185

Division III Championship

March 19-20 in Northfield, Vt.

Semifinals

St. Norbert (Wis.) 4 . . . . Plattsburgh St. (NY) 1
Middlebury (Vt.) 3 . . . . . . 2OT . . . . Norwich (Vt.) 2

Championship

Middlebury 1 . . . . OT . . . . St. Norbert 0

Final records: Middlebury (27-3-0); St. Norbert (27-3-2); Norwich (24-4-0); Plattsburgh St. (23-5-3).

Women's College Hockey

NCAA Division I Frozen Four

Held March 26 and 28 at the Dunkin' Dounts Center in Providence, R.I. Overall seeds in parentheses.

Semifinals

(1) Minnesota 5 . . . . (4) Dartmouth 1
(2) Harvard 2 . . . . (3) St. Lawrence 1

Third Place

St. Lawrence 2 . . . . Dartmouth 1

Championship

Minnesota 6 . . . . Harvard 2

Final records: Minnesota (30-4-2); Harvard (30-4-1); St. Lawrence (28-10-1); Dartmouth (24-8-2).

Most Outstanding Player: Krissy Wendell, Minnesota sophomore forward; three goals and one assist in semifinal game, one goal and three assists in championship game.

All-Tournament Team: Wendell, forward Natalie Darwitz, forward Kelly Stephens, defenseman Allie Sanchez and goalie Jody Horak of Minnesota; defenseman Angela Ruggiero of Harvard.

NCAA Division III Championship

First round games held on campus sites of higher seed. Semifinals, Championship and Third Place games held March 19-20 at Kenyon Arena in Middlebury, Vt.

First Round

Wis.-Stevens Point 3 . . . . . 2OT . . at Gustavus Adolphus 2
at Plattsburgh St. 2 . . . . Bowdoin 1
at Middlebury 2 . . . . Elmira 1

Semifinals

Wis.-Stevens Point 4 . . . . Manhattanville 1
Middlebury 2 . . . . Plattsburgh St. 1

Third Place

Plattsburgh St. 4 . . . . Manhattanville 2

Championship

Middlebury 2 . . . . Wis.-Stevens Point 1

Final records: Middlebury (24-4-0); Wis.-Stevens Point (19-7-4); Plattsburgh St. (22-6-2); Manhattanville (23-4-2).

Patty Kazmaier Award

Awarded by the USA Hockey Foundation to the women's college hockey player of the Year. Voting is done by a 13-member panel of national media, varsity college coaches, and one USA Hockey member.

			Cl	Pos
Winner:	Angela Ruggiero, Harvard		Sr	D

MINOR LEAGUE HOCKEY

American Hockey League

Division champions (*) and playoff qualifiers (†) are noted. T denotes any game that was tied after regulation play and a five-minute overtime period. OL signifies any game that was tied after regulation play but lost in overtime. They are each worth one point in the standings.

Eastern Conference

Atlantic Division

Team (Affiliate)	W	L	T	OL	Pts	GF	GA
*Hartford (NYR)	44	22	12	2	102	198	153
†Manchester (LA)	40	28	7	5	92	223	181
†Worcester (St.L)	37	27	13	3	90	207	186
†Providence (Bos)	36	29	11	4	87	170	170
†Portland (Wash)	32	27	13	8	85	156	160
Lowell (Car/Calg)	32	36	6	6	76	208	242
Springfield (Pho/TB)	26	43	9	2	63	179	234

East Division

Team (Affiliate)	W	L	T	OL	Pts	GF	GA
*Philadelphia (Phi)	46	25	7	2	101	216	168
†Bridgeport (NYI)	41	23	12	4	98	178	140
†Wilkes-Barre (Pit)	34	28	10	8	86	197	197
†Binghamton (Ott)	34	34	9	3	80	210	216
†Norfolk (Chi)	35	36	4	5	79	172	187
Hershey (TB/Col)	33	34	8	5	78	203	218
Albany (NJ)	21	39	11	9	62	182	257

Western Conference

North Division

Team (Affiliate)	W	L	T	OL	Pts	GF	GA
*Hamilton (Mon)	41	25	10	4	96	235	191
†Syracuse (Clb)	38	25	10	7	93	239	235
†Rochester (Buf)	37	28	10	5	89	207	188
†Cleveland (SJ)	37	28	8	7	89	235	220
†Toronto (Edm)	35	34	8	3	81	219	224
Manitoba (Van)	32	35	11	2	77	214	232
St. John's (Tor)	32	36	8	4	76	225	265

West Division

Team (Affiliate)	W	L	T	OL	Pts	GF	GA
*Milwaukee (Nash)	46	24	7	3	102	269	191
†Grand Rapids (Det)	44	28	8	0	96	195	166
†Chicago (Atl)	42	26	9	3	96	246	208
†Houston (Min)	28	34	14	4	74	197	220
†Cincinnati (Ana)	29	37	13	1	72	188	211
San Antonio (Fla)	30	42	8	0	68	191	231
Utah (Dal)	27	42	6	5	65	162	230

Scoring Leaders

	Gm	G	A	Pts	PM
Pavel Rosa, Man.	77	39	49	88	32
Domenic Pittis, Roch	75	20	57	77	137
Miroslav Zalesak, Cle	72	35	40	75	80
Eric Perrin, Her.	71	21	54	75	49
Kirby Law, Phi	74	32	41	73	139

Goaltending Leaders

(At least 1590 minutes)	GP	GAA	Sv%	Record
Wade Dubielewicz, Bri	33	1.38	.946	20-8-5
Jason LaBarbera, Har	59	1.59	.936	34-9-9
Tim Thomas, Pro	43	1.84	.941	20-16-6

Calder Cup Finals

	W-L	GF	Leading Scorers
Milwaukee	4-0	19	Gamache (2-7–9)
Wilkes-Barre	0-4	8	Boileau (1-3–4)

Date	Winner	Home Ice
June 1	Milwaukee, 2-1 (OT)	at Milwaukee
June 2	Milwaukee, 8-4	at Milwaukee
June 4	Milwaukee, 2-1 (OT)	at Wilkes-Barre
June 6	Milwaukee, 7-2	at Wilkes-Barre

Playoff MVP

Wade Flaherty, Milwaukee, G
16-5, 1.93 GAA, .932 save pct., 1 ShO

2004 IIHF World Hockey Championships

MEN

Held April 24-May 9 in Prague and Ostrava, CZE.

Quarterfinals

Sweden 4	Latvia 1
United States 3 OT	Czech Republic 2
Canada 5 OT	Finland 4
Slovakia 3	Switzerland 1

Semifinals

Canada 2	Slovakia 1
Sweden 3	United States 2

Bronze Medal Game

United States 1 OT	Slovakia 0

Gold Medal Game

Canada 5	Sweden 3

All-Tournament First Team (selected by media): **G—** Henrik Lundqvist, Sweden; **D—** Zdeno Chara, Slovakia and Dick Tarnstrom, Sweden; **F—** Dany Heatley, Canada (MVP), Ville Peltonen, Finland and Jaromir Jagr, Czech Republic.

WOMEN

Held March 30-April 6 in Halifax and Dartmouth, Nova Scotia, CAN.

Bronze Medal Game

Finland 3	Sweden 2

Gold Medal Game

Canada 2	United States 0

All-Tournament First Team (selected by media): **G—** Pam Dreyer, United States; **D—** Angela Ruggiero, United States and Gunilla Anderson, Sweden; **F—** Jennifer Botterill, Canada (MVP), Natalie Darwitz, United States and Jayna Hefford, Canada.

2004 WORLD CUP OF HOCKEY

The second World Cup of Hockey, held in North America (Toronto, Montreal and St. Paul) and Europe (Stockholm, Helsinki, Prague and Cologne) from August 30 to Sept. 14. The tournament featured the top players from eight of the top hockey nations in the world and was a joint venture between the NHL and NHL Players' Association in cooperation with the International Ice Hockey Federation (IIHF).

All teams advance to the single-elimination quarterfinals after round-robin play. Round-robin standings determined the seedings and sites for the quarterfinal round.

Semifinal games were predetermined to be held at the XCel Energy Center in St. Paul and the Air Canada Centre in Toronto. The site of the championship game was determined by a coin toss (Canada won the toss so the game was held at the Air Canada Centre).

Final Round Robin Standings

European Pool	W-L-T	Pts	GF	GA
Finland	2-0-1	5	11	4
Sweden	2-0-1	5	13	9
Czech Republic	1-2-0	2	10	10
Germany	0-3-0	0	4	15

Note: While Finland and Sweden each ended the round-robin competition with five points, Finland was awarded the top seed due to a better goal differential (+7 to +4).

North American Pool	W-L-T	Pts	GF	GA
Canada	3-0-0	6	10	3
Russia	2-1-0	4	9	6
United States	1-2-0	2	5	6
Slovakia	0-3-0	0	4	13

Quarterfinals

European

(1) Finland 2	(4) Germany 1
(3) Czech Republic 6	(2) Sweden 1

North American

(1) Canada 5	(4) Slovakia 0
(3) United States 5	(2) Russia 3

Semifinals

Finland 2 ....United States 1
Canada 4 ....OT ......Czech Republic 3

Championship Game

Canada 3 ....Finland 2

Tournament MVP
Vincent Lecavalier, F, Canada

All-Tournament Team
Forwards:	Vincent Lecavalier, Canada
	Saku Koivu, Finland
	Fredrik Modin, Sweden
Defensemen:	Kimmo Timonen, Finland
	Adam Foote, Canada
Goaltender:	Martin Brodeur, Canada

Scoring Leaders

	Gm	G	A	Pts	PM
Fredrik Modin, Sweden	4	4	4	8	2
Vincent Lecavalier, Canada	6	2	5	7	8
Keith Tkachuk, United States	5	5	1	6	23
Joe Sakic, Canada	6	4	2	6	2
Martin Havlat, Czech Republic	5	3	3	6	2
Kimmo Timonen, Finland	6	1	5	6	2
Joe Thornton, Canada	6	1	5	6	0
Mike Modano, United States	5	0	6	6	0
Daniel Alfredsson, Sweden	4	0	6	6	2
Patrik Elias, Czech Republic	5	3	2	5	10
Milan Hejduk, Czech Republic	4	3	2	5	2
Tomas Holmstrom, Sweden	4	3	2	5	8
Mario Lemieux, Canada	6	1	4	5	2
Mats Sundin, Sweden	4	1	4	5	0

Twelve tied with 4 pts. each.

Goaltending Leaders

(At least 120 minutes)	Gm	Min	Sv%	GAA
Martin Brodeur, Canada	5	300	.961	**1.00**
Miikka Kiprusoff, Finland	6	363	.940	**1.48**
Ilja Bryzgalov, Russia	3	179	.897	**2.34**
Robert Esche, United States	4	237	.909	**2.53**
Tomas Vokoun, Czech Republic	5	302	.881	**2.98**
Olaf Kolzig, Germany	3	179	.905	**3.34**
Mikael Tellqvist, Sweden	3	178	.875	**4.03**
Jan Lasak, Slovakia	3	151	.833	**4.75**

Championship Game Box
Canada, 3-2

Tuesday, Sept. 14 at the Air Canada Centre in Toronto

Finland	1	1	0	**—2**
Canada	1	1	1	**—3**

1st Period: CAN—Joe Sakic 4 (Mario Lemieux, Eric Brewer), 0:52; FIN—Riku Hahl 1 (Toni Lydman, Aki Berg), 6:34.

2nd Period: CAN—Scott Niedermayer 1 (Chris Draper, Joe Thornton), 3:15; FIN—Tuomo Ruutu 1 (Lydman), 19:00.

3rd Period: CAN—Shane Doan 1 (Thornton, Adam Foote), 0:34.

Shots on Goal: Finland—7-12-10—29; Canada—9-12-12—33. **Power plays:** Finland 0-1; Canada 0-1.

Goalies: Finland—Miikka Kiprusoff (33 shots, 30 saves); Canada—Martin Brodeur (29 shots, 27 saves).

Attendance: 19,370.

1893-2004
Through the Years

SPORTS ALMANAC

The Stanley Cup

The Stanley Cup was originally donated to the Canadian Amateur Hockey Association by Sir Frederick Arthur Stanley, Lord Stanley of Preston and 16th Earl of Derby, who had become interested in the sport while Governor General of Canada from 1888 to 1893. Stanley wanted the trophy to be a challenge cup, contested for each year by the best amateur hockey teams in Canada.

In 1893, the Cup was presented without a challenge to the AHA champion Montreal Amateur Athletic Association team. Every year since, however, there has been a playoff. In 1914, Cup trustees limited the field challenging for the trophy to the champion of the eastern professional National Hockey Association (NHA, organized in 1910) and the western professional Pacific Coast Hockey Association (PCHA, organized in 1912).

The NHA disbanded in 1917 and the National Hockey League (NHL) was formed. From 1918 to 1926, the NHL and PCHA champions played for the Cup with the Western Canada Hockey League (WCHL) champion joining in a three-way challenge in 1923 and '24. The PCHA disbanded in 1924, while the WCHL became the Western Hockey League (WHL) for the 1925-26 season and folded the following year. The NHL playoffs have decided the winner of the Stanley Cup ever since.

Champions, 1893-1917

Multiple winners: Montreal Victorias and Montreal Wanderers (4); Montreal Amateur Athletic Association and Ottawa Silver Seven (3); Montreal Shamrocks, Ottawa Senators, Quebec Bulldogs and Winnipeg Victorias (2).

Year		Year		Year	
1893	Montreal AAA	1901	Winnipeg Victorias	1909	Ottawa Senators
1894	Montreal AAA	1902	Montreal AAA	1910	Montreal Wanderers
1895	Montreal Victorias	1903	Ottawa Silver Seven	1911	Ottawa Senators
1896	(Feb.) Winnipeg Victorias	1904	Ottawa Silver Seven	1912	Quebec Bulldogs
	(Dec.) Montreal Victorias	1905	Ottawa Silver Seven	1913	Quebec Bulldogs
1897	Montreal Victorias	1906	Montreal Wanderers	1914	Toronto Blueshirts (NHA)
1898	Montreal Victorias	1907	(Jan.) Kenora Thistles	1915	Vancouver Millionaires (PCHA)
1899	Montreal Shamrocks		(Mar.) Montreal Wanderers	1916	Montreal Canadiens (NHA)
1900	Montreal Shamrocks	1908	Montreal Wanderers	1917	Seattle Metropolitans (PCHA)

Champions Since 1918

Multiple winners: Montreal Canadiens (23); Toronto Arenas-St. Pats-Maple Leafs (13); Detroit Red Wings (10); Boston Bruins and Edmonton Oilers (5); NY Islanders, NY Rangers and Ottawa Senators (4); Chicago Blackhawks and New Jersey Devils (3); Colorado Avalanche, Montreal Maroons, Philadelphia Flyers and Pittsburgh Penguins (2).

Year	Winner	Head Coach	Series	Loser	Head Coach
1918	Toronto Arenas	Dick Carroll	3-2 (WLWLW)	Vancouver (PCHA)	Frank Patrick
1919	No Decision*				
1920	Ottawa	Pete Green	3-2 (WWLLW)	Seattle (PCHA)	Pete Muldoon
1921	Ottawa	Pete Green	3-2 (LWWLW)	Vancouver (PCHA)	Frank Patrick
1922	Toronto St. Pats	Eddie Powers	3-2 (LWLWW)	Vancouver (PCHA)	Frank Patrick
1923	Ottawa	Pete Green	3-1 (WLWW)	Vancouver (PCHA)	Frank Patrick
			2-0	Edmonton (WCHL)	K.C. McKenzie
1924	Montreal	Leo Dandurand	2-0	Vancouver (PCHA)	Frank Patrick
			2-0	Calgary (WCHL)	Eddie Oatman
1925	Victoria (WCHL)	Lester Patrick	3-1 (WWLW)	Montreal	Leo Dandurand
1926	Montreal Maroons	Eddie Gerard	3-1 (WWLW)	Victoria (WHL)	Lester Patrick
1927	Ottawa	Dave Gill	2-0-2 (TWTW)	Boston	Art Ross
1928	NY Rangers	Lester Patrick	3-2 (LWLWW)	Montreal Maroons	Eddie Gerard
1929	Boston	Cy Denneny	2-0	NY Rangers	Lester Patrick
1930	Montreal	Cecil Hart	2-0	Boston	Art Ross
1931	Montreal	Cecil Hart	3-2 (WLLWW)	Chicago	Art Duncan
1932	Toronto	Dick Irvin	3-0	NY Rangers	Lester Patrick
1933	NY Rangers	Lester Patrick	3-1 (WWLW)	Toronto	Dick Irvin
1934	Chicago	Tommy Gorman	3-1 (WWLW)	Detroit	Jack Adams
1935	Montreal Maroons	Tommy Gorman	3-0	Toronto	Dick Irvin
1936	Detroit	Jack Adams	3-1 (WWLW)	Toronto	Dick Irvin
1937	Detroit	Jack Adams	3-2 (LWLWW)	NY Rangers	Lester Patrick
1938	Chicago	Bill Stewart	3-1 (WWLW)	Toronto	Dick Irvin
1939	Boston	Art Ross	4-1 (WLWWW)	Toronto	Dick Irvin

* The 1919 finals were cancelled after five games due to an influenza epidemic with Montreal and Seattle (PCHA) tied at 2-2-1.

The Stanley Cup (Cont.)

Year	Winner	Head Coach	Series	Loser	Head Coach
1940	NY Rangers	Frank Boucher	4-2 (WWLLWW)	Toronto	Dick Irvin
1941	Boston	Cooney Weiland	4-0	Detroit	Jack Adams
1942	Toronto	Hap Day	4-3 (LLLWWWW)	Detroit	Jack Adams
1943	Detroit	Ebbie Goodfellow	4-0	Boston	Art Ross
1944	Montreal	Dick Irvin	4-0	Chicago	Paul Thompson
1945	Toronto	Hap Day	4-3 (WWWLLLW)	Detroit	Jack Adams
1946	Montreal	Dick Irvin	4-1 (WWWLW)	Boston	Dit Clapper
1947	Toronto	Hap Day	4-2 (LWWWLW)	Montreal	Dick Irvin
1948	Toronto	Hap Day	4-0	Detroit	Tommy Ivan
1949	Toronto	Hap Day	4-0	Detroit	Tommy Ivan
1950	Detroit	Tommy Ivan	4-3 (WLWLLWW)	NY Rangers	Lynn Patrick
1951	Toronto	Joe Primeau	4-1 (WLWWW)	Montreal	Dick Irvin
1952	Detroit	Tommy Ivan	4-0	Montreal	Dick Irvin
1953	Montreal	Dick Irvin	4-1 (WLWWW)	Boston	Lynn Patrick
1954	Detroit	Tommy Ivan	4-3 (WLWLLWW)	Montreal	Dick Irvin
1955	Detroit	Jimmy Skinner	4-3 (WWLLWLW)	Montreal	Dick Irvin
1956	Montreal	Toe Blake	4-1 (WWLWW)	Detroit	Jimmy Skinner
1957	Montreal	Toe Blake	4-1 (WWLWW)	Boston	Milt Schmidt
1958	Montreal	Toe Blake	4-2 (WLWLWW)	Boston	Milt Schmidt
1959	Montreal	Toe Blake	4-1 (WWLWW)	Toronto	Punch Imlach
1960	Montreal	Toe Blake	4-0	Toronto	Punch Imlach
1961	Chicago	Rudy Pilous	4-2 (WLWLWW)	Detroit	Sid Abel
1962	Toronto	Punch Imlach	4-2 (WWLLWW)	Chicago	Rudy Pilous
1963	Toronto	Punch Imlach	4-1 (WWLWW)	Detroit	Sid Abel
1964	Toronto	Punch Imlach	4-3 (WLLWLWW)	Detroit	Sid Abel
1965	Montreal	Toe Blake	4-3 (WWLLWLW)	Chicago	Billy Reay
1966	Montreal	Toe Blake	4-2 (LLWWWW)	Detroit	Sid Abel
1967	Toronto	Punch Imlach	4-2 (LWWLWW)	Montreal	Toe Blake
1968	Montreal	Toe Blake	4-0	St. Louis	Scotty Bowman
1969	Montreal	Claude Ruel	4-0	St. Louis	Scotty Bowman
1970	Boston	Harry Sinden	4-0	St. Louis	Scotty Bowman
1971	Montreal	Al MacNeil	4-3 (LLWWLWW)	Chicago	Billy Reay
1972	Boston	Tom Johnson	4-2 (WWLWLW)	NY Rangers	Emile Francis
1973	Montreal	Scotty Bowman	4-2 (WWLWLW)	Chicago	Billy Reay
1974	Philadelphia	Fred Shero	4-2 (LWWWLW)	Boston	Bep Guidolin
1975	Philadelphia	Fred Shero	4-2 (WWLLWW)	Buffalo	Floyd Smith
1976	Montreal	Scotty Bowman	4-0	Philadelphia	Fred Shero
1977	Montreal	Scotty Bowman	4-0	Boston	Don Cherry
1978	Montreal	Scotty Bowman	4-2 (WWLLWW)	Boston	Don Cherry
1979	Montreal	Scotty Bowman	4-1 (LWWWW)	NY Rangers	Fred Shero
1980	NY Islanders	Al Arbour	4-2 (WLWWLW)	Philadelphia	Pat Quinn
1981	NY Islanders	Al Arbour	4-1 (WWWLW)	Minnesota	Glen Sonmor
1982	NY Islanders	Al Arbour	4-0	Vancouver	Roger Neilson
1983	NY Islanders	Al Arbour	4-0	Edmonton	Glen Sather
1984	Edmonton	Glen Sather	4-1 (WLWWW)	NY Islanders	Al Arbour
1985	Edmonton	Glen Sather	4-1 (LWWWW)	Philadelphia	Mike Keenan
1986	Montreal	Jean Perron	4-1 (LWWWW)	Calgary	Bob Johnson
1987	Edmonton	Glen Sather	4-3 (WWLWLLW)	Philadelphia	Mike Keenan
1988	Edmonton	Glen Sather	4-0	Boston	Terry O'Reilly
1989	Calgary	Terry Crisp	4-2 (WLLWWW)	Montreal	Pat Burns
1990	Edmonton	John Muckler	4-1 (WWLWW)	Boston	Mike Milbury
1991	Pittsburgh	Bob Johnson	4-2 (LWLWLWW)	Minnesota	Bob Gainey
1992	Pittsburgh	Scotty Bowman	4-0	Chicago	Mike Keenan
1993	Montreal	Jacques Demers	4-1 (LWWWW)	Los Angeles	Barry Melrose
1994	NY Rangers	Mike Keenan	4-3 (LWWWLLW)	Vancouver	Pat Quinn
1995	New Jersey	Jacques Lemaire	4-0	Detroit	Scotty Bowman
1996	Colorado	Marc Crawford	4-0	Florida	Doug MacLean
1997	Detroit	Scotty Bowman	4-0	Philadelphia	Terry Murray
1998	Detroit	Scotty Bowman	4-0	Washington	Ron Wilson
1999	Dallas	Ken Hitchcock	4-2 (LWWLWW)	Buffalo	Lindy Ruff
2000	New Jersey	Larry Robinson	4-2 (WLWWLW)	Dallas	Ken Hitchcock
2001	Colorado	Bob Hartley	4-3 (WLWLLWW)	New Jersey	Larry Robinson
2002	Detroit	Scotty Bowman	4-1 (LWWWW)	Carolina	Paul Maurice
2003	New Jersey	Pat Burns	4-3 (WWLLWLW)	Anaheim	Mike Babcock
2004	Tampa Bay	John Tortorella	4-3 (LWLWLWW)	Calgary	Darryl Sutter

M.J. O'Brien Trophy

Donated by Canadian mining magnate M.J. O'Brien, whose son Ambróse founded the National Hockey Association in 1910. Originally presented to the NHA champion until the league's demise in 1917, the trophy then passed to the NHL champion through 1927. It was awarded to the NHL's Canadian Division winner from 1927-38 and the Stanley Cup runner-up from 1939-50 before being retired in 1950.

NHA winners included the Montreal Wanderers (1910), original Ottawa Senators (1911 and '15), Quebec Bulldogs (1912 and '13), Toronto Blueshirts (1914) and Montreal Canadiens (1916 and '17).

Conn Smythe Trophy

The Most Valuable Player of the Stanley Cup Playoffs, as selected by the Pro Hockey Writers Association. Presented since 1965 by Maple Leaf Gardens Limited in the name of the former Toronto coach, GM and owner, Conn Smythe. Winners who did not play for the Cup champion are in **bold** type.

Multiple winners: Patrick Roy (3); Wayne Gretzky, Mario Lemieux, Bobby Orr and Bernie Parent (2).

Year		Year		Year	
1965	Jean Beliveau, Mon., C	1979	Bob Gainey, Mon., LW	1993	Patrick Roy, Mon., G
1966	**Roger Crozier**, Det., G	1980	Bryan Trottier, NYI, C	1994	Brian Leetch, NYR, D
1967	Dave Keon, Tor., C	1981	Butch Goring, NYI, C	1995	Claude Lemieux, NJ, RW
1968	**Glenn Hall**, St.L., G	1982	Mike Bossy, NYI, RW	1996	Joe Sakic, Col., C
1969	Serge Savard, Mon., D	1983	Billy Smith, NYI, G	1997	Mike Vernon, Det., G
1970	Bobby Orr, Bos., D	1984	Mark Messier, Edm., LW	1998	Steve Yzerman, Det., C
1971	Ken Dryden, Mon., G	1985	Wayne Gretzky, Edm., C	1999	Joe Nieuwendyk, Dal., C
1972	Bobby Orr, Bos., D	1986	Patrick Roy, Mon., G	2000	Scott Stevens, NJ, D
1973	Yvan Cournoyer, Mon., RW	1987	**Ron Hextall**, Phi., G	2001	Patrick Roy, Col., G
1974	Bernie Parent, Phi., G	1988	Wayne Gretzky, Edm., C	2002	Nicklas Lidstrom, Det., D
1975	Bernie Parent, Phi., G	1989	Al MacInnis, Calg., D	2003	**J-S Giguere**, Ana., G
1976	**Reggie Leach**, Phi., RW	1990	Bill Ranford, Edm., G	2004	Brad Richards, TB, C
1977	Guy Lafleur, Mon., RW	1991	Mario Lemieux, Pit., C		
1978	Larry Robinson, Mon., D	1992	Mario Lemieux, Pit., C		

Note: Ken Dryden (1971) and Patrick Roy (1986) are the only players to win as rookies.

All-Time Stanley Cup Playoff Leaders

CAREER

Stanley Cup Playoff leaders through 2004. Years listed indicate number of playoff appearances. Players active in 2004 are in **bold** type; (DNP) indicates player that was active in 2004 but did not participate in playoffs.

Scoring

Points

		Yrs	Gm	G	A	Pts
1	Wayne Gretzky	16	208	122	260	382
2	**Mark Messier** (DNP)	17	236	109	186	295
3	Jari Kurri	14	200	106	127	233
4	Glenn Anderson	15	225	93	121	214
5	Paul Coffey	16	194	59	137	196
6	**Brett Hull**	19	202	103	87	190
7	Doug Gilmour	17	182	60	128	188
8	Bryan Trottier	17	221	71	113	184
9	**Steve Yzerman**	19	192	70	111	181
10	Ray Bourque	21	214	41	139	180
11	Jean Beliveau	17	162	79	97	176
12	Denis Savard	16	169	66	109	175
13	**Mario Lemieux** (DNP)	8	107	76	96	172
14	**Joe Sakic**	11	153	78	91	169
15	Denis Potvin	14	185	56	108	164
16	**Sergei Fedorov** (DNP)	13	162	50	113	163
17	Mike Bossy	10	129	85	75	160
	Gordie Howe	20	157	68	92	160
	Bobby Smith	13	184	64	96	160
	Al MacInnis (DNP)	19	177	39	121	160
21	Claude Lemieux	17	233	80	78	158
22	**Adam Oates** (DNP)	15	163	42	114	156
23	**Jaromir Jagr** (DNP)	12	146	67	87	154
	Peter Forsberg	10	133	57	97	154
25	Larry Murphy	20	215	37	115	152

Goals

		Yrs	Gm	G
1	Wayne Gretzky	16	208	122
2	**Mark Messier** (DNP)	17	236	109
3	Jari Kurri	15	200	106
4	**Brett Hull**	19	202	103
5	Glenn Anderson	15	225	93
6	Mike Bossy	10	129	85
7	Maurice Richard	15	133	82
8	Claude Lemieux	17	233	80
9	Jean Beliveau	17	162	79
10	**Joe Sakic**	11	153	78

Assists

		Yrs	Gm	A
1	Wayne Gretzky	16	208	260
2	**Mark Messier** (DNP)	17	236	186
3	Ray Bourque	21	214	139
4	Paul Coffey	16	194	137
5	Doug Gilmour	17	182	128
6	Jari Kurri	15	200	127
7	Glenn Anderson	15	225	121
	Al MacInnis (DNP)	19	177	121
9	Larry Robinson	20	227	116
10	Larry Murphy	20	215	115

The Stanley Cup (Cont.)

Goaltending
Wins

		Gm	W-L	Pct	GAA
1	Patrick Roy	247	151-94	.616	2.30
2	Grant Fuhr	150	92-50	.648	2.92
3	Billy Smith	132	88-36	.710	2.73
	Ed Belfour	161	88-68	.564	2.17
5	**Martin Brodeur**	144	84-60	.583	1.87
6	Ken Dryden	112	80-32	.714	2.40
7	Mike Vernon	138	77-56	.579	2.68
8	Jacques Plante	112	71-37	.657	2.17
9	Andy Moog	132	68-57	.544	3.04
10	**Curtis Joseph**	131	62-66	.484	2.44

Shutouts

		Gm	GAA	No
1	Patrick Roy	247	2.30	23
2	**Martin Brodeur**	144	1.87	20
3	**Curtis Joseph**	131	2.44	16
4	Clint Benedict	48	1.80	15
	Jacques Plante	112	2.17	15

Appearances in Cup Finals
Standings of all teams that have reached the Stanley Cup championship round, since 1918.

App		Cups	Last Won
32	Montreal Canadiens	23 *	1993
22	Detroit Red Wings	10	2002
21	Toronto Maple Leafs	13 †	1967
17	Boston Bruins	5	1972
10	New York Rangers	4	1994
10	Chicago Blackhawks	3	1961
7	Philadelphia Flyers	2	1975
6	Edmonton Oilers	5	1990
5	New York Islanders	4	1983
5	Vancouver Millionaires (PCHA)	0	—
4	(original) Ottawa Senators	4	1927
4	Minnesota/Dallas (North) Stars	1	1999
4	New Jersey Devils	3	2003
3	Montreal Maroons	2	1935
3	Calgary Flames	1	1989
3	St. Louis Blues	0	—
2	Colorado Avalanche	2	2001
2	Pittsburgh Penguins	2	1992
2	Victoria Cougars (WCHL-WHL)	1	1925
2	Buffalo Sabres	0	—
2	Seattle Metropolitans (PCHA)	0	—
2	Vancouver Canucks	0	—
1	Tampa Bay Lightning	1	2004
1	Mighty Ducks of Anaheim	0	—
1	Calgary Tigers (WCHL)	0	—
1	Carolina Hurricanes	0	—
1	Edmonton Eskimos (WCHL)	0	—
1	Florida Panthers	0	—
1	Los Angeles Kings	0	—
1	Washington Capitals	0	—

*Les Canadiens also won the Cup in 1916 for a total of 24. Also, their final with Seattle in 1919 was cancelled due to an influenza epidemic that claimed the life of the Habs' Joe Hall.
†Toronto has won the Cup under three nicknames—Arenas (1918), St. Pats (1922) and Maple Leafs (1932,42,45,47-49,51,62-64,67).
Teams now defunct (7): Calgary Tigers, Edmonton Eskimos, Montreal Maroons, (original) Ottawa Senators, Seattle, Vancouver Millionaires and Victoria. Edmonton (1923) and Calgary (1924) represented the WCHL and later the WHL, while Vancouver (1918,1921-24) and Seattle (1919-20) played out of the PCHA.

Goals Against Average
Minimum of 50 games played

		Gm	Min	GA	GAA
1	**Martin Brodeur**	144	9000	280	1.87
2	George Hainsworth	52	3486	112	1.93
3	Turk Broda	101	6389	211	1.98
4	**Dominik Hasek** (DNP)	97	5972	202	2.03
5	Jacques Plante	112	6652	240	2.16
6	**Ed Belfour**	161	9945	359	2.17
7	**Chris Osgood**	87	5085	190	2.24
8	**Nikolai Khabibulin**	57	3464	131	2.27
9	Patrick Roy	247	15209	584	2.30
10	Ken Dryden	112	6846	274	2.40

Note: Clint Benedict had an average of 1.80 but played in only 48 games.

Games Played

		Yrs	Gm
1	Patrick Roy, Mon-Col	17	247
2	**Ed Belfour**, Chi-Dal-Tor	13	161
3	Grant Fuhr, Edm-Buf-St.L	14	150
4	**Martin Brodeur**, New Jersey	11	144
5	Mike Vernon, Calg-Det-SJ-Fla	14	138

Miscellaneous
Championships

		Yrs	Cups
1	Henri Richard, Montreal	18	11
2	Yvan Cournoyer, Montreal	15	10
	Jean Beliveau, Montreal	17	10
4	Claude Provost, Montreal	14	9
5	Jacques Lemaire, Montreal	11	8
	Maurice Richard, Montreal	15	8
	Red Kelly, Detroit-Toronto	19	8

Years in Playoffs

		Yrs	Gm
1	Ray Bourque, Boston-Colorado	21	214
2	Gordie Howe, Detroit-Hartford	20	157
	Larry Robinson, Montreal-Los Angeles	20	227
	Larry Murphy, LA-Wash-Min-Pit-Tor-Det	20	215
	Scott Stevens, Wash-St.L-NJ (DNP)	20	233
	Chris Chelios, Mon-Chi-Det	20	222

Games Played

		Yrs	Gm
1	**Mark Messier**, Edm-NYR-Van (DNP)	17	236
2	Claude Lemieux, Mon-NJ-Col-Pho-Dal	17	233
	Scott Stevens, Wash-St.L-NJ (DNP)	20	233
4	Guy Carbonneau, Mon-St.L-Dal	17	231
5	Larry Robinson, Montreal-Los Angeles	20	227

Penalty Minutes

		Yrs	Gm	Min
1	Dale Hunter, Que-Wash-Col	18	186	729
2	Chris Nilan, Mon-NYR-Bos-Mon	12	111	541
3	Claude Lemieux, Mon-NJ-Col-Pho-Dal	17	233	529
4	Rick Tocchet, Phi-Pit-Bos-Pho	13	145	471
5	Willi Plett, Atl-Calg-Min-Bos	10	83	466

Five Longest Playoff Overtime Games

The 5 longest overtime games in Stanley Cup history. Note the following Series initials: SF (semifinals), CQF (conference quarterfinal), CSF (conference semifinal), DSF (division semifinal), QF (quarterfinal) and Final (Cup final). Series winners are in **bold** type; (*) indicates deciding game of series.

		OTs	Elapsed Time	Goal Scorer	Date	Series	Location
1	**Detroit** 1, Montreal Maroons 0	6	176:30	Mud Bruneteau	3/24/36	SF, Gm 1	Montreal
2	**Toronto** 1, Boston 0	6	164:46	Ken Doraty	4/3/33	SF, Gm 5	Toronto
3	**Philadelphia** 2, Pittsburgh 1	5	152:01	Keith Primeau	5/4/00	CSF, Gm 4	Pittsburgh
4	**Anaheim** 4, Dallas 3	5	140:48	Petr Sykora	4/24/03	CSF, Gm 1	Dallas
5	**Pittsburgh** 3 Washington 2	4	139:15	Petr Nedved	4/24/96	CQF, Gm 4	Washington

SINGLE SEASON

Points

		Year	Gm	G	A	Pts
1	Wayne Gretzky, Edm	1985	18	17	30	47
2	Mario Lemieux, Pit	1991	23	16	28	44
3	Wayne Gretzky, Edm	1988	19	12	31	43
4	Wayne Gretzky, LA	1993	24	15	25	40
5	Wayne Gretzky, Edm	1983	16	12	26	38
6	Paul Coffey, Edm	1985	18	12	25	37
7	Mike Bossy, NYI	1981	18	17	18	35
	Wayne Gretzky, Edm	1984	19	13	22	35
	Doug Gilmour, Tor	1993	21	10	25	35
10	Six tied with 34 each.					

Goals

		Year	Gm	No
1	Reggie Leach, Philadelphia	1976	16	19
	Jari Kurri, Edmonton	1985	18	19
3	Joe Sakic, Colorado	1996	22	18
4	Seven tied with 17 each, incl. 3 times by Mike Bossy.			

Assists

		Year	Gm	No
1	Wayne Gretzky, Edmonton	1988	19	31
2	Wayne Gretzky, Edmonton	1985	18	30
3	Wayne Gretzky, Edmonton	1987	21	29
4	Mario Lemieux, Pittsburgh	1991	23	28
5	Wayne Gretzky, Edmonton	1983	16	26

Goaltending

Wins

1 Sixteen tied with 16 each.

Shutouts

		Year	Gm	No
1	Martin Brodeur, New Jersey	2003	24	7
2	Dominik Hasek, Detroit	2002	23	6
3	J-S Giguere, Anaheim	2003	21	5
	Nikolai Khabibulin, Tampa Bay	2004	23	5
	Miikka Kiprusoff, Calgary	2004	26	5

Goals Against Average

(Min. 8 games played)	Year	Gm	Min	GA	GAA
1 Terry Sawchuk, Det	1952	8	480	5	0.63
2 Clint Benedict, Mon-M	1928	9	555	8	0.89
3 Turk Broda, Tor	1951	9	509	9	1.06
4 Dave Kerr, NYR	1937	9	553	10	1.11
5 Jacques Plante, Mon	1960	8	489	11	1.35

Note: Average determined by games played through 1942-43 season and by minutes played since then.

SINGLE SERIES

Points

		Year	Rd	G-A—Pts
Rick Middleton, Bos vs Buf		1983	DF	5-14—19
Wayne Gretzky, Edm vs Chi		1985	CF	4-14—18
Mario Lemieux, Pit vs Wash		1992	DSF	7-10—17
Barry Pederson, Bos vs Buf		1983	DF	7-9—16
Doug Gilmour, Tor vs SJ		1994	CSF	3-13—16

Goals

	Year	Rd	No
Jari Kurri, Edm vs Chi	1985	CF	12
Newsy Lalonde, Mon vs Ott	1919	SF*	11
Tim Kerr, Phi vs Pit	1989	DF	10
Five tied with 9 each.			

*NHL final prior to Stanley Cup series with Seattle (PCHA).

Assists

	Year	Rd	No
Rick Middleton, Bos vs Buf	1983	DF	14
Wayne Gretzky, Edm vs Chi	1985	CF	14
Wayne Gretzky, Edm vs LA	1987	DSF	13
Doug Gilmour, Tor vs SJ	1994	CSF	13
Four tied with 11 each.			

SINGLE GAME

Points

	Date	G	A	Pts
Patrik Sundstrom, NJ vs Wash	4/22/88	3	5	8
Mario Lemieux, Pit vs Phi	4/25/89	5	3	8
Wayne Gretzky, Edm at Calg	4/17/83	4	3	7
Wayne Gretzky, Edm at Win	4/25/85	3	4	7
Wayne Gretzky, Edm vs LA	4/9/87	1	6	7

Goals

	Date	No
Newsy Lalonde, Mon vs Ott	3/1/19	5
Maurice Richard, Mon vs Tor	3/23/44	5
Darryl Sittler, Tor vs Phi	4/22/76	5
Reggie Leach, Phi vs Bos	5/6/76	5
Mario Lemieux, Pit vs Phi	4/25/89	5

Assists

	Date	No
Mikko Leinonen, NYR vs Phi	4/8/82	6
Wayne Gretzky, Edm vs LA	4/9/87	6
11 tied with 5 each.		

NHL All-Star Game

Three benefit NHL All-Star Games were staged in the 1930s for forward Ace Bailey and the families of Howie Morenz and Babe Siebert. Bailey, of Toronto, suffered a fractured skull on a career-ending check by Boston's Eddie Shore. Morenz, the Montreal Canadiens' legend, died of a heart attack at 35 after a severely broken leg ended his career. Siebert, who played with both Montreal teams, drowned at age 35.

The All-Star Game was revived at the start of the 1947-48 season as an annual exhibition match between the defending Stanley Cup champion and all-stars from the league's other five teams. The format has changed several times since then. The game was moved to midseason in 1966-67 and became an East vs. West contest in 1968-69. The Eastern (East, 1968-1974; Wales, 1975-93) Conference leads the series 19-8-1. From 1998-2002, the East-West format was abandoned for one pitting North America vs. the rest of the world (N. America leads that series 3-2). In 2003 the game returned to East vs. West.

NHL All-Star Game (Cont.)
Benefit Games

Date	Occasion		Host	Coaches
2/14/34	Ace Bailey Benefit	Toronto 7, All-Stars 3	Toronto	Dick Irvin, Lester Patrick
11/3/37	Howie Morenz Memorial	All-Stars 6, Montreals* 5	Montreal	Jack Adams, Cecil Hart
10/29/39	Babe Siebert Memorial	All-Stars 5, Canadiens 3	Montreal	Art Ross, Pit Lepine

*Combined squad of Montreal Canadiens and Montreal Maroons.

All-Star Games

Multiple MVP winners: Wayne Gretzky and Mario Lemieux (3); Bobby Hull and Frank Mahovlich (2).

Year		Host	Coaches	Most Valuable Player
1947	All-Stars 4, Toronto 3	Toronto	Dick Irvin, Hap Day	No award
1948	All-Stars 3, Toronto 1	Chicago	Tommy Ivan, Hap Day	No award
1949	All-Stars 3, Toronto 1	Toronto	Tommy Ivan, Hap Day	No award
1950	Detroit 7, All-Stars 1	Detroit	Tommy Ivan, Lynn Patrick	No award
1951	1st Team 2, 2nd Team 2	Toronto	Joe Primeau, Hap Day	No award
1952	1st Team 1, 2nd Team 1	Detroit	Tommy Ivan, Dick Irvin	No award
1953	All-Stars 3, Montreal 1	Montreal	Lynn Patrick, Dick Irvin	No award
1954	All-Stars 2, Detroit 2	Detroit	King Clancy, Jim Skinner	No award
1955	Detroit 3, All-Stars 1	Detroit	Jim Skinner, Dick Irvin	No award
1956	All-Stars 1, Montreal 1	Montreal	Jim Skinner, Toe Blake	No award
1957	All-Stars 5, Montreal 3	Montreal	Milt Schmidt, Toe Blake	No award
1958	Montreal 6, All-Stars 3	Montreal	Toe Blake, Milt Schmidt	No award
1959	Montreal 6, All-Stars 1	Montreal	Toe Blake, Punch Imlach	No award
1960	All-Stars 2, Montreal 1	Montreal	Punch Imlach, Toe Blake	No award
1961	All-Stars 3, Chicago 1	Chicago	Sid Abel, Rudy Pilous	No award
1962	Toronto 4, All-Stars 1	Toronto	Punch Imlach, Rudy Pilous	Eddie Shack, Tor., RW
1963	All-Stars 3, Toronto 3	Toronto	Sid Abel, Punch Imlach	Frank Mahovlich, Tor., LW
1964	All-Stars 3, Toronto 2	Toronto	Sid Abel, Punch Imlach	Jean Beliveau, Mon., C
1965	All-Stars 5, Montreal 2	Montreal	Billy Reay, Toe Blake	Gordie Howe, Det., RW
1966	No game (see below)			
1967	Montreal 3, All-Stars 0	Montreal	Toe Blake, Sid Abel	Henri Richard, Mon., C
1968	Toronto 4, All-Stars 3	Toronto	Punch Imlach, Toe Blake	Bruce Gamble, Tor., G
1969	West 3, East 3	Montreal	Scotty Bowman, Toe Blake	Frank Mahovlich, Det., LW
1970	East 4, West 1	St. Louis	Claude Ruel, Scotty Bowman	Bobby Hull, Chi., LW
1971	West 2, East 1	Boston	Scotty Bowman, Harry Sinden	Bobby Hull, Chi., LW
1972	East 3, West 2	Minnesota	Al MacNeil, Billy Reay	Bobby Orr, Bos., D
1973	East 5, West 4	NY Rangers	Tom Johnson, Billy Reay	Greg Polis, Pit., LW
1974	West 6, East 4	Chicago	Billy Reay, Scotty Bowman	Garry Unger, St.L., C
1975	Wales 7, Campbell 1	Montreal	Bep Guidolin, Fred Shero	Syl Apps Jr., Pit., C
1976	Wales 7, Campbell 5	Philadelphia	Floyd Smith, Fred Shero	Peter Mahovlich, Mon., C
1977	Wales 4, Campbell 3	Vancouver	Scotty Bowman, Fred Shero	Rick Martin, Buf., LW
1978	Wales 3, Campbell 2 (OT)	Buffalo	Scotty Bowman, Fred Shero	Billy Smith, NYI, G
1979	No game (see below)			
1980	Wales 6, Campbell 3	Detroit	Scotty Bowman, Al Arbour	Reggie Leach, Phi., RW
1981	Campbell 4, Wales 1	Los Angeles	Pat Quinn, Scotty Bowman	Mike Liut, St.L., G
1982	Wales 4, Campbell 2	Washington	Al Arbour, Glen Sonmor	Mike Bossy, NYI, RW
1983	Campbell 9, Wales 3	NY Islanders	Roger Neilson, Al Arbour	Wayne Gretzky, Edm., C
1984	Wales 7, Campbell 6	New Jersey	Al Arbour, Glen Sather	Don Maloney, NYR, LW
1985	Wales 6, Campbell 4	Calgary	Al Arbour, Glen Sather	Mario Lemieux, Pit., C
1986	Wales 4, Campbell 3 (OT)	Hartford	Mike Keenan, Glen Sather	Grant Fuhr, Edm., G
1987	No game (see below)			
1988	Wales 6, Campbell 5 (OT)	St. Louis	Mike Keenan, Glen Sather	Mario Lemieux, Pit., C
1989	Campbell 9, Wales 5	Edmonton	Glen Sather, Terry O'Reilly	Wayne Gretzky, LA, C
1990	Wales 12, Campbell 7	Pittsburgh	Pat Burns, Terry Crisp	Mario Lemieux, Pit., C
1991	Campbell 11, Wales 5	Chicago	John Muckler, Mike Milbury	Vincent Damphousse, Tor., LW
1992	Campbell 10, Wales 6	Philadelphia	Bob Gainey, Scotty Bowman	Brett Hull, St.L., RW
1993	Wales 16, Campbell 6	Montreal	Scotty Bowman, Mike Keenan	Mike Gartner, NYR, RW
1994	East 9, West 8	NY Rangers	Jacques Demers, Barry Melrose	Mike Richter, NYR, G
1995	No game (see below)			
1996	East 5, West 4	Boston	Doug MacLean, Scotty Bowman	Ray Bourque, Bos., D
1997	East 11, West 7	San Jose	Doug MacLean, Ken Hitchcock	Mark Recchi, Mon., RW
1998	North America 8, World 7	Vancouver	Jacques Lemaire, Ken Hitchcock	Teemu Selanne, Ana., RW
1999	North America 8, World 6	Tampa	Ken Hitchcock, Lindy Ruff	Wayne Gretzky, NYR, C
2000	World 9, North America 4	Toronto	Scotty Bowman, Pat Quinn	Pavel Bure, Fla., RW
2001	North America 14, World 12	Denver	Joel Quenneville, Jacques Martin	Bill Guerin, Bos., RW
2002	World 8, North America 5	Los Angeles	Scotty Bowman, Pat Quinn	Eric Daze, Chi., LW
2003	West 6, East 5 (OT)†	Florida	Marc Crawford, Jacques Martin	Dany Heatley, Atl., RW
2004	East 6, West 4	Minnesota	Pat Quinn, Dave Lewis	Joe Sakic, Col., C

†After a five-minute scoreless overtime, the game was settled by a shootout. The West outscored the East, 3-1.

No All-Star Game: in 1966 (moved from start of season to mid-season); in 1979 (replaced by Challenge Cup series with USSR); in 1987 (replaced by Rendez-Vous '87 series with USSR); and in 1995 (cancelled when NHL lockout shortened season to 48 games).

NHL Franchise Origins

Here is what the current 30 teams in the National Hockey League have to show for the years they have put in as members of the NHL, the early National Hockey Association (NHA) and the more recent World Hockey Association (WHA). League titles and Stanley Cup championships are noted by year won. The Stanley Cup has automatically gone to the NHL champion since the 1926-27 season. Following the 1992-93 season, the NHL renamed the Clarence Campbell Conference the Western Conference, while the Prince of Wales Conference became the Eastern Conference.

Western Conference

	First Season	League Titles	Franchise Stops
Anaheim, Mighty Ducks of	1993-94 (NHL)	None	•Anaheim, CA (1993—)
Calgary Flames	1972-73 (NHL)	1 Cup (1989)	•Atlanta (1972-80)
			Calgary (1980—)
Chicago Blackhawks	1926-27 (NHL)	3 Cups (1934,38,61)	•Chicago (1926—)
Colorado Avalanche	1972-73 (WHA)	1 WHA (1977)	•Quebec City (1972-95)
		2 Cups (1996, 2001)	Denver (1995—)
Columbus Blue Jackets	2000-01 (NHL)	None	•Columbus, OH (2000—)
Dallas Stars	1967-68 (NHL)	1 Cup (1999)	•Bloomington, MN (1967-93)
			Dallas (1993—)
Detroit Red Wings	1926-27 (NHL)	10 Cups (1936-37,43,50,52,54-55,97,98, 2002)	•Detroit (1926—)
Edmonton Oilers	1972-73 (WHA)	5 Cups (1984-85,87-88,90)	•Edmonton (1972—)
Los Angeles Kings	1967-68 (NHL)	None	•Inglewood, CA (1967-99)
			Los Angeles (1999—)
Minnesota Wild	2000-01 (NHL)	None	•St. Paul, MN (2000—)
Nashville Predators	1998-99 (NHL)	None	•Nashville, TN (1998—)
Phoenix Coyotes	1972-73 (WHA)	3 WHA (1976, 78-79)	•Winnipeg (1972-96)
			Phoenix (1996—)
St. Louis Blues	1967-68 (NHL)	None	•St. Louis (1967—)
San Jose Sharks	1991-92 (NHL)	None	•San Francisco (1991-93)
			San Jose (1993—)
Vancouver Canucks	1970-71 (NHL)	None	•Vancouver (1970—)

Eastern Conference

	First Season	League Titles	Franchise Stops
Atlanta Thrashers	1999-00 (NHL)	None	•Atlanta (1999—)
Boston Bruins	1924-25 (NHL)	5 Cups (1929,39,41,70,72)	•Boston (1924—)
Buffalo Sabres	1970-71 (NHL)	None	•Buffalo (1970—)
Carolina Hurricanes	1972-73 (WHA)	1 WHA (1973)	•Boston (1972-74)
			W. Springfield, MA (1974-75)
			Hartford, CT (1975-78)
			Springfield, MA (1978-80)
			Hartford (1980-97)
			Greensboro, NC (1997-99)
			Raleigh, NC (1999—)
Florida Panthers	1993-94 (NHL)	None	•Miami (1993-98)
			Sunrise, FL (1998—)
Montreal Canadiens	1909-10 (NHA)	2 NHA (1916-17)	•Montreal (1909—)
		2 NHL (1924-25)	
		24 Cups (1916,24,30-31,44,46,53,56-60,65-66,68-69,71,73,76-79,86,93)	
New Jersey Devils	1974-75 (NHL)	3 Cups (1995, 2000,03)	•Kansas City (1974-76)
			Denver (1976-82)
			E. Rutherford, NJ (1982—)
New York Islanders	1972-73 (NHL)	4 Cups (1980-83)	•Uniondale, NY (1972—)
New York Rangers	1926-27 (NHL)	4 Cups (1928,33,40,94)	•New York (1926—)
Ottawa Senators	1992-93 (NHL)	None	•Ottawa (1992-1996)
			Kanata, Ont. (1996—)
Philadelphia Flyers	1967-68 (NHL)	2 Cups (1974-75)	•Philadelphia (1967—)
Pittsburgh Penguins	1967-68 (NHL)	2 Cups (1991-92)	•Pittsburgh (1967—)
Tampa Bay Lightning	1992-93 (NHL)	1 Cup (2004)	•Tampa, FL (1992-93)
			St. Petersburg, FL (1993-96)
			Tampa, FL (1996—)
Toronto Maple Leafs	1916-17 (NHA)	2 NHL (1918,22)	•Toronto (1916—)
		13 Cups (1918,22,32,42,45, 47-49,51,62-64,67)	
Washington Capitals	1974-75 (NHL)	None	•Landover, MD (1974-97)
			Washington, D.C. (1997—)

Note: The Hartford Civic Center roof collapsed after a snowstorm in January 1978, forcing the Whalers to move their home games to Springfield, Mass., for two years.

The Growth of the NHL

Of the four franchises that comprised the National Hockey League (NHL) at the start of the 1917-18 season, only two remain—the Montreal Canadiens and the Toronto Maple Leafs (originally the Toronto Arenas). From 1919-26, eight new teams joined the league, but only four—the Boston Bruins, Chicago Blackhawks (originally Black Hawks), Detroit Red Wings (originally Cougars) and New York Rangers—survived.

It was 41 years before the NHL expanded again, doubling in size for the 1967-68 season with new teams in Bloomington (Minn.), Los Angeles, Oakland, Philadelphia, Pittsburgh and St. Louis. The league had 16 clubs by the start of the 1972-73 season, but it also had a rival in the **World Hockey Association,** which debuted that year with 12 teams.

The NHL added two more teams in 1974 and merged the struggling Cleveland Barons (originally the Oakland Seals) and Minnesota North Stars in 1978, before absorbing four WHA clubs—the Edmonton Oilers, Hartford Whalers, Quebec Nordiques and Winnipeg Jets—in time for the 1979-80 season. Seven expansion teams joined the league in the 1990s, with two more being added in 2000 to make it an even 30.

Expansion/Merger Timetable

For teams currently in NHL.

1919—Quebec Bulldogs finally take the ice after sitting out NHL's first two seasons; **1924**—Boston Bruins and Montreal Maroons; **1925**—New York Americans and Pittsburgh Pirates; **1926**—Chicago Black Hawks (now Blackhawks), Detroit Cougars (now Red Wings) and New York Rangers; **1932**—Ottawa Senators return after sitting out 1931-32 season.

1967—California-Oakland Seals (later Cleveland Barons), Los Angeles Kings, Minnesota North Stars, Philadelphia Flyers, Pittsburgh Penguins and St. Louis Blues.

1970—Buffalo Sabres and Vancouver Canucks; **1972**—Atlanta Flames (now Calgary) and New York Islanders; **1974**—Kansas City Scouts (now New Jersey Devils) and Washington Capitals; **1978**—Cleveland Barons merge with Minnesota North Stars (now Dallas Stars) and team remains in Minnesota; **1979**—added WHA's Edmonton Oilers, Hartford Whalers (now Carolina Hurricanes), Quebec Nordiques (now Colorado Avalanche) and Winnipeg Jets (now Phoenix Coyotes).

1991—San Jose Sharks; **1992**—Ottawa Senators and Tampa Bay Lightning; **1993**—Mighty Ducks of Anaheim and Florida Panthers; **1998**—Nashville Predators; **1999**—Atlanta Thrashers.

2000—Columbus Blue Jackets and Minnesota Wild.

City and Nickname Changes

1919—Toronto Arenas renamed St. Pats; **1920**—Quebec Bulldogs move to Hamilton and become Tigers (will fold in 1925); **1926**—Toronto St. Pats renamed Maple Leafs; **1929**—Detroit Cougars renamed Falcons.

1930—Pittsburgh Pirates move to Philadelphia and become Quakers (will fold in 1931); **1932**—Detroit Falcons renamed Red Wings; **1934**—Ottawa Senators move to St. Louis and become Eagles (will fold in 1935); **1941**—New York Americans renamed Brooklyn Americans (will fold in 1942).

1967—California Seals renamed Oakland Seals three months into first season; **1970**—Oakland Seals renamed California Golden Seals; **1975**—California Golden Seals renamed Seals; **1976**—California Seals move to Cleveland and become Barons, while Kansas City Scouts move to Denver and become Colorado Rockies; **1978**—Cleveland Barons merge with Minnesota North Stars and become Minnesota North Stars.

1980—Atlanta Flames move to Calgary; **1982**—Colorado Rockies move to East Rutherford, N.J., and become New Jersey Devils; **1986**—Chicago Black Hawks renamed Blackhawks; **1993**—Minnesota North Stars move to Dallas and become Stars. **1995**—Quebec Nordiques move to Denver and become Colorado Avalanche; **1996**—Winnipeg Jets move to Phoenix and become Coyotes; **1997**—Hartford Whalers move to Greensboro, N.C. and become Carolina Hurricanes; **1999**—Carolina Hurricanes move to Raleigh, N.C.

Defunct NHL Teams

Teams that once played in the NHL, but no longer exist.

Brooklyn—Americans (1941-42, formerly NY Americans from 1925-41); **Cleveland**—Barons (1976-78, originally California-Oakland Seals from 1967-76); **Hamilton (Ont.)**—Tigers (1920-25, originally Quebec Bulldogs from 1919-20); **Montreal**—Maroons (1924-38) and Wanderers (1917-18); **New York**—Americans (1925-41, later Brooklyn Americans for 1941-42); **Oakland**—Seals (1967-76, also known as California Seals and Golden Seals and later Cleveland Barons from 1976-78); **Ottawa**—Senators (1917-31 and 1932-34, later St. Louis Eagles for 1934-35); **Philadelphia**—Quakers (1930-31, originally Pittsburgh Pirates from 1925-30); **Pittsburgh**—Pirates (1925-30, later Philadelphia Quakers for 1930-31); **Quebec**—Bulldogs (1919-20, later Hamilton Tigers from 1920-25); **St. Louis**—Eagles (1934-35), originally Ottawa Senators (1917-31 and 1932-34).

WHA Teams (1972-79)

Baltimore—Blades (1975); **Birmingham**—Bulls (1976-78); **Calgary**—Cowboys (1975-77); **Chicago**—Cougars (1972-75); **Cincinnati**—Stingers (1975-79); **Cleveland**—Crusaders (1972-76, moved to Minnesota); **Denver**—Spurs (1975-76, moved to Ottawa); **Edmonton**—Oilers (1972-79, originally called Alberta Oilers in 1972-73); **Houston**—Aeros (1972-78); **Indianapolis**—Racers (1974-78).

Los Angeles—Sharks (1972-74, moved to Michigan); **Michigan**—Stags (1974-75, moved to Baltimore); **Minnesota**—Fighting Saints (1972-76) and New Fighting Saints (1976-77); **New England**—Whalers (1972-79, played in Boston from 1972-74, West Springfield, MA from 1974-75, Hartford from 1975-78 and Springfield, MA in 1979); **New Jersey**—Knights (1973-74, moved to San Diego); **New York**—Raiders (1972-73, renamed Golden Blades in 1973, moved to New Jersey).

Ottawa—Nationals (1972-73, moved to Toronto) and Civics (1976); **Philadelphia**—Blazers (1972-73, moved to Vancouver); **Phoenix**—Roadrunners (1974-77); **Quebec**—Nordiques (1972-79); **San Diego**—Mariners (1974-77); **Toronto**—Toros (1973-76, moved to Birmingham, AL); **Vancouver**—Blazers (1973-75, moved to Calgary); **Winnipeg**—Jets (1972-79).

Annual NHL Leaders

Art Ross Trophy (Scoring)

Given to the player who leads the league in points scored and named after the former Boston Bruins general manager-coach. First presented in 1948, names of prior leading scorers have been added retroactively. A tie for the scoring championship is broken three ways: 1. total goals; 2. fewest games played; 3. first goal scored.

Multiple winners: Wayne Gretzky (10); Gordie Howe and Mario Lemieux (6); Phil Esposito and Jaromir Jagr (5); Stan Mikita (4); Bobby Hull and Guy Lafleur (3); Max Bentley, Charlie Conacher, Bill Cook, Babe Dye, Bernie Geoffrion, Elmer Lach, Newsy Lalonde, Joe Malone, Dickie Moore, Howie Morenz, Bobby Orr and Sweeney Schriner (2).

Year		Gm	G	A	Pts	Year		Gm	G	A	Pts
1918	Joe Malone, Mon	20	44	0	44	1962	Bobby Hull, Chi	70	50	34	84
1919	Newsy Lalonde, Mon	17	23	9	32	1963	Gordie Howe, Det	70	38	48	86
						1964	Stan Mikita, Chi	70	39	50	89
1920	Joe Malone, Que	24	39	6	45	1965	Stan Mikita, Chi	70	28	59	87
1921	Newsy Lalonde, Mon	24	33	8	41	1966	Bobby Hull, Chi	65	54	43	97
1922	Punch Broadbent, Ott	24	32	14	46	1967	Stan Mikita, Chi	70	35	62	97
1923	Babe Dye, Tor	22	26	11	37	1968	Stan Mikita, Chi	72	40	47	87
1924	Cy Denneny, Ott	21	22	1	23	1969	Phil Esposito, Bos	74	49	77	126
1925	Babe Dye, Tor	29	38	6	44	1970	Bobby Orr, Bos	76	33	87	120
1926	Nels Stewart, Maroons	36	34	8	42	1971	Phil Esposito, Bos	78	76	76	152
1927	Bill Cook, NYR	44	33	4	37	1972	Phil Esposito, Bos	76	66	67	133
1928	Howie Morenz, Mon	43	33	18	51	1973	Phil Esposito, Bos	78	55	75	130
1929	Ace Bailey, Tor	44	22	10	32	1974	Phil Esposito, Bos	78	68	77	145
1930	Cooney Weiland, Bos	44	43	30	73	1975	Bobby Orr, Bos	80	46	89	135
1931	Howie Morenz, Mon	39	28	23	51	1976	Guy Lafleur, Mon	80	56	69	125
1932	Busher Jackson, Tor	48	28	25	53	1977	Guy Lafleur, Mon	80	56	80	136
1933	Bill Cook, NYR	48	28	22	50	1978	Guy Lafleur, Mon	79	60	72	132
1934	Charlie Conacher, Tor	42	32	20	52	1979	Bryan Trottier, NYI	76	47	87	134
1935	Charlie Conacher, Tor	47	36	21	57	1980	Marcel Dionne, LA	80	53	84	137
1936	Sweeney Schriner, NYA	48	19	26	45	1981	Wayne Gretzky, Edm	80	55	109	164
1937	Sweeney Schriner, NYA	48	21	25	46	1982	Wayne Gretzky, Edm	80	92	120	212
1938	Gordie Drillon, Tor	48	26	26	52	1983	Wayne Gretzky, Edm	80	71	125	196
1939	Toe Blake, Mon	48	24	23	47	1984	Wayne Gretzky, Edm	74	87	118	205
1940	Milt Schmidt, Bos	48	22	30	52	1985	Wayne Gretzky, Edm	80	73	135	208
1941	Bill Cowley, Bos	46	17	45	62	1986	Wayne Gretzky, Edm	80	52	163	215
1942	Bryan Hextall, NYR	48	24	32	56	1987	Wayne Gretzky, Edm	79	62	121	183
1943	Doug Bentley, Chi	50	33	40	73	1988	Mario Lemieux, Pit	77	70	98	168
1944	Herbie Cain, Bos	48	36	46	82	1989	Mario Lemieux, Pit	76	85	114	199
1945	Elmer Lach, Mon	50	26	54	80	1990	Wayne Gretzky, LA	73	40	102	142
1946	Max Bentley, Chi	47	31	30	61	1991	Wayne Gretzky, LA	78	41	122	163
1947	Max Bentley, Chi	60	29	43	72	1992	Mario Lemieux, Pit	64	44	87	131
1948	Elmer Lach, Mon	60	30	31	61	1993	Mario Lemieux, Pit	60	69	91	160
1949	Roy Conacher, Chi	60	26	42	68	1994	Wayne Gretzky, LA	81	38	92	130
1950	Ted Lindsay, Det	69	23	55	78	1995	Jaromir Jagr, Pit	48	32	38	70
1951	Gordie Howe, Det	70	43	43	86	1996	Mario Lemieux, Pit	70	69	92	161
1952	Gordie Howe, Det	70	47	39	86	1997	Mario Lemieux, Pit	76	50	72	122
1953	Gordie Howe, Det	70	49	46	95	1998	Jaromir Jagr, Pit	77	35	67	102
1954	Gordie Howe, Det	70	33	48	81	1999	Jaromir Jagr, Pit	81	44	83	127
1955	Bernie Geoffrion, Mon	70	38	37	75	2000	Jaromir Jagr, Pit	63	42	54	96
1956	Jean Beliveau, Mon	70	47	41	88	2001	Jaromir Jagr, Pit	81	52	69	121
1957	Gordie Howe, Det	70	44	45	89	2002	Jarome Iginla, Calg	82	52	44	96
1958	Dickie Moore, Mon	70	36	48	84	2003	Peter Forsberg, Col	75	29	77	106
1959	Dickie Moore, Mon	70	41	55	96	2004	Martin St. Louis, TB	82	38	56	94
1960	Bobby Hull, Chi	70	39	42	81						
1961	Bernie Geoffrion, Mon	64	50	45	95						

Note: The three times players have tied for total points in one season the player with more goals has won the trophy. In 1961-62, Hull outscored Andy Bathgate of NY Rangers, 50 goals to 28. In 1979-80, Dionne outscored Wayne Gretzky of Edmonton, 53-51. In 1995, Jagr outscored Eric Lindros of Philadelphia, 32-29.

Goals

Multiple winners: Bobby Hull (7); Phil Esposito (6); Charlie Conacher, Wayne Gretzky, Gordie Howe and Maurice Richard (5); Bill Cooke, Babe Dye, Brett Hull, Mario Lemieux, Pavel Bure and Teemu Selanne (3); Jean Beliveau, Doug Bentley, Peter Bondra, Mike Bossy, Bernie Geoffrion, Bryan Hextall, Jarome Iginla, Joe Malone and Nels Stewart (2).

Year		No	Year		No	Year		No
1918	Joe Malone, Mon	44	1927	Bill Cook, NYR	33	1936	Charlie Conacher, Tor	23
1919	Odie Cleghorn, Mon	23	1928	Howie Morenz, Mon	33		& Bill Thoms, Tor	23
	& Newsy Lalonde, Mon	23	1929	Ace Bailey, Tor	22	1937	Larry Aurie, Det	23
1920	Joe Malone, Que	39	1930	Cooney Weiland, Bos	43		& Nels Stewart, NYA	23
1921	Babe Dye, Ham-Tor	35	1931	Charlie Conacher, Tor	31	1938	Gordie Drillon, Tor	26
1922	Punch Broadbent, Ott	32	1932	Charlie Conacher, Tor	34	1939	Roy Conacher, Bos	26
1923	Babe Dye, Tor	26		& Bill Cook, NYR	34	1940	Bryan Hextall, NYR	24
1924	Cy Denneny, Ott	22	1933	Bill Cook, NYR	28	1941	Bryan Hextall, NYR	26
1925	Babe Dye, Tor	38	1934	Charlie Conacher, Tor	32	1942	Lynn Patrick, NYR	32
1926	Nels Stewart, Maroons	34	1935	Charlie Conacher, Tor	36	1943	Doug Bentley, Chi	33

Annual NHL Leaders (Cont.)

Year		No	Year		No	Year		No
1944	Doug Bentley, Chi.	38	1965	Norm Ullman, Tor	42	1986	Jari Kurri, Edm	68
1945	Maurice Richard, Mon	50	1966	Bobby Hull, Chi	54	1987	Wayne Gretzky, Edm	62
1946	Gaye Stewart, Tor	37	1967	Bobby Hull, Chi	52	1988	Mario Lemieux, Pit	70
1947	Maurice Richard, Mon	45	1968	Bobby Hull, Chi	44	1989	Mario Lemieux, Pit	85
1948	Ted Lindsay, Det	33	1969	Bobby Hull, Chi	58	1990	Brett Hull, St.L	72
1949	Sid Abel, Det	28	1970	Phil Esposito, Bos	43	1991	Brett Hull, St.L	86
1950	Maurice Richard, Mon	43	1971	Phil Esposito, Bos	76	1992	Brett Hull, St.L	70
1951	Gordie Howe, Det	43	1972	Phil Esposito, Bos	66	1993	Alexander Mogilny, Buf.	76
1952	Gordie Howe, Det	47	1973	Phil Esposito, Bos	55		& Teemu Selanne, Win	76
1953	Gordie Howe, Det	49	1974	Phil Esposito, Bos	68	1994	Pavel Bure, Van	60
1954	Maurice Richard, Mon	37	1975	Phil Esposito, Bos	61	1995	Peter Bondra, Wash	34
1955	Bernie Geoffrion, Mon	38	1976	Reggie Leach, Phi	61	1996	Mario Lemieux, Pit	69
	& Maurice Richard, Mon.	38	1977	Steve Shutt, Mon	60	1997	Keith Tkachuk, Pho	52
1956	Jean Beliveau, Mon	47	1978	Guy Lafleur, Mon	60	1998	Teemu Selanne, Ana.	52
1957	Gordie Howe, Det	44	1979	Mike Bossy, NYI	69		& Peter Bondra, Wash	52
1958	Dickie Moore, Mon	36	1980	Danny Gare, Buf	56	1999	Teemu Selanne, Ana.	47
1959	Jean Beliveau, Mon	45		Charlie Simmer, LA	56	2000	Pavel Bure, Fla.	58
1960	Bronco Horvath, Bos.	39		& Blaine Stoughton, Hart.	56	2001	Pavel Bure, Fla.	59
	& Bobby Hull, Chi	39	1981	Mike Bossy, NYI	68	2002	Jarome Iginla, Calg.	52
1961	Bernie Geoffrion, Mon	50	1982	Wayne Gretzky, Edm	92	2003	Milan Hejduk, Col.	50
1962	Bobby Hull, Chi	50	1983	Wayne Gretzky, Edm	71	2004	Jarome Iginla, Calg.	41
1963	Gordie Howe, Det	38	1984	Wayne Gretzky, Edm	87		Ilya Kovalchuk, Atl	41
1964	Bobby Hull, Chi	43	1985	Wayne Gretzky, Edm	73		& Rick Nash, Clb	41

Assists

Multiple winners: Wayne Gretzky (16); Bobby Orr (5); Adam Oates, Frank Boucher, Bill Cowley, Phil Esposito, Gordie Howe, Jaromir Jagr, Elmer Lach, Mario Lemieux, Stan Mikita and Joe Primeau (3); Syl Apps, Andy Bathgate, Jean Beliveau, Doug Bentley, Art Chapman, Bobby Clarke, Ron Francis, Ted Lindsay, Bert Olmstead, Henri Richard and Bryan Trottier (2).

Year		No	Year		No	Year		No
1918	No official records kept.		1949	Doug Bentley, Chi.	43	1979	Bryan Trottier, NYI	87
1919	Newsy Lalonde, Mon	9	1950	Ted Lindsay, Det	55	1980	Wayne Gretzky, Edm	86
1920	Corbett Denneny, Tor	12	1951	Gordie Howe, Det	43	1981	Wayne Gretzky, Edm	109
1921	Louis Berlinquette, Mon	9		& Teeder Kennedy, Tor	43	1982	Wayne Gretzky, Edm	120
	Harry Cameron, Tor . :	9	1952	Elmer Lach, Mon	50	1983	Wayne Gretzky, Edm	125
	& Joe Matte, Ham	9	1953	Gordie Howe, Det	46	1984	Wayne Gretzky, Edm	118
1922	Punch Broadbent, Ott	14	1954	Gordie Howe, Det	48	1985	Wayne Gretzky, Edm	135
	& Leo Reise, Ham.	14	1955	Bert Olmstead, Mon	48	1986	Wayne Gretzky, Edm	163
1923	Ed Bouchard, Ham	12	1956	Bert Olmstead, Mon	56	1987	Wayne Gretzky, Edm	121
1924	King Clancy, Ott	8	1957	Ted Lindsay, Det.	55	1988	Wayne Gretzky, Edm	109
1925	Cy Denneny, Ott	15	1958	Henri Richard, Mon	52	1989	Wayne Gretzky, LA	114
1926	Frank Nighbor, Ott.	13	1959	Dickie Moore, Mon	55		& Mario Lemieux, Pit	114
1927	Dick Irvin, Chi	18	1960	Don McKenney, Bos	49	1990	Wayne Gretzky, LA	102
1928	Howie Morenz, Mon	18	1961	Jean Beliveau, Mon	58	1991	Wayne Gretzky, LA	122
1929	Frank Boucher, NYR	16	1962	Andy Bathgate, NYR	56	1992	Wayne Gretzky, LA	90
1930	Frank Boucher, NYR	36	1963	Henri Richard, Mon	50	1993	Adam Oates, Bos	97
1931	Joe Primeau, Tor	32	1964	Andy Bathgate, NYR-Tor	58	1994	Wayne Gretzky, LA	92
1932	Joe Primeau, Tor.	37	1965	Stan Mikita, Chi.	59	1995	Ron Francis, Pit	48
1933	Frank Boucher, NYR	28	1966	Jean Beliveau, Mon	48	1996	Ron Francis, Pit	92
1934	Joe Primeau, Tor.	32		Stan Mikita, Chi.	48		& Mario Lemieux, Pit	92
1935	Art Chapman, NYA	34		& Bobby Rousseau, Mon.	48	1997	Mario Lemieux, Pit	72
1936	Art Chapman, NYA	28	1967	Stan Mikita, Chi.	62		& Wayne Gretzky, NYR	72
1937	Syl Apps, Tor	29	1968	Phil Esposito, Bos	49	1998	Jaromir Jagr, Pit	67
1938	Syl Apps, Tor.	29	1969	Phil Esposito, Bos	77		& Wayne Gretzky, NYR	67
1939	Bill Cowley, Bos	34	1970	Bobby Orr, Bos	87	1999	Jaromir Jagr, Pit	83
1940	Milt Schmidt, Bos	30	1971	Bobby Orr, Bos	102	2000	Mark Recchi, Phi	63
1941	Bill Cowley, Bos	45	1972	Bobby Orr, Bos	80	2001	Jaromir Jagr, Pit	69
1942	Phil Watson, NYR.	37	1973	Phil Esposito, Bos	75		& Adam Oates, Wash	69
1943	Bill Cowley, Bos	45	1974	Bobby Orr, Bos	90	2002	Adam Oates, Wash-Phi.	64
1944	Clint Smith, Chi	49	1975	Bobby Clarke, Phi	89	2003	Peter Forsberg, Col.	77
1945	Elmer Lach, Mon	54		& Bobby Orr, Bos.	89	2004	Scott Gomez, NJ	56
1946	Elmer Lach, Mon	34	1976	Bobby Clarke, Phi	89		& Martin St. Louis, TB	56
1947	Billy Taylor, Det.	46	1977	Guy Lafleur, Mon	80			
1948	Doug Bentley, Chi.	37	1978	Bryan Trottier, NYI	77			

Goals Against Average

Average determined by games played through 1942-43 season and by minutes played since then. Minimum of 15 games from 1917-18 season through 1925-26; minimum of 25 games since 1926-27 season. Not to be confused with the Vezina Trophy. Goaltenders who posted the season's lowest goals against average, but did not win the Vezina are in **bold** type.

Multiple winners: Jacques Plante (9); Clint Benedict and Bill Durnan (6); Johnny Bower, Ken Dryden and Tiny Thompson (4); Patrick Roy and Georges Vezina (3); Ed Belfour, Frankie Brimsek, Turk Broda, George Hainsworth, Dominik Hasek, Harry Lumley, Bernie Parent, Pete Peeters, Terry Sawchuk and Marty Turco (2).

Year	GAA	Year	GAA	Year	GAA
1918 Georges Vezina, Mon	3.82	1947 Bill Durnan, Mon	2.30	1976 Ken Dryden, Mon	2.03
1919 Clint Benedict, Ott	2.94	1948 Turk Broda, Tor	2.38	1977 Bunny Larocque, Mon	2.09
1920 Clint Benedict, Ott	2.67	1949 Bill Durnan, Mon	2.10	1978 Ken Dryden, Mon	2.05
1921 Clint Benedict, Ott	3.13	1950 Bill Durnan, Mon	2.20	1979 Ken Dryden, Mon	2.30
1922 Clint Benedict, Ott	3.50	1951 Al Rollins, Tor	1.77	1980 Bob Sauve, Buf	2.36
1923 Clint Benedict, Ott	2.25	1952 Terry Sawchuk, Det	1.90	1981 Richard Sevigny, Mon	2.40
1924 Georges Vezina, Mon	2.00	1953 Terry Sawchuk, Det	1.90	1982 **Denis Herron,** Mon	2.64
1925 Georges Vezina, Mon	1.87	1954 Harry Lumley, Tor	1.86	1983 Pete Peeters, Bos	2.36
1926 Alex Connell, Ott	1.17	1955 **Harry Lumley,** Tor	1.94	1984 **Pat Riggin,** Wash	2.66
1927 **Clint Benedict,** Mon-M	1.51	1956 Jacques Plante, Mon	1.86	1985 **Tom Barrasso,** Buf	2.66
1928 Geo. Hainsworth, Mon	1.09	1957 Jacques Plante, Mon	2.02	1986 **Bob Froese,** Phi	2.55
1929 Geo. Hainsworth, Mon	0.98	1958 Jacques Plante, Mon	2.11	1987 **Brian Hayward,** Mon	2.81
1930 Tiny Thompson, Bos	2.23	1959 Jacques Plante, Mon	2.16	1988 Pete Peeters, Wash	2.78
1931 Roy Worters, NYA	1.68	1960 Jacques Plante, Mon	2.54	1989 Patrick Roy, Mon	2.47
1932 Chuck Gardiner, Chi	1.92	1961 Johnny Bower, Tor	2.50	1990 **Mike Liut,** Hart-Wash	2.53
1933 Tiny Thompson, Bos	1.83	1962 Jacques Plante, Mon	2.37	1991 Ed Belfour, Chi	2.47
1934 **Wilf Cude,** Det-Mon	1.57	1963 **Jacques Plante,** Mon	2.49	1992 Patrick Roy, Mon	2.36
1935 Lorne Chabot, Chi	1.83	1964 **Johnny Bower,** Tor	2.11	1993 **Felix Potvin,** Tor	2.50
1936 Tiny Thompson, Bos	1.71	1965 Johnny Bower, Tor	2.38	1994 Dominik Hasek, Buf	1.95
1937 Norm Smith, Det	2.13	1966 **Johnny Bower,** Tor	2.25	1995 Dominik Hasek, Buf	2.11
1938 Tiny Thompson, Bos	1.85	1967 Glenn Hall, Chi	2.38	1996 **Ron Hextall,** Phi	2.17
1939 Frankie Brimsek, Bos	1.58	1968 Gump Worsley, Mon	1.98	1997 **Martin Brodeur,** NJ	1.88
1940 Dave Kerr, NYR	1.60	1969 **Jacques Plante,** St.L	1.96	1998 **Ed Belfour,** Dal	1.88
1941 Turk Broda, Tor	2.06	1970 **Ernie Wakely,** St.L	2.11	1999 **Ron Tugnutt,** Ott	1.79
1942 Frankie Brimsek, Bos	2.45	1971 **Jacques Plante,** Tor	1.88	2000 **Brian Boucher,** Phi	1.91
1943 John Mowers, Det	2.47	1972 Tony Esposito, Chi	1.77	2001 **Marty Turco,** Dal	1.90
1944 Bill Durnan, Mon	2.18	1973 Ken Dryden, Mon	2.26	2002 **Patrick Roy,** Col	1.94
1945 Bill Durnan, Mon	2.42	1974 Bernie Parent, Phi	1.89	2003 **Marty Turco,** Dal	1.72
1946 Bill Durnan, Mon	2.60	1975 Bernie Parent, Phi	2.03	2004 **Miikka Kiprusoff,** Calg	1.69

Penalty Minutes

Multiple winners: Red Horner (8); Gus Mortson and Dave Schultz (4); Bert Corbeau, Lou Fontinato and Tiger Williams (3); Matthew Barnaby, Billy Boucher, Carl Brewer, Red Dutton, Pat Egan, Bill Ezinicki, Joe Hall, Tim Hunter, Keith Magnuson, Chris Nilan, Jimmy Orlando and Rob Ray (2).

Year	Min	Year	Min	Year	Min
1918 Joe Hall, Mon	60	1947 Gus Mortson, Tor	133	1976 Steve Durbano, Pit-KC	370
1919 Joe Hall, Mon	85	1948 Bill Barilko, Tor	147	1977 Tiger Williams, Tor	338
1920 Cully Wilson, Tor	79	1949 Bill Ezinicki, Tor	145	1978 Dave Schultz, LA-Pit	405
1921 Bert Corbeau, Mon	86	1950 Bill Ezinicki, Tor	144	1979 Tiger Williams, Tor	298
1922 Sprague Cleghorn, Mon	63	1951 Gus Mortson, Tor	142	1980 Jimmy Mann, Win	287
1923 Billy Boucher, Mon	52	1952 Gus Kyle, Bos	127	1981 Tiger Williams, Van	343
1924 Bert Corbeau, Tor	55	1953 Maurice Richard, Mon	112	1982 Paul Baxter, Pit	409
1925 Billy Boucher, Mon	92	1954 Gus Mortson, Chi	132	1983 Randy Holt, Wash	275
1926 Bert Corbeau, Tor	121	1955 Fern Flaman, Bos	150	1984 Chris Nilan, Mon	338
1927 Nels Stewart, Mon-M	133	1956 Lou Fontinato, NYR	202	1985 Chris Nilan, Mon	358
1928 Eddie Shore, Bos	165	1957 Gus Mortson, Chi	147	1986 Joey Kocur, Det	377
1929 Red Dutton, Mon-M	139	1958 Lou Fontinato, NYR	152	1987 Tim Hunter, Calg	361
1930 Joe Lamb, Ott	119	1959 Ted Lindsay, Chi	184	1988 Bob Probert, Det	398
1931 Harvey Rockburn, Det	118	1960 Carl Brewer, Tor	150	1989 Tim Hunter, Calg	375
1932 Red Dutton, NYA	107	1961 Pierre Pilote, Chi	165	1990 Basil McRae, Min	351
1933 Red Horner, Tor	144	1962 Lou Fontinato, Mon	167	1991 Rob Ray, Buf	350
1934 Red Horner, Tor	146	1963 Howie Young, Det	273	1992 Mike Peluso, Chi	408
1935 Red Horner, Tor	125	1964 Vic Hadfield, NYR	151	1993 Marty McSorley, LA	399
1936 Red Horner, Tor	167	1965 Carl Brewer, Tor	177	1994 Tie Domi, Win	347
1937 Red Horner, Tor	124	1966 Reg Fleming, Bos-NYR	166	1995 Enrico Ciccone, TB	225
1938 Red Horner, Tor	82	1967 John Ferguson, Mon	177	1996 Matthew Barnaby, Buf	335
1939 Red Horner, Tor	85	1968 Barclay Plager, St.L	153	1997 Gino Odjick, Van	371
1940 Red Horner, Tor	87	1969 Forbes Kennedy, Phi-Tor	219	1998 Donald Brashear, Van	372
1941 Jimmy Orlando, Det	99	1970 Keith Magnuson, Chi	213	1999 Rob Ray, Buf	261
1942 Pat Egan, NYA	124	1971 Keith Magnuson, Chi	291	2000 Denny Lambert, Atl	219
1943 Jimmy Orlando, Det	99	1972 Bryan Watson, Pit	212	2001 Matthew Barnaby, Pit-TB	265
1944 Mike McMahon, Mon	98	1973 Dave Schultz, Phi	259	2002 Peter Worrell, Fla	354
1945 Pat Egan, Bos	86	1974 Dave Schultz, Phi	348	2003 Jody Shelley, Clb	249
1946 Jack Stewart, Det	73	1975 Dave Schultz, Phi	472	2004 Sean Avery, LA	261

All-Time NHL Regular Season Leaders

Through 2004 regular season.

CAREER

Players active during 2004 season in **bold** type.

Points

		Yrs	Gm	G	A	Pts
1	Wayne Gretzky	20	1487	894	1963	2857
2	**Mark Messier**	25	1756	694	1193	1887
3	Gordie Howe	26	1767	801	1049	1850
4	**Ron Francis**	23	1731	549	1249	1798
5	Marcel Dionne	18	1348	731	1040	1771
6	**Steve Yzerman**	21	1453	678	1043	1721
7	**Mario Lemieux**	16	889	683	1018	1701
8	Phil Esposito	18	1282	717	873	1590
9	Ray Bourque	22	1612	410	1169	1579
10	Paul Coffey	21	1409	396	1135	1531
11	Stan Mikita	22	1394	541	926	1467
12	Bryan Trottier	18	1279	524	901	1425
13	**Adam Oates**	19	1337	341	1079	1420
14	Doug Gilmour	20	1474	450	964	1414
15	Dale Hawerchuk	16	1188	518	891	1409
16	**Joe Sakic**	16	1155	542	860	1402
17	Jari Kurri	17	1251	601	797	1398
18	**Brett Hull**	19	1264	741	649	1390
19	**Luc Robitaille**	18	1366	653	717	1370
20	John Bucyk	23	1540	556	813	1369
21	Guy Lafleur	17	1126	560	793	1353
22	Denis Savard	17	1196	473	865	1338
23	Mike Gartner	19	1432	708	627	1335
24	Gilbert Perreault	17	1191	512	814	1326
25	**Dave Andreychuk**	22	1597	634	686	1320
26	**Jaromir Jagr**	14	1027	537	772	1309
27	Alex Delvecchio	24	1549	456	825	1281
28	**Pierre Turgeon**	17	1215	495	779	1274
	Al MacInnis	23	1416	340	934	1274
30	Jean Ratelle	21	1281	491	776	1267

Goals

		Yrs	Gm	No
1	Wayne Gretzky	20	1487	894
2	Gordie Howe	26	1767	801
3	**Brett Hull**	19	1264	741
4	Marcel Dionne	18	1348	731
5	Phil Esposito	18	1282	717
6	Mike Gartner	19	1432	708
7	**Mark Messier**	25	1756	694
8	**Mario Lemieux**	16	889	683
9	**Steve Yzerman**	21	1453	678
10	**Luc Robitaille**	18	1366	653
11	**Dave Andreychuk**	22	1597	634
12	Bobby Hull	16	1063	610
13	Dino Ciccarelli	19	1232	608
14	Jari Kurri	17	1251	601
15	Mike Bossy	10	752	573
16	Guy Lafleur	17	1126	560
17	**Brendan Shanahan**	17	1268	558
18	John Bucyk	23	1540	556
19	**Ron Francis**	23	1731	549
20	Michel Goulet	15	1089	548
21	Maurice Richard	18	978	544
22	**Joe Sakic**	16	1155	542
23	Stan Mikita	22	1394	541
24	**Jaromir Jagr**	14	1027	537
25	**Joe Nieuwendyk**	18	1177	533
	Frank Mahovlich	18	1181	533
27	Bryan Trottier	18	1279	524
28	Pat Verbeek	20	1424	522
29	Dale Hawerchuk	16	1188	518
30	Gilbert Perreault	17	1191	512

Assists

		Yrs	Gm	No
1	Wayne Gretzky	20	1487	1963
2	**Ron Francis**	23	1731	1249
3	**Mark Messier**	25	1756	1193
4	Ray Bourque	22	1612	1169
5	Paul Coffey	21	1409	1135
6	**Adam Oates**	19	1337	1079
7	Gordie Howe	26	1767	1049
8	**Steve Yzerman**	21	1453	1043
9	Marcel Dionne	18	1348	1040
10	**Mario Lemieux**	16	889	1018
11	Doug Gilmour	20	1474	964
12	**Al MacInnis**	23	1416	934
13	Larry Murphy	21	1615	929
14	Stan Mikita	22	1394	926
15	Bryan Trottier	18	1279	901
16	Phil Housley	21	1495	894
17	Dale Hawerchuk	16	1188	891
18	Phil Esposito	18	1281	873
19	Denis Savard	17	1196	865
20	**Joe Sakic**	16	1155	860

Penalty Minutes

		Yrs	Gm	Min
1	Tiger Williams	14	962	3966
2	Dale Hunter	19	1407	3565
3	**Tie Domi**	15	943	3406
4	Marty McSorley	17	961	3381
5	Bob Probert	16	935	3300
6	**Rob Ray**	15	900	3207
7	Craig Berube	17	1054	3149
8	Tim Hunter	16	815	3146
9	Chris Nilan	13	688	3043
10	Rick Tocchet	18	1144	2972
11	Pat Verbeek	20	1424	2905
12	Dave Manson	16	1103	2792
13	**Scott Stevens**	22	1635	2785
14	**Chris Chelios**	21	1395	2695
15	Willi Plett	12	834	2572

NHL-WHA Top 10

All-time regular season scoring leaders, including games played in World Hockey Association (1972-79). NHL players with WHA experience are listed in CAPITAL letters. Players active during 2004 are in **bold** type.

Points

		Yrs	G	A	Pts
1	WAYNE GRETZKY	21	940	2027	2967
2	GORDIE HOWE	32	975	1383	2358
3	**MARK MESSIER**	26	695	1203	1898
4	BOBBY HULL	23	913	895	1808
5	**Ron Francis**	23	549	1249	1798
6	Marcel Dionne	18	731	1040	1771
7	**Steve Yzerman**	21	678	1043	1721
8	**Mario Lemieux**	16	683	1018	1701
9	Phil Esposito	18	717	873	1590
10	Ray Bourque	22	410	1169	1579

WHA Totals: GRETZKY (1 yr, 80 gm, 46-64—110); HOWE (6 yrs, 419 gm, 174-334—508); MESSIER (1 yr, 52 gm, 1-10—11); HULL (7 yrs, 411 gm, 303-335—638).

Years Played

		Yrs	Career	Gm
1	Gordie Howe	26	1946-71, 79-80	1767
2	**Mark Messier**	25	1979–	1756
3	Alex Delvecchio	24	1950-74	1549
	Tim Horton	24	1949-50, 51-74	1446
5	**Ron Francis**	23	1981–	1731
	John Bucyk	23	1955-78	1540
	Al MacInnis	23	1982–	1416
8	**Scott Stevens**	22	1982–	1635
	Ray Bourque	22	1979-2001	1612
	Dave Andreychuk	22	1982–	1597
	Stan Mikita	22	1958-80	1394
	Doug Mohns	22	1953-75	1390
	Dean Prentice	22	1952-74	1378
14	Fifteen tied with 21 years each.			

Note: Combined NHL-WHA years played: Howe (32); Messier (26); Howell (24); Bobby Hull (23); Norm Ullman, Eric Nesterenko, Frank Mahovlich and Dave Keon (22).

Games Played

		Yrs	Career	Gm
1	Gordie Howe	26	1946-71, 79-80	1767
2	**Mark Messier**	25	1979–	1756
3	Ron Francis	23	1981–	1731
4	Scott Stevens	22	1982–	1635
5	Larry Murphy	21	1980-2001	1615
6	Ray Bourque	22	1979-2001	1612
7	**Dave Andreychuk**	22	1982–	1597
8	Alex Delvecchio	24	1950-74	1549
9	John Bucyk	23	1955-78	1540
10	Phil Housley	21	1982-2003	1495
11	Wayne Gretzky	20	1979-99	1487
12	Doug Gilmour	20	1983-2003	1474
13	**Steve Yzerman**	21	1983–	1453
14	Tim Horton	24	1949-50, 51-74	1446
15	Mike Gartner	19	1979-98	1432

Note: Combined NHL-WHA games played: Howe (2,186); Messier (1808), Dave Keon (1,597), Harry Howell (1,581), Gretzky (1,567), Norm Ullman (1,554), Gartner (1,510) and Bobby Hull (1,474).

Goaltending

Wins

		Yrs	Gm	W	L	T	Pct
1	Patrick Roy	19	1029	**551**	315	131	.618
2	Terry Sawchuk	21	971	**447**	330	172	.562
3	**Ed Belfour**	16	856	**435**	281	111	.593
4	Jacques Plante	18	837	**434**	247	146	.614
5	Tony Esposito	16	886	**423**	306	152	.566
6	Glenn Hall	18	906	**407**	326	163	.545
7	**Martin Brodeur**	12	740	**403**	217	105	.628
	Grant Fuhr	19	868	**403**	295	114	.567
8	**Curtis Joseph**	15	798	**396**	289	90	.569
10	Mike Vernon	19	781	**385**	273	92	.575
11	John Vanbiesbrouck	20	882	**374**	346	119	.517
12	Andy Moog	18	713	**372**	209	88	.622
13	Tom Barrasso	19	777	**369**	277	86	.563
14	Rogie Vachon	16	795	**355**	291	127	.541
15	Gump Worsley	21	861	**335**	352	150	.490
16	Harry Lumley	16	804	**330**	329	143	.501
17	**Chris Osgood**	11	568	**305**	177	66	.617
	Billy Smith	18	680	**305**	233	105	.556
19	**Sean Burke**	16	762	**304**	321	101	.488
20	Turk Broda	12	629	**302**	224	101	.562

Losses

		Yrs	Gm	W	L	T	Pct
1	Gump Worsley	21	861	335	**352**	150	.490
2	Gilles Meloche	18	788	270	**351**	131	.446
3	John Vanbiesbrouck	20	882	374	**346**	119	.517
4	Terry Sawchuk	21	971	447	**330**	172	.562
5	Harry Lumley	16	804	330	**329**	143	.501

Shutouts

		Yrs	Games	No
1	Terry Sawchuk	21	971	103
2	George Hainsworth	11	465	94
3	Glenn Hall	18	906	84
4	Jacques Plante	18	837	82
5	Alex Connell	12	417	81
	Tiny Thompson	12	553	81
7	Tony Esposito	16	886	76
8	**Ed Belfour**	16	856	75
	Martin Brodeur	12	740	75
10	Lorne Chabot	11	411	73
11	Harry Lumley	16	804	71
12	Roy Worters	12	484	66
	Patrick Roy	19	1029	66
14	**Dominik Hasek**	13	595	63
15	Turk Broda	14	629	62

Goals Against Average
Minimum of 300 games played.

Before 1950

		Gm	Min	GA	GAA
1	George Hainsworth	465	29,415	937	1.91
2	Alex Connell	417	26,050	830	1.91
3	Chuck Gardiner	316	19,687	664	2.02
4	Lorne Chabot	411	25,307	860	2.04
5	Tiny Thompson	553	34,175	1183	2.08

Since 1950

		Gm	Min	GA	GAA
1	**Martin Brodeur**	740	43,511	1573	2.17
2	**Dominik Hasek**	595	34,562	1284	2.23
3	Ken Dryden	397	23,352	870	2.24
4	**Roman Turek**	328	19,095	734	2.31
5	Jacques Plante	837	49,533	1965	2.38
6	**Patrick Lalime**	322	18,553	738	2.39
7	**Ed Belfour**	856	49,509	2006	2.43
8	**Chris Osgood**	568	32,604	1324	2.44
9	Glen Hall	906	53,484	2222	2.49
10	Terry Sawchuk	971	57,194	2389	2.51

All-Time NHL Regular Season Leaders (Cont.)
SINGLE SEASON

Scoring
Points

		Season	G	A	Pts
1	Wayne Gretzky, Edm	1985-86	52	163	215
2	Wayne Gretzky, Edm	1981-82	92	120	212
3	Wayne Gretzky, Edm	1984-85	73	135	208
4	Wayne Gretzky, Edm	1983-84	87	118	205
5	Mario Lemieux, Pit	1988-89	85	114	199
6	Wayne Gretzky, Edm	1982-83	71	125	196
7	Wayne Gretzky, Edm	1986-87	62	121	183
8	Mario Lemieux, Pit	1987-88	70	98	168
	Wayne Gretzky, LA	1988-89	54	114	168
10	Wayne Gretzky, Edm	1980-81	55	109	164
11	Wayne Gretzky, LA	1990-91	41	122	163
12	Mario Lemieux, Pit	1995-96	69	92	161
13	Mario Lemieux, Pit	1992-93	69	91	160
14	Steve Yzerman, Det	1988-89	65	90	155
15	Phil Esposito, Bos	1970-71	76	76	152
16	Bernie Nicholls, LA	1988-89	70	80	150
17	Jaromir Jagr, Pit	1995-96	62	87	149
	Wayne Gretzky, Edm	1987-88	40	109	149
19	Pat LaFontaine, Buf	1992-93	53	95	148
20	Mike Bossy, NYI	1981-82	64	83	147

WHA 150 points or more: 154—Marc Tardif, Que. (1977-78).

Goals

		Season	Gm	No
1	Wayne Gretzky, Edm	1981-82	80	92
2	Wayne Gretzky, Edm	1983-84	74	87
3	Brett Hull, St.L	1990-91	78	86
4	Mario Lemieux, Pit	1988-89	76	85
5	Alexander Mogilny, Buf.	1992-93	77	76
	Phil Esposito, Bos	1970-71	78	76
	Teemu Selanne, Win	1992-93	84	76
8	Wayne Gretzky, Edm	1984-85	80	73
9	Brett Hull, St.L	1989-90	80	72
10	Jari Kurri, Edm	1984-85	73	71
	Wayne Gretzky, Edm	1982-83	80	71
12	Brett Hull, St.L	1991-92	73	70
	Mario Lemieux, Pit	1987-88	77	70
	Bernie Nicholls, LA	1988-89	79	70
15	Mario Lemieux, Pit	1992-93	60	69
	Mario Lemieux, Pit	1995-96	70	69
	Mike Bossy, NYI	1978-79	80	69
18	Phil Esposito, Bos	1973-74	78	68
	Jari Kurri, Edm	1985-86	78	68
	Mike Bossy, NYI	1980-81	79	68

WHA 70 goals or more: 77—Bobby Hull, Win. (1974-75); 75—Real Cloutier, Que. (1978-79); 71—Marc Tardif, Que. (1975-76); 70—Anders Hedberg, Win. (1976-77).

Assists

		Season	Gm	No
1	Wayne Gretzky, Edm	1985-86	80	163
2	Wayne Gretzky, Edm	1984-85	80	135
3	Wayne Gretzky, Edm	1982-83	80	125
4	Wayne Gretzky, LA	1990-91	78	122
5	Wayne Gretzky, Edm	1986-87	79	121
6	Wayne Gretzky, Edm	1981-82	80	120
7	Wayne Gretzky, Edm	1983-84	74	118
8	Mario Lemieux, Pit	1988-89	76	114
	Wayne Gretzky, LA	1988-89	78	114
10	Wayne Gretzky, Edm	1987-88	64	109
	Wayne Gretzky, Edm	1980-81	80	109
12	Wayne Gretzky, LA	1989-90	73	102
	Bobby Orr, Bos	1970-71	78	102
14	Mario Lemieux, Pit	1987-88	77	98
15	Adam Oates, Bos	1992-93	84	97

WHA 95 assists or more: 106—Andre Lacroix, San Diego (1974-75).

Goaltending
Wins

		Season	Record
1	Bernie Parent, Phi	1973-74	47-13-12
2	Bernie Parent, Phi	1974-75	44-14-9
	Terry Sawchuk, Det	1950-51	44-13-13
	Terry Sawchuk, Det	1951-52	44-14-12
5	Martin Brodeur, NJ	1999-00	43-20- 8
	Martin Brodeur, NJ	1997-98	43-17- 8
	Tom Barrasso, Pit	1992-93	43-14- 5
	Ed Belfour, Chi	1990-91	43-19- 7
9	Jacques Plante, Mon	1955-56	42-12-10
	Jacques Plante, Mon	1961-62	42-14-14
	Ken Dryden, Mon	1975-76	42-10- 8
	Mike Richter, NYR	1993-94	42-12- 6
	Roman Turek, St.L	1999-00	42-15- 9
	Martin Brodeur, NJ	2000-01	42-17-11

Most WHA wins in one season: 44—Richard Brodeur, Que. (1975-76).

Losses

		Season	Record
1	Gary Smith, Cal	1970-71	19-48- 4
2	Al Rollins, Chi	1953-54	12-47- 7
3	Peter Sidorkiewicz, Ott	1992-93	8-46- 3
4	Harry Lumley, Chi	1951-52	17-44-9
5	Three tied with 41 losses each.		

Most WHA losses in one season: 36—Don McLeod, Van. (1974-75) and Andy Brown, Ind. (1974-75).

Shutouts

		Season	Gm	No
1	George Hainsworth, Mon	1928-29	44	22
2	Alex Connell, Ott	1925-26	36	15
	Alex Connell, Ott	1927-28	44	15
	Hal Winkler, Bos	1927-28	44	15
	Tony Esposito, Chi	1969-70	63	15

Most WHA shutouts in one season: 5—Gerry Cheevers, Cle. (1972-73) and Joe Daly, Win. (1975-76).

Goals Against Average
Before 1950

		Season	Gm	GAA
1	George Hainsworth, Mon	1928-29	44	0.98
2	George Hainsworth, Mon	1927-28	44	1.09
3	Alex Connell, Ott	1925-26	36	1.17
4	Tiny Thompson, Bos	1928-29	44	1.18
5	Roy Worters, NY Americans	1928-29	38	1.21

Since 1950

		Season	Gm	GAA
1	Miikka Kiprusoff, Calg	2003-04	38	1.69
2	Marty Turco, Dal	2002-03	55	1.72
3	Tony Esposito, Chi	1971-72	48	1.77
4	Al Rollins, Tor	1950-51	40	1.77
5	Ron Tugnutt, Ott	1998-99	43	1.79

Penalty Minutes

		Season	PM
1	Dave Schultz, Phi	1974-75	472
2	Paul Baxter, Pit	1981-82	409
3	Mike Peluso, Chi	1991-92	408
4	Dave Schultz, LA-Pit	1977-78	405
5	Marty McSorley, LA	1992-93	399
6	Bob Probert, Det	1987-88	398
7	Basil McRae, Min	1987-88	382
8	Joey Kocur, Det	1985-86	377
9	Tim Hunter, Calg	1988-89	375
10	Donald Brashear, Van	1997-98	372

WHA 355 minutes or more: 365—Curt Brackenbury, Min-Que. (1975-76).

SINGLE GAME

Points

	Date	G-A—Pts
Darryl Sittler, Tor vs Bos	2/7/76	6-4—10
Maurice Richard, Mon vs Det	12/28/44	5-3— 8
Bert Olmstead, Mon vs Chi	1/9/54	4-4— 8
Tom Bladon, Phi vs Cle	12/11/77	4-4— 8
Bryan Trottier, NYI vs NYR	12/23/78	5-3— 8
Peter Stastny, Que at Wash	2/22/81	4-4— 8
Anton Stastny, Que at Wash	2/22/81	3-5— 8
Wayne Gretzky, Edm vs NJ	11/19/83	3-5— 8
Wayne Gretzky, Edm vs Min	1/4/84	4-4— 8
Paul Coffey, Edm vs Det	3/14/86	2-6— 8
Mario Lemieux, Pit vs St.L	10/15/88	2-6— 8
Bernie Nicholls, LA vs Tor	12/1/88	2-6— 8
Mario Lemieux, Pit vs NJ	12/31/88	5-3— 8

Goals

	Date	No
Joe Malone, Que vs Tor	1/31/20	7
Newsy Lalonde, Mon vs Tor	1/10/20	6
Joe Malone, Que vs Ott	3/10/20	6
Corb Denneny, Tor vs Ham	1/26/21	6
Cy Denneny, Ott vs Ham	3/7/21	6
Syd Howe, Det vs NYR	2/3/44	6
Red Berenson, St.L at Phi	11/7/68	6
Darryl Sittler, Tor vs Bos	2/7/76	6

Assists

	Date	No
Billy Taylor, Det at Chi	3/16/47	7
Wayne Gretzky, Edm vs Wash	2/15/80	7
Wayne Gretzky, Edm at Chi	12/11/85	7
Wayne Gretzky, Edm vs Que	2/14/86	7
24 players tied with 6 each.		

Penalty Minutes

	Date	Min
Randy Holt, LA at Phi	3/11/79	67
Brad Smith, Tor vs Det	11/15/86	57
Reed Low, St.L at Calg	2/28/02	57
Frank Bathe, Phi vs LA	3/11/79	55
Reed Low, St.L at Det	12/31/02	53
Russ Anderson, Pit vs Edm	1/19/80	51

Penalties

	Date	No
Chris Nilan, Bos vs Har	3/31/91	10*
Nine tied with 9 each.		

* Nilan accumulated six minors, two majors, one 10-minute misconduct and one game misconduct.

All-Time Winningest NHL Coaches

Top 20 NHL career victories through the 2003-04 season. Career, regular season and playoff records are noted along with NHL titles won. Coaches active during 2003-04 season in **bold** type. **Note:** In the following tables, overtime losses are considered losses.

		Career					Regular Season				Playoffs				
		Yrs	W	L	T	Pct	W	L	T	Pct	W	L	T	Pct	Stanley Cups
1	Scotty Bowman	30	**1467**	714	313	.651	1244	584	313	.654	223	130	0	.632	9 (1973, 76-79, 92, 97-98, 2002)
2	Al Arbour	22	**904**	663	248	.566	781	577	248	.564	123	86	0	.589	4 (1980-83)
3	Dick Irvin	26	**790**	609	228	.556	690	521	226	.559	100	88	2	.532	4 (1932,44,46,53)
4	Pat Quinn	18	**710**	555	154	.555	616	466	154	.561	94	89	0	.514	None
5	**Mike Keenan**	18	**675**	560	147	.542	584	491	147	.538	91	69	0	.569	1 (1994)
6	Billy Reay	16	**599**	445	175	.563	542	385	175	.571	57	60	0	.487	None
7	**Glen Sather**	13	**586**	351	122	.611	497	314	121	.598	89	37	1	.705	4 (1984-85,87-88)
8	Toe Blake	13	**582**	292	159	.640	500	255	159	.634	82	37	0	.689	8 (1956-60,65-66,68)
9	**Pat Burns**	14	**579**	438	151	.560	501	367	151	.566	78	71	0	.523	1 (2003)
10	Bryan Murray	14	**547**	457	131	.540	513	413	131	.547	34	44	0	.436	None
11	Roger Neilson	17	**511**	436	159	.540	460	381	159	.540	51	55	0	.481	None
12	**Brian Sutter**	13	**479**	477	140	.501	451	437	140	.507	28	40	0	.412	None
13	Jack Adams	21	**465**	442	162	.511	413	390	161	.512	52	52	1	.500	3 (1936-37, 43)
14	Jacques Demers	14	**464**	510	130	.479	409	467	130	.471	55	43	0	.561	1 (1993)
15	Fred Shero	10	**451**	272	119	.606	390	225	119	.612	61	47	0	.565	2 (1974-75)
16	**Jacques Martin**	11	**445**	373	119	.538	407	326	119	.548	38	47	0	.447	None
17	Punch Imlach	15	**439**	384	148	.538	395	336	148	.534	44	48	0	.478	4 (1962-64,67)
18	Emile Francis	13	**433**	326	112	.561	393	273	112	.577	40	53	0	.430	None
19	**Jacques Lemaire**	11	**427**	353	124	.541	370	309	124	.538	57	44	0	.564	1 (1995)
20	**Ken Hitchcock**	9	**426**	264	88	.604	362	217	88	.609	64	47	0	.577	1 (1999)

Where They Coached

Adams—Toronto (1922-23), Detroit (1927-47); **Arbour**—St. Louis (1970-73), NY Islanders (1973-86,88-94); **Blake**—Montreal (1955-68); **Bowman**—St. Louis (1967-71), Montreal (1971-79), Buffalo (1979-87), Pittsburgh (1991-93), Detroit (1993-2002); **Burns**—Montreal (1988-92), Toronto (1992-96), Boston (1997-2000), New Jersey (2002–); **Demers**—Quebec (1979-80), St. Louis (1983-86), Detroit (1986-90), Montreal (1992-95), Tampa Bay (1997-99); **Francis**—NY Rangers (1965-75), St. Louis (1976-77,81-83).

Hitchcock—Dallas (1996-2002), Philadelphia (2002–); **Imlach**—Toronto (1958-69), Buffalo (1970-72), Toronto (1979-81); **Irvin**—Chicago (1930-31,55-56), Toronto (1931-40), Montreal (1940-55); **Keenan**—Philadelphia (1984-88), Chicago (1988-92), NY Rangers (1993-94), St. Louis (1994-96), Vancouver (1997-99), Boston (2000-01), Florida (2001-03); **Lemaire**—Montreal (1984-85), New Jersey (1993-98), Minnesota (2000–); **Martin**—St. Louis (1986-88), Ottawa (1995-2004), Florida (2004–); **Murray**—Washington (1982-90), Detroit (1990-93), Florida (1997-98), Anaheim (2001-02), Ottawa (2004–).

Neilson—Toronto (1977-79), Buffalo (1979-81), Vancouver (1982-83), Los Angeles (1984), NY Rangers (1989-93), Florida (1993-95), Philadelphia (1998-00), Ottawa (2002); **Quinn**—Philadelphia (1978-82), Los Angeles (1984-87), Vancouver (1990-94, 96), Toronto (1998–); **Reay**—Toronto (1957-59), Chicago (1963-77); **Sather**—Edmonton (1979-89, 93-94), NY Rangers (2003-04); **Shero**—Philadelphia (1971-78), NY Rangers (1978-81); **Sutter**—St. Louis (1988-92), Boston (1992-95), Calgary (1997-2000), Chicago (2001–).

Top Winning Percentages

Minimum of 275 victories, including playoffs.

		Yrs	W	L	T	Pct.
1	Scotty Bowman	30	1467	714	313	**.651**
2	Toe Blake	13	582	292	159	**.640**
3	Glen Sather	13	586	351	122	**.611**
4	Fred Shero	10	451	272	119	**.606**
5	**Ken Hitchcock**	9	426	264	88	**.604**
6	Don Cherry	6	281	177	77	**.597**
7	Tommy Ivan	9	324	205	111	**.593**
8	**Bob Hartley**	6	294	205	61	**.579**
9	**Joel Quenneville**	8	341	243	77	**.574**
10	Al Arbour	22	904	663	248	**.566**
11	Billy Reay	16	599	445	175	**.563**
12	**Marc Crawford**	10	412	309	103	**.563**
13	Emile Francis	13	433	326	112	**.561**
14	**Pat Burns**	14	579	438	151	**.560**
15	Hap Day	10	308	237	81	**.557**
16	Dick Irvin	26	790	609	228	**.556**
17	**Pat Quinn**	18	710	555	154	**.555**
18	Lester Patrick	13	312	242	115	**.552**
19	Art Ross	18	393	310	95	**.552**
20	Bob Johnson	6	275	223	58	**.547**
21	Terry Murray	11	406	331	89	**.545**
22	**Mike Keenan**	18	675	560	147	**.542**
23	**Jacques Lemaire**	11	427	353	124	**.541**
24	Bryan Murray	14	547	457	131	**.540**
25	**Jacques Martin**	11	445	373	119	**.538**
26	Roger Neilson	16	511	436	159	**.534**
27	Punch Imlach	15	439	384	148	**.528**
28	**Darryl Sutter**	10	407	364	101	**.525**
29	Terry Crisp	9	310	296	78	**.518**
30	**Lindy Ruff**	7	285	265	78	**.516**

Active Coaches' Victories

Through 2003-04 season, including playoffs.

		Yrs	W	L	T	Pct.
1	Pat Quinn, Tor.	18	**710**	555	154	.555
2	Pat Burns, NJ	14	**579**	438	151	.560
3	Bryan Murray, Ott.	14	**547**	457	131	.540
4	Brian Sutter, Chi.	13	**479**	477	140	.501
5	Jacques Martin, Fla.	11	**445**	373	119	.538
6	Jacques Lemaire, Min.	11	**427**	353	124	.541
7	Ken Hitchcock, Phi.	9	**426**	264	88	.604
8	Marc Crawford, Van.	10	**412**	309	103	.563
9	Darryl Sutter, Calg.	10	**407**	364	101	.525
10	Ron Wilson, SJ	11	**403**	401	101	.501
11	Joel Quenneville, Col	8	**341**	243	77	.574
12	Bob Hartley, Atl.	6	**294**	205	61	.579
13	Lindy Ruff, Buf.	7	**285**	265	78	.516
14	Andy Murray, LA	5	**188**	188	58	.500
15	Barry Trotz, Nash.	6	**185**	253	60	.432
16	Craig MacTavish, Edm.	4	**153**	140	47	.519
17	John Tortorella, TB	5	**142**	148	37	.491
18	Rick Bowness, Pho.	9	**131**	299	48	.324
19	Dave Lewis, Det.	3	**106**	58	21	.630
20	Peter Laviolette, Car.	3	**101**	102	25	.498
21	Dave Tippett, Dal.	2	**94**	59	28	.597
22	Mike Babcock, Ana.	2	**84**	82	19	.505
23	Claude Julien, Mon.	2	**57**	62	10	.481
24	Mike Sullivan, Bos.	1	**44**	30	15	.579
	Tom Renney, NYR	3	**44**	68	9	.401
26	Steve Stirling, NYI	1	**39**	37	11	.511
27	Ed Olczyk, Pit.	1	**23**	51	8	.329
28	Gerard Gallant, Clb.	1	**16**	25	4	.400
29	Glen Hanlon, Wash.	1	**15**	30	9	.361
30	Mike Kitchen, St.L	1	**11**	11	4	.500

Annual Awards
Hart Memorial Trophy

Awarded to the player "adjudged to be the most valuable to his team" and named after Cecil Hart, the former manager-coach of the Montreal Canadiens. Winners selected by Pro Hockey Writers Assn. (PHWA). Winners' scoring statistics or goaltender W-L records and goals against average are provided; (*) indicates led or tied for league lead.

Multiple winners: Wayne Gretzky (9); Gordie Howe (6); Eddie Shore (4); Bobby Clarke, Mario Lemieux, Howie Morenz and Bobby Orr (3); Jean Beliveau, Bill Cowley, Phil Esposito, Dominik Hasek, Bobby Hull, Guy Lafleur, Mark Messier, Stan Mikita and Nels Stewart (2).

Year		G	A	Pts	Year		G	A	Pts
1924	Frank Nighbor, Ottawa, C	10	3	13	1952	Gordie Howe, Det., RW	47	39	86*
1925	Billy Burch, Hamilton, C	20	4	24	1953	Gordie Howe, Det., RW	49	46	95*
1926	Nels Stewart, Maroons, C	34	8	42*	1954	Al Rollins, Chi., G	12-47-7;		3.23
1927	Herb Gardiner, Mon., C	6	6	12	1955	Ted Kennedy, Tor., C	10	42	52
1928	Howie Morenz, Mon., C	33	18	51	1956	Jean Beliveau, Mon., C	47	41	88
1929	Roy Worters, NYA, G	16-13-9;		1.21	1957	Gordie Howe, Det., RW	44	45	89*
1930	Nels Stewart, Maroons, C	39	16	55	1958	Gordie Howe, Det., RW	33	44	77
1931	Howie Morenz, Mon., C	28	23	51*	1959	Andy Bathgate, NYR, RW	40	48	88
1932	Howie Morenz, Mon., C	24	25	49	1960	Gordie Howe, Det., RW	28	45	73
1933	Eddie Shore, Bos., D	8	27	35	1961	Bernie Geoffrion, Mon., RW	50	45	95*
1934	Aurel Joliat, Mon., LW	22	15	37	1962	Jacques Plante, Mon., G	42-14-14;		2.37*
1935	Eddie Shore, Bos., D	7	26	33	1963	Gordie Howe, Det., RW	38	48	86*
1936	Eddie Shore, Bos., D	3	16	19	1964	Jean Beliveau, Mon., C	28	50	78
1937	Babe Siebert, Mon., D	8	20	28	1965	Bobby Hull, Chi., LW	39	32	71
1938	Eddie Shore, Bos., D	3	14	17	1966	Bobby Hull, Chi., LW	54	43	97*
1939	Toe Blake, Mon., LW	24	23	47*	1967	Stan Mikita, Chi., C	35	62	97*
1940	Ebbie Goodfellow, Det., D	11	17	28	1968	Stan Mikita, Chi., C	40	47	87*
1941	Bill Cowley, Bos., C	17	45	62*	1969	Phil Esposito, Bos., C	49	77	126*
1942	Tommy Anderson, NYA, D	12	29	41	1970	Bobby Orr, Bos., D	33	87	120*
1943	Bill Cowley, Bos., C	27	45	72	1971	Bobby Orr, Bos., D	37	102	139
1944	Babe Pratt, Tor., D	17	40	57	1972	Bobby Orr, Bos., D	37	80	117
1945	Elmer Lach, Mon., C	26	54	80*	1973	Bobby Clarke, Phi., C	37	67	104
1946	Max Bentley, Chi., C	31	30	61*	1974	Phil Esposito, Bos., C	68	77	145*
1947	Maurice Richard, Mon., RW	45	26	71	1975	Bobby Clarke, Phi., C	27	89	116
1948	Buddy O'Connor, NYR, C	24	36	60	1976	Bobby Clarke, Phi., C	30	89	119
1949	Sid Abel, Det., C	28	26	54	1977	Guy Lafleur, Mon., RW	56	80	136*
1950	Chuck Rayner, NYR, G	28-30-11;		2.62	1978	Guy Lafleur, Mon., RW	60	72	132*
1951	Milt Schmidt, Bos., C	22	39	61	1979	Bryan Trottier, NYI., C	47	87	134*

Year		G	A	Pts
1980	Wayne Gretzky, Edm., C	51	86	137*
1981	Wayne Gretzky, Edm., C	55	109	164*
1982	Wayne Gretzky, Edm., C	92	120	212*
1983	Wayne Gretzky, Edm., C	71	125	196*
1984	Wayne Gretzky, Edm., C	87	118	205*
1985	Wayne Gretzky, Edm., C	73	135	208*
1986	Wayne Gretzky, Edm., C	52	163	215*
1987	Wayne Gretzky, Edm., C	62	121	183*
1988	Mario Lemieux, Pit., C	70	98	168*
1989	Wayne Gretzky, LA, C	54	114	168
1990	Mark Messier, Edm., C	45	84	129
1991	Brett Hull, St. L., RW	86	45	131
1992	Mark Messier, NYR, C	35	72	107
1993	Mario Lemieux, Pit., C	69	91	160*
1994	Sergei Fedorov, Det., C	56	64	120
1995	Eric Lindros, Phi., C	29	41	70*
1996	Mario Lemieux, Pit., C	69	92	161*
1997	Dominik Hasek, Buf., G	37-20-10;		2.27
1998	Dominik Hasek, Buf., G	33-23-13;		2.09
1999	Jaromir Jagr, Pit., RW	44	83	127*
2000	Chris Pronger, St.L, D	14	48	62
2001	Joe Sakic, Col., C	54	64	118
2002	Jose Theodore, Mon., G	30-24-10;		2.11
2003	Peter Forsberg, Col., C	29	77	106*
2004	Martin St. Louis, TB, RW	38	56	94*

Calder Memorial Trophy

Awarded to the most outstanding rookie of the year and named after Frank Calder, the late NHL president (1917-43). Since the 1990-91 season, all eligible candidates must not have attained their 26th birthday by Sept. 15 of their rookie year. Winners selected by PHWA. Winners' scoring statistics or goaltender W-L record & goals against average are provided.

Year		G	A	Pts
1933	Carl Voss, NYR-Det., C	8	15	23
1934	Russ Blinco, Maroons, C	14	9	23
1935	Sweeney Schriner, NYA, LW	18	22	40
1936	Mike Karakas, Chi., G	21-19-8;		1.92
1937	Syl Apps, Tor., C	16	29	45
1938	Cully Dahlstrom, Chi., C	10	9	19
1939	Frankie Brimsek, Bos., G	33-9-1;		1.58
1940	Kilby MacDonald, NYR, LW	15	13	28
1941	John Quilty, Mon., C	18	16	34
1942	Knobby Warwick, NYR, RW	16	17	33
1943	Gaye Stewart, Tor., LW	24	23	47
1944	Gus Bodnar, Tor., C	22	40	62
1945	Frank McCool, Tor., G	24-22-4;		3.22
1946	Edgar Laprade, NYR, C	15	19	34
1947	Howie Meeker, Tor., RW	27	18	45
1948	Jim McFadden, Det., C	24	24	48
1949	Penny Lund, NYR, RW	14	16	30
1950	Jack Gelineau, Bos., G	22-30-15;		3.28
1951	Terry Sawchuk, Det., G	44-13-13;		1.99
1952	Bernie Geoffrion, Mon., RW	30	24	54
1953	Gump Worsley, NYR, G	13-29-8;		3.06
1954	Camille Henry, NYR, LW	24	15	39
1955	Ed Litzenberger, Mon-Chi., RW	23	28	51
1956	Glenn Hall, Det., G	30-24-16;		2.11
1957	Larry Regan, Bos., RW	14	19	33
1958	Frank Mahovlich, Tor., LW	20	16	36
1959	Ralph Backstrom, Mon., C	18	22	40
1960	Billy Hay, Chi., C	18	37	55
1961	Dave Keon, Tor., C	20	25	45
1962	Bobby Rousseau, Mon., RW	21	24	45
1963	Kent Douglas, Tor., D	7	15	22
1964	Jacques Laperriere, Mon., D	2	28	30
1965	Roger Crozier, Det., G	40-23-7;		2.42
1966	Brit Selby, Tor., LW	14	13	27
1967	Bobby Orr, Bos., D	13	28	41
1968	Derek Sanderson, Bos., C	24	25	49
1969	Danny Grant, Min., LW	34	31	65
1970	Tony Esposito, Chi., G	38-17-8;		2.17
1971	Gilbert Perreault, Buf., C	38	34	72
1972	Ken Dryden, Mon., G	39-8-15;		2.24
1973	Steve Vickers, NYR, LW	30	23	53
1974	Denis Potvin, NYI, D	17	37	54
1975	Eric Vail, Atl., LW	39	21	60
1976	Bryan Trottier, NYI, C	32	63	95
1977	Willi Plett, Atl., RW	33	23	56
1978	Mike Bossy, NYI, RW	53	38	91
1979	Bobby Smith, Min., C	30	44	74
1980	Ray Bourque, Bos., D	17	48	65
1981	Peter Stastny, Que., C	39	70	109
1982	Dale Hawerchuk, Win., C	45	58	103
1983	Steve Larmer, Chi., RW	43	47	90
1984	Tom Barrasso, Buf., G	26-12-3;		2.84
1985	Mario Lemieux, Pit., C	43	57	100
1986	Gary Suter, Calg., D	18	50	68
1987	Luc Robitaille, LA, LW	45	39	84
1988	Joe Nieuwendyk, Calg., C	51	41	92
1989	Brian Leetch, NYR, D	23	48	71
1990	Sergei Makarov, Calg., RW	24	62	86
1991	Ed Belfour, Chi., G	43-19-7;		2.47
1992	Pavel Bure, Van., RW	34	26	60
1993	Teemu Selanne, Win., RW	76	56	132
1994	Martin Brodeur, NJ, G	27-11-8;		2.40
1995	Peter Forsberg, Que., C	15	35	50
1996	Daniel Alfredsson, Ott., RW	26	35	61
1997	Bryan Berard, NYI, D	8	40	48
1998	Sergei Samsonov, Bos., LW	22	25	47
1999	Chris Drury, Col., C	20	24	44
2000	Scott Gomez, NJ, C	19	51	70
2001	Evgeni Nabokov, SJ, G	32-21-7;		2.19
2002	Dany Heatley, Atl., RW	26	41	67
2003	Barret Jackman, St.L, D	3	16	19
2004	Andrew Raycroft, Bos., G	29-18-9;		2.05

Vezina Trophy

From 1927-80, given to the principal goaltender(s) on the team allowing the fewest goals during the regular season. Trophy named after 1920's goalie Georges Vezina of the Montreal Canadiens, who died of tuberculosis in 1926. Since the 1980-81 season, the trophy has been awarded to the most outstanding goaltender of the year as selected by the league's general managers.

Multiple Winners: Jacques Plante (7, one of them shared); Bill Durnan and Dominik Hasek (6); Ken Dryden (5, three shared); Bunny Larocque (4, all shared); Terry Sawchuk (4, one shared); Tiny Thompson (4); Tony Esposito (3, one shared); George Hainsworth (3); Glenn Hall (3, two shared); Patrick Roy (3); Ed Belfour (2); Johnny Bower (2, one shared); Frankie Brimsek (2); Turk Broda (2); Martin Brodeur (2); Chuck Gardiner (2); Charlie Hodge (2, one shared); Bernie Parent (2, one shared); Gump Worsley (2, both shared).

Year		Record	GAA
1927	George Hainsworth, Mon	28-14-2	1.52
1928	George Hainsworth, Mon	26-11-7	1.09
1929	George Hainsworth, Mon	22-7-15	0.98
1930	Tiny Thompson, Bos	38-5-1	2.23
1931	Roy Worters, NYA	18-16-10	1.68
1932	Chuck Gardiner, Chi	18-19-11	1.92
1933	Tiny Thompson, Bos	25-15-8	1.83
1934	Chuck Gardiner, Chi	20-17-11	1.73

Annual Awards (Cont.)

Year		Record	GAA	Year		Record	GAA
1935	Lorne Chabot, Chi	26-17-5	1.83	1972	Tony Esposito, Chi	31-10-6	1.77
1936	Tiny Thompson, Bos	22-20-6	1.71		& Gary Smith, Chi	14-5-6	2.42
1937	Norm Smith, Det	25-14-9	2.13	1973	Ken Dryden, Mon	33-7-13	2.26
1938	Tiny Thompson, Bos	30-11-7	1.85	1974	(Tie) Bernie Parent, Phi	47-13-12	1.89
1939	Frankie Brimsek, Bos	33-9-1	1.58		Tony Esposito, Chi	34-14-21	2.04
1940	Dave Kerr, NYR	27-11-10	1.60	1975	Bernie Parent, Phi	44-14-10	2.03
1941	Turk Broda, Tor	28-14-6	2.06	1976	Ken Dryden, Mon	42-10-8	2.03
1942	Frankie Brimsek, Bos	24-17-6	2.45	1977	Ken Dryden, Mon	41-6-8	2.14
1943	John Mowers, Det	25-14-11	2.47		& Bunny Larocque, Mon	19-2-4	2.09
1944	Bill Durnan, Mon	38-5-7	2.18	1978	Ken Dryden, Mon	37-7-7	2.05
1945	Bill Durnan, Mon	38-8-4	2.42		& Bunny Larocque, Mon	22-3-4	2.67
1946	Bill Durnan, Mon	24-11-5	2.60	1979	Ken Dryden, Mon	30-10-7	2.30
1947	Bill Durnan, Mon	34-16-10	2.30		& Bunny Larocque, Mon	22-7-4	2.84
1948	Turk Broda, Tor	32-15-13	2.38	1980	Bob Sauve, Buf	20-8-4	2.36
1949	Bill Durnan, Mon	28-23-9	2.10		& Don Edwards, Buf.	27-9-12	2.57
1950	Bill Durnan, Mon	26-21-17	2.20	1981	Richard Sevigny, Mon	20-4-3	2.40
1951	Al Rollins, Tor	27-5-8	1.77		Denis Herron, Mon	6-9-6	3.50
1952	Terry Sawchuk, Det	44-14-12	1.90		& Bunny Larocque, Mon.	16-9-3	3.03
1953	Terry Sawchuk, Det	32-15-16	1.90	1982	Billy Smith, NYI	32-9-4	2.97
1954	Harry Lumley, Tor	32-24-13	1.86	1983	Pete Peeters, Bos	40-11-9	2.36
1955	Terry Sawchuk, Det	40-17-11	1.96	1984	Tom Barrasso, Buf.	26-12-3	2.84
1956	Jacques Plante, Mon	42-12-10	1.86	1985	Pelle Lindbergh, Phi	40-17-7	3.02
1957	Jacques Plante, Mon	31-18-12	2.02	1986	John Vanbiesbrouck, NYR	31-21-5	3.32
1958	Jacques Plante, Mon	34-14-8	2.11	1987	Ron Hextall, Phi	37-21-6	3.00
1959	Jacques Plante, Mon	38-16-13	2.16	1988	Grant Fuhr, Edm.	40-24-9	3.43
1960	Jacques Plante, Mon	40-17-12	2.54	1989	Patrick Roy, Mon	33-5-6	2.47
1961	Johnny Bower, Tor	33-15-10	2.50	1990	Patrick Roy, Mon	31-16-5	2.53
1962	Jacques Plante, Mon	42-14-14	2.37	1991	Ed Belfour, Chi.	43-19-7	2.47
1963	Glenn Hall, Chi	30-20-16	2.55	1992	Patrick Roy, Mon.	36-22-8	2.36
1964	Charlie Hodge, Mon	33-18-11	2.26	1993	Ed Belfour, Chi.	41-18-11	2.59
1965	Johnny Bower, Tor	13-13-8	2.38	1994	Dominik Hasek, Buf	30-20-6	1.95
	& Terry Sawchuk, Tor	17-13-6	2.56	1995	Dominik Hasek, Buf	19-14-7	2.11
1966	Gump Worsley, Mon	29-14-6	2.36	1996	Jim Carey, Wash	35-24-9	2.26
	& Charlie Hodge, Mon	12-7-2	2.58	1997	Dominik Hasek, Buf	37-20-10	2.27
1967	Glenn Hall, Chi	19-5-5	2.38	1998	Dominik Hasek, Buf	33-23-13	2.09
	& Denis DeJordy, Chi	22-12-7	2.46	1999	Dominik Hasek, Buf	30-18-14	1.87
1968	Gump Worsley, Mon	19-9-8	1.98	2000	Olaf Kolzig, Wash	41-20-11	2.24
	& Rogie Vachon, Mon	23-13-2	2.48	2001	Dominik Hasek, Buf	37-24-4	2.11
1969	Jacques Plante, St.L	18-12-6	1.96	2002	Jose Theodore, Mon.	30-24-10	2.11
	& Glenn Hall, St.L	19-12-8	2.17	2003	Martin Brodeur, NJ.	41-23-9	2.02
1970	Tony Esposito, Chi	38-17-8	2.17	2004	Martin Brodeur, NJ.	38-26-11	2.03
1971	Ed Giacomin, NYR	27-10-7	2.16				
	& Gilles Villemure, NYR	22-8-4	2.30				

Lady Byng Memorial Trophy

Awarded to the player "adjudged to have exhibited the best type of sportsmanship and gentlemanly conduct combined with a high standard of playing ability" and named after Lady Evelyn Byng, the wife of former Canadian Governor General (1921-26) Baron Byng of Vimy. Winners selected by PHWA.

Multiple winners: Frank Boucher (7); Wayne Gretzky (5); Red Kelly (4); Bobby Bauer, Mike Bossy, Alex Delvecchio and Ron Francis (3); Johnny Bucyk, Marcel Dionne, Paul Kariya, Dave Keon, Stan Mikita, Joey Mullen, Frank Nighbor, Jean Ratelle, Clint Smith and Sid Smith (2).

Year		Year		Year	
1925	Frank Nighbor, Ott., C	1943	Max Bentley, Chi., C	1961	Red Kelly, Tor., D
1926	Frank Nighbor, Ott., C	1944	Clint Smith, Chi., C	1962	Dave Keon, Tor., C
1927	Billy Burch, NYA, C	1945	Bill Mosienko, Chi., RW	1963	Dave Keon, Tor., C
1928	Frank Boucher, NYR, C	1946	Toe Blake, Mon., LW	1964	Ken Wharram, Chi., RW
1929	Frank Boucher, NYR, C	1947	Bobby Bauer, Bos., RW	1965	Bobby Hull, Chi., LW
1930	Frank Boucher, NYR, C	1948	Buddy O'Connor, NYR, C	1966	Alex Delvecchio, Det., LW
1931	Frank Boucher, NYR, C	1949	Bill Quackenbush, Det., D	1967	Stan Mikita, Chi., C
1932	Joe Primeau, Tor., C	1950	Edgar Laprade, NYR, C	1968	Stan Mikita, Chi., C
1933	Frank Boucher, NYR, C	1951	Red Kelly, Det., D	1969	Alex Delvecchio, Det., LW
1934	Frank Boucher, NYR, C	1952	Sid Smith, Tor., LW	1970	Phil Goyette, St.L., C
1935	Frank Boucher, NYR, C	1953	Red Kelly, Det., D	1971	Johnny Bucyk, Bos., LW
1936	Doc Romnes, Chi., F	1954	Red Kelly, Det., D	1972	Jean Ratelle, NYR, C
1937	Marty Barry, Det., C	1955	Sid Smith, Tor., LW	1973	Gilbert Perreault, Buf., C
1938	Gordie Drillon, Tor., RW	1956	Earl Reibel, Det., C	1974	Johnny Bucyk, Bos., LW
1939	Clint Smith, NYR, C	1957	Andy Hebenton, NYR, RW	1975	Marcel Dionne, Det., C
1940	Bobby Bauer, Bos., RW	1958	Camille Henry, NYR, LW	1976	Jean Ratelle, NY-Bos., C
1941	Bobby Bauer, Bos., RW	1959	Alex Delvecchio, Det., LW	1977	Marcel Dionne, LA, C
1942	Syl Apps, Tor., C	1960	Don McKenney, Bos., C	1978	Butch Goring, LA, C

Year		Year		Year	
1979	Bob MacMillan, Atl., RW	1988	Mats Naslund, Mon., LW	1997	Paul Kariya, Ana., LW
1980	Wayne Gretzky, Edm., C	1989	Joey Mullen, Calg., RW	1998	Ron Francis, Pit., C
1981	Rick Kehoe, Pit., RW	1990	Brett Hull, St.L., RW	1999	Wayne Gretzky, NYR, C
1982	Rick Middleton, Bos., RW	1991	Wayne Gretzky, LA, C	2000	Pavol Demitra, St.L, RW
1983	Mike Bossy, NYI, RW	1992	Wayne Gretzky, LA, C	2001	Joe Sakic, Col., C
1984	Mike Bossy, NYI, RW	1993	Pierre Turgeon, NYI, C	2002	Ron Francis, Car., C
1985	Jari Kurri, Edm., C	1994	Wayne Gretzky, LA, C	2003	Alexander Mogilny, Tor., RW
1986	Mike Bossy, NYI, RW	1995	Ron Francis, Pit., C	2004	Brad Richards, TB, C
1987	Joey Mullen, Calg., RW	1996	Paul Kariya, Ana., LW		

Note: Bill Quackenbush and Red Kelly are the only defensemen to win the Lady Byng.

James Norris Memorial Trophy

Awarded to the most outstanding defenseman of the year and named after James Norris, the late Detroit Red Wings owner-president. Winners selected by PHWA.

Multiple winners: Bobby Orr (8); Doug Harvey (7); Ray Bourque (5); Chris Chelios, Paul Coffey, Nicklas Lidstrom, Pierre Pilote and Denis Potvin (3); Rod Langway, Brian Leetch and Larry Robinson (2).

Year		Year		Year	
1954	Red Kelly, Detroit	1971	Bobby Orr, Boston	1988	Ray Bourque, Boston
1955	Doug Harvey, Montreal	1972	Bobby Orr, Boston	1989	Chris Chelios, Montreal
1956	Doug Harvey, Montreal	1973	Bobby Orr, Boston		
1957	Doug Harvey, Montreal	1974	Bobby Orr, Boston	1990	Ray Bourque, Boston
1958	Doug Harvey, Montreal	1975	Bobby Orr, Boston	1991	Ray Bourque, Boston
1959	Tom Johnson, Montreal	1976	Denis Potvin, NY Islanders	1992	Brian Leetch, NY Rangers
		1977	Larry Robinson, Montreal	1993	Chris Chelios, Chicago
1960	Doug Harvey, Montreal	1978	Denis Potvin, NY Islanders	1994	Ray Bourque, Boston
1961	Doug Harvey, Montreal	1979	Denis Potvin, NY Islanders	1995	Paul Coffey, Detroit
1962	Doug Harvey, NY Rangers	1980	Larry Robinson, Montreal	1996	Chris Chelios, Chicago
1963	Pierre Pilote, Chicago	1981	Randy Carlyle, Pittsburgh	1997	Brian Leetch, NY Rangers
1964	Pierre Pilote, Chicago	1982	Doug Wilson, Chicago	1998	Rob Blake, Los Angeles
1965	Pierre Pilote, Chicago	1983	Rod Langway, Washington	1999	Al MacInnis, St. Louis
1966	Jacques Laperriere, Montreal	1984	Rod Langway, Washington	2000	Chris Pronger, St. Louis
1967	Harry Howell, NY Rangers	1985	Paul Coffey, Edmonton	2001	Nicklas Lidstrom, Detroit
1968	Bobby Orr, Boston	1986	Paul Coffey, Edmonton	2002	Nicklas Lidstrom, Detroit
1969	Bobby Orr, Boston	1987	Ray Bourque, Boston	2003	Nicklas Lidstrom, Detroit
1970	Bobby Orr, Boston			2004	Scott Niedermayer, NJ

Frank Selke Trophy

Awarded to the outstanding defensive forward of the year and named after the late Montreal Canadiens general manager. Winners selected by the PHWA.

Multiple winners: Bob Gainey (4); Guy Carbonneau and Jere Lehtinen (3); Sergei Fedorov and Michael Peca (2).

Year		Year		Year	
1978	Bob Gainey, Mon., LW	1987	Dave Poulin, Phi., C	1996	Sergei Fedorov, Det., C
1979	Bob Gainey, Mon., LW	1988	Guy Carbonneau, Mon., C	1997	Michael Peca, Buf., C
1980	Bob Gainey, Mon., LW	1989	Guy Carbonneau, Mon., C	1998	Jere Lehtinen, Dal., RW
1981	Bob Gainey, Mon., LW	1990	Rick Meagher, St.L., C	1999	Jere Lehtinen, Dal., RW
1982	Steve Kasper, Bos., C	1991	Dirk Graham, Chi., RW	2000	Steve Yzerman, Det., C
1983	Bobby Clarke, Phi., C	1992	Guy Carbonneau, Mon., C	2001	John Madden, NJ, LW
1984	Doug Jarvis, Wash., C	1993	Doug Gilmour, Tor., C	2002	Michael Peca, NYI, C
1985	Craig Ramsay, Buf., LW	1994	Sergei Fedorov, Det., C	2003	Jere Lehtinen, Dal., RW
1986	Troy Murray, Chi., C	1995	Ron Francis, Pit., C	2004	Kris Draper, Det., C

Jack Adams Award

Awarded to the coach "adjudged to have contributed the most to his team's success" and named after the late Detroit Red Wings coach and general manager. Winners selected by NHL Broadcasters' Assn.; (*) indicates division champion.

Multiple winners: Pat Burns (3); Scotty Bowman, Jacques Demers and Pat Quinn (2).

Year		Improvement		Year		Improvement	
1974	Fred Shero, Phi	37-30-11	to	50-16-12*	1990	Bob Murdoch, Win	26-42-12 to 37-32-11
1975	Bob Pulford, LA	41-14-23	to	37-35-8	1991	Brian Sutter, St.L	37-34-9 to 47-22-11
1976	Don Cherry, Bos	40-26-14	to	48-15-17*	1992	Pat Quinn, Van	28-43-9 to 42-26-12*
1977	Scotty Bowman, Mon	58-11-11*	to	60-8-12*	1993	Pat Burns, Tor	30-43-7 to 44-29-11
1978	Bobby Kromm, Det	6-55-9	to	32-34-14	1994	Jacques Lemaire, NJ	40-37-7 to 47-25-12
1979	Al Arbour, NYI	48-17-15*	to	51-15-14*	1995	Marc Crawford, Que	34-42-8 to 30-13-5*
1980	Pat Quinn, Phi	40-25-15	to	48-12-20*	1996	Scotty Bowman, Det	33-11-4* to 62-13-7*
1981	Red Berenson, St.L	34-34-12	to	45-18-17*	1997	Ted Nolan, Buf	33-42-7 to 40-30-12*
1982	Tom Watt, Win	9-57-14	to	33-33-14	1998	Pat Burns, Bos	26-47-9 to 39-30-13
1983	Orval Tessier, Chi	30-38-12	to	47-23-10	1999	Jacques Martin, Ott	34-33-15 to 44-23-15*
1984	Bryan Murray, Wash	39-25-16	to	48-27-5	2000	Joel Quenneville, St.L.	37-32-13 to 51-20-11*
1985	Mike Keenan, Phi	44-26-10	to	53-20-7*	2001	Bill Barber, Phi	45-25-12 to 43-25-11-3
1986	Glen Sather, Edm	49-20-11*	to	56-17-7*	2002	Bob Francis, Pho	35-27-17-3 to 40-27-9-6
1987	Jacques Demers, Det	17-57-6	to	34-36-10	2003	Jacques Lemaire, Minn.	26-35-12-9 to 42-29-10-1
1988	Jacques Demers, Det	34-36-10	to	41-28-11*	2004	John Tortorella, TB.	36-25-16-5 to 46-22-8-6*
1989	Pat Burns, Mon	45-22-13	to	53-18-9*			

Annual Awards (Cont.)
Lester B. Pearson Award

Awarded to the season's most outstanding player and named after the former diplomat, Nobel Peace Prize winner and Canadian prime minister. Winners selected by the NHL Players Association.

Multiple winners: Wayne Gretzky (5); Mario Lemieux (4); Guy Lafleur (3); Marcel Dionne, Phil Esposito, Dominik Hasek, Jaromir Jagr and Mark Messier (2).

Year		Year		Year	
1971	Phil Esposito, Bos., C	1983	Wayne Gretzky, Edm., C	1995	Eric Lindros, Phi., C
1972	Jean Ratelle, NYR, C	1984	Wayne Gretzky, Edm., C	1996	Mario Lemieux, Pit., C
1973	Bobby Clarke, Phi., C	1985	Wayne Gretzky, Edm., C	1997	Dominik Hasek, Buf., G
1974	Phil Esposito, Bos., C	1986	Mario Lemieux, Pit., C	1998	Dominik Hasek, Buf., G
1975	Bobby Orr, Bos., D	1987	Wayne Gretzky, Edm., C	1999	Jaromir Jagr, Pit., RW
1976	Guy Lafleur, Mon., RW	1988	Mario Lemieux, Pit., C	2000	Jaromir Jagr, Pit., RW
1977	Guy Lafleur, Mon., RW	1989	Steve Yzerman, Det., C	2001	Joe Sakic, Col., C
1978	Guy Lafleur, Mon., RW	1990	Mark Messier, Edm., C	2002	Jarome Iginla, Calg., RW
1979	Marcel Dionne, LA, C	1991	Brett Hull, St.L., RW	2003	Markus Naslund, Van., LW
1980	Marcel Dionne, LA, C	1992	Mark Messier, NYR, C	2004	Martin St. Louis, TB, RW
1981	Mike Liut, St.L., G	1993	Mario Lemieux, Pit., C		
1982	Wayne Gretzky, Edm., C	1994	Sergei Fedorov, Det., C		

King Clancy Memorial Trophy

Awarded to the player who "best exemplifies leadership on and off the ice and who has made a noteworthy humanitarian contribution to his community" and named after former player, coach, official and executive Frank "King" Clancy. Presented by the NHL's Board of Governors.

Year		Year		Year	
1988	Lanny McDonald, Calg., RW	1994	Adam Graves, NYR, LW	2000	Curtis Joseph, Tor., G
1989	Bryan Trottier, NYI, C	1995	Joe Nieuwendyk, Calg., C	2001	Shjon Podein, Col., LW
1990	Kevin Lowe, Edm., D	1996	Kris King, Win., LW	2002	Ron Francis, Car., C
1991	Dave Taylor, LA, RW	1997	Trevor Linden, Van., C	2003	Brendan Shanahan, Det., LW
1992	Ray Bourque, Bos., D	1998	Kelly Chase, St.L, RW	2004	Jarome Iginla, Calg., RW
1993	Dave Poulin, Bos., C	1999	Rob Ray, Buf., RW		

Bill Masterton Trophy

Awarded to the player who "best exemplifies the qualities of perseverance, sportsmanship and dedication to hockey" and named after the 29-year-old rookie center of the Minnesota North Stars who died of a head injury sustained in a 1968 NHL game. Presented by the PHWA.

Year		Year		Year	
1968	Claude Provost, Mon., RW	1981	Blake Dunlop, St.L., C	1994	Cam Neely, Bos., RW
1969	Ted Hampson, Oak., C	1982	Chico Resch, Colo., G	1995	Pat LaFontaine, Buf., C
1970	Pit Martin, Chi., C	1983	Lanny McDonald, Calg., RW	1996	Gary Roberts, Calg., LW
1971	Jean Ratelle, NYR, C	1984	Brad Park, Det., D	1997	Tony Granato, SJ, LW
1972	Bobby Clarke, Phi., C	1985	Anders Hedberg, NYR, RW	1998	Jamie McLennan, St.L, G
1973	Lowell MacDonald, Pit., RW	1986	Charlie Simmer, Bos., LW	1999	John Cullen, TB, C
1974	Henri Richard, Mon., C	1987	Doug Jarvis, Hart., C	2000	Ken Daneyko, NJ, D
1975	Don Luce, Buf., C	1988	Bob Bourne, LA, C	2001	Adam Graves, NYR, LW
1976	Rod Gilbert, NYR, RW	1989	Tim Kerr, Phi., C	2002	Saku Koivu, Mon., C
1977	Ed Westfall, NYI, RW	1990	Gord Kluzak, Bos., D	2003	Steve Yzerman, Det., C
1978	Butch Goring, LA, C	1991	Dave Taylor, LA, RW	2004	Bryan Berard, Chi., D
1979	Serge Savard, Mon., D	1992	Mark Fitzpatrick, NYI, G		
1980	Al MacAdam, Min., RW	1993	Mario Lemieux, Pit., C		

Number One Draft Choices

Overall first choices in the NHL draft since the league staged its first universal amateur draft in 1969. Players are listed with team that selected them; those who became Rookie of the Year are in **bold** type.

Year		Year		Year	
1969	Rejean Houle, Mon., LW	1982	Gord Kluzak, Bos., D	1995	**Bryan Berard,** Ott., D
1970	**Gilbert Perreault,** Buf., C	1983	Brian Lawton, Min., C	1996	Chris Phillips, Ott., D
1971	Guy Lafleur, Mon., RW	1984	**Mario Lemieux,** Pit., C	1997	Joe Thornton, Bos., C
1972	Billy Harris, NYI, RW	1985	Wendel Clark, Tor., LW/D	1998	Vincent Lecavalier, TB, C
1973	**Denis Potvin,** NYI, D	1986	Joe Murphy, Det., C	1999	Patrik Stefan, Atl., C
1974	Greg Joly, Wash., D	1987	Pierre Turgeon, Buf., C	2000	Rick DiPietro, NYI, G
1975	Mel Bridgman, Phi., C	1988	Mike Modano, Min., C	2001	Ilya Kovalchuk, Atl., RW
1976	Rick Green, Wash., D	1989	Mats Sundin, Que., RW	2002	Rick Nash, Clb., LW
1977	Dale McCourt, Det., C	1990	Owen Nolan, Que., RW	2003	Marc-Andre Fleury, Pit., G
1978	**Bobby Smith,** Min., C	1991	Eric Lindros, Que., C	2004	Alexander Ovechkin, Wash., LW
1979	Rob Ramage, Colo., D	1992	Roman Hamrlik, TB, D		
1980	Doug Wickenheiser, Mon., C	1993	Alexandre Daigle, Ott., C		
1981	**Dale Hawerchuk,** Win., C	1994	Ed Jovanovski, Fla., D		

World Hockey Association

WHA Finals

The World Hockey Association began play in 1972-73 as a 12-team rival of the 56-year-old NHL. The WHA played for the AVCO World Trophy in its seven playoff finals (Avco Financial Services underwrote the playoffs).

Multiple winners: Winnipeg (3); Houston (2).

Year	Winner	Head Coach	Series	Loser	Head Coach
1973	New England Whalers	Jack Kelley	4-1 (WWLWW)	Winnipeg Jets	Bobby Hull
1974	Houston Aeros	Bill Dineen	4-0	Chicago Cougars	Pat Stapleton
1975	Houston Aeros	Bill Dineen	4-0	Quebec Nordiques	Jean-Guy Gendron
1976	Winnipeg Jets	Bobby Kromm	4-0	Houston Aeros	Bill Dineen
1977	Quebec Nordiques	Marc Boileau	4-3 (LWLWWLW)	Winnipeg Jets	Bobby Kromm
1978	Winnipeg Jets	Larry Hillman	4-0	NE Whalers	Harry Neale
1979	Winnipeg Jets	Larry Hillman	4-2 (WWLWLW)	Edmonton Oilers	Glen Sather

Playoff MVPs—1973—No award; **1974**—No award; **1975**—Ron Grahame, Houston, G; **1976**—Ulf Nilsson, Winnipeg, C; **1977**—Serg Bernier, Quebec, C; **1978**—Bobby Guindon, Winnipeg, C; **1979**—Rich Preston, Winnipeg, RW.

Most Valuable Player

(Gordie Howe Trophy, 1976-79)

Year		G	A	Pts
1973	Bobby Hull, Win., LW	.51	52	103
1974	Gordie Howe, Hou., RW	.31	69	100
1975	Bobby Hull, Win., LW	.77	65	142
1976	Marc Tardif, Que., LW	.71	77	148
1977	Robbie Ftorek, Pho., C	.46	71	117
1978	Marc Tardif, Que., LW	.65	89	154
1979	Dave Dryden, Edm., G	.41-17-2; 2.89		

Scoring Leaders

Year		Gm	G	A	Pts
1973	Andre Lacroix, Phi	.78	50	74	124
1974	Mike Walton, Min	.78	57	60	117
1975	Andre Lacroix, S. Diego	.78	41	106	147
1976	Marc Tardif, Que	.81	71	77	148
1977	Real Cloutier, Que	.76	66	75	141
1978	Marc Tardif, Que	.78	65	89	154
1979	Real Cloutier, Que	.77	75	54	129

Note: In 1979, 18 year-old Rookie of the Year Wayne Gretzky finished third in scoring (46-64—110).

Rookie of the Year

Year		G	A	Pts
1973	Terry Caffery, N. Eng., C	.39	61	100
1974	Mark Howe, Hou., LW	.38	41	79
1975	Anders Hedberg, Win., RW	.53	47	100
1976	Mark Napier, Tor., RW	.43	50	93
1977	George Lyle, N. Eng., LW	.39	33	72
1978	Kent Nilsson, Win., C	.42	65	107
1979	Wayne Gretzky, Ind.-Edm., C	.46	64	110

Best Goaltender

Year		Record	GAA
1973	Gerry Cheevers, Cleveland	.32-20-0	2.84
1974	Don McLeod, Houston	.33-13-3	2.56
1975	Ron Grahame, Houston	.33-10-0	3.03
1976	Michel Dion, Indianapolis	.14-15-1	2.74
1977	Ron Grahame, Houston	.27-10-2	2.74
1978	Al Smith, New England	.30-20-3	3.22
1979	Dave Dryden, Edmonton	.41-17-2	2.89

Best Defenseman

Year	
1973	J.C. Tremblay, Quebec
1974	Pat Stapleton, Chicago
1975	J.C. Tremblay, Quebec
1976	Paul Shmyr, Cleveland
1977	Ron Plumb, Cincinnati
1978	Lars-Erik Sjoberg, Winnipeg
1979	Rick Ley, New England

Coach of the Year

Year			Improvement
1973	Jack Kelley, N. Eng		46-30-2*
1974	Billy Harris, Tor	.35-39-4 to	41-33-4
1975	Sandy Hucul, Pho	.Expan. to	39-31-8
1976	Bobby Kromm, Win	.38-35-5 to	52-27-2*
1977	Bill Dineen, Hou	.53-27-0 * to	50-24-6*
1978	Bill Dineen, Hou	.50-24-6 * to	42-34-4
1979	John Brophy, Birm	.36-41-3 to	32-42-6

*Won Division.

WHA All-Star Game

The WHA All-Star Game was an Eastern Division vs Western Division contest from 1973-75. In 1976, the league's five Canadian-based teams played the nine teams in the US. Over the final three seasons—East played West in 1977; AVCO Cup champion Quebec played a WHA All-Star team in 1978; and in 1979, a full WHA All-Star team played a three-game series with Moscow Dynamo of the Soviet Union.

Year	Result	Host	Coaches	Most Valuable Player
1973	East 6, West 2	Quebec	Jack Kelley, Bobby Hull	Wayne Carleton, Ottawa
1974	East 8, West 4	St. Paul, MN	Jack Kelley, Bobby Hull	Mike Walton, Minnesota
1975	West 6, East 4	Edmonton	Bill Dineen, Ron Ryan	Rejean Houle, Quebec
1976	Canada 6, USA 1	Cleveland	Jean-Guy Gendron, Bill Dineen	Can—Real Cloutier, Que. USA—Paul Shmyr, Cleve.
1977	East 4, West 2	Hartford	Jacques Demers, Bobby Kromm	East—L. Levasseur, Min. West—W. Lindstrom, Win.
1978	Quebec 5, WHA 4	Quebec	Marc Boileau, Bill Dineen	Quebec—Marc Tardif WHA—Mark Howe, NE
1979	WHA def. Moscow Dynamo 3 games to none (4-2, 4-2, 4-3)	Edmonton	Larry Hillman, P. Iburtovich	No awards

World Championship
Men

The World Hockey Championship tournament has been played regularly since 1930. The International Ice Hockey Federation (IIHF), which governs both the World and Winter Olympic tournaments, considers the Olympic champions from 1920-68 to also be the World champions. However the IIHF has not recognized an Olympic champion as World champion since 1968. The IIHF has sanctioned separate World Championships in Olympic years four times—in 1972, 1976, 1992 and 2002. The world championship is officially vacant for the three Olympic years from 1980-88.

Multiple winners: Soviet Union/Russia and Canada (23); Sweden (7); Czechoslovakia (6) Czech Republic (4), USA (2).

Year		Year		Year		Year	
1920	Canada	1951	Canada	1969	Soviet Union	1987	Sweden
1924	Canada	1952	Canada	1970	Soviet Union	1988	Not held
1928	Canada	1953	Sweden	1971	Soviet Union	1989	Soviet Union
1930	Canada	1954	Soviet Union	1972	Czechoslovakia	1990	Soviet Union
1931	Canada	1955	Canada	1973	Soviet Union	1991	Sweden
1932	Canada	1956	Soviet Union	1974	Soviet Union	1992	Sweden
1933	United States	1957	Sweden	1975	Soviet Union	1993	Russia
1934	Canada	1958	Canada	1976	Czechoslovakia	1994	Canada
1935	Canada	1959	Canada	1977	Czechoslovakia	1995	Finland
1936	Great Britain	1960	United States	1978	Soviet Union	1996	Czech Republic
1937	Canada	1961	Canada	1979	Soviet Union	1997	Canada
1938	Canada	1962	Sweden	1980	Not held	1998	Sweden
1939	Canada	1963	Soviet Union	1981	Soviet Union	1999	Czech Republic
1940-46	Not held	1964	Soviet Union	1982	Soviet Union	2000	Czech Republic
1947	Czechoslovakia	1965	Soviet Union	1983	Soviet Union	2001	Czech Republic
1948	Canada	1966	Soviet Union	1984	Not held	2002	Slovakia
1949	Czechoslovakia	1967	Soviet Union	1985	Czechoslovakia	2003	Canada
1950	Canada	1968	Soviet Union	1986	Soviet Union	2004	Canada

Women

The women's World Hockey Championship tournament is governed by the International Ice Hockey Federation (IIHF).

Multiple winners: Canada (8).

Year		Year		Year		Year	
1990	Canada	1994	Canada	1999	Canada	2001	Canada
1992	Canada	1997	Canada	2000	Canada	2004	Canada

Canada vs. USSR Summits

The first competition between the Soviet National Team and the NHL took place Sept. 2-28, 1972. A team of NHL All-Stars emerged as the winner of the heralded 8-game series, but just barely—winning with a record of 4-3-1 after trailing 1-3-1.

Two years later a WHA All-Star team played the Soviet Nationals and could win only one game and tie three others in eight contests. Two other Canada vs USSR series took place during NHL All-Star breaks: the three-game Challenge Cup at New York in 1979, and the two-game Rendez-Vous '87 in Quebec City in 1987.

The NHL All-Stars played the USSR in a three-game Challenge Cup series in 1979.

1972 Team Canada vs. USSR

NHL All-Stars vs Soviet National Team.

Date	City	Result	Goaltenders
9/2	Montreal	USSR, 7-3	Tretiak/Dryden
9/4	Toronto	Canada, 4-1	Esposito/Tretiak
9/6	Winnipeg	Tie, 4-4	Tretiak/Esposito
9/8	Vancouver	USSR, 5-3	Tretiak/Dryden
9/22	Moscow	USSR, 5-4	Tretiak/Esposito
9/24	Moscow	Canada, 3-2	Dryden/Tretiak
9/26	Moscow	Canada, 4-3	Esposito/Tretiak
9/28	Moscow	Canada, 6-5	Dryden/Tretiak

Standings

	W	L	T	Pts	GF	GA
Team Canada (NHL)	4	3	1	9	32	32
Soviet Union	3	4	1	7	32	32

Leading Scorers

1. Phil Esposito, Canada, (7-6—13); **2.** Aleksandr Yakushev, USSR (7-4—11); **3.** Paul Henderson, Canada (7-2—9); **4.** Boris Shadrin, USSR (3-5—8); **5.** Valeri Kharlamov, USSR (3-4—7) and Vladimir Petrov, USSR (3-4—7).

1974 Team Canada vs. USSR

WHA All-Stars vs Soviet National Team.

Date	City	Result	Goaltenders
9/17	Quebec City	Tie, 3-3	Tretiak/Cheevers
9/19	Toronto	Canada, 4-1	Cheevers/Tretiak
9/21	Winnipeg	USSR, 8-5	Tretiak/McLeod
9/23	Vancouver	Tie, 5-5	Tretiak/Cheevers
10/1	Moscow	USSR, 3-2	Tretiak/Cheevers
10/3	Moscow	USSR, 5-2	Tretiak/Cheevers
10/5	Moscow	Tie, 4-4	Cheevers/Tretiak
10/6	Moscow	USSR, 3-2	Sidelinkov/Cheevers

Standings

	W	L	T	Pts	GF	GA
Soviet Union	4	1	3	11	32	27
Team Canada (WHA)	1	4	3	5	27	34

Leading Scorers

1. Bobby Hull, Canada (7-2—9); **2.** Aleksandr Yakushev, USSR (6-2—8), Ralph Backstrom, Canada (4-4—8) and Valeri Kharlamov, USSR (2-6—8); **5.** Gordie Howe, Canada (3-4—7), Andre Lacroix, Canada (1-6—7) and Vladimi Petrov, USSR (1-6—7).

1979 Challenge Cup Series

NHL All-Stars vs Soviet National Team

Date	City	Result	Goaltenders
2/8	New York	NHL, 4-2	K. Dryden/Tretiak
2/10	New York	USSR, 5-4	Tretiak/K. Dryden
2/11	New York	USSR, 6-0	Myshkin/Cheevers

Rendez-Vous '87

NHL All-Stars vs Soviet National Team

Date	City	Result	Goaltenders
2/11	Quebec	NHL, 4-3	Fuhr/Belosheykhin
2/13	Quebec	USSR, 5-3	Belosheykhin/Fuhr

The Canada Cup

After organizing the historic 8-game Team Canada-Soviet Union series of 1972, NHL Players Association executive director Alan Eagleson and the NHL created the Canada Cup in 1976. For the first time, the best players from the world's six major hockey powers—Canada, Czechoslovakia, Finland, Russia, Sweden and the USA—competed together in one tournament.

1976
Round Robin Standings

	W	L	T	Pts	GF	GA
Canada	4	1	0	8	22	6
Czechoslovakia	3	1	1	7	19	9
Soviet Union	2	2	1	5	23	14
Sweden	2	2	1	5	16	18
United States	1	3	1	3	14	21
Finland	1	4	0	2	16	42

Finals (Best of 3)

Date	City	Score
9/13	Toronto	Canada 6, Czechoslovakia 0
9/15	Montreal	Canada 5, Czechoslovakia 4 (OT)

Note: Darryl Sittler scored the winning goal for Canada at 11:33 in overtime to clinch the Cup, 2 games to none.

Leading Scorers

1. Victor Hluktov, USSR (5-4—9), Bobby Orr, Canada (2-7—9) and Denis Potvin, Canada (1-8—9); **4.** Bobby Hull, Canada (5-3—8) and Milan Novy, Czechoslovakia (5-3—8).

Team MVPs

Canada—Rogie Vachon
Czech.—Milan Novy
USSR—Alexandr Maltsev
Sweden—Borje Salming
USA—Robbie Ftorek
Finland—Matti Hagman
Tournament MVP—Bobby Orr, Canada

1981
Round Robin Standings

	W	L	T	Pts	GF	GA
Canada	4	0	1	9	32	13
Soviet Union	3	1	1	7	20	13
Czechoslovakia	2	1	2	6	21	13
United States	2	2	1	5	17	19
Sweden	1	4	0	2	13	20
Finland	0	4	1	1	6	31

Semifinals

Date	City	Score
9/11	Ottawa	USSR 4, Czechoslovakia 1
9/11	Montreal	Canada 4, United States 1

Finals

Date	City	Score
9/13	Montreal	USSR 8, Canada 1

Leading Scorers

1. Wayne Gretzky, Canada (5-7—12); **2.** Mike Bossy, Canada (8-3—11), Bryan Trottier, Canada (3-8—11), Guy Lafleur, Canada (2-9—11), Alexei Kasatonov, USSR (1-10—11).

All-Star Team

Goal—Vladislav Tretiak, USSR; **Defense**—Arnold Kadlec, Czech., and Alexei Kasatonov, USSR; **Forwards**—Mike Bossy, Canada, Gil Perreault, Canada, and Sergei Shepelev, USSR. **Tournament MVP**—Tretiak.

1984
Round Robin Standings

	W	L	T	Pts	GF	GA
Soviet Union	5	0	0	10	22	7
United States	3	1	1	7	21	13
Sweden	3	2	0	6	15	16
Canada	2	2	1	5	23	18
West Germany	0	4	1	1	13	29
Czechoslovakia	0	4	1	1	10	21

Semifinals

Date	City	Score
9/12	Edmonton	Sweden 9, United States 2
9/15	Montreal	Canada 3, USSR 2 (OT)

Note: Mike Bossy scored the winning goal for Canada at 12:29 in overtime.

Finals (Best of 3)

Date	City	Score
9/16	Calgary	Canada 5, Sweden 2
9/18	Edmonton	Canada 6, Sweden 5

Leading Scorers

1. Wayne Gretzky, Canada (5-7—12); **2.** Michel Goulet, Canada (5-6—11), Kent Nilsson, Sweden (3-8—11), Paul Coffey, Canada (3-8—11); **5.** Hakan Loob, Sweden (6-4—10).

All-Star Team

Goal—Vladimir Myshkin, USSR; **Defense**—Paul Coffey, Canada and Rod Langway, USA; **Forwards**—Wayne Gretzky, Canada, John Tonelli, Canada, and Sergei Makarov, USSR. **Tournament MVP**—Tonelli.

1987
Round Robin Standings

	W	L	T	Pts	GF	GA
Canada	3	0	2	8	19	13
Soviet Union	3	1	1	7	22	13
Sweden	3	2	0	6	17	14
Czechoslovakia	2	2	1	5	12	15
United States	2	3	0	4	13	14
Finland	0	5	0	0	9	23

Semifinals

Date	City	Score
9/8	Hamilton	USSR 4, Sweden 2
9/9	Montreal	Canada 5, Czechoslovakia 3

Finals (Best of 3)

Date	City	Score
9/11	Montreal	USSR 6, Canada 5 (OT)
9/13	Hamilton	Canada 6, USSR 5 (2 OT)
9/15	Hamilton	Canada 6, USSR 5

Note: In Game 1, Alexander Semak of USSR scored at 5:33 in overtime. In Game 2, Mario Lemieux of Canada scored at 10:01 in the second overtime period. Lemieux also won Game 3 on a goal with 1:26 left in regulation time.

Leading Scorers

1. Wayne Gretzky, Canada (3-18—21); **2.** Mario Lemieux, Canada (11-7—18); **3.** Sergei Makarov, USSR (7-8—15); **4.** Vladimir Krutov, USSR (7-7—14); **5.** Viacheslav Bykov, USSR (2-7—9); **6.** Ray Bourque, Canada (2-6—8).

All-Star Team

Goal—Grant Fuhr, Canada; **Defense**—Ray Bourque, Canada and Viacheslav Fetisov, USSR; **Forwards**—Wayne Gretzky, Canada, Mario Lemieux, Canada, and Vladimir Krutov, USSR. **Tournament MVP**—Gretzky.

1991

Round Robin Standings

	W	L	T	Pts	GF	GA
Canada	3	0	2	8	21	11
United States	4	1	0	8	19	15
Finland	2	2	1	5	10	13
Sweden	2	3	0	4	13	17
Soviet Union	1	3	1	3	14	14
Czechoslovakia	1	4	0	2	11	18

Semifinals

Date	City	Score
9/11	Hamilton	United States 7, Finland 3
9/12	Toronto	Canada 4, Sweden 0

Finals (Best of 3)

Date	City	Score
9/14	Montreal	Canada 4, United States 1
9/16	Hamilton	Canada 4, United States 2

Leading Scorers

1. Wayne Gretzky, Canada (4-8—12); **2.** Steve Larmer, Canada (6-5—11); **3.** Brett Hull, USA (2-7—9); **4.** Mike Modano, USA (2-7—9); **5.** Mark Messier, Canada (2-6—8).

All-Star Team

Goal—Bill Ranford, Canada; **Defense**—Al MacInnis, Canada and Chris Chelios, USA; **Forwards**—Wayne Gretzky, Canada, Jeremy Roenick, USA and Mats Sundin, Sweden. **Tournament MVP**—Bill Ranford.

The World Cup

Formed jointly by the NHL and the NHL Players Association in cooperation with the International Ice Hockey Federation. The inaugural World Cup held games in nine different cities throughout North America and Europe, the most ever by a single international hockey tournament.

1996

Round Robin Standings

European Pool	W	L	T	Pts	GF	GA
Sweden	3	0	0	6	14	3
Finland	2	1	0	4	17	11
Germany	1	2	0	2	11	15
Czech Republic	0	3	0	0	4	17

North American Pool	W	L	T	Pts	GF	GA
United States	3	0	0	6	19	8
Canada	2	1	0	4	11	10
Russia	1	2	0	2	12	14
Slovakia	0	3	0	0	10	18

Semifinals

Date	City	Score
9/7	Philadelphia	Canada 3, Sweden 2 (OT)
9/8	Ottawa	United States 5, Russia 2

Finals (Best of 3)

Date	City	Score
9/10	Philadelphia	Canada 4, United States 3 (OT)
9/12	Montreal	United States 5, Canada 2
9/14	Montreal	United States 5, Canada 2

Leading Scorers

1. Brett Hull, USA (7-4—11); **2.** John LeClair, USA (6-4—10); **3.** Mats Sundin, Sweden (4-3—7); Wayne Gretzky, Canada (2-5—7); Doug Weight, USA (3-4—7); Paul Coffey, Canada (0-7—7); Brian Leetch, USA (0-7—7).

All-Tournament Team

Goal—Mike Richter, USA; **Defense**—Calle Johansson, Sweden and Chris Chelios, USA; **Forwards**—Brett Hull, USA; John LeClair, USA and Mats Sundin, Sweden. **Tournament MVP**—Mike Richter, USA.

2004

Round Robin Standings

European Pool	W	L	T	Pts	GF	GA
Finland	2	0	1	5	11	4
Sweden	2	0	1	5	13	9
Czech Republic	1	2	0	2	10	10
Germany	0	3	0	0	4	15

North American Pool	W	L	T	Pts	GF	GA
Canada	3	0	0	6	10	3
Russia	2	1	0	4	9	6
United States	1	2	0	2	5	6
Slovakia	0	3	0	0	4	13

Semifinals

Date	City	Score
9/10	St. Paul, Minn.	Finland 2, United States 1
9/11	Toronto	Canada 4, Czech Rep. 3 (OT)

Championship Game

Date	City	Score
9/14	Toronto	Canada 3, Finland 2

Leading Scorers

1. Fredrik Modin, Sweden (4-4—8); **2.** Vincent Lecavalier, Canada (2-5—7); **3.** Keith Tkachuk, USA (5-1—6); Joe Sakic, Canada (4-2—6); Martin Havlat, Czech Republic (3-3—6); Kimmo Timonen, Finland (1-5—6); Joe Thornton, Canada (1-5—6); Mike Modano, USA (0-6—6); Daniel Alfredsson, Sweden (0-6—6).

All-Tournament Team

Goal—Martin Brodeur, Canada; **Defense**—Kimmo Timonen, Finland and Adam Foote, Canada; **Forwards**—Vincent Lecavalier, Canada; Saku Koivu, Finland and Fredrik Modin, Sweden. **Tournament MVP**—Vincent Lecavalier, Canada.

U.S. DIVISION I COLLEGE HOCKEY

NCAA Men's Frozen Four

The NCAA Division I hockey tournament began in 1948 and was played at the Broadmoor Ice Palace in Colorado Springs from 1948-57. Since 1958, the tournament has moved around the country, stopping for consecutive years only at Boston Garden from 1949-89 and discontinued in 1990. Consolation games to determine third place were played from 1972-74.

Multiple winners: Michigan (9); North Dakota (7); Denver (6); Minnesota (5); Boston University (4); Lake Superior St. and Michigan Tech (3); Boston College, Colorado College, Cornell, Maine, Michigan St. and RPI (2).

Year	Champion	Head Coach	Score	Runner-up	Third Place
1948	Michigan	Vic Heyliger	8-4	Dartmouth	Colorado College and Boston College

Year	Champion	Head Coach	Score	Runner-up	Third Place	Score	Fourth Place
1949	Boston College	Snooks Kelley	4-3	Dartmouth	Michigan	10-4	Colorado Col.
1950	Colorado College	Cheddy Thompson	13-4	Boston Univ.	Michigan	10-6	Boston College
1951	Michigan	Vic Heyliger	7-1	Brown	Boston Univ.	7-4	Colorado College
1952	Michigan	Vic Heyliger	4-1	Colorado Col.	Yale	4-1	St. Lawrence
1953	Michigan	Vic Heyliger	7-3	Minnesota	RPI	6-3	Boston Univ.
1954	RPI	Ned Harkness	5-4 *	Minnesota	Michigan	7-2	Boston College
1955	Michigan	Vic Heyliger	5-3	Colorado Col.	Harvard	6-3	St. Lawrence
1956	Michigan	Vic Heyliger	7-5	Michigan Tech	St. Lawrence	6-2	Boston College
1957	Colorado College	Tom Bedecki	13-6	Michigan	Clarkson	2-1†	Harvard
1958	Denver	Murray Armstrong	6-2	North Dakota	Clarkson	5-1	Harvard
1959	North Dakota	Bob May	4-3 *	Michigan St.	Boston College	7-6†	St. Lawrence
1960	Denver	Murray Armstrong	5-3	Michigan Tech	Boston Univ.	7-6	St. Lawrence
1961	Denver	Murray Armstrong	12-2	St. Lawrence	Minnesota	4-3	RPI
1962	Michigan Tech	John MacInnes	7-1	Clarkson	Michigan	5-1	St. Lawrence
1963	North Dakota	Barry Thorndycraft	6-5	Denver	Clarkson	5-3	Boston College
1964	Michigan	Allen Renfrew	6-3	Denver	RPI	2-1	Providence
1965	Michigan Tech	John MacInnes	8-2	Boston College	North Dakota	9-5	Brown
1966	Michigan St.	Amo Bessone	6-1	Clarkson	Denver	4-3	Boston Univ.
1967	Cornell	Ned Harkness	4-1	Boston Univ.	Michigan St.	6-1	North Dakota
1968	Denver	Murray Armstrong	4-0	North Dakota	Cornell	6-1	Boston College
1969	Denver	Murray Armstrong	4-3	Cornell	Harvard	6-5†	Michigan Tech
1970	Cornell	Ned Harkness	6-4	Clarkson	Wisconsin	6-5	Michigan Tech
1971	Boston Univ.	Jack Kelley	4-2	Minnesota	Denver	1-0	Harvard
1972	Boston Univ.	Jack Kelley	4-0	Cornell	Wisconsin	5-2	Denver
1973	Wisconsin	Bob Johnson	4-2	Denver	Boston College	3-1	Cornell
1974	Minnesota	Herb Brooks	4-2	Michigan Tech	Boston Univ.	7-5	Harvard
1975	Michigan Tech	John MacInnes	6-1	Minnesota	Boston Univ.	10-5	Harvard
1976	Minnesota	Herb Brooks	6-4	Michigan Tech	Brown	8-7	Boston Univ.
1977	Wisconsin	Bob Johnson	6-5 *	Michigan	Boston Univ.	-6-5	N. Hampshire
1978	Boston Univ.	Jack Parker	5-3	Boston College	Bowl. Green	4-3	Wisconsin
1979	Minnesota	Herb Brooks	4-3	North Dakota	Dartmouth	7-3	N. Hampshire
1980	North Dakota	Gino Gasparini	5-2	N. Michigan	Dartmouth	8-4	Cornell
1981	Wisconsin	Bob Johnson	6-3	Minnesota	Mich. Tech	5-2	N. Michigan
1982	North Dakota	Gino Gasparini	5-2	Wisconsin	Northeastern	10-4	N. Hampshire
1983	Wisconsin	Jeff Sauer	6-2	Harvard	Providence	4-3	Minnesota
1984	Bowling Green	Jerry York	5-4 *	Minn-Duluth	North Dakota	6-5†	Michigan St.
1985	RPI	Mike Addesa	2-1	Providence	Minn. Duluth	7-6†	Boston College
1986	Michigan St.	Ron Mason	6-5	Harvard	Minnesota	6-4	Denver
1987	North Dakota	Gino Gasparini	5-3	Michigan St.	Minnesota	6-3	Harvard
1988	Lake Superior St.	Frank Anzalone	4-3 *	St. Lawrence	Maine	5-2	Minnesota
1989	Harvard	Billy Cleary	4-3 *	Minnesota	Michigan St.	7-4	Maine

Year	Champion	Head Coach	Score	Runner-up	Third Place
1990	Wisconsin	Jeff Sauer	7-3	Colgate	Boston College and Boston Univ.
1991	Northern Michigan	Rick Comley	8-7 *	Boston Univ.	Maine and Clarkson
1992	Lake Superior St.	Jeff Jackson	5-3	Wisconsin	Michigan and Michigan St.
1993	Maine	Shawn Walsh	5-4	Lake Superior St.	Boston Univ. and Michigan
1994	Lake Superior St.	Jeff Jackson	9-1	Boston Univ.	Harvard and Minnesota
1995	Boston Univ.	Jack Parker	6-2	Maine	Michigan and Minnesota
1996	Michigan	Red Berenson	3-2 *	Colorado Col.	Vermont and Boston Univ.
1997	North Dakota	Dean Blais	6-4	Boston Univ.	Colorado College and Michigan
1998	Michigan	Red Berenson	3-2 *	Boston College	New Hampshire and Ohio St.
1999	Maine	Shawn Walsh	3-2 *	New Hampshire	Boston College and Michigan St.
2000	North Dakota	Dean Blais	4-2	Boston College	St. Lawrence and Maine
2001	Boston College	Jerry York	3-2 *	North Dakota	Michigan and Michigan St.
2002	Minnesota	Don Lucia	4-3 *	Maine	Michigan and New Hampshire
2003	Minnesota	Don Lucia	5-1	New Hampshire	Michigan and Cornell
2004	Denver	George Gwozdecky	1-0	Maine	Minnesota Duluth and Boston College

*Championship game overtime goals: **1954**—1:54; **1959**—4:22; **1977**—0: 23; **1984**—7:11 in 4th OT; **1988**—4:46; **1989**—4:16; **1991**—1:57 in 3rd OT; **1996**—3:35; **1998**—17:51; **1999**—10:50; **2001**—4:43; **2002**—16:58.
†Consolation game overtimes ended in 1st OT except in 1957, '59, and '69, which all ended in 2nd OT.
Note: Runners-up Denver (1973) and Wisconsin (1992) had participation voided by the NCAA for using ineligible players.

U.S. Division I College Hockey (Cont.)

Tournament Most Outstanding Player

The Most Outstanding Players of each NCAA Div. I tournament since 1948. Winners of the award who did not play for the tournament champion are in **bold** type. In 1960, three players, none on the winning team, shared the award.

Multiple winners: Lou Angotti and Marc Behrend (2).

Year	Year	Year
1948 Joe Riley, Dartmouth, F	1966 Gaye Cooley, Mich. St., G	1986 Mike Donnelly, Mich. St., F
1949 **Dick Desmond,** Dart., G	1967 Walt Stanowski, Cornell, D	1987 Tony Hrkac, N. Dakota, F
1950 **Ralph Bevins,** Boston U., G	1968 Gerry Powers, Denver, G	1988 Bruce Hoffort, Lk. Superior, G
1951 **Ed Whiston,** Brown, G	1969 Keith Magnuson, Denver, D	1989 Ted Donato, Harvard, F
1952 **Ken Kinsley,** Colo. Col., G	1970 Dan Lodboa, Cornell, D	1990 Chris Tancill, Wisconsin, F
1953 John Matchefts, Mich., F	1971 Dan Brady, Boston U., G	1991 Scott Beattie, No. Mich., F
1954 Abbie Moore, RPI, F	1972 Tim Regan, Boston U., G	1992 Paul Constantin, Lk. Superior, F
1955 **Phil Hilton,** Colo. Col., F	1973 Dean Talafous, Wisc., F	1993 Jim Montgomery, Maine, F
1956 Lorne Howes, Mich., G	1974 Brad Shelstad, Minn., G	1994 Sean Tallaire, Lk. Superior, F
1957 Bob McCusker, Colo. Col., F	1975 Jim Warden, Mich. Tech, G	1995 Chris O'Sullivan, Boston U., F
1958 Murray Massier, Denver, F	1976 Tom Vannelli, Minn., F	1996 Brendan Morrison, Michigan, F
1959 Reg Morelli, N. Dakota, F	1977 Julian Baretta, Wisc., G	1997 Matt Henderson, N. Dakota, F
1960 **Lou Angotti,** Mich. Tech, F;	1978 Jack O'Callahan, Boston U., D	1998 Marty Turco, Michigan, G
Bob Marquis, Boston U., F;	1979 Steve Janaszak, Minn., G	1999 Alfie Michaud, Maine, G
& **Barry Urbanski,** BU, G	1980 Doug Smail, N. Dakota, F	2000 Lee Goren, N. Dakota, F
1961 Bill Masterton, Denver, F	1981 Marc Behrend, Wisc., G	2001 Chuck Kobasew, Boston College, F
1962 Lou Angotti, Mich. Tech, F	1982 Phil Sykes, N. Dakota, F	2002 Grant Potulny, Minnesota, F
1963 Al McLean, N. Dakota, F	1983 Marc Behrend, Wisc., G	2003 Thomas Vanek, Minnesota, F
1964 Bob Gray, Michigan, G	1984 Gary Kruzich, Bowl. Green, G	2004 Adam Berkhoel, Denver, G
1965 Gary Milroy, Mich. Tech, F	1985 **Chris Terreri**, Prov., G	

Hobey Baker Award

College hockey's Player of the Year award; voted on by a national panel of sportswriters, broadcasters, college coaches and pro scouts (plus a fan vote beginning in 2003). First presented in 1981 by the Decathlon Athletic Club of Bloomington, Minn., in the name of the Princeton collegiate hockey and football star who was killed in a plane crash.

Year	Year	Year
1981 Neal Broten, Minnesota, F	1989 Lane MacDonald, Harvard, F	1997 Brendan Morrison, Michigan, F
1982 George McPhee, Bowl. Green, F	1990 Kip Miller, Michigan St., F	1998 Chris Drury, Boston U., F
1983 Mark Fusco, Harvard, D	1991 Dave Emma, Boston College, F	1999 Jason Krog, UNH, F
1984 Tom Kurvers, Minn. Duluth, D	1992 Scott Pellerin, Maine, F	2000 Mike Mottau, Boston College, D
1985 Bill Watson, Minn. Duluth, F	1993 Paul Kariya, Maine, F	2001 Ryan Miller, Michigan St., G
1986 Scott Fusco, Harvard, F	1994 Chris Marinucci, Minn. Duluth, F	2002 Jordan Leopold, Minnesota, D
1987 Tony Hrkac, North Dakota, F	1995 Brian Holzinger, Bowl. Green, F	2003 Peter Sejna, Colorado Coll., F
1988 Robb Stauber, Minnesota, G	1996 Brian Bonin, Minnesota, F	2004 Junior Lessard, Minn. Duluth, F

NCAA Women's Frozen Four

Women's college hockey was officially introduced as an NCAA Division I sport in 2000-01.

Multiple winner: Minnesota-Duluth (3).

Year	Champion	Head Coach	Score	Runner-up	Third Place	Score	Fourth Place
2001	Minnesota Duluth	Shannon Miller	4-2	St. Lawrence	Harvard	3-2	Dartmouth
2002	Minnesota Duluth	Shannon Miller	3-2	Brown	(tie) Niagara and Minnesota, 2-2		
2003	Minnesota Duluth	Shannon Miller	4-3*	Harvard	Dartmouth	4-2	Minnesota
2004	Minnesota	Laura Halldorson	6-2	Harvard	St. Lawrence	2-1	Dartmouth

*Championship game overtime goal: 2003—4:19 in 2nd OT.

Tournament Most Outstanding Player

The Most Outstanding Players of each NCAA Women's Division I tournament since 2001. Winner of the award who did not play for the tournament champion in **bold** type.

Year	Year	Year
2001 Maria Rooth, Minn. Duluth, F	2003 Caroline Ouellette, Minn. Duluth, F	2004 Krissy Wendell, Minnesota, F
2002 **Kristy Zamora**, Brown, F		

Patty Kazmaier Award

Awarded annually to the women's Division I player who displays the highest standards of personal and team excellence during the season; voted on by a 13-member panel of national media, college coaches and one USA Hockey member. First presented in 1998, in the name of the Princeton collegiate hockey and lacrosse star who died in 1990 of a rare blood disease.

Multiple winner: Jennifer Botterill (2).

Year	Year	Year
1998 Brandy Fisher, New Hampshire, F	2001 Jennifer Botterill, Harvard, F	2004 Angela Ruggiero, Harvard, D
1999 A.J. Mleczko, Harvard, F	2002 Brooke Whitney, Northeastern, F	
2000 Ali Brewer, Brown, G	2003 Jennifer Botterill, Harvard, F	

College Sports

Pitt fans express their thoughts on Virginia Tech (along with Miami and BC) jumping ship to the ACC.

AP/Wide World Photos

Falling Dominoes

The ACC's quest for expansion and better football sent shock waves through the rest of the NCAA.

Michael Morrison
is co-editor of the ESPN Sports Almanac.

The Atlantic Coast Conference started it all in the spring of 2003 by wooing Big East members Miami, Syracuse and Boston College. What followed was a seemingly unending game of conference musical chairs not seen since the breakup of the Southwest Conference in 1996.

When the dust settled, seven of the NCAA's 11 Division I-A football conferences were impacted and approximately 20 percent of the 117 teams were realigned (or slated to be realigned) over the next three years. Reasons for the movement were plentiful, but as one might expect, money was at the center of it all. And as with most multimillion-dollar transactions, dealings grew contentious, previously strong relationships cooled and multiple lawsuits were filed.

Follow along carefully:

The ACC ultimately decided on the Big East's Miami and Virginia Tech,
followed by Boston College (who will switch in 2005).

The Big East then set its sights on Conference USA, grabbing Cincinnati, Louisville and South Florida (all joining in 2005) and accelerated Connecticut football's move to the conference one season earlier than previously announced.

Conference USA, also losing TCU to the Mountain West, Army football to Independent, and Charlotte and Saint Louis basketball to the Atlantic Sun, responded by going after the Mid American Conference (Marshall and Central Florida) and the Western Athletic Conference (Rice, SMU, Tulsa and UTEP).

The WAC took it out on the Sun Belt, attracting Idaho, New Mexico State and Utah State.

The Sun Belt then replenished its roster by going after I-AA independents, Florida Atlantic and Florida International.

*ACC Commissioner **John Swofford**, center, officially welcomes Boston College president **Rev. William Leahy**, left, and athletic director, **Gene DeFilippo** to the conference.*

The MAC, previously loaded with 14 teams, seemed content with its new lineup of 12 and thus the cycle was stopped.

For the most part, conference administrators and affected school athletic directors were civil while the juggling was going on, most seeing the moves as unavoidable once the ACC knocked over the first domino. But any bonds between long-time NCAA members, the ACC and the Big East may have been damaged beyond repair.

Back in May, 2003 when the initial rumors were flying, the five presumed football-playing Big East schools left standing (Virginia Tech, West Virginia, Pittsburgh, Rutgers and Connecticut) filed suit against the ACC for damages. Big East officials were concerned that by losing three of its top football programs, it would lose automatic bid status to the Bowl Championship Series and potentially millions of dollars in the process.

Big East commissioner Mike Tranghese went as far as to call the ACC's pillaging of his conference, "the most disastrous blow to intercollegiate athletics in my lifetime." Included in the suit were Miami and

AP/Wide World Photos

*Mississippi State made Green Bay Packers assistant **Sylvester Croom** the first African-American head football coach in the 72-year history of the Southeastern Conference.*

Boston College, which were alleged to have secretly planned to move while publicly saying otherwise. Syracuse was not named because it made no promises to stay.

Oddly, while the suit was being filed, Charles Steger, president of plaintiff Virginia Tech, reportedly visited the ACC offices and according to ACC commissioner John Swofford, "expressed a desire to join the Atlantic Coast Conference." The plot thickened.

Soon after, ACC presidents voted to invite Miami and Virginia Tech, presumably leaving Syracuse and Boston College standing at the altar. Predictably, Virginia Tech dropped its lawsuit against the ACC.

The ACC wasn't finished, however. Just four months later, ACC presidents realized it would be financially prudent to add one more school for a total of 12, the amount required by the NCAA to stage a lucrative league championship football game.

Boston College was a unanimous choice. The school was offered an invitation and given roughly three weeks to decide its intentions. It took

continued on page 446 ▶

The Ten Biggest Stories
of the Year in College Sports

10 Women's bowling officially becomes the NCAA's 88th Championship sport. Between 400-450 spectators pack the Emerald Bowl in Houston to witness Nebraska's stirring come-from-behind win over Central Missouri State to win the inaugural title.

9 Oklahoma State wins its record 32nd Division I wrestling title in St. Louis. Matt Gentry wins the 157-pound class for Stanford's first-ever individual championship, while Harvard's Jesse Jantzen becomes the first Crimson winner since 1938.

8 In what would be a preview of the Olympic Games in Athens, nine world records are set at the NCAA Swimming & Diving Championships in East Meadow, N.Y. Texas Olympians Aaron Peirsol, Brendan Hansen and Ian Crocker dominate their individual events while Auburn successfully defends both its men's and women's team titles.

7 Stanford wins its tenth consecutive Directors' Cup as the NCAA's best overall Division I program. Grand Valley St., Mich. (Division II), Williams, Mass. (Division III) and Simon Fraser, B.C. (NAIA) also win their respective divisions.

6 Head coaches George O'Leary (Central Florida football), Larry Eustachy (Southern Miss basketball) and Mike Price (UTEP football) are all given second chances after losing their jobs over the last two years amidst controversy.

5 Southeast Missouri State announces that after more than 80 years, it will no longer use "Indians" and "Otahkians" as its nicknames. By the spring of 2005 they will be known as the "Redhawks." Additionally several NCAA institutions, including the University of Iowa, will no longer compete against schools with Indians as their mascot.

4 Reigning freestyle skiing world champion Jeremy Bloom officially loses his eligibility to play football at the University of Colorado when an NCAA panel turns down his last-ditch appeal. He had been accepting endorsements in order to prepare for the 2006 Winter Olympics.

3 NFL assistant and Alabama alum Sylvester Croom, 49, takes over the football program at Mississippi State and becomes the first African-American head football coach in Southeastern Conference history.

2 The NCAA refuses to reinstate Mike Williams after the former USC star receiver hired an agent and announced his intention to turn pro. After announcing his eligibility for the 2004 NFL draft, an appeals court overturned a prior ruling that allowed players out of high school less than three years into the draft.

1 When Miami, Virginia Tech and later Boston College announce their exodus from the Big East for the ACC, a parade of conference changes follows, affecting seven major conferences.

school officials four hours to send their reply. Boston College, a charter member of the Big East, was ACC-bound. Tranghese and remaining Big East presidents were once again disgusted.

"Our membership is very surprised that the ACC presidents continue to come back into our league for membership" said Tranghese.

Yet another lawsuit was filed on behalf of Connecticut, West Virginia, Rutgers and Pittsburgh, this one against Boston College, athletic director Gene DiFilippo, the ACC

and Miami. It claimed that B.C.'s departure was part of a "back room conspiracy" designed to damage the Big East Conference.

All claims were subsequently dismissed but the damage may be irreparable. When all is said and done, conference and school administrators, coaches, players and fans may all be better off with the new conference configurations from a financial, competitive and geographic standpoint. But it won't take away the bitter feelings incurred while the migrations were occurring.

Their Cup Runneth Over

Since 1993-94, the NACDA Director's Cup has ranked every NCAA institution according to their postseason performance. Listed are the top three schools in each division, by points, since the Cup's existence. **Source**: NCAA News

Div. I	Pts
Stanford	12,514.80
UCLA	9,844.05
Florida	8,889.50

Div. II	Pts
Cal-State Bakersfield	4,202.00
Abilene Christian, TX	3,806.00
North Dakota	3,759.00

Div. III	Pts
Williams, MA	7,666.00
College of New Jersey	5,842.75
Middlebury, VT	5,065.00

Golden State Warriors

California led all states in 2003-04 with 12 NCAA national team champions. Rivals USC and UCLA led the way with four each. The top10 states are listed below. Note that championships encompass all divisions. There are 88 NCAA championships in all.

Source: NCAA News

State	Team Titles
California	12
Texas	6
New York	5
Ohio	5
Vermont	5
Wisconsin	5
Missouri	4
Pennsylvania	4
Six states tied with 3 each.	

NCAA Schools & Champions

SPORTS ALMANAC

NCAA Division I-A Football Schools

2004 Season

Conferences and coaches as of Sept. 30, 2004.

Joining ACC in 2004: MIAMI-FL and VIRGINIA TECH from Big East.
Joining Big East in 2004: CONNECTICUT from Independent.
Joining Sun Belt in 2004: TROY from Independent.
Joining ACC in 2005: BOSTON COLLEGE from Big East.
Joining Big East in 2005: CINCINNATI, LOUISVILLE and SOUTH FLORIDA from Conference USA.
Joining Conference USA in 2005: MARSHALL and CENTRAL FLORIDA from Mid-American; RICE, SMU, TULSA and UTEP from the WAC.
Joining Mountain West in 2005: TCU from Conference USA.
Joining Sun Belt in 2005: FLORIDA ATLANTIC and FLORIDA INTERNATIONAL from I-AA Independent (2004 transition).
Joining WAC in 2005: IDAHO, NEW MEXICO STATE and UTAH ST from Sun Belt.
To I-A Independent from conferences in 2005: TEMPLE from Big East and ARMY from Conference USA.

	Nickname	Conference	Head Coach	Location	Colors
Air Force	Falcons	Mountain West	Fisher DeBerry	Colo. Springs, CO	Blue/Silver
Akron	Zips	Mid-American	J.D. Brookhart	Akron, OH	Blue/Gold
Alabama	Crimson Tide	SEC-West	Mike Shula	Tuscaloosa, AL	Crimson/White
Arizona	Wildcats	Pac-10	Mike Stoops	Tucson, AZ	Cardinal/Navy
Arizona St.	Sun Devils	Pac-10	Dirk Koetter	Tempe, AZ	Maroon/Gold
Arkansas	Razorbacks	SEC-West	Houston Nutt	Fayetteville, AR	Cardinal/White
Arkansas St.	Indians	Sun Belt	Steve Roberts	State Univ., AR	Scarlet/Black
Army	Cadets, Black Knights	USA	Bobby Ross	West Point, NY	Black/Gold/Gray
Auburn	Tigers	SEC-West	Tommy Tuberville	Auburn, AL	Orange/Blue
Ball St.	Cardinals	Mid-American	Brady Hoke	Muncie, IN	Cardinal/White
Baylor	Bears	Big 12	Guy Morriss	Waco, TX	Green/Gold
Boise St.	Broncos	WAC	Dan Hawkins	Boise, ID	Orange/Blue
Boston College	Eagles	Big East	Tom O'Brien	Chestnut Hill, MA	Maroon/Gold
Bowling Green	Falcons	Mid-American	Gregg Brandon	Bowling Green, OH	Orange/Brown
Brigham Young	Cougars	Mountain West	Gary Crowton	Provo, UT	Royal Blue/White
Buffalo	Bulls	Mid-American	Jim Hofher	Buffalo, NY	Royal Blue/White
California	Golden Bears	Pac-10	Jeff Tedford	Berkeley, CA	Blue/Gold
Central Florida	Golden Knights	Mid-American	George O'Leary	Orlando, FL	Black/Gold
Central Michigan	Chippewas	Mid-American	Brian Kelly	Mt. Pleasant, MI	Maroon/Gold
Cincinnati	Bearcats	USA	Mark Dantonio	Cincinnati, OH	Red/Black
Clemson	Tigers	ACC	Tommy Bowden	Clemson, SC	Purple/Orange
Colorado	Buffaloes	Big 12	Gary Barnett	Boulder, CO	Silver/Gold/Black
Colorado St.	Rams	Mountain West	Sonny Lubick	Ft. Collins, CO	Green/Gold
Connecticut	Huskies	Big East	Randy Edsall	Storrs, CT	Blue/White
Duke	Blue Devils	ACC	Ted Roof	Durham, NC	Royal Blue/White
East Carolina	Pirates	USA	John Thompson	Greenville, NC	Purple/Gold
Eastern Michigan	Eagles	Mid-American	Jeff Genyk	Ypsilanti, MI	Green/White
Florida	Gators	SEC-East	Ron Zook	Gainesville, FL	Orange/Blue
Florida St.	Seminoles	ACC	Bobby Bowden	Tallahassee, FL	Garnet/Gold
Fresno St.	Bulldogs	WAC	Pat Hill	Fresno, CA	Cardinal/Blue
Georgia	Bulldogs	SEC-East	Mark Richt	Athens, GA	Red/Black
Georgia Tech	Yellow Jackets	ACC	Chan Gailey	Atlanta, GA	Old Gold/White
Hawaii	Warriors	WAC	June Jones	Honolulu, HI	Green/White
Houston	Cougars	USA	Art Briles	Houston, TX	Scarlet/White
Idaho	Vandals	Sun Belt	Nick Holt	Moscow, ID	Silver/Gold
Illinois	Fighting Illini	Big Ten	Ron Turner	Champaign, IL	Orange/Blue
Indiana	Hoosiers	Big Ten	Gerry DiNardo	Bloomington, IN	Cream/Crimson
Iowa	Hawkeyes	Big Ten	Kirk Ferentz	Iowa City, IA	Old Gold/Black
Iowa St.	Cyclones	Big 12	Dan McCarney	Ames, IA	Cardinal/Gold
Kansas	Jayhawks	Big 12	Mark Mangino	Lawrence, KS	Crimson/Blue
Kansas St.	Wildcats	Big 12	Bill Snyder	Manhattan, KS	Purple/White
Kent St.	Golden Flashes	Mid-American	Doug Martin	Kent, OH	Navy Blue/Gold
Kentucky	Wildcats	SEC-East	Rich Brooks	Lexington, KY	Blue/White
LSU	Fighting Tigers	SEC-West	Nick Saban	Baton Rouge, LA	Purple/Gold
LA-Lafayette	Ragin' Cajuns	Sun Belt	Rickey Bustle	Lafayette, LA	Vermilion/White

	Nickname	Conference	Head Coach	Location	Colors
LA-Monroe	Indians	Sun Belt	Charlie Weatherbie	Monroe, LA	Maroon/Gold
Louisiana Tech	Bulldogs	WAC	Jack Bicknell III	Ruston, LA	Red/Blue
Louisville	Cardinals	USA	Bob Petrino	Louisville, KY	Red/Black/White
Marshall	Thundering Herd	Mid-American	Bob Pruett	Huntington, WV	Green/White
Maryland	Terrapins, Terps	ACC	Ralph Friedgen	College Park, MD	Red/White/Black/Gold
Memphis	Tigers	USA	Tommy West	Memphis, TN	Blue/Gray
Miami-FL	Hurricanes	ACC	Larry Coker	Coral Gables, FL	Orange/Grn./Wt.
Miami-OH	RedHawks	Mid-American	Terry Hoeppner	Oxford, OH	Red/White
Michigan	Wolverines	Big Ten	Lloyd Carr	Ann Arbor, MI	Maize/Blue
Michigan St.	Spartans	Big Ten	John L. Smith	E. Lansing, MI	Green/White
Middle Tenn. St.	Blue Raiders	Sun Belt	Andy McCollum	Murfreesboro, TN	Blue/White
Minnesota	Golden Gophers	Big Ten	Glen Mason	Minneapolis, MN	Maroon/Gold
Mississippi	Ole Miss, Rebels	SEC-West	David Cutcliffe	Oxford, MS	Cardinal/Navy Bl.
Mississippi St.	Bulldogs	SEC-West	Sylvester Croom	Starkville, MS	Maroon/White
Missouri	Tigers	Big 12	Gary Pinkel	Columbia, MO	Old Gold/Black
Navy	Midshipmen	Independent	Paul Johnson	Annapolis, MD	Navy Blue/Gold
Nebraska	Cornhuskers	Big 12	Bill Callahan	Lincoln, NE	Scarlet/Cream
Nevada	Wolf Pack	WAC	Chris Ault	Reno, NV	Silver/Blue
New Mexico	Lobos	Mountain West	Rocky Long	Albuquerque, NM	Cherry/Silver
New Mexico St.	Aggies	Sun Belt	Tony Samuel	Las Cruces, NM	Crimson/White
North Carolina	Tar Heels	ACC	John Bunting	Chapel Hill, NC	Carolina Blue/Wt.
North Carolina St.	Wolfpack	ACC	Chuck Amato	Raleigh, NC	Red/White
North Texas	Mean Green	Sun Belt	Darrell Dickey	Denton, TX	Green/White
Northern Illinois	Huskies	Mid-American	Joe Novak	De Kalb, IL	Cardinal/Black
Northwestern	Wildcats	Big Ten	Randy Walker	Evanston, IL	Purple/White
Notre Dame	Fighting Irish	Independent	Tyrone Willingham	Notre Dame, IN	Gold/Blue
Ohio University	Bobcats	Mid-American	Brian Knorr	Athens, OH	Hunter Green/Wt.
Ohio St.	Buckeyes	Big Ten	Jim Tressel	Columbus, OH	Scarlet/Gray
Oklahoma	Sooners	Big 12	Bob Stoops	Norman, OK	Crimson/Cream
Oklahoma St.	Cowboys	Big 12	Les Miles	Stillwater, OK	Orange/Black
Oregon	Ducks	Pac-10	Mike Bellotti	Eugene, OR	Green/Yellow
Oregon St.	Beavers	Pac-10	Mike Riley	Corvallis, OR	Orange/Black
Penn St.	Nittany Lions	Big Ten	Joe Paterno	University Park, PA	Blue/White
Pittsburgh	Panthers	Big East	Walt Harris	Pittsburgh, PA	Blue/Gold
Purdue	Boilermakers	Big Ten	Joe Tiller	W. Lafayette, IN	Old Gold/Black
Rice	Owls	WAC	Ken Hatfield	Houston, TX	Blue/Gray
Rutgers	Scarlet Knights	Big East	Greg Schiano	New Brunswick, NJ	Scarlet
San Diego St.	Aztecs	Mountain West	Tom Craft	San Diego, CA	Scarlet/Black
San Jose St.	Spartans	WAC	Fitz Hill	San Jose, CA	Gold/White/Blue
South Carolina	Gamecocks	SEC-East	Lou Holtz	Columbia, SC	Garnet/Black
South Florida	Bulls	USA	Jim Leavitt	Tampa, FL	Green/Gold
SMU	Mustangs	WAC	Phil Bennett	Dallas, TX	Red/Blue
Southern Miss.	Golden Eagles	USA	Jeff Bower	Hattiesburg, MS	Black/Gold
Stanford	Cardinal	Pac-10	Buddy Teevens	Stanford, CA	Cardinal/White
Syracuse	Orange	Big East	Paul Pasqualoni	Syracuse, NY	Orange
Temple	Owls	Big East	Bobby Wallace	Philadelphia, PA	Cherry/White
Tennessee	Volunteers	SEC-East	Phillip Fulmer	Knoxville, TN	Orange/White
Texas	Longhorns	Big 12	Mack Brown	Austin, TX	Burnt Orange/Wt.
Texas A&M	Aggies	Big 12	Dennis Franchione	College Station, TX	Maroon/White
TCU	Horned Frogs	USA	Gary Patterson	Ft. Worth, TX	Purple/White
Texas Tech	Red Raiders	Big 12	Mike Leach	Lubbock, TX	Scarlet/Black
Toledo	Rockets	Mid-American	Tom Amstutz	Toledo, OH	Blue/Gold
Troy	Trojans	Sun Belt	Larry Blakeney	Troy, AL	Cardinal/Slvr./Blk.
Tulane	Green Wave	USA	Chris Scelfo	New Orleans, LA	Olive Grn./Sky Bl.
Tulsa	Golden Hurricane	WAC	Steve Kragthorpe	Tulsa, OK	Blue/Gold
UAB	Blazers	USA	Watson Brown	Birmingham, AL	Green/Gold
UCLA	Bruins	Pac-10	Karl Dorrell	Los Angeles, CA	Blue/Gold
UNLV	Rebels	Mountain West	John Robinson	Las Vegas, NV	Scarlet/Gray
USC	Trojans	Pac-10	Pete Carroll	Los Angeles, CA	Cardinal/Gold
Utah	Utes	Mountain West	Urban Meyer	Salt Lake City, UT	Crimson/White
Utah St.	Aggies	Sun Belt	Mick Dennehy	Logan, UT	Navy Blue/White
UTEP	Miners	WAC	Mike Price	El Paso, TX	Orange/Blue/Wt.
Vanderbilt	Commodores	SEC-East	Bobby Johnson	Nashville, TN	Black/Gold
Virginia	Cavaliers	ACC	Al Groh	Charlottesville, VA	Orange/Blue
Virginia Tech	Hokies, Gobblers	ACC	Frank Beamer	Blacksburg, VA	Orange/Maroon
Wake Forest	Demon Deacons	ACC	Jim Grobe	Winston-Salem, NC	Old Gold/Black
Washington	Huskies	Pac-10	Keith Gilbertson	Seattle, WA	Purple/Gold
Washington St.	Cougars	Pac-10	Bill Doba	Pullman, WA	Crimson/Gray
West Virginia	Mountaineers	Big East	Rich Rodriguez	Morgantown, WV	Old Gold/Blue
Western Michigan	Broncos	Mid-American	Gary Darnell	Kalamazoo, MI	Brown/Gold
Wisconsin	Badgers	Big Ten	Barry Alvarez	Madison, WI	Cardinal/White
Wyoming	Cowboys	Mountain West	Joe Glenn	Laramie, WY	Brown/Yellow

NCAA Division I-AA Football Schools
2004 Season
Conferences and coaches as of Sept. 30, 2004.

Joining Atlantic 10 in 2004: TOWSON from Patriot.

New Conference in 2004: Great West Football Conference (6 teams)—CAL POLY, NORTHERN COLORADO, SOUTH-ERN UTAH and UC-DAVIS from I-AA Independent; NORTH DAKOTA ST. and SOUTH DAKOTA ST. from Division II.

Leaving Metro Atlantic in 2004: SIENA (program discontinued).

Leaving Southern in 2004: EAST TENNESSEE ST. (program discontinued).

Leaving Division I-AA Independent in 2004: ST. MARY'S-CA (program discontinued).

Joining Southland in 2005: SOUTHEASTERN LOUISIANA from Independent.

Joining Mid-Eastern in 2005: FLORIDA A&M from Independent (former Mid-Eastern member is spending 2004 as an Independent after an aborted move to Division I-A).

	Nickname	Conference	Head Coach	Location	Colors
Alabama A&M	Bulldogs	SWAC	Anthony Jones	Huntsville, AL	Maroon/White
Alabama St.	Hornets	SWAC	Charles Coe	Montgomery, AL	Black/Gold
Albany	Great Danes	Northeast	Bob Ford	Albany, NY	Purple/Gold
Alcorn St.	Braves	SWAC	Johnny Thomas	Lorman, MS	Purple/Gold
Appalachian St.	Mountaineers	Southern	Jerry Moore	Boone, NC	Black/Gold
Ark.-Pine Bluff	Golden Lions	SWAC	Mo Forte	Pine Bluff, AR	Black/Gold
Austin Peay St.	Governors	Pioneer	Carroll McCray	Clarksville, TN	Red/White
Bethune-Cookman	Wildcats	Mid-Eastern	Alvin Wyatt	Daytona Beach, FL	Maroon/Gold
Brown	Bears	Ivy	Phil Estes	Providence, RI	Brown/Red/White
Bucknell	Bison	Patriot	Tim Landis	Lewisburg, PA	Orange/Blue
Butler	Bulldogs	Pioneer	Kit Cartwright	Indianapolis, IN	Blue/White
Cal Poly	Mustangs	Great West	Rich Ellerson	San Luis Obispo, CA	Green/Gold
Central Conn. St.	Blue Devils	Northeast	Tom Masella	New Britain, CT	Blue/White
Charleston So.	Buccaneers	Big South	Jay Mills	Charleston, SC	Blue/Gold
Chattanooga	Mocs	Southern	Rodney Allison	Chattanooga, TN	Navy Blue/Old Gold
The Citadel	Bulldogs	Southern	John Zernhelt	Charleston, SC	Blue/White
Coastal Carolina	Chanticleers	Big South	David Bennett	Conway, SC	Green/Bronze/Black
Colgate	Raiders	Patriot	Dick Biddle	Hamilton, NY	Maroon/White/Gray
Columbia	Lions	Ivy	Bob Shoop	New York, NY	Lt. Blue/White
Cornell	Big Red	Ivy	Jim Knowles	Ithaca, NY	Carnelian/White
Dartmouth	Big Green	Ivy	John Lyons	Hanover, NH	Green/White
Davidson	Wildcats	Pioneer	Mike Toop	Davidson, NC	Red/Black
Dayton	Flyers	Pioneer	Mike Kelly	Dayton, OH	Red/Blue
Delaware	Blue Hens	Atlantic 10	K.C. Keeler	Newark, DE	Blue/Gold
Delaware St.	Hornets	Mid-Eastern	Al Lavan	Dover, DE	Red/Blue
Drake	Bulldogs	Pioneer	Rob Ash	Des Moines, IA	Blue/White
Duquesne	Dukes	Metro Atlantic	Greg Gattuso	Pittsburgh, PA	Red/Blue
Eastern Illinois	Panthers	Ohio Valley	Bob Spoo	Charleston, IL	Blue/Gray
Eastern Kentucky	Colonels	Ohio Valley	Danny Hope	Richmond, KY	Maroon/White
Eastern Washington	Eagles	Big Sky	Paul Wulff	Cheney, WA	Red/White
Elon	Phoenix	Southern	Paul Hamilton	Elon, NC	Maroon/Gold
Florida A&M	Rattlers	Independent	Billy Joe	Tallahassee, FL	Orange/Green
Florida Atlantic	Owls	Independent	H. Schnellenberger	Boca Raton, FL	Blue/Red
Florida Int'l	Golden Panthers	Independent	Don Strock	Miami, FL	Blue/Gold
Fordham	Rams	Patriot	Ed Foley	Bronx, NY	Maroon/White
Furman	Paladins	Southern	Bobby Lamb	Greenville, SC	Purple/White
Gardner-Webb	Bulldogs	Big South	Steve Patton	Boiling Springs, NC	Scarlet/Black
Georgetown	Hoyas	Patriot	Bob Benson	Washington, DC	Blue/Gray
Georgia Southern	Eagles	Southern	Mike Sewak	Statesboro, GA	Blue/White
Grambling St.	Tigers	SWAC	Melvin Spears	Grambling, LA	Black/Gold
Hampton	Pirates	Mid-Eastern	Joe Taylor	Hampton, VA	Royal Blue/White
Harvard	Crimson	Ivy	Tim Murphy	Cambridge, MA	Crimson/Black/White
Hofstra	Pride	Atlantic 10	Joe Gardi	Hempstead, NY	Gold/White/Blue
Holy Cross	Crusaders	Patriot	Tom Gilmore	Worcester, MA	Royal Purple
Howard	Bison	Mid-Eastern	Rayford T. Petty	Washington, DC	Blue/Wt./Red
Idaho St.	Bengals	Big Sky	Larry Lewis	Pocatello, ID	Orange/Black
Illinois St.	Redbirds	Gateway	Denver Johnson	Normal, IL	Red/White
Indiana St.	Sycamores	Gateway	Tim McGuire	Terre Haute, IN	Royal Blue/White
Iona	Gaels	Metro Atlantic	Fred Mariani	New Rochelle, NY	Maroon/Gold
Jackson St.	Tigers	SWAC	James Bell	Jackson, MS	Blue/White
Jacksonville	Dolphins	Pioneer	Steve Gilbert	Jacksonville, FL	Green/White
Jacksonville St.	Gamecocks	Ohio Valley	Jack Crowe	Jacksonville, AL	Red/White
James Madison	Dukes	Atlantic 10	Mickey Matthews	Harrisonburg, VA	Purple/Gold
Lafayette	Leopards	Patriot	Frank Tavani	Easton, PA	Maroon/White

	Nickname	Conference	Head Coach	Location	Colors
La Salle	Explorers	Metro Atlantic	Phil Longo	Philadelphia, PA	Blue/Gold
Lehigh	Mountain Hawks	Patriot	Pete Lembo	Bethlehem, PA	Brown/White
Liberty	Flames	Big South	Ken Karcher	Lynchburg, VA	Red/White/Blue
Maine	Black Bears	Atlantic 10	Jack Cosgrove	Orono, ME	Blue/White
Marist	Red Foxes	Metro Atlantic	Jim Parady	Poughkeepsie, NY	Red/White
Massachusetts	Minutemen	Atlantic 10	Don Brown	Amherst, MA	Maroon/White
McNeese St.	Cowboys	Southland	Tommy Tate	Lake Charles, LA	Blue/Gold
Miss. Valley St.	Delta Devils	SWAC	Willie Totten	Itta Bena, MS	Green/White
Monmouth	Hawks	Northeast	Kevin Callahan	W. Long Branch, NJ	Royal Blue/White
Montana	Grizzlies	Big Sky	Bobby Hauck	Missoula, MT	Maroon/Silver
Montana St.	Bobcats	Big Sky	Mike Kramer	Bozeman, MT	Blue/Gold
Morehead St.	Eagles	Pioneer	Matt Ballard	Morehead, KY	Blue/Gold
Morgan St.	Bears	Mid-Eastern	Donald Hill-Eley	Baltimore, MD	Blue/Orange
Murray St.	Racers	Ohio Valley	Joe Pannunzio	Murray, KY	Blue/Gold
New Hampshire	Wildcats	Atlantic 10	Sean McDonnell	Durham, NH	Blue/White
Nicholls St.	Colonels	Southland	Jay Thomas	Thibodaux, LA	Red/Gray
Norfolk State	Spartans	Mid-Eastern	Willie Gillus	Norfolk, VA	Green/Gold
North Carolina A&T	Aggies	Mid-Eastern	George Small	Greensboro, NC	Blue/Gold
North Dakota St.	Bison	Great West	Craig Bohl	Fargo, ND	Green/Yellow
Northeastern	Huskies	Atlantic 10	Rocky Hager	Boston, MA	Red/Black
Northern Arizona	Lumberjacks	Big Sky	Jerome Souers	Flagstaff, AZ	Blue/Gold
Northern Colorado	Bears	Great West	O. Kay Dalton	Greeley, CO	Blue/Gold
Northern Iowa	Panthers	Gateway	Mark Farley	Cedar Falls, IA	Purple/Old Gold
Northwestern St.	Demons	Southland	Scott Stoker	Natchitoches, LA	Purple/White
Pennsylvania	Quakers	Ivy	Al Bagnoli	Philadelphia, PA	Red/Blue
Portland St.	Vikings	Big Sky	Tim Walsh	Portland, OR	Green/White
Prairie View A&M	Panthers	SWAC	Henry Frazier	Prairie View, TX	Purple/Gold
Princeton	Tigers	Ivy	Roger Hughes	Princeton, NJ	Orange/Black
Rhode Island	Rams	Atlantic 10	Tim Stowers	Kingston, RI	Light Blue/Navy/Wt.
Richmond	Spiders	Atlantic 10	Dave Clawson	Richmond, VA	Red/Blue
Robert Morris	Colonials	Northeast	Joe Walton	Moon Township, PA	Blue/White
Sacramento St.	Hornets	Big Sky	Steve Mooshagian	Sacramento, CA	Green/Gold
Sacred Heart	Pioneers	Northeast	Paul Gorham	Fairfield, CT	Scarlet/White
St. Francis-PA	Red Flash	Northeast	Dave Opfar	Loretto, PA	Red/White
Saint Peter's	Peacocks	Metro Atlantic	Chris Taylor	Jersey City, NJ	Blue/White
Sam Houston St.	Bearkats	Southland	Ron Randleman	Huntsville, TX	Orange/White
Samford	Bulldogs	Ohio Valley	Bill Gray	Birmingham, AL	Crimson/Blue
San Diego	Toreros	Pioneer	Jim Harbaugh	San Diego, CA	Lt. Blue/Navy
Savannah St.	Tigers	Independent	Richard Basil	Savannah, GA	Orange/Blue
South Carolina St.	Bulldogs	Mid-Eastern	Oliver Pough	Orangeburg, SC	Garnet/Blue
South Dakota St.	Jackrabbits	Great West	John Stiegelmeier	Brookings, SD	Yellow/Blue
SE Missouri St.	Redhawks	Ohio Valley	Tim Billings	Cape Girardeau, MO	Red/Black
SE Louisiana	Lions	Independent	Hal Mumme	Hammond, LA	Green/Gold
Southern-BR	Jaguars	SWAC	Pete Richardson	Baton Rouge, LA	Blue/Gold
Southern Illinois	Salukis	Gateway	Jerry Kill	Carbondale, IL	Maroon/White
Southern Utah	Thunderbirds	Great West	Wes Meier	Cedar City, UT	Scarlet/White
SW Missouri St.	Bears	Gateway	Randy Ball	Springfield, MO	Maroon/White
S.F. Austin St.	Lumberjacks	Southland	Mike Santiago	Nacogdoches, TX	Purple/White
Stony Brook	Seawolves	Northeast	Sam Kornhauser	Stony Brook, NY	Scarlet/Gray
Tennessee-Martin	Skyhawks	Ohio Valley	Matt Griffin	Martin, TN	Orange/White/Blue
Tennessee St.	Tigers	Ohio Valley	James Reese	Nashville, TN	Blue/White
Tennessee Tech	Golden Eagles	Ohio Valley	Mike Hennigan	Cookeville, TN	Purple/Gold
Texas Southern	Tigers	SWAC	Steve Wilson	Houston, TX	Maroon/Gray
Texas St.-San Marcos	Bobcats	Southland	David Bailiff	San Marcos, TX	Maroon/Gold
Towson	Tigers	Atlantic 10	Gordy Combs	Towson, MD	Gold/White
UC-Davis	Aggies	Great West	Bob Biggs	Davis, CA	Yale Blue/Gold
Valparaiso	Crusaders	Pioneer	Tom Horne	Valparaiso, IN	Brown/Gold
Villanova	Wildcats	Atlantic 10	Andy Talley	Villanova, PA	Blue/White
VMI	Keydets	Big South	Cal McCombs	Lexington, VA	Red/White/Yellow
Wagner	Seahawks	Northeast	Walt Hameline	Staten Island, NY	Green/White
Weber St.	Wildcats	Big Sky	Jerry Graybeal	Ogden, UT	Royal Purple/White
Western Carolina	Catamounts	Southern	Kent Briggs	Cullowhee, NC	Purple/Gold
Western Illinois	Leathernecks	Gateway	Don Patterson	Macomb, IL	Purple/Gold
Western Kentucky	Hilltoppers	Gateway	David Elson	Bowling Green, KY	Red/White
William & Mary	Tribe	Atlantic 10	Jimmye Laycock	Williamsburg, VA	Green/Gold/Silver
Wofford	Terriers	Southern	Mike Ayers	Spartanburg, SC	Old Gold/Black
Yale	Bulldogs, Elis	Ivy	Jack Siedlecki	New Haven, CT	Yale Blue/White
Youngstown St.	Penguins	Gateway	Jon Heacock	Youngstown, OH	Red/White

NCAA Division I Basketball Schools
2004-2005 Season
Conferences and coaches as of Sept. 30, 2004.

Joining ACC in 2004-05: MIAMI-FL and VIRGINIA TECH from Big East.
Joining Big West in 2004-05: UC-DAVIS from Independent.
To Div. I Independent in 2004-05: NORTH DAKOTA ST. and SOUTH DAKOTA ST. from Div. II.
Joining ACC in 2005-06: BOSTON COLLEGE from Big East.
Joining Atlantic Sun in 2005-06: EAST TENNESSEE STATE from Southern.
Joining Atlantic 10 in 2005-06: CHARLOTTE and SAINT LOUIS from Conference USA.
Joining Big East in 2005-06: CINCINNATI, DEPAUL, LOUISVILLE, MARQUETTE and SOUTH FLORIDA from C-USA,
Joining Colonial Athletic Association in 2005-06: NORTHEASTERN from America East.
Joining Conference USA in 2005-06: MARSHALL from Mid-American; RICE, SMU, TULSA and UTEP from the WAC;
CENTRAL FLORIDA from Atlantic Sun.
Joining Mountain West in 2005-06: TCU from Conference USA.
Joining Sun Belt in 2005-06: TROY from Atlantic Sun.
Joining WAC in 2005-06: NEW MEXICO ST. from Sun Belt; IDAHO and UTAH STATE from Big West.
Joining Colonial Athletic Association in 2006-07: GEORGIA STATE from Atlantic Sun.
Joining Sun Belt in 2006-07: FLORIDA ATLANTIC from Atlantic Sun; LA-MONROE from Southland.

	Nickname	Conference	Head Coach	Location	Colors
Air Force	Falcons	Mountain West	Chris Mooney	Colo. Springs, CO	Blue/Silver
Akron	Zips	Mid-American	Keith Dambrot	Akron, OH	Blue/Gold
Alabama	Crimson Tide	SEC-West	Mark Gottfried	Tuscaloosa, AL	Crimson/White
Alabama A&M	Bulldogs	SWAC	Vann Pettaway	Huntsville, AL	Maroon/White
Alabama St.	Hornets	SWAC	Rob Spivery	Montgomery, AL	Black/Gold
Albany	Great Danes	America East	Will Brown	Albany, NY	Purple/Gold
Alcorn St.	Braves	SWAC	Samuel West	Lorman, MS	Purple/Gold
American	Eagles	Patriot	Jeff Jones	Washington, DC	Red/Blue
Appalachian St.	Mountaineers	Southern	Houston Fancher	Boone, NC	Black/Gold
Arizona	Wildcats	Pac-10	Lute Olson	Tucson, AZ	Cardinal/Navy
Arizona St.	Sun Devils	Pac-10	Rob Evans	Tempe, AZ	Maroon/Gold
Arkansas	Razorbacks	SEC-West	Stan Heath	Fayetteville, AR	Cardinal/White
Ark.-Little Rock	Trojans	Sun Belt	Steve Shields	Little Rock, AR	Silver/Black/Maroon
Ark.-Pine Bluff	Golden Lions	SWAC	Van Holt	Pine Bluff, AR	Black/Gold
Arkansas St.	Indians	Sun Belt	Dickey Nutt	State Univ., AR	Scarlet/Black
Army	Black Knights	Patriot	Jim Crews	West Point, NY	Black/Gold/Gray
Auburn	Tigers	SEC-West	Jeff Lebo	Auburn, AL	Orange/Blue
Austin Peay St.	Governors	Ohio Valley	Dave Loos	Clarksville, TN	Red/White
Ball St.	Cardinals	Mid-American	Tim Buckley	Muncie, IN	Cardinal/White
Baylor	Bears	Big 12	Scott Drew	Waco, TX	Green/Gold
Belmont	Bruins	Atlantic Sun	Rick Byrd	Nashville, TN	Navy Blue/Red
Bethune-Cookman	Wildcats	Mid-Eastern	Clifford Reed	Daytona Beach, FL	Maroon/Gold
Binghamton	Bearcats	America East	Al Walker	Binghamton, NY	Green/Black/White
Birmingham Southern	Panthers	Big South	Duane Reboul	Birmingham, AL	Black/Gold
Boise St.	Broncos	WAC	Greg Graham	Boise, ID	Orange/Blue
Boston College	Eagles	Big East	Al Skinner	Chestnut Hill, MA	Maroon/Gold
Boston University	Terriers	America East	Dennis Wolff	Boston, MA	Scarlet/White
Bowling Green	Falcons	Mid-American	Dan Dakich	Bowling Green, OH	Orange/Brown
Bradley	Braves	Mo. Valley	Jim Les	Peoria, IL	Red/White
Brigham Young	Cougars	Mountain West	Steve Cleveland	Provo, UT	Royal Blue/White
Brown	Bears	Ivy	Glen Miller	Providence, RI	Brown/Cardinal/White
Bucknell	Bison	Patriot	Pat Flannery	Lewisburg, PA	Orange/Blue
Buffalo	Bulls	Mid-American	R. Witherspoon	Buffalo, NY	Royal Blue/White
Butler	Bulldogs	Horizon	Todd Lickliter	Indianapolis, IN	Blue/White
California	Golden Bears	Pac-10	Ben Braun	Berkeley, CA	Blue/Gold
Cal Poly	Mustangs	Big West	Kevin Bromley	San Luis Obispo, CA	Green/Gold
CS-Fullerton	Titans	Big West	Bob Burton	Fullerton, CA	Blue/Orange/White
CS-Northridge	Matadors	Big West	Bobby Braswell	Northridge, CA	Red/White/Black
Campbell	Camels	Atlantic Sun	Robbie Laing	Buies Creek, NC	Orange/Black
Canisius	Golden Griffins	Metro Atlantic	Mike MacDonald	Buffalo, NY	Blue/Gold
Centenary	Gents, Gentlemen	Mid-Continent	Kevin Johnson	Shreveport, LA	Maroon/White
Central Conn. St.	Blue Devils	Northeast	Howie Dickenman	New Britain, CT	Blue/White
Central Florida	Golden Knights	Atlantic Sun	Kirk Speraw	Orlando, FL	Black/Gold
Central Michigan	Chippewas	Mid-American	Jay Smith	Mt. Pleasant, MI	Maroon/Gold
Charleston So.	Buccaneers	Big South	Jim Platt	Charleston, SC	Blue/Gold
Charlotte	49ers	USA	Bobby Lutz	Charlotte, NC	Green/White
Chattanooga	Mocs	Southern	John Shulman	Chattanooga, TN	Navy Blue/Old Gold
Chicago St.	Cougars	Mid-Continent	Kevin Jones	Chicago, IL	Green/White
Cincinnati	Bearcats	USA	Bob Huggins	Cincinnati, OH	Red/Black
The Citadel	Bulldogs	Southern	Pat Dennis	Charleston, SC	Blue/White
Clemson	Tigers	ACC	Oliver Purnell	Clemson, SC	Purple/Orange
Cleveland St.	Vikings	Horizon	Mike Garland	Cleveland, OH	Forest Green/White

NCAA Division I Basketball Schools (Cont.)

	Nickname	Conference	Head Coach	Location	Colors
Coastal Carolina	Chanticleers	Big South	Pete Strickland	Conway, SC	Green/Bronze/Black
Colgate	Raiders	Patriot	Emmett Davis	Hamilton, NY	Maroon/Gray/White
College of Charleston	Cougars	Southern	Tom Herrion	Charleston, SC	Maroon/White
Colorado	Buffaloes	Big 12	Ricardo Patton	Boulder, CO	Silver/Gold/Black
Colorado St.	Rams	Mountain West	Dale Layer	Ft. Collins, CO	Green/Gold
Columbia	Lions	Ivy	Joseph Jones	New York, NY	Lt. Blue/White
Connecticut	Huskies	Big East	Jim Calhoun	Storrs, CT	Blue/White
Coppin St.	Eagles	Mid-Eastern	Ron Mitchell	Baltimore, MD	Royal Blue/Gold
Cornell	Big Red	Ivy	Steve Donahue	Ithaca, NY	Carnelian/White
Creighton	Bluejays	Mo. Valley	Dana Altman	Omaha, NE	Blue/White
Dartmouth	Big Green	Ivy	Terry Dunn	Hanover, NH	Green/White
Davidson	Wildcats	Southern	Bob McKillop	Davidson, NC	Red/Black
Dayton	Flyers	Atlantic 10	Brian Gregory	Dayton, OH	Red/Blue
Delaware	Fightin' Blue Hens	Colonial	David Henderson	Newark, DE	Blue/Gold
Delaware St.	Hornets	Mid-Eastern	Greg Jackson	Dover, DE	Red/Columbia Blue
Denver	Pioneers	Sun Belt	Terry Carroll	Denver, CO	Crimson/Gold
DePaul	Blue Demons	USA	Dave Leitao	Chicago, IL	Scarlet/Blue
Detroit Mercy	Titans	Horizon	Perry Watson	Detroit, MI	Red/White/Blue
Drake	Bulldogs	Mo. Valley	Tom Davis	Des Moines, IA	Blue/White
Drexel	Dragons	Colonial	Bruiser Flint	Philadelphia, PA	Navy Blue/Gold
Duke	Blue Devils	ACC	Mike Krzyzewski	Durham, NC	Royal Blue/White
Duquesne	Dukes	Atlantic 10	Danny Nee	Pittsburgh, PA	Red/Blue
East Carolina	Pirates	USA	Bill Herrion	Greenville, NC	Purple/Gold
East Tenn. St.	Buccaneers	Southern	Murry Bartow	Johnson City, TN	Blue/Gold
Eastern Illinois	Panthers	Ohio Valley	Rick Samuels	Charleston, IL	Blue/Gray
Eastern Kentucky	Colonels	Ohio Valley	Travis Ford	Richmond, KY	Maroon/White
Eastern Michigan	Eagles	Mid-American	Jim Boone	Ypsilanti, MI	Green/White
Eastern Washington	Eagles	Big Sky	Mike Burns	Cheney, WA	Red/White
Elon	Phoenix	Southern	Ernie Nestor	Elon, NC	Maroon/Gold
Evansville	Aces	Mo. Valley	Steve Merfeld	Evansville, IN	Purple/White
Fairfield	Stags	Metro Atlantic	Tim O'Toole	Fairfield, CT	Cardinal Red
Fairleigh Dickinson	Knights	Northeast	Tom Green	Teaneck, NJ	Maroon/Blue
Florida	Gators	SEC-East	Billy Donovan	Gainesville, FL	Orange/Blue
Florida A&M	Rattlers	Mid-Eastern	Mike Gillespie	Tallahassee, FL	Orange/Green
Florida Atlantic	Owls	Atlantic Sun	Sidney Green	Boca Raton, FL	Blue/Red
Florida Int'l	Golden Panthers	Sun Belt	Sergio Rouco	Miami, FL	Blue/Gold
Florida St.	Seminoles	ACC	Leonard Hamilton	Tallahassee, FL	Garnet/Gold
Fordham	Rams	Atlantic 10	Dereck Whittenburg	Bronx, NY	Maroon/White
Fresno St.	Bulldogs	WAC	Ray Lopes	Fresno, CA	Cardinal/Blue
Furman	Paladins	Southern	Larry Davis	Greenville, SC	Purple/White
Gardner-Webb	Bulldogs	Atlantic Sun	Rick Scruggs	Boiling Springs, NC	Scarlet/Black
George Mason	Patriots	Colonial	Jim Larranaga	Fairfax, VA	Green/Gold
George Washington	Colonials	Atlantic 10	Karl Hobbs	Washington, DC	Buff/Blue
Georgetown	Hoyas	Big East	John Thompson III	Washington, DC	Blue/Gray
Georgia	Bulldogs, 'Dawgs	SEC-East	Dennis Felton	Athens, GA	Red/Black
Georgia Southern	Eagles	Southern	Jeff Price	Statesboro, GA	Blue/White
Georgia St.	Panthers	Atlantic Sun	Michael Perry	Atlanta, GA	Roy. Blue/White
Georgia Tech	Yellow Jackets	ACC	Paul Hewitt	Atlanta, GA	Old Gold/White
Gonzaga	Bulldogs, Zags	West Coast	Mark Few	Spokane, WA	Blue/White/Red
Grambling St.	Tigers	SWAC	Larry Wright	Grambling, LA	Black/Gold
Hampton	Pirates	Mid-Eastern	Bobby Collins	Hampton, VA	Royal Blue/White
Hartford	Hawks	America East	Larry Harrison	W. Hartford, CT	Scarlet/White
Harvard	Crimson	Ivy	Frank Sullivan	Cambridge, MA	Crimson/Black/White
Hawaii	Rainbow Warriors	WAC	Riley Wallace	Honolulu, HI	Green/White
High Point	Panthers	Big South	Bart Lundy	High Point, NC	Purple/White
Hofstra	Pride	Colonial	Tom Pecora	Hempstead, NY	Blue/Gold/White
Holy Cross	Crusaders	Patriot	Ralph Willard	Worcester, MA	Royal Purple
Houston	Cougars	USA	Tom Penders	Houston, TX	Scarlet/White
Howard	Bison	Mid-Eastern	Frankie Allen	Washington, DC	Blue/White/Red
Idaho	Vandals	Big West	Leonard Perry	Moscow, ID	Silver/Gold
Idaho St.	Bengals	Big Sky	Doug Oliver	Pocatello, ID	Orange/Black
Illinois	Fighting Illini	Big Ten	Bruce Weber	Champaign, IL	Orange/Blue
Illinois-Chicago	Flames	Horizon	Jim Collins	Chicago, IL	Navy Blue/Red
Illinois St.	Redbirds	Mo. Valley	Porter Moser	Normal, IL	Red/White
Indiana	Hoosiers	Big Ten	Mike Davis	Bloomington, IN	Cream/Crimson
IPFW	Mastodons	Independent	Doug Noll	Fort Wayne, IN	Royal Blue/White
IUPUI	Jaguars	Mid-Continent	Ron Hunter	Indianapolis, IN	Red/Gold
Indiana St.	Sycamores	Mo. Valley	Royce Waltman	Terre Haute, IN	Blue/White
Iona	Gaels	Metro Atlantic	Jeff Ruland	New Rochelle, NY	Maroon/Gold

Nickname	Conference	Head Coach	Location	Colors
Iowa . . . . Hawkeyes	Big Ten	Steve Alford	Iowa City, IA	Old Gold/Black
Iowa St. . . . . Cyclones	Big 12	Wayne Morgan	Ames, IA	Cardinal/Gold
Jackson St. . . . . Tigers	SWAC	Tevester Anderson	Jackson, MS	Blue/White
Jacksonville . . . . Dolphins	Atlantic Sun	Hugh Durham	Jacksonville, FL	Green/White
Jacksonville St. . . . . . Gamecocks	Ohio Valley	Mike LaPlante	Jacksonville, AL	Red/White
James Madison . . . . Dukes	Colonial	Dean Keener	Harrisonburg, VA	Purple/Gold
Kansas . . . . Jayhawks	Big 12	Bill Self	Lawrence, KS	Crimson/Blue
Kansas St. . . . . Wildcats	Big 12	Jim Wooldridge	Manhattan, KS	Purple/White
Kent St. . . . . . . Golden Flashes	Mid-American	Jim Christian	Kent, OH	Navy Blue/Gold
Kentucky . . . . Wildcats	SEC-East	Tubby Smith	Lexington, KY	Blue/White
La Salle . . . . Explorers	Atlantic 10	John Giannini	Philadelphia, PA	Blue/Gold
Lafayette . . . . Leopards	Patriot	Fran O'Hanlon	Easton, PA	Maroon/White
Lamar . . . . Cardinals	Southland	Billy Tubbs	Beaumont, TX	Red/White
Lehigh . . . . Mountain Hawks	Patriot	Bill Taylor	Bethlehem, PA	Brown/White
Liberty . . . . Flames	Big South	Randy Dunton	Lynchburg, VA	Red/White/Blue
Lipscomb . . . . Bisons	Atlantic Sun	Scott Sanderson	Nashville, TN	Purple/Gold
Long Beach St. 49ers	Big West	Larry Reynolds	Long Beach, CA	Black/Gold
Longwood . . . . Lancers	Independent	Mike Gillian	Farmville, VA	Blue/White
LIU-Brooklyn . . . . . . Blackbirds	Northeast	Jim Ferry	Brooklyn, NY	Black/Silver/Blue
LSU . . . . Fighting Tigers	SEC-West	John Brady	Baton Rouge, LA	Purple/Gold
LA-Lafayette . . . . . Ragin' Cajuns	Sun Belt	Robert Lee	Lafayette, LA	Vermilion/White
LA-Monroe . . . . Indians	Southland	Mike Vining	Monroe, LA	Maroon/Gold
Louisiana Tech . . . . . . Bulldogs	WAC	Keith Richard	Ruston, LA	Red/Blue
Louisville . . . . Cardinals	USA	Rick Pitino	Louisville, KY	Red/Black/White
Loyola Chicago . . . . . Ramblers	Horizon	Jim Whitesell	Chicago, IL	Maroon/Gold
Loyola Maryland . Greyhounds	Metro Atlantic	Jimmy Patsos	Baltimore, MD	Green/Gray
Loyola Marymount . . . . . Lions	West Coast	Steve Aggers	Los Angeles, CA	Crimson/Blue
Maine . . . . Black Bears	America East	Ted Woodward	Orono, ME	Blue/White
Manhattan . . . . Jaspers	Metro Atlantic	Bobby Gonzalez	Riverdale, NY	Kelly Green/White
Marist . . . . Red Foxes	Metro Atlantic	Matt Brady	Poughkeepsie, NY	Red/White
Marquette . . . . . Golden Eagles	USA	Tom Crean	Milwaukee, WI	Blue/Gold
Marshall . . . . . Thundering Herd	Mid-American	Ron Jirsa	Huntington, WV	Green/White
Maryland . . . . . Terrapins, Terps	ACC	Gary Williams	College Park, MD	Red/Wt./Black/Gold
MD-Balt. County . . . . Retrievers	America East	Randy Monroe	Baltimore, MD	Black/Gold/Red
MD-Eastern Shore . . . . . Hawks	Mid-Eastern	Larry Lessett	Princess Anne, MD	Maroon/Gray
Massachusetts . . . . . Minutemen	Atlantic 10	Steve Lappas	Amherst, MA	Maroon/White
McNeese St. . . . . Cowboys	Southland	Tic Price	Lake Charles, LA	Blue/Gold
Memphis . . . . Tigers	USA	John Calipari	Memphis, TN	Blue/Gray
Mercer . . . . Bears	Atlantic Sun	Mark Slonaker	Macon, GA	Orange/Black
Miami-FL . . . . Hurricanes	ACC	Frank Haith	Coral Gables, FL	Orange/Grn./White
Miami-OH . . . . RedHawks	Mid-American	Charlie Coles	Oxford, OH	Red/White
Michigan . . . . Wolverines	Big Ten	Tommy Amaker	Ann Arbor, MI	Maize/Blue
Michigan St. . . . . Spartans	Big Ten	Tom Izzo	East Lansing, MI	Green/White
Middle Tenn. St. . . . Blue Raiders	Sun Belt	Kermit Davis Jr.	Murfreesboro, TN	Blue/White
Minnesota . . . . Golden Gophers	Big Ten	Dan Monson	Minneapolis, MN	Maroon/Gold
Mississippi . . . . Ole Miss, Rebels	SEC-West	Rod Barnes	Oxford, MS	Red/Blue
Mississippi St. . . . . Bulldogs	SEC-West	Rick Stansbury	Starkville, MS	Maroon/White
Miss. Valley St. . . . . Delta Devils	SWAC	Lafayette Stribling	Itta Bena, MS	Green/White
Missouri . . . . Tigers	Big 12	Quin Snyder	Columbia, MO	Old Gold/Black
Missouri-KC . . . . Kangaroos	Mid-Continent	Rich Zvosec	Kansas City, MO	Blue/Gold
Monmouth . . . . Hawks	Northeast	Dave Calloway	W. Long Branch, NJ	Midnight Blue/White
Montana . . . . Grizzlies	Big Sky	Larry Krystkowiak	Missoula, MT	Copper/Silver/Gold
Montana St. . . . . Bobcats	Big Sky	Mick Durham	Bozeman, MT	Blue/Gold
Morehead St. . . . . Eagles	Ohio Valley	Kyle Macy	Morehead, KY	Blue/Gold
Morgan St. . . . . Bears	Mid-Eastern	Butch Beard	Baltimore, MD	Blue/Orange
Mt. St. Mary's . . . Mountaineers	Northeast	Milan Brown	Emmitsburg, MD	Blue/White
Murray St. . . . . Racers	Ohio Valley	Mick Cronin	Murray, KY	Blue/Gold
Navy . . . . Midshipmen	Patriot	Billy Lange	Annapolis, MD	Navy Blue/Gold
Nebraska . . . . Cornhuskers	Big 12	Barry Collier	Lincoln, NE	Scarlet/Cream
Nevada . . . . Wolf Pack	WAC	Mark Fox	Reno, NV	Silver/Blue
New Hampshire . . . . Wildcats	America East	Phil Rowe	Durham, NH	Blue/White
New Mexico . . . . Lobos	Mountain West	Ritchie McKay	Albuquerque, NM	Cherry/Silver
New Mexico St. . . . . Aggies	Sun Belt	Lou Henson	Las Cruces, NM	Crimson/White
New Orleans . . . . Privateers	Sun Belt	Monte Towe	New Orleans, LA	Royal Blue/Silver
Niagara . . . . Purple Eagles	Metro Atlantic	Joe Mihalich	Lewiston, NY	Purple/White/Gold
Nicholls St. . . . . Colonels	Southland	Ricky Blanton	Thibodaux, LA	Red/Gray
Norfolk State . . . . Spartans	Mid-Eastern	Dwight Freeman	Norfolk, VA	Green/Gold
North Carolina . . . . . . Tar Heels	ACC	Roy Williams	Chapel Hill, NC	Carolina Blue/Wht.
North Carolina A&T . . . . Aggies	Mid-Eastern	Jerry Eaves	Greensboro, NC	Blue/Gold
North Carolina St. . . . Wolfpack	ACC	Herb Sendek	Raleigh, NC	Red/White
NC-Asheville . . . . Bulldogs	Big South	Eddie Biedenbach	Asheville, NC	Royal Blue/White

NCAA Division I Basketball Schools (Cont.)

	Nickname	Conference	Head Coach	Location	Colors
NC-Greensboro	Spartans	Southern	Fran McCaffrey	Greensboro, NC	Gold/White/Navy
NC-Wilmington	Seahawks	Colonial	Brad Brownell	Wilmington, NC	Green/Gold/Navy
North Dakota St.	Bison	Independent	Tim Miles	Fargo, ND	Yellow/Green
North Texas	Mean Green	Sun Belt	Johnny Jones	Denton, TX	Green/White
Northeastern	Huskies	America East	Ron Everhart	Boston, MA	Red/Black
Northern Arizona	Lumberjacks	Big Sky	Mike Adras	Flagstaff, AZ	Blue/Gold
Northern Colorado	Bears	Independent	Craig Rasmuson	Greeley, CO	Blue/Gold
Northern Illinois	Huskies	Mid-American	Rob Judson	De Kalb, IL	Cardinal/Black
Northern Iowa	Panthers	Mo. Valley	Greg McDermott	Cedar Falls, IA	Purple/Old Gold
Northwestern	Wildcats	Big Ten	Bill Carmody	Evanston, IL	Purple/White
Northwestern St.	Demons	Southland	Mike McConathy	Natchitoches, LA	Purple/Orange/Wt.
Notre Dame	Fighting Irish	Big East	Mike Brey	Notre Dame, IN	Gold/Blue
Oakland-MI	Golden Grizzlies	Mid-Continent	Greg Kampe	Rochester, MI	Black/Gold
Ohio University	Bobcats	Mid-American	Tim O'Shea	Athens, OH	Hunter Green/White
Ohio St.	Buckeyes	Big Ten	Thad Matta	Columbus, OH	Scarlet/Gray
Oklahoma	Sooners	Big 12	Kelvin Sampson	Norman, OK	Crimson/Cream
Oklahoma St.	Cowboys	Big 12	Eddie Sutton	Stillwater, OK	Orange/Black
Old Dominion	Monarchs	Colonial	Blaine Taylor	Norfolk, VA	Slate Blue/Silver
Oral Roberts	Golden Eagles	Mid-Continent	Scott Sutton	Tulsa, OK	Navy Blue/White
Oregon	Ducks	Pac-10	Ernie Kent	Eugene, OR	Green/Yellow
Oregon St.	Beavers	Pac-10	Jay John	Corvallis, OR	Orange/Black
Pacific	Tigers	Big West	Bob Thomason	Stockton, CA	Orange/Black
Pennsylvania	Quakers	Ivy	Fran Dunphy	Philadelphia, PA	Red/Blue
Penn St.	Nittany Lions	Big Ten	Ed DeChellis	University Park, PA	Blue/White
Pepperdine	Waves	West Coast	Paul Westphal	Malibu, CA	Blue/Orange
Pittsburgh	Panthers	Big East	Jamie Dixon	Pittsburgh, PA	Gold/Blue
Portland	Pilots	West Coast	Mike Holton	Portland, OR	Purple/White
Portland St.	Vikings	Big Sky	Heath Schroyer	Portland, OR	Green/White
Prairie View A&M	Panthers	SWAC	Jerry Francis	Prairie View, TX	Purple/Gold
Princeton	Tigers	Ivy	Joe Scott	Princeton, NJ	Orange/Black
Providence	Friars	Big East	Tim Welsh	Providence, RI	Black/White
Purdue	Boilermakers	Big Ten	Gene Keady	W. Lafayette, IN	Old Gold/Black
Quinnipiac	Bobcats	Northeast	Joe DeSantis	Hamden, CT	Navy/Gold
Radford	Highlanders	Big South	Byron Samuels	Radford, VA	Blue/Red/Green/Wt.
Rhode Island	Rams	Atlantic 10	Jim Baron	Kingston, RI	Lt. Blue/White/Navy
Rice	Owls	WAC	Willis Wilson	Houston, TX	Blue/Gray
Richmond	Spiders	Atlantic 10	Jerry Wainwright	Richmond, VA	Red/Blue
Rider	Broncs	Metro Atlantic	Don Harnum	Lawrenceville, NJ	Cranberry/White
Robert Morris	Colonials	Northeast	Mark Schmidt	Moon Township, PA	Blue/Red/White
Rutgers	Scarlet Knights	Big East	Gary Waters	New Brunswick, NJ	Scarlet
Sacramento St.	Hornets	Big Sky	Jerome Jenkins	Sacramento, CA	Green/Gold
Sacred Heart	Pioneers	Northeast	Dave Bike	Fairfield, CT	Scarlet/White
St. Bonaventure	Bonnies	Atlantic 10	Anthony Solomon	St. Bonaventure, NY	Brown/White
St. Francis-NY	Terriers	Northeast	Ron Ganulin	Brooklyn, NY	Red/Blue
St. Francis-PA	Red Flash	Northeast	Bobby Jones	Loretto, PA	Red/White
St. John's	Red Storm	Big East	Norm Roberts	Jamaica, NY	Red/White
Saint Joseph's	Hawks	Atlantic 10	Phil Martelli	Philadelphia, PA	Crimson/Gray
Saint Louis	Billikens	USA	Brad Soderberg	St. Louis, MO	Blue/White
Saint Mary's-CA	Gaels	West Coast	Randy Bennett	Moraga, CA	Red/Blue
Saint Peter's	Peacocks	Metro Atlantic	Bob Leckie	Jersey City, NJ	Blue/White
Sam Houston St.	Bearkats	Southland	Bob Marlin	Huntsville, TX	Orange/White
Samford	Bulldogs	Ohio Valley	Jimmy Tillette	Birmingham, AL	Red/Blue
San Diego	Toreros	West Coast	Brad Holland	San Diego, CA	Lt. Blue/Navy
San Diego St.	Aztecs	Mountain West	Steve Fisher	San Diego, CA	Scarlet/Black
San Francisco	Dons	West Coast	Jessie Evans	San Francisco, CA	Green/Gold
San Jose St.	Spartans	WAC	Phil Johnson	San Jose, CA	Gold/White/Blue
Santa Clara	Broncos	West Coast	Dick Davey	Santa Clara, CA	Bronco Red/White
Savannah St.	Tigers	Independent	Edward Daniels	Savannah, GA	Orange/Blue
Seton Hall	Pirates	Big East	Louis Orr	South Orange, NJ	Blue/White
Siena	Saints	Metro Atlantic	Rob Lanier	Loudonville, NY	Green/Gold
South Alabama	Jaguars	Sun Belt	John Pelphrey	Mobile, AL	Red/White/Blue
South Carolina	Gamecocks	SEC-East	Dave Odom	Columbia, SC	Garnet/Black
South Carolina St.	Bulldogs	Mid-Eastern	Benjamin Betts Jr.	Orangeburg, SC	Garnet/Blue
South Dakota St.	Jackrabbits	Independent	Scott Nagy	Brookings, SD	Yellow/Blue
South Florida	Bulls	USA	Robert McCullum	Tampa, FL	Green/Gold
SE Missouri St.	Redhawks	Ohio Valley	Gary Garner	Cape Girardeau, MO	Red/Black
SE Louisiana	Lions	Southland	Billy Kennedy	Hammond, LA	Green/Gold
Southern-BR	Jaguars	SWAC	Michael Grant	Baton Rouge, LA	Blue/Gold
Southern Illinois	Salukis	Mo. Valley	Chris Lowery	Carbondale, IL	Maroon/White

	Nickname	Conference	Head Coach	Location	Colors
SMU	Mustangs	WAC	Jimmy Tubbs	Dallas, TX	Red/Blue
Southern Miss	Golden Eagles	USA	Larry Eustachy	Hattiesburg, MS	Black/Gold
Southern Utah	Thunderbirds	Mid-Continent	Bill Evans	Cedar City, UT	Scarlet/White
SW Missouri St.	Bears	Mo. Valley	Barry Hinson	Springfield, MO	Maroon/White
Stanford	Cardinal	Pac-10	Trent Johnson	Stanford, CA	Cardinal/White
S.F. Austin St.	Lumberjacks	Southland	Danny Kaspar	Nacogdoches, TX	Purple/White
Stetson	Hatters	Atlantic Sun	Derek Waugh	DeLand, FL	Green/White
Stony Brook	Seawolves	America East	Nick Macarchuk	Stony Brook, NY	Scarlet/Gray
Syracuse	Orange	Big East	Jim Boeheim	Syracuse, NY	Orange
Temple	Owls	Atlantic 10	John Chaney	Philadelphia, PA	Cherry/White
Tennessee	Volunteers	SEC-East	Buzz Peterson	Knoxville, TN	Orange/White
Tenn-Martin	Skyhawks	Ohio Valley	Bret Campbell	Martin, TN	Orange/Wt./Blue
Tennessee St.	Tigers	Ohio Valley	Cy Alexander	Nashville, TN	Blue/White
Tennessee Tech	Golden Eagles	Ohio Valley	Mike Sutton	Cookeville, TN	Purple/Gold
Texas	Longhorns	Big 12	Rick Barnes	Austin, TX	Burnt Orange/White
Texas A&M	Aggies	Big 12	Billy Gillispie	College Station, TX	Maroon/White
TX A&M Corpus-Christi	Islanders	Independent	Ronnie Arrow	Corpus Christi, TX	Blue/Green/Silver
TCU	Horned Frogs	USA	Neil Dougherty	Ft. Worth, TX	Purple/White
Texas Southern	Tigers	SWAC	Ronnie Courtney	Houston, TX	Maroon/Gray
Texas St.-San Marcos	Bobcats	Southland	Dennis Nutt	San Marcos, TX	Maroon/Gold
Texas Tech	Red Raiders	Big 12	Bob Knight	Lubbock, TX	Scarlet/Black
TX-Arlington	Mavericks	Southland	Eddie McCarter	Arlington, TX	Royal Blue/White
TX-Pan American	Broncs	Independent	Robert Davenport	Edinburg, TX	Green/White
TX-San Antonio	Roadrunners	Southland	Tim Carter	San Antonio, TX	Orange/Navy/White
Toledo	Rockets	Mid-American	Stan Joplin	Toledo, OH	Blue/Gold
Towson	Tigers	Colonial	Pat Kennedy	Towson, MD	Gold/White/Black
Troy	Trojans	Atlantic Sun	Don Maestri	Troy, AL	Cardinal/Silver/Black
Tulane	Green Wave	USA	Shawn Finney	New Orleans, LA	Olive Grn./Sky Blue
Tulsa	Golden Hurricane	WAC	John Phillips	Tulsa, OK	Blue/Red/Gold
UAB	Blazers	USA	Mike Anderson	Birmingham, AL	Green/Gold
UC-Irvine	Anteaters	Big West	Pat Douglass	Irvine, CA	Blue/Gold
UCLA	Bruins	Pac-10	Ben Howland	Los Angeles, CA	Blue/Gold
UC-Davis	Aggies	Big West	Gary Stewart	Davis, CA	Yale Blue/Gold
UC-Riverside	Highlanders	Big West	John Masi	Riverside, CA	Blue/Gold
UC-Santa Barbara	Gauchos	Big West	Bob Williams	Santa Barbara, CA	Blue/Gold
UNLV	Runnin' Rebels	Mountain West	Lon Kruger	Las Vegas, NV	Scarlet/Gray
USC	Trojans	Pac-10	Henry Bibby	Los Angeles, CA	Cardinal/Gold
Utah	Utes	Mountain West	Ray Giacoletti	Salt Lake City, UT	Crimson/White
Utah St.	Aggies	Big West	Stew Morrill	Logan, UT	Navy Blue/White
Utah Valley St.	Wolverines	Independent	Dick Hunsaker	Orem, UT	Green/Gold/White
UTEP	Miners	WAC	Doc Sadler	El Paso, TX	Orange/Blue/White
Valparaiso	Crusaders	Mid-Continent	Homer Drew	Valparaiso, IN	Brown/Gold
Vanderbilt	Commodores	SEC-East	Kevin Stallings	Nashville, TN	Black/Gold
Vermont	Catamounts	America East	Tom Brennan	Burlington, VT	Green/Gold
Villanova	Wildcats	Big East	Jay Wright	Villanova, PA	Blue/White
Virginia	Cavaliers	ACC	Pete Gillen	Charlottesville, VA	Orange/Blue
VCU	Rams	Colonial	Jeff Capel III	Richmond, VA	Black/Gold
VMI	Keydets	Big South	Bart Bellairs	Lexington, VA	Red/White/Yellow
Virginia Tech	Hokies, Gobblers	ACC	Seth Greenberg	Blacksburg, VA	Orange/Maroon
Wagner	Seahawks	Northeast	Mike Deane	Staten Island, NY	Green/White
Wake Forest	Demon Deacons	ACC	Skip Prosser	Winston-Salem, NC	Old Gold/Black
Washington	Huskies	Pac-10	Lorenzo Romar	Seattle, WA	Purple/Gold
Washington St.	Cougars	Pac-10	Dick Bennett	Pullman, WA	Crimson/Gray
Weber St.	Wildcats	Big Sky	Joe Cravens	Ogden, UT	Purple/White
West Virginia	Mountaineers	Big East	John Beilein	Morgantown, WV	Old Gold/Blue
Western Carolina	Catamounts	Southern	Steve Shurina	Cullowhee, NC	Purple/Gold
Western Illinois	Leathernecks	Mid-Continent	Derek Thomas	Macomb, IL	Purple/Gold
Western Kentucky	Hilltoppers	Sun Belt	Darrin Horn	Bowling Green, KY	Red/White
Western Michigan	Broncos	Mid-American	Steve Hawkins	Kalamazoo, MI	Brown/Gold
Wichita St.	Shockers	Mo. Valley	Mark Turgeon	Wichita, KS	Yellow/Black
William & Mary	Tribe	Colonial	Tony Shaver	Williamsburg, VA	Green/Gold/Silver
Winthrop	Eagles	Big South	Gregg Marshall	Rock Hill, SC	Garnet/Gold
Wisconsin	Badgers	Big Ten	Bo Ryan	Madison, WI	Cardinal/White
WI-Green Bay	Phoenix	Horizon	Tod Kowalczyk	Green Bay, WI	Green/White/Red
WI-Milwaukee	Panthers	Horizon	Bruce Pearl	Milwaukee, WI	Black/Gold
Wofford	Terriers	Southern	Mike Young	Spartanburg, SC	Old Gold/Black
Wright St.	Raiders	Horizon	Paul Biancardi	Dayton, OH	Green/Gold
Wyoming	Cowboys	Mountain West	Steve McClain	Laramie, WY	Brown/Yellow
Xavier	Musketeers	Atlantic 10	Sean Miller	Cincinnati, OH	Blue/Gray/White
Yale	Bulldogs, Elis	Ivy	James Jones	New Haven, CT	Yale Blue/White
Youngstown St.	Penguins	Horizon	John Robic	Youngstown, OH	Red/White

| Mississippi St.
Sylvester Croom
Packers to Miss. St. | Arizona
Mike Stoops
Oklahoma to Arizona | Central Florida
George O'Leary
Vikings to UCF | Northeastern
Rocky Hager
Temple to Northeastern |

Coaching Changes

New head coaches were named at 14 Division 1-A and 22 Division 1-AA football schools while 37 Division 1 basketball schools changed head coaches after the 2003-04 season. Coaching changes listed below are as of September 30, 2004.

Division I-A Football

	Old Coach	Record	Why Left?	New Coach	Old Job
Akron	Lee Owens	7-5	fired	J.D. Brookhart	Off. coord., Pittsburgh
Arizona	John Mackovic	2-10 †	fired	Mike Stoops	Def. coord., Oklahoma
Army	Todd Berry	0-13@	fired	Bobby Ross	Former coach, NFL Detroit
Central Florida . .	Mike Kruczek	3-9 #	fired	George O'Leary	Def. coord., NFL Minnesota
Central Michigan .	Mike DeBord	3-9	resigned	Brian Kelly	Coach, Grand Valley St.
Cincinnati	Rick Minter	5-7	fired	Mark Dantonio	Def. coord., Ohio St.
Duke	Carl Franks	4-8&	fired	Ted Roof	Def. coord., Duke
Eastern Michigan	Jeff Woodruff	3-9 $	fired	Jeff Genyk	Asst., Northwestern
Idaho	Tom Cable	3-9	fired	Nick Holt	Asst., USC
Kent St.	Dean Pees	5-7	to NFL New Eng.**	Doug Martin	Off. coord., Kent St.
Mississippi St. . . .	Jackie Sherrill	2-10	retired	Sylvester Croom	Asst., NFL Green Bay
Nebraska	Frank Solich	10-3	fired	Bill Callahan	Coach, NFL Oakland
Nevada	Chris Tormey	6-6	fired	Chris Ault	Athletic Director, Nevada
UTEP	Gary Nord	2-11	fired	Mike Price	Former coach, Wash. St.

** as assistant coach

† Mackovic (1-4) was fired on Sept. 28, 2003 and replaced on an interim basis by defensive coordinator Mike Hankwitz (1-6) .
@ Berry (0-6) was fired on Oct. 13, 2003 and replaced on an interim basis by defensive line coach John Mumford (0-6).
# Kruczek (3-7) was fired on Nov. 10, 2003 and replaced on an interim basis by assistant Alan Gooch (0-2).
& Franks (2-5) was fired on Oct. 19, 2003 and replaced by defensive coordinator Roof (2-3).
$ Woodruff (1-8) was fired on Nov. 3, 2003 and replaced on an interim basis by assistant coach Al Lavan (2-1).
+ Solich (9-3) was fired on Nov. 30, 2003. Defensive coordinator Bo Pelini (0-1) coached the team in the Alamo Bowl.

Division I-AA Football

	Old Coach	Record	Why Left?	New Coach	Old Job
Ark.-Pine Bluff . .	Lee Hardman	4-7	resigned	Mo Forte	Former coach, Norfolk St.
Central Conn. St. .	Paul Schudel	3-8	fired	Tom Masella	Def. coord., Massachusetts
The Citadel	Ellis Johnson	6-6	to Miss. St.**	John Zernhelt	Off. coord., The Citadel
Cornell	Tim Pendergast	1-9	fired	Jim Knowles	Asst., Mississippi
Delaware St.	Ben Blacknall	1-10@	fired	Al Lavan	Asst., Eastern Michigan
Elon	Al Seagraves	2-10	fired	Paul Hamilton	Coach, East Tennessee
Fordham	Dave Clawson	9-3	to Richmond*	Ed Foley	Off. coord., Fordham
Grambling St.	Doug Williams	9-3	to NFL Tampa Bay	Melvin Spears	Off. coord., Grambling St.
Holy Cross	Dan Allen	1-11	Reassigned	Tom Gilmore	Def. coord., Lehigh
La Salle	Archie Stalcup	3-8	Resigned	Phil Longo	Off. coord., La Salle
Massachusetts . . .	Mark Whipple	10-3	to NFL Pittsburgh**	Don Brown	Coach, Northeastern
Nicholls St.	Daryl Daye	5-6	fired	Jay Thomas	Def. Coord., Nicholls St.
Northeastern	Don Brown	8-4	to Massachusetts*	Rocky Hager	Asst., Temple
Prairie View	C.L. Whittington	1-9	fired	Henry Frazier	Coach, Bowie St.
Richmond	Jim Reid	2-9	to Syracuse**	Dave Clawson	Coach, Fordham
Saint Peter's	Scott Kochman	0-1 +	fired	Chris Taylor	Asst., Saint Peter's
San Diego	Kevin McGarry	8-2 &	fired	Jim Harbaugh	Asst., NFL Oakland
Sacred Heart	Bill Lacey	6-5	resigned	Paul Gorham	Asst., Massachusetts
Savannah St.	Ken Pettiford	0-12 #	fired	Richard Basil	Asst., Savannah St.
Southern Utah . . .	Gary Andersen	4-7	to Utah**	Wes Meier	Asst., Southern Utah
Texas Southern . .	Bill Thomas	5-6	resigned	Steve Wilson	Def. coord., Bowie St.
Texas St.	Manny Matsakis	4-8	fired	David Bailiff	Def. coord., TCU

* as head coach   ** as assistant coach   † as a personnel executive.

+ Kochman (0-1) was fired on Sept. 10, 2004 and replaced by defensive line coach Chris Taylor.
& McGarry (5-1) was fired on Oct. 17 and replaced on an interim basis by defensive coordinator Jason DesJarlais (3-1).
& McGarry (5-1) was fired on Oct. 17 and replaced on an interim basis by defensive coordinator Jason DesJarlais (3-1).
# Pettiford (0-5) was fired on Sept. 29, 2003 and replaced by assistant Richard Basil (0-7).

Georgetown
John Thompson III
Princeton to Georgetown

Ohio St.
Thad Matta
Xavier to Ohio St.

Stanford
Trent Johnson
Nevada to Stanford

UNLV
Lon Kruger
Knicks to UNLV

Division I Basketball

	Old Coach	Record	Why Left?	New Coach	Old Job
Air Force	Joe Scott	22-7	to Princeton*	Chris Mooney	Asst., Air Force
Akron	Dan Hipsher	13-15	fired	Keith Dambrot	Asst., Akron
Auburn	Cliff Ellis	14-14	fired	Jeff Lebo	Coach, Chattanooga
Chattanooga	Jeff Lebo	19-11	to Auburn*	John Shulman	Asst., Chattanooga
Dartmouth	Dave Faucher	3-25	resigned	Terry Dunn	Asst., Colorado
Eastern Wash.	Ray Giacoletti	17-13	to Utah*	Mike Burns	Asst., Washington St.
Florida Int'l	Donnie Marsh	5-22	fired	Sergio Rouco	Asst., UTEP
Georgetown	Craig Esherick	13-15	fired	John Thompson III	Coach, Princeton
Houston	Ray McCallum	9-18	reassigned	Tom Penders	Former coach, Geo. Wash.
James Madison	Sherman Dillard	7-21	resigned	Dean Keener	Asst., Georgia Tech
La Salle	Billy Hahn	10-20	resigned	John Giannini	Coach, Maine
LA-Lafayette	Jessie Evans	20-9	to San Francisco*	Glynn Cyprien	Asst., Oklahoma St.
	Glynn Cyprien	—	fired†	Robert Lee	Asst., LA-Lafayette
Loyola Chicago	Larry Farmer	9-20	fired	Jim Whitesell	Coach, Lewis
Loyola Maryland	Scott Hicks	1-27	fired	Jimmy Patsos	Asst., Maryland
Maine	John Giannini	20-10	to La Salle*	Ted Woodward	Asst., Maine
Marist	Dave Magarity	6-22	resigned	Matt Brady	Asst., Saint Joseph's
MD-Balt. County	Tom Sullivan	7-21	resigned	Randy Monroe	Asst., MD-Balt. County
MD-Eastern Shore	Thomas Trotter	8-21	fired	Larry Lessett	International scout
Miami-FL	Perry Clark	14-16	fired	Frank Haith	Asst., Texas
Montana	Pat Kennedy	10-18	to Towson*	Larry Krystkowiak	Coach, CBA Idaho
Navy	Don DeVoe	5-23	resigned	Billy Lange	Asst., Villanova
Nevada	Trent Johnson	25-9	to Stanford*	Mark Fox	Asst., Nevada
Ohio St.	Jim O'Brien	14-16	fired	Thad Matta	Coach, Xavier
Princeton	John Thompson III	20-8	to Georgetown*	Joe Scott	Coach, Air Force
St. John's	Mike Jarvis	6-21@	fired	Norm Roberts	Asst., Kansas
San Francisco	Philip Mathews	17-14	fired	Jessie Evans	Coach, LA-Lafayette
Southern Illinois	Matt Painter	25-5	to Purdue**	Chris Lowery	Asst., Illinois
SMU	Mike Dement	12-18#	fired	Jimmy Tubbs	Asst., Oklahoma
Southern Miss	James Green	13-15$	resigned	Larry Eustachy	Former coach, Iowa St.
Stanford	Mike Montgomery	30-2	to NBA Golden St.*	Trent Johnson	Coach, Nevada
Texas A&M	Melvin Watkins	7-21	resigned	Billy Gillispie	Coach, UTEP
TX-Pan American	Bob Hoffman	14-14	to Oklahoma**	Robert Davenport	Asst., TX-Pan American
Towson	Michael Hunt	8-21	resigned	Pat Kennedy	Coach, Montana
UNLV	Charlie Spoonhour	18-13+	resigned	Lon Kruger	Asst., NBA NY Knicks
Utah	Rick Majerus	24-9%	resigned	Ray Giacoletti	Coach, Eastern Wash.
UTEP	Billy Gillispie	24-8	to Texas A&M*	Doc Sadler	Asst., UTEP
Xavier	Thad Matta	26-11	to Ohio St.*	Sean Miller	Asst., Xavier

* as head coach
** as assistant coach
† Cyprien was hired on May 5, 2004 but was relieved of his duties on July 16 when discrepancies on his resume were uncovered.
@ Jarvis (2-4) was fired on Dec. 19, 2003 and replaced on an interim basis by associate head coach Kevin Clark (4-17).
# Dement (10-15) was fired on Feb. 27, 2004 and replaced on an interim basis by assistant Robert Lineburg (2-3).
$ Green (13-13) resigned on March 5, 2004 and was replaced on an interim basis by assistant Jeff Norwood (0-2).
+ Spoonhour (12-9) resigned on Feb. 17, 2004 due to health issues and was replaced on an interim basis by assistant Jay Spoonhour (6-4).
% Majerus (15-5) resigned on Jan. 27, 2004 due to health issues and was replaced on an interim basis by assistant Kerry Rupp (9-4).

2003-04 Directors' Cup

Sponsored by the United States Sports Academy (USSA). Developed as a joint effort between the National Association of Collegiate Directors of Athletics (NACDA) and USA Today. Introduced in 1993-94 to honor the nation's best overall NCAA Division I athletic department (combining men's and women's sports). Winners in NCAA Division II and III and NAIA were named for the first time following the 1995-96 season.

Standings are computed by NACDA with points awarded for each Div. I school's finish in 20 sports (top 10 scoring sports for both men and women). Div. II schools are awarded points in 14 sports (top 7 scoring sports for both men and women). Div III schools are awarded points in 18 sports (top 9 scoring sports for both men and women). NAIA schools are awarded points in 12 sports (top 6 scoring sports for both men and women). National champions in each sport earn 100 points, while 2nd through 64th-place finishers earn decreasing points depending on the size of the tournament field. Division I-A football points are based on the final ESPN/*USA Today* Coaches' Top 25 poll. Listed below are team conferences (for Div. I only), combined Final Four finishes (1st through 4th place) for men's and women's programs, overall points in **bold** type, and the previous year's ranking (for Div. I only).

Multiple winners: Stanford (10); Williams, MA (8); Simon Fraser, BC and UC-Davis (6); Lindenwood, MO (2).

Division I

		Conf	1-2-3-4	Pts	02-03 Rank			Conf	1-2-3-4	Pts	02-03 Rank
1	Stanford	Pac-10	3-1-2-0	**1337.3**	1	15	Oklahoma	Big 12	0-1-1-0	**728.75**	20
2	Michigan	Big Ten	0-0-2-1	**1226.3**	4	16	Texas A&M	Big 12	0-0-0-0	**714**	28
3	UCLA	Pac-10	4-3-1-0	**1178.8**	6	17	Arizona St.	Pac-10	0-0-0-0	**708**	10
4	Ohio St.	Big Ten	1-0-1-3	**1026.5**	3	18	Duke	ACC	0-1-2-0	**706.5**	21
5	Georgia	SEC	0-2-1-0	**1005.3**	15	19	Notre Dame	Big East	0-0-1-0	**705**	13
6	Florida	SEC	0-4-0-1	**993.25**	7	20	Minnesota	Big Ten	0-0-2-0	**687**	11
7	North Carolina	ACC	1-0-0-0	**925**	8	21	USC	Pac-10	1-1-1-0	**683.5**	13
8	Washington	Pac-10	0-0-0-0	**919.5**	17	22	Florida St.	ACC	0-0-1-0	**623**	38
9	California	Pac-10	1-1-0-2	**899.5**	9	23	Auburn	SEC	2-0-0-0	**616.75**	12
10	Texas	Big 12	0-1-1-3	**880.25**	2	24	Maryland	ACC	0-0-2-0	**599**	22
11	LSU	SEC	3-1-3-0	**867.75**	23	25	Illinois	Big Ten	0-0-2-0	**597**	30
12	Arizona	Pac-10	0-0-2-1	**799.5**	16						
13	Penn St.	Big Ten	1-1-0-0	**795.5**	5						
14	Tennessee	SEC	0-1-0-1	**755.75**	27						

Division II

		1-2-3-4	Pts			1-2-3-4	Pts
1	Grand Valley St., MI	1-1-2-0	**810**	14	Indianapolis	0-0-0-0	**440**
2	California-San Diego	0-0-2-0	**663**	15	Abilene Christian, TX	2-1-1-1	**438.5**
3	Truman St., MO	1-0-0-0	**603**	16	Nebraska-Omaha	1-0-1-0	**436.5**
4	North Dakota	0-1-1-0	**574.5**	16	Drury, MO	0-3-0-0	**432**
5	California St.-Chico	0-2-0-2	**574**	18	Western St., CO	0-1-0-1	**431.75**
6	Rollins, FL	1-0-2-0	**570**	19	Kennesaw St., GA	2-0-0-0	**430.5**
7	California St.-Bakersfield	1-0-0-1	**503**	20	Minnesota St.-Mankato	0-0-0-0	**415**
8	North Dakota St.	0-1-2-1	**498.5**	21	North Florida	0-0-1-0	**412**
9	South Dakota St.	0-0-0-0	**474.5**	22	Central Missouri St.	0-0-1-0	**410.5**
10	Northern Kentucky	0-0-0-0	**472.5**	23	Nebraska-Kearney	0-0-0-0	**402.5**
11	South Dakota	0-0-0-0	**452.5**	24	Bryant, RI	0-0-0-0	**399.25**
	St. Cloud St., MN	0-0-1-0	**452.5**	25	Barry, FL	0-0-1-0	**387**
13	Adams St., CO	2-2-1-1	**444**				

Division III

		1-2-3-4	Pts			1-2-3-4	Pts
1	Williams, MA	0-2-1-2	**1081.75**	14	Trinity, TX	1-0-0-0	**492**
2	Emory, GA	1-2-1-1	**811**	15	Wisconsin-Oshkosh	2-0-1-0	**480.75**
3	Middlebury, VT	3-1-1-0	**779.5**	16	Johns Hopkins, MD	0-0-1-0	**469.5**
4	New Jersey	0-1-2-0	**751**	17	Wheaton, MA	0-1-2-0	**458.75**
5	Wisconsin-Stevens Point	1-1-2-1	**730**	18	New York	0-1-0-0	**435.5**
6	Amherst, MA	0-1-1-1	**686.75**	19	Washington & Lee, VA	0-0-0-1	**421**
7	Wisconsin-La Crosse	2-0-0-1	**640**	20	Bowdoin, ME	0-1-0-0	**416.5**
8	Cortland St., NY	0-0-1-0	**627.5**	21	Wheaton, IL	0-0-0-0	**390**
9	Washington, MO	1-0-0-0	**610.5**	22	Denison, OH	0-0-1-1	**383**
10	Gustavus Adolphus, MN	1-0-0-0	**583**	23	Calvin, MI	1-1-0-0	**382.5**
11	Ithaca, NY	0-0-0-0	**553.5**	24	Chicago	0-1-0-0	**377**
12	Salisbury, MD	2-0-2-0	**537**	25	Wisconsin-Whitewater	0-1-2-0	**374.25**
13	Wartburg, IA	1-0-0-1	**504.25**				

NAIA

		1-2-3-4	Pts			1-2-3-4	Pts
1	Simon Fraser, BC	.3-2-2-0	**842.25**	14	Minot St., ND	.1-0-0-0	**447.5**
2	Azusa Pacific, CA	.3-2-1-0	**700**	15	Cumberland, KY	.0-0-1-0	**443**
3	Lindenwood, MO	.0-3-0-1	**673**	16	Oklahoma Baptist	.0-0-2-0	**442**
4	Oklahoma City	.1-3-1-0	**573**	17	Northwood, FL	.0-0-1-0	**425**
5	Dickinson St., ND	.1-0-0-0	**545.5**	18	Malone, OH	.0-0-1-0	**420.5**
	Mary, ND	.0-0-1-0	**545.5**	19	Biola, CA	.0-0-1-0	**420**
7	Pt. Loma Nazarene, CA	.0-0-1-0	**542.75**	20	Mobile, AL	.0-0-0-1	**419**
8	Berry, GA	.0-0-1-0	**519**	21	Flagler, FL	.0-0-0-0	**412**
9	Southern Nazarene, OK	.1-0-1-0	**486**	22	Lindsey Wilson, KY	.0-1-0-0	**411**
10	Cedarville, OH	.0-1-0-0	**471**	23	California St.-San Marcos	.0-0-1-1	**402.75**
11	Embry-Riddle, FL	.0-0-1-0	**468**	24	Spring Hill, AL	.0-0-1-0	**402**
12	Indiana Wesleyan	.0-0-0-1	**456**	25	Cornerstone, MI	.0-0-0-0	**399.5**
13	British Columbia	.1-0-0-1	**452.25**				

NCAA Division I Schools on Probation

As of Sept. 30, 2004, there were 29 Division I member institutions serving NCAA probations.

School	Sport	Yrs	Penalty To End	School	Sport	Yrs	Penalty To End
Howard	Baseball	3	11/26/04	Villanova	M Basketball	2	7/7/06
	M & W Swimming	3	11/26/04	St. Bonaventure	M Basketball	3	7/14/06
	& M & W Basketball	3	11/26/04	Utah	M Basketball	3	7/29/06
UNLV	M Basketball	4	12/11/04	Jacksonville	M Soccer	5	8/29/06
Kentucky	Football	3	1/30/05		& W Rowing	5	8/29/06
Washington	M Basketball	2	2/9/05	Wisconsin	M Basketball	5	9/30/06
San Diego St.	Football	2	2/23/05		& Football	5	9/30/06
Miami-FL	Baseball	2	2/26/05	Minnesota	W Basketball	4	10/22/06
Stetson	W. Tennis	1	5/8/05		& M Basketball	6	10/22/06
Jackson St.	M Track and XC	5	5/16/05	Tennessee St.	M Basketball	3	10/23/06
New Mexico St.	M Basketball	4	6/19/05	Fresno St.	M & W Basketball	4	12/3/06
LA-Monroe	W Tennis	1	9/29/05		& M & W Soccer	4	12/3/06
Chicago St.	W Basketball	2	12/16/05	Alabama	Football	5	1/31/07
Marshall	Football	4	12/20/05	Gardner-Webb	Baseball	3	3/3/07
	& M Basketball	4	12/20/05		M & W Basketball	3	3/3/07
California	Football	5	3/7/06		M Soccer	3	3/3/07
Arkansas	Football	3	4/15/06		& W Track	3	3/3/07
	& M Basketball	3	4/15/06	Michigan	M Basketball	4	5/6/07
Auburn	M Basketball	2	4/26/06	CS-Northridge	M Basketball	3	6/1/07
Oregon	Football	2	6/22/06	Georgia	M Basketball	4	4/16/08

Remaining postseason and TV sanctions

2004-2005 postseason bans: none.
2004-2005 television bans: None.

NCAA Graduation Rates

The following table compares graduation rates of NCAA Division I student athletes with the entire student body in those schools. Years given denote the year in which students entered college. Rates are based on students who enrolled as freshmen, received an athletics scholarship and graduated in six years or less. All figures are percentages.
Source: NCAA Graduation-Rates Report, 2003.

	1991	1992	1993	1994	1995	1996
All Student Athletes	57	58	58	58	60	62
Entire Student Body	56	56	56	56	58	59
Male Student Athletes	51	52	51	51	54	55
Male Student Body	53	54	54	54	56	56
Female Student Athletes	67	68	68	69	69	70
Female Student Body	58	59	59	59	61	62
Div. I-A Football Players	50	51	48	51	53	54
Male Basketball Players	41	41	42	40	43	44
Female Basketball Players	66	62	63	65	65	66

2003-04 NCAA Team Champions

Multiple winners: Five—MIDDLEBURY, VT (Div. III women's cross country, men's and women's ice hockey, women's lacrosse and men's tennis). **Four**—UCLA (National Div. women's gymnastics, Div. I women's golf, women's outdoor track and softball); USC (Div I-A football, Div. I women's volleyball, National Div. men's and women's water polo). **Three**—LSU (Div. I-A football, Div. I men's and women's indoor track); STANFORD (Div. I men's and women's cross country and women's tennis).
Two—ABILENE CHRISTIAN (Div. II men's indoor and outdoor track); ADAMS ST., CO (Div. II men's and women's cross country); AUBURN (Div. I men's and women's swimming & diving); CONNECTICUT (Div. I men's and women's basketball); KENNESAW ST., GA (Div. II women's soccer and men's basketball); KENYON, OH (Div. III men's and women's swimming & diving); LINCOLN, MO (Div. II women's indoor and outdoor track); SALISBURY, MD (Div. III women's field hockey and men's lacrosse); WIS-LA CROSSE (Div. III men's indoor and outdoor track); WIS-OSHKOSH (Div. III women's indoor and outdoor track).
Overall titles in parentheses; (*) indicates defending champions.

FALL

Cross Country
Men

Div.	Winner		Runner-Up	Score
I	Stanford*	(4)	Wisconsin	24-174
II	Adams St., CO	(5)	Abilene Christian	40-68
III	Calvin, MI	(2)	Wis.-Stevens Point	48-128

Women

Div.	Winner		Runner-Up	Score
I	Stanford	(2)	Brigham Young*	120-128
II	Adams St., CO	(9)	Western St., CO*	38-101
III	Middlebury, VT	(3)	Trinity, CT	135-174

Field Hockey

Div.	Winner		Runner-Up	Score
I	Wake Forest*	(2)	Duke	3-1
II	Bloomsburg, PA*	(8)	UMass-Lowell	4-1
III	Salisbury, MD	(2)	Middlebury, VT	4-1

Football

Div.	Winner		Runner-Up	Score
I-A	USC	(9)	LSU	AP Poll
	LSU	(3)	USC	ESPN/USA Today
I-AA	Delaware	(6)	Colgate	40-0
II	Grand Valley St., MI*	(2)	North Dakota	10-3
III	St. John's, MN	(2)	Mt. Union, OH*	24-6

Note: There is no official Div. I-A playoff.

Soccer
Men

Div.	Winner		Runner-Up	Score
I	Indiana	(6)	St. John's, NY	2-1
II	Lynn, FL	(1)	Cal State-Chico	2-1
III	Trinity, TX	(1)	Drew, NJ	2-1

Women

Div.	Winner		Runner-Up	Score
I	North Carolina	(17)	Connecticut	6-0
II	Kennesaw St., GA	(1)	Franklin Pierce, NH	2-0
III	Oneonta St., NY	(1)	Chicago	2-1 (OT)

Volleyball
Women

Div.	Winner		Runner-Up	Score
I	USC*	(3)	Florida	3-1
II	North Alabama	(1)	Concordia-St. Paul, MN	3-0
III	Washington, MO	(8)	New York University	3-0

Water Polo
Men

Div.	Winner		Runner-Up	Score
National	USC	(2)	Stanford*	9-7 (2OT)

WINTER

Basketball
Men

Div.	Winner		Runner-Up	Score
I	Connecticut	(2)	Georgia Tech	82-73
II	Kennesaw St., GA	(1)	Southern Indiana	84-59
III	Wis.-Stevens Point	(1)	Williams, MA*	84-82

Women

Div.	Winner		Runner-Up	Score
I	Connecticut*	(5)	Tennessee	70-61
II	California, PA	(1)	Drury, MO	75-72
III	Wilmington, OH	(1)	Bowdoin, ME	59-53

Bowling
Women

Div.	Winner		Runner-Up	Score
National	Nebraska	(1)	Central Missouri St.	4-2

Note: In 2003-04, women's bowling became an official NCAA sport.

Fencing

Div.	Winner		Runner-Up	Score
Combined	Ohio St.	(1)	Penn St.	194-160

Gymnastics

Div.	Winner		Runner-Up	Margin
Men	Penn St.	(11)	Oklahoma*	by 1.050
Women	UCLA*	(5)	Georgia	by .925

Ice Hockey
Men

Div.	Winner		Runner-Up	Score
I	Denver	(6)	Maine	1-0
III	Middlebury, VT	(6)	St. Norbert, WI	1-0 (OT)

Women

Div.	Winner		Runner-Up	Score
I	Minnesota	(1)	Harvard	6-2
III	Middlebury, VT	(1)	Wis.-Stevens Point	2-1

Rifle

Div.	Winner		Runner-Up	Score
Combined	AK-Fairbanks*	(7)	Nevada	6273-6185

Skiing

Div.	Winner		Runner-Up	Score
Combined	New Mexico	(1)	Utah*	623-581

Swimming & Diving
Men

Div.	Winner		Runner-Up	Score
I	Auburn*	(4)	Stanford	634-377½
II	Cal St.-Bakersfield	(13)	Drury, MO	718½-586
III	Kenyon, OH*	(25)	Emory, GA	678½-446

Women

Div.	Winner		Runner-Up	Score
I	Auburn*	(3)	Georgia	569-431
II	Truman St., MO*	(4)	Drury, MO	641-561
III	Kenyon, OH*	(20)	Emory, GA	507-362

Indoor Track
Men

Div.	Winner		Runner-Up	Score
I	LSU	(2)	Arkansas*	44½-38
II	Abilene Christian*	(11)	St. Augustine's, NC	55-50
III	Wis.-La Crosse*	(11)	(tie) Lincoln, PA & Wis.-Whitewater	70-29

Women

Div.	Winner		Runner-Up	Score
I	LSU*	(11)	Florida	52-51
II	Lincoln, MO	(1)	Adams St., CO	64-50
III	Wis.-Oshkosh	(4)	Wheaton, MA*	56½-28

Wrestling
Men

Div.	Winner		Runner-Up	Score
I	Oklahoma St.*	(32)	Iowa	123½-82
II	Nebraska-Omaha	(6)	North Dakota St.	97½-95
III	Wartburg, IA*	(4)	Augsburg, MN	156½-140½

SPRING
Baseball

Div.	Winner		Runner-Up	Score
I	Cal St.-Fullerton	(4)	Texas	6-4, 3-2
II	Delta St., MS	(1)	Grand Valley St., MI	12-8
III	George Fox, OR	(1)	Eastern Conn St.	6-3

Note: The Division I Championship Series is best-of-three.

Golf
Men

Div.	Winner		Runner-Up	Score
I	California	(1)	UCLA	1134-1140
II	S. Carolina-Aiken	(1)	Cal St.-Chico	1191-1200
III	Gustavus Adolphus	(1)	Redlands, CA	1178-1190

Women

Div.	Winner		Runner-Up	Score
I	UCLA	(2)	Oklahoma St.	1148-1151
II	Rollins, FL*	(2)	(tie) Ferris St., MI & Florida Southern	1196-1264
III	Methodist, NC*	(8)	Mary Hardin-Baylor	1303-1305

Lacrosse
Men

Div.	Winner		Runner-Up	Score
I	Syracuse	(8)	Navy	14-13
II	Le Moyne, NY	(1)	Limestone, SC	11-10 (2OT)
III	Salisbury, MD*	(5)	Nazareth, NY	13-9

Women

Div.	Winner		Runner-Up	Score
I	Virginia	(3)	Princeton*	10-4
II	Adelphi, NY	(1)	West Chester, PA	12-11
III	Middlebury, VT	(5)	New Jersey	13-11 (OT)

Rowing
Women

Div.	Winner		Runner-Up	Score
I	Brown	(4)	Yale	70-58
II	Mercyhurst, PA	(1)	Humboldt St., CA	18-17
III	Ithaca, NY	(1)	Smith, MA	7-10

Softball

Div.	Winner		Runner-Up	Score
I	UCLA*	(10)	California	3-1
II	Angelo St., TX	(1)	Florida Southern	7-3
III	St. Thomas, MN	(1)	Moravian, PA	2-0

Tennis

Note that both Div. II tournaments were team-only.

Men

Div.	Winner		Runner-Up	Score
I	Baylor	(1)	UCLA	4-0
II	West Florida	(1)	Valdosta St., GA	5-2
III	Middlebury, VT	(1)	Williams, MA	4-3

Women

Div.	Winner		Runner-Up	Score
I	Stanford	(13)	UCLA	4-1
II	BYU-Hawaii*	(5)	Lynn, FL	5-1
III	Emory, GA*	(3)	Amherst, MA	5-0

Outdoor Track
Men

Div.	Winner		Runner-Up	Score
I	Arkansas*	(11)	LSU	65½-31
II	Abilene Christian*	(14)	St. Augustine's, NC	75-74
III	Wis.-La Crosse*	(9)	Neb.-Wesleyan	101-39

Women

Div.	Winner		Runner-Up	Score
I	UCLA	(3)	LSU*	69-68
II	Lincoln, MO*	(2)	Adams St., CO	85-81
III	Wis-Oshkosh	(6)	Calvin, MI	57-54.3

Volleyball
Men

Div.	Winner		Runner-Up	Score
National	Brigham Young	(3)	Long Beach St.	3-2

Water Polo
Women

Div.	Winner		Runner-Up	Score
National	USC	(1)	Loyola-Marymount	10-8

All-time Team Champions
Division I - Top Ten

Combined NCAA Division I men's, women's and coed team champions through spring 2004.

	School	Men's	Women's	Coed	Total
1	UCLA	67	27	0	**94**
2	Stanford	57	31	0	**88**
3	USC	72	11	0	**83**
4	Oklahoma St.	45	0	0	**45**
5	Arkansas	40	0	0	**40**
	LSU	16	24	0	**40**
7	Texas	16	20	0	**36**
8	Michigan	30	1	0	**31**
9	North Carolina	8	22	0	**30**
	Penn State	17	4	9	**30**

Note: Totals above do not reflect Division I-A football championships, which are not conducted by the NCAA. Coed championships include rifle, skiing and fencing (since 1990).

Source: NCAA

North Carolina
Shalane Flanagan
Cross Country

Alabama
Jeana Rice
Gymnastics

Harvard
Jesse Jantzen
Wrestling

UNLV
Ryan Moore
Golf

2003-04 Division I Individual Champions
Repeat champions in **bold** type.

FALL

Cross Country

Men (10,000 meters)		**Time**
1	Dathan Ritzenhein, Colorado	29:14.1
2	Ryan Hall, Stanford	29:15.4
3	Gavin Thompson, Eastern Michigan	29:17.4

Women (6,000 meters)		**Time**
1	**Shalane Flanagan**, North Carolina	19:30.4
2	Kim Smith, Providence	19:42.7
3	Sara Bei, Stanford	19:49.1

WINTER

Fencing

Men

Event		Score
Foil	Boaz Ellis, Ohio St.	15-8
Epee	Arpad Horvath, St. John's	15-7
Sabre	**Adam Crompton**, Ohio St.	15-14

Women

Event		Score
Foil	**Alicja Kryczalo**, Notre Dame	15-7
Epee	Anna Garina, Wayne St.	15-10
Sabre	Valerie Providenza, Notre Dame	15-8

Gymnastics

Men

Event		Points
All-Around	Luis Vargas, Penn St.	56.475
Floor Exercise	Graham Ackerman, California	9.687
Pommel Horse	Bob Rogers, Illinois	9.775
Rings	**Kevin Tan**, Penn St.	9.812
Vault	Graham Ackerman, California	9.687
Parallel Bars	Ramon Jackson, Wm. & Mary	9.200
Horizontal Bar	Justin Spring, Illinois	9.775

Women

Event		Points
All-Around	Jeana Rice, Alabama	39.650
Vault	**Ashley Miles**, Alabama	9.9438
Uneven Bars	Elise Ray, Michigan	9.9750
Balance Beam	Ashley Kelly, Arizona St.	9.9500
Floor Exercise	Ashley Miles, Alabama	9.9375

Rifle
Combined
Number in parentheses denotes inner tens.

Smallbore

		Points
1	Matthew Rawlings, AK-Fairbanks	1179
2	Joseph Hein, AK-Fairbanks	1178
3	Jamie Beyerle, AK-Fairbanks	1177

Air Rifle

		Points
1	Morgan Hicks, Murray St.	398
2	Matthew Rawlings, AK-Fairbanks	396
3	Jamie Beyerle, AK-Fairbanks	395

Skiing
Men

Event		Time
Slalom	Paul McDonald, Dartmouth	1:14.09
Giant Slalom	**Ben Thornhill**, Utah	1:52.24
10-k Freestyle	Henning Dybendal, Utah	21:27.9
20-k Classic	Henning Dybendal, Utah	53:11.9

Women

Event		Time
Slalom	Pia Rivelsrud, Denver	1:22.80
Giant Slalom	Jennifer Delich, New Mexico	1:59.18
5-k Freestyle	Sigrid Aas, AK-Fairbanks	11:55.5
15-k Classic	Sigrid Aas, AK-Fairbanks	53:04.7

Wrestling

Wgt	Champion	Runner-Up
125	Jason Powell, Nebraska	K. Ott, Illinois
133	Zach Robertson, Iowa St.	J. Moore, Penn St.
141	Cliff Moore, Iowa	M. Murray, Nebraska
149	Jesse Jantzen, Harvard	Z. Esposito, Okla. St.
157	Matt Gentry, Stanford	J. Percival, Ohio
165	Troy Letters, Lehigh	T. Lewis, Okla. St.
174	Chris Pendleton, Okla. St.	B. Askren, Missouri
184	Greg Jones, W. Virginia	B. Heizer, N. Illinois
197	**Damion Hahn**, Minnesota	R. Fulsaas, Iowa
Hvy	Tommy Rowlands, Ohio St.	P. Cummins, Penn St.

Brendan Hansen
Texas
Swimming

Alistair Cragg
Arkansas
Track & Field/XC

Muna Lee
LSU
Track & Field

Amber Liu
Stanford
Tennis

Swimming & Diving

(*) indicates meet record. (†) indicates world record.
(Races held in a 25-meter pool)

Men

Event (yards)	Time
50 free ....**Fred Bousquet**, Auburn	21.10†
100 free ....Ian Crocker, Texas	46.25†
200 free ...... Jayme Cramer, Stanford	1:45.04
400 free ......Peter Vanderkaay, Michigan	3:40.78
1500 free ......Peter Vanderkaay, Michigan	14:44.53
100 back ......**Peter Marshall**, Stanford	50.32†
200 back ....**Aaron Peirsol**, Texas	1:50.64†
100 breast ....**Brendan Hansen**, Texas	58.19
200 breast ......**Brendan Hansen**, Texas	2:04.73*
100 butterfly ....**Ian Crocker**, Texas	49.07†
200 butterfly ....Rainer Kendrick, Texas	1:54.97*
200 IM ....**George Bovell**, Auburn	1:53.93†
400 IM ....Ryan Lochte, Florida	4:04.52*
200 free relay ....Auburn	1:23.75*
400 free relay ....Auburn	3:08.85*
800 free relay ....Michigan	7:01.42*
200 medley relay ....Auburn	1:34.25†
400 medley relay ....**Texas**	3:25.38*

Diving	Points
1-meter .... Jevon Tarantino, Tennessee	388.65
3-meter .... Joona Puhakka, Arizona St.	647.30
Platform ....**Caesar Garcia**, Auburn	635.05

Women

Event (yards)	Time
50 free ....Kara Lynn Joyce, Georgia	24.24*
100 free ....Kara Lynn Joyce, Georgia	53.15*
200 free ....Margaret Hoelzer, Auburn	1:56.16*
400 free ....Emily Mason, Arizona	4:01.58*
1500 free ....Kalyn Keller, USC	15:49.14*
100 back ....**Natalie Coughlin**, California	57.51*
200 back ....Kirsty Coventry, Auburn	2:03.86*
100 breast ....**Tara Kirk**, Stanford	1:04.79†
200 breast ....**Tara Kirk**, Stanford	2:20.70*
100 butterfly .**Natalie Coughlin**, California	56.88*
200 butterfly ..**Mary DeScenza**, Georgia	2:06.02*
200 IM ....Kaitlin Sandeno, USC	2:08.11*
400 IM ....Kaitlin Sandeno, USC	4:30.44*
200 free relay ....**Georgia**	1:37.27†
400 free relay ....Georgia	3:35.14*
800 free relay ....California	7:50.94*
200 medley relay ....**Auburn**	1:49.02*
400 medley relay ....Georgia	3:56.48*

Diving	Points
1-meter .....Allison Brennan, South Carolina	307.20
3-meter ....Lane Bassham, Alabama	557.75
Platform ....Nicole Pohorenec, Texas	482.20

Indoor Track

(*) indicates meet record

Men

Event	Time
60 meters .....DaBryan Blanton, Oklahoma	6.59
200 meters ....**Leo Bookman**, Kansas	20.42
400 meters ...... Jeremy Wariner, Baylor	45.39*
800 meters ....**Nate Brannen**, Michigan	1:47.61
Mile .... Sean Jefferson, Indiana	4:00.16
3000 meters ...**Alistair Cragg**, Arkansas	7:55.29
5000 meters ...**Alistair Cragg**, Arkansas	13:39.63
60-m hurdles .....Antwon Hicks, Mississippi	7.61
4x400-m relay ....Baylor	3:03.96*
Distance medley relay ....Michigan	9:27.77*

Event	Hgt/Dist
High Jump ....Andra Manson, Texas	7-3¾
Pole Vault .....**Brad Walker**, Washington	18-8¼
Long Jump ....John Moffitt, LSU	26-9¾
Triple Jump ....Lejuan Simon, LSU	55-11¼
Shot Put ....Dan Taylor, Ohio St.	66-3
35-lb Throw ....Dan Taylor, Ohio St.	77-7½
Heptathlon ......Donovan Kilmartin, Texas	6136 pts.*

Women

Event	Time
60 meters ....**Muna Lee**, LSU	7.21
200 meters ....Veronica Campbell, Arkansas	22.43*
400 meters ....Sanya Richards, Texas	50.82*
800 meters ....Nicole Cook, Tennessee	2:03.27
Mile .....Tiffany McWilliams, Mississippi St.	4:32.24
3000 meters ......Kim Smith, Providence	8:49.18*
5000 meters ......Kim Smith, Providence	15:14.18*
60-m hurdles .....Priscilla Lopes, Nebraska	7.96
4x400-m relay ....**Texas**	3:28.69
Distance medley relay ....Tennessee	11:06.07

Event	Hgt/Dist
High Jump .Chaunte Howard, Georgia Tech	6-3½
Pole Vault ....Fanni Juhasz, Georgia	13-11¼
Long Jump ......Hyleas Fountain, Georgia	21-7¼
Triple Jump .....Ineta Radevica, Nebraska	44-10¾
Shot Put .**Laura Gerraughty**, N. Carolina	62-10*
20-lb Throw ....Candice Scott, Florida	75-7½*
Pentathlon ......Hyleas Fountain, Georgia	4412 pts.

SPRING
Golf
Men

		Total
1	Ryan Moore, UNLV ....67-70-64-66—267	
2	Bill Haas, Wake Forest ....70-68-67-68—273	
	Chris Nallen, Arizona.........69-67-67-70—273	

Golf (cont.)
Women

		Total
1	Sarah Huarte, California	73-69-67-69 — 278
2	Karin Sjodin, Oklahoma St.	71-69-68-71 — 279
3	Susie Mathews, UCLA	71-69-68-72 — 280

Tennis
Men

Singles— Benjamin Becker (Baylor) def. Michael Kogan (Tulane), 6-4, 7-6 (10-8).

Doubles— KC Corkery & Sam Warburg (Stanford) def. Bo Hodge & John Isner (Georgia), 6-2, 6-7, 6-4.

Women

Singles— Amber Liu (Stanford) def. Jelena Pandzic (Fresno St.), 6-4, 0-6, 6-3.

Doubles— Daniela Bercek & Lauren Fisher (UCLA) def. Jessica Johnson & Ashley Kroh (Marshall), 6-4, 6-4.

Outdoor Track
(*) indicates meet record
Men

Event		Time
100 meters	Tyson Gay, Arkansas	10.06
200 meters	Wallace Spearmon, Arkansas	20.12
400 meters	Jeremy Wariner, Baylor	44.71
800 meters	Jonathan Johnson, Texas Tech	1:46.39
1500 meters	Chris Mulvaney, Arkansas	3:44.72
5000 meters	Robert Cheseret, Arizona	13:49.85
10,000 meters	Alistair Cragg, Arkansas	29:22.43
110-m hurdles	Josh Walker, Florida	13.32
400-m hurdles	Kerron Clement, Florida	49.05
3000-m steeple	Jordan Desilets, E. Michigan	8:42.64
4x100-m relay	Florida	39.11
4x400-m relay	Baylor	3:01.03

Event		Hgt/Dist
High Jump	Andra Manson, Texas	7-7¼
Pole Vault	Tommy Skipper, Oregon	18-8¼
Long Jump	John Moffitt, LSU	27-6¾
Triple Jump	Leevan Sands, Auburn	56-2
Shot Put	**Carl Myerscough**, Nebraska	67-8¾
Discus	**Hannes Hopley**, SMU	203-5
Javelin	Gabriel Wallin, Boise St.	264-9
Hammer	Thomas Freeman, Manhattan	232-2
Decathlon	Ryan Harlan, Rice	8171 pts.

Women

Event		Time
100 meters	Lauryn Williams, Miami	10.97
200 meters	LaShaunte'a Moore, Arkansas	22.37
400 meters	Dee Dee Trotter, Tennessee	50.32
800 meters	Neisha Bernard-Thomas, LSU	2:02.86
1500 meters	**Tiffany McWilliams**, Miss. St.	4:11.59
5000 meters	Kim Smith, Providence	15:48.86
10,000 meters	**Alicia Craig**, Stanford	33:58.27
100-m hurdles	Nichole Denby, Texas	12.62*
400-m hurdles	**Sheena Johnson**, UCLA	53.54*
3000-m steeple	Ida Nilsson, N. Arizona	9:48.29
4x100-m relay	**LSU**	42.61
4x400-m relay	LSU	3:25.26*

Event		Hgt/Dist
High Jump	Chaunte Howard, Georgia Tech	6-4
Pole Vault	Chelsea Johnson, UCLA	14-1¼
Long Jump	Hyleas Fountain, Georgia	21-8¼
Triple Jump	**Ineta Radevica**, Nebraska	45-6¼
Shot Put	Laura Gerraughty, N. Carolina	59-11
Discus	Becky Breisch, Nebraska	204-5
Javelin	Katy Doyle, Texas A&M	185-7
Hammer	**Candice Scott**, Florida	225-10
Heptathlon	Jacquelyn Johnson, Arizona St.	5807 pts.

Championships
Most Outstanding Players
Men

Baseball	Jason Windsor, Cal St.-Fullerton
Basketball	Emeka Okafor, Connecticut
Cross Country	Dathan Ritzenhein, Colorado*
Golf	Ryan Moore, UNLV*
Gymnastics	Luis Vargas, Penn St.*
Ice Hockey	Adam Berkhoel, Denver
Lacrosse	Michael Powell, Syracuse
Soccer: Offense	Jacob Peterson, Indiana
Soccer: Defense	Jay Nolly, Indiana
Swimming & Diving	Ian Crocker, Texas
	Caesar Garcia, Auburn
Tennis	Benjamin Becker, Baylor*
Track: Indoor	Alistair Cragg, Arkansas* & Dan Taylor, Ohio St.*
Track: Outdoor	Jeremy Wariner, Baylor*
Volleyball	Carlos Moreno, Brigham Young
Water Polo	Bozidar Damjanovic, USC & Tony Azevedo, Stanford
Wrestling	Jesse Jantsen Harvard

Women

Basketball	Diana Taurasi, Connecticut
Bowling	Shannon Pluhowsky, Nebraska
Cross Country	Shalane Flanagan, North Carolina*
Golf	Sarah Huarte, California*
Gymnastics	Jeana Rice, Alabama*
Ice Hockey	Krissy Wendell, Minnesota
Lacrosse	Andrea Pfeiffer, Virginia
Soccer: Offense	Heather O'Reilly, N. Carolina
Soccer: Defense	Catherine Reddick, N. Carolina
Softball	Kristin Schmidt, LSU
Swimming & Diving	Tara Kirk, Stanford
	Lane Bassham, Alabama
Tennis	Amber Liu, Stanford*
Track: Indoor	Kim Smith, Providence & Hyleas Fountain, Georgia*
Track: Outdoor	Hyleas Fountain, Georgia*
Volleyball	Keao Burdine, USC
Water Polo	Brittany Hayes, USC

(*) indicates won individual or all-around NCAA championship; There were no official Outstanding Players in fencing, field hockey, I-AA football, riflery, rowing and skiing. Outstanding players in indoor and outdoor track are the individuals earning the most points in the Championships.

2003-04 NAIA Team Champions
Total NAIA titles in parentheses.

Cross Country: MEN'S–Minot St., ND (2); WOMEN'S–Simon Fraser, BC (6). **Football:** MEN'S–Carroll, MT (2). **Soccer:** MEN'S–Rio Grande, OH (1); WOMEN'S– Westmont, CA (5). **Volleyball:** WOMEN'S–Fresno Pacific, CA (2).

WINTER

Basketball: MEN'S–Division I: Mountain St., WV (1) and Division II: Oregon Tech (1); WOMEN'S–Division I: Southern Nazarene, OK (7) and Division II: Morningside, IA (1). **Swimming & Diving:** MEN'S–Simon Fraser, BC (16); WOMEN'S– Simon Fraser, BC (10). **Indoor Track:** MEN'S–Azusa Pacific, CA (4); WOMEN'S–Azusa Pacific, CA (2). **Wrestling:** MEN'S–Montana St.-Northern (6).

SPRING

Baseball: MEN'S–Cumberland, TN (1). **Golf:** MEN'S–Okla. City (4); WOMEN'S–Brit. Columbia (2). **Softball:** WOMEN'S–Thomas, GA (1). **Tennis:** MEN'S–Auburn-Montgomery (5); WOMEN'S–Auburn-Montgomery (5). **Outdoor Track:** MEN'S–Dickinson St., ND (1); WOMEN'S–Azusa Pacific, CA (2).

Annual NCAA Division I Team Champions

Men's and women's NCAA Division I team champions from cross country to wrestling. Also see team champions for baseball, basketball, bowling, football, golf, ice hockey, soccer and tennis in the appropriate chapters throughout the almanac. See pages 462-464 for list of 2003-04 individual champions.

CROSS COUNTRY

Men

The Stanford harriers made it look easy, placing four runners in the top six en route to their second consecutive Division I cross country title. Ryan Hall paced the Cardinal with a second place finish while teammates Grant Robison, Ian Dobson and Louis Luchini followed closely behind in fourth, fifth and sixth, respectively. Stanford finished with a miniscule point total of 24 to trounce runner-up Wisconsin (174) and third-place Northern Arizona (190). (*Waterloo, IA; Nov. 24, 2003.*)

Multiple winners: Arkansas (11); Michigan St. (8); UTEP (7); Oregon, Stanford and Villanova (4); Drake, Indiana, Penn St. and Wisconsin (3); Iowa St., San Jose St. and Western Michigan (2).

Year		Year		Year		Year		Year	
1938	Indiana	1951	Syracuse	1965	Western Mich.	1979	UTEP	1993	Arkansas
1939	Michigan St.	1952	Michigan St.	1966	Villanova	1980	UTEP	1994	Iowa St.
1940	Indiana	1953	Kansas	1967	Villanova	1981	UTEP	1995	Arkansas
1941	Rhode Island	1954	Oklahoma St.	1968	Villanova	1982	Wisconsin	1996	Stanford
1942	Indiana	1955	Michigan St.	1969	UTEP	1983	Vacated	1997	Stanford
	& Penn St.	1956	Michigan St.	1970	Villanova	1984	Arkansas	1998	Arkansas
1943	Not held	1957	Notre Dame	1971	Oregon	1985	Wisconsin	1999	Arkansas
1944	Drake	1958	Michigan St.	1972	Tennessee	1986	Arkansas	2000	Arkansas
1945	Drake	1959	Michigan St.	1973	Oregon	1987	Arkansas	2001	Colorado
1946	Drake	1960	Houston	1974	Oregon	1988	Wisconsin	2002	Stanford
1947	Penn St.	1961	Oregon St.	1975	UTEP	1989	Iowa St.	2003	Stanford
1948	Michigan St.	1962	San Jose St.	1976	UTEP	1990	Arkansas		
1949	Michigan St.	1963	San Jose St.	1977	Oregon	1991	Arkansas		
1950	Penn St.	1964	Western Mich.	1978	UTEP	1992	Arkansas		

Women

Stanford coach Dena Evans may have said it best, "If you want to win this thing, you have to beat BYU." Her Cardinal squad did just that, edging the two-time defending champions 120-128. Stanford placed four runners in the top 23, led by a third-place finish from junior Sara Bei and a sixth-place finish by Alicia Craig. North Carolina's Shalane Flanagan successfully defended her individual crown, winning with a time of 19:30.4 over the 6,000-meter course (*Waterloo, IA; Nov. 24, 2003.*)

Multiple winners: Villanova (7); BYU (4); Oregon, Stanford, Virginia and Wisconsin (2).

Year		Year		Year		Year		Year	
1981	Virginia	1986	Texas	1991	Villanova	1996	Stanford	2001	BYU
1982	Virginia	1987	Oregon	1992	Villanova	1997	BYU	2002	BYU
1983	Oregon	1988	Kentucky	1993	Villanova	1998	Villanova	2003	Stanford
1984	Wisconsin	1989	Villanova	1994	Villanova	1999	BYU		
1985	Wisconsin	1990	Villanova	1995	Providence	2000	Colorado		

FENCING

Men & Women

Behind individual event victories by sophomore Adam Crompton and freshman Boaz Ellis, the Ohio State Buckeyes grabbed their first NCAA national fencing title. Crompton edged Columbia's Sergey Isayenko, 15-14 to win the Sabre discipline for the second straight year, while Ellis beat Yale's Cory Werk, 15-8 to win the Foil. The Buckeyes (194 pts.) outdistanced runner-up Penn State (160), who has now placed either first or second in every championship since 1990. (*Waltham, MA; Mar. 25-28, 2004.*)

Multiple winners: Penn St. (9); Columbia/Barnard and Notre Dame (2). **Note:** Prior to 1990, men and women held separate championships. Men's multiple winners included: NYU (12); Columbia (11); Wayne St. (7); Navy, Notre Dame and Penn (3); Illinois (2). Women's multiple winners included: Wayne St. (3); Yale (2).

Year		Year		Year		Year	
1990	Penn St.	1994	Notre Dame	1998	Penn St.	2002	Penn St.
1991	Penn St.	1995	Penn St.	1999	Penn St.	2003	Notre Dame
1992	Columbia/Barnard	1996	Penn St.	2000	Penn St.	2004	Ohio St.
1993	Columbia/Barnard	1997	Penn St.	2001	St. John's		

FIELD HOCKEY

Women

Senior Katie Ackerman scored two first-half goals to vault Wake Forest to a hard-fought 3-1 victory over Duke and its second straight title. Goaltender Katie Ridd stopped four shots for Wake Forest with her Duke counterpart Christy Morgan made seven saves. Duke's Gracie Sorbello scored early in the second half to cut the lead to one but Wake Forest freshman Kristi Harshman netted a much-needed insurance goal with just over seven minutes left. (*Amherst, MA; Nov. 23, 2003.*)

Multiple winners: Old Dominion (9); North Carolina (4); Maryland (3); Connecticut and Wake Forest (2).

Year		Year		Year		Year		Year	
1981	Connecticut	1986	Iowa	1991	Old Dominion	1996	North Carolina	2001	Michigan
1982	Old Dominion	1987	Maryland	1992	Old Dominion	1997	North Carolina	2002	Wake Forest
1983	Old Dominion	1988	Old Dominion	1993	Maryland	1998	Old Dominion	2003	Wake Forest
1984	Old Dominion	1989	North Carolina	1994	J. Madison	1999	Maryland		
1985	Connecticut	1990	Old Dominion	1995	North Carolina	2000	Old Dominion		

Annual NCAA Division I Team Champions (Cont.)

GYMNASTICS
Men

Penn State edged two-time defending champion Oklahoma, 223.350-222.300, to win its 11th National Division men's gymnastics team title and first since 2000. Host Illinois placed third with 222.225 points. Bolstered by a strong overall performance on the pommel horse and an exceptional display by Kevin Tan on the rings, the Nittany Lions put themselves in prime position for the championship, needing only an average score in the final event, the vault. (Champaign, IL; Apr. 2-4, 2004.)

Multiple winners: Penn St. (11); Illinois (9); Nebraska (8); Oklahoma (5); California and So. Illinois (4); Iowa St., Michigan, Ohio St. and Stanford (3); Florida St and UCLA (2).

Year	Year	Year	Year	Year
1938 Chicago	1956 Illinois	1969 Iowa	1980 Nebraska	1994 Nebraska
1939 Illinois	1957 Penn St.	& Michigan (T)	1981 Nebraska	1995 Stanford
1940 Illinois	1958 Michigan St.	1970 Michigan	1982 Nebraska	1996 Ohio St.
1941 Illinois	& Illinois	& Michigan (T)	1983 Nebraska	1997 California
1942 Illinois	1959 Penn St.	1971 Iowa St.	1984 UCLA	1998 California
1943-47 Not held	1960 Penn St.	1972 So. Illinois	1985 Ohio St.	1999 Michigan
1948 Penn St.	1961 Penn St.	1973 Iowa St.	1986 Arizona St.	2000 Penn St.
1949 Temple	1962 USC	1974 Iowa St.	1987 UCLA	2001 Ohio St.
1950 Illinois	1963 Michigan	1975 California	1988 Nebraska	2002 Oklahoma
1951 Florida St.	1964 So. Illinois	1976 Penn St.	1989 Illinois	2003 Oklahoma
1952 Florida St.	1965 Penn St.	1977 Indiana St.	1990 Nebraska	2004 Penn St.
1953 Penn St.	1966 So. Illinois	& Oklahoma	1991 Oklahoma	(T) indicates won tram-
1954 Penn St.	1967 So. Illinois	1978 Oklahoma	1992 Stanford	poline competition
1955 Illinois	1968 California	1979 Nebraska	1993 Stanford	(1969-70).

Women

Host UCLA amassed a championships-record 198.125 points to claim its second consecutive women's gymnastics title and fifth overall. Georgia placed second with 197.200 points while Alabama and Stanford tied for third with 197.125. Led by seniors Jeanette Antolin, Jamie Dantzcher, Kristen Maloney and Yvonne Tousek, the incredibly balanced Bruins squad recorded top marks in the floor exercise, balance beam, vault and uneven bars. Alabama's Jeana Rice took the individual all-around title over runners-up Antolin and LSU's April Burkholder. (Los Angeles, CA; Apr. 15-17, 2004.)

Multiple winners: Utah (9); Georgia and UCLA (5); Alabama (4).

Year	Year	Year	Year	Year
1982 Utah	1987 Georgia	1992 Utah	1997 UCLA	2002 Alabama
1983 Utah	1988 Alabama	1993 Georgia	1998 Georgia	2003 UCLA
1984 Utah	1989 Georgia	1994 Utah	1999 Georgia	2004 UCLA
1985 Utah	1990 Utah	1995 Utah	2000 UCLA	
1986 Utah	1991 Alabama	1996 Alabama	2001 UCLA	

LACROSSE
Men

Four-time first team All-American Michael Powell scored the game-winning goal with one minute left in the game to give Syracuse a 14-13 win over Navy in the Division I men's lacrosse championship game. It is the Orange's eighth title overall and third in the last five years. Powell also dished out five assists and was named the game's most outstanding player. Syracuse goalie Jay Pfeifer turned away 15 Navy shots. Brian Nee and Brian Crockett added hat tricks for Syracuse while Jon Birsner led the Midshipmen with two goals and three assists. (Baltimore, MD; May 31, 2004.)

Multiple winners: Syracuse (8); Johns Hopkins (7); Princeton (6); North Carolina (4); Cornell and Virginia (3); Maryland (2).

Year	Year	Year	Year	Year
1971 Cornell	1978 Johns Hopkins	1985 Johns Hopkins	1992 Princeton	1999 Virginia
1972 Virginia	1979 Johns Hopkins	1986 North Carolina	1993 Syracuse	2000 Syracuse
1973 Maryland	1980 Johns Hopkins	1987 Johns Hopkins	1994 Princeton	2001 Princeton
1974 Johns Hopkins	1981 North Carolina	1988 Syracuse	1995 Syracuse	2002 Syracuse
1975 Maryland	1982 North Carolina	1989 Syracuse	1996 Princeton	2003 Virginia
1976 Cornell	1983 Syracuse	1990 Syracuse*	1997 Princeton	2004 Syracuse
1977 Cornell	1984 Johns Hopkins	1991 North Carolina	1998 Princeton	

*Title was later vacated due to action by the NCAA Committee on Infractions.

Women

Virginia jumped out to a 5-1 first half lead and never looked back, dominating two-time defending champion Princeton, 10-4, in the Division I women's lacrosse championship game. It is their third overall title and a measure of revenge for the Cavaliers, who lost the 2003 title game to Princeton in overtime. Amy Appeldt netted four goals and Caitlin Banks added three more to pace Virginia. Standout goaltender Andrea Pfeiffer made 19 saves to garner most outstanding player honors. Elizabeth Pillion scored twice for the Tigers. (Princeton, NJ; May 23, 2004.)

Multiple winners: Maryland (9); Princeton and Virginia (3); Penn St. and Temple (2).

Year	Year	Year	Year	Year
1982 Massachusetts	1987 Penn St.	1992 Maryland	1997 Maryland	2002 Princeton
1983 Delaware	1988 Temple	1993 Virginia	1998 Maryland	2003 Princeton
1984 Temple	1989 Penn St.	1994 Princeton	1999 Virginia	2004 Virginia
1985 New Hampshire	1990 Harvard	1995 Maryland	2000 Maryland	
1986 Maryland	1991 Virginia	1996 Maryland	2001 Maryland	

RIFLE
Men & Women

The mastery continues. Alaska-Fairbanks won both the smallbore and air rifle disciplines to ease to its sixth consecutive NCAA rifle championship and seventh overall. The Nanooks recorded 6273 aggregate points to better runner-up Nevada (6185) and third-place Navy (6182). Matthew Rawlings was the top scorer for Alaska-Fairbanks with 1577 points, followed by Jamie Beyerle (1570), Joseph Hein (1567) and Karl Olsson (1559). (Murray, KY; Mar. 12-13, 2004.)

Multiple winners: West Virginia (13); Alaska-Fairbanks (7); Tennessee Tech (3); Murray St. (2).

Year		Year		Year		Year		Year	
1980	Tenn. Tech	1985	Murray St.	1990	West Virginia	1995	West Virginia	2000	AK-Fairbanks
1981	Tenn. Tech	1986	West Virginia	1991	West Virginia	1996	West Virginia	2001	AK-Fairbanks
1982	Tenn. Tech	1987	Murray St.	1992	West Virginia	1997	West Virginia	2002	AK-Fairbanks
1983	West Virginia	1988	West Virginia	1993	West Virginia	1998	West Virginia	2003	AK-Fairbanks
1984	West Virginia	1989	West Virginia	1994	AK-Fairbanks	1999	AK-Fairbanks	2004	AK-Fairbanks

ROWING
NCAA Championships
Women

After a second place finish in last year's championship, Brown returned to its familiar spot as NCAA Division I rowing champion. The Bears solidified their title with a victory in the Varsity Eights, completing the 2000-meter course in 6:32.9, edging second-place Yale (6:34.6) by just 1.7 seconds. Brown also won the second Varsity Eights event while Virginia raced to victories in the second Varsity Eights Petite final and the Varsity Fours. Brown accumulated a total of 70 points for the overall team title to outpace runner-up Yale (58) and third-place finisher, Michigan (52). (Sacramento, CA; May 28-31, 2004).

Multiple winners: Brown (4); Washington (3).

Year	Overall winner	Varsity Eights	Year	Overall winner	Varsity Eights
1997	Washington	Washington	2001	Washington	Washington
1998	Washington	Washington	2002	Brown	Washington
1999	Brown	Brown	2003	Harvard	Harvard
2000	Brown	Brown	2004	Brown	Brown

Intercollegiate Rowing Association Regatta
VARSITY EIGHTS
Men

For the second straight year Harvard proved itself as the most dominant crew in the nation, cruising to victory in the Varsity Eights in 5:53.18 at the 102nd IRA Championships Regatta. Due to academic and scheduling conflicts, it was just Harvard's fifth appearance at the IRA Championships. Last year's runner-up Washington came in second again in 5:48.03 while California placed third in 5:59.49. (Cooper River, Camden, NJ; June 3-5, 2004.)

The IRA was formed in 1895 by several Northeastern colleges after Harvard and Yale quit the Rowing Association (established in 1871) to stage an annual race of their own. Since then the IRA Regatta has been contested over courses of varying lengths in Poughkeepsie, N.Y., Marietta, Ohio, Syracuse, N.Y. and Camden, N.J.

Distances: 4 miles (1895-97,1899-1916,1925-41); 3 miles (1898,1921-24,1947-49,1952-63,1965-67); 2 miles (1920,1950-51); 2000 meters (1964, since 1968).

Multiple winners: Cornell (24); California (14); Navy (13); Washington (11); Penn (9); Brown and Wisconsin (7); Syracuse (6); Columbia (4); Princeton (3); Harvard and Northeastern (2).

Year		Year		Year		Year		Year	
1895	Columbia	1916	Syracuse	1939	California	1964	California	1985	Princeton
1896	Cornell	1917-19	Not held	1940	Washington	1965	Navy	1986	Brown
1897	Cornell			1941	Washington	1966	Wisconsin	1987	Brown
1898	Penn	1920	Syracuse	1942-46	Not held	1967	Penn	1988	Northeastern
1899	Penn	1921	Navy	1947	Navy	1968	Penn	1989	Penn
		1922	Navy	1948	Washington	1969	Penn		
1900	Penn	1923	Washington	1949	California			1990	Wisconsin
1901	Cornell	1924	Washington			1970	Washington	1991	Northeastern
1902	Cornell	1925	Navy	1950	Washington	1971	Cornell	1992	Dartmouth,
1903	Cornell	1926	Washington	1951	Wisconsin	1972	Penn		Navy & Penn†
1904	Syracuse	1927	Columbia	1952	Navy	1973	Wisconsin	1993	Brown
1905	Cornell	1928	California	1953	Navy	1974	Wisconsin	1994	Brown
1906	Cornell	1929	Columbia	1954	Navy*	1975	Wisconsin	1995	Brown
1907	Cornell			1955	Cornell	1976	California	1996	Princeton
1908	Syracuse	1930	Cornell	1956	Cornell	1977	Cornell	1997	Washington
1909	Cornell	1931	Navy	1957	Cornell	1978	Syracuse	1998	Princeton
		1932	California	1958	Cornell	1979	Brown	1999	California
1910	Cornell	1933	Not held	1959	Wisconsin				
1911	Cornell	1934	California			1980	Navy	2000	California
1912	Cornell	1935	California	1960	California	1981	Cornell	2001	California
1913	Syracuse	1936	Washington	1961	California	1982	Cornell	2002	California
1914	Columbia	1937	Washington	1962	Cornell	1983	Brown	2003	Harvard
1915	Cornell	1938	Navy	1963	Cornell	1984	Navy	2004	Harvard

*In 1954, Navy was disqualified because of an ineligible coxswain; no trophies were given.
†First dead heat in history of IRA Regatta.

Annual NCAA Division I Team Champions (Cont.)

National Rowing Championship
VARSITY EIGHTS
Men

National championship raced annually from 1982-96 in Bantam, Ohio over a 2,000-meter course on Lake Harsha. Winner received the Herschede Cup. Regatta discontinued in 1997.
Multiple winners: Harvard (6); Brown (3); Wisconsin (2).

Year	Champion	Time	Runner-up	Time	Year	Champion	Time	Runner-up	Time
1982	Yale	5:50.8	Cornell	5:54.15	1990	Wisconsin	5:52.5	Harvard	5:56.84
1983	Harvard	5:59.6	Washington	6:00.0	1991	Penn	5:58.21	Northeastern	5:58.48
1984	Washington	5:51.1	Yale	5:55.6	1992	Harvard	5:33.97	Dartmouth	5:34.28
1985	Harvard	5:44.4	Princeton	5:44.87	1993	Brown	5:54.15	Penn	5:56.98
1986	Wisconsin	5:57.8	Brown	5:59.9	1994	Brown	5:24.52	Harvard	5:25.83
1987	Harvard	5:35.17	Brown	5:35.63	1995	Brown	5:23.40	Princeton	5:25.83
1988	Harvard	5:35.98	Northeastern	5:37.07	1996	Princeton	5:57.47	Penn	6:03.28
1989	Harvard	5:36.6	Washington	5:38.93	1997	discontinued			

Women

National championship held over various distances at 10 different venues from 1979-96. Distances— 1000 meters (1979-81); 1500 meters (1982-83); 1000 meters (1984); 1750 meters (1985); 2000 meters (1986-88, 1991-96); 1852 meters (1989-90). Winner received the Ferguson Bowl. Regatta discontinued in 1997.
Multiple winners: Washington (7); Princeton (4); Boston University (2).

Year	Champion	Time	Runner-up	Time	Year	Champion	Time	Runner-up	Time
1979	Yale	3:06	California	3:08.6	1988	Washington	6:41.0	Yale	6:42.37
1980	California	3:05.4	Oregon St.	3:05.8	1989	Cornell	5:34.9	Wisconsin	5:37.5
1981	Washington	3:20.6	Yale	3:22.9	1990	Boston Univ.	7:03.2	Cornell	7:06.21
1982	Washington	4:56.4	Wisconsin	4:59.83	1991	Boston Univ.	6:28.79	Cornell	6:32.79
1983	Washington	4:57.5	Dartmouth	5:03.02	1992	Princeton	6:40.75	Washington	6:43.86
1984	Washington	3:29.48	Radcliffe	3:31.08	1993	Princeton	6:11.38	Yale	6:14.46
1985	Washington	5:28.4	Wisconsin	5:32.0	1994	Princeton	6:11.98	Washington	6:12.69
1986	Wisconsin	6:53.28	Radcliffe	6:53.34	1995	Brown	6:45.7	Princeton	6:49.3
1987	Washington	6:33.8	Yale	6:37.4	1996	discontinued			

The Harvard-Yale Regatta

Harvard made it five in a row and 18 of the last 20 by sweeping Yale at the 139th running of the Harvard/Yale Regatta on June 12, 2004. The win gave the Harvard crew is second consecutive undefeated season. In rough, windy conditions, Harvard's Varsity Eights squad finished the four-mile course on the Thames River in New London, Conn. in 18:42.1, just two-tenths off the upstream course record. Yale's crew came in 24.7 seconds later in 19:06.8. The Harvard/Yale Regatta is the nation's oldest intercollegiate sporting event. Harvard holds an 86-53 series edge.

SKIING
Men & Women

New Mexico won its first NCAA skiing championship and first NCAA team title in any sport, with a stunning 42-point victory over defending champion Utah. The Lobos amassed 623 points to overwhelm Utah (581) and perennial powerhouse Denver (568). Senior Jennifer Delich won the women's Giant Slalom for the Lobos' only individual title. Peter Roering placed second in the men's GS while Trine Lundamo and Geir-Endre Rogn took thirds in the 15-k Classic and 20-k Classic, respectively. The championships' only double-winners came in the Nordic events as Utah's Henning Dybendal won the men's 10-k Freestyle and 20-k Classic, while Sigrid Aas of Alaska-Fairbanks took the women's 5-k freestyle and 15-k Classic. Utah's Ben Thornhill was the only repeat winner, successfully defending his title in the men's Giant Slalom. (*Truckee, CA; March 10-13, 2004*)
Multiple winners: Denver (17); Colorado (15); Utah (10); Vermont (5); Dartmouth and Wyoming (2).

Year		Year		Year		Year		Year	
1954	Denver	1965	Denver	1976	Colorado	1986	Utah	1997	Utah
1955	Denver	1966	Denver		& Dartmouth	1987	Utah	1998	Colorado
1956	Denver	1967	Denver	1977	Colorado	1988	Utah	1999	Colorado
1957	Denver	1968	Wyoming	1978	Colorado	1989	Vermont	2000	Denver
1958	Dartmouth	1969	Denver	1979	Colorado	1990	Vermont	2001	Denver
1959	Colorado	1970	Denver	1980	Vermont	1991	Colorado	2002	Denver
1960	Colorado	1971	Denver	1981	Utah	1992	Vermont	2003	Utah
1961	Denver	1972	Colorado	1982	Colorado	1993	Utah	2004	New Mexico
1962	Denver	1973	Colorado	1983	Utah	1994	Vermont		
1963	Denver	1974	Colorado	1984	Utah	1995	Colorado		
1964	Denver	1975	Colorado	1985	Wyoming	1996	Utah		

SOFTBALL
Women

Pinch-hitter Kristen Dedmon laced a tie-breaking two-run single in the bottom of fifth inning to propel UCLA to its second consecutive NCAA Division I softball championship with a 3-1 victory over California. It's the tenth overall softball title for UCLA. California jumped out to a 1-0, first-inning lead and pitcher Kelly Anderson kept the UCLA bats in check early on. In the fifth, however, first baseman Claire Sua led off with a home run to tie the game. After a hit batter, a walk and a sacrifice gave the Bruins second and third, Dedmon came through with a single to center to give her team a lead it wouldn't relinquish. UCLA hurler Keira Goerl won the championship game for the second straight year, allowing one run on seven hits to follow last year's nine-inning no-hitter against California. (*Oklahoma City, OK; May 27-31, 2004.*)

Multiple winners: UCLA (10); Arizona (6); Texas A&M (2).

Year	Year	Year	Year	Year
1982 UCLA	1987 Texas A&M	1992 UCLA	1997 Arizona	2002 California
1983 Texas A&M	1988 UCLA	1993 Arizona	1998 Fresno St.	2003 UCLA
1984 UCLA	1989 UCLA	1994 Arizona	1999 UCLA	2004 UCLA
1985 UCLA	1990 UCLA	1995 UCLA*	2000 Oklahoma	
1986 CS-Fullerton	1991 Arizona	1996 Arizona	2001 Arizona	

*Title was later vacated due to action by the NCAA Committee on Infractions.

SWIMMING & DIVING
Men

Auburn scored an NCAA Division I men's record 634 points to win its second consecutive championship in dominating fashion. Stanford was runner-up with 377½ points while Texas placed third with 374. The 256½ point margin of victory is the second-largest in men's championship history. Seven world records were broken in the 25-meter pool, three by Auburn.

Fred Bousquet and George Bovell successfully defended their titles with world records in the 50-meter freestyle and 200-meter individual medley, respectively. The Tigers' 200 medley relay foursome of Doug Van Wie, Bousquet, Mark Gangloff and Derek Gibb set a new world mark (1:34.25) in edging Texas' powerhouse relay team. Auburn netted six individual titles overall, while Texas did them one better with seven. Brendan Hansen won the 100- and 200-meter breaststrokes for the fourth consecutive year, Aaron Piersol repeated as champion in the 200-meter backstroke and Ian Crocker won the 100-meter butterfly for the third straight year and added a title in the 100-meter freestyle, setting world marks in each. (*East Meadow, NY; Mar. 25-27, 2004.*)

Multiple winners: Michigan and Ohio St. (11); Texas and USC (9); Stanford (8); Indiana (6); Auburn and Yale (4); California and Florida (2).

Year	Year	Year	Year	Year
1937 Michigan	1951 Yale	1965 USC	1979 California	1993 Stanford
1938 Michigan	1952 Ohio St.	1966 USC	1980 California	1994 Stanford
1939 Michigan	1953 Yale	1967 Stanford	1981 Texas	1995 Michigan
1940 Michigan	1954 Ohio St.	1968 Indiana	1982 UCLA	1996 Texas
1941 Michigan	1955 Ohio St.	1969 Indiana	1983 Florida	1997 Auburn
1942 Yale	1956 Ohio St.	1970 Indiana	1984 Florida	1998 Stanford
1943 Ohio St.	1957 Michigan	1971 Indiana	1985 Stanford	1999 Auburn
1944 Yale	1958 Michigan	1972 Indiana	1986 Stanford	2000 Texas
1945 Ohio St.	1959 Michigan	1973 Indiana	1987 Stanford	2001 Texas
1946 Ohio St.	1960 USC	1974 USC	1988 Texas	2002 Texas
1947 Ohio St.	1961 Michigan	1975 USC	1989 Texas	2003 Auburn
1948 Michigan	1962 Ohio St.	1976 USC	1990 Texas	2004 Auburn
1949 Ohio St.	1963 USC	1977 USC	1991 Texas	
1950 Ohio St.	1964 USC	1978 Tennessee	1992 Stanford	

Women

Individual titles by Kirsty Coventry and Margaret Hoelzer carried the Auburn Tigers to their third consecutive NCAA women's swimming and diving title. After second place finishes in the last three years, Coventry finally broke through with a surprising win over previously unbeaten Natalie Coughlin of California in the 200-meter backstroke. Hoelzer set an NCAA record in the 200-meter freestyle, rocketing to a time of 1:56.16. Auburn also added a third victory by defending its title in the 200-meter medley relay. The Tigers finished with 569 points to crush runner-up Georgia (431) and Arizona (369).

Stanford's Tara Kirk won the 100-meter breaststoke for the fourth straight year and the 200-meter breaststroke for the third straight and was named swimmer of the meet. Her time of 1:04.79 in the 100 set a new world record. Despite her loss to Coventry in the 200 free, Coughlin was hardly shut out, repeating as champion in the 100-meter backstroke and 100-meter butterfly. Georgia set a new world record (1:37.27) in the 200-meter freestyle relay. (*College Station, TX; Mar. 18-20, 2004.*)

Multiple winners: Stanford (8); Texas (7); Auburn and Georgia (3).

Year	Year	Year	Year	Year
1982 Florida	1987 Texas	1992 Stanford	1997 USC	2002 Auburn
1983 Stanford	1988 Texas	1993 Stanford	1998 Stanford	2003 Auburn
1984 Texas	1989 Stanford	1994 Stanford	1999 Georgia	2004 Auburn
1985 Texas	1990 Texas	1995 Stanford	2000 Georgia	
1986 Texas	1991 Texas	1996 Stanford	2001 Georgia	

Annual NCAA Division I Team Champions (Cont.)

INDOOR TRACK

Men

Buoyed by two field event victories, LSU stormed to its second title at the NCAA Division I championships. The Tigers accumulated 44½ points to better Florida and defending champ Arkansas, who tied for second with 38. LeJuan Simon recorded a leap of 55-11¼ in the triple jump to earn the victory and lead an astounding 1-2-3 LSU sweep in the event. John Moffitt, who had LSU's other individual title in the long jump, finished in second while Willie Bradley rounded out the top three. Kansas' Leo Bookman (200-meters), Michigan's Nate Brannen (800-meters) and Washington's Brad Walker (pole vault) were repeat champions while Arkansas' Alistair Cragg won the 3000-meters for the second straight year and 5000-meters for the third straight. (Fayetteville, AR; Mar. 12-13, 2004.)

Multiple winners: Arkansas (17); UTEP (7); Kansas and Villanova (3); LSU and USC (2).

Year	Year	Year	Year	Year
1965 Missouri	1973 Manhattan	1981 UTEP	1989 Arkansas	1997 Arkansas
1966 Kansas	1974 UTEP	1982 UTEP	1990 Arkansas	1998 Arkansas
1967 USC	1975 UTEP	1983 SMU	1991 Arkansas	1999 Arkansas
1968 Villanova	1976 UTEP	1984 UTEP	1992 Arkansas	2000 Arkansas
1969 Kansas	1977 Washington St.	1985 Arkansas	1993 Arkansas	2001 LSU
1970 Kansas	1978 UTEP	1986 Arkansas	1994 Arkansas	2002 Tennessee
1971 Villanova	1979 Villanova	1987 Arkansas	1995 Arkansas	2003 Arkansas
1972 USC	1980 UTEP	1988 Arkansas	1996 George Mason	2004 LSU

Women

A second-place finish in the 4x400-meter relay and Muna Lee's second consecutive 60-meter victory led LSU to its third straight women's track and field championship and 11th overall. The Lady Tigers' performance in the relay, the meet's final event, was enough to give them a one-point victory over runner-up Florida, 52-51. LSU becomes the first school to sweep both the men's and women's titles in Division I indoor track history. Lee's individual title was the fourth of her illustrious indoor championships career. North Carolina's Laura Gerraughty was the meet's other individual repeat winner with her NCAA meet record in the shot put. Providence's Kim Smith swept the distance events with meet records in the 3000- and 5000-meters while Georgia's Hyleas Fountain won the long jump and the pentathlon. (Fayetteville, AR; Mar. 12-13, 2004.)

Multiple winners: LSU (11); Texas (5); Nebraska and UCLA (2).

Year	Year	Year	Year	Year
1983 Nebraska	1988 Texas	1993 LSU	1998 Texas	2003 LSU
1984 Nebraska	1989 LSU	1994 LSU	1999 Texas	2004 LSU
1985 Florida St.	1990 Texas	1995 LSU	2000 UCLA	
1986 Texas	1991 LSU	1996 LSU	2001 UCLA	
1987 LSU	1992 Florida	1997 LSU	2002 LSU	

OUTDOOR TRACK

Men

Arkansas won its second straight title and tenth in the last 13 years at the NCAA Division I track and field championships. They finished with 65½ points to finish well ahead of runner-up LSU (31). Typically distance powerhouses, the Razorbacks were surprisingly led to victory by their sprinters. Freshman Wallace Spearman won the 200-meter event in 20.12 while teammate Tyson Gay took the 100 in 10.06. No Razorback had ever won either event. The Arkansas distance squad couldn't let the sprinters have all the glory, however, as Chris Mulvaney won the 1500 meters with a time of 3:44.72 while Alistair Cragg won the 10-k in 29:22.43. The meet's only repeat champions were Nebraska's Carl Myerscough in the shot put and SMU's Hannes Hopley in the discus. (Austin, TX; June 9-12, 2004.)

Multiple winners: USC (26); Arkansas (11); UCLA (8); UTEP (6); Illinois and Oregon (5); LSU and Stanford (4); Kansas and Tennessee (3); SMU (2).

Year	Year	Year	Year	Year
1921 Illinois	1938 USC	1955 USC	1971 UCLA	1988 UCLA
1922 California	1939 USC	1956 UCLA	1972 UCLA	1989 LSU
1923 Michigan	1940 USC	1957 Villanova	1973 UCLA	
1924 Not held	1941 USC	1958 USC	1974 Tennessee	1990 UCLA
1925 Stanford*	1942 USC	1959 Kansas	1975 UTEP	1991 Tennessee
1926 USC*	1943 USC	1960 Kansas	1976 USC	1992 Arkansas
1927 Illinois*	1944 Illinois	1961 USC	1977 Arizona St.	1993 Arkansas
1928 Stanford	1945 Navy	1962 Oregon	1978 UCLA & UTEP	1994 Arkansas
1929 Ohio St.	1946 Illinois	1963 USC	1979 UTEP	1995 Arkansas
	1947 Illinois	1964 Oregon		1996 Arkansas
1930 USC	1948 Minnesota	1965 Oregon & USC	1980 UTEP	1997 Arkansas
1931 USC	1949 USC	1966 UCLA	1981 UTEP	1998 Arkansas
1932 Indiana		1967 USC	1982 UTEP	1999 Arkansas
1933 LSU	1950 USC	1968 USC	1983 SMU	
1934 Stanford	1951 USC	1969 San Jose St.	1984 Oregon	2000 Stanford
1935 USC	1952 USC	1970 BYU, Kansas	1985 Arkansas	2001 Tennessee
1936 USC	1953 USC	& Oregon	1986 SMU	2002 LSU
1937 USC	1954 USC		1987 UCLA	2003 Arkansas
				2004 Arkansas

(*) indicates unofficial championship.

AP/Wide World Photos

*UCLA senior and Athens olympian **Sheena Johnson** made it back-to-back 400-meter hurdle national titles to lead the Bruins to their first outdoor championship since 1983.*

Women

After eight runner-up finishes in the last 15 years, UCLA finally broke through with it's first women's outdoor track and field championship since 1983. As it normally does, the championship came down to the final event on the final night, the 4x400-meter relay. LSU won the event with a meet-record time of 3:25.26, but UCLA's fourth place finish was enough for an overall one-point victory. The Bruins registed 69 points to squeak by the Lady Tigers (68). Nebraska placed third with 58.

UCLA's Sheena Johnson won the 400-meter hurdles for the second straight year with a time of 53.54, the second fastest mark ever by a collegian. Pole vaulter Chelsea Johnson added the only other UCLA victory, with a leap of 14-1¼. LSU lost a much-needed six points when 200-meter runner-up Stephanie Durst was disqualified for running out of her lane. LSU appealed but to no avail. (*Austin, TX; June 9-12, 2004.*)

Multiple winners: LSU (13); Texas and UCLA (3).

Year	Year	Year	Year	Year
1982 UCLA	1987 LSU	1992 LSU	1997 LSU	2002 South Carolina
1983 UCLA	1988 LSU	1993 LSU	1998 Texas	2003 LSU
1984 Florida St.	1989 LSU	1994 LSU	1999 Texas	2004 UCLA
1985 Oregon	1990 LSU	1995 LSU	2000 LSU	
1986 Texas	1991 LSU	1996 LSU	2001 USC	

VOLLEYBALL

Men

BYU marched to a five-game victory over Long Beach State to win its third National men's volleyball title in the last six years. It was a see-saw affair as the Cougars rallied from behind to record the 15-30, 30-18, 20-30, 32-30, 19-17 victory. The tournament's most outstanding player Carlos Moreno guided BYU with 51 assists, three kills and four block-assists. Joe Hillman led BYU with 14 kills while Jonathan Alleman added 13, including four in the decisive fifth game. Scott Touzinsky led Long Beach with 17 kills and Tyler Hildebrand dished out 65 assists. BYU raised its record to 29-4 while Long Beach closed out its season at 28-7, with four of its losses coming at the hands of BYU. (*Honolulu, HI; May 8, 2004.*)

Multiple winners: UCLA (18); Pepperdine and USC (4); BYU (3).

Year	Year	Year	Year	Year
1970 UCLA	1978 Pepperdine	1986 Pepperdine	1994 Penn St.	2002 Hawaii†
1971 UCLA	1979 UCLA	1987 UCLA	1995 UCLA	2003 Lewis, IL*
1972 UCLA	1980 USC	1988 USC	1996 UCLA	2004 BYU
1973 San Diego St.	1981 UCLA	1989 UCLA	1997 Stanford	*Division II
1974 UCLA	1982 UCLA	1990 USC	1998 UCLA	†Title was later vacat-
1975 UCLA	1983 UCLA	1991 Long Beach St.	1999 BYU	ed due to action by
1976 UCLA	1984 UCLA	1992 Pepperdine	2000 UCLA	the NCAA Committee
1977 USC	1985 Pepperdine	1993 UCLA	2001 BYU	on Infractions.

Annual NCAA Division I Team Champions (Cont.)
Women

USC made it two in a row with a four-game victory over Florida in the NCAA women's volleyball championship match. The Gators grabbed Game 1 before the Women of Troy got down to business, winning three straight games to register the 25-30, 30-27, 30-19, 30-26 victory. For the second consecutive year, USC's Keao Burdine was voted Most Outstanding Player of the tournament, pounding 23 kills and playing stellar defense. Aury Cruz led Florida with 18 kills and 18 digs. USC closed out its season with a perfect 35-0 mark and ran its unbeaten streak to 47 matches. (Dallas, TX; Dec. 20, 2003.)
Multiple winners: Stanford (5); Hawaii, Long Beach St., UCLA and USC (3); Nebraska and Pacific (2).

Year	Year	Year	Year	Year
1981 USC	1986 Pacific	1991 UCLA	1996 Stanford	2001 Stanford
1982 Hawaii	1987 Hawaii	1992 Stanford	1997 Stanford	2002 USC
1983 Hawaii	1988 Texas	1993 Long Beach St.	1998 Long Beach St.	2003 USC
1984 UCLA	1989 Long Beach St.	1994 Stanford	1999 Penn St.	
1985 Pacific	1990 UCLA	1995 Nebraska	2000 Nebraska	

WATER POLO
Men

Top-ranked USC scored a thrilling, 9-7, double-overtime victory over two-time defending champ Stanford to capture its first water polo title since 1998 and second overall. Predrag Damjanov netted three goals for the Trojans, including the insurance goal in overtime. The Cardinal were ahead, 7-6, late in the game until Gadi Hadar tied it up with 1:31 left to send it to overtime. Trevor Clark scored the game-winner for USC. Tony Azevedo led Stanford with four goals. (Stanford, CA; Dec. 7, 2003.)
Multiple winners: California (11); Stanford (10); UCLA (7); UC-Irvine (3); USC (2).

Year	Year	Year	Year	Year
1969 UCLA	1976 Stanford	1983 California	1990 California	1997 Pepperdine
1970 UC-Irvine	1977 California	1984 California	1991 California	1998 USC
1971 UCLA	1978 Stanford	1985 Stanford	1992 California	1999 UCLA
1972 UCLA	1979 UC-S. Barbara	1986 Stanford	1993 Stanford	2000 UCLA
1973 California	1980 Stanford	1987 California	1994 Stanford	2001 Stanford
1974 California	1981 Stanford	1988 California	1995 UCLA	2002 Stanford
1975 California	1982 UC-Irvine	1989 UC-Irvine	1996 UCLA	2003 USC

Women

USC put the icing on the cake, finishing off their perfect 29-0 season with a 10-8 victory over Loyola Marymount in the women's national water polo championship. Most Outstanding Player Brittany Hayes tallied three goals for the Trojans and Kelly Graff backboned the defense with nine saves. Freshman Cara Colton scored four goals for Loyola Marymount to spark a late comeback that ultimately fell short. It was the first title game appearance for both teams. (Stanford, CA; May 9, 2004.)
Multiple winner: UCLA (2).

Year	Year	Year	Year
2001 UCLA	2002 Stanford	2003 UCLA	2004 USC

WRESTLING
Men

Oklahoma State added to its legend, winning its second straight, and 32nd overall, Division I wrestling title. The Cowboys collected 123½ points, well ahead of runner-up Iowa (82) and third place finishers Lehigh and Ohio State (77½). Chris Pendleton delivered the only individial title for Oklahoma State, defeating Ben Askren of Missouri in the 174-pound final. Favorite Tyrone Lewis was runner-up to Lehigh's Troy Letters at 165 pounds, and Zack Esposito lost in the finals of the 149-pound bracket to Harvard's Jesse Jantzen. Jantzen is Harvard's first individual champ since 1938. (St. Louis, MO; Mar. 18-20, 2004.)
Multiple winners: Oklahoma St. (32); Iowa (20); Iowa St. (8); Oklahoma (7); Minnesota (2).

Year	Year	Year	Year	Year
1928 Okla. A&M*	1943-45 Not held	1961 Okla. St.	1977 Iowa St.	1993 Iowa
1929 Okla. A&M	1946 Okla. A&M	1962 Okla. St.	1978 Iowa	1994 Okla. St.
1930 Okla. A&M	1947 Cornell Col.	1963 Oklahoma	1979 Iowa	1995 Iowa
1931 Okla. A&M*	1948 Okla. A&M	1964 Okla. St.	1980 Iowa	1996 Iowa
1932 Indiana*	1949 Okla. A&M	1965 Iowa St.	1981 Iowa	1997 Iowa
1933 Okla. A&M*	1950 Northern Iowa	1966 Okla. St.	1982 Iowa	1998 Iowa
& Iowa St.*	1951 Oklahoma	1967 Michigan St.	1983 Iowa	1999 Iowa
1934 Okla. A&M	1952 Oklahoma	1968 Okla. St.	1984 Iowa	2000 Iowa
1935 Okla. A&M	1953 Penn St.	1969 Iowa St.	1985 Iowa	2001 Minnesota
1936 Oklahoma	1954 Okla. A&M	1970 Iowa St.	1986 Iowa	2002 Minnesota
1937 Okla. A&M	1955 Okla. A&M	1971 Okla. St.	1987 Iowa St.	2003 Okla. St.
1938 Okla. A&M	1956 Okla. A&M	1972 Iowa St.	1988 Arizona St.	2004 Okla. St.
1939 Okla. A&M	1957 Oklahoma	1973 Iowa St.	1989 Okla. St.	
1940 Okla. A&M	1958 Okla. St.	1974 Oklahoma	1990 Okla. St.	
1941 Okla. A&M	1959 Okla. St.	1975 Iowa	1991 Iowa	
1942 Okla. A&M	1960 Oklahoma	1976 Iowa	1992 Iowa	

(*) indicates unofficial champions. **Note:** Oklahoma A&M became Oklahoma St. in 1958.

Halls of Fame & Awards

Tennis great **Steffi Graf** was inducted into the International Tennis Hall of Fame in 2004. Her husband Andre will have to wait a while.

BASEBALL

National Baseball Hall of Fame & Museum

Established in 1935 by Major League Baseball to celebrate the game's 100th anniversary. **Address:** P.O. Box 590, Cooperstown, NY 13326. **Telephone:** (607) 547-7200.

Eligibility: In August 2001, the Hall of Fame announced changes in the way players are elected via the Veterans Committee. The voting done by Baseball Writers' Association of America remains unchanged. Nominated players must have played at least parts of 10 seasons in the major leagues and be retired for at least five. Certain nominated players not elected by the writers can become eligible via the Veterans Committee. The new Veterans Committee will be comprised of all living Hall of Famers (currently 58 people) as well as all living winners of the Ford Frick (13) and J.G. Taylor Spink (12) Awards and three members of the old 15-member Veterans Committee with unexpired terms. There was no Veterans Committee vote in 2002. Beginning in 2003 the new Veterans Committee votes every two years on former players and every four years on managers, umpires and executives. Previously, the committee voted annually.

Also, the eligibility of all players that had been dropped from the ballots for not receiving five percent of the vote was restored and those players can now be immediately considered by the new Veterans Committee. The players on baseball's ineligible list are still excluded from consideration. Pete Rose is the only living ex-player on that list.

Class of 2004 (2): BBWAA vote— **Paul Molitor**, Milwaukee (1978-92), Toronto (1993-95), Minnesota (1996-98); **Dennis Eckersley**, Cleveland (1975-77), Boston (1978-84, 98), Chicago Cubs (1984-86), Oakland (1987-95), St. Louis (1996-97).

2004 Top 10 vote-getters (506 BBWAA ballots cast, 380 needed to elect): 1. **Paul Molitor** (431), 2. **Dennis Eckersley** (421), 3. **Ryne Sandberg** (309), 4. **Bruce Sutter** (301), 5. **Jim Rice** (276), 6. **Andre Dawson** (253), 7. **Rich Gossage** (206), 8. **Lee Smith** (185), 9. **Bert Blyleven** (179), 10. **Jack Morris** (133).

Elected first year on ballot (40): Hank Aaron, Ernie Banks, Johnny Bench, George Brett, Lou Brock, Rod Carew, Steve Carlton, Ty Cobb, Dennis Eckersley, Bob Feller, Bob Gibson, Reggie Jackson, Walter Johnson, Al Kaline, Sandy Koufax, Mickey Mantle, Christy Mathewson, Willie Mays, Willie McCovey, Paul Molitor, Joe Morgan, Eddie Murray, Stan Musial, Jim Palmer, Kirby Puckett, Brooks Robinson, Frank Robinson, Jackie Robinson, Babe Ruth, Nolan Ryan, Mike Schmidt, Tom Seaver, Ozzie Smith, Warren Spahn, Willie Stargell, Honus Wagner, Ted Williams, Dave Winfield, Carl Yastrzemski and Robin Yount.

Members are listed with years of induction; (+) indicates deceased members.

Catchers

Bench, Johnny 1989	+ Cochrane, Mickey 1947	+ Hartnett, Gabby 1955
Berra, Yogi 1972	+ Dickey, Bill 1954	+ Lombardi, Ernie 1986
+ Bresnahan, Roger 1945	+ Ewing, Buck 1939	+ Schalk, Ray 1955
+ Campanella, Roy 1969	+ Ferrell, Rick 1984	
Carter, Gary 2003	Fisk, Carlton 2000	

1st Basemen

+ Anson, Cap 1939	+ Connor, Roger 1976	McCovey, Willie 1986
+ Beckley, Jake 1971	+ Foxx, Jimmie 1951	+ Mize, Johnny 1981
+ Bottomley, Jim 1974	+ Gehrig, Lou 1939	Murray, Eddie 2003
+ Brouthers, Dan 1945	+ Greenberg, Hank 1956	Perez, Tony 2000
Cepeda, Orlando 1999	+ Kelly, George 1973	+ Sisler, George 1939
+ Chance, Frank 1946	Killebrew, Harmon 1984	+ Terry, Bill 1954

2nd Basemen

Carew, Rod 1991	+ Herman, Billy 1975	+ Robinson, Jackie 1962
+ Collins, Eddie 1939	+ Hornsby, Rogers 1942	Schoendienst, Red 1989
Doerr, Bobby 1986	+ Lajoie, Nap 1937	
+ Evers, Johnny 1946	+ Lazzeri, Tony 1991	**Designated Hitters**
+ Fox, Nellie 1997	Mazeroski, Bill 2001	
+ Frisch, Frankie 1947	+ McPhee, Bid 2000	Molitor, Paul 2004
+ Gehringer, Charlie 1949	Morgan, Joe 1990	

Shortstops

Aparicio, Luis 1984	+ Jackson, Travis 1982	+ Tinker, Joe 1946
+ Appling, Luke 1964	+ Jennings, Hugh 1945	+ Vaughan, Arky 1985
+ Bancroft, Dave 1971	+ Maranville, Rabbit 1954	+ Wagner, Honus 1936
Banks, Ernie 1977	+ Reese, Pee Wee 1984	+ Wallace, Bobby 1953
+ Boudreau, Lou 1970	Rizzuto, Phil 1994	+ Ward, Monte 1964
+ Cronin, Joe 1956	+ Sewell, Joe 1977	Yount, Robin 1999
+ Davis, George 1998	Smith, Ozzie 2002	

3rd Basemen

+ Baker, Frank 1955	Kell, George 1983	Robinson, Brooks 1983
Brett, George 1999	+ Lindstrom, Fred 1976	Schmidt, Mike 1995
+ Collins, Jimmy 1945	+ Mathews, Eddie 1978	+ Traynor, Pie 1948

Center Fielders

+ Ashburn, Richie 1995	+ Doby, Larry 1998	+ Roush, Edd 1962
+ Averill, Earl 1975	+ Duffy, Hugh 1945	Snider, Duke 1980
+ Carey, Max 1961	+ Hamilton, Billy 1961	+ Speaker, Tris 1937
+ Cobb, Ty 1936	+ Mantle, Mickey 1974	+ Waner, Lloyd 1967
+ Combs, Earle 1970	Mays, Willie 1979	+ Wilson, Hack 1979
+ DiMaggio, Joe 1955	Puckett, Kirby 2001	

Left Fielders

Brock, Lou	.1985	+ Kelley, Joe	.1971	+ Simmons, Al	.1953
+ Burkett, Jesse	.1946	Kiner, Ralph	.1975	+ Stargell, Willie	.1988
+ Clarke, Fred	.1945	+ Manush, Heinie	.1964	+ Wheat, Zack	.1959
+ Delahanty, Ed	.1945	+ Medwick, Joe	.1968	Williams, Billy	.1987
+ Goslin, Goose	.1968	Musial, Stan	.1969	+ Williams, Ted	.1966
+ Hafey, Chick	.1971	+ O'Rourke, Jim	.1945	Yastrzemski, Carl	.1989

Right Fielders

Aaron, Hank	.1982	Kaline, Al	.1980	+ Ruth, Babe	.1936
+ Clemente, Roberto	.1973	+ Keeler, Willie	.1939	+ Slaughter, Enos	.1985
+ Crawford, Sam	.1957	+ Kelly, King	.1945	+ Thompson, Sam	.1974
+ Cuyler, Kiki	.1968	+ Klein, Chuck	.1980	+ Waner, Paul	.1952
+ Flick, Elmer	.1963	+ McCarthy, Tommy	.1946	Winfield, Dave	.2001
+ Heilmann, Harry	.1952	+ Ott, Mel	.1951	+ Youngs, Ross	.1972
+ Hooper, Harry	.1971	+ Rice, Sam	.1963	
Jackson, Reggie	.1993	Robinson, Frank	.1982	

Pitchers

+ Alexander, Grover	.1938	+ Dean, Dizzy	.1953	Gibson, Bob	.1981
+ Bender, Chief	.1953	+ Drysdale, Don	.1984	+ Gomez, Lefty	.1972
+ Brown, Mordecai	.1949	Eckersley, Dennis	.2004	+ Grimes, Burleigh	.1964
Bunning, Jim	.1996	+ Faber, Red	.1964	+ Grove, Lefty	.1947
Carlton, Steve	.1994	Feller, Bob	.1962	+ Haines, Jess	.1970
+ Chesbro, Jack	.1946	Fingers, Rollie	.1992	+ Hoyt, Waite	.1969
+ Clarkson, John	.1963	Ford, Whitey	.1974	
+ Coveleski, Stan	.1969	+ Galvin, Jim	.1965	

Major League Baseball's All-Time Team—Then and Now

The Baseball Writers' Association of America originally selected an all-time team as part of major league baseball's 100th anniversary, announcing the outcome of its vote on July 21, 1969. Vote totals were not released. Recently, another vote was released when a panel of 36 BWAA members picked an all-time team for the Classic Sports Network just before the 1997 All-Star Game. This time vote totals were given, the single outfield category was divided into three (left, center and right) and two recently popularized positions—the designated hitter and relief pitcher—were added. In the most recent vote two points were awarded for first-place votes and one point for second place. Point totals follow the names with the number of first-place votes in parentheses. All-time team members are listed in **bold** type.

1969 Vote

C	**Mickey Cochrane**, Bill Dickey, Roy Campanella	RHP	**Walter Johnson**, Christy Mathewson, Cy Young
1B	**Lou Gehrig**, George Sisler, Stan Musial	LHP	**Lefty Grove**, Sandy Koufax, Carl Hubbell
2B	**Rogers Hornsby**, Charlie Gehringer, Eddie Collins	Mgr.	**John McGraw**, Casey Stengel, Joe McCarthy
SS	**Honus Wagner**, Joe Cronin, Ernie Banks		
3B	**Pie Traynor**, Brooks Robinson, Jackie Robinson	1969 Vote All-Time Outstanding Player: **Ruth**, Cobb,
OF	**Babe Ruth, Ty Cobb, Joe DiMaggio**, Ted Williams, Tris Speaker, Willie Mays		Wagner, DiMaggio

1997 Vote

C **Johnny Bench** (24) 52; Yogi Berra (4) 22; Roy Campanella (4) 17; Mickey Cochrane (1) 5; Bill Dickey (1) 4; Gabby Hartnett (1) 3; Carlton Fisk 2.

1B **Lou Gehrig** (31) 661/2; Jimmie Foxx (3) 19; George Sisler (2) 8; Willie McCovey 6; Hank Greenberg 21/2; Stan Musial, Eddie Murray, Mark McGwire and Frank Thomas 1.

2B **Rogers Hornsby** (17) 44; Joe Morgan (6) 23; Jackie Robinson (6) 15; Charley Gehringer (4) and Napoleon Lajoie (3) 11; Eddie Collins (1) 3; Rod Carew 2; Ryne Sandberg 1.

SS **Honus Wagner** (23) 55; Cal Ripken Jr. (6) 24; Ozzie Smith (5) 16; Ernie Banks (1) 8; Lou Boudreau and Luke Appling 1.

3B **Mike Schmidt** (21) 50; Brooks Robinson (13) 37; Eddie Mathews 5; George Brett (1) 8; Pie Traynor 3; Pete Rose (1) 2; Frank Baker, Al Rosen and Wade Boggs 1.

LF **Ted Williams** (32) 68; Stan Musial (4) 36; Pete Rose, Ralph Kiner, Rickey Henderson and Barry Bonds 1.

CF **Willie Mays** (25) 57; Ty Cobb (7) 22; Joe DiMaggio (3) 17; Mickey Mantle (1) 10; Tris Speaker 2.

RF **Babe Ruth** (31) 67; Hank Aaron (5) 36; Frank Robinson 2; Al Kaline, Roberto Clemente and Tony Gwynn 1.

DH **Paul Molitor** (22) 48; Harold Baines (3) 12; Don Baylor (1) 10; Edgar Martinez (2) 9; Ty Cobb (2) 6; Hal McRae (1) 5; Mickey Mantle (1) and Dave Parker (1) 3; Joe DiMaggio (1) 2; Lee May, Frank Robinson and Tony Oliva 1.

RHP **Walter Johnson** (9) 30; Cy Young (12) 25; Christy Mathewson (5) 18; Bob Feller (4) 10; Bob Gibson (2) 9; Nolan Ryan (2) 7; Tom Seaver (1) 3; Greg Maddux (1), Grover Cleveland Alexander and Juan Marichal 2.

LHP **Sandy Koufax** (11) 32; Warren Spahn (11) 28; Lefty Grove (8) 25; Steve Carlton (4) 12; Carl Hubbell 6; Whitey Ford (1) 3; Eddie Plank (1) 2.

RP **Dennis Eckersley** (16) 40; Rollie Fingers (9) 29; Lee Smith (4) 13; Hoyt Wilhelm (3) 10; Rich Gossage (3) 9; Bruce Sutter (1) 6, Dan Quisenberry 1.

Mgr. **Casey Stengel** (6) 22; Joe McCarthy (6) 18; Connie Mack (7) 17; John McGraw (6) 14; Sparky Anderson (3) 11; Leo Durocher (2) 6; Dick Williams (1) 4; Billy Martin (1) 3; Al Lopez (1), Ned Hanlon (1), Whitey Herzog (1), Earl Weaver and Bobby Cox 2; Tony La Russa 1.

Baseball (Cont.)

+ Hubbell, Carl 1947	Niekro, Phil 1997	Seaver, Tom 1992
+ Hunter, Catfish 1987	+ Newhouser, Hal 1992	+ Spahn, Warren 1973
Jenkins, Ferguson 1991	+ Nichols, Kid 1949	Sutton, Don 1998
+ Johnson, Walter 1936	Palmer, Jim 1990	+ Vance, Dazzy 1955
+ Joss, Addie 1978	+ Pennock, Herb 1948	+ Waddell, Rube 1946
+ Keefe, Tim 1964	Perry, Gaylord 1991	+ Walsh, Ed 1946
Koufax, Sandy 1972	+ Plank, Eddie 1946	+ Welch, Mickey 1973
+ Lemon, Bob 1976	+ Radbourne, Old Hoss ...1939	+ Wilhelm, Hoyt 1985
+ Lyons, Ted 1955	+ Rixey, Eppa 1963	+ Willis, Vic 1995
Marichal, Juan 1983	Roberts, Robin 1976	+ Wynn, Early 1972
+ Marquard, Rube 1971	+ Ruffing, Red 1967	+ Young, Cy 1937
+ Mathewson, Christy 1936	+ Rusie, Amos 1977	
+ McGinnity, Joe 1946	Ryan, Nolan 1999	

Managers

+ Alston, Walter 1983	Lasorda, Tommy 1997	+ Robinson, Wilbert 1945
Anderson, Sparky 2000	Lopez, Al 1977	+ Selee, Frank 1999
+ Durocher, Leo 1994	+ Mack, Connie 1937	+ Stengel, Casey 1966
+ Hanlon, Ned 1996	+ McCarthy, Joe 1957	Weaver, Earl 1996
+ Harris, Bucky 1975	+ McGraw, John 1937	
+ Huggins, Miller 1964	+ McKechnie, Bill 1962	

Umpires

+ Barlick, Al 1989	+ Connolly, Tom 1953	+ Klem, Bill 1953
+ Chylak, Nestor 1999	+ Evans, Billy 1973	+ McGowan, Bill 1992
+ Conlan, Jocko 1974	+ Hubbard, Cal 1976	

From Negro Leagues

+ Bell, Cool Papa (OF) ...1974	+ Foster, Willie (P) 1996	+ Paige, Satchel (P) 1971
+ Charleston, Oscar (1B-OF) .1976	+ Gibson, Josh (C) 1972	+ Rogan, Wilber (P) 1998
+ Dandridge, Ray (3B) ...1987	Irvin, Monte (OF) 1973	+ Smith, Hilton 2001
+ Day, Leon (P-OF-2B) 1995	+ Johnson, Judy (3B) 1975	+ Stearnes, Turkey (OF) ...2000
+ Dihigo, Martin (P-OF) ...1977	+ Leonard, Buck (1B) 1972	+ Wells, Willie (SS) 1997
+ Foster, Rube (P-Mgr) 1981	+ Lloyd, Pop (SS) 1977	+ Williams, Joe (P) 1999

Pioneers and Executives

+ Barrow, Ed 1953	+ Giles, Warren 1979	+ Rickey, Branch 1967
+ Bulkeley, Morgan 1937	+ Griffith, Clark 1946	+ Spalding, Al 1939
+ Cartwright, Alexander ...1938	+ Harridge, Will 1972	+ Veeck, Bill 1991
+ Chadwick, Henry 1938	+ Hulbert, William 1995	+ Weiss, George 1971
+ Chandler, Happy 1982	+ Johnson, Ban 1937	+ Wright, George 1937
+ Comiskey, Charles 1939	+ Landis, Kenesaw 1944	+ Wright, Harry 1953
+ Cummings, Candy 1939	+ MacPhail, Larry 1978	+ Yawkey, Tom 1980
+ Frick, Ford 1970	MacPhail, Lee 1998	

Ford Frick Award

First presented in 1978 by the Hall of Fame for meritorious contributions by baseball broadcasters. Named in honor of the late newspaper reporter, broadcaster, National League president and commissioner, the Frick Award does not constitute induction into the Hall of Fame.

Year		Year		Year	
1978	Mel Allen & Red Barber	1987	Jack Buck	1996	Herb Carneal
1979	Bob Elson	1988	Lindsey Nelson	1997	Jimmy Dudley
1980	Russ Hodges	1989	Harry Caray	1998	Jaime Jarrin
1981	Ernie Harwell	1990	Byrum Saam	1999	Arch McDonald
1982	Vin Scully	1991	Joe Garagiola	2000	Marty Brennaman
1983	Jack Brickhouse	1992	Milo Hamilton	2001	Felo Ramirez
1984	Curt Gowdy	1993	Chuck Thompson	2002	Harry Kalas
1985	Buck Canel	1994	Bob Murphy	2003	Bob Uecker
1986	Bob Prince	1995	Bob Wolff	2004	Lon Simmons

J.G. Taylor Spink Award

First presented in 1962 by the Baseball Writers' Association of America for meritorious contributions by members of the BBWAA. Named in honor of the late publisher of *The Sporting News*, the Spink Award does not constitute induction into the Hall of Fame. Winners are honored in the year following their selection.

Year		Year		Year	
1962	J.G. Taylor Spink	1972	Dan Daniel, Fred Lieb	1978	Tim Murnane & Dick Young
1963	Ring Lardner		& J. Roy Stockton	1979	Bob Broeg & Tommy Holmes
1964	Hugh Fullerton	1973	Warren Brown, John	1980	Joe Reichler & Milt Richman
1965	Charley Dryden		Drebinger & John F. Kieran	1981	Bob Addie & Allen Lewis
1966	Grantland Rice	1974	John Carmichael	1982	Si Burick
1967	Damon Runyon		& James Isaminger	1983	Ken Smith
1968	H.G. Salsinger	1975	Tom Meany & Shirley Povich	1984	Joe McGuff
1969	Sid Mercer	1976	Harold Kaese & Red Smith	1985	Earl Lawson
1970	Heywood C. Broun	1977	Gordon Cobbledick	1986	Jack Lang
1971	Frank Graham		& Edgar Munzel	1987	Jim Murray

Year		Year		Year	
1988	Bob Hunter & Ray Kelly	1993	John Wendell Smith	1999	Hal Lebovitz
1989	Jerome Holtzman	1994	No award	2000	Ross Newhan
1990	Phil Collier	1995	Joseph Durso	2001	Joe Falls
1991	Ritter Collett	1996	Charley Feeney	2002	Hal McCoy
1992	Leonard Koppett & Buzz Saidt	1997	Sam Lacy	2003	Murray Chass
		1998	Bob Stevens		

BASKETBALL

Naismith Memorial Basketball Hall of Fame

Established in 1949 by the National Association of Basketball Coaches in memory of the sport's inventor, Dr. James Naismith. Original Hall opened in 1968 and a renovated version of the Hall opened in 1985. A completely new building opened Sept. 28, 2002. **Address:** 1000 West Columbus Avenue, Springfield, MA 01105. **Telephone:** (413) 781-6500.

Eligibility: Nominated players and referees must be retired for five years, coaches must have coached 25 years or be retired for five, and contributors must have already completed their noteworthy service to the game. Voting done by 24-member honors committee made up of media representatives, Hall of Fame members and trustees. Any nominee not elected after five years becomes eligible for consideration by the Veterans' Committee after a five-year wait.

Class of 2004 (6): PLAYERS—forward **Clyde Drexler**, Portland (1983-95), Houston (1995-98); forward **Lynette Woodard**, Kansas University (1978-81); CONTRIBUTOR—**Jerry Colangelo**; COACH—**Bill Sharman**. INTERNATION-AL—**Drazen Dalipagic**; VETERAN—**Maurice Stokes**.

2004 finalists (nominated but not elected): PLAYERS—Bobby Jones, Gus Johnson, Bernard King and Chet Walker. COACHES—Jim Calhoun, Gene Keady and Harley Redin. CONTRIBUTOR—Dick Vitale. VETERAN—John Kerr. INTERNA-TIONAL—Hortencia Marcari.

Note: John Wooden, Lenny Wilkens and **Bill Sharman** who was rehonored by the Hall in 2004, are the only members to be inducted as both a player and a coach.

Members are listed with years of induction; (+) indicates deceased members.

Men

	Abdul-Jabbar, Kareem	1995		Greer, Hal	1981		Monroe, Earl	1990
	Archibald, Nate	1991	+	Gruenig, Robert	1963		Murphy, Calvin	1993
	Arizin, Paul	1977	+	Hagan, Cliff	1977	+	Murphy, Charles (Stretch)	1960
+	Barlow, Thomas (Babe)	1980	+	Hanson, Victor	1960		Page, Harlan (Pat)	1962
	Barry, Rick	1987		Havlicek, John	1983		Parish, Robert	2003
	Baylor, Elgin	1976		Hawkins, Connie	1992	+	Petrovic, Drazen	2002
+	Beckman, John	1972		Hayes, Elvin	1990		Pettit, Bob	1970
	Bellamy, Walt	1993		Haynes, Marques	1998	+	Phillip, Andy	1961
	Belov, Sergei	1992		Heinsohn, Tom	1986		Pollard, Jim	1977
	Bing, Dave	1990	+	Holman, Nat	1964		Ramsey, Frank	1981
	Bird, Larry	1998		Houbregs, Bob	1987		Reed, Willis	1981
+	Borgmann, Bennie	1961		Howell, Bailey	1997		Risen, Arnie	1998
	Bradley, Bill	1982	+	Hyatt, Chuck	1959		Robertson, Oscar	1979
+	Brennan, Joe	1974		Issel, Dan	1993		Roosma, John	1961
	Cervi, Al	1984	+	Jeannette, Buddy	1994		Russell, Bill	1974
+	Chamberlain, Wilt	1978	+	Johnson, Bill (Skinny)	1976	+	Russell, John (Honey)	1964
+	Cooper, Charles (Tarzan)	1976		Johnson, Earvin (Magic)	2002	+	Schayes, Dolph	1972
+	Cosic, Kresimir	1996	+	Johnston, Neil	1990	+	Schmidt, Ernest J	1973
	Cousy, Bob	1970		Jones, K. C	1989	+	Schommer, John	1959
	Cowens, Dave	1991		Jones, Sam	1983	+	Sedran, Barney	1962
	Cunningham, Billy	1986	+	Krause, Edward (Moose)	1975		Sharman, Bill	1975
+	Davies, Bob	1969		Kurland, Bob	1961	+	Steinmetz, Christian	1961
+	DeBernardi, Forrest	1961		Lanier, Bob	1992		Thomas, Isiah	2000
+	DeBusschere, Dave	1982	+	Lapchick, Joe	1966		Thompson, David	1996
+	Dehnert, Dutch	1968		Lovellette, Clyde	1988	+	Thompson, John (Cat)	1962
	Drexler, Clyde	2004		Lucas, Jerry	1979		Thurmond, Nate	1984
+	Endacott, Paul	1971		Luisetti, Hank	1959		Twyman, Jack	1982
	English, Alex	1997		Macauley, Ed	1960		Unseld, Wes	1988
	Erving, Julius (Dr. J)	1993		Malone, Moses	2001	+	Vandivier, Robert (Fuzzy)	1974
+	Foster, Bud	1964	+	Maravich, Pete	1987	+	Wachter, Ed	1961
	Frazier, Walt	1987		Martin, Slater	1981		Walton, Bill	1993
+	Friedman, Marty	1971		McAdoo, Bob	2000		Wanzer, Bobby	1987
+	Fulks, Joe	1977	+	McCracken, Branch	1960		West, Jerry	1979
+	Gale, Laddie	1976	+	McCracken, Jack	1962		Wilkens, Lenny	1989
+	Gallatin, Harry	1991	+	McDermott, Bobby	1988		Wooden, John	1960
+	Gates, William (Pop)	1989		McGuire, Dick	1993		Worthy, James	2003
	Gervin, George	1996		McHale, Kevin	1999	+	Yardley, George	1996
	Gola, Tom	1975		Mikan, George	1959			
	Goodrich, Gail	1996		Mikkelsen, Vern	1995			

Women

Blazejowski, Carol	1994	Harris-Stewart, Lucia	1992	Semenova, Uljana	1993
Crawford, Joan	1997	Lieberman, Nancy	1996	White, Nera	1992
Curry, Denise	1997	Meyers, Ann	1993	Woodard, Lynette	2004
Donovan, Anne	1995	Miller, Cheryl	1995		

Basketball (Cont.)

Teams

Buffalo Germans 1961
First Team 1959

Harlem Globetrotters 2002
New York Renaissance 1963

Original Celtics 1959

Referees

+ Enright, Jim 1978
+ Hepbron, George 1960
+ Hoyt, George 1961
+ Kennedy, Pat 1959

+ Leith, Lloyd 1982
+ Mihalik, Red 1986
+ Nucatola, John 1977
+ Quigley, Ernest (Quig) . . .1961

+ Shirley, J. Dallas 1979
+ Strom, Earl 1995
+ Tobey, Dave 1961
+ Walsh, David 1961

Coaches

+ Allen, Forrest (Phog) 1959
+ Anderson, Harold (Andy) . .1984
  Auerbach, Red 1968
  Barmore, Leon 2003
+ Barry, Sam 1978
+ Blood, Ernest (Prof) 1960
  Brown, Larry 2002
+ Cann, Howard 1967
+ Carlson, Henry (Doc) 1959
  Carnesecca, Lou 1992
  Carnevale, Ben 1969
  Carril, Pete 1997
+ Case, Everett 1981
  Chaney, John 2001
  Conradt, Jody 1998
  Crum, Denny 1994
  Daly, Chuck 1994
+ Dean, Everett 1966
+ Diaz-Miguel, Antonio 1997
+ Diddle, Ed 1971
+ Drake, Bruce 1972
  Gaines, Clarence (Bighouse) .1981
+ Gardner, Jack 1983
+ Gill, Amory (Slats) 1967

  Gomelsky, Aleksandr 1995
+ Hannum, Alex 1998
  Harshman, Marv 1984
  Haskins, Don 1997
+ Hickey, Eddie 1978
+ Hobson, Howard (Hobby) . .1965
+ Holzman, Red 1986
+ Iba, Hank 1968
+ Julian, Alvin (Doggie) 1967
+ Keaney, Frank 1960
+ Keogan, George 1961
  Knight, Bob 1991
  Krzyzewski, Mike 2001
  Kundla, John 1995
+ Lambert, Ward (Piggy) 1960
+ Litwack, Harry 1975
+ Loeffler, Ken 1964
+ Lonborg, Dutch 1972
+ McCutchan, Arad 1980
+ McGuire, Al 1992
+ McGuire, Frank 1976
+ McLendon, John 1978
+ Meanwell, Walter (Doc) . . .1959

  Meyer, Ray 1978
+ Miller, Ralph 1988
  Moore, Billie 1999
  Newell, Pete 1978
+ Nikolic, Aleksandar 1998
  Olson, Lute 2002
  Ramsay, Jack 1992
  Rubini, Cesare 1994
+ Rupp, Adolph 1968
+ Sachs, Leonard 1961
  Sharman, Bill 2004
+ Shelton, Everett 1979
  Smith, Dean 1982
  Summitt, Pat 2000
+ Taylor, Fred 1986
  Thompson, John 1999
+ Wade, Margaret 1984
  Watts, Stan 1985
  Wilkens, Lenny 1998
  Wooden, John 1972
+ Woolpert, Phil 1992
  Wootten, Morgan 2000
  Yow, Kay 2002

Contributors

+ Abbott, Senda Berenson . . .1984
+ Bee, Clair 1967
+ Biasone, Danny 2000
+ Brown, Walter A 1965
+ Bunn, John 1964
  Colangelo, Jerry 2004
+ Douglas, Bob 1971
+ Duer, Al 1981
  Embry, Wayne 1999
+ Fagan, Clifford B 1983
+ Fisher, Harry 1973
+ Fleisher, Larry 1991
+ Gottlieb, Eddie 1971
+ Gulick, Luther 1959
+ Harrison, Les 1979
+ Hearn, Francis (Chick) 2003
+ Hepp, Ferenc 1980

+ Hickox, Ed 1959
+ Hinkle, Tony 1965
+ Irish, Ned 1964
+ Jones, R. William 1964
+ Kennedy, Walter 1980
  Lemon, Meadowlark 2003
+ Liston, Emil (Liz) 1974
+ Mokray, Bill 1965
+ Morgan, Ralph 1959
+ Morgenweck, Frank (Pop) . .1962
+ Naismith, James 1959
  Newton, Charles M. 2000
+ O'Brien, John J. (Jack) 1961
+ O'Brien, Larry 1991
+ Olsen, Harold G 1959
+ Podoloff, Maurice 1973

+ Porter, Henry (H.V.) 1960
+ Reid, William A 1963
+ Ripley, Elmer 1972
+ St. John, Lynn W 1962
+ Saperstein, Abe 1970
+ Schabinger, Arthur 1961
+ Stagg, Amos Alonzo 1959
  Stankovic, Boris 1991
+ Steitz, Ed 1983
+ Taylor, Chuck 1968
+ Teague, Bertha 1984
+ Tower, Oswald 1959
+ Trester, Arthur (A.L.) 1961
+ Wells, Cliff 1971
+ Wilke, Lou 1982
+ Zollner, Fred 1999

Curt Gowdy Award

First presented in 1990 by the Hall of Fame Board of Trustees for meritorious contributions by the media. Named in honor of the former NBC sportscaster, the Gowdy Award does not constitute induction into the Hall of Fame.

Year		Year		Year	
1990	Curt Gowdy & Dick Herbert	1997	Marv Albert & Bob Ryan	2003	Sid Hartman
1991	Dave Dorr & Marty Glickman	1998	Dick Vitale, Larry Donald		& Hot Rod Hundley
1992	Sam Goldaper & Chick Hearn		& Dick Weiss	2004	Phil Jasner & Max Falkenstien
1993	Leonard Lewin & Johnny Most	1999	Smith Barrier & Bob Costas		
1994	Leonard Koppett	2000	Dave Kindred & Hubie Brown		
	& Cawood Ledford	2001	Dick Stockton		
1995	Dick Enberg & Bob Hammel		& Curry Kirkpatrick		
1996	Billy Packer & Bob Hentzen	2002	Jim Nantz & Jim O'Connell		

BOWLING

International Bowling Hall of Fame & Museum

The National Bowling Hall is one museum with separate wings for honorees of the American Bowling Congress (ABC), Professional Bowlers' Association (PBA) and Women's International Bowling Congress (WIBC). The museum does not include the Pro Women Bowlers Hall of Fame, which is located in Las Vegas. **Address:** 111 Stadium Plaza, St. Louis, MO 63102. **Telephone:** (314) 231-6340.

Professional Bowlers Association

Established in 1975. **Eligibility:** The criteria was revamped in 2002. Nominees must now be retired from full-time competition on the PBA Tour for a minimum of at least five years, or reached the age of 50, and must have won a minimum of 10 PBA Tour titles or two major titles.

Class of 2004 (2): MERITORIOUS SERVICE—**Matt Fiorito** and **Mort Luby Jr.**.
Members are listed with years of induction; (+) indicates deceased members.

Performance

+ Allen, Bill 1983	+ Fazio, Buzz 1976	Roth, Mark 1987
+ Anthony, Earl 1986	Ferraro, Dave 1997	Salvino, Carmen 1975
Aulby, Mike 1996	+ Godman, Jim 1987	Semiz, Teata 1998
Berardi, Joe 1990	Hardwick, Billy 1977	Smith, Harry 1975
Bluth, Ray 1975	Holman, Marshall 1990	Soutar, Dave 1979
Bohn, Parker III 2000	Hudson, Tommy 1989	Stefanich, Jim 1980
Buckley, Roy 1992	Husted, Dave 1996	Voss, Brian 1994
Burton, Nelson Jr 1979	Johnson, Don 1977	Webb, Wayne 1993
Carter, Don 1975	Laub, Larry 1985	Weber, Dick 1975
Colwell, Paul 1991	Monacelli, Amleto 1997	Weber, Pete 1998
Cook, Steve 1993	Ozio, David 1995	+ Welu, Billy 1975
Davis, Dave 1978	Pappas, George 1986	Williams, Mark 1999
Dickinson, Gary 1988	Petraglia, John 1982	Williams, Walter Ray Jr. . . .1995
Durbin, Mike 1984	Ritger, Dick 1978	Zahn, Wayne 1981

Veterans

Allison, Glenn 1984	+ Joseph, Joe 1985	Schlegel, Ernie 1997
Asher, Barry 1988	Limongello, Mike 1994	+ St. John, Jim 1989
Baker, Tom 1999	Marzich, Andy 1990	Strampe, Bob 1987
Foremsky, Skee 1992	McCune, Don 1991	
Guenther, Johnny 1986	McGrath, Mike 1988	

Meritorious Service

+ Antenora, Joe 1993	+ Fitzgerald, Jim 2000	Nakano, Keijiro 1999
Archibald, John 1989	+ Frantz, Lou 1978	Pezzano, Chuck 1975
Clemens, Chuck 1994	Golden, Harry 1983	Reichert, Jack 1992
+ Elias, Eddie 1976	Hoffman, Ted Jr 1985	+ Richards, Joe 1976
Esposito, Frank 1975	Jowdy, John 1988	Schenkel, Chris 1976
Evans, Dick 1986	Kelley, Joe 1989	Stitzlein, Lorraine 1980
Fiorito, Matt 2004	Lichstein, Larry 1996	Thompson, Al 1991
Firestone, Raymond 1987	Luby, Mort Jr. 2004	Zeller, Roger 1995
Fisher, E.A. (Bud) 1984	+ Nagy, Steve 1977	

American Bowling Congress

Established in 1941 and open to professional and amateur bowlers. **Eligibility:** Nominated bowlers must have competed in at least 20 years of ABC tournaments. Voting done by 170-member panel made up of ABC officials, Hall of Fame members and media representatives..

Class of 2004 (3): PERFORMANCE—**Pete Couture, Mark Lewis** and **Bob Hanson**.
Members are listed with years of induction; (+) indicates deceased members.

Performance

Allison, Glenn 1979	+ Brosius, Eddie 1976	Davis, Dave 1990
+ Anthony, Earl 1986	+ Bujack, Fred 1967	+ Daw, Charlie 1941
Asher, Barry 1998	Bunetta, Bill 1968	+ Day, Ned 1952
+ Asplund, Harold 1978	Burton, Nelson Jr 1981	Dickinson, Gary 1992
Aulby, Mike 2001	+ Burton, Nelson Sr 1964	Duke, Norm 2002
Baer, Gordy 1987	+ Campi, Lou 1968	+ Easter, Sarge 1963
Beach, Bill 1991	+ Carlson, Adolph 1941	Ellis, Don 1981
+ Benkovic, Frank 1958	Carter, Don 1970	+ Falcaro, Joe 1968
Berlin, Mike 1994	+ Caruana, Frank 1977	+ Faragalli, Lindy 1968
+ Billick, George 1982	+ Cassio, Marty 1972	+ Fazio, Buzz 1963
+ Blouin, Jimmy 1953	+ Castellano, Graz 1976	Fehr, Steve 1993
Bluth, Ray 1973	+ Clause, Frank 1980	+ Gersonde, Russ 1968
+ Bodis, Joe 1941	Cohn, Alfred 1985	+ Gibson, Therm 1965
+ Bomar, Buddy 1966	Colwell, Paul 1999	+ Godman, Jim 1987
Bower, Gary 2001	Couture, Pete 2004	Goike, Robert 1996
+ Brandt, Allie 1960	+ Crimmins, Johnny 1962	+ Golembiewski, Billy 1979

Bowling (Cont.)

Griffo, Greg 1995	+ Lindsey, Mort 1941	Smith, Harry 1978
Guenther, Johnny 1988	+ Lippe, Harry 1989	+ Smith, Jimmy 1941
Hanson, Bob 2004	Lubanski, Ed 1971	Soutar, Dave 1985
Hardwick, Billy 1985	+ Lucci, Vince Sr 1978	+ Sparando, Tony 1968
Hart, Bob 1994	+ Marino, Hank 1941	Spigner, Bill 2001
+ Hennessey, Tom 1976	+ Martino, John 1969	+ Spinella, Barney 1968
Hoover, Dick 1974	Marzich, Andy 1993	+ Steers, Harry 1941
Horn, Bud 1992	McGrath, Mike 1993	Stefanich, Jim 1983
Howard, George 1986	+ McMahon, Junie 1967	+ Stein, Otto Jr 1971
Jackson, Eddie 1988	+ Meisel, Darold 1998	Stoudt, Bud 1991
+ Jackson, Lowell 2003	+ Mercurio, Skang 1967	Strampe, Bob 1977
+ Johnson, Don 1982	+ Meyers, Norm 1984	+ Thoma, Sykes 1971
Johnson, Earl 1987	+ Nagy, Steve 1963	Toft, Rod 1991
+ Joseph, Joe 1969	+ Norris, Joe 1954	+ Totsky, Mike 1996
+ Jouglard, Lee 1979	+ O'Donnell, Chuck 1968	Tountas, Pete 1989
+ Kartheiser, Frank 1967	Pappas, George 1989	Tucker, Bill 1988
+ Kawolics, Ed 1968	+ Patterson, Pat 1974	Tuttle, Tommy 1995
+ Kissoff, Joe 1976	+ Powell, John (Junior) 2000	+ Varipapa, Andy 1957
+ Klares, John 1982	Ritger, Dick 1984	+ Ward, Walter 1959
+ Knox, Billy 1954	+ Rogoznica, Andy 1993	Weber, Dick . . . . r . .1970
+ Koster, John 1941	Salvino, Carmen 1979	Weber, Pete 2002
+ Krems, Eddie 1973	Schissler, Les 1991	+ Welu, Billy 1975
Kristof, Joe 1968	Schlegel, Ernie 1997	Wilcox, John 1999
+ Krumske, Paul 1968	Schroeder, Jim 1990	+ Wilman, Joe 1951
+ Lange, Herb 1941	+ Schwoegler, Connie 1968	+ Wolf, Phil 1961
+ Lauman, Hank 1976	Scudder, Don 1999	Wonders, Rich 1990
Lewis, Mark 2004	Semiz, Teata 1991	+ Young, George 1959
Lillard, Bill 1972	+ Sielaff, Lou 1968	Zahn, Wayne 1980
Lindemann, Tony 1979	+ Sinke, Joe 1977	Zikes, Les 1983
	+ Sixty, Billy 1961	+ Zunker, Gil 1941

Pioneers

+ Allen, Lafayette Jr. 1994	+ Hall, William Sr. 1994	+ Satow, Masao 1994
+ Briell, Frank 1996	Hirashima, Hiroto 1995	+ Schutte, Louis 1993
+ Carow, Rev. Charles 1995	+ Karpf, Samuel 1993	Shimada, Fuzzy 1997
+ Celestine, Sydney 1993	+ Moore, Henry 1996	+ Stein, Louis 1997
+ Curtis, Thomas 1993	+ Pasdeloup, Frank 1993	+ Thompson, William V. 1993
+ de Freitas, Eric 1994	+ Rhodman, Bill 1997	+ Timm, Dr. Henry 1993

Meritorious Service

+ Allen, Harold 1966	+ Franklin, Bill 1992	+ Petersen, Louie 1963
Archibald, John 1996	+ Hagerty, Jack 1963	Pezzano, Chuck 1982
+ Baker, Frank 1975	+ Hattstrom, H.A. (Doc) 1980	Picchietti, Remo 1993
+ Baumgarten, Elmer 1963	+ Hermann, Cornelius 1968	Pluckhahn, Bruce 1989
+ Bellisimo, Lou 1986	+ Howley, Pete 1941	+ Raymer, Milt 1972
+ Bensinger, Bob 1969	Jensen, Mark 2002	+ Reed, Elmer 1978
Borden, Fred 2002	Jowdy, John 2001	Reichert, Jack 1998
+ Chase, LeRoy 1972	+ Kennedy, Bob 1981	Rudo, Milt 1984
+ Coker, John 1980	+ Langtry, Abe 1963	Schenkel, Chris 1988
+ Collier, Chuck 1963	+ Levine, Sam 1971	Skelton, Max 2002
+ Cruchon, Steve 1983	+ Luby, David 1969	+ Sweeney, Dennis 1974
+ Ditzen, Walt 1973	+ Luby, Mort Jr. 1988	Tessman, Roger 1994
+ Dobs, Darold 1999	+ Luby, Mort Sr. 1974	+ Thum, Joe 1980
+ Doehrman, Bill 1968	Matzelle, Al 1995	Weinstein, Sam 1970
+ Elias, Eddie 1985	+ McCullough, Howard 1971	+ Whitney, Eli 1975
Esposito, Frank 1997	Mormando, Nick 2003	+ Wolf, Fred 1976
Evans, Dick 1992	+ Patterson, Morehead 1985	

Women's International Bowling Congress

Established in 1953. **Eligibility:** Performance nominees must have won at least one WIBC Championship Tournament title, a WIBC Queens tournament title or an international competition title and have bowled in at least 15 national WIBC Championship Tournaments (unless injury or illness cut career short).

Class of 2004 (2): PERFORMANCE—**Cora Fiebig**; MERITORIOUS SERVICE—**Dorothy Rowe**.

Members are listed with years of induction; (+) indicates deceased members.

Performance

Abel, Joy 1984	Buckner, Pam 1990	Coburn, Doris 1976
Adamek, Donna 1996	+ Burling, Catherine 1958	Coburn-Carroll, Cindy 1998
Ann, Patty 1995	+ Burns, Nina 1977	Costello, Pat 1986
Bolt, Mae 1978	Cantaline, Anita 1979	Costello, Patty 1989
Bouvia, Gloria 1987	Carter, LaVerne 1977	Daniels, Cheryl 2002
Boxberger, Loa 1984	Carter, Paula 1994	Dryer, Pat 1978

Duval, Helen 1970	Kelly, Annese 1985	+ Robinson, Leona 1969
+ Fellmeth, Catherine 1970	Kelly, Linda 2003	Romeo, Robin 1995
Fiebig, Cora 2004	+ Knechtges, Doris 1983	+ Rump, Anita 1962
Fothergill, Dotty 1980	Kuczynski, Betty 1981	+ Ruschmeyer, Addie 1961
+ Fulton, Louise 2001	Ladewig, Marion 1964	+ Ryan, Esther 1963
+ Fritz, Deane 1966	+ Matthews, Merle 1974	+ Sablatnik, Ethel 1979
Garms, Shirley 1971	+ McCutcheon, Floretta 1956	Sandelin, Lucy 1999
Gianulias, Nikki 1997	Merrick, Marge 1980	+ Schulte, Myrtle 1965
+ Gloor, Olga 1976	+ Mikiel, Val 1979	+ Shablis, Helen 1977
Gonzalez, Ashie 1998	Miller-Mackey, Dana 2000	Sill, Aleta 1996
Graham, Linda 1992	Miller, Carol 1997	+ Simon, Violet (Billy) 1960
Graham, Mary Lou 1989	+ Miller, Dorothy 1954	+ Small, Tess 1971
+ Greenwald, Goldie 1953	Mivelaz, Betty 1991	+ Smith, Grace 1968
Grinfelds, Vesma 1991	Mohacsi, Mary 1994	Soutar, Judy 1976
+ Harman, Janet 1985	Morris, Betty 1983	+ Stockdale, Louise 1953
+ Hartrick, Stella 1972	Naccarato, Jeanne 1999	Toepfer, Elvira 1976
+ Hatch, Grayce 1953	Nichols, Lorrie Koch 1989	+ Twyford, Sally 1964
Havlish, Jean 1987	Norman, Carol 2001	Wagner, Lisa 2000
+ Hoffman, Martha 1979	Norman, Edie Jo 1993	+ Warmbier, Marie 1953
Holm, Joan 1974	Norton, Virginia 1988	Wene-Martin, Sylvia 1966
+ Humphreys, Birdie 1979	Notaro, Phyllis 1979	Wilkinson, Dorothy 1990
Ignizio, Millie Martorella ..1975	Ortner, Bev 1972	+ Winandy, Cecelia 1975
Jacobson, D.D 1981	+ Powers, Connie 1973	Zimmerman, Donna 1982
+ Jaeger, Emma 1953	Reichley, Susie 2000	
Johnson, Tish 2002	Rickard, Robbie 1994	

Meritorious Service

+ Baetz, Helen 1977	Hagin, Elaine 2000	+ Phaler, Emma 1965
+ Baker, Helen 1989	+ Herold, Mitzi 1998	+ Porter, Cora 1986
+ Banker, Gladys 1994	+ Higley, Margaret 1969	+ Quin, Zoe 1979
+ Bayley, Clover 1992	+ Hochstadter, Bee 1967	+ Rishling, Gertrude 1972
Bennie, Bernice 2003	+ Kay, Nora 1964	Robinson, Jeanette 2000
+ Berger, Winifred 1976	Keller, Pearl 1999	Rowe, Dorothy 2004
+ Bohlen, Philena 1955	+ Kelly, Ellen 1979	Simone, Anne 1991
Borschuk, Lo 1988	Kelone, Theresa 1978	Sloan, Catherine 1985
+ Botkin, Freda 1986	+ Knepprath, Jeannette 1963	+ Speck, Berdie 1966
+ Chapman, Emily 1957	+ Lasher, Iolia 1967	Spitalnick, Mildred 1994
Chapman, Nancy 2002	+ Marrs, Mabel 1979	+ Spring, Alma 1979
+ Crowe, Alberta 1982	+ McBride, Bertha 1968	+ Switzer, Pearl 1973
Deitch, Joyce 2003	McLeary, Hazel 2000	+ Todd, Trudy 1993
+ Dornblaser, Gertrude 1979	+ Menne, Catherine 1979	+ Veatch, Georgia 1974
Duffy, Agnes 1987	Mitchell, Flora 1996	+ White, Mildred 1975
Finke, Gertrude 1990	Morton, Clara 2001	+ Wood, Ann 1970
+ Fisk, Rae 1983	+ Mraz, Jo 1959	
+ Haas, Dorothy 1977	O'Connor, Billie 1992	

Professional Women Bowlers Hall of Fame

Established in 1995 by the Ladies Pro Bowlers Tour. The LPBT has since been renamed the Professional Women Bowlers Association. **Address:** Sam's Town Hotel, Gambling Hall and Bowling Center, 5111 Boulder Highway, Las Vegas, NV 89122. **Telephone:** (815) 332-5756.

Eligibility: Nominees in performance category must have at least five titles from organizations including All-Star, World Invitational, LPBT, WPBA, PWBA, TPA and LPBA. Voting done by 10-member committee of bowling writers appointed by PWBA president John Falzone.

Members are listed with year of induction; (+) indicates deceased member.

Performance

Adamek, Donna 1995	Grinfelds, Vesma 1997	Nichols, Lorrie 1996
Coburn-Carroll, Cindy 1997	Johnson, Tish 1998	Norton, Virginia 2003
Costello, Pat 1997	Ladewig, Marion 1995	Romeo, Robin 1996
Costello, Patty 1995	Martorella, Millie 1995	Sill, Aleta 1998
Duggan, Anne-Marie 2003	Miller-Mackie, Dana 2002	Wagner, Lisa 1996
Fothergill, Dotty 1995	Morris, Betty 1995	
Gianulias, Nikki 1996	Naccarato, Jeanne 2002	

Pioneers

Able, Joy 1998	Coburn, Doris 1996	Ortner, Bev 1998
Boxberger, Loa 1997	Duval, Helen 1995	Soutar, Judy 1997
Carter, LaVerne 1995	Garms, Shirley 1995	Zimmerman, Donna 1996

Builders

+ Buehler, Janet 1996	Robinson, Jeanette 1996	+ Veatch, Georgia 1995
Keller, Pearl 1997	Sommer Jr., John 1997	

BOXING

International Boxing Hall of Fame

Established in 1984 and opened in 1989. **Address:** 1 Hall of Fame Drive, Canastota, NY 13032. **Tel.:** (315) 697-7095.

Eligibility: All nominees must be retired for five years. Voting done by 142-member panel made up of Boxing Writers' Association members and world-wide boxing historians.

Class of 2004 (15): MODERN ERA—**Azumah Nelson, Carlos Palomino, Dwight Muhammad Qawi** and **Daniel Zaragoza**. OLD TIMERS—**Baby Arizmendi, Young Corbet III, Jackie Fields** and **Willie Ritchie**. PIONEER—**Billy Edwards**. NON-PARTICIPANTS—**Umberto Branchini, Stanley Christodoulou, J. Russell Peltz** and **Lou Viscusi**. OBSERVERS—**W.C. Heinz** and **Barney Nagler**.

Members are listed with year of induction; (+) indicates deceased member.

Modern Era

Ali, Muhammad .... .1990	Gavilan, Kid .... .1990	+ Olson, Carl (Bobo) ...... .2000
+ Angott, Sammy .... .1998	Giardello, Joey .... .1993	Ortiz, Carlos .... .1991
+ Apostoli, Fred .... .2003	Gomez, Wilfredo .... .1995	+ Ortiz, Manuel .... .1996
Arguello, Alexis .... .1992	+ Graham, Billy .... .1992	Palomino, Carlos ...... .2004
+ Armstrong, Henry ...... .1990	+ Graziano, Rocky ...... .1991	Papp, Laszlo .... .2001
Basilio, Carmen .... .1990	Griffith, Emile .... .1990	+ Pastrano, Willie .... .2001
Benitez, Wilfredo ...... .1996	Hagler, Marvelous Marvin .1993	Patterson, Floyd .... .1991
Benvenuti, Nino .... .1992	Harada, Masahiko (Fighting) 1995	Pedroza, Eusebio ...... .1999
+ Berg, Jackie (Kid) ...... .1994	Jack, Beau .... .1991	Pep, Willie .... .1990
Bivins, Jimmy .... .1999	+ Jenkins, Lew .... .1999	+ Perez, Pascual .... .1995
+ Brown, Joe .... .1996	Jofre, Eder .... .1992	Pryor, Aaron .... .1996
Buchanan, Ken .... .2000	Johansson, Ingemar .... .2002	Qawi, Dwight Muhammad .2004
+ Burley, Charley .... .1992	Johnson, Harold .... .1993	Ramos, Ultiminio ...... .2001
Canto, Miguel .... .1998	Laguna, Ismael .... .2001	+ Robinson, Sugar Ray ... .1990
+ Carter, Jimmy .... .2000	LaMotta, Jake .... .1990	+ Rodriguez, Luis .... .1997
+ Cerdan, Marcel .... .1991	Leonard, Sugar Ray ..... .1997	+ Saddler, Sandy .... .1990
Cervantes, Antonio ..... .1998	+ Liston, Sonny .... .1991	+ Saldivar, Vicente ...... .1999
Chandler, Jeff .... .2000	Locche, Nicolino .... .2003	+ Sanchez, Salvador ..... .1991
+ Charles, Ezzard .... .1990	+ Louis, Joe .... .1990	Schmeling, Max .... .1992
Cokes, Curtis .... .2003	+ Marciano, Rocky ...... .1990	Spinks, Michael .... .1994
+ Conn, Billy .... .1990	+ Maxim, Joey .... .1994	+ Tiger, Dick .... .1991
Cuevas, Pipino .... .2002	McCallum, Mike .... .2003	Torres, Jose .... .1997
+ Elorde, Gabriel (Flash) ... .1993	+ Montgomery, Bob ..... .1995	+ Turpin, Randy .... .2001
Fenech, Jeff .... .2002	+ Monzon, Carlos .... .1990	+ Walcott, Jersey Joe .... .1990
Foreman, George ...... .2003	+ Moore, Archie .... .1990	+ Williams, Ike .... .1990
Foster, Bob .... .1990	Muhammad, Matthew Saad 1998	+ Wright, Chalky .... .1997
Frazier, Joe .... .1990	Napoles, Jose .... .1990	+ Zale, Tony .... .1991
Fullmer, Gene .... .1991	Nelson, Azumah .... .2004	Zaragoza, Daniel ...... .2004
Galaxy, Khaosai .... .1999	Norton, Ken .... .1992	Zarate, Carlos .... .1994
+ Galindez, Victor .... .2002	Olivares, Ruben .... .1991	+ Zivic, Fritzie .... .1993

Old-Timers

+ Ambers, Lou .... .1992	+ Dundee, Johnny ...... .1991	+ Loughran, Tommy ...... .1991
+ Arizmendi, Baby ...... .2004	+ Escobar, Sixto .... .2002	+ Lynch, Benny .... .1998
+ Attell, Abe .... .1990	+ Fields, Jackie .... .2004	+ Mandell, Sammy ...... .1998
+ Baer, Max .... .1995	+ Fitzsimmons, Bob ...... .1990	+ McAuliffe, Jack .... .1995
+ Barry, Jimmy .... .2000	+ Flowers, Theodore (Tiger) ..1993	+ McCoy, Charles (Kid) .... .1991
+ Bass, Benny .... .2002	+ Gans, Joe .... .1990	+ McFarland, Packey ..... .1992
+ Battalino, Battling ..... .2003	+ Genaro, Frankie ...... .1998	+ McGovern, Terry ...... .1990
+ Berlenbach, Paul ...... .2001	+ Gibbons, Mike .... .1992	McLarnin, Jimmy ...... .1991
+ Britton, Jack .... .1990	+ Gibbons, Tommy ...... .1993	+ McVey, Sam .... .1999
+ Brown, Aaron (Dixie Kid) .2002	+ Greb, Harry .... .1990	+ Miller, Freddie .... .1997
+ Brown, Panama Al ...... .1992	+ Griffo, Young .... .1991	+ Mitchell, Charley ...... .2002
+ Burns, Tommy .... .1996	+ Harris, Harry .... .2002	+ Moran, Owen .... .2002
+ Canzoneri, Tony ...... .1990	+ Herman, Pete .... .1997	+ Nelson, Battling .... .1992
+ Carpentier, Georges .... .1991	+ Jackson, Peter .... .1990	+ O'Brien, Philadelphia Jack .1994
+ Chocolate, Kid .... .1991	+ Jeanette, Joe .... .1997	+ Papke, Billy .... .2001
+ Choynski, Joe .... .1998	+ Jeffries, James J .... .1990	+ Petrolle, Billy .... .2000
+ Corbett, James J. ...... .1990	+ Johnson, Jack .... .1990	+ Ritchie, Willie .... .2004
+ Corbett III, Young ...... .2004	+ Kaplan, Louis (Kid) ..... .2003	+ Rosenbloom, Maxie ..... .1993
+ Coulon, Johnny .... .1999	+ Ketchel, Stanley .... .1990	+ Ross, Barney .... .1990
+ Darcy, Les .... .1993	+ Kilbane, Johnny .... .1995	+ Ryan, Tommy .... .1991
+ Delaney, Jack .... .1996	+ LaBarba, Fidel .... .1996	+ Sharkey, Jack .... .1994
+ Dempsey, Jack .... .1990	+ Langford, Sam .... .1990	+ Sharkey, Tom .... .2003
+ Dempsey, Jack (Nonpareil) .1992	+ Lavigne, George (Kid) ... .1998	+ Steele, Freddie .... .1999
+ Dillon, Jack .... .1995	+ Leonard, Benny .... .1990	+ Stribling, Young .... .1996
+ Dixon, George .... .1990	+ Levinsky, Battling ...... .2000	+ Tendler, Lew .... .1999
+ Driscoll, Jim .... .1990	+ Lewis, John Henry ..... .1994	+ Tunney, Gene .... .1990
	+ Lewis, Ted (Kid) ...... .1992	+ Villa, Pancho .... .1994

+ Walcott, Joe (Barbados) ...1991
+ Walker, Mickey 1990
+ Welsh, Freddie 1997

+ Wilde, Jimmy 1990
+ Willard, Jess 2003
+ Williams, Kid 1996

+ Wills, Harry 1992
+ Wolgast, Ad 2000
+ Wolgast, Midget 2001

Pioneers

+ Aaron, Barney 2001
+ Baldwin, Caleb 2003
+ Belcher, Jem 1992
+ Brain, Ben 1994
+ Broughton, Jack 1990
+ Burke, James (Deaf) 1992
+ Chambers, Arthur 2000
+ Cribb, Tom 1991
+ Donovan, Prof. Mike 1998
+ Duffy, Paddy 1994
+ Goss, Joe 2003

+ Edwards, Billy 2004
+ Figg, James 1992
+ Heenan, John C. 2002
+ Jackson, Gentleman John ..1992
+ Johnson, Tom 1995
+ King, Tom 1992
+ Langham, Nat 1992
+ Mace, Jem 1990
+ Mendoza, Daniel 1990
+ Molineaux, Tom 1997
+ Morrissey, John 1996

+ Pearce, Henry 1993
+ Richmond, Bill 1999
+ Sam, Dutch 1997
+ Sam, Young Dutch 2002
+ Sayers, Tom 1990
+ Spring, Tom 1992
+ Sullivan, John L 1990
+ Thompson, William 1991
+ Ward, Jem 1995

Non-Participants

+ Andrews, Thomas S 1992
+ Arcel, Ray 1991
  Arum, Bob 1999
+ Ballarati, Giuseppe 1999
  Benton, George 2001
+ Blackburn, Jack 1992
+ Brady, William A. 1998
+ Branchini, Umberto 2004
  Brenner, Teddy 1993
+ Chambers, John Graham .1990
  Chargin, Don 2001
  Christodoulou, Stanley ..2004
  Clancy, Gil 1993
+ Coffroth, James W. 1991
+ Cohen, Irving 2002
+ D'Amato, Cus. 1995
  Dickson, Jeff 2000
+ Donovan, Arthur 1993
  Duff, Mickey 1999
  Dundee, Angelo 1992
+ Dundee, Chris 1994
+ Dunphy, Don 1993

+ Duva, Dan 2003
  Duva, Lou 1998
+ Eaton, Aileen 2002
+ Egan, Pierce 1991
+ Fleischer, Nat 1990
+ Fox, Richard K. 1997
+ Fragetta, Dewey 2003
+ Futch, Eddie 1994
+ Goldman, Charley 1992
+ Goldstein, Ruby 1994
  Goodman, Murray 1999
+ Humphreys, Joe 1997
+ Ichinose, Sam 2001
+ Jacobs, Jimmy 1993
+ Jacobs, Mike 1990
+ Johnston, Jimmy 1999
+ Kearns, Jack (Doc) 1990
  King, Don 1997
  Lectoure, Tito 2000
+ Liebling, A.J 1992
+ Lonsdale, Lord 1990
+ Markson, Harry 1992

  Mercante, Arthur 1995
+ Morgan, Dan 2000
+ Muldoon, William 1996
  Odd, Gilbert 1995
+ O'Rourke, Tom 1999
+ Parker, Dan 1996
+ Parnassus, George 1991
  Peltz, J. Russell 2004
+ Queensberry, Marquis of .1990
+ Rickard, Tex 1990
+ Rudd, Irving 1999
+ Siler, George 1995
+ Silverman, Sam 2002
+ Solomons, Jack 1995
  Steward, Emanuel 1996
+ Taub, Sam 1994
+ Taylor, Herman 1998
+ Viscusi, Lou 2004
+ Walker, James J. (Jimmy) .1992
+ Weill, Al 2003

Observers

+ Bromberg, Lester 2001
+ Cannon, Jimmy 2002
  Citro, Ralph 2001
  Gallo, Bill 2001

  Gutteridge, Reg 2002
  Heinz, W.C. 2004
  Fiske, Jack 2003
+ Nagler, Barney 2004

+ Runyon, Damon 2002
  Schulberg, Budd 2003

Old *Ring* Hall Members Not in Int'l. Boxing Hall

Nat Fleischer, the late founder and editor-in-chief of *The Ring*, established his magazine's Boxing Hall of Fame in 1954, but it was abandoned after the 1987 inductions. One hundred and twenty-nine members of the old *Ring* Hall have been elected to the International Hall since 1989. The 25 boxers and one sportswriter who have yet to be elected to the International Hall are listed below with their year of induction into the *Ring* Hall.

Modern Group

+ Garcia, Ceferino 1977

+ Lesnevich, Gus 1973

+ Shirai, Yoshio 1977

Old-Timers

+ Britt, Jimmy 1976
+ Chaney, George (K.O.) ...1974
+ Corbett, Young II 1965
+ Houck, Leo 1969

+ Jeffra, Harry 1982
+ Klaus, Frank 1974
+ Maher, Peter 1978
+ Root, Jack 1961

+ Smith, Jeff 1969
+ Taylor, Bud 1986

Pioneers

+ Chandler, Tom 1972
+ Clark, Nobby 1971
+ Collyer, Sam 1964
+ Donnelly, Dan 1960
+ Gully, John 1959

+ Hyer, Jacob 1968
+ Hyer, Tom 1954
+ Jackling, Thomas 1985
+ Kilrain, Jack 1965
+ Price, Ned 1962

+ Ryan, Paddy 1973

Non-Participant

+ Daniel, Dan (sportswriter) ..1977

FOOTBALL

College Football Hall of Fame

Established in 1955 by the National Football Foundation. **Address:** 111 South St. Joseph St., South Bend, IN 46601. **Telephone:** (574) 235-9999.

Eligibility: Nominated players must be out of college 10 years and a first team All-America pick by a major selector during their careers; coaches must be retired three years. Voting done by 12-member panel of athletic directors, conference and bowl officials and media representatives. The first year representatives from NCAA Div. I-AA, II, and III, and the NAIA were eligible for induction was 1996.

Class of 2004 (23): LARGE COLLEGE—RB **Bob P. Anderson**, Army (1957-59); G **Tony Casillas**, Oklahoma (1982-85); LB **Frank Emanuel**, Tennessee (1963-65); P **Ray Guy**, SMU (1970-72); G/LB **Wayne Harris**, Arkansas (1958-60); QB **Joe Kapp**, California (1956-58); TE **Joe Mandich**, Michigan (1967-69); RB **Lydell Mitchell**, Penn St. (1969-71); DT **Tracy Rocker**, Auburn (1985-88); DB **Jack Tatum**, Ohio St. (1968-70); QB **Andre Ware**, Houston (1987-89); TE **Charles Young**, USC (1970-72). COACHES—**LaVell Edwards**, BYU (1972-2000); **George Welsh**, Navy (1973-81), Virginia (1982-2000). SMALL COLLEGE—HB **Harold Davis**, Westminster (1953-56); CB **Darrell Green**, Texas A&I (1978-82); HB **Garney Henley**, Huron (1956-59); HB **Jackie Hunt**, Marshall (1938-41); TE **Dan Ross**, Northeastern (1975-78); WR **Bill Stromberg**, Johns Hopkins (1978-81). SMALL COLLEGE COACHES—**Tom Beck**, Illinois Benedictine (1970-74), Elmhurst (1976-83), Grand Valley St. (1985-90); **Charlie Richard**, Baker (1980-1990, 1992-94); **Dick Strahm**, Findlay (1975-98).

Note: Bobby Dodd and **Amos Alonzo Stagg** are the only members to be honored as both players and coaches. Players are listed with final year they played in college and coaches are listed with year of induction; (+) indicates deceased members.

Players

+ Abell, Earl-Colgate	1915
Agase, Alex-Purdue/Ill	1946
+ Agganis, Harry-Boston U	1952
Albert, Frank-Stanford	1941
+ Aldrich, Ki-TCU	1938
+ Aldrich, Malcolm-Yale	1921
+ Alexander, Joe-Syracuse	1920
Allen, Marcus-USC	1981
Alworth, Lance-Arkansas	1961
+ Ameche, Alan-Wisconsin	1954
+ Ames, Knowlton-Princeton	1889
+ Amling, Warren-Ohio St	1946
Anderson, Bob P.-Army	1959
Anderson, Dick-Colorado	1967
Anderson, Donny-Tex.Tech	1965
+ Anderson, Hunk-N.Dame	1921
Arnett, Jon-USC	1956
Atkins, Doug-Tennessee	1952
Babich, Bob-Miami-OH	1968
+ Bacon, Everett-Wesleyan	1912
+ Bagnell, Reds-Penn	1950
+ Baker, Hobey-Princeton	1913
+ Baker, John-USC	1931
+ Baker, Moon-N'western	1926
Baker, Terry-Oregon St	1962
+ Ballin, Harold-Princeton	1914
+ Banker, Bill-Tulane	1929
Banonis, Vince-Detroit	1941
+ Barnes, Stan-California	1921
+ Barrett, Charles-Cornell	1915
+ Baston, Bert-Minnesota	1916
+ Battles, Cliff-WV Wesleyan	1931
Baugh, Sammy-TCU	1936
Baughan, Maxie-Ga.Tech	1959
+ Bausch, James-Wichita/Kansas	1930
Beagle, Ron-Navy	1955
Beasley, Terry-Auburn	1971
Beban, Gary-UCLA	1967
Bechtol, Hub-Tex.Tech/Texas	1946
Beck, Ray-Ga. Tech	1951
+ Beckett, John-Oregon	1916
Bednarik, Chuck-Penn	1948
Behm, Forrest-Nebraska	1940
Bell, Bobby-Minnesota	1962
Bell, Ricky-USC	1976
Bellino, Joe-Navy	1960
Below, Marty-Wisconsin	1923

+ Benbrook, Al-Michigan	1910
+ Berry, Charlie-Lafayette	1924
+ Bertelli, Angelo-N.Dame	1943
+ Berwanger, Jay-Chicago	1935
+ Bettencourt, L.-St.Mary's	1927
Biletnikoff, Fred-Fla.St.	1964
Blanchard, Doc-Army	1946
+ Blozis, Al-Georgetown	1941
Bock, Ed-Iowa St	1938
Bomar, Lynn-Vanderbilt	1924
+ Bomeisler, Bo-Yale	1912
+ Booth, Albie-Yale	1931
+ Borries, Fred-Navy	1934
+ Bosley, Bruce-West Va	1955
Bosseler, Don-Miami,FL	1956
Bottari, Vic-California	1938
Bowden, Murry-Dartmouth	1970
+ Boynton, Ben-Williams	1920
+ Brewer, Charles-Harvard	1895
+ Bright, Johnny-Drake	1951
Brodie, John-Stanford	1956
+ Brooke, George-Penn	1895
Brosky, Al-Illinois	1952
Brown, Bob-Nebraska	1963
Brown, Geo-Navy/S.Diego St	1947
+ Brown, Gordon-Yale	1900
Brown, Jim-Syracuse	1956
+ Brown, John, Jr.-Navy	1913
+ Brown, Johnny Mack-Ala	1925
+ Brown, Tay-USC	1932
Brown, Tom-Minnesota	1960
Browner, Ross-Notre Dame	1977
Budde, Brad-USC	1979
+ Bunker, Paul-Army	1902
Burford, Chris-Stanford	1959
+ Burris, Kurt-Oklahoma	1954
Burton, Ron-N'western	1959
Butkus, Dick-Illinois	1964
Butler, Kevin-Georgia	1984
+ Butler, Robert-Wisconsin	1913
+ Cafego, George-Tenn	1939
+ Cagle, Red-SWLa/Army	1929
+ Cain, John-Alabama	1932
Cameron, Ed-Wash.& Lee	1924
+ Campbell, David-Harvard	1901
Campbell, Earl-Texas	1977
+ Cannon, Jack-N.Dame	1929
Cappelletti, John-Penn St	1973

+ Carideo, Frank-N.Dame	1930
+ Carney, Charles-Illinois	1921
Caroline, J.C.-Illinois	1954
Carpenter, Bill-Army	1959
+ Carpenter, Hunter-No. Carolina/Virginia Tech	1905
Carroll, Chas.-Washington	1928
Carter, Anthony-Michigan	1982
Casanova, Tommy-LSU	1971
+ Casey, Edward-Harvard	1919
Casillas, Tony-Oklahoma	1985
Cassady, Howard-Ohio St	1955
+ Chamberlin, Guy-Neb.Wesleyan/Nebraska	1915
Chapman, Sam-California	1937
Chappuis, Bob-Michigan	1947
+ Christman, Paul-Missouri	1940
+ Clark, Dutch-Colo. Col.	1929
Cleary, Paul-USC	1947
+ Clevenger, Zora-Indiana	1903
Cloud, Jack-Wm. & Mary	1949
+ Cochran, Gary-Princeton	1897
+ Cody, Josh-Vanderbilt	1919
Coleman, Don-Mich.St	1951
+ Conerly, Charlie-Miss	1947
Connor, George-HC/ND	1947
+ Corbin, William-Yale	1888
Corbus, William-Stanford	1933
Covert, Jimbo-Pittsburgh	1983
+ Cowan, Hector-Princeton	1889
+ Coy, Edward (Ted)-Yale	1909
+ Crawford, Fred-Duke	1933
Crow, John David-Tex.A&M	1957
+ Crowley, Jim-Notre Dame	1924
Csonka, Larry-Syracuse	1967
Cutter, Slade-Navy	1934
+ Czarobski, Ziggie-N.Dame	1947
Dale, Carroll-Va.Tech	1959
+ Dalrymple, Gerald-Tulane	1931
+ Dalton, John-Navy	1911
+ Daly, Chas.-Harvard/Army	1902
Daniell, Averell-Pitt	1936
+ Daniell, James-Ohio St	1941
+ Davies, Tom-Pittsburgh	1921
Davis, Ernie-Syracuse	1961
Davis, Glenn-Army	1946
Davis, Robert-Ga.Tech	1947
Dawkins, Pete-Army	1958

College Football Hall of Fame (Cont.)

Selmon, Lee Roy-Okla 1975	+ Stydahar, Joe-West Va 1935	+ Wedemeyer, H.-St. Mary's .1947
Sewell, Harley-Texas 1952	+ Suffridge, Bob-Tennessee . . .1940	+ Weekes, Harold-Columbia .1902
+ Shakespeare, Bill-N.Dame . .1935	+ Suhey, Steve-Penn St 1947	Wehrli, Roger-Missouri 1968
Shell, Donnie-S.Carolina St. .1998	Sullivan, Pat-Auburn 1971	Weiner, Art-N. Carolina . . .1949
+ Shelton, Murray-Cornell . . .1915	+ Sundstrom, Frank-Cornell . .1923	+ Weir, Ed-Nebraska 1925
+ Shevlin, Tom-Yale 1905	Swann, Lynn-USC 1973	+ Welch, Gus-Carlisle 1914
+ Shively, Bernie-Illinois 1926	+ Swanson, Clarence-Neb 1921	+ Weller, John-Princeton 1935
+ Simons, Monk-Tulane 1934	+ Swiacki, Bill-Columbia/HC .1947	+ Wendell, Percy-Harvard 1912
Simpson, O.J.-USC 1968	Swink, Jim-TCU 1956	+ West, Belford-Colgate 1919
Sims, Billy-Oklahoma 1979	+ Talboom, Eddie-Wyoming . . .1950	+ Westfall, Bob-Michigan 1941
Singletary, Mike-Baylor 1980	Taliaferro, Geo.-Indiana . . .1948	+ Weyand, Babe-Army 1915
Sington, Fred-Alabama 1930	Tarkenton, Fran-Georgia . . .1960	+ Wharton, Buck-Penn 1896
+ Sinkwich, Frank-Georgia . . .1942	Tatum, Jack-Ohio St. 1970	+ Wheeler, Arthur-Princeton . .1894
Sisemore, Jerry-Texas 1972	+ Tavener, John-Indiana 1944	+ White, Byron-Colorado 1937
+ Sitko, Emil-Notre Dame 1949	+ Taylor, Chuck-Stanford 1942	White, Charles-USC 1979
+ Skladany, Joe-Pittsburgh . . .1933	Theismann, Joe-Notre Dame 1970	White, Danny-Ariz. St. 1973
+ Slater, Duke-Iowa 1921	Thomas, Aurelius-Ohio St .1957	White, Ed-Cal.Berkeley 1968
Smith, Billy Ray-Arkansas . .1982	+ Thompson, Joe-Geneva/	White, Randy-Maryland 1974
+ Smith, Bruce-Minnesota 1941	Pittsburgh 1906	+ White, Reggie-Tennessee 1983
+ Smith, Bubba-Michigan St . .1966	+ Thorne, Samuel-Yale 1895	Whitmire, Don-Navy/Ala . .1944
+ Smith, Clipper-N.Dame 1927	+ Thorpe, Jim-Carlisle 1912	+ Wickhorst, Frank-Navy 1926
+ Smith, Ernie-USC 1932	+ Ticknor, Ben-Harvard 1930	Widseth, Ed-Minnesota 1936
Smith, Harry-USC 1939	+ Tigert, John-Vanderbilt 1903	+ Wildung, Dick-Minnesota . .1942
Smith, Jim Ray-Baylor 1954	+ Tinsley, Gaynell-LSU 1936	Williams, Bob-N. Dame 1950
Smith, Riley-Alabama 1935	+ Tipton, Eric-Duke 1938	Williams, Froggie-Rice 1949
+ Smith, Vernon-Georgia 1931	+ Tonnemaker, Clayton-Minn .1949	Willis, Bill-Ohio St 1944
+ Snow, Neil-Michigan 1901	+ Torrey, Bob-Pennsylvania . . .1905	+ Wilson, Bobby-SMU 1935
Spani, Gary-Kansas St. 1977	+ Travis, Brick-Tarkio/Missouri 1920	+ Wilson, George-Lafayette . . .1928
Sparlis, Al-UCLA 1945	Trippi, Charley-Georgia 1946	+ Wilson, George-Wash 1925
+ Spears, Clarence-Knox/Dart 1915	+ Tryon, Edward-Colgate 1925	+ Wilson, Harry-Army/Penn St .1927
Spears, W.D.-Vanderbilt . . .1927	Tubbs, Jerry-Oklahoma 1956	Wilson, Marc-BYU 1979
+ Sprackling, Wm.-Brown 1911	Turner, Bulldog-H.Simmons .1939	Wilson, Mike-Lafayette 1928
+ Sprague, Bud-Army/Texas . .1928	Twilley, Howard-Tulsa 1965	Winslow, Kellen-Missouri . . .1978
Spurrier, Steve-Florida 1966	+ Utay, Joe-Texas A&M 1907	Wistert, Albert-Michigan . . .1942
Stafford, Harrison-Texas 1932	+ Van Brocklin, Norm-Ore 1948	Wistert, Alvin-Michigan 1949
+ Stagg, Amos Alonzo-Yale . . .1889	Van Pelt, Brad-Michigan St. .1972	+ Wistert, Whitey-Michigan . . .1933
Stanfill, Bill-Georgia 1968	+ Van Sickel, Dale-Florida 1929	+ Wojciechowicz, Alex-Fordham 1937
+ Starcevich, Max-Wash 1936	+ Van Surdam, H.-Wesleyan . . .1905	+ Wood, Barry-Harvard 1931
Staubach, Roger-Navy 1964	+ Very, Dexter-Penn St 1912	+ Wyatt, Andy-Bucknell/
+ Steffen, Walter-Chicago 1908	+ Vessels, Billy-Oklahoma 1952	Chicago 1894
Steffy, Joe-Tenn/Army 1947	+ Vick, Ernie-Michigan 1921	+ Wyatt, Bowden-Tenn 1938
Stein, Herbert-Pitt 1921	+ Wagner, Hube-Pittsburgh . . .1913	+ Wyckoff, Clint-Cornell 1895
Steuber, Bob-Missouri/	Walker, Doak-SMU 1949	+ Yarr, Tommy-N.Dame 1931
DePauw 1943	Walker, Herschel-Georgia . .1982	Yary, Ron-USC 1967
+ Stevens, Mal-Washburn/Yale 1923	+ Wallace, Bill-Rice 1935	+ Yoder, Lloyd-Carnegie 1926
+ Stevenson, Vincent-Penn 1905	+ Walsh, Adam-N.Dame 1924	Young, Charles-USC 1972
Stillwagon, Jim-Ohio St. 1970	+ Warburton, Cotton, USC 1934	+ Young, Claude-Illinois 1946
+ Stinchcomb, Pete-Ohio St. . .1920	Ward, Bob-Maryland 1951	+ Young, Harry-Wash.& Lee . .1916
Strom, Brock-Air Force 1959	Ware, Andre-Houston 1989	Young, Steve-Brigham Young .1983
+ Strong, Ken-NYU 1928	+ Warner, William-Cornell 1902	+ Young, Waddy-Okla 1938
+ Strupper, Ev-Ga.Tech 1917	+ Washington, Kenny-UCLA . .1939	Youngblood, Jack-Florida . .1970
+ Stuhldreher, Harry-N.Dame .1924	+ Weatherall, Jim-Okla. 1951	+ Younger, Tank-Grambling . .1948
+ Sturhahn, Herb-Yale 1926	Webster, George-Mich. St .1966	Zarnas, Gustave-Ohio St. . .1937

Coaches

+ Aillet, Joe 1989	+ Bryant, Paul (Bear) 1986	+ Dobie, Gil 1951
+ Alexander, Bill 1951	+ Butts, Wally 1997	+ Dodd, Bobby 1993
+ Anderson, Ed 1971	+ Caldwell, Charlie 1961	Donahue, Tom 2000
+ Armstrong, Ike 1957	+ Camp, Walter 1951	+ Donohue, Michael 1951
+ Bachman, Charlie 1978	Casanova, Len 1977	Dooley, Vince 1994
+ Banks, Earl 1992	+ Cavanaugh, Frank 1954	+ Dorais, Gus 1954
+ Baujan, Harry 1990	+ Claiborne, Jerry 1999	+ Edwards, Bill 1986
+ Bell, Matty 1955	+ Colman, Dick 1990	Edwards, LaVell 2004
+ Bezdek, Hugo 1954	Coryell, Don 1999	+ Engle, Rip 1973
+ Bible, Dana X 1951	Cozza, Carmen 2002	Evashevski, Forest 2000
+ Bierman, Bernie 1955	+ Crisler, Fritz 1954	Faurot, Don 1961
Blackman, Bob 1987	+ Daugherty, Duffy 1984	Fry, Hayden 2003
+ Blaik, Earl (Red) 1965	+ Devaney, Bob 1981	+ Gaither, Jake 1973
Broyles, Frank 1983	+ Devine, Dan 1985	Gillman, Sid 1989
Bruce, Earle 2002	Dickey, Doug 2003	+ Godfrey, Ernest 1972

College Football Hall of Fame (Cont.)
Coaches (Cont.)

	Graves, Ray	1990	+	McLaughry, Tuss	1962	+	Schmidt, Francis	1971

Graves, Ray 1990
+ Gustafson, Andy 1985
+ Hall, Edward 1951
+ Harding, Jack 1980
+ Harlow, Richard 1954
+ Harman, Harvey 1981
+ Harper, Jesse 1971
+ Haughton, Percy 1951
+ Hayes, Woody 1983
+ Heisman, John W 1954
+ Higgins, Robert 1954
+ Hollingberry, Babe 1979
+ Howard, Frank 1989
+ Ingram, Bill 1973
  James, Don 1997
+ Jennings, Morley 1973
+ Jones, Biff 1954
+ Jones, Howard 1951
+ Jones, Tad 1958
+ Jordan, Lloyd 1978
+ Jordan, Ralph (Shug) 1982
+ Kerr, Andy 1951
  Kush, Frank 1995
+ Leahy, Frank 1970
+ Little, George 1955
+ Little, Lou 1960
+ Madigan, Slip 1974
  Maurer, Dave 1991
+ McClendon, Charley 1986
+ McCracken, Herb 1973
+ McGugin, Dan 1951
+ McKay, John 1988
+ McKeen, Allyn 1991

+ McLaughry, Tuss 1962
+ Merritt, John 1994
+ Meyer, Dutch 1956
+ Mollenkopf, Jack 1988
+ Moore, Bernie 1954
+ Moore, Scrappy 1980
+ Morrison, Ray 1954
+ Munger, George 1976
+ Munn, Clarence (Biggie) . . .1959
+ Murray, Bill 1974
+ Murray, Frank 1983
+ Mylin, Ed (Hooks) 1974
+ Neale, Earle (Greasy) 1967
+ Neely, Jess 1971
+ Nelson, David 1987
+ Neyland, Robert 1956
+ Norton, Homer 1971
+ O'Neill, Frank (Buck) 1951
+ Osborne, Tom 1998
+ Owen, Bennie 1951
  Parseghian, Ara 1980
+ Perry, Doyt 1988
+ Phelan, Jimmy 1973
+ Prothro, Tommy 1991
  Ralston, John 1992
+ Robinson, E.N. 1955
+ Rockne, Knute 1951
+ Romney, Dick 1954
+ Roper, Bill 1951
  Royal, Darrell 1983
+ Sanders, Henry (Red) 1996
+ Sanford, George 1971
  Schembechler, Bo 1993

+ Schmidt, Francis 1971
+ Schwartzwalder, Ben 1982
+ Shaughnessy, Clark 1968
+ Shaw, Buck 1972
+ Smith, Andy 1951
+ Snavely, Carl 1965
+ Stagg, Amos Alonzo 1951
+ Sutherland, Jock 1951
  Switzer, Barry 2001
+ Tatum, Jim 1984
  Teaff, Grant 2001
+ Thomas, Frank 1951
+ Vann, Thad 1987
  Vaught, Johnny 1979
+ Wade, Wallace 1955
+ Waldorf, Lynn (Pappy) 1966
+ Warner, Glenn (Pop) 1951
  Welsh, George 2004
+ Wieman, E.E. (Tad) 1956
+ Wilce, John 1954
+ Wilkinson, Bud 1969
+ Williams, Henry 1951
+ Woodruff, George 1963
+ Woodson, Warren 1989
+ Wyatt, Bowden 1997
  Yeoman, Bill 2001
+ Yost, Fielding (Hurry Up) . .1951
  Young, Jim 1999
+ Zuppke, Bob 1951

Small College
Players

  Bailey, Johnny-Texas A&I . .1989
  Bentrim, Jeff-N.Dakota St. . .1986
+ Blazine, Tony-Ill Wesleyan . .1934
  Bork, George-N. Illinois 1963
  Bradshaw, Terry-La. Tech . .1969
  Bruner, Teel-Centre KY 1985
+ Buchanon, Buck-Grambling .1962
  Calip, Brad-E. Central 1984
  Carson, Harry, S.C. State . . .1975
  Cason, Rod, Angelo St. 1971
  Cichy, Joe-N.Dakota St. 1970
  Cooper, Bill-Muskinghum . . .1960
  Crawford, Brad-Franklin 1977
  Davis, Harold-Wesminster . . .1956
  Deery, Tom-Widener 1981
+ Delaney, Joe-N'western St. . .1980
  Dement, Kenneth-SE Mo St. .1954
  Den Herder, Vern-Central IA .1970
  Dryer, Fred-San Diego St. . . .1968
  Dudek, Joe-Plymouth St. 1985
  Floyd, George-E. Kentucky . .1981

  Galimore, Willie-Fla. A&M . .1956
  Gamble, Kenny-Colgate 1987
  Green, Charlie-Wittenberg . . .1964
  Green, Darrell-Texas A&I . . .1982
  Grinnell, Williams-Tufts 1934
  Haslett, Jim-Indiana, PA 1978
  Hawkins, Frank-Nevada 1980
  Henley, Garney-Huron 1959
  Holt, Pierce-Angelo St. 1987
+ Hunt, Jackie-Marshall 1941
  Johnson, Billy-Widener 1973
  Johnson, Gary-Grambling . . .1974
  Lanier, Willie-Morgan St. . . .1966
  LeClair, Jim-North Dakota . . .1971
  Lackbaum, Gordie-Holy Cross 1987
  Lomax, Neil-Portland 1980
  McGriff, Tyrone-Jackson St. . .1974
  Montgomery, Wilbert-
    Abilene Christian 1976
  Nix, Dwayne-Texas A&I 1968
  O'Brien, Ken-UC Davis 1982

+ Payton, Walter-Jackson St. . .1974
  Pugh, Larrry-Westminster . . .1964
  Reasons, Gary-N'western St. 1983
  Redell, Bill-Occidental 1963
  Reppert, Scott-Lawrence 1982
  Richardson, Willie-Jackson St. 1962
  Ritchie, Richard-Texas A&I . .1976
+ Roberts, Calvin-
    Gustavus Adolphus 1952
  Ross, Dan-Northeastern 1978
  Scott, Freddie-Amherst 1973
  Shell, Donnie-S.C. State 1973
+ Stevenson, Ben-Tuskegee . . .1930
  Stromberg, Bill-Johns Hopkins 1981
  Taylor, Bruce-Boston U. 1969
  Thomsen, Lynn-Augustana . .1986
  Trautman, Randy-Boise St. . .1964
  Williams, Doug-Grambling . .1977
  Youngblood, Jim-Tenn. Tech .1972
  Younger, Paul-Grambling . . .1948

Coaches

  Ault, Chris 2002
  Beck, Tom 2004
+ Burry, Harold 1996
  Butterfield, Jim 1997
  Casem, Marino 2003
  Fusco, Joe 2001
  Hoerneman, Paul 1997
  Huerta, Marcelino 2002
  Keade, Bob 1998

  Kidd, Roy 2003
  Klausing, Chuck 1998
  Martinelli, Fred 1993
  Mudra, Darrell 2000
+ Mumford, Ace 2001
  Nicks, Billy 1999
  Raymond, Tubby 2003
  Reade, Bob 1998
  Robinson, Eddie G. 1997

+ Richard, Charlie 2004
  Rutschman, Ad 1998
  Schipper, Ron 2000
  Sherman, Edgar 1996
  Sochor, James 1999
+ Steinke, Gilbert 1996
  Strahm, Dick 2004
+ Tressel, Lee 1996
  Waters, Frank 2000

Pro Football Hall of Fame

Established in 1963 by National Football League to commemorate the sport's professional origins. **Address:** 2121 George Halas Drive NW, Canton, OH 44708. **Telephone:** (330) 456-8207.

Eligibility: Nominated players must be retired five years, coaches must be retired, and contributors can still be active. Voting done by 39-member panel made up of media representatives from all 31 NFL cities (two from New York), one PFWA representative and six selectors-at-large.

Class of 2004 (4): PLAYERS—OT **Bob "Boomer" Brown**, Philadelphia (1964-68), L.A Rams (1969-70), Oakland (1971-73); DE **Carl Eller**, Minnesota (1964-78), Seattle (1979); QB **John Elway**, Denver (1983-98) and RB **Barry Sanders**, Detroit (1989-98).

Quarterbacks

Baugh, Sammy 1963	+ Graham, Otto 1965	Parker, Clarence (Ace) 1972
Blanda, George (also PK) ..1981	Griese, Bob 1990	Starr, Bart 1977
Bradshaw, Terry 1989	+ Herber, Arnie 1966	Staubach, Roger 1985
+ Clark, Dutch 1963	Jurgensen, Sonny 1983	Tarkenton, Fran 1986
+ Conzelman, Jimmy 1964	Kelly, Jim 2002	Tittle, Y.A 1971
Dawson, Len 1987	+ Layne, Bobby 1967	+ Unitas, Johnny 1979
+ Driscoll, Paddy 1965	+ Luckman, Sid 1965	+ Van Brocklin, Norm 1971
Elway, John 2004	Montana, Joe 2000	+ Waterfield, Bob 1965
Fouts, Dan 1993	Namath, Joe 1985	

Running Backs

Allen, Marcus 2003	+ Hinkle, Clarke 1964	+ Payton, Walter 1993
+ Battles, Cliff 1968	Hornung, Paul 1986	Perry, Joe 1969
Brown, Jim 1971	Johnson, John Henry 1987	Riggins, John 1992
Campbell, Earl 1991	Kelly, Leroy 1994	Sanders, Barry 2004
Canadeo, Tony 1974	+ Leemans, Tuffy 1978	Sayers, Gale 1977
Csonka, Larry 1987	Matson, Ollie 1972	Simpson, O.J 1985
Dickerson, Eric 1999	McAfee, George 1966	+ Strong, Ken 1967
Dorsett, Tony 1994	McElhenny, Hugh 1970	Taylor, Jim 1976
Dudley, Bill 1966	+ McNally, Johnny (Blood) ..1963	+ Thorpe, Jim 1963
Gifford, Frank 1977	Moore, Lenny 1975	Trippi, Charley 1968
+ Grange, Red 1963	+ Motley, Marion 1968	Van Buren, Steve 1965
+ Guyon, Joe 1966	+ Nagurski, Bronko 1963	+ Walker, Doak 1986
Harris, Franco 1990	+ Nevers, Ernie 1963	

Ends & Wide Receivers

Alworth, Lance 1978	+ Hutson, Don 1963	Newsome, Ozzie 1999
+ Badgro, Red 1981	Joiner, Charlie 1996	Pihos, Pete 1970
Berry, Raymond 1973	Largent, Steve 1995	Smith, Jackie 1994
Biletnikoff, Fred 1988	Lavelli, Dante 1975	Stallworth, John 2002
Casper, Dave 2002	Lofton, James 2003	Swann, Lynn 2001
+ Chamberlin, Guy 1965	Mackey, John 1992	Taylor, Charley 1984
Ditka, Mike 1988	Maynard, Don 1987	Warfield, Paul 1983
Fears, Tom 1970	McDonald, Tommy 1998	Winslow, Kellen 1995
+ Hewitt, Bill 1971	+ Millner, Wayne 1968	
Hirsch, Elroy (Crazylegs) ..1968	Mitchell, Bobby 1983	

Linemen (pre-World War II)

+ Edwards, Turk (T) 1969	+ Hubbard, Cal (T) 1963	+ Musso, George (T-G) 1982
+ Fortmann, Dan (G) 1985	+ Kiesling, Walt (G) 1966	+ Stydahar, Joe (T) 1967
+ Healey, Ed (T) 1964	+ Kinard, Bruiser (T) 1971	+ Trafton, George (C) 1964
+ Hein, Mel (C) 1963	+ Lyman, Link (T) 1964	+ Turner, Bulldog (C) 1966
+ Henry, Pete (T) 1963	+ Michalske, Mike (G) 1964	+ Wojciechowicz, Alex (C) ..1968

Offensive Linemen

Bednarik, Chuck (C-LB) 1967	Langer, Jim (C) 1987	Ringo, Jim (C) 1981
Brown, Bob (T) 2004	Little, Larry (G) 1993	St. Clair, Bob (T) 1990
Brown, Roosevelt (T) 1975	Mack, Tom (G) 1999	Shaw, Billy (G) 1999
DeLamielleure, Joe (G) 2003	McCormack, Mike (T) 1984	Shell, Art (T) 1989
Dierdorf, Dan (T) 1996	Mix, Ron (T-G) 1979	Slater, Jackie (T) 2001
Gatski, Frank (C) 1985	Munchak, Mike (G) 2001	Stephenson, Dwight (C) ..1998
Gregg, Forrest (T-G) 1977	Munoz, Anthony (T) 1998	Upshaw, Gene (G) 1987
Groza, Lou (T-PK) 1974	+ Musso, George (T-G) 1982	Yary, Ron (T) 2001
Hannah, John (G) 1991	Otto, Jim (C) 1980	+ Webster, Mike (C) 1997
Jones, Stan (T-G-DT) 1991	Parker, Jim (G) 1973	

Defensive Linemen

Atkins, Doug	1982	
Bethea, Elvin	2003	
+ Buchanan, Buck	1990	
Creekmur, Lou	1996	
Davis, Willie	1981	
Donovan, Art	1968	
Eller, Carl	2004	
+ Ford, Len	1976	
Greene, Joe	1987	

Hampton, Dan	2002
Jones, Deacon	1980
+ Jordan, Henry	1995
Lilly, Bob	1980
Long, Howie	2000
Marchetti, Gino	1972
+ Nomellini, Leo	1969
Olsen, Merlin	1982
Page, Alan	1988

Robustelli, Andy	1971
Selmon, Lee Roy	1995
Stautner, Ernie	1969
+ Weinmeister, Arnie	1984
White, Randy	1994
Willis, Bill	1977
Youngblood, Jack	2001

Linebackers

Bell, Bobby	1983
Buoniconti, Nick	2001
Butkus, Dick	1979
Connor, George (DT-OT)	1975
+ George, Bill	1974

Ham, Jack	1988
Hendricks, Ted	1990
Huff, Sam	1982
Lambert, Jack	1990
Lanier, Willie	1986

+ Nitschke, Ray	1978
Schmidt, Joe	1973
Singletary, Mike	1998
Taylor, Lawrence	1999
Wilcox, Dave	2000

Defensive Backs

Adderley, Herb	1980
Barney, Lem	1992
Blount, Mel	1989
Brown, Willie	1984
+ Christiansen, Jack	1970
Haynes, Michael	1997

Houston, Ken	1986
Johnson, Jimmy	1994
Krause, Paul	1998
+ Lane, Dick (Night Train)	1974
Lary, Yale	1979
Lott, Ronnie	2000

Renfro, Mel	1996
+ Tunnell, Emlen	1967
Wilson, Larry	1978
Wood, Willie	1989

Placekicker

Stenerud, Jan	1991

Coaches

+ Allen, George	2002
+ Brown, Paul	1967
+ Ewbank, Weeb	1978
+ Flaherty, Ray	1976
Gibbs, Joe	1996
Gillman, Sid	1983

Grant, Bud	1994
+ Halas, George	1963
+ Lambeau, Curly	1963
+ Landry, Tom	1990
Levy, Marv	2001
+ Lombardi, Vince	1971

+ Neale, Earle (Greasy)	1969
Noll, Chuck	1993
+ Owen, Steve	1966
Shula, Don	1997
Stram, Hank	2003
Walsh, Bill	1993

Contributors

+ Bell, Bert	1963
+ Bidwill, Charles	1967
+ Carr, Joe	1963
Davis, Al	1992
+ Finks, Jim	1995
+ Halas, George	1963

Hunt, Lamar	1972
+ Mara, Tim	1963
Mara, Wellington	1997
+ Marshall, George	1963
+ Ray, Hugh (Shorty)	1966
+ Reeves, Dan	1967

+ Rooney, Art	1964
Rooney, Dan	2000
+ Rozelle, Pete	1985
Schramm, Tex	1991

NFL's All-Time Team

Selected by the Pro Football Hall of Fame voters and released Aug. 1, 2000 as part of the NFL Century celebration.

Offense

Wide Receivers: Don Hutson and Jerry Rice
Tight End: John Mackey
Tackles: Roosevelt Brown and Anthony Munoz
Guards: John Hannah and Jim Parker
Center: Mike Webster
Quarterback: Johnny Unitas
Running Backs: Jim Brown and Walter Payton

Defense

Ends: Deacon Jones and Reggie White
Tackles: Joe Greene and Bob Lilly
Linebackers: Dick Butkus, Jack Ham and Lawrence Taylor
Cornerbacks: Mel Blount and Dick (Night Train) Lane
Safeties: Ronnie Lott and Larry Wilson

Specialists

Placekicker: Jan Stenerud
Punter: Ray Guy
Kick Returner: Gale Sayers

Punt Returner: Deion Sanders
Special Teams: Steve Tasker

GOLF

World Golf Hall of Fame

The World Golf Hall of Fame opened its doors in 1998 at the World Golf Village outside of Jacksonville, Fla. **Address:** One World Golf Place, St. Augustine, FL 32092. **Telephone:** (904) 940-4000. **Eligibility:** Professionals have three avenues into the WGHF. A PGA Tour player qualifies for the ballot if he has at least 10 victories in approved tournaments, or at least two victories among The Players Championship, Masters, U.S. Open, British Open and PGA Championship, is at least 40 years old and has been a member of the Tour for 10 years. A senior PGA Tour player qualifies if he has been a Senior Tour member for five years and has 20 wins between the PGA Tour and Senior Tour or five wins among the PGA majors, the Players Championship and the senior majors (U.S. Senior Open, Tradition, PGA Seniors' Championship and Senior Players Championship). Final selections for both Veteran's and Lifetime Achievement Categories are made by the Executive Committee of the World Golf Hall of Fame, which includes leaders from the major golf organizations.

Any player qualifying for the LPGA Hall automatically qualifies for the WGHF. Until 1999, nominees must have had played 10 years on the LPGA tour and won 30 official events, including two major championships; 35 official events and one major; or 40 official events and no majors. The eligibility requirements were loosened somewhat in 1999. The new guidelines are based on a system which awards two points for winning a major and one point for winning other tournaments, the Vare trophy (for lowest scoring average) and the player of the year award. Players must win at least one major, Vare trophy, or player of the year award and accumulate a total of 27 points to be inducted. For players not eligible for either the PGA Tour or the LPGA Hall of Fame, a body of over 300 international golf writers and historians will vote each year.

Members are listed with year of induction; (+) indicates deceased members.

Class of 2004 (4): MEN—**Isao Aoki, Tom Kite** and **Charlie Sifford**; WOMEN—**Marlene Stewart Streit**.

Note: Karrie Webb (2005) already has enough points for entrance into the Hall but will be inducted after her 10th LPGA season.

Men

+ Anderson, Willie 1975	Faldo, Nick 1997	Nicklaus, Jack 1974
Aoki, Isao 2004	Floyd, Ray 1989	Norman, Greg 2001
+ Armour, Tommy 1976	+ Guldahl, Ralph 1981	+ Ouimet, Francis 1974
+ Ball, John, Jr 1977	+ Hagen, Walter 1974	Palmer, Arnold 1974
Ballesteros, Seve 1999	+ Hilton, Harold 1978	Player, Gary 1974
+ Barnes, Jim 1989	+ Hogan, Ben 1974	Price, Nick 2003
Beman, Deane 2000	Irwin, Hale 1992	+ Robertson, Allan 2001
Bolt, Tommy 2002	Jacklin, Tony 2002	+ Runyan, Paul 1990
Bonallack, Sir Michael 2000	Jacobs, John 2000	+ Sarazen, Gene 1974
+ Boros, Julius 1982	+ Jones, Bobby 1974	Sifford, Charlie 2004
+ Braid, James 1976	Kite, Tom 2004	+ Smith, Horton 1990
Burke, Jack Jr. 2000	Langer, Bernhard 2002	+ Snead, Sam 1974
Casper, Billy 1978	+ Little, Lawson 1980	+ Stewart, Payne 2001
Coles, Neil 2000	Littler, Gene 1990	+ Taylor, John H 1975
+ Cooper, Lighthorse Harry . .1992	+ Locke, Bobby 1977	Thomson, Peter 1988
+ Cotton, Sir Henry 1980	+ Mangrum, Lloyd 1998	+ Travers, Jerry 1976
Crenshaw, Ben 2002	+ Middlecoff, Cary 1986	+ Travis, Walter 1979
+ Demaret, Jimmy 1983	Miller, Johnny 1996	Trevino, Lee 1981
De Vicenzo, Roberto 1989	+ Morris, Tom Jr 1975	+ Vardon, Harry 1974
+ Diegel, Leo 2003	+ Morris, Tom Sr 1976	Watson, Tom 1988
+ Evans, Chick 1975	Nelson, Byron 1974	

Women

Alcott, Amy 1999	+ Howe, Dorothy C.H 1978	Sorenstam, Annika 2003
Berg, Patty 1974	Inkster, Julie 2000	Streit, Marlene Stewart 2004
Bradley, Pat 1986	Jameson, Betty 1951	Suggs, Louise 1979
Carner, JoAnne 1985	King, Betsy 1995	+ Vare, Glenna Collett 1975
Caponi, Donna 2001	Lopez, Nancy 1989	+ Wethered, Joyce 1975
Daniel, Beth 1999	Mann, Carol 1977	Whitworth, Kathy 1982
Hagge, Marlene 2002	Rankin, Judy 2000	Wright, Mickey 1976
Haynie, Sandra 1977	Rawls, Betsy 1987	+ Zaharias, Babe Didrikson . .1974
Higuchi, Chako 2003	Sheehan, Patty 1993	

Contributors

Bell, Judy 2001	+ Harlow, Robert 1988	+ Ross, Donald 1977
Campbell, William 1990	+ Hope, Bob 1983	+ Solheim, Karsten 2001
+ Corcoran, Fred 1975	+ Jones, Robert Trent 1987	+ Shore, Dinah 1994
+ Crosby, Bing 1978	+ Penick, Harvey 2002	+ Tufts, Richard 1992
+ Dey, Joe 1975	+ Roberts, Clifford 1978	
+ Graffis, Herb 1977	Rodriguez, Chi Chi 1992	

HOCKEY

Hockey Hall of Fame

Established in 1945 by the National Hockey League and opened in 1961. **Address:** BCE Place, 30 Yonge Street, Toronto, Ontario, M5E 1X8. **Telephone:** (416) 360-7735.

Eligibility: Nominated players and referees must be retired three years. However that waiting period has now been waived 10 times. Players that have had the waiting period waived are indicated with an asterisk. Voting done by 18-member panel made up of pro and amateur hockey personalities and media representatives. A 15-member Veterans Committee that selected older players was eliminated in 2000.

Class of 2004 (4): PLAYERS—D **Ray Bourque**, Boston (1979-2000), Colorado (2000-01); D **Paul Coffey**, Edmonton (1980-87), Pittsburgh (1987-92), Los Angeles (1991-1993), Detroit (1992-96), Hartford (1996), Philadelphia (1996-98), Chicago (1998), Carolina (1998-2000), Boston (2000-01); D **Larry Murphy**, Los Angeles (1980-83), Washington (1983-89), Minnesota (1998-91), Pittsburgh (1990-95), Toronto (1995-97), Detroit (1997-2001). BUILDER—**Cliff Fletcher**, executive.

Members are listed with year of induction; (+) indicates deceased members.

Forwards

+ Abel, Sid 1969	+ Gardner, Jimmy 1962	+ Nighbor, Frank 1947
+ Adams, Jack 1959	Gartner, Mike 2001	+ Noble, Reg 1962
+ Apps, Syl 1961	Geoffrion, Bernie 1972	+ O'Connor, Buddy 1988
Armstrong, George 1975	+ Gerard, Eddie 1945	+ Oliver, Harry 1967
+ Bailey, Ace 1975	Gilbert, Rod 1982	Olmstead, Bert 1985
+ Bain, Dan 1945	Gillies, Clark 2002	+ Patrick, Lynn 1980
+ Baker, Hobey 1945	+ Gilmour, Billy 1962	Perreault, Gilbert 1990
Barber, Bill 1990	Goulet, Michel 1998	+ Phillips, Tom 1945
+ Barry, Marty 1965	Gretzky, Wayne* 1999	+ Primeau, Joe 1963
Bathgate, Andy 1978	+ Griffis, Si 1950	Pulford, Bob 1991
+ Bauer, Bobby 1996	Hawerchuk, Dale 2001	+ Rankin, Frank 1961
Beliveau, Jean* 1972	+ Hay, George 1958	Ratelle, Jean 1985
+ Bentley, Doug 1964	+ Hextall, Bryan 1969	Richard, Henri 1979
+ Bentley, Max 1966	+ Hooper, Tom 1962	+ Richard, Maurice (Rocket)* .1961
+ Blake, Toe 1966	Howe, Gordie* 1972	+ Richardson, George 1950
Bossy, Mike 1991	+ Howe, Syd 1965	+ Roberts, Gordie 1971
+ Boucher, Frank 1958	Hull, Bobby 1983	+ Russel, Blair 1965
+ Bowie, Dubbie 1945	+ Hyland, Harry 1962	+ Russell, Ernie 1965
+ Broadbent, Punch 1962	+ Irvin, Dick 1958	+ Ruttan, Jack 1962
Bucyk, John (Chief) 1981	+ Jackson, Busher 1971	Savard, Denis 2000
+ Burch, Billy 1974	+ Joliat, Aurel 1947	+ Scanlan, Fred 1965
Clarke, Bobby 1987	+ Keats, Duke 1958	Schmidt, Milt 1961
+ Colville, Neil 1967	Kennedy, Ted (Teeder) 1966	+ Schriner, Sweeney 1962
+ Conacher, Charlie 1961	Keon, Dave 1986	+ Seibert, Oliver 1961
Conacher, Roy 1998	Kurri, Jari 2001	Shutt, Steve 1993
+ Cook, Bill 1952	Lach, Elmer 1966	+ Siebert, Babe 1964
+ Cook, Bun 1995	Lafleur, Guy 1988	Sittler, Darryl 1989
Cournoyer, Yvan 1982	LaFontaine, Pat 2003	+ Smith, Alf 1962
Cowley, Bill 1968	+ Lalonde, Newsy 1950	Smith, Clint 1991
+ Crawford, Rusty 1962	Laprade, Edgar 1993	+ Smith, Hooley 1972
+ Darragh, Jack 1962	Lemaire, Jacques 1984	+ Smith, Tommy 1973
+ Davidson, Scotty 1950	Lemieux, Mario* 1997	+ Stanley, Barney 1962
+ Day, Hap 1961	+ Lewis, Herbie 1989	Stastny, Peter 1998
Delvecchio, Alex 1977	Lindsay, Ted* 1966	+ Stewart, Nels 1962
+ Denneny, Cy 1959	+ MacKay, Mickey 1952	+ Stuart, Bruce 1961
Dionne, Marcel 1992	Mahovlich, Frank 1981	+ Taylor, Fred (Cyclone) 1947
+ Drillon, Gordie 1975	+ Malone, Joe 1950	+ Trihey, Harry 1950
+ Drinkwater, Graham 1950	+ Marshall, Jack 1965	Trottier, Bryan 1997
Dumart, Woody 1992	+ Maxwell, Fred 1962	Ullman, Norm 1982
+ Dunderdale, Tommy 1974	McDonald, Lanny 1992	+ Walker, Jack 1960
+ Dye, Babe 1970	+ McGee, Frank 1945	+ Walsh, Marty 1962
Esposito, Phil 1984	+ McGimsie, Billy 1962	+ Watson, Harry (Whipper) . .1994
+ Farrell, Arthur 1965	Mikita, Stan 1983	+ Watson, Harry (Moose) . . .1962
Federko, Bernie 2002	Moore, Dickie 1974	+ Weiland, Cooney 1971
+ Foyston, Frank 1958	+ Morenz, Howie 1945	+ Westwick, Harry (Rat) 1962
+ Frederickson, Frank 1958	+ Mosienko, Bill 1965	+ Whitcroft, Fred 1962
Gainey, Bob 1992	Mullen, Joe 2000	

+ Benedict, Clint 1965
Bower, Johnny 1976
+ Brimsek, Frankie 1966
+ Broda, Turk 1967
Cheevers, Gerry 1985
+ Connell, Alex 1958
Dryden, Ken 1983
+ Durnan, Bill 1964
Esposito, Tony 1988
Fuhr, Grant 2003
+ Gardiner, Chuck 1945

Boivin, Leo 1986
+ Boon, Dickie 1952
+ Bouchard, Butch 1966
+ Boucher, George 1960
Bourque, Ray 2004
+ Cameron, Harry 1962
+ Clancy, King 1958
+ Clapper, Dit* 1947
+ Cleghorn, Sprague 1958
Coffey, Paul 2004
+ Conacher, Lionel 1994
+ Coulter, Art 1974
+ Dutton, Red 1958
Fetisov, Viacheslav 2001
Flaman, Fernie 1990
Gadsby, Bill 1970
+ Gardiner, Herb 1958
+ Goheen, F.X. (Moose) 1952
+ Goodfellow, Ebbie 1963
+ Grant, Mike 1950

Armstrong, Neil 1991
Ashley, John 1981
Chadwick, Bill 1964
D'Amico, John 1993
+ Elliott, Chaucer 1961

+ Adams, Charles 1960
+ Adams, Weston W. Sr 1972
+ Ahearn, Frank 1962
+ Ahearne, J.F. (Bunny) 1977
+ Allan, Sir Montagu 1945
Allen, Keith 1992
Arbour, Al 1996
+ Ballard, Harold 1977
+ Bauer, Fr. David 1989
+ Bickell, J.P. 1978
Bowman, Scotty 1991
+ Brown, George 1961
+ Brown, Walter 1962
+ Buckland, Frank 1975
Bush, Walter 2000
Butterfield, Jack 1980
+ Calder, Frank 1945
+ Campbell, Angus 1964
+ Campbell, Clarence 1966
+ Cattarinich, Joseph 1977
+ Dandurand, Leo 1963
+ Dilio, Frank 1964
+ Dudley, George 1958
+ Dunn, James 1968
Fletcher, Cliff 2004
Francis, Emile 1982
+ Gibson, Jack 1976
+ Gorman, Tommy 1963
+ Griffiths, Frank A. 1993
+ Hanley, Bill 1986
+ Hay, Charles 1984
+ Hendy, Jim 1968

Goaltenders

Giacomin, Eddie 1987
+ Hainsworth, George 1961
Hall, Glenn 1975
+ Hern, Riley 1962
+ Holmes, Hap 1972
+ Hutton, J.B. (Bouse) 1962
+ Lehman, Hughie 1958
+ LeSueur, Percy 1961
+ Lumley, Harry 1980
+ Moran, Paddy 1958

Defensemen

+ Green, Wilf (Shorty) 1962
+ Hall, Joe 1961
+ Harvey, Doug 1973
Horner, Red 1965
+ Horton, Tim 1977
Howell, Harry 1979
+ Johnson, Ching 1958
+ Johnson, Ernie 1952
Johnson, Tom 1970
Kelly, Red* 1969
Langway, Rod 2002
Laperriere, Jacques 1987
Lapointe, Guy 1993
+ Laviolette, Jack 1962
+ Mantha, Sylvio 1960
+ McNamara, George 1958
Murphy, Larry 2004
Orr, Bobby* 1979
Park, Brad 1988
+ Patrick, Lester 1947

Referees & Linesmen

+ Hayes, George 1988
+ Hewitson, Bobby 1963
+ Ion, Mickey 1961
Pavelich, Matt 1987
+ Rodden, Mike 1962

Builders

+ Hewitt, Foster 1965
+ Hewitt, W.A. 1945
+ Hume, Fred 1962
+ Ilitch, Mike 2003
+ Imlach, Punch 1984
+ Ivan, Tommy 1964
+ Jennings, Bill 1975
+ Johnson, Bob 1992
+ Juckes, Gordon 1979
+ Kilpatrick, John 1960
Kilrea, Brian 2003
+ Knox, Seymour III 1993
+ Leader, Al 1969
+ LeBel, Bob 1970
+ Lockhart, Tom 1965
+ Loicq, Paul 1961
+ Mariucci, John 1985
Mathers, Frank 1992
+ McLaughlin, Frederic 1963
+ Milford, Jake 1984
+ Molson, Hartland 1973
Morrison, Ian (Scotty) 1999
+ Murray, Athol (Pere) 1998
+ Nelson, Francis 1945
+ Neilson, Roger 2002
+ Norris, Bruce 1969
+ Norris, James D 1962
+ Norris, James Sr 1958
+ Northey, William 1945
+ O'Brien, J.A 1962
O'Neill, Brian 1994
Page, Fred 1993

Parent, Bernie 1984
+ Plante, Jacques 1978
+ Rayner, Chuck 1973
+ Sawchuk, Terry* 1971
Smith, Billy 1993
+ Thompson, Tiny 1959
Tretiak, Vladislav 1989
+ Vezina, Georges 1945
Worsley, Gump 1980
+ Worters, Roy 1969

Pilote, Pierre 1975
+ Pitre, Didier 1962
Potvin, Denis 1991
+ Pratt, Babe 1966
Pronovost, Marcel 1978
+ Pulford, Harvey 1945
+ Quackenbush, Bill 1976
Reardon, Kenny 1966
Robinson, Larry 1995
+ Ross, Art 1945
Salming, Borje 1996
Savard, Serge 1986
+ Seibert, Earl 1963
+ Shore, Eddie 1947
+ Simpson, Joe 1962
Stanley, Allan 1981
+ Stewart, Jack 1964
+ Stuart, Hod 1945
+ Wilson, Gordon (Phat) 1962

+ Smeaton, J. Cooper 1961
Storey, Red 1967
Udvari, Frank 1973
van Hellemond, Andy 1999

Patrick, Craig 2001
+ Patrick, Frank 1958
+ Pickard, Allan 1958
+ Pilous, Rudy 1985
Poile, Bud 1990
Pollock, Sam 1978
+ Raymond, Donat 1958
+ Robertson, John Ross 1945
+ Robinson, Claude 1945
+ Ross, Philip 1976
+ Sabetzki, Gunther 1995
Sather, Glen 1997
+ Selke, Frank 1960
Sinden, Harry 1983
+ Smith, Frank 1962
+ Smythe, Conn 1958
Snider, Ed 1988
+ Stanley, Lord of Preston . . .1945
+ Sutherland, James 1945
+ Tarasov, Anatoli 1974
Torrey, Bill 1995
+ Turner, Lloyd 1958
+ Tutt, William Thayer 1978
+ Voss, Carl 1974
+ Waghorne, Fred 1961
+ Wirtz, Arthur 1971
Wirtz, Bill 1976
Ziegler, John 1987

Note: Alan Eagleson was inducted into the Hockey Hall of Fame in 1989 but resigned in 1998 after being found guilty of fraud.

U.S. Hockey Hall of Fame

Established in 1968 by the Eveleth (Minn.) Civic Association Project H Committee and opened in 1973. **Address:** 801 Hat Trick Ave., P.O. Box 657, Eveleth, MN 55734. **Telephone:** (218) 744-5167.

Eligibility: Nominated players and referees must be American-born and retired five years; coaches must be American-born and must have coached predominantly American teams. Voting done by 12-member panel made up of Hall of Fame members and U.S. hockey officials.

Class of 2004 (4): PLAYERS—**Paul Coppo, Phil Housley** and **Mark Johnson**. OWNER—**Mike Ilitch**.

Members are listed with year of induction; (+) indicates deceased members.

Players

+ Abel, Clarence (Taffy) 1973	Fusco, Mark 2002	Mayasich, John 1976
+ Baker, Hobey 1973	Fusco, Scott 2002	McCartan, Jack 1983
Bartholome, Earl 1977	+ Garrison, John 1974	Moe, Bill 1974
+ Bessone, Peter 1978	Garrity, Jack 1986	Morrow, Ken 1995
Blake, Bob 1985	+ Goheen, Frank (Moose) . . .1973	+ Moseley, Fred 1975
Boucha, Henry 1995	Grant, Wally 1994	Mullen, Joe 1998
+ Brimsek, Frankie 1973	+ Harding, Austie 1975	+ Murray, Hugh (Muzz) Sr . . .1987
Broten, Neal 2000	Housley, Phil 2004	+ Nelson, Hub 1978
Cavanagh, Joe 1994	Howe, Mark 2003	+ Nyrop, William D. 1997
+ Chaisson, Ray 1974	Iglehart, Stewart 1975	Olson, Eddie 1977
Chase, John 1973	Ikola, Willard 1990	+ Owen, George 1973
Christian, Bill 1984	Johnson, Mark 2004	+ Palmer, Winthrop 1973
Christian, Dave 2001	Johnson, Paul 2001	Paradise, Bob 1989
Christian, Roger 1989	Johnson, Virgil 1974	+ Purpur, Clifford (Fido) 1974
Cleary, Bill 1976	+ Karakas, Mike 1973	Ramsey, Mike 2001
Cleary, Bob 1981	Kirrane, Jack 1987	Riley, Bill 1977
+ Conroy, Tony 1975	LaFontaine, Pat 2003	Riley, Joe 2002
Coppo, Paul 2004	+ Lane, Myles 1973	+ Romnes, Elwin (Doc) 1973
Curran, Mike 1998	Langevin, Dave 1993	+ Rondeau, Dick 1985
+ Dahlstrom, Carl (Cully) 1973	Langway, Rod 1999	Sheehy, Timothy 1997
+ Desjardins, Vic 1974	Larson, Reed 1996	Watson, Gordie 1999
+ Desmond, Richard 1988	+ Linder, Joe 1975	+ Williams, Tom 1981
+ Dill, Bob 1979	+ LoPresti, Sam 1973	+ Winters, Frank (Coddy) 1973
Dougherty, Richard 2003	+ Mariucci, John 1973	+ Yackel, Ken 1986
+ Everett, Doug 1974	Matchefts, John 1991	
Ftorek, Robbie 1991	+ Mather, Bruce 1998	

Coaches

+ Almquist, Oscar 1983	Heyliger, Vic 1974	Pleban, Connie 1990
Bessone, Amo 1992	+ Holt Jr., Charles E. 1997	Ramsay, Mike 2001
+ Brooks, Herb 1990	Ikola, Willard 1990	Riley, Jack 1979
Ceglarski, Len 1992	+ Jeremiah, Eddie 1973	+ Ross, Larry 1988
Cunniff, John 2003	+ Johnson, Bob 1991	+ Thompson, Cliff 1973
+ Fullerton, James 1992	Johnson, Paul 2001	+ Stewart, Bill 1982
Gambucci, Sergio 1996	Kelley, Jack 1993	Watson, Sid 1999
+ Gordon, Malcolm 1973	+ Kelly, John (Snooks) 1974	+ Winsor, Ralph 1973
Harkness, Ned 1994	Nanne, Lou 1998	Woog, Doug 2002

Referee

Chadwick, Bill 1974

Contributor

+ Schulz, Charles M. 1993

Administrators

+ Brown, George 1973	+ Jennings, Bill 1981	Ridder, Bob 1976
+ Brown, Walter 1973	+ Kahler, Nick 1980	Trumble, Hal 1970
Bush, Walter 1980	+ Lockhart, Tom 1973	+ Tutt, Thayer 1973
+ Clark, Don 1978	Marvin, Cal 1982	Wirtz, Bill 1967
Claypool, Jim 1995	Palazzari, Doug 2000	+ Wright, Lyle 1973
+ Gibson, J.L. (Doc) 1973	Patrick, Craig 1996	
Ilitch, Mike 2004	Pleau, Larry 2000	

Members of Both Hockey and U.S. Hockey Halls of Fame

Players	**Coach**		**Builders**
Hobey Baker	Bob Johnson	George Brown	Bill Jennings
Frankie Brimsek		Walter Brown	Tom Lockhart
Frank (Moose) Goheen	**Referee**	Walter Bush	Craig Patrick
Pat LaFontaine	Bill Chadwick	Doc Gibson	Thayer Tutt
Rod Langway		Mike Ilitch	Bill Wirtz
John Mariucci			
Joe Mullen			

HORSE RACING

National Museum of Racing and Hall of Fame

Established in 1950 by the Saratoga Springs Racing Association and opened in 1955. **Address:** National Museum of Racing and Hall of Fame, 191 Union Ave., Saratoga Springs, NY 12866. **Telephone:** (518) 584-0400.

Eligibility: Nominated horses must be retired five years; jockeys must be active at least 15 years; trainers must be active at least 25 years. Voting done by 125-member panel of horse racing media.

Class of 2004 (4): JOCKEY—**Kent Desormeaux**. TRAINER—**Shug McGaughey**. HORSES—**Flawlessly** and **Skip Away**.

Members are listed with year of induction; (+) indicates deceased members.

Jockeys

+ Adams, Frank (Dooley)* 1970	Fishback, Jerry* 1992	+ Parke, Ivan 1978
+ Adams, John 1965	+ Garner, Andrew (Mack) 1969	+ Patrick, Gil 1970
+ Aitcheson, Joe Jr.* 1978	+ Garrison, Snapper 1955	Pincay, Laffit Jr. 1975
+ Arcaro, Eddie 1958	+ Gomez, Avelino 1982	+ Purdy, Sam 1970
Atkinson, Ted 1957	+ Griffin, Henry 1956	+ Reiff, John 1956
Baeza, Braulio 1976	+ Guerin, Eric 1972	+ Robertson, Alfred 1971
Bailey, Jerry 1995	Hartack, Bill 1959	Rotz, John L. 1983
+ Barbee, George 1996	Hawley, Sandy 1992	+ Sande, Earl 1955
+ Bassett, Carroll* 1972	+ Johnson, Albert 1971	+ Shilling, Carroll 1970
Baze, Russell 1999	+ Knapp, Willie 1969	+ Shoemaker, Bill 1958
+ Blum, Walter 1987	Krone, Julie 2000	+ Simms, Willie 1977
+ Bostwick, George H.* 1968	+ Kummer, Clarence 1972	+ Sloan, Todhunter 1955
+ Boulmetis, Sam 1973	+ Kurtsinger, Charley 1967	Smith, Mike 2003
+ Brooks, Steve 1963	+ Loftus, Johnny 1959	+ Smithwick, A. Patrick* 1973
Brumfield, Don 1996	Longden, Johnny 1958	Stevens, Gary 1997
+ Burns, Tommy 1983	Maher, Danny 1955	+ Stout, James 1968
+ Butwell, Jimmy 1984	+ McAtee, Linus 1956	+ Taral, Fred 1955
+ Byers, J.D. (Dolly) 1967	McCarron, Chris 1989	+ Tuckerman, Bayard Jr.* 1973
Cauthen, Steve 1994	+ McCreary, Conn 1975	Turcotte, Ron 1979
+ Coltiletti, Frank 1970	+ McKinney, Rigan 1968	+ Turner, Nash 1955
Cordero, Angel Jr. 1988	+ McLaughlin, James 1955	Ussery, Robert 1980
+ Crawford, Robert (Specs)* ..1973	+ Miller, Walter 1955	Vasquez, Jacinto 1998
Day, Pat 1991	+ Murphy, Isaac 1955	Velasquez, Jorge 1990
Delahoussaye, Eddie 1993	+ Neves, Ralph 1960	+ Westrope, Jack 2002
Desormeaux, Kent 2004	+ Notter, Joe 1963	+ Woolf, George 1955
+ Ensor, Lavelle (Buddy) 1962	+ O'Connor, Winnie 1956	+ Workman, Raymond 1956
+ Fator, Laverne 1955	+ Odom, George 1955	Ycaza, Manuel 1977
Fires, Earlie 2001	+ O'Neill, Frank 1956	*Steeplechase jockey

Harness Racing Museum & Hall of Fame

Established by the U.S. Harness Writers Association (USHWA) in 1958. **Address:** Trotting Horse Museum, 240 Main Street, P.O. Box 590, Goshen, NY 10924; **Telephone:** (845) 294-6330.

Eligibility: Open to all harness racing drivers, trainers and executives. Voting done by USHWA membership. There are 88 members of the Living Hall of Fame, but only the 48 drivers and trainer-drivers are listed below.

Class of 2004 (1): TRAINER/DRIVERS—**John Simpson Jr.**

Members are listed with years of induction; (+) indicates deceased members.

Trainer-Drivers

Abbatiello, Carmine 1986	Farrington, Bob 1980	Miller, Del 1969
Abbatiello, Tony 1995	Filion, Herve 1976	+ O'Brien, Joe 1971
Ackerman, Doug 1995	+ Garnsey, Glen 1983	O'Donnell, Bill 1991
+ Avery, Earle 1975	Galbraith, Clint 1990	Patterson, John Sr 1994
+ Baldwin, Ralph 1972	Gilmour, Buddy 1990	+ Pownall, Harry 1971
Beissinger, Howard 1975	Harner, Levi 1986	Remmen, Ray 1998
Bostwick, Dunbar 1989	Harvey, Harry M. 2002	Riegle, Gene 1992
+ Cameron, Del 1975	+ Haughton, Billy 1969	+ Russell, Sanders 1971
Campbell, John 1991	+ Hodgins, Clint 1973	+ Shively, Bion 1968
+ Chapman, John 1980	Insko, Del 1981	Sholty, George 1985
Cruise, Jimmy 1987	Kopas, Jack 1996	Simpson, John Sr 1972
Dancer, Stanley 1970	Lachance, Mike 1996	Simpson, John Jr. 2004
Dancer, Vernon 2001	Lindstedt, Berndt 2003	+ Smart, Curly 1970
Dennis, Jim 2002	Magee, Dave 2001	Sylvester, Charles 1998
Doherty, James 2003	Manzi, Catello 2002	Waples, Keith 1987
+ Ervin, Frank 1969	McIntosh, Robert 2003	Waples, Ron 1994

Horse Racing (Cont.)
Trainers

+ Barrera, Laz ...1979
+ Bedwell, H. Guy ...1971
+ Brown, Edward D. ...1984
Burch, Elliot ...1980
+ Burch, Preston M. ...1963
+ Burch, W.P. ...1955
+ Burlew, Fred ...1973
+ Childs, Frank E. ...1968
+ Clark, Henry ...1982
+ Cocks, W. Burling ...1985
Conway, James P. ...1996
Croll, Jimmy ...1994
Delp, Bud ...2002
Drysdale, Neil ...2000
+ Duke, William ...1956
+ Feustel, Louis ...1964
+ Fitzsimmons, J. (Sunny Jim) ...1958
Frankel, Bobby ...1995
+ Gaver, John M. ...1966
+ Healey, Thomas ...1955
+ Hildreth, Samuel ...1955
+ Hine, Hubert (Sonny) ...2003
+ Hirsch, Max ...1959
+ Hirsch, W.J. (Buddy) ...1982
+ Hitchcock, Thomas Sr. ...1973
+ Hughes, Hollie ...1973

+ Hyland, John ...1956
+ Jacobs, Hirsch ...1958
+ Jerkens, H. Allen ...1975
Johnson, Philip ...1997
+ Johnson, William R. ...1986
+ Jolley, LeRoy ...1987
+ Jones, Ben A. ...1958
+ Jones, H.A. (Jimmy) ...1959
+ Joyner, Andrew ...1955
Kelly, Tom ...1993
+ Laurin, Lucien ...1977
+ Lewis, J. Howard ...1969
Lukas, D. Wayne ...1999
+ Luro, Horatio ...1980
Mandella, Richard ...2001
+ Madden, John ...1983
+ Maloney, Jim ...1989
Martin, Frank (Pancho) ...1981
McAnally, Ron ...1990
+ McDaniel, Henry ...1956
McGaughey, Shug ...2004
+ Miller, MacKenzie ...1987
+ Molter, William, Jr. ...1960
Mott, Bill ...1998
+ Mulholland, Winbert ...1967
+ Neloy, Eddie ...1983

Nerud, John ...1972
+ Parke, Burley ...1986
+ Penna, Angel Sr. ...1988
+ Pincus, Jacob ...1988
+ Rogers, John ...1955
+ Rowe, James Sr. ...1955
Schulhofer, Scotty ...1992
Sheppard, Jonathan ...1990
+ Smith, Robert A. ...1976
Smith, Tom ...2001
+ Smithwick, Mike ...1976
+ Stephens, Woody ...1976
Tenny, Mesh ...1991
+ Thompson, H.J. ...1969
+ Trotsek, Harry ...1984
Van Berg, Jack ...1985
+ Van Berg, Marion ...1970
+ Veitch, Sylvester ...1977
+ Walden, Robert ...1970
Walsh, Michael ...1997
+ Ward, Sherrill ...1978
+ Whiteley, Frank Jr. ...1978
+ Whittingham, Charlie ...1974
+ Williamson, Ansel ...1998
Winfrey, W.C. (Bill) ...1971

Horses
Year foaled in parentheses.

A.P. Indy (1989) ...2000
+ Ack Ack (1966) ...1986
Affectionately (1960) ...1989
+ Affirmed (1975) ...1980
All-Along (1979) ...1990
+ Alsab (1939) ...1976
+ Alydar (1975) ...1989
Alysheba (1984) ...1993
+ American Eclipse (1814) ...1970
+ Armed (1941) ...1963
+ Artful (1902) ...1956
+ Arts and Letters (1966) ...1994
+ Assault (1943) ...1964
+ Battleship (1927) ...1969
+ Bayakoa (1984) ...1998
+ Bed O'Roses (1947) ...1976
+ Beldame (1901) ...1956
+ Ben Brush (1893) ...1955
+ Bewitch (1945) ...1977
+ Bimelech (1937) ...1990
+ Black Gold (1919) ...1989
+ Black Helen (1932) ...1991
+ Blue Larkspur (1926) ...1957
+ Bold 'n Determined (1977) ...1997
+ Bold Ruler (1954) ...1973
+ Bon Nouvel (1960) ...1976
+ Boston (1833) ...1955
+ Broomstick (1901) ...1956
+ Buckpasser (1963) ...1970
+ Busher (1942) ...1964
+ Bushranger (1930) ...1967
+ Cafe Prince (1970) ...1985
+ Carry Back (1958) ...1975
+ Cavalcade (1931) ...1993
+ Challendon (1936) ...1977
+ Chris Evert (1971) ...1988
+ Cicada (1959) ...1967
Cigar (1990) ...2002
+ Citation (1945) ...1959
+ Coaltown (1945) ...1983
+ Colin (1905) ...1956
+ Commando (1898) ...1956

+ Count Fleet (1940) ...1961
+ Crusader (1923) ...1995
+ Dahlia (1971) ...1981
+ Damascus (1964) ...1974
Dance Smartly (1989) ...2003
+ Dark Mirage (1965) ...1974
+ Davona Dale (1976) ...1985
+ Desert Vixen (1970) ...1979
+ Devil Diver (1939) ...1980
+ Discovery (1931) ...1969
+ Domino (1891) ...1955
+ Dr. Fager (1964) ...1971
Easy Goer (1986) ...1997
+ Eight 30 (1936) ...1994
+ Elkridge (1938) ...1966
+ Emperor of Norfolk (1885) ...1988
+ Equipoise (1928) ...1957
+ Exceller (1973) ...1999
+ Exterminator (1915) ...1957
+ Fairmount (1921) ...1985
+ Fair Play (1905) ...1956
+ Firenze (1885) ...1981
Flatterer (1979) ...1994
Flawlessly (1989) ...2004
+ Foolish Pleasure (1972) ...1995
+ Forego (1971) ...1979
+ Fort Marcy (1964) ...1998
+ Gallant Bloom (1966) ...1977
+ Gallant Fox (1927) ...1957
+ Gallant Man (1954) ...1987
+ Gallorette (1942) ...1962
+ Gamely (1964) ...1980
Genuine Risk (1977) ...1986
+ Good and Plenty (1900) ...1956
+ Go For Wand (1987) ...1996
+ Granville (1933) ...1997
+ Grey Lag (1918) ...1957
+ Gun Bow (1960) ...1999
+ Hamburg (1895) ...1986
+ Hanover (1884) ...1955
+ Henry of Navarre (1891) ...1985
+ Hill Prince (1947) ...1991

+ Hindoo (1878) ...1955
Holy Bull (1991) ...2001
+ Imp (1894) ...1965
+ Jay Trump (1957) ...1971
John Henry (1975) ...1990
+ Johnstown (1936) ...1992
+ Jolly Roger (1922) ...1965
+ Kingston (1884) ...1955
+ Kelso (1957) ...1967
+ Kentucky (1861) ...1983
Lady's Secret (1982) ...1992
+ La Prevoyante (1970) ...1995
+ L'Escargot (1963) ...1977
+ Lexington (1850) ...1955
+ Longfellow (1867) ...1971
+ Luke Blackburn (1877) ...1956
+ Majestic Prince (1966) ...1988
+ Man o' War (1917) ...1957
Maskette (1906) ...2001
Miesque (1984) ...1999
+ Miss Woodford (1880) ...1967
+ Myrtlewood (1933) ...1979
+ Nashua (1952) ...1965
+ Native Dancer (1950) ...1963
+ Native Diver (1959) ...1978
+ Needles (1953) ...2000
+ Neji (1950) ...1966
+ Noor (1945) ...2002
+ Northern Dancer (1961) ...1976
+ Oedipus (1941) ...1978
+ Old Rosebud (1911) ...1968
+ Omaha (1932) ...1965
+ Pan Zareta (1910) ...1972
+ Parole (1873) ...1984
Personal Ensign (1984) ...1993
Paseana (1987) ...2001
+ Peter Pan (1904) ...1956
Precisionist (1983) ...2003
Princess Rooney (1980) ...1991
+ Real Delight (1949) ...1987
+ Regret (1912) ...1957
+ Reigh Count (1925) ...1978

Riva Ridge (1969) 1998
+ Roamer (1911) 1981
+ Roseben (1901) 1956
+ Round Table (1954) 1972
+ Ruffian (1972) 1976
+ Ruthless (1864) 1975
+ Salvator (1886) 1955
+ Sarazen (1921) 1957
+ Seabiscuit (1933) 1958
+ Searching (1952) 1978
+ Seattle Slew (1974) 1981
+ Secretariat (1970) 1974
Serena's Song (1992) 2002

+ Shuvee (1966) 1975
+ Silver Spoon (1956) 1978
+ Sir Archy (1805) 1955
+ Sir Barton (1916) 1957
Skip Away (1993) 2004
Slew o' Gold (1980) 1992
+ Sun Beau (1925) 1996
+ Sunday Silence (1986) 1996
+ Stymie (1941) 1975
+ Susan's Girl (1969) 1976
+ Swaps (1952) 1966
+ Sword Dancer (1956) 1977
+ Sysonby (1902) 1956

+ Ta Wee (1966) 1994
+ Tim Tam (1955) 1985
+ Tom Fool (1949) 1960
+ Top Flight (1929) 1966
+ Tosmah (1961) 1984
+ Twenty Grand (1928) 1957
+ Twilight Tear (1941) 1963
+ War Admiral (1934) 1958
+ Whirlaway (1938) 1959
+ Whisk Broom II (1907) 1979
Winning Colors (1985) 2000
Zaccio (1976) 1990
+ Zev (1920) 1983

Exemplars of Racing

+ Hanes, John W 1982
+ Jeffords, Walter M 1973

+ Mellon, Paul 1989

Widener, George D 1971

MEDIA

National Sportscasters and Sportswriters Hall of Fame

Established in 1959 by the National Sportscasters and Sportswriters Association. A permanent museum for the NSSA Hall of Fame opened on May 1, 2000. **Address:** 322 East Innes St., Salisbury, NC 28144. **Telephone:** (704) 633-4275.
Eligibility: Nominees must be active for at least 25 years. Voting done by NSSA membership and other media representatives.
Class of 2004 (2): **Joe Garagiola** and **Jerome Holtzman.**
Members are listed with year of induction; (+) indicates deceased members.

Sportscasters

+ Allen, Mel 1972
+ Barber, Walter (Red) 1973
+ Brickhouse, Jack 1983
+ Buck, Jack 1990
+ Caray, Harry 1989
+ Cosell, Howard 1993
+ Dean, Dizzy 1976
+ Dunphy, Don 1986
+ Elson, Bob 1995
Enberg, Dick 1996
Garagiola, Joe 2004
+ Glickman, Marty 1992

Gowdy, Curt 1981
Harwell, Ernie 1989
+ Hearn, Chick 1997
+ Hodges, Russ 1975
+ Hoyt, Waite 1987
+ Husing, Ted 1963
Jackson, Keith 1995
+ McCarthy, Clem 1970
McKay, Jim 1987
+ McNamee, Graham 1964
Michaels, Al 1998
Miller, Jon 1999

Murphy, Bob 2002
+ Nelson, Lindsey 1979
+ Prince, Bob 1986
Schenkel, Chris 1981
+ Scott, Ray 1982
Scully, Vin 1991
Simpson, Jim 2000
+ Stern, Bill 1974
Summerall, Pat 1994
Whitaker, Jack 2001
Wolff, Bob 2003

Sportswriters

Anderson, Dave 1990
Bisher, Furman 1989
Broeg, Bob 1997
+ Burick, Si 1985
+ Cannon, Jimmy 1986
+ Carmichael, John P. 1994
Collins, Bud 2002
+ Connor, Dick 1992
+ Considine, Bob 1980
+ Daley, Arthur 1976
Deford, Frank 1998
Durslag, Mel 1995
+ Gould, Alan 1990

+ Graham, Frank Sr. 1995
+ Grimsley, Will 1987
Heinz, W.C. 2001
Holtzman, Jerome 2004
Izenberg, Jerry 2000
Jenkins, Dan 1996
+ Kieran, John 1971
+ Lardner, Ring 1967
+ McDonough, Will 2003
+ Murphy, Jack 1988
+ Murray, Jim 1978
Olderman, Murray 1993
+ Parker, Dan 1975

Pope, Edwin 1994
+ Povich, Shirley 1984
+ Rice, Grantland 1962
+ Runyon, Damon 1964
Russell, Fred 1988
Sherrod, Blackie 1991
+ Smith, Walter (Red) 1977
+ Spink, J.G. Taylor 1969
+ Steadman, John 1999
Vecsey, George 2001
+ Ward, Arch 1973
+ Woodward, Stanley 1974

MOTORSPORTS

Motorsports Hall of Fame of America

Established in 1989. **Mailing Address:** P.O. Box 194, Novi, MI 48376. **Telephone:** (248) 349-7223.
Eligibility: Nominees must be retired at least three years or engaged in their area of motorsports for at least 20 years. Areas include: open wheel, stock car, dragster, sports car, motorcycle, off road, power boat, air racing, land speed records, historic and at-large.
Class of 2004 (7): DRIVERS—**Joe Amato** (drag racing), **Geoff Brabham** (open wheel), **Johnnie Parsons** (open wheel), **Bobby Rahal** (open wheel), **Don Vesco** (motorcycles). CONTRIBUTORS—**Bill France Jr.** and **Shav Glick.**
Members are listed with year of induction; (+) indicates deceased members.

Drivers

Allison, Bobby 1992
Amato, Joe 2004
Andretti, Mario 1990
Arfons, Art 1991
+ Baker, Buck 1998
+ Baker, Cannonball 1989
+ Bettenhausen, Tony 1997
Brabham, Geoff 2004

Breedlove, Craig 1993
Bryan, Jimmy 1999
+ Campbell, Sir Malcolm 1994
+ Cantrell, Bill 1992
+ Chenoweth, Dean 1991
+ Chevrolet, Gaston 2002
Chrisman, Art 1997
+ Clark, Jim 1990

+ Cook, Betty 1996
+ Cooper, Earl 2001
Cunningham, Briggs 1997
+ Davis, Jim 1997
+ D'Eath, Tom 2000
DeCoster, Roger 1994
+ DePalma, Ralph 1992
+ DePaolo, Peter 1995

Motorsports (Cont.)

+ Donahue, Mark 1990	Kenyon, Mel 2003	+ Petrali, Joe 1992
+ Earnhardt, Dale 2002	+ Kurtis, Frank 1999	+ Petty, Lee 1996
Fittipaldi, Emerson 2001	Lawson, Eddie 2002	Petty, Richard 1989
Flock, Tim 1999	Leonard, Joe 1991	Prudhomme, Don 1991
Follmer, George 1999	+ Lockhart, Frank 1999	Rahal, Bobby 2004
Foyt, A.J 1989	Lorenzen, Fred 2001	Resweber, Carroll 1998
Garlits, Don 1989	+ McLaren, Bruce 1995	Redman, Brian 2002
Glidden, Bob 1994	Mann, Dick 1993	+ Revson, Peter 1996
+ Gregg, Peter 2000	Markle, Bart 1999	+ Roberts, Fireball 1995
Gurney, Dan 1991	+ Mays, Rex 1995	Roberts, Kenny 1990
Hanauer, Chip 1995	McEwen, Tom 2001	Rutherford, Johnny 1996
Hannah, Bob 2000	Mears, Rick 1998	Seebold, Bill 1999
+ Hanks, Sam 2000	+ Meyer, Louis 1993	+ Shaw, Wilbur 1991
+ Harroun, Ray 2000	+ Miles, Ken 2001	Slovak, Mira 2001
Hart, C.J. 1999	+ Milton, Tommy 1998	Smith, Malcolm 1996
Hill, Eddie 2002	Muldowney, Shirley 1990	Spencer, Freddie 2001
Hill, Phil 1989	+ Muncy, Bill 1989	+ Thompson, Mickey 1990
+ Hinnershitz, Tommy 2003	+ Murphy, Jimmy 1998	Unser, Al 1991
+ Holbert, Al 1993	+ Musson, Ron 1993	Unser, Bobby 1994
+ Horn, Ted 1993	Nickelson, Don 1998	Vesco, Don 2004
+ Hulme, Denis 1998	Nixon, Gary 2003	+ Vukovich, Bill Sr 1992
Jarrett, Ned 1997	+ Nordskog, Bob 1997	Waltrip, Darrell 2003
Jenkins, Bill (Grumpy) 1996	+ Oldfield, Barney 1989	Ward, Rodger 1995
Johncock, Gordon 2002	Ongais, Danny 2000	+ Wood, Gar 1990
Johnson, Junior 1991	Parks, Wally 1993	Yarborough, Cale 1994
Jones, Parnelli 1992	+ Parsons, Johnnie 2004	
Kalitta, Connie 1992	Pearson, David 1993	

Contributors

+ Agajanian, J.C 1992	France, Bill Jr. 2004	+ Offenhauser, Fred 2002
Bignotti, George 1993	+ France, Bill Sr. 1990	Penske, Roger 1995
+ Black, Keith 1995	Glick, Shav 2004	+ Rickenbacker, Eddie 1994
Bondurant, Bob 2003	Granatelli, Andy 2001	+ Rose, Mauri 1996
+ Brawner, Clint 1998	Hall, Jim 1994	Shelby, Carroll 1992
Chapman, Colin 1997	+ Hulman, Tony 1991	Simpson, Bill 2003
+ Chevrolet, Louis 1995	+ Jones, Ted 2003	Watson, A.J. 1996
+ Donovan, Ed 2003	+ Kiekhaefer, Carl 1998	Wood, Glen 2000
Duesenberg, Fred 1997	Little, Bernie 1994	Wood, Leonard 2000
Economaki, Chris 1994	+ Miller, Harry 1999	+ Yunick, Smokey 2000
+ Ford, Henry 1996		

International Motorsports Hall of Fame

Established in 1990 by the International Motorsports Hall of Fame Commission. **Mailing Address:** P.O. Box 1018, Talladega, AL 35160. **Telephone:** (256) 362-5002.

Eligibility: Nominees must be retired from their specialty in motorsports for five years. Voting done by 150-member panel made up of the world-wide auto racing media. Members are listed with year of induction; (+) indicates deceased members.

Class of 2004 (5): DRIVERS—**Charles "Red" Farmer** (stock cars), **Shirley Muldowney** (drag racing), **Bill Muncey** (hydroplane racing), **Bobby Rahal** (open wheel). CONTRIBUTORS—**Bill France Jr.**.

Drivers

Allison, Bobby 1993	+ Holbert, Al 1993	Prodhomme, Don 2000
Andretti, Mario 2000	+ Hulme, Denis 2002	Prost, Alain 1999
+ Ascari, Alberto 1992	Ickx, Jacky 2002	Rahal, Bobby 2004
+ Baker, Buck 1990	+ Isaac, Bobby 1996	+ Richmond, Tim 2002
Bonnett, Neil 2001	Jarrett, Ned 1991	+ Roberts, Fireball 1990
+ Bettenhausen, Tony 1991	Johncock, Gordon 1999	Roberts, Kenny 1992
Brabham, Jack 1990	Johnson, Junior 1990	Rose, Mauri 1994
Bryan, Jimmy 2001	Jones, Parnelli 1990	Rutherford, Johnny 1996
+ Campbell, Sir Malcolm 1990	Kenyon, Mel 2003	Scott, Wendell 1999
+ Caracciola, Rudolph 1998	+ Kulwicki, Alan 2002	+ Senna, Ayrton 2000
+ Clark, Jim 1990	Lauda, Niki 1993	+ Shaw, Wilbur 1991
+ DePalma, Ralph 1991	Lorenzen, Fred 1991	Smith, Louise 1999
+ Donahue, Mark 1990	+ Lund, Tiny 1994	Stewart, Jackie 1990
+ Evans, Richie 1996	+ Mays, Rex 1993	Surtees, John 1996
+ Fangio, Juan Manuel 1990	+ McLaren, Bruce 1991	+ Thomas, Herb 1994
Farmer, Charles 2004	+ Meyer, Louis 1992	+ Turner, Curtis 1992
Fittipaldi, Emerson 2003	Moss, Stirling 1990	Unser, Al Sr. 1998
+ Flock, Tim 1991	Muldowney, Shirley 2004	Unser, Bobby 1990
Foyt, A.J. 2000	+ Muncey, Bill 2004	+ Vukovich, Bill 1991
+ Gregg, Peter 1992	+ Nuvolari, Tazio 1998	Ward Rodger 1992
Gurney, Dan 1990	+ Oldfield, Barney 1990	+ Weatherly, Joe 1994
Hailwood, Mike 2001	Parsons, Benny 1994	Wood, Glen 2002
+ Haley, Donald 1996	Pearson, David 1993	Yarborough, Cale 1993
+ Hill, Graham 1990	+ Petty, Lee 1990	
Hill, Phil 1991	Piquet, Nelson 2000	

Contributors

Bignotti, George 1993	France, Bill Jr. 2004	Parks, Wally 1992
Breedlove, Craig 2000	+ France, Bill Sr 1990	Penske, Roger 1998
+ Bugatti, Ettore 2002	Granatelli, Andy 1992	+ Porsche, Ferdinand 1996
+ Chapman, Colin 1994	+ Hulman, Tony 1990	+ Rickenbacker, Eddie 1992
+ Chevrolet, Louis 1992	+ Hyde, Harry 1999	Shelby, Carroll 1991
+ Cunningham, Briggs 2003	Marcum, John 1994	+ Thompson, Mickey 1990
+ Ferrari, Enzo 1994	+ Matthews, Banjo 1998	Watson, A.J. 2003
+ Ford, Henry 1993	Moody, Ralph 1994	+ Yunick, Smokey 1990
Fox, Ray 2003	+ Offenhauser, Fred 2001	

OLYMPICS

U.S. Olympic Hall of Fame

Established in 1983 by the United States Olympic Committee. **Mailing Address:** U.S. Olympic Committee, 1750 East Boulder Street, Colorado Springs, CO 80909. Plans for a permanent museum site have been suspended due to lack of funding. **Telephone:** (719) 866-4529.

Eligibility: Nominated athletes must be four years removed from their last Olympic competition. Voting for membership in the Hall was suspended in 1993 but resumed in 2004. Voting from 1983-92 was done by National Sportscasters and Sportswriters Association, Hall of Fame members and the USOC board members of directors. Beginning in 2004 the voting weight was divided among U.S. Olympians, select U.S. Olympic family/media and fans.

Members are listed with year of induction; (+) indicates deceased members.

Teams

1956 Basketball Dick Boushka, Carl Cain, Chuck Darling, Bill Evans, Gib Ford, Burdy Haldorson, Bill Hougland, Bob Jeangerard, K.C. Jones, Bill Russell, Ron Tomsic, +Jim Walsh and coach +Gerald Tucker.
1960 Basketball Jay Arnette, Walt Bellamy, Bob Boozer, Terry Dischinger, Burdy Haldorson, Darrall Imhoff, Allen Kelley, +Lester Lane, Jerry Lucas, Oscar Robertson, Adrian Smith, Jerry West and coach Pete Newell.
1964 Basketball Jim Barnes, Bill Bradley, Larry Brown, Joe Caldwell, Mel Counts, Richard Davies, Walt Hazzard, Luke Jackson, John McCaffrey, Jeff Mullins, Jerry Shipp, George Wilson and coach +Hank Iba.
1960 Ice Hockey Billy Christian, Roger Christian, Billy Cleary, Bob Cleary, Gene Grazia, Paul Johnson, Jack Kirrane, John Mayasich, Jack McCartan, Bob McKay, Dick Meredith, Weldon Olson, Ed Owen, Rod Paavola, Larry Palmer, Dick Rodenheiser, +Tom Williams and coach Jack Riley.
1980 Ice Hockey Bill Baker, Neal Broten, Dave Christian, Steve Christoff, Jim Craig, Mike Eruzione, John Harrington, Steve Janaszak, Mark Johnson, Ken Morrow, Rob McClanahan, Jack O'Callahan, Mark Pavelich, Mike Ramsey, Buzz Schneider, Dave Silk, Eric Strobel, Bob Suter, Phil Verchota, Mark Wells and coach Herb Brooks.
1996 Women's Soccer Michelle Akers, Brandi Chastain, Amanda Cromwell, Joy Fawcett, Julie Foudy, Carin Gabarra, Mia Hamm, Mary Harvey, Kristine Lilly, Shannon MacMillan, Tiffeny Milbrett, Carla Overbeck, Cindy Parlow, Tiffany Roberts, Briana Scurry, Thori Staples Bryan, Tisha Venturini, Saskia Webber, Staci Wilson and coach Tony DiCicco.

Alpine Skiing

Mahre, Phil 1992

Bobsled

+ Eagan, Eddie (see Boxing) .1983

Boxing

Clay, Cassius* 1983
+ Eagan, Eddie (see Bobsled) .1983
Foreman, George 1990
Frazier, Joe 1989
Leonard, Sugar Ray 1985
Patterson, Floyd 1987
*Clay changed name to Muhammad Ali in 1964.

Cycling

Carpenter-Phinney, Connie .1992

Diving

King, Miki 1992
Lee, Sammy 1990
Louganis, Greg 1985
McCormick, Pat 1985

Figure Skating

Albright, Tenley 1988
Button, Dick 1983
Fleming, Peggy 1983
Hamill, Dorothy 1991
Hamilton, Scott 1990

Gymnastics

Conner, Bart 1991
Retton, Mary Lou 1985
Vidmar, Peter 1991

Rowing

+ Kelly, Jack Sr. 1990

Speed Skating

Blair, Bonnie 2004
Heiden, Eric 1983
Jansen, Dan 2004

Swimming

Babashoff, Shirley 1987
Biondi, Matt 2004
Caulkins, Tracy 1990
+ Daniels, Charles 1988
de Varona, Donna 1987
Evans, Janet 2004
+ Kahanamoku, Duke 1984
+ Madison, Helene 1992
Meyer, Debbie 1986
Naber, John 1984
Schollander, Don 1983
Spitz, Mark 1983
+ Weissmuller, Johnny 1983

Track & Field

Beamon, Bob 1983
Boston, Ralph 1985
+ Calhoun, Lee 1991
Campbell, Milt 1992
Coachman, Alice 2004
+ Davenport, Willie 1991
Davis, Glenn 1986
+ Didrikson, Babe 1983
Dillard, Harrison 1983
Evans, Lee 1989
+ Ewry, Ray 1983
Fosbury, Dick 1992
Jenner, Bruce 1986
Johnson, Rafer 1983
+ Joyner, Florence Griffith . . .2004
Joyner-Kersee, Jackie 2004
+ Kraenzlein, Alvin 1985

Lewis, Carl 1985
Mathias, Bob 1983
Mills, Billy 1984
Morrow, Bobby 1989
Moses, Edwin 1985
O'Brien, Parry 1984
Oerter, Al 1983
+ Owens, Jesse 1983
+ Paddock, Charley 1991
Richards, Bob 1983
+ Rudolph, Wilma 1983
+ Sheppard, Mel 1989
Shorter, Frank 1984
+ Thorpe, Jim 1983
Toomey, Bill 1984
Tyus, Wyomia 1985
Whitfield, Mal 1988
+ Wykoff, Frank 1984

Weight Lifting

+ Davis, John 1989
Kono, Tommy 1990

Wrestling

Gable, Dan 1985

Contributors

+ Arledge, Roone 1989
+ Brundage, Avery 1983
+ Bushnell, Asa 1990
Greenspan, Bud 2004
Hull, Col. Don 1992
+ Iba, Hank 1985
+ Kane, Robert 1986
+ Kelly, Jack Jr. 1992
McKay, Jim 1988
Miller, Don 1984
+ Simon, William 1991
Walker, LeRoy 1987

SOCCER

International Football Hall of Champions

Established in 1998 by FIFA, soccer's international governing body. Located at Disneyland Paris.

Eligibility: Nominated players and coaches must be retired at least five years. Nominations made by a committee composed of FIFA members, the Hall of Champions management and three ad hoc members then submit a list to a panel of 32 soccer journalists from around the world who also have the chance to add nominees of their own as well as voting for a specific number of candidates in each category.

Note: There have been no inductions since 2001.

Players

+ Andrade, José Leandro (URU) 2001
 Beckenbauer, Franz (W. Ger) 1998
 Best, George (N. Ire) 2000
 Charlton, Sir Bobby (ENG) .1998
 Cruyff, Johan (NED) 1998
+ Didi (BRA) 2000
 Distefano, Alfredo (ARG/SPA) 1998
 Eusebio (POR) 1998
 Fontaine, Just (FRA) 1999
+ Garrincha (BRA) 1999
+ Matthews, Sir Stanley (ENG) .1998
+ Meazza, Giuseppe (ITA) ...2001
+ Moore, Bobby (ENG) 1999
 Müller, Gerd (W. Ger) 1999
 Pele (BRA) 1998
 Plantini, Michel (FRA) 1998
 Puskas, Ferenc (HUN/SPA) .1998
 Van Basten, Marko (HOL) ...2000

+ Yashin, Lev (RUS) 1998
 Zico (BRA) 2000
 Zoff, Dino (ITA) 1999

Managers

+ Busby, Sir Matt (SCO) 1998
 Michels, Rinus (NED) 1998
+ Pozzo, Vittorio (ITA) 2001
+ Shankly, Bill (SCO) 1999

Referees

 Taylor, Jack (ENG) 1999
 Vautrot, Michel (FRA) 1998

Pioneers

 Havelange, Joao (BRA) 1999
+ Rimet, Jules (FRA) 1998

Club Teams

 Ajax Amsterdam (NED) 1999
 FC Barcelona (SPA) 2000
 Real Madrid (SPA) 1998

National Teams

 Argentina 2001
 Brazil 1998
 Germany 1999
 Italy 2000

Media

 Ferran, Jacques (FRA) 1999
 Goddett, Jacques (FRA) ...1998

For the Good of the Game

+ Dassler, Horst (GER) 1998
+ Sastre, Fernard (FRA) 1999

National Soccer Hall of Fame

Established in 1950 by the Philadelphia Oldtimers Association. First exhibit unveiled in Oneonta, NY in 1982. Moved into new Hall of Fame building in the summer of 1999. **Address:** 18 Stadium Circle, Oneonta, NY 13820. **Telephone:** (607) 432-3351.

Eligibility: Nominated players must have represented the U.S. in international competition and be retired five years; other categories include Meritorious Service and Special Commendation.

Nominations made by state organizations and a veterans' committee. Voting done by nine-member committee made up of Hall of Famers, U.S. Soccer officials and members of the national media.

Class of 2004 (3): **Michelle Akers, Paul Caligiuri** and **Eric Wynalda**.

Members are listed with home state and year of induction; (+) indicates deceased members.

Members

 Abronzino, Umberto (CA) ..1971
 Aimi, Milton (TX) 1991
 Akers, Michelle (CA) 2004
 Alberto, Carlos (Bra) 2003
+ Alonso, Julie (NY) 1972
+ Andersen, William (NY) ...1956
 Annis, Robert (MO) 1976
+ Ardizzone, John (CA) 1971
+ Armstrong, James (NY) ...1952
+ Auld, Andrew (RI) 1986
 Bachmeier, Adolph (IL) ...2002
 Bahr, Walter (PA) 1976
+ Barr, George (NY) 1983
+ Barriskill, Joe (NY) 1953
+ Beardsworth, Fred (MA) ...1965
 Beckenbauer, Franz (Ger) .1998
 Berling, Clay (CA) 1995
 Bernabei, Ray (PA) 1978
+ Best, John O. (CA) 1982
 Bogicevic, Vladislav (Yug) .2002
+ Bookie, Michael (PA) 1986
+ Booth, Joseph (CT) 1952
 Borghi, Frank (MO) 1976
 Boulos, Frenchy (NY) 1980
+ Boxer, Matt (CA) 1961
 Bradley, Gordon (Eng) 1996
+ Briggs, Lawrence E. (MA) ..1978
+ Brittan, Harold (PA) 1951
+ Brock, John (MA) 1950
+ Brown, Andrew M. (OH) ...1950
+ Brown, David (NJ) 1951
 Brown, George (NJ) 1995
+ Brown, James (NY) 1986
+ Cahill, Thomas W (NY) ...1950

 Caligiuri, Paul (CA) 2004
+ Carenza, Joe (MO) 1982
+ Caraffi, Ralph (OH) 1959
 Chacurian, Chico (CT) 1992
+ Chesney, Stan (NY) 1966
 Child, Paul (Eng) 2003
 Chinaglia, Giorgio (Italy) ..2000
+ Chyzowych, Walter (PA) ..1997
+ Coll, John (NY) 1986
+ Collins, George M. (MA) ..1951
+ Collins, Peter (NY) 1998
+ Colombo, Charlie (MO) ...1976
+ Commander, Colin (OH) ...1967
 Coombes, Geoff (MI) 1976
+ Cordery, Ted (CA) 1975
+ Craddock, Robert (PA) ...1959
 Craddock Jr., Robert (PA) .1976
+ Craggs, Edmund (WA) 1969
 Craggs, George (WA) 1981
+ Cummings, Wilfred R. (IL) .1953
 Danilo, Paul (PA) 1997
 Davis, Rick (CA) 2001
+ Delach, Joseph (PA) 1973
 DeLuca, Enzo (NY) 1979
+ Dick, Walter (CA) 1989
 Diorio, Nick (PA) 1974
+ Donaghy, Edward J. (NY) .1951
+ Donelli, Buff (PA) 1954
+ Donnelly, George (NY) ...1989
+ Douglas, Jimmy (NJ) 1953
+ Dresmich, John W. (PA) ...1968
+ Duff, Duncan (CA) 1972
+ Duggan, Thomas (NJ) 1951
+ Dunn, James (MO) 1974

+ Edwards, Gene (WI) 1985
+ Ely, Alexander (PA) 1997
+ Epperlein, Rudy (NJ) 1951
 Ertegun, Ahmet (NY) 2003
 Ertegun, Nesuhi (NY) 2003
+ Fairfield, Harry (PA) 1951
 Feibusch, Ernst (CA) 1984
+ Ferguson, John (PA) 1950
+ Fernley, John A. (MA) 1951
+ Ferro, Charles (NY) 1958
+ Fishwick, George E. (IL) ..1974
+ Flamhaft, Jack (NY) 1964
+ Fleming, Harry G. (PA) ...1967
+ Florie, Thomas (NJ) 1986
+ Foulds, Pal (MA) 1953
+ Foulds, Sam (MA) 1969
+ Fowler, Dan (NY) 1970
+ Fowler, Peg (NY) 1979
+ Fricker, Werner (PA) 1992
+ Fryer, William J. (NJ) 1951
 Gabarra, Carin (CA) 2000
+ Gaetjens, Joe (NY) 1976
+ Gallagher, James (NY) ...1986
+ Garcia, Pete (MO) 1964
 Gard, Gino (IL) 1976
+ Gentle, James (PA) 1986
 Getzinger, Rudy (IL) 1991
+ Giesler, Walter (MO) 1962
+ Glover, Teddy (NY) 1965
+ Gonsalves, Billy (MA) 1950
 Gormley, Bob (PA) 1989
+ Gould, David L. (PA) 1953
+ Govier, Sheldon (IL) 1950
 Granitza, Karl-Heinz (Ger) .2003

+ Greer, Don (CA) 1985	+ McGhee, Bart (NY) 1986	+ Rottenberg, Jack (NJ) 1971
Gryzik, Joe (IL) 1973	+ McGrath, Frank (MA) 1978	Roy, Willy (IL) 1989
+ Guelker, Bob (MO) 1980	+ McGuire, Jimmy (NY) 1951	+ Ryan, Hun (PA) 1958
Guennel, Joe (CO) 1980	+ McGuire, John (NY) 1951	+ Sager, Tom (PA) 1968
Harker, Al (PA) 1979	+ McIlveney, Eddie (PA) 1976	Saunders, Harry (NY) 1981
+ Healey, George (MI) 1951	McLaughlin, Bennie (PA) 1977	Schaller, Willy (IL) 1995
Heilpern, Herb (NY) 1988	+ McSkimming, Dent (MO) 1951	Schellscheidt, Mannie (NJ) . .1990
Heinrichs, April (CO) 1998	Merovich, Pete (PA) 1971	+ Schillinger, Emil (PA) 1960
+ Hemmings, William (IL) 1961	+ Mieth, Werner (NJ) 1974	+ Schroeder, Elmer (PA) 1951
Hermann, Robert (MO) 2001	+ Millar, Robert (NY) 1950	+ Scwarcz, Erno (NY) 1951
Higgins, Shannon (NC) 2002	Miller, Al (OH) 1995	+ Shields, Fred (PA) 1968
Howard, Ted (NY) 2003	+ Miller, Milton (NY) 1971	+ Single, Erwin (NY) 1981
+ Hudson, Maurice (CA) 1966	+ Mills, Jimmy (PA) 1954	Slone, Philip (NY) 1986
Hunt, Lamar (TX) 1982	Monsen, Lloyd (NY) 1994	+ Smith, Alfred (PA) 1951
Hynes, John (NY) 1977	+ Moore, James F. (MO) 1971	Smith, Patrick (OH) 1998
+ Iglehart, Alfredda (MD) 1951	Moore, Johnny (CA) 1997	+ Souza, Ed (MA) 1976
+ Japp, John (PA) 1953	+ Moorehouse, George (NY) . . .1986	Souza, Clarkie (MA) 1976
+ Jeffrey, William (PA) 1951	+ Morrison, Robert (PA) 1951	+ Spalding, Dick (PA) 1951
+ Johnston, Jack (IL) 1952	+ Morrissette, Bill (MA) 1967	Spath, Reinhold (NY) 1997
+ Kabanica, Mike (WI) 1987	Murphy, Edward (IL) 1998	+ Stark, Archie (NJ) 1950
Kehoe, Bob (MO) 1990	Nanoski, Jukey (PA) 1993	+ Steelink, Nicolaas (CA) 1971
+ Kelly, Frank (NJ) 1994	+ Netto, Fred (IL) 1958	Stern, Lee (IL) 2003
+ Kempton, George (WA) 1950	Newman, Ron (CA) 1992	+ Steur, August (NY) 1969
+ Keough, Harry (MO) 1976	+ Niotis, D.J. (IL) 1963	+ Stewart, Douglas (PA) 1950
+ Klein, Paul (NJ) 1953	Ntsoelengoe, Ace (S.Afr.) . .2003	+ Stone, Robert T. (CO) 1971
Kleinaitis, Al (IN) 1995	+ O'Brien, Shamus (NY) 1990	+ Swords, Thomas (MA) 1951
+ Kozma, Oscar (CA) 1964	Olaff, Gene (NJ) 1971	+ Tintle, Joseph (NJ) 1952
+ Kracher, Frank (IL) 1983	+ Oliver, Arnie (MA) 1968	Toye, Clive (NY) 2003
Kraft, Granny (MD) 1984	Oliver, Len (PA) 1996	+ Tracey, Ralph (MO) 1986
+ Kraus, Harry (NY) 1963	+ Palmer, William (PA) 1952	+ Triner, Joseph (IL) 1951
Kropfelder, Nicholas 1996	Pariani, Gino (MO) 1976	+ Vaughn, Frank (MO) 1986
+ Kunter, Rudy (NY) 1963	+ Patenaude, Bert (MA) 1971	+ Walder, Jimmy (PA) 1971
+ Lamm, Kurt (NY) 1979	+ Pearson, Eddie (GA) 1990	+ Wallace, Frank (MO) 1976
Lang, Millard (MD) 1950	+ Peel, Peter (IL) 1951	+ Washauer, Adolph (CA) 1977
Larson, Bert (CT) 1988	Pel|fe (Brazil) 1993	+ Webb, Tom (WA) 1987
Lenarduzzi, Bob (Can) . . .2003	+ Peters, Wally (NJ) 1967	+ Weir, Alex (NY) 1975
+ Lewis, H. Edgar (PA) 1950	Phillipson, Don (CO) 1987	+ Weston, Victor (WA) 1956
Lombardo, Joe (NY) 1984	+ Piscopo, Giorgio (NY) 1978	Willey, Alan (Eng) 2003
Long, Denny (MO) 1993	Pomeroy, Edgar (CA) 1955	Wilson, Bruce (Can) 2003
Looby, Bill (MO) 2001	+ Ramsden, Arnold (TX) 1957	+ Wilson, Peter (NJ) 1950
+ MacEwan, John J. (MI) 1953	+ Ratican, Harry (MO) 1950	Wolanin, Adam (IL) 1976
+ Maca, Joe (NY) 1976	+ Reese, Doc (MD) 1957	+ Wood, Alex (MI) 1986
+ Magnozzi, Enzo (NY) 1977	+ Renzulli, Pete (NY) 1951	+ Woods, John W. (IL) 1952
+ Maher, Jack (IL) 1970	Ringsdorf, Gene (MD) 1979	Woosnam, Phil (GA) 1997
+ Manning, Dr. Randolf (NY) . .1950	Robbie, Elizabeth (FL) 2003	Wynalda, Eric (CA) 2004
+ Marre, John (MO) 1953	+ Robbie, Joe (FL) . . . : 2003	Yeagley, Jerry (IN) 1989
Mausser, Arnie (RI) 2003	+ Roe, Jimmy (MO) 1997	+ Young, John (CA) 1958
McBride, Pat (MO) 1994	Ross, Steve (NY) 2003	+ Zampini, Dan (PA) 1963
+ McClay, Allan (MA) 1971	Roth, Werner (NY) 1989	Zerhusen, Al (CA) 1978

SWIMMING

International Swimming Hall of Fame

Established in 1965 by the U.S. College Coaches' Swim Forum. **Address:** One Hall of Fame Drive, Ft. Lauderdale, FL 33316. **Telephone:** (954) 462-6536.

Categories for induction are: swimming, diving, water polo, synchronized swimming, coaching, pioneers and contributors. Coaches and contributors are not included in the following list. Only U.S. men and women listed below.

Class of 2004 (1): U.S. WOMEN—**Becky Dyroen-Lancer.**

Members are listed with year of induction; (+) indicates deceased members.

U.S. Men

+ Anderson, Miller 1967	+ Daniels, Charlie 1965	+ Glancy, Harrison 1990
Barrowman, Mike 1997	Degener, Dick 1971	Goodell, Brian 1986
Biondi, Matt 1997	DeMont, Rick 1990	+ Goodwin, Budd 1971
+ Boggs, Phil 1985	Dempsey, Frank 1996	Graef, Jed 1988
Breen, George 1975	+ Desjardins, Pete 1966	Haines, George 1977
+ Browning, Skippy 1975	Dysdale, Taylor 1994	Hall Sr., Gary 1981
Bruner, Mike 1988	Edgar, David 1996	+ Harlan, Bruce 1973
Burton, Mike 1977	+ Faricy, John 1990	Harper, Don 1998
+ Cann, Tedford 1967	+ Farrell, Jeff 1968	+ Hebner, Harry 1968
Carey, Rick 1993	+ Fick, Peter 1978	+ Heidenreich, Jerry 1992
Clark, Earl 1972	+ Flanagan, Ralph 1978	Hencken, John 1988
Clark, Steve 1966	Ford, Alan 1966	Hickcox, Charles 1976
Cleveland, Dick 1991	Furniss, Bruce 1987	Higgins, John 1971
Clotworthy, Robert 1980	Gaines, Rowdy 1995	+ Holiday, Harry 1991
+ Crabbe, Buster 1965	Garton, Tim 1997	Hough, Richard 1970

Irwin, Juno Stover	1980	
Graham, Johnston	1998	
Jager, Tom	2001	
Jastremski, Chet	1977	
+ Kahanamoku, Duke	1965	
+ Kealoha, Warren	1968	
Kiefer, Adolph	1965	
Kinsella, John	1986	
+ Kojac, George	1968	
Konno, Ford	1972	
+ Kruger, Stubby	1986	
+ Kuehn, Louis	1988	
+ Langer, Ludy	1988	
+ Langner, G. Harold	1995	
Larson, Lance	1980	
Laufer, Walter	1973	
Lee, Dr. Sammy	1968	
Lemmon, Kelley	1999	
+ LeMoyne, Harry	1988	
Lenzi, Mark	2003	
Louganis, Greg	1993	
Lundquist, Steve	1990	
Mann, Thompson	1984	
+ Martin, G. Harold	1999	
McCormick, Pat	1965	
+ McDermott, Turk	1969	
+ McGillivray, Perry	1981	
McKee, Tim	1998	

McKenzie, Don	1989	
McKinney, Frank	1975	
McLane, Jimmy	1970	
+ Medica, Jack	1966	
Montgomery, Jim	1986	
Morales, Pablo	1998	
Mulliken, Bill	1984	
Naber, John	1982	
Nakama, Keo	1975	
+ O'Connor, Wally	1966	
Oyakawa, Yoshi	1973	
+ Patnik, Al	1969	
Prew, William	1998	
+ Riley, Mickey	1977	
+ Ris, Wally	1966	
Robie, Carl	1976	
Ross, Clarence	1988	
+ Ross, Norman	1967	
Roth, Dick	1987	
Rouse, Jeff	2001	
+ Ruddy Sr., Joe	1986	
Russell, Doug	1985	
Saari, Roy	1976	
+ Schaeffer, E. Carroll	1968	
Scholes, Clarke	1980	
Schollander, Don	1965	
Schroeder, Terry	2002	
Shaw, Tim	1989	

+ Sheldon, George	1989	
Sitzberger, Ken	1994	
+ Skelton, Robert	1988	
Smith, Bill	1966	
+ Smith, Dutch	1979	
+ Smith, Jimmy	1992	
Spitz, Mark	1977	
+ Stack, Allen	1979	
Stewart, Melvin	2002	
Stickles, Ted	1995	
Stock, Tom	1989	
+ Swendsen, Clyde	1991	
Taft, Ray	1996	
Tobian, Gary	1978	
Troy, Mike	1971	
Vande Weghe, Albert	1990	
Vassallo, Jesse	1997	
+ Verdeur, Joe	1966	
Vogel, Matt	1996	
+ Vollmer, Hal	1990	
+ Wayne, Marshall	1981	
Webster, Bob	1970	
+ Weissmuller, Johnny	1965	
+ White, Al	1965	
Wiggins, Al	1994	
Wrightson, Bernie	1984	
Yorzyk, Bill	1971	

U.S. Women

Andersen, Teresa	1986	
Atwood, Sue	1992	
Babashoff, Shirley	1982	
Babb-Sprague, Kristen	1999	
Ball, Catie	1976	
+ Bauer, Sybil	1967	
Bean, Dawn Pawson	1996	
Belote, Melissa	1983	
Bleibtrey, Ethelda	1967	
+ Boyle, Charlotte	1988	
Bruner, Jayne Owen	1998	
Burke, Lynn	1978	
Bush, Lesley	1986	
Callen, Gloria	1984	
Caretto, Patty	1987	
Carr, Cathy	1988	
Caulkins, Tracy	1990	
+ Chadwick, Florence	1970	
Chandler, Jennifer	1987	
Cohen, Tiffany	1996	
+ Coleman, Georgia	1966	
Cone, Carin	1984	
Costie, Candy	1995	
Cox, Lynne	2000	
Crlenkovich, Helen	1981	
Curtis, Ann	1966	
Daniel, Ellie	1997	
de Varona, Donna	1969	
Dean, Penny	1996	
+ Dorfner, Olga	1970	
Draves, Vickie	1969	
Duenkel, Ginny	1985	
Dunbar, Barbara	2000	
Dyroen-Lancer, Becky	2004	
Ederle, Gertrude	1965	
Ellis, Kathy	1991	
Elsener, Patty	2002	
Evans, Janet	2001	
Fauntz, Jane	1991	
Ferguson, Cathy	1978	

Finneran, Sharon	1985	
+ Fulton, Patty Robinson	2001	
+ Galligan, Claire	1970	
+ Garatti-Seville, Eleanor	1992	
Gestring, Marjorie	1976	
Gossick, Sue	1988	
+ Guest, Irene	1990	
Gundling, Buelah	1965	
Hall, Kaye	1979	
Henne, Jan	1979	
Hogan, Peg	2002	
Hogshead, Nancy	1994	
Holm, Eleanor	1966	
Hunt-Newman, Virginia	1993	
Johnson, Gail	1983	
Josephson, Karen	1997	
Josephson, Sarah	1997	
+ Kaufman, Beth	1967	
+ Kight, Lenore	1981	
King, Micki	1978	
Kolb, Claudia	1975	
+ Lackie, Ethel	1969	
+ Landon, Alice Lord	1993	
Linehan, Kim	1997	
+ Madison, Helene	1966	
Mann, Shelly	1966	
McCormick, Kelly	1999	
McGrath, Margo	1989	
McKim, Josephine	1991	
Meagher, Mary T.	1993	
+ Meany, Helen	1971	
Merlino, Maxine	1999	
Meyer, Debbie	1977	
Mitchell, Betsy	1998	
Mitchell, Michele	1995	
Moe, Karen	1992	
Morris, Pam	1965	
Mueller, Ardeth	1996	
Neilson, Sandra	1986	
Neyer, Megan	1997	

+ Norelius, Martha	1967	
Olsen, Zoe Ann	1989	
O'Rourke, Heidi	1980	
+ Osipowich, Albina	1986	
Pedersen, Susan	1995	
Pinkston, Betty Becker	1967	
Pope, Paula Jean Meyers	1979	
Potter, Cynthia	1987	
+ Poynton, Dorothy	1968	
+ Rawls, Katherine	1965	
Redmond, Carol	1989	
Riggin, Aileen	1967	
Roper, Gail	1997	
Ross, Anne	1984	
Rothhammer, Keena	1991	
Ruiz-Conforto, Tracie	1993	
Ruuska, Sylvia	1976	
Sanders, Summer	2002	
Schuler, Carolyn	1989	
Seller, Peg	1988	
+ Smith, Caroline	1988	
Steinseifer, Carrie	1999	
Sterkel, Jill	2002	
Stouder, Sharon	1972	
+ Toner, Vee	1995	
Val, Laura	2003	
+ Vilen, Kay	1978	
Von Saltza, Chris	1966	
+ Wainwright, Helen	1972	
Walker, Clara Lamore	1995	
+ Watson, Lillian (Pokey)	1984	
Wayte, Mary	2000	
Wehselau, Mariechen	1989	
Welshons, Kim	1988	
Wichman, Sharon	1991	
Williams, Esther	1966	
+ Woodbridge, Margaret	1989	
Woodhead, Cynthia	1994	
Wyland, Wendy	2001	

TENNIS

International Tennis Hall of Fame

Originally the National Tennis Hall of Fame. Established in 1953 by James Van Alen and sanctioned by the U.S. Tennis Association in 1954. Renamed the International Tennis Hall of Fame in 1976. **Address:** 194 Bellevue Ave., Newport, RI 02840. **Telephone:** (401) 849-3990.

Eligibility: Nominated players must be five years removed from being a "significant factor" in competitive tennis. Voting done by members of the international tennis media.

Class of 2004 (3): **Steffi Graf, Stefan Edberg** and **Dorothy "Dodo" Cheney**.

Members are listed with year of induction; (+) indicates deceased members.

Men

+ Adee, George 1964	+ Griffin, Clarence 1970	Pietrangeli, Nicola 1986
+ Alexander, Fred 1961	+ Hackett, Harold 1961	+ Quist, Adrian 1984
+ Allison, Wilmer 1963	Hewitt, Bob 1992	Ralston, Dennis 1987
+ Alonso, Manuel 1977	+ Hoad, Lew 1980	+ Renshaw, Ernest 1983
Anderson, Malcolm 2000	+ Hovey, Fred 1974	+ Renshaw, William 1983
Ashe, Arthur 1985	+ Hunt, Joe 1966	+ Richards, Vincent 1961
+ Austin, Bunny 1997	+ Hunter, Frank 1961	+ Riggs, Bobby 1967
Becker, Boris 2003	+ Johnston, Bill 1958	Roche, Tony 1986
+ Behr, Karl 1969	+ Jones, Perry 1970	Rose, Mervyn 2001
Borg, Bjorn 1987	Kelleher, Robert 2000	Rosewall, Ken 1980
+ Borotra, Jean 1976	+ Kodes, Jan 1990	Santana, Manuel 1984
+ Bromwich, John 1984	Kramer, Jack 1968	Savitt, Dick 1976
+ Brookes, Norman 1977	+ Lacoste, Rene 1976	Schroeder, Ted 1966
+ Brugnon, Jacques 1976	+ Larned, William 1956	+ Sears, Richard 1955
+ Budge, Don 1964	Larsen, Art 1969	Sedgman, Frank 1979
+ Campbell, Oliver 1955	Laver, Rod 1981	Segura, Pancho 1984
+ Chace, Malcolm 1961	Lendl, Ivan 2001	Seixas, Vic 1971
+ Clark, Clarence 1983	+ Lott, George 1964	+ Shields, Frank 1964
+ Clark, Joseph 1955	Mako, Gene 1973	+ Slocum, Henry 1955
+ Clothier, William 1956	McEnroe, John 1999	Smith, Stan 1987
+ Cochet, Henri 1976	McGregor, Ken 1999	Stolle, Fred 1985
Connors, Jimmy 1998	+ McKinley, Chuck 1986	+ Talbert, Bill 1967
Cooper, Ashley 1991	+ McLoughlin, Maurice . . .1957	+ Tilden, Bill 1959
+ Crawford, Jack 1979	McMillan, Frew 1992	Trabert, Tony 1970
+ David, Herman 1998	+ McNeill, Don 1965	+ Van Ryn, John 1963
+ Doeg, John 1962	+ Mulloy, Gardnar 1972	Vilas, Guillermo 1991
+ Doherty, Lawrence 1980	+ Murray, Lindley 1958	+ Vines, Ellsworth 1962
+ Doherty, Reginald 1980	+ Myrick, Julian 1963	+ von Cramm, Gottfried 1977
+ Drobny, Jaroslav 1983	Nastase, Ilie 1991	+ Ward, Holcombe 1956
+ Dwight, James 1955	Newcombe, John 1986	+ Washburn, Watson 1965
Edberg, Stefan 2004	+ Nielsen, Arthur 1971	+ Whitman, Malcolm 1955
Emerson, Roy 1982	Olmedo, Alex 1987	Wilander, Mats 2002
+ Etchebaster, Pierre 1978	+ Osuna, Rafael 1979	+ Wilding, Anthony 1978
Falkenburg, Bob 1974	+ Parker, Frank 1966	+ Williams, Richard 2nd . . .1957
Fraser, Neale 1984	+ Patterson, Gerald 1989	Wood, Sidney 1964
+ Garland, Chuck 1969	+ Patty, Budge 1977	+ Wrenn, Robert 1955
+ Gonzales, Pancho 1968	+ Perry, Fred 1975	+ Wright, Beals 1956
+ Grant, Bryan (Bitsy) 1972	+ Pettitt, Tom 1982	

Women

+ Atkinson, Juliette 1974	Fry Irvin, Shirley 1970	Mortimer Barrett, Angela . .1993
Austin, Tracy 1992	+ Gibson, Althea 1971	Navratilova, Martina . . .2000
+ Barger-Wallach, Maud 1958	Goolagong Cawley, Evonne 1988	+ Nuthall Shoemaker, Betty . .1977
Betz Addie, Pauline 1965	Graf, Steffi 2004	Osborne duPont, Margaret .1967
+ Bjurstedt Mallory, Molla . . .1958	+ Hansell, Ellen 1965	+ Palfrey Danzig, Sarah 1963
Bowrey, Lesley Turner 1997	Hard, Darlene 1973	Richey, Nancy 2003
Brough Clapp, Louise 1967	Hart, Doris 1969	+ Roosevelt, Ellen 1975
+ Browne, Mary 1957	Haydon Jones, Ann 1985	+ Round Little, Dorothy 1986
Bueno, Maria 1978	Heldman, Gladys 1979	+ Ryan, Elizabeth 1972
+ Cahill, Mabel 1976	+ Hotchkiss Wightman, Hazel 1957	+ Sears, Eleanora 1968
Casals, Rosie 1996	+ Jacobs, Helen Hull 1962	Shriver, Pam 2002
Cheney, Dorothy (Dodo) . . .2004	King, Billie Jean 1987	Smith Court, Margaret . . .1979
+ Connolly Brinker, Maureen .1968	+ Lenglen, Suzanne 1978	+ Sutton Bundy, May 1956
+ Dod, Charlotte (Lottie) . . .1983	Mandlikova, Hana 1994	+ Townsend Toulmin, Bertha .1974
+ Douglass Chambers, Dorothy 1981	+ Marble, Alice 1964	Wade, Virginia 1989
Dürr, Françoise 2003	+ McKane Godfree, Kitty . . .1978	+ Wagner, Marie 1969
Evert, Chris 1995	+ Moore, Elisabeth 1971	+ Wills Moody Roark, Helen .1959

Contributors

+ Baker, Lawrence Sr 1975	+ Hester, W.E. (Slew) 1981	+ Outerbridge, Mary 1981
+ Chatrier, Philippe 1992	+ Hopman, Harry 1978	+ Pell, Theodore 1966
Collins, Bud 1994	Hunt, Lamar 1993	+ Tingay, Lance 1982
+ Cullman, Joseph F. 3rd 1990	+ Laney, Al 1979	+ Tinling, Ted 1986
+ Danzig, Allison 1968	Martin, Alastair 1973	Tobin, John 2003
+ Davis, Dwight 1956	+ Martin, William M. 1982	+ Van Alen, James 1965
+ Gray, David 1985	+ Maskell, Dan 1996	+ Wingfield, Walter Clopton .1997
+ Gustaf, V (King of Sweden) .1980		

TRACK & FIELD

National Track & Field Hall of Fame

Established in 1974 by the The Athletics Congress (now USA Track & Field). Originally located in Charleston, WV, the Hall moved to Indianapolis in 1983 and opened at the Hoosier Dome (now RCA Dome) in 1986. The Hall moved to Manhattan and reopened at the 168th Street Armory in early 2004. **Address:** 216 Fort Washington Ave., New York, NY 10032. **Telephone:** (212) 923-1803, ext. 10.

Eligibility: Nominated athletes must be retired three years and coaches must have coached at least 20 years if retired or 35 years if still coaching. Voting done by 800-member panel made up of Hall of Fame and USA Track & Field officials, Hall of Fame members, current U.S. champions and members of the Track & Field Writers of America.

Class of 2003 (4): MEN—**John Carlos** (sprinter), **Larry James** (sprinter), **Mike Larrabee** (sprinter). WOMEN—**Mary Slaney** (middle distance). Members are listed with year of induction; (+) indicates deceased members.

Men

+ Albritton, Dave 1980	James, Larry 2003	Prinstein, Meyer 2000
Ashenfelter, Horace 1975	Jenkins, Charlie 1992	+ Ray, Joie 1976
Banks, Willie 1999	Jenner, Bruce 1980	+ Rice, Greg 1977
+ Bausch, James 1979	+ Johnson, Cornelius 1994	Richards, Rev. Bob 1975
Beamon, Bob 1977	Johnson, Rafer 1974	Robinson, Arnie 2000
Beatty, Jim 1990	Jones, Hayes 1976	Rodgers, Bill 1999
Bell, Earl 2002	+ Kelley, John A. 1980	+ Rose, Ralph 1976
Bell, Greg 1988	+ Kiviat, Abel 1985	Ryun, Jim 1980
+ Boeckmann, Dee 1976	+ Kraenzlein, Alvin 1974	Salazar, Alberto 2001
Boston, Ralph 1974	Laird, Ron 1986	+ Scholz, Jackson 1977
Borican, Jonn 2000	Larrabee, Mike 2003	Schul, Bob 1991
Bragg, Don 1996	+ Lash, Don 1995	Scott, Steve 2002
+ Calhoun, Lee 1974	+ Laskau, Henry 1997	Seagren, Bob 1986
Campbell, Milt 1989	Lewis, Carl 2001	+ Sheppard, Mel 1976
Carlos, John 2003	Liquori, Marty 1995	+ Sheridan, Martin 1988
Carr, Henry 1997	Long, Dr. Dallas 1996	Shorter, Frank 1989
+ Clark, Ellery 1991	Marsh, Henry 2001	Silvester, Jay 1998
Connolly, Harold 1984	Mathias, Bob 1974	Sime, Dave 1981
Courtney, Tom 1978	Matson, Randy 1984	+ Simpson, Robert 1974
+ Cunningham, Glenn 1974	McCluskey, Joe 1996	Smith, Tommie 1978
+ Curtis, William 1979	+ Meadows, Earle 1996	+ Stanfield, Andy 1977
+ Davenport, Willie 1982	+ Meredith, Ted 1982	Steers, Les 1974
Davis, Glenn 1974	+ Metcalfe, Ralph 1975	Stones, Dwight 1998
Davis, Harold 1974	+ Milburn, Rod 1993	+ Taylor, Frederick Morgan .2000
Dillard, Harrison 1974	Mills, Billy 1976	+ Tewksbury, Dr. Walter ...1996
Dumas, Charles 1990	Moore, Charles 1999	Thomas, John 1985
Evans, Lee 1983	Moore, Tom 1988	+ Thomson, Earl 1977
+ Ewell, Barney 1986	Morrow, Bobby 1975	+ Thorpe, Jim 1975
+ Ewry, Ray 1974	+ Mortensen, Jess 1992	+ Tolan, Eddie 1982
+ Flanagan, John 1975	Moses, Edwin 1994	Toomey, Bill 1975
Fosbury, Dick 1981	+ Myers, Lawrence 1974	+ Towns, Forrest (Spec) ...1976
Foster, Greg 1998	Myricks, Larry 2001	Warmerdam, Cornelius ...1974
+ Gordien, Fortune 1979	Nehemiah, Renaldo 1997	Whitfield, Mal 1974
Greene, Charles 1992	O'Brien, Parry 1974	Wilkins, Mac 1993
+ Hahn, Archie 1983	Oerter, Al 1974	+ Williams, Archie 1992
Hardin, Glenn 1978	+ Osborn, Harold 1974	Wohlhuter, Rick 1990
Hayes, Bob 1976	+ Owens, Jesse 1974	Woodruff, John 1978
Held, Bud 1987	Paddock, Charlie 1976	Wottle, Dave 1982
Hines, Jim 1979	Patton, Mel 1985	+ Wykoff, Frank 1977
+ Houser, Bud 1979	+ Peacock, Eulace 1987	Young, George 1981
+ Hubbard, DeHart 1979	+ Prefontaine, Steve 1976	Young, Larry 2002

Women

Ashford, Evelyn 1997	Heritage, Doris Brown ...1990	Schmidt, Kate 1994
Brisco, Valerie 1995	+ Jackson, Nell 1989	Seidler, Maren 2000
Cheeseborough, Chandra .2000	Larrieu Smith, Francie ...1998	+ Shiley Newhouse, Jean ..1993
Coachman, Alice 1975	Manning-Mims, Madeline .1984	Slaney, Mary 2003
+ Copeland, Lillian 1994	McDaniel, Mildred 1983	+ Stephens, Helen 1975
+ Didrikson, Babe 1974	McGuire, Edith 1979	Torrence, Gwen 2002
+ Faggs, Mae 1976	Ritter, Louise 1995	Tyus, Wyomia 1980
Ferrell, Barbara 1988	+ Robinson, Betty 1977	+ Walsh, Stella 1975
+ Griffith Joyner, Florence .1995	+ Rudolph, Wilma 1974	Watson, Martha 1987
+ Hall Adams, Evelyne ...1988		White, Willye 1981

Coaches

+ Abbott, Cleve 1996	+ Easton, Bill 1975	+ Hurt, Edward 1975
+ Baskin, Weems 1982	+ Ellis, Larry 1999	+ Hutsell, Wilbur 1975
+ Beard, Percy 1981	+ Elliott, Jumbo 1981	+ Jones, Thomas 1977
Bell, Sam 1992	+ Giegengack, Bob 1978	Jordan, Payton 1982
+ Botts, Tom 1983	+ Hamilton, Brutus 1974	+ Littlefield, Clyde 1981
+ Bowerman, Bill 1981	+ Haydon, Ted 1975	+ Moakley, Jack 1988
Bush, Jim 1987	+ Hayes, Billy 1976	+ Murphy, Michael 1974
+ Cromwell, Dean 1974	+ Haylett, Ward 1979	Rosen, Mel 1995
Dellinger, Bill 2000	+ Higgins, Ralph 1982	+ Snyder, Larry 1978
+ Doherty, Ken 1976	+ Hillman, Harry 1976	Temple, Ed 1989

+ Templeton, Dink 1976
  Walker, LeRoy 1983
+ Wilt, Fred 1981

+ Winter, Bud 1985
+ Wolfe, Vern 1996

  Wright, Stan 1993
+ Yancy, Joseph 1984

+ Abramson, Jesse 1981
  Andersen, Roxanne 1991
+ Bakjian, Andy 1986
+ Brundage, Avery 1974

Contributors

+ Ferris, Dan 1974
+ Griffith, John 1979
+ Lebow, Fred 1994

+ Nelson, Bert 1991
  Nelson, Cordner 1988
+ Sullivan, James 1977

WOMEN

International Women's Sports Hall of Fame

Established in 1980 by the Women's Sports Foundation. **Address:** Women's Sports Foundation, Eisenhower Park, East Meadow, NY 11554. **Telephone:** (516) 542-4700.

Eligibility: Nominees' achievements and commitment to the development of women's sports must be internationally recognized. Athletes are elected in two categories—Pioneer (before 1960) and Contemporary (since 1960). Members are divided below by sport for the sake of easy reference; (*) indicates member inducted in Pioneer category. Coaching nominees must have coached at least 10 years. Members are listed with year of induction; (+) indicates deceased members.

Class of 2003 (4): CONTEMPORARY—**Jackie Joyner-Kersee** (track and field) and **Min Gao** (diving); PIONEER—**Heather McKay** (squash); COACH—**Linda Vollstedt** (golf).

Note: Charlotte Dod is inducted for tennis, as well as archery and golf; **Marie Marvingt** is inducted for aviation, as well as mountaineering; **Eleanora Sears** is inducted for golf, as well as polo and squash.

Alpine Skiing

Cranz, Christl* 1991
+ Golden Brosnihan, Diana . .1997
  Lawrence, Andrea Mead* . .1983
  Moser-Proell, Annemarie . .1982

Auto Racing

Guthrie, Janet 1980

Aviation

+ Coleman, Bessie* 1992
+ Earhart, Amelia* 1980
+ Marvingt, Marie* 1987

Badminton

Hashman, Judy Devlin* . . .1995

Baseball

Stone, Toni* 1993

Basketball

Meyers, Ann 1985
Miller, Cheryl 1991

Bowling

Ladewig, Marion* 1984

Cycling

Carpenter Phinney, Connie .1990

Diving

Gao, Min 2003
King, Micki 1983
McCormick, Pat* 1984
Riggin, Aileen* 1988

Equestrian

Hartel, Lis 1994

Fencing

Schacherer-Elek, Ilona* . . .1989

Figure Skating

Albright, Tenley* 1983
+ Blanchard, Theresa Weld* .1989
  Fleming, Peggy 1981
  Heiss Jenkins, Carol* 1992
+ Henie, Sonja* 1982
  Protopopov, Ludmila 1992
  Rodnina, Irena 1988
  Scott-King, Barbara Ann* . .1997
  Torvill, Jayne 2002

Golf

Berg, Patty* 1980
Carner, JoAnne 1987
Haynie, Sandra 1999
Hicks, Betty* 1995
Jameson, Betty* 1999

Mann, Carol 1982
Rawls, Betsy* 1986
+ Sears, Eleanora 1984
  Suggs, Louise* 1987
+ Vare, Glenna Collett* 1981
  Whitworth, Kathy 1984
  Wright, Mickey 1981

Golf/Track & Field

+ Zaharias, Babe Didrikson* .1980

Gymnastics

Caslavska, Vera 1991
Comaneci, Nadia 1990
Korbut, Olga 1982
Latynina, Larysa* 1985
Retton, Mary Lou 1993
Tourischeva, Lyudmila 1987

Orienteering

Kringstad, Annichen 1995

Shooting

Murdock, Margaret 1988

Softball

Joyce, Joan 1989

Speed Skating

+ Klein Outland, Kit* 1993
  Young, Sheila 1981

Squash

McKay, Heather* 2003

Swimming

Caulkins, Tracy 1986
+ Chadwick, Florence* 1996
  Curtis Cuneo, Ann* 1985
  de Varona, Donna 1983
  Ederle, Gertrude* 1980
  Fraser, Dawn 1985
  Holm, Eleanor* 1980
  Meagher, Mary T. 1993
  Meyer-Reyes, Debbie 1987
  Ruiz-Confronto, Tracie 2001

Tennis

+ Connolly, Maureen* 1987
+ Dod, Charlotte (Lottie)* 1986
  Evert, Chris 1981
+ Gibson, Althea* 1980
  Goolagong Cawley, Evonne 1989
+ Hotchkiss Wightman, Hazel*1986
  King, Billie Jean 1980

+ Lenglen, Suzanne* 1984
  Navratilova, Martina 1984
  Osbourne du Pont,Margaret*1998
+ Sears, Eleanora* 1984
  Smith Court, Margaret 1986

Track & Field

Ashford, Evelyn 1997
Blankers-Koen, Fanny* 1982
Brisco, Valerie 2002
Cheng, Chi 1994
Coachman Davis, Alice* . . .1991
Cuthbert, Betty* 2002
+ Faggs Star, Aeriwentha Mae* 1996
+ Griffith Joyner, Florence . . .1998
  Joyner-Kersee, Jackie 2003
  Manning Mims, Madeline . .1987
  Nelson, Marjorie Jackson* .2001
+ Rudolph, Wilma 1980
  Samuelson, Joan Benoit . . .1999
+ Stephens, Helen* 1983
  Strickland de la Hunty, Shirley*1998
  Szewinska, Irena 1992
  Tyus, Wyomia 1981
  Waitz, Grete 1995
  White, Willye 1988

Volleyball

+ Hyman, Flo 1986

Water Skiing

McGuire, Willa Worthington* 1990

Coaches

+ Applebee, Constance 1991
  Backus, Sharron 1993
  Carver, Chris 2001
  Conradt, Judy 1995
  Emery, Gail 1997
  Franke, Nikki 2002
  Green, Tina Sloan 1999
  Grossfeld, Muriel 1991
  Holum, Diana 1996
  Jacket, Barbara 1995
+ Jackson, Nell 1990
  Kanakogi, Rusty 1994
  Summitt, Pat Head 1990
  VanDerveer, Tara 1998
  Vollstedt, Linda 2003
+ Wade, Margaret 1992

RETIRED NUMBERS
Major League Baseball

The New York Yankees have retired the most uniform numbers (14) in the major leagues; followed by the Brooklyn/Los Angeles Dodgers (10), the St. Louis Cardinals (9), the Chicago White Sox and the Pittsburgh Pirates (8) and the New York/San Francisco Giants (7). **Jackie Robinson** had his #42 retired by Major League Baseball in 1997. Players who were already wearing the number were allowed to continue to do so. Los Angeles had already retired Robinson's number so he's only listed with the Dodgers below. **Nolan Ryan** has had his number retired by three teams—#34 by Texas and Houston and #30 by California (now Anaheim). Six players and a manager have had their numbers retired by two teams: **Hank Aaron**—#44 by the Boston/Milwaukee/Atlanta Braves and the Milwaukee Brewers; **Rod Carew**—#29 by Minnesota and California (now Anaheim); **Rollie Fingers**—#34 by Milwaukee and Oakland; **Carlton Fisk**—#27 by Boston and #72 by the Chicago White Sox; **Reggie Jackson**—#9 by the Oakland Athletics and #44 by the New York Yankees; **Frank Robinson**—#20 by Cincinnati and Baltimore; **Casey Stengel**—#37 by the New York Yankees and New York Mets.

    Number retired in 2004 (3): MONTREAL EXPOS—#30 worn by **Tim Raines** (1979-90, 2001 with Expos); OAKLAND ATHLETICS—#9 worn by **Reggie Jackson** (1968-75, 1987 with A's); SAN DIEGO PADRES—#19 worn by **Tony Gwynn** (1982-2001 with Padres).

American League

Two AL teams—the Seattle Mariners and the Toronto Blue Jays—have not retired any numbers. The Blue Jays have a "level of excellence" which includes Joe Carter (#29), Tony Fernandez (#1), Dave Stieb (#11), George Bell (#37), and Cito Gaston (#43). All numbers have been used in recent years, however.

Anaheim Angels
11	Jim Fregosi
26	Gene Autry
29	Rod Carew
30	Nolan Ryan
50	Jimmie Reese

Baltimore Orioles
4	Earl Weaver
5	Brooks Robinson
8	Cal Ripken Jr.
20	Frank Robinson
22	Jim Palmer
33	Eddie Murray

Boston Red Sox
1	Bobby Doerr
4	Joe Cronin
8	Carl Yastrzemski
9	Ted Williams
27	Carlton Fisk

Chicago White Sox
2	Nellie Fox
3	Harold Baines
4	Luke Appling
9	Minnie Minoso
11	Luis Aparicio
16	Ted Lyons
19	Billy Pierce
72	Carlton Fisk

Cleveland Indians
3	Earl Averill
5	Lou Boudreau
14	Larry Doby
18	Mel Harder
19	Bob Feller
21	Bob Lemon
455	Fans (# of consecutive sellouts)

Detroit Tigers
2	Charlie Gehringer
5	Hank Greenberg
6	Al Kaline
16	Hal Newhouser
23	Willie Horton

Kansas City Royals
5	George Brett
10	Dick Howser
20	Frank White

Minnesota Twins
3	Harmon Killebrew
6	Tony Oliva
14	Kent Hrbek
29	Rod Carew
34	Kirby Puckett

Oakland Athletics
9	Reggie Jackson
27	Catfish Hunter
34	Rollie Fingers

New York Yankees
1	Billy Martin
3	Babe Ruth
4	Lou Gehrig
5	Joe DiMaggio
7	Mickey Mantle
8	Yogi Berra & Bill Dickey
9	Roger Maris
10	Phil Rizzuto
15	Thurman Munson
16	Whitey Ford
23	Don Mattingly
32	Elston Howard
37	Casey Stengel
44	Reggie Jackson
49	Ron Guidry

Tampa Bay Devil Rays
12	Wade Boggs

Texas Rangers
34	Nolan Ryan

National League

Two NL teams—the Arizona Diamondbacks and Colorado Rockies—have not retired any numbers. San Francisco has honored former NY Giants Christy Mathewson and John McGraw even though they played before numbers were worn. As did the Philadelphia Phillies for Grover Cleveland Alexander and Chuck Klein.

Atlanta Braves
3	Dale Murphy
21	Warren Spahn
35	Phil Niekro
41	Eddie Mathews
44	Hank Aaron

Chicago Cubs
10	Ron Santo
14	Ernie Banks
26	Billy Williams

Cincinnati Reds
1	Fred Hutchinson
5	Johnny Bench
8	Joe Morgan
18	Ted Kluszewski
20	Frank Robinson
24	Tony Perez

Florida Marlins
5	Carl Barger

Houston Astros
25	Jose Cruz
32	Jim Umbricht
33	Mike Scott
34	Nolan Ryan
40	Don Wilson
49	Larry Dierker

Los Angeles Dodgers
1	Pee Wee Reese
2	Tommy Lasorda
4	Duke Snider
19	Jim Gilliam
20	Don Sutton
24	Walter Alston
32	Sandy Koufax
39	Roy Campanella
42	Jackie Robinson
53	Don Drysdale

Milwaukee Brewers
4	Paul Molitor
19	Robin Yount
34	Rollie Fingers
44	Hank Aaron

Montreal Expos
8	Gary Carter
10	Rusty Staub & Andre Dawson
30	Tim Raines

New York Mets
14	Gil Hodges
37	Casey Stengel
41	Tom Seaver

Philadelphia Phillies
1	Richie Ashburn
14	Jim Bunning
20	Mike Schmidt
32	Steve Carlton
36	Robin Roberts

Pittsburgh Pirates
1	Billy Meyer
4	Ralph Kiner
8	Willie Stargell
9	Bill Mazeroski
20	Pie Traynor
21	Roberto Clemente
33	Honus Wagner
40	Danny Murtaugh

St. Louis Cardinals
1	Ozzie Smith
2	Red Schoendienst
6	Stan Musial
9	Enos Slaughter
14	Ken Boyer
17	Dizzy Dean
20	Lou Brock
45	Bob Gibson
85	August (Gussie) Busch

San Diego Padres
6	Steve Garvey
19	Tony Gwynn
31	Dave Winfield
35	Randy Jones

San Francisco Giants
3	Bill Terry
4	Mel Ott
11	Carl Hubbell
24	Willie Mays
27	Juan Marichal
30	Orlando Cepeda
44	Willie McCovey

National Basketball Association

Boston has retired the most numbers (21) in the NBA, followed by Portland (9); the Rochester/Cincinnati Royals/K.C./Sacramento Kings, Syracuse Nats/Philadelphia 76ers and New York Knicks (8); Detroit, Los Angeles Lakers, Milwaukee and Phoenix Suns have (7); Cleveland and New Jersey have (6). **Wilt Chamberlain** is the only player to have his number retired by three teams: #13 by the LA Lakers, Golden State and Philadelphia; Nine players have had their numbers retired by two teams: **Kareem Abdul-Jabbar**—#33 by LA Lakers and Milwaukee; **Charles Barkley**—#34 by Philadelphia and Phoenix; **Clyde Drexler**—#22 by Houston and Portland; **Julius Erving**—#6 by Philadelphia and #32 by New Jersey; **Michael Jordan**—#23 by Chicago and Miami (in his honor); **Bob Lanier**—#16 by Detroit and Milwaukee; **Pete Maravich**—#7 by Utah and New Orleans; **Oscar Robertson**—#1 by Milwaukee and #14 by Sacramento; **Nate Thurmond**—#42 by Cleveland and Golden State.

Numbers retired in 2003-04 (3): PHOENIX—#34 worn by **Charles Barkley** (1992-95 with Suns); SACRAMENTO—#2 worn by **Mitch Richmond** (1991-98 with Kings); UTAH—#12 worn by **John Stockton** (1984-2003 with Jazz).

Eastern Conference

Two Eastern teams—the Charlotte Bobcats and Toronto Raptors—have not retired any numbers.

Atlanta Hawks
- **9** Bob Pettit
- **21** Dominique Wilkins
- **23** Lou Hudson

Boston Celtics
- **1** Walter A. Brown
- **2** Red Auerbach
- **3** Dennis Johnson
- **6** Bill Russell
- **10** Jo Jo White
- **14** Bob Cousy
- **15** Tom Heinsohn
- **16** Tom (Satch) Sanders
- **17** John Havlicek
- **18** Dave Cowens
- **19** Don Nelson
- **21** Bill Sharman
- **22** Ed Macauley
- **23** Frank Ramsey
- **24** Sam Jones
- **25** K.C. Jones
- **31** Cedric Maxwell
- **32** Kevin McHale
- **33** Larry Bird
- **35** Reggie Lewis
- **00** Robert Parish
- **Loscy** Jim Loscutoff (#18)
- **Radio mic** Johnny Most

Chicago Bulls
- **4** Jerry Sloan
- **10** Bob Love
- **23** Michael Jordan

Cleveland Cavaliers
- **7** Bingo Smith
- **22** Larry Nance
- **25** Mark Price
- **34** Austin Carr
- **42** Nate Thurmond
- **43** Brad Daugherty

Detroit Pistons
- **2** Chuck Daly
- **4** Joe Dumars
- **11** Isiah Thomas
- **15** Vinnie Johnson
- **16** Bob Lanier
- **21** Dave Bing
- **40** Bill Laimbeer

Indiana Pacers
- **30** George McGinnis
- **34** Mel Daniels
- **35** Roger Brown
- **529** Bob "Slick" Leonard

Miami Heat
- **23** Michael Jordan

Milwaukee Bucks
- **1** Oscar Robertson
- **2** Junior Bridgeman
- **4** Sidney Moncrief
- **14** Jon McGlocklin
- **16** Bob Lanier
- **32** Brian Winters
- **33** Kareem Abdul-Jabbar

New York Knicks
- **10** Walt Frazier
- **12** Dick Barnett
- **15** Dick McGuire
- **19** & Earl Monroe
- **19** Willis Reed
- **22** Dave DeBusschere
- **24** Bill Bradley
- **33** Patrick Ewing
- **613** Red Holzman

New Jersey Nets
- **3** Drazen Petrovic
- **4** Wendell Ladner
- **23** John Williamson
- **25** Bill Melchionni
- **32** Julius Erving
- **52** Buck Williams

New Orleans Hornets
- **7** Pete Maravich
- **13** Bobby Phills

Orlando Magic
- **6** Fans ("Sixth Man")

Philadelphia 76ers
- **2** Moses Malone
- **6** Julius Erving
- **10** Maurice Cheeks
- **13** Wilt Chamberlain
- **15** Hal Greer
- **24** Bobby Jones
- **32** Billy Cunningham
- **34** Charles Barkley
- **P.A. mic** Dave Zinkoff

Washington Wizards
- **11** Elvin Hayes
- **25** Gus Johnson
- **41** Wes Unseld

Western Conference

Two Western teams—the Los Angeles Clippers and Memphis Grizzlies—have not retired any numbers.

Dallas Mavericks
- **15** Brad Davis
- **22** Rolando Blackman

Denver Nuggets
- **2** Alex English
- **33** David Thompson
- **40** Byron Beck
- **44** Dan Issel
- **432** Doug Moe

Golden St. Warriors
- **13** Wilt Chamberlain
- **14** Tom Meschery
- **16** Al Attles
- **24** Rick Barry
- **42** Nate Thurmond

Houston Rockets
- **22** Clyde Drexler
- **23** Calvin Murphy
- **24** Moses Malone
- **34** Hakeem Olajuwon
- **45** Rudy Tomjanovich

Los Angeles Lakers
- **13** Wilt Chamberlain
- **22** Elgin Baylor
- **25** Gail Goodrich
- **32** Magic Johnson
- **33** Kareem Abdul-Jabbar
- **42** James Worthy
- **44** Jerry West
- **Radio mic** Chick Hearn

Minnesota Timberwolves
- **2** Malik Sealy

Phoenix Suns
- **5** Dick Van Arsdale
- **6** Walter Davis
- **7** Kevin Johnson
- **9** Dan Majerle
- **24** Tom Chambers
- **33** Alvan Adams
- **34** Charles Barkley
- **42** Connie Hawkins
- **44** Paul Westphal

Portland Trail Blazers
- **1** Larry Weinberg
- **13** Dave Twardzik
- **15** Larry Steele
- **20** Maurice Lucas
- **22** Clyde Drexler
- **32** Bill Walton
- **36** Lloyd Neal
- **45** Geoff Petrie
- **77** Jack Ramsay

Sacramento Kings
- **1** Nate Archibald
- **2** Mitch Richmond
- **6** Fans ("Sixth Man")
- **11** Bob Davies
- **12** Maurice Stokes
- **14** Oscar Robertson
- **27** Jack Twyman
- **44** Sam Lacey

San Antonio Spurs
- **13** James Silas
- **44** George Gervin
- **50** David Robinson
- **00** Johnny Moore

Seattle SuperSonics
- **10** Nate McMillan
- **19** Lenny Wilkens
- **32** Fred Brown
- **43** Jack Sikma
- **Radio mic** Bob Blackburn

Utah Jazz
- **1** Frank Layden
- **7** Pete Maravich
- **12** John Stockton
- **14** Jeff Hornacek
- **35** Darrell Griffith
- **53** Mark Eaton

Retired Numbers (Cont.)
National Football League

The Chicago Bears have retired the most uniform numbers (13) in the NFL; followed by the New York Giants (11); the Dallas Texans/Kansas City Chiefs, Boston-New England Patriots and San Francisco (8); the Baltimore-Indianapolis Colts (7); Detroit and Philadelphia (6); Cleveland (5). No player has ever had his number retired by more than one NFL team. The NFL has recently discouraged (though not eliminated) the practice of retiring numbers. As a result, the Green Bay Packers retired the jersey (but not the #92) of defensive end Reggie White in 1999. Nonetheless, Packers GM Ron Wolf announced that there are no plans to reissue the number.

Number retired in 2003-04 (2): ARIZONA—#40 worn by **Pat Tillman** (1998-2001 with Cardinals); SAN FRANCISCO—#42 worn by **Ronnie Lott** (1981-90 with 49ers).

AFC

Four AFC teams—the Baltimore Ravens, Houston Texans, Jacksonville Jaguars and Oakland Raiders—have not retired any numbers.

Buffalo Bills		**Indianapolis Colts**		**Miami Dolphins**		**New York Jets**	
12	Jim Kelly	19	Johnny Unitas	12	Bob Griese	12	Joe Namath
Cincinnati Bengals		22	Buddy Young	13	Dan Marino	13	Don Maynard
54	Bob Johnson	24	Lenny Moore	39	Larry Csonka		
Cleveland Browns		70	Art Donovan	**New England**		**Pittsburgh Steelers**	
14	Otto Graham	77	Jim Parker	**Patriots**		70	Ernie Stautner
32	Jim Brown	82	Raymond Berry	20	Gino Cappelletti	**San Diego Chargers**	
45	Ernie Davis	89	Gino Marchetti	40	Mike Haynes	14	Dan Fouts
46	Don Fleming	**Kansas City Chiefs**		56	Andre Tippett	**Tennessee Titans**	
76	Lou Groza	3	Jan Stenerud	57	Steve Nelson	34	Earl Campbell
Denver Broncos		16	Len Dawson	73	John Hannah	43	Jim Norton
7	John Elway	28	Abner Haynes	78	Bruce Armstrong	63	Mike Munchak
18	Frank Tripucka	33	Stone Johnson	79	Jim Lee Hunt	65	Elvin Bethea
44	Floyd Little	36	Mack Lee Hill	89	Bob Dee		
		63	Willie Lanier				
		78	Bobby Bell				
		86	Buck Buchanan				

NFC

Dallas and the Carolina Panthers are the only NFC teams that haven't officially retired any numbers. The Falcons haven't issued uniform #10 (Steve Bartkowski) and #78 (Mike Kenn) since those players retired. The Cowboys have a "Ring of Honor" at Texas Stadium that includes 10 players, one coach and one president/GM—Tony Dorsett, Bob Hayes, Chuck Howley, Lee Roy Jordan, Tom Landry, Bob Lilly, Don Meredith, Don Perkins, Mel Renfro, Tex Schramm, Roger Staubach and Randy White. The Panthers have a Hall of Fame that includes Mike McCormack and Sam Mills.

Arizona Cardinals		**Detroit Lions**		**New York Giants**		**St. Louis Rams**	
8	Larry Wilson	7	Dutch Clark	1	Ray Flaherty	7	Bob Waterfield
40	Pat Tillman	22	Bobby Layne	4	Tuffy Leemans	29	Eric Dickerson
77	Stan Mauldin	37	Doak Walker	7	Mel Hein	74	Merlin Olsen
88	J.V. Cain	56	Joe Schmidt	11	Phil Simms	78	Jackie Slater
99	Marshall Goldberg	85	Chuck Hughes	14	Y.A. Tittle	85	Jack Youngblood
Atlanta Falcons		88	Charlie Sanders	16	Frank Gifford	**San Francisco 49ers**	
31	William Andrews	**Green Bay Packers**		32	Al Blozis	12	John Brodie
57	Jeff Van Note	3	Tony Canadeo	40	Joe Morrison	16	Joe Montana
60	Tommy Nobis	14	Don Hutson	42	Charlie Conerly	34	Joe Perry
Chicago Bears		15	Bart Starr	50	Ken Strong	37	Jimmy Johnson
3	Bronko Nagurski	66	Ray Nitschke	56	Lawrence Taylor	39	Hugh McElhenny
5	George McAfee	**Minnesota Vikings**		**Philadelphia Eagles**		42	Ronnie Lott
7	George Halas	10	Fran Tarkenton	15	Steve Van Buren	70	Charlie Krueger
28	Willie Galimore	53	Mick Tingelhoff	40	Tom Brookshier	73	Leo Nomellini
34	Walter Payton	70	Jim Marshall	44	Pete Retzlaff	79	Bob St. Clair
40	Gale Sayers	77	Korey Stringer	60	Chuck Bednarik	87	Dwight Clark
41	Brian Piccolo	80	Cris Carter	70	Al Wistert	**Seattle Seahawks**	
42	Sid Luckman	88	Alan Page	99	Jerome Brown	12	Fans ("12th Man")
51	Dick Butkus	**New Orleans Saints**				80	Steve Largent
56	Bill Hewitt	31	Jim Taylor			**Tampa Bay Bucs**	
61	Bill George	81	Doug Atkins			63	Lee Roy Selmon
66	Bulldog Turner					**Wash. Redskins**	
77	Red Grange					33	Sammy Baugh

National Hockey League

The Boston Bruins have retired the most uniform numbers (10) in the NHL; followed by Montreal (7); N.Y. Islanders (6); Chicago and Detroit (5). Following his retirement in 1999, the NHL announced that the league would retire **Wayne Gretzky**'s #99. Three other players have had their numbers retired by two teams: **Gordie Howe**—#9 by Detroit and Hartford; **Bobby Hull**—#9 by Chicago and Winnipeg (now Phoenix); and **Ray Bourque**—#77 by Boston and Colorado.

Numbers retired in 2003-04 (2): COLORADO—#33 worn by **Patrick Roy** (1995-2003 with Avalanche); EDMONTON—#31 worn by **Grant Fuhr** (1981-91 with Oilers).

Eastern Conference

Five Eastern teams—the Atlanta Thrashers, Carolina Hurricanes, Florida Panthers, New Jersey Devils and Tampa Bay Lightning—have not retired any numbers. The Hartford Whalers had retired three numbers: #2 Rick Ley, #9 Gordie Howe and #19 John McKenzie. Mario Lemieux's retired #66 with Pittsburgh has been temporarily unretired during his recent comeback.

Boston Bruins
2 Eddie Shore
3 Lionel Hitchman
4 Bobby Orr
5 Dit Clapper
7 Phil Esposito
8 Cam Neely
9 John Bucyk
15 Milt Schmidt
24 Terry O'Reilly
77 Ray Bourque

Buffalo Sabres
2 Tim Horton
7 Rick Martin
11 Gilbert Perreault
14 Rene Robert

Montreal Canadiens
1 Jacques Plante
2 Doug Harvey
4 Jean Beliveau
7 Howie Morenz
9 Maurice Richard
10 Guy Lafleur
16 Henri Richard

New York Islanders
5 Denis Potvin
9 Clark Gillies
19 Bryan Trottier
22 Mike Bossy
23 Bob Nystrom
31 Billy Smith

New York Rangers
1 Eddie Giacomin
7 Rod Gilbert
35 Mike Richter

Ottawa Senators
8 Frank Finnigan

Philadelphia Flyers
1 Bernie Parent
4 Barry Ashbee
7 Bill Barber
16 Bobby Clarke

Pittsburgh Penguins
21 Michel Briere
66 Mario Lemieux

Toronto Maple Leafs
5 Bill Barilko
6 Ace Bailey

Washington Capitals
5 Rod Langway
7 Yvon Labre
32 Dale Hunter

Western Conference

Four Western teams—the Columbus Blue Jackets, Mighty Ducks of Anaheim, Nashville Predators and San Jose Sharks—have not retired any numbers. Note, the Quebec Nordiques retired the numbers of J.C. Tremblay (3), Marc Tardif (8) and Michel Goulet (16) but these numbers have been worn since the team moved to Colorado. Detroit has not officially retired the number of Larry Aurie (6) but has kept it "out of circulation."

Calgary Flames
9 Lanny McDonald

Chicago Blackhawks
1 Glenn Hall
9 Bobby Hull
18 Denis Savard
21 Stan Mikita
35 Tony Esposito

Colorado Avalanche
33 Patrick Roy
77 Ray Bourque

Dallas Stars
7 Neal Broten
8 Bill Goldsworthy
19 Bill Masterton

Detroit Red Wings
1 Terry Sawchuk
7 Ted Lindsay
9 Gordie Howe
10 Alex Delvecchio
12 Sid Abel

Edmonton Oilers
3 Al Hamilton
17 Jari Kurri
31 Grant Fuhr
99 Wayne Gretzky

Los Angeles Kings
16 Marcel Dionne
18 Dave Taylor
30 Rogie Vachon
99 Wayne Gretzky

Minnesota Wild
1 Fans

Phoenix Coyotes
9 Bobby Hull
25 Thomas Steen

St. Louis Blues
3 Bob Gassoff
8 Barclay Plager
11 Brian Sutter
24 Bernie Federko

Vancouver Canucks
12 Stan Smyl

AWARDS

Associated Press Athletes of the Year

Selected annually by AP newspaper sports editors since 1931.

Male

Lance Armstrong won his fifth consecutive Tour de France and second straight AP Male Athlete of the Year Award in 2003. Armstrong also tied the record for most Tour de France victories, picking himself up after a nasty fall in a late mountain stage and bested his main rival Jan Ullrich by 62 seconds. San Francisco slugger Barry Bonds finished in second in the voting behind Armstrong for the second consecutive year.

The top 5 vote-getters (first place votes in parentheses): 1. **Lance Armstrong**, cycling (26), 174 pts; 2. **Barry Bonds**, baseball (10), 59 pts; 3. **Tim Duncan**, basketball (5), 47 pts; 4. **LeBron James**, basketball (2), 39 pts; 5. **Carmelo Anthony**, basketball (2), 21 pts.

Multiple winners: Michael Jordan and Tiger Woods (3); Lance Armstrong, Don Budge, Sandy Koufax, Carl Lewis, Joe Montana and Byron Nelson (2).

Year		Year		Year	
1931	**Pepper Martin**, baseball	1941	**Joe DiMaggio**, baseball	1951	**Dick Kazmaier**, col. football
1932	**Gene Sarazen**, golf	1942	**Frank Sinkwich**, col. football	1952	**Bob Mathias**, track
1933	**Carl Hubbell**, baseball	1943	**Gunder Haegg**, track	1953	**Ben Hogan**, golf
1934	**Dizzy Dean**, baseball	1944	**Byron Nelson**, golf	1954	**Willie Mays**, baseball
1935	**Joe Louis**, boxing	1945	**Byron Nelson**, golf	1955	**Hopalong Cassady**, col. football
1936	**Jesse Owens**, track	1946	**Glenn Davis**, college football		
1937	**Don Budge**, tennis	1947	**Johnny Lujack**, col. football	1956	**Mickey Mantle**, baseball
1938	**Don Budge**, tennis	1948	**Lou Boudreau**, baseball	1957	**Ted Williams**, baseball
1939	**Nile Kinnick**, college football	1949	**Leon Hart**, college football	1958	**Herb Elliott**, track
1940	**Tom Harmon**, college football	1950	**Jim Konstanty**, baseball	1959	**Ingemar Johansson**, boxing

Awards (Cont.)

Year		Year		Year	
1960	**Rafer Johnson**, track	1976	**Bruce Jenner**, track	1992	**Michael Jordan**, pro basketball
1961	**Roger Maris**, baseball	1977	**Steve Cauthen**, horse racing	1993	**Michael Jordan**, pro basketball
1962	**Maury Wills**, baseball	1978	**Ron Guidry**, baseball	1994	**George Foreman**, boxing
1963	**Sandy Koufax**, baseball	1979	**Willie Stargell**, baseball	1995	**Cal Ripken Jr.**, baseball
1964	**Don Schollander**, swimming	1980	**U.S. Olympic hockey team**	1996	**Michael Johnson**, track
1965	**Sandy Koufax**, baseball	1981	**John McEnroe**, tennis	1997	**Tiger Woods**, golf
1966	**Frank Robinson**, baseball	1982	**Wayne Gretzky**, hockey	1998	**Mark McGwire**, baseball
1967	**Carl Yastrzemski**, baseball	1983	**Carl Lewis**, track	1999	**Tiger Woods**, golf
1968	**Denny McLain**, baseball	1984	**Carl Lewis**, track	2000	**Tiger Woods**, golf
1969	**Tom Seaver**, baseball	1985	**Dwight Gooden**, baseball	2001	**Barry Bonds**, baseball
1970	**George Blanda**, pro football	1986	**Larry Bird**, pro basketball	2002	**Lance Armstrong**, cycling
1971	**Lee Trevino**, golf	1987	**Ben Johnson**, track	2003	**Lance Armstrong**, cycling
1972	**Mark Spitz**, swimming	1988	**Orel Hershiser**, baseball		
1973	**O.J. Simpson**, pro football	1989	**Joe Montana**, pro football		
1974	**Muhammad Ali**, boxing	1990	**Joe Montana**, pro football		
1975	**Fred Lynn**, baseball	1991	**Michael Jordan**, pro basketball		

Female

Swedish golfer Annika Sorenstam won two majors, the LPGA Championship and Women's British Open, in 2003 and became the first woman in 58 years to play on the PGA Tour with two rounds at the Colonial, before missing the cut. She also led Europe to victory at a Solheim Cup played for the first time in her native country, was inducted into the World Golf Hall of Fame and won her first AP Female Athlete of the Year award.

The top 5 vote-getters (first place votes in parentheses) are: 1. **Annika Sorenstam**, golf (47) 249 pts; 2. **Diana Taurasi**, basketball (6), 102 pts; 3. **Justine Henin-Hardenne**, tennis, 44 pts; 4. **Mia Hamm**, soccer, 31 pts; 5. **Julie Krone**, horse racing, 11 pts.

Multiple winners: Babe Didrikson Zaharias (6); Chris Evert (4); Patty Berg and Maureen Connolly (3); Tracy Austin, Althea Gibson, Billie Jean King, Nancy Lopez, Alice Marble, Martina Navratilova, Wilma Rudolph, Monica Seles, Kathy Whitworth and Mickey Wright (2).

Year		Year		Year	
1931	**Helene Madison**, swimming	1956	**Pat McCormick**, diving	1981	**Tracy Austin**, tennis
1932	**Babe Didrikson**, track	1957	**Althea Gibson**, tennis	1982	**Mary Decker Tabb**, track
1933	**Helen Jacobs**, tennis	1958	**Althea Gibson**, tennis	1983	**Martina Navratilova**, tennis
1934	**Virginia Van Wie**, golf	1959	**Maria Bueno**, tennis	1984	**Mary Lou Retton**, gymnastics
1935	**Helen Wills Moody**, tennis	1960	**Wilma Rudolph**, track	1985	**Nancy Lopez**, golf
1936	**Helen Stephens**, track	1961	**Wilma Rudolph**, track	1986	**Martina Navratilova**, tennis
1937	**Katherine Rawls**, swimming	1962	**Dawn Fraser**, swimming	1987	**Jackie Joyner-Kersee**, track
1938	**Patty Berg**, golf	1963	**Mickey Wright**, golf	1988	**Florence Griffith Joyner**, track
1939	**Alice Marble**, tennis	1964	**Mickey Wright**, golf	1989	**Steffi Graf**, tennis
1940	**Alice Marble**, tennis	1965	**Kathy Whitworth**, golf	1990	**Beth Daniel**, golf
1941	**Betty Hicks Newell**, golf	1966	**Kathy Whitworth**, golf	1991	**Monica Seles**, tennis
1942	**Gloria Callen**, swimming	1967	**Billie Jean King**, tennis	1992	**Monica Seles**, tennis
1943	**Patty Berg**, golf	1968	**Peggy Fleming**, skating	1993	**Sheryl Swoopes**, basketball
1944	**Ann Curtis**, swimming	1969	**Debbie Meyer**, swimming	1994	**Bonnie Blair**, speed skating
1945	**Babe Didrikson Zaharias**, golf	1970	**Chi Cheng**, track	1995	**Rebecca Lobo**, col. basketball
1946	**Babe Didrikson Zaharias**, golf	1971	**Evonne Goolagong**, tennis	1996	**Amy Van Dyken**, swimming
1947	**Babe Didrikson Zaharias**, golf	1972	**Olga Korbut**, gymnastics	1997	**Martina Hingis**, tennis
1948	**Fanny Blankers-Koen**, track	1973	**Billie Jean King**, tennis	1998	**Se Ri Pak**, golf
1949	**Marlene Bauer**, golf	1974	**Chris Evert**, tennis	1999	**U.S. Soccer Team**
1950	**Babe Didrikson Zaharias**, golf	1975	**Chris Evert**, tennis	2000	**Marion Jones**, track
1951	**Maureen Connolly**, tennis	1976	**Nadia Comaneci**, gymnastics	2001	**Jennifer Capriati**, tennis
1952	**Maureen Connolly**, tennis	1977	**Chris Evert**, tennis	2002	**Serena Williams**, tennis
1953	**Maureen Connolly**, tennis	1978	**Nancy Lopez**, golf	2003	**Annika Sorenstam**, golf
1954	**Babe Didrikson Zaharias**, golf	1979	**Tracy Austin**, tennis		
1955	**Patty Berg**, golf	1980	**Chris Evert Lloyd**, tennis		

USOC Sportsman & Sportswoman of the Year

To the outstanding overall male and female athletes from within the U.S. Olympic Committee member organizations. Winners are chosen from nominees of the national governing bodies for Olympic and Pan American Games and affiliated organizations. Voting is done by members of the national media, USOC board of directors and Athletes' Advisory Council.

Sportsman

Multiple winners: Lance Armstrong (4); Eric Heiden and Michael Johnson (3); Matt Biondi and Greg Louganis (2).

Year		Year		Year	
1974	**Jim Bolding**, track	1984	**Edwin Moses**, track	1994	**Dan Jansen**, speed skating
1975	**Clint Jackson**, boxing	1985	**Willie Banks**, track	1995	**Michael Johnson**, track
1976	**John Naber**, swimming	1986	**Matt Biondi**, swimming	1996	**Michael Johnson**, track
1977	**Eric Heiden**, speed skating	1987	**Greg Louganis**, diving	1997	**Pete Sampras**, tennis
1978	**Bruce Davidson**, equestrian	1988	**Matt Biondi**, swimming	1998	**Jonny Moseley**, skiing
1979	**Eric Heiden**, speed skating	1989	**Roger Kingdom**, track	1999	**Lance Armstrong**, cycling
1980	**Eric Heiden**, speed skating	1990	**John Smith**, wrestling	2000	**Rulon Gardner**, wrestling
1981	**Scott Hamilton**, fig. skating	1991	**Carl Lewis**, track	2001	**Lance Armstrong**, cycling
1982	**Greg Louganis**, diving	1992	**Pablo Morales**, swimming	2002	**Lance Armstrong**, cycling
1983	**Rick McKinney**, archery	1993	**Michael Johnson**, track	2003	**Lance Armstrong**, cycling

Sportswoman

Multiple winners: Bonnie Blair, Tracy Caulkins, Jackie Joyner-Kersee, Picabo Street and Sheila Young Ochowicz (2).

Year		Year		Year	
1974	**Shirley Babashoff**, swimming	1984	**Tracy Caulkins**, swimming	1995	**Picabo Street**, skiing
1975	**Kathy Heddy**, swimming	1985	**Mary Decker Slaney**, track	1996	**Amy Van Dyken**, swimming
1976	**Sheila Young**, speedskating	1986	**Jackie Joyner-Kersee**, track	1997	**Tara Lipinski,** figure skating
1977	**Linda Fratianne**, fig. skating	1987	**Jackie Joyner-Kersee**, track	1998	**Picabo Street**, skiing
1978	**Tracy Caulkins**, swimming	1988	**Florence Griffith Joyner**, track	1999	**Jenny Thompson**, swimming
1979	**Sippy Woodhead**, swimming	1989	**Janet Evans**, swimming	2000	**Marion Jones**, track
1980	**Beth Heiden**, speed skating	1990	**Lynn Jennings**, track	2001	**Jennifer Capriati**, tennis
1981	**Sheila Ochowicz**, speed skating & cycling	1991	**Kim Zmeskal**, gymnastics	2002	**Sarah Hughes**, figure skating
1982	**Melanie Smith**, equestrian	1992	**Bonnie Blair**, speed skating	2003	**Michelle Kwan**, figure skating
1983	**Tamara McKinney**, skiing	1993	**Gail Devers**, track		
		1994	**Bonnie Blair**, speed skating		

UPI International Athletes of the Year

Selected annually by United Press International's European newspaper sports editors from 1974-95.

Male

Multiple winners: Sebastian Coe, Alberto Juantorena and Carl Lewis (2).

Year		Year		Year	
1974	**Muhammad Ali**, boxing	1982	**Daley Thompson**, track	1990	**Stefan Edberg**, tennis
1975	**Joao Oliveira**, track	1983	**Carl Lewis**, track	1991	**Sergei Bubka**, track
1976	**Alberto Juantorena**, track	1984	**Carl Lewis**, track	1992	**Kevin Young**, track
1977	**Alberto Juantorena**, track	1985	**Steve Cram**, track	1993	**Miguel Indurain**, cycling
1978	**Henry Rono**, track	1986	**Diego Maradona**, soccer	1994	**Johann Olav Koss**, speed skating
1979	**Sebastian Coe**, track	1987	**Ben Johnson**, track	1995	**Jonathan Edwards**, track
1980	**Eric Heiden**, speed skating	1988	**Matt Biondi**, swimming	1996	discontinued
1981	**Sebastian Coe**, track	1989	**Boris Becker**, tennis		

Female

Multiple winners: Nadia Comaneci, Steffi Graf, Marita Koch and Monica Seles (2).

Year		Year		Year	
1974	**Irena Szewinska**, track	1982	**Marita Koch**, track	1990	**Merlene Ottey**, track
1975	**Nadia Comaneci**, gymnastics	1983	**Jarmila Kratochvilova**, track	1991	**Monica Seles**, tennis
1976	**Nadia Comaneci**, gymnastics	1984	**Martina Navratilova**, tennis	1992	**Monica Seles**, tennis
1977	**Rosie Ackermann**, track	1985	**Mary Decker Slaney**, track	1993	**Wang Junxia**, track
1978	**Tracy Caulkins**, swimming	1986	**Heike Drechsler**, track	1994	**Le Jingyi**, swimming
1979	**Marita Koch**, track	1987	**Steffi Graf**, tennis	1995	**Gwen Torrence**, track
1980	**Hanni Wenzel**, alpine skiing	1988	**Florence Griffith Joyner**, track	1996	discontinued
1981	**Chris Evert Lloyd**, tennis	1989	**Steffi Graf**, tennis		

American-International Athlete Trophy

Formerly known as the Jesse Owens International Trophy, the trophy has been presented annually by the International Amateur Athletic Association since 1981 and selected by a worldwide panel of electors.

Multiple winners: Lance Armstrong, Michael Johnson and Marion Jones (2).

Year		Year		Year	
1981	**Eric Heiden**, speed skating	1990	**Roger Kingdom**, track	1997	**Michael Johnson**, track
1982	**Sebastian Coe**, track	1991	**Greg LeMond**, cycling	1998	**Haile Gebrselassie**, track
1983	**Mary Decker**, track	1992	**Mike Powell**, track	1999	**Marion Jones**, track
1984	**Edwin Moses**, track	1993	**Vitaly Scherbo**, gymnastics	2000	**Lance Armstrong**, cycling
1985	**Carl Lewis**, track	1994	**Wang Junxia**, track	2001	**Marion Jones**, track
1986	**Said Aouita**, track	1995	**Johann Olva Koss**, speed skating	2002	**Ian Thorpe**, swimming
1987	**Greg Louganis**, diving			2003	**Lance Armstrong**, cycling
1988	**Ben Johnson**, track	1996	**Michael Johnson**, track	2004	**Michael Phelps**, swimming

Honda-Broderick Cup

To the outstanding collegiate woman athlete of the year in NCAA competition. Winner is chosen from nominees in each of the NCAA's 10 competitive sports. Final voting is done by member athletic directors. Award is named after founder and sportswear manufacturer Thomas Broderick.

Multiple winner: Tracy Caulkins (2).

Year		Year		
1977	**Lucy Harris**, Delta St . . . . .basketball	1987	**Mary T. Meagher**, California . . . . . .swimming
1978	**Ann Meyers**, UCLA . . . . .basketball	1988	**Teresa Weatherspoon**, La. Tech . . . .basketball
1979	**Nancy Lieberman**, Old Dominion . . .basketball	1989	**Vicki Huber**, Villanova . . . . .track
1980	**Julie Shea**, N.C. State . . . . .track & field	1990	**Suzy Favor**, Wisconsin . . . . .track
1981	**Jill Sterkel**, Texas . . . . .swimming	1991	**Dawn Staley**, Virginia . . . . .basketball
1982	**Tracy Caulkins**, Florida . . . . .swimming	1992	**Missy Marlowe**, Utah . . . . .gymnastics
1983	**Deitre Collins**, Hawaii . . . . .volleyball	1993	**Lisa Fernandez**, UCLA . . . . .softball
1984	**Tracy Caulkins**, Florida . . . . .swimming	1994	**Mia Hamm**, North Carolina . . . . .soccer
	& **Cheryl Miller**, USC . . . . .basketball	1995	**Rebecca Lobo**, UConn . . . . .basketball
1985	**Jackie Joyner**, UCLA . . . . .track & field	1996	**Jennifer Rizzotti**, UConn . . . . .basketball
1986	**Kamie Ethridge**, Texas . . . . .basketball	1997	**Cindy Daws**, Notre Dame . . . . .soccer

Awards (Cont.)

Year		
1998 **Chamique Holdsclaw**, Tennessee . . .basketball		
1999 **Misty May**, Long Beach St. . . . . .volleyball		
2000 **Cristina Teuscher**, Columbia . . . . . .swimming		
2001 **Jackie Stiles**, SW Missouri St. . . . . .basketball		

Year		
2002 **Angela Williams**, USC . . . . .track		
2003 **Natasha Watley**, UCLA . . . . .softball		
2004 **Tara Kirk**, Stanford . . . . .swimming		

Flo Hyman Award

Presented annually since 1987 by the Women's Sports Foundation for "exemplifying dignity, spirit and commitment to excellence" and named in honor of the late captain of the 1984 U.S. Women's Volleyball team. Voting by WSF members.

Year	Year	Year
1987 **Martina Navratilova**, tennis	1993 **Lynette Woodard**, basketball	1999 **Bonnie Blair**, speed skating
1988 **Jackie Joyner-Kersee**, track	1994 **Patty Sheehan**, golf	2000 **Monica Seles**, tennis
1989 **Evelyn Ashford**, track	1995 **Mary Lou Retton**, gymnastics	2001 **Lisa Leslie**, basketball
1990 **Chris Evert**, tennis	1996 **Donna de Varona**, swimming	2002 **Dot Richardson**, softball
1991 **Diana Golden**, skiing	1997 **Billie Jean King**, tennis	2003 **Nawal El Moutawakel**, track
1992 **Nancy Lopez**, golf	1998 **Nadia Comaneci**, gymnastics	

James E. Sullivan Memorial Award

Presented annually by the Amateur Athletic Union since 1930. The Sullivan Award is named after the former AAU president and given to the athlete who, "by his or her performance, example and influence as an amateur, has done the most during the year to advance the cause of sportsmanship." An athlete cannot win the award more than once.

Nineteen year-old swimmer **Michael Phelps** won the 2003 Sullivan Award. He became the first male to win five U.S. titles at one meet, setting a world record in the 200 individual medley and set five records at the world championships. The four additional finalists are listed alphabetically: **LeBron James**, basketball; **Apolo Anton Ohno**, short track speed skating; **Philippa Raschker**, track and field, and **Diana Taurasi**, basketball. Vote totals were not released.

Year	Year	Year
1930 **Bobby Jones**, golf	1956 **Pat McCormick**, diving	1982 **Mary Decker**, track
1931 **Barney Berlinger**, track	1957 **Bobby Morrow**, track	1983 **Edwin Moses**, track
1932 **Jim Bausch**, track	1958 **Glenn Davis**, track	1984 **Greg Louganis**, diving
1933 **Glenn Cunningham**, track	1959 **Parry O'Brien**, track	1985 **Joan B. Samuelson**, track
1934 **Bill Bonthron**, track	1960 **Rafer Johnson**, track	1986 **Jackie Joyner-Kersee**, track
1935 **Lawson Little**, golf	1961 **Wilma Rudolph**, track	1987 **Jim Abbott**, baseball
1936 **Glenn Morris**, track	1962 **Jim Beatty**, track	1988 **Florence Griffith Joyner**, track
1937 **Don Budge**, tennis	1963 **John Pennel**, track	1989 **Janet Evans**, swimming
1938 **Don Lash**, track	1964 **Don Schollander**, swimming	1990 **John Smith**, wrestling
1939 **Joe Burk**, rowing	1965 **Bill Bradley**, basketball	1991 **Mike Powell**, track
1940 **Greg Rice**, track	1966 **Jim Ryun**, track	1992 **Bonnie Blair**, speed skating
1941 **Leslie MacMitchell**, track	1967 **Randy Matson**, track	1993 **Charlie Ward**, football
1942 **Cornelius Warmerdam**, track	1968 **Debbie Meyer**, swimming	1994 **Dan Jansen**, speed skating
1943 **Gilbert Dodds**, track	1969 **Bill Toomey**, track	1995 **Bruce Baumgartner**, wrestling
1944 **Ann Curtis**, swimming	1970 **John Kinsella**, swimming	1996 **Michael Johnson**, track
1945 **Doc Blanchard**, football	1971 **Mark Spitz**, swimming	1997 **Peyton Manning**, football
1946 **Arnold Tucker**, football	1972 **Frank Shorter**, track	1998 **Chamique Holdsclaw**,
1947 **John B. Kelly, Jr.**, rowing	1973 **Bill Walton**, basketball	basketball
1948 **Bob Mathias**, track	1974 **Rich Wohlhuter**, track	1999 **Coco and Kelly Miller**,
1949 **Dick Button**, skating	1975 **Tim Shaw**, swimming	basketball
1950 **Fred Wilt**, track	1976 **Bruce Jenner**, track	2000 **Rulon Gardner**, wrestling
1951 **Bob Richards**, track	1977 **John Naber**, swimming	2001 **Michelle Kwan**, figure skating
1952 **Horace Ashenfelter**, track	1978 **Tracy Caulkins**, swimming	2002 **Sarah Hughes**, figure skating
1953 **Sammy Lee**, diving	1979 **Kurt Thomas**, gymnastics	2003 **Michael Phelps**, swimming
1954 **Mal Whitfield**, track	1980 **Eric Heiden**, speed skating	
1955 **Harrison Dillard**, track	1981 **Carl Lewis**, track	

ESPY Awards

The ESPY Awards, which represent the convergence of the sports and entertainment communities, were created by ESPN in 1993 and are given for Excellence in Sports Performance in more than 30 categories. ESPYs are awarded by a panel of sports executives, journalists and retired athletes whose decisions are based on the performances of the nominees during the year preceding the awards ceremony. Note that not all categories are listed below.

Breakthrough Athlete

Year	Year
1993 Gary Sheffield, San Diego Padres	2000 Kurt Warner, St. Louis Rams
1994 Mike Piazza, Los Angeles Dodgers	2001 Daunte Culpepper, Minnesota Vikings
1995 Jeff Bagwell, Houston Astros	2002 Tom Brady, New England Patriots
1996 Hideo Nomo, Los Angeles Dodgers	2003 Alfonso Soriano, New York Yankees
1997 Tiger Woods, golf	2004 LeBron James, Cleveland Cavaliers
1998 Nomar Garciaparra, Boston Red Sox	
1999 Randy Moss, Minnesota Vikings	

Best Coach/Manager

Year	
1993	Jimmy Johnson, Dallas Cowboys
1994	Jimmy Johnson, Dallas Cowboys
1995	George Siefert, San Francisco 49ers
1996	Gary Barnett, Northwestern
1997	Joe Torre, New York Yankees
1998	Jim Leyland, Florida Marlins
1999	Joe Torre, New York Yankees
2000	Joe Torre, New York Yankees
2001	Joe Torre, New York Yankees
2002	Phil Jackson, Los Angeles Lakers
2003	Jon Gruden, Tampa Bay Buccaneers
2004	Larry Brown, Detroit Pistons

Best Comeback Athlete

Year	
1993	Dave Winfield, Toronto Blue Jays
1994	Mario Lemieux, Pittsburgh Penguins
1995	Dan Marino, Miami Dolphins
1996	Michael Jordan, Chicago Bulls
1997	Evander Holyfield, boxer
1998	Roger Clemens, Toronto Blue Jays
1999	Eric Davis, Baltimore Orioles
2000	Lance Armstrong, cycling
2001	Andres Galarraga, baseball
2002	Jennifer Capriati, tennis
2003	Tommy Maddox, Pittsburgh Steelers
2004	Bethany Hamilton, surfing

Best Female Athlete

Year	
1993	Monica Seles, tennis
1994	Julie Krone, jockey
1995	Bonnie Blair, speed skater
1996	Rebecca Lobo, basketball
1997	Amy Van Dyken, swimming
1998	Mia Hamm, soccer
1999	Chamique Holdsclaw, college basketball
2000	Mia Hamm, soccer
2001	Marion Jones, track
2002	Venus Williams, tennis
2003	Serena Williams, tennis
2004	Diana Taurasi, basketball

Best Male Athlete

Year	
1993	Michael Jordan, Chicago Bulls
1994	Barry Bonds, San Francisco Giants
1995	Steve Young, San Francisco 49ers
1996	Cal Ripken, Baltimore Orioles
1997	Michael Johnson, Olympic sprinter
1998	Tiger Woods, golf
1999	Mark McGwire, St. Louis Cardinals
2000	Tiger Woods, golf
2001	Tiger Woods, golf
2002	Tiger Woods, golf
2003	Lance Armstrong, cycling
2004	Lance Armstrong, cycling

Outstanding Performance Under Pressure

Year	
1993	Christian Laettner, Duke
1994	Joe Carter, Toronto Blue Jays
1995	Mark Messier, New York Rangers
1996	Martin Brodeur, New Jersey Devils
1997	Kerri Strug, Olympic gymnast
1998	Terrell Davis, Denver Broncos
1999	Mark O'Meara, golf
2000	discontinued

Best Team

Year	
1993	Dallas Cowboys
1994	Toronto Blue Jays
1995	New York Rangers
1996	UConn women's hoops
1997	New York Yankees
1998	Denver Broncos
1999	New York Yankees
2000	U.S. Women's World Cup Soccer Team
2001	New York Yankees & Oklahoma football
2002	Los Angeles Lakers
2003	Anaheim Angels
2004	Detroit Pistons

Best Baseball Player

Year	
1993	Dennis Eckersley, Oakland A's
1994	Barry Bonds, San Francisco Giants
1995	Jeff Bagwell, Houston Astros
1996	Greg Maddux, Atlanta Braves
1997	Ken Caminiti, San Diego Padres
1998	Larry Walker, Colorado Rockies
1999	Mark McGwire, St. Louis Cardinals
2000	Pedro Martinez, Boston Red Sox
2001	Pedro Martinez, Boston Red Sox
2002	Barry Bonds, San Francisco Giants
2003	Barry Bonds, San Francisco Giants
2004	Barry Bonds, San Francisco Giants

Best NFL Player

Year	
1993	Emmitt Smith, Dallas Cowboys
1994	Emmitt Smith, Dallas Cowboys
1995	Barry Sanders, Detroit Lions
1996	Brett Favre, Green Bay Packers
1997	Brett Favre, Green Bay Packers
1998	Barry Sanders, Detroit Lions
1999	Terrell Davis, Denver Broncos
2000	Kurt Warner, St. Louis Rams
2001	Marshall Faulk, St. Louis Rams
2002	Marshall Faulk, St. Louis Rams
2003	Michael Vick, Atlanta Falcons
2004	Peyton Manning, Indianapolis Colts

Best NBA Player

Year	
1993	Michael Jordan, Chicago Bulls
1994	Charles Barkley, Phoenix Suns
1995	Hakeem Olajuwon, Houston Rockets
1996	Hakeem Olajuwon, Houston Rockets
1997	Michael Jordan, Chicago Bulls
1998	Michael Jordan, Chicago Bulls
1999	Michael Jordan, Chicago Bulls
2000	Tim Duncan, San Antonio Spurs
2001	Shaquille O'Neal, Los Angeles Lakers
2002	Shaquille O'Neal, Los Angeles Lakers
2003	Tim Duncan, San Antonio Spurs
2004	Kevin Garnett, Minnesota Timberwolves

Best WNBA Player

Year	
1998	Cynthia Cooper, Houston Comets
1999	Cynthia Cooper, Houston Comets
2000	Cynthia Cooper, Houston Comets
2001	Sheryl Swoopes, Houston Comets
2002	Lisa Leslie, Los Angeles Sparks
2003	Lisa Leslie, Los Angeles Sparks
2004	Lauren Jackson, Seattle Storm

Best NHL Player

Year	
1993	Mario Lemieux, Pittsburgh Penguins
1994	Mario Lemieux, Pittsburgh Penguins
1995	Mark Messier, New York Rangers
1996	Eric Lindros, Philadelphia Flyers
1997	Joe Sakic, Colorado Avalanche
1998	Mario Lemieux, Pittsburgh Penguins
1999	Dominik Hasek, Buffalo Sabres
2000	Dominik Hasek, Buffalo Sabres
2001	Chris Pronger, St. Louis Blues
2002	Jarome Iginla, Calgary Flames
2003	Jean-Sebastien Giguere, Anaheim Mighty Ducks
2004	Jarome Iginla, Calgary Flames

Outstanding College Football Performer of the Year

Year	
1993	Garrison Hearst, Georgia
1994	Charlie Ward, Florida State
1995	Rashaan Salaam, Colorado
1996	Eddie George, Ohio State
1997	Danny Wuerffel, Florida
1998	Peyton Manning, Tennessee
1999	Ricky Williams, Texas
2000	Michael Vick, Virginia Tech
2001	Chris Weinke, Florida State
2002	discontinued

Outstanding College Basketball Performer of the Year

Year	
1993	Christian Laettner, Duke
1994	Bobby Hurley, Duke
1995	Grant Hill, Duke
1996	Ed O'Bannon, UCLA
1997	Tim Duncan, Wake Forest
1998	Keith Van Horn, Utah
1999	Antawn Jamison, North Carolina
2000	Elton Brand, Duke
2001	Kenyon Martin, Cincinnati
2002	discontinued

Outstanding Women's College Hoops Performer of the Year

Year	
1993	Dawn Staley, Virginia
1994	Sheryl Swoopes, Texas Tech
1995	Charlotte Smith, North Carolina
1996	Rebecca Lobo, Connecticut
1997	Saudia Roundtree, Georgia
1998	Chamique Holdsclaw, Tennessee
1999	Chamique Holdsclaw, Tennessee
2000	Chamique Holdsclaw, Tennessee
2001	Tamika Catchings, Tennessee
2002	discontinued

Best Men's Tennis Player

Year	
1993	Jim Courier
1994	Pete Sampras
1995	Pete Sampras
1996	Pete Sampras
1997	Pete Sampras
1998	Pete Sampras
1999	Pete Sampras
2000	Andre Agassi
2001	Pete Sampras
2002	Lleyton Hewitt
2003	Andre Agassi
2004	Andy Roddick

Best Women's Tennis Player

Year	
1993	Monica Seles
1994	Steffi Graf
1995	A. Sanchez Vicario
1996	Steffi Graf
1997	Steffi Graf
1998	Martina Hingis
1999	Lindsay Davenport
2000	Lindsay Davenport
2001	Venus Williams
2002	Venus Williams
2002	Venus Williams
2003	Serena Williams
2004	Serena Williams

Best Men's Golfer

Year	
1993	Fred Couples
1994	Nick Price
1995	Nick Price
1996	Corey Pavin
1997	Tom Lehman
1998	Tiger Woods
1999	Mark O'Meara
2000	Tiger Woods
2001	Tiger Woods
2002	Tiger Woods
2003	Tiger Woods
2004	Phil Mickelson

Best Women's Golfer

Year	
1993	Dottie Mochrie
1994	Betsy King
1995	Laura Davies
1996	Annika Sorenstam
1997	Karrie Webb
1998	Annika Sorenstam
1999	Annika Sorenstam
2000	Julie Inkster
2001	Karrie Webb
2002	Annika Sorenstam
2003	Annika Sorenstam
2004	Annika Sorenstam

Best Jockey

Year	
1994	Mike Smith
1995	Chris McCarron
1996	Jerry Bailey
1997	Jerry Bailey
1998	Gary Stevens
1999	Kent Desormeaux
2000	Chris Antley
2001	Kent Desormeaux
2002	Victor Espinoza
2003	Jose Santos
2004	Stewart Elliot

Best Bowler

Year	
1995	Norm Duke
1996	Mike Aulby
1997	Bob Learn Jr.
1998	Walter Ray Williams Jr.
1999	Walter Ray Williams Jr.
2000	Parker Bohn III
2001	Walter Ray Williams Jr.
2002	Pete Weber
2003	Walter Ray Williams Jr.
2004	Pete Weber

Best Driver

Year	
1993	Nigel Mansell
1994	Nigel Mansell
1995	Al Unser Jr.
1996	Jeff Gordon
1997	Jimmy Vasser
1998	Jeff Gordon
1999	Jeff Gordon
2000	Dale Jarrett
2001	Bobby Labonte
2002	Michael Schumacher
2003	Tony Stewart
2004	Dale Earnhardt Jr.

Best Men's Track Athlete

Year	
1993	Kevin Young
1994	Michael Johnson
1995	Dennis Mitchell
1996	Michael Johnson
1997	Michael Johnson
1998	Wilson Kipketer
1999	Maurice Greene
2000	Michael Johnson
2001	Maurice Greene
2002	Maurice Greene
2003	Tim Montgomery
2004	Tom Pappas

Best Women's Track Athlete

Year	
1993	Evelyn Ashford
1994	Gail Devers
1995	Gwen Torrence
1996	Kim Batten
1997	Marie-Jose Perec
1998	Marion Jones
1999	Marion Jones
2000	Marion Jones
2001	Marion Jones
2002	Marion Jones
2003	Gail Devers
2004	Gail Devers

Game of the Year

Year	
1996	AFC championship between Colts and Steelers
1997	Rose Bowl, Ohio State edges Arizona St.
1998	Super Bowl XXXII, Broncos over Packers
1999-2001	not awarded
2002	World Series Game 7, Diamondbacks-Yankees
2003	Fiesta Bowl, Ohio State beat Miami-FL in OT
2004	Super Bowl XXXVIII, Patriots over Panthers

Best Play

Year	
2002	Derek Jeter's throw in World Series Game 3.
2003	LSU's Hail Mary TD.
2004	New Orleans Saints' lateral

Best Boxer

Year	
1993	Riddick Bowe
1994	Evander Holyfield
1995	George Foreman
1996	Roy Jones Jr.
1997	Evander Holyfield
1998	Evander Holyfield
1999	Oscar De La Hoya
2000	Roy Jones Jr.
2001	Felix Trinidad
2002	Lennox Lewis
2003	Roy Jones Jr.
2004	Antonio Tarver

Best Male College Athlete

Year	
2002	Cael Sanderson, Iowa St. wrestling
2003	Carmelo Anthony, Syracuse basketball
2004	Emeka Okafor, UConn basketball

Best Female College Athlete

Year	
2002	Sue Bird, UConn basketball
2003	Diana Taurasi, UConn basketball
2004	Diana Taurasi, UConn basketball

Best Male Soccer Player

Year	
2002	Landon Donovan
2003	Ronaldo
2004	David Beckham

Best Female Soccer Player

Year	
2002	Tiffeny Milbrett
2003	Katia
2004	Mia Hamm

Best Outdoors Athlete

Year	
2002	Kevin VanDam, fishing
2003	Jay Yelas, fishing
2004	Tina Bosworth, log rolling

Best Action Sports Athlete

Year	
2002	Kelly Clark, snowboarding
2003	Shaun White, snowboarding
2004	Award split into female and male categories

Best Male Action Sports Athlete

Year	
2004	Ryan Nyquist, bike

Best Female Action Sports Athlete

Year	
2004	Dallas Friday, wakeboarding

Arthur Ashe Award for Courage

Presented since 1993 on the annual ESPN "ESPYs" telecast. Given to a member of the sports community who has exemplified the same courage, spirit and determination to help others despite personal hardship that characterized Arthur Ashe, the late tennis champion and humanitarian. Voting done by select 26-member committee of media and sports personalities.

Year		Year		Year	
1993	**Jim Valvano**, basketball	1998	**Dean Smith**, college basketball	2002	**Todd Beamer, Mark Bingham, Tom Burnett** and
1994	**Steve Palermo**, baseball	1999	**Billie Jean King**, tennis		**Jeremy Glick**, Flight 93
1995	**Howard Cosell**, TV & radio	2000	**Dave Sanders**, Columbine	2003	**Pat Tillman**, football
1996	**Loretta Clairborne**, special		H.S. coach		**& Kevin Tillman**, baseball
	olympics	2001	**Cathy Freeman**, track	2004	**George Weah**, soccer
1997	**Muhammad Ali**, boxing				

Presidential Medal of Freedom

Since President John F. Kennedy established the Medal of Freedom as America's highest civilian honor in 1963, only 12 sports figures have won the award. Note that (*) indicates the presentation was made posthumously.

Year		President	Year		President
1963	**Bob Kiphuth**, swimming	Kennedy	1991	**Ted Williams**, baseball	G. Bush
1976	**Jesse Owens**, track & field	Ford	1992	**Richard Petty**, auto racing	G. Bush
1977	**Joe DiMaggio**, baseball	Ford	1993	**Arthur Ashe***, tennis	Clinton
1983	**Paul (Bear) Bryant***, football	Reagan	2002	**Hank Aaron**, baseball	G.W. Bush
1984	**Jackie Robinson***, baseball	Reagan	2003	**John Wooden**, basketball	G.W. Bush
1986	**Earl (Red) Blaik**, football	Reagan	2004	**Arnold Palmer**, golf	G.W. Bush

The Hickok Belt

Officially known as the S. Rae Hickok Professional Athlete of the Year Award and presented by the Kickik Manufacturing Co. of Arlington, Texas, from 1950-76. The trophy was a large belt of gold, diamonds and other jewels, reportedly worth $30,000 in 1976, the last year it was handed out. Voting was done by 270 newspaper sports editors from around the country.
Multiple winner: Sandy Koufax (2).

Year		Year		Year	
1950	**Phil Rizzuto**, baseball	1960	**Arnold Palmer**, golf	1970	**Brooks Robinson**, baseball
1951	**Allie Reynolds**, baseball	1961	**Roger Maris**, baseball	1971	**Lee Trevino**, golf
1952	**Rocky Marciano**, boxing	1962	**Maury Wills**, baseball	1972	**Steve Carlton**, baseball
1953	**Ben Hogan**, golf	1963	**Sandy Koufax**, baseball	1973	**O.J. Simpson**, football
1954	**Willie Mays**, baseball	1964	**Jim Brown**, football	1974	**Muhammad Ali**, boxing
1955	**Otto Graham**, football	1965	**Sandy Koufax**, baseball	1975	**Pete Rose**, baseball
1956	**Mickey Mantle**, baseball	1966	**Frank Robinson**, baseball	1976	**Ken Stabler**, football
1957	**Carmen Basilio**, boxing	1967	**Carl Yastrzemski**, baseball	1977	Discontinued
1958	**Bob Turley**, baseball	1968	**Joe Namath**, football		
1959	**Ingemar Johansson**, boxing	1969	**Tom Seaver**, baseball		

ABC's "Wide World of Sports" Athlete of the Year

Selected annually by the producers of ABC Sports since 1962.
Multiple winners: Greg LeMond and Tiger Woods (2).

Year		Year		Year	
1962	**Jim Beatty**, track	1975	**Jack Nicklaus**, golf	1989	**Greg LeMond**, cycling
1963	**Valery Brumel**, track	1976	**Nadia Comaneci**, gymnastics	1990	**Greg LeMond**, cycling
1964	**Don Schollander**, swimming	1977	**Steve Cauthen**, horse racing	1991	**Carl Lewis**, track
1965	**Jim Clark**, auto racing	1978	**Ron Guidry**, baseball		& **Kim Zmeskal**, gymnastics
1966	**Jim Ryun**, track	1979	**Willie Stargell**, baseball	1992	**Bonnie Blair**, speed skating
1967	**Peggy Fleming**, figure skating	1980	**U.S. Olympic hockey team**	1993	**Evander Holyfield**, boxing
1968	**Bill Toomey**, track	1981	**Sugar Ray Leonard**, boxing	1994	**Al Unser Jr.**, auto racing
1969	**Mario Andretti**, auto racing	1982	**Wayne Gretzky**, hockey	1995	**Miguel Induráin**, cycling
1970	**Willis Reed**, basketball	1983	**Australia II**, yachting	1996	**Michael Johnson**, track
1971	**Lee Trevino**, golf	1984	**Edwin Moses**, track	1997	**Tiger Woods**, golf
1972	**Olga Korbut**, gymnastics	1985	**Pete Rose**, baseball	1998	**Mark McGwire**, baseball
1973	**O.J. Simpson**, football	1986	**Debi Thomas**, figure skating	1999	**Lance Armstrong**, cycling
	& **Jackie Stewart**, auto racing	1987	**Dennis Conner**, yachting	2000	**Tiger Woods**, golf
1974	**Muhammad Ali**, boxing	1988	**Greg Louganis**, diving	2001	discontinued

Time Person of the Year

Since Charles Lindbergh was named _Time_ magazine's first Man of the Year for 1927, two individuals with significant sports credentials have won the honor.

Year
1984 **Peter Ueberroth**, president of the Los Angeles Olympic Organizing Committee.
1991 **Ted Turner**, owner-president of Turner Broadcasting System, founder of CNN cable news network, owner of the Atlanta Braves (NL) and Atlanta Hawks (NBA), and former winning America's Cup skipper.

TROPHY CASE

From the first organized track meet at Olympia in 776 B.C., to the Athens Summer Olympics over 2,700 years later, championships have been officially recognized with prizes that are symbolically rich and eagerly pursued. Here are 15 of the most coveted trophies in America.
(Illustrations by Lynn Mercer Michaud)

America's Cup

First presented by England's Royal Yacht Squadron to the winner of an invitational race around the Isle of Wight on Aug. 22, 1851 . . . originally called the Hundred Guinea Cup . . . renamed after the U.S. boat America, winner of the first race . . . made of sterling silver and designed by London jewelers R. & G. Garrard . . . measures 2 feet, 3 inches high and weighs 16 lbs . . . originally cost 100 guineas ($500), now valued at $250,000 . . . bell-shaped base added in 1958 . . . challenged for every three to four years . . . trophy held by yacht club sponsoring winning boat . . . Cup was badly damaged when a Maori protester repeatedly smashed it with a sledgehammer on March 14, 1997. It was sent back to the original maker and fully restored.

Vince Lombardi Trophy

First presented at the AFL-NFL World Championship Game (now Super Bowl) on Jan. 15, 1967 . . . originally called the World Championship Game Trophy . . . renamed in 1971 in honor of former Green Bay Packers GM-coach and two-time Super Bowl winner Vince Lombardi, who died in 1970 as coach of Washington . . . made of sterling silver and designed by Tiffany & Co. of New York . . . measures 21 inches high and weighs 7 lbs (football depicted is regulation size) . . . valued at $12,500 . . . competed for annually . . . winning team keeps trophy.

Olympic Gold Medal

First presented by International Olympic Committee in 1908 (until then winners received silver medals) . . . second and third place finishers also got medals of silver and bronze for first time in 1908 . . . each medal must be at least 2.4 inches in diameter and 0.12 inches thick . . . the gold medal is actually made of silver, but must be gilded with at least 6 grams (0.21 ounces) of pure gold . . . the medals for the 1996 Atlanta Games were designed by Malcolm Grear Designers and produced by Reed & Barton of Taunton, Mass . . 604 gold, 604 silver and 630 bronze medals were made . . . competed for every two years as Winter and Summer Games alternate . . . winners keep medals.

Awards (Cont.)

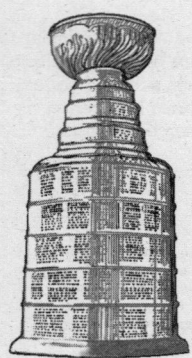

Stanley Cup

Donated by Lord Stanley of Preston, the Governor General of Canada and first presented in 1893 . . . original cup was made of sterling silver by an unknown London silversmith and measured 7 inches high with an 11½-inch diameter . . . in order to accommodate all the rosters of winning teams, the cup now measures 35½ inches high with a base 54 inches around and weighs 32 lbs . . . in order to add new names each year, bands on the trophy are often retired and displayed at the Hall of Fame . . . originally bought for 10 guineas ($48.67), it is now insured for $75,000 . . . actual cup retired to Hall of Fame and replaced in 1970 . . . presented to NHL playoff champion since 1918 . . . trophy loaned to winning team for one year.

World Cup

First presented by the Federation Internationale de Football Association (FIFA) . . . originally called the World Cup Trophy . . . renamed the Jules Rimet Cup (after the then FIFA president) in 1946, but retired by Brazil after that country's third title in 1970 . . . new World Cup trophy created in 1974 . . . designed by Italian sculptor Silvio Gazzaniga and made of solid 18 carat gold with two malachite rings inlaid at the base . . . measures 14.2 inches high and weighs 11 lbs . . . insured for $200,000 (U.S.) . . . competed for every four years . . . winning team gets gold-plated replica.

Commissioner's Trophy

First presented by the Commissioner of baseball to the winner of the 1967 World Series . . . also known as the World Championship Trophy . . . made of brass and gold plate with an ebony base and a baseball in the center made of pewter with a silver finish . . . designed by Balfour & Co. of Attleboro, Mass . . . 30 pennants represent 14 AL and 16 NL teams . . . measures 30 inches high and 36 inches around at the base and weighs 30 lbs . . . valued at $15,000 . . . competed for annually . . . winning team keeps trophy.

Larry O'Brien Trophy

First presented in 1978 to winner of NBA Finals . . . originally called the Walter A. Brown Trophy after the league pioneer and Boston Celtics owner (an earlier NBA championship bowl was also named after Brown) . . . renamed in 1984 in honor of outgoing commissioner O'Brien, who served from 1975-84 . . . made of sterling silver with 24 carat gold overlay and designed by Tiffany & Co. of New York . . . measures 2 feet high and weighs 14½ lbs (basketball depicted is regulation size) . . . valued at $13,500 . . . competed for annually . . . winning team keeps trophy.

Heisman Trophy

First presented in 1935 to the best college football player east of the Mississippi by the Downtown Athletic Club of New York . . . players across the entire country eligible since 1936 . . . originally called the DAC Trophy . . . renamed in 1936 following the death of DAC athletic director and former college coach John W. Heisman . . . made of bronze and designed by New York sculptor Frank Eliscu, it measures 13½ in. high, 6½ in. wide and 14 in. long at the base and weighs 25 lbs . . . valued at $2,000 . . . voting done by national media and former Heisman winners . . . trophy sponsor American Suzuki announced plans for limited fan voting starting in 1999 . . . awarded annually . . . winner keeps trophy.

James E. Sullivan Memorial Award

First presented by the Amateur Athletic Union (AAU) in 1930 as a gold medal and given to the nation's outstanding amateur athlete . . . trophy given since 1933 . . . named after the amateur sports movement pioneer, who was a founder and past president of AAU and the director of the 1904 Olympic Games in St. Louis . . . made of bronze with a marble base, it measures 17½ in. high and 11 in. wide at the base and weighs 13½ lbs . . . valued at $2,500 . . . voting done by AAU and USOC officials, former winners and selected media . . . awarded annually . . . winner keeps trophy.

Ryder Cup

Donated in 1927 by English seed merchant Samuel Ryder, who offered the gold cup for a biennial match between teams of golfing pros from Great Britain and the United States . . . the format changed in 1977 to include the best players on the European PGA Tour . . . made of 14 carat gold on a wood base and designed by Mappin and Webb of London . . . the golfer depicted on the top of the trophy is Ryder's friend and teaching pro Abe Mitchell . . . the cup measures 16 in. high and weighs 4 lbs . . . insured for $50,000 . . . competed for every two years at alternating European and U.S. sites . . . the cup is held by the PGA headquarters of the winning side.

Davis Cup

Donated by American college student and U.S. doubles champion Dwight F. Davis in 1900 and presented by the International Tennis Federation (ITF) to the winner of the annual 16-team men's competition . . . officially called the International Lawn Tennis Challenge Trophy . . . made of sterling silver and designed by Shreve, Crump and Low of Boston, the cup has a matching tray (added in 1921) and a very heavy two-tiered base containing rosters of past winning teams . . . it stands 34½ in. high and 108 in. around at the base and weighs 400 lbs . . . insured for $150,000 . . . competed for annually . . . trophy loaned to winning country for one year.

Borg-Warner Trophy

First presented by the Borg-Warner Automotive Co. of Chicago in 1936 to the winner of the Indianapolis 500 . . . replaced the Wheeler-Schebler Trophy which went to the 400-mile leader from 1911-32 . . . made of sterling silver with bas-relief sculptured heads of each winning driver and a gold bas-relief head of Tony Hulman, the owner of the Indy Speedway from 1945-77 . . . designed by Robert J. Hill and made by Gorham, Inc. of Rhode Island . . . measures 51½ in. high and weighs over 80 lbs . . . new base added in 1988 and the entire trophy restored in 1991 . . . competed for annually . . . insured for $1 million . . . trophy stays at Speedway Hall of Fame . . . winner gets a 14-in. high replica valued at $30,000.

NCAA Championship Trophy

First presented in 1952 by the NCAA to all 1st, 2nd and 3rd place teams in sports with sanctioned tournaments . . . 1st place teams receive gold-plated awards, 2nd place award is silver-plated and 3rd is bronze . . . replaced silver cup given to championship teams from 1939-51 . . . made of walnut, the trophy stands 24¾ in. high, 14⅛ in. wide and 4½ in. deep at the base and weighs 15 lbs . . . designed by Medallic Art Co. of Danbury, Conn. and made by House of Usher of Kansas City since 1990 . . . valued at $500 . . . competed for annually . . . winning teams keep trophies.

World Championship Belt

First presented in 1921 by the World Boxing Association, one of the three organizations (the World Boxing Council and International Boxing Federation are the others) generally accepted as sanctioning legitimate world championship fights . . . belt weighs 8 lbs. and is made of hand tanned leather . . . the outsized buckle measures 10½ in. high and 8 in. wide, is made of pewter with 24 carat gold plate and contains crystal and semi-precious stones . . . side panels of polished brass are for engraving title bout results . . . currently made by Champbelts by Ronn Scala in Pittsburgh . . . champions keep belts even if they lose their title.

World Championship Ring

Rings decorated with gems and engraving date back to ancient Egypt where the wealthy wore heavy gold and silver rings to indicate social status . . . championship rings in sports serve much the same purpose, indicating the wearer is a champion . . . As an example, the Dallas Cowboys' ring for winning Superbowl XXX on Jan. 28, 1996 was designed by Diamond Cutters International of Houston . . . each ring is made of 14 carat yellow gold, weighs 48-51 penny weights and features five trimmed marquis diamonds interlocking in the shape of the Cowboys' star logo as well as five more marquis diamonds (for the team's five Super Bowl wins) on a bed of 51 smaller diamonds . . . rings were appraised at over $30,000 each.

Who's Who

Stock car king **Richard Petty** won 200 races and countless fans during his illustrious NASCAR career.

Sports Personalities

Nine hundred thirty-six entries dating back to the 19th century. Entries updated through Oct. 13, 2004.

Hank Aaron (b. Feb. 5, 1934): Baseball OF; led NL in HRs and RBI 4 times each and batting twice with Milwaukee and Atlanta Braves; MVP in 1957; played in 24 All-Star Games, all-time leader in HRs (755), RBI (2,297), total bases (6,856), 3rd in hits (3,771); won 3 Gold Gloves; executive with Braves.

Kareem Abdul-Jabbar (b. Lew Alcindor, Apr. 16, 1947): Basketball C; led UCLA to 3 NCAA titles (1967-69); Final 4 MOP 3 times; Player of Year twice; led Milwaukee (1) and LA Lakers (5) to 6 NBA titles; playoff MVP twice (1971,85), regular season MVP 6 times (1971-72,74,76-77,80); retired in 1989 after 20 seasons as all-time leader in over 20 categories.

Andre Agassi (b. Apr. 29, 1970): Tennis; 59 career tournament wins including the career grand slam; Wimbledon (1992), U.S. Open (1994,99), Australian Open (1995,2000,01,03), French Open (1999); helped U.S. win 2 Davis Cup finals (1990,92); regained the world No. 1 ranking in 1999 for the first time since 1996.

Troy Aikman (b. Nov. 21, 1966): Football QB; consensus All-America at UCLA (1988); 1st overall pick in 1989 NFL Draft (by Dallas); led Cowboys to 3 Super Bowl titles (1992,93,95 seasons); MVP of Super Bowl XXVII.

Marv Albert (b. June 12, 1941): Radio-TV; NBC announcer and radio broadcaster for the New York Knicks, Rangers and Giants who pleaded guilty to a misdemeanor assault charge amid embarrassing allegations of his sex life. Rehired to MSG and Turner networks in 1998 and NBC in '99.

Tenley Albright (b. July 18, 1935): Figure skater; 2-time world champion (1953,55); won Olympic silver (1952) and gold (1956) medals; became a surgeon.

Amy Alcott (b. Feb. 22, 1956): Golfer; 29 career wins, including five majors; inducted into World Golf Hall of Fame in 1999.

Grover Cleveland (Pete) Alexander (b. Feb. 26, 1887, d. Nov. 4, 1950): Baseball RHP; won 20 or more games 9 times; 373 career wins and 90 shutouts.

Muhammad Ali (b. Cassius Clay, Jan. 17, 1942): Boxer; 1960 Olympic light heavyweight champion; 3-time world heavyweight champ (1964-67, 1974-78,1978-79); defeated Sonny Liston (1964), George Foreman (1974) and Leon Spinks (1978) for title; fought Joe Frazier in 3 memorable bouts (1971-75), winning twice; adopted Black Muslim faith in 1964 and changed name; stripped of title in 1967 after conviction for refusing induction into U.S. Army; verdict reversed by Supreme Court in 1971; career record of 56-5 with 37 KOs and 19 successful title defenses; lit the flaming cauldron to signal the beginning of the 1996 Summer Olympics in Atlanta.

Forrest (Phog) Allen (b. Nov. 18, 1885, d. Sept. 16, 1974): Basketball; college coach 48 years; directed Kansas to NCAA title (1952); 746 wins.

Bobby Allison (b. Dec. 3, 1937): Auto racer; 3-time winner of Daytona 500 (1978,82,88); NASCAR national champ in 1983; father of Davey.

Davey Allison (b. Feb. 25, 1961, d. July 13, 1993): Auto racer; stock car Rookie of Year (1987); winner of 19 NASCAR races, including 1992 Daytona 500; killed at age 32 in helicopter accident at Talladega Superspeedway; son of Bobby.

Roberto Alomar (b. Feb. 5, 1968): Baseball; 10-time Gold Glove second baseman; MVP of 1992 ALCS; became known well beyond baseball for spitting in the face of umpire John Hirschbeck during final week-end of 1996 season; named MVP of 1998 All-Star Game.

Walter Alston (b. Dec. 1, 1911, d. Oct. 1, 1984): Baseball; managed Brooklyn-LA Dodgers 23 years, won 7 pennants and 4 World Series (1955,59,63,65); retired after 1976 season with 2,063 wins (2,040 regular season and 23 postseason).

Gary Anderson (b. July 16, 1959): Football K; all-time leading scorer in NFL history; had perfect regular season in 1998 (59/59 PAT, 35/35 FG); held NFL record for consecutive FG made (40, broken by M. Vanderjagt's 42); led AFC in scoring 3 times (1983-85 with Steelers) and NFC once (1998 with Vikings).

Sparky Anderson (b. Feb. 22, 1934): Baseball; only manager to win World Series in each league—Cincinnati in NL (1975-76) and Detroit in AL (1984); 3rd-ranked skipper on all-time career list with 2,228 wins (2,194 regular season and 34 postseason); inducted into the Baseball Hall of Fame in 2000.

Mario Andretti (b. Feb. 28, 1940): Auto racer; 4-time USAC-CART national champion (1965-66,69,84); only driver to win Daytona 500 (1967), Indy 500 (1969) and Formula One world title (1978); Indy 500 Rookie of Year (1965); retired after 1994 racing season ranked 1st in poles (67) and starts (407) and 2nd in wins (52) on all-time CART list; father of Michael and Jeff, uncle of John.

Michael Andretti (b. Oct. 5, 1962): Auto racer; 1991 CART national champion with single-season record 8 wins; Indy 500 Rookie of Year (1984); left IndyCar circuit for ill-fated Formula One try in 1993; returned to IndyCar in 1994; son of Mario.

Earl Anthony (b. Apr. 27, 1938, d. Aug. 14, 2001): Bowler; 6-time PBA Bowler of Year; 41 career titles; first to earn $100,000 in 1 season (1975); first to earn $1 million in career; won 10 Majors (2 Tournament of Champions, 6 PBA National Championships and 2 ABC Masters).

Said Aouita (b. Nov. 2, 1959): Moroccan runner; won gold (5000m) and bronze (800m) in 1984 Olympics; won 5000m at 1987 World Championships; formerly held 2 world records recognized by IAAF—2000m and 5000m.

Luis Aparicio (b. Apr. 29, 1934): Baseball SS; retired as all-time leader in most games, assists and double plays by shortstop; led AL in stolen bases 9 times (1956-64); 506 career steals.

Al Arbour (b. Nov. 1, 1932): Hockey; coached NY Islanders to 4 straight Stanley Cup titles (1980-83); retired after 1993-94 season; 2nd on all-time career list with 904 wins (781 regular season and 123 postseason); elected to Hockey Hall of Fame in 1996.

Eddie Arcaro (b. Feb. 19, 1916, d. Nov. 14, 1997): Jockey; 2-time Triple Crown winner (Whirlaway in 1941, Citation in '48); won Kentucky Derby 5 times, Preakness and Belmont 6 times each.

Roone Arledge (b. July 8, 1931, d. Dec. 5, 2002): Sports TV pioneer; innovator of live events, anthology shows, Olympic coverage, "Monday Night Football" and "Wide World of Sports"; ran ABC Sports from 1968-86; ran ABC News from 1977-98.

Henry Armstrong (b. Dec. 12, 1912, d. Oct. 22, 1988): Boxer; held feather-, light- and welterweight titles simultaneously in 1938; pro record 152-21-8 with 100 KOs.

Lance Armstrong (b. Sept. 18, 1971): Cyclist; Texan who made cycling history as the first 6-time winner of the Tour de France (1999-2004) as member of the U.S. Postal Service team; returned from treatment for testicular cancer to become the world's top cyclist; only the 2nd American winner (Greg Lemond) in the race's history.

Arthur Ashe (b. July 10, 1943, d. Feb. 6, 1993): Tennis; first black man to win U.S. Championship (1968) and Wimbledon (1975); 1st U.S. player to earn $100,000 in 1 year (1970); won Davis Cup as player (1968-70) and captain (1981-82); wrote black sports history, *Hard Road to Glory*; announced in 1992 that he was infected with AIDS virus from a blood transfusion during 1983 heart surgery; in 1997, the new home for the U.S. Open was named Arthur Ashe Stadium.

Evelyn Ashford (b. Apr. 15, 1957): Track & Field; winner of 4 Olympic gold medals—100m in 1984, and 4x100m in 1984, '88 and '92; also won silver medal in 100m in '88; member of 5 U.S. Olympic teams (1976-92); Inducted into Track and Field and Women's Sports Halls of Fame in 1997.

Red Auerbach (b. Sept. 20, 1917): Basketball; 4th winningest coach (regular season and playoffs) in NBA history; won 1,037 times in 20 years; as coach-GM, led Boston to 9 NBA titles, including 8 in a row (1959-66); also coached defunct Washington Capitols (1946-49); NBA Coach of the Year award named after him; retired as Celtics coach in 1966 and as GM in '84; club president from 1970 to 1997 and then again beginning in 2001.

Tracy Austin (b. Dec. 12, 1962): Tennis; youngest player to win U.S. Open (age 16 in 1979); won 2nd U.S. Open in '81; named AP Female Athlete of Year twice before she was 20; recurring neck and back injuries shortened career after 1983; youngest player ever inducted into Tennis Hall of Fame (age 29 in 1992).

Paul Azinger (b. Jan. 6, 1960): Golf; PGA Player of Year (1987); 12 career wins, including '93 PGA Championship; missed most of '94 season overcoming lymphoma (a form of cancer) in right shoulder blade; member of 4 U.S. Ryder Cup teams (1989,91,93,2002).

Bob Baffert (b. Jan. 13, 1953): Horse racing; 3-time Eclipse Award winner as outstanding trainer (1997-99); trained 3 Kentucky Derby winners (1997,98,02), 4 Preakness winners (1997,98,01,02) and 1 Belmont Stakes winner (2001); 4-time leading annual money leader for trainers (1998-01).

Donovan Bailey (b. Dec. 16, 1967): Track; Jamaican-born Canadian sprinter who set world record in the 100m (9.84) in a gold medal-winning performance at 1996 Olympics which stood until '99; set indoor record in 50m (5.56) in 1996; member of Canadian 4x100 relay that won gold in 1996 Olympics.

Oksana Baiul (b. Feb. 26, 1977): Ukrainian figure skater; 1993 world champion at age 15; edged Nancy Kerrigan by a 5-4 judges' vote for 1994 Olympic gold medal.

Hobey Baker (b. Jan. 15, 1892, d. Dec. 21, 1918): Football and hockey star at Princeton (1911-14); member of college football and pro hockey Halls of Fame; college hockey Player of Year award named after him; killed in plane crash.

Seve Ballesteros (b. Apr. 9, 1957): Spanish golfer; has won British Open 3 times (1979,84,88) and Masters twice (1980,83); 3-time European Golfer of Year (1986,88,91); has led Europe to 5 Ryder Cup titles (1985,87,89,95,97).

Ernie Banks (b. Jan. 31, 1931): Baseball SS-1B; led NL in home runs and RBI twice each; 2-time MVP (1958-59) with Chicago Cubs; 512 career HRs.

Roger Bannister (b. Mar. 23, 1929): British runner; first to run mile in less than 4 minutes (3:59.4 on May 6, 1954).

Walter (Red) Barber (b. Feb. 17, 1908, d. Oct. 22, 1992): Radio-TV; renowned baseball play-by-play broadcaster for Cincinnati, Brooklyn and N.Y. Yankees from 1934-66; won Peabody Award for radio commentary in 1991.

Charles Barkley (b. Feb. 20, 1963): Basketball F; 5-time All-NBA 1st team with Philadelphia and Phoenix; U.S. Olympic Dream Team member in '92; NBA regular season MVP in 1993; currently a basketball announcer for TNT.

Leon Barmore (b. June 3, 1944): college basketball coach; respected coach of Louisiana Tech Lady Techsters; retired in Aug. 2002; career win pct. of .869 (576-87, 20 yrs) is best all-time; won national championship with Louisiana Tech in 1988.

Rick Barry (b. Mar. 28, 1944): Basketball F; only player to lead both NBA and ABA in scoring; 5-time All-NBA 1st team; Finals MVP with Golden St. in 1975. Perfected the underhand foul shot.

Sammy Baugh (b. Mar. 17, 1914): Football QB-DB-P; led Washington to NFL titles in 1937 (his rookie year) and '42; led league in passing 6 times, punting 4 times and interceptions once.

Elgin Baylor (b. Sept. 16, 1934): Basketball F; MOP of Final 4 in 1958; led Minneapolis-LA Lakers to 8 NBA Finals; 10-time All-NBA 1st team (1959-65,67-69); LA Clippers' vice president of basketball operations.

Bob Beamon (b. Aug. 29, 1946): Track & Field; won 1968 Olympic gold medal in long jump with world record (29-ft, 2½in.) that shattered old mark by nearly 2 feet; record finally broken by 2 inches in 1991 by Mike Powell.

Franz Beckenbauer (b. Sept. 11, 1945): Soccer; captain of West German World Cup champions in 1974 then coached West Germany to World Cup title in 1990; invented sweeper position; played in U.S. for NY Cosmos (1977-80,83); Member of International Soccer Hall of Champions.

Boris Becker (b. Nov. 22, 1967): German tennis player; 3-time Wimbledon champ (1985-86,89); youngest male (17) to win Wimbledon; led country to 1st Davis Cup win in 1988; has also won U.S. (1989) and Australian (1991,96) Opens.

Chuck Bednarik (b. May 1, 1925): Football C-LB; 2-time All-America at Penn and 7-time All-Pro with NFL Eagles as both center (1950) and linebacker (1951-56); missed only 3 games in 14 seasons; led Eagles to 1960 NFL title as a 35-year-old two-way player.

Clair Bee (b. Mar. 2, 1896, d. May 20, 1983): Basketball coach who led LIU to 2 undefeated seasons (1936,39) and 2 NIT titles (1939,41); his teams won 95 percent of their games between 1931-51, including 43 in a row from 1935-37; coached NBA Baltimore Bullets from 1952-54, but was only 34-116; contributions to game include 1-3-1 zone defense, 3-second rule and NBA 24-second clock.

Jean Beliveau (b. Aug. 31, 1931): Hockey C; led Montreal to 10 Stanley Cups in 17 playoffs; playoff MVP (1965); 2-time regular season MVP (1956,64).

Bert Bell (b. Feb. 25, 1895, d. Oct. 11, 1959): Football; team owner and 2nd NFL commissioner (1946-59); proposed college draft in 1935 and instituted TV blackout rule.

James (Cool Papa) Bell (b. May 17, 1903, d. Mar. 8, 1991): Baseball; member of the Negro Leagues; widely considered the fastest player ever to play baseball; also coached for the Kansas City Monarchs, teaching such players as Jackie Robinson; member of the National Baseball Hall of Fame.

Deane Beman (b. Apr. 22, 1938): Golf; 1st commissioner of PGA Tour (1974-94); introduced "stadium golf" and created The Players Championship; as player, won U.S. Amateur twice and British Amateur once; inducted into the World Golf Hall of Fame in 2000.

Johnny Bench (b. Dec. 7, 1947): Baseball C; led NL in HRs twice and RBI 3 times; 2-time regular season MVP (1970,72) with Cincinnati, World Series MVP in 1976; 389 career HRs.

Patty Berg (b. Feb. 13, 1918): Golfer; 60 career pro wins, including 15 majors; 3-time AP Female Athlete of Year (1938,43,55).

Chris Berman (b. May 10, 1955): Radio-TV; 6-time National Sportscaster of Year famous for his nicknames and jovial studio anchoring on ESPN; play-by-play man only year Brown University football team won the Ivy League (1976).

Yogi Berra (b. May 12, 1925): Baseball C; played on 10 World Series winners with NY Yankees; holds WS records for games played (75), at bats (259) and hits (71); 3-time AL MVP (1951,54-55); managed both Yankees (1964) and NY Mets (1973) to pennants.

Jay Berwanger (b. Mar. 19, 1914, d. June 26, 2002): Football HB; Univ. of Chicago star; won 1st Heisman Trophy in 1935; top selection in the 1st-ever NFL Draft (1936).

Gary Bettman (b. June 2, 1952): Hockey; former NBA executive, who was named first commissioner of NHL on Dec. 11, 1992; took office on Feb. 1, 1993; announced NHL lockout on Sept. 15, 2004.

Abebe Bikila (b. Aug. 7, 1932, d. Oct. 25, 1973): Ethiopian runner; 1st to win consecutive Olympic marathons (1960,64).

Matt Biondi (b. Oct. 8, 1965): Swimmer; won 7 medals in 1988 Olympics, including 5 gold (2 individual, 3 relay); won a total of 11 medals (8 gold, 2 silver and a bronze) in 3 Olympics (1984,88,92).

Larry Bird (b. Dec. 7, 1956): Basketball F; college Player of Year (1979) at Indiana St.; 1980 NBA Rookie of Year; 9-time All-NBA 1st team; 3-time regular season MVP (1984-86); led Boston to 3 NBA titles (1981,84, 86); 2-time Finals MVP (1984,86); U.S. Olympic Dream Team member in '92; inducted into Hall of Fame in 1998; in 1997, named coach of Indiana Pacers and won Coach of the Year honors in first season; led the Pacers to the NBA Finals in 2000 but lost in 6 games to the Lakers and retired; named president of basketball operations of Pacers in 2003.

The Black Sox: Eight Chicago White Sox players who were banned from baseball for life in 1921 for allegedly throwing the 1919 World Series— RHP Eddie Cicotte (1884-1969), OF Happy Felsch (1891-1964), 1B Chick Gandil (1887-1970), OF Shoeless Joe Jackson (1889-1951), INF Fred McMullin (1891-1952), SS Swede Risberg (1894-1975), 3B-SS Buck Weaver (1890-1956), and LHP Lefty Williams (1893-1959).

Earl (Red) Blaik (b. Feb. 15, 1897, d. May 6, 1989): Football; coached Army to consecutive national titles in 1944-45; 166 career wins and 3 Heisman winners (Blanchard, Davis, Dawkins).

Bonnie Blair (b. Mar. 18, 1964): Speed skater; only American woman to win 5 Olympic gold medals in Winter Games; won 500-meters in 1988, then 500m and 1,000m in both 1992 and '94; added 1,000m bronze in 1988; Sullivan Award winner (1992); retired on 31st birthday as reigning world sprint champ.

Hector (Toe) Blake (b. Aug. 21, 1912, d. May 17, 1995): Hockey LW; led Montreal to 3 Stanley Cups as a player and 8 more as coach; regular season MVP in 1939.

Felix (Doc) Blanchard (b. Dec. 11, 1924): Football FB; 3-time All-America; led Army to national titles in 1944-45; Glenn Davis' running mate; won Heisman Trophy and Sullivan Award in 1945.

George Blanda (b. Sept. 17, 1927): Football QB-PK; was pro football's all-time leading scorer (2,002 points) until 2000 when he was finally passed by kicker Gary Anderson; led Houston to 2 AFL titles (1960-61); played 26 pro seasons; retired at age 48.

Fanny Blankers-Koen (b. Apr. 26, 1918): Dutch sprinter; 30-year-old mother of two, who won 4 gold medals (100m, 200m, 800m hurdles and 4x100m relay) at 1948 Olympics.

Drew Bledsoe (b. Feb. 14, 1972): Football QB; 1st overall pick in 1993 NFL draft (by New England); holds NFL season record for most passes attempted (691) and game records for most passes completed (45) and attempted (70); traded to Buffalo before 2002 season.

Wade Boggs (b. June 15, 1958): Baseball 3B; 5 AL batting titles (1983,85-88) with Boston Red Sox; 11-time All-Star; two Gold Gloves; later played with NY Yankees and Tampa Bay; got 3000th career hit with a home run Aug. 7, 1999 against Cleveland.

Barry Bonds (b. July 24, 1964): Baseball OF; set MLB single-season HR record in 2001 with 73; 6-time NL MVP, 2 with Pittsburgh (1990,92) and 4 with San Francisco (1993,2001-03); one of only 3 men with 40 HRs and 40 SBs in same season (1996); became the 3rd player to reach 700 career HRs in Sept. 2004; holds major league record for single season (2004) and career walks; hit .370 in 2002 at age 38; check baseball chapter for career HR total through 2004; son of Bobby.

Bjorn Borg (b. June 6, 1956): Swedish tennis player; 2-time Player of Year (1979-80); won 6 French Opens and 5 straight Wimbledons (1976-80); led Sweden to 1st Davis Cup win in 1975; retired in 1983 at age 26; attempted unsuccessful comeback in 1991.

Mike Bossy (b. Jan. 22, 1957): Hockey RW; led NY Isles to 4 Stanley Cups; playoff MVP in 1982; 50 goals or more 9 straight years; 573 career goals.

Ralph Boston (b. May 9, 1939): Track & Field; medaled in 3 consecutive Olympic long jumps— gold (1960), silver (1964), bronze (1968).

Ray Bourque (b. Dec. 28, 1960): Hockey D; 12-time All-NHL 1st team; won 5 Norris Trophies (1987-88,1990-91,94) with Boston; '96 All-Star Game MVP; all-time leader for points and assists by a defenseman; won 2001 Stanley Cup with Colorado then retired ranked 8th in scoring (1,579 points) and 3rd in games played (1,612); elected to Hall of Fame in 2004.

Bobby Bowden (b. Nov. 8, 1929): Football; coached Florida St. to 2 national titles (1993,99); entered 2004 season as all-time wins leader in college football history with 342 victories including a 18-8-1 bowl record in 38 years as coach at Samford, West Va. and FSU; father of Clemson head coach Tommy and former Auburn coach Terry.

Riddick Bowe (b. Aug. 10, 1967): Boxer; won world heavyweight title with unanimous dec. over champion Evander Holyfield on Nov. 13, 1992; lost title to Holyfield on maj. dec. Nov. 6, 1993; served 17 months in prison for kidnapping his first wife and their 5 kids in 1998; began unlikely comeback in 2004 at age 37.

Scotty Bowman (b. Sept. 18, 1933): Hockey coach; all-time winningest NHL coach in both regular season (1,244) and playoffs (223) over 30 seasons; coached a record nine Stanley Cup winners with Montreal (1973,76-79), Pittsburgh (1992) and Detroit (1997,98,2002); retired after 2001-02 season.

Jack Brabham (b. Apr. 2, 1926): Australian auto racer; 3-time Formula One champion (1959-60,66); 14 career wins; member of the Hall of Fame.

Bill Bradley (b. July 28, 1943): Basketball F; 2-time All-America at Princeton; Player of the Year and Final 4 MOP in 1965; captain of gold medal-winning 1964 U.S. Olympic team; Sullivan Award winner (1965); led NY Knicks to 2 NBA titles (1970,73); U.S. Senator (D, N.J.) 1979-95; ran for President in 2000.

Pat Bradley (b. Mar. 24, 1951): Golfer; 2-time LPGA Player of Year (1986,91); has won all four majors on LPGA tour, including 3 du Maurier Classics; inducted into the LPGA Hall of Fame on Jan. 18, 1992; among all-time LPGA money leaders and tournament winners (31); captained the 2000 U.S. Solheim Cup team.

Terry Bradshaw (b. Sept. 2, 1948): Football QB; led Pittsburgh to 4 Super Bowl titles (1975-76,79-80); 2-time Super Bowl MVP (1979-80) and regular season MVP in 1978; Fox TV studio analyst.

George Brett (b. May 15, 1953): Baseball 3B-1B; AL batting champion in 3 different decades (1976,80,90); MVP in 1980; led KC to World Series title in 1985; retired after 1993 season with 3,154 hits and .305 average; inducted into Hall of Fame in 1999.

Valerie Brisco-Hooks (b. July 6, 1960): Track & Field; won three gold medals at the 1984 Olympics (200 meters, 400 meters and 4x100 relay); first athlete to ever win the 200 and 400 in the same Olympics.

Lou Brock (b. June 18, 1939): Baseball OF; former all-time stolen base leader (938); led NL in steals 8 times; led St. Louis to 2 World Series titles (1964,67); had 3,023 career hits.

Herb Brooks (b. Aug. 5, 1937, d. Aug. 11, 2003): Hockey; former U.S. Olympic player (1964,68) who coached 1980 "Miracle on Ice" team to gold medal and 2002 U.S. team to silver medal; coached Minnesota to 3 NCAA titles (1974,76,78); also coached NY Rangers, Minnesota, New Jersey and Pittsburgh in NHL.

Jim Brown (b. Feb. 17, 1936): Football FB; All-America at Syracuse (1956) and NFL Rookie of Year (1957); led NFL in rushing 8 times; 8-time All-Pro (1957-61,63-65); 3-time MVP (1958,63,65) with Cleveland; ran for 12,312 yards and scored 126 touchdowns in just 9 seasons; went to jail for 4 mos in 2002 after he was convicted of vandalizing his wife's car and refused court ordered counseling.

Larry Brown (b. Sept. 14, 1940): Basketball; played in ACC, AAU, 1964 Olympics and ABA; 3-time assist leader (1968-70) and 3-time Coach of Year (1973,75-76) in ABA; coached ABA's Carolina and Denver and NBA's Denver, N.J., San Antonio, LA Clippers, Indiana, Philadelphia and Detroit, winning the 2004 NBA title with Pistons; also coached UCLA to NCAA Final (1980), Kansas to NCAA title (1988) and the USA men's basketball team to a disappointing bronze medal in Athens in 2004.

Mordecai (Three-Finger) Brown (b. Oct. 18, 1876, d. Feb. 14, 1948): Baseball; nickname derived from injury in a childhood accident that left him with three digits on right hand; injury gave him a particularly nasty curve ball; won the decisive game of the the 1907 World Series as a Chicago Cub; in 1908, first pitcher to record 4 consecutive shutouts and finished at 29-9; career record of 239-130 with lifetime ERA of 2.06; member of Hall of Fame.

Paul Brown (b. Sept. 7, 1908, d. Aug. 5, 1991): Football innovator; coached Ohio St. to national title in 1942; in pros, directed Cleveland Browns to 4 straight AAFC titles (1946-49) and 3 NFL titles (1950,54-55); formed Cincinnati Bengals as head coach and part owner in 1968 (reached playoffs in '70).

Valery Brumel (b. Apr. 14, 1942): Soviet high jumper; dominated event from 1961-64; broke world record 5 times; won silver medal in 1960 Olympics and gold in 1964; highest jump was 7-5¾.

Avery Brundage (b. Sept. 28, 1887, d. May 5, 1975): Amateur sports czar for over 40 years as president of AAU (1928-35), U.S. Olympic Committee (1929-53) and Int'l Olympic Committee (1952-72).

Kobe Bryant (b. Aug. 23, 1978): Basketball; G/F for the LA Lakers; graduated from Lower Merion (Penn.) HS and made the jump directly to the NBA; youngest player (18 yrs., 2 mos., 11 days) ever to appear in an NBA game; became the youngest all-star in NBA history in 1998 and scored a team-high 18 points; won 3 consecutive titles with the Lakers (2000,01,02); accused of rape in 2003 but charges were dropped in 2004.

Paul (Bear) Bryant (b. Sept. 11, 1913, d. Jan. 26, 1983): Football; coached at 4 colleges over 38 years; directed Alabama to 6 national titles (1961,64-65,73,78-79); retired as the winningest coach of all-time (323-85-17 record) finally passed by Joe Paterno in 2001; 15 bowl wins, including 8 Sugar Bowls.

Sergey Bubka (b. Dec. 4, 1963): Ukrainian pole vaulter; 1st man to clear 20 feet both indoors and out (1991); holder of indoor (20-2) and outdoor (20-1¾) world records as of Sept. 30, 2004; 6-time world champion (1983,87,91,93,95,97); won Olympic gold medal in 1988, but failed to clear any height in 1992 Games.

Buck Buchanan (b. Sept. 10, 1940, d. July 16, 1992): Football; played both ways in college at Grambling; first player chosen in the first AFL draft by the Dallas Texans who later became the KC Chiefs; missed one game in a 13-year pro career; played in six AFL All-Star games and two Pro Bowls at def. tackle; defensive star of the Chiefs team that won Super Bowl IV; later coached for the New Orleans Saints and Cleveland Browns; member of Pro Football Hall of Fame.

Jack Buck (b. Aug. 21, 1924, d. June 18, 2002): Radio-TV; broadcast baseball games for St. Louis Cardinals from 1954-2001; CBS Radio voice for Monday Night Football (1978-96) and announcer for 1st televised AFL game in 1960; recipient of Baseball Hall of Fame's Ford Frick Award (1987) and Football Hall of Fame's Pete Rozelle Award (1996); received the Purple Heart in WWII; father of sportscaster Joe.

Don Budge (b. June 13, 1915, d. Jan. 26, 2000): Tennis; in 1938 became 1st player to win the Grand Slam— the French, Wimbledon, U.S. and Australian titles in 1 year; led U.S. to 2 Davis Cups (1937-38); turned pro in late '38.

Maria Bueno (b. Oct. 11, 1939): Brazilian tennis player; won 4 U.S. Championships (1959,63-64,66) and 3 Wimbledons (1959-60,64).

Leroy Burrell (b. Feb. 21, 1967): Track & Field; set former world record of 9.85 in 100 meters, July 6, 1994; previously held record (9.90) in 1991; member of 4 world record-breaking 4x100m relay teams.

Susan Butcher (b. Dec. 26, 1956): Sled Dog racer; 4-time winner of Iditarod Trail race (1986-88,90).

Dick Butkus (b. Dec. 9, 1942): Football LB; 2-time All-America at Illinois (1963-64); All-Pro 7 of 9 NFL seasons with Chicago Bears; worked with XFL in 2001.

Dick Button (b. July 18, 1929): Figure skater; 5-time world champion (1948-52); 2-time Olympic champ (1948,52); Sullivan Award winner (1949); won Emmy Award as Best Analyst for 1980-81 TV season.

Walter Byers (b. Mar. 13, 1922): College athletics; 1st exec. director of NCAA, serving from 1951-88.

Frank Calder (b. Nov. 17, 1877, d. Feb. 4, 1943): Hockey; 1st NHL president (1917-43); guided league through its formative years; NHL's Rookie of the Year named after him.

Jim Calhoun (b. May 10, 1942): Basketball; has coached UConn to 2 NCAA titles (1999, 2004).

Lee Calhoun (b. Feb. 23, 1933, d. June 22, 1989): Track & Field; won consecutive Olympic gold medals in the 110m hurdles (1956,60).

Walter Camp (b. Apr. 7, 1859, d. Mar. 14, 1925): Football coach and innovator; established scrimmage line, center snap, downs, 11 players per side; selected 1st All-America team (1889).

Roy Campanella (b. Nov. 19, 1921, d. June 26, 1993): Baseball C; 3-time NL MVP (1951,53,55); led Brooklyn to 5 pennants and 1st World Series title (1955); career cut short when 1958 car accident left him paralyzed.

Clarence Campbell (b. July 9, 1905, d. June 24, 1984): Hockey; 3rd NHL president (1946-77), league tripled in size from 6 to 18 teams during his tenure.

Earl Campbell (b. Mar. 29, 1955): Football RB; won Heisman Trophy in 1977; led NFL in rushing 3 times; 3-time All-Pro; 2-time MVP (1978-79) at Houston.

John Campbell (b. Apr. 8, 1955): Harness racing; 5-time winner of Hambletonian (1987,88,90,95,98); 3-time Driver of Year; first driver to go over $100 million in career winnings.

Milt Campbell (b. Dec. 9, 1933): Track & Field; won silver medal in 1952 Olympic decathlon and gold medal in '56.

Jimmy Cannon (b. 1910, d. Dec. 5, 1973): Tough, opinionated New York sportswriter and essayist who viewed sports as an extension of show business; protégé of Damon Runyon; covered World War II for *Stars & Stripes*.

Jose Canseco (b. July 2, 1964): Baseball OF/DH; AL Rookie of the Year in 1986 and MVP in 1988 with the Oakland A's; in 1988 became the 1st player in MLB history with 40 HRs and 40 steals in a season; retired in 2003 with 462 career HRs.

Tony Canzoneri (b. Nov. 6, 1908, d. Dec. 9, 1959): Boxer; 2-time world lightweight champion (1930-33,35-36); pro record 141-24-10 with 44 KOs.

Jennifer Capriati (b. Mar. 29, 1976): Tennis; youngest Grand Slam semifinalist ever (age 14 in 1990 French Open); surprise gold medalist at 1992 Olympics; left Tour from 1994-96 due to personal problems including an arrest for marijuana possession; waged successful comeback, winning French Open (2001) and 2 Australian Opens (2001,02).

Harry Caray (b. Mar. 1, 1917, d. Feb. 18, 1998): Radio-TV; baseball play-by-play broadcaster for St. Louis Cardinals, Oakland, Chicago White Sox and Cubs 1945-98; father of sportscaster Skip and grandfather of sportscaster Chip.

Rod Carew (b. Oct. 1, 1945): Baseball 2B-1B; led AL in batting 7 times (1969,72-75,77-78) with Minnesota; MVP in 1977; had 3,053 career hits.

Steve Carlton (b. Dec. 22, 1944): Baseball LHP; won 20 or more games 6 times; 4-time Cy Young winner (1972,77,80,82) with Philadelphia; 329-244 career record; 4,136 career Ks.

JoAnne Carner (b. Apr. 4, 1939): Golfer; 5-time U.S. Amateur champion; 2-time U.S. Open champ; 3-time LPGA Player of Year (1974,81-82); 43 career wins.

Cris Carter (b. Nov. 25, 1965): Football; WR with Philadelphia (1987-89), Minnesota (1990-2001) and Miami (2002); twice caught 122 passes in a season (1994, '95), the first time establishing an NFL record for catches in a season that was beaten a year later; 2nd player to reach 1000 career catches.

Don Carter (b. July 29, 1926): Bowler; 6-time Bowler of Year (1953-54,57-58,60,62); voted Greatest of All-Time in 1970.

Joe Carter (b. Mar. 7, 1960): Baseball OF; 3-time All-America at Wichita St. (1979-81); won 1993 World Series for Toronto with 3-run HR in bottom of the 9th of Game 6.

Alexander Cartwright (b. Apr. 17, 1820, d. July 12, 1892): Baseball; engineer and draftsman who spread gospel of baseball from New York City to California gold fields; widely regarded as the father of modern game; his guidelines included setting 3 strikes for an out and 3 outs for each half inning.

Billy Casper (b. June 24, 1931): Golfer; 2-time PGA Player of Year (1966,70); has won U.S. Open (1959,66), Masters (1970), U.S. Senior Open (1983); compiled 51 PGA Tour wins and 9 on Senior Tour.

Tracy Caulkins (b. Jan. 11, 1963): Swimmer; won 3 gold medals (2 individual) at 1984 Olympics; set 5 world records and won 48 U.S. national titles from 1978-84; Sullivan Award winner (1978); 2-time Honda Broderick Cup winner (1982,84).

Steve Cauthen (b. May 1, 1960): Jockey; became youngest jockey (18) to win the Triple Crown with Affirmed in 1978; won a record $6.1 million in 1977, winning the Eclipse Award as the nation's top rider and the award for AP male athlete of the year.

Evonne Goolagong Cawley (b. July 31, 1951): Australian tennis player; won Australian Open 4 times, Wimbledon twice (1971,80), French once (1971).

Florence Chadwick (b. Nov. 9, 1917, d. Mar. 15, 1995): Dominant distance swimmer of 1950s; set English Channel records from France to England (1950) and England to France (1951 and '55).

Wilt Chamberlain (b. Aug. 21, 1936, d. Oct. 12, 1999): Basketball C; consensus All-America in 1957 and '58 at Kansas; Final Four MOP in 1957; led NBA in scoring 7 times and rebounding 11 times; 7-time All-NBA first team; 4-time MVP (1960,66-68) in Philadelphia; scored 100 points vs. NY Knicks in Hershey, Pa., Mar. 2, 1962; led 76ers (1967) and LA Lakers (1972) to NBA titles; Finals MVP in 1972.

A.B. (Happy) Chandler (b. July 14, 1898, d. June 15, 1991): Baseball; former Kentucky governor and U.S. Senator who succeeded Judge Landis as commissioner in 1945; backed Branch Rickey's move in 1947 to make Jackie Robinson 1st black player in major leagues; deemed too pro-player and ousted by owners in 1951.

Michael Chang (b. Feb. 22, 1972): Tennis; won the 1989 French Open, becoming the youngest men's champion of a grand slam event (17 years, 3 months.); went 11 consecutive years (1988-98) with at least one title; finished in top 10 in the ATP year-end rankings from 1992-97 (career high no. 2 in 1996).

Julio Cesar Chavez (b. July 12, 1962): Mexican boxer; world jr. welterweight champ (1989-94); also held titles as jr. lightweight (1984-87) and lightweight (1987-89); won over 100 bouts; 90-bout unbeaten streak ended 1/29/94 when Frankie Randall won title on split decision; Chavez won title back 4 months later.

Linford Christie (b. Apr. 2, 1960): British sprinter; won 100-meter gold medals at both 1992 Olympics (9.96) and '93 World Championships (9.87).

Jim Clark (b. Mar. 14, 1936, d. Apr. 7, 1968): Scottish auto racer; 2-time Formula One world champion (1963,65); won Indy 500 in 1965; killed in car crash.

Bobby Clarke (b. Aug. 13, 1949): Hockey C; led Philadelphia Flyers to consecutive Stanley Cups in 1974-75; 3-time regular season MVP (1973,75-76); currently Flyers GM.

Ron Clarke (b. Feb. 21, 1937): Australian runner; from 1963-70 set 17 world records in races from 2 miles to 20,000m; never won Olympic gold medal.

Roger Clemens (b. Aug. 4, 1962): Baseball RHP; twice fanned MLB record 20 batters in 9-inning game (April 29, 1986 and Sept. 18, 1996); won a record 6 Cy Young Awards with Boston (1986-87,91), Toronto (1997,98) and N.Y. Yankees (2001); AL MVP in 1986; won 2 World Series with Yankees (1999-2000); got 300th win in 2003; pitched for Houston Astros in 2004 and named All-Star game starter.

Roberto Clemente (b. Aug. 18, 1934, d. Dec. 31, 1972): Baseball OF; hit over .300 13 times with Pittsburgh; led NL in batting 4 times; World Series MVP in 1971; regular season MVP in 1966; had 3,000 career hits; killed in plane crash; MLB Man of the Year award is named for him.

Alice Coachman (b. Nov. 9, 1923): Track & Field; became the first black woman to win an Olympic gold medal with her win in the high jump in 1948 (London); broke the high school and college high jump records despite not wearing any shoes; member of the National Track & Field Hall of Fame.

Ty Cobb (b. Dec. 18, 1886, d. July 17, 1961): Baseball OF; all-time highest career batting average (.367); hit over .400 3 times; led AL in batting 12 times and stolen bases 6 times with Detroit; MVP in 1911; had 4,191 career hits, 2,245 career runs and 892 steals; played 24 years (22 with Detroit, 2 with Philadelphia); nicknamed "The Georgia Peach"; part of baseball Hall of Fame's inaugural class.

Mickey Cochrane (b. Apr. 6, 1903, d. June 28, 1962): Baseball C; led Philadelphia A's (1929-30) and Detroit (1935) to 3 World Series titles; 2-time AL MVP (1928,34).

Sebastian Coe (b. Sept. 29, 1956): British runner; won gold medal in 1500m and silver medal in 800m at both 1980 and '84 Olympics; long-time world record holder in 800m and 1000m; elected to Parliament as Conservative in 1992.

Paul Coffey (b. June 1, 1961): Hockey D; 3-time Norris Trophy winner; member of 4 Stanley Cup champions at Edmonton (1984-85,87) and Pittsburgh (1991); ranks 10th on NHL all-time scoring list; elected to Hall of Fame in 2004.

Rocky Colavito (b. August 10, 1933): Baseball OF; six-time all-star who hit 374 HRs over his 14-year career; hugely popular in Cleveland where he played from 1955-59 and then 1965-67; led the league in HRs in 1959 with 42 and RBI in 1965 with 108; hit four consecutive HRs in one game.

Eddie Collins (b. May 2, 1887, d. Mar. 25, 1951): Baseball 2B; led Philadelphia A's (1910-11) and Chicago White Sox (1917) to 3 World Series titles; AL MVP in 1914; had 3,311 career hits and 743 stolen bases.

Nadia Comaneci (b. Nov. 12, 1961): Romanian gymnast; first to record perfect 10 in Olympics; won 3 individual golds at 1976 Olympics and 2 more in '80.

Lionel Conacher (b. May 24, 1901, d. May 26, 1954): Canada's greatest all-around athlete; NHL hockey (2 Stanley Cups), CFL football (1 Grey Cup), minor league baseball, soccer, lacrosse, track, amateur boxing champion; member of Parliament (1949-54).

Tony Conigliaro (b. Jan. 7, 1945, d. Feb. 24, 1990): Baseball OF; youngest (20 years old) to lead the AL in HRs (32 in 1965); hit in the face with a fastball in 1967; came back to hit 36 HRs in 1970 but was never the same.

Gene Conley (b. Nov. 10, 1930): Baseball and Basketball; played for World Series and NBA champions with Milwaukee Braves (1957) and Boston Celtics (1959-61); losing pitcher in 1954 All-Star Game and winning pitcher in 1955 Game; 91-96 record in 11 seasons.

Billy Conn (b. Oct. 8, 1917, d. May 29, 1993): Boxer; Pittsburgh native and world light heavyweight champion from 1939-41; nearly upset heavyweight champ Joe Louis in 1941 title bout, but was knocked out in 13th round; pro record 63-11-1 with 14 KOs.

Dennis Conner (b. Sept. 16, 1942): Sailing; 3-time America's Cup-winning skipper aboard *Freedom* (1980), *Stars & Stripes* (1987) and the *Stars & Stripes* catamaran (1988); only American skipper to lose Cup, first in 1983 when *Australia II* beat *Liberty* and again in '95 when New Zealand's *Black Magic* swept Conner and his *Stars & Stripes* crew aboard the borrowed *Young America*.

Maureen Connolly (b. Sept. 17, 1934, d. June 21, 1969): Tennis; 1st woman to win Grand Slam in 1953 at age 18); horse riding accident ended her career in '54 at age 19; won 3 Wimbledons (1952-54), 3 U.S. Opens (1951-53), 2 French Opens (1953-54) and 1 Australian Open (1953); 3-time AP Female Athlete of Year (1951-53).

Jimmy Connors (b. Sept. 2, 1952): Tennis; No.1 player in world 5 times (1974-78); won 5 U.S. Opens, 2 Wimbledons and 1 Australian; rose from No. 936 at the close of 1990 to U.S. Open semifinals in 1991 at age 39; NCAA singles champ (1971); all-time leader in pro singles titles (109) and matches won at U.S. Open (98) and Wimbledon (84).

Jack Kent Cooke (b. Oct. 25, 1912, d. April 6, 1997): Football; sole owner of NFL Washington Redskins from 1985-97; teams won 2 Super Bowls (1988,92); also owned NBA Lakers and NHL Kings in LA; built LA Forum for $12 million in 1967.

Cynthia Cooper (b. April 14, 1963): Women's basketball G; won two NCAA basketball titles at USC (1983-84); won gold medal with U.S. team in 1988; 2-time WNBA MVP and 4-time league champion with Houston Comets; coach of WNBA's Phoenix Mercury 2001-02.

Angel Cordero Jr. (b. Nov. 8, 1942): Jockey; retired third on all-time list with 7,057 wins in 38,646 starts; won Kentucky Derby 3 times (1974,76,85), Preakness twice and Belmont once; 2-time Eclipse Award winner (1982-83).

Howard Cosell (b. Mar. 25, 1920, d. Apr. 23, 1995): Radio-TV; former ABC commentator on *Monday Night Football* and *Wide World of Sports*, who energized TV sports journalism with abrasive "tell it like it is" style.

Bob Costas (b. Mar. 22, 1952): Radio-TV; NBC broadcaster who has been anchor for NBA, NFL and Summer Olympics as well as baseball play-by-play man; 13-time Emmy winner as studio host/play-by-play and 8-time National Sportscaster of Year.

James (Doc) Counsilman (b. Dec. 28, 1920): Swimming; coached Indiana men's swim team to 6 NCAA championships (1968-73); coached the 1964 and '76 U.S. men's Olympic teams that won a combined 21 of 24 gold medals; in 1979 became oldest person (59) to swim English Channel; retired in 1990 with dual meet record of 287-36-1.

Fred Couples (b. Oct. 3, 1959): Golfer; 2-time PGA Tour Player of the Year (1991,92); 15 Tour victories, including 1992 Masters.

Jim Courier (b. Aug. 17, 1970): Tennis; No. 1 player in world in 1992; won 2 Australian Opens (1992-93) and 2 French Opens (1991-92); played on 1992 Davis Cup winner; Nick Bollettieri Academy classmate of Andre Agassi.

Margaret Smith Court (b. July 16, 1942): Australian tennis player; won Grand Slam in both singles (1970) and mixed doubles (1963 with Ken Fletcher); record 24 Grand Slam singles titles—11 Australian, 5 U.S., 5 French and 3 Wimbledon.

Bob Cousy (b. Aug. 9, 1928): Basketball G; led NBA in assists 8 times; 10-time All-NBA 1st team; 1957 MVP; led Boston to 6 NBA titles (1957,59-63); elected to Hall of Fame in 1970, one of NBA's 50 Greatest Players.

Buster Crabbe (b. Feb. 7, 1908, d. Apr. 23, 1983): Swimmer; 2-time Olympic freestyle medalist with bronze in 1928 (1500m) and gold in '32 (400m); became movie star and King of Serials as Flash Gordon and Buck Rogers.

Ben Crenshaw (b. Jan. 11, 1952): Golfer; co-NCAA champion with Tom Kite in 1972; battled Graves' disease in mid-1980s; 19 career Tour victories; won Masters for second time in 1995 and dedicated it to 90-year-old mentor Harvey Penick, who had died a week earlier; captain of 1999 Ryder Cup team.

Joe Cronin (b. Oct. 12, 1906, d. Sept. 7, 1984): Baseball SS; hit over .300 and drove in over 100 runs 8 times each; player-manager in Washington and Boston (1933-47); AL president (1959-73).

Larry Csonka (b. Dec. 25, 1946): Football RB; powerful runner and blocker who gained 8,081 yards in 11 seasons in the AFL and NFL; won two consecutive Super Bowls with the Miami Dolphins (1973-74) and was named MVP in the latter, rushing for 145 yards and two TDs; member of the College and Pro Football Halls of Fame.

Ann Curtis (b. Mar. 6, 1926): Swimming; won 2 gold medals and 1 silver in 1948 Olympics; set 4 world and 18 U.S. records during career; 1st woman and swimmer to win Sullivan Award (1944).

Betty Cuthbert (b. Apr. 20, 1938): Australian runner; won gold medals in 100 and 200 meters and 4x100m relay at 1956 Olympics; also won 400m gold at 1964 Olympics.

Bjorn Dählie (b. June 19, 1967): Norwegian cross-country skier; winner of a record eight gold and 12 overall Winter Olympic medals from 1992-98.

Chuck Daly (b. July 20, 1930): Basketball; coached Detroit to two NBA titles (1989-90) before leaving in 1992 to coach New Jersey; coached NBA "Dream Team" to gold medal in 1992 Olympics; retired in 1994 but returned in 1997 to coach Orlando Magic for two seasons.

John Daly (b. Apr. 28, 1966): Golfer; this big hitter was the surprise winner of 1991 PGA Championship as unknown 25-year old; battled through personal troubles in 1994 to return in '95 and win 2nd major at British Open, beating Italy's Costantino Rocca in 4-hole playoff; won first PGA Tour event in nine years at 2004 Buick Invitational.

Stanley Dancer (b. July 25, 1927): Harness racing; winner of 4 Hambletonians; trainer-driver of Triple Crown winners in trotting (Nevele Pride in 1968 and Super Bowl in '72) and pacing (Most Happy Fella in 1970).

Beth Daniel (b. Oct. 14, 1956): Golfer; 33 career wins, including 1 major; inducted into World Golf Hall of Fame in 1999.

Alvin Dark (b. Jan. 7, 1922): Baseball IF and MGR; hit .322 to win the NL Rookie of the Year award in 1948 with the Boston Braves; traded to the N.Y. Giants where he led the league in doubles (41) in 1951; won 994 games as a manager and led the Oakland A's to a World Series win in 1974.

Tamas Darnyi (b. June 3, 1967): Hungarian swimmer; 2-time double gold medal winner in 200m and 400m individual medley at 1988 and '92 Olympics; also won both events in 1986 and '91 world championships; set world records in both at '91 worlds; 1st swimmer to break 2 minutes in 200m IM (1:59:36).

Lindsay Davenport (b. June 8, 1976): Tennis player; became first American female to be ranked No. 1 in the world (1998) since Chris Evert in 1985; won U.S. Open (1998), Wimbledon (1999) and Australian Open (2000); Olympic gold medalist at Atlanta in 1996.

Al Davis (b. July 4, 1929): Football; GM-coach of Oakland 1963-66; helped force AFL-NFL merger as AFL commissioner in 1966; returned to Oakland as managing general partner and directed club to 3 Super Bowl wins (1977,81,84); defied fellow NFL owners and moved Raiders to LA in 1982; turned down owners' 1995 offer to build him a new stadium in LA and moved back to Oakland instead.

Dwight Davis (b. July 5, 1879, d. Nov. 28, 1945): Tennis; donor of Davis Cup; played for winning U.S. team in 1st two Cup finals (1900,02); won U.S. and Wimbledon doubles titles in 1901; Secretary of War (1925-29) under President Coolidge.

Ernie Davis (b. Dec. 14, 1939, d. May 18, 1963): Football; star running back at Syracuse University; first black player to win the Heisman Trophy in 1961; drafted by the Washington Redskins and traded to Cleveland but died the following year of leukemia before playing a pro game.

Glenn Davis (b. Dec. 26, 1924): Football HB; 3-time All-America; led Army to national titles in 1944-45; Doc Blanchard's running mate; won Heisman Trophy in 1946.

John Davis (b. Jan. 12, 1921, d. July 13, 1984): Weightlifting; 6-time world champion; 2-time Olympic super-heavyweight champ (1948,52); undefeated from 1938-53.

Terrell Davis (b. Oct. 28, 1972): Football RB; 1998 NFL MVP, rushing for a league-leading 2,008 yards (4th all-time); played for two Super Bowl winners in Denver (XXXII and XXXIII), earning MVP honors in the former with Super Bowl-record 3 rushing TDs.

Pat Day (b. Oct. 13, 1953): Jockey; 4-time Eclipse award winner; became all-time leader in earnings in 2002; over 8,000 career victories; won Kentucky Derby (1992), 5 Preaknesses (1985,90,94-96) and 3 Belmonts (1989,94,2000); inducted into Hall of Fame in 1991.

Ron Dayne (b. Mar. 14, 1978): Football RB; NCAA Div. I-A all-time leading rusher, gaining 6,397 yards at Wisconsin (1996-99); 1999 Heisman Trophy winner; selected in 1st round (11th overall) of 2000 NFL draft by NY Giants.

Dizzy Dean (b. Jan. 16 1911, d. July 17, 1974): Baseball RHP; led NL in strikeouts and complete games 4 times; last NL pitcher to win 30 games (30-7 in 1934); MVP in 1934 with St. Louis; 150-83 record.

Dave DeBusschere (b. Oct. 16, 1940, d. May, 14, 2003): Basketball F; youngest coach in NBA history (24 in 1964); player-coach of Detroit Pistons (1964-67); played in 8 All-Star games; won 2 NBA titles as player with NY Knicks (1970, 73); ABA commissioner (1975-76); also pitched 2 seasons for Chicago White Sox (1962-63) with 3-4 record.

Pierre de Coubertin (b. Jan. 1, 1863, d. Sept. 2, 1937): French educator; father of the Modern Olympic Games; IOC president from 1896-1925.

Anita DeFrantz (b. Oct. 4, 1952): Olympics; attorney who became the International Olympic Committee's first female vice president in 1997; first woman to represent U.S. on IOC (elected in 1986); member of USOC Executive Committee; member of bronze medal U.S. women's eight-oared shell at Montreal in 1976.

Oscar De La Hoya (b. Feb. 4, 1973): Boxer; 1992 Olympic gold medallist (lightweight); has held world titles in 4 weight classes (lightweight, super lightweight, welterweight and jr. middleweight); was unbeaten until losing WBC Welterweight belt to Felix Trinidad in a majority decision in 1999; later moved to jr. middleweight and won WBA and WBC belts; TKO'd in 9th round by Bernard Hopkins in their undisputed middleweight title fight in September 2004.

Cedric Dempsey (b. Apr. 14, 1932): College sports; succeeded Dick Schultz as NCAA executive director (title later changed to president) in 1993 and served until the end of 2002; former athletic director at Pacific (1967-79), San Diego St. (1979), Houston (1979-82) and Arizona (1983-93).

Jack Dempsey (b. June 24, 1895, d. May 31, 1983): Boxer; world heavyweight champion from 1919-26; lost title to Gene Tunney, then lost "Long Count" rematch in 1927 when he floored Tunney in 7th round but failed to retreat to neutral corner; pro record 64-6-9 with 49 KOs.

Bob Devaney (b. April 13, 1915, d. May 9, 1997): Football; head coach at Wyoming from 1957-1961; from 1962 to 1972 built Nebraska into a college football power; won two consecutive national championships in 1970-71; won eight Big Eight Conference titles; later served as Nebraska's athletic director.

Donna de Varona (b. Apr. 26, 1947): Swimming; won gold medals in 400 IM and 400 freestyle relay at 1964 Olympics; set 18 world records during career; co-founder of Women's Sports Foundation in 1974.

Gail Devers (b. Nov. 19, 1966): Track & Field; won Olympic gold medal in 100 meters in 1992 and '96; world champion in 100 meters (1993) and 100-meter hurdles (1993,95,99); overcame thyroid disorder (Graves' disease) that sidelined her in 1989-90 and nearly resulted in having both feet amputated.

Klaus Dibiasi (b. Oct. 6, 1947): Italian diver; won 3 consecutive Olympic gold medals in platform event (1968,72,76).

Eric Dickerson (b. Sept. 2, 1960): Football RB; led NFL in rushing 4 times (1983-84,86,88); ran for single-season record 2,105 yards in 1984; NFC Rookie of Year in 1983; All-Pro 5 times; traded from LA Rams to Indianapolis (Oct. 31, 1987) in 3-team, 10-player deal (including draft picks) that also involved Buffalo; 4th on all-time career rushing list with 13,259 yards in 11 seasons.

Harrison Dillard (b. July 8, 1923): Track & Field; only man to win Olympic gold medals in both sprints (100m in 1948) and hurdles (110m in 1952).

Joe DiMaggio (b. Nov. 25, 1914, d. Mar. 8, 1999): Baseball OF; hit safely in 56 straight games (1941); led AL in batting, HRs and RBI twice each; 3-time MVP (1939,41,47); hit .325 with 361 HRs over 13 seasons; led NY Yankees to 10 World Series titles.

Marcel Dionne (b. Aug. 3, 1951): Hockey C; fifth on NHL's all-time points list (1,771) and fourth on goals list (731) through 2004; tied Wayne Gretzky for the league lead in points (137) in 1980; scored 50 goals in a season 6 times; won the Lady Byng Trophy for gentlemanly play in 1975 and 1977; member of the Hockey Hall of Fame.

Mike Ditka (b. Oct. 18, 1939): Football; All-America at Pitt (1960); NFL Rookie of Year (1961); 5-time Pro Bowl tight end for Chicago Bears; returned to Chicago as head coach in 1982 and won Super Bowl XX in 1986; left Bears in 1992 and worked as a broadcaster at NBC for four years; coached the New Orleans Saints from 1997-99; compiled 127-101-0 record in 14 seasons; currently an analyst on ESPN.

Larry Doby (b. Dec. 13, 1924, d. June 18, 2003): Baseball OF; first black player in the AL; joined the Cleveland Indians in July 1947, three months after Jackie Robinson entered the Majors with the NL's Brooklyn Dodgers; an all-star centerfielder from 1949-55; managed the Chicago White Sox in 1978, becoming the second black major league manager; inducted into the Hall of Fame in 1998.

Charlotte (Lottie) Dod (b. Sept. 24, 1871, d. June 27, 1960): British athlete; was 5-time Wimbledon singles champion (1887-88,91-93); youngest player ever to win Wimbledon (15 in 1887); archery silver medalist at 1908 Olympics; member of national field hockey team in 1899; British Amateur golf champ in 1904.

Tony Dorsett (b. Apr. 7, 1954): Football RB; won Heisman Trophy and national title in 1976; 3rd all-time in NCAA Div. I-A rushing with 6,082 yards; led Dallas to Super Bowl title as NFC Rookie of Year (1977); NFC Player of Year (1981); rushed for 12,739 yards in 12 years.

James (Buster) Douglas (b. Apr. 7, 1960): Boxer; 42-1 shot who knocked out undefeated Mike Tyson in 10th round on Feb. 10, 1990 to win heavyweight title in Tokyo; 8½ months later, lost only title defense to Evander Holyfield by KO in 3rd round.

Vicki Manalo Draves (b. Dec. 31, 1924): Diver; First woman in olympic history to win gold medals in both platform diving and springboard diving; inducted into Int'l Swimming Hall of Fame in 1969.

The Dream Team Head coach Chuck Daly's "Best Ever" 12-man NBA All-Star squad that headlined the 1992 Summer Olympics in Barcelona and easily won the basketball gold medal; co-captained by Larry Bird and Magic Johnson, with veterans Charles Barkley, Clyde Drexler, Patrick Ewing, Michael Jordan, Karl Malone, Chris Mullin, Scottie Pippen, David Robinson, John Stockton and Duke's Christian Laettner.

Heike Drechsler (b. Dec. 16, 1964): German long jumper and sprinter; East German before reunification in 1991; set world long jump record (24-2¼) in 1988; won long jump gold medals at 1992 Olympics and 1983 and '93 World Championships; won silver medal in long jump and bronze medals in both 100- and 200-meter sprints at 1988 Olympics.

Ken Dryden (b. Aug. 8, 1947): Hockey G; led Montreal to 6 Stanley Cup titles; playoff MVP as rookie in 1971; won or shared 5 Vezina trophies; 2.24 career GAA.

Don Drysdale (b. July 23, 1936, d. July 3, 1993): Baseball RHP; led NL in strikeouts 3 times and games started 4 straight years; pitched record 6 shutouts in a row in 1968; won Cy Young (1962); had 209-166 record and hit 29 HRs in 14 years.

Charley Dumas (b. Feb. 12, 1937): U.S. high jumper; first man to clear 7 feet (7-0½) on June 29, 1956; won gold medal at 1956 Olympics.

Tim Duncan (b. Apr. 25, 1976): Basketball C/F; This 7-foot shot-blocker and shot-maker is a 2-time NBA Finals MVP (1999, 2003); 2-time NBA MVP (2002-03); 1997 College Player of the Year at Wake Forest; #1 overall pick by San Antonio (1997); 1998 NBA Rookie of the Year.

Margaret Osborne du Pont (b. Mar. 4, 1918): Tennis; won 5 French, 7 Wimbledon and an unprecedented 25 U.S. national titles in singles, doubles and mixed doubles from 1941-62.

Roberto Duran (b. June 16, 1951): Panamanian boxer; one of only 6 fighters to hold 4 different world titles— lightweight (1972-79), welterweight (1980), junior middleweight (1983) and middleweight (1989-90); lost famous "No Mas" welterweight title bout when he quit in 8th round against Sugar Ray Leonard (1980); finally retired in 2002 at the age of 50 with a record of 104-16 (69 KOs).

Leo Durocher (b. July 27, 1905, d. Oct. 7, 1991): Baseball; managed in NL 24 years; won 2,015 games, including postseason; 3 pennants with Brooklyn (1941) and NY Giants (1951,54); won World Series in 1954.

Eddie Eagan (b. Apr. 26, 1898, d. June 14, 1967): Only athlete to win gold medals in both Summer and Winter Olympics (Boxing–1920, Bobsled–1932).

Alan Eagleson (b. Apr. 24, 1933): Hockey; Toronto lawyer, agent and 1st executive director of NHL Players Assn. (1967-90); midwived Team Canada vs. Soviet series (1972) and Canada Cup; charged with racketeering and defrauding NHLPA in indictment handed down by U.S. grand jury in 1994; was sentenced to 18 months in jail in Jan. 1998 after pleading guilty but only served 6 months; resigned from Hall of Fame in 1998.

Dale Earnhardt (b. Apr. 29, 1951, d. Feb. 18, 2001): Auto racer; 7-time NASCAR national champion (1980,86-87,90-91,93-94); Rookie of Year in 1979; was all-time NASCAR money leader with over $34 million won and 76 career wins when he died; finally won Daytona 500 in 1998 on 20th attempt; died in last lap crash at the 2001 Daytona 500.

James Easton (b. July 26, 1935): Olympics; archer and sporting goods manufacturer (Easton softball bats); one of 4 American delegates to the International Olympic Committee; president of International Archery Federation (FITA); member of LA Olympic Organizing Committee in 1984.

Dennis Eckersley (b. Oct. 3, 1954): Baseball P; began his career as a starter in 1975 with Cleveland; no-hit Angels in 1977; won 20 games in 1978 with Boston; moved to the bullpen after 12 seasons as a starter and became one of the best closers of all-time with Oakland; won 1992 AL Cy Young and MVP.

Stefan Edberg (b. Jan. 19, 1966): Swedish tennis player; 2-time No.1 player (1990-91); 2-time winner of Australian Open (1985,87), Wimbledon (1988,90) and U.S. Open (1991-92).

Gertrude Ederle (b. Oct. 23, 1906): Swimmer; 1st woman to swim English Channel, breaking men's record by 2 hours in 1926; won 3 medals in 1924 Olympics.

Krisztina Egerszegi (b. Aug. 16, 1974): Hungarian swimmer; 3-time gold medal winner (100m and 200m backstroke and 400m IM) at 1992 Olympics; also won a gold (200m back) and silver (100m back) at 1988 Games; youngest (14) ever to win swimming gold. Won fifth gold medal (200m back) at '96 Games.

Lee Elder (b. July 14, 1934): Golf; in 1975, became the first black golfer to play in the Masters Tournament; also played in the 1977 Masters; member of the 1979 U.S. Ryder Cup team; played in South Africa's first integrated tournament in 1972.

Todd Eldredge (b. Aug. 28, 1971): Figure Skater; 6-time U.S. champion (1990,91,95,97,98,2002); 1996 World Champion; won U.S. titles at all three levels (novice, junior and senior); most decorated American figure skater without an Olympic medal.

Bill Elliott (b. Oct. 8, 1955): Auto racer; 2-time winner of Daytona 500 (1985,87); NASCAR national champ in 1988; 44 NASCAR wins as of Sept. 2004.

Herb Elliott (b. Feb. 25, 1938): Australian runner; undefeated from 1958-60; ran 17 sub-4:00 miles; 3 world records; won gold medal in 1500 meters at 1960 Olympics; retired at age 22.

Ernie Els (b. Oct. 17, 1969): Golfer; sweet swinging South African; 1994 PGA Tour Rookie of the Year and European Golfer of the Year; 2-time U.S. Open winner (1994,97); won 3rd major in 2002 British Open playoff; 14 PGA Tour wins through Sept. 2004.

John Elway (b. June 28, 1960): Football QB; All-American at Stanford; #1 overall pick in the famous quarterback draft of 1983; known for his last-minute, game-winning scoring drives; led Broncos to 3 Super Bowl losses before back-to-back wins in Super Bowl XXXII and XXXIII; 1987 NFL MVP; 4-time Pro Bowler; one of only two quarterbacks (Marino) to throw for over 50,000 yards.

Roy Emerson (b. Nov. 3, 1936): Australian tennis player; won 12 majors in singles— 6 Australian, 2 French, 2 Wimbledon and 2 U.S. from 1961-67.

Kornelia Ender (b. Oct. 25, 1958): East German swimmer; 1st woman to win 4 gold medals at one Olympics (1976), all in world-record time.

Julius Erving (b. Feb. 22, 1950): Basketball F; "Dr. J"; in ABA (1971-76)— 3-time MVP, 2-time playoff MVP, led NY Nets to 2 titles (1974,76); in NBA (1976-87)— 5-time All-NBA 1st team, MVP in 1981, led Philadelphia 76ers to title in 1983.

Phil Esposito (b. Feb. 20, 1942): Hockey C; 1st NHL player to score 100 points in a season (126 in 1969); 6-time All-NHL 1st team with Boston (1969-74); 2-time MVP (1969,74); 5-time scoring champ; star of 1972 Canada-Soviet series; former president-GM of Tampa Bay Lightning.

Janet Evans (b. Aug. 28, 1971): Swimmer; won 3 individual gold medals (400m & 800m freestyle, 400m IM) at 1988 Olympics; 1989 Sullivan Award winner; won 1 gold (800m) and 1 silver (400m) at 1992 Olympics.

Lee Evans (b. Feb. 25, 1947): Track & Field; dominant quarter-miler in world from 1966-72; world record in 400m set at 1968 Olympics stood 20 years.

Chris Evert (b. Dec. 21, 1954): Tennis; No. 1 player in world 5 times (1975-77,80-81); won at least 1 Grand Slam singles title every year from 1974-86; 18 majors in all— 7 French, 6 U.S., 3 Wimbledon and 2 Australian; retired after 1989 season with 154 singles titles and $8,896,195 in career earnings.

Weeb Ewbank (b. May 6, 1907, d. Nov. 18, 1998): Football; only coach to win NFL and AFL titles; led Baltimore to 2 NFL titles (1958-59) and NY Jets to Super Bowl III win.

Patrick Ewing (b. Aug. 5, 1962): Basketball C; 3-time All-America; led Georgetown to 3 NCAA Finals and 1984 title; Final 4 MOP in '84; 1986 NBA Rookie of Year with New York; All-NBA (1990); on U.S. Olympic gold medal-winning teams in 1984 and '92; named one of the NBA's 50 Greatest Players.

Ray Ewry (b. Oct. 14, 1873, d. Sept. 29, 1937): Track & Field; won 10 gold medals (although 2 are not recognized by IOC) over 4 consecutive Olympics (1900,04,06,08); all events he won (Standing HJ, LJ and TJ) were discontinued in 1912.

Nick Faldo (b. July 18, 1957): British golfer; 3-time winner of British Open (1987,90,92) and Masters (1989, 90, 96); 3-time European Golfer of Year (1989-90,92); PGA Player of Year in 1990.

Juan Manuel Fangio (b. June 24, 1911, d. July 17, 1995): Argentine auto racer; 5-time Formula One world champion (1951,54-57); 24 career wins, retired in 1958.

Marshall Faulk (b. Feb. 26, 1973): Football RB; 3-time consensus All-America at San Diego St.; 2-time NCAA Div. I-A rushing leader (1991-92); 2nd overall pick (Indianapolis) of the 1994 NFL draft; traded to St.L Rams in 1999; 3-time AP Offensive Player of the Year (1999-2001); NFL MVP in 2000 (AP/PFWA) and 2001 (Bell/PFWA); set NFL single season record with 26 TDs in 2000 (broken by P. Holmes's 27 in 2003).

Brett Favre (b. Oct. 10, 1969): Football; Strong-armed Southern Miss. QB drafted in 1991 in the 2nd round (33rd overall) by Atlanta; traded to Green Bay in 1992; NFL's only 3-time league MVP (1995-97); 8-time Pro Bowl QB; led Packers to Super Bowl victory in 1997; has started an NFL quarterback record 189 consecutive games entering the 2004 season.

Sergei Fedorov (b. Dec. 13, 1969): Hockey C; first Russian to win NHL Hart Trophy as 1993-94 regular season MVP; 5-time All-Star and 3-time Stanley Cup winner (1997,98,2002) with Detroit.

Donald Fehr (b. July 18, 1948): Baseball labor leader; protégé of Marvin Miller; executive director and general counsel of Major League Players Assn. since 1983; led players in 1994 "salary cap" strike that lasted eight months and resulted in first cancellation of World Series since 1904.

Bob Feller (b. Nov. 3, 1918): Baseball RHP; Hall of Fame fire-baller who led AL in strikeouts 7 times and wins 6 times with Cleveland Indians; threw 3 no-hitters and major league record 12 one-hitters; 266-162 record; amassed 2,581 Ks despite missing four seasons to military service during WWII.

Tom Ferguson (b. Dec. 20, 1950): Rodeo; 6-time All-Around champion (1974-79); 1st cowboy to win $100,000 in one season (1978); 1st to win $1 million in career (1986).

Herve Filion (b. Feb. 1, 1940): Harness racing; 10-time Driver of Year; all-time leader in races won with 15,017 in 37 years.

Rollie Fingers (b. Aug. 25, 1946): Baseball RHP; mustachioed relief ace with 341 career saves; won AL MVP and Cy Young awards in 1981 with Milwaukee; World Series MVP in 1974 with Oakland; elected to Hall of Fame in 1992.

Charles O. Finley (b. Feb. 22, 1918, d. Feb, 19, 1997): Baseball owner; moved KC A's to Oakland in 1968; won 3 straight World Series from 1972-74; also owned teams in NHL and ABA.

Bobby Fischer (b. Mar. 9, 1943): Chess; at 15, became youngest international grandmaster in chess history; only American to hold world championship (1972-75); was stripped of title in 1975 after refusing to defend against Anatoly Karpov and became recluse; re-emerged to defeat old foe and former world champion Boris Spassky in 1992.

Carlton Fisk (b. Dec. 26, 1947): Baseball C; holds all-time major league record for games caught (2,229); also held HR record for catchers (351) until 2004 (Mike Piazza); AL Rookie of Year (1972) and 10-time All-Star; hit epic, 12th-inning Game 6 homer for Boston Red Sox in 1975 World Series; elected to the Hall of Fame in 2000.

Emerson Fittipaldi (b. Dec. 12, 1946): Brazilian auto racer; 2-time Formula One world champion (1972,74); 2-time winner of Indy 500 (1989,93); won overall IndyCar title in 1989.

Bob Fitzsimmons (b. May 26, 1863, d. Oct. 22, 1917): British boxer; held three world titles— middleweight (1881-97), heavyweight (1897-99) and light heavyweight (1903-05); pro record 40-11 with 32 KOs.

James (Sunny Jim) Fitzsimmons (b. July 23, 1874, d. Mar. 11, 1966): Horse racing; trained horses that won over 2,275 races, including 2 Triple Crown winners—Gallant Fox in 1930 and Omaha in '35.

Jim Fixx (b. Apr. 23, 1932, d. July 20, 1984): Running; author who popularized the sport of running; his 1977 bestseller The Complete Book of Running, is credited with helping start America's fitness revolution; ironically died of a heart attack while running.

Larry Fleisher (b. Sept. 26, 1930, d. May 4, 1989): Basketball; led NBA players union from 1961-89; increased average yearly salary from $9,400 in 1967 to $600,000 without a strike.

Peggy Fleming (b. July 27, 1948): Figure skating; 3-time world champion (1966-68); won Olympic gold medal in 1968.

Curt Flood (b. Jan. 18, 1938, d. Jan. 20, 1997): Baseball OF; played 15 years (1956-69,71) mainly with St. Louis; hit over .300 6 times with 7 Gold Gloves; refused trade to Phillies in 1969; lost challenge to baseball's reserve clause in Supreme Court in 1972 but his case helped bring free agency to MLB.

Ray Floyd (b. Sept. 14, 1942): Golfer; has 22 PGA victories in 4 decades; joined Senior PGA Tour in 1992 and has 14 Senior wins; has won Masters (1976), U.S. Open (1986), PGA twice (1969,82) and PGA Seniors Championship (1995); first player to win on PGA and Senior tours in same year (1992); member of 8 Ryder Cup teams and captain in 1989.

Doug Flutie (b. Oct. 23, 1962): Football QB; Boston College QB who threw famous 48-yard "Hail Mary" to defeat Miami on Nov. 23, 1984; 1984 Heisman Trophy winner; has played in USFL, NFL and CFL; 6-time CFL MVP with B.C. Lions (1991), Calgary (1992-94) and Toronto (1996-97); led Calgary (1992) and Toronto (1996-97) to Grey Cup titles.

Whitey Ford (b. Oct. 21, 1928): Baseball LHP; all-time leader in World Series wins (10); led AL in wins 3 times; won Cy Young and World Series MVP in 1961 with NY Yankees; 236-106 record.

George Foreman (b. Jan. 10, 1949): Boxer; Olympic heavyweight champ (1968); world heavyweight champ (1973-74, 94-95); lost title to Muhammad Ali (KO-8th) in '74; recaptured it on Nov. 5, 1994 at age 45 with a 10-round KO of WBA/IBF champ Michael Moorer, becoming the oldest man to win heavyweight crown; named AP Male Athlete of Year 20 years after losing title to Ali; stripped of WBA title in 1995 after declining to fight No. 1 contender; successfully defended title at age 46 against 26-year-old Axel Schulz in controversial maj. decision; gave up IBF title after refusing rematch with Schulz.

Dick Fosbury (b. Mar. 6, 1947): Track & Field; revolutionized high jump with back-first "Fosbury Flop"; won gold medal at 1968 Olympics.

Greg Foster (b. Aug. 4, 1958): Track & Field; 3-time winner of World Championship in 110-m hurdles (1983,87,91); won silver in 1984 Olympics; world indoor champion in 1991.

The Four Horsemen Senior backfield that led Notre Dame to national collegiate football championship in 1924; put together as sophomores by Irish coach Knute Rockne; immortalized by sportswriter Grantland Rice, whose report of the Oct. 19, 1924, Notre Dame-Army game began: "Outlined against a blue, gray October sky the Four Horsemen rode again..."; HB Jim Crowley (b. Sept. 10, 1902, d. Jan. 15, 1986), FB Elmer Layden (b. May 4, 1903, d. June 30, 1973), HB Don Miller (b. May 30, 1902, d. July 28, 1979) and QB Harry Stuhldreher (b. Oct. 14, 1901, d. Jan. 26, 1965).

The Four Musketeers French quartet that dominated men's tennis in 1920s and '30s, winning 8 straight French singles titles (1925-32), 6 Wimbledons in a row (1924-29) and 6 consecutive Davis Cups (1927-32) — Jean Borotra (b. Aug. 13, 1898, d. July 17, 1994), Jacques Brugnon (b. May 11, 1895, d. Mar. 20, 1978), Henri Cochet (b. Dec. 14, 1901, d. Apr. 1, 1987), Rene Lacoste (b. July 2, 1905, d. Oct. 13, 1996).

Nellie Fox (b. Dec. 25, 1927, d. Dec. 1, 1975): Baseball 2B; batted .306 in 1959 to win the AL MVP award with the pennant-winning Chicago White Sox; led the league in fielding percentage six times, hits four times and triples once; ended his 19-year career with 2,663 hits, 1,279 runs and .288 average.

Jimmie Foxx (b. Oct. 22, 1907, d. July 21, 1967): Baseball 1B; led AL in HRs 4 times and batting twice; won Triple Crown in 1933; 3-time MVP (1932-33,38) with Philadelphia and Boston; hit 30 HRs or more 12 years in a row; 534 career HRs.

A.J. Foyt (b. Jan. 16, 1935): Auto racer; 7-time USAC-CART national champion (1960-61,63-64, 67,75,79); 4-time Indy 500 winner (1961,64, 67,77); only driver in history to win Indy 500, Daytona 500 (1972) and 24 Hours of LeMans (1967 with Dan Gurney); retired in 1993 as all-time CART wins leader with 67.

Bill France Sr. (b. Sept. 26, 1909, d. June 7, 1992): Stock car driver and promoter; founded NASCAR in 1948; guided race circuit through formative years; built both Daytona (Fla.) Int'l Speedway and Talladega (Ala.) Superspeedway.

Dawn Fraser (b. Sept. 4, 1937): Australian swimmer; won gold medals in 100m freestyle at 3 consecutive Olympics (1956,60,64).

Joe Frazier (b. Jan. 12, 1944): Boxer; 1964 Olympic heavyweight champion; world heavyweight champ (1970-73); decisioned former champ Muhammad Ali in March 1971 in one of the most anticipated prizefights in history, fought Ali twice more, losing both times including the "Thrilla in Manila" in 1975; pro record 32-4-1 with 27 KOs.

Walt Frazier (b. March 29, 1945): Basketball G; won the NBA championship twice (1970 and 73) with the New York Knicks; stole spotlight from teammate Willis Reed in Game 7 of 1970 Finals vs. the Lakers with 36 points, 19 assists and 5 steals; averaged 18.9 PPG and 6.1 APG over his career; four-time all-NBA and a member of the Hall of Fame; nicknamed "Clyde" after well-dressed gangster Clyde Barrow.

Cathy Freeman (b. Feb. 16, 1973): Track & Field; Australian Aborigine who lit the cauldron at the start of the 2000 Olympic Games in Sydney and later won gold in the 400-meters on her home soil; 2-time world champion in the 400-meters (1997,99); won silver in the 400 at the 1996 Olympics in Atlanta.

Ford Frick (b. Dec. 19, 1894, d. Apr. 8, 1978): Baseball; sportswriter and radio announcer who served as NL president (1934-51) and commissioner (1951-65); convinced record-keepers to list Roger Maris' and Babe Ruth's season records separately; major leagues moved to West Coast and expanded from 16 to 20 teams during his tenure.

Frankie Frisch (b. Sept. 9, 1898, d. Mar. 12, 1973): Baseball 2B; played on 8 NL pennant winners in 19 years with NY and St. Louis; hit .300 or better 11 years in a row (1921-31); MVP in 1931; player-manager from 1933-37.

Dan Gable (b. Oct. 25, 1948): Wrestling; career wrestling record of 118-1 (Larry Owings beat him in his final collegiate match) at Iowa St., where he was a 2-time NCAA champ (1968,69) and tourney MVP in 1969 (137 lbs); won gold medal (149 lbs) at 1972 Olympics; coached U.S. freestyle team in 1988; coached Iowa to 9 straight NCAA titles (1978-86) and 15 overall in 21 years.

Eddie Gaedel (b. June 8, 1925, d. June 18, 1961): Baseball PH; St. Louis Browns' 3-foot-7 player whose career lasted one at bat (he walked) on Aug 19, 1951; hired as a publicity stunt by eccentric owner Bill Veeck.

Clarence (Big House) Gaines (b. May 21, 1924): Basketball; retired as coach of Div. II Winston-Salem after 1992-93 season with 828-447 record in 47 years.

Alonzo (Jake) Gaither (b. Apr. 11, 1903, d. Feb. 18, 1994): Football; head coach at Florida A&M for 25 years; led Rattlers to 6 national black college titles; retired after 1969 season with record of 203-36-4 and a winning percentage of .844; coined phrase, "I like my boys agile, mobile and hostile."

Cito Gaston (b. Mar. 17, 1944): Baseball; managed Toronto to consecutive World Series titles (1992-93); first black manager to win Series; shared *The Sporting News* 1993 Man of Year award with Blue Jays GM Pat Gillick.

Rulon Gardner (b. Aug. 16, 1971): Olympic wrestler; surprise winner of the super heavyweight Greco-Roman wrestling gold medal at the 2000 Sydney Games; beat unbeatable Russian legend Alexandre Kareline, 1-0; won 2000 Sullivan Award and USOC Sportsman of the Year Award; lost a toe to frostbite in 2002 but still took bronze medal in Athens (2004), retired following the match.

Lou Gehrig (b. June 19, 1903, d. June 2, 1941): Baseball 1B; played in 2,130 consecutive games from 1925-39 a major league record until Cal Ripken Jr. surpassed it in 1995; led AL in RBI 5 times and HRs 3 times; drove in 100 runs or more 13 years in a row; 2-time MVP (1927,36); hit .340 with 493 HRs over 17 seasons; led NY Yankees to 6 World Series titles; died at age 37 of Amyotrophic Lateral Sclerosis (ALS), a rare and incurable disease of the nervous system now better known as Lou Gehrig's disease.

Bernie Geoffrion (b. Feb. 14, 1931): Hockey RW; credited with popularizing the slap shot, earning his nickname "Boom Boom"; scored 30 goals in 1952 to win the NHL's Calder Trophy (Rookie of the Year Award); won the MVP award (Hart) in 1955; became the second player in history to score 50 goals in one season; led the league in points in 1955 and 61; won 6 Stanley Cups with Montreal; member of the Hockey Hall of Fame.

George Gervin (b. April 27, 1952): Basketball G/F; joined the ABA in 1972 and came to the NBA with San Antonio in 1976; a five-time NBA all-star; led the league in scoring four times; scored 26,595 points with an average of 25.1 per game; known as the "Iceman" because of his cool style; elected to the Hall of Fame in 1996.

A. Bartlett Giamatti (b. Apr. 14, 1938, d. Sept. 1, 1989): Scholar and 7th commissioner of baseball; banned Pete Rose for life for betting on Major League games and associating with known gamblers; also served as president of Yale (1978-86) and National League (1986-89).

Joe Gibbs (b. Nov. 25, 1940): Football; coached Washington to 140 victories and 3 Super Bowl titles in 12 seasons before retiring in 1993; owner of NASCAR racing team that won 1993 Daytona 500 and 2000 Winston Cup title; returned to coach Redskins in 2004.

Althea Gibson (b. Aug. 25, 1927, d. Sept. 28, 2003): Tennis; won both Wimbledon and U.S. championships in 1957 and '58; 1st black to play in either tourney in 1958 to win each title.

Bob Gibson (b. Nov. 9, 1935): Baseball RHP; won 20 or more games 5 times; won 2 NL Cy Youngs (1968,70); MVP in 1968; led St. Louis to 2 World Series titles (1964,67); his ERA of 1.12 in 1968 is the lowest for a starter since 1914; 251-174 record.

Josh Gibson (b. Dec. 21, 1911, d. Jan. 20, 1947): Baseball C; the "Babe Ruth of the Negro Leagues"; Satchel Paige's battery mate with Pittsburgh Crawfords. The Negro Leagues did not keep accurate records but Gibson hit 84 home runs in one season and his Baseball Hall of Fame plaque says he hit "almost 800" home runs in his seventeen-year career.

Kirk Gibson (b. May 28, 1957): Baseball OF; All-America flanker at Mich. St. in 1978; chose baseball career and was AL playoff MVP with Detroit in 1984 and NL regular season MVP with Los Angeles in 1988; hit famous pinch-hit home run against Oakland's Dennis Eckersley in Game 1 of the 1988 World Series to vault the Dodgers to the title.

Frank Gifford (b. Aug. 16, 1930): Football HB; 4-time All-Pro (1955-57,59); NFL MVP in 1956; led NY Giants to 3 NFL title games; longtime TV sportscaster, beginning career in 1958 while still a player; scandal struck the married Gifford after he was videotaped in a compromising position with a former stewardess in 1997.

Sid Gillman (b. Oct. 26, 1911): Football innovator; coach elected to both College and Pro Football Halls of Fame; led college teams at Miami-OH and Cincinnati to combined 81-19-2 record from 1944-54; coached LA Rams (1955-59) in NFL, then led LA-San Diego Chargers to 5 Western titles and 1 league championship in first six years of AFL.

George Gipp (b. Feb. 18, 1895, d. Dec. 14, 1920): Football FB; died of throat infection 2 weeks before he made All-America; rushed for 2,341 yards, scored 156 points and averaged 38 yards a punt in 4 years (1917-20).

Marc Girardelli (b. July 18, 1963): Luxembourg Alpine skier; Austrian native who refused to join Austrian Ski Federation because he wanted to be coached by his father; won unprecedented 5th overall World Cup title in 1993; winless at Olympics, although he won 2 silver medals in 1992.

Tom Glavine (b. Mar. 26, 1966): Baseball LHP; led the majors in wins from 1991-95 with 91; NL Cy Young winner in 1991 and '98; seven-time All-Star and was the NL starter twice; World Series MVP with Atlanta in 1995.

Tom Gola (b. Jan. 13, 1933): Basketball F; 4-time All-America and 1955 Player of Year at La Salle; MOP in 1952 NIT and '54 NCAA Final 4, leading Explorers to both titles; won NBA title as rookie with Philadelphia Warriors in 1956; 4-time NBA All-Star.

Marshall Goldberg (b. Oct. 24, 1917): Football HB; 2-time consensus All-America at Pittsburgh (1937-38); led Pitt to national championship in 1937; played with NFL champion Chicago Cardinals 10 years later.

Lefty Gomez (b. Nov. 26, 1908, d. Feb. 17, 1989): Baseball LHP; 4-time 20-game winner with NY Yankees; holds World Series record for most wins (6) without a defeat; pitched on 5 world championship clubs in 1930s.

Pancho Gonzales (b. May 9, 1928, d. July 3, 1995): Tennis; won consecutive U.S. Championships in 1948-49 before turning pro at 21; dominated pro tour from 1950-61; in 1969 at age 41, played longest Wimbledon match ever (5:12), beating Charlie Pasarell 22-24,1-6,16-14,6-3,11-9.

Bob Goodenow (b. Oct. 29, 1952): Hockey; succeeded Alan Eagleson as executive director of NHL Players Assn. in 1990; led players out on 10-day strike (Apr. 1-10) in 1992, during 103-day owners' lockout in 1994-95 and lockout in 2004.

Gail Goodrich (b. April 23, 1943): Basketball G; starred at UCLA and won two national championships in 1964 and 1965 under legendary coach John Wooden's tutelage; won the NBA championship with the L.A. Lakers in 1972 and led the team in scoring (25.9 ppg); averaged 18.6 ppg over his 14-year career.

Jeff Gordon (b. Aug. 4, 1971): Auto racer; NASCAR Rookie of Year (1993); 4-time Winston Cup champion (1995,97,98,2001); won inaugural Brickyard 400 in 1994; in 1997, at 25 became youngest winner of the Daytona 500; in 1998 he tied Richard Petty for the modern-era record for wins in a single season with 13; NASCAR's all-time leading money winner.

Rich (Goose) Gossage (b. July 5, 1951): Baseball RHP; Nine-time All-Star (1975-78, 80-82, 84-85); intimidating relief pitcher; Fireman of the Year in 1975 with White Sox and 1978 with Yankees; led AL in saves with 26 (1975), 27 (1978); 1,002 career appearances; 310 saves.

Shane Gould (b. Nov. 23, 1956): Australian swimmer; set world records in 5 different women's freestyle events between July 1971 and Jan. 1972; won 3 gold medals, a silver and bronze in 1972 Olympics then retired at age 16.

Alf Goullet (b. Apr. 5, 1891, d. Mar. 11, 1995): Cycling; Australian who gained fame and fortune early in century as premier performer on U.S. 6-day bike race circuit; won 8 annual races at Madison Square Garden with 6 different partners from 1913-23.

Curt Gowdy (b. July 31, 1919): Radio-TV; former radio voice of NY Yankees and then Boston Red Sox from 1949-66; TV play-by-play man for AFL, NFL and major league baseball; has broadcast World Series, All-Star Games, Rose Bowls, Super Bowls, Olympics and NCAA Final Fours for 3 networks; hosted "The American Sportsman."

Steffi Graf (b. June 14, 1969): German tennis player; won Grand Slam and Olympic gold medal in 1988 at age 19; won three of four majors in 1993, '95 and '96; won 22 Grand Slam singles titles— 7 at Wimbledon, 6 French, 5 U.S. and 4 Australian Opens, retired in 1999 as 3rd all-time with 107 career singles titles and as all-time tour leader in career earnings with over $21 million in prize money; married to tennis great Andre Agassi.

Otto Graham (b. Dec. 6, 1921, d. Dec. 17, 2003): Football QB and basketball All-America at Northwestern; in pro ball, led Cleveland Browns to 7 league titles in 10 years, winning 4 AAFC championships (1946-49) and 3 NFL (1950,54-55); 5-time All-Pro; 2-time NFL MVP (1953,55).

Cammi Granato (b. Mar. 25, 1971): Hockey; American women's hockey pioneer; captain of U.S. team that won gold at the inaugural Olympic women's hockey competition in 1998 at Nagano; sister of NHL veteran Tony.

Red Grange (b. June 13, 1903, d. Jan. 28, 1991): Football HB; 3-time All-America at Illinois who brought 1st huge crowds to pro football when he signed with Chicago Bears in 1925; formed 1st AFL with manager-promoter C.C. Pyle in 1926, but league folded and he returned to Bears.

Bud Grant (b. May 20, 1927): Football and Basketball; only coach to win 100 games in both CFL and NFL and only member of both CFL and U.S. Pro Football Halls of Fame; led Winnipeg to 4 Grey Cup titles (1958-59,61-62) in 6 appearances, but his Minnesota Vikings lost all 4 Super Bowl attempts in 1970s; accumulated 122 CFL wins and 168 NFL wins; also All-Big Ten at Minnesota in both football and basketball in late 1940s; a 3-time CFL All-Star offensive end; also member of 1950 NBA champion Minneapolis Lakers.

Rocky Graziano (b. June 7, 1922, d. May 22, 1990): Boxer; world middleweight champion (1946-47); fought Tony Zale for title 3 times in 21 months, losing twice; pro record 67-10-6 with 52 KOs; movie "Somebody Up There Likes Me" based on his life.

Hank Greenberg (b. Jan. 1, 1911, d. Sept. 4, 1986): Baseball 1B/LF; slugging right-hander who led AL in HRs and RBI 4 times each; 2-time MVP (1935, 40) with Detroit; 331 career HRs, including 58 in 1938; elected to Hall of Fame in 1956.

Joe Greene (b. Sept. 24, 1946): Football DT; 5-time All-Pro (1972-74,77,79); led Pittsburgh to 4 Super Bowl titles in 1970s; nicknamed "Mean Joe."

Maurice Greene (b. July 23, 1974): Track & Field; world 100m champion in 1997, 99 and 2001 and 200m champion in 1999; former world record holder (9.79) in the 100m; won the gold medal in the 100m and 4x100m at the 2000 Sydney Olympics; took 100m bronze at 2004 Athens Olympics.

Bud Greenspan (b. Sept. 18, 1926): Filmmaker specializing in the Olympic Games; has won Emmy awards for 22-part "The Olympiad" (1976-77) and historical vignettes for ABC-TV's coverage of 1980 Winter Games; won 1994 Emmy award for edited special on Lillehammer Winter Olympics; won The Peabody Award in 1996 for his outstanding service in chronicling the Olympic Games.

Wayne Gretzky (b. Jan. 26, 1961): Hockey C; 10-time NHL scoring champion; 9-time regular season MVP (1979-87,89) and 9-time All-NHL first team; scored 200 points or more in a season 4 times; led Edmonton to 4 Stanley Cups (1984-85,87-88); 2-time playoff MVP (1985,88); traded to LA Kings (Aug. 9, 1988); broke Gordie Howe's all-time NHL goal scoring record of 801 on Mar. 23, 1994; all-time NHL leader in points (2857), goals (894) and assists (1963); also all-time Stanley Cup leader in points, goals and assists; spent the end of the 1996 season with the St. Louis Blues and then signed a free agent contract with the New York Rangers; retired in 1999 at age 38 with 61 NHL scoring records in 20 seasons; became part-owner of NHL's Coyotes in 2000.

Bob Griese (b. Feb. 3, 1945): Football QB; 2-time All-Pro (1971,77); led Miami to undefeated season (17-0) in 1972 and consecutive Super Bowl titles (1973-74); father of Brian.

Ken Griffey Jr. (b. Nov. 21, 1969): Baseball OF; overall 1st pick of 1987 draft by Seattle; 10-time Gold Glove winner; 11-time All-Star; 1997 AL MVP; Mariners all-time leader in home runs and RBIs; MVP of 1992 All-Star game at age 23; hit home runs in 8 consecutive games in 1993; son of Ken Sr. and in 1990 they became the first father-son combination to appear in the same major league lineup; traded to the Cincinnati Reds before the 2000 season but has been plagued with injuries since.

Archie Griffin (b. Aug. 21, 1954): Football RB; only college player to win two Heisman Trophies (1974-75); rushed for 5,177 yards in career at Ohio St. and played in four straight Rose Bowls; drafted by Cincinnati Bengals and played 8 years in NFL.

Emile Griffith (b. Feb. 3, 1938): Boxer; world welterweight champion (1961,62-63,63-65); world middleweight champ (1966-67,67-68); pro record 85-24-2 with 23 KOs.

Dick Groat (b. Nov. 4, 1930): Basketball G and Baseball SS; 2-time basketball All-America at Duke and college Player of Year in 1951; won NL MVP award as shortstop with Pittsburgh in 1960; won World Series with Pirates (1960) and St. Louis (1964).

Lefty Grove (b. Mar. 6, 1900, d. May 23, 1975): Baseball LHP; won 20 or more games 8 times; led AL in ERA 9 times and strikeouts 7 times; 31-4 record and MVP in 1931 with Philadelphia; 300-141 record; real name: Robert Moses Grove.

Lou Groza (b. Jan. 25, 1924, d. Nov. 29, 2000): Football T-PK; 6-time All-Pro; played in 13 championship games for Cleveland from 1946-67; kicked winning field goal in 1950 NFL title game; 1,608 career points (1,349 in NFL).

Janet Guthrie (b. Mar. 7, 1938): Auto racer; in 1977, became 1st woman to race in Indianapolis 500; placed 9th at Indy in 1978.

Tony Gwynn (b. May 9, 1960): Baseball OF; 8-time NL batting champion (1984,87-89,94-97) with San Diego, 15-time All-Star; got 3,000th career hit Aug. 6, 1999 at Montreal; played basketball at San Diego St. leaving as school's all-time assist leader; drafted in 10th round of 1981 NBA draft by then San Diego Clippers; retired with 3,141 career hits.

Harvey Haddix (b. Sept. 18, 1925, d. Jan. 9, 1994): Baseball LHP; pitched 12 perfect innings for Pittsburgh, but lost to Milwaukee in the 13th, 1-0 (May 26, 1959); won Game 7 of 1960 World Series.

Walter Hagen (b. Dec. 21, 1892, d. Oct. 5, 1969): Pro golf pioneer; won 2 U.S. Opens (1914,19), 4 British Opens (1922,24,28-29), 5 PGA Championships (1921,24-27) and 5 Western Opens; 44 career PGA wins; 6-time U.S. Ryder Cup captain.

Marvin Hagler (b. May 23, 1954): Boxer; hard-punching world middleweight champion from 1980-87; enjoyed his nickname "Marvelous Marvin" so much he had his name legally changed; pro record of 62-3-2 with 52 KOs; retired after suffering 1987 upset loss to Sugar Ray Leonard.

Mika Hakkinen (b. Sept. 28, 1968): Finnish auto racer; won two consecutive Formula One world drivers championships in 1998 and '99; recorded eight wins in '98 and five in '99; 20 career F1 wins.

George Halas (b. Feb. 2, 1895, d. Oct. 31, 1983): Football pioneer; MVP in 1919 Rose Bowl; player-coach-owner of Chicago Bears from 1920-83; signed Red Grange in 1925; coached Bears for 40 seasons and won 8 NFL titles (1921,32-33,40-41,43,46,63); 2nd on all-time career list with 324 wins; elected to NFL Hall of Fame in 1963.

Dorothy Hamill (b. July 26, 1956): Figure skater; won Olympic gold medal and world championship in 1976; Ice Capades headliner from 1977-84; bought the financially-strapped Ice Capades in 1993 and sold it several years later.

Scott Hamilton (b. Aug. 28, 1958): Figure skater; 4-time world champion (1981-84); won gold medal at 1984 Olympics.

Mia Hamm (b. Mar. 17, 1972): Soccer F; all-time leading international scorer with 154 goals; member of 3 U.S. Olympic team (1996,2000,04), and 4 U.S. World Cup teams (1991,95,99,2003); made the U.S. National Team at 15; a three-time collegiate All-American; led UNC to 4 national titles (1989,90, 92,93); Two-time FIFA Women's World Player of the Year (2001-02); married to baseball's Nomar Garciaparra.

Tonya Harding (b. Nov. 12, 1970): Figure skater; 1991 and 1994 U.S. women's champion; involved in plot hatched by ex-husband Jeff Gillooly to injure rival Nancy Kerrigan and keep her off Olympic team; won '94 U.S. title in Kerrigan's absence; denied any role in assault and sued USOC to keep her spot in Olympics; finished 8th at Lillehammer (Kerrigan recovered and won silver medal); pleaded guilty on Mar. 16 to conspiracy to hinder investigation; stripped of 1994 title by U.S. Figure Skating Association.

Tom Harmon (b. Sept. 28, 1919, d. Mar. 17, 1990): Football HB; 2-time All-America at Michigan; won Heisman Trophy in 1940; played with AFL NY Americans in 1941 and NFL LA Rams (1946-47); World War II fighter pilot who won Silver Star and Purple Heart; became radio-TV commentator.

Franco Harris (b. Mar. 7, 1950): Football RB; ran for over 1,000 yards in a season 8 times; rushed for 12,120 yards in 13 years; led Pittsburgh to 4 Super Bowl titles.

Leon Hart (b. Nov. 2, 1928, d. Sept. 24, 2002): Football E; only player to win 3 national championships in college and 3 more in the NFL; won his titles at Notre Dame (1946-47,49) and with Detroit Lions (1952-53,57); 3-time All-America and last lineman to win Heisman Trophy (1949); All-Pro on both offense and defense in 1951.

Bill Hartack (b. Dec. 9, 1932): Jockey; won Kentucky Derby 5 times (1957,60,62,64,69), Preakness 3 times (1956,64,69), and the Belmont once (1960).

Doug Harvey (b. Dec. 19, 1924, d. Dec. 26, 1989): Hockey D; 10-time All-NHL 1st team; won Norris Trophy 7 times (1955-58,60-62); led Montreal to 6 Stanley Cups.

Dominik Hasek (b. Jan. 29, 1965): Czech hockey goaltender; 2-time NHL MVP (1997,98) with Buffalo; 6-time Vezina Trophy winner (1994,95,97,98,99, 2001); led Czech Republic to Olympic gold medal in 1998 at Nagano; won Stanley Cup with Detroit in 2002.

Billy Haughton (b. Nov. 2, 1923, d. July 15, 1986): Harness racing; 4-time winner of Hambletonian; trainer-driver of one Pacing Triple Crown winner (1968); 4,910 career wins.

João Havelange (b. May 8, 1916): Soccer; Brazilian-born president of Federation Internationale de Football Assoc. (FIFA) 1974-98; also member of International Olympic Committee.

John Havlicek (b. Apr. 8, 1940): Basketball F; played in 3 NCAA Finals at Ohio St. (1960-62); led Boston to 8 NBA titles (1963-66,68-69,74,76); Finals MVP in 1974; 4-time All-NBA 1st team.

Bob Hayes (b. Dec. 20, 1942, d. Sept. 18, 2002): Track & Field and Football; won gold medal in 100m at 1964 Olympics; all-pro SE for Dallas in 1966; won Super Bowl with Cowboys in 1972; convicted of drug trafficking in 1979 and served 18 months of a 5-year sentence.

Elvin Hayes (b. Nov. 17, 1945): Basketball C; Known as "the Big E"; Overall number one pick of the 1968 NBA draft; three-time All-NBA first team (1975,77,79); 1978 Finals MVP; 12-time NBA all-star (1969-80); named to NBA's 50 Greatest Players; amassed 27,313 points and 16,279 rebounds; member of basketball Hall of Fame.

Woody Hayes (b. Feb. 14, 1913, d. Mar. 12, 1987): Football; coached Ohio St. to 6 national titles (1954,57,61,68,70) and 4 Rose Bowl victories; 238 career wins in 28 seasons at Denison, Miami-OH and OSU; his coaching career ended abruptly in 1978 after he attacked an opposing player on the sidelines.

Thomas Hearns (b. Oct. 18, 1958): Boxer; held world titles as welterweight, junior middleweight, middleweight and light heavyweight; four career losses came against Ray Leonard, Marvin Hagler and twice to Iran Barkley; pro record of 59-4-1, 46 KOs.

Eric Heiden (b. June 14, 1958): Speed skater; 3-time overall world champion (1977-79); won all 5 men's speed skating gold medals at 1980 Olympics; setting records in each; Sullivan Award winner (1980).

Mel Hein (b. Aug. 22, 1909, d. Jan. 31, 1992): Football C; NFL All-Pro 8 straight years (1933-40); MVP in 1938 with Giants; didn't miss a game in 15 years.

John W. Heisman (b. Oct. 23, 1869, d. Oct. 3, 1936): Football; coached at 9 colleges from 1892-1927; won 185 games; Director of Athletics at Downtown Athletic Club in NYC (1928-36); DAC named Heisman Trophy after him.

Carol Heiss (b. Jan. 20, 1940): Figure skater; 5-time world champion (1956-60); won Olympic silver medal in 1956 and gold in '60; married 1956 men's gold medalist Hayes Jenkins.

Rickey Henderson (b. Dec. 25, 1958): Baseball OF; AL playoff MVP (1989) and AL regular season MVP (1990); set single-season base stealing record of 130 in 1982; led AL in steals a record 12 times; broke Lou Brock's all-time record of 938 on May 1, 1991; all-time MLB leader in runs, steals, and HRs as leadoff batter.

Sonja Henie (b. Apr. 8, 1912, d. Oct. 12, 1969): Norwegian figure skater; 10-time world champion (1927-36); won 3 consecutive Olympic gold medals (1928,32,36); became movie star.

Foster Hewitt (b. Nov. 21, 1902, d. Apr. 21, 1985): Radio-TV; Canada's premier hockey play-by-play broadcaster from 1923-81; coined phrase, "He shoots, he scores!"

Damon Hill (b. Sept. 17, 1960): British auto racer; 1996 Formula One champion; 22 F1 wins places him 10th all-time; retired following 1999 season; son of Graham.

Graham Hill (b. Feb. 15, 1929, d. Nov. 29, 1975): British auto racer; 2-time Formula One champion (1962,68); won Indy 500 in 1966; killed in plane crash; father of Damon.

Phil Hill (b. Apr. 20, 1927): Auto racer; first U.S. driver to win Formula One championship (1961); 3 career wins (1958-64).

Martina Hingis (b. Sept. 30, 1980): Swiss tennis player; in March 1997 at 16 years, 6 months, she became the youngest No. 1 ranked player since the ranking system began in 1975; won Wimbledon (1997), U.S. Open (1997) and 3 Australian Opens (1997,98,99); first woman to surpass the $3 million mark in earnings for one season (1997).

Max Hirsch (b. July 30, 1880, d. Apr. 3, 1969): Horse racing; trained 1,933 winners from 1908-68; won Triple Crown with Assault in 1946.

Tommy Hitchcock (b. Feb. 11, 1900, d. Apr. 19, 1944): Polo; world class player at 20; achieved 10-goal rating 18 times from 1922-40.

Lew Hoad (b. Nov. 23, 1934, d. July 3, 1994): Australian tennis player; 2-time Wimbledon winner (1956-57); won Australian, French and Wimbledon titles in 1956, but missed capturing Grand Slam at Forest Hills when beaten by Ken Rosewall in 4-set final.

Gil Hodges (b. Apr. 4, 1924, d. Apr. 2, 1972): Baseball 1B-Manager; tied Major League record with four home runs in one game on Aug 31, 1950; won three Gold Gloves (1957-59); drove in 100 runs in seven consecutive seasons (1949-55); hit 370 home runs and 1,274 RBIs lifetime; won 660 games as a manager (Senators and Mets).

Ben Hogan (b. Aug. 13, 1912, d. July 25, 1997): Golfer; 4-time PGA Player of Year; one of only five players to win all four Grand Slam titles (others are Nicklaus, Player, Sarazen and Woods); won 4 U.S. Opens, 2 Masters, 2 PGAs and 1 British Open between 1946-53; nearly killed in Feb. 2, 1949 car accident, but came back to win 1950 U.S. Open just 16 months later; one of only two players (Woods) to win three of the four current majors in one year when he won Masters, U.S. Open and British Open in 1953 at age 41; third on all-time list with 64 career wins.

Chamique Holdsclaw (b. Aug. 9, 1977): Basketball F; 2-time national player of the year, leading Tennessee to 3 straight national championships (1996-98); 1998 Sullivan Award winner; top selection by the Washington Mystics in the 1999 WNBA draft; 1999 WNBA Rookie of the Year.

Eleanor Holm (b. Dec. 6, 1913): Swimmer; won gold medal in 100m backstroke at 1932 Olympics; thrown off '36 U.S. team for drinking champagne in public and shooting craps on boat to Germany.

Nat Holman (b. Oct. 18, 1896, d. Feb. 12, 1995): Basketball pioneer; played with Original Celtics (1920-28); coached CCNY to both NCAA and NIT titles in 1950 (a year later, several of his players were caught up in a point-shaving scandal); 423 career wins.

Larry Holmes (b. Nov. 3, 1949): Boxer; heavyweight champion (WBC or IBF) from 1978-85; successfully defended title 20 times before losing to Michael Spinks; returned from first retirement in 1988 and was KO'd in 4th by champ Mike Tyson; launched second comeback in 1991; fought and lost title bids against Evander Holyfield in '92 and Oliver McCall in '95; pro record of 69-6 and 44 KOs.

Lou Holtz (b. Jan. 6, 1937): Football; coached Notre Dame to national title in 1988; 2-time Coach of Year (1977,88); has coached six schools in all—William & Mary (3 years), N.C. State (4), Arkansas (7), Minnesota (2), ND (11) and South Carolina (6+); also coached NFL's NY Jets for 13 games (3-10) in 1976.

Evander Holyfield (b. Oct. 19, 1962): Boxer; only man in history to win (and lose) world heavyweight title 4 times; Wore belt off and on from 1990-2001; defeated former champ Mike Tyson in 1996 to win WBA belt; in 1997 rematch, Tyson was DQ'd for twice biting his ear; former undisputed cruiserweight world (1987-88) champ before moving to heavyweight.

Red Holzman (b. Aug. 10, 1920, d. Nov. 13, 1998): Basketball; played for NBL and NBA champions at Rochester (1,946,51); coached NY Knicks to 2 NBA titles (1970,73); Coach of Year (1970); 754 career NBA wins.

Bernard Hopkins (b. Jan. 15, 1965): Boxer; became first undisputed world middleweight champion since Marvin Hagler when he upset undefeated Felix Trinidad with a 12th-round TKO in 2001 to unify belts; defended belts for 18th time with TKO of Oscar De La Hoya in 2004.

Rogers Hornsby (b. Apr. 27, 1896, d. Jan. 5, 1963): Baseball 2B; hit .400 3 times, including .424 in 1924; led NL in batting 7 times; 2-time MVP (1925,29); career BA of .358 over 23 years is highest in NL.

Paul Hornung (b. Dec. 23, 1935): Football HB-PK; only Heisman Trophy winner to play for losing team (2-8 Notre Dame in 1956); 3-time NFL scoring leader (1959-61) at Green Bay; 176 points in 1960, an all-time record; MVP in 1961; suspended by NFL for 1963 season for betting on his own team.

Gordie Howe (b. Mar. 31, 1928): Hockey RW; played 32 seasons in NHL and WHA from 1946-80; led NHL in scoring 6 times; All-NHL 1st team 12 times; MVP 6 times in NHL (1952-53,57-58,60,63) with Detroit and once in WHA (1974) with Houston; ranks 2nd on all-time NHL list in goals (801) and 3rd in points (1,850); played with sons Mark and Marty at Houston (1973-77) and New England-Hartford (1977-80).

Cal Hubbard (b. Oct. 31, 1900, d. Oct. 17, 1977): Member of college football, pro football and baseball halls of fame; 9 years in NFL; 4-time All-Pro at end and tackle; AL umpire (1936-51).

William DeHart Hubbard (b. Nov. 25, 1903, d. June 23, 1976): Track & Field; won the long jump at the 1924 Olympics, becoming the first black athlete to win an Olympic gold medal in an individual event; set the long jump world record in 1925 (25-10¾) and tied the 100-yard dash record (9.6) in 1926.

Carl Hubbell (b. June 22, 1903, d. Nov. 21, 1988): Baseball LHP; led NL in wins and ERA 3 times each; 2-time MVP (1933,36) with NY Giants; fanned Ruth, Gehrig, Foxx, Simmons and Cronin in succession in 1934 All-Star Game; 253-154 career record.

Sam Huff (b. Oct. 4, 1934): Football LB; glamorized NFL's middle linebacker position with NY Giants from 1956-63; subject of "The Violent World of Sam Huff" TV special in 1961; helped club win 6 division titles and a world championship (1956).

Miller Huggins (b. Mar. 27, 1878, d. Sept. 25, 1929): Baseball; managed NY Yankees from 1918 until his death late in '29 season; led Yanks to 6 pennants and 3 World Series titles from 1921-28.

Bobby Hull (b. Jan. 3, 1939): Hockey LW; led NHL in scoring 3 times; 2-time MVP (1965-66) with Chicago; All-NHL first team 10 times; jumped to WHA in 1972, 2-time MVP there (1973,75) with Winnipeg; scored 913 goals in both leagues; father of Brett.

Brett Hull (b. Aug. 9, 1964): Hockey RW; NHL MVP in 1991 with St. Louis; holds single season RW scoring record with 86 goals; he and father Bobby have both won Hart (MVP), Lady Byng (sportsmanship) and All-Star Game MVP trophies; won Stanley Cup with Dallas in 1999 and Detroit in 2002.

Lamar Hunt (b. Aug. 2, 1932): Football/Soccer; Founder of the Kansas City Chiefs (formerly Dallas Texans); instrumental in forming the AFL in 1959 and merging the league with NFL in 1966; elected to the Pro Football Hall of Fame in 1972; AFC Championship trophy bear his name; investor/operator in Major League Soccer.

Jim (Catfish) Hunter (b. Apr. 8, 1946, d. Sept. 9, 1999): Baseball RHP; won 20 games or more 5 times (1971-75); played on 5 World Series winners with Oakland and NY Yankees; threw perfect game in 1968; won AL Cy Young Award in 1974; 224-166 career record.

Ibrahim Hussein (b. June 3, 1958): Kenyan distance runner; 3-time winner of Boston Marathon (1988,91-92) and 1st African runner to win in Boston; won New York Marathon in 1987.

Don Hutson (b. Jan. 31, 1913, d. June 24, 1997): Football E-PK; led NFL in receptions 8 times and interceptions once; 9-time All-Pro (1936,38-45) for Green Bay; 99 career TD catches.

Flo Hyman (b. July 31, 1954, d. Jan. 24, 1986): Volleyball; 3-time All-America spiker at Houston and captain of 1984 U.S. Women's Olympic team; died of heart attack caused by Marfan Syndrome during a match in Japan in 1986; namesake of award given out annually by the Women's Sports Foundation.

Hank Iba (b. Aug. 6, 1904, d. Jan. 15, 1993): Basketball; coached Oklahoma A&M to 2 straight NCAA titles (1945-46); 767 career wins in 41 years; coached U.S. Olympic team to 2 gold medals (1964,68), but lost to Soviets in controversial '72 final.

Punch Imlach (b. Mar. 15, 1918, d. Dec. 1, 1987): Hockey; directed Toronto to 4 Stanley Cups (1962-64,67) in 11 seasons as GM-coach.

Miguel Induráin (b. July 16, 1964): Spanish cyclist; won 5 straight Tour de Frances (1991-95), won gold in time trial at '96 Olympics; retired in 1997.

Juli Inkster (b. June 24, 1960): Golfer; 30 career LPGA victories; winner of 7 major LPGA tournaments and 3 consecutive U.S. Women's Amateur tournaments (1980-82); inducted into the World Golf Hall of Fame in 2000; LPGA Rookie of the Year in 1984.

Hale Irwin (b. June 3, 1945): Golfer; oldest player ever to win U.S. Open (45 in 1990); NCAA champion in 1967; 20 PGA victories, including 3 U.S. Opens (1974,79,90); 5-time Ryder Cup team member; joined Senior PGA Tour in 1995 and has already won 40 titles.

Allen Iverson (b. June 7, 1975): Basketball G; former Georgetown Hoya chosen first overall by the Philadelphia 76ers in the 1996 NBA Draft; NBA Rookie of the Year (1997); 2-time NBA scoring leader (2001-02) and steals leader (2001-02); voted regular season MVP in 2001 and led 76ers to NBA Finals.

Bo Jackson (b. Nov. 30, 1962): Baseball OF and Football RB; won Heisman Trophy in 1985 and MVP of baseball All-Star Game in 1989; starter for both baseball's KC Royals and NFL's LA Raiders in 1988 and '89; severely injured left hip Jan. 13, 1991, in NFL playoffs; waived by Royals but signed by Chicago White Sox in 1991; missed entire 1992 season recovering from hip surgery; played for White Sox in 1993 and California in '94 before retiring.

Joe Jackson (b. July 16, 1889, d. Dec. 5, 1951): Baseball OF; hit .300 or better 11 times; nicknamed "Shoeless Joe"; career average of .356, third highest all-time; was placed on MLB's ineligible list in 1921 following the Black Sox scandal in which he and 7 teammates were accused of fixing 1919 World Series.

Phil Jackson (b. Sept. 17, 1945): Basketball; NBA champion as reserve forward with New York in 1973 (injured when Knicks won in '70); coached Chicago to six NBA titles in eight years (1991-93, 96-98); coach of the year in 1996 and 97; returned to coach the LA Lakers in 1999 and won 3 more titles (2000,01,02); all-time leader in winning pct. for NBA coaches with 350 or more wins; left Lakers after 2004 Finals loss to Detroit; all-time NBA leader in playoff wins (175).

Reggie Jackson (b. May 18, 1946): Baseball OF; led AL in HRs 4 times; MVP in 1973; played on 5 World Series winners with Oakland and NY Yankees; 1977 Series MVP with 5 HRs; 563 career HRs; all-time strikeout leader (2,597); member of the Hall of Fame.

Dr. Robert Jackson (b. Aug. 6, 1932): Surgeon; revolutionized sports medicine by popularizing the use of arthroscopic surgery to treat injuries; learned technique from Japanese physician that allowed athletes to return quickly from potentially career-ending injuries.

Helen Jacobs (b. Aug. 6, 1908, d. June 2, 1997): Tennis; 4-time winner of U.S. Championship (1932-35); Wimbledon winner in 1936; lost 4 Wimbledon finals to arch-rival Helen Wills Moody.

Jaromir Jagr (b. Feb. 15, 1972): Czech Hockey RW; fifth overall pick by Pittsburgh (1990); NHL All-Rookie team (1991); NHL MVP (1999); Won Art Ross Trophy (1995,98,99,00,01); 7-time All-NHL First Team; NHL single season record for most points by a right wing (149); NHL single season record for most assists by a RW (87).

LeBron James (b. Dec. 30, 1984): Basketball; mega-hyped top overall pick in 2003 NBA Draft (Cleveland) out of St. Vincent-St. Mary high school in Akron, Ohio; 2004 NBA Rookie of the Year.

Dan Jansen (b. June 17, 1965): Speed skater; fell in 500m and 1,000m in 1988 Olympics just after sister Jane's death; placed 4th in 500m and didn't attempt 1,000m in 1992; fell in 500m at '94 Games, but finally won an Olympic medal with world record (1:12.43) effort in 1,000m, then took victory lap with baby daughter Jane in his arms; won 1994 Sullivan Award.

Dale Jarrett (b. Nov. 26, 1956): Auto racer; 1999 Winston Cup champion; 3-time Daytona 500 champion (1993,96,2000); son of former Ned Jarrett.

James J. Jeffries (b. Apr. 15, 1875, d. Mar. 3, 1953): Boxer; world heavyweight champion (1899-1905); retired undefeated but came back to fight Jack Johnson in 1910 and lost (KO, 15th).

David Jenkins (b. June 29, 1936): Figure skater; brother of Hayes; 3-time world champion (1957-59); won gold medal at 1960 Olympics.

Hayes Jenkins (b. Mar. 23, 1933): Figure skater; 4-time world champion (1953-56); won gold medal at 1956 Olympics; married 1960 women's gold medalist Carol Heiss.

Bruce Jenner (b. Oct. 28, 1949): Track & Field; won gold medal in 1976 Olympic decathlon.

Jackie Jensen (b. Mar. 9, 1927, d. July 14, 1982): Football RB and Baseball OF; All-America at Cal in 1948; AL MVP with Boston Red Sox in 1958.

Ben Johnson (b. Dec. 30, 1961): Canadian sprinter; set 100m world record (9.83) at 1987 World Championships; won 100m at 1988 Olympics, but flunked drug test and forfeited gold medal; 1987 world record revoked in '89 for admitted steroid use; returned drug-free in 1991, but performed poorly; banned for life by IAAF in 1993 for testing positive again.

Bob Johnson (b. Mar. 4, 1931, d. Nov. 26, 1991): Hockey; coached Pittsburgh Penguins to 1st Stanley Cup title in 1991; led Wisconsin to 3 NCAA titles (1973,77,81); also coached 1976 U.S. Olympic team and NHL Calgary Flames (1982-87).

Earvin (Magic) Johnson (b. Aug. 14, 1959): Basketball G; led Michigan St. to NCAA title in 1979 and was Final 4 MOP; All-NBA 1st team 9 times; 3-time MVP (1987,89-90); led LA Lakers to 5 NBA titles; 3-time Finals MVP (1980, 82, 87); 3rd all-time in NBA assists with 10,141; retired on Nov. 7, 1991 after announcing he was HIV-positive; returned to score 25 points in 1992 NBA All-Star Game; U.S. Olympic Dream Team co-captain; announced NBA comeback then retired again before start of 1992-93 season; named head coach of Lakers on Mar. 23, 1994, but finished season at 5-11 and quit; later became minority owner of team; came back a final time and played 32 games during 1995-96 season.

Jack Johnson (b. Mar. 31, 1878, d. June 10, 1946): Boxer; controversial heavyweight champion (1908-15) and 1st black to hold title; defeated Tommy Burns for crown at age 30; fled to Europe in 1913 after Mann Act conviction; lost title to Jess Willard in Havana, but claimed to have taken a dive; pro record 78-8-12 with 45 KOs.

Jimmy Johnson (b. July 16, 1943): Football; All-SWC defensive lineman on Arkansas' 1964 national championship team; coached Miami-FL to national title in 1987; college record of 81-34-3 in 10 years; hired by old friend Jerry Jones to succeed Tom Landry in 1989; went 1-15 in '89, then led Cowboys to consecutive Super Bowl victories (1993-94); quit in 1994 after feuding with Jones; replaced Don Shula as Miami Dolphins head coach from 1996-99.

Judy Johnson (b. Oct. 26, 1899, d. June 13, 1989): Baseball IF; one of the great stars of the Negro Leagues; a terrific fielding third baseman who regularly batted over .300; when baseball integrated Johnson's playing days were over but he coached and scouted for the Philadelphia Athletics, Boston Braves and Philadelphia Phillies; member of Hall of Fame.

Junior Johnson (b. June 28, 1931): Auto Racing; won Daytona 500 in 1960; also won 13 NASCAR races in 1965, including the Rebel 300 at Darlington; retired from racing to become a highly successful car owner; his first driver was Bobby Allison.

Michael Johnson (b. Sep 13, 1967): Track & Field; Shattered world record in 200m (19.32) and set Olympic record in 400m (43.49) to become first man to win the gold in both races in the same Olympic Games at Atlanta in 1996; two-time world champion in 200 (1991,95) and four-time world champ in 400 (1993,95,97,99); set world record in 400m (43.18) at '99 world championships in Seville; won the 400 in Sydney in 2000 to become the only man to win the event in two consecutive Olympics; retired in 2001.

Rafer Johnson (b. Aug. 18, 1935): Track & Field; won silver medal in 1956 Olympic decathlon and gold medal in 1960.

Randy Johnson (b. Sept. 10, 1963): Baseball LHP; 6'10" flamethrower; struck out over 300 batters 6 times (1993,98,99,00,01,02); led AL in Ks 4 times (1992-95) and NL 5 times (1999-2002,04); struck out 20 batters in a game (5/8/01); 5-time Cy Young Award winner (AL-1995, NL-1999,00,01,02); traded to Houston in 1998 and signed as a free agent with Arizona in 1999; won 3 games and co-MVP honors (Curt Schilling) in 2001 World Series; became oldest in baseball history to pitch a perfect game at age 40 on May 18, 2004 against Atlanta.

Walter Johnson (b. Nov. 6, 1887, d. Dec. 10, 1946): Baseball RHP; won 20 games or more 10 straight years; led AL in ERA 5 times, wins 6 times and strikeouts 12 times; twice MVP (1913, 24) with Washington; all-time leader in shutouts (110) and 2nd in wins (417); nicknamed "Big Train."

Ben A. Jones (b. Dec. 31, 1882, d. June 13, 1961): Horse racing; Calumet Farm trainer (1939-47); saddled 6 Kentucky Derby champions, including 2 Triple Crown winners—Whirlaway in 1941 and Citation in '48.

Bobby Jones (b. Mar. 17, 1902, d. Dec. 18, 1971): Won U.S. and British Opens plus U.S. and British Amateurs in 1930 to become golf's only Grand Slam winner ever; from 1922-30, won 4 U.S. Opens, 5 U.S. Amateurs, 3 British Opens, and played in 6 Walker Cups; founded Masters tournament in 1934.

Deacon Jones (b. Dec. 9, 1938): Football DE; 5-time All-Pro (1965-69) with LA Rams; unofficially 3rd all-time in NFL sacks with 173½ in 14 years; inducted into Pro Football Hall of Fame in 1980.

Jerry Jones (b. Oct. 13, 1942): Football; owner-GM of Dallas Cowboys; maverick who bought declining team (3-13) and Texas Stadium for $140 million in 1989; hired pal Jimmy Johnson to replace legendary Tom Landry as coach; their partnership led to 2 Super Bowl titles (1993-94); when feud developed in 1994, he fired Johnson and hired Barry Switzer and won Super Bowl in 1996; defied NFL by signing separate sponsorship deals with Pepsi and Nike in 1995, causing NFL to file a $300 million lawsuit against him, Jones countersued and both sides eventually settled; hired proven winner Bill Parcells as head coach in 2003 following three losing seasons.

Marion Jones (b. Oct. 12, 1975): Track & Field; American sprinter who won 3 golds (100m, 200m, 4x100m) at 2000 Sydney Olympics; 5-time world champion: 100m (1997,99), 200m (2001), 4x100m (1997, 2001); voted Women's Athlete of the Year by *Track & Field News* in 1997,98 and 2000; 1999 Jesse Owens Award winner; 2000 AP and USOC Female Athlete of the Year.

Roy Jones Jr. (b. Jan. 16, 1969): Boxing; robbed of gold medal at 1988 Olympics on a scoring error; still voted Outstanding Boxer of the Games; won IBF middleweight crown, beating Bernard Hopkins in 1993; moved up to super middleweight and won IBF title from James Toney in 1994; moved up to light heavyweight, winning WBC (1997), WBA (1998) and IBF titles (1999); made temporary move to heavyweight in 2003 and decisioned John Ruiz for WBA belt; lost WBC light heavyweight belt to Antonio Tarver in a 2nd round KO in 2004; knocked out in 9th round of comeback fight with Glen Johnson in Sept. 2004.

Michael Jordan (b. Feb. 17, 1963): Basketball G; College Player of Year with North Carolina in 1984; NBA Rookie of the Year (1985); led NBA in scoring 7 years in a row (1987-93) and also 1996-98; 10-time All-NBA 1st team; 5-time regular season MVP (1988,91-92,96,98) and 6-time MVP of NBA Finals (1991-93,96-98); 3-time AP Male Athlete of Year; led U.S. Olympic team to gold in 1984 and '92; stunned sports world when he retired at age 30 on Oct. 6, 1993; signed as OF with Chi. White Sox and spent summer of '94 in AA with Birmingham; struggled with .204 average; made one of the most anticipated comebacks in sports history when he returned to the Bulls lineup on Mar. 19, 1995 but Bulls were eliminated by Orlando in 2nd round of playoffs later that season; led Bulls to NBA titles for the next 3 years for 6 titles in all (1991-93,96-98); retired in 1999; became pres. of Wash. Wizards before unretiring again in 2001 and returning to play with Wizards for 2 seasons.

Florence Griffith Joyner (b. Dec. 21, 1959, d. Sept. 21, 1998): Track & Field; set world records in 100 and 200m in 1988; won 3 gold medals at '88 Olympics (100m, 200m, 4x100m relay); Sullivan Award winner (1988); retired in 1989; named as co-chairperson of President's Council on Physical Fitness and Sports in 1993; sister-in-law of Jackie Joyner-Kersee; died of suffocation during an epileptic seizure in 1998.

Jackie Joyner-Kersee (b. Mar. 3, 1962): Track & Field; 2-time world champion in both long jump (1987,91) and heptathlon (1987,93); won heptathlon gold medals at 1988 and '92 Olympics and LJ gold at '88 Games; also won Olympic silver (1984) in heptathlon and bronze (1992,96) in LJ; Sullivan Award winner (1986); only woman to receive *The Sporting News* Man of Year award.

Alberto Juantorena (b. Nov. 21, 1950): Cuban runner; won both 400m and 800m gold medals at 1976 Olympics.

Sonny Jurgensen (b. Aug. 23, 1934): Football QB; played 18 seasons with Philadelphia and Washington; led NFL in passing twice (1967,69); All-Pro in 1961; 255 career TD passes.

Duke Kahanamoku (b. Aug. 24, 1890, d. Jan. 22, 1968): Swimmer; won 3 gold medals and 2 silver over 3 Olympics (1912,20,24); also surfing pioneer.

Al Kaline (b. Dec. 19, 1934): Baseball; youngest player (at age 20) to win batting title (led AL with .340 in 1955); had 3,007 hits, 399 HRs in 22 years with Detroit.

Paul Kariya (b. Oct. 16, 1974): Hockey LW; first-ever selection of Anaheim (4th overall in 1993); led Maine to an NCAA Div. I national title in 1993; won Hobey Baker Award in 1993 as a freshman.

Anatoly Karpov (b. May 23, 1951): Chess; Soviet world champion from 1975-85; regained International Chess Federation (FIDE) championship in 1993 when countryman Garry Kasparov was stripped of title after forming new Professional Chess Association; held FIDE title until 1999.

Garry Kasparov (b. Apr. 13, 1963): Chess; Azerbaijani who became youngest player (22 years, 210 days) ever to win world championship as Soviet in 1985; defeated countryman Anatoly Karpov for title; split with International Chess Federation (FIDE) to form Professional Chess Association (PCA) in 1993; stripped of FIDE title in '93 but successfully defended PCA title against Briton Nigel Short; beat IBM supercomputer "Deep Blue" 4 games to 2 in 1996 much-publicized match in New York; lost rematch to computer in 1997; finally lost world title to Vladimir Kramnik in 2000.

Mike Keenan (b. Oct. 21, 1949): Hockey; coach who finally led NY Rangers to Stanley Cup title in 1994 after 53 unsuccessful years; ranked 5th all-time on NHL coaching wins list.

Kipchoge (Kip) Keino (b. Jan. 17, 1940): Kenyan runner; policeman who beat USA's Jim Ryun to win 1,500m gold medal at 1968 Olympics; won again in steeplechase at 1972 Summer Games; his success spawned long line of distance champions from Kenya.

Johnny A. Kelley (b. Sept. 6, 1907, d. Oct. 7, 2004): Distance runner; ran in his 61st and final Boston Marathon at age 84 in 1992, finishing in 5:58:36; won Boston twice (1935,45) and was 2nd seven times.

Jim Kelly (b. Feb. 14, 1960): Football QB; led Buffalo to four straight Super Bowls, and is only QB to lose four times; named to AFC Pro Bowl team 5 times; inducted into Pro Football Hall of Fame in 2002.

Leroy Kelly (b. May 20, 1942): Football; replaced Jim Brown in the Cleveland Browns backfield; in 1967, he led the NFL in rushing yards (1,205), rushing average (5.1 per carry) and rushing touchdowns (11).

Walter Kennedy (b. June 8, 1912, d. June 26, 1977): Basketball; 2nd NBA commissioner (1963-75), league doubled in size to 18 teams during his tenure.

Nancy Kerrigan (b. Oct. 13, 1969): Figure skating; 1993 U.S. women's champion and Olympic medalist in 1992 (bronze) and '94 (silver); victim of Jan. 6, 1994 assault at U.S. nationals in Detroit when Shane Stant clubbed her in right knee with metal baton after a practice session; conspiracy hatched by Jeff Gillooly, ex-husband of rival Tonya Harding; although unable to compete in nationals, she recovered and was granted berth on Olympic team; finished 2nd in Lillehammer to Oksana Baiul of Ukraine by a 5-4 judges' vote.

Billy Kidd (b. Apr. 13, 1943): Skiing; the first great American male Alpine skier; first American male to win an Olympic medal when he won a silver in the slalom and a bronze in the Alpine combined in 1964; competed respectably with the great Jean-Claude Killy; won the world Alpine combined event in 1970, which was the first world championship for an American male.

Harmon Killebrew (b. June 29, 1936): Baseball 3B-1B; led AL in HRs 6 times and RBI 3 times; MVP in 1969 with Minnesota; 573 career HRs.

Jean-Claude Killy (b. Aug. 30, 1943): French alpine skier; 2-time World Cup champion (1967-68); won 3 gold medals at 1968 Olympics in Grenoble; co-president of 1992 Winter Games in Albertville; president of coordination commission for 2006 Turin Games.

Ralph Kiner (b. Oct. 27, 1922): Baseball OF; led NL in home runs 7 straight years (1946-52) with Pittsburgh; 369 career HRs and 1,015 RBI in 10 seasons; long-time NY Mets announcer.

Betsy King (b. Aug. 13, 1955): Golfer; 2-time LPGA Player of Year (1984,89); 3-time winner of Dinah Shore (1987,90,97) and 2-time winner of U.S. Open (1989,90); 34 overall Tour wins; 1st player in LPGA history to break $5 million mark in career earnings; member of LPGA Hall of Fame.

Billie Jean King (b. Nov. 22, 1943): Tennis; women's rights pioneer; Wimbledon singles champ 6 times; U.S. champ 4 times; first woman athlete to earn $100,000 in one year (1971); beat 55-year-old Bobby Riggs 6-4,6-3,6-3, in "Battle of the Sexes" to win $100,000 at Astrodome in 1973; founded the Women's Sports Foundation in 1974; captained the U.S. Olympic team in 1996 and 2000.

Don King (b. Aug. 20, 1931): Boxing promoter; first major black promoter who has controlled heavyweight title off and on since 1978; first big promotion was Muhammad Ali's fight against George Foreman in 1974; former numbers operator who served 4 years for manslaughter (1967-70); acquitted of tax evasion and fraud in 1985; also promoted Larry Holmes, Mike Tyson, Evander Holyfield, Roberto Duran and Julio Cesar Chavez among others; has been accused of bilking his fighters out of money; famous for his gravity-defying hairstyle and his catchphrase "Only in America!".

Karch Kiraly (b. Nov. 3, 1960): Volleyball; USA's preeminent volleyball player; led UCLA to three NCAA championships (1979,81,82); played on US national teams that won Olympic gold medals in 1984 and '88, world championships in '82 and '86; won the inaugural gold medal for Olympic beach volleyball with Kent Steffes in 1996.

Tom Kite (b. Dec. 9, 1949): Golfer; co-NCAA champion with Ben Crenshaw (1972); PGA Rookie of Year (1973); PGA Player of Year (1989); finally won 1st major with victory in 1992 U.S. Open at Pebble Beach; captain of 1997 US Ryder Cup team; 19 career PGA wins, played on the Senior tour since 2000.

Gene Klein (b. Jan. 29, 1921, d. Mar. 12, 1990): Horseman; won 3 Eclipse awards as top owner (1985-87); his filly Winning Colors won 1988 Kentucky Derby; also owned San Diego Chargers football team (1966-84).

Bob Knight (b. Oct. 25, 1940): Basketball; coached Indiana to 3 NCAA titles (1976,81,87); 3-time Coach of Year (1975-76,89); coached 1984 U.S. Olympic team to gold medal; his volatile temper finally cost him when he was fired from Indiana in Sept. 2000 after a string of unacceptable incidents that included choking one of his players; returned to coaching with Texas Tech in 2001; 3rd on all-time NCAA list with 832 wins in 38 years.

Phil Knight (b. Feb. 24, 1938): Founder and chairman of Nike, Inc., the multi-billion dollar shoe and fitness company founded in 1972 and based in Beaverton, Ore.; named "The Most Powerful Man in Sports" by *The Sporting News* in 1992.

Bill Koch (b. June 7, 1955): Cross country skiing; first highly accomplished American male in his sport; first American male to win a cross country Olympic medal when he took home a silver in the 30-kilometer race in 1976; in 1982, he was the first American male to win the Nordic World Cup.

Tommy Kono (b. June 27, 1930): weight lifter; won 2 olympic gold medals for U.S. (1952,56) and 1 silver (1960); all 3 medals were in different weight classes; set world records in four different classes; inducted into U.S. Olympic Hall of Fame in 1990.

Olga Korbut (b. May 16, 1955): Soviet gymnast; became the media darling of the 1972 Olympics in Munich by winning 3 gold medals (balance beam, floor exercise and team all-around); came back in the 1976 Olympics in Montreal and was a part of the USSR's gold medal winning all-around team; first to perform back somersault on balance beam; was inducted into the International Women's Sports Hall of Fame in 1982, the first gymnast to be inducted.

Johann Olav Koss (b. Oct. 29, 1968): Norwegian speed skater; won three gold medals at 1994 Olympics in Lillehammer with world records in the 1,500m, 5,000m and 10,000m; also won 1,500m gold and 10,000m silver in 1992 Games; retired shortly after '94 Olympics.

Sandy Koufax (b. Dec. 30, 1935): Baseball LHP; led NL in strikeouts 4 times and ERA 5 straight years; won 3 Cy Young Awards (1963,65,66) with LA Dodgers; MVP in 1963; 2-time World Series MVP (1963, 65); threw perfect game against Chicago Cubs (1-0, Sept. 9, 1965) and had 3 other no-hitters, 40 shutouts and 137 complete games in a career that ended prematurely due to an arm injury.

Alvin Kraenzlein (b. Dec. 12, 1876, d. Jan. 6, 1928): Track & Field; won 4 individual gold medals in 1900 Olympics (60m, long jump and the 110m and 200m hurdles).

Jack Kramer (b. Aug. 1, 1921): Tennis; Wimbledon singles champ 1947; U.S. champ 1946-47; promoter and Open pioneer.

Lenny Krayzelburg (b. Sept. 28, 1975): Swimmer; born in Ukraine but became American citizen in 1995; won gold for U.S. in the 100m and 200m backstrokes at the 2000 Sydney Games; was also part of U.S. team that set a world record in the 4x100m medley relay in Sydney.

Ingrid Kristiansen (b. Mar. 21, 1956): Norwegian runner; 2-time Boston Marathon winner (1986,89); won New York City Marathon in 1989; former world record holder in the marathon.

Julie Krone (b. July 24, 1963): Jockey; only woman to ride winner in a Triple Crown race when she took 1993 Belmont Stakes aboard Colonial Affair; retired in 1999 as all-time winningest female jockey with over 3,000 wins; became the first female jockey named to hall of fame in 2000; came out of retirement in 2002, winning 2003 Breeders Cup race aboard Halfbridled.

Mike Krzyzewski (b. Feb. 13, 1947): Basketball; has coached Duke to 10 Final Four appearances and 3 NCAA titles (1991-92,2001); has coached at Army (1976-80) and Duke (1981–); inducted into Hall of Fame in 2001.

Bowie Kuhn (b. Oct. 28, 1926): Baseball Commissioner; Elected commissioner on Feb. 4, 1969 and served until Sept. 30, 1984; kept Willie Mays and Mickey Mantle out of baseball for their employment with casinos; handed down one-year suspensions of several players for drug involvement; nixed Charlie Finley's sale of three players for $3.5 million; baseball enjoyed unprecedented attendance and television contracts during his reign.

Alan Kulwicki (b. Dec. 14, 1954, d. Apr. 1, 1993): Auto racer; 1992 NASCAR national champion; 1st college grad and Northerner to win title; NASCAR Rookie of Year in 1986; famous for driving car backwards on victory lap; killed at age 38 in plane crash near Bristol, Tenn.

Michelle Kwan (b. July 7, 1980): Figure Skater; 1998 Olympic silver medalist at Nagano and 2002 bronze medalist at Salt Lake City; 8-time U.S. Champion (1996,98-04) and 5-time World Champ (1996,98,00,01,03); holds U.S. record with 8 career overall medals at the World Championships (5 gold, 3 silver); was U.S. alternate to the Olympics in 1994 as a 13-year-old.

Marion Ladewig (b. Oct. 30, 1914): Bowler; named Woman Bowler of the Year 9 times (1950-54,57-59,63).

Guy Lafleur (b. Sept. 20, 1951): Hockey RW; led NHL in scoring 3 times (1976-78); 2-time MVP (1977-78), played for 5 Stanley Cup winners in Montreal; playoff MVP in 1977; returned to NHL as player in 1988 after election to Hall of Fame; retired again in 1991 with 560 goals and 1,353 points.

Napoleon (Nap) Lajoie (b. Sept. 5, 1874, d. Feb. 7, 1959): Baseball 2B; led AL in batting 3 times (1901,03-04); batted .422 in 1901; hit .339 for career with 3,251 hits.

Jack Lambert (b. July 8, 1952): Football LB; 6-time All-Pro (1975-76,79-82); led Pittsburgh to 4 Super Bowl titles.

Kenesaw Mountain Landis (b. Nov. 20, 1866, d. Nov. 25, 1944): U.S. District Court judge who became first baseball commissioner (1920-44); banned eight Chicago "Black Sox" from baseball for life for throwing 1919 World Series.

Tom Landry (b. Sept. 11, 1924, d. Feb. 12, 2000): Football; All-Pro DB for NY Giants (1954); coached Dallas for 29 years (1960-88); won 2 Super Bowls (1972,78); 3rd on NFL all-time list with 270 wins.

Steve Largent (b. Sept. 28, 1954): Football WR; retired in 1989 after 14 years in Seattle with then NFL records in passes caught (819) and TD passes caught (100); elected to U.S. House of Representatives (R, Okla.) in 1994 and Pro Football Hall of Fame in '95; ran for governor of Oklahoma in 2002 but suffered a narrow defeat.

Don Larsen (b. Aug. 7, 1929): Baseball RHP; NY Yankees hurler who pitched the only perfect game in World Series history—a 2-0 victory over Brooklyn in Game 5 of the 1956 Series (Oct. 8); Series MVP that year; had career record of 81-91 in 14 seasons with 6 clubs.

Tommy Lasorda (b. Sept. 22, 1927): Baseball; managed LA Dodgers to 2 World Series titles (1981,88) in 4 appearances; retired as manager during 1996 season with 1,599 regular-season wins in 21 years; named interim GM of Dodgers in 1998; member of Baseball Hall of Fame; managed gold-medal winning U.S. Olympic team in 2000 at Sydney.

Larissa Latynina (b. Dec. 27, 1934): Soviet gymnast; won total of 18 medals, (9 gold) in 3 Olympics (1956,60,64).

Nikki Lauda (b. Feb. 22, 1949): Austrian auto racer; 3-time world Formula One champion (1975, 77,84); 25 career wins from 1971-85.

Rod Laver (b. Aug. 9, 1938): Australian tennis player; undersized but big-hitting left-hander is only player to win Grand Slam twice (1962,69); Wimbledon champion 4 times; 1st to earn $1 million in career prize money, won 11 Grand Slam and 47 professional singles titles.

Andrea Mead Lawrence (b. Apr. 19, 1932): Alpine skier; won 2 gold medals at 1952 Olympics.

Bobby Layne (b. Dec. 19, 1926, d. Dec. 1, 1986): Football QB; college star at Texas; master of 2-minute offense; led Detroit to 4 divisional titles and 3 NFL championships in 1950s.

Frank Leahy (b. Aug. 27, 1908, d. June 21, 1973): Football; coached Notre Dame to four national titles (1943,46-47,49); career record of 107-13-9 for a winning pct. of .864.

Jeanette Lee (b. July 9, 1971): Billiards; nicknamed "The Black Widow"; won the 1994 Women's Professional Billiards Assoc. (WPBA) National Championship and vaulted to the No. 1 women's player in the world; voted 1994 WPBA Player of the Year.

Sammy Lee (b. Aug. 1, 1920): Diving; won Olympic gold medals for U.S. in the platform diving event in 1948 and 1952, the first male diver in history to win 2 golds in that event; Sullivan Award winner (1953); former doctor in U.S. Army; trained Greg Louganis.

Brian Leetch (b. Mar. 3, 1968): Hockey D; NHL Rookie of Year in 1989; won Norris Trophy as top defenseman in 1992; Conn Smythe Trophy winner as playoffs' MVP in 1994 when he helped lead NY Rangers to 1st Stanley Cup title in 54 years.

Jacques Lemaire (b. Sept. 7, 1945): Hockey C; member of 8 Stanley Cup champions in Montreal; scored 366 goals in 12 seasons; coached Canadiens (1983-85) and NJ Devils (1993-98), won 1995 Stanley Cup with New Jersey; returned to coaching with the expansion Minnesota Wild in 2000.

Mario Lemieux (b. Oct. 5, 1965): Hockey C; 6-time NHL scoring leader (1988-89,92-93,96-97); Rookie of Year (1985); 4-time All-NHL 1st-team (1988-89,93,96); 3-time regular season MVP (1988,93,96); 3-time All-Star Game MVP; led Pittsburgh to consecutive Stanley Cup titles (1991 and '92) and was playoff MVP both years; won 1993 scoring title despite missing 24 games to undergo radiation treatments for Hodgkin's disease; missed 62 games during 1993-94 season and entire 94-95 season due to back injuries and fatigue; returned in 1995-96 to lead NHL in scoring and win the MVP trophy; retired after 1996-97 season and inducted into the Hall of Fame; headed group of investors that bought bankrupt Penguins in 1999; made surprising return to the ice in 2001.

Greg LeMond (b. June 26, 1961): American cyclist; 3-time Tour de France winner (1986,89-90); only non-European to win the event until Lance Armstrong in 1999; retired in Dec. 1994 after being diagnosed with a rare muscular disease known as mitochondria myopathy.

Ivan Lendl (b. Mar. 7, 1960): Czech tennis player; No. 1 player in world 4 times (1985-87,89); won both French and U.S. Opens 3 times and Australian twice; owns 94 career tournament wins.

Suzanne Lenglen (b. May 24, 1899, d. July 4, 1938): French tennis player; dominated women's tennis from 1919-26; won both Wimbledon and French singles titles 6 times.

Sugar Ray Leonard (b. May 17, 1956): Boxer; light welterweight Olympic champ (1976); won world welterweight title in 1979 and 4 more titles; in 1987 he upset Marvin Hagler for the middleweight crown; retired and unretired several times, before ending his career for good in 1997 with record of 36-3-1 and 25 KOs following a TKO loss to Hector Camacho.

Walter (Buck) Leonard (b. Sept. 8, 1907, d. Nov. 27, 1997): Baseball 1B; won Negro League championship nine years in a row with the Homestead Grays; hit .391 in 1948 to lead the league; usually batted cleanup behind Josh Gibson; retired at the age of 48; member of the National Baseball Hall of Fame.

Lisa Leslie (b. July 7, 1972): Basketball C; 2-time WNBA Finals MVP (2001-02) with the champion Los Angeles Sparks; 2001 regular season MVP; 3-time WNBA All-Star Game MVP (1999,2001-02); 3-time Olympic gold medalist (1996,2000,2004); consensus National Player of the Year at USC (1994).

Marv Levy (b. Aug. 3, 1928): Football; coached Buffalo to four consecutive Super Bowls, but is one of two coaches who are 0-4 (Bud Grant is the other); won 50 games and two CFL Grey Cups with Montreal (1974,77).

Bill Lewis (b. Nov. 30, 1868, d. Jan. 1, 1949): Football; college star at Amherst College and then Harvard; first black player to be selected as an All-American (1892-93); also the first black admitted to the American Bar Association (1911); was U.S. Assistant Attorney General.

Carl Lewis (b. July 1, 1961): Track & Field; won 9 Olympic gold medals; 4 in 1984 (100m, 200m, 4x100m, LJ), 2 in '88 (100m, LJ), 2 in '92 (4x100m, LJ) and 1 in '96 (LJ); has record 8 World Championship titles and 9 medals in all; Sullivan Award winner (1981); two-time AP Athlete of the Year (1983-84); in 1991, set world record in 100m with a 9.86 (since broken).

Lennox Lewis (b. Sept. 2, 1965): British boxer; won 1988 Olympic super heavyweight gold medal for Canada; was awarded WBC heavyweight belt when Riddick Bowe tossed it in a London trash can in 1993; lost title in a 2nd round TKO loss to Oliver McCall; won rematch 3 years later when McCall suffered emotional breakdown in the ring; unified titles in his rematch with Evander Holyfield in Nov. 1999; lost belts in upset loss to Hasim Rahman in April 2001 but took them back 7 months later; recorded 8th-round KO of Mike Tyson in June 2002.

Nancy Lieberman (b. July 1, 1958): Basketball; 3-time All-America and 2-time Player of Year (1979-80); led Old Dominion to consecutive AIAW titles in 1979 and '80; played in defunct WPBL and WABA and became 1st woman to play in men's pro league (USBL) in 1986; played in the inaugural season of the WNBA for the Phoenix Mercury and served as coach/GM of Detroit Shock (1998-2000).

Eric Lindros (b. Feb. 28, 1973): Hockey C; No. 1 pick in 1991 NHL draft by Quebec but sat out 1991-92 season rather than play for Nordiques; traded to Philadelphia in 1992 for 6 players, 2 No. 1 picks and $15 million; elected Flyers captain at age 22; won Hart Trophy as league MVP in 1995; suffered series of concussions in 1999-00 and was traded to NY Rangers in 2001.

Tara Lipinski (b. June 10, 1982): Figure Skater; won the 1998 women's figure skating gold medal at the Olympics in Nagano, becoming the youngest in history (15 yrs., 7 mos.) to do so; she and Michelle Kwan gave the U.S. its first 1-2 finish in that event since 1956; 1997 U.S. and World champion; turned pro in April 1998.

Sonny Liston (b. May 8, 1932, d. Dec. 30, 1970): Boxer; heavyweight champion (1962-64), who knocked out Floyd Patterson twice in the first round, then lost title to Muhammad Ali (then Cassius Clay) in 1964; pro record of 50-4 with 39 KOs.

Vince Lombardi (b. June 11, 1913, d. Sept. 3, 1970): Football; coached Green Bay to 5 NFL titles; won first 2 Super Bowls (1967-68); died as NFL's all-time winningest coach with percentage of .740 (105-35-6); Super Bowl trophy named in his honor.

Johnny Longden (b. Feb. 14, 1907): Jockey; first to win 6,000 races; rode Count Fleet to Triple Crown in 1943.

Jeannie Longo (b. Oct. 31, 1958): French cyclist; 12-time world cycling champion and 1996 olympic road race gold medallist.

Nancy Lopez (b. Jan. 6, 1957): Golfer; 4-time LPGA Player of the Year (1978-79,85,88); Rookie of Year (1977); 3-time winner of LPGA Championship; reached Hall of Fame by age 30 with 35 victories; 48 career wins.

Donna Lopiano (b. Sept. 11, 1946): Former basketball and softball star who was women's AD at Texas for 18 years before leaving to become executive director of Women's Sports Foundation in 1992.

Greg Louganis (b. Jan. 29, 1960): U.S. diver; widely considered the greatest diver in history; won platform and springboard gold medals at both 1984 and '88 Olympics; also won a silver medal at the 1976 Olympics at the age of 16; won five world championships and 47 U.S. National Diving titles; revealed on Feb. 22, 1995 that he has AIDS.

Joe Louis (b. May 13, 1914, d. Apr. 12, 1981): Boxer; world heavyweight champion from June 22, 1937 to Mar. 1, 1949; his reign of 11 years, 8 months longest in division history; successfully defended title 25 times; retired in 1949, but returned to lose title shot against successor Ezzard Charles in 1950 and then to Rocky Marciano in '51; pro record of 63-3 with 49 KOs.

Sid Luckman (b. Nov. 21, 1916, d. July 5, 1998): Football QB; 6-time All-Pro; led Chicago Bears to 4 NFL titles (1940-41,43,46); MVP in 1943.

Hank Luisetti (b. June 16, 1916): Basketball F; 3-time All-America at Stanford (1936-38); revolutionized game with one-handed shot.

Johnny Lujack (b. Jan. 4, 1925): Football QB; led Notre Dame to three national titles (1943,46-47); won Heisman Trophy in 1947.

Darrell Wayne Lukas (b. Sept. 2, 1935): Horse racing; 4-time Eclipse-winning trainer who saddled Horses of Year Lady's Secret in 1988 and Criminal Type in 1990; first trainer to earn over $100 million in purses; led nation in earnings 14 times since 1983; Grindstone's Kentucky Derby win in 1996 gave him six Triple Crown wins in a row; has won Preakness 5 times, Kentucky Derby 4 times and Belmont 4 times; his most recent Triple Crown victory came in the 2000 Belmont with Commendable; leads all Breeders' Cup trainers with 16 victories.

Gen. Douglas MacArthur (b. Jan. 26, 1880, d. Apr. 5, 1964): Controversial U.S. general of World War II and Korea; president of U.S. Olympic Committee (1927-28); college football devotee, National Football Foundation MacArthur Bowl named after him.

Connie Mack (b. Dec. 22, 1862, d. Feb. 8, 1956): Baseball owner; managed Philadelphia A's until he was 87 (1901-50); all-time major league wins leader with 3,755, including World Series; won 9 AL pennants and 5 World Series (1910-11,13,29-30); also finished last 17 times.

Andy MacPhail (b. Apr. 5, 1953): Baseball; Chicago Cubs president/CEO who was GM of 2 World Series champions in Minnesota (1987,91); won first title at age 34; son of Lee, grandson of Larry.

Larry MacPhail (b. Feb. 3, 1890, d. Oct. 1, 1975): Baseball exec. and innovator; introduced major leagues to night games at Cincinnati (May 24, 1935); won pennant in Brooklyn (1941) and World Series with NY Yankees (1947); father of Lee, grandfather of Andy.

Lee MacPhail (b. Oct. 25, 1917): Baseball; AL president (1974-83); president of owners' Player Relations Committee (1984-85); also GM of Baltimore (1959-65) and NY Yankees (1967-74); son of Larry and father of Andy.

Wendy Macpherson (b. Jan. 28, 1968): Bowling; voted Bowler of the Decade for the 1990s; Major titles include the 1986 BPAA U.S. Open, 1988, 2000 and 2003 WIBC Queens and 1999 Sam's Town Invitational; annual PWBA money winner 4 times (1996, 97,99,2000).

John Madden (b. Apr. 10, 1936): Football and Radio-TV; won 112 games and a Super Bowl (1976 season) as coach of Oakland Raiders; has won 14 Emmy Awards since 1982 as NFL analyst; signed 4-year, $32 million deal with Fox in 1994— a richer contract than any NFL player at the time; joined Al Michaels in ABC's Monday Night Football booth in 2002 after 21 seasons alongside Pat Summerall.

Greg Maddux (b. Apr. 14, 1966): Baseball RHP; won unprecedented 4 straight NL Cy Young Awards with Cubs (1992) and Atlanta (1993-95); has led NL in ERA four times (1993-95,98); won 13th straight gold glove in 2002; only pitcher to win at least 15 games in 17 straight seasons (1988-2004); got his 300th win in 2004.

Larry Mahan (b. Nov. 21, 1943): Rodeo; 6-time All-Around world champion cowboy (1966-70,73).

Phil Mahre (b. May 10, 1957): Alpine skier; 3-time World Cup overall champ (1981-83); finished 1-2 with twin brother Steve in 1984 Olympic slalom.

Karl Malone (b. July 24, 1963): Basketball F; 11-time All-NBA 1st team (1989-99) with Utah; 2-time NBA MVP (1997,99); all-time NBA leader in free throws made (9,787), 2nd in career points (36,928) and field goals made (13,528); member of the 1992 and '96 Olympic gold medal teams; named one of the NBA's 50 greatest players.

Moses Malone (b. Mar. 23, 1955): Basketball C; signed with Utah of ABA out of high school at age 19; led NBA in rebounding 6 times; 4-time All-NBA 1st team; 3-time NBA MVP (1979,82-83); Finals MVP with Philadelphia in 1983; played in 21st pro season in 1994-95.

Nigel Mansell (b. Aug. 8, 1953): British auto racer; won 1992 Formula One driving championship with record 9 victories and 14 poles; quit Grand Prix circuit to race Indy cars in 1993; 1st rookie to win IndyCar title; 3rd driver to win IndyCar and F1 titles; returned to F1 after 1994 IndyCar season and won '94 Australian Grand Prix; left F1 again on May 23, 1995 with 31 wins and 32 poles in 15 years.

Mickey Mantle (b. Oct. 20, 1931, d. Aug. 13, 1995): Baseball CF; led AL in home runs 4 times; won Triple Crown in 1956; hit 52 HRs in 1956 and 54 in '61; 3-time MVP (1956-57,62); hit 536 career HRs; played in 12 World Series with NY Yankees and won 7 times; all-time World Series leader in HRs (18), RBI (40), runs (42) and strikeouts (54); inducted into Baseball Hall of Fame in 1974.

Diego Maradona (b. Oct. 30, 1960): Soccer F; captain and MVP of 1986 World Cup champion Argentina; also led national team to 1990 World Cup final; consensus Player of Decade in 1980s; led Napoli to 2 Italian League titles (1987,90) and UEFA Cup (1989); tested positive for cocaine and suspended 15 months by FIFA in 1991; returned to World Cup as Argentine captain in 1994, but was kicked out after two games when test found 5 banned substances in his urine.

Pete Maravich (b. June 27, 1947, d. Jan. 5, 1988): Basketball; NCAA scoring leader 3 times at LSU (1968-70); averaged NCAA-record 44.2 points a game over career; Player of Year in 1970; NBA scoring champ in '77 with New Orleans.

Alice Marble (b. Sept. 28, 1913, d. Dec. 13, 1990): Tennis; 4-time U.S. champion (1936,38-40); won Wimbledon in 1939; swept U.S. singles, doubles and mixed doubles from 1938-40.

Gino Marchetti (b. Jan. 2, 1927): Football DE; 8-time NFL All-Pro (1957-64) with Baltimore Colts.

Rocky Marciano (b. Sept. 1, 1923, d. Aug. 31, 1969): Boxer; heavyweight champion (1952-56); only heavyweight champ in history to retire undefeated; pro record of 49-0 with 43 KOs; killed in plane crash.

Juan Marichal (b. Oct. 20, 1938): Baseball RHP; won 21 or more games 6 times for S.F. Giants from 1963-69; ended 16-year career at 243-142.

Dan Marino (b. Sept. 15, 1961): Football QB; all-time NFL leader in career TD passes (420), passing yards (61,361), attempts (8,358) and completions (4,967); 4-time leading passer in AFC (1983-84,86,89); set NFL single-season records for TD passes (48) and passing yards (5,084) in 1984.

Roger Maris (b. Sept. 10, 1934, d. Dec. 14, 1985): Baseball OF; broke Babe Ruth's season HR record with 61 in 1961 and held record until 1998 (Mark McGwire); 2-time AL MVP (1960-61) with NY Yankees; 275 HRs in 12 years.

Jim Marshall (b. Dec. 30, 1937): Football; long-time Vikings DE and NFL ironman; played in an NFL-record 282 consecutive games (1960-1979); also famous for picking up a fumble and running 66 yards the wrong way into the opponent's (49ers) endzone.

Billy Martin (b. May 16, 1928, d. Dec. 25, 1989): Baseball; 5-time manager of NY Yankees; won 2 pennants and 1 World Series (1977); also managed Minnesota, Detroit, Texas and Oakland; played on 5 Yankee world champions in 1950s.

Casey Martin (b. June 2, 1972): Golfer; suffers from a birth defect in his right leg known as Klippel-Trenauney-Webber Syndrome; won lawsuit against the PGA Tour for the right to use a golf cart during competition under the Americans with Disabilities Act.

Pedro Martinez (b. Oct. 25, 1971): Baseball RHP; one of baseball's premier pitchers; won 1997 NL Cy Young award with Montreal; traded to Boston Red Sox in Nov. 1997; 2-time AL Cy Young Award winner with Boston (1999,2000).

Eddie Mathews (b. Oct. 13, 1931, d. Feb. 18, 2001): Baseball 3B; led NL in HRs twice (1953,59); hit 30 or more home runs 9 straight years; 512 career HRs.

Christy Mathewson (b. Aug. 12, 1880, d. Oct. 7, 1925): Baseball RHP; won 22 or more games 12 straight years (1903-14); 373 career wins; pitched 3 shutouts in 1905 World Series.

Bob Mathias (b. Nov. 17, 1930): Track & Field; youngest winner of decathlon with gold medal in 1948 Olympics at age 17; first to repeat as decathlon champ in 1952; Sullivan Award winner (1948); 4-term member of U.S. Congress (R, Calif.) from 1967-74.

Ollie Matson (b. May 1, 1930): Football HB; All-America at San Francisco (1951); bronze medal winner in 400m at 1952 Olympics; 4-time All-Pro for NFL Chicago Cardinals (1954-57); traded to LA Rams for 9 players in 1959; accounted for 12,884 all-purpose yards and scored 73 TDs in 14 seasons.

Don Mattingly (b. Apr. 20, 1961): Baseball 1B; AL MVP (1985); won AL batting title in 1984 (.343); led majors with 145 RBI in 1985; led AL with 238 hits (Yankee record) and 53 doubles in 1986; won 9 Gold Glove Awards at 1B (1985-89, 91-94).

Willie Mays (b. May 6, 1931): Baseball OF; nicknamed the "Say Hey Kid;" led NL in HRs and stolen bases 4 times each; 2-time MVP (1954,65) with NY-SF Giants; Hall of Famer who played in 24 All-Star Games, earning MVP honors twice (1963,68); 12-time Gold Glove winner; 660 HRs and 3,283 hits in career.

Bill Mazeroski (b. Sept. 5, 1936): Baseball 2B; career .260 hitter who won the 1960 World Series for Pittsburgh with a lead-off HR in the bottom of the 9th inning of Game 7; the pitcher was Ralph Terry of the NY Yankees, the count was 1-0 and the score was tied 9-9; also a sure-fielder, Maz won 8 Gold Gloves in 17 seasons.

Bob McAdoo (b. Sept. 25, 1951): Basketball F/C; 1972 Sporting News First Team All-American; NBA Rookie of the Year (1973); NBA MVP (1975); All-NBA First Team (1975); Led NBA in scoring three consecutive years (1974-76); 5-time All-Star (1974-78); two championships with LA Lakers (1982,85).

Joe McCarthy (b. Apr. 21, 1887, d. Jan. 13, 1978): Baseball; first manager to win pennants in both leagues (Chicago Cubs in 1929 and NY Yankees in 1932); greatest success came with Yankees when he won seven pennants and six World Series championships from 1936 to 1943; first manager to win four World Series in a row (1936-39); finished his career with the Boston Red Sox (1948-'50); lifetime record of 2125-1333; member of Baseball Hall of Fame.

Pat McCormick (b. May 12, 1930): U.S. diver; won women's platform and springboard gold medals in both 1952 and '56 Olympics.

Willie McCovey (b. Jan. 10, 1938): Baseball 1B; led NL in HRs 3 times and RBI twice; MVP in 1969 with SF; 521 career HRs; indicted for tax evasion in July 1995, pled guilty; "McCovey Cove," the bay outside the rightfield fence at San Francisco's Pacific Bell Park is named for him.

John McEnroe (b. Feb. 16, 1959): Tennis; No.1 player in the world 4 times (1981-84); 4-time U.S. Open champ (1979-81,84); 3-time Wimbledon champ (1981,83-84); played on 5 Davis Cup winners (1978,79,81,82,92); won NCAA singles title (1978); finished career with 77 singles championships, 77 more in men's doubles (including 9 Grand Slam titles), and U.S. Davis Cup records for years played (13) and singles matches won (41).

John McGraw (b. Apr. 7, 1873, d. Feb. 25, 1934): Baseball; managed NY Giants to 9 NL pennants between 1905-24; won 3 World Series (1905,21-22); 2nd on all-time career list with 2,866 wins in 33 seasons (2,840 regular season and 26 World Series).

Frank McGuire (b. Nov. 8, 1916, d. Oct. 11, 1994): Basketball; winner of 731 games as high school, college and pro coach; won at least 100 games at 3 colleges— St. John's (103), North Carolina (164) and South Carolina (283); won 550 games in 30 college seasons; 1957 UNC team went 32-0 and beat Kansas 54-53 in triple OT to win NCAA title; coached NBA Philadelphia Warriors to 49-31 record in 1961-62 season, but refused to move with team to San Francisco.

Mark McGwire (b. Oct. 1, 1963): Baseball 1B; Sporting News college player of the year (1984); Member of 1984 U.S. Olympic baseball team; won AL Rookie of the Year and hit rookie-record 49 HRs in 1987; shattered Roger Maris' season home run record (61) in 1998 with St. Louis (70); followed that magical season with 65 HRs and 147 RBI in 1999.

Jim McKay (b. Sept. 24, 1921): Radio-TV; host and commentator of ABC's Olympic coverage and "Wide World of Sports" show since 1961; 12-time Emmy winner; also given Peabody Award in 1988 and Life Achievement Emmy in 1990; became part owner of Baltimore Orioles in 1993.

Tamara McKinney (b. Oct. 16, 1962): Skiing; first American woman to win overall Alpine World Cup championship (1983); won World Cup slalom (1984) and giant slalom titles twice (1981,83).

Denny McLain (b. Mar. 29, 1944): Baseball RHP; last pitcher to win 30 games (1968); 2-time Cy Young winner (1968-69) with Detroit; convicted of racketeering, extortion and drug possession in 1985, served 29 months of 25-year jail term, sentence overturned when court ruled he had not received a fair trial; he has faced subsequent legal troubles.

Rick Mears (b. Dec. 3, 1951): Auto racer; 3-time CART national champ (1979,81-82); 4-time winner of Indy 500 (1979,84,88,91) and only driver to win 6 Indy 500 poles; Indy 500 Rookie of Year (1978); retired in 1992 with 29 CART wins and 40 poles.

Mark Messier (b. Jan. 18, 1961): Hockey C; 2-time NHL MVP with Edmonton (1990) and NY Rangers (1992); captain of 1994 Rangers team that won 1st Stanley Cup since 1940; ranks 2nd in all-time playoff points, goals and assists; 2nd on all-time regular season points list (1,887).

Debbie Meyer (b. Aug. 14, 1952): Swimmer; 1st swimmer to win 3 individual gold medals at one Olympics (1968).

Ann Meyers (b. Mar. 26, 1955): Basketball G; In 1974, became first high schooler to play for U.S. national team; 4-time All-American at UCLA (1976-79); member of 1976 U.S. Olympic team; Broderick Award and Cup winner (1978); Signed $50,000 no cut contract with NBA's Indiana Pacers (1980); married Dodger great Don Drysdale.

George Mikan (b. June 18, 1924): Basketball C; 3-time All-America (1944-46); led DePaul to NIT title (1945); led Minneapolis Lakers to 5 NBA titles in 6 years (1949-54); first commissioner of ABA (1967-69).

Stan Mikita (b. May 20, 1940): Hockey C; led NHL in scoring 4 times; won both MVP and Lady Byng awards in 1967 and '68 with Chicago.

Bode Miller (b. Oct. 12, 1977): Alpine Skier; won 2 silver medals at 2002 Winter Games; 2 golds, 1 silver at 2003 World Championships; 2nd overall in 2003 World Cup standings; 2004 Giant Slalom World Cup champion.

Cheryl Miller (b. Jan. 3, 1964): Basketball; 3-time College Player of Year (1984-86); led USC to NCAA title and U.S. to Olympic gold medal in 1984; coached USC to 44-14 record in 2 years; coached WNBA's Phoenix Mercury for 4 years; sister of NBA's Reggie.

Del Miller (b. July 5, 1913, d. Aug. 19, 1996): Harness racing; driver, trainer, owner, breeder, seller and track owner; drove to 2,441 wins from 1929-90.

Marvin Miller (b. Apr. 14, 1917): Baseball labor leader; executive director of Players' Assn. from 1966-82; increased average salary from $19,000 to over $240,000; led 13-day strike in 1972 and 50-day walkout in '81.

Shannon Miller (b. Mar. 10, 1977): Gymnast; won 5 medals in 1992 Olympics and 2 golds in '96 Games; All-Around world champion in 1993 and '94.

Billy Mills (b. June 30, 1938): Track & Field; Native American who was upset winner of 10,000m gold medal at 1964 Olympics.

Bora Milutinovic (b. Sept. 7, 1944): Soccer; Serbian who coached United States national team from 1991-95; led Mexico (1986), Costa Rica ('90), USA ('94) and Nigeria ('98) into the 2nd round of the World Cup.

Tommy Moe (b. Feb. 17, 1970): Alpine skier; won Downhill gold and Super-G silver at 1994 Winter Olympics; 1st U.S. man to win 2 Olympic alpine medals in one year.

Paul Molitor (b. Aug. 22, 1956): Baseball DH-1B; All-America SS at Minnesota in 1976; spent 15 years with Milwaukee, then 3 each with Toronto and Minnesota; led Blue Jays to 2nd straight World Series title as MVP (1993); hit .418 in 2 Series appearances (1982,93); holds World Series record with five hits in one game.

Joe Montana (b. June 11, 1956): Football QB; led Notre Dame to national title in 1977; led San Francisco to 4 Super Bowl titles in 1980s; only 3-time Super Bowl MVP; 2-time NFL MVP (1989-90); led NFL in passing 5 times; traded to K.C. in 1993; ranks 3rd all-time in passing efficiency (92.3), 273 career TD passes and 40,551 passing yards; inducted into Pro Football Hall of Fame in 2000.

Tim Montgomery (b. Jan. 25, 1975): American sprinter; broke world record in 100m with a 9.78 on Sept. 14, 2002; failed to qualify for 2004 Olympics.

Helen Wills Moody (b. Oct. 6, 1905, d. Jan. 1, 1998): Tennis; won 8 Wimbledon singles titles, 7 U.S. and 4 French from 1923-38.

Warren Moon (b. Nov. 18, 1956): Football QB; MVP of 1978 Rose Bowl with Washington; MVP of CFL with Edmonton in 1983; led Eskimos to 5 consecutive Grey Cup titles (1978-82) and was playoff MVP twice (1980,82); entered NFL in 1984 and played for 4 different teams; picked for 9 Pro Bowls.

Archie Moore (b. Dec. 13, 1913, d. Dec. 9, 1998): Boxer; world light heavyweight champion (1952-60); pro record 199-26-8 with a record 145 KOs.

Noureddine Morceli (b. Feb. 28, 1970): Algerian runner; 3-time world champion at 1,500 meters (1991,93,95) and 1996 Olympic gold medal winner; former holder of world records in several middle distance events.

Howie Morenz (b. June 21, 1902, d. Mar. 8, 1937): Hockey C; 3-time NHL MVP (1928,31,32); led Montreal Canadiens to 3 Stanley Cups; voted Outstanding Player of the Half-Century in 1950.

Joe Morgan (b. Sept. 19, 1943): Baseball 2B; regular-season MVP both years he led Cincinnati to World Series titles (1975-76); 1,865 career walks; led NL in walks 4 times.

Bobby Morrow (b. Oct. 15, 1935): Track & Field; won 3 gold medals at 1956 Olympics (100m, 200m and 4x400m relay).

Willie Mosconi (b. June 27, 1913, d. Sept. 12, 1993): Pocket Billiards; 14-time world champion from 1941-57.

Annemarie Moser-Pröll (b. Mar. 27, 1953): Austrian alpine skier; won World Cup overall title 6 times (1971-75,79); all-time women's World Cup leader in career wins with 61; won Downhill in 1980 Olympics.

Edwin Moses (b. Aug. 31, 1955): Track & Field; won 400m hurdles at 1976 and '84 Olympics, bronze medal in '88; also winner of 122 consecutive races from 1977-87.

Stirling Moss (b. Sept. 17, 1929): Auto racer; won 194 of 466 career races and 16 Formula One events, but was never world champion.

Marion Motley (b. June 5, 1920, d. June 27, 1999): Football FB/LB; hard-charging runner who was all-time leading AAFC rusher; ran for over 4,700 yards and 31 TDs for Cleveland Browns (1946-53), leading the NFL in 1950; first black member of the Pro Football Hall of Fame.

Shirley Muldowney (b. June 19, 1940): Drag Racer; "Cha Cha"; women's racing pioneer; 3-time Winston drag racing Top Fuel champion (1977,80,82); recorded 18 career NHRA National Event Victories.

Anthony Munoz (b. Aug. 19, 1958): Football OT; drafted 3rd overall in 1980 out of USC; 11-time All-Pro with Cincinnati; member of NFL 75th Anniv. All-Time Team; elected to Hall of Fame in 1998.

Calvin Murphy (b. May 9, 1948): Basketball G; NBA All-Rookie team (1971); holds NBA single season free throw percentage (.958); third all-time career free throw pct. (.892); elected to Basketball Hall of Fame in 1992; though only 5'9" and 165 pounds, he is regarded as one of the best guards ever.

Dale Murphy (b. Mar. 12, 1956): Baseball OF; led NL in HRs and RBI twice; 2-time MVP (1982-83) with Atlanta; also played with Philadelphia and Colorado; retired in 1993 with 398 HRs.

Jack Murphy (b. Feb. 5, 1923, d. Sept. 24, 1980): Sports editor and columnist of *The San Diego Union* from 1951-80; instrumental in bringing AFL Chargers south from LA in 1961, landing Padres as NL expansion team in '69; and lobbying for San Diego stadium that would later bear his name.

Eddie Murray (b. Feb. 24, 1956): Baseball 1B-DH; AL Rookie of Year in 1977; became 20th player in history, but only 2nd switch hitter (after Pete Rose) to get 3,000 hits; one of only 3 men (Aaron and Mays) with 500 HRs and 3,000 hits.

Jim Murray (b. Dec. 29, 1919, d. Aug. 16, 1998): Sports columnist for *LA Times* 1961-98; 14-time Sportswriter of the Year; won Pulitzer Prize for commentary in 1990.

Ty Murray (b. Oct. 11, 1969): Rodeo cowboy; 7-time All-Around world champion (1989-94,98); Rookie of Year in 1988; youngest (age 20) to win All-Around title; set single season earnings mark with $297,896 in 1993; career hampered by injury.

Stan Musial (b. Nov. 21, 1920): Baseball OF-1B; led NL in batting 7 times and RBI 2 times; 3-time MVP (1943,46,48) with St. Louis; played in 24 All-Star Games; had 3,630 career hits (4th all-time) and .331 average.

John Naber (b. Jan. 20, 1956): Swimmer; won 4 gold medals and a silver in 1976 Olympics.

Bronko Nagurski (b. Nov. 3, 1908, d. Jan. 7, 1990): Football FB-T; All-America at Minnesota (1929); All-Pro with Chicago Bears (1932-34); charter member of college and pro Halls of Fame.

James Naismith (b. Nov. 6, 1861, d. Nov. 28, 1939): Canadian physical education instructor who invented basketball in 1891 at the YMCA Training School (now Springfield College) in Springfield, Mass.

Joe Namath (b. May 31, 1943): Football QB; signed for unheard-of $400,000 as rookie with AFL's NY Jets in 1965; 2-time All-AFL (1968-69) and All-NFL (1972); led Jets to Super Bowl upset as MVP in '69 after making brash prediction of victory.

Ilie Nastase (b. July 19, 1946): Romanian tennis player; No.1 in the world twice (1972-73); won U.S. (1972) and French (1973) Opens; has since entered Romanian politics.

Martina Navratilova (b. Oct. 18, 1956): Tennis player; No.1 player in the world 7 times (1978-79,82-86); won her record 9th Wimbledon singles title in 1990; also won 4 U.S. Opens, 3 Australian and 2 French; in all, won 18 Grand Slam singles titles, 40 Grand Slam doubles titles; all-time leader among men and women in singles titles (167); 2nd all-time (Steffi Graf) on women's career money list with over $21 million; still active in limited competition; inducted into International Tennis Hall of Fame in 2000.

Cosmas Ndeti (b. Nov. 24, 1971): Kenyan distance runner; winner of three consecutive Boston Marathons (1993-95); set what is still the course record of 2:07:15 in 1994.

Earle (Greasy) Neale (b. Nov. 5, 1891, d. Nov. 2, 1973): Baseball and Football; hit .357 for Cincinnati in 1919 World Series; also played with pre-NFL Canton Bulldogs; later coached Philadelphia Eagles to 2 NFL titles (1948-49).

Primo Nebiolo (b. July 14, 1923, d. Nov. 7, 1999): Italian president of International Amateur Athletic Federation (IAAF) since 1981; also an at-large member of International Olympic Committee; regarded as dictatorial, but credited with elevating track & field to world class financial status.

Byron Nelson (b. Feb. 4, 1912): Golfer; 2-time winner of both Masters (1937,42) and PGA (1940,45); also U.S. Open champion in 1939; won 19 tournaments in 1945, including 11 in a row; also set all-time PGA stroke average with 68.33 strokes per round over 120 rounds in '45.

Lindsey Nelson (b. May 25, 1919, d. June 10, 1995): Radio-TV; all-purpose play-by-play broadcaster for CBS, NBC and others; 4-time Sportscaster of the Year (1959-62); voice of Cotton Bowl for 25 years and NY Mets from 1962-78; given Life Achievement Emmy Award in 1991.

Ernie Nevers (b. June 11, 1903, d. May 3, 1976): Football FB; earned 11 letters in four sports at Stanford; played pro football, baseball and basketball; scored 40 points for Chicago Cardinals in one NFL game (1929).

Paula Newby-Fraser (b. June 2, 1962): Zimbabwean triathlete; 8-time winner of Ironman Triathlon in Hawaii; established women's record of 8:55:28 in 1992.

John Newcombe (b. May 23, 1944): Australian tennis player; No.1 player in world 3 times (1967,70-71); won Wimbledon 3 times and U.S. and Australian championships twice each.

Pete Newell (b. Aug. 31, 1915): Basketball; coached at Univ. of San Francisco, Michigan St. and the Univ. of California; first coach to win NIT (San Francisco-1949), NCAA (California-1959) and Olympic gold medal (1960); later served as the general manager of the San Diego Rockets and LA Lakers in the NBA; member of Basketball Hall of Fame.

Jack Nicklaus (b. Jan. 21, 1940): Golfer; all-time leader in major tournament wins with 18— 6 Masters, 5 PGAs, 4 U.S. Opens and 3 British Opens; oldest player to win Masters (46 in 1986); PGA Player of Year 5 times (1967,72-73,75-76); named Golfer of the Century by PGA in 1988; 6-time Ryder Cup player and 2-time captain (1983,87); won NCAA title (1961) and 2 U.S. Amateurs (1959,61); 73 PGA Tour wins (2nd to Sam Snead's 82); fourth win in Tradition in 1996 gave him 8 majors on Senior PGA Tour; nicknamed "the Golden Bear."

Chuck Noll (b. Jan. 5, 1932): Football; coached Pittsburgh to 4 Super Bowl titles (1975-76,79-80); retired after 1991 season with 209 career wins (including playoffs) in 23 years.

Greg Norman (b. Feb. 10, 1955): Australian golfer; 73 tournament wins worldwide including 20 PGA Tour victories; 2-time British Open winner (1986,93); lost Masters by a stroke in both 1986 (to Jack Nicklaus) and '87 (to Larry Mize in sudden death); 1995 PGA Tour Player of the Year.

James D. Norris (b. Nov. 6, 1906, d. Feb. 25, 1966): Boxing promoter and NHL owner; president of International Boxing Club from 1949 until U.S. Supreme Court ordered its break-up (for anti-trust violations) in 1958; only NHL owner to win Stanley Cups in two cities: Detroit (1936-37,43) and Chicago (1961).

Paavo Nurmi (b. June 13, 1897, d. Oct. 2, 1973): Finnish runner; won 9 gold medals (6 individual) in 1920, '24 and '28 Olympics; from 1921-31 broke 23 world outdoor records in events ranging from 1,500 to 20,000 meters.

Dan O'Brien (b. July 18, 1966): Track & Field; Olympic decathlon gold medalist (1996); set world record in decathlon (8,891 pts) in 1992, after shockingly failing to qualify for event at U.S. Olympic Trials; three-time gold medalist at World Championships (1991,93,95).

Larry O'Brien (b. July 7, 1917, d. Sept. 27, 1990): Basketball; former U.S. Postmaster General and 3rd NBA commissioner (1975-84); league absorbed 4 ABA teams and created salary cap during his term in office.

Parry O'Brien (b. Jan. 28, 1932): Track & Field; in 4 consecutive Olympics, won two gold medals, a silver and placed 4th in the shot put (1952-64).

Al Oerter (b. Sept. 19, 1936): Track & Field; his 4 discus gold medals in consecutive Olympics from 1956-68 is an unmatched Olympic record.

Sadaharu Oh (b. May 20, 1940): Baseball 1B; led Japan League in HRs 15 times; 9-time MVP for Tokyo Giants; hit 868 HRs in 22 years.

Hakeem Olajuwon (b. Jan. 21, 1963): Basketball C; Nigerian native who was All-America in 1984 and Final Four MOP in 1983 for Houston; overall 1st pick by Houston Rockets in 1984 NBA draft; led Rockets to back-to-back NBA titles (1994-95); regular season MVP (1994) and 2-time Finals MVP ('94,95); 6-time All-NBA 1st team (1987-89,93-95); all-time NBA blocks leader.

Jose Maria Olazabal (b. Feb. 5, 1966): Spanish golfer; has 28 worldwide victories including 2 Masters (1994,99); played on 6 European Ryder Cup teams.

Barney Oldfield (b. Jan. 29, 1878, d. Oct. 4, 1946): Auto racing pioneer; drove cars built by Henry Ford; first man to drive car a mile per minute (1903).

Walter O'Malley (b. Oct. 9, 1903, d. Aug. 9, 1979): Baseball owner; moved Brooklyn Dodgers to Los Angeles after 1957 season; won 4 World Series (1955,59,63,65).

Shaquille O'Neal (b. Mar. 6, 1972): Basketball C; 2-time All-America at LSU (1991-92); overall 1st pick (as a junior) by Orlando in 1992 NBA draft; Rookie of Year in 1993; 2-time NBA scoring leader (1995,2000); regular season MVP (2000) and 3-time NBA Finals MVP (2000,01,02); named one of the NBA's 50 Greatest Players; traded to Miami in 2004.

Bobby Orr (b. Mar. 20, 1948): Hockey D; league's only 8-time Norris Trophy winner as best defenseman (1968-75); credited with revolutionizing the position; 3-time Hart Trophy winner as NHL regular season MVP (1970-72); led NHL in scoring twice and assists 5 times; All-NHL 1st team 8 times; playoff MVP twice (1970,72) with Boston.

Tom Osborne (b. Feb. 23, 1937): Football; Nebraska head coach from 1973-97; career record of 255-49-3; his win pct. of .836 is fifth all-time; won national championships in 1994 and '95 and shared national title with Michigan in '97; elected to U.S. Congress (R., Neb.) in 2000.

Mel Ott (b. Mar. 2, 1909, d. Nov. 21, 1958): Baseball OF; joined NY Giants at age 16; led NL in HRs 6 times; had 511 HRs and 1,860 RBI in 22 years.

Kristin Otto (b. Feb. 7, 1966): East German swimmer; 1st woman to win 6 gold medals (4 individual) at one Olympics (1988).

Francis Ouimet (b. May 8, 1893, d. Sept. 3, 1967): Golfer; won 1913 U.S. Open as 20-year-old amateur playing on Brookline, Mass. course where he used to caddie; won U.S. Amateur twice; 8-time Walker Cup player.

Steve Owen (b. Apr. 21, 1898, d. May 17, 1964): Football; All-Pro guard (1927); coached NY Giants for 23 years (1931-53); won 153 career games and 2 NFL titles (1934,38).

Jesse Owens (b. Sept. 12, 1913, d. Mar. 31, 1980): Track & Field; set 4 world records in one afternoon competing for Ohio State at the Big Ten Championships (May 25, 1935); a year later, he soundly debunked Adolf Hitler's "master race" claims, winning 4 gold medals (100m, 200m, 4x100m relay and long jump) at 1936 Summer Olympics in Berlin.

Alan Page (b. Aug. 7, 1945): Football DE; All-America at Notre Dame in 1966 and member of two national championship teams; 6-time NFL All-Pro and 1971 Player of Year with Minnesota Vikings; later a lawyer who was elected to Minnesota Supreme Court in 1992.

Satchel Paige (b. July 7, 1906, d. June 6, 1982): Baseball RHP; pitched 55 career no-hitters over 20 seasons in Negro Leagues; entered major leagues with Cleveland in 1948 at age 42; had 28-31 record in 5 years; returned to AL at age 59 to start 1 game for Kansas City in 1965 (went 3 innings, gave up a hit and got a strikeout); elected to Baseball Hall of Fame in 1971.

Se Ri Pak (b. Sept. 28, 1977): Golfer; won two Majors as an LPGA rookie in 1998 (LPGA Championship and U.S. Open); youngest player to win the U.S. Open (20); won British Open in 2001 and added her 2nd LPGA Championship in 2002.

Arnold Palmer (b. Sept. 10, 1929): Golfer; winner of 4 Masters, 2 British Opens and a U.S. Open; 2-time PGA Player of Year (1960,62); 1st player to earn over $1 million in career (1968); annual PGA Tour money leader award named after him; 62 wins on PGA Tour and 10 more on Senior Tour; made 48 consecutive Masters starts.

Jim Palmer (b. Oct. 15, 1945): Baseball RHP; 3-time Cy Young Award winner (1973,75-76); won 20 or more games 8 times with Baltimore; elected to Baseball Hall of Fame in 1990; 1991 comeback attempt at age 45 scrubbed in spring training.

Bill Parcells (b. Aug. 22, 1941): Football; coached NY Giants to 2 Super Bowl titles (1987,91); retired after 1990 season then returned in 1993 as coach of New England; took hapless Pats from 2-14 in 1992 to Super Bowl (loss to Green Bay) in 1997; left Patriots after Super Bowl to coach the New York Jets; coached 3 seasons with the Jets (1997-99), turning them from 1-15 doormat to AFC East champ in 2 years; retired again in 2000 but returned to the sidelines in 2003 as head coach of the Dallas Cowboys.

Jack Pardee (b. Apr. 19, 1936): Football; All-America LB at Texas A&M; All-Pro with LA Rams (1963) and Washington (1971); 2-time NFL Coach of Year (1976,79); won 87 games in 11 seasons; only man hired as head coach in NFL, WFL, USFL and CFL.

Bernie Parent (b. Apr. 3, 1945): Hockey G; led Philadelphia Flyers to 2 Stanley Cups as playoff MVP (1974,75); 2-time Vezina Trophy winner; posted 55 career shutouts and 2.55 GAA in 13 seasons.

Joe Paterno (b. Dec. 21, 1926): Football; passed Bear Bryant in 2001 as all-time wins leader in college football (since passed himself by Bobby Bowden); coached Penn St. to 339-109-3 record, 20-10-1 bowl record and 2 national titles (1982,86) in 38 years; also had three unbeaten teams that didn't finish No. 1; 4-time Coach of Year (1968,78,82,86).

Craig Patrick (b. May 20, 1946): Hockey; 3rd generation Patrick to have name inscribed on Stanley Cup; GM of 2-time Cup champion Pittsburgh Penguins (1991-92); also captain of 1969 NCAA champion at Denver; assistant coach-GM of 1980 gold medal-winning U.S. Olympic team; grandson of Lester.

Lester Patrick (b. Dec. 30, 1883, d. June 1, 1960): Hockey; pro hockey pioneer as player, coach and general manager for 43 years; led NY Rangers to Stanley Cups as coach (1928,33) and GM (1940); grandfather of Craig.

Carly Patterson (b. Feb. 4, 1988): American gymnast; Olympic all-around champ at Athens in 2004.

Floyd Patterson (b. Jan. 4, 1935): Boxer; Olympic middleweight champ in 1952; world heavyweight champion (1956-59,60-62); 1st to regain heavyweight crown; fought Ingemar Johansson 3 times in 22 months from 1959-61 and won last two; pro record 55-8-1 with 40 KOs.

Walter Payton (b. July 25, 1954, d. Nov. 1, 1999): Football RB; formerly NFL's all-time leading rusher with 16,726 yards (1984-2002; passed by Emmitt Smith); scored 125 career TDs; All-Pro 7 times with Chicago; led NFL in rushing 5 times (1976-80); league MVP in 1977 (AP & PFWA) and 1985 (Bell); won ring with Bears in Super Bowl XX; known as superb runner, receiver and blocker; nicknamed "Sweetness".

Calvin Peete (b. July 18, 1943): Golf; began playing golf at the age of 23; earned over $2 million in career earnings; selected to the U.S. Ryder Cup teams in 1983 and 1985.

Pelé (b. Oct. 23, 1940): Brazilian soccer F; given name— Edson Arantes do Nascimento; led Brazil to 3 World Cup titles (1958,62,70); came to U.S. in 1975 to play for NY Cosmos in NASL; scored 1,281 goals in 22 years including 12 goals in the World Cup; served as Brazil's minister of sport (1990-98); named IOC Athlete of the Century and FIFA's co-Player of the Century (along with Diego Maradona).

Roger Penske (b. Feb. 20, 1937): Auto racing; national sports car driving champion (1964); established racing team in 1961; co-founder of Championship Auto Racing Teams (CART); Penske Racing has won 13 Indianapolis 500s and 11 CART points titles; announced surprising move to IRL for 2002 season.

Willie Pep (b. Sept. 19, 1922): Boxer; 2-time world featherweight champion (1942-48,49-50); pro record 230-11-1 with 65 KOs.

Marie-Jose Perec (b. 1968): Track & Field; French sprinter who became 2nd woman to win the 200m and 400m events in the same Olympics (1996); her time in the 400 (48.25) set an Olympic record; also won the 400 in 1992 Games.

Fred Perry (b. May 18, 1909, d. Feb. 2, 1995): British tennis player; 3-time Wimbledon champ (1934-36); first player to win all four Grand Slam singles titles, though not in same year; last native to win All-England men's title.

Gaylord Perry (b. Sept. 15, 1938): Baseball RHP; was only pitcher to win Cy Young Award in both leagues until 1999 (Randy Johnson and Pedro Martinez); retired in 1983 with 314-265 record and 3,534 strikeouts over 22 years with 8 teams; brother Jim won 215 games for family total of 529.

Bob Pettit (b. Dec. 12, 1932): Basketball F; All-NBA 1st team 10 times (1955-64); 2-time MVP (1956,59) with St. Louis Hawks; first player to score 20,000 points.

Richard Petty (b. July 2, 1937): Auto racer; 7-time winner of Daytona 500; 7-time NASCAR national champ (1964,67,71-72,74-75,79); first stock car driver to win $1 million in career; all-time NASCAR leader in races won (200), poles (126) and wins in a single season (27 in 1967); son of Lee (55 career wins), father of Kyle (8 career wins), grandfather of Adam; nicknamed "The King".

Michael Phelps (b. June 30, 1985): American swimmer who attempted to break Mark Spitz's Olympic record of 7 gold medals in 2004 but "settled" for 6 golds and two bronzes in Athens.

Mike Piazza (b. Sept. 4, 1968): Baseball C; slugger who broke Carlton Fisk's MLB record for HRs by a catcher in 2004 with his 352nd; 10-time All-Star.

Laffit Pincay Jr. (b. Dec. 29, 1946): Jockey; 5-time Eclipse Award winner (1971,73-74,79,85); winner of 3 Belmonts and 1 Kentucky Derby (aboard Swale in 1984); retired as all-time winningest jockey with 9,531 career wins.

Scottie Pippen (b. Sept. 25, 1965): Basketball F; started on 6 NBA champions with Chicago (1991-93, 96-98); 3-time All-NBA first team (1994-96). Voted one of NBA's 50 Greatest Players.

Uta Pippig (b. Sept. 7, 1965): German marathoner; won three-straight Boston Marathons (1994,95,96); set a new course record in '94 (since broken in 2002).

Nelson Piquet (b. Aug. 17, 1952): Brazilian auto racer; 3-time Formula One world champion (1981,83, 87); left circuit in 1991 with 23 career wins.

Rick Pitino (b. Sept. 18, 1952): Basketball; won 1996 NCAA title at Kentucky and in 1997, became coach and president of Boston Celtics but was unsuccessful and resigned in 2001, returning to college coaching in Louisville.

Jacques Plante (b. Jan. 17, 1929, d. Feb. 27, 1986): Hockey G; led Montreal to 6 Stanley Cups (1953,56-60); won 7 Vezina Trophies; MVP in 1962; first goalie to regularly wear a mask; posted 82 shutouts with 2.38 GAA.

Gary Player (b. Nov. 1, 1936): South African golfer; 3-time winner of Masters (1961,74,78) and British Open (1959,68,74); one of only 5 players to win career Grand Slam (Hogan, Nicklaus, Sarazen and Woods); also won 2 PGAs, a U.S. Open and 2 U.S. Senior Opens.

Jim Plunkett (b. Dec. 5, 1947): Football QB; Heisman Trophy winner (Stanford) in 1970; AFL Rookie of the Year in 1971; led Oakland-LA Raiders to Super Bowl wins in 1981 and '84; MVP in '81.

Maurice Podoloff (b. Aug. 18, 1890, d. Nov. 24, 1985): Basketball; engineered merger of Basketball Assn. of America and National Basketball League into NBA in 1949; NBA commissioner (1949-63); league MVP trophy named after him.

Fritz Pollard (b. Jan. 27, 1894, d. May 11, 1986): Football; 1st black All-America RB (1916 at Brown); 1st black to play in Rose Bowl; 7-year NFL pro (1920-26); 1st black NFL coach, at Milwaukee and Hammond, Ind.

Sam Pollock (b. Dec. 15, 1925): Hockey GM; managed NHL Montreal Canadiens to 9 Stanley Cups in 14 years (1965-78).

Denis Potvin (b. Oct. 29, 1953): Hockey D; won Norris Trophy 3 times (1976,78-79); 5-time All-NHL 1st-team; led NY Islanders to 4 Stanley Cups.

Mike Powell (b. Nov. 10, 1963): Track & Field; broke Bob Beamon's 23-year-old long jump world record by 2 inches with leap of 29-ft., 4½ in. at the 1991 World Championships; Sullivan Award winner (1991); won long jump silver medals in 1988 and '92 Olympics; repeated as world champ in 1993.

Steve Prefontaine (b. Jan. 25, 1951, d. May 30, 1975): Track & Field; All-America distance runner at Oregon; first athlete to win same event at NCAA championships 4 straight years (5,000 meters from 1970-73); finished 4th in 5,000 at 1972 Munich Olympics; first athlete to endorse Nike running shoes; killed in a one-car accident.

Nick Price (b. Jan. 28, 1957): Zimbabwean golfer; PGA Tour Player of Year in 1993 and '94; became 1st since Nick Faldo in 1990 to win 2 Grand Slam titles in same year when he took British Open and PGA Championship in 1994; also won PGA in '92.

Alain Prost (b. Feb. 24, 1955): French auto racer; 4-time Formula One world champion (1985-86,89,93); sat out 1992 then returned to win title in 1993; retired after '93 season as all-time leader with 51 F1 wins (passed by Michael Schumacher in 2001).

Kirby Puckett (b. Mar. 14, 1961): Baseball OF; led Minnesota Twins to World Series titles in 1987 and '91; retired in 1996 due to an eye ailment with a batting title (1989), 2,304 hits and a .318 career average in 12 seasons; elected to Hall of Fame in 2001.

C.C. Pyle (b. 1882, d. Feb. 3, 1939): Promoter; known as "Cash and Carry"; hyped Red Grange's pro football debut by arranging 1925 barnstorming tour with Chicago Bears; had Grange bolt NFL for new AFL in 1926 (AFL folded in '27); also staged two transcontinental footraces (1928-29), known as "Bunion Derbies."

Bobby Rahal (b. Jan. 10, 1953): Auto racer; 3-time PPG Cup champ (1986,87,92); 24 career Indy-Car wins, including 1986 Indy 500; current IRL team owner with TV's David Letterman; acted as interim president-CEO of CART in 2000 but resigned to assume position with Jaguar Formula One team.

Jack Ramsay (b. Feb. 21, 1925): Basketball; coach who won 239 college games with St. Joe's-PA in 11 seasons and 906 NBA games (including playoffs) with 4 teams over 21 years; led Portland to 1977 NBA title; placed 3rd in 1961 Final Four (later vacated).

Bill Rassmussen (b. Oct. 15, 1932): Radio-TV; unemployed radio broadcaster who founded ESPN, the nation's first 24-hour all-sports cable-TV network, in 1978; bought out by Getty Oil in 1981.

Willis Reed (b. June 25, 1942): Basketball C; led NY Knicks to NBA titles in 1970 and '73, Finals MVP both years; regular season MVP 1970. Voted one of NBA's 50 Greatest Players.

Pee Wee Reese (b. July 23, 1918, d. Aug. 14, 1999): Baseball SS; member of Brooklyn/Los Angeles Dodgers from 1940-58; led NL in runs scored (132) in 1949 and stolen bases (30) in 1952; hit over .300 in a season once (.309 in 1954); led the NL in putouts four times; real name was Harold H. Reese.

Mary Lou Retton (b. Jan. 24, 1968): Gymnast; won gold medal in women's All-Around at the 1984 Olympics; also won 2 silvers and 2 bronzes.

Manon Rheaume (b. Feb. 24, 1972): Hockey; 2-time gold medallist (1992,94) at the Women's World Hockey Championships as goaltender for Canada; first woman to sign a professional hockey contract; started in goal in an exhibition game for the Tampa Bay Lightning on Sept. 23, 1992 to become the only woman to play in an NHL game.

Grantland Rice (b. Nov. 1, 1880, d. July 13, 1954): First celebrated American sportswriter; chronicled the Golden Age of Sport in 1920s; immortalized Notre Dame's "Four Horsemen."

Jerry Rice (b. Oct. 13, 1962): Football WR; 2-time Div. I-AA All-America at Mississippi Valley St. (1983-84); won 3 Super Bowls with San Francisco (1989,90,95); 10-time All-Pro; regular season MVP in 1987 and Super Bowl MVP in 1989; NFL all-time regular season and Super Bowl leader in touchdowns, receptions and receiving yards.

Henri Richard (b. Feb. 29, 1936): Hockey C; leap year baby who played on more Stanley Cup championship teams (11) than anybody else; at 5-foot-7, known as the "Pocket Rocket"; brother of Maurice.

Maurice Richard (b. Aug. 4, 1921, d. May 27, 2000): Hockey RW; the "Rocket"; 8-time NHL 1st team All-Star; MVP in 1947; 1st to score 50 goals in one season (1944-45); 544 career goals; played on 8 Stanley Cup winners in Montreal.

Bob Richards (b. Feb. 2, 1926): Track & Field; pole vaulter, ordained minister and original *Wheaties* pitchman, remains only 2-time Olympic pole vault champ (1952,56).

Nolan Richardson (b. Dec. 27, 1941): Basketball; coached Arkansas to consecutive NCAA finals, beating Duke in 1994 and losing to UCLA in '95; school bought out his contract in 2002, ending his 17-year reign.

Tex Rickard (b. Jan. 2, 1870, d. Jan. 6, 1929): Promoter who handled boxing's first $1 million gate (Dempsey vs. Carpentier in 1921); built Madison Square Garden in 1925; founded NY Rangers as Garden tenant in 1926 and named NHL team after himself (Tex's Rangers); also built Boston Garden in 1928.

Eddie Rickenbacker (b. Oct. 8, 1890, d. July 23, 1973): Mechanic and auto racer; became America's top flying ace (22 kills) in World War I; owned Indianapolis Speedway (1927-45) and ran Eastern Air Lines (1938-59).

Branch Rickey (b. Dec. 20, 1881, d. Dec. 9, 1965): Baseball innovator; revolutionized game with creation of modern farm system while GM of St. Louis Cardinals (1917-42); integrated major leagues in 1947 as president-GM of Brooklyn Dodgers when he brought up Jackie Robinson (whom he had signed on Oct. 23, 1945); later GM of Pittsburgh Pirates.

Leni Riefenstahl (b. Aug. 22, 1902, d. Sept. 8, 2003): German filmmaker of 1930s; directed classic sports documentary "Olympia" on 1936 Berlin Summer Olympics; infamous, however, for also making 1934 Hitler propaganda film "Triumph of the Will."

Roy Riegels (b. Apr. 4, 1908, d. Mar. 26, 1993): Football; California center who picked up fumble in 2nd quarter of 1929 Rose Bowl and raced 70 yards in the wrong direction to set up a 2-point safety in 8-7 loss to Georgia Tech.

Bobby Riggs (b. Feb. 25, 1918, d. Oct. 25, 1995): Tennis; won Wimbledon once (1939) and U.S. title twice (1939,41); legendary hustler who made his biggest score in 1973 as 55-year-old male chauvinist challenging the best women players; beat No. 1 Margaret Smith Court 6-2,6-1, but was thrashed by No. 2 Billie Jean King, 6-4,6-3,6-3 in nationally televised "Battle of the Sexes" on Sept. 20, before 30,492 at the Astrodome.

Pat Riley (b. Mar. 20, 1945): Basketball; coached LA Lakers to 4 of their 5 NBA titles in 1980s (1982,85,87-88); coached New York Knicks from 1991-95; then signed with Miami Heat as coach, team president and part-owner; 3-time Coach of Year (1990,93,97); 2nd on list of all-time coaching victories behind Lenny Wilkens.

Cal Ripken Jr. (b. Aug. 24, 1960): Baseball SS; broke Lou Gehrig's major league Iron Man record of 2,130 consecutive games on Sept. 6, 1995; record streak began on May 30, 1982 and ended Sept. 19, 1998 after 2,632 games; 2-time AL MVP (1983,91) for Baltimore; AL Rookie of Year (1982); AL starter in All-Star Game from 1984-2001; 2-time All-Star Game MVP (1991,2001); holds record for career home runs by a shortstop.

Phil Rizzuto (b. Sept. 25, 1918): Baseball SS; nicknamed "the Scooter"; AL MVP with the Yankees in 1950; 5-time All-Star; retired in 1956 and became Yankees radio and television announcer; elected to the Hall of Fame in 1994.

Oscar Robertson (b. Nov. 24, 1938): Basketball G; 3-time College Player of Year (1958-60) at Cincinnati; led 1960 U.S. Olympic team to gold medal; NBA Rookie of Year (1961); 9-time All-NBA 1st team; MVP in 1964 with Cincinnati Royals; NBA champion in 1971 with Milwaukee Bucks; 6-time annual NBA assist leader; 4th in career assists with 9,887; 8th in career points with 26,710.

Paul Robeson (b. Apr. 8, 1898, d. Jan. 23, 1976): Black 4-sport star and 2-time football All-America (1917-18) at Rutgers; 3-year NFL pro; also scholar, lawyer, singer, actor and political activist; long-tainted by Communist sympathies, he was finally inducted into College Football Hall of Fame in 1995.

Brooks Robinson (b. May 18, 1937): Baseball 3B; led AL in fielding 12 times from 1960-72 with Baltimore; AL MVP in 1964; World Series MVP in 1970; 16 Gold Gloves; entered Hall of Fame in 1983.

David Robinson (b. Aug. 6, 1965): Basketball C; 1987 College Player of Year at Navy; overall 1st pick by San Antonio in 1987 NBA draft; served in military (1987-89); NBA Rookie of Year (1990) and MVP (1995); 2-time All-NBA 1st team (1991,92); led NBA in scoring in 1994; member of 1988, '92 and '96 U.S. Olympic teams; won 2 NBA titles (1999, 2003).

Eddie Robinson (b. Feb. 13, 1919): Football; head coach at Div. I-AA Grambling from 1941-97; retired as winningest coach in college history (408-165-15), since passed by St. John's-Minn. (Div. III) coach John Gagliardi; led Tigers to 8 national black college titles.

Frank Robinson (b. Aug. 31, 1935): Baseball OF; won MVP in NL (1961) and AL (1966); Triple Crown winner and World Series MVP in 1966 with Baltimore; 5th on all-time home run list with 586; 1st black manager in major leagues with Cleveland in 1975; also managed in SF, Baltimore and Montreal; served as the league's VP of on-field operations (2000-01).

Jackie Robinson (b. Jan. 31, 1919, d. Oct. 24, 1972): Baseball 1B-2B-3B; 4-sport athlete at UCLA (baseball, basketball, football and track); hit .387 with Kansas City Monarchs of Negro Leagues in 1945; signed by Brooklyn Dodgers' Branch Rickey on Oct. 23, 1945. Played in minors (Montreal) in 1946 and broke Major League Baseball's color line in 1947; Rookie of Year in 1947 and NL's MVP in 1949; hit .311 over 10 seasons. His #42 was retired by Major League Baseball in 1997.

Sugar Ray Robinson (b. May 3, 1921, d. Apr. 12, 1989): Boxer; arguably the greatest pound-for-pound prizefighter of all-time; world welterweight champion (1946-51); 5-time middleweight champ; retired at age 45 after 25 years in the ring; pro record 174-19-6 with 109 KOs.

Knute Rockne (b. Mar. 4, 1888, d. Mar. 31, 1931): Football; coached Notre Dame to 3 consensus national titles (1924,29,30), highest winning percentage in college history (.881) with record of 105-12-5 over 13 seasons; killed in plane crash.

Bill Rodgers (b. Dec. 23, 1947): Distance runner; won Boston and New York City marathons 4 times each from 1975-80.

Dennis Rodman (b. May 13, 1961): Basketball F; superb rebounder and defender; known for dyeing his hair various colors and for getting suspended regularly; in 1997, he was suspended for 11 games for kicking a cameraman; led NBA in rebounding 7 straight years (1992-98); member of 5 NBA champion teams with Detroit (1989,90) and Chicago (1996-98); 2-time defensive player of the year (1990-91).

Irina Rodnina (b. Sept. 12, 1949): Soviet figure skater; won 10 world championships and 3 Olympic gold medals in pairs competition from 1969-80.

Alex Rodriguez (b. July 27, 1975): Baseball 3B; led AL in hitting (.358) his first full season in the majors (1996); in 1998 became third player ever with 40 HRs and 40 steals in one season; signed a 10-year, $252m deal (the biggest in U.S. sports history) with Texas in 2000, won AL MVP in 2003 but was traded to NY Yankees in 2004.

Juan (Chi Chi) Rodriguez (b. Oct. 23, 1935): Golfer; popular player with 8 PGA Tour victories and 22 Senior Tour wins; 1973 U.S. Ryder Cup Team.

Ronaldo (b. Sept. 22, 1976): Brazilian soccer F; named to the Brazilian National Team when he was 17; 3-time FIFA World Player of the Year (1996,97,2002); European Player of the Year in 1997 and 2002; named 1998 World Cup MVP; led Brazil to World Cup title in 2002, scoring 8 times including both of Brazil's goals in its win over Germany in the final.

Art Rooney (b. Jan. 27, 1901, d. Aug. 25, 1988): Race track legend and pro football pioneer; bought Pittsburgh Steelers franchise in 1933 for $2,500; finally won NFL title with 1st of 4 Super Bowls in 1974 season.

Theodore Roosevelt (b. Oct. 27, 1858, d. Jan. 6, 1919): 26th President of the U.S.; physical fitness buff who boxed as undergraduate at Harvard; credited with presidential assist in forming of Intercollegiate Athletic Assn. (now NCAA) in 1905-06.

Mauri Rose (b. May 26, 1906, d. Jan. 1, 1981): Auto racer; 3-time winner of Indy 500 (1941,47-48).

Murray Rose (b. Jan. 6, 1939): Australian swimmer; won 3 gold medals at 1956 Olympics; added a gold, silver and bronze in 1960.

Pete Rose (b. Apr. 14, 1941): Baseball OF-IF; all-time hits leader with 4,256 and games leader with 3562; led NL in batting 3 times; regular-season MVP in 1973; World Series MVP in 1975; had 44-game hitting streak in '78; managed Cincinnati (1984-89); banned for life in 1989 for conduct detrimental to baseball (betting on baseball); convicted of tax evasion in 1990 and sentenced to 5 months in prison.

Ken Rosewall (b. Nov. 2, 1934): Tennis; won French and Australian singles titles at age 18; U.S. champ twice, but never won Wimbledon.

Mark Roth (b. Apr. 10, 1951): Bowler; 4-time PBA Player of Year (1977-79,84); has 34 tournament wins and over $1.6 million in career earnings; U.S. Open champ in 1984.

Alan Rothenberg (b. Apr. 10, 1939): Soccer; president of U.S. Soccer 1990-98; surprised European skeptics by directing hugely successful 1994 World Cup tournament; successfully got oft-delayed outdoor Major League Soccer off ground in 1996.

Chad Rowan (Akebono) (b. May 8, 1969): Sumo Wrestling; 6-foot-9, 510-pound naturalized Japanese citizen born in Hawaii; first foreign grand champion in sumo wrestling's 2,000-year history; retired in 2001.

Patrick Roy (b. Oct. 5, 1965): Hockey G; led Montreal to 2 Stanley Cup titles (1986,93) and won 3rd and 4th Cups with Colorado (1996,2001); 3-time playoff MVP (as rookie in 1986,93,2001); won Vezina Trophy 3 times (1989-90,92); led NHL in goals against average 3 times (1989,92,2002); all-time leader in career regular season wins (551) and playoff wins (151).

Pete Rozelle (b. Mar. 1, 1926, d. December 6, 1996): Football; NFL Commissioner from 1960-89; presided over growth of league from 12 to 28 teams, merger with AFL, creation of Super Bowl and advent of huge TV rights fees.

Wilma Rudolph (b. June 23, 1940, d. Nov. 12, 1994): Track & Field; won 3 gold medals (100m, 200m and 4x100m relay) at 1960 Olympics; also won relay silver in '56 Games at age 16; 2-time AP Athlete of Year (1960-61) and Sullivan Award winner in 1961; suffered from polio and wore leg braces until she was 9.

John Ruiz (b. Jan. 4, 1972): Boxer; defeated Evander Holyfield to decision in 2001 for the WBA heavyweight title; the first-ever Hispanic heavyweight champ; lost belt to Roy Jones Jr. on unanimous dec. in 2003.

Damon Runyon (b. Oct. 4, 1884, d. Dec. 10, 1946): Kansas native who gained fame as New York journalist, sports columnist and short-story writer; best known for 1932 story collection, "Guys and Dolls."

Adolph Rupp (b. Sept. 2, 1901, d. Dec. 10, 1977): Basketball; 2nd in all-time college coaching wins with 876; led Kentucky to 4 NCAA championships (1948-49,51,58) and 1 NIT title (1946).

Bill Russell (b. Feb. 12, 1934): Basketball C; won titles in college (with San Francisco in 1955,56), Olympics (1956) and pros; 5-time NBA MVP (1958,61,62,63,65); led Boston Celtics to an amazing 11 titles from 1957-69; all-time NBA rebound leader (1958-59,64-65); 2nd on all-time rebound list with 21,620; became first black NBA (and major professional sports) head coach in 1966.

Babe Ruth (b. Feb. 6, 1895, d. Aug. 16, 1948): Baseball LHP-OF; two-time 20-game winner with Boston Red Sox (1916-17); had a 94-46 record with a 2.28 ERA, while he was 3-0 in the World Series with an ERA of 0.87; sold to New York Yankees for $100,000 in 1920; AL MVP in 1923; led AL in slugging average 13 times, HRs 12 times, RBI 6 times and batting once (.378 in 1924); hit 60 HRs in 1927 and at least 54 3 other times; ended career with Boston Braves in 1935 with 714 HRs, 2,211 RBI, 2,062 walks and a batting average of .342; remains all-time leader in slugging percentage (.690); member of the Hall of Fame's inaugural class of 1936.

Johnny Rutherford (b. Mar. 12, 1938): Auto racer; 3-time winner of Indy 500 (1974,76,80); CART national champion in 1980.

Nolan Ryan (b. Jan. 31, 1947): Baseball RHP; recorded 7 no-hitters against Kansas City and Detroit (1973), Minnesota (1974), Baltimore (1975), LA Dodgers (1981), Oakland A's (1990) and Toronto (1991 at age 44); 2-time 20-game winner (1973-74); 2-time NL leader in ERA (1981,87); led AL in strikeouts 9 times and NL twice in 27 years; retired after 1993 season with 324 wins, 292 losses and all-time records for strikeouts (5,714) and walks (2,795); never won Cy Young Award; had his number retired by three teams (California, Houston, Texas).

Samuel Ryder (b. Mar. 24, 1858, d. Jan. 2, 1936): Golf; English seed merchant who donated the Ryder Cup in 1927 for competition between pro golfers from Great Britain and the U.S.; made his fortune by coming up with idea of selling seeds in small packages.

Toni Sailer (b. Nov. 17, 1935): Austrian skier; 1st to win 3 alpine gold medals in Winter Olympics—taking downhill, slalom and giant slalom events in 1956.

Alberto Salazar (b. Aug. 7, 1958): Track and Field; set one world and six U.S. records during his career; broke 12-year-old record at New York Marathon in 1981 and broke Boston Marathon record in 1982; won three straight NY Marathons (1980-82); qualified for the 1980 and 1984 U.S. Olympic teams.

Juan Antonio Samaranch (b. July 17, 1920): president of International Olympic Committee (1980-2001); the native of Barcelona was re-elected in 1996 after IOC's move in '95 to bump membership age limit to 80; replaced by Belgian Jacques Rogge.

Pete Sampras (b. Aug. 12, 1971): Tennis; No.1 in world (1993-98); youngest ever U.S. Open men's champ (19 years, 28 days) in 1990; his win at 2002 U.S. Open was record 14th grand slam singles title; won 2 Australian Opens (1994,97), 7 Wimbledons (1993-95, 1997-2000) and 5 U.S. Opens (1990,93, 95-96,2002); career money leader on ATP Tour.

Joan Benoit Samuelson (b. May 16, 1957): Distance runner; won Boston Marathon twice (1979,83); won first women's Olympic marathon in 1984 Games; Sullivan Award recipient in 1985.

Arantxa Sanchez-Vicario (b. Dec. 18, 1971): Spanish tennis player; won 29 singles titles including 3 French Opens (1989,94,98) and 1 U.S. Open (1994); 6 doubles and 4 mixed doubles grand slam titles.

Earl Sande (b. Nov. 13, 1898, d. Aug. 19, 1968): Jockey; rode Gallant Fox to Triple Crown in 1930; won 5 Belmonts and 3 Kentucky Derbies.

Barry Sanders (b. July 16, 1968): Football RB; won 1988 Heisman Trophy as junior at Oklahoma St.; all-time NCAA single season leader in rushing (2,628 yards), scoring (234 points) and TDs (39); 4-time NFL rushing leader with Detroit Lions (1990,94,96,97); NFC Rookie of Year (1988); 2-time NFL Player of Year (1991,97); NFC MVP (1994); rushed for 2,053 yards in 1997; No. 3 all-time rusher (15,269 yds); abruptly retired just prior to 1999 season; inducted into Pro Football Hall of Fame in 2004.

Deion Sanders (b. Aug. 9, 1967): Baseball OF and Football DB-KR-WR; 2-time All-America at Florida St. in football (1987-88); 7-time NFL All-Pro CB with Atlanta, San Fran. and Dallas (1991-94,96-98); led majors in triples (14) with Braves in 1992 and hit .533 in World Series that year; played on 2 Super Bowl winners (SF in XXIX, and Dallas in XXX); first 2-way starter in NFL since 1962 (Chuck Bednarik); only athlete to play in both World Series and Super Bowl.

Cael Sanderson (b. June 20, 1979): Wrestling; first 4-time undefeated NCAA college wrestling champion (1999-2002); went 159-0 during 4-year career at Iowa State; 4-time NCAA Most Outstanding Wrestler; won gold medal at Athens Games in 2004.

Abe Saperstein (b. July 4, 1901, d. Mar. 15, 1966): Basketball; founded all-black, Harlem Globetrotters barnstorming team in 1927; coached sharpshooting comedians to 1940 world pro title in Chicago and established troupe as game's foremost goodwill ambassadors; also served as 1st commissioner of American Basketball League (1961-62).

Gene Sarazen (b. Feb. 27, 1902, d. May 13, 1999): Golfer; one of only five players to win all four Grand Slam titles (others are Hogan, Nicklaus, Player and Woods); won Masters, British Open, 2 U.S. Opens and 3 PGA titles between 1922-35; invented sand wedge in 1930.

Glen Sather (b. Sept. 2, 1943): Hockey; GM-coach of 4 Stanley Cup winners in Edmonton (1984-85,87-88) and GM-only for another in 1990; ranks 7th on all-time NHL coaching list with 586 wins (including playoffs); entered Hockey Hall of Fame in 1997; named Pres-GM of NY Rangers in 2000.

Terry Sawchuk (b. Dec. 28, 1929, d. May 31, 1970): Hockey G; recorded 103 shutouts in 21 NHL seasons; 4-time Vezina Trophy winner; played on 4 Stanley Cup winners at Detroit and Toronto; posted career 2.52 GAA.

Gale Sayers (b. May 30, 1943): Football HB; 2-time All-America at Kansas; NFL Rookie of Year (1965) and 5-time All-Pro with Chicago; scored then-record 22 TDs in rookie year; led league in rushing twice (1966,69).

Chris Schenkel (b. Aug. 21, 1923): Radio-TV; 4-time Sportscaster of Year; easy-going baritone who covered basketball, bowling, football, golf and the Olympics for ABC and CBS; host of ABC's Pro Bowlers Tour for 33 years; received lifetime achievement Emmy Award in 1992.

Vitaly Scherbo (b. Jan. 13, 1972): Russian gymnast; winner of unprecedented 6 gold medals in gymnastics, including men's All-Around, for Unified Team in 1992 Olympics; also won 3 bronze in '96 Games.

Curt Schilling (b. Nov. 14, 1966): Baseball RHP; led majors in strikeouts twice (1997-98) with Philadelphia Phillies; traded to Arizona in 2000; 3-time 20-game winner (2001-02,04); shared 2001 World Series MVP award with Diamondbacks teammate Randy Johnson; traded to Boston after 2003 season.

Mike Schmidt (b. Sept. 27, 1949): Baseball 3B; led NL in HRs 8 times; 3-time MVP (1980,81,86) with Philadelphia; 548 career HRs and 10 Gold Gloves; inducted into Hall of Fame in 1995.

Don Schollander (b. Apr. 30, 1946): Swimming; won 4 gold medals at 1964 Olympics, plus one gold and one silver in 1968; won Sullivan Award in 1964.

Dick Schultz (b. Sept. 5, 1929): Reform-minded executive director of NCAA from 1988-93; announced resignation on May 11, 1993 in wake of special investigator's report citing Univ. of Virginia with improper student-athlete loan program during Schultz's tenure as athletic director (1981-87); executive director of the USOC 1995-2000.

Michael Schumacher (b. Jan. 3, 1969): German auto racer; Formula One's all-time win leader with 82 grand prix victories (and counting); 7-time world champion (1994-95,2000-04); broke his own F1 single-season record with 12 wins as of Sept. 2004.

Bob Seagren (b. Oct. 17, 1946): Track & Field; won gold medal in pole vault at 1968 Olympics; broke world outdoor record 5 times.

Tom Seaver (b. Nov. 17, 1944): Baseball RHP; won 3 Cy Young Awards (1969,73,75); led NL in K 5 times (1970,71,73,75,76); pitched no-hitter in 1978 for Cin.; had 311 wins, 3,640 strikeouts and 2.86 ERA over 20 years.

Peter Seitz (b. May 17, 1905, d. Oct. 17, 1983): Baseball arbitrator; ruled on Dec. 23, 1975 that players who perform for one season without a signed contract can become free agents; decision ushered in big money era for players.

Monica Seles (b. Dec. 2, 1973): Tennis; No. 1 in the world in 1991 and '92 after winning Australian, French and U.S. Opens both years; won 4 Australian, 3 French and 2 US Opens; winner of 30 singles titles in just 5 years before she was stabbed in the back by Steffi Graf fan Gunter Parche on Apr. 30, 1993 during match in Hamburg, Germany; spent remainder of 1993, all of '94 and most of '95 recovering; returned to tennis with win at the 1995 Canadian Open; won 1996 Australian Open; winner of 53 WTA tournaments.

Bud Selig (b. July 30, 1934): Baseball; Milwaukee car dealer who bought AL Seattle Pilots for $10.8 million in 1970 and moved team to Midwest; as de facto commissioner, he presided over 232-day players' strike that resulted in cancellation of World Series for first time since 1904; officially named baseball's ninth commissioner on July 2, 1998; made the controversial decision to end the 2002 All-Star Game after 11 inns., tied 7-7.

Frank Selke (b. May 7, 1893, d. July 3, 1985): Hockey; GM of 6 Stanley Cup champions in Montreal (1953,56-60); the annual NHL trophy for best defensive forward bears his name.

Ayrton Senna (b. Mar. 21, 1960, d. May 1, 1994): Brazilian auto racer; 3-time Formula One champion (1988,90-91); died as all-time F1 leader in poles (65) and 2nd in wins (41, currently in 3rd); killed in crash at Imola, Italy in 1994 San Marino GP.

Wilbur Shaw (b. Oct. 13, 1902, d. Oct. 30, 1954): Auto racer; 3-time winner and 3-time runner-up of Indy 500 from 1933-1940.

Patty Sheehan (b. Oct. 27, 1956): Golfer; LPGA Player of Year in 1983; clinched entry into LPGA Hall of Fame with her 30th career win in 1993; her 6 major titles include 3 LPGA Champ. (1983-84,93), 2 U.S. Opens (1992,94) 1 Dinah Shore (1996).

Bill Shoemaker (b. Aug. 19, 1931, d. Oct. 12, 2003): Jockey; ranks second all-time in career wins with 8,833 (passed by Laffit Pincay Jr. in Dec. 1999); 3-time Eclipse Award winner as jockey (1981) and special award recipient (1976,81); won Belmont 5 times, Kentucky Derby 4 times and Preakness twice; oldest jockey to win Kentucky Derby (age 54, aboard Ferdinand in 1986); retired in 1990 to become trainer; paralyzed in 1991 auto accident but continued to train horses.

Eddie Shore (b. Nov. 25, 1902, d. Mar. 16, 1985): Hockey D; only NHL defenseman to win Hart Trophy as MVP 4 times (1933,35-36,38); led Boston Bruins to Stanley Cup titles in 1929 and '39; had 105 goals and 1,047 penalty minutes in 14 seasons.

Frank Shorter (b. Oct. 31, 1947): Track & Field; won gold medal in marathon at 1972 Olympics, 1st American to win in 64 years.

Don Shula (b. Jan. 4, 1930): Football; retired after 1995 season with an NFL-record 347 career wins (including playoffs) and a winning percentage of .665; took six teams to Super Bowl and won twice with Miami (VII, VIII); 4-time Coach of Year, twice with Baltimore (1964,68) and twice with Miami (1970-71); coached 1972 Dolphins to 17-0 record, the only undefeated team in NFL history.

Charlie Sifford (b. June 2, 1922): Golf; won the Hartford Open in 1967 with a final-round 64, becoming the first black player to win a PGA event; won the PGA Seniors Championship in 1975; amassed over $1 million in career earnings; published his autobiography "Just Let Me Play" in 1992.

Al Simmons (b. May 22, 1902, d. May 26, 1956): Baseball OF; led AL in batting twice (1930-31) with Philadelphia A's and knocked in 100 runs or more 11 straight years (1924-34).

O.J. Simpson (b. July 9, 1947): Football RB; won Heisman Trophy in 1968 at USC; ran for 2,003 yards in NFL in 1973; All-Pro 5 times; MVP in 1973; rushed for 11,236 career yards; TV analyst and actor after career ended; arrested June 17, 1994 as suspect in double murder of ex-wife Nicole Brown Simpson and her friend Ronald Goldman; acquitted on Oct. 3, 1995 by a Los Angeles jury in criminal trial but forced to make financial reparations after losing wrongful death suit.

Vijay Singh (b. Feb. 22, 1963): Fijian golfer; dethroned Tiger Woods as world's top-ranked player in 2004; has 23 career PGA Tour wins including 1998 PGA championship and 2000 Masters; 2003-04 PGA Tour money leader.

George Sisler (b. Mar. 24, 1893, d. Mar. 26, 1973): Baseball 1B; hit over .400 twice (1920,22) and batted over .300 in 13 of his 15 seasons; his MLB record of 257 hits (1920) was finally broken by Seattle's Ichiro Suzuki (262) in 2004; played most of his career with the St. Louis Browns; inducted into Baseball Hall of Fame in 1939.

Mary Decker Slaney (b. Aug. 4, 1958): U.S. middle distance runner; has held 7 separate American track & field records from the 800 to 10,000 meters; won both 1,500 and 3,000 meters at 1983 World Championships in Helsinki, but no Olympic medals.

Raisa Smetanina (b. Feb. 29, 1952): Russian Nordic skier; all-time leading female Winter Olympics medalist with 10 cross country medals (4 gold, 5 silver and a bronze) in 5 appearances (1976,80,84, 88,92) for USSR and Unified Team.

Billy Smith (b. Dec. 12, 1950): Hockey G; led NY Islanders to 4 consecutive Stanley Cups (1980-83); won Vezina Trophy in 1982; Stanley Cup MVP in 1983.

Dean Smith (b. Feb. 28, 1931): Basketball; No. 1 on all-time NCAA coaches victory list (879 wins); led North Carolina to 25 NCAA tournaments in 34 years, reaching Final Four 10 times and winning championship twice (1982,93); coached U.S. Olympic team to gold medal in 1976.

Emmitt Smith (b. May 15, 1969): Football RB; passed Walter Payton in 2002 to become the NFL's all-time leading rusher; also holds all-time record for rushing TDs (155); 4-time NFL rushing leader (1991-93,95); 11 straight 1,000-yard seasons (1991-2001); regular season and Super Bowl MVP in 1993; played on three Super Bowl champions (1993,94,96).

John Smith (b. Aug. 9, 1965): Wrestler; 2-time NCAA champion for Oklahoma St. at 134 lbs (1987-88) and Most Outstanding Wrestler of '88 championships; 3-time world champion; gold medal winner at 1988 and '92 Olympics at 137 lbs; won Sullivan Award (1990); coached Oklahoma St. to 1994 NCAA title and brother Pat was Most Outstanding Wrestler.

Lee Smith (b. Dec. 4, 1957): Baseball RHP; 3-time NL saves leader (1983,91-92); retired as all-time saves leader with 478 and an ERA of 3.03; 10 seasons with 30+ saves and 3 times saved over 40.

Michelle Smith deBruin (b. Apr. 7, 1969): Irish swimmer; won three gold medals at the 1996 Olympics; accused of using performance-enhancing drugs but passed all tests until she was suspended for 4 years by FINA in 1998 for tampering with a urine sample.

Ozzie Smith (b. Dec. 26, 1954): Baseball SS; won 13 straight Gold Gloves (1980-92); played in 12 straight All-Star Games (1981-92); MVP of 1985 NL playoffs; all-time MLB assist leader (8,375); inducted into Baseball Hall of Fame in 2002.

Walter (Red) Smith (b. Sept. 25, 1905, d. Jan. 15, 1982): Sportswriter for newspapers in Philadelphia and New York from 1936-82; won Pulitzer Prize for commentary in 1976.

Conn Smythe (b. Feb. 1, 1895, d. Nov. 18, 1980): Hockey pioneer; built Maple Leaf Gardens in 1931; managed Toronto to 7 Stanley Cups.

Sam Snead (b. May 27, 1912, d. May 23, 2002): Golfer; won both Masters and PGA 3 times and British Open once; runner-up in U.S. Open 4 times; PGA Player of Year in 1949; oldest player (52 years, 10 months) to win PGA event with Greater Greensboro Open title in 1965; all-time PGA Tour career victory leader with 82.

Peter Snell (b. Dec. 17, 1938): Track & Field; New Zealander who won gold medal in 800m at 1960 Olympics, then won both the 800m and 1,500m at 1964 Games.

Duke Snider (b. Sept. 19, 1926): Baseball OF; hit 40 or more home runs five straight seasons (1953-57); led the league in runs scored 1953-55; played in six World Series with the Dodgers and batted .286 with 11 home runs; nicknamed "Duke of Flatbush"; in 18 seasons hit 407 home runs, scored 1,259 runs and had 1,333 RBI.

Annika Sorenstam (b. Oct. 9, 1970): Swedish golfer; has won 7 women's majors through 2004; 6-time Rolex Player of the Year (1995,97-98, 2001-03); shot an LPGA-record 59 in round 2 of the 2001 Standard Register Ping; LPGA all-time leading money winner; in 2003 she became first woman in 58 years to play on men's PGA Tour (via a sponsor's exemption); shot 71-74 but missed the cut at the Colonial by 4 strokes.

Sammy Sosa (b. Nov. 12, 1968): Baseball OF; slugging Chicago Cub who surpassed Roger Maris' season home run record (61), just after Mark McGwire did in 1998 and finished the year with 66; followed that up with seasons of 63, 50 and 64 HRs; 1998 NL MVP; 7-time All-Star (1995,98-2002,2004).

Javier Sotomayor (b. Oct. 13, 1967): Cuban high jumper; first man to clear 8 feet (8-0) on July 29, 1989; won gold medal at 1992 Olympics with jump of only 7-ft, 8-in.; broke world record with leap of 8-0½ in 1993; had a controversial drug suspension reduced, which allowed him to participate in 2000 Olympics; won the silver medal in Sydney with a leap of 7-7¼.

Warren Spahn (b. Apr. 23, 1921, d. Nov. 23, 2003): Baseball LHP; led NL in wins 8 times; won 20 or more games 13 times; Cy Young winner in 1957; most career wins (363) by a lefthander.

Tris Speaker (b. Apr. 4, 1888, d. Dec. 8, 1958): Baseball OF; all-time leader in outfield assists (449) and doubles (792); had a .344 career BA and 3,515 hits.

J.G. Taylor Spink (b. Nov. 6, 1888, d. Dec. 7, 1962): Publisher of *The Sporting News* from 1914-62; BBWAA annual meritorious service award named after him.

Leon Spinks (b. July 11, 1953): Boxing; won heavyweight crown in split decision over Muhammad Ali in Feb. 1978; Ali regained title seven months later; won gold medal in light heavyweight division at 1976 Olympics; brother Michael won the heavyweight title in 1983; were the only brothers to hold world titles; known more for frequent traffic violations and lavish lifestyle than bouts late in career; filed for bankruptcy in 1986.

Mark Spitz (b. Feb. 10, 1950): American swimmer; set 23 world and 35 U.S. records; won all-time record 7 gold medals (4 individual, 3 relay) in 1972 Olympics; also won 4 medals (2 gold, a silver and a bronze) in 1968 Games for a total of 11; comeback attempt at age 41 foundered in 1991.

Latrell Sprewell (b. Sept. 8, 1970): Basketball G; former NBA All-Star who made headlines in 1997 after being suspended by the NBA for attacking Golden State Warriors head coach P.J. Carlesimo during a practice.

Lyn St. James (b. Mar. 13, 1947): Auto racer; one of just 3 women to qualify for the Indianapolis 500; best finish in the race came in 1992 when she came in 11th and won Indianapolis 500 Rookie of the Year.

Amos Alonzo Stagg (b. Aug. 16, 1862, d. Mar. 17, 1965): Football innovator; coached at U. of Chicago for 41 seasons and College of the Pacific for 14 more; 314-199-35 record; elected to both college football and basketball Halls of Fame.

Willie Stargell (b. Mar. 6, 1940, d. Apr. 9, 2001): Baseball OF-1B; "Pops"; led NL in home runs twice (1971,73); 475 career HRs; NL co-MVP and World Series MVP in 1979.

Bart Starr (b. Jan. 9, 1934): Football QB; led Green Bay to 5 NFL titles and 2 Super Bowl wins from 1961-67; regular season MVP in 1966; MVP of Super Bowls I and II.

Roger Staubach (b. Feb. 5, 1942): Football QB; Heisman Trophy winner as Navy junior in 1963; led Dallas to 2 Super Bowl wins (1972,78) and was Super Bowl MVP in 1972; 5-time leading passer in NFC (1971,73,77-79).

George Steinbrenner (b. July 4, 1930): Baseball; principal owner of NY Yankees since 1973; teams have won 10 pennants and 6 World Series (1977-78,96,98,99,00); has changed managers 21 times and GMs 11 times in 31 years; ordered by baseball commish Fay Vincent in 1990 to surrender control of club for dealings with small-time gambler; reinstated in 1993.

Casey Stengel (b. July 30, 1890, d. Sept. 29, 1975): Baseball; player for 14 years and manager for 25; outfielder and lifetime .284 hitter with 5 clubs (1912-25); guided NY Yankees to 10 AL pennants and 7 World Series titles from 1949-60; 1st NY Mets skipper from 1962-65.

Ingemar Stenmark (b. Mar. 18, 1956): Swedish alpine skier; 3-time World Cup overall champ (1976-78); posted 86 World Cup wins in 16 years; won 2 gold medals at 1980 Olympics.

Helen Stephens (b. Feb. 3, 1918, d. Jan. 17, 1994): Track & Field; set 3 world records in 100-yard dash and 4 more in 100 meters in 1935-36; won gold medals in 100 meters and 4x100-meter relay in 1936 Olympics; retired in 1937.

Woody Stephens (b. Sept. 1, 1913, d. Aug. 22, 1998): Horse racing; trainer who saddled an unprecedented 5 straight winners in Belmont Stakes (1982-86); also had two Kentucky Derby winners (1974,84) and one Preakness winner (1952); trained 1982 Horse of Year Conquistador Cielo; won Eclipse award as nation's top trainer in 1983.

David Stern (b. Sept. 22, 1942): Basketball; marketing expert and NBA commissioner since 1984; took office the year Michael Jordan turned pro; league has grown from 23 teams to 30 during his watch and opened offices worldwide; oversaw launch of WNBA in 1997.

Teófilo Stevenson (b. Mar. 29, 1952): Cuban boxer; won 3 consecutive gold medals as Olympic heavyweight (1972,76,80); was denied a chance to win a fourth when Cuba boycotted 1984 Los Angeles Games; did not turn pro.

Jackie Stewart (b. June 11, 1939): Auto racer; won 27 Formula One races and 3 world driving titles from 1965-73.

John Stockton (b. Mar 26, 1962): Basketball G; all-time NBA leader in every major assist category, including most in a season (1,164) and most in a career (15,806); also the NBA's all-time leader in steals (3,265); All-NBA team in '94 and '95; member of 1992 and '96 US Olympic basketball teams; 10-time All-Star; played 19 seasons with Utah Jazz—18 of them with Karl Malone—perfecting the pick and roll.

Curtis Strange (b. Jan. 30, 1955): Golfer; won consecutive U.S. Open titles (1988-89); 3-time leading money winner on PGA Tour (1985,87-88); first PGA player to win $1 million in one year (1988); captain of the 2002 U.S. Ryder Cup team.

Picabo Street (b. Apr. 3, 1971): Skiing; 2-time Olympic medalist, gold (Super G in 1998) and silver (downhill in 1994); her 1995 World Cup downhill series title first-ever by U.S. woman, she repeated the feat in 1996.

Kerri Strug (b. Nov. 19, 1977): Gymnastics; delivered the most dramatic moment of the 1996 Summer Olympics when she completed a vault (9.712) after spraining her ankle; the second vault helped assure the first all-around gold medal for a US Women's gymnastics team.

Louise Suggs (b. Sept. 7, 1923): Golfer; won 11 majors and 58 LPGA events overall from 1949-62.

James E. Sullivan (b. Nov. 18, 1862, d. Sept. 16, 1914): Track & Field; pioneer who founded Amateur Athletic Union (AAU) in 1888; director of St. Louis Olympic Games in 1904; AAU's annual Sullivan Award for performance and sportsmanship named after him.

John L. Sullivan (b. Oct. 15, 1858, d. Feb. 2, 1918): Boxer; nicknamed "The Boston Strong Boy"; world heavyweight champion (1882-92); last of bare-knuckle champions, beating Jake Kilrain after 75 rounds in 1889; was knocked out by "Gentleman" Jim Corbett in the 21st round in 1892, never fought again.

Pat Summitt (b. June 14, 1952): Basketball; women's basketball coach at Tennessee (1974—); entered 2004-05 season as all-time leader in career victories with 852; coached 1984 US women's basketball team to its first Olympic gold medal; coached Lady Vols to 6 national championships (1987, 89,91,96,97,98).

Don Sutton (b. April 2, 1945): Baseball RHP; won 324 games and tossed 58 shutouts in his 23-year career; recorded NL record five career 1-hitters; played with Dodgers, Astros, Brewers, Athletics, Angels and was a 4-time All-Star; elected to Hall of Fame in 1998.

Ichiro Suzuki (b. Oct. 22, 1973): Baseball OF; became the 2nd player (Fred Lynn) to win AL Rookie of the Year and MVP in same year (2001); 1st Japanese-born position player to play in the majors; won 7 consecutive Japanese batting titles (1994-2000) and has won two more in AL (2001,04); broke George Sisler's 84-year-old MLB season hits record in 2004.

Lynn Swann (b. Mar. 7, 1952): Football WR; played nine seasons with Pittsburgh (1974-82); appeared in four Super Bowls and had 16 catches for 364 yards and three TDs; named MVP of Super Bowl X for 4 catch, 161 yard, 1 TD performance.

Barry Switzer (b. Oct. 5, 1937): Football; coached Oklahoma to 3 national titles (1974-75,85); 4th in all-time winning pct list at .837 (157-29-4); resigned in 1989 after OU was slapped with 3-year NCAA probation; hired as Dallas Cowboys head coach in 1994 and led team to victory in Super Bowl XXX in 1996.

Sheryl Swoopes (b. Mar. 25, 1971): Basketball; forward for WNBA's Houston Comets; 3-time WNBA regular season MVP (2000,02,03); Defensive Player of the Year in 2000, 3-time Olympic gold medalist (1996,2000,2004); led Texas Tech to Div. I NCAA championship in 1993; consensus National Player of the Year in 1993.

Paul Tagliabue (b. Nov. 24, 1940): Football; NFL attorney who was elected league's 4th commissioner in 1989; ushered in salary cap in 1994; the league has expanded from 28 teams to 32 in his tenure.

Anatoli Tarasov (b. 1918, d. June 23, 1995): Hockey; coached Soviet Union to 9 straight world championships and 3 Olympic gold medals (1964, 68,72).

Jerry Tarkanian (b. Aug. 30, 1930): Basketball; amassed 778 wins in 31 years at Long Beach St., UNLV and Fresno St.; led UNLV to 4 Final Fours and 1 national title (1990); fought battle with NCAA over purity of UNLV program; quit as coach after giving 26-2 in 1991-92; fired after 20 games (9-11) as coach of NBA San Antonio Spurs in 1992.

Fran Tarkenton (b. Feb. 3, 1940): Football QB; scrambling two-time NFL All-Pro (1973,75); 1975 Player of the Year; threw for 47,003 yards and 342 TDs (both former NFL records) in 18 seasons with Vikings and N.Y. Giants; selected to 9 Pro Bowls; inducted into Pro Football Hall of Fame in 1986.

Chuck Taylor (b. June 24, 1901, d. June 23, 1969): Converse traveling salesman whose name came to grace the classic, high-top canvas basketball sneakers known as "Chucks"; over 750 million pairs have been sold since 1917; he also ran clinics worldwide and edited Converse Basketball Yearbook (1922-68).

Lawrence Taylor (b. Feb. 4, 1959): Football LB; All-America at North Carolina (1980); only defensive player in NFL history to be consensus Player of Year (1986); led N.Y. Giants to Super Bowl titles in 1986 and '90 seasons; played in 10 Pro Bowls (1981-90); retired after 1993 season with 132½ sacks; had several drug-related arrests in retirement; inducted into Hall of Fame in 1999.

Marshall (Major) Taylor (b. Nov. 26, 1878, d. June 21, 1932): Cyclist; Considered one of the first African-American sports heroes; held seven world cycling records at the turn of the century, racing mostly in Europe, Australia and New Zealand after being barred from many events in the U.S. due to racial prejudices; won the world one-mile championship in 1899.

Gustavo Thoeni (b. Feb. 28, 1951): Italian alpine skier; 4-time World Cup overall champion (1971-73,75); won giant slalom at 1972 Olympics.

Isiah Thomas (b. Apr. 30, 1961): Basketball; led Indiana to NCAA title as sophomore and Final 4 MOP in 1981; consensus All-America guard in '81; led Detroit to 2 NBA titles (1989,1990); NBA Finals MVP in 1990; 3-time All-NBA 1st team (1984-86); elected to Hall of Fame in 2000; currently president of the N.Y. Knicks.

Thurman Thomas (b. May 16, 1966): Football RB; 3-time AFC rushing leader (1990-91,93); 2-time All-Pro (1990-91); 1991 NFL Player of Year; led Buffalo to 4 straight Super Bowls (1991-94).

Daley Thompson (b. July 30, 1958): British Track & Field; won consecutive gold medals in decathlon at 1980 and '84 Olympics.

Jenny Thompson (b. Feb. 26, 1973): American swimmer; 8-time Olympic gold medalist (all in relays) and winner of 12 Olympic medals overall, more than any other American; competed in 5 Olympic Games (1988,92,96,2000,04) won 3 golds (4x100 free, 4x200 free, 4x100 medley) and 1 bronze (100m freestyle) at Sydney.

John Thompson (b. Sept. 2, 1941): Basketball; coached centers Patrick Ewing, Alonzo Mourning and Dikembe Mutombo at Georgetown; reached NCAA tourney final 3 out of 4 years with Ewing, winning title in 1984; also led Hoyas to 6 Big East tourney titles; coached 1988 U.S. Olympic team to bronze medal; retired abruptly during 1999 season with 27-year mark of 596-239.

Bobby Thomson (b. Oct. 25, 1923): Baseball OF; career .270 hitter who won the 1951 NL pennant for the NY Giants with a 1-out, 3-run HR in the bottom of the 9th inning of Game 3 of a best-of-3 playoff with Brooklyn; the pitcher was Ralph Branca, the count was 0-1 and the Dodgers were ahead 4-2; the Giants had trailed Brooklyn by 13½ games on Aug. 11.

Ian Thorpe (b. Oct. 13, 1982): Australian swimmer; 5-time gold medalist; won 400m free at Sydney Olympics (breaking his own world record) and silver in 200m free; won gold and broke the world record in the 4x100m and 4x200 free relays; won 200m free and 400m free Olympic gold at Athens in 2004; 2002 Jesse Owens Award winner.

Jim Thorpe (b. May 28, 1887, d. Mar. 28, 1953): Native American multi-sport superstar; 2-time All-America halfback at Carlisle; won both pentathlon and decathlon gold medals at 1912 Olympics; stripped of medals a month later for playing semi-pro baseball prior to Games (medals restored in 1982); played major league baseball (1913-19) and pro football (1920-26,28); became first president of NFL (then known as the APFA) in 1920; chosen "Athlete of the Half Century" by AP in 1950.

Bill Tilden (b. Feb. 10, 1893, d. June 5, 1953): Tennis; won 7 U.S. and 3 Wimbledon titles in 1920s; led U.S. to 7 straight Davis Cup victories (1920-26).

Tinker to Evers to Chance Chicago Cubs double play combination from 1903-10; immortalized in poem by New York sportswriter Franklin P. Adams — SS Joe Tinker (1880-1948), 2B Johnny Evers (1883-1947) and 1B Frank Chance (1877-1924); all 3 managed the Cubs and made the Hall of Fame.

Y.A. Tittle (b. Oct. 24, 1926): Football QB; Yelberton Abraham Tittle played 17 years in AAFC and NFL; All-Pro 4 times; league MVP with San Francisco (1957) and NY Giants (1962, 63); passed for 28,339 career yards.

Alberto Tomba (b. Dec. 19, 1966): Italian alpine skier; winner of 5 Olympic medals (3 gold, 2 silver); became 1st alpine skier to win gold medals in 2 consecutive Winter Games when he won the slalom and giant slalom in 1988 then repeated in the GS in '92; also won silvers in slalom in 1992 and '94.

Dara Torres (b. April 15, 1967): Swimmer; her 9 career Olympic medals (4G, 1S, 4B) are 2nd-most for an American woman; took a 7-year hiatus before returning to the pool to win 5 medals in Sydney in 2000; participated in 4 Olympic Games overall (1984,88,92,2000).

Vladislav Tretiak (b. Apr. 25, 1952): Hockey G; led USSR to Olympic gold medals in 1972 and '76; starred for Soviets against Team Canada in 1972, and again in 2 Canada Cups (1976,81).

Lee Trevino (b. Dec. 1, 1939): Golfer; 2-time winner of 3 majors—U.S. Open (1968, 71), British Open (1971-72) and PGA (1974,84); Player of Year once on PGA Tour (1971) and 3 times with Seniors (1990,92,94); 29 PGA Tour and 29 Senior Tour wins.

Felix Trinidad (b. Jan. 10, 1973): Puerto Rican boxer; former WBC/IBF welterweight champion; won WBC belt with a majority decision over Oscar De La Hoya in Sept., 1999; stepped up to junior middleweight and won the WBA title from David Reid in March, 2000; moved to middleweight and lost in a 12th-round TKO to Bernard Hopkins in Sept. 2001; knocked out Ricardo Mayorga in 2004 comeback fight.

Bryan Trottier (b. July 17, 1956): Hockey C; led NY Islanders to 4 straight Stanley Cups (1980-83); Rookie of Year (1976); scoring champion (134 points) and regular season MVP in 1979; playoff MVP (1980); added 5th and 6th Cups with Pittsburgh in 1991 and '92; entered Hockey Hall of Fame in 1997; head coach of NY Rangers in 2002, fired in 2003.

Gene Tunney (b. May 25, 1897, d. Nov. 7, 1978): Boxer; world heavyweight champion from 1926-28; beat 31-year-old champ Jack Dempsey in unanimous 10 round decision in 1926; beat him again in famous "long count" rematch in '27; quit while still champion in 1928 with 65-1-1 record and 47 KOs.

Ted Turner (b. Nov. 19, 1938): Sportsman and TV mogul; skippered *Courageous* to America's Cup win in 1977; one-time owner of MLB Atlanta Braves, NBA Hawks and NHL Thrashers; founder of CNN, TNT and TBS; founder of Goodwill Games; 1991 *Time* Man of Year.

Mike Tyson (b. June 30, 1966): Boxer; youngest (age 19) to win heavyweight title (WBC in 1986); undisputed champ from 1987 until upset loss to 42-1 shot Buster Douglas on Feb. 10, 1990, in Tokyo; found guilty on Feb. 10, 1992, of raping 18-year-old Miss Black America contestant Desiree Washington in Indianapolis on July 19, 1991; sentenced to 6-year prison term; released May 9, 1995 after serving 3 years; reclaimed WBC and WBA belts with wins over Frank Bruno and Bruce Seldon in 1996; lost WBA title to Evander Holyfield in 1996; he bit Holyfield's ear twice during their 1997 WBA title rematch; was KO'd in 8th round by Lennox Lewis in 2002; despite earning $300m in his career, he filed for bankruptcy in 2003.

Wyomia Tyus (b. Aug. 29, 1945): Track & Field; 1st woman to win consecutive Olympic gold medals in 100m (1964-68).

Peter Ueberroth (b. Sept. 2, 1937): Organizer of 1984 Summer Olympics in LA; 1984 *Time* Man of Year; baseball commissioner from 1984-89; headed Rebuild Los Angeles for one year after 1992 riots; currently chairman of USOC.

Johnny Unitas (b. May 7, 1933, d. Sept. 11, 2002): Football QB; Big-game field general who led Baltimore Colts to 2 NFL titles (1958-59) and a Super Bowl win (1971); All-Pro 5 times; 3-time MVP (1959,64,67); selected to 10 Pro Bowls; passed for 40,239 career yards and 290 TDs.

Al Unser Jr. (b. Apr. 19, 1962): Auto racer; 2-time CART-IndyCar national champion (1990,94); 2-time Indy 500 winer (1992,94), giving Unser family 9 overall titles at the Brickyard; retired in 2004 with 31 CART wins in 19 years; left CART for Indy Racing League in 2000; son of Al and nephew of Bobby.

Al Unser Sr. (b. May 29, 1939): Auto racer; 3-time USAC-CART national champion (1970,83,85); 4-time winner of Indy 500 (1970-71,78,87); retired in 1994 with 39 wins; younger brother of Bobby and father of Al Jr.

Bobby Unser (b. Feb. 20, 1934): Auto racer; 2-time USAC-CART national champion (1968,74); 3-time winner of Indy 500 (1968,75,81); retired after 1981 season; fifth all-time with 35 career wins.

Gene Upshaw (b. Aug. 15, 1945): Football G; 2-time All-AFL and 3-time All-NFL selection with Oakland; helped lead Raiders to 2 Super Bowl titles in 1976 and '80 seasons; executive director of NFL Players Assn. since 1987; agreed to application of salary cap in 1994.

Jim Valvano (b. Mar. 10, 1946, d. Apr. 28, 1993): Basketball; coach at N.C. State whose team upset Houston to win national title in 1983; in 19 seasons as a coach appeared in 8 NCAA tournaments; twice voted ACC Coach of the Year; career record 346-212; AD at N.C. State (1986-89) when a recruiting and admissions scandal forced him out of the job; worked as a broadcaster for ESPN and ABC; died after a year-long battle with cancer; The V Foundation for cancer research is named for him.

Norm Van Brocklin (b. Mar. 15, 1926, d. May 2, 1983): Football QB-P; led NFL in passing 3 times and punting twice; led LA Rams (1951) and Philadelphia (1960) to NFL titles; MVP in 1960.

Amy Van Dyken (b. Feb. 17, 1973): Swimming; first American woman to win four gold medals in one Olympics (1996); won the individual 50m freestyle, 100m butterfly, and was on the US team for the 4x100 freestyle and 4x50 medley; won gold at Sydney in 2000 as part of the US 4x100 freestyle relay.

Johnny Vander Meer (b. Nov. 2, 1914, d. Oct. 6, 1997): Baseball LHP; only major leaguer to pitch consecutive no-hitters (June 11 & 15, 1938).

Harold S. Vanderbilt (b. July 6, 1884, d. July 4, 1970): Sportsman; successfully defended America's Cup 3 times (1930, 34,37); also invented contract bridge in 1926.

Glenna Collett Vare (b. June 20, 1903, d. Feb. 10, 1989): Golfer; won record 6 U.S. Women's Amateur titles from 1922-35; "the female Bobby Jones."

Andy Varipapa (b. Mar. 31, 1891, d. Aug. 25, 1984): Bowler; trick-shot artist; won consecutive All-Star match game titles (1947-48) at age 55 and 56.

Bill Veeck (b. Feb. 9, 1914, d. Jan. 2, 1986): Maverick baseball executive; owned AL teams in Cleveland, St. Louis and Chicago from 1946-80; introduced ballpark giveaways, exploding scoreboards, Wrigley Field's ivy-covered walls and midget Eddie Gaedel; won World Series with Indians (1948) and pennant with White Sox (1959).

Jacques Villeneuve (b. Apr. 9, 1971): Canadian auto racer; Indianapolis 500 runner-up and Indy-Car Rookie of Year in 1994; won 500 and IndyCar driving championship in 1995; jumped to Formula One racing in 1996 and won the F1 title in 1997.

Fay Vincent (b. May 29, 1938): Baseball; became 8th commissioner after death of A. Bartlett Giamatti in 1989; presided over World Series earthquake, owners' lockout and banishment of NY Yankees owner George Steinbrenner in his first year on the job; contentious relationship with owners resulted in his resignation on Sept. 7, 1992, four days after 18-9 "no confidence" vote.

Lasse Viren (b. July 22, 1949): Finnish runner; won gold medals at 5,000 and 10,000 meters in 1972 Munich Olympics; repeated 5,000/10,000 double in 1976 Games and added a fifth place finish in the marathon.

Dick Vitale (b. June 9, 1939): Broadcaster; Radio and television commentator for ESPN and ABC Sports known for his enthusiastic, almost spastic style; had successful college and pro basketball coaching career with the University of Detroit (1973-77) and the Detroit Pistons (1978-79).

Lanny Wadkins (b. Dec. 5, 1949): Golfer; member of 8 U.S. Ryder Cup teams and captain of 1995 team; 21 PGA Tour wins.

Honus Wagner (b. Feb. 24, 1874, d. Dec. 6, 1955): Baseball SS; hit .300 for 17 consecutive seasons (1897-1913) with Louisville and Pittsburgh; led NL in batting 8 times; ended career with 3,430 career hits, a .329 average and 722 stolen bases.

Lisa Wagner (b. May 19, 1961): Bowler; 4-time LPBT Player of Year (1983,86,88,93); 1980's Bowler of Decade; first woman to earn $100,000 in a season; winner of 32 pro titles.

Grete Waitz (b. Oct. 1, 1953): Norwegian runner; 9-time winner of New York City Marathon from 1978-88; won silver medal at 1984 Olympics.

Jersey Joe Walcott (b. Jan. 31, 1914, d. Feb. 27, 1994): Boxer; oldest heavyweight (37) to win the championship (until George Foreman beat his record in 1994); lost two championship bouts before knocking out Ezzard Charles in the seventh round in 1951; lost the title the following year to Rocky Marciano; won 50 bouts, 30 by knockout, lost 17 and fought one draw as a professional; later became sheriff of Camden County, NJ.

Doak Walker (b. Jan. 1, 1927, d. Sept. 27, 1998): Football HB; won Heisman Trophy as SMU junior in 1948; led Detroit to 2 NFL titles (1952-53); All-Pro 4 times in 6 years.

Herschel Walker (b. Mar. 3, 1962): Football RB; led Georgia to national title as freshman in 1980; won Heisman in 1982 then jumped to upstart USFL in '83; signed by Dallas Cowboys after USFL folded; led NFL in rushing in 1988; traded to Minnesota in 1989 for 5 players and 6 draft picks.

Rusty Wallace (b. Aug. 14, 1956): Auto racing; NASCAR Winston Cup champion in 1989 and runner-up in 1980, 1988 and 1993; recorded 55 victories and has won over $30 million in earnings in 25 years of racing.

Bill Walsh (b. Nov. 30, 1931): Football; Hall of Fame coach and GM of 3 Super Bowl winners with San Francisco (1982,85,89); retired after 1989 Super Bowl; returned to college coaching in 1992 for his second stint at Stanford; retired again after 1994 season; returned as 49er GM from 1999-2001.

Bill Walton (b. Nov. 5, 1952): Basketball C; 3-time College Player of Year (1972-74); led UCLA to 2 national titles (1972-73); led Portland to NBA title as MVP in 1977; regular season MVP in 1978; won 1986 NBA title with Boston.

Darrell Waltrip (b. Feb. 5, 1947): Auto racing; 3-time NASCAR Winston Cup champion (1981,82,85); 84 career Winston Cup wins and 59 poles.

Arch Ward (b. Dec. 27, 1896, d. July 9, 1955): Promoter and sports editor of *Chicago Tribune* from 1930-55; founder of baseball All-Star Game (1933), Chicago College All-Star Football Game (1934) and the All-America Football Conference (1946-49).

Charlie Ward (b. Oct. 12, 1970): Football QB and Basketball G; 1993 Heisman winner with national champion Florida St.; won Sullivan Award (1993); 3-year starter for FSU basketball team; not taken in NFL draft (made it clear he was pursuing NBA career); 1st round pick of NY Knicks in 1994 NBA draft.

Glenn (Pop) Warner (b. Apr. 5, 1871, d. Sept. 7, 1954): Football innovator; coached at 7 colleges over 49 years; 319 career wins, fourth all-time; produced 47 All-Americas, including Jim Thorpe and Ernie Nevers.

Kurt Warner (b. June 22, 1971): Football QB; former Arena leaguer who led the St. Louis Rams to 2000 Super Bowl win; threw for a record 414 yards and was voted Super Bowl MVP; lost Super Bowl in 2002 with Rams; 2-time NFL MVP (1999,2001).

Tom Watson (b. Sept. 4, 1949): Golfer; 6-time PGA Player of the Year (1977-80,82,84); has won 5 British Opens, 2 Masters and a U.S. Open; 4-time Ryder Cup member and captain of 1993 team; 39 PGA tour wins.

Earl Weaver (b. Aug. 14, 1930): Baseball; managed the Baltimore Orioles to 6 Eastern Division titles, four AL pennants and a World Series victory in 1970; was ejected 91 times and suspended four times for outbursts against umpires; record of 1,480-1,060 from 1968-82 and 1985-86.

Alan Webb (b. Jan. 13, 1983): Track; on May 27, 2001 at the Prefontaine Classic, he ran a mile in 3:53.43 to break Jim Ryun's 36-year-old national high school record.

Karrie Webb (b. Dec. 21, 1974): Australian golfer; youngest woman (26) to win career Grand Slam; her win in the 2002 British Open made her the first player to win the "Super Grand Slam" (5 different majors) and gave her 6 major titles; 2-time Rolex Player of the Year (1999-2000)

Dick Weber (b. Dec. 23, 1929): Bowler; 3-time PBA Bowler of the Year (1961,63,65); won 30 PBA titles in 4 decades; father of Pete.

Pete Weber (b. Aug. 21, 1962): Bowler; 2nd on all-time PBA money list; 1990 PBA Rookie of the Year; inducted into PBA Hall of Fame (1998); has 31 PBA titles; son of Dick.

Johnny Weissmuller (b. June 2, 1904, d. Jan. 20 1984): American swimmer; won 3 gold medals (100m free, 400m free, 4x200m free) at 1924 Olympics and 2 more at 1928 Games (100m free and 4x200m free); set 51 world records; became Hollywood's most famous Tarzan.

Jerry West (b. May 28, 1938): Basketball G; 2-time All-America and NCAA Final 4 MOP (1959) at West Virginia; led 1960 U.S. Olympic team to gold medal; 10-time All-NBA 1st-team; NBA finals MVP (1969); led LA Lakers to NBA title once as player (1972) and then 6 more times (1980,82,85,87,88,00) as an executive in various positions with the club; hired as President of Basketball Ops. by Memphis Grizzlies in 2002; his silhouette serves as the NBA's logo.

Pernell Whitaker (b. Jan. 2, 1964): Boxer; won Olympic gold medal as lightweight in 1984; won 4 world championships as lightweight, jr. welterweight, welterweight and jr. middleweight; outfought but failed to beat Julio Cesar Chavez when 1993 welterweight title defense ended in controversial draw; pro record of 41-3-1 (17 KOs); nicknamed "Sweet Pea".

Bill White (b. Jan. 28, 1934): Baseball; former NL president and highest ranking black executive in sports from 1989-94; as 1st baseman, won 7 Gold Gloves and hit .286 with 202 HRs in 13 seasons.

Byron (Whizzer) White (b. June 8, 1917, d. Apr. 15, 2002): Football; All-America HB at Colorado (1937); signed with Pittsburgh in 1938 for the then largest contract in pro history ($15,800); took Rhodes Scholarship in 1939; returned to NFL in 1940 to lead league in rushing and retired in 1941; named to U.S. Supreme Court by President Kennedy in 1962 and stepped down in 1993.

Reggie White (b. Dec. 19, 1961): Football DE; consensus All-America in 1983 at Tennessee; 7-time All-NFL (1986-92) with Philadelphia; signed as free agent with Green Bay in 1993; made headlines in 1998 after making controversial public comments about gays and minorities; 2nd all-time in NFL sacks (198).

Kathy Whitworth (b. Sept. 27, 1939): Golf; 7-time LPGA Player of the Year (1966-69,71-73); won 6 majors; 88 tour wins, most on LPGA or PGA tour.

Hoyt Wilhelm (b. July 26, 1923, d. Aug. 23, 2002): Baseball RHP; Knuckleballer who is 4th all-time in games pitched (1,070) and 1st in games finished (651) and games won in relief (123); career ERA of 2.52 and 227 saves; 1st reliever inducted into Hall of Fame (1985); threw no-hitter vs. NY Yankees (1958); also hit lone HR of career in first major league at bat (1952); won Purple Heart at the Battle of the Bulge.

Lenny Wilkens (b. Oct. 28, 1937): Basketball; NBA's all-time winningest coach; MVP of 1960 NIT as Providence guard; played 15 years in NBA, including 4 as player-coach; 9-time All-Star and MVP of 1971 game; coached Seattle to 1979 NBA title; Coach of Year in 1994 with Atlanta; career record of 1395-1231 including playoffs with 6 NBA teams; coached USA basketball team to gold medal in 1996; member of the basketball hall of fame as player and coach.

Dominique Wilkins (b. Jan. 12, 1960): Basketball F; prolific scorer and ferocious dunker who led NBA in scoring (30.3 ppg) in 1986 with Atlanta; All-NBA 1st team in 1986; 2-time NBA slam dunk champion; nicknamed "The Human Highlight Film".

Bud Wilkinson (b. Apr. 23, 1916, d. Feb. 9, 1994): Football; played on 1936 national championship team at Minnesota; coached Oklahoma to 3 national titles (1950, 55, 56); won 4 Orange and 2 Sugar Bowls; teams had winning streaks of 47 (1953-57) and 31 (1948-50); retired after 1963 season with 145-29-4 record in 17 years; also coached St. Louis of NFL to 9-20 record from 1978-79.

Ricky Williams (b. May 21, 1977): Football RB; became all-time NCAA Div. I-A leader in rushing yards (6,279) and TDs (75) at Texas but has been passed in both categories; 1998 Heisman Trophy winner; Mike Ditka and New Orleans Saints traded their entire draft to take him fifth overall in 1999 NFL draft; traded to Miami Dolphins in 2002; retired suddenly just prior to 2004 season.

Serena Williams (b. Sept. 26, 1981): Tennis; beat Martina Hingis for 1999 U.S. Open championship to become the first African-American woman to win a Grand Slam title since Althea Gibson in 1958; won Wimbledon, the French Open and U.S. Open in 2002 and Australian and Wimbledon in 2003, defeating big sister Venus in the final of each; has won career doubles grand slam with Venus.

Ted Williams (b. Aug. 30, 1918, d. July 5, 2002): Baseball OF; led AL in batting 6 times, and HRs and RBI 4 times each; won Triple Crown twice (1942,47); 2-time MVP (1946,49); last player to bat .400 when he hit .406 in 1941; Marine Corps combat pilot who missed 3 full seasons during WWII (1943-45) and most of two others (1952-53) during Korean War; hit .344 lifetime with 521 HRs in 19 years with Boston Red Sox; also known as avid fisherman; furor erupted following his death when plans to keep his body frozen at a cryogenic lab were made public.

Venus Williams (b. June 17, 1980): Tennis; won career doubles grand slam with sister Serena; winner of 2 Wimbledon (2000,01) and 2 U.S. Open (2000, 01) singles titles; 2000 Olympic singles and doubles (with sister Serena) gold medalist; recorded fastest serve in WTA history with 127 mph blast in 1998.

Walter Ray Williams Jr. (b. Oct. 6, 1959): Bowling and Horseshoes; 6-time PBA Bowler of Year (1986,93,96,97,98,2003); all-time leading money winner on the PBA Tour; has 39 PBA titles; won 6 World Horseshoe Pitching titles.

Hack Wilson (b. Apr. 26, 1900, d. Nov. 23, 1948): Baseball; as a Chicago Cub, he produced one of baseball's most outstanding seasons in 1930 with 56 home runs, .356 batting average, 105 walks and, most amazingly, a major league record 191 RBIs that still stands; finished career with 1,461 hits, 244 homers, 1,062 RBIs; member of Baseball Hall of Fame.

Dave Winfield (b. Oct. 3, 1951): Baseball OF-DH; selected in 4 major sports league drafts in 1973—NFL, NBA, ABA, and MLB; chose baseball and played in 12 All-Star Games over 22-year career; at age 41, helped lead Toronto to World Series title in 1992; 3,110 hits and 465 HRs.

Katarina Witt (b. Dec. 3, 1965): East German figure skater; 4-time world champion (1984-85,87-88); won consecutive Olympic gold medals (1984,88).

John Wooden (b. Oct. 14, 1910): Basketball; College Player of Year at Purdue in 1932; coached UCLA to 88 straight wins (1971-74), 10 national titles (1964-65,67-73,75); inducted into the Hall of Fame as both player and coach; career college coaching record of 664-162 over 29 years.

Tiger Woods (b. Dec. 30, 1975): Golfer; 3-time winner of U.S. Amateur (1994-96); in first full year on the PGA Tour, he won 6 events and broke the single season money record; won 1997 Masters by a record 18 under par and 13 stroke margin of victory; won second major at 1999 PGA Championship; in 2000 won the U.S. Open at Pebble Beach by a record 15 strokes, the British Open by 8 strokes and the PGA Championship in a playoff; one of only five players to win all four Grand Slam titles (others are Hogan, Nicklaus, Player and Sarazen); held all 4 Major titles simultaneously with his win at 2001 Masters; won 2 more majors in 2002 (Masters and U.S. Open); the all-time career money leader on the PGA Tour.

Mickey Wright (b. Feb. 14, 1935): Golfer; won 3 of 4 majors (LPGA, U.S. Open, Titleholders) in 1961; 4-time winner of both U.S. Open and LPGA titles; 82 career wins including 13 majors.

Early Wynn (b. Jan. 6, 1920, d. Mar. 4, 1999): Baseball RHP; won 20 games 5 times; Cy Young winner in 1959; 300-244 record in 23 years.

Kristi Yamaguchi (b. July 12, 1971): Figure Skating; finished second in the 1991 American nationals but won the world title that year; dominated the sport in 1992 by winning the national, world and Olympic titles and then turned professional.

Cale Yarborough (b. Mar. 27, 1940): Auto racer; 3-time NASCAR national champion (1976-78); 4-time winner of Daytona 500 (1968,77,83-84); 83 career NASCAR wins.

Carl Yastrzemski (b. Aug. 22, 1939): Baseball OF; led AL in batting 3 times; won Triple Crown and MVP in 1967; had 3,419 hits and 452 HRs in 23 years with Boston Red Sox; member of Hall of Fame.

Cy Young (b. Mar. 29, 1867, d. Nov. 4, 1955): Baseball RHP; all-time leader in wins (511), losses (313), complete games (751) and innings pitched (7,356); had career 2.63 ERA in 22 years (1890-1911); 30-game winner 5 times and 20-game winner 11 other times; threw three no-hitters and a perfect game (1904); annual AL and NL pitching awards named after him.

Dick Young (b. Oct. 17, 1917, d. Aug. 31, 1987): Confrontational sportswriter for 44 years with NY tabloids; as baseball beat writer and columnist, he led change from flowery prose to hard-nosed reporting.

Sheila Young (b. Oct. 14, 1950): Speed skater and cyclist; 1st U.S. athlete to win 3 medals at Winter Olympics (1976); won speed skating overall and sprint cycling world titles in 1976.

Steve Young (b. Oct. 11, 1961): Football QB; All-America at BYU (1983); NFL Player of Year (1992) with SF 49ers; only QB to lead NFL in passer rating 4 straight years (1991-94); rating of 112.8 in 1994 is highest ever; threw record 6 TD passes in MVP performance in Super Bowl XXIX; retired with NFL records for highest passer rating (96.8) and completion pct. (64.4); 232 career TD passes and 33,124 yards.

Robin Yount (b. Sept. 16, 1955): Baseball SS-OF; AL MVP at 2 positions—as SS in 1982 and OF in '89; retired after 1993 season with 3,142 hits, 251 HRs and a major-league-record 123 sacrifice flies after 20 seasons with Brewers; inducted into Hall of Fame in 1999.

Steve Yzerman (b. May 9, 1965): Hockey C; Captained the Detroit Red Wings to 3 Stanley Cup wins (1997-98,2002); won the Conn Smythe Trophy as the playoff MVP in 1998; one of only 14 NHL players to score more than 600 goals; 1,721 career points.

Mario Zagalo (b. Aug. 9, 1931): Soccer; Brazilian forward who is one of only two men (Franz Beckenbauer is the other) to serve as both captain (1962) and coach (1970,94) of World Cup champion.

Babe Didrikson Zaharias (b. June 26, 1911, d. Sept. 27, 1956): All-around athlete who was chosen AP Female Athlete of Year 6 times from 1932-54; won 2 gold medals (javelin and 80-meter hurdles) and a silver (high jump) at 1932 Olympics; played baseball and acquired the nickname "Babe" for her tape measure home runs; real first name was Mildred; took up golf in 1935 and went on to win 55 pro and amateur events; won 10 majors, including 3 U.S. Opens (1948,50,54); helped found LPGA in 1949; chosen female "Athlete of the Half Century" by AP in 1950; when asked if there was anything she didn't play, she replied, "Yeah, dolls."

Tony Zale (b. May 29, 1913, d. March 20, 1997): Boxer; 2-time world middleweight champion (1941-47,48); fought Rocky Graziano for title 3 times in 21 months in 1947-48, winning twice; pro record 67-18-2 with 44 KOs.

Frank Zamboni (b. Jan. 16, 1901, d. July 27, 1988): Mechanic, ice salesman and skating rink owner in Paramount, Calif.; invented ice-resurfacing machine in 1949; now there are few skating rinks without one as thousands have been sold in over 35 countries.

Emil Zatopek (b. Sept. 19, 1922, d. Nov. 22, 2000): Czech distance runner; winner of 1948 Olympic gold medal at 10,000 meters; 4 years later, won unprecedented Olympic triple crown (5,000 meters, 10,000 meters and marathon) at 1952 Games in Helsinki.

Zinedine Zidane (b. June 23, 1972): French soccer player; 2-time FIFA World Player of the Year (1998, 2000); led host nation France to 1998 World Cup title, scoring twice in final against Brazil; a record $64m transfer fee sent the midfielder from Juventus to Real Madrid in 2001.

John Ziegler (b. Feb. 9, 1934): Hockey; NHL president from 1977-92; negotiated settlement with rival WHA in 1979 that led to inviting four WHA teams (Edmonton, Hartford, Quebec and Winnipeg) to join NHL; stepped down June 12, 1992, 2 months after settling 10-day players' strike.

Nick Zito (b. Feb. 6, 1948): Horse racing; trainer who has saddled 2 Kentucky Derby winners (Strike the Gold in 1991 and Go for Gin in 1994), 1996 Preakness Stakes winner (Louis Quartoze) and 2004 Belmont Stakes winner (Birdstone).

Pirmin Zurbriggen (b. Feb. 4, 1963): Swiss alpine skier; 4-time World Cup overall champ (1984,87-88,90) and 3-time runner-up; 40 World Cup wins in 10 years; won gold and bronze medals at 1988 Olympics.

Ballparks & Arenas

Phillies' legend Mike Schmidt has a statue in his honor outside Philadelphia's new **Citizens Bank Park**.

AP/Wide World Photos

Coming Attractions

SPORTS ALMANAC

2004

BASEBALL

Philadelphia (NL): Citizens Bank Park (Citizens Bank is the title sponsor) officially opened on April 12 for the Phillies home-opening 4-1 loss to the Cincinnati Reds. The baseball-only, grass-field park is located adjacent to Veterans Stadium in South Philadelphia on the north side of Pattison Avenue, between 11th and Darien Streets and offers scenic views of the Philadelphia skyline. The ballpark seats 43,500, including 4,700 club seats and 71 luxury suites. Final cost of project is $458 million. One of the more impressive design features of the new park is a 50-foot high neon Liberty Bell that lights up and rings following Phillies home runs.

San Diego (NL): PETCO Park (PETCO Animal Supplies, Inc. is the title sponsor) held its first game on Mar. 12 with a regular-season game between San Diego St. and the University of Houston (SDSU won, 4-0) four weeks before the Padres' home opener. The crowd of 40,106 was the largest in college baseball history. The Padres christened the park on Apr. 8 with a 10-inning, 4-3 win over upstate rival San Francisco. The open-air, grass-field park is located on a one-square-block downtown lot and part of a larger redevelopment project that includes a new hotel, office space and retail space. The park seats approximately 42,000, including 6,000 club seats and 58 luxury suites, and cost $474 million. The adjacent historic Western Metal Supply Company building was incorporated as a portion of the left field wall and foul pole.

NBA BASKETBALL

Memphis (East): The opening of FedExForum (FedEx Corp. is the title sponsor) was set for September 2004. The new $250 million home of the Grizzlies, located between Third and Fourth Streets and Lt. George W. Lee and Linden Avenues, will seat 18,400 for basketball (including 64 luxury suites) and 12,500 for hockey. The project includes a new home for the Rock 'n' Soul Museum, an affiliate of the Smithsonian. The first major event at FedExForum (yes, it's all one word) was an Usher concert on Sept. 17.

2005

NBA BASKETBALL

Charlotte (expansion): Construction on the new Charlotte Arena (title sponsor pending) for the NBA expansion Charlotte Bobcats and the WNBA Charlotte Sting began with a ceremonial "groundblasting" on July 29, 2003. The arena, which will seat 18,500 for basketball (including 60 luxury suites) and 14,100 for hockey, is being built by the City of Charlotte and will cost an estimated $200 million. The building will be located in Center City Charlotte bounded by East Trade, Fifth and North Caldwell streets and the South Corridor Light Rail Line. The Bobcats will begin play in the NBA in 2004 and will play their first season at the Charlotte Coliseum before moving to the new Charlotte Arena in November 2005 for the start of their second season.

2006

BASEBALL

St. Louis (NL): The Cardinals broke ground on the site of the new Busch Stadium (Anheuser-Busch Cos. Inc. is the title sponsor) on Dec. 19, 2003. The site is on the northern edge of current Busch Stadium (Walnut Street) to the base of the elevated Interstate 40/64 highway (Poplar Street). The open-air, baseball-only ballpark will offer a spectacular view of the Gateway Arch and St. Louis skyline. The seating capacity will be approximately 46,000. Estimated cost (including a new Cardinals Hall of Fame and Museum) is $387.5 million. Opening is scheduled for April 2006.

NFL FOOTBALL

Arizona (NFC): Construction on a new home for the Arizona Cardinals and Fiesta Bowl is well underway. The 63,000-seat stadium will be located in Glendale, Ariz. (15 miles west of Phoenix) on a site on the Loop 101 (Agua Fria Freeway) south of Glendale Avenue and adjacent to the new home of the NHL's Coyotes. The stadium will feature a bold design, with a partially retractable roof and wall and feature a natural grass field that can be rolled out into the adjoining parking lot in order to help it grow. The stadium would include 88 luxury suites and 7,000 club seats; estimated cost: $370.6 million. Earliest Cardinals' home opener will be fall 2006.

NHL HOCKEY

New Jersey (East): New arena for the Devils is stalled in the planning stages. Funding from a new lease on Newark Airport would help pay for the project. Arena would be located in downtown Newark near Penn Station; estimated cost: $310 million of which the city would reportedly contribute $210 million. Earliest opening would be fall 2006.

2007

BASEBALL

Florida (NL): The team is currently in discussions with the state and local governments involving financing for a new retractable-roofed ballpark for the Marlins. Preliminary plans call for a $325 million, 38,000-seat ballpark to be built in Miami-Dade County. Miami-Dade County has reportedly promised $73 million in tourist taxes to the project and the team has committed $137 million, leaving the plan $115 million short.

No realistic timetable has been set forth but the earliest home opener would likely be no earlier than April 2007.

NBA BASKETBALL

New Jersey (East): An ownership group headed by Brooklyn developer Bruce Ratner was cleared by the NBA to purchase the Nets. The new owners will presumably move the team to Brooklyn where Ratner plans to build a 19,000-seat, Frank Gehry-designed arena that will be part of a $2.5 billion office, residential and shopping complex.

The plans face opposition from area residents and the arena is expected to be open for business no sooner than 2007. The entire project is expected to take 10 years to complete.

The San Diego Padres opened the doors to **PETCO Park** in 2004. The Padres christened the new downtown ballpark with an extra-innings win over the San Francisco Giants.

2008

BASEBALL

Minnesota (AL): The Twins unveiled plans for a new ballpark in 2004. The new park would seat 42,000 including 72 suites and 4,000 club seats and feature a retractable roof. The site has yet to be determined and the team could potentially move to St. Paul. The financing proposals stalled in the state legislature in 2004 and the immediate future of the plans are unclear, but the earliest Twins home opener would likely be no earlier than 2008.

Washington (NL): The latest plans call for a $440 million bond package that would pay for a new ballpark along the Anacostia River at South Capitol and M Streets for the relocated (and renamed) Expos. The proposal also includes a $13 million renovation of RFK Stadium, where the team will play for three seasons until the new park is ready. The earliest home opener will likely be no earlier than 2008.

2009

BASEBALL

New York (AL): The Yankees recently unveiled plans for a new 50,000-seat ballpark. The new retro-styled park would be located right across 161st Street from the existing Yankee Stadium and would be entirely financed by the team. Although the new park would have fewer seats than "The House that Ruth Built" it would have an increase in the number of luxury suites. The cost of the new stadium is estimated at $700 million, lower than previous estimates because the team has decided to eschew a retractable roof. There is no official timetable for the project but it's expected that the park would be completed no earlier than 2009. In 2001, the Yankees unveiled a plan to build a futuristic retractable-dome stadium in Macombs Dam Park, with taxpayers and the team sharing the $800 million cost. The new ballpark would reportedly have a more retro appearance, modeled on the old Yankee Stadium, prior to its 1974 face-lift. Under the latest proposal, the state and city would pay for any infrastructure and nonstadium improvements, such as a new Metro-North stop, a ferry landing and a hotel and conference center. Estimated cost for said improvements is between $300-400 million. Plans for the long term future of the existing Yankee Stadium include converting it to a parking garage and soccer stadium.

NFL FOOTBALL

New York (AFC): Plans for a new stadium for the New York Jets have been proposed. The $1.4 billion stadium, known as the New York Sports and Convention Center would be located on the Far West Side of Manhattan. It would be built over rail yards located between 30th and 33rd Streets and 11th and 12th Avenues. With a retractable roof and moveable seating, the facility would operate primarily as a 200,000 square foot, column-free exhibition hall with 30,000 square feet of meeting space, but could also serve as a plenary hall seating up to 40,000 people or as a stadium seating 75,000. It would also serve as the new home to the Jets and, if New York City were selected as the host to the 2012 Summer Olympic Games, as the Olympic Stadium. The Jets would pay $800 million for the facility's construction and the city and state will each invest $300 million to cover the cost of building the platform over the rail yards and the roof that allows for year-round use as a convention facility.

Dallas (NFC): Plans for a new stadium for the Cowboys were unveiled in 2004. The 75,000-seat stadium would be located south of the Tom Landry Freeway, next door to the Texas Rangers' Ameriquest Field in Arlington. The retractable-roof stadium would be expandable to hold up to 90,000 fans and cost an estimated $650 million. The plan which would be partly financed through an increase in sales, hotel and car-rental taxes, was set to go to the voters on Nov. 2, 2004. Earliest home opener would be in the fall of 2009.

Other Ballparks & Stadia in the Works

Portland, Ore. officials continue to make plans for a new ballpark despite the fact that the Montreal Expos are headed to the Washington, D.C. area. The 38,000-seat stadium would only be built if and when a Major League team agrees to move there...New Orleans Saints owner Tom Benson is still looking for a new stadium for his team and may get it through a combined convention center/stadium in the *Big Easy*...The San Diego Chargers and the city agreed to renegotiate their lease agreement with an eye toward eventually *replacing Qualcomm Stadium* and thereby keeping the team in town for the long term...The Pittsburgh Penguins are seeking a license to *operate a slot machine parlor* to fund their plans for a $250 million replacement of 43-year-old Mellon Arena...Stay tuned.

Home, Sweet Home

The home fields, home courts and home ice of the AL, NL, NBA, NFL, NHL, NCAA Division I-A college football and Division I basketball. Also included are MLS stadiums, Formula One, CART, Indy Racing League and NASCAR auto racing tracks.

Attendance figures for the 2003 NFL regular season and the 2003-04 NBA and NHL regular seasons are provided. See Baseball chapter for 2004 AL and NL attendance figures.

MAJOR LEAGUE BASEBALL

American League

		Built	Capacity	LF	LCF	CF	RCF	RF	Field
Anaheim Angels	Angel Stadium of Anaheim	1966	**45,030**	365	387	400	370	365	Grass
Baltimore Orioles	Oriole Park at Camden Yards	1992	**48,190**	337	376	406	391	320	Grass
Boston Red Sox	Fenway Park	1912	**34,892**	310	379	390*	380	302	Grass
Chicago White Sox	U.S. Cellular Field	1991	**41,000**	330	377	400	372	335	Grass
Cleveland Indians	Jacobs Field	1994	**43,068**	325	370	405	375	325	Grass
Detroit Tigers	Comerica Park	2000	**40,120**	345	395	420	365	330	Grass
Kansas City Royals	Kauffman Stadium	1973	**40,793**	330	375	400	375	330	Grass
Minnesota Twins	Hubert H. Humphrey Metrodome	1982	**48,678**	343	385	408	367	327	Turf
New York Yankees	Yankee Stadium	1923	**57,478**	318	399	408	385	314	Grass
Oakland Athletics	McAfee Coliseum	1966	**43,662**	330	367	400	367	330	Grass
Seattle Mariners	SAFECO Field	1999	**47,116**	331	390	405	387	327	Grass
Tampa Bay Devil Rays	Tropicana Field	1990	**43,761**	315	370	404	370	322	Turf
Texas Rangers	Ameriquest Field in Arlington	1994	**49,115**	332	390	400	381	325	Grass
Toronto Blue Jays	SkyDome	1989	**50,516**	328	375	400	375	328	Turf

*The straightaway center-field fence at Fenway Park is 390 feet from home plate but the deepest part of center-field, a.k.a. "the Triangle," is 420 feet away. The left-field fence, known as "the Green Monster," is 37 feet tall. Two hundred and seventy seats were added to the top of the wall in 2003 replacing the 23-foot screen that previously topped the Monster.

National League

		Built	Capacity	LF	LCF	CF	RCF	RF	Field
Arizona Diamondbacks	Bank One Ballpark	1998	**49,033**	330	376	407	376	334	Grass
Atlanta Braves	Turner Field	1996	**50,091**	335	380	401	390	330	Grass
Chicago Cubs	Wrigley Field	1914	**39,111**	355	368	400	368	353	Grass
Cincinnati Reds	Great American Ballpark	2003	**42,059**	328	379	404	370	325	Grass
Colorado Rockies	Coors Field	1995	**50,449**	347	390	415	375	350	Grass
Florida Marlins	Pro Player Stadium	1987	**36,331**	330	385	434	385	345	Grass
Houston Astros	Minute Maid Park	2000	**40,950**	315	362	436	373	326	Grass
Los Angeles Dodgers	Dodger Stadium	1962	**56,000**	330	385	395	385	330	Grass
Milwaukee Brewers	Miller Park	2001	**42,400**	340	374	400	378	345	Grass
New York Mets	Shea Stadium	1964	**56,749**	338	378	410	378	338	Grass
Philadelphia Phillies	Citizens Bank Park	2004	**43,000**	329	369	401*	369	330	Grass
Pittsburgh Pirates	PNC Park	2001	**37,898**	326	368	399*	375	324	Grass
St. Louis Cardinals	Busch Stadium	1966	**49,814**	330	372	402	372	330	Grass
San Diego Padres	PETCO Park	2004	**46,000**	334	367	396*	387	322	Grass
San Francisco Giants	SBC Park	2000	**41,467**	339	364	399	421	309	Grass
Washington	RFK Stadium	1961	**45,016***	TBD	TBD	TBD	TBD	TBD	Grass

*The deepest part of PNC Park is 410 feet between straightaway center and left-center. The deepest part of Citizens Bank Park is 409 feet in part of left-center. The deepest part of PETCO Park is 411 feet in part of right-center. Also, the capacity of RFK stadium listed above is what it was in the Washington Senators' final season there in 1971 before the team moved to Texas and became the Rangers.

Rank by Capacity

AL		NL	
New York	.57,478	New York	.56,749
Toronto	.50,516	Los Angeles	.56,000
Texas	.49,115	Colorado	.50,449
Minnesota	.48,678	Atlanta	.50,091
Baltimore	.48,190	St. Louis	.49,814
Seattle	.47,116	Arizona	.49,033
Anaheim	.45,030	San Diego	.46,000
Tampa Bay	.43,761	Washington	.45,016
Oakland	.43,662	Philadelphia	.43,000
Cleveland	.43,068	Milwaukee	.42,400
Chicago	.41,000	Cincinnati	.42,059
Kansas City	.40,793	San Francisco	.41,467
Detroit	.40,120	Houston	.40,950
Boston	.34,892	Chicago	.39,111
		Pittsburgh	.37,898
		Florida	.36,331

Rank by Age

AL		NL	
Boston	.1912	Chicago	.1914
New York	.1923	Washington	.1961
Anaheim	.1966	Los Angeles	.1962
Oakland	.1966	New York	.1964
Kansas City	.1973	St. Louis	.1966
Minnesota	.1982	Florida	.1987
Toronto	.1989	Atlanta	.1993
Tampa Bay	.1990	Colorado	.1995
Chicago	.1991	Arizona	.1998
Baltimore	.1992	Houston	.2000
Cleveland	.1994	San Francisco	.2000
Texas	.1994	Milwaukee	.2001
Seattle	.1999	Pittsburgh	.2001
Detroit	.2000	Cincinnati	.2003
Note: New York's Yankee Stadium (AL) was rebuilt in 1976.		Philadelphia	.2004
		San Diego	.2004

Home Fields

Listed below are the principal home fields used through the years by current American and National League teams. The NL became a major league in 1876, the AL in 1901.

The capacity figures in the right-hand column indicate the largest seating capacity of the ballpark while the club played there. Capacity figures before 1915 (and the introduction of concrete grandstands) are sketchy at best and have been left blank.

American League

Anaheim Angels
1961	Wrigley Field (Los Angeles)	20,457
1962-65	Dodger Stadium	56,000
1966–	Angel Stadium of Anaheim	45,030
	(1966 capacity—43,250)	

Baltimore Orioles
1901	Lloyd Street Grounds (Milwaukee)	—
1902–53	Sportsman's Park II (St. Louis)	30,500
1954–91	Memorial Stadium (Baltimore)	53,371
1992–	Oriole Park at Camden Yards	48,190

Boston Red Sox
1901–11	Huntington Ave. Grounds	
1912–	Fenway Park	34,892
	(1934 capacity—27,000)	

Chicago White Sox
1901–10	Southside Park	—
1910–90	Comiskey Park I	43,931
1991–	U.S. Cellular Field	41,000
	(2003 capacity—46,943)	

Cleveland Indians
1901–09	League Park I	—
1910–46	League Park II	21,414
1932–93	Cleveland Stadium	74,483
1994–	Jacobs Field	43,068

Detroit Tigers
1901–11	Bennett Park	—
1912–99	Tiger Stadium	46,945
2000–	Comerica Park	40,120
	(1912 capacity—23,000)	

Kansas City Royals
1969–72	Municipal Stadium	35,020
1973–	Kauffman Stadium	40,793
	(1973 capacity—40,762)	

Minnesota Twins
1901-02	American League Park (Washington, DC)	—
1903-60	Griffith Stadium	27,410
1960-81	Metropolitan Stadium (Bloomington, MN)	45,919
1982–	HHH Metrodome (Minneapolis)	48,678
	(1982 capacity—54,000)	

New York Yankees
1901-02	Oriole Park (Baltimore)	—
1903–12	Hilltop Park (New York)	—
1913–22	Polo Grounds II	38,000
1923–73	Yankee Stadium I	67,224
1974–75	Shea Stadium	55,101
1976–	Yankee Stadium II	57,478
	(1976 capacity—57,145)	

Oakland Athletics
1901–08	Columbia Park (Philadelphia)	—
1909–54	Shibe Park	33,608
1955–67	Municipal Stadium (Kansas City)	35,020
1968–	McAfee Coliseum	43,662
	(1968 capacity—48,621)	

Seattle Mariners
1977–99	The Kingdome	59,166
1999–	SAFECO Field	47,116

Tampa Bay Devil Rays
1990–	Tropicana Field	43,761

Texas Rangers
1961	Griffith Stadium (Washington, DC)	27,410
1962–71	RFK Stadium	45,016
1972–93	Arlington Stadium (Texas)	43,521
1994–	Ameriquest Field in Arlington	49,115

Toronto Blue Jays
1977–89	Exhibition Stadium	43,737
1989–	SkyDome	50,516
	(1989 capacity—49,500)	

Ballpark Name Changes: ANAHEIM—**Angel Stadium of Anaheim**, originally Anaheim Stadium (1966-98), then Edison International Field of Anaheim (1998-2003); CHICAGO—**Comiskey Park I** originally White Sox Park (1910-12), then Comiskey Park in 1913, then White Sox Park again in 1962, then Comiskey Park again in 1976; **U.S. Cellular Field** originally Comiskey Park (1991-2002); CLEVELAND—**League Park** renamed Dunn Field in 1920, then League Park again in 1928; **Cleveland Stadium** originally Municipal Stadium (1932-74); DETROIT—**Tiger Stadium** originally Navin Field (1912-37), then Briggs Stadium (1938-60); KANSAS CITY—**Kauffman Stadium** originally Royals Stadium (1973-93); LOS ANGELES—**Dodger Stadium** referred to as Chavez Revine by AL while Angels played there (1962-65); OAKLAND—**McAfee Coliseum** originally Oakland Alameda Coliseum (1968-98), then Network Associates Coliseum (1998-2004); PHILADELPHIA—**Shibe Park** renamed Connie Mack Stadium in 1953; ST. LOUIS—**Sportsman's Park** renamed Busch Stadium in 1953; WASHINGTON—**Griffith Stadium** originally National Park (1892-1920), **RFK Stadium** originally D.C. Stadium (1961-68); TEXAS—**Ameriquest Field in Arlington** originally The Ballpark in Arlington (1994-2004).

National League

Arizona Diamondbacks
1998–	Bank One Ballpark	49,033

Atlanta Braves
1876–94	South End Grounds I (Boston)	—
1894–1914	South End Grounds II	—
1915–52	Braves Field	40,000
1953–65	County Stadium (Milwaukee)	43,394
1966–96	Atlanta-Fulton County Stadium	52,769
	(1966 capacity—50,000)	
1997–	Turner Field	50,091

Chicago Cubs
1876–77	State Street Grounds	—
1878–84	Lakefront Park	—
1885–91	West Side Park	—
1891–93	Brotherhood Park	—
1893–1915	West Side Grounds	—
1916–	Wrigley Field	39,111
	(1916 capacity—16,000)	

Cincinnati Reds
1876–79	Avenue Grounds	—
1880	Bank Street Grounds	—
1890–1901	Redland Field I	—
1902–11	Palace of the Fans	—
1912–70	Crosley Field	29,603
1970–2002	Cinergy Field	40,007
	(1970 capacity—52,000)	
2003–	Great American Ballpark	42,059

Major League Baseball (Cont.)

Colorado Rockies

1993–94	Mile High Stadium (Denver)	76,100
1995–	Coors Field	50,449

Florida Marlins

1993–	Pro Player Stadium (Miami)	36,331
	(1993 capacity—47,662)	

Houston Astros

1962–64	Colt Stadium	32,601
1965–99	The Astrodome	54,370
	(1965 capacity—45,011)	
2000–	Minute Maid Park	40,950

Los Angeles Dodgers

1890	Washington Park I (Brooklyn)	—
1891–97	Eastern Park	—
1898–1912	Washington Park II	—
1913–55	Ebbets Field	31,497
1956–57	Ebbets Field	31,497
	& Roosevelt Stadium (Jersey City)	24,167
1958–61	Memorial Coliseum (Los Angeles)	93,600
1962–	Dodger Stadium	56,000

Milwaukee Brewers

1969	Sick's Stadium (Seattle)	59,166
1970–	County Stadium (Milwaukee)	53,192
2000	(1970 capacity—46,620)	
2001–	Miller Park	42,400

New York Mets

1962–63	Polo Grounds	55,987
1964–	Shea Stadium	56,749
	(1964 capacity—55,101)	

Philadelphia Phillies

1883–86	Recreation Park	—
1887–94	Huntingdon Ave. Grounds	—
1895–1938	Baker Bowl	18,800
1938–70	Shibe Park	33,608
1971–2003	Veterans Stadium	62,418
2004–	Citizens Bank Park	43,000

Pittsburgh Pirates

1887–90	Recreation Park	—
1891–1909	Exposition Park	—
1909–70	Forbes Field	35,000
1970–2000	Three Rivers Stadium	47,687
	(1970 capacity—50,235)	
2001–	PNC Park	37,898

St. Louis Cardinals

1876–77	Sportsman's Park I	—
1885–86	Vandeventer Lot	—
1892–1920	Robison Field	18,000
1920–66	Sportsman's Park II	30,500
1966–	Busch Stadium	49,814
	(1966 capacity—50,126)	

San Diego Padres

1969–2003	Qualcomm Stadium	66,083
2004–	PETCO Park	46,000

San Francisco Giants

1876	Union Grounds (Brooklyn)	—
1883–88	Polo Grounds I (New York)	—
1889–90	Manhattan Field	—
1891–1957	Polo Grounds II	55,987
1958–59	Seals Stadium (San Francisco)	22,900
1960–99	3Com Park	63,000
	(1960 capacity—42,553)	
2000–	SBC Park	41,467

Washington

1969–76	Jarry Park (Montreal)	28,000
1977–2002	Olympic Stadium	46,500
2003–04	Olympic Stadium	46,500
	& Hiram Bithon Stadium (San Juan)	18,000
2005–	RFK Stadium (Washington, D.C.)	45,016

Ballpark Name Changes: ATLANTA—**Atlanta-Fulton County Stadium** originally Atlanta Stadium (1966-74), **Turner Field** originally Centennial Olympic Stadium (1996); CHICAGO—**Wrigley Field** originally Weeghman Park (1914-17), then Cubs Park (1918-25); CINCINNATI—**Redland Field** originally League Park (1890-93), **Crosley Field** originally Redland Field II (1912-33) and **Cinergy Field** originally Riverfront Stadium (1970-96); FLORIDA—**Pro Player Stadium** originally Joe Robbie Stadium (1987-96); HOUSTON—**Astrodome** originally Harris County Domed Stadium before it opened in 1965; **Enron Field** renamed Astros Field briefly and then Minute Maid Park in 2002; PHILADELPHIA—**Baker Field** originally Philadelphia Park (1895-1912), **Shibe Park** renamed Connie Mack Stadium in 1953; ST. LOUIS—**Robison Field** originally Vandeventer Lot, then League Park, then Cardinal Park all before becoming Robison Field in 1901, **Sportsman's Park** renamed Busch Stadium in 1953, and **Busch Stadium** originally Busch Memorial Stadium (1966-82); SAN DIEGO—**Qualcomm Stadium** originally San Diego Stadium (1967-81) and San Diego/Jack Murphy Stadium (1982-96); SAN FRANCISCO—**3Com Park** originally Candlestick Park (1960-95), **SBC Park** originally Pacific Bell Park (2000-03).

NATIONAL BASKETBALL ASSOCIATION

Western Conference

		Location	Built	Capacity
Dallas Mavericks	**American Airlines Center**	Dallas, Texas	2001	**19,200**
Denver Nuggets	**Pepsi Center**	Denver, Colo.	1999	**19,099**
Golden State Warriors	**The Arena in Oakland**	Oakland, Calif.	1997	**19,596**
Houston Rockets	**Toyota Center**	Houston, Texas	2003	**18,300**
Los Angeles Clippers	**Staples Center**	Los Angeles, Calif.	1999	**18,694**
Los Angeles Lakers	**Staples Center**	Los Angeles, Calif.	1999	**18,997**
Memphis Grizzlies	**FedExForum**	Memphis, Tenn.	2004	**18,400**
Minnesota Timberwolves	**Target Center**	Minneapolis, Minn.	1990	**19,006**
New Orleans Hornets	**New Orleans Arena**	New Orleans, La.	1999	**18,500**
Phoenix Suns	**America West Arena**	Phoenix, Ariz.	1992	**19,023**
Portland Trail Blazers	**Rose Garden**	Portland, Ore.	1995	**19,980**
Sacramento Kings	**ARCO Arena**	Sacramento, Calif.	1988	**17,317**
San Antonio Spurs	**SBC Center**	San Antonio, Texas	2002	**18,500**
Seattle SuperSonics	**KeyArena at Seattle Center**	Seattle, Wash.	1962	**17,072**
Utah Jazz	**Delta Center**	Salt Lake City, Utah	1991	**19,911**

Notes: Seattle's KeyArena was originally the Seattle Center Coliseum before being rebuilt in 1995; The Staples Center has different listed capacities for Clippers games and Lakers games because of different floor seating arrangements.

Eastern Conference

Team	Arena	Location	Built	Capacity
Atlanta Hawks	Philips Arena	Atlanta, Ga.	1999	**19,445**
Boston Celtics	FleetCenter	Boston, Mass.	1995	**18,624**
Charlotte Bobcats	Charlotte Coliseum	Charlotte, N.C.	1988	**19,925**
Chicago Bulls	United Center	Chicago, Ill.	1994	**21,711**
Cleveland Cavaliers	Gund Arena	Cleveland, Ohio	1994	**20,562**
Detroit Pistons	The Palace of Auburn Hills	Auburn Hills, Mich.	1988	**22,076**
Indiana Pacers	Conseco Fieldhouse	Indianapolis, Ind.	1999	**18,345**
Miami Heat	AmericanAirlines Arena	Miami, Fla.	1999	**16,500**
Milwaukee Bucks	Bradley Center	Milwaukee, Wisc.	1988	**18,717**
New Jersey Nets	Continental Airlines Arena	E. Rutherford, N.J.	1981	**20,049**
New York Knicks	Madison Square Garden	New York, N.Y.	1968	**19,763**
Orlando Magic	TD Waterhouse Centre	Orlando, Fla.	1989	**17,248**
Philadelphia 76ers	Wachovia Center	Philadelphia, Penn.	1996	**20,444**
Toronto Raptors	Air Canada Centre	Toronto, Ont.	1999	**19,800**
Washington Wizards	MCI Center	Washington, D.C.	1997	**20,674**

Note: The expansion Charlotte Bobcats will play the 2004-05 NBA season at the Charlotte Coliseum before moving to the new Charlotte Arena in late 2005.

Rank by Capacity

Western		Eastern	
Portland	19,980	Detroit	22,076
Utah	19,911	Chicago	21,711
Golden State	19,596	Washington	20,674
Dallas	19,200	Cleveland	20,562
Denver	19,099	Philadelphia	20,444
Phoenix	19,023	New Jersey	20,049
Minnesota	19,006	Charlotte	19,925
LA Lakers	18,997	Toronto	19,800
LA Clippers	18,694	New York	19,763
San Antonio	18,500	Atlanta	19,445
New Orleans	18,500	Milwaukee	18,717
Memphis	18,400	Boston	18,624
Houston	18,300	Indiana	18,345
Sacramento	17,317	Orlando	17,248
Seattle	17,072	Miami	16,500

Rank by Age

Western		Eastern	
Seattle	1962	New York	1968
Sacramento	1988	New Jersey	1981
Minnesota	1990	Charlotte	1988
Utah	1991	Detroit	1988
Phoenix	1992	Milwaukee	1988
Portland	1995	Orlando	1989
Golden St.	1997	Chicago	1994
Denver	1999	Cleveland	1994
LA Clippers	1999	Boston	1995
LA Lakers	1999	Philadelphia	1996
New Orleans	1999	Washington	1997
Dallas	2001	Toronto	1999
San Antonio	2002	Atlanta	1999
Houston	2003	Indiana	1999
Memphis	2004	Miami	1999

Note: The Seattle Center Coliseum was rebuilt and renamed KeyArena in 1995.

2003-04 NBA Attendance

Official overall attendance in the NBA for the 2003-04 season was 20,283,156 for an average per game crowd of 17,059 over 1,189 games. Teams in each conference are ranked by attendance over 41 home games based on total tickets distributed. Rank column refers to rank in entire league. Numbers in parentheses indicate conference rank in 2002-03.

Western Conference

	Team	Attendance	Rank	Average
1	Dallas (1)	825,954	2	20,136
2	Utah (3)	785,570	6	19,160
3	LA Lakers (4)	777,657	7	18,967
4	San Antonio (5)	739,706	10	18,042
5	Minnesota (9)	723,161	11	17,638
6	Denver (13)	721,476	12	17,597
7	Sacramento (6)	709,997	13	17,317
8	Portland (2)	684,038	15	16,684
9	Phoenix (8)	670,385	17	16,351
10	Golden St. (11)	665,648	18	16,235
11	LA Clippers (7)	665,396	19	16,229
12	Houston (14)	640,794	22	15,629
13	Seattle (10)	631,349	23	15,399
14	Memphis (12)	622,723	25	15,188
	TOTAL	9,863,854	—	17,184

Eastern Conference

	Team	Attendance	Rank	Average
1	Detroit (1)	872,902	1	21,290
2	Chicago (4)	809,171	3	19,736
3	Philadelphia (3)	788,128	4	19,223
4	New York (5)	785,739	5	19,164
5	Toronto (6)	750,608	8	18,308
6	Cleveland (15)	749,790	9	18,288
7	Milwaukee (9)	690,180	14	16,834
8	Indiana (8)	683,125	16	16,662
9	Boston (7)	664,248	20	16,201
10	Washington (2)	645,363	21	15,741
11	Miami (11)	624,812	24	15,239
12	New Jersey (12)	613,051	26	14,952
13	Orlando (13)	589,194	27	14,371
14	New Orleans (10)	587,613	28	14,332
15	Atlanta (14)	565,738	29	13,798
	TOTAL	10,419,302	—	16,942

National Basketball Association (Cont.)
Home Courts

Listed below are the principal home courts used through the years by current NBA teams. The largest capacity of each arena is noted in the right-hand column. ABA arenas (1967-76) are included for Denver, Indiana, New Jersey and San Antonio.

Western Conference

Dallas Mavericks

1980–2000	Reunion Arena	18,187
2001–	American Airlines Center	19,200

Denver Nuggets

1967–75	Auditorium Arena	6,841
1975–99	McNichols Sports Arena	17,171
	(1975 capacity—16,700)	
1999–	Pepsi Center	19,099

Golden State Warriors

1946–52	Philadelphia Arena	7,777
1952–62	Convention Hall (Philadelphia)	9,200
	& Philadelphia Arena	7,777
1962–64	Cow Palace (San Francisco)	13,862
1964–66	Civic Auditorium	7,500
	& (USF Memorial Gym)	6,000
1966–67	Cow Palace, Civic Auditorium	
	& Oakland Coliseum Arena	15,000
1967–71	Cow Palace	14,500
1971–96	Oakland Coliseum Arena	15,025
	(1971 capacity—12,905)	
1996–97	San Jose Arena	18,500
1997–	The Arena in Oakland	19,596

Houston Rockets

1967–71	San Diego Sports Arena	14,000
1971–72	Hofheinz Pavilion (Houston)	10,218
1972–73	Hofheinz Pavilion	10,218
	& HemisFair Arena (San Antonio)	10,446
1973–75	Hofheinz Pavilion	10,218
1975–2002	Compaq Center	16,285
2003–	Toyota Center	18,300

Los Angeles Clippers

1970–78	Memorial Auditorium (Buffalo)	17,300
1978–84	San Diego Sports Arena	12,167
1985–94	Los Angeles Sports Arena	16,005
1994–99	Los Angeles Sports Arena	16,021
	& Arrowhead Pond	18,211
1999–	Staples Center	18,694

Los Angeles Lakers

1948–60	Minneapolis Auditorium	10,000
1960–67	Los Angeles Sports Arena	14,781
1967–99	Great Western Forum (Inglewood, CA)	17,505
	(1967 capacity—17,086)	
1999–	Staples Center	18,997

Memphis Grizzlies

1995–2001	General Motors Place (Vancouver)	19,193
2001–03	The Pyramid (Memphis, TN)	19,342
2004–	FedExForum	18,400

Minnesota Timberwolves

1989–90	Hubert H. Humphrey Metrodome	23,000
1990–	Target Center	19,006

New Orleans Hornets

1988–	Charlotte Coliseum	19,925
2002	(1988 capacity—23,500)	
2002–	New Orleans Arena	18,500

Phoenix Suns

1968–92	Arizona Veterans' Memorial Coliseum	14,487
1992–	America West Arena	19,023

Portland Trail Blazers

1970–95	Memorial Coliseum	12,888
1995–	Rose Garden	19,980
	(1995 capacity—21,538)	

Sacramento Kings

1948–55	Edgarton Park Arena (Rochester, NY)	5,000
1955–58	Rochester War Memorial	10,000
1958–72	Cincinnati Gardens	11,438
1972–74	Municipal Auditorium (Kansas City)	9,929
	& Omaha (NE) Civic Auditorium	9,136
1974–78	Kemper Arena (Kansas City)	16,785
	& Omaha Civic Auditorium	9,136
1978–85	Kemper Arena	16,886
1985–88	ARCO Arena I	10,333
1988–	ARCO Arena II	17,317
	(1988 capacity—16,517)	

San Antonio Spurs

1967–70	Memorial Auditorium (Dallas)	8,088
	& Moody Coliseum (Dallas)	8,500
1970–71	Moody Coliseum	8,500
	Tarrant County	
	Convention Center (Ft. Worth)	13,500
	& Municipal Coliseum (Lubbock)	10,400
1971–73	Moody Coliseum	9,500
	& Memorial Auditorium	8,088
1973–93	HemisFair Arena (San Antonio)	16,057
1993–2002	The Alamodome	20,557
2002–	SBC Center	18,500

Seattle SuperSonics

1967–78	Seattle Center Coliseum	14,098
1978–85	Kingdome	40,192
1985–94	Seattle Center Coliseum	14,252
1994–95	Tacoma Dome	19,000
1995–	KeyArena at Seattle Center	17,072

Utah Jazz

1974–75	Municipal Auditorium (New Orleans)	7,853
	& Louisiana Superdome	47,284
1975–79	Superdome	47,284
1979–83	Salt Palace (Salt Lake City)	12,519
1983–84	Salt Palace	12,519
	& Thomas & Mack Center (Las Vegas)	18,500
1984–91	Salt Palace	12,616
1991–	Delta Center	19,911

Note: The Sacramento (then Kansas City) Kings played 30 home games at Kansas City Municipal Auditorium during the 1979-80 season after the Kemper Auditorium roof collapsed during a severe rain and wind storm on June 4, 1979.

Eastern Conference

Atlanta Hawks

1949–51	Wharton Field House (Moline, IL)	6,000
1951–55	Milwaukee Arena	11,000
1955–68	Kiel Auditorium (St. Louis)	10,000
1968–72	Alexander Mem. Coliseum (Atlanta)	7,166
1972–96	The Omni	16,378
1997–99	Georgia Dome	21,570
	& Alexander Mem. Coliseum	9,300
1999–	Philips Arena	19,445

Boston Celtics

1946–95	Boston Garden	14,890
1995–	FleetCenter	18,624

Note: From 1975-95 the Celtics played some regular season games at the Hartford Civic Center (15,418).

Charlotte Bobcats

2004–	Charlotte Coliseum	19,925

Chicago Bulls

1966–67	Chicago Amphitheater	11,002
1967–94	Chicago Stadium	18,676
1994–	United Center	21,711

Cleveland Cavaliers

1970–74	Cleveland Arena	11,000
1974–94	The Coliseum (Richfield, OH)	20,273
1994–	Gund Arena	20,562

Detroit Pistons

1948–52	North Side H.S. Gym (Ft. Wayne, IN)	3,800
1952–57	Memorial Coliseum (Ft. Wayne)	9,306
1957–61	Olympia Stadium (Detroit)	14,000
1961–78	Cobo Arena	11,147
1978–88	Silverdome (Pontiac, MI)	22,366
1988–	The Palace of Auburn Hills	22,076

Indiana Pacers

1967–74	State Fairgrounds (Indianapolis)	9,479
1974–99	Market Square Arena	16,530
	(1974 capacity—17,287)	
1999–	Conseco Fieldhouse	18,345

Miami Heat

1988–99	Miami Arena	15,200
2000–	AmericanAirlines Arena	16,500

Milwaukee Bucks

1968–88	Milwaukee Arena (The Mecca)	11,052
1988–	Bradley Center	18,717

New Jersey Nets

1967–68	Teaneck (NJ) Armory	3,500

1968–69	Long Island Arena (Commack, NY)	6,500
1969–71	Island Garden (W. Hempstead, NY)	5,200
1971–77	Nassau Coliseum (Uniondale, NY)	15,500
1977–81	Rutgers Ath. Center (Piscataway, NJ)	9,050
1981–	Continental Airlines Arena (E. Ruth., NJ)	20,049

New York Knicks

1946–68	Madison Sq. Garden III (50th St.)	18,496
1968–	Madison Sq. Garden IV (33rd St.)	19,763
	(1968 capacity—19,694)	

Orlando Magic

1989–	TD Waterhouse Centre	17,248

Philadelphia 76ers

1949–51	State Fair Coliseum (Syracuse, NY)	7,500
1951–63	Onondaga County (NY) War Memorial	8,000
1963–67	Convention Hall (Philadelphia)	12,000
	& Philadelphia Arena	7,777
1967–96	CoreStates Spectrum	18,136
1996–	Wachovia Center	20,444

Toronto Raptors

1995–99	SkyDome	20,125
1999–	Air Canada Centre	19,800

Washington Wizards

1961–62	Chicago Amphitheater	11,000
1962–63	Chicago Coliseum	7,100
1963–73	Baltimore Civic Center	12,289
1973–97	USAir Arena (Landover, MD)	18,756
1997–	MCI Center	20,674

Note: From 1988-96 the Wizards (then Bullets) played four regular season games at Baltimore Arena (12,756).

Building Name Changes: HOUSTON—**Compaq Center** originally The Summit (1975-97); NEW JERSEY—**Continental Airlines Arena** originally Byrne Meadowlands Arena (1981-96); ORLANDO—**TD Waterhouse Centre** originally Orlando Arena (1989-99); PHILADELPHIA—**Wachovia Center** originally the CoreStates Center (1996-98), then the First Union Center (1998-2003) and **CoreStates Spectrum** originally The Spectrum (1967-94); WASHINGTON—**USAir Arena** originally Capital Centre (1973-93).

NATIONAL FOOTBALL LEAGUE

American Football Conference

		Location	Built	Capacity	Field
Baltimore Ravens	**Ravens Stadium**	Baltimore, Md.	1998	**69,084**	Grass
Buffalo Bills	**Ralph Wilson Stadium**	Orchard Park, N.Y.	1973	**73,967**	Turf
Cincinnati Bengals	**Paul Brown Stadium**	Cincinnati, Ohio	2000	**65,352**	Grass
Cleveland Browns	**Cleveland Browns Stadium**	Cleveland, Ohio	1999	**73,200**	Grass
Denver Broncos	**INVESCO Field at Mile High**	Denver, Colo.	2001	**76,125**	Grass
Houston Texans	**Reliant Stadium**	Houston, Tex.	2002	**69,500**	Grass
Indianapolis Colts	**RCA Dome**	Indianapolis, Ind.	1984	**56,127**	Turf
Jacksonville Jaguars	**ALLTEL Stadium**	Jacksonville, Fla.	1995	**73,000**	Grass
Kansas City Chiefs	**Arrowhead Stadium**	Kansas City, Mo.	1972	**79,451**	Grass
Miami Dolphins	**Pro Player Stadium**	Miami, Fla.	1987	**75,540**	Grass
New England Patriots	**Gillette Stadium**	Foxboro, Mass.	2002	**68,000**	Grass
New York Jets	**Giants Stadium**	E. Rutherford, N.J.	1976	**80,062**	Turf
Oakland Raiders	**McAfee Coliseum**	Oakland, Calif.	1966	**63,132**	Grass
Pittsburgh Steelers	**Heinz Field**	Pittsburgh, Pa.	2001	**64,450**	Grass
San Diego Chargers	**Qualcomm Stadium**	San Diego, Calif.	1967	**71,000**	Grass
Tennessee Titans	**The Coliseum**	Nashville, Tenn.	1999	**68,798**	Grass

National Football Conference

		Location	Built	Capacity	Field
Arizona Cardinals	**Sun Devil Stadium**	Tempe, Ariz.	1958	**73,273**	Grass
Atlanta Falcons	**Georgia Dome**	Atlanta, Ga.	1992	**71,228**	Turf
Carolina Panthers	**Ericsson Stadium**	Charlotte, N.C.	1996	**73,500**	Grass
Chicago Bears	**Soldier Field**	Chicago, Ill.	1924	**63,000**	Grass
Dallas Cowboys	**Texas Stadium**	Irving, Tex.	1971	**65,639**	Turf
Detroit Lions	**Ford Field**	Detroit, Mich.	2002	**65,000**	Turf
Green Bay Packers	**Lambeau Field**	Green Bay, Wis.	1957	**72,515**	Grass
Minnesota Vikings	**Hubert H. Humphrey Metrodome**	Minneapolis, Minn.	1982	**64,121**	Turf
New Orleans Saints	**Louisiana Superdome**	New Orleans, La.	1975	**68,395**	Turf
New York Giants	**Giants Stadium**	E. Rutherford, N.J.	1976	**80,062**	Grass
Philadelphia Eagles	**Lincoln Financial Field**	Philadelphia, Pa.	2003	**68,532**	Grass
St. Louis Rams	**Edward Jones Dome**	St. Louis, Mo.	1995	**66,000**	Turf
San Francisco 49ers	**Monster Park**	San Francisco, Calif.	1960	**69,400**	Grass
Seattle Seahawks	**Qwest Field**	Seattle, Wash.	2002	**67,000**	Grass
Tampa Bay Buccaneers	**Raymond James Stadium**	Tampa, Fla.	1998	**65,657**	Grass
Washington Redskins	**FedExField**	Raljon, Md.	1997	**91,665**	Grass

National Football League (Cont.)

Rank by Capacity

AFC		NFC	
NY Jets	80,062	Washington	91,665
Kansas City	79,451	NY Giants	80,062
Denver	76,125	Arizona	73,273
Miami	75,540	Carolina	73,500
Buffalo	73,967	Green Bay	72,515
Cleveland	73,200	Atlanta	71,228
Jacksonville	73,000	San Francisco	69,400
San Diego	71,000	Philadelphia	68,532
Houston	69,500	New Orleans	68,395
Baltimore	69,084	Seattle	67,000
Tennessee	68,798	St. Louis	66,000
New England	68,000	Tampa Bay	65,657
Cincinnati	65,352	Dallas	65,639
Pittsburgh	64,450	Detroit	65,000
Oakland	63,132	Minnesota	64,121
Indianapolis	56,127	Chicago	63,000

Rank by Age

AFC		NFC	
Oakland	1966	Chicago	1924
San Diego	1967	Green Bay	1957
Kansas City	1972	Arizona	1958
Buffalo	1973	San Francisco	1960
NY Jets	1976	Dallas	1971
Indianapolis	1984	New Orleans	1975
Miami	1987	NY Giants	1976
Jacksonville	1995	Minnesota	1982
Baltimore	1998	Atlanta	1992
Cleveland	1999	St. Louis	1995
Tennessee	1999	Carolina	1996
Cincinnati	2000	Washington	1997
Denver	2001	Tampa Bay	1998
Pittsburgh	2001	Seattle	2002
New England	2002	Detroit	2002
Houston	2002	Philadelphia	2003

Notes: Chicago's Soldier Field was rebuilt and Green Bay's Lambeau Field was renovated in 2003.

2003 NFL Attendance

Official overall paid attendance in the NFL for the 2003 season was 16,913,584 for an average per game crowd of 66,328 over 256 games. Teams in each conference are ranked by attendance over eight home games. Rank column indicates rank in entire league. Numbers in parentheses indicate conference rank in 2002.

AFC

		Attendance	Rank	Average
1	Kansas City (2)	627,840	3	78,480
2	N.Y. Jets (1)	622,255	4	77,781
3	Denver (3)	607,167	5	75,895
4	Miami (5)	587,787	6	73,473
5	Cleveland (4)	585,564	7	73,195
6	Buffalo (9)	584,122	8	73,015
7	Houston (6)	563,748	10	70,468
8	Baltimore (7)	556,634	13	69,579
9	Tennessee (8)	550,472	14	68,809
10	New England (10)	547,488	16	68,436
11	San Diego (11)	492,165	25	61,520
12	Cincinnati (16)	479,488	27	59,936
13	Pittsburgh (12)	477,584	28	59,698
14	Indianapolis (14)	454,138	29	56,767
15	Oakland (13)	440,063	30	55,007
16	Jacksonville (15)	428,072	31	53,509
	TOTAL	8,604,227	—	67,221

NFC

		Attendance	Rank	Average
1	Washington (1)	643,997	1	80,499
2	NY Giants (2)	628,960	2	78,620
3	Carolina (3)	582,566	9	72,820
4	Atlanta (4)	563,676	11	70,459
5	Green Bay (11)	562,819	12	70,352
6	New Orleans (5)	548,894	15	68,611
7	Philadelphia (9)	544,349	17	68,043
8	San Francisco (6)	540,644	18	67,580
9	St. Louis (7)	528,456	19	66,057
10	Tampa Bay (8)	524,352	20	65,544
11	Minnesota (10)	513,437	21	64,179
12	Seattle (13)	512,150	22	64,018
13	Dallas (12)	511,224	23	63,903
14	Chicago (15)	492,420	24	61,552
15	Detroit (14)	490,442	26	61,305
16	Arizona (16)	288,499	32	36,062
	TOTAL	8,309,357	—	64,917

Home Fields

Listed below are the principal home fields used through the years by current NFL teams. The largest capacity of each stadium is noted in the right-hand column. All-America Football Conference stadiums (1946-49) are included for Cleveland and San Francisco.

AFC

Baltimore Ravens

1996–97	Memorial Stadium	65,000
1998–	Ravens Stadium	69,084

Buffalo Bills

1960–72	War Memorial Stadium	45,748
1973–	Ralph Wilson Stadium (Orchard Park, NY)	73,967
	(1973 capacity—80,020)	

Cincinnati Bengals

1968–69	Nippert Stadium (Univ. of Cincinnati)	26,500
1970–99	Cinergy Field	60,389
	(1970 capacity—56,200)	
2000–	Paul Brown Stadium	65,352

Cleveland Browns

1946–95	Cleveland Stadium	78,512
	(1946 capacity—85,703)	
1999–	Cleveland Browns Stadium	73,200

Denver Broncos

1960–	Mile High Stadium	76,123
2000	(1960 capacity—34,000)	
2001–	INVESCO Field at Mile High	76,125

Houston Texans

2002–	Reliant Stadium	69,500

Indianapolis Colts

1953–83	Memorial Stadium (Baltimore)	60,020
1984–	RCA Dome (Indianapolis)	56,127
	(1984 capacity—60,127)	

Jacksonville Jaguars
1995–	ALLTEL Stadium	.73,000

Kansas City Chiefs
1960–62	Cotton Bowl (Dallas)	.72,000
1963–71	Municipal Stadium (Kansas City)	.47,000
1972–	Arrowhead Stadium	.79,451
	(1972 capacity—78,097)	

Miami Dolphins
1966–86	Orange Bowl	.75,206
1987–	Pro Player Stadium	.75,540

New England Patriots
1960–62	Nickerson Field (Boston Univ.)	.17,369
1963–68	Fenway Park	.33,379
1969	Alumni Stadium (Boston College)	.26,000
1970	Harvard Stadium	.37,300
1971-2001	Foxboro Stadium	.60,292
	(1971 capacity—61,114)	
2002–	Gillette Stadium	.68,000

New York Jets
1960–63	Polo Grounds	.55,987
1964–83	Shea Stadium	.60,372
1984–	Giants Stadium (E. Rutherford, NJ)	.80,062

Oakland Raiders
1960	Kesar Stadium (San Francisco)	.59,636
1961	Candlestick Park	.42,500
1962–65	Frank Youell Field (Oakland)	.20,000
1966–81	Oakland-Alameda County Coliseum	.54,587
1982–94	Memorial Coliseum (Los Angeles)	.67,800
1995–	McAfee Coliseum	.63,132

Pittsburgh Steelers
1933–57	Forbes Field	.35,000
1958–63	Forbes Field	.35,000
	& Pitt Stadium	.54,500
1964–69	Pitt Stadium	.54,500
1970– 2000	Three Rivers Stadium	.59,600
	(1970 capacity—49,000)	
2001–	Heinz Field	.64,450

San Diego Chargers
1960	Memorial Coliseum (Los Angeles)	.92,604
1961–66	Balboa Stadium (San Diego)	.34,000
1967–	Qualcomm Stadium	.71,000
	(1967 capacity—54,000)	

Tennessee Titans
1960–64	Jeppesen Stadium (Houston)	.23,500
1965–67	Rice Stadium (Rice Univ.)	.70,000
1968–96	Astrodome	.59,969
1997	Liberty Bowl (Memphis)	.62,380
1998	Vanderbilt Stadium (Nashville)	.41,600
1999–	The Coliseum (Nashville)	.68,798

Ballpark Name Changes: BALTIMORE—PSInet Stadium originally named Ravens Stadium (1998-99) and renamed **Ravens Stadium** in 2002; BUFFALO—**Ralph Wilson Stadium** originally Rich Stadium (1973-99); CINCINNATI—**Cinergy Field** originally Riverfront Stadium (1970-96); CLEVELAND—**Cleveland Stadium** originally Municipal Stadium (1932-74); DENVER—**Mile High Stadium** originally Bears Stadium (1948-66); INDIANAPOLIS—**RCA Dome** originally Hoosier Dome (1984-94); JACKSONVILLE—**ALLTEL Stadium** originally Jacksonville Municipal Stadium (1995-97); MIAMI—**Pro Player Stadium** originally Joe Robbie Stadium (1987-96); NEW ENGLAND—**Foxboro Stadium** originally Schaefer Stadium (1971-82), then Sullivan Stadium (1983-89); **Gillette Stadium** originally CMGI Field; OAKLAND—**McAfee Coliseum** originally Oakland Alameda Coliseum (1995-99), Network Associates Coliseum (1999-2004); SAN DIEGO—**Qualcomm Stadium** originally San Diego Stadium (1967-81) then San Diego/Jack Murphy Stadium (1981-96); TENNESSEE—**The Coliseum** originally Adelphia Coliseum (1999-2001).

NFC

Arizona Cardinals
1920–21	Normal Field (Chicago)	.7,500
1922–25	Comiskey Park	.28,000
1926–28	Normal Field	.7,500
1929–59	Comiskey Park	.52,000
1960–65	Busch Stadium (St. Louis)	.34,000
1966–87	Busch Memorial Stadium	.54,392
1988–	Sun Devil Stadium (Tempe, AZ)	.73,273

Atlanta Falcons
1966-91	Atlanta-Fulton County Stadium	.59,643
1992–	Georgia Dome	.71,228

Carolina Panthers
1995	Memorial Stadium (Clemson, SC)	.81,473
1996–	Ericsson Stadium	.73,500

Chicago Bears
1920	Staley Field (Decatur, IL)	—
1921–70	Wrigley Field (Chicago)	.37,741
1971–2001	Soldier Field	.66,944
	(1971 capacity—55,049)	
2002	Memorial Stadium (Champaign, IL)	.69,249
2003–	Soldier Field	.63,000

Dallas Cowboys
1960–70	Cotton Bowl	.72,132
1971–	Texas Stadium (Irving, TX)	.65,639
	(1971 capacity—65,101)	

Detroit Lions
1930–33	Spartan Stadium (Portsmouth, OH)	.8,200
1934–37	Univ. of Detroit Stadium	.25,000
1938–74	Tiger Stadium	.54,468
1975-2001	Pontiac Silverdome	.80,311
	(1975 capacity—80,638)	
2002–	Ford Field	.65,000

Green Bay Packers
1921–22	Hagemeister Brewery Park	—
1923–24	Bellevue Park	—
1925–56	City Stadium I	.24,800
1957–	Lambeau Field	.72,515
	(1957 capacity—32,150)	
	(2002 capacity—62,500)	

Note: The Packers played games in Milwaukee from 1933-94: at Borchert Field, State Fair Park and Marquette Stadium (1933-52), and County Stadium (1953-94).

Minnesota Vikings
1961–81	Metropolitan Stadium (Bloomington)	.48,446
1982–	HHH Metrodome (Minneapolis)	.64,121
	(1982 capacity—62,220)	

New Orleans Saints
1967–74	Tulane Stadium	.80,997
1975–	Louisiana Superdome	.68,395
	(1975 capacity—74,472)	

New York Giants
1925–55	Polo Grounds II	.55,200
1956–73	Yankee Stadium I	.63,800
1973–74	Yale Bowl (New Haven, CT)	.70,896
1975	Shea Stadium	.60,372
1976	Giants Stadium (E. Rutherford, NJ)	.80,062
	(1976 capacity—76,800)	

National Football League (Cont.)

Philadelphia Eagles

1933–35	Baker Bowl	18,800
1936–39	Municipal Stadium	73,702
1940	Shibe Park	33,608
1941	Municipal Stadium	73,702
1942	Shibe Park	33,608
1943	Forbes Field (Pittsburgh)	34,528
1944–57	Shibe Park	33,608
1958–70	Franklin Field (Univ. of Penn.)	60,546
1971–2002	Veterans Stadium	65,352
2003–	Lincoln Financial Field	68,532

St. Louis Rams

1937–42	Municipal Stadium (Cleveland)	85,703
1937	League Park (Cleveland)	—
1938	Shaw Stadium (Cleveland)	—
1937	League Park	—
1943	Suspended operations for one year.	
1944–45	Municipal Stadium	85,703
1946–79	Memorial Coliseum (Los Angeles)	92,604
1980–94	Anaheim Stadium	69,008
1995	Busch Stadium	60,000
1995–	Edward Jones Dome	66,000

San Francisco 49ers

1946–70	Kezar Stadium	59,636
1971–	Monster Park	69,400
	(1971 capacity—61,246)	

Seattle Seahawks

1976–94	Kingdome	66,000
1994	Kingdome	66,400
	& Husky Stadium	72,500
1995–99	Kingdome	66,400
2000-01	Husky Stadium	72,500
2002-	Qwest Field	67,000

Tampa Bay Buccaneers

1976–97	Houlihan's Stadium	74,300
1998–	Raymond James Stadium	65,657

Washington Redskins

1932	Braves Field (Boston)	40,000
1933–36	Fenway Park	27,000
1937–60	Griffith Stadium (Washington, DC)	35,000
1961–97	RFK Stadium	56,454
1997–	FedExField (Raljon, MD)	91,665
	(2003 capacity—86,484)	

Ballpark Name Changes: ATLANTA—**Atlanta-Fulton County Stadium** originally Atlanta Stadium (1966-74); CHICAGO—**Wrigley Field** originally Cubs Park (1916-25); DETROIT—**Tiger Stadium** originally Navin Field (1912-37), then Briggs Stadium (1938-60), also, **Pontiac Silverdome** originally Pontiac Metropolitan Stadium (1975); GREEN BAY—**Lambeau Field** originally City Stadium II (1957-64); PHILADELPHIA—**Shibe Park** renamed Connie Mack Stadium in 1953; ST. LOUIS—**Busch Memorial Stadium** renamed Busch Stadium in 1983, **Edward Jones Dome** originally Trans World Dome (1995-99), then The Dome at America's Center (2000-01); SAN FRANCISCO—**Monster Park** originally Candlestick Park (1960-94, 2001-04), then 3Com Park (1995-2001); SEATTLE—**Qwest Field** originally Seahawks Stadium (2002-03); TAMPA BAY—**Raymond James Stadium** originally Tampa Stadium (1976-96), then **Houlihan's Stadium** (1996-98); WASHINGTON—**RFK Stadium** originally D.C. Stadium (1961-68), also, **FedEx Field** originally Jack Kent Cooke Stadium (1997-99).

NATIONAL HOCKEY LEAGUE

Western Conference

		Location	Built	Capacity
Anaheim, Mighty Ducks of	**Arrowhead Pond**	Anaheim, Calif.	1993	**17,174**
Calgary Flames	**Pengrowth Saddledome**	Calgary, Alb.	1983	**17,135**
Chicago Blackhawks	**United Center**	Chicago, Ill.	1994	**20,500**
Colorado Avalanche	**Pepsi Center**	Denver, Colo.	1999	**18,007**
Columbus Blue Jackets	**Nationwide Arena**	Columbus, Ohio	2000	**18,136**
Dallas Stars	**American Airlines Center**	Dallas, Texas	2001	**18,532**
Detroit Red Wings	**Joe Louis Arena**	Detroit, Mich.	1979	**20,058**
Edmonton Oilers	**Skyreach Centre**	Edmonton, Alb.	1974	**16,839**
Los Angeles Kings	**Staples Center**	Los Angeles, Calif.	1999	**18,118**
Minnesota Wild	**Xcel Energy Center**	St. Paul, Minn.	2000	**18,064**
Nashville Predators	**Gaylord Entertainment Center**	Nashville, Tenn.	1994	**17,113**
Phoenix Coyotes	**Glendale Arena**	Glendale, Ariz.	2003	**17,500**
St. Louis Blues	**Savvis Center**	St. Louis, Mo.	1994	**19,022**
San Jose Sharks	**HP Pavilion at San Jose**	San Jose, Calif.	1993	**17,496**
Vancouver Canucks	**General Motors Place**	Vancouver, B.C.	1995	**18,422**

Eastern Conference

		Location	Built	Capacity
Atlanta Thrashers	**Philips Arena**	Atlanta, Ga.	1999	**18,545**
Boston Bruins	**FleetCenter**	Boston, Mass.	1995	**17,565**
Buffalo Sabres	**HSBC Arena**	Buffalo, N.Y.	1996	**18,690**
Carolina Hurricanes	**RBC Center**	Raleigh, N.C.	1999	**18,730**
Florida Panthers	**Office Depot Center**	Sunrise, Fla.	1998	**19,250**
Montreal Canadiens	**Bell Centre**	Montreal, Que.	1996	**21,273**
New Jersey Devils	**Continental Airlines Arena**	E. Rutherford, N.J.	1981	**19,040**
New York Islanders	**Nassau Veterans' Mem. Coliseum**	Uniondale, N.Y.	1972	**16,234**
New York Rangers	**Madison Square Garden**	New York, N.Y.	1968	**18,200**
Ottawa Senators	**Corel Centre**	Kanata, Ont.	1996	**18,500**
Philadelphia Flyers	**Wachovia Center**	Philadelphia, Penn.	1996	**18,523**
Pittsburgh Penguins	**Mellon Arena**	Pittsburgh, Penn.	1961	**16,958**
Tampa Bay Lightning	**St. Pete Times Forum**	Tampa Bay, Fla.	1996	**19,758**
Toronto Maple Leafs	**Air Canada Centre**	Toronto, Ont.	1999	**18,819**
Washington Capitals	**MCI Center**	Washington, D.C.	1997	**18,672**

Rank by Capacity

Western		Eastern	
Chicago	.20,500	Montreal	.21,273
Detroit	.20,058	Tampa Bay	.19,758
St. Louis	.19,022	Florida	.19,250
Dallas	.18,532	New Jersey	.19,040
Vancouver	.18,422	Toronto	.18,819
Columbus	.18,136	Carolina	.18,730
Los Angeles	.18,118	Buffalo	.18,690
Minnesota	.18,064	Washington	.18,672
Colorado	.18,007	Atlanta	.18,545
Phoenix	.17,500	Philadelphia	.18,523
San Jose	.17,496	Ottawa	.18,500
Anaheim	.17,174	NY Rangers	.18,200
Calgary	.17,135	Boston	.17,565
Nashville	.17,113	Pittsburgh	.16,958
Edmonton	.16,839	NY Islanders	.16,234

Rank by Age

Western		Eastern	
Edmonton	.1974	Pittsburgh	.1961
Detroit	.1979	NY Rangers	.1968
Calgary	.1983	NY Islanders	.1972
Anaheim	.1993	New Jersey	.1981
San Jose	.1993	Boston	.1995
Chicago	.1994	Montreal	.1996
St. Louis	.1994	Ottawa	.1996
Nashville	.1994	Buffalo	.1996
Vancouver	.1995	Philadelphia	.1996
Colorado	.1999	Tampa Bay	.1996
Los Angeles	.1999	Washington	.1997
Columbus	.2000	Florida	.1998
Minnesota	.2000	Toronto	.1999
Dallas	.2001	Carolina	.1999
Phoenix	.2003	Atlanta	.1999

2003-04 NHL Attendance

Official overall paid attendance for the 2003-04 season according to the NHL accounting office was 20,336,817 (paid tickets) for an average per game crowd of 16,534 over 1,230 games. Teams in each conference are ranked by attendance over 41 home games. Rank column refers to rank in entire league. Numbers in parentheses indicate conference rank in 2002-03.

Western Conference

		Attendance	Rank	Average
1	Detroit (1)	.822,646	2	20,065
2	Vancouver (5)	.763,867	5	18,631
3	St. Louis (2)	.760,976	6	18,560
4	Minnesota (4)	.759,776	7	18,531
5	Dallas (3)	.752,556	8	18,355
6	Colorado (6)	.738,287	10	18,007
7	Los Angeles (8)	.733,185	11	17,883
8	Edmonton (10)	.724,780	14	17,678
9	Columbus (7)	.712,145	15	17,369
10	Calgary (11)	.679,767	16	16,580
11	San Jose (9)	.649,261	18	15,836
12	Phoenix (14)	.634,242	19	15,469
13	Anaheim (13)	.614,504	24	14,988
14	Chicago (12)	.543,374	27	13,253
15	Nashville (15)	.539,900	28	13,168
	TOTAL	.10,429,266	—	16,958

Eastern Conference

		Attendance	Rank	Average
1	Montreal (1)	.842,767	1	20,555
2	Toronto (3)	.794,439	3	19,377
3	Philadelphia (2)	.794,388	4	19,375
4	NY Rangers (4)	.741,302	9	18,081
5	Tampa Bay (6)	.730,634	12	17,820
6	Ottawa (5)	.728,101	13	17,759
7	Florida (9)	.653,380	17	15,936
8	Buffalo (15)	.626,903	20	15,290
9	Boston (10)	.620,469	21	15,133
10	Atlanta (14)	.619,965	22	15,121
11	New Jersey (12)	.617,459	23	15,060
12	Washington (7)	.603,528	25	14,720
13	NY Islanders (11)	.551,711	26	13,456
14	Carolina (8)	.495,544	29	12,086
15	Pittsburgh (13)	.486,961	30	11,877
	TOTAL	.9,907,551	—	16,110

Home Ice

Listed below are the principal home buildings used through the years by current NHL teams. The largest capacity of each arena is noted in the right hand column. World Hockey Association arenas (1972-79) are included for Edmonton, Hartford (now Carolina), Quebec (now Colorado) and Winnipeg (now Phoenix).

Western Conference

Anaheim, Mighty Ducks of

1993–	Arrowhead Pond	.17,174

Calgary Flames

1972–80	The Omni (Atlanta)	.15,278
1980–83	Calgary Corral	.7,424
1983–	Pengrowth Saddledome	.17,135
	(1983 capacity—16,674)	

Chicago Blackhawks

1926–29	Chicago Coliseum	.5,000
1929–94	Chicago Stadium	.17,317
1994–	United Center	.20,500

Colorado Avalanche

1972–95	Le Coliseé de Quebec	.15,399
1995–99	McNichols Arena (Denver)	.16,061
1999–	Pepsi Center	.18,007

Columbus Blue Jackets

2000–	Nationwide Arena	.18,136

Dallas Stars

1967–93	Met Center (Bloomington, MN)	.15,174
1993–2000	Reunion Arena (Dallas)	.17,001
2001–	American Airlines Center	.18,532

Detroit Red Wings

1926–27	Border Cities Arena (Windsor, Ont.)	.3,200
1927–79	Olympia Stadium (Detroit)	.16,700
1979–	Joe Louis Arena	.20,058

Edmonton Oilers

1972–74	Edmonton Gardens	.7,200
1974–	Skyreach Centre	.16,839
	(1974 capacity—15,513)	

Los Angeles Kings

1967–99	Great Western Forum (Inglewood)	.16,005
	(1967 capacity—15,651)	
1999–	Staples Center	.18,118

Note: The Kings played 17 games at Long Beach Sports Arena and LA Sports Arena at the start of the 1967-68 season.

National Hockey League (Cont.)

Minnesota Wild

2000–	Xcel Energy Center (St. Paul)	18,064

Nashville Predators

1998–	Gaylord Entertainment Center	17,113

Phoenix Coyotes

1972–96	Winnipeg Arena	15,393
	(1972 capacity—10,177)	
1996–2002	America West (Phoenix)	16,210
2003–	Glendale Arena (Glendale, Ariz.)	17,500

St. Louis Blues

1967–94	St. Louis Arena	17,188
1994–	Savvis Center	19,022

San Jose Sharks

1991–93	Cow Palace (Daly City, CA)	11,100
1993–	HP Pavilion at San Jose	17,496

Vancouver Canucks

1970–95	Pacific Coliseum	16,150
1995–	General Motors Place	18,422

Building Name Changes: CALGARY—**Pengrowth Saddledome** formerly named Canadian Airlines Saddledome (1996-2000) which was originally Olympic Saddledome (1983-95); DALLAS—**Met Center** in Minneapolis originally Metropolitan Sports Center (1967-82); EDMONTON—**Skyreach Centre** formerly named Edmonton Coliseum (1995-99) which was originally Northlands Coliseum (1974-94); LOS ANGELES—**Great Western Forum** originally The Forum (1967-88); NASHVILLE—**Gaylord Entertainment Center** originally Nashville Arena (1994-99); ST. LOUIS—**Savvis Center** originally Kiel Center (1994-2000), **St. Louis Arena** renamed The Checkerdome in 1977, then St. Louis Arena again in 1982; SAN JOSE—**HP Pavilion at San Jose** originally San Jose Arena (1993-2000), then Compaq Center at San Jose (2000-03).

Eastern Conference

Atlanta Thrashers

1999–	Philips Arena	18,545

Boston Bruins

1924–28	Boston Arena	6,200
1928–95	Boston Garden	14,448
1995–	FleetCenter	17,565

Buffalo Sabres

1970–96	Memorial Auditorium (The Aud)	16,284
	(1970 capacity—10,429)	
1996–	HSBC Arena	18,690

Carolina Hurricanes

1972–73	Boston Garden	14,442
1973–74	Boston Garden (regular season)	14,442
	West Springfield (MA) Big E (playoffs)	5,513
1974–75	West Springfield Big E	5,513
	& Hartford (CT) Civic Center	10,507
1975–77	Hartford Civic Center	10,507
1977–78	Hartford Civic Center	10,507
	& Springfield (MA) Civic Center	7,725
1978–79	Springfield Civic Center	7,725
1979–80	Springfield Civic Center	7,725
	& Hartford Civic Center II	14,250
1980–97	Hartford Civic Center II	15,635
1997–99	Greensboro Coliseum	21,500
1999–	RBC Center	18,730

Note: The Hartford Civic Center roof caved in January 1978, forcing the Whalers to move their home games to Springfield, MA for two years.

Florida Panthers

1993–98	Miami Arena	14,703
1998–	Office Depot Center	19,250

Montreal Canadiens

1910–21	Jubilee Arena	3,200
1913–18	Montreal Arena (Westmount)	6,000
1918–26	Mount Royal Arena	6,750
1926–68	Montreal Forum I	15,500
1968–96	Montreal Forum II	17,959
1996–	Bell Centre	21,273

New Jersey Devils

1974–76	Kemper Arena (Kansas City)	16,300
1976–82	McNichols Arena (Denver)	15,900
1982–	Continental Airlines Arena	19,040
	(1982 capacity—19,023)	

New York Islanders

1972–	Nassau Veterans' Mem. Coliseum	16,234
	(1972 capacity—14,500)	

New York Rangers

1925–68	Madison Square Garden III	15,925
1968–	Madison Square Garden IV	18,200
	(1968 capacity—17,250)	

Ottawa Senators

1992–96	Ottawa Civic Center	10,755
1996–	Corel Centre (Kanata)	18,500

Philadelphia Flyers

1967–96	CoreStates Spectrum	17,380
	(1967 capacity—14,558)	
1996–	Wachovia Center	18,523

Pittsburgh Penguins

1967–	Mellon Arena	16,958
	(1967 capacity—12,508)	

Tampa Bay Lightning

1992–93	Expo Hall (Tampa)	10,500
1993–96	ThunderDome (St. Petersburg)	26,000
1996–	St. Pete Times Forum	19,758

Toronto Maple Leafs

1917–31	Mutual Street Arena	8,000
1931–99	Maple Leaf Gardens	15,746
	(1931 capacity—13,542)	
1999–	Air Canada Centre	18,819

Washington Capitals

1974–97	USAir Arena (Landover, MD)	18,130
1997–	MCI Center	18,672

Building Name Changes: BUFFALO—**HSBC Arena** originally Marine Midland Arena (1996-99); CALGARY—**Pengrowth Saddledome** originally Canadian Airlines Arena (1983-2000); CAROLINA—**RBC Center** originally Raleigh Entertainment and Sports Arena (1999-2002); DALLAS—**American Airlines Center** originally Reunion Arena (1993-2000); FLORIDA—**Office Depot Center** originally National Car Rental Center (1998-2002); MONTREAL—**Bell Centre** originally Molson Centre (1996-2002); NEW JERSEY—**Continental Airlines Arena** originally Meadowlands Arena (1982-96); PHILADELPHIA—**Wachovia Center** originally the CoreStates Center (1996-98), then First Union Center (1998-2003) and **CoreStates Spectrum** originally The Spectrum (1967-94); PITTSBURGH—**Mellon Arena** originally Civic Arena (1967-2000); TAMPA BAY—**St. Pete Times Forum** originally Ice Palace (1996-2002); WASHINGTON—**USAir Arena** originally Capital Centre (1974-93).

AUTO RACING

Formula One, NASCAR Winston Cup, Champ Car and Indy Racing League (IRL) racing circuits. Qualifying records accurate as of Sept. 30, 2004. Capacity figures for NASCAR, Champ Car and IRL tracks are approximate and pertain to grandstand seating only. Standing room and hillside terrain seating featured at most road courses are not included.

Champ Car World Series

	Location	Miles	Qual.mph record	Set by	Seats
Burke Lakefront Airport	Cleveland, Ohio	2.106**	134.385	Jimmy Vasser (1998)	36,000
Concord Pacific Place	Vancouver, B.C.	1.781**	106.260	Cristiano da Matta (2002)	65,000
EuroSpeedway	Lausitz, Germany	2.023	153.553	Kenny Brack (2001)	120,000
Exhibition Place	Toronto, Ont.	1.755**	110.565	Gil de Ferran (1999)	60,000
Fundidora Park	Monterrey, Mexico	2.104*	102.474	Sebastien Bourdais (2004)	61,871
Circuit Gilles Villeneuve	Montreal, Que.	2.709*	122.726	Cristiano da Matta (2002)	
Grand Prix of Denver	Denver, Colo.	1.647**	99.516	Sebastien Bourdais (2004)	
Mazda Raceway at Laguna Seca	Monterey, Calif.	2.238*	118.969	Helio Castroneves (2000)	8,000
Las Vegas Motor Speedway	Las Vegas, Nev.	1.500	TBD	first race in late 2004	126,000
Long Beach	Long Beach, Calif.	1.968**	104.969	Gil de Ferran (2000)	63,000
Mexico Gran Premio	Mexico City, Mexico	2.75*	116.703	Bruno Junqueira (2002)	
The Milwaukee Mile	West Allis, Wisc.	1.032	185.500	Patrick Carpentier (1998)	45,000
Portland International Raceway	Portland, Ore.	1.969*	122.768	Helio Castroneves (2000)	50,000
Road America	Elkhart Lake, Wisc.	4.048*	145.924	Dario Franchitti (2000)	10,000
Grand Prix of Seoul	Seoul, South Korea	NA	TBD	first race in late 2004	
Surfers Paradise	Queensland, Australia	2.795**	111.547	Cristiano da Matta (2002)	55,000

*Road courses (not ovals). **Temporary street circuits. †Indicates world closed-course record for auto racing.

Indy Racing League

Founded by Indianapolis Motor Speedway president Tony George, the Indy Racing League fielded 16 races, anchored by the Indianapolis 500, in 2004. Note that the track records listed are for normally-aspirated IRL cars unless otherwise noted by an asterisk.

	Location	Miles	Qual.mph Record	Set by	Seats
California Speedway	Fontana, Calif.	2.0	221.422	Eddie Cheever Jr. (2002)	92,109
Chicagoland Speedway	Joliet, Ill.	1.5	222.137	Robbie Buhl (2001)	75,000
Homestead-Miami Speedway	Homestead, Fla.	1.5	217.388	Buddy Rice (2004)	65,000
Indianapolis Motor Speedway	Indianapolis, Ind.	2.5	237.498	Arie Luyendyk (1996)*	250,000
Kansas Speedway	Kansas City, Kan.	1.5	218.085	Scott Dixon (2003)	75,000
Kentucky Speedway	Sparta, Ky.	1.5	219.191	Scott Goodyear (2000)	70,000
Michigan Intl. Speedway	Brooklyn, Mich.	2.0	222.458	Tomas Scheckter (2003)	136,373
The Milwaukee Mile	West Allis, Wisc.	1.032	169.338	Victor Meira (2004)	45,000
Nashville Superspeedway	Nashville, Tenn.	1.33	206.211	Scott Dixon (2003)	50,000
Nazareth Speedway	Nazareth, Penn.	1.0	172.778	Gil de Ferran (2002)	44,044
Phoenix International Raceway	Phoenix, Ariz.	1.0	183.599	Arie Luyendyk (1996)*	78,450
Pikes Peak Int'l. Raceway	Fountain, Colo.	1.0	179.874	Greg Ray (2000)	42,787
Richmond International Raceway	Richmond, Va.	0.75	171.202	Helio Castroneves (2004)	95,920
Texas Motor Speedway	Fort Worth, Texas	1.5	225.979	Billy Boat (1998)	154,861
Twin Ring Motegi	Motegi, Japan	1.549	206.996	Scott Dixon (2003)	50,000

NASCAR

	Location	Miles	Qual.mph Record	Set by	Seats
Atlanta Motor Speedway	Hampton, Ga.	1.54	197.478	Geoff Bodine (1997)	124,000
Bristol Motor Speedway	Bristol, Tenn.	0.533	128.709	Ryan Newman (2003)	147,000
California Speedway	Fontana, Calif.	2.0	187.432	Ryan Newman (2002)	92,000
Chicagoland Speedway	Joliet, Ill.	1.5	184.786	Tony Stewart (2003)	75,000
Darlington International Raceway	Darlington, S.C.	1.366	173.797	Ward Burton (1996)	65,000
Daytona International Speedway	Daytona Beach, Fla.	2.5	210.364	Bill Elliott (1987)	168,000
Dover International Speedway	Dover, Del.	1.0	161.522	Jeremy Mayfield (2004)	140,000
Homestead-Miami Speedway	Homestead, Fla.	1.5	156.440	Steve Park (2000)	72,000
Indianapolis Motor Speedway	Indianapolis, Ind.	2.5	186.293	Casey Mears (2004)	250,000+
Infineon Raceway	Sonoma, Calif.	1.949*	99.309	Rusty Wallace (2000)	42,500
Kansas Speedway	Kansas City, Kan.	1.5	177.924	Dale Earnhardt Jr. (2002)	75,000
Las Vegas Motor Speedway	Las Vegas, Nev.	1.5	174.904	Kasey Kahne (2004)	126,000
Lowe's Motor Speedway	Concord, N.C.	1.5	187.052	Jimmie Johnson (2004)	167,000
Martinsville Speedway	Martinsville, Va.	0.526	95.371	Tony Stewart (2000)	91,000
Michigan Speedway	Brooklyn, Mich.	2.0	191.149	Dale Earnhardt Jr. (2000)	136,384
New Hampshire Int'l Speedway	Loudon, N.H.	1.058	132.360	Ryan Newman (2004)	91,000
North Carolina Speedway	Rockingham, N.C.	1.017	158.035	Rusty Wallace (2000)	60,113
Phoenix International Raceway	Phoenix, Ariz.	1.0	134.178	Rusty Wallace (2000)	76,812
Pocono Raceway	Long Pond, Penn.	2.5	172.533	Kasey Kahne (2004)	77,000

Auto Racing (Cont.)

	Location	Miles	Qual.mph Record	Set by	Seats
Richmond International Raceway	Richmond, Va.	0.75	129.983	Brian Vickers (2004)	100,000+
Talladega Superspeedway	Talladega, Ala.	2.66	212.809	Bill Elliott (1987)	143,000
Texas Motor Speedway	Ft. Worth, Texas	1.5	194.224	Bill Elliott (2002)	154,861
Watkins Glen International	Watkins Glen, N.Y.	2.45*	124.580	Jeff Gordon (2003)	40,000

*Road courses (not ovals).

Note: Richmond sells reserved seats only (no infield) for Winston Cup races.

Formula One

Race track capacity figures unavailable.

Grand Prix		Miles	Qual.mph Record	Set by
Australian	**Albert Park** (Melbourne)	3.295	140.537	Michael Schumacher (2004)
Austrian	**A1-Ring** (Zeltwig, Austria)	2.684	141.595	Rubens Barrichello (2002)
Bahrain	**Bahrain International** (Sakhir)	3.366	134.432	Michael Schumacher (2004)
Belgian	**Spa-Francorchamps**	4.333	143.418	Mika Hakkinen (1998)
Brazilian	**Interlagos** (Sao Paulo)	2.684	193.747	Rubens Barrichello (2003)
British	**Silverstone** (Towcester)	3.194	148.043	Nigel Mansell (1992)
Canadian	**Circuit Gilles Villeneuve** (Montreal)	2.747	133.941	Juan Montoya (2002)
China	**Shanghai International**	3.3.87	TBD	inaugural race in late 2004
European	**Nürburgring** (Nürburg, Germany)	2.822	135.959	Michael Schumacher (2001)
French	**Magny Cours** (Nevers)	2.641	159.757	Juan Montoya (2002)
German	**Hockenheim** (Germany)	2.796	204.450	Michael Schumacher (2002)
Hungarian	**Hungaroring** (Budapest)	2.468	120.984	Rubens Barrichello (2002)
Italian	**Autodromo Nazionale di Monza** (Milan)	3.585	159.951	Ayrton Senna (1991)
Japanese	**Suzuka** (Nagoya)	3.644	138.515	Gerhard Berger (1991)
Malaysian	**Sepang** (Kuala Lumpur)	3.444	133.220	Michael Schumacher (2004)
Monaco	**Monte Carlo** (Monaco)	2.082	141.595	Rubens Barrichello (2002)
San Marino	**Autodromo Enzo e Dino Ferrari** (Imola, Italy)	3.063	138.362	Jenson Button (2004)
Spanish	**Catalunya** (Barcelona)	2.937	140.935	Michael Schumacher (2004)
United States	**Indianapolis Motor Speedway**	2.606	126.355	Michael Schumacher (2000)

SOCCER

World's Premier Soccer Stadiums

(Listed alphabetically by city)

Stadium	Location	Seats	Stadium	Location	Seats
New Olympic	Athens, Greece	72,000	Estadio Azteca	Mexico City, Mexico	106,000
Eden Park	Auckland, New Zealand	50,000	Meazza (San Siro)	Milan, Italy	85,700
Nou Camp	Barcelona, Spain	98,000	Centenario	Montevideo, Uruguay	73,609
Workers'	Beijing, China	72,000	Luzhniki Stadion	Moscow, Russia	80,840
Olympiastadion	Berlin, Germany	76,243	Olympiastadion	Munich, Germany	63,000
Népstadion	Budapest, Hungary	65,000	San Paolo	Naples, Italy	78,210
Antonio Liberti	Buenos Aires, Argentina	76,689	Stade de France	Paris, France	80,000
National	Cairo, Egypt	90,000	Rungnado (May Day)	Pyongyang, N. Korea	150,000
Salt Lake	Calcutta, India	120,000	Maracana	Rio de Janeiro, Brazil	122,268
Millennium	Cardiff, Wales	72,500	King Fahd II	Riyadh, Saudi Arabia	79,000
Westfalenstadion	Dortmund, Germany	68,600	Olimpico	Rome, Italy	82,307
Lansdowne Road	Dublin, Ireland	48,000	Nacional	Santiago, Chile	77,000
Celtic Park	Glasgow, Scotland	60,506	Morumbi	Sao Paulo, Brazil	80,000
Hampden Park	Glasgow, Scotland	52,670	Chasmil	Seoul, S. Korea	100,000
FNB Stadium	Johannesburg, S. Africa	90,000	Stadium Australia	Sydney, Australia	80,000
Olympic Stadium	Kiev, Ukraine	83,160	Azadi	Tehran, Iran	100,000
new Estadio da Luz	Lisbon, Portugal	65,000	Delle Alpi	Turin, Italy	69,041
Santiago Bernabeu	Madrid, Spain	87,000	Ernst Happel	Vienna, Austria	47,500
Old Trafford	Manchester, England	67,650	International	Yokohama, Japan	77,000

Major League Soccer

The 12-team MLS is the only U.S. Division I professional outdoor league sanctioned by FIFA and U.S. Soccer. Note that all capacity figures are approximate given the adjustments of football stadium seating to soccer.

Western Conference

	Stadium	Built	Seats	Field
CD Chivas USA	Home Depot Center	2003	27,000	Grass
Colorado Rapids	INVESCO Field	2001	17,500	Grass
FC Dallas	Cotton Bowl	1935	22,528	Grass
Kansas City Wizards	Arrowhead	1972	20,571	Grass
L.A. Galaxy	Home Depot Center	2003	27,000	Grass
San Jose Earthquakes	Spartan	1933	26,000	Grass

Eastern Conference

	Stadium	Built	Seats	Field
Chicago Fire	Soldier Field	1924	25,000	Grass
Columbus Crew	Columbus Crew	1999	22,555	Grass
D.C. United	RFK	1961	26,169	Grass
Metro Stars (N.Y./N.J.)	Giants	1976	25,576	Grass
N.E. Revolution	Gillette	2002	21,000	Grass
Real Salt Lake	Rice-Eccles	1927	45,634	Grass

Horse Racing
Triple Crown race tracks

Race	Racetrack	Seats	Infield
Kentucky Derby	Churchill Downs	48,500	65,000
Preakness Stakes	Pimlico Race Course	13,047	60,000
Belmont Stakes	Belmont Park	32,941	N/A

Record crowds: Kentucky Derby—163,628 (1974); Preakness—112,668 (2004); Belmont—120,139 (2004).
Note: Belmont Park does not open infield for Belmont Stakes.

Tennis
Grand Slam center courts

Event	Main Stadium	Seats
Australian Open	Melbourne Park	15,021
French Open	Stade Roland Garros	16,300
Wimbledon	Centre Court	13,813
U.S. Open	Arthur Ashe Stadium	22,547

COLLEGE BASKETBALL

The 50 Largest Arenas

The 50 largest arenas in Division I for the 2004-05 NCAA regular season. Note that (*) indicates part-time home court.

		Seats	Home Team			Seats	Home Team
1	Carrier Dome	33,000	Syracuse	26	Herb Kohl Center	17,142	Wisconsin
2	Thompson-Boling Arena	24,535	Tennessee	27	Assembly Hall	16,450	Illinois
3	Rupp Arena	23,500	Kentucky	28	Frank Erwin Center	16,331	Texas
4	Marriott Center	22,700	BYU	29	Allen Fieldhouse	16,300	Kansas
5	Dean Smith Center	21,750	N. Carolina	30	Hartford Civic Center	16,294	UConn*
6	MCI Center	20,674	Georgetown*	31	L.A. Sports Arena	16,161	USC
7	Continental Airlines Arena	20,049	Seton Hall	32	Carver-Hawkeye Arena	15,500	Iowa
8	Savvis Center	20,000	Saint Louis		Pepsi Arena	15,500	Siena
9	The Rose Garden	19,980	Portland St.*	34	Bryce Jordan Center	15,261	Penn St.
10	RBC Center	19,722	N.C. State	35	United Spirit Arena	15,050	Texas Tech
11	Value City Arena	19,500	Ohio St.	36	Coleman Coliseum	15,043	Alabama
12	Bud Walton Arena	19,200	Arkansas	37	Arena-Auditorium	15,028	Wyoming
13	Wachovia Center	19,010	Villanova*	38	Huntsman Center	15,000	Utah
14	Freedom Hall	18,865	Louisville	39	Breslin Events Center	14,992	Michigan St.
15	Bradley Center	18,717	Marquette	40	LJVM Coliseum	14,665	Wake Forest
16	Thomas & Mack Center	18,500	UNLV	41	Williams Arena	14,625	Minnesota
17	Madison Square Garden	18,470	St. John's*	42	McKale Center	14,545	Arizona
18	FedEx Forum	18,400	Memphis	43	Maravich Assembly Ctr	14,236	LSU
19	University Arena (The Pit)	18,018	New Mexico	44	Wells Fargo Arena	14,198	Arizona St.
20	Alltel Arena	18,000	Arkansas-Little Rock	45	Memorial Gym	14,168	Vanderbilt
21	Comcast Center	17,950	Maryland	46	Mackey Arena	14,123	Purdue
22	New Orleans Arena	17,832	Tulane*	47	James H. Hilton Coliseum	14,092	Iowa St.
23	Carolina Center	17,600	South Carolina	48	WVU Coliseum	14,000	West Virginia
24	Allstate Arena	17,500	DePaul	49	Crisler Arena	13,751	Michigan
25	Assembly Hall	17,257	Indiana	50	CSU Convocation Center	13,610	Cleveland St.

Division I Conference Home Courts

NCAA Division I conferences for the 2004-05 season. Teams with home games in more than one arena are noted.

America East

	Home Floor	Seats
Albany	Rec & Convocation Ctr.	5,000
Binghamton	Events Center	4,500
Boston University	Case Gym	1,800
	& Agganis Arena	6,300
Hartford	Reich Family Pavilion	3,977
Maine	Alfond Arena	5,712
MD-Balt. County	Retriever Activity Center	4,024
New Hampshire	Lundholm Gym	3,500
Northeastern	Solomon Court	1,500
Stony Brook	USB Sports Complex	4,103
Vermont	Patrick Gym	3,228

Atlantic Sun

	Home Floor	Seats
Belmont	Municipal Auditorium	5,000
Campbell	Carter Gym	1,050
Central Fla.	UCF Arena	5,100
Fla. Atlantic	FAU Gym	5,000
Gardner-Webb	Paul Porter Arena	5,000
Georgia St.	GSU Sports Arena	5,500
Jacksonville	Swisher Gym	1,500
Lipscomb	Lipscomb U. Arena	5,028
Mercer	University Center	3,200
Stetson	Edmunds Center	5,000
Troy	Trojan Arena	3,000

Atlantic Coast

	Home Floor	Seats
Clemson	Littlejohn Coliseum	11,020
Duke	Cameron Indoor Stadium	9,314
Florida St.	Tallahassee-Leon County Civic Center	12,100
Georgia Tech	Alexander Memorial Coliseum	9,191
Maryland	Comcast Center	17,950
Miami-FL	Convocation Center	7,000
North Carolina	Dean Smith Center	21,750
N.C. State	RBC Center	19,722
Virginia	University Hall	8,864
Virginia Tech	Cassell Coliseum	10,052
Wake Forest	LJVM Coliseum	14,665

Atlantic 10

	Home Floor	Seats
Dayton	U. of Dayton Arena	13,266
Duquesne	Palumbo Center	6,200
Fordham	Rose Hill Gym	3,470
George Washington	Smith Center	5,000
La Salle	Tom Gola Arena	4,000
Massachusetts	Mullins Center	9,493
Rhode Island	Ryan Center	7,800
Richmond	Robins Center	9,171
St. Bonaventure	Reilly Center	6,000
St. Joseph's-PA	Alumni Mem. Fieldhouse	3,200
Temple	Liacouras Center	10,206
Xavier-OH	Cintas Center	10,200

College Basketball (Cont.)

Big East

	Home Floor	Seats
Boston College	Conte Forum	8,606
Connecticut	Gampel Pavilion	10,027
	& Hartford Civic Center	16,294
Georgetown	MCI Center	20,674
	& McDonough Arena	2,500
Notre Dame	Joyce Center	11,418
Pittsburgh	Petersen Event Center	12,500
Providence	Dunkin Donuts Center	12,993
Rutgers	Louis Brown Athletic Center	9,000
St. John's	Alumni Hall	6,008
	& Madison Square Garden	18,470
Seton Hall	Continental Airlines Arena	20,049
Syracuse	Carrier Dome	33,000
Villanova	The Pavilion	6,500
	& Wachovia Center	19,010
West Virginia	WVU Coliseum	14,000

Big Sky

	Home Floor	Seats
Eastern Wash	Reese Court	6,000
Idaho St.	Reed Gym	3,600
Montana	Adams Center	7,500
Montana St.	Worthington Arena	7,250
Northern Arizona	Walkup Skydome	7,000
Portland St.	Rose Garden	19,980
	& Stott Center	1,775
Sacramento St.	Hornet Gym	1,500
Weber St.	Dee Events Center	12,000

Big South

	Home Floor	Seats
Birmingham-Southern	Bill Battle Coliseum	2,000
Charleston Southern	CSU Fieldhouse	1,500
Coastal Carolina	Kimbel Gymnasium	1,037
High Point	Millis Center	3,000
Liberty	Vines Center	9,000
NC-Asheville	Justice Center	1,100
	& Asheville Civic Center	6,000
Radford	Dedmon Center	5,000
VMI	Cameron Hall	5,029
Winthrop	Winthrop Coliseum	6,100

Big Ten

	Home Floor	Seats
Illinois	Assembly Hall	16,450
Indiana	Assembly Hall	17,257
Iowa	Carver-Hawkeye Arena	15,500
Michigan	Crisler Arena	13,751
Michigan St.	Breslin Events Center	14,759
Minnesota	Williams Arena	14,625
Northwestern	Welsh-Ryan Arena	8,117
Ohio St.	Value City Arena	19,200
Penn St.	Bryce Jordan Center	15,261
Purdue	Mackey Arena	14,123
Wisconsin	Kohl Center	17,142

Big 12

	Home Floor	Seats
Colorado	Coors Events Conference Ctr.	11,076
Iowa St.	Hilton Coliseum	14,092
Kansas	Allen Fieldhouse	16,300
Kansas St.	Bramlage Coliseum	13,500
Missouri	Paige Sports Arena	15,000
Nebraska	Devaney Sports Center	13,500
Baylor	Ferrell Center	10,284
Oklahoma	Lloyd Noble Center	11,100
Oklahoma St.	Gallagher-Iba Arena	13,611
Texas	Erwin Center	16,175
Texas A&M	Reed Arena	12,700
Texas Tech	United Spirit Arena	15,050

Big West

	Home Floor	Seats
Cal Poly	Mott Gym	3,032
CS-Fullerton	Titan Gym	3,500
CS-Northridge	The Matadome	1,600
Idaho	Cowan Spectrum	7,000
Long Beach St.	The Pyramid	5,000
Pacific	Spanos Center	6,150
UC-Davis	The Pavilion	7,200
UC-Irvine	Bren Events Center	5,000
UC-Riverside	Student Rec. Center	3,168
UC-Santa Barbara	The Thunderdome	6,000
Utah St.	The Smith Spectrum	10,270

Colonial

	Home Floor	Seats
Delaware	Bob Carpenter Center	5,000
Drexel	Daskalis Athletic Center	2,300
George Mason	Patriot Center	10,000
Hofstra	Hofstra Arena	5,124
James Madison	JMU Convocation Center	7,156
NC-Wilmington	Trask Coliseum	6,100
Old Dominion	Ted Constant Convocation Ctr.	8,650
Towson	Towson Center	5,000
VCU	Siegel Center	7,500
Wm. & Mary	William &Mary Hall	8,600

Conference USA

	Home Floor	Seats
UAB	Bartow Arena	8,500
Charlotte	Halton Arena	9,105
Cincinnati	Shoemaker Center	13,176
DePaul	Allstate Arena	17,500
East Carolina	Minges Coliseum	8,000
Houston	Hofheinz Pavilion	8,479
Louisville	Freedom Hall	18,865
Marquette	Bradley Center	18,717
Memphis	FedEx Forum	18,400
Saint Louis	Savvis Center	20,000
South Florida	Sun Dome	10,411
Southern Miss	Reed Green Coliseum	8,095
TCU	Daniel-Meyer Coliseum	7,166
Tulane	New Orleans Arena	17,832
	& Fogelman Arena	3,600

Horizon League

	Home Floor	Seats
Butler	Hinkle Fieldhouse	11,043
Cleveland St.	CSU Convocation Center	13,610
Detroit Mercy	Calihan Hall	8,837
IL-Chicago	UIC Pavilion	8,000
Loyola-IL	Gentile Center	5,200
WI-Green Bay	Rush Center	10,400
WI-Milwaukee	Klotsche Center	5,000
Wright St.	Nutter Center	10,632
Youngstown St.	Beeghly Center	8,000

Ivy League

	Home Floor	Seats
Brown	Pizzitola Sports Center	2,800
Columbia	Levien Gymnasium	3,408
Cornell	Newman Arena	4,473
Dartmouth	Leede Arena	2,200
Harvard	Lavietes Pavilion	2,195
Penn	The Palestra	8,700
Princeton	Jadwin Gymnasium	6,854
Yale	Payne Whitney Gym	3,100

Metro Atlantic

	Home Floor	Seats
Canisius	Koessler Athletic Center	2,176
Fairfield	Bridgeport Center	9,500
Iona	Mulcahy Center	3,200
Loyola-MD	Reitz Arena	3,000
Manhattan	Draddy Gymnasium	3,000
Marist	McCann Center	3,944
Niagara	Gallagher Center	2,400
Rider	Alumni Gymnasium	1,650
St. Peter's	Yanitelli Center	3,200
Siena	Pepsi Arena	15,500

Mid-American

	Home Floor	Seats
Akron	JAR Arena	5,942
Ball St.	John E. Wortham Arena	11,500
Bowling Green	Anderson Arena	5,000
Buffalo	Alumni Arena	8,500
Central Mich.	Rose Arena	5,200
Eastern Mich.	Convocation Center	8,824
Kent St.	MAC Center	6,327
Marshall	Cam Henderson Center	9,043
Miami-OH	Millett Hall	9,200
Northern Illinois	Convocation Center	9,100
Ohio Univ.	Convocation Center	13,000
Toledo	Savage Hall	9,000
Western Mich.	University Arena	5,800

Mid-Continent

	Home Floor	Seats
Centenary	Gold Dome	3,000
Chicago St.	Dickens Athletic Center	2,500
IUPUI	IUPUI Gym	2,000
Missouri-KC	Municipal Auditorium	9,287
Oakland	Oakland Arena	3,000
Oral Roberts	Mabee Center	10,575
Southern Utah	Centrum	5,300
Valparaiso	Athletics-Recreation Center	4,500
Western Ill.	Western Hall	5,139

Mid-Eastern Athletic

	Home Floor	Seats
Bethune-Cookman	Moore Gym	3,000
Coppin St.	Coppin Center	3,000
Delaware St.	Memorial Hall	3,000
Florida A&M	Gaither Gym	3,365
Hampton	Hampton Convocation Center	7,500
Howard	Burr Gym	2,200
MD-East.Shore	W.P. Hytche Center	5,500
Morgan St.	Hill Fieldhouse	4,500
Norfolk St.	Echols Hall	7,600
N. Carolina A&T	Corbett Sports Center	6,700
South Carolina St.	SHM Center	3,200

Missouri Valley

	Home Floor	Seats
Bradley	Carver Arena	11,300
Creighton	Omaha Civic Auditorium	9,377
Drake	Knapp Center	7,002
Evansville	Roberts Stadium	12,144
Illinois St.	Redbird Arena	10,200
Indiana St.	Hulman Center	10,200
Northern Iowa	UNI-Dome	10,000
Southern Ill.	SIU Arena	10,000
SW Missouri St.	Hammons Student Center	8,846
Wichita St.	Levitt Arena	10,556

Mountain West

	Home Floor	Seats
Air Force	Clune Arena	6,002
BYU	Marriott Center	22,700
Colorado St.	Moby Arena	8,745
UNLV	Thomas & Mack Center	18,500
New Mexico	The Pit	18,018
San Diego St.	Cox Arena at the Aztec Bowl	12,414
Utah	Huntsman Center	15,000
Wyoming	Arena-Auditorium	15,028

Northeast

	Home Floor	Seats
Central Conn. St.	Detrick Gym	3,200
Farleigh Dickinson	Rothman Center	5,000
LIU-Brooklyn	Schwartz Athletic Center	1,200
Monmouth	Boylan Gym	2,500
Mt. St. Mary's	Knott Arena	3,196
Quinnipiac	Burt Kahn Court	1,500
Robert Morris	Sewall Center	3,056
Sacred Heart	Pitt Center	2,100
St. Francis-NY	Pope Center	1,200
St. Francis-PA	DeGol Arena	3,500
Wagner	Spiro Sports Center	2,100

Ohio Valley

	Home Floor	Seats
Austin Peay	Dunn Center	9,000
Eastern Illinois	Lantz Gym	5,300
Eastern Ky.	McBrayer Arena	6,500
Jacksonville St.	Mathews Coliseum	5,500
Morehead St.	Johnson Arena	6,500
Murray St.	Regional Special Events Ctr.	8,600
Samford	Seibert Hall	4,000
SE Missouri St.	Show Me Center	7,000
Tennessee-Martin	Skyhawk Arena	6,700
Tennessee St.	Gentry Complex	10,500
Tennessee Tech	Eblen Center	10,152

Pacific-10

	Home Floor	Seats
Arizona	McKale Center	14,545
Arizona St.	Wells Fargo Arena	14,198
California	Haas Pavilion	12,172
Oregon	McArthur Court	9,087
Oregon St.	Gill Coliseum	10,400
Stanford	Maples Pavilion	7,500
UCLA	Pauley Pavilion	12,819
USC	LA Sports Arena	16,161
Washington	Bank of America Arena	10,000
Washington. St.	Friel Court	12,058

Patriot League

	Home Floor	Seats
American	Bender Arena	5,000
Army	Christl Arena	5,043
Bucknell	The Rack Pavilion	4,000
Colgate	Cotterell Court	3,000
Holy Cross	Hart Recreation Center	3,600
Lafayette	Kirby Field House	3,500
Lehigh	Stabler Arena	5,600
Navy	Alumni Hall	5,710

College Basketball (Cont.)

Southeastern

Eastern	Home Floor	Seats
Florida	O'Connell Center	12,000
Georgia	Stegeman Coliseum	10,523
Kentucky	Rupp Arena	23,500
South Carolina	Carolina Center	17,600
Tennessee	Thompson-Boling Arena	24,535
Vanderbilt	Memorial Gymnasium	14,168
Western	**Home Floor**	**Seats**
Alabama	Coleman Coliseum	15,316
Arkansas	Bud Walton Arena	19,200
Auburn	Eaves-Memorial Coliseum	10,500
LSU	Maravich Assembly Center	14,164
Mississippi	Tad Smith Coliseum	8,135
Mississippi St.	Humphrey Coliseum	10,500

Southern

	Home Floor	Seats
Appalachian St.	Seby Jones Arena	8,300
Chattanooga	McKenzie Arena	11,218
The Citadel	McAlister Field House	6,200
Coll. of Charleston	John Kresse Arena	5,000
Davidson	Belk Arena	5,700
E. Tenn. St.	Memorial Center	12,000
Elon	Koury Center	2,000
Furman	Timmons Arena	5,000
Ga. Southern	Hanner Fieldhouse	5,500
NC-Greensboro	Fleming Gymnasium	2,320
W. Carolina	Ramsey Center	7,286
Wofford	Johnson Arena	3,500

Southland

	Home Floor	Seats
Lamar	Montagne Center	10,080
Louisiana-Monroe	Fant-Ewing Coliseum	8,000
McNeese St.	Burton Coliseum	8,000
Nicholls St.	Stopher Gym	3,800
Northwestern St.	Prather Coliseum	4,300
Sam Houston St.	Johnson Coliseum	6,172
SE Louisiana	University Center	7,500
S.F. Austin St.	W.R. Johnson Coliseum	7,200
TX-Arlington	Texas Hall	4,200
TX-San Antonio	Convocation Center	5,100
Texas St.-San Marcos	Strahan Coliseum	7,200

Southwestern Athletic

	Home Floor	Seats
Alabama A&M	Elmore Healh/Science Building	6,000
Alabama St.	Joe Reed Acadome	8,000
Alcorn St.	Whitney Complex	7,000
Arkansas-Pine Bluff	HPER Complex	4,500
Grambling St.	Tiger Memorial Gym	4,500
Jackson St.	Williams Center	8,000
Miss.Valley St.	Harrison HPER Athletic Complex	6,000
Prairie View A&M	The Baby Dome	6,600
Southern-BR	Clark Activity Center	7,500
TX Southern	Health & P.E. Building	8,100

Sun Belt

	Home Floor	Seats
Arkansas-Little Rock	Alltel Arena	18,000
Arkansas St	Convocation Center	10,563
Denver	Magness Arena	7,200
Florida International	Golden Panther Arena	5,000
LA-Lafayette	The Cajundome	12,800
Middle Tenn. St.	Murphy Center	11,520
New Mexico St.	Pan American Center	13,071
New Orleans	Lakefront Arena	10,000
North Texas	The Super Pit	10,000
South Alabama	Mitchell Center	10,000
Western Ky.	E.A. Diddle Arena	11,300

West Coast

	Home Floor	Seats
Gonzaga	McCarthey Athletic Center	6,000
Loyola Marymount	Gersten Pavilion	4,156
Pepperdine	Firestone Fieldhouse	3,104
Portland	Chiles Center	5,000
St. Mary's-CA	McKeon Pavilion	3,500
San Diego	Jenny Craig Pavilion	5,100
San Francisco	War Memorial Gym	5,300
Santa Clara	Leavy Center	5,000

Western Athletic

	Home Floor	Seats
Boise St.	BSU Pavilion	12,380
Fresno St.	Selland Arena	10,220
Hawaii	Stan Sherif Center	10,300
Louisiana Tech	Thomas Assembly Center	8,000
Nevada	Lawlor Events Center	11,200
Rice	Autry Court	5,000
San Jose St.	The Events Center	5,000
SMU	Moody Coliseum	8,998
Tulsa	Reynolds Center	8,355
UTEP	Haskins Center	12,000

Independents

	Home Floor	Seats
IPFW	Hilliard Gates Sports Center	2,700
Longwood	Henry I. Willet Jr. Hall	2,522
North Dakota St.	Bison Sports Arena	7,500
Northern Colorado	Butler-Hancock Hall	4,500
Savannah St.	Wiley Gym	2,100
South Dakota St.	Frost Arena	8,500
Texas A&M-Corpus Christi	Memorial Coliseum	4,000
Texas-Pan Am	Health/PE Fieldhouse	3,500
Utah Valley St.	McKay Center	8,000

Future NCAA Final Four Sites

Men

Year	Arena	Seats	Location
2005	Edward Jones Dome	66,000	St. Louis
2006	RCA Dome	47,100	Indianapolis
2007	Georgia Dome	40,000	Atlanta
2008	Alamodome	20,557*	San Antonio
2009	Ford Field	TBA	Detroit
2010	RCA Dome	47,100	Indianapolis
2011	Reliant Stadium	TBA	Houston

Women

Year	Arena	Seats	Location
2005	RCA Dome	56,127	Indianapolis
2006	FleetCenter	18,624	Boston
2007	Gund Arena	20,562	Cleveland
2008	St. Pete Times Forum	TBA	Tampa
2009	Edward Jones Dome	TBA	St. Louis
2010	Alamodome	20,557*	San Antonio

*This was the listed capacity for Spurs games at the Alamodome before they moved to the SBC Center. It is likely that the seating will be reconfigured to fit more spectators for the Final Four.

COLLEGE FOOTBALL

The 40 Largest I-A Stadiums

The 40 largest stadiums in NCAA Division I-A college football heading into the 2004 season. Note that (*) indicates stadium not on campus.

		Location	Seats	Home Team	Conference	Built	Field
1	Michigan Stadium	Ann Arbor, Mich.	107,501	Michigan	Big Ten	1927	Turf
2	Beaver Stadium	University Park, Penn.	107,282	Penn St.	Big Ten	1960	Grass
3	Neyland Stadium	Knoxville, Tenn.	104,079	Tennessee	SEC-East	1921	Grass
4	Ohio Stadium	Columbus, Ohio	101,568	Ohio St.	Big Ten	1922	Grass
5	Rose Bowl*	Pasadena, Calif.	98,636	UCLA	Pac-10	1922	Grass
6	Sanford Stadium	Athens, Ga.	92,020	Georgia	SEC-East	1929	Grass
7	LA Memorial Coliseum*	Los Angeles, Calif.	92,000	USC	Pac-10	1923	Grass
8	Tiger Stadium	Baton Rouge, La.	91,644	LSU	SEC-West	1924	Grass
9	Ben Hill Griffin Stadium at Florida Field	Gainesville, Fla.	88,548	Florida	SEC-East	1929	Grass
10	Jordan-Hare Stadium	Auburn, Ala.	86,063	Auburn	SEC-West	1939	Grass
11	Stanford Stadium	Stanford, Calif.	85,500	Stanford	Pac-10	1921	Grass
12	Bryant-Denny Stadium	Tuscaloosa, Ala.	83,818	Alabama	SEC-West	1929	Grass
13	Legion Field*	Birmingham, Ala.	83,091	UAB	USA	1927	Grass
14	Kyle Field	College Station, Texas	82,600	Texas A&M	Big 12-South	1925	Grass
15	Gaylord Family-Oklahoma Memorial Stadium	Norman, Okla.	82,112	Oklahoma	Big 12-South	1924	Grass
16	Doak Campbell Stadium	Tallahasse, Fla.	82,000	Florida St.	ACC	1950	Grass
17	Memorial Stadium	Clemson, S.C.	81,474	Clemson	ACC	1942	Grass
18	Camp Randall Stadium	Madison, Wis.	81,318	Wisconsin	Big Ten	1917	Turf
19	Notre Dame Stadium	Notre Dame, Ind.	80,795	Notre Dame	Independent	1930	Grass
20	Williams-Brice Stadium	Columbia, S.C.	80,250	South Carolina	SEC-East	1934	Grass
21	Darrell K. Royal-Texas Memorial Stadium	Austin, Texas	80,082	Texas	Big 12-South	1924	Grass
22	Memorial Stadium	Lincoln, Neb.	73,918	Nebraska	Big 12-North	1923	Turf
23	Sun Devil Stadium	Tempe, Ariz.	73,379	Arizona St.	Pac-10	1959	Grass
24	Memorial Stadium	Berkeley, Calif.	73,347	California	Pac-10	1923	Turf
25	Husky Stadium	Seattle, Wash.	72,500	Washington	Pac-10	1920	Turf
26	Orange Bowl*	Miami, Fla.	72,319	Miami-FL	ACC	1935	Grass
27	Spartan Stadium	East Lansing, Mich.	72,027	Michigan St.	Big Ten	1957	Turf
28	Donald W. Reynolds Razorback Stadium	Fayetteville, Ark.	72,000	Arkansas	SEC-West	1938	Grass
29	Qualcomm Stadium	San Diego, Calif.	70,561	San Diego St.	Mountain West	1967	Grass
30	Kinnick Stadium	Iowa City, Iowa	70,397	Iowa	Big Ten	1929	Grass
31	Citrus Bowl*	Orlando, Fla.	70,188	Central Florida	Mid-American	1936	Grass
32	Rice Stadium	Houston, Texas	70,000	Rice	WAC	1950	Turf
33	Superdome*	New Orleans, La.	69,767	Tulane	USA	1975	Turf
34	Memorial Stadium	Champaign, Ill.	69,249	Illinois	Big Ten	1923	Turf
35	Lincoln Financial Field*	Philadelphia, Penn.	68,532	Temple	Big East	2003	Grass
36	Commonwealth	Lexington, Ky.	67,606	Kentucky	SEC-East	1973	Grass
37	Lane Stadium	Blacksburg, Va.	65,115	Va. Tech	ACC	1965	Grass
38	LaVell Edwards Stadium	Provo, Utah	65,000	BYU	Mountain West	1964	Grass
39	Heinz Field*	Pittsburgh, Penn.	64,450	Pittsburgh	Big East	2001	Grass
40	HHH Metrodome*	Minneapolis, Minn.	64,172	Minnesota	Big Ten	1982	Turf

Note: The capacities for several stadiums including the Rose Bowl, Louisiana Superdome and Sun Devil Stadium are often listed differently for other events, such as bowl games, which they host.

2004 Conference Home Fields

NCAA Division I-A conference by conference listing includes member teams heading into the 2004 season. Note that (*) indicates stadium is not on campus.

Atlantic Coast

	Stadium	Built	Seats	Field
Clemson	Memorial	1942	81,474	Grass
Duke	Wallace Wade	1929	33,941	Grass
Florida St.	Doak Campbell	1950	82,000	Grass
Ga. Tech	Bobby Dodd Stadium at Historic Grant Field	1913	55,000	Grass
Maryland	Byrd	1950	48,055	Grass
Miami-FL	Orange Bowl*	1935	72,319	Grass
N. Carolina	Kenan Memorial	1927	60,000	Grass
N.C. State	Carter-Finley	1966	53,800	Grass
Virginia	Scott	1931	61,500	Grass
Va. Tech	Lane	1965	65,115	Grass
Wake Forest	Groves	1968	31,500	Grass

Big East

	Stadium	Built	Seats	Field
Boston College	Alumni	1957	44,500	Turf
Connecticut	Rentschler Field*	2003	40,000	Grass
Pittsburgh	Heinz Field*	2001	64,450	Grass
Rutgers	Rutgers	1994	41,500	Grass
Syracuse	Carrier Dome	1980	49,550	Turf
Temple	Lincoln Financial Field*	2003	68,532	Grass
West Va.	Milan Puskar	1980	63,500	Turf

College Football (Cont.)

Big Ten

	Stadium	Built	Seats	Field
Illinois	Memorial	1923	69,249	Turf
Indiana	Memorial	1960	52,354	Turf
Iowa	Kinnick	1929	70,397	Grass
Michigan	Michigan	1927	107,501	Turf
Michigan St.	Spartan	1957	72,027	Turf
Minnesota	HHH Metrodome*	1982	64,172	Turf
Northwestern	Ryan Field	1926	47,130	Grass
Ohio St.	Ohio	1922	101,568	Grass
Penn St.	Beaver	1960	107,282	Grass
Purdue	Ross-Ade	1924	66,295	Grass
Wisconsin	Camp Randall	1917	76,634	Turf

Big 12

NORTH	Stadium	Built	Seats	Field
Colorado	Folsom Field	1924	53,750	Turf
Iowa St.	Jack Trice Field	1975	45,814	Grass
Kansas	Memorial	1921	50,250	Turf
Kansas St.	Wagner Field	1968	50,000	Turf
Missouri	Faurot Field	1926	62,000	Turf
Nebraska	Memorial	1923	73,918	Turf
SOUTH	**Stadium**	**Built**	**Seats**	**Field**
Baylor	Floyd Casey	1950	50,000	Grass
Oklahoma	Gaylord Family-Oklahoma Memorial	1924	81,000	Grass
Oklahoma St.	Lewis Field	1920	48,000	Turf
Texas	Royal-Memorial	1924	80,082	Grass
Texas A&M	Kyle Field	1925	82,600	Grass
Texas Tech	Jones SBC	1947	53,702	Turf

Note: The annual Oklahoma-Texas game has been played at the Cotton Bowl (capacity 68,252) in Dallas since 1937.

Conference USA

	Stadium	Built	Seats	Field
UAB	Legion Field	1927	83,091	Grass
Army	Michie	1924	39,929	Turf
Cincinnati	Nippert	1924	35,000	Turf
E. Carolina	Dowdy-Ficklen	1963	43,000	Grass
Houston	Robertson	1942	32,000	Grass
Louisville	Papa John's Cardinal	1998	42,000	Turf
Memphis	Liberty Bowl*	1965	62,380	Grass
S. Florida	Raymond James*	1988	41,444	Grass
Southern Miss	M.M. Roberts	1976	33,000	Grass
TCU	Amon G. Carter	1929	44,008	Grass
Tulane	Superdome*	1975	69,767	Turf

Mid-American

	Stadium	Built	Seats	Field
Akron	Rubber Bowl*	1940	35,202	Turf
Ball St.	Ball State	1967	21,581	Grass
Bowling Green	Doyt Perry	1966	30,599	Grass
Buffalo	UB	1993	31,000	Grass
C. Florida	Citrus Bowl	1936	70,188	Grass
Central Mich.	Kelly/Shorts	1972	30,199	Turf
Eastern Mich.	Rynearson	1969	30,200	Turf
Kent St.	Dix	1969	30,520	Turf
Marshall	Joan C. Edwards	1991	38,016	Turf
Miami-OH	Fred Yager	1983	30,012	Grass
Northern Ill.	Huskie	1965	31,000	Turf
Ohio Univ.	Peden	1929	24,000	Grass
Toledo	Glass Bowl	1937	26,248	Turf
Western Mich.	Waldo	1939	30,200	Grass

Mountain West

	Stadium	Built	Seats	Field
Air Force	Falcon	1962	52,480	Grass
BYU	LaVell Edwards	1964	65,000	Grass
Colorado St.	Hughes	1968	30,000	Grass
New Mexico	University	1960	37,370	Grass
San Diego St.	Qualcomm*	1967	70,561	Grass
UNLV	Sam Boyd*	1971	36,800	Grass
Utah	Rice-Eccles	1927	45,634	Grass
Wyoming	War Memorial	1950	33,500	Grass

Pacific-10

	Stadium	Built	Seats	Field
Arizona	Arizona	1928	56,002	Grass
Arizona St.	Sun Devil	1958	73,379	Grass
California	Memorial	1923	75,028	Grass
Oregon	Autzen	1967	53,800	Turf
Oregon St.	Reser	1953	35,362	Turf
Stanford	Stanford	1921	85,500	Grass
UCLA	Rose Bowl*	1922	98,636	Grass
USC	LA Memorial Coliseum*	1923	92,000	Grass
Washington	Husky	1920	72,500	Grass
Washington St.	Martin	1972	37,600	Turf

Southeastern

EAST	Stadium	Built	Seats	Field
Florida	Florida Field	1929	90,000	Grass
Georgia	Sanford	1929	92,020	Grass
Kentucky	Commonwealth	1973	67,530	Grass
S. Carolina	Williams-Brice	1934	80,250	Grass
Tennessee	Neyland	1921	104,079	Grass
Vanderbilt	Vanderbilt	1981	41,600	Grass
WEST	**Stadium**	**Built**	**Seats**	**Field**
Alabama	Bryant-Denny & Legion Field	1929 1927	83,818 83,091	Grass Grass
Arkansas	Donald W. Reynolds Razorback & War Memorial*	1938 1948	72,000 53,727	Grass Grass
Auburn	Jordan-Hare	1939	86,063	Grass
LSU	Tiger	1924	91,600	Grass
Mississippi	Vaught-Hemingway	1915	60,580	Grass
Miss. St.	Davis-Wade	1915	52,884	Grass

Note: EAST–Vanderbilt Stadium was rebuilt in 1981.

Sun Belt

	Stadium	Built	Seats	Field
Arkansas St.	Indian	1974	33,410	Grass
Idaho	Kibbie Dome	1975	16,000	Turf
LA-Lafayette	Cajun Field	1971	31,000	Grass
LA-Monroe	Malone	1978	30,427	Grass
Middle Tennessee St.	Johnny Red Floyd	1933	30,788	Turf
New Mexico St.	Aggie Memorial	1978	30,343	Grass
North Texas	Fouts Field	1952	30,500	Turf
Troy	Movie Gallery Veterans	1950	30,000	Turf
Utah St.	Romney	1968	30,257	Grass

Western Athletic

	Stadium	Built	Seats	Field
Boise St.	Bronco	1970	30,000	Turf
Fresno St.	Bulldog	1980	41,031	Grass
Hawaii	Aloha*	1975	50,000	Turf
Louisiana Tech	Joe Aillet	1968	30,600	Grass
Nevada	Mackay	1967	31,545	Grass
Rice	Rice	1950	70,000	Turf
San Jose St.	Spartan	1933	30,456	Grass
SMU	Gerald J. Ford Stadium	2000	32,000	Grass
Tulsa	Skelly	1930	40,385	Turf
UTEP	Sun Bowl*	1963	51,500	Turf

I-A Independents

	Stadium	Built	Seats	Field
Navy	Navy-Marine Corps Memorial	1959	30,000	Grass
Notre Dame	Notre Dame	1930	80,795	Grass

Business

The Yankees' trade for **Alex Rodriguez**, right, boosted the team's payroll past $180 million in 2004.

AP/Wide World Photos

2003-04 Top 75 TV Sports Events

Final 2003-04 network television ratings for the top nationally telecast sports events, according to Nielsen Media Research. Covers period from Sept. 1, 2003 through Aug. 31, 2004. Events are listed with ratings points and audience share; each ratings point represents 1,084,000 households and shares indicate percentage of TV sets in use.

Multiple entries: SPORTS—NFL Football (43); Summer Olympics (17); Major League Baseball (10); NBA Finals and NCAA Football bowl games (2). NETWORKS—FOX (27); NBC (18); ABC (17); CBS (13).

		Date	Net	Rtg/Sh
1	**Super Bowl XXXVIII** (Patriots vs Panthers)	2/1/04	CBS	41.4/63
2	**AFC Championship Game** (Colts at Patriots)	1/18/04	CBS	24.7/46
3	**NFC Div. Playoff Game** (Packers at Eagles)	1/11/04	FOX	23.8/40
4	**NFC Championship Game** (Panthers at Eagles)	1/18/04	FOX	23.2/45
5	**AFC Div. Playoff Game** (Colts at Chiefs)	1/11/04	CBS	19.7/42
6	**Summer Olympics** (Women's gymnastics individual all-around final, men's/women's swim finals, beach volleyball)	8/19/04	NBC	19.3/32
7	**NFC Wild Card Game** (Seahawks at Packers)	1/4/04	FOX	19.1/39
8	**Summer Olympics** (Women's gymnastics team final, men's/women's swim finals, beach volleyball)	8/17/04	NBC	18.3/30
9	**Summer Olympics** (Men's gymnastics individual all-around final, men's/women's swim finals, men's shot put final)	8/18/04	NBC	17.3/29
10	**MLB ALCS—Game 7** (Red Sox at Yankees)	10/16/03	FOX	17.1/28
11	**MLB NLCS—Game 7** (Marlins at Cubs)	10/15/03	FOX	16.9/27
12	**NFC Div. Playoff Game** (Panthers at Rams)	1/10/04	FOX	16.6/32
	Summer Olympics (Men's gymnastics team final, men's/women's swim finals, women's diving synchronized platform final)	8/16/04	NBC	16.6/27
14	**AFC Wild Card Game** (Broncos at Colts)	1/4/04	CBS	16.5/30
15	**Summer Olympics** (Men's/women's gymnastics individual event finals, men's/women's track & field finals, beach volleyball semifinal)	8/23/04	NBC	16.4/27
16	**AFC Div. Playoff Game** (Titans at Patriots)	1/10/04	CBS	15.9/27
17	**Summer Olympics** (Men's/women's gymnastics individual event finals, men's/women's track & field finals incl. men's 100m, wom. diving platform final)	8/22/04	NBC	15.8/28
18	**Summer Olympics** (Gymnastics champions gala, women's beach volleyball final, women's diving springboard final, men's/women's T&F finals)	8/24/04	NBC	15.7/26
19	**NFC Div. Playoff Game** (Cowboys at Panthers)	1/3/04	ABC	15.4/25
	Summer Olympics (Women's gymnastics team preliminaries, men's/women's swimming finals, beach volleyball)	8/15/04	NBC	15.4/26
21	**Summer Olympics** (Women's track & field finals: 400m hurd. and 200m, wrestling 120kg Greco-Roman final, women's triathlon)	8/22/04	NBC	15.3/26
22	**NFL Regular Season Late Game** (Various teams)	12/7/03	CBS	15.1/28
23	**Sugar Bowl** (LSU vs. Oklahoma)	1/4/04	ABC	14.8/23
24	**AFC Div. Playoff Game** (Titans at Ravens)	1/3/04	ABC	14.6/29

Janet Jackson's "wardrobe malfunction" during halftime of Super Bowl XXXVIII was seen in almost 45 million households.

		Date	Net	Rtg/Sh
	Summer Olympics (Opening ceremonies)	8/13/04	NBC	14.6/27
26	**NFL Regular Season Late Game** (Various teams)	11/16/03	FOX	14.4/27
	Summer Olympics (Men's/women's swim finals, women's platform diving, women's volleyball: USA vs. Russia)	8/20/04	NBC	14.4/27
28	**Rose Bowl** (USC vs. Michigan)	1/1/04	ABC	14.3/25
29	**MLB World Series—Game 6** (Marlins at Yankees)	10/25/03	FOX	13.9/25
30	**NBA Finals—Game 5** (Lakers at Pistons)	6/15/04	ABC	13.8/23
	Summer Olympics (Women's track & field 100m finals, men's/women's swimming finals, women's diving and beach volleyball)	8/21/04	NBC	13.6/26
32	**MLB World Series—Game 4** (Yankees at Marlins)	10/22/03	FOX	13.6/23
	Summer Olympics (Men's/women's swim finals, women's platform diving, women's volleyball: USA vs. Russia)	8/21/04	NBC	13.6/26
34	**NFL Regular Season Late Game** (Various teams)	11/9/03	CBS	13.4/26
	NFL Regular Season Late Game (Various teams)	12/28/03	CBS	13.4/27
36	**NFL Regular Season Late Game** (Various teams)	10/19/03	FOX	13.3/28
37	**MLB World Series—Game 5** (Yankees at Marlins)	10/23/03	FOX	13.2/21

	Date	Net	Rtg/Sh
NFL Regular Season Late Game			
(Various teams) 11/2/03	FOX	13.2/24
39 **NFL Monday Night Football**			
(Buccaneers at Eagles) 9/8/03	ABC	13.0/22
NFL Regular Season Late Game			
(Various teams) 12/21/03	FOX	13.0/26
Belmont Stakes			
(Smarty Jones in second) . .6/5/04	NBC	13.0/29
42 **NFL Thursday Night Football**			
(Jets at Redskins) 9/4/03	ABC	12.9/22
NFL Monday Night Football			
(Cowboys at Giants) 9/15/03	ABC	12.9/22
NFL Regular Season Late Game			
(Various teams) 11/30/03	CBS	12.9/24
NFL Regular Season Late Game			
(Various teams) 12/14/03	FOX	12.9/23
46 **NFL Thanksgiving Day Early Game**			
(Packers at Lions) 11/27/03	FOX	12.8/32
47 **NBA Finals—Game 4**			
(Lakers at Pistons) 6/13/04	ABC	12.7/22
48 **MLB NLCS—Game 6**			
(Marlins at Cubs) 10/14/03	FOX	12.6/20
MLB World Series—Game 2			
(Marlins at Yankees) . . .10/19/03	FOX	12.6/20
NFL Monday Night Football			
(Eagles at Dolphins) 12/15/03	ABC	12.6/21
51 **NFL Regular Season Late Game**			
(Various teams) 9/7/03	FOX	12.5/27
MLB World Series—Game 3			
(Yankees at Marlins) . . .10/21/03	FOX	12.5/21
NFL Monday Night Football			
(Eagles at Packers) 11/10/03	ABC	12.5/21
NFL Regular Season Late Game			
(Various teams) 11/23/03	CBS	12.5/23
NFL Thanksgiving Day Late Game			
(Dolphins at Cowboys) . .11/27/03	CBS	12.5/32
Summer Olympics			
(Men's/women's track & field finals,			
men's platform diving) . . .8/27/04	NBC	12.5/23
57 **NFL Regular Season Early Game**			
(Various teams) 11/23/03	FOX	12.4/27
58 **NFL Regular Season Late Game**			
(Various teams) 10/26/03	CBS	12.2/23
59 **NFL Monday Night Football**			
(Packers at Bears) 9/29/03	ABC	12.1/20
NFL Regular Season Early Game			
(Various teams) 10/26/03	FOX	12.1/27
61 **MLB ALCS Game 1 & NLCS Game 2**			
(Red Sox and Yankees,			
Marlins at Cubs) 10/8/03	FOX	12.0/20
62 **NFL Monday Night Football**			
(Raiders at Broncos) 9/22/03	ABC	11.9/20
NFL Regular Season Late Game			
(Various teams) 10/5/03	FOX	11.9/24
NFL Monday Night Football			
(Chiefs at Raiders) 10/20/03	ABC	11.9/20
Summer Olympics			
(Closing ceremonies) . . .8/29/04	NBC	11.9/20
66 **NFL Regular Season Late Game**			
(Various teams) 9/28/03	FOX	11.8/24
NFL Regular Season Early Game			
(Various teams) 12/7/03	FOX	11.8/26
Summer Olympics			
(Men's gymnastics team preliminaries,			
men's/women's swim finals, men's synchro.			
diving platform final) 8/14/04	NBC	11.8/23
69 **NFL Regular Season Late Game**			
(Various teams) 9/14/03	CBS	11.7/23
70 **MLB ALCS—Game 4**			
(Yankees at Red Sox) . . .10/13/03	FOX	11.6/18
NFL Monday Night Football			
(Patriots at Broncos) 11/3/03	ABC	11.6/20
72 **NFL Monday Night Football**			
(Steelers at 49ers) 11/17/03	ABC	11.1/18
NFL Monday Night Football			
(Packers at Raiders) 12/22/03	ABC	11.1/19
NFL Regular Season Early Game			
(Various teams) 12/28/03	FOX	11.1/26
Summer Olympics			
(Men's/women's track & field finals,			
men's platform diving final, wrestling			
freestyle finals) 8/28/04	NBC	11.1/21

AP/Wide World Photos

Fans at a sports bar in Royal Oak, Mich. celebrate the Pistons' Game 5 victory over the Lakers to clinch the NBA Championship. It was the 30th most-watched sports event of the year.

All-Time Top-Rated TV Programs

NFL Football dominates television's All-Time Top-Rated 50 Programs with 22 Super Bowls and the 1981 NFC Championship Game making the list. Rankings based on surveys taken from January 1961 through August 31, 2004; include only sponsored programs seen on individual networks; and programs under 30 minutes scheduled duration are excluded. Programs are listed with ratings points, audience share and number of households watching, according to Nielsen Media Research.

Multiple entries: The Super Bowl (22); "Roots" (7); "The Beverly Hillbillies" and "The Thorn Birds" (3); "The Bob Hope Christmas Show," "The Ed Sullivan Show," "Gone With The Wind" and 1994 Winter Olympics (2).

	Program	Episode/Game	Net	Date	Rating	Share	Households
1	M*A*S*H (series)	Final episode	CBS	2/28/83	**60.2**	77	50,150,000
2	Dallas (series)	"Who Shot J.R.?"	CBS	11/21/80	**53.3**	76	41,470,000
3	Roots (mini-series)	Part 8	ABC	1/30/77	**51.1**	71	36,380,000
4	**Super Bowl XVI**	49ers 26, Bengals 21	CBS	1/24/82	**49.1**	73	40,020,000
5	**Super Bowl XVII**	Redskins 27, Dolphins 17	NBC	1/30/83	**48.6**	69	40,480,000
6	**XVII Winter Olympics**	Women's Figure Skating	CBS	2/23/94	**48.5**	64	45,690,000
7	**Super Bowl XX**	Bears 46, Patriots 10	NBC	1/26/86	**48.3**	70	41,490,000
8	Gone With the Wind (movie)	Part 1	NBC	11/7/76	**47.7**	65	33,960,000
9	Gone With the Wind (movie)	Part 2	NBC	11/8/76	**47.4**	64	33,750,000
10	**Super Bowl XII**	Cowboys 27, Broncos 10	CBS	1/15/78	**47.2**	67	34,410,000
11	**Super Bowl XIII**	Steelers 35, Cowboys 31	NBC	1/21/79	**47.1**	74	35,090,000
12	Bob Hope Special	Christmas Show	NBC	1/15/70	**46.6**	64	27,260,000
13	**Super Bowl XVIII**	Raiders 38, Redskins 9	CBS	1/22/84	**46.4**	71	38,800,000
	Super Bowl XIX	49ers 38, Dolphins 16	ABC	1/20/85	**46.4**	63	39,390,000
15	**Super Bowl XIV**	Steelers 31, Rams 19	CBS	1/20/80	**46.3**	67	35,330,000
16	**Super Bowl XXX**	Cowboys 27, Steelers 17	NBC	1/28/96	**46.0**	68	44,114,400
	ABC Theater (special)	"The Day After"	ABC	11/20/83	**46.0**	62	38,550,000
18	Roots (mini-series)	Part 6	ABC	1/28/77	**45.9**	66	32,680,000
	The Fugitive (series)	Final episode	ABC	8/29/67	**45.9**	72	25,700,000
20	**Super Bowl XXI**	Giants 39, Broncos 20	CBS	1/25/87	**45.8**	66	40,030,000
21	Roots (mini-series)	Part 5	ABC	1/27/77	**45.7**	71	32,540,000
22	**Super Bowl XXVIII**	Cowboys 30, Bills 13	NBC	1/30/94	**45.5**	66	42,860,000
	Cheers (series)	Final episode	NBC	5/20/93	**45.5**	64	42,360,500
24	The Ed Sullivan Show	Beatles' 1st appearance	CBS	2/9/64	**45.3**	60	23,240,000
25	**Super Bowl XXVII**	Cowboys 52, Bills 17	NBC	1/31/93	**45.1**	66	41,988,100
26	Bob Hope Special	Christmas Show	NBC	1/14/71	**45.0**	61	27,050,000
27	Roots (mini-series)	Part 3	ABC	1/25/77	**44.8**	68	31,900,000
28	**Super Bowl XXXII**	Broncos 31, Packers 24	NBC	1/25/98	**44.5**	67	43,630,000
29	**Super Bowl XI**	Raiders 32, Vikings 14	NBC	1/9/77	**44.4**	73	31,610,000
	Super Bowl XV	Raiders 27, Eagles 10	NBC	1/25/81	**44.4**	63	34,540,000
31	**Super Bowl VI**	Cowboys 24, Dolphins 3	CBS	1/16/72	**44.2**	74	27,450,000
32	**XVII Winter Olympics**	Women's Figure Skating	CBS	2/25/94	**44.1**	64	41,540,000
	Roots (mini-series)	Part 2	ABC	1/24/77	**44.1**	62	31,400,000
34	The Beverly Hillbillies (series)	Regular episode	CBS	1/8/64	**44.0**	65	22,570,000
35	Roots (mini-series)	Part 4	ABC	1/26/77	**43.8**	66	31,190,000
	The Ed Sullivan Show	Beatles' 2nd appearance	CBS	2/16/64	**43.8**	60	22,445,000
37	**Super Bowl XXIII**	49ers 20, Bengals 16	NBC	1/22/89	**43.5**	68	39,320,000
38	The Academy Awards	John Wayne wins Oscar	ABC	4/7/70	**43.4**	78	25,390,000
39	**Super Bowl XXXI**	Packers 35, Patriots 21	FOX	1/26/97	**43.3**	65	42,000,000
	Super Bowl XXXIV	Rams 23, Titans 16	ABC	1/30/00	**43.3**	63	43,618,000
41	The Thorn Birds (mini-series)	Part 3	ABC	3/29/83	**43.2**	62	35,990,000
42	The Thorn Birds (mini-series)	Part 4	ABC	3/30/83	**43.1**	62	35,900,000
43	**NFC Championship Game**	49ers 28, Cowboys 27	CBS	1/10/82	**42.9**	62	34,940,000
44	The Beverly Hillbillies (series)	Regular episode	CBS	1/15/64	**42.8**	62	21,960,000
45	**Super Bowl VII**	Dolphins 14, Redskins 7	NBC	1/14/73	**42.7**	72	27,670,000
46	The Thorn Birds (mini-series)	Part 2	ABC	3/28/83	**42.5**	59	35,400,000
47	**Super Bowl IX**	Steelers 16, Vikings 6	NBC	1/12/75	**42.4**	72	29,040,000
	The Beverly Hillbillies (series)	Regular episode	CBS	2/26/64	**42.4**	60	21,750,000
49	**Super Bowl X**	Steelers 21, Cowboys 17	CBS	1/18/76	**42.3**	78	29,440,000
	ABC Sunday Night Movie	"Airport"	ABC	11/11/73	**42.3**	63	28,000,000
	ABC Sunday Night Movie	"Love Story"	ABC	10/1/72	**42.3**	62	27,410,000
	Cinderella	Musical special	CBS	2/22/65	**42.3**	59	22,250,000
	Roots (mini-series)	Part 7	ABC	1/29/77	**42.3**	65	30,120,000

All-Time Top-Rated Cable TV Sports Events

All-time cable television for sports events, according to ESPN, Turner Sports research and *The Sports Business Daily*. Covers period from Sept. 1, 1980 through Aug. 31, 2004.

NFL Telecasts

		Date	Net	Rtg
1	Chicago at Minnesota	12/6/87	ESPN	17.6
2	Detroit at Miami	12/25/94	ESPN	15.1
3	Chicago at Minnesota	12/3/89	ESPN	14.7
4	Cleveland at San Fran	11/29/87	ESPN	14.2
5	Pittsburgh at Houston	12/30/90	ESPN	13.8

Non-NFL Telecasts

		Date	Net	Rtg
1	MLB: Chicago (NL)-St. Louis	9/7/98	ESPN	9.5
2	NBA: Detroit-Boston	6/1/88	TBS	8.8
3	NBA: Chicago-Detroit	5/31/89	TBS	8.2
4	NBA: Detroit-Boston	5/26/88	TBS	8.1
5	MLB: Giants-Chicago (NL)	9/28/98	ESPN	8.0

Teams Bought in 2004

Seven major league clubs acquired new majority owners from Sept. 26, 2003 through Sept. 25, 2004.

Major League Baseball

Los Angeles Dodgers: On Jan. 29, 2004 MLB owners unanimously approved the sale of the Dodgers from Fox's News Corp. to Boston real estate developer Frank McCourt for $430 million. McCourt reportedly paid in excess of $200 million in cash and took a $205 million loan from Fox to complete the deal. The transaction also included Dodger Stadium and surrounding Chavez Ravine property, plus training sites in Vero Beach and the Dominican Republic. News Corp retains a minority share.

NBA Basketball

Atlanta Hawks: The sale of the Hawks, the NHL's Atlanta Thrashers and the rights to Philips Arena from Time Warner to Atlanta Spirit LLC closed on March 31, 2004. According to Time Warner, the value of the deal is approximately $250 million, including $142 million in Philips Arena debt. While Atlanta Spirit LLC is a partnership of nine investors, partner Steven Belkin will serve as the Hawks governor while Bruce Levenson will head the Thrashers. Time Warner retains a 15 percent passive equity stake.

New Jersey Nets: On Aug. 11, 2004 the NBA Board of Governors unanimously approved the sale of the Nets from Community Youth Organization and holding company YankeeNets to Brooklyn real estate developer Bruce Ratner. Financial terms were not disclosed but Ratner's original offer in 2003 was $300 million. Ratner and his ownership group plan to move the team to a proposed 19,000-seat arena in downtown Brooklyn as early as 2007-08.

Phoenix Suns: On June 30, 2004 the NBA Board of Governors unanimously approved the sale of the Suns from Jerry Colangelo to Arizona native Robert Sarver for an NBA-record $401 million. The transaction also includes the WNBA's Phoenix Mercury, the Arena Football League's Arizona Rattlers and the management contract for America West Arena. Sarver is chairman and CEO of Western Alliance Bancorporation and founder of real estate company, Southwest Value Partners.

NHL Hockey

Atlanta Thrashers: The sale of the Thrashers, the NBA's Atlanta Hawks and the rights to Philips Arena from Time Warner to Atlanta Spirit LLC closed on March 31, 2004. According to Time Warner, the value of the deal is approximately $250 million, including $142 million in Philips Arena debt. While Atlanta Spirit LLC is a partnership of nine investors, partner Steven Belkin will serve as the Hawks governor while Bruce Levenson will head the Thrashers. Time Warner retains a 15 percent passive equity stake.

Also of Note

New Jersey Devils: Jeffrey Vanderbeek, a minority owner of the Devils since 2000 and an executive with Lehman Brothers investment firm, was set to become the principal owner of the club. At press time, however, the deal still needed approval from the NHL Board of Governors. The team had been owned by Puck Holdings and the now-dissolved conglomerate YankeeNets.

NFL Football

Baltimore Ravens: Art Modell's 43-year reign as majority owner came to a close on April 8, 2004 with the completion of the $600 million sale to 44-year-old Steve Bisciotti. The transaction originally began in late 1999 when Bisciotti paid $275 million for 49 percent of the team and was finalized in April with the transfer of the remaining $325 million. Modell retains a one percent ownership stake in the club. Bisciotti is the founder of Aerotek (now known as Allegis Group), a technical staffing firm.

Top 10 Salaries In Each Sport

The top 10 highest paid athletes over the 2003-04 season for the NBA and NHL, 2004 (opening day) for Major League Baseball and the 2003 season for the NFL (including signing bonuses). Figures are in millions of dollars.

Sources: USA Today, Street & Smith's SportsBusiness Journal, NHLPA and AP.

NFL

		Position	Team	Salary
1	Brian Urlacher	Linebacker	Chicago	$15.056
2	Laveranues Coles	Receiver	Washington	13.528
3	Torry Holt	Receiver	St. Louis	13.080
4	Daunte Culpepper	Quarterback	Minnesota	12.440
5	K. Gbaja-Biamila	Def. Lineman	Green Bay	11.654
6	Kyle Turley	Off. Lineman	St. Louis	11.469
7	Peyton Manning	Quarterback	Indianapolis	11.328
8	Keith Brooking	Linebacker	Atlanta	11.206
9	Carson Palmer	Quarterback	Cincinnati	11.080
10	Peerless Price	Receiver	Atlanta	10.535
	League Avg			1.260

MLB

		Position	Team	Salary
1	Manny Ramirez	Left Field	Boston	$22.500
2	Alex Rodriguez	Third Base	NY Yankees	22.000
3	Carlos Delgado	First Base	Toronto	19.700
4	Derek Jeter	Shortstop	NY Yankees	18.600
5	Barry Bonds	Left Field	San Fran.	18.000
6	Pedro Martinez	Pitcher	Boston	17.500
7	Mo Vaughn	First Base	NY Mets	17.167
8	Shawn Green	Right Field	Los Angeles	16.667
9	Mike Piazza	Catcher	NY Mets	16.071
10	Four tied at $16,000,000.			
	League Avg			2.490

NBA

		Position	Team	Salary
1	Kevin Garnett	Forward	Minnesota	$28.000
2	Shaquille O'Neal	Center	LA Lakers	26.518
3	Rasheed Wallace	Center	Port.-Det.	16.990
4	Allan Houston	Guard	New York	15.938
	Chris Webber	Forward	Sacramento	15.938
6	Damon Stoudamire	Guard	Portland	14.375
7	Ten tied at $13,500,000.			
	League Avg			4.920

NHL

		Position	Team	Salary
1	Peter Forsberg	Center	Colorado	$11.000
2	Jaromir Jagr	Right Wing	Wash.-NYR	11.000
3	Pavel Bure	Right Wing	NY Rangers	11.000
	Sergei Fedorov	Center	Anaheim	10.000
	Nicklas Lidstrom	Defenseman	Detroit	10.000
	Keith Tkachuk	Left Wing	St. Louis	10.000
7	Joe Sakic	Center	Colorado	9.881
8	Chris Pronger	Defenseman	St. Louis	9.500
9	Rob Blake	Defenseman	Colorado	9.327
10	Three tied at $9,000,000.			
	League Avg			1.790

2003-04 Team Payrolls

Team payrolls for active players during the 2003-04 season for the NBA and NHL, the 2003 season for the NFL and the 2004 season (as of opening day) for Major League Baseball. Figures are in millions of dollars. **Note:** The NFL and NBA use a salary cap to set payroll. In 2003, the NFL's cap was $75.1 million. In 2003-04 the NBA's cap was $43.84 million. Teams can circumvent the cap, however, via bonuses and other exceptions. **Sources:** USA Today, NHLPA, NFLPA and AP.

	NBA		MLB		NHL		NFL
1	New York $84.5	1	NY Yankees ...$184.2	1	Detroit $77.9	1	New Orleans ...$95.1
2	Portland 84.3	2	Boston 127.3	2	NY Rangers ...76.5	2	Tampa Bay 88.1
3	Dallas 79.1	3	Anaheim 100.5	3	Dallas 68.6	3	Minnesota 85.7
4	Minnesota 72.4	4	NY Mets 96.7	4	Philadelphia ...68.2	4	Cincinnati 85.5
5	Sacramento ...69.6	5	Philadelphia ...93.2	5	Colorado 63.4	5	Atlanta 84.9
6	LA Lakers 65.5	6	Los Angeles ...92.9	6	Toronto 62.5	6	Washington 84.8
7	Phoenix 65.2	7	Chicago-NL 90.6	7	St. Louis 61.7	7	Seattle 84.2
8	Atlanta 63.5	8	Atlanta 90.2	8	Los Angeles ...53.8	8	Chicago 82.8
9	Toronto 60.3	9	St. Louis 83.2	9	Anaheim 53.3	9	New England ...82.1
10	Boston 59.1	10	San Francisco ..82.0	10	Washington 50.9	10	Dallas 81.0
11	Memphis 58.2	11	Seattle 81.5	11	New Jersey 48.9	11	Arizona 81.0
12	Philadelphia ...57.7	12	Houston 75.4	12	Boston 46.6	12	St. Louis 80.2
13	Indiana 57.5	13	Arizona 69.8	13	Vancouver 42.1	13	Jacksonville 78.7
14	Detroit 52.9	14	Colorado 65.4	14	NY Islanders ...40.9	14	NY Giants 78.1
15	Houston 52.4	15	Chicago-AL 65.2	15	Ottawa 39.6	15	Detroit 77.7
16	Chicago 52.2	16	Oakland 59.4	16	Phoenix 39.2	16	Houston 77.6
17	Golden St. 51.8	17	San Diego 55.4	17	Montreal 38.9	17	Philadelphia ...77.4
18	Seattle 50.6	18	Texas 55.1	18	Calgary 36.4	18	Kansas City 77.4
19	New Jersey 48.6	19	Minnesota 53.6	19	Carolina 35.9	19	Green Bay 77.2
20	New Orleans ...48.1	20	Baltimore 51.6	20	San Jose 34.5	20	Baltimore 76.2
21	Orlando 47.7	21	Toronto 50.0	21	Tampa Bay 34.1	21	Tennessee 75.6
22	San Antonio ...46.9	22	Kansas City 47.6	22	Columbus 34.0	22	Carolina 75.0
23	Cleveland 46.5	23	Detroit 46.8	23	Edmonton 33.4	23	Indianapolis ...75.0
24	Washington ...45.7	24	Cincinnati 46.6	24	Buffalo 33.0	24	Oakland 74.9
25	Miami 45.5	25	Florida 42.1	25	Chicago 30.9	25	Buffalo 73.3
26	Milwaukee 42.5	26	Montreal 41.2	26	Atlanta 28.5	26	San Diego 73.2
27	LA Clippers 37.5	27	Cleveland 34.3	27	Minnesota 27.2	27	NY Jets 69.2
28	Denver 36.0	28	Pittsburgh 32.2	28	Florida 26.1	28	Miami 67.4
29	Utah 28.3	29	Tampa Bay 29.6	29	Pittsburgh 23.4	29	Denver 64.8
		30	Milwaukee 27.5	30	Nashville 21.9	30	Pittsburgh 63.6
						31	San Francisco ..60.5
						32	Cleveland 53.8

Highest and Lowest Ticket Prices

The most expensive and least expensive average ticket prices for NFL and MLB franchises for the 2004 season, and NBA and NHL franchises for the 2003-04 season. Note that average ticket prices for each league are as follows: **NFL** $54.75, **MLB** $19.82, **NBA** $44.68 and **NHL** $43.57. **Source:** Team Marketing Report

NFL

	Highest	Venue	Avg. Price
1	New England ....Gillette Stadium		$75.33
2	Washington ....FedExField		68.12
3	Kansas City ....Arrowhead Stadium		67.26
4	NY Giants ....Giants Stadium		66.67
5	NY Jets ....Giants Stadium		66.39

	Lowest	Venue	Avg. Price
1	Buffalo ....Ralph Wilson Stadium		$37.13
2	Arizona ....Sun Devil Stadium		39.72
3	Jacksonville ....ALLTEL Stadium		40.80
4	New Orleans ....Louisiana Superdome		42.36
5	Seattle ....Qwest Field		42.80

MLB

	Highest	Venue	Avg. Price
1	Boston ....Fenway Park		$40.77
2	Chicago Cubs ....Wrigley Field		28.45
3	Philadelphia ....Citizens Bank Park		26.08
4	NY Yankees ....Yankee Stadium		24.86
5	Seattle ....Safeco Field		24.01

	Lowest	Venue	Avg. Price
1	Montreal ....Olympic Stadium		$10.82
2	Florida ....Pro Player Stadium		12.78
3	Kansas City ......Kauffman Stadium		13.42
4	Minnesota ....HHH Metrodome		14.42
5	Colorado ....Coors Field		15.10

NBA

	Highest	Venue	Avg. Price
1	LA Lakers ....Staples Center		$75.40
2	New York .....Madison Sq. Garden		64.10
3	Sacramento ....ARCO Arena		63.20
4	Houston ....Toyota Center		59.05
5	Boston ....FleetCenter		57.02

	Lowest	Venue	Avg. Price
1	Golden St. ....The Arena in Oakland		$26.38
2	Denver ....Pepsi Center		32.77
3	New Orleans ....New Orleans Arena		33.35
4	Detroit ....The Palace		33.60
5	Seattle ....KeyArena		34.01

NHL

	Highest	Venue	Avg. Price
1	Detroit ....Joe Louis Arena		$57.11
2	Philadelphia ....Wachovia Center		57.06
3	Toronto ....Air Canada Centre		56.90
4	New Jersey ..Continental Airlines Arena		54.67
5	Boston ....FleetCenter		54.10

	Lowest	Venue	Avg. Price
1	Florida ....Office Depot Center		$29.76
2	Phoenix ....Glendale Arena		31.32
3	Carolina ....RBC Center		31.77
4	Atlanta ....Philips Arena		34.87
5	Buffalo ....HSBC Arena		35.46

The Rights Stuff

Major sports and their television deals as of Sept. 1, 2004.

League	Network	Yrs (Ends)	Amount	League	Network	Yrs (Ends)	Amount
NFL	ESPN	8 (2006)	$4.8 billion	NCAA Women's Hoops			
	FOX	8 (2006)	4.4 billion	Tournament	ESPN	11 (2013)	$200 million@
	ABC	8 (2006)	4.4 billion	NCAA Football BCS	ABC	8 (2006)	$930 million%
	CBS	8 (2006)	4.0 billion	NASCAR	NBC/Turner	6 (2006)	$1.2 billion
NBA	ABC/ESPN	6 (2008)	$2.4 billion		FOX	8 (2008)	1.6 billion
	TNT	6 (2008)	2.2 billion	Olympics	NBC	13 (2008)	$3.5 billion #
MLB	FOX	6 (2006)	$2.5 billion		NBC	9 (2012)	2.2 billion #
	ESPN	6 (2005)	undisclosed *	PGA Tour	ABC, CBS,		
NHL	NBC	2 (2006)	— †		NBC, ESPN, USA		
	ESPN	1 (2005)	$60 million	and The Golf Channel		4 (2006)	$850 million
NCAA Men's Hoops				WNBA	ABC/ESPN	6 (2008)	undisclosed
Tournament	CBS	1-1 (2013)	$6.0 billion				

* Terms of the deal are undisclosed but estimated to be valued at more than $850 million.
† NBC and the NHL agreed to a two-year deal whereby the two entities share advertising revenues. NBC paid no rights fees and has an option to renew the deal for an additional two years. ESPN also holds an option to renew its deal for an additional two years for a reported $70 million per year.
@ Also included are all rights to the College World Series and various other NCAA championships.
% ABC and the Rose Bowl agreed to a new eight-year deal (2007-2014) for approximately $300 million to include eight Rose Bowls and two other BCS title games. Negotiations for the other BCS bowls were to begin in September 2004.
# NBC has a deal with the Olympics worth approximately $3.5 billion, which gave them exclusive rights to the 1996 Summer Games (Atlanta), the 2000 Summer Games (Sydney), the 2002 Winter Games (Salt Lake City), the 2004 Summer Games (Athens), the 2006 Winter Games (Torino), and the 2008 Summer Games (Beijing). In July 2003, NBC announced a new deal which also gave them rights to the 2010 Winter Games (Vancouver) and the 2012 Summer Games (TBA).
Note: The NFL, NBA and MLB also have their own league-owned channels. The NFL Network shows preseason games, NBA TV offers 96 NBA regular season games during the 2004-05 while MLB's Baseball Channel begins in 2005 and will be limited to spring training games until at least 2006.

AWARDS

The Peabody Award

Presented annually since 1940 for outstanding achievement in radio and television broadcasting. Named after Georgia banker and philanthropist George Foster Peabody, the awards are administered by the Henry W. Grady College of Journalism and Mass Communication at the University of Georgia.

Television

Year
1960 **CBS** for coverage of 1960 Winter and Summer Olympic Games
1966 ABC's **"Wide World of Sports"** (for Outstanding Achievement in Promotion of International Understanding).
1968 **ABC Sports** coverage of both the 1968 Winter and Summer Olympic Games.
1972 **ABC Sports** coverage of the 1972 Summer Olympics in Munich.
1973 **Joe Garagiola** of NBC Sports (for "The Baseball World of Joe Garagiola").
1976 **ABC Sports** coverage of both the 1976 Winter and Summer Olympic Games.
1984 **Roone Arledge**, president of ABC News & Sports (for significant contributions to news and sports programming).
1986 **WFAA-TV**, Dallas for its investigation of the Southern Methodist University football program.
1988 **Jim McKay** of ABC Sports (for pioneering efforts and career accomplishments in the world of TV sports).
1991 **CBS Sports** coverage of the 1991 Masters golf tournament
 & **HBO Sports** and **Black Canyon Productions** for the baseball special "When It Was A Game."
1995 **Kartemquin Educational Films** and **KTCA-TV** in St. Paul, MN, presented on PBS for "Hoop Dreams"
 & **Turner Original Productions** for the baseball special "Hank Aaron: Chasing the Dream."
1996 **HBO Sports** for its documentary "The Journey of the African-American Athlete."
 & **Bud Greenspan**, a personal award for excellence in chronicling the Olympic Games.
1997 **HBO Pictures** and **The Thomas Carter Company** for the original movie "Don King: Only in America."
1998 **KTVX-TV**, Salt Lake City for its investigation into the policies and practices of the IOC during the Olympic bribery scandal & **HBO Sports** for its ongoing series of sports documentaries.
1999 **WCPO-TV**, Cincinnati for its investigation of fraud and misrepresentation in the construction of new sports stadiums,
 HBO Sports for its documentary "Dare to Compete: The Struggle of Women in Sports," and its documentary "Fists of Freedom: The Story of the '68 Summer Games" & **ESPN** for its "SportsCentury" series.
2000 **HBO Sports** for its documentary "Ali-Frazier 1: One Nation...Divisible."
2001 **The Ciesla Foundation** and **Cinemax** for the documentary "The Life and Times of Hank Greenberg."
2002 **ESPN** for "The Complete Angler," its documentary celebrating nature, art and fly-fishing.

Radio

Year
1974 **WSB** radio in Atlanta for "Henry Aaron: A Man with a Mission."
1991 **Red Barber** of National Public Radio (for his six decades as a broadcaster and his 10 years as a commentator on NPR's "Morning Edition").

National Emmy Awards
Sports Programming

Presented by the Academy of Television Arts and Sciences since 1948. Eligibility period covered the calendar year from 1948-57 and since 1988.

Multiple major award winners: ABC "Wide World of Sports" (20), NFL Films Football coverage (14); ABC Olympics coverage, CBS NFL Football coverage, HBO "Real Sports with Bryant Gumbel," NBC Olympics coverage (9); ABC "Monday Night Football," ESPN "Outside the Lines," ESPN "SportsCenter" and FOX MLB coverage (8); CBS NCAA Basketball coverage, CBS "NFL Today" and ESPN "GameDay/Sunday NFL Countdown (5); ABC "The American Sportsman," ABC Indianapolis 500 coverage, CBS Tour de France coverage, ESPN "SportsCentury" series and FOX "NFL Sunday" (3); ABC Kentucky Derby coverage, ABC "Sportsbeat," Bud Greenspan Olympic specials, CBS Olympics coverage, CBS Golf coverage, ESPN "Speedworld," ESPN Sunday Night Football, MTV Sports series, The NBA on NBC, NBC Ironman Triathlon coverage and NBC World Series coverage (2).

1949
Coverage—"Wrestling" (KTLA, Los Angeles)

1950
Program—"Rams Football" (KNBH-TV, Los Angeles)

1954
Program—"Gillette Cavalcade of Sports" (NBC)

1965-66
Programs—"Wide World of Sports" (ABC), "Shell's Wonderful World of Golf" (NBC) and "CBS Golf Classic" (CBS)

1966-67
Program—"Wide World of Sports" (ABC)

1967-68
Program—"Wide World of Sports" (ABC)

1968-69
Program—"1968 Summer Olympics" (ABC)

1969-70
Programs—"NFL Football" (CBS) and "Wide World of Sports" (ABC)

1970-71
Program—"Wide World of Sports" (ABC)

1971-72
Program—"Wide World of Sports" (ABC)

1972-73
News Special—"Coverage of Munich Olympic Tragedy" (ABC)
Sports Programs—"1972 Summer Olympics" (ABC) and "Wide World of Sports" (ABC)

1973-74
Program—"Wide World of Sports" (ABC)

1974-75
Non-Edited Program— "Jimmy Connors vs. Rod Laver Tennis Challenge" (CBS)
Edited Program— "Wide World of Sports" (ABC)

1975-76
Live Special—"1975 World Series: Cincinnati vs. Boston" (NBC)
Live Series—"NFL Monday Night Football" (ABC)
Edited Specials—"1976 Winter Olympics" (ABC) and "Triumph and Tragedy: The Olympic Experience" (ABC)
Edited Series—"Wide World of Sports" (ABC)

1976-77
Live Special—"1976 Summer Olympics" (ABC)
Live Series—"The NFL Today/NFL Football" (CBS)
Edited Special—"1976 Summer Olympics Preview" (ABC)
Edited Series—"The Olympiad" (PBS)

1977-78
Live Special—"Muhammad Ali vs. Leon Spinks Heavyweight Championship Fight" (CBS)
Live Series—"The NFL Today/NFL Football" (CBS)
Edited Special—"The Impossible Dream: Ballooning Across the Atlantic" (CBS)
Edited Series—"The Way It Was" (PBS)

1978-79
Live Special—"Super Bowl XIII: Pittsburgh vs Dallas" (NBC)
Live Series—"NFL Monday Night Football" (ABC)
Edited Special—"Spirit of '78: The Flight of Double Eagle II" (ABC)
Edited Series—"The American Sportsman" (ABC)

1979-80
Live Special—"1980 Winter Olympics" (ABC)
Live Series—"NCAA College Football" (ABC)
Edited Special—"Gossamer Albatross: Flight of Imagination" (CBS)
Edited Series—"NFL Game of the Week" (NFL Films)

1980-81
Live Special—"1981 Kentucky Derby" (ABC)
Live Series—"PGA Golf Tour" (CBS)
Edited Special—"Wide World of Sports 20th Anniversary Show" (ABC)
Edited Series—"The American Sportsman" (ABC)

1981-82
Live Special—"1982 NCAA Basketball Final: North Carolina vs Georgetown" (CBS)
Live Series—"NFL Football" (CBS)
Edited Special—"1982 Indianapolis 500" (ABC)
Edited Series—"Wide World of Sports" (ABC)

1982-83
Live Special—"1982 World Series: St. Louis vs Milwaukee" (NBC)
Live Series—"NFL Football" (CBS)
Edited Special—"Wimbledon '83" (NBC)
Edited Series—"Wide World of Sports" (ABC)
Journalism—"ABC Sportsbeat" (ABC)

1983-84
No awards given

1984-85

Live Special—"1984 Summer Olympics" (ABC)
Live Series—No award given
Edited Special—"Road to the Super Bowl '85" (NFL Films)
Edited Series—"The American Sportsman" (ABC)
Journalism—"ABC Sportsbeat" (ABC), "CBS Sports Sunday" (CBS), Dick Schaap features (ABC) and 1984 Summer Olympic features (ABC)

1985-86

No awards given

1986-87

Live Special—"1987 Daytona 500" (CBS)
Live Series—"NFL Football" (CBS)
Edited Special—"Wide World of Sports 25th Anniversary Special" (ABC)
Edited Series—"Wide World of Sports" (ABC)

1987-88

Live Special—"1987 Kentucky Derby" (ABC)
Live Series—"NFL Monday Night Football" (ABC)
Edited Special—"Paris-Roubaix Bike Race" (CBS)
Edited Series—"Wide World of Sports" (ABC)

1988

Live Special—"1988 Summer Olympics" (NBC)
Live Series—"1988 NCAA Basketball" (CBS)
Edited Special—"Road to the Super Bowl '88" (NFL Films)
Edited Series—"Wide World of Sports" (ABC)
Studio Show—"NFL GameDay" (ESPN)
Journalism—1988 Summer Olympic reporting (NBC)

1989

Live Special—"1989 Indianapolis 500" (ABC)
Live Series—"NFL Monday Night Football" (ABC)
Edited Special—"Trans-Antarctica! The International Expedition" (ABC)
Edited Series—"This is the NFL" (NFL Films)
Studio Show—"NFL Today" (CBS)
Journalism—1989 World Series Game 3 earthquake coverage (ABC)

1990

Live Special—"1990 Indianapolis 500" (ABC)
Live Series—"1990 NCAA Basketball Tournament" (CBS)
Edited Special—"Road to Super Bowl XXIV" (NFL Films)
Edited Series—"Wide World of Sports" (ABC)
Studio Show—"SportsCenter" (ESPN)
Journalism—"Outside the Lines: The Autograph Game" (ESPN)

1991

Live Special—"1991 NBA Finals: Chicago vs LA Lakers" (NBC)
Live Series—"1991 NCAA Basketball Tournament" (CBS)
Edited Special—"Wide World of Sports 30th Anniversary Special" (ABC)
Edited Series—"This is the NFL" (NFL Films)
Studio Show—"NFL GameDay" (ESPN) and "NFL Live" (NBC)
Journalism—"Outside the Lines: Steroids—Whatever It Takes" (ESPN)

1992

Live Special—"1992 Breeders' Cup" (NBC)
Live Series—"1992 NCAA Basketball Tournament" (CBS)
Edited Special—"1992 Summer Olympics" (NBC)
Edited Series—"MTV Sports" (MTV)
Studio Show—"The NFL Today" (CBS)
Journalism—"Outside the Lines: Portraits in Black and White" (ESPN)

1993

Live Special—"1993 World Series" (CBS)
Live Series—"Monday Night Football" (ABC)
Edited Special—"Road to the Super Bowl" (NFL Films)
Edited Series—"This is the NFL" (NFL Films)
Studio Show—"The NFL Today" (CBS)
Journalism (TIE)—"Outside the Lines: Mitch Ivey Feature" (ESPN) and "SportsCenter: University of Houston Football" (ESPN).
Feature—"Arthur Ashe: His Life, His Legacy" (NBC).

1994

Live Special—"NHL Stanley Cup Finals" (ESPN)
Live Series—"Monday Night Football" (ABC)
Edited Special—"Lillehammer '94: 16 Days of Glory" (Disney/Cappy Productions)
Edited Series—"MTV Sports" (MTV)
Studio Show—"NFL GameDay" (ESPN)
Journalism—"1994 Winter Olympic Games: Mossad feature" (CBS)
Feature (TIE)—"Heroes of Telemark" on Winter Olympic Games (CBS); and "SportsCenter: Vanderbilt running back Brad Gaines" (ESPN).

1995

Live Special—"Cal Ripken 2131" (ESPN)
Live Series—"ESPN Speedworld" (ESPN)
Edited Special (quick turn-around)—"Outside the Lines: Play-ball–Opening Day in America" (ESPN)
Edited Special (long turn-around)—"Lillehammer, an Olympic Diary" (CBS)
Edited Series—"NFL Films Presents" (NFL Films)
Studio Show (TIE)—"NFL GameDay" (ESPN) and "FOX NFL Sunday" (FOX)
Journalism—"Real Sports with Bryant Gumbel: Broken Promises" (HBO)
Feature (TIE)—"SportsCenter: Jerry Quarry" (ESPN) and "Real Sports with Bryant Gumbel: Coach" (HBO).

1996

Live Special—"1996 World Series" (FOX)
Live Series—"ESPN Speedworld" (ESPN)
Edited Special—"Football America" (TNT/NFL Films)
Edited Series—"NFL Films Presents" (NFL Films)
Live Event Turnaround—"The Centennial Olympic Games" (NBC)
Studio Show—"SportsCenter" (ESPN)
Journalism—"Outside the Lines: AIDS in Sports" (ESPN)
Feature—"Real Sports with Bryant Gumbel: 1966 Texas Western NCAA Champs" (HBO).

"Baseball" Wins Prime Time Emmy

Ken Burns's miniseries "Baseball" won the 1994 Emmy Award for Outstanding Informational Series. The nine-part documentary aired from Sept. 18-28, 1994 and ran more than 18 hours, drawing the largest audience in PBS history.

National Emmy Awards (Cont.)

1997

Live Special—"The NBA Finals" (NBC)
Live Series—"NFL Monday Night Football" (ABC)
Edited Special—"Ironman Triathlon World Championship" (NBC/World Triathlon Corporation)
Edited Series—"NFL Films Presents" (NFL Films)
Live Event Turnaround—"Outside The Lines: Inside The Kentucky Derby" (ESPN)
Studio Show—"FOX NFL Sunday" (FOX)
Journalism—"Real Sports with Bryant Gumbel: Pros and Cons" (HBO)
Feature—"NFL Films Presents: Eddie George" (NFL Films).

1998

Live Special—"McGwire's 62nd Home Run Game" (FOX)
Live Series—"NBC Golf Tour" (NBC)
Edited Special—"A Cinderella Season: The Lady Vols Fight Back" (HBO)
Edited Series—"Real Sports with Bryant Gumbel" (HBO)
Live Event Turnaround—"Wimbledon '98" (NBC)
Studio Show—"FOX NFL Sunday" (FOX)
Journalism (TIE)—"Real Sports with Bryant Gumbel: Winning At All Costs" (HBO) and "Real Sports with Bryant Gumbel: Diamond Bucks" (HBO)
Feature—"NFL Films Presents: Steve Mariucci" (ESPN2 and NFL Films).

1999

Live Special—"2000 MLB All-Star Game" (FOX)
Live Series—"MLB Regular Season" (FOX)
Edited Special—"Ironman Triathlon World Championship" (NBC)
Edited Series—"SportsCentury: 50 Greatest Athletes" (ESPN)
Live Event Turnaround—"The World Track & Field Championships" (NBC)
Studio Show—"MLB Pre-Game Show" (FOX)
Journalism—"Real Sports with Bryant Gumbel: Fake Golf Clubs" (HBO)
Feature—"NFL Films Presents: Lt. Kalsu" (ESPN2)

2000

Live Special—"2000 World Series" (FOX)
Live Series—"NFL Sunday Night Football" (ESPN)
Edited Special—"Hoops and Hoosiers: The Story of the Final Four 2000" (CBS)
Edited Series—"SportsCentury: The Top 50 & Beyond" (ESPN)
Live Event Turnaround—"The Games of the XXVII Olympiad" (NBC)
Studio Show—"FOX NFL Sunday" (FOX)
Journalism—"Real Sports with Bryant Gumbel: Dominican Free-For-All" (HBO)
Feature—"The Games of the XXVII Olympiad" (NBC)

2001

Live Special—"2001 World Series" (FOX)
Live Series—"NASCAR on FOX" (FOX)
Edited Special—"ABC's Wide World of Sports 40th Anniversary Special" (ABC)
Edited Series—"SportsCentury" (ESPN Classic)
Live Event Turnaround—"Tour de France" (CBS)
Studio Show—Weekly—"Sunday NFL Countdown" (ESPN)
Studio Show—Daily—"Inside the NBA" (TNT/TBS)
Journalism—"Real Sports with Bryant Gumbel: Amare Stoudemire" (HBO)
Feature—"NFL Films Presents: Gerry Faust—The Golden Dream" (ESPN2)
Documentary—"Do You Believe in Miracles? The Story of the 1980 U.S. Hockey Team" (HBO)

AP/Wide World Photos
NFL Films president **Steve Sabol** and founder, Ed Sabol, won the Lifetime Achievement Emmy Award in 2003.

2002

Live Special—"XIX Olympic Winter Games" (NBC)
Live Series—"The NBA on NBC" (NBC)
Edited Special—"America's Heroes: The Bravest vs. The Finest" (NBC)
Edited Series—"Real Sports with Bryant Gumbel" (HBO)
Live Event Turnaround—"Tour de France" (CBS)
Studio Show—Weekly—"Inside the NFL" (HBO & NFL Films)
Studio Show—Daily—"Baseball Tonight" (ESPN)
Journalism—"Outside the Lines, Weekly: Eligibility for Sale" (ESPN) and "Outside the Lines, Weekly: Iraqi Athletes, Tales of Torture" (ESPN)
Long Feature—"SportsCenter: Flight 93" (ESPN)
Short Feature—"SportsCenter: Chris Paul" (ESPN), "XIX Olympic Winter Games: Bill Johnson" (NBC) and "XIX Olympic Winter Games: The Sheas" (NBC)
Documentary—"Our Greatest Hopes, Our Worst Fears: The Tragedy of the Munich Games" (ABC)

2003

Live Special— "MLB on FOX: Post Season" (FOX)
Live Series— "ESPN NFL Sunday Night Football" (ESPN)
Edited Special— "Ironman Triathlon World Championship" (NBC/World Triathlon Corporation)
Edited Series/Anthology—Legendary Nights" (HBO)
Live Event Turnaround— "Tour de France" (CBS)
Studio Show—Weekly— "Sunday NFL Countdown" (ESPN)
Studio Show—Daily— "SportsCenter" (ESPN)
Journalism—"Real Sports with Bryant Gumbel: Marcus Dixon" (HBO)
Editing—"Jim McKay — My World in My Words " (HBO)
The Dick Schaap Outstanding Writing Award—
"Wimbledon — Where is Wimbledon?" (ESPN)
Long Feature—"NFL Films Presents on The NFL Network: Big Charlie's" (NFL Network/NFL Films) and "Real Sports with Bryant Gumbel: Alex Zanardi" (HBO)
Short Feature—"SportsCenter: Picking Up Butch" (HBO)
Documentary—"The Curse of the Bambino" (HBO/Black Canyon Productions/Clear Channel Entertainment Television)

Sportscasters of the Year
National Emmy Awards

An Emmy Award for Sportscasters was first introduced in 1968 and given for Outstanding Host/Commentator for the 1967-68 TV season. Two awards, one for Outstanding Host or Play-by-Play and the other for Outstanding Analyst, were first presented in 1981 for the 1980-81 season. Three awards, for Outstanding Studio Host, Play-by-Play and Studio Analyst, have been given since the 1993 season, and one more, Sports Event Analyst, was added in 1997.

Multiple winners: John Madden (14); Bob Costas (13); Jim McKay (9); Joe Buck, Cris Collinsworth, Dick Enberg and Al Michaels (4); Keith Jackson and Tim McCarver (3); Terry Bradshaw and James Brown (2). Note that Jim McKay has won a total of 12 Emmy awards: eight for Host/Commentator, one for Host/Play-by-Play, two for Sports Writing, and one for News Commentary.

Season	Host/Commentator	Season	Host/Play-by-Play	Season	Analyst
1967-68	Jim McKay, ABC	1980-81	Dick Enberg, NBC	1980-81	Dick Button, ABC
1968-69	No award	1981-82	Jim McKay, ABC	1981-82	John Madden, CBS
1969-70	No award	1982-83	Dick Enberg, NBC	1982-83	John Madden, CBS
1970-71	Jim McKay, ABC	1983-84	No award	1983-84	No award
	& Don Meredith, ABC	1984-85	George Michael, NBC	1984-85	No award
1971-72	No award	1985-86	No award	1985-86	No award
1972-73	Jim McKay, ABC	1986-87	Al Michaels, ABC	1986-87	John Madden, CBS
1973-74	Jim McKay, ABC	1987-88	Bob Costas, NBC	1987-88	John Madden, CBS
1974-75	Jim McKay, ABC	1988	Bob Costas, NBC	1988	John Madden, CBS
1975-76	Jim McKay, ABC	1989	Al Michaels, ABC	1989	John Madden, CBS
1976-77	Frank Gifford, ABC	1990	Dick Enberg, NBC	1990	John Madden, CBS
1977-78	Jack Whitaker, CBS	1991	Bob Costas, NBC	1991	John Madden, CBS
1978-79	Jim McKay, ABC	1992	Bob Costas, NBC	1992	John Madden, CBS
1979-80	Jim McKay, ABC				

Studio Host

Year		Year		Year	
1993	Bob Costas, NBC	1997	Dan Patrick, ESPN	2001	Bob Costas, HBO &
1994	Bob Costas, NBC	1998	James Brown, FOX		Ernie Johnson, TNT/TBS
1995	Bob Costas, NBC	1999	James Brown, FOX	2002	Bob Costas, HBO/NBC
1996	Bob Costas, NBC	2000	Bob Costas, NBC	2003	Bob Costas, HBO/NBC

Play-by-Play

Year		Year		Year	
1993	Dick Enberg, NBC	1997	Bob Costas, NBC	2001	Joe Buck, FOX
1994	Keith Jackson, ABC	1998	Keith Jackson, ABC	2002	Joe Buck, FOX
1995	Al Michaels, ABC	1999	Joe Buck, FOX	2003	Joe Buck, FOX
1996	Keith Jackson, ABC	2000	Al Michaels, ABC		

Studio Analyst

Year		Year		Year	
1993	Billy Packer, CBS	1997	Cris Collinsworth, HBO/NBC	2001	Terry Bradshaw, FOX
1994	John Madden, FOX	1998	Cris Collinsworth, HBO/FOX	2002	Cris Collinsworth, HBO
1995	John Madden, FOX	1999	Terry Bradshaw, FOX	2003	Cris Collinsworth, HBO
1996	Howie Long, FOX	2000	Steve Lyons, FOX		

Sports Events Analyst

Year		Year		Year	
1997	Joe Morgan, ESPN	2000	Tim McCarver, FOX	2003	John Madden, ABC
1998	John Madden, FOX	2001	Tim McCarver, FOX		
1999	John Madden, FOX	2002	Tim McCarver, FOX		

Lifetime Achievement Emmy Award

Year		Year		Year		Year	
1989	Jim McKay	1993	Pat Summerall	1997	Jim Simpson	2001	Herb Granath
1990	Lindsey Nelson	1994	Howard Cosell	1998	Keith Jackson	2002	Roone Arledge*
1991	Curt Gowdy	1995	Vin Scully	1999	Jack Buck	2003	Ed and Steve Sabol
1992	Chris Schenkel	1996	Frank Gifford	2000	Dick Enberg		

*Arledge is the only recipient of two Lifetime Achievement Emmy Awards. In addition to sports, he won the lifetime award for "News and Documentary" in 2002.

National Sportscasters and Sportswriters Assn. Award

Sportscaster of the Year presented annually since 1959 by the National Sportcasters and Sportswriters Association, based in Salisbury, N.C. Voting is done by NSSA members and selected national media.

Multiple winners: Bob Costas (8); Chris Berman (6) Keith Jackson (5); Lindsey Nelson and Chris Schenkel (4); Dick Enberg, Al Michaels and Vin Scully (3); Joe Buck, Curt Gowdy and Ray Scott (2).

Year		Year		Year		Year	
1959	Lindsey Nelson	1971	Ray Scott	1982	Vin Scully	1994	Chris Berman
1960	Lindsey Nelson	1972	Keith Jackson	1983	Al Michaels	1995	Bob Costas
1961	Lindsey Nelson	1973	Keith Jackson	1984	John Madden	1996	Chris Berman
1962	Lindsey Nelson	1974	Keith Jackson	1985	Bob Costas	1997	Bob Costas
1963	Chris Schenkel	1975	Keith Jackson	1986	Al Michaels	1998	Jim Nantz
1964	Chris Schenkel	1976	Keith Jackson	1987	Bob Costas	1999	Dan Patrick
1965	Vin Scully	1977	Pat Summerall	1988	Bob Costas	2000	Bob Costas
1966	Curt Gowdy	1978	Vin Scully	1989	Chris Berman	2001	Chris Berman
1967	Chris Schenkel	1979	Dick Enberg	1990	Chris Berman	2002	Joe Buck
1968	Ray Scott	1980	Dick Enberg & Al Michaels	1991	Bob Costas	2003	Joe Buck
1969	Curt Gowdy			1992	Bob Costas		
1970	Chris Schenkel	1981	Dick Enberg	1993	Chris Berman		

The Pulitzer Prize

The Pulitzer Prizes for journalism, letters, drama and music have been presented annually since 1917 in the name of Joseph Pulitzer (1847-1911), the publisher of the New York World. Prizes are awarded by the president of Columbia University on the recommendation of a board of review. Sixteen Pulitzers have been awarded for newspaper sports reporting, sports commentary and sports photography.

News Coverage

1935 **Bill Taylor,** NY Herald Tribune, for his reporting on the 1934 America's Cup yacht races.

Special Citation

1952 **Max Kase,** NY Journal-American, for his reporting on the 1951 college basketball point-shaving scandal.

Meritorious Public Service

1954 **Newsday** (Garden City, N.Y.) for its expose of New York State's race track scandals and labor racketeering.

General Reporting

1956 **Arthur Daley,** NY Times, for his 1955 columns.

Investigative Reporting

1981 **Clark Hallas** & **Robert Lowe,** (Tucson) Arizona Daily Star, for their 1980 investigation of the University of Arizona athletic department.

1986 **Jeffrey Marx** & **Michael York,** Lexington (Ky.) Herald-Leader, for their 1985 investigation of the basketball program at the University of Kentucky and other major colleges.

Photography

1949 **Nat Fein,** NY Herald Tribune, for his photo, "Babe Ruth Bows Out."

1952 **John Robinson** & **Don Ultang,** Des Moines (Iowa) Register and Tribune, for their sequence of six pictures of the 1951 Drake-Oklahoma A&M football game, in which Drake's Johnny Bright had his jaw broken.

Specialized Reporting

1985 **Randall Savage** & **Jackie Crosby,** Macon (Ga.) Telegraph and News, for their 1984 investigation of athletics and academics at the University of Georgia and Georgia Tech.

Beat Reporting

2000 **George Dohrmann,** St. Paul (Min.) Pioneer Press, for his investigation that revealed academic fraud in the men's basketball program at the University of Minnesota.

Feature Writing

1997 **Lisa Pollak,** Baltimore Sun, for her story about baseball umpire John Hirschbeck dealing with the death of one son and the illness of another from the same disease.

Commentary

1976 **Red Smith,** NY Times, for his 1975 columns.
1981 **Dave Anderson,** NY Times, for his 1980 columns.
1990 **Jim Murray,** LA Times, for his 1989 columns.

1985 **The Photography Staff** of the Orange County (Calif.) Register, for their coverage of the 1984 Summer Olympics in Los Angeles.

1993 **William Snyder** & **Ken Geiger,** The Dallas Morning News, for their coverage of the 1992 Summer Olympics in Barcelona, Spain.

Red-Smith Award

Presented annually by the Associated Press Sports Editors (APSE) to a person who has made "major contributions to sports journalism" and named in honor of the late newspaper columnist for the New York Herald-Tribune and New York Times.

Year		Year		Year	
1981	Red Smith, NY Times	1990	Dave Smith, Dallas Morning News	1999	Bud Collins, Boston Globe
1982	Jim Murray, LA Times	1991	Dave Kindred, Nat'l Sports Daily	2000	Jerry Izenberg, Newark Star Ledger
1983	Shirley Povich, Washington Post	1992	Ed Storin, Miami Herald		
1984	Fred Russell, Nashville Banner	1993	Tom McEwen, Tampa Tribune	2001	John Steadman, Baltimore Sun
1985	Blackie Sherrod, Dallas Morning News	1994	Dave Anderson, NY Times	2002	Dick Schaap, ESPN "The Sports Reporters"
		1995	Richard Sandler, Newsday		
1986	Si Burick, Dayton Daily News	1996	Bill Dwyre, LA Times	2003	George Solomon, Washington Post
1987	Will Grimsley, AP	1997	Jerome Holtzman, Chicago Tribune		
1988	Furman Bisher, Atlanta Journal			2004	Jimmy Cannon, New York City Columnist
1989	Edwin Pope, Miami Herald	1998	Sam Lacy, Baltimore Afro-American		

Sportswriter of the Year
NSSA Award

Presented annually since 1959 by the National Sportscasters and Sportswriters Association, based in Salisbury, N.C. Voting is done by NSSA members and selected national media.

Multiple winners: Jim Murray (14); Rick Reilly (9); Frank Deford (6); Red Smith (5); Will Grimsley (4); Peter Gammons (3).

Year		Year		Year	
1959	Red Smith, NY Herald-Tribune	1976	Jim Murray, LA Times	1993	Peter Gammons, Boston Globe
1960	Red Smith, NY Herald-Tribune	1977	Jim Murray, LA Times	1994	Rick Reilly, Sports Ill.
1961	Red Smith, NY Herald-Tribune	1978	Will Grimsley, AP	1995	Rick Reilly, Sports Ill.
1962	Red Smith, NY Herald-Tribune	1979	Jim Murray, LA Times	1996	Rick Reilly, Sports Ill.
1963	Arthur Daley, NY Times	1980	Will Grimsley, AP	1997	Dave Kindred, The Sporting News
1964	Jim Murray, LA Times	1981	Will Grimsley, AP		
1965	Red Smith, NY Herald-Tribune	1982	Frank Deford, Sports Ill.	1998	Mitch Albom, Detroit Free Press
1966	Jim Murray, LA Times	1983	Will Grimsley, AP	1999	Rick Reilly, Sports Ill.
1967	Jim Murray, LA Times	1984	Frank Deford, Sports Ill.	2000	Bob Ryan, Boston Globe
1968	Jim Murray, LA Times	1985	Frank Deford, Sports Ill.	2001	Rick Reilly, Sports Ill.
1969	Jim Murray, LA Times	1986	Frank Deford, Sports Ill.	2002	Rick Reilly, Sports Ill.
1970	Jim Murray, LA Times	1987	Frank Deford, Sports Ill.	2003	Rick Reilly, Sports Ill.
1971	Jim Murray, LA Times	1988	Frank Deford, Sports Ill.		
1972	Jim Murray, LA Times	1989	Peter Gammons, Sports Ill.		
1973	Jim Murray, LA Times	1990	Peter Gammons, Boston Globe		
1974	Jim Murray, LA Times	1991	Rick Reilly, Sports Ill.		
1975	Jim Murray, LA Times	1992	Rick Reilly, Sports Ill.		

Best Newspaper Sports Sections of 2003

Winners of the annual Associated Press Sports Editors contest for best daily and Sunday sports sections. Awards are divided into different categories, based on circulation figures. Selections are made by a committee of APSE members.

Circulation Over 250,000

Top 10 Daily		Top 10 Sunday	
Atlanta Journal-Constitution	Kansas City Star	Atlanta Journal-Constitution	Los Angeles Times
Boston Globe	Los Angeles Times	Boston Globe	Miami Herald
Chicago Tribune	Miami Herald	Dallas Morning News	Daily News (NY)
Dallas Morning News	Minneapolis Star Tribune	Denver Post	Orlando Sentinel
Fort Worth Star-Telegram	Star-Ledger (Newark, NJ)	Kansas City Star	South Florida Sun Sentinel

Circulation 100,000-250,000

Top 10 Daily		Top 10 Sunday	
Daily Herald (Arlington Heights, IL)	Palm Beach Post	Charlotte Observer	Louisville Courier Journal
	Raleigh News & Observer	The State (Columbia, SC)	Palm Beach Post
The State (Columbia, SC)	Seattle Post-Intelligencer	Detroit News	Raleigh News & Observer
	Seattle Times	Hartford Courant	Seattle Times
Hartford Courant	Tampa Tribune	Lexington Herald-Leader	Tacoma News Tribune
The Tennessean (Nashville)	Washington Times		

Best Sportswriting of 2003

Winners of the annual Associated Press Sports Editors Contest for best sportswriting in 2003. Eventual winners were chosen from five finalists in each writing division. Selections are made by a committee of APSE members. Note the investigative writing division included all circulation categories.

Circulation over 250,000

Column:	Sally Jenkins, Washington Post	**Explanatory:**	Jo-Ann Barnas, Detroit Free Press
Game story:	Steve Campbell, Houston Chronicle	**Project:**	Randy Covits, Bob Dutton, Jeffrey Flanagan,
Feature:	Joe Posnanski, Kansas City Star		Dick Kaegel, Joe Posnanski and Wright
News story:	Bill Pennington, New York Times		Thompson, Kansas City Star

Circulation 100,000-250,000

Column:	Ian O'Connor, Westchester Journal News (White Plains, NY)	**News story:**	Eric Crawford and Pat Forde, Louisville Courier Journal
Game story:	Sam Weinman, Westchester Journal News (White Plains, NY)	**Explanatory:** **Project:**	Carter Strickland, Spokane Spokesman-Review Zack McMillin, The Commercial Appeal (Memphis)
Feature:	Janet Patton, Lexington Herald-Leader		

All Categories

Investigative: Maureen O'Hagan and Christine Willmsen, Seattle Times

Directory of Organizations

Listing of the major sports organizations, teams and media addresses and officials as of Sept. 30, 2004.

AUTO RACING

Champ Car World Series
5350 Lakeview Pkwy South Drive
Indianapolis, IN 46268
(317) 715-4100　　　　　　　www.champcarworldseries.com
President . . . . .Richard P. Eidswick
V.P. of Communications . . . . .Wendy Gabers

IRL
(Indy Racing League)
4565 West 16th St., Indianapolis, IN 46222
(317) 484-6526　　　　　　　　　　www.indyracing.com
President-CEO . . . . .Tony George
Sr. V.P. of Operations . . . . .Brian Barnhart
Director of Public Relations . . . . .Tom Savage

FIA—Formula One
(Federation Internationale de L'Automobile)
8 Place de la Concorde, Paris 75008 France
TEL: 011-33-1-43-12-58-15　　　　　　　www.fia.com
President . . . . .Max Mosley
Deputy President (Sport) . . . . .Marco Piccinini

NASCAR
(National Assn. for Stock Car Auto Racing)
P.O. Box 2875, Daytona Beach, FL 32120
(386) 253-0611　　　　　　　　　　　www.nascar.com
Chairman-CEO . . . . .Brian France
President . . . . .Michael Helton
V.P. of Corporate Comm./Regional Touring . . . Jim Hunter

NHRA
(National Hot Rod Association)
2035 Financial Way, Glendora, CA 91741
(626) 914-4761　　　　　　　　　　　www.nhra.com
President . . . . .Tom Compton
Sr. V.P. of Racing Operations . . . . .Graham Light
V.P. of Communications . . . . .Jerry Archambeault

MAJOR LEAGUE BASEBALL

Office of the Commissioner
245 Park Ave., 31st Floor, New York, NY 10167
(212) 931-7800　　　　　　　　　　　www.mlb.com
Commissioner . . . . .Bud Selig
President-COO . . . . .Robert DuPuy
Exec. V.P. of Baseball Ops. . . . . .Sandy Alderson
Sr. V.P./General Counsel . . . . .Thomas Ostertag
Sr. V.P. of Public Relations . . . . .Richard Levin
V.P. of Media Relations . . . . .Patrick Courtney

Player Relations Committee
245 Park Ave.
New York, NY 10160
(212) 931-7800
Executive V.P. for Labor Relations . . . . .Rob Manfred
Chief Labor Negotiator . . . . .Frank Coonelly

Major League Baseball Players Association
12 East 49th St., 24th Floor
New York, NY 10017
(212) 931-7800　　　　　　　　　www.bigleaguers.com
Exec. Director & General Counsel . . . . .Donald Fehr
Chief Operating Officer . . . . .Gene Orza
Director of Communications . . . . .Greg Bouris

AL

American League Office
245 Park Ave., 31st Floor, New York, NY 10167
(212) 931-7800

Anaheim Angels
2000 Gene Autry Way, Anaheim, CA 92806
(714) 940-2000　　　　　　　　www.angelsbaseball.com
Owner . . . . .Arturo Moreno
President . . . . .Dennis Kuhl
V.P. & General Manager . . . . .Bill Stoneman
V.P. of Communications . . . . .Tim Mead

Baltimore Orioles
333 West Camden St., Baltimore, MD 21201
(410) 685-9800　　　　　　　　　　www.theorioles.com
CEO . . . . .Peter Angelos
Vice Chairman & COO . . . . .Joseph Foss
Exec. V.P. of Baseball Operations . . . . .Jim Beattie
V.P. of Baseball Operations . . . . .Mike Flanagan
Director of Public Relations . . . . .Bill Stetka

Boston Red Sox
Fenway Park, 4 Yawkey Way, Boston, MA 02215
(617) 267-9440　　　　　　　　　　　www.redsox.com
Principal Owner .John Henry
President-CEO . . . . .Larry Lucchino
Senior V.P./General Manager . . . . .Theo Epstein
Director of Public Relations . . . . .Glenn Geffner

Chicago White Sox
U.S. Cellular Field, 333 W. 35th St., Chicago, IL 60616
(312) 674-1000　　　　　　　　　　　www.whitesox.com
Chairman . . . . .Jerry Reinsdorf
Vice Chairman . . . . .Eddie Einhorn
Senior V.P./General Manager . . . . .Ken Williams
V.P. of Communications . . . . .Scott Reifert

Cleveland Indians
Jacobs Field, 2401 Ontario St., Cleveland, OH 44115
(216) 420-4200　　　　　　　　　　　www.indians.com
Owner/CEO . . . . .Lawrence Dolan
President . . . . .Paul Dolan
Exec. V.P./General Manager . . . . .Mark Shapiro
Director, Media Relations . . . . .Bart Swain

Detroit Tigers
Comerica Park, 2100 Woodward Ave., Detroit, MI 48201
(313) 962-4000　　　　　　　　　　www.detroittigers.com
Owner and Director . . . . .Mike Ilitch
President/CEO/GM . . . . .Dave Dombrowski
Sr. Dir. of Communications . . . . .Cliff Russell

Kansas City Royals
One Royal Way, Kansas City, MO 64129
(816) 921-8000　　　　　　　　　　www.kcroyals.com
Owner/CEO . . . . .David Glass
President . . . . .Dan Glass
Senior V.P./General Manager . . . . .Allard Baird
V.P. of Broadcasting and Public Relations . . . .David Witty

Minnesota Twins
Hubert H. Humphrey Metrodome
34 Kirby Puckett Place, Minneapolis, MN 55415
(612) 375-1366　　　　　　　　　　　www.mntwins.com
Owner . . . . .Carl Pohlad
President . . . . .Dave St. Peter
V.P./General Manager . . . . .Terry Ryan
Director of Communications . . . . .Brad Ruiter

New York Yankees
Yankee Stadium, 161st St. and River Ave., Bronx, NY 10451
(718) 293-4300   www.yankees.com
Principal Owner . . . . .George Steinbrenner
President . . . . .Randy Levine
Sr. V.P./General Manager . . . . .Brian Cashman
Sr. Dir. of Media Relations . . . . .Rick Cerrone

Oakland Athletics
7000 Coliseum Way
Oakland, CA 94621
(510) 638-4900   www.oaklandathletics.com
Co-Owners . . . . .Steve Schott and Ken Hofmann
President . . . . .Mike Crowley
V.P./General Manager . . . . .Billy Beane
Baseball Information Manager . . . . .Mike Selleck

Seattle Mariners
Safeco Field, P.O. Box 4100 , Seattle, WA 98104
(206) 346-4000   www.mariners.org
Chairman-CEO . . . . .Howard Lincoln
President . . . . .Chuck Armstrong
Executive V.P./General Manager . . . . .Bill Bavasi
Director of Baseball Information . . . . .Tim Hevly

Tampa Bay Devil Rays
Tropicana Field, One Tropicana Drive
St. Petersburg, FL 33705
(727) 825-3137   www.devilrays.com
Managing General Partner/CEO . . . . .Vincent J. Naimoli
Senior V.P., Baseball Ops./GM . . . . .Chuck LaMar
V.P. of Public Relations . . . . .Rick Vaughn

Texas Rangers
1000 Ballpark Way #400, Arlington, TX 76011
(817) 273-5222   www.texasrangers.com
Owner/Chairman . . . . .Thomas Hicks
Executive V.P., General Manager . . . . .John Hart
Senior Dir., Baseball Media Relations . . . . . .Gregg Elkin

Toronto Blue Jays
SkyDome, One Blue Jays Way, Suite 3200
Toronto, Ontario M5V 1J1
(416) 341-1000   www.bluejays.com
Majority Owner . . . . .Rogers Communications
President & CEO . . . . .Paul Godfrey
Sr. V.P. of Baseball Ops./GM . . . . .J.P. Ricciardi
Director of Communications . . . . .Jay Stenhouse

NL

National League Office
245 Park Ave., 31st Floor, New York, NY 10167
(212) 931-7800

Arizona Diamondbacks
401 E. Jefferson St., Phoenix, AZ 85004
(602) 462-6500   www.azdiamondbacks.com
CEO . . . . .Jeff Moorad
President .Richard H. Dozer
V.P./General Manager . . . . .Joe Garagiola Jr.
Director of Public Relations . . . . .Mike Swanson

Atlanta Braves
755 Hank Aaron Drive, Atlanta, GA 30315
(404) 522-7630   www.atlantabraves.com
President/Chairman . . . . .Terry McGuirk
Exec. V.P./General Manager . . . . .John Schuerholz
Media Relations Manager . . . . .Brad Hainje

Chicago Cubs
1060 West Addison St., Chicago, IL 60613
(773) 404-2827   www.cubs.com
Owner . . . . .The Tribune Company
President/CEO . . . . .Andy MacPhail
V.P./General Manager . . . . .Jim Hendry
Director of Media Relations . . . . .Sharon Pannozzo

Cincinnati Reds
Great American Ballpark, 100 Main St., Cincinnati, OH 45202
(513) 765-7000   www.cincinnatireds.com
Majority Owner-CEO . . . . .Carl H. Lindner
General Manager . . . . .Dan O'Brien
Director of Media Relations . . . . .Rob Butcher

Colorado Rockies
Coors Field, 2001 Blake St., Denver, CO 80205
(303) 292-0200   www.coloradorockies.com
Chairman/CEO . . . . .Charles Monfort
President . . . . .Keli McGregor
Executive V.P./General Manager . . . . .Dan O'Dowd
Sr. Director Comm./PR . . . . .Jay Alves

Florida Marlins
2267 Dan Marino Blvd., Miami, FL 33056
(305) 626-7400   www.flamarlins.com
Owner/Chairman/CEO . . . . .Jeffrey Loria
President . . . . .David Samson
Senior V.P./General Manager . . . . .Larry Beinfest
Director of Media Relations . . . . .Steve Copses

Houston Astros
Minute Maid Park, P.O. Box 288, Houston, TX 77001
(713) 259-8900   www.astros.com
Chairman-CEO . . . . .Drayton McLane Jr.
President of Baseball Ops. . . . . .Tal Smith
General Manager . . . . .Gerry Hunsicker
Senior V.P., Communications . . . . .Jay Lucas

Los Angeles Dodgers
1000 Elysian Park Ave., Los Angeles, CA 90012
(323) 224-1500   www.dodgers.com
Chairman .Frank McCourt
Chief Operating Officer . . . . .Martin Greenspun
Executive V.P./General Manager . . . . . . .Paul DePodesta
Director of Public Relations . . . . .John Olguin

Milwaukee Brewers
Miller Park, One Brewers Way, Milwaukee, WI 53214
(414) 902-4400   www.milwaukeebrewers.com
Chairwoman . . . . .Wendy Selig-Prieb
Executive V.P./General Manager . . . . .Doug Melvin
Director of Media Relations . . . . .Jon Greenberg

New York Mets
123-01 Roosevelt Ave., Flushing, NY 11368
(718) 507-6387   www.mets.com
Chairman/CEO . . . . .Fred Wilpon
President . . . . .Saul Katz
G.M./Exec. V.P. of Baseball Ops. . . . . . . .Omar Minaya
V.P. of Media Relations . . . . .Jay Horwitz

Philadelphia Phillies
One Citizens Bank Way, Philadelphia, PA 19148
(215) 463-6000   www.phillies.com
General Partner/Pres./CEO . . . . . . .David Montgomery
Chairman . . . . .Bill Giles
General Manager & V.P. . . . . .Ed Wade
V.P. of Public Relations . . . . .Larry Shenk

Pittsburgh Pirates
115 Federal St., Pittsburgh, PA 15212
(412) 323-5000   www.pirateball.com
CEO/Managing General Partner . . . . . .Kevin McClatchy
Senior V.P. & General Manager . . . . .Dave Littlefield
Director of Media Relations . . . . .Jim Trdinich

St. Louis Cardinals
250 Stadium Plaza, St. Louis, MO 63102
(314) 421-3060   www.stlcardinals.com
Chairman/General Partner . . . . .William O. DeWitt Jr.
President . . . . .Mark Lamping
Senior V.P./General Manager . . . . .Walt Jocketty
Director of Media Relations . . . . .Brian Bartow

San Diego Padres
100 Park Blvd., San Diego, CA 92101
(619) 795-5000   www.padres.com
Chairman . . . . .John Moores
President-CEO .Dick Freeman
Executive V.P./General Manager . . . . .Kevin Towers
Director of Media Relations . . . . .Luis Garcia

San Francisco Giants
24 Willie Mays Plaza, San Francisco, CA 94107
(415) 972-2000   www.sfgiants.com
President/Managing Gen. Partner . . . . .Peter Magowan
Executive V.P./COO . . . . .Larry Baer
Senior V.P./General Manager . . . . .Brian Sabean
Manager of Media Relations . . . . .Jim Moorehead

Washington (unnamed as of Sept. 30, 2004)
(moving from Montreal for the 2005 season, pending
owner's vote and ballpark vote by Wash. City Council)
RFK Stadium, 2400 E. Capitol St., SE, Washington DC 20003
(202) 547-9077   www.montrealexpos.com
President . . . . .Tony Tavares
General Manager . . . . .TBA
Dir. Baseball Information . . . . .John Dever

PRO BASKETBALL

NBA

League Office
Olympic Tower, 645 Fifth Ave., New York, NY 10022
(212) 407-8000   www.nba.com
Commissioner .David Stern
Senior V.P. of Basketball Ops. . . . . .Stuart Jackson
Deputy Commissioner . . . . .Russell Granik
Sr. V.P. Sports Media Relations . . . . .Brian McIntyre
Executive V.P. Global Media . . . . .Heidi Ueberroth

NBA Players Association
Two Penn Plaza, Suite 2430, New York, NY 10121
(212) 655-0880   www.nbpa.com
Executive Director . . . . .Billy Hunter
Associate General Counsel . . . . .Ron Klempner
President . . . . .Michael Curry
Director of Communications . . . . .Dan Wasserman

Atlanta Hawks
Centennial Tower, 101 Marietta St. NW, Suite 1900
Atlanta, GA 30303
(404) 827-3800   www.hawks.com
Owner . . . . .Atlanta Spirit, LLC
President/CEO .Bernie Mullin
General Manager . . . . .Billy Knight
V.P. of Communications . . . . .Arthur Triche

Boston Celtics
151 Merrimac St., Boston, MA 02114
(617) 854-8000   www.celtics.com
CEO/Managing Partner . . . . .Wyc Grousbeck
President . . . . .Red Auerbach
Exec. Director of Basketball Ops. . . . . .Danny Ainge
Vice President of Communications . . . . . .Bill Bonsiewicz

Charlotte Bobcats
129 West Trade St., Suite 700, Charlotte, NC 28202
(704) 424-4120   www.bobcatsbasketball.com
Majority Owner . . . . .Robert L. Johnson
President/COO .Ed Tapscott
General Manager/Head Coach . . . . . . .Bernie Bickerstaff
Public Relations Director . . . . .Scott Leightman

Chicago Bulls
United Center, 1901 West Madison St., Chicago, IL 60612
(312) 455-4000   www.bulls.com
Chairman . . . . .Jerry Reinsdorf
Exec V.P. of Basketball Operations . . . . .John Paxson
Sr. Dir. of Public & Media Relations . . . . .Tim Hallam

Cleveland Cavaliers
Gund Arena, One Center Court, Cleveland, OH 44115
(216) 420-2000   www.cavs.com
Owner-Chairman . . . . .Gordon Gund
President . . . . .Len Komoroski
President & General Manager . . . . .Jim Paxson
Director of Public Relations . . . . .Amanda Mercado

Dallas Mavericks
2909 Taylor St., Dallas, TX 75226
(214) 747-6287   www.dallasmavericks.com
Owner . . . . .Mark Cuban
President/CEO . . . . .Terdema Ussery
GM & Head Coach . . . . .Don Nelson
Sr. V.P., Marketing and Communications . . .Matt Fitzgerald

Denver Nuggets
1000 Chopper Cir., Denver, CO 80204
(303) 405-1100   www.nuggets.com
Owner . . . . .Stan Kroenke
General Manager . . . . .Kiki Vandeweghe
Sr. Dir. of Communications . . . . .Teri Washington

Detroit Pistons
The Palace of Auburn Hills
Two Championship Dr., Auburn Hills, MI 48326
(248) 377-0100   www.pistons.com
Managing Partner . . . . .William Davidson
President/CEO .Tom Wilson
President of Basketball Operations . . . . . .Joe Dumars
V.P. of Public Relations . . . . .Matt Dobek

Golden State Warriors
1011 Broadway, Oakland, CA 94607
(510) 986-2200   www.warriors.com
Owner-CEO .Chris Cohan
President . . . . .Robert Rowell
Exec. V.P. of Basketball Operations . . . . . . .Chris Mullin
General Manager . . . . .Rod Higgins
Director of Public Relations . . . . .Raymond Ridder

Houston Rockets
Toyota Center, 1510 Polk Street, Houston, TX 77002
(713) 758-7200   www.rockets.com
Owner . . . . .Leslie L. Alexander
President-CEO . . . . .George Postolos
General Manager . . . . .Carroll Dawson
Director of Media Relations . . . . .Nelson Luis

Indiana Pacers
125 S. Pennsylvania Street, Indianapolis, IN 46204
(317) 917-2500   www.pacers.com
Owners . . . . .Melvin Simon & Herb Simon
CEO/President . . . . .Donnie Walsh
President of Basketball Ops. . . . . .Larry Bird
Director of Public Information . . . . .David Benner

Los Angeles Clippers
Staples Center, 1111 S. Figueroa St., Suite 1100
Los Angeles, CA 90015
(213) 742-7500   www.clippers.com
Owner-Chairman . . . . .Donald T. Sterling
Executive V.P. .Andy Roeser
V.P., Basketball Operations . . . . .Elgin Baylor
V.P. of Communications . . . . .Joe Safety

Los Angeles Lakers
555 N. Nash St., El Segundo, CA 90245
(310) 426-6000   www.lakers.com
Owner . . . . .Jerry Buss
General Manager . . . . .Mitch Kupchak
Director of Public Relations . . . . .John Black

Memphis Grizzlies
175 Toyota Plaza, Suite 150
Memphis, TN 38103
(901) 888-4667   www.grizzlies.com
Owner ....Michael Heisley
President of Basketball Ops. ....Jerry West
General Manager ....Dick Versace
Media Relations Director ....Kirk Clayborn

Miami Heat
AmericanAirlines Arena, 601 Biscayne Blvd.
Miami, FL 33132
(786) 777-4328   www.heat.com
Managing General Partner ....Micky Arison
President ....Pat Riley
General Manager & President Basketball Ops. .Randy Pfund
V.P. of Sports Media Relations ....Tim Donovan

Milwaukee Bucks
1001 N. Fourth St., Milwaukee, WI 53203
(414) 227-0500   www.bucks.com
President ....Sen. Herb Kohl (D., Wisc.)
General Manager ....Larry Harris
Director of Public Relations ....Cheri Hanson

Minnesota Timberwolves
Target Center
600 First Ave. North, Minneapolis, MN 55403
(612) 673-1600   www.timberwolves.com
Owner ....Glen Taylor
CEO ....Rob Moor
V.P., Basketball Operations ....Kevin McHale
V.P. of Communications ....Ted Johnson

New Jersey Nets
390 Murray Hill Pkwy., East Rutherford, NJ 07073
(201) 935-8888   www.njnets.com
Owner ....Bruce Ratner
President/CEO ....Rod Thorn
General Manager ....Ed Stefanski
Director of Public Relations ....Gary Sussman

New Orleans Hornets
1501 Girod St., New Orleans, LA 70113
(504) 301-4000   www.hornets.com
Majority Owner ....George Shinn
Executive V.P./COO ....Jack Capella
General Manager ....Allan Bristow
V.P. of Public Relations ....Harold Kaufman

New York Knickerbockers
Madison Square Garden
Two Penn Plaza, 14th Floor, New York, NY 10121
(212) 465-6471   www.knicks.com
Owner ....Cablevision Systems Inc.
President/CEO (Cablevision) ....James Dolan
President of Basketball Ops. ....Isiah Thomas
V.P. of Communications ....Joe Favorito

Orlando Magic
2 Magic Place
8701 Maitland Summit Blvd., Orlando, FL 32810
(407) 916-2400   www.orlandomagic.com
Owner ....Rich DeVos
President ....Bob Vander Weide
General Manager ....John Weisbrod
Director of Media Relations ....Joel Glass

Philadelphia 76ers
Wachovia Center
3601 S. Broad St., Philadelphia, PA 19148
(215) 339-7600   www.76ers.com
Owner ....Comcast-Spectacor
Chairman ....Ed Snider
President/General Manager ....Billy King
V.P. of Communications ....Karen Frascona

Phoenix Suns
201 E Jefferson St., Phoenix, AZ 85004
(602) 379-7900   www.suns.com
Majority Owner ....Robert Sarver
Chairman-CEO ....Jerry Colangelo
President/General Manager ....Bryan Colangelo
Sr. Executive V.P. ....Dick Van Arsdale
V.P. of Basketball Communications ....Julie Fie

Portland Trail Blazers
One Center Court, Suite 200, Portland, OR 97227
(503) 234-9291   www.blazers.com
Owner-Chairman ....Paul Allen
President ....Steve Patterson
General Manager ....John Nash
Executive Dir. of Communications ......Mike Hanson

Sacramento Kings
One Sports Parkway, Sacramento, CA 95834
(916) 928-0000   www.kings.com
Owners ....Joe and Gavin Maloof
President, Basketball Operations ....Geoff Petrie
V.P., Basketball Operations ....Wayne Cooper
Director of Media Relations ....Troy Hanson

San Antonio Spurs
One SBC Center
San Antonio, TX 78219
(210) 444-5000   www.spurs.com
Chairman/CEO ....Peter Holt
Exec. V.P. of Basketball Ops./Head Coach ..Gregg Popovich
General Manager ...................R.C. Buford
Director of Media Services ....Tom James

Seattle SuperSonics
351 Elliott Ave. West, Suite 500
Seattle, WA 98119
(206) 281-5800   www.supersonics.com
Chairman ....Howard Schultz
President & CEO ....Wally Walker
General Manager ....Rick Sund
Director of Media Relations ....Marc Moquin

Toronto Raptors
40 Bay St., Suite 400
Toronto, Ontario M5J 2X2
(416) 815-5600   www.raptors.com
Chairman ....Larry Tanenbaum
President/CEO ....Richard Peddie
General Manager ....Rob Babcock
Director of Media Relations ....Jim LaBumbard

Utah Jazz
301 West South Temple
Salt Lake City, UT 84101
(801) 325-2500   www.utahjazz.com
Owner ....Larry Miller
President ....Dennis Haslam
Sr. V.P. of Basketball Operations ......Kevin O'Connor
Director of Media Relations ....Kim Turner

Washington Wizards
MCI Center, 601 F Street NW
Washington, D.C., 20004
(202) 661-5000   www.washingtonwizards.com
Chairman ....Abe Pollin
President ....Susan O'Malley
President of Basketball Ops. ....Ernie Grunfeld
Director of Player Personnel ....Milt Newton
Director of Public Relations ....TBA

Other Men's Pro Leagues

Continental Basketball Association
1412 W. Idaho St., Ste. 235
Boise, ID 83702
(208) 429-0101   www.cbahoopsonline.com
Commissioner . . . . Gary Hunter
Dir. of Public/Media Relations . . . . Todd Anderson
   Member teams (8): Dakota Wizards, Gary Steelheads, Great Lakes Storm, Idaho Stampede, Michigan Mayhem, Rockford Lightning, Sioux Falls Skyforce and Yakima Sun Kings.

United States Basketball League
46 Quirk Road, Milford, CT 06460
(203) 877-9508   www.usbl.com
Commissioner . . . . Daniel T. Meisenheimer III
Dir. of Public Relations . . . . Dennis Truax
   Member teams (11): Adirondack (NY) Wildcats, Brevard (FL) Blue Ducks, Brooklyn Kings, Cedar Rapids River Raiders, Dodge City Legend, Florence Flyers, Kansas Cagerz, Oklahoma Storm, Pennsylvania ValleyDawgs, St. Louis Skyhawks and Westchester (NY) Wildfire.

National Basketball Development League
24 Vardry Street, Suite 201, Greenville, SC 29601
(843) 460-1001   www.nbdl.com
President . . . . Philip Evans
Director of Communications . . . . Kent Partridge
   Member teams (6): Asheville (NC) Altitude; Columbus (GA) Riverdragons; Fayetteville (NC) Patriots; Florida Flame, Huntsville (AL) Flight; Roanoke (VA) Dazzle.

WNBA

League Office
645 5th Ave., New York, NY 10022
(212) 688-9622   www.wnba.com
President . . . . Val Ackerman
Chief Operating Officer . . . . Ann Sarnoff
V.P. of Player Personnel . . . . Renee Brown
Sr. Director of Communications . . . . Sharon Robustelli

Charlotte Sting
129 W. Trade Street, Suite 700, Charlotte, NC 28202
(704) 357-0252   www.charlottesting.com
Owner/President . . . . Robert L. Johnson
General Manager/Head Coach . . . . Trudi Lacey
Director of Public Relations . . . . Karen Kase

Connecticut Sun
One Mohegan Sun Blvd., Uncasville, CT 06382
(860) 862-4000   www.wnba.com/sun
CEO . . . . Mitchell Etess
General Manager . . . . Christopher Sienko
Media Relations Manager . . . . Bill Tavares

Detroit Shock
The Palace of Auburn Hills
Two Championship Dr., Auburn Hills, MI 48326
(248) 377-0100   www.detroitshock.com
President . . . . Thomas S. Wilson
Head Coach/Dir. of Player Personnel . . . . . . Bill Laimbeer
Director of Media Relations . . . . Paul Hickey

Houston Comets
1510 Polk Street
Houston, TX 77002
(713) 627-9622   www.houstoncomets.com
Owner/President . . . . Leslie L. Alexander
General Manager/Head Coach . . . . Van Chancellor
Director of Media Relations . . . . Nelson Luis

Indiana Fever
125 S. Pennsylvania St., Indianapolis, IN 46204
(317) 917-2500   www.wnba.com/fever
CEO/President . . . . Donnie Walsh
COO/General Manager . . . . Kelly Krauskopf
Director of Media Relations . . . . Kevin Messenger

Los Angeles Sparks
2151 E. Grand Ave., Suite 100, El Segundo, CA 90245
(310) 341-1000   www.lasparks.com
Chairman . . . . Jerry Buss
General Manager . . . . Penny Toler
Director of Communications . . . . Kristal Shipp

Minnesota Lynx
Target Center
600 First Ave. N., Minneapolis, MN 55403
(612) 673-8400   www.wnba.com/lynx
Owner . . . . Glen Taylor
Head Coach . . . . Suzie McConnell Serio
Manager of Media Relations . . . . Mike Cristaldi

New York Liberty
Madison Square Garden
Two Penn Plaza, New York, NY 10121
(212) 564-9622   www.nyliberty.com
Owner . . . . Cablevision Systems Inc.
Senior V.P/General Manager . . . . Carol Blazejowski
V.P., Marketing & Communications . . . . Amy Scheer

Phoenix Mercury
201 E. Jefferson St., Phoenix, AZ 85004
(602) 514-8333   www.phoenixmercury.com
President . . . . Bryan Colangelo
V.P., General Manager . . . . Seth Sulka
Director of Communications . . . . Tami Nealy

Sacramento Monarchs
ARCO Arena, One Sports Parkway
Sacramento, CA 95834
(916) 928-0000   www.sacramentomonarchs.com
President, Basketball Ops. . . . . John Thomas
General Manager/Head Coach . . . . . . John Whisenant
Manager of Media Relations . . . . Kimberly Williams

San Antonio Silver Stars
One SBC Center
San Antonio, TX 78219
(210) 444-5000   www.wnba.com/silverstars
Chairman/CEO . . . . Peter Holt
COO . . . . Clarissa Davis-Wrightsil
Manager, Media Services . . . . Kris Davis

Seattle Storm
351 Elliott Ave. W., Suite 500
Seattle, WA 98119
(206) 281-5800   www.wnba.com/storm
President & CEO . . . . Wally Walker
Chief Operating Officer . . . . Karen Bryant
Public Relations Director . . . . Valerie O'Neil

Washington Mystics
MCI Center, 601 F St. NW
Washington D.C. 20004
(202) 661-5000   www.wnba.com/mystics
President . . . . Susan O'Malley
Sr. V.P. Business & Basketball Ops. . . . . Judy Holland-Burton
Dir. of Public Relations . . . . Dyani Gordon

BOWLING

ABC
(American Bowling Congress)
5301 South 76th St., Greendale, WI 53129
(800) 514-2695   www.bowl.com/bowl/abc
Executive Director . . . . Roger Dalkin
President . . . . Paul Egbers

BPAA
(Bowling Proprietors' Assn. of America)
P.O. Box 5802, Arlington, TX 76011
(817) 649-5105   www.bpaa.com
President .... Jeff Boje
Executive Director .... John F. Berglund
Director of Public Relations .... Cary Richmond

PBA
(Professional Bowlers Association)
719 Second Ave., Suite 701
Seattle, WA 98104
(206) 332-9688   www.pba.com
Chairman .... Chris Peters
President/CEO .... Steve Miller
Commissioner .... Fred Schreyer
Manager of Public Relations .... Jason Carr

USBC
(United States Bowling Congress)
5301 South 76th St., Greendale, WI 53129
(414) 421-9000   www.bowl.com
President .... Michael Carroll
Vice President .... Sam Lantto
Note: On Jan. 1, 2005, ABC, WIBC, YABA (Young
American Bowling Alliance) and USA Bowling will merge
into the United States Bowling Congress.

WIBC
(Women's International Bowling Congress, Inc.)
5301 South 76th St., Greendale, WI 53129
(414) 421-9000   www.bowl.com/bowl/wibc
President .... Sylvia Broyles
Executive Director .... Roseann Kuhn

BOXING

IBF
(International Boxing Federation)
516 Main Street, 2nd Floor, East Orange, NJ 07018
(973) 414-0300   www.ibf-usba-boxing.com
President .... Marian Muhammad
Treasurer-Ratings Chairman .... Daryl Peoples

WBA
(World Boxing Association)
P.O. Box 377, Maracay 2101-A, Estado Aragua
Venezuela
TEL: 011-58-244-663-1584   www.wbaonline.com
President .... Gilberto Mendoza
Ratings Chairman .... Jose Oliver Gomez
                              TEL: (507) 638-0527

WBC
(World Boxing Council)
Cuzco 872, Col. Lindavista
C.P. 07300, Mexico City, D.F.
TEL: 011 (52.55) 5119-52-74   www.wbcboxing.com
President .... Jose Sulaiman
Ratings Chairman .... Frank Quill
Note: The WBC entered bankruptcy liquidation proceed-
ings in June, 2004.

WBO
(World Boxing Organization)
1st Federal Bldg.
1056 Ave Munoz Rivera, Suite 711
San Juan, P.R. 00927
(787) 765-4444   www.wbo-int.com
President .... Francisco "Paco" Valcarcel
Past Pres./Chairman Champ. Committee ... Luis Batista Salas
Ratings Chairman .... Luis Perez

Don King Productions, Inc.
501 Fairway Dr.
Deerfield Beach, FL 33441
(954) 418-5800   www.donking.com
President .... Don King
V.P. of Boxing Ops. .... Dana Jamison
V.P., Boxing Ops./Public Relations .... Bob Goodman

Top Rank
3980 Howard Hughes Pkwy. Ste. 580
Las Vegas, NV 89109
(702) 732-2717   www.toprank.com
Chairman .... Bob Arum
Director of Public Relations .... Lee Samuels

COLLEGE SPORTS

NAIA
(National Assn. of Intercollegiate Athletics)
23500 W. 105th Street, Olathe, KS 66051
(913) 791-0044   www.naia.org
President-CEO .... Steve Baker
Director of Sports Information .... Dawn Harmon

NCAA
(National Collegiate Athletic Association)
700 W. Washington St.
P.O. Box 6222, Indianapolis, IN 46206
(317) 917-6222   www.ncaa.org
President .... Myles Brand
V.P. of Enforcement .... David Price
Managing Dir. of Public Relations .... Jeff Howard

WSF
(Women's Sports Foundation)
Eisenhower Park, East Meadow, NY 11554
(516) 542-4700   www.womenssportsfoundation.org
Founder .... Billie Jean King
Executive Director .... Donna Lopiano
President (beginning Jan. 2005) .... Dominique Dawes
Dir. of Public Relations .... Eloise Longobardi

Major NCAA Conferences

See pages 447-455 for football coaches, basketball
coaches, nicknames and colors of all Division I-A and I-AA
football schools and Division I basketball schools.

ATLANTIC COAST CONFERENCE
P.O. Drawer ACC
Greensboro, NC 27417-6724
(336) 854-8787   www.theacc.com
Founded: 1953
Commissioner .... John Swofford
Asst. Commis. of Media Relations ...... Brian Morrison
   2004-05 members: BASKETBALL & FOOTBALL (11)—
Clemson, Duke, Florida St., Georgia Tech, Maryland, Miami-
FL, North Carolina, N.C. State, Virginia, Virginia Tech and
Wake Forest.

Clemson University
Clemson, SC 29633
SID: (864) 656-2114   www.clemsontigers.com
Founded: 1889 .... Enrollment: 15,873
President .... James F. Barker
Athletic Director .... Terry Don Phillips
Asst. AD, Sports Information .... Tim Bourret

Duke University
Durham, NC 27708
SID: (919) 684-2633   www.goduke.com
Founded: 1838   Enrollment: 6,522
President .... Richard H. Brodhead
Athletic Director .... Joe Alleva
Sports Information Director .... Jon Jackson

Florida State University
Tallahassee, FL 32306
SID: (850) 644-1403 www.seminoles.com
Founded: 1851 Enrollment: 37,328
President . . . . .Dr. T.K. Wetherell
Athletic Director . . . . .Dave Hart Jr.
Sports Information.Director . . . . .Rob Wilson

Georgia Tech
Atlanta, GA 30332
SID: (404) 894-5445 www.ramblinwreck.com
Founded: 1885 Enrollment: 15,000
President . . . . .Dr. G. Wayne Clough
Athletic Director . . . . .Dave Braine
Sports Information Director . . . . .Allison George

University of Maryland
College Park, MD 20741
SID: (301) 314-7064 www.umterps.com
Founded: 1807 Enrollment: 33,066
President . . . . .Dr. Clayton D. Mote Jr.
Athletic Director . . . . .Deborah Yow
Assoc. AD, Media Relations . . . . .Doug Dull

University of Miami
Coral Gables, FL 33146
SID: (305) 284-3244 www.hurricanesports.com
Founded: 1926 Enrollment: 15,248
President .Dr. Donna E. Shalala
Athletic Director . . . . .Paul Dee
Asst. Athletic Director/Communications . . . . . .Mark Pray

University of North Carolina
Chapel Hill, NC 27514
SID: (919) 962-2123 www.tarheelblue.com
Founded: 1789 Enrollment: 25,972
Chancellor . . . . .James Moeser
Athletic Director .Dick Baddour
Sports Information Director . . . . .Steve Kirschner

North Carolina State University
Raleigh, NC 27695
SID: (919) 515-2102 www.gopack.com
Founded: 1887 Enrollment: 29,637
Interim Chancellor . . . . .Robert A. Barnhardt
Athletic Director . . . . .Lee Fowler
Asst. AD for Media Relations . . . . . . .Annabelle Vaughan

University of Virginia
Charlottesville, VA 22903
SID: (434) 982-5500 www.virginiasports.com
Founded: 1819 Enrollment: 19,643
President . . . . .John T. Casteen III
Athletic Director . . . . .Craig Littlepage
Sports Information Director . . . . .Rich Murray

Virginia Tech
Blacksburg, VA 24061
SID: (540) 231-6726 www.hokiesports.com
Founded: 1872 Enrollment: 28,000
President . . . . .Charles W. Steger
Athletic Director . . . . .Jim Weaver
Sports Information Director . . . . .Dave Smith

Wake Forest University
Winston-Salem, NC 27109
SID: (336) 758-5640 www.wakeforestsports.com
Founded: 1834 Enrollment: 6,444
President . . . . .Dr. Thomas K. Hearn Jr.
Athletic Director .Ron Wellman
Asst. Athletic Director/Media Relations . . . . .Dean Buchan

* * *

BIG EAST CONFERENCE
222 Richmond Street, Suite 110
Providence, RI 02903
(401) 272-9108 www.bigeast.org
Founded: 1979
Commissioner . . . . .Mike Tranghese
Assoc. Commissioner/Communications . . . John Paquette
   2004-05 members: BASKETBALL (12)—Boston
College, Connecticut, Georgetown, Notre Dame, Pittsburgh,
Providence, Rutgers, St. John's, Seton Hall, Syracuse,
Villanova and West Virginia; FOOTBALL (7)—Boston
College, Connecticut, Pittsburgh, Rutgers, Syracuse, Temple
and West Virginia.

Boston College
Chestnut Hill, MA 02467
SID: (617) 552-3004 www.bceagles.com
Founded: 1863 Enrollment: 14,500
President . . . . .Rev. William P. Leahy, S.J.
Athletic Director . . . . .Gene DeFilippo
Sports Information Director . . . . .Chris Cameron

University of Connecticut
Storrs, CT 06269
SID: (860) 486-3531 www.uconnhuskies.com
Founded:1881 Enrollment: 19,287
President . . . . .Philip Austin
Athletic Director . . . . .Jeffrey Hathaway
Sports Information Director . . . . .Michael Enright

Georgetown University
Washington, DC 20057
SID: (202) 687-2492 www.guhoyas.com
Founded: 1789 Enrollment: 6,332
President . . . . .John J. DeGioia, Ph. D.
Interim Athletic Director . . . . .Adam Brick
Sr. Sports Communication Director . . . . . . .Bill Shapland

University of Notre Dame
Notre Dame, IN 46556
SID: (574) 631-7516 www.und.com
Founded: 1842 Enrollment: 8,261
President . . . . .Rev. Edward (Monk) Malloy
President-Elect (June 30, 2005) . . . . . . .Rev. John I. Jenkins
Athletic Director . . . . .Kevin White
Sports Information Director . . . . .John Heisler

University of Pittsburgh
Pittsburgh, PA 15260
SID: (412) 648-8240 www.pittsburghpanthers.com
Founded: 1787 Enrollment: 33,792
Chancellor . . . . .Mark A. Nordenberg
Athletic Director . . . . .Jeff Long
Sports Information Director . . . . .E.J. Borghetti

Providence College
Providence, RI 02918
SID: (401) 865-2272 www.friars.com
Founded: 1917 Enrollment: 3,700
President . . . . .Philip A. Smith, O.P.
Athletic Director . . . . .Robert Driscoll
Sports Information Director . . . . .Arthur Parks

Rutgers University
New Brunswick, NJ 08903
SID: (732) 445-4200 www.scarletknights.com
Founded: 1766 Enrollment: 33,500
President . . . . .Richard L. McCormick
Athletic Director . . . . .Robert E. Mulcahy III
Sports Information Director . . . . .John Wooding

St. John's University
Jamaica, NY 11439
SID: (718) 990-1520 www.redstormsports.com
Founded: 1870 Enrollment: 18,300
President . . . . .Rev. Donald J. Harrington, CM
Athletic Director . . . . .David Wegrzyn
Sports Information Director . . . . .Dominic Scianna

Seton Hall University
South Orange, NJ 07079
SID: (973) 761-9493
Founded: 1856
President . . . . .Monsignor Robert Sheeran
Athletic Director .Jeff Fogelson
Assistant AD/Communications . . . . .Jeff Andriesse

www.shupirates.com
Enrollment: 9,604

Syracuse University
Syracuse, NY 13244
SID: (315) 443-2608
Founded: 1870
Chancellor . . . . .Nancy Cantor
Athletic Director . . . . .Jake Crouthamel
Sports Information Director . . . . .Sue Edson

www.suathletics.com
Enrollment: 10,000

Temple University
Philadelphia, PA 19122
SID: (215) 204-7445
Founded: 1884
President . . . . .Dr. David Adamany
Athletic Director . . . . .Bill Bradshaw
Sports Information Director . . . . .Kevin Lorincz

www.owlsports.com
Enrollment: 30,000

Villanova University
Villanova, PA 19085
SID: (610) 519-4120
Founded: 1842
President . . . . .Rev. Edmund J. Dobbin, OSA
Athletic Director . . . . .Vince Nicastro
Sports Information Director . . . . .Dean Kenefick

www.villanova.com
Enrollment: 6,295

West Virginia University
Morgantown, WV 26507
SID: (304) 293-2821
Founded: 1867
President . . . . .David Hardesty
Athletic Director . . . . .Ed Pastilong
Sports Information Director . . . . .Shelly Poe

www.msnsportsnet.com
Enrollment: 23,492

*　　　*　　　*

BIG 12 CONFERENCE
2201 Stemmons Fwy., 28th Floor
Dallas, TX 75207
(214) 742-1212
Founded: 1996
Commissioner . . . . .Kevin Weiberg
Asst. Commiss. for Communications . . . . .Bob Burda
  2004-05 members: BASKETBALL & FOOTBALL (12)—
Baylor, Colorado, Iowa St., Kansas, Kansas St., Missouri,
Nebraska, Oklahoma, Oklahoma St., Texas, Texas A&M
and Texas Tech.

www.big12sports.com

Baylor University
Waco, TX 76711
SID: (254) 710-2743
Founded: 1845
President . . . . .Robert B. Sloan Jr.
Athletic Director .Ian McCaw
Assoc. AD for Media Relations . . . . .Nick Joos

www.baylorbears.com
Enrollment: 13,937

University of Colorado
Boulder, CO 80309
SID: (303) 492-5626
Founded: 1876
President . . . . .Dr. Elizabeth Hoffman
Athletic Director . . . . .Richard Tharp
Sports Information Director . . . . .Dave Plati

www.cubuffs.com
Enrollment: 27,954

Iowa State University
Ames, IA 50011
SID: (515) 294-3372
Founded: 1858
President . . . . .Dr. Gregory L. Geoffroy
Athletic Director . . . . .Bruce Van De Velde
Sports Information Director . . . . .Tom Kroeschell

www.cyclones.com
Enrollment: 27,380

University of Kansas
Lawrence, KS 66045
SID: (785) 864-3417
Founded: 1866
Chancellor . . . . .Robert Hemenway
Athletic Director .Lew Perkins
Asst. AD for Media Relations . . . . .Chris Theisen

www.kuathletics.com
Enrollment: 28,849

Kansas State University
Manhattan, KS 66502
SID: (785) 532-6735
Founded: 1863
President . . . . .Dr. Jon Wefald
Athletic Director .Tim Weiser
Sports Information Director . . . . .Garry Bowman

www.kstatesports.com
Enrollment: 23,050

University of Missouri
Columbia, MO 65205
SID: (573) 882-0712
Founded: 1839
President . . . . .Dr. Elson S. Floyd
Athletic Director . . . . .Michael Alden
Media Relations Director . . . . .Chad Moller

www.mutigers.com
Enrollment: 26,805

University of Nebraska
Lincoln, NE 68588
SID: (402) 472-2263
Founded: 1869
Chancellor . . . . .Harvey Perlman
Athletic Director . . . . .Steve Pederson
Associate AD for Communications . . . . . . .Chris Anderson

www.huskers.com
Enrollment: 25,000

University of Oklahoma
Norman, OK 73019
SID: (405) 325-8231
Founded: 1890
President . . . . .David Boren
Athletic Director . . . . .Joe Castiglione
Asst. AD for Media Relations . . . . .Kenny Mossman

www.soonersports.com
Enrollment: 28,954

Oklahoma State University
Stillwater, OK 74078
SID: (405) 744-7714
Founded: 1890
President . . . . .Dr. David J. Schimdly
Athletic Director . . . . .Harry Birdwell
Assoc. AD, Media Relations . . . . .Steve Buzzard

www.okstate.com
Enrollment: 21,000

University of Texas
Austin, TX 78713
SID: (512) 471-7437
Founded: 1883
President . . . . .Dr. Larry Faulkner
Athletic Director . . . . .DeLoss Dodds
Asst. AD for Media Relations . . . . .John Bianco

www.texassports.com
Enrollment: 51,438

Texas A&M University
College Station, TX 77843
SID: (979) 845-5725
Founded: 1876
President .Dr. Robert Gates
Athletic Director .Bill Byrne
Asst. AD for Media Relations . . . . .Alan Cannon

www.aggieathletics.com
Enrollment: 45,083

Texas Tech University
Lubbock, TX 79409
SID: (806) 742-2770
Founded: 1923
Chancellor . . . . .David R. Smith
Athletic Director . . . . .Gerald Myers
Asst. AD for Media Relations . . . . .Chris Cook

www.texastech.com
Enrollment: 27,000

*　　　*　　　*

BIG TEN CONFERENCE
1500 West Higgins Road
Park Ridge, IL 60068-6300
(847) 696-1010   www.bigten.org
Founded: 1896
Commissioner . . . . .James E. Delany
Director of Communications . . . . .Scott Chipman
    2004-05 members: BASKETBALL & FOOTBALL (11)—
Illinois, Indiana, Iowa, Michigan, Michigan St., Minnesota,
Northwestern, Ohio St., Penn St., Purdue and Wisconsin.

University of Illinois
Champaign, IL 61820
SID: (217) 244-6533
www.fightingillini.com
Founded: 1867   Enrollment: 38,000
President .James J. Stukel
Athletic Director . . . . .Ron Guenther
Director of Communications . . . . .Kent Brown

Indiana University
Bloomington, IN 47408
SID: (812) 855-9399
www.iuhoosiers.com
Founded: 1820   Enrollment: 38,589
President . . . . .Dr. Adam W. Herbert
Athletic Director . . . . .Rick Greenspan
Assoc. Dir. of Media Relations . . . . .Pete Rhoda

University of Iowa
Iowa City, IA 52242
SID: (319) 335-9411   www.hawkeyesports.com
Founded: 1847   Enrollment: 29,745
President . . . . .David Skorton
Athletic Director . . . . .Bob Bowlsby
Sports Information Director . . . . .Phil Haddy

University of Michigan
Ann Arbor, MI 48109
SID: (734) 763-4423
www.mgoblue.com
Founded: 1817   Enrollment: 36,787
President . . . . .Mary Sue Coleman
Athletic Director . . . . .William Martin
Sports Information Director . . . . .Bruce Madej

Michigan State University
East Lansing, MI 48824
SID: (517) 355-2271
www.msuspartans.com
Founded: 1855   Enrollment: 44,937
President . . . . .Peter McPherson
Athletic Director . . . . .Ron Mason
Asst. AD for Media Relations . . . . . . .John Lewandowski

University of Minnesota
Minneapolis, MN 55455
SID: (612) 625-4090   www.gophersports.com
Founded: 1851   Enrollment: 47,518
President . . . . .Robert Bruininks
Athletic Director . . . . .Joel Maturi
Director of Media Relations . . . . .Mike Lockrem

Northwestern University
Evanston, IL 60208
SID: (847) 491-7503
www.nusports.com
Founded: 1851   Enrollment: 7,700
President . . . . .Henry S. Bienen
Athletic Director . . . . .Mark Murphy
Asst. Athletic Director/Media Services . . . . . .Mike Wolf

Ohio State University
Columbus, OH 43210
SID: (614) 292-6861   www.ohiostatebuckeyes.com
Founded: 1870   Enrollment: 55,043
President . . . . .Karen A. Holbrook
Athletic Director . . . . .Andy Geiger
Assoc. AD, Athletic Communications . . . . . .Steve Snapp

Penn State University
University Park, PA 16802
SID: (814) 865-1757   www.gopsusports.com
Founded: 1855   Enrollment: 41,445
President . . . . .Graham Spanier
Athletic Director . . . . .Tim Curley
Assoc. AD, Communications . . . . .Jeff Nelson

Purdue University
West Lafayette, IN 47907
SID: (765) 494-3201   www.purduesports.com
Founded: 1869   Enrollment: 38,564
President . . . . .Martin C. Jischke
Athletic Director . . . . .Morgan Burke
Sports Information Director . . . . .Tom Schott

University of Wisconsin
Madison, WI 53711
SID: (608) 262-1811   www.uwbadgers.com
Founded: 1848   Enrollment: 41,522
Chancellor . . . . .John Wiley
Athletic Director . . . . .Barry Alvarez
Director of Athletic Communications . . . . . .Justin Doherty

          *   *   *

CONFERENCE USA
5201 North O'Connor, Suite 300, Irving, TX 75039
(214) 774-1300   www.conferenceusa.com
Founded: 1995
Commissioner . . . . .Britton Banowsky
Asst. Comm. for Media Relations . . . . .Russell Anderson
    2004-05 members: BASKETBALL (14)—UAB, Char-
lotte, Cincinnati, DePaul, East Carolina, Houston, Louisville,
Marquette, Memphis, Saint Louis, South Florida, Southern
Miss, TCU and Tulane; FOOTBALL (11)—UAB, Army, Cincin-
nati, East Carolina, Houston, Louisville, Memphis, South
Florida, Southern Miss, TCU and Tulane.

University of Alabama at Birmingham
Birmingham, AL 35294
SID: (205) 934-0723   www.uabsports.com
Founded: 1969   Enrollment: 16,357
President . . . . .Carol Z. Garrison
Athletic Director . . . . .Watson Brown
Asst. AD for Media Relations . . . . .Norm Reilly

Army—U.S. Military Academy
West Point, NY 10996
SID: (845) 938-3303   www.goarmysports.com
Founded: 1802   Enrollment: 4,000
Superintendent . . . . .Lt. Gen. William J. Lennox, Jr.
Interim Athletic Director . . . . .Col. James Knowlton
Assoc. AD for Media Relations . . . . .Bob Beretta

University of Cincinnati
Cincinnati, OH 45221
SID: (513) 556-5191   www.ucbearcats.com
Founded: 1819   Enrollment: 34,000
President . . . . .Dr. Nancy L. Zimpher
Athletic Director . . . . .Bob Goin
Asst. AD for Media Relations . . . . .Tom Hathaway

DePaul University
Chicago, IL 60614
SID: (773) 325-7525   www.depaulbluedemons.com
Founded: 1898   Enrollment: 25,300
President . . . . .Rev. Dennis H. Holtschneider, C.M.
Athletic Director . . . . .Jean Lenti Ponsetto
Sports Information Director . . . . .Scott Reed

East Carolina University
Greenville, NC 27858
SID: (252) 328-4522   www.ecupirates.com
Founded: 1907   Enrollment: 21,979
Chancellor .Dr. Steve Ballard
Athletic Director . . . . .Terry Holland
Director of Athletic Media Relations . . . . .Tom McClellan

University of Houston
Houston, TX 77204
SID: (713) 743-9404   www.uhcougars.com
Founded: 1927   Enrollment: 32,296
President . . . . .Dr. Jay Gogue
Athletic Director . . . . .Dave Maggard
Sports Information Director . . . . .Chris Burkhalter

University of Louisville
Louisville, KY 40292
SID: (502) 852-6581   www.uoflsports.com
Founded: 1798   Enrollment: 21,000
President .Dr. James Ramsey
Athletic Director . . . . .Tom Jurich
Sports Information Director . . . . .Kenny Klein

Marquette University
Milwaukee, WI 53233
SID: (414) 288-7447   www.gomarquette.com
Founded: 1881   Enrollment: 11,000
President . . . . .Rev. Robert A. Wild S.J.
Athletic Director .Bill Cords
Asst. AD for Media Relations . . . . .Mike Broeker

University of Memphis
Memphis, TN 38152
SID: (901) 678-2337   www.gotigersgo.com
Founded: 1912   Enrollment: 20,332
President .Dr. Shirley Raines
Athletic Director . . . . .R.C. Johnson
Asst. AD, Media Relations . . . . .Bob Winn

University of North Carolina at Charlotte
Charlotte, NC 28223
SID: (704) 687-6312   www.charlotte49ers.com
Founded: 1946   Enrollment: 19,608
Chancellor .James Woodward
Athletic Director . . . . .Judy Rose
Asst. AD, Media Relations . . . . .Tom Whitestone

Saint Louis University
St. Louis, MO 63103
SID: (314) 977-3462   www.slubillikens.com
Founded: 1818   Enrollment: 11,100
President . . . . .Rev. Lawrence Biondi, S.J.
Athletic Director . . . . .Cheryl Levick
Sport Information Director . . . . .Doug McIlhagga

University of South Florida
Tampa, FL 33620
SID: (813) 974-4086   www.gousfbulls.com
Founded: 1956   Enrollment: 40,000
President . . . . .Judy Genshaft
Athletic Director . . . . .Doug Woolard
Sports Information Director . . . . .John Gerdes

University of Southern Mississippi
Hattiesburg, MS 39406
SID: (601) 266-4507   www.southernmiss.com
Founded: 1910   Enrollment: 15,259
President .Dr. Shelby Thames
Athletic Director . . . . .Rich Giannini
Asst. AD for Media Relations . . . . .Mike Montoro

TCU—Texas Christian University
Fort Worth, TX 76129
SID: (817) 257-7969   www.gofrogs.com
Founded: 1873   Enrollment: 7,500
Chancellor .Dr. Victor Boschini
Athletic Director . . . . .Eric Hyman
Director of Media Relations . . . . .Steve Fink

Tulane University
New Orleans, LA 70118
SID: (504) 865-5506   www.tulanegreenwave.com
Founded: 1834   Enrollment: 12,381
President .Dr. Scott S. Cowen
Athletic Director . . . . .Rick Dickson
Asst. AD for Media Relations . . . . .Donna Turner

*   *   *

MID-AMERICAN CONFERENCE
24 Public Square, 15th Floor, Cleveland, OH 44113
(216) 566-4622   www.mac-sports.com
Founded: 1946
Commissioner .Rick Chryst
Asst. Commissioner for Media Relations . . . . .Gary Richter
   2004-05 members: FOOTBALL (14)—Akron, Ball St.,
Bowling Green, Buffalo, Central Florida, Central Michigan,
Eastern Michigan, Kent St., Marshall, Miami-OH, Northern
Illinois, Ohio University, Toledo and Western Michigan;
BASKETBALL (13)—all except Central Florida.

University of Akron
Akron, OH 44325
SID: (330) 972-7468   www.gozips.com
Founded: 1870   Enrollment: 24,300
President .Dr. Luis Proenza
Athletic Director . . . . .Michael J. Thomas
Director of Media Relations . . . . .Shawn Nestor

Ball State University
Muncie, IN 47306
SID: (765) 285-8242   www.ballstatesports.com
Founded: 1918   Enrollment: 18,528
President .Dr. Jo Ann M. Gora
Athletic Director . . . . .Lawrence "Bubba" Cunningham
Assoc. AD for External Affairs . . . . .Joe Hernandez

Bowling Green State University
Bowling Green, OH 43403
SID: (419) 372-7075   www.bgsufalcons.com
Founded: 1910   Enrollment: 20,276
President .Dr. Sidney Ribeau
Athletic Director . . . . .Paul Krebs
Director of Athletic Communications . . . . .J.D. Campbell

University of Buffalo
Buffalo, NY 14260
SID: (716) 645-6311   www.buffalobulls.com
Founded: 1846   Enrollment: 25,838
President .John B. Simpson, Ph.D
Interim Athletic Director . . . . .William Maher
Sports Information Director . . . . .Paul Vecchio

University of Central Florida
Orlando, FL 32816
SID: (407) 823-2729   www.ucfathletics.com
Founded: 1963   Enrollment: 40,000
President .Dr. John C. Hitt
Athletic Director . . . . .Steve Orsini
Asst. AD for Media Relations . . . . .John Marini

Central Michigan University
Mt. Pleasant, MI 48859
SID: (989) 774-3277   www.cmuchippewas.com
Founded: 1892   Enrollment: 28,003
President . . . . .Michael Rao
Athletic Director . . . . .Herb Deromedi
Sports Information Director . . . . .Fred Stabley Jr.

Eastern Michigan University
Ypsilanti, MI 48197
SID: (734) 487-0317   www.emich.edu/goeagles
Founded: 1849   Enrollment: 24,000
Interim President . . . . .Craig Willis
Athletic Director . . . . .Dr. David Diles
Sports Information Director . . . . Jim Streeter

Kent State University
Kent, OH 44242
SID: (330) 672-2110   www.kent.edu/athletics
Founded: 1910   Enrollment: 33,000
President . . . . .Carol Cartwright
Athletic Director . . . . .Laing Kennedy
Dir. of Athletic Communications . . . . Jeff Schaefer

Marshall University
Huntington, WV 25715
SID: (304) 696-5275   www.herdzone.com
Founded: 1837   Enrollment: 16,551
President . . . . .Dan Angel
Athletic Director . . . . .Bob Marcum
Asst. AD for Media Relations . . . . .Randy Burnside

Miami University
Oxford, OH 45056
SID: (513) 529-4327   www.muredhawks.com
Founded: 1809   Enrollment: 16,300
President . . . . James C. Garland
Athletic Director . . . . .Brad Bates
Asst. AD for External Affairs . . . . .Mike Harris

Northern Illinois University
DeKalb, IL 60115
SID: (815) 753-1706   www.niuhuskies.com
Founded: 1895   Enrollment: 25,260
President . . . . .John G. Peters
Athletic Director . . . . Jim Phillips
Sports Information Director . . . . .Michael Korcek

Ohio University
Athens, OH 45701
SID: (740) 593-1298   www.ohiobobcats.com
Founded: 1804   Enrollment: 28,598
President . . . . .Dr. Roderick J. McDavis
Athletic Director . . . . .Tom Boeh
Asst. AD for External Affairs . . . . .Derek Scott

University of Toledo
Toledo, OH 43606
SID: (419) 530-4920   www.utrockets.com
Founded: 1872   Enrollment: 19,019
President .Dr. Daniel Johnson
Athletic Director . . . . .Mike O'Brien
Assoc. AD, Media Relations . . . . .Paul Helgren

Western Michigan University
Kalamazoo, MI 49008
SID: (616) 387-4138   www.wmubroncos.com
Founded: 1903   Enrollment: 28,931
President . . . . .Dr. Judith I. Bailey
Athletic Director . . . . .Kathy Beauregard
Sports Information Director . . . . .Dan Jankowski

*   *   *

MOUNTAIN WEST CONFERENCE
15455 Gleneagle Drive, Suite 200
Colorado Springs, CO 80921
(719) 488-4040   www.themwc.com
Founded: 1999
Commissioner .Craig Thompson
Asst. Comm. for Communications . . . . Javan Hedlund
    2004-05 members: BASKETBALL & FOOTBALL (8)—
Air Force, BYU, Colorado St., UNLV, New Mexico, San
Diego St., Utah and Wyoming.

U.S. Air Force Academy
US Academy, CO 80840
SID: (719) 333-9263   www.airforcesports.com
Founded: 1959   Enrollment: 4,000
Superintendent . . . . .Lt. Gen. John W. Rosa Jr.
Athletic Director . . . . .Dr. Hans J. Mueh
Asst. AD for Media Relations . . . . .Troy Garnhart

Brigham Young University
Provo, UT 84602
SID: (801) 422-4910   www.byucougars.com
Founded: 1875   Enrollment: 32,122
President .Cecil O. Samuelson
Athletic Director . . . . .TBA
Assoc. Director, Communications . . . . .Duff Tittle

Colorado State University
Fort Collins, CO 80523
SID: (970) 491-5067   www.csurams.com
Founded: 1870   Enrollment: 23,934
President . . . . .Dr. Larry Penley
Athletic Director . . . . .Mark Driscoll
Asst. AD, Media Relations Director . . . . . . .Gary Ozzello

University of New Mexico
Albuquerque, NM 87131
SID: (505) 925-5520   www.golobos.com
Founded: 1889   Enrollment: 24,250
President . . . . .Louis Caldera
Athletic Director . . . . .Rudy Davalos
Assoc. AD, Media Relations . . . . .Greg Remington

San Diego State University
San Diego, CA 92182
SID: (619) 594-5547   www.goaztecs.com
Founded: 1897   Enrollment: 33,400
President .Dr. Stephen L. Weber
Athletic Director . . . . .Mike Bohn
Assoc. AD, Media Relations . . . . .Kevin Klintworth

UNLV—University of Nevada, Las Vegas
Las Vegas, NV 89154
SID: (702) 895-3207   www.unlvrebels.com
Founded: 1957   Enrollment: 25,000
President . . . . .Dr. Carol Harter
Athletic Director . . . . .Mike Hamrick
Sports Information Director . . . . .Andy Grossman

University of Utah
Salt Lake City, UT 84112
SID: (801) 581-3510.   www.utahutes.com
Founded: 1850   Enrollment: 28,300
President .Michael K. Young
Athletic Director . . . . .Dr. Chris Hill
Asst. AD, Sports Information . . . . .Liz Abel

University of Wyoming
Laramie, WY 82071
SID: (307) 766-2256   www.wyomingathletics.com
Founded: 1886   Enrollment: 13,162
President . . . . .Dr. Philip L. Dubois
Athletic Director . . . . .Gary Barta
Assoc. AD/Sports Info. Director . . . . .Kevin McKinney

*   *   *

PACIFIC-10 CONFERENCE
800 South Broadway, Suite 400
Walnut Creek, CA 94596
(925) 932-4411   www.pac-10.org
Founded: 1915
Commissioner .Thomas Hansen
Asst. Commissioner, Public Relations . . . . . . Jim Muldoon
    2004-05 members: BASKETBALL & FOOTBALL (10)—
Arizona, Arizona St., California, Oregon, Oregon St.,
Stanford, UCLA, USC, Washington and Washington St.

University of Arizona
Tucson, AZ 85721
SID: (520) 621-4163 — www.arizonaathletics.com
Founded: 1885 — Enrollment: 37,000
President . . . . .Dr. Peter Likins
Athletic Director . . . . Jim Livengood
Sports Information Director . . . . .Tom Duddleston Jr.

Arizona State University
Tempe, AZ 85287
SID: (480) 965-5799 — www.thesundevils.com
Founded: 1885 — Enrollment: 45,693
President . . . . .Dr. Michael Crow
Athletic Director . . . . .Gene Smith
Asst. AD/Sports Information Director . . . . . .Mark Brand

University of California
Berkeley, CA 94720
SID: (510) 642-5363 — www.calbears.com
Founded: 1868 — Enrollment: 33,000
Chancellor . . . . .Dr. Robert J. Birgeneau
Athletic Director .Sandy Barbour
Exec. Assoc. AD for Communications . . . . .Bob Rose

University of Oregon
Eugene, OR 97401
SID: (541) 346-5488 — www.goducks.com
Founded: 1876 — Enrollment: 20,033
President . . . . .Dave Frohnmayer
Athletic Director . . . . .Bill Moos
Asst. AD/Sports Information Director . . . . .Dave Williford

Oregon State University
Corvallis, OR 97331
SID: (541) 737-3720 — www.osubeavers.com
Founded: 1868 — Enrollment: 19,000
President . . . . .Dr. Edward Ray
Athletic Director . . . . .Bob De Carolis
Sports Information Director . . . . .Steve Fenk

Stanford University
Stanford, CA 94305
SID: (650) 723-4418 — www.gostanford.com
Founded: 1891 — Enrollment: 13,075
President . . . . .John L. Hennessy
Athletic Director . . . . .Ted Leland
Sports Information Director . . . . .Gary Migdol

UCLA—Univ. of California, Los Angeles
Los Angeles, CA 90024
SID: (310) 206-6831 — www.uclabruins.com
Founded: 1919 — Enrollment: 36,890
Chancellor . . . . .Albert Carnesale
Athletic Director . . . . .Dan Guerrero
Sports Information Director . . . . .Marc Dellins

USC—Univ. of Southern California
Los Angeles, CA 90089
SID: (213) 740-8480 — www.usctrojans.com
Founded: 1880 — Enrollment: 30,000
President . . . . .Steven Sample
Athletic Director .Mike Garrett
Sports Information Director . . . . .Tim Tessalone

University of Washington
Seattle, WA 98195
SID: (206) 543-2230 — www.gohuskies.com
Founded: 1861 — Enrollment: 42,000
President . . . . .Dr. Mark A. Emmert
Athletic Director . . . . .Todd Turner
Asst. AD for Media Relations . . . . Jim Daves

Washington State University
Pullman, WA 99164
SID: (509) 335-2684 — www.wsucougars.com
Founded: 1890 — Enrollment: 21,000
President . . . . .V. Lane Rawlins
Athletic Director . . . . .Jim Sterk
Asst. AD/Dir. of Media Relations . . . . .Rod Commons

          *   *   *

SOUTHEASTERN CONFERENCE
2201 Richard Arrington Blvd. North
Birmingham, AL 35203
(205) 458-3010 — www.secsports.com
Founded: 1933
Commissioner . . . . .Mike Slive
Assoc. Commis. of Media Relations . . . . .Charles Bloom
    2004-05 members: BASKETBALL & FOOTBALL (12)—
Alabama, Arkansas, Auburn, Florida, Georgia, Kentucky,
LSU, Mississippi St., Ole Miss, South Carolina, Tennessee
and Vanderbilt.

University of Alabama
Tuscaloosa, AL 35487
SID: (205) 348-6084 — www.rolltide.com
Founded: 1831 — Enrollment: 20,033
President . . . . .Dr. Robert Witt
Athletic Director . . . . .Mal Moore
Assoc. AD for Media Relations . . . . .Larry White

University of Arkansas
Fayetteville, AR 72701 — www.hogwired.com
SID: (479) 575-2751 — www.ladybacks.com
Founded: 1871 — Enrollment: 16,449
Chancellor . . . . .Dr. John White
Athletic Director . . . . .Frank Broyles
Women's Athletic Director . . . . .Bev Lewis
Asst. AD, Sports Information . . . . .Kevin Trainor

Auburn University
Auburn, AL 36831
SID: (334) 844-9800 — www.auburntigers.com
Founded: 1856 — Enrollment: 23,152
Interim President . . . . .Dr. Ed Richardson
Athletic Director (retires Jan. '05) . . . . .David Housel
Asst. AD, Media Relations . . . . .Meredith Jenkins

University of Florida
Gainesville, FL 32604
SID: (352) 375-4683 ext. 6100 — www.gatorzone.com
Founded: 1853 — Enrollment: 48,373
President .Dr. J. Bernard Machen
Athletic Director .Jeremy Foley
Asst. AD for Sports Information . . . . .Steve McClain

University of Georgia
Athens, GA 30603
SID: (706) 542-1621 — www.georgiadogs.com
Founded: 1785 — Enrollment: 33,878
President .Dr. Michael F. Adams
Athletic Director .Damon Evans
Assoc. AD for Sports Communications . . . . .Claude Felton

University of Kentucky
Lexington, KY 40506
SID: (859) 257-3838 — www.ukathletics.com
Founded: 1865 — Enrollment: 25,397
President . . . . .Dr. Lee Todd
Athletic Director .Mitch Barnhart
Asst. AD/Media Relations . . . . .Scott Stricklin

LSU—Louisiana State University
Baton Rouge, LA 70894
SID: (225) 578-8226 — www.lsusports.net
Founded: 1860 — Enrollment: 31,582
Interim Chancellor . . . . .Dr. William L. Jenkins
Athletic Director .Skip Bertman
Asst. AD for Sports Information . . . . . . .Michael Bonnette

Mississippi State University
Starkville, MS 39762
SID: (662) 325-2703 — www.mstateathletics.com
Founded: 1878 — Enrollment: 16,236
President . . . . .Dr. J. Charles Lee
Athletic Director .Larry Templeton
Assoc. AD, Media & Public Relations . . . . .Mike Nemeth

Ole Miss—University of Mississippi
University, MS 38677
SID: (662) 915-7522   www.olemisssports.com
Founded: 1848   Enrollment: 16,080
Chancellor . . . . .Dr. Robert C. Khayat
Athletic Director . . . . .Pete Boone
Assoc. AD for Media Relations . . . . . . .Langston Rogers

University of South Carolina
Columbia, SC 29208
SID: (803) 777-5204   www.uscsports.com
Founded: 1801   Enrollment: 26,000
President . . . . .Dr. Andrew Sorensen
Athletic Director . . . . .Dr. Mike McGee
Assoc. AD/Sports Information Director . . . . . .Kerry Tharp

University of Tennessee
Knoxville, TN 37996   www.utsports.com
SID: (865) 974-1212   www.utladyvols.com
Founded: 1794   Enrollment: 25,058
President . . . . .Dr. John D. Petersen
Athletic Director . . . . .Mike Hamilton
Women's Athletic Director . . . . Joan Cronan
Sports Information Director . . . . .Bud Ford

Vanderbilt University
Nashville, TN 37212
SID: (615) 322-4121   www.vucommodores.com
Founded: 1873   Enrollment: 6,319
Chancellor . . . . .Gordon Gee
Vice Chancellor . . . . .David Williams
Assoc. AD, Communications . . . . .Rod Williamson

          *   *   *

SUN BELT CONFERENCE
601 Poydras Street, Suite 2355
New Orleans, LA 70130
(504) 299-9066   www.sunbeltsports.org
Founded: 1976
Commissioner . . . . .Wright Waters
Asst. Commissioner/Media Relations . . . . . . .Judy Wilson
    2004-05 members: BASKETBALL (11)—Arkansas-Little Rock, Arkansas St., Denver, Florida International, LA-Lafayette, Middle Tenn. St., New Mexico St., New Orleans, North Texas, South Alabama and Western Kentucky; FOOTBALL (9)—Arkansas St., Idaho, LA-Lafayette, LA-Monroe, Middle Tenn. State, New Mexico St., North Texas, Troy and Utah St.

Arkansas-Little Rock
Little Rock, AR 72204
SID: (501) 569-3449   www.ualrtrojans.com
Founded: 1927   Enrollment: 11,798
Chancellor . . . . .Dr. Joel E. Anderson
Athletic Director .Chris Peterson
Sports Information Director . . . . .Kevin Tankersley

Arkansas State
Jonesboro, AR 72467
SID: (870) 972-2541   www.asuindians.com
Founded: 1909   Enrollment: 10,429
President .Dr. J. Leslie Wyatt
Athletic Director . . . . .Dr. Dean Lee
Asst. AD/Media Relations . . . . .Gina Bowman

University of Denver
Denver, CO 80208
SID: (303) 871-4990   www.denverpioneers.com
Founded: 1864   Enrollment: 9,689
Chancellor .Daniel L. Ritchie
Interim Athletic Director . . . . .Stu Halsall
Director of Sports Media Relations . . . . .Marla Rodriguez

Florida International University
Miami, FL 33199
SID: (305) 348-3164   www.fiusports.com
Founded: 1972   Enrollment: 34,000
President . . . . .Modesto A. Maidique
Athletic Director .Rick Mello
Asst. AD/Media Relations . . . . .Rich Kelch

University of Idaho
Moscow, ID 83844
SID: (208) 885-0245   www.uiathletics.com
Founded: 1889   Enrollment: 12,894
President . . . . .Dr. Tim White
Athletic Director . . . . .Dr. Rob Spear
Asst. AD/Media Relations . . . . .Becky Paull

University of Louisiana at Lafayette
Lafayette, LA 70506
SID: (337) 851-2255   www.ragincajuns.com
Founded: 1898   Enrollment: 15,343
President . . . . .Dr. Ray P. Authement
Athletic Director . . . . .Nelson Schexnayder
Sports Information Director . . . . .Daryl Cetnar

University of Louisiana at Monroe
Monroe, LA 71209
SID: (318) 342-5442   www.ulmathletics.com
Founded: 1931   Enrollment: 8,563
President . . . . .Dr. James E. Cofer
Athletic Director . . . . .Bobby Staub
Interim SID . . . . .Fred Sington

Middle Tennessee State
Murfreesboro, TN 37132
SID: (615) 898-2450   www.goblueraiders.com
Founded: 1911   Enrollment: 21,741
President . . . . .Dr. Sidney A. McPhee
Athletic Director . . . . .Boots Donnelly
Asst. AD/Media Relations Director . . . . . . .Mark Owens

New Mexico State
Las Cruces, NM 88003
SID: (505) 646-3929   www.nmstatesports.com
Founded: 1888   Enrollment: 16,158
President .Michael V. Martin
Athletic Director . . . . .Brian Faison
Asst. AD/Media Relations . . . . .Sean Johnson

University of New Orleans
New Orleans, LA 70148
SID: (504) 280-6284   www.unoprivateers.com
Founded: 1958   Enrollment: 17,360
Chancellor . . . . .Dr. Timothy P. Ryan
Athletic Director .Jim Miller
Sports Information Director . . . . .Jack Duggan

University of North Texas
Denton, TX 76203
SID: (940) 565-2476   www.meangreensports.com
Founded: 1890   Enrollment: 31,112
President . . . . .Dr. Norval F. Pohl
Athletic Director . . . . .Rick Villarreal
Asst. AD/Media Relations . . . . .Eric Capper

University of South Alabama
Mobile, AL 36688
SID: (251) 460-7035   www.usajaguars.com
Founded: 1963   Enrollment: 13,238
President . . . . .V. Gordon Moulton
Athletic Director . . . . .Joe Gottfried
Director of Athletic Media Relations . . . . .Matt Smith

Troy University
Troy, AL 36082
SID: (334) 670-3229 www.troystate.com
Founded: 1887 Enrollment: 18,222
Chancellor . . . . .Dr. Jack Hawkins Jr.
Athletic Director . . . . .Johnny Williams
Athletics Media Relations Dir. . . . . .Ricky Hazel

Utah State University
Logan, UT 84322
SID: (435) 797-1361 www.utahstateaggies.com
Founded: 1888 Enrollment: 21,490
President . . . . .Dr. Kermit L. Hall
Athletic Director . . . . .Randy Spetman
Asst. AD for Media Relations . . . . .Mike Strauss

Western Kentucky University
Bowling Green, KY 42101
SID: (270) 745-4298 www.wkusports.com
Founded: 1906 Enrollment: 17,331
President . . . . .Dr. Gary Ransdell
Athletic Director . . . . .Dr. Camden Wood Selig
Dir. of Athletic Media Relations . . . . .Brian Fremund

* * *

WESTERN ATHLETIC CONFERENCE
9250 East Costilla Ave., Suite 300
Englewood, CO 80112
(303) 799-9221 www.wacsports.com
Founded: 1962
Commissioner . . . . .Karl Benson
Asst. Commiss./Media Relations . . . . .Dave Chaffin
2004-05 members: BASKETBALL & FOOTBALL (10)—
Boise St., Fresno St., Hawaii, Louisiana Tech, Nevada,
Rice, San Jose St., SMU, Tulsa and UTEP.

Boise State
Boise, ID 83725
SID: (208) 426-1515 www.broncosports.com
Founded: 1932 Enrollment: 18,447
President . . . . .Dr. Robert Kustra
Athletic Director . . . . .Gene Bleymaier
Asst. AD/Media Relations . . . . .Max Corbet

Fresno State University
Fresno, CA 93740
SID: (559) 278-2509 www.gobulldogs.com
Founded: 1911 Enrollment: 21,389
President . . . . .Dr. John D. Welty
Athletic Director . . . . .Scott Johnson
Asst. AD/Communications . . . . .Steve Weakland

University of Hawaii
Honolulu, HI 96822
SID: (808) 956-7523 www.hawaiiathletics.com
Founded: 1907 Enrollment: 17,828
Chancellor . . . . .Peter Englert
Athletic Director . . . . .Herman Frazier
Media Relations Director . . . . .Lois Manin

Louisiana Tech University
Ruston, LA 71272
SID: (318) 257-3144 www.latechsports.com
Founded: 1894 Enrollment: 11,975
President . . . . .Dan Reneau
Athletic Director . . . . .Jim Oakes
Sports Information Director . . . . .Malcolm Butler

University of Nevada
Reno, NV 89557
SID: (775) 784-6900 www.nevadawolfpack.com
Founded: 1874 Enrollment: 16,000
President .Dr. John Lilley
Athletic Director . . . . .Cary Groth
Director of Media Services . . . . .Jamie Klund

Rice University
Houston, TX 77005
SID: (713) 348-5775 www.riceowls.com
Founded: 1912 Enrollment: 4,785
President . . . . .Dr. David W. Leebron
Athletic Director . . . . .Bobby May
Asst. AD/Sports Information Director . . . . . . .Bill Cousins

San Jose State University
San Jose, CA 95192
SID: (408) 924-1217 www.sjsuspartans.com
Founded: 1857 Enrollment: 30,067
Acting President . . . . .Don Kassing
Athletic Director . . . . .Chuck Bell
Sports Information Director . . . . .Lawrence Fan

SMU—Southern Methodist University
Dallas, TX 75275
SID: (214) 768-2883 www.smumustangs.com
Founded: 1911 Enrollment: 10,038
President . . . . .Dr. R. Gerald Turner
Athletic Director . . . . .Jim Copeland
Asst. AD/Media Relations . . . . .Brad Sutton

University of Tulsa
Tulsa, OK 74104
SID: (918) 631-2395 www.tulsahurricane.com
Founded: 1894 Enrollment: 4,100
President . . . . .Dr. Steadman Upham
Athletic Director . . . . .Judy MacLeod
Asst. AD/Media Relations . . . . .Don Tomkalski

UTEP—University of Texas at El Paso
El Paso, TX 79902
SID: (915) 747-6653 www.utepathletics.com
Founded: 1914 Enrollment: 18,542
President . . . . .Dr. Diana Natalicio
Athletic Director . . . . .Bob Stull
Assoc. AD/Media Relations . . . . .Jeff Darby

* * *

Major Independents
Division I-A football independents in 2004.

Navy—U.S. Naval Academy
Annapolis, MD 21402
SID: (410) 293-2700 www.navysports.com
Founded: 1845 Enrollment: 4,000
Superintendent . . . . . . .Vice Adm. Rodney P. Rempt, USN
Athletic Director . . . . .Chet Gladchuk
Asst. AD/Sports Information Director . . . .Scott Strasemeier

University of Notre Dame
Notre Dame, IN 46556
SID: (574) 631-7516 www.und.com
Founded: 1842 Enrollment: 8,261
President . . . . .Rev. Edward (Monk) Malloy
President-Elect (June 30, 2005) . . . . . . .Rev. John I. Jenkins
Athletic Director . . . . .Kevin White
Sports Information Director . . . . .John Heisler

* * *

Other Major Division I Conferences
Conferences that play either Division I basketball or Division
I-AA football, or both.

America East
10 High St., Suite 860, Boston, MA 02110
(617) 695-6369 www.americaeast.com
Founded: 1979
Commissioner . . . . .Chris Monasch
Dir. of Communications . . . . .Matt Bourque
2004-05 members: BASKETBALL (10)—Albany, Binghamton, Boston University, Hartford, Maine, Maryland-Balti-
more County, New Hampshire, Northeastern, Stony Brook
and Vermont.

Atlantic Sun Conference
3370 Vineville Ave., Suite 108-B
Macon, GA 31204
(478) 474-3394   www.atlanticsun.org
Founded: 1978
Commissioner ....Bill Bibb
Asst. Commissioner ....Devlin Pierce
    2004-05 members: BASKETBALL (11)—Belmont, Campbell, Central Florida, Florida Atlantic, Gardner-Webb, Georgia St., Jacksonville, Lipscomb, Mercer, Stetson and Troy.

Atlantic 10 Conference
230 S. Broad St., Suite 1700
Philadelphia, PA 19102
(215) 545-6678   www.atlantic10.org
Founded: 1976   A-10 Football founded: 1997
Commissioner ....Linda Bruno
Asst. Commissioner/P.R. ....Ray Cella
    2004-05 members: BASKETBALL (12)—Dayton, Duquesne, Fordham, George Washington, La Salle, Massachusetts, Rhode Island, Richmond, St. Bonaventure, St. Joseph's-PA, Temple and Xavier-OH. FOOTBALL (12)—Delaware, Hofstra, James Madison, Maine, Massachusetts, New Hampshire, Northeastern, Rhode Island, Richmond, Towson, Villanova and William & Mary.

Big Sky Conference
2491 Washington Blvd. Suite 201
Ogden, UT 84401
(801) 392-1978   www.bigskyconf.com
Founded: 1963
Commissioner ....Douglas Fullerton
Asst. Commissioner, Media Relations ....Dusty Clements
    2004-05 members: BASKETBALL & FOOTBALL (8)—Eastern Washington, Idaho St., Montana, Montana St., Northern Arizona, Portland St., Sacramento St., and Weber St.

Big South Conference
7233 Pineville-Matthews Rd., Suite 100
Charlotte, NC 28226
(704) 341-7990   www.bigsouthsports.com
Founded: 1983
Commissioner ....Kyle B. Kallander
Director of Public Relations ....Mark Simpson
    2004-05 members: BASKETBALL (9)—Birmingham Southern, Charleston Southern, Coastal Carolina, High Point, Liberty, NC-Asheville, Radford, VMI and Winthrop. FOOTBALL (5)—Charleston Southern, Coastal Carolina, Gardner-Webb, Liberty and VMI.

Big West Conference
Two Corporate Park, Suite 206
Irvine, CA 92606
(949) 261-2525   www.bigwest.org
Founded: 1969
Commissioner ....Dennis Farrell
Information Director ....Rob Washburn
    2004-05 members: BASKETBALL (11)—CS-Fullerton, CS-Northridge, Cal Poly, Idaho, Long Beach St., Pacific, UC-Davis, UC-Irvine, UC-Riverside, UC-Santa Barbara and Utah St.

Colonial Athletic Association
8625 Patterson Ave.,
Richmond, VA 23229
(804) 754-1616   www.caasports.com
Founded: 1985
Commissioner ....Thomas E. Yeager
Asst. Commissioner/Commun. ....Rob Washburn
    2004-05 members: BASKETBALL (10)—Delaware, Drexel, George Mason, Hofstra, James Madison, NC-Wilmington, Old Dominion, Towson, Virginia Commonwealth and William & Mary.

Gateway Football Conference
1818 Chouteau Ave.
St. Louis, MO 63103
(314) 421-2268   www.gatewayfootball.org
Founded: 1985
Commissioner ....Patty Viverito
Asst. Commissioner ....Mike Kern
    2004 members: FOOTBALL (8)—Illinois St., Indiana St., Northern Iowa, Southern Illinois, SW Missouri St., Western Illinois, Western Kentucky and Youngstown St.

Great West Football Conference
Harris Center, 351 W. Center
Cedar City, UT 84720
(435) 865-8354   www.greatwestfootball.com
Founded: 2004
Executive Committee Chair ....Tom Douple
External Relations Chair ....Jim Fallis
    2004 members: FOOTBALL (6)—Cal Poly, North Dakota St., Northern Colorado, South Dakota St., Southern Utah and UC-Davis.

Horizon League
201 South Capitol Ave., Suite 500
Indianapolis, IN 46225
(317) 237-5622   www.horizonleague.org
Founded: 1979
Commissioner ....Jon LeCrone
Asst. Commiss. for Communications ....Will Roleson
    2004-05 members: BASKETBALL (9)—Butler, Cleveland St., Detroit Mercy, Illinois-Chicago, Loyola-Chicago, Wisconsin-Green Bay, Wisconsin-Milwaukee, Wright St. and Youngstown St.

Ivy League
228 Alexander Street
Princeton, NJ 08544
(609) 258-6426   www.ivyleaguesports.com
Founded: 1954
Executive Director ....Jeffrey Orleans
Assistant Director ....Brett Hoover
    2004-05 members: BASKETBALL & FOOTBALL (8)—Brown, Columbia, Cornell, Dartmouth, Harvard, Pennsylvania, Princeton and Yale.

Metro Atlantic Athletic Conference
712 Amboy Avenue
Edison, NJ 08837
(732) 738-5455   www.maacsports.com
Founded: 1980
Commissioner ....Richard Ensor
Director of Media Relations ....Jill Skotarczak
    2004-05 members: BASKETBALL (10)—Canisius, Fairfield, Iona, Loyola-MD, Manhattan, Marist, Niagara, Rider, St. Peter's and Siena. FOOTBALL (5)—Duquesne, Iona, La Salle, Marist and St. Peter's.

Mid-Continent Conference
340 West Butterfield Rd., Ste 3D
Elmhurst, IL 60126
(630) 516-0661   www.mid-con.com
Founded: 1982
Commissioner ....Ron Bertovich
Director of Media Relations ....Tony Hamilton
    2004-05 members: BASKETBALL (9)—Centenary, Chicago St., IUPUI, UMKC, Oakland, Oral Roberts, Southern Utah, Valparaiso and Western Illinois.

Mid-Eastern Athletic Conference
102 North Elm St.
SE Building, Suite 401
Greensboro, NC 27402
(336) 275-9961   www.meacsports.com
Founded: 1970
Commissioner . . . . .Dr. Dennis Thomas
Director of Media Relations . . . . .Michelle Jinks
   2004-05 members: BASKETBALL (11)—Bethune-Cookman, Coppin St., Delaware St., Florida A&M, Hampton, Howard, MD-Eastern Shore, Morgan St., Norfolk St., North Carolina A&T and South Carolina St.; FOOTBALL (8)—all but Coppin St., Florida A&M and MD-Eastern Shore.

Missouri Valley Conference
1818 Chouteau Ave.
St. Louis, MO 63103
(314) 421-0339   www.mvc-sports.com
Founded: 1907
Commissioner . . . . .Doug Elgin
Assoc. Commissioner, Communications . . . . . .Mike Kern
   2004-05 members: BASKETBALL (10)—Bradley, Creighton, Drake, Evansville, Illinois St., Indiana St., Northern Iowa, Southern Illinois, SW Missouri St. and Wichita St.

Northeast Conference
200 Cottontail Lane, Vantage Court North
Somerset, NJ 08873
(732) 469-0440   www.northeastconference.org
Founded: 1981
Commissioner . . . . .John Iamarino
Associate Commissioner . . . . .Ron Ratner
   2004-05 members: BASKETBALL (11)—Cent. Conn. St., Fairleigh Dickinson, LIU-Brooklyn, Monmouth, Mount St. Mary's, Quinnipiac, Robert Morris, Sacred Heart, St. Francis-NY, St. Francis-PA and Wagner. FOOTBALL (8)—Albany, Cent. Conn. St., Monmouth, Robert Morris, Sacred Heart, St. Francis-PA, Stony Brook and Wagner.

Ohio Valley Conference
215 Centerview Drive, Suite 115
Brentwood, TN 37027
(615) 371-1698   www.ovcsports.com
Founded: 1948
Commissioner . . . . .Dr. Jon A. Steinbrecher
Asst. Commissioner for Media Relations . . . . .Kim Melcher
   2004-05 members: BASKETBALL (11)—Austin Peay St., Eastern Illinois, Eastern Kentucky, Jacksonville St., Morehead St., Murray St., Samford, SE Missouri St., Tennessee-Martin, Tennessee St. and Tennessee Tech; FOOTBALL (9)—all but Austin Peay St. and Morehead St.

Patriot League
3773 Corporate Pkwy, Suite 190
Center Valley, PA 18034
(610) 289-1950   www.patriotleague.com
Founded: 1984
Executive Director . . . . .Carolyn Schlie Femovich
Asst. Exec. Dir. for Media Relations . . . . .Tom Byrnes
   2004-05 members: BASKETBALL (8)—American, Army, Bucknell, Colgate, Holy Cross, Lafayette, Lehigh and Navy; FOOTBALL (8)—Bucknell, Colgate, Fordham, Georgetown, Holy Cross, Lafayette and Lehigh.

Pioneer Football League
1818 Chouteau Ave.
St. Louis, MO 63103
(314) 421-2268   www.pioneer-football.org
Founded: 1993
Commissioner .Patty Viverito
Sports Information Director . . . . .Cody Bush
   2004 members: FOOTBALL (9): Austin Peay St., Butler, Davidson, Dayton, Drake, Jacksonville, Morehead St., San Diego and Valparaiso.

Southern Conference
905 East Main St.
Spartanburg, SC 29302
(864) 591-5100   www.soconsports.com
Founded: 1921
Commissioner . . . . .Dr. Daniel B. Morrison Jr.
Assoc. Commissioner for Public Affairs . . . . . .Steve Shutt
   2004-05 members: BASKETBALL (12)—Appalachian St., Chattanooga, The Citadel, College of Charleston, Davidson, East Tennessee St., Elon, Furman, Georgia Southern, NC-Greensboro, Western Carolina and Wofford; FOOTBALL (8)—all except College of Charleston, Davidson, East Tennessee St. and NC-Greensboro.

Southland Conference
1700 Alma Drive, Suite 550
Plano, TX 75075
(972) 422-9500   www.southland.org
Founded: 1963
Commissioner .Tom Burnett
Asst. Commissioner for Media Relations . . . .Bruce Ludlow
   2004-05 members: BASKETBALL (11)—Lamar, LA-Monroe, McNeese St., Nicholls St., Northwestern St., Sam Houston St., SE Louisiana, Stephen F. Austin St., Texas-Arlington, Texas-San Antonio and Texas St.-San Marcos; FOOTBALL (6)—McNeese St., Nicholls St., Northwestern St., Sam Houston St., Stephen F. Austin St. and Texas St.-San Marcos.

Southwestern Athletic Conference
1527 Fifth Ave. North
Birmingham, AL 35204
(205) 251-7573   www.swac.org
Founded: 1920
Commissioner . . . . .Robert C. Vowels Jr.
Asst. Comm. for Media Relations   Wallace Dooley Jr.
   2004-05 members: BASKETBALL & FOOTBALL (10)—Alabama A&M, Alabama St., Alcorn St., Arkansas-Pine Bluff, Grambling St., Jackson St., Mississippi Valley St., Prairie View A&M, Southern-Baton Rouge and Texas Southern.

West Coast Conference
1200 Bayhill Dr., Suite 302
San Bruno, CA 94066
(650) 873-8622   www.wccsports.com
Founded: 1952
Commissioner . . . . .Michael Gilleran
Asst. Commissioner . . . . .Brad Walker
   2004-05 members: BASKETBALL (8)—Gonzaga, Loyola Marymount, Pepperdine, Portland, Saint Mary's-CA, San Diego, San Francisco and Santa Clara.

PRO FOOTBALL

National Football League

League Office
280 Park Ave.
New York, NY 10017
(212) 450-2000   www.nfl.com
Commissioner . . . . .Paul Tagliabue
Exec. Vice President/League Counsel . . . . .Jeff Pash
Exec. V.P. for Labor Relations . . . . . . .Harold Henderson
Exec. V.P., Communications, Public Affairs . . .Joe Browne
AFC Info. Coordinator . . . . .Steve Alic
NFC Info. Coordinator . . . . .Mike Signora

NFL Players Association
2021 L Street NW, Suite 600
Washington, DC 20036
(202) 463-2200   www.nflpa.org
Executive Director . . . . .Gene Upshaw
Asst. Exec. Director . . . . .Doug Allen
General Counsel . . . . .Richard Berthelsen
Director of Communications . . . . .Carl Francis

AFC

Baltimore Ravens
11001 Owings Mills Blvd.
Owings Mills, MD 21117
(410) 654-6200   www.baltimoreravens.com
Owner .Stephen J. Bisciotti
President .Richard W. Cass
GM/Executive V.P. . . . . .Ozzie Newsome
Sr. V.P. of Public & Community Relations . . . . .Kevin Byrne

Buffalo Bills
One Bills Drive, Orchard Park, NY 14127
(716) 648-1800   www.buffalobills.com
Chairman & Owner . . . . .Ralph C. Wilson Jr.
President & GM .Tom Donahoe
V.P. of Communications . . . . . : . . . . .Scott Berchtold

Cincinnati Bengals
One Paul Brown Stadium, Cincinnati, OH 45202
(513) 621-3550   www.bengals.com
President . . . . .Mike Brown
Sr. Vice President .Pete Brown
Public Relations Director . . . . .Jack Brennan

Cleveland Browns
76 Lou Groza Blvd., Berea, OH 44017
(440) 891-5000   www.clevelandbrowns.com
Owner/Chairman . . . . .Randolph Lerner
President/CEO .John Collins
Vice President, Communications . . . . .Julia Payne

Denver Broncos
13655 Broncos Parkway, Englewood, CO 80112
(303) 649-9000   www.denverbroncos.com
Owner-President-CEO . . . . .Pat Bowlen
Exec. V.P. of Football Ops./Head Coach . . .Mike Shanahan
General Manager . . . . .Ted Sundquist
V.P. of Public Relations . . . . : . . . . .Jim Saccomano

Houston Texans
Two Reliant Park, Houston, TX 77054
(832) 667-2000   www.houstontexans.com
Chairman & CEO . . . . .Robert C. McNair
Sr. V.P. & GM of Football Ops. . . . . . . .Charley Casserly
V.P. of Communications . . . . .Tony Wyllie

Indianapolis Colts
7001 W 56th St., Indianapolis, IN 46254
(317) 297-2658   www.colts.com
Owner-CEO . . . . .Jim Irsay
President . . . . .Bill Polian
Dir. of Football Operations . . . . .Dom Anile
V.P. of Public Relations . . . . .Craig Kelley

Jacksonville Jaguars
One ALLTEL Stadium Place
Jacksonville, FL 32202
(904) 633-6000   www.jaguars.com
Chairman & CEO . . . . .Wayne Weaver
Sr. V.P., Football Operations . . . . .Paul Vance
V.P. of Communications & Media . . . . .Dan Edwards

Kansas City Chiefs
One Arrowhead Drive, Kansas City, MO 64129
(816) 920-9300   www.kcchiefs.com
Owner-Founder .Lamar Hunt
Chairman . . . . .Jack Steadman
President-CEO-General Manager . . . . .Carl Peterson
Director of Public Relations . . . . .Bob Moore

Miami Dolphins
7500 SW 30th St., Davie, FL 33329
(954) 452-7000   www.miamidolphins.com
Owner-Chairman . . . . .H. Wayne Huizenga
President . . . . .Eddie Jones
Sr. V.P. Football Ops & Player Personnel . . .Rick Spielman
Sr. V.P. of Media Relations . . . . .Harvey Greene

New England Patriots
One Patriot Place, Foxboro, MA 02035
(508) 543-8200   www.patriots.com
Owner & Chairman . . . . .Bob Kraft
Dir. of Player Personnel . . . . .Scott Pioli
Director of Media Relations . . . . .Stacey James

New York Jets
1000 Fulton Ave., Hempstead, NY 11550
(516) 560-8100   www.newyorkjets.com
Owner & Chairman . . . . .Robert Wood Johnson IV
President . . . . .Terry Bradway
V.P. of Public Relations . . . . .Ron Colangelo

Oakland Raiders
1220 Harbor Bay Parkway, Alameda, CA 94502
(510) 864-5000   www.raiders.com
Owner — Manager of General Partners . . . . . . .Al Davis
CEO . . . . .Amy Trask
Director of Player Personnel . . . . .Mike Lombardi
Director of Public Relations . . . . .Mike Taylor

Pittsburgh Steelers
3400 South Water Street, Pittsburgh, PA 15203
(412) 432-7800   www.steelers.com
Chairman . . . . .Dan Rooney
President . . . . .Art Rooney II
Director of Football Operations . . . . .Kevin Colbert
Communications Coordinator . . . . .Ron Wahl

San Diego Chargers
4020 Murphy Canyon Rd.
San Diego, CA 92123
(858) 874-4500   www.chargers.com
Owner-Chairman . . . . .Alex Spanos
President-CEO .Dean Spanos
Exec. V.P./General Manager . . . . .A.J. Smith
Director of Public Relations . . . . .Bill Johnston

Tennessee Titans
460 Great Circle Road, Nashville, TN 37228
(615) 565-4000   www.titansonline.com
Owner/Chairman/President/CEO . . .K.S. (Bud) Adams Jr.
Exec. V.P./General Manager . . . . .Floyd Reese
Exec. V.P./Head Coach . . . . .Jeff Fisher
Director of Media Services . . . . .Robbie Bohren

NFC

Arizona Cardinals
8701 S. Hardy Drive, Tempe, AZ 85284
(602) 379-0101   www.azcardinals.com
Owner-President . . . . .Bill Bidwill Sr.
V.P. of Football Operations . . . . .Rod Graves
Director of Public Relations . . . . .Mark Dalton

Atlanta Falcons
4400 Falcon Pkwy
Flowery Branch, GA 30542
(770) 965-3115   www.atlantafalcons.com
Owner-CEO . . . . .Arthur Blank
President/GM .Rich McKay
V.P. of Football Communications . . . . .Reggie Roberts

Carolina Panthers
800 South Mint St., Charlotte, NC 28202-1502
(704) 358-7000   www.panthers.com
Founder-Owner . . . . .Jerry Richardson
President .Mark Richardson
General Manager . . . . .Marty Hurney
Director of Communications . . . . .Charlie Dayton

Chicago Bears
1000 Football Drive, Lake Forest, IL 60045
(847) 295-6600 www.chicagobears.com
Chairman .Michael McCaskey
President-CEO . . . . .Ted Phillips
General Manager . . . . .Jerry Angelo
Sr. Dir. of Corp. Communications . . . . .Scott Hagel

Dallas Cowboys
Cowboys Center, One Cowboys Parkway
Irving, TX 75063
(972) 556-9900 www.dallascowboys.com
Owner/GM . . . . .Jerry Jones
Exec. V.P./Dir. of Player Personnel/COO . . .Stephen Jones
Public Relations Director . . . . .Rich Dalrymple

Detroit Lions
222 Republic Drive, Allen Park, MI 48101
(313) 216-4000 www.detroitlions.com
Owner . . . . .William Clay Ford
President & CEO .Matt Millen
Dir. of Pro Personnel . . . . .Sheldon White
Director of Media Relations . . . . .Matt Barnhart

Green Bay Packers
1265 Lombardi Ave.
Green Bay, WI 54304
(920) 496-5700 www.packers.com
President & CEO . . . . .Bob Harlan
Exec. V.P./GM & Head Coach . . . . .Mike Sherman
Director of Public Relations . . . . .Jeff Blumb

Minnesota Vikings
9520 Viking Drive, Eden Prairie, MN 55344
(952) 828-6500 www.vikings.com
Owner . . . . .Red McCombs
President . . . . .Gary Woods
Executive Vice President . . . . .Michael Kelly
Director of Public Relations . . . . .Bob Hagan

New Orleans Saints
5800 Airline Drive, Metairie, LA 70003
(504) 731-1799 www.neworleanssaints.com
Owner . . . . .Tom Benson
Exec. V.P./GM of Football Ops. . . . . .Mickey Loomis
Dir. of Player Personnel . . . . .Rick Mueller
Director of Media/Public Relations . . . . .Greg Bensel

New York Giants
Giants Stadium
East Rutherford, NJ 07073
(201) 935-8111 www.giants.com
President/co-CEO . . . . .Wellington Mara
Chairman/co-CEO . . . . .Preston Robert Tisch
Senior V.P. & General Manager . . . . .Ernie Accorsi
V.P. of Communications . . . . .Pat Hanlon

Philadelphia Eagles
NovaCare Complex
One NovaCare Way
Philadelphia, PA 19145
(215) 463-2500 www.philadelphiaeagles.com
Owner-Chairman-CEO . . . . .Jeffrey Lurie
President/COO .Joe Banner
Head Coach/Exec. V.P. of Football Ops. . . . . .Andy Reid
Dir. of Football Media Services . . . . .Derek Boyko

St. Louis Rams
One Rams Way, St. Louis, MO 63045
(314) 982-7267 www.stlouisrams.com
Owner-Chairman . . . . .Georgia Frontiere
Owner-Vice Chairman . . . . .Stan Kroenke
President . . . . .John Shaw
Pres. of Football Operations . . . . .Jay Zygmunt
Director of Football Media . . . . .Duane Lewis

San Francisco 49ers
4949 Centennial Blvd., Santa Clara, CA 95054
(408) 562-4949 www.sf49ers.com
Owner . . . . .Denise DeBartolo-York
Owner . . . . .John York
General Manager . . . . .Terry Donahue
Director of Public Relations . . . . .Kirk Reynolds

Seattle Seahawks
11220 NE 53rd Street, Kirkland, WA 98033
(425) 827-9777 www.seahawks.com
Owner . . . . .Paul Allen
President . . . . .Bob Whitsitt
General Manager . . . . .Bob Ferguson
Public Relations Director . . . . .Dave Pearson

Tampa Bay Buccaneers
One Buccaneer Place, Tampa, FL 33607
(813) 870-2700 www.buccaneers.com
Owner-President . . . . .Malcolm Glazer
General Manager . . . . .Bruce Allen
Communications Manager . . . . .Jeff Kamis

Washington Redskins
21300 Redskins Park , Ashburn, VA 20147
(703) 726-7000 www.redskins.com
Owner . . . . .Daniel M. Snyder
V.P. of Football Operations . . . . .Vinny Cerrato
Director of Public Relations . . . . .Michelle Tessier

Canadian Football League

League Office
50 Wellington St. East, 3rd Floor
Toronto, Ontario M5E 1C8
(416) 322-9650 www.cfl.ca
Commissioner . . . . .Tom Wright
V.P. of Football Operations . . . . .Ed Chalupka
Director, Football Media . . . . .Shawn Lackie
Member teams (9): West Division—British Columbia Lions, Calgary Stampeders, Edmonton Eskimos, Saskatchewan Roughriders and Winnipeg Blue Bombers. East Division—Hamilton Tiger-Cats, Montreal Alouettes, Ottawa Renegades and Toronto Argonauts.

NFL Europe

New York Office
280 Park Avenue
New York, NY 10017
(212) 450-2000 www.nfleurope.com
Sr. Vice President of Football Ops. . . . . .Art Shell
Managing Director . . . . .Jim Connelly
Director of Public Relations . . . . .David Tossell
Public Relations Assistant . . . . .Neil Reynolds
Member teams (6): Amsterdam Admirals, Berlin Thunder, Cologne Centurions, Frankfurt Galaxy, Rhein Fire (Dusseldorf), Scottish Claymores (Edinburgh).

Arena Football League

20 North Wacker Dr., Suite 1231
Chicago, IL 60606
(312) 621-7000 www.arenafootball.com
(212) 252-8100 (N.Y. office)
Commissioner . . . . .C. David Baker
V.P. of Football Operations . . . . .Jerry Trice
Senior V.P. of Communications . . . . .Chris McCloskey
Member teams (17): American Conference—Arizona Rattlers, Chicago Rush, Colorado Crush, Columbus Destroyers, Grand Rapids Rampage, Las Vegas Gladiators, Los Angeles Avengers and San Jose SaberCats. National Conference—Austin Wranglers, Dallas Desperados, Georgia Force, Nashville Kats, New Orleans Voodoo, New York Dragons, Orlando Predators, Philadelphia Soul and Tampa Bay Storm.

GOLF

LPGA Tour
(Ladies' Professional Golf Association)
100 International Golf Drive
Daytona Beach, FL 32124
(386) 274-6200
Commissioner . . . . .Ty Votaw
Director of Media Relations . . . . .Connie Wilson

PGA of America
100 Avenue of the Champions
Palm Beach Gardens, FL 33410
(561) 624-8400   www.pga.com
President . . . . .M.G. Orender
CEO . . . . Jim Awtrey
Director of Public/Media Relations . . . . Julius Mason

PGA European Tour
Wentworth Drive, Virginia Water
Surrey, England GU25 4LX
TEL: 011-44-1344-840400   www.europeantour.com
Executive Director . . . . .Ken Schofield
Director of P.R./Corporate Affairs . . . . .Mitchell Platts
Director of Communications . . . . .Gordon Simpson

PGA Tour
112 PGA Tour Blvd.
Ponte Vedra, FL 32082
(904) 285-3700   www.pgatour.com
Commissioner . . . . .Tim Finchem
Senior V.P./Chief of Operations . . . . .Henry Hughes
Senior V.P. of Communications . . . . .Bob Combs

USGA
(United States Golf Association)
P.O. Box 708, Liberty Corner Road
Far Hills, NJ 07931
(908) 234-2300   www.usga.org
President . . . . .Fred S. Ridley
Executive Director . . . . .David Fay
Sr. Director of Communications . . . . .Marty Parkes

PRO HOCKEY

NHL
National Hockey League

Commissioner . . . . .Gary Bettman
Pres., NHL Enterprises . . . . .Ed Horne
Exec. V.P., Dir. of Hockey Ops. . . . . .Colin Campbell
Exec. V.P., Chief Legal Officer . . . . .Bill Daly
V.P. of Media Relations . . . . .Frank Brown

League Offices

Montreal
1800 McGill College Ave., Suite 2600
Montreal, Quebec H3A 3J6
(514) 841-9220

New York
1251 Avenue of the Americas, 47th Floor, New York, NY 10020
(212) 789-2000

Toronto
50 Bay St., 11th Floor
Toronto, Ontario M5J 2X8
(416) 981-2777   www.nhl.com

NHL Players' Association
777 Bay St., Suite 2400
P.O. Box 121
Toronto, Ontario M5G 2C8
(416) 408-4040   www.nhlpa.com
Executive Director . . . . .Bob Goodenow
Senior Director . . . . .Ted Saskin
Media Relations . . . . .Jonathan Weatherdon

Anaheim, Mighty Ducks of
Arrowhead Pond of Anaheim
2695 Katella Ave.
Anaheim, CA 92806
(714) 940-2900   www.mightyducks.com
Owner . . . . '. . . Walt Disney Co.
Governor . . . . .Jay Rasulo
Sr. V.P./Interim General Manager . . . . .Al Coates
Director, Comm. and Team Services . . . . . . .Alex Gilchrist

Atlanta Thrashers
Centennial Tower
101 Marietta Street NW, Suite 1900
Atlanta, GA 30303
(404) 827-5300   www.atlantathrashers.com
Owner . . . . .Atlanta Spirit, LLC
President/CEO . . . . .Bernie Mullin
Exec. V.P./General Manager . . . . .Don Waddell
Sr. V.P. of Communications . . . . .Tom Hughes

Boston Bruins
1 FleetCenter, Suite 250
Boston, MA 02114
(617) 624-1900   www.bostonbruins.com
Owner . . . . .Jeremy Jacobs
President . . . . .Harry Sinden
V.P. & General Manager . . . . .Mike O'Connell
Director of Media Relations . . . . .Heidi Holland

Buffalo Sabres
HSBC Arena
One Seymour H. Knox III Plaza
Buffalo, NY 14203-3096
(716) 855-4100   www.sabres.com
Owner . . . . .B. Thomas Golisano
General Manager . . . . .Darcy Regier
Director of Public Relations . . . . .Michael Gilbert

Calgary Flames
P.O. Box 1540, Station M
Calgary, Alberta T2P 3B9
(403) 777-2177   www.calgaryflames.com
Owners . . . . .Harley Hotchkiss, Murray Edwards,
Alvin G. Libin, Allan P. Markin, J.R. McCaig,
Clay Riddell, Byron and Daryl Seamen
President & CEO . . . . .Ken King
General Manager/Head Coach . . . . .Darryl Sutter
Director of Communications . . . . .Peter Hanlon

Carolina Hurricanes
RBC Center
1400 Edwards Mill Rd., Raleigh, NC 27607
(919) 467-7825   www.caneshockey.com
CEO/Owner/Governer . . . . .Peter Karmanos Jr.
President & General Manager . . . . .Jim Rutherford
Dir., Media Relations . . . . .Mike Sundheim

Chicago Blackhawks
United Center, 1901 West Madison St.
Chicago, IL 60612
(312) 455-7000   www.chicagoblackhawks.com
Owner-President . . . . .William Wirtz
Senior V.P./General Manager . . . . .Bob Pulford
Executive Director of Communications . . . . .Jim DeMaria

Colorado Avalanche
1000 Chopper Cir., Denver, CO 80204
(303) 405-1100   www.coloradoavalanche.com
Owner ....Stan Kroenke
President/GM/Alt. Governor ....Pierre Lacroix
V.P. of Comm. & Team Services .... Jean Martineau

Columbus Blue Jackets
200 W. Nationwide Boulevard
Columbus, OH 43215
(614) 246-4625   www.bluejackets.com
Majority Owner .... John H. McConnell
President/General Manager ....Doug MacLean
Director of Communications ....Todd Sharrock

Dallas Stars
2601 Avenue of the Stars, Frisco, TX 75034
(214) 387-5600   www.dallasstars.com
Owner/Chairman ....Thomas O. Hicks
President ....Jim Lites
General Manager ....Doug Armstrong
Sr. Director of Hockey Comm. ....Rob Scichili

Detroit Red Wings
Joe Louis Arena, 600 Civic Center Drive
Detroit, MI 48226
(313) 396-7544   www.detroitredwings.com
Owner/Governor ....Mike Ilitch
Owner/Secretary-Treasurer ....Marian Ilitch
General Manager ....Ken Holland
Sr. Director of Communications ....John Hahn

Edmonton Oilers
11230 110th St., Edmonton, Alberta, T5G 3H7
(780) 414-4000   www.edmontonoilers.com
Owners ....Edmonton Investors Group, Ltd.
President & CEO ....Patrick LaForge
Exec. V.P./General Manager ....Kevin Lowe
V.P./Public Relations ....Bill Tuele

Florida Panthers
Office Depot Center
One Panther Parkway, Sunrise, FL 33323
(954) 835-7000   www.flpanthers.com
Chairman/CEO ....Alan Cohen
President ....Jordan Zimmerman
General Manager ....Mike Keenan
Director of Media Relations ....Randy Sieminski

Los Angeles Kings
1111 S. Figueroa, Los Angeles, CA 90015
(213) 742-7100   www.lakings.com
Majority Owners .... Philip Anschutz and Ed Roski
President/Governor ....Tim Leiweke
Sr. V.P. & General Manager ....Dave Taylor
V.P. of Comm. & Broadcasting ....Mike Altieri

Minnesota Wild
317 Washington Street, St. Paul, MN 55102
(651) 602-6000   www.wild.com
Owner ....Bob Naegele Jr.
CEO ....Jac Sperling
President/General Manager ....Doug Risebrough
V.P. of Comm. & Broadcasting ....Bill Robertson

Montreal Canadiens
Bell Centre, 1260 Gauchetiere St. West
Montreal, Quebec H3B 5E8
(514) 989-2829   www.canadiens.com
Owner ....George N. Gillett Jr.
President ....Pierre Boivin
Exec. V.P./General Manager ....Bob Gainey
V.P. of Communications ....Donald Beauchamp

Nashville Predators
501 Broadway, Nashville, TN 37203
(615) 770-2300   www.nashvillepredators.com
Owner/Chairman/Governor ....Craig Leipold
President/COO ....Jack Diller
Exec. V.P. & General Manager ....David Poile
V.P., Communications & Development ......Gerry Helper

New Jersey Devils
Continental Airlines Arena, P.O. Box 504
East Rutherford, NJ 07073
(201) 935-6050   www.newjerseydevils.com
Chairman .... Jeff Vanderbeek
President/CEO/General Manager ....Lou Lamoriello
Director of Public Relations ....Jeff Altstadter

New York Islanders
1535 Old Country Road, Plainview, NY 11083
(516) 501-6700   www.newyorkislanders.com
Owner ....Charles Wang & Sanjay Kumar
General Manager ....Mike Milbury
V.P. of Communications ....Chris Botta

New York Rangers
2 Pennsylvania Plaza, New York, NY 10121
(212) 465-6486   www.newyorkrangers.com
Owner ....Cablevision Systems Inc.
President (MSG) ....James Dolan
President/General Manager ....Glen Sather
V.P. of Public Relations ....John Rosasco

Ottawa Senators
1000 Palladium Dr., Kanata, Ontario, K2V 1A5
(613) 599-0250   www.ottawasenators.com
Owner/Chairman/Governor ....Eugene Melnyk
President & CEO ....Roy Mlakar
General Manager ....John Muckler
Director of Communications ....Steve Keogh

Philadelphia Flyers
3601 S. Broad St., Philadelphia, PA 19148
(215) 465-4500   www.philadelphiaflyers.com
Chairman ....Ed Snider
President ....Ron Ryan
General Manager ....Bob Clarke
Sr. Director of Communications ....Zack Hill

Phoenix Coyotes
5800 W. Glenn Drive, Suite 350, Glendale, AZ 85301
(623) 463-8800   www.phoenixcoyotes.com
Chairman/Governor ....Steve Ellman
President/COO/Alt. Governor ....Douglas Moss
General Manager/Alt. Governor ....Michael Barnett
V.P. of Communications ....Richard Nairn

Pittsburgh Penguins
Mellon Arena, 66 Mario Lemieux Place
Pittsburgh, PA 15219
(412) 642-1800   www.pittsburghpenguins.com
Owner/Chairman/CEO ....Mario Lemieux
President/Governor ....Ken Sawyer
Exec. V.P. & General Manager ....Craig Patrick
V.P. of Communications ....Tom McMillan

St. Louis Blues
Savvis Center, 1401 Clark Ave.
St. Louis, MO 63103
(314) 622-2500   www.stlouisblues.com
Owner/Chairman ....Bill Laurie
President/CEO ....Mark Sauer
Senior V.P./General Manager ....Larry Pleau
Director of Communications ....Chuck Menke

San Jose Sharks

525 West Santa Clara St., San Jose, CA 95113
(408) 287-7070   www.sjsharks.com
Owner . . . .San Jose Sports and Entertainment Enterprises
President-CEO . . . . .Greg Jamison
Exec. V.P. & General Manager . . . . .Doug Wilson
Sr. Dir. of Communications . . . . .Ken Arnold

Tampa Bay Lightning

401 Channelside Drive, Tampa, FL 33602
(813) 301-6600   www.tampabaylightning.com
Owner . . . . .Palace Sports & Ent.
CEO & Governor . . . . .Tom Wilson
Exec. V.P. & General Manager . . . . .Jay Feaster
Director of Public Relations . . . . Jay Preble

Toronto Maple Leafs

Air Canada Centre
40 Bay Street, Ste. 400, Toronto, Ontario M5J 2X2
(416) 815-5500   www.mapleleafs.com
Owner . . . . .Maple Leaf Sports & Entertainment, Ltd
Chairman .Larry Tanenbaum
President/CEO . . . . .Richard Peddie
General Manager . . . . .John Ferguson
Director of Media Relations . . . . .Pat Park

Vancouver Canucks

General Motors Place, 800 Griffiths Way
Vancouver, B.C. V6B 6G1
(604) 899-4600   www.canucks.com
Chairman . . . . .John E. McCaw Jr.
President/CEO . . . . .Stanley McCammon
Sr. V.P. & General Manager . . . . .Dave Nonis
Manager of Media Relations . . . . .Chris Brumwell

Washington Capitals

MCI Center, 401 Ninth St., Suite 750
Washington, D.C. 20004
(202) 266-2200   www.washingtoncaps.com
Majority Owner/Chairman . . . . .Ted Leonsis
Owner/President .Dick Patrick
V.P./General Manager . . . . .George McPhee
Manager of Media Relations . . . . .Brian Potter

Other Leagues/Organizations

American Hockey League

One Monarch Place, Springfield, MA 01144
(413) 781-2030   www.theahl.com
President/CEO . . . . .David Andrews
V.P. of Hockey Operations . . . . Jim Mill
Director of Public Relations . . . . .Jason Chaimovitch
   Member teams (28): Eastern Conference—Albany
River Rats, Binghamton Senators, Bridgeport Sound Tigers,
Hartford Wolf Pack, Hershey Bears, Lowell Lock Monsters,
Manchester Monarchs, Norfolk Admirals, Philadelphia Phan-
toms, Portland Pirates, Providence Bruins, Springfield Falcons,
Wilkes-Barre/Scranton Penguins and Worcester IceCats.
   Western Conference—Chicago Wolves, Cincinnati
Mighty Ducks, Cleveland Barons, Edmonton Road Runners,
Grand Rapids Griffins, Hamilton Bulldogs, Houston Aeros,
Manitoba Moose, Milwaukee Admirals, Rochester Ameri-
cans, St. John's Maple Leafs, San Antonio Rampage, Syra-
cuse Crunch and Utah Grizzlies.
   Joining the league in 2005-06: Iowa Stars

International Ice Hockey Federation

Brandschenkestrasse 50, Postfach
CH-8039 Zurich, Switzerland
TEL: 011-411-562-2200   www.iihf.com
President . . . . .Rene Fasel
General Secretary . . . . .Jan-Ake Edvinsson
Director of P.R./Marketing . . . . .Kimmo Leinonen

Original Stars Hockey League

15-6400 Millcreek Drive, Suite 353
Mississauga, Ontario L5N 3E7
(647) 226-3372   www.oshl.ca
President . . . . .Randall Gumbley
V.P. of Public Relations . . . . .Doug Philpott
   Member teams (6): Boston, Chicago, Detroit, Montreal,
New York and Toronto.
   Note: While teams are named after the original six
National Hockey League teams, games are actually played at
various sites throughout Canada.

HORSE RACING

NTRA
(National Thoroughbred Racing Association)

Commissioner . . . . .D.G. Van Clief Jr.
President & COO . . . . .Greg Avioli
V.P. of Marketing & Industry Relations . . . . .Keith Chamblin
Sr. Director of Media Relations . . . . .Eric Wing

New York Office

800 Third Ave., Suite 901
New York, NY 10022
(212) 230-9500   www.ntra.com

Kentucky Office

2525 Harrodsburg Rd.
Lexington, KY 40504
(859) 223-5444

TRA
(Thoroughbred Racing Associations of N. America, Inc.)

420 Fair Hill Drive, Suite 1, Elkton, MD 21921
(410) 392-9200   www.tra-online.com
President . . . . .Joe Harper
Executive Vice President . . . . .Christopher N. Scherf
Director of Services . . . . .Tony DeMarco

USTA
(United States Trotting Association)

750 Michigan Ave., Columbus, OH 43215
(614) 224-2291   www.ustrotting.com
President . . . . .F. Phillip Langley
Executive V.P. (to retire March 2005) . . . . .Fred Noe
Director of Public Relations . . . . John Pawlak

MEDIA

PERIODICALS

ESPN, The Magazine

19 E 34th St., New York, NY 10016
(888) 267-3684   www.espnmag.com
Editor in Chief .Gary Hoenig
Executive Editors . .Gary Belsky, Neil Fine and Steve Wulf
Sr. Vice President/GM . . . . .Geoff Reiss
Sr. Vice President/Editorial Director . . . . . . John Papanek

Sports Illustrated

135 West 50th St., New York, NY 10020
(212) 522-9797   www.si.com
President . . . . .John Squires
Managing Editor . . . . .Terry McDonell
Executive Editors . . . . .Michael Bevans, Rob Fleder
                                    and Charlie Leerhsen

The Sporting News

10176 Corporate Square Dr., Suite 200
St. Louis, MO 63132
(314) 997-7111   www.sportingnews.com
Senior V.P./Editorial Director . . . . .John D. Rawlings
President/CEO . . . . .Rick Allen

The Sports Business Daily
120 West Morehead St., Ste. 220
Charlotte, NC 28202
(704) 973-1500 www.sportsbizdaily.com
Executive Editor . . . . .Abe Madkour
Editor-at-Large . . . . .Terry Lefton
Media Relations Manager . . . . .Bill Magrath

USA Today
7950 Jones Branch Drive, McLean, VA 22108
(703) 854-3400 www.usatoday.com
Owner . . . . .Gannett Co.
President/Publisher . . . . .Craig Moon
Editor . . . . .Ken Paulson
Managing Editor/Sports . . . . .Monte Lorell

WIRE SERVICES

Associated Press
450 West 33rd Street
New York, NY 10001
(212) 621-1500 www.ap.org
President/CEO . . . . .Tom Curley
Sports Editor . . . . .Terry Taylor
Deputy Sports Editor . . . . .Aaron Watson

United Press International
1510 H Street NW
Washington, DC 20005
(202) 898-8000 www.upi.com
Managing Editor, Sports . . . . .Ron Colbert

The Sports Network
2200 Byberry Rd., Suite 200
Hatboro, PA 19040
(215) 441-8444 www.sportsnetwork.com
CEO/President . . . . .Mickey Charles
Director of Operations . . . . .Phil Sokol
Press Secretary . . . . .Maureen McGillian-Galeone

Sportsticker
ESPN Plaza, Building B, 4th Floor
Bristol, CT 06010
(860) 766-1899 www.sportsticker.com
Mgr., Customer Marketing & Communication . .Lou Monaco
(212) 515-1163

TV NETWORKS

ABC Sports
47 West 66th St., 13th Floor
New York, NY 10023
(212) 456-4867 www.abcsports.com
President . . . . .George Bodenheimer
Senior V.P., Executive Producer . . . . .Mike Pearl
V.P. of Media Relations . . . . .Mark Mandel

CBC Sports
250 Front St. West, P.O. Box 500, Station A
Toronto, Ontario M5W 1E6
(416) 205-6523 www.cbc.ca/sports
Executive Director-Sports . . . . .Nancy Lee
Sr. Executive Producer . . . . .Mike Brannagan

CBS Sports
51 West 52nd St., 25th Floor
New York, NY 10019
(212) 975-5230 www.cbs.sportsline.com
President . . . . .Sean McManus
Executive Producer . . . . .Tony Petitti
Sr. V.P., Programming . . . . .Rob Correa and Mike Aresco
V.P., Communications . . . . .Leslie Anne Wade

ESPN
ESPN Plaza, Bristol, CT 06010
(860) 766-2000 www.espn.go.com
President . . . . .George Bodenheimer
Sr. V.P. & Executive Editor . . . . .John Walsh
Executive V.P. of Programming . . . . .Mark Shapiro
Vice President/Director of News . . . . .Vince Doria
Director of Communications . . . . .Mike Soltys

FOX Sports
10201 W. Pico Blvd., Los Angeles, CA 90035
(310) 369-6000 www.foxsports.com
Chairman-CEO . . . . .David Hill
President . . . . .Ed Goren
Sr. V.P. of Communications (NYC) . . . . .Lou D'Ermilio
(212) 556-2573

The Golf Channel
7580 Commerce Center Drive
Orlando, FL 32819
(407) 363-4653 www.thegolfchannel.com
Co-founder & Chairman . . . . .Arnold Palmer
President-CEO . . . . .David-Manougian
V.P. of Production/Executive Producer . . . . .Tony Tortorici
Director of Public Relations . . . . .Dan Higgins

HBO Sports
1100 Ave. of the Americas
New York, NY 10036
(212) 512-1987 www.hbo.com/sports
President-CEO . . . . .Ross Greenburg
Sr. V.P./Exec. Producer . . . . .Rick Bernstein
Sr. V.P., Programming . . . . .Kery Davis
Director of Publicity . . . . .Ray Stallone

NBC Sports
30 Rockefeller Plaza, New York, NY 10112
(212) 664-2160 www.nbcsports.com
Chairman . . . . .Dick Ebersol
President . . . . .Ken Schanzer
Executive Producer . . . . .Tommy Roy
V.P. of Communications . . . . .Kevin Sullivan

NFL Network
280 Park Ave.
New York, NY 10017
(212) 450-2000 www.nfl.com/nflnetwork
President/CEO . . . . .Steve Bornstein
V.P. of Programming . . . . .Charles Coplin
Director of Media Services . . . . .Seth Palansky

TSN—The Sports Network
Nine Channel Nine Court
Scarborough, Ontario, M1S 4B5
(416) 332-7660 www.tsn.ca
President . . . . .Phil King
Communications Manager . . . . .Andrea Goldstein

Turner Sports
One CNN Center
13th Floor, Atlanta, GA 30303
(404) 827-1735 www.si.com/turnersports
President . . . . .David R. Levy
Senior V.P./Coordinating Producer . . . . .Jeff Behnke
Senior V.P. of Public Relations . . . . .Greg Hughes

USA Network
1230 Ave. of the Americas, New York, NY 10020
(212) 413-5000 www.usanetwork.com
Sr. V.P., Exec. Producer . . . . .Gordon Beck
V.P., Sports Programming . . . . .Kevin Landy
Sports Publicity . . . . .Tom Caraccioli

OLYMPICS

IOC
(International Olympic Committee)
Chateau de Vidy
CH-1007 Lausanne, Switzerland
TEL: 011-41-21-621-6111   www.olympic.org
President . . . . .Jacques Rogge
Director General . . . . .Urs Lacotte
Director of Communications . . . . .Giselle Davies

COC
(Canadian Olympic Committee)
21 St. Clair Avenue E., Suite 900
Toronto, Ontario M4T 1L9
(416) 962-0262   www.olympic.ca
CEO . . . . .Chris Rudge
President . . . . .Michael Chambers
IOC members . . . . . . .Charmaine Crooks, Paul Henderson,
       Richard Pound, James Worrall (Honourary)
Director of Communications . . . . .Jackie DeSouza

USOC
(United States Olympic Committee)
One Olympic Plaza
Colorado Springs, CO 80909
(719) 632-5551   www.usolympicteam.com
Chairman .Peter Ueberroth
Interim CEO .Jim Scherr
IOC members . . .Anita DeFrantz, James Easton & Bob Ctvrlik
Chief Communications Officer . . . . .Darryl Seibel

2006 WINTER GAMES

Torino Olympic Organizing Committee
Via Nizza 262/58
10126 Torino, Italy
TEL: 011-39-011-63-10-511   www.torino2006.org
President . . . . .Valentino Castellani
Deputy President . . . . .Evelina Christillin
CEO . . . . .Paolo Rota
Chairman of Coord. Commission . . . . . Jean Claude-Killy
Media Relations Manager . . . . .Giuseppe Gattino
Director of Press Operations . . . . .Cristiano Carlutti
    (XXth Olympic Winter Games, Feb. 10-26)

2008 SUMMER GAMES

Beijing Olympic Organizing Committee
24 Dongsi Shitiao St.
Beijing, China 100007
TEL: 86-10-65-28-20-09   www.beijing-2008.org
President . . . . .Liu Qi
Executive President . . . . .Yuan Weimin
Executive President . . . . .Wang Qishan
Executive President . . . . .Deng Pufang
Vice President/Secretary General . . . . .Wang Wei
    (XXIXth Olympic Summer Games, Aug. 8-24)

2010 WINTER GAMES

Vancouver Olympic Organizing Committee
Suite 400 — 1095 West Pender Street
Vancouver, B.C. Canada V6E 2M6
TEL: (604) 408-2010   www.vancouver2010.com
CEO . . . . .John Furlong
Sr. Vice President, Sport . . . . .Cathy Priestner Allinger
Sr. V.P., Revenue, Mktg., Communications . . . .Dave Cobb
Communications Director . . . .Sam Corea (604-806-1019)
    (XXIth Olympic Winter Games, Feb. 12-28)

U.S. OLYMPICS TRAINING CENTERS

Colorado Springs Training Center
One Olympic Plaza, Colorado Springs, CO 80909
(719) 866-4500
Director . . . . .John P. Smyth

Lake Placid Training Center
196 Old Military Road, Lake Placid, NY 12946
(518) 523-2600
Director . . . . .Jack Favro

Chula Vista Training Center
2800 Olympic Parkway, Chula Vista, CA 91915
(619) 656-1500
Director . . . . .Patrice Milkovich

U.S. OLYMPIC ORGANIZATIONS

National Archery Association
One Olympic Plaza, Colorado Springs, CO 80909
(719) 866-4576   www.usarchery.org
President . . . . .Darrell Pace
Executive Director . . . . .Brad Camp
Comm./Media Relations Mgr. . . . . . .Mary Beth Vorwerk

U.S. Badminton Association
One Olympic Plaza, Colorado Springs, CO 80909
(719) 866-4808   www.usabadminton.org
President . . . . .Cliff Peters
Executive Director . . . . .Dan Cloppas
Media Contact . . . . .Cecil Bleiker

USA Baseball
PO Box 1131, Durham, NC 27702
(919) 474-8721   www.usabaseball.com
President . . . . .Mike Gaski
Executive Director & CEO . . . . .Paul Seiler
Dir. of Communications . . . . .David Fannucchi

USA Basketball
5465 Mark Dabling Blvd.
Colorado Springs, CO 80918
(719) 590-4800   www.usabasketball.com
President . . . . .Tom Jernstedt
Executive Director . . . . .James Tooley
Asst. Exec. Director, Communications . . . . . . .Craig Miller

U.S. Biathlon Association
29 Ethan Allen Ave.
Colchester, VT 05446
(802) 654-7833   www.usbiathlon.org
President . . . . .Lyle Nelson
Exec. Director . . . . .Stephen Sands
Program Director . . . . .Max Cobb
Media Coordinator . . . . .Jerry Kokesh

U.S. Bobsled and Skeleton Federation
421 Old Military Road
Lake Placid, NY 12946
(518) 523-1842   www.usbsf.com
President . . . . .Bob Pokelwaldt
Executive Director . . . . .Claire DelNegro
Media/P.R. Manager . . . . .Tom LaDue

USA Boxing
One Olympic Plaza
Colorado Springs, CO 80909
(719) 866-4506   www.usaboxing.org
President . . . . .Dr. Robert Voy
Executive Director . . . . .Eric Parthen
Director of Media/Public Relations . . . . .Julie Goldsticker

U.S. Canoe and Kayak Team
230 South Tyron St., Suite 220, Charlotte, NC 28202
(704) 348-4330   www.usack.org
President ....Anne Blanchard
Executive Director ....David Yarborough
Press Officer ....Melissa Fletcher

USA Curling
1100 CenterPoint Drive, PO Box 866
Stevens Point, WI 54481
(715) 344-1199   www.usacurl.org
President ....Robert Fenson
Executive Director ....David Garber
Communications Director ....Rick Patzke

USA Cycling
One Olympic Plaza, Colorado Springs, CO 80909
(719) 866-4581   www.usacycling.org
President ....Jim Ochowicz
Executive Director/CEO ....Gerard Bisceglia
Communications Director ....Andy Lee
Communications Coordinator ....Keri Fagan

United States Diving, Inc.
201 South Capitol Avenue, Suite 430
Indianapolis, IN 46225
(317) 237-5252   www.usadiving.org
President ....Dave Burgering
Executive Director ....Todd Smith
Director of Communications ....Kelli Servizzi

U.S. Equestrian Federation
4047 Iron Works Pkwy., Lexington, KY 40511
(859) 258-2472   www.usef.org
CEO ....John Long
President ....David O'Connor
Sr. V.P., Marketing & Communications ....Maria Partlow

U.S. Fencing Association
One Olympic Plaza, Colorado Springs, CO 80909
(719) 866-4511   www.usfencing.org
President ....Stacey Johnson
Executive Director ....Michael Massik
Media Relations Contact ....Cindy Bent Findlay

U.S. Field Hockey Association
One Olympic Plaza, Colorado Springs, CO 80909
(719) 866-4567   www.usfieldhockey.com
President ....Sharon Taylor
Executive Director ....Sheila Walker
Director of Sport/Public Info. ....Howard Thomas

U.S. Figure Skating Association
20 First Street, Colorado Springs, CO 80906
(719) 635-5200   www.usfsa.org
President ....Chuck Foster
Interim Executive Director ....Jerry Lace
Sr. Dir., Sponsorships & Communications ...Kristin Matta
Director of Media Services ....Lindsay DeWall

USA Gymnastics (Artistic, Rhythmic, Trampoline)
201 South Capitol Avenue, Indianapolis, IN 46225
(317) 237-5050   www.usa-gymnastics.org
Chairman ....Ron Froehlich
President-Exec. Director ....Robert V. Colarossi
Communications Manager ....Brian Eaton

USA Hockey, Inc.
1775 Bob Johnson Dr., Colorado Springs, CO 80906
(719) 576-8724   www.usahockey.com
President ....Ron DeGregorio
Executive Director ....Doug Palazzari
Dir. of Public and Media Relations ....TBA

United States Judo, Inc.
One Olympic Plaza, Suite 202
Colorado Springs, CO 80909
(719) 866-4730   www.usjudo.org
President ....Dr. Ron Tripp
Exec. Director ....William Rosenberg
Director of Operations ....John Miller

U.S. Luge Association
35 Church Street, Lake Placid, NY 12946
(518) 523-2071   www.usaluge.org
President ....Doug Bateman
Executive Director ....Ron Rossi
Public/Media Relations Manager ....Jon Lundin

U.S. Modern Pentathlon
5415 Bandera Rd., Suite 512
San Antonio, TX 78238
(210) 229-2004   www.usapentathlon.org
President ....Ralph Bender
Executive Director ....Robert Marbut
Media Coordinator ....Olivier Bourgoin

USRowing
201 South Capitol Avenue, Suite 400
Indianapolis, IN 46225
(317) 237-5656   www.usrowing.org
President ....Donovan Langford
Executive Director ....John Dane
Director of Communications ....Brett Johnson

U.S. Sailing Association
P.O. Box 1260, 15 Maritime Drive, Portsmouth, RI 02871
(401) 683-0800   www.ussailing.org
President ....Janet C. Baxter
Executive Director ....Nick Craw
Communications Manager .....Marlieke de Lange Eaton

USA Shooting
One Olympic Plaza, Colorado Springs, CO 80909
(719) 866-4670   www.usashooting.com
Chairman ....Michael English
Executive Director ....Robert Mitchell
Media Director ....Sara Greenlee

U.S. Ski & Snowboard Association
P.O. Box 100, 1500 Kearns Blvd.
Park City, UT 84060
(435) 649-9090   www.ussa.org
Chairman ....Chuck Ferries
CEO/President ....Bill Marolt
V.P. of Public Relations/Member Svcs. ....Tom Kelly

U.S. Soccer Federation
1801 South Prairie Ave.
Chicago, IL 60616
(312) 808-1300   www.ussoccer.com
President ....Dr. S. Robert Contiguglia
Secretary General ....Dan Flynn
Director of Communications ....Jim Moorhouse

Amateur Softball Association
2801 N.E. 50th Street
Oklahoma City, OK 73111
(405) 424-5266   www.softball.org
President ............................E.T. Colvin
Executive Director ....Ron Radigonda
Director of Communications ....Brian McCall

U.S. Speed Skating
P.O. Box 450639, Westlake, OH 44145
(440) 899-0128   www.usspeedskating.org
President ....Andy Gabel
Executive Director ....Katie Marquard
Public Relations Director ....Bill Kellick

USA Swimming
One Olympic Plaza, Colorado Springs, CO 80909
(719) 866-4578   www.usaswimming.org
President ....Ron Van Pool
Executive Director ....Chuck Wielgus
Communications Director ....Mary Wagner

U.S. Synchronized Swimming, Inc.
201 South Capitol Avenue, Suite 901
Indianapolis, IN 46225
(317) 237-5700   www.usasynchro.org
President ....Betty Hazle
Executive Director ....Terry Harper
Media Relations Director ....Amy McClintock

USA Table Tennis
One Olympic Plaza, Colorado Springs, CO 80909
(719) 866-4583   www.usatt.org
President ....Sheri Soderberg Pittman
Executive Director ....Doru Gheorghe
Program and Marketing Coord. ....Tommy Perkins

U.S. Taekwondo Union
One Olympic Plaza, Suite 104-C
Colorado Springs, CO 80909
(719) 866-4632   www.ustu.org
CEO/Secretary General ....Bob Gambardella
Director of National Events ....Monica Paul

USA Team Handball
One Olympic Plaza
Colorado Springs, CO 80909
(719) 866-4036   www.usateamhandball.org
President ....Bob Djokovich
Executive Director ....Mike Cavanaugh
Program Directors ....Lindalisa Severo, Kim Miller

U.S. Tennis Association
70 West Red Oak Lane
White Plains, NY 10604
(914) 696-7000   www.usta.com
Chairman/President (as of Jan.1) .....Franklin R. Johnson
Executive Director/COO ....D. Lee Hamilton
Communications Coordinator ....Randy Walker

USA Track and Field
One RCA Dome, Suite 140
Indianapolis, IN 46225
(317) 261-0500   www.usatf.org
President ....Bill Roe
CEO ....Craig Masback
Director of Communications ....Jill Geer

USA Triathlon
1365 Garden of the Gods Road
Colorado Springs, CO 80907
(719) 597-9090   www.usatriathlon.org
President ....Brad Davison
Communications Director ........B.J. Hoeptner-Evans

USA Volleyball
715 South Circle Drive
Colorado Springs, CO 80910
(719) 228-6800   www.usavolleyball.org
President ....Albert Monaco
CEO ....Rebecca Howard
Manager P.R./Publications ....Paul Soriano

United States Water Polo
1685 W. Uintah St., Colorado Springs, CO 80904
(719) 634-0699   www.usawaterpolo.com
President ....Rich Foster
Executive Director ....Tom Seitz
Dir. of Media/Marketing ....Eric Velazquez

USA Weightlifting
One Olympic Plaza, Colorado Springs, CO 80909
(719) 866-4508   www.usaweightlifting.org
President ....Dennis Snethen
Exec. Director ....Wes Barnett
Communications Coordinator ....Beth Connolly

USA Wrestling
6155 Lehman Drive, Colorado Springs, CO 80918
(719) 598-8181   www.themat.com
President ....Stan Dziedzic
Executive Director ....Rich Bender
Dir. of Comm./Special Projects ....Gary Abbott

SOCCER

FIFA

(Federation Internationale de Football Assn.)
P.O. Box 85, 8030 Zurich, Switzerland
TEL: 011-41-43-222-7777   www.fifa.com
President ....Joseph S. Blatter
General Secretary ....Dr. Urs Linsi
Director of Communications ....Markus Siegler

MLS

Major League Soccer
110 E. 42nd Street, 10th Floor
New York, NY 10017
(212) 450-1200   www.mlsnet.com
Founder ....Alan I. Rothenberg
Commissioner ....Don Garber
Senior Dir. of Communications ....Trey Fitz-Gerald

Chicago Fire
980 N. Michigan Ave., Suite 1998
Chicago, IL 60611
(312) 705-7200   www.chicago-fire.com
Investor/Operator ....Philip F. Anschutz (AEG)
General Manager ....Peter Wilt
Director of Communications ....Diana Lopez

Colorado Rapids
1000 Chopper Circle, Denver, CO 80204
(303) 405-1100   www.coloradorapids.com
Investor/Operator ....Kroenke Sports Enterprises
General Manager ....Dan Counce
Director of Media Relations ....Jurgen Mainka

Columbus Crew
Columbus Crew Stadium
One Black & Gold Blvd., Columbus, OH 43211
(614) 447-2739   www.thecrew.com
Investor/Operator ....Hunt Sports Group
Interim General Manager ....Mark McCullers
Director of Public Relations ....Jeff Wuerth

Dallas Burn
(changing name to FC Dallas for the 2005 season)
14800 Quorum Drive, Suite 300
Dallas, TX 75254
(214) 979-0303   www.dallasburn.com
Investor/Operator ....Hunt Sports Group
President/GM ....Greg Elliott
Sr. Director of Media Services ....Chris Ward

D.C. United
2400 East Capitol St. SE, Washington, D.C. 20003
(202) 587-5000   www.dcunited.com
Investor/Operator ....Philip F. Anschutz (AEG)
President/CEO ....Kevin Payne
V.P., Communications ....Doug Hicks

Kansas City Wizards
2 Arrowhead Drive
Kansas City, MO 64129
(816) 920-9300   www.kcwizards.com
Investor/Operator . . . . .Hunt Sports Group
General Manager .Curt Johnson
Assoc. Manager of Public Relations . Justin Gorman, Staci
                                                        Schottman

Los Angeles Galaxy
18400 Avalon Blvd., Ste. 200
Carson, CA 90746
(310) 630-2200   www.lagalaxy.com
Investor/Operator . . . . .Philip F. Anschutz (AEG)
President/General Manager . . . . .Doug Hamilton
Manager of Communications . . . . .Patrick Donnelly

MetroStars
One Harmon Plaza, 3rd Floor
Secaucus, NJ 07094
(201) 583-7000   www.metrostars.com
Investor/Operator . . . . .Philip F. Anschutz (AEG)
President/GM .Nick Sakiewicz
Manager of Communications . . . . .Matthew Chmura

New England Revolution
Gillette Stadium, One Patriot Place
Foxboro, MA 02035
(508) 543-5001   www.revolutionsoccer.net
Investor/Operator . . . . .Robert Kraft/Jonathan Kraft
General Manager . . . . .Craig Tornberg
Managing Director .Sunil Gulati

San Jose Earthquakes
100 North Almaden Ave., San Jose, CA 95110
(408) 241-9922   www.sjearthquakes.com
Investor/Operator . . . . .Philip F. Anschutz (AEG)
President/General Manager . . . . .Alexi Lalas
Director of Media Relations . . . . .Jed Mettee

Note: MLS will add two expansion teams for the 2005
season—in Los Angeles (Club Deportivo Chivas USA) and
Salt Lake City (Real Salt Lake).

Other Soccer

CONCACAF
(Confederation of North, Central American & Caribbean Association Football)
725 Fifth Ave., 17th Floor, New York, NY 10022
(212) 308-0044   www.concacaf.com
President .Jack Austin Warner
General Secretary . . . . .Chuck Blazer
Press Officer . . . . .Steven Torres

U.S. Soccer
(United States Soccer Federation)
1801 South Prairie Ave., Chicago, IL 60616
(312) 808-1300   www.ussoccer.com
President . . . . .Dr. S. Robert Contiguglia
Secretary General .Dan Flynn
Director of Communications . . . . .Jim Moorhouse

MISL
(Major Indoor Soccer League)
1175 Post Road East, Westport, CT 06880
(203) 222-4900   www.misl.net
Commissioner . . . . .Steve Ryan
Vice President, Soccer Operations . . . . . .David Grimaldi
Director of Communications . . . . .Jaye Cavallo
  Member teams (11): Baltimore Blast, California
Cougars (beginning in 2005), Chicago Storm, Cleveland
Force, Dallas Sidekicks, Kansas City Comets, Milwaukee
Wave, Monterrey (Mex.) Fury, Philadelphia Kixx, St. Louis
Steamers and San Diego Sockers.

FINA
(Federation Internationale de Natation Amateur)
4 ave de l'Avante Poste
1005 Lausanne, Switzerland
TEL: 011-4121-310-4710   www.fina.org
President . . . .,. . . .Mustapha Larfaoui
Executive Director . . . . .Cornel Marculescu
Honorary Secretary . . . . .Bartolo Consolo

USA Swimming
One Olympic Plaza
Colorado Springs, CO 80909
(719) 866-4578   www.usswim.org
President . . . . .Ron Van Pool
Executive Director . . . . .Chuck Wielgus
Communications Director . . . . .Mary Wagner

ATP Tour
(Association of Tennis Professionals)
201 ATP Boulevard
Ponte Vedra Beach, FL 32082
(904) 285-8000   www.atptennis.com
Chief Executive Officer . . . . .Mark Miles
Chairman, ATP Properties . . . . . . .Christopher E. Clouser
Senior V.P., Communications . . . . .David Higdon
Dir. of Public Relations . . . . .J.J. Carter

ITF
(International Tennis Federation)
Bank Lane, Roehampton
London, England SW15 5XZ
TEL: 011-44-208-878-6464   www.itftennis.com
President .Francesco Ricci Bitti
Executive V.P. . . . . .Juan Margets
Head of Communications . . . . .Barbara Travers

World TeamTennis
250 Park Ave. South, 9th Floor
New York, NY 10003
(212) 979-0202   www.wtt.com
Director/Co-Founder . . . . .Billie Jean King
Commissioner & CEO . . . . .Ilana Kloss
Public Relations . . . . . . .Katie Fassbinder—GEM Group
                                                  (303-237-0616)
  Member teams (10): Delaware Smash, Hartford
FoxForce, Kansas City Explorers, New York Buzz, New York
Sportimes, Newport Beach Breakers, Philadelphia Freedoms,
Sacramento Capitals, Springfield (Mo.) Lasers and St. Louis
Aces.

U.S. Tennis Association
70 West Red Oak Lane
White Plains, NY 10604
(914) 696-7000   www.usta.com
Chairman/President (as of Jan.1) . . . . .Franklin R. Johnson
Executive Director . . . . .D. Lee Hamilton
Communications Coordinator . . . . .Randy Walker

WTA Tour
(Women's Tennis Association)
One Progress Plaza, Suite 1500, St. Petersburg, FL 33701
(727) 895-5000   www.wtatour.com
Chairman/CEO . . . . .Larry Scott
Senior V.P., Tour Operations . . . . .Peachy Kellmeyer
V.P., Communications . . . . .Susan Lomax
Dir. of Corporate Communications . . . . .Darrell Fry

TRACK & FIELD

IAAF
(International Association of Athletics Federations)
17 rue Princesse Florestine, BP 359
MC 98007 Monaco
TEL: 011-377-93-10-8888   www.iaaf.org
President ....Lamine Diack
Senior V.P. ....Dr. Arne Ljungqvist
General Secretary ....Istvan Gyulai

USA Track & Field
One RCA Dome, Suite 140
Indianapolis, IN 46225
(317) 261-0500   www.usatf.org
President ....Bill Roe
CEO ....Craig Masback
Director of Communications ....Jill Geer

MISCELLANEOUS

AAU
(Amateur Athletic Union)
P.O. Box 22409
Lake Buena Vista, FL 32830
(407) 934-7200   www.aausports.org
President/CEO ....Bobby Dodd
Media/Public Relations Director ....Melissa Wilson

All-American Soap Box Derby
P.O. Box 7225, Akron, OH 44306
(330) 733-8723   www.aasbd.org
Executive Director ....Tony DeLuca
General Manager ....Jeff Iula
Public Relations Director ....Bob Troyer

American Power Boat Association
17640 East Nine Mile Road
Eastpointe, MI 48021
(586) 773-9700   www.apba.org
President ....Steve Hearn
Executive Administrator ....Gloria Urbin

Association of Surfing Professionals
P.O. Box 1095, Coolangatta
Queensland, Australia 4225
011-61-7-5599-1550   www.aspworldtour.com
President/CEO ....Wayne "Rabbit" Bartholomew
Media Director ....Jesse Faen

BASS, Inc.
(Bass Anglers Sportsmen Society)
5845 Carmichael Road
Montgomery, AL 36141
(334) 272-9530   www.bassmaster.com
Owner ....ESPN
V.P., General Manager ....Dean Kessel
Tournament Director ....Trip Weldon
Director of Communications ....George McNeilly

Iditarod Trail Committee
P.O. Box 870800
Wasilla, AK 99687
(907) 376-5155   www.iditarod.com
Executive Director ....Stan Hooley
Race Director ....Joanne Potts

Little League Baseball, Incorporated
P.O. Box 3485, Williamsport, PA 17701
(570) 326-1921   www.littleleague.org
CEO-President ....Stephen Keener
Sr. Communications Executive ....Lance Van Auken

Major League Lacrosse
20 Guest St., Suite 125, Brighton, MA 02135
(617) 746-9980   www.majorleaguelacrosse.com
Commissioner ....David Gross
Dir. of Public Relations ....Mike Lieberman
    Member teams (6): Baltimore Bayhawks, Boston
Cannons, Long Island Lizards, New Jersey Pride, Philadelphia Barrage and Rochester Rattlers.

National Lacrosse League
1212 Avenue of the Americas, 5th Floor
New York, NY 10036
(917) 510-9200   www.nll.com
Commissioner ....Jim Jennings
V.P. of Communications ....Doug Fritts
    Member teams (11): Anaheim Storm, Arizona Sting, Buf-
falo Bandits, Calgary Roughnecks, Colorado Mammoth, Minnesota (TBA), Philadelphia Wings, Rochester Knighthawks,
San Jose Stealth, Toronto Rock and Vancouver Ravens.

Professional Rodeo Cowboys Association
101 Pro Rodeo Drive
Colorado Springs, CO 80919
(719) 593-8840   www.prorodeo.com
Commissioner ....Steven J. Hatchell
Director of Communications ....Leslie King

Special Olympics
1325 G St., NW Suite 500
Washington, DC 20005
(202) 628-3630   www.specialolympics.org
Founder/Honorary Chairman ....Eunice Kennedy Shriver
Chairman Emeritus ....Sargent Shriver
Chairman/CEO ....Timothy P. Shriver
Media Relations Coordinator ......Jo-Ann Enwezor

U.S. Association of Blind Athletes
33 N. Institute St.
Colorado Springs, CO 80903
(719) 630-0422   www.usaba.org
Executive Director ....Mark Lucas
Communications Director ....Nicole Jomantas

U.S. Chess Federation
3068 US Rt. 9W, Suite 100
New Windsor, NY 12553
(845) 562-8350   www.uschess.org
President ....Beatriz Marinello
Media Coordinator ....Joan DuBois

U.S. Polo Association
771 Corporate Dr., Suite 505
Lexington, KY 40503
(859) 219-1000   www.us-polo.org
Chairman ....Jack L. Shelton
Interim Executive Director ....Peter Rizzo

USA Rugby
1033 Walnut St., Suite 200
Boulder, CO 80302
(303) 539-0300   www.usarugby.org
CEO ....Doug Arnot
Manager of Operations ....Dan Lyle

Wheelchair Sports, USA
1668 320th Way
Earlham, IA 50072
(515) 833-2450   www.wsusa.org
Chairman ....Paul DePace
COO ....Dennis Runyan

Women's Professional Billiard Association
3306-C North Davidson Street
Charlotte, NC 28205
(704) 344-8664   www.wpba.com
President ....Ewa Mataya Laurance

International Sports

Austria's **Hermann Maier** returned from a serious injury to win skiing's World Cup overall title in 2004.

AP/Wide World Photos

Six

Lance Armstrong reaches the peak of the cycling mountain, winning his unprecedented sixth Tour de France.

Gerry Brown *is co-editor of the ESPN Sports Almanac.*

Now the French *really* can't stand us.

In 2004, American Lance Armstrong put his name at le tippy top of the list of the biggest winners in the history of that country's biggest sporting event, the Tour de France.

Armstrong is, with the possible exception of Jerry Lewis, the most famous American in France. It's the American equivalent of a foreigner dominating a distinctly American sporting event like say, the Boston Marathon. Or someone from another country breaking our national pastime's record for most hits in a season. Or if the Dream Team didn't win the gold medal at the Olympics. Never mind.

Armstrong's story should be getting pretty old by now but it never seems to. That is, unless you are a proud Gallic sports fan.

For those of you who are just coming out of your Y2K-scare bunkers here's the backstory...

Armstrong was a talented young cyclist before he was diagnosed with testicular cancer in 1996 but he gave no real sign that he would someday dominate the sport to this extent. The aggressive cancer spread quickly and by most accounts, Armstrong should be pushing up daisies by now rather than pushing down the fastest pedals on the planet.

Instead, you may recall, it was the summer of 1999 that he made his big splash, becoming just the second American (Greg LeMond) to win cycling's marquee race. It was a great story but no one was thinking it was the beginning of a new era in pro cycling.

Then he came back to defend his title in 2000 and won the dang thing again. Then again and again and again and, now, again.

In today's world sporting climate, especially in the post-BALCO world, eyebrows raise whenever an athlete dominates to such an extent. And Armstrong has had to endure a lot more than elevated eyebrows and repetitive questions from the European press. Some of them reportedly tried to break into his hotel room while he was out racing in search of smoking syringes.

AP/Wide World Photos

Lance Armstrong signals his record-breaking sixth Tour de France victory in 2004.

But worst of all were some of the spectators, who spit on and tossed their drinks at Armstrong, calling him a cheater on the long ascents up the French Alps.

Armstrong, who is well known for his insane training routine, is fast to reply that he has never failed a test. Nevertheless, a book *L.A. Confidential: The Secrets of Lance Armstrong* by London's *Sunday Times* journalist David Walsh and French cycling writer Pierre Ballester alleges he used performance enhancers, particularly the banned blood booster erythropoietin (EPO).

Even fellow American LeMond has publicly questioned Armstrong's honesty on the issue, alleging that he has likely used some sort of banned substances.

The one year where he, by his own admission, may have eased off a little on the training—2003—he had his toughest Tour and nearly had the win streak stopped at four.

In preparation for the 2004 Tour Armstrong rededicated himself and kicked it into a higher gear.

It showed.

Although his margin of victory has been larger in some previous Tour wins, he was never more dominant than he was in his record sixth straight win.

He won six stages and the prologue, controlling the peloton without mercy. One rider, Filippo Simeoni, who had once crossed Armstrong by testifying about banned drugs to an Italian judge and then, when Armstrong called him a liar, sued him for defamation, broke

AP/Wide World Photos

*A federal indictment was handed down by a San Francisco grand jury in 2004 alleging that **BALCO Laboratories** in Burlingame, Calif. supplied performance-enhancing drugs to major league baseball and NFL players, as well as American track and field stars.*

away from the pack in a bid to win the 18th stage. Armstrong let his displeasure with Simeoni show by immediately chasing him down and denying him the chance at even a little glory.

On another stage Armstrong pulled back a bit so that teammate and loyal soldier Floyd Landis could take home a stage win, but Floyd was caught and passed by Germans Jan Ullrich and Andreas Klöden. Armstrong took this personally, stood up on his pedals and surged past an obviously stunned Klöden at the finish line.

Following the stage, Armstrong saw Bernard Hinault, a fellow five-time Tour de France champ and the last Frenchman to win the race. Hinault smiled and said, "Perfect. No gifts."

The question of whether Lance will go for a seventh win has already been asked plenty but he has yet to officially put it to rest. He admits that it's very likely, but also talks about the time it takes away from his kids and his desire to try the Giro d'Italia in 2005.

And while Armstrong is no doubt an army of one he has not achieved this record success all by himself. His team of supporting riders is one of the best ever assembled and teams with such talent are tricky to keep together.

Armstrong will almost certainly be back to torture the French fans at least once more, whether it be in 2005 or beyond. One thing they can count on when he returns is that there will be no gifts.

The Ten Biggest Stories
of the Year in International Sports

10 England beats host-nation and defending champions Australia, 20-17, in extra-time to win the 2003 Rugby World Cup in November. The Brits become the first northern hemisphere team to win the world title.

9 Kenyans Timothy Cherigat and Catherine Ndereba beat the 85-degree heat and 20,000 others to win the 108th Boston Marathon. Cherigat takes the men's division with a relatively slow winning time of 2:10:37 while Ndereba came from behind and edges out Ethiopia's Elfenesh Alemu for the women's division by 16 seconds for her third Boston win.

8 Austria's Stephan Eberharter wins the downhill title for the third straight year in the 2004 World Cup season (and finishes in second place in the overall standings) and later announces his retirement from skiing in September. Eberharter won four Olympic medals (a gold, two silvers and a bronze), four world championship medals, and 29 World Cup races in his 16-year career.

7 Russian Yelena Isinbayeva breaks the women's pole vault record five times in 2004, most recently with a vault of 16-1¾ on Sept. 3, and wins the IAAF Female Athlete of the Year Award to go along with her gold from Athens.

6 Japan's Shizuka Arakawa beats out Americans Sahsa Cohen (second) and five-time world champion Michelle Kwan (third) to take the gold medal in the women's division at the 2004 World Figure Skating Championships in Dortmund, Germany. Russia sweeps gold in the men's (Evgeni Plushenko), pairs (Tatiana Totmianina and Maxim Marinin) and ice dance (Tatiana Navka and Roman Kostomarov).

5 Austrian ski god Hermann Maier completes his amazing comeback from a career-threatening injury suffered in a 2001 motorcycle accident and claims his fourth overall World Cup title and the unofficial title of world's greatest skier. New Hampshire's Bode Miller takes the men's giant slalom season title to keep the Austrians from a clean sweep.

4 Ethiopia's Kenenisa Bekele shatters two world records in nine days, besting his countryman Haile Gebrselassie's world marks in the 5,000 meters (May 31) and the 10,000 meters (June 8) by more than two seconds apiece. Bekele tries to make Olympic history by winning gold in both events but falls just short, taking silver in the 5,000 after setting an Olympic record in his gold-medal run in the 10,000.

3 Top American sprinters (and sweethearts) Tim Montgomery and Marion Jones both fail to qualify for Athens in the 100-meter dash. Montgomery, the world record holder in the distance, has languished under a cloud of steroid suspicion and he fails to make the U.S. Olympic team with his seventh place finish at the trials. Jones manages to qualify in the long jump but is unable to defend her 100m gold.

2 The specter of a massive doping crisis looms over U.S. track and field as more and more athletes are suspected. American sprinter Kelli White is stripped of the gold medals she won in the 100 and 200 meter dashes at the 2003 World Championships in Paris and is banned from competition for two years by the International Association of Athletics Federation (IAAF) after accepting the ban for her use of performance-enhancing drugs. The reigning U.S. 1,500-meter champion Regina Jacobs is suspended for four years and loses her U.S. title for testing positive for the banned steroid THG.

1 The world's greatest bike rider, Lance Armstrong, does it yet again, claiming an unreal sixth straight victory in the Tour de France, securing his spot atop the list of the greatest cyclists in history.

INSIDE the numbers

Miller's Time

American skier Bode Miller won six races on the World Cup circuit in 2004 and captured the World Cup giant slalom title, becoming the first American in 21 years (Phil Mahre) to win a World Cup title. Here's a look at the Americans with the most career World Cup race victories.

	World Cup Wins
Phil Mahre	27
Tamara McKinney	18
Bode Miller	12
Steve Mahre	9
Picabo Street	9

Straight, No Chaser

Spaniard Miguel Indurain and American Lance Armstrong shared the record of consecutive Tour de France victories with five—until Lance won his sixth straight in 2004. Here's a look at the top two win streaks in the race's long history.

	L. Armstrong	M. Indurain
Wins	6	5
Years	1999-2004	1991-95
Total Margin	35:00	23:24
Stages Won	21	12

2003-2004 Season in Review

SPORTS ALMANAC

TRACK & FIELD

2004 IAAF World Athletics Final

The 2nd annual IAAF World Athletics Final held in Monaco, Sept. 18-19, 2004 (with the hammer competition taking place on Sept. 5 in Szombathely, Hungary). Participants are decided according to the IAAF rankings in each event. Athletes who are in the top seven positions (top-11 for the 1500m race and longer) are automatic qualifiers. Note that (WR) indicates world record and (CR) indicates championship meet record.

MEN

Event		Time	
100 meters	Asafa Powell, Jamaica	9.98	CR
200 meters	Asafa Powell, Jamaica	20.06	CR
400 meters	Michael Blackwood, Jamaica	44.95	CR
800 meters	Youssef Saad Kamel, Bahrain	1:45.91	CR
1500 meters	Ivan Heshko, Ukraine	3:44.92	
3000 meters	Eliud Kipchoge, Kenya	7:38.67	
5000 meters	Sileshi Sihine, Ethiopia	13:06.95	CR
110m hurdles	Allen Johnson, USA	13.16	
400m hurdles	Bershawn Jackson, USA	47.86	
3000m steeple	Saaeed Saif Shaheen, Qatar	7:56.94	CR

Event		Hgt/Dist	
High Jump	Stefan Holm, Sweden	7-7¾	CR
Pole Vault	Timothy Mack, USA	19-8¾	CR
Long Jump	Ignisious Gaisah, Ghana	27-3¾	CR
Triple Jump	Christian Olsson, Sweden	57-11¼	CR
Shot Put	Joachim Olsen, Denmark	70-5	CR
Discus	Mario Pestano, Spain	210-4	
Hammer	Olli-Pekka Karjalainen, Finland	267-2	
Javelin	Breaux Greer, USA	287-8	CR

WOMEN

Event		Time	
100 meters	Veronica Campbell, Jamaica	10.91	
200 meters	Veronica Campbell, Jamaica	22.64	
400 meters	Ana Guevara, Mexico	50.13	
800 meters	Hasna Benhassi, Morocco	2:01.42	
1500 meters	Kelly Holmes, Gr. Britain	4:04.55	
3000 meters	Meseret Defar, Ethiopia	8:36.46	CR
5000 meters	Elvan Abeylegesse, Turkey	14:59.19	
100m hurdles	Joanna Hayes, USA	12.58	
400m hurdles	Sandra Glover, USA	54.57	

Event		Hgt/Dist	
High Jump	Yelena Slesarenko, Russia	6-7	CR
Pole Vault	Yelena Isinbayeva, Russia	15-10	CR
Long Jump	Irina Simagina, Russia	22-1¼	
Triple Jump	F. Mbango Etone, Cameroon	49-3	
Shot Put	Nadezhda Ostapchuk, Belarus	63-1	
Discus	V. Pospisilova-Cechlova, Czech Rep.	216-1	CR
Hammer	Olga Kuzenkova, Russia	239-2	
Javelin	Osleidys Menendez, Cuba	217-2	CR

2004 IAAF World Cross Country Championships

The 32nd IAAF World Cross Country Championships held in Brussels, Belgium (March 20-21).

MEN

12 km	1. Kenenisa Bekele, Ethiopia 35:52
(7.45 mi)	2. Gebre-egziabher Gebremariam, Ethiopia 36:10
	3. Sileshi Sihine, Ethiopia 36:11
	Best USA—Abdihakem Abdirahman, 34th 38:09

WOMEN

8 km	1. Benita Johnson, Australia 27:17
(4.97 mi)	2. Ejegayehu Dibaba, Ethiopia 27:29
	3. Werknesh Kidane, Ethiopia 27:34
	Best USA—Kate O'Neill, 15th 28:37

World Outdoor Records Set in 2004

World outdoor records set or equaled between Sept. 29, 2003 and Sept. 28, 2004; (p) indicates record is pending ratification by the IAAF; (†) indicates the IAAF does not officially recognize world records in that event.

MEN

Event	Name	Record	Old Mark	Former Holder
5000 meters	Kenenisa Bekele, ETH	12:37.35	12:39.36	Haile Gebrselassie, ETH (1998)
10,000 meters	Kenenisa Bekele, ETH	26:20.31	26:22.75	Haile Gebrselassie, ETH (1998)
110m hurdles	(TIE) Xiang Liu, CHN	12.91p	12.91	(TIE) Colin Jackson, GBR (1993)
3000m steeplechase	Saif Saaeed Shaheen, QAT	7:53.63	7:55.28*	Brahim Boulami, MAR (2001)
50k walk	Denis Nizhegorodov, RUS	3:35:29p	3:36:03	Robert Korzeniowski, POL (2003)

*Boulami's record run of 7:53.17 on Aug. 16, 2002 was removed from the record books after he tested positive for EPO.

WOMEN

Event	Name	Record	Old Mark	Former Holder
5000 meters	Elvan Abeylegesse, TUR	14:24:68	14:28:09	Jiang Bo, CHN (1997)
3000m steeplechase	Gulnara Samitova, RUS	9:01.59	9:08.33	Gulnara Samitova, RUS (2003)
Pole Vault	Yelena Isinbayeva, RUS	16-1¾ p	16-1¼	Yelena Isinbayeva, RUS (2004)

Note: The women's pole vault world record was broken seven times in 2004. Isinbayeva held the record (15-9¾) heading into 2004. American Stacey Dragila jumped 15-10 on June 8, Isinbayeva jumped 15-11¾ on June 27, Svetlana Feofanova of Russia jumped 16-0 on July 4, Isinbayeva jumped 16-0½ on July 25, Isinbayeva jumped 16-0¾ on July 30, Isinbayeva jumped 16-1¼ at the Olympics on Aug. 24, then Isinbayeva jumped 16-1¾ on Sept. 3.

World, Olympic and American Records
As of Sept. 28, 2004

World outdoor records officially recognized by the International Amateur Athletics Federation (IAAF); (p) indicates record is pending ratification.

MEN
Running

Event		Time		Date Set	Location
100 meters:	World	9.78	**Tim Montgomery**, USA	Sept. 14, 2002	Paris
	Olympic	9.84	Donovan Bailey, Canada	July 27, 1996	Atlanta
	American	9.78	Montgomery (same as World)	—	—
200 meters:	World	19.32	**Michael Johnson**, USA	Aug. 1, 1996	Atlanta
	Olympic	19.32	Johnson (same as World)	—	—
	American	19.32	Johnson (same as World)	—	—
400 meters:	World	43.18	**Michael Johnson**, USA	Aug. 26, 1999	Seville
	Olympic	43.49	Michael Johnson, USA	July 29, 1996	Atlanta
	American	43.18	Johnson (same as World)	—	—
800 meters:	World	1:41.11	**Wilson Kipketer**, Denmark	Aug. 24, 1997	Cologne
	Olympic	1:42.58	Vebjoern Rodal, Norway	July 31, 1996	Atlanta
	American	1:42.60	Johnny Gray	Aug. 28, 1985	Koblenz, W. Ger.
1000 meters:	World	2:11.96	**Noah Ngeny**, Kenya	Sept. 5, 1999	Rieti, ITA
	Olympic		Not an event		
	American	2:13.9	Rick Wohlhuter	July 30, 1974	Oslo
1500 meters:	World	3:26.00	**Hicham El Guerrouj**, Morocco	July 14, 1998	Rome
	Olympic	3:32.07	Noah Ngeny, Kenya	Sept. 29, 2000	Sydney
	American	3:29.77	Sydney Maree	Aug. 25, 1985	Cologne
Mile:	World	3:43.13	**Hicham El Guerrouj**, Morocco	July 7, 1999	Rome
	Olympic		Not an event		
	American	3:47.69	Steve Scott	July 7, 1982	Oslo
2000 meters:	World	4:44.79	**Hicham El Guerrouj**, Morocco	Sept. 7, 1999	Berlin
	Olympic		Not an event		
	American	4:52.44	Jim Spivey	Sept. 15, 1987	Lausanne, SWI
3000 meters:	World	7:20.67	**Daniel Komen**, Kenya	Sept. 1, 1996	Rieti, ITA
	Olympic		Not an event		
	American	7:30.84	Bob Kennedy	Aug. 8, 1998	Monte Carlo
5000 meters:	World	12:37.35	**Kenenisa Bekele**, Ethiopia	May 31, 2004	Hengelo, NED
	Olympic	13:05.59	Said Aouita, Morocco	Aug. 11, 1984	Los Angeles
	American	12:58.21	Bob Kennedy	Aug. 14, 1996	Zurich
10,000 meters:	World	26:20.31	**Kenenisa Bekele**, Ethiopia	June 8, 2004	Ostrava, CZR
	Olympic	27:05.10	Kenenisa Bekele, Ethiopia	Aug. 20, 2004	Athens
	American	27:13.98	Meb Keflezighi	May 4, 2001	Stanford, Calif.
20,000 meters:	World	56:55.6	**Arturo Barrios**, Mexico	Mar. 30, 1991	La Fleche, FRA
	Olympic		Not an event	—	—
	American	58:15.0	Bill Rodgers	Aug. 9, 1977	Boston
Marathon:	World	2:04:55†	**Paul Tergat**, KEN	Sept. 28, 2003	Berlin
	Olympic	2:09:21	Carlos Lopes, Portugal	Aug. 12, 1984	Los Angeles
	American	2:05:38	Khalid Khannouchi	Apr. 14, 2002	London

Note: The Mile run is 1,609.344 meters and the Marathon is 42,194.988 meters (26 miles, 385 yards).
†Marathon records are not officially recognized by the IAAF.

Relays

Event		Time		Date Set	Location
4 x 100m:	World	37.40	**USA** (Marsh, Burrell, Mitchell, C. Lewis)	Aug. 8, 1992	Barcelona
		37.40	**USA** (Drummond, Cason, Mitchell, Burrell)	Aug. 21, 1993	Stuttgart
	Olympic	37.40	USA (same as World - 1992)	—	—
	American	37.40	USA (same as World)	—	—
4 x 200m:	World	1:18.68	**USA** (Marsh, Burrell, Heard, C. Lewis)	Apr. 17, 1994	Walnut, Calif.
	Olympic		Not an event	—	—
	American	1:18.68	USA (same as World)	—	—
4 x 400m:	World	2:54.20	**USA** (Young, Pettigrew, Washington, Johnson)	July 22,1998	Uniondale, N.Y.
	Olympic	2:55.74	USA (Valmon, Watts, Johnson, S. Lewis)	Aug. 8, 1992	Barcelona
	American	2:54.20	USA (same as World)	—	—
4 x 800m:	World	7:03.89	**Great Britain** (Elliott, Cook, Cram, Coe)	Aug. 30, 1982	London
	Olympic		Not an event	—	—
	American	7:06.5	Santa Monica TC (J. Robinson, Mack, E. Jones, Gray)	Apr. 26, 1986	Walnut, Calif.
4 x 1500m:	World	14:38.8	**West Germany** (Wessinghage, Hudak, Lederer, Fleschen)	Aug.17, 1977	Cologne
	Olympic		Not an event	—	—
	American	14:46.3	USA (Aldredge, Clifford, Harbour, Duits)	June 24, 1979	Bourges, FRA

Hurdles

Event		Time		Date Set	Location
110 meters:	World	12.91	**Colin Jackson**, Great Britain	Aug. 20, 1993	Stuttgart
		12.91p	**Xiang Liu**, China	Aug. 27, 2004	Athens
	Olympic	12.91	Liu (same as World)	—	—
	American	12.92	Roger Kingdom	Aug. 16, 1989	Zurich
		12.92	Allen Johnson	June 23, 1996	Atlanta
400 meters:	World	46.78	**Kevin Young**, USA	Aug. 6, 1992	Barcelona
	Olympic	46.78	Young (same as World)	—	—
	American	46.78	Young (same as World)	—	—

Note: The 10 hurdles at 110 meters are 3 feet, 6 inches high and those at 400 meters are 3 feet.

Walking

Event		Time		Date Set	Location
20 km:	World	1:17:21	**Jefferson Perez**, Ecuador	Aug. 23, 2003	Paris
	Olympic	1:18:59	Robert Korzeniowski, Poland	Sept. 22, 2000	Sydney
	American	1:22:02	Tim Seaman	May 22, 2004	Copenhagen, DEN
50 km:	World	3:35:29p	**Denis Nizhegorodov**, Russia	June 13, 2004	Cheboksary, RUS
	Olympic	3:38:29	Vyacheslav Ivanenko, USSR	Sept. 30, 1988	Seoul
	American	3:48:04	Curt Clausen	May 2, 1999	Deauville, FRA

Steeplechase

Event		Time		Date Set	Location
3000 meters:	World	7:53.63 p	**Saif Saaeed Shaheen**, Qatar	Sept. 3, 2004	Brussels
	Olympic	8:05.51	Julius Kariuki, Kenya	Sept. 30, 1988	Seoul
	American	8:09.17	Henry Marsh	Aug. 28, 1985	Koblenz, W. Ger

Note: A men's steeplechase course consists of 28 hurdles (3 feet high) and seven water jumps (12 feet long).

Field Events

Event		Mark		Date Set	Location
High Jump:	World	8-0½	**Javier Sotomayor**, Cuba	July 27, 1993	Salamanca, SPA
	Olympic	7-10	Charles Austin, USA	July 28, 1996	Atlanta
	American	7-10½	Charles Austin	Aug. 7, 1991	Zurich
Pole Vault:	World	20-1¾	**Sergey Bubka**, Ukraine	July 31, 1994	Sestriere, ITA
	Olympic	19-6¼	Tim Mack, USA	Aug. 27, 2004	Athens
	American	19-9¼	Jeff Hartwig	June 14, 2000	Jonesboro, Ark.
Long Jump:	World	29-4½	**Mike Powell**, USA	Aug. 30, 1991	Tokyo
	Olympic	29-2½	Bob Beamon, USA	Oct. 18, 1968	Mexico City
	American	29-4½	Powell (same as World)	—	—
Triple Jump:	World	60- 0¼	**Jonathan Edwards**, GBR	Aug. 7, 1995	Göteborg, SWE
	Olympic	59-4¼	Kenny Harrison, USA	July 27, 1996	Atlanta
	American	59-4¼	Kenny Harrison (same as Olympic)	—	—
Shot Put:	World	75-10¼	**Randy Barnes**, USA	May 20, 1990	Los Angeles
	Olympic	73- 8¾	Ulf Timmermann, East Germany	Sept. 23, 1988	Seoul
	American	75-10¼	Barnes (same as World)	—	—
Discus:	World	243-0	**Jurgen Schult**, East Germany	June 6, 1986	Neubrandenburg
	Olympic	229-3½	Virgilijus Alekna, Lithuania	Aug. 23, 2004	Athens
	American	237-4	Ben Plucknett	July 7, 1981	Stockholm
Javelin:	World	323-1	**Jan Zelezny**, Czech Republic	May 25, 1996	Jena, GER
	Olympic	295-10	Jan Zelezny, Czech Republic	Sept. 23, 2000	Sydney
	American	287-8	Breaux Greer	Sept 19, 2004	Monaco
Hammer:	World	284-7	**Yuriy Sedykh**, USSR	Aug. 30, 1986	Stuttgart
	Olympic	278-2	Sergey Litvinov, USSR	Sept. 26, 1988	Seoul
	American	270-9	Lance Deal	Sept. 7, 1996	Milan

Note: The international weights for men—**Shot** (16 lbs); **Discus** (4 lbs/6.55 oz); **Javelin** (minimum 1 lb/12¼ oz.); **Hammer** (16 lbs).

Decathlon

Event		Points		Date Set	Location
Ten Events:	World	9026	**Roman Sebrle**, Czech Republic	May 26-27, 2001	Gotzis, AUT
	Olympic	8893	Roman Sebrle, Czech Republic	Aug. 23-24, 2004	Athens
	American	8891	Dan O'Brien	Sept. 4-5, 1992	Talence, FRA

Note: Sebrle's WR times and distances, in order over two days—**100m** (10.64); **LJ** (26-7¼); **Shot** (50-3½); **HJ** (6-11½); **400m** (47.79); **110m H** (13.92); **Discus** (157-3); **PV** (15-9); **Jav** (230-2); **1500m** (4:21.98).

WOMEN
Running

Event		Time		Date Set	Location
100 meters:	World	10.49	**Florence Griffith Joyner**, USA	July 16, 1988	Indianapolis
	Olympic	10.62	Florence Griffith Joyner, USA	Sept. 24, 1988	Seoul
	American	10.49	Griffith Joyner (same as World)	—	—
200 meters:	World	21.34	**Florence Griffith Joyner**, USA	Sept. 29, 1988	Seoul
	Olympic	21.34	Griffith Joyner (same as World)	—	—
	American	21.34	Griffith Joyner (same as World)	—	—

World, Olympic and American Outdoor Records (Cont.)

Event		Time		Date Set	Location
400 meters:	World	47.60	**Marita Koch**, East Germany	Oct. 6, 1985	Canberra, AUS
	Olympic	48.25	Marie-Jose Perec, France	July 29, 1996	Atlanta
	American	48.83	Valerie Brisco	Aug. 6, 1984	Los Angeles
800 meters:	World	1:53.28	**Jarmila Kratochvilova**, Czech.	July 26, 1983	Munich
	Olympic	1:53.42	Nadezhda Olizarenko, USSR	July 27, 1980	Moscow
	American	1:56.40	Jearl Miles-Clark	Aug. 11, 1999	Zurich
1000 meters:	World	2:28.98	**Svetlana Masterkova**, Russia	Aug. 23, 1996	Brussels
	Olympic		Not an event	—	—
	American	2:31.80	Regina Jacobs	July 3, 1999	Brunswick, Me.
1500 meters:	World	3:50.46	**Qu Yunxia**, China	Sept. 11, 1993	Beijing
	Olympic	3:53.96	Paula Ivan, Romania	Oct. 1, 1988	Seoul
	American	3:57.12	Mary Slaney	July 26, 1983	Stockholm
Mile:	World	4:12.56	**Svetlana Masterkova**, Russia	Aug. 14, 1996	Zurich
	Olympic		Not an event	—	—
	American	4:16.71	Mary Slaney	Aug. 21, 1985	Zurich
2000 meters:	World	5:25.36	**Sonia O'Sullivan**, Ireland	July 8, 1994	Edinburgh
	Olympic		Not an event	—	—
	American	5:32.7	Mary Slaney	Aug. 3, 1984	Eugene, Ore.
3000 meters:	World	8:06.11	**Wang Junxia**, China	Sept. 13, 1993	Beijing
	Olympic	8:26.53	Tatyana Samolenko, USSR	Sept. 25, 1988	Seoul
	American	8:25.83	Mary Slaney	Sept. 7, 1985	Rome
5000 meters:	World	14:24.68	**Elvan Abeylegesse**, Turkey	June 11, 2004	Bergen, NOR
	Olympic	14:40.79	Gabriela Szabo, Romania	Sept. 25, 2000	Sydney
	American	14:45.35	Regina Jacobs	July 27, 2000	Sacramento
10,000 meters:	World	29:31.78	**Wang Junxia**, China	Sept. 8, 1993	Beijing
	Olympic	30:17.49	Derartu Tulu, Ethiopia	Sept. 30, 2000	Sydney
	American	30:50.32p	Deena Drossin	May 3, 2002	Stanford, Calif.
Marathon:	World	2:15:25†	**Paula Radcliffe**, Great Britain	Apr. 13, 2003	London
	Olympic	2:23:14	Naoko Takahashi, Japan	Sept. 24, 2000	Sydney
	American	2:21:16	Deena Drossin	Apr. 13, 2003	London

Note: The Mile run is 1,609.344 meters and the Marathon is 42,194.988 meters (26 miles, 385 yards).
†Marathon records are not officially recognized by the IAAF.

Relays

Event		Time		Date Set	Location
4 x 100m:	World	41.37	**East Germany** (Gladisch, Rieger, Auerswald, Gohr)	Oct. 6, 1985	Canberra, AUS
	Olympic	41.60	East Germany (Muller, Wockel, Auerswald, Gohr)	Aug. 1, 1980	Moscow
	American	41.47	USA (Gaines, Jones, Miller, Devers)	Aug. 9, 1997	Athens
4 x 200m:	World	1:27.46	USA (Jenkins, Colander-Richardson, Perry, Jones)	Apr. 29, 2000	Philadelphia
	Olympic		Not an event	—	—
	American	1:27.46	USA (same as World)	—	—
4 x 400m:	World	3:15.17	**USSR** (Ledovskaya, Nazarova, Pinigina, Bryzgina)	Oct. 1, 1988	Seoul
	Olympic	3:15.17	USSR (same as World)	—	—
	American	3:15.51	USA (Howard, Dixon, Brisco, Griffith Joyner)	Oct. 1, 1988	Seoul
4 x 800m:	World	7:50.17	**USSR** (Olizarenko, Gurina, Borisova, Podyalovskaya)	Aug. 5, 1984	Moscow
	Olympic		Not an event	—	—
	American	8:17.09	Athletics West (Addison, Arbogast, Decker Slaney, Mullen)	Apr. 24, 1983	Walnut, Calif.

Hurdles

Event		Time		Date Set	Location
100 meters:	World	12.21	**Yordanka Donkova**, Bulgaria	Aug. 20, 1988	Stara Zagora, BUL
	Olympic	12.37	Joanna Hayes, USA	Aug. 24, 2004	Athens
	American	12.33	Gail Devers	July 23, 2000	Sacramento
400 meters:	World	52.34	**Yuliya Pechonkina**, Russia	Aug. 8, 2003	Tula, RUS
	Olympic	52.77	Fani Halkia, Greece	Aug. 22, 2004	Athens
	American	52.61	Kim Batten	Aug. 11, 1995	Göteborg, SWE

Note: The 10 hurdles at 110 meters are 3 feet, 6 inches high and those at 400 meters are 3 feet.

Walking

Event		Time		Date Set	Location
20 km:	World	1:26:22	**Wang Yan**, China	Nov. 19, 2001	Guangzhou, CHN
	Olympic	1:29:05	Wang Liping, China	Sept. 28, 2000	Sydney
	American	1:31:51	Michelle Rohl	May 13, 2000	Kenosha, Wis.

Steeplechase

Event	Time		Date Set	Location
3000 meters: **World** 9:01.59		**Gulnara Samitova**, Russia	July 4, 2004	Heraklion, GRE
Olympic		Not an event	—	—
American . . 9:29.32		Briana Shook	July 31, 2004	Heusden-Zolder, BEL

Note: A women's steeplechase course consists of 28 hurdles (30 inches high) and seven water jumps (10 feet long).

Field Events

Event	Mark		Date Set	Location
High Jump:	**World** 6-10¼	**Stefka Kostadinova,** Bulgaria	Aug. 30, 1987	Rome
	Olympic 6-9	Yelena Slesarenko, Russia	Aug. 28, 2004	Athens
	American. 6-8	Louise Ritter	July 8, 1988	Austin, Texas
Pole Vault:	**World** 16-1¾p	**Yelena Isinbayeva**, Russia	Sept. 3, 2004	Brussels
	Olympic 16-1¼	Yelena Isinbayeva, Russia	Aug. 24, 2004	Athens
	American . . 15-10	Stacy Dragila	June 8, 2004	Ostrava, CZR
Long Jump:	**World** 24-8¼	**Galina Chistyakova**, USSR	June 11, 1988	Leningrad
	Olympic 24-3¼	Jackie Joyner-Kersee, USA	Sept. 29, 1988	Seoul
	American. 24-7	Jackie Joyner-Kersee	May 22, 1994	New York
Triple Jump:	**World** 50-10¼	**Inessa Kravets**, Ukraine	Aug. 10, 1995	Göteborg, SWE
	Olympic . . . 50-3½	Inessa Kravets, Ukraine	July 31, 1996	Atlanta
	American 47-5	Tiombe Hurd	July 11, 2004	Sacramento, Calif.
Shot Put:	**World** 74-3	**Natalya Lisovskaya**, USSR	June 7, 1987	Moscow
	Olympic . . 73-6¼	Ilona Slupianek, E. Germany	July 24, 1980	Moscow
	American. . . 66-2½	Ramona Pagel	June 25, 1988	San Diego
Discus:	**World** . . . 252-0	**Gabriele Reinsch**, E. Germany	July 9, 1988	Neubrandenburg
	Olympic . . 237-2½	Martina Hellmann, E. Germany	Sept. 29, 1988	Seoul
	American. . 227-10	Suzy Powell	Apr. 27, 2002	La Jolla, Calif.
Javelin:	**World** . . . 234-8	**Osleidys Menendez**, Cuba	July 1, 2001	Rethymno, GRE
	Olympic . . . 234-8	Osleidys Menendez, Cuba	Aug. 27, 2004	Athens
	American. . 199-8	Kim Kreiner	Aug. 7, 2003	Santo Domingo
Hammer:	**World** . . . 249-7	**Mihaela Melinte**, Romania	Aug. 29, 1999	Rudlingen, SWI
	Olympic . . 246-1	Olga Kuzenkova, Russia	Aug. 25, 2004	Athens
	American. . 236-7	Erin Gilreath	Apr. 10, 2004	Tempe, Ariz.

Note: The international weights for women—**Shot** (8 lbs/13 oz); **Discus** (2 lbs/3.27 oz); **Javelin** (minimum 1 lb/5.16 oz); **Hammer** (8 lbs/13 oz).

Heptathlon

Event	Points		Date Set	Location
Seven Events:	**World** 7291	**Jackie Joyner-Kersee**, USA	Sept. 23-24, 1988	Seoul
	Olympic 7291	Joyner-Kersee (same as World)	—	—
	American . . . 7291	Joyner-Kersee (same as World)	—	—

Note: Joyner-Kersee's WR times and distances, in order over two days—**100m H** (12.69); **HJ** (61¼); **Shot** (51-10); **200m** (22.56); **LJ** (2310¼); **Jav** (149-10); **800m** (2:08.51).

AP/Wide World Photos

*Russian **Yelena Isinbayeva** clears 16-1¾ at the IAAF Golden League meet in Brussels on Sept. 3 to break the world pole vault record she set 10 days earlier at the Olympics.*

World and American Indoor Records
As of Sept. 28, 2004

World indoor records officially recognized by the International Amateur Athletics Federation (IAAF); (p) indicates record is pending ratification by the IAAF; (a) indicates record was set at an altitude over 1000 meters.

MEN
Running

Event		Time		Date Set	Location
50 meters:	World	5.56a	**Donovan Bailey**, Canada	Feb. 9, 1996	Reno, Nev.
		5.56	**Maurice Greene**, USA	Feb. 13, 1999	Los Angeles
	American	5.56	Greene (same as World)	Feb. 13, 1999	Los Angeles
60 meters:	World	6.39	**Maurice Greene**, USA	Feb. 3, 1998	Madrid
		6.39	**Maurice Greene**, USA	Mar. 3, 2001	Atlanta
	American	6.39	Greene (same as World)	—	
200 meters:	World	19.92	**Frankie Fredericks**, Namibia	Feb. 18, 1996	Lievin, FRA
	American	20.26	John Capel	Mar. 11, 2000	Fayetteville, Ark.
		20.26	Shawn Crawford	Mar. 11, 2000	Fayetteville, Ark.
400 meters:	World	44.63	**Michael Johnson**, USA	Mar. 4, 1995	Atlanta
	American	44.63	Johnson (same as World)	—	
800 meters:	World	1:42.67	**Wilson Kipketer**, Denmark	Mar. 9, 1997	Paris
	American	1:45.00	Johnny Gray	Mar. 8, 1992	Sindelfingen, GER
1000 meters:	World	2:14.96	**Wilson Kipketer**, Denmark	Feb. 20, 2000	Birmingham, ENG
	American	2:17.86	David Krummenacker	Jan. 27, 2002	Boston
1500 meters:	World	3:31.18	**Hicham El Guerrouj**, Morocco	Feb. 2, 1997	Stuttgart
	American	3:38.12	Jeff Atkinson	Mar. 5, 1989	Budapest
Mile:	World	3:48.45	**Hicham El Guerrouj**, Morocco	Feb. 12, 1997	Ghent, BEL
	American	3:51.8	Steve Scott	Feb. 20, 1981	San Diego
3000 meters:	World	7:24.90	**Daniel Komen**, Kenya	Feb. 6, 1998	Budapest
	American	7:39.23	Tim Broe	Jan. 27, 2002	Boston
5000 meters:	World	12:49.6Q	**Kenenisa Bekele**, Ethiopia	Feb. 20, 2004	Birmingham, ENG
	American	13:20.55	Doug Padilla	Feb. 12, 1982	New York

Note: The Mile run is 1,609.344 meters.

Hurdles

Event		Time		Date Set	Location
50 meters:	World	6.25	**Mark McKoy**, Canada	Mar. 5, 1986	Kobe, JPN
	American	6.35	Greg Foster	Jan. 27, 1985	Rosemont, Ill.
		6.35	Greg Foster	Jan. 31, 1987	Ottawa
60 meters:	World	7.30	**Colin Jackson**, Great Britain	Mar. 6, 1994	Sindelfingen, GER
	American	7.36	Greg Foster	Jan. 16, 1987	Los Angeles
		7.36	Allen Johnson	March 6, 2004	Budapest

Note: The hurdles for both distances are 3 feet, 6 inches high. There are four hurdles in the 50 meters and five in the 60.

Walking

Event		Time		Date Set	Location
5000 meters:	World	18:07.08	**Mikhail Shchennikov**, Russia	Feb. 14, 1995	Moscow
	American	19:18.40	Tim Lewis	Mar. 7, 1987	Indianapolis

Relays

Event		Time		Date Set	Location
4 x 200 meters:	World	1:22.11	**Great Britain**	Mar. 3, 1991	Glasgow
	American	1:22.71	National Team	Mar. 3, 1991	Glasgow
4 x 400 meters:	World	3:02.83	**United States**	Mar. 7, 1999	Maebashi, JPN
	American	3:02.83	National Team (same as World)	Mar. 7, 1999	Maebashi, JPN
4 x 800 meters:	World	7:13.94	**United States**	Feb. 6, 2000	Boston
	American	7:13.94	Global Athletics (same as World)	Feb. 6, 2000	Boston

World Indoor Records Set in 2004
World indoor records set or equaled between Sept. 29, 2003 and Sept. 28, 2004.

MEN

Event	Name	Record	Old Mark	Former Holder
5000 meters	**Kenenisa Bekele**, ETH	12:49.60	12:50.38	Haile Gebrselassie, ETH (1999)
Triple Jump	(TIE) **Christian Olsson**, SWE	58-6	58-6	(TIE) Aliecer Urrutia, CUB (1997)

WOMEN

Event	Name	Record	Old Mark	Former Holder
5000 meters	**Berhane Adere**, ETH	14:39.29	14:47.35	Gabriela Szabo, ROM (1999)
4 x 400m relay	**Russia**	3:23.88	3:24.25	Russia (1999)
Pole Vault	**Yelena Isinbayeva**, RUS	15-11¼	15-11	Svetlana Feofanova, RUS (2004)
Triple Jump	**Tatyana Lebedeva**, RUS	50-4¾	49-9	Ashia Hansen, GBR (1998)

Note: The women's pole vault world record was broken three times in 2004. Feofanova held the record (15-9) heading into 2004. Isinbayeva jumped 15-10 on Feb. 15, Feofanova jumped 15-11 on Feb. 22 and Isinbayeva jumped 15-11¼ on March 6.

Field Events

Event		Mark		Date Set	Location
High Jump:	World	7-11½	**Javier Sotomayor**, Cuba	Mar. 4, 1989	Budapest
	American	7-10½	Hollis Conway	Mar. 10, 1991	Seville
Pole Vault:	World	20-2	**Sergey Bubka**, Ukraine	Feb. 21, 1993	Donyetsk, UKR
	American	19-9	Jeff Hartwig	Mar. 10, 2002	Sindelfingen, GER
Long Jump:	World	28-10¼	**Carl Lewis**, USA	Jan. 27, 1984	New York
	American	28-10¼	Lewis (same as World)	—	—
Triple Jump:	World	58-6	**Aliecer Urrutia**, Cuba	Mar. 1, 1997	Sindelfingen, GER
		58-6	**Christian Olsson**, Sweden	Mar. 7, 2004	Budapest
	American	58-3¼	Mike Conley	Feb. 27, 1987	New York
Shot Put:	World	74-4¼	**Randy Barnes**, USA	Jan. 20, 1989	Los Angeles
	American	74-4¼	Barnes (same as World)	—	—

Note: The international shot put weight for men is 16 lbs.

Heptathlon

Event		Points		Date Set	Location
Seven Events:	World	6476	**Dan O'Brien**, USA	Mar. 13-14, 1993	Toronto
	American	6476	O'Brien (same as World)	—	—

Note: O'Brien's WR times and distances, in order over two days—**60m** (6.67); **LJ** (25-8¾); **SP** (52-6¾); **HJ** (6-11¾); **60m H** (7.85); **PV** (17-0¾); **1000m** (2:57.96).

WOMEN
Running

Event		Time		Date Set	Location
50 meters:	World	5.96	**Irina Privalova**, Russia	Feb. 9, 1995	Madrid
	American	6.02	Gail Devers	Feb. 21, 1999	Lievin, FRA
60 meters:	World	6.92	**Irina Privalova**, Russia	Feb. 11, 1993	Madrid
		6.92	**Irina Privalova**, Russia	Feb. 9, 1995	Madrid
	American	6.95	Gail Devers	Mar. 12, 1993	Toronto
		6.95	Marion Jones	Mar. 7, 1998	Maebashi, JPN
200 meters:	World	21.87	**Merlene Ottey**, Jamaica	Feb. 13, 1993	Lievin, FRA
	American	22.18	Michelle Collins	Mar. 15, 2003	Birmingham, ENG
400 meters:	World	49.59	**Jarmila Kratochvilova**, Czech.	Mar. 7, 1982	Milan
	American	50.64	Diane Dixon	Mar. 10, 1991	Seville
800 meters:	World	1:55.82	**Jolanda Ceplak**, Slovenia	Mar. 3, 2002	Vienna
	American	1:58.71	Nicole Teter	Mar. 2, 2002	New York
1000 meters:	World	2:30.94	**Maria Mutola**, Mozambique	Feb. 25, 1999	Stockholm
	American	2:34.19	Jennifer Toomey	Feb. 20, 2004	Birmingham, ENG
1500 meters:	World	3:59.98	**Regina Jacobs**, USA	Feb. 1, 2003	Boston
	American	3:59.98	Jacobs (same as World)	—	—
Mile:	World	4:17.14	**Doina Melinte**, Romania	Feb. 9, 1990	E. Rutherford, N.J.
	American	4:20.5	Mary Slaney	Feb. 19, 1982	San Diego
3000 meters:	World	8:29.15	**Berhane Adere**, Ethiopia	Feb. 3, 2002	Stuttgart
	American	8:39.14	Regina Jacobs	Mar. 7, 1999	Maebashi, JPN
5000 meters:	World	14:39.29	**Berhane Adere**, Ethiopia	Jan. 31, 2004	Stuttgart
	American	15:07.33	Marla Runyan	Feb. 18, 2001	New York City

Note: The Mile run is 1,609.344 meters.

Hurdles

Event		Time		Date Set	Location
50 meters:	World	6.58	**Cornelia Oschkenat**, E. Ger.	Feb. 20, 1988	East Berlin
	American	6.67a	Jackie Joyner-Kersee	Feb. 10, 1995	Reno, Nev.
60 meters:	World	7.69	**Ludmila Engquist**, USSR	Feb. 4, 1990	Chelyabinsk, USSR
	American	7.74	Gail Devers	Mar. 1, 2003	Boston

Note: The hurdles for both distances are 2 feet, 9 inches high. There are four hurdles in the 50 meters and five in the 60.

Walking

Event		Time		Date Set	Location
3000 meters:	World	11:35.34p	**Gillian O'Sullivan**, IRL	Feb. 15, 2003	Belfast
	American	12:20.79	Debbi Lawrence	Mar. 12, 1993	Toronto

Relays

Event		Time		Date Set	Location
4 x 200 meters:	World	1:32.55	**West Germany**	Feb. 20, 1988	Dortmund, W. Ger.
		1:32.55	Germany	Feb. 21, 1999	Karlsruhe, GER
	American	1:33.24	National Team	Feb. 12, 1994	Glasgow
4 x 400 meters:	World	3:23.88	**Russia**	Mar. 7, 2004	Budapest
	American	3:27.59	National Team	Mar. 7, 1999	Maebashi, JPN
4 x 800 meters:	World	8:18.71	**Russia**	Feb. 4, 1994	Moscow
	American	8:25.5	Villanova	Feb. 7, 1987	Gainesville, Fla.

World and American Indoor Records (Cont.)
Field Events

Event		Mark		Date Set	Location
High Jump:	**World**	6-9½	Heike Henkel, Germany	Feb. 9, 1992	Karlsruhe, GER
	American	6-7	Tisha Waller	Feb. 28, 1998	Atlanta
Pole Vault:	**World**	15-11¼	**Yelena Isinbayeva**, Russia	Mar. 6, 2004	Budapest
	American	15-9¼	Stacy Dragila, USA	Mar. 6, 2004	Budapest
Long Jump:	**World**	24-2¼	**Heike Drechsler**, E. Germany	Feb. 13, 1988	Vienna
	American	23-4¾	Jackie Joyner-Kersee	Mar. 5, 1994	Atlanta
Triple Jump:	**World**	50-4¾	**Tatyana Lebedeva**, Russia	Mar. 6, 2004	Budapest
	American	46-8¼	Sheila Hudson	Mar. 4, 1995	Atlanta
Shot Put:	**World**	73-10	**Helena Fibingerova**, Czech.	Feb. 19, 1977	Jablonec, CZE
	American	65-0¾	Ramona Pagel	Feb. 20, 1987	Inglewood, Calif.

Note: The international shotput weight for women is 8 lbs. and 13 oz.

Pentathlon

		Points		Date Set	Location
Five Events:	**World**	4991	**Irina Byelova**, Russia	Feb. 14-15, 1992	Berlin
	American	4753	DeDee Nathan	Mar. 4-5, 1999	Maebashi, JPN

Note: Byelova's WR times and distances, in order over two days—**60m H** (8.22); **HJ** (6-4); **SP** (43-5¾); **LJ** (21-1¾); **800m** (2:10.26).

2004 IAAF World Indoor Championships

The 10th IAAF World Indoor Championships in Athletics held in Budapest, Hungary, Mar. 5-7, 2004. Note that (WR) indicates world record and (CR) indicates championships meet record.

Final Medal Leaders

		G	S	B	Total			G	S	B	Total
1	Russia	8	6	5	19	10	Canada	1	1	0	2
2	United States	4	5	1	10		Portugal	1	1	0	2
3	Jamaica	1	2	2	5		Bahamas	1	0	1	2
4	Ethiopia	2	1	1	4		Great Britain & N.I.	1	0	1	2
	Sweden	2	1	1	4		Brazil	0	1	1	2
	Ukraine	1	2	1	4		Cuba	0	0	2	2
7	Kenya	2	0	1	3		Greece	0	0	2	2
	Czech Republic	1	1	1	3		Romania	0	0	2	2
	Belarus	0	2	1	3	18	Fifteen countries tied with one medal each.				

MEN

Event		Time	
60 meters	Jason Gardener, GBR	6.49	
200 meters	Dominic Demeritte, BAH	20.66	
400 meters	Alleyne Francique, GRN	45.88	
800 meters	Mbulaeni Mulaudzi, RSA	1:45.71	
1500 meters	Paul Korir, KEN	3:52.31	
3000 meters	Bernard Lagat, KEN	7:56.34	
60m hurdles	Allen Johnson, USA	7.36	CR
4 x 400m relay	Jamaica (Haughton, Colquhoun, McDonald, Clarke)	3:05.21	
200m blind	Janos Hajner, HUN	32.14	

Event		Hgt/Dist	
High Jump	Stefan Holm, SWE	7-8½	
Pole Vault	Igor Pavlov, RUS	19-0½	
Long Jump	Savante Stringfellow, USA	27-6¾	
Triple Jump	Christian Olsson, SWE	58-6	WR
Shot Put	Christian Cantwell, USA	70-6¼	
Heptathlon	Roman Sebrle, CZR	6438 pts	

WOMEN

Event		Time	
60 meters	Gail Devers, USA	7.08	
200 meters	Natalya Safronnikova, BLR	23.13	
400 meters	Natalya Nazarova, RUS	50.19	CR
800 meters	M. de Lourdes Mutola, MOZ	1:58.50	
1500 meters	Kutre Dulecha, ETH	4:06.40	
3000 meters	Meseret Defar, ETH	9:11.22	
60m hurdles	Perdita Felicien, CAN	7.75	CR
4 x 400m relay	Russia (Krasnomovets, Kotlyarova, Levina, Nazarova)	3:23.88	WR
200m blind	Flora Buranyi, HUN	39.07	

Event		Hgt/Dist	
High Jump	Yelena Slesarenko, RUS	6-8¼	
Pole Vault	Yelena Isinbayeva, RUS	15-11¼	WR
Long Jump	Tatyana Lebedeva, RUS	22-10½	
Triple Jump	Tatyana Lebedeva, RUS	50-4¾	WR
Shot Put	Svetlana Krivelyova, RUS	65-3½	
Pentathlon	Naide Gomes, POR	4759 pts	

SWIMMING

World, Olympic and American Records
As of September 28, 2004

World long course records officially recognized by the Federation Internationale de Natation Amateur (FINA). Note that (p) indi - cates preliminary heat; (r) relay lead-off split; and (s) indicates split time. Note that (*) denotes that a record is awaiting ratification.

MEN

Freestyle

Distance	Time		Date Set	Location
50 meters:	World 21.64	**Aleksandr Popov**, Russia	June 16, 2000	Moscow
	Olympic. 21.91	Aleksandr Popov, Unified Team	July 30, 1992	Barcelona
	American 21.76	Gary Hall Jr.	Aug. 15, 2000	Indianapolis
100 meters:	World 47.84p	**P. van den Hoogenband**, NED	Sept. 19, 2000	Sydney
	Olympic. 47.84p	P. van den Hoogenband, NED (same as World)	—	—
	American 48.17p	Jason Lezak	July 10, 2004	Long Beach, Calif.
200 meters:	World 1:44.06	**Ian Thorpe**, Australia	July 25, 2001	Fukuoka, JPN
	Olympic . . . 1:44.71	Ian Thorpe, Australia	Aug. 16, 2004	Athens
	American . . 1:45.32	Michael Phelps	Aug. 16, 2004	Athens
400 meters:	World 3:40.08	**Ian Thorpe**, Australia	July 30, 2002	Manchester, GBR
	Olympic . . . 3:40.59	Ian Thorpe, Australia	Sept. 16, 2000	Sydney
	American . . 3:44.11	Klete Keller	Aug. 14, 2004	Athens
800 meters:	World 7:39.16	**Ian Thorpe**, Australia	July 24, 2001	Fukuoka, JPN
	Olympic	Not an event	—	—
	American . . 7:48.09	Larsen Jensen	July 25, 2003	Barcelona
1500 meters:	World . . . 14:34.56	**Grant Hackett**, Australia	July 29, 2001	Fukuoka, JPN
	Olympic . . 14:43.40	Grant Hackett, Australia	Aug. 21, 2004	Athens
	American . 14:45.29	Larsen Jensen	Aug. 21, 2004	Athens

Backstroke

Distance	Time		Date Set	Location
50 meters:	World 24.80	**Thomas Rupprath**, Germany	July 27, 2003	Barcelona
	Olympic	Not an event	—	—
	American . . . 24.99	Lenny Krayzelburg	Aug. 28, 1999	Sydney
100 meters:	World 53.45r	**Aaron Peirsol**, USA	Aug. 21, 2004	Athens
	Olympic. 53.45r	Peirsol (same as World)	—	—
	American . . . 53.45r	Peirsol (same as World)	—	—
200 meters:	World 1:54.74	**Aaron Peirsol**, USA	July 12, 2004	Long Beach, Calif.
	Olympic . . . 1:54.95	Aaron Peirsol, USA	Aug. 19, 2004	Athens
	American . . 1:54.74	Peirsol (same as World)	—	—

Breaststroke

Distance	Time		Date Set	Location
50 meters:	World 27.18	**Oleg Lisogor**, Ukraine	Aug. 1, 2002	Berlin
	Olympic	Not an event	—	—
	American 27.39	Ed Moses	Mar. 31, 2001	Austin, Texas
100 meters:	World 59.30	**Brendan Hansen**, USA	July 8, 2004	Long Beach, Calif.
	Olympic . . . 1:00.01p	Brendan Hansen, USA	Aug. 14, 2004	Athens
	American 59.30	Hansen (same as Olympic)	—	—
200 meters:	World . . . 2:09.04	**Brendan Hansen**, USA	July 11, 2004	Long Beach, Calif.
	Olympic . . . 2:09.44	Kosuke Kitajima, Japan	Aug. 18, 2004	Athens
	American . . 2:09.04	Hansen (same as Olympic)	—	—

Butterfly

Distance	Time		Date Set	Location
50 meters:	World 23.30	**Ian Crocker**, USA	Feb. 29, 2004	Austin, Texas
	Olympic	Not an event	—	—
	American . . . 23.30	Crocker (same as World)	—	—
100 meters:	World 50.76	**Ian Crocker**, USA	July 13, 2004	Long Beach, Calif.
	Olympic. 51.25	Michael Phelps	Aug. 20, 2004	Athens
	American . . . 50.76	Crocker (same as World)	—	—
200 meters:	World 1:53.93p	**Michael Phelps**, USA	July 22, 2003	Barcelona
	Olympic . . . 1:54.04	Michael Phelps, USA	Aug. 17, 2004	Athens
	American . . 1:53.93p	Phelps (same as World)	—	—

Individual Medley

Distance	Time		Date Set	Location
200 meters:	World . . . 1:55.94	**Michael Phelps**, USA	Aug. 9, 2003	College Park, Md.
	Olympic . . . 1:57.14	Michael Phelps, USA	Aug. 19, 2004	Athens
	American . . 1:55.94	Phelps (same as World)	—	—
400 meters:	World 4:08.26	**Michael Phelps**, USA	Aug. 14, 2004	Athens
	Olympic . . . 4:08.26	Phelps (same as World)	—	—
	American . . 4:08.26	Phelps (same as World)	—	—

Swimming (Cont.)

Relays

Distance		Time		Date Set	Location
4x100m free:	World	3:13.17	**South Africa** (Schoeman, Ferns, Townsend, Neethling)	Aug. 15, 2004	Athens
	Olympic	3:13.17	South Africa (same as world)	—	—
	American	3:13.86	USA (Ervin, Walker, Lezak, Hall Jr.)	Sept. 16, 2000	Sydney
4x200m free:	World	7:04.66	**Australia** (Hackett, Klim, Kirby, Thorpe)	July 27, 2001	Fukuoka, JPN
	Olympic	7:07.05	Australia (Thorpe, Klim, Pearson, Kirby)	Sept. 19, 2000	Sydney
	American	7:07.33	USA (Phelps, Lochte, Vanderkaay, Keller)	Aug. 17, 2004	Athens
4x100m medley:	World	3:30.68	**USA** (Peirsol, Hansen, Crocker, Lezak)	Aug. 21, 2004	Athens
	Olympic	3:30.68	USA (same as World)	—	—
	American	3:30.68	USA (same as World)	—	—

WOMEN

Freestyle

Distance		Time		Date Set	Location
50 meters:	World	24.13p	**Inge de Bruijn**, Netherlands	Sept. 22, 2000	Sydney
	Olympic	24.13p	de Bruijn (same as World)	—	—
	American	24.63	Dara Torres	Sept. 23, 2000	Sydney
100 meters:	World	53.52p	**Jodie Henry**, Australia	Aug. 18, 2004	Athens
	Olympic	53.52p	Henry (same as World)	—	—
	American	53.99	Natalie Coughlin	Aug. 29, 2002	Yokohama, JPN
200 meters:	World	1:56.64	**Franziska van Almsick**, Ger.	Aug. 3, 2002	Berlin
	Olympic	1:57.65	Heike Friedrich, E. Germany	Sept. 21, 1988	Seoul
	American	1:57.41r	Lindsay Benko	July 24, 2003	Barcelona
400 meters:	World	4:03.85	**Janet Evans**, USA	Sept. 22, 1988	Seoul
	Olympic	4:03.85	Evans (same as World)	—	—
	American	4:03.85	Evans (same as World)	—	—
800 meters:	World	8:16.22	**Janet Evans**, USA	Aug. 20, 1989	Tokyo
	Olympic	8:19.67	Brooke Bennett, USA	Sept. 22, 2000	Sydney
	American	8:16.22	Evans (same as World)	—	—
1500 meters:	World	15:52.10	**Janet Evans**, USA	Mar. 26, 1988	Orlando
	Olympic		Not an event	—	—
	American	15:52.10	Evans (same as World)	—	—

Backstroke

Distance		Time		Date Set	Location
50 meters:	World	28.25	**Sandra Volker**, Germany	June 17, 2000	Berlin
	Olympic		Not an event	—	—
	American	28.49p	Natalie Coughlin	July 23, 2001	Fukuoka, JPN
100 meters:	World	59.58	**Natalie Coughlin**, USA	Aug. 13, 2002	Ft. Lauderdale, Fla.
	Olympic	59.68r	Natalie Coughlin, USA	Aug. 21, 2004	Athens
	American	59.58	Coughlin (same as World)	—	—
200 meters:	World	2:06.62	**Krisztina Egerszegi**, Hungary	Aug. 25, 1991	Athens
	Olympic	2:07.06	Krisztina Egerszegi, Hungary	July 31, 1992	Barcelona
	American	2:08.53	Natalie Coughlin	Aug. 16, 2002	Ft. Lauderdale, Fla.

Breaststroke

Distance		Time		Date Set	Location
50 meters:	World	30.57	**Zoe Baker**, Great Britain	July 30, 2002	Manchester, GBR
	Olympic		Not an event	—	—
	American	31.34p	Megan Quann	Aug. 11, 2000	Indianapolis
100 meters:	World	1:06.37p	**Leisel Jones**, Australia	July 21, 2003	Barcelona
	Olympic	1:06.64	Luo Xuejuan, China	Aug. 16, 2004	Athens
	American	1:07.05	Megan Quann	Sept. 18, 2000	Sydney
200 meters:	World	2:22.44	**Amanda Beard**, USA	July 12, 2004	Long Beach, Calif.
	Olympic	2:23.37	Amanda Beard, USA	Aug. 19, 2004	Athens
	American	2:22.44	Beard (same as World)	—	—

World Swimming Records Set in 2004

World long course records set or equaled between Oct. 1, 2003 and Sept. 28, 2004; (*) indicates record is awaiting ratification. (r) indicates relay leadoff split.

MEN

Event	Name	Record	Old Mark	Former Holder
100m backstroke	**Aaron Peirsol**, USA	53.45r	53.60	Lenny Krayzelburg, USA (1999)
200m backstroke	**Aaron Peirsol**, USA	1:54.74	1:55.15	Aaron Peirsol, USA (2002)
100m breaststroke	**Brendan Hansen**, USA	59.30	59.78	Kosuke Kitajima, JPN (2003)
200m breaststroke	**Brendan Hansen**, USA	2:09.04	2:09.42	Kosuke Kitajima, JPN (2003)
50m butterfly	**Ian Crocker**, USA	23.30	23.43	Matthew Welsh, AUS (2003)
100m butterfly	**Ian Crocker**, USA	50.76	50.98	Ian Crocker, USA (2003)
400m IM (1)	**Michael Phelps**, USA	4:08.41	4:09.09	Michael Phelps, USA (2003)
400m IM (2)	**Michael Phelps**, USA	4:08.26	4:08.41	Michael Phelps, USA (2004)
4x100m freestyle	**South Africa**—Schoeman, Ferns, Townsend, Neethling	3:13.17	3:13.67	AUS—Klim, Fydler, Callus, Thorpe (2000)
4x100m medley	**USA**—Peirsol, Hansen, Crocker, Lezak	3:30.68	3:31.54	USA—Peirsol, Hansen, Crocker, Lezak (2003)

WOMEN

Event	Name	Record	Old Mark	Former Holder
100m freestyle (1)	**Lisbeth Lenton**, AUS	53.66	53.77	Inge de Bruijn, NED (2000)
100m freestyle (2)	**Jodie Henry**, AUS	53.52	53.66	Lisbeth Lenton, AUS (2004)
200m breaststroke (1)	**Leisel Jones**, AUS	2:22.96	2:22.99	Hui Qi, CHN (2001) Amanda Beard, USA (2003)
200m breaststroke (2)	**Amanda Beard**, USA	2:22.44	2:22.96	Leisel Jones, AUS (2004)
4x100m freestyle	**Australia**—Mills, Lenton, Thomas, Henry	3:35.94	3:36.00	GER—Meissner, Dallmann, Volker, van Almsick (2002)
4x200m freestyle	**USA**—Coughlin, Piper, Vollmer, Sandeno	7:53.42	7:55.47	E. GER—Stellmach, Strauss, Mohring, Friedrich (1987)
4x100m medley	**Australia**—Rooney, Jones, Thomas, Henry	3:57.32	3:58.30	USA—Bedford, Quann, Thompson, Torres (2000)

Butterfly

Distance		Time		Date Set	Location
50 meters:	World	25.57	**Anna-Karin Kammerling**, SWE	July 30, 2002	Berlin
	Olympic		Not an event	—	—
	American	26.00	Jenny Thompson	July 26, 2003	Barcelona
100 meters:	World	56.61	**Inge de Bruijn**, Netherlands	Sept. 17, 2000	Sydney
	Olympic	56.61	de Bruijn (same as World)	—	—
	American	57.58p	Dara Torres	Aug. 9, 2000	Indianapolis
200 meters:	World	2:05.78	**Otylia Jedrejczak**, Poland	Aug. 4, 2002	Berlin
	Olympic	2:05.88	Misty Hyman, USA	Sept. 20, 2000	Sydney
	American	2:05.88	Hyman (same as Olympic)	—	—

Individual Medley

Distance		Time		Date Set	Location
200 meters:	World	2:09.72	**Wu Yanyan**, China	Oct. 17, 1997	Shanghai
	Olympic	2:10.68	Yana Klochkova, Ukraine	Sept. 19, 2000	Sydney
	American	2:11.70	Amanda Beard	Aug. 17, 2004	Athens
400 meters:	World	4:33.59	**Yana Klochkova**, Ukraine	Sept. 16, 2000	Sydney
	Olympic	4:33.59	Klochkova, UKR (same as World)	—	—
	American	4:34.95	Kaitlin Sandeno	Aug. 14, 2004	Athens

Relays

Distance		Time		Date Set	Location
4x100m free:	World	3:35.94	**Australia** (Mills, Lenton, Thomas, Henry)	Aug. 14, 2004	Athens
	Olympic	3:35.94	Australia (same as World)	—	—
	American	3:36.39	USA (Joyce, Coughlin, Weir, Thompson)	Aug. 14, 2004	Athens
4x200m free:	World	7:53.42	**USA** (Coughlin, Piper, Vollmer, Sandeno)	Aug. 18, 2004	Athens
	Olympic	7:53.42	USA (same as World)	—	—
	American	7:53.42	USA (same as World)	—	—
4x100m medley:	World	3:57.32	**Australia** (Rooney, Jones, Thomas, Henry)	Aug. 21, 2004	Athens
	Olympic	3:57.32	Australia (same as World)	—	—
	American	3:58.30	USA (Bedford, Quann, Thompson, Torres)	Sept. 23, 2000	Sydney

Alpine Skiing
World Cup Champions
Top Five Standings
MEN

Overall 1. Hermann Maier, AUT (1265 pts); 2. Stephan Eberharter, AUT (1223); 3. Benjamin Raich, AUT (1139); 4. Bode Miller, USA (1134); 5. Daron Rahlves, USA (1004).

Downhill 1. Stephan Eberharter, AUT (831 pts); 2. Daron Rahlves, USA (627); 3. Hermann Maier, AUT (537); 4. Fritz Strobl, AUT (512); 5. Michael Walchhofer, AUT (503).

Slalom 1. Rainer Schoenfelder, AUT (630 pts); 2. Kalle Palander, FIN (595); 3. Benjamin Raich, AUT (468); 4. Giorgio Rocca, ITA (429); 5. Bode Miller, USA (376).

Giant Slalom 1. Bode Miller, USA (410 pts); 2. Kalle Palander, FIN (349); 3. Massimiliano Blardone, ITA (266); 4. Benjamin Raich, AUT (255); 5. Davide Simoncelli, ITA (238).

Super G 1. Hermann Maier, AUT (580 pts); 2. Daron Rahlves, USA (340); 3. Stephan Eberharter, AUT (312); 4. Bjarne Solbakken, NOR (298); 5. Michael Walchhofer, AUT (243).

Combined 1. Bode Miller, USA (200 pts); 2. Benjamin Raich, AUT (160); 3. Lasse Kjus, NOR (120); 4. Pierrick Bourgeat, FRA (90); 5. Michael Walchhofer, AUT (82).

Nation's Cup Champion: Austria

WOMEN

Overall 1. Anja Paerson, SWE (1561 pts); 2. Renate Goetschl, AUT (1344); 3. Maria Riesch, GER (977); 4. Hilde Gerg, GER (962); 5. Carole Montillet-Carles, FRA (957). *Best USA*—Kirsten Clark (13th, 456 pts).

Downhill 1. Renate Goetschl, AUT (680 pts); 2. Hilde Gerg, GER (546); 3. Carole Montillet-Carles, FRA (492); 4. Isolde Kostner, ITA (348); 5. Michaela Dorfmeister, AUT (334). *Best USA*—Kirsten Clark (9th, 228 pts).

Slalom 1. Anja Paerson, SWE (770 pts); 2. Marlies Schild, AUT (447); 3. Monika Bergmann-Schmuderer, GER (437); 4. Tanja Poutiainen, FIN (390); 5. Elisabeth Goergl, AUT (339). *Best USA*—Kristina Koznick (8th, 297 pts).

Giant Slalom 1. Anja Paerson, SWE (630 pts); 2. Denise Karbon, ITA (343); 3. Maria Jose Rienda Contreras, SPA (339); 4. Elisabeth Goergl, AUT (293); 5. Tanja Poutiainen, FIN (279).
Best USA—Sarah Schleper (12th, 201 pts).

Super G 1. Renate Goetschl, AUT (467 pts); 2. Carole Montillet-Carles, FRA (402); 3. Michaela Dorfmeister, AUT (391); 4. Hilde Gerg, GER (390); 5. Maria Riesch, GER (338). *Best USA*—Caroline Lalive (11th, 178 pts).

Nation's Cup Champion: Austria

2004 U.S. Alpine Championships
at Alyeska, Alaska (March 19-23)
MEN

Downhill	Bryon Friedman, Park City, Utah
Slalom	James Cochran, Keene, N.H.
Giant Slalom	James Cochran, Keene, N.H.
Super G	Daron Rahlves, Sugar Bowl, CA
Combined	Bryon Friedman, Park City, UT

WOMEN

Downhill	Jonna Mendes, Heavenly, Calif.
Slalom	Lindsey Kildow, Vail, Colo.
Giant Slalom	Libby Ludlow, Bellevue, Wash.
Super G	Lindsey Kildow, Vail, Colo.
Combined	Julia Mancuso, Olympic Valley, Calif.

Freestyle Skiing
World Cup Champions
MEN

Overall	Steve Omischl, Canada
Aerials	Steve Omischl, Canada
Moguls	Janne Lahtela, Finland
Halfpipe	Mathias Wecxsteen, France
Ski Cross	Jesper Brugge, Sweden

WOMEN

Overall	Kari Traa, Norway
Aerials	Alisa Camplin, Australia
Moguls	Jennifer Heil, Canada
Halfpipe	Marie Martinod, France
Ski Cross	Ophelie David, France

2004 U.S. Freestyle Championships
at Heavenly, Calif. (March 26-28)
MEN

Aerials	Jeret Peterson, Boise, Idaho
Moguls	Travis Cabral, South Lake Tahoe, Calif.
Dual Moguls	Travis Cabral, South Lake Tahoe, Calif.

WOMEN

Aerials	Kelly Hilliman, Tonawanda, N.Y.
Moguls	Jillian Vogtli, Ellicotville, N.Y.
Dual Moguls	Shelly Robertson, Reno, Nev.

Nordic Skiing
World Cup Champions
MEN

Cross Country - Overall	Rene Sommerfeldt, Germany
Cross Country - Distance	Rene Sommerfeldt, Germany
Cross Country - Sprint	Thobias Fredriksson, Sweden
Ski Jumping - Overall	Janne Ahonen, Finland
Ski Jumping - Four Hills	Sigurd Pettersen, Norway
Nordic Combined - Overall	Hannu Manninen, Finland
Nordic Combined - Sprint	Hannu Manninen, Finland

WOMEN

Cross Country - Overall	Gabriella Paruzzi, Italy
Cross Country - Distance	Valentina Shevchenko, Ukraine
Cross Country - Sprint	Marit Bjoergen, Norway

2004 U.S. Cross Country Championships
at Rumford, Maine (Jan. 3-11)
MEN

Sprint	Leif Zimmerman, Bozeman, Mont.
10-k Classic	Carl Swenson, Boulder, Colo.
30-k Classic	Carl Swenson, Boulder, Colo.
10-k Freestyle	Carl Swenson, Boulder, Colo.
50-k Freestyle	Lars Flora, Anchorage, Alaska

WOMEN

Sprint	Kikkan Randall, Anchorage, Alaska
5-k Classic	Rebecca Dussault, Gunnison, Colo.
15-k Classic	Rebecca Dussault, Gunnison, Colo.
5-k Freestyle	Rebecca Dussault, Gunnison, Colo.
30-k Freestyle	Sarah Konrad, Laramie, Wyo.

2004 U.S. Ski Jumping/
Nordic Combined Championships
at Steamboat Springs, Colo. (March 20-21)
MEN

Nordic Combined
(K90 jump/10-k ski) Todd Lodwick, Steamboat Springs, Colo.
Normal Hill (K90) . .Todd Lodwick, Steamboat Springs, Colo.
Large Hill (K114) . .Todd Lodwick, Steamboat Springs, Colo.

WOMEN

Normal Hill (K90) . . . . .Lindsey Van, Park City, Utah
Large Hill (K114) . . . . .Lindsey Van, Park City, Utah

Snowboarding
World Cup Champions
MEN

Overall . . . . Jasey Jay Anderson, Canada
Halfpipe . . . . .Risto Mattila, Finland
Parallel Slalom . . . . .Siegfried Grabner, Austria
Snowboardcross . . . . .Xavier Delerue, France
Big Air . . . . .Simon Ax, Sweden

WOMEN

Overall . . . . Julie Pomagalski, France
Halfpipe . . . . .Soko Yamaoka, Japan
Parallel Slalom . . . . .Daniela Meuli, Switzerland
Snowboardcross . . . . .Karine Ruby, France

2004 U.S. Open Snowboarding
Championships
at Stratton, Vt. (March 19-21)
MEN

Halfpipe . . . . .Danny Kass, Hamburg, N.J.
Rail Jam . . . . .Rahm Klampert, Mammoth Lakes, Calif.
Slopestyle . . . . Jake Blauvelt, Waterbury Center, Vt.

WOMEN

Halfpipe . . . . .Kelly Clark, Mount Snow, Vt.
Rail Jam . . . . .Leanne Pelosi, Whistler, B.C., Canada
Slopestyle . . . . . .Priscilla Levac, Pemberton, B.C., Canada

2004 Snowboarding Alpine Finals
at Breckenridge, Colo. (March 20-21)

Men's Slalom . . . . .Phillipe Berube, Canada
Men's Parallel GS . . . . .Chris Klug, Aspen, Colo.
Women's Slalom . . . . .Tomoka Takeuchi, Japan
Women's Parallel GS   . .Michelle Gorgone, Sudbury, Mass.

Speed Skating
World Cup Champions
MEN

100 meters .Yu Fengton, China
500 meters . . . . .Jeremy Wotherspoon, Canada
1000 meters . . . . .Erben Wennemars, Netherlands
1500 meters . . . . .Mark Tuitert, Netherlands
5000/10,000 meters . . . . .Bob de Jong, Netherlands

WOMEN

100 meters . . . . .Shihomi Shinya, Japan
500 meters . . . . .Wang Manli, China
1000 meters . . . . .Jennifer Rodriguez, USA
1500 meters . . . . .Anni Friesinger, Germany
3000/5000 meters . . . . . . .Claudia Pechstein, Germany

2004 World Allround Championships
at Hamar, Norway (Feb. 7-8)
MEN

500 meters . . . . .Yevgeny Lalenkov, Russia
1500 meters . . . . .Shani Davis, USA
5000 meters . . . . .Carl Verheijen, Netherlands
10,000 meters . . . . .Carl Verheijen, Netherlands
All-Around . . . . .Chad Hedrick, USA

WOMEN

500 meters . . . . .Jennifer Rodriguez, United States
1500 meters . . . . .Jennifer Rodriguez, United States
3000 meters . . . . .Renate Groenewold, Netherlands
5000 meters . . . . .Gretha Smit, Netherlands
All-Around . . . . .Renate Groenewold, Netherlands

2004 World Short Track
Championships
at Goteborg, Sweden (March 19-21)
MEN

500 meters . . . . .Song Suk-Woo, S. Korea
1000 meters . . . . .Ahn Hyun-Soo, S. Korea
1500 meters . . . . .Ahn Hyun-Soo, S. Korea
3000 meters . . . . .Ahn Hyun-Soo, S. Korea
5000 meter relay . . . . .S. Korea
All-Around . . . . .Ahn Hyun-Soo, S. Korea

WOMEN

500 meters . . . . .Wang Meng, China
1000 meters . . . . .Choi Eun-Kyung, S. Korea
1500 meters . . . . .Choi Eun-Kyung, S. Korea
3000 meters . . . . .Byun Chun-Sa, S. Korea
3000 meter relay . . . . .S. Korea
All-Around . . . . .Choi Eun-Kyung, S. Korea

Figure Skating

World Championships
at Dortmund, Germany (March 22-28)

Men's —1. Evgeni Plushenko, Russia; 2. Brian Joubert, France; 3. Stefan Lindemann, Germany; 4. Stephane Lambiel, Switzerland; 5. Johnny Weir, USA.

Women's —1. Shizuka Arakawa, Japan; 2. Sasha Cohen, USA; 3. Michelle Kwan, USA; 4. Miki Ando, Japan; 5. Carolina Kostner, Italy.

Pairs —1. Tatiana Totmianina & Maxim Marinin, Russia; 2. Xue Shen & Hongbo Zhao, China; 3. Qing Pang & Jian Tong, China; 4. Maria Petrova & Alexei Tikhonov, Russia; 5. Dan Zhang & Hao Zhang, China.

Ice Dance —1. Tatiana Navka & Roman Kostomarov, Russia; 2. Albena Denkova & Maxim Staviyski, Bulgaria; 3. Kati Winkler & Rene Lohse, Germany; 4. Elena Grushina & Ruslan Goncharov, Ukraine; 5. Tanith Belbin & Benjamin Agosto, USA.

U.S. Championships
at Atlanta, Ga. (Jan. 3-11)

Men's . . . . .Johnny Weir
Women's . . . . .Michelle Kwan
Pairs . . . . .Rena Inoue
& John Baldwin
Ice Dance . . . . .Tanith Belbin
& Benjamin Agosto

European Championships
at Budapest, Hungary (Feb. 2-8)

Men's .Brian Joubert, France
Women's . . . . .Julia Sebestyen, Hungary
Pairs . . . . .Tatiana Totmianina
& Maxim Marinin, Russia
Ice Dance . . . . .Tatiana Navka
& Roman Kostomarov, Russia

SUMMER SPORTS

Cycling
2004 Tour de France

The 91st Tour de France (July 3-25) ran 20 stages plus a prologue, covering 3,391 kilometres (2,107 miles) starting in the Belgian city of Liege, winding through the French countryside, passing through the Alps and Pyrenees and finishing in Paris on the Avenue des Champs-Elysees. U.S. Postal Service rider Lance Armstrong won his unprecedented sixth consecutive Tour, completing the grueling event in 83 hours, 36 minutes and two seconds He defeated his closest rival, Andreas Kloden of Germany, by just over six minutes. While the margin of victory wasn't his largest (7:37 in 1999), Armstrong's five solo stage wins, one team trial win and usual brilliance in the mountains would indicate this year may have been his most dominant.

	Team	Behind			Team	Behind
1 Lance Armstrong, USA	U.S. Postal	—	6	Francisco Mancebo, ESP	Illes Balears	18:01
2 Andreas Kloden, GER	T-Mobile	6:19	7	Georg Totschnig, AUT	Gerolsteiner	18:27
3 Ivan Basso, ITA	CSC	6:40	8	Carlos Sastre, ESP	CSC	19:51
4 Jan Ullrich, GER	T-Mobile	8:50	9	Levi Leipheimer, USA	Rabobank	20:12
5 Jose Azevedo, POR	U.S. Postal	14:30	10	Oscar Pereiro Sio, ESP	Phonak Hearing	22:54

Other Worldwide Champions

2004 Major UCI (Union Cycliste Internationale) Road results through Sept. 26. Note that in some instances, the date shown below is the final day of that particular race.

MEN

Race	Winner	Race	Winner
Jan. 25: Tour Down Under (AUS)	Patrick Jonker, AUS	Apr. 7: Ghent-Wevelgem (BEL)	Tom Boonen, BEL
Feb. 15: Tour de Langwaki (MAS)	Freddy Gonzalez, COL	Apr. 11: Paris-Roubaix (FRA)	Magnus Backstedt, SWE
Feb. 15: Mediterranean Tour (FRA)	Jorg Jaksche, GER	Apr. 21: Fleche Wallonne (BEL)	Davide Rebellin, ITA
Feb. 19: Ruta del Sol (ESP)	Juan Carlos Dominguez, ESP	May 2: Tour de Romandie (SWI)	Tyler Hamilton, USA
Mar. 1: Tour de Valencia (ESP)	Alejandro Valverde, ESP	May 9: Four Days of Dunkirk (FRA)	Sylvain Chavanel, FRA
Feb. 28: Omloop Het Volk (BEL)	cancelled (snow)	May 30: Giro d'Italia (ITA)	Damiano Cunego, ITA
Mar. 14: Paris-Nice (FRA)	Jorg Jaksche, GER	June 13: Dauphine Libere (FRA)	Iban Mayo, ESP
Mar. 16: Tirreno-Adriatico (ITA)	Paolo Bettini, ITA	June 20: Tour of Switzerland (SWI)	Jan Ullrich, GER
Mar. 20: Milan-San Remo (ITA)	Oscar Freire Gomez, ESP	Aug. 14: Olympics Road Race (GRE)	Paolo Bettini, ITA
Mar. 26: Setmana Catalana (ESP)	Joaquin Rodriguez, ESP	Aug. 18: Olympics Time Trial (GRE)	Tyler Hamilton, USA
Mar. 28: Criterium Int'l (FRA)	Jens Voigt, GER	Aug. 28: Tour of the Netherlands (NED)	Erik Dekker, NED
Apr. 4: Tour de Flanders (BEL)	Steffen Wesemann, GER	Sept. 26: Tour of Spain (ESP)	Roberto Heras, ESP

WOMEN

Race	Winner	Race	Winner
Feb. 25: Geelong World Cup (AUS)	Oenone Wood, AUS	July 11: Giro d'Italia Femminile (ITA)	Nicole Cooke, GBR
Mar. 20: Primavera Rosa (ITA)	Zoulfia Zabirova, RUS	Aug. 15: Olympics Road Race (GRE)	Sara Carrigan, AUS
Apr. 4: Tour de Flanders (BEL)	Zoulfia Zabirova, RUS	Aug. 18: Olympics Time Trial (GRE)	Leontien
Apr. 21: Fleche Wallonne (BEL)	Sonia Huguet, FRA		Zijlaard-van Moorsel, NED
May 23: Tour de L'Aude (FRA)	Trixi Worrack, GER	Aug. 28: GP Ouest France (FRA)	Edita Pucinskaite, LTU
May 29: Montreal World Cup (CAN)	G. Jeanson, CAN	Sept. 5: Rotterdam Tour (NED)	Petra Rossner, GER
June 6: Wachovia Liberty Classic (USA)	Petra Rossner, GER	Sept. 12: Tour of Nuremberg (GER)	Petra Rossner, GER

Gymnastics
2004 U.S. Championships
at Nashville, Tenn. (June 2-5)

MEN

All-Around	Paul Hamm
High Bar	Paul Hamm
Parallel Bars	Alexander Artemev
Vault	David Sender
Pommel Horse	Brett McClure
Rings	Raj Bhavsar
Floor Exercise	Paul Hamm
Trampoline	Ryan Weston
Trampoline: Double Mini	Derek Stangel
Trampoline: Synchronized	Ryan Weston & Chris Estrada
Tumbling	Casey Finley

Note: The 38th Artistic Gymnastics World Championships will be held in Melbourne, Australia, Nov. 21-27, 2005.

WOMEN

All-Around	(TIE) Carly Patterson & Courtney Kupets
Vault	Liz Tricase
Uneven Bars	Courtney Kupets
Balance Beam	Courtney Kupets
Floor Exercise	Carly Patterson
Trampoline	Jennifer Parilla
Trampoline: Double Mini	Krista Mahoney
Trampoline: Synchronized	Jenny Wescott & Brittany Dircks
Tumbling	Leanne Seitzinger
Rhythmic: All-Around	Mary Sanders
Rhythmic: Club	Olga Karmansky
Rhythmic: Hoop	Mary Sanders
Rhythmic: Ball	Mary Sanders
Rhythmic: Ribbon	Olga Karmansky

Marathons
2004 Boston Marathon

The 108th edition of the Boston Marathon was held Monday, April 19, 2004 and run, as always, from Hopkinton through Ashland, Framingham, Natick, Wellesley, Newton and Brookline to Boston, Mass. On a brutally hot, 85-degree afternoon, powerhouse Kenya claimed the top four finishers, seven of the top ten and was led by 27-year-old race winner Timothy Cherigat (2:10:37). It was the 13th time in the last 14 years that a Kenyan has won the world's oldest annual marathon.

In the women's division, 31-year-old Kenyan Catherine Ndereba returned to the winner's podium for the third time with a 16-second victory over Ethiopian Elfenesh Alemu. It was the closest 1-2 women's finish in Boston history. **Distance:** 26.2 miles.

MEN

		Time
1	Timothy Cherigat, Kenya	2:10:37
2	Robert Cheboror, Kenya	2:11:49
3	Martin Lel, Kenya	2:13:38
4	Stephen Kiogora, Kenya	2:14:34
5	Hailu Negussie, Ethiopia	2:17:30

Best USA: 13th—Christopher Zieman, California, 2:25:45

WOMEN

		Time
1	Catherine Ndereba, Kenya	2:24:27
2	Elfenesh Alemu, Ethiopia	2:24:43
3	Olivera Jevtic, Serbia & Montenegro	2:27:34
4	Jelena Prokopcuka, Latvia	2:30:16
5	Nuta Olaru, Romania	2:30:44

Best USA: 16th—Julie S. Spencer, Wisconsin, 2:56:39

Other 2004 Winners

Tokyo

Feb. 8	Men	Daniel Njenga, KEN	2:08:43

(No women's division)

Los Angeles

Mar. 7	Men	David Kirui, KEN	2:13:41
	Women	Tatyana Pozdnyakova, UKR	2:30:17

Paris

Apr. 4	Men	Ambesa Tolosa, ETH	2:08:56
	Women	Salina Kosgei, KEN	2:24:32

Rotterdam

Apr. 4	Men	Felix Limo, KEN	2:06:14
	Women	Zhor El Kamch, MAR	2:26:10

London

Apr. 18	Men	Evans Rutto, KEN	2:06:18
	Women	Margaret Okaya, KEN	2:22:35

Olympics (Athens)

Aug. 29	Men	Stefano Baldini, ITA	2:10:55
Aug. 22	Women	Mizuki Noguchi, JPN	2:26:20

Late 2003

Chicago

Oct. 12	Men	Evans Rutto, KEN	2:05:50
	Women	Svetlana Zakharova, RUS	2:23:07

New York City

Nov. 3	Men	Martin Lel, KEN	2:10:30
	Women	Margaret Okayo, KEN	2:22:31

Tokyo Women's

Nov. 16	Women	Elfenesh Alemu, ETH	2:24:47

Fukuoka

Dec. 7	Men	Tomoaki Kunichika, JPN	2:07:52

(No women's division)

2003 Rugby World Cup

The fourth World Cup tournament held Oct. 10-Nov. 22 throughout Australia. Note that (*) indicates teams that advanced to the quarterfinals (top two teams from each pool). PF denotes Points For while PA denotes Points Against.

Pool A	W	L	T	Pts	PF	PA
*Australia	4	0	0	18	273	32
*Ireland	3	1	0	15	141	56
Argentina	2	2	0	11	140	57
Romania	1	3	0	5	65	192
Namibia	0	4	0	0	28	310

Pool B	W	L	T	Pts	PF	PA
*France	4	0	0	20	204	70
*Scotland	3	1	0	14	102	97
Fiji	2	2	0	10	98	114
United States	1	3	0	6	86	125
Japan	0	4	0	0	79	163

Pool C	W	L	T	Pts	PF	PA
*England	4	0	0	19	255	47
*South Africa	3	1	0	15	184	60
Samoa	2	4	0	10	138	117
Uruguay	1	3	0	4	56	255
Georgia	0	4	0	0	46	200

Pool D	W	L	T	Pts	PF	PA
*New Zealand	4	0	0	20	282	57
*Wales	3	1	0	14	132	98
Italy	2	2	0	8	77	123
Canada	1	3	0	5	54	135
Tonga	0	4	0	1	46	178

Quarterfinals

New Zealand 29 . . . . .South Africa 9
Australia 33 .Scotland 16
France 43 . . . . .Ireland 21
England 28 . . . . .Wales 17

Semifinals

Australia 22 . . . . .New Zealand 10
England 24 . . . . .France 7

Third Place

New Zealand 40 .France 13

Championship

England 20 . . . . .Australia 17

Awards

Player of the Year . . . . .Jonny Wilkinson, England
Coach of the Year . . . . .Clive Woodward, England

1882-2004
Through the Years

TRACK & FIELD

IAAF World Championships

While the Summer Olympics have served as the unofficial world outdoor championships for track and field throughout the centuries, a separate World Championship meet was started in 1983 by the International Amateur Athletic Federation (IAAF). The meet was held every four years from 1983-91, but began an every-other-year cycle in 1993. World Championship sites include Helsinki (1983), Rome (1987), Tokyo (1991), Stuttgart (1993), Göteborg, Sweden (1995), Athens (1997), Seville, Spain (1999), Edmonton (2001) and Paris (2003). Looking forward, the Championships will be held in Helsinki (2005) and Osaka, Japan (2007). Note that (WR) indicates world record and (CR) indicates championship meet record.

MEN

Multiple gold medals (including relays): Michael Johnson (9); Carl Lewis (8); Sergey Bubka (6); Maurice Greene and Lars Riedel (5); Hicham El Guerrouj, Haile Gebrselassie, Allen Johnson, Ivan Pedroso, Antonio Pettigrew and Calvin Smith (4); Donovan Bailey, Tomas Dvorak, Greg Foster, John Godina, Werner Gunthor, Wilson Kipketer, Moses Kiptanui, Robert Korzeniowski, Dennis Mitchell, Noureddine Morceli, Dan O'Brien, Butch Reynolds, Jerome Young and Jan Zelezny (3); Andrey Abduvaliyev, Abel Anton, Derrick Brew, Leroy Burrell, John Capel, Andre Cason, Maurizio Damilano, Jon Drummond, Jonathan Edwards, Colin Jackson, Ismael Kirui, Billy Konchellah, Sergey Litvinov, Tim Montgomery, Edwin Moses, Mike Powell, Felix Sanchez, Javier Sotomayor, Angelo Taylor and Bernard Williams (2).

100 Meters

Year		Time	
1983	Carl Lewis, USA	10.07	
1987	Carl Lewis, USA	9.93	
1991	Carl Lewis, USA	9.86	**WR**
1993	Linford Christie, GBR	9.87	
1995	Donovan Bailey, CAN	9.97	
1997	Maurice Greene, USA	9.86	
1999	Maurice Greene, USA	9.80	**CR**
2001	Maurice Greene, USA	9.82	
2003	Kim Collins, SKN	10.07	

Note: Ben Johnson was the original winner in 1987, but was stripped of his title and world record time (9.83) following his 1989 admission of drug taking.

200 Meters

Year		Time	
1983	Calvin Smith, USA	20.14	
1987	Calvin Smith, USA	20.16	
1991	Michael Johnson, USA	20.01	
1993	Frank Fredericks, NAM	19.85	
1995	Michael Johnson, USA	19.79	**CR**
1997	Ato Boldon, USA	20.04	
1999	Maurice Greene, USA	19.90	
2001	Konstantinos Kenteris, GRE	20.04	
2003	John Capel, USA	20.30	

400 Meters

Year		Time	
1983	Bert Cameron, JAM	45.05	
1987	Thomas Schonlebe, E. Ger	44.33	
1991	Antonio Pettigrew, USA	44.57	
1993	Michael Johnson, USA	43.65	
1995	Michael Johnson, USA	43.39	
1997	Michael Johnson, USA	44.12	
1999	Michael Johnson, USA	43.18	**WR**
2001	Avard Moncur, BAH	44.64	
2003	Jerome Young, USA	44.50	

800 Meters

Year		Time	
1983	Willi Wülbeck, W. Ger	1:43.65	
1987	Billy Konchellah, KEN	1:43.06	**CR**
1991	Billy Konchellah, KEN	1:43.99	
1993	Paul Ruto, KEN	1:44.71	
1995	Wilson Kipketer, DEN	1:45.08	
1997	Wilson Kipketer, DEN	1:43.38	
1999	Wilson Kipketer, DEN	1:43.30	
2001	Andre Bucher, SWI	1:43.70	
2003	Djabir Said-Guerni, ALG	1:44.81	

1500 Meters

Year		Time	
1983	Steve Cram, GBR	3:41.59	
1987	Abdi Bile, SOM	3:36.80	
1991	Noureddine Morceli, ALG	3:32.84	
1993	Noureddine Morceli, ALG	3:34.24	
1995	Noureddine Morceli, ALG	3:33.73	
1997	Hicham El Guerrouj, MOR	3:35.83	
1999	Hicham El Guerrouj, MOR	3:27.65	**CR**
2001	Hicham El Guerrouj, MOR	3:30.68	
2003	Hicham El Guerrouj, MOR	3:31.77	

5000 Meters

Year		Time	
1983	Eammon Coghlan, IRL	13:28.53	
1987	Said Aouita, MOR	13:26.44	
1991	Yobes Ondieki, KEN	13:14.45	
1993	Ismael Kirui, KEN	13:02.75	
1995	Ismael Kirui, KEN	13:16.77	
1997	Daniel Komen, KEN	13:07.38	
1999	Salah Hissou, MOR	12:58.13	
2001	Richard Limo, KEN	13:00.77	
2003	Eliud Kipchoge, KEN	12:52.79	**CR**

10,000 Meters

Year		Time	
1983	Alberto Cova, ITA	28:01.04	
1987	Paul Kipkoech, KEN	27:38.63	
1991	Moses Tanui, KEN	27:38.74	
1993	Haile Gebrselassie, ETH	27:46.02	
1995	Haile Gebrselassie, ETH	27:12.95	
1997	Haile Gebrselassie, ETH	27:24.58	
1999	Haile Gebrselassie, ETH	27:57.27	
2001	Charles Kamathi, KEN	27:53.25	
2003	Kenenisa Bekele, ETH	26:49.57	**CR**

Marathon

Year		Time	
1983	Rob de Castella, AUS	2:10:03	
1987	Douglas Wakiihuri, KEN	2:11:48	
1991	Hiromi Taniguchi, JPN	2:14:57	
1993	Mark Plaatjes, USA	2:13:57	
1995	Martin Fiz, SPA	2:11:41	
1997	Abel Anton, SPA	2:13:16	
1999	Abel Anton, SPA	2:13:36	
2001	Gezahegne Abera, ETH	2:12:42	
2003	Jaouad Gharib, MOR	2:08:31	CR

110-Meter Hurdles

Year		Time	
1983	Greg Foster, USA	13.42	
1987	Greg Foster, USA	13.21	
1991	Greg Foster, USA	13.06	
1993	Colin Jackson, GBR	12.91	WR
1995	Allen Johnson, USA	13.00	
1997	Allen Johnson, USA	12.93	
1999	Colin Jackson, GBR	13.04	
2001	Allen Johnson, USA	13.04	
2003	Allen Johnson, USA	13.12	

400-Meter Hurdles

Year		Time	
1983	Edwin Moses, USA	47.50	
1987	Edwin Moses, USA	47.46	
1991	Samuel Matete, ZAM	47.64	
1993	Kevin Young, USA	47.18	CR
1995	Derrick Adkins, USA	47.98	
1997	Stephane Diagana, FRA	47.70	
1999	Fabrizio Mori, ITA	47.72	
2001	Felix Sanchez, DOM	47.49	
2003	Felix Sanchez, DOM	47.25	

3000-Meter Steeplechase

Year		Time	
1983	Patriz Ilg, W. Ger	8:15.06	
1987	Francesco Panetta, ITA	8:08.57	
1991	Moses Kiptanui, KEN	8:12.59	
1993	Moses Kiptanui, KEN	8:06.36	
1995	Moses Kiptanui, KEN	8:04.16	CR
1997	Wilson B. Kipketer, KEN	8:05.84	
1999	Christopher Koskei, KEN	8:11.76	
2001	Reuben Kosgei, KEN	8:15.16	
2003	Saif Saaeed Shaheen, QAT	8:04.39	

4 x 100-Meter Relay

Year		Time	
1983	United States	37.86	WR
1987	United States	37.90	
1991	United States	37.50	WR
1993	United States	37.48	CR
1995	Canada	38.31	
1997	Canada	37.86	
1999	United States	37.59	
2001	United States	37.96	
2003	United States	38.06	

4 x 400-Meter Relay

Year		Time	
1983	Soviet Union	3:00.79	
1987	United States	2:57.29	
1991	Great Britain	2:57.53	
1993	United States	2:54.29	WR
1995	United States	2:57.32	
1997	United States	2:56.47	
1999	United States	2:56.45	
2001	United States	2:57.54	
2003	United States	2:58.88	

20-Kilometer Walk

Year		Time	
1983	Ernesto Canto, MEX	1:20.49	
1987	Maurizio Damilano, ITA	1:20.45	
1991	Maurizio Damilano, ITA	1:19.37	
1993	Valentin Massana, SPA	1:22.31	
1995	Michele Didoni, ITA	1:19.59	
1997	Daniel Garcia, MEX	1:21:43	
1999	Ilya Markov, RUS	1:23:34	
2001	Roman Rasskazov, RUS	1:20:31	
2003	Jefferson Perez, ECU	1:17:21	WR

50-Kilometer Walk

Year		Time	
1983	Ronald Weigel, E. Ger	3:43:08	
1987	Hartwig Gauder, E. Ger	3:40:53	
1991	Aleksandr Potashov, USSR	3:53:09	
1993	Jesus Angel Garcia, SPA	3:41:41	
1995	Valentin Kononen, FIN	3:43.42	
1997	Robert Korzeniowski, POL	3:44:46	
1999	Ivano Brugnetti, ITA	3:47:54	
2001	Robert Korzeniowski, POL	3:42:08	
2003	Robert Korzeniowski, POL	3:36:03	WR

* Original winner German Skurygin, RUS, was stripped of his 1999 title after testing positive for a banned substance.

High Jump

Year		Height	
1983	Gennedy Avdeyenko, USSR	7-7¼	
1987	Patrik Sjoberg, SWE	7-9¾	
1991	Charles Austin, USA	7-9¾	
1993	Javier Sotomayor, CUB	7-10½	CR
1995	Troy Kemp, BAH	7-9¼	
1997	Javier Sotomayor, CUB	7-9¼	
1999	Vyacheslav Voronin, RUS	7-9¼	
2001	Martin Buss, GER	7-8¾	
2003	Jacques Freitag, RSA	7-8½	

Pole Vault

Year		Height	
1983	Sergey Bubka, USSR	18-8¼	
1987	Sergey Bubka, USSR	19-2¼	
1991	Sergey Bubka, USSR	19-6¼	
1993	Sergey Bubka, UKR	19-8¼	
1995	Sergey Bubka, UKR	19-5	
1997	Sergey Bubka, UKR	19-8½	
1999	Maksim Tarasov, RUS	19-9	
2001	Dmitri Markov, AUS	19-10¼	CR
2003	Giuseppe Gibilisco, ITA	19-4¼	

Long Jump

Year		Distance	
1983	Carl Lewis, USA	28-0¾	
1987	Carl Lewis, USA	28-0¼	
1991	Mike Powell, USA	29-4½	WR
1993	Mike Powell, USA	28-2¼	
1995	Ivan Pedroso, CUB	28-6½	
1997	Ivan Pedroso, CUB	27-7½	
1999	Ivan Pedroso, CUB	28-1	
2001	Ivan Pedroso, CUB	27-6¾	
2003	Dwight Phillips, USA	27-3¾	

Triple Jump

Year		Distance	
1983	Zdzislaw Hoffmann, POL	57-2	
1987	Khristo Markov, BUL	58-9	
1991	Kenny Harrison, USA	58-4	
1993	Mike Conley, USA	58-7¼	
1995	Jonathan Edwards, GBR	60-0¼	WR
1997	Yoelvis Quesada, CUB	58-6¾	
1999	Charles Michael Friedek, GER	57-8½	
2001	Jonathan Edwards, GBR	58-9½	
2003	Christian Olsson, SWE	58-1¾	

Track & Field (Cont.)

Shot Put

Year		Distance	
1983	Edward Sarul, POL	.70- 2¼	
1987	Werner Günthör, SWI	.72-11¼	CR
1991	Werner Günthör, SWI	.71- 1¼	
1993	Werner Günthör, SWI	.72- 1	
1995	John Godina, USA	.70- 5¼	
1997	John Godina, USA	.70- 4¼	
1999	C.J. Hunter, USA	.71- 6	
2001	John Godina, USA	.71- 9	
2003	Andrei Mikhnevich, BLR	.71- 2	

Discus

Year		Distance	
1983	Imrich Bugar, CZE	.222- 2	
1987	Jurgen Schult, E. Ger	.225- 6	
1991	Lars Riedel, GER	.217- 2	
1993	Lars Riedel, GER	.222- 2	
1995	Lars Riedel, GER	.225- 7	
1997	Lars Riedel, GER	.224-10	
1999	Anthony Washington, USA	.226- 7	
2001	Lars Riedel, GER	.228- 9	
2003	Virgilijus Alekena, LTA	.228- 7	CR

Decathlon

Year		Points
1983	Daley Thompson, GBR	.8714
1987	Torsten Voss, E. Ger	.8680
1991	Dan O'Brien, USA	.8812
1993	Dan O'Brien, USA	.8817
1995	Dan O'Brien, USA	.8695

Hammer Throw

Year		Distance	
1983	Sergey Litvinov, USSR	.271- 3	
1987	Sergey Litvinov, USSR	.272- 6	
1991	Yuri Sedykh, USSR	.268- 0	
1993	Andrey Abduvaliyev, TAJ	.267-10	
1995	Andrey Abduvaliyev, TAJ	.267- 7	
1997	Heinz Weis, GER	.268- 4	
1999	Karsten Kobs, GER	.263- 3	
2001	Szymon Ziolkowski, POL	.273- 7	CR
2003	Ivan Tikhon, BLR	.272- 5	

Javelin

Year		Distance	
1983	Detlef Michel, E. Ger	.293-7	
1987	Seppo Raty, FIN	.274-1	
1991	Kimmo Kinnunen, FIN	.297-11	
1993	Jan Zelezny, CZR	.282-1	
1995	Jan Zelezny, CZR	.293-11	
1997	Marius Corbett, S. Afr.	.290-0	
1999	Aki Parviainen, FIN	.293-8	
2001	Jan Zelezny, CZR	.304- 5	CR
2003	Sergey Makarov, RUS	.280- 3	

Year		Points	
1997	Tomas Dvorak, CZR	.8837	
1999	Tomas Dvorak, CZR	.8744	
2001	Tomas Dvorak, CZR	.8902	CR
2003	Tom Pappas, USA	.8750	

WOMEN

Multiple gold medals (including relays): Gail Devers (5), Jearl Miles Clark, Jackie Joyner-Kersee and Marion Jones (4); Tatyana Samolenko Dorovskikh, Silke Gladisch, Marita Koch, Astrid Kumbernuss, Maria Mutola, Merlene Ottey, Gabriela Szabo and Gwen Torrence (3); Hassiba Boulmerka, Sabine Braun, Olga Bryzgina, Hestrie Cloete, Mary Decker, Stacy Dragila, Heike Daute Drechsler, Lyudmila Narozhilenko Enquist, Cathy Freeman, Chryste Gaines, Trine Hattestad, Inger Miller, Martina Optiz Hellmann, Stefka Kostadinova, Katrin Krabbe, Jarmila Kratochvilova, Tatyana Lebedeva, Mirela Manjani, Fiona May, Yipsi Moreno, Marie-José Pérec, Zhanna Pintusevich-Block, Ana Quirot and Huang Zhihong (2).

100 Meters

Year		Time	
1983	Marlies Gohr, E. Ger	.10.97	
1987	Silke Gladisch, E. Ger	.10.90	
1991	Katrin Krabbe, GER	.10.99	
1993	Gail Devers, USA	.10.81	CR
1995	Gwen Torrence, USA	.10.85	
1997	Marion Jones, USA	.10.83	
1999	Marion Jones, USA	.10.70	CR
2001	Zhanna Pintusevich-Block, UKR	.10.82	
2003	Torri Edwards, USA	.10.93*	

*Original winner Kelli White, USA, was stripped of her medal.

200 Meters

Year		Time	
1983	Marita Koch, E. Ger	.22.13	
1987	Silke Gladisch, E. Ger	.21.74	CR
1991	Katrin Krabbe, GER	.22.09	
1993	Merlene Ottey, JAM	.21.98	
1995	Merlene Ottey, JAM	.22.12	
1997	Zhanna Pintusevich, UKR	.22.32	
1999	Inger Miller, USA	.21.77	
2001	Marion Jones, USA	.22.39	
2003	Anastasiya Kapachinskaya, RUS	.22.38*	

*Original winner Kelli White, USA, was stripped of her medal.

400 Meters

Year		Time	
1983	Jarmila Kratochvilova, CZE	.47.99	WR
1987	Olga Bryzgina, USSR	.49.38	
1991	Marie-José Pérec, FRA	.49.13	
1993	Jearl Miles, USA	.49.82	
1995	Marie-José Pérec, FRA	.49.28	
1997	Cathy Freeman, AUS	.49.77	
1999	Cathy Freeman, AUS	.49.67	
2001	Amy Mbacke Thiam, SEN	.49.86	
2003	Ana Guevara, MEX	.48.89	

800 Meters

Year		Time	
1983	Jarmila Kratochvilova, CZE	1:54.68	CR
1987	Sigrun Wodars, E. Ger	1:55.26	
1991	Lilia Nurutdinova, USSR	1:57.50	
1993	Maria Mutola, MOZ	1:55.43	
1995	Ana Quirot, CUB	1:56.11	
1997	Ana Quirot, CUB	1:57.14	
1999	Ludmila Formanova, CZR	1:56.68	
2001	Maria Mutola, MOZ	1:57.17	
2003	Maria Mutola, MOZ	1:59.89	

1500 Meters

Year		Time	
1983	Mary Decker, USA	4:00.90	
1987	Tatiana Samolenko, USSR	3:58.56	
1991	Hassiba Boulmerka, ALG	4:02.21	
1993	Liu Dong, CHN	4:00.50	
1995	Hassiba Boulmerka, ALG	4:02.42	
1997	Carla Sacramento, POR	4:04.24	
1999	Svetlana Masterkova, RUS	3:59.53	
2001	Gabriela Szabo, ROM	4:00.57	
2003	Tatyana Tomashova, RUS	3:58.52	CR

5000 Meters

Held as 3000-meter race from 1983-93

Year		Time	
1983	Mary Decker, USA	8:34.62	
1987	Tatyana Samolenko, USSR	8:38.73	
1991	T. Samolenko Dorovskikh, USSR	8:35.82	
1993	Qu Yunxia, CHN	8:28.71	
1995	Sonia O'Sullivan, IRL	14:46.47	
1997	Gabriela Szabo, ROM	14:57.68	
1999	Gabriela Szabo, ROM	14:41.82	CR
2001	Olga Yegorova, RUS	15:03.39	
2003	Tirunesh Dibaba, ETH	14:51.72	

10,000 Meters

Year		Time
1983	Not held	
1987	Ingrid Kristiansen, NOR	31:05.85
1991	Liz McColgan, GBR	31:14.31
1993	Wang Junxia, CHN	30:49.30
1995	Fernanda Ribeiro, POR	31:04.99
1997	Sally Barsosio, KEN	31:32.92
1999	Gete Wami, ETH	30:24.56
2001	Derartu Tulu, ETH	31:48.81
2003	Berhane Adere, ETH	30:04.18 CR

Marathon

Year		Time
1983	Grete Waitz, NOR	2:28:09
1987	Rose Mota, POR	2:25:17
1991	Wanda Panfil, POL	2:29:53
1993	Junko Asari, JPN	2:30:03
1995	Manuela Machado, POR	2:25:39
1997	Hiromi Suzuki, JPN	2:29:48
1999	Jong Song-Ok, N. Kor	2:26:59
2001	Lidia Simon, ROM	2:26:01
2003	Catherine Ndereba, KEN	2:23:55 CR

100-Meter Hurdles

Year		Time
1983	Bettine Jahn, E. Ger	12.35ʷ
1987	Ginka Zagorcheva, BUL	12.34 CR
1991	Lyudmila Narozhilenko, USSR	12.59
1993	Gail Devers, USA	12.46
1995	Gail Devers, USA	12.68
1997	Ludmila Enquist, SWE	12.50
1999	Gail Devers, USA	12.37
2001	Anjanette Kirkland, USA	12.42
2003	Perdita Felicien, CAN	12.53

ʷ indicates wind-aided.

400-Meter Hurdles

Year		Time
1983	Yekaterina Fesenko, USSR	54.14
1987	Sabine Busch, E. Ger	53.62
1991	Tatiana Ledovskaya, USSR	53.11
1993	Sally Gunnell, GBR	52.74 WR
1995	Kim Batten, USA	52.61 WR
1997	Nezha Bidouane, MOR	52.97
1999	Daima Pernia, CUB	52.89
2001	Nezha Bidouane, MOR	53.34
2003	Jana Pittman, AUS	53.22

4 x 100-Meter Relay

Year		Time
1983	East Germany	41.76
1987	United States	41.58
1991	Jamaica	41.94
1993	Russia	41.49
1995	United States	42.12
1997	United States	41.47 CR
1999	Bahamas	41.92
2001	Germany	42.32*
2003	France	41.78

*The United States was stripped of its 2001 gold after lead runner Kelli White tested positive for a stimulant. As a result, Chryste Gaines, Inger Miller and Marion Jones also lost their gold.

4 x 400-Meter Relay

Year		Time
1983	East Germany	3:19.73
1987	East Germany	3:18.63
1991	Soviet Union	3:18.43
1993	United States	3:16.71 CR
1995	United States	3:22.39
1997	Germany	3:20.92
1999	Russia	3:21.98
2001	Jamaica	3:20.65
2003	United States	3:22.63

20-Kilometer Walk

Held as 10-Kilometer race from 1987-97

Year		Time
1983	Not held	
1987	Irina Strakhova, USSR	44:12
1991	Alina Ivanova, USSR	42:57
1993	Sari Essayah, FIN	42:59
1995	Irina Stankina, RUS	42:13
1997	Anna Sidoti, ITA	42:55
1999	Hongyu Liu, CHN	1:30:50
2001	Olimpiada Ivanova, RUS	1:27:48
2003	Yelena Nikolayeva, RUS	1:26:52 CR

High Jump

Year		Height
1983	Tamara Bykova, USSR	6- 7
1987	Stefka Kostadinova, BUL	6-10¼ WR
1991	Heike Henkel, GER	6- 8¾
1993	Ioamnet Quintero, CUB	6- 6¼
1995	Stefka Kostadinova, BUL	6- 7
1997	Hanne Haugland, NOR	6- 6¼
1999	Inga Babakova, UKR	6- 6¼
2001	Hestrie Cloete, RSA	6- 6¾
2003	Hestrie Cloete, RSA	6- 9

Pole Vault

Year		Height
1999	Stacy Dragila, USA	15- 1
2001	Stacy Dragila, USA	15- 7 CR
2003	Svetlana Feofanova, RUS	15- 7 CR

Long Jump

Year		Distance
1983	Heike Daute, E. Ger	23-10¼ʷ
1987	Jackie Joyner-Kersee, USA	24- 1¾ CR
1991	Jackie Joyner-Kersee, USA	24- 0¼
1993	Heike Drechsler, GER	23- 4
1995	Fiona May, ITA	22-10¾ʷ
1997	Lyudmila Galkina, RUS	23- 1¾
1999	Niurka Montalvo, SPA	23- 2
2001	Fiona May, ITA	23- 0½
2003	Eunice Barber, FRA	22-11¼

ʷ indicates wind-aided.

Triple Jump

Year		Distance
1993	Ana Biryukova, RUS	46- 6¼ WR
1995	Inessa Kravets, UKR	50- 10¾ WR
1997	Sarka Kasparkova, CZR	49- 10½
1999	Paraskevi Tsiamita, GRE	48- 10
2001	Tatyana Lebedeva, RUS	50- 0½
2003	Tatyana Lebedeva, RUS	49- 9¾

Shot Put

Year		Distance
1983	Helena Fibingerova, CZE	69- 0
1987	Natalia Lisovskaya, USSR	69- 8 CR
1991	Huang Zhihong, CHN	68- 4
1993	Huang Zhihong, CHN	67- 6
1995	Astrid Kumbernuss, GER	69- 7½
1997	Astrid Kumbernuss, GER	67- 11½
1999	Astrid Kumbernuss, GER	65- 1½
2001	Yanina Korolchik, BLR	67- 7½
2003	Svetlana Krivelyova, RUS	67- 8¼

Discus

Year		Distance
1983	Martina Opitz, E. Ger	226- 2
1987	Martina Opitz Hellmann, E. Ger	235- 0 CR
1991	Tsvetanka Khristova, BUL	233- 0
1993	Olga Burova, RUS	221- 1
1995	Ellina Zvereva, BLR	225- 2
1997	Beatrice Faumuina, NZE	219- 3
1999	Franka Dietzsch, GER	223- 6
2001	Natalya Sadova, RUS	224-11
2003	Irina Yatchenko, BLR	220-10

Track & Field (Cont.)

Hammer Throw

Year		Distance	
1999	Mihaela Melinte, ROM	246-8¾	CR
2001	Yipsi Moreno, CUB	231-9	
2003	Yipsi Moreno, CUB	240-7	

Javelin

Year		Distance	
1983	Tiina Lillak, FIN	232-4	
1987	Fatima Whitbread, GBR	251-5	CR
1991	Xu Demei, CHN	225-8	
1993	Trine Hattestad, NOR	227-0	
1995	Natalya Shikolenko, BLR	221-8	
1997	Trine Hattestad, NOR	225-8	
1999	Mirela Manjani-Tzelili, GRE	220-1	
2001	Osleidys Menendez, CUB	228-1	CR
2003	Mirela Manjani, GRE	218-3	

Heptathlon

Year		Points	
1983	Ramona Neubert, E. Ger	6770	
1987	Jackie Joyner-Kersee, USA	7128	CR
1991	Sabine Braun, GER	6672	
1993	Jackie Joyner-Kersee, USA	6837	
1995	Ghada Shouaa, SYR	6651	
1997	Sabine Braun, GER	6739	
1999	Eunice Barber, FRA	6861	
2001	Yelena Prokhorova, RUS.	6694	
2003	Carolina Kluft, SWE	7001	

World Cross Country Championships

MEN

Multiple winners: John Ngugi and Paul Tergat (5); Kenenisa Bekele and Carlos Lopes (3); Mohammed Mourhit, Khalid Skah, William Sigei, John Treacy and Craig Virgin (2).

Year		Year		Year	
1973	Pekka Paivarinta, Finland	1984	Carlos Lopes, Portugal	1995	Paul Tergat, Kenya
1974	Eric DeBeck, Belgium	1985	Carlos Lopes, Portugal	1996	Paul Tergat, Kenya
1975	Ian Stewart, Scotland	1986	John Ngugi, Kenya	1997	Paul Tergat, Kenya
1976	Carlos Lopes, Portugal	1987	John Ngugi, Kenya	1998	Paul Tergat, Kenya
1977	Leon Schots, Belgium	1988	John Ngugi, Kenya	1999	Paul Tergat, Kenya
1978	John Treacy, Ireland	1989	John Ngugi, Kenya	2000	Mohammed Mourhit, Belgium
1979	John Treacy, Ireland	1990	Khalid Skah, Morocco	2001	Mohammed Mourhit, Belgium
1980	Craig Virgin, USA	1991	Khalid Skah, Morocco	2002	Kenenisa Bekele, Ethiopia
1981	Craig Virgin, USA	1992	John Ngugi, Kenya	2003	Kenenisa Bekele, Ethiopia
1982	Mohammed Kedir, Ethiopia	1993	William Sigei, Kenya	2004	Kenenisa Bekele, Ethiopia
1983	Bekele Debele, Ethiopia	1994	William Sigei, Kenya		

WOMEN

Multiple winners: Grete Waitz (5); Lynn Jennings and Derartu Tulu (3); Zola Budd, Paola Cacchi, Maricica Puica, Paula Radcliffe, Annette Sergent, Carmen Valero and Gete Wami (2).

Year		Year		Year	
1973	Paola Cacchi, Italy	1984	Maricica Puica, Romania	1995	Derartu Tulu, Ethiopia
1974	Paola Cacchi, Italy	1985	Zola Budd, England	1996	Gete Wami, Ethiopia
1975	Julie Brown, USA	1986	Zola Budd, England	1997	Derartu Tulu, Ethiopia
1976	Carmen Valero, Spain	1987	Annette Sergent, France	1998	Sonia O'Sullivan, Ireland
1977	Carmen Valero, Spain	1988	Ingrid Kristiansen, Norway	1999	Gete Wami, Ethiopia
1978	Grete Waitz, Norway	1989	Annette Sergent, France	2000	Derartu Tulu, Ethiopia
1979	Grete Waitz, Norway	1990	Lynn Jennings, USA	2001	Paula Radcliffe, Gr. Britain
1980	Grete Waitz, Norway	1991	Lynn Jennings, USA	2002	Paula Radcliffe, Gr. Britain
1981	Grete Waitz, Norway	1992	Lynn Jennings, USA	2003	Werknesh Kidane, Ethiopia
1982	Maricica Puica, Romania	1993	Albertina Dias, Portugal	2004	Benita Johnson, Australia
1983	Grete Waitz, Norway	1994	Helen Chepngeno, Kenya		

Marathons

Boston

America's oldest regularly contested foot race, the Boston Marathon is held on Patriots' Day every April. It has been run at four different distances: 24 miles, 1232 yards (1897-1923); 26 miles, 209 yards (1924-26); 26 miles, 385 yards (1927-52, since 1957); 25 miles, 958 yards (1953-56).

MEN

Multiple winners: Clarence DeMar (7); Gerard Cote and Bill Rodgers (4); Ibrahim Hussein, Cosmas Ndeti, Eino Oksanen and Leslie Pawson (3); Tarzan Brown, Jim Caffrey, John A. Kelley, John Miles, Toshihiko Seko, Geoff Smith, Moses Tanui and Aurele Vandendriessche (2).

Year		Time	Year		Time
1897	John McDermott, New York	2:55:10	1903	J.C. Lorden, Massachusetts	2:41:29
1898	Ronald McDonald, Massachusetts	2:42:00	1904	Mike Spring, New York	2:38:04
1899	Lawrence Brignolia, Massachusetts	2:54:38	1905	Fred Lorz, New York	2:38:25
1900	Jim Caffrey, Canada	2:39:44	1906	Tim Ford, Massachusetts	2:45:45
1901	Jim Caffrey, Canada	2:29:23	1907	Tom Longboat, Canada	2:24:24
1902	Sam Mellor, New York	2:43:12	1908	Tom Morrissey, New York	2:25:43
			1909	Henri Renaud, New Hampshire	2:53:36

Year		Time	Year		Time
1910	Fred Cameron, Nova Scotia	2:28:52	1958	Franjo Mihalic, Yugoslavia	2:25:54
1911	Clarence DeMar, Massachusetts	2:21:39	1959	Eino Oksanen, Finland	2:22:42
1912	Mike Ryan, Illinois	2:21:18			
1913	Fritz Carlson, Minnesota	2:25:14	1960	Paavo Kotila, Finland	2:20:54
1914	James Duffy, Canada	2:25:01	1961	Eino Oksanen, Finland	2:23:39
1915	Edouard Fabre, Canada	2:31:41	1962	Eino Oksanen, Finland	2:23:48
1916	Arthur Roth, Massachusetts	2:27:16	1963	Aurele Vandendriessche, Belgium	2:18:58
1917	Bill Kennedy, New York	2:28:37	1964	Aurele Vandendriessche, Belgium	2:19:59
1918	World War relay race		1965	Morio Shigematsu, Japan	2:16:33
1919	Carl Linder, Massachusetts	2:29:13	1966	Kenji Kimihara, Japan	2:17:11
			1967	David McKenzie, New Zealand	2:15:45
1920	Peter Trivoulidas, New York	2:29:31	1968	Amby Burfoot, Connecticut	2:22:17
1921	Frank Zuna, New Jersey	2:18:57	1969	Yoshiaki Unetani, Japan	2:13:49
1922	Clarence DeMar, Massachusetts	2:18:10			
1923	Clarence DeMar, Massachusetts	2:23:37	1970	Ron Hill, England	2:10:30
1924	Clarence DeMar, Massachusetts	2:29:40	1971	Alvaro Mejia, Colombia	2:18:45
1925	Charles Mellor, Illinois	2:33:00	1972	Olavi Suomalainen, Finland	2:15:39
1926	John Miles, Nova Scotia	2:25:40	1973	Jon Anderson, Oregon	2:16:03
1927	Clarence DeMar, Massachusetts	2:40:22	1974	Neil Cusack, Ireland	2:13:39
1928	Clarence DeMar, Massachusetts	2:37:07	1975	Bill Rodgers, Massachusetts	2:09:55
1929	John Miles, Nova Scotia	2:33:08	1976	Jack Fultz, Pennsylvania	2:20:19
			1977	Jerome Drayton, Canada	2:14:46
1930	Clarence DeMar, Massachusetts	2:34:48	1978	Bill Rodgers, Massachusetts	2:10:13
1931	James Henigan, Massachusetts	2:46:45	1979	Bill Rodgers, Massachusetts	2:09:27
1932	Paul deBruyn, Germany	2:33:36			
1933	Leslie Pawson, Rhode Island	2:31:01	1980	Bill Rodgers, Massachusetts	2:12:11
1934	Dave Komonen, Canada	2:32:53	1981	Toshihiko Seko, Japan	2:09:26
1935	John A. Kelley, Massachusetts	2:32:07	1982	Alberto Salazar, Oregon	2:08:52
1936	Ellison (Tarzan) Brown, Rhode Island	2:33:40	1983	Greg Meyer, New Jersey	2:09:00
1937	Walter Young, Canada	2:33:20	1984	Geoff Smith, England	2:10:34
1938	Leslie Pawson, Rhode Island	2:35:34	1985	Geoff Smith, England	2:14:05
1939	Ellison (Tarzan) Brown, Rhode Island	2:28:51	1986	Rob de Castella, Australia	2:07:51
			1987	Toshihiko Seko, Japan	2:11:50
1940	Gerard Cote, Canada	2:28:28	1988	Ibrahim Hussein, Kenya	2:08:43
1941	Leslie Pawson, Rhode Island	2:30:38	1989	Abebe Mekonnen, Ethiopia	2:09:06
1942	Joe Smith, Massachusetts	2:26:51			
1943	Gerard Cote, Canada	2:28:25	1990	Gelindo Bordin, Italy	2:08:19
1944	Gerard Cote, Canada	2:31:50	1991	Ibrahim Hussein, Kenya	2:11:06
1945	John A. Kelley, Massachusetts	2:30:40	1992	Ibrahim Hussein, Kenya	2:08:14
1946	Stylianos Kyriakides, Greece	2:29:27	1993	Cosmas Ndeti, Kenya	2:09:33
1947	Yun Bok Suh, Korea	2:25:39	1994	Cosmas Ndeti, Kenya	2:07:15*
1948	Gerard Cote, Canada	2:31:02	1995	Cosmas Ndeti, Kenya	2:09:22
1949	Karle Leandersson, Sweden	2:31:50	1996	Moses Tanui, Kenya	2:09:16
			1997	Lameck Aguta, Kenya	2:10:34
1950	Kee Yonh Ham, Korea	2:32:39	1998	Moses Tanui, Kenya	2:07:34
1951	Shigeki Tanaka, Japan	2:27:45	1999	Joseph Chebet, Kenya	2:09:52
1952	Doroteo Flores, Guatemala	2:31:53			
1953	Keizo Yamada, Japan	2:18:51	2000	Elijah Lagat, Kenya	2:09:47
1954	Veiko Karvonen, Finland	2:20:39	2001	Lee Bong-Ju, South Korea	2:09:43
1955	Hideo Hamamura, Japan	2:18:22	2002	Rodgers Rop, Kenya	2:09:02
1956	Antti Viskari, Finland	2:14:14	2003	Robert Kipoech Cheruiyot, Kenya	2:10:11
1957	John J. Kelley, Connecticut	2:20:05	2004	Timothy Cherigat, Kenya	2:10:37
				*Course record.	

WOMEN

Multiple winners: Rosa Mota, Catherine Ndereba, Uta Pippig and Fatuma Roba (3); Joan Benoit, Miki Gorman, Ingrid Kristiansen and Olga Markova (2).

Year		Time	Year		Time
1972	Nina Kuscsik, New York	3:08:58	1989	Ingrid Kristiansen, Norway	2:24:33
1973	Jacqueline Hansen, California	3:05:59	1990	Rosa Mota, Portugal	2:25:23
1974	Miki Gorman, California	2:47:11	1991	Wanda Panfil, Poland	2:24:18
1975	Liane Winter, West Germany	2:42:24	1992	Olga Markova, CIS	2:23:43
1976	Kim Merritt, Wisconsin	2:47:10	1993	Olga Markova, Russia	2:25:27
1977	Miki Gorman, California	2:48:33	1994	Uta Pippig, Germany	2:21:45
1978	Gayle Barron, Georgia	2:44:52	1995	Uta Pippig, Germany	2:25:11
1979	Joan Benoit, Maine	2:35:15	1996	Uta Pippig, Germany	2:27:12
1980	Jacqueline Gareau, Canada	2:34:28	1997	Fatuma Roba, Ethiopia	2:26:23
1981	Allison Roe, New Zealand	2:26:46	1998	Fatuma Roba, Ethiopia	2:23:21
1982	Charlotte Teske, West Germany	2:29:33	1999	Fatuma Roba, Ethiopia	2:23:25
1983	Joan Benoit, Maine	2:22:43	2000	Catherine Ndereba, Kenya	2:26:11
1984	Lorraine Moller, New Zealand	2:29:28	2001	Catherine Ndereba, Kenya	2:23:53
1985	Lisa Larsen Weidenbach, Mass	2:34:06	2002	Margaret Okayo, Kenya	2:20:43*
1986	Ingrid Kristiansen, Norway	2:24:55	2003	Svetlana Zakharova, Russia	2:25:20
1987	Rosa Mota, Portugal	2:25:21	2004	Catherine Ndereba, Kenya	2:24:27
1988	Rosa Mota, Portugal	2:24:30		*Course record.	

Track & Field (Cont.)
New York City

Started in 1970, the New York City Marathon is run in the fall, usually on the first Sunday in November. The route winds through all of the city's five boroughs and finishes in Central Park.

MEN

Multiple winners: Bill Rodgers (4); Alberto Salazar (3); Tom Fleming, John Kagwe, Orlando Pizzolato and German Silva (2).

Year		Time	Year		Time	Year		Time
1970	Gary Muhrcke, USA	2:31:38	1982	Alberto Salazar, USA	2:09:29	1994	German Silva, MEX	2:11:21
1971	Norman Higgins, USA	2:22:54	1983	Rod Dixon, NZE	2:08:59	1995	German Silva, MEX	2:11:00
1972	Sheldon Karlin, USA	2:27:52	1984	Orlando Pizzolato, ITA	2:14:53	1996	Giacomo Leone, ITA	2:09:54
1973	Tom Fleming, USA	2:21:54	1985	Orlando Pizzolato, ITA	2:11:34	1997	John Kagwe, KEN	2:08:12
1974	Norbert Sander, USA	2:26:30	1986	Gianni Poli, ITA	2:11:06	1998	John Kagwe, KEN	2:08:45
1975	Tom Fleming, USA	2:19:27	1987	Ibrahim Hussein, KEN	2:11:01	1999	Joseph Chebet, KEN	2:09:14
1976	Bill Rodgers, USA	2:10:09	1988	Steve Jones, WAL	2:08:20	2000	Abdelkhader El Mouaziz,	
1977	Bill Rodgers, USA	2:11:28	1989	Juma Ikangaa, TAN	2:08:01		MOR	2:10:08
1978	Bill Rodgers, USA	2:12:12	1990	Douglas Wakiihuri, KEN	2:12:39	2001	Tesfaye Jifar, ETH	2:07:43*
1979	Bill Rodgers, USA	2:11:42	1991	Salvador Garcia, MEX	2:09:28	2002	Rodgers Rop, KEN	2:08:07
1980	Alberto Salazar, USA	2:09:41	1992	Willie Mtolo, S. Afr.	2:09:29	2003	Martin Lel, KEN	2:10:30
1981	Alberto Salazar, USA	2:08:13	1993	Andres Espinosa, MEX	2:10:04	*Course record.		

WOMEN

Multiple winners: Grete Waitz (9); Miki Gorman, Nina Kuscsik, Margaret Okayo and Tegla Loroupe (2).

Year		Time	Year		Time	Year		Time
1970	No Finisher		1982	Grete Waitz, NOR	2:27:14	1994	Tegla Loroupe, KEN	2:27:37
1971	Beth Bonner, USA	2:55:22	1983	Grete Waitz, NOR	2:27:00	1995	Tegla Loroupe, KEN	2:28:06
1972	Nina Kuscsik, USA	3:08:41	1984	Grete Waitz, NOR	2:29:30	1996	Anuta Catuna, ROM	2:28:18
1973	Nina Kuscsik, USA	2:57:07	1985	Grete Waitz, NOR	2:28:34	1997	F. Rochat-Moser, SWI	2:28:43
1974	Katherine Switzer, USA	3:07:29	1986	Grete Waitz, NOR	2:28:06	1998	Franca Fiacconi, ITA	2:25:17
1975	Kim Merritt, USA	2:46:14	1987	Priscilla Welch, GBR	2:30:17	1999	Adriana Fernandez, MEX	2:25:06
1976	Miki Gorman, USA	2:39:11	1988	Grete Waitz, NOR	2:28:07	2000	Ludmila Petrova, RUS	2:25:45
1977	Miki Gorman, USA	2:43:10	1989	Ingrid Kristiansen, NOR	2:25:30	2001	Margaret Okayo, KEN	2:24:21
1978	Grete Waitz, NOR	2:32:30	1990	Wanda Panfil, POL	2:30:45	2002	Joyce Chepchumba, KEN	2:25:56
1979	Grete Waitz, NOR	2:27:33	1991	Liz McColgan, GBR	2:27:23	2003	Margaret Okayo, KEN	2:22:31*
1980	Grete Waitz, NOR	2:25:41	1992	Lisa Ondieki, AUS	2:24:40	*Course record.		
1981	Allison Roe, NZE	2:25:29	1993	Uta Pippig, GER	2:26:24			

Annual Awards
Track & Field News Athletes of the Year

Voted on by an international panel of track and field experts and presented since 1959 for men and 1974 for women.

MEN

Multiple winners: Hicham El Guerrouj and Carl Lewis (3); Sergey Bubka, Sebastian Coe, Haile Gebrselassie, Michael Johnson, Alberto Juantorena, Noureddine Morceli, Jim Ryun and Peter Snell (2).

Year		Event	Year		Event
1959	Martin Lauer, W. Germany	110H/Decathlon	1982	Carl Lewis, USA	100/200/Long Jump
1960	Rafer Johnson, USA	Decathlon	1983	Carl Lewis, USA	100/200/Long Jump
1961	Ralph Boston, USA	Long Jump/110 Hurdles	1984	Carl Lewis, USA	100/200/Long Jump
1962	Peter Snell, New Zealand	800/1500	1985	Said Aouita, Morocco	1500/5000
1963	C.K. Yang, Taiwan	Decathlon/Pole Vault	1986	Yuri Sedykh, USSR	Hammer Throw
1964	Peter Snell, New Zealand	800/1500	1987	Ben Johnson, Canada	100
1965	Ron Clarke, Australia	5000/10,000	1988	Sergey Bubka, USSR	Pole Vault
1966	Jim Ryun, USA	800/1500	1989	Roger Kingdom, USA	110 Hurdles
1967	Jim Ryun, USA	1500	1990	Michael Johnson, USA	200/400
1968	Bob Beamon, USA	Long Jump	1991	Sergey Bubka, USSR	Pole Vault
1969	Bill Toomey, USA	Decathlon	1992	Kevin Young, USA	400 Hurdles
1970	Randy Matson, USA	Shot Put	1993	Noureddine Morceli, Algeria	Mile/1500/3000
1971	Rod Milburn, USA	110 Hurdles	1994	Noureddine Morceli, Algeria	Mile/1500/3000
1972	Lasse Viren, Finland	5000/10,000	1995	Haile Gebrselassie, Ethiopia	5000/10,000
1973	Ben Jipcho, Kenya	1500/5000/Steeplechase	1996	Michael Johnson, USA	200/400
1974	Rick Wohlhuter, USA	800/1500	1997	Wilson Kipketer, Denmark	800
1975	John Walker, New Zealand	800/1500	1998	Haile Gebrselassie, Ethiopia	3000/5000/10,000
1976	Alberto Juantorena, Cuba	400/800	1999	Hicham El Guerrouj, Morocco	Mile/1500
1977	Alberto Juantorena, Cuba	400/800	2000	Virgilijus Alekna, Lithuania	Discus
1978	Henry Rono, Kenya	5000/10,000/Steeplechase	2001	Hicham El Guerrouj, Morocco	Mile/1500
1979	Sebastian Coe, Great Britain	800/1500	2002	Hicham El Guerrouj, Morocco	Mile/1500
1980	Edwin Moses, USA	400 Hurdles	2003	Felix Sanchez, Dominican Republic	400 Hurdles
1981	Sebastian Coe, Great Britain	800/1500			

WOMEN

Multiple winners: Marita Koch (4); Marion Jones and Jackie Joyner-Kersee (3); Evelyn Ashford (2).

Year		Event
1974	Irena Szewinska, Poland	100/200/400
1975	Faina Melnik, USSR	Shot Put/Discus
1976	Tatiana Kazankina, USSR	800/1500
1977	Rosemarie Ackermann, E. Germany	High Jump
1978	Marita Koch, E. Germany	100/200/400
1979	Marita Koch, E. Germany	100/200/400
1980	Ilona Briesenick, E. Germany	Shot Put
1981	Evelyn Ashford, USA	100/200
1982	Marita Koch, E. Germany	100/200/400
1983	Jarmila Kratochvilova, Czech	200/400/800
1984	Evelyn Ashford, USA	100
1985	Marita Koch, E. Germany	100/200/400
1986	Jackie Joyner-Kersee, USA	Heptathlon/Long Jump
1987	Jackie Joyner-Kersee, USA	100H/Heptathlon/LJ
1988	Florence Griffith Joyner, USA	100/200
1989	Ana Quirot, Cuba	400/800
1990	Merlene Ottey, Jamaica	100/200
1991	Heike Henkel, Germany	High Jump
1992	Heike Drechsler, Germany	Long Jump
1993	Wang Junxia, China	1500/3000/10,000
1994	Jackie Joyner-Kersee, USA	100H/Heptathlon/LJ
1995	Sonia O'Sullivan, Ireland	1500/3000/5000
1996	Svetlana Masterkova, Russia	800/1500
1997	Marion Jones, USA	100/200
1998	Marion Jones, USA	100/200/LJ
1999	Gabriela Szabo, Romania	3000/5000
2000	Marion Jones, USA	100/200/LJ
2001	Stacy Dragila, USA	Pole Vault
2002	Paula Radcliffe, Gr. Britain	3000/5000/10k/Mar
2003	Maria Mutola, Mozambique	800

SWIMMING & DIVING

FINA World Championships

While the Summer Olympics have served as the unofficial world championships for swimming and diving throughout the centuries, a separate World Championship meet was started in 1973 by the Federation Internationale de Natation Amateur (FINA). The meet has varied between being held every two years, every three years or every four years. Currently it is held every two years. Sites have been Belgrade (1973); Cali, COL (1975); West Berlin (1978); Guayaquil, ECU (1982); Madrid (1986); Perth (1991 & 98); Rome (1994), Fukuoka, JPN (2001) and Barcelona (2003). Looking forward, the Championships will be held in Montreal (2005) and Melbourne (2007).

MEN

Most gold medals (including relays): Ian Thorpe (11); Grant Hackett and Jim Montgomery (7); Matt Biondi, Michael Klim and Aleksandr Popov (6); Rowdy Gaines (5); Joe Bottom, Tamas Darnyi, Michael Gross, Tom Jager, David McCagg, Aaron Peirsol, Michael Phelps, Vladimir Salnikov, Tim Shaw and Matt Welsh (4); Billy Forrester, Andras Hargitay, Roland Matthes, John Murphy, Jeff Rouse, Norbert Rozsa and David Wilkie (3).

50-Meter Freestyle

Year		Time	
1973-82	Not held		
1986	Tom Jager, USA	22.49	
1991	Tom Jager, USA	22.16	
1994	Aleksandr Popov, RUS	22.17	
1998	Bill Pilczuk, USA	22.29	
2001	Anthony Ervin, USA	22.09	
2003	Aleksandr Popov, RUS	21.92	**CR**

100-Meter Freestyle

Year		Time	
1973	Jim Montgomery, USA	51.70	
1975	Tim Shaw, USA	51.25	
1978	David McCagg, USA	50.24	
1982	Jorg Woithe, E. Ger	50.18	
1986	Matt Biondi, USA	48.94	
1991	Matt Biondi, USA	49.18	
1994	Aleksandr Popov, RUS	49.12	
1998	Aleksandr Popov, RUS	48.93	
2001	Anthony Ervin, USA	48.33	**CR**
2003	Aleksandr Popov, RUS	48.42	

200-Meter Freestyle

Year		Time	
1973	Jim Montgomery, USA	1:53.02	
1975	Tim Shaw, USA	1:52.04	
1978	Billy Forrester, USA	1:51.02	
1982	Michael Gross, W. Ger	1:49.84	
1986	Michael Gross, W. Ger	1:47.92	
1991	Giorgio Lamberti, ITA	1:47.27	
1994	Antti Kasvio, FIN	1:47.32	
1998	Michael Klim, AUS	1:47.41	
2001	Ian Thorpe, AUS	1:44.06	**WR**
2003	Ian Thorpe, AUS	1:45.14	

400-Meter Freestyle

Year		Time	
1973	Rick DeMont, USA	3:58.18	
1975	Tim Shaw, USA	3:54.88	
1978	Vladimir Salnikov, USSR	3:51.94	
1982	Vladimir Salnikov, USSR	3:51.30	
1986	Rainer Henkel, W. Ger	3:50.05	
1991	Jorg Hoffman, GER	3:48.04	
1994	Kieren Perkins, AUS	3:43.80	**WR**
1998	Ian Thorpe, AUS	3:46.29	
2001	Ian Thorpe, AUS	3:40.17	**WR**
2003	Ian Thorpe, AUS	3:42.58	

800-Meter Freestyle

Year		Time	
1973-98	Not held		
2001	Ian Thorpe, AUS	7:39.16	**WR**
2003	Grant Hackett, AUS	7:43.82	

1500-Meter Freestyle

Year		Time	
1973	Stephen Holland, AUS	15:31.85	
1975	Tim Shaw, USA	15:28.92	
1978	Vladimir Salnikov, USSR	15:03.99	
1982	Vladimir Salnikov, USSR	15:01.77	
1986	Rainer Henkel, W. Ger	15:05.31	
1991	Jorg Hoffman, GER	14:50.36	**WR**
1994	Kieren Perkins, AUS	14:50.52	
1998	Grant Hackett, AUS	14:51.70	
2001	Grant Hackett, AUS	14:34.56	**WR**
2003	Grant Hackett, AUS	14:43.14	

50-Meter Backstroke

Year		Time	
1973-98	Not held		
2001	Randall Bal, USA	25.34	
2003	Thomas Rupprath, GER	24.80	**WR**

Swimming & Diving (Cont.)

100-Meter Backstroke

Year		Time	
1973	Roland Matthes, E. Ger	.57.47	
1975	Roland Matthes, E. Ger	.58.15	
1978	Bob Jackson, USA	.56.36	
1982	Dirk Richter, E. Ger	.55.95	
1986	Igor Polianski, USSR	.55.58	
1991	Jeff Rouse, USA	.55.23	
1994	Martin Lopez-Zubero, SPA	.55.17	
1998	Lenny Krayzelburg, USA	.55.00	
2001	Matt Welsh, AUS	.54.31	
2003	Aaron Peirsol, USA	.53.61	**CR**

200-Meter Backstroke

Year		Time	
1973	Roland Matthes, E. Ger	2:01.87	
1975	Zoltan Varraszto, HUN	2:05.05	
1978	Jesse Vassallo, USA	2:02.16	
1982	Rick Carey, USA	2:00.82	
1986	Igor Polianski, USSR	1:58.78	
1991	Martin Zubero, SPA	1:59.52	
1994	Vladimir Selkov, RUS	1:57.42	
1998	Lenny Krayzelburg, USA	1:58.84	
2001	Aaron Peirsol, USA	1:57.13	
2003	Aaron Peirsol, USA	1:55.92	

50-Meter Breaststroke

Year		Time
1973-98	Not held	
2001	Oleg Lisogor, UKR	.27.52
2003	James Gibson, GBR	.27.56

100-Meter Breaststroke

Year		Time	
1973	John Hencken, USA	1:04.02	
1975	David Wilkie, GBR	1:04.26	
1978	Walter Kusch, W. Ger	1:03.56	
1982	Steve Lundquist, USA	1:02.75	
1986	Victor Davis, CAN	1:02.71	
1991	Norbert Rozsa, HUN	1:01.45	
1994	Norbert Rozsa, HUN	1:01.24	
1998	Frederik deBurghgraeve, BEL	1:01.34	
2001	Roman Sloudnov, RUS	1:00.16	
2003	Kosuke Kitajima, JPN	.59.78	**WR**

200-Meter Breaststroke

Year		Time	
1973	David Wilkie, GBR	2:19.28	
1975	David Wilkie, GBR	2:18.23	
1978	Nick Nevid, USA	2:18.37	
1982	Victor Davis, CAN	2:14.77	**WR**
1986	Jozsef Szabo, HUN	2:14.27	
1991	Mike Barrowman, USA	2:11.23	**WR**
1994	Norbert Rozsa, HUN	2:12.81	
1998	Kurt Grote, USA	2:13.40	
2001	Brendan Hansen, USA	2:10.69	
2003	Kosuke Kitajima, JPN	2:09.42	**WR**

50-Meter Butterfly

Year		Time	
1973-98	Not held		
2001	Geoff Huegill, AUS	.23.50	
2003	Matt Welsh, AUS	.23.43	**WR**

100-Meter Butterfly

Year		Time	
1973	Bruce Robertson, CAN	.55.69	
1975	Greg Jagenburg, USA	.55.63	
1978	Joe Bottom, USA	.54.30	
1982	Matt Gribble, USA	.53.88	
1986	Pablo Morales, USA	.53.54	
1991	Anthony Nesty, SUR	.53.29	
1994	Rafal Szukala, POL	.53.51	
1998	Michael Klim, AUS	.52.25	
2001	Lars Frolander, SWE	.52.10	
2003	Ian Crocker, USA	.50.98	**WR**

200-Meter Butterfly

Year		Time	
1973	Robin Backhaus, USA	2:03.32	
1975	Billy Forrester, USA	2:01.95	
1978	Mike Bruner, USA	1:59.38	
1982	Michael Gross, W. Ger	1:58.85	
1986	Michael Gross, W. Ger	1:56.53	
1991	Melvin Stewart, USA	1:55.69	**WR**
1994	Denis Pankratov, RUS	1:56.54	
1998	Denys Sylantyev, UKR	1:56.61	
2001	Michael Phelps, USA	1:54.58	**WR**
2003	Michael Phelps, USA	1:54.35	

200-Meter Individual Medley

Year		Time	
1973	Gunnar Larsson, SWE	2:08.36	
1975	Andras Hargitay, HUN	2:07.72	
1978	Graham Smith, CAN	2:03.65	**WR**
1982	Alexander Sidorenko, USSR	2:03.30	
1986	Tamás Darnyi, HUN	2:01.57	
1991	Tamás Darnyi, HUN	1:59.36	**WR**
1994	Janis Sievinen, FIN	1:58.16	**WR**
1998	Marcel Wouda, NET	2:01.18	
2001	Massimiliano Rosolino, ITA	1:59.71	
2003	Michael Phelps, USA	1:56.04	**WR**

400-Meter Individual Medley

Year		Time	
1973	Andras Hargitay, HUN	4:31.11	
1975	Andras Hargitay, HUN	4:32.57	
1978	Jesse Vassallo, USA	4:20.05	**WR**
1982	Ricardo Prado, BRA	4:19.78	**WR**
1986	Tamás Darnyi, HUN	4:18.98	
1991	Tamás Darnyi, HUN	4:12.36	**WR**
1994	Tom Dolan, USA	4:12.30	**WR**
1998	Tom Dolan, USA	4:14.95	
2001	Alessio Boggiatto, ITA	4:13.15	
2003	Michael Phelps, USA	4:09.09	**WR**

4 x 100-Meter Freestyle Relay

Year		Time	
1973	United States	3:27.18	
1975	United States	3:24.85	
1978	United States	3:19.74	
1982	United States	3:19.26	**WR**
1986	United States	3:19.98	
1991	United States	3:17.15	
1994	United States	3:16.90	
1998	United States	3:16.69	
2001	Australia	3:14.10	
2003	Russia	3:14.06	**WR**

4 x 200-Meter Freestyle Relay

Year		Time	
1973	United States	7:33.22	**WR**
1975	West Germany	7:39.44	
1978	United States	7:20.82	
1982	United States	7:21.09	
1986	East Germany	7:15.91	
1991	Germany	7:13.50	**CR**
1994	Sweden	7:17.34	
1998	Australia	7:12.48	
2001	Australia	7:04.66	**WR**
2003	Australia	7:08.58	

4 x 100-Meter Medley Relay

Year		Time	
1973	United States	3:49.49	
1975	United States	3:49.00	
1978	United States	3:44.63	
1982	United States	3:40.84	**WR**
1986	United States	3:41.25	
1991	United States	3:39.66	
1994	United States	3:37.74	
1998	Australia	3:37.98	
2001	Australia	3:35.35	
2003	United States	3:31.54	**WR**

WOMEN

Most gold medals (including relays): Kornelia Ender (8); Kristin Otto (7); Jenny Thompson (6); Inge De Bruijn, Hannah Stockbauer and Luo Xuejuan (5); Tracy Caulkins, Heike Friedrich, Le Jingyi, Jana Klochkova, Rosemarie Kother and Ulrike Richter (4); Hannalore Anke, Lu Bin, He Cihong, Janet Evans, Nicole Haislett, Lui Limin, Birgit Meineke, Joan Pennington, Manuela Stellmach, Petria Thomas, Amy Van Dyken, Renate Vogel and Cynthia Woodhead (3).

50-Meter Freestyle

Year		Time	
1973-82	Not held		
1986	Tamara Costache, ROM	.25.28	**WR**
1991	Zhuang Yong, CHN	.25.47	
1994	Le Jingyi, CHN	.24.51	**WR**
1998	Amy Van Dyken, USA	.25.15	
2001	Inge de Bruijn, NED	.24.47	
2003	Inge de Bruijn, NED	.24.47	

100-Meter Freestyle

Year		Time	
1973	Kornelia Ender, E. Ger	.57.54	
1975	Kornelia Ender, E. Ger	.56.50	
1978	Barbara Krause, E. Ger	.55.68	
1982	Birgit Meineke, E. Ger	.55.79	
1986	Kristin Otto, E. Ger	.55.05	
1991	Nicole Haislett, USA	.55.17	
1994	Le Jingyi, CHN	.54.01	**WR**
1998	Jenny Thompson, USA	.54.95	
2001	Inge de Bruijn, NED	.54.18	
2003	Hanna-Maria Seppala, FIN	.54.37	

200-Meter Freestyle

Year		Time	
1973	Keena Rothhammer, USA	2:04.99	
1975	Shirley Babashoff, USA	2:02.50	
1978	Cynthia Woodhead, USA	1:58.53	**WR**
1982	Annemarie Verstappen, NED	1:59.53	
1986	Heike Friedrich, E. Ger	1:58.26	
1991	Hayley Lewis, AUS	2:00.48	
1994	Franziska Van Almsick, GER	1:56.78	**WR**
1998	Claudia Poll, CRC	1:58.90	
2001	Giaan Rooney, AUS	1:58.57	
2003	Alena Popchenko, BLR	1:58.32	

400-Meter Freestyle

Year		Time	
1973	Heather Greenwood, USA	4:20.28	
1975	Shirley Babashoff, USA	4:22.70	
1978	Tracey Wickham, AUS	4:06.28	**WR**
1982	Carmela Schmidt. E. Ger	4:08.98	
1986	Heike Friedrich, E. Ger	4:07.45	
1991	Janet Evans, USA	4:08.63	
1994	Yang Aihua, CHN	4:09.64	
1998	Yan Chen, CHN	4:06.72	
2001	Yana Klochkova, UKR	4:07.30	
2003	Hannah Stockbauer, GER	4:06.75	

800-Meter Freestyle

Year		Time	
1973	Novella Calligaris, ITA	8:52.97	
1975	Jenny Turrall, AUS	8:44.75	
1978	Tracey Wickham, AUS	8:25.94	
1982	Kim Linehan, USA	8:27.48	
1986	Astrid Strauss, E. Ger	8:28.24	
1991	Janet Evans, USA	8:24.05	
1994	Janet Evans, USA	8:29.85	
1998	Brooke Bennett, USA	8:28.71	
2001	Hannah Stockbauer, GER	8:24.66	
2003	Hannah Stockbauer, GER	8:23.66	**CR**

1500-Meter Freestyle

Year		Time	
1973-98	Not held		
2001	Hannah Stockbauer, GER	16:01.02	
2003	Hannah Stockbauer, GER	16:00.18	**CR**

50-Meter Backstroke

Year		Time	
1973-98	Not held		
2001	Haley Cope, USA	.28.51	
2003	Nina Zhivanevskaya, ESP	.28.48	**CR**

100-Meter Backstroke

Year		Time	
1973	Ulrike Richter, E. Ger	1:05.42	
1975	Ulrike Richter, E. Ger	1:03.30	
1978	Linda Jezek, USA	1:02.55	
1982	Kristin Otto, E. Ger	1:01.30	
1986	Betsy Mitchell, USA	1:01.74	
1991	Krisztina Egerszegi, HUN	1:01.78	
1994	He Cihong, CHN	1:00.57	**WR**
1998	Lea Maurer, USA	1:01.16	
2001	Natalie Coughlin, USA	1:00.37	
2003	Antje Buschschulte, GER	1:00.50	

200-Meter Backstroke

Year		Time	
1973	Melissa Belote, USA	2:20.52	
1975	Birgit Treiber, E. Ger	2:15.46	**WR**
1978	Linda Jezek, USA	2:11.93	**WR**
1982	Cornelia Sirch, E. Ger	2:09.91	**WR**
1986	Cornelia Sirch, E. Ger	2:11.37	
1991	Krisztina Egerszegi, HUN	2:09.15	
1994	He Cihong, CHN	2:07.40	
1998	Roxana Maracineanu, FRA	2:11.26	
2001	Diana Iuliana Mocanu, ROM	2:09.94	
2003	Katy Sexton, GBR	2:08.74	

50-Meter Breaststroke

Year		Time	
1973-82	Not held		
2001	Luo Xuejuan, CHN	.30.84	
2003	Luo Xuejuan, CHN	.30.67	

100-Meter Breaststroke

Year		Time	
1973	Renate Vogel, E. Ger	1:13.74	
1975	Hannalore Anke, E. Ger	1:12.72	
1978	Julia Bogdanova, USSR	1:10.31	**WR**
1982	Ute Geweniger, E. Ger	1:09.14	
1986	Sylvia Gerasch, E. Ger	1:08.11	**WR**
1991	Linley Frame, AUS	1:08.81	
1994	Samantha Riley, AUS	1:07.69	**WR**
1998	Kristy Kowal, USA	1:08.42	
2001	Luo Xuejuan, CHN	1:07.18	**CR**
2003	Luo Xuejuan, CHN	1:06.80	

200-Meter Breaststroke

Year		Time	
1973	Renate Vogel, E. Ger	2:40.01	
1975	Hannalore Anke, E. Ger	2:37.25	
1978	Lina Kachushite, USSR	2:31.42	**WR**
1982	Svetlana Varganova, USSR	2:28.82	
1986	Silke Hoerner, E. Ger	2:27.40	**WR**
1991	Elena Volkova, USSR	2:29.53	
1994	Samantha Riley, AUS	2:26.87	
1998	Agnes Kovacs, HUN	2:25.45	
2001	Agnes Kovacs, HUN	2:24.90	
2003	Amanda Beard, USA	2:22.99	**WR**

50-Meter Butterfly

Year		Time	
1973-98	Not held		
2001	Inge de Bruijn, NED	.25.90	
2003	Inge de Bruijn, NED	.25.84	**CR**

Swimming & Diving (Cont.)

100-Meter Butterfly

Year		Time	
1973	Kornelia Ender, E. Ger	1:02.53	
1975	Kornelia Ender, E. Ger	1:01.24	WR
1978	Joan Pennington, USA	1:00.20	
1982	Mary T. Meagher, USA	.59.41	
1986	Kornelia Gressler, E. Ger	.59.51	
1991	Qian Hong, CHN	.59.68	
1994	Liu Limin, CHN	.58.98	
1998	Jenny Thompson, USA	.58.46	
2001	Petria Thomas, AUS	.58.27	
2003	Jenny Thompson, USA	.57.96	

200-Meter Butterfly

Year		Time	
1973	Rosemarie Kother, E. Ger	2:13.76	
1975	Rosemarie Kother, E. Ger	2:15.92	
1978	Tracy Caulkins, USA	2:09.78	WR
1982	Ines Geissler, E. Ger	2:08.66	
1986	Mary T. Meagher, USA	2:08.41	
1991	Summer Sanders, USA	2:09.24	
1994	Liu Limin, CHN	2:07.25	CR
1998	Susie O'Neill, AUS	2:07.93	
2001	Petria Thomas, AUS	2:06.73	CR
2003	Otylia Jedrzejczak, POL	2:07.56	

200-Meter Individual Medley

Year		Time	
1973	Andre Huebner, E. Ger	2:20.51	
1975	Kathy Heddy, USA	2:19.80	
1978	Tracy Caulkins, USA	2:19.80	WR
1982	Petra Schneider, E. Ger	2:11.79	
1986	Kristin Otto, E. Ger	2:15.56	
1991	Lin Li, CHN	2:13.40	
1994	Lu Bin, CHN	2:12.34	
1998	Yanyan Wu, CHN	2:10.88	
2001	Maggie Bowen, USA	2:11.93	
2003	Yana Klochkova, UKR	2:10.75	

400-Meter Individual Medley

Year		Time	
1973	Gudrun Wegner, E. Ger	4:57.71	
1975	Ulrike Tauber, E. Ger	4:52.76	
1978	Tracy Caulkins, USA	4:40.83	WR
1982	Petra Schneider, E. Ger	4:36.10	WR
1986	Kathleen Nord, E. Ger	4:43.75	
1991	Lin Li, CHN	4:41.45	
1994	Dai Guohong, CHN	4:39.14	
1998	Yan Chen, CHN	4:36.66	
2001	Yana Klochkova, UKR	4:36.98	
2003	Yana Klochkova, UKR	4:36.74	

4 x 100-Meter Freestyle Relay

Year		Time	
1973	East Germany	3:52.45	
1975	East Germany	3:49.37	
1978	United States	3:43.43	WR
1982	East Germany	3:43.97	
1986	East Germany	3:40.57	
1991	United States	3:43.26	
1994	China	3:37.91	WR
1998	United States	3:42.11	
2001	Germany	3:39.58	
2003	United States	3:38.09	

4 x 200-Meter Freestyle Relay

Year		Time	
1973-82 Not held			
1986	East Germany	7:59.33	WR
1991	Germany	8:02.56	
1994	China	7:57.96	
1998	Germany	8:01.46	
2001	Great Britain	7:58.69	
2003	United States	7:55.70	CR

4 x 100-Meter Medley Relay

Year		Time		Year		Time	
1973	East Germany	4:16.84		1991	United States	4:06.51	
1975	East Germany	4:14.74		1994	China	4:01.67	CR
1978	United States	4:08.21		1998	United States	4:01.93	
1982	East Germany	4:05.80	WR	2001	Australia	4:01.50	CR
1986	East Germany	4:04.82		2003	China	3:59.89	CR

Diving

Multiple Gold Medals: MEN–Greg Louganis and Dmitri Sautin (5); Phil Boggs (3); Klaus Dibiasi, Tian Liang and Yu Zhuocheng (2). WOMEN–Guo Jingjing (4); Irina Kalinina and Gao Min (3); Irina Lashko, Fu Mingxia and Wu Mingxia (2).

MEN

1-Meter Springboard

Year		Pts
1973-86 Not Held		
1991	Edwin Jongejans, NED	588.51
1994	Evan Stewart, ZIM	382.14
1998	Yu Zhuocheng, CHN	417.54
2001	Wang Feng, CHN	444.03
2003	Xu Xiang, CHN	431.94

3-Meter Springboard

Year		Pts
1973	Phil Boggs, USA	618.57
1975	Phil Boggs, USA	597.12
1978	Phil Boggs, USA	913.95
1982	Greg Louganis, USA	752.67
1986	Greg Louganis, USA	750.06
1991	Kent Ferguson, USA	650.25
1994	Yu Zhuocheng, CHN	655.44

Year		Pts
1998	Dmitri Sautin, RUS	746.79
2001	Dmitri Sautin, RUS	725.82
2003	Alexander Dobroskok, RUS	788.37

Platform

Year		Pts
1973	Klaus Dibiasi, ITA	559.53
1975	Klaus Dibiasi, ITA	547.98
1978	Greg Louganis, USA	844.11
1982	Greg Louganis, USA	634.26
1986	Greg Louganis, USA	668.58
1991	Sun Shuwei, CHN	626.79
1994	Dmitri Sautin, RUS	634.71
1998	Dmitri Sautin, RUS	750.99
2001	Tian Liang, CHN	688.77
2003	Alexandre Despatie, CAN	716.91

3-Meter Synchronized

Year		Pts
1973-98	Not held	
2001	Peng Bo & Wang Kenan, CHN	342.63
2003	Alexander Dobroskok & Dmitri Sautin, RUS	369.18

10-Meter Synchronized

Year		Pts
1973-98	Not held	
2001	Tian Liang & Hu Jia, CHN	361.41
2003	Mathew Helm & Robert Newbery, AUS	384.60

WOMEN

1-Meter Springboard

Year		Pts
1973-86	Not held	
1991	Gao Min, CHN	478.26
1994	Chen Lixia, CHN	279.30
1998	Irina Lashko, RUS	296.07
2001	Blythe Hartley, CAN	300.81
2003	Irina Lashko, AUS	299.97

3-Meter Springboard

Year		Pts
1973	Christa Koehler, E. Ger	442.17
1975	Irina Kalinina, USSR	489.81
1978	Irina Kalinina, USSR	691.43
1982	Megan Neyer, USA	501.03
1986	Gao Min, CHN	582.90
1991	Gao Min, CHN	539.01
1994	Tan Shuping, CHN	548.49
1998	Yulia Pakhalina, RUS	544.52
2001	Guo Jingjing, CHN	596.67
2003	Guo Jingjing, CHN	617.94

Platform

Year		Pts
1973	Ulrike Knape, SWE	406.77
1975	Janet Ely, USA	403.89

Year		Pts
1978	Irina Kalinina, USSR	412.71
1982	Wendy Wyland, USA	438.79
1986	Chen Lin, CHN	449.67
1991	Fu Mingxia, CHN	426.51
1994	Fu Mingxia, CHN	434.04
1998	Olena Zhupyna	550.41
2001	Xu Mian, CHN	532.65
2003	Emilie Heymans, CAN	597.45

3-Meter Synchronized

Year		Pts
1973-98	Not held	
2001	Wu Minxia & Guo Jingjing, CHN	347.31
2003	Wu Minxia & Guo Jingjing, CHN	357.30

10-Meter Synchronized

Year		Pts
1973-98	Not held	
2001	Duan Qing & Sang Xue, CHN	329.94
2003	Lao Lishi & Li Ting, CHN	344.58

ALPINE SKIING

World Cup Overall Champions

World Cup Overall Champions (downhill and slalom events combined) since the tour was organized in 1967.

MEN

Multiple winners: Marc Girardelli (5); Hermann Maier, Gustavo Thoeni and Pirmin Zurbriggen (4); Phil Mahre and Ingemar Stenmark (3); Stephan Eberharter, Jean-Claude Killy, Lasse Kjus and Karl Schranz (2).

Year		Year		Year	
1967	Jean-Claude Killy, France	1980	Andreas Wenzel, Liechtenstein	1993	Marc Girardelli, Luxembourg
1968	Jean-Claude Killy, France	1981	Phil Mahre, USA	1994	Kjetil Andre Aamodt, Norway
1969	Karl Schranz, Austria	1982	Phil Mahre, USA	1995	Alberto Tomba, Italy
1970	Karl Schranz, Austria	1983	Phil Mahre, USA	1996	Lasse Kjus, Norway
1971	Gustavo Thoeni, Italy	1984	Pirmin Zurbriggen, Switzerland	1997	Luc Alphand, France
1972	Gustavo Thoeni, Italy	1985	Marc Girardelli, Luxembourg	1998	Hermann Maier, Austria
1973	Gustavo Thoeni, Italy	1986	Marc Girardelli, Luxembourg	1999	Lasse Kjus, Norway
1974	Piero Gros, Italy	1987	Pirmin Zurbriggen, Switzerland	2000	Hermann Maier, Austria
1975	Gustavo Thoeni, Italy	1988	Pirmin Zurbriggen, Switzerland	2001	Hermann Maier, Austria
1976	Ingemar Stenmark, Sweden	1989	Marc Girardelli, Luxembourg	2002	Stephan Eberharter, Austria
1977	Ingemar Stenmark, Sweden	1990	Pirmin Zurbriggen, Switzerland	2003	Stephan Eberharter, Austria
1978	Ingemar Stenmark, Sweden	1991	Marc Girardelli, Luxembourg	2004	Hermann Maier, Austria
1979	Peter Luescher, Switzerland	1992	Paul Accola, Switzerland		

WOMEN

Multiple winners: Annemarie Moser-Proell (6); Petra Kronberger and Vreni Schneider (3); Janica Kostelic, Michela Figini, Nancy Greene, Erika Hess, Katja Seizinger, Maria Walliser and Hanni Wenzel (2).

Year		Year		Year	
1967	Nancy Greene, Canada	1980	Hanni Wenzel, Liechtenstein	1993	Anita Wachter, Austria
1968	Nancy Greene, Canada	1981	Marie-Therese Nadig, SWI	1994	Vreni Schneider, Switzerland
1969	Gertrud Gabi, Austria	1982	Erika Hess, Switzerland	1995	Vreni Schneider, Switzerland
1970	Michele Jacot, France	1983	Tamara McKinney, USA	1996	Katja Seizinger, Germany
1971	Annemarie Pröll, Austria	1984	Erika Hess, Switzerland	1997	Pernilla Wiberg, Sweden
1972	Annemarie Pröll, Austria	1985	Michela Figini, Switzerland	1998	Katja Seizinger, Germany
1973	Annemarie Pröll, Austria	1986	Maria Walliser, Switzerland	1999	Alexandra Meissnitzer, Austria
1974	Annemarie Pröll, Austria	1987	Maria Walliser, Switzerland	2000	Renate Goetschl, Austria
1975	Annemarie Moser-Pröll, Austria	1988	Michela Figini, Switzerland	2001	Janica Kostelic, Croatia
1976	Rosi Mittermaier, W. Germany	1989	Vreni Schneider, Switzerland	2002	Michaela Dorfmeister, Austria
1977	Lise-Marie Morerod, Switzerland	1990	Petra Kronberger, Austria	2003	Janica Kostelic, Croatia
1978	Hanni Wenzel, Liechtenstein	1991	Petra Kronberger, Austria	2004	Anja Paerson, Sweden
1979	Annemarie Moser-Pröll, Austria	1992	Petra Kronberger, Austria		

Alpine Skiing (Cont.)
World Cup Event Champions
World Cup Champions in each individual event since the tour was organized in 1967.
MEN
Downhill

Multiple winners: Franz Klammer (5); Luc Alphand, Stephan Eberharter, Franz Heinzer and Peter Muller (3); Roland Collumbin, Marc Girardelli, Helmut Hoflehner, Hermann Maier, Bernard Russi, Karl Schranz and Pirmin Zurbriggen (2).

Year		Year		Year	
1967	Jean-Claude Killy, France	1980	Peter Muller, Switzerland	1993	Franz Heinzer, Switzerland
1968	Gerhard Nenning, Austria	1981	Harti Weirather, Austria	1994	Marc Girardelli, Luxembourg
1969	Karl Schranz, Austria	1982	Steve Podborski, Canada	1995	Luc Alphand, France
1970	Karl Schranz, Austria		Peter Muller, Switzerland	1996	Luc Alphand, France
	Karl Cordin, Austria	1983	Franz Klammer, Austria	1997	Luc Alphand, France
1971	Bernard Russi, Switzerland	1984	Urs Raber, Switzerland	1998	Andreas Schifferer, Austria
1972	Bernard Russi, Switzerland	1985	Helmut Hoflehner, Austria	1999	Lasse Kjus, Norway
1973	Roland Collumbin, Switzerland	1986	Peter Wirnsberger, Austria	2000	Hermann Maier, Austria
1974	Roland Collumbin, Switzerland	1987	Pirmin Zurbriggen, Switzerland	2001	Hermann Maier, Austria
1975	Franz Klammer, Austria	1988	Pirmin Zurbriggen, Switzerland	2002	Stephan Eberharter, Austria
1976	Franz Klammer, Austria	1989	Marc Girardelli, Luxembourg	2003	Stephan Eberharter, Austria
1977	Franz Klammer, Austria	1990	Helmut Hoflehner, Austria	2004	Stephan Eberharter, Austria
1978	Franz Klammer, Austria	1991	Franz Heinzer, Switzerland		
1979	Peter Muller, Switzerland	1992	Franz Heinzer, Switzerland		

Slalom

Multiple winners: Ingemar Stenmark (8); Alberto Tomba (4); Jean-Noel Augert and Marc Girardelli (3); Armin Bittner, Thomas Sykora and Gustavo Thoeni (2).

Year		Year		Year	
1967	Jean-Claude Killy, France	1979	Ingemar Stenmark, Sweden	1992	Alberto Tomba, Italy
1968	Domeng Giovanoli, Switzerland	1980	Ingemar Stenmark, Sweden	1993	Tomas Fogdo, Sweden
1969	Jean-Noel Augert, France	1981	Ingemar Stenmark, Sweden	1994	Alberto Tomba, Italy
1970	Patrick Russel, France	1982	Phil Mahre, USA	1995	Alberto Tomba, Italy
	Alain Penz, France	1983	Ingemar Stenmark, Sweden	1996	Sebastien Amiez, France
1971	Jean-Noel Augert, France	1984	Marc Girardelli, Luxembourg	1997	Thomas Sykora, Austria
1972	Jean-Noel Augert, France	1985	Marc Girardelli, Luxembourg	1998	Thomas Sykora, Austria
1973	Gustavo Thoeni, Italy	1986	Rok Petrovic, Yugoslavia	1999	Thomas Stangassinger, Austria
1974	Gustavo Thoeni, Italy	1987	Bojan Krizaj, Yugoslavia	2000	Kjetil Andre Aamodt, Norway
1975	Ingemar Stenmark, Sweden	1988	Alberto Tomba, Italy	2001	Benjamin Raich, Austria
1976	Ingemar Stenmark, Sweden	1989	Armin Bittner, West Germany	2002	Ivica Kostelic, Croatia
1977	Ingemar Stenmark, Sweden	1990	Armin Bittner, West Germany	2003	Kalle Palander, Finland
1978	Ingemar Stenmark, Sweden	1991	Marc Girardelli, Luxembourg	2004	Rainer Schoenfelder, Austria

Giant Slalom

Multiple winners: Ingemar Stenmark (8); Michael von Gruenigen and Alberto Tomba (4); Hermann Maier and Pirmin Zurbriggen (3); Joel Gaspoz, Jean-Claude Killy, Phil Mahre and Gustavo Thoeni (2).

Year		Year		Year	
1967	Jean-Claude Killy, France	1980	Ingemar Stenmark, Sweden	1991	Alberto Tomba, Italy
1968	Jean-Claude Killy, France	1981	Ingemar Stenmark, Sweden	1992	Alberto Tomba, Italy
1969	Karl Schranz, Austria	1982	Phil Mahre, USA	1993	Kjetil Andre Aamodt, Norway
1970	Gustavo Thoeni, Italy	1983	Phil Mahre, USA	1994	Christian Mayer, Austria
1971	Patrick Russel, France	1984	Ingemar Stenmark, Sweden	1995	Alberto Tomba, Italy
1972	Gustavo Thoeni, Italy		Pirmin Zurbriggen, Switzerland	1996	Michael von Gruenigen, SWI
1973	Hans Hinterseer, Austria	1985	Marc Girardelli, Luxembourg	1997	Michael von Gruenigen, SWI
1974	Piero Gros, Italy	1986	Joel Gaspoz, Switzerland	1998	Hermann Maier, Austria
1975	Ingemar Stenmark, Sweden	1987	Joel Gaspoz, Switzerland	1999	Michael von Gruenigen, SWI
1976	Ingemar Stenmark, Sweden		Pirmin Zurbriggen, Switzerland	2000	Hermann Maier, Austria
1977	Heini Hemmi, Switzerland	1988	Alberto Tomba, Italy	2001	Hermann Maier, Austria
	Ingemar Stenmark, Sweden	1989	Pirmin Zurbriggen, Switzerland	2002	Frederic Covili, France
1978	Ingemar Stenmark, Sweden	1990	Ole-Cristian Furuseth, Norway	2003	Michael von Gruenigen, SWI
1979	Ingemar Stenmark, Sweden		Gunther Mader, Austria	2004	Bode Miller, USA

Super G

Multiple winners: Hermann Maier (5); Pirmin Zurbriggen (4); Stephan Eberharter (2).

Year		Year		Year	
1986	Markus Wasmeier, W. Ger.	1993	Kjetil Andre Aamodt, Norway	2000	Hermann Maier, Austria
1987	Pirmin Zurbriggen, Switzerland	1994	Jan Einar Thorsen, Norway	2001	Hermann Maier, Austria
1988	Pirmin Zurbriggen, Switzerland	1995	Peter Runggaldier, Italy	2002	Stephan Eberharter, Austria
1989	Pirmin Zurbriggen, Switzerland	1996	Atle Skaardal, Norway	2003	Stephan Eberharter, Austria
1990	Pirmin Zurbriggen, Switzerland	1997	Luc Alphand, France	2004	Hermann Maier, Austria
1991	Franz Heinzer, Switzerland	1998	Hermann Maier, Austria		
1992	Paul Accola, Switzerland	1999	Hermann Maier, Austria		

Combined

Multiple winners: Marc Girardelli and Andreas Wenzel (4); Kjetil Andre Aamodt and Phil Mahre (3); Bode Miller and Pirmin Zurbriggen (2).

Year		Year		Year	
1979	Andreas Wenzel, Liechtenstein	1987	Pirmin Zurbriggen, Switzerland	1995	Marc Girardelli, Luxembourg
1980	Andreas Wenzel, Liechtenstein	1988	Hubert Strolz, Austria	1996	Gunther Mader, Austria
1981	Phil Mahre, USA	1989	Marc Girardelli, Luxembourg	1997-99	Not awarded
1982	Phil Mahre, USA	1990	Pirmin Zurbriggen, Switzerland	2000	Kjetil Andre Aamodt, Norway
1983	Phil Mahre, USA	1991	Marc Girardelli, Luxembourg	2001	Lasse Kjus, Norway
1984	Andreas Wenzel, Liechtenstein	1992	Paul Accola, Switzerland	2002	Kjetil Andre Aamodt, Norway
1985	Andreas Wenzel, Liechtenstein	1993	Marc Girardelli, Luxembourg	2003	Bode Miller, USA
1986	Markus Wasmeier, W. Ger	1994	Kjetil Andre Aamodt, Norway	2004	Bode Miller, USA

WOMEN
Downhill

Multiple winners: Annemarie Moser-Pröll (7); Michela Figini and Katja Seizinger (4); Renate Goetschl (3); Isolde Kostner, Isabelle Mir, Marie-Therese Nadig, Picabo Street, Bridgitte Totschnig-Habersatter and Maria Walliser (2).

Year		Year		Year	
1967	Marielle Goitschel, France	1979	Annemarie Moser-Pröll, Austria	1992	Katja Seizinger, Germany
1968	Isabelle Mir, France	1980	Marie-Therese Nadig, SWI	1993	Katja Seizinger, Germany
	Olga Pall, Austria	1981	Marie-Therese Nadig, SWI	1994	Katja Seizinger, Germany
1969	Wiltrud Drexel, Austria	1982	Marie-Cecile Gros-Gaudenier, FRA	1995	Picabo Street, USA
1970	Isabelle Mir, France	1983	Doris De Agostini, Switzerland	1996	Picabo Street, USA
1971	Annemarie Pröll, Austria	1984	Maria Walliser, Switzerland	1997	Renate Goetschl, Austria
1972	Annemarie Pröll, Austria	1985	Michela Figini, Switzerland	1998	Katja Seizinger, Germany
1973	Annemarie Pröll, Austria	1986	Maria Walliser, Switzerland	1999	Renate Goetschl, Austria
1974	Annemarie Pröll, Austria	1987	Michela Figini, Switzerland	2000	Regina Haeusl, Germany
1975	Annemarie Moser-Pröll, Austria	1988	Michela Figini, Switzerland	2001	Isolde Kostner, Italy
1976	Bridgitte Totschnig-Habersatter, AUT	1989	Michela Figini, Switzerland	2002	Isolde Kostner, Italy
1977	Bridgitte Totschnig-Habersatter, AUT	1990	Katrin Gutensohn-Knopf, GER	2003	Michaela Dorfmeister, Austria
1978	Annemarie Moser-Pröll, Austria	1991	Chantal Bournissen, SWI	2004	Renate Goetschl, Austria

Slalom

Multiple winners: Vreni Schneider (6); Erika Hess (5); Janica Kostelic, Marielle Goitschel, Britt Lafforgue, Lisa-Marie Morerod and Roswitha Steiner (2).

Year		Year		Year	
1967	Marielle Goitschel, France	1981	Erika Hess, Switzerland	1993	Vreni Schneider, Switzerland
1968	Marielle Goitschel, France	1982	Erika Hess, Switzerland	1994	Vreni Schneider, Switzerland
1969	Gertrud Gabl, Austria	1983	Erika Hess, Switzerland	1995	Vreni Schneider, Switzerland
1970	Ingrid Lafforgue, France	1984	Tamara McKinney, USA	1996	Elfi Eder, Austria
1971	Britt Lafforgue, France	1985	Erika Hess, Switzerland	1997	Pernilla Wiberg, Sweden
1972	Britt Lafforgue, France	1986	Roswitha Steiner, Austria	1998	Ylva Nowen, Sweden
1973	Patricia Emonet, France		Erika Hess, Switzerland	1999	Sabine Egger, Austria
1974	Christa Zechmeister, W. Germany	1987	Corrine Schmidhauser,	2000	Spela Pretnar, Slovenia
1975	Lisa-Marie Morerod, Switzerland		Switzerland	2001	Janica Kostelic, Croatia
1976	Rosi Mittermaier, W. Germany	1988	Roswitha Steiner, Austria	2002	Laure Pequegnot, France
1977	Lisa-Marie Morerod, Switzerland	1989	Vreni Schneider, Switzerland	2003	Janica Kostelic, Croatia
1978	Hanni Wenzel, Liechtenstein	1990	Vreni Schneider, Switzerland	2004	Anja Paerson, Sweden
1979	Regina Sackl, Austria	1991	Petra Kronberger, Austria		
1980	Perrine Pelene, France	1992	Vreni Schneider, Switzerland		

Giant Slalom

Multiple winners: Vreni Schneider (5); Lisa-Marie Morerod and Annemarie Moser-Pröll (3); Martina Ertl, Nancy Greene, Carole Merle, Sonja Nef, Anja Paerson, Anita Wachter and Hanni Wenzel (2).

Year		Year		Year	
1967	Nancy Greene, Canada	1980	Hanni Wenzel, Liechtenstein	1992	Carole Merle, France
1968	Nancy Greene, Canada	1981	Marie-Therese Nadig, SWI	1993	Carole Merle, France
1969	Marilyn Cochran, USA	1982	Irene Epple, West Germany	1994	Anita Wachter, Austria
1970	Michele Jacot, France	1983	Tamara McKinney, USA	1995	Vreni Schneider, Switzerland
	Francoise Macchi, France	1984	Erika Hess, Switzerland	1996	Martina Ertl, Germany
1971	Annemarie Pröll, Austria	1985	Maria Keihl, West Germany	1997	Deborah Compagnoni, Italy
1972	Annemarie Pröll, Austria		Michela Figini, Switzerland	1998	Martina Ertl, Germany
1973	Monika Kaserer, Austria	1986	Vreni Schneider, Switzerland	1999	Alexandra Meissnitzer, Austria
1974	Hanni Wenzel, Liechtenstein	1987	Vreni Schneider, Switzerland	2000	Michaela Dorfmeister, Austria
1975	Annemarie Moser-Pröll, Austria		Maria Walliser, Switzerland	2001	Sonja Nef, Switzerland
1976	Lisa-Marie Morerod, SWI	1988	Mateja Svet, Yugoslavia	2002	Sonja Nef, Switzerland
1977	Lisa-Marie Morerod, SWI	1989	Vreni Schneider, Switzerland	2003	Anja Paerson, Sweden
1978	Lisa-Marie Morerod, SWI	1990	Anita Wachter, Austria	2004	Anja Paerson, Sweden
1979	Christa Kinshofer, W. Ger.	1991	Vreni Schneider, Switzerland		

Alpine Skiing (Cont.)

Super G

Multiple winners: Katja Seizinger (5); Carole Merle (4); Hilde Gerg and Renate Goetschl (2).

Year		Year		Year	
1986	Maria Kiehl, West Germany	1993	Katja Seizinger, Germany	2000	Renate Goetschl, Austria
1987	Maria Walliser, Switzerland	1994	Katja Seizinger, Germany	2001	Regine Cavagnoud, France
1988	Michela Figini, Switzerland	1995	Katja Seizinger, Germany	2002	Hilde Gerg, Germany
1989	Carole Merle, France	1996	Katja Seizinger, Germany	2003	Carole Montillet, France
1990	Carole Merle, France	1997	Hilde Gerg, Germany	2004	Renate Goetschl, Austria
1991	Carole Merle, France	1998	Katja Seizinger, Germany		
1992	Carole Merle, France	1999	Alexandra Meissnitzer, Austria		

Combined

Multiple winners: Brigitte Oertli (5); Anita Wachter and Hanni Wenzel (3); Sabine Ginther, Renate Goetschl, Janica Kostelic and Pernilla Wiberg (2).

Year		Year		Year	
1979	Annemarie Moser-Pröll, Austria	1986	Maria Walliser, Switzerland	1994	Pernilla Wiberg, Sweden
	Hanni Wenzel, Liechtenstein	1987	Brigitte Oertli, Switzerland	1995	Pernilla Wiberg, Sweden
1980	Hanni Wenzel, Liechtenstein	1988	Brigitte Oertli, Switzerland	1996	Anita Wachter, Austria
1981	Maria-Therese Nadig,	1989	Brigitte Oertli, Switzerland	1997–99	Not Awarded
	Switzerland	1989	Brigitte Oertli, Switzerland	2000	Renate Goetschl, Austria
1982	Irene Epple, West Germany	1990	Anita Wachter, Austria	2001	Janica Kostelic, Croatia
1983	Hanni Wenzel, Liechtenstein	1991	Sabine Ginther, Austria	2002	Renate Goetschl, Austria
1984	Erika Hess, Switzerland	1992	Sabine Ginther, Austria	2003	Janica Kostelic, Croatia
1985	Brigitte Oertli, Switzerland	1993	Anita Wachter, Austria	2004	Not Awarded

TOUR DE FRANCE

The world's premier cycling event, the Tour de France is staged throughout the country (sometimes passing through neighboring countries) over four weeks. The 1946 Tour, however, the first after World War II, was only a five-day race.

Multiple winners: Lance Armstrong (6); Jacques Anquetil, Bernard Hinault, Miguel Induráin and Eddy Merckx (5); Louison Bobet, Greg LeMond and Philippe Thys (3); Gino Bartali Ottavio Bottecchia, Fausto Coppi, Laurent Fignon, Nicholas Frantz, Firmin Lambot, André Leducq, Sylvere Maes, Antonin Magne, Lucien Petit-Breton and Bernard Thevenet (2):

Year		Year		Year	
1903	Maurice Garin, France	1938	Gino Bartali, Italy	1975	Bernard Thevenet, France
1904	Henri Cornet, France	1939	Sylvere Maes, Belgium	1976	Lucien van Impe, Belgium
1905	Louis Trousselier, France	1940-45	Not held	1977	Bernard Thevenet, France
1906	René Pottier, France	1946	Jean Lazarides, France	1978	Bernard Hinault, France
1907	Lucien Petit-Breton, France	1947	Jean Robic, France	1979	Bernard Hinault, France
1908	Lucien Petit-Breton, France	1948	Gino Bartali, Italy		
1909	Francois Faber, Luxembourg	1949	Fausto Coppi, Italy	1980	Joop Zoetemelk, Netherlands
1910	Octave Lapize, France	1950	Ferdinand Kubler, Switzerland	1981	Bernard Hinault, France
1911	Gustave Garrigou, France	1951	Hugo Koblet, Switzerland	1982	Bernard Hinault, France
1912	Odile Defraye, Belgium	1952	Fausto Coppi, Italy	1983	Laurent Fignon, France
1913	Philippe Thys, Belgium	1953	Louison Bobet, France	1984	Laurent Fignon, France
1914	Philippe Thys, Belgium	1954	Louison Bobet, France	1985	Bernard Hinault, France
1915-18	Not held	1955	Louison Bobet, France	1986	Greg LeMond, USA
1919	Firmin Lambot, Belgium	1956	Roger Walkowiak, France	1987	Stephen Roche, Ireland
1920	Philippe Thys, Belgium	1957	Jacques Anquetil, France	1988	Pedro Delgado, Spain
1921	Léon Scieur, Belgium	1958	Charly Gaul, Luxembourg	1989	Greg LeMond, USA
1922	Firmin Lambot, Belgium	1959	Federico Bahamontes, Spain	1990	Greg LeMond, USA
1923	Henri Pelissier, France	1960	Gastone Nencini, Italy	1991	Miguel Induráin, Spain
1924	Ottavio Bottecchia, Italy	1961	Jacques Anquetil, France	1992	Miguel Induráin, Spain
1925	Ottavio Bottecchia, Italy	1962	Jacques Anquetil, France	1993	Miguel Induráin, Spain
1926	Lucien Buysse, Belgium	1963	Jacques Anquetil, France	1994	Miguel Induráin, Spain
1927	Nicholas Frantz, Luxembourg	1964	Jacques Anquetil, France	1995	Miguel Induráin, Spain
1928	Nicholas Frantz, Luxembourg	1965	Felice Gimondi, Italy	1996	Bjarne Riis, Denmark
1929	Maurice Dewaele, Belgium	1966	Lucien Aimar, France	1997	Jan Ullrich, Germany
1930	André Leducq, France	1967	Roger Pingeon, France	1998	Marco Pantani, Italy
1931	Antonin Magne, France	1968	Jan Janssen, Netherlands	1999	Lance Armstrong, USA
1932	André Leducq, France	1969	Eddy Merckx, Belgium	2000	Lance Armstrong, USA
1933	Georges Speicher, France	1970	Eddy Merckx, Belgium	2001	Lance Armstrong, USA
1934	Antonin Magne, France	1971	Eddy Merckx, Belgium	2002	Lance Armstrong, USA
1935	Romain Maes, Belgium	1972	Eddy Merckx, Belgium	2003	Lance Armstrong, USA
1936	Sylvere Maes, Belgium	1973	Luis Ocana, Spain	2004	Lance Armstrong, USA
1937	Roger Lapebie, France	1974	Eddy Merckx, Belgium		

FIGURE SKATING
World Champions
Skaters who won World and Olympic championships in the same year are listed in **bold** type.

MEN

Multiple winners: Ulrich Salchow (10); Karl Schafer (7); Dick Button (5); Willy Bockl, Kurt Browning, Scott Hamilton and Hayes Jenkins and Alexei Yagudin (4); Emmerich Danzer, Gillis Grafstrom, Gustav Hugel, David Jenkins, Fritz Kachler, Ondrej Nepela, Evgeni Plushenko and Elvis Stojko (3); Brian Boitano, Gilbert Fuchs, Jan Hoffmann, Felix Kaspar, Vladimir Kovalev and Tim Wood (2).

Year		Year		Year	
1896	Gilbert Fuchs, Germany	1935	Karl Schafer, Austria	1973	Ondrej Nepela, Czechoslovakia
1897	Gustav Hugel, Austria	1936	**Karl Schafer**, Austria	1974	Jan Hoffmann, E. Germany
1898	Henning Grenander, Sweden	1937	Felix Kaspar, Austria	1975	Sergie Volkov, USSR
1899	Gustav Hugel, Austria	1938	Felix Kaspar, Austria	1976	**John Curry**, Britain
1900	Gustav Hugel, Austria	1939	Graham Sharp, Britain	1977	Vladimir Kovalev, USSR
1901	Ulrich Salchow, Sweden	1940-46	Not held	1978	Charles Tickner, USA
1902	Ulrich Salchow, Sweden	1947	Hans Gerschwiler, Switzerland	1979	Vladimir Kovalev, USSR
1903	Ulrich Salchow, Sweden	1948	**Dick Button**, USA	1980	Jan Hoffmann, E. Germany
1904	Ulrich Salchow, Sweden	1949	Dick Button, USA	1981	Scott Hamilton, USA
1905	Ulrich Salchow, Sweden	1950	Dick Button, USA	1982	Scott Hamilton, USA
1906	Gilbert Fuchs, Germany	1951	Dick Button, USA	1983	Scott Hamilton, USA
1907	Ulrich Salchow, Sweden	1952	**Dick Button**, USA	1984	**Scott Hamilton**, USA
1908	**Ulrich Salchow**, Sweden	1953	Hayes Jenkins, USA	1985	Alexander Fadeev, USSR
1909	Ulrich Salchow, Sweden	1954	Hayes Jenkins, USA	1986	Brian Boitano, USA
1910	Ulrich Salchow, Sweden	1955	Hayes Jenkins, USA	1987	Brian Orser, Canada
1911	Ulrich Salchow, Sweden	1956	**Hayes Jenkins**, USA	1988	**Brian Boitano**, USA
1912	Fritz Kachler, Austria	1957	David Jenkins, USA	1989	Kurt Browning, Canada
1913	Fritz Kachler, Austria	1958	David Jenkins, USA	1990	Kurt Browning, Canada
1914	Gosta Sandhal, Sweden	1959	David Jenkins, USA	1991	Kurt Browning, Canada
1915-21	Not held	1960	Alan Giletti, France	1992	**Viktor Petrenko**, CIS
1922	Gillis Grafstrom, Sweden	1961	Not held	1993	Kurt Browning, Canada
1923	Fritz Kachler, Austria	1962	Donald Jackson, Canada	1994	Elvis Stojko, Canada
1924	**Gillis Grafstrom,** Sweden	1963	Donald McPherson, Canada	1995	Elvis Stojko, Canada
1925	Willy Bockl, Austria	1964	**Manfred Schnelldorfer**,	1996	Todd Eldredge, USA
1926	Willy Bockl, Austria		W. Germany	1997	Elvis Stojko, Canada
1927	Willy Bockl, Austria	1965	Alain Calmat, France	1998	Alexei Yagudin, Russia
1928	Willy Bockl, Austria	1966	Emmerich Danzer, Austria	1999	Alexei Yagudin, Russia
1929	Gillis Grafstrom, Sweden	1967	Emmerich Danzer, Austria	2000	Alexei Yagudin, Russia
1930	Karl Schafer, Austria	1968	Emmerich Danzer, Austria	2001	Evgeni Plushenko, Russia
1931	Karl Schafer, Austria	1969	Tim Wood, USA	2002	**Alexei Yagudin**, Russia
1932	**Karl Schafer**, Austria	1970	Tim Wood, USA	2003	Evgeni Plushenko, Russia
1933	Karl Schafer, Austria	1971	Ondrej Nepela, Czechoslovakia	2004	Evgeni Plushenko, Russia
1934	Karl Schafer, Austria	1972	**Ondrej Nepela**, Czechoslovakia		

WOMEN

Multiple winners: Sonja Henie (10); Carol Heiss, Michelle Kwan and Herma Planck Szabo (5); Lily Kronberger and Katarina Witt (4); Sjoukje Dijkstra, Peggy Fleming and Meray Horvath (3); Tenley Albright, Linda Fratianne, Anett Poetzsch, Beatrix Schuba, Barbara Ann Scott, Gabriele Seyfert, Megan Taylor, Alena Vrzanova and Kristi Yamaguchi (2).

Year		Year		Year	
1906	Madge Syers, Britain	1932	**Sonja Henie**, Norway	1958	Carol Heiss, USA
1907	Madge Syers, Britain	1933	Sonja Henie, Norway	1959	Carol Heiss, USA
1908	Lily Kronberger, Hungary	1934	Sonja Henie, Norway	1960	**Carol Heiss**, USA
1909	Lily Kronberger, Hungary	1935	Sonja Henie, Norway	1961	Not held
1910	Lily Kronberger, Hungary	1936	**Sonja Henie**, Norway	1962	Sjoukje Dijkstra, Netherlands
1911	Lily Kronberger, Hungary	1937	Cecilia Colledge, Britain	1963	Sjoukje Dijkstra, Netherlands
1912	Meray Horvath, Hungary	1938	Megan Taylor, Britain	1964	**Sjoukje Dijkstra**, Netherlands
1913	Meray Horvath, Hungary	1939	Megan Taylor, Britain	1965	Petra Burka, Canada
1914	Meray Horvath, Hungary	1940-46	Not held	1966	Peggy Fleming, USA
1915-21	Not held	1947	Barbara Ann Scott, Canada	1967	Peggy Fleming, USA
1922	Herma Planck-Szabo, Austria	1948	**Barbara Ann Scott**, Canada	1968	**Peggy Fleming**, USA
1923	Herma Planck-Szabo, Austria	1949	Alena Vrzanova, Czechoslovakia	1969	Gabriele Seyfert, E. Germany
1924	**Herma Planck-Szabo**, AUT	1950	Alena Vrzanova, Czechoslovakia	1970	Gabriele Seyfert, E. Germany
1925	Herma Planck-Szabo, Austria	1951	Jeannette Altwegg, Britain	1971	Beatrix Schuba, Austria
1926	Herma Planck-Szabo, Austria	1952	Jacqueline Du Bief, France	1972	**Beatrix Schuba**, Austria
1927	Sonja Henie, Norway	1953	Tenley Albright, USA	1973	Karen Magnussen, Canada
1928	**Sonja Henie**, Norway	1954	Gundi Busch, W. Germany	1974	Christine Errath, E. Germany
1929	Sonja Henie, Norway	1955	Tenley Albright, USA	1975	Dianne DeLeeuw, Netherlands
1930	Sonja Henie, Norway	1956	Carol Heiss, USA	1976	**Dorothy Hamill**, USA
1931	Sonja Henie, Norway	1957	Carol Heiss, USA	1977	Linda Fratianne, USA

Figure Skating (Cont.)

Year		Year		Year	
1978	Anett Poetzsch, E. Germany	1987	Katarina Witt, E. Germany	1996	Michelle Kwan, USA
1979	Linda Fratianne, USA	1988	**Katarina Witt**, E. Germany	1997	Tara Lipinski, USA
1980	**Anett Poetzsch**, E. Germany	1989	Midori Ito, Japan	1998	Michelle Kwan, USA
1981	Denise Biellmann, Switzerland	1990	Jill Trenary, USA	1999	Maria Butyrskaya, Russia
1982	Elaine Zayak, USA	1991	Kristi Yamaguchi, USA	2000	Michelle Kwan, USA
1983	Rosalyn Sumners, USA	1992	**Kristi Yamaguchi**, USA	2001	Michelle Kwan, USA
1984	**Katarina Witt**, E. Germany	1993	Oksana Baiul, Ukraine	2002	Irina Slutskaya, Russia
1985	Katarina Witt, E. Germany	1994	Yuka Sato, Japan	2003	Michelle Kwan, USA
1986	Debi Thomas, USA	1995	Lu Chen, China	2004	Shizuka Arakawa, Japan

PAIRS

Year		Year		Year	
1908	**Anna Hubler** & **Heinrich Burger**, GER	1949	Andrea Kekessy & Ede Kiraly, HUN	1977	Irina Rodnina & Aleksandr Zaitsev, USSR
1909	Phyllis Johnson & James H. Johnson, GBR	1950	Karol Kennedy & Peter Kennedy, USA	1978	Irina Rodnina & Aleksandr Zaitsev, USSR
1910	Anna Hubler & Heinrich Burger, GER	1951	Ria Baran & Paul Falk, W. Ger	1979	Tai Babilonia & Randy Gardner, USA
1911	Ludowika Eilers, GER & Walter Jakobsson, FIN	1952	**Ria Falk-Baran** & **Paul Falk**, W. Ger	1980	Maria Cherkasova & Sergei Shakhrai, USSR
1912	Phyllis Johnson & James H. Johnson, GBR	1953	Jennifer Nicks & John Nicks, GBR	1981	Irina Vorobieva & Igor Lisovsky, USSR
1913	Helene Engelmann & Karl Majstrik, AUT	1954	Frances Dafoe & Norris Bowden, CAN	1982	Sabine Baess & Tassilio Thierbach, E. Ger
1914	Ludowika Jakobsson-Eilers & Walter Jakobsson-Eilers, FIN	1955	Frances Dafoe & Norris Bowden, CAN	1983	Elena Valova & Oleg Vasiliev, USSR
1915-21	Not held	1956	**Elisabeth Schwarz** & **Kurt Oppelt**, AUT	1984	Barbara Underhill & Paul Martini, CAN
1922	**Helene Engelmann** & **Alfred Berger**, AUT	1957	Barbara Wagner & Robert Paul, CAN	1985	Elena Valova & Oleg Vasiliev, USSR
1923	Ludowika Jakobsson-Eilers & Walter Jakobsson-Eilers, FIN	1958	Barbara Wagner & Robert Paul, CAN	1986	Ekaterina Gordeeva & Sergei Grinkov, USSR
1924	Helene Engelmann & Alfred Berger, GER	1959	Barbara Wagner & Robert Paul, CAN	1987	Ekaterina Gordeeva & Sergei Grinkov, USSR
1925	Herma Jaross-Szabo & Ludwig Wrede, AUT	1960	**Barbara Wagner** & **Robert Paul**, CAN	1988	Elena Valova & Oleg Vasiliev, USSR
1926	Andree Joly & Pierre Brunet, FRA	1961	Not held	1989	Ekaterina Gordeeva & Sergei Grinkov, USSR
1927	Herma Jaross-Szabo & Ludwig Wrede, AUT	1962	Maria Jelinek & Otto Jelinek, CAN	1990	Ekaterina Gordeeva & Sergei Grinkov, USSR
1928	**Andree Joly** & **Pierre Brunet**, FRA	1963	Marika Kilius & H.J. Baumler, W. Ger	1991	Natalya Mishkutienok & Arhtur Dmitriev, USSR
1929	Lilly Scholz & Otto Kaiser, AUT	1964	Marika Kilius & H.J. Baumler, W. Ger	1992	**Natalya Mishkutienok** & **Arthur Dmitriev**, USSR
1930	Andree Brunet-Joly & Pierre Brunet-Joly, FRA	1965	Ludmila Protopopov & Oleg Protopopov, USSR	1993	Isabelle Brasseur & Lloyd Eisler, CAN
1931	Emilie Rotter & Laszlo Szollas, HUN	1966	Ludmila Protopopov & Oleg Protopopov, USSR	1994	Evgenia Shishkova & Vadim Naumov, RUS
1932	**Andree Brunet-Joly** & **Pierre Brunet-Joly**, FRA	1967	Ludmila Protopopov & Oleg Protopopov, USSR	1995	Radka Kovarikova & Rene Novotny, CZR
1933	Emilie Rotter & Laszlo Szollas, HUN	1968	**Ludmila Protopopov** & **Oleg Protopopov**, USSR	1996	Marina Eltsova & Andrey Buskhov, RUS
1934	Emilie Rotter & Laszlo Szollas, HUN	1969	Irina Rodnina & Alexsei Ulanov, USSR	1997	Mandy Wotzel & Ingo Steuer, GER
1935	Emilie Rotter & Laszlo Szollas, HUN	1970	Irina Rodnina & Aleksei Ulanov, USSR	1998	Jenni Meno & Todd Sand, USA
1936	**Maxi Herber** & **Ernst Baier**, GER	1971	Irina Rodnina & Aleksei Ulanov, USSR	1999	Elena Berezhnaya & Anton Sikharulidze, RUS
1937	Maxi Herber & Ernst Baier, GER	1972	**Irina Rodnina** & **Aleksei Ulanov**, USSR	2000	Maria Petrova & Alexei Tikhonov, RUS
1938	Maxi Herber & Ernst Baier, GER	1973	Irina Rodnina & Aleksandr Zaitsev, USSR	2001	Jamie Sale & David Pelletier, CAN
1939	Maxi Herber & Ernst Baier, GER	1974	Irina Rodnina & Aleksandr Zaitsev, USSR	2002	Xue Shen & Hongbo Zhao, CHN
1940-46	Not held	1975	Irina Rodnina & Aleksandr Zaitsev, USSR	2003	Xue Shen & Hongbo Zhao, CHN
1947	Micheline Lannoy & Pierre Baugniet, BEL	1976	**Irina Rodnina** & **Aleksandr Zaitsev**, USSR	2004	Tatiana Totmianina & Maxim Marinin, RUS
1948	**Micheline Lannoy** & **Pierre Baugniet**, BEL				

AP/Wide World Photos

*Five-time world champ **Carol Heiss**, top, shakes hands with Austrian runners-up Ingrid Wendl, left, and Hanna Walter after retaining her world title on Feb. 15, 1958.*

DANCE

Year		Year		Year	
1950	Lois Waring & Michael McGean, USA	1969	Diane Towler & Bernard Ford, GBR	1987	Natalia Bestemianova & Andrei Bukin, USSR
1951	Jean Westwood & Lawrence Demmy, GBR	1970	Lyudmila Pakhomova & Aleksandr Gorshkov, USSR	1988	**Natalia Bestemianova & Andrei Bukin**, USSR
1952	Jean Westwood & Lawrence Demmy, GBR	1971	Lyudmila Pakhomova & Aleksandr Gorshkov, USSR	1989	Marina Klimova & Sergei Ponomarenko, USSR
1953	Jean Westwood & Lawrence Demmy, GBR	1972	Lyudmila Pakhomova & Aleksandr Gorshkov, USSR	1990	Marina Klimova & Sergei Ponomarenko, USSR
1954	Jean Westwood & Lawrence Demmy, GBR	1973	Lyudmila Pakhomova & Aleksandr Gorshkov, USSR	1991	Isabelle Duchesnay & Paul Duchesnay, FRA
1955	Jean Westwood & Lawrence Demmy, GBR	1974	Lyudmila Pakhomova & Aleksandr Gorshkov, USSR	1992	**Marina Klimova & Sergei Ponomarenko**, USSR
1956	Pamela Wieght & Paul Thomas, GBR	1975	Irina Moiseeva & Andreij Minenkov, USSR	1993	Renee Roca & Gorsha Sur, USA
1957	June Markham & Courtney Jones, GBR	1976	**Lyudmila Pakhomova & Aleksandr Gorshkov**, USSR	1994	**Oksana Grishuk & Evgeny Platov**, RUS
1958	June Markham & Courtney Jones, GBR	1977	Irina Moiseeva & Andreij Minenkov, USSR	1995	Oksana Grishuk & Evgeny Platov, RUS
1959	Doreen D. Denny & Courtney Jones, GBR	1978	Natalia Linichuk & Gennadi Karponosov, USSR	1996	Oksana Grishuk & Evgeny Platov, RUS
1960	Doreen D. Denny & Courtney Jones, GBR	1979	Natalia Linichuk & Gennadi Karponosov, USSR	1997	Oksana Grishuk & Evgeny Platov, RUS
1961	Not held	1980	Krisztina Regoeczy & Andras Sallai, HUN	1998	Anjelika Krylova & Oleg Ovsyannikov, RUS
1962	Eva Romanova & Pavel Roman, CZE	1981	Jayne Torvill & Christopher Dean, GBR	1999	Anjelika Krylova & Oleg Ovsyannikov, RUS
1963	Eva Romanova & Pavel Roman, CZE	1982	Jayne Torvill & Christopher Dean, GBR	2000	Marina Anissina & Gwendal Peizerat, FRA
1964	Eva Romanova & Pavel Roman, CZE	1983	Jayne Torvill & Christopher Dean, GBR	2001	Barbara Fusar Poli & Maurizio Margaglio, ITA
1965	Eva Romanova & Pavel Roman, CZE	1984	**Jayne Torvill & Christopher Dean**, GBR	2002	Irina Lobacheva & Ilia Averbukh, RUS
1966	Diane Towler & Bernard Ford, GBR	1985	Natalia Bestemianova & Andrei Bukin, USSR	2003	Shae-Lynn Bourne & Victor Kraatz, CAN
1967	Diane Towler & Bernard Ford, GBR	1986	Natalia Bestemianova & Andrei Bukin, USSR	2004	Tatiana Navka & Roman Kostomarov, RUS
1968	Diane Towler & Bernard Ford, GBR				

U.S. Champions
Skaters who won U.S., World and Olympic championships in same year are in **bold** type.
MEN

Multiple winners: Dick Button and Roger Turner (7); Todd Eldredge (6); Sherwin Badger and Robin Lee (5); Brian Boitano, Scott Hamilton, Hayes Jenkins and Charles Tickner (4); Gordon McKellen, Nathaniel Niles, Michael Weiss and Tim Wood (3); Scott Allen, Christopher Bowman, Scott Davis, Eugene Turner and Gary Visconti (2).

Year		Year		Year		Year	
1914	Norman Scott	1938	Robin Lee	1961	Bradley Lord	1983	Scott Hamilton
1915-17	Not held	1939	Robin Lee	1962	Monty Hoyt	1984	**Scott Hamilton**
1918	Nathaniel Niles	1940	Eugene Turner	1963	Thomas Litz	1985	Brian Boitano
1919	Not held	1941	Eugene Turner	1964	Scott Allen	1986	Brian Boitano
1920	Sherwin Badger	1942	Robert Specht	1965	Gary Visconti	1987	Brian Boitano
1921	Sherwin Badger	1943	Arthur Vaughn	1966	Scott Allen	1988	**Brian Boitano**
1922	Sherwin Badger	1944-45	Not held	1967	Gary Visconti	1989	Christopher Bowman
1923	Sherwin Badger	1946	Dick Button	1968	Tim Wood	1990	Todd Eldredge
1924	Sherwin Badger	1947	Dick Button	1969	Tim Wood	1991	Todd Eldredge
1925	Nathaniel Niles	1948	**Dick Button**	1970	Tim Wood	1992	Christopher Bowman
1926	Chris Christenson	1949	Dick Button	1971	John (Misha) Petkevich	1993	Scott Davis
1927	Nathaniel Niles	1950	Dick Button	1972	Ken Shelley	1994	Scott Davis
1928	Roger Turner	1951	Dick Button	1973	Gordon McKellen	1995	Todd Eldredge
1929	Roger Turner	1952	**Dick Button**	1974	Gordon McKellen	1996	Rudy Galindo
1930	Roger Turner	1953	Hayes Jenkins	1975	Gordon McKellen	1997	Todd Eldredge
1931	Roger Turner	1954	Hayes Jenkins	1976	Terry Kubicka	1998	Todd Eldredge
1932	Roger Turner	1955	Hayes Jenkins	1977	Charles Tickner	1999	Michael Weiss
1933	Roger Turner	1956	**Hayes Jenkins**	1978	Charles Tickner	2000	Michael Weiss
1934	Roger Turner	1957	David Jenkins	1979	Charles Tickner	2001	Tim Goebel
1935	Robin Lee	1958	David Jenkins	1980	Charles Tickner	2002	Todd Eldredge
1936	Robin Lee	1959	David Jenkins	1981	Scott Hamilton	2003	Michael Weiss
1937	Robin Lee	1960	David Jenkins	1982	Scott Hamilton	2004	Johnny Weir

WOMEN

Multiple winners: Maribel Vinson (9); Michelle Kwan (8); Theresa Weld Blanchard and Gretchen Merrill (6); Tenley Albright, Peggy Fleming and Janet Lynn (5); Linda Fratianne and Carol Heiss (4); Dorothy Hamill, Beatrix Loughran, Rosalyn Summers, Joan Tozzer and Jill Trenary (3); Yvonne Sherman and Debi Thomas (2).

Year		Year		Year		Year	
1914	Theresa Weld	1939	Joan Tozzer	1962	Barbara Pursley	1985	Tiffany Chin
1915-17	Not held	1940	Joan Tozzer	1963	Lorraine Hanlon	1986	Debi Thomas
1918	Rosemary Beresford	1941	Jane Vaughn	1964	Peggy Fleming	1987	Jill Trenary
1919	Not held	1942	Jane Sullivan	1965	Peggy Fleming	1988	Debi Thomas
1920	Theresa Weld	1943	Gretchen Merrill	1966	Peggy Fleming	1989	Jill Trenary
1921	Theresa Blanchard	1944	Gretchen Merrill	1967	Peggy Fleming	1990	Jill Trenary
1922	Theresa Blanchard	1945	Gretchen Merrill	1968	**Peggy Fleming**	1991	Tonya Harding
1923	Theresa Blanchard	1946	Gretchen Merrill	1969	Janet Lynn	1992	**Kristi Yamaguchi**
1924	Theresa Blanchard	1947	Gretchen Merrill	1970	Janet Lynn	1993	Nancy Kerrigan
1925	Beatrix Loughran	1948	Gretchen Merrill	1971	Janet Lynn	1994	vacated*
1926	Beatrix Loughran	1949	Yvonne Sherman	1972	Janet Lynn	1995	Nicole Bobek
1927	Beatrix Loughran	1950	Yvonne Sherman	1973	Janet Lynn	1996	Michelle Kwan
1928	Maribel Vinson	1951	Sonya Klopfer	1974	Dorothy Hamill	1997	Tara Lipinski
1929	Maribel Vinson	1952	Tenley Albright	1975	Dorothy Hamill	1998	Michelle Kwan
1930	Maribel Vinson	1953	Tenley Albright	1976	**Dorothy Hamill**	1999	Michelle Kwan
1931	Maribel Vinson	1954	Tenley Albright	1977	Linda Fratianne	2000	Michelle Kwan
1932	Maribel Vinson	1955	Tenley Albright	1978	Linda Fratianne	2001	Michelle Kwan
1933	Maribel Vinson	1956	Tenley Albright	1979	Linda Fratianne	2002	Michelle Kwan
1934	Suzanne Davis	1957	Carol Heiss	1980	Linda Fratianne	2003	Michelle Kwan
1935	Maribel Vinson	1958	Carol Heiss	1981	Elaine Zayak	2004	Michelle Kwan
1936	Maribel Vinson	1959	Carol Heiss	1982	Rosalyn Sumners		
1937	Maribel Vinson	1960	**Carol Heiss**	1983	Rosalyn Sumners		
1938	Joan Tozzer	1961	Laurence Owen	1984	Rosalyn Sumners		

* Tonya Harding was stripped of the 1994 women's title and banned from membership in the U.S. Figure Skating Assn. for life on June 30, 1994 for violating the USFSA Code of Ethics after she pleaded guilty to a charge of conspiracy to hinder the prosecution related to the Jan. 6, 1994 attack on Nancy Kerrigan.

RUGBY
World Cup
The inaugural Rugby World Cup was held in 1987. Like soccer's World Cup, it is held every four years. Sixteen national teams were assembled for the first three tournaments but beginning in 1999, 20 teams played for the William Webb Ellis Cup, named for the game's inventor. The Rugby World Cup is now billed as the world's third largest athletic event, behind the Olympics and the soccer World Cup.

Year	Winner	Score	Runner up	Host Country
1987	New Zealand	29-9	France	Australia & New Zealand
1991	Australia	12-6	England	United Kingdom & France
1995	South Africa	15-12	New Zealand	South Africa
1999	Australia	35-12	France	Wales
2003	England	20-17	Australia	Australia

Olympics

Gymnast Paul Hamm celebrates his gold medal in the men's all-around. Hamm's spirits were not as high later when his win came into question.

AP/Wide World Photos

Greeks give golden Games

After all the fears and hype, Athens and Michael Phelps both delivered another great Summer Games.

Seth Wickersham
is a reporter for *ESPN The Magazine.*

What didn't happen at the Athens Games is almost as important as what did.

There were no terrorist attacks. No sniffs of violence. All the venues were completed. OK, except the roof to the swimming stadium. But who cared? Being roofless only meant that Michael Phelps had a tan when collecting his medals.

There were no traffic pileups, no power outages, no unsafe tourists. Instead, Athens scored a 9.9 in hosting the Games. There was an Iraqi soccer team nearly medalling, a Greek woman waving to the crowd with her shoes off and a new Mary Lou Retton crowned. There was Paul Hamm's gold-medal controversy. There was the USA Softball team not losing a game and the USA men's basketball team losing too many. It cost 1.2 billion euros to keep the Games safe, but the best parts about the 2004 Olympics were free.

Free: Watching American Justin Gatlin tear up on the track after winning his surprise gold medal in the 100, or watching softball pitcher Jennie Finch do the same after winning her gold, or watching Allyson Felix silver in the 200 meters—a forecast to 2008.

Free: Watching Fani Halkia, shoeless, circling the track crying, waving to 70,000 hometown fans shouting "Hell-as" with her every step.

Free: The Iraqi soccer team nearly playing for a medal, and the lone Iraqi female, sprinter Ala'a Jassim, finishing last in her 100 meter sprint but transcending so much in the process.

People kept wondering if the Olympics still mattered as much, as if the only sports that count have versions to play on an XBox. But despite the security concerns and the BALCO investigations, the Games found a way into the Neilsen rat-

AP/Wide World Photos

*American **Michael Phelps** didn't eclipse Spitz but he won an amazing eight medals, including six golds and led the charge for the U.S. Olympic team who won 103 medals at Athens.*

ings. And into America's hearts. They always do.

First, it was Phelps' ambitious pursuit of eight gold medals at a single Games, which would have broken Mark Spitz's Olympic record from 1972. Phelps swam an astounding 17 races in one week of competition at Athens.

No, he didn't break Spitz's record, but on his way to getting eight total medals (six golds, two bronze) might have done something better: He benched himself in the 4 x 100 medley relay final, giving his spot to teammate Ian Crocker, who had battled depression prior to qual-

ifying for the Olympics. That sort of selflessness only comes around every four years.

Then came gymnastics, where both the USA men's and women's teams silvered with Carly Patterson winning her individual all-around gold medal outright and Hamm winning his in controversy. He nearly fell off onto the judges table on his vault attempt, and entered his final event needing a ridiculous 9.825 to tie for the gold medal.

He twisted off a 9.837, and suddenly had pulled off what seemed unbelievable. But what happened next was.

AP/Wide World Photos

Greece's **Fani Halkia** exults as she wins gold in the women's 400-meter hurdles in front of a stadium packed full of her cheering countrymen.

South Korea's Yang Tae Young entered his parallel bars routine with a 9.9 start value, instead of the 10.0 it had in qualifiers, and that tenth of a point gave him a bronze medal instead of a gold. Under pressure to forfeit his medal, Hamm left Athens as soon as he could, days before closing ceremonies, and it's hard to remember a gold-medal winner who was more dejected and angry.

Speaking of dejected and angry, the USA men's basketball team, wearing the label of Dream Team that even the players knew wasn't deserved, stumbled and for the first time since 1988 (the last time NBA players didn't compete) did not win the gold medal.

But they were bailed out. USA softball didn't lose a single game. Neither did USA women's soccer, led by the departing Mia Hamm and newcomer Abby Wambach.

And just when all the BALCO investigations got everyone down on track, Felix, just 18, gave the sport a clean superstar who will be endlessly promoted in Beijing in 2008.

When those Games arrive, hopefully everyone will still remember why the 2004 Olympics were great.

Athens proved that these Games still matter. For all the right reasons.

The Ten Biggest Stories of the 2004 Summer Games

10 USA women's soccer: The team that made it cool for women to be athletic, strong, dominant, and good looking won gold again. It was the last game for many of the team leaders that ushered the popularity of women's soccer in America, perhaps most notably Mia Hamm.

9 Fani Halkia: Bulbs flashed. Fans cried. People screamed, "Hell-as! Hell-as!" And when Greece's Fani Halkia trotted barefoot, waving to her fellow citizens after winning the 400m hurdles, she helped cleanse every Greek athlete after so many were suspended for positive drug tests.

8 USA softball team: Pitcher Lisa Fernandez not only went 3-0 with an invisible 0.29 ERA but also hit .545, best of the Games. Playing for coach Mike Candrea's wife, Sue, who died suddenly, the U.S. women's team cruised to the gold medal.

7 Athens' competence: With fears of terrorism, unfinished venues and a lackadaisical approach to the Games, the city of Athens won an underdog gold. The Games were more efficient than Atlanta in 1996 and the venues were better than Sydney in 2000, even if the swimming stadium didn't have a roof.

6 Carly Patterson's all-around gold. Twenty years after Mary Lou became the first U.S. woman to win individual gold, Patterson, a 16-year-old from Baton Rouge, did it by upstaging Russia's Svetlana Khorkina with a 9.712 floor finish.

5 Iraq soccer: One year removed from the torture regimes of Uday Hussein, the Iraqi soccer team stunned Portugal, 4-2, in their first match, and as violence scarred their country back home, eventually made it to the medal round before falling to traditional soccer power Italy in the bronze-medal match.

4 USA men's basketball: No jump shooters, no breaks from the referees, and no adjustments by head coach Larry Brown led to a regrettable performance by this year's "Dream" team. At least the Americans looked happy as they were awarded their bronze medals. Oh, wait, they didn't look happy.

3 Hamm's medal mess: Nice move by the International Gymnastics Federation: Mess up the score of South Korea's Yang Tae Young's parallel bars routine, then shift all the pressure to American Paul Hamm to give up his gold medal. No wonder Hamm couldn't wait to leave Athens.

2 A Changing of the Guard in Track and Field.
On their way out: Gail Devers, Allen Johnson and Marion Jones. On their way in: Lauren Williams, Jeremy Wariner and Allyson Felix. The Beijing Summer Games in 2008 should be a coronation of the American track and field athletes that broke out in Athens.

1 American Dominance in Swimming. The marquee man of the Games, Michael Phelps didn't break Mark Spitz's famous record, but he not only led a USA white-washing of the rest of the world, winning six gold medals (and eight total), he also showed true sports-manship by giving up his spot on the final relay team to teammate Ian Crocker.

Soft ball, Tough team
The U.S. softball team simply destroyed the competition at the 2004 Summer Games in Athens. Here's a look at some of the astounding numbers they put up in their nine-game victory parade to the gold medal.

	USA	Opponents
Wins	9	0
Runs	51	1
Hits	73	18
HRs	9	0

Note: The team recorded eight consecutive shutouts before finally allowing its first (and only) run in the gold-medal game with Australia.

A Pattern Diverges
Whatever the reason (the USA had no jump-shooters, the improvement of the global game, or the NBA stars don't mesh as a cohesive unit), the long-running pattern of American domination in Olympic men's basketball was flipped on its head in 2004. Take a look at these numbers from the past and present in USA Men's Basketball.

	1936-2000	2004
Olympic W-L	109-2	5-3
P.P.G. Allowed	60.6	83.5

Athens 2004
Games in Review

Final Medal Standings

National Medal Standings are not recognized by the IOC. The unofficial point totals are based on three points for every gold medal, two for each silver and one for each bronze.

		G	S	B	Total	Points			G	S	B	Total	Points
1	**United States**	35	39	29	103	212	39	Georgia	2	2	0	4	10
2	Russia	27	27	38	92	173		Jamaica	2	1	2	5	10
3	China	32	17	14	63	144		Uzbekistan	2	1	2	5	10
4	Australia	17	16	16	49	99		Argentina	2	0	4	6	10
5	Germany	14	16	18	48	92	43	North Korea	0	4	1	5	9
6	Japan	16	9	12	37	78		Croatia	1	2	2	5	9
7	France	11	9	13	33	64	45	Switzerland	1	1	3	5	8
8	Italy	10	11	11	32	63		Latvia	0	4	0	4	8
9	South Korea	9	12	9	30	60	47	Morocco	2	1	0	3	7
10	Great Britain	9	9	12	30	57		Azerbaijan	1	0	4	5	7
11	Cuba	9	7	11	27	52		Indonesia	1	1	2	4	7
12	Ukraine	9	5	9	23	46		Mexico	0	3	1	4	7
13	Romania	8	5	6	19	40	51	Zimbabwe	1	1	1	3	6
14	Hungary	8	6	3	17	39	52	Slovenia	0	1	3	4	5
	Netherlands	4	9	9	22	39		Belgium	1	0	2	3	5
16	Spain	3	11	5	19	36		Portugal	0	2	1	3	5
17	Greece	6	6	4	16	34		Lithuania	1	2	0	3	5
18	Belarus	2	6	7	15	25	56	Bahamas	1	0	1	2	4
19	Canada	3	6	3	12	24		Israel	1	0	1	2	4
20	Brazil	4	3	3	10	21		Finland	0	2	0	2	4
21	Turkey	3	3	4	10	19		Serbia & Montenegro	0	2	0	2	4
22	Poland	3	2	5	10	18		Estonia	0	1	2	3	4
23	Bulgaria	2	1	9	12	17	61	Ireland	1	0	0	1	3
24	Norway	5	0	1	6	16		Cameroon	1	0	0	1	3
	Sweden	4	1	2	7	16		Dominican Republic	1	0	0	1	3
26	Thailand	3	1	4	8	15		United Arab Emirates	1	0	0	1	3
	Austria	2	4	1	7	15	65	Hong Kong	0	1	0	1	2
28	Ethiopia	2	3	2	7	14		India	0	1	0	1	2
	Kazakhstan	1	4	3	8	14		Nigeria	0	0	2	2	2
30	New Zealand	3	2	0	5	13		Paraguay	0	1	0	1	2
	Czech Republic	1	3	4	8	13		Venezuela	0	0	2	2	2
	Kenya	1	4	2	7	13	70	Colombia	0	0	1	1	1
33	Iran	2	2	2	6	12		Eritrea	0	0	1	1	1
	Slovakia	2	2	2	6	12		Mongolia	0	0	1	1	1
	Denmark	2	0	6	8	12		Syria	0	0	1	1	1
37	Chinese Taipei	2	2	1	5	11		Trinidad & Tobago	0	0	1	1	1
	South Africa	1	3	2	6	11							

Leading Medal Winners

(*) indicates at least one medal earned as preliminary member of eventual medal-winning relay team. USA medalists in bold type.

Men

No		Sport	G-S-B	No		Sport	G-S-B
8*	**Michael Phelps**, USA	Swimming	6-0-2	3	Marian Dragulescu, ROM	Gymnastics	0-1-2
4	Ian Thorpe, AUS	Swimming	2-1-1	2	Ryan Bayley, AUS	Cycling	2-0-0
3	**Aaron Peirsol**, USA	Swimming	3-0-0	2	Graeme Brown, AUS	Cycling	2-0-0
3	Kosuke Kitajima, JPN	Swimming	2-1-0	2	Hicham El Guerrouj, MOR	Track and Field	2-0-0
3	Grant Hackett, AUS	Swimming	1-2-0	2	Nicolas Massu, CHI	Tennis	2-0-0
3	**Paul Hamm**, USA	Gymnastics	1-2-0	2	Kenenisa Bekele, ETH	Track and Field	1-1-0
3	**Brendan Hansen**, USA	Swimming	1-1-1	2	David Cal, SPA	Canoeing	1-1-0
3	**Ian Crocker**, USA	Swimming	1-1-1	2	**Shawn Crawford**, USA	Track and Field	1-1-0
3	**Justin Gatlin**, USA	Track and Field	1-1-1	2	Andrea Dittmer, GER	Canoeing	1-1-0
3	Roland Mark Schoeman, RSA	Swimming	1-1-1	2	**Otis Harris Jr.**, USA	Track and Field	1-1-0
3	Bradley Wiggins, GBR	Cycling	1-1-1	2	**Ryan Lochte**, USA	Swimming	1-1-0

Leading Medal Winners (Cont.)

No		Sport	G-S-B	No		Sport	G-S-B
2	Brad McGee, AUS	Cycling	1-1-0	2	Rene Wolff, GER	Cycling	1-0-1
2	Aldo Montano, ITA	Fencing	1-1-0	2	Isao Yoneda, JPN	Gymnastics	1-0-1
2	Mikhail Nestruev, RUS	Shooting	1-1-0	2	Nathan Baggaley, AUS	Canoeing	0-2-0
2	Salvatore Sanzo, ITA	Fencing	1-1-0	2	Marcus Rogan, AUT	Swimming	0-2-0
2	Hiroyuki Tomita, JPN	Gymnastics	1-1-0	2	**Maurice Greene**, USA	Track and Field	0-1-1
2	Pieter van den Hoogenband, NED	Swimming	1-1-0	2	Rob Hayles, GBR	Cycling	0-1-1
2	**Derrick Brew**, USA	Track and Field	1-0-1	2	Mathew Helm, AUS	Diving	0-1-1
2	Andrea Cassara, ITA	Fencing	1-0-1	2	Alexander Kostoglod, RUS	Canoeing	0-1-1
2	Fernando Gonzalez, CHI	Tennis	1-0-1	2	Alexander Kovalev, RUS	Canoeing	0-1-1
2	Takehiro Kashima, JPN	Gymnastics	1-0-1	2	Marius Daniel Urzica, ROM	Gymnastics	0-1-1
2	**Klete Keller**, USA	Swimming	1-0-1	2	Takashi Yamamoto, JPN	Swimming	0-1-1
2	**Jason Lezak**, USA	Swimming	1-0-1	2	Arnaud Tournant, FRA	Cycling	0-1-1
2	Stefan Nimke, GER	Cycling	1-0-1	2	Sergi Escobar, SPA	Cycling	0-0-2
2	Adam van Koeverden, CAN	Canoeing	1-0-1	2	Tomomi Morita, JPN	Swimming	0-0-2
2	Eirik Veraas Larsen, NOR	Canoeing	1-0-1	2	Robert Newbery, AUS	Diving	0-0-2
2	**Neil Walker**, USA	Swimming	1-0-1				

Women

No		Sport	G-S-B	No		Sport	G-S-B
5	**Natalie Coughlin**, USA	Swimming	2-2-1	2	Lao Lishi, CHN	Diving	1-1-0
4	Petria Thomas, AUS	Swimming	3-1-0	2	Olga Slyusareva, RUS	Cycling	1-1-0
4	Inge de Bruijn, NED	Swimming	1-1-2	2	Nicoleta Daniela Sofronie, ROM	Gymnastics	1-1-0
3	Jodie Henry, AUS	Swimming	3-0-0	2	Alexandra Georgiana Eremia, ROM	Gymnastics	1-0-1
3	Catalina Ponor, ROM	Gymnastics	3-0-0	2	Maria Grozdeva, BUL	Shooting	1-0-1
3	Veronica Campbell, JAM	Track and Field	2-0-1	2	Tatyana Lebedeva, RUS	Track and Field	1-0-1
3	**Amanda Beard**, USA	Swimming	1-2-0	2	Lisbeth Lenton, AUS	Swimming	1-0-1
3	Otylia Jedrzejczak, POL	Swimming	1-2-0	2	Anna Meares, AUS	Cycling	1-0-1
3	**Carly Patterson**, USA	Gymnastics	1-2-0	2	Chantelle Newbery, AUS	Diving	1-0-1
3	Kirsty Coventry, ZIM	Swimming	1-1-1	2	Leontien Zijlaard-van Moorsel, NED	Cycling	1-0-1
3	Leisel Jones, AUS	Swimming	1-1-1	2	**Annia Hatch**, USA	Gymnastics	0-2-0
3	Laure Manaudoue, FRA	Swimming	1-1-1	2	**Terin Humphrey**, USA	Gymnastics	0-2-0
3	**Kaitlin Sandeno**, USA	Swimming	1-1-1	2	**Kara Lynn Joyce**, USA	Swimming	0-2-0
2	Georgeta Andrunache-Damian, ROM	Rowing	2-0-0	2	Miho Takeda, JPN	Synch. Swimming	0-2-0
2	Anastasia Davydova, RUS	Synch. Swimming	2-0-0	2	**Jenny Thompson**, USA	Swimming	0-2-0
2	Anastasia Ermakova, RUS	Synch. Swimming	2-0-0	2	**Alison Bartosik**, USA	Synch. Swimming	0-0-2
2	Kelly Holmes, GBR	Track and Field	2-0-0	2	**Anna Kozlova**, USA	Synch. Swimming	0-0-2
2	Park Sung Hyun, S. KOR	Archery	2-0-0	2	Anna Pavlova, RUS	Gymnastics	0-0-2
2	Natasa Janics, HUN	Canoeing	2-0-0	2	Natalya Antyukh, RUS	Track and Field	0-1-1
2	Yana Klochkova, UKR	Swimming	2-0-0	2	Laura Flessel-Colovic, FRA	Fencing	0-1-1
2	Monica Rosu, ROM	Gymnastics	2-0-0	2	Svetlana Khorkina, RUS	Gymnastics	0-1-1
2	Viorica Susanu, ROM	Rowing	2-0-0	2	**Courtney Kupets**, USA	Gymnastics	0-1-1
2	Zhang Yining, CHN	Table Tennis	2-0-0	2	Lee Bo Na, S. KOR	Shooting	0-1-1
2	Birgit Fischer, GER	Canoeing	1-1-0	2	Julia Pakhalina, RUS	Diving	0-1-1
2	Lee Sung Jin, S. KOR	Archery	1-1-0	2	Antje Buschschulte, GER	Swimming	0-0-2
2	Katalin Kovacs, HUN	Canoeing	1-1-0	2	Maureen Nisima, FRA	Fencing	0-0-2
2	Carolin Leonhardt, GER	Canoeing	1-1-0	2	Franziska van Almsick, GER	Swimming	0-0-2
2	Gao Ling, CHN	Badminton	1-1-0				

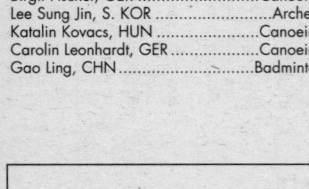

The United States has now won 6 straight and 11 of 12 gold medals in the Men's Swimming 4x100m Medley Relay (the only exception was the 1980 boycott). **Did you know**, the record for the longest national win streak in a single event is 16 (USA — Pole Vault from 1896-1968. Excluding the unofficial 1906 Games)?

MEDAL SPORTS

Medal winners in individual sports contested at Athens, Greece from Aug. 13-29, 2004. Team Sports summaries from Baseball to Water Polo begin on page 676.

ARCHERY

(70 meters)

MEN

Individual: 1. Marco Galiazzo, ITA def. **2.** Hiroshi Yamamoto, JPN (111-109); **3.** Tim Cuddihy, AUS def. Laurence Godfrey, GBR (113-112).

Team: 1. South Korea (Jang Yonng Ho, Park Kyung Mo, Im Dong Hyun) def. **2.** Chinese Taipei (251-245); **3.** Ukraine def. USA (237-235).

WOMEN

Individual: 1. Park Sung Hyun, S. KOR def. **2.** Lee Sung Jin, S. KOR (110-108); **3.** Alison Williamson, GBR def. Yuan Shu Chi, TPE (105-104).

Team: 1. South Korea (Park Sung Hyun, Yun Mi Jin, Lee Sung Jin) def. **2.** China (241-240); **3.** Chinese Taipei def. France (242-228).

BADMINTON

MEN

Singles: 1. Taufik Hidayat, INA, def. **2.** Shon Seung Mo, S. KOR (15-8, 15-7); **3.** Soni Dwi Kuncoro, INA, def. Boonsak Ponsana, THA (15-11, 17-16).

Doubles: 1. Kim Dong Moon & Ha Tae Kwon, S. KOR def. **2.** Lee Dong Soo & Yoo Young Sung, S. KOR (15-11, 15-4); **3.** Eng Hian & Flandy Limpele, INA def. Jens Eriksen & H. Martin Lundgaard, DEN (15-13, 15-7).

WOMEN

Singles: 1. Zhang Ning, CHN def. **2.** Mia Audina, NED (8-11, 11-6, 11-7); **3.** Zhou Mi, CHN def. Gong Ruin, CHN (11-2, 8-11, 11-6).

Doubles: 1. Zhang Jiewen & Yang Wei, CHN def. **2.** Huang Sui & Gao Ling, CHN (7-15, 15-4, 15-8); **3.** Ra Kyung Min & Lee Kyung Won, S. KOR def. Zhao Tingting & Wei Yili, CHN (10-15, 15-9, 15-7).

MIXED

Doubles: 1. Zhang Jun & Gao Ling, CHN def. **2.** Nathan Robertson & Gail Emms, GBR (15-1, 12-15, 15-12); **3.** Jen Eriksen & Mette Schjoldager, DEN def. Jonas Rasmussen & Rikke Olsen, DEN (15-5, 15-5).

BEACH VOLLEYBALL

Men: 1. Ricardo Alex Santos & Emanuel Rego, BRA def. **2.** Javier Bosma & Pablo Herrera, SPA (21-16, 21-15); **3.** Stefan Kobel & Patrick Heuscher, SUI def. Julien Prosser & Mark Williams, AUS (19-21, 21-17, 15-13).

Women: 1. Kerri Walsh & Misty May, USA def. **2.** Adriana Behar & Shelda Bede, BRA (21-17, 21-11); **3.** Holly McPeak & Elaine Youngs, USA def. Natalie Cook & Nicole Sanderson, AUS (21-18, 15-21, 15-9).

BOXING

Light Flyweight (106 lbs)**: 1.** Yan Bhartelemy Varela, CUB dec. **2.** Atagun Yalcinkaya, TUR (21-16); **3.** Sergey Kazakov, RUS, and Zou Shiming, CHN.

Flyweight (112 lbs)**: 1.** Yuriorkis Gamboa Toledano, CUB dec. **2.** Jerome Thomas, FRA (38-23); **3.** Rustamhodza Rahimov, GER, and Fuad Aslanov, AZE.

Batamweight (119 lbs)**: 1.** Guillermo Rigondeaux Ortis, CUB dec. **2.** Worapoj Petchkoom, THA (22-13); **3.** Bahodirjon Sooltonov, UZB, and Aghasi Mammadov, AZE.

Featherweight (125 lbs)**: 1.** Alexei Tichtchenko, RUS dec. **2.** Kim Song Guk, N. KOR (39-17); **3.** Vitali Tajbert, GER, and Jo Seok Hwan, S. KOR.

Lightweight (132 lbs)**: 1.** Mario-Cesar Kindelan, CUB dec. **2.** Amir Khan, GBR (30-22); **3.** Serik Yeleuov, KAZ, and Murat Khrachev, RUS.

Light Welterweight (141 lbs)**: 1.** Manus Boonjumnong, THA dec. **2.** Yudel Johnson Cedeno, CUB (17-11); **3.** Marian Simion, ROM, and Daniel Santos, PUR.

Welterweight (152 lbs)**: 1.** Bakhtiyar Artayev, KAZ dec. **2.** Lorenzo Aragon Armenteros, CUB; **3.** Kim Jung Joo, S. KOR, and Oleg Saitov, RUS.

Middleweight (165 lbs)**: 1.** Gaydarbek Gaydarbekov, RUS dec. **2.** Genndiy Golovkin, KAZ (28-18); **3.** Andre Dirrell, USA and Suriya Prasathinphimai, THA.

Light Heavyweight (178 lbs)**: 1.** Andre Ward, USA dec. **2.** Magomed Aripgadjiev, BLR (20-13); **3.** Utkirebek Haydarov, UZB, and Ahmed Ismail, EGY.

Heavyweight (201 lbs)**: 1.** Odlanier Solis Fonte, CUB dec. **2.** Viktar Zuyev, BLR (22-13); **3.** Naser Al Shami, SYR, and Mohamed Elsayed, EGY.

Super Heavyweight (over 201 lbs)**: 1.** Alexander Povetkin, RUS def. **2.** Mohamed Aly, EGY (walkover); **3.** Roberto Cammarelle, ITA, and Michel Lopez Nunez, CUB.

CANOE/KAYAK

MEN'S FLATWATER

Canoe 500m Singles: 1. Andreas Dittmer, GER (1:46.38); **2.** David Cal, SPA (1:46.72); **3.** Maxim Opalev, RUS (1:47.77).

Canoe 1000m Singles: 1. David Cal, SPA (3:46.20); **2.** Andreas Dittmer, GER (3:56.72); **3.** Attila Vajda, HUN (3:49.03).

Canoe 500m Doubles: 1. Meng Guanliang & Yang Wejun, CHN (1:40.28); **2.** Ibrahim Rojas Blanco & Ledis Frank Balceiro Pajon, CUB (1:40.35); **3.** Alexander Kostoglod & Alexander Kovalev, RUS (1:40.44).

Canoe 1000m Doubles: 1. Christian Gille & Tomasz Wylenzek, GER (3:41.80); **2.** Alexander Kostoglod & Alexander Kovalev, RUS (3:42.99); **3.** Gyorgy Kozmann & Gyorgy Kolonics, HUN (3:43.11).

Kayak 500m Singles: 1. Adam van Koeverden, CAN (1:37.92); **2.** Nathan Baggaley, AUS (1:38.47); **3.** Ian Wynne, GBR (1:38.55).

Kayak 500m Doubles: 1. Ronald Rauhe & Tim Wieskoetter, GER (1:27.040 pts); **2.** Clint Robinson & Nathan Baggaley, AUS (1:27.920); **3.** Raman Piatrushenka & Vadzim Makhneu, BLR (1:27.996).

Kayak 500m Singles: 1. Antonio Rossi, ITA (1:37.42); **2.** Knut Holmann, NOR (1:38.33); **3.** Piotr Markiewicz, POL (1:38.61).

Kayak 1000m Singles: 1. Eirik Veraas Larsen, NOR (3:25.897); **2.** Ben Fouhy, AUS (3:27.413); **3.** Adam van Koeverden, CAN (3:28.218).

Kayak 1000m Doubles: 1. Markus Oscarsson & Henrik Nilsson, SWE (3:18.420); **2.** Antonio Rossi & Beniamino Bonomi, ITA (3:19.484); **3.** Eirik Verass Larsen & Nils Olav Fjeldheim, NOR (3:19.528).

Kayak 1000m Fours: 1. Hungary (2:56.919); **2.** Germany (2:58.659); **3.** Slovakia (2:59.314).

WOMEN'S FLAT WATER

Kayak 500m Singles: 1. Natasa Janics, HUN (1:47.741); **2.** Josefa Idem, ITA (1:49.729); **3.** Caroline Brunet, CAN (1:50.601).

Kayak 500m Doubles: 1. Katalin Kovacs & Natasa Janic, HUN (1:38.101); **2.** Birgit Fischer & Carolin Leonhart, GER (1:39.533); **3.** Aneta Pastuszka & Beata Sokolowska Kulesza, POL (1:40.077).

Kayak Sprint 500m Fours: 1. Germany (1:34.340); **2.** Hungary (1:34.536); **3.** Ukraine (1:36.192).

MEN'S SLALOM

Canoe Singles: 1. Tony Estanguet, FRA (189.16 pts); **2.** Michal Martikan, SVK (189.28); **3.** Stefan Pfannmoeller, GER (191.56).

Canoe Doubles: 1. Pavol Hochschorner & Peter Hochschorner, SVK (207.16 pts); **2.** Marcus Becker & Stefan Henze, GER (210.98); **3.** Jaroslav Volf & Ondrej Stepanek, CZE (212.86).

Kayak Singles: 1. Benoit Peschier, FRA (187.96 pts); **2.** Campbell Walsh, GBR (190.17); **3.** Fabien Lefevre, FRA (190.99).

WOMEN'S SLALOM

Kayak Singles: 1. Elena Kaliska, SVK (210.03 pts); **2.** Rebecca Giddens, USA (214.62); **3.** Helen Reeves, GBR (218.77).

CYCLING

MEN
Mountain Bike

Cross Country (43.3 km)**: 1.** Julien Absalon, FRA (2:15:02); **2.** Jose Antonio Hermida, SPA (2:16:02); **3.** Bart Brentjens, NED (2:17:05).

Road

Individual Road Race (224.4 km)**: 1.** Paolo Bettini, ITA (5:41:44); **2.** Sergio Paulinho, POR (5:41:45); **3.** Axel Merckx, BEL (5:41:52).

Individual Time Trial (48 km)**: 1.** Tyler Hamilton, USA (57:31.74); **2.** Viatcheslav Ekimov, RUS (57:50.58); **3.** Bobby Julich, USA (57:58.19).

Track

Time Trial (1 km)**: 1.** Chris Hoy, GBR (1:00.711); **2.** Arnaud Tournant, FRA (1:00.896); **3.** Stefan Nimke, GER (1:01.186).

Individual Match Sprint (3 laps)**: 1.** Ryan Bayley, AUS; **2.** Theo Bos, NED; 3. Rene Wolff, GER.

Keirin (8 laps)**: 1.** Ryan Bayley, AUS; **2.** Jose Escuredo, SPA; **3.** Shane Kelly, AUS.

Individual Points Race (40 km)**: 1.** Mikhail Ignatyev, RUS (93 pts); **2.** Joan Llaneras, SPA (82); **3.** Guido Fulst, GER (79).

Individual Pursuit (4000 m)**: 1.** Bradley Wiggins, GBR (4:16.304) def. ; **2.** Brad McGee, AUS (4:20.436); **3.** Sergi Escobar, SPA (4:17.947) def. Rob Hayles, GBR (4:22.291).

Team Sprint (3 laps)**: 1.** Germany (43.980) def. **2.** Japan (44.246); **3.** France (44.359) def. Australia (44.404).

Team Pursuit (4 km)**: 1.** Australia (3:58.233) def. **2.** Great Britain (4:01.760); **3.** Spain (4:05.523) def. Germany (4:07.193).

Madison (50 km)**: 1.** Graeme Brown & Stuart O'Grady, AUS (22 pts); **2.** Franco Marvulli & Bruno Risi, SUI (15); **3.** Rob Hayles & Bradley Wiggins, GBR (12).

WOMEN
Mountain Bike

Cross Country (31.3 km)**: 1.** Gunn-Rita Dahle, NOR (1:56:51); **2.** Marie-Helene Premont, CAN (1:57:50); **3.** Sabine Spitz, GER (1:59:21).

Road

Individual Road Race (118.8 km)**: 1.** Sara Carrigan, AUS (3:24:24); **2.** Judith Arndt, GER (3:24:31); **3.** Olga Slyusareva, RUS (3:25:03).

Individual Time Trial (26 km)**: 1.** Leontien Zijlaard-van Moorsel, NED (31:11.53); 2. Deirdre Demet-Barry, USA (31:35.62); 3. Karin Thuerig, SUI (31:54.89).

Track

Time Trial (500 m)**: 1.** Anna Meares, AUS (33.952 **WR**); **2.** Jiang Yonghua (34.112); **3.** Nataliia Tsylinskaya, BLR (34.167).

Individual Match Sprint (3 laps)**: 1.** Lori-Ann Muenzer, CAN; **2.** Tamilla Abassova, RUS; **3.** Anna Meares, AUS.

Individual Pursuit (3 km)**: 1.** Sarah Ulmer, NZL (3:24.537) def. **2.** Katie Mactier, AUS (3:27.650); **3.** Leontien Zijlaard-van Moorsel, NED (3:27.037) def. Katherine Bates, AUS (3:31.715).

Individual Points Race (25 km)**: 1.** Olga Slyusareva, RUS (20 pts); **2.** Belem Guerrero Mendez, MEX (14); **3.** Erin Mirabella, USA (9).

DIVING

MEN

3m Springboard: 1. Peng Bo, CHN (787.38 pts); **2.** Alexandre Despatie, CAN (755.97); **3.** Dmitri Sautin, RUS (753.27).

10m Platform: 1. Hu Jia, CHN (748.08 pts); **2.** Mathew Helm, AUS (730.56); **3.** Tian Liang, CHN (729.66).

Synchronized 3m Springboard: 1. Nikolaos Siranidis & Thomas Bimis, GRE (353.34 pts); **2.** Andreas Wels & Tobias Schellenberg, GER (350.01); **3.** Robert Newbery & Steve Barnett, AUS (349.59).

Synchronized 10m Platform: 1. Tian Liang & Yang Jinghui, CHN (383.88 pts); **2.** Peter Waterfield & Leon Taylor, GBR (371.52); **3.** Mathew Helm & Robert Newbery, AUS (366.84).

WOMEN

3m Springboard: 1. Guo Jingjing, CHN (633.15 pts); **2.** Wu Minxia, CHN (612.00); **3.** Yulia Pakhalina, RUS (610.62).

10m Platform: 1. Chantelle Newbery, AUS (590.31 pts); **2.** Lao Lishi, CHN (576.30); **3.** Loudy Tourky, AUS (561.66).

Synchronized 3m Springboard: 1. Wu Minxia & Guo Jingjing, CHN (336.90 pts); **2.** Vera Ilyina & Yulia Pakhalina, RUS (330.84); **3.** Irina Lashko & Chantelle Newbery, AUS (309.30).

Synchronized 10m Platform: 1. Lao Lishi & Li Ting, CHN (352.14 pts); **2.** Natalia Goncharova & Yulia Koltunova, RUS (340.92); **3.** Blythe Hartley & Emilie Heymans, CAN (327.78).

EQUESTRIAN

Horses in parentheses.

Individual Dressage: 1. Anky Van Grunsven, (Salinero) NED (79.278); **2.** Ulla Salzgeber (Rusty) GER (78.833); **3.** Beatriz Ferrer-Salat (Beauvalais) SPA (76.667).

Team Dressage: 1. Germany (74.653); **2.** Spain (72.917); **3.** United States (71.500).

Individual Show Jumping: 1. Cian O'Connor, (Waterford Crystal) IRL (4 pts) **2.** Rodrigo Pessoa, (Baloubet Du Rouet) BRA (8); **3.** Chris Kappler, (Royal Kaliber) USA (8).

Team Show Jumping: 1. Germany; **2.** United States (12.00); **3.** Sweden (17.25).

Individual 3-Day Eventing: 1. Leslie Law, (Shear L'Eau) GBR (44.40); **2.** Kimberly Severson, (Winsome Adante) USA (45.20); **3.** Phillipa Funnell, (Primmore's Pride) GBR (46.60).

Team 3-Day Eventing: 1. France (140.40); **2.** Great Britain (143.00); **3.** United States (145.60).

USA Entry: Kim Severson, Amy Tryon, Darren Chiacchia, John Williams, Julie Richards.

Note: Germany's **Bettina Hoy** was stripped of her individual eventing gold and Germany lost the team eventing gold when the Court of Arbirtration for Sports ruled that she should be given extra penalty points for crossing the starting line twice on her run.

FENCING

MEN

Individual Epée: 1. Marcel Fischer, SUI def. **2.** Wang Lei, CHN (15-9); **3.** Pavel Kolobkov, RUS def. Eric Boisse, FRA (15-8).

Team Epée: 1. France def. **2.** Hungary (43-32); **3.** Germany def. Russia (37-29).

Individual Foil: 1. Brice Guyart, FRA, def. **2.** Salvatore Sanzo, ITA (15-13); **3.** Andrea Cassara, ITA def. Renal Gannev, RUS (15-12).

Team Foil: 1. Italy def. **2.** China (45-42); **3.** Russia def. United States (45-38).

Individual Sabre: 1. Aldo Montano, ITA, def. **2.** Zsolt Nemcsik, HUN (15-14); **3.** Vladislav Tretiak, UKR def. Dmitri Lapkes, BLR (15-11).

Team Sabre: 1. France def. **2.** Italy (45-42); **3.** Russia def. United States (45-44).

WOMEN

Individual Epée: 1. Timea Nagy, HUN, def. **2.** Laura Flessel-Colovic, FRA (15-10); **3.** Maureen Nisima, FRA def. Ildiko Mincza-Nebald, (15-12).

Team Epée: 1. Russia def. **2.** Germany (34-28); **3.** France def. Canada (45-37).

Individual Foil: 1. Valentina Vezzali, ITA def. **2.** Giovanni Trillini (15-11); **3.** Sylwia Gruchala, POL, def. Aida Mohammed, HUN (15-9).

Individual Sabre: 1. Mariel Zagunis, USA def. **2.** Tan Xue, CHN (15-9); **3.** Sada Jacobson, USA def. Catalina Gheorghitoaia (15-7).

GYMNASTICS

MEN
All-Around

		Points
1	Paul Hamm, USA	57.823
2	Kim Dae Eun, S. KOR	57.811
3	Yang Tae Young, S. KOR	57.774

Other Top 10 USA: 9th—Brett McClure (57.248).

Floor Exercise

		Points
1	Kyle Shewfelt, CAN	9.787
2	Marian Dragulescu, ROM	9.787
3	Jordan Jovtchev, BUL	9.775

Top 10 USA: 5th—Paul Hamm (9.712).

Horizontal Bar

		Points
1	Igor Cassina, ITA	9.812
2	Paul Hamm, USA	9.812
3	Isao Yoneda, JPN	9.787

Other Top 10 USA: 4th—Morgan Hamm (9.787).

Parallel Bars

		Points
1	Valeri Goncharov, UKR	9.787
2	Hiroyuki Tomita, JPN	9.775
3	Li Xiaopeng, CHN	9.762

Top 10 USA: 7th—Paul Hamm (9.737).

Pommel Horse

		Points
1	Teng Haibin, CHN	9.837
2	Marius Daniel Urzica, ROM	9.825
3	Takehiro Kashima, JPN	9.787

Top 10 USA: 6th—Paul Hamm (9.737).

Rings

		Points
1	Dimosthenis Tampakos, GRE	9.862
2	Jordan Jovtchev, BUL	9.850
3	Yuri Chechi, ITA	9.812

Vault

		Points
1	Gervasio Deferr, SPA	9.737
2	Evgeni Sapronenko, LAT	9.706
3	Marian Dragulescu, ROM	9.612

Team

		Points
1	Japan	173.821
2	United States	172.933
3	Romania	172.384

USA entry: Jason Gatson, Morgan Hamm, Paul Hamm, Brett McClure, Blaine Wilson and Guard Young.

WOMEN
All-Around

		Points
1	Carly Patterson, USA	38.387
2	Svetlana Khorkina, RUS	38.211
3	Zhang Nan, CHN	38.049

Other Top 10 USA: 9th—Courtney Kupets (37.112).

Floor Exercise

		Points
1	Catalina Ponor, ROM	9.750
2	Nicoleta Daniela Sofronie, ROM	9.562
3	Patricia Moreno, SPA	9.487

Top 8 USA: 6th—Mohini Bhardwaj (9.312).

Balance Beam

		Points
1	Catalina Ponor, ROM	9.787
2	Carly Patterson, USA	9.775
3	Alexandra Georgiana Eremia, ROM	9.700

Other Top 8 USA: 5th—Courtney Kupets (9.375).

Uneven Bars

		Points
1	Emilie Lepennec, FRA	9.687
2	Terin Humphrey, USA	9.662
3	Courtney Kupets, USA	9.637

Vault

		Points
1	Monica Rosu, ROM	9.656
2	Annia Hatch, USA	9.481
3	Anna Pavlova, RUS	9.475

Team

		Points
1	Romania	114.283
2	United States	113.584
3	Russia	113.235

USA entry: Mohini Bhardwaj, Annia Hatch, Terin Humphrey, Courtney Kupets, Courtney McCool, Carly Patterson.

RHYTHMIC GYMNASTICS

Individual All-Around

		Points
1	Alina Kabaeva, RUS	105.875
2	Irina Tchachina, RUS	105.675
3	Anna Bessonova, UKR	104.725

Team

		Points
1	Russia	49.875
2	Italy	48.175
3	Bulgaria	46.900

TRAMPOLINE

Men

		Points
1	Yuri Nikitin, UKR	41.50
2	Alexander Moskalenko, RUS	41.20
3	Henrik Stehlik, GER	40.80

Women

		Points
1	Anna Dogonadze, GER	39.60
2	Karen Cockburn, CAN	39.20
3	Huang Shanshan, CHN	39.00

JUDO

MEN

Extra Lightweight (132 lbs): **1.** Tadahiro Nomura, JPN **2.** Nestor Khergiani, GEO; **3.** Khashbaatar Tsagaanbaatar, MGL and Choi Min Ho, S. KOR.

Half-Lightweight (143 lbs): **1.** Masato Uchishiba, JPN; **2.** Jozef Krnac, SVK; **3.** Georgi Georgiev, BUL and Yordanis Arencibia, CUB.

Lightweight (157 lbs): **1.** Lee Won Hee, S. KOR; **2.** Vitaliy Makarov, RUS; **3.** Leandro Guilherio, BRA and James Pedro, USA.

Half-Middleweight (172 lbs): **1.** Ilias Iliadis, GRE; **2.** Roman Gontyuk, UKR; **3.** Dmitri Nossov, RUS and Flavio Canto, BRA.

Middleweight (190 lbs): **1.** Zurab Zviadauri, GEO; **2.** Hiroshi Izumi, JPN; **3.** Khasanbi Taov, RUS and Mark Huizinga, NED.

Half-Heavyweight (209 lbs): **1.** Ihar Makarau, BLR; 2. Jang Sung Ho, S.KOR; 3. Michael Jurack, GER and Ariel Zeevi, ISR.

Heavyweight (over 209 lbs): **1.** Keiji Suzuki, JPN; **2.** Tamerlan Tmenov, RUS; **3.** Dennis van Der Geest, NED and Indrek Pertelson, EST.

WOMEN

Extra Lightweight (106 lbs): **1.** Ryoko Tani, JPN; **2.** Frederique Jossinet, FRA; **3.** Julia Matijass, GER and Feng Gao, CHN.

Half-Lightweight (115 lbs): **1.** Xian Dongmei, CHN; **2.** Yuki Yokosawa, JPN; **3.** Amarilys Savon, CUB and Ilse Heylen, BEL.

Lightweight (123 lbs): **1.** Yvonne Boenisch, GER; **2.** Kye Sun Hui, N.KOR; **3.** Deborah Gravenstijn, NED and Yurisleidy Lupetey, CUB.

Half-Middleweight (134 lbs): **1.** Ayumi Tanimoto, JPN; **2.** Claudia Heill, AUT; **3.** Urska Zolnir, SLO and Driulys Gonzalez, CUB.

Middleweight (146 lbs): **1.** Masae Ueno, JPN; **2.** Edith Bosch, NED; **3.** Dongya Qin, CHN and Annett Boehm, GER.

Half-Heavyweight (159 lbs): **1.** Noriko Anno, JPN; **2.** Liu Xia, CHN; **3.** Lucia Morico, ITA and Yurisel Laborde, CUB.

Heavyweight (over 159 lbs): **1.** Maki Tsukada JPN; **2.** Dayma Beltran, CUB; **3.** Tea Donguzashvili, RUS and Sun Fuming, CHN.

MODERN PENTATHLON

Five events in one day—shooting (4.5mm air pistol), fencing (one-touch epée), swimming (200m freestyle), riding (450m stadium course with 15 jumps), and running (3,000m cross-country).

MEN

1. Andrey Moiseev (5,480 pts); **2.** Andrejus Zadneprovskis, LTU (5428); **3.** Libor Capalini, CZE (5392).

Top USA entrant—9th-Vakhtang Iagorashvili (5,276).

WOMEN

1. Zsuzsanna Voros, HUN (5,448 pts); **2.** Jelena Rublevska, LAT (5,380); **3.** Georgina Harland (5,344).

Top USA entrant—15th- Mary Beth Iagorashvili (5,052).

ROWING

(2000-meter course)

MEN

Single Sculls: 1. Olar Tufte, NOR (6:49.30); **2.** Jueri Jaanson, EST (6:51.42); **3.** Ivo Yanakiev, BUL (6:52.80).

Lightweight Double Sculls: 1. Tomasz Kucharski & Robert Sycz, POL (6:20.93); **2.** Frederic Dufour & Pascal Touron, FRA (6:21.46); **3.** Vasileios Polymeros & Nikolaos Skiathitis, GRE (6:23.23).

Double Sculls: 1. Sebastien Vieilledent & Adrien Hardy, FRA (6:29.00); **2.** Luka Spik & Iztok Cop, SLO (6:31.72); **3.** Rossano Galtarossa & Alessio Sartori, ITA (6:32.93).

Quadruple Sculls: 1. Russia (5:56.85); **2.** Czech Republic (5:57.43); **3.** Ukraine (5:58.87).

Coxless Pairs: 1. Drew Ginn & James Tomkins, AUS (6:30.76); **2.** Sinisa Skelin & Niksa Skelin (6:32.64); **3.** Donvan Cech & Roman di Clemente, RSA (6:33.40).

Lightweight Coxless Fours: 1. Denmark (6:01.39); **2.** Austria (6:02.79); **3.** Italy (6:03.74).

Coxless Fours: 1. Great Britain (6:06.98); **2.** Canada (6:07.06); **3.** Italy (6:10.41).

Coxed Eight: 1. United States (5:42.48); **2.** Netherlands (5:43.75); **3.** Australia (5:45.38). **USA entry:** Jason Read, Allen Wyatt, Chris Ahrens, Joseph Hansen, Matt Deakin, Dan Beery, Beau Hoopman, Bryan Volpenhein, Pete Cipollone.

WOMEN

Single Sculls: 1. Katrin Rutschow-Stomporowski, GER (7:18.12); **2.** Ekaterina Karsten (7:22.04); **3.** Rumyana Neykova, BUL (7:23.10).

Lightweight Double Sculls: 1. Constanta Burcica & Angela Alupei, ROM (6:56.05); **2.** Daniela Reimer & Claudia Blasberg, GER (6:57.33); **3.** Kirsten van Der Kolk & Marit van Eupen, NED (6:58.54).

Double Sculls: 1. Georgina Evers-Swindell & Caroline Evers-Swindell, NZL (7:01.79); **2.** Peggy Waleska & Britta Oppelt, GER (7:02.78); **3.** Sarah Winckless & Elise Laverick, GBR (7:07.58).

Quadruple Sculls: 1. Germany (6:29.29); **2.** Great Britain (6:31.26); **3.** Australia (6:34.73).

Coxless Pairs: 1. Georgeta Damian & Viorica Susanu, ROM (7:06.55); **2.** Katherine Grainger & Cath Bishop, GBR (7:08.66); **3.** Yuliya Bichyk & Natallia Helakh, BLR (7:09.86).

Coxed Eights: 1. Romania (6:17.70); **2.** United States (6:19.56); **3.** Netherlands (6:19.85). **USA entry:** 2nd— Kate Johnson, Samantha Magee, Megan Dirkmaat, Alison Cox, Anna Mickelson, Laurel Korholz, Caryn Davies, Lianne Nelson, Mary Whipple.

SAILING

OPEN

Laser: 1. Robert Scheidt, BRA; **2.** Andreas Geritzer, AUT; **3.** Vasilij Zbogar, SLO.

Tornado: 1. Roman Hagara & Hans Peter Steinacher, AUT; **2.** John Lovell & Charlie Ogletree, USA; **3.** Carlos Espinola & Santiago Lange, ARG.

49er: 1. Xavier Fernandez & Iker Martinez, SPA; **2.** George Leonchuk & Rodion Luka, UKR; **3.** Chris Draper & Simon Hiscocks, GBR.

MEN

Finn: 1. Ben Ainslie, GBR; **2.** Rafael Trujillo, SPA; **3.** Mateusz Kusznierewicz, POL.

Mistral: 1. Gal Fridman, ISR; **2.** Nikolaos Kaklamanakis, GRE; **3.** Nick Dempsey, GBR.

470: 1. Kevin Burnham & Paul Foerster, USA; **2.** Joe Glanfield & Nick Rogers, GBR; **3.** Kazuto Seki & Kenjiro Todoroki, JPN.

Star: 1. Marcelo Ferreira & Torben Grael, BRA; **2.** Ross MacDonald & Mike Wolfs, CAN; **3.** Pascal Rambeau & Xavier Rohart, FRA.

WOMEN

Europe: 1. Siren Sundby, NOR; **2.** Lenka Smidova, CZE; **3.** Signe Livbjerg, DEN.

Mistral: 1. Faustine Merret, FRA; **2.** Jian Yin, CHN; **3.** Alessandra Sensini, ITA.

470: 1. Sofia Bekatorou & Aimilia Tsoulfa, GRE; **2.** Sandra Azon & Natalia Via Dufresne, SPA; **3.** Therese Torgersson & Vendela Zachrisson, SWE.

Yngling: 1. Great Britain; **2.** Ukraine; **3.** Denmark.

SHOOTING

MEN

50m Free Pistol: 1. Mikhail Nestruev, RUS (663.3 pts); **2.** Jin Jong Oh, S. KOR (661.5); **3.** Kim Jong Su, N. KOR (657.7).

50m Free Rifle/3 Positions: 1. Zhanbo Jia, CHN (1264.5 pts); **2.** Michael Anti, USA (1263.1); **3.** Christian Planer, AUT (1262.8).

50m Free Rifle/Prone: 1. Matthew Emmons, USA (703.3 pts); **2.** Christian Lusch, GER (702.2); **3.** Sergei Martynov, BLR (701.6).

25m Rapid Fire Pistol: 1. Ralf Schumann, GER (694.9 pts); **2.** Sergei Poliakov, RUS (692.7); **3.** Sergei Alifirenko, RUS (692.3).

10m Running Game Target: 1. Manfred Kurzer, GER (682.4 pts); **2.** Alexander Blinov, RUS (678.0); **3.** Dimitri Lykin, RUS (677.1).

10m Air Pistol: 1. Wang Yifu, CHN (690.0 pts); **2.** Mikhail Nestruev, RUS (689.8); **3.** Vladimir Isakov, RUS (684.3).

10m Air Rifle: 1. Zhu Qinan, CHN (702.7 pts); **2.** Li Jie, CHN (701.3); **3.** Jozef Gonci, SVK (697.4).

Trap: 1. Alexei Alipov, RUS (149 pts); **2.** Giovanni Pellielo, ITA (146); **3.** Adam Vella, AUS (145).

Double Trap: 1. Ahmed Almaktoum, UAE (189 pts); **2.** Rajyavardhan Singh Rathore, IND (179); **3.** Wang Zheng, CHN (178).

Skeet: 1. Andrea Benelli, ITA (149 pts, won shoot-off); **2.** Marko Kemppainen, FIN (149); **3.** Juan Miguel Rodriguez, CUB (147).

WOMEN

25m Sport Pistol: 1. Maria Grozdeva, BUL (688.2 pts); **2.** Lenka Hykova, CZE (687.8); **3.** Irada Ashumova, AZB (687.3).

10m Air Pistol: 1. Olga Klochneva, RUS (483.3 pts, won shoot-off); **2.** Jasna Sekaric, SBM (483.3); **3.** Maria Grozdeva, BUL (482.3).

50m smallbore/3 Positions: 1. Lioubov Galkina, RUS (688.4 pts); **2.** Valentina Turisini, ITA (685.9); **3.** Wang Chengyi, CHN (685.4.

10m Air Rifle: 1. Du Li, CHN (502.0 pts); **2.** Lioubov Galkina, RUS (501.5); **3.** Katerina Kurkoba, CZE (501.1).

Double Trap: 1. Kim Rhode, USA (146 pts); **2.** Lee Bo Na, S. KOR (145); **3.** Gao E, CHN (142).

Skeet: 1. Diana Igaly, Hungary (97 pts); **2.** Wei Ning, CHN (93); **3.** Zemfira Meftakhetdinova, AZB (93).

SWIMMING

MEN
50-meter Freestyle

		Time
1	Gary Hall Jr., USA	21.93
2	Duje Draganja, CRO	21.94
3	Roland Mark Schoeman, RSA	22.02

100-meter Freestyle

		Time
1	Pieter van den Hoogenband, NED	48.17
2	Roland Mark Schoeman, RSA	48.23
3	Ian Thorpe, AUS	48.56

200-meter Freestyle

		Time	
1	Ian Thorpe, AUS	1:44.71	OR
2	Pieter van den Hoogenband, NED	1:45.23	
3	Michael Phelps, USA	1:45.32	

400-meter Freestyle

		Time
1	Ian Thorpe, AUS	3:43.10
2	Grant Hackett, AUS	3:43.36
3	Klete Keller, USA	3:44.11

1500-meter Freestyle

		Time	
1	Grant Hackett, AUS	14:43.40	OR
2	Larsen Jensen, USA	14:45.29	
3	David Davies, GBR	14:45.95	

100-meter Backstroke

		Time
1	Aaron Peirsol, USA	54.06
2	Markus Rogan, AUT	54.35
3	Tomomi Morita, JPN	54.36

200-meter Backstroke

		Time	
1	Aaron Peirsol, USA	1:54.95	OR
2	Markus Rogan, AUT	1:57.35	
3	Razvan Florea, ROM	1:57.56	

100-meter Breaststroke

		Time
1	Kosuke Kitajima, JPN	1:00.08
2	Brendan Hansen, USA	1:00.25
3	Hugues Duboscq, FRA	1:00.88

200-meter Breaststroke

		Time	
1	Kosuke Kitajima, JPN	2:09.44	OR
2	Daniel Gyurta, HUN	2:10.80	
3	Brendan Hansen, USA	2:10.87	

100-meter Butterfly

		Time	
1	Michael Phelps, USA	51.25	OR
2	Ian Crocker, USA	51.29	
3	Andriy Serdinov, UKR	51.36	

200-meter Butterfly

		Time	
1	Michael Phelps, USA	1:54.04	OR
2	Takashi Yamamoto, JPN	1:54.56	
3	Stephen Parry, GBR	1:55.52	

200-meter Individual Medley

		Time	
1	Michael Phelps, USA	1:57.14	OR
2	Ryan Lochte, USA	1:58.78	
3	George Bovell, TRI	1:58.80	

400-meter Individual Medley

		Time	
1	Michael Phelps USA	4:08.26	WR
2	Erik Vendt, USA	4:11.81	
3	Lasklo Cseh, HUN	4:12.15	

4x100-meter Freestyle Relay

		Time	
1	South Africa	3:13.17	WR
2	Netherlands	3:14.36	
3	United States	3:14.62	

RSA—Roland Mark Schoeman, Lyndon Ferns, Darian Townsend, Ryk Neethling.; **NED**—Johan Kenkhuis, Mitja Zastrow, Klaas-Erik Zwering, Pieter van den Hoogenband; **USA**—Ian Crocker, Michael Phelps, Neil Walker, Jason Lezak.

4x200-meter Freestyle Relay

		Time
1	United States	7:07.33
2	Australia	7:07.46
3	Italy	7:11.83

USA—Michael Phelps, Ryan Lochte, Peter Vanderkaay, Klete Keller; **AUS**—Grant Hackett, Michael Klim, Nicholas Sprenger, Ian Thorpe; **ITA**—Emiliano Brembilla, Massimiliano Rosolino, Simone Cercato, Filippo Magnini.

4x100-meter Medley Relay

		Time	
1	United States	3:30.68	WR
2	Germany	3:33.62	
3	Japan	3:35.22	

USA—Aaron Perisol, Brendan Hansen, Ian Crocker, Jason Lezak; **GER**—Steffen Driesen, Jens Kruppa, Thomas Rupprath, Lars Conrad; **JPN**—Tomomi Morita, Kosuke Kitajima, Takashi Yamamoto, Yoshihiro Okumaura.

WOMEN
50-meter Freestyle

		Time
1	Inge de Bruijn, NED	24.58
2	Malia Metella, FRA	24.89
3	Lisbeth Lenton, AUS	24.91

100-meter Freestyle

		Time
1	Jodie Henry, AUS	53.84
2	Inge de Bruijn, NED	54.16
3	Natalie Coughlin, USA	54.40

200-meter Freestyle

		Time
1	Camelia Potec, ROM	1:58.03
2	Federica Pellegrini, ITA	1:58.22
3	Solenne Figues, FRA	1:58.45

400-meter Freestyle

		Time
1	Laure Manaudou, FRA	4:05.34
2	Otylia Jedrzejczak, POL	4:05.84
3	Kaitlin Sandeno, USA	4:06.19

800-meter Freestyle

		Time
1	Ai Shibata, JPN	8:24.54
2	Laure Manaudou, FRA	8:24.96
3	Diana Munz, USA	8:26.61

100-meter Backstroke

		Time
1	Natalie Coughlin, USA	1:00.37
2	Kirsty Coventry, ZIM	1:00.50
3	Laure Manaudou, FRA	1:00.88

200-meter Backstroke

		Time
1	Kirsty Coventry, ZIM	2:09.19
2	Stanislava Komarova, RUS	2:09.72
3	Reiko Nakamura, JPN	2:09.88

100-meter Breaststroke

		Time	
1	Luo Xuejuan, CHN	1:06.64	OR
2	Brooke Hansen, AUS	1:07.15	
3	Leisel Jones, AUS	1:07.16	

200-meter Breaststroke

		Time	
1	Amanda Beard, USA	2:23.37	OR
2	Leisel Jones, AUS	2:23.60	
3	Anne Poleska, GER	2:25.82	

100-meter Butterfly

		Time
1	Petria Thomas, AUS	57.72
2	Otylia Jedrzejczak, POL	57.84
3	Inge de Bruijn, NED	57.99

200-meter Butterfly

		Time
1	Otylia Jedrzejczak, POL	2:06.05
2	Petria Thomas, AUS	2:06.36
3	Anne Poleska, GER	2:25.82

200-meter Individual Medley

		Time
1	Yana Klochkova, UKR	2:11.14
2	Amanda Beard, USA	2:11.70
3	Kirsty Coventry, ZIM	2:12.72

400-meter Individual Medley

		Time
1	Yana Klochkova, UKR	4:34.83
2	Kaitlin Sandeno, USA	4:34.95
3	Georgina Bardach, ARG	4:37.51

4x 100-meter Freestyle Relay

		Time	
1	Australia	3:35.94	WR
2	United States	3:36.39	
3	Netherlands	3:37.59	

AUS—Alice Mills, Lisbeth Lenton, Petria Thomas, Jodie Henry; **USA**—Kara Lynn Joyce, Natalie Coughlin, Amanda Weir, Jenny Thompson; **NED**—Chantal Groot, Inge Dekker, Marleen Veldhuis, Inge de Bruijn.

4x 200-meter Freestyle Relay

		Time	
1	United States	7:53.42	WR
2	China	7:55.97	
3	Germany	7:57.35	

USA—Natalie Coughlin, Carly Piper, Dana Vollmer, Kaitlin Sandeno; **CHN**—Zhu Yingwen, Xu Yanwei, Yang Yu, Pang Jiaying; **GER**—Franziska van Almsick, Petra Dallmann, Antje Buschschulte, Hannah Stockbauer.

4x 100-meter Medley Relay

		Time	
1	Australia	3:57.32	WR
2	United States	3:59.12	
3	Germany	4:00.72	

AUS—Giaan Rooney, Leisel Jones, Petria Thomas, Jodie Henry; **USA**—Natalie Coughlin, Amanda Beard, Jenny Thompson, Kara Lynn Joyce; **GER**—Antje Buschschulte, Sarah Poewe, Franziska van Almsick, Daniela Gotz.

Synchronized Swimming

Duet: 1. Anastasia Davydova & Anastasia Ermakova, RUS (99.334 pts); **2.** Miya Tachibana & Miho Takeda, JPN (98.417); **3.** Alison Bartosik & Anna Kozlova, USA (96.918)

Team: 1. Russia (99.667 pts); **2.** Japan (98.667); **3.** United States (97.667).

USA Entry—Alison Bartosik, Tamara Crow, Rebecca Jasontek, Anna Kozlova, Sara Lowe, Lauren McFall, Stephanie Nesbitt, Kendra Zanotto.

TABLE TENNIS

MEN

Singles: 1. Ryu Seung Min, S. KOR def. **2.** Wang Hao, CHN (4 games to 2); **3.** Wang Liqin, CHN def. Jan-Ove Waldner, SWE (4 games to 1).

Doubles: 1. Chen Qi & Ma Lin, CHN, def. **2.** Ko Lai Chak & Li Ching, HKG (4 games to 2); **3.** Michael Maze & Finn Tugwell, DEN, def. Dimitrij Mazunov & Alexei Smirnov, RUS (4 games to 2).

WOMEN

Singles: 1. Zhang Yining, CHN, def. **2.** Kim Hyang Mi, N.KOR (4 games to 0); **3.** Kim Kyung Ah, S.KOR, def. Li Jia Wei, SIN (4 games to 1).

Doubles: 1. Wang Nan & Zhang Yining, CHN, def. **2.** Lee Eun Sil & Seok Eun Mi, S.KOR (4 games to 0); **3.** Guo Yue & Niu Jianfeng, CHN, def. Kim Bok Rae & Kim Kyung Ah, S.KOR (4 games to 3).

TAEKWONDO

MEN

128 pounds: 1. Ten Chu Mu, TPE def. **2.** Oscar Franiso Salazar Blanco, MEX (5-1); **3.** Tamer Bayoumi, EGY def. Juan Ramos, SPA (9-4).

150 pounds: 1. Hadi Saei Bonehkohal, IRI def. **2.** Hsiung Huang Chih, TPE (4-3); **3.** Seob Song Myeong, S.KOR def. Diogo Silva, BRA (12-7).

176 pounds: 1. Steve Lopez, USA def. **2.** Bahri Tanrikulu, CHN (3-1); **3.** Yossef Karami, IRI def. Rashad Ahmadov, AZB (9-8).

Over 176 pounds: 1. Sung Moon Dae, S.KOR def. **2.** Alexandros Nikolaidis, GRE (3-0); **3.** Pascal Gentil, FRA def. Ibrahim Kamal (6-2).

Taekwondo (Cont.)

WOMEN

108 pounds: 1. Hsin Chen Shih, TPE def. **2.** Yanelis Yuliet Labrada Diaz , CUB (5-4); **3.** Yaowapa Boorapolchai, THA def. Gladys Alicia Mora Romero, COL (2-1).

125 pounds: 1. Won Jang Ji, S.KOR def. **2.** Nia Abdallah, USA (2-1); **3.** Iridia Salazar Blanco, MEX def. Sonia Reyes, SPA (2-1).

147 pounds: 1. Wei Luo, CHN def. **2.** Elisavet Mystakidou, GRE (7-6); **3.** Sun Hwang Kyung, S.KOR def. Heidy Juarez, GUA (5-8).

Over 147 pounds: 1. Zhong Chen, CHN def. **2.** Myriam Baverel, FRA (12-5); **3.** Adriana Carmona, VEN def. Natalia Silva, BRA (7-4).

TENNIS

MEN

Singles: 1. Nicolas Massu, CHI, def. **2.** Mardy Fish, USA 6-3, 3-6, 2-6, 6-3,6-4; **3.** Leander Paes, IND def. Fernando Meligeni, BRA 3-6, 6-2, 6-4.

Doubles: 1. Fernando Gonzalez & Nicolas Massu, CHI, def. **2.** Nicolas Kiefer & Rainer Schuettler, GER 6-2, 4-6, 3-6, 7-6 (9-7), 6-4; **3.** Mario Ancic & Ivan Ljubicic, CRO def. Mahesh Bhupathi & Leander Paes, IND 7-6 (7-5), 4-6. 16-14.

WOMEN

Singles: 1. Justine Henin-Hardenne, BEL def. **2.** Amelie Mauresmo, FRA 6-3, 6-3; **3.** Alicia Molik, AUS def. Anastasia Myskina, RUS 6-3, 6-4.

Doubles: 1. Li Ting & Sun Tian Tian, CHN, def. **2.** Conchita Martinez & Virginia Ruano Pascual, SPA, 6-3, 6-3; **3.** Paola Suarez & Patricia Tarabini, ARG def. Shinobu Asagoe & Ai Sugiyama, JPN 6-3, 6-3.

TRACK & FIELD

MEN

100 meters

		Time
1	Justin Gatlin, USA	9.85
2	Francis Obikwelu, POR	9.86
3	Maurice Greene, USA	9.87

Other Top 8 USA—4th Shawn Crawford (9.89).

200 meters

		Time
1	Shawn Crawford, USA	19.79
2	Bernard Williams, USA	20.01
3	Justin Gatlin, USA	20.03

400 meters

		Time
1	Jeremy Wariner, USA	44.00
2	Otis Harris, USA	44.16
3	Derrick Brew, USA	44.42

800 meters

		Time
1	Yuriy Borzakovskiy, RUS	1:44.45
2	Mbulaeni Mulaudzi, RSA	1:44.61
3	Wilson Kipketer, DEN	1:44.65

1500 meters

		Time
1	Hicham El Guerrouj, MAR	3:34.18
2	Bernard Lagat, KEN	3:34.30
3	Rui Silva, POR	3:34.68

5000 meters

		Time
1	Hicham El Guerrouj, MAR	13:14.39
2	Kenenisa Bekele, ETH	13:14.59
3	Eliud Kipchoge, KEN	13:15.10

10,000 meters

		Time	
1	Kenenisa Bekele, ETH	27:05.10	OR
2	Sileshi Sihine, ETH	27:09.39	
3	Zarsenay Tadesse, ERI	27:22.57	

Marathon

		Time
1	Stefano Baldini, ITA	2:10:55
2	Mebrahtom Keflezighi, USA	2:11:29
3	Vanderlei Lima, BRA	2:12:11

Other Top USA—12th Alan Culpepper (2:15:26); 65th Daniel Browne (2:27:17).

4x100-meter Relay

		Time
1	Great Britain	38.07
2	United States	38.08
3	Nigeria	38.23

GBR—Jason Gardner, Darren Campbell, Marlon Devonish, Mark Lewis-Francis; **USA**—Shawn Crawford, Justin Gatlin, Coby Miller, Maurice Greene; **NGR**—Olusoji A. Fasuba, Uchenna Emedolu, Aaron Egbele, Deji Aliu.

4x400-meter Relay

		Time
1	United States	2:55.91
2	Australia	3:00.60
3	Nigeria	3:00.90

USA—Otis Harris, Derrick Brew, Jeremy Wariner, Darold Williamson; **AUS**—John Steffensen, Mark Ormrod, Patrick Dwyer, Clinton Hill; **NGR**—James Godday, Musa Audu, Saul Weigopwa, Enefiok Udo Obong.

110-meter Hurdles

		Time	
1	Liu Xiang, CHN	12.91	OR
2	Terrence Trammell, USA	13.18	
3	Anier Garcia, CUB	13.20	

400-meter Hurdles

		Time
1	Felix Sanchez, DOM	47.63
2	Danny McFarlane, JAM	48.11
3	Naman Keita, FRA	48.26

3000-meter Steeplechase

		Time
1	Ezekiel Kemboi, KEN	8:05.81
2	Brimin Kipruto, KEN	8:06.11
3	Paul Kipsiele Koech, KEN	8:06.64

USA Top 15—11th Daniel Lincoln (8:16.86).

20-kilometer Walk

		Time
1	Ivano Brugnetti, ITA	1:19:40
2	Francisco Javier Fernandez, SPA	1:19:45
3	Nathan Deakes, AUS	1:20:02

USA Entrants—20th Timothy Seaman (1:25:17), 21st Kevin Eastler (1:25:20); 26th John Nunn (1:27:38).

50-kilometer Walk

		Time
1	Robert Korzeniowski, POL	3:38:46
2	Denis Nizhegorodov, RUS	3:42:50
3	Aleksey Voyevodin, RUS	3:43:34

USA Entrants—32nd Curt Clausen (4:11:31), 35th Phillip Dunn (4:12:49).

High Jump

		Height
1	Stefan Holm, SWE	7-8¾
2	Matthew Hemingway, USA	7-8
3	Jaroslav Baba, CZE	7-8

Note: Second, third and fourth place (**Jamie Nieto**, USA) all cleared the same height, order of finish was decided by number of misses.

Pole Vault

		Height
1	Timothy Mack, USA	19-6¼ **OR**
2	Toby Stevenson, USA	19-4¼
3	Giuseppe Gibilisco, ITA	19-2¼

Long Jump

		Distance
1	Dwight Phillips, USA	28-2¼
2	John Moffitt, USA	27-9½
3	Joan Lino Martinez, SPA	27-3¾

Triple Jump

		Distance
1	Christian Olsson, SWE	58-4½
2	Marian Oprea, ROM	57-7
3	Danila Burkenya, RUS	57-4¼

Top 10 USA—9th Kenwood Bell (55-5½)

Shot Put

		Distance
1	Yuriy Bilonog, UKR	69-5¼
2	Adam Nelson, USA	69-5¼
3	Joachim Olsen, DEN	69-1½

Other Top 10 USA—9th John Godina (66-3).

Discus

		Distance
1	Virgilijius Alekna, LTU	229-3
2	Zoltan Kovago, HUN	219-11
3	Aleksander Tammert, EST	218-8

Note: Hungary's **Robert Fazekas** had a throw of 232 feet, 8 inches, and was initially declared the winner, but he was disqualified for failing to submit to a drug test following the competition.

Top 10 USA—7th Casey Malone (211-0)

Hammer Throw

		Distance
1	Koji Murofushi, JPN	272-0
2	Ivan Tikhon, BLR	261-10
3	Esref Apak, TUR	260-10

Note: Hungary's **Adrian Annus** was initially awarded the gold medal for his throw of 272-11, but after questions were raised about the legitimacy of his post-competition drug test, and he failed to submit to a follow-up test, he was disqualified and stripped of the gold.

Javelin

		Distance
1	Andreas Thorkildsen, NOR	283-9
2	Vadims Vasilevskis, LAT	278-8
3	Sergey Makarov, RUS	278-4

Decthalon

Ten events held over two days: 100m dash, long jump, shot put, high jump, 400m run, 110m hurdles, discus, pole vault, javelin, 1500m run

		Points
1	Roman Sebrle, CZE	8893
2	Bryan Clay, USA	8820
3	Dmitriy Karpov, KAZ	8725

WOMEN

100 meters

		Time
1	Yuliya Nesterenko, BLR	10.93
2	Lauryn Williams, USA	10.96
3	Veronica Campbell, JAM	10.97

Other Top 8 USA—8th LaTasha Colander (11.18)

200 meters

		Time
1	Veronica Campbell, JAM	22.05
2	Allyson Felix, USA	22.18
3	Debbie Ferguson, BAH	22.30

Other Top 8 USA—7th Muna Lee (22.87)

400 meters

		Time
1	Tonique Williams-Darling, BAH	49.41
2	Ana Guevara, MEX	49.56
3	Natalya Antyukh, RUS	49.89

Top 8 USA—4th Monique Hennagan (49.97), 5th DeeDee Trotter (50.00), 6th Sanya Richards (50.19).

800 meters

		Time
1	Kelly Holmes, GBR	1:56.38
2	Hasna Benhassi, MAR	1:56.43
3	Jolanda Ceplak, SLO	1:56.43

1500 meters

		Time
1	Kelly Holmes, GBR	3:57.90
2	Tatyana Tomashova, RUS	3:58.12
3	Maria Cioncan, ROM	3:58.39

5000 meters

		Time
1	Meseret Defar, ETH	14:45.65
2	Isabella Ochichi, KEN	14:48.19
3	Tirunesh Dibaba, ETH	14:51.83

10,000 meters

		Time
1	Xing Huina, CHN	30:24.36
2	Ejegayehu Dibaba, ETH	30:24.98
3	Derartu Tulu, ETH	30:26.42

Marathon

		Time
1	Mizuki Noguchi, JPN	2:26:20
2	Catherine Ndereba, KEN	2:26:32
3	Deena Kastor, USA	2:27:20

Other Top USA—34th Jennifer Rhines (2:43:52), 39th Colleen de Reuck (2:46:30).

4x100-meter Relay

		Time
1	Jamaica	41.73
2	Russia	42.27
3	France	42.54

JAM—Tayna Lawrence, Sherone Simpson, Aleen Bailey, Veronica Campbell; **RUS**—Olga Fyodorova, Yulita Tabakova, Irina Khabarova, Larisa Kruglova; **FRA**—Veronique Mang, Muriel Hurtis, Sylviane Felix, Christine Arron.

4x400-meter Relay

		Time
1	United States	3:19.01
2	Russia	3:20.16
3	Jamaica	3:22.00

USA—DeeDee Trotter, Monique Henderson, Sanya Richards, Monique Hennagan; **RUS**—Olesya Krasnomovets, Natalya Nazarova, Olesya Zykina, Natalya Antyukh; **JAM**—Novlene Williams, Michelle Burgher, Nadia Davy, Sandie Richards.

100-meter Hurdles

		Time	
1	Joanna Hayes, USA	12.37	OR
2	Olena Krasovska, UKR	12.45	
3	Melissa Morrison, USA	12.56	

400-meter Hurdles

		Time
1	Fani Halkia, GRE	52.82
2	Ionela Tirlea-Manolache, ROM	53.38
3	Tetiana Tereshchuk-Antipova, UKR	53.44

Top 8 USA—4th Sheena Johnson (53.83), 7th Brenda Taylor (54.97)

20-kilometer Walk

		Time
1	Athanasia Tsoumeleka, GRE	1:29:12
2	Olimpiada Ivanova, RUS	1:29:16
3	Jane Saville, AUS	1:29:25

Top USA—43rd Teresa Vaill (1:38:17).

High Jump

		Height	
1	Yelena Slesarenko, RUS	6-9	OR
2	Hestrie Suzette Cloete, RSA	6-7½	
3	Vita Styopina, UKR	6-7½	

Top USA—4th Amy Acuff (6-6¼).

Pole Vault

		Height	
1	Yelena Isinbayeva, RUS	16-1¼	WR
2	Svetlana Feofanova, RUS	15-7	
3	Anna Rogowska, POL	15-5	

Long Jump

		Distance
1	Tatyana Lebedeva, RUS	23-2½
2	Irina Simagina, RUS	23-1¾
3	Tatyanaa Kotova, RUS	23-1¾

Top USA—5th Marion Jones (22-5¾), 10th Grace Upshaw (21-9½)

Triple Jump

		Distance
1	Francoise Mbango Etone, CMR	50-2½
2	Chrysopigi Devetzi, GRE	50-0½
3	Tatyana Lebedeva, RUS	49-8¼

Shot Put

		Distance
1	Yumileidi Cumba, CUB	64-3¼
2	Nadine Kleinert, GER	64-1¾
3	Svetlana Krivelyova, RUS	63-11½

Note: Russia's **Irina Korzhanenko** (69-1¼) was initially awarded the gold medal but was later stripped of it for failing a post-competition drug test.

Discus

		Distance
1	Natalya Sadova, RUS	219-10
2	Anastasia Kelesidou, GRE	218-9
3	Iryna Yatchenko. BLR	217-1

Hammer Throw

		Distance	
1	Olga Kuzenkova, RUS	246-1	OR
2	Yipsi Moreno, CUB	240-8¼	
3	Yunaika Crawford, CUB	240-0½	

Javelin

		Distance	
1	Osleidys Menedez, CUB	234-8	OR
2	Steffi Nerius, GER	215-11	
3	Mirela Manjani, GRE	210-11	

Heptathlon

Seven events held over two days: 100m hurdles, high jump, shot put, 200m dash, long jump, javelin, 800m run

		Points
1	Carolina Kluft, SWE	6952
2	Austra Skujyte, LTU	6435
3	Kelly Sotherton, GBR	6424

Top USA—4th Shelly Burrell (6296), 14th Michelle Perry (6124).

AP/Wide World Photos

*Gold-medalist **Hossein Reza Zadeh** of Iran celebrates after lifting 581 pounds for a world record in the clean and jerk at the 2004 Summer Olympics in Athens.*

TRIATHLON

1.5k swim, 40k bike, 10k run

MEN

1. Hamish Carter, NZL (1:51:07.73); **2.** Bevan Docherty, NZL (1:51:15.60); **3.** Sven Riederer, SUI (1:51:33.26)

Top USA—9th Hunter Kemper (1:52:46.33), 22nd Andy Potts (1:55:36.47)

WOMEN

1. Kate Allen, AUT (2:04:43.45); **2.** Loretta Harrop, AUS (2:04:50.17); **3.** Susan Williams, USA (2:05:08.92)

Other Top USA—9th Barbara Lindquist (2:06:25.49), 23rd Sheila Taormina, USA (2:09:21.08)

WEIGHTLIFTING

MEN

123 lbs (56kg): **1.** Halil Mutlu, TUR (650 lbs); **2.** Wu Meijin, CHN (634); **3.** Sedat Artuc, TUR (617).

136 lbs (62kg): **1.** Shi Zhiyong, CHN (717 lbs); **2.** Le Maosheng, CHN (689); **3.** Israel Jose Rubio*, VEN (650).

***Leonidas Sampanis** (689 lbs) of Greece originally won the bronze medal in the 136-pound division but was stripped of the medal after testing positive for twice the legal limit of testosterone.

152 lbs (69kg): **1.** Zhang Guozheng, CHN (766 lbs); **2.** Lee Bae Young, S.KOR (755); **3.** Nikolay Pechalov, CRO (744).

169 lbs (77kg): **1.** Taner Sagir, TUR (827 lbs); **2.** Sergey Filimonov, KAZ (821); **3.** Oleg Perepetchenov, RUS (805).

187 lbs (85kg): **1.** George Asanidze, GEO (843 lbs); **2.** Andrei Rybakou, BLR (838); **3.** Pyrros Dimas, GRE (832).

207 lbs (94kg): **1.** Milon Dobrev, BUL (899 lbs); **2.** Khadjimourad Akkaev, RUS (893); **3.** Eduard Tjukin, RUS (875).

231 lbs (105kg): **1.** Dmitry Berestov, RUS (937 lbs); **2.** Igor Razoronov*, UKR (926); **3.** Gleb Pisarevskiy*, RUS (915).

***Hungary's Ferenc Gyurkovics** (926 lbs) originally won the silver medal in the 231-pound division but was stripped for testing positive for steroids

Over 231 lbs (105+kg): **1.** Hossein Reza Zadeh, IRN (1042 lbs); **2.** Viktors Scerbatihs, LAT (1003); **3.** Velichko Cholakov, BUL (987).

WOMEN

106 lbs (48kg): **1.** Nurcan Taylan, TUR (463 lbs); **2.** Zhuo Li , CHN (452); **3.** Aree Wiratthaworn , THA (441).

123 lbs (53kg): **1.** Udomporn Polsak, THA (491 lbs); **2.** Raema Lisa Rumbewas, INA (463); **3.** Mabel Mosquera Mena, COL (435).

128 lbs (58kg): **1.** Chen Yanqing , TUR (524 lbs); **2.** Ri Song Hui, N.KOR (513); **3.** Wandee Kameaim, THA (507).

139 lbs (63kg): **1.** Nataliya Skakun, UKR (535 lbs); **2.** Hanna Batsiushka, BLR (535); **3.** Tatsiana Stukalava, BLR (491).

152 lbs (69kg): **1.** Liu Chunhong, CHN (606 lbs); **2.** Eszter Krutzler, HUN (579); **3.** Zarema Kasaeva, RUS (579).

165 lbs (75kg): **1.** Pawina Thongsuk, THA (601 lbs); **2.** Natalia Zabolotnaia, RUS (601); **3.** Valentina Popova, RUS (584).

Over 165 lbs (75+kg): **1.** Tang Gonghong, CHN (673 lbs); **2.** Jang Mi Ran, S.KOR (667); **3.** Agata Wrobel, POL (639).

WRESTLING

Freestyle

MEN

121 lbs (55 kg): **1.** Mavlet Batirov, RUS def. **2.** Stephen Abas, USA (9-1); **3.** Chikara Tanabe, JPN def. Armiran Karntanov, GER (7-0).

132 lbs (60 kg): **1.** Yandro Miguel Quintana Rivalta, CUB def. **2.** Masuod Mostafa Gokar, IRA (4-0); **3.** Kenji Inoue, JPN def. Vasyl Fedoryshyn, UKR (6-5).

145 lbs (66 kg): **1.** Elbrus Tedeyev, UKR def. **2.** Jamill Kelly, USA (5-1); **3.** Makhach Murtazaliev, RUS def. Leonid Spiridonov, KAZ (2-1).

163 lbs (74 kg): **1.** Buvaysa Saytiev, RUS def. **2.** Gennadiy Laliyev, KAZ (7-0); **3.** Ivan Fundora Zaldivar, CUB def. Krystian Brzozowski, POL (3-0).

184 lbs (84 kg): **1.** Cael Sanderson, USA def. **2.** Moon Eui Jae, S. KOR (3-1); **3.** Sazhid Sazhidov, RUS def. Yoel Romero Palacios, CUB (5-3).

211 lbs (96 kg): **1.** Khadjimourat Gatsalov, RUS def. **2.** Magomed Ibragimov, UZB (4-1); **3.** Alireza Heidari, IRA def. Daniel Cormier, USA (3-2).

264 lbs (120 kg): **1.** Artur Taymazov, UZB def. **2.** Alireza Rezaei, IRA (by fall, 4:33); **3.** Aydin Polatci, TUR def. Marid Mutalimov, KAZ (3-1).

WOMEN

106 lbs (48 kg): **1.** Irinin Merleni, UKR def. **2.** Chiharu Icho, JPN (2-2, ref's decision); **3.** Patricia Miranda, USA def. Angelique Berthenet, FRA (12-4).

121 lbs (55 kg): **1.** Saori Yoshida, JPN def. **2.** Tonya Verbeek, CAN (6-0); **3.** Anna Gomis, FRA def. Ida-Theres Karlsson, SWE (6-0).

139 lbs (63 kg): **1.** Kaori Icho, JPN def. **2.** Sara McMann, USA (3-2); **3.** Lisa Legrand, FRA def. Stavroula Zygouri, GRE (by fall, 2:04).

158 lbs (72 kg): **1.** Wang Xu, CHN def. **2.** Gouzel Maniourova, RUS (7-2); **3.** Kyoko Hamaguchi, JPN def. Svitlana Sayenko, UKR (4-0).

Greco-Roman

MEN

121 lbs (55 kg): **1.** Istvan Majoros, HUN def. **2.** Gueidar Mamedaliev, RUS (3-1); **3.** Artiom Kiouregkian, GRE def. Oleksiy Vakulenko, UKR (6-1)

132 lbs (60 kg): **1.** Jung Ji Hyun, S.KOR def. **2.** Roberto Monzon Gonzalez, CUB (3-0); **3.** Armen Nazarian, BUL def. Alexey Shevtsov, RUS (4-3).

145 lbs (66 kg): **1.** Farid Mansurov, AZB def. **2.** Seref Eroglu, TUR (4-3); **3.** Mkkhitar Manukyan, KAZ def. Jimmy Samielsson, SWE (8-1).

163 lbs (74 kg): **1.** Alexandr Dokturishivili, UZB def. **2.** Marko Yli-Hannuksela, FIN (4-1); **3.** Varteres Samourgachev, RUS def. Reto Bucher, SUI (10-0).

185 lbs (84 kg): **1.** Alexei Michine, RUS def. **2.** Ara Abrahamian, SWE (1-1, ref's decision); **3.** Viachaslau Makaranka, BLR def. Hamza Yerlikaya, TUR (2-1).

211 lbs (96 kg): **1.** Karam Ibrahim, EGY def. **2.** Ramaz Nozadze, GEO (12-1); **3.** Mehmet Ozal, TUR def. Masoud Hashem Zadeh, IRA (DQ).

264 lbs (120 kg): **1.** Khasan Baroev, RUS def. **2.** Georgiy Tsurtasumia, KAZ (4-2); **3.** Rulon Gardner, USA def. Sajar Barzi, IRA (3-0).

TEAM SPORTS

BASEBALL

Round Robin Standings

Top four teams advance to medal round. Note that RF stands for Runs For and RA stands for Runs Against.

	Gm	W	L	Pct	RF	RA	Medal Round
*Japan	7	6	1	.857	49	20	1-1
*Cuba	7	6	1	.857	41	17	2-0
*Canada	7	5	2	.714	39	17	0-2
*Australia	7	4	3	.571	49	30	1-1
Chinese Taipei	7	3	4	.429	24	28	—
Netherlands	7	2	5	.286	29	55	—
Greece	7	1	6	.143	24	49	—
Italy	7	1	6	.143	19	58	—

Semifinals

Cuba 8 .... Canada 5
Australia 1 .... Japan 0

Bronze Medal

Japan 11 .... Canada 2

Gold Medal

Cuba 6 .... Australia 2

BASKETBALL

Round Robin Standings

Top four teams advance to medal round.

MEN

Group A	Gm	W	L	Pts	Per Game For	Per Game Opp	Medal Round
*Spain	5	5	0	10	81.0	69.8	0-1
*Italy	5	3	2	8	74.2	68.2	2-1
*Argentina	5	3	2	8	82.8	79.2	3-0
*China	5	2	3	7	60.6	76.4	0-1
New Zealand	5	1	4	6	79.8	82.6	—
Serbia & Montenegro	5	1	4	6	75.4	77.6	—

Group B	Gm	W	L	Pts	Per Game For	Per Game Opp	Medal Round
*Lithuania	5	5	0	10	93.6	68.2	1-2
*Greece	5	3	2	8	77.8	68.6	0-1
*Puerto Rico	5	3	2	8	82.0	82.2	0-1
*United States	5	3	2	8	83.6	77.8	2-1
Australia	5	1	4	6	76.6	82.2	—
Angola	5	0	5	5	64.2	84.2	—

Quarterfinals

United States 102 .... Spain 94
Lithuania 95 .... China 75
Italy 83 .... Puerto Rico 70
Argentina 69 .... Greece 64

Semifinals

Argentina 89 .... United States 81
Italy 100 .... Lithuania 91

Bronze Medal

United States 104 .... Lithuania 96

Gold Medal

Argentina 84 .... Italy 69

WOMEN

Group A	Gm	W	L	Pts	Per Game For	Opp	Medal Round
*Australia	5	5	0	10	83.6	62.6	2-1
*Russia	5	4	1	9	77.8	66.6	2-1
*Brazil	5	3	2	8	86.0	72.2	1-2
*Greece	5	2	3	7	70.6	78.4	0-1
Japan	5	1	4	6	76.2	97.0	—
Nigeria	5	0	5	5	67.0	84.4	—

Group B	Gm	W	L	Pts	Per Game For	Opp	Medal Round
*United States	5	5	0	10	86.0	57.0	3-0
*Spain	5	4	1	9	73.6	66.8	0-1
*Czech Republic	5	3	2	8	81.6	75.0	0-1
*New Zealand	5	2	3	7	64.2	82.8	0-1
China	5	1	4	6	53.0	81.2	—
South Korea	5	0	5	5	64.0	78.6	—

Quarterfinals

Russia 70 .... Czech Republic 49
United States 102 .... Greece 72
Brazil 67 .... Spain 63
Australia 94 .... New Zealand 55

Semifinals

United States 66 .... Russia 62
Australia 88 .... Brazil 75

Bronze Medal

Russia 71 .... Brazil 62

Gold Medal

United States 74 .... Australia 63

Team USA Men's Statistics

	Gm	FG%	FT%	—Per Game— Min	Pts	Reb	Ast
Allen Iverson	8	.378	.711	27.1	13.8	1.6	2.5
Tim Duncan	8	.567	.750	26.0	12.9	9.1	1.6
Stephon Marbury	8	.423	.737	26.0	10.5	1.3	3.4
Shawn Marion	8	.531	.778	19.6	9.9	5.9	0.8
Lamar Odom	8	.569	.522	22.0	9.3	5.8	1.4
Carlos Boozer	8	.625	.656	17.1	7.6	6.1	0.4
Dwyane Wade	8	.382	.696	17.5	7.3	1.9	2.4
Richard Jefferson	8	.321	.545	18.5	6.8	2.8	1.0
LeBron James	8	.594	1.00	11.4	5.4	1.0	1.6
Amare Stoudemire	8	.563	.500	7.1	2.8	1.8	0.1
Carmelo Anthony	7	.250	.500	6.7	2.4	1.6	0.0
Emeka Okafor	2	.000	.000	7.0	0.0	1.5	0.0
TEAM USA	8	.459	.668	200.0	88.1	38.9	15.1
OPPONENTS	8	.482	.678	200.0	83.5	28.1	11.0

Team USA Women's Statistics

	Gm	FG%	FT%	—Per Game— Min	Pts	Reb	Ast
Lisa Leslie	8	.588	.733	22.9	15.6	8.0	1.4
Tina Thompson	8	.500	.773	24.4	14.1	5.0	1.4
Sheryl Swoopes	8	.408	.857	24.4	9.1	4.0	1.6
Diana Taurasi	8	.377	.714	19.3	8.5	3.0	1.0
Yolanda Griffith	8	.605	.571	17.3	8.5	6.6	0.1
Tamika Catchings	8	.404	.833	24.8	6.9	5.4	0.4
Shannon Johnson	8	.391	1.00	16.5	6.1	2.5	1.9
Swin Cash	7	.457	.800	14.4	6.3	4.4	0.3
Dawn Staley	8	.522	.889	17.9	4.1	0.5	2.9
Ruth Riley	7	.667	.800	8.3	3.4	2.4	0.3
Sue Bird	7	.300	.000	12.9	2.9	0.9	1.0
Katie Smith	3	.000	.000	4.3	0.0	0.3	0.3
TEAM USA	8	.470	.763	200.0	84.0	41.9	12.3
OPPONENTS	8	.367	.721	200.0	60.3	24.1	9.5

FIELD HOCKEY

Round Robin Standings

Top two teams advance to medal round.

MEN

Group A	Gm	W	L	T	Pts	GF	GA	Medal Round
*Spain	5	3	0	2	11	14	3	0-2
*Germany	5	3	0	2	11	15	6	1-1
Pakistan	5	3	2	0	9	19	8	—
South Korea	5	2	1	2	8	17	8	—
Great Britain	5	1	4	0	3	9	21	—
Egypt	5	0	5	0	0	2	30	—

Group B	Gm	W	L	T	Pts	GF	GA	Medal Round
*Netherlands	5	5	0	0	15	16	9	1-1
*Australia	5	3	1	1	10	14	10	2-0
New Zealand	5	3	2	0	9	13	11	—
India	5	1	3	1	4	11	13	—
South Africa	5	1	4	0	3	9	15	—
Argentina	5	0	3	2	2	8	13	—

Semifinals

Australia 6 .... Spain 3
Netherlands 3 .... Germany 2

Bronze Medal

Germany 4 .... Spain 3

Gold Medal

Australia 2 .... Netherlands 1

WOMEN

Group A	Gm	W	L	T	Pts	GF	GA	Medal Round
*China	4	4	0	0	12	11	2	0-2
*Argentina	4	3	1	0	9	12	4	1-1
Japan	4	2	2	0	6	5	7	—
New Zealand	4	1	3	0	3	3	9	—
Spain	4	0	4	0	0	3	12	—

Group B	Gm	W	L	T	Pts	GF	GA	Medal Round
*Netherlands	4	4	0	0	12	14	5	1-1
*Germany	4	2	2	0	6	6	10	2-0
South Korea	4	1	2	1	4	9	8	—
Australia	4	1	2	1	4	6	5	—
South Africa	4	1	3	0	3	5	12	—

Semifinals

Netherlands 2 .... Argentina 2
Netherlands won shoot-out 4-2
Germany 0 .... China 0
Germany won shoot-out 4-3

Bronze Medal

Argentina 1 .... China 0

Gold Medal

Germany 2 .... Netherlands 1

AP/Wide World Photos

*The **USA softball team** practiced world domination at the 2004 Summer Olympics, allowing just one run in nine games on their way to the gold medal.*

SOCCER

MEN

Group A	Gm	W	L	T	Pts	GF	GA	Medal Round
*Mali	3	1	0	2	5	5	3	0-1
*South Korea	3	1	0	2	5	6	5	0-1
Mexico	3	1	1	1	4	3	3	—
Greece	3	0	2	1	1	4	7	—

Group B	Gm	W	L	T	Pts	GF	GA	Medal Round
*Paraguay	3	2	1	0	6	6	5	2-1
*Italy	3	1	1	1	4	5	5	2-1
Ghana	3	1	1	1	4	4	4	—
Japan	3	1	2	0	3	6	7	—

Group C	Gm	W	L	T	Pts	GF	GA	Medal Round
*Argentina	3	3	0	0	9	9	0	3-0
*Australia	3	1	1	1	4	6	3	0-1
Tunisia	3	1	1	1	4	4	5	—
Serbia/ Montenegro	3	0	3	0	0	3	14	—

Group D	Gm	W	L	T	Pts	GF	GA	Medal Round
*Iraq	3	2	1	0	6	7	4	1-2
*Costa Rica	3	1	1	1	4	4	4	0-1
Morocco	3	1	1	1	4	3	3	—
Portugal	3	1	2	0	3	6	9	—

Quarterfinals

Italy 1 ....OT.......................Mali 0
Argentina 4 ....Costa Rica 0
Iraq 1 ....Australia 0
Paraguay 3 ....South Korea 2

Semifinals

Argentina 3 ....Italy 0
Paraguay 3 ....Iraq 1

Bronze Medal

Italy 1 ....Iraq 0

Gold Medal

Argentina 1 ....Paraguay 0

WOMEN

Group E	Gm	W	L	T	Pts	GF	GA	Medal Round
*Sweden	2	1	1	0	3	2	2	1-2
*Nigeria	2	1	1	0	3	2	2	0-1
Japan	2	1	1	0	3	1	1	—

Group F	Gm	W	L	T	Pts	GF	GA	Medal Round
*Germany	2	2	0	0	6	10	0	2-1
*Mexico	2	0	1	1	1	3	0-1	
China	2	0	1	1	1	1	9	—

Group G	Gm	W	L	T	Pts	GF	GA	Medal Round
*United States	3	2	0	1	7	6	1	3-0
*Brazil	3	2	1	0	6	8	2	2-1
Australia	3	1	1	1	4	2	2	—
Greece	3	0	3	0	0	0	11	—

Quarterfinals

United States 2.....................................Japan 1
Germany 2...Nigeria 1
Sweden 2...Australia 1
Brazil 5..Mexico 0

Semifinals

Brazil 1 ....Sweden 0
United States 2 ....OT......................Germany 1

Bronze Medal

Germany 1 ....Sweden 0

Gold Medal

United States 2 ....OT......................Brazil 1

SOFTBALL

Top four teams advance to semifinals.

	Gm	W	L	RF	RA	Medal Round
*United States	7	7	0	41	0	2-0
*Australia	7	6	1	22	14	1-2
*Japan	7	4	3	17	8	1-1
*China	7	3	4	15	20	0-1
Canada	7	3	4	6	14	—
Chinese Taipei	7	2	5	3	13	—
Greece	7	2	5	6	24	—
Italy	7	1	6	8	25	—

Semifinals

United States 5 ....Australia 0
Japan 1 ....China 0

Bronze Medal
(loser gets medal)

Australia 5..Japan 0

Gold Medal

United States 5 ....Australia 1

TEAM HANDBALL

Top four teams in each group advance to medal round.

MEN

Group A	Gm	W	L	T	Pts	GF	GA	Medal Round
*Croatia	5	5	0	0	10	146	129	3-0
*Spain	5	4	1	0	8	154	137	0-1
*South Korea	5	2	3	0	4	148	148	0-1
*Russia	5	2	3	0	4	145	145	2-1
Iceland	5	1	4	0	2	143	158	—
Slovenia	5	1	4	0	2	130	149	—

Group B	Gm	W	L	T	Pts	GF	GA	Medal Round
*France	5	5	0	0	10	135	108	0-1
*Hungary	5	4	1	0	8	132	124	1-2
*Germany	5	3	2	0	6	139	110	2-1
*Greece	5	2	3	0	4	117	130	0-1
Brazil	5	1	4	0	2	105	133	—
Egypt	5	0	5	0	0	110	133	—

Quarterfinals

Hungary 30..South Korea 25
Croatia 33..Greece 27
Germany 32..Spain 30
Russia 26..France 24

Semifinals

Croatia 33..Hungary 31
Germany 21..Russia 15

Bronze Medal

Russia 28..Hungary 26

Gold Medal

Croatia 26..Germany 24

WOMEN

Group A	Gm	W	L	T	Pts	GF	GA	Medal Round
*Ukraine	4	4	0	0	8	99	82	2-1
*Hungary	4	3	1	0	6	118	93	0-1
*China	4	2	2	0	4	106	90	0-1
*Brazil	4	1	3	0	2	97	105	0-1
Greece	4	0	4	0	0	74	124	—

Group B	Gm	W	L	T	Pts	GF	GA	Medal Round
*South Korea	4	3	0	1	7	135	103	2-1
*Denmark	4	3	0	1	7	125	98	3-0
*France	4	2	2	0	4	105	106	1-2
*Spain	4	0	3	1	1	86	110	0-1
Angola	4	0	3	1	1	97	131	—

Quarterfinals

Ukraine 25..Spain 23
France 25..Hungary 23
South Korea 26..Brazil 24
Denmark 32..China 28

Semifinals

South Korea 32..France 31
Denmark 32..Ukraine 28

Bronze Medal

Ukraine 21..France 18

Gold Medal

Denmark 38..South Korea 36

VOLLEYBALL

Top four teams advance to quarterfinals. Note that SF stands for Sets For and SA stands for Sets Against.

MEN

Group A	Gm	W	L	Pts	SF	SA	Medal Round
*Serbia/Montenegro	5	4	1	9	12	5	0-1
*Greece	5	3	2	8	12	9	0-1
*Argentina	5	3	2	8	12	9	0-1
*Poland	5	3	2	8	10	9	0-1
France	5	2	3	7	8	10	—
Tunisia	5	0	5	5	4	15	—

Group B	Gm	W	L	Pts	SF	SA	Medal Round
*Brazil	5	4	1	9	13	7	3-0
*Italy	5	3	2	8	13	7	2-1
*United States	5	3	2	8	11	8	1-2
*Russia	5	3	2	8	11	9	2-1
Netherlands	5	2	3	7	7	11	—
Australia	5	0	5	5	2	15	—

Quarterfinals

Russia 3 ....Serbia/Montenegro 1
(29-27, 23-25, 27-25, 28-26)
Italy 3..Argentina 1
(22-25, 25-22, 26-24, 26-28)
United States 3..Greece 2
(25-20, 22-25, 25-27, 25-23, 17-15)
Brazil 3..Poland 0
(25-20, 27-25, 25-18)

Volleyball (Cont.)

Semifinals

Italy 3 ....Russia 0
(25-16, 25-17, 25-16)
Brazil 3 ....United States 0
(25-16, 25-17, 25-23)

Bronze Medal

Russia 3 ....United States 0
(25-22, 27-25, 25-16)

Gold Medal

Brazil 3 ....Italy 1
(25-15, 24-26, 25-20, 25-22)

WOMEN

Group A	Gm	W	L	Pts	SF	SA	Medal Round
*Brazil	5	5	0	10	15	2	1-2
*Italy	5	4	1	9	14	3	0-1
South Korea	5	3	2	8	9	7	0-1
Japan	5	2	3	7	6	10	0-1
Greece	5	1	4	6	5	12	—
Kenya	5	0	5	5	0	15	—

Group B	Gm	W	L	Pts	SF	SA	Medal Round
*China	5	4	1	9	14	4	3-0
*Russia	5	3	2	8	11	8	2-1
*Cuba	5	3	2	8	11	10	2-1
*United States	5	2	3	7	11	10	0-1
Germany	5	2	3	7	7	11	—
Dominican Republic	5	1	4	6	3	14	—

Quarterfinals

Brazil 3 ....United States 2
(25-22, 25-20, 22-25, 25-27, 15-6)
Russia 3 ....South Korea 0
(25-17, 25-15, 25-22)
Cuba 3 ....Italy 2
(25-23, 14-25, 22-25, 25-14, 15-12)
China 3 ....Japan 0
(25-20, 25-22, 25-20)

Semifinals

Russia 3 ....Brazil 2
(18-25, 21-25, 25-22, 28-26, 16-14)
China 3 ....Cuba 2
(25-22, 25-20, 17-25, 23-25, 15-10)

Bronze Medal

Cuba 3 ....Brazil 1
(25-22, 25-22, 14-25, 25-17)

Gold Medal

China 3 ....Russia 2
(28-30, 25-27, 25-20, 25-23, 15-12)

WATER POLO

Round Robin Standings

Top three teams in each group advance to medal round, the top team in each group gets a bye into the semifinals.

MEN

Group A	Gm	W	L	T	Pts	GF	GA	Medal Round
*Hungary	5	5	0	0	10	44	27	2-0
*Serbia/ Montenegro	5	4	1	0	8	37	26	2-1
*Russia	5	3	2	0	6	32	28	2-1
United States	5	2	3	0	4	32	37	—
Croatia	5	1	4	0	2	35	41	—
Kazakhstan	5	0	5	0	0	21	42	—

Group B	Gm	W	L	T	Pts	GF	GA	Medal Round
*Greece	5	4	1	0	8	43	27	0-2
*Germany	5	3	1	1	7	40	28	0-1
*Spain	5	3	2	0	6	35	31	0-1
Italy	5	3	2	0	6	39	24	—
Australia	5	1	3	1	3	37	35	—
Egypt	5	0	5	0	0	18	67	—

Quarterfinals

Russia 12 ....Germany 5
Serbia/Montenegro 7 ....Spain 5

Semifinal

Hungary 7 ....Russia 5
Serbia/Montenegro 7 ....Greece 3

Bronze Medal

Russia 6 ....Greece 5

Gold Medal

Hungary 8 ....Serbia/Montenegro 7

WOMEN

Group A	Gm	W	L	T	Pts	GF	GA	Medal Round
*Australia	3	2	0	1	5	22	16	0-2
*Italy	3	2	1	0	4	20	14	3-0
*Greece	3	1	1	1	3	17	20	2-1
Kazakhstan	3	0	3	0	0	16	25	—

Group B	Gm	W	L	T	Pts	GF	GA	Medal Round
*United States	3	2	1	0	4	20	16	1-1
*Russia	2	1	0	0	4	21	22	0-1
*Hungary	3	1	2	0	2	19	20	0-1
Canada	3	1	2	0	2	16	18	—

Quarterfinals

Greece 7 ....Russia 4
Italy 8 ....Hungary 5

Semifinals

Italy 6 ....United States 5
Greece 6 ....Australia 2

Bronze Medal

United States 6 ....Australia 5

Gold Medal

Italy 10 ....Greece 9

1896-2004
Through the Years

SPORTS ALMANAC

Modern Olympic Games

The original Olympic Games were celebrated as a religious festival from 776 B.C. until 393 A.D., when Roman emperor Theodosius I banned all pagan festivals (the Olympics celebrated the Greek god Zeus). On June 23, 1894, French educator Baron Pierre de Coubertin, speaking at the Sorbonne in Paris to a gathering of international sports leaders, proposed that the ancient games be revived on an international scale. The idea was enthusiastically received and the Modern Olympics were born. The first Olympics were held two years later in Athens, where 245 athletes from 14 nations competed in the ancient Panathenaic stadium to large and ardent crowds. Americans captured nine out of 12 track and field events, but Greece won the most medals with 47.

The Summer Olympics

Year	No	Location	Dates	Nations	Most medals	USA medals	
1896	I	Athens, GRE	Apr. 6-15	14	Greece (10-19-18—47)	11- 6- 2 — 19	(2nd)
1900	II	Paris, FRA	May 20-Oct. 28	26	France (26-37-32—95)	18-14-15 — 47	(2nd)
1904	III	St. Louis, USA. . . .	July 1-Nov. 23	13	USA (78-84-82—244)	78-84-82—244	(1st)
1906-**a**	—	Athens, GRE	Apr. 22-May 2	20	France (15-9-16—40)	12-6- 6 — 24	(3rd)
1908	IV	London, GBR	Apr. 27-Oct. 31	·22	Britain (54-46-38 — 138)	23-12-12 — 47	(2nd)
1912	V	Stockholm, SWE	May 5-July 22	28	Sweden (23-24-17—64)	25-18-20— 63	(2nd)
1916	VI	Berlin, GER	Cancelled (WWI)				
1920	VII	Antwerp, BEL	Apr. 20-Sept. 12	29	USA (41-27-27—95)	41-27-27— 95	(1st)
1924	VIII	Paris, FRA	May 4-July 27	44	USA (45-27-27—99)	45-27-27— 99	(1st)
1928	IX	Amsterdam, NED .	May 17-Aug. 12	46	USA (22-18-16—56)	22-18-16— 56	(1st)
1932	X	Los Angeles, USA. .	July 30-Aug. 14	37	USA (41-32-30—103)	41-32-30—103	(1st)
1936	XI	Berlin, GER	Aug. 1-16	49	Germany (33-26-30—89)	24-20-12— 56	(2nd)
1940-**b**	XII	Tokyo, JPN	Cancelled (WWII)				
1944	XIII	London, GBR	Cancelled (WWII)				
1948	XIV	London, GBR	July 29-Aug. 14	59	USA (38-27-19—84)	38-27-19— 84	(1st)
1952-**cd**	XV	Helsinki, FIN	July 19-Aug. 3	69	USA (40-19-17—76)	40-19-17— 76	(1st)
1956-**e**	XVI	Melbourne, AUS . .	Nov. 22-Dec. 8	72	USSR (37-29-32—98)	32-25-17— 74	(2nd)
1960	XVII	Rome, ITA	Aug. 25-Sept. 11	83	USSR (43-29-31—103)	34-21-16— 71	(2nd)
1964	XVIII	Tokyo, JPN	Oct. 10-24	93	USSR (30-31-35—96)	36-26-28— 90	(2nd)
1968-**f**	XIX	Mexico City, MEX ·	Oct. 12-27	112	USA (45-28-34—107)	45-28-34—107	(1st)
1972	XX	Munich, W. GER . .	Aug. 26-Sept. 10	121	USSR (50-27-22—99)	33-31-30— 94	(2nd)
1976-**g**	XXI	Montreal, CAN . . .	July 17-Aug. 1	92	USSR (49-41-35—125)	34-35-25— 94	(3rd)
1980-**h**	XXII	Moscow, USSR . . .	July 19-Aug. 3	80	USSR (80-69-46—195)	Boycotted games	
1984-**i**	XXIII	Los Angeles, USA .	July 28-Aug. 12	140	USA (83-61-30—174)	83-61-30—174	(1st)
1988	XXIV	Seoul, S. KOR	Sept. 17-Oct. 2	159	USSR (55-31-46—132)	36-31-27— 94	(3rd)
1992-**j**	XXV	Barcelona, SPA . . .	July 25-Aug. 9	169	UT (45-38-29—112)	37-34-37—108	(2nd)
1996	XXVI	Atlanta, USA	July 20-Aug. 4	197	USA (44-32-25—101)	44-32-25—101	(1st)
2000	XXVII	Sydney, AUS	Sept. 15-Oct. 1	199	USA (40-24-33—97)	40-24-33—97	(1st)
2004	XXVIII	Athens, GRE	Aug. 13-29	202	USA (35-39-29—103)	35-39-29—103	(1st)
2008	XXIX	Beijing, CHN	Aug. 8-24				

a—The 1906 Intercalated Games in Athens are considered unofficial by the IOC because they did not take place in the four-year cycle established in 1896. However, most record books include these interim games with the others.

b—The 1940 Summer Games are originally scheduled for Tokyo, but Japan resigns as host after the outbreak of the Sino-Japanese War in 1937. Helsinki is the next choice, but the IOC cancels the Games after Soviet troops invade Finland in 1939.

c—Germany and Japan are allowed to rejoin the Olympic community for the first Summer Games since 1936. Though a divided country, the Germans send a joint East-West team until 1964.

d—The Soviet Union (USSR) participates in its first Olympics, Winter or Summer, since the Russian revolution in 1917 and takes home the second most medals (22-30-19—71).

e—Due to Australian quarantine laws, the equestrian events for the 1956 Games are held in Stockholm, June 10-17.

f—East Germany and West Germany send separate teams for the first time and will continue to do so through 1988.

g—The 1976 Games are boycotted by 32 nations, most of them from black Africa, because the IOC will not ban New Zealand. Earlier that year, a rugby team from New Zealand had toured racially segregated South Africa.

h—The 1980 Games are boycotted by 64 nations, led by the USA, to protest the Soviet invasion of Afghanistan on Dec. 27, 1979.

i—The 1984 Games are boycotted by 14 Eastern Bloc nations, led by the USSR, to protest America's overcommercialization of the Games, inadequate security and an anti-Soviet attitude by the U.S. government. Most believe, however, the communist walkout is simply revenge for 1980.

j—Germany sends a single team after East and West German reunification in 1990 and the USSR competes as the Unified Team after the breakup of the Soviet Union in 1991.

Event-by-Event

Gold medal winners from 1896-2004 in the following events: Baseball, Basketball, Boxing, Diving, Field Hockey, Gymnastics, Soccer, Softball, Swimming, Tennis and Track & Field.

BASEBALL

Multiple gold medals: Cuba (3).

Year		Year	
1992	**Cuba**, Taiwan, Japan	2000	**United States**, Cuba, South Korea
1996	**Cuba**, Japan, United States	2004	**Cuba**, Australia, Japan

U.S. Medal-Winning Baseball Teams

1996 (bronze medal): P–Kris Benson, R.A. Dickey, Seth Greisinger, Billy Koch, Braden Looper, Jim Parque and Jeff Weaver; C–A.J. Hinch, Matt LeCroy and Brian Lloyd; INF–Troy Glaus, Kip Harkrider, Travis Lee, Warren Morris, Augie Ojeda and Jason Williams; OF–Chad Allen, Chad Green, Jacque Jones and Mark Kotsay; Manager–Skip Bertman. Final: Cuba over Japan, 13-9

2000 (gold medal): P–Kurt Ainsworth, Ryan Franklin, Chris George, Shane Heams, Rick Krivda, Roy Oswalt, Jon Rauch, Bobby Seay, Ben Sheets, Todd Williams and Tim Young; C–Pat Borders, Marcus Jensen and Mike Kinkade; INF–Brent Abernathy, Sean Burroughs, John Cotton, Gookie Dawkins, Adam Everett and Doug Mientkiewicz; OF–Mike Neill, Anthony Sanders, Brad Wilkerson and Ernie Young; Manager–Tommy Lasorda. Final: USA over Cuba, 4-0.

BASKETBALL

MEN

Multiple gold medals: USA (12), USSR (2).

Year		Year	
1936	**United States**, Canada, Mexico	1976	**United States**, Yugoslavia, Soviet Union
1948	**United States**, France, Brazil	1980	**Yugoslavia**, Italy, Soviet Union
1952	**United States**, Soviet Union, Uruguay	1984	**United States**, Spain, Yugoslavia
1956	**United States**, Soviet Union, Uruguay	1988	**Soviet Union**, Yugoslavia, United States
1960	**United States**, Soviet Union, Brazil	1992	**United States**, Croatia, Lithuania
1964	**United States**, Soviet Union, Brazil	1996	**United States**, Yugoslavia, Lithuania
1968	**United States**, Yugoslavia, Soviet Union	2000	**United States**, France, Lithuania
1972	**Soviet Union**, United States, Cuba	2004	**Argentina**, Italy, United States

U.S. Medal-Winning Men's Basketball Teams

1936 (gold medal): Sam Balter, Ralph Bishop, Joe Fortenberry, Tex Gibbons, Francis Johnson, Carl Knowles, Frank Lubin, Art Mollner, Don Piper, Jack Ragland, Carl Shy, Willard Schmidt, Duane Swanson and William Wheatley. Coach–Jim Needles; Assistant–Gene Johnson. Final: USA over Canada, 19-8.

1948 (gold medal): Cliff Barker, Don Barksdale, Ralph Beard, Louis Beck, Vince Boryla, Gordon Carpenter, Alex Groza, Wallace Jones, Bob Kurland, Ray Lumpp, R.C. Pitts, Jesse Renick, Robert (Jackie) Robinson and Ken Rollins. Coach–Omar Browning; Assistant–Adolph Rupp. Final: USA over France, 65-21.

1952 (gold medal): Ron Bontemps, Mark Freiberger, Wayne Glasgow, Charlie Hoag, Bill Hougland, John Keller, Dean Kelley, Bob Kenney, Bob Kurland, Bill Lienhard, Clyde Lovellette, Frank McCabe, Dan Pippin and Howie Williams. Coach–Warren Womble; Assistant–Forrest (Phog) Allen. Final: USA over USSR, 36-25.

1956 (gold medal): Dick Boushka, Carl Cain, Chuck Darling, Bill Evans, Gib Ford, Burdy Haldorson, Bill Hougland, Bob Jeangerard, K.C. Jones, Bill Russell, Ron Tomsic and Jim Walsh. Coach–Gerald Tucker; Assistant–Bruce Drake. Final: USA over USSR, 89-55.

1960 (gold medal): Jay Arnette, Walt Bellamy, Bob Boozer, Terry Dischinger, Jerry Lucas, Oscar Robertson, Adrian Smith, Burdy Haldorson, Darrall Imhoff, Allen Kelley, Lester Lane and Jerry West. Coach–Pete Newell; Assistant–Warren Womble. Final round: USA defeated USSR (81-57), Italy (112-81) and Brazil (90-63) in round robin.

1964 (gold medal): Jim (Bad News) Barnes, Bill Bradley, Larry Brown, Joe Caldwell, Mel Counts, Dick Davies, Walt Hazzard, Lucious Jackson, Pete McCaffrey, Jeff Mullins, Jerry Shipp and George Wilson. Coach–Hank Iba; Assistant–Henry Vaughn. Final: USA over USSR, 73-59.

1968 (gold medal): Mike Barrett, John Clawson, Don Dee, Cal Fowler, Spencer Haywood, Bill Hosket, Jim King, Glynn Saulters, Charlie Scott, Mike Silliman, Ken Spain, and Jo Jo White. Coach–Hank Iba; Assistant–Henry Vaughn. Final: USA over Yugoslavia, 65-50.

1972 (silver medal refused): Mike Bantom, Jim Brewer, Tom Burleson, Doug Collins, Kenny Davis, Jim Forbes, Tom Henderson, Bobby Jones, Dwight Jones, Kevin Joyce, Tom McMillen and Ed Ratleff. Coach–Hank Iba; Assistants– John Bach and Don Haskins. Final: USSR over USA, 51-50.

1976 (gold medal): Tate Armstrong, Quinn Buckner, Kenny Carr, Adrian Dantley, Walter Davis, Phil Ford, Ernie Grunfeld, Phil Hubbard, Mitch Kupchak, Tommy LaGarde, Scott May and Steve Sheppard. Coach–Dean Smith; Assistants–Bill Guthridge and John Thompson. Final: USA over Yugoslavia, 95-74.

1980 (no medal): USA boycotted Moscow Games. Final: Yugoslavia over Italy, 86-77.

1984 (gold medal): Steve Alford, Patrick Ewing, Vern Fleming, Michael Jordan, Joe Kleine, Jon Koncak, Chris Mullin, Sam Perkins, Alvin Robertson, Wayman Tisdale, Jeff Turner and Leon Wood. Coach–Bobby Knight; Assistants– Don Donoher and George Raveling. Final: USA over Spain, 96-65.

1988 (bronze medal): Stacey Augmon, Willie Anderson, Bimbo Coles, Jeff Grayer, Hersey Hawkins, Dan Majerle, Danny Manning, Mitch Richmond, J.R. Reid, David Robinson, Charles D. Smith and Charles E. Smith. Coach–John Thompson; Assistants–George Raveling and Mary Fenlon. Final: USSR over Yugoslavia, 76-63.

1992 (gold medal): Charles Barkley, Larry Bird, Clyde Drexler, Patrick Ewing, Magic Johnson, Michael Jordan, Christian Laettner, Karl Malone, Chris Mullin, Scottie Pippen, David Robinson and John Stockton. Coach–Chuck Daly; Assistants–Lenny Wilkens, Mike Krzyzewski and P.J. Carlesimo. Final: USA over Croatia, 117-85.

1996 (gold medal): Charles Barkley, Anfernee Hardaway, Grant Hill, Karl Malone, Reggie Miller, Hakeem Olajuwon, Shaquille O'Neal, Gary Payton, Scottie Pippen, David Robinson and John Stockton. Coach–Lenny Wilkens; Assistants–Bobby Cremins, Clem Haskins and Jerry Sloan. Final: USA over Yugoslavia, 95-69.

2000 (gold medal): Shareef Abdur-Rahim, Ray Allen, Vin Baker, Vince Carter, Kevin Garnett, Tim Hardaway, Allan Houston, Jason Kidd, Antonio McDyess, Alonzo Mourning, Gary Payton and Steve Smith. Coach–Rudy Tomjanovich; Assistants–Larry Brown, Gene Keady and Tubby Smith. Final: USA over France, 85-75.

2004 (bronze medal): Carmelo Anthony, Carlos Boozer, Tim Duncan, Allen Iverson, LeBron James, Richard Jefferson, Stephon Marbury, Shawn Marion, Lamar Odom, Emeka Okafor, Amare Stoudemire, Dwyane Wade. Coach—Larry Brown; Assistants—Gregg Popovich, Roy Williams, Oliver Purnell, Dr. Sheldon Burns. Final—USA over Lithuania, 104-96.

WOMEN

Multiple gold medals: USA (4), USSR/UT (3).

Year		Year	
1976	**Soviet Union**, United States, Bulgaria	1992	**Unified Team**, China, United States
1980	**Soviet Union**, Bulgaria, Yugoslavia	1996	**United States**, Brazil, Australia
1984	**United States**, South Korea, China	2000	**United States**, Australia, Brazil
1988	**United States**, Yugoslavia, Soviet Union	2004	**United States**, Australia, Russia

U.S. Gold Medal-Winning Women's Basketball Teams

1984 (gold medal): Cathy Boswell, Denise Curry, Anne Donovan, Teresa Edwards, Lea Henry, Janice Lawrence, Pamela McGee, Carol Menken-Schaudt, Cheryl Miller, Kim Mulkey, Cindy Noble and Lynette Woodard. Coach—Pat Summitt; Assistant—Kay Yow. Final: USA over South Korea, 85-55.

1988 (gold medal): Cindy Brown, Vicky Bullett, Cynthia Cooper, Anne Donovan, Teresa Edwards, Kamie Ethridge, Jennifer Gillom, Bridgette Gordon, Andrea Lloyd, Katrina McClain, Suzie McConnell and Teresa Weatherspoon. Coach—Kay Yow; Assistants—Sylvia Hatchell and Susan Yow. Final: USA over Yugoslavia, 77-70.

1996 (gold medal): Jennifer Azzi, Ruthie Bolton, Teresa Edwards, Venus Lacy, Lisa Leslie, Rebecca Lobo, Katrina McClain, Nikki McCray, Carla McGee, Dawn Staley, Katy Steding and Sheryl Swoopes. Coach—Tara VanDerveer; Assistants—Ceal Barry, Nancy Darsch and Marian Washington. Final: USA over Brazil, 111-87.

2000 (gold medal): Ruthie Bolton-Holyfield, Teresa Edwards, Yolanda Griffith, Chamique Holdsclaw, Lisa Leslie, Nikki McCray, DeLisha Milton, Katie Smith, Dawn Staley, Sheryl Swoopes, Natalie Williams and Kara Wolters. Coach—Nell Fortner; Assistants—Geno Auriemma and Peggie Gillom. Final: USA over Australia, 76-54.

2004 (gold medal): Sue Bird, Swin Cash, Tamika Catchings, Yolanda Griffith, Shannon Johnson, Lisa Leslie, Ruth Riley, Katie Smith, Dawn Staley, Sheryl Swoopes, Diana Taurasi, Tina Thompson. Coach—Van Chancellor; Assistants—Anne Donovan, Gail Goestenkors, C. Vivian Stringer. Final: USA over Australia, 74-63.

BOXING

Multiple gold medals: László Papp, Felix Savon and Teófilo Stevenson (3); Ariel Hernandez, Angel Herrera, Mario Kindelan, Oliver Kirk, Jerzy Kulej, Boris Lagutin, Harry Mallin, Guillermo Rigondeaux, Oleg Saitov and Hector Vinent (2). All fighters won titles in consecutive Olympics, except Kirk, who won both the bantamweight and featherweight titles in 1904 (he only had to fight once in each division).

Light Flyweight (106 lbs)

Year		Final Match	Year		Final Match
1968	Francisco Rodriguez, VEN	Decision, 3-2	1988	Ivailo Hristov, BUL	Decision, 5-0
1972	György Gedó, HUN	Decision, 5-0	1992	Rogelio Marcelo, CUB	Decision, 24-10
1976	Jorge Hernandez, CUB	Decision, 4-1	1996	Daniel Petrov Bojilov, BUL	Decision, 19-6
1980	Shamil Sabyrov, USSR	Decision, 3-2	2000	Brahim Asloum, FRA	Decision, 23-10
1984	Paul Gonzales, USA	Default	2004	Yan Bhartelemy, CUB	Decision, 21-16

Flyweight (112 lbs)

Year		Final Match	Year		Final Match
1904	George Finnegan, USA	Stopped, 1st	1968	Ricardo Delgado, MEX	Decision, 5-0
1920	Frank Di Gennara, USA	Decision	1972	Georgi Kostadinov, BUL	Decision, 5-0
1924	Fidel LaBarba, USA	Decision	1976	Leo Randolph, USA	Decision, 3-2
1928	Antal Kocsis, HUN	Decision	1980	Peter Lessov, BUL	Stopped, 2nd
1932	István Énekes, HUN	Decision	1984	Steve McCrory, USA	Decision, 4-1
1936	Willi Kaiser, GER	Decision	1988	Kim Kwang-Sun, S. Kor	Decision, 4-1
1948	Pascual Perez, ARG	Decision	1992	Su Choi-Chol, N. Kor	Decision, 12-2
1952	Nate Brooks, USA	Decision, 3-0	1996	Maikro Romero, CUB	Decision, 12-11
1956	Terence Spinks, GBR	Decision	2000	Wijan Ponlid, THA	Decision, 19-12
1960	Gyula Török, HUN	Decision, 3-2	2004	Yuriorkis Gamboa, CUB	Decision, 38-23
1964	Fernando Atzori, ITA	Decision, 4-1			

Bantamweight (119 lbs)

Year		Final Match	Year		Final Match
1904	Oliver Kirk, USA	Stopped, 3rd	1964	Takao Sakurai, JPN	Stopped, 2nd
1908	Henry Thomas, GBR	Decision	1968	Valery Sokolov, USSR	Stopped, 2nd
1920	Clarence Walker, RSA	Decision	1972	Orlando Martinez, CUB	Decision, 5-0
1924	William Smith, RSA	Decision	1976	Gu Yong-Ju, N. Kor	Decision, 5-0
1928	Vittorio Tamagnini, ITA	Decision	1980	Juan Hernandez, CUB	Decision, 5-0
1932	Horace Gwynne, CAN	Decision	1984	Maurizio Stecca, ITA	Decision, 4-1
1936	Ulderico Sergo, ITA	Decision	1988	Kennedy McKinney, USA	Decision, 5-0
1948	Tibor Csik, HUN	Decision	1992	Joel Casamayor, CUB	Decision, 14-8
1952	Pentti Hämäläinen, FIN	Decision, 2-1	1996	Istvan Kovacs, HUN	Decision, 14-7
1956	Wolfgang Behrendt, GER	Decision	2000	Guillermo Rigondeaux, CUB	Decision, 18-12
1960	Oleg Grigoryev, USSR	Decision	2004	Guillermo Rigondeaux, CUB	Decision, 22-13

Boxing (Cont.)
Featherweight (125 lbs)

Year		Final Match	Year		Final Match
1904	Oliver Kirk, USA	Decision	1964	Stanislav Stepashkin, USSR	Decision, 3-2
1908	Richard Gunn, GBR	Decision	1968	Antonio Roldan, MEX	Won on Disq.
1920	Paul Fritsch, FRA	Decision	1972	Boris Kousnetsov, USSR	Decision, 3-2
1924	John Fields, USA	Decision	1976	Angel Herrera, CUB	KO, 2nd
1928	Lambertus van Klaveren, NED	Decision	1980	Rudi Fink, E. Ger	Decision, 4-1
1932	Carmelo Robledo, ARG	Decision	1984	Meldrick Taylor, USA	Decision, 5-0
1936	Oscar Casanovas, ARG	Decision	1988	Giovanni Parisi, ITA	Stopped, 1st
1948	Ernesto Formenti, ITA	Decision	1992	Andreas Tews, GER	Decision, 16-7
1952	Jan Zachara, CZE	Decision, 2-1	1996	Somluck Kamsing, THA	Decision, 8-5
1956	Vladimir Safronov, USSR	Decision	2000	Bekzat Sattarkhanov, KAZ	Decision, 22-14
1960	Francesco Musso, ITA	Decision, 4-1	2004	Alexei Tichtchenko, RUS	Decision, 39-17

Lightweight (132 lbs)

Year		Final Match	Year		Final Match
1904	Harry Spanger, USA	Decision	1964	Józef Grudzien, POL	Decision
1908	Frederick Grace, GBR	Decision	1968	Ronnie Harris, USA	Decision, 5-0
1920	Samuel Mosberg, USA	Decision	1972	Jan Szczepanski, POL	Decision, 5-0
1924	Hans Nielsen, DEN	Decision	1976	Howard Davis, USA	Decision, 5-0
1928	Carlo Orlandi, ITA	Decision	1980	Angel Herrera, CUB	Stopped, 3rd
1932	Lawrence Stevens, S. Afr	Decision	1984	Pernell Whitaker, USA	Foe quit, 2nd
1936	Imre Harangi, HUN	Decision	1988	Andreas Zuelow, E. Ger	Decision, 5-0
1948	Gerald Dreyer, S. Afr	Decision	1992	Oscar De La Hoya, USA	Decision, 7-2
1952	Aureliano Bolognesi, ITA	Decision, 2-1	1996	Hocine Soltani, ALG	Tiebreak, 3-3
1956	Richard McTaggart, GBR	Decision	2000	Mario Kindelan, CUB	Decision, 14-4
1960	Kazimierz Pazdzior, POL	Decision, 4-1	2004	Mario Kindelan, CUB	Decision, 30-22

Light Welterweight (141 lbs)

Year		Final Match	Year		Final Match
1952	Charles Adkins, USA	Decision, 2-1	1980	Patrizio Oliva, ITA	Decision, 4-1
1956	Vladimir Yengibaryan, USSR	Decision	1984	Jerry Page, USA	Decision, 5-0
1960	Bohumil Nemecek, CZE	Decision, 5-0	1988	Vyacheslav Yanovsky, USSR	Decision, 5-0
1964	Jerzy Kulej, POL	Decision, 5-0	1992	Hector Vinent, CUB	Decision, 11-1
1968	Jerzy Kulej, POL	Decision, 3-2	1996	Hector Vinent, CUB	Decision, 20-13
1972	Ray Seales, USA	Decision, 3-2	2000	Mahamadkadyz Abdullaev, UZB	Decision, 27-20
1976	Ray Leonard, USA	Decision, 5-0	2004	Manus Boonjumnong, THA	Decision, 17-11

Welterweight (152 lbs)

Year		Final Match	Year		Final Match
1904	Albert Young, USA	Decision	1968	Manfred Wolke, E. Ger	Decision, 4-1
1920	Bert Schneider, CAN	Decision	1972	Emilio Correa, CUB	Decision, 5-0
1924	Jean Delarge, BEL	Decision	1976	Jochen Bachfeld, E. Ger	Decision, 3-2
1928	Edward Morgan, NZE	Decision	1980	Andrés Aldama, CUB	Decision, 4-1
1932	Edward Flynn, USA	Decision	1984	Mark Breland, USA	Decision, 5-0
1936	Sten Suvio, FIN	Decision	1988	Robert Wangila, KEN	KO, 2nd
1948	Julius Torma, CZE	Decision	1992	Michael Carruth, IRE	Decision, 13-10
1952	Zygmunt Chychla, POL	Decision, 3-0	1996	Oleg Saitov, RUS	Decision, 14-9
1956	Nicolae Linca, ROM	Decision, 3-2	2000	Oleg Saitov, RUS	Decision, 24-16
1960	Nino Benvenuti, ITA	Decision, 4-1	2004	Bakhtiyar Artayev, KAZ	Decision, 36-26
1964	Marian Kasprzyk, POL	Decision, 4-1			

Light Middleweight (156 lbs)

Year		Final Match	Year		Final Match
1952	László Papp, HUN	Decision, 3-0	1980	Armando Martinez, CUB	Decision, 4-1
1956	László Papp, HUN	Decision	1984	Frank Tate, USA	Decision, 5-0
1960	Skeeter McClure, USA	Decision, 4-1	1988	Park Si-Hun, S. Kor	Decision, 3-2
1964	Boris Lagutin, USSR	Decision, 4-1	1992	Juan Lemus, CUB	Decision, 6-1
1968	Boris Lagutin, USSR	Decision, 5-0	1996	David Reid, USA	KO, 3rd
1972	Dieter Kottysch, W. Ger	Decision, 3-2	2000	Yermakhan Ibraimov, KAZ	Decision, 25-23
1976	Jerzy Rybicki, POL	Decision, 5-0	2004	weight class eliminated.	

Middleweight (165 lbs)

Year		Final Match	Year		Final Match
1904	Charles Mayer, USA	Stopped, 3rd	1964	Valery Popenchenko, USSR	Stopped, 1st
1908	John Douglas, GBR	Decision	1968	Christopher Finnegan, GBR	Decision, 3-2
1920	Harry Mallin, GBR	Decision	1972	Vyacheslav Lemechev, USSR	KO, 1st
1924	Harry Mallin, GBR	Decision	1976	Michael Spinks, USA	Stopped, 3rd
1928	Piero Toscani, ITA	Decision	1980	José Gomez, CUB	Decision, 4-1
1932	Carmen Barth, USA	Decision	1984	Shin Joon-Sup, S. Kor	Decision, 3-2
1936	Jean Despeaux, FRA	Decision	1988	Henry Maske, E. Ger	Decision, 5-0
1948	László Papp, HUN	Decision	1992	Ariel Hernandez, CUB	Decision, 12-7
1952	Floyd Patterson, USA	KO, 1st	1996	Ariel Hernandez, CUB	Decision, 11-3
1956	Gennady Schatkov, USSR	KO, 1st	2000	Jorge Gutierrez, CUB	Decision, 17-15
1960	Eddie Crook, USA	Decision, 3-2	2004	Gaydarbek Gaydarbekov, RUS	Decision, 28-18

Light Heavyweight (178 lbs)

Year		Final Match	Year		Final Match
1920	Eddie Eagan, USA	Decision	1968	Dan Poznjak, USSR	Default
1924	Harry Mitchell, GBR	Decision	1972	Mate Parlov, YUG	Stopped, 2nd
1928	Victor Avendaño, ARG	Decision	1976	Leon Spinks, USA	Stopped, 3rd
1932	David Carstens, S. Afr	Decision	1980	Slobodan Kacar, YUG	Decision, 4-1
1936	Roger Michelot, FRA	Decision	1984	Anton Josipovic, YUG	Default
1948	George Hunter, S. Afr	Decision	1988	Andrew Maynard, USA	Decision, 5-0
1952	Norvel Lee, USA	Decision, 3-0	1992	Torsten May, GER	Decision, 8-3
1956	Jim Boyd, USA	Decision	1996	Vasilii Jirov, KAZ	Decision, 17-4
1960	Cassius Clay, USA	Decision, 5-0	2000	Alexander Lebziak, RUS	Decision, 20-6
1964	Cosimo Pinto, ITA	Decision, 3-2	2004	Andre Ward, USA	Decision, 20-13

Note: Cassius Clay changed his name to Muhammad Ali after winning the world heavyweight championship in 1964.

Heavyweight (201 lbs)

Year		Final Match	Year		Final Match
1984	Henry Tillman, USA	Decision, 5-0	1996	Felix Savon, CUB	Decision, 20-2
1988	Ray Mercer, USA	KO, 1st	2000	Felix Savon, CUB	Decision, 21-13
1992	Felix Savon, CUB	Decision, 14-1	2004	Odlanier Solis, CUB	Decision, 22-13

Super Heavyweight (Unlimited)

Year		Final Match	Year		Final Match
1904	Samuel Berger, USA	Decision	1964	Joe Frazier, USA	Decision, 3-2
1908	Albert Oldham, GBR	KO, 1st	1968	George Foreman, USA	Stopped, 2nd
1920	Ronald Rawson, GBR	Decision	1972	Teófilo Stevenson, CUB	Default
1924	Otto von Porat, NOR	Decision	1976	Teófilo Stevenson, CUB	KO, 3rd
1928	Arturo Rodriguez Jurado, ARG	Stopped, 1st	1980	Teófilo Stevenson, CUB	Decision, 4-1
1932	Santiago Lovell, ARG	Decision	1984	Tyrell Biggs, USA	Decision, 4-1
1936	Herbert Runge, GER	Decision	1988	Lennox Lewis, CAN	Stopped, 2nd
1948	Rafael Iglesias, ARG	KO, 2nd	1992	Roberto Balado, CUB	Decision, 13-2
1952	Ed Sanders, USA	Won on Disq.*	1996	Vladimir Klichko, UKR	Decision, 7-3
1956	Pete Rademacher, USA	Stopped, 1st	2000	Audley Harrison, GBR	Decision, 30-16
1960	Franco De Piccoli, ITA	KO, 1st	2004	Alexander Povetkin, RUS	walkover†

*Sanders' opponent, Ingemar Johansson, was disqualified in 2nd round for not trying.
†Povetkin was awarded the gold when his opponet Mohamed Aly failed a pre-fight physical due to a shoulder injury.
Note: Super Heavyweight was called heavyweight through 1980.

DIVING

MEN

Multiple gold medals: Greg Louganis (4); Klaus Dibiasi and Xiong Ni (3); Pete Desjardins, Sammy Lee, Tian Liang, Bob Webster and Albert White (2).

Springboard

Year		Points	Year		Points
1908	Albert Zürner, GER	85.5	1964	Ken Sitzberger, USA	159.90
1912	Paul Günther, GER	79.23	1968	Bernie Wrightson, USA	170.15
1920	Louis Kuehn, USA	675.4	1972	Vladimir Vasin, USSR	594.09
1924	Albert White, USA	696.4	1976	Phil Boggs, USA	619.05
1928	Pete Desjardins, USA	185.04	1980	Aleksandr Portnov, USSR	905.03
1932	Michael Galitzen, USA	161.38	1984	Greg Louganis, USA	754.41
1936	Richard Degener, USA	163.57	1988	Greg Louganis, USA	730.80
1948	Bruce Harlan, USA	163.64	1992	Mark Lenzi, USA	676.53
1952	David Browning, USA	205.29	1996	Xiong Ni, CHN	701.46
1956	Bob Clotworthy, USA	159.56	2000	Xiong Ni, CHN	708.72
1960	Gary Tobian, USA	170.00	2004	Peng Bo, CHN	787.38

Platform

Year		Points	Year		Points
1904	George Sheldon, USA	12.66	1960	Bob Webster, USA	165.56
1906	Gottlob Walz, GER	156.0	1964	Bob Webster, USA	148.58
1908	Hjalmar Johansson, SWE	83.75	1968	Klaus Dibiasi, ITA	164.18
1912	Erik Adlerz, SWE	73.94	1972	Klaus Dibiasi, ITA	504.12
1920	Clarence Pinkston, USA	100.67	1976	Klaus Dibiasi, ITA	600.51
1924	Albert White, USA	97.46	1980	Falk Hoffmann, E. Ger	835.65
1928	Pete Desjardins, USA	98.74	1984	Greg Louganis, USA	710.91
1932	Harold Smith, USA	124.80	1988	Greg Louganis, USA	638.61
1936	Marshall Wayne, USA	113.58	1992	Sun Shuwei, CHN	677.31
1948	Sammy Lee, USA	130.05	1996	Dmitri Sautin, RUS	692.34
1952	Sammy Lee, USA	156.28	2000	Tian Liang, CHN	724.53
1956	Joaquin Capilla, MEX	152.44	2004	Hu Jia, CHN	748.08

Diving (Cont.)

Synchronized Platform

Year		Points	Year		Points
2000	Igor Louckachine & Dmitri Sautin, RUS	365.04	2004	Tian Liang & Yang Jinghui, CHN	383.88

Synchronized Springboard

Year		Points	Year		Points
2000	Xiao Hailiang & Xiong Ni, CHN	365.58	2004	Nikolaos Siranidis & Thomas Bimis, GRE	353.34

WOMEN

Multiple gold medals: Pat McCormick and Fu Mingxia (4); Ingrid Engel-Krämer (3); Vicki Draves, Dorothy Poynton Hill, Guo Jingjing and Gao Min (2).

Springboard

Year		Points	Year		Points
1920	Aileen Riggin, USA	539.9	1968	Sue Gossick, USA	150.77
1924	Elizabeth Becker, USA	474.5	1972	Micki King, USA	450.03
1928	Helen Meany, USA	78.62	1976	Jennifer Chandler, USA	506.19
1932	Georgia Coleman, USA	87.52	1980	Irina Kalinina, USSR	725.91
1936	Marjorie Gestring, USA	89.27	1984	Sylvie Bernier, CAN	530.70
1948	Vicki Draves, USA	108.74	1988	Gao Min, CHN	580.23
1952	Pat McCormick, USA	147.30	1992	Gao Min, CHN	572.40
1956	Pat McCormick, USA	142.36	1996	Fu Mingxia, CHN	547.68
1960	Ingrid Krämer, GER	155.81	2000	Fu Mingxia, CHN	609.42
1964	Ingrid Engel-Krämer, GER	145.00	2004	Guo Jingjing, CHN	633.15

Platform

Year		Points	Year		Points
1912	Greta Johansson, SWE	39.9	1968	Milena Duchková, CZE	109.59
1920	Stefani Fryland-Clausen, DEN	34.6	1972	Ulrika Knape, SWE	390.00
1924	Caroline Smith, USA	33.2	1976	Elena Vaytsekhovskaya, USSR	406.59
1928	Elizabeth Becker Pinkston, USA	31.6	1980	Martina Jäschke, E. Ger	596.25
1932	Dorothy Poynton, USA	40.26	1984	Zhou Jihong, CHN	435.51
1936	Dorothy Poynton Hill, USA	33.93	1988	Xu Yanmei, CHN	445.20
1948	Vicki Draves, USA	68.87	1992	Fu Mingxia, CHN	461.43
1952	Pat McCormick, USA	79.37	1996	Fu Mingxia, CHN	521.58
1956	Pat McCormick, USA	84.85	2000	Laura Wilkinson, USA	543.75
1960	Ingrid Krämer, GER	91.28	2004	Chantelle Newberry, AUS	590.31
1964	Lesley Bush, USA	99.80			

Synchronized Platform

Year		Points	Year		Points
2000	Li Na & Sang Xue, CHN	345.12	2004	Lao Lishi & Li Ting, CHN	53.40

Synchronized Springboard

Year		Points	Year		Points
2000	Vera Ilyina & Yulia Pakhalina, RUS	332.64	2004	Wu Minxia & Guo Jingjing, CHN	336.90

FIELD HOCKEY

MEN

Multiple gold medals: India (8); Great Britain and Pakistan (3); West Germany/Germany and Netherlands (2).

Year		Year	
1908	**Great Britain**, Ireland, Scotland	1968	**Pakistan**, Australia, India
1920	**Great Britain**, Denmark, Belgium	1972	**West Germany**, Pakistan, India
1928	**India**, Netherlands, Germany	1976	**New Zealand**, Australia, Pakistan
1932	**India**, Japan, United States	1980	**India**, Spain, Soviet Union
1936	**India**, Germany, Netherlands	1984	**Pakistan**, West Germany, Great Britain
1948	**India**, Great Britain, Netherlands	1988	**Great Britain**, West Germany, Netherlands
1952	**India**, Netherlands, Great Britain	1992	**Germany**, Australia, Pakistan
1956	**India**, Pakistan, Germany	1996	**Netherlands**, Spain, Australia
1960	**Pakistan**, India, Spain	2000	**Netherlands**, South Korea, Australia
1964	**India**, Pakistan, Australia	2004	**Australia**, Netherlands, Germany

WOMEN

Multiple gold medals: Australia (3).

Year		Year	
1980	**Zimbabwe**, Czechoslovakia, Soviet Union	1996	**Australia**, South Korea, Netherlands
1984	**Netherlands**, West Germany, United States	2000	**Australia**, Argentina, Netherlands
1988	**Australia**, South Korea, Netherlands	2004	**Germany**, Netherlands, Argentina
1992	**Spain**, Germany, Great Britain		

GYMNASTICS

MEN

At least 4 gold medals (including team events): Sawao Kato (8); Nikolai Andrianov, Viktor Chukarin and Boris Shakhlin (7); Akinori Nakayama and Vitaly Scherbo (6); Yukio Endo, Anton Heida, Mitsuo Tsukahara and Takashi Ono (5); Vladimir Artemov, Georges Miez, Valentin Muratov and Alexei Nemov (4).

All-Around

Year		Points	Year		Points
1900	Gustave Sandras, FRA	.302	1960	Boris Shakhlin, USSR	115.95
1904	Julius Lenhart, AUT	69.80	1964	Yukio Endo, JPN	115.95
1906	Pierre Payssé, FRA	97.0	1968	Sawao Kato, JPN	115.9
1908	Alberto Braglia, ITA	317.0	1972	Sawao Kato, JPN	114.650
1912	Alberto Braglia, ITA	135.0	1976	Nikolai Andrianov, USSR	116.65
1920	Giorgio Zampori, ITA	88.35	1980	Aleksandr Dityatin, USSR	118.65
1924	Leon Stukelj, YUG	110.340	1984	Koji Gushiken, JPN	118.7
1928	Georges Miez, SWI	247.500	1988	Vladimir Artemov, USSR	119.125
1932	Romeo Neri, ITA	140.625	1992	Vitaly Scherbo, UT	59.025
1936	Alfred Schwarzmann, GER	113.100	1996	Li Xiaosahuang, CHN	58.423
1948	Veikko Huhtanen, FIN	229.7	2000	Alexei Nemov, RUS	58.474
1952	Viktor Chukarin, USSR	115.7	2004	Paul Hamm, USA	57.823
1956	Viktor Chukarin, USSR	114.25			

High Bar

Year		Points	Year		Points
1896	Hermann Weingärtner, GER	–	1968	(TIE) Akinori Nakayama, JPN	19.55
1904	(TIE) Anton Heida, USA	40		& Mikhail Voronin, USSR	19.55
	& Edward Hennig, USA	40	1972	Mitsuo Tsukahara, JPN	19.725
1924	Leon Stukelj, YUG	19.73	1976	Mitsuo Tsukahara, JPN	19.675
1928	Georges Miez, SWI	19.17	1980	Stoyan Deltchev, BUL	19.825
1932	Dallas Bixler, USA	18.33	1984	Shinji Morisue, JPN	20.00
1936	Aleksanteri Saarvala, FIN	19.367	1988	(TIE) Vladimir Artemov, USSR	19.900
1948	Josef Stalder, SWI	19.85		& Valeri Lyukin, USSR	19.900
1952	Jack Günthard, SWI	19.55	1992	Trent Dimas, USA	9.875
1956	Takashi Ono, JPN	19.60	1996	Andreas Wecker, GER	9.850
1960	Takashi Ono, JPN	19.60	2000	Alexei Nemov, RUS	9.787
1964	Boris Shakhlin, USSR	19.625	2004	Igor Cassina, ITA	9.812

Parallel Bars

Year		Points	Year		Points
1896	Alfred Flatow, GER	–	1968	Akinori Nakayama, JPN	19.475
1904	George Eyser, USA	44	1972	Sawao Kato, JPN	19.475
1924	August Güttinger, SWI	21.63	1976	Sawao Kato, JPN	19.675
1928	Ladislav Vácha, CZE	18.83	1980	Aleksandr Tkachyov, USSR	19.775
1932	Romeo Neri, ITA	18.97	1984	Bart Conner, USA	19.95
1936	Konrad Frey, GER	19.067	1988	Vladimir Artemov, USSR	19.925
1948	Michael Reusch, SWI	19.75	1992	Vitaly Scherbo, UT	9.900
1952	Hans Eugster, SWI	19.65	1996	Rustam Sharipov, UKR	9.837
1956	Viktor Chukarin, USSR	19.20	2000	Li Xiaopeng, CHN	9.825
1960	Boris Shakhlin, USSR	19.40	2004	Valeri Goncharov, UKR	9.787
1964	Yukio Endo, JPN	19.675			

Vault

Year		Points	Year		Points
1896	Karl Schumann, GER	–	1964	Haruhiro Yamashita, JPN	19.60
1904	(TIE) George Eyser, USA	36	1968	Mikhail Voronin, USSR	19.00
	& Anton Heida, USA	36	1972	Klaus Köste, E. Ger	18.85
1924	Frank Kriz, USA	9.98	1976	Nikolai Andrianov, USSR	19.45
1928	Eugen Mack, SWI	9.58	1980	Nikolai Andrianov, USSR	19.825
1932	Savino Guglielmetti, ITA	18.03	1984	Lou Yun, CHN	19.95
1936	Alfred Schwarzmann, GER	19.20	1988	Lou Yun, CHN	19.875
1948	Paavo Aaltonen, FIN	19.55	1992	Vitaly Scherbo, UT	9.856
1952	Viktor Chukarin, USSR	19.20	1996	Alexei Nemov, RUS	9.787
1956	(TIE) Helmut Bantz, GER	18.85	2000	Gervasio Deferr, SPA	9.712
	& Valentin Muratov, USSR	18.85	2004	Gervasio Deferr, SPA	9.737
1960	(TIE) Takashi Ono, JPN	19.35			
	& Boris Shakhlin, USSR	19.35			

Gymnastics (Cont.)

Pommel Horse

Year		Points	Year		Points
1896	Louis Zutter, SWI	.–	1968	Miroslav Cerar, YUG	19.325
1904	Anton Heida, USA	.42	1972	Viktor Klimenko, SOV	19.125
1924	Josef Wilhelm, SWI	21.23	1976	Zoltán Magyar, HUN	19.70
1928	Hermann Hänggi, SWI	19.75	1980	Zoltán Magyar, HUN	19.925
1932	Istvän Pelle, HUN	19.07	1984	(TIE) Li Ning, CHN	19.95
1936	Konrad Frey, GER	19.333		& Peter-Vidmar, USA	19.95
1948	(TIE) Paavo Aaltonen, FIN	19.35	1988	(TIE) Dmitri Bilozerchev, USSR,	19.95
	Veikko Huhtanen, FIN	19.35		Zsolt Borkai, HUN	19.95
	& Heikki Savolainen, FIN	19.35		& Lyubomir Geraskov, BUL	19.95
1952	Viktor Chukarin, USSR	19.50	1992	(TIE) Pae Gil-Su, N. Kor	9.925
1956	Boris Shakhlin, USSR	19.25		& Vitaly Scherbo, UT	9.925
1960	(TIE) Eugen Ekman, FIN	19.375	1996	Li Donghua, SWI	9.875
	& Boris Shakhlin, USSR	19.375	2000	Marius Urzica, ROM	9.862
1964	Miroslav Cerar, YUG	19.525	2004	Teng Haibin, CHN	9.837

Rings

Year		Points	Year		Points
1896	Ioannis Mitropoulos, GRE	.–	1972	Akinori Nakayama, JPN	19.35
1904	Hermann Glass, USA	.45	1976	Nikolai Andrianov, USSR	19.65
1924	Francesco Martino, ITA	21.553	1980	Aleksandr Dityatin, USSR	19.875
1928	Leon Stukelj, YUG	19.25	1984	(TIE) Koji Gushiken, JPN	19.85
1932	George Gulack, USA	18.97		& Li Ning, CHN	19.85
1936	Alois Hudec, CZE	19.433	1988	(TIE) Holger Behrendt, E. Ger	19.925
1948	Karl Frei, SWI	19.80		& Dmitri Bilozerchev, USSR	19.925
1952	Grant Shaginyan, USSR	19.75	1992	Vitaly Scherbo, UT	9.937
1956	Albert Azaryan, USSR	19.35	1996	Yuri Chechi, ITA	9.887
1960	Albert Azaryan, USSR	19.725	2000	Szilveszter Csollany, HUN	9.850
1964	Takuji Haytta, JPN	19.475	2004	Dimonsthenis Tampakos, GRE	9.862
1968	Akinori Nakayama, JPN	19.45			

Floor Exercise

Year		Points	Year		Points
1932	Istvan Pelle, HUN	9.60	1976	Nikolai Andrianov, USSR	19.45
1936	Georges Miez, SWI	18.666	1980	Roland Brückner, E. Ger	19.75
1948	Ferenc Pataki, HUN	19.35	1984	Li Ning, CHN	19.925
1952	William Thoresson, SWE	19.25	1988	Sergei Kharkov, USSR	19.925
1956	Valentin Muratov, USSR	19.20	1992	Li Xiaosahuang, CHN	9.925
1960	Nobuyuki Aihara, JPN	19.45	1996	Ioannis Melissanidis, GRE	9.850
1964	Franco Menichelli, ITA	19.45	2000	Igors Vihrovs, LAT	9.812
1968	Sawao Kato, JPN	19.475	2004	Kyle Shewfelt, CAN	9.787
1972	Nikolai Andrianov, USSR	19.175			

Team Combined Exercises

Year		Points	Year		Points
1904	United States	374.43	1960	Japan	575.20
1906	Norway	19.00	1964	Japan	577.95
1908	Sweden	.438	1968	Japan	575.90
1912	Italy	265.75	1972	Japan	571.25
1920	Italy	359.855	1976	Japan	576.85
1924	Italy	839.058	1980	Soviet Union	598.60
1928	Switzerland	1718.625	1984	United States	591.40
1932	Italy	541.850	1988	Soviet Union	593.35
1936	Germany	657.430	1992	Unified Team	585.45
1948	Finland	1358.30	1996	Russia	576.778
1952	Soviet Union	574.40	2000	China	231.919
1956	Soviet Union	568.25	2004	Japan	173.821

WOMEN

At least 4 gold medals (including team events): Larissa Latynina (9); Vera Cáslavská (7); Polina Astakhova, Nadia Comaneci, Agnes Keleti and Nelli Kim (5); Olga Korbut, Ecaterina Szabó and Lyudmila Tourischeva (4).

All-Around

Year		Points	Year		Points
1952	Maria Gorokhovskaya, USSR	76.78	1980	Yelena Davydova, USSR	79.15
1956	Larissa Latynina, USSR	74.933	1984	Mary Lou Retton, USA	79.175
1960	Larissa Latynina, USSR	77.031	1988	Yelena Shushunova, USSR	79.662
1964	Vera Cáslavská, CZE	77.564	1992	Tatiana Gutsu, UT	39.737
1968	Vera Cáslavská, CZE	78.25	1996	Lilia Podkopayeva, UKR	39.255
1972	Lyudmila Tourischeva, USSR	77.025	2000	Simona Amanar, ROM*	38.642
1976	Nadia Comaneci, ROM	79.275	2004	Carly Patterson, USA	38.387

*Amanar finished second to **Andreea Raducan**, Romania, who was disqualified for testing positive for pseudo-ephedrine, a drug banned by the IOC and found in Nurofen—an over-the-counter medicine she purportedly took to treat a cold.

Vault

Year		Points	Year		Points
1952	Yekaterina Kalinchuk, USSR	19.20	1984	Ecaterina Szabó, ROM	19.875
1956	Larissa Latynina, USSR	18.833	1988	Svetlana Boginskaya, USSR	19.905
1960	Margarita Nikolayeva, USSR	19.316	1992	(TIE) Henrietta Onodi, HUN	9.925
1964	Vera Cáslavská, CZE	19.483		& Lavinia Milosovici, ROM	9.925
1968	Vera Cáslavská, CZE	19.775	1996	Simona Amanar, ROM	9.775
1972	Karin Janz, E. Ger	19.525	2000	Elena Zamolodtchikova, RUS	9.731
1976	Nelli Kim, USSR	19.80	2004	Monica Rosu, ROM	9.656
1980	Natalia Shaposhnikova, USSR	19.725			

Uneven Bars

Year		Points	Year		Points
1952	Margit Korondi, HUN	19.40	1984	(TIE) Julianne McNamora, USA	19.95
1956	Agnes Keleti, HUN	18.966		& Ma Yanhong, CHN	19.95
1960	Polina Astakhova, USSR	19.616	1988	Daniela Silivas, ROM	20.00
1964	Polina Astakhova, USSR	19.332	1992	Lu Li, CHN	10.00
1968	Vera Cáslavská, CZE	19.65	1996	Svetlana Khorkina, RUS	9.850
1972	Karin Janz, E. Ger	19.675	2000	Svetlana Khorkina, RUS	9.862
1976	Nadia Comaneci, ROM	20.00	2004	Emilie Lepennec, FRA	9.687
1980	Maxi Gnauck, E. Ger	19.875			

Balance Beam

Year		Points	Year		Points
1952	Nina Bocharova, USSR	19.22	1984	(TIE) Simona Pauca, ROM	19.80
1956	Agnes Keleti, HUN	18.80		& Ecaterina Szabó, ROM	19.80
1960	Eva Bosakova, CZE	19.283	1988	Daniela Silivas, ROM	19.924
1964	Vera Cáslavská, CZE	19.449	1992	Tatiana Lyssenko, UT	9.975
1968	Natalya Kuchinskaya, USSR	19.65	1996	Shannon Miller, USA	9.862
1972	Olga Korbut, USSR	19.40	2000	Liu Xuan, CHN	9.825
1976	Nadia Comaneci, ROM	19.95	2004	Catalina Ponor, ROM	9.787
1980	Nadia Comaneci, ROM	19.80			

Floor Exercise

Year		Points	Year		Points
1952	Agnes Keleti, HUN	19.36	1980	(TIE) Nadia Comaneci, ROM	19.875
1956	(TIE) Agnes Keleti, HUN	18.733		& Nelli Kim, USSR	19.875
	& Larissa Latynina, USSR	18.733	1984	Ecaterina Szabó, ROM	19.975
1960	Larissa Latynina, USSR	19.583	1988	Daniela Silivas, ROM	19.937
1964	Larissa Latynina, USSR	19.599	1992	Lavinia Milosovici, UKR	10.000
1968	(TIE) Vera Cáslavská, CZE	19.675	1996	Lilia Podkopayeva, UKR	9.887
	& Larissa Petrik, USSR	19.675	2000	Elena Zamolodtchikova, RUS	9.850
1972	Olga Korbut, USSR	19.575	2004	Catalina Ponor, ROM	9.750
1976	Nelli Kim, USSR	19.85			

Team Combined Exercises

Year		Points	Year		Points
1928	Netherlands	316.75	1976	Soviet Union	466.00
1936	Germany	506.50	1980	Soviet Union	394.90
1948	Czechoslovakia	445.45	1984	Romania	392.02
1952	Soviet Union	527.03	1988	Soviet Union	395.475
1956	Soviet Union	444.800	1992	Unified Team	395.666
1960	Soviet Union	382.320	1996	United States	389.225
1964	Soviet Union	280.890	2000	Romania	154.608
1968	Soviet Union	382.85	2004	Romania	114.283
1972	Soviet Union	380.50			

SOCCER

MEN

Multiple gold medals: Great Britain and Hungary (3); Uruguay and USSR (2).

Year		Year	
1900	**Great Britain**, France, Belgium	1960	**Yugoslavia**, Denmark, Hungary
1904	**Canada**, USA I, USA II	1964	**Hungary**, Czechoslovakia, Germany
1906	**Denmark**, Smyrna (Int'l entry), Greece	1968	**Hungary**, Bulgaria, Japan
1908	**Great Britain**, Denmark, Netherlands	1972	**Poland**, Hungary, East Germany & Soviet Union
1912	**Great Britain**, Denmark, Netherlands	1976	**East Germany**, Poland, Soviet Union
1920	**Belgium**, Spain, Netherlands	1980	**Czechoslovakia**, East Germany, Soviet Union
1924	**Uruguay**, Switzerland, Sweden	1984	**France**, Brazil, Yugoslavia
1928	**Uruguay**, Argentina, Italy	1988	**Soviet Union**, Brazil, West Germany
1936	**Italy**, Austria, Norway	1992	**Spain**, Poland, Ghana
1948	**Sweden**, Yugoslavia, Denmark	1996	**Nigeria**, Argentina, Brazil
1952	**Hungary**, Yugoslavia, Sweden	2000	**Cameroon**, Spain, Chile
1956	**Soviet Union**, Yugoslavia, Bulgaria	2004	**Argentina**, Paraguay, Italy

WOMEN

Multiple gold medals: United States (2).

Year		Year	
1996	**United States**, China, Norway	2004	**United States**, Brazil, Germany
2000	**Norway**, United States, Germany		

SOFTBALL

Multiple gold medals: United States (3).

Year		Year	
1996	**United States**, China, Australia	2004	**United States**, Australia, Japan
2000	**United States**, Japan, Australia		

U.S. Medal-Winning Softball Teams

1996 (gold medal): P–Lisa Fernandez, Michele Granger, Lori Harrigan and Michele Smith; C–Gillian Boxx and Shelly Stokes; INF–Sheila Cornell, Kim Maher, Leah O'Brien, Dot Richardson, Julie Smith and Dani Tyler; OF–Laura Berg, Dionna Harris; Manager–Ralph Raymond. Final: USA over China, 3-1.

2000 (gold medal): P–Lisa Fernandez, Lori Harrigan, Danielle Henderson, Michele Smith and Stacey Williams; C–Stacey Nuveman and Michelle Venturella; INF–Jennifer Brundage, Crystl Bustos, Sheila Douty, Jennifer McFalls and Dot Richardson; OF–Christie Ambrosi, Laura Berg, Leah O'Brien-Amico; Manager–Ralph Raymond. Final: USA over Japan, 2-1.

2004 (gold medal): P–Lisa Fernandez, Jennie Finch, Lori Harrigan and Catherine Osterman; C–Stacey Nuveman and Jenny Topping; INF–Crystl Bustos, Jaime Clark, Lovieanne Jung and Natasha Watley; OF–Laura Berg, Nicole Giordano, Kelly Kretschman, Jessica Mendoza and Leah O'Brien-Amico; UT–Tairia Flowers, Amanda Freed and Lauren Lappin ; Manager–Mike Candrea. Final: USA over Australia, 5-1.

SWIMMING

World and Olympic records below that appear to be broken or equaled by winning times in subsequent years, but are not so indicated, were all broken in preliminary heats leading up to the finals. Some events were not held at every Olympics.

MEN

At least 4 gold medals (including relays): Mark Spitz (9); Matt Biondi (8); Gary Hall Jr. and Michael Phelps (6); Charles Daniels, Tom Jager, Don Schollander, Ian Thorpe and Johnny Weissmuller (5); Tamás Darnyi, Roland Matthes, John Naber, Aleksandr Popov, Murray Rose, Vladimir Salnikov and Henry Taylor (4).

50-meter Freestyle

Year	Time		Year	Time	
1904 Zoltán Halmay, HUN (50 yds)	28.0		1996 Aleksandr Popov, RUS	22.13	
1906-84 Not held			2000 (TIE) Anthony Ervin, USA	21.98	
1988 Matt Biondi, USA	22.14	**WR**	& Gary Hall Jr., USA	21.98	
1992 Aleksandr Popov, UT	21.91	**OR**	2004 Gary Hall Jr., USA	21.93	

100-meter Freestyle

Year	Time		Year	Time	
1896 Alfréd Hajós, HUN	1:22.2	**OR**	1936 Ferenc Csik, HUN	57.6	
1904 Zoltán Halmay, HUN (100 yds)	1:02.8		1948 Wally Ris, USA	57.3	**OR**
1906 Charles Daniels, USA	1:13.4		1952 Clarke Scholes, USA	57.4	
1908 Charles Daniels, USA	1:05.6	**WR**	1956 Jon Henricks, AUS	55.4	**OR**
1912 Duke Kahanamoku, USA	1:03.4		1960 John Devitt, AUS	55.2	**OR**
1920 Duke Kahanamoku, USA	1:00.4	**WR**	1964 Don Schollander, USA	53.4	**OR**
1924 Johnny Weissmuller, USA	59.0	**OR**	1968 Michael Wenden, AUS	52.2	**WR**
1928 Johnny Weissmuller, USA	58.6	**OR**	1972 Mark Spitz, USA	51.22	**WR**
1932 Yasuji Miyazaki, JPN	58.2		1976 Jim Montgomery, USA	49.99	**WR**

Year		Time		Year		Time	
1980	Jorg Woithe, E. Ger	.50.40		1996	Aleksandr Popov, RUS	.48.74	
1984	Rowdy Gaines, USA	.49.80	OR	2000	Pieter van den Hoogenband, NED	.48.30	
1988	Matt Biondi, USA	.48.63	OR	2004	Pieter van den Hoogenband, NED	.48.17	
1992	Aleksandr Popov, UT	.49.02					

200-meter Freestyle

Year		Time		Year		Time	
1900	Frederick Lane, AUS (220 yds)	2:25.2	OR	1984	Michael Gross, W. Ger	1:47.44	WR
1904	Charles Daniels, USA (220 yds)	2:44.2		1988	Duncan Armstrong, AUS	1:47.25	WR
1968	Michael Wenden, AUS	1:55.2	OR	1992	Yevgeny Sadovyi, UT	1:46.70	OR
1972	Mark Spitz, USA	1:52.78	WR	1996	Danyon Loader, NZE	1:47.63	
1976	Bruce Furniss, USA	1:50.29	WR	2000	Pieter van den Hoogenband, NED	1:45.35	WR
1980	Sergei Kopliakov, USSR	1:49.81	OR	2004	Ian Thorpe, AUS	1:44.71	OR

400-meter Freestyle

Year		Time		Year		Time	
1896	Paul Neumann, AUT (550m)	8:12.6		1960	Murray Rose, AUS	4:18.3	OR
1904	Charles Daniels, USA (440 yds)	6:16.2		1964	Don Schollander, USA	4:12.2	WR
1906	Otto Scheff, AUT	6:23.8		1968	Mike Burton, USA	4:09.0	OR
1908	Henry Taylor, GBR	5:36.8		1972	Bradford Cooper, AUS*	4:00.27	OR
1912	George Hodgson, CAN	5:24.4		1976	Brian Goodell, USA	3:51.93	WR
1920	Norman Ross, USA	5:26.8		1980	Vladimir Salnikov, USSR	3:51.31	OR
1924	Johnny Weissmuller, USA	5:04.2	OR	1984	George DiCarlo, USA	3:51.23	OR
1928	Alberto Zorilla, ARG	5:01.6	OR	1988	Uwe Dassler, E. Ger	3:46.95	WR
1932	Buster Crabbe, USA	4:48.4	OR	1992	Yevgeny Sadovyi, UT	3:45.00	WR
1936	Jack Medica, USA	4:44.5	OR	1996	Danyon Loader, NZE	3:47.97	
1948	Bill Smith, USA	4:41.0	OR	2000	Ian Thorpe, AUS	3:40.59	WR
1952	Jean Boiteux, FRA	4:30.7	OR	2004	Ian Thorpe, AUS	3:43.10	
1956	Murray Rose, AUS	4:27.3	OR				

*Cooper finished second to Rick DeMont of the U.S., who was disqualified when he flunked the post-race drug test (his asthma medication was on the IOC's banned list).

1500-meter Freestyle

Year		Time		Year		Time	
1896	Alfréd Hajós, HUN (1200m)	18:22.2	OR	1956	Murray Rose, AUS	17:58.9	
1900	John Arthur Jarvis, GBR (1000m)	13:40.2		1960	Jon Konrads, AUS	17:19.6	OR
1904	Emil Rausch, GER (1 mile)	27:18.2		1964	Robert Windle, AUS	17:01.7	OR
1906	Henry Taylor, GBR (1 mile)	28:28.0		1968	Mike Burton, USA	16:38.9	OR
1908	Henry Taylor, GBR	22:48.4	WR	1972	Mike Burton, USA	15:52.58	WR
1912	George Hodgson, CAN	22:00.0	WR	1976	Brian Goodell, USA	15:02.40	WR
1920	Norman Ross, USA	22:23.2		1980	Vladimir Salnikov, USSR	14:58.27	WR
1924	Andrew (Boy) Charlton, AUS	20:06.6	WR	1984	Mike O'Brien, USA	15:05.20	
1928	Arne Borge, SWE	19:51.8	OR	1988	Vladimir Salnikov, USSR	15:00.40	
1932	Kusuo Kitamura, JPN	19:12.4	OR	1992	Kieren Perkins, AUS	14:43.48	WR
1936	Noboru Terada, JPN	19:13.7		1996	Kieren Perkins, AUS	14:56.40	
1948	James McLane, USA	19:18.5		2000	Grant Hackett, AUS	14:48.33	
1952	Ford Konno, USA	18:30.3	OR	2004	Grant Hackett, AUS	14:43.40	OR

100-meter Backstroke

Year		Time		Year		Time	
1904	Walter Brack, GER (100 yds)	1:16.8		1960	David Theile, AUS	1:01.9	OR
1908	Arno Bieberstein, GER	1:24.6	WR	1968	Roland Matthes, E. Ger	.58.7	OR
1912	Harry Hebner, USA	1:21.2		1972	Roland Matthes, E. Ger	.56.58	OR
1920	Warren Kealoha, USA	1:15.2		1976	John Naber, USA	.55.49	WR
1924	Warren Kealoha, USA	1:13.2	OR	1980	Bengt Baron, SWE	.56.33	
1928	George Kojac, USA	1:08.2	WR	1984	Rick Carey, USA	.55.79	
1932	Masaji Kiyokawa, JPN	1:08.6		1988	Daichi Suzuki, JPN	.55.05	
1936	Adolf Kiefer, USA	1:05.9	OR	1992	Mark Tewksbury, CAN	.53.98	OR
1948	Allen Stack, USA	1:06.4		1996	Jeff Rouse, USA	.54.10	
1952	Yoshinobu Oyakawa, USA	1:05.4	OR	2000	Lenny Krayzelburg, USA	.53.72	OR
1956	David Theile, AUS	1:02.2	OR	2004	Aaron Peirsol, USA	.54.06	

200-meter Backstroke

Year		Time		Year		Time	
1900	Ernst Hoppenberg, GER	2:47.0		1984	Rick Carey, USA	2:00.23	
1964	Jed Graef, USA	2:10.3	WR	1988	Igor Poliansky, USSR	1:59.37	
1968	Roland Matthes, E. Ger	2:09.6	OR	1992	Martin Lopez-Zubero, SPA	1:58.47	OR
1972	Roland Matthes, E. Ger	2:02.82	=WR	1996	Brad Bridgewater, USA	1:58.54	
1976	John Naber, USA	1:59.19	WR	2000	Lenny Krayzelburg, USA	1:56.76	OR
1980	Sándor Wládar, HUN	2:01.93		2004	Aaron Peirsol, USA	1:54.95	OR

100-meter Breaststroke

Year		Time		Year		Time	
1968	Don McKenzie, USA	1:07.7		1988	Adrian Moorhouse, GBR	1:02.04	
1972	Nobutaka Taguchi, JPN	1:04.94	**WR**	1992	Nelson Diebel, USA	1:01.50	**OR**
1976	John Hencken, USA	1:03.11	**WR**	1996	Fred deBurghgraeve, BEL	1:00.60	
1980	Duncan Goodhew, GBR	1:03.44		2000	Domenico Fioravanti, ITA	1:00.46	**OR**
1984	Steve Lundquist, USA	1:01.65	**WR**	2004	Kosuke Kitajima, JPN	1:00.08	

200-meter Breaststroke

Year		Time		Year		Time	
1908	Frederick Holman, GBR	3:09.2	**WR**	1964	Ian O'Brien, AUS	2:27.8	**WR**
1912	Walter Bathe, GER	3:01.8	**OR**	1968	Felipe Muñoz, MEX	2:28.7	
1920	Hakan Malmroth, SWE	3:04.4		1972	John Hencken, USA	2:21.55	**WR**
1924	Robert Skelton, USA	2:56.6		1976	David Wilkie, GBR	2:15.11	**WR**
1928	Yoshiyuki Tsuruta, JPN	2:48.8	**OR**	1980	Robertas Zhulpa, USSR	2:15.85	
1932	Yoshiyuki Tsuruta, JPN	2:45.4		1984	Victor Davis, CAN	2:13.34	**WR**
1936	Tetsuo Hamuro, JPN	2:41.5	**OR**	1988	József Szabó, HUN	2:13.52	
1948	Joseph Verdeur, USA	2:39.3	**OR**	1992	Mike Barrowman, USA	2:10.16	**WR**
1952	John Davies, AUS	2:34.4	**OR**	1996	Norbert Rozsa, HUN	2:12.57	
1956	Masaru Furukawa, JPN	2:34.7*	**OR**	2000	Domenico Fioravanti, ITA	2:10.87	
1960	Bill Mulliken, USA	2:37.4		2004	Kosuke Kitajima, JPN	2:09.44	**OR**

*In 1956, the butterfly stroke and breaststroke were separated into two different events.

100-meter Butterfly

Year		Time		Year		Time	
1968	Doug Russell, USA	55.9	**OR**	1988	Anthony Nesty, SUR	53.0	**OR**
1972	Mark Spitz, USA	54.27	**WR**	1992	Pablo Morales, USA	53.32	
1976	Matt Vogel, USA	54.35		1996	Dennis Pankratov, RUS	52.27	
1980	Pär Arvidsson, SWE	54.92		2000	Lars Frolander, SWE	52.00	
1984	Michael Gross, W. Ger	53.08	**WR**	2004	Michael Phelps, USA	51.25	**OR**

200-meter Butterfly

Year		Time		Year		Time	
1956	Bill Yorzyk, USA	2:19.3	**OR**	1980	Sergei Fesenko, USSR	1:59.76	
1960	Mike Troy, USA	2:12.8	**WR**	1984	Jon Sieben, AUS	1:57.04	**WR**
1964	Kevin Berry, AUS	2:06.6	**WR**	1988	Michael Gross, W. Ger	1:56.94	**OR**
1968	Carl Robie, USA	2:08.7		1992	Melvin Stewart, USA	1:56.26	**OR**
1972	Mark Spitz, USA	2:00.70	**WR**	1996	Dennis Pankratov, RUS	1:56.51	
1976	Mike Bruner, USA	1:59.23	**WR**	2000	Tom Malchow, USA	1:55.35	**OR**
				2004	Michael Phelps, USA	1:54.04	**OR**

200-meter Individual Medley

Year		Time		Year		Time	
1968	Charles Hickcox, USA	2:12.0	**OR**	1992	Tamás Darnyi, HUN	2:00.76	
1972	Gunnar Larsson, SWE	2:07.17	**WR**	1996	Attila Czene, HUN	1:59.91	
1984	Alex Baumann, CAN	2:01.42	**WR**	2000	Massimiliano Rosolino, ITA	1:58.98	**OR**
1988	Tamás Darnyi, HUN	2:00.17	**WR**	2004	Michael Phelps, USA	1:57.14	**OR**

400-meter Individual Medley

Year		Time		Year		Time	
1964	Richard Roth, USA	4:45.4	**WR**	1988	Tamás Darnyi, HUN	4:14.75	**WR**
1968	Charles Hickcox, USA	4:48.4		1992	Tamás Darnyi, HUN	4:14.23	**OR**
1972	Gunnar Larsson, SWE	4:31.98	**OR**	1996	Tom Dolan, USA	4:14.90	
1976	Rod Strachan, USA	4:23.68	**WR**	2000	Tom Dolan, USA	4:11.76	**WR**
1980	Aleksandr Sidorenko, USSR	4:22.89	**OR**	2004	Michael Phelps, USA	4:08.26	**WR**
1984	Alex Baumann, CAN	4:17.41	**WR**				

4x100-meter Freestyle Relay

Year		Time		Year		Time	
1964	United States	3:32.2	**WR**	1988	United States	3:16.53	**WR**
1968	United States	3:31.7	**WR**	1992	United States	3:16.74	
1972	United States	3:26.42	**WR**	1996	United States	3:15.41	
1976-80	Not held			2000	Australia	3:13.67	**WR**
1984	United States	3:19.03	**WR**	2004	South Africa	3:13.17	**WR**

4x200-meter Freestyle Relay

Year		Time		Year		Time	
1906	Hungary (x250m)	16:52.4		1948	United States	8:46.0	**WR**
1908	Great Britain	10:55.6	**WR**	1952	United States	8:31.1	**OR**
1912	Australia/New Zealand	10:11.6	**WR**	1956	Australia	8:23.6	**WR**
1920	United States	10:04.4	**WR**	1960	United States	8:10.2	**WR**
1924	United States	9:53.4	**WR**	1964	United States	7:52.1	**WR**
1928	United States	9:36.2	**WR**	1968	United States	7:52.33	
1932	Japan	8:58.4	**WR**	1972	United States	7:35.78	**WR**
1936	Japan	8:51.5	**WR**	1976	United States	7:23.22	**WR**

Year		Time		Year		Time	
1980	Soviet Union	7:23.50		1996	United States	7:14.84	
1984	United States	7:15.69	**WR**	2000	Australia	7:07.05	**WR**
1988	United States	7:12.51	**WR**	2004	United States	7:07.33	
1992	Unified Team	7:11.95	**WR**				

4x100-meter Medley Relay

Year		Time		Year		Time	
1960	United States	4:05.4	**WR**	1984	United States	3:39.30	**WR**
1964	United States	3:58.4	**WR**	1988	United States	3:36.93	**WR**
1968	United States	3:54.9	**WR**	1992	United States	3:36.93	**=WR**
1972	United States	3:48.16	**WR**	1996	United States	3:34.84	
1976	United States	3:42.22	**WR**	2000	United States	3:33.73	
1980	Australia	3:45.70		2004	United States	3:30.68	**WR**

WOMEN

At least 4 gold medals (including relays): Jenny Thompson (8); Kristin Otto and Amy Van Dyken (6); Krisztina Egerszegi (5), Kornelia Ender, Janet Evans, Dawn Fraser and Dara Torres (4).

50-meter Freestyle

Year		Time		Year		Time	
1988	Kristin Otto, E. Ger	25.49	**OR**	2000	Inge de Bruijn, NED	24.32	
1992	Yang Wenyi, CHN	24.79	**WR**	2004	Inge de Bruijn, NED	24.58	
1996	Amy Van Dyken, USA	24.87					

100-meter Freestyle

Year		Time		Year		Time	
1912	Fanny Durack, AUS	1:22.2		1968	Jan Henne, USA	1:00.0	
1920	Ethelda Bleibtrey, USA	1:13.6	**WR**	1972	Sandra Neilson, USA	58.59	**OR**
1924	Ethel Lackie, USA	1:12.4		1976	Kornelia Ender, E. Ger	55.65	**WR**
1928	Albina Osipowich, USA	1:11.0	**OR**	1980	Barbara Krause, E. Ger	54.79	**WR**
1932	Helene Madison, USA	1:06.8	**OR**	1984	(TIE) Nancy Hogshead, USA	55.92	
1936	Rie Mastenbroek, NED	1:05.9	**OR**		& Carrie Steinseifer, USA	55.92	
1948	Greta Andersen, DEN	1:06.3		1988	Kristin Otto, E. Ger	54.93	
1952	Katalin Szöke, HUN	1:06.8		1992	Zhuang Yong, CHN	54.65	**OR**
1956	Dawn Fraser, AUS	1:02.0	**WR**	1996	Le Jingyi, CHN	54.50	
1960	Dawn Fraser, AUS	1:01.2	**OR**	2000	Inge de Bruijn, NED	53.83	
1964	Dawn Fraser, AUS	59.5	**OR**	2004	Jodie Henry, AUS	53.84	

200-meter Freestyle

Year		Time		Year		Time	
1968	Debbie Meyer, USA	2:10.5	**OR**	1988	Heike Friedrich, E. Ger	1:57.65	**OR**
1972	Shane Gould, AUS	2:03.56	**WR**	1992	Nicole Haislett, USA	1:57.90	
1976	Kornelia Ender, E. Ger	1:59.26	**WR**	1996	Claudia Poll, CRC	1:58.16	
1980	Barbara Krause, E. Ger	1:58.33	**OR**	2000	Susie O'Neill, AUS	1:58.24	
1984	Mary Wayte, USA	1:59.23		2004	Camelia Potec, ROM	1:58.03	

400-meter Freestyle

Year		Time		Year		Time	
1920	Ethelda Bleibtrey, USA (300m)	4:34.0	**WR**	1968	Debbie Meyer, USA	4:31.8	**OR**
1924	Martha Norelius, USA	6:02.2	**WR**	1972	Shane Gould, AUS	4:19.44	**WR**
1928	Martha Norelius, USA	5:42.8	**WR**	1976	Petra Thümer, E. Ger	4:09.89	**WR**
1932	Helene Madison, USA	5:28.5	**WR**	1980	Ines Diers, E. Ger	4:08.76	**OR**
1936	Rie Mastenbroek, NED	5:26.4	**OR**	1984	Tiffany Cohen, USA	4:07.10	**OR**
1948	Ann Curtis, USA	5:17.8	**OR**	1988	Janet Evans, USA	4:03.85	**WR**
1952	Valéria Gyenge, HUN	5:12.1	**OR**	1992	Dagmar Hase, GER	4:07.18	
1956	Lorraine Crapp, AUS	4:54.6	**OR**	1996	Michelle Smith, IRE	4:07.25	
1960	Chris von Saltza, USA	4:50.6	**OR**	2000	Brooke Bennett, USA	4:05.80	
1964	Ginny Duenkel, USA	4:43.3	**OR**	2004	Laure Manaudou, FRA	4:05.34	

800-meter Freestyle

Year		Time		Year		Time	
1968	Debbie Meyer, USA	9:24.0	**OR**	1988	Janet Evans, USA	8:20.20	**OR**
1972	Keena Rothhammer, USA	8:53.68	**WR**	1992	Janet Evans, USA	8:25.52	
1976	Petra Thümer, E. Ger	8:37.14	**WR**	1996	Brooke Bennett, USA	8:27.89	
1980	Michelle Ford, AUS	8:28.90	**OR**	2000	Brooke Bennett, USA	8:19.67	**OR**
1984	Tiffany Cohen, USA	8:24.95	**OR**	2004	Ai Shibata, JPN	8:24.54	

100-meter Backstroke

Year		Time		Year		Time	
1924	Sybil Bauer, USA	1:23.2	**OR**	1972	Melissa Belote, USA	1:05.78	**OR**
1928	Maria Braun, NED	1:22.0		1976	Ulrike Richter, E. Ger	1:01.83	**OR**
1932	Eleanor Holm, USA	1:19.4		1980	Rica Reinisch, E. Ger	1:00.86	**WR**
1936	Dina Senff, NED	1:18.9		1984	Theresa Andrews, USA	1:02.55	
1948	Karen-Margrete Harup, DEN	1:14.4	**OR**	1988	Kristin Otto, E. Ger	1:00.89	
1952	Joan Harrison, S. Afr.	1:14.3		1992	Krisztina Egerszegi, HUN	1:00.68	**OR**
1956	Judy Grinham, GBR	1:12.9	**OR**	1996	Beth Botsford, USA	1:01.19	
1960	Lynn Burke, USA	1:09.3	**OR**	2000	Diana Mocanu, ROM	1:00.21	**OR**
1964	Cathy Ferguson, USA	1:07.7	**WR**	2004	Natalie Coughlin, USA	1:03.37	
1968	Kaye Hall, USA	1:06.2	**WR**				

200-meter Backstroke

Year		Time		Year		Time	
1968	Pokey Watson, USA	2:24.8		1988	Krisztina Egerszegi, HUN	2:09.29	OR
1972	Melissa Belote, USA	2:19.19	WR	1992	Krisztina Egerszegi, HUN	2:07.06	OR
1976	Ulrike Richter, E. Ger	2:13.43	OR	1996	Krisztina Egerszegi, HUN	2:07.83	
1980	Rica Reinisch, E. Ger	2:11.77	WR	2000	Diana Mocanu, ROM	2:08.16	
1984	Jolanda de Rover, NED	2:12.38		2004	Kirsty Coventry, ZIM	2:09.19	

100-meter Breaststroke

Year		Time		Year		Time	
1968	Djurdjica Bjedov, YUG	1:15.8	OR	1988	Tania Dangalakova, BUL	1:07.95	OR
1972	Cathy Carr, USA	1:13.58	WR	1992	Yelena Rudkovskaya, UT	1:08.00	
1976	Hannelore Anke, E. Ger	1:11.16		1996	Penny Heyns, RSA.	1:07.73	
1980	Ute Geweniger, E. Ger	1:10.22		2000	Megan Quann, USA	1:07.05	
1984	Petra van Staveren, NED	1:09.88	OR	2004	Luo Xuejuan, CHN	1:06.64	OR

200-meter Breaststroke

Year		Time		Year		Time	
1924	Lucy Morton, GBR	3:33.2	OR	1972	Beverley Whitfield, AUS	2:41.71	OR
1928	Hilde Schrader, GER	3:12.6		1976	Marina Koshevaya, USSR	2:33.35	WR
1932	Clare Dennis, AUS	3:06.3	OR	1980	Lina Kaciusyte, USSR	2:29.54	OR
1936	Hideko Maehata, JPN	3:03.6		1984	Anne Ottenbrite, CAN	2:30.38	
1948	Petronella van Vliet, NED	2:57.2		1988	Silke Hörner, E. Ger	2:26.71	WR
1952	éva Székely, HUN	2:51.7	OR	1992	Kyoko Iwasaki, JPN	2:26.65	OR
1956	Ursula Happe, GER	2:53.1	OR	1996	Penny Heyns, RSA	2:25.41	
1960	Anita Lonsbrough, GBR	2:49.5	WR	2000	Agnes Kovacs, HUN	2:24.35	
1964	Galina Prozumenshikova, USSR	2:46.4	OR	2004	Amanda Beard, USA	2:23.37	OR
1968	Sharon Wichman, USA	2:44.4	OR				

100-meter Butterfly

Year		Time		Year		Time	
1956	Shelley Mann, USA	1:11.0	OR	1984	Mary T. Meagher, USA	.59.26	
1960	Carolyn Schuler, USA	1:09.5	OR	1988	Kristin Otto, E. Ger	.59.00	OR
1964	Sharon Stouder, USA	1:04.7	WR	1992	Qian Hong, CHN	.58.62	OR
1968	Lynn McClements, AUS	1:05.5		1996	Amy Van Dyken, USA	.59.13	
1972	Mayumi Aoki, JPN	1:03.34	WR	2000	Inge de Bruijn, NED	.56.61	WR
1976	Kornelia Ender, E. Ger	1:00.13	=WR	2004	Petria Thomas, AUS	.57.72	
1980	Caren Metschuck, E. Ger	1:00.42					

200-meter Butterfly

Year		Time		Year		Time	
1968	Ada Kok, NED	2:24.7	OR	1988	Kathleen Nord, E. Ger	2:09.51	
1972	Karen Moe, USA	2:15.57	OR	1992	Summer Sanders, USA	2:08.67	
1976	Andrea Pollack, E. Ger	2:11.41	OR	1996	Susie O'Neill, AUS	2:07.76	
1980	Ines Geissler, E. Ger	2:10.44	OR	2000	Misty Hyman, USA	2:05.88	OR
1984	Mary T. Meagher, USA	2:06.90	OR	2004	Otylia Jedrzejczak, POL	2:06.05	

200-meter Individual Medley

Year		Time		Year		Time	
1968	Claudia Kolb, USA	2:24.7	OR	1992	Lin Li, CHN	2:11.65	WR
1972	Shane Gould, AUS	2:23.07	WR	1996	Michelle Smith, IRE	2:13.93	
1984	Tracy Caulkins, USA	2:12.64	OR	2000	Yana Klochkova, UKR	2:10.68	OR
1988	Daniela Hunger, E. Ger	2:12.59	OR	2004	Yana Klochkova, UKR	2:11.14	

400-meter Individual Medley

Year		Time		Year		Time	
1964	Donna de Varona, USA	5:18.7	OR	1988	Janet Evans, USA	4:37.76	
1968	Claudia Kolb, USA	5:08.5	OR	1992	Krisztina Egerszegi, HUN	4:36.54	
1972	Gail Neall, AUS	5:02.97	WR	1996	Michelle Smith, IRE	4:39.18	
1976	Ulrike Tauber, E. Ger	4:42.77	WR	2000	Yana Klochkova, UKR	4:33.59	WR
1980	Petra Schneider, E. Ger	4:36.29	WR	2004	Yana Klochkova, UKR	4:34.83	
1984	Tracy Caulkins, USA	4:39.24					

4x100-meter Freestyle Relay

Year		Time		Year		Time	
1912	Great Britain	5:52.8	WR	1968	United States	4:02.5	OR
1920	United States	5:11.6	WR	1972	United States	3:55.19	WR
1924	United States	4:58.8	WR	1976	United States	3:44.82	WR
1928	United States	4:47.6	WR	1980	East Germany	3:42.71	WR
1932	United States	4:38.0	WR	1984	United States	3:43.43	
1936	Netherlands	4:36.0	OR	1988	East Germany	3:40.63	OR
1948	United States	4:29.2	OR	1992	United States	3:39.46	WR
1952	Hungary	4:24.4	WR	1996	United States	3:39.29	
1956	Australia	4:17.1	WR	2000	United States	3:36.61	WR
1960	United States	4:08.9	WR	2004	Australia	3:35.94	WR
1964	United States	4:03.8	WR				

4x200-meter Freestyle Relay

Year		Time		Year		Time	
1996	United States	7:59.87		2004	United States	7:53.42	**WR**
2000	United States	7:57.80	**OR**				

4x100-meter Medley Relay

Year		Time		Year		Time	
1960	United States	4:41.1	**WR**	1984	United States	4:08.34	
1964	United States	4:33.9	**WR**	1988	East Germany	4:03.74	**OR**
1968	United States	4:28.3	**OR**	1992	United States	4:02.54	**WR**
1972	United States	4:20.75	**WR**	1996	United States	4:02.88	
1976	East Germany	4:07.95	**WR**	2000	United States	3:58.30	**WR**
1980	East Germany	4:06.67	**WR**	2004	Australia	3:57.32	**WR**

TENNIS

MEN

Multiple gold medals (including men's doubles): John Boland, Max Decugis, Laurie Doherty, Reggie Doherty, Arthur Gore, Andre Grobert, Nicolas Massu, Vincent Richards, Charles Winslow and Beals Wright (2).

Singles

Year			Year		
1896	John Boland	Great Britain/Ireland	1920	Louis Raymond	South Africa
1900	Laurie Doherty,	Great Britain	1924	Vincent Richards	United States
1904	Beals Wright	United States	1928-84	Not held	
1906	Max Decugis	France	1988	Miloslav Mecir	Czechoslovakia
1908	Josiah Ritchie	Great Britain	1992	Marc Rosset	Switzerland
	(Indoor) Arthur Gore	Great Britain	1996	Andre Agassi	United States
1912	Charles Winslow	South Africa	2000	Yevgeny Kafelnikov	Russia
	(Indoor) André Gobert	France	2004	Nicolas Massu	Chile

Doubles

Year		Year	
1896	John Boland, IRE & Fritz Traun, GER	1920	Noel Turnbull & Max Woosnam, GBR
1900	Laurie and Reggie Doherty, GBR	1924	Vincent Richards & Frank Hunter, USA
1904	Edgar Leonard & Beals Wright, USA	1928-84	Not held
1906	Max Decugis & Maurice Germot, FRA	1988	Ken Flach & Robert Seguso, USA
1908	George Hillyard & Reggie Doherty, GBR	1992	Boris Becker & Michael Stich, GER
	(Indoor) Arthur Gore & Herbert Barrett, GBR	1996	Todd Woodbridge & Mark Woodforde, AUS
1912	Charles Winslow & Harold Kitson, S. Afr.	2000	Sebastien Lareau & Daniel Nestor, CAN
	(Indoor) Andre Gobert & Maurice Germot, FRA	2004	Fernando Gonzalez & Nicolas Massu, CHI

WOMEN

Multiple gold medals (including women's doubles): Helen Wills, Gigi Fernandez, Mary Joe Fernandez and Venus Williams (2).

Singles

Year			Year		
1900	Charlotte Cooper	Great Britain	1924	Helen Wills	United States
1906	Esmee Simiriotou	Greece	1928-84	Not held	
1908	Dorothea Chambers	Great Britain	1988	Steffi Graf	West Germany
	(Indoor) Gwen Eastlake-Smith	Great Britain	1992	Jennifer Capriati	United States
1912	Marguerite Broquedis	France	1996	Lindsay Davenport	United States
	(Indoor) Edith Hannam	Great Britain	2000	Venus Williams	United States
1920	Suzanne Lenglen	France	2004	Justine Henin-Hardenne	Belgium

Doubles

Year		Year	
1920	Winifred McNair & Kitty McKane, GBR	1992	Gigi Fernandez & Mary Joe Fernandez, USA
1924	Hazel Wightman & Helen Wills, USA	1996	Gigi Fernandez & Mary Joe Fernandez, USA
1928-84	Not held	2000	Serena Williams & Venus Williams, USA
1988	Pam Shriver & Zina Garrison, USA	2004	Li Ting & Sun Tian Tian, CHN

TRACK & FIELD

World and Olympic records below that appear to be broken or equaled by winning times, heights and distances in subsequent years, but are not so indicated, were all broken in preliminary races and field events leading up to the finals.

MEN

At least 4 gold medals (including relays and discontinued events): Ray Ewry (10); Carl Lewis and Paavo Nurmi (9); Ville Ritola and Martin Sheridan (5); Harrison Dillard, Archie Hahn, Michael Johnson, Hannes Kolehmainen, Alvin Kraenzlein, Eric Lemming, Jim Lightbody, Al Oerter, Jesse Owens, Meyer Prinstein, Mel Sheppard, Lasse Viren and Emil Zátopek (4). Note that all of Ewry's gold medals came before 1912, in the Standing High Jump, Standing Long Jump and Standing Triple Jump.

100 meters

Year		Time		Year		Time	
1896	Tom Burke, USA	12.0		1960	Armin Hary, GER	10.2	OR
1900	Frank Jarvis, USA	11.0		1964	Bob Hayes, USA	10.0	=WR
1904	Archie Hahn, USA	11.0		1968	Jim Hines, USA	9.95	WR
1906	Archie Hahn, USA	11.2		1972	Valery Borzov, USSR	10.14	
1908	Reggie Walker, S. Afr.	10.8	=OR	1976	Hasely Crawford, TRI	10.06	
1912	Ralph Craig, USA	10.8		1980	Allan Wells, GBR	10.25	
1920	Charley Paddock, USA	10.8		1984	Carl Lewis, USA*	9.99	
1924	Harold Abrahams, GBR	10.6	=OR	1988	Carl Lewis, USA*	9.92	WR
1928	Percy Williams, CAN	10.8		1992	Linford Christie, GBR	9.96	
1932	Eddie Tolan, USA	10.3	OR	1996	Donovan Bailey, CAN	9.84	WR
1936	Jesse Owens, USA	10.3ᵂ		2000	Maurice Greene, USA	9.87	
1948	Harrison Dillard, USA	10.3	=OR	2004	Justin Gatlin, USA	9.85	
1952	Lindy Remigino, USA	10.4					
1956	Bobby Morrow, USA	10.5					

ᵂindicates wind-aided.

*Lewis finished second to Ben Johnson of Canada, who set a world record of 9.79 seconds. Two days later, Johnson was stripped of his gold medal and his record when he tested positive for steroid use in a post-race drug test.

200 meters

Year		Time		Year		Time	
1900	Walter Tewksbury, USA	22.2		1960	Livio Berruti, ITA	20.5	=WR
1904	Archie Hahn, USA	21.6	OR	1964	Henry Carr, USA	20.3	OR
1908	Bobby Kerr, CAN	22.6		1968	Tommie Smith, USA	19.83	WR
1912	Ralph Craig, USA	21.7		1972	Valery Borzov, USSR	20.00	
1920	Allen Woodring, USA	22.0		1976	Donald Quarrie, JAM	20.23	
1924	Jackson Scholz, USA	21.6		1980	Pietro Mennea, ITA	20.19	
1928	Percy Williams, CAN	21.8		1984	Carl Lewis, USA	19.80	OR
1932	Eddie Tolan, USA	21.2	OR	1988	Joe DeLoach, USA	19.75	OR
1936	Jesse Owens, USA	20.7	OR	1992	Mike Marsh, USA	20.01	
1948	Mel Patton, USA	21.1		1996	Michael Johnson, USA	19.32	WR
1952	Andy Stanfield, USA	20.7		2000	Konstantinos Kenteris, GRE	20.09	
1956	Bobby Morrow, USA	20.6	OR	2004	Shawn Crawford, USA	19.79	

400 meters

Year		Time		Year		Time	
1896	Tom Burke, USA	54.2		1956	Charley Jenkins, USA	46.7	
1900	Maxey Long, USA	49.4	OR	1960	Otis Davis, USA	44.9	WR
1904	Harry Hillman, USA	49.2	OR	1964	Mike Larrabee, USA	45.1	
1906	Paul Pilgrim, USA	53.2		1968	Lee Evans, USA	43.86	WR
1908	Wyndham Halswelle, GBR	50.0		1972	Vince Matthews, USA	44.66	
1912	Charlie Reidpath, USA	48.2	OR	1976	Alberto Juantorena, CUB	44.26	
1920	Bevil Rudd, S. Afr.	49.6		1980	Viktor Markin, USSR	44.60	
1924	Eric Liddell, GBR	47.6	OR	1984	Alonzo Babers, USA	44.27	
1928	Ray Barbuti, USA	47.8		1988	Steve Lewis, USA	43.87	
1932	Bill Carr, USA	46.2	WR	1992	Quincy Watts, USA	43.50	OR
1936	Archie Williams, USA	46.5		1996	Michael Johnson, USA	43.49	OR
1948	Arthur Wint, JAM	46.2		2000	Michael Johnson, USA	43.84	
1952	George Rhoden, JAM	45.9	OR	2004	Jeremy Wariner, USA	44.00	

800 meters

Year		Time		Year		Time	
1896	Teddy Flack, AUS	2:11.0	–	1956	Tom Courtney, USA	1:47.7	OR
1900	Alfred Tysoe, USA	2:01.2		1960	Peter Snell, NZE	1:46.3	OR
1904	Jim Lightbody, USA	1:56.0	OR	1964	Peter Snell, NZE	1:45.1	OR
1906	Paul Pilgrim, USA	2:01.5		1968	Ralph Doubell, AUS	1:44.3	=WR
1908	Mel Sheppard, USA	1:52.8	WR	1972	Dave Wottle, USA	1:45.9	
1912	Ted Meredith, USA	1:51.9	WR	1976	Alberto Juantorena, CUB	1:43.50	WR
1920	Albert Hill, GBR	1:53.4		1980	Steve Ovett, GBR	1:45.4	
1924	Douglas Lowe, GBR	1:52.4		1984	Joaquim Cruz, BRA	1:43.00	OR
1928	Douglas Lowe, GBR	1:51.8	OR	1988	Paul Ereng, KEN	1:43.45	
1932	Tommy Hampson, GBR	1:49.7	WR	1992	William Tanui, KEN	1:43.66	
1936	John Woodruff, USA	1:52.9		1996	Vebjoern Rodal, NOR	1:42.58	OR
1948	Mal Whitfield, USA	1:49.2	OR	2000	Nils Schumann, GER	1:45.08	
1952	Mal Whitfield, USA	1:49.2	=OR	2004	Yuriy Borzakovskiy, RUS	1:44.45	

1500 meters

Year		Time		Year		Time	
1896	Teddy Flack, AUS	4:33.2		1956	Ron Delany, IRE	3:41.2	**OR**
1900	Charles Bennett, GBR	4:06.2	**WR**	1960	Herb Elliott, AUS	3:35.6	**WR**
1904	Jim Lightbody, USA	4:05.4	**WR**	1964	Peter Snell, NZE	3:38.1	
1906	Jim Lightbody, USA	4:12.0		1968	Kip Keino, KEN	3:34.9	**OR**
1908	Mel Sheppard, USA	4:03.4	**OR**	1972	Pekka Vasala, FIN	3:36.3	
1912	Arnold Jackson, GBR	3:56.8	**OR**	1976	John Walker, NZE	3:39.17	
1920	Albert Hill, GBR	4:01.8		1980	Sebastian Coe, GBR	3:38.4	
1924	Paavo Nurmi, FIN	3:53.6	**OR**	1984	Sebastian Coe, GBR	3:32.53	**OR**
1928	Harry Larva, FIN	3:53.2	**OR**	1988	Peter Rono, KEN	3:35.96	
1932	Luigi Beccali, ITA	3:51.2	**OR**	1992	Fermin Cacho, SPA	3:40.12	
1936	John Lovelock, NZE	3:47.8	**WR**	1996	Noureddine Morceli, ALG	3:35.78	
1948	Henry Eriksson, SWE	3:49.8		2000	Noah Ngeny, KEN	3:32.07	**OR**
1952	Josy Barthel, LUX	3:45.1	**OR**	2004	Hicham El Guerrouj, MOR	3:34.18	

5000 meters

Year		Time		Year		Time	
1912	Hannes Kolehmainen, FIN	14:36.6	**WR**	1968	Mohamed Gammoudi, TUN	14:05.0	
1920	Joseph Guillemot, FRA	14:55.6		1972	Lasse Viren, FIN	13:26.4	**OR**
1924	Paavo Nurmi, FIN	14:31.2	**OR**	1976	Lasse Viren, FIN	13:24.76	
1928	Ville Ritola, FIN	14:38.0		1980	Miruts Yifter, ETH	13:21.0	
1932	Lauri Lehtinen, FIN	14:30.0	**OR**	1984	Said Aouita, MOR	13:05.59	**OR**
1936	Gunnar Höckert, FIN	14:22.2	**OR**	1988	John Ngugi, KEN	13:11.70	
1948	Gaston Reiff, BEL	14:17.6	**OR**	1992	Dieter Baumann, GER	13:12.52	
1952	Emil Zátopek, CZE	14:06.6	**OR**	1996	Venuste Niyongabo, BUR	13:07.96	
1956	Vladimir Kuts, USSR	13:39.6	**OR**	2000	Millon Wolde, ETH	13:35.49	
1960	Murray Halberg, NZE	13:43.4		2004	Hicham El Guerrouj, MOR	13:14.39	
1964	Bob Schul, USA	13:48.8					

10,000 meters

Year		Time		Year		Time	
1912	Hannes Kolehmainen, FIN	31:20.8		1968	Naftali Temu, KEN	29:27.4	
1920	Paavo Nurmi, FIN	31:45.8		1972	Lasse Viren, FIN	27:38.4	**WR**
1924	Ville Ritola, FIN	30:23.2	**WR**	1976	Lasse Viren, FIN	27:40.38	
1928	Paavo Nurmi, FIN	30:18.8	**OR**	1980	Miruts Yifter, ETH	27:42.7	
1932	Janusz Kusocinski, POL	30:11.4	**OR**	1984	Alberto Cova, ITA	27:47.54	
1936	Ilmari Salminen, FIN	30:15.4		1988	Brahim Boutaib, MOR	27:21.46	**OR**
1948	Emil Zátopek, CZE	29:59.6	**OR**	1992	Khalid Skah, MOR	27:46.70	
1952	Emil Zátopek, CZE	29:17.0	**OR**	1996	Haile Gebrselassie, ETH	27:07.34	**OR**
1956	Vladimir Kuts, USSR	28:45.6	**OR**	2000	Haile Gebrselassie, ETH	27:18.20	
1960	Pyotr Bolotnikov, USSR	28:32.2	**OR**	2004	Kenenisa Bekele, ETH	27:05.10	**OR**
1964	Billy Mills, USA	28:24.4	**OR**				

Marathon

Year		Time		Year		Time	
1896	Spiridon Louis, GRE	2:58:50		1956	Alain Mimoun, FRA	2:25:00.0	
1900	Michel Théato, FRA	2:59:45		1960	Abebe Bikila, ETH	2:15:16.2	**WB**
1904	Thomas Hicks, USA	3:28:53		1964	Abebe Bikila, ETH	2:12:11.2	**WB**
1906	Billy Sherring, CAN	2:51:23.6		1968	Mamo Wolde, ETH	2:20:26.4	
1908	Johnny Hayes, USA*	2:55:18.4	**OR**	1972	Frank Shorter, USA	2:12:19.8	
1912	Kenneth McArthur, S. Afr.	2:36:54.8		1976	Waldemar Cierpinski, E. Ger	2:09:55.0	**OR**
1920	Hannes Kolehmainen, FIN	2:32:35.8	**WB**	1980	Waldemar Cierpinski, E. Ger	2:11:03.0	
1924	Albin Stenroos, FIN	2:41:22.6		1984	Carlos Lopes, POR	2:09:21.0	**OR**
1928	Boughéra El Ouafi, FRA	2:32:57.0		1988	Gelindo Bordin, ITA	2:10:32	
1932	Juan Carlos Zabala, ARG	2:31:36.0	**OR**	1992	Hwang Young-Cho, S. Kor	2:13:23	
1936	Sohn Kee-Chung, JPN†	2:29:19.2	**OR**	1996	Josia Thugwane, RSA	2:12:36	
1948	Delfo Cabrera, ARG	2:34:51.6		2000	Gezahenge Abera, ETH	2:10:11	
1952	Emil Zátopek, CZE	2:23:03.2	**OR**	2004	Stefano Baldini, ITA	2:10:55	

*Dorando Pietri of Italy placed first, but was disqualified for being helped across the finish line.
†Sohn was a Korean, but he was forced to compete under the name Kitei Son by Japan, which occupied Korea at the time.
Note: Marathon distances–40,000 meters (1896,1904); 40,260 meters (1900); 41,860 meters (1906); 42,195 meters (1908 and since 1924); 40,200 meters (1912); 42,750 meters (1920). Current distance of 42,195 meters measures 26 miles, 385 yards.

110-meter Hurdles

Year		Time		Year		Time	
1896	Tom Curtis, USA	17.6		1956	Lee Calhoun, USA	13.5	**OR**
1900	Alvin Kraenzlein, USA	15.4	**OR**	1960	Lee Calhoun, USA	13.8	
1904	Frederick Schule, USA	16.0		1964	Hayes Jones, USA	13.6	
1906	Robert Leavitt, USA	16.2		1968	Willie Davenport, USA	13.3	**OR**
1908	Forrest Smithson, USA	15.0	**WR**	1972	Rod Milburn, USA	13.24	**=WR**
1912	Frederick Kelly, USA	15.1		1976	Guy Drut, FRA	13.30	
1920	Earl Thomson, CAN	14.8	**WR**	1980	Thomas Munkelt, E. Ger	13.39	
1924	Daniel Kinsey, USA	15.0		1984	Roger Kingdom, USA	13.20	**OR**
1928	Syd Atkinson, S. Afr.	14.8		1988	Roger Kingdom, USA	12.98	**OR**
1932	George Saling, USA	14.6		1992	Mark McKoy, CAN	13.12	
1936	Forrest (Spec) Towns, USA	14.2		1996	Allen Johnson, USA	12.95	**OR**
1948	William Porter, USA	13.9	**OR**	2000	Anier Garcia, CUB	13.00	
1952	Harrison Dillard, USA	13.7	**OR**	2004	Liu Xiang, CHN	12.91	**OR**

400-meter Hurdles

Year		Time		Year		Time	
1900	Walter Tewksbury, USA	.57.6		1964	Rex Cawley, USA	.49.6	
1904	Harry Hillman, USA	.53.0		1968	David Hemery, GBR	.48.12	**WR**
1908	Charley Bacon, USA	.55.0	**WR**	1972	John Akii-Bua, UGA	.47.82	**WR**
1920	Frank Loomis, USA	.54.0	**WR**	1976	Edwin Moses, USA	.47.64	**WR**
1924	Morgan Taylor, USA	.52.6		1980	Volker Beck, E. Ger	.48.70	
1928	David Burghley, GBR	.53.4	**OR**	1984	Edwin Moses, USA	.47.75	
1932	Bob Tisdall, IRE	.51.7		1988	Andre Phillips, USA	.47.19	**OR**
1936	Glenn Hardin, USA	.52.4		1992	Kevin Young, USA	.46.78	**WR**
1948	Roy Cochran, USA	.51.1	**OR**	1996	Derrick Adkins, USA	.47.54	
1952	Charley Moore, USA	.50.8	**OR**	2000	Angelo Taylor, USA	.47.50	
1956	Glenn Davis, USA	.50.1	**=OR**	2004	Felix Sanchez, DOM	.47.63	
1960	Glenn Davis, USA	.49.3	**OR**				

3000-meter Steeplechase

Year		Time		Year		Time	
1900	George Orton, CAN	.7:34.4		1964	Gaston Roelants, BEL	.8:30.8	**OR**
1904	Jim Lightbody, USA	.7:39.6		1968	Amos Biwott, KEN	.8:51.0	
1908	Arthur Russell, GBR	.10:47.8		1972	Kip Keino, KEN	.8:23.6	**OR**
1920	Percy Hodge, GBR	.10:00.4	**OR**	1976	Anders Gärderud, SWE	.8:08.2	**WR**
1924	Ville Ritola, FIN	.9:33.6	**OR**	1980	Bronislaw Malinowski, POL	.8:09.7	
1928	Toivo Loukola, FIN	.9:21.8	**WR**	1984	Julius Korir, KEN	.8:11.80	
1932	Volmari Iso-Hollo, FIN	.10:33.4*		1988	Julius Kariuki, KEN	.8:05.51	**OR**
1936	Volmari Iso-Hollo, FIN	.9:03.8	**WR**	1992	Matthew Birir, KEN	.8:08.84	
1948	Thore Sjöstrand, SWE	.9:04.6		1996	Joseph Keter,KEN	.8:07.12	
1952	Horace Ashenfelter, USA	.8:45.4	**WR**	2000	Reuben Kosgei, KEN	.8:21.43	
1956	Chris Brasher, GBR	.8:41.2	**OR**	2004	Ezekiel Kemboi, KEN	.8:05.81	
1960	Zdzislaw Krzyszkowiak, POL	.8:34.2	**OR**				

*Iso-Hollo ran one extra lap due to lap counter's mistake.
Note: Other steeplechase distances– 2500 meters (1900); 2590 meters (1904); 3200 meters (1908) and 3460 meters (1932).

4x100-meter Relay

Year		Time		Year		Time	
1912	Great Britain	.42.4		1968	United States	.38.23	**WR**
1920	United States	.42.2	**WR**	1972	United States	.38.19	**WR**
1924	United States	.41.0	**=WR**	1976	United States	.38.33	
1928	United States	.41.0	**=WR**	1980	Soviet Union	.38.26	
1932	United States	.40.0	**WR**	1984	United States	.37.83	**WR**
1936	United States	.39.8	**WR**	1988	Soviet Union	.38.19	
1948	United States	.40.6		1992	United States	.37.40	**WR**
1952	United States	.40.1		1996	Canada	.37.69	
1956	United States	.39.5	**WR**	2000	United States	.37.61	
1960	Germany	.39.5	**=WR**	2004	Great Britain	.38.07	
1964	United States	.39.0	**WR**				

4x400-meter Relay

Year		Time		Year		Time	
1908	United States	.3:29.4		1964	United States	.3:00.7	**WR**
1912	United States	.3:16.6	**WR**	1968	United States	.2:56.16	**WR**
1920	Great Britain	.3:22.2		1972	Kenya	.2:59.8	
1924	United States	.3:16.0	**WR**	1976	United States	.2:58.65	
1928	United States	.3:14.2	**WR**	1980	Soviet Union	.3:01.1	
1932	United States	.3:08.2	**WR**	1984	United States	.2:57.91	
1936	Great Britain	.3:09.0		1988	United States	.2:56.16	**=WR**
1948	United States	.3:10.4		1992	United States	.2:55.74	**WR**
1952	Jamaica	.3:03.9	**WR**	1996	United States	.2:55.99	
1956	United States	.3:04.8		2000	United States	.2:56.35	
1960	United States	.3:02.2	**WR**	2004	United States	.2:55.91	

20-kilometer Walk

Year		Time		Year		Time	
1956	Leonid Spirin, USSR	.1:31:27.4		1984	Ernesto Canto, MEX	.1:23:13	**OR**
1960	Vladimir Golubnichiy, USSR	.1:34:07.2		1988	Jozef Pribilinec, CZE	.1:19:57	**OR**
1964	Ken Matthews, GBR	.1:29:34.0	**OR**	1992	Daniel Plaza Montero, SPA	.1:21:45	
1968	Vladimir Golubnichiy, USSR	.1:33:58.4		1996	Jefferson Perez, ECU	.1:20:07	
1972	Peter Frenkel, E. Ger	.1:26:42.4	**OR**	2000	Robert Korzeniowski, POL	.1:18:59	**OR**
1976	Daniel Bautista, MEX	.1:24:40.6	**OR**	2004	Ivano Brugnetti, ITA	.1:19:40	
1980	Maurizio Damilano, ITA	.1:23:35.5	**OR**				

50-kilometer Walk

Year		Time		Year		Time	
1932	Thomas Green, GBR	4:50:10		1976	Not held		
1936	Harold Whitlock, GBR	4:30:41.4	OR	1980	Hartwig Gauder, E. Ger	3:49:24.0	OR
1948	John Ljunggren, SWE	4:41:52		1984	Raul Gonzalez, MEX	3:47:26	OR
1952	Giuseppe Dordoni, ITA	4:28:07.8	OR	1988	Vyacheslav Ivanenko, USSR	3:38:29	OR
1956	Norman Read, NZE	4:30:42.8		1992	Andrei Perlov, UT	3:50:13	
1960	Don Thompson, GBR	4:25:30.0	OR	1996	Robert Korzeniowski, POL	3:43:30	
1964	Abdon Pamich, ITA	4:11:12.4	OR	2000	Robert Korzeniowski, POL	3:42:22	
1968	Christoph Höhne, E. Ger	4:20:13.6		2004	Robert Korzeniowski, POL	3:38:46	
1972	Bernd Kannenberg, W. Ger	3:56:11.6	OR				

High Jump

Year		Height		Year		Height	
1896	Ellery Clark, USA	5-11¼		1956	Charley Dumas, USA	6-11½	OR
1900	Irving Baxter, USA	6- 2¾	OR	1960	Robert Shavlakadze, USSR	7- 1	OR
1904	Sam Jones, USA	5-11		1964	Valery Brumel, USSR	7- 1¾	OR
1906	Cornelius Leahy, GBR/IRE	5-10		1968	Dick Fosbury, USA	7- 4¼	OR
1908	Harry Porter, USA	6- 3	OR	1972	Yuri Tarmak, USSR	7- 3¾	
1912	Alma Richards, USA	6- 4	OR	1976	Jacek Wszola, POL	7- 4½	OR
1920	Richmond Landon, USA	6- 4	=OR	1980	Gerd Wessig, E. Ger	7- 8¾	WR
1924	Harold Osborn, USA	6- 6	OR	1984	Dietmar Mögenburg, W. Ger	7- 8½	
1928	Bob King, USA	6- 4½		1988	Gennady Avdeyenko, USSR	7- 9¾	OR
1932	Duncan McNaughton, CAN	6- 5½		1992	Javier Sotomayor, CUB	7- 8	
1936	Cornelius Johnson, USA	6- 8	OR	1996	Charles Austin, USA	7-10	OR
1948	John Winter, AUS	6- 6		2000	Sergey Klugin, RUS	7- 8½	
1952	Walt Davis, USA	6- 8½	OR	2004	Stefan Holm, SWE	7- 8¾	

Pole Vault

Year		Height		Year		Height	
1896	William Hoyt, USA	10-10		1956	Bob Richards, USA	14-11½	OR
1900	Irving Baxter, USA	10-10		1960	Don Bragg, USA	15- 5	OR
1904	Charles Dvorak, USA	11- 5¾		1964	Fred Hansen, USA	16- 8¾	OR
1906	Fernand Gonder, FRA	11- 5¾		1968	Bob Seagren, USA	17-8½	OR
1908	(TIE) Edward Cooke, USA	12- 2		1972	Wolfgang Nordwig, E. Ger	18- 0½	OR
	& Alfred Gilbert, USA	12- 2	OR	1976	Tadeusz Slusarski, POL	18- 0½	=OR
1912	Harry Babcock, USA	12-11½	OR	1980	Wladyslaw Kozakiewicz, POL	18-11½	WR
1920	Frank Foss, USA	13- 5	WR	1984	Pierre Quinon, FRA	18-10¼	
1924	Lee Barnes, USA	12-11½		1988	Sergey Bubka, USSR	19- 4¼	OR
1928	Sabin Carr, USA	13- 9¼	OR	1992	Maksim Tarasov, UT	19-0¼	
1932	Bill Miller, USA	14-1¾	OR	1996	Jean Galfione, FRA	19- 5¼	OR
1936	Earle Meadows, USA	14- 3¼	OR	2000	Nick Hysong, USA	19-4¼	
1948	Guinn Smith, USA	14-1¼		2004	Timothy Mack, USA	19-6¼	OR
1952	Bob Richards, USA	14-11	OR				

Long Jump

Year		Distance		Year		Distance	
1896	Ellery Clark, USA	20-10		1956	Greg Bell, USA	25- 8¼	
1900	Alvin Kraenzlein, USA	23- 6¾	OR	1960	Ralph Boston, USA	26-7¾	OR
1904	Meyer Prinstein, USA	24- 1	OR	1964	Lynn Davies, GBR	26- 5¾	
1906	Meyer Prinstein, USA	23- 7½		1968	Bob Beamon, USA	29- 2½	WR
1908	Frank Irons, USA	24- 6½	OR	1972	Randy Williams, USA	27-0½	
1912	Albert Gutterson, USA	24-11¼	OR	1976	Arnie Robinson, USA	27- 4¾	
1920	William Petersson, SWE	23-5½		1980	Lutz Dombrowski, E. Ger	28- 0¼	
1924	De Hart Hubbard, USA	24- 5		1984	Carl Lewis, USA	28-0¼	
1928	Ed Hamm, USA	25- 4½	OR	1988	Carl Lewis, USA	28- 7¼	
1932	Ed Gordon, USA	25- 0¾		1992	Carl Lewis, USA	28- 5½	
1936	Jesse Owens, USA	26-5½	OR	1996	Carl Lewis, USA	27-10¾	
1948	Willie Steele, USA	25- 8		2000	Ivan Pedroso, CUB	28- 0¾	
1952	Jerome Biffle, USA	24-10		2004	Dwight Phillips, USA	28- 2¼	

Triple Jump

Year		Distance		Year		Distance	
1896	James Connolly, USA	44-11¾		1960	Józef Schmidt, POL	55- 2	
1900	Meyer Prinstein, USA	47- 5¾	OR	1964	Józef Schmidt, POL	55-3½	OR
1904	Meyer Prinstein, USA	47- 1		1968	Viktor Saneyev, USSR	57- 0¾	WR
1906	Peter O'Connor, GBR/IRE	46-2¼		1972	Viktor Saneyev, USSR	56-11¼	
1908	Timothy Ahearne, GBR/IRE	48-11¼	OR	1976	Viktor Saneyev, USSR	56- 8¾	
1912	Gustaf Lindblom, SWE	48-5¼		1980	Jack Uudmäe, USSR	56-11¼	
1920	Vilho Tuulos, FIN	47- 7		1984	Al Joyner, USA	56-7½	
1924	Nick Winter, AUS	50-11¼	WR	1988	Khristo Markov, BUL	57- 9¼	OR
1928	Mikio Oda, JPN	49-11		1992	Mike Conley, USA	59-7½ᵂ	OR
1932	Chuhei Nambu, JPN	51- 7	WR	1996	Kenny Harrison, USA	59-4¼	OR
1936	Naoto Tajima, JPN	52- 6	WR	2000	Jonathan Edwards, GBR	58-1¼	
1948	Arne Ahman, SWE	50- 6¼		2004	Christian Olsson, SWE	58-4½	
1952	Adhemar da Silva, BRA	53-2¾	WR	ᵂindicates wind-aided.			
1956	Adhemar da Silva, BRA	53- 7¾	OR				

Shot Put

Year		Distance		Year		Distance	
1896	Bob Garrett, USA	36- 9¾		1956	Parry O'Brien, USA	60-11¼	OR
1900	Richard Sheldon, USA	46- 3¼	OR	1960	Bill Nieder, USA	64-6¾	OR
1904	Ralph Rose, USA	48- 7	WR	1964	Dallas Long, USA	66- 8½	OR
1906	Martin Sheridan, USA	40- 5¼		1968	Randy Matson, USA	67-4¾	
1908	Ralph Rose, USA	46- 7½		1972	Wladyslaw Komar, POL	69- 6	OR
1912	Patrick McDonald, USA	50- 4	OR	1976	Udo Beyer, E. Ger	69- 0¾	
1920	Ville Pörhölä, FIN	48-7¼		1980	Vladimir Kiselyov, USSR	70- 0½	OR
1924	Bud Houser, USA	49- 2¼		1984	Alessandro Andrei, ITA	69- 9	
1928	John Kuck, USA	52- 0¾	WR	1988	Ulf Timmermann, E. Ger	73- 8¾	OR
1932	Leo Sexton, USA	52- 6		1992	Mike Stulce, USA	71-2½	
1936	Hans Woellke, GER	53- 1¾	OR	1996	Randy Barnes, USA	70-11¼	
1948	Wilbur Thompson, USA	56- 2	OR	2000	Arsi Harju, FIN	69-10¼	
1952	Parry O'Brien, USA	57- 1½	OR	2004	Yuriy Bilonog, UKR	69-5¼	

Discus Throw

Year		Distance		Year		Distance	
1896	Bob Garrett, USA	95- 7½		1956	Al Oerter, USA	184-11	OR
1900	Rudolf Bauer, HUN	118- 3	OR	1960	Al Oerter, USA	194- 2	OR
1904	Martin Sheridan, USA	128-10½	OR	1964	Al Oerter, USA	200- 1	OR
1906	Martin Sheridan, USA	136-0		1968	Al Oerter, USA	212- 6	OR
1908	Martin Sheridan, USA	134- 2	OR	1972	Ludvik Danek, CZE	211- 3	
1912	Armas Taipale, FIN	148- 3	OR	1976	Mac Wilkins, USA	221- 5	
1920	Elmer Niklander, FIN	146- 7		1980	Viktor Rashchupkin, USSR	218- 8	
1924	Bud Houser, USA	151- 4	OR	1984	Rolf Danneberg, W. Ger	218- 6	
1928	Bud Houser, USA	155- 3	OR	1988	Jürgen Schult, E. Ger	225- 9	OR
1932	John Anderson, USA	162- 4	OR	1992	Romas Ubartas, LIT	213- 8	
1936	Ken Carpenter, USA	165- 7	OR	1996	Lars Riedel, GER	227-8	
1948	Adolfo Consolini, ITA	173- 2	OR	2000	Virgilijus Alekna, LIT	227-4	
1952	Sim Iness, USA	180- 6	OR	2004	Virgilijus Alekna, LIT*	229-3	OR

*Hungary's **Robert Fazekas** had a throw of 232 feet, 8 inches, and was initially declared the winner, but he was disqualified for failing to submit to a drug test following the competition.

Hammer Throw

Year		Distance		Year		Distance	
1900	John Flanagan, USA	163- 1		1960	Vasily Rudenkov, USSR	220- 2	OR
1904	John Flanagan, USA	168- 1	OR	1964	Romuald Klim, USSR	228-10	OR
1908	John Flanagan, USA	170- 4	OR	1968	Gyula Zsivótzky, HUN	240- 8	OR
1912	Matt McGrath, USA	179- 7	OR	1972	Anatoly Bondarchuk, USSR	247- 8	OR
1920	Pat Ryan, USA	173- 5		1976	Yuri Sedykh, USSR	254- 4	OR
1924	Fred Tootell, USA	174-10		1980	Yuri Sedykh, USSR	268- 4	WR
1928	Pat O'Callaghan, IRE	168- 7		1984	Juha Tiainen, FIN	256- 2	
1932	Pat O'Callaghan, IRE	176-11		1988	Sergey Litvinov, USSR	278- 2	OR
1936	Karl Hein, GER	185- 4	OR	1992	Andrei Abduvaliyev, UT	270- 9	
1948	Imre Németh, HUN	183-11		1996	Balazs Kiss, HUN	266-6	
1952	József Csérmák, HUN	197-11	WR	2000	Szymon Ziolkowski, POL	262-6	
1956	Harold Connolly, USA	207- 3	OR	2004	Koji Murofushi, JPN*	272-0	

Hungary's **Adrian Annus** was initially awarded the gold medal for his throw of 272-11, but after questions were raised about the legitimacy of his post-competition drug test, and he failed to submit to a follow-up test, he was disqualified and stripped of the gold.

Javelin Throw

Year		Distance	
1908	Eric Lemming, SWE	179-10	**WR**
1912	Eric Lemming, SWE	198-11	**WR**
1920	Jonni Myyrä, FIN	215-10	**OR**
1924	Jonni Myyrä, FIN	206-7	
1928	Erik Lundkvist, SWE	218-6	**OR**
1932	Matti Järvinen, FIN	238-6	**OR**
1936	Gerhard Stöck, GER	235-8	
1948	Kai Tapio Rautavaara, FIN	228-10	
1952	Cy Young, USA	242-1	**OR**
1956	Egil Danielson, NOR	281-2	**WR**
1960	Viktor Tsibulenko, USSR	277-8	

Year		Distance	
1964	Pauli Nevala, FIN	271-2	
1968	Jänis Lüsis, USSR	295-7	**OR**
1972	Klaus Wolfermann, W. Ger	296-10	**OR**
1976	Miklos Németh, HUN	310-4	**WR**
1980	Dainis Kula, USSR	299-2	
1984	Arto Härkönen, FIN	284-8	
1988	Tapio Korjus, FIN	276-6	
1992	Jan Zelezny, CZE	294-2*	**OR**
1996	Jan Zelezny, CZR	289-3	
2000	Jan Zelezny, CZR	295-10	**OR**
2004	Andreas Thorkildsen, NOR	283-9	

*In 1986 the balance point of the javelin was modified and new records have been kept since.

Decathlon

Year		Points	
1904	Thomas Kiely, IRE	6036	
1906-08	Not held		
1912	Jim Thorpe, USA	8412	**WR**
1920	Helge Lövland, NOR	6803	
1924	Harold Osborn, USA	7711	**WR**
1928	Paavo Yrjölä, FIN	8053	**WR**
1932	Jim Bausch, USA	8462	**WR**
1936	Glenn Morris, USA	7900	**WR**
1948	Bob Mathias, USA	7139	
1952	Bob Mathias, USA	7887	**WR**
1956	Milt Campbell, USA	7937	**OR**
1960	Rafer Johnson, USA	8392	**OR**

Year		Points	
1964	Willi Holdorf, GER	7887	
1968	Bill Toomey, USA	8193	**OR**
1972	Nikolai Avilov, USSR	8454	**WR**
1976	Bruce Jenner, USA	8617	**WR**
1980	Daley Thompson, GBR	8495	
1984	Daley Thompson, GBR	8798	**=WR**
1988	Christian Schenk, E. Ger	8488	
1992	Robert Zmelik, CZE	8611	
1996	Dan O'Brien, USA	8824	
2000	Erki Nool, EST	8641	
2004	Roman Sebrle, CZE	8893	**OR**

WOMEN

At least 4 gold medals (including relays): Evelyn Ashford, Fanny Blankers-Koen, Betty Cuthbert and Bärbel Eckert Wöckel (4).

100 meters

Year		Time	
1928	Betty Robinson, USA	12.2	**=WR**
1932	Stella Walsh, POL*	11.9	**=WR**
1936	Helen Stephens, USA	11.5ᵂ	
1948	Fanny Blankers-Koen, NED	11.9	
1952	Marjorie Jackson, AUS	11.5	**=WR**
1956	Betty Cuthbert, AUS	11.5	
1960	Wilma Rudolph, USA	11.0ᵂ	
1964	Wyomia Tyus, USA	11.4	
1968	Wyomia Tyus, USA	11.08	**WR**

Year		Time	
1972	Renate Stecher, E. Ger	11.07	
1976	Annegret Richter, W. Ger	11.08	
1980	Lyudmila Kondratyeva, USSR	11.06	
1984	Evelyn Ashford, USA	10.97	**OR**
1988	Florence Griffith Joyner, USA	10.54ᵂ	
1992	Gail Devers, USA	10.82	**OR**
1996	Gail Devers, USA	10.94	
2000	Marion Jones, USA	10.75	
2004	Yuliya Nesterenko, BLR	10.93	

*An autopsy performed after Walsh's death in 1980 revealed that she was a man.
ᵂindicates wind-aided.

200 meters

Year		Time	
1948	Fanny Blankers-Koen, NED	24.4	
1952	Marjorie Jackson, AUS	23.7	**OR**
1956	Betty Cuthbert, AUS	23.4	**=OR**
1960	Wilma Rudolph, USA	24.0	
1964	Edith McGuire, USA	23.0	**O**
1968	Irena Szewinska, POL	22.5	**WR**
1972	Renate Stecher, E. Ger	22.40	**=WR**
1976	Bärbel Eckert, E. Ger	22.37	**OR**

Year		Time	
1980	Bärbel Eckert Wockel, E. Ger	22.03	**OR**
1984	Valerie Brisco-Hooks, USA	21.81	**OR**
1988	Florence Griffith Joyner, USA	21.34	**WR**
1992	Gwen Torrence, USA	21.81	
1996	Marie-Jose Perec, FRA	22.12	
2000	Marion Jones, USA	21.84	
2004	Veronica Campbell, JAM	22.05	

400 meters

Year		Time	
1964	Betty Cuthbert, AUS	52.0	
1968	Colette Besson, FRA	52.03	**=OR**
1972	Monika Zehrt, E. Ger	51.08	**OR**
1976	Irena Szewinska, POL	49.29	**WR**
1980	Marita Koch, E. Ger	48.88	**OR**
1984	Valerie Brisco-Hooks, USA	48.83	**OR**

Year		Time	
1988	Olga Bryzgina, USSR	48.65	**OR**
1992	Marie-Jose Perec, FRA	48.83	
1996	Marie-Jose Perec, FRA	48.25	**OR**
2000	Cathy Freeman, AUS	49.11	
2004	Tonique Williams-Darling, BAH	49.41	

800 meters

Year		Time	
1928	Lina Radke, GER	2:16.8	**WR**
1932-56	Not held		
1960	Lyudmila Shevtsova, USSR	2:04.3	**=WR**
1964	Ann Packer, GBR	2:01.1	**OR**
1968	Madeline Manning, USA	2:00.9	**OR**
1972	Hildegard Falck, W. Ger	1:58.55	**OR**
1976	Tatyana Kazankina, USSR	1:54.94	**WR**

Year		Time	
1980	Nadezhda Olizarenko, USSR	1:53.42	**WR**
1984	Doina Melinte, ROM	1:57.60	
1988	Sigrun Wodars, E. Ger	1:56.10	
1992	Ellen van Langen, NED	1:55.54	
1996	Svetlana Masterkova, RUS	1:57.73	
2000	Maria Mutola, MOZ	1:56.15	
2004	Kelly Holmes, GBR	1:56.38	

1500 meters

Year		Time		Year		Time	
1972	Lyudmila Bragina, USSR	4:01.4	WR	1992	Hassiba Boulmerka, ALG	3:55.30	
1976	Tatyana Kazankina, USSR	4:05.48		1996	Svetlana Masterkova, RUS	4:00.83	
1980	Tatyana Kazankina, USSR	3:56.6	OR	2000	Nouria Merah-Benida, ALG	4:05.10	
1984	Gabriella Dorio, ITA	4:03.25		2004	Kelly Holmes, GBR	3:57.90	
1988	Paula Ivan, ROM	3:53.96	OR				

5000 meters

Year		Time		Year		Time	
1984	Maricica Puica, ROM	8:35.96		1996	Wang Junxia, CHN	14:59.88	
1988	Tatyana Samolenko, USSR	8:26.53	OR	2000	Gabriela Szabo, ROM	14:40.79	OR
1992	Elena Romanova, UT	8:46.04		2004	Meseret Defar, ETH	14:45.65	

Note: Event held over 3000 meters from 1984-92.

10,000 meters

Year		Time		Year		Time	
1988	Olga Bondarenko, USSR	31:05.21	OR	2000	Derartu Tulu, ETH	30:17.49	OR
1992	Derartu Tulu, ETH	31:06.02		2004	Xing Huina, CHN	30:24.36	
1996	Fernanda Ribeiro, POR	31:01.63	OR				

Marathon

Year		Time	Year		Time
1984	Joan Benoit, USA	2:24:52	1996	Fatuma Roba, ETH	2:26:05
1988	Rosa Mota, POR	2:25:40	2000	Naoko Takahashi, JPN	2:23:14
1992	Valentina Yegorova, UT	2:32:41	2004	Mizuki Noguchi, JPN	2:26:20

100-meter Hurdles

Year		Time		Year		Time	
1932	Babe Didrikson, USA	11.7	WR	1980	Vera Komisova, USSR	12.56	OR
1936	Trebisonda Valla, ITA	11.7		1984	Benita Fitzgerald-Brown, USA	12.84	
1948	Fanny Blankers-Koen, NED	11.2	OR	1988	Yordanka Donkova, BUL	12.38	OR
1952	Shirley Strickland, AUS	10.9	WR	1992	Paraskevi Patoulidou, GRE	12.64	
1956	Shirley Strickland, AUS	10.7	OR	1996	Ludmila Enquist, SWE	12.58	
1960	Irina Press, USSR	10.8		2000	Olga Shishigina, KAZ	12.65	
1964	Karin Balzer, GER	10.5ᵂ		2004	Joanna Hayes, USA	12.37	OR
1968	Maureen Caird, AUS	10.3	OR				
1972	Annelie Ehrhardt, E. Ger	12.59	WR				
1976	Johanna Schaller, E. Ger	12.77					

ᵂindicates wind-aided.

Note: Event held over 80 meters from 1932-68.

400-meter Hurdles

Year		Time		Year		Time	
1984	Nawal El Moutawakel, MOR	54.61	OR	1996	Deon Hemmings, JAM	52.82	OR
1988	Debra Flintoff-King, AUS	53.17	OR	2000	Irina Privalova, RUS	53.02	
1992	Sally Gunnell, GBR	53.23		2004	Fani Halkia, GRE	52.82	

4x100-meter Relay

Year		Time		Year		Time	
1928	Canada	48.4	WR	1972	West Germany	42.81	WR
1932	United States	46.9	WR	1976	East Germany	42.55	OR
1936	United States	46.9		1980	East Germany	41.60	WR
1948	Holland	47.5		1984	United States	41.65	
1952	United States	45.9	WR	1988	United States	41.98	
1956	Australia	44.5	WR	1992	United States	42.11	
1960	United States	44.5		1996	United States	41.95	
1964	Poland	43.6		2000	Bahamas	42.20	
1968	United States	42.87	WR	2004	Jamaica	41.73	

4x400-meter Relay

Year		Time		Year		Time	
1972	East Germany	3:23.0	WR	1992	Unified Team	3:20.20	
1976	East Germany	3:19.23	WR	1996	United States	3:20.91	
1980	Soviet Union	3:20.2		2000	United States	3:22.62	
1984	United States	3:18.29	OR	2004	United States	3:19.01	
1988	Soviet Union	3:15.18	WR				

20-kilometer Walk

Year		Time	Year		Time
1992	Chen Yueling, CHN	44:32	2000	Wang Liping, CHN	1:29:05
1996	Yelena Ninikolayeva, RUS	41:49	2004	Athanasia Tsoumeleka, GRE	1:29:12

Note: Event was held over 10 kilometers from 1992-96.

Pole Vault

Year		Height		Year		Height	
2000	Stacy Dragila, USA	15-1	OR	2004	Yelena Isinbayeva, RUS	16-1¼	WR

High Jump

Year		Height		Year		Height	
1928	Ethel Catherwood, CAN	5-2½		1972	Ulrike Meyfarth, W. Ger	6-3½	=WR
1932	Jean Shiley, USA	5-5¼	WR	1976	Rosemarie Ackermann, E. Ger	6-4	OR
1936	Ibolya Csák, HUN	5-3		1980	Sara Simeoni, ITA	6-5½	OR
1948	Alice Coachman, USA	5-6	OR	1984	Ulrike Meyfarth, W. Ger	6-7½	OR
1952	Esther Brand, RSA	5-5¾		1988	Louise Ritter, USA	6-8	OR
1956	Mildred McDaniel, USA	5-9¼	WR	1992	Heike Henkel, GER	6-7½	
1960	Iolanda Balas, ROM	6-0¾	OR	1996	Stefka Kostadinova, BUL	6-8¾	
1964	Iolanda Balas, ROM	6-2¾	OR	2000	Yelena Yelesina, RUS	6-7	
1968	Miloslava Rezkova, CZE	5-11½		2004	Yelena Slesarenko, RUS	6-9	OR

Long Jump

Year		Distance		Year		Distance	
1948	Olga Gyarmati, HUN	18-8¼		1980	Tatyana Kolpakova, USSR	23-2	OR
1952	Yvette Williams, NZE	20-5¾	OR	1984	Anisoara Cusmir-Stanciu, ROM	22-10	
1956	Elzbieta Krzesinska, POL	20-10	=WR	1988	Jackie Joyner-Kersee, USA	24-3¼	OR
1960	Vyera Krepkina, USSR	20-10¾	WR	1992	Heike Drechsler, GER	23-5¼	
1964	Mary Rand, GBR	22-2¼	WR	1996	Chioma Ajunwa, NGR	23-4½	
1968	Viorica Viscopoleanu, ROM	22-4½	WR	2000	Heike Drechsler, GER	22-11¼	
1972	Heidemarie Rosendahl, W. Ger	22-3		2004	Tatyana Lebedeva, RUS	23-2½	
1976	Angela Voigt, E. Ger	22-0¾					

Triple Jump

Year		Distance		Year		Distance	
1996	Inessa Kravets, UKR	50-3½		2004	Francoise Mbango Etone, CMR	50-2½	
2000	Tereza Marinova, BUL	49-10½					

Shot Put

Year		Distance		Year		Distance	
1948	Micheline Ostermeyer, FRA	45-1½		1980	Ilona Slupianek, E. Ger	73-6¼	OR
1952	Galina Zybina, USSR	50-1¾	WR	1984	Claudia Losch, W. Ger	67-2¼	
1956	Tamara Tyshkevich, USSR	54-5	OR	1988	Natalia Lisovskaya, USSR	72-11¾	
1960	Tamara Press, USSR	56-10	OR	1992	Svetlana Krivaleva, UT	69-1¼	
1964	Tamara Press, USSR	59-6¼	OR	1996	Astrid Kumbernuss, GER	67-5½	
1968	Margitta Gummel, E. Ger	64-4	WR	2000	Yanina Korolchik, BLR	67-5½	
1972	Nadezhda Chizhova, USSR	69-0	WR	2004	Yumileidi Cumba, CUB*	64-3¼	
1976	Ivanka Hristova, BUL	69-5¼	OR				

*Russia's Irina Korzhanenko (69-1¼) was stripped of the gold for failing a post-competition drug test.

Discus Throw

Year		Distance		Year		Distance	
1928	Halina Konopacka, POL	129-11¾	WR	1972	Faina Melnik, USSR	218-7	OR
1932	Lillian Copeland, USA	133-2	OR	1976	Evelin Schlaak, E. Ger	226-4	OR
1936	Gisela Mauermayer, GER	156-3	OR	1980	Evelin Schlaak Jahl, E. Ger	229-6	OR
1948	Micheline Ostermeyer, FRA	137-6		1984	Ria Stalman, NED	214-5	
1952	Nina Romaschkova, USSR	168-8	OR	1988	Martina Hellmann, E. Ger	237-2½	OR
1956	Olga Fikotová, CZE	176-1	OR	1992	Maritza Marten, CUB	229-10	
1960	Nina Ponomaryeva, USSR	180-9	OR	1996	Ilke Wyludda, GER	228-6	
1964	Tamara Press, USSR	187-10	OR	2000	Ellina Zvereva, BLR	224-5	
1968	Lia Manoliu, ROM	191-2	OR	2004	Natalya Sadova, RUS	219-10	

Hammer Throw

Year		Distance		Year		Distance	
2000	Kamila Skolimowska, POL	233-5¾	OR	2004	Olga Kuzenkova, RUS	246-1	OR

Javelin Throw

Year		Distance		Year		Distance	
1932	Babe Didrikson, USA	143-4		1976	Ruth Fuchs, E. Ger	216-4	OR
1936	Tilly Fleischer, GER	148-3	OR	1980	Maria Colon Rueñes, CUB	224-5	OR
1948	Herma Bauma, AUT	149-6	OR	1984	Tessa Sanderson, GBR	228-2	OR
1952	Dana Zátopková, CZE	165-7	OR	1988	Petra Felke, E. Ger	245-0	OR
1956	Ineze Jaunzeme, USSR	176-8	OR	1992	Silke Renk, GER	224-2	
1960	Elvira Ozolina, USSR	183-8	OR	1996	Heli Rantanen, FIN	222-11	
1964	Mihaela Penes, ROM	198-7	OR	2000	Trine Hattestad, NOR	226-1	OR
1968	Angéla Németh, HUN	198-0	OR	2004	Osleidys Menendez, CUB	234-8	OR
1972	Ruth Fuchs, E. Ger	209-7	OR				

Heptathlon

Year		Points		Year		Points	
1964	Irina Press, USSR	5246	WR	1988	Jackie Joyner-Kersee, USA	7291	WR
1968	Ingrid Becker, W. Ger	5098		1992	Jackie Joyner-Kersee, USA	7044	
1972	Mary Peters, GBR	4801	WR	1996	Ghada Shouaa, SYR	6780	
1976	Siegrun Siegl, E. Ger	4745		2000	Denise Lewis, GBR	6584	
1980	Nadezhda Tkachenko, USSR	5083	WR	2004	Carolina Klüft, SWE	6952	
1984	Glynis Nunn, AUS	6390	OR				

Note: Seven-event Heptathlon replaced five-event Pentathlon in 1984.

All-Time Leading Medal Winners – Single Games

Athletes who have won the most medals in a single Summer Olympics. Totals include individual, relay and team medals. U.S. athletes are in **bold** type.

MEN

No		Sport	G-S-B	No		Sport	G-S-B
8†	**Michael Phelps**, USA (2004)	Swim	6-0-2	6	Takashi Ono, JPN (1960)	Gym	3-1-2
8	Aleksandr Dityatin, USSR (1980)	Gym	3-4-1	6	Viktor Chukarin, USSR (1956)	Gym	4-2-0
7	**Mark Spitz**, USA (1972)	Swim	7-0-0	6	Konrad Frey, GER (1936)	Gym	3-1-2
7	**Willis Lee**, USA (1920)	Shoot	5-1-1	6	Ville Ritola, FIN (1924)	Track	4-2-0
7	**Matt Biondi**, USA (1988)	Swim	5-1-1	6	Hubert Van Innis, BEL (1920)	Arch	4-2-0
7	Boris Shakhlin, USSR (1960)	Gym	4-2-1	6	**Carl Osburn**, USA (1920)	Shoot	4-1-1
7	**Lloyd Spooner**, USA (1920)	Shoot	4-1-2	6	Louis Richardet, SWI (1906)	Shoot	3-3-0
7	Mikhail Voronin, USSR (1968)	Gym	2-4-1	6	**Anton Heida**, USA (1904)	Gym	5-1-0
7	Nikolai Andrianov, USSR (1976)	Gym	2-4-1	6	**George Eyser**, USA (1904)	Gym	3-2-1
6	Vitaly Scherbo, UT (1992)	Gym	6-0-0	6	**Burton Downing**, USA (1904)	Cycle	2-3-1
6	Li Ning, CHN (1984)	Gym	3-2-1	6	Alexei Nemov, RUS (1996)	Gym	2-1-3
6	Akinori Nakayama, JPN (1968)	Gym	4-1-1	6	Alexei Nemov, RUS (2000)	Gym	2-1-3

†Includes gold medal as preliminary member of 1st-place relay team.

WOMEN

No		Sport	G-S-B	No		Sport	G-S-B
7	Maria Gorokhovskaya, USSR (1952)	Gym	2-5-0	5	Shane Gould, AUS (1972)	Swim	3-1-1
6	Kristin Otto, E. Ger (1988)	Swim	6-0-0	5	Nadia Comaneci, ROM (1976)	Gym	3-1-1
6	Agnes Keleti, HUN (1956)	Gym	4-2-0	5	Karin Janz, E. Ger (1972)	Gym	2-2-1
6	Vera Cáslavská, CZE (1968)	Gym	4-2-0	5	Ines Diers, E. Ger (1980)	Swim	2-2-1
6	Larisa Latynina, USSR (1956)	Gym	4-1-1	5	**Shirley Babashoff**, USA (1976)	Swim	1-4-0
6	Larisa Latynina, USSR (1960)	Gym	3-2-1	5	**Mary Lou Retton**, USA (1984)	Gym	1-2-2
6	Daniela Silivas, ROM (1988)	Gym	3-2-1	5	**Shannon Miller**, USA (1992)	Gym	0-2-3
6	Larisa Latynina, USSR (1964)	Gym	2-2-2	5	**Marion Jones**, USA (2000)	Track	3-0-2
6	Margit Korondi, HUN (1956)	Gym	1-1-4	5	**Dara Torres**, USA (2000)	Swim	2-0-3
5	Kornelia Ender, E. Ger (1976)	Swim	4-1-0	5	**Natalie Coughlin**, USA (2004)	Swim	2-2-1
5	Ecaterina Szabó, ROM (1984)	Gym	4-1-0				

All-Time Leading Medal Winners – Career

MEN

No		Sport	G-S-B	No		Sport	G-S-B
15	Nikolai Andrianov, USSR	Gymnastics	7-5-3	10	**Carl Lewis**, USA	Track/Field	9-1-0
13	Boris Shakhlin, USSR	Gymnastics	7-4-2	10	Aladár Gerevich, HUN	Fencing	7-1-2
13	Edoardo Mangiarotti, ITA	Fencing	6-5-2	10	Akinori Nakayama, JPN	Gymnastics	6-2-2
13	Takashi Ono, JPN	Gymnastics	5-4-4	10	Aleksandr Dityatin, USSR	Gymnastics	3-6-1
12	Paavo Nurmi, FIN	Track/Field	9-3-0	9	Vitaly Scherbo, BLR	Gymnastics	6-0-3
12	Sawao Kato, JPN	Gymnastics	8-3-1	9	**Gary Hall Jr.**, USA	Swimming	5-3-1
12	Alexei Nemov, RUS	Gymnastics	4-2-6	9*	**Martin Sheridan**, USA	Track/Field	5-3-1
11	**Mark Spitz**, USA	Swimming	9-1-1	9*	Zoltán Halmay, HUN	Swimming	3-5-1
11†	**Matt Biondi**, USA	Swimming	8-2-1	9	Giulio Gaudini, ITA	Fencing	3-4-2
11	Viktor Chukarin, USSR	Gymnastics	7-3-1	9	Mikhail Voronin, USSR	Gymnastics	2-6-1
11	**Carl Osburn**, USA	Shooting	5-4-2	9	Heikki Savolainen, FIN	Gymnastics	2-1-6
10*	**Ray Ewry**, USA	Track/Field	10-0-0	9	Yuri Titov, USSR	Gymnastics	1-5-3

†Includes gold medal as preliminary member of 1st-place relay team.
*Medals won by Ewry (2-0-0), Sheridan (2-3-0) and Halmay (1-1-0) at the 1906 Intercalated games are not officially recognized by the IOC.

Games Participated In

Andrianov (1972,76,80); **Biondi** (1984,88,92); **Chukarin** (1952,56); **Dityatin** (1976,80); **Ewry** (1900,04,06,08); **Gerevich** (1932,36,48,52,56,60); **Gaudini** (1928,32,36); **Hall Jr.** (1996,2000,04); **Halmay** (1900,04,06,08); **Kato** (1968,72,76); **Lewis** (1984,88,92,96); **Mangiarotti** (1936,48,52,56,60); **Nakayama** (1968,72); **Nemov** (1996,2000) **Nurmi** (1920,24,28); **Ono** (1952,56,60,64); **Osburn** (1912,20, 24); **Savolainen** (1928,32,36,48,52); **Scherbo** (1992,96); **Shakhlin** (1956,60,64); **Sheridan** (1904,06,08); **Spitz** (1968,72); **Titov** (1956,60,64); **Voronin** (1968,72).

Most Individual Medals

Not including team competition.

	Sport	G-S-B
Men: 12-Nikolai Andrianov, USSR	Gym	6-3-3
Women: 15-Larissa Latynina, USSR	Gym	7-5-3

WOMEN

No		Sport	G-S-B
18	Larissa Latynina, USSR	Gymnastics	9-5-4
12	**Jenny Thompson**, USA	Swimming	8-3-1
11	Vera Cáslavská, CZE	Gymnastics	7-4-0
10	Birgit Fischer, GER	Canoe/Kayak	7-3-0
10	Agnes Keleti, HUN	Gymnastics	5-3-2
10	Polina Astakhova, USSR	Gymnastics	5-2-3
9	Nadia Comaneci, ROM	Gymnastics	5-3-1
9	Lyudmila Tourischeva, USSR	Gymnastics	4-3-2
9	**Dara Torres**, USA	Swimming	4-1-4
8	Kornelia Ender, E. Ger	Swimming	4-4-0
8	Dawn Fraser, AUS	Swimming	4-4-0

No		Sport	G-S-B
8	**Shirley Babashoff**, USA	Swimming	2-6-0
8	Sofia Muratova, USSR	Gymnastics	2-2-4
8	Inge de Bruijn, NED	Swimming	4-2-2
7	Krisztina Egerszegi, HUN	Swimming	5-1-1
7	Irena Kirszenstein Szewinska, POL	Track/Field	3-2-2
7	Shirley Strickland, AUS	Track/Field	3-1-3
7	Maria Gorokhovskaya, USSR	Gymnastics	2-5-0
7	Ildiko Sagine-Ujlaki-Rejto, HUN	Fencing	2-3-2
7	**Shannon Miller**, USA	Gymnastics	2-2-3
7	Susie O'Neill, AUS	Swimming	2-4-1
7	Merlene Ottey, JAM	Track/Field	0-2-5

Games Participated In

Astakhova (1956,60,64); **Babashoff** (1972,76); **Cáslavská** (1960,64,68); **Comaneci** (1976,80); **de Bruijn** (2000,04); **Egerszegi** (1988,92,96); **Ender** (1972,76); **Fischer** (1980,92,96,2000); **Fraser** (1956,60,64); **Gorokhovskaya** (1952); **Keleti** (1952,56); **Latynina** (1956,60,64); **Miller** (1992,96); **Muratova** (1956,60); **O'Neill** (1996,2000) **Ottey** (1980,84,88,92,96) **Sagine-Ujlaki-Rejto** (1960,64,68,72,76); **Strickland** (1948,52,56); **Szewinska** (1964,68,72,76,80); **Thompson** (1992,96,2000,04); **Torres** (1984,88,92,2000) **Tourischeva** (1968, 72,76).

Most Gold Medals

MEN

No		Sport	G-S-B
10*	**Ray Ewry**, USA	Track/Field	10-0-0
9	Paavo Nurmi, FIN	Track/Field	9-3-0
9	**Mark Spitz**, USA	Swimming	9-1-1
9	**Carl Lewis**, USA	Track/Field	9-1-0
8	Sawao Kato, JPN	Gymnastics	8-3-1
8†	**Matt Biondi**, USA	Swimming	8-2-1
7	Nikolai Andrianov, USSR	Gymnastics	7-5-3

No		Sport	G-S-B
7	Boris Shakhlin, USSR	Gymnastics	7-4-2
7	Viktor Chukarin, USSR	Gymnastics	7-3-1
7	Aladar Gerevich, HUN	Fencing	7-1-2

*Medals won by Ewry (2-0-0) at the 1906 Intercalated games are not officially recognized by the IOC.

†Includes gold medal as preliminary member of 1st-place relay team.

WOMEN

No		Sport	G-S-B
9	Larissa Latynina, USSR	Gymnastics	9-5-4
8	**Jenny Thompson**, USA	Swimming	8-3-1
7	Vera Cáslavská, CZE	Gymnastics	7-4-0
7	Birgit Fischer, GER	Canoe/Kayak	7-3-0
6†	Kristin Otto, E. Ger	Swimming	6-0-0
6†	**Amy Van Dyken**, USA	Swimming	6-0-0
5	Agnes Keleti, HUN	Gymnastics	5-3-2
5	Nadia Comaneci, ROM	Gymnastics	5-3-1
5	Polina Astakhova, USSR	Gymnastics	5-2-3
5	Krisztina Egerszegi, HUN	Swimming	5-1-1
4	Kornelia Ender, E. Ger	Swimming	4-4-0
4	Dawn Fraser, AUS	Swimming	4-4-0

No		Sport	G-S-B
4	Lyudmila Tourischeva, USSR	Gymnastics	4-3-2
4	**Dara Torres**, USA	Swimming	4-1-4
4	**Evelyn Ashford**, USA	Track/Field	4-1-0
4	**Janet Evans**, USA	Swimming	4-1-0
4	Fu Mingxia, CHN	Diving	4-1-0
4	Fanny Blankers-Koen, NED	Track/Field	4-0-0
4	Betty Cuthbert, AUS	Track/Field	4-0-0
4	**Pat McCormick**, USA	Diving	4-0-0
4	Bärbel Eckert Wäckel, E. Ger	Track/Field	4-0-0
4	Inge de Bruijn, NED	Swimming	4-2-2

†Includes gold medal as preliminary member of 1st-place relay team.

All-Time Leading Medal Winners – Career (Cont.)
Most Silver Medals

	MEN				WOMEN		
No		Sport	G-S-B	No		Sport	G-S-B
6	Alexandr Dityatin, USSR	Gymnastics	3-6-1	6	**Shirley Babashoff**, USA	Swimming	2-6-0
6	Mikhail Voronin, USSR	Gymnastics	2-6-1	5	Larissa Latynina, USSR	Gymnastics	9-5-4
5	Nikolai Andrianov, USSR	Gymnastics	7-5-3	5	Maria Gorokhovskaya, USSR	Gymnastics	2-5-0
5	Edoardo Mangiarotti, ITA	Fencing	6-5-2	4	Vera Cáslavská, CZE	Gymnastics	7-4-0
5	Zoltán Halmay, HUN	Swimming	3-5-1	4	Kornelia Ender, E. Ger	Swimming	4-4-0
5	Gustavo Marzi, ITA	Fencing	2-5-0	4	Dawn Fraser, AUS	Swimming	4-4-0
5	Yuri Titov, USSR	Gymnastics	1-5-3	4	Erica Zuchold, E. Ger	Gymnastics	0-4-1
5	Viktor Lisitsky, USSR	Gymnastics	0-5-0				

Most Bronze Medals

	MEN				WOMEN		
No		Sport	G-S-B	No		Sport	G-S-B
6	Alexei Nemov, RUS	Gymnastics	4-2-6	5	Merlene Ottey, JAM	Track/Field	0-2-5
6	Heikki Savolainen, FIN	Gymnastics	2-1-6	4	Larissa Latynina, USSR	Gymnastics	9-5-4
5	Daniel Revenu, FRA	Fencing	1-0-5	4	**Dara Torres**, USA	Swimming	4-1-4
5	Philip Edwards, CAN	Track/Field	0-0-5	4	Sofia Muratova, USSR	Gymnastics	2-2-4
5	Adrianus Jong, NED	Fencing	0-0-5				

All-Time Leading USA Medal Winners
Most Overall Medals
MEN

No		Sport	G-S-B	No		Sport	G-S-B
11	Mark Spitz	Swimming	9-1-1	6	Anton Heida	Gymnastics	5-1-0
11†	Matt Biondi	Swimming	8-2-1	6	Don Schollander	Swimming	5-1-0
11	Carl Osburn	Shooting	5-4-2	6	Johnny Weissmuller	Swim/Water Polo	5-0-1
10*	Ray Ewry	Track/Field	10-0-0	6	Alfred Lane	Shooting	5-0-1
10	Carl Lewis	Track/Field	9-1-0	6	Jim Lightbody	Track/Field	4-2-0
9	Gary Hall Jr.	Swimming	5-3-1	6	George Eyser	Gymnastics	3-2-1
9*	Martin Sheridan	Track/Field	5-3-1	6	Ralph Rose	Track/Field	3-2-1
8†	Michael Phelps	Swimming	6-0-2	6	Michael Plumb	Equestrian	2-4-0
8	Charles Daniels	Swimming	5-1-2	6	Burton Downing	Cycling	2-3-1
7‡	Tom Jager	Swimming	5-1-1	6	Bob Garrett	Track/Field	2-2-2
7	Willis Lee	Shooting	5-1-1				
7	Lloyd Spooner	Shooting	4-1-2				

†Includes gold medal as prelim. member of 1st-place relay team.
*Medals won by Ewry (2-0-0) and Sheridan (2-3-0) at the 1906 Intercalated games are not officially recognized by the IOC.
‡Includes 3 gold medals as prelim. member of 1st-place relay teams.

Games Participated In
Biondi (1984,88,92); **Daniels** (1904,06,08); **Downing** (1904); **Ewry** (1900,04,06,08); **Eyser** (1904); **Garrett** (1896,1900); **Hall Jr.** (1996,2000,04) **Heida** (1904); **Jager** (1984,88,92); **Lane** (1912,20); **Lee** (1920); **Lewis** (1984,88,92,96); **Lightbody** (1904,06); **Osburn** (1912,20,24); **Phelps** (2004), **Plumb** (1960, 64,68,72,76,84); **Rose** (1904,08,12); **Schollander** (1964, 68); **Sheridan** (1904,06,08); **Spitz** (1968,72); **Spooner** (1920); **Weissmuller** (1924,28).

WOMEN

No		Sport	G-S-B	No		Sport	G-S-B
12	Jenny Thompson	Swimming	8-3-1	5	Evelyn Ashford	Track/Field	4-1-0
9	Dara Torres	Swimming	4-1-4	5	Janet Evans	Swimming	4-1-0
8	Shirley Babashoff	Swimming	2-6-0	5	Florence Griffith Joyner	Track/Field	3-2-0
7	Shannon Miller	Gymnastics	2-2-3	5†	Mary T. Meagher	Swimming	3-1-1
7	Amanda Beard	Swimming	2-4-1	5	Gwen Torrence	Track/Field	3-2-0
6†	Amy Van Dyken	Swimming	6-0-0	5	Marion Jones	Track/Field	3-0-2
6	Jackie Joyner-Kersee	Track/Field	3-1-2	5	Mary Lou Retton	Gymnastics	1-2-2
6	Angel Martino	Swimming	3-0-3	5	Natalie Coughlin	Swimming	2-2-1

†Includes gold medal as prelim. member of 1st-place relay team.

Games Participated In
Ashford (1976,84,88,92); **Babashoff** (1972,76); **Beard** (1996;2000,04); **Coughlin** (2004), **Evans** (1988,92,96); **Griffith Joyner** (1984,88); **Jones** (2000); **Joyner-Kersee** (1984,88,92,96); **Martino** (1992,96); **McCormick** (1952,56); **Meagher** (1984,88); **Miller** (1992, 96); **Retton** (1984); **Thompson** (1988,92,96,2000,04); **Torrence** (1988,92,96); **Torres** (1984,88,92,2000); **Van Dyken** (1996,2000).

Most Gold Medals

No	MEN	Sport	G-S-B
10*	Raymond Ewry	Track/Field	10-0-0
9	Mark Spitz	Swimming	9-1-1
9	Carl Lewis	Track/Field	9-1-0
8†	Matt Biondi	Swimming	8-2-1
6†	Michael Phelps	Swimming	6-0-2
5	Carl Osburn	Shooting	5-4-2
5*	Martin Sheridan	Track/Field	5-3-1
5	Charles Daniels	Swimming	5-1-2
5‡	Tom Jager	Swimming	5-1-1
5	Willis Lee	Shooting	5-1-1
5	Anton Heida	Gymnastics	5-1-0
5	Don Schollander	Swimming	5-1-0
5	Johnny Weissmuller	Swim/Water Polo	5-0-1
5	Alfred Lane	Shooting	5-0-1
5	Morris Fisher	Shooting	5-0-0
5	Gary Hall Jr.	Swimming	5-3-1
4	Jim Lightbody	Track/Field	4-2-0
4	Lloyd Spooner	Shooting	4-1-2
4	Greg Louganis	Diving	4-1-0
4	John Naber	Swimming	4-1-0
4	Meyer Prinstein	Track/Field	4-1-0
4	Mel Sheppard	Track/Field	4-1-0
4	Marcus Hurley	Cycling	4-0-1
4†	Jon Olsen	Swimming	4-0-1
4	Archie Hahn	Track/Field	4-0-0
4	Alvin Kraenzlein	Track/Field	4-0-0
4	Al Oerter	Track/Field	4-0-0
4	Jesse Owens	Track/Field	4-0-0

*Medals won by Ewry (2-0-0) and Sheridan (2-3-0) at the 1906 Intercalated games are not officially recognized by the IOC.
†Includes gold medal as preliminary member of 1st-place relay team.
‡Includes 3 gold medals as preliminary member of 1st-place relay teams.

No	WOMEN	Sport	G-S-B
8	Jenny Thompson	Swimming	8-3-1
6†	Amy Van Dyken	Swimming	6-0-0
4	Dara Torres	Swimming	4-1-4
4	Evelyn Ashford	Track/Field	4-1-0
4	Janet Evans	Swimming	4-1-0
4	Pat McCormick	Diving	4-0-0
3	Florence Griffith Joyner	Track/Field	3-2-0
3	Jackie Joyner-Kersee	Track/Field	3-1-2
3†	Mary T. Meagher	Swimming	3-1-1
3	Gwen Torrence	Track/Field	3-1-1
3	Valerie Brisco-Hooks	Track/Field	3-1-0
3	Nancy Hogshead	Swimming	3-1-0
3	Sharon Stouder	Swimming	3-1-0
3	Wyomia Tyus	Track/Field	3-1-0
3	Chris von Saltza	Swimming	3-1-0
3	Wilma Rudolph	Track/Field	3-0-1
3	Melissa Belote	Swimming	3-0-0
3	Ethelda Bleibtrey	Swimming	3-0-0
3	Tracy Caulkins	Swimming	3-0-0
3†	Nicole Haislett	Swimming	3-0-0
3	Helen Madison	Swimming	3-0-0
3	Debbie Meyer	Swimming	3-0-0
3	Sandra Neilson	Swimming	3-0-0
3	Martha Norelius	Swimming	3-0-0
3†	Carrie Steinseifer	Swimming	3-0-0
3‡	Ashley Tappin	Swimming	3-0-0

†Includes gold medal as preliminary member of 1st-place relay team.
‡Includes 3 gold medals as preliminary member of 1st-place relay teams

Most Silver Medals

MEN

No		Sport	G-S-B
4	Carl Osburn	Shooting	5-4-2
4	Michael Plumb	Equestrian	2-4-0
3	Martin Sheridan	Track/Field	5-3-1
3	Burton Downing	Cycling	2-3-1
3	Irving Baxter	Track/Field	2-3-0

No		Sport	G-S-B
3	Earl Thomson	Equestrian	2-3-0
3	Alexander McKee	Swimming	0-3-0

WOMEN

No		Sport	G-S-B
6	Shirley Babashoff	Swimming	2-6-0

All-Time Medal Standings, 1896-2004

All-time Summer Games medal standings, based on *The Golden Book of the Olympic Games.* Medal counts include the 1906 Intercalated Games, which are not recognized by the IOC.

		G	S	B	Total
1	**United States**	907	697	615	2219
2	USSR (1952-88)	395	319	296	1010
3	Great Britain	189	242	237	668
4	France	199	202	230	631
5	Italy	189	154	168	511
6	Germany (1896-64,92-)	151	154	178	483
7	Sweden	140	157	179	476
8	Hungary	158	141	161	460
9	East Germany (1968-88)	153	150	136	445
10	Australia	119	126	154	399
11	Japan	113	106	114	333
12	West Germany (1968-88)	77	104	120	301
13	Finland	101	83	114	298
14	China	112	96	78	286
15	Romania	82	88	114	284
16	Poland	59	74	118	251
17	Russia (1896-1912, 96-)	85	79	84	248
18	Canada	54	87	101	242

		G	S	B	Total
19	Netherlands	65	76	94	234
20	Bulgaria	50	83	74	207
21	Switzerland	48	76	64	188
22	South Korea	55	64	65	184
23	Denmark	42	63	64	169
24	Cuba	64	51	49	164
25	Belgium	38	51	54	143
26	Czechoslovakia (1924-92)	49	49	44	142
	Greece	38	54	50	142
28	Norway	54	44	42	140
29	Unified Team (1992)	45	38	29	112
30	Spain	28	39	27	94
31	Yugoslavia (1924-88,96-2000)	28	32	33	93
	Austria	22	36	35	93
33	New Zealand	33	14	32	79
34	Brazil	16	22	38	76
35	Turkey	36	19	19	74
36	Rep. of S. Africa (1904-60, 92-)	20	23	26	69

All-Time Medal Standings, 1896-2004 (Cont.)

		G	S	B	Total
37	Kenya	17	24	20	61
38	Argentina	15	23	22	60
39	Mexico	10	18	23	51
40	Iran	10	15	21	46
	Ukraine	12	15	19	46
42	Jamaica	7	21	14	42
43	North Korea	8	11	16	35
44	Belarus	5	9	18	32
45	Ethiopia	14	5	12	31
46	Estonia	8	7	14	29
47	Czech Republic	7	9	11	27
48	Ireland	9	6	6	21
	Egypt	7	6	8	21
50	Great Britain/Ireland	6	11	3	20
	Portugal	3	6	11	20
	Indonesia	5	8	7	20
53	Nigeria	2	8	9	19
	Morocco	6	4	9	19
55	India	8	4	5	17
	Thailand	5	2	10	17
57	Mongolia	0	5	10	15
	Chinese Taipei	2	6	7	15
	Kazakhstan	4	8	3	15
60	Latvia	1	10	3	14
	Slovakia	4	6	4	14
62	Algeria	4	1	7	12
	Trinidad & Tobago	1	3	8	12
	Lithuania	4	2	6	12
	Chile	2	6	4	12
	Georgia	2	2	8	12
	Croatia	3	4	5	12
68	Uzbekistan	3	3	5	11
69	Pakistan	3	3	4	10
	Uruguay	2	2	6	10
	Venezuela	1	2	7	10
	Slovenia	2	3	5	10
73	Azerbaijan	3	1	5	9
	Philippines	0	2	7	9
75	Bahamas	3	2	3	8
	Colombia	1	2	5	8
77	Uganda	1	3	2	6
	Tunisia	1	2	3	6
	Bohemia	0	1	5	6
	Puerto Rico	0	1	5	6
	Israel	1	1	4	6
82	Cameroon	2	1	1	4
	Zimbabwe	2	1	1	4
	Peru	1	3	0	4
	Costa Rica	1	1	2	4
	Namibia	0	4	0	4
	Lebanon	0	2	2	4
	Moldova	0	2	2	4
	Ghana	0	1	3	4
90	Luxembourg	2	1	0	3
	Armenia	1	1	1	3
	Iceland	0	1	2	3
	Malaysia	0	1	2	3
	Syria	1	1	1	3

		G	S	B	Total
95	Hong Kong	1	1	0	2
	Dominican Republic	1	0	1	2
	Japan/Korea	1	0	1	2
	Mozambique	1	0	1	2
	Surinam	1	0	1	2
	Serbia & Montenegro	0	2	0	2
	Tanzania	0	2	0	2
	Great Britain/USA	0	1	1	2
	Haiti	0	1	1	2
	Russia/Estonia	0	1	1	2
	Saudi Arabia	0	1	1	2
	United Arab Republic	0	1	1	2
	Zambia	0	1	1	2
	The Antilles	0	0	2	2
	Panama	0	0	2	2
	Qatar	0	0	2	2
111	Australia/New Zealand	1	0	0	1
	Burkina Faso	1	0	0	1
	Cuba/USA	1	0	0	1
	Denmark/Sweden	1	0	0	1
	Ecuador	1	0	0	1
	Gr. Britain/Ireland/Germany	1	0	0	1
	Gr. Britain/Ireland/USA	1	0	0	1
	Ireland/USA	1	0	0	1
	United Arab Emirates	1	0	0	1
	Belgium/Greece	0	1	0	1
	Ceylon	0	1	0	1
	France/USA	0	1	0	1
	France/Gr. Britain/Ireland	0	1	0	1
	Ivory Coast	0	1	0	1
	Netherlands Antilles	0	1	0	1
	Paraguay	0	1	0	1
	Senegal	0	1	0	1
	Singapore	0	1	0	1
	Smyrna	0	1	0	1
	Tonga	0	1	0	1
	Vietnam	0	1	0	1
	Virgin Islands	0	1	0	1
	Australia/Great Britain	0	0	1	1
	Barbados	0	0	1	1
	Bermuda	0	0	1	1
	Bohemia/Great Britain	0	0	1	1
	Djibouti	0	0	1	1
	Eritrea	0	0	1	1
	France/Great Britain	0	0	1	1
	Guyana	0	0	1	1
	Iraq	0	0	1	1
	Kuwait	0	0	1	1
	Kyrgyzstan	0	0	1	1
	Macedonia	0	0	1	1
	Mexico/Spain	0	0	1	1
	Niger	0	0	1	1
	Scotland	0	0	1	1
	Sri Lanka	0	0	1	1
	Thessalonika	0	0	1	1
	Wales	0	0	1	1

Combined totals:	G	S	B	Total
USSR/UT/Russia	525	436	409	1370
Germany/E. Ger/W. Ger	388	408	434	1230

Notes: Athletes from the USSR participated in the Summer Games from 1952-88, returned as the Unified Team in 1992 after the breakup of the Soviet Union (in 1991) and have competed as independent republics since the 1994 Winter Games. Germany was barred from the Olympics in 1924 and 1948 following World Wars I and II. Divided into East and West Germany after WWII, both countries competed together from 1952-64, then separately from 1968-88. Germany was reunified in 1990. Czechoslovakia split into Slovakia and the Czech Republic in 1993. Croatia and Bosnia-Herzegovina gained independence from Yugoslavia in 1991. Yugoslavia was not invited to the 1992 games (though Serbian and Montenegrin athletes were allowed to compete as independent athletes) but returned in 1996 and competed under the name Serbia & Montenegro starting in 2004. South Africa was banned from 1964-88 for using the apartheid policy in the selection of its teams. It returned in 1992 as the Republic of South Africa (RSA).

1924-2002
Through the Years

SPORTS ALMANAC

The Winter Olympics

The move toward a winter version of the Olympics began in 1908 when figure skating made an appearance at the Summer Games in London. Ten-time world champion Ulrich Salchow of Sweden, who originated the backwards, one revolution jump that bears his name, and Madge Syers of Britain were the first singles champions. Germans Anna Hubler and Heinrich Berger won the pairs competition.

Organizers of the 1916 Summer Games in Berlin planned to introduce a "Skiing Olympia," featuring nordic events in the Black Forest, but the Games were cancelled after the outbreak of World War I in 1914.

The Games resumed in 1920 at Antwerp, Belgium, where figure skating returned and ice hockey was added as a medal event. Sweden's Gillis Grafstrom and Magda Julin took individual honors, while Ludovika and Walter Jakobsson were the top pair. In hockey, Canada won the gold medal with the United States second and Czechoslovakia third.

Despite the objections of Modern Olympics' founder Baron Pierre de Coubertin and the resistance of the Scandinavian countries, which had staged their own Nordic championships every four or five years from 1901-26 in Sweden, the International Olympic Committee sanctioned an "International Winter Sports Week" at Chamonix, France, in 1924. The 11-day event, which included nordic skiing, speed skating, figure skating, ice hockey and bobsledding, was a huge success and was retroactively called the first Olympic Winter Games.

Seventy years after those first cold weather Games, the 17th edition of the Winter Olympics took place in Lillehammer, Norway, in 1994. The event ended the four-year Olympic cycle of staging both Winter and Summer Games in the same year and began a new schedule that calls for the two Games to alternate every two years.

Year	No	Location	Dates	Nations	Most medals	USA medals
1924	I	Chamonix, FRA	Jan. 25-Feb. 4	16	Norway (4-7-6–17)	1-2-1–4 (3rd)
1928	II	St. Moritz, SWI	Feb. 11-19	25	Norway (6-4-5–15)	2-2-2– 6 (2nd)
1932	III	Lake Placid, USA	Feb. 4-15	17	USA (6-4-2–12)	6-4-2–12 (1st)
1936	IV	Garmisch-Partenkirchen, GER .	Feb. 6-16	28	Norway (7-5-3–15)	1-0-3– 4 (T-5th)
1940-**a**	–	Sapporo, JPN	Cancelled (WWII)			
1944	–	Cortina d'Ampezzo, ITA	Cancelled (WWII)			
1948	V	St. Moritz, SWI	Jan. 30-Feb. 8	28	Norway (4-3-3–10), Sweden (4-3-3–10) & Switzerland (3-4-3–10)	3-4-2– 9 (4th)
1952-**b**	VI	Oslo, NOR	Feb. 14-25	30	Norway (7-3-6–16)	4-6-1–11 (2nd)
1956-**c**	VII	Cortina d'Ampezzo, ITA	Jan. 26-Feb. 5	32	USSR (7-3-6–16)	2-3-2– 7 (T-4th)
1960	VIII	Squaw Valley, USA	Feb. 18-28	30	USSR (7-5-9–21)	3-4-3–10 (2nd)
1964	IX	Innsbruck, AUT	Jan. 29-Feb. 9	36	USSR (11-8-6–25)	1-2-3– 6 (7th)
1968-**d**	X	Grenoble, FRA	Feb. 6-18	37	Norway (6-6-2–14)	1-5-1– 7 (T-7th)
1972	XI	Sapporo, JPN	Feb. 3-13	35	USSR (8-5-3–16)	3-2-3– 8 (6th)
1976-**e**	XII	Innsbruck, AUT	Feb. 4-15	37	USSR (13-6-8–27)	3-3-4–10 (T-3rd)
1980	XIII	Lake Placid, USA	Feb. 14-23	37	E. Germany (9-7-7–23)	6-4-2–12 (3rd)
1984	XIV	Sarajevo, YUG	Feb. 7-19	49	USSR (6-10-9–25)	4-4-0– 8 (T-5th)
1988	XV	Calgary, CAN	Feb. 13-28	57	USSR (11-9-9–29)	2-1-3– 6 (T-8th)
1992-**f**	XVI	Albertville, FRA	Feb. 8-23	63	Germany (10-10-6–26)	5-4-2–11 (6th)
1994-**g**	XVII	Lillehammer, NOR	Feb. 12-27	67	Norway (10-11-5–26)	6-5-2–13 (T-5th)
1998	XVIII	Nagano, JPN	Feb. 7-22	72	Germany (12-9-8–29)	6-3-4–13 (5th)
2002	XIX	Salt Lake City, USA	Feb. 8-24	78	Germany (12-16-7–35)	10-13-11–34 (2nd)
2006	XX	Turin, ITA	Feb. 10-26			
2010	XXI	Vancouver, CAN	Feb. 12-28			

a—The 1940 Winter Games are originally scheduled for Sapporo, but Japan resigns as host in 1937 when the Sino-Japanese war breaks out. St. Moritz is the next choice, but the Swiss feel that ski instructors should not be considered professionals and the IOC withdraws its offer. Finally, Garmisch-Partenkirchen is asked to serve again as host, but the Germans invade Poland in 1939 and the Games are eventually cancelled.

b—Germany and Japan are allowed to rejoin the Olympic community for the first time since World War II. Though a divided country, the Germans send a joint East-West team through 1964.

c—The Soviet Union (USSR) participates in its first Winter Olympics and takes home the most medals, including the gold medal in ice hockey.

d—East Germany and West Germany officially send separate teams for the first time and will continue to do so through 1988.

e—The IOC grants the 1976 Winter Games to Denver in May 1970, but in 1972 Colorado voters reject a $5 million bond issue to finance the undertaking. Denver immediately withdraws as host and the IOC selects Innsbruck, the site of the 1964 Games, to take over.

f—Germany sends a single team after East and West German reunification in 1990 and the USSR competes as the Unified Team after the breakup of the Soviet Union in 1991.

g—The IOC moves the Winter Games' four-year cycle ahead two years in order to separate them from the Summer Games and alternate Olympics every two years.

Event-by-Event

Gold medal winners from 1924-2002 in the following events: Alpine Skiing, Biathlon, Bobsled, Cross Country Skiing, Curling, Figure Skating, Freestyle Skiing, Ice Hockey, Luge, Nordic Combined, Skeleton, Ski Jumping, Snowboarding and Speed Skating.

ALPINE SKIING

MEN

Multiple gold medals: Kjetil Andre Aamodt, Jean-Claude Killy, Toni Sailer and Alberto Tomba (3); Hermann Maier, Henri Oreiller, Ingemar Stenmark and Markus Wasmeier (2).

Downhill

Year		Time	Year		Time
1948	Henri Oreiller, FRA	2:55.0	1980	Leonhard Stock, AUS	1:45.50
1952	Zeno Colò, ITA	2:30.8	1984	Bill Johnson, USA	1:45.59
1956	Toni Sailer, AUT	2:52.2	1988	Pirmin Zurbriggen, SWI	1:59.63
1960	Jean Vuarnet, FRA	2:06.0	1992	Patrick Ortlieb, AUT	1:50.37
1964	Egon Zimmermann, AUT	2:18.16	1994	Tommy Moe, USA	1:45.75
1968	Jean-Claude Killy, FRA	1:59.85	1998	Jean-Luc Cretier, FRA	1:50.11
1972	Bernhard Russi, SWI	1:51.43	2002	Fritz Strobl, AUT	1:39.13
1976	Franz Klammer AUT	1:45.73			

Slalom

Year		Time	Year		Time
1948	Edi Reinalter, SWI	2:10.3	1980	Ingemar Stenmark, SWE	1:44.26
1952	Othmar Schneider, AUT	2:00.0	1984	Phil Mahre, USA	1:39.41
1956	Toni Sailer, AUT	3:14.7	1988	Alberto Tomba, ITA	1:39.47
1960	Ernst Hinterseer, AUT	2:08.9	1992	Finn Christian Jagge, NOR	1:44.39
1964	Pepi Stiegler, AUT	2:11.13	1994	Thomas Stangassinger, AUT	2:02.02
1968	Jean-Claude Killy, FRA	1:39.73	1998	Hans-Petter Buraas, NOR	1:49.31
1972	Francisco Ochoa, SPA	1:49.27	2002	Jean-Pierre Vidal, FRA	1:41.06
1976	Piero Gros, ITA	2:03.29			

Giant Slalom

Year		Time	Year		Time
1952	Stein Eriksen, NOR	2:25.0	1980	Ingemar Stenmark, SWE	2:40.74
1956	Toni Sailer, AUT	3:00.1	1984	Max Julen, SWI	2:41.18
1960	Roger Staub, SWI	1:48.3	1988	Alberto Tomba, ITA	2:06.37
1964	Francois Bonlieu, FRA	1:46.71	1992	Alberto Tomba, ITA	2:06.98
1968	Jean-Claude Killy, FRA	3:29.28	1994	Markus Wasmeier, GER	2:52.46
1972	Gustav Thöni, ITA	3:09.62	1998	Hermann Maier, AUT	2:38.51
1976	Heini Hemmi, SWI	3:26.97	2002	Stephan Eberharter, AUT	2:23.28

Super G

Year		Time	Year		Time
1988	Frank Piccard, FRA	1:39.66	1998	Hermann Maier, AUT	1:34.82
1992	Kjetil Andre Aamodt, NOR	1:13.04	2002	Kjetil Andre Aamodt, NOR	1:21.58
1994	Markus Wasmeier, GER	1:32.53			

Alpine Combined

Year		Points	Year		Time
1936	Franz Pfnür, GER	99.25	1994	Lasse Kjus, NOR	3:17.53
1948	Henri Oreiller, FRA	3.27	1998	Mario Reiter, AUT	3:08.06
1952-84 Not held			2002	Kjetil Andre Aamodt, NOR	3:17.56
1988	Hubert Strolz, AUT	36.55			
1992	Josef Polig, ITA	14.58			

WOMEN

Multiple gold medals: Deborah Compagnoni, Janica Kostelic, Vreni Schneider and Katja Seizinger (3); Marielle Goitschel, Trude Jochum-Beiser, Petra Kronberger, Andrea Mead Lawrence, Rosi Mittermaier, Marie-Theres Nadig, Hanni Wenzel and Pernilla Wiberg (2).

Downhill

Year		Time	Year		Time
1948	Hedy Schlunegger, SWI	2:28.3	1980	Annemarie Moser-Pröll, AUT	1:37.52
1952	Trude Jochum-Beiser, AUT	1:47.1	1984	Michela Figini, SWI	1:13.36
1956	Madeleine Berthod, SWI	1:40.7	1988	Marina Kiehl, W. Ger	1:25.86
1960	Heidi Biebl, GER	1:37.6	1992	Kerrin Lee-Gartner, CAN	1:52.55
1964	Christl Haas, AUT	1:55.39	1994	Katja Seizinger, GER	1:35.93
1968	Olga Pall, AUT	1:40.87	1998	Katja Seizinger, GER	1:28.89
1972	Marie-Theres Nadig, SWI	1:36.68	2002	Carole Montillet, FRA	1:39.56
1976	Rosi Mittermaier, W. Ger	1:46.16			

Slalom

Year		Time	Year		Time
1948	Gretchen Fraser, USA	1:57.2	1980	Hanni Wenzel, LIE	1:25.09
1952	Andrea Mead Lawrence, USA	2:10.6	1984	Paoletta Magoni, ITA	1:36.47
1956	Renée Colliard, SWI	1:52.3	1988	Vreni Schneider, SWI	1:36.69
1960	Anne Heggtveit, CAN	1:49.6	1992	Petra Kronberger, AUT	1:32.68
1964	Christine Goitschel, FRA	1:29.86	1994	Vreni Schneider, SWI	1:56.01
1968	Marielle Goitschel, FRA	1:25.86	1998	Hilde Gerg, GER	1:32.40
1972	Barbara Cochran, USA	1:31.24	2002	Janica Kostelic, CRO	1:46.10
1976	Rosi Mittermaier, W. Ger	1:30.54			

Giant Slalom

Year		Time	Year		Time
1952	Andrea Mead Lawrence, USA	2:06.8	1980	Hanni Wenzel, LIE	2:41.66
1956	Ossi Reichert, GER	1:56.5	1984	Debbie Armstrong, USA	2:20.98
1960	Yvonne Rügg, SWI	1:39.9	1988	Vreni Schneider, SWI	2:06.49
1964	Marielle Goitschel, FRA	1:52.24	1992	Pernilla Wiberg, SWE	2:12.74
1968	Nancy Greene, CAN	1:51.97	1994	Deborah Compagnoni, ITA	2:30.97
1972	Marie-Theres Nadig, SWI	1:29.90	1998	Deborah Compagnoni, ITA	2:50.59
1976	Kathy Kreiner, CAN	1:29.13	2002	Janica Kostelic, CRO	2:30.01

Super G

Year		Time	Year		Time
1988	Sigrid Wolf, AUT	1:19.03	1998	Picabo Street, USA	1:18.02
1992	Deborah Compagnoni, ITA	1:21.22	2002	Daniela Ceccarelli, ITA	1:13.59
1994	Diann Roffe-Steinrotter, USA	1:22.15			

Alpine Combined

Year		Points	Year		Time
1936	Christl Cranz, GER	97.06	1994	Pernilla Wiberg, SWE	3:05.16
1948	Trude Beiser, AUT	6.58	1998	Katja Seizinger, GER	2:40.74
1952-84	Not held		2002	Janica Kostelic, CRO	2:43.28
1988	Anita Wachter, AUT	29.25			
1992	Petra Kronberger, AUT	2.55			

BIATHLON

MEN

Multiple gold medals (including relays): Ole Einar Bjoerndalen (5); Aleksandr Tikhonov (4); Mark Kirchner and Ricco Gross (3); Anatoly Alyabyev, Ivan Biakov, Sergei Chepikov, Sven Fischer, Halvard Hanevold, Frank Luck, Viktor Mamatov, Frank-Peter Roetsch, Magnar Solberg and Dmitri Vasilyev (2).

10 kilometers

Year		Time	Year		Time
1980	Frank Ulrich, E. Ger	32:10.69	1994	Sergei Chepikov, RUS	28:07.0
1984	Erik Kvalfoss, NOR	30:53.8	1998	Ole Einar Bjoerndalen, NOR	27:16.2
1988	Frank-Peter Roetsch, E. Ger	25:08.1	2002	Ole Einar Bjoerndalen, NOR	24:51.3
1992	Mark Kirchner, GER	26:02.3			

12.5 kilometers

Year		Time
2002	Ole Einar Bjoerndalen, NOR	32:34.6

20 kilometers

Year		Time	Year		Time
1960	Klas Lestander, SWE	1:33:21.6	1984	Peter Angerer, W. Ger	1:11:52.7
1964	Vladimir Melanin, USSR	1:20:26.8	1988	Frank-Peter Roetsch, E. Ger	56:33.3
1968	Magnar Solberg, NOR	1:13:45.9	1992	Yevgeny Redkine, UT	57:34.4
1972	Magnar Solberg, NOR	1:15:55.50	1994	Sergei Tarasov, RUS	57:25.3
1976	Nikolai Kruglov, USSR	1:14:12.26	1998	Halvard Hanevold, NOR	56:16.4
1980	Anatoly Alyabyev, USSR	1:08:16.31	2002	Ole Einar Bjoerndalen, NOR	51:03.3

4x7.5-kilometer Relay

Year		Time	Year		Time	Year		Time
1968	Soviet Union	2:13:02.4	1984	Soviet Union	1:38:51.7	1998	Germany	1:21:36.2
1972	Soviet Union	1:51:44.92	1988	Soviet Union	1:22:30.0	2002	Norway	1:23:42.3
1976	Soviet Union	1:57:55.64	1992	Germany	1:24:43.5			
1980	Soviet Union	1:34:03.27	1994	Germany	1:30:22.1			

BIATHLON (Cont.)
WOMEN

Multiple gold medals (including relays): Myriam Bedard, Andrea Henkel, Anfisa Reztsova and Kati Wilhelm (2). Note that Reztsova won a third gold medal in 1988 in the cross country 4x5-kilometer relay.

7.5 kilometers

Year		Time	Year		Time
1992	Anfisa Reztsova, UT	24:29.2	1998	Galina Koukleva, RUS	23:08.0
1994	Myriam Bedard, CAN	26:08.8	2002	Kati Wilhelm, GER	20:41.4

10 kilometers

Year		Time
2002	Olga Pyleva, RUS	31:07.7

15 kilometers

Year		Time	Year		Time
1992	Antje Misersky, GER	51:47.2	1998	Ekaterina Dafovska, BUL	54:52.0
1994	Myriam Bedard, CAN	52:06.6	2002	Andrea Henkel, GER	47:29.1

4x7.5-kilometer Relay

Year		Time	Year		Time
1992	France	1:15:55.6	1998	Germany	1:40:13.6
1994	Russia	1:47:19.5	2002	Germany	1:27:55.0

Note: Event featured three skiers per team in 1992.

BOBSLED

A two-woman bobsled event was added in 2002. Only drivers are listed in parentheses.

Multiple gold medals: DRIVERS—Meinhard Nehmer (3); Billy Fiske, Wolfgang Hoppe, Christoph Langen, Eugenio Monti, Andreas Ostler and Gustav Weder (2). CREW—Bernard Germeshausen (3); Donat Acklin, Luciano De Paolis, Cliff Gray, Lorenz Nieberl and Dietmar Schauerhammer (2).

Two-Man

Year		Time	Year		Time
1932	United States (Hubert Stevens)	8:14.74	1976	East Germany (Meinhard Nehmer)	3:44.42
1936	United States (Ivan Brown)	5:29.29	1980	Switzerland (Erich Schärer)	4:09.36
1948	Switzerland (Felix Endrich)	5:29.2	1984	East Germany (Wolfgang Hoppe)	3:25.56
1952	Germany (Andreas Ostler)	5:24.54	1988	Soviet Union (Janis Kipurs)	3:54.19
1956	Italy (Lamberto Dalla Costa)	5:30.14	1992	Switzerland I (Gustav Weder)	4:03.26
1960	Not held		1994	Switzerland I (Gustav Weder)	3:30.81
1964	Great Britain (Anthony Nash)	4:21.90	1998	(TIE) Italy I (Guenther Huber)	3:37.24
1968	Italy (Eugenio Monti)	4:41.54		& Canada I (Pierre Lueders)	3:37.24
1972	West Germany (Wolfgang Zimmerer)	4:57.07	2002	Germany I (Christoph Langen)	3:10.11

Two-Woman

Year		Time
2002	United States II (Jill Bakken)	1:37.76

Four-Man

Year		Time	Year		Time
1924	Switzerland (Eduard Scherrer)	5:45.54	1972	Switzerland (Jean Wicki)	4:43.07
1928	United States (Billy Fiske)	3:20.5	1976	East Germany (Meinhard Nehmer)	3:40.43
1932	United States (Billy Fiske)	7:53.68	1980	East Germany (Meinhard Nehmer)	3:59.92
1936	Switzerland (Pierre Musy)	5:19.85	1984	East Germany (Wolfgang Hoppe)	3:20.22
1948	United States (Francis Tyler)	5:20.1	1988	Switzerland (Ekkehard Fasser)	3:47.51
1952	Germany (Andreas Ostler)	5:07.84	1992	Austria I (Ingo Appelt)	3:53.90
1956	Switzerland (Franz Kapus)	5:10.44	1994	Germany II (Harald Czudaj)	3:27.78
1960	Not held		1998	Germany II (Christoph Langen)	2:39.41
1964	Canada (Vic Emery)	4:14.46	2002	Germany II (Andre Lange)	3:07.51
1968	Italy (Eugenio Monti)	2:17.39			

Note: Five-man sleds were used in 1928.

CROSS COUNTRY SKIING

Starting with the 1988 Winter Games in Calgary, the classical and freestyle (i.e., skating) techniques were designated for specific events. The Pursuit race was introduced in 1992 and revamped after the 1998 Nagano Games. The Sprint was added in 2002.

MEN

Multiple gold medals (including relays): Bjorn Dählie (8); Thomas Alsgaard, Sixten Jernberg, Gunde Svan, Thomas Wassberg and Nikolai Zimyatov (4); Veikko Hakulinen, Eero Mäntyranta and Vegard Ulvang (3); Hallgeir Brenden, Harald Grönningen, Thorleif Haug, Johann Muehlegg, Jan Ottoson, Kristen Skjeldal, Pål Tyldum and Vyacheslav Vedenine (2).

Multiple gold medals (including Nordic Combined): Johan Gröttumsbråten and Thorleif Haug (3).

1.5-kilometer Sprint
New event in 2002.

Year		Time
2002	Tor Arne Hetland, NOR	2:56.9

10 kilometers
Held as a classical event.

Year		Time	Year		Time
1992	Vegard Ulvang, NOR	27:36.0	1998	Bjorn Dählie, NOR	27:24.5
1994	Bjorn Dählie, NOR	24:20.1	2002	Not held	

Combined Pursuit (10km)
From 1992-98 the pursuit included a 10-km classical race and a 15-km freestyle race contested on separate days. Beginning in 2002, the pursuit was shortened to two 5-kilometer races held on the same day.

Year		Time	Year		Time
1992	Bjorn Dählie, NOR	1:05:37.9	1998	Thomas Alsgaard, NOR	1:07:01.7
1994	Bjorn Dählie, NOR	1:00:08.8	2002	Johann Muehlegg, SPA	49:20.4

15 kilometers
Held over 18 kilometers from 1924-52. Held as a classical event from 1956-88, and since 2002. Replaced by the 15-km combined pursuit (1992-98).

Year		Time	Year		Time
1924	Thorleif Haug, NOR	1:14:31.0	1968	Harald Grönningen, NOR	47:54.2
1928	Johan Gröttumsbräten, NOR	1:37:01.0	1972	Sven-Ake Lundback, SWE	45:28.24
1932	Sven Utterström, SWE	1:23:07.0	1976	Nikolai Bazhukov, USSR	43:58.47
1936	Erik-August Larsson, SWE	1:14:38.0	1980	Thomas Wassberg, SWE	41:57.63
1948	Martin Lundström, SWE	1:13:50.0	1984	Gunde Svan, SWE	41:25.6
1952	Hallgeir Brenden, NOR	1:01:34.0	1988	Mikhail Devyatyarov, USSR	41:18.9
1956	Hallgeir Brenden, NOR	49:39.0	1992-98	Not held	
1960	Hakon Brusveen, NOR	51:55.5	2002	Andrus Veerpalu, EST	37:07.4
1964	Eero Mäntyranta, FIN	50:54.1			

30 kilometers
Held as a freestyle event from 1956-94, and since 2002. Held as a classical event in 1998.

Year		Time	Year		Time
1956	Veikko Hakulinen, FIN	1:44:06.0	1984	Nikolai Zimyatov, USSR	1:28:56.3
1960	Sixten Jernberg, SWE	1:51:03.9	1988	Alexei Prokurorov, USSR	1:24:26.3
1964	Eero Mäntyranta, FIN	1:30:50.7	1992	Vegard Ulvang, NOR	1:22:27.8
1968	Franco Nones, ITA	1:35:39.2	1994	Thomas Alsgaard, NOR	1:12:26.4
1972	Vyacheslav Vedenine, USSR	1:36:31.15	1998	Mika Myllylae, FIN	1:33:55.8
1976	Sergei Saveliev, USSR	1:30:29.38	2002	Johann Muehlegg, SPA	1:09:28.9
1980	Nikolai Zimyatov, USSR	1:27:02.80			

50 kilometers
Held as a classical event from 1924-94, and since 2002. Held as a freestyle event in 1998.

Year		Time	Year		Time
1924	Thorleif Haug, NOR	3:44:32.0	1972	Päl Tyldum, NOR	2:43:14.75
1928	Per Erik Hedlund, SWE	4:52:03.0	1976	Ivar Formo, NOR	2:37:30.05
1932	Veli Saarinen, FIN	4:28:00.0	1980	Nikolai Zimyatov, USSR	2:27:24.60
1936	Elis Wiklund, SWE	3:30:11.0	1984	Thomas Wassberg, SWE	2:15:55.8
1948	Nils Karlsson, SWE	3:47:48.0	1988	Gunde Svan, SWE	2:04:30.9
1952	Veikko Hakulinen, FIN	3:33:33.0	1992	Bjorn Dählie, NOR	2:03:41.5
1956	Sixten Jernberg, SWE	2:50:27.0	1994	Vladimir Smirnov, KAZ	2:07:20.3
1960	Kalevi Hämäläinen, FIN	2:59:06.3	1998	Bjorn Dählie, NOR	2:05:08.2
1964	Sixten Jernberg, SWE	2:43:52.6	2002	Mikhail Ivanov, RUS*	2:06:20.8
1968	Ole Ellefsaeter, NOR	2:28:45.8			

*Ivanov finished second to Johann Muehlegg of Spain, who was disqualified for failing a drug test.

4x10-kilometer Mixed Relay
Two classical and two freestyle legs.

Year		Time	Year		Time	Year		Time
1936	Finland	2:41:33.0	1968	Norway	2:08:33.5	1992	Norway	1:39:26.0
1948	Sweden	2:32:08.0	1972	Soviet Union	2:04:47.94	1994	Italy	1:41:15.0
1952	Finland	2:20:16.0	1976	Finland	2:07:59.72	1998	Norway	1:40:55.7
1956	Soviet Union	2:15:30.0	1980	Soviet Union	1:57:03.46	2002	Norway	1:32:45.5
1960	Finland	2:18:45.6	1984	Sweden	1:55:06.3			
1964	Sweden	2:18:34.6	1988	Sweden	1:43:58.6			

CROSS COUNTRY SKIING (Cont.)
WOMEN

Multiple gold medals (including relays): Lyubov Egorova (6); Larissa Lazutina (5); Galina Kulakova and Raisa Smetanina (4); Claudia Boyarskikh, Olga Danilova and Marja-Liisa Hämäläinen and Elena Valbe (3); Stefania Belmondo, Manuela Di Centa, Nina Gavriluk, Toini Gustafsson, Barbara Petzold and Julija Tchepalova (2).

Multiple gold medals (including relays and Biathlon): Anfisa Reztsova (2).

1.5-kilometer Sprint

New event in 2002.

Year		Time
2002	Julija Tchepalova, RUS	3:10.6

5 kilometers

Held as a classical event from 1964-98. From 1992-98 it was half of the combined pursuit event. Discontinued after 1998.

Year		Time	Year		Time
1964	Claudia Boyarskikh, USSR	17:50.5	1984	Marja-Liisa Hämäläinen, FIN	17:04.0
1968	Toini Gustafsson, SWE	16:45.2	1988	Marjo Matikainen, FIN	15:04.0
1972	Galina Kulakova, USSR	17:00.50	1992	Marjut Lukkarinen, FIN	14:13.8
1976	Helena Takalo, FIN	15:48.69	1994	Lyubov Egorova, RUS	14:08.8
1980	Raisa Smetanina, USSR	15:06.92	1998	Larissa Lazutina, RUS	17:37.9

Combined Pursuit (10km)

From 1992-98 the pursuit consisted of a 10-km freestyle race in which the starting order was determined by order of finish in the 5-km classical race contested on separate days. Beginning in 2002, the pursuit was shortened to a 5-km classical race followed by a 5-km freestyle race contested on the same day. The 5-km classical is no longer a separate medal event.

Year		Time	Year		Time
1992	Lyubov Egorova, UT	40:07.7	1998	Larissa Lazutina, RUS	46:06.9
1994	Lyubov Egorova, RUS	41:38.1	2002	Olga Danilova, RUS	24:52.1

10 kilometers

Held as a classical event from 1952-88, and since 2002. Replaced by 10-km combined pursuit from 1992-98.

Year		Time	Year		Time
1952	Lydia Wideman, FIN	41:40.0	1976	Raisa Smetanina, USSR	30:13.41
1956	Lyubov Kosyreva, USSR	38:11.0	1980	Barbara Petzold, E. Ger	30:31.54
1960	Maria Gusakova, USSR	39:46.6	1984	Marja-Liisa Hämäläinen, FIN	31:44.2
1964	Claudia Boyarskikh, USSR	40:24.3	1988	Vida Venciene, USSR	30:08.3
1968	Toini Gustafsson, SWE	36:46.5	1992-98	Not held	
1972	Galina Kulakova, USSR	34:17.82	2002	Bente Skari, NOR	28:05.6

15 kilometers

Held as a freestyle event from 1992-94, and since 2002. Held as a classical event in 1998.

Year		Time	Year		Time
1992	Lyubov Egorova, UT	42:20.8	1998	Olga Danilova, RUS	46:55.4
1994	Manuela Di Centa, ITA	39:44.5	2002	Stefania Belmondo, ITA	39:54.4

20 kilometers

Held as a classical event from 1984-88. Discontinued in 1992 and replaced by the 30-kilometer freestyle.

Year		Time	Year		Time
1984	Marja-Liisa Hämäläinen, FIN	1:01:45.0	1988	Tamara Tikhonova, USSR	55:53.6

30 kilometers

Replaced 20-km classical event in 1992. Held as a freestyle event 1992-98. Held as a classical event since 2002.

Year		Time	Year		Time
1992	Stefania Belmondo, ITA	1:22:30.1	1998	Julija Tchepalova, RUS	1:22:01.5
1994	Manuela Di Centa, ITA	1:25:41.6	2002	Gabriella Paruzzi, ITA*	1:30:57.1

*Paruzzi finished second to Larissa Lazutina of Russia, who was disqualified after failing a drug test.

4x5-kilometer Relay

Two classical and two freestyle legs since 1992. Event featured three skiers per team from 1956-72.

Year		Time	Year		Time	Year		Time
1956	Finland	1:09:01.0	1976	Soviet Union	1:07:49.75	1994	Russia	57:12.5
1960	Sweden	1:04:21.4	1980	East Germany	1:02:11.10	1998	Russia	55:13.5
1964	Soviet Union	59:20.2	1984	Norway	1:06:49.7	2002	Germany	49:30.6
1968	Norway	57:30.0	1988	Soviet Union	59:51.1			
1972	Soviet Union	48:46.15	1992	Unified Team	59:34.8			

CURLING

MEN	WOMEN
Year	**Year**
1998 **Switzerland**, Canada, Norway	1998 **Canada**, Denmark, Sweden
2002 **Norway**, Canada, Switzerland	2002 **Great Britain**, Switzerland, Canada

FIGURE SKATING

MEN

Multiple gold medals: Gillis Grafström (3); Dick Button and Karl Schäfer (2).

Year		Year		Year	
1908	Ulrich Salchow ....SWE	1952	Dick Button ....USA	1984	Scott Hamilton ....USA
1912	Not held	1956	Hayes Alan Jenkins .....USA	1988	Brian Boitano ....USA
1920	Gillis Grafström ......SWE	1960	David Jenkins ....USA	1992	Victor Petrenko ....UT
1924	Gillis Grafström ......SWE	1964	Manfred Schnelldorfer ....GER	1994	Alexei Urmanov ....RUS
1928	Gillis Grafström ......SWE	1968	Wolfgang Schwarz .....AUT	1998	Ilia Kulik ....RUS
1932	Karl Schäfer ....AUT	1972	Ondrej Nepela ....CZE	2002	Alexei Yagudin ....RUS
1936	Karl Schäfer ....AUT	1976	John Curry ....GBR		
1948	Dick Button ....USA	1980	Robin Cousins ....GBR		

WOMEN

Multiple gold medals: Sonja Henie (3); Katarina Witt (2).

Year		Year		Year	
1908	Madge Syers ....GBR	1952	Jeanette Altwegg ....GBR	1984	Katarina Witt ....E. Ger
1912	Not held	1956	Tenley Albright ....USA	1988	Katarina Witt ....E. Ger
1920	Magda Julin-Mauroy ....SWE	1960	Carol Heiss ....USA	1992	Kristi Yamaguchi ....USA
1924	Herma Planck-Szabó .....AUT	1964	Sjoukje Dijkstra ....NED	1994	Oksana Baiul ....UKR
1928	Sonja Henie ....NOR	1968	Peggy Fleming ....USA	1998	Tara Lipinski ....USA
1932	Sonja Henie ....NOR	1972	Beatrix Schuba ....AUT	2002	Sarah Hughes ....USA
1936	Sonja Henie ....NOR	1976	Dorothy Hamill ....USA		
1948	Barbara Ann Scott ......CAN	1980	Anett Poetzsch ....E. Ger		

Pairs

Multiple gold medals: MEN–Pierre Brunet, Artur Dmitriev, Sergei Grinkov, Oleg Protopopov and Aleksandr Zaitsev (2). WOMEN–Irina Rodnina (3); Ludmila Belousova, Ekaterina Gordeeva and Andree Joly Brunet (2).

Year			Year		
1908	Anna Hübler & Heinrich Burger	Germany	1968	Ludmila Belousova & Oleg Protopopov .....USSR
1912	Not held		1972	Irina Rodnina & Aleksei Ulanov ....USSR
1920	Ludovika & Walter Jakobsson ....Finland		1976	Irina Rodnina & Aleksandr Zaitsev ....USSR
1924	Helene Engelmann & Alfred Berger ....Austria		1980	Irina Rodnina & Aleksandr Zaitsev ....USSR
1928	Andrée Joly & Pierre Brunet ....France		1984	Elena Valova & Oleg Vasiliev ....USSR
1932	Andrée & Pierre Brunet ....France		1988	Ekaterina Gordeeva & Sergei Grinkov .....USSR
1936	Maxi Herber & Ernst Baier ....Germany		1992	Natalia Mishkutienok & Arthur Dmitriev .....UT
1948	Micheline Lannoy & Pierre Baugniet .....Belgium		1994	Ekaterina Gordeeva & Sergei Grinkov .....RUS
1952	Ria & Paul Falk ....Germany		1998	Oksana Kazakova & Artur Dmitriev ......RUS
1956	Elisabeth Schwartz & Kurt Oppelt ....Austria		2002	Elena Berezhnaya & Anton Sikharulidze ...RUS
1960	Barbara Wagner & Robert Paul ....Canada			Jamie Sale & David Pelletier* ....CAN
1964	Ludmila Belousova & Oleg Protopopov .....USSR			

*Originally awarded silver medals, Sale & Pelletier later had them upgraded to gold after an investigation by the International Olympic Committee and the International Skating Union concluded that a judge was guilty of misconduct.

Ice Dancing

Multiple gold medals: Oksana Grishuk & Yevgeny Platov (2).

Year		Year	
1976	Lyudmila Pakhomova & Aleksandr Gorshkov ..USSR	1992	Marina Klimova & Sergei Ponomarenko ......UT
1980	Natalia Linichuk & Gennady Karponosov ....USSR	1994	Oksana Grishuk & Yevgeny Platov ....RUS
1984	Jayne Torvill & Christopher Dean .....Great Britain	1998	Oksana Grishuk & Yevgeny Platov ....RUS
1988	Natalia Bestemianova & Andrei Bukin ......USSR	2002	Marina Anissina & Gwendal Peizerat ....FRA

FREESTYLE SKIING

MEN		WOMEN	
Aerials		**Aerials**	
Year	**Points**	**Year**	**Points**
1994 Andreas Schoebaechler, SWI 234.67		1994 Lina Cherjazova, UZB 166.84	
1998 Eric Bergoust, USA 255.64		1998 Nikki Stone, USA 193.00	
2002 Ales Valenta, CZR 257.02		2002 Alisa Camplin, AUS 193.47	
Moguls		**Moguls**	
Year	**Points**	**Year**	**Points**
1994 Jean-Luc Brassard, CAN 27.24		1994 Stine Lise Hattestad, NOR 25.97	
1998 Jonny Moseley, USA 26.93		1998 Tae Satoya, JPN 25.06	
2002 Janne Lahtela, FIN 27.97		2002 Kari Traa, NOR 25.94	

ICE HOCKEY

MEN

Multiple gold medals: Soviet Union/Unified Team (8); Canada (7); United States (2).

Year		Year	
1920	**Canada**, United States Czechoslovakia	1980	**United States**, Soviet Union, Sweden
1924	**Canada**, United States, Great Britain	1984	**Soviet Union**, Czechoslovakia, Sweden
1928	**Canada**, Sweden, Switzerland	1988	**Soviet Union**, Finland, Sweden
1932	**Canada**, United States, Germany	1992	**Unified Team**, Canada, Czechoslovakia
1936	**Great Britain**, Canada, United States	1994	**Sweden**, Canada, Finland
1948	**Canada**, Czechoslovakia, Switzerland	1998	**Czech Republic**, Russia, Finland
1952	**Canada**, United States, Sweden	2002	**Canada**, United States, Russia
1956	**Soviet Union**, United States, Canada		
1960	**United States**, Canada, Soviet Union		
1964	**Soviet Union**, Sweden, Czechoslovakia		**WOMEN**
1968	**Soviet Union**, Czechoslovakia, Canada	Year	
1972	**Soviet Union**, United States, Czechoslovakia	1998	**United States**, Canada, Finland
1976	**Soviet Union**, Czechoslovakia, West Germany	2002	**Canada**, United States, Sweden

U.S. Gold Medal Hockey Teams
1960

Forwards: Billy Christian, Roger Christian, Billy Cleary, Gene Grazia, Paul Johnson, Bob McVey, Dick Meredith, Weldy Olson, Dick Rodenheiser and Tom Williams. **Defensemen:** Bob Cleary, Jack Kirrane (captain), John Mayasich, Bob Owen and Rod Paavola. **Goaltenders:** Jack McCartan and Larry Palmer. **Coach:** Jack Riley.

1980

Forwards: Neal Broten, Steve Christoff, Mike Eruzione (captain), John Harrington, Mark Johnson, Rob McClanahan, Mark Pavelich, Buzz Schneider, Dave Silk, Eric Strobel, Phil Verchota and Mark Wells. **Defensemen:** Bill Baker, Dave Christian, Ken Morrow, Jack O'Callahan, Mike Ramsey and Bob Suter. **Goaltenders:** Jim Craig and Steve Janaszak. **Coach:** Herb Brooks.

1998

Forwards: Laurie Baker, Alana Blahoski, Lisa Brown-Miller, Karen Bye, Tricia Dunn, Cammi Granato, Katie King, Shelley Looney, A.J. Mleczko, Jenny Schmidgall, Gretchen Ulion, Sandra Whyte. **Defensemen:** Chris Bailey, Colleen Coyne, Sue Mertz, Tara Mounsey, Vicki Movessian, Angela Ruggiero. **Goaltenders:** Sarah DeCosta and Sarah Tueting. **Coach:** Ben Smith.

LUGE

MEN

Multiple gold medals: (including doubles): Georg Hackl (3); Jan Behrendt, Norbert Hahn, Paul Hildgartner, Thomas Köhler, Stefan Krausse and Hans Rinn (2).

Singles

Year		Time	Year		Time
1964	Thomas Köhler, GER	3:26.77	1988	Jens Müller, E. Ger	3:05.548
1968	Manfred Schmid, AUT	2:52.48	1992	Georg Hackl, GER	3:02.363
1972	Wolfgang Scheidel, E. Ger	3:27.58	1994	Georg Hackl, GER	3:21.571
1976	Dettlef Günther, E. Ger	3:27.688	1998	Georg Hackl, GER	3:18.436
1980	Bernhard Glass, E. Ger	2:54.796	2002	Armin Zoeggeler, ITA	2:57.941
1984	Paul Hildgartner, ITA	3:04.258			

Doubles

Year		Time	Year		Time
1964	Josef Feistmantl & Manfred Stengl, AUT	1:41.62	1988	Joerg Hoffmann & Jochen Pietzsch, E. Ger.	1:31.940
1968	Klaus Bonsack & Thomas Köhler, E. Ger.	1:35.85	1992	Jan Behrendt & Stefan Krausse, GER	1:32.053
1972	(TIE) Paul Hildgartner/Walter Plaikner, ITA	1:28.35	1994	Kurt Brugger & Wilfred Huber, ITA	1:36.720
	& Richard Bredow/Horst Hornlein, E. Ger.	1:28.35	1998	Jan Behrendt & Stefan Krausse, GER	1:41.105
1976	Norbert Hahn & Hans Rinn, E. Ger.	1:25.604	2002	Patric-Fritz Leitner & Alexander Resch, GER	1:26.082
1980	Norbert Hahn & Hans Rinn, E. Ger.	1:19.331			
1984	Hans Stangassinger & Franz Wembacher, W. Ger.	1:23.620			

WOMEN

Multiple gold medals: Steffi Martin Walter (2).

Singles

Year		Time	Year		Time
1964	Ortrun Enderlein, GER	3:24.67	1988	Steffi Martin Walter, E. Ger	3:03.973
1968	Erica Lechner, ITA	2:28.66	1992	Doris Neuner, AUT	3:06.696
1972	Anna-Maria Müller, E. Ger	2:59.18	1994	Gerda Weissensteiner, ITA	3:15.517
1976	Margit Schumann, E. Ger	2:50.621	1998	Silke Kraushaar, GER	3:23.779
1980	Vera Zozulya, USSR	2:36.537	2002	Sylke Otto, GER	2:52.464
1984	Steffi Martin, E. Ger	2:46.570			

NORDIC COMBINED

Ski jumping followed by a cross country race. Judges stopped converting cross country times into points after the 1994 Games. The times listed are final cross country times adjusted to include the competitors' staggered start time. The staggered start is determined by the Gundersen Method, which is a table that converts final ski jumping point differentials into time intervals.

Multiple gold medals: Samppa Lajunen and Ulrich Wehling (3); Bjarte Engen Vik, Johan Gröttumsbråten, Fred Boerre Lundberg, Takanori Kono and Kenji Ogiwara (2).

Individual

Year		Points	Year		Points
1924	Thorleif Haug, NOR	18.906	1972	Ulrich Wehling, E. Ger	413.340
1928	Johan Gröttumsbråten, NOR	17.833	1976	Ulrich Wehling, E. Ger	423.39
1932	Johan Gröttumsbråten, NOR	446.00	1980	Ulrich Wehling, E. Ger	432.200
1936	Oddbjörn Hagen, NOR	430.3	1984	Tom Sandberg, NOR	422.595
1948	Heikki Hasu, FIN	448.80	1988	Hippolyt Kempf, SWI	432.230
1952	Simon Slattvik, NOR	451.621	1992	Fabrice Guy, FRA	426.470
1956	Sverre Stenersen, NOR	455.000	1994	Fred Boerre Lundberg, NOR	457.970
1960	Georg Thoma, GER	457.952			**Time**
1964	Tormod Knutsen, NOR	469.28	1998	Bjarte Engen Vik, NOR	41:21.1
1968	Franz Keller, W. Ger	449.04	2002	Samppa Lajunen, FIN	39:11.7

Sprint

New event in 2002.

Year		Time
2002	Samppa Lajunen, FIN	16:40.1

Team

Year		Points	Year		Time
1988	West Germany	792.08	1998	Norway	54:11.5
1992	Japan	1247.180	2002	Finland	48:42.2
1994	Japan	1368.860			

SKELETON

| **MEN** | | | **WOMEN** | | |
Singles			**Singles**		
Year		Time	Year		Time
1928	Jennison Heaton, USA	3:01.8	2002	Tristan Gale, USA	1:45.11
1932-36 Not held					
1948	Nino Bibbia, ITA	5:23.2			
1952-98 Not held					
2002	Jim Shea, USA	1:41.96			

Note: This event was called Cresta when it was held in 1928 and 1948.

SKI JUMPING

Multiple gold medals (including team jumping): Matti Nykänen (4); Jens Weissflog (3); Simon Ammann, Birger Ruud and Toni Nieminen (2).

Normal Hill–90 Meters

Year		Points	Year		Points
1924-60 Not held			1984	Jens Weissflog, E. Ger	215.2
1964	Veikko Kankkonen, FIN	229.9	1988	Matti Nykänen, FIN	229.1
1968	Jiri Raska, CZE	216.5	1992	Ernst Vettori, AUT	222.8
1972	Yukio Kasaya, JPN	244.2	1994	Espen Bredesen, NOR	282.0
1976	Hans-Georg Aschenbach, E. Ger	252.0	1998	Jani Soininen, FIN	234.5
1980	Anton Innauer, AUT	266.3	2002	Simon Ammann, SWI	269.0

Note: Jump held at 70 meters from 1964-92.

Large Hill–120 Meters

Year		Points	Year		Points
1924	Jacob Tullin Thams, NOR	18.960	1972	Wojciech Fortuna, POL	219.9
1928	Alf Andersen, NOR	19.208	1976	Karl Schäabl, AUT	234.8
1932	Birger Ruud, NOR	228.1	1980	Jouko Törmänen, FIN	271.0
1936	Birger Ruud, NOR	232.0	1984	Matti Nykänen, FIN	231.2
1948	Petter Hugsted, NOR	228.1	1988	Matti Nykänen, FIN	224.0
1952	Arnfinn Bergmann, NOR	226.0	1992	Toni Nieminen, FIN	239.5
1956	Antti Hyvärinen, NOR	227.0	1994	Jens Weissflog, GER	274.5
1960	Helmut Recknagel, GER	227.2	1998	Kazuyoshi Funaki, JPN	272.3
1964	Toralf Engan, NOR	230.7	2002	Simon Ammann, SWI	281.4
1968	Vladimir Beloussov, USSR	231.3			

Note: Jump held at various lengths from 1924-56; at 80 meters from 1960-64; and at 90 meters from 1968-88.

SKI JUMPING (Cont.)
Team Large Hill

Year		Points	Year		Points
1988	Finland	.634.4	1998	Japan	.933.0
1992	Finland	.644.4	2002	Germany	.974.1
1994	Germany	.970.1			

SNOWBOARDING

MEN
Halfpipe

Year		Points	Year		Points
1998	Gian Simmen, SWI	.85.2	1998	Nicola Thost, GER	.74.6
2002	Ross Powers, USA	.46.1	2002	Kelly Clark, USA	.47.9

WOMEN
Halfpipe

Giant Slalom (Discont.)
Discontinued after 1998, replaced by Parallel Giant Slalom.

Year		Time	Year		Time
1998	Ross Rebagliati, CAN	.2:03.96	1998	Karine Ruby, FRA	.2:17.34

Discontinued after 1998, replaced by Parallel Giant Slalom.

Parallel Giant Slalom

Year			Year		
2002	Philipp Schoch	.SWI	2002	Isabelle Blanc	.FRA

SPEED SKATING

MEN

Multiple gold medals: Eric Heiden and Clas Thunberg (5); Ivar Ballangrud, Yevgeny Grishin and Johann Olav Koss (4); Hjalmar Andersen, Tomas Gustafson, Irving Jaffee and Ard Schenk (3); Gaétan Boucher, Knut Johannesen, Erhard Keller, Uwe-Jens Mey, Gianni Romme, Jack Shea and Jochem Uytdehaage (2). Note that Thunberg's total includes the All-Around, which was contested for the only time in 1924.

500 meters

Year		Time		Year		Time	
1924	Charles Jewtraw, USA	.44.0		1968	Erhard Keller, W. Ger	.40.3	
1928	(TIE) Bernt Evensen, NOR	.43.4	OR	1972	Erhard Keller, W. Ger	.39.44	OR
	& Clas Thunberg, FIN	.43.4	OR	1976	Yevgeny Kulikov, USSR	.39.17	OR
1932	Jack Shea, USA	.43.4	=OR	1980	Eric Heiden, USA	.38.03	OR
1936	Ivar Ballangrud, NOR	.43.4	=OR	1984	Sergei Fokichev, USSR	.38.19	
1948	Finn Helgesen, NOR	.43.1	OR	1988	Uwe-Jens Mey, E. Ger	.36.45	WR
1952	Ken Henry, USA	.43.2		1992	Uwe-Jens Mey, GER	.37.14	
1956	Yevgeny Grishin, USSR	.40.2	=WR	1994	Aleksandr Golubev, RUS	.36.33	OR
1960	Yevgeny Grishin, USSR	.40.2	=WR	1998	Hiroyasu Shimizu, JPN	.71.35*	OR
1964	Terry McDermott, USA	.40.1	OR	2002	Casey FitzRandolph, USA	.69.23	OR

*The two-race final was introduced; skater with the lowest combined time wins gold.

1000 meters

Year		Time		Year		Time	
1924-72	Not held			1992	Olaf Zinke, GER	.1:14.85	
1976	Peter Mueller, USA	.1:19.32		1994	Dan Jansen, USA	.1:12.43	WR
1980	Eric Heiden, USA	.1:15.18	OR	1998	Ids Postma, NED	.1:10.64	OR
1984	Gaétan Boucher, CAN	.1:15.80		2002	Gerard van Velde, NED	.1:07.18	WR
1988	Nikolai Gulyaev, USSR	.1:13.03	OR				

1500 meters

Year		Time		Year		Time	
1924	Clas Thunberg, FIN	.2:20.8		1968	Kees Verkerk, NED	.2:03.4	OR
1928	Clas Thunberg, FIN	.2:21.1		1972	Ard Schenk, NED	.2:02.96	OR
1932	Jack Shea, USA	.2:57.5		1976	Jan Egil Storholt, NOR	.1:59.38	OR
1936	Charles Mathisen, NOR	.2:19.2	OR	1980	Eric Heiden, USA	.1:55.44	OR
1948	Sverre Farstad, NOR	.2:17.6	OR	1984	Gaétan Boucher, CAN	.1:58.36	
1952	Hjalmar Andersen, NOR	.2:20.4		1988	Andre Hoffman, E. Ger	.1:52.06	WR
1956	(TIE) Yevgeny Grishin, USSR	.2:08.6	WR	1992	Johann Olav Koss, NOR	.1:54.81	
	& Yuri Mikhailov, USSR	.2:08.6	WR	1994	Johann Olav Koss, NOR	.1:51.29	WR
1960	(TIE) Roald Aas, NOR	.2:10.4		1998	Aadne Sondral, NOR	.1:47.87	WR
	& Yevgeny Grishin, USSR	.2:10.4		2002	Derek Parra, USA	.1:43.95	WR
1964	Ants Antson, USSR	.2:10.3					

5000 meters

Year		Time		Year		Time	
1924	Clas Thunberg, FIN	.8:39.0		1932	Irving Jaffee, USA	.9:40.8	
1928	Ivar Ballangrud, NOR	.8:50.5		1936	Ivar Ballangrud, NOR	.8:19.6	OR

Year		Time		Year		Time	
1948	Reidar Liaklev, NOR	8:29.4		1980	Eric Heiden, USA	7:02.29	OR
1952	Hjalmar Andersen, NOR	8:10.6	OR	1984	Tomas Gustafson, SWE	7:12.28	
1956	Boris Shilkov, USSR	7:48.7	OR	1988	Tomas Gustafson, SWE	6:44.63	WR
1960	Viktor Kosichkin, USSR	7:51.3		1992	Geir Karlstad, NOR	6:59.97	
1964	Knut Johannesen, NOR	7:38.4	OR	1994	Johann Olav Koss, NOR	6:34.96	WR
1968	Fred Anton Maier, NOR	7:22.4	WR	1998	Gianni Romme, NED	6:22.20	WR
1972	Ard Schenk, NED	7:23.61		2002	Jochem Uytdehaage, NED	6:14.66	WR
1976	Sten Stensen, NOR	7:24.48					

10,000 meters

Year		Time		Year		Time	
1924	Julius Skutnabb, FIN	18:04.8		1972	Ard Schenk, NED	15:01.35	OR
1928	Irving Jaffee, USA*	18:36.5		1976	Piet Kleine, NED	14:50.59	OR
1932	Irving Jaffee, USA	19:13.6		1980	Eric Heiden, USA	14:28.13	WR
1936	Ivar Ballangrud, NOR	17:24.3	OR	1984	Igor Malkov, USSR	14:39.90	
1948	Ake Seyffarth, SWE	17:26.3		1988	Tomas Gustafson, SWE	13:48.20	WR
1952	Hjalmar Andersen, NOR	16:45.8	OR	1992	Bart Veldkamp, NED	14:12.12	
1956	Sigvard Ericsson, SWE	16:35.9	OR	1994	Johann Olav Koss, NOR	13:30.55	WR
1960	Knut Johannesen, NOR	15:46.6	WR	1998	Gianni Romme, NED	13:15.33	WR
1964	Jonny Nilsson, SWE	15:50.1		2002	Jochem Uytdehaage, NED	12:58.92	WR
1968	Johnny Höglin, SWE	15:23.6	OR				

*Unofficial, according to the IOC. Jaffee recorded the fastest time, but the event was called off in progress due to thawing ice.

WOMEN

Multiple gold medals: Lydia Skoblikova (6); Bonnie Blair (5); Claudia Pechstein (4); Karin Enke, Gunda Niemann-Stirnemann and Yvonne van Gennip (3); Tatiana Averina, Catriona Lemay-Doan, Christa Rothenburger and Marianne Timmer (2).

500 meters

Year		Time		Year		Time	
1960	Helga Haase, GER	45.9		1984	Christa Rothenburger, E. Ger	41.02	OR
1964	Lydia Skoblikova, USSR	45.0	OR	1988	Bonnie Blair, USA	39.10	WR
1968	Lyudmila Titova, USSR	46.1		1992	Bonnie Blair, USA	40.33	
1972	Anne Henning, USA	43.33	OR	1994	Bonnie Blair, USA	39.25	
1976	Sheila Young, USA	42.76	OR	1998	Catriona Lemay-Doan, CAN	76.60*	OR
1980	Karin Enke, E. Ger	41.78	OR	2002	Catriona Lemay-Doan, CAN	74.75	OR

*The two-race final was introduced; skater with the lowest combined time wins gold.

1000 meters

Year		Time		Year		Time	
1960	Klara Guseva, USSR	1:34.1		1984	Karin Enke, E. Ger	1:21.61	OR
1964	Lydia Skoblikova, USSR	1:33.2	OR	1988	Christa Rothenburger, E. Ger	1:17.65	WR
1968	Carolina Geijssen, NED	1:32.6	OR	1992	Bonnie Blair, USA	1:21.90	
1972	Monika Pflug, W. Ger	1:31.40	OR	1994	Bonnie Blair, USA	1:18.74	
1976	Tatiana Averina, USSR	1:28.43	OR	1998	Marianne Timmer, NED	1:16.51	OR
1980	Natalia Petruseva, USSR	1:24.10	OR	2002	Chris Witty, USA	1:13.83	WR

1500 meters

Year		Time		Year		Time	
1960	Lydia Skoblikova, USSR	2:25.2	WR	1984	Karin Enke, E. Ger	2:03.42	WR
1964	Lydia Skoblikova, USSR	2:22.6	OR	1988	Yvonne van Gennip, NED	2:00.68	OR
1968	Kaija Mustonen, FIN	2:22.4	OR	1992	Jacqueline Börner, GER	2:05.87	
1972	Dianne Holum, USA	2:20.85	OR	1994	Emese Hunyady, AUT	2:02.19	
1976	Galina Stepanskaya, USSR	2:16.58	OR	1998	Marianne Timmer, NED	1:57.58	WR
1980	Annie Borckink, NED	2:10.95	OR	2002	Anni Friesinger, GER	1:54.02	WR

3000 meters

Year		Time		Year		Time	
1960	Lydia Skoblikova, USSR	5:14.3		1984	Andrea Schöne, E. Ger	4:24.79	OR
1964	Lydia Skoblikova, USSR	5:14.9		1988	Yvonne van Gennip, NED	4:11.94	WR
1968	Johanna Schut, NED	4:56.2	OR	1992	Gunda Niemann, GER	4:19.90	
1972	Christina Baas-Kaiser, NED	4:52.14	OR	1994	Svetlana Bazhanova, RUS	4:17.43	
1976	Tatiana Averina, USSR	4:45.19	OR	1998	Gunda Niemann-Stirnemann, GER	4:07.29	OR
1980	Bjorg Eva Jensen, NOR	4:32.13	OR	2002	Claudia Pechstein, GER	3:57.70	WR

5000 meters

Year		Time		Year		Time	
1960-84 Not held				1994	Claudia Pechstein, GER	7:14.37	
1988	Yvonne van Gennip, NED	7:14.13	WR	1998	Claudia Pechstein, GER	6:59.61	WR
1992	Gunda Niemann, GER	7:31.57		2002	Claudia Pechstein, GER	6:46.91	WR

SHORT TRACK SPEED SKATING

MEN

Multiple gold medals (including relays): Marc Gagnon and Kim Ki-Hoon (3).

500 meters

Year		Time
1994	Chae Ji-Hoon, S. Kor.	.43.45
1998	Takafumi Nishitani, JPN	.42.862
2002	Marc Gagnon, CAN	.41.802 **OR**

1000 meters

Year		Time
1992	Kim Ki-Hoon, S. Kor.	1:30.76 **WR**
1994	Kim Ki-Hoon, S. Kor.	1:34.57
1998	Kim Dong-Sung, S. Kor.	1:32.375
2002	Steven Bradbury, AUS	1:29.109

1500 meters

Year		Time
2002	Apolo Anton Ohno, USA*	2:18.541

*Ohno finished second to South Korea's Kim Dong-Sung, who was disqualifed for cross-tracking.

5000-m Relay

Year		Time
1992	South Korea	.7:14.02 **WR**
1994	Italy	.7:11.74 **OR**
1998	Canada	.7:06.075
2002	Canada	.6:51.579

WOMEN

Multiple gold medals (including relays): Chun Lee-Kyung (4); Kim Yun-Mi, Annie Perrault, Cathy Turner, Won Hye-Kyung and Yang Yang (A) (2)

500 meters

Year		Time
1992	Cathy Turner, USA	.47.04
1994	Cathy Turner, USA	.45.98 **OR**
1998	Annie Perrault, CAN	.46.568
2002	Yang Yang (A), CHN	.44.187

1000 meters

Year		Time
1994	Chun Lee-Kyung, S. Kor.	1:36.87
1998	Chun Lee-Kyung, S. Kor.	1:42.776
2002	Yang Yang (A), CHN	1:36.391

1500 meters

Year		Time
2002	Ko Gi-Hyun, S. Kor.	2:31.581

3000-m Relay

Year		Time
1992	Canada	.4:36.62
1994	South Korea	.4:26.64 **WR**
1998	South Korea	.4:16.260 **WR**
2002	South Korea	.4:12.793 **WR**

Athletes with Winter and Summer Medals

Only three athletes have won medals in both the Winter and Summer Olympics:
Eddie Eagan, USA–Light Heavyweight Boxing gold (1920) and Four-man Bobsled gold (1932).
Jacob Tullin Thams, Norway–Ski Jumping gold (1924) and 8-meter Yachting silver (1936).
Christa Luding-Rothenburger, East Germany–Speed Skating gold at 500 meters (1984) and 1,000m (1988), silver at 500m (1988) and bronze at 500m (1992) and Match Sprint Cycling silver (1988). Luding-Rothenburger is the only athlete to ever win medals in both Winter and Summer Games in the same year.

All-Time Leading Medal Winners
MEN

No		Sport	G-S-B
12	Bjorn Dählie, NOR	Cross Country	8-4-0
9	Sixten Jernberg, SWE	Cross Country	4-3-2
7	Clas Thunberg, FIN	Speed Skating	5-1-1
7	Ivar Ballangrud, NOR	Speed Skating	4-2-1
7	Ricco Gross, GER	Biathlon	3-3-1
7	Veikko Hakulinen, FIN	Cross Country	3-3-1
7	Kjetil Andre Aamodt, NOR	Alpine	3-2-2
7	Eero Mäntyranta, FIN	Cross Country	3-2-2
7	Bogdan Musiol, E. Ger/GER	Bobsled	1-5-1
6	Ole Einar Bjoerndalen, NOR	Biathlon	5-1-0
6	Thomas Alsgaard, NOR	Cross Country	4-2-0
6	Gunde Svan, SWE	Cross Country	4-1-1
6	Vegard Ulvang, NOR	Cross Country	3-2-1
6	Johan Gröttumsbråten, NOR	Nordic	3-1-2
6	Wolfgang Hoppe, E. Ger/GER	Bobsled	2-3-1
6	Eugenio Monti, ITA	Bobsled	2-2-2
6	Vladimir Smirnov, USSR/UT/KAZ	X-country	1-4-1
6	Mika Myllylae, FIN	Cross Country	1-1-4
6	Roald Larsen, NOR	Speed Skating	0-2-4
6	Harri Kirvesniemi, FIN	Cross Country	0-0-6
5	**Eric Heiden, USA**	Speed Skating	5-0-0
5	Yevgeny Grishin, USSR	Speed Skating	4-1-0
5	Johann Olav Koss, NOR	Speed Skating	4-1-0
5	Matti Nykänen, FIN	Ski Jumping	4-1-0
5	Aleksandr Tikhonov, USSR	Biathlon	4-1-0
5	Nikolai Zimyatov, USSR	Cross Country	4-1-0
5	Georg Hackl, GER	Luge	3-2-0
5	Samppa Lajunen, FIN	Cross Country	3-2-0
5	Alberto Tomba, ITA	Alpine	3-2-0
5	Marc Gagnon, CAN	ST Sp. Skating	3-0-2
5	Harald Grönningen, NOR	Cross Country	2-3-0
5	Frank Luck, GER	Biathlon	2-3-0
5	Pål Tyldum, NOR	Cross Country	2-3-0
5	Sven Fischer, GER	Biathlon	2-2-1
5	Knut Johannesen, NOR	Speed Skating	2-2-1
5	Lasse Kjus, NOR	Alpine	1-3-1
5	Peter Angerer, W. Ger/GER	Biathlon	1-2-2
5	Juha Mieto, FIN	Cross Country	1-2-2
5	Fritz Feierabend, SWI	Bobsled	0-3-2
5	Rintje Ritsma, NED	Speed Skating	0-2-3

WOMEN

No		Sport	G-S-B
10	Raisa Smetanina, USSR/UT	Cross Country	4-5-1
9	Lyubov Egorova, UT/RUS	Cross Country	6-3-0
9	Larissa Lazutina, UT/RUS	Cross Country	5-3-1
9	Stefania Belmondo, ITA	Cross Country	2-3-4
8	Galina Kulakova, USSR	Cross Country	4-2-2
8	Karin (Enke) Kania, E. Ger	Speed Skating	3-4-1
8	Gunda Neimann-Stirnemann, GER	Speed Skating	3-4-1
8	Ursula Disl, GER	Biathlon	2-4-2
7	Claudia Pechstein, GER	Speed Skating	4-1-2
7	Marja-Liisa (Hämäläinen) Kirvesniemi, FIN	Cross Country	3-0-4

No		Sport	G-S-B	No		Sport	G-S-B
7	Elena Valbe, UT/RUS	Cross Country	3-0-4	5	Anfisa Reztsova, USSR/UT	CC/Biathlon	3-1-1
7	Andrea (Mitscherlich, Schöne) Ehrig, E. Ger	Speed Skating	1-5-1	5	Vreni Schneider, SWI	Alpine	3-1-1
6	Lydia Skoblikova, USSR	Speed Skating	6-0-0	5	Katja Seizinger, GER	Alpine	3-0-2
6	**Bonnie Blair, USA**	Speed Skating	5-0-1	5	Helena Takalo, FIN	Cross Country	1-3-1
6	Manuela Di Centa, ITA	Cross Country	2-2-2	5	Bente (Martinsen) Skari, NOR	Cross Country	1-2-2
5	Lee-Kyung Chun, S. Kor	ST Sp. Skating	4-0-1	5	Alevtina Kolchina, USSR	Cross Country	1-1-3
5	Olga Danilova, RUS	Cross Country	3-2-0	5	Yang Yang (S), CHN	ST Sp. Skating	0-4-1
				5	Anita Moen, NOR	Cross Country	0-3-2

Games Medaled In

MEN–Aamodt (1992,94,2002); **Alsgaard** (1994,98,2002); **Angerer** (1980,84,88); **Ballangrud** (1928,32,36); **Bjoerndalen** (1998,2002); **Dählie** (1992,94,98); **Feierabend** (1936,48,52); **Fischer** (1994,98,2002); **Gagnon** (1994,98,2002); **Grishin** (1956,60,64); **Gross** (1992,94,98,2002); **Gröttumsbråten** (1924,28,32); **Grönningen** (1960,64,68); **Hackl** (1988,92,94,98,2002) **Hakulinen** (1952,56,60); **Heiden** (1980); **Hoppe** (1984,88,92,94); **Jernberg** (1956,60,64); **Johannesen** (1956,60,64); **Kirvesniemi** (1980,84,92,94,98); **Kjus** (1994,98,2002); **Koss** (1992,94); **Lajunen** (1998,2002);**Larsen** (1924,28); **Luck** (1994,98,2002); **Mäntyranta** (1960,64,68); **Mieto** (1976,80,84); **Monti** (1956,60,64,68); **Musiol** (1980,84,88,92); **Myllylae** (1994,98); **Nykänen** (1984,88); **Ritsma** (1994,98); **Smirnov** (1988,92,94,98); **Svan** (1984,88); **Thunberg** (1924,28); **Tikhonov** (1968,72,76,80); **Tomba** (1988,92,94); **Tyldum** (1968,72,76); **Ulvang** (1988,92,94); **Zimyatov** (1980,84).

WOMEN–Belmondo (1992,94,98,2002); **Blair** (1988,92,94); **Chun** (1994,98); **Danilova** (1998,2002); **Di Centa** (1992,94); **Disl** (1992,94,98,2002); **Egorova** (1992,94); **Ehrig** (1976,80,84,88); **Kania** (1980,84,88); **Kirvesniemi** (1984,88,94); **Kolchina** (1956,64,68); **Kulakova** (1968,72,76,80); **Lazutina** (1992,94,98,2002); **Moen** (1994,98,2002); **Niemann-Stirnemann** (1992,94,98); **Pechstein** (1992,94,98,2002); **Reztsova** (1988,92,94); **Schneider** (1988,92,94); **Seizinger** (1992,94,98); **Skari** (1998,2002); **Skoblikova** (1960,64); **Smetanina** (1976,80,84,88,92); **Takalo** (1972,76,80); **Valbe** (1992,94,98); **Yang** (1998,2002).

Most Gold Medals
MEN

No		Sport	G-S-B	No		Sport	G-S-B
8	Bjorn Dählie, NOR	Cross Country	8-4-0	4	Thomas Wassberg, SWE	Cross Country	4-0-0
5	Clas Thunberg, FIN	Speed Skating	5-1-1				
5	Ole Einar Bjoerndalen, NOR	Biathlon	5-1-0		### WOMEN		
5	**Eric Heiden, USA**	Speed Skating	5-0-0	No		Sport	G-S-B
4	Sixten Jernberg, SWE	Cross Country	4-3-2	6	Lyubov Egorova, UT/RUS	Cross Country	6-3-0
4	Ivar Ballangrud, NOR	Speed Skating	4-2-1	6	Lydia Skoblikova, USSR	Speed Skating	6-0-0
4	Thomas Alsgaard, NOR	Cross Country	4-2-0	5	Larissa Lanina, USSR/UT	Cross Country	4-5-1
4	Gunde Svan, SWE	Cross Country	4-1-1	4	Galina Kulakova, USSR	Cross Country	4-2-2
4	Yevgeny Grishin, USSR	Speed Skating	4-1-0	4	Claudia Pechstein, GER	ST Sp. Skating	4-1-2
4	Johann Olav Koss, NOR	Speed Skating	4-1-0	4	Lee-Kyung Chun, S. Kor.	ST Sp. Skating	4-0-1
4	Matti Nykänen, FIN	Ski Jumping	4-1-0				
4	Aleksandr Tikhonov, USSR	Biathlon	4-1-0				
4	Nikolai Zimyatov, USSR	Cross Country	4-1-0				

All-Time Leading USA Medalists
MEN

No		Sport	G-S-B	No		Sport	G-S-B
5	Eric Heiden	Speed Skating	5-0-0	2	Terry McDermott	Speed Skating	1-1-0
3*	Irving Jaffee	Speed Skating	3-0-0	2	Dick Meredith	Ice Hockey	1-1-0
3	Pat Martin	Bobsled	1-2-0	2	Tommy Moe	Alpine	1-1-0
3	John Heaton	Bobsled/Skeleton	0-2-1	2	Weldy Olson	Ice Hockey	1-1-0
2	Dick Button	Figure Skating	2-0-0	2	Derek Parra	Speed Skating	1-1-0
2†	Eddie Eagan	Boxing/Bobsled	2-0-0	2	Dick Rodenheiser	Ice Hockey	1-1-0
2	Billy Fiske	Bobsled	2-0-0	2	Ross Powers	Snowboarding	1-0-1
2	Cliff Gray	Bobsled	2-0-0	2	Stan Benham	Bobsled	0-2-0
2	Jack Shea	Speed Skating	2-0-0	2	Herb Drury	Ice Hockey	0-2-0
2	Apolo Anton Ohno	ST Sp. Skating	1-1-0	2	Eric Flaim	Sp. Skate/ST Sp. Skate	0-2-0
2	Billy Cleary	Ice Hockey	1-1-0	2	Bode Miller	Alpine	0-2-0
2	Jennison Heaton	Bobsled/Skeleton	1-1-0	2	Frank Synott	Ice Hockey	0-2-0
2	David Jenkins	Figure Skating	1-1-0	2	John Garrison	Ice Hockey	0-1-1
2	John Mayasich	Ice Hockey	1-1-0				

*Jaffee is generally given credit for a third gold medal in the 10,000-meter Speed Skating race of 1928. He had the fastest time before the race was cancelled due to thawing ice. The IOC considers the race unofficial.
†Eagan won the light heavyweight boxing title at the 1920 Summer Games in Antwerp and the four-man Bobsled at the 1932 Winter Games in Lake Placid. He is the only athlete ever to win gold medals in both the Winter and Summer Olympics.

WOMEN

No		Sport	G-S-B	No		Sport	G-S-B
6	Bonnie Blair	Speed Skating	5-0-1	2	Carol Heiss	Figure Skating	1-1-0
4	Cathy Turner	ST Sp. Skating	2-1-1	2	Katie King	Ice Hockey	1-1-0
4	Dianne Holum	Speed Skating	1-2-1	2	Shelley Looney	Ice Hockey	1-1-0
3	Chris Witty	Speed Skating	1-1-1	2	Sue Merz	Ice Hockey	1-1-0
3	Sheila Young	Speed Skating	1-1-1	2	A.J. Mleczko	Ice Hockey	1-1-0
3	Leah Poulos Mueller	Speed Skating	0-3-0	2	Tara Mounsey	Ice Hockey	1-1-0
3	Beatrix Loughran	Figure Skating	0-2-1	2	Diann Roffe-Steinrotter	Alpine	1-1-0
3	Amy Peterson	ST Sp. Skating	0-2-1	2	Angela Ruggiero	Ice Hockey	1-1-0
2	Andrea Mead Lawrence	Alpine	2-0-0	2	Picabo Street	Alpine	1-1-0
2	Tenley Albright	Figure Skating	1-1-0	2	Sarah Teuting	Ice Hockey	1-1-0
2	Chris Bailey	Ice Hockey	1-1-0	2	Anne Henning	Speed Skating	1-0-1
2	Laurie Baker	Ice Hockey	1-1-0	2	Penny Pitou	Alpine	0-2-0
2	Karyn Bye	Ice Hockey	1-1-0	2	Nancy Kerrigan	Figure Skating	0-1-1
2	Sara DeCosta	Ice Hockey	1-1-0	2	Michelle Kwan	Figure Skating	0-1-1
2	Tricia Dunn	Ice Hockey	1-1-0	2	Jean Saubert	Alpine	0-1-1
2	Gretchen Fraser	Alpine	1-1-0	2	Nikki Ziegelmeyer	ST Sp. Skating	0-1-1
2	Cammi Granato	Ice Hockey	1-1-0	2	Jennifer Rodriguez	Speed Skating	0-0-2

Note: The term ST Sp. Skating refers to Short Track (or pack) Speed Skating.

All-Time Medal Standings, 1924-2002

All-time Winter Games medal standings, according to *The Golden Book of the Olympic Games*. Medal counts include figure skating medals (1908 and '20) and hockey medals (1920) awarded at the Summer Games. National medal standings for the Winter and Summer Games are not recognized by the IOC.

		G	S	B	Total			G	S	B	Total
1	Norway	94	94	75	263	25	Czech Republic (1998–)	2	1	2	5
2	Soviet Union (1956-88)	78	57	59	194		Kazakhstan (1994–)	1	2	2	5
3	**United States**	69	72	52	193		Belgium	1	1	3	5
4	Austria	41	57	64	162		Bulgaria	1	1	3	5
5	Finland	42	51	49	142		Belarus (1994–)	0	2	3	5
6	Germany (1928-36, 52-64, 92–)	47	46	32	125	30	Croatia	3	1	0	4
							Spain	3	0	1	4
7	East Germany (1968-88)	43	39	36	118		Australia	2	0	2	4
8	Sweden	39	30	39	108		Yugoslavia (1924-88)	0	3	1	4
9	Switzerland	32	33	38	103		Slovenia	0	0	4	4
10	Canada	31	28	37	96	35	Estonia	1	1	1	3
11	Italy	31	31	27	89		Ukraine (1994–)	1	1	1	3
12	France	22	22	28	72		Slovenia (1992–)	0	0	3	3
13	Netherlands	22	28	19	69	38	Luxembourg	0	2	0	2
14	Russia (1994–)	27	20	11	58		North Korea	0	1	1	2
15	West Germany (1968-88)	18	20	19	57	40	Uzbekistan (1994–)	1	0	0	1
16	Japan	8	10	13	31		Denmark	0	1	0	1
17	Great Britain	8	4	14	26		New Zealand	0	1	0	1
	Czechoslovakia (1924-92)	2	8	16	26		Romania	0	0	1	1
19	Unified Team (1992)	9	6	8	23						
20	China	2	12	8	22	**Combined totals**		**G**	**S**	**B**	**Total**
21	South Korea	11	5	4	20	Germany/E. Ger/W. Ger		108	105	87	300
22	Liechtenstein	2	2	5	9	USSR/UT/Russia		114	83	78	275
23	Poland	1	2	3	6						
	Hungary	0	2	4	6						

Notes: Athletes from the USSR participated in the Winter Games from 1956-88, returned as the Unified Team in 1992 after the breakup of the Soviet Union (in 1991) and then competed for the independent republics of Belarus, Kazakhstan, Russia, Ukraine, Uzbekistan and three others in 1994. Yugoslavia divided into Croatia and Bosnia-Herzegovina in 1992, while Czechoslovakia split into Slovakia and the Czech Republic in 1993.

Germany was barred from the Olympics in 1924 and 1948 as an aggressor nation in both World Wars I and II. Divided into East and West Germany after WWII, both countries competed under one flag from 1952-64, then as separate teams from 1968-88. Germany was reunified in 1990.

Soccer

Fourteen-year-old **Freddy Adu** was drafted first
overall by the D.C. United and made a successful
MLS debut in 2004.

AP/Wide World Photos

Nothing Gold Can Stay

Led by a group of veterans and a dominating newcomer, the core of the USA women's team said goodbye at the Athens.

Gerry Brown
is co-editor of the ESPN Sports Almanac

Anything short of the gold medal would have been a total loss. Coming off perhaps the worst year in the recent history of women's soccer in the United States, Team USA wanted this one, *needed* this one, for a happy ending.

It was the preamble to the farewell tour, the beginning of the end, for a key group of veterans, players who saw the rise in prominence of women's soccer that would have been thought unlikely 10 years ago. After all, soccer doesn't sell in the United States, so says the gospel of sports. And women's soccer? C'mon.

Then came Mia Hamm with the quickness, the ball-hawking and rocket shot along with a fresh face and a certain grace. The goals followed in great number, as did the wins.

The leading lady of women's soccer over the last decade and a half was Hamm but she wasn't alone or even the first. Players like Michelle Akers set the stage for Hamm and her teammates to come on and usher women's soccer into the spotlight.

The five veterans of the inaugural Women's World Cup Team in 1991 still active—Brandi Chastain, Joy Fawcett, Kristine Lilly, Julie Foudy and Hamm—made plans to say goodbye after one more act. They had won two World Cups (1991 and 1999) and an Olympic gold medal (1996) but 2003 had flipped the script and—out of nowhere—things seemed headed in the wrong direction.

It was a year that started with great promise. The 2003 Women's World Cup was relocated from China to the United States due to the SARS scare in Asia and the team looked for home-field advantage to put them over the top.

Just before the Cup was set to start, the three-year-old WUSA, the world's top league for female professionals and primary employer for the USA national team players, folded and then the other cleat dropped in the World Cup with a semifinal loss to eventual champion Germany and a disappointing third-place finish on their home soil.

AP/Wide World Photos

*Out-going national team veterans **Julie Foudy, Joy Fawcett, Mia Hamm, Kristine Lilly** and **Brandi Chastain** get a golden parachute with their championship run at the 2004 Summer Olympics in Athens.*

This year, playing on the world's biggest stage, the team had a perfect opportunity to make those bad memories fade a bit.

Before the Olympics began however, the WUSA, still breathing, held two soccer "festivals" consisting of youth clinics, coaching seminars and games between teams of WUSA players, including most of the national teamers.

The attendance of the first festival, held in Blaine, Minn., was not as big as might have been hoped but the numbers improved for their second festival held a week later at the Home Depot Center outside Los Angeles in Carson, Calif.

The future of the WUSA is murky at best but the founding mothers of U.S. soccer have done their part.

Unlike the 2003 World Cup, the 2004 Summer Games in Athens went right according to plan.

The team beat host-nation Greece, 3-0, in the opening match of the Games, then shut out Brazil, 2-0, behind Hamm's record 153rd international goal (on a penalty kick) in the second half and a clincher by young striker Abby Wambach.

The team tied Australia, 1-1, before moving to the medal round and getting by Japan, 2-1, in the quarterfinals to set up a rematch with Germany, the team that ended its World Cup in 2003.

Kristine Lilly, the world's all-time leader in caps, who has appeared in nearly 90 percent of the matches ever played by the U.S. women, gave the

AP/Wide World Photos

*Even if it hadn't hosted the Summer Olympics it would have been a big year for **Greece**, who shocked Europe with their championship run at the 2004 European Championships in Portugal.*

U.S. the lead in the first half on a point-blank, one-timer from Wambach. It looked like Lilly's goal would be the decider until Germany broke through two minutes into stoppage time to score the last-gasp equalizer and force overtime on a pin-ball shot past long-time U.S. goalkeeper Brianna Scurry.

In overtime, the U.S. bounced back and teenager Heather O'Reilly got a ball in front from Hamm and slipped it home. The 2-1 win was a satisfying payback for 2003 but the job was not finished and it wouldn't be until they all had gold around their necks.

The gold-medal game with Brazil was another thriller and wasn't decided until two more overtimes were played. Twenty-year-old Lindsay Tarpley scored early on an assist from 1999 World Cup hero Brandi Chastain and after Brazil tied it in the second half the teams were headed to overtime.

Finally in the game's 112th minute, Lilly came up big one more time and lifted a perfect corner kick onto the head of a leaping Wambach, who nodded home the gold-medal winner.

While it was a curtain call for those five aforementioned national team stars, it was next-generation players like Wambach, O'Reilly and Tarpley, who shared center stage and offered a reassuring glimpse into the future.

However it was the glorious past and present that the U.S. national team and the five ladies who helped built it were focused on as they kissed their gold medals on the Olympic podium.

Tomorrow is another day.

The Ten Biggest
Stories of the Year in Soccer

10 Major League Soccer announces it will add two expansion teams for the 2005 season. The debut of Mexican-run Club Deportivo Chivas USA in Los Angeles will create an instant intra-city rivalry with the L.A. Galaxy. Real Salt Lake, the league's 12th team, is owned by long-time NBA executive and Utah-native Dave Checketts. The league is also planning to add two teams for the 2006 season, one of which will almost certainly be located in Seattle.

9 Argentina's most famous club, Boca Juniors, the champions of South America, beat European champions AC Milan, 3-1, in a penalty shoot-out to win professional soccer's world championship at the 2003 European/South American Cup in Tokyo.

8 Portuguese league champions FC Porto wins the 2004 UEFA Champions League, beating France's AS Monaco, 3-0. Porto knocked out some of Europe's top clubs, including England's Manchester United and Spain's Deportivo La Coruna, on their way to their second-ever European championship. A victim of their own success, Porto loses their highly regarded young manager Jose Mourinho to England's Chelsea just a week later.

7 FIFA, as part of its new plan to rotate the World Cup among the six continents (thankfully, Antarctica is not part of this plan), awards the 2010 Cup to South Africa. It is the first time the World Cup will be played in Africa. The South African delegation includes three Nobel Peace Prize winners—former president Nelson Mandela, F.W. de Klerk, the last apartheid-era president and Archbishop Desmond Tutu.

6 North Carolina crushes UConn, 6-0, in the NCAA women's College Cup championship game to complete their perfect (27-0-0) season. The Tar Heels have now won 17 of the 22 NCAA Division I women's championships ever awarded.

5 Teen-age phenom Freddy Adu makes his MLS debut for the D.C. United. Adu, just 14 years old as the season begins, mostly comes in off the bench but more than holds his own with the grown men and is named to the MLS All-Star team as a reserve. Adu finishes the regular season with five goals and an assist.

4 Argentina wins the men's Olympic gold medal at the Summer Games in Athens beating Paraguay, 1-0. It's the first ever soccer gold for Argentina and the silver is the first medal for Paraguay in any sport.

Argentine striker Carlos Tevez scores eight goals in the tournament, including the game-winner against Paraguay. Italy takes the bronze medal, beating the surprising Iraqi team, 1-0.

3 Greece shocks the rest of Europe by winning the 2004 European championship, beating their gracious hosts Portugal, 1-0, in the championship match. Greece becomes the first team in European Championship history to beat the host-nation and the defending champions (France) on their way to the title.

2 Eight-seed Indiana beats St. John's, 2-1, to win a sixth NCAA men's championship for their retiring hall of fame head coach Jerry Yeagley, who goes out on top as the all-time winningest coach in Div. I soccer history with a career record of 544-101-45.

1 The United States women's national team bounces back from its disappointing finish in the 2003 World Cup and wins the gold medal at Athens. It's the final game for several long-time national team stars including all-time leading scorer Mia Hamm.

Setting Goals

USA forward Mia Hamm padded her sizeable lead on the all-time list of leading goal-scorers in men's and women's international soccer in 2004, and even though she retired, she is not in jeopardy of losing her record anytime soon. The closest person is 49 goals shy of her—and retired herself.

	Goals
Mia Hamm, USA	156
Elisabetta Vignotta, Italy	107
Michelle Akers, USA	105
Carolina Morace, Italy	104

Note: As of Oct. 15, 2004 Iran's Ali Daei (still active) was the men's all-time leader in international goals with 98. The retired Ferenc Puskás of Hungary was second with 84 goals and the world famous (and retired) Pelé of Brazil was third with 77.

Nice Hat, Mr. Johnson

Twenty-year-old national team substitute Ed Johnson scored three goals in the second half of the USA's 6-0 win over Panama in a World Cup qualifying match in October 2004. Here's a look at the eight hat tricks scored in U.S. men's national team history.

	Date
Ed Johnson vs. Panama	Oct. 9, 2004
Landon Donovan vs. Cuba	July 19, 2003
Brian McBride vs. El Salvador	Jan. 27, 2002
Joe-Max Moore vs. El Salvador	Dec. 5, 1993
Peter Millar vs. Bermuda	Nov. 2, 1968
Aldo "Buff" Donelli vs. Mexico	May 24, 1934
Bert Patenaude vs. Paraguay*	July 17, 1930
Archie Stark vs. Canada	June 27, 1925

*World Cup match.

2003-2004
Season in Review

SPORTS ALMANAC

2004 European Championship

The UEFA European Championship is held every four years to determine the best men's national team in Europe. Contested June 12-July 4, 2004 for the 12th time since its inception in 1960.

First Round

Round robin; each team played the other three teams in its group once. Note that three points were awarded for a win and one point for a tie. (*) indicates team advanced to second round.

Group A	W	L	T	Pts	GF	GA
Portugal	2	1	0	6	4	2
Greece	1	1	1	4	4	4
Spain	1	1	1	4	2	2
Russia	1	2	0	3	2	4

Results
Date	Site	Result
June 12	Porto	Greece 2, Portugal 1
June 12	Faro-Loulé	Spain 1, Russia 0
June 16	Porto	Greece 1, Spain 1
June 16	Lisbon	Portugal 2, Russia 0
June 20	Lisbon	Portugal 1, Spain 0
June 20	Faro-Loulé	Russia 2, Greece 1

Group B	W	L	T	Pts	GF	GA
France	2	0	1	7	7	4
England	2	1	0	6	8	4
Croatia	0	1	2	2	4	6
Switzerland	0	2	1	1	1	6

Results
Date	Site	Result
June 13	Leiria	Switzerland 0, Croatia 0
June 13	Lisbon	France 2, England 1
June 17	Coimbra	England 3, Switzerland 0
June 17	Leiria	Croatia 2, France 2
June 21	Lisbon	England 4, Croatia 2
June 21	Coimbra	France 3, Switzerland 1

Group C	W	L	T	Pts	GF	GA
Sweden	1	0	2	5	8	3
Denmark	1	0	2	5	4	2
Italy	1	0	2	5	3	2
Bulgaria	0	3	0	0	1	9

Results
Date	Site	Result
June 14	Guimarães	Denmark 0, Italy 0
June 14	Lisbon	Sweden 5, Bulgaria 0
June 18	Braga	Denmark 2, Bulgaria 0
June 18	Porto	Italy 1, Sweden 1
June 22	Guimarães	Italy 2, Bulgaria 1
June 22	Porto	Denmark 2, Sweden 2

Group D	W	L	T	Pts	GF	GA
Czech Republic	3	0	0	9	7	4
Netherlands	1	1	1	4	6	4
Germany	0	1	2	2	2	3
Latvia	0	2	1	1	1	5

Results
Date	Site	Result
June 15	Porto	Germany 1, Netherlands 1
June 15	Aveiro	Czech Republic 2, Latvia 1
June 19	Porto	Latvia 0, Germany 0
June 19	Aveiro	Czech Republic 3, Netherlands 2
June 23	Braga	Netherlands 3, Latvia 0
June 23	Lisbon	Czech Republic 2, Germany 1

Quarterfinals
Date	Site	Result
June 24	Lisbon	Portugal 2, England 2
	Portugal advances, 6-5, on penalty kicks	
June 25	Lisbon	Greece 1, France 0
June 26	Faro-Loulé	Netherlands 0, Sweden 0
	Netherlands advances, 5-4, on penalty kicks	
June 27	Porto	Czech Republic 3, Denmark 0

Semifinals
Date	Site	Result
June 30	Lisbon	Portugal 2, Netherlands 1
July 1	Porto	Greece 1, Czech Republic 0 OT

Final
Date	Site	Result
July 4	Lisbon	Greece 1, Portugal 0

Goal: Greece—Angelos Charisteas (57th).

Top Scorers
Goals Scored
	Goals
Milan Baros, Czech Republic	5
Wayne Rooney, England	4
Ruud Van Nistelrooij, Netherlands	4
Frank Lampard, England	3
Henrik Larsson, Sweden	3
Jon Dahl Tomasson, Denmark	3
Zinédine Zidane, France	3

Assists
	Assists
Karel Poborsky, Czech Republic	4
Arjen Robben, Netherlands	3
Five players tied with 2 each.	

Most Valuable Player
Theodoros Zagorakis, Greece, MF

Euro 2004 All-Star Team

GK—Petr Cech, Czech Rep.; Antonios Nikopolidis, Greece; **D**—Sol Campbell, England; Ashley Cole, England; Traianos Dellas, Greece; Ricardo Carvalho, Portugal; Georgios Seitaridis, Greece; Gianluca Zambrotta, Italy; **MF**—Michael Ballack, Germany; Luis Figo, Portugal; Frank Lampard, England; Maniche, Portugal; Pavel Nedved, Czech Rep.; Theodoros Zagorakis, Greece; Zinédine Zidane, France; **F**—Milan Baros, Czech Rep.; Angelos Charisteas, Greece; Henrik Larsson, Sweden; Cristiano Ronaldo, Portugal; Wayne Rooney, England; Jon Dahl Tomasson, Denmark; Ruud Van Nistelrooy, Netherlands.

FIFA Top 50 World Rankings

FIFA announced a new monthly world ranking system on Aug. 13, 1993 designed to "provide a constant international comparison of national team performances." The rankings are based on a mathematical formula that weighs strength of schedule, importance of matches and goals scored for and against. Games considered include World Cup qualifying and final rounds, Continental championship qualifying and final rounds, and friendly matches.

The formula was altered slightly in January 1999. Now the rankings annually take into account a team's seven best matches of the last eight years, thereby favoring some teams that have been consistent over a long period of time but that may have stumbled just recently. At the end of the year, FIFA designates a Team of the Year. Teams of the Year so far have been Germany (1993), Brazil (1994-2000, 2002-03) and France (2001). The USA reached their highest-ever ranking (8th) in Sept. 2002.

2003

		Points	2002 Rank			Points	2002 Rank			Points	2002 Rank
1	Brazil	848	1		Portugal	682	11	35	Nigeria	623	29
2	France	827	2	19	Sweden	677	25	36	South Africa	618	30
3	Spain	798	3	20	Croatia	673	32	37	Ecuador	615	31
4	Netherlands	752	6	21	Uruguay	671	28	38	Morocco	614	35
5	Argentina	744	5	22	South Korea	664	20	39	Colombia	612	37
6	Czech Republic	743	15		Paraguay	664	18	40	Finland	610	43
7	Mexico	740	8	24	Russia	659	23	41	Serbia & Montenegro	605	19
8	Turkey	738	9	25	Poland	656	33	42	Norway	604	26
	England	738	7	26	Saudi Arabia	655	38	43	Iraq	595	53
10	Italy	734	13	27	Romania	653	24	44	Switzerland	592	44
11	USA	732	10	28	Iran	649	33	45	Tunisia	580	41
12	Germany	729	4	29	Japan	646	22	46	Jamaica	569	51
13	Denmark	715	12	30	Greece	641	48	47	Jordan	567	77
14	Ireland	712	14	31	Slovenia	637	36	48	Kuwait	566	83
	Cameroon	712	16	32	Egypt	634	39	49	Honduras	564	40
16	Belgium	696	17	33	Senegal	628	27	50	Slovakia	557	55
17	Costa Rica	682	21	34	Bulgaria	627	42				

2004 (as of Oct. 6)

		Points	2003 Rank			Points	2003 Rank			Points	2003 Rank
1	Brazil	845	1	18	Nigeria	701	35	35	Belgium	635	16
2	France	799	2	19	Japan	699	29	36	Tunisia	630	45
3	Argentina	778	5	20	Iran	698	28	37	Norway	610	42
4	Spain	774	3	21	Cameroon	690	14	38	Jordan	609	47
5	Netherlands	755	4	22	Sweden	687	19	39	Iraq	607	43
6	Czech Republic	751	6	23	Croatia	686	20	40	South Africa	604	36
7	England	739	8		Paraguay	686	22	41	Bulgaria	601	34
8	Portugal	735	17	25	South Korea	664	22	42	Switzerland	596	44
	Italy	735	10	26	Romania	657	24	43	Slovenia	595	31
10	Mexico	734	7	27	Saudi Arabia	662	38	44	Mali	590	54
11	USA	717	11	28	Colombia	660	39	45	Finland	585	40
12	Turkey	711	8	29	Poland	652	25		Cote d'Ivoire	585	70
13	Germany	706	12	30	Egypt	649	32	47	Bahrain	584	64
14	Ireland	705	14	31	Senegal	643	33	48	Ecuador	583	37
15	Denmark	704	13	32	Costa Rica	642	17	49	China	579	86
16	Greece	703	30	33	Russia	641	24	50	Oman	578	62
17	Uruguay	702	21	34	Morocco	639	38				

FIFA Women's World Rankings

As part of its growing recognition of women's soccer FIFA began ranking the women's national teams in 2002 following the inaugural FIFA Women's U19 World Championship in Canada. The rankings are currently released four times a year and are calculated in a similar manner to the men's rankings. The first women's international was held on April 17, 1971 (France vs. the Netherlands). The Top 30 teams are listed below.

2004 (as of Aug. 30)

		Points	2003 Rank			Points	2003 Rank			Points	2003 Rank
1	Germany	2184	1	11	Russia	1893	12	21	Spain	1756	20
2	USA	2177	2	12	Canada	1890	11	22	New Zealand	1755	21
3	Norway	2145	3	13	Japan	1883	14	23	Nigeria	1749	24
4	Brazil	2053	6	14	England	1857	13	24	Chinese Taipei	1742	23
5	Sweden	2039	4	15	Australia	1836	16	25	Mexico	1728	30
6	China	2033	5	16	Netherlands	1821	15	26	South Korea	1725	25
7	France	1992	9	17	Iceland	1791	26	27	Hungary	1701	26
8	North Korea	1988	7	18	Finland	1786	19		Belgium	1701	27
9	Denmark	1985	8	19	Ukraine	1778	18	29	Switzerland	1699	28
10	Italy	1948	10	20	Czech Republic	1760	22	30	Scotland	1685	30

U.S. Women's National Team
2004 Schedule and Results

Through Oct. 16, 2004. Games in **bold type** are Olympic matches.

Date		Result	USA Goals	Site
Jan. 30	Sweden	W, 3-0	Boxx, Tarpley (2)	Shenzhen, China
Feb. 1	China	T, 0-0	—	Shenzhen, China
Feb. 3	Canada	W, 2-0	Tarpley, Fawcett	Shenzhen, China
Feb. 25	Trinidad & Tobago	W, 7-0	Boxx (3), Lilly, Hamm (2), Wambach	San Jose, Costa Rica
Feb. 27	Haiti	W, 8-0	Wagner, Parlow (3), MacMillan, Tarpley	Heredia, Costa Rica
Feb. 29	Mexico	W, 2-0	own goal, Wambach	San Jose, Costa Rica
Mar. 3	Costa Rica	W, 4-0	Wagner, Wambach, Lilly, Boxx	San Jose, Costa Rica
Mar. 5	Mexico	W, 3-2	Tarpley, Wambach, Foudy	Heredia, Costa Rica
Mar 14	France	W, 5-1	Wambach, Hamm, Hucles (2), Tarpley	Ferreiras, Portugal
Mar. 16	Denmark	W, 1-0	Hucles	Quarteira, Portugal
Mar. 17	Sweden	L, 1-3	Reddick	Lagos, Portugal
Mar. 20	Norway	W, 4-1	Wambach (3), Tarpley	Faro, Portugal
Apr. 24	Brazil	W, 5-1	Foudy, Wambach (2), Welsh, Hamm	Birmingham, Alabama
May 9	Mexico	W, 3-0	Parlow, Hamm, Chalupny	Albuquerque, N.M.
June 6	Japan	T, 1-1	Wambach	Louisville, Ky.
July 3	Canada	W, 1-0	Mitts	Nashville, Tenn.
July 21	Australia	W, 3-1	Boxx, Hamm, Wambach	Blaine, Minn.
Aug. 1	China	W, 3-1	Wagner, Hamm, Wambach	E. Hartford, Conn.
Aug. 11	**Greece**	W, 3-0	Boxx, Wambach, Hamm	Heraklio, Greece
Aug. 14	**Brazil**	W, 2-0	Hamm, Wambach	Thessaloniki, Greece
Aug. 17	**Australia**	T, 1-1	Lilly	Thessaloniki, Greece
Aug. 20	**Japan**	W, 2-1	Lilly, Wambach	Thessaloniki, Greece
Aug. 23	**Germany**	W, 2-1 (OT)	Lilly, O'Reilly	Heraklio, Greece
Aug. 26	**Brazil**	W, 2-1 (OT)	Tarpley, Wambach	Athens, Greece
Sept. 25	Iceland	W, 4-3	Wambach (2), Hamm, Mitts	Rochester, N.Y.
Sept. 29	Iceland	W, 3-0	Parlow, Wambach, Lilly	Pittsburgh, Penn.
Oct. 3	New Zealand	W, 5-0	Hamm (2), Wambach, Lilly, Reddick	Portland, Ore.
Oct. 10	New Zealand	W, 6-0	Hamm, Lilly, Wagner, Foudy, Parlow (2)	Cincinnati, Ohio
Oct. 16	Mexico	W, 1-0	Hucles	Kansas City, Mo.

Overall record: 25-1-3.
Team Scoring: Goals for–87; Goals against–18.

2004 U.S. Women's National Team Statistics

Individual records through Oct. 16, 2004. Note that the column labeled "Career C/G" refers to career caps and goals.

Forwards	GP	GS	Mins	G	A	Pts	Career C/G
Mia Hamm	25	23	1853	13	16	42	270/157
Shannon MacMillan	15	5	602	1	6	7	174/60
Heather O'Reilly	11	0	265	1	2	4	29/4
Cindy Parlow	19	8	865	7	8	22	153/72
Abby Wambach	28	23	1958	22	11	55	50/36
Christie Welsh	2	0	56	1	1	3	23/13

Defenders	GP	GS	Mins	G	A	Pts	Career C/G
Kylie Bivens	1	1	45	0	0	0	17/0
Brandi Chastain	15	9	809	0	2	2	187/30
Joy Fawcett	15	15	1341	1	1	3	239/27
Amy LePeilbet	6	4	437	0	1	1	6/0
Kate Markgraf	28	28	2452	0	3	3	132/0
Heather Mitts	23	16	1587	2	0	4	28/2
Christie Rampone	23	21	1860	0	0	0	131/4
Cat Reddick	27	24	2167	2	0	4	69/5

Midfielders	GP	GS	Mins	G	A	Pts	Career C/G
Nicole Barnhart	1	0	4	0	0	0	1/0
Shannon Boxx	27	26	2264	7	4	18	36/11
Lori Chalupny	4	1	96	1	0	2	8/1
Julie Foudy	27	24	2029	3	4	10	266/45
Angela Hucles	17	7	799	4	2	10	41/5
Kristine Lilly	23	22	2024	8	7	23	286/101
Leslie Osborne	9	6	493	0	0	0	9/0
Tiffany Roberts	5	0	159	0	0	0	110/7
Lindsay Tarpley	24	13	1216	8	3	19	32/8
Aly Wagner	22	15	1314	4	3	11	74/16

Goalkeepers	GP	GS	Mins	W-L-T	SO	GAA	Caps
Siri Mullinix	4	4	360	4-0-0	3	0.50	45
Kristin Luckenbill	9	2	442	2-0-1	2	0.61	9
Briana Scurry	23	23	1868	18-1-2	7	0.63	149

Yellow Cards: Hamm (5); Boxx, Parlow, Wagner, Wambach (3); Lilly, Markgraf, Scurry (2); Chastain, Foudy, LePeilbet, Osborne, Rampone, Tarpley.
Red Cards: none.

Head coach: April Heinrichs

U.S. Men's National Team
2004 Schedule and Results

Through Oct. 13, 2004. Games in **bold** type are 2006 World Cup qualifying matches.

Date		Result	USA Goals	Site
Jan. 18	Denmark	T, 1-1	Donovan	Carson, Calif.
Feb. 18	Netherlands	L, 0-1	—	Amsterdam
Mar. 13	Haiti	T, 1-1	Califf	Miami, Fla.
Mar. 31	Poland	W, 1-0	Beasley	Plock, Poland
Apr. 28	Mexico	W, 1-0	Pope	Dallas, Texas
June 2	Honduras	W, 4-0	McBride (2), Lewis, Sanneh	Foxboro, Mass.
June 13	Grenada	W, 3-0	Beasley (2), Vanney	Columbus, Ohio
June 20	Grenada	W, 3-2	Donovan, Wolff, Beasley	St. George's, Grenada
July 11	Poland	T, 1-1	Bocanegra	Chicago, Ill.
Aug. 18	**Jamaica**	T, 1-1	Ching	Kingston, Jamaica
Sept. 4	**El Salvador**	W, 2-0	Ching, Donovan	Foxboro, Mass.
Sept. 9	**Panama**	T, 1-1	Jones	Panama City, Panama
Oct. 10	**El Salvador**	W, 2-0	McBride, Johnson	San Salvador, El Salvador
Oct. 13	**Panama**	W, 6-0	Donovan (2), Johnson (3) own goal	Washington, D.C.

Overall record: 8-1-5. Team scoring: Goals For–27; Goals Against–8.

2004 Copa America

Unofficially, the championship of South America. Contested for the 41st time since its inception in 1916. Held July 6-25, 2004 in Peru.

First Round

Round robin; each team played the other three teams in its group once. Note that three points were awarded for a win and one point for a tie. (*) indicates team advanced to second round.

Group A	W	L	T	Pts	GF	GA
*Colombia	2	0	1	7	4	2
*Peru	1	0	2	5	7	5
Bolivia	0	1	2	2	3	4
Venezuela	0	2	1	1	2	5

Group B	W	L	T	Pts	GF	GA
*Mexico	2	0	1	7	5	3
*Argentina	2	1	0	6	10	4
Uruguay	1	1	1	4	6	7
Ecuador	0	3	0	0	3	10

Group C	W	L	T	Pts	GF	GA
*Paraguay	2	0	1	7	4	2
*Brazil	2	1	0	6	3	3
Costa Rica	1	2	0	3	3	6
Chile	0	2	1	1	2	4

Quarterfinals

Date	Site	Result
July 17	Chiclayo	Argentina 1, Peru 0
July 17	Trujillo	Colombia 2, Costa Rica 0
July 18	Tacna	Uruguay 3, Paraguay 1
July 18	Piura	Brazil 4, Mexico 0

Semifinals

Date	Site	Result
July 20	Lima	Argentina 3, Colombia 0
July 21	Lima	Brazil 1, Uruguay 1

Brazil advanced, 5-3, on penalty kicks

Third Place

Date	Site	Result
July 24	Cusco	Uruguay 2, Colombia 1

Final

Date	Site	Result
July 25	Lima	Brazil 2, Argentina 2

Brazil wins Copa America, 4-2, on penalty kicks

Club Team Competition

2003 European/South American Cup

Also known as the Toyota Cup and the Intercontinental Cup; a year-end match for the Club World Championship between the UEFA Champions League (formerly the European Cup) and Copa Libertadores winners. Its winner is generally recognized as the Club World Champion but with the recent advent of FIFA's Club World Championship that will change. The FIFA World Club Championship will replace the European/South American Cup in 2005. The six-team format will be held in December in Tokyo. The 2004 (and final) edition of the European/South American Cup was set to be played between Once Caldas (Colombia) and FC Porto (Portugal).

Final

Dec. 14 at International Stadium, Yokohama, Japan. **Attendance:** 66,070

Boca Juniors (Argentina) 1 . . . . AC Milan (Italy) 0

Boca Juniors win, 3-1, on penalty kicks

Scoring: AC Milan—Jon Dahl Tomasson (24th); Boca Juniors—Matias Donnet (29th).

Referee: Valentin Ivanov, Russia

2004 Libertadores Cup

Contested by the league champions of South America's football union. Two-leg Semifinals and two-leg Final; home teams listed first. Winner Once Caldas of Colombia was to play UEFA Champions League winner FC Porto of Portugal in the 2004 Europe/South America Cup in Yokohama, Japan in December.

Final Four: Once Caldas (Colombia), Boca Juniors (Argentina), River Plate (Argentina) and São Paulo (Brazil).

Semifinals

Boca Juniors vs. River Plate

Boca Juniors 1 . . . . .River Plate 0
River Plate 2 . . . . .Boca Juniors 1
Boca Juniors won 5-4 on penalty kicks

São Paulo vs. Once Caldas

São Paulo 0 . . . . .Once Caldas 0
Once Caldas 2 . . . . .São Paulo 1
Once Caldas won 2-1 on aggregate

Final

Matches played June 26 in Buenos Aires, Argentina and July 1 in Manizales, Colombia.

Boca Juniors 0 .Once Caldas 0
Once Caldas 1 .Boca Juniors 1
Once Caldas won 2-0 on penalty kicks

There are two major European club competitions sanctioned by the Union of European Football Associations (UEFA). The constantly evolving **Champions League** is currently a 74-team tournament made up from UEFA member countries. The teams are ranked 1-74 depending on how they finish in their own domestic leagues. UEFA ranks the quality of the 52 European national football associations (from number one Spain to number 52 San Marino) and assigns each association a number weighted by their respective ranking (UEFA calls this number a coefficient). Each team's domestic league finish is then multiplied by the coefficient and the teams are finally ranked (countries can enter a maximum of four teams).

The defending champions AC Milan and the other 15 highest-ranked teams form Group 1 and are given a direct entry into the League but the remaining 16 teams are determined by dividing teams 17-74 into three groups—Group 2 (teams 17-34), Group 3 (35-50) and Group 4 (51-74). The 24 teams in the lowest Group (Group 4) play two-leg, total goal elimination series. The 12 survivors advance to the Second Qualifying Phase and join the 16 teams from Group 3 to play 14 two-leg, total goal elimination series. The 14 clubs that survive this phase join the 18 teams from Group 2 to play in the Third Qualifying Phase. The winning clubs from the 16 two-leg, total goal elimination series advance to the Champions League for the right to play against the top-ranked 16 teams in Europe.

The 32 teams are separated into eight groups of four and play a round-robin series of home-and-home matches. Starting for the 2003-04 Champions League, the eight group winners and eight group runners-up advance to the next round where they are paired and play two home-and-home matches. The home-and-home series are played through the sem-finals until ultimately ah single championship match for the European club championship is held. Winner FC Porto of Portugal plays Libertadores Cup champion Once Caldas of Colombia in the 2004 European/South American Cup in Japan.

The updated **UEFA Cup**, which is basically a combination of the what was known as the Cup Winners' Cup (played between national cup champions) and the old UEFA Cup (sort of a "best of the rest" tournament), is single-elimination throughout and features 121 additional teams plus teams that have been already eliminated from the Champions League.

2003-04 Champions League

Following the first three qualifying phases, the first group phase starts with six-game double round-robin format in eight four-team groups (Sept. 13-Nov. 13); top two teams in each group advance to second group phase (Nov. 26-Mar. 19) where four, four-team groups compete in the same format. Group winners and runners-up advance to the quarterfinals. While the third-place team from each of the eight groups moves to the third round of the UEFA Cup tournament. (*) indicates team advanced to the next round (of the Champions League). Note that in results listing under each table the home team is listed first.

Group Phase

Group A	W	L	T	GF	GA	Pts
*Lyon (France)	3	2	1	7	7	10
*Bayern Munich (Germany)	2	1	3	6	5	9
Celtic (Scotland)	2	3	1	8	7	7
Anderlecht (Belgium)	2	3	1	4	5	7

RESULTS: **Sept. 17**–Lyon 1, Anderlecht 0; Bayern Munich 2, Celtic 0; **Sept. 30**–Celtic 2, Lyon 0; Anderlecht 1, Bayern Munich 1; **Oct. 21**–Anderlecht 1, Celtic 0; Lyon 1, Bayern Munich 1; **Nov. 5**–Celtic 3, Anderlecht 1; Bayern Munich 1, Lyon 2; **Nov. 25**–Anderlecht 1, Lyon 0; Celtic 0, Bayern Munich 0; **Dec. 10**–Lyon 3, Celtic 2; Bayern Munich 1, Anderlicht 0.

Group B	W	L	T	GF	GA	Pts
*Arsenal (England)	3	2	1	9	6	10
*Lokomotiv Moskva (Russia)	2	2	2	7	7	8
Internazionale (Italy)	2	2	2	8	11	8
Dynamo Kyiv (Ukraine)	2	3	1	8	8	7

RESULTS: **Sept. 17**–Dynamo Kyiv 2, Lokomotiv 0; Arsenal 0, Internazionale 3; **Sept. 30**–Internazionale 2, Dynamo Kyiv 1; Lokomotiv 0, Arsenal 0; **Oct. 21**–Lokomotiv 3, Internazionale 0; Dynamo Kyiv 2, Arsenal 1; **Nov. 5**–Internazionale 1, Lokomotiv 1; Arsenal 1, Dynamo Kyiv 0; **Nov. 25**–Lokomotiv 3, Dynamo Kyiv 0; Internazionale 1, Arsenal 5; **Dec. 10**–Dynamo Kyiv 1, Internazionale 1; Arsenal 2, Lokomotov 0.

UEFA Champions League (Cont.)

Group C	W	L	T	GF	GA	Pts
*Monaco (France)	.3	1	2	15	6	11
*Deportivo La Coruna (Spain)	.3	2	1	12	10	10
PSV Eindhoven (Netherlands)	.3	2	1	8	7	10
AEK (Greece)	.0	4	2	1	11	2

RESULTS: **Sept. 17**–AEK 1, Deportivo 1; PSV 1, Monaco 2; **Sept. 30**–Monaco 4, AEK 0; Deportivo 2, PSV 0; **Oct. 21**–Deportivo 2, PSV 0; Deportivo 1, Monaco 0; **Nov. 5**–Monaco 8, Deportivo 3; PSV 2, AEK 0; **Nov. 25**–Deportivo 3, AEK 0; Monaco 1, PSV 1; **Dec. 10**–AEK 0, Monaco 0; PSV 3, Deportivo 2.

Group D	W	L	T	GF	GA	Pts
*Juventus (Italy)	.4	1	1	15	6	13
*Real Sociedad (Spain)	.2	1	3	8	8	9
Galatasaray (Turkey)	.2	3	1	6	8	7
Olympiakos (Greece)	.1	4	1	6	13	4

RESULTS: **Sept. 17**–Juventus 2, Galatasaray 1; Real Sociedad 1, Olympiakos 0; **Sept. 30**–Olympiakos 1, Juventus 2; Real Sociedad 2, Galatasaray 1; **Oct. 21**–Galatasaray 1, Olympiakos 0; Juventus 4, Real Sociedad 0; **Nov. 5**–Olympiakos 3, Galatasaray 0; Real Sociedad 0, Juventus 0; **Nov. 25**–Olympiakos 2, Real Sociedad 2; **Dec. 2**– Galatasaray 2, Juventus 0; **Dec. 10**–Juventus 7, Olympiakos 0; Real Sociedad 1, Galatasaray 1.

Group E	W	L	T	GF	GA	Pts
*Manchester United (England)	.5	1	0	13	2	15
*Stuttgart (Germany)	.4	2	0	9	6	12
Panathinaikos (Greece)	.1	4	1	5	13	4
Rangers (Scotland)	.1	4	1	4	10	4

RESULTS: **Sept. 16**–Rangers 2, Stuttgart 1; Manchester 5, Panathinaikos 0; **Oct. 1**–Panathinaikos 1, Rangers 1; Stuttgart 2, Manchester 1; **Oct. 22**–Stuttgart 2, Manchester 1; Rangers 0, Manchester 1; **Nov. 4**–Panathinaikos 1, Stuttgart 3; Manchester 2, Rangers 1; **Nov. 26**–Stuttgart 1, Rangers 0l Panathinaikos 0, Manchester 1; **Dec. 9**–Rangers 1, Panathinaikos 3; Manchester 2, Stuttgart 0.

Group F	W	L	T	GF	GA	Pts
*Real Madrid (Spain)	.4	0	2	11	5	14
*FC Porto (Portugal)	.3	1	2	9	8	11
Marseille (France)	.1	4	1	9	11	4
Partizan (Serbia & Monte.) . .	.0	3	3	3	8	3

RESULTS: **Sept. 16**–Real Madrid 4, Marseille 2; Partizan 1, Porto 1; **Oct. 1**–Porto 1, Real Madrid 3; Marseille 3, Partizan 0; **Oct. 22**–Marseille 2, Porto 3; Real Madrid 1, Partizan 0; **Nov. 4**–Porto 1, Marseille 0; Partizan 0, Real Madrid 0; **Nov. 26**–Marseille 1, Real Madrid 2; Porto 2, Partizan 1; **Dec. 9**–Real Madrid 1, Porto 1; Partizan 1, Marseille 1.

Group G	W	L	T	GF	GA	Pts
*Chelsea (England)	.4	1	1	9	3	13
*Sparta (Czech Republic)	.2	2	2	5	5	8
Besiktas (Turkey)	.2	3	1	5	7	7
Lazio (Italy)	.1	3	2	6	10	5

RESULTS: **Sept. 16**–Sprta 0, Chelsea 1; Besiktas 0, Lazio 2; **Oct. 1**–Lazio 2, Sparta 2; Chelsea 0, Besiktas 2; **Oct. 22**–Chelsea 0, Besiktas 2; Chelsea 2, Lazio 1; **Nov. 4**–Lazio 0, Chelsea 4; Besiktas 1, Sparta 0; **Nov. 26**–Chelsea 0, Sparta 0; Lazio 1, Besiktas 1; **Dec. 9**–Sparta 1, Lazio 0; Besiktas 0, Chelsea 2.

Group H	W	L	T	GF	GA	Pts
*AC Milan (Italy)	.3	2	1	4	3	10
*Celta (Spain)	.2	1	3	7	6	9
Club Brugge (Belgium)	.2	2	2	5	6	8
Ajax (Netherlands)	.2	4	0	6	7	6

RESULTS: **Sept. 16**–Milan 1, Ajax 0; Club Brugge 1, Celta 1; **Oct. 1**–Celta 0, Milan 1; Ajax 2, Club Brugge 0; **Oct. 22**–Ajax 2, Celta 0; Milan 0, Club Brugge 1; **Nov. 4**–Celta 3, Ajax 2; Club Brugge 0, Milan 1; **Nov. 26**–Ajax 0, Milan 1; Celta 1, Club Brugge 1; **Dec. 9**–Milan 1, Celta 2; Brugge 2, Ajax 1.

Round of 16
Two legs, total goals; home team listed first.

Arsenal vs. Celta
Feb. 24   Celta 2 .Arsenal 3
Mar. 10   Arsenal 2 .Celta 0
Arsenal wins 5-2 on aggregate

FC Porto vs. Manchester United
Feb. 25   FC Porto 2 . . . . .Manchester United 1
Mar. 9   Manchester United 1 . . . . .FC Porto 1
FC Porto wins 3-2 on aggregate

Real Sociedad vs. Lyon
Feb. 25   Real Sociedad 0 . . . . .Lyon 1
Mar. 9   Lyon 1 . . . . .Real Sociedad 0
Lyon wins 2-0 on aggregate

Chelsea vs. Stuttgart
Feb. 24   Stuttgart 0 . . . . .Chelsea 1
Mar. 9   Chelsea 0 . . . . .Stuttgart 0
Chelsea wins 1-0 on aggregate

Real Madrid vs. Bayern Munich
Feb. 24   Bayern Munich 1 . . . . .Real Madrid 1
Mar. 10   Real Madrid 1 . . . . .Bayern Munich 0
Real Madrid wins 2-1 on aggregate

Sparta vs. AC Milan
Feb. 24   Sparta 0 . . . . .AC Milan 0
Mar. 10   AC Milan 4 . . . . .Sparta 1
AC Milan wins 4-1 on aggregate

Deportivo vs. Juventus
Feb. 25   Deportivo 1 . . . . .Juventus 0
Mar. 9   Juventus 0 . . . . .Deportivo 1
Deportivo wins 2-0 on aggregate

Lokomotiv Moskva vs. Monaco
Feb. 24   Lokomotiv 2 . . . . .Monaco 1
Mar. 9   Monaco 1 . . . . .Lokomotiv 0
Aggregate tied 2-2, Monaco advances on away goals.

Quarterfinals
Two legs, total goals; home team listed first.

FC Porto vs. Lyon
Mar. 23 FC Porto 2 . . . . .Lyon 0
Apr. 7   Lyon 2 .FC Porto 2
FC Porto wins 4-2 on aggregate

Chelsea vs. Arsenal
Mar. 24 Chelsea 1 . . . . .Arsenal 1
Apr. 6   Arsenal 1 . . . . .Chelsea 2
Chelsea wins 3-2 on aggregate

Real Madrid vs. Monaco
Mar. 24 Real Madrid 4 . . . . .Monaco 2
Apr. 6   Monaco 3 . . . . .Real Madrid 1
Aggregate tied 5-5, Monaco advances on away goals

AC Milan vs. Deportivo
Mar. 23 AC Milan 4 . . . . .Deportivo 1
Apr. 7   Deportivo 4 . . . . .AC Milan 0
Deportivo wins 5-4 on aggregate

Semifinals
Two legs, total goals; home team listed first.

Monaco vs. Chelsea
Apr. 20 Monaco 3 . . . . .Chelsea 1
May 4   Chelsea 2 . . . . .Monaco 2
Monaco wins 5-3 on aggregate

FC Porto vs. Deportivo
Apr. 21 FC Porto 0 . . . . .Deportivo 0
May 4   Deportivo 0 . . . . .FC Porto 1
FC Porto wins 1-0 on aggregate

Final
FC Porto vs. Monaco
May 26, 2004 at Arena Auf Schalke Stadium, Gelsenkirchen, Germany.
Attendance: 52,000

FC Porto 3 . . . . .Monaco 0

Goals: FC Porto—Carlos Alberto 39th, Deco Souza 71st, Dmitri Alenichev 75th)

2004 UEFA Cup
Two-leg Quarterfinals and Semifinals, one-game Final; home team listed first.

Final Eight: Bordeaux (France), Celtic (Scotland), Internazionale (Italy), Marseille (France), Newcastle (England), PSV Eindhoven (Netherlands), Valencia (Spain), Villarreal (Spain).

Quarterfinals

Bordeaux vs. Valencia
Apr. 8   Bordeaux 1 . . . . .Valencia 2
Apr. 14 Valencia 2 . . . . .Bordeaux 1
Valencia wins 4-2 on aggregate

Celtic vs. Villarreal
Apr. 8   Celtic 1 . . . . .Villarreal 1
Apr. 14 Villarreal 2 . . . . .Celtic 0
Villarreal wins 3-1 on aggregate

Marseille vs. Internazionale
Apr. 8   Marseille 1 . . . . .Internazionale 0
Apr. 14 Internazionale 0 . . . . .Marseille 1
Marseille wins 2-0 on aggregate

PSV Eindhoven vs. Newcastle
Apr. 8   PSV Eindhoven 1 . . . . .Newcastle 1
Apr. 14 Newcastle 2 . . . . .PSV Eindhoven 1
Newcastle wins 3-2 on aggregate

Semifinals

Newcastle vs. Marseille
Apr 22 Newcastle 0 . . . . .Marseille 0
May 6   Marseille 2 . . . . .Newcastle 0
Marseille wins 2-0 on aggregate

Villarreal vs. Valencia
Apr. 22 Villarreal 0 . . . . .Valencia 0
May 6   Valencia 1 . . . . .Villarreal 0
Valencia wins 1-0 on aggregate

Final
Valencia vs. Marseille
May 19 in Gothenburg, Sweden. **Attendance:** 43,000

Valencia 2 . . . . .Marseille 0

Goals: Valencia—Vincente (45th-pen) Mista (58th)

2004 U.S. Open Cup
Dating back to 1914, the U.S. Open Cup is the oldest soccer competition in the United States and is among the oldest in the world. The U.S. Open Cup is a single-elimination tournament open to all amateur and professional teams in the United States. Forty teams competed for the 92-year-old Dewar Cup trophy in the 2004 U.S. Open Cup.

Quarterfinals
Charleston Battery def. Rochester Raging Rhinos, 1-0
Chicago Fire def. Richmond Kickers, 1-0
Minnesota Thunder def. San Jose Earthquakes, on PKs
Kansas City Wizards def. Dallas Burn, 4-2

Semifinals
Chicago Fire def. Charleston Battery, 1-0
Kansas City Wizards def. San Jose Earthquakes, 1-0

Final
Kansas City Wizards def. Chicago Fire, 1-0 (OT)

Major League Soccer
2004 Final Regular Season Standings

Conference champions (*) and playoff qualifiers (†) are noted. Teams receive three points for a win and one for a tie. The GF and GA columns refer to Goals For and Goals Against in regulation play. Number of seasons listed after each head coach refers to current tenure with club through the 2004 season.

Eastern Conference

Team	W	L	T	Pts	GF	GA
*Columbus Crew	12	5	13	49	40	32
†D.C. United	11	10	9	42	43	42
†MetroStars	11	12	7	40	47	49
†N.E. Revolution	8	13	9	33	42	43
Chicago Fire	8	13	9	33	36	44

Head Coaches: Clb—Greg Andrulis (4th season); **DC**—Peter Nowak (1st); **Met**—Bob Bradley (2nd); **NE**—Steve Nicol (4th); **Chi**—Dave Sarachan (2nd).

Western Conference

Team	W	L	T	Pts	GF	GA
*Kansas City Wizards	14	9	7	49	38	30
†Los Angeles Galaxy	11	9	10	43	42	40
†Colorado Rapids	10	9	11	41	29	32
†San Jose Earthquakes	9	10	11	38	41	35
Dallas Burn	10	14	6	36	34	45

Head Coaches: KC—Bob Gansler (6th season); **LA**—Sigi Schmid (6th); **Colo**—Tim Hankinson (4th); **SJ**—Dominic Kinnear (1st); **Dal**—Colin Clarke (2nd).

Leading Scorers

Points

	Gm	G	A	Pts
Pat Noonan, NE	29	11	8	30
Amado Guevara, Met	24	10	10	30
Brian Ching, SJ	25	12	4	28
Jaime Moreno, DC	27	7	14	28
Eddie Johnson, Dal	26	12	3	27
Josh Wolff, KC	26	10	7	27
Davy Arnaud, KC	30	9	8	26
Damani Ralph, Chi	26	11	3	25
Edson Buddle, Clb	24	11	2	24
Carlos Ruiz, LA	20	11	2	24
John Wolyniec, Met	30	10	3	23
Jeff Cunningham, Clb	30	9	4	22
Landon Donovan, SJ	23	6	10	22
Alecko Eskandarian, DC	24	10	2	22
Steve Ralston, NE	30	7	8	22
Eddie Gaven, Met	29	7	7	21
Taylor Twellman, NE	23	9	1	19

Goals

	Gm	No
Brian Ching, SJ	25	12
Eddie Johnson, Dal	26	12
Edson Buddle, Clb	24	11
Pat Noonan, NE	29	11
Damani Ralph, Chi	26	11
Carlos Ruiz, LA	20	11
Alecko Eskandarian, DC	24	10
Amado Guevara, Met	24	10
Josh Wolff, KC	26	10
John Wolyniec, Met	30	10

Assists

	Gm	No
Jaime Moreno, DC	27	14
Jose Cancela, NE	25	10
Landon Donovan, SJ	23	10
Simon Elliott, Clb	27	10
Amado Guevara, Met	24	10
Dema Kovalenko, DC	25	10
Ronnie O'Brien, Dal	29	10
Andy Williams, Chi	25	9
six players tied with 8 each.		

Shots

	Gm	No
Damani Ralph, Chi	26	89
Eddie Johnson, Dal	26	75
Pat Noonan, NE	29	75
Taylor Twellman, NE	23	70
Andreas Herzog, LA	27	68
Ronnie O'Brien, Dal	29	67
Edson Buddle, Clb	24	65
Amado Guevara, Met	24	65
Jeff Cunningham, Clb	30	63
Carlos Ruiz, LA	20	63

Shots on Goal

	Gm	No
Taylor Twellman, NE	23	39
Pat Noonan, NE	29	37
Damani Ralph, Chi	26	36
Carlos Ruiz, LA	20	36
Josh Wolff, KC	26	33
Alecko Eskandarian, DC	24	32
Eddie Johnson, Dal	26	32
Edson Buddle, Clb	24	31
Amado Guevara, Met	24	30
Ronnie O'Brien, Dal	29	30

Game-Winning Goals

	Gm	GWG
Eddie Johnson, Dal	26	7
Edson Buddle, Clb	24	5
Alecko Eskandarian, DC	24	5
John Wolyniec, Met	30	5
Jovan Kirovski, LA	24	4
Brian Ching, SJ	25	3
Jordan Cila, Col	21	3
Brian Ching, SJ	25	3
Amado Guevara, Met	24	3
Diego Gutierrez, KC	28	3
Damani Ralph, Chi	26	3
Taylor Twellman, NE	23	3
Josh Wolff, KC	26	3

MLS All-Star Game
East 3, West 2

Played Saturday, July 31, 2004 at RFK Stadium in Washington, D.C.; **Attendance:** 21,378; **Coaches:** Peter Nowak, East and Sigi Schmid, West; **MVP:** Amado Guevara, East (MetroStars).

	1	2	Final
West	1	1	—2
East	2	1	—3

Scoring

1st Half: EAST—Amdao Guevara (Damani Ralph) 20th; EAST—Guevara (penalty kick) 22nd; WEST—Brian Ching (Richard Mulrroney, Landon Donovan) 43rd.

2nd Half: EAST—Alecko Eskandarian (Guevara, Shalrie Joseph) 74th. WEST—Jason Kreis (Donovan) 89th.

Fouls Committed

	Gm	No
Simo Valakari, Dal	26	73
Brian Mullan, SJ	28	68
Bryan Namoff, DC	27	62
Marcelo Saragosa, LA	26	62
Amadao Guevara, Met	24	58
Ben Olsen, DC	25	58
Kyle Beckerman, Col	29	57
Diego Gutierrez, KC	28	53
Ronnie O'Brien, Dal	29	53
Davy Arnaud, KC	30	52

Fouls Suffered

	Gm	No
Davy Arnaud, KC	30	111
Richard Mulrooney, SJ	30	89
Kyle Martino, Clb	29	84
Andy Williams, Chi	25	83
Eddie Gaven, Met	29	79
Jose Cancela, NE	25	73
Brian Ching, SJ	25	73
Brian Mullan, SJ	28	69
Clint Dempsey, NE	24	68
Marcelo Saragosa, LA	26	60

Offsides

	Gm	Offs
Taylor Twellman, NE	23	35
Jean Philippe Peguero, Col	18	34
Damani Ralph, Chi	26	28
Jeff Cunningham, Clb	30	27
Eddie Johnson, Dal	26	27
Davy Arnaud, KC	30	25
Carlos Ruiz, LA	20	25
Chris Henderson, Col	29	23
Josh Wolff, KC	26	22

Cautions

	Gm	No
Alecko Eskandarian, D.C.	24	8
Chris Gbandi, Dal	23	8
Amado Guevara, Met	24	8
Diego Gutierrez, KC	28	8
Ryan Suarez, LA	26	8
Simo Valakari, Dal	26	8

Eight tied with seven each.

Corner Kicks

	Gm	CKs
Jose Cancela, NE	25	118
Andreas Herzog, LA	27	97
Brad Davis, Dal	29	91
Antonio de la Torre, Col	28	87
Simon Elliott, Clb	27	87
Richard Mulrooney, SJ	30	87
Jeff Agoos, SJ	24	79
Chris Klein, KC	19	64
Earnie Stewart, DC	26	59
Mike Magee, Met	22	58

Minutes Played

	Mins
Joe Cannon, Col	2700
Jim Curtin, Chi	2700
Richard Mulrooney, SJ	2700
Steve Ralston, NE	2700
Kevin Hartman, LA	2655
Davy Arnaud, KC	2626
Nat Borchers, Col	2610
Jon Busch, Clb	2610
Jimmy Conrad, KC	2610
Chris Leitch, Met	2610

2004 MLS Attendance

Number in parentheses indicates last year's rank.

	Gm	Total	Avg
Los Angeles (1)	15	357,137	23,809
D.C. United (6)	15	258,484	17,232
MetroStars (4)	15	257,923	17,195
Chicago (8)	15	257,295	17,153
Columbus (3)	15	253,079	16,872
Kansas City (5)	15	222,235	14,816
Colorado (2)	15	212,925	14,195
San Jose (9)	15	195,015	13,001
New England (7)	15	183,385	12,226
Dallas (10)	15	136,319	9,088
TOTAL	150	2,333,797	15,559

Leading Goaltenders

Goals Against Average

	Gm	Min	Shts	Svs	GAA	W-L-T
Nick Rimando, DC	13	1170	39	26	**1.00**	7-3-3
Tony Meola, KC	21	1890	98	76	**1.05**	9-7-5
Joe Cannon, Col	30	2700	182	150	**1.07**	10-9-11
Jon Busch, Clb	29	2610	163	132	**1.07**	12-5-12
Pat Onstad, SJ	25	2250	130	98	**1.28**	7-8-10
Kevin Hartman, LA	30	2655	156	117	**1.32**	11-8-10
Matt Reis, NE	24	2115	129	97	**1.36**	7-10-7
Henry Ring, NE	24	2520	168	128	**1.43**	7-12-9
Jeff Cassar, Dal	19	1632	92	65	**1.49**	7-8-4
Scott Garlick, Dal	12	1068	70	52	**1.52**	3-6-2
Jonny Walker, Met	28	2520	144	99	**1.61**	10-11-7
Troy Perkins, DC	16	1440	78	52	**1.63**	4-6-6

Save Percentage

	Svs	SOG	SV Pct
Joe Cannon, Col	150	187	80.2
Jon Busch, Clb	132	169	78.1
Henry Ring, Chi	128	170	75.3
Bo Oshoniyi, KC	42	56	75.0
Tony Meola, KC	76	102	74.5
Pat Onstad, SJ	98	132	74.2
Matt Reis, NE	97	134	72.4

Saves

	Gm	No
Joe Cannon, Col	30	150
Jon Busch, Clb	29	132
Henry Ring, Chi	28	128
Kevin Hartman, LA	30	117
Jonny Walker, Met	28	99

Shutouts

	Gm	No
Jon Busch, Clb	29	10
Joe Cannon, Col	30	10
Kevin Hartman, LA	30	7
Tony Meola, KC	21	7
Henry Ring, Chi	28	7

Catches & Punches

	Gm	C/P
Joe Cannon, Col	30	126
Jon Busch, Clb	29	124
Matt Reis, NE	24	110
Tony Meola, KC	21	107
Jeff Cassar, Dal	19	105
Pat Onstad, SJ	25	101
Kevin Hartman, LA	30	96

Major League Soccer (Cont.)
Team-by-Team Statistics
Players who played with more than one club during the season are listed with final team.

Eastern Conference
Chicago Fire

	Pos	Gm	Min	G	A	Pts
Damani Ralph	F	26	2250	11	3	25
Andy Williams	M	25	2023	4	9	17
Nate Jaqua	F/M	26	1836	4	4	12
Justin Mapp	M	24	1627	3	4	10
Ante Razov	F	13	996	4	2	10
Chris Armas	M	21	1821	1	7	9
Andy Herron	F	4	310	4	0	8
Dipsy Selolwane	F	19	627	2	0	4
DaMarcus Beasley	M	15	1290	0	3	3
Scott Buete	M	13	702	0	2	2
Craig Capano	M	13	440	1	0	2
Kelly Gray	D/M	25	2112	1	0	2
Logan Pause	M/D	21	1482	0	2	2
C.J. Brown	D	24	2130	0	1	1
Jim Curtin	D	30	2700	0	1	1
Orlando Perez	M/D	17	1075	0	1	1
Evan Whitfield	M/D	23	1655	0	1	1
Alexandre Boucicaut	M	5	164	0	0	0
Chris Carrieri	F	1	34	0	0	0
Denny Clanton	D	10	500	0	0	0
Leonard Griffin	D	9	330	0	0	0
Sumed Ibrahim	M	3	82	0	0	0
Jesse Marsch	M	10	681	0	0	0

Goalkeepers	Gm	Min	W-L-T	Shts	Svs	GAA
Henry Ring	28	2520	7-12-9	7	128	1.43
D.J. Countess	2	180	1-1-0	0	4	2.00

Columbus Crew

	Pos	Gm	Min	G	A	Pts
Edson Buddle	F	24	1721	11	2	24
Jeff Cunningham	F	30	1856	9	4	22
Ross Paule	M	25	2059	7	2	16
Kyle Martino	M	29	2301	5	2	12
Simon Elliott	M	27	2353	0	10	10
Duncan Oughton	M/F	28	2020	2	1	5
Tony Sanneh	M	6	513	2	1	5
Frankie Hejduk	D/M	20	1644	2	0	4
Manny Lagos	M	18	766	1	2	4
Michael Ritch	F	12	397	1	1	3
Eric Denton	M/D	18	1310	0	2	2
Chris Wingert	M	22	1488	0	2	2
Chad Marshall	D	22	1488	0	2	2
Danny Szetela	M	8	374	0	1	1
David Testo	F	16	443	0	1	1
Nelson Akwari	D	19	1400	0	0	0
Devin Barclay	F	3	72	0	0	0
Robin Fraser	D	28	2520	0	0	0
Stephen Herdsman	D	8	675	0	0	0
Brian Maisonneuve	M	9	427	0	0	0
Erick Scott	F	6	143	0	0	0
Jamal Sutton	F	1	5	0	0	0
Dante Washington	F	1	19	0	0	0

Goalkeepers	Gm	Min	W-L-T	Shts	Svs	GAA
Jon Busch	29	2610	12-5-12	10	132	1.07
Matt Jordan	1	90	0-0-1	0	5	1.00

MetroStars

	Pos	Gm	Min	G	A	Pts
Amado Guevara	M	24	2110	10	10	30
John Wolyniec	F	30	2051	10	3	23
Eddie Gaven	M	29	2578	7	7	21
Cornell Glen	F	18	966	6	2	14
Fabian Taylor	F	21	883	5	1	11
Mike Magee	F/M	22	1536	3	4	10
Sergio Galvan Rey	F	20	871	2	1	5
Mark Lisi	M	11	695	0	4	4
Ricardo Clark	M	26	1769	1	1	3
Jeff Parke	D	28	2409	1	1	3
Joselito Vaca	M	21	1673	1	1	3
Kenny Arena	D	10	707	1	0	2
Chris Leitch	D	29	2610	0	2	2
Craig Ziadie	M	15	1289	0	2	2
Gilberto Flores	M	7	451	0	1	1
Tenywa Bonseu	M	14	1164	0	0	0
Pablo Brenes	M/D	14	709	0	0	0
Eddie Pope	D	22	1928	0	0	0
Tim Regan	D/M	12	578	0	0	0
Seth Stammler	D	1	1	0	0	0

Goalkeepers	Gm	Min	W-L-T	Shts	Svs	GAA
Jonny Walker	28	2520	10-11-7	5	99	1.61
Zach Wells	2	180	1-1-0	0	4	2.00

D.C. United

	Pos	Gm	Min	G	A	Pts
Jaime Moreno	F	27	2279	7	14	28
Alecko Eskandarian	F	24	1627	10	2	22
Dema Kovalenko	M	25	2163	2	10	14
Freddy Adu	F	30	1440	5	3	13
Ben Olsen	M	25	2046	3	4	10
Earnie Stewart	M	26	2093	3	4	10
Christian Gomez	M	9	582	4	0	8
Joshua Gros	M	29	2087	1	4	6
Ronald Cerritos	F	10	545	2	1	5
Ryan Nelsen	D	17	1417	2	0	4
Bobby Convey	M	10	823	0	3	3
Bryan Namoff	D	27	2384	0	2	2
Mike Petke	D	26	2027	1	0	2
Brian Carroll	M	30	2438	0	1	1
Kevin Ara	M	6	114	0	0	0
Ezra Hendrickson	D	12	787	0	0	0
Nana Kuffor	F	5	90	0	0	0
Brandon Prideaux	D	23	1458	0	0	0
Santino Quaranta	M	1	23	0	0	0
David Stokes	D	11	410	0	0	0
Jason Thompson	F	1	60	0	0	0

Goalkeepers	Gm	Min	W-L-T	Shts	Svs	GAA
Troy Perkins	16	1440	4-6-6	3	52	1.62
Nick Rimando	13	1170	7-3-3	4	26	1.00
Doug Warren	1	90	0-1-0	0	6	3.00

New England Revolution

	Pos	Gm	Min	G	A	Pts
Pat Noonan	F	29	2545	11	8	30
Steve Ralston	M	30	2700	7	8	22
Taylor Twellman	F	23	2050	9	1	19
Jose Cancela	M	25	1957	3	10	16
Clint Dempsey	M/F	24	2024	7	1	15
Richie Baker	M	20	1052	0	6	6
Andy Dorman	M	20	365	2	1	5
Felix Brillant	M/F	19	856	1	2	4
Jay Heaps	D	28	2415	1	2	4
Shalrie Joseph	M	23	2032	0	3	3
Joe Franchino	M/D	20	1693	1	0	2
Brian Kamler	M/D	22	1653	0	2	2
Joe-Max Moore	F	3	246	0	2	2
Marshall Leonard	D	25	1992	0	1	1
Steve Howey	D	3	193	0	0	0
Avery John	D	21	1808	0	0	0
Rusty Pierce	D	14	1179	0	0	0
Luke Vercollone	M	1	60	0	0	0

Goalkeepers	Gm	Min	W-L-T	Shts	Svs	GAA
Matt Reis	24	2115	7-10-7	3	97	1.33
Adin Brown	7	585	1-3-2	1	39	1.57

Western Conference

Colorado Rapids

	Pos	Gm	Min	G	A	Pts
Jean Phillipe Peguero	F	18	1389	7	4	18
Chris Henderson	M	29	2562	3	5	11
Mark Chung	M	22	1914	3	4	10
Jordan Cila	M	21	1310	4	2	10
John Spencer	F	22	1752	4	1	9
Matt Crawford	D/M	30	2534	1	4	6
Nat Borchers	D	29	2610	2	1	5
Antonio de La Torre	D	28	2409	0	5	5
Alberto Delgado	F	13	742	1	3	5
Kyle Beckerman	M	29	2241	1	2	4
Seth Trembly	M/D	24	761	1	1	3
Zizi Roberts	F	5	363	1	0	2
Joey DiGiamarino	M	8	413	0	1	1
Ritchie Kotschau	D	28	2351	0	1	1
Rey Angel Martinez	F	7	314	0	1	1
Ricky Lewis	D	5	289	0	0	0
Pablo Mastroeni	D/M	17	1467	0	0	0
Darryl Powell	M	13	1013	0	0	0
Gary Sullivan	D	16	339	0	0	0

Goalkeepers	Gm	Min	W-L-T	Shts	Svs	GAA
Joe Cannon	30	2700	10-9-11	10	150	1.07

Dallas Burn

	Pos	Gm	Min	G	A	Pts
Eddie Johnson	F	26	2269	12	3	27
Toni Nhleko	F	23	1186	6	2	14
Ronnie O'Brien	M	29	2581	2	10	14
Jason Kreis	F	25	1703	5	2	12
Oscar Pareja	M	24	1096	1	6	8
Brad Davis	M	29	1945	2	2	6
Bobby Rhine	F	19	693	2	2	6
Simo Valakari	M	26	2297	1	4	6
Eric Quill	M	23	1377	1	3	5
Matt Behncke	D	17	1239	1	0	2
Steve Jolley	D	28	2428	1	0	2
Chris Gbandi	D	23	1771	0	1	1
Cory Gibbs	D	21	1850	0	1	1
Carey Talley	D/M	23	1688	0	1	1
Clarence Goodson	D	5	247	0	0	0
Ramon Nunez	M	8	107	0	0	0
Milton Reyes	D/M	12	828	0	0	0
Philip Salyer	D	17	1407	0	0	0
Jordan Stone	M	5	145	0	0	0

Goalkeepers	Gm	Min	W-L-T	Shts	Svs	GAA
Jeff Cassar	19	1632	7-8-4	4	65	1.42
Scott Garlick	12	1068	3-6-2	4	52	1.50

Kansas City Wizards

	Pos	Gm	Min	G	A	Pts
Josh Wolff	F	26	2252	10	7	27
Davy Arnaud	M	30	2626	9	8	26
Chris Klein	M	19	1694	4	8	16
Diego Gutierrez	D/M	28	2520	3	4	10
Matt Talylor	M	17	524	3	1	7
Jack Jewsbury	M	22	1406	2	2	6
Jose Burciaga Jr.	D	24	1876	1	1	3
Jimmy Conrad	D	29	2610	1	0	2
Francisco Gomez	M	23	1097	1	0	2
Taylor Graham	D	17	750	1	0	2
Igor Simutenkov	M/F	9	456	1	0	2
Shavar Thomas	D	25	1880	1	0	2
Kerry Zavagnin	M	24	2160	0	2	2
Nick Garcia	D	26	2295	0	1	-1
Justin Detter	F	6	162	0	0	0
Preki	M	2	90	0	0	0
Vuk Rasovic	D	1	45	0	0	0
Khari Stephenson	M	3	44	0	0	0
Diego Walsh	M/F	15	688	0	0	0
Alex Zotinca	D	25	1779	0	0	0

Goalkeepers	Gm	Min	W-L-T	Shts	Svs	GAA
Tony Meola	21	1890	9-7-5	7	76	1.05
Bo Oshoniyi	9	810	5-2-2	5	42	0.89

Los Angeles Galaxy

	Pos	Gm	Min	G	A	Pts
Carlos Ruiz	F	20	1587	11	2	24
Jovan Kirovski	F	24	1984	8	2	18
Andreas Herzog	M/F	27	2048	4	7	15
Alejandro Moreno	F	25	1297	6	2	14
Joseph Ngwenya	F/M	22	880	4	2	10
Sasha Victorine	M	26	2265	3	3	9
Chris Albright	M/F	24	2111	1	6	8
Ned Grabavoy	M	15	928	1	3	5
Cobi Jones	M/F	23	1751	0	5	5
Tyrone Marshall	D	18	1449	2	1	5
Arturo Torres	D	18	599	1	2	4
Ricky Lewis	D	13	855	0	2	2
Paul Broome	D/M	22	1758	0	1	1
Marcelo Saragosa	M	26	2123	0	1	1
Peter Vagenas	M	12	913	0	1	1
Chris Aloisi	D	4	281	0	0	0
Danny Califf	D	13	855	0	0	0
Josh Gardner	M	2	25	0	0	0
Guillermo Gonzalez	M	6	114	0	0	0
Alan Gordon	F	3	142	0	0	0
Hong Myung-Bo	D	13	858	0	0	0
Ryan Suarez	D	26	2154	0	0	0
Scot Thompson	D	1	1	0	0	0

Goalkeepers	Gm	Min	W-L-T	Shts	Svs	GAA
Kevin Hartman	30	2655	11-8-10	7	117	1.30
Dan Popik	1	45	0-1-0	0	2	1.00

San Jose Earthquakes

	Pos	Gm	Min	G	A	Pts
Brian Ching	F	25	1954	12	4	28
Landon Donovan	F/M	23	2018	6	10	22
Brian Mullan	M/F	28	2408	3	8	14
Dwayne De Rosario	F	21	1214	5	3	13
Ronnie Ekelund	M	26	2018	4	3	11
Richard Mulrooney	M	30	2700	1	8	10
Ramiro Corrales	M/D	29	2475	3	1	7
Jeff Agoos	D	24	2152	1	4	6
Chris Brown	M/F	11	561	2	1	5
Craig Waibel	D	23	2005	1	1	3
Arturo Alvarez	M/F	11	374	1	0	2
Troy Dayak	D	16	1367	1	0	2
Ryan Cochrane	D	18	1459	0	1	1
Ian Russell	M/F	22	1091	0	1	1
Tighe Dombrowski	M	4	44	0	0	0
Todd Dunivant	D	16	1212	0	0	0
Wes Hart	D	18	1180	0	0	0
Eddie Robinson	D	8	458	0	0	0
Jamil Walker	F	10	237	0	0	0

Goalkeepers	Gm	Min	W-L-T	Shts	Svs	GAA
Pat Onstad	25	2250	7-8-10	6	98	1.28
Jon Conway	5	450	2-2-1	2	15	0.60

A-League

The A-League serves as a minor league system for Major League Soccer. The division II outdoor league is part of the United Systems of Independent Soccer Leagues (USISL) and is recognized by U.S. Soccer. MLS and the USISL have an agreement where MLS teams can assign players to the A-League and call-up A-League players when desired. Conference champions (†) and playoff qualifiers (*) are noted.

2004 Final Standings

Western Conference

Team	W	T	L	GF	GA	Pts
†Portland Timbers	18	3	7	58	30	57
*Vancouver Whitecaps	14	5	9	38	29	47
*Minnesota Thunders	13	6	9	33	23	45
*Seattle Sounders	13	4	11	40	34	43
Milwaukee Wave United	12	4	12	44	48	40
Edmonton FC	4	6	18	19	56	18
Calgary Mustangs	4	6	18	30	51	18

Eastern Conference

Team	W	T	L	GF	GA	Pts
†Montreal Impact	17	5	6	36	15	56
*Richmond Kickers	17	3	8	44	29	54
*Syracuse Salty Dogs	15	5	8	40	29	50
*Rochester Raging Rhinos	15	3	10	36	32	48
Atlanta Silverbacks	14	3	11	41	38	45
Virginia Beach Mariners	11	3	14	43	41	36
Toronto Lynx	10	2	16	38	50	32
Charleston Battery	7	6	15	30	39	27
Puerto Rico Islanders	5	6	17	22	48	21

Playoffs

First Round (Total Goals)

Western Conference

Portland vs. Seattle

Sept. 1	Portland 2, Seattle 1	at Portland
Sept. 5	Seattle 2, Portland 0 (OT)	at Seattle
	Seattle wins 3-2 on aggregate	

Minnesota vs. Vancouver

Sept. 3	Vancouver 2, Minnesota 0	at Vancouver
Sept. 5	Vancouver 1, Minnesota 0	at Minnesota
	Seattle wins 3-0 on aggregate	

Eastern Conference

Richmond vs. Syracuse

Sept. 3	Syracuse 1, Richmond 0	at Richmond
Sept. 5	Richmond 2, Syracuse 1	at Syracuse
	Aggregate tied 2-2, Syracuse wins 5-4 on penalty kicks	

Montreal vs. Rochester

Sept. 3	Montreal 1, Rochester 0	at Rochester
Sept. 5	Montreal 1, Rochester 0	at Montreal
	Montreal wins 2-0 on aggregate	

Semifinals (Total Goals)

Western Conference

Vancouver vs. Seattle

Sept. 10	Seattle 1, Vancouver 0	at Seattle
Sept. 12	Seattle 1, Vancouver 1	at Vancouver
	Seattle wins 2-1 on aggregate	

Eastern Conference

Montreal vs. Syracuse

Sept. 10	Montreal 2, Syracuse 0	at Syracuse
Sept. 12	Montreal 1, Syracuse 1	at Montreal
	Montreal wins 3-1 on aggregate	

Final

Sept. 18 at Claude-Robillard Stadium, Montreal, Canada
Attendance: 13,648

Montreal 2 . . . . Seattle 0

Goals: MON—Mauricio Vincello (Ze Roberto), 33rd minute; MON—Frederick Commodore (Nevio Pizzolitto), 78th

---

WUSA Festivals

The Women's United Soccer Association (WUSA) ceased operations indefinitely following its 2003 season but in an effort to "keep the dream alive," the league held two soccer "festivals" in 2004 at separate locations (Blaine, Minn. and Carson, Calif.) featuring many of the league's marquee players. Each of the league's eight teams appeared in exhibition matches.

Blaine, Minnesota

	1st	2nd	F
New York Power	0	2	2
Atlanta Beat	0	2	2

Scoring: ATL-Maribel Dominguez (Charmaine Hooper) 73rd minute; NY-Shannon Boxx (Many Clemens) 74th; NY-Boxx (penalty kick) 80th; ATL-Hooper (penalty) 90th.

	1st	2nd	F
Washington Freedom	3	0	3
Boston Breakers	1	2	3

Scoring: WAS-Mia Hamm (Angela Hucles) 3rd minute; WAS-Hamm (unassisted) 34th; BOS-Marinette Pinchon (Kristine Lilly) 44th; WAS-Abby Wambach (unassisted) 45th; BOS-Sarah Popper (Rebekah Splaine); BOS-Kelly Smith (Splaine) 82nd

Carson, California

	1st	2nd	F
San Diego Spirit	0	2	2
Carolina Courage	0	1	1

Scoring: SD-Angela Hucles (Julie Fleeting) 27th minute; SD-Abby Wambach (Kerry Connors) 61st; CAR-Charmaine Hooper (penalty) 67th.

	1st	2nd	F
San Jose CyberRays	0	0	0
Philadelphia Charge	1	1	2

Scoring: PHI-Marinette Pichon (Kelly Smith) 27th minute; PHI-Kristine Lilly (Pichon) 52nd.

Colleges
MEN
2003 Final Soccer America Top 25

Final 2003 regular season poll including games through Nov. 16. Conducted by the national weekly *Soccer America* and released on Nov. 17. Listing includes records through conference playoffs as well as NCAA tournament record and team lost to. Teams in **bold** type went on to reach NCAA Final Four. All tournament games decided by penalty kicks are considered ties.

	Nov. 16 Record	NCAA Recap		Nov. 16 Record	NCAA Recap
1 UCLA	18-1-1	2-1 (Indiana)	14 North Carolina	12-3-4	0-1 (Coas. Carolina)
2 **Maryland**	17-2-1	3-1 (St. John's)	15 Virginia Tech	14-4-2	1-1 (VCU)
3 Notre Dame	15-3-3	1-0-1 (Michigan)	16 CS-Northridge	14-3-2	0-0-1 (Fla. Int'l)
4 Wake Forest	15-4-0	0-1 (Virginia)	17 SMU	13-6-2	0-0-1 (Santa Clara)
5 **Indiana**	12-3-5	5-0	18 Oregon St.	13-6-0	0-1 (Portland)
6 **Santa Clara**	13-3-3	3-1-1 (Indiana)	19 San Diego	12-4-3	0-0-1 (Creighton)
7 **St. John's**	14-5-2	3-1-1 (Indiana)	20 Brown	10-3-3	0-1 (St. Peter's)
8 St. Louis	14-5-2	2-1 (Maryland)	21 Akron	14-4-2	1-1 (Maryland)
9 VCU	16-4-0	1-1 (Indiana)	22 Virginia	9-9-2	2-1 (Creighton)
10 Old Dominion	14-3-1	1-1 (Maryland)	23 UC-Santa Barbara	15-4-1	1-1 (St. John's)
11 Florida International	13-4-2	1-1-1 (Indiana)	24 Hartwick	15-2-1	DNP
12 Coastal Carolina	18-2-0	2-1 (Santa Clara)	25 Tulsa	12-5-2	1-1 (UCLA)
13 Washington	12-4-2	1-1 (St. Louis)			

NCAA Division I Tournament

First Round (Nov. 21 or 22)

at Tulsa 3 .... Oakland 2
at Florida International 3 .... Central Florida 1
at Virginia Tech 3 .... Clemson 3
Va. Tech advanced on PKs
at Kentucky 0 .... Cincinnati 0
Kentucky advanced on PKs
at Wisc-Milwaukee 4 .... Western Michigan 1
St. Peter's 2 .... at Brown 0
at Santa Clara 1 .... SMU 1
Santa Clara advanced on PKs
at Coastal Carolina 3 .... Davidson 0
at Virginia 2 .... Seton Hall 0
at Creighton 6 .... UMKC 0
at California 2 .... San Jose St. 0
at Connecticut 3 .... Rhode Island 0
Binghamton 1 .... at Fairleigh Dickinson 0
Portland 3 .... at Oregon St. 2
at Rutgers 3 .... Lafayette 1
at Old Dominion 6 .... N.C. State 3

Second Round (Nov. 26)

at UCLA 3 .... Tulsa 2
at Florida International 1 .... CS-Northridge 1
Florida International advanced on PKs
at Virginia Commonwealth 5 ..... Virginia Tech 2
at Indiana .... 2 OT .... Kentucky 1
at Notre Dame 4 .... Wisc-Milwaukee 1
at Michigan 6 .... St. Peter's 2
Santa Clara 1 .... OT ..at Loyola Marymount 0
Coastal Carolina 3 .... at North Carolina 0
Virginia 2 .... at Wake Forest 0
Creighton 1 .... at San Diego 0
Creighton advanced on PKs
at UC-Santa Barbara 2 .... California 0
at St. John's 0 .... at Connecticut 0
St. John's advanced on PKs
at St. Louis 1 .... OT .... Binghamton 0
at Washington 1 .... Portland 0
at Akron 3 .... Rutgers 2
at Maryland 2 .... Old Dominion 1

Third Round (Nov. 30)

at UCLA 2 .... Florida International 0
at Indiana 5 .... Virginia Commonwealth 0
Michigan 1 .... at Notre Dame 1
Michigan advanced on PKs
at Santa Clara 3 .... OT ..... Coastal Carolina 2
Creighton 3 .... at Virginia 1
at St. John's 3 ...... 2 OT .... UC-Santa Barbara 2
at St. Louis 3 .... OT .... Washington 2
at Maryland 1 .... Akron 0

Quarterfinals (Dec. 6 or 7)

Indiana 2 .... at UCLA 1
at Santa Clara 3 .... Michigan 1
at Maryland 4 .... St. Louis 2
at St. John's 3 .... Creighton 2

2003 College Cup
at Columbus, Ohio (Dec. 12 & 14)

Semifinals

St. John's 1 .... Maryland 0
Indiana 1 .... 2 OT .... Santa Clara 0

Championship

Indiana 2 .... St. John's 1

Scoring
1st Half: Indiana—Ned Grabavoy (16th min), Jacob Peterson (20th)
2nd Half: St. John's—Ashley Kozicki (78th)
Attendance: 5,330
Final records: Indiana (15-3-5); St. John's (17-6-3).
Offensive MVP: Jacob Peterson, Indiana, F
Defensive MVP: Jay Nolly, Indiana, GK

All-Tournament Team: GK—Jay Nolly, Ind.; D—Jed Zayner, Ind.; Seth Stammler, Maryland; Christopher Wingert, St. John's; Drew Shinabarger, Ind.; M—Will Weatherley, Santa Clara; Josh Tudela, Ind.; Danny O'Rourke, Ind.; Sumed Ibrahim, Maryland; F—Jacob Peterson, Ind.; Ned Grabavoy, Ind.

WOMEN
2003 Final *Soccer America* Top 25

Final 2003 regular season poll including games through Nov. 9. Conducted by the national weekly *Soccer America* and released on Nov. 10. Listing includes records through conference playoffs as well as NCAA tournament record and team lost to. Teams in **bold** type went on to reach NCAA Final Four. All tournament games decided by penalty kicks are considered ties.

	Nov. 9 Record	NCAA Recap		Nov. 9 Record	NCAA Recap
1 **North Carolina**	21-0-0	6-0	14 Arizona St.	12-4-3	1-1 (Santa Clara)
2 UCLA	16-1-3	4-1 (North Carolina)	15 Illinois	16-3-2	0-1 (W. Michigan)
3 Santa Clara	12-3-5	2-1-1 (No. Carolina)	16 Villanova	14-5-3	1-0-2 (BYU)
4 Portland	16-3-1	2-0-1 (Santa Clara)	17 Clemson	11-6-2	0-1 (Georgia)
5 Notre Dame	19-2-1	1-1 (Michigan)	18 Colorado	15-3-1	0-1 (BYU)
6 **Florida St.**	13-7-1	4-1 (UConn)	19 Utah	16-2-1	0-0-1 (Idaho St.)
7 Penn St.	16-2-3	3-1 (UCLA)	20 Cal Poly	18-1-2	0-1 (Arizona St.)
8 Florida	16-3-2	3-1 (Florida St.)	21 Texas A&M	12-5-2	2-1-1 (Penn St.)
9 West Virginia	15-3-2	2-1 (Florida St.)	22 Maryland	11-8-1	0-0-1 (Rutgers)
10 Virginia	12-5-2	0-0-2 (Villanova)	23 **Connecticut**	10-5-3	5-1 (North Carolina)
11 Tennessee	15-4-2	2-1 (Florida)	24 Pepperdine	13-5-1	1-1 (UCLA)
12 Duke	13-6-1	1-1 (Texas A&M)	25 Washington	11-6-3	0-1 (Nebraska)
13 Boston College	15-2-3	0-1 (C. Conn. St.)			

NCAA Division I Tournament

First Round (Nov. 13 or 14)

at North Carolina 8			High Point 0
NC-Greensboro 2			Wake Forest 1
Purdue 2			DePaul 1
Western Michigan 2			at Illinois 1
Arizona St. 3			Cal Poly 1
at Santa Clara 1			Stanford 0
Nebraska 2			Washington 1
at Portland 1			Denver 0
Rutgers 1			Maryland 1

Rutgers advanced on PKs

at Penn St. 5			Navy 1
Duke 3			Stephen F. Austin 0
at Texas A&M 1			SMU 1

Texas A&M advanced on PKs

Kansas 3			Illinois St. 1
at Missouri 1			Eastern Illinois 0
Pepperdine 1			Southern California 0
at UCLA 2			San Diego 0
Mississippi 1			Texas 0
at Florida 3	2 OT		Central Florida 2
Georgia 2			Clemson 1
at Tennessee 1			Oklahoma 0
Auburn 1			Oklahoma St. 0
at Florida St. 5			Dartmouth 0
Ohio St. 3			Dayton 1
at West Virginia 4			Loyola (Md.) 2
at Virginia 1			William & Mary 1

Virginia advanced on PKs

Villanova 2			Princeton 1
BYU 2			Colorado 0
Idaho St. 0			at Utah 0

Idaho St. advanced on PKs

Connecticut 1			Boston University 0
Central Connecticut St. 1			at Boston College 0
Michigan 1			Oakland 0
at Notre Dame 5			Loyola (Ill.) 0

Second Round (Nov. 15 or 16)

at North Carolina 5			NC-Greensboro 0
Purdue 3			at Western Michigan 1
at Santa Clara 1			Arizona St. 0
at Portland 4			Nebraska 1
at Penn St. 3			Rutgers 1
at Texas A&M 2			Duke 1
Kansas 2			at Missouri 0
at UCLA 2			Pepperdine 0
at Florida 4	2 OT		Mississippi 3
Tennessee 1			Georgia 0
at Florida St. 2			Auburn 1

at West Virginia 3			Ohio St. 0
Villanova 0			at Virginia 0

Villanova advanced on PKs

BYU 2			Idaho St. 0
Connecticut 3	2 OT	Central Connecticut St. 2
Michigan 1			at Notre Dame 0

Third Round (Nov. 21-23)

at North Carolina 7			Purdue 0
Santa Clara 0			Portland 0

Santa Clara advanced on PKs

at Penn St. 3			Texas A&M 0
at UCLA 1			Kansas 0
at Florida 1			Tennessee 0
Florida St. 3	2 OT		at West Virginia 2
BYU 0			Villanova 0

BYU advanced on PKs

Connecticut 5			Michigan 0

Quarterfinals (Nov. 29-Dec. 1)

at North Carolina 3			Santa Clara 0
at UCLA 4			Penn St. 0
Florida St. 2			at Florida 1
at Connecticut 3			BYU 1

2003 College Cup
at Cary, N.C. (Dec. 5 & 7)

Semifinals

Connecticut 2		Florida St. 0
North Carolina 3		UCLA 0

Championship

North Carolina 6		Connecticut 0

Scoring

1st Half: NC—Lindsay Tarpley (8th min.), Lori Chalupny (31st). **2nd Half:** NC—Heather O'Reilly (57th), Maggie Tomecka (59th), O'Reilly (61st), Alyssa Ramsey (90th).

Attendance: 10,042

Final records: No. Carolina (27-0-0); UConn (15-6-3).

Offensive MVP: Heather O'Reilly, NC, F

Defensive MVP: Catherine Reddick, NC, D

All Tournament Team: Lori Chalupny, NC; Jessica Gjertsen, UConn; Kristen Graczyk, UConn; Heather O'Reilly, NC; Nandi Pryce, UCLA; Alyssa Ramsey, NC; Catherine Reddick, NC; Lindsay Tarpley, NC; Maggie Tomecka, NC; India Trotter, Florida St.; Carmen Watley, NC.

2003 Annual Awards

Men's Players of the Year

MAC/Hermann Trophy . . . . . .Chris Wingert, St. John's, D
Soccer America . . . Joseph Ngwenya, Coastal Carolina, F
NCAA Div. II . . . . .Ross Lumsden, Lynn
NCAA Div. III . . . . Joshua Smith, Trinity
NAIA . . . . .Fabricio Cordeceira, Fresno Pacific
JuCo Div. I . . . . .Ramon-Dee L. Bailey, Mercer Co. CC
JuCo Div. III . . . . Jesus Rodriguez, Richland

Women's Players of the Year

MAC/Hermann Trophy .Catherine Reddick, N. Carolina, D
Soccer America . . . . .Lindsay Tarpley, N. Carolina, F/MF
NCAA Div. II . . . . .Laura Hislop, Franklin Pierce
NCAA Div. III . . . . .Renee Neuner, Univ. of Chicago
NAIA . . . . .Karin Sullivan, Westmont College
JuCo Div. I . . . . .Nicole Anderson, Dixie State
JuCo Div. III .Ashely DeAlejandro, Long Beach City College

NSCAA Coaches of the Year

Women's Div. I . . . . .Anson Dorrance, North Carolina
Men's Div. I . . . . Jerry Yeagley, Indiana
Women's Div. II . . . . .Rob King, Kennesaw St.
Men's Div. II . . . . .Mike O'Malley, Chico St.
Women's Div. III . . . . .Tracy Ranieri, Oneonta St.
Men's Div. III . . . . .Lenny Armuth, Drew
Women's NAIA . . . . .Mike Giuliano, Wesmont
Men's NAIA . . . . .Scott Morrissey, Rio Grande
Men's Juco Div. I . . . . .Stephen Peck Jr., East Central
Men's JuCo Div. III . . . . .Sean Worley, Richland
Women's JuCo Div. I . . . . .Linda Huddleston, Dixie St.
Women's JuCo Div. III .Mauricio Ingrassia, Long Beach City

Division I All-America Teams

MEN

The 2003 first team All-America selections of the National Soccer Coaches Association of America (NSCAA). Holdovers from the 2002 NSCAA All-America team are in **bold** type.

GOALKEEPER—Will Hesmer, Wake Forest.

DEFENDERS—**Chris Wingert**, St. John's; Leonard Griffin, UCLA; Trevor McEachron, Old Dominion.

MIDFIELDERS—**Sumed Ibrahim**, Maryland; Scott Buete, Maryland; C.J. Klaas, Washington.

FORWARDS—Adom Crew, Brown; Ned Grabavoy, Indiana; Vedad Ibisevic, St. Louis; Joseph Ngwenya, Coastal Carolina

WOMEN

The 2003 first team All-America selections of the National Soccer Coaches Association of America (NSCAA). Holdovers from the 2002 NSCAA All-America team are in **bold** type.

GOALKEEPER—Leisha Alcia, Illinois.

DEFENDERS—**Catherine Reddick**, North Carolina; **Nandi Pryce**, UCLA; Keeley Dowling, Tennesse; Becky Sauerbrunn, Virginia.

MIDFIELDERS—**Joanna Lohman**, Penn St.; Sarah Rahko, Boston College; Lisa Stoia, West Virginia.

FORWARDS—Iris Mora, UCLA; Lindsay Tarpley, North Carolina; Amy Warner, Notre Dame; Tiffany Weimer, Penn St.

Small College Final Fours

MEN

NCAA Division II
at Virginia Beach, Va. (Dec. 5-7)

Semifinals: Lynn def. Dowling, 3-2; Cal St. Chico def. Findlay, 2-0.
Championship: Lynn def. Cal St. Chico, 2-1. Final records: Lynn (22-0-1), Cal St. Chico (21-5-1).

NCAA Division III
at Madison, N.J. (Nov. 29-30)

Semifinals: Trinity (Texas) def. Wisc-Oshkosh, 3-2 (2OT); Drew ties Wheaton (Mass.), 1-1 (2OT) Drew advances on penalty kicks, 3-2.
Championship: Trinity def. Drew, 2-1; Final records: Trinity (23-0-0), Drew (20-1-3).

NAIA
at Olathe, Kan. (Nov. 24-25)

Semifinals: Fresno Pacific (Calif.) def. Berry (Ga.), 4-1; Rio Grande (Ohio) def. Hastings (Neb.), 1-0.
Championship: Rio Grande def. Fresno Pacific, 1-0; Final records: Rio Grande (24-0-1), Fresno Pacific (22-2-0).

WOMEN

NCAA Division II
at Virginia Beach, Va. (Dec. 4-6)

Semifinals: Kennesaw St. def. Nebraska-Omaha, 1-0; Franklin Pierce def. UC San Diego, 2-1 (OT).
Championship: Kennesaw St. def. Franklin Pierce, 2-0. Final records: Kennsaw St. (25-1-0), Franklin Pierce (22-3-0).

NCAA Division III
at Oneonta, N.Y. (Nov. 29-30)

Semifinals: Chicago def. DePauw, 2-1 (2OT); Oneonta St. def. TCNJ, 2-1.
Championship: Oneonta St. def. Chicago, 2-1 (OT). Final records: Oneonta St. (20-1-3), Chicago (17-1-3).

NAIA
at Santa Barbara, Calif. (Nov. 24-25)

Semifinals: Lindsey Wilson (Ky.) def. Concordia (Ore.), 2-0; Westmont (Calif.) def. William Jewell (Mo.), 5-1.
Championship: Westmont def. Lindsey Wilson, 2-1 (7OT); Final records: Westmont (22-1-1), Azusa Pacific (25-2-0).

1900-2004
Through the Years

SPORTS ALMANAC

The World Cup

The Federation Internationale de Football Association (FIFA) began the World Cup championship tournament in 1930 with a 13-team field in Uruguay. Sixty-four years later, 138 countries competed in qualifying rounds to fill 24 berths in the 1994 World Cup finals. FIFA increased the World Cup '98 tournament field from 24 to 32 teams, and it remained at 32 in 2002 including automatic berths for defending champion France and co-hosts Japan and South Korea. The other 29 slots were allotted by region: Europe (13), Africa (5), South America (4), CONCACAF (3), Asia (2), the two remaining positions were determined via two home-and-away playoff series. One was between the #14 European team (Ireland) and the #3 Asian team (Iran) and the other was between the #5 South American team (Uruguay) and the champion of Oceania (Australia).

Tournaments have been played once in Asia (Japan/South Korea), three times in North America (Mexico 2 and U.S.), four times in South America (Argentina, Chile, Brazil and Uruguay) and nine times in Europe (France 2, Italy 2, England, Spain, Sweden, Switzerland and West Germany). Following an outcry when Germany was awarded the 2006 World Cup over South Africa, FIFA announced that, starting in 2010, the World Cup will be rotated among six continents.

Brazil retired the first World Cup (called the Jules Rimet Trophy after FIFA's first president) in 1970 after winning it for the third time. The new trophy, first presented in 1974, is known as simply the World Cup.

Multiple winners: Brazil (5); Italy and West Germany (3); Argentina and Uruguay (2).

Year	Champion	Manager	Score	Runner-up	Host Country	Third Place
1930	Uruguay	Alberto Suppici	4-2	Argentina	Uruguay	No game
1934	Italy	Vittório Pozzo	2-1*	Czechoslovakia	Italy	Germany 3, Austria 2
1938	Italy	Vittório Pozzo	4-2	Hungary	France	Brazil 4, Sweden 2
1942-46	Not held					
1950	Uruguay	Juan Lopez	2-1	Brazil	Brazil	No game
1954	West Germany	Sepp Herberger	3-2	Hungary	Switzerland	Austria 3, Uruguay 1
1958	Brazil	Vicente Feola	5-2	Sweden	Sweden	France 6, W. Ger. 3
1962	Brazil	Aimoré Moreira	3-1	Czechoslovakia	Chile	Chile 1, Yugoslavia 0
1966	England	Alf Ramsey	4-2*	W. Germany	England	Portugal 2, USSR 1
1970	Brazil	Mario Zagalo	4-1	Italy	Mexico	W. Ger. 1, Uruguay 0
1974	West Germany	Helmut Schoen	2-1	Netherlands	W. Germany	Poland 1, Brazil 0
1978	Argentina	Cesar Menotti	3-1*	Netherlands	Argentina	Brazil 2, Italy 1
1982	Italy	Enzo Bearzot	3-1	W. Germany	Spain	Poland 3, France 2
1986	Argentina	Carlos Bilardo	3-2	W. Germany	Mexico	France 4, Belgium 2*
1990	West Germany	Franz Beckenbauer	1-0	Argentina	Italy	Italy 2, England 1
1994	Brazil	Carlos Parreira	0-0†	Italy	USA	Sweden 4, Bulgaria 0
1998	France	Aimé Jacquet	3-0	Brazil	France	Croatia 2, Netherlands 1
2002	Brazil	Luiz Felipe Scolari	2-0	Germany	Japan/S. Korea	Turkey 3, S. Korea 2
2006	at Germany (June 9-July 9)					
2010	at South Africa (TBD)					

*Winning goals scored in overtime (no sudden death); †Brazil defeated Italy in shootout (3-2) after scoreless overtime period.

All-Time World Cup Leaders

Career Goals

World Cup scoring leaders through 2002. Years listed are years played in World Cup.

	No
Gerd Müller, West Germany (1970, 74)	14
Just Fontaine, France (1958)	13
Pelé, Brazil (1958, 62, 66, 70)	12
Ronaldo, Brazil (1994, 98, 2002)	12
Sandor Kocsis, Hungary (1954)	11
Juergen Klinsmann, Germany (1990, 94, 98)	11
Helmut Rahn, West Germany (1954, 58)	10
Teofilo Cubillas, Peru (1970, 78)	10
Gregorz Lato, Poland (1974, 78, 82)	10
Gary Lineker, England (1986, 90)	10

Most Valuable Player

Officially, the Golden Ball Award, the Most Valuable Player of the World Cup tournament has been selected since 1982 by a panel of international soccer journalists.

Year		Year	
1982	Paolo Rossi, Italy	1994	Romario, Brazil
1986	Diego Maradona, Arg.	1998	Ronaldo, Brazil
1990	Toto Schillaci, Italy	2002	Oliver Kahn, Germany

Single Tournament Goals

World Cup tournament scoring leaders through 2002.

Year		Gm	No
1930	Guillermo Stabile, Argentina	4	8
1934	Angelo Schiavio, Italy	3	4
	Oldrich Nejedly, Czechoslovakia	4	4
	Edmund Conen, Germany	4	4
1938	Leônidas, Brazil	3	8
1950	Ademir, Brazil	6	7
1954	Sandor Kocsis, Hungary	5	11
1958	Just Fontaine, France	6	13
1962	Drazen Jerkovic, Yugoslavia	6	5
1966	Eusébio, Portugal	6	9
1970	Gerd Müller, West Germany	6	10
1974	Grzegorz Lato, Poland	7	7
1978	Mario Kempes, Argentina	7	6
1982	Paolo Rossi, Italy	7	6
1986	Gary Lineker, England	5	6
1990	Toto Schillaci, Italy	7	6
1994	Oleg Salenko, Russia	3	6
	Hristo Stoitchkov, Bulgaria	7	6
1998	Davor Suker, Croatia	7	6
2002	Ronaldo, Brazil	7	8

All-Time World Cup Ranking Table

Since the first World Cup in 1930, Brazil is the only country to play in all 17 final tournaments. The FIFA all-time table below ranks all nations that have ever qualified for a World Cup final tournament by points earned through 2002. Victories, which earned two points from 1930-90, were awarded three points starting in 1994. Note that Germany's appearances include 10 made by West Germany from 1954-90. Participants in the 2002 World Cup final are in **bold** type.

		App	Gm	W	L	T	Pts	GF	GA
1	**Brazil**	17	87	60	13	14	141	191	82
2	**Germany**	15	85	50	17	18	123	176	106
3	**Italy**	15	70	39	14	17	96	110	67
4	**Argentina**	13	60	30	19	11	72	102	71
5	**England**	11	50	26	13	15	61	68	45
6	**Spain**	11	45	20	15	10	54	71	53
7	**France**	11	44	21	16	7	49	86	61
8	**Sweden**	10	42	15	16	10	42	71	65
9	**Russia**	9	37	17	14	6	41	64	44
10	Yugoslavia	9	37	16	13	8	40	60	46
	Uruguay	10	40	15	15	10	40	65	57
12	Netherlands	7	31	14	9	9	37	56	36
13	**Poland**	6	28	14	9	5	34	42	36
14	Hungary	9	32	15	14	3	33	87	57
	Mexico	12	41	10	20	11	33	43	80
16	**Belgium**	11	36	10	17	9	30	46	63
17	Austria	7	29	12	13	4	28	43	47
18	Czech Republic	8	30	11	14	5	27	44	45
19	Romania	7	21	8	8	5	21	30	32
20	Chile	7	25	7	12	6	20	31	40
21	**Paraguay**	6	19	5	8	6	18	25	34
	Denmark	3	13	7	4	2	18	24	18
23	**South Korea**	6	21	4	12	5	17	19	49
24	**Cameroon**	5	17	4	6	7	16	15	29
	USA	7	22	6	14	2	16	25	45
26	**Portugal**	3	12	7	5	0	15	25	16
	Scotland	8	23	4	12	7	15	25	41
	Switzerland	7	22	6	13	3	15	33	51
	Turkey	2	10	4	4	1	15	20	17
30	Bulgaria	7	26	3	15	8	14	22	53
31	**Croatia**	2	10	6	4	0	13	13	8
32	**Ireland**	3	13	2	4	7	12	10	10
33	Peru	4	15	4	8	3	11	19	31
	No. Ireland	3	13	3	5	5	11	13	23
35	**Nigeria**	3	11	4	6	1	9	14	16
36	Morocco	4	13	2	7	4	8	12	18
	Colombia	4	13	3	8	2	8	14	23
	Costa Rica	2	7	3	3	1	8	9	12
	Senegal	1	5	2	1	2	8	7	6
40	Norway	2	8	2	3	3	7	7	8
	Japan	2	7	2	4	1	7	6	7
42	East Germany	1	6	2	2	2	6	5	5
	South Africa	2	6	1	2	3	6	8	11
44	**Saudi Arabia**	3	10	2	7	1	5	7	25
	Algeria	2	6	2	3	1	5	6	10
	Wales	1	5	1	1	3	5	4	4
	Tunisia	3	9	1	5	3	5	5	11
48	Iran	2	6	1	4	1	3	4	12
	North Korea	1	4	1	2	1	3	5	9
	Cuba	1	3	1	1	1	3	5	12
	Jamaica	1	3	1	2	0	3	3	9
52	**Ecuador**	1	3	1	2	0	2	2	4
	Egypt	2	4	0	2	2	2	3	6
	Honduras	1	3	0	1	2	2	2	3
	Israel	1	3	0	1	2	2	1	3
56	Bolivia	3	6	0	5	1	1	1	20
	Australia	1	3	0	2	1	1	0	5
	Kuwait	1	3	0	2	1	1	2	6
59	El Salvador	2	6	0	6	0	0	1	22
	Canada	1	3	0	3	0	0	0	5
	East Indies	1	1	0	1	0	0	0	6
	Greece	1	3	0	3	0	0	0	10
	Haiti	1	3	0	3	0	0	2	14
	Iraq	1	3	0	3	0	0	1	4
	Slovenia	1	3	0	3	0	0	2	7
	New Zealand	1	3	0	3	0	0	2	12
	UAE	1	3	0	3	0	0	2	11
	China	1	3	0	3	0	0	0	9
	Zaire	1	3	0	3	0	0	0	14

The United States in the World Cup

While the United States has fielded a national team every year of the World Cup, only seven of those teams have been able to make it past the preliminary competition and qualify for the final World Cup tournament. The 1994 national team automatically qualified because the U.S. served as host of the event for the first time. The U.S. played in three of the first four World Cups (1930, '34 and '50) and each of the last four (1990, '94, '98 and 2002). The Americans have a record of 6-14-2 in 22 World Cup matches.

1930
1st Round Matches
United States 3 . . . . Belgium 0
United States 3 . . . . Paraguay 0

Semifinals
Argentina 6 . . . . United States 1

U.S. Scoring—Bert Patenaude (3), Bart McGhee (2), James Brown and Thomas Florie.

1934
1st Round Match
Italy 7 . . . . United States 1

U.S. Scoring—Buff Donelli (who later became a noted college and NFL football coach).

1950
1st Round Matches
Spain 3 . . . . United States 1
United States 1 . . . . England 0
Chile 5 . . . . United States 2

U.S. Scoring—Joe Gaetjens, Joe Maca, John Souza and Frank Wallace.

1990
1st Round Matches
Czechoslovakia 5 . . . . United States 1
Italy 1 . . . . United States 0
Austria 2 . . . . United States 1

U.S. Scoring—Paul Caligiuri and Bruce Murray.

1994
1st Round Matches
United States 1 . . . . Switzerland 1
United States 2 . . . . Colombia 1
Romania 1 . . . . United States 0

Round of 16
Brazil 1 . . . . United States 0

U.S. Scoring—Eric Wynalda, Earnie Stewart and own goal (Colombia defender Andres Escobar).

1998
1st Round Matches

Germany 2 . . . . United States 0
Iran 2 . . . . United States 1
Yugoslavia 1 . . . . United States 0

U.S. Scoring–Brian McBride.

2002
1st Round Matches

United States 3 . . . . Portugal 2
United States 1 . . . . So. Korea 1
Poland 3 . . . . United States 1

Round of 16

United States 2 . . . . Mexico 0

Round of 8

Germany 1 . . . . United States 0

U.S. Scoring– Landon Donovan (2), Brian McBride (2), John O'Brien, own goal (Portugal defender Jorge Costa) and Clint Mathis.

World Cup Finals

Brazil and Germany (formerly West Germany) have played in the most Cup finals with seven but faced each other for the first time in a final in 2002. Note that a four-team round robin determined the 1950 championship–the deciding game turned out to be the last one of the tournament between Uruguay and Brazil.

1930
Uruguay 4, Argentina 2
(at Montevideo, Uruguay)

		1	2–T
July 30	Uruguay (4-0)	1	3–4
	Argentina (4-1)	2	0–2

Goals: Uruguay–Pablo Dorado (12th minute), Pedro Cea (54th), Santos Iriarte (68th), Castro (89th); Argentina–Carlos Peucelle (20th), Guillermo Stabile (37th).

Uruguay–Ballesteros, Nasazzi, Mascheroni, Andrade, Fernandez, Gestido, Dorado, Scarone, Castro, Cea, Iriarte.

Argentina–Botasso, Della Torre, Paternoster, J. Evaristo, Monti, Suarez, Peucelle, Varallo, Stabile, Ferreira, M. Evaristo.

Attendance: 90,000. **Referee:** Langenus (Belgium).

1934
Italy 2, Czechoslovakia 1 (OT)
(at Rome)

		1	2	OT–T
June 10	Italy (4-0-1)	0	1	1–2
	Czechoslovakia (3-1)	0	1	0–1

Goals: Italy–Raimondo Orsi (80th minute), Angelo Schiavio (95th); Czechoslovakia–Puc (70th).

Italy–Combi, Monzeglio, Allemandi, Ferraris IV, Monti, Bertolini, Guaita, Meazza, Schiavio, Ferrari, Orsi.

Czechoslovakia–Planicka, Zenisek, Ctyroky, Kostalek, Cambal, Krcil, Junek, Svoboda, Sobotka, Nejedly, Puc.

Attendance: 55,000. **Referee:** Eklind (Sweden).

1938
Italy 4, Hungary 2
(at Paris)

		1	2–T
June 19	Italy (4-0)	3	1–4
	Hungary (3-1)	1	1–2

Goals: Italy–Gino Colaussi (5th minute), Silvio Piola (16th), Colaussi (35th), Piola (82nd); Hungary–Titkos (7th), Georges Sarosi (70th).

Italy–Olivieri, Foni, Rava, Serantoni, Andreolo, Locatelli, Biavati, Meazza, Piola, Ferrari, Colaussi.

Hungary–Szabo, Polgar, Biro, Szalay, Szucs, Lazar, Sas, Vincze, G. Sarosi, Szengeller, Titkos.

Attendance: 65,000. **Referee:** Capdeville (France).

1950
Uruguay 2, Brazil 1
(at Rio de Janeiro)

		1	2–T
July 16	Uruguay (3-0-1)	0	2–2
	Brazil (4-1)	0	1–1

Goals: Uruguay–Juan Schiaffino (66th minute), Chico Ghiggia (79th); Brazil–Friaca (47th).

Uruguay–Maspoli, M. Gonzales, Tejera, Gambetta, Varela, Andrade, Ghiggia, Perez, Miguez, Schiaffino, Moran.

Brazil–Barbosa, Augusto, Juvenal, Bauer, Danilo, Bigode, Friaça, Zizinho, Ademir, Jair, Chico.

Attendance: 199,854. **Referee:** Reader (England).

1954
West Germany 3, Hungary 2
(at Berne, Switzerland)

		1	2–T
July 4	West Germany (4-1)	2	1–3
	Hungary (4-1)	2	0–2

Goals: West Germany–Max Morlock (10th minute), Helmut Rahn (18th), Rahn (84th); Hungary–Ferenc Puskas (4th), Zoltan Czibor (9th).

West Germany–Turek, Posipal, Liebrich, Kohlmeyer, Eckel, Mai, Rahn, Morlock, O. Walter, F. Walter, Schaefer.

Hungary–Grosics, Buzansky, Lorant, Lantos, Bozsik, Zakarias, Czibor, Kocsis, Hidegkuti, Puskas, J. Toth.

Attendance: 60,000. **Referee:** Ling (England).

1958
Brazil 5, Sweden 2
(at Stockholm)

		1	2–T
June 29	Brazil (5-0-1)	2	3–5
	Sweden (4-1-1)	1	1–2

Goals: Brazil–Vava (9th minute), Vava (32nd), Pelé (55th), Mario Zagalo (68th), Pelé (90th); Sweden–Nils Liedholm (3rd), Agne Simonsson (80th).

Brazil–Gilmar, D. Santos, N. Santos, Zito, Bellini, Orlando, Garrincha, Didi, Vava, Pelé, Zagalo.

Sweden–Svensson, Bergmark, Axbom, Boerjesson, Gustavsson, Parling, Hamrin, Gren, Simonsson, Liedholm, Skoglund.

Attendance: 49,737. **Referee:** Guigue (France).

World Cup Finals (Cont.)

1962
Brazil 3, Czechoslovakia 1
(at Santiago, Chile)

		1	2–T
June 17	Brazil (5-0-1)	1	2–3
	Czechoslovakia (3-2-1)	1	0–1

Goals: Brazil–Amarildo (17th minute), Zito (68th), Vava (77th); Czechoslovakia–Josef Masopust (15th).
Brazil–Gilmar, D. Santos, N. Santos, Zito, Mauro, Zozimo, Garrincha, Didi, Vava, Amarildo, Zagalo.
Czechoslovakia–Schroiff, Tichy, Novak, Pluskal, Popluhar, Masopust, Pospichal, Scherer, Kvasniak, Kadraba, Jelinek.
Attendance: 68,679. **Referee:** Latishev (USSR).

1966
England 4, West Germany 2 (OT)
(at London)

		1	2	OT–T
July 30	England (5-0-1)	1	1	2–4
	West Germany (4-1-1)	1	1	0–2

Goals: England–Geoff Hurst (18th minute), Martin Peters (78th), Hurst (101st), Hurst (120th); West Germany–Helmut Haller (12th), Wolfgang Weber (90th).
England–Banks, Cohen, Wilson, Stiles, J. Charlton, Moore, Ball, Hurst, B. Charlton, Hunt, Peters.
West Germany–Tilkowski, Hottges, Schnellinger, Beckenbauer, Schulz, Weber, Haller, Seeler, Held, Overath, Emmerich.
Attendance: 93,802. **Referee:** Dienst (Switzerland).

1970
Brazil 4, Italy 1
(at Mexico City)

		1	2–T
June 21	Brazil (6-0)	1	3–4
	Italy (3-1-2)	1	0–1

Goals: Brazil–Pelé (18th minute), Gerson (65th), Jairzinho (70th), Carlos Alberto (86th); Italy–Roberto Boninsegna (37th).
Brazil–Felix, C. Alberto, Everaldo, Clodoaldo, Brito, Piazza, Jairzinho, Gerson, Tostão, Pelé, Rivelino.
Italy–Albertosi, Burgnich, Facchetti, Bertini (Juliano, 73rd), Rosato, Cera, Domenghini, Mazzola, Boninsegna (Rivera, 84th), De Sisti, Riva.
Attendance: 107,412. **Referee:** Glockner (E. Germany).

1974
West Germany 2, Netherlands 1
(at Munich)

		1	2–T
July 7	West Germany (6-1)	2	0–2
	Netherlands (5-1-1)	1	0–1

Goals: West Germany–Paul Breitner (25th minute, penalty kick), Gerd Müller (43rd); Netherlands–Johan Neeskens (1st, penalty kick).
West Germany–Maier, Beckenbauer, Vogts, Breitner, Schwarzenbeck, Overath, Bonhof, Hoeness, Grabowski, Muller, Holzenbein.
Netherlands–Jongbloed, Suurbier, Rijsbergen (De Jong, 58th), Krol, Haan, Jansen, Van Hanegem, Neeskens, Rep, Cruyff, Rensenbrink (R. Van de Kerkhof, 46th).
Attendance: 77,833. **Referee:** Taylor (England).

1978
Argentina 3, Netherlands 1 (OT)
(at Buenos Aires)

		1	2	OT–T
June 25	Argentina (5-1-1)	1	0	2–3
	Netherlands (3-2-2)	0	1	0–1

Goals: Argentina–Mario Kempes (37th minute), Kempes (104th), Daniel Bertoni (114th); Netherlands–Dirk Nanninga (81st).
Argentina–Fillol, Olguin, L. Galvan, Passarella, Tarantini, Ardiles (Larrosa, 65th), Gallego, Kempes, Luque, Bertoni, Ortiz (Houseman, 77th).
Netherlands–Jongbloed, Jansen (Suurbier, 72nd), Brandts, Krol, Poortvliet, Haan, Neeskens, W. Van de Kerkhof, R. Van de Kerkhof, Rep (Nanninga, 58th), Rensenbrink.
Attendance: 77,260. **Referee:** Gonella (Italy).

1982
Italy 3, West Germany 1
(at Madrid)

		1	2–T
July 11	Italy (4-0-3)	0	3–3
	West Germany (4-2-1)	0	1–1

Goals: Italy–Paolo Rossi (57th minute), Marco Tardelli (68th), Alessandro Altobelli (81st); West Germany–Paul Breitner (83rd).
Italy–Zoff, Scirea, Gentile, Cabrini, Collovati, Bergomi, Tardelli, Oriali, Conti, Rossi, Graziani (Altobelli, 8th, and Causio, 89th).
West Germany–Schumacher, Stielike, Kaltz, Briegel, K.H. Forster, B. Forster, Breitner, Dremmler (Hrubesch, 61st), Littbarski, Fischer, Rummenigge (Muller, 69th).
Attendance: 90,080. **Referee:** Coelho (Brazil).

1986
Argentina 3, West Germany 2
(at Mexico City)

		1	2–T
June 29	Argentina (6-0-1)	1	2–3
	West Germany (4-2-1)	0	2–2

Goals: Argentina–Jose Brown (22nd minute), Jorge Valdano (55th), Jorge Burruchaga (83rd); West Germany–Karl-Heinz Rummenigge (73rd), Rudi Voller (81st).
Argentina–Pumpido, Cuciuffo, Olarticoechea, Ruggeri, Brown, Batista, Burruchaga (Trobbiani, 89th), Giusti, Enrique, Maradona, Valdano.
West Germany–Schumacher, Jakobs, B. Forster, Berthold, Briegel, Eder, Brehme, Matthaus, Rummenigge, Magath (Hoeness, 61st), Allofs (Voller, 46th).
Attendance: 114,590. **Referee:** Filho (Brazil).

1990
West Germany 1, Argentina 0
(at Rome)

		1	2–T
July 8	West Germany (6-0-1)	0	1–1
	Argentina (4-2-1)	0	0–0

Goals: West Germany–Andreas Brehme (85th minute, penalty kick).
West Germany–Illgner, Berthold (Reuter, 73rd), Kohler, Augenthaler, Buchwald, Brehme, Haessler, Matthaus, Littbarski, Klinsmann, Voller.
Argentina: Goycoechea, Ruggeri (Monzon, 46th), Simon, Serrizuela, Lorenzo, Basualdo, Troglio, Burruchaga (Calderon, 53rd), Sensini, Dezotti, Maradona.
Attendance: 73,603. **Referee:** Codesal (Mexico).

1994

Brazil 0, Italy 0 (Shootout)

(at Pasadena, Calif.)

		1	2	OT–	T
July 17	Brazil (6-0-1)	0	0	0–	0*
	Italy (4-2-1)	0	0	0–	0

*Brazil wins shootout, 3-2.

Shootout (five shots each, alternating): ITA–Baresi (miss, 0-0); BRA–Santos (blocked, 0-0); ITA– Albertini (goal, 1-0); BRA–Romario (goal, 1-1); ITA–Evani (goal, 2-1); BRA–Branco (goal, 2-2); ITA–Massaro (blocked, 2-2); BRA–Dunga (goal, 2-3); ITA–R. Baggio (miss, 2-3).

Brazil–Taffarel, Jorginho (Cafu, 21st minute), Branco, Aldair, Santos, Mazinho, Silva, Dunga, Zinho (Viola, 106th), Bebeto, Romario.

Italy–Pagliuca, Mussi (Apolloni, 35th minute), Baresi, Benarrivo, Maldini, Albertini, D. Baggio (Evani, 95th), Berti, Donadoni, R. Baggio, Massaro.

Attendance: 94,194. **Referee:** Puhl (Hungary).

1998

France 3, Brazil 0

(at Paris)

		1	2–	T
July 12	Brazil (6-1)	0	0–	0
	France (7-0)	2	1–	3

Goals: France–Zinedine Zidane (27th and 46th minutes), Petit (92).

Brazil–Taffarel, Cafu, Aldair, Baiano, Carlos, Sampaio (Edmundo, 74th minute), Dunga, Rivaldo, Leonardo (Denilson, 46th minute), Bebeto, Ronaldo.

France–Barthez, Lizarazu, Desailly, Thuram, Leboeuf, Djorkaeff (Viera, 75th minute), Deschamps, Zidane, Petit, Karembeu (Boghossian, 57th minute), Guivarc'h, Dugarry.

Attendance: 75,000. **Referee:** Belqola (Morocco).

2002

Brazil 2, Germany 0

(at Yokohama, Japan)

		1	2–	T
June 30	Germany (5-2)	0	0–	0
	Brazil (7-0)	0	2–	2

Goals: Brazil–Ronaldo (67th and 79th minutes).

Germany–Kahn, Linke, Ramelow, Neuville, Hamann, Klose (Bierhoff, 74th minute), Jeremies (Asamoah, 77th minute), Bode (Ziege, 84th minute), Schneider, Metzelder, Frings.

Brazil–Marcos, Cafu, Lucio, Junior, Edmilson, Carlos, Silva, Ronaldo (Denilson, 90th minute), Rivaldo, Ronaldinho (Paulista, 85th minute), Kleberson.

Attendance: 69,029. **Referee:** Collina (Italy).

Year-by-Year Comparisons

How the 17 World Cup tournaments have compared in nations qualifying, matches played, players participating, goals scored, average goals per game, overall attendance and attendance per game.

Year	Host	Continent	Nations	Matches	Players	Goals Scored	Per Game	Attendance Overall	Per Game
1930	Uruguay	So. America	13	18	189	70	3.8	589,300	32,739
1934	Italy	Europe	16	17	208	70	4.1	361,000	21,235
1938	France	Europe	15	18	210	84	4.7	376,000	20,889
1942-46	Not held								
1950	Brazil	So. America	13	22	192	88	4.0	1,044,763	47,489
1954	Switzerland	Europe	16	26	233	140	5.3	872,000	33,538
1958	Sweden	Europe	16	35	241	126	3.6	819,402	23,411
1962	Chile	So. America	16	32	252	89	2.8	892,812	27,900
1966	England	Europe	16	32	254	89	2.8	1,464,944	45,780
1970	Mexico	No. America	16	32	270	95	3.0	1,690,890	52,840
1974	West Germany	Europe	16	38	264	97	2.6	1,809,953	47,630
1978	Argentina	So. America	16	38	277	102	2.7	1,685,602	44,358
1982	Spain	Europe	24	52	396	146	2.8	2,108,723	40,552
1986	Mexico	No. America	24	52	414	132	2.5	2,393,031	46,020
1990	Italy	Europe	24	52	413	115	2.2	2,516,354	48,391
1994	United States	No. America	24	52	437	140	2.7	3,587,088	68,982
1998	France	Europe	32	64	704	171	2.7	2,775,400	43,366
2002	Japan/So. Korea	Asia	32	64	736	161	2.5	2,705,197	42,269

World Cup Shootouts

Introduced in 1982; winning sides in **bold** type.

Year	Round		Final	SO	Year	Round		Final	SO
1982	Semi	**W. Germany** vs. France	3-3	(5-4)	1994	Second	**Bulgaria** vs. Mexico	1-1	(3-1)
1986	Quarter	**Belgium** vs. Spain	1-1	(5-4)		Quarter	**Sweden** vs. Romania	2-2	(5-4)
	Quarter	**France** vs. Brazil	1-1	(4-3)		Final	**Brazil** vs. Italy	0-0	(3-2)
	Quarter	**W. Germany** vs. Mexico	0-0	(4-1)	1998	Second	**Argentina** vs. England	2-2	(4-3)
1990	Second	**Ireland** vs. Romania	0-0	(5-4)		Quarter	**France** vs. Italy	0-0	(4-3)
	Quarter	**Argentina** vs. Yugoslavia	0-0	(3-2)	2002	Second	**Spain** vs. Ireland	1-1	(3-2)
	Semi	**Argentina** vs. Italy	1-1	(4-3)		Quarter	**So. Korea** vs. Spain	0-0	(5-3)
	Semi	**W. Germany** vs. England	1-1	(4-3)					

World Team of the 20th Century

The team, comprised of the century's best players, was voted on by a panel that included 250 international soccer journalists and released on June 10, 1998 in conjunction with the opening of the 1998 World Cup. The panel first selected the European and South American Teams of the Century and then chose the World Team from those two lists.

World Team

Pos		Pos	
GK	Lev Yashin, Soviet Union	MF	Alfredo Di Stefano, Argentina
D	Carlos Alberto, Brazil	MF	Michel Platini, France
D	Franz Beckenbauer, West Germany	F	Pele, Brazil
D	Bobby Moore, England	F	Garrincha, Brazil
D	Nilton Santos, Brazil	F	Diego Maradona, Argentina
MF	Johan Cruyff, Netherlands		

European Team

South American Team

Pos		Pos	
GK	Lev Yashin, Soviet Union	GK	Ubaldo Fillol, Argentina
D	Paolo Maldini, Italy	D	Carlos Alberto, Brazil
D	Franz Beckenbauer, West Germany	D	Elias Figueroa, Chile
D	Bobby Moore, England	D	Daniel Passarella, Argentina
D	Franco Baresi, Italy	D	Nilton Santos, Brazil
MF	Johan Cruyff, Netherlands	MF	Didi, Brazil
MF	Eusebio, Portugal	MF	Alfredo Di Stefano, Argentina
MF	Michel Platini, France	MF	Rivelino, Brazil
F	Ferenc Puskas, Hungary	F	Pele, Brazil
F	Bobby Charlton, England	F	Garrincha, Brazil
F	Marco Van Basten, Netherlands	F	Diego Maradona, Argentina

OTHER WORLDWIDE COMPETITION

The Olympic Games

Held every four years since 1896, except during World War I (1916) and World War II (1940-44). Soccer was not a medal sport in 1896 at Athens or in 1932 at Los Angeles. By agreement between FIFA and the IOC, Olympic soccer competition is currently limited to players 23 years old and under with a few exceptions.

Multiple winners: England and Hungary (3); Soviet Union and Uruguay (2).

MEN

Year		Year	
1900	**England**, France, Belgium	1964	**Hungary**, Czechoslovakia, Germany
1904	**Canada**, USA I, USA II	1968	**Hungary**, Bulgaria, Japan
1906	**Denmark**, Smyrna (Int'l entry), Greece	1972	**Poland**, Hungary, East Germany & Soviet Union
1908	**England**, Denmark, Netherlands	1976	**East Germany**, Poland, Soviet Union
1912	**England**, Denmark, Netherlands	1980	**Czechoslovakia**, East Germany, Soviet Union
1920	**Belgium**, Spain, Netherlands	1984	**France**, Brazil, Yugoslavia
1924	**Uruguay**, Switzerland, Sweden	1988	**Soviet Union**, Brazil, West Germany
1928	**Uruguay**, Argentina, Italy	1992	**Spain**, Poland, Ghana
1936	**Italy**, Austria, Norway	1996	**Nigeria**, Argentina, Brazil
1948	**Sweden**, Yugoslavia, Denmark	2000	**Cameroon**, Spain, Chile
1952	**Hungary**, Yugoslavia, Sweden	2004	**Argentina**, Paraguay, Italy
1956	**Soviet Union**, Yugoslavia, Bulgaria	2008	(at Beijing, China)
1960	**Yugoslavia**, Denmark, Hungary		

WOMEN

Multiple winners: United States (2).

Year		Year	
1996	**USA**, China, Norway	2004	**USA**, Brazil, Germany
2000	**Norway**, USA, Germany	2008	(at Beijing, China)

The Under-20 World Cup

Held every two years since 1977. Officially, the FIFA World Youth Championship.

Multiple winners: Argentina (4); Brazil (3); Portugal (2).

Year		Year	
1977	Soviet Union	1991	Portugal
1979	Argentina	1993	Brazil
1981	West Germany	1995	Argentina
1983	Brazil	1997	Argentina
1985	Brazil	1999	Spain
1987	Yugoslavia	2001	Argentina
1989	Portugal	2003	Brazil

The Under-17 World Cup

Held every two years since 1985. Officially, the FIFA U-17 World Championship.

Multiple winners: Brazil (3); Ghana and Nigeria (2).

Year		Year	
1985	Nigeria	1995	Ghana
1987	Soviet Union	1997	Brazil
1989	Saudi Arabia	1999	Brazil
1991	Ghana	2001	France
1993	Nigeria	2003	Brazil

Indoor World Championship

First held in 1989. Officially. the FIFA Futsal World Championship. **Multiple winner:** Brazil (3).

Year		Year	
1989	Brazil	2000	Spain
1992	Brazil	2004	(at Chinese Taipei)
1996	Brazil		

Women's World Cup

First held in 1991. Officially, the FIFA Women's World Championship. **Multiple winner:** United States (2).

Year		Year	
1991	United States	1999	United States
1995	Norway	2003	Germany

Confederations Cup

First held in 1992. Contested by the Continental champions of Africa, Asia, Europe, North America and South America and originally called the Intercontinental Championship for the King Fahd Cup until it was redubbed the FIFA/Confederations Cup for the King Fahd Trophy in 1997.

Year		Year	
1992	Argentina	1999	Mexico
1995	Denmark	2001	France
1997	Brazil	2003	France

CONTINENTAL COMPETITION

European Championship

Held every four years since 1960. Officially, the European Football Championship. Winners receive the Henri Delaunay trophy, named for the Frenchman who first proposed the idea of a European Soccer Championship in 1927. The first one would not be played until five years after his death in 1955.

Multiple winners: Germany/West Germany (3); France (2).

Year		Year		Year		Year	
1960	Soviet Union	1972	West Germany	1984	France	1996	Germany
1964	Spain	1976	Czechoslovakia	1988	Netherlands	2000	France
1968	Italy	1980	West Germany	1992	Denmark	2004	Greece

Copa America

Held irregularly since 1916. Unofficially, the Championship of South America.

Multiple winners: Argentina and Uruguay (14); Brazil (6); Paraguay and Peru (2).

Year		Year		Year		Year		Year	
1916	Uruguay	1926	Uruguay	1946	Argentina	1963	Bolivia	1995	Uruguay
1917	Uruguay	1927	Argentina	1947	Argentina	1967	Uruguay	1997	Brazil
1919	Brazil	1929	Argentina	1949	Brazil	1975	Peru	1999	Brazil
1920	Uruguay	1935	Uruguay	1953	Paraguay	1979	Paraguay	2001	Colombia
1921	Argentina	1937	Argentina	1955	Argentina	1983	Uruguay	2004	Brazil
1922	Brazil	1939	Peru	1956	Uruguay	1987	Uruguay		
1923	Uruguay	1941	Argentina	1957	Argentina	1989	Brazil		
1924	Uruguay	1942	Uruguay	1958	Argentina	1991	Argentina		
1925	Argentina	1945	Argentina	1959	Uruguay	1993	Argentina		

African Nations Cup

Contested since 1957 and held every two years since 1968.

Multiple winners: Cameroon, Egypt and Ghana (4); Congo/Zaire (3); Nigeria (2).

Year		Year		Year		Year		Year	
1957	Egypt	1968	Zaire	1978	Ghana	1988	Cameroon	1998	Egypt
1959	Egypt	1970	Sudan	1980	Nigeria	1990	Algeria	2000	Cameroon
1962	Ethiopia	1972	Congo	1982	Ghana	1992	Ivory Coast	2002	Cameroon
1963	Ghana	1974	Zaire	1984	Cameroon	1994	Nigeria	2004	Tunisia
1965	Ghana	1976	Morocco	1986	Egypt	1996	South Africa		

CONCACAF Gold Cup

The Confederation of North, Central American and Caribbean Football Championship. Contested irregularly from 1963-81 and revived as CONCACAF Gold Cup in 1991.

Multiple winners: Mexico (7); Costa Rica (2).

Year		Year		Year		Year		Year	
1963	Costa Rica	1969	Costa Rica	1977	Mexico	1993	Mexico	2000	Canada
1965	Mexico	1971	Mexico	1981	Honduras	1996	Mexico	2003	Mexico
1967	Guatemala	1973	Haiti	1991	United States	1998	Mexico		

CLUB COMPETITION
European/South American Cup

Also known as the Toyota Cup and Intercontinental Cup. Contested annually in December between the winners of the European Champions League (formerly European Cup) and South America's Copa Libertadores for the unofficial World Club Championship. Four European Cup winners refused to participate in the championship match in the 1970s and were replaced each time by the European Cup runner-up: Panathinaikos (Greece) for Ajax Amsterdam (Netherlands) in 1971; Juventus (Italy) for Ajax in 1973; Atlético Madrid (Spain) for Bayern Munich (West Germany) in 1974; and Malmo (Sweden) for Nottingham Forest (England) in 1979. Another European Cup winner, Marseille of France, was prohibited by the Union of European Football Associations (UEFA) from playing for the 1993 Toyota Cup because of its involvement in a match-rigging scandal.

Best-of-three game format from 1960-68, then a two-game/total goals format from 1969-79. Toyota became Cup sponsor in 1980, changed the format to a one-game championship and moved it to Toyko.

Multiple winners: AC Milan, Boca Juniors, Nacional, Penarol and Real Madrid (3); Ajax Amsterdam, Bayern Munich, Independiente, Inter Milan, Juventus, Santos and Sao Paulo (2).

Year		Year		Year	
1960	Real Madrid (Spain)	1975	Not held	1990	AC Milan (Italy)
1961	Penarol (Uruguay)	1976	Bayern Munich (W. Germany)	1991	Red Star (Yugoslavia)
1962	Santos (Brazil)	1977	Boca Juniors (Argentina)	1992	Sao Paulo (Brazil)
1963	Santos (Brazil)	1978	Not held	1993	Sao Paulo (Brazil)
1964	Inter Milan (Italy)	1979	Olimpia (Paraguay)	1994	Velez Sarsfield (Argentina)
1965	Inter Milan (Italy)	1980	Nacional (Uruguay)	1995	Ajax Amsterdam (Netherlands)
1966	Penarol (Uruguay)	1981	Flamengo (Brazil)	1996	Juventus (Italy)
1967	Racing Club (Argentina)	1982	Penarol (Uruguay)	1997	Borussia Dortmund (Germany)
1968	Estudiantes (Argentina)	1983	Gremio (Brazil)	1998	Real Madrid (Spain)
1969	AC Milan (Italy)	1984	Independiente (Argentina)	1999	Manchester United (England)
1970	Feyenoord (Netherlands)	1985	Juventus (Italy)	2000	Boca Juniors (Argentina)
1971	Nacional (Uruguay)	1986	River Plate (Argentina)	2001	Bayern Munich (Germany)
1972	Ajax Amsterdam (Netherlands)	1987	FC Porto (Portugal)	2002	Real Madrid (Spain)
1973	Independiente (Argentina)	1988	Nacional (Uruguay)	2003	Boca Juniors (Argentina)
1974	Atlético Madrid (Spain)	1989	AC Milan (Italy)		

European Cup/UEFA Champions League

Contested annually since the 1955-56 season by the league champions of the member countries of the Union of European Football Associations (UEFA). In 1999, UEFA announced the formation of a new competition called the UEFA Champions League to take the place of the Cup competition.

Multiple winners: Real Madrid (9); AC Milan (6); Ajax Amsterdam, Bayern Munich and Liverpool (4); Benfica, FC Porto, Inter Milan, Juventus and Nottingham Forest (2).

Year		Year		Year	
1956	Real Madrid (Spain)	1973	Ajax Amsterdam (Netherlands)	1990	AC Milan (Italy)
1957	Real Madrid (Spain)	1974	Bayern Munich (W. Germany)	1991	Red Star Belgrade (Yugo.)
1958	Real Madrid (Spain)	1975	Bayern Munich (W. Germany)	1992	Barcelona (Spain)
1959	Real Madrid (Spain)	1976	Bayern Munich (W. Germany)	1993	Marseille (France)*
1960	Real Madrid (Spain)	1977	Liverpool (England)	1994	AC Milan (Italy)
1961	Benfica (Portugal)	1978	Liverpool (England)	1995	Ajax Amsterdam (Netherlands)
1962	Benfica (Portugal)	1979	Nottingham Forest (England)	1996	Juventus (Italy)
1963	AC Milan (Italy)	1980	Nottingham Forest (England)	1997	Borussia Dortmund (Germany)
1964	Inter Milan (Italy)	1981	Liverpool (England)	1998	Real Madrid (Spain)
1965	Inter Milan (Italy)	1982	Aston Villa (England)	1999	Manchester United (England)
1966	Real Madrid (Spain)	1983	SV Hamburg (W. Germany)	2000	Real Madrid (Spain)
1967	Glasgow Celtic (Scotland)	1984	Liverpool (England)	2001	Bayern Munich (Germany)
1968	Manchester United (England)	1985	Juventus (Italy)	2002	Real Madrid (Spain)
1969	AC Milan (Italy)	1986	Steaua Bucharest (Romania)	2003	AC Milan (Italy)
1970	Feyenoord (Netherlands)	1987	FC Porto (Portugal)	2004	FC Porto (Portugal)
1971	Ajax Amsterdam (Netherlands)	1988	PSV Eindhoven (Netherlands)		*title vacated
1972	Ajax Amsterdam (Netherlands)	1989	AC Milan (Italy)		

European Cup Winner's Cup

Contested annually from the 1960-61 season through the 1999-2000 season by the cup winners of the member countries of the Union of European Football Associations (UEFA). The Cup Winner's Cup was absorbed by the UEFA Cup in 2000.

Multiple winners: Barcelona (4); AC Milan, RSC Anderlecht, Chelsea and Dinamo Kiev (2).

Year		Year		Year	
1961	Fiorentina (Italy)	1972	Glasgow Rangers (Scotland)	1983	Aberdeen (Scotland)
1962	Atletico Madrid (Spain)	1973	AC Milan (Italy)	1984	Juventus (Italy)
1963	Tottenham Hotspur (England)	1974	FC Magdeburg (E. Germany)	1985	Everton (England)
1964	Sporting Lisbon (Portugal)	1975	Dinamo Kiev (USSR)	1986	Dinamo Kiev (USSR)
1965	West Ham United (England)	1976	RSC Anderlecht (Belgium)	1987	Ajax Amsterdam (Netherlands)
1966	Borussia Dortmund (W.Germany)	1977	SV Hamburg (W. Germany)	1988	Mechelen (Belgium)
1967	Bayern Munich (W. Germany)	1978	RSC Anderlecht (Belgium)	1989	Barcelona (Spain)
1968	AC Milan (Italy)	1979	Barcelona (Spain)	1990	Sampdoria (Italy)
1969	Slovan Bratislava (Czech.)	1980	Valencia (Spain)	1991	Manchester United (England)
1970	Manchester City (England)	1981	Dinamo Tbilisi (USSR)	1992	Werder Bremen (Germany)
1971	Chelsea (England)	1982	Barcelona (Spain)	1993	Parma (Italy)

Year		Year		Year	
1994	Arsenal (England)	1997	Barcelona (Spain)	1999	Lazio (Italy)
1995	Real Zaragoza (Spain)	1998	Chelsea (England)	2000	discontinued
1996	Paris St. Germain (France)				

UEFA Cup

Contested annually since the 1957-58 season by teams other than league champions and cup winners of the Union of European Football Associations (UEFA). Teams selected by UEFA based on each country's previous performance in the tournament. Teams from England were banned from UEFA Cup play from 1985-90 for the criminal behavior of their supporters. In 1999, with the formation of the new Champions League, UEFA announced that the UEFA Cup would be expanded and include any teams that would have normally played in the Cup Winner's Cup.

Multiple winners: Barcelona, Inter Milan, Juventus, Liverpool and Valencia (3); Borussia Mönchengladbach, Feyenoord, IFK Göteborg, Leeds United, Parma, Real Madrid and Tottenham Hotspur (2).

Year		Year		Year	
1958	Barcelona (Spain)	1975	Borussia Mönchengladbach (W. Germany)	1990	Juventus (Italy)
1959	Not held	1976	Liverpool (England)	1991	Inter Milan (Italy)
1960	Barcelona (Spain)	1977	Juventus (Italy)	1992	Ajax Amsterdam (Netherlands)
1961	AS Roma (Italy)	1978	PSV Eindhoven (Netherlands)	1993	Juventus (Italy)
1962	Valencia (Spain)	1979	Borussia Mönchengladbach (W. Germany)	1994	Inter Milan (Italy)
1963	Valencia (Spain)			1995	Parma (Italy)
1964	Real Zaragoza (Spain)	1980	Eintracht Frankfurt (W. Germany)	1996	Bayern Munich (Germany)
1965	Ferencvaros (Hungary)	1981	Ipswich Town (England)	1997	Schalke 04 (Germany)
1966	Barcelona (Spain)	1982	IFK Göteborg (Sweden)	1998	Inter Milan (Italy)
1967	Dinamo Zagreb (Yugoslavia)	1983	RSC Anderlecht (Belgium)	1999	Parma (Italy)
1968	Leeds United (England)	1984	Tottenham Hotspur (England)	2000	Galatasaray (Turkey)
1969	Newcastle United (England)	1985	Real Madrid (Spain)	2001	Liverpool (England)
1970	Arsenal (England)	1986	Real Madrid (Spain)	2002	Feyenoord (Netherlands)
1971	Leeds United (England)	1987	IFK Göteborg (Sweden)	2003	FC Porto (Portugal)
1972	Tottenham Hotspur (England)	1988	Bayer Leverkusen (W. Germany)	2004	Valencia (Spain)
1973	Liverpool (England)	1989	Napoli (Italy)		
1974	Feyenoord (Netherlands)				

Copa Libertadores

Contested annually since the 1955-56 season by the league champions of South America's football union.

Multiple winners: Independiente (7); Boca Juniors and Peñarol (5); Estudiantes, Nacional-Uruguay and Olimpia (3); Cruzeiro, Gremio, River Plate, Santos and São Paulo (2).

Year		Year		Year	
1960	Peñarol (Uruguay)	1975	Independiente (Argentina)	1990	Olimpia (Paraguay)
1961	Peñarol (Uruguay)	1976	Cruzeiro (Brazil)	1991	Colo Colo (Chile)
1962	Santos (Brazil)	1977	Boca Juniors (Argentina)	1992	São Paulo (Brazil)
1963	Santos (Brazil)	1978	Boca Juniors (Argentina)	1993	São Paulo (Brazil)
1964	Independiente (Argentina)	1979	Olimpia (Paraguay)	1994	Velez Sarsfield (Argentina)
1965	Independiente (Argentina)			1995	Gremio (Brazil)
1966	Peñarol (Uruguay)	1980	Nacional (Uruguay)	1996	River Plate (Argentina)
1967	Racing Club (Argentina)	1981	Flamengo (Brazil)	1997	Cruzeiro (Brazil)
1968	Estudiantes de la Plata (Argentina)	1982	Peñarol (Uruguay)	1998	Vasco da Gama (Brazil)
1969	Estudiantes de la Plata (Argentina)	1983	Gremio (Brazil)	1999	Palmeiras (Brazil)
1970	Estudiantes de la Plata (Argentina)	1984	Independiente (Argentina)	2000	Boca Juniors (Argentina)
1971	Nacional (Uruguay)	1985	Argentinos Jrs. (Argentina)	2001	Boca Juniors (Argentina)
1972	Independiente (Argentina)	1986	River Plate (Argentina)	2002	Olimpia (Paraguay)
1973	Independiente (Argentina)	1987	Peñarol (Uruguay)	2003	Boca Juniors (Argentina)
1974	Independiente (Argentina)	1988	Nacional (Uruguay)	2004	Once Caldas (Colombia)
		1989	Nacional Medellin (Colombia)		

Annual Awards
World Player of the Year

Presented by FIFA, the European Sports Magazine Association (ESM) and Adidas, the sports equipment manufacturer, since 1991. Winners are selected by national team coaches from around the world.

Multiple winners: Ronaldo and Zinedine Zidane (3).

Year		Nat'l Team	Year		Nat'l Team
1991	Lothar Matthäus, Inter Milan	Germany	1998	Zinedine Zidane, Juventus	France
1992	Marco Van Basten, AC Milan	Netherlands	1999	Rivaldo, Barcelona	Brazil
1993	Roberto Baggio, Juventus	Italy	2000	Zinedine Zidane, Juventus	France
1994	Romario, Barcelona	Brazil	2001	Luis Figo, Real Madrid	Portugal
1995	George Weah, AC Milan	Liberia	2002	Ronaldo, Real Madrid	Brazil
1996	Ronaldo, Barcelona	Brazil	2003	Zinedine Zidane, Real Madrid	France
1997	Ronaldo, Inter Milan	Brazil			

Women's World Player of the Year

Presented by FIFA since 2001. Winners are selected by national team coaches from around the world.
Multiple winner: Mia Hamm (2).

Year		Nat'l Team	Year		Nat'l Team
2001	Mia Hamm, Washington Freedom	USA	2003	Birgit Prinz, FFC Frankfurt	Germany
2002	Mia Hamm, Washington Freedom	USA			

European Player of the Year

Officially, the "Ballon d'Or," or "Golden Ball," and presented by *France Football* magazine since 1956. Candidates are limited to European players in European leagues and winners are selected by a poll of European soccer journalists.
Multiple winners: Johan Cruyff, Michel Platini and Marco Van Basten (3); Franz Beckenbauer, Alfredo di Stéfano, Kevin Keegan, Ronaldo and Karl-Heinz Rummenigge (2).

Year		Nat'l Team	Year		Nat'l Team
1956	Stanley Matthews, Blackpool	England	1980	K.H. Rummenigge, Bayern Munich	W. Ger.
1957	Alfredo di Stéfano, Real Madrid	Arg./Spain	1981	K.H. Rummenigge, Bayern Munich	W. Ger.
1958	Raymond Kopa, Real Madrid	France	1982	Paolo Rossi, Juventus	Italy
1959	Alfredo di Stéfano, Real Madrid	Arg./Spain	1983	Michel Platini, Juventus	France
1960	Luis Suarez, Barcelona	Spain	1984	Michel Platini, Juventus	France
1961	Enrique Sivori, Juventus	Arg./Italy	1985	Michel Platini, Juventus	France
1962	Josef Masopust, Dukla Prague	Czech.	1986	Igor Belanov, Dinamo Kiev	Soviet Union
1963	Lev Yashin, Dinamo Moscow	Soviet Union	1987	Ruud Gullit, AC Milan	Netherlands
1964	Denis Law, Manchester United	Scotland	1988	Marco Van Basten, AC Milan	Netherlands
1965	Eusébio, Benfica	Portugal	1989	Marco Van Basten, AC Milan	Netherlands
1966	Bobby Charlton, Manchester United	England	1990	Lothar Matthäus, Inter Milan	W. Ger.
1967	Florian Albert, Ferencvaros	Hungary	1991	Jean-Pierre Papin, Marseille	France
1968	George Best, Manchester United	No. Ireland	1992	Marco Van Basten, AC Milan	Netherlands
1969	Gianni Rivera, AC Milan	Italy	1993	Roberto Baggio, Juventus	Italy
1970	Gerd Müller, Bayern Munich	W. Ger.	1994	Hristo Stoitchkov, Barcelona	Bulgaria
1971	Johan Cruyff, Ajax Amsterdam	Netherlands	1995	George Weah, AC Milan	Liberia
1972	Franz Beckenbauer, Bayern Munich	W. Ger.	1996	Matthias Sammer, Bor. Dortmund	Germany
1973	Johan Cruyff, Barcelona	Netherlands	1997	Ronaldo, Inter Milan	Brazil
1974	Johan Cruyff, Barcelona	Netherlands	1998	Zinedine Zidane, Juventus	France
1975	Oleg Blokhin, Dinamo Kiev	Soviet Union	1999	Rivaldo, Barcelona	Brazil
1976	Franz Beckenbauer, Bayern Munich	W. Ger.	2000	Luis Figo, Real Madrid	Portugal
1977	Allan Simonsen, B. Mönchengladbach	Denmark	2001	Michael Owen, Liverpool	England
1978	Kevin Keegan, SV Hamburg	England	2002	Ronaldo, Real Madrid	Brazil
1979	Kevin Keegan, SV Hamburg	England	2003	Pavel Nedved, Juventus	Czech Republic

South American Player of the Year

Presented by *El Mundo* of Venezuela from 1971-1985 and *El Pais* of Uruguay since 1986. Candidates are limited to South American players in South American leagues and winners are selected by a poll of South American sports editors.
Multiple winners: Elias Figueroa and Zico (3); Enzo Francescoli, Diego Maradona and Carlos Valderrama (2).

Year		Nat'l Team	Year		Nat'l Team
1971	Tostao, Cruzeiro	Brazil	1988	Ruben Paz, Racing Buenos Aires	Uruguay
1972	Teofilo Cubillas, Alianza Lima	Peru	1989	Bebeto, Vasco da Gama	Brazil
1973	Pelé, Santos	Brazil	1990	Raul Amarilla, Olimpia	Paraguay
1974	Elias Figueroa, Internacional	Chile	1991	Oscar Ruggeri, Velez Sarsfield	Argentina
1975	Elias Figueroa, Internacional	Chile	1992	Rai, Sao Paulo	Brazil
1976	Elias Figueroa, Internacional	Chile	1993	Carlos Valderrama, Atl. Junior	Colombia
1977	Zico, Flamengo	Brazil	1994	Cafu, Sao Paulo	Brazil
1978	Mario Kempes, Valencia	Argentina	1995	Enzo Francescoli, River Plate	Uruguay
1979	Diego Maradona, Argentinos Juniors	Argentina	1996	Jose Luis Chilavert, Velez Sarsfield	Paraguay
1980	Diego Maradona, Boca Juniors	Argentina	1997	Marcelo Salas, River Plate	Chile
1981	Zico, Flamengo	Brazil	1998	Martin Palermo, Boca Juniors	Argentina
1982	Zico, Flamengo	Brazil	1999	Javier Saviola, River Plate	Argentina
1983	Socrates, Corinthians	Brazil	2000	Romario, Vasco da Gama	Brazil
1984	Enzo Francescoli, River Plate	Uruguay	2001	Juan Roman Riquelme, Boca Juniors	Argentina
1985	Julio Cesar Romero, Fluminense	Paraguay	2002	Jose Cardozo, Toluca	Paraguay
1986	Antonio Alzamendi, River Plate	Uruguay	2003	Carlos Tevez, Boca Juniors	Argentina
1987	Carlos Valderrama, Deportivo Cali	Colombia			

Asian Player of the Year

Presented by the Asian Football Confederation since 1994. Prior to 1994 it was awarded unofficially.
Multiple winners: Kim Joo-Sung (3); Hidetoshi Nakata (2).

Year		Year		Year	
1988	Ahmed Radhi, Iraq	1994	Saeed Al-Owairan, S. Arabia	2000	Nawaf Al-Temyat, S. Arabia
1989	Kim Joo-Sung, South Korea	1995	Masami Ihara, Japan	2001	Fan Zhiyi, China
1990	Kim Joo-Sung, South Korea	1996	Khodadad Azizi, Iran	2002	Shinji Ono, Japan
1991	Kim Joo-Sung, South Korea	1997	Hidetoshi Nakata, Japan	2003	Mehdi Mahdavikia, Iran
1992	no award	1998	Hidetoshi Nakata, Japan		
1993	Kazuyoshi Miura, Japan	1999	Ali Daei, Iran		

African Player of the Year

Officially, the African "Ballon d'Or" and presented by *France Football* magazine from 1970-96. The Arican Player of the Year award has been presented by the CAF (African Football Confederation) since 1997. All African players are eligible for the award.

Multiple winners: George Weah and Abedi Pelé (3); El Hadji Diouf, Nwankwo Kanu, Roger Milla and Thomas N'Kono (2).

Year		Year		Year	
1970	Salif Keita, Mali	1982	Thomas N'Kono, Cameroon	1994	George Weah, Liberia
1971	Ibrahim Sunday, Ghana	1983	Mahmoud Al-Khatib, Egypt	1995	George Weah, Liberia
1972	Cherif Souleymane, Guinea	1984	Theophile Abega, Cameroon	1996	Nwankwo Kanu, Nigeria
1973	Tshimimu Bwanga, Zaire	1985	Mohamed Timoumi, Morocco	1997	Victor Ikpeba, Nigeria
1974	Paul Moukila, Congo	1986	Badou Zaki, Morocco	1998	Mustapha Hadji, Morocco
1975	Ahmed Faras, Morocco	1987	Rabah Madjer, Algeria	1999	Nwankwo Kanu, Nigeria
1976	Roger Milla, Cameroon	1988	Kalusha Bwalya, Zambia	2000	Patrick Mboma, Cameroon
1977	Dhiab Tarak, Tunisia	1989	George Weah, Liberia	2001	El Hadji Diouf, Senegal
1978	Abdul Razak, Ghana	1990	Roger Milla, Cameroon	2002	El Hadji Diouf, Senegal
1979	Thomas N'Kono, Cameroon	1991	Abedi Pelé, Ghana	2003	Samuel Eto'o Fils, Cameroon
1980	Jean Manga Onguene, Cameroon	1992	Abedi Pelé, Ghana		
1981	Lakhdar Belloumi, Algeria	1993	Abedi Pelé, Ghana		

U.S. Player of the Year

Presented by Honda and the Spanish-speaking radio show "Futbol de Primera" since 1991. Candidates are limited to American players who have played with the U.S. National Team and winners are selected by a panel of U.S. soccer journalists.

Multiple winners: Landon Donovan and Eric Wynalda (2).

Year		Year		Year		Year	
1991	Hugo Perez	1995	Alexi Lalas	1999	Kasey Keller	2003	Landon Donovan
1992	Eric Wynalda	1996	Eric Wynalda	2000	Claudio Reyna		
1993	Thomas Dooley	1997	Eddie Pope	2001	Earnie Stewart		
1994	Marcelo Balboa	1998	Cobi Jones	2002	Landon Donovan		

U.S. PRO LEAGUES

OUTDOOR
Major League Soccer

Sanctioned by U.S. Soccer and FIFA, the international soccer federation. MLS was founded on the heels of the successful 1994 World Cup tournament hosted by the United States and it remains the only FIFA-sanctioned division I outdoor league in the United States. The annual MLS title game is known as the MLS Cup.

Multiple winner: D.C. United (3).

MLS Cup

Year	Winner	Head Coach	Score	Loser	Head Coach	Site
1996	D.C. United	Bruce Arena	3-2 OT	Los Angeles Galaxy	Lothar Osiander	Foxboro, Mass.
1997	D.C. United	Bruce Arena	2-1	Colorado Rapids	Glen Myernick	Washington, D.C.
1998	Chicago Fire	Bob Bradley	2-0	D.C. United	Bruce Arena	Pasadena, Calif.
1999	D.C. United	Thomas Rongen	2-0	Los Angeles Galaxy	Sigi Schmid	Foxboro, Mass.
2000	K.C. Wizards	Bob Gansler	1-0	Chicago Fire	Bob Bradley	Washington, D.C.
2001	San Jose Earthquakes	Frank Yallop	2-1 OT	Los Angeles Galaxy	Sigi Schmid	Columbus, Ohio
2002	Los Angeles Galaxy	Sigi Schmid	1-0 2OT	N.E. Revolution	Steve Nicol	Foxboro, Mass.
2003	San Jose	Frank Yallop	4-2	Chicago	Dave Sarachan	Carson, Calif.

MLS Cup '96
D.C. United, 3-2 (OT)
Oct. 20 at Foxboro Stadium, Foxboro, Mass.
Attendance: 34,643

	1	2	OT	
Los Angeles Galaxy	1	1	0	—2
D.C. United	0	2	1	—3

First Half: LA—Eduardo Hurtado (Mauricio Cienfuegos), 5th minute.

Second Half: LA—Chris Armas (unassisted), 56th; DC—Tony Sanneh (Marco Etcheverry), 73rd; DC—Shawn Medved (unassisted), 82nd.

Overtime: DC—Eddie Pope (Etcheverry), 94th.

MVP: Marco Etcheverry, D.C. United, Midfielder

MLS Cup '97
D.C. United, 2-1
Oct. 26 at RFK Stadium, Washington, D.C.
Attendance: 57,431

	1	2	
Colorado Rapids	0	1	—1
D.C. United	1	1	—2

First Half: DC—Jaime Moreno (Tony Sanneh, David Vaudreuil), 37th minute.

Second Half: DC—Sanneh (John Harkes, Richie Williams), 68th; COL—Adrian Paz (David Patino, Matt Kmosko), 75th.

MVP: Jaime Moreno, D.C. United, Forward

MLS Cup '98
Chicago Fire, 2-0
Oct. 25 at the Rose Bowl, Pasadena, Calif.
Attendance: 51,350

	1	2	
D.C. United	0	0	—0
Chicago	2	0	—2

First Half: CHI–Jerzy Podbrozny (Peter Nowak, Ante Razov), 29th minute; CHI–Diego Gutierrez (Nowak), 45th.
MVP: Nowak, Chicago, Midfielder

MLS Cup '99
D.C. United, 2-0
Nov. 21 at Foxboro Stadium, Foxboro, Mass.
Attendance: 44,910

	1	2	
D.C. United	2	0	—2
Los Angeles	0	0	—0

First Half: DC–Jaime Moreno (Roy Lassiter), 19th minute; DC–Ben Olsen (unassisted), 48th
MVP: Olsen, D.C. United, Midfielder

MLS Cup 2000
Kansas City Wizards, 1-0
Oct. 15 at RFK Stadium, Washington, D.C.
Attendance: 39,159

	1	2	
Chicago	0	0	—0
Kansas City	1	0	—1

First Half: DC– Miklos Molnar (Chris Klein), 11th minute.
MVP: Tony Meola, Kansas City, Goalkeeper

MLS Cup 2001
San Jose Earthquakes, 2-1 (OT)
Oct. 21 at Crew Stadium, Columbus, Ohio
Attendance: 21,626

	1	2	OT	
San Jose	1	0	1	—2
Los Angeles	1	0	0	—1

First Half: LA–Luis Hernandez (Greg Vanney, Kevin Hartman), 21st minute; SJ–Landon Donovan (Ian Russell, Richard Mulrooney), 43rd. **Overtime:** SJ–Dwayne DeRosario (Ronnie Ekelund, Zak Ibsen), 96th.
MVP: Dwayne DeRosario, San Jose, Forward

MLS Cup 2002
Los Angeles Galaxy, 1-0 (2 OT)
Oct. 20 at Gillette Stadium, Foxboro, Mass.
Attendance: 61,316

	1	2	1OT	2OT	F
Los Angeles	0	0	0	1	—1
New England	0	0	0	0	—0

2nd OT: LA–Carlos Ruiz, (Tyrone Marshall, Chris Albright), 113th minute.
MVP: Carlos Ruiz, Los Angeles, F

MLS Cup 2003
San Jose Earthquakes, 4-2
Nov. 23 at Home Depot Center, Carson, Calif.
Attendance: 27,000

	1	2	
San Jose	2	2	—4
Chicago	0	2	—2

First Half: SJ– Ronnie Ekelund (unassisted), 5th minute; SJ–Landon Donovan (Jamil Walker), 38th. **Second Half:** CHI–DaMarcus Beasley (Andy Williams), 49th; SJ–Richard Mulrooney (Craig Waibel), 50th; CHI–own goal (Chris Roner), 54th; SJ–Donovan (Dwayne De Rosario, Brian Mullan), 71st.
MVP: Landon Donovan, San Jose, F

Regular Season

MLS Most Valuable Player
Multiple winner: Preki (2).
1996 Carlos Valderrama, Tampa Bay
1997 Preki, Kansas City
1998 Marco Etcheverry, D.C.
1999 Jason Kreis, Dallas
2000 Tony Meola, Kansas City
2001 Alex Pineda Chacón, Miami
2002 Carlos Ruiz, LA
2003 Preki, Kansas City

MLS Leading Scorer
Multiple winner: Preki (2).

		G	A	Pts
1996	Roy Lassiter, Tampa Bay	27	4	58
1997	Preki, Kansas City	12	17	41
1998	Stern John, Columbus	26	5	57
1999	Jason Kreis, Dallas	18	15	51
2000	Mamadou Diallo, Tampa Bay	26	4	56
2001	Alex Pineda Chacón	19	9	47
2002	Taylor Twellman, New England	23	6	52
2003	Preki, Kansas City	12	17	41
2004	Pat Noonan, New England	11	8	30
	& Amado Guevara, MetroStars	10	10	30

Women's United Soccer Association (2001-03)

The eight-team WUSA was formed in 2000 as the top women's outdoor professional league and play began in 2001. The league championship game is known as the Founders Cup. The league folded following the 2003 season.

Founders Cup

Year	Winner	Score	Loser	Site
2001	Bay Area CyberRays	3-3*	Atlanta Beat	Foxboro, Mass.
2002	Carolina Courage	3-2	Washington Freedom	Atlanta, Ga.
2003	Washington Freedom	2-1 OT	Atlanta Beat	San Diego, Calif.

*Bay Area won shoot-out, 4-2.

Regular Season

WUSA Most Valuable Player
2001 Tiffeny Milbrett, New York
2002 Marinette Pichon, Philadelphia
2003 Maren Meinert, Boston

WUSA Leading Scorer

		G	A	Pts
2001	Tiffeny Milbrett, New York	16	3	35
2002	Katia, San Jose	15	5	35
2003	Mia Hamm, Washington	11	11	33
	& Abby Wambach, Washington	13	7	33

Other U.S. Pro Leagues (Cont.)

National Professional Soccer League (1967)

Not sanctioned by FIFA, the international soccer federation. The NPSL recruited individual players to fill the rosters of its 10 teams. The league lasted only one season.

	Playoff Final			Regular Season			
Year	Winner	Scores	Loser	Leading Scorer	G	A	Pts
1967	Oakland Clippers	0-1, 4-1	Baltimore Bays	Yanko Daucik, Toronto 20		8	48

United Soccer Association (1967)

Sanctioned by FIFA. Originally called the North American Soccer League; it became the USA to avoid being confused with the National Professional Soccer League (see above). Instead of recruiting individual players, the USA imported 12 entire teams from Europe to represent its 12 franchises. It, too, only lasted a season. The league champion Los Angeles Wolves were actually Wolverhampton of England and the runner-up Washington Whips were Aberdeen of Scotland.

	Playoff Final			Regular Season			
Year	Winner	Score	Loser	Leading Scorer	G	A	Pts
1967	Los Angeles Wolves	6-5 (OT)	Washington Whips	Roberto Boninsegna, Chicago 10		1	21

North American Soccer League (1968-84)

The NPSL and USA merged to form the NASL in 1968 and the new league lasted through 1984. The NASL championship was known as the Soccer Bowl from 1975-84. One game decided the NASL title every year but five. There were no playoffs in 1969; a two-game/aggregate goals format was used in 1968 and '70; and a best-of-three games format was used in 1971 and '84; (*) indicates overtime and (†) indicates game decided by shootout.

Multiple winners: NY Cosmos (5); Chicago (2).

	Playoff Final			Regular Season			
Year	Winner	Score(s)	Loser	Leading Scorer	G	A	Pts
1968	Atlanta Chiefs	0-0,3-0	San Diego Toros	John Kowalik, Chicago 30		9	69
1969	Kansas City Spurs	No game	Atlanta Chiefs	Kaiser Motaung, Atlanta 16		4	36
1970	Rochester Lancers	3-0,1-3	Washington Darts	Kirk Apostolidis, Dallas 16		3	35
1971	Dallas Tornado	1-2*,4-1,2-0	Atlanta Chiefs	Carlos Metidieri, Rochester 19		8	46
1972	New York Cosmos	2-1	St. Louis Stars	Randy Horton, New York 9		4	22
1973	Philadelphia Atoms	2-0	Dallas Tornado	Kyle Rote Jr., Dallas 10		10	30
1974	Los Angeles Aztecs	3-3†	Miami Toros	Paul Child, San Jose 15		6	36
1975	Tampa Bay Rowdies	2-0	Portland Timbers	Steve David, Miami 23		6	52
1976	Toronto Metros	3-0	Minnesota Kicks	Giorgio Chinaglia, New York 19		11	49
1977	New York Cosmos	2-1	Seattle Sounders	Steve David, Los Angeles 26		6	58
1978	New York Cosmos	3-1	Tampa Bay Rowdies	Giorgio Chinaglia, New York 34		11	79
1979	Vancouver Whitecaps	2-1	Tampa Bay Rowdies	Oscar Fabbiani, Tampa Bay 25		8	58
1980	New York Cosmos	3-0	Ft. Laud. Strikers	Giorgio Chinaglia, New York 32		13	77
1981	Chicago Sting	0-0†	New York Cosmos	Giorgio Chinaglia, New York 29		16	74
1982	New York Cosmos	1-0	Seattle Sounders	Giorgio Chinaglia, New York 20		15	55
1983	Tulsa Roughnecks	2-0	Toronto Blizzard	Roberto Cabanas, New York 25		16	66
1984	Chicago Sting	2-1,3-2	Toronto Blizzard	Steve Zungul, Golden Bay 20		10	50

Note: In 1969, Kansas City won the NASL regular season championship with 110 points to 109 for Atlanta. There were no playoffs.

Regular Season MVP

Regular season Most Valuable Player as designated by the NASL.

Multiple winner: Carlos Metidieri (2).

Year		Year		Year	
1967	Rueben Navarro, Phila (NPSL)	1973	Warren Archibald, Miami	1979	Johan Cruyff, Los Angeles
1968	John Kowalik, Chicago	1974	Peter Silvester, Baltimore	1980	Roger Davies, Seattle
1969	Cirilio Fernandez, KC	1975	Steve David, Miami	1981	Giorgio Chinaglia, New York
1970	Carlos Metidieri, Rochester	1976	Pelé, New York	1982	Peter Ward, Seattle
1971	Carlos Metidieri, Rochester	1977	Franz Beckenbauer, New York	1983	Roberto Cabanas, New York
1972	Randy Horton, New York	1978	Mike Flanagan, New England	1984	Steve Zungul, Golden Bay

A-League (American Professional Soccer League)

The American Professional Soccer League was formed in 1990 with the merger of the Western Soccer League and the New American Soccer League. The APSL was officially sanctioned as an outdoor pro league in 1992 and changed its name to the A-League in 1995.

Multiple winners: Rochester (3); Colorado, Milwaukee, Montreal and Seattle (2).

Year		Year		Year	
1990	Maryland Bays	1995	Seattle Sounders	2000	Rochester Rhinos
1991	SF Bay Blackhawks	1996	Seattle Sounders	2001	Rochester Rhinos
1992	Colorado Foxes	1997	Milwaukee Rampage	2002	Milwaukee Rampage
1993	Colorado Foxes	1998	Rochester Rhinos	2003	Charleston Battery
1994	Montreal Impact	1999	Minnesota Thunder	2004	Montreal Impact

INDOOR
Major Soccer League (1978-92)

Originally the Major Indoor Soccer League from 1978-79 season through 1989-90. The MISL championship was decided by one game in 1980 and 1981; a best-of-three games series in 1979, best-of-five games in 1982 and 1983; and best-of-seven games since 1984. The MSL folded after the 1991-92 season.

Multiple winners: San Diego (8); New York (4).

Playoff Final

Year	Winner	Series	Loser
1979	New York Arrows	2-0	Philadelphia
1980	New York Arrows	7-4 (1 game)	Houston
1981	New York Arrows	6-5 (1 game)	St. Louis
1982	New York Arrows	3-2 (LWWLW)	St. Louis
1983	San Diego Sockers	3-2 (WWLLW)	Baltimore
1984	Baltimore Blast	4-1 (LWWWW)	St. Louis
1985	San Diego Sockers	4-1 (WWLWW)	Baltimore
1986	San Diego Sockers	4-3 (WLLLWWW)	Minnesota
1987	Dallas Sidekicks	4-3 (LLWWLWW)	Tacoma
1988	San Diego Sockers	4-0	Cleveland
1989	San Diego Sockers	4-3 (LWWWLLW)	Baltimore
1990	San Diego Sockers	4-2 (LWWWLW)	Baltimore
1991	San Diego Sockers	4-2 (WLWLWW)	Cleveland
1992	San Diego Sockers	4-2 (WWWLLW)	Dallas

Regular Season

Leading Scorer	G	A	Pts
Fred Grgurev, Philadelphia 46	28	74	
Steve Zungul, New York 90	46	136	
Steve Zungul, New York 108	44	152	
Steve Zungul, New York 103	60	163	
Steve Zungul, NY/Golden Bay 75	47	122	
Stan Stamenkovic, Baltimore 34	63	97	
Steve Zungul, San Diego 68	68	136	
Steve Zungul, Tacoma 55	60	115	
Tatu, Dallas 73	38	111	
Eric Rasmussen, Wichita 55	57	112	
Preki, Tacoma 51	53	104	
Tatu, Dallas 64	49	113	
Tatu, Dallas 78	66	144	
Zoran Karic, Cleveland 39	63	102	

Playoff MVPs

MSL playoff Most Valuable Players, selected by a panel of soccer media covering the playoffs.

Multiple winners: Steve Zungul (4); Brian Quinn (2).

Year		Year	
1979	Shep Messing, NY	1986	Brian Quinn, SD
1980	Steve Zungul, NY	1987	Tatu, Dallas
1981	Steve Zungul, NY	1988	Hugo Perez, SD
1982	Steve Zungul, NY	1989	Victor Nogueira, SD
1983	Juli Veee, SD	1990	Brian Quinn, SD
1984	Scott Manning, Bal.	1991	Ben Collins, SD
1985	Steve Zungul, SD	1992	Thompson Usiyan, SD

Regular Season MVPs

MSL regular season Most Valuable Players, selected by a panel of soccer media from every city in the league.

Multiple winners: Steve Zungul (6); Victor Nogueira and Tatu (2).

Year		Year	
1979	Steve Zungul, NY	1986	Steve Zungul, SD/Tac.
1980	Steve Zungul, NY	1987	Tatu, Dallas
1981	Steve Zungul, NY	1988	Erik Rasmussen, Wich.
1982	Steve Zungul, NY & Stan Terlecki, Pit.	1989	Preki, Tacoma
1983	Alan Mayer, SD	1990	Tatu, Dallas
1984	Stan Stamenkovic, Bal.	1991	Victor Nogueira, SD
1985	Steve Zungul, SD	1992	Victor Nogueira, SD

NASL Indoor Champions (1980-84)

The North American Soccer League started an indoor league in the fall of 1979. The indoor NASL, which featured many of the same teams and players who played in the outdoor NASL, crowned champions from 1980-82 before suspending play. It was revived for the 1983-84 indoor season but folded for good in 1984. The NASL held indoor tournaments in 1975 (San Jose Earthquakes won) and 1976 (Tampa Bay Rowdies won) before the indoor league was started.

Multiple winner: San Diego (2).

Year		Year		Year		Year	
1980	Tampa Bay Rowdies	1982	San Diego Sockers	1983	Play suspended	1984	San Diego Sockers
1981	Edmonton Drillers						

Major Indoor Soccer League

The winter indoor MISL began as the American Indoor Soccer Association in 1984-85, then changed its name to the National Professional Soccer League in 1989-90 and was known as the NPSL until 2001 when the name was changed again and the league was relaunched as the MISL.

Multiple winners: Canton (5); Cleveland and Milwaukee (3); Baltimore and Kansas City (2).

Year		Year		Year		Year	
1985	Canton (OH) Invaders	1990	Canton Invaders	1995	St. Louis Ambush	2000	Milwaukee Wave
1986	Canton Invaders	1991	Chicago Power	1996	Cleveland Crunch	2001	Milwaukee Wave
1987	Louisville Thunder	1992	Detroit Rockers	1997	Kansas City Attack	2002	Philadelphia Kixx
1988	Canton Invaders	1993	Kansas City Attack	1998	Milwaukee Wave	2003	Baltimore Blast
1989	Canton Invaders	1994	Cleveland Crunch	1999	Cleveland Crunch	2004	Baltimore Blast

Continental Indoor Soccer League (1993-97)

The summer indoor CISL played its first season in 1993 and folded following the 1997 season.

Multiple winner: Monterrey (2).

Year		Year		Year	
1993	Dallas Sidekicks	1995	Monterrey La Raza	1997	Seattle Seadogs
1994	Las Vegas Dustdevils	1996	Monterrey La Raza		

U.S. COLLEGES

NCAA Men's Division I Champions

NCAA Division I champions since the first title was contested in 1959. The championship has been shared three times–in 1967, 1968 and 1989. There was a playoff for third place from 1974-81.

Multiple winners: Saint Louis (10); Indiana (6); San Francisco and Virginia (5); UCLA (4); Clemson, Connecticut, Howard and Michigan St. (2).

Year	Winner	Head Coach	Score	Runner-up	Host/Site	Semifinalists
1959	Saint Louis	Bob Guelker	5-2	Bridgeport	Connecticut	West Chester, CCNY
1960	Saint Louis	Bob Guelker	3-2	Maryland	Brooklyn	West Chester, Connecticut
1961	West Chester	Mel Lorback	2-0	Saint Louis	Saint Louis	Bridgeport, Rutgers
1962	Saint Louis	Bob Guelker	4-3	Maryland	Saint Louis	Mich. St., Springfield
1963	Saint Louis	Bob Guelker	3-0	Navy	Rutgers	Army, Maryland
1964	Navy	F.H. Warner	1-0	Michigan St.	Brown	Army, Saint Louis
1965	Saint Louis	Bob Guelker	1-0	Michigan St.	Saint Louis	Army, Navy
1966	San Francisco	Steve Negoesco	5-2	LIU-Brooklyn	California	Army, Mich. St.
1967-**a**	Michigan St. & Saint Louis	Gene Kenney Harry Keough	0-0	–	Saint Louis	LIU-Bklyn, Navy
1968-**b**	Michigan St. & Maryland	Gene Kenney Doyle Royal	2-2 (2 OT)	–	Ga. Tech	Brown, San Jose St.
1969	Saint Louis	Harry Keough	4-0	San Francisco	San Jose St.	Harvard, Maryland
1970	Saint Louis	Harry Keough	1-0	UCLA	SIU-Ed'sville	Hartwick, Howard
1971-**c**	Howard	Lincoln Phillips	3-2	Saint Louis	Miami	Harvard, San Fran.
1972	Saint Louis	Harry Keough	4-2	UCLA	Miami	Cornell, Howard
1973	Saint Louis	Harry Keough	2-1 (OT)	UCLA	Miami	Brown, Clemson

Year	Winner	Head Coach	Score	Runner-up	Host/Site	Third Place
1974	Howard	Lincoln Phillips	2-1 (4OT)	Saint Louis	Saint Louis	Hartwick 3, UCLA 1
1975	San Francisco	Steve Negoesco	4-0	SIU-Ed'sville	SIU-Ed'sville	Brown 2, Howard 0
1976	San Francisco	Steve Negoesco	1-0	Indiana	Penn	Hartwick 4, Clemson 3
1977	Hartwick	Jim Lennox	2-1	San Francisco	California	SIU-Ed'sville 3, Brown 2
1978-**d**	San Francisco	Steve Negoesco	4-3 (OT)	Indiana	Tampa	Clemson 6, Phi. Textile 2
1979	SIU-Ed'sville	Bob Guelker	3-2	Clemson	Tampa	Penn St. 2, Columbia 1
1980	San Francisco	Steve Negoesco	4-3 (OT)	Indiana	Tampa	Ala. A&M 2, Hartwick 0
1981	Connecticut	Joe Morrone	2-1 (OT)	Alabama A&M	Stanford	East. Ill. 4, Phi. Textile 2

Year	Winner	Head Coach	Score	Runner-up	Host/Site	Semifinalists
1982	Indiana	Jerry Yeagley	2-1 (8 OT)	Duke	Ft. Lauderdale	Connecticut, SIU-Ed'sville
1983	Indiana	Jerry Yeagley	1-0 (2 OT)	Columbia	Ft. Lauderdale	Connecticut, Virginia
1984	Clemson	I.M. Ibrahim	2-1	Indiana	Seattle	Hartwick, UCLA
1985	UCLA	Sigi Schmid	1-0 (8 OT)	American	Seattle	Evansville, Hartwick
1986	Duke	John Rennie	1-0	Akron	Tacoma	Fresno St., Harvard
1987	Clemson	I.M. Ibrahim	2-0	San Diego St.	Clemson	Harvard, N. Carolina
1988	Indiana	Jerry Yeagley	1-0	Howard	Indiana	Portland, S. Carolina
1989-**e**	Santa Clara & Virginia	Steve Sampson Bruce Arena	1-1 (2 OT)	–	Rutgers	Indiana, Rutgers
1990-**f**	UCLA	Sigi Schmid	0-0 (PKs)	Rutgers	South Fla.	Evansville, N.C. State
1991-**g**	Virginia	Bruce Arena	0-0 (PKs)	Santa Clara	Tampa	Indiana, Saint Louis
1992	Virginia	Bruce Arena	2-0	San Diego	Davidson	Davidson, Duke
1993	Virginia	Bruce Arena	2-0	South Carolina	Davidson	CS-Fullerton, Princeton
1994	Virginia	Bruce Arena	1-0	Indiana	Davidson	Rutgers, UCLA
1995	Wisconsin	Jim Launder	2-0	Duke	Richmond	Portland, Virginia
1996	St. John's	Dave Masur	4-1	Fla. International	Richmond	Creighton, NC-Charlotte
1997	UCLA	Sigi Schmid	2-0	Virginia	Richmond	Indiana, Saint Louis
1998	Indiana	Jerry Yeagley	3-1	Stanford	Richmond	Maryland, Santa Clara
1999	Indiana	Jerry Yeagley	1-0	Santa Clara	Charlotte	Connecticut, UCLA
2000	Connecticut	Ray Reid	2-0	Creighton	Charlotte	Indiana, Southern Methodist
2001	North Carolina	Elmar Bolowich	2-0	Indiana	Columbus	St. John's, Stanford
2002	UCLA	Tom Fitzgerald	1-0	Stanford	Dallas	Creighton, Maryland
2003	Indiana	Jerry Yeagley	2-1	St. John's	Columbus	Maryland, Santa Clara

a–game declared a draw due to inclement weather after regulation time; **b**–game declared a draw after two overtimes; **c**–Howard vacated title for using ineligible player; **d**–San Francisco vacated title for using ineligible player; **e**–game declared a draw due to inclement weather after two overtimes. **f**–UCLA wins on penalty kicks (4-3) after four overtimes; **g**–Virginia wins on penalty kicks (3-1) after four overtimes.

Women's NCAA Division I Champions

NCAA Division I women's champions since the first tournament was contested in 1982.

Multiple winner: North Carolina (17).

Year	Winner	Coach	Score	Runner-up	Host/Site
1982	North Carolina	Anson Dorrance	2-0	Central Florida	Central Florida
1983	North Carolina	Anson Dorrance	4-0	George Mason	Central Florida
1984	North Carolina	Anson Dorrance	2-0	Connecticut	North Carolina
1985	George Mason	Hank Leung	2-0	North Carolina	George Mason
1986	North Carolina	Anson Dorrance	2-0	Colorado College	George Mason
1987	North Carolina	Anson Dorrance	1-0	Massachusetts	Massachusetts
1988	North Carolina	Anson Dorrance	4-1	N.C. State	North Carolina
1989	North Carolina	Anson Dorrance	2-0	Colorado College	N.C. State
1990	North Carolina	Anson Dorrance	6-0	Connecticut	North Carolina
1991	North Carolina	Anson Dorrance	3-1	Wisconsin	North Carolina
1992	North Carolina	Anson Dorrance	9-1	Duke	North Carolina
1993	North Carolina	Anson Dorrance	6-0	George Mason	North Carolina
1994	North Carolina	Anson Dorrance	5-0	Notre Dame	Portland
1995	Notre Dame	Chris Petrucelli	1-0 (3OT)	Portland	North Carolina
1996	North Carolina	Anson Dorrance	1-0 (2OT)	Notre Dame	Santa Clara
1997	North Carolina	Anson Dorrance	2-0	Connecticut	NC-Greensboro
1998	Florida	Becky Burleigh	1-0	North Carolina	NC-Greensboro
1999	North Carolina	Anson Dorrance	2-0	Notre Dame	San Jose, Calif.
2000	North Carolina	Anson Dorrance	2-1	UCLA	San Jose, Calif.
2001	Santa Clara	Jerry Smith	1-0	North Carolina	Dallas
2002	Portland	Clive Charles	2-1 (2OT)	Santa Clara	Austin
2003	North Carolina	Anson Dorrance	6-0	Connecticut	Cary, N.C.

Annual Awards
MEN
Hermann Trophy

College Player of the Year. Voted on by Division I college coaches and selected sportswriters and first presented in 1967 in the name of Robert Hermann, one of the founders of the North American Soccer League.

Multiple winners: Mike Fisher, Mike Seerey, Ken Snow and Al Trost (2).

Year		Year		Year	
1967	Dov Markus, LIU	1980	Joe Morrone, Jr. Connecticut	1991	Alexi Lalas, Rutgers
1968	Manuel Hernandez, San Jose St.	1981	Armando Betancourt, Indiana	1994	Brian Maisonneuve, Indiana
1969	Al Trost, Saint Louis	1982	Joe Ulrich, Duke	1995	Mike Fisher, Virginia
1970	Al Trost, Saint Louis	1983	Mike Jeffries, Duke	1996	Mike Fisher, Virginia
1971	Mike Seerey, Saint Louis	1984	Amr Aly, Columbia	1997	Johnny Torres, Creighton
1972	Mike Seerey, Saint Louis	1985	Tom Kain, Duke	1998	Wojtek Krakowiak, Clemson
1973	Dan Counce, Saint Louis	1986	John Kerr, Duke	1999	Ali Curtis, Duke
1974	Farrukh Quraishi, Oneonta St.	1987	Bruce Murray, Clemson	2000	Chris Gbandi, Connecticut
1975	Steve Ralbovsky, Brown	1988	Ken Snow, Indiana	2001	Luchi Gonzalez, SMU
1976	Glenn Myernick, Hartwick	1989	Tony Meola, Virginia	2002	Alecko Eskandarian, Virginia
1977	Billy Gazonas, Hartwick	1990	Ken Snow, Indiana	2003	Chris Wingert, St. John's
1978	Angelo DiBernardo, Indiana	1992	Brad Friedel, UCLA		
1979	Jim Stamatis, Penn St.	1993	Claudio Reyna, Virginia		

Missouri Athletic Club Award

College Player of the Year. Voted on by men's team coaches around the country from Division I to junior college level and first presented in 1986 by the Missouri Athletic Club of St. Louis.

Multiple winners: Claudio Reyna and Ken Snow (2).

Year		Year		Year	
1986	John Kerr, Duke	1992	Claudio Reyna, Virginia	1998	Jay Heaps, Duke
1987	John Harkes, Virginia	1993	Claudio Reyna, Virginia	1999	Sasha Victorine, UCLA
1988	Ken Snow, Indiana	1994	Todd Yeagley, Indiana	2000	Ali Curtis, Duke
1989	Tony Meola, Virginia	1995	Matt McKeon, St. Louis	2001	Luchi Gonzalez, SMU
1990	Ken Snow, Indiana	1996	Mike Fisher, Virginia	2002	merged with Hermann Trophy.
1991	Alexi Lalas, Rutgers	1997	Johnny Torres, Creighton		

Coach of the Year

Men's Coach of the Year. Voted on by the National Soccer Coaches Association of America. From 1973-81 all Senior College coaches were eligible. In 1982, the award was split into several divisions. The Division I Coach of the Year is listed since 1982.
Multiple winner: Jerry Yeagley (6).

Year		Year		Year	
1973	Robert Guelker, SIU-Edwardsville	1984	James Lennox, Hartwick	1995	Jim Launder, Wisconsin
1974	Jack MacKenzie, Quincy College	1985•Peter Mehleft, American	1996	Dave Masur, St. John's
1975	Paul Reinhardt, Vermont	1986	Steve Parker, Akron	1997	Sigi Schmid, UCLA
1976	Jerry Yeagley, Indiana	1987	Anson Dorrance, N. Carolina	1998	Jerry Yeagley, Indiana
1977	Klass Deboer, Cleveland St.	1988	Keith Tucker, Howard	1999	Jerry Yeagley, Indiana
1978	Cliff McCrath, Seattle Pacific	1989	Steve Sampson, Santa Clara	2000	Ray Reid, Connecticut
1979	Walter Bahr, Penn St.	1990	Bob Reasso, Rutgers	2001	Elmar Bolowich, North Carolina
1980	Jerry Yeagley, Indiana	1991	Mitch Murray, Santa Clara	2002	Tom Fitzgerald, UCLA
1981	Schellas Hyndman, E. Illinois	1992	Charles Slagle, Davidson	2003	Jerry Yeagley, Indiana
1982	John Rennie, Duke	1993	Bob Bradley, Princeton		
1983	Dieter Ficken, Columbia	1994	Jerry Yeagley, Indiana		

WOMEN
Hermann Trophy

Women's College Player of the year. Voted on by Division I college coaches and selected sportswriters and first presented in 1988 in the name of Robert Hermann, one of the founders of the North American Soccer League.
Multiple winners: Mia Hamm and Cindy Parlow (2).

Year		Year		Year	
1988	Michelle Akers, Central Fla.	1994	Tisha Venturini, N. Carolina	2000	Anne Makinen, Notre Dame
1989	Shannon Higgins, N. Carolina	1995	Shannon McMillan, N. Carolina	2001	Christie Welsh, Penn St.
1990	April Kater, Massachusetts	1996	Cindy Daws, Notre Dame	2002	Aly Wagner, Santa Clara
1991	Kristine Lilly, N. Carolina	1997	Cindy Parlow, N. Carolina	2003	Catherine Reddick, N. Carolina
1992	Mia Hamm, N. Carolina	1998	Cindy Parlow, N. Carolina		
1993	Mia Hamm, N. Carolina	1999	Mandy Clemens, Santa Clara		

Missouri Athletic Club Award

Women's College Player of the Year. Voted on by women's team coaches around the country from Division I to junior college level and first presented in 1991 by the Missouri Athletic Club of St. Louis.
Multiple winners: Mia Hamm and Cindy Parlow (2).

Year		Year		Year	
1991	Kristine Lilly, N. Carolina	1995	Shannon McMillan, Portland	1999	Mandy Clemens, Santa Clara
1992	Mia Hamm, N. Carolina	1996	Cindy Daws, Notre Dame	2000	Anne Makinen, Notre Dame
1993	Mia Hamm, N. Carolina	1997	Cindy Parlow, N. Carolina	2001	Christie Welsh, Penn St.
1994	Tisha Venturini, N. Carolina	1998	Cindy Parlow, N. Carolina	2002	merged with Hermann Trophy.

Coach of the Year

Women's Coach of the Year. Voted on by the National Soccer Coaches Association of America. From 1982-87 all Senior College coaches were eligible. In 1988, the award was split into several divisions. The Division I Coach of the Year is listed since 1988.
Multiple winners: Anson Dorrance (3); Kalenkeni M. Banda and Chris Petrucelli (2).

Year		Year		Year	
1982	Anson Dorrance, N. Carolina	1990	Lauren Gregg, Virginia	1998	Becky Burleigh, Florida
1983	David Lombardo, Keene St.	1991	Greg Ryan, Wisc-Madison	1999	Patrick Farmer, Penn St.
1984	Phillip Picince, Brown	1992	Bell Hempen, Duke	2000	Jillian Ellis, UCLA
1985	Kalenkeni M. Banda, UMass	1993	Jac Cicala, George Mason	2001	Jerry Smith, Santa Clara
1986	Anson Dorrance, N. Carolina	1994	Chris Petrucelli, Norte Dame	2002	Clive Charles, Portland
1987	Kalenkeni M. Banda, UMass	1995	Chris Petrucelli, Norte Dame	2003	Anson Dorrance, N. Carolina
1988	Larry Gross, N.C. State	1996	John Walker, Nebraska		
1989	Austin Daniels, Hartford	1997	Len Tsantiris, Connecticut		

Bowling

Tom Baker won the season-ending PBA World Championship, his first major title.

PBA Tour

Fantastic, Finnish

Finland's Mika Koivuniemi becomes the first European to become PBA Player of the Year.

Michael Morrison
is co-editor of the ESPN Sports Almanac.

When you think of Finland, what's generally the first thing that comes to mind?

Ski jumping? Hockey? Maybe. Nokia? Possibly. Bowling? Doubtful. But Mika Koivuniemi might just change that.

The 37-year-old Koivuniemi is widely known in international bowling circles, having recorded victories in ten countries and winning the 1991 FIQ World Championship. He showed signs of things to come in 2000 with a win in the ABC Masters, then followed that up in 2001 with a U.S. Open title, making him the first foreign-born bowler to win those events. But in the 2003-04 season, it was time to shine on the PBA Tour.

He led the Tour in average (222.73) and earnings ($238,590), two categories that are normally off-limits unless your name is Walter Ray Williams Jr. or Parker Bohn III. For his efforts, he was voted Chris Schenkel PBA Player of the Year by his peers.

He was the model of consistency, with the occasional burst of brilliance. Of the 21 official PBA Tour events in 2003-04, Koivuniemi reached the championship round in seven of them, more than anyone else on the Tour. He won two of those tournaments and finished runner-up in three more.

In early December at the Cambridge Credit Classic in Windsor Locks, Conn., Koivuniemi showed the rest of the Tour, not to mention the entire ESPN audience, the reaches of his talent. The six-foot-four former electrician notched three perfect games over the course of the tournament. His third, a 300-248 masterpiece over Jason Couch in the wild card match, was the 16th televised 300 game in the history of the PBA.

He would go on to defeat Patrick Allen in the title match, 259-237, for his first victory of the season. Koivuniemi's performance is regarded as one of the most impressive in recent years.

PBA Tour

*It all came together in 2003-04 for Finland native and Ann Arbor resident **Mika Koivuniemi**, who led all PBA bowlers in earnings and average.*

Consider this—during the three games of the championship round, he threw a total of 35 shots. He struck on 32 of them. His 836 three-game total was 14 pins shy of Bob Learn Jr.'s all-time TV record set at the Flagship Open in 1996.

"I was not that concerned about the 300 game," Koivuniemi said. "I was on a mission. Now that I have won, mission accomplished."

Koivuniemi was on a mission once again the following month at the National Bowling Stadium in Reno, where the finals of the ABC Masters and the Reno Open would be played within a span of five days. As expected, he reached the championship round in each. After finishing third in the Masters (won by Williams Jr.), he roared through match-play competition at the Reno Open, making short work of Brad Angelo in the title match, 258-181, to win his second tournament of the season.

The proverbial icing on the cake would be a victory at the season-ending PBA World Championship in Michigan. A win would give him the third major title of his career, add an additional $120,000 to his tour-leading total, and solidify his chances at winning Player of the Year honors.

PBA Tour

*Hall of famer **Pete Weber**, left, won his third U.S. Open title in February while **Tom Baker**, right, defeated Mika Koivuniemi at the season-ending PBA World Championship in March.*

It came down to the tournament's final frame. Koivuniemi defeated Wes Malott in the semis to set up a finals showdown with Buffalo-native Tom Baker. Koivuniemi put the pressure on, forcing Baker to mark in the tenth frame to win. And mark he did. Baker spared, then struck with his final ball to record the hard-fought 246-239 victory. Koivuniemi "settled" for second place and the accompanying $50,000 prize.

Bowler of the Year honors were far from a sure thing. Illinois' Steve Jaros won three events in 2003-04, more than any other bowler on the Tour, and also became the PBA's 28th career million-aire. Like Koivuniemi, hall of famer Pete

Weber added two titles to his growing list, including his third U.S. Open, to put himself in the running.

And of course, there's always Walter Ray, who added to his legend by rebounding from a slow start to pick up two more wins and two runner-ups. Williams Jr. now needs just three more titles to overtake Earl Anthony as the PBA's all-time leader.

In the end, however, PBA members simply couldn't look past Koivuniemi's earnings and consistency and made him the first European bowler to win the Schenkel Award. Given his perform-ances with the television cameras on him, it likely won't be his last.

The Ten Biggest Stories of the Year in Bowling

10 PBA hall of famer Mike Aulby says goodbye, retiring from the Tour after 25 years, 27 Tour titles, seven majors and over $2 million in career earnings. The 1979 Rookie of the Year and two-time Player of the Year is the only bowler to win an event in four separate decades.

9 Women's bowling becomes the NCAA's 88th official championship. Nebraska comes from behind to defeat Central Missouri State at Emerald Bowl in Houston to become the inaugural titlist.

8 With a second-place finish at the Toledo Open and a rookie-leading $45,260 in earnings, six-foot-two Texan Chris Johnson is named the Harry Golden PBA Rookie of the Year. Johnson leads all rookies with two championship round appearances and 12 cashes in 19 events.

7 At the International Bowl Expo in August, the Women's International Bowling Congress (WIBC) announces that it has acquired all rights and assets of the Professional Women's Bowling Association (PWBA). As part of the deal, the WIBC now oversees all PWBA records, as well as the possibility of a new national women's tour and other sponsorship and television opportunities.

6 Three-time defending Tournament of Champions winner Jason Couch is ousted in the round of 16 of the 2004 event by Randy Pedersen, 3 games to 0, opening the door for a new champion. Patrick Healey Jr. walks right through that door, defeating Pedersen in the title match, 222-188, for the first major title of his career.

5 The finals of the 61st U.S. Open sees a battle of two hall of famers, Brian Voss and Pete Weber. Voss' open seventh frame ultimately does him in as Weber takes his third U.S. Open title and seventh overall major with a 231-178 victory.

4 The PBA's new "exempt" format begins with the 2004-05 season, meaning each of the 16 standard tournaments will include only 64 bowlers. Fifty of those 64 entries come directly from performances in the 2003-04 season. For more, see box on page 768.

3 Walter Ray Williams Jr. shakes off an early-season slump to record two victories over the last half of the season. His second title of the year comes at the 54th ABC Masters, where he strikes in his first six frames and takes down Chris Barnes, 268-239, in the championship game. The win gives him 39 for his career, placing him just two shy of Earl Anthony's all-time win record.

2 In one of the largest non-profit mergers in United States history, the country's top bowling organizations (WIBC, USA Bowling, American Bowling Congress and Young American Bowling Alliance) agree to merge into a single organization known as the United States Bowling Congress (USBC). The merger officially takes place on Jan. 1, 2005 and the new entity will have a membership of roughly 3.2 million people.

1 Finland's Mika Koivuniemi takes the PBA Tour by storm, winning his third and fourth career tournaments, leading the Tour in earnings and average and taking home the PBA Player of the Year Award. In his Dec. 7 victory at the Cambridge Credit Classic, Koivuniemi is nearly flawless in the final round, bowling 32 strikes in the three games and recording the 16th perfect game in PBA television history.

One MILLION Dollars

During the 2003-04 season, a PBA-record five bowlers passed the $1 million mark for career earnings. There are now 30 PBA Tour millionaires, as of October, 2004.

	Tournament	Date
Steve Hoskins	Banquet Open	10/12/03
Doug Kent	Reno Open	1/29/04
Steve Jaros	Days Inn Open	2/22/04
Ryan Shafer	Baby Ruth	2/29/04
Dave D'Entremont	Uniroyal	3/7/04

Source: Professional Bowlers Association

Everything but the Trophy

Brad Angelo earned $115,250 during the 2003-04 season, good enough for ninth place on the season money list, but he's still looking for his first Tour victory. Listed are the top single-season earners without a title.

	Earnings	Season
Pete McCordic	$156,476	1987
Marshall Holman	152,563	1987
Patrick Healey Jr.	139,708	2001-02
Dave Ferraro	137,907	1989

Source: Professional Bowlers Association

300 Times Four

Mika Koivuniemi recorded three perfect games at the Cambridge Credit Classic in December. With one more he would have tied the PBA mark of four in one tournament, currently held by three players.

	Year
Walter Ray Williams Jr.	1993
Dave D'Entremont	1995
John Bauerle Jr.	1999

Source: Professional Bowlers Association

2003-2004
Season in Review

SPORTS ALMANAC

Tournament Results

Winners of stepladder finals in all PBA, Seniors and PWBA tournaments from Sept. 15, 2003 through Sept. 28, 2004; major tournaments in **bold** type. Note (a) indicates amateur.

PBA
2003-04 Season

Final	Event	Winner	Earnings	Score	Runner-up
Sept. 15	Dream Bowl 2003 (Yokohama)	Walter Ray Williams Jr.	$25,000	445-421	Yasuyuki Sadamatsu
Sept. 21	Japan Cup	Chris Barnes	40,000	210-179	Tommy Jones
Oct. 12	Banquet Open	Robert Smith	40,000	244-187	Michael Machuga
Oct. 19	Greater Kansas City Classic	Norm Duke	40,000	197-194	Mika Koivuniemi
Oct. 26	Miller High Life Open	Brian Himmler	40,000	230-215	Mika Koivuniemi
Nov. 2	Pepsi Open	Jason Couch	40,000	187-177	Steve Wilson
Nov. 9	Toledo Open	Steve Jaros	40,000	224-222	Chris Johnson
Nov. 16	Greater Philadelphia Open	Patrick Allen	40,000	200-178	Danny Wiseman
Nov. 23	Empire State Open	Ryan Shafer	40,000	217-215	Chris Barnes
Nov. 30	Geico Open	Patrick Healey Jr.	40,000	235-214	Ryan Shafer
Dec. 7	Cambridge Credit Classic	Mika Koivuniemi	50,300	259-237	Patrick Allen
Dec. 14	**Dexter Tournament of Champions at Mohegan Sun**	Patrick Healey Jr.	100,000	222-188	Randy Pedersen
Jan. 11	Earl Anthony Classic	Walter Ray Williams Jr.	40,000	211-205	Lonnie Waliczek
Jan. 18	Medford Open	Pete Weber	40,000	265-256	Tommy Delutz Jr.
Jan. 25	**ABC Masters**	Walter Ray Williams Jr.	100,000	268-239	Chris Barnes
Jan. 29	Reno Open	Mika Koivuniemi	40,000	258-181	Brad Angelo
Feb. 8	**U.S. Open** presented by Jackson Hewitt Tax Service	Pete Weber	100,000	231-178	Brian Voss
Feb. 15	Odor-Eaters Open	Robert Smith	40,000	227-218	Walter Ray Williams Jr.
Feb. 22	Days Inn Open	Steve Jaros	40,000	260-235	David Traber
Feb. 29	Baby Ruth Real Deal Classic	Mike Scroggins	40,000	270-248	Walter Ray Williams Jr.
Mar. 7	Uniroyal Tire Classic	Steve Jaros	40,000	257-195	Dave D'Entremont
Mar. 21	**PBA World Championship**	Tom Baker	120,000	246-239	Mika Koivuniemi

Note: Dream Bowl 2003 is not an official PBA Tour event.

2004-05 PBA Tour Schedule

Major tournaments are in **bold** type. See Updates chapter for results through mid-October.

September—Japan Cup, Yokohama, JPN (Sept. 14-21).

October—**Miller High Life Masters presented by the American Bowling Congress**, Milwaukee, Wis. (Oct. 24-31).

November—Chicago Open, Vernon Hills, Ill. (Nov. 3-7); Uniroyal Tire Classic, Wickliffe, Ohio (Nov. 10-14); BowlersParadise.com Open, Valley Park, Mo. (Nov. 17-21); Pepsi Open, Wichita, Kan. (Nov. 23-28).

December—Denver Open, Lakewood, Colo. (Dec. 1-5); Earl Anthony Medford Classic, Medford, Ore. (Dec. 8-12); Orange County Classic presented by Storm, Fountain Valley, Calif. (Dec. 15-19).

January 2005—Geico Open, Mesa, Ari. (Jan. 5-9); El Paso Classic, El Paso, Texas (Jan. 12-16); Dallas Open, Dallas, Texas (Jan. 19-23); Birmingham Open, Trussville, Ala. (Jan. 26-30).

February—Atlanta Classic, Norcross, Ga. (Feb. 2-6); Jackson Hewitt Tax Service Open, Fairlawn, Ohio (Feb. 9-13); **U.S. Open presented by Odor-Eaters**, North Brunswick, N.J. (Feb. 13-20); Cambridge Credit Classic, West Babylon, N.Y. (Feb. 23-27).

March—Baby Ruth Real Deal Classic, Indianapolis, Ind. (Mar. 2-6); Banquet Open, Grand Rapids, Mich. (Mar. 16-20).

April— **PBA World Championship**, Taylor, Mich. (Mar. 26-Apr. 3); **Dexter Tournament of Champions**, Uncasville, Conn. (Apr. 6-10).

Tournament Results (Cont.)

PBA Majors

Dexter Tournament of Champions

Edition: 38th   **Dates:** Dec. 11-13, 2003
Site: Mohegan Sun in Uncasville, Conn.
Prize Fund: $230,000

Championship Round

		Total pins	Earnings
1	Patrick Healey Jr.	432 (2 games)	$100,000
2	Randy Pedersen	466 (2 games)	30,000
3	Brian Himmler	227 (1 game)	10,000
	Chris Barnes	192 (1 game)	10,000

Playoff Results: Healey Jr. def. Barnes, 210-192; Pedersen def. Himmler, 278-227; and in the championship game, Healey Jr. def. Pedersen, 222-188.

ABC Masters

Edition: 54th   **Dates:** Jan. 20-25, 2004
Site: National Bowling Stadium in Reno, Nev.
Prize Fund: $350,000

Championship Round

		Total pins	Earnings
1	Walter Ray Williams Jr.	505 (2 games)	$100,000
2	Chris Barnes	239 (1 game)	50,000
3	Mika Koivuniemi	651 (3 games)	25,000
4	D.J. Archer	149 (1 game)	15,000
5	Patrick Allen	173 (1 game)	10,000

Playoff Results: Koivuniemi def. Allen, 214-173; Koivuniemi def. Archer, 224-149; Williams Jr. def. Koivuniemi, 237-213; and in the championship game, Williams Jr. def. Barnes, 268-239.

U.S. Open

Edition: 61st   **Dates:** Feb. 2-8, 2004.
Site: Fountain Bowl in Fountain Valley, Calif.
Prize Fund: $350,000

Championship Round

		Total pins	Earnings
1	Pete Weber	231 (1 game)	$100,000
2	Brian Voss	652 (3 games)	50,100
3	Chris Barnes	193 (1 game)	25,000
4	Walter Ray Williams Jr.	442 (2 games)	15,000
5	Osku Palermaa	198 (1 game)	10,000

Playoff Results: Williams Jr. def. Palermaa, 228-198; Voss def. Williams Jr., 260-214; Voss def. Barnes, 214-193; and in the championship game, Weber def. Voss, 231-178.

PBA World Championship

Edition: 45th   **Dates:** Mar. 15-21, 2004
Site: Taylor Lanes in Taylor, Mich.
Prize Fund: $438,000

Championship Round

		Total pins	Earnings
1	Tom Baker	523 (2 games)	$120,000
2	Mika Koivuniemi	464 (2 games)	50,000
3	Wes Malott	193 (2 games)	20,000
	Brad Angelo	243 (1 game)	20,000

Playoff Results: Baker def. Angelo, 277-243; Koivuniemi def. Malott, 225-193; and in the championship game, Baker def. Koivuniemi, 246-239.

Senior PBA

2004 Spring/Summer Tour

Final	Event	Winner	Earnings	Score	Runner-up
Mar. 31	Epicenter Classic	Robert Glass	$8,000	3 games to 2	Don Sylvia
Apr. 9	**ABC Senior Masters**	Gary Dickinson	20,000	638-580	Roy Buckley
Apr. 27	Clarksville Open presented by Georgia Boot	Gary Hiday	8,000	2 games to 1	Bob Chamberlain
May 4	Chillicothe Open	Robert Glass	8,100	2 games to 1	Gary Skidmore
May 14	**Senior U.S. Open** presented by Days Inn	David Ozio	20,100	189-167	Steve Neff
May 19	Manassas Open	George Pappas	8,000	2 games to 0	Tim Kauble
Aug. 4	Don Carter Classic presented by Storm	Doug Evans	8,000	2 games to 1	Tommy Nevitt
Aug. 11	St. Petersburg/Clearwater Open	Jeff Bellinger	8,000	2 games to 0	Gary Hiday
Aug. 18	Jackson Open	Vince Mazzanti Jr.	8,000	2 games to 0	Roger Bowker
Aug. 26	Lake County Open	Roger Kossert	8,000	2 games to 0	Pete Couture

Note: In 2004, all tournaments on the Senior PBA Tour followed a best-of-three match-play final-round format with the exception of the Senior U.S. Open, which used a traditional step-ladder single-match final round. The ABC Senior Masters used a best-of-three match format, however each match was comprised of three games.

PBA Tour goes exempt in 2004-05

Beginning with the 2004-05 season, the PBA Tour will be structured as an all-exempt field. Each of the 16 standard tournaments (majors not included) will be limited to 64 bowlers, 58 of whom will have exempt status for the entire Tour season.

Of the 58 who have exemption for the entire season, 50 will come directly as a result of their performance during the 2003-04 season (16 standard event champions, four major champions and the remaining 30 from a new season point list). The remaining eight season-long qualifiers come from the PBA Tour Trials, held June 1-6 in Merrillville, Ind.

The other six bowlers (bringing the weekly total to 64) will change from week to week. Five will come from a "Weekly Qualifier" held on the Wednesday morning of each tournament. The final weekly participant will be chosen by the Commissioner in what is known as the "Weekly Commissioner Exemption."

Tour Leaders

Official standings for 2003-04. Note that (TB) indicates Tournaments Bowled; (CR) Championship Rounds as Stepladder or Match-play Finalist; and (1st) Titles Won.

PBA
2003-04

	Top 10 Money Winners	TB	CR	1st	Earnings		Top 10 Averages	TB	Games	Avg
1	Mika Koivuniemi	20	7	2	$238,590	1	Mika Koivuniemi	20	487	222.73
2	Walter Ray Williams Jr.	21	5	2	233,950	2	Patrick Allen	20	505	221.98
3	Pete Weber	21	4	2	206,217	3	Walter Ray Williams Jr.	21	510	221.87
4	Chris Barnes	21	7	1	191,550	4	Chris Barnes	21	489	221.33
5	Patrick Healey Jr.	19	3	2	174,600	5	Brad Angelo	20	574	221.00
6	Steve Jaros	21	5	3	166,300	6	Jason Couch	20	441	220.94
7	Tom Baker	19	1	1	134,633	7	Mike Scroggins	19	452	220.62
8	Patrick Allen	20	4	1	118,550	8	Norm Duke	13	278	220.37
9	Brad Angelo	20	5	0	115,250	9	Michael Haugen Jr.	19	443	219.34
10	Robert Smith	20	3	2	108,750	10	Ryan Shafer	21	437	219.29

Note: Earnings include ABC Masters and U.S. Open. Dream Bowl not included.

Senior PBA
2004

	Top 10 Money Winners	TB	CR	1st	Earnings		Top 10 Averages	TB	Games	Avg
1	Robert Glass	9	3	2	$28,600	1	David Ozio	6	180	226.47
2	David Ozio	6	2	1	27,900	2	Gary Skidmore	6	146	217.16
3	Gary Dickinson	6	1	1	26,700	3	Bob Chamberlain	9	290	216.65
4	Gary Hiday	10	3	1	25,150	4	George Pappas	8	169	216.37
5	Bob Chamberlain	9	4	0	24,050	5	Roger Bowker	9	243	216.12
6	Roy Buckley	9	2	0	18,700	6	Bob Handley	6	169	214.92
7	Ron Winger	10	2	0	17,350	7	Ron Winger	10	275	214.59
8	Jeff Bellinger	7	2	1	16,910	8	Gary Dickinson	6	181	214.46
9	Steve Neff	6	1	0	15,600	9	Jeff Bellinger	7	180	214.32
10	George Pappas	8	2	1	15,200	10	Guppy Troup	6	170	214.25

Note: Earnings include ABC Senior Masters.

Women's Bowling

Note: The Professional Women's Bowling Association (PWBA) national tour was cancelled in the fall of 2003 due to a lack of operating funds. There was no national tour in 2004.

Majors

WIBC Queens

Edition: 44th
Site: Northrock Lanes in Wichita, Kan.
Prize Fund: $105,500
Dates: May 15-19, 2004

Championship Round

		Total pins	Earnings
1	Marianne DiRupo	419 (2 games)	$13,500
2	Michelle Feldman	924 (4 games)	10,000
3	Olivia Sandham	159 (1 game)	7,500
4	Takiko Naganawa	436 (2 games)	6,500
5	Liz Johnson	192 (1 game)	5,000

Playoff Results: Naganawa def. Johnson, 213-192; Feldman def. Naganawa, 235-223; Feldman def. Sandham, 245-159; Feldman def. DiRupo, 242-193; and in the championship game, DiRupo def. Feldman, 226-202.

NCAA Women's Bowling Championship

Nebraska fought off elimination three times on the final day of competition to win the inaugural NCAA women's bowling championship at Emerald Bowl in Houston, Texas. The Huskers defeated New Jersey City, then Central Missouri State to set up a winner-take-all title match, also against Central Missouri State. Nebraska quickly fell behind, two games to one, in the best-of-seven title match before roaring back to win three straight to claim the title, four games to two. Junior Shannon Pluhowsky rolled the championship-clinching ball for Nebraska and was named the tournament's first MVP. (Houston, TX; April 8-10, 2004.)

1942-2004
Through the Years

SPORTS ALMANAC

Major Championships
MEN
U.S. Open

Started in 1941 by the Bowling Proprietors' Association of America, 18 years before the founding of the Professional Bowlers Association. Originally the BPAA All-Star Tournament, it became the U.S. Open in 1971.

Multiple winners: Don Carter and Dick Weber (4); Dave Husted and Pete Weber (3); Del Ballard Jr., Marshall Holman, Junie McMahon, Connie Schwoegler, Andy Varipapa and Walter Ray Williams Jr. (2).

Year		Year		Year		Year	
1942	John Crimmins	1958	Don Carter	1974	Larry Laub	1990	Ron Palombi Jr.
1943	Connie Schwoegler	1959	Billy Welu	1975	Steve Neff	1991	Pete Weber
1944	Ned Day	1960	Harry Smith	1976	Paul Moser	1992	Robert Lawrence
1945	Buddy Bomar	1961	Bill Tucker	1977	Johnny Petraglia	1993	Del Ballard Jr.
1946	Joe Wilman	1962	Dick Weber	1978	Nelson Burton Jr.	1994	Justin Hromek
1947	Andy Varipapa	1963	Dick Weber	1979	Joe Berardi	1995	Dave Husted
1948	Andy Varipapa	1964	Bob Strampe	1980	Steve Martin	1996	Dave Husted
1949	Connie Schwoegler	1965	Dick Weber	1981	Marshall Holman	1997	Not held
1950	Junie McMahon	1966	Dick Weber	1982	Dave Husted	1998	Walter Ray Williams Jr.
1951	Dick Hoover	1967	Les Schissler	1983	Gary Dickinson	1999	Bob Learn Jr.
1952	Junie McMahon	1968	Jim Stefanich	1984	Mark Roth	2000	Robert Smith
1953	Don Carter	1969	Billy Hardwick	1985	Marshall Holman	2001	Miko Koivuniemi
1954	Don Carter	1970	Bobby Cooper	1986	Steve Cook	2003	Walter Ray Williams Jr.
1955	Steve Nagy	1971	Mike Limongello	1987	Del Ballard Jr.	2004	Pete Weber
1956	Bill Lillard	1972	Don Johnson	1988	Pete Weber		
1957	Don Carter	1973	Mike McGrath	1989	Mike Aulby		

PBA World Championship

The Professional Bowlers Association was formed in 1958 and its first national championship tournament was held in Memphis in 1960. Formerly known as the PBA National Championship, the name was changed in 2002. The tournament was held in various locations (1960-80), Toledo, Ohio (1981-2002) and Taylor, Mich. (2003-).

Multiple winners: Earl Anthony (6); Mike Aulby, Dave Davis, Mike McGrath, Pete Weber, Walter Ray Williams Jr. and Wayne Zahn (2).

Year		Year		Year		Year	
1960	Don Carter	1972	Johnny Guenther	1984	Bob Chamberlain	1996	Butch Soper
1961	Dave Soutar	1973	Earl Anthony	1985	Mike Aulby	1997	Rick Steelsmith
1962	Carmen Salvino	1974	Earl Anthony	1986	Tom Crites	1998	Pete Weber
1963	Billy Hardwick	1975	Earl Anthony	1987	Randy Pedersen	1999	Tim Criss
1964	Bob Strampe	1976	Paul Colwell	1988	Brian Voss	2000	Norm Duke
1965	Dave Davis	1977	Tommy Hudson	1989	Pete Weber	2001	Walter Ray Williams Jr.
1966	Wayne Zahn	1978	Warren Nelson	1990	Jim Pencak	2002	Doug Kent
1967	Dave Davis	1979	Mike Aulby	1991	Mike Miller	2003	Walter Ray Williams Jr.
1968	Wayne Zahn	1980	Johnny Petraglia	1992	Eric Forkel	2004	Tom Baker
1969	Mike McGrath	1981	Earl Anthony	1993	Ron Palombi Jr.		
1970	Mike McGrath	1982	Earl Anthony	1994	David Traber		
1971	Mike Limongello	1983	Earl Anthony	1995	Scott Alexander		

Tournament of Champions

Originally the Firestone Tournament of Champions (1965-93), the tournament has also been sponsored by General Tire (1994), Brunswick Corp. (1995-2000) and Dexter (2002-). Held in Akron, Ohio in 1965, then Fairlawn, Ohio (1966-94), Lake Zurich, Ill. (1995-96, 2000), Reno, N.V. (1997), Overland Park, Kan. (1998-99) and Uncasville, Conn. (2002-).

Multiple winners: Jason Couch and Mike Durbin (3); Earl Anthony, Dave Davis, Jim Godman, Marshall Holman and Mark Williams (2).

Year		Year		Year		Year	
1965	Billy Hardwick	1975	Dave Davis	1985	Mark Williams	1995	Mike Aulby
1966	Wayne Zahn	1976	Marshall Holman	1986	Marshall Holman	1996	Dave D'Entremont
1967	Jim Stefanich	1977	Mike Berlin	1987	Pete Weber	1997	John Gant
1968	Dave Davis	1978	Earl Anthony	1988	Mark Williams	1998	Bryan Goebel
1969	Jim Godman	1979	George Pappas	1989	Del Ballard Jr.	1999	Jason Couch
1970	Don Johnson	1980	Wayne Webb	1990	Dave Ferraro	2000	Jason Couch
1971	Johnny Petraglia	1981	Steve Cook	1991	David Ozio	2001	Not held
1972	Mike Durbin	1982	Mike Durbin	1992	Marc McDowell	2002	Jason Couch
1973	Jim Godman	1983	Joe Berardi	1993	George Branham III	2003	Patrick Healey Jr.
1974	Earl Anthony	1984	Mike Durbin	1994	Norm Duke		

ABC Masters Tournament

Sponsored by the American Bowling Congress, the Masters became an official PBA Tour title event in 1998. It is open to qualified pros and amateurs.

Multiple winners: Mike Aulby (3); Earl Anthony, Billy Golembiewski, Dick Hoover and Billy Welu (2).

Year		Year		Year		Year	
1951	Lee Jouglard	1965	Billy Welu	1979	Doug Myers	1993	Norm Duke
1952	Willard Taylor	1966	Bob Strampe	1980	Neil Burton	1994	Steve Fehr
1953	Rudy Habetler	1967	Lou Scalia	1981	Randy Lightfoot	1995	Mike Aulby
1954	Red Elkins	1968	Pete Tountas	1982	Joe Berardi	1996	Ernie Schlegel
1955	Buzz Fazio	1969	Jim Chestney	1983	Mike Lastowski	1997	Jason Queen
1956	Dick Hoover	1970	Don Glover	1984	Earl Anthony	1998	Mike Aulby
1957	Dick Hoover	1971	Jim Godman	1985	Steve Wunderlich	1999	Brian Boghosian
1958	Tom Hennessey	1972	Bill Beach	1986	Mark Fahy	2000	Mika Koivuniemi
1959	Ray Bluth	1973	Dave Soutar	1987	Rick Steelsmith	2001	Parker Bohn III
1960	Billy Golembiewski	1974	Paul Colwell	1988	Del Ballard Jr.	2002	Brett Wolfe
1961	Don Carter	1975	Eddie Ressler Jr.	1989	Mike Aulby	2003	Bryon Smith
1962	Billy Golembiewski	1976	Nelson Burton Jr.	1990	Chris Warren	2004	Walter Ray Williams Jr.
1963	Harry Smith	1977	Earl Anthony	1991	Doug Kent		
1964	Billy Welu	1978	Frank Ellenburg	1992	Ken Johnson		

WOMEN
U.S. Open

Started by the Bowling Proprietors' Association of America in 1949. Originally the BPAA Women's All-Star Tournament (1949-70); and U.S. Open since 1971. There were two BPAA All-Star tournaments in 1955, in January and December.

Multiple winners: Marion Ladewig (8); Donna Adamek, Paula Sperber Carter, Pat Costello, Dotty Fothergill, Dana Miller-Mackie, Aleta Sill and Sylvia Wene (2).

Year		Year		Year		Year	
1949	Marion Ladewig	1963	Marion Ladewig	1978	Donna Adamek	1993	Dede Davidson
1950	Marion Ladewig	1964	LaVerne Carter	1979	Diana Silva	1994	Aleta Sill
1951	Marion Ladewig	1965	Ann Slattery	1980	Patty Costello	1995	Cheryl Daniels
1952	Marion Ladewig	1966	Joy Abel	1981	Donna Adamek	1996	Liz Johnson
1953	Not held	1967	Gloria Simon	1982	Shinobu Saitoh	1997	Not held
1954	Marion Ladewig	1968	Dotty Fothergill	1983	Dana Miller	1998	Aleta Sill
1955	Sylvia Wene	1969	Dotty Fothergill	1984	Karen Ellingsworth	1999	Kim Adler
1955	Anita Cantaline	1970	Mary Baker	1985	Pat Mercatanti	2000	Tennelle Grijalva
1956	Marion Ladewig	1971	Paula Sperber	1986	Wendy Macpherson	2001	Kim Terrell
1957	Not held	1972	Lorrie Koch	1987	Carol Norman	2002	Not held
1958	Merle Matthews	1973	Millie Martorella	1988	Lisa Wagner	2003	Kelly Kulick
1959	Marion Ladewig	1974	Patty Costello	1989	Robin Romeo	2004	Not held
1960	Sylvia Wene	1975	Paula Sperber Carter	1990	Dana Miller-Mackie		
1961	Phyllis Notaro	1976	Patty Costello	1991	Anne Marie Duggan		
1962	Shirley Garms	1977	Betty Morris	1992	Tish Johnson		

WIBC Queens

Sponsored by the Women's International Bowling Congress, the Queens is open to qualified pros and amateurs.

Multiple winners: Wendy Macpherson and Millie Martorella (3); Donna Adamek, Dotty Fothergill, Aleta Sill and Katsuko Sugimoto (2).

Year		Year		Year		Year	
1961	Janet Harman	1972	Dotty Fothergill	1983	Aleta Sill	1994	Anne Marie Duggan
1962	Dorothy Wilkinson	1973	Dotty Fothergill	1984	Kazue Inahashi	1995	Sandra Postma
1963	Irene Monterosso	1974	Judy Soutar	1985	Aleta Sill	1996	Lisa Wagner
1964	D.D. Jacobson	1975	Cindy Powell	1986	Cora Fiebig	1997	Sandra Jo Odom
1965	Betty Kuczynski	1976	Pam Rutherford	1987	Cathy Almeida	1998	Lynda Norry
1966	Judy Lee	1977	Dana Stewart	1988	Wendy Macpherson	1999	Leanne Barrette
1967	Millie Martorella	1978	Loa Boxberger	1989	Carol Gianotti	2000	Wendy Macpherson
1968	Phyllis Massey	1979	Donna Adamek	1990	Patty Ann	2001	Carolyn Dorin-Ballard
1969	Ann Feigel	1980	Donna Adamek	1991	Dede Davidson	2002	Kim Terrell
1970	Millie Martorella	1981	Katsuko Sugimoto	1992	Cindy Coburn-Carroll	2003	Wendy Macpherson
1971	Millie Martorella	1982	Katsuko Sugimoto	1993	Jan Schmidt	2004	Marianne DiRupo

WPBA National Championship (1960-1980)

The Women's Professional Bowling Association National Championship tournament was discontinued when the WPBA broke up in 1981. The WPBA changed its name from the Professional Women Bowlers Association (PWBA) in 1978.

Multiple winners: Patty Costello (3); Dotty Fothergill (2).

Year		Year		Year		Year	
1960	Marion Ladewig	1966	Judy Lee	1972	Patty Costello	1978	Toni Gillard
1961	Shirley Garms	1967	Betty Mivelaz	1973	Betty Morris	1979	Cindy Coburn
1962	Stephanie Balogh	1968	Dotty Fothergill	1974	Pat Costello	1980	Donna Adamek
1963	Janet Harman	1969	Dotty Fothergill	1975	Pam Buckner		
1964	Betty Kuczynski	1970	Bobbe North	1976	Patty Costello		
1965	Helen Duval	1971	Patty Costello	1977	Vesma Grinfelds		

Annual Leaders
Average
PBA Tour

The George Young Memorial Award, named after the late ABC Hall of Fame bowler. Based on at least 16 national PBA tournaments from 1959-78, and at least 400 games of tour competition since 1979.

Multiple winners: Mark Roth (6); Earl Anthony and Walter Ray Williams Jr. (5); Marshall Holman (3); Parker Bohn III, Norm Duke, Billy Hardwick, Don Johnson and Wayne Zahn (2).

Year		Avg	Year		Avg	Year		Avg
1962	Don Carter	212.84	1976	Mark Roth	215.97	1990	Amleto Monacelli	218.16
1963	Billy Hardwick	210.35	1977	Mark Roth	218.17	1991	Norm Duke	218.21
1964	Ray Bluth	210.51	1978	Mark Roth	219.83	1992	Dave Ferraro	219.70
1965	Dick Weber	211.90	1979	Mark Roth	221.66	1993	Walter Ray Williams Jr.	222.98
1966	Wayne Zahn	208.63	1980	Earl Anthony	218.54	1994	Norm Duke	222.83
1967	Wayne Zahn	212.14	1981	Mark Roth	216.70	1995	Mike Aulby	225.49
1968	Jim Stefanich	211.90	1982	Marshall Holman	216.15	1996	Walter Ray Williams Jr.	225.37
1969	Billy Hardwick	212.96	1983	Earl Anthony	216.65	1997	Walter Ray Williams Jr.	222.00
1970	Nelson Burton Jr.	214.91	1984	Marshall Holman	213.91	1998	Walter Ray Williams Jr.	226.13
1971	Don Johnson	213.98	1985	Mark Baker	213.72	1999	Parker Bohn III	228.04
1972	Don Johnson	215.29	1986	John Gant	214.38	2000	Chris Barnes	220.93
1973	Earl Anthony	215.80	1987	Marshall Holman	216.80	2002	Parker Bohn III	221.54
1974	Earl Anthony	219.34	1988	Mark Roth	218.04	2003	Walter Ray Williams Jr.	224.94
1975	Earl Anthony	219.06	1989	Pete Weber	215.43	2004	Mika Koivuniemi	222.73

Note: After its first nine events of 2001, the PBA instituted a new September-to-March schedule with the statistics for those first nine tournaments rolled over into players' final 2001-02 statistics.

PWBA Tour

The Professional Women's Bowling Association (PWBA) went by the name Ladies Professional Bowling Tour (LPBT) from 1981-97 and the Women's Professional Bowling Association prior to that. This table is based on at least 282 games of tour competition, with the expection of 2003 when the minimum was 122 games. In 2003 the fall season was unexpectedly cancelled, shortening the year to eight tournaments. There was no PWBA Tour in 2004.

Multiple winners: Leanne Barrette (4); Nikki Gianulias, Wendy Macpherson and Lisa Rathgeber Wagner (3); Carolyn Dorin-Ballard, Anne Marie Duggan and Aleta Sill (2).

Year		Avg	Year		Avg	Year		Avg
1981	Nikki Gianulias	213.71	1989	Lisa Wagner	211.87	1997	Wendy Macpherson	214.68
1982	Nikki Gianulias	210.63	1990	Leanne Barrette	211.53	1998	Dede Davidson	217.25
1983	Lisa Rathgeber	208.50	1991	Leanne Barrette	211.48	1999	Wendy Macpherson	218.85
1984	Aleta Sill	210.68	1992	Leanne Barrette	211.36	2000	Cara Honeychurch	215.18
1985	Aleta Sill	211.10	1993	Tish Johnson	215.39	2001	Carolyn Dorin-Ballard	214.73
1986	Nikki Gianulias	213.89	1994	Anne Marie Duggan	213.47	2002	Leanne Barrette	216.45
1987	Wendy Macpherson	211.11	1995	Anne Marie Duggan	215.79	2003	Carolyn Dorin-Ballard	215.22
1988	Lisa Wagner	213.02	1996	Tammy Turner	215.23			

Money Won
PBA Tour

Multiple winners: Earl Anthony and Walter Ray Williams Jr. (6); Mark Roth and Dick Weber (4); Mike Aulby (3); Parker Bohn III, Don Carter and Norm Duke (2).

Year		Earnings	Year		Earnings	Year		Earnings
1959	Dick Weber	$7,672	1974	Earl Anthony	$99,585	1989	Mike Aulby	$298,237
1960	Don Carter	22,525	1975	Earl Anthony	107,585	1990	Amleto Monacelli	204,775
1961	Dick Weber	26,280	1976	Earl Anthony	110,833	1991	David Ozio	225,585
1962	Don Carter	49,972	1977	Mark Roth	105,583	1992	Marc McDowell	176,215
1963	Dick Weber	46,333	1978	Mark Roth	134,500	1993	Walter Ray Williams Jr.	296,370
1964	Bob Strampe	33,592	1979	Mark Roth	124,517	1994	Norm Duke	273,752
1965	Dick Weber	47,675	1980	Wayne Webb	116,700	1995	Mike Aulby	219,792
1966	Wayne Zahn	54,720	1981	Earl Anthony	164,735	1996	Walter Ray Williams Jr.	244,630
1967	Dave Davis	54,165	1982	Earl Anthony	134,760	1997	Walter Ray Williams Jr.	240,544
1968	Jim Stefanich	67,375	1983	Earl Anthony	135,605	1998	Walter Ray Williams Jr.	238,225
1969	Billy Hardwick	64,160	1984	Mark Roth	158,712	1999	Parker Bohn III	232,595
1970	Mike McGrath	52,049	1985	Mike Aulby	201,200	2000	Norm Duke	136,900
1971	Johnny Petraglia	85,065	1986	Walter Ray Williams Jr.	145,550	2002	Parker Bohn III	245,200
1972	Don Johnson	56,648	1987	Pete Weber	179,516	2003	Walter Ray Williams Jr.	419,700
1973	Don McCune	69,000	1988	Brian Voss	225,485	2004	Mika Koivuniemi	238,590

Note: After its first nine events of 2001, the PBA instituted a new September-to-March schedule with the statistics for those first nine tournaments rolled over into players' final 2001-02 statistics.

WPBA and PWBA Tours

WPBA leaders through 1980; PWBA leaders since 1981. Totals include the WIBC Queens, but do not include TV incentives. In 2003 the fall season was unexpectedly cancelled, shortening the year to eight tournaments. There was no PWBA Tour in 2004.

Multiple winners: Aleta Sill (6); Donna Adamek and Wendy Macpherson (4); Patty Costello, Tish Johnson and Betty Morris (3); Carolyn Dorin-Ballard and Dotty Fothergill (2).

Year		Earnings	Year		Earnings	Year		Earnings
1965	Betty Kuczynski	$ 3,792	1978	Donna Adamek	$31,000	1991	Leanne Barrette	$87,618
1966	Joy Abel	5,795	1979	Donna Adamek	26,280	1992	Tish Johnson	96,872
1967	Shirley Garms	4,920	1980	Donna Adamek	31,907	1993	Aleta Sill	57,995
1968	Dotty Fothergill	16,170	1981	Donna Adamek	41,270	1994	Aleta Sill	126,325
1969	Dotty Fothergill	9,220	1982	Nikki Gianulias	45,875	1995	Tish Johnson	123,440
1970	Patty Costello	9,317	1983	Aleta Sill	42,525	1996	Wendy Macpherson	107,230
1971	Vesma Grinfelds	4,925	1984	Aleta Sill	81,452	1997	Wendy Macpherson	165,425
1972	Patty Costello	11,350	1985	Aleta Sill	52,655	1998	Carol Gianotti-Block	150,350
1973	Judy Cook	11,200	1986	Aleta Sill	36,212	1999	Wendy Macpherson	86,265
1974	Betty Morris	30,037	1987	Betty Morris	55,095	2000	Wendy Macpherson	108,525
1975	Judy Soutar	20,395	1988	Lisa Wagner	105,500	2001	Carolyn Dorin-Ballard	135,045
1976	Patty Costello	39,585	1989	Robin Romeo	113,750	2002	Michelle Feldman	80,905
1977	Betty Morris	23,802	1990	Tish Johnson	94,420	2003	Carolyn Dorin-Ballard	53,750

All-Time Leaders

All-time leading money winners on the PBA and PWBA tours, through Sept. 30, 2004. PBA figures date back to 1959, while PWBA figures include Women's Pro Bowlers Association (WPBA) earnings through 1980. National tour titles are also listed.

Money Won

PBA Top 20

		Titles	Earnings
1	Walter Ray Williams Jr.	39	$3,236,132
2	Pete Weber	31	2,585,168
3	Parker Bohn III	29	2,201,964
4	Mike Aulby	27	2,094,060
5	Brian Voss	22	2,055,077
6	Amleto Monacelli	18	1,915,223
7	Norm Duke	21	1,883,041
8	Marshall Holman	22	1,699,390
9	Dave Husted	14	1,612,723
10	Mark Roth	34	1,611,886
11	Earl Anthony	41	1,441,061
12	Wayne Webb	20	1,399,341
13	David Ozio	11	1,387,266
14	Gary Dickinson	8	1,284,806
15	Tom Baker	10	1,268,882
16	Jason Couch	11	1,177,813
17	Del Ballard Jr.	12	1,170,232
18	Mark Williams	7	1,169,527
19	Dave Soutar	17	1,114,537
20	Bob Learn Jr.	5	1,088,535

WPBA-PWBA Top 10

		Titles	Earnings
1	Wendy Macpherson	20	$1,238,960
2	Tish Johnson	25	1,098,563
3	Aleta Sill	31	1,071,194
4	Leanne Barrette	26	1,028,994
5	Anne Marie Duggan	15	955,809
6	Carol Gianotti-Block	16	918,777
7	Carolyn Dorin-Ballard	20	916,477
8	Lisa (Rathgeber) Wagner	32	853,796
9	Kim Adler	15	827,493
10	Cheryl Daniels	10	754,545

Senior PBA Top 5

		Titles	Earnings
1	Dave Soutar	7	$464,815
2	Gene Stus	11	461,180
3	Gary Dickinson	11	446,746
4	John Handegard	14	444,593
5	Teata Semiz	8	395,213

Annual Awards
MEN
BWAA Bowler of the Year

Winners selected by Bowling Writers Association of America.

Multiple winners: Walter Ray Williams Jr. (7); Earl Anthony and Don Carter (6); Mark Roth (4); Mike Aulby and Dick Weber (3); Parker Bohn III, Buddy Bomar, Ned Day, Norm Duke, Billy Hardwick, Don Johnson and Steve Nagy (2).

Year		Year		Year		Year	
1942	John Crimmins	1958	Don Carter	1974	Earl Anthony	1990	Amleto Monacelli
1943	Ned Day	1959	Ed Lubanski	1975	Earl Anthony	1991	David Ozio
1944	Ned Day	1960	Don Carter	1976	Earl Anthony	1992	Marc McDowell
1945	Buddy Bomar	1961	Dick Weber	1977	Mark Roth	1993	Walter Ray Williams Jr.
1946	Joe Wilman	1962	Don Carter	1978	Mark Roth	1994	Norm Duke
1947	Buddy Bomar	1963	Dick Weber	1979	Mark Roth	1995	Mike Aulby
1948	Andy Varipapa	1964	Billy Hardwick	1980	Wayne Webb	1996	Walter Ray Williams Jr.
1949	Connie Schwoegler	1965	Dick Weber	1981	Earl Anthony	1997	Walter Ray Williams Jr.
1950	Junie McMahon	1966	Wayne Zahn	1982	Earl Anthony	1998	Walter Ray Williams Jr.
1951	Lee Jouglard	1967	Dave Davis	1983	Earl Anthony	1999	Parker Bohn III
1952	Steve Nagy	1968	Jim Stefanich	1984	Mark Roth	2000	Norm Duke
1953	Don Carter	1969	Billy Hardwick	1985	Mike Aulby	2001	Parker Bohn III
1954	Don Carter	1970	Nelson Burton Jr.	1986	Walter Ray Williams Jr.	2002	Walter Ray Williams Jr.
1955	Steve Nagy	1971	Don Johnson	1987	Marshall Holman	2003	Walter Ray Williams Jr.
1956	Bill Lillard	1972	Don Johnson	1988	Brian Voss		
1957	Don Carter	1973	Don McCune	1989	Mike Aulby		

Annual Awards (Cont.)
PBA Player of the Year

Named after longtime broadcaster Chris Schenkel, winners are selected by members of Professional Bowlers Association. The PBA Player of the Year has differed from the BWAA Bowler of the Year four times—in 1963, '64, '89 and '92.

Multiple winners: Earl Anthony and Walter Ray Williams Jr. (6); Mark Roth (4); Mike Aulby, Parker Bohn III, Norm Duke, Billy Hardwick, Don Johnson and Amleto Monacelli (2).

Year		Year		Year		Year	
1963	Billy Hardwick	1974	Earl Anthony	1985	Mike Aulby	1996	Walter Ray Williams Jr.
1964	Bob Strampe	1975	Earl Anthony	1986	Walter Ray Williams Jr.	1997	Walter Ray Williams Jr.
1965	Dick Weber	1976	Earl Anthony	1987	Marshall Holman	1998	Walter Ray Williams Jr.
1966	Wayne Zahn	1977	Mark Roth	1988	Brian Voss	1999	Parker Bohn III
1967	Dave Davis	1978	Mark Roth	1989	Amleto Monacelli	2000	Norm Duke
1968	Jim Stefanich	1979	Mark Roth	1990	Amleto Monacelli	2002	Parker Bohn III
1969	Billy Hardwick	1980	Wayne Webb	1991	David Ozio	2003	Walter Ray Williams Jr.
1970	Nelson Burton Jr.	1981	Earl Anthony	1992	Dave Ferraro	2004	Mika Koivuniemi
1971	Don Johnson	1982	Earl Anthony	1993	Walter Ray Williams Jr.		
1972	Don Johnson	1983	Earl Anthony	1994	Norm Duke		
1973	Don McCune	1984	Mark Roth	1995	Mike Aulby		

Note: After its first nine events of 2001, the PBA instituted a new September-to-March schedule with the statistics for those first nine tournaments rolled over into players' final 2001-02 statistics. Individual awards were handed out in 2002.

PBA Rookie of the Year

Named after PBA Hall of Famer Harry Golden, who was the PBA's national tournament director for 30 years. Winners selected by members of Professional Bowlers Association.

Year		Year		Year		Year	
1964	Jerry McCoy	1974	Cliff McNealy	1984	John Gant	1994	Tony Ament
1965	Jim Godman	1975	Guy Rowbury	1985	Tom Crites	1995	Billy Myers Jr.
1966	Bobby Cooper	1976	Mike Berlin	1986	Marc McDowell	1996	C.K. Moore
1967	Mike Durbin	1977	Steve Martin	1987	Ryan Shafer	1997	Anthony Lombardo
1968	Bob McGregor	1978	Joseph Groskind	1988	Rick Steelsmith	1998	Chris Barnes
1969	Larry Lichstein	1979	Mike Aulby	1989	Steve Hoskins	1999	Paul Fleming
1970	Denny Krick	1980	Pete Weber	1990	Brad Kiszewski	2000	Joe Ciccone
1971	Tye Critchlow	1981	Mark Fahy	1991	Ricky Ward	2002	Tommy Jones
1972	Tommy Hudson	1982	Mike Steinbach	1992	Jason Couch	2003	Brad Angelo
1973	Steve Neff	1983	Toby Contreras	1993	Mark Scroggins	2004	Chris Johnson

Note: After its first nine events of 2001, the PBA instituted a new September-to-March schedule with the statistics for those first nine tournaments rolled over into players' final 2001-02 statistics. Individual awards were handed out in 2002.

WOMEN
BWAA Bowler of the Year

Winners selected by Bowling Writers Association of America.

Multiple winners: Marion Ladewig (9); Donna Adamek, Lisa Rathgeber Wagner and Wendy Macpherson (4); Tish Johnson and Betty Morris (3); Leanne Barrette, Patty Costello, Carolyn Dorin-Ballard, Dotty Fothergill, Shirley Garms, Val Mikiel, Aleta Sill, Judy Soutar and Sylvia Wene (2).

Year		Year		Year		Year	
1948	Val Mikiel	1962	Shirley Garms	1976	Patty Costello	1990	Tish Johnson
1949	Val Mikiel	1963	Marion Ladewig	1977	Betty Morris	1991	Leanne Barrette
1950	Marion Ladewig	1964	LaVerne Carter	1978	Donna Adamek	1992	Tish Johnson
1951	Marion Ladewig	1965	Betty Kuczynski	1979	Donna Adamek	1993	Lisa Wagner
1952	Marion Ladewig	1966	Joy Abel	1980	Donna Adamek	1994	Anne Marie Duggan
1953	Marion Ladewig	1967	Millie Martorella	1981	Donna Adamek	1995	Tish Johnson
1954	Marion Ladewig	1968	Dotty Fothergill	1982	Nikki Gianulias	1996	Wendy Macpherson
1955	Sylvia Wene	1969	Dotty Fothergill	1983	Lisa Rathgeber	1997	Wendy Macpherson
1956	Anita Cantaline	1970	Mary Baker	1984	Aleta Sill	1998	Carol Gianotti-Block
1957	Marion Ladewig	1971	Paula Sperber	1985	Aleta Sill	1999	Wendy Macpherson
1958	Marion Ladewig	1972	Patty Costello	1986	Lisa Wagner	2000	Wendy Macpherson
1959	Marion Ladewig	1973	Judy Soutar	1987	Betty Morris	2001	Carolyn Dorin-Ballard
1960	Sylvia Wene	1974	Betty Morris	1988	Lisa Wagner	2002	Leanne Barrette
1961	Shirley Garms	1975	Judy Soutar	1989	Robin Romeo	2003	Carolyn Dorin-Ballard

PWBA Player of the Year

Winners selected by members of Professional Women's Bowling Association. The PWBA Player of the Year has differed from the BWAA Bowler of the Year four times—in 1985, '86, '90 and 2002. This award was known as the LPBT Player of the Year Award from 1983-97. In 2003, PWBA suspended operations due to a lack of operating funds. No award was handed out.

Multiple winners: Wendy Macpherson (4); Lisa Rathgeber Wagner (3); Leanne Barrette and Tish Johnson (2).

Year		Year		Year		Year	
1983	Lisa Rathgeber	1988	Lisa Wagner	1993	Lisa Wagner	1998	Carol Gianotti-Block
1984	Aleta Sill	1989	Robin Romeo	1994	Anne Marie Duggan	1999	Wendy Macpherson
1985	Patty Costello	1990	Leanne Barrette	1995	Tish Johnson	2000	Wendy Macpherson
1986	Jeanne Maiden	1991	Leanne Barrette	1996	Wendy Macpherson	2001	Carolyn Dorin-Ballard
1987	Betty Morris	1992	Tish Johnson	1997	Wendy Macpherson	2002	Michelle Feldman

Horse Racing

Smarty Jones *missed being the first Triple Crown winner since 1978 by one length.*

Smart Money

Smarty Jones wins the Kentucky Derby and the Preakness but comes up short in his courageous Triple Crown bid.

Michael Morrison
is co-editor of the ESPN Sports Almanac.

Not again! Like Funny Cide (2003) and War Emblem (2002) before him, Pennsylvania-bred Smarty Jones became the sixth horse in the last eight years, and third in the last three, to win the first two legs of thoroughbred racing's Triple Crown, only to be thwarted in the last.

And so the drought continues—26 years and counting since jockey Steve Cauthen rode Affirmed to victory in the 1978 Kentucky Derby, Preakness and Belmont Stakes.

While the comparisons to Seabiscuit have become almost cliché, they're simply too blatant to ignore. Had he completed his quest at the Belmont, *Smarty Jones*, the movie may already be in theaters.

In his three years, this horse has already seen its share of tough times. Owner Roy Chapman, a 78-year-old former car sales-man, suffers from emphysema and is hooked up to oxygen 24 hours a day. He had never even been to the Kentucky Derby, much less entered a horse in one.

His original trainer and breeder was Bobby Camac. In late 2001, Camac and wife, Maryann, were fatally shot by Maryann's son (from a former marriage), allegedly in a dispute over money. After the murder of their trainer, the despondent Chapman and his wife, Pat, sold off the majority of their horses. One of the keepers, however, was Smarty Jones because Pat saw something special in his eyes.

They called upon trainer John Servis, who had been highly regarded by Camac, and 39-year-old jockey Stewart Elliott, a journeyman from Philadelphia with over 3,000 career wins but a relative newcomer to the national scene. Elliott had seen plenty of struggles over the course of his career as well, battling with his weight like many jockeys, and getting caught up in a series of alcohol-fueled incidents several years ago.

During a training session at the starting gate at Philadelphia Park in July 2003, Smarty Jones jerked upright and smacked

AP/Wide World Photos

Celebrating Smarty Jones' Derby win is trainer John Servis, left, owners Pat Chapman, 2nd from left, and Roy Chapman, lower center, Kentucky Gov. Ernie Fletcher, 2nd from right and jockey Stewart Elliott.

his head on a metal bar. He fractured his skull, broke his eye socket and broke his nasal passage. He crumpled to the ground unconscious with blood streaming from his nose. According to Servis, his survival was "touch and go." But after a few weeks in the hospital and a few more in recovery, Smarty Jones was back in fine form.

While 2003 darling Funny Cide barely got a pre-race mention in last year's Derby, Smarty Jones was not just the sentimental favorite in the 2004 race, but a betting favorite as well. He entered the Derby having run six prior races…and winning each one. He was attempting to become the first undefeated Derby winner since Seattle Slew in 1977.

As if that and a blanket of roses weren't enough incentive, there was also a $5 million bonus on the line, offered by Oaklawn Park in Arkansas for any horse that won the Rebel Stakes, Arkansas Derby and Kentucky Derby. So far, Smarty Jones was two for two. The win bonus would immediately vault him to sixth place on the all-time earnings list (see page 799).

A rainy Derby Day made the track sloppy, but Elliott didn't mind, having ridden Smarty Jones to victory in the rainy Arkansas Derby a month prior. He certainly didn't start from the most enviable post position, No. 13, but quickly shot to the four-spot behind early leader Lion Heart under jockey Mike Smith.

AP/Wide World Photos

Missed it by that much. **Birdstone**, *with jockey Edgar Prado aboard, edges Smarty Jones by a length at the Belmont Stakes to spoil the party.*

Entering the final turn, Elliott shook the reins in search of another gear. And he got it, chasing down Lion Heart and pulling away for a definitive 2 3/4-length victory.

It was on to the Preakness two weeks later, where Smarty Jones was initially pegged as an 8-5 favorite. By post time, those odds had drastically shortened to 3-5. Ten horses lined up at the starting gates at Pimlico, but by the mile mark, it had turned into a one-horse show.

As in the Kentucky Derby, Smith guided Lion Heart to the front of the pack from the get-go and held a one-length lead at the 3/4-mile mark. Then Elliott decided it was time to coax that next gear out of his colt.

He cut to the inside at the top of the stretch and quickly built a five-length lead with ease. At the wire, it had grown to an astonishing 11 1/2 lengths, the widest margin of victory in the 129-year history of the Preakness. Lion Heart faded to fourth as Rock Hard Ten and Eddington took second and third, respectively.

Now only if he could handle Belmont's stamina-busting mile-and-a-half track that had done in so many elite horses before him.

Referring to Belmont's backstretch, Elliott said, "It looks like you're looking down a beach in South Carolina or something. And there's no end to it."

continued on page 780 ▶

The Ten Biggest Stories of the Year in Horse Racing

10 Since it happened too late to get into the 2003 top-ten list, it gets a mention here. Trainer Richard Mandella makes history at the 2003 Breeders' Cup Championships at Santa Anita by saddling four winners. One of those winners, Halfbridled, is ridden by hall of famer Julie Krone, who becomes the first female to win a Breeders' Cup race.

9 Two-time Eclipse Award winning jockey Kent Desormeaux is elected to the National Museum of Racing's Hall of Fame with trainer Shug McGaughey and horses Flawlessly and Skip Away.

8 New York Racing Association announces it is splitting up NBC's Triple Crown coverage by moving the Belmont Stakes back to ABC, where it had been from 1986-2000. ABC's coverage begins with the 2006 race.

7 Just two days before the Kentucky Derby, a federal judge hands down a ruling declaring it legal for jockeys to display ads on their riding pants. While the actual ruling applies only to the five jockeys that originally sued, Churchill Downs decides to allow ads for all jockeys at the Derby as long as they weren't offensive.

6 Windsong's Legacy sweeps the Yonkers Trot, Hambletonian and the Kentucky Futurity to become harness racing's first Triple Crown-winning trotter since Super Bowl in 1972.

5 In early October, Funny Cide returns to Belmont Park, the site of his third-place finish in the 2003 Belmont Stakes, and wins the $1 million Jockey Club Gold Cup. It is his first win since the 2003 Preakness.

4 Kristin Mulhall, 21, trains Imperialism to a third-place finish in the Kentucky Derby. She was attempting to become the youngest trainer of a Derby winner, and the first female in history. Two weeks later at the Preakness, a record three women trained starters— Mulhall with Imperialism, Jennifer Pedersen with Song of the Sword and Linda Albert with Water Cannon.

3 Fresh off his Breeders' Cup Classic victory in October 2003, Pleasantly Perfect wins three of the four races he enters in 2004 (through Sept.), including the $6 million Dubai World Cup and the $1 million Pacific Classic.

2 Birdstone disappoints throngs of racing fans hoping to see an end to thoroughbred racing's 25-year Triple Crown drought, upsetting Smarty Jones by a length at the Belmont Stakes. The win gives trainer Nick Zito his first Belmont victory in 12 tries.

1 Smarty Jones, who recovered from a near-fatal training accident in 2003, wins the Kentucky Derby and the Preakness (by a record 11½ lengths), setting up yet another Triple Crown bid.

And yet he remained confident.

"I don't think the mile-and-one-half will be a problem for him...because he'll do whatever I want him to do," said Elliott.

He went off as a 1-5 favorite, about as close to a sure thing as you can get. Sadly, as evidenced by the wall-to-wall carpet of torn up betting slips after every race day, there are no sure things in horse racing.

As expected, Todd Pletcher's Purge jumped out of the gate to an early lead and held it until the backstretch. Smarty Jones shot to the front, though neither Servis nor Elliott were confident, each realizing the horse didn't look settled. Nevertheless, he fought off numerous charges and carried a four-length lead as the horses entered the stretch where Nick Zito's Birdstone came up on him. Elliott gave it all he had, but in the end, it was Birdstone by a length.

Unlike 2003 when trainer Bobby Frankel proclaimed, "I don't feel bad that Funny Cide didn't win the Triple Crown," after his horse Empire Maker sent a crowd of 100,000-plus home in disappointment, Birdstone's handlers actually apologized for stealing the glory.

"I'm sorry, I'm sorry, I'm sorry that Smarty Jones didn't win," said owner Marylou Whitney. "We kept telling [jockey] Edgar Prado, 'Be Second.'"

Zito, a native New Yorker, finally won his first Belmont after finishing runner-up five times. As they did to Frankel a year prior, the crowd (a record of 120,139) booed Zito and Birdstone as they entered the winner's circle. Even Zito couldn't blame them. It wasn't the right ending to the movie.

INSIDE the numbers

Perfectionists

Smarty Jones was a perfect six-for-six entering the Kentucky Derby, making him the fifth Derby winner to enter the race undefeated.

Year	Horse	Pre-race record
2004	Smarty Jones	6-0
1977	Seattle Slew	6-0
1969	Majestic Prince	7-0
1922	Morvich	11-0
1915	Regret	3-0

All By Himself

With his 11½-length romp at the Preakness, Smarty Jones broke the record for largest margin of victory that stood since the first Preakness in 1873.

Year	Horse	Margin (in lengths)
2004	Smarty Jones	11½
1873	Survivor	10
2003	Funny Cide	9¾
1889	Buddhist	8
1943	Count Fleet	8

2003-2004
Season in Review

SPORTS ALMANAC

Thoroughbred Racing
Major Stakes Races
Winners of major stakes races from Nov. 29, 2003 through Sept. 25, 2004; (T) indicates turf race course; F indicates furlongs.

Late 2003

Date	Race	Track	Miles	Winner	Jockey	Purse
Nov. 29	Citation Handicap	Hollywood Park	1 1/16	Redattore	Julie Krone	$400,000
Nov. 30	Japan Cup*	Nakayama	1 1/2 (T)	Tap Dance City	Tetsuzo Sato	4,327,273
Nov. 30	Matriarch Stakes	Hollywood Park	1 1/8 (T)	Heat Haze	John Velazquez	500,000
Nov. 30	Hollywood Derby	Hollywood Park	1 1/8 (T)	Sweet Return	Julie Krone	600,000
Dec. 14	Hong Kong Cup*	Sha Tin	1 1/4 (T)	Falbrav	Frankie Dettori	2,300,000

2004 (through Sept. 25)

Date	Race	Track	Miles	Winner	Jockey	Purse
Jan. 24	Sunshine Millions Classic	Santa Anita	1 1/8	Southern Image	Victor Espinoza	$1,000,000
Feb. 7	Charles H. Strub Stakes	Santa Anita	1 1/8	Domestic Dispute	Kent Desormeaux	300,000
Feb. 7	San Vicente Stakes	Santa Anita	7 F	Imperialism	Victor Espinoza	150,000
Feb. 7	Donn Handicap	Gulfstream	1 1/8	Medaglia d'Oro	Jerry Bailey	500,000
Feb. 14	Hutcheson Stakes	Gulfstream	7 F	Limehouse	John Velazquez	150,000
Feb. 14	Fountain of Youth Stakes	Gulfstream	1 1/16	Read the Footnotes	Jerry Bailey	250,000
Mar. 6	San Rafael Stakes	Santa Anita	1	Imperialism	Victor Espinoza	200,000
Mar. 6	Santa Anita Handicap	Santa Anita	1 1/4	Southern Image	Victor Espinoza	1,000,000
Mar. 7	Louisiana Derby	Fair Grounds	1 1/16	Wimbledon	Javier Santiago	600,000
Mar. 13	El Camino Real Derby	Golden Gate	1 1/16	Kilgowan	Chance Rollins	200,000
Mar. 13	Santa Anita Oaks	Santa Anita	1 1/16	Silent Sighs	David Flores	300,000
Mar. 13	Florida Derby	Gulfstream	1 1/8	Friend's Lake	Richard Migliore	1,000,000
Mar. 13	Swale Stakes	Gulfstream	7 F	Wynn Dot Comma	Edgar Prado	150,000
Mar. 14	San Felipe Stakes	Santa Anita	1 1/16	Preachinatthebar	Javier Santiago	250,000
Mar. 14	Tampa Bay Derby	Tampa Bay	1 1/16	Limehouse	Pat Day	250,000
Mar. 14	Santa Margarita Handicap	Santa Anita	1 1/8	Adoration	Mike Smith	300,000
Mar. 20	Lane's End Stakes	Turfway	1 1/8	Sinister G	Paul Toscano	500,000
Mar. 20	Rebel Stakes	Turfway	1 1/16	Smarty Jones	Stewart Elliott	200,000
Mar. 27	UAE Derby	Nad al-Sheba	1 1/8	Lundy's Liability	Weiching Marwing	2,000,000
Mar. 27	Dubai World Cup	Nad al-Sheba	1 1/4	Pleasantly Perfect	Alex Solis	6,000,000
Mar. 28	WinStar Derby	Sunland	1 1/16	Hi Teck Man	Ricardo Jaime	500,000
Apr. 3	Santa Anita Derby	Santa Anita	1 1/8	Castledale	Jose Valdivia Jr.	750,000
Apr. 3	Ashland Stakes	Keeneland	1 1/16	Madcap Escapade	Rene Douglas	500,000
Apr. 3	The Oaklawn Handicap	Oaklawn	1 1/8	Peace Rules	Jerry Bailey	500,000
Apr. 3	Apple Blossom Handicap	Oaklawn	1 1/16	Azeri	Mike Smith	500,000
Apr. 3	Illinois Derby	Hawthorne	1 1/8	Pollard's Vision	Eibar Coa	500,000
Apr. 10	Wood Memorial	Aqueduct	1 1/8	Tapit	Ramon Dominguez	750,000
Apr. 10	Blue Grass Stakes	Keeneland	1 1/8	The Cliff's Edge	Shane Sellers	750,000
Apr. 10	Arkansas Derby	Oaklawn	1 1/8	Smarty Jones	Stewart Elliott	1,000,000
Apr. 17	Coolmore Lexington Stakes	Keeneland	1 1/16	Quinton's Gold Rush	Jerry Bailey	325,000
Apr. 25	Queen Elizabeth II Cup*	Sha Tin	1 1/4 (T)	River Dancer	Glyn Schofield	1,790,000
April 30	Kentucky Oaks	Churchill Downs	1 1/8	Ashado	John Velazquez	572,000
April 30	Louisville Breeders' Cup H	Churchill Downs	1 1/16	Lead Story	Calvin Borel	327,000
May 1	**Kentucky Derby**	Churchill Downs	1 1/4	Smarty Jones	Stewart Elliott	6,154,800#
May 9	Vanity Handicap	Hollywood Park	1 1/8	Victory Encounter	Alex Solis	250,000
May 14	Black-Eyed Susan Stakes	Pimlico	1 1/8	Yearly Report	Jerry Bailey	200,000
May 14	Pimlico Special	Pimlico	1 3/16	Southern Image	Victor Espinoza	500,000
May 15	**Preakness Stakes**	Pimlico	1 3/16	Smarty Jones	Stewart Elliott	1,000,000
May 16	Singapore Airlines Cup*	Singapore	1 1/4 (T)	Epalo	Andrasch Starke	1,710,000
May 22	Peter Pan Stakes	Belmont	1 1/8	Purge	John Velazquez	200,000
May 31	Gamely BC Handicap	Hollywood Park	1 1/8 (T)	Noches De Rosa	Mike Smith	324,250
May 31	Shoemaker BC Mile	Hollywood Park	1 (T)	Designed for Luck	Patrick Valenzuela	456,000
May 31	Metropolitan Handicap	Belmont	1	Pico Central	Alex Solis	750,000
June 4	Acorn Stakes	Belmont	1	Island Sand	Terry Thompson	250,000
June 5	**Belmont Stakes**	Belmont	1 1/2	Birdstone	Edgar Prado	1,000,000
June 5	Manhattan Handicap	Belmont	1 1/4 (T)	Meteor Storm	Jose Valdivia Jr.	400,000
June 5	Vodafone English Derby	Epsom Downs	1 1/2 (T)	North Light	Kieren Fallon	2,300,000

Major Stakes Races (Cont.)

Date	Race	Track	Miles	Winner	Jockey	Purse
June 12	Charles Whittingham H	Hollywood Park	1¼ (T)	Sabiango	Tyler Baze	$350,000
June 12	Stephen Foster Handicap	Churchill Downs	1⅛	Colonial Colony	Rafael Bejarano	810,750
June 19	Ogden Phipps Handicap	Belmont	1¹⁄₁₆	Sightseek	Jerry Bailey	300,000
June 19	Massachusetts Handicap	Suffolk Downs	1⅛	Offlee Wild	Edgar Prado	500,000
June 21	Ohio Derby	Thistledown	1⅛	Brass Hat	Willie Martinez	350,000
June 22	Queen's Plate	Woodbine	1¼	Niigon	Robert Landry	1,000,000
June 26	Mother Goose Stakes	Belmont	1⅛	Stellar Jayne	Robby Albarado	300,000
June 27	Irish Derby	Curragh	1½ (T)	Grey Swallow	Pat Smullen	1,536,219
July 3	Suburban Handicap	Belmont	1¼	Peace Rules	Jerry Bailey	500,000
July 3	American Oaks	Hollywood Park	1¼ (T)	Ticker Tape	Kent Desormeaux	750,000
July 10	Hollywood Gold Cup	Hollywood Park	1¼	Total Impact	Mike Smith	750,000
July 10	Swaps Stakes	Hollywood Park	1⅛	Rock Hard Ten	Corey Nakatani	421,300
July 10	Virginia Derby	Colonial Downs	1¼ (T)	Kitten's Joy	Edgar Prado	500,000
July 18	Delaware Handicap	Delaware	1¼	Summer Wind Dancer	Victor Espinoza	750,900
July 24	Coaching Club Am. Oaks	Belmont	1½	Ashado	John Velazquez	500,000
July 24	K. George VI and Q. Elizabeth Diamond Stakes*	Ascot	1½ (T)	Doyen	Frankie Dettori	1,400,000
July 24	John C. Mabee Handicap	Del Mar	1⅛ (T)	Musical Chimes	Kent Desormeaux	400,000
July 25	Eddie Read Handicap	Del Mar	1⅛ (T)	Special Ring	Victor Espinoza	400,000
July 31	Washington Park Handicap	Arlington	1³⁄₁₆	Eye of the Tiger	Eddie Razo Jr.	350,000
July 31	Test Stakes	Saratoga	7 F	Society Selection	Edgar Prado	250,000
July 31	Diana Handicap	Saratoga	1⅛ (T)	Wonder Again	Edgar Prado	500,000
Aug. 1	Go for Wand Handicap	Saratoga	1⅛	Azeri	Pat Day	250,000
Aug. 7	Whitney Handicap	Saratoga	1⅛	Roses in May	Edgar Prado	750,000
Aug. 7	West Virginia Derby	Mountaineer Park	1⅛	Sir Shackleton	Rafael Bejarano	600,000
Aug. 8	Jim Dandy Stakes	Saratoga	1⅛	Purge	John Velazquez	500,000
Aug. 8	Haskell Invitational	Monmouth	1⅛	Lion Heart	Joe Bravo	1,000,000
Aug. 14	Sword Dancer Invitational	Saratoga	1½ (T)	Better Talk Now	Ramon Dominguez	500,000
Aug. 14	Arlington Million*	Arlington	1¼ (T)	Kicken Kris	Kent Desormeaux	1,000,000
Aug. 14	Beverly D. Stakes	Arlington	1³⁄₁₆ (T)	Crimson Palace	Frankie Dettori	750,000
Aug. 14	Secretariat Stakes	Arlington	1¼ (T)	Kitten's Joy	Jerry Bailey	400,000
Aug. 21	Alabama Stakes	Saratoga	1¼	Society Selection	Cornelio Velasquez	750,000
Aug. 22	Pacific Classic	Del Mar	1¼	Pleasantly Perfect	Jerry Bailey	1,000,000
Aug. 27	Personal Ensign Handicap	Saratoga	1¼	Storm Flag Flying	John Velazquez	400,000
Aug. 28	Travers Stakes	Saratoga	1¼	Birdstone	Edgar Prado	1,000,000
Sept. 5	Grosser Preis von Baden*	Baden-Baden	1½ (T)	Warrsan	Kerrin McEvoy	988,240
Sept. 6	Pennsylvania Derby	Philadelphia	1⅛	Love of Money	Robby Albarado	750,000
Sept. 11	Gazelle Handicap	Belmont	1⅛	Stellar Jayne	Robby Albarado	250,000
Sept. 11	Man o' War Stakes	Belmont	1⅜ (T)	Magistretti	Edgar Prado	500,000
Sept. 11	The Woodward Stakes	Belmont	1⅛	Ghostzapper	Javier Castellano	500,000
Sept. 11	Irish Champion Stakes*	Leopardstown	1¼ (T)	Azamour	Michael Kinane	1,290,000
Sept. 18	Kentucky Cup Classic	Turfway	1¹⁄₈	Roses in May	John Velazquez	350,000
Sept. 19	Atto Mile	Woodbine	1 (T)	Soaring Free	Todd Kabel	1,000,000
Sept. 19	Matron Stakes	Belmont	1	Sense of Style	Edgar Prado	300,000
Sept. 19	Futurity Stakes	Belmont	1	Park Avenue Ball	Javier Castellano	300,000
Sept. 19	Ruffian Handicap	Belmont	1¹⁄₁₆	Sightseek	John Velazquez	300,000
Sept. 25	Super Derby XXV	Louisiana Downs	1⅛	Fantasticat	Gerard Melancon	500,000

*World Series Racing Championship series race.
Includes a $5 million bonus awarded to Smarty Jones for winning the Rebel Stakes, Arkansas Derby and Kentucky Derby.

NTRA National Thoroughbred Poll

The NTRA Thoroughbred Poll conducted by National Thoroughbred Racing Association, covering races through Sept. 26, 2004. Rankings are based on the votes of horse racing media representatives on a 10-9-8-7-6-5-4-3-2-1 basis. First place votes are in parentheses.

		Pts	Age	Sex	'04 Record Sts—1-2-3	Owner	Trainer
1	Pleasantly Perfect (16)	169	6	Horse	4–3-1-0	Diamond A Racing Corp.	Richard Mandella
2	Ghostzapper	128	4	Colt	3–3-0-0	Stronach Stables	Bobby Frankel
3	Roses in May (1)	119	4	Colt	5–5-0-0	Ken & Sarah Ramsey	Dale Romans
4	Birdstone	102	3	Colt	5–3-0-0	Marylou Whitney Stables	Nick Zito
5	Speightstown	66	6	Horse	4–4-0-0	Eugene & Laura Melnyk	Todd Pletcher
6	Azeri	60	6	Mare	6–2-2-0	Allen Paulson Living Trust	D. Wayne Lukas
7	Sightseek	48	5	Mare	6–3-1-0	Juddmonte Farms, Inc.	Bobby Frankel
8	Kitten's Joy	44	3	Colt	6–5-1-0	Ken & Sarah Ramsey	Dale Romans
9	Southern Image	39	4	Colt	4–3-1-0	Blahut Stables, Kagele Bros. & Tepper	Mike Machowsky
10	Pico Central	33	5	Horse	5–4-0-0	Gary Tanaka	Paulo Lobo

Others receiving votes: 11. Ashado (29 points); **12.** Peace Rules (13); **14.** Magistretti (13); **14.** Soaring Free (12); **15.** Kela (8); **16.** Perfect Drift, Saint Liam and Storm Flag Flying (7); **19.** Society Selection (6); **20.** Choctaw Nation; **21.** Declan's Moon and Special Ring (4); **23.** Artie Schiller, Midas Eyes and Pomeroy (3); **26.** Bear Fan and Blackdoun (1).

The 2004 Triple Crown

130TH KENTUCKY DERBY

Grade I for three-year-olds; 10th race at Churchill Downs in Louisville. **Date**—May 1, 2004; **Distance**—1 ¼ miles; **Stakes Purse**—$1,154,800; **Value of Race**—$6,154,800 ($5,854,800 to winner including $5 million racing series bonus; $170,000 for 2nd; $85,000 for 3rd; $45,000 for 4th); **Track**—Sloppy, **Off**—6:12 p.m. EDT. **Favorite**—Smarty Jones (4-1 odds). **Time**—2:04.06; **Start**—Good for all; **Won**—Driving; **Sire**—Elusive Quality (Gone West); **Dam**—I'll Get Along (Smile); **Record** (going into race)—6 starts, 6 wins, 0 second, 0 third; **Last start**—1st in Arkansas Derby (Apr. 10); **Breeder**—Someday Farm (Pa.).

Order of Finish	Jockey	PP	1/4	1/2	3/4	Mile	Stretch	Finish	To $1
Smarty Jones	Stewart Elliott	13	4-½	4-1½	2-hd	2-4	1-hd	1-2¾	4.10
Lion Heart	Mike Smith	3	1-1½	1-2	1-1½	1-hd	2-3½	2-3¼	5.40
Imperialism	Kent Desormeaux	8	15-½	17-3	13-hd	10-½	6-½	3-2	10.90
Limehouse	Jose Santos	1	7-hd	8-hd	6-½	6-½	3-2	4-4½	41.70
The Cliff's Edge	Shane Sellers	9	16-½	15-hd	17-2	17-20	5-1	5-1¼	8.20
Action This Day	David Flores	4	18	18	18	14-2	12-hd	6-1	43.40
Read the Footnotes	Robby Albarado	12	5-½	6-hd	4-½	3-1	4-hd	7-½	22.50
Birdstone	Edgar Prado	11	14-2	11-½	10-hd	9-½	9-½	8-½	21.20
Tapit	Ramon Dominguez	16	17-3	16-hd	12-½	7-hd	10-1½	9-½	6.40
Borrego	Victor Espinoza	10	9-hd	7-2	9-½	4-hd	7-hd	10-¼	14.20
Song of the Sword	Norberto Arroyo Jr.	2	11-½	13-½	7-½	12-1½	11-1½	11-1	55.90
Master David	Alex Solis	7	8-hd	9-hd	14-hd	11-1½	13-3	12-1½	10.60
Pro Prado	John McKee	17	10-2	10-1½	8-hd	5-hd	8-hd	13-5¼	53.50
Castledale	Jose Valdivia Jr.	14	13-hd	12-hd	15-hd	16-½	14-3	14-11½	21.90
Friends Lake	Richard Migliore	5	12-hd	14-1	16-1½	15-hd	15-½	15-½	18.50
Minister Eric	Pat Day	6	6-1½	5-hd	3-½	13-½	17-20	16-3½	22.50
Pollard's Vision	John Velazquez	15	3-hd	2-½	5-1	8-2	16-hd	17-20	24.00
Quinton's Gold Rush	Corey Nakatani	18	2-hd	3-hd	11-hd	18	18	18	51.20

Times—22.99; 46.73; 1:11.80; 1:37.35; 2:04.06.
$2 Mutuel Prices—#15 Smarty Jones ($10.20, $6.20, $4.80); #3 Lion Heart ($8.20, $5.80); #10 Imperialism ($6.20).
Exacta—(15-3) for $65.20; **Trifecta**—(15-3-10) for $987.60; **Superfecta**—(15-3-10-1) for $41,380.20; **Pick Six**—(1-1/3/7-2-5-10-5/9/15) 5 correct for $6,878.00; **Scratched**—Wimbledon, St Averil; **Overweights**—none.
Attendance—140,054; **TV Rating**—8.3/18 share (NBC).

Trainers & Owners (by finish): **1**—John Servis & Someday Farm; **2**—Patrick Biancone & Derrick Smith/Michael Tabor; **3**—Kristin Mulhall & Steve Taub; **4**—Todd Pletcher & Dogwood Stable; **5**—Nick Zito & Robert LaPenta; **6**—Richard Mandella & B. Wayne Hughes; **7**—Richard Violette & Klaravich Stables, Inc.; **8**—Nick Zito & Marylou Whitney Stables; **9**—Michael Dickinson & Winchell Thoroughbreds LLC; **10**—Beau Greely & Kelly Ralls and Scott Foster LLC et al; **11**—Jennifer Pedersen & Paraneck Stable; **12**—Bobby Frankel & Georgica Stable/Stephen Mack/Star Crown Stable; **13**—Robert Holthus & Mrs. James Winn; **14**—Jeff Mullins & Frank Lyons/Greg Knee; **15**—John Kimmel & Mary/Chester Broman; **16**—Richard Mandella & Diamond A Racing Corp.; **17**—Todd Pletcher & Edgewood Farm; **18**—Steve Asmussen & Padua Stables/Jay Manoogian.

129TH PREAKNESS STAKES

Grade I for three-year-olds; 12th race at Pimlico in Baltimore. **Date**—May 15, 2004; **Distance**—1 3/16 miles; **Stakes Purse**—$1,000,000 ($650,000 to winner; $200,000 for 2nd; $100,000 for 3rd; $50,000 for 4th); **Track**—Fast; **Off**—6:25 p.m. EDT. **Favorite**—Smarty Jones (3-5 odds). **Winner**—Smarty Jones; **Field**—10 horses; **Time**—1:55.59; **Start**—Good for all but Little Matth Man; **Won**—Driving; **Sire**—Elusive Quality (Gone West); **Dam**—I'll Get Along (Smile); **Record** (going into race)—7 starts, 7 wins, 0 second, 0 third; **Last start**—1st in Kentucky Derby (May 1); **Breeder**—Someday Farm (Pa.).

Order of Finish	Jockey	PP	1/4	1/2	3/4	Stretch	Finish	To $1
Smarty Jones	Stewart Elliott	6	2-½	2-2	2-2½	1-5	1-11½	0.70
Rock Hard Ten	Gary Stevens	9	7-1½	7-hd	6-1	2-hd	2-2	6.90
Eddington	Jerry Bailey	8	6-1	6-2	8-3½	7-5	3-hd	13.20
Lion Heart	Mike Smith	1	1-1½	1-2½	1-1	3-4½	4-hd	4.90
Imperialism	Kent Desormeaux	7	3-1	4-hd	5-½	4-2	5-1	6.60
Sir Shackleton	Rafael Bejarano	5	5-½	5-½	4-hd	5-hd	6-¾	37.50
Borrego	Victor Espinoza	2	8-2½	8-4	7-hd	6-½	7-5½	12.80
Little Matth Man	Richard Migliore	3	10	10	10	8-2½	8-2	45.00
Song of the Sword	Jorge Chavez	4	4-hd	3-hd	3-½	9-2	9-3½	51.00
Water Cannon	Ryan Fogelsonger	10	9-3½	9-½	9-½	10	10	39.50

Times—23.65; 47.32; 1:11.53; 1:36.44; 1:55.59.
$2 Mutuel Prices—#7 Smarty Jones ($3.40, $3.00, $2.60); #10 Rock Hard Ten ($5.00, $4.00); #9 Eddington ($5.20).
Exacta—(7-10) for $24.60; **Trifecta**—(7-10-9) for $177.20; **Superfecta**—(7-10-9-1) for $230.70; **Pick Three**—(7-4-4/7) for $143.20; **Scratched**—The Cliff's Edge; **Overweights**—none.
Attendance—112,668; **TV Rating**—7.2/16 share (NBC).

Trainers & Owners (by finish): **1**—John Servis & Someday Farm; **2**—Jason Orman & Mercedes Stable LLC/Madeleine Paulson; **3**—Mark Hennig & Willmott Stables Inc.; **4**—Patrick Biancone & Derrick Smith/Michael Tabor; **5**—Kristin Mulhall & Steve Taub; **6**—Nick Zito & Tracy Farmer; **7**—Beau Greely & Kelly Ralls and Scott Foster LLC et al; **8**—Martin Ciresa & Vincent Papandrea; **9**—Jennifer Pedersen & Paraneck Stable; **10**—Linda Albert & The Nonsequitur Stable LLC.

The 2004 Triple Crown (Cont.)

136TH BELMONT STAKES

Grade I for three-year-olds; 11th race at Belmont Park in Elmont, N.Y. **Date**—June 5, 2004; **Distance**—1½ miles; **Stakes Purse**—$1,000,000 ($600,000 to winner; $200,000 for 2nd; $110,000 for 3rd; $60,000 for 4th; $30,000 for 5th); **Track**—Fast; **Off**—6:48 p.m. EDT; **Favorite**—Smarty Jones (1-5 odds). **Winner**—Birdstone; **Field**—9 horses; **Time**—2:27.50; **Start**—Good for all; **Won**—Driving; **Sire**—Grindstone (Unbridled); **Dam**—Dear Birdie (Storm Bird); **Record** (going into race)—6 starts, 3 wins, 0 second, 0 third; **Last Start**—8th in Kentucky Derby (May 1); **Breeder**—Marylou Whitney Stables (Ky.).

Order of Finish	Jockey	PP	1/4	1/2	Mile	1-1/4	Stretch	Finish	To $1
Birdstone	Edgar Prado	4	7-1½	5-½	4-6	2-1½	2-6	1-1	36.00
Smarty Jones	Stewart Elliott	9	3-½	3-½	1-½	1-3½	1-1½	2-8	0.35
Royal Assault	Pat Day	6	6-hd	6-1½	6-1	5-2	5-10	3-3	27.75
Eddington	Jerry Bailey	8	5-hd	4-1½	3-3½	4-8	4-6	4-no	14.20
Rock Hard Ten	Alex Solis	5	2-½	2-1	2-1	3-2	3-2½	5-14	6.70
Tap Dancer	Javier Castellano	7	9	9	8-10	7-½	6-hd	6-4¼	40.50
Master David	Jose Santos	1	8-1	8-hd	7-hd	6-hd	7-8	7-1	24.50
Caiman	Ramon Dominguez	3	4-hd	7-hd	9	9	9	8-6¼	49.75
Purge	John Velazquez	2	1-½	1-hd	5-6	8-6	8-2	9	9.60

Times—24.33; 48.65; 1:11.76; 1:35.44; 2:00.52; 2:27.50.

$2 Mutuel Prices—#4 Birdstone ($74.00, $14.00, $8.60); #9 Smarty Jones ($3.30, $2.60); #6 Royal Assault ($6.10). **Exacta**—(4-9) for $139.00; **Trifecta**—(4-9-6) for $1,589.00; **Superfecta**—(4-9-6-8) for $11,679.00; **Pick Six**—(4-3-1-3-5-4) for $47,421.00; **Scratched**—none; **Overweights**—none; **Attendance**—120,139; **TV Rating**—13.0/29 share (NBC).

Trainers & Owners (by finish): **1**—Nick Zito & Marylou Whitney Stables; **2**—John Servis & Someday Farm; **3**—Nick Zito & Tracy Farmer; **4**—Mark Hennig & Willmott Stables Inc.; **5**—Jason Orman & Mercedes Stables LLC/Madeleine Paulson; **6**—Edward Allard & Gilbert Campbell; **7**—Bobby Frankel & Georgica Stable/Stephen Mack/Star Crown Stable; **8**—Angel Medina & Victor Achar; **9**—Todd Pletcher & Starlight Stables LLC/Paul Saylor/Johns Martin.

2003-04 Money Leaders

Official Top 10 standings for 2003 and unofficial Top 10 standings for 2004, through Sept. 25. Results are based on North American races, plus all World Series Racing Championship series races. Source: *Equibase Company.*

FINAL 2003

HORSES	Age	Sts	1-2-3	Earnings
Moon Ballad (IRE)	4	3	1-0-0	$3,651,101
Pleasantly Perfect	5	4	2-0-1	2,470,000
Tap Dance City	6	1	1-0-0	2,316,001
Mineshaft	4	9	7-2-0	2,209,686
Wando	3	8	5-1-0	2,017,323
Medaglia d'Oro	4	5	3-2-0	1,990,000
Funny Cide	3	8	2-2-2	1,963,200
Empire Maker	3	6	3-3-0	1,936,200
Peace Rules	3	7	3-1-1	1,850,000
Falbrav (IRE)	5	4	1-1-1	1,787,249

JOCKEYS	Mts	1st	Earnings
Jerry Bailey	776	206	$23,354,960
Edgar Prado	1478	259	18,475,582
John Velazquez	1309	306	16,625,501
Alex Solis	1117	203	16,304,252
Patrick Valenzuela	1447	287	15,697,352
Pat Day	985	215	13,378,292
Jose Santos	1157	176	11,472,287
Ramon Dominguez	1627	453	11,359,767
Todd Kabel	836	160	11,323,313
Patrick Husbands	882	168	11,168,817

TRAINERS	Sts	1st	Earnings
Bobby Frankel	413	114	$19,143,289
Todd Pletcher	827	199	13,556,924
Steve Asmussen	1949	452	11,725,782
Richard Mandella	254	51	9,869,548
Bob Baffert	674	127	9,442,281
Scott Lake	2009	455	9,163,599
Bill Mott	719	138	6,866,920
Doug O'Neill	760	133	6,438,799
Jerry Hollendorfer	1216	282	6,260,305
Saeed bin Suroor	23	4	6,034,130

2004 (Through Sept. 25)

HORSES	Age	Sts	1-2-3	Earnings
Smarty Jones	3	7	6-1-0	$7,563,535
Pleasantly Perfect	6	4	3-1-0	4,400,000
Southern Image	4	4	3-1-0	1,612,150
Medaglia d'Oro	5	2	1-1-0	1,500,000
Birdstone	3	5	3-0-0	1,236,600
Epalo (GER)	5	3	1-1-1	1,122,041
Lion Heart	3	7	2-3-0	1,080,000
Ashado	3	6	3-2-1	1,069,640
Diaghilev (IRE)	5	1	1-0-0	1,025,600
Peace Rules	4	6	3-0-0	1,024,288

JOCKEYS	Mts	1st	Earnings
Edgar Prado	1190	232	$14,411,549
John Velazquez	1048	270	13,794,754
Victor Espinoza	1051	188	12,557,835
Jerry Bailey	578	133	12,537,970
Stewart Elliott	1037	202	12,108,484
Alex Solis	556	120	11,554,851
Corey Nakatani	844	173	8,912,167
Todd Kabel	509	129	8,830,743
Rafael Bejarano	1488	375	8,386,571
Tyler Baze	1075	178	8,113,241

TRAINERS	Sts	1st	Earnings
Todd Pletcher	712	188	$11,698,859
Bobby Frankel	353	103	10,047,485
Steve Asmussen	1610	387	9,768,108
John Servis	205	48	8,433,694
Bob Baffert	440	83	6,528,724
Jeff Mullins	404	119	5,992,956
Richard Mandella	111	16	5,798,738
Scott Lake	1231	265	5,349,426
Richard Dutrow Jr.	450	122	5,317,323
Nick Zito	340	57	5,098,911

Harness Racing
2003-04 Major Stakes Races

Winners of major stakes races from Oct. 19, 2003 through Sept. 23, 2004; all paces and trots cover one mile; (BC) indicates year-end Breeders' Crown series.

Late 2003

Date	Race	Raceway	Winner	Time	Driver	Purse
Nov. 29	BC 3-Yr-Old Colt Pace	Meadowlands	No Pan Intended	1:50³/₅	David Miller	$542,500
Nov. 29	BC 3-Yr-Old Filly Pace	Meadowlands	Burning Point	1:51⁴/₅	Kevin Wallis	670,000
Nov. 29	BC 3-Yr-Old Colt Trot	Meadowlands	Mr. Muscleman	1:54²/₅	Ron Pierce	585,000
Nov. 29	BC 3-Yr-Old Filly Trot	Meadowlands	Stroke Play	1:55²/₅	Brian Sears	500,000
Nov. 29	BC 2-Yr-Old Colt Pace	Meadowlands	I Am A Fool	1:52²/₅	Ron Pierce	540,000
Nov. 29	BC 2-Yr-Old Filly Pace	Meadowlands	Pans Culottes	1:54³/₅	Dan Dube	470,000
Nov. 29	BC 2-Yr-Old Colt Trot	Meadowlands	Cantab Hall	1:56⁴/₅	Mike Lachance	420,000
Nov. 29	BC 2-Yr-Old Filly Trot	Meadowlands	Forever Starlet	1:57⁴/₅	David Miller	480,000

2004 (through Sept. 23)

Date	Race	Raceway	Winner	Time	Driver	Purse
May 29	Hoosier Cup	Hoosier Park	Skydancer Hanover	1:51²/₅	Dan Dube	$500,000
May 29	New Jersey Classic	Meadowlands	Modern Art	1:50²/₅	David Miller	500,000
June 19	North America Cup	Woodbine	Mantacular	1:51²/₅	Cat Manzi	1,189,535
July 10	William Haughton Open Pace	Meadowlands	Four Starzzz Shark	1:48¹/₅	Mike Lachance	700,000
July 16	Stanley Dancer Trot	Meadowlands	Windsong's Legacy	1:53	T. Smedshammer	382,000
July 17	Meadowlands Pace	Meadowlands	Holborn Hanover	1:49	Jim Morrill Jr.	1,000,000
July 31	BC Open Pace	Meadowlands	Boulder Creek	1:48¹/₅	Ron Pierce	552,500
July 31	BC Mare Trot	Meadowlands	Armbro Affair	1:54¹/₅	Ron Pierce	250,000
July 31	BC Open Trot	Meadowlands	HP Paque	1:52²/₅	Brian Sears	800,000
July 31	BC Mare Pace	Meadowlands	Always Cam	1:49²/₅	David Miller	300,000
Aug. 5	Peter Haughton Memorial	Meadowlands	New York Yank	1:58²/₅	Ron Pierce	420,000
Aug. 5	Merrie Annabelle Final	Meadowlands	Reinvent	1:57¹/₅	Ron Pierce	450,620
Aug. 6	Sweetheart Pace	Meadowlands	Fox Valley Shaker	1:53³/₅	George Brennan	443,200
Aug. 6	Woodrow Wilson Pace	Meadowlands	Village Jolt	1:51³/₅	Ron Pierce	432,000
Aug. 7	**Hambletonian**	Meadowlands	Windsong's Legacy	1:54¹/₅	T. Smedshammer	1,000,000
Aug. 7	Hambletonian Oaks	Meadowlands	Silver Springs	1:53³/₅	George Brennan	500,000
Aug. 7	Mistletoe Shalee	Meadowlands	Kikikatie	1:51¹/₅	David Miller	350,000
Aug. 7	Nat Ray	Meadowlands	Revenue	1:53	Lutfi Kolgjini	300,000
Aug. 14	Coors Del Miller Adios	The Meadows	Timesarechanging	1:49³/₅	Ron Pierce	350,350
Aug. 28	Fan Hanover Pace	Woodbine	Rainbow Blue	1:51¹/₅	Ron Pierce	543,543
Aug. 22	Confederation Cup XXVIII	Flamboro	Sparkler	1:53¹/₅	Paul MacDonell	436,590
Aug. 28	**Yonkers Trot**	Hawthorne	Windsong's Legacy	1:53¹/₅	T. Smedshammer	391,200
Sept. 4	Metro Pace	Woodbine	Rocknroll Hanover	1:49¹/₅	Brian Sears	933,086
Sept. 4	Canadian Pacing Derby	Woodbine	Casimir Camotion	1:48³/₅	Patrick Lachance	708,400
Sept. 4	World Trotting Derby	DuQuoin	Tom Ridge	1:50²/₅	Ron Pierce	530,000
Sept. 6	**Cane Pace**	Freehold	Timesarechanging	1:52³/₅	Ron Pierce	334,875
			Western Terror (dead heat)		John Campbell	
Sept. 14	**Messenger Stakes**	Delaware	Metropolitan	1:52²/₅	John Campbell	340,950
Sept. 18	Maple Leaf Trot	Mohawk	Mr. Muscleman	1:53²/₅	Ron Pierce	851.500
Sept. 23	**Little Brown Jug**	Delaware	Timesarechanging	1:51³/₅	Ron Pierce	571,500

2003-04 Money Leaders

Official Top 10 standings for 2003 and unofficial Top 10 standings for 2004 through Sept. 23.

FINAL 2003

HORSES	Age	Sts	1-2-3	Earnings
No Pan Intended	3ph	21	17-3-0	$1,465,852
Mr. Muscleman	3tg	17	8-4-2	1,178,115
I Am A Fool	2ph	15	9-2-2	1,159,062
Art Major	4ph	11	8-3-0	1,082,930
Eternal Camnation	6pm	20	11-4-0	908,346
Amigo Hall	3th	16	8-4-3	896,209
Burning Point	3pm	29	22-4-1	861,252
McArdle	4ph	17	7-3-5	849,222
Allamerican Theory	3ph	19	9-3-1	827,565
Yankee Cruiser	3ph	22	5-5-4	807,129

DRIVERS	Mts	1st	Earnings
David Miller	2415	426	$11,490,590
Ron Pierce	1962	280	9,361,745
Chris Christoforou	3201	580	8,492,464
Luc Ouellette	2167	316	8,120,602
Mike Lachance	1876	208	7,876,334
John Campbell	875	119	6,035,930
Randall Waples	2759	512	6,009,832
George Brennan	2351	338	5,580,064
Cat Manzi	2724	415	5,509,422
James Morrill Jr.	2117	350	5,233,189

2004 (through Sept. 23)

HORSES	Age	Sts	1-2-3	Earnings
Windsong's Legacy	3th	10	7-2-1	$1,497,506
Timesarechanging	3pg	16	9-5-1	1,007,105
Cantab Hall	3th	10	3-5-1	792,116
Mantacular	3ph	18	2-3-5	767,223
Metropolitan	3ph	13	4-4-2	767,183
Four Starzzz Shark	6ph	11	9-1-0	766,945
Rainbow Blue	3pm	16	15-0-0	716,767
Royal Mattjesty	5ph	25	7-6-5	679,386
Holborn Hanover	3pg	17	4-2-2	646,699
Casimir Camotion	4pg	26	12-6-4	627,220

DRIVERS	Mts	1st	Earnings
Ron Pierce	1785	323	$9,103,110
Brian Sears	1673	277	7,091,757
David Miller	1902	260	6,177,466
Cat Manzi	2440	436	5,855,109
Mike Lachance	1510	160	5,654,583
George Brennan	1774	273	5,642,147
Luc Ouellette	1724	298	5,331,809
John Campbell	728	114	4,852,156
Paul MacDonell	1363	177	4,308,285
Chris Christoforou	1766	306	4,204,159

1867-2004
Through the Years

SPORTS ALMANAC

Thoroughbred Racing

The Triple Crown

The term "Triple Crown" was coined by sportswriter Charles Hatton while covering the 1930 victories of Gallant Fox in the Kentucky Derby, Preakness Stakes and Belmont Stakes. Before then, only Sir Barton (1919) had won all three races in the same year. Since then, nine horses have won the Triple Crown. Two trainers, James (Sunny Jim) Fitzsimmons and Ben A. Jones, have saddled two Triple Crown champions, while Eddie Arcaro is the only jockey to ride two champions.

Year		Jockey	Trainer	Owner	Sire/Dam
1919	**Sir Barton**	Johnny Loftus	H. Guy Bedwell	J.K.L. Ross	Star Shoot/Lady Sterling
1930	**Gallant Fox**	Earl Sande	J.E. Fitzsimmons	Belair Stud	Sir Gallahad III/Marguerite
1935	**Omaha**	Willie Saunders	J.E. Fitzsimmons	Belair Stud	Gallant Fox/Flambino
1937	**War Admiral**	Charley Kurtsinger	George Conway	Samuel Riddle	Man o' War/Brushup
1941	**Whirlaway**	Eddie Arcaro	Ben A. Jones	Calumet Farm	Blenheim II/Dustwhirl
1943	**Count Fleet**	Johnny Longden	Don Cameron	Mrs. J.D. Hertz	Reigh Count/Quickly
1946	**Assault**	Warren Mehrtens	Max Hirsch	King Ranch	Bold Venture/Igual
1948	**Citation**	Eddie Arcaro	Ben A. Jones	Calumet Farm	Bull Lea/Hydroplane II
1973	**Secretariat**	Ron Turcotte	Lucien Laurin	Meadow Stable	Bold Ruler/Somethingroyal
1977	**Seattle Slew**	Jean Cruguet	Billy Turner	Karen Taylor	Bold Reasoning/My Charmer
1978	**Affirmed**	Steve Cauthen	Laz Barrera	Harbor View Farm	Exclusive Native/Won't Tell You

Note: Gallant Fox (1930) is the only Triple Crown winner to sire another Triple Crown winner, Omaha (1935). Wm. Woodward Sr., owner of Belair Stud, was breeder-owner of both horses and both were trained by Sunny Jim Fitzsimmons.

Triple Crown Near Misses

Forty-eight horses have won two legs of the Triple Crown. Of those, eighteen won the Kentucky Derby (KD) and Preakness Stakes (PS) only to be beaten in the Belmont Stakes (BS). Two others, Burgoo King (1932) and Bold Venture (1936), won the Derby and Preakness, but were forced out of the Belmont with the same injury–a bowed tendon–that effectively ended their racing careers. In 1978, Alydar finished second to Affirmed in all three races, the only time that has happened. Note that the Preakness preceded the Kentucky Derby in 1922, '23 and '31; (*) indicates won on disqualification.

Year		KD	PS	BS	Year		KD	PS	BS
1877	**Cloverbrook**	DNS	won	won	1966	**Kauai King**	won	won	4th
1878	**Duke of Magenta**	DNS	won	won	1967	**Damascus**	3rd	won	won
1880	**Grenada**	DNS	won	won	1968	**Forward Pass**	won*	won	2nd
1881	**Saunterer**	DNS	won	won	1969	**Majestic Prince**	won	won	2nd
1895	**Belmar**	DNS	won	won	1971	**Canonero II**	won	won	4th
1920	**Man o' War**	DNS	won	won	1972	**Riva Ridge**	won	4th	won
1922	**Pillory**	DNS	won	won	1974	**Little Current**	5th	won	won
1923	**Zev**	won	12th	won	1976	**Bold Forbes**	won	3rd	won
1931	**Twenty Grand**	won	2nd	won	1979	**Spectacular Bid**	won	won	3rd
1932	**Burgoo King**	won	won	DNS	1981	**Pleasant Colony**	won	won	3rd
1936	**Bold Venture**	won	won	DNS	1984	**Swale**	won	7th	won
1939	**Johnstown**	won	5th	won	1987	**Alysheba**	won	won	4th
1940	**Bimelech**	2nd	won	won	1988	**Risen Star**	3rd	won	won
1942	**Shut Out**	won	5th	won	1989	**Sunday Silence**	won	won	2nd
1944	**Pensive**	won	won	2nd	1991	**Hansel**	10th	won	won
1949	**Capot**	2nd	won	won	1994	**Tabasco Cat**	6th	won	won
1950	**Middleground**	won	2nd	won	1995	**Thunder Gulch**	won	3rd	won
1953	**Native Dancer**	2nd	won	won	1997	**Silver Charm**	won	won	2nd
1955	**Nashua**	2nd	won	won	1998	**Real Quiet**	won	won	2nd
1956	**Needles**	2nd	won	won	1999	**Charismatic**	won	won	3rd
1958	**Tim Tam**	won	won	2nd	2001	**Point Given**	5th	won	won
1961	**Carry Back**	won	won	7th	2002	**War Emblem**	won	won	8th
1963	**Chateaugay**	won	2nd	won	2003	**Funny Cide**	won	won	3rd
1964	**Northern Dancer**	won	won	3rd	2004	**Smarty Jones**	won	won	2nd

The Triple Crown Challenge (1987-93)

Seeking to make the Triple Crown more than just a media event and to insure that owners would not be attracted to more lucrative races, officials at Churchill Downs, the Maryland Jockey Club and the New York Racing Association created Triple Crown Productions in 1985 and announced that a $1 million bonus would be given to the horse that performs best in the Kentucky Derby, Preakness Stakes and Belmont Stakes. Furthermore, a bonus of $5 million would be presented to any horse winning all three races.

Revised in 1991, the rules stated that the winning horse must: 1. finish all three races; 2. earn points by finishing first, second, third or fourth in at least one of the three races; and 3. earn the highest number of points based on the following system—10 points to win, five to place, three to show and one to finish fourth. In the event of a tie, the $1 million is distributed equally among the top point-getters. From 1987-90, the system was five points to win, three to place and one to show. The Triple Crown Challenge was discontinued in 1994.

Year		KD	PS	BS	Pts	Year		KD	PS	BS	Pts
1987	1 Bet Twice	2nd	2nd	1st—	11	1991	1 Hansel	10th	1st	1st—	20
	2 Alysheba	1st	1st	4th—	10		2 Strike the Gold	1st	6th	2nd—	15
	3 Cryptoclearance	4th	3rd	2nd—	4		3 Mane Minister	3rd	3rd	3rd—	9
1988	1 Risen Star	3rd	1st	1st—	11	1992	1 Pine Bluff	5th	1st	3rd—	13
	2 Winning Colors	1st	3rd	6th—	6		2 Casual Lies	2nd	3rd	5th—	8
	3 Brian's Time	6th	2nd	3rd—	4		(No other horses ran all three races.)					
1989	1 Sunday Silence	1st	1st	2nd—	13	1993	1 Sea Hero	1st	5th	7th—	10
	2 Easy Goer	2nd	2nd	1st—	11		2 Wild Gale	3rd	8th	3rd—	6
	3 Hawkster	5th	5th	5th—	0		(No other horses ran all three races.)					
1990	1 Unbridled	1st	2nd	4th—	8							
	2 Summer Squall	2nd	1st	DNR—	8							
	3 Go and Go	DNR	DNR	1st—	5							
	(Unbridled was only horse to run all three races.)											

Kentucky Derby

For three-year-olds. Held the first Saturday in May at Churchill Downs in Louisville, Ky. Inaugurated in 1875.

Originally run at 1½ miles (1875-95), shortened to present 1¼ miles in 1896.

Trainers with most wins: Ben Jones (6); D. Wayne Lukas and Dick Thompson (4); Bob Baffert, Sunny Jim Fitzsimmons and Max Hirsch (3).

Jockeys with most wins: Eddie Arcaro and Bill Hartack (5); Bill Shoemaker (4); Angel Cordero Jr., Issac Murphy, Earl Sande and Gary Stevens (3).

Winning fillies: Regret (1915), Genuine Risk (1980) and Winning Colors (1988).

Year	Winner (Margin)	Time	Jockey	Trainer	2nd place	3rd place
1875	Aristides (1)	2:37¾	Oliver Lewis	Ansel Anderson	Volcano	Verdigris
1876	Vagrant (2)	2:38¼	Bobby Swim	James Williams	Creedmore	Harry Hill
1877	Baden-Baden (2)	2:38	Billy Walker	Ed Brown	Leonard	King William
1878	Day Star (2)	2:37¼	Jimmy Carter	Lee Paul	Himyar	Leveler
1879	Lord Murphy (1)	2:37	Charlie Shauer	George Rice	Falsetto	Strathmore
1880	Fonso (1)	2:37½	George Lewis	Tice Hutsell	Kimball	Bancroft
1881	Hindoo (4)	2:40	Jim McLaughlin	James Rowe Sr.	Lelex	Alfambra
1882	Apollo (½)	2:40¼	Babe Hurd	Green Morris	Runnymede	Bengal
1883	Leonatus (3)	2:43	Billy Donohue	John McGinty	Drake Carter	Lord Raglan
1884	Buchanan (2)	2:40¼	Isaac Murphy	William Bird	Loftin	Audrain
1885	Joe Cotton (nk)	2:37¼	Babe Henderson	Alex Perry	Bersan	Ten Booker
1886	Ben Ali (½)	2:36½	Paul Duffy	Jim Murphy	Blue Wing	Free Knight
1887	Montrose (2)	2:39¼	Isaac Lewis	John McGinty	Jim Gore	Jacobin
1888	MacBeth II (1)	2:38¼	George Covington	John Campbell	Gallifet	White
1889	Spokane (ns)	2:34½	Thomas Kiley	John Rodegap	Proctor Knott	Once Again
1890	Riley (2)	2:45	Isaac Murphy	Edward Corrigan	Bill Letcher	Robespierre
1891	Kingman (1)	2:52¼	Isaac Murphy	Dud Allen	Balgowan	High Tariff
1892	Azra (ns)	2:41½	Lonnie Clayton	John Morris	Huron	Phil Dwyer
1893	Lookout (5)	2:39¼	Eddie Kunze	Wm. McDaniel	Plutus	Boundless
1894	Chant (2)	2:41	Frank Goodale	Eugene Leigh	Pearl Song	Sigurd
1895	Halma (3)	2:37½	Soup Perkins	Byron McClelland	Basso	Laureate
1896	Ben Brush (ns)	2:07¾	Willie Simms	Hardy Campbell	Ben Eder	Semper Ego
1897	Typhoon II (hd)	2:12½	Buttons Garner	J.C. Cahn	Ornament	Dr. Catlett
1898	Plaudit (nk)	2:09	Willie Simms	John E. Madden	Lieber Karl	Isabey
1899	Manuel (2)	2:12	Fred Taral	Robert Walden	Corsini	Mazo
1900	Lieut. Gibson (4)	2:06¼	Jimmy Boland	Charles Hughes	Florizar	Thrive
1901	His Eminence (2)	2:07¾	Jimmy Winkfield	F.B. Van Meter	Sannazarro	Driscoll
1902	Alan-a-Dale (ns)	2:08¾	Jimmy Winkfield	T.C. McDowell	Inventor	The Rival
1903	Judge Himes (¾)	2:09	Hal Booker	J.P. Mayberry	Early	Bourbon
1904	Elwood (½)	2:08½	Shorty Prior	C.E. Durnell	Ed Tierney	Brancas
1905	Agile (3)	2:10¾	Jack Martin	Robert Tucker	Ram's Horn	Layson
1906	Sir Huon (2)	2:08⅘	Roscoe Troxler	Pete Coyne	Lady Navarre	James Reddick
1907	Pink Star (2)	2:12⅗	Andy Minder	W.H. Fizer	Zal	Ovelando
1908	Stone Street (1)	2:15⅕	Arthur Pickens	J.W. Hall	Sir Cleges	Dunvegan
1909	Wintergreen (4)	2:08⅕	Vincent Powers	Charles Mack	Miami	Dr. Barkley

Kentucky Derby (Cont.)

Year	Winner (Margin)	Time	Jockey	Trainer	2nd place	3rd place
1910	Donau (½)	2:06⅖	Fred Herbert	George Ham	Joe Morris	Fighting Bob
1911	Meridian (¾)	2:05	George Archibald	Albert Ewing	Governor Gray	Colston
1912	Worth (nk)	2:09⅖	C.H. Shilling	Frank Taylor	Duval	Flamma
1913	Donerail (½)	2:04⅘	Roscoe Goose	Thomas Hayes	Ten Point	Gowell
1914	Old Rosebud (8)	2:03⅖	John McCabe	F.D. Weir	Hodge	Bronzewing
1915	Regret (2)	2:05⅖	Joe Notter	James Rowe Sr.	Pebbles	Sharpshooter
1916	George Smith (nk)	2:04	Johnny Loftus	Hollie Hughes	Star Hawk	Franklin
1917	Omar Khayyam (2)	2:04⅗	Charles Borel	C.T. Patterson	Ticket	Midway
1918	Exterminator (1)	2:10⅘	William Knapp	Henry McDaniel	Escoba	Viva America
1919	SIR BARTON (5)	2:09⅘	Johnny Loftus	H. Guy Bedwell	Billy Kelly	Under Fire
1920	Paul Jones (hd)	2:09	Ted Rice	Billy Garth	Upset	On Watch
1921	Behave Yourself (hd)	2:04⅕	Charles Thompson	Dick Thompson	Black Servant	Prudery
1922	Morvich (1½)	2:04⅗	Albert Johnson	Fred Burlew	Bet Mosie	John Finn
1923	Zev (1½)	2:05⅖	Earl Sande	David Leary	Martingale	Vigil
1924	Black Gold (½)	2:05⅕	John Mooney	Hanly Webb	Chilhowee	Beau Butler
1925	Flying Ebony (1½)	2:07⅗	Earl Sande	William Duke	Captain Hal	Son of John
1926	Bubbling Over (5)	2:03⅘	Albert Johnson	Dick Thompson	Bagenbaggage	Rock Man
1927	Whiskery (hd)	2:06	Linus McAtee	Fred Hopkins	Osmand	Jock
1928	Reigh Count (3)	2:10⅖	Chick Lang	Bert Michell	Misstep	Toro
1929	Clyde Van Dusen (2)	2:10⅘	Linus McAtee	Clyde Van Dusen	Naishapur	Panchio
1930	GALLANT FOX (2)	2:07⅗	Earl Sande	Jim Fitzsimmons	Gallant Knight	Ned O.
1931	Twenty Grand (4)	2:01⅘	Charley Kurtsinger	James Rowe Jr.	Sweep All	Mate
1932	Burgoo King (5)	2:05⅕	Eugene James	Dick Thompson	Economic	Stepenfetchit
1933	Brokers Tip (ns)	2:06⅘	Don Meade	Dick Thompson	Head Play	Charley O.
1934	Cavalcade (2½)	2:04	Mack Garner	Bob Smith	Discovery	Agrarian
1935	OMAHA (1½)	2:05	Willie Saunders	Jim Fitzsimmons	Roman Soldier	Whiskolo
1936	Bold Venture (hd)	2:03⅗	Ira Hanford	Max Hirsch	Brevity	Indian Broom
1937	WAR ADMIRAL (1¾)	2:03⅕	Charley Kurtsinger	George Conway	Pompoon	Reaping Reward
1938	Lawrin (1)	2:04⅘	Eddie Arcaro	Ben Jones	Dauber	Can't Wait
1939	Johnstown (8)	2:03⅖	James Stout	Jim Fitzsimmons	Challedon	Heather Broom
1940	Gallahadion (1½)	2:05	Carroll Bierman	Roy Waldron	Bimelech	Dit
1941	WHIRLAWAY (8)	2:01⅖	Eddie Arcaro	Ben Jones	Staretor	Market Wise
1942	Shut Out (2½)	2:04⅖	Wayne Wright	John Gaver	Alsab	Valdina Orphan
1943	COUNT FLEET (3)	2:04	Johnny Longden	Don Cameron	Blue Swords	Slide Rule
1944	Pensive (4½)	2:04⅕	Conn McCreary	Ben Jones	Broadcloth	Stir Up
1945	Hoop Jr (6)	2:07	Eddie Arcaro	Ivan Parke	Pot O'Luck	Darby Dieppe
1946	ASSAULT (8)	2:06⅗	Warren Mehrtens	Max Hirsch	Spy Song	Hampden
1947	Jet Pilot (hd)	2:06⅘	Eric Guerin	Tom Smith	Phalanx	Faultless
1948	CITATION (3½)	2:05⅖	Eddie Arcaro	Ben Jones	Coaltown	My Request
1949	Ponder (3)	2:04⅕	Steve Brooks	Ben Jones	Capot	Palestinian
1950	Middleground (1¼)	2:01⅗	William Boland	Max Hirsch	Hill Prince	Mr. Trouble
1951	Count Turf (4)	2:02⅗	Conn McCreary	Sol Rutchick	Royal Mustang	Ruhe
1952	Hill Gail (2)	2:01⅗	Eddie Arcaro	Ben Jones	Sub Fleet	Blue Man
1953	Dark Star (hd)	2:02	Hank Moreno	Eddie Hayward	Native Dancer	Invigorator
1954	Determine (1½)	2:03	Raymond York	Willie Molter	Hasty Road	Hasseyampa
1955	Swaps (1½)	2:01⅘	Bill Shoemaker	Mesh Tenney	Nashua	Summer Tan
1956	Needles (¾)	2:03⅖	David Erb	Hugh Fontaine	Fabius	Come On Red
1957	Iron Liege (ns)	2:02⅕	Bill Hartack	Jimmy Jones	Gallant Man	Round Table
1958	Tim Tam (½)	2:05	Ismael Valenzuela	Jimmy Jones	Lincoln Road	Noureddin
1959	Tomy Lee (ns)	2:02⅕	Bill Shoemaker	Frank Childs	Sword Dancer	First Landing
1960	Venetian Way (3½)	2:02⅖	Bill Hartack	Victor Sovinski	Bally Ache	Victoria Park
1961	Carry Back (¾)	2:04	John Sellers	Jack Price	Crozier	Bass Clef
1962	Decidedly (2¼)	2:00⅖	Bill Hartack	Horatio Luro	Roman Line	Ridan
1963	Chateaugay (1¼)	2:01⅘	Braulio Baeza	James Conway	Never Bend	Candy Spots
1964	Northern Dancer (nk)	2:00	Bill Hartack	Horatio Luro	Hill Rise	The Scoundrel
1965	Lucky Debonair (nk)	2:01⅕	Bill Shoemaker	Frank Catrone	Dapper Dan	Tom Rolfe
1966	Kauai King (½)	2:02	Don Brumfield	Henry Forrest	Advocator	Blue Skyer
1967	Proud Clarion (1)	2:00⅗	Bobby Ussery	Loyd Gentry	Barbs Delight	Damascus
1968	Forward Pass* (nk)	—	Ismael Valenzuela	Henry Forrest	Francie's Hat	T.V. Commercial
1969	Majestic Prince (nk)	2:01⅘	Bill Hartack	Johnny Longden	Arts and Letters	Dike
1970	Dust Commander (5)	2:03⅖	Mike Manganello	Don Combs	My Dad George	High Echelon
1971	Canonero II (3¼)	2:03⅕	Gustavo Avila	Juan Arias	Jim French	Bold Reason
1972	Riva Ridge (3¼)	2:01⅘	Ron Turcotte	Lucien Laurin	No Le Hace	Hold Your Peace
1973	SECRETARIAT (2½)	1:59⅖	Ron Turcotte	Lucien Laurin	Sham	Our Native
1974	Cannonade (2¼)	2:04	Angel Cordero Jr.	Woody Stephens	Hudson County	Agitate
1975	Foolish Pleasure (1¾)	2:02	Jacinto Vasquez	LeRoy Jolley	Avatar	Diabolo
1976	Bold Forbes (1)	2:01⅗	Angel Cordero Jr.	Laz Barrera	Honest Pleasure	Elocutionist
1977	SEATTLE SLEW (1¾)	2:02⅕	Jean Cruguet	Billy Turner	Run Dusty Run	Sanhedrin
1978	AFFIRMED (1½)	2:01⅕	Steve Cauthen	Laz Barrera	Alydar	Believe It

Year	Winner (Margin)	Time	Jockey	Trainer	2nd place	3rd place
1979	**Spectacular Bid** (2¾)	2:02⅖	Ron Franklin	Bud Delp	General Assembly	Golden Act
1980	**Genuine Risk** (1)	2:02	Jacinto Vasquez	LeRoy Jolley	Rumbo	Jaklin Klugman
1981	**Pleasant Colony** (¾)	2:02	Jorge Velasquez	John Campo	Woodchopper	Partez
1982	**Gato Del Sol** (2½)	2:02⅖	E. Delahoussaye	Eddie Gregson	Laser Light	Reinvested
1983	**Sunny's Halo** (2)	2:02⅕	E. Delahoussaye	David Cross Jr.	Desert Wine	Caveat
1984	**Swale** (3¼)	2:02⅖	Laffit Pincay Jr.	Woody Stephens	Coax Me Chad	At The Threshold
1985	**Spend A Buck** (5¼)	2:00⅕	Angel Cordero Jr.	Cam Gambolati	Stephan's Odyssey	Chief's Crown
1986	**Ferdinand** (2¼)	2:02⅘	Bill Shoemaker	Chas. Whittingham	Bold Arrangement	Broad Brush
1987	**Alysheba** (¾)	2:03⅖	Chris McCarron	Jack Van Berg	Bet Twice	Avies Copy
1988	**Winning Colors** (nk)	2:02⅕	Gary Stevens	D. Wayne Lukas	Forty Niner	Risen Star
1989	**Sunday Silence** (2½)	2:05	Pat Valenzuela	Chas. Whittingham	Easy Goer	Awe Inspiring
1990	**Unbridled** (3½)	2:02	Craig Perret	Carl Nafzger	Summer Squall	Pleasant Tap
1991	**Strike the Gold** (1¾)	2:03	Chris Antley	Nick Zito	Best Pal	Mane Minister
1992	**Lil E. Tee** (1)	2:03	Pat Day	Lynn Whiting	Casual Lies	Dance Floor
1993	**Sea Hero** (2½)	2:02⅖	Jerry Bailey	Mack Miller	Prairie Bayou	Wild Gale
1994	**Go For Gin** (2)	2:03⅗	Chris McCarron	Nick Zito	Strodes Creek	Blumin Affair
1995	**Thunder Gulch** (2¼)	2:01⅕	Gary Stevens	D. Wayne Lukas	Tejano Run	Timber Country
1996	**Grindstone** (ns)	2:01	Jerry Bailey	D. Wayne Lukas	Cavonnier	Prince of Thieves
1997	**Silver Charm** (hd)	2:02⅖	Gary Stevens	Bob Baffert	Captain Bodgit	Free House
1998	**Real Quiet** (½)	2:02⅕	Kent Desormeaux	Bob Baffert	Victory Gallop	Indian Charlie
1999	**Charismatic** (nk)	2:03⅕	Chris Antley	D. Wayne Lukas	Menifee	Cat Thief
2000	**Fusaichi Pegasus** (1½)	2:01⅕	Kent Desormeaux	Neil Drysdale	Aptitude	Impeachment
2001	**Monarchos** (4¾)	1:59⅘	Jorge Chavez	John Ward Jr.	Invisible Ink	Congaree
2002	**War Emblem** (4)	2:01	Victor Espinoza	Bob Baffert	Proud Citizen	Perfect Drift
2003	**Funny Cide** (1¾)	2:01	Jose Santos	Barclay Tagg	Empire Maker	Peace Rules
2004	**Smarty Jones** (2¾)	2:04	Stewart Elliott	John Servis	Lion Heart	Imperialism

*Dancer's Image finished first (in 2:02½), but was disqualified after traces of prohibited medication were found in his system.

Preakness Stakes

For three-year-olds. Held two weeks after the Kentucky Derby at Pimlico Race Course in Baltimore. Inaugurated 1873. Note that the 1918 race was held over two divisions. Originally run at 1½ miles (1873-88), then at 1¼ miles (1889), 1½ miles (1890), $1\frac{1}{16}$ miles (1894-1900), 1 mile & 70 yards (1901-07), $1\frac{1}{16}$ miles (1908), 1 mile (1909-1910), 1⅛ miles (1911-24), and the present $1\frac{3}{16}$ miles since 1925.

Trainers with most wins: Robert W. Walden (7); T.J. Healey and D. Wayne Lukas (5); Bob Baffert, Sunny Jim Fitzsimmons and Jimmy Jones (4); J. Whalen (3).

Jockeys with most wins: Eddie Arcaro (6); Pat Day (5); G. Barbee, Bill Hartack and Lloyd Hughes (3).

Winning fillies: Flocarline (1903), Whimsical (1906), Rhine Maiden (1915) and Nellie Morse (1924).

Year	Winner (Margin)	Time	Jockey	Trainer	2nd place	3rd place
1873	**Survivor** (10)	2:43	G. Barbee	A.D. Pryor	John Boulger	Artist
1874	**Culpepper** (¾)	2:56½	W. Donohue	H. Gaffney	King Amadeus	Scratch
1875	**Tom Ochiltree** (2)	2:43½	L. Hughes	R.W. Walden	Viator	Bay Final
1876	**Shirley** (4)	2:44¾	G. Barbee	W. Brown	Rappahannock	Compliment
1877	**Cloverbrook** (2)	2:45½	C. Holloway	J. Walden	Bombast	Lucifer
1878	**Duke of Magenta** (2)	2:41¾	C. Holloway	R.W. Walden	Bayard	Albert
1879	**Harold** (1)	2:40½	L. Hughes	R.W. Walden	Jericho	Rochester
1880	**Grenada** (¾)	2:40½	L. Hughes	R.W. Walden	Oden	Emily F.
1881	**Saunterer** (½)	2:40½	T. Costello	R.W. Walden	Compensation	Baltic
1882	**Vanguard** (nk)	2:44½	T. Costello	R.W. Walden	Heck	Col. Watson
1883	**Jacobus** (4)	2:42½	G. Barbee	R. Dwyer	Parnell	(2-horse race)
1884	**Knight of Ellerslie** (2)	2:39½	S. Fisher	T.B. Doswell	Welcher	(2-horse race)
1885	**Tecumseh** (2)	2:49	Jim McLaughlin	C. Littlefield	Wickham	John C.
1886	**The Bard** (3)	2:45	S. Fisher	J. Huggins	Eurus	Elkwood
1887	**Dunboyne** (1)	2:39½	W. Donohue	W. Jennings	Mahoney	Raymond
1888	**Refund** (3)	2:49	F. Littlefield	R.W. Walden	Bertha B.*	Glendale
1889	**Buddhist** (8)	2:17½	W. Anderson	J. Rogers	Japhet	(2-horse race)
1890	**Montague** (3)	2:36¾	W. Martin	E. Feakes	Philosophy	Barrister
1891-93	Not held					
1894	**Assignee** (3)	1:49¼	F. Taral	W. Lakeland	Potentate	Ed Kearney
1895	**Belmar** (1)	1:50½	F. Taral	E. Feakes	April Fool	Sue Kittie
1896	**Margrave** (1)	1:51	H. Griffin	Byron McClelland	Hamilton II	Intermission
1897	**Paul Kauvar** (1½)	1:51¼	T. Thorpe	T.P. Hayes	Elkins	On Deck
1898	**Sly Fox** (2)	1:49¾	W. Simms	H. Campbell	The Huguenot	Nuto
1899	**Half Time** (1)	1:47	R. Clawson	F. McCabe	Filigrane	Lackland
1900	**Hindus** (hd)	1:48⅖	H. Spencer	J.H. Morris	Sarmatian	Ten Candles
1901	**The Parader** (2)	1:47⅕	F. Landry	T.J. Healey	Sadie S.	Dr. Barlow
1902	**Old England** (ns)	1:45⅘	L. Jackson	G.B. Morris	Maj. Daingerfield	Namtor
1903	**Flocarline** (½)	1:44⅘	W. Gannon	H.C. Riddle	Mackey Dwyer	Rightful
1904	**Bryn Mawr** (1)	1:44⅕	E. Hildebrand	W.F. Presgrave	Wotan	Dolly Spanker
1905	**Cairngorm** (hd)	1:45⅘	W. Davis	A.J. Joyner	Kiamesha	Coy Maid
1906	**Whimsical** (4)	1:45	Walter Miller	T.J. Gaynor	Content	Larabie

Preakness Stakes (Cont.)

Year	Winner (Margin)	Time	Jockey	Trainer	2nd place	3rd place
1907	**Don Enrique** (1)	1:45⅖	G. Mountain	J. Whalen	Ethon	Zambesi
1908	**Royal Tourist** (4)	1:46⅖	Eddie Dugan	A.J. Joyner	Live Wire	Robert Cooper
1909	**Effendi** (1)	1:39⅘	Willie Doyle	F.C. Frisbie	Fashion Plate	Hill Top
1910	**Layminster** (½)	1:40⅗	R. Estep	J.S. Healy	Dalhousie	Sager
1911	**Watervale** (1)	1:51	Eddie Dugan	J. Whalen	Zeus	The Nigger
1912	**Colonel Holloway** (5)	1:56⅗	C. Turner	D. Woodford	Bwana Tumbo	Tipsand
1913	**Buskin** (nk)	1:53⅖	James Butwell	J. Whalen	Kleburne	Barnegat
1914	**Holiday** (¾)	1:53⅘	A. Schuttinger	J.S. Healy	Brave Cunarder	Defendum
1915	**Rhine Maiden** (1½)	1:58	Douglas Hoffman	F. Devers	Half Rock	Runes
1916	**Damrosch** (1½)	1:54⅘	Linus McAtee	A.G. Weston	Greenwood	Achievement
1917	**Kalitan** (2)	1:54⅖	E. Haynes	Bill Hurley	Al M. Dick	Kentucky Boy
1918	**War Cloud** (¾)	1:53⅗	Johnny Loftus	W.B. Jennings	Sunny Slope	Lanius
1918	**Jack Hare Jr** (2)	1:53⅖	Charles Peak	F.D. Weir	The Porter	Kate Bright
1919	**SIR BARTON** (4)	1:53	Johnny Loftus	H. Guy Bedwell	Eternal	Sweep On
1920	**Man o' War** (1½)	1:51⅗	Clarence Kummer	L. Feustel	Upset	Wildair
1921	**Broomspun** (¾)	1:54⅕	F. Coltiletti	James Rowe Sr.	Polly Ann	Jeg
1922	**Pillory** (hd)	1:51⅗	L. Morris	Thomas Healey	Hea	June Grass
1923	**Vigil** (1¼)	1:53⅗	B. Marinelli	Thomas Healey	General Thatcher	Rialto
1924	**Nellie Morse** (1½)	1:57⅕	John Merimee	A.B. Gordon	Transmute	Mad Play
1925	**Coventry** (4)	1:59	Clarence Kummer	William Duke	Backbone	Almadel
1926	**Display** (hd)	1:59⅘	John Maiben	Thomas Healey	Blondin	Mars
1927	**Bostonian** (½)	2:01⅗	Whitey Abel	Fred Hopkins	Sir Harry	Whiskery
1928	**Victorian** (ns)	2:00⅕	Sonny Workman	James Rowe Jr.	Toro	Solace
1929	**Dr. Freeland** (1)	2:01⅗	Louis Schaefer	Thomas Healey	Minotaur	African
1930	**GALLANT FOX** (¾)	2:00⅗	Earl Sande	Jim Fitzsimmons	Crack Brigade	Snowflake
1931	**Mate** (1½)	1:59	George Ellis	J.W. Healy	Twenty Grand	Ladder
1932	**Burgoo King** (hd)	1:59⅘	Eugene James	Dick Thompson	Tick On	Boatswain
1933	**Head Play** (4)	2:02	Charley Kurtsinger	Thomas Hayes	Ladysman	Utopian
1934	**High Quest** (ns)	1:58⅕	Robert Jones	Bob Smith	Cavalcade	Discovery
1935	**OMAHA** (6)	1:58⅖	Willie Saunders	Jim Fitzsimmons	Firethorn	Psychic Bid
1936	**Bold Venture** (ns)	1:59	George Woolf	Max Hirsch	Granville	Jean Bart
1937	**WAR ADMIRAL** (hd)	1:58⅖	Charley Kurtsinger	George Conway	Pompoon	Flying Scot
1938	**Dauber** (7)	1:59⅘	Maurice Peters	Dick Handlen	Cravat	Menow
1939	**Challedon** (1¼)	1:59⅘	George Seabo	Louis Schaefer	Gilded Knight	Volitant
1940	**Bimelech** (3)	1:58⅗	F.A. Smith	Bill Hurley	Mioland	Gallahadion
1941	**WHIRLAWAY** (5½)	1:58⅘	Eddie Arcaro	Ben Jones	King Cole	Our Boots
1942	**Alsab** (1)	1:57	Basil James	Sarge Swenke	Requested & Sun Again (dead heat)	
1943	**COUNT FLEET** (8)	1:57⅖	Johnny Longden	Don Cameron	Blue Swords	Vincentive
1944	**Pensive** (¾)	1:59⅕	Conn McCreary	Ben Jones	Platter	Stir Up
1945	**Polynesian** (2½)	1:58⅘	W.D. Wright	Morris Dixon	Hoop Jr.	Darby Dieppe
1946	**ASSAULT** (nk)	2:01⅖	Warren Mehrtens	Max Hirsch	Lord Boswell	Hampden
1947	**Faultless** (1¼)	1:59	Doug Dodson	Jimmy Jones	On Trust	Phalanx
1948	**CITATION** (5½)	2:02⅖	Eddie Arcaro	Jimmy Jones	Vulcan's Forge	Bovard
1949	**Capot** (hd)	1:56	Ted Atkinson	J.M. Gaver	Palestinian	Noble Impulse
1950	**Hill Prince** (5)	1:59⅕	Eddie Arcaro	Casey Hayes	Middleground	Dooly
1951	**Bold** (7)	1:56⅖	Eddie Arcaro	Preston Burch	Counterpoint	Alerted
1952	**Blue Man** (3½)	1:57⅖	Conn McCreary	Woody Stephens	Jampol	One Count
1953	**Native Dancer** (nk)	1:57⅘	Eric Guerin	Bill Winfrey	Jamie K.	Royal Bay Gem
1954	**Hasty Road** (nk)	1:57⅖	Johnny Adams	Harry Trotsek	Correlation	Hasseyampa
1955	**Nashua** (1)	1:54⅗	Eddie Arcaro	Jim Fitzsimmons	Saratoga	Traffic Judge
1956	**Fabius** (¾)	1:58⅖	Bill Hartack	Jimmy Jones	Needles	No Regrets
1957	**Bold Ruler** (2)	1:56⅕	Eddie Arcaro	Jim Fitzsimmons	Iron Liege	Inside Tract
1958	**Tim Tam** (1½)	1:57⅕	Ismael Valenzuela	Jimmy Jones	Lincoln Road	Gone Fishin'
1959	**Royal Orbit** (4)	1:57	William Harmatz	R. Cornell	Sword Dancer	Dunce
1960	**Bally Ache** (4)	1:57⅗	Bobby Ussery	Jimmy Pitt	Victoria Park	Celtic Ash
1961	**Carry Back** (¾)	1:57⅗	Johnny Sellers	Jack Price	Globemaster	Crozier
1962	**Greek Money** (ns)	1:56⅕	John Rotz	V.W. Raines	Ridan	Roman Line
1963	**Candy Spots** (3½)	1:56⅕	Bill Shoemaker	Mesh Tenney	Chateaugay	Never Bend
1964	**Northern Dancer** (2¼)	1:56⅘	Bill Hartack	Horatio Luro	The Scoundrel	Hill Rise
1965	**Tom Rolfe** (nk)	1:56⅕	Ron Turcotte	Frank Whiteley	Dapper Dan	Hail To All
1966	**Kauai King** (1¾)	1:55⅖	Don Brumfield	Henry Forrest	Stupendous	Amberoid
1967	**Damascus** (2¼)	1:55⅕	Bill Shoemaker	Frank Whiteley	In Reality	Proud Clarion
1968	**Forward Pass** (6)	1:56⅘	Ismael Valenzuela	Henry Forrest	Out Of the Way	Nodouble
1969	**Majestic Prince** (hd)	1:55⅗	Bill Hartack	Johnny Longden	Arts and Letters	Jay Ray
1970	**Personality** (nk)	1:56⅕	Eddie Belmonte	John Jacobs	My Dad George	Silent Screen
1971	**Canonero II** (1½)	1:54	Gustavo Avila	Juan Arias	Eastern Fleet	Jim French
1972	**Bee Bee Bee** (1¼)	1:55⅗	Eldon Nelson	Red Carroll	No Le Hace	Key To The Mint
1973	**SECRETARIAT** (2½)	1:54⅖	Ron Turcotte	Lucien Laurin	Sham	Our Native

Year	Winner (Margin)	Time	Jockey	Trainer	2nd place	3rd place
1974	**Little Current** (7)	1:54⅗	Miguel Rivera	Lou Rondinello	Neapolitan Way	Cannonade
1975	**Master Derby** (1)	1:56⅖	Darrel McHargue	Smiley Adams	Foolish Pleasure	Diabolo
1976	**Elocutionist** (3½)	1:55	John Lively	Paul Adwell	Play The Red	Bold Forbes
1977	**SEATTLE SLEW** (1½)	1:54⅖	Jean Cruguet	Billy Turner	Iron Constitution	Run Dusty Run
1978	**AFFIRMED** (nk)	1:54⅖	Steve Cauthen	Laz Barrera	Alydar	Believe It
1979	**Spectacular Bid** (3½)	1:54⅕	Ron Franklin	Bud Delp	Golden Act	Screen King
1980	**Codex** (4¾)	1:54⅕	Angel Cordero Jr.	D. Wayne Lukas	Genuine Risk	Colonel Moran
1981	**Pleasant Colony** (1)	1:54⅗	Jorge Velasquez	John Campo	Bold Ego	Paristo
1982	**Aloma's Ruler** (½)	1:55⅖	Jack Kaenel	John Lenzini Jr.	Linkage	Cut Away
1983	**Deputed Testamony** (2¾)	1:55⅖	Donald Miller Jr.	Bill Boniface	Desert Wine	High Honors
1984	**Gate Dancer** (1½)	1:53⅗	Angel Cordero Jr.	Jack Van Berg	Play On	Fight Over
1985	**Tank's Prospect** (hd)	1:53⅖	Pat Day	D. Wayne Lukas	Chief's Crown	Eternal Prince
1986	**Snow Chief** (4)	1:54⅘	Alex Solis	Melvin Stute	Ferdinand	Broad Brush
1987	**Alysheba** (½)	1:55⅘	Chris McCarron	Jack Van Berg	Bet Twice	Cryptoclearance
1988	**Risen Star** (1¼)	1:56⅕	E. Delahoussaye	Louie Roussel III	Brian's Time	Winning Colors
1989	**Sunday Silence** (ns)	1:53⅘	Pat Valenzuela	Chas. Whittingham	Easy Goer	Rock Point
1990	**Summer Squall** (2¼)	1:53⅗	Pat Day	Neil Howard	Unbridled	Mister Frisky
1991	**Hansel** (7)	1:54	Jerry Bailey	Frank Brothers	Corporate Report	Mane Minister
1992	**Pine Bluff** (¾)	1:55⅗	Chris McCarron	Tom Bohannan	Alydeed	Casual Lies
1993	**Prairie Bayou** (½)	1:56⅗	Mike Smith	Tom Bohannan	Cherokee Run	El Bakan
1994	**Tabasco Cat** (¾)	1:56⅖	Pat Day	D. Wayne Lukas	Go For Gin	Concern
1995	**Timber Country** (½)	1:54⅖	Pat Day	D. Wayne Lukas	Oliver's Twist	Thunder Gulch
1996	**Louis Quatorze** (3¼)	1:53⅖	Pat Day	Nick Zito	Skip Away	Editor's Note
1997	**Silver Charm** (hd)	1:54⅖	Gary Stevens	Bob Baffert	Free House	Captain Bodgit
1998	**Real Quiet** (2¼)	1:54⅘	Kent Desormeaux	Bob Baffert	Victory Gallop	Classic Cat
1999	**Charismatic** (1½)	1:55⅕	Chris Antley	D. Wayne Lukas	Menifee	Badge
2000	**Red Bullet** (3¾)	1:56	Jerry Bailey	Joe Orseno	Fusaichi Pegasus	Impeachment
2001	**Point Given** (2¼)	1:55⅖	Gary Stevens	Bob Baffert	A P Valentine	Congaree
2002	**War Emblem** (¾)	1:56⅕	Victor Espinoza	Bob Baffert	Magic Weisner	Proud Citizen
2003	**Funny Cide** (9¾)	1:55⅗	Jose Santos	Barclay Tagg	Midway Road	Scrimshaw
2004	**Smarty Jones** (11½)	1:55⅖	Stewart Elliott	John Servis	Rock Hard Ten	Eddington

* Later named Judge Murray.

AP/Wide World Photos

*Jockey Eddie Arcaro waves from atop **Citation** after his 5½-length victory in the Preakness on May 15, 1948. From left are owner Warren Wright, trainer Jimmy Jones and an unidentified groom.*

Belmont Stakes

For three-year-olds. Held three weeks after Preakness Stakes at Belmont Park in Elmont, N.Y. Inaugurated in 1867 at Jerome Park, moved to Morris Park in 1890 and then to Belmont Park in 1905.

Originally run at 1 mile and 5 furlongs (1867-89), then 1¼ miles (1890-1905), 1⅜ miles (1906-25), and the present 1½ miles since 1926.

Trainers with most wins: James Rowe Sr. (8); Sam Hildreth (7); Sunny Jim Fitzsimmons (6); Woody Stephens (5); Max Hirsch, D. Wayne Lukas and Robert W. Walden (4); Elliott Burch, Lucien Laurin, F. McCabe and D. McDaniel (3).

Jockeys with most wins: Eddie Arcaro and Jim McLaughlin (6); Earl Sande and Bill Shoemaker (5); Braulio Baeza, Pat Day, Laffit Pincay Jr., Gary Stevens and James Stout (3).

Winning fillies: Ruthless (1867) and Tanya (1905).

Year	Winner (Margin)	Time	Jockey	Trainer	2nd place	3rd place
1867	**Ruthless** (½)	3:05	J. Gilpatrick	A.J. Minor	DeCourcey	Rivoli
1868	**General Duke** (2)	3:02	Bobby Swim	A. Thompson	Northumberland	Fanny Ludlow
1869	**Fenian** (6)	3:04¼	C. Miller	J. Pincus	Glenelg	Invercauld
1870	**Kingfisher** (nk)	2:59½	W. Dick	R. Colston	Foster	Midday
1871	**Harry Bassett** (3)	2:56	W. Miller	D. McDaniel	Stockwood	By the Sea
1872	**Joe Daniels** (¾)	2:58¼	James Roe	D. McDaniel	Meteor	Shylock
1873	**Springbok** (¾)	3:01¾	James Roe	D. McDaniel	Count d'Orsay	Strachino
1874	**Saxon** (nk)	2:39½	G. Barbee	W. Prior	Grinstead	Aaron Pennington
1875	**Calvin** (2)	2:42¼	Bobby Swim	A. Williams	Aristides	Milner
1876	**Algerine** (½)	2:40½	Billy Donohue	Major Doswell	Fiddlesticks	Barricade
1877	**Cloverbrook** (1)	2:46	C. Holloway	J. Walden	Loiterer	Baden-Baden
1878	**Duke of Magenta** (2)	2:43½	L. Hughes	R.W. Walden	Bramble	Sparta
1879	**Spendthrift** (6)	2:42¾	George Evans	T. Puryear	Monitor	Jericho
1880	**Grenada** (nk)	2:47	L. Hughes	R.W. Walden	Ferncliffe	Turenne
1881	**Saunterer** (nk)	2:47	T. Costello	R.W. Walden	Eole	Baltic
1882	**Forester** (5)	2:43	Jim McLaughlin	L. Stuart	Babcock	Wyoming
1883	**George Kinney** (3)	2:42½	Jim McLaughlin	James Rowe Sr.	Trombone	Renegade
1884	**Panique** (nk)	2:42	Jim McLaughlin	James Rowe Sr.	Knight of Ellerslie	Himalaya
1885	**Tyrant** (3)	2:43	Paul Duffy	W. Claypool	St. Augustine	Tecumseh
1886	**Inspector B** (1)	2:41	Jim McLaughlin	F. McCabe	The Bard	Linden
1887	**Hanover** (15)	2:43½	Jim McLaughlin	F. McCabe	Oneko	(2-horse race)
1888	**Sir Dixon** (15)	2:40¼	Jim McLaughlin	F. McCabe	Prince Royal	(2-horse race)
1889	**Eric** (½)	2:47¼	W. Hayward	J. Huggins	Diablo	Zephyrus
1890	**Burlington** (2)	2:07¾	Pike Barnes	A. Cooper	Devotee	Padishah
1891	**Foxford** (nk)	2:08¾	Ed Garrison	M. Donavan	Montana	Laurestan
1892	**Patron** (6)	2:12	W. Hayward	L. Stuart	Shellbark	(2-horse race)
1893	**Commanche** (hd)	1:53¼	Willie Simms	G. Hannon	Dr. Rice	Rainbow
1894	**Henry of Navarre** (1½)	1:56½	Willie Simms	B. McClelland	Prig	Assignee
1895	**Belmar** (hd)	2:11½	Fred Taral	E. Feakes	Counter Tenor	Nanki Poo
1896	**Hastings** (hd)	2:24½	H. Griffin	J.J. Hyland	Handspring	Hamilton II
1897	**Scottish Chieftain** (1)	2:23¼	J. Scherrer	M. Byrnes	On Deck	Octagon
1898	**Bowling Brook** (6)	2:32	F. Littlefield	R.W. Walden	Previous	Hamburg
1899	**Jean Beraud** (hd)	2:23	R. Clawson	Sam Hildreth	Half Time	Glengar
1900	**Ildrim** (ns)	2:21¼	Nash Turner	H.E. Leigh	Petruchio	Missionary
1901	**Commando** (2)	2:21	H. Spencer	James Rowe Sr.	The Parader	All Green
1902	**Masterman** (2)	2:22⅗	John Bullman	J.J. Hyland	Renald	King Hanover
1903	**Africander** (2)	2:21¾	John Bullman	R. Miller	Whorler	Red Knight
1904	**Delhi** (4)	2:06⅗	George Odom	James Rowe Sr.	Graziallo	Rapid Water
1905	**Tanya** (½)	2:08	E. Hildebrand	J.W. Rogers	Blandy	Hot Shot
1906	**Burgomaster** (4)	2:20	Lucien Lyne	J.W. Rogers	The Quail	Accountant
1907	**Peter Pan** (1)	N/A	G. Mountain	James Rowe Sr.	Superman	Frank Gill
1908	**Colin** (hd)	N/A	Joe Notter	James Rowe Sr.	Fair Play	King James
1909	**Joe Madden** (8)	2:21⅗	E. Dugan	Sam Hildreth	Wise Mason	Donald MacDonald
1910	**Sweep** (6)	2:22	James Butwell	James Rowe Sr.	Duke of Ormonde	(2-horse race)
1911-12	Not held					
1913	**Prince Eugene** (½)	2:18	Roscoe Troxler	James Rowe Sr.	Rock View	Flying Fairy
1914	**Luke McLuke** (8)	2:20	Merritt Buxton	J.F. Schorr	Gainer	Charlestonian
1915	**The Finn** (4)	2:18⅖	George Byrne	E.W. Heffner	Half Rock	Pebbles
1916	**Friar Rock** (3)	2:22	E. Haynes	Sam Hildreth	Spur	Churchill
1917	**Hourless** (10)	2:17⅘	James Butwell	Sam Hildreth	Skeptic	Wonderful
1918	**Johren** (2)	2:20⅖	Frank Robinson	A. Simons	War Cloud	Cum Sah
1919	**SIR BARTON** (5)	2:17⅖	John Loftus	H. Guy Bedwell	Sweep On	Natural Bridge
1920	**Man o' War** (20)	2:14⅕	Clarence Kummer	L. Feustel	Donnacona	(2-horse race)
1921	**Grey Lag** (3)	2:16⅘	Earl Sande	Sam Hildreth	Sporting Blood	Leonardo II
1922	**Pillory** (2)	2:18⅘	C.H. Miller	T.J. Healey	Snob II	Hea
1923	**Zev** (1½)	2:19	Earl Sande	Sam Hildreth	Chickvale	Rialto
1924	**Mad Play** (2)	2:18⅘	Earl Sande	Sam Hildreth	Mr. Mutt	Modest
1925	**American Flag** (8)	2:16⅘	Albert Johnson	G.R. Tompkins	Dangerous	Swope

Year	Winner (Margin)	Time	Jockey	Trainer	2nd place	3rd place
1926	**Crusader** (1)	2:32⅕	Albert Johnson	George Conway	Espino	Haste
1927	**Chance Shot** (1½)	2:32⅖	Earl Sande	Pete Coyne	Bois de Rose	Flambino
1928	**Vito** (3)	2:33⅕	Clarence Kummer	Max Hirsch	Genie	Diavolo
1929	**Blue Larkspur** (¾)	2:32⅘	Mack Garner	C. Hastings	African	Jack High
1930	**GALLANT FOX** (3)	2:31⅗	Earl Sande	Jim Fitzsimmons	Whichone	Questionnaire
1931	**Twenty Grand** (10)	2:29⅗	Charley Kurtsinger	James Rowe Jr.	Sun Meadow	Jamestown
1932	**Faireno** (1½)	2:32⅘	Tom Malley	Jim Fitzsimmons	Osculator	Flag Pole
1933	**Hurryoff** (1½)	2:32⅗	Mack Garner	H. McDaniel	Nimbus	Union
1934	**Peace Chance** (6)	2:29⅕	W.D. Wright	Pete Coyne	High Quest	Good Goods
1935	**OMAHA** (1½)	2:30⅗	Willie Saunders	Jim Fitzsimmons	Firethorn	Rosemont
1936	**Granville** (ns)	2:30	James Stout	Jim Fitzsimmons	Mr. Bones	Hollyrood
1937	**WAR ADMIRAL** (3)	2:28⅗	Charley Kurtsinger	George Conway	Sceneshifter	Vamoose
1938	**Pasteurized** (nk)	2:29⅖	James Stout	George Odom	Dauber	Cravat
1939	**Johnstown** (5)	2:29⅗	James Stout	Jim Fitzsimmons	Belay	Gilded Knight
1940	**Bimelech** (¾)	2:29⅗	Fred Smith	Bill Hurley	Your Chance	Andy K.
1941	**WHIRLAWAY** (2½)	2:31	Eddie Arcaro	Ben Jones	Robert Morris	Yankee Chance
1942	**Shut Out** (2)	2:29⅕	Eddie Arcaro	John Gaver	Alsab	Lochinvar
1943	**COUNT FLEET** (25)	2:28⅕	Johnny Longden	Don Cameron	Fairy Manhurst	Deseronto
1944	**Bounding Home** (½)	2:32⅕	G.L. Smith	Matt Brady	Pensive	Bull Dandy
1945	**Pavot** (5)	2:30⅕	Eddie Arcaro	Oscar White	Wildlife	Jeep
1946	**ASSAULT** (3)	2:30⅘	Warren Mehrtens	Max Hirsch	Natchez	Cable
1947	**Phalanx** (5)	2:29⅖	R. Donoso	Syl Veitch	Tide Rips	Tailspin
1948	**CITATION** (8)	2:28⅕	Eddie Arcaro	Jimmy Jones	Better Self	Escadru
1949	**Capot** (½)	2:30⅕	Ted Atkinson	John Gaver	Ponder	Palestinian
1950	**Middleground** (1)	2:28⅗	William Boland	Max Hirsch	Lights Up	Mr. Trouble
1951	**Counterpoint** (4)	2:29	David Gorman	Syl Veitch	Battlefield	Battle Morn
1952	**One Count** (2½)	2:30⅕	Eddie Arcaro	Oscar White	Blue Man	Armageddon
1953	**Native Dancer** (nk)	2:28⅗	Eric Guerin	Bill Winfrey	Jamie K.	Royal Bay Gem
1954	**High Gun** (nk)	2:30⅘	Eric Guerin	Max Hirsch	Fisherman	Limelight
1955	**Nashua** (9)	2:29	Eddie Arcaro	Jim Fitzsimmons	Blazing Count	Portersville
1956	**Needles** (nk)	2:29⅘	David Erb	Hugh Fontaine	Career Boy	Fabius
1957	**Gallant Man** (8)	2:26⅗	Bill Shoemaker	John Nerud	Inside Tract	Bold Ruler
1958	**Cavan** (6)	2:30⅕	Pete Anderson	Tom Barry	Tim Tam	Flamingo
1959	**Sword Dancer** (¾)	2:28⅖	Bill Shoemaker	Elliott Burch	Bagdad	Royal Orbit
1960	**Celtic Ash** (5½)	2:29⅕	Bill Hartack	Tom Barry	Venetian Way	Disperse
1961	**Sherluck** (2¼)	2:29⅕	Braulio Baeza	Harold Young	Globemaster	Guadalcanal
1962	**Jaipur** (ns)	2:28⅘	Bill Shoemaker	B. Mulholland	Admiral's Voyage	Crimson Satan
1963	**Chateaugay** (2½)	2:30⅕	Braulio Baeza	James Conway	Candy Spots	Choker
1964	**Quadrangle** (2)	2:28⅖	Manuel Ycaza	Elliott Burch	Roman Brother	Northern Dancer
1965	**Hail to All** (nk)	2:28⅖	John Sellers	Eddie Yowell	Tom Rolfe	First Family
1966	**Amberoid** (2½)	2:29⅗	William Boland	Lucien Laurin	Buffle	Advocator
1967	**Damascus** (2½)	2:28⅘	Bill Shoemaker	F.Y. Whiteley Jr.	Cool Reception	Gentleman James
1968	**Stage Door Johnny** (1¼)	2:27⅕	Gus Gustines	John Gaver	Forward Pass	Call Me Prince
1969	**Arts and Letters** (5½)	2:28⅘	Braulio Baeza	Elliott Burch	Majestic Prince	Dike
1970	**High Echelon** (¾)	2:34	John Rotz	John Jacobs	Needles N Pens	Naskra
1971	**Pass Catcher** (¾)	2:30⅖	Walter Blum	Eddie Yowell	Jim French	Bold Reason
1972	**Riva Ridge** (7)	2:28	Ron Turcotte	Lucien Laurin	Ruritania	Cloudy Dawn
1973	**SECRETARIAT** (31)	2:24	Ron Turcotte	Lucien Laurin	Twice A Prince	My Gallant
1974	**Little Current** (7)	2:29⅕	Miguel Rivera	Lou Rondinello	Jolly Johu	Cannonade
1975	**Avatar** (nk)	2:28⅕	Bill Shoemaker	Tommy Doyle	Foolish Pleasure	Master Derby
1976	**Bold Forbes** (nk)	2:29	Angel Cordero Jr.	Laz Barrera	McKenzie Bridge	Great Contractor
1977	**SEATTLE SLEW** (4)	2:29⅗	Jean Cruguet	Billy Turner	Run Dusty Run	Sanhedrin
1978	**AFFIRMED** (hd)	2:26⅘	Steve Cauthen	Laz Barrera	Alydar	Darby Creek Road
1979	**Coastal** (3¼)	2:28⅗	Ruben Hernandez	David Whiteley	Golden Act	Spectacular Bid
1980	**Temperence Hill** (2)	2:29⅘	Eddie Maple	Joseph Cantey	Genuine Risk	Rockhill Native
1981	**Summing** (nk)	2:29	George Martens	Luis Barerra	Highland Blade	Pleasant Colony
1982	**Conquistador Cielo** (14)	2:28⅕	Laffit Pincay Jr.	Woody Stephens	Gato Del Sol	Illuminate
1983	**Caveat** (3½)	2:27⅘	Laffit Pincay Jr.	Woody Stephens	Slew o' Gold	Barberstown
1984	**Swale** (4)	2:27⅕	Laffit Pincay Jr.	Woody Stephens	Pine Circle	Morning Bob
1985	**Creme Fraiche** (½)	2:27	Eddie Maple	Woody Stephens	Stephan's Odyssey	Chief's Crown
1986	**Danzig Connection** (1¼)	2:29⅘	Chris McCarron	Woody Stephens	Johns Treasure	Ferdinand
1987	**Bet Twice** (14)	2:28⅕	Craig Perret	Jimmy Croll	Cryptoclearance	Gulch
1988	**Risen Star** (14¾)	2:26⅖	E. Delahoussaye	Louie Roussel III	Kingpost	Brian's Time
1989	**Easy Goer** (8)	2:26	Pat Day	Shug McGaughey	Sunday Silence	Le Voyageur
1990	**Go And Go** (8¼)	2:27⅕	Michael Kinane	Dermot Weld	Thirty Six Red	Baron de Vaux
1991	**Hansel** (hd)	2:28	Jerry Bailey	Frank Brothers	Strike the Gold	Mane Minister
1992	**A.P. Indy** (¾)	2:26	E. Delahoussaye	Neil Drysdale	My Memoirs	Pine Bluff
1993	**Colonial Affair** (2)	2:29⅘	Julie Krone	Scotty Schulhofer	Kissin Kris	Wild Gale
1994	**Tabasco Cat** (2)	2:26⅘	Pat Day	D. Wayne Lukas	Go For Gin	Strodes Creek
1995	**Thunder Gulch** (2)	2:32	Gary Stevens	D. Wayne Lukas	Star Standard	Citadeed

Belmont Stakes (Cont.)

Year	Winner (Margin)	Time	Jockey	Trainer	2nd place	3rd place
1996	**Editor's Note** (1)	2:28⅘	Rene Douglas	D. Wayne Lukas	Skip Away	My Flag
1997	**Touch Gold** (¾)	2:28⅘	Chris McCarron	David Hofmans	Silver Charm	Free House
1998	**Victory Gallop** (ns)	2:29	Gary Stevens	Elliott Walden	Real Quiet	Thomas Jo
1999	**Lemon Drop Kid** (hd)	2:27⅘	Jose Santos	Scotty Schulhofer	Vision and Verse	Charismatic
2000	**Commendable** (1½)	2:31⅕	Pat Day	D. Wayne Lukas	Aptitude	Unshaded
2001	**Point Given** (12¼)	2:26⅖	Gary Stevens	Bob Baffert	A P Valentine	Monarchos
2002	**Sarava** (½)	2:29⅗	Edgar Prado	Ken McPeek	Medaglia d'Oro	Sunday Break
2003	**Empire Maker** (¾)	2:28⅕	Jerry Bailey	Bobby Frankel	Ten Most Wanted	Funny Cide
2004	**Birdstone** (1)	2:27⅖	Edgar Prado	Nick Zito	Smarty Jones	Royal Assault

Breeders' Cup Championship

Inaugurated on Nov. 10, 1984, the Breeders' Cup World Thoroughbred Championships consists of eight races on one track on one day late in the year to determine thoroughbred racing's principle champions.

The Breeders' Cup has been (will be) held at the following tracks (in alphabetical order): Aqueduct Racetrack (N.Y.) in 1985; Arlington Park (Ill.) in 2002; Belmont Park (N.Y.) in 1990, '95, 2001 and '05; Churchill Downs (Ky.) in 1988, '91, '94, '98, 2000 and '06; Gulfstream Park (Fla.) in 1989, '92 and '99; Hollywood Park (Calif.) in 1984, '87 and '97; Lone Star Park (Texas) in 2004; Monmouth Park (N.J.) in 2007; Santa Anita Park (Calif.) in 1986, '93 and 2003 and Woodbine (Toronto) in 1996.

Horses with most wins: Bayakoa, Da Hoss, High Chaparral, Lure, Miesque and Tiznow (2).

Trainers with most wins: D. Wayne Lukas (17); Shug McGaughey (8); Neil Drysdale and Richard Mandella (6); Bill Mott (5); Ron McAnally (4); Bob Baffert, Pascal Bary, Francois Boutin, Patrick Byrne, Andre Fabre, Aidan O'Brien and Sir Michael Stoute (3).

Jockeys with most wins: Jerry Bailey (14); Pat Day (12); Mike Smith (10); Chris McCarron (9); Gary Stevens (8); Eddie Delahoussaye, Laffit Pincay Jr., Jose Santos and Pat Valenzuela (7); Corey Nakatani (5); Angel Cordero Jr., Craig Perret and John Velazquez (4); Frankie Dettori, Michael Kinane, Randy Romero and Alex Solis (3).

Juvenile

Distances: one mile (1984-85, 87); 1 1/16 miles (1986, 1988-2001, 2003), 1⅛ miles (2002).

Year	Winner (Margin)	Time	Jockey	Trainer	2nd place	3rd place
1984	**Chief's Crown** (¾)	1:36⅕	Don MacBeth	Roger Laurin	Tank's Prospect	Spend A Buck
1985	**Tasso** (ns)	1:36⅕	Laffit Pincay Jr.	Neil Drysdale	Storm Cat	Scat Dancer
1986	**Capote** (1¼)	1:43⅘	Laffit Pincay Jr.	D. Wayne Lukas	Qualify	Alysheba
1987	**Success Express** (1¾)	1:35⅕	Jose Santos	D. Wayne Lukas	Regal Classic	Tejano
1988	**Is It True** (1¼)	1:46⅗	Laffit Pincay Jr.	D. Wayne Lukas	Easy Goer	Tagel
1989	**Rhythm** (2)	1:43⅗	Craig Perret	Shug McGaughey	Grand Canyon	Slavic
1990	**Fly So Free** (3)	1:43⅖	Jose Santos	Scotty Schulhofer	Take Me Out	Lost Mountain
1991	**Arazi** (4¾)	1:44⅗	Pat Valenzuela	Francois Boutin	Bertrando	Snappy Landing
1992	**Gilded Time** (¾)	1:43⅖	Chris McCarron	Darrell Vienna	It'sali'lknownfact	River Special
1993	**Brocco** (5)	1:42⅘	Gary Stevens	Randy Winick	Blumin Affair	Tabasco Cat
1994	**Timber Country** (½)	1:44⅖	Pat Day	D. Wayne Lukas	Eltish	Tejano Run
1995	**Unbridled's Song** (nk)	1:41⅗	Mike Smith	James Ryerson	Hennessy	Editor's Note
1996	**Boston Harbor** (nk)	1:43⅖	Jerry Bailey	D. Wayne Lukas	Acceptable	Ordway
1997	**Favorite Trick** (5½)	1:41⅖	Pat Day	Patrick Byrne	Dawson's Legacy	Nationalore
1998	**Answer Lively** (hd)	1:44	Jerry Bailey	Bobby Barnett	Aly's Alley	Cat Thief
1999	**Anees** (2½)	1:42⅕	Gary Stevens	Alex Hassinger Jr.	Chief Seattle	High Yield
2000	**Macho Uno** (ns)	1:42	Jerry Bailey	Joe Orseno	Point Given	Street Cry
2001	**Johannesburg** (2¼)	1:42⅕	Michael Kinane	Aidan O'Brien	Repent	Siphonic
2002	**Vindication** (2¾)	1:49⅗	Mike Smith	Bob Baffert	Kafwain	Hold That Tiger
2003	**Action This Day** (2¼)	1:43⅗	David Flores	Richard Mandella	Minister Eric	Chapel Royal

Breeders' Cup Leaders

The all-time money-winning horses and jockeys in the history of the Breeders' Cup through 2003.

Top 10 Horses

		Sts	1-2-3	Earnings
1	Tiznow	2	2-0-0	$4,560,400
2	Awesome Again	1	1-0-0	2,662,400
3	Skip Away	2	1-0-0	2,288,000
4	Cat Thief	3	1-0-1	2,200,000
5	Alysheba	3	1-1-1	2,133,000
6	Alphabet Soup	1	1-0-0	2,080,000
	Pleasantly Perfect	1	1-0-0	2,080,000
	Volponi	1	1-0-0	2,080,000
9	Cigar	2	1-0-1	2,040,000
10	High Chaparral	2	2-0-0	2,021,600

Top 10 Jockeys

		Sts	1-2-3	Earnings
1	Pat Day	112	12-17-11	$22,913,360
2	Chris McCarron	101	9-12-7	17,669,600
3	Jerry Bailey	89	14-8-10	17,632,540
4	Gary Stevens	93	8-15-10	13,441,160
5	Mike Smith	52	10-6-3	10,505,760
6	Jose Santos	57	7-2-4	7,948,800
7	Eddie Delahoussaye	68	7-3-6	7,775,000
8	Corey Nakatani	48	5-7-7	7,340,280
9	Laffit Pincay Jr.	61	7-4-9	6,811,000
10	Pat Valenzuela	46	7-0-3	6,274,280

Juvenile Fillies

Distances: one mile (1984-85, 87); 1 1/16 miles (1986, 1988-2001, 2003); 1⅛ miles (2002).

Year	Winner (Margin)	Time	Jockey	Trainer	2nd place	3rd place
1984	**Outstandingly***	1:37⅘	Walter Guerra	Pancho Martin	Dusty Heart	Fine Spirit
1985	**Twilight Ridge** (1)	1:35⅘	Jorge Velasquez	D. Wayne Lukas	Family Style	Steal A Kiss
1986	**Brave Raj** (5½)	1:43⅕	Pat Valenzuela	Melvin Stute	Tappiano	Saros Brig
1987	**Epitome** (ns)	1:36⅖	Pat Day	Phil Hauswald	Jeanne Jones	Dream Team
1988	**Open Mind** (1¾)	1:46⅗	Angel Cordero Jr.	D. Wayne Lukas	Darby Shuffle	Lea Lucinda
1989	**Go for Wand** (2¾)	1:44⅕	Randy Romero	Wm. Badgett Jr.	Sweet Roberta	Stella Madrid
1990	**Meadow Star** (5)	1:44	Jose Santos	LeRoy Jolley	Private Treasure	Dance Smartly
1991	**Pleasant Stage** (nk)	1:46⅖	E. Delahoussaye	Chris Speckert	La Spia	Cadillac Women
1992	**Eliza** (nk)	1:42⅘	Pat Valenzuela	Alex Hassinger	Educated Risk	Boots 'n Jackie
1993	**Phone Chatter** (hd)	1:43	Laffit Pincay Jr.	Richard Mandella	Sardula	Heavenly Prize
1994	**Flanders** (hd)	1:45⅕	Pat Day	D. Wayne Lukas	Serena's Song	Stormy Blues
1995	**My Flag** (½)	1:42⅖	Jerry Bailey	Shug McGaughey	Cara Rafaela	Golden Attraction
1996	**Storm Song** (4½)	1:43⅗	Craig Perret	Nick Zito	Love That Jazz	Critical Factor
1997	**Countess Diana** (8½)	1:42⅕	Shane Sellers	Patrick Byrne	Career Collection	Primaly
1998	**Silverbulletday** (½)	1:43⅗	Gary Stevens	Bob Baffert	Excellent Meeting	Three Ring
1999	**Cash Run** (1¼)	1:43⅕	Jerry Bailey	D. Wayne Lukas	Chilukki	Surfside
2000	**Caressing** (½)	1:42⅗	John Velazquez	David Vance	Platinum Tiara	She's a Devil Due
2001	**Tempera** (1½)	1:41⅖	David Flores	Eoin Harty	Imperial Gesture	Bella Bellucci
2002	**Storm Flag Flying** (½)	1:49⅗	John Velazquez	Shug McGaughey	Composure	Santa Catarina
2003	**Halfbridled** (2½)	1:42⅗	Julie Krone	Richard Mandella	Ashado	Victory U.S.A.

*In 1984, winner Fran's Valentine was disqualified for interference in the stretch and placed 10th.

Sprint

Distance: six furlongs (since 1984).

Year	Winner (Margin)	Time	Jockey	Trainer	2nd place	3rd place
1984	**Eillo** (ns)	1:10⅕	Craig Perret	Budd Lepman	Commemorate	Fighting Fit
1985	**Precisionist** (¾)	1:08⅖	Chris McCarron	L.R. Fenstermaker	Smile	Mt. Livermore
1986	**Smile** (1¼)	1:08⅖	Jacinto Vasquez	Scotty Schulhofer	Pine Tree Lane	Bedside Promise
1987	**Very Subtle** (4)	1:08⅘	Pat Valenzuela	Melvin Stute	Groovy	Exclusive Enough
1988	**Gulch** (¾)	1:10⅖	Angel Cordero Jr.	D. Wayne Lukas	Play The King	Afleet
1989	**Dancing Spree** (nk)	1:09	Angel Cordero Jr.	Shug McGaughey	Safely Kept	Dispersal
1990	**Safely Kept** (nk)	1:09⅗	Craig Perret	Alan Goldberg	Dayjur	Black Tie Affair
1991	**Sheikh Albadou** (nk)	1:09⅕	Pat Eddery	Alexander Scott	Pleasant Tap	Robyn Dancer
1992	**Thirty Slews** (nk)	1:08⅕	Eddie Delahoussaye	Bob Baffert	Meafara	Rubiano
1993	**Cardmania** (nk)	1:08⅗	Eddie Delahoussaye	Derek Meredith	Meafara	Gilded Time
1994	**Cherokee Run** (nk)	1:09⅖	Mike Smith	Frank Alexander	Soviet Problem	Cardmania
1995	**Desert Stormer** (nk)	1:09	Kent Desormeaux	Frank Lyons	Mr. Greeley	Lit de Justice
1996	**Lit de Justice** (1¼)	1:08⅗	Corey Nakatani	Jenine Sahadi	Paying Dues	Honour and Glory
1997	**Elmhurst** ½)	1:08⅕	Corey Nakatani	Jenine Sahadi	Hesabull	Bet On Sunshine
1998	**Reraise** (2)	1:09	Corey Nakatani	Craig Dollase	Grand Slam	Kona Gold
1999	**Artax** (½)	1:07⅘	Jorge Chavez	Louis Albertrani	Kona Gold	Big Jag
2000	**Kona Gold** (½)	1:07⅗	Alex Solis	Bruce Headley	Honest Lady	Bet On Sunshine
2001	**Squirtle Squirt** (½)	1:08⅖	Jerry Bailey	Bobby Frankel	Xtra Heat	Caller One
2002	**Orientate** (½)	1:08⅘	Jerry Bailey	D. Wayne Lukas	Thunderello	Crafty C.T.
2003	**Cajun Beat** (2¼)	1:07⅗	Cornelio Velasquez	Stephen Margolis	Bluesthestandard	Shake You Down

Mile

Year	Winner (Margin)	Time	Jockey	Trainer	2nd place	3rd place
1984	**Royal Heroine** (1½)	1:32⅗	Fernando Toro	John Gosden	Star Choice	Cozzene
1985	**Cozzene** (2¼)	1:35	Walter Guerra	Jan Nerud	Al Mamoon*	Shadeed
1986	**Last Tycoon** (hd)	1:35⅕	Yves St.-Martin	Robert Collet	Palace Music	Fred Astaire
1987	**Miesque** (3½)	1:32⅘	Freddie Head	Francois Boutin	Show Dancer	Sonic Lady
1988	**Miesque** (4)	1:38⅗	Freddie Head	Francois Boutin	Steinlen	Simply Majestic
1989	**Steinlen** (¾)	1:37⅕	Jose Santos	D. Wayne Lukas	Sabona	Most Welcome
1990	**Royal Academy** (nk)	1:35⅕	Lester Piggott	M.V. O'Brien	Itsallgreektome	Priolo
1991	**Opening Verse** (2¼)	1:37⅖	Pat Valenzuela	Dick Lundy	Val des Bois	Star of Cozzene
1992	**Lure** (3)	1:32⅘	Mike Smith	Shug McGaughey	Paradise Creek	Brief Truce
1993	**Lure** (2¼)	1:33⅖	Mike Smith	Shug McGaughey	Ski Paradise	Fourstars Allstar
1994	**Barathea** (hd)	1:34⅖	Frankie Dettori	Luca Cumani	Johann Quatz	Unfinished Symph
1995	**Ridgewood Pearl** (2)	1:43⅗	John Murtagh	John Oxx	Fastness	Sayyedati
1996	**Da Hoss** (1½)	1:35⅘	Gary Stevens	Michael Dickinson	Spinning World	Same Old Wish
1997	**Spinning World** (2)	1:32⅗	Cash Asmussen	Jonathan Pease	Geri	Decorated Hero
1998	**Da Hoss** (hd)	1:35⅕	John Velazquez	Michael Dickinson	Hawksley Hill	Labeeb
1999	**Silic** (nk)	1:34⅕	Corey Nakatani	Julio Canani	Tuzla	Docksider
2000	**War Chant** (nk)	1:34⅗	Gary Stevens	Neil Drysdale	North East Bound	Dansili
2001	**Val Royal** (1¾)	1:32	Jose Valdivia	Julio Canani	Forbidden Apple	Bach
2002	**Domedriver** (¾)	1:36⅘	Thierry Thulliez	Pascal Bary	Rock of Gibraltar	Good Journey
2003	**Six Perfections** (¾)	1:33⅘	Jerry Bailey	Pascal Bary	Touch of the Blues	Century City

*In 1985, 2nd place finisher Palace Music was disqualified for interference and placed 9th.

Breeders' Cup Championship (Cont.)

Distaff

Distances: 1¼ miles (1984-87); 1⅛ miles (since 1988).

Year	Winner (Margin)	Time	Jockey	Trainer	2nd place	3rd place
1984	**Princess Rooney** (7)	2:02⅖	Eddie Delahoussaye	Neil Drysdale	Life's Magic	Adored
1985	**Life's Magic** (6¼)	2:02	Angel Cordero Jr.	D. Wayne Lukas	Lady's Secret	DontstopThemusic
1986	**Lady's Secret** (2½)	2:01⅕	Pat Day	D. Wayne Lukas	Fran's Valentine	Outstandingly
1987	**Sacahuista** (2¼)	2:02⅘	Randy Romero	D. Wayne Lukas	Clabber Girl	Oueee Bebe
1988	**Personal Ensign** (ns)	1:52	Randy Romero	Shug McGaughey	Winning Colors	Goodbye Halo
1989	**Bayakoa** (1½)	1:47⅖	Laffit Pincay Jr.	Ron McAnally	Gorgeous	Open Mind
1990	**Bayakoa** (6¾)	1:49⅕	Laffit Pincay Jr.	Ron McAnally	Colonial Waters	Valay Maid
1991	**Dance Smartly** (½)	1:50⅘	Pat Day	Jim Day	Versailles Treaty	Brought to Mind
1992	**Paseana** (4)	1:48	Chris McCarron	Ron McAnally	Versailles Treaty	Magical Maiden
1993	**Hollywood Wildcat** (ns)	1:48⅕	Eddie Delahoussaye	Neil Drysdale	Paseana	Re Toss
1994	**One Dreamer** (nk)	1:50⅗	Gary Stevens	Thomas Proctor	Heavenly Prize	Miss Dominique
1995	**Inside Information** (13½)	1:46	Mike Smith	Shug McGaughey	Heavenly Prize	Lakeway
1996	**Jewel Princess** (1½)	1:48⅕	Corey Nakatani	Wallace Dollase	Serena's Song	Different
1997	**Ajina** (2)	1:47⅕	Mike Smith	Bill Mott	Sharp Cat	Escena
1998	**Escena** (ns)	1:49⅘	Gary Stevens	Bill Mott	Banshee Breeze	Keeper Hill
1999	**Beautiful Pleasure** (¾)	1:47⅖	Jorge Chavez	John Ward Jr.	Banshee Breeze	Heritage of Gold
2000	**Spain** (1½)	1:47⅗	Victor Espinoza	D. Wayne Lukas	Surfside	Heritage of Gold
2001	**Unbridled Elaine** (hd)	1:49⅕	Pat Day	Dallas Stewart	Spain	Two Item Limit
2002	**Azeri** (5)	1:48⅗	Mike Smith	Laura de Seroux	Farda Amiga	Imperial Gesture
2003	**Adoration** (4½)	1:49⅕	Pat Valenzuela	David Hofmans	Elloluv	Got Koko

Turf

Distance: 1½ miles (since 1984).

Year	Winner (Margin)	Time	Jockey	Trainer	2nd place	3rd place
1984	**Lashkari** (nk)	2:25⅕	Yves St.-Martin	de Royer-Dupre	All Along	Raami
1985	**Pebbles** (nk)	2:27	Pat Eddery	Clive Brittain	StrawberryRoad II	Mourjane
1986	**Manila** (nk)	2:25⅖	Jose Santos	Leroy Jolley	Theatrical	Estrapade
1987	**Theatrical** (½)	2:24⅖	Pat Day	Bill Mott	Trempolino	Village Star II
1988	**Gt. Communicator** (½)	2:35⅕	Ray Sibille	Thad Ackel	Sunshine Forever	Indian Skimmer
1989	**Prized** (hd)	2:28	Eddie Delahoussaye	Neil Drysdale	Sierra Roberta	Star Lift
1990	**In The Wings** (½)	2:29⅗	Gary Stevens	Andre Fabre	With Approval	El Senor
1991	**Miss Alleged** (2)	2:30⅘	Eric Legrix	Pascal Bary	Itsallgreektome	Quest for Fame
1992	**Fraise** (ns)	2:24	Pat Valenzuela	Bill Mott	Sky Classic	Quest for Fame
1993	**Kotashaan** (½)	2:25	Kent Desormeaux	Richard Mandella	Bien Bien	Luazur
1994	**Tikkanen** (1½)	2:26⅖	Mike Smith	Jonathan Pease	Hatoof	Paradise Creek
1995	**Northern Spur** (nk)	2:42	Chris McCarron	Ron McAnally	Freedom Cry	Carnegie
1996	**Pilsudski** (1¼)	2:30⅕	Walter Swinburn	Sir Michael Stoute	Singspiel	Swain
1997	**Chief Bearhart** (¾)	2:24	Jose Santos	Mark Frostad	Borgia	Flag Down
1998	**Buck's Boy** (1¼)	2:28⅗	Shane Sellers	Noel Hickey	Yagli	Dushyantor
1999	**Daylami** (2½)	2:24⅗	Frankie Dettori	Saeed bin Suroor	Royal Anthem	Buck's Boy
2000	**Kalanisi** (½)	2:26⅘	John Murtagh	Sir Michael Stoute	Quiet Resolve	John's Call
2001	**Fantastic Light** (¾)	2:24⅕	Frankie Dettori	Saeed bin Suroor	Milan	Timboroa
2002	**High Chaparral** (1¼)	2:30⅕	Michael Kinane	Aidan O'Brien	With Anticipation	Falcon Flight
2003	**High Chaparral***	2:24⅕	Michael Kinane	Aidan O'Brien	—	Falbrav
	& **Johar***	2:24⅕	Alex Solis	Richard Mandella		

*High Chaparral and Johar finished in a dead heat, the first in Breeders' Cup history.

Filly & Mare Turf

Distance: 1⅜ miles (1999-2000); 1¼ miles (since 2001).

Year	Winner (Margin)	Time	Jockey	Trainer	2nd place	3rd place
1999	**Soaring Softly** (¾)	2:13⅘	Jerry Bailey	James J. Toner	Coretta	Zomarradah
2000	**Perfect Sting** (¾)	2:13	Jerry Bailey	Joe Orseno	Tout Charmant	Catella
2001	**Banks Hill** (5½)	2:00⅕	Olivier Peslier	Andre Fabre	Spook Express	Spring Oak
2002	**Starine** (1½)	2:03⅗	John Velazquez	Bobby Frankel	Banks Hill	Islington
2003	**Islington** (nk)	1:59	Kieren Fallon	Sir Michael Stoute	L'Ancresse	Yesterday

Classic

Distance: 1¼ miles (since 1984).

Year	Winner (Margin)	Time	Jockey	Trainer	2nd place	3rd place
1984	**Wild Again** (hd)	2:03⅖	Pat Day	Vincent Timphony	Slew o' Gold	Gate Dancer*
1985	**Proud Truth** (hd)	2:00⅘	Jorge Velasquez	John Veitch	Gate Dancer	Turkoman
1986	**Skywalker** (1¼)	2:00⅖	Laffit Pincay Jr.	M. Whittingham	Turkoman	Precisionist
1987	**Ferdinand** (ns)	2:01⅖	Bill Shoemaker	C. Whittingham	Alysheba	Judge Angelucci
1988	**Alysheba** (ns)	2:04⅘	Chris McCarron	Jack Van Berg	Seeking the Gold	Waquoit
1989	**Sunday Silence** (½)	2:00⅕	Chris McCarron	C. Whittingham	Easy Goer	Blushing John

Year	Winner (Margin)	Time	Jockey	Trainer	2nd place	3rd place
1990	**Unbridled** (1)	2:02⅕	Pat Day	Carl Nafzger	Ibn Bey	Thirty Six Red
1991	**Black Tie Affair** (1¼)	2:02⅘	Jerry Bailey	Ernie Poulos	Twilight Agenda	Unbridled
1992	**A.P. Indy** (2)	2:00⅕	Eddie Delahoussaye	Neil Drysdale	Pleasant Tap	Jolypha
1993	**Arcangues** (2)	2:00⅘	Jerry Bailey	Andre Fabre	Bertrando	Kissin Kris
1994	**Concern** (nk)	2:02⅖	Jerry Bailey	Richard Small	Tabasco Cat	Dramatic Gold
1995	**Cigar** (2½)	1:59⅖	Jerry Bailey	Bill Mott	L'Carriere	Unaccounted For
1996	**Alphabet Soup** (ns)	2:01	Chris McCarron	David Hofmans	Louis Quatorze	Cigar
1997	**Skip Away** (6)	1:59⅕	Mike Smith	Hubert Hine	Deputy Commander	Dowty
1998	**Awesome Again** (¾)	2:02	Pat Day	Patrick Byrne	Silver Charm	Swain
1999	**Cat Thief** (1¼)	1:59⅖	Pat Day	D. Wayne Lukas	Budroyale	Golden Missile
2000	**Tiznow** (nk)	2:00⅗	Chris McCarron	Jay Robbins	Giant's Causeway	Captain Steve
2001	**Tiznow** (ns)	2:00⅗	Chris McCarron	Jay Robbins	Sakhee	Albert the Great
2002	**Volponi** (6½)	2:01⅖	Jose Santos	Philip Johnson	Medaglia d'Oro	Milwaukee Brew
2003	**Pleasantly Perfect** (1½)	1:59⅘	Alex Solis	Richard Mandella	Medaglia d'Oro	Dynever

*In 1984, 2nd place finisher Gate Dancer was disqualified for interference and placed 3rd.

Annual Money Leaders

Horses

Annual money-leading horses since 1910, according to *The American Racing Manual.*

Multiple leaders: Round Table, Buckpasser, Alysheba and Cigar (2).

Year	Horse	Age	Sts	1-2-3	Earnings
1910	Novelty	2	16	11—	$72,630
1911	Worth	2	13	10—	16,645
1912	Star Charter	4	17	6—	14,655
1913	Old Rosebud	2	14	12—	19,057
1914	Roamer	3	16	12—	29,105
1915	Borrow	7	9	4—	20,195
1916	Campfire	2	9	6—	49,735
1917	Sun Briar	2	9	5—	59,505
1918	Eternal	2	8	6—	56,173
1919	Sir Barton	3	13	8-3-2	88,250
1920	Man o' War	3	11	11-0-0	166,140
1921	Morvich	2	11	11-0-0	115,234
1922	Pillory	3	7	4-1-1	95,654
1923	Zev	3	14	12-1-0	272,008
1924	Sarzen	3	12	8-1-1	95,640
1925	Pompey	2	10	7-2-0	121,630
1926	Crusader	3	15	9-4-0	166,033
1927	Anita Peabody	2	7	6-0-1	111,905
1928	High Strung	2	6	5-0-0	153,590
1929	Blue Larkspur	3	6	4-1-0	153,450
1930	Gallant Fox	3	10	9-1-0	308,275
1931	Gallant Flight	2	7	7-0-0	219,000
1932	Gusto	3	16	4-3-2	145,940
1933	Singing Wood	2	9	3-2-2	88,050
1934	Cavalcade	3	7	6-1-0	111,235
1935	Omaha	3	9	6-1-2	142,255
1936	Granville	3	11	7-3-0	110,295
1937	Seabiscuit	4	15	11-2-2	168,580
1938	Stagehand	3	15	8-2-3	189,710
1939	Challedon	3	15	9-2-3	184,535
1940	Bimelech	3	7	4-2-1	110,005
1941	Whirlaway	3	20	13-5-2	272,386
1942	Shut Out	3	12	8-2-0	238,872
1943	Count Fleet	3	6	6-0-0	174,055
1944	Pavot	2	8	8-0-0	179,040
1945	Busher	3	13	10-2-1	273,735
1946	Assault	3	15	8-2-3	424,195
1947	Armed	6	17	11-4-1	376,325
1948	Citation	3	20	19-1-0	709,470
1949	Ponder	3	21	9-5-2	321,825
1950	Noor	5	12	7-4-1	346,940
1951	Counterpoint	3	15	7-2-1	250,525
1952	Crafty Admiral	4	16	9-4-1	277,225
1953	Native Dancer	3	10	9-1-0	513,425
1954	Determine	3	15	10-3-2	328,700
1955	Nashua	3	12	10-1-1	752,550
1956	Needles	3	8	4-2-0	440,850
1957	Round Table	3	22	15-1-3	$600,383
1958	Round Table	4	20	14-4-0	662,780
1959	Sword Dancer	3	13	8-4-0	537,004
1960	Bally Ache	3	15	10-3-1	445,045
1961	Carry Back	3	16	9-1-3	565,349
1962	Never Bend	2	10	7-1-2	402,969
1963	Candy Spots	3	12	7-2-1	604,481
1964	Gun Bow	4	16	8-4-2	580,100
1965	Buckpasser	2	11	9-1-0	568,096
1966	Buckpasser	3	14	13-1-0	669,078
1967	Damascus	3	16	12-3-1	817,941
1968	Forward Pass	3	13	7-2-0	546,674
1969	Arts and Letters	3	14	8-5-1	555,604
1970	Personality	3	18	8-2-1	444,049
1971	Riva Ridge	2	9	7-0-0	503,263
1972	Droll Role	4	19	7-3-4	471,633
1973	Secretariat	3	12	9-2-1	860,404
1974	Chris Evert	3	8	5-1-2	551,063
1975	Foolish Pleasure	3	11	5-4-1	716,278
1976	Forego	6	8	6-1-1	401,701
1977	Seattle Slew	3	7	6-1-1	641,370
1978	Affirmed	3	11	8-2-0	901,541
1979	Spectacular Bid	3	12	10-1-1	1,279,334
1980	Temperence Hill	3	17	8-3-1	1,130,452
1981	John Henry	6	10	8-0-0	1,798,030
1982	Perrault (GBR)	5	8	4-1-2	1,197,400
1983	All Along (FRA)	4	7	4-1-1	2,138,963
1984	Slew o' Gold	4	6	5-1-0	2,627,944
1985	Spend A Buck	3	7	5-1-1	3,552,704
1986	Snow Chief	3	9	6-1-1	1,875,200
1987	Alysheba	3	10	3-3-1	2,511,156
1988	Alysheba	4	9	7-1-0	3,808,600
1989	Sunday Silence	3	9	7-2-0	4,578,454
1990	Unbridled	3	11	4-3-2	3,718,149
1991	Dance Smartly	3	8	8-0-0	2,876,821
1992	A.P. Indy	3	7	5-0-1	2,622,560
1993	Kotashaan (FRA)	5	10	6-3-0	2,619,014
1994	Paradise Creek	5	11	8-2-1	2,610,187
1995	Cigar	5	10	10-0-0	4,819,800
1996	Cigar	6	8	5-2-1	4,910,000
1997	Skip Away	4	11	4-5-2	4,089,000
1998	Silver Charm	4	9	6-2-0	4,696,506
1999	Almutawakel	4	4	1-1-1	3,290,000
2000	Dubai Millennium (GBR)	4	1	1-0-0	3,600,000
2001	Captain Steve	4	6	2-1-1	4,201,200
2002	Street Cry (IRE)	4	3	2-1-0	4,266,615
2003	Moon Ballad (IRE)	4	3	1-0-0	3,651,101

Annual Money Leaders (Cont.)

Jockeys

Annual money-leading jockeys since 1910, according to *The American Racing Manual.*

Multiple leaders: Bill Shoemaker (10); Laffit Pincay Jr. (7); Eddie Arcaro and Jerry Bailey (6); Braulio Baeza (5); Chris McCarron and Jose Santos (4); Angel Cordero Jr. and Earl Sande (3); Ted Atkinson, Pat Day, Laverne Fator, Mack Garner, Bill Hartack, Charley Kurtsinger, Johnny Longden, Mike Smith, Gary Stevens, Sonny Workman and Wayne Wright (2).

Year		Mts	Wins	Earnings	Year		Mts	Wins	Earnings
1910	Carroll Shilling	506	172	$176,030	1958	Bill Shoemaker	1133	300	$2,961,693
1911	Ted Koerner	813	162	88,308	1959	Bill Shoemaker	1285	347	2,843,133
1912	Jimmy Butwell	684	144	79,843	1960	Bill Shoemaker	1227	274	2,123,961
1913	Merritt Buxton	887	146	82,552	1961	Bill Shoemaker	1256	304	2,690,819
1914	J. McCahey	824	155	121,845	1962	Bill Shoemaker	1126	311	2,916,844
1915	Mack Garner	775	151	96,628	1963	Bill Shoemaker	1203	271	2,526,925
1916	John McTaggart	832	150	155,055	1964	Bill Shoemaker	1056	246	2,649,553
1917	Frank Robinson	731	147	148,057	1965	Braulio Baeza	1245	270	2,582,702
1918	Lucien Luke	756	178	201,864	1966	Braulio Baeza	1341	298	2,951,022
1919	John Loftus	177	65	252,707	1967	Braulio Baeza	1064	256	3,088,888
1920	Clarence Kummer	353	87	292,376	1968	Braulio Baeza	1089	201	2,835,108
1921	Earl Sande	340	112	263,043	1969	Jorge Velasquez	1442	258	2,542,315
1922	Albert Johnson	297	43	345,054	1970	Laffit Pincay Jr.	1328	269	2,626,526
1923	Earl Sande	430	122	569,394	1971	Laffit Pincay Jr.	1627	380	3,784,377
1924	Ivan Parke	844	205	290,395	1972	Laffit Pincay Jr.	1388	289	3,225,827
1925	Laverne Fator	315	81	305,775	1973	Laffit Pincay Jr.	1444	350	4,093,492
1926	Laverne Fator	511	143	361,435	1974	Laffit Pincay Jr.	1278	341	4,251,060
1927	Earl Sande	179	49	277,877	1975	Braulio Baeza	1190	196	3,674,398
1928	Linus McAtee	235	55	301,295	1976	Angel Cordero Jr.	1534	274	4,709,500
1929	Mack Garner	274	57	314,975	1977	Steve Cauthen	2075	487	6,151,750
1930	Sonny Workman	571	152	420,438	1978	Darrel McHargue	1762	375	6,188,353
1931	Charley Kurtsinger	519	93	392,095	1979	Laffit Pincay Jr.	1708	420	8,183,535
1932	Sonny Workman	378	87	385,070	1980	Chris McCarron	1964	405	7,666,100
1933	Robert Jones	471	63	226,285	1981	Chris McCarron	1494	326	8,397,604
1934	Wayne Wright	919	174	287,185	1982	Angel Cordero Jr.	1838	397	9,702,520
1935	Silvio Coucci	749	141	319,760	1983	Angel Cordero Jr.	1792	362	10,116,807
1936	Wayne Wright	670	100	264,000	1984	Chris McCarron	1565	356	12,038,213
1937	Charley Kurtsinger	765	120	384,202	1985	Laffit Pincay Jr.	1409	289	13,415,049
1938	Nick Wall	658	97	385,161	1986	Jose Santos	1636	329	11,329,297
1939	Basil James	904	191	353,333	1987	Jose Santos	1639	305	12,407,355
1940	Eddie Arcaro	783	132	343,661	1988	Jose Santos	1867	370	14,877,298
1941	Don Meade	1164	210	398,627	1989	Jose Santos	1459	285	13,847,003
1942	Eddie Arcaro	687	123	481,949	1990	Gary Stevens	1504	283	13,881,198
1943	Johnny Longden	871	173	573,276	1991	Chris McCarron	1440	265	14,456,073
1944	Ted Atkinson	1539	287	899,101	1992	Kent Desormeaux	1568	361	14,193,006
1945	Johnny Longden	778	180	981,977	1993	Mike Smith	1510	343	14,024,815
1946	Ted Atkinson	1377	233	1,036,825	1994	Mike Smith	1484	317	15,979,820
1947	Douglas Dodson	646	141	1,429,949	1995	Jerry Bailey	1367	287	16,311,876
1948	Eddie Arcaro	726	188	1,686,230	1996	Jerry Bailey	1187	298	19,465,376
1949	Steve Brooks	906	209	1,316,817	1997	Jerry Bailey	1136	269	18,206,013
1950	Eddie Arcaro	888	195	1,410,160	1998	Gary Stevens	869	178	19,358,840
1951	Bill Shoemaker	1161	257	1,329,890	1999	Pat Day	1265	254	18,092,845
1952	Eddie Arcaro	807	188	1,859,591	2000	Pat Day	1219	267	17,479,838
1953	Bill Shoemaker	1683	485	1,784,187	2001	Jerry Bailey	912	227	22,597,720
1954	Bill Shoemaker	1251	380	1,876,760	2002	Jerry Bailey	833	214	22,871,814
1955	Eddie Arcaro	820	158	1,864,796	2003	Jerry Bailey	776	206	23,354,960
1956	Bill Hartack	1387	347	2,343,955					
1957	Bill Hartack	1238	341	3,060,501					

Trainers

Annual money-leading trainers since 1908, according to *The American Racing Manual.*

Multiple Leaders: D. Wayne Lukas (14); Sam Hildreth (9); Charlie Whittingham (7); Sunny Jim Fitzsimmons and Jimmy Jones (5); Bob Baffert, Laz Barrera, Ben Jones and Willie Molter (4); Hirsch Jacobs, Eddie Neloy and James Rowe Sr. (3); H. Guy Bedwell, Bobby Frankel, Jack Gaver, John Schorr, Humming Bob Smith, Silent Tom Smith and Mesh Tenney (2).

Year		Wins	Earnings	Year		Wins	Earnings
1908	James Rowe Sr.	50	$284,335	1914	R.C. Benson	45	$59,315
1909	Sam Hildreth	73	123,942	1915	James Rowe Sr.	19	75,596
1910	Sam Hildreth	84	148,010	1916	Sam Hildreth	39	70,950
1911	Sam Hildreth	67	49,418	1917	Sam Hildreth	23	61,698
1912	John Schorr	63	58,110	1918	H. Guy Bedwell	53	80,296
1913	James Rowe Sr.	18	45,936	1919	H. Guy Bedwell	63	208,728

Year		Wins	Earnings
1920	Louis Feustel	.22	$186,087
1921	Sam Hildreth	.85	262,768
1922	Sam Hildreth	.74	247,014
1923	Sam Hildreth	.75	392,124
1924	Sam Hildreth	.77	255,608
1925	G.R. Tompkins	.30	199,245
1926	Scott Harlan	.21	205,681
1927	W.H. Bringloe	.63	216,563
1928	John Schorr	.65	258,425
1929	James Rowe Jr.	.25	314,881
1930	Sunny Jim Fitzsimmons	.47	397,355
1931	Big Jim Healy	.33	297,300
1932	Sunny Jim Fitzsimmons	.68	266,650
1933	Humming Bob Smith	.53	135,720
1934	Humming Bob Smith	.43	249,938
1935	Bud Stotler	.87	303,005
1936	Sunny Jim Fitzsimmons	.42	193,415
1937	Robert McGarvey	.46	209,925
1938	Earl Sande	.15	226,495
1939	Sunny Jim Fitzsimmons	.45	266,205
1940	Silent Tom Smith	.14	269,200
1941	Ben Jones	.70	475,318
1942	Jack Gaver	.48	406,547
1943	Ben Jones	.73	267,915
1944	Ben Jones	.60	601,660
1945	Silent Tom Smith	.52	510,655
1946	Hirsch Jacobs	.99	560,077
1947	Jimmy Jones	.85	1,334,805
1948	Jimmy Jones	.81	1,118,670
1949	Jimmy Jones	.76	978,587
1950	Preston Burch	.96	637,754
1951	Jack Gaver	.42	616,392
1952	Ben Jones	.29	662,137
1953	Harry Trotsek	.54	1,028,873
1954	Willie Molter	.136	1,107,860
1955	Sunny Jim Fitzsimmons	.66	1,270,055
1956	Willie Molter	.142	1,227,402
1957	Jimmy Jones	.70	1,150,910
1958	Willie Molter	.69	1,116,544
1959	Willie Molter	.71	847,290
1960	Hirsch Jacobs	.97	748,349
1961	Jimmy Jones	.62	759,856
1962	Mesh Tenney	.58	1,099,474

Year		Sts	Wins	Earnings
1963	Mesh Tenney	.192	40	$860,703
1964	Bill Winfrey	.287	61	1,350,534
1965	Hirsch Jacobs	.610	91	1,331,628
1966	Eddie Neloy	.282	93	2,456,250
1967	Eddie Neloy	.262	72	1,776,089
1968	Eddie Neloy	.212	52	1,233,101
1969	Elliott Burch	.156	26	1,067,936
1970	Charlie Whittingham	.551	82	1,302,354
1971	Charlie Whittingham	.393	77	1,737,115
1972	Charlie Whittingham	.429	79	1,734,020
1973	Charlie Whittingham	.423	85	1,865,385
1974	Pancho Martin	.846	166	2,408,419
1975	Charlie Whittingham	.487	3	2,437,244
1976	Jack Van Berg	.2362	496	2,976,196
1977	Laz Barrera	.781	127	2,715,848
1978	Laz Barrera	.592	100	3,307,164
1979	Laz Barrera	.492	98	3,608,517
1980	Laz Barrera	.559	99	2,969,151
1981	Charlie Whittingham	.376	74	3,993,302
1982	Charlie Whittingham	.410	63	4,587,457
1983	D. Wayne Lukas	.595	78	4,267,261
1984	D. Wayne Lukas	.805	131	5,835,921
1985	D. Wayne Lukas	.1140	218	11,155,188
1986	D. Wayne Lukas	.1510	259	12,345,180
1987	D. Wayne Lukas	.1735	343	17,502,110
1988	D. Wayne Lukas	.1500	318	17,842,358
1989	D. Wayne Lukas	.1398	305	16,103,998
1990	D. Wayne Lukas	.1396	267	14,508,871
1991	D. Wayne Lukas	.1497	289	15,942,223
1992	D. Wayne Lukas	.1349	230	9,806,436
1993	Bobby Frankel	.345	79	8,933,252
1994	Bobby Frankel	.693	147	9,247,457
1995	D. Wayne Lukas	.837	194	12,834,483
1996	D. Wayne Lukas	.1006	192	15,966,344
1997	D. Wayne Lukas	.824	169	9,993,569
1998	Bob Baffert	.538	139	15,000,870
1999	Bob Baffert	.735	169	16,934,607
2000	Bob Baffert	.678	146	11,831,605
2001	Bob Baffert	.660	138	16,354,996
2002	Bobby Frankel	.480	117	17,748,340
2003	Bobby Frankel	.413	114	19,143,289

All-Time Leaders

The all-time money-winning horses, trainers and race-winning jockeys of North America, according to the *Equibase Company*. Records include all available earnings from races in foreign countries. Horses must have had at least one start in the United States or Canada.

Top 30 Horses—Money Won

Note that horses who raced in 2004 are in **bold** type. Records are through Sept. 29, 2004.

		Sts	1st	2nd	3rd	Earnings			Sts	1st	2nd	3rd	Earnings
1	Cigar	.33	19	4	5	$9,999,815	16	**High Chaparral** (IRE)	13	10	1	2	$5,331,231
2	Skip Away	.38	18	10	6	9,616,360	17	Street Cry (IRE)	.12	5	6	1	5,150,837
3	Fantastic Light	.25	12	5	3	8,486,957	18	**Preeminence** (JPN)	.50	13	9	7	5,042,956
4	**Smarty Jones**	.9	8	1	0	7,613,155	19	Jim and Tonic (FRA)	.39	13	13	4	4,975,807
5	**Pleasantly Perfect**	17	9	3	1	7,349,880	20	Sunday Silence	.14	9	5	0	4,968,554
6	Silver Charm	.24	12	7	2	6,944,369	21	Easy Goer	.20	14	5	1	4,873,770
7	Captain Steve	.25	9	3	7	6,828,356	22	Daylami (IRE)	.21	11	3	4	4,614,762
8	Alysheba	.26	11	8	2	6,679,242	23	Behrens	.27	9	8	3	4,563,500
9	John Henry	.83	39	15	9	6,591,860	24	Unbridled	.24	8	6	6	4,489,475
10	Tiznow	.15	8	4	2	6,427,830	25	Awesome Again	.12	9	0	2	4,374,590
11	Singspiel (IRE)	.20	9	8	0	5,952,825	26	**Moon Ballad** (IRE)	.14	5	3	1	4,364,791
12	**Falbrav** (IRE)	.26	13	5	5	5,825,517	27	**Sulamani** (IRE)	.16	8	3	1	4,352,368
13	**Medaglia d'Oro**	.17	8	7	0	5,754,720	28	Spend A Buck	.15	10	3	2	4,220,689
14	Best Pal	.47	18	11	4	5,668,245	29	Pilsudski (IRE)	.22	10	6	2	4,080,297
15	Taiki Blizzard	.23	6	8	2	5,523,549	30	Creme Fraiche	.64	17	12	13	4,024,727

All-Time Leaders (Cont.)

Top 30 Jockeys—Races Won

Note that jockeys active in 2004 are in **bold** type. Records are through Sept. 29, 2004.

		Yrs	Wins	Earnings			Yrs	Wins	Earnings
1	Laffit Pincay Jr.	.37	9531	$236,851,825	16	**Mario Pino**	.27	5428	$86,297,965
2	Bill Shoemaker	.42	8833	123,375,524	17	Jacinto Vasquez	.37	5228	85,754,115
3	**Pat Day**	.32	8728	293,221,817	18	Ron Ardoin	.31	5226	58,908,059
4	**Russell Baze**	.31	8693	129,019,330	19	**Edgar Prado**	.21	5176	145,005,851
5	David Gall	.43	7396	24,972,821	20	**Rick Wilson**	.32	4939	77,288,270
6	Chris McCarron	.29	7141	263,985,505	21	Rudy Baez	.25	4875	30,474,225
7	Angel Cordero Jr.	.35	7057	164,561,227	22	**Anthony Black**	.34	4795	54,026,591
8	Jorge Velasquez	.33	6795	125,544,379	23	Eddie Arcaro	.31	4779	30,039,543
9	Sandy Hawley	.31	6449	88,481,292	24	**Gary Stevens**	.26	4773	210,512,280
10	Larry Snyder	.35	6388	47,207,289	25	**Perry Wayne Ouzts**	32	4666	26,293,296
11	Eddie Delahoussaye	.36	6384	195,884,940	26	**Mark Guidry**	.31	4638	80,553,893
12	Carl Gambardella	.39	6349	29,389,041	27	Don Brumfield	.37	4573	43,567,861
13	**Earlie Fires**	.40	6326	82,282,240	28	**Tim Doocy**	.31	4473	54,389,496
14	John Longden	.41	6032	24,665,800	29	**Kent Desormeaux**	.19	4456	172,713,862
15	**Jerry Bailey**	.30	5704	274,200,851	30	Steve Brooks	.34	4451	18,239,817

Top 10 Trainers—Money Won

Note that trainers active in 2004 are in **bold** type. Records are through Sept. 29, 2004.

		Wins	Earnings			Wins	Earnings
1	**D. Wayne Lukas**	.4284	$238,366,498	6	**Bob Baffert**	.1426	$105,299,201
2	**Bobby Frankel**	.3096	166,866,561	7	**Richard Mandella**	.1645	97,457,062
3	**Bill Mott**	.3263	133,457,615	8	**H. Allen Jerkens**	.3566	86,504,574
4	**Ron McAnally**	.2415	112,190,820	9	**Claude McGaughey III**	.1397	85,176,298
5	Charles Whittingham	.2534	109,215,527	10	**Jack Van Berg**	.6341	80,298,699

Eclipse Awards

The Eclipse Awards, honoring the Horse of the Year and other champions of the sport, are sponsored by the National Thoroughbred Racing Association (NTRA), *Daily Racing Form* and the National Turf Writers Assn. In 1998, the NTRA replaced the Thoroughbred Racing Associations of North America as co-sponsor.

The awards are named after the 18th century racehorse and sire, Eclipse, who began racing at age five and was unbeaten in 18 starts (eight wins were walkovers). As a stallion, Eclipse sired winners of 344 races, including three Epsom Derby champions.

Horses listed in CAPITAL letters won the Triple Crown that year. Age of horse in parentheses where necessary.

Multiple winners: (horses): Forego (8); John Henry (7); Affirmed, Lonesome Glory and Secretariat (5); Cigar, Flatterer, Seattle Slew, Skip Away and Spectacular Bid (4); Ack Ack, Azeri, Susan's Girl, Tiznow and Zaccio (3); All Along, Alysheba, Bayakoa, Black Tie Affair, Cafe Prince, Charismatic, Conquistador Cielo, Desert Vixen, Favorite Trick, Ferdinand, Flawlessly, Flat Top, Go for Wand, High Chaparral, Holy Bull, Housebuster, Kotashaan, Lady's Secret, Life's Magic, Miesque, Mineshaft, Morley Street, Open Mind, Paseana, Point Given, Riva Ridge, Silverbulletday, Slew o' Gold and Spend A Buck (2).

Multiple winners: (people): Jerry Bailey (7); Juddmonte Farms and Laffit Pincay Jr. (6); Bobby Frankel (5); Laz Barrera, Pat Day, John Franks, D. Wayne Lukas, Allen Paulson, Ogden Phipps and Frank Stronach (4); Bob Baffert, Steve Cauthen, Harbor View Farm, Fred W. Hooper, Nelson Bunker Hunt, Mr. & Mrs. Gene Klein, Dan Lasater, John & Betty Mabee, Paul Mellon, Bill Shoemaker, Edward Taylor and Charlie Whittingham (3); Braulio Baeza, C.T. Chenery, Claiborne Farm, Angel Cordero Jr., Kent Desormeaux, Richard Englander, William S. Farish, John W. Galbreath, Chris McCarron, Bill Mott and Mike Smith (2).

Horse of the Year

Year		Year		Year		Year	
1971	Ack Ack (5)	1980	Spectacular Bid (4)	1989	Sunday Silence (3)	1998	Skip Away (5)
1972	Secretariat (2)	1981	John Henry (6)	1990	Criminal Type (5)	1999	Charismatic (3)
1973	SECRETARIAT (3)	1982	Conquistador Cielo (3)	1991	Black Tie Affair (5)	2000	Tiznow (3)
1974	Forego (4)	1983	All Along (4)	1992	A.P. Indy (3)	2001	Point Given (3)
1975	Forego (5)	1984	John Henry (9)	1993	Kotashaan (5)	2002	Azeri (4)
1976	Forego (6)	1985	Spend A Buck (3)	1994	Holy Bull (3)	2003	Mineshaft (4)
1977	SEATTLE SLEW (3)	1986	Lady's Secret (4)	1995	Cigar (5)		
1978	AFFIRMED (3)	1987	Ferdinand (4)	1996	Cigar (6)		
1979	Affirmed (4)	1988	Alysheba (4)	1997	Favorite Trick (2)		

Older Male

Year		Year		Year		Year	
1971	Ack Ack (5)	1980	Spectacular Bid (4)	1989	Blushing John (4)	1998	Skip Away (5)
1972	Autobiography (4)	1981	John Henry (6)	1990	Criminal Type (5)	1999	Victory Gallop (4)
1973	Riva Ridge (4)	1982	Lemhi Gold (4)	1991	Black Tie Affair (5)	2000	Lemon Drop Kid (4)
1974	Forego (4)	1983	Bates Motel (4)	1992	Pleasant Tap (5)	2001	Tiznow (4)
1975	Forego (5)	1984	Slew o' Gold (4)	1993	Bertrando (4)	2002	Left Bank (5)
1976	Forego (6)	1985	Vanlandingham (4)	1994	The Wicked North (4)	2003	Mineshaft (4)
1977	Forego (7)	1986	Turkoman (4)	1995	Cigar (5)		
1978	Seattle Slew (4)	1987	Ferdinand (4)	1996	Cigar (6)		
1979	Affirmed (4)	1988	Alysheba (4)	1997	Skip Away (4)		

Older Female

Year		Year		Year		Year	
1971	Shuvee (5)	1980	Glorious Song (4)	1989	Bayakoa (5)	1998	Escena (5)
1972	Typecast (6)	1981	Relaxing (5)	1990	Bayakoa (6)	1999	Beautiful Pleasure (4)
1973	Susan's Girl (4)	1982	Track Robbery (6)	1991	Queena (5)	2000	Riboletta (5)
1974	Desert Vixen (4)	1983	Amb. of Luck (4)	1992	Paseana (5)	2001	Gourmet Girl (6)
1975	Susan's Girl (6)	1984	Princess Rooney (4)	1993	Paseana (6)	2002	Azeri (4)
1976	Proud Delta (4)	1985	Life's Magic (4)	1994	Sky Beauty (4)	2003	Azeri (5)
1977	Cascapedia (4)	1986	Lady's Secret (4)	1995	Inside Information (4)		
1978	Late Bloomer (4)	1987	North Sider (5)	1996	Jewel Princess (4)		
1979	Waya (5)	1988	Personal Ensign (4)	1997	Hidden Lake (4)		

3-Year-Old Male

Year		Year		Year		Year	
1971	Canonero II	1980	Temperence Hill	1989	Sunday Silence	1998	Real Quiet
1972	Key to the Mint	1981	Pleasant Colony	1990	Unbridled	1999	Charismatic
1973	SECRETARIAT	1982	Conquistador Cielo	1991	Hansel	2000	Tiznow
1974	Little Current	1983	Slew o' Gold	1992	A.P. Indy	2001	Point Given
1975	Wajima	1984	Swale	1993	Prairie Bayou	2002	War Emblem
1976	Bold Forbes	1985	Spend A Buck	1994	Holy Bull	2003	Funny Cide
1977	SEATTLE SLEW	1986	Snow Chief	1995	Thunder Gulch		
1978	AFFIRMED	1987	Alysheba	1996	Skip Away		
1979	Spectacular Bid	1988	Risen Star	1997	Silver Charm		

3-Year-Old Filly

Year		Year		Year		Year	
1971	Turkish Trousers	1980	Genuine Risk	1989	Open Mind	1998	Banshee Breeze
1972	Susan's Girl	1981	Wayward Lass	1990	Go for Wand	1999	Silverbulletday
1973	Desert Vixen	1982	Christmas Past	1991	Dance Smartly	2000	Surfside
1974	Chris Evert	1983	Heartlight No. One	1992	Saratoga Dew	2001	Xtra Heat
1975	Ruffian	1984	Life's Magic	1993	Hollywood Wildcat	2002	Farda Amiga
1976	Revidere	1985	Mom's Command	1994	Heavenly Prize	2003	Bird Town
1977	Our Mims	1986	Tiffany Lass	1995	Serena's Song		
1978	Tempest Queen	1987	Sacahuista	1996	Yanks Music		
1979	Davona Dale	1988	Winning Colors	1997	Ajina		

Horse of the Year (1936-70)

In 1971, the *Daily Racing Form*, the Thoroughbred Racing Associations, and the National Turf Writers Assn. joined forces to create the Eclipse Awards. Before then, however, the *Racing Form* (1936-70) and the TRA (1950-70) issued separate selections for Horse of the Year. Their picks differed only four times from 1950-70 and are so noted. Horses listed in CAPITAL letters are Triple Crown winners; (f) indicates female.

Multiple winners: Kelso (5); Challedon, Native Dancer and Whirlaway (2).

Year		Year		Year		Year	
1936	Granville	1946	ASSAULT	1955	Nashua	1964	Kelso
1937	WAR ADMIRAL	1947	Armed	1956	Swaps	1965	Roman Brother (DRF)
1938	Seabiscuit	1948	CITATION	1957	Bold Ruler (DRF)		Moccasin (TRA)
1939	Challedon	1949	Capot		Dedicate (TRA)	1966	Buckpasser
1940	Challedon	1950	Hill Prince	1958	Round Table	1967	Damascus
1941	WHIRLAWAY	1951	Counterpoint	1959	Sword Dancer	1968	Dr. Fager
1942	Whirlaway	1952	One Count (DRF)	1960	Kelso	1969	Arts and Letters
1943	COUNT FLEET		Native Dancer (TRA)	1961	Kelso	1970	Fort Marcy (DRF)
1944	Twilight Tear (f)	1953	Tom Fool	1962	Kelso		Personality (TRA)
1945	Busher (f)	1954	Native Dancer	1963	Kelso		

Eclipse Awards (Cont.)

2-Year-Old Male

Year		Year		Year		Year	
1971	Riva Ridge	1980	Lord Avie	1989	Rhythm	1998	Answer Lively
1972	Secretariat	1981	Deputy Minister	1990	Fly So Free	1999	Anees
1973	Protagonist	1982	Roving Boy	1991	Arazi	2000	Macho Uno
1974	Foolish Pleasure	1983	Devil's Bag	1992	Gilded Time	2001	Johannesburg
1975	Honest Pleasure	1984	Chief's Crown	1993	Dehere	2002	Vindication
1976	Seattle Slew	1985	Tasso	1994	Timber Country	2003	Action This Day
1977	Affirmed	1986	Capote	1995	Maria's Mon		
1978	Spectacular Bid	1987	Forty Niner	1996	Boston Harbor		
1979	Rockhill Native	1988	Easy Goer	1997	Favorite Trick		

2-Year-Old Filly

Year		Year		Year		Year	
1971	Numbered Account	1979	Smart Angle	1988	Open Mind	1997	Countess Diana
1972	La Prevoyante	1980	Heavenly Cause	1989	Go for Wand	1998	Silverbulletday
1973	Talking Picture	1981	Before Dawn	1990	Meadow Star	1999	Chilukki
1974	Ruffian	1982	Landaluce	1991	Pleasant Stage	2000	Caressing
1975	Dearly Precious	1983	Althea	1992	Eliza	2001	Tempera
1976	Sensational	1984	Outstandingly	1993	Phone Chatter	2002	Storm Flag Flying
1977	Lakeville Miss	1985	Family Style	1994	Flanders	2003	Halfbridled
1978	(TIE) Candy Eclair	1986	Brave Raj	1995	Golden Attraction		
	& It's in the Air	1987	Epitome	1996	Storm Song		

Champion Turf Horse

Year		Year		Year		Year	
1971	Run the Gantlet (3)	1973	SECRETARIAT (3)	1975	Snow Knight (4)	1977	Johnny D (3)
1972	Cougar II (6)	1974	Dahlia (4)	1976	Youth (3)	1978	Mac Diarmida (3)

Champion Male Turf Horse

Year		Year		Year		Year	
1979	Bowl Game (5)	1986	Manila (3)	1993	Kotashaan (5)	2000	Kalanisi (4)
1980	John Henry (5)	1987	Theatrical (5)	1994	Paradise Creek (5)	2001	Fantastic Light (5)
1981	John Henry (6)	1988	Sunshine Forever (3)	1995	Northern Spur (4)	2002	High Chaparral (3)
1982	Perrault (5)	1989	Steinlen (6)	1996	Singspiel (5)	2003	High Chaparral (4)
1983	John Henry (8)	1990	Itsallgreektome (3)	1997	Chief Bearhart (4)		
1984	John Henry (9)	1991	Tight Spot (4)	1998	Buck's Boy (5)		
1985	Cozzene (4)	1992	Sky Classic (5)	1999	Daylami (5)		

Champion Female Turf Horse

Year		Year		Year		Year	
1979	Trillion (5)	1986	Estrapade (6)	1993	Flawlessly (5)	2000	Perfect Sting (4)
1980	Just A Game II (4)	1987	Miesque (3)	1994	Hatoof (5)	2001	Banks Hill (3)
1981	De La Rose (3)	1988	Miesque (4)	1995	Possibly Perfect (5)	2002	Golden Apples (4)
1982	April Run (4)	1989	Brown Bess (7)	1996	Wandesta (5)	2003	Islington (5)
1983	All Along (4)	1990	Laugh and Be Merry (5)	1997	Ryafan (3)		
1984	Royal Heroine (4)	1991	Miss Alleged (4)	1998	Fiji (4)		
1985	Pebbles (4)	1992	Flawlessly (4)	1999	Soaring Softly (4)		

Sprinter

Year		Year		Year		Year	
1971	Ack Ack (5)	1979	Star de Naskra (4)	1988	Gulch (4)	1997	Smoke Glacken (3)
1972	Chou Croute (4)	1980	Plugged Nickle (3)	1989	Safely Kept (3)	1998	Reraise (3)
1973	Shecky Greene (3)	1981	Guilty Conscience (5)	1990	Housebuster (3)	1999	Artax (4)
1974	Forego (4)	1982	Gold Beauty (3)	1991	Housebuster (4)	2000	Kona Gold (6)
1975	Gallant Bob (3)	1983	Chinook Pass (4)	1992	Rubiano (5)	2001	Squirtle Squirt (3)
1976	My Juliet (4)	1984	Eillo (4)	1993	Cardmania (7)	2002	Orientate (4)
1977	What a Summer (4)	1985	Precisionist (4)	1994	Cherokee Run (4)	2003	Aldebaran (5)
1978	(TIE) Dr. Patches (4)	1986	Smile (4)	1995	Not Surprising (4)		
	& J.O. Tobin (4)	1987	Groovy (4)	1996	Lit de Justice (6)		

Steeplechase or Hurdle Horse

Year		Year		Year		Year	
1971	Shadow Brook (7)	1980	Zaccio (4)	1989	Highland Bud (4)	1998	Flat Top (5)
1972	Soothsayer (5)	1981	Zaccio (5)	1990	Morley Street (6)	1999	Lonesome Glory (11)
1973	Athenian Idol (5)	1982	Zaccio (6)	1991	Morley Street (7)	2000	All Gong (6)
1974	Gran Kan (8)	1983	Flatterer (4)	1992	Lonesome Glory (4)	2001	Pompeyo (8)
1975	Life's Illusion (4)	1984	Flatterer (5)	1993	Lonesome Glory (5)	2002	Flat Top (9)
1976	Straight and True (6)	1985	Flatterer (6)	1994	Warm Spell (6)	2003	McDynamo (6)
1977	Cafe Prince (7)	1986	Flatterer (7)	1995	Lonesome Glory (7)		
1978	Cafe Prince (8)	1987	Inlander (6)	1996	Correggio (5)		
1979	Martie's Anger (4)	1988	Jimmy Lorenzo (6)	1997	Lonesome Glory (9)		

Outstanding Jockey

Year		Year		Year		Year	
1971	Laffit Pincay Jr.	1980	Chris McCarron	1989	Kent Desormeaux	1998	Gary Stevens
1972	Braulio Baeza	1981	Bill Shoemaker	1990	Craig Perret	1999	Jorge Chavez
1973	Laffit Pincay Jr.	1982	Angel Cordero Jr.	1991	Pat Day	2000	Jerry Bailey
1974	Laffit Pincay Jr.	1983	Angel Cordero Jr.	1992	Kent Desormeaux	2001	Jerry Bailey
1975	Braulio Baeza	1984	Pat Day	1993	Mike Smith	2002	Jerry Bailey
1976	Sandy Hawley	1985	Laffit Pincay Jr.	1994	Mike Smith	2003	Jerry Bailey
1977	Steve Cauthen	1986	Pat Day	1995	Jerry Bailey		
1978	Darrel McHargue	1987	Pat Day	1996	Jerry Bailey		
1979	Laffit Pincay Jr.	1988	Jose Santos	1997	Jerry Bailey		

Outstanding Apprentice Jockey

Year		Year		Year		Year	
1971	Gene St. Leon	1981	Richard Migliore	1991	Mickey Walls	2000	Tyler Baze
1972	Thomas Wallis	1982	Alberto Delgado	1992	Rosemary Homeister	2001	Jeremy Rose
1973	Steve Valdez	1983	Declan Murphy	1993	Juan Umana	2002	Ryan Fogelsonger
1974	Chris McCarron	1984	Wesley Ward	1994	Dale Beckner	2003	Eddie Castro
1975	Jimmy Edwards	1985	Art Madrid Jr.	1995	Ramon B. Perez		
1976	George Martens	1986	Allen Stacy	1996	Neil Poznansky		
1977	Steve Cauthen	1987	Kent Desormeaux	1997	Roberto Rosado		
1978	Ron Franklin	1988	Steve Capanas		& Philip Teator		
1979	Cash Asmussen	1989	Michael Luzzi	1998	Shaun Bridgmohan		
1980	Frank Lovato Jr.	1990	Mark Johnston	1999	Ariel Smith		

Outstanding Trainer

Year		Year		Year		Year	
1971	Charlie Whittingham	1980	Bud Delp	1989	Charlie Whittingham	1998	Bob Baffert
1972	Lucien Laurin	1981	Ron McAnally	1990	Carl Nafzger	1999	Bob Baffert
1973	H. Allen Jerkens	1982	Charlie Whittingham	1991	Ron McAnally	2000	Bobby Frankel
1974	Sherill Ward	1983	Woody Stephens	1992	Ron McAnally	2001	Bobby Frankel
1975	Steve DiMauro	1984	Jack Van Berg	1993	Bobby Frankel	2002	Bobby Frankel
1976	Laz Barrera	1985	D. Wayne Lukas	1994	D. Wayne Lukas	2003	Bobby Frankel
1977	Laz Barrera	1986	D. Wayne Lukas	1995	Bill Mott		
1978	Laz Barrera	1987	D. Wayne Lukas	1996	Bill Mott		
1979	Laz Barrera	1988	Shug McGaughey	1997	Bob Baffert		

Outstanding Owner

Year		Year		Year		Year	
1971	Mr. & Mrs. E.E. Fogleson	1980	Mr. & Mrs. Bertram Firestone	1988	Ogden Phipps	1997	Carolyn Hine
1972-73	No award	1981	Dotsam Stable	1989	Ogden Phipps	1998	Frank Stronach
1974	Dan Lasater	1982	Viola Sommer	1990	Frances Genter	1999	Frank Stronach
1975	Dan Lasater	1983	John Franks	1991	Sam-Son Farms	2000	Frank Stronach
1976	Dan Lasater	1984	John Franks	1992	Juddmonte Farms	2001	Richard Englander
1977	Maxwell Gluck	1985	Mr. & Mrs. Gene Klein	1993	John Franks	2002	Richard Englander
1978	Harbor View Farm	1986	Mr. & Mrs. Gene Klein	1994	John Franks	2003	Juddmonte Farms
1979	Harbor View Farm	1987	Mr. & Mrs. Gene Klein	1995	Allen Paulson		
				1996	Allen Paulson		

Outstanding Breeder

Year		Year		Year		Year	
1971	Paul Mellon	1980	Mrs. Henry Paxson	1989	North Ridge Farm	1998	John & Betty Mabee
1972	C.T. Chenery	1981	Golden Chance Farm	1990	Calumet Farm	1999	William S. Farish
1973	C.T. Chenery	1982	Fred W. Hooper	1991	John & Betty Mabee	2000	Frank Stronach
1974	John W. Galbreath	1983	Edward P. Taylor	1992	William S. Farish	2001	Juddmonte Farms
1975	Fred W. Hooper	1984	Claiborne Farm	1993	Allan Paulson	2002	Juddmonte Farms
1976	Nelson Bunker Hunt	1985	Nelson Bunker Hunt	1994	William T. Young	2003	Juddmonte Farms
1977	Edward P. Taylor	1986	Paul Mellon	1995	Juddmonte Farms		
1978	Harbor View Farm	1987	Nelson Bunker Hunt	1996	Farnsworth Farms		
1979	Claiborne Farm	1988	Ogden Phipps	1997	John & Betty Mabee		

Eclipse Awards (Cont.)
Award of Merit

Year		Year		Year		Year	
1976	Jack J. Dreyfus	1985	Keene Daingerfield	1992	Joe Hirsch	1998	D.G. Van Clief Jr.
1977	Steve Cauthen	1986	Herman Cohen		& Robert P. Strub	2000	Jim McKay
1978	Dinny Phipps	1987	J.B. Faulconer	1993	Paul Mellon	2001	Pete Pederson
1979	Jimmy Kilroe	1988	John Forsythe	1994	Alfred G. Vanderbilt		& Harry T. Mangurian
1980	John D. Shapiro	1989	Michael Sandler	1995	Ted Bassett III	2002	Ogden Phipps
1981	Bill Shoemaker	1990	Warner L. Jones	1996	Allen Paulson		& Howard Battle
1984	John Gaines	1991	Fred W. Hooper	1997	Bob & Beverly Lewis	2003	Richard Duchossois

Special Award

Year		Year		Year		Year	
1971	Robert J. Kleberg	1985	Arlington Park	1995	Russell Baze	2001	Sheikh Mohammed
1974	Charles Hatton	1987	Anheuser-Busch	1998	Oak Tree Racing		al-Maktoum
1976	Bill Shoemaker	1988	Edward J. DeBartolo Sr.		Assoc.	2002	Keeneland Library
1980	John T. Landry	1989	Richard Duchossois	1999	Laffit Pincay Jr.		
	& Pierre E. Bellocq	1994	Eddie Arcaro	2000	John Hettinger		
1984	C.V. Whitney		& John Longden				

HARNESS RACING

Triple Crown Winners
PACERS

Ten three-year-olds have won the Cane Pace, Little Brown Jug and Messenger Stakes in the same year since the Pacing Triple Crown was established in 1956. No trainer or driver has won it more than once.

Year		Driver	Trainer	Owner
1959	**Adios Butler**	Clint Hodgins	Paige West	Paige West & Angelo Pellillo
1965	**Bret Hanover**	Frank Ervin	Frank Ervin	Richard Downing
1966	**Romeo Hanover**	Bill Myer & George Sholty*	Jerry Silverman	Lucky Star Stables & Morton Finder
1968	**Rum Customer**	Billy Haughton	Billy Haughton	Kennilworth Farms & L.C. Mancuso
1970	**Most Happy Fella**	Stanley Dancer	Stanley Dancer	Egyptian Acres Stable
1980	**Niatross**	Clint Galbraith	Clint Galbraith	Niagara Acres, Niatross Stables & Clint Galbraith
1983	**Ralph Hanover**	Ron Waples	Stew Firlotte	Waples Stable, Pointsetta Stable, Grant's Direct Stable & P.J. Baugh
1997	**Western Dreamer**	Mike Lachance	Bill Robinson Stable	Matthew, Daniel and Patrick Daly
1999	**Blissful Hall**	Ron Pierce	Benn Wallace	Daniel Plouffe
2003	**No Pan Intended**	David Miller	Ivan Sugg	Bob Glazer

*Myer drove Romeo Hanover in the Cane, Sholty in the other two races.

TROTTERS

Six three-year-olds have won the Yonkers Trot, Hambletonian and Kentucky Futurity in the same year since the Trotting Triple Crown was established in 1955. Stanley Dancer is the only driver/trainer to win it twice. **Note:** As of closing time for the Horse Racing chapter, Windsong's Legacy had won the Yonkers Trot and the Hambletonian. See *Updates* for results from Ky. Futurity.

Year		Driver/Trainer	Owner
1955	**Scott Frost**	Joe O'Brien	S.A. Camp Farms
1963	**Speedy Scot**	Ralph Baldwin	Castleton Farms
1964	**Ayres**	John Simpson Sr.	Charlotte Sheppard
1968	**Nevele Pride**	Stanley Dancer	Nevele Acres & Lou Resnick
1969	**Lindy's Pride**	Howard Beissinger	Lindy Farms
1972	**Super Bowl**	Stanley Dancer	Rachel Dancer & Rose Hild Breeding Farm

Triple Crown Near Misses
PACERS

Nine horses have won the first two legs of the Triple Crown, but not the third. The Cane Pace (CP), Little Brown Jug (LBJ), and Messenger Stakes (MS) have not always been run in the same order so numbers after races won indicate sequence for that year.

Year		CP	LBJ	MS	Year		CP	LBJ	MS
1957	**Torpid**	won, 1	won, 2	DNF*	1990	**Jake and Elwood**	won, 1	NE	won, 2
1960	**Countess Adios**	won, 2	NE	won, 1	1992	**Western Hanover**	won, 1	2nd*	won, 2
1971	**Albatross**	won, 2	2nd*	won, 1	1993	**Rijadh**	won, 1	2nd*	won, 2
1976	**Keystone Ore**	won, 1	won, 2	2nd*	1998	**Shady Character**	won, 1	won, 2	6th*
1986	**Barberry Spur**	won, 1	won, 2	2nd*					

Winning horses: Meadow Lands (1957), Nansemond (1971), Windshield Wiper (1976), Amity Chef (1986), Fake Left (1992), Life Sign (1993), Fit for Life (1998).

Note: Torpid (1957) scratched before the final heat; Countess Adios (1960) and Jake and Elwood (1990) not eligible for Little Brown Jug.

TROTTERS

Eight horses have won the first two legs of the Triple Crown– the Yonkers Trot (YT) and the Hambletonian (Ham)–but not the third. The winner of the Kentucky Futurity (KF) is listed.

Year		YT	Ham	KF	Year		YT	Ham	KF
1962	**A.C.'s Viking**	won	won	Safe Mission	1987	**Mack Lobell**	won	won	Napoletano
1976	**Steve Lobell**	won	won	Quick Pay	1993	**American Winner**	won	won	Pine Chip
1977	**Green Speed**	won	won	Texas	1996	**Continentalvictory**	won	won	Running Sea
1978	**Speedy Somolli**	won	won	Doublemint	1998	**Muscles Yankee**	won	won	Trade Balance

Note: Green Speed (1977) was not eligible for the Kentucky Futurity; Continentalvictory (1996) was withdrawn from the Kentucky Futurity due to a leg injury.

The Hambletonian

For three-year-old trotters. Inaugurated in 1926 and has been held in Syracuse, N.Y.; Lexington, Ky.; Goshen, N.Y.; Yonkers, N.Y.; Du Quoin, Ill.; and since 1981 at The Meadowlands in East Rutherford, N.J.

Run at one mile since 1947. Winning horse must win two heats.

Drivers with most wins: John Campbell (5); Stanley Dancer, Billy Haughton, Mike Lachance and Ben White (4); Howard Beissinger, Del Cameron and Henry Thomas (3).

Year		Driver	Fastest Heat	Year		Driver	Fastest Heat
1926	**Guy McKinney**	Nat Ray	2:04¾	1968	**Nevele Pride**	Stanley Dancer	1:59²/₅
1927	**Iosola's Worthy**	Marvin Childs	2:03¾	1969	**Lindy's Pride**	Howard Beissinger	1:57³/₅
1928	**Spencer**	W.H. Lessee	2:02½	1970	**Timothy T**	John Simpson Jr.	1:58²/₅
1929	**Walter Dear**	Walter Cox	2:02¾	1971	**Speedy Crown**	Howard Beissinger	1:57²/₅
1930	**Hanover's Bertha**	Tom Berry	2:03	1972	**Super Bowl**	Stanley Dancer	1:56²/₅
1931	**Calumet Butler**	R.D. McMahon	2:03¼	1973	**Flirth**	Ralph Baldwin	1:57¹/₅
1932	**The Marchioness**	Will Caton	2:01¼	1974	**Christopher T**	Billy Haughton	1:58³/₅
1933	**Mary Reynolds**	Ben White	2:03¾	1975	**Bonefish**	Stanley Dancer	1:59
1934	**Lord Jim**	Doc Parshall	2:02¾	1976	**Steve Lobell**	Billy Haughton	1:56²/₅
1935	**Greyhound**	Sep Palin	2:02¼	1977	**Green Speed**	Billy Haughton	1:55³/₅
1936	**Rosalind**	Ben White	2:01¾	1978	**Speedy Somolli**	Howard Beissinger	1:55
1937	**Shirley Hanover**	Henry Thomas	2:01½	1979	**Legend Hanover**	George Sholty	1:56¹/₅
1938	**McLin Hanover**	Henry Tomas	2:02¼	1980	**Burgomeister**	Billy Haughton	1:56³/₅
1939	**Peter Astra**	Doc Parshall	2:04¼	1981	**Shiaway St. Pat**	Ray Remmen	2:01¹/₅
1940	**Spencer Scott**	Fred Egan	2:02	1982	**Speed Bowl**	Tommy Haughton	1:56⁴/₅
1941	**Bill Gallon**	Lee Smith	2:05	1983	**Duenna**	Stanley Dancer	1:57²/₅
1942	**The Ambassador**	Ben White	2:04	1984	**Historic Freight**	Ben Webster	1:56²/₅
1943	**Volo Song**	Ben White	2:02½	1985	**Prakas**	Bill O'Donnell	1:54³/₅
1944	**Yankee Maid**	Henry Thomas	2:04	1986	**Nuclear Kosmos**	Ulf Thoresen	1:55²/₅
1945	**Titan Hanover**	Harry Pownall Sr.	2:04	1987	**Mack Lobell**	John Campbell	1:53²/₅
1946	**Chestertown**	Thomas Berry	2:02½	1988	**Armbro Goal**	John Campbell	1:54³/₅
1947	**Hoot Mon**	Sep Palin	2:00	1989	**Park Avenue Joe** & **Probe** *	Ron Waples / Bill Fahy	1:54³/₅
1948	**Demon Hanover**	Harrison Hoyt	2:02				
1949	**Miss Tilly**	Fred Egan	2:01²/₅				
1950	**Lusty Song**	Del Miller	2:02	1990	**Harmonious**	John Campbell	1:54¹/₅
1951	**Mainliner**	Guy Crippen	2:02³/₅	1991	**Giant Victory**	Jack Moiseyev	1:54⁴/₅
1952	**Sharp Note**	Bion Shively	2:02³/₅	1992	**Alf Palema**	Mickey McNichol	1:56²/₅
1953	**Helicopter**	Harry Harvey	2:01³/₅	1993	**American Winner**	Ron Pierce	1:53¹/₅
1954	**Newport Dream**	Del Cameron	2:02⁴/₅	1994	**Victory Dream**	Mike Lachance	1:54¹/₅
1955	**Scott Frost**	Joe O'Brien	2:00³/₅	1995	**Tagliabue**	John Campbell	1:54⁴/₅
1956	**The Intruder**	Ned Bower	2:01²/₅	1996	**Continentalvictory**	Mike Lachance	1:52⁴/₅
1957	**Hickory Smoke**	John Simpson Sr.	2:00¹/₅	1997	**Malabar Man**	Mal Burroughs	1:55
1958	**Emily's Pride**	Flave Nipe	1:59⁴/₅	1998	**Muscles Yankee**	John Campbell	1:52²/₅
1959	**Diller Hanover**	Frank Ervin	2:01¹/₅	1999	**Self Possessed**	Mike Lachance	1:51³/₅
1960	**Blaze Hanover**	Joe O'Brien	1:59³/₅	2000	**Yankee Paco**	Trevor Ritchie	1:53²/₅
1961	**Harlan Dean**	James Arthur	1:58²/₅	2001	**Scarlet Knight**	Stefan Melander	1:53⁴/₅
1962	**A.C.'s Viking**	Sanders Russell	1:59³/₅	2002	**Chip Chip Hooray**	Eric Ledford	1:53³/₅
1963	**Speedy Scot**	Ralph Baldwin	1:57³/₅	2003	**Amigo Hall**	Mike Lachance	1:54
1964	**Ayres**	John Simpson Sr.	1:56⁴/₅	2004	**Windsong's Legacy**	T. Smedshammer	1:54¹/₅
1965	**Egyptian Candor**	Del Cameron	2:03⁴/₅				
1966	**Kerry Way**	Frank Ervin	1:58⁴/₅				
1967	**Speedy Streak**	Del Cameron	2:00				

*In 1989, Park Avenue Joe and Probe finished in a dead heat in the race-off. They were later declared co-winners, but Park Avenue Joe was awarded 1st place money because his three-race summary (2-1-1) was better than Probe's (1-9-1).

Harness Racing (Cont.)
All-Time Leaders

The all-time winning trotters, pacers and drivers through 2003, according to *The Trotting and Pacing Guide*. Purses for horses include races in foreign countries. Earnings and wins for drivers include only races held in North America.

Top 15 Horses—Money Won

		T/P	Yrs	Earnings
1	Varenne	.T	1998-2002	$5,636,255
2	Moni Maker	.T	1995-2000	5,589,256
3	Gallo Blue Chip	.P	1999-2003	4,164,469
4	Peace Corps	.T	1988-93	4,137,737
5	Ourasi	.T	1988-90	4,010,105
6	Mack Lobell	.T	1986-91	3,917,594
7	Victory Tilly	.T	1997-2003	3,745,896
8	Reve d'Udon	.T	1985-92	3,611,351
9	Magician	.T	1997-2003	3,579,103
10	Zoogin	.T	1992-99	3,513,324
11	Eternal Camnation	.P	1999-2003	3,385,398
12	General du Pommeau	T	1996-2002	3,247,727
13	Nihilator	.P	1984-85	3,225,653
14	Real Desire	.P	2000-02	3,159,814
15	Sea Cove	.T	1989-95	3,138,986

Top 15 Drivers—Races Won

		Yrs	1st	Earnings
1	Herve Filion	.37	15,017	$86,883,736
2	Walter Case Jr.	.26	11,027	43,680,566
3	Cat Manzi	.36	10,066	94,153,367
4	Mike Lachance	.36	9,475	155,812,691
5	Dave Magee	.31	9,474	75,370,241
6	Dave Palone	.22	9,384	41,011,259
7	John Campbell	.32	9,265	219,812,569
8	Tony Morgan	.30	8,595	55,104,718
9	Jack Moiseyev	.28	8,505	93,518,733
10	Bill (Zeke) Parker Jr.	.33	8,429	20,770,224
11	Eddie Davis	.40	8,318	47,392,227
12	Doug Brown	.31	7,898	82,130,423
13	Carmine Abbatiello	.47	7,170	50,328,868
14	Kevin Wallis	.29	7,146	30,178,423
15	Leigh Fitch	.41	7,084	7,838,324

Annual Awards
Harness Horse of the Year

Selected since 1947 by U.S. Trotting Association and the U.S. Harness Writers Association; age of winning horse is noted; (t) indicates trotter and (p) indicates pacer.

Multiple winners: Bret Hanover and Nevele Pride (3); Adios Butler, Albatross, Cam Fella, Good Time, Mack Lobell, Moni Maker, Niatross and Scott Frost (2).

Year		Year		Year		Year	
1947	Victory Song (4t)	1963	Speedy Scot (3t)	1979	Niatross (2p)	1995	CR Kay Suzie (3t)
1948	Rodney (4t)	1964	Bret Hanover (2p)	1980	Niatross (3p)	1996	Continentalvictory (3t)
1949	Good Time (3p)	1965	Bret Hanover (3p)	1981	Fan Hanover (3p)	1997	Malabar Man (3t)
1950	Proximity (8t)	1966	Bret Hanover (4p)	1982	Cam Fella (3p)	1998	Moni Maker (5t)
1951	Pronto Don (6t)	1967	Nevele Pride (2t)	1983	Cam Fella (4p)	1999	Moni Maker (6t)
1952	Good Time (6p)	1968	Nevele Pride (3t)	1984	Fancy Crown (3t)		
1953	Hi Lo's Forbes (5p)	1969	Nevele Pride (4t)	1985	Nihilator (3p)	2000	Gallo Blue Chip (3p)
1954	Stenographer (3t)	1970	Fresh Yankee (7t)	1986	Forrest Skipper (4p)	2001	Bunny Lake (3p)
1955	Scott Frost (3t)	1971	Albatross (3p)	1987	Mack Lobell (3t)	2002	Real Desire (4p)
1956	Scott Frost (4t)	1972	Albatross (4p)	1988	Mack Lobell (4t)	2003	No Pan Intended (3p)
1957	Torpid (3p)	1973	Sir Dalrae (4p)	1989	Matt's Scooter (4p)		
1958	Emily's Pride (3t)	1974	Delmonica Hanover (5t)	1990	Beach Towel (3p)		
1959	Bye Bye Byrd (4p)	1975	Savoir (7t)	1991	Precious Bunny (3p)		
1960	Adios Butler (4p)	1976	Keystone Ore (3p)	1992	Artsplace (4p)		
1961	Adios Butler (5p)	1977	Green Speed (3t)	1993	Staying Together (4p)		
1962	Su Mac Lad (8t)	1978	Abercrombie (3p)	1994	Cam's Card Shark (3p)		

Driver of the Year

Determined by Universal Driving Rating System (UDR) and presented by the Harness Tracks of America since 1968. Eligible drivers must have at least 1,000 starts for the season.

Multiple winners: Herve Filion (10); John Campbell, Walter Case Jr., Mike Lachance and Dave Palone (3); Tony Morgan, Bill O'Donnell, Luc Ouellette and Ron Waples (2).

Year		Year		Year		Year	
1968	Stanley Dancer	1978	Carmine Abbatiello	1987	Mike Lachance	1996	Tony Morgan
1969	Herve Filion		& Herve Filion	1988	John Campbell		& Luc Ouellette
1970	Herve Filion	1979	Ron Waples	1989	Herve Filion	1997	Tony Morgan
1971	Herve Filion	1980	Ron Waples	1990	John Campbell	1998	Walter Case Jr.
1972	Herve Filion	1981	Herve Filion	1991	Walter Case Jr.	1999	Dave Palone
1973	Herve Filion	1982	Bill O'Donnell	1992	Walter Case Jr.		
1974	Herve Filion	1983	John Campbell	1993	Jack Moiseyev	2000	Dave Palone
1975	Joe O'Brien	1984	Bill O'Donnell	1994	Dave Magee	2001	Stephane Bouchard
1976	Mike Lachance	1985	Mike Lachance	1995	Luc Ouellette	2002	Tony Morgan
1977	Donald Dancer	1986	Mike Lachance			2003	Dave Palone

Tennis

Chile's **Nicolas Massu** is wiped out after winning
the men's tennis gold medal at Athens in 2004.

AP/Wide World Photos

Roger and the Russians

Roger Federer takes three of four Grand Slams and the Russians do the same in the women's game.

Gerry Brown
is co-editor of the ESPN Sports Almanac.

Switzerland's Roger Federer had an historic season, winning three of four Grand Slam men's singles titles. With his straight set win over Australian Lleyton Hewitt at the U.S. Open, he became the first player since Swede Mats Wilander in 1988 to win three of tennis's four majors in one season.

Only three other men have done it in history. American Don Budge won the 1938 Grand Slam, Australia's Rod Laver won the Grand Slam in 1962 and 1969 and American Jimmy Connors won the Australian Open, Wimbledon and U.S. Open in 1974, missing out on the French Open when he was banned by the ATP for signing to play with a rival tour.

Federer lost in the third round to three-time champ Gustavo Kuerten in the 2004 French Open but the 23-year-old Federer has four career Grand Slam titles (including his 2003 Wimbledon title) and plenty of time to work on his clay game in order to seriously threaten Pete Sampras's career record of 14 Grand Slam titles. Of course, Sampras never won the French Open either.

Many observers, including tennis guru Bud Collins, feel that Federer, who took the world's No. 1 ranking from Andy Roddick in February, has a shot at matching Budge and Laver in winning a Grand Slam, that all he needs is time to figure out the surface at Roland Garros.

Aside from France, the only other place where Federer, who won 10 tournaments as of October, met real disappointment on the court in 2004 was at the Summer Olympics in Athens. Federer did not hide his desire to win a gold medal, saying that it was more important to him than winning the U.S. Open which was to be held just a few weeks following.

Some top players, including Hewitt and eight-time Grand Slam winner and 1996 Olympic gold medallist Andre Agassi, passed up Athens in order to focus on the U.S. Open but Federer had other priorities, playing both singles and doubles for two chances at gold. He lost both on the same day.

AP/Wide World Photos

*Switzerland's **Roger Federer** did something in 2004 that hadn't been done in men's tennis for 16 years when he came within a French Open of winning the Grand Slam.*

First in singles competition he self-destructed and lost in just the second round to 74th-ranked Czech teenager Thomas Berdych, 4-6, 7-5, 7-5, and then he, and Swiss doubles teammate Yves Allegro, lost to a pair from India.

There was no Olympic hangover however and Federer regained his form to overpower a rested and ready Hewitt, 6-0, 7-6, 6-0, in the men's final at the U.S. Open.

Roddick, the top American men's player nowadays, has a power game to meet (and exceed) Federer and a long career in front of him as well. The two could combine to form tennis' next great rivalry in the line going back through Agassi-Sampras, Edberg-Becker, Lendl-McEnroe, Borg-Connors and Laver-Rosewall.

In women's tennis, the Russians are not only coming, they're here. The recently anticipated Russian invasion landed with a big splash on the lawns near London in 2004.

Tall teenager Maria Sharapova broke the Williams sisters' four-year choke hold on the Wimbledon women's title with a 6-1, 6-4 shocker over defending champion Serena.

Sharapova's breakthrough win and model's good looks gave her the media attention and the endorsement deals but she's not even the top-ranked Russian player on the women's tour. In fact, she's not second or even third.

As of Oct. 18, four of the world's top 10 were Russians: Anastasia Myskina, Svetlana Kuznetsova, Elena Dementieva and Sharapova.

AP/Wide World Photos

Maria Sharapova *was on the front lines of the so-called Russian invasion of women's tennis in 2004. She upset American Serena Williams in the ladies finals at Wimbledon.*

Myskina won the 2004 French Open in under an hour, 6-1, 6-2, over compatriot Dementieva in the first all-Russian Grand Slam final ever. It didn't take very long for the second however.

Kuznetsova kept the vodka flowing at Flushing Meadows with her win over Dementieva, becoming the lowest seeded (ninth) U.S. Open winner in the open era.

When it will be Dementieva's turn to become prima ballerina is not known but with the invincibility of Venus and Serena apparently a thing of the past, a Russian dynasty could be on the horizon.

Despite the success of the Russian ladies in 2004 and the fact that it was the first year in 16 that no American woman or man won a Grand Slam event, former No. 1 Lindsay Davenport was able to regain the world No. 1 ranking in October, dethroning France's Amelie Mauresmo after just four weeks on top.

Belgium's former No. 1 and 2003 player of the year, Justine Henin-Hardenne, was worn out from a tremendous run in recent years and shut down her season early but not before winning a gold medal at the Summer Games in Athens.

If Davenport stumbles in 2005, there will be no shortage of talented players from points around the world ready to pounce.

The Ten Biggest Stories of the Year in Tennis

10 Australian doubles master Todd Woodbridge partners with Jonas Bjorkman and wins his ninth men's doubles titles at Wimbledon but misses out on his 11th overall Wimbledon title when he and partner Alicia Molik take an early one-set lead but then lose to Zimbabwean siblings Wayne and Cara Black in the mixed doubles finals.

9 Former long-time No. 1 ranked Steffi Graf, winner of 22 Grand Slam singles titles, is inducted into the International Tennis Hall of Fame.

8 Austria upsets the United States in the quarterfinals of the Fed Cup, handing Martina Navratilova her first loss in 41 Fed Cup matches. Barbara Schwartz, ranked 324th in the world, surprises 30th-ranked Lisa Raymond to clinch the best-of-five series.

7 No Americans win a Grand Slam title for the first time in 16 years. The last year without an American-born player winning a Grand Slam event was 1988 when Germany's Steffi Graf won all four, and Mats Wilander (who won three) and Stefan Edberg won on the men's side. In the open era there have been only four years without an American-born winner in a Grand Slam event (2004, 1988, 1987 and 1969).

6 Lindsay Davenport regains the No. 1 ranking late in the 2004 season, dethroning France's Amelie Mauresmo, who became the first French person ever to be ranked No. 1. Davenport, who regained the top spot by advancing into the quarterfinals of the Kremlin Cup, was last ranked No. 1 on Jan. 13, 2002 but the American has since struggled, mostly due to injury.

5 Belgium's Justine Henin-Hardenne, winner of two Grand Slam singles titles in 2003 and the year-end No. 1 ranked women's player, starts the season with a win at the 2004 Australian Open but stumbles somewhat with early exits at the French Open and U.S. Open. Henin-Hardenne salvages the season with her Olympic gold medal in Athens.

4 Nicolas Massu of Chile ends American Mardy Fish's amazing Olympic run, 6-3, 3-6, 2-6, 6-3, 6-4, in an epic, four-hour gold medal match in Athens. Massu goes on to win doubles gold as well with Chilean teammate Fernando Gonzalez.

3 Unseeded Gaston Gaudio completes his cinderella run with a come-from-behind win over countryman Guillermo Coria in the all-Argentine final at the French Open. Gaudio took advantage of his opponent's muscle cramps to fight back from two sets down, saving two match points to win, 0-6, 3-6, 6-4, 6-1, 8-6, and become the first Argentine men's winner of a grand slam event since Guillermo Villas won the Australian Open in 1979.

2   Six-foot teenager Maria Sharapova leads a veritable Russian invasion of the women's tennis tour in 2004, highlighted by her surprising singles title win at Wimbledon. Fellow Russians Anastasia Mysinka (French Open) and Svetlana Kuznetsova (U.S. Open) also win Grand Slam events. Sharapova has been called the "anti-Kournikova" because she has stunning looks but, unlike Kournikova, actually wins tournaments.

1   Roger Federer wins three of the four Grand Slam events in 2004, becoming the first man to accomplish the feat since Mats Wilander in 1988. Federer is one of only two active men (Andre Agassi) to win at least three different majors in his career. Federer also joins retired stars John McEnroe and Bjorn Borg as the only players in the last 25 years to win 12 straight ATP finals with his win over Andy Roddick at the Thailand Open in October.

Sharapova Shines

Russia's Maria Sharapova became the first Russian and one of the youngest women of any nationality to win the Wimbledon women's singles title in 2004. Here's a look at the youngest ladies' champions in Wimbledon's long history.

Year		Age Years-Days
1887	Lottie Dodd	15-285
1997	Martina Hingis	16-278
2004	Maria Sharapova	17- 75
1952	Maureen Connelly	17-292

From Russia with Love

Russian women won three Grand Slams in 2004. Prior to this season they had never won a slam in the open era. Here's a look at the numbers that Russians have put up in Grand Slam events this year and the previous 36 years of the open era combined.

	1968-2003	2004
Players	2	4
Finals App.	3	5
Titles	0	3*

*Anastasia Myskina, Maria Sharapova and Svetlana Kuznetsova

2003-2004
Season in Review

Tournament Results

Winners of men's and women's pro singles championships from Nov. 2, 2003 through Sept. 26, 2004.

Men's ATP Tour
Late 2003

Finals	Tournament	Winner	Earnings	Runner-Up	Score
Nov. 2	TMS—Paris	Tim Henman	$526,800	A. Pavel	62 76 76
Nov. 17	Tennis Masters Cup (Houston)	Roger Federer	700,000	A. Agassi	63 60 64
Nov. 30	Davis Cup Final (Paris)	Australia	—	Spain	3-1

2004

Finals	Tournament	Winner	Earnings	Runner-Up	Score
Jan. 10	Qatar ExxonMobil Open (Doha)	Nicolas Escude	$142,000	I. Ljubicic	63 76
Jan. 11	AAPT Championships (Adelaide)	Dominik Hrbaty	52,000	M. Llodra	64 60
Jan. 11	Tata Open (Chennai)	Carlos Moya	52,000	P. Srichaphan	64 36 76
Jan. 17	adidas International (Sydney)	Lleyton Hewitt	48,600	C. Moya	43 (ret.)
Jan. 17	Heineken Open (Auckland)	Dominik Hrbaty	48,600	R. Nadal	46 62 75
Feb. 1	**Australian Open** (Melbourne)	Roger Federer	917,277	M. Safin	76 64 62
Feb. 15	Milan Indoors	Antony Dupuis	52,000	M. Ancic	64 67 76
Feb. 15	Siebel Open (San Jose)	Andy Roddick	52,000	M. Fish	76 64
Feb. 15	BellSouth Open (Vina Del Mar)	Fernando Gonzalez	45,000	G. Kuerten	75 64
Feb. 22	Kroger St. Jude (Memphis)	Joachim Johansson	128,000	N. Kiefer	76 63
Feb. 22	ABN/AMRO World Tennis Tournament (Rotterdam)	Lleyton Hewitt	202,522	J.C. Ferrero	67 75 64
Feb. 22	ATP Buenos Aires	Guillermo Coria	52,000	C. Moya	64 61
Feb. 29	Marseille Open	Dominik Hrbaty	102,075	R. Soderling	46 64 64
Feb. 29	Brasil Open (Costa Do Sauipe)	Gustavo Kuerten	52,000	A. Calleri	36 62 63
Mar. 7	Mexican Open (Acapulco)	Carlos Moya	128,000	F. Verdasco	63 60
Mar. 7	Dubai Tennis Championships	Roger Federer	187,500	F. Lopez	46 61 62
Mar. 7	Franklin Templeton Classic (Scottsdale)	Vincent Spadea	52,000	N. Kiefer	75 67 63
Mar. 21	TMS—Pacific Life Open (Indian Wells)	Roger Federer	421,600	T. Henman	63 63
Apr. 4	TMS—Nasdaq 100 Open (Miami)	Andy Roddick	533,350	G. Coria	67 63 61 (ret.)
Apr. 18	Valencia Open	Fernando Verdasco	52,000	A. Montanes	76 63
Apr. 18	Estoril Open	Juan Ignacio Chela	86,531	M. Safin	67 63 63
Apr. 18	U.S. Clay Court Championships (Houston)	Tommy Haas	52,000	A. Roddick	63 64
Apr. 25	TMS—Monte Carlo	Guillermo Coria	474,646	R. Schuettler	62 61 63
May 2	Open Seat Godo (Barcelona)	Tommy Robredo	181,756	G. Coria	63 46 62 36 63
May 2	BMW Open by Credit Suisse (Munich)	Nikolay Davydenko	61,608	M. Verkerk	64 75
May 9	TMS—Telecom Italia Masters (Rome)	Carlos Moya	396,000	D. Nalbandian	63 63 61
May 16	TMS—Hamburg	Roger Federer	467,360	G. Coria	46 64 62 63
May 22	Int'l Raiffeisen Grand Prix (St. Poelten)	Filippo Volandri	61,840	X. Malisse	61 64
May 22	Grand Prix Hassan II (Casablanca)	Santiago Ventura	61,840	D. Hrbaty	63 16 64
May 22	ATP World Team Championship (Dusseldorf)	Chile	515,490	Australia	2-1
June 5	**French Open** (Roland Garros)	Gaston Gaudio	1,043,610	G. Coria	06 36 64 61 86
June 13	Gerry Weber Open (Halle)	Roger Federer	135,253	M. Fish	60 63
June 13	Stella Artois Championships (London)	Andy Roddick	112,602	S. Grosjean	76 64
June 19	Nottingham Open	Paradorn Srichaphan	66,360	T. Johansson	16 76 63
June 20	Ordina Open ('s-Hertogenbosch)	Michael Llodra	62,618	G. Coria	63 64
July 4	**Wimbledon** (London)	Roger Federer	1,096,550	A. Roddick	46 75 76 64
July 11	Allianz Swiss Open (Gstaad)	Roger Federer	94,013	I. Andreev	62 63 57 63
July 11	Hall of Fame Championships (Newport)	Greg Rusedski	52,000	A. Popp	76 76
July 11	Synsam Swedish Open (Bastad)	Mariano Zabaleta	62,538	G. Gaudio	61 46 76
July 18	Dutch Open (Amersfoort)	Martin Verkerk	62,538	F. Gonzalez	76 46 64
July 18	Mercedes Cup (Stuttgart)	Guillermo Canas	128,608	G. Gaudio	57 62 60 16 63
July 18	Mercedes-Benz Cup (Los Angeles)	Tommy Haas	52,000	N. Kiefer	76 64
July 25	Croatia Open (Umag)	Guillermo Canas	66,576	F. Volandri	75 63
July 25	Generali Open (Kitzbuhel)	Nicolas Massu	165,924	G. Gaudio	64 76
July 25	RCA Championships (Indianapolis)	Andy Roddick	74,250	N. Kiefer	62 63

Tournament Results (Cont.)

Finals	Tournament	Winner	Earnings	Runner-Up	Score
Aug. 1	TMS—Tennis Masters Canada (Toronto)	Roger Federer	$410,500	A. Roddick	75 63
Aug. 8	TMS—Western & Southern Financial Group Masters (Cincinnati)	Andre Agassi	400,000	L. Hewitt	63 36 62
Aug. 15	Idea Prokom Open (Sopot)	Rafael Nadal	67,966	J. Acasuso	63 64
Aug. 22	Olympic Games (Athens)	Nicolas Massu	—	M. Fish	63 36 26 63 64
Aug. 22	Legg Mason Classic (Washington D.C.)	Lleyton Hewitt	69,200	G. Muller	63 64
Aug. 29	TD Waterhouse Cup (Long Island)	Lleyton Hewitt	52,000	L. Horna	63 61
Sept. 12	**U.S. Open** (Flushing)	Roger Federer	1,000,000	L. Hewitt	60 76 60
Sept. 19	China Open (Beijing)	Marat Safin	69,200	M. Youzhny	76 75
Sept. 19	Int'l Tennis Champs. (Delray Beach)	Ricardo Mello	52,000	V. Spadea	76 63
Sept. 19	Romanian Open (Bucharest)	Jose Acasuso	63,258	I. Andreev	63 60

Note: TMS indicates tournament is part of the ATP Tennis Masters Series.

Women's WTA Tour

Late 2003

Finals	Tournament	Winner	Earnings	Runner-Up	Score
Nov. 2	Advanta Championships (Philadelphia)	Amelie Mauresmo	$93,000	A. Myskina	57 60 62
Nov. 2	Bell Challenge (Quebec)	Maria Sharapova	27,000	M. Sequera	62 (ret.)
Nov. 9	Volvo Open (Pattaya City)	Henrieta Nagyova	16,000	L. Kurhajcova	64 62
Nov. 10	WTA Championships (Los Angeles)	Kim Clijsters	1,000,000	A. Mauresmo	62 60
Nov. 23	Fed Cup Final	France	—	United States	4-1

2004

Finals	Tournament	Winner	Earnings	Runner-Up	Score
Jan. 10	Uncle Toby's Hardcourts (Gold Coast)	Ai Sugiyama	$27,000	N. Petrova	16 61 64
Jan. 10	ASB Bank Classic (Auckland)	Eleni Daniilidou	22,000	A. Harkleroad	63 62
Jan. 16	Moorilla International (Hobart)	Amy Frazier	16,000	S. Asagoe	63 63
Jan. 17	Canberra Women's Classic	Paola Suarez	16,000	S. Farina Elia	36 64 76
Jan. 17	adidas International (Sydney)	Justine Henin-Hardenne	93,000	A. Mauresmo	64 64
Jan. 31	**Australian Open** (Melbourne)	Justine Henin-Hardenne	917,277	K. Clijsters	63 46 63
Feb. 8	Toray Pan Pacific Open (Tokyo)	Lindsay Davenport	189,000	M. Maleeva	64 61
Feb. 15	Open Gaz de France (Paris)	Kim Clijsters	93,000	M. Pierce	62 61
Feb. 22	Proximus Diamond Games (Antwerp)	Kim Clijsters	93,000	S. Farina Elia	63 60
Feb. 22	Indian Open (Hyderabad)	Nicole Pratt	22,000	M. Kirilenko	76 61
Feb. 22	Kroger St. Jude and Cellular South Cup (Memphis)	Vera Zvonareva	28,900	L. Raymond	46 64 75
Feb. 28	Dubai Duty Free Women's Open	Justine Henin-Hardenne	93,000	S. Kuznetsova	76 63
Feb. 29	Copa Colsanitas (Bogota)	Fabiola Zuluaga	27,000	M. Sanchez Lorenzo	36 64 62
Mar. 7	Qatar Open (Doha)	Anastasia Myskina	94,000	S. Kuznetsova	46 64 64
Mar. 7	Mexican Open (Acapulco)	Iveta Benesova	27,000	F. Pennetta	76 64
Mar. 21	Pacific Life Open (Indian Wells)	Justine Henin-Hardenne	332,000	L. Davenport	61 64
Apr. 4	Nasdaq 100 Open (Miami)	Serena Williams	400,000	E. Dementieva	61 61
Apr. 11	Grand Prix De S.A.R. (Casablanca)	Emilie Loit	16,000	L. Cervanova	62 62
Apr. 11	Bausch & Lomb Championships (Amelia Island)	Lindsay Davenport	93,000	A. Mauresmo	64 64
Apr. 19	Family Circle Cup (Charleston)	Venus Williams	189,000	C. Martinez	26 62 61
Apr. 19	Estoril Open	Emilie Loit	16,000	I. Benesova	75 76
May 2	J&S Cup (Warsaw)	Venus Williams	93,000	S. Kuznetsova	61 64
May 2	Tippmix Budapest Grand Prix	Jelena Jankovic	16,000	M. Sucha	76 63
May 9	German Open (Berlin)	Amelie Mauresmo	189,000	V. Williams	(win by default)
May 16	Italian Masters (Rome)	Amelie Mauresmo	189,000	J. Capriati	36 63 76
May 22	Strasbourg International	Claudine Schaul	27,000	L. Davenport	26 60 63
May 22	Wien Energie Grand Prix (Vienna)	A. Smashnova-Pistolesi	27,000	A. Molik	62 36 63
June 5	**French Open** (Roland Garros)	Anastasia Myskina	1,017,520	E. Dementieva	61 62
June 13	DFS Classic (Birmingham)	Maria Sharapova	27,000	T. Golovin	46 62 61
June 19	Ordina Open ('s-Hertogenbosch)	Mary Pierce	27,000	K. Koukalova	76 62
June 19	Hastings Direct Int'l Champs (Eastbourne) . .	Svetlana Kuznetsova	93,000	D. Hantuchova	26 76 64
July 4	**Wimbledon** (London)	Maria Sharapova	1,020,110	S. Williams	61 64
July 18	Bank of the West Classic (Stanford)	Lindsay Davenport	93,000	V. Williams	76 57 76
July 25	Palermo International	A. Medina Garrigues	16,000	F. Pennetta	64 64
July 25	JP Morgan Chase Open (Los Angeles)	Lindsay Davenport	93,000	S. Williams	61 63
Aug. 1	Acura Classic (San Diego)	Lindsay Davenport	189,000	A. Myskina	61 61
Aug. 8	Nordea Nordic Light Open (Stockholm)	Alicia Molik	22,000	T. Perebiynis	61 61
Aug. 8	Rogers AT&T Cup (Montreal)	Amelie Mauresmo	189,000	E. Likhovtseva	61 60

Finals	Tournament	Winner	Earnings	Runner-Up	Score
Aug. 14	Idea Prokom Polish Open (Sopot)	Flavia Pennetta	$50,000	K. Koukalova	75 36 63
Aug. 15	Odlum Brown Vancouver Women's Open . . .	Nicole Vaidisova	16,000	L. Granville	26 64 62
Aug. 22	Western & Southern Financial Group Women's Open (Cincinnati)	Lindsay Davenport	27,000	V. Zvonareva	63 62
Aug. 21	Olympic Games (Athens)	Justine Henin-Hardenne	—	A. Mauresmo	63 63
Aug. 28	Pilot Pen Tennis (New Haven)	Elena Bovina	29,000	N. Dechy	62 26 75
Aug. 28	Forest Hills Women's Tennis Classic	Elena Likhovtseva	16,000	I. Benesova	62 62
Sept. 12	**U.S. Open** (Flushing)	Svetlana Kuznetsova	1,000,000	E. Dementieva	63 75
Sept. 19	Wismilak International (Bali)	Svetlana Kuznetsova	35,000	M. Weingartner	61 64
Sept. 26	China Open (Beijing)	Serena Williams	93,000	S. Kuznetsova	46 75 64

2004 Grand Slam Tournaments

Australian Open

MEN'S SINGLES

FINAL EIGHT—#1 Andy Roddick; #2 Roger Federer; #3 Juan Carlos Ferrero; #4 Andre Agassi; #8 David Nalbandian; #9 Sebastein Grosjean; plus unseeded Hicham Arazi and Marat Safin.

Quarterfinals

Safin def. Roddick	26 63 75 67(0) 64
Agassi def. Grosjean	62 20 (ret.)
Federer def. Nalbandian	75 64 57 63
Ferrero def. Arazi	61 76(6) 76(5)

Semifinals

Safin def. Agassi	76(6) 76(6) 57 16 63
Federer def. Ferrero	64 61 64

Final

Federer def. Safin	76(3) 64 62

WOMEN'S SINGLES

FINAL EIGHT—#1 Justine Henin-Hardenne; #2 Kim Clijsters; #4 Amelie Mauresmo; #5 Lindsay Davenport; #6 Anastasia Myskina; #22 Patty Schnyder; # 25 Lisa Raymond and #32 Fabiola Zuluaga.

Quarterfinals

Henin-Hardenne def. Davenport	75 63
Zuluaga def. Mauresmo	(walkover)
Clijsters def. Myskina	62 76(9)
Schnyder def. Raymond	76(2) 63

Semifinals

Henin-Hardenne def. Zuluaga	62 62
Clijsters def. Schnyder	62 76(2)

Final

Henin-Hardenne def. Clijsters	63 46 63

DOUBLES FINALS

Men—#5 Michael Llodra & Fabrice Santoro def. #1 Bob Bryan & Mike Bryan, 7-6 (7-4), 6-3.

Women—#1 Virginia Ruano Pascual & Paola Suarez def. #2 Svetlana Kuznetsova & Elena Likhovtseva, 6-4, 6-3.

Mixed—Elena Bovina & Nenad Zimonjic def. #4 Martina Navratilova & Leander Paes, 6-1, 7-6 (7-3).

French Open

MEN'S SINGLES

FINAL EIGHT—#3 Guillermo Coria; #5 Carlos Moya; #8 David Nalbandian; #9 Tim Henman; #12 Lleyton Hewitt; #22 Juan Ignacio Chela; #28 Gustavo Kuerten; plus unseeded Gaston Gaudio.

Quarterfinals

Nalbandian def. Kuerten	62 36 64 76(6)
Gaudio def. Hewitt	63 62 62
Coria def. Moya	75 76(3) 63
Henman def. Chela	62 64 64

Semifinals

Gaudio def. Nalbandian	63 76(5) 60
Coria def. Henman	36 64 60 75

Final

Gaudio def. Coria	06 36 64 61 86

WOMEN'S SINGLES

FINAL EIGHT—#2 Serena Williams; #3 Amelie Mauresmo; #4 Venus Williams; #6 Anastasia Myskina; #7 Jennifer Capriati; #9 Elena Dementieva; #14 Paola Suarez and #18 Maria Sharapova.

Quarterfinals

Capriati def. S. Williams	63 26 63
Dementieva def. Mauresmo	64 63
Myskina def. V. Williams	63 64
Suarez def. Sharapova	61 63

Semifinals

Myskina def. Capriati	62 62
Dementieva def. Suarez	60 75

Final

Myskina def. Dementieva	61 62

DOUBLES FINALS

Men—Xavier Malisse & Olivier Rochus def. #6 Michael Llodra & Fabrice Santoro, 7-5, 7-5.

Women—#1 Virginia Ruano Pascual & Paola Suarez def. Svetlana Kuznetsova & Elena Likhovtseva, 6-0, 6-3.

Mixed—Tatiana Golovin & Richard Gasquet def. #4 Cara Black & Wayne Black, 6-3, 6-4.

Wimbledon

MEN'S SINGLES

FINAL EIGHT—#1 Roger Federer; #2 Andy Roddick; #5 Tim Henman; #7 Lleyton Hewitt; #10 Sebastien Grosjean; #12 Sjeng Schalken; plus unseeded Mario Ancic and Florian Mayer.

Quarterfinals

Federer def. Hewitt . . . . .61 67(1) 60 64
Grosjean def. Mayer 75 64 62
Ancic def. Henman . . . . .76(5) 64 62
Roddick def. Schalken . . . . .76(4) 76(9) 63

Semifinals

Federer def. Grosjean . . . . .62 63 76(6)
Roddick def. Ancic 64 46 75 75

Final

Federer def. Roddick . . . . .46 75 76(3) 64

WOMEN'S SINGLES

FINAL EIGHT—#1 Serena Williams; #4 Amelie Mauresmo; #5 Lindsay Davenport; #7 Jennifer Capriati; #9 Paola Suarez; #11 Ai Sugiyama; #13 Maria Sharapova; plus unseeded Karolina Sprem.

Quarterfinals

S. Williams def. Capriati 61 61
Mauresmo def. Suarez 60 57 61
Davenport def. Sprem 62 62
Sharapova def. Sugiyama 57 75 61

Semifinals

S. Williams def. Mauresmo . . . . .67(4) 75 64
Sharapova def. Davenport . . . . .26 76(5) 61

Final

Sharapova def. S. Williams 61 64

DOUBLES FINALS

Men—#1 Jonas Bjorkman & Todd Woodbridge def. #16 Julian Knowle & Nenad Zimonjic, 6-1, 6-4, 4-6, 6-4.

Women—#6 Cara Black & Rennae Stubbs def. #5 Liezel Huber & Ai Sugiyama, 6-3, 7-6 (7-5).

Mixed—Cara Black & Wayne Black def. Alicia Molik & Todd Woodbridge, 3-6, 7-6 (10-8), 6-4.

U.S. Open

MEN'S SINGLES

FINAL EIGHT—#1 Roger Federer; #2 Andy Roddick; #4 Lleyton Hewitt; #5 Tim Henman; #6 Andre Agassi; #22 Dominik Hrbaty; #28 Joachim Johansson; plus unseeded Tommy Haas.

Quarterfinals

Federer def. Agassi 63 26 75 36 63
Johansson def. Roddick 64 64 36 26 64
Hewitt def. Haas 62 62 62
Henman def. Hrbaty 61 75 57 62

Semifinals

Federer def. Henman 63 64 64
Hewitt def. Johansson 64 75 63

Final

Federer def. Hewitt . . . . .60 76(3) 60

WOMEN'S SINGLES

FINAL EIGHT—#2 Amelie Mauresmo; #3 Serena Williams; #5 Lindsay Davenport; #6 Elena Dementieva; #8 Jennifer Capriati; #9 Svetlana Kuznetsova; #14 Nadia Petrova; plus unseeded Shinobu Asagoe.

Quarterfinals

Davenport def. Asagoe 61 61
Kuznetsova def. Petrova . . . . .76(4) 63
Dementieva def. Mauresmo . . . . .46 64 76(1)
Capriati def. S. Williams 26 64 64

Semifinals

Kuznetsova def. Davenport 16 62 64
Dementieva def. Capriati . . . . .60 26 76(5)

Final

Kuznetsova def. Dementieva 63 75

DOUBLES FINALS

Men—#3 Mark Knowles & Daniel Nestor def. #13 Leander Paes & David Rikl, 6-3, 6-3.

Women—#1 Virginia Ruano Pascual & Paola Suarez def. #2 Svetlana Kuznetsova & Elena Likhovtseva, 6-4, 7-5.

Mixed—#4 Vera Zvonareva & Bob Bryan def. #5 Alicia Molik & Todd Woodbridge, 6-3, 6-4.

Fed Cup

Originally the Federation Cup and started in 1963 by the International Tennis Federation as the Davis Cup of women's tennis.

2003 FINAL
France 4, United States 1
at Moscow, Russia (Nov. 22-23)

Singles—Amelie Mauresmo (FRA) def. Lisa Raymond (USA) 6-4, 6-3; Mary Pierce (FRA) def. Meghann Shaughnessy (USA) 6-3, 3-6, 8-6; Mauresmo (FRA) def. Shaughnessy (USA) 6-2, 6-1; Emilie Loit (FRA) def. Alexandra Stevenson (USA) 6-4, 6-2.

Doubles—Martina Navratilova & Raymond (USA) def. Loit & Stephanie Cohen-Aloro (FRA) 6-4, 6-0.

2004 Early Rounds
First Round
(April 24-25)

Winner	Loser
United States 4	at Slovenia 1
at Austria 3	Slovakia 2
at Russia 4	Australia 1
at Argentina 4	Japan 1
at Italy 3	Czech Republic 1

Winner	Loser
at France 5	Germany 0
at Spain 3	Switzerland 2
at Belgium 3	Croatia 2

Quarterfinals
(July 10-11)

Winner	Loser
at Austria 4	United States 1
Russia 4	at Argentina 1
France 3	at Italy 2
at Spain 3	Belgium 2

SEMIFINALS & FINAL

The 2004 Fed Cup semifinals and final were to be held indoors at the brand new 5,200-seat Krylatskoe Ice Stadium in Moscow, Russia from Nov. 22-28. Austria was to play host Russia, while defending champ France was to take on Spain in the semifinals.

Singles Leaders

Official Top 20 rankings and money leaders of men's and women's tours for 2003 and unofficial rankings for 2004 (through Sept. 26), as compiled by the ATP Tour (Association of Tennis Professionals) and WTA (Women's Tennis Association). Note that money lists include doubles earnings.

Final 2003 Rankings and Money Won

Listed are events won and times a finalist and semifinalist (Finish, 1-2-SF), match record (W-L), and earnings for the year.

MEN

		Finish 1-2-SF	W-L	Earnings
1	Andy Roddick	6-2-6	72-19	$3,227,342
2	Roger Federer	7-2-3	78-17	4,000,680
3	Juan Carlos Ferrero	4-3-2	67-21	3,026,760
4	Andre Agassi	4-1-3	47-10	2,530,929
5	Guillermo Coria	5-2-1	61-16	1,971,162
6	Rainer Schuettler	2-2-6	71-30	1,875,002
7	Carlos Moya	3-2-2	58-22	1,322,935
8	David Nalbandian	0-2-2	42-20	1,280,383
9	Mark Philippoussis	1-2-1	38-20	931,963
10	Sebastien Grosjean	0-2-2	36-21	780,607
11	Paradorn Srichaphan	2-1-3	50-28	794,362
12	Jiri Novak	1-2-1	46-27	932,786
13	Younes El Aynaoui	0-1-3	41-25	783,849
14	Tim Henman	2-0-2	31-17	921,609
15	Gustavo Kuerten	2-1-3	41-21	768,447
16	Lleyton Hewitt	2-1-2	37-10	873,598
17	Sjeng Schalken	2-0-1	41-24	736,739
18	Nicolas Massu	2-3-0	36-20	814,391
19	Martin Verkerk	1-1-1	25-25	879,616
20	Mardy Fish	1-3-0	39-25	663,993

WOMEN

		Finish 1-2-SF	W-L	Earnings
1	Justine Henin-Hardenne	8-3-6	75-11	$3,667,430
2	Kim Clijsters	9-6-5	90-12	4,466,345
3	Serena Williams	4-1-2	38-3	2,504,871
4	Amelie Mauresmo	2-4-3	56-16	1,560,341
5	Lindsay Davenport	1-5-3	47-12	1,632,909
6	Jennifer Capriati	1-2-7	42-18	1,942,015
7	Anastasia Myskina	4-1-0	46-22	1,025,355
8	Elena Dementieva	3-0-4	47-24	869,740
9	Chanda Rubin	2-3-2	45-20	945,288
10	Ai Sugiyama	2-0-4	44-24	1,254,283
11	Venus Williams	1-3-0	26-4	1,126,555
12	Nadia Petrova	0-1-4	43-21	686,794
13	Vera Zvonareva	1-0-3	46-24	502,712
14	Paola Suarez	1-0-2	35-22	1,050,691
15	Jelena Dokic	0-1-1	27-30	824,798
16	Anna Smashnova-Pistolesi	2-0-2	35-20	361,297
17	Meghann Shaughnessy	1-0-1	35-25	495,113
18	Conchita Martinez	0-1-1	28-20	496,178
19	Daniela Hantuchova	0-0-1	28-23	579,804
20	Francesca Schiavone	0-1-2	31-24	392,746

2004 Tour Rankings (through Sept. 26)

Listed are tournaments won and times a finalist and semifinalist (Finish, 1-2-SF), match record (W-L), and points earned (Pts). The **ATP Champions Race** replaced the men's pro tennis tour's 27-year-old computer ranking system in 2000. Under the new system players start from zero on Jan. 1 and accumulate points during the calendar year with the player accumulating the most points becoming the World No. 1. Points are awarded in 18 tournaments: nine Tennis Masters Series events, four Grand Slams and five other International Series events. The Tennis Master Cup will count as a 19th tournament for those that qualify.

MEN

Final ATP Tour singles rankings will be based on points earned from 18 tournaments played in 2004. Tournaments, titles and match won-lost records are for 2004 only.

Rank 04	(03)		Finish 1-2-SF	W-L	Pts
1	2	Roger Federer	9-0-0	64-6	1087
2	1	Andy Roddick	4-3-2	66-13	647
3	16	Lleyton Hewitt	4-3-2	60-14	611
4	7	Carlos Moya	3-2-2	56-17	484
5	5	Guillermo Coria	2-4-0	39-11	480
6	14	Tim Henman	0-1-4	39-17	432
7	33	Gaston Gaudio	1-4-0	36-19	383
8	66	Marat Safin	1-2-1	34-18	351
9	4	Andre Agassi	1-0-4	30-11	348
10	10	Sebastien Grosjean	0-1-1	28-15	274
11	8	David Nalbandian	0-1-1	23-10	268
12	21	Tommy Robredo	1-0-3	40-21	267
13	57	Dominik Hrbaty	3-1-1	39-21	262
14	150	Joachim Johansson	1-0-1	27-18	254
15	55	Nicolas Kiefer	0-4-1	37-20	248
16	34	Fernando Gonzalez	1-1-3	42-18	245
17	18	Nicolas Massu	2-0-1	34-22	234
18	38	Juan Ignacio Chela	1-0-1	35-22	225
19	29	Vincent Spadea	1-1-1	34-24	215
20	71	Mario Ancic	0-1-4	27-20	204
—		Tommy Haas	2-0-0	28-18	204

WOMEN

WTA Tour singles ranking system based on total Round and Quality Points for each tournament played during the last 12 months (capped at 17 tournaments). Tournaments, titles and match won-lost records, however, are for 2004 only.

Rank 04	(03)		Finish 1-2-SF	W-L	Pts
1	4	Amelie Mauresmo	3-3-2	50-9	4527
2	5	Lindsay Davenport	6-2-3	55-7	4057
3	1	Justine Henin-Hardenne	5-0-2	35-4	3845
4	7	Anastasia Myskina	2-1-4	42-14	3779
5	36	Svetlana Kuznetsova	3-4-0	54-17	3333
6	8	Elena Dementieva	0-3-3	29-17	3078
7	2	Kim Clijsters	2-1-0	18-1	2689
8	32	Maria Sharapova	2-0-2	37-13	2603
9	6	Jennifer Capriati	0-2-3	28-11	2598
10	3	Serena Williams	2-2-1	36-6	2596
11	13	Vera Zvonareva	1-1-6	47-19	2191
12	11	Venus Williams	2-2-1	38-9	2145
13	12	Nadia Petrova	0-1-3	32-20	2095
14	10	Ai Sugiyama	1-0-1	29-21	1888
15	23	Patty Schnyder	0-0-3	30-18	1674
16	14	Paola Suarez	1-0-2	37-14	1592
17	21	Elena Bovina	1-0-0	24-12	1476
18	59	Karolina Sprem	0-0-3	33-19	1415
19	20	Francesca Schiavone	0-0-2	33-21	1319
20	35	Alicia Molik	1-1-1	34-18	1291

2004 Money Winners

Amounts include singles and doubles earnings through Sept. 26, 2004.

MEN

		Earnings			Earnings			Earnings
1	Roger Federer	$4,753,222	11	Sebastien Grosjean	$755,795	21	Rainer Schuettler	$615,054
2	Andy Roddick	2,081,440	12	Jonas Bjorkman	720,309	22	Michael Llodra	592,057
3	Lleyton Hewitt	1,977,421	13	Fernando Gonzalez	715,951	23	Vincent Spadea	574,855
4	Guillermo Coria	1,607,155	14	David Nalbandian	710,020	24	Mario Ancic	537,220
5	Gaston Gaudio	1,514,589	15	Nicolas Massu	705,333	25	Andrei Pavel	523,444
6	Carlos Moya	1,238,209	16	Juan Ignacio Chela	679,756	26	Xavier Malisse	512,069
7	Tim Henman	1,212,577	17	Fabrice Santoro	673,578	27	Feliciano Lopez	501,377
8	Andre Agassi	1,011,154	18	Joachim Johansson	670,014	28	Daniel Nestor	489,745
9	Marat Safin	961,333	19	Dominik Hrbaty	666,064	29	Max Mirnyi	488,911
10	Tommy Robredo	763,207	20	Nicolas Kiefer	626,439	30	Juan Carlos Ferrero	487,375

WOMEN

		Earnings			Earnings			Earnings
1	Svetlana Kuznetsova	$1,828,878	11	V. Ruano Pascual	$791,454	21	Fabiola Zuluaga	$440,963
2	Lindsay Davenport	1,697,011	12	Venus Williams	755,028	22	Meghann Shaughnessy	425,696
3	Anastasia Myskina	1,481,863	13	Vera Zvonareva	717,649	23	Francesca Schiavone	411,884
4	J. Henin-Hardenne	1,425,406	14	Nadia Petrova	699,285	24	Silvia Farina Elia	405,989
5	Elena Dementieva	1,391,420	15	Elena Likhovtseva	688,762	25	Magdalena Maleeva	403,819
6	Serena Williams	1,317,198	16	Ai Sugiyama	646,011	26	Nathalie Dechy	393,758
7	Amelie Mauresmo	1,299,236	17	Kim Clijsters	596,116	27	Conchita Martinez	391,680
8	Maria Sharapova	1,297,380	18	Patty Schnyder	543,607	28	Alicia Molik	379,725
9	Paola Suarez	1,157,526	19	Cara Black	520,120	29	Elena Daniilidou	369,212
10	Jennifer Capriati	809,961	20	Lisa Raymond	447,253	30	Karolina Sprem	359,443

Davis Cup

Mark Philippoussis' thrilling five-set victory over Juan Carlos Ferrero lifted Australia to its 22nd Davis Cup title and first since 1999 (Australasia also won six titles from 1907-1919). A shoulder injury nearly forced Philippoussis to retire after the fourth set, but he battled through the pain to shut Ferrero out in the fifth set, 6-0, and clinch the victory for his team.

2003 FINAL
Australia 3, Spain 1
at Melbourne, Australia (Nov. 28-30)

Day One—Lleyton Hewitt (AUS) def. Juan Carlos Ferrero (ESP) 3-6, 6-3, 3-6, 7-6 (7-0), 6-2; Carlos Moya (ESP) def. Mark Philippoussis (AUS) 6-4, 6-4, 4-6, 7-6 (7-4).

Day Two—Wayne Arthurs & Todd Woodbridge (AUS) def. Alex Corretja & Feliciano Lopez (ESP) 6-3, 6-1, 6-3.

Day Three—Philippoussis (AUS) def. Ferrero (ESP) 7-5, 6-3, 1-6, 2-6, 6-0; Hewitt (AUS) vs. Moya (ESP) not played.

2004 Early Rounds
FIRST ROUND
(Feb. 6-8)

Winner	Loser
at United States 5	Austria 0
Sweden 4	at Australia 1
at Belarus 3	Russia 2
Argentina 5	at Morocco 0
Switzerland 3	at Romania 2
at France 4	Croatia 1
at Netherlands 4	Canada 1
Spain 3	at Czech Republic 2

QUARTERFINALS
(Apr. 9-11)

Winner	Loser
at United States 4	Sweden 1
at Belarus 5	Argentina 0
France 3	at Switzerland 2
at Spain 4	Netherlands 1

SEMIFINALS
United States 4, Belarus 0
at Charleston, S.C. (Sept. 24-26)

Day One—Andy Roddick (USA) def. Vladimir Voltchkov (BLR) 6-1, 6-4, 6-4; Mardy Fish (USA) def. Max Mirnyi (BLR) 7-5, 6-2, 3-6, 6-3.

Day Two—Bob Bryan & Mike Bryan (USA) def. Mirnyi & Voltchkov (BLR) 6-1, 6-3, 7-5.

Day Three—Roddick (USA) def. Alexander Skrypko (BLR) 6-4, 6-2; Fish (USA) vs. Andrei Karatchenia (BLR) was called off due to rain with Fish leading 3-0 in the first set.

Spain 4, France 1
at Alicante, Spain (Sept. 24-26)

Day One—Paul-Henri Mathieu (FRA) def. Carlos Moya (ESP) 6-3, 3-6, 2-6, 6-3, 6-3; Juan Carlos Ferrero (ESP) def. Fabrice Santoro (FRA) 6-3, 6-1, 1-6, 6-3.

Day Two—Rafael Nadal & Tommy Robredo (ESP) def. Michael Llodra & Arnaud Clement (FRA) 7-6 (7-4), 4-6, 6-2, 2-6, 6-3.

Day Three—Nadal (ESP) def. Clement (FRA) 6-4, 6-1, 6-2; Robredo (ESP) def. Mathieu (FRA) 6-4, 6-4.

2004 FINAL

The 2004 Davis Cup final between the United States and Spain was to be held from Dec. 3-5 on the clay courts of the Olympic Stadium of La Cartuja in Seville, Spain. The two nations have never met in a David Cup final. Host Spain, the 2003 runner-up, last won a Davis Cup title in 2000, while the Americans' last win was in 1995.

1877-2004
Through the Years

Grand Slam Championships
Australian Open
MEN

Became an Open Championship in 1969. Two tournaments were held in 1977; the first in January, the second in December. Tournament moved back to January in 1987, so no championship was decided in 1986. **Surface:** Synpave Rebound Ace (hardcourt surface composed of polyurethane and synthetic rubber).

Multiple winners: Roy Emerson (6); Andre Agassi, Jack Crawford and Ken Rosewall (4); James Anderson, Rod Laver, Adrian Quist, Mats Wilander and Pat Wood (3); Boris Becker, Jack Bromwich, Ashley Cooper, Jim Courier, Stefan Edberg, Rodney Heath, Johan Kriek, Ivan Lendl, John Newcombe, Pete Sampras, Frank Sedgman, Guillermo Vilas and Tony Wilding (2).

Year	Winner	Loser	Score
1905	Rodney Heath	A. Curtis	46 63 64 64
1906	Tony Wilding	H. Parker	60 64 64
1907	Horace Rice	H. Parker	63 64 64
1908	Fred Alexander	A. Dunlop	36 36 60 62 63
1909	Tony Wilding	E. Parker	61 75 62
1910	Rodney Heath	H. Rice	64 63 62
1911	Norman Brookes	H. Rice	61 62 63
1912	J. Cecil Parke	A. Beamish	36 63 16 61 75
1913	Ernie Parker	H. Parker	26 61 62 63
1914	Pat Wood	G. Patterson	64 63 57 61
1915	Gordon Lowe	H. Rice	46 61 61 64
1916-18 Not held World War I.			
1919	A.R.F. Kingscote	E. Pockley	64 60 63
1920	Pat Wood	R. Thomas	63 46 68 61 63
1921	Rhys Gemmell	A. Hedeman	75 61 64
1922	James Anderson	G. Patterson	60 36 36 63 62
1923	Pat Wood	C.B. St. John	61 61 63
1924	James Anderson	R. Schlesinger	63 64 36 57 63
1925	James Anderson	G. Patterson	11-9 26 62 63
1926	John Hawkes	J. Willard	61 63 61
1927	Gerald Patterson	J. Hawkes	36 64 36 18-16 63
1928	Jean Borotra	R.O. Cummings	64 61 46 57 63
1929	John Gregory	R. Schlesinger	62 62 57 75
1930	Gar Moon	H. Hopman	63 61 63
1931	Jack Crawford	H. Hopman	64 62 26 61
1932	Jack Crawford	H. Hopman	46 63 36 63 61
1933	Jack Crawford	K. Gledhill	26 75 63 62
1934	Fred Perry	J. Crawford	63 75 61
1935	Jack Crawford	F. Perry	26 64 64 64
1936	Adrian Quist	J. Crawford	62 63 46 36 97
1937	Viv McGrath	J. Bromwich	63 16 60 26 61
1938	Don Budge	J. Bromwich	64 62 61
1939	Jack Bromwich	A. Quist	64 61 63
1940	Adrian Quist	J. Crawford	63 61 62
1941-45 Not held World War II.			
1946	Jack Bromwich	D. Pails	57 63 75 36 62
1947	Dinny Pails	J. Bromwich	46 64 36 75 86
1948	Adrian Quist	J. Bromwich	64 36 63 26 63
1949	Frank Sedgman	J. Bromwich	63 63 62
1950	Frank Sedgman	K. McGregor	63 64 46 61
1951	Dick Savitt	K. McGregor	63 26 63 61
1952	Ken McGregor	F. Sedgman	75 12-10 26 62
1953	Ken Rosewall	M. Rose	60 63 64
1954	Mervyn Rose	R. Hartwig	62 06 64 62
1955	Ken Rosewall	L. Hoad	97 64 64
1956	Lew Hoad	K. Rosewall	64 36 64 75
1957	Ashley Cooper	N. Fraser	63 9-11 64 62
1958	Ashley Cooper	M. Anderson	75 63 64
1959	Alex Olmedo	N. Fraser	61 62 36 63
1960	Rod Laver	N. Fraser	57 36 63 86 86
1961	Roy Emerson	R. Laver	16 63 75 64
1962	Rod Laver	R. Emerson	86 06 64 64
1963	Roy Emerson	K. Fletcher	63 63 61
1964	Roy Emerson	F. Stolle	63 64 62
1965	Roy Emerson	F. Stolle	79 26 64 75 61
1966	Roy Emerson	A. Ashe	64 68 62 63
1967	Roy Emerson	A. Ashe	64 61 61
1968	Bill Bowrey	J. Gisbert	75 26 97 64
1969	Rod Laver	A. Gimeno	63 64 75
1970	Arthur Ashe	D. Crealy	64 97 62
1971	Ken Rosewall	A. Ashe	61 75 63
1972	Ken Rosewall	M. Anderson	76 63 75
1973	John Newcombe	O. Parun	63 67 75 61
1974	Jimmy Connors	P. Dent	76 64 46 63
1975	John Newcombe	J. Connors	75 36 64 75
1976	Mark Edmondson	J. Newcombe	67 63 76 61
1977	Roscoe Tanner	G. Vilas	63 63 63
	Vitas Gerulaitis	J. Lloyd	63 76 57 36 62
1978	Guillermo Vilas	J. Marks	64 64 36 63
1979	Guillermo Vilas	J. Sadri	76 63 62
1980	Brian Teacher	K. Warwick	75 76 63
1981	Johan Kriek	S. Denton	62 76 67 64
1982	Johan Kriek	S. Denton	63 63 62
1983	Mats Wilander	I. Lendl	61 64 64
1984	Mats Wilander	K. Curren	67 64 76 62
1985	Stefan Edberg	M. Wilander	64 63 63
1986 Not held			
1987	Stefan Edberg	P. Cash	63 64 36 57 63
1988	Mats Wilander	P. Cash	63 67 36 61 86
1989	Ivan Lendl	M. Mecir	62 62 62
1990	Ivan Lendl	S. Edberg	46 76 52 (ret.)
1991	Boris Becker	I. Lendl	16 64 64 64
1992	Jim Courier	S. Edberg	63 36 64 62
1993	Jim Courier	S. Edberg	62 61 26 75
1994	Pete Sampras	T. Martin	76 64 64
1995	Andre Agassi	P. Sampras	46 61 76 64
1996	Boris Becker	M. Chang	62 64 26 62
1997	Pete Sampras	C. Moya	62 63 63
1998	Petr Korda	M. Rios	62 62 62
1999	Yevgeny Kafelnikov	T. Enqvist	46 60 63 76
2000	Andre Agassi	Y. Kafelnikov	36 63 62 64
2001	Andre Agassi	A. Clement	64 62 62
2002	Thomas Johansson	M. Safin	36 64 64 76
2003	Andre Agassi	R. Schuettler	62 62 61
2004	Roger Federer	M. Safin	76 64 62

WOMEN

Became an Open Championship in 1969. Two tournaments were held in 1977, the first in January, the second in December. Tournament moved back to January in 1987, so no championship was decided in 1986.

Multiple winners: Margaret Smith Court (11); Nancye Wynne Bolton (6); Daphne Akhurst (5); Evonne Goolagong Cawley, Steffi Graf and Monica Seles (4); Joan Hartigan, Martina Hingis and Martina Navratilova (3); Coral Buttsworth, Jennifer Capriati, Chris Evert Lloyd, Thelma Long, Hana Mandlikova, Mall Molesworth and Mary Carter Reitano (2).

Year	Winner	Loser	Score	Year	Winner	Loser	Score
1922	Mall Molesworth	E. Boyd	63 10-8	1966	Margaret Smith	N. Richey	walkover
1923	Mall Molesworth	E. Boyd	61 75	1967	Nancy Richey	L. Turner	61 64
1924	Sylvia Lance	E. Boyd	63 36 64	1968	Billie Jean King	M. Smith	61 62
1925	Daphne Akhurst	E. Boyd	16 86 64	1969	Margaret Court	B.J. King	64 61
1926	Daphne Akhurst	E. Boyd	61 63	1970	Margaret Court	K. Melville	61 63
1927	Esna Boyd	S. Harper	57 61 62	1971	Margaret Court	E. Goolagong	26 76 75
1928	Daphne Akhurst	E. Boyd	75 62	1972	Virginia Wade	E. Goolagong	64 64
1929	Daphne Akhurst	L. Bickerton	61 57 62	1973	Margaret Court	E. Goolagong	64 75
1930	Daphne Akhurst	S. Harper	10-8 26 75	1974	Evonne Goolagong	C. Evert	76 46 60
1931	Coral Buttsworth	M. Crawford	16 63 64	1975	Evonne Goolagong	M. Navratilova	63 62
1932	Coral Buttsworth	K. Le Messurier	97 64	1976	Evonne Cawley	R. Tomanova	62 62
1933	Joan Hartigan	C. Buttsworth	64 63	1977	Kerry Reid	D. Balestrat	75 62
1934	Joan Hartigan	M. Molesworth	61 64		Evonne Cawley	H. Gourlay	63 60
1935	Dorothy Round	N. Lyle	16 61 63	1978	Chris O'Neil	B. Nagelsen	63 76
1936	Joan Hartigan	N. Wynne	64 64	1979	Barbara Jordan	S. Walsh	63 63
1937	Nancye Wynne	E. Westacott	63 57 64	1980	Hana Mandlikova	W. Turnbull	60 75
1938	Dorothy Bundy	D. Stevenson	63 62	1981	Martina Navratilova	C. Evert Lloyd	67 64 75
1939	Emily Westacott	N. Hopman	61 62	1982	Chris Evert Lloyd	M. Navratilova	63 26 63
1940	Nancye Wynne	T. Coyne	57 64 60	1983	Martina Navratilova	K. Jordan	62 76
1941-45 Not held World War II				1984	Chris Evert Lloyd	H. Sukova	67 61 63
1946	Nancye Bolton	J. Fitch	64 64	1985	Martina Navratilova	C. Evert Lloyd	62 46 62
1947	Nancye Bolton	N. Hopman	63 62	1986 Not held			
1948	Nancye Bolton	M. Toomey	63 61	1987	Hana Mandlikova	M. Navratilova	75 76
1949	Doris Hart	N. Bolton	63 64	1988	Steffi Graf	C. Evert	61 76
1950	Louise Brough	D. Hart	64 36 64	1989	Steffi Graf	H. Sukova	64 64
1951	Nancye Bolton	T. Long	61 75	1990	Steffi Graf	M.J. Fernandez	63 64
1952	Thelma Long	H. Angwin	62 63	1991	Monica Seles	J. Novotna	57 63 61
1953	Maureen Connolly	J. Sampson	63 62	1992	Monica Seles	M.J. Fernandez	62 63
1954	Thelma Long	J. Staley	63 64	1993	Monica Seles	S. Graf	46 63 62
1955	Beryl Penrose	T. Long	64 63	1994	Steffi Graf	A.S. Vicario	60 62
1956	Mary Carter	T. Long	36 62 97	1995	Mary Pierce	A.S. Vicario	63 62
1957	Shirley Fry	A. Gibson	63 64	1996	Monica Seles	A. Huber	64 61
1958	Angela Mortimer	L. Coghlan	63 64	1997	Martina Hingis	M. Pierce	62 62
1959	Mary Reitano	R. Schuurman	62 63	1998	Martina Hingis	C. Martinez	63 63
1960	Margaret Smith	J. Lehane	75 62	1999	Martina Hingis	A. Mauresmo	62 63
1961	Margaret Smith	J. Lehane	61 64	2000	Lindsay Davenport	M. Hingis	61 75
1962	Margaret Smith	J. Lehane	60 62	2001	Jennifer Capriati	M. Hingis	64 63
1963	Margaret Smith	J. Lehane	62 62	2002	Jennifer Capriati	M. Hingis	46 76 62
1964	Margaret Smith	L. Turner	63 62	2003	Serena Williams	V. Williams	76 36 64
1965	Margaret Smith	M. Bueno	57 64 52 (ret)	2004	J. Henin-Hardenne	K. Clijsters	63 46 63

French Open
MEN

From 1891 to 1925, entry was restricted to members of French clubs. Became an Open Championship in 1968, but closed to contract pros in 1972. Note that Max Decugis won eight tournaments before 1925 (1903-04, 1907-09, 1912-14) to lead all men. **Surface:** Red clay.

Multiple winners (since 1925): Bjorn Borg (6); Henri Cochet (4); Gustavo Kuerten, Rene Lacoste, Ivan Lendl and Mats Wilander (3); Sergi Bruguera, Jim Courier, Jaroslav Drobny, Roy Emerson, Jan Kodes, Rod Laver, Frank Parker, Nicola Pietrangeli, Ken Rosewall, Manuel Santana, Tony Trabert and Gottfried von Cramm (2).

Year	Winner	Loser	Score	Year	Winner	Loser	Score
1925	Rene Lacoste	J. Borotra	75 61 64	1938	Don Budge	R. Menzel	63 62 64
1926	Henri Cochet	R. Lacoste	62 64 63	1939	Don McNeill	B. Riggs	75 60 63
1927	Rene Lacoste	B. Tilden	64 46 57 63 11-9	1940-45 Not held World War II			
1928	Henri Cochet	R. Lacoste	57 63 61 63	1946	Marcel Bernard	J. Drobny	36 26 61 64 63
1929	Rene Lacoste	J. Borotra	63 26 60 26 86	1947	Joseph Asboth	E. Sturgess	86 75 64
1930	Henri Cochet	B. Tilden	36 86 63 61	1948	Frank Parker	J. Drobny	64 75 57 86
1931	Jean Borotra	C. Boussus	26 86 63 61	1949	Frank Parker	B. Patty	63 16 61 64
1932	Henri Cochet	G. de Stefani	60 64 46 63	1950	Budge Patty	J. Drobny	61 62 36 57 75
1933	Jack Crawford	H. Cochet	86 61 63	1951	Jaroslav Drobny	E. Sturgess	63 63 63
1934	Gottfried von Cramm	J. Crawford	64 79 36 75 63	1952	Jaroslav Drobny	F. Sedgman	62 60 36 64
1935	Fred Perry	G. von Cramm	63 36 61 63	1953	Ken Rosewall	V. Seixas	63 64 16 62
1936	Gottfried von Cramm	F. Perry	60 26 62 26 60	1954	Tony Trabert	A. Larsen	64 75 61
1937	Henner Henkel	H. Austin	61 64 63	1955	Tony Trabert	S. Davidson	26 61 64 62

Year	Winner	Loser	Score
1956	Lew Hoad	S. Davidson	64 86 63
1957	Sven Davidson	H. Flam	63 64 64
1958	Mervyn Rose	L. Ayala	63 64 64
1959	Nicola Pietrangeli	I. Vermaak	36 63 64 61
1960	Nicola Pietrangeli	L. Ayala	36 63 64 46 63
1961	Manuel Santana	N. Pietrangeli	46 61 36 60 62
1962	Rod Laver	R. Emerson	36 26 63 97 62
1963	Roy Emerson	P. Darmon	36 61 64 64
1964	Manuel Santana	N. Pietrangeli	63 61 46 75
1965	Fred Stolle	T. Roche	36 60 62 63
1966	Tony Roche	I. Gulyas	61 64 75
1967	Roy Emerson	T. Roche	61 64 26 62
1968	Ken Rosewall	R. Laver	63 61 26 62
1969	Rod Laver	K. Rosewall	64 63 64
1970	Jan Kodes	Z. Franulovic	62 64 60
1971	Jan Kodes	I. Nastase	86 62 26 75
1972	Andres Gimeno	P. Proisy	46 63 61 61
1973	Ilie Nastase	N. Pilic	63 63 60
1974	Bjorn Borg	M. Orantes	26 67 60 61 61
1975	Bjorn Borg	G. Vilas	62 63 64
1976	Adriano Panatta	H. Solomon	61 64 46 76
1977	Guillermo Vilas	B. Gottfried	60 63 60
1978	Bjorn Borg	G. Vilas	61 61 63
1979	Bjorn Borg	V. Pecci	63 61 67 64
1980	Bjorn Borg	V. Gerulaitis	64 61 62
1981	Bjorn Borg	I. Lendl	61 46 62 36 61
1982	Mats Wilander	G. Vilas	16 76 60 64
1983	Yannick Noah	M. Wilander	62 75 76
1984	Ivan Lendl	J. McEnroe	36 26 64 75 75
1985	Mats Wilander	I. Lendl	36 64 62 62
1986	Ivan Lendl	M. Pernfors	63 62 64
1987	Ivan Lendl	M. Wilander	75 62 36 76
1988	Mats Wilander	H. Leconte	75 62 61
1989	Michael Chang	S. Edberg	61 36 46 64 62
1990	Andres Gomez	A. Agassi	63 26 64 64
1991	Jim Courier	A. Agassi	36 64 26 61 64
1992	Jim Courier	P. Korda	75 62 61
1993	Sergi Bruguera	J. Courier	64 26 62 36 63
1994	Sergi Bruguera	A. Berasategui	63 75 26 61
1995	Thomas Muster	M. Chang	75 62 64
1996	Yevgeny Kafelnikov	M. Stich	76 75 76
1997	Gustavo Kuerten	S. Bruguera	63 64 62
1998	Carlos Moya	A. Corretja	63 75 63
1999	Andre Agassi	A. Medvedev	16 26 64 63 64
2000	Gustavo Kuerten	M. Norman	62 63 26 76
2001	Gustavo Kuerten	A. Corretja	67 75 62 60
2002	Albert Costa	J. C. Ferrero	61 60 46 63
2003	Juan Carlos Ferrero	M. Verkerk	61 63 62
2004	Gaston Gaudio	G. Coria	06 36 64 61 86

WOMEN

From 1897 to 1925, entry was restricted to members of French clubs. Became an Open Championship in 1968, but closed to contract pros in 1972. Note that Suzanne Lenglen won two titles prior to 1925, giving her six total.

Multiple winners (since 1925): Chris Evert Lloyd (7); Steffi Graf (6); Margaret Smith Court (5); Helen Wills Moody (4); Arantxa Sanchez Vicario, Monica Seles and Hilde Sperling (3); Maureen Connolly, Margaret Osborne du Pont, Doris Hart, Ann Haydon Jones, Suzanne Lenglen, Simone Mathieu, Margaret Scriven, Martina Navratilova and Lesley Turner (2).

Year	Winner	Loser	Score
1925	Suzanne Lenglen	K. McKane	61 62
1926	Suzanne Lenglen	M. Browne	61 60
1927	Kea Bouman	I. Peacock	62 64
1928	Helen Wills	E. Bennett	61 62
1929	Helen Wills	S. Mathieu	63 64
1930	Helen Moody	H. Jacobs	62 61
1931	Cilly Aussem	B. Nuthall	86 61
1932	Helen Moody	S. Mathieu	75 61
1933	Margaret Scriven	S. Mathieu	62 46 64
1934	Margaret Scriven	H. Jacobs	75 46 61
1935	Hilde Sperling	S. Mathieu	62 61
1936	Hilde Sperling	S. Mathieu	63 64
1937	Hilde Sperling	S. Mathieu	62 64
1938	Simone Mathieu	N. Landry	60 63
1939	Simone Mathieu	J. Jedrzejowska	63 86
1940-45	Not held World War II		
1946	Margaret Osborne	P. Betz	16 86 75
1947	Patricia Todd	D. Hart	63 36 64
1948	Nelly Landry	S. Fry	62 06 60
1949	Margaret du Pont	N. Adamson	75 62
1950	Doris Hart	P. Todd	64 46 62
1951	Shirley Fry	D. Hart	63 36 63
1952	Doris Hart	S. Fry	64 64
1953	Maureen Connolly	D. Hart	62 64
1954	Maureen Connolly	G. Bucaille	64 61
1955	Angela Mortimer	D. Knode	26 75 10-8
1956	Althea Gibson	A. Mortimer	60 12-10
1957	Shirley Bloomer	D. Knode	61 63
1958	Suzi Kormoczi	S. Bloomer	64 16 62
1959	Christine Truman	S. Kormoczi	64 75
1960	Darlene Hard	Y. Ramirez	63 64
1961	Ann Haydon	Y. Ramirez	62 61
1962	Margaret Smith	L. Turner	63 36 75
1963	Lesley Turner	A. Jones	26 63 75
1964	Margaret Smith	M. Bueno	57 61 62
1965	Lesley Turner	M. Smith	63 64
1966	Ann Jones	N. Richey	63 61
1967	Francoise Durr	L. Turner	46 63 64
1968	Nancy Richey	A. Jones	57 64 61
1969	Margaret Court	A. Jones	61 46 63
1970	Margaret Court	H. Niessen	62 64
1971	Evonne Goolagong	H. Gourlay	63 75
1972	Billie Jean King	E. Goolagong	63 63
1973	Margaret Court	C. Evert	67 76 64
1974	Chris Evert	O. Morozova	61 62
1975	Chris Evert	M. Navratilova	26 62 61
1976	Sue Barker	R. Tomanova	62 06 62
1977	Mima Jausovec	F. Mihai	62 67 61
1978	Virginia Ruzici	M. Jausovec	62 62
1979	Chris Evert Lloyd	W. Turnbull	62 60
1980	Chris Evert Lloyd	V. Ruzici	60 63
1981	Hana Mandlikova	S. Hanika	62 64
1982	Martina Navratilova	A. Jaeger	76 61
1983	Chris Evert Lloyd	M. Jausovec	61 62
1984	Martina Navratilova	C. Evert Lloyd	63 61
1985	Chris Evert Lloyd	M. Navratilova	63 67 75
1986	Chris Evert Lloyd	M. Navratilova	26 63 63
1987	Steffi Graf	M. Navratilova	64 46 86
1988	Steffi Graf	N. Zvereva	60 60
1989	A. Sanchez Vicario	S. Graf	76 36 75
1990	Monica Seles	S. Graf	76 64
1991	Monica Seles	A.S. Vicario	63 64
1992	Monica Seles	S. Graf	62 36 10-8
1993	Steffi Graf	M.J. Fernandez	46 62 64
1994	A. Sanchez Vicario	M. Pierce	64 64
1995	Steffi Graf	A.S. Vicario	76 46 60
1996	Steffi Graf	A.S. Vicario	63 67 10-8
1997	Iva Majoli	M. Hingis	64 62
1998	A. Sanchez Vicario	M. Seles	76 06 62
1999	Steffi Graf	M. Hingis	46 75 62
2000	Mary Pierce	C. Martinez	62 75
2001	Jennifer Capriati	K. Clijsters	16 64 1210
2002	Serena Williams	V. Williams	75 63
2003	J. Henin-Hardenne	K. Clijsters	60 64
2004	Anastasia Myskina	E. Dementieva	61 62

Wimbledon
MEN

Officially called "The Lawn Tennis Championships" at the All England Club, Wimbledon. Challenge round system (defending champion qualified for following year's final) used from 1877-1921. Became an Open Championship in 1968, but closed to contract pros in 1972. **Surface:** Grass.

Multiple winners: Willie Renshaw and Pete Sampras (7); Bjorn Borg and Laurie Doherty (5); Reggie Doherty, Rod Laver and Tony Wilding (4); Wilfred Baddeley, Boris Becker, Arthur Gore, John McEnroe, John Newcombe, Fred Perry and Bill Tilden (3); Jean Borotra, Norman Brookes, Don Budge, Henri Cochet, Jimmy Connors, Stefan Edberg, Roy Emerson, Roger Federer, John Hartley, Lew Hoad, Rene Lacoste, Gerald Patterson and Joshua Pim (2).

Year	Winner	Loser	Score	Year	Winner	Loser	Score
1877	Spencer Gore	W. Marshall	61 62 64	1940-45	Not held World War II		
1878	Frank Hadow	S. Gore	75 61 97	1946	Yvon Petra	G. Brown	62 64 79 57 64
1879	John Hartley	V. St. L. Goold	62 64 62	1947	Jack Kramer	T. Brown	61 63 62
1880	John Hartley	H. Lawford	60 62 26 63	1948	Bob Falkenburg	J. Bromwich	75 06 62 36 75
1881	Willie Renshaw	J. Hartley	60 61 61	1949	Ted Schroeder	J. Drobny	36 60 63 46 64
1882	Willie Renshaw	E. Renshaw	61 26 46 62 62	1950	Budge Patty	F. Sedgman	61 8-10 62 63
1883	Willie Renshaw	E. Renshaw	26 63 63 46 63	1951	Dick Savitt	K. McGregor	64 64 64
1884	Willie Renshaw	H. Lawford	60 64 97	1952	Frank Sedgman	J. Drobny	46 62 63 62
1885	Willie Renshaw	H. Lawford	75 62 46 75	1953	Vic Seixas	K. Nielsen	97 63 64
1886	Willie Renshaw	H. Lawford	60 57 63 64	1954	Jaroslav Drobny	K. Rosewall	13-11 46 62 97
1887	Herbert Lawford	E. Renshaw	16 63 36 64 64	1955	Tony Trabert	K. Nielsen	63 75 61
1888	Ernest Renshaw	H. Lawford	63 75 60	1956	Lew Hoad	K. Rosewall	62 46 75 64
1889	Willie Renshaw	E. Renshaw	64 61 36 60	1957	Lew Hoad	A. Cooper	62 61 62
1890	Willoughby Hamilton	W. Renshaw	68 62 36 61 61	1958	Ashley Cooper	N. Fraser	36 63 64 13-11
1891	Wilfred Baddeley	J. Pim	64 16 75 60	1959	Alex Olmedo	R. Laver	64 63 64
1892	Wilfred Baddeley	J. Pim	46 63 63 62	1960	Neale Fraser	R. Laver	64 36 97 75
1893	Joshua Pim	W. Baddeley	36 61 63 62	1961	Rod Laver	C. McKinley	63 61 64
1894	Joshua Pim	W. Baddeley	10-8 62 86	1962	Rod Laver	M. Mulligan	62 62 61
1895	Wilfred Baddeley	W. Eaves	46 28 86 62 63	1963	Chuck McKinley	F. Stolle	97 61 64
1896	Harold Mahony	W. Baddeley	62 68 57 86 63	1964	Roy Emerson	F. Stolle	64 12-10 46 63
1897	Reggie Doherty	H. Mahony	64 64 63	1965	Roy Emerson	F. Stolle	62 64 64
1898	Reggie Doherty	L. Doherty	63 63 26 57 61	1966	Manuel Santana	D. Ralston	64 11-9 64
1899	Reggie Doherty	A. Gore	16 46 62 63 63	1967	John Newcombe	W. Bungert	63 61 61
1900	Reggie Doherty	S. Smith	68 63 61 62	1968	Rod Laver	T. Roche	63 64 62
1901	Arthur Gore	R. Doherty	46 75 64 64	1969	Rod Laver	J. Newcombe	64 57 64 64
1902	Laurie Doherty	A. Gore	64 63 36 60	1970	John Newcombe	K. Rosewall	57 63 62 36 61
1903	Laurie Doherty	F. Riseley	75 63 60	1971	John Newcombe	S. Smith	63 57 26 64 64
1904	Laurie Doherty	F. Riseley	61 75 86	1972	Stan Smith	I. Nastase	46 63 63 46 75
1905	Laurie Doherty	N. Brookes	86 62 64	1973	Jan Kodes	A. Metreveli	61 98 63
1906	Laurie Doherty	F. Riseley	64 46 62 63	1974	Jimmy Connors	K. Rosewall	61 61 64
1907	Norman Brookes	A. Gore	64 62 62	1975	Arthur Ashe	J. Connors	61 61 57 64
1908	Arthur Gore	R. Barrett	63 62 46 36 64	1976	Bjorn Borg	I. Nastase	64 62 97
1909	Arthur Gore	M. Ritchie	68 16 62 62 62	1977	Bjorn Borg	J. Connors	36 62 61 57 64
1910	Tony Wilding	A. Gore	64 75 46 62	1978	Bjorn Borg	J. Connors	62 62 63
1911	Tony Wilding	R. Barrett	64 46 26 62 (ret)	1979	Bjorn Borg	R. Tanner	67 61 36 63 64
1912	Tony Wilding	A. Gore	64 64 46 64	1980	Bjorn Borg	J. McEnroe	16 75 63 67 86
1913	Tony Wilding	M. McLoughlin	86 63 10-8	1981	John McEnroe	B. Borg	46 76 76 64
1914	Norman Brookes	T. Wilding	64 64 75	1982	Jimmy Connors	J. McEnroe	36 63 67 76 64
1915-18	Not held World War I			1983	John McEnroe	C. Lewis	62 62 62
1919	Gerald Patterson	N. Brookes	63 75 62	1984	John McEnroe	J. Connors	61 61 62
1920	Bill Tilden	G. Patterson	26 63 62 64	1985	Boris Becker	K. Curren	63 67 76 64
1921	Bill Tilden	B. Norton	46 26 61 60 75	1986	Boris Becker	I. Lendl	64 63 75
1922	Gerald Patterson	R. Lycett	63 64 62	1987	Pat Cash	I. Lendl	76 62 75
1923	Bill Johnston	F. Hunter	60 63 61	1988	Stefan Edberg	B. Becker	46 76 64 62
1924	Jean Borotra	R. Lacoste	61 36 61 36 64	1989	Boris Becker	S. Edberg	60 76 64
1925	Rene Lacoste	J. Borotra	63 63 46 86	1990	Stefan Edberg	B. Becker	62 62 36 36 64
1926	Jean Borotra	H. Kinsey	86 61 63	1991	Michael Stich	B. Becker	64 76 64
1927	Henri Cochet	J. Borotra	46 46 63 64 75	1992	Andre Agassi	G. Ivanisevic	67 64 64 16 64
1928	Rene Lacoste	H. Cochet	61 46 64 62	1993	Pete Sampras	J. Courier	76 76 36 63
1929	Henri Cochet	J. Borotra	64 63 64	1994	Pete Sampras	G. Ivanisevic	76 76 60
1930	Bill Tilden	W. Allison	63 97 64	1995	Pete Sampras	B. Becker	67 62 64 62
1931	Sidney Wood	F. Shields	walkover	1996	Richard Krajicek	M. Washington	63 64 63
1932	Ellsworth Vines	H. Austin	64 62 60	1997	Pete Sampras	C. Pioline	64 62 64
1933	Jack Crawford	E. Vines	46 11-9 62 26 64	1998	Pete Sampras	G. Ivanisevic	67 76 64 36 62
1934	Fred Perry	J. Crawford	63 60 75	1999	Pete Sampras	A. Agassi	63 64 75
1935	Fred Perry	G. von Cramm	62 64 64	2000	Pete Sampras	P. Rafter	67 76 64 62
1936	Fred Perry	G. von Cramm	61 61 60	2001	Goran Ivanisevic	P. Rafter	63 36 63 26 97
1937	Don Budge	G. von Cramm	63 64 62	2002	Lleyton Hewitt	D. Nalbandian	61 63 62
1938	Don Budge	H. Austin	61 60 63	2003	Roger Federer	M. Philippoussis	76 62 76
1939	Bobby Riggs	E. Cooke	26 86 36 63 62	2004	Roger Federer	A. Roddick	46 75 76 64

WOMEN

Officially called "The Lawn Tennis Championships" at the All England Club, Wimbledon. Challenge round system (defending champion qualified for following year's final) used from 1877-1921. Became an Open Championship in 1968, but closed to contract pros in 1972.

Multiple winners: Martina Navratilova (9); Helen Wills Moody (8); Dorothea Douglass Chambers and Steffi Graf (7); Blanche Bingley Hillyard, Billie Jean King and Suzanne Lenglen (6); Lottie Dod and Charlotte Cooper Sterry (5); Louise Brough (4); Maria Bueno, Maureen Connolly, Margaret Smith Court and Chris Evert Lloyd (3); Evonne Goolagong Cawley, Althea Gibson, Kitty McKane Godfree, Dorothy Round, May Sutton, Maud Watson, Serena Williams and Venus Williams (2).

Year	Winner	Loser	Score	Year	Winner	Loser	Score
1884	Maud Watson	L. Watson	68 63 63	1949	Louise Brough	M. du Pont	10-8 16 10-8
1885	Maud Watson	B. Bingley	61 75	1950	Louise Brough	M. du Pont	61 36 61
1886	Blanche Bingley	M. Watson	63 63	1951	Doris Hart	S. Fry	61 60
1887	Lottie Dod	B. Bingley	62 60	1952	Maureen Connolly	L. Brough	75 63
1888	Lottie Dod	B. Hillyard	63 63	1953	Maureen Connolly	D. Hart	86 75
1889	Blanche Hillyard	L. Rice	46 86 64	1954	Maureen Connolly	L. Brough	62 75
1890	Lena Rice	M. Jacks	64 61	1955	Louise Brough	B. Fleitz	75 86
1891	Lottie Dod	B. Hillyard	62 61	1956	Shirley Fry	A. Buxton	63 61
1892	Lottie Dod	B. Hillyard	61 61	1957	Althea Gibson	D. Hard	63 62
1893	Lottie Dod	B. Hillyard	68 61 64	1958	Althea Gibson	A. Mortimer	86 62
1894	Blanche Hillyard	E. Austin	61 61	1959	Maria Bueno	D. Hard	64 63
1895	Charlotte Cooper	H. Jackson	75 86	1960	Maria Bueno	S. Reynolds	86 60
1896	Charlotte Cooper	A. Pickering	62 63	1961	Angela Mortimer	C. Truman	46 64 75
1897	Blanche Hillyard	C. Cooper	57 75 62	1962	Karen Susman	V. Sukova	64 64
1898	Charlotte Cooper	L. Martin	64 64	1963	Margaret Smith	B.J. Moffitt	63 64
1899	Blanche Hillyard	C. Cooper	62 63	1964	Maria Bueno	M. Smith	64 79 63
1900	Blanche Hillyard	C. Cooper	46 64 64	1965	Margaret Smith	M. Bueno	64 75
1901	Charlotte Sterry	B. Hillyard	62 62	1966	Billie Jean King	M. Bueno	63 36 61
1902	Muriel Robb	C. Sterry	75 61	1967	Billie Jean King	A. Jones	63 64
1903	Dorothea Douglass	E. Thomson	46 64 62	1968	Billie Jean King	J. Tegart	97 75
1904	Dorothea Douglass	C. Sterry	60 63	1969	Ann Jones	B.J. King	36 63 62
1905	May Sutton	D. Douglass	63 64	1970	Margaret Court	B.J. King	14-12 11-9
1906	Dorothea Douglass	M. Sutton	63 97	1971	Evonne Goolagong	M. Court	64 61
1907	May Sutton	D. Chambers	61 64	1972	Billie Jean King	E. Goolagong	63 63
1908	Charlotte Sterry	A. Morton	64 64	1973	Billie Jean King	C. Evert	60 75
1909	Dora Boothby	A. Morton	64 46 86	1974	Chris Evert	O. Morozova	60 64
1910	Dorothea Chambers	D. Boothby	62 62	1975	Billie Jean King	E. Cawley	60 61
1911	Dorothea Chambers	D. Boothby	60 60	1976	Chris Evert	E. Cawley	63 46 86
1912	Ethel Larcombe	C. Sterry	63 61	1977	Virginia Wade	B. Stove	46 63 61
1913	Dorothea Chambers	R. McNair	60 64	1978	Martina Navratilova	C. Evert	26 64 75
1914	Dorothea Chambers	E. Larcombe	75 64	1979	Martina Navratilova	C. Evert Lloyd	64 64
1915-18	Not held World War I			1980	Evonne Cawley	C. Evert Lloyd	61 76
1919	Suzanne Lenglen	D. Chambers	10-8 46 97	1981	Chris Evert Lloyd	H. Mandlikova	62 62
1920	Suzanne Lenglen	D. Chambers	63 60	1982	Martina Navratilova	C. Evert Lloyd	61 36 62
1921	Suzanne Lenglen	E. Ryan	62 60	1983	Martina Navratilova	A. Jaeger	60 63
1922	Suzanne Lenglen	M. Mallory	62 60	1984	Martina Navratilova	C. Evert Lloyd	76 62
1923	Suzanne Lenglen	K. McKane	62 62	1985	Martina Navratilova	C. Evert Lloyd	46 63 62
1924	Kitty McKane	H. Wills	46 64 64	1986	Martina Navratilova	H. Mandlikova	76 63
1925	Suzanne Lenglen	J. Fry	62 60	1987	Martina Navratilova	S. Graf	75 63
1926	Kitty Godfree	L. de Alvarez	62 46 63	1988	Steffi Graf	M. Navratilova	57 62 61
1927	Helen Wills	L. de Alvarez	62 64	1989	Steffi Graf	M. Navratilova	62 67 61
1928	Helen Wills	L. de Alvarez	62 63	1990	Martina Navratilova	Z. Garrison	64 61
1929	Helen Wills	H. Jacobs	61 62	1991	Steffi Graf	G. Sabatini	64 36 86
1930	Helen Moody	E. Ryan	62 62	1992	Steffi Graf	M. Seles	62 61
1931	Cilly Aussem	H. Krahwinkel	62 75	1993	Steffi Graf	J. Novotna	76 16 64
1932	Helen Moody	H. Jacobs	63 61	1994	Conchita Martinez	M. Navratilova	64 36 63
1933	Helen Moody	D. Round	64 68 63	1995	Steffi Graf	A.S. Vicario	46 61 75
1934	Dorothy Round	H. Jacobs	62 57 63	1996	Steffi Graf	A.S. Vicario	63 75
1935	Helen Moody	H. Jacobs	63 36 75	1997	Martina Hingis	J. Novotna	26 63 63
1936	Helen Jacobs	H.K. Sperling	62 46 75	1998	Jana Novotna	N. Tauziat	64 76
1937	Dorothy Round	J. Jedrzejowska	62 26 75	1999	Lindsay Davenport	S. Graf	64 75
1938	Helen Moody	H. Jacobs	64 60	2000	Venus Williams	L. Davenport	63 76
1939	Alice Marble	K. Stammers	62 60	2001	Venus Williams	J. Henin	61 36 60
1940-45	Not held World War II			2002	Serena Williams	V. Williams	76 63
1946	Pauline Betz	L. Brough	62 64	2003	Serena Williams	V. Williams	46 64 62
1947	Margaret Osborne	D. Hart	62 64	2004	Maria Sharapova	S. Williams	61 64
1948	Louise Brough	D. Hart	63 86				

U.S. Open
MEN

Challenge round system (defending champion qualified for following year's final) used from 1884 to 1911. Known as the Patriotic Tournament in 1917 during World War I. Amateur and Open Championships held in 1968 and '69. Became an exclusively Open Championship in 1970. **Surface:** Decoturf II (acrylic cement).

Multiple winners: Bill Larned, Richard Sears and Bill Tilden (7); Jimmy Connors and Pete Sampras (5); John McEnroe and Robert Wrenn (4); Oliver Campbell, Ivan Lendl, Fred Perry and Malcolm Whitman (3); Andre Agassi, Don Budge, Stefan Edberg, Roy Emerson, Neale Fraser, Pancho Gonzales, Bill Johnston, Jack Kramer, Rene Lacoste, Rod Laver, Maurice McLoughlin, Lindley Murray, John Newcombe, Frank Parker, Patrick Rafter, Bobby Riggs, Ken Rosewall, Frank Sedgman, Henry Slocum Jr., Tony Trabert, Ellsworth Vines and Dick Williams (2).

Year	Winner	Loser	Score	Year	Winner	Loser	Score
1881	Richard Sears	W. Glyn	60 63 62	1944	Frank Parker	B. Talbert	64 36 63 63
1882	Richard Sears	C. Clark	61 64 60	1945	Frank Parker	B. Talbert	14-12 61 62
1883	Richard Sears	J. Dwight	62 60 97	1946	Jack Kramer	T. Brown, Jr.	97 63 60
1884	Richard Sears	H. Taylor	60 16 60 62	1947	Jack Kramer	F. Parker	46 26 61 60 63
1885	Richard Sears	G. Brinley	63 46 60 63	1948	Pancho Gonzales	E. Sturgess	62 63 14-12
1886	Richard Sears	R. Beeckman	46 61 63 64	1949	Pancho Gonzales	F. Schroeder	16-18 26 61 62 64
1887	Richard Sears	H. Slocum Jr.	61 63 62	1950	Arthur Larsen	H. Flam	63 46 57 64 63
1888	Henry Slocum Jr.	H. Taylor	64 61 60	1951	Frank Sedgman	V. Seixas	64 61 61
1889	Henry Slocum Jr.	Q. Shaw	63 61 46 62	1952	Frank Sedgman	G. Mulloy	61 62 63
1890	Oliver Campbell	H. Slocum Jr.	62 46 63 61	1953	Tony Trabert	V. Seixas	63 62 63
1891	Oliver Campbell	C. Hobart	26 75 79 61 62	1954	Vic Seixas	R. Hartwig	36 62 64 64
1892	Oliver Campbell	F. Hovey	.75 36 63 75	1955	Tony Trabert	K. Rosewall	97 63 63
1893	Robert Wrenn	F. Hovey	64 36 64 64	1956	Ken Rosewall	L. Hoad	46 62 63 63
1894	Robert Wrenn	M. Goodbody	68 61 64 64	1957	Mal Anderson	A. Cooper	10-8 75 64
1895	Fred Hovey	R. Wrenn	63 62 64	1958	Ashley Cooper	M. Anderson	62 36 46 10-8 86
1896	Robert Wrenn	F. Hovey	75 36 60 16 61	1959	Neale Fraser	A. Olmedo	63 57 62 64
1897	Robert Wrenn	W. Eaves	46 86 63 26 62	1960	Neale Fraser	R. Laver	64 64 97
1898	Malcolm Whitman	D. Davis	36 62 62 61	1961	Roy Emerson	R. Laver	75 63 62
1899	Malcolm Whitman	P. Paret	61 62 36 75	1962	Rod Laver	R. Emerson	62 64 57 64
1900	Malcolm Whitman	B. Larned	64 16 62 62	1963	Rafael Osuna	F. Froehling	75 64 62
1901	Bill Larned	B. Wright	62 68 64 64	1964	Roy Emerson	F. Stolle	64 62 64
1902	Bill Larned	R. Doherty	46 62 64 86	1965	Manuel Santana	C. Drysdale	62 79 75 61
1903	Laurie Doherty	B. Larned	60 63 10-8	1966	Fred Stolle	J. Newcombe	46 12-10 63 64
1904	Holcombe Ward	B. Clothier	10-8 64 97	1967	John Newcombe	C. Graebner	64 64 86
1905	Beals Wright	H. Ward	62 61 11-9	1968	Am-Arthur Ashe	B. Lutz	46 63 8-10 60 64
1906	Bill Clothier	B. Wright	63 60 64		Op-Arthur Ashe	T. Okker	14-12 57 63 36 63
1907	Bill Larned	R. LeRoy	62 62 64	1969	Am-Stan Smith	B. Lutz	97 63 61
1908	Bill Larned	B. Wright	61 62 86		Op-Rod Laver	T. Roche	79 61 63 62
1909	Bill Larned	B. Clothier	61 62 57 16 61	1970	Ken Rosewall	T. Roche	26 64 76 63
1910	Bill Larned	T. Bundy	61 57 60 68 61	1971	Stan Smith	J. Kodes	36 63 62 76
1911	Bill Larned	M. McLoughlin	64 64 62	1972	Ilie Nastase	A. Ashe	36 63 67 64 63
1912	Maurice McLoughlin	W.F. Johnson	36 26 62 64 62	1973	John Newcombe	J. Kodes	64 16 46 62 63
1913	Maurice McLoughlin	R. Williams	64 57 63 61	1974	Jimmy Connors	K. Rosewall	61 60 61
1914	Dick Williams	M. McLoughlin	63 86 10-8	1975	Manuel Orantes	J. Connors	64 63 63
1915	Bill Johnston	M. McLoughlin	16 60 75 10-8	1976	Jimmy Connors	B. Borg	64 36 76 64
1916	Dick Williams	B. Johnston	46 64 06 62 64	1977	Guillermo Vilas	J. Connors	26 63 76 60
1917	Lindley Murray	N. Niles	57 86 63 63	1978	Jimmy Connors	B. Borg	64 62 62
1918	Lindley Murray	B. Tilden	63 61 75	1979	John McEnroe	V. Gerulaitis	75 63 63
1919	Bill Johnston	B. Tilden	64 64 63	1980	John McEnroe	B. Borg	76 61 67 57 64
1920	Bill Tilden	B. Johnston	61 16 75 57 63	1981	John McEnroe	B. Borg	46 62 64 63
1921	Bill Tilden	W. Johnson	61 63 61	1982	Jimmy Connors	I. Lendl	63 62 46 64
1922	Bill Tilden	B. Johnston	46 36 62 63 64	1983	Jimmy Connors	I. Lendl	63 67 75 60
1923	Bill Tilden	B. Johnston	64 61 64	1984	John McEnroe	I. Lendl	63 64 61
1924	Bill Tilden	B. Johnston	61 97 62	1985	Ivan Lendl	J. McEnroe	76 63 64
1925	Bill Tilden	B. Johnston	46 11-9 63 46 63	1986	Ivan Lendl	M. Mecir	64 62 60
1926	Rene Lacoste	J. Borotra	64 60 64	1987	Ivan Lendl	M. Wilander	67 60 76 64
1927	Rene Lacoste	B. Tilden	11-9 63 11-9	1988	Mats Wilander	I. Lendl	64 46 63 57 64
1928	Henri Cochet	F. Hunter	46 64 36 75 63	1989	Boris Becker	I. Lendl	76 16 63 76
1929	Bill Tilden	F. Hunter	36 63 46 62 64	1990	Pete Sampras	A. Agassi	64 63 62
1930	John Doeg	F. Shields	10-8 16 64 16-14	1991	Stefan Edberg	J. Courier	62 64 60
1931	Ellsworth Vines	G. Lott Jr.	79 63 97 75	1992	Stefan Edberg	P. Sampras	36 64 76 62
1932	Ellsworth Vines	H. Cochet	64 64 64	1993	Pete Sampras	C. Pioline	64 64 63
1933	Fred Perry	J. Crawford	63 11-13 46 60 61	1994	Andre Agassi	M. Stich	61 76 75
1934	Fred Perry	W. Allison	64 63 16 86	1995	Pete Sampras	A. Agassi	64 63 46 75
1935	Wilmer Allison	S. Wood	62 62 63	1996	Pete Sampras	M. Chang	61 64 76
1936	Fred Perry	D. Budge	26 62 86 16 10-8	1997	Patrick Rafter	G. Rusedski	63 62 46 75
1937	Don Budge	G. von Cramm	61 79 61 36 61	1998	Patrick Rafter	M. Philippoussis	63 36 62 60
1938	Don Budge	G. Mako	63 68 62 61	1999	Andre Agassi	T. Martin	64 67 67 63 62
1939	Bobby Riggs	S.W. van Horn	64 62 64	2000	Marat Safin	P. Sampras	64 63 63
1940	Don McNeill	B. Riggs	46 68 63 63 75	2001	Lleyton Hewitt	P. Sampras	76 61 61
1941	Bobby Riggs	F. Kovacs	57 61 63 63	2002	Pete Sampras	A. Agassi	63 64 57 64
1942	Fred Schroeder	F. Parker	86 75 36 46 62	2003	Andy Roddick	J.C. Ferrero	63 76 63
1943	Joe Hunt	J. Kramer	63 68 10-8 60	2004	Roger Federer	L. Hewitt	60 76 60

WOMEN

Challenge round system used from 1887-1918. Five set final played from 1887 to 1901. Amateur and Open Championships held in 1968 and '69. Became an exclusively Open Championship in 1970.

Multiple winners: Molla Bjurstedt Mallory (8); Helen Wills Moody (7); Chris Evert Lloyd (6); Margaret Smith Court and Steffi Graf (5); Pauline Betz, Maria Bueno, Helen Jacobs, Billie Jean King, Alice Marble, Elisabeth Moore, Martina Navratilova and Hazel Hotchkiss Wightman (4); Juliette Atkinson, Mary Browne, Maureen Connolly and Margaret Osborne du Pont (3); Tracy Austin, Mabel Cahill, Sarah Palfrey Cooke, Althea Gibson, Darlene Hard, Doris Hart, Marion Jones, Monica Seles, Bertha Townsend, Serena Williams and Venus Williams (2).

Year	Winner	Loser	Score	Year	Winner	Loser	Score
1887	Ellen Hansell	L. Knight	61 60	1947	Louise Brough	M. Osborne	86 46 61
1888	Bertha Townsend	E. Hansell	63 65	1948	Margaret du Pont	L. Brough	46 64 15-13
1889	Bertha Townsend	L. Voorhes	75 62	1949	Margaret du Pont	D. Hart	64 61
1890	Ellen Roosevelt	B. Townsend	62 62	1950	Margaret du Pont	D. Hart	64 63
1891	Mabel Cahill	E. Roosevelt	64 61 46 63	1951	Maureen Connolly	S. Fry	63 16 64
1892	Mabel Cahill	E. Moore	57 63 64 46 62	1952	Maureen Connolly	D. Hart	63 75
1893	Aline Terry	A. Schultz	61 63	1953	Maureen Connolly	D. Hart	62 64
1894	Helen Hellwig	A. Terry	75 36 60 36 63	1954	Doris Hart	L. Brough	68 61 86
1895	Juliette Atkinson	H. Hellwig	64 62 61	1955	Doris Hart	P. Ward	64 62
1896	Elisabeth Moore	J. Atkinson	64 46 62 62	1956	Shirley Fry	A. Gibson	63 64
1897	Juliette Atkinson	E. Moore	63 63 46 36 63	1957	Althea Gibson	L. Brough	63 62
1898	Juliette Atkinson	M. Jones	63 57 64 26 75	1958	Althea Gibson	D. Hard	36 61 62
1899	Marion Jones	M. Banks	61 61 75	1959	Maria Bueno	C. Truman	61 64
1900	Myrtle McAteer	E. Parker	62 62 60	1960	Darlene Hard	M. Bueno	64 10-12 64
1901	Elisabeth Moore	M. McAteer	64 36 75 26 62	1961	Darlene Hard	A. Haydon	63 64
1902	Marion Jones	E. Moore	61 10(ret)	1962	Margaret Smith	D. Hard	97 64
1903	Elisabeth Moore	M. Jones	75 86	1963	Maria Bueno	M. Smith	75 64
1904	May Sutton	E. Moore	61 62	1964	Maria Bueno	C. Graebner	61 60
1905	Elisabeth Moore	H. Homans	64 57 61	1965	Margaret Smith	B.J. Moffitt	86 75
1906	Helen Homans	M. Barger-Wallach	64 63	1966	Maria Bueno	N. Richey	63 61
1907	Evelyn Sears	C. Neely	63 62	1967	Billie Jean King	A. Jones	11-9 64
1908	Maud B. Wallach	Ev. Sears	63 16 63	1968	Am-Margaret Court	M. Bueno	62 62
1909	Hazel Hotchkiss	M. Barger-Wallach	60 61		Op-Virginia Wade	B.J. King	64 62
1910	Hazel Hotchkiss	L. Hammond	64 62	1969	Am-Margaret Court	V. Wade	46 63 60
1911	Hazel Hotchkiss	F. Sutton	8-10 61 97		Op-Margaret Court	N. Richey	62 62
1912	Mary Browne	E. Sears	64 62	1970	Margaret Court	R. Casals	62 26 61
1913	Mary Browne	D. Green	62 75	1971	Billie Jean King	R. Casals	64 76
1914	Mary Browne	M. Wagner	62 16 61	1972	Billie Jean King	K. Melville	63 75
1915	Molla Bjurstedt	H. Wightman	46 62 60	1973	Margaret Court	E. Goolagong	76 57 62
1916	Molla Bjurstedt	L. Raymond	60 61	1974	Billie Jean King	E. Goolagong	36 63 75
1917	Molla Bjurstedt	M. Vanderhoef	46 60 62	1975	Chris Evert	E. Cawley	57 64 62
1918	Molla Bjurstedt	E. Goss	64 63	1976	Chris Evert	E. Cawley	63 60
1919	Hazel Wightman	M. Zinderstein	61 62	1977	Chris Evert	W. Turnbull	76 62
1920	Molla Mallory	M. Zinderstein	63 61	1978	Chris Evert	P. Shriver	75 64
1921	Molla Mallory	M. Browne	46 64 62	1979	Tracy Austin	C. Evert Lloyd	64 63
1922	Molla Mallory	H. Wills	63 61	1980	Chris Evert Lloyd	H. Mandlikova	57 61 61
1923	Helen Wills	M. Mallory	62 61	1981	Tracy Austin	M. Navratilova	16 76 76
1924	Helen Wills	M. Mallory	61 63	1982	Chris Evert Lloyd	H. Mandlikova	63 61
1925	Helen Wills	K. McKane	36 60 62	1983	Martina Navratilova	C. Evert Lloyd	61 63
1926	Molla Mallory	E. Ryan	46 64 97	1984	Martina Navratilova	C. Evert Lloyd	46 64 64
1927	Helen Wills	B. Nuthall	61 64	1985	Hana Mandlikova	M. Navratilova	76 16 76
1928	Helen Wills	H. Jacobs	62 61	1986	Martina Navratilova	H. Sukova	63 62
1929	Helen Wills	P. Watson	64 62	1987	Martina Navratilova	S. Graf	76 61
1930	Betty Nuthall	A. Harper	61 64	1988	Steffi Graf	G. Sabatini	63 36 61
1931	Helen Moody	E. Whittingstall	64 61	1989	Steffi Graf	M. Navratilova	36 75 61
1932	Helen Jacobs	C. Babcock	62 62	1990	Gabriela Sabatini	S. Graf	62 76
1933	Helen Jacobs	H. Moody	86 36 30(ret)	1991	Monica Seles	M. Navratilova	76 61
1934	Helen Jacobs	S. Palfrey	61 64	1992	Monica Seles	A.S. Vicario	63 63
1935	Helen Jacobs	S. Fabyan	62 64	1993	Steffi Graf	H. Sukova	63 63
1936	Alice Marble	H. Jacobs	46 63 62	1994	A. Sanchez Vicario	S. Graf	16 76 64
1937	Anita Lizana	J. Jedrzejowska	64 62	1995	Steffi Graf	M. Seles	76 06 63
1938	Alice Marble	N. Wynne	64 62	1996	Steffi Graf	M. Seles	75 64
1939	Alice Marble	H. Jacobs	60 8-10 64	1997	Martina Hingis	V. Williams	60 64
1940	Alice Marble	H. Jacobs	62 63	1998	Lindsay Davenport	M. Hingis	63 75
1941	Sarah Cooke	P. Betz	75 62	1999	Serena Williams	M. Hingis	63 76
1942	Pauline Betz	L. Brough	46 61 64	2000	Venus Williams	L. Davenport	64 75
1943	Pauline Betz	L. Brough	63 57 63	2001	Venus Williams	S. Williams	62 64
1944	Pauline Betz	M. Osborne	63 86	2002	Serena Williams	V. Williams	64 63
1945	Sarah Cooke	P. Betz	36 86 64	2003	J. Henin-Hardenne	K. Clijsters	75 61
1946	Pauline Betz	P. Canning	11-9 63	2004	Svetlana Kuznetsova	E. Dementieva	63 75

Grand Slam Summary

Singles winners of the four Grand Slam tournaments–Australian, French, Wimbledon and United States–since the French was opened to all comers in 1925. Note that there were two Australian Opens in 1977 and none in 1986.

MEN

Three wins in one year: Jack Crawford (1933); Fred Perry (1934); Tony Trabert (1955); Lew Hoad (1956); Ashley Cooper (1958); Roy Emerson (1964); Jimmy Connors (1974); Mats Wilander (1988); Roger Federer (2004).

Two wins in one year: Roy Emerson and Pete Sampras (4 times); Bjorn Borg (3 times); Rene Lacoste, Ivan Lendl, John Newcombe and Fred Perry (twice); Andre Agassi, Boris Becker, Don Budge, Henri Cochet, Jimmy Connors, Jim Courier, Neale Fraser, Jack Kramer, John McEnroe, Alex Olmedo, Budge Patty, Bobby Riggs, Ken Rosewall, Dick Savitt, Frank Sedgman and Guillermo Vilas (once).

Year	Australian	French	Wimbledon	U.S.
1925	Anderson	Lacoste	Lacoste	Tilden
1926	Hawkes	Cochet	Borotra	Lacoste
1927	Patterson	Lacoste	Cochet	Lacoste
1928	Borotra	Cochet	Lacoste	Cochet
1929	Gregory	Lacoste	Cochet	Tilden
1930	Moon	Cochet	Tilden	Doeg
1931	Crawford	Borotra	Wood	Vines
1932	Crawford	Cochet	Vines	Vines
1933	Crawford	Crawford	Crawford	Perry
1934	Perry	von Cramm	Perry	Perry
1935	Crawford	Perry	Perry	Allison
1936	Quist	von Cramm	Perry	Perry
1937	McGrath	Henkel	Budge	Budge
1938	**Budge**	**Budge**	**Budge**	**Budge**
1939	Bromwich	McNeill	Riggs	Riggs
1940	Quist	—	—	McNeill
1941	—	—	—	Riggs
1942	—	—	—	Schroeder
1943	—	—	—	Hunt
1944	—	—	—	Parker
1945	—	—	—	Parker
1946	Bromwich	Bernard	Petra	Kramer
1947	Pails	Asboth	Kramer	Kramer
1948	Quist	Parker	Falkenburg	Gonzales
1949	Sedgman	Parker	Schroeder	Gonzales
1950	Sedgman	Patty	Patty	Larsen
1951	Savitt	Drobny	Savitt	Sedgman
1952	McGregor	Drobny	Sedgman	Sedgman
1953	Rosewall	Rosewall	Seixas	Trabert
1954	Rose	Trabert	Drobny	Seixas
1955	Rosewall	Trabert	Trabert	Trabert
1956	Hoad	Hoad	Hoad	Rosewall
1957	Cooper	Davidson	Hoad	Anderson
1958	Cooper	Rose	Cooper	Cooper
1959	Olmedo	Pietrangeli	Olmedo	Fraser
1960	Laver	Pietrangeli	Fraser	Fraser
1961	Emerson	Santana	Laver	Emerson
1962	**Laver**	**Laver**	**Laver**	**Laver**
1963	Emerson	Emerson	McKinley	Osuna
1964	Emerson	Santana	Emerson	Emerson
1965	Emerson	Stolle	Emerson	Santana

Year	Australian	French	Wimbledon	U.S.
1966	Emerson	Roche	Santana	Stolle
1967	Emerson	Emerson	Newcombe	Newcombe
1968	Bowrey	Rosewall	Laver	Ashe
1969	**Laver**	**Laver**	**Laver**	**Laver**
1970	Ashe	Kodes	Newcombe	Rosewall
1971	Rosewall	Kodes	Newcombe	Smith
1972	Rosewall	Gimeno	Smith	Nastase
1973	Newcombe	Nastase	Kodes	Newcombe
1974	Connors	Borg	Connors	Connors
1975	Newcombe	Borg	Ashe	Orantes
1976	Edmondson	Panatta	Borg	Connors
1977	Tanner & Gerulaitis	Vilas	Borg	Vilas
1978	Vilas	Borg	Borg	Connors
1979	Vilas	Borg	Borg	McEnroe
1980	Teacher	Borg	Borg	McEnroe
1981	Kriek	Borg	McEnroe	McEnroe
1982	Kriek	Wilander	Connors	Connors
1983	Wilander	Noah	McEnroe	Connors
1984	Wilander	Lendl	McEnroe	McEnroe
1985	Edberg	Wilander	Becker	Lendl
1986	—	Lendl	Becker	Lendl
1987	Edberg	Lendl	Cash	Lendl
1988	Wilander	Wilander	Edberg	Wilander
1989	Lendl	Chang	Becker	Becker
1990	Lendl	Gomez	Edberg	Sampras
1991	Becker	Courier	Stich	Edberg
1992	Courier	Courier	Agassi	Edberg
1993	Courier	Bruguera	Sampras	Sampras
1994	Sampras	Bruguera	Sampras	Agassi
1995	Agassi	Muster	Sampras	Sampras
1996	Becker	Kafelnikov	Krajicek	Sampras
1997	Sampras	Kuerten	Sampras	Rafter
1998	Korda	Moya	Sampras	Rafter
1999	Kafelnikov	Agassi	Sampras	Agassi
2000	Agassi	Kuerten	Sampras	Safin
2001	Agassi	Kuerten	Ivanisevic	Hewitt
2002	Johansson	Costa	Hewitt	Sampras
2003	Agassi	Ferrero	Federer	Roddick
2004	Federer	Gaudio	Federer	Federer

Men's, Women's & Mixed Doubles Grand Slam

The tennis Grand Slam has only been accomplished in doubles competition six times in the same calendar year. Here are the doubles teams to accomplish the feat. The two men and three women to win the singles Grand Slam are noted in the Grand Slam Summary tables.

Men's Doubles

1951 . . . . .Frank Sedgman, Australia
& Ken McGregor, Australia

Mixed Doubles

1963 . . . . Ken Fletcher, Australia
& Margaret Smith, Australia

1967 . . . . .Owen Davidson and two partners*

*Davidson's partners: AUS–Lesley Turner; FR, WIM, U.S.–Billie Jean King.

Women's Doubles

1960 . . . . .Maria Bueno, Brazil & two partners†

1984 . . . . .Martina Navratilova, USA
& Pam Shriver, USA

1998 . . . .Martina Hingis, Switzerland & two partners#

†Bueno's partners: AUS–Christine Truman; FR, WIM, U.S.–Darlene Hard.

#Hingis' partners: AUS–Mirjana Lucic; FR, WIM, U.S.–Jana Novotna.

WOMEN

Three in one year: Helen Wills Moody (1928 and '29); Margaret Smith Court (1962, '65, '69 and '73); Billie Jean King (1972); Martina Navratilova (1983 and '84); Steffi Graf (1989, '93, '95 and '96); Monica Seles (1991 and '92); Martina Hingis (1997) and Serena Williams (2002).

Two in one year: Chris Evert Lloyd (5 times); Helen Wills Moody and Martina Navratilova (3 times); Maria Bueno, Maureen Connolly, Margaret Smith Court, Althea Gibson, Billie Jean King and Venus Williams (twice); Cilly Aussem, Pauline Betz, Louise Brough, Jennifer Capriati, Evonne Goolagong Cawley, Margaret Osborne du Pont, Shirley Fry, Darlene Hard, Justine Henin-Hardenne, Suzanne Lenglen, Alice Marble, Arantxa Sanchez Vicario and Serena Williams (once).

Year	Australian	French	Wimbledon	U.S.	Year	Australian	French	Wimbledon	U.S.
1925	Akhurst	Lenglen	Lenglen	Wills	1967	Richey	Durr	King	King
1926	Akhurst	Lenglen	Godfree	Mallory	1968	King	Richey	King	Wade
1927	Boyd	Bouman	Wills	Wills	1969	Court	Court	Jones	Court
1928	Akhurst	Wills	Wills	Wills	1970	**Court**	**Court**	**Court**	**Court**
1929	Akhurst	Wills	Wills	Wills	1971	Court	Goolagong	Goolagong	King
1930	Akhurst	Moody	Moody	Nuthall	1972	Wade	King	King	King
1931	Buttsworth	Aussem	Aussem	Moody	1973	Court	Court	King	Court
1932	Buttsworth	Moody	Moody	Jacobs	1974	Goolagong	Evert	Evert	King
1933	Hartigan	Scriven	Moody	Jacobs	1975	Goolagong	Evert	King	Evert
1934	Hartigan	Scriven	Round	Jacobs	1976	Cawley	Barker	Evert	Evert
1935	Round	Sperling	Moody	Jacobs	1977	Jausovec	Wade	Evert	Evert
1936	Hartigan	Sperling	Jacobs	Marble		& Cawley			
1937	Wynne	Sperling	Round	Lizana	1978	O'Neil	Ruzici	Navratilova	Evert
1938	Bundy	Mathieu	Moody	Marble	1979	Jordan	Evert Lloyd	Navratilova	Austin
1939	Westacott	Mathieu	Marble	Marble	1980	Mandlikova	Evert Lloyd	Cawley	Evert Lloyd
1940	Wynne	—	—	Marble	1981	Navratilova	Mandlikova	Evert Lloyd	Austin
1941	—	—	—	Cooke	1982	Evert Lloyd	Navratilova	Navratilova	Evert Lloyd
1942	—	—	—	Betz	1983	Evert Lloyd	Navratilova	Navratilova	Navratilova
1943	—	—	—	Betz	1984	Evert Lloyd	Navratilova	Navratilova	Navratilova
1944	—	—	—	Betz	1985	Navratilova	Evert Lloyd	Navratilova	Mandlikova
1945	—	—	—	Cooke	1986	–	Evert Lloyd	Navratilova	Navratilova
1946	Bolton	Osborne	Betz	Betz	1987	Mandlikova	Graf	Navratilova	Navratilova
1947	Bolton	Todd	Osborne	Brough	1988	**Graf**	**Graf**	**Graf**	**Graf**
1948	Bolton	Landry	Brough	du Pont	1989	Graf	Vicario	Graf	Graf
1949	Hart	du Pont	Brough	du Pont	1990	Graf	Seles	Navratilova	Sabatini
1950	Brough	Hart	Brough	du Pont	1991	Seles	Seles	Graf	Seles
1951	Bolton	Fry	Hart	Connolly	1992	Seles	Seles	Graf	Seles
1952	Long	Hart	Connolly	Connolly	1993	Seles	Graf	Graf	Graf
1953	**Connolly**	**Connolly**	**Connolly**	**Connolly**	1994	Graf	Vicario	Martinez	Vicario
1954	Long	Connolly	Connolly	Hart	1995	Pierce	Graf	Graf	Graf
1955	Penrose	Mortimer	Brough	Hart	1996	Seles	Graf	Graf	Graf
1956	Carter	Gibson	Fry	Fry	1997	Hingis	Majoli	Hingis	Hingis
1957	Fry	Bloomer	Gibson	Gibson	1998	Hingis	Vicario	Novotna	Davenport
1958	Mortimer	Kormoczi	Gibson	Gibson	1999	Hingis	Graf	Davenport	S. Williams
1959	Reitano	Truman	Bueno	Bueno	2000	Davenport	Pierce	V. Williams	V. Williams
1960	Smith	Hard	Bueno	Hard	2001	Capriati	Capriati	V. Williams	V. Williams
1961	Smith	Haydon	Mortimer	Hard	2002	Capriati	S. Williams	S. Williams	S. Williams
1962	Smith	Smith	Susman	Smith	2003	S. Williams	Henin-Hardenne	S. Williams	Henin-Hardenne
1963	Smith	Turner	Smith	Bueno	2004	Henin-Hardenne	Myskina	Sharapova	Kuznetsova
1964	Smith	Smith	Bueno	Bueno					
1965	Smith	Turner	Smith	Smith					
1966	Smith	Jones	King	Bueno					

Overall Leaders

All-Time Grand Slam titleists including all singles and doubles championships at the four major tournaments. Titles listed under each heading are singles, doubles and mixed doubles. Players active in 2004 are in **bold** type.

		MEN						Total
		Career	Australian	French	Wimbledon	U.S.	S-D-M	Titles
1	Roy Emerson 1959-71		6-3-0	2-6-0	2-3-0	2-4-0	12-16-0	28
2	John Newcombe 1965-76		2-5-0	0-3-0	3-6-0	2-3-1	7-17-1	25
3	Frank Sedgman 1949-52		2-2-2	0-2-2	1-3-2	2-2-2	5-9-8	22
	Todd Woodbridge . . . . .1988—		0-3-1	0-1-1	0-9-1	0-3-3	0-16-6	22
5	Bill Tilden 1913-30		*	0-0-1	3-1-0	7-5-4	10-6-5	21
6	Rod Laver 1959-71		3-4-0	2-1-1	4-1-2	2-0-0	11-6-3	20
7	Jack Bromwich 1938-50		2-8-1	0-0-0	0-2-2	0-3-1	2-13-4	19
	Neale Fraser 1957-62		0-3-1	0-3-0	1-2-1	2-3-3	3-11-5	19
9	Ken Rosewall 1953-72		4-3-0	2-2-0	0-2-0	2-2-1	8-9-1	18
	Jean Borotra 1925-36		1-1-1	1-5-2	2-3-1	0-0-1	4-9-5	18
	Fred Stolle 1962-69		0-3-1	1-2-0	0-2-3	1-3-2	2-10-6	18
12	John McEnroe 1977-93		0-0-0	0-0-1	3-5-0	4-4-0	7-9-1	17
	Jack Crawford 1929-35		4-4-3	1-1-1	1-1-1	0-0-0	6-6-5	17
	Mark Woodforde 1985-2000		0-2-2	0-1-1	0-6-1	0-3-1	0-12-5	17
	Adrian Quist 1936-50		3-10-0	0-1-0	0-2-0	0-1-0	3-14-0	17

Grand Slam Overall Leaders (Cont.)
WOMEN

		Career	Australian	French	Wimbledon	U.S.	S-D-M	Total Titles
1	Margaret Smith Court	1960-75	11-8-2	5-4-4	3-2-5	5-5-8	24-19-19	62
2	**Martina Navratilova**	1974-95, 2000—	3-8-1	2-7-2	9-7-4	4-9-2	18-31-9	58
3	Billie Jean King	1961-81	1-0-1	1-1-2	6-10-4	4-5-4	12-16-11	39
4	Margaret du Pont	1941-62	*	2-3-0	1-5-1	3-13-9	6-21-10	37
5	Louise Brough	1942-57	1-1-0	0-3-0	4-5-4	1-12-4	6-21-8	35
	Doris Hart	1948-55	1-1-2	2-5-3	1-4-5	2-4-5	6-14-15	35
7	Helen Wills Moody	1923-38	*	4-2-0	8-3-1	7-4-2	19-9-3	31
8	Elizabeth Ryan	1914-34	*	0-4-0	0-12-7	0-1-2	0-17-9	26
9	Suzanne Lenglen	1919-26	*	6-2-2	6-6-3	0-0-0	12-8-5	25
10	Steffi Graf	1982-99	4-0-0	6-0-0	7-1-0	5-0-0	22-1-0	23
11	Pam Shriver	1981-97	0-7-0	0-4-1	0-5-0	0-5-0	0-21-1	22
12	Chris Evert	1974-89	2-0-0	7-2-0	3-1-0	6-0-0	18-3-0	21
	Darlene Hard	1958-69	*	1-3-2	0-4-3	2-6-0	3-13-5	21
14	Natasha Zvereva	1989-2002	0-3-2	0-6-0	0-5-0	0-4-0	0-18-2	20
	Nancye Wynne Bolton	1935-52	6-10-4	0-0-0	0-0-0	0-0-0	6-10-4	20
	Maria Bueno	1958-68	0-1-0	0-1-1	3-5-0	4-5-0	7-12-1	20

All-Time Grand Slam Singles Titles

Men and women with the most singles championships in the Australian, French, Wimbledon and U.S. championships, through 2004. Note that (*) indicates player never played in that particular Grand Slam event; and players active in singles play in 2004 are in **bold** type.

Top 10 Men

		Aus	Fre	Wim	US	Total
1	Pete Sampras	2	0	7	5	14
2	Roy Emerson	6	2	2	2	12
3	Bjorn Borg	0	6	5	0	11
	Rod Laver	3	2	4	2	11
5	Bill Tilden	*	0	3	7	10
6	**Andre Agassi**	4	1	1	2	8
	Jimmy Connors	1	0	2	5	8
	Ivan Lendl	2	3	0	3	8
	Fred Perry	1	1	3	3	8
	Ken Rosewall	4	2	0	2	8

Top 10 Women

		Aus	Fre	Wim	US	Total
1	Margaret Smith Court	11	5	3	5	24
2	Steffi Graf	4	6	7	5	22
3	Helen Wills Moody	*	4	8	7	19
4	Chris Evert	2	7	3	6	18
	Martina Navratilova	3	2	9	4	18
6	Billie Jean King	1	1	6	4	12
	Suzanne Lenglen	*	6	6	0	12
8	Maureen Connolly	1	2	3	3	9
	Monica Seles	4	3	0	2	9
10	Molla Bjurstedt Mallory	*	*	0	8	8

Annual Number One Players

Unofficial world rankings for men and women determined by the *London Daily Telegraph* from 1914-72. Since then, official world rankings computed by men's and women's tours. Rankings included only amateur players from 1914 until the arrival of open (professional) tennis in 1968. No rankings were released during World Wars I and II.

MEN

Multiple winners: Pete Sampras and Bill Tilden (6); Jimmy Connors (5); Henri Cochet, Rod Laver, Ivan Lendl and John McEnroe (4); John Newcombe and Fred Perry (3); Bjorn Borg, Don Budge, Ashley Cooper, Stefan Edberg, Roy Emerson, Neale Fraser, Lleyton Hewitt, Jack Kramer, Rene Lacoste, Ilie Nastase, Frank Sedgman and Tony Trabert (2).

Year		Year		Year		Year	
1914	Maurice McLoughlin	1938	Don Budge	1964	Roy Emerson	1985	Ivan Lendl
1915-18	No rankings	1939	Bobby Riggs	1965	Roy Emerson	1986	Ivan Lendl
1919	Gerald Patterson	1940-45	No rankings	1966	Manuel Santana	1987	Ivan Lendl
1920	Bill Tilden	1946	Jack Kramer	1967	John Newcombe	1988	Mats Wilander
1921	Bill Tilden	1947	Jack Kramer	1968	Rod Laver	1989	Ivan Lendl
1922	Bill Tilden	1948	Frank Parker	1969	Rod Laver	1990	Stefan Edberg
1923	Bill Tilden	1949	Pancho Gonzales	1970	John Newcombe	1991	Stefan Edberg
1924	Bill Tilden	1950	Budge Patty	1971	John Newcombe	1992	Jim Courier
1925	Bill Tilden	1951	Frank Sedgman	1972	Ilie Nastase	1993	Pete Sampras
1926	Rene Lacoste	1952	Frank Sedgman	1973	Ilie Nastase	1994	Pete Sampras
1927	Rene Lacoste	1953	Tony Trabert	1974	Jimmy Connors	1995	Pete Sampras
1928	Henri Cochet	1954	Jaroslav Drobny	1975	Jimmy Connors	1996	Pete Sampras
1929	Henri Cochet	1955	Tony Trabert	1976	Jimmy Connors	1997	Pete Sampras
1930	Henri Cochet	1956	Lew Hoad	1977	Jimmy Connors	1998	Pete Sampras
1931	Henri Cochet	1957	Ashley Cooper	1978	Jimmy Connors	1999	Andre Agassi
1932	Ellsworth Vines	1958	Ashley Cooper	1979	Bjorn Borg	2000	Gustavo Kuerten
1933	Jack Crawford	1959	Neale Fraser	1980	Bjorn Borg	2001	Lleyton Hewitt
1934	Fred Perry	1960	Neale Fraser	1981	John McEnroe	2002	Lleyton Hewitt
1935	Fred Perry	1961	Rod Laver	1982	John McEnroe	2003	Andy Roddick
1936	Fred Perry	1962	Rod Laver	1983	John McEnroe		
1937	Don Budge	1963	Rafael Osuna	1984	John McEnroe		

WOMEN

Multiple winners: Helen Wills Moody (9); Steffi Graf (8); Margaret Smith Court and Martina Navratilova (7); Chris Evert Lloyd and Billie Jean King (5); Margaret Osborne du Pont (4); Maureen Connolly, Martina Hingis and Monica Seles (3); Maria Bueno, Lindsay Davenport, Althea Gibson and Suzanne Lenglen (2).

Year		Year		Year		Year	
1925	Suzanne Lenglen	1949	Margaret du Pont	1968	Billie Jean King	1987	Steffi Graf
1926	Suzanne Lenglen	1950	Margaret du Pont	1969	Margaret Court	1988	Steffi Graf
1927	Helen Wills	1951	Doris Hart	1970	Margaret Court	1989	Steffi Graf
1928	Helen Wills	1952	Maureen Connolly	1971	Evonne Goolagong	1990	Steffi Graf
1929	Helen Wills Moody	1953	Maureen Connolly	1972	Billie Jean King	1991	Monica Seles
1930	Helen Wills Moody	1954	Maureen Connolly	1973	Margaret Court	1992	Monica Seles
1931	Helen Wills Moody	1955	Louise Brough	1974	Billie Jean King	1993	Steffi Graf
1932	Helen Wills Moody	1956	Shirley Fry	1975	Chris Evert	1994	Steffi Graf
1933	Helen Wills Moody	1957	Althea Gibson	1976	Chris Evert	1995	Steffi Graf
1934	Dorothy Round	1958	Althea Gibson	1977	Chris Evert		& Monica Seles*
1935	Helen Wills Moody	1959	Maria Bueno	1978	Martina Navratilova	1996	Steffi Graf
1936	Helen Jacobs	1960	Maria Bueno	1979	Martina Navratilova	1997	Martina Hingis
1937	Anita Lizana	1961	Angela Mortimer	1980	Chris Evert Lloyd	1998	Lindsay Davenport
1938	Helen Wills Moody	1962	Margaret Smith	1981	Chris Evert Lloyd	1999	Martina Hingis
1939	Alice Marble	1963	Margaret Smith	1982	Martina Navratilova		
1940-45	No rankings	1964	Margaret Smith	1983	Martina Navratilova	2000	Martina Hingis
1946	Pauline Betz	1965	Margaret Smith	1984	Martina Navratilova	2001	Lindsay Davenport
1947	Margaret Osborne	1966	Billie Jean King	1985	Martina Navratilova	2002	Serena Williams
1948	Margaret du Pont	1967	Billie Jean King	1986	Martina Navratilova	2003	Justine Henin-Hardenne

*Upon her return to the WTA Tour on Aug. 15, 1995, Seles retained her #1 ranking and was co-ranked at #1 through her first six tournaments (August '95–May '96). Seles was on leave since April 1993 when she was stabbed by a fan during a match.

Annual Top 10 World Rankings (since 1968)

Year by year Top 10 world computer rankings for men (ATP Tour) and women (WTA Tour) since the arrival of open tennis in 1968. Rankings from 1968-72 made by Lance Tingay of the *London Daily Telegraph*. Since 1973 the WTA Tour and ATP tour had compiled its own computer rankings. Since 2000, the men's rankings reflect the final standings of the ATP Champions Race.

MEN

1968	1971	1974	1977	1980
1 Rod Laver	1 John Newcombe	1 Jimmy Connors	1 Jimmy Connors	1 Bjorn Borg
2 Arthur Ashe	2 Stan Smith	2 John Newcombe	2 Guillermo Vilas	2 John McEnroe
3 Ken Rosewall	3 Rod Laver	3 Bjorn Borg	3 Bjorn Borg	3 Jimmy Connors
4 Tom Okker	4 Ken Rosewall	4 Rod Laver	4 Vitas Gerulaitis	4 Gene Mayer
5 Tony Roche	5 Jan Kodes	5 Guillermo Vilas	5 Brian Gottfried	5 Guillermo Vilas
6 John Newcombe	6 Arthur Ashe	6 Tom Okker	6 Eddie Dibbs	6 Ivan Lendl
7 Clark Graebner	7 Tom Okker	7 Arthur Ashe	7 Manuel Orantes	7 Harold Solomon
8 Dennis Ralston	8 Marty Riessen	8 Ken Rosewall	8 Raul Ramirez	8 Jose-Luis Clerc
9 Cliff Drysdale	9 Cliff Drysdale	9 Stan Smith	9 Ilie Nastase	9 Vitas Gerulaitis
10 Pancho Gonzales	10 Ilie Nastase	10 Ilie Nastase	10 Dick Stockton	10 Eliot Teltscher

1969	1972	1975	1978	1981
1 Rod Laver	1 Stan Smith	1 Jimmy Connors	1 Jimmy Connors	1 John McEnroe
2 Tony Roche	2 Ken Rosewall	2 Guillermo Vilas	2 Bjorn Borg	2 Ivan Lendl
3 John Newcombe	3 Ilie Nastase	3 Bjorn Borg	3 Guillermo Vilas	3 Jimmy Connors
4 Tom Okker	4 Rod Laver	4 Arthur Ashe	4 John McEnroe	4 Bjorn Borg
5 Ken Rosewall	5 Arthur Ashe	5 Manuel Orantes	5 Vitas Gerulaitis	5 Jose-Luis Clerc
6 Arthur Ashe	6 John Newcombe	6 Ken Rosewall	6 Eddie Dibbs	6 Guillermo Vilas
7 Cliff Drysdale	7 Bob Lutz	7 Ilie Nastase	7 Brian Gottfried	7 Gene Mayer
8 Pancho Gonzales	8 Tom Okker	8 John Alexander	8 Raul Ramirez	8 Eliot Teltscher
9 Andres Gimeno	9 Marty Riessen	9 Roscoe Tanner	9 Harold Solomon	9 Vitas Gerulaitis
10 Fred Stolle	10 Andres Gimeno	10 Rod Laver	10 Corrado Barazzutti	10 Peter McNamara

1970	1973	1976	1979	1982
1 John Newcombe	1 Ilie Nastase	1 Jimmy Connors	1 Bjorn Borg	1 John McEnroe
2 Ken Rosewall	2 John Newcombe	2 Bjorn Borg	2 Jimmy Connors	2 Jimmy Connors
3 Tony Roche	3 Jimmy Connors	3 Ilie Nastase	3 John McEnroe	3 Ivan Lendl
4 Rod Laver	4 Tom Okker	4 Manuel Orantes	4 Vitas Gerulaitis	4 Guillermo Vilas
5 Arthur Ashe	5 Stan Smith	5 Raul Ramirez	5 Roscoe Tanner	5 Vitas Gerulaitis
6 Ilie Nastase	6 Ken Rosewall	6 Guillermo Vilas	6 Guillermo Vilas	6 Jose-Luis Clerc
7 Tom Okker	7 Manuel Orantes	7 Adriano Panatta	7 Arthur Ashe	7 Mats Wilander
8 Roger Taylor	8 Rod Laver	8 Harold Solomon	8 Harold Solomon	8 Gene Mayer
9 Jan Kodes	9 Jan Kodes	9 Eddie Dibbs	9 Jose Higueras	9 Yannick Noah
10 Cliff Richey	10 Arthur Ashe	10 Brian Gottfried	10 Eddie Dibbs	10 Peter McNamara

Annual Top 10 World Rankings (since 1968) (Cont.)
MEN

1983	**1989**	**1995**	**2001**
1 John McEnroe	1 Ivan Lendl	1 Pete Sampras	1 Lleyton Hewitt
2 Ivan Lendl	2 Boris Becker	2 Andre Agassi	2 Gustavo Kuerten
3 Jimmy Connors	3 Stefan Edberg	3 Thomas Muster	3 Andre Agassi
4 Mats Wilander	4 John McEnroe	4 Boris Becker	4 Yevgeny Kafelnikov
5 Yannick Noah	5 Michael Chang	5 Michael Chang	5 Juan Carlos Ferrero
6 Jimmy Arias	6 Brad Gilbert	6 Yevgeny Kafelnikov	6 Sebastien Grosjean
7 Jose Higueras	7 Andre Agassi	7 Thomas Enqvist	7 Patrick Rafter
8 Jose-Luis Clerc	8 Aaron Krickstein	8 Jim Courier	8 Tommy Haas
9 Kevin Curren	9 Alberto Mancini	9 Wayne Ferreira	9 Tim Henman
10 Gene Mayer	10 Jay Berger	10 Goran Ivanisevic	10 Pete Sampras

1984	**1990**	**1996**	**2002**
1 John McEnroe	1 Stefan Edberg	1 Pete Sampras	1 Lleyton Hewitt
2 Jimmy Connors	2 Boris Becker	2 Michael Chang	2 Andre Agassi
3 Ivan Lendl	3 Ivan Lendl	3 Yevgeny Kafelnikov	3 Marat Safin
4 Mats Wilander	4 Andre Agassi	4 Goran Ivanisevic	4 Juan Carlos Ferrèro
5 Andres Gomez	5 Pete Sampras	5 Thomas Muster	5 Carlos Moya
6 Anders Jarryd	6 Andres Gomez	6 Boris Becker	6 Roger Federer
7 Henrik Sundstrom	7 Thomas Muster	7 Richard Krajicek	7 Jiri Novak
8 Pat Cash	8 Emilio Sanchez	8 Andre Agassi	8 Tim Henman
9 Eliot Teltscher	9 Goran Ivanisevic	9 Thomas Enqvist	9 Albert Costa
10 Yannick Noah	10 Brad Gilbert	10 Wayne Ferreira	10 Andy Roddick

1985	**1991**	**1997**	**2003**
1 Ivan Lendl	1 Stefan Edberg	1 Pete Sampras	1 Andy Roddick
2 John McEnroe	2 Jim Courier	2 Patrick Rafter	2 Roger Federer
3 Mats Wilander	3 Boris Becker	3 Michael Chang	3 Juan Carlos Ferrero
4 Jimmy Connors	4 Michael Stich	4 Jonas Bjorkman	4 Andre Agassi
5 Stefan Edberg	5 Ivan Lendl	5 Yevgeny Kafelnikov	5 Guillermo Coria
6 Boris Becker	6 Pete Sampras	6 Greg Rusedski	6 Rainer Schuettler
7 Yannick Noah	7 Guy Forget	7 Carlos Moya	7 Carlos Moya
8 Anders Jarryd	8 Karel Novacek	8 Sergi Bruguera	8 David Nalbandian
9 Miloslav Mecir	9 Petr Korda	9 Thomas Muster	9 Mark Philippoussis
10 Kevin Curren	10 Andre Agassi	10 Marcelo Rios	10 Sebastien Grosjean

1986	**1992**	**1998**
1 Ivan Lendl	1 Jim Courier	1 Pete Sampras
2 Boris Becker	2 Stefan Edberg	2 Marcelo Rios
3 Mats Wilander	3 Pete Sampras	3 Alex Corretja
4 Yannick Noah	4 Goran Ivanisevic	4 Patrick Rafter
5 Stefan Edberg	5 Boris Becker	5 Carlos Moya
6 Henri Leconte	6 Michael Chang	6 Andre Agassi
7 Joakim Nystrom	7 Petr Korda	7 Tim Henman
8 Jimmy Connors	8 Ivan Lendl	8 Karol Kucera
9 Miloslav Mecir	9 Andre Agassi	9 Greg Rusedski
10 Andres Gomez	10 Richard Krajicek	10 Richard Krajicek

1987	**1993**	**1999**
1 Ivan Lendl	1 Pete Sampras	1 Andre Agassi
2 Stefan Edberg	2 Michael Stich	2 Yevgeny Kafelnikov
3 Mats Wilander	3 Jim Courier	3 Pete Sampras
4 Jimmy Connors	4 Sergi Bruguera	4 Thomas Enqvist
5 Boris Becker	5 Stefan Edberg	5 Gustavo Kuerten
6 Miloslav Mecir	6 Andrei Medvedev	6 Nicolas Kiefer
7 Pat Cash	7 Goran Ivanisevic	7 Todd Martin
8 Yannick Noah	8 Michael Chang	8 Nicolas Lapentti
9 Tim Mayotte	9 Thomas Muster	9 Marcelo Rios
10 John McEnroe	10 Cedric Pioline	10 Richard Krajicek

1988	**1994**	**2000**
1 Mats Wilander	1 Pete Sampras	1 Gustavo Kuerten
2 Ivan Lendl	2 Andre Agassi	2 Marat Safin
3 Andre Agassi	3 Boris Becker	3 Pete Sampras
4 Boris Becker	4 Sergi Bruguera	4 Magnus Norman
5 Stefan Edberg	5 Goran Ivanisevic	5 Yevgeny Kafelnikov
6 Kent Carlsson	6 Michael Chang	6 Andre Agassi
7 Jimmy Connors	7 Stefan Edberg	7 Lleyton Hewitt
8 Jakob Hlasek	8 Alberto Berasategui	8 Alex Corretja
9 Henri Leconte	9 Michael Stich	9 Thomas Enqvist
10 Tim Mayotte	10 Todd Martin	10 Tim Henman

WOMEN

1968
1 Billie Jean King
2 Virginia Wade
3 Nancy Richey
4 Maria Bueno
5 Margaret Court
6 Ann Jones
7 Judy Tegart
8 Annette du Plooy
9 Leslie Bowrey
10 Rosie Casals

1969
1 Margaret Court
2 Ann Jones
3 Billie Jean King
4 Nancy Richey
5 Julie Heldman
6 Rosie Casals
7 Kerry Melville
8 Peaches Bartkowicz
9 Virginia Wade
10 Leslie Bowrey

1970
1 Margaret Court
2 Billie Jean King
3 Rosie Casals
4 Virginia Wade
5 Helga Niessen
6 Kerry Melville
7 Julie Heldman
8 Karen Krantczke
9 Francoise Durr
10 Nancy R. Gunter

1971
1 Evonne Goolagong
2 Billie Jean King
3 Margaret Court
4 Rosie Casals
5 Kerry Melville
6 Virginia Wade
7 Judy Tegart
8 Francoise Durr
9 Helga N. Masthoff
10 Chris Evert

1972
1 Billie Jean King
2 Evonne Goolagong
3 Chris Evert
4 Margaret Court
5 Kerry Melville
6 Virginia Wade
7 Rosie Casals
8 Nancy R. Gunter
9 Francoise Durr
10 Linda Tuero

1973
1 Margaret S. Court
2 Billie Jean King
3 Evonne G. Cawley
4 Chris Evert
5 Rosie Casals
6 Virginia Wade
7 Kerry Reid
8 Nancy Richey
9 Julie Heldman
10 Helga Masthoff

1974
1 Billie Jean King
2 Evonne G. Cawley
3 Chris Evert
4 Virginia Wade
5 Julie Heldman
6 Rosie Casals
7 Kerry Reid
8 Olga Morozova
9 Lesley Hunt
10 Francoise Durr

1975
1 Chris Evert
2 Billie Jean King
3 Evonne G. Cawley
4 Martina Navratilova
5 Virginia Wade
6 Margaret S. Court
7 Olga Morozova
8 Nancy Richey
9 Francoise Durr
10 Rosie Casals

1976
1 Chris Evert
2 Evonne G. Cawley
3 Virginia Wade
4 Martina Navratilova
5 Sue Barker
6 Betty Stove
7 Dianne Balestrat
8 Mima Jausovec
9 Rosie Casals
10 Francoise Durr

1977
1 Chris Evert
2 Billie Jean King
3 Martina Navratilova
4 Virginia Wade
5 Sue Barker
6 Rosie Casals
7 Betty Stove
8 Dianne Balestrat
9 Wendy Turnbull
10 Kerry Reid

1978
1 Martina Navratilova
2 Chris Evert Lloyd
3 Evonne G. Cawley
4 Virginia Wade
5 Billie Jean King
6 Tracy Austin
7 Wendy Turnbull
8 Kerry Reid
9 Betty Stove
10 Dianne Balestrat

1979
1 Martina Navratilova
2 Chris Evert Lloyd
3 Tracy Austin
4 Evonne G. Cawley
5 Billie Jean King
6 Dianne Balestrat
7 Wendy Turnbull
8 Virginia Wade
9 Kerry Reid
10 Sue Barker

1980
1 Chris Evert Lloyd
2 Tracy Austin
3 Martina Navratilova
4 Hana Mandlikova
5 Evonne G. Cawley
6 Billie Jean King
7 Andrea Jaeger
8 Wendy Turnbull
9 Pam Shriver
10 Greer Stevens

1981
1 Chris Evert Lloyd
2 Tracy Austin
3 Martina Navratilova
4 Andrea Jaeger
5 Hana Mandlikova
6 Sylvia Hanika
7 Pam Shriver
8 Wendy Turnbull
9 Bettina Bunge
10 Barbara Potter

1982
1 Martina Navratilova
2 Chris Evert Lloyd
3 Andrea Jaeger
4 Tracy Austin
5 Wendy Turnbull
6 Pam Shriver
7 Hana Mandlikova
8 Barbara Potter
9 Bettina Bunge
10 Sylvia Hanika

1983
1 Martina Navratilova
2 Chris Evert Lloyd
3 Andrea Jaeger
4 Pam Shriver
5 Sylvia Hanika
6 Jo Durie
7 Bettina Bunge
8 Wendy Turnbull
9 Tracy Austin
10 Zina Garrison

1984
1 Martina Navratilova
2 Chris Evert Lloyd
3 Hana Mandlikova
4 Pam Shriver
5 Wendy Turnbull
6 Manuela Maleeva
7 Helena Sukova
8 Claudia Kohde-Kilsch
9 Zina Garrison
10 Kathy Jordan

1985
1 Martina Navratilova
2 Chris Evert Lloyd
3 Hana Mandlikova
4 Pam Shriver
5 Claudia Kohde-Kilsch
6 Steffi Graf
7 Manuela Maleeva
8 Zina Garrison
9 Helena Sukova
10 Bonnie Gadusek

1986
1 Martina Navratilova
2 Chris Evert Lloyd
3 Steffi Graf
4 Hana Mandlikova
5 Helena Sukova
6 Pam Shriver
7 Claudia Kohde-Kilsch
8 M. Maleeva-Fragniere
9 Zina Garrison
10 Gabriela Sabatini

1987
1 Steffi Graf
2 Martina Navratilova
3 Chris Evert
4 Pam Shriver
5 Hana Mandlikova
6 Gabriela Sabatini
7 Helena Sukova
8 M. Maleeva-Fragniere
9 Zina Garrison
10 Claudia Kohde-Kilsch

1988
1 Steffi Graf
2 Martina Navratilova
3 Chris Evert
4 Gabriela Sabatini
5 Pam Shriver
6 M. Maleeva-Fragniere
7 Natalia Zvereva
8 Helena Sukova
9 Zina Garrison
10 Barbara Potter

1989
1 Steffi Graf
2 Martina Navratilova
3 Gabriela Sabatini
4 Z. Garrison-Jackson
5 A. Sanchez Vicario
6 Monica Seles
7 Conchita Martinez
8 Helena Sukova
9 M. Maleeva-Fragniere
10 Chris Evert

1990
1 Steffi Graf
2 Monica Seles
3 Martina Navratilova
4 Mary Joe Fernandez
5 Gabriela Sabatini
6 Katerina Maleeva
7 A. Sanchez Vicario
8 Jennifer Capriati
9 M. Maleeva-Fragniere
10 Z. Garrison-Jackson

1991
1 Monica Seles
2 Steffi Graf
3 Gabriela Sabatini
4 Martina Navratilova
5 A. Sanchez Vicario
6 Jennifer Capriati
7 Jana Novotna
8 Mary Joe Fernandez
9 Conchita Martinez
10 M. Maleeva-Fragniere

1992
1 Monica Seles
2 Steffi Graf
3 Gabriela Sabatini
4 A. Sanchez Vicario
5 Martina Navratilova
6 Mary Joe Fernandez
7 Jennifer Capriati
8 Conchita Martinez
9 M. Maleeva-Fragniere
10 Jana Novotna

1993
1 Steffi Graf
2 A. Sanchez Vicario
3 Martina Navratilova
4 Conchita Martinez
5 Gabriela Sabatini
6 Jana Novotna
7 Mary Joe Fernandez
8 Monica Seles
9 Jennifer Capriati
10 Anke Huber

1994
1 Steffi Graf
2 A. Sanchez Vicario
3 Conchita Martinez
4 Jana Novotna
5 Mary Pierce
6 Lindsay Davenport
7 Gabriela Sabatini
8 Martina Navratilova
9 Kimiko Date
10 Natasha Zvereva

1995
1 Steffi Graf
  Monica Seles*
2 Conchita Martinez
3 A. Sanchez Vicario
4 Kimiko Date
5 Mary Pierce
6 Magdalena
  Maleeva
7 Gabriela
  Sabatini
8 Mary Joe Fernandez
9 Iva Majoli
10 Anke Huber

1996
1 Steffi Graf
2 Monica Seles†
  A. Sanchez Vicario
3 Jana Novotna
4 Martina Hingis
5 Conchita Martinez
6 Anke Huber
7 Iva Majoli
8 Kimiko Date
9 Lindsay Davenport
10 Barbara Paulus

Annual Top 10 World Rankings (since 1968) (Cont.)
WOMEN

1997	1999	2001	2003
1 Martina Hingis	1 Martina Hingis	1 Lindsay Davenport	1 Justine Henin-Hardenne
2 Jana Novotna	2 Lindsay Davenport	2 Jennifer Capriati	2 Kim Clijsters
3 Lindsay Davenport	3 Venus Williams	3 Venus Williams	3 Serena Williams
4 Amanda Coetzer	4 Serena Williams	4 Martina Hingis	4 Amelie Mauresmo
5 Monica Seles	5 Mary Pierce	5 Kim Clijsters	5 Lindsay Davenport
6 Iva Majoli	6 Monica Seles	6 Serena Williams	6 Jennifer Capriati
7 Mary Pierce	7 Nathalie Tauziat	7 Justine Henin	7 Anastasia Myskina
8 Irina Spirlea	8 Barbara Schett	8 Jelena Dokic	8 Elena Dementieva
9 A. Sanchez Vicario	9 Julie Halard-Decugis	9 Amelie Mauresmo	9 Chanda Rubin
10 Mary Joe Fernandez	10 Amelie Mauresmo	10 Monica Seles	10 Ai Sugiyama

1998	2000	2002	
1 Lindsay Davenport	1 Martina Hingis	1 Serena Williams	
2 Martina Hingis	2 Lindsay Davenport	2 Venus Williams	
3 Jana Novotna	3 Venus Williams	3 Jennifer Capriati	
4 A. Sanchez Vicario	4 Monica Seles	4 Kim Clijsters	
5 Venus Williams	5 Conchita Martinez	5 Justine Henin-Hardenne	
6 Monica Seles	6 Serena Williams	6 Amelie Mauresmo	
7 Mary Pierce	7 Mary Pierce	7 Monica Seles	
8 Conchita Martinez	8 Anna Kournikova	8 Daniela Hantuchova	
9 Steffi Graf	9 A. Sanchez Vicario	9 Jelena Dokic	
10 Nathalie Tauziat	10 Nathalie Tauziat	10 Martina Hingis	

*Returning to the WTA Tour on Aug. 15, 1995, Seles was co-ranked #1 for her first six tournaments. Seles had been absent from the Tour since April 1993 when she was stabbed by a fan during a match. She was ranked #1 at the time of the stabbing.
†Seles' ranking was revised in May 1996. The revision stipulated that her new modified ranking would be calculated using a divisor of the actual number of tournaments she had played (13), and she would be co-ranked with the player whose average is immediately below her average (Sanchez Vicario).

All-Time Leaders

Tournaments Won (singles)

All-time tournament wins from the arrival of open tennis in 1968 through 2004 (through Sept. 26). Men's totals include ATP Tour, Grand Prix and WCT tournaments. Players active in singles play in 2004 are in **bold** type.

MEN

		Total			Total			Total
1	Jimmy Connors	109	11	Thomas Muster	44	21	Vitas Gerulaitis	27
2	Ivan Lendl	94	12	Stefan Edberg	41	22	Yevgeny Kafelnikov	26
3	John McEnroe	77	13	Stan Smith	39	23	Jose-Luis Clerc	25
4	Pete Sampras	64	14	Michael Chang	34		Brian Gottfried	25
5	Bjorn Borg	62	15	Arthur Ashe	33	25	Jim Courier	23
	Guillermo Vilas	62		Mats Wilander	33		**Lleyton Hewitt**	23
7	**Andre Agassi**	59	17	John Newcombe	32		Yannick Noah	23
8	Ilie Nastase	57		Manuel Orantes	32	28	Eddie Dibbs	22
9	Boris Becker	49		Ken Rosewall	32		**Goran Ivanisevic**	22
10	Rod Laver	47	20	Tom Okker	31		Harold Solomon	22

WOMEN

		Total			Total			Total
1	Martina Navratilova	167	12	Olga Morozova	31	22	**Kim Clijsters**	21
2	Chris Evert	154		**Venus Williams**	31		Pam Shriver	21
3	Steffi Graf	107	14	Tracy Austin	30	24	Julie Heldman	20
4	Margaret Smith Court	92	15	Arantxa Sanchez-Vicario	29	25	**J. Henin-Hardenne**	19
5	E. Goolagong Cawley	68	16	Hana Mandlikova	27		M. Maleeva-Fragniere	19
6	Billie Jean King	67		Gabriela Sabatini	27		Nancy Richey	19
7	Virginia Wade	55	18	Nancy Richey	25	28	Virginia Ruzici	17
8	Monica Seles	53		**Serena Williams**	25		Regina Marsikova	17
9	**Lindsay Davenport**	44	20	Jana Novotna	24	30	Ann Jones	16
10	Martina Hingis	40	21	Kerry Melville Reid	22		**Mary Pierce**	16
11	**Conchita Martinez**	32						

Money Won

All-time money winners from the arrival of open tennis in 1968 through 2004 (through Sept. 26). Totals include doubles earnings.

MEN

		Earnings				Earnings				Earnings
1	Pete Sampras	. . . . $43,280,489	10	Jim Courier	. . . . . . $14,033,132	19	Jonas Bjorkman	. . . $10,915,233
2	Andre Agassi	. . . 29,200,579	11	Lleyton Hewitt	 13,713,820	20	Petr Korda	 10,448,450
3	Boris Becker	 25,080,956	12	Michael Stich	 12,592,483	21	Alex Corretja	 10,339,509
4	Yevgeny Kafelnikov	. 23,883,797	13	John McEnroe	 12,539,622	22	Tim Henman	 10,321,240
5	Ivan Lendl	 21,262,417	14	Roger Federer	 12,491,230	23	Thomas Enqvist	. . . 10,290,743
6	Stefan Edberg	 20,630,941	15	Thomas Muster	 12,224,410	24	Richard Krajicek	. . . 10,077,425
7	Goran Ivanisevic	. . 19,876,579	16	Sergi Bruguera	. . . 11,632,199	25	Wayne Ferreira	 9,969,617
8	Michael Chang	 19,145,632	17	Patrick Rafter	 11,127,058			
9	Gustavo Kuerten	. . . 14,609,954	18	Carlos Moya	: 10,937,296			

WOMEN

		Earnings				Earnings				Earnings
1	Steffi Graf	. . . . . . $21,895,277	10	Conchita Martinez	$11,005,339	19	Helena Sukova	. . . . $6,391,245
2	Mart. Navratilova	. . 21,194,804	11	Jennifer Capriati	. . . 9,726,539	20	Amelie Mauresmo	. . . 6,024,213
3	Martina Hingis	 18,344,660	12	Chris Evert	 8,896,195	21	Amanda Coetzer	. . . 5,582,821
4	Lindsay Davenport	. . 18,171,981	13	Gabriela Sabatini	. . 8,785,850	22	Lisa Raymond	 5,501,821
5	A. Sanchez-Vicario	. 16,938,363	14	Kim Clijsters	 8,711,741	23	Pam Shriver	 5,460,566
6	Monica Seles	 14,891,762	15	Natasha Zvereva	. . 7,792,503	24	Mary Joe Fernandez	. 5,258,471
7	Serena Williams	. . . 13,864,061	16	J. Henin-Hardenne	. . 7,518,086	25	Ai Sugiyama	 5,020,457
8	Venus Williams	 13,784,491	17	Mary Pierce	 7,009,293			
9	Jana Novotna	 11,249,284	18	Nathalie Tauziat	 6,649,907			

Year-end Tournaments
MEN
Tennis Masters Cup

The year-end championship featuring the top eight players in the Tennis Masters Series rankings. Two groups of four players square off in a round-robin tournament followed by a single-elimination semifinals and finals. Originally called the Masters in 1970, the tournament followed a round-robin format, but was revised in 1972 to include a round-robin to decide the four semi-finalists then a single elimination format after that. Replaced by ATP Tour World Championship from 1990 through 1999.

Multiple Winners: Ivan Lendl and Pete Sampras (5); Ilie Nastase (4); Boris Becker and John McEnroe (3); Bjorn Borg and Lleyton Hewitt (2).

Year	Winner		Runner-Up		Year	Winner	Loser	Score
1970	Stan Smith (4-1) *		Rod Laver (4-1)		1987	Ivan Lendl	M. Wilander	62 62 63
1971	Ilie Nastase (6-0)		Stan Smith (4-2)		1988	Boris Becker	I. Lendl	57 76 36 62 76
					1989	Stefan Edberg	B. Becker	46 76 63 61
Year	Winner	Loser		Score	1990	Andre Agassi	S. Edberg	57 76 75 62
1972	Ilie Nastase	S. Smith	63 62 36 26 63		1991	Pete Sampras	J. Courier	36 76 63 64
1973	Ilie Nastase	T. Okker	63 75 46 63		1992	Boris Becker	J. Courier	64 63 75
1974	Guillermo Vilas	I. Nastase	76 62 36 36 64		1993	Michael Stich	P. Sampras	76 26 76 62
1975	Ilie Nastase	B. Borg	62 62 61		1994	Pete Sampras	B. Becker	46 63 75 64
1976	Manuel Orantes	W. Fibak	57 62 06 76 61		1995	Boris Becker	M. Chang	76 60 76
1978	Jimmy Connors	B. Borg	64 16 64		1996	Pete Sampras	B. Becker	36 76 76 67 64
1979	John McEnroe	A. Ashe	67 63 75		1997	Pete Sampras	Y. Kafelnikov	63 62 62
1980	Bjorn Borg	V. Gerulaitis	62 62		1998	Alex Corretja	C. Moya	36 36 75 63 75
1981	Bjorn Borg	I. Lendl	64 62 62		1999	Pete Sampras	A. Agassi	61 75 64
1982	Ivan Lendl	V. Gerulaitis	67 26 76 62 64		2000	Gustavo Kuerten	A. Agassi	64 64 64
1983	Ivan Lendl	J. McEnroe	64 64 62		2001	Lleyton Hewitt	S. Grosjean	63 63 64
1984	John McEnroe	I. Lendl	75 60 64		2002	Lleyton Hewitt	J.C. Ferrero	75 75 26 26 64
1985	John McEnroe	I. Lendl	76 60 64		2003	Roger Federer	A. Agassi	63 60 64
1986	Ivan Lendl	B. Becker	62 76 63					
1986	Ivan Lendl	B. Becker	64 64 64					

*Smith was declared the winner because he beat Laver in their round-robin match (4-6, 6-3, 6-4).
Note: The tournament switched from December to January in 1977-78, then back to December in 1986.

Playing Sites

1970—Tokyo; **1971**—Paris; **1972**—Barcelona; **1973**—Boston; **1974**—Melbourne; **1975**—Stockholm; **1976, 2003-04**—Houston; **1977-89**—New York City; **1990-95**—Frankfurt, GER; **1996-99**—Hannover, GER; **2000**—Lisbon, POR; **2001**—Sydney, AUS; **2002**—Shanghai, CHN.

WCT Championship (1971-89)

World Championship Tennis was established in 1967 to promote professional tennis and led the way into the open era. Its major singles and doubles championships were held every May among the top eight regular season finishers on the circuit from 1971 until the WCT folded in 1989.

Multiple winners: John McEnroe (5), Jimmy Connors, Ivan Lendl and Ken Rosewall (2).

Year	Winner	Loser	Score	Year	Winner	Loser	Score
1971	Ken Rosewall	R. Laver	64 16 76 76	1973	Stan Smith	A. Ashe	63 63 46 64
1972	Ken Rosewall	R. Laver	46 60 63 67 76	1974	John Newcombe	B. Borg	46 63 63 62

Year-end Tournaments (Cont.)

Year	Winner	Loser	Score	Year	Winner	Loser	Score
1975	Arthur Ashe	B. Borg	36 64 64 60	1983	John McEnroe	I. Lendl	62 46 63 67 76
1976	Bjorn Borg	G. Vilas	16 61 75 61	1984	John McEnroe	J. Connors	61 62 63
1977	Jimmy Connors	D. Stockton	67 61 64 63	1985	Ivan Lendl	T. Mayotte	76 64 61
1978	Vitas Gerulaitis	E. Dibbs	63 62 61	1986	Anders Jarryd	B. Becker	67 61 61 64
1979	John McEnroe	B. Borg	75 46 62 76	1987	Miloslav Mecir	J. McEnroe	60 36 62 62
1980	Jimmy Connors	J. McEnroe	26 76 61 62	1988	Boris Becker	S. Edberg	64 16 75 62
1981	John McEnroe	J. Kriek	61 62 64	1989	John McEnroe	B. Gilbert	63 63 76
1982	Ivan Lendl	J. McEnroe	62 36 63 63				

WOMEN
WTA Championships

The WTA Tour's year-end tournament took place in March from 1972 until 1986 when the WTA decided to adopt a January-to-November playing season. Given the changeover, two championships were held in 1986. Held in Boca Raton (1972-73), Los Angeles (1974-76, 2002–), New York (1977, 1979-2000), Oakland (1978), Munich (2001).

Multiple winners: Martina Navratilova (8); Steffi Graf (5); Chris Evert (4); Monica Seles (3); Kim Clijsters, Evonne Goolagong, Martina Hingis and Gabriela Sabatini (2).

Year	Winner	Loser	Score	Year	Winner	Loser	Score
1972	Chris Evert	K. Reid	75 64	1988	Gabriela Sabatini	P. Shriver	75 62 62
1973	Chris Evert	N. Richey	63 63	1989	Steffi Graf	M. Navratilova	64 75 26 62
1974	Evonne Goolagong	C. Evert	63 64	1990	Monica Seles	G. Sabatini	64 57 36 64 62
1975	Chris Evert	M. Navratilova	64 62	1991	Monica Seles	M. Navratilova	64 36 75 60
1976	Evonne Goolagong	C. Evert	63 57 63	1992	Monica Seles	M. Navratilova	75 63 61
1977	Chris Evert	S. Barker	26 61 61	1993	Steffi Graf	A. S. Vicario	61 64 36 61
1978	M. Navratilova	E. Goolagong	76 64	1994	Gabriela Sabatini	L. Davenport	63 62 64
1979	M. Navratilova	T. Austin	63 36 62	1995	Steffi Graf	A. Huber	61 26 61 46 63
1980	Tracy Austin	M. Navratilova	62 26 62	1996	Steffi Graf	M. Hingis	63 46 60 46 60
1981	M. Navratilova	A. Jaeger	63 76	1997	Jana Novotna	M. Pierce	76 62 63
1982	Sylvia Hanika	M. Navratilova	16 63 64	1998	Martina Hingis	L. Davenport	75 64 46 62
1983	M. Navratilova	C. Evert	62 60	1999	Lindsay Davenport	M. Hingis	64 62
1984	M. Navratilova	C. Evert	63 75 61	2000	Martina Hingis	M. Seles	67 64 64
1985	M. Navratilova	H. Sukova	63 75 64	2001	Serena Williams	L. Davenport	walkover
1986	M. Navratilova	H. Mandlikova	62 60 36 61	2002	Kim Clijsters	S. Williams	75 63
1986	M. Navratilova	S. Graf	76 63 62	2003	Kim Clijsters	A. Mauresmo	62 60
1987	Steffi Graf	G. Sabatini	46 64 60 64				

Note: The final was best-of-five sets from 1984-98 and best-of-three sets from 1972-83 and since 1999.

Davis Cup

Established in 1900 as an annual international tournament by American player Dwight Davis. Originally called the International Lawn Tennis Challenge Trophy. Challenge round system until 1972. Since 1981, the top 16 nations in the world have played a straight knockout tournament over the course of a year. The format is a best-of-five match of two singles, one doubles and two singles over three days. Note that from 1900-24 Australia and New Zealand competed together as Australasia.

Multiple winners: USA (31); Australia (22); France (9); Sweden (7); Australasia (6); British Isles (5); Britain (4); Germany (3).

Challenge Rounds

Year	Winner	Loser	Score	Site	Year	Winner	Loser	Score	Site
1900	USA	British Isles	3-0	Boston	1927	France	USA	3-2	Philadelphia
1901	Not held				1928	France	USA	4-1	Paris
1902	USA	British Isles	3-2	New York	1929	France	USA	3-2	Paris
1903	British Isles	USA	4-1	Boston	1930	France	USA	4-1	Paris
1904	British Isles	Belgium	5-0	Wimbledon	1931	France	Britain	3-2	Paris
1905	British Isles	USA	5-0	Wimbledon	1932	France	USA	3-2	Paris
1906	British Isles	USA	5-0	Wimbledon	1933	Britain	France	3-2	Paris
1907	Australasia	British Isles	3-2	Wimbledon	1934	Britain	USA	4-1	Wimbledon
1908	Australasia	USA	3-2	Melbourne	1935	Britain	USA	5-0	Wimbledon
1909	Australasia	USA	5-0	Sydney	1936	Britain	Australia	3-2	Wimbledon
1910	Not held				1937	USA	Britain	4-1	Wimbledon
1911	Australasia	USA	5-0	Christchurch, NZ	1938	USA	Australia	3-2	Philadelphia
1912	British Isles	Australasia	3-2	Melbourne	1939	Australia	USA	3-2	Philadelphia
1913	USA	British Isles	3-2	Wimbledon	1940-45	Not held World War II			
1914	Australasia	USA	3-2	New York	1946	USA	Australia	5-0	Melbourne
1915-18	Not held World War I				1947	USA	Australia	4-1	New York
1919	Australasia	British Isles	4-1	Sydney	1948	USA	Australia	5-0	New York
1920	USA	Australasia	5-0	Auckland, NZ	1949	USA	Australia	4-1	New York
1921	USA	Japan	5-0	New York	1950	Australia	USA	4-1	New York
1922	USA	Australasia	4-1	New York	1951	Australia	USA	3-2	Sydney
1923	USA	Australasia	4-1	New York	1952	Australia	USA	4-1	Adelaide
1924	USA	Australia	5-0	Philadelphia	1953	Australia	USA	3-2	Melbourne
1925	USA	France	5-0	Philadelphia	1954	USA	Australia	3-2	Sydney
1926	USA	France	4-1	Philadelphia	1955	Australia	USA	5-0	New York

Year	Winner	Loser	Score	Site	Year	Winner	Loser	Score	Site
1956	Australia	USA	5-0	Adelaide	1962	Australia	Mexico	5-0	Brisbane
1957	Australia	USA	3-2	Melbourne	1963	USA	Australia	3-2	Adelaide
1958	USA	Australia	3-2	Brisbane	1964	Australia	USA	3-2	Cleveland
1959	Australia	USA	3-2	New York	1965	Australia	Spain	4-1	Sydney
1960	Australia	Italy	4-1	Sydney	1966	Australia	India	4-1	Melbourne
1961	Australia	Italy	5-0	Melbourne	1967	Australia	Spain	4-1	Brisbane

Final Rounds

Year	Winner	Loser	Score	Site	Year	Winner	Loser	Score	Site
1968	USA	Australia	4-1	Adelaide	1986	Australia	Sweden	3-2	Melbourne
1969	USA	Romania	5-0	Cleveland	1987	Sweden	India	5-0	Göteborg
1970	USA	W. Germany	5-0	Cleveland	1988	W. Germany	Sweden	4-1	Göteborg
1971	USA	Romania	3-2	Charlotte	1989	W. Germany	Sweden	3-2	Stuttgart
1972	USA	Romania	3-2	Bucharest	1990	USA	Australia	3-2	St. Petersburg
1973	Australia	USA	5-0	Cleveland	1991	France	USA	3-1	Lyon
1974	So. Africa	India	walkover	Not held	1992	USA	Switzerland	3-1	Ft. Worth
1975	Sweden	Czech.	3-2	Stockholm	1993	Germany	Australia	4-1	Dusseldorf
1976	Italy	Chile	4-1	Santiago	1994	Sweden	Russia	4-1	Moscow
1977	Australia	Italy	3-1	Sydney	1995	USA	Russia	3-2	Moscow
1978	USA	Britain	4-1	Palm Springs	1996	France	Sweden	3-2	Malmo
1979	USA	Italy	5-0	San Francisco	1997	Sweden	USA	5-0	Göteborg
1980	Czech.	Italy	4-1	Prague	1998	Sweden	Italy	4-1	Milan
1981	USA	Argentina	3-1	Cincinnati	1999	Australia	France	3-2	Nice
1982	USA	France	4-1	Grenoble	2000	Spain	Australia	3-1	Barcelona
1983	Australia	Sweden	3-2	Melbourne	2001	France	Australia	3-2	Melbourne
1984	Sweden	USA	4-1	Göteborg	2002	Russia	France	3-2	Paris
1985	Sweden	W. Germany	3-2	Munich	2003	Australia	Spain	3-1	Melbourne

Note: In 1974, India refused to play the final as a protest against the South African government's policies of apartheid.

Fed Cup

Originally the Federation Cup started by the International Tennis Federation as the Davis Cup of women's tennis. Played by 32 teams over one week at one site from 1963-94. Tournament changed to Davis Cup-style format of four rounds and home site in 1995. Currently 16 teams compete in a home-and-away knockout format, with the top four teams advancing to "finals week" at a single location.

Multiple winners: USA (17); Australia (7); Czechoslovakia and Spain (5); France and Germany (2).

Year	Winner	Loser	Score	Site	Year	Winner	Loser	Score	Site
1963	USA	Australia	2-1	London	1984	Czech.	Australia	2-1	Brazil
1964	Australia	USA	2-1	Philadelphia	1985	Czech.	USA	2-1	Japan
1965	Australia	USA	2-1	Melbourne	1986	USA	Czech.	3-0	Prague
1966	USA	W. Germany	3-0	Italy	1987	W. Germany	USA	2-1	Vancouver
1967	USA	Britain	2-0	W. Germany	1988	Czech.	USSR	2-1	Melbourne
1968	Australia	Holland	3-0	Paris	1989	USA	Spain	3-0	Tokyo
1969	USA	Australia	2-1	Athens	1990	USA	USSR	2-1	Atlanta
1970	Australia	Britain	3-0	W. Germany	1991	Spain	USA	2-1	Nottingham
1971	Australia	Britain	3-0	Perth	1992	Germany	Spain	2-1	Frankfurt
1972	So. Africa	Britain	2-1	So. Africa	1993	Spain	Australia	3-0	Frankfurt
1973	Australia	So. Africa	3-0	W. Germany	1994	Spain	USA	3-0	Frankfurt
1974	Australia	USA	2-1	Italy	1995	Spain	USA	3-2	Valencia
1975	Czech.	Australia	3-0	France	1996	USA	Spain	5-0	Atlantic City
1976	USA	Australia	2-1	Philadelphia	1997	France	Netherlands	4-1	Netherlands
1977	USA	Australia	2-1	Eastbourne	1998	Spain	Switzerland	3-2	Geneva
1978	USA	Australia	2-1	Melbourne	1999	USA	Russia	4-1	Palo Alto
1979	USA	Australia	3-0	Spain	2000	USA	Spain	5-0	Las Vegas
1980	USA	Australia	3-0	W. Germany	2001	Belgium	Russia	2-1	Madrid
1981	USA	Britain	3-0	Tokyo	2002	Slovakia	Spain	3-1	Canary Islands
1982	USA	W. Germany	3-0	Santa Clara	2003	France	USA	4-1	Moscow
1983	Czech.	W. Germany	2-1	Zurich					

COLLEGES

NCAA team titles were not sanctioned until 1946. NCAA women's individual and team championships started in 1982.

Men's NCAA Individual Champions (1883-1945)

Multiple winners: Malcolm Chace and Pancho Segura (3); Edward Chandler, George Church, E.B. Dewhurst, Fred Hovey, Frank Guernsey, W.P. Knapp, Robert LeRoy, P.S. Sears, Cliff Sutter, Ernest Sutter and Richard Williams (2).

Year		Year		Year	
1883	J. Clark, Harvard (spring)	1887	P.S. Sears, Harvard	1891	Fred Hovey, Harvard
	H. Taylor, Harvard (fall)	1888	P.S. Sears, Harvard	1892	William Larned, Cornell
1884	W.P. Knapp, Yale	1889	R.P. Huntington Jr., Yale	1893	Malcolm Chace, Brown
1885	W.P. Knapp, Yale	1890	Fred Hovey, Harvard	1894	Malcolm Chace, Yale
1886	G.M. Brinley, Trinity, CT	1891	Fred Hovey, Harvard	1895	Malcolm Chace, Yale

Colleges (Cont.)

Year		Year		Year	
1896	Malcolm Whitman, Harvard	1912	George Church, Princeton	1930	Cliff Sutter, Tulane
1897	S.G. Thompson, Princeton	1913	Richard Williams, Harv.	1931	Keith Gledhill, Stanford
1898	Leo Ware, Harvard	1914	George Church, Princeton	1932	Cliff Sutter, Tulane
1899	Dwight Davis, Harvard	1915	Richard Williams, Harv.	1933	Jack Tidball, UCLA
1900	Ray Little, Princeton	1916	G.C. Caner, Harvard	1934	Gene Mako, USC
1901	Fred Alexander, Princeton	1917-1918	Not held	1935	Wilbur Hess, Rice
1902	William Clothier, Harvard	1919	Charles Garland, Yale	1936	Ernest Sutter, Tulane
1903	E.B. Dewhurst, Penn	1920	Lascelles Banks, Yale	1937	Ernest Sutter, Tulane
1904	Robert LeRoy, Columbia	1921	Philip Neer, Stanford	1938	Frank Guernsey, Rice
1905	E.B. Dewhurst, Penn	1922	Lucien Williams, Yale	1939	Frank Guernsey, Rice
1906	Robert LeRoy, Columbia	1923	Carl Fischer, Phi. Osteo.		
1907	G.P. Gardner Jr., Harvard	1924	Wallace Scott, Wash.	1940	Don McNeill, Kenyon
1908	Nat Niles, Harvard	1925	Edward Chandler, Calif.	1941	Joseph Hunt, Navy
1909	Wallace Johnson, Penn	1926	Edward Chandler, Calif.	1942	Ted Schroeder, Stanford
		1927	Wilmer Allison, Texas	1943	Pancho Segura, Miami-FL
1910	R.A. Holden Jr., Yale	1928	Julius Seligson, Lehigh	1944	Pancho Segura, Miami-FL
1911	E.H. Whitney, Harvard	1929	Berkeley Bell, Texas	1945	Pancho Segura, Miami-FL

NCAA Men's Division I Champions

Multiple winners (Teams): Stanford (17); USC (16); UCLA (15); Georgia (4); William & Mary (2). (Players): Matias Boeker, Alex Olmedo, Mikael Pernfors, Dennis Ralston and Ham Richardson (2).

Year	Team winner	Individual Champion	Year	Team winner	Individual Champion
1946	USC	Bob Falkenburg, USC	1976	USC & UCLA	Bill Scanlon, Trinity-TX
1947	Wm. & Mary	Gardner Larned, Wm. & Mary	1977	Stanford	Matt Mitchell, Stanford
1948	Wm. & Mary	Harry Likas, San Francisco	1978	Stanford	John McEnroe, Stanford
1949	San Francisco	Jack Tuero, Tulane	1979	UCLA	Kevin Curren, Texas
1950	UCLA	Herbert Flam, UCLA	1980	Stanford	Robert Van't Hof, USC
1951	USC	Tony Trabert, Cincinnati	1981	Stanford	Tim Mayotte, Stanford
1952	UCLA	Hugh Stewart, USC	1982	UCLA	Mike Leach, Michigan
1953	UCLA	Ham Richardson, Tulane	1983	Stanford	Greg Holmes, Utah
1954	UCLA	Ham Richardson, Tulane	1984	UCLA	Mikael Pernfors, Georgia
1955	USC	Jose Aguero, Tulane	1985	Georgia	Mikael Pernfors, Georgia
1956	UCLA	Alex Olmedo, USC	1986	Stanford	Dan Goldie, Stanford
1957	Michigan	Barry MacKay, Michigan	1987	Georgia	Andrew Burrow, Miami-FL
1958	USC	Alex Olmedo, USC	1988	Stanford	Robby Weiss, Pepperdine
1959	Tulane & Notre Dame	Whitney Reed, San Jose St.	1989	Stanford	Donni Leaycraft, LSU
1960	UCLA	Larry Nagler, UCLA	1990	Stanford	Steve Bryan, Texas
1961	UCLA	Allen Fox, UCLA	1991	USC	Jared Palmer, Stanford
1962	USC	Rafael Osuna, USC	1992	Stanford	Alex O'Brien Stanford
1963	USC	Dennis Ralston, USC	1993	USC	Chris Woodruff, Tennessee
1964	USC	Dennis Ralston, USC	1994	USC	Mark Merklein, Florida
1965	UCLA	Arthur Ashe, UCLA	1995	Stanford	Sargis Sargsian, Ariz. St.
1966	USC	Charlie Pasarell, UCLA	1996	Stanford	Cecil Mamiit, USC
1967	USC	Bob Lutz, USC	1997	Stanford	Luke Smith, UNLV
1968	USC	Stan Smith, USC	1998	Stanford	Bob Bryan, Stanford
1969	USC	Joaquin Loyo-Mayo, USC	1999	Georgia	Jeff Morrison, Florida
1970	UCLA	Jeff Borowiak, UCLA	2000	Stanford	Alex Kim, Stanford
1971	UCLA	Jimmy Connors, UCLA	2001	Georgia	Matias Boeker, Georgia
1972	Trinity-TX	Dick Stockton, Trinity-TX	2002	USC	Matias Boeker, Georgia
1973	Stanford	Alex Mayer, Stanford	2003	Illinois	Amer Delic, Illinois
1974	Stanford	John Whitlinger, Stanford	2004	Baylor	Benjamin Becker, Baylor
1975	UCLA	Bill Martin, UCLA			

NCAA Women's Division I Champions

Multiple winners (Teams): Stanford (13); Florida (4); Georgia, Texas and USC (2). (Players): Sandra Birch, Patty Fendick, Laura Granville, Amber Liu and Lisa Raymond (2).

Year	Team winner	Individual Champion	Year	Team winner	Individual Champion
1982	Stanford	Alycia Moulton, Stanford	1994	Georgia	Angela Lettiere, Georgia
1983	USC	Beth Herr, USC	1995	Texas	Keri Phoebus, UCLA
1984	Stanford	Lisa Spain, Georgia	1996	Florida	Jill Craybas, Florida
1985	USC	Linda Gates, Stanford	1997	Florida	Lilia Osterloh, Stanford
1986	Stanford	Patty Fendick, Stanford	1998	Florida	Vanessa Webb, Duke
1987	Stanford	Patty Fendick, Stanford	1999	Stanford	Zuzana Lesenarova, S. Diego
1988	Stanford	Shaun Stafford, Florida	2000	Georgia	Laura Granville, Stanford
1989	Stanford	Sandra Birch, Stanford	2001	Stanford	Laura Granville, Stanford
1990	Stanford	Debbie Graham, Stanford	2002	Stanford	Bea Bielik, Wake Forest
1991	Stanford	Sandra Birch, Stanford	2003	Florida	Amber Liu, Stanford
1992	Florida	Lisa Raymond, Florida	2004	Stanford	Amber Liu, Stanford
1993	Texas	Lisa Raymond, Florida			

Golf

Hard-working **Vijay Singh** grabbed the world's
No. 1 ranking from Tiger in 2004.

Right On, Lefty!

In his 47th major tournament, Phil Mickelson finally removes the monkey with a win at the Masters.

Scott Van Pelt
is an analyst for ESPN's golf coverage.

One putt. That's what changed everything for Phil Mickelson. The difference between one and none, is only one. But it was more than enough to silence the critics and give his throng of supporters the occasion to lift their collective voices to the heavens. The support Mickelson received at Augusta, and everywhere else for that matter, is really remarkable. Somehow this good-looking, wealthy, immensely talented guy became embraced by everyone from blue-blooded country clubbers to the guys who wear wife beaters and jean shorts on the golf course.

It was never more evident than on one of the most electric Sundays ever seen at Augusta National, which, by the way, has seen its share of electric Sundays. Mickelson charged home with five birdies in seven holes and won the green jacket.

It was as dramatic a finish as we've seen and it was authored by the man every patron on the grounds seemed to be cheering for. There are different roars at Augusta—birdie roars, eagle roars, Jack roars and Arnie roars. We heard the latter as the King said so long after 50 straight trips down Magnolia Lane. This year they invented a new roar—a Phil roar.

The one man who wasn't cheering was Ernie Els. He did nothing wrong that Sunday, shot 67, his best final-round ever at the Masters, and simply got beaten.

His chance for redemption came quickly. Els played himself into the final group Sunday at the U.S. Open two months later. He couldn't have imagined what was in store that day. No one could. Shinnecock wasn't over the edge—it was off the cliff. The USGA, in its endless pursuit of the toughest test in golf, basically ruined one of the greatest courses in the world. Twenty-seven men failed to break 80 in the final round. Els was one of them. Retief Goosen put on one of the sickest displays of clutch putting you'll ever see as he edged Mickelson by two strokes. If ever there was a doubt what the Masters meant

AP/Wide World Photos

Phil Mickelson's *birdie putt on the 72nd hole at Augusta gives him a well-deserved Masters title and a green jacket of his very own.*

to Mickelson, it was put to bed at the U.S. Open. His three-putt from inside of 10 feet on the 71st hole opened the door for Goosen to walk through and win his second U.S. Open. Turns out that green jacket doubled as a bullet-proof vest. Without that ONE major, he would have been trashed by the press yet again.

My favorite event each year is the British Open. The R & A just get it. They set up the course so that if the wind doesn't blow and the champ is 20-under-par, so be it. The yellow leader boards, the bad food, the people—there is nothing quite like it. Again it appeared Els was the man of the moment but he was topped by the relatively unknown Todd Hamilton. For the

final two days, and then the four-hole play-off, these men walked together. Hamilton told me after the third round he had an eerie sense of calm. It showed. Though he had never been on a stage as grand, he had won around the world and never doubted himself as many Scots wondered aloud who he was.

After losing by a putt on the 72nd hole at Augusta, Els had his own putt on the final hole to win the Claret Jug. Perfect symmetry. It went begging. It's a cruel game, and it wasn't done with Els just yet.

In the final major of the year, the PGA Championship, Els missed out on a playoff by a shot. Mickelson, who missed the playoff at Royal Troon by a shot, missed this

AP/Wide World Photos

The **European team** trounced the Americans in Bloomfield Hills, Mich. to win its second straight Ryder Cup and four out of the last five.

one by two. They both played spectacularly in all four majors, but at Whistling Straits, they couldn't top the man who owned this season.

At 41, Vijay Singh is a man in full. From the remote golfing outpost of Fiji, he has risen to the top of the golfing world. His swing is elegant, his temperament much better than you might have been led to believe. He closes down driving ranges the way drunks close bars and he just authored the greatest season for anyone north of 40 in history.

Wins? All-time earnings in a season? Player of the year? Pick a question and the answer in 2004 was Vijay. And he's now the world's top-ranked player. It was only appropriate that the official change came after Singh won in Boston, in the event Tiger Woods hosts. They played together in the final round. That meant a great deal to Singh. These two are not friends, but respect goes both ways. Tiger knows Veej is a great player. Veej knows Tiger works as hard as anyone out there. They have not seen the last of each other.

Maybe now that he's married to a Swede, Tiger might lobby to play for the European side in the Ryder Cup. How much longer until the men from that side of the Atlantic are finally, and correctly, recognized as the favorites? They have won four of the last five, and only that historic Brookline comeback prevented a clean sweep.

The Ten Biggest Stories
of the Year in Golf

10 Big-hitter John Daly, who had fallen into relative obscurity and a 299th-place world ranking, finds his swing at the Buick Invitational in February. He wins a three-man playoff for his first Tour victory in eight-plus years. He narrowly misses his second win of the year with a second-place finish to Vijay Singh at the Buick Open in August.

9 Welcome Michelle Wie. The six-foot, 14-year-old amateur finishes fourth at the LPGA's Kraft Nabisco Championship, four shots off tournament winner Grace Park. At the Sony Open in January, and that would be on the *men's* Tour, she cards a 72-68, missing the cut by one stroke.

8 PGA Tour player Jeff Julian, 42, and long-time Tom Watson caddie, Bruce Edwards, 49, die from ALS (Lou Gehrig's Disease).

7 England's Karen Stupples wins the Weetabix British Open in grand style. Her 19-under-par 269 ties for the lowest score in tournament history and her final-round 64 ties the record for low score in any major. Just a few months earlier in Tucson, she broke the LPGA record for best 72-hole score with a 258.

6 Todd Hamilton, a 38-year-old PGA Tour rookie, outplays Phil Mickelson and survives a four-hole play-off with Ernie Els to win the British Open at Royal Troon. Els is done in by a bogey on the third playoff hole.

5 Annika Sorenstam shoots a third-round 64 at the rain-soaked LPGA Championship, then holds on to win the seventh major championship of her hall-of-fame career.

4 It was never even close. Captain Bernhard Langer's European team jumps out to a 6½-1½ first-day lead and coasts to a 18½-9½ demolition of the U.S. team to retain the Ryder Cup. The controversial "dream team" pairing of Tiger Woods and Phil Mickelson loses both matches.

3 A gusty wind and ridiculously difficult pin placements give golfers fits at the U.S. Open at Shinnecock Hills in June. Calm and collected South African Retief Goosen perseveres for his second career U.S. title. Countryman Ernie Els, in contention through three rounds, cards an 80 on Sunday.

2 Vijay Singh wins eight tournaments through early October (including his third major at the PGA Championship), breaks the PGA Tour's single-season earnings mark formerly held by Tiger Woods, then in early September claims the world No. 1 ranking that Woods had held for five years.

1 Finally! In dramatic fashion, Phil Mickelson rolls in a 20-foot birdie put on the 72nd hole of the Masters to beat Ernie Els by a stroke and win the first major of his career.

While Colin Montgomerie is still searching for a major, I would suggest that his record in the Ryder Cup, which includes an unbeaten mark in singles play for his entire career, has to equal a major of some sort. He has been the rock of the European side during the time that saw the entire pendulum of this competition swing from U.S. dominance to European. He is not without flaws, but he has been a giant in this game.

Any remembrance of this year would be incomplete without mentioning Bruce Edwards and Jeff Julian. A caddie and a relatively anonymous pro. Both men lost battles to ALS this year, and the PGA family lost two fine brothers from its fraternity. I was lucky enough to know Bruce and while I can't say the same about Jeff, I know the game of golf is better because of both of them. They were beloved by family, peers and friends and battled bravely until the end. I'm not one to romanticize the game too much. But I do believe that on a sunny day on whatever green fairway you might be walking on, you won't have to search too far to find the spirit and soul of Jeff and Bruce.

Worth the Wait

Phil Mickelson, who had his share of near-misses at major tournaments, finally broke through with a title on his 47th try. He hasn't exactly been a slouch, however, winning 22 PGA titles before his Masters win, placing him third on the list of most wins without a major.

Wins before first major

	Wins	1st major title
Ben Hogan	30	1946 PGA Champ.
Sam Snead	27	1942 PGA Champ.
Phil Mickelson	22	2004 Masters

Dethroned

Vijay Singh's three-stroke victory over Adam Scott and Tiger Woods at the Deutche Bank Championship in September vaulted him to the world No. 1 ranking, a title Woods had held since Aug. 8, 1999. Listed are the records for most consecutive weeks with the top spot (rankings began in 1986).

	Years	Weeks
Tiger Woods	1999-2004	264
Greg Norman	1995-97	96
Nick Faldo	1992-94	81

Note: During Tiger's 264-week run atop the World Golf Rankings, his earnings totaled $36,387,088.

2003-2004
Season In Review

SPORTS ALMANAC

Tournament Results
Schedules and results of PGA, European PGA, Champions and LPGA tournaments from Nov. 2, 2003 through Oct. 3, 2004.

PGA Tour
Late 2003

Last Rd	Tournament	Winner	Earnings	Runner-Up
Nov. 2	Chrysler Championship	Retief Goosen (272)	$900,000	V. Singh (275)
Nov. 9	The Tour Championship	Chad Campbell (268)	1,080,000	C. Howell III (271)
Nov. 14@	Franklin Templeton Shootout	Jeff Sluman/ Hank Kuehne*	275,000 (each)	C. Campbell/S. Micheel & B. Faxon/S. McCarron
Nov. 16@	WGC: World Cup	RSA—Trevor Immelman/ Rory Sabbatini (275)	700,000 (each)	Eng.—J. Rose/ P. Casey (279)
Nov. 23@	The Presidents Cup	International 17, USA 17 (Match called due to darkness. Cup is shared.)		
Nov. 23@	UBS Cup	Rest of the World 12, USA 12 (USA retains the Cup.)		
Nov. 30@	Skins Game	Fred Couples (8 skins)	605,000	A. Sorenstam (5 skins)
Dec. 6@	PGA Grand Slam†	Jim Furyk (135)	400,000	M. Weir (143)
Dec. 14@	Target World Challenge	Davis Love III (277)	1,200,000	T. Woods (279)

***Playoffs: Franklin Templeton**—Sluman/Kuehne won on 2nd hole.
@ Unofficial PGA Tour money event.
† 36-hole event exclusively for the winners of the tour's four major tournaments.

2004 (through Oct. 3)

Last Rd	Tournament	Winner	Earnings	Runner-Up
Jan. 11	Mercedes Championships	Stuart Appleby (270)	$1,060,000	V. Singh (271)
Jan. 18	Sony Open in Hawaii	Ernie Els (262)*	864,000	H. Frazar (262)
Jan 25	Bob Hope Chrysler Classic	Phil Mickelson (330)*+	810,000	S. Kendall (330)
Feb. 1	FBR Open	Jonathan Kaye (266)	936,000	C. DiMarco (268)
Feb. 8	AT&T Pebble Beach Pro-Am	Vijay Singh (272)	954,000	J. Maggert (275)
Feb. 15	Buick Invitational	John Daly (278)*	864,000	L. Donald & C. Riley (278)
Feb. 22	Nissan Open	Mike Weir (267)	864,000	S. Maruyama (268)
Feb. 29	WGC: Accenture Match Play Championship	Tiger Woods (3&2)	1,200,000	D. Love III
Feb. 29	Chrysler Classic of Tucson	Heath Slocum (266)	540,000	A. Baddeley (267)
Mar. 7	Ford Championship at Doral	Craig Parry (271)*	900,000	S. Verplank (271)
Mar. 14	Honda Classic	Todd Hamilton (276)	900,000	D. Love III (277)
Mar. 21	Bay Hill Invitational	Chad Campbell (270)	900,000	S. Appleby (276)
Mar. 28	The Players Championship	Adam Scott (276)	1,440,000	P. Harrington (277)
Apr. 4	BellSouth Classic	Zach Johnson (275)	810,000	M. Hensby (276)
Apr. 11	**The Masters** (Augusta, Ga.)	Phil Mickelson (279)	1,170,000	E. Els (280)
Apr. 18	MCI Heritage	Stewart Cink (274)*	864,000	T. Purdy (274)
Apr. 25	Shell Houston Open	Vijay Singh (277)	900,000	S. Hoch (279)
May 2	HP Classic of New Orleans	Vijay Singh (266)	918,000	J. Ogilvie & P. Mickelson (267)
May 9	Wachovia Championship	Joey Sindelar (277)*	1,080,000	A. Oberholser (277)
May 16	EDS Byron Nelson Championship	Sergio Garcia (263)*	1,044,000	R. Damron & D. Hart (270)
May 23	Bank of America Colonial	Steve Flesch (269)	954,000	C. Campbell (270)
May 30	FedEx St. Jude Classic	David Toms (268)	846,000	B. Estes (274)
June 6	The Memorial Tournament	Ernie Els (270)	945,000	F. Couples (274)
June 13	Buick Classic	Sergio Garcia (272)*	945,000	P. Harrington & R. Sabbatini (272)
June 20	**U.S. Open** (Southampton, N.Y.)	Retief Goosen (276)	1,125,000	P. Mickelson (278)
June 27	Booz Allen Classic	Adam Scott (263)	864,000	C. Howell III (267)
July 4	Cialis Western Open	Stephen Ames (274)	864,000	S. Lowery (274)
July 11	John Deere Classic	Mark Hensby (268)*	684,000	J. Morgan (268)
July 18	**British Open** (Royal Troon, Scot.)	Todd Hamilton (274)*	1,348,272	E. Els (274)
July 18	B.C. Open	Jonathan Byrd (268)	540,000	T. Purdy (269)
July 25	U.S. Bank Championship	Carlos Franco (267)	630,000	F. Funk & B. Quigley (269)
Aug. 1	Buick Open	Vijay Singh (265)	810,000	J. Daly (266)
Aug. 8	The International†	Rod Pampling (+31)	900,000	A. Cejka (+29)
Aug. 15	**PGA Championship** (Kohler, Wis.)	Vijay Singh (280)*	1,125,000	C. DiMarco & J. Leonard (280)
Aug. 22	WGC: NEC Invitational	Stewart Cink (269)	1,200,000	T. Woods & R. Sabbatini (273)

PGA Tour Results (Cont.)

Last Rd	Tournament	Winner	Earnings	Runner-Up
Aug. 22	Reno-Tahoe Open	Vaughn Taylor (278)	$540,000	3-way tie (278)
Aug. 29	Buick Championship	Woody Austin (270)*	756,000	T. Herron (270)
Sept. 6	Deutsche Bank Championship	Vijay Singh (268)	900,000	A. Scott & T. Woods (271)
Sept. 12	Bell Canadian Open	Vijay Singh (275)*	810,000	M. Weir (275)
Sept. 19	Valero Texas Open	Bart Bryant (261)	630,000	P. Sheehan (264)
Sept. 19	Ryder Cup (Bloomfield Hills, Mich.) . . .	Europe (18½)	—	USA (9½)
Sept. 26	84 Lumber Classic of Pennsylvania	Vijay Singh (273)	756,000	S. Cink (274)
Oct. 3	WGC: American Express Championship	Ernie Els (270)	1,200,000	T. Bjorn (271)
Oct. 3	Southern Farm Bureau Classic	Fred Funk (266)	540,000	R. Palmer (267)

+This is a five-round, 90-hole event played over five days.

†The scoring for The International is based on a modified Stableford system (8 points for a double eagle, 5 for an eagle, 2 for a birdie, 0 for a par, −1 for a bogey, −3 for double bogey or worse).

*Playoffs: Sony—Els won on 3rd hole; **Bob Hope**—Mickelson won on 1st hole; **Buick Invit.**—Daly won on 1st hole; **Ford Championship**—Parry won on 1st hole; **MCI Heritage**—Cink won on 5th hole; **Wachovia**—Sindelar won on 2nd hole; **EDS Byron Nelson**—Garcia won on 1st hole; **Buick Classic**—Garcia def. Harrington on 2nd hole and Sabbatini on 3rd; **John Deere**—Hensby won on 2nd hole; **British Open**—Hamilton won the 4-hole playoff; **PGA Championship**—Singh won the 3-hole playoff; **Reno-Tahoe**—Taylor won on 1st hole; **Buick Championship**—Austin won on 1st hole; **Bell Canadian**—Singh won on 3rd hole.

Second place ties (3 players or more): 3-WAY—**Reno-Tahoe** (C. McCarron, S. Allan, H. Mahan).

PGA Majors

The Masters

Edition: 68th   **Dates:** April 8–11
Site: Augusta National GC, Augusta, Ga.
Par: 36-36—72 (7290 yards) **Purse:** $6,000,000

		1	2	3	4	Tot	Earnings
1	Phil Mickelson	72	69	69	69	— 279	$1,170,000
2	Ernie Els	70	72	71	67	— 280	702,000
3	K.J. Choi	71	70	72	69	— 282	442,000
4	Bernhard Langer . . .	71	73	69	72	— 285	286,000
	Sergio Garcia	72	72	75	66	— 285	286,000
6	Fred Couples	73	69	74	70	— 286	189,893
	Davis Love III	75	67	74	70	— 286	189,893
	Nick Price	72	73	71	70	— 286	189,893
	Kirk Triplett	71	74	69	72	— 286	189,893
	Chris DiMarco	69	73	68	76	— 286	189,893
	Vijay Singh	75	73	69	69	— 286	189,893
	Paul Casey	75	69	68	74	— 286	189,893

Early round leaders: 1st—Justin Rose (67); 2nd—Rose (138); 3rd—Mickelson & DiMarco (210).
Top amateur: Casey Wittenberg (288).

U.S. Open

Edition: 104th   **Dates:** June 17–20
Site: Shinnecock Hills Golf Club, Southampton, N.Y.
Par: 35-35—70 (6996 yards) **Purse:** $6,250,000

		1	2	3	4	Tot	Earnings
1	Retief Goosen	70	66	69	71	— 276	$1,125,000
2	Phil Mickelson	68	66	73	71	— 278	675,000
3	Jeff Maggert	68	67	74	72	— 281	424,604
4	Mike Weir	69	70	71	74	— 284	267,756
	Shigeki Maruyama . .	66	68	74	76	— 284	267,756
6	Fred Funk	70	66	72	77	— 285	212,444
7	Steve Flesch	68	74	70	74	— 286	183,828
	Robert Allenby	70	72	74	70	— 286	183,828
9	Jay Haas	66	74	76	71	— 287	145,282
	Stephen Ames	74	66	73	74	— 287	145,282
	Chris DiMarco	71	71	70	75	— 287	145,282
	Ernie Els	70	67	70	80	— 287	145,282

Early round leaders: 1st—Haas & Maruyama (66); 2nd—Mickelson & Maruyama (134); 3rd—Goosen (205).
Top amateur: Spencer Levin (288).

British Open

Edition: 133rd   **Dates:** July 15–18
Site: Royal Troon Golf Club, Troon, Scotland
Par: 36-35—71 (7175 yards) **Purse:** $7,490,400

		1	2	3	4	Tot	Earnings
1	Todd Hamilton*	71	67	67	69	— 274	$1,348,272
2	Ernie Els*	69	69	68	68	— 274	805,218
3	Phil Mickelson	73	66	68	68	— 275	514,965
4	Lee Westwood	72	71	68	67	— 278	393,246
5	Davis Love III	72	69	71	67	— 279	298,679
	Thomas Levet	66	70	71	72	— 279	298,679
7	Scott Verplank	69	70	70	71	— 280	220,030
	Retief Goosen	69	70	68	73	— 280	220,030
9	Tiger Woods	70	71	68	72	— 281	167,597
	Mike Weir	71	68	71	71	— 281	167,597

Early round leaders: 1st—Levet & Paul Casey (66); 2nd—Skip Kendall (135); 3rd—Hamilton (205).
Top amateur: Stuart Wilson (296).

* Hamilton (4-4-3-4—15) defeated Els (4-4-4-4—16) in a 4-hole playoff (played on holes 1, 2, 17 and 18).

PGA Championship

Edition: 86th   **Dates:** Aug. 12–15
Site: Whistling Straits, Kohler, Wis.
Par: 36-36—72 (7514 yards) **Purse:** $6,250,000

		1	2	3	4	Tot	Earnings
1	Vijay Singh*	67	68	69	76	— 280	$1,125,000
2	Chris DiMarco*	68	70	71	71	— 280	550,000
	Justin Leonard*	66	69	70	75	— 280	550,000
4	Ernie Els	66	70	72	73	— 281	267,500
	Chris Riley	69	70	69	73	— 281	267,500
6	Paul McGinley	69	74	70	69	— 282	196,000
	K.J. Choi	68	71	73	70	— 282	196,000
	Phil Mickelson	69	72	67	74	— 282	196,000
9	Robert Allenby	71	70	72	70	— 283	152,000
	Ben Crane	70	74	69	70	— 283	152,000
	Adam Scott	71	71	69	72	— 283	152,000
	Stephen Ames	71	71	66	75	— 283	152,000

Early round leaders: 1st—Darren Clarke (65); 2nd—Singh & Leonard (135); 3rd—Singh (204).
Top amateur: none.

* Singh (3-3-4—10) defeated DiMarco (4-3-DNF) and Leonard (4-3-DNF) in a 3-hole playoff (played on holes 10, 17 and 18).

The Official World Golf Ranking

Begun in 1986, the Official World Golf Ranking (formerly the Sony World Ranking) combines the best golfers on the world's six leading professional tours (U.S. PGA Tour, European Tour, Japan Golf Tour, South African PGA Tour, Asian PGA Tour and the PGA Tour of Australasia) in conjunction with the Canadian, Nationwide and Challenge Tours. Rankings are based on a rolling two-year period and weighted in favor of more recent results. Points are awarded after each worldwide tournament according to finish. Final points-per-tournament averages are determined by dividing a player's total points by the number of tournaments played over that two-year period (through Oct. 3, 2004).

	Avg		Avg		Avg
1 Vijay Singh, FIJ	14.14	6 Davis Love III, USA	7.04	11 Adam Scott, AUS	4.95
2 Ernie Els, RSA	12.48	7 Mike Weir, CAN	6.77	12 Jim Furyk, USA	4.69
3 Tiger Woods, USA	11.54	8 Padraig Harrington, IRE	5.98	13 Darren Clarke, N. IRE	4.64
4 Phil Mickelson, USA	8.55	9 Stewart Cink, USA	5.33	14 Chris DiMarco, USA	4.48
5 Retief Goosen, RSA	7.26	10 Sergio Garcia, ESP	4.96	15 Stuart Appleby, AUS	4.48

European PGA Tour

Official money won on the European Tour is presented in euros (E).

Late 2003

Last Rd	Tournament	Winner	Earnings	Runner-Up
Nov. 2	Volvo Masters Andalucia	Fredrik Jacobson (276)*	E583,330	C. Rodiles (276)
Nov. 9	The Seve Trophy	Great Britain & Ireland (15)	—	Continental Europe (13)
Nov. 16	WGC: World Cup	RSA—Trevor Immelman/ Rory Sabbatini (275)	569,661 (each)	Eng.—J. Rose/ P. Casey (279)
Dec. 7	Omega Hong Kong Open	Padraig Harrington (269)	94,205	H. Otto (270)

*Playoffs: Volvo Masters—Jacobson won on 4th hole.

2004 (through Oct. 3)

Last Rd	Tournament	Winner	Earnings	Runner-Up
Jan. 18	South African Airways Open	Trevor Immelman (276)	E113,536	S. Webster & A. Forsyth (279)
Jan. 25	Dunhill Championship	Marcel Siem (266)*	114,698	R. Jacquelin & G. Havret (266)
Feb. 1	Johnnie Walker Classic	Miguel Angel Jimenez (271)	240,580	J. Randhawa & T. Bjorn (273)
Feb. 8	Heineken Classic	Ernie Els (268)	232,049	A. Scott (269)
Feb. 15	ANZ Championship†	Brian Davis (+44)	200,583	P. Casey (+43)
Feb. 22	Carlsberg Malaysian Open	Thongchai Jaidee (274)	158,153	B. Kennedy (276)
Feb. 29	WGC: Accenture Match Play Championship	Tiger Woods (3&2)	955,185	D. Love III
Mar. 7	Dubai Desert Classic	Mark O'Meara (271)	267,929	P. McGinley (272)
Mar. 14	Qatar Masters	Joakim Haeggman (272)	201,596	N. Sato (273)
Mar. 21	Caltex Singapore Masters	Colin Montgomerie (272)	123,041	G. Hanrahan (275)
Mar. 28	Madeira Island Open	Christopher Hanell (284)	100,000	3-way tie (285)
Apr. 4	Algarve Portugal Open	Miguel Angel Jimenez (272)	208,330	T. Price (273)
Apr. 11	The Masters Tournament	Phil Mickelson (279)	966,227	E. Els (280)
Apr. 18	Open de Sevilla	Ricardo Gonzalez (274)	166,660	J. Lomas & S. Gallacher (276)
Apr. 25	Canarias Open	Christian Cevaer (271)	275,000	3-way tie (272)
May 2	Italian Open	Graeme McDowell (197)*#	200,000	Thomas Levet (197)
May 9	British Masters	Barry Lane (272)	395,123	E. Romero & A. Cabrera (275)
May 16	BMW Asian Open	Miguel Angel Jimenez (274)	210,349	S. Dyson (277)
May 23	Deutsche Bank-SAP Open TPC	Trevor Immelman (271)	500,000	P. Harrington (272)
May 30	Volvo PGA Championship	Scott Drummond (269)	625,000	A. Cabrera (271)
June 6	Celtic Manor Wales Open	Simon Khan (267)*	375,092	P. Casey (267)
June 13	Diageo Championship	Miles Tunnicliff (275)	349,615	G. McDowell (280)
June 20	U.S. Open	Retief Goosen (276)	915,527	P. Mickelson (278)
June 20	Aa St. Omer Open	Philippe Lima (279)	66,660	A. Tadini (280)
June 27	French Open	Jean-Francois Remesy (272)	500,000	R. Green & N. O'Hern (279)
July 4	Smurfit European Open	Retief Goosen (275)	550,005	3-way tie (280)
July 11	The Barclays Scottish Open	Thomas Levet (269)	545,208	M. Campbell (270)
July 18	British Open	Todd Hamilton (274)*	1,078,430	E. Els (274)
July 25	Nissan Irish Open	Brett Rumford (274)	316,660	P. Harrington & R. Jacquelin (278)
Aug. 1	Scandinavian Masters	Luke Donald (272)	266,660	P. Hanson & H. Stenson (277)
Aug. 8	KLM Open	David Lynn (264)	200,000	R. Green & P. McGinley (267)
Aug. 15	PGA Championship	Vijay Singh (280)*	916,724	C. DiMarco & J. Leonard (280)
Aug. 15	BMW Russian Open	Gary Emerson (269)	67,903	M. Brier (274)
Aug. 22	WGC: NEC Invitational	Stewart Cink (269)	971,341	T. Woods & R. Sabbatini (273)
Aug. 29	BMW International Open	Miguel Angel Jimenez (267)	300,000	T. Levet (269)
Sept. 5	Omega European Masters	Luke Donald (265)	266,660	M.A. Jimenez (270)
Sept. 12	Linde German Masters	Padraig Harrington (275)	500,000	N. O'Hern (278)

European PGA Tour Results (Cont.)

Last Rd	Tournament	Winner	Earnings	Runner-Up
Sept. 19	Ryder Cup (Bloomfield Hills, Mich.) . . .	Europe (18½)	—	USA (9½)
Sept. 26	The Heritage	Henrik Stenson (269)	E333,330	C. Rodiles (273)
Oct. 3	WGC: American Express Championship	Ernie Els (270)	979,113	T. Bjorn (271)

†The scoring for the ANZ Championship is based on a modified Stableford system (8 points for a double eagle, 5 for an eagle, 2 for a birdie, 0 for a par, −1 for a bogey, −3 for double bogey or worse).

#Weather-shortened.

*Playoffs: **Dunhill Championship**—Siem def. Havret on 2nd hole and Jacquelin on 3rd; **Italian Open**—McDowell won on 4th hole; **Wales Open**—Khan won on 2nd hole; **British Open**—Hamilton won the 4-hole playoff; **PGA Championship**—Singh won the 3-hole playoff.

Second place ties (3 players or more): 3-WAY—**Madeira Island** (B. Kennedy, S. Jeppesen, R. Rashell); **Canarias Open** (P. Hedblom, R. Gonzalez, D. Park); **European Open** (R. Green, P. O'Malley, L. Westwood).

Champions Tour
(formerly Senior PGA Tour)

Late 2003

Last Rd	Tournament	Winner	Earnings	Runner-Up
Nov. 23@	UBS Cup	Rest of the World 12, USA 12 (USA retains the Cup.)		
Dec. 7@	Office Depot Father/Son Challenge . .	Hale/Steve Irwin (123)*	$100,000 (each)	Jack/Jackie Nicklaus (124)

2004 (through Oct. 3)

Last Rd	Tournament	Winner	Earnings	Runner-Up
Jan. 25	MasterCard Championship	Fuzzy Zoeller (196)	$268,000	D. Quigley (197)
Feb. 1@	Wendy's Champions Skins Game	Tom Watson (10 skins)	400,000	A. Palmer (5 skins)
Feb. 8	Royal Caribbean Classic	Bruce Fleisher (210)	217,500	D. Quigley (211)
Feb. 15	ACE Group Classic	Craig Stadler (206)*	240,000	T. Watson & G. Koch (206)
Feb. 22	Outback Steakhouse Pro-Am	Mark McNulty (200)	241,000	L. Nelson (201)
Mar. 7	MasterCard Classic	Ed Fiori (210)*	300,000	G. Marsh (210)
Mar. 14	SBC Classic	Gil Morgan (202)	225,000	L. Nelson (204)
Mar. 21	Toshiba Senior Classic	Tom Purtzer (198)	240,000	M. Hatalsky (199)
Apr. 18	Blue Angels Classic	Tom Jenkins (196)	225,000	R. Davis (201)
Apr. 25@	Liberty Mutual Legends of Golf	Hale Irwin (205)	350,000	G. Koch & G. Morgan (206)
May 2	Bruno's Memorial Classic	Bruce Fleisher (200)	225,000	B. Lietzke & D.A. Weibring (207)
May 9	FedEx Kinko's Classic	Larry Nelson (209)	240,000	B. Lietzke (210)
May 23	Allianz Championship	D.A. Weibring (204)	225,000	T. Jenkins (207)
May 30	**Senior PGA Championship** (Louisville, Ky.)	Hale Irwin (276)	360,000	J. Haas (277)
June 6	Farmers Charity Classic	Jim Thorpe (203)	240,000	F. Gibson (204)
June 13	Bayer Advantage Celebrity Pro-Am . .	Allen Doyle (131)#	247,500	J. Pate (132)
June 27	Bank of America Championship	Craig Stadler (201)	232,500	3-way tie (205)
July 4	Commerce Bank Long Island Classic . .	Jim Thorpe (201)	225,000	3-way tie (202)
July 11	**Ford Senior Players Championship** (Dearborn, Mich.)	Mark James (275)	375,000	J.M. Canizares (276)
July 25	**Senior British Open** (Portrush, N. Ireland)	Pete Oakley (284)	289,153	T. Kite & E. Romero (285)
Aug. 1	**U.S. Senior Open** (St. Louis, Mo.)	Peter Jacobsen (272)	470,000	H. Irwin (273)
Aug. 8	3M Championship	Tom Kite (203)	262,500	C. Stadler (204)
Aug. 22	Greater Hickory Classic	Doug Tewell (202)	240,000	B. Fleisher (203)
Aug. 29	**JELD-WEN Tradition** (Aloha, Ore.)	Craig Stadler (275)	345,000	J. Pate & A. Doyle (276)
Sept. 5	The First Tee Open at Pebble Beach . .	Craig Stadler (201)	300,000	J. Haas (204)
Sept. 12	Kroger Classic	Bruce Summerhays (201)	225,000	3-way tie (202)
Sept. 26	SAS Championship	Craig Stadler (199)	270,000	T. Jenkins (205)
Oct. 3	Constellation Energy Classic	Wayne Levi (200)	240,000	H. Irwin (202)

#Weather-shortened.

@Unofficial Champions Tour money event.

*Playoffs: **ACE Group Classic**—Stadler won on 1st hole; **MasterCard Classic**—Fiori won on 3rd hole;.

Second place ties (3 players or more): 3-WAY—**Bank of America Championships** (T. Kite, T. Purtzer, D.A. Weibring); **Long Island Classic** (A. Bean, W. Levi, B. Wadkins); **Kroger Classic** (G. Morgan, D. Tewell, J. Thorpe).

Champions Tour Majors

Senior PGA Championship

Edition: 65th **Dates:** May 27-30
Site: Valhalla Golf Club, Louisville, Ky.
Par: 35-36—71 (6990 yards) **Purse:** $2,000,000

		1 2 3 4	Tot	Earnings
1	Hale Irwin	67-69-69-71—	276	$360,000
2	Jay Haas	67-71-69-70—	277	216,000
3	Craig Stadler	69-71-70-69—	279	136,000
4	Dave Barr	69-70-69-74—	282	79,333
	Mark James	69-71-73-69—	282	79,333
	Tom Watson	67-72-70-73—	282	79,333
7	Mark McNulty	70-71-71-71—	283	60,000
	Gil Morgan	67-71-74-71—	283	60,000
9	John Harris	70-67-71-76—	284	54,000
10	Raymond Floyd	73-72-69-71—	285	46,000
	Wayne Levi	69-68-76-72—	285	46,000
	Jerry Pate	73-72-68-72—	285	46,000

Early round leaders: 1st—Irwin, Haas, Watson & Morgan (67); 2nd—Irwin (136); 3rd—Irwin (205).
Top amateur: none.

Ford Sr. Players Championship

Edition: 22nd **Dates:** July 8-11
Site: TPC of Michigan, Dearborn, Mich.
Par: 36-36—72 (7069 yards) **Purse:** $2,500,000

		1 2 3 4	Tot	Earnings
1	Mark James	68-67-67-73—	275	$375,000
2	Jose Maria Canizares	68-66-71-71—	276	219,000
3	Bruce Fleisher	68-69-69-71—	277	180,000
4	Bruce Lietzke	70-67-70-71—	278	150,000
5	Gary McCord	70-64-71-74—	279	110,000
	Dana Quigley	68-67-72-72—	279	110,000
7	Tom Kite	72-68-69-71—	280	85,000
	Jim Thorpe	70-69-68-73—	280	85,000
9	Allen Doyle	68-70-70-73—	281	62,500
	Hale Irwin	69-74-66-72—	281	62,500
	Mark McNulty	69-72-69-71—	281	62,500
	Gil Morgan	65-70-75-71—	281	62,500

Early round leaders: 1st—Morgan (65); 2nd—Canizares & McCord (134); 3rd—James (202).
Top amateur: none.

Senior British Open

Edition: 18th (2nd as major) **Dates:** July 22-25
Site: Royal Portrush Golf Club, Portrush, N. Ireland
Par: 36-36—72 (6845 yards) **Purse:** $1,830,000

		1 2 3 4	Tot	Earnings
1	Pete Oakley	73-68-73-70—	284	$289,153
2	Tom Kite	71-71-74-69—	285	150,715
	Eduardo Romero	69-75-74-67—	285	150,715
4	Mark James	72-70-74-70—	286	86,764
5	Mark McNulty	72-69-74-72—	287	67,121
	Don Pooley	69-72-74-72—	287	67,121
7	Bill Longmuir	71-71-76-72—	290	52,040
8	Carl Mason	70-71-81-69—	291	43,336
9	Graham Marsh	76-73-72-71—	292	33,799
	Sam Torrance	72-73-78-69—	292	33,799
	Bruce Summerhays	73-73-75-71—	292	33,799
	Bobby Lincoln	78-69-73-72—	292	33,799

Early round leaders: 1st—Romero, Pooley, John Chillas & Jim Rhodes (69); 2nd—Oakley, McNulty, Pooley & Mason (141); 3rd—Oakley (214).
Top amateur: Roy Smethurst (301).

U.S. Senior Open

Edition: 25th **Dates:** July 29-Aug. 1
Site: Bellerive Country Club, St. Louis, Mo.
Par: 36-35—71 (7117 yards) **Purse:** $2,600,000

		1 2 3 4	Tot	Earnings
1	Peter Jacobsen	65-70-69-68—	272	$470,000
2	Hale Irwin	71-67-67-68—	273	280,000
3	Jay Haas	67-70-69-68—	274	149,920
	Tom Kite	69-68-65-72—	274	149,920
5	Bob Gilder	68-69-67-71—	275	99,702
6	D.A. Weibring	71-66-73-67—	277	88,402
7	Doug Tewell	70-70-71-67—	278	70,557
	Walter Hall	69-71-69-69—	278	70,557
	Fuzzy Zoeller	71-66-70-71—	278	70,557
	Craig Stadler	66-69-73-70—	278	70,557

Early round leaders: 1st—Jacobsen (65); 2nd—Jacobsen & Stadler (135); 3rd—Kite (202).
Top amateur: Pat Tallent (296).

JELD-WEN Tradition

Edition: 16th **Dates:** Aug. 26-29
Site: The Reserve Vineyards & Golf Club, Aloha, Ore.
Par: 36-36—72 (6998 yards) **Purse:** $2,300,000

		1 2 3 4	Tot	Earnings			1 2 3 4	Tot	Earnings
1	Craig Stadler	70-70-68-67—	275	$345,000	Tom Kite	72-71-65-69—	277	88,714
2	Allen Doyle	69-72-64-71—	276	183,540	Doug Tewell	69-70-69-69—	277	88,714
	Jerry Pate	73-71-66-66—	276	183,540	Vicente Fernandez	67-71-66-73—	277	88,714
4	Andy Bean	69-69-72-67—	277	88,714	Peter Jacobsen	69-66-69-73—	277	88,714
	Bruce Fleisher	71-70-70-66—	277	88,714	D.A. Weibring	69-69-69-70—	277	88,714

Early round leaders: 1st—Fernandez, Jose Maria Canizares & Bruce Summerhays (67); 2nd—Jacobsen (135); 3rd—Fernandez & Jacobsen (204).
Top amateur: none.

LPGA Tour
Late 2003

Last Rd	Tournament	Winner	Earnings	Runner-Up
Nov. 2	Sports Today CJ Nine Bridges Classic	Shi Hyun Ahn (204)	$187,500	4-way tie (207)
Nov. 9	Mizuno Classic	Annika Sorenstam (192)	169,500	3-way tie (201)
Nov. 16	Mobile Tournament of Champions	Dorothy Delasin (280)*	122,000	H-W Han (280)
Nov. 23	ADT Tour Championship	Meg Mallon (281)	215,000	A. Sorenstam (282)

*Playoffs: Mobile TOC—Delasin won on 1st hole.

Second place ties (3 players or more): 4-WAY—**Nine Bridges** (Gl. Park, S.R. Pak, L. Davies, Gr. Park); 3-WAY—**Mizuno** (S. Gustafson, Gr. Park, S.R. Pak).

2004 (through Oct. 3)

Last Rd	Tournament	Winner	Earnings	Runner-Up
Mar. 14	Welch's/Fry's Championship	Karen Stupples (258)	$120,000	J Y Lee & Gr. Park (263)
Mar. 21	Safeway International	Annika Sorenstam (270)	180,000	C. Kerr (274)
Mar. 28	**Kraft Nabisco Championship** (Rancho Mirage, Calif.)	Grace Park (277)	240,000	A. Song (278)
Apr. 4	Office Depot Championship	Annika Sorenstam (207)	262,500	A. Bunch & M. Mallon (210)
Apr. 17	Takefuji Classic	Cristie Kerr (209)*	165,000	S-A Jeon (209)
May 2	Chick-fil-A Charity Championship	Jennifer Rosales (274)	240,000	4-way tie (275)
May 9	Michelob Ultra Open	Se Ri Pak (275)	330,000	J. Inkster & L. Ochoa (277)
May 16	Franklin American Mortgage Champ.	Lorena Ochoa (272)	135,000	W. Ward (273)
May 23	Sybase Classic	Sherri Steinhauer (272)	187,500	Gr. Park (274)
May 30	Corning Classic	Annika Sorenstam (270)	150,000	V. Goetze-Ackerman & M. Estill (272)
June 6	Kellogg-Keebler Classic	Karrie Webb (200)	180,000	3-way tie (205)
June 13	**McDonald's LPGA Championship** (Wilmington, Del.)	Annika Sorenstam (271)	240,000	S H Ahn (274)
June 20	ShopRite Classic	Cristie Kerr (202)	195,000	P. Creamer & G. Sergas (203)
June 27	Wegmen's Rochester	Kim Saiki (274)	225,000	M H Kim & R. Jones (278)
July 4	**U.S. Women's Open** (South Hadley, Mass.)	Meg Mallon (274)	560,000	A. Sorenstam (276)
July 11	BMO Canadian Women's Open	Meg Mallon (270)	195,000	B. Daniel (274)
July 18	Giant Eagle Classic	Moira Dunn (204)	150,000	Y-A Yang (206)
July 24	Evian Masters	Wendy Doolan (270)	375,000	A. Sorenstam (271)
Aug. 1	**Weetabix Women's British Open** (Berkshire, England)	Karen Stupples (269)	290,880	R. Teske (274)
Aug. 8	Jamie Farr Owens Corning Classic	Meg Mallon (274)	165,000	S R Pak & K. Stupples (278)
Aug. 22	Wendy's Championship for Children	Catriona Matthew (278)*	165,000	H-W Han (278)
Aug. 29	Wachovia Classic	Lorena Ochoa (269)	150,000	Gr. Park (271)
Sept. 5	State Farm Classic	Cristie Kerr (264)	180,000	C. Kim (265)
Sept. 12	John Q. Hammons Hotel Classic	Annika Sorenstam (204)	150,000	S H Ahn (208)
Sept. 19	Safeway Classic	Hee-Won Han (207)*	180,000	L. Kane (207)
Sept. 26	Longs Drugs Challenge	Christina Kim (266)	150,000	K. Webb (267)

*Playoffs: Takefuji—Kerr won on 7th hole; **Wendy's**—Matthew won on 1st hole; **Safeway**—Han won on 1st hole.

Second place ties (3 players or more): 4-WAY—**Chick-fil-A** (J Y Lee, R. Jones, B. Morgan, Gr. Park); 3-WAY—**Kellogg-Keebler** (S-A Lim, A. Sorenstam, J. Jang).

LPGA Majors

Kraft Nabisco Championship

Edition: 33rd **Dates:** March 25-28
Site: Mission Hills CC, Rancho Mirage, Calif.
Par: 36-36—72 (6542 yards) **Purse:** $1,600,000

	1 2 3 4	Tot	Earnings
1 Grace Park	72-69-67-69—	277	$240,000
2 Aree Song	66-73-69-70—	278	146,826
3 Karrie Webb	68-71-71-69—	279	106,512
4 a-Michelle Wie	69-72-69-71—	281	amateur
5 Cristie Kerr	71-71-71-69—	282	74,358
Catriona Matthew	67-75-70-70—	282	74,358
7 Mi-Hyun Kim	71-70-71-71—	283	54,261
8 Lorena Ochoa	67-76-74-67—	284	36,737
Candie Kung	69-75-71-69—	284	36,737
Christina Kim	72-72-70-70—	284	36,737
Rosie Jones	67-73-71-73—	284	36,737
Jung Yeon Lee	69-69-71-75—	284	36,737

Early round leaders: 1st—Song (66); 2nd—Dottie Pepper & Lee (138); 3rd—Park & Song (208).

McDonald's LPGA Championship

Edition: 50th **Dates:** June 10-13
Site: DuPont CC, Wilmington, Del.
Par: 35-36—71 (6408 yards) **Purse:** $1,600,000

	1 2 3 4	Tot	Earnings
1 Annika Sorenstam	68-67-64-72—	271	$240,000
2 Shi Hyun Ahn	69-70-69-66—	274	147,780
3 Grace Park	68-70-70-68—	276	105,028
4 Angela Stanford	69-71-67-71—	278	73,322
Gloria Park	67-72-68-71—	278	73,322
6 Christina Kim	74-69-64-72—	279	49,145
Juli Inkster	70-66-70-73—	279	49,145
8 Wendy Doolan	73-70-65-72—	280	35,538
Soo-Yun Kang	69-68-71-72—	280	35,538
Lorena Ochoa	71-67-67-75—	280	35,538

Early round leaders: 1st—Jennifer Rosales (66); 2nd—Sorenstam (135); 3rd—Sorenstam (199).
Top amateur: none.

U.S. Women's Open

Edition: 59th   **Dates:** July 1-4
Site: Orchards Golf Club, South Hadley, Mass.
Par: 36-35-71 (6473 yds)   **Purse:** $3,100,000

		1 2 3 4	Tot	Earnings
1	Meg Mallon	73-69-67-65	274	$560,000
2	Annika Sorenstam	71-68-70-67	276	335,000
3	Kelly Robbins	74-67-68-69	278	208,863
4	Jennifer Rosales	70-67-69-75	281	145,547
5	Michele Redman	70-72-73-67	282	111,173
	Candie Kung	70-68-74-70	282	111,173
7	Jeong Jang	72-74-71-66	283	86,744
	Moira Dunn	73-67-72-71	283	86,744
	Pat Hurst	70-71-71-71	283	86,744
10	Carin Koch	72-67-75-70	284	68,813
	Michelle Ellis	70-69-72-73	284	68,813
	Rachel Teske	71-69-70-74	284	68,813

Early round leaders: 1st—Brittany Lincicome (66); 2nd—Rosales (137); 3rd—Rosales (206).
Top amateur: Paula Creamer & Michelle Wie (285).

Weetabix Women's British Open

Edition: 11th   **Dates:** July 29-Aug. 1
Site: Sunningdale Golf Club, Berkshire, England
Par: 36-36—72 (6392 yards)   **Purse:** $1,600,000

		1 2 3 4	Tot	Earnings
1	Karen Stupples	65-70-70-64	269	$290,880
2	Rachel Teske	70-69-65-70	274	181,800
3	Heather Bowie	70-69-65-71	275	127,260
4	Lorena Ochoa	69-71-66-70	276	99,990
5	Michele Redman	70-71-70-66	277	72,114
	Giulia Sergas	72-71-67-67	277	72,114
	Beth Daniel	69-69-71-68	277	72,114
8	Jung Yeon Lee	67-72-70-69	278	52,722
	Minea Blomqvist	68-78-62-70	278	52,722
	Laura Davies	70-69-69-70	278	52,722

Early round leaders: 1st—Stupples (65); 2nd—Stupples (135); 3rd—Teske & Bowie (204).
Top amateur: Louise Stahle (290).

National Team Competition
2004 Ryder Cup

The 35th Ryder Cup tournament, Sept. 17-19, at Oakland Hills Country Club, Bloomfield Hills, Mich.

Rosters

The 2004 U.S. Team was chosen on the basis of points awarded for wins and top-10 finishes at official PGA events from Jan. 3, 2002 through the 2004 PGA Championship on Aug. 15. The top 10 finishers on the points list automatically qualified for the 12-member team, and U.S. Captain Hal Sutton selected the final two players.

The 2004 European Team was chosen as follows: the top five players on The Ryder Cup World Points list as of Aug. 23, 2004, as well as the top five players on the European Ryder Cup points list as of Aug. 29, 2004 were automatic qualifiers for the 12-member team. European Team captain Bernhard Langer selected the final two players.

United States: Qualifiers—Tiger Woods, Phil Mickelson, Davis Love III, Jim Furyk, Kenny Perry, David Toms, Chad Campbell, Chris DiMarco, Fred Funk and Chris Riley; Captain's selections—Jay Haas and Stewart Cink.

Europe: Qualifiers—Padraig Harrington (Ireland), Sergio Garcia (Spain), Darren Clarke (N. Ireland), Miguel Angel Jimenez (Spain), Lee Westwood (England), Thomas Levet (France), Paul Casey (England), David Howell (England), Paul McGinley (Ireland), Ian Poulter (England); Captain's selections—Colin Montgomerie (Scotland) and Luke Donald (England).

First Day

Four-Ball Match Results

Winner	Score	Loser
Montgomerie/Harrington	2&1	Woods/Mickelson
Clarke/Jimenez	5&4	Love III/Campbell
Riley/Cink	halved	McGinley/Donald
Garcia/Westwood	5&3	Toms/Furyk

Europe wins morning, 3½-½

Foursome Match Results

Winner	Score	Loser
DiMarco/Haas	3&2	Jimenez/Levet
Montgomerie/Harrington	4&2	Love III/Funk
Clarke/Westwood	1-up	Woods/Mickelson
Garcia/Donald	2&1	Perry/Cink

Europe wins afternoon, 3-1; (Europe leads, 6½-1½)

Second Day

Four-Ball Match Results

Winner	Score	Loser
Haas/DiMarco	halved	Garcia/Westwood
Woods/Riley	4&3	Clarke/Poulter
Casey/Howell	1-up	Furyk/Campbell
Cink/Love III	3&2	Montgomerie/Harrington

USA wins morning, 2½-1½; (Europe leads, 8-4)

Foursome Match Results

Winner	Score	Loser
Clarke/Westwood	5&4	DiMarco/Haas
Mickelson/Toms	4&3	Jimenez/Levet
Donald/Garcia	1-up	Funk/Furyk
Harrington/McGinley	4&3	Love III/Woods

Europe wins afternoon, 3-1; (Europe leads, 11-5)

Third Day
Singles Match Results

Winner	Score	Loser
Woods	3&2	Casey
Garcia	3&2	Mickelson
Love III	halved	Clarke
Furyk	6&4	Howell
Westwood	1-up	Perry
Montgomerie	1-up	Toms

Winner	Score	Loser
Campbell	5&3	Donald
DiMarco	1-up	Jimenez
Levet	1-up	Funk
Poulter	3&2	Riley
Harrington	1-up	Haas
McGinley	3&2	Cink

Europe wins day, 7½-4½

Europe wins Ryder Cup, 18½-9½

Money Leaders

Official money leaders of PGA, European PGA, Champions and LPGA tours for 2003 and unofficial money leaders for 2004, through Oct. 3, as compiled by the PGA, European PGA and LPGA. All European amounts are in euros (E).

PGA

Arnold Palmer Award standings: listed are tournaments played (TP); cuts made (CM); 1st, 2nd and 3rd place finishes; and earnings for the year.

FINAL 2003

		TP	CM	Finish 1-2-3	Earnings
1	Vijay Singh	27	26	4-5-0	$7,573,907
2	Tiger Woods	18	18	5-2-0	6,673,413
3	Davis Love III	23	20	4-1-1	6,081,896
4	Jim Furyk	27	25	2-1-1	5,182,865
5	Mike Weir	21	20	3-0-4	4,918,910
6	Kenny Perry	26	24	3-1-1	4,400,122
9	Chad Campbell	27	25	1-3-0	3,912,064
7	David Toms	26	19	2-1-0	3,710,905
8	Ernie Els	17	17	2-0-0	3,371,237
10	Retief Goosen	19	17	1-1-3	3,166,373

2004 (through Oct. 3)

		TP	CM	Finish 1-2-3	Earnings
1	Vijay Singh	26	25	8-1-1	$9,455,566
2	Phil Mickelson	19	18	2-2-3	5,672,323
3	Ernie Els	15	14	3-2-1	5,629,025
4	Tiger Woods	18	18	1-2-3	4,717,472
5	Stewart Cink	26	23	2-1-0	4,344,670
6	Adam Scott	15	11	2-1-1	3,619,384
7	Sergio Garcia	15	15	2-0-0	3,115,415
8	Davis Love III	21	18	0-2-1	3,075,092
9	Stephen Ames	24	18	1-0-1	3,014,679
10	Todd Hamilton	26	18	2-0-0	2,970,178

European PGA

Volvo Order of Merit standings: listed are tournaments played (TP); cuts made (CM); 1st, 2nd and 3rd place finishes; and earnings for the year.

FINAL 2003

		TP	CM	Finish 1-2-3	Earnings
1	Ernie Els	16	16	4-3-0	E2,975,374
2	Darren Clarke	18	16	1-1-0	2,210,051
3	Padraig Harrington	20	17	2-2-0	1,555,623
4	Fredrik Jacobson	18	15	3-0-0	1,521,303
5	Ian Poulter	30	21	2-1-2	1,500,855
6	Paul Casey	24	21	2-1-1	1,360,456
7	Lee Westwood	25	16	2-0-0	1,330,713
8	Thomas Bjorn	22	17	0-3-0	1,327,148
9	Brian Davis	31	25	0-2-1	1,245,513
10	Phillip Price	20	15	1-1-0	1,234,018

2004 (through Oct. 3)

		TP	CM	Finish 1-2-3	Earnings
1	Ernie Els	13	13	2-2-2	E3,368,122
2	Retief Goosen	11	11	2-0-0	2,168,879
3	Padraig Harrington	17	15	2-0-0	1,666,390
4	Miguel Angel Jimenez	24	20	4-1-0	1,644,000
5	Thomas Levet	25	19	1-2-2	1,582,796
6	Darren Clarke	17	13	0-0-3	1,474,132
7	Nick O'Hern	20	17	0-0-3	1,285,273
8	Angel Cabrera	13	10	0-2-0	1,224,293
9	David Howell	23	21	0-0-3	1,206,570
10	Graeme McDowell	28	21	1-1-2	1,153,932

Champions Tour

FINAL 2003

		TP	CM	Finish 1-2-3	Earnings
1	Tom Watson	14	14	2-5-0	$1,853,108
2	Jim Thorpe	30	30	3-0-1	1,830,306
3	Gil Morgan	25	25	1-4-0	1,620,206
4	Bruce Lietzke	22	21	2-2-1	1,610,826
5	Hale Irwin	22	22	2-2-2	1,607,391
6	Tom Kite	27	25	0-4-1	1,549,819
7	Tom Jenkins	30	30	1-1-0	1,415,503
8	Larry Nelson	24	24	1-4-2	1,365,973
9	Allen Doyle	30	30	1-1-1	1,349,272
10	Bruce Fleisher	29	29	1-3-1	1,306,013

2004 (through Oct. 3)

		TP	CM	Finish 1-2-3	Earnings
1	Craig Stadler	18	18	5-1-2	$2,179,666
2	Hale Irwin	20	20	2-2-1	1,771,897
3	Gil Morgan	24	24	1-2-3	1,536,819
4	Tom Kite	24	24	1-2-2	1,459,211
5	Bruce Fleisher	25	24	2-1-1	1,405,228
6	D.A. Weibring	23	23	1-2-0	1,302,995
7	Jim Thorpe	23	22	2-1-0	1,207,547
8	Doug Tewell	24	24	1-1-2	1,139,457
9	Larry Nelson	22	21	1-2-1	1,113,224
10	Wayne Levi	24	24	1-1-2	1,072,664

LPGA

FINAL 2003

		TP	CM	Finish 1-2-3	Earnings
1	Annika Sorenstam	17	17	6-4-1	$2,029,506
2	Se Ri Pak	26	25	3-6-0	1,611,928
3	Grace Park	26	24	1-5-4	1,417,702
4	Hee-Won Han	27	26	2-3-2	1,111,860
5	Juli Inkster	21	18	2-1-0	1,028,205
6	Candie Kung	30	25	3-1-0	938,079
7	Rachel Teske	27	26	2-2-1	924,667
8	Beth Daniel	22	20	1-2-1	917,654
9	Lorena Ochoa	24	23	0-2-3	823,740
10	Rosie Jones	19	19	1-0-2	808,785

2004 (through Oct. 3)

		TP	CM	Finish 1-2-3	Earnings
1	Annika Sorenstam	14	14	5-3-0	$1,864,608
2	Meg Mallon	19	17	3-1-0	1,313,623
3	Lorena Ochoa	21	21	2-1-4	1,263,043
4	Grace Park	18	17	1-4-3	1,003,845
5	Cristie Kerr	20	18	3-1-0	986,936
6	Mi-Hyun Kim	24	22	0-1-1	886,608
7	Karen Stupples	20	20	2-1-0	845,200
8	Hee-Won Han	23	19	1-1-1	746,870
9	Se Ri Pak	17	15	1-1-0	648,860
10	Jennifer Rosales	18	18	1-0-0	619,394

1860-2004
Through the Years

SPORTS ALMANAC

Major Golf Championships
MEN
The Masters

The Masters has been played every year (except during World War II) since 1934 at the Augusta National Golf Club in Augusta, Ga. Both the course and the tournament were created by Bobby Jones; (*) indicates playoff winner.

Multiple winners: Jack Nicklaus (6); Arnold Palmer (4); Jimmy Demaret, Nick Faldo, Gary Player, Sam Snead and Tiger Woods (3); Seve Ballesteros, Ben Crenshaw, Ben Hogan, Bernhard Langer, Byron Nelson, Jose Maria Olazabal, Horton Smith and Tom Watson (2).

Year	Winner	Score	Runner-up
1934	Horton Smith	284	Craig Wood (285)
1935	Gene Sarazen*	282	Craig Wood (282)
1936	Horton Smith	285	Harry Cooper (286)
1937	Byron Nelson	283	Ralph Guldahl (285)
1938	Henry Picard	285	Ralph Guldahl
			& Harry Cooper (287)
1939	Ralph Guldahl	279	Sam Snead (280)
1940	Jimmy Demaret	280	Lloyd Mangrum (284)
1941	Craig Wood	280	Byron Nelson (283)
1942	Byron Nelson*	280	Ben Hogan (280)
1943-45	Not held		World War II
1946	Herman Keiser	282	Ben Hogan (283)
1947	Jimmy Demaret	281	Frank Stranahan
			& Byron Nelson (283)
1948	Claude Harmon	279	Cary Middlecoff (284)
1949	Sam Snead	282	Lloyd Mangrum
			& Johnny Bulla (285)
1950	Jimmy Demaret	283	Jim Ferrier (285)
1951	Ben Hogan	280	Skee Riegel (282)
1952	Sam Snead	286	Jack Burke Jr. (290)
1953	Ben Hogan	274	Porky Oliver (279)
1954	Sam Snead*	289	Ben Hogan (289)
1955	Cary Middlecoff	279	Ben Hogan (286)
1956	Jack Burke Jr.	289	Ken Venturi (290)
1957	Doug Ford	283	Sam Snead (286)
1958	Arnold Palmer	284	Doug Ford
			& Fred Hawkins (285)
1959	Art Wall Jr.	284	Cary Middlecoff (285)
1960	Arnold Palmer	282	Ken Venturi (283)
1961	Gary Player	280	Arnold Palmer
			& Charles R. Coe (281)
1962	Arnold Palmer*	280	Dow Finsterwald
			& Gary Player (280)
1963	Jack Nicklaus	286	Tony Lema (287)
1964	Arnold Palmer	276	Jack Nicklaus
			& Dave Marr (282)
1965	Jack Nicklaus	271	Arnold Palmer
			& Gary Player (280)
1966	Jack Nicklaus*	288	Gay Brewer Jr.
			& Tommy Jacobs (288)
1967	Gay Brewer Jr.	280	Bobby Nichols (281)
1968	Bob Goalby	277	Roberto DeVicenzo (278)
1969	George Archer	281	Billy Casper,
			George Knudson
			& Tom Weiskopf (282)
1970	Billy Casper*	279	Gene Littler (279)
1971	Charles Coody	279	Jack Nicklaus
			& Johnny Miller (281)

Year	Winner	Score	Runner-up
1972	Jack Nicklaus	286	Bruce Crampton,
			Bobby Mitchell
			& Tom Weiskopf (289)
1973	Tommy Aaron	283	J.C. Snead (284)
1974	Gary Player	278	Tom Weiskopf,
			& Dave Stockton (280)
1975	Jack Nicklaus	276	Johnny Miller
			& Tom Weiskopf (277)
1976	Ray Floyd	271	Ben Crenshaw (279)
1977	Tom Watson	276	Jack Nicklaus (278)
1978	Gary Player	277	Hubert Green,
			Rod Funseth
			& Tom Watson (278)
1979	Fuzzy Zoeller*	280	Ed Sneed
			& Tom Watson (280)
1980	Seve Ballesteros	275	Gibby Gilbert
			& Jack Newton (279)
1981	Tom Watson	280	Jack Nicklaus
			& Johnny Miller (282)
1982	Craig Stadler*	284	Dan Pohl (284)
1983	Seve Ballesteros	280	Ben Crenshaw
			& Tom Kite (284)
1984	Ben Crenshaw	277	Tom Watson (279)
1985	Bernhard Langer	282	Curtis Strange,
			Seve Ballesteros
			& Ray Floyd (284)
1986	Jack Nicklaus	279	Greg Norman
			& Tom Kite (280)
1987	Larry Mize*	285	Seve Ballesteros
			& Greg Norman (285)
1988	Sandy Lyle	281	Mark Calcavecchia (282)
1989	Nick Faldo*	283	Scott Hoch (283)
1990	Nick Faldo*	278	Ray Floyd (278)
1991	Ian Woosnam	277	J.M. Olazabal (278)
1992	Fred Couples	275	Ray Floyd (277)
1993	Bernhard Langer	277	Chip Beck (281)
1994	J.M. Olazabal	279	Tom Lehman (281)
1995	Ben Crenshaw	274	Davis Love III (275)
1996	Nick Faldo	276	Greg Norman (281)
1997	Tiger Woods	270	Tom Kite (282)
1998	Mark O'Meara	279	Fred Couples
			& David Duval (280)
1999	J.M. Olazabal	280	Davis Love III (282)
2000	Vijay Singh	278	Ernie Els (281)
2001	Tiger Woods	272	David Duval (274)
2002	Tiger Woods	276	Retief Goosen (279)
2003	Mike Weir*	281	Len Mattiace (281)
2004	Phil Mickelson	279	Ernie Els (280)

The Masters (Cont.)

*PLAYOFFS:

1935: Gene Sarazen (144) def. Craig Wood (149) in 36 holes. **1942:** Byron Nelson (69) def. Ben Hogan (70) in 18 holes.
1954: Sam Snead (70) def. Ben Hogan (71) in 18 holes. **1962:** Arnold Palmer (68) def. Gary Player (71) and Dow Finsterwald (77) in 18 holes. **1966:** Jack Nicklaus (70) def. Tommy Jacobs (72) and Gay Brewer Jr. (78) in 18 holes. **1970:** Billy Casper (69) def. Gene Littler (74) in 18 holes. **1979:** Fuzzy Zoeller (4-3) def. Ed Sneed (4-4) and Tom Watson (4-4) on 2nd hole of sudden death. **1982:** Craig Stadler (4) def. Dan Pohl (5) on 1st hole of sudden death. **1987:** Larry Mize (4-3) def. Greg Norman (4-4) and Seve Ballesteros (5) on 2nd hole of sudden death. **1989:** Nick Faldo (5-3) def. Scott Hoch (5-4) on 2nd hole of sudden death. **1990:** Nick Faldo (4-4) def. Raymond Floyd (4) on 2nd hole of sudden death. **2003:** Mike Weir (5) def. Len Mattiace (6) on 1st hole of sudden death.

U.S. Open

Played at a different course each year, the U.S. Open was launched by the new U.S. Golf Association in 1895. The Open was a 36-hole event from 1895-97 and has been 72 holes since then. It switched from a 3-day, 36-hole Saturday finish to 4 days of play in 1965. Note that (*) indicates playoff winner and (a) indicates amateur.

Multiple winners: Willie Anderson, Ben Hogan, Bobby Jones and Jack Nicklaus (4); Hale Irwin (3); Julius Boros, Billy Casper, Ernie Els, Retief Goosen, Ralph Guldahl, Walter Hagen, Lee Janzen, John McDermott, Cary Middlecoff, Andy North, Gene Sarazen, Alex Smith, Payne Stewart, Curtis Strange, Lee Trevino and Tiger Woods (2).

Year	Winner	Score	Runner-up	Course	Location
1895	Horace Rawlins	173	Willie Dunn (175)	Newport GC	Newport, R.I.
1896	James Foulis	152	Horace Rawlins (155)	Shinnecock Hills GC	Southampton, N.Y.
1897	Joe Lloyd	162	Willie Anderson (163)	Chicago GC	Wheaton, Ill.
1898	Fred Herd	328	Alex Smith (335)	Myopia Hunt Club	Hamilton, Mass.
1899	Willie Smith	315	George Low, W.H. Way & Val Fitzjohn (326)	Baltimore CC	Baltimore
1900	Harry Vardon	313	J.H. Taylor (315)	Chicago GC	Wheaton, Ill.
1901	Willie Anderson*	331	Alex Smith (331)	Myopia Hunt Club	Hamilton, Mass.
1902	Laurie Auchterlonie	307	Stewart Gardner (313)	Garden City GC	Garden City, N.Y.
1903	Willie Anderson*	307	David Brown (307)	Baltusrol GC	Springfield, N.J.
1904	Willie Anderson	303	Gil Nicholls (308)	Glen View Club	Golf, Ill.
1905	Willie Anderson	314	Alex Smith (316)	Myopia Hunt Club	Hamilton, Mass.
1906	Alex Smith	295	Willie Smith (302)	Onwentsia Club	Lake Forest, Ill.
1907	Alec Ross	302	Gil Nicholls (304)	Phila. Cricket Club	Chestnut Hill, Pa.
1908	Fred McLeod*	322	Willie Smith (322)	Myopia Hunt Club	Hamilton, Mass.
1909	George Sargent	290	Tom McNamara (294)	Englewood GC	Englewood, N.J.
1910	Alex Smith*	298	Macdonald Smith & John McDermott (298)	Phila. Cricket Club	Chestnut Hill, Pa.
1911	John McDermott*	307	George Simpson & Mike Brady (307)	Chicago GC	Wheaton, Ill.
1912	John McDermott	294	Tom McNamara (296)	CC of Buffalo	Buffalo
1913	a-Francis Ouimet*	304	Harry Vardon & Ted Ray (304)	The Country Club	Brookline, Mass.
1914	Walter Hagen	290	a-Chick Evans (291)	Midlothian CC	Blue Island, Ill.
1915	a-John Travers	297	Tom McNamara (298)	Baltusrol GC	Springfield, N.J.
1916	a-Chick Evans	286	Jock Hutchinson (288)	Minikahda Club	Minneapolis
1917-18	Not held		World War I		
1919	Walter Hagen*	301	Mike Brady (301)	Brae Burn CC	West Newton, Mass.
1920	Ted Ray	295	Jock Hutchison, Jack Burke, Leo Diegel & Harry Vardon (296)	Inverness Club	Toledo, Ohio
1921	Jim Barnes	289	Walter Hagen & Fred McLeod (298)	Columbia CC	Chevy Chase, Md.
1922	Gene Sarazen	288	a-Bobby Jones & John Black (289)	Skokie CC	Glencoe, Ill.
1923	a-Bobby Jones*	296	Bobby Cruickshank (296)	Inwood CC	Inwood, N.Y.
1924	Cyril Walker	297	a-Bobby Jones (300)	Oakland Hills CC	Birmingham, Mich.
1925	Willie Macfarlane*	291	a-Bobby Jones (291)	Worcester CC	Worcester, Mass.
1926	a-Bobby Jones	293	Joe Turnesa (294)	Scioto CC	Columbus, Ohio
1927	Tommy Armour*	301	Harry Cooper (301)	Oakmont CC	Oakmont, Pa.
1928	Johnny Farrell*	294	a-Bobby Jones (294)	Olympia Fields CC	Matteson, Ill.
1929	a-Bobby Jones*	294	Al Espinosa (294)	Winged Foot CC	Mamaroneck, N.Y.
1930	a-Bobby Jones	287	Macdonald Smith (289)	Interlachen CC	Hopkins, Minn.
1931	Billy Burke*	292	George Von Elm (292)	Inverness Club	Toledo, Ohio
1932	Gene Sarazen	286	Bobby Cruickshank & Phil Perkins (289)	Fresh Meadow CC	Flushing, N.Y.
1933	a-Johnny Goodman	287	Ralph Guldahl (288)	North Shore GC	Glenview, Ill.
1934	Olin Dutra	293	Gene Sarazen (294)	Merion Cricket Club	Ardmore, Pa.
1935	Sam Parks Jr.	299	Jimmy Thomson (301)	Oakmont CC	Oakmont, Pa.
1936	Tony Manero	282	Harry E. Cooper (284)	Baltusrol GC	Springfield, N.J.
1937	Ralph Guldahl	281	Sam Snead (283)	Oakland Hills CC	Birmingham, Mich.
1938	Ralph Guldahl	284	Dick Metz (290)	Cherry Hills CC	Denver

Year	Winner	Score	Runner-up	Course	Location
1939	Byron Nelson*	284	Craig Wood & Denny Shute (284)	Philadelphia CC	Philadelphia
1940	Lawson Little*	287	Gene Sarazen (287)	Canterbury GC	Cleveland
1941	Craig Wood	284	Denny Shute (287)	Colonial Club	Ft. Worth
1942-45	Not held		World War II		
1946	Lloyd Mangrum*	284	Byron Nelson & Vic Ghezzi (284)	Canterbury GC	Cleveland
1947	Lew Worsham*	282	Sam Snead (282)	St. Louis CC	Clayton, Mo.
1948	Ben Hogan	276	Jimmy Demaret (278)	Riviera CC	Los Angeles
1949	Cary Middlecoff	286	Clayton Heafner & Sam Snead (287)	Medinah CC	Medinah, Ill.
1950	Ben Hogan*	287	Lloyd Mangrum & George Fazio (287)	Merion Golf Club	Ardmore, Pa.
1951	Ben Hogan	287	Clayton Heafner (289)	Oakland Hills CC	Birmingham, Mich.
1952	Julius Boros	281	Porky Oliver (285)	Northwood Club	Dallas
1953	Ben Hogan	283	Sam Snead (289)	Oakmont CC	Oakmont, Pa.
1954	Ed Furgol	284	Gene Littler (285)	Baltusrol GC	Springfield, N.J.
1955	Jack Fleck*	287	Ben Hogan (287)	Olympic CC	San Francisco
1956	Cary Middlecoff	281	Ben Hogan & Julius Boros (282)	Oak Hill CC	Rochester, N.Y.
1957	Dick Mayer*	282	Cary Middlecoff (282)	Inverness Club	Toledo, Ohio
1958	Tommy Bolt	283	Gary Player (287)	Southern Hills CC	Tulsa
1959	Billy Casper	282	Bob Rosburg (283)	Winged Foot GC	Mamaroneck, N.Y.
1960	Arnold Palmer	280	Jack Nicklaus (282)	Cherry Hills CC	Denver
1961	Gene Littler	281	Doug Sanders & Bob Goalby (282)	Oakland Hills CC	Birmingham, Mich.
1962	Jack Nicklaus*	283	Arnold Palmer (283)	Oakmont CC	Oakmont, Pa.
1963	Julius Boros*	293	Arnold Palmer & Jacky Cupit (293)	The Country Club	Brookline, Mass.
1964	Ken Venturi	278	Tommy Jacobs (282)	Congressional CC	Bethesda, Md.
1965	Gary Player*	282	Kel Nagle (282)	Bellerive CC	St. Louis
1966	Billy Casper*	278	Arnold Palmer (278)	Olympic CC	San Francisco
1967	Jack Nicklaus	275	Arnold Palmer (279)	Baltusrol GC	Springfield, N.J.
1968	Lee Trevino	275	Jack Nicklaus (279)	Oak Hill CC	Rochester, N.Y.
1969	Orville Moody	281	Al Geiberger, Deane Beman & Bob Rosburg (282)	Champions GC	Houston
1970	Tony Jacklin	281	Dave Hill (288)	Hazeltine National GC	Chaska, Minn.
1971	Lee Trevino*	280	Jack Nicklaus (280)	Merion GC	Ardmore, Pa.
1972	Jack Nicklaus	290	Bruce Crampton (293)	Pebble Beach GL	Pebble Beach, Calif.
1973	Johnny Miller	279	John Schlee (280)	Oakmont CC	Oakmont, Pa.
1974	Hale Irwin	287	Forest Fezler (289)	Winged Foot GC	Mamaroneck, N.Y.
1975	Lou Graham*	287	John Mahaffey (287)	Medinah CC	Medinah, Ill.
1976	Jerry Pate	277	Al Geiberger & Tom Weiskopf (279)	Atlanta AC	Duluth, Ga.
1977	Hubert Green	278	Lou Graham (279)	Southern Hills CC	Tulsa
1978	Andy North	285	Dave Stockton & J.C. Snead (286)	Cherry Hills CC	Denver
1979	Hale Irwin	284	Gary Player & Jerry Pate (286)	Inverness Club	Toledo, Ohio
1980	Jack Nicklaus	272	Isao Aoki (274)	Baltusrol GC	Springfield, N.J.
1981	David Graham	273	George Burns & Bill Rogers (276)	Merion GC	Ardmore, Pa.
1982	Tom Watson	282	Jack Nicklaus (284)	Pebble Beach GL	Pebble Beach, Calif.
1983	Larry Nelson	280	Tom Watson (281)	Oakmont CC	Oakmont, Pa.
1984	Fuzzy Zoeller*	276	Greg Norman (276)	Winged Foot GC	Mamaroneck, N.Y.
1985	Andy North	279	Dave Barr, T.C. Chen & Denis Watson (280)	Oakland Hills CC	Birmingham, Mich.
1986	Ray Floyd	279	Lanny Wadkins & Chip Beck (281)	Shinnecock Hills GC	Southampton, N.Y.
1987	Scott Simpson	277	Tom Watson (278)	Olympic Club	San Francisco
1988	Curtis Strange*	278	Nick Faldo (278)	The Country Club	Brookline, Mass.
1989	Curtis Strange	278	Chip Beck, Ian Woosnam & Mark McCumber (279)	Oak Hill CC	Rochester, N.Y.
1990	Hale Irwin*	280	Mike Donald (280)	Medinah CC	Medinah, Ill.
1991	Payne Stewart*	282	Scott Simpson (282)	Hazeltine National GC	Chaska, Minn.
1992	Tom Kite	285	Jeff Sluman (287)	Pebble Beach GL	Pebble Beach, Calif.
1993	Lee Janzen	272	Payne Stewart (274)	Baltusrol GC	Springfield, N.J.
1994	Ernie Els*	279	Colin Montgomerie (279) & Loren Roberts (279)	Oakmont CC	Oakmont, Pa.
1995	Corey Pavin	280	Greg Norman (282)	Shinnecock Hills GC	Southampton, N.Y.

U.S. Open (Cont.)

Year	Winner	Score	Runner-up	Course	Location
1996	Steve Jones	.278	Davis Love III & Tom Lehman (279)	Oakland Hills CC	Bloomfield Hills, Mich.
1997	Ernie Els	.276	Colin Montgomerie (277)	Congressional CC	Bethesda, Md.
1998	Lee Janzen	.280	Payne Stewart (281)	Olympic Club	San Francisco
1999	Payne Stewart	.279	Phil Mickelson (280)	Pinehurst CC	Pinehurst, N.C.
2000	Tiger Woods	.272	Miguel Angel Jimenez & Ernie Els (287)	Pebble Beach GL	Pebble Beach, Calif.
2001	Retief Goosen*	.276	Mark Brooks (276)	Southern Hills CC	Tulsa
2002	Tiger Woods	.277	Phil Mickelson (280)	Bethpage Black	Farmingdale, N.Y.
2003	Jim Furyk	.272	Stephen Leaney (275)	Olympia Fields CC	Olympia Fields, Ill.
2004	Retief Goosen	.276	Phil Mickelson (278)	Shinnecock Hills GC	Southampton, N.Y.

*PLAYOFFS:

1901: Willie Anderson (85) def. Alex Smith (86) in 18 holes. **1903:** Willie Anderson (82) def. David Brown (84) in 18 holes. **1908:** Fred McLeod (77) def. Willie Smith (83) in 18 holes. **1910:** Alex Smith (71) def. John McDermott (75) & Macdonald Smith (77) in 18 holes. **1911:** John McDermott (80) def. Mike Brady (82) & George Simpson (85) in 18 holes. **1913:** Francis Ouimet (72) def. Harry Vardon (77) & Edward Ray (78) in 18 holes. **1919:** Walter Hagen (77) def. Mike Brady (78) in 18 holes. **1923:** Bobby Jones (76) def. Bobby Cruickshank (78) in 18 holes. **1925:** Willie Macfarlane (75-72—147) def. Bobby Jones (75-73—148) in 36 holes. **1927:** Tommy Armour (76) def. Harry Cooper (79) in 18 holes. **1928:** Johnny Farrell (70-73—143) def. Bobby Jones (73-71—144) in 36 holes. **1929:** Bobby Jones (141) def. Al Espinosa (164) in 36 holes. **1931:** Billy Burke (149-148) def. George Von Elm (149-149) in 72 holes. **1939:** Byron Nelson (68-70) def. Craig Wood (68-73) and Denny Shute (76) in 36 holes. **1940:** Lawson Little (70) def. Gene Sarazen (73) in 18 holes. **1946:** Lloyd Mangrum (72-72—144) def. Byron Nelson (72-73—145) and Vic Ghezzi (72-73—145) in 36 holes. **1947:** Lew Worsham (69) def. Sam Snead (70) in 18 holes. **1950:** Ben Hogan (69) def. Lloyd Mangrum (73) & George Fazio (75) in 18 holes. **1955:** Jack Fleck (69) def. Ben Hogan (72) in 18 holes. **1957:** Dick Mayer (72) def. Cary Middlecoff (79) in 18 holes. **1962:** Jack Nicklaus (71) def. Arnold Palmer (74) in 18 holes. **1963:** Julius Boros (70) def. Jacky Cupit (73) & Arnold Palmer (76) in 18 holes. **1965:** Gary Player (71) def. Kel Nagle (74) in 18 holes. **1966:** Billy Casper (69) def. Arnold Palmer (73) in 18 holes. **1971:** Lee Trevino (68) def. Jack Nicklaus (71) in 18 holes. **1975:** Lou Graham (71) def. John Mahaffey (73) in 18 holes. **1984:** Fuzzy Zoeller (67) def. Greg Norman (75) in 18 holes. **1988:** Curtis Strange (71) def. Nick Faldo (75) in 18 holes. **1990:** Hale Irwin (74-3) def. Mike Donald (74-4) on 1st hole of sudden death after 18 holes. **1991:** Payne Stewart (75) def. Scott Simpson (77) in 18 holes. **1994:** Ernie Els (74-4-4) def. Loren Roberts (74-4-5) and Colin Montgomerie (78) on 2nd hole of sudden death after 18 holes; **2001:** Goosen (70) def. Brooks (72) in 18 holes.

British Open

The oldest of the Majors, the Open began in 1860 to determine "the champion golfer of the world." While only professional golfers participated in the first year of the tournament, amateurs have been invited ever since. Competition was extended from 36 to 72 holes in 1892. Conducted by the Royal and Ancient Golf Club of St. Andrews, the Open is rotated among select golf courses in England and Scotland. Note that (*) indicates playoff winner and (a) indicates amateur winner.

Multiple winners: Harry Vardon (6); James Braid, J.H. Taylor, Peter Thomson and Tom Watson (5); Walter Hagen, Bobby Locke, Tom Morris Sr., Tom Morris Jr. and Willie Park (4); Jamie Anderson, Seve Ballesteros, Henry Cotton, Nick Faldo, Bob Ferguson, Bobby Jones, Jack Nicklaus and Gary Player (3); Harold Hilton, Bob Martin, Greg Norman, Arnold Palmer, Willie Park Jr. and Lee Trevino (2).

Year	Winner	Score	Runner-up	Course	Location
1860	Willie Park	.174	Tom Morris Sr. (176)	Prestwick Club	Ayrshire, Scotland
1861	Tom Morris Sr.	.163	Willie Park (167)	Prestwick Club	Ayrshire, Scotland
1862	Tom Morris Sr.	.163	Willie Park (176)	Prestwick Club	Ayrshire, Scotland
1863	Willie Park	.168	Tom Morris Sr. (170)	Prestwick Club	Ayrshire, Scotland
1864	Tom Morris Sr.	.167	Andrew Strath (169)	Prestwick Club	Ayrshire, Scotland
1865	Andrew Strath	.162	Willie Park (164)	Prestwick Club	Ayrshire, Scotland
1866	Willie Park	.169	David Park (171)	Prestwick Club	Ayrshire, Scotland
1867	Tom Morris Sr.	.170	Willie Park (172)	Prestwick Club	Ayrshire, Scotland
1868	Tom Morris Jr.	.157	Robert Andrew (159)	Prestwick Club	Ayrshire, Scotland
1869	Tom Morris Jr.	.154	Tom Morris Sr. (157)	Prestwick Club	Ayrshire, Scotland
1870	Tom Morris Jr.	.149	Bob Kirk (161)	Prestwick Club	Ayrshire, Scotland
1871	Not held				
1872	Tom Morris Jr.	.166	David Strath (169)	Prestwick Club	Ayrshire, Scotland
1873	Tom Kidd	.179	Jamie Anderson (180)	St. Andrews	St. Andrews, Scotland
1874	Mungo Park	.159	Tom Morris Jr. (161)	Musselburgh	Musselburgh, Scotland
1875	Willie Park	.166	Bob Martin (168)	Prestwick Club	Ayrshire, Scotland
1876	Bob Martin*	.176	David Strath (176)	St. Andrews	St. Andrews, Scotland
1877	Jamie Anderson	.160	Bob Pringle (162)	Musselburgh	Musselburgh, Scotland
1878	Jamie Anderson	.157	Bob Kirk (159)	Prestwick Club	Ayrshire, Scotland
1879	Jamie Anderson	.169	Andrew Kirkaldy & James Allan (172)	St. Andrews	St. Andrews, Scotland
1880	Bob Ferguson	.162	Peter Paxton (167)	Musselburgh	Musselburgh, Scotland
1881	Bob Ferguson	.170	Jamie Anderson (173)	Prestwick Club	Ayrshire, Scotland
1882	Bob Ferguson	.171	Willie Fernie (174)	St. Andrews	St. Andrews, Scotland
1883	Willie Fernie*	.159	Bob Ferguson (159)	Musselburgh	Musselburgh, Scotland

Year	Winner	Score	Runner-up	Course	Location
1884	Jack Simpson	160	Douglas Rolland & Willie Fernie (164)	Prestwick Club	Ayrshire, Scotland
1885	Bob Martin	171	Archie Simpson (172)	St. Andrews	St. Andrews, Scotland
1886	David Brown	157	Willie Campbell (159)	Musselburgh	Musselburgh, Scotland
1887	Willie Park Jr.	161	Bob Martin (162)	Prestwick Club	Ayrshire, Scotland
1888	Jack Burns	171	David Anderson & Ben Sayers (172)	St. Andrews	St. Andrews, Scotland
1889	Willie Park Jr.*	155	Andrew Kirkaldy (155)	Musselburgh	Musselburgh, Scotland
1890	a-John Ball	164	Willie Fernie (167) & A. Simpson (167)	Prestwick Club	Ayrshire, Scotland
1891	Hugh Kirkaldy	166	Andrew Kirkaldy & Willie Fernie (168)	St. Andrews	St. Andrews, Scotland
1892	a-Harold Hilton	305	John Ball, Sandy Herd & Hugh Kirkaldy (308)	Muirfield	Gullane, Scotland
1893	Willie Auchterlonie	322	Johnny Laidley (324)	Prestwick Club	Ayrshire, Scotland
1894	J.H. Taylor	326	Douglas Rolland (331)	Royal St. George's	Sandwich, England
1895	J.H. Taylor	322	Sandy Herd (326)	St. Andrews	St. Andrews, Scotland
1896	Harry Vardon*	316	J.H. Taylor (316)	Muirfield	Gullane, Scotland
1897	a-Harold Hilton	314	James Braid (315)	Hoylake	Hoylake, England
1898	Harry Vardon	307	Willie Park Jr. (308)	Prestwick Club	Ayrshire, Scotland
1899	Harry Vardon	310	Jack White (315)	Royal St. George's	Sandwich, England
1900	J.H. Taylor	309	Harry Vardon (317)	St. Andrews	St. Andrews, Scotland
1901	James Braid	309	Harry Vardon (312)	Muirfield	Gullane, Scotland
1902	Sandy Herd	307	Harry Vardon (308)	Hoylake	Hoylake, England
1903	Harry Vardon	300	Tom Vardon (306)	Prestwick Club	Ayrshire, Scotland
1904	Jack White	296	James Braid (297)	Royal St. George's	Sandwich, England
1905	James Braid	318	J.H. Taylor (323) & Rowland Jones (323)	St. Andrews	St. Andrews, Scotland
1906	James Braid	300	J.H. Taylor (304)	Muirfield	Gullane, Scotland
1907	Arnaud Massy	312	J.H. Taylor (314)	Hoylake	Hoylake, England
1908	James Braid	291	Tom Ball (299)	Prestwick Club	Ayrshire, Scotland
1909	J.H. Taylor	295	James Braid (299)	Deal	Deal, England
1910	James Braid	299	Sandy Herd (303)	St. Andrews	St. Andrews, Scotland
1911	Harry Vardon*	303	Arnaud Massy (303)	Royal St. George's	Sandwich, England
1912	Ted Ray	295	Harry Vardon (299)	Muirfield	Gullane, Scotland
1913	J.H. Taylor	304	Ted Ray (312)	Hoylake	Hoylake, England
1914	Harry Vardon	306	J.H. Taylor (309)	Prestwick Club	Ayrshire, Scotland
1915-19 Not held			World War I		
1920	George Duncan	303	Sandy Herd (305)	Deal	Deal, England
1921	Jock Hutchison*	296	Roger Wethered (296)	St. Andrews	St. Andrews, Scotland
1922	Walter Hagen	300	George Duncan & Jim Barnes (301)	Royal St. George's	Sandwich, England
1923	Arthur Havers	295	Walter Hagen (296)	Royal Troon	Troon, Scotland
1924	Walter Hagen	301	Ernest Whitcombe (302)	Hoylake	Hoylake, England
1925	Jim Barnes	300	Archie Compston & Ted Ray (301)	Prestwick Club	Ayrshire, Scotland
1926	a-Bobby Jones	291	Al Watrous (293)	Royal Lytham	Lytham, England
1927	a-Bobby Jones	285	Aubrey Boomer (291)	St. Andrews	St. Andrews, Scotland
1928	Walter Hagen	292	Gene Sarazen (294)	Royal St. George's	Sandwich, England
1929	Walter Hagen	292	Johnny Farrell (298)	Muirfield	Gullane, Scotland
1930	a-Bobby Jones	291	Macdonald Smith & Leo Diegel (293)	Hoylake	Hoylake, England
1931	Tommy Armour	296	Jose Jurado (297)	Carnoustie	Carnoustie, Scotland
1932	Gene Sarazen	283	Macdonald Smith (288)	Prince's	Prince's, England
1933	Denny Shute*	292	Craig Wood (292)	St. Andrews	St. Andrews, Scotland
1934	Henry Cotton	283	Sid Brews (288)	Royal St. George's	Sandwich, England
1935	Alf Perry	283	Alf Padgham (287)	Muirfield	Gullane, Scotland
1936	Alf Padgham	287	Jimmy Adams (288)	Hoylake	Hoylake, England
1937	Henry Cotton	290	Reg Whitcombe (292)	Carnoustie	Carnoustie, Scotland
1938	Reg Whitcombe	295	Jimmy Adams (297)	Royal St. George's	Sandwich, England
1939	Dick Burton	290	Johnny Bulla (292)	St. Andrews	St. Andrews, Scotland
1940-45 Not held			World War II		
1946	Sam Snead	290	Bobby Locke (294) & Johnny Bulla (294)	St. Andrews	St. Andrews, Scotland
1947	Fred Daly	293	Frank Stranahan & Reg Horne (294)	Hoylake	Hoylake, England
1948	Henry Cotton	284	Fred Daly (289)	Muirfield	Gullane, Scotland
1949	Bobby Locke*	283	Harry Bradshaw (283)	Royal St. George's	Sandwich, England
1950	Bobby Locke	279	Roberto de Vicenzo (281)	Royal Troon	Troon, Scotland
1951	Max Faulkner	285	Tony Cerda (287)	Royal Portrush	Portrush, Ireland

British Open (Cont.)

Year	Winner	Score	Runner-up	Course	Location
1952	Bobby Locke	.287	Peter Thomson (288)	Royal Lytham	Lytham, England
1953	Ben Hogan	.282	Frank Stranahan, Dai Rees, Tony Cerda & Peter Thomson (286)	Carnoustie	Carnoustie, Scotland
1954	Peter Thomson	.283	Sid Scott, Dai Rees & Bobby Locke (284)	Royal Birkdale	Southport, England
1955	Peter Thomson	.281	Johny Fallon (283)	St. Andrews	St. Andrews, Scotland
1956	Peter Thomson	.286	Flory Van Donck (289)	Hoylake	Hoylake, England
1957	Bobby Locke	.279	Peter Thomson (282)	St. Andrews	St. Andrews, Scotland
1958	Peter Thomson*	.278	Dave Thomas (278)	Royal Lytham	Lytham, England
1959	Gary Player	.284	Flory Van Donck & Fred Bullock (286)	Muirfield	Gullane, Scotland
1960	Kel Nagle	.278	Arnold Palmer (279)	St. Andrews	St. Andrews, Scotland
1961	Arnold Palmer	.284	Dai Rees (285)	Royal Birkdale	Southport, England
1962	Arnold Palmer	.276	Kel Nagle (282)	Royal Troon	Troon, Scotland
1963	Bob Charles*	.277	Phil Rodgers (277)	Royal Lytham	Lytham, England
1964	Tony Lema	.279	Jack Nicklaus (284)	St. Andrews	St. Andrews, Scotland
1965	Peter Thomson	.285	Christy O'Connor & Brian Huggett (287)	Royal Birkdale	Southport, England
1966	Jack Nicklaus	.282	Doug Sanders & Dave Thomas (283)	Muirfield	Gullane, Scotland
1967	Roberto de Vicenzo	.278	Jack Nicklaus (280)	Hoylake	Hoylake, England
1968	Gary Player	.289	Jack Nicklaus & Bob Charles (291)	Carnoustie	Carnoustie, Scotland
1969	Tony Jacklin	.280	Bob Charles (282)	Royal Lytham	Lytham, England
1970	Jack Nicklaus*	.283	Doug Sanders (283)	St. Andrews	St. Andrews, Scotland
1971	Lee Trevino	.278	Lu Liang Huan (279)	Royal Birkdale	Southport, England
1972	Lee Trevino	.278	Jack Nicklaus (279)	Muirfield	Gullane, Scotland
1973	Tom Weiskopf	.276	Johnny Miller & Neil Coles (279)	Royal Troon	Troon, Scotland
1974	Gary Player	.282	Peter Oosterhuis (286)	Royal Lytham	Lytham, England
1975	Tom Watson*	.279	Jack Newton (279)	Carnoustie	Carnoustie, Scotland
1976	Johnny Miller	.279	Seve Ballesteros & Jack Nicklaus (285)	Royal Birkdale	Southport, England
1977	Tom Watson	.268	Jack Nicklaus (269)	Turnberry	Turnberry, Scotland
1978	Jack Nicklaus	.281	Tom Kite, Ray Floyd, Ben Crenshaw & Simon Owen (283)	St. Andrews	St. Andrews, Scotland
1979	Seve Ballesteros	.283	Jack Nicklaus & Ben Crenshaw (286)	Royal Lytham	Lytham, England
1980	Tom Watson	.271	Lee Trevino (275)	Muirfield	Gullane, Scotland
1981	Bill Rogers	.276	Bernhard Langer (280)	Royal St. George's	Sandwich, England
1982	Tom Watson	.284	Peter Oosterhuis & Nick Price (285)	Royal Troon	Troon, Scotland
1983	Tom Watson	.275	Hale Irwin & Andy Bean (276)	Royal Birkdale	Southport, England
1984	Seve Ballesteros	.276	Bernhard Langer & Tom Watson (278)	St. Andrews	St. Andrews, Scotland
1985	Sandy Lyle	.282	Payne Stewart (283)	Royal St. George's	Sandwich, England
1986	Greg Norman	.280	Gordon J. Brand (285)	Turnberry	Turnberry, Scotland
1987	Nick Faldo	.279	Paul Azinger & Rodger Davis (280)	Muirfield	Gullane, Scotland
1988	Seve Ballesteros	.273	Nick Price (275)	Royal Lytham	Lytham, England
1989	Mark Calcavecchia*	.275	Greg Norman & Wayne Grady (275)	Royal Troon	Troon, Scotland
1990	Nick Faldo	.270	Payne Stewart & Mark McNulty (275)	St. Andrews	St. Andrews, Scotland
1991	Ian Baker-Finch	.272	Mike Harwood (274)	Royal Birkdale	Southport, England
1992	Nick Faldo	.272	John Cook (273)	Muirfield	Gullane, Scotland
1993	Greg Norman	.267	Nick Faldo (269)	Royal St. George's	Sandwich, England
1994	Nick Price	.268	Jesper Parnevik (269)	Turnberry	Turnberry, Scotland
1995	John Daly*	.282	Costantino Rocca (282)	St. Andrews	St. Andrews, Scotland
1996	Tom Lehman	.271	Mark McCumber & Ernie Els (273)	Royal Lytham	Lytham, England
1997	Justin Leonard	.272	Jesper Parnevik & Darren Clarke (275)	Royal Troon	Troon, Scotland
1998	Mark O'Meara*	.280	Brian Watts (280)	Royal Birkdale	Southport, England
1999	Paul Lawrie*	.290	Justin Leonard & Jean Van de Velde (290)	Carnoustie	Carnoustie, Scotland

Year	Winner	Score	Runner-up	Course	Location
2000	Tiger Woods	269	Thomas Bjorn & Ernie Els (277)	St. Andrews	St. Andrews, Scotland
2001	David Duval	274	Niclas Fasth (277)	Royal Lytham	Lytham, England
2002	Ernie Els*	278	Thomas Levet, Stuart Appleby & Steve Elkington (278)	Muirfield	Gullane, Scotland
2003	Ben Curtis	283	Vijay Singh & Thomas Bjorn (284)	Royal St. George's	Sandwich, England
2004	Todd Hamilton*	274	Ernie Els (274)	Royal Troon	Troon, Scotland

*PLAYOFFS:

1876: Bob Martin awarded title when David Strath refused playoff. **1883:** Willie Fernie (158) def. Robert Ferguson (159) in 36 holes. **1889:** Willie Park Jr. (158) def. Andrew Kirkaldy (163) in 36 holes. **1896:** Harry Vardon (157) def. John H. Taylor (161) in 36 holes. **1911:** Harry Vardon won when Arnaud Massy conceded at 35th hole. **1921:** Jock Hutchison (150) def. Roger Wethered (159) in 36 holes. **1933:** Denny Shute (149) def. Craig Wood (154) in 36 holes. **1949:** Bobby Locke (135) def. Harry Bradshaw (147) in 36 holes. **1958:** Peter Thomson (139) def. Dave Thomas (143) in 36 holes. **1963:** Bob Charles (140) def. Phil Rodgers (148) in 36 holes. **1970:** Jack Nicklaus (72) def. Doug Sanders (73) in 18 holes. **1975:** Tom Watson (71) def. Jack Newton (72) in 18 holes. **1989:** Mark Calcavecchia (4-3-3-3—13) def. Wayne Grady (4-4-4-4—16) and Greg Norman (3-3-4) in 4 holes. **1995:** John Daly (3-4-4-4—15) def. Costantino Rocca (4-5-7-3—19) in 4 holes. **1998:** Mark O'Meara (4-4-5-4—17) def. Brian Watts (5-4-5-5—19) in 4 holes. **1999:** Paul Lawrie (5-4-3-3—15) def. Justin Leonard (5-4-4-5—18) and Jean Van de Velde (6-4-3-5—18) in 4 holes. **2002:** Els (4-3-5-4—16) and Levet (4-2-5-5—16) remained tied after a four-hole playoff that also included Appleby (4-4-4-5—17) and Elkington (5-3-4-5—17). The pair moved on to sudden death, where Els (4) def. Levet (5) on the 1st hole. **2004:** Todd Hamilton (4-4-3-4—15) def. Ernie Els (4-4-4-4—16) in 4 holes.

PGA Championship

The PGA Championship began in 1916 as a professional golfers match play tournament, but switched to stroke play in 1958. Conducted by the PGA of America, the tournament is played on a different course each year.

Multiple winners: Walter Hagen and Jack Nicklaus (5); Gene Sarazen and Sam Snead (3); Jim Barnes, Leo Diegel, Ray Floyd, Ben Hogan, Byron Nelson, Larry Nelson, Gary Player, Nick Price, Paul Runyan, Denny Shute, Vijay Singh, Dave Stockton, Lee Trevino and Tiger Woods (2).

Year	Winner	Score	Runner-up	Course	Location
1916	Jim Barnes	1-up	Jock Hutchison	Siwanoy CC	Bronxville, N.Y.
1917-18	Not held		World War I		
1919	Jim Barnes	6 & 5	Fred McLeod	Engineers CC	Roslyn, N.Y.
1920	Jock Hutchison	1-up	J. Douglas Edgar	Flossmoor CC	Flossmoor, Ill.
1921	Walter Hagen	3 & 2	Jim Barnes	Inwood CC	Inwood, N.Y.
1922	Gene Sarazen	4 & 3	Emmet French	Oakmont CC	Oakmont, Pa.
1923	Gene Sarazen*	1-up/38	Walter Hagen	Pelham CC	Pelham, N.Y.
1924	Walter Hagen	2-up	Jim Barnes	French Lick CC	French Lick, Ind.
1925	Walter Hagen	6 & 5	Bill Mehlhorn	Olympia Fields CC	Matteson, Ill.
1926	Walter Hagen	5 & 3	Leo Diegel	Salisbury GC	Westbury, N.Y.
1927	Walter Hagen	1-up	Joe Turnesa	Cedar Crest CC	Dallas
1928	Leo Diegel	6 & 5	Al Espinosa	Five Farms CC	Baltimore
1929	Leo Diegel	6 & 4	John Farrell	Hillcrest CC	Los Angeles
1930	Tommy Armour	1-up	Gene Sarazen	Fresh Meadow CC	Flushing, N.Y.
1931	Tom Creavy	2 & 1	Denny Shute	Wannamoisett CC	Rumford, R.I.
1932	Olin Dutra	4 & 3	Frank Walsh	Keller GC	St. Paul, Minn.
1933	Gene Sarazen	5 & 4	Willie Goggin	Blue Mound CC	Milwaukee
1934	Paul Runyan*	1-up/38	Craig Wood	Park CC	Williamsville, N.Y.
1935	Johnny Revolta	5 & 4	Tommy Armour	Twin Hills CC	Oklahoma City
1936	Denny Shute	3 & 2	Jimmy Thomson	Pinehurst CC	Pinehurst, N.C.
1937	Denny Shute*	1-up/37	Harold McSpaden	Pittsburgh FC	Aspinwall, Pa.
1938	Paul Runyan	8 & 7	Sam Snead	Shawnee CC	Shawnee-on-Del, Pa.
1939	Henry Picard*	1-up/37	Byron Nelson	Pomonok CC	Flushing, N.Y.
1940	Byron Nelson	1-up	Sam Snead	Hershey CC	Hershey, Pa.
1941	Vic Ghezzi*	1-up/38	Byron Nelson	Cherry Hills CC	Denver
1942	Sam Snead	2 & 1	Jim Turnesa	Seaview CC	Atlantic City, N.J.
1943	Not held		World War II		
1944	Bob Hamilton	1-up	Byron Nelson	Manito G & CC	Spokane, Wash.
1945	Byron Nelson	4 & 3	Sam Byrd	Morraine CC	Dayton, Ohio
1946	Ben Hogan	6 & 4	Porky Oliver	Portland GC	Portland, Ore.
1947	Jim Ferrier	2 & 1	Chick Harbert	Plum Hollow CC	Detroit
1948	Ben Hogan	7 & 6	Mike Turnesa	Norwood Hills CC	St. Louis
1949	Sam Snead	3 & 2	John Palmer	Hermitage CC	Richmond, Va.
1950	Chandler Harper	4 & 3	Henry Williams Jr.	Scioto CC	Columbus, Ohio
1951	Sam Snead	7 & 6	Walter Burkemo	Oakmont CC	Oakmont, Pa.
1952	Jim Turnesa	1-up	Chick Harbert	Big Spring CC	Louisville
1953	Walter Burkemo	2 & 1	Felice Torza	Birmingham CC	Birmingham, Mich.
1954	Chick Harbert	4 & 3	Walter Burkemo	Keller GC	St. Paul, Minn.
1955	Doug Ford	4 & 3	Cary Middlecoff	Meadowbrook CC	Detroit
1956	Jack Burke	3 & 2	Ted Kroll	Blue Hill CC	Boston

PGA Championship (Cont.)

Year	Winner	Score	Runner-up	Course	Location
1957	Lionel Hebert	2 & 1	Dow Finsterwald	Miami Valley GC	Dayton, Ohio
1958	Dow Finsterwald	276	Billy Casper (278)	Llanerch CC	Havertown, Pa.
1959	Bob Rosburg	277	Jerry Barber & Doug Sanders (278)	Minneapolis GC	St. Louis Park, Minn.
1960	Jay Hebert	281	Jim Ferrier (282)	Firestone CC	Akron, Ohio
1961	Jerry Barber**	277	Don January (277)	Olympia Fields CC	Matteson, Ill.
1962	Gary Player	278	Bob Goalby (279)	Aronimink GC	Newtown Square, Pa.
1963	Jack Nicklaus	279	Dave Ragan (281)	Dallas AC	Dallas
1964	Bobby Nichols	271	Jack Nicklaus & Arnold Palmer (274)	Columbus CC	Columbus, Ohio
1965	Dave Marr	280	Jack Nicklaus & Billy Casper (282)	Laurel Valley GC	Ligonier, Pa.
1966	Al Geiberger	280	Dudley Wysong (284)	Firestone CC	Akron, Ohio
1967	Don January**	281	Don Massengale (281)	Columbine CC	Littleton, Colo.
1968	Julius Boros	281	Arnold Palmer & Bob Charles (282)	Pecan Valley CC	San Antonio
1969	Ray Floyd	276	Gary Player (277)	NCR GC	Dayton, Ohio
1970	Dave Stockton	279	Arnold Palmer & Bob Murphy (281)	Southern Hills CC	Tulsa
1971	Jack Nicklaus	281	Billy Casper (283)	PGA National GC	Palm Beach Gardens, Fla.
1972	Gary Player	281	Jim Jamieson & Tommy Aaron (283)	Oakland Hills GC	Birmingham, Mich.
1973	Jack Nicklaus	277	Bruce Crampton (281)	Canterbury GC	Cleveland
1974	Lee Trevino	276	Jack Nicklaus (277)	Tanglewood GC	Winston-Salem, N.C.
1975	Jack Nicklaus	276	Bruce Crampton (278)	Firestone CC	Akron, Ohio
1976	Dave Stockton	281	Don January & Ray Floyd (282)	Congressional CC	Bethesda, Md.
1977	Lanny Wadkins**	282	Gene Littler (282)	Pebble Beach GL	Pebble Beach, Calif.
1978	John Mahaffey**	276	Jerry Pate & Tom Watson (276)	Oakmont CC	Oakmont, Pa.
1979	David Graham**	272	Ben Crenshaw (272)	Oakland Hills CC	Birmingham, Mich.
1980	Jack Nicklaus	274	Andy Bean (281)	Oak Hill CC	Rochester, N.Y.
1981	Larry Nelson	273	Fuzzy Zoeller (277)	Atlanta AC	Duluth, Ga.
1982	Ray Floyd	272	Lanny Wadkins (275)	Southern Hills CC	Tulsa
1983	Hal Sutton	274	Jack Nicklaus (275)	Riviera CC	Los Angeles
1984	Lee Trevino	273	Lanny Wadkins & Gary Player (277)	Shoal Creek	Birmingham, Ala.
1985	Hubert Green	278	Lee Trevino (280)	Cherry Hills CC	Denver
1986	Bob Tway	276	Greg Norman (278)	Inverness Club	Toledo, Ohio
1987	Larry Nelson**	287	Lanny Wadkins (287)	PGA National	Palm Beach Gardens, Fla.
1988	Jeff Sluman	272	Paul Azinger 275)	Oak Tree GC	Edmond, Okla.
1989	Payne Stewart	276	Andy Bean, Mike Reid & Curtis Strange (277)	Kemper Lakes GC	Hawthorn Woods, Ill.
1990	Wayne Grady	282	Fred Couples (285)	Shoal Creek	Birmingham, Ala.
1991	John Daly	276	Bruce Lietzke (279)	Crooked Stick GC	Carmel, Ind.
1992	Nick Price	278	Nick Faldo, John Cook, Jim Gallagher & Gene Sauers (281)	Bellerive CC	St. Louis
1993	Paul Azinger**	272	Greg Norman (272)	Inverness Club	Toledo, Ohio
1994	Nick Price	269	Corey Pavin (275)	Southern Hills CC	Tulsa
1995	Steve Elkington**	267	Colin Montgomerie (267)	Riviera CC	Pacific Palisades, Calif.
1996	Mark Brooks**	277	Kenny Perry (277)	Valhalla GC	Louisville, Ky.
1997	Davis Love III	269	Justin Leonard (274)	Winged Foot GC	Mamaroneck, N.Y.
1998	Vijay Singh	271	Steve Stricker (273)	Sahalee CC	Redmond, Wash.
1999	Tiger Woods	277	Sergio Garcia (278)	Medinah CC	Medinah, Ill.
2000	Tiger Woods**	270	Bob May (270)	Valhalla GC	Louisville, Ky.
2001	David Toms	265	Phil Mickelson (266)	Atlanta AC	Duluth, Ga.
2002	Rich Beem	278	Tiger Woods (279)	Hazeltine National GC	Chaska, Minn.
2003	Shaun Micheel	276	Chad Campbell (278)	Oak Hill CC	Rochester, N.Y.
2004	Vijay Singh**	280	Chris DiMarco & Justin Leonard (280)	Whistling Straits	Kohler, Wis.

*While the PGA Championship was a match play tournament from 1916-57, the two finalists played 36 holes for the title. In the five years that a playoff was necessary, the match was decided on the 37th or 38th hole.

**PLAYOFFS:
1961: Jerry Barber (67) def. Don January (68) in 18 holes. **1967:** Don January (69) def. Don Massengale (71) in 18 holes. **1977:** Lanny Wadkins (4-4-4) def. Gene Littler (4-4-5) on 3rd hole of sudden death. **1978:** John Mahaffey (4-3) def. Jerry Pate (4-4) and Tom Watson (4-5) on 2nd hole of sudden death. **1979:** David Graham (4-4-2) def. Ben Crenshaw (4-4-4) on 3rd hole of sudden death. **1987:** Larry Nelson (4) def. Lanny Wadkins (5) on 1st hole of sudden death. **1993:** Paul Azinger

(4-4) def. Greg Norman (4-5) on 2nd hole of sudden death. **1995:** Steve Elkington (3) def. Colin Montgomerie (4) on 1st hole of sudden death. **1996:** Mark Brooks (4) def. Kenny Perry (5) on 1st hole of sudden death. **2000:** Tiger Woods (3-4-5—12) won a three-hole playoff over Bob May (4-4-5—13). **2004:** Vijay Singh (3-3-4—10) won a three-hole playoff over Chris DiMarco (4-3-DNF) and Justin Leonard (4-3-DNF).

Grand Slam Summary

The only golfer ever to win a recognized Grand Slam—four major championships in a single season—was Bobby Jones in 1930. That year, Jones won the U.S. and British Opens as well as the U.S. and British Amateurs.

The men's professional Grand Slam—the Masters, U.S. Open, British Open and PGA Championship—did not gain acceptance until 30 years later when Arnold Palmer won the 1960 Masters and U.S. Open. The media wrote that the popular Palmer was chasing the "new" Grand Slam and would have to win the British Open and the PGA to claim it. He did not, but then nobody has before nor since.

Three wins in one year (2): Ben Hogan (1953) and Tiger Woods (2000). **Two wins in one year** (20): Jack Nicklaus (5 times); Ben Hogan, Arnold Palmer, Tom Watson and Tiger Woods (twice); Nick Faldo, Mark O'Meara, Gary Player, Nick Price, Sam Snead, Lee Trevino and Craig Wood (once).

Year	Masters	US Open	Brit. Open	PGA	Year	Masters	US Open	Brit. Open	PGA
1934	H. Smith	Dutra	Cotton	Runyan	1970	Casper	Jacklin	Nicklaus	Stockton
1935	Sarazen	Parks	Perry	Revolta	1971	Coody	Trevino	Trevino	Nicklaus
1936	H. Smith	Manero	Padgham	Shute	1972	Nicklaus	Nicklaus	Trevino	Player
1937	B. Nelson	Guldahl	Cotton	Shute	1973	Aaron	J. Miller	Weiskopf	Nicklaus
1938	Picard	Guldahl	Whitcombe	Runyan	1974	Player	Irwin	Player	Trevino
1939	Guldahl	B. Nelson	Burton	Picard	1975	Nicklaus	L. Graham	T. Watson	Nicklaus
1940	Demaret	Little	—	B. Nelson	1976	Floyd	J. Pate	Miller	Stockton
1941	Wood	Wood	—	Ghezzi	1977	T. Watson	H. Green	T. Watson	L. Wadkins
1942	B. Nelson	—	—	Snead	1978	Player	North	Nicklaus	Mahaffey
1943	—	—	—	—	1979	Zoeller	Irwin	Ballesteros	D. Graham
1944	—	—	—	Hamilton	1980	Ballesteros	Nicklaus	T. Watson	Nicklaus
1945	—	—	—	B. Nelson	1981	T. Watson	D. Graham	Rogers	L. Nelson
1946	Keiser	Mangrum	Snead	Hogan	1982	Stadler	T. Watson	T. Watson	Floyd
1947	Demaret	Worsham	F. Daly	Ferrier	1983	Ballesteros	L. Nelson	T. Watson	Sutton
1948	Harmon	Hogan	Cotton	Hogan	1984	Crenshaw	Zoeller	Ballesteros	Trevino
1949	Snead	Middlecoff	Locke	Snead	1985	Langer	North	Lyle	H. Green
1950	Demaret	Hogan	Locke	Harper	1986	Nicklaus	Floyd	Norman	Tway
1951	Hogan	Hogan	Faulkner	Snead	1987	Mize	S. Simpson	Faldo	L. Nelson
1952	Snead	Boros	Locke	Turnesa	1988	Lyle	Strange	Ballesteros	Sluman
1953	Hogan	Hogan	Hogan	Burkemo	1989	Faldo	Strange	Calcavecchia	Stewart
1954	Snead	Furgol	Thomson	Harbert	1990	Faldo	Irwin	Faldo	Grady
1955	Middlecoff	Fleck	Thomson	Ford	1991	Woosnam	Stewart	Baker-Finch	J. Daly
1956	Burke	Middlecoff	Thomson	Burke	1992	Couples	Kite	Faldo	Price
1957	Ford	Mayer	Locke	L. Hebert	1993	Langer	Janzen	Norman	Azinger
1958	Palmer	Bolt	Thomson	Finsterwald	1994	Olazabal	Els	Price	Price
1959	Wall	Casper	Player	Rosburg	1995	Crenshaw	Pavin	Daly	Elkington
1960	Palmer	Palmer	Nagle	J. Hebert	1996	Faldo	S. Jones	Lehman	Brooks
1961	Player	Littler	Palmer	J. Barber	1997	Woods	Els	Leonard	Love
1962	Palmer	Nicklaus	Palmer	Player	1998	O'Meara	Janzen	O'Meara	Singh
1963	Nicklaus	Boros	Charles	Nicklaus	1999	Olazabal	Stewart	Lawrie	Woods
1964	Palmer	Venturi	Lema	Nichols	2000	Singh	Woods	Woods	Woods
1965	Nicklaus	Player	Thomson	Marr	2001	Woods	Goosen	Duval	Toms
1966	Nicklaus	Casper	Nicklaus	Geiberger	2002	Woods	Woods	Els	Beem
1967	Brewer Jr.	Nicklaus	De Vicenzo	January	2003	Weir	Furyk	Curtis	Micheel
1968	Goalby	Trevino	Player	Boros	2004	Mickelson	Goosen	Hamilton	Singh
1969	Archer	Moody	Jacklin	Floyd					

Major Championship Leaders

Through 2004; active PGA players in **bold** type.

	US Open	British Open	PGA	Masters	US Am	British Am	Total
Jack Nicklaus 4		3	5	6	2	0	**20**
Bobby Jones 4		3	0	0	5	1	**13**
Walter Hagen 2		4	5	0	0	0	**11**
Tiger Woods 2		1	2	3	3	0	**11**
Ben Hogan 4		1	2	2	0	0	**9**
Gary Player 1		3	2	3	0	0	**9**
John Ball 0		1	0	0	0	8	**9**
Arnold Palmer 1		2	0	4	1	0	**8**
Tom Watson 1		5	0	2	0	0	**8**
Harold Hilton 0		2	0	0	1	4	**7**
Gene Sarazen 2		1	3	1	0	0	**7**
Sam Snead 0		1	3	3	0	0	**7**
Harry Vardon 1		6	0	0	0	0	**7**

Tournaments: U.S. Open, British Open, PGA Championship, Masters, U.S. Amateur and British Amateur.

U.S. Amateur

Match play from 1895-64, stroke play from 1965-72, match play 1973-79, 36-hole stroke-play qualifying before match play since 1979.

Multiple winners: Bobby Jones (5); Jerry Travers (4); Walter Travis and Tiger Woods (3); Deane Beman, Charles Coe, Gary Cowan, H. Chandler Egan, Chick Evans, Lawson Little, Jack Nicklaus, Francis Ouimet, Jay Sigel, William Turnesa, Bud Ward, Harvie Ward, and H.J. Whigham (2).

Year		Year		Year		Year	
1895	Charles Macdonald	1923	Max Marston	1953	Gene Littler	1980	Hal Sutton
1896	H.J. Whigham	1924	Bobby Jones	1954	Arnold Palmer	1981	Nathaniel Crosby
1897	H.J. Whigham	1925	Bobby Jones	1955	Harvie Ward	1982	Jay Sigel
1898	Findlay Douglas	1926	George Von Elm	1956	Harvie Ward	1983	Jay Sigel
1899	H.M. Harriman	1927	Bobby Jones	1957	Hillman Robbins	1984	Scott Verplank
1900	Walter Travis	1928	Bobby Jones	1958	Charles Coe	1985	Sam Randolph
1901	Walter Travis	1929	Harrison Johnston	1959	Jack Nicklaus	1986	Buddy Alexander
1902	Louis James	1930	Bobby Jones	1960	Deane Beman	1987	Billy Mayfair
1903	Walter Travis	1931	Francis Ouimet	1961	Jack Nicklaus	1988	Eric Meeks
1904	H. Chandler Egan	1932	Ross Somerville	1962	Labron Harris	1989	Chris Patton
1905	H. Chandler Egan	1933	George Dunlap	1963	Deane Beman	1990	Phil Mickelson
1906	Eben Byers	1934	Lawson Little	1964	Bill Campbell	1991	Mitch Voges
1907	Jerry Travers	1935	Lawson Little	1965	Bob Murphy	1992	Justin Leonard
1908	Jerry Travers	1936	John Fischer	1966	Gary Cowan	1993	John Harris
1909	Robert Gardner	1937	John Goodman	1967	Bob Dickson	1994	Tiger Woods
1910	W.C. Fownes Jr.	1938	William Turnesa	1968	Bruce Fleisher	1995	Tiger Woods
1911	Harold Hilton	1939	Bud Ward	1969	Steve Melnyk	1996	Tiger Woods
1912	Jerry Travers	1940	Richard Chapman	1970	Lanny Wadkins	1997	Matt Kuchar
1913	Jerry Travers	1941	Bud Ward	1971	Gary Cowan	1998	Hank Kuehne
1914	Francis Ouimet	1942-45	Not held	1972	Vinny Giles	1999	David Gossett
1915	Robert Gardner	1946	Ted Bishop	1973	Craig Stadler	2000	Jeff Quinney
1916	Chick Evans	1947	Skee Riegel	1974	Jerry Pate	2001	Bubba Dickerson
1917-18	Not held	1948	William Turnesa	1975	Fred Ridley	2002	Ricky Barnes
1919	Davidson Herron	1949	Charles Coe	1976	Bill Sander	2003	Nick Flanagan
1920	Chick Evans	1950	Sam Urzetta	1977	John Fought	2004	Ryan Moore
1921	Jesse Guilford	1951	Billy Maxwell	1978	John Cook		
1922	Jess Sweetser	1952	Jack Westland	1979	Mark O'Meara		

British Amateur

Match play since 1885.

Multiple winners: John Ball (8); Michael Bonallack (5); Harold Hilton (4); Joe Carr (3); Horace Hutchinson, Ernest Holderness, Trevor Homer, Johnny Laidley, Lawson Little, Peter McEvoy, Dick Siderowf, Frank Stranahan, Freddie Tait, Cyril Tolley and Gary Wolstenholme (2).

Year		Year		Year		Year	
1885	Allen MacFie	1913	Harold Hilton	1950	Frank Stranahan	1978	Peter McEvoy
1886	Horace Hutchinson	1914	J.L.C. Jenkins	1951	Richard Chapman	1979	Jay Sigel
1887	Horace Hutchinson	1915-19	Not held	1952	Harvie Ward	1980	Duncan Evans
1888	John Ball	1920	Cyril Tolley	1953	Joe Carr	1981	Phillipe Ploujoux
1889	Johnny Laidley	1921	William Hunter	1954	Douglas Bachli	1982	Martin Thompson
1890	John Ball	1922	Ernest Holderness	1955	Joe Conrad	1983	Philip Parkin
1891	Johnny Laidley	1923	Roger Wethered	1956	John Beharrell	1984	Jose-Maria Olazabal
1892	John Ball	1924	Ernest Holderness	1957	Reid Jack	1985	Garth McGimpsey
1893	Peter Anderson	1925	Robert Harris	1958	Joe Carr	1986	David Curry
1894	John Ball	1926	Jess Sweetser	1959	Deane Beman	1987	Paul Mayo
1895	Leslie Balfour-Melville	1927	William Tweddell	1960	Joe Carr	1988	Christian Hardin
1896	Freddie Tait	1928	Thomas Perkins	1961	Michael Bonallack	1989	Stephen Dodd
1897	Jack Allan	1929	Cyril Tolley	1962	Richard Davies	1990	Rolf Muntz
1898	Freddie Tait	1930	Bobby Jones	1963	Michael Lunt	1991	Gary Wolstenholme
1899	John Ball	1931	Eric Smith	1964	Gordon Clark	1992	Stephen Dundas
1900	Harold Hilton	1932	John deForest	1965	Michael Bonallack	1993	Ian Pyman
1901	Harold Hilton	1933	Michael Scott	1966	Bobby Cole	1994	Lee James
1902	Charles Hutchings	1934	Lawson Little	1967	Bob Dickson	1995	Gordon Sherry
1903	Robert Maxwell	1935	Lawson Little	1968	Michael Bonallack	1996	Warren Bladon
1904	Walter Travis	1936	Hector Thomson	1969	Michael Bonallack	1997	Craig Watson
1905	Arthur Barry	1937	Robert Sweeny Jr.	1970	Michael Bonallack	1998	Sergio Garcia
1906	James Robb	1938	Charles Yates	1971	Steve Melnyk	1999	Graeme Storm
1907	John Ball	1939	Alexander Kyle	1972	Trevor Homer	2000	Mikko Ilonen
1908	E.A. Lassen	1940-45	Not held	1973	Dick Siderowf	2001	Michael Hoey
1909	Robert Maxwell	1946	James Bruen	1974	Trevor Homer	2002	Alejandro Larrazabal
1910	John Ball	1947	William Turnesa	1975	Vinny Giles	2003	Gary Wolstenholme
1911	Harold Hilton	1948	Frank Stranahan	1976	Dick Siderowf	2004	Stuart Wilson
1912	John Ball	1949	Samuel McCready	1977	Peter McEvoy		

WOMEN
Nabisco Championship

Formerly known as the Colgate Dinah Shore (1972-81) and the Nabisco Dinah Shore (1982-99), the tournament became the LPGA's fourth designated major championship in 1983. Shore's name, which was dropped from the tournament in 2000, is preserved with the Nabisco Dinah Shore Trophy, which is awarded to the winner. The tourney has been played at Mission Hills CC in Rancho Mirage, Calif., since it began; (*) indicates playoff winner.

Multiple winners: (as a major): Amy Alcott and Betsy King (3); Juli Inkster, Dottie Pepper and Annika Sorenstam (2).

Year	Winner	Score	Runner-up	Year	Winner	Score	Runner-up
1972	Jane Blalock	213	Carol Mann	1990	Betsy King	283	Kathy Postlewait
			& Judy Rankin (216)				& Shirley Furlong (285)
1973	Mickey Wright	284	Joyce Kazmierski (286)	1991	Amy Alcott	273	Dottie Pepper (281)
1974	Jo Anne Prentice*	289	Jane Blalock	1992	Dottie Pepper*	279	Juli Inkster (279)
			& Sandra Haynie (289)	1993	Helen Alfredsson	284	Amy Benz
1975	Sandra Palmer	283	Kathy McMullen (284)				& Tina Barrett (286)
1976	Judy Rankin	285	Betty Burfeindt (288)	1994	Donna Andrews	276	Laura Davies (277)
1977	Kathy Whitworth	289	JoAnne Carner	1995	Nanci Bowen	285	Susie Redman (286)
			& Sally Little (290)	1996	Patty Sheehan	281	Kelly Robbins,
1978	Sandra Post*	283	Penny Pulz (283)				Meg Mallon
1979	Sandra Post	276	Nancy Lopez (277)				& Annika Sorenstam
1980	Donna Caponi	275	Amy Alcott (277)				(276)
1981	Nancy Lopez	277	Carolyn Hill (279)	1997	Betsy King	276	Kris Tschetter (278)
1982	Sally Little	278	Hollis Stacy	1998	Pat Hurst	281	Helen Dobson (282)
			& Sandra Haynie (281)	1999	Dottie Pepper	269	Meg Mallon (275)
1983	Amy Alcott	282	Beth Daniel	2000	Karrie Webb	274	Dottie Pepper (284)
			& Kathy Whitworth (284)	2001	Annika Sorenstam	281	Akiko Fukushima, Janice
1984	Juli Inkster*	280	Pat Bradley (280)				Moodie, Dottie Pepper,
1985	Alice Miller	275	Jan Stephenson (278)				Rachel Teske
1986	Pat Bradley	280	Val Skinner (282)				& Karrie Webb (284)
1987	Betsy King*	283	Patty Sheehan (283)	2002	Annika Sorenstam	280	Liselotte Neumann (281)
1988	Amy Alcott	274	Colleen Walker (276)	2003	P. Meunier-Lebouc	281	Annika Sorenstam (282)
1989	Juli Inkster	279	Tammie Green	2004	Grace Park	277	Aree Song (278)
			& JoAnne Carner (284)				

*PLAYOFFS:

1974: Jo Ann Prentice def. Jane Blalock in sudden death. **1978:** Sandra Post def. Penny Pulz in sudden death. **1984:** Juli Inkster def. Pat Bradley in sudden death. **1987:** Betsy King def. Patty Sheehan in sudden death. **1992:** Dottie Pepper def. Juli Inkster in sudden death.

U.S. Women's Open

The U.S. Women's Open began under the direction of the defunct Women's Professional Golfers Assn. in 1946, passed to the LPGA in 1949 and to the USGA in 1953. The tournament used a match play format its first year then switched to stroke play; (*) indicates playoff winner and (a) indicates amateur.

Multiple winners: Betsy Rawls and Mickey Wright (4); Susie Maxwell Berning, Hollis Stacy and Babe Zaharias (3); JoAnne Carner, Donna Caponi, Juli Inkster, Betsy King, Meg Mallon, Patty Sheehan, Annika Sorenstam, Louise Suggs and Karrie Webb (2).

Year	Winner	Score	Runner-up	Course	Location
1946	Patty Berg	5&4	Betty Jameson	Spokane CC	Spokane, Wash.
1947	Betty Jameson	295	a-Sally Sessions	Starmount Forest CC	Greensboro, N.C.
			& a-Polly Riley (301)		
1948	Babe Zaharias	300	Betty Hicks (308)	Atlantic City CC	Northfield, N.J.
1949	Louise Suggs	291	Babe Zaharias (305)	Prince Georges CC	Landover, Md.
1950	Babe Zaharias	291	a-Betsy Rawls (300)	Rolling Hills CC	Wichita, Kan.
1951	Betsy Rawls	293	Louise Suggs (298)	Druid Hills GC	Atlanta, Ga.
1952	Louise Suggs	284	Marlene Hagge (291)	Bala GC	Philadelphia, Penn.
1953	Betsy Rawls*	302	Jackie Pung (302)	CC of Rochester	Rochester, N.Y.
1954	Babe Zaharias	291	Betty Hicks (303)	Salem CC	Peabody, Mass.
1955	Fay Crocker	299	Mary Lena Faulk (303)	Wichita CC	Wichita, Kan.
1956	Kathy Cornelius*	302	Barbara McIntire (302)	Northland CC	Duluth, Minn.
1957	Betsy Rawls	299	Patty Berg (305)	Winged Foot GC	Mamaroneck, N.Y.
1958	Mickey Wright	290	Louise Suggs (295)	Forest Lake CC	Detroit, Mich.
1959	Mickey Wright	287	Louise Suggs (289)	Churchill Valley CC	Pittsburgh, Penn.
1960	Betsy Rawls	292	Joyce Ziske (293)	Worcester CC	Worcester, Mass.
1961	Mickey Wright	293	Betsy Rawls (299)	Baltusrol GC	Springfield, N.J.
1962	Murle Breer	301	Jo Anne Prentice	Dunes GC	Myrtle Beach, S.C.
			& Ruth Jessen (303)		
1963	Mary Mills	289	Sandra Haynie	Kenwood CC	Cincinnati, Ohio
			& Louise Suggs (292)		
1964	Mickey Wright*	290	Ruth Jessen (290)	San Diego CC	Chula Vista, Calif.
1965	Carol Mann	290	Kathy Cornelius (292)	Atlantic City CC	Northfield, N.J.
1966	Sandra Spuzich	297	Carol Mann (298)	Hazeltine National GC	Chaska, Minn.
1967	a-Catherine LaCoste	294	Susie Berning	Hot Springs GC	Hot Springs, Va.
			& Beth Stone (296)		

U.S. Women's Open (Cont.)

Year	Winner	Score	Runner-up	Course	Location
1968	Susie Berning	289	Mickey Wright (292)	Moselem Springs GC	Fleetwood, Penn.
1969	Donna Caponi	294	Peggy Wilson (295)	Scenic Hills CC	Pensacola, Fla.
1970	Donna Caponi	287	Sandra Haynie (288)	Muskogee CC	Muskogee, Okla.
1971	JoAnne Carner	288	Kathy Whitworth (295)	Kahkwa CC	Erie, Penn.
1972	Susie Berning	299	Kathy Ahern, Pam Barnett & Judy Rankin (300)	Winged Foot GC	Mamaroneck, N.Y.
1973	Susie Berning	290	Gloria Ehret (295)	CC of Rochester	Rochester, N.Y.
1974	Sandra Haynie	295	Carol Mann & Beth Stone (296)	La Grange CC	La Grange, Ill.
1975	Sandra Palmer	295	JoAnne Carner, a-Nancy Lopez & Sandra Post (299)	Atlantic City CC	Northfield, N.J.
1976	JoAnne Carner*	292	Sandra Palmer (292)	Rolling Green CC	Springfield, Penn.
1977	Hollis Stacy	292	Nancy Lopez (294)	Hazeltine National GC	Chaska, Minn.
1978	Hollis Stacy	289	JoAnne Carner & Sally Little (290)	CC of Indianapolis	Indianapolis, Ind.
1979	Jerilyn Britz	284	Debbie Massey & Sandra Palmer (286)	Brooklawn CC	Fairfield, Conn.
1980	Amy Alcott	280	Hollis Stacy (289)	Richland CC	Nashville, Tenn.
1981	Pat Bradley	279	Beth Daniel (280)	La Grange CC	La Grange, Ill.
1982	Janet Anderson	283	Beth Daniel, Sandra Haynie & Donna White (289)	Del Paso CC	Sacramento, Calif.
1983	Jan Stephenson	290	JoAnne Carner (291)	Cedar Ridge CC	Tulsa, Okla.
1984	Hollis Stacy	290	Rosie Jones (291)	Salem CC	Peabody, Mass.
1985	Kathy Baker	280	Judy Dickenson (283)	Baltusrol GC	Springfield, N.J.
1986	Jane Geddes*	287	Sally Little (287)	NCR GC	Dayton, Ohio
1987	Laura Davies*	285	Ayako Okamoto & JoAnne Carner (285)	Plainfield CC	Plainfield, N.J.
1988	Liselotte Neumann	277	Patty Sheehan (280)	Baltimore CC	Baltimore, Md.
1989	Betsy King	278	Nancy Lopez (282)	Indianwood GC	Lake Orion, Mich.
1990	Betsy King	284	Patty Sheehan (285)	Atlanta Athletic Club	Duluth, Ga.
1991	Meg Mallon	283	Pat Bradley (285)	Colonial CC	Ft. Worth, Texas
1992	Patty Sheehan*	280	Juli Inkster (280)	Oakmont CC	Oakmont, Penn.
1993	Lauri Merten	280	Donna Andrews & Helen Alfredsson (281)	Crooked Stick GC	Carmel, Ind.
1994	Patty Sheehan	277	Tammie Green (278)	Indianwood CC	Lake Orion, Mich.
1995	Annika Sorenstam	278	Meg Mallon (279)	The Broadmoor	Colorado Springs, Colo.
1996	Annika Sorenstam	272	Kris Tschetter (278)	Pine Needles Lodge & GC	Southern Pines, N.C.
1997	Alison Nicholas	274	Nancy Lopez (275)	Pumpkin Ridge GC	Cornelius, Ore.
1998	Se Ri Pak*	290	a-Jenny Chuasiriporn (290)	Blackwolf Run GC	Kohler, Wis.
1999	Juli Inkster	272	Sherri Turner (277)	Old Waverly GC	West Point, Miss.
2000	Karrie Webb	282	Cristie Kerr & Meg Mallon (287)	Merit Club	Libertyville, Ill.
2001	Karrie Webb	273	Se Ri Pak (281)	Pine Needles Lodge & GC	Southern Pines, N.C.
2002	Juli Inkster	276	Annika Sorenstam (278)	Prairie Dunes CC	Hutchinson, Kan.
2003	Hilary Lunke*	283	Angela Stanford & Kelly Robbins (283)	Pumpkin Ridge GC	North Plains, Ore.
2004	Meg Mallon	274	Annika Sorenstam (276)	Orchards GC	South Hadley, Mass.

*PLAYOFFS:

1953: Betsy Rawls (70) def. Jackie Pung (77) in 18 holes. **1956:** Kathy Cornelius (75) def. Barbara McIntire (82) in 18 holes. **1964:** Mickey Wright (70) def. Ruth Jessen (72) in 18 holes. **1976:** JoAnne Carner (76) def. Sandra Palmer (78) in 18 holes. **1986:** Jane Geddes (71) def. Sally Little (73) in 18 holes. **1987:** Laura Davies (71) def. Ayako Okamoto (73) and JoAnne Carner (74) in 18 holes. **1992:** Patty Sheehan (72) def. Juli Inkster (74) in 18 holes. **1998:** Se Ri Pak def. Jenny Chuasiriporn on the second sudden death hole after both players were tied after an 18-hole playoff. **2003:** Hilary Lunke (70) def. Angela Stanford (71) and Kelly Robbins (73) in 18 holes.

LPGA Championship

Officially the McDonald's LPGA Championship since 1994 (Mazda was the title sponsor from 1987-93), the tournament began in 1955 and has had extended stays at the Stardust CC in Las Vegas (1961-66), Pleasant Valley CC in Sutton, Mass. (1967-68), the Jack Nicklaus Sports Center at Kings Island, Ohio (1978-89), Bethesda CC in Maryland (1990-93) and DuPont CC in Wilmington, Del. (since 1994); (*) indicates playoff winner and (#) weather-shortened.

Multiple winners: Mickey Wright (4); Nancy Lopez, Patty Sheehan and Kathy Whitworth (3); Donna Caponi, Laura Davies, Sandra Haynie, Juli Inkster, Mary Mills, Se Ri Pak, Betsy Rawls and Annika Sorenstam (2).

Year	Winner	Score	Runner-up	Year	Winner	Score	Runner-up
1955	Beverly Hanson	220	Louise Suggs (223)	1959	Betsy Rawls	288	Patty Berg (289)
1956	Marlene Hagge*	291	Patty Berg (291)	1960	Mickey Wright	292	Louise Suggs (295)
1957	Louise Suggs	285	Wiffi Smith (288)	1961	Mickey Wright	287	Louise Suggs (296)
1958	Mickey Wright	288	Fay Crocker (294)	1962	Judy Kimball	282	Shirley Spork (286)

Year	Winner	Score	Runner-up
1963	Mickey Wright	294	Mary Lena Faulk & Mary Mills (296)
1964	Mary Mills	278	Mickey Wright (280)
1965	Sandra Haynie	279	Clifford A. Creed (280)
1966	Gloria Ehret	282	Mickey Wright (285)
1967	Kathy Whitworth	284	Shirley Englehorn (285)
1968	Sandra Post	294	Kathy Whitworth (294)
1969	Betsy Rawls	293	Susie Berning & Carol Mann (297)
1970	Shirley Englehorn	285	Kathy Whitworth (285)
1971	Kathy Whitworth	288	Kathy Ahern (292)
1972	Kathy Ahern	293	Jane Blalock (299)
1973	Mary Mills	288	Betty Burfeindt (289)
1974	Sandra Haynie	288	JoAnne Carner (290)
1975	Kathy Whitworth	288	Sandra Haynie (289)
1976	Betty Burfeindt	287	Judy Rankin (288)
1977	Chako Higuchi	279	Pat Bradley, Sandra Post & Judy Rankin (282)
1978	Nancy Lopez	275	Amy Alcott (281)
1979	Donna Caponi	279	Jerilyn Britz (282)
1980	Sally Little	285	Jane Blalock (288)
1981	Donna Caponi	280	Jerilyn Britz & Pat Meyers (281)
1982	Jan Stephenson	279	JoAnne Carner (281)
1983	Patty Sheehan	279	Sandra Haynie (281)
1984	Patty Sheehan	272	Beth Daniel & Pat Bradley (282)

Year	Winner	Score	Runner-up
1985	Nancy Lopez	273	Alice Miller (281)
1986	Pat Bradley	277	Patty Sheehan (278)
1987	Jane Geddes	275	Betsy King (275)
1988	Sherri Turner	281	Amy Alcott (282)
1989	Nancy Lopez	274	Ayako Okamoto (277)
1990	Beth Daniel	280	Rosie Jones (281)
1991	Meg Mallon	274	Pat Bradley & Ayako Okamoto (275)
1992	Betsy King	267	JoAnne Carner, Karen Noble & Liselotte Neumann (278)
1993	Patty Sheehan	275	Lauri Merten (276)
1994	Laura Davies	279	Alice Ritzman (280)
1995	Kelly Robbins	274	Laura Davies (275)
1996	Laura Davies#	213	Julie Piers (214)
1997	Chris Johnson*	281	Leta Lindley (281)
1998	Se Ri Pak	273	Donna Andrews & Lisa Hackney (276)
1999	Juli Inkster	268	Liselotte Neumann (272)
2000	Juli Inkster*	281	Stefania Croce (281)
2001	Karrie Webb	270	Laura Diaz (272)
2002	Se Ri Pak	279	Beth Daniel (282)
2003	Annika Sorenstam*	278	Grace Park (278)
2004	Annika Sorenstam	271	Shi Hyun Ahn (274)

*PLAYOFFS:

1956: Marlene Hagge def. Patti Berg in sudden death. **1968:** Sandra Post (68) def. Kathy Whitworth (75) in 18 holes. **1970:** Shirley Englehorn def. Kathy Whitworth in sudden death. **1997:** Chris Johnson def. Leta Lindley in sudden death. **2000:** Juli Inkster def. Stefania Croce in sudden death. **2003:** Annika Sorenstam def. Grace Park in sudden death.

Women's British Open

Sponsored by Weetabix, this has been an official stop on the LPGA Tour since 1994, and it became the fourth designated major championship in 2001 when it replaced the du Maurier Classic.
Multiple winners Karrie Webb (3); and Sherri Steinhauer (2); (as a major): none.

Year	Winner	Score	Runner-up	Course	Location
1994	Liselotte Neumann	280	Dottie Mochrie & Annika Sorenstam (283)	Woburn G&CC	Milton Keynes, England
1995	Karrie Webb	278	Annika Sorenstam & Jill McGill (284)	Woburn G&CC	Milton Keynes, England
1996	Emilee Klein	277	Penny Hammel & Amy Alcott (284)	Woburn G&CC	Milton Keynes, England
1997	Karrie Webb	269	Rosie Jones (277)	Sunningdale GC	Berkshire, England
1998	Sherri Steinhauer	292	Sophie Gustafson & Brandie Burton (293)	Royal Lytham	Lytham, England
1999	Sherri Steinhauer	283	Annika Sorenstam (284)	Woburn G&CC	Milton Keynes, England
2000	Sophie Gustafson	282	Kirsty Taylor, Liselotte Neumann, Becky Iverson & Meg Mallon (284)	Royal Birkdale	Southport, England
2001	Se Ri Pak	277	Mi Hyun Kim (279)	Sunningdale GC	Berkshire, England
2002	Karrie Webb	273	Michelle Ellis & Paula Marti (275)	Turnberry GC	Turnberry, Scotland
2003	Annika Sorenstam	278	Se Ri Pak (279)	Royal Lytham	Lytham, England
2004	Karen Stupples	269	Rachel Teske (274)	Sunningdale GC	Berkshire, England

du Maurier Classic (1979-2000)

The du Maurier Classic was considered a major title on the women's tour from 1979-2000; (*) indicates playoff winner.
Multiple winners (as a major): Pat Bradley (3); Brandie Burton (2).

Year		Year		Year		Year	
1973	Jocelyne Bourassa	1980	Pat Bradley	1987	Jody Rosenthal	1994	Martha Nause
1974	Carole Jo Skala	1981	Jan Stephenson	1988	Sally Little	1995	Jenny Lidback
1975	JoAnne Carner	1982	Sandra Haynie	1989	Tammie Green	1996	Laura Davies
1976	Donna Caponi	1983	Hollis Stacy	1990	Cathy Johnston	1997	Colleen Walker
1977	Judy Rankin	1984	Juli Inkster	1991	Nancy Scranton	1998	Brandie Burton
1978	JoAnne Carner	1985	Pat Bradley	1992	Sherri Steinhauer	1999	Karrie Webb
1979	Amy Alcott	1986	Pat Bradley*	1993	Brandie Burton*	2000	Meg Mallon

Titleholders Championship (1937-72)

The Titleholders was considered a major title on the women's tour until it was discontinued after the 1972 tournament.

Multiple winners: Patty Berg (7); Louise Suggs (4); Babe Zaharias (3); Dorothy Kirby, Marilynn Smith, Kathy Whitworth and Mickey Wright (2).

Year		Year		Year		Year	
1937	Patty Berg	1947	Babe Zaharias	1955	Patty Berg	1963	Marilynn Smith
1938	Patty Berg	1948	Patty Berg	1956	Louise Suggs	1964	Marilynn Smith
1939	Patty Berg	1949	Peggy Kirk	1957	Patty Berg	1965	Kathy Whitworth
1940	Betty Hicks	1950	Babe Zaharias	1958	Beverly Hanson	1966	Kathy Whitworth
1941	Dorothy Kirby	1951	Pat O'Sullivan	1959	Louise Suggs	1967-71	Not held
1942	Dorothy Kirby	1952	Babe Zaharias	1960	Fay Crocker	1972	Sandra Palmer
1943-45	Not held	1953	Patty Berg	1961	Mickey Wright		
1946	Louise Suggs	1954	Louise Suggs	1962	Mickey Wright		

Western Open (1930-67)

The Western Open was considered a major title on the women's tour until it was discontinued after the 1967 tournament.

Multiple winners: Patty Berg (7); Louise Suggs and Babe Zaharias (4); Mickey Wright (3); June Beebe, Opal Hill, Betty Jameson and Betsy Rawls (2).

Year		Year		Year		Year	
1930	Mrs. Lee Mida	1940	Babe Zaharias	1950	Babe Zaharias	1960	Joyce Ziske
1931	June Beebe	1941	Patty Berg	1951	Patty Berg	1961	Mary Lena Faulk
1932	Jane Weiller	1942	Betty Jameson	1952	Betsy Rawls	1962	Mickey Wright
1933	June Beebe	1943	Patty Berg	1953	Louise Suggs	1963	Mickey Wright
1934	Marian McDougall	1944	Babe Zaharias	1954	Betty Jameson	1964	Carol Mann
1935	Opal Hill	1945	Babe Zaharias	1955	Patty Berg	1965	Susie Maxwell
1936	Opal Hill	1946	Louise Suggs	1956	Beverly Hanson	1966	Mickey Wright
1937	Betty Hicks	1947	Louise Suggs	1957	Patty Berg	1967	Kathy Whitworth
1938	Bea Barrett	1948	Louise Suggs	1958	Patty Berg		
1939	Helen Dettweiler	1949	Louise Suggs	1959	Betsy Rawls		

Grand Slam Summary

From 1955-66, the U.S. Open, LPGA Championship, Western Open and Titleholders tournaments served as the Women's Grand Slam. From 1983-2000 the U.S. Open, LPGA, du Maurier Classic and Nabisco Championship were the major events. In 2001, the Weetabix Women's British Open replaced the du Maurier Classic as the tour's fourth major. No one has won a four-event Grand Slam on the women's tour.

Three wins in one year (3): Babe Zaharias (1950), Mickey Wright (1961) and Pat Bradley (1986).

Two wins in one year (19): Patty Berg and Mickey Wright (3 times); Juli Inkster, Louise Suggs and Karrie Webb (twice); Laura Davies, Sandra Haynie, Betsy King, Meg Mallon, Se Ri Pak, Betsy Rawls, Annika Sorenstam and Kathy Whitworth (once).

Year	LPGA	US Open	T'holders	Western	Year	LPGA	US Open	T'holders	Western
1937	—	—	Berg	Hicks	1944	—	—	—	Zaharias
1938	—	—	Berg	Barrett	1945	—	—	—	Zaharias
1939	—	—	Berg	Dettweiler	1946	—	Berg	Suggs	Suggs
1940	—	—	Hicks	Zaharias	1947	—	Jameson	Zaharias	Suggs
1941	—	—	Kirby	Berg	1948	—	Zaharias	Berg	Berg
1942	—	—	Kirby	Jameson	1949	—	Suggs	Kirk	Suggs
1943	—	—	—	Berg	1950	—	Zaharias	Zaharias	Zaharias

Major Championship Leaders

Through 2004; active LPGA players in **bold** type.

	US Open	LPGA	Nabisco	British Open	duM	Title	Western	US Am	Brit Am	Total
Patty Berg	1	0	0	0	0	7	7	1	0	**16**
Mickey Wright	4	4	0	0	0	2	3	0	0	**13**
Louise Suggs	2	1	0	0	0	4	4	1	1	**13**
Babe Didrikson Zaharias	3	0	0	0	0	3	4	1	1	**12**
Juli Inkster	2	2	2	0	1	0	0	3	0	**10**
Betsy Rawls	4	2	0	0	0	0	2	0	0	**8**
Annika Sorenstam	2	2	2	1	0	0	0	0	0	**7**
JoAnne Carner	2	0	0	0	0	0	0	5	0	**7**
Kathy Whitworth	0	3	0	0	0	2	1	0	0	**6**
Pat Bradley	1	1	1	0	3	0	0	0	0	**6**
Betsy King	2	1	3	0	0	0	0	0	0	**6**
Patty Sheehan	2	3	1	0	0	0	0	0	0	**6**
Glenna C. Vare	0	0	0	0	0	0	0	6	0	**6**
Karrie Webb	2	1	1	1	1	0	0	0	0	**6**

Tournaments: U.S. Open, LPGA Championship, Nabisco Championship, British Open, du Maurier Classic (1979-2000), Titleholders (1930-72), Western Open (1937-67), U.S. Amateur and British Amateur.

Year	LPGA	US Open	T'holders	Western	Year	LPGA	US Open	duMaurier	Nabisco
1951	—	Rawls	O'Sullivan	Berg	1979	Caponi	Britz	Alcott	—
1952	—	Suggs	Zaharias	Rawls	1980	Little	Alcott	Bradley	—
1953	—	Rawls	Berg	Suggs	1981	Caponi	Bradley	Stephenson	—
1954	—	Zaharias	Suggs	Jameson	1982	Stephenson	Anderson	Haynie	—
1955	Hanson	Crocker	Berg	Berg	1983	Sheehan	Stephenson	Stacy	Alcott
1956	Hagge	Cornelius	Suggs	Hanson	1984	Sheehan	Stacy	Inkster	Inkster
1957	Suggs	Rawls	Berg	Berg	1985	Lopez	Baker	Bradley	Miller
1958	Wright	Wright	Hanson	Berg	1986	Bradley	Geddes	Bradley	Bradley
1959	Rawls	Wright	Suggs	Berg	1987	Geddes	Davies	Rosenthal	King
1960	Wright	Rawls	Crocker	Ziske	1988	Turner	Neumann	Little	Alcott
1961	Wright	Wright	Wright	Faulk	1989	Lopez	King	Green	Inkster
1962	Kimball	Lindstrom	Wright	Wright	1990	Daniel	King	Johnston	King
1963	Wright	Mills	M. Smith	Wright	1991	Mallon	Mallon	Scranton	Alcott
1964	Mills	Wright	M. Smith	Mann	1992	King	Sheehan	Steinhauer	Pepper
1965	Haynie	Mann	Whitworth	Maxwell	1993	Sheehan	Merten	Burton	Alfredsson
1966	Ehret	Whitworth	Whitworth	Wright	1994	Davies	Sheehan	Nause	Andrews
1967	Whitworth	a-LaCoste	—	Whitworth	1995	Robbins	Sorenstam	Lidback	Bowen
1968	Post	Berning	—	—	1996	Davies	Sorenstam	Davies	Sheehan
1969	Rawls	Caponi	—	—	1997	Johnson	Nicholas	Walker	King
1970	Englehorn	Caponi	—	—	1998	Pak	Pak	Burton	Hurst
1971	Whitworth	Carner	—	—	1999	Inkster	Inkster	Webb	Pepper
1972	Ahern	Berning	Palmer	—	2000	Inkster	Webb	Mallon	Webb
1973	Mills	Berning	—	—	**Year**	**LPGA**	**US Open**	**Brit. Open**	**Nabisco**
1974	Haynie	Haynie	—	—	2001	Webb	Webb	Pak	Sorenstam
1975	Whitworth	Palmer	—	—	2002	Pak	Inkster	Webb	Sorenstam
1976	Burfeindt	Carner	—	—	2003	Sorenstam	Lunke	Sorenstam	Meunier-Lebouc
1977	Higuchi	Stacy	—	—	2004	Sorenstam	Mallon	Stupples	Park
1978	Lopez	Stacy	—	—					

U.S. Women's Amateur

Stroke play in 1895, match play since 1896.

Multiple winners: Glenna Collett Vare (6); JoAnne Gunderson (5); Margaret Curtis, Beatrix Hoyt, Dorothy Campbell Hurd, Juli Inkster, Alexa Stirling, Virginia Van Wie, Anne Quast Decker Welts (3); Kay Cockerill, Beth Daniel, Vicki Goetze, Katherine Harley, Genevieve Hecker, Betty Jameson, Kelli Kuehne and Barbara McIntire (2).

Year		Year		Year		Year	
1895	Mrs. C.S. Brown	1924	Dorothy C. Hurd	1955	Patricia Lesser	1983	Joanne Pacillo
1896	Beatrix Hoyt	1925	Glenna Collett	1956	Marlene Stewart	1984	Deb Richard
1897	Beatrix Hoyt	1926	Helen Stetson	1957	JoAnne Gunderson	1985	Michiko Hattori
1898	Beatrix Hoyt	1927	Miriam Burns Horn	1958	Anne Quast	1986	Kay Cockerill
1899	Ruth Underhill	1928	Glenna Collett	1959	Barbara McIntire	1987	Kay Cockerill
1900	Frances Griscom	1929	Glenna Collett	1960	JoAnne Gunderson	1988	Pearl Sinn
1901	Genevieve Hecker	1930	Glenna Collett	1961	Anne Quast Decker	1989	Vicki Goetze
1902	Genevieve Hecker	1931	Helen Hicks	1962	JoAnne Gunderson	1990	Pat Hurst
1903	Bessie Anthony	1932	Virginia Van Wie	1963	Anne Quast Welts	1991	Amy Fruhwirth
1904	Georgianna Bishop	1933	Virginia Van Wie	1964	Barbara McIntire	1992	Vicki Goetze
1905	Pauline Mackay	1934	Virginia Van Wie	1965	Jean Ashley	1993	Jill McGill
1906	Harriot Curtis	1935	Glenna Collett Vare	1966	JoAnne G. Carner	1994	Wendy Ward
1907	Margaret Curtis	1936	Pamela Barton	1967	Mary Lou Dill	1995	Kelli Kuehne
1908	Katherine Harley	1937	Estelle Lawson	1968	JoAnne G. Carner	1996	Kelli Kuehne
1909	Dorothy Campbell	1938	Patty Berg	1969	Catherine Lacoste	1997	Silvia Cavalleri
1910	Dorothy Campbell	1939	Betty Jameson	1970	Martha Wilkinson	1998	Grace Park
1911	Margaret Curtis	1940	Betty Jameson	1971	Laura Baugh	1999	Dorothy Delasin
1912	Margaret Curtis	1941	Elizabeth Hicks	1972	Mary Budke	2000	Marcy Newton
1913	Gladys Ravenscroft	1942-45	Not held	1973	Carol Semple	2001	Meredith Duncan
1914	Katherine Harley	1946	Babe D. Zaharias	1974	Cynthia Hill	2002	Becky Lucidi
1915	Florence Vanderbeck	1947	Louise Suggs	1975	Beth Daniel	2003	V. Nirapathpongporn
1916	Alexa Stirling	1948	Grace Lenczyk	1976	Donna Horton	2004	Jane Park
1917-18	Not held	1949	Dorothy Porter	1977	Beth Daniel		
1919	Alexa Stirling	1950	Beverly Hanson	1978	Cathy Sherk		
1920	Alexa Stirling	1951	Dorothy Kirby	1979	Carolyn Hill		
1921	Marion Hollins	1952	Jacqueline Pung	1980	Juli Inkster		
1922	Glenna Collett	1953	Mary Lena Faulk	1981	Juli Inkster		
1923	Edith Cummings	1954	Barbara Romack	1982	Juli Inkster		

British Women's Amateur
Match play since 1893.

Multiple winners: Cecil Leitch and Joyce Wethered (4); May Hezlet, Lady Margaret Scott, Jessie Anderson Valentine, Brigitte Varangot and Enid Wilson (3); Rhona Adair, Pam Barton, Dorothy Campbell, Elizabeth Chadwick, Helen Holm, Rebecca Hudson, Marley Spearman, Frances Stephens and Michelle Walker (2).

Year		Year		Year		Year	
1893	Lady Margaret Scott	1923	Doris Chambers	1954	Frances Stephens	1980	Anne Quast Sander
1894	Lady Margaret Scott	1924	Joyce Wethered	1955	Jessie Valentine	1981	Belle Robertson
1895	Lady Margaret Scott	1925	Joyce Wethered	1956	Wiffi Smith	1982	Kitrina Douglas
1896	Amy Pascoe	1926	Cecil Leitch	1957	Philomena Garvey	1983	Jill Thornhill
1897	Edith Orr	1927	Simone de la Chaume	1958	Jessie Valentine	1984	Jody Rosenthal
1898	Lena Thomson	1928	Nanette le Blan	1959	Elizabeth Price	1985	Lillian Behan
1899	May Hezlet	1929	Joyce Wethered	1960	Barbara McIntire	1986	Marnie McGuire
1900	Rhona Adair	1930	Diana Fishwick	1961	Marley Spearman	1987	Janet Collingham
1901	Mary Graham	1931	Enid Wilson	1962	Marley Spearman	1988	Joanne Furby
1902	May Hezlet	1932	Enid Wilson	1963	Brigitte Varangot	1989	Helen Dobson
1903	Rhona Adair	1933	Enid Wilson	1964	Carol Sorenson		
1904	Lottie Dod	1934	Helen Holm	1965	Brigitte Varangot	1990	Julie Wade Hall
1905	Bertha Thompson	1935	Wanda Morgan	1966	Elizabeth Chadwick	1991	Valerie Michaud
1906	Mrs. W. Kennion	1936	Pam Barton	1967	Elizabeth Chadwick	1992	Bernille Pedersen
1907	May Hezlet	1937	Jessie Anderson	1968	Brigitte Varangot	1993	Catriona Lambert
1908	Maud Titterton	1938	Helen Holm	1969	Catherine Lacoste	1994	Emma Duggleby
1909	Dorothy Campbell	1939	Pam Barton			1995	Julie Wade Hall
				1970	Dinah Oxley	1996	Kelli Kuehne
1910	Elsie Grant-Suttie	1940-45	Not held	1971	Michelle Walker	1997	Alison Rose
1911	Dorothy Campbell	1946	Jean Hetherington	1972	Michelle Walker	1998	Kim Rostron
1912	Gladys Ravenscroft	1947	Babe Zaharias	1973	Ann Irvin	1999	Marine Monnet
1913	Muriel Dodd	1948	Louise Suggs	1974	Carol Semple		
1914	Cecil Leitch	1949	Frances Stephens	1975	Nancy Roth Syms	2000	Rebecca Hudson
1915-19	Not held			1976	Cathy Panton	2001	Marta Prieto
		1950	Lally de St. Sauveur	1977	Angela Uzielli	2002	Rebecca Hudson
1920	Cecil Leitch	1951	Catherine MacCann	1978	Edwina Kennedy	2003	Elisa Serramia
1921	Cecil Leitch	1952	Moira Paterson	1979	Maureen Madill	2004	Louise Stahle
1922	Joyce Wethered	1953	Marlene Stewart				

Champions Tour
(formerly Senior PGA Tour)

Senior PGA Championship
First played in 1937. Two championships played in 1979 and 1984.

Multiple winners: Sam Snead (6); Hale Irwin (4); Gary Player, Al Watrous and Eddie Williams (3); Julius Boros, Jock Hutchison, Don January, Arnold Palmer, Paul Runyan, Gene Sarazen and Lee Trevino (2).

Year		Year		Year		Year	
1937	Jock Hutchison	1956	Pete Burke	1974	Roberto De Vicenzo	1990	Gary Player
1938	Fred McLeod*	1957	Al Watrous	1975	Charlie Sifford*	1991	Jack Nicklaus
1939	Not held	1958	Gene Sarazen	1976	Pete Cooper	1992	Lee Trevino
1940	Otto Hackbarth*	1959	Willie Goggin	1977	Julius Boros	1993	Tom Wargo*
1941	Jack Burke	1960	Dick Metz	1978	Joe Jiminez*	1994	Lee Trevino
1942	Eddie Williams	1961	Paul Runyan	1979	Jack Fleck*	1995	Ray Floyd
1943-44	Not held	1962	Paul Runyan	1979	Don January	1996	Hale Irwin
1945	Eddie Williams	1963	Herman Barron	1980	Arnold Palmer*	1997	Hale Irwin
1946	Eddie Williams*	1964	Sam Snead	1981	Miller Barber	1998	Hale Irwin
1947	Jock Hutchison	1965	Sam Snead	1982	Don January	1999	Allen Doyle
1948	Charles McKenna	1966	Fred Haas	1983	Not held	2000	Doug Tewell
1949	Marshall Crichton	1967	Sam Snead	1984	Arnold Palmer	2001	Tom Watson
1950	Al Watrous	1968	Chandler Harper	1984	Peter Thomson	2002	Fuzzy Zoeller
1951	Al Watrous*	1969	Tommy Bolt	1985	Not held	2003	John Jacobs
1952	Ernest Newnham	1970	Sam Snead	1986	Gary Player	2004	Hale Irwin
1953	Harry Schwab	1971	Julius Boros	1987	Chi Chi Rodriguez		
1954	Gene Sarazen	1972	Sam Snead	1988	Gary Player		
1955	Mortie Dutra	1973	Sam Snead	1989	Larry Mowry		

*PLAYOFFS:
1938: Fred McLeod def. Otto Hackbarth in 18 holes. **1940:** Otto Hackbarth def. Jock Hutchison in 36 holes. **1946:** Eddie Williams def. Jock Hutchison in 18 holes. **1951:** Al Watrous def. Jock Hutchison in 18 holes. **1975:** Charlie Sifford def. Fred Wampler on 1st extra hole **1978:** Joe Jiminez def. Paul Harney on 1st extra hole. **1979:** Jack Fleck def. Bill Johnston on 1st extra hole. **1980:** Arnold Palmer def. Paul Harney on 1st extra hole. **1993:** Tom Wargo def. Bruce Crampton on 2nd extra hole.

U.S. Senior Open

Established in 1980 for senior players 55 years old and over, the minimum age was dropped to 50 (the Champions Tour entry age) in 1981. Arnold Palmer, Billy Casper, Hale Irwin, Orville Moody, Jack Nicklaus and Lee Trevino are the only golfers who have won both the U.S. Open and U.S. Senior Open.

Multiple winners: Miller Barber (3); Hale Irwin, Jack Nicklaus and Gary Player (2).

Year		Year		Year		Year	
1980	Roberto De Vicenzo	1987	Gary Player	1994	Simon Hobday	2001	Bruce Fleisher
1981	Arnold Palmer*	1988	Gary Player*	1995	Tom Weiskopf	2002	Don Pooley*
1982	Miller Barber	1989	Orville Moody	1996	Dave Stockton	2003	Bruce Lietzke
1983	Bill Casper*	1990	Lee Trevino	1997	Graham Marsh	2004	Peter Jacobsen
1984	Miller Barber	1991	Jack Nicklaus*	1998	Hale Irwin		
1985	Miller Barber	1992	Larry Laoretti	1999	Dave Eichelberger		
1986	Dale Douglass	1993	Jack Nicklaus	2000	Hale Irwin		

*PLAYOFFS:

1981: Arnold Palmer (70) def. Bob Stone (74) and Billy Casper (77) in 18 holes. **1983:** Tied at 75 after 18-hole playoff, Casper def. Rod Funseth with a birdie on the 1st extra hole. **1988:** Gary Player (68) def. Bob Charles (70) in 18 holes. **1991:** Jack Nicklaus (65) def. Chi Chi Rodriguez (69) in 18 holes. **2002:** Don Pooley and Tom Watson remained tied after a three hole playoff and Pooley won on the second hole of sudden death.

Senior Players Championship

Sponsored by Ford since 1993. First played in 1983 and contested in Cleveland (1983-86), Ponte Vedra, Fla. (1987-89) and Dearborn, Mich. (since 1990).

Multiple winners: Ray Floyd, Arnold Palmer and Dave Stockton (2).

Year		Year		Year		Year	
1983	Miller Barber	1989	Orville Moody	1995	J.C. Snead*	2001	Allen Doyle*
1984	Arnold Palmer	1990	Jack Nicklaus	1996	Ray Floyd	2002	Stewart Ginn
1985	Arnold Palmer	1991	Jim Albus	1997	Larry Gilbert	2003	Craig Stadler
1986	Chi Chi Rodriguez	1992	Dave Stockton	1998	Gil Morgan	2004	Mark James
1987	Gary Player	1993	Jim Colbert	1999	Hale Irwin		
1988	Billy Casper	1994	Dave Stockton	2000	Ray Floyd		

*PLAYOFFS:

1995: J.C. Snead def. Jack Nicklaus on 1st extra hole. **2001:** Allen Doyle def. Doug Tewell on 1st extra hole.

The Tradition

Sponsored by window and door manufacturer JELD-WEN since 2003, it was formerly called The Tradition at Desert Mountain (1989-91), The Tradition (1992-99) and The Countrywide Tradition (2000-02). Held at GC at Desert Mountain in Scottsdale, Ariz. (1989-2001), Superstition Mountain (Ariz.) G & CC (2002) and The Reserve Vineyards & GC in Aloha, Ore. (2003—).

Multiple winners: Jack Nicklaus (4); Gil Morgan (2).

Year		Year		Year		Year	
1989	Don Bies	1993	Tom Shaw	1997	Gil Morgan	2001	Doug Tewell
1990	Jack Nicklaus	1994	Ray Floyd*	1998	Gil Morgan	2002	Jim Thorpe*
1991	Jack Nicklaus	1995	Jack Nicklaus*	1999	Graham Marsh	2003	Tom Watson
1992	Lee Trevino	1996	Jack Nicklaus	2000	Tom Kite	2004	Craig Stadler

*PLAYOFFS:

1994: Ray Floyd def. Dale Douglass on 1st extra hole. **1995:** Jack Nicklaus def. Isao Aoki on 3rd extra hole; **2002:** Jim Thorpe def. John Jacobs on 1st extra hole.

Senior British Open

First played in 1987 and contested in Turnberry, Scotland (1987-90, 2003), Lytham, England (1991-94), Portrush, Ireland (1995-99) and Newcastle, Ireland (2000-02). In 2003 it became the fifth designated major championship on the Champions Tour.

Multiple winners: Gary Player (3); Brian Barnes, Bob Charles and Christy O'Connor Jr. (2). (as a major): none.

Year		Year		Year		Year	
1987	Neil Coles	1992	John Fourie	1997	Gary Player	2002	Noboru Sugai
1988	Gary Player	1993	Bob Charles	1998	Brian Huggett	2003	Tom Watson*
1989	Bob Charles	1994	Tom Wargo	1999	Christy O'Connor Jr.	2004	Pete Oakley
1990	Gary Player	1995	Brian Barnes	2000	Christy O'Connor Jr.		
1991	Bobby Verwey	1996	Brian Barnes	2001	Ian Stanley		

*PLAYOFF (as a Major)— **2003:** Tom Watson def. Carl Mason on 2nd extra hole.

Major Senior Championship Leaders

Through 2004. All players are still active. **Note:** The Senior British Open became the Champions Tour's fifth major in 2003.

	Senior PGA	US Open	Senior Players	Trad	Total		Senior PGA	US Open	Senior Players	Trad	Total
1 Jack Nicklaus	1	2	1	4	8	4 Ray Floyd	1	0	2	1	4
2 Hale Irwin	4	2	1	0	7	Lee Trevino	2	1	0	1	4
3 Gary Player	3	2	1	0	6						

Champions Tour (Cont.)
Grand Slam Summary

The Senior Grand Slam had officially consisted of The Tradition, the Senior PGA Championship, the Senior Players Championship and the U.S. Senior Open from 1990-2002. In 2003, the Senior British Open was added. Jack Nicklaus won three of the four events in 1991, but no one has won all four (or now five) in one season.

Three wins in one year: Jack Nicklaus (1991). **Two wins in one year** (8): Gary Player (twice); Hale Irwin, Gil Morgan, Orville Moody, Jack Nicklaus, Arnold Palmer, Lee Trevino and Tom Watson (once).

Year	Tradition	Sr. PGA	Players	US Open	Year	Tradition	Sr. PGA	Players	US Open
1983	—	—	M. Barber	Casper	1993	Shaw	Wargo	Colbert	Nicklaus
1984	—	Palmer	Palmer	M. Barber	1994	Floyd	Trevino	Stockton	Hobday
1985	—	Thomson	Palmer	M. Barber	1995	Nicklaus	Floyd	Snead	Weiskopf
1986	—	Player	Rodriguez	Douglass	1996	Nicklaus	Irwin	Floyd	Stockton
1987	—	Rodriguez	Player	Player	1997	Morgan	Irwin	Gilbert	Marsh
1988	—	Player	Casper	Player	1998	Morgan	Irwin	Morgan	Irwin
1989	Bies	Mowry	Moody	Moody	1999	Marsh	Doyle	Irwin	Eichelberger
1990	Nicklaus	Player	Nicklaus	Trevino	2000	Kite	Tewell	Floyd	Irwin
1991	Nicklaus	Nicklaus	Albus	Nicklaus	2001	Tewell	Watson	Doyle	Fleisher
1992	Trevino	Trevino	Stockton	Laoretti	2002	Thorpe	Zoeller	Ginn	Pooley

Year	Tradition	Sr. PGA	Players	US Open	Sr. Brit. Open
2003	Watson	Jacobs	Stadler	Lietzke	Watson
2004	Stadler	Irwin	James	Jacobsen	Oakley

Annual Money Leaders

Official annual money leaders on the PGA, European PGA, Champions and LPGA tours.

PGA

Multiple leaders: Jack Nicklaus (8); Ben Hogan, Tom Watson and Tiger Woods (5); Arnold Palmer (4); Greg Norman, Sam Snead and Curtis Strange (3); Julius Boros, Billy Casper, Tom Kite, Byron Nelson and Nick Price (2).

Year		Earnings	Year		Earnings	Year		Earnings
1934	Paul Runyan	$6,767	1958	Arnold Palmer	$42,608	1982	Craig Stadler	$446,462
1935	Johnny Revolta	9,543	1959	Art Wall	53,168	1983	Hal Sutton	426,668
1936	Horton Smith	7,682	1960	Arnold Palmer	75,263	1984	Tom Watson	476,260
1937	Harry Cooper	14,139	1961	Gary Player	64,540	1985	Curtis Strange	542,321
1938	Sam Snead	19,534	1962	Arnold Palmer	81,448	1986	Greg Norman	653,296
1939	Henry Picard	10,303	1963	Arnold Palmer	128,230	1987	Curtis Strange	925,941
1940	Ben Hogan	10,655	1964	Jack Nicklaus	113,285	1988	Curtis Strange	1,147,644
1941	Ben Hogan	18,358	1965	Jack Nicklaus	140,752	1989	Tom Kite	1,395,278
1942	Ben Hogan	13,143	1966	Billy Casper	121,945	1990	Greg Norman	1,165,477
1943	No records kept		1967	Jack Nicklaus	188,998	1991	Corey Pavin	979,430
1944	Byron Nelson	37,968	1968	Billy Casper	205,169	1992	Fred Couples	1,344,188
1945	Byron Nelson	63,336	1969	Frank Beard	164,707	1993	Nick Price	1,478,557
1946	Ben Hogan	42,556	1970	Lee Trevino	157,037	1994	Nick Price	1,499,927
1947	Jimmy Demaret	27,937	1971	Jack Nicklaus	244,491	1995	Greg Norman	1,654,959
1948	Ben Hogan	32,112	1972	Jack Nicklaus	320,542	1996	Tom Lehman	1,780,159
1949	Sam Snead	31,594	1973	Jack Nicklaus	308,362	1997	Tiger Woods	2,066,833
1950	Sam Snead	35,759	1974	Johnny Miller	353,022	1998	David Duval	2,591,031
1951	Lloyd Mangrum	26,089	1975	Jack Nicklaus	298,149	1999	Tiger Woods	6,616,585
1952	Julius Boros	37,033	1976	Jack Nicklaus	266,439	2000	Tiger Woods	9,188,321
1953	Lew Worsham	34,002	1977	Tom Watson	310,653	2001	Tiger Woods	5,687,777
1954	Bob Toski	65,820	1978	Tom Watson	362,429	2002	Tiger Woods	6,912,625
1955	Julius Boros	63,122	1979	Tom Watson	462,636	2003	Vijay Singh	7,573,907
1956	Ted Kroll	72,836	1980	Tom Watson	530,808			
1957	Dick Mayer	65,835	1981	Tom Kite	375,699			

Note: In 1944-45, Nelson's winnings were in War Bonds.

Champions Tour

Multiple leaders: Hale Irwin and Don January (3); Miller Barber, Bob Charles, Jim Colbert, Dave Stockton and Lee Trevino (2).

Year		Earnings	Year		Earnings	Year		Earnings
1980	Don January	$44,100	1988	Bob Charles	$533,929	1996	Jim Colbert	$1,627,890
1981	Miller Barber	83,136	1989	Bob Charles	725,887	1997	Hale Irwin	2,343,364
1982	Miller Barber	106,890	1990	Lee Trevino	1,190,518	1998	Hale Irwin	2,861,945
1983	Don January	237,571	1991	Mike Hill	1,065,657	1999	Bruce Fleisher	2,515,705
1984	Don January	328,597	1992	Lee Trevino	1,027,002	2000	Larry Nelson	2,708,005
1985	Peter Thomson	386,724	1993	Dave Stockton	1,175,944	2001	Allen Doyle	2,553,582
1986	Bruce Crampton	454,299	1994	Dave Stockton	1,402,519	2002	Hale Irwin	3,028,304
1987	Chi Chi Rodriguez	509,145	1995	Jim Colbert	1,444,386	2003	Tom Watson	1,853,108

European PGA

Official money in the Volvo Order of Merit was awarded in British pounds from 1961-98 and euros (E) since 1999.

Multiple leaders: Colin Montgomerie (7); Seve Ballesteros (6); Sandy Lyle (3); Gay Brewer Jr., Nick Faldo, Retief Goosen, Bernard Hunt, Bernhard Langer, Peter Thomson and Ian Woosnam (2).

Year		Earnings	Year		Earnings	Year		Earnings
1961	Bernard Hunt	£4,492	1976	Seve Ballesteros	£39,504	1991	Seve Ballesteros	£790,811
1962	Peter Thomson	5,764	1977	Seve Ballesteros	46,436	1992	Nick Faldo	1,220,540
1963	Bernard Hunt	7,209	1978	Seve Ballesteros	54,348	1993	Colin Montgomerie	798,145
1964	Neil Coles	7,890	1979	Sandy Lyle	49,233	1994	Colin Montgomerie	920,647
1965	Peter Thomson	7,011	1980	Greg Norman	74,829	1995	Colin Montgomerie	1,038,718
1966	Bruce Devlin	13,205	1981	Bernhard Langer	95,991	1996	Colin Montgomerie	1,034,752
1967	Gay Brewer Jr.	20,235	1982	Sandy Lyle	86,141	1997	Colin Montgomerie	1,583,904
1968	Gay Brewer Jr.	23,107	1983	Nick Faldo	140,761	1998	Colin Montgomerie	1,082,833
1969	Billy Casper	23,483	1984	Bernhard Langer	160,883	1999	C. Montgomerie	E2,066,885
1970	Christy O'Connor	31,532	1985	Sandy Lyle	254,711	2000	Lee Westwood	3,125,147
1971	Gary Player	11,281	1986	Seve Ballesteros	259,275	2001	Retief Goosen	2,862,806
1972	Bob Charles	18,538	1987	Ian Woosnam	439,075	2002	Retief Goosen	2,360,128
1973	Tony Jacklin	24,839	1988	Seve Ballesteros	502,000	2003	Ernie Els	2,975,374
1974	Peter Oosterhuis	32,127	1989	Ronan Rafferty	465,981			
1975	Dale Hayes	20,507	1990	Ian Woosnam	737,977			

LPGA

Multiple leaders: Kathy Whitworth (8); Annika Sorenstam (5); Mickey Wright (4); Patty Berg, JoAnne Carner, Beth Daniel, Betsy King, Nancy Lopez and Karrie Webb (3); Pat Bradley, Judy Rankin, Betsy Rawls, Louise Suggs and Babe Zaharias (2).

Year		Earnings	Year		Earnings	Year		Earnings
1950	Babe Zaharias	$14,800	1968	Kathy Whitworth	$48,379	1986	Pat Bradley	$492,021
1951	Babe Zaharias	15,087	1969	Carol Mann	49,152	1987	Ayako Okamoto	466,034
1952	Betsy Rawls	14,505	1970	Kathy Whitworth	30,235	1988	Sherri Turner	350,851
1953	Louise Suggs	19,816	1971	Kathy Whitworth	41,181	1989	Betsy King	654,132
1954	Patty Berg	16,011	1972	Kathy Whitworth	65,063	1990	Beth Daniel	863,578
1955	Patty Berg	16,492	1973	Kathy Whitworth	82,864	1991	Pat Bradley	763,118
1956	Marlene Hagge	20,235	1974	JoAnne Carner	87,094	1992	Dottie Pepper	693,335
1957	Patty Berg	16,272	1975	Sandra Palmer	76,374	1993	Betsy King	595,992
1958	Beverly Hanson	12,639	1976	Judy Rankin	150,734	1994	Laura Davies	687,201
1959	Betsy Rawls	26,774	1977	Judy Rankin	122,890	1995	Annika Sorenstam	666,533
1960	Louise Suggs	16,892	1978	Nancy Lopez	189,814	1996	Karrie Webb	1,002,000
1961	Mickey Wright	22,236	1979	Nancy Lopez	197,489	1997	Annika Sorenstam	1,236,789
1962	Mickey Wright	21,641	1980	Beth Daniel	231,000	1998	Annika Sorenstam	1,092,748
1963	Mickey Wright	31,269	1981	Beth Daniel	206,998	1999	Karrie Webb	1,591,959
1964	Mickey Wright	29,800	1982	JoAnne Carner	310,400	2000	Karrie Webb	1,876,853
1965	Kathy Whitworth	28,658	1983	JoAnne Carner	291,404	2001	Annika Sorenstam	2,105,868
1966	Kathy Whitworth	33,517	1984	Betsy King	266,771	2002	Annika Sorenstam	2,863,904
1967	Kathy Whitworth	32,937	1985	Nancy Lopez	416,472	2003	Annika Sorenstam	2,029,506

All-Time Leaders

PGA, Champions Tour and LPGA leaders through Oct. 3, 2004. **Note:** In Sept. 2002, the PGA Tour board approved the retroactive awarding of an official victory to British Open winners prior to 1995. The list below reflects the new totals.

Tournaments Won

	PGA	No		Champions	No		LPGA	No
1	Sam Snead	82	1	Hale Irwin	40	1	Kathy Whitworth	88
2	Jack Nicklaus	73	2	Lee Trevino	29	2	Mickey Wright	82
3	Ben Hogan	64	3	Miller Barber	24	3	Patty Berg	60
4	Arnold Palmer	62	4	Bob Charles	23	4	Louise Suggs	58
5	Byron Nelson	52		Gil Morgan	23	5	Betsy Rawls	55
6	Billy Casper	51	6	Don January	22	6	Annika Sorenstam	53
7	Walter Hagen	44		Chi Chi Rodriguez	22	7	Nancy Lopez	48
8	Cary Middlecoff	40	8	Bruce Crampton	20	8	JoAnne Carner	43
	Tiger Woods	40		Jim Colbert	20	9	Sandra Haynie	42
10	Gene Sarazen	39	10	George Archer	19	10	Babe Zaharias	41
	Tom Watson	39		Gary Player	19	11	Carol Mann	38
12	Lloyd Mangrum	36	12	Mike Hill	18	12	Patty Sheehan	35
13	Horton Smith	32		Larry Nelson	18	13	Betsy King	34
14	Harry Cooper	31		Bruce Fleisher	18	14	Beth Daniel	33
	Jimmy Demaret	31	15	Dave Stockton	14	15	Pat Bradley	31
16	Leo Diegel	30		Raymond Floyd	14	16	Juli Inkster	30
17	Gene Littler	29	17	Jim Dent	12		Karrie Webb	30
	Paul Runyan	29	18	Dale Douglass	11	18	Amy Alcott	29
	Lee Trevino	29		Orville Moody	11	19	Jane Blalock	27
20	Henry Picard	26		Bob Murphy	11	20	Judy Rankin	26
				Peter Thomson	11		Marlene Hagge	26

All-Time Leaders (Cont.)
Money Won
All-time earnings through Oct. 3, 2004.
PGA

		Earnings			Earnings			Earnings
1	Tiger Woods	$44,494,737	10	Justin Leonard	$17,586,648	19	Fred Funk	$14,859,518
2	Vijay Singh	35,310,489	11	Fred Couples	16,544,574	20	Tom Lehman	14,836,499
3	Phil Mickelson	29,445,428	12	David Duval	16,339,549	21	Loren Roberts	14,035,943
4	Davis Love III	29,207,838	13	Mark Calcavecchia	16,240,545	22	Stewart Cink	13,998,988
5	Ernie Els	24,308,792	14	Kenny Perry	15,671,778	23	Greg Norman	13,946,089
6	Nick Price	19,715,533	15	Jeff Sluman	15,403,402	24	Mark O'Meara	13,687,545
7	Jim Furyk	19,643,382	16	Mike Weir	15,358,744	25	Jay Haas	13,500,059
8	Scott Hoch	18,455,984	17	Brad Faxon	15,295,723			
9	David Toms	18,408,565	18	Hal Sutton	15,249,365			

European PGA
Official earnings in Euros (E) for European Tour members only.

		Earnings			Earnings			Earnings
1	C. Montgomerie	E16,916,815	10	J. Maria Olazabal	E8,897,136	19	Paul Lawrie	E5,580,782
2	Ernie Els	15,205,219	11	Thomas Bjorn	8,758,949	20	Barry Lane	5,522,613
3	Darren Clarke	13,728,223	12	M. Angel Jimenez	8,686,103	21	Sam Torrance	5,440,205
4	Retief Goosen	12,077,241	13	Nick Faldo	7,828,838	22	Sergio Garcia	5,370,405
5	Bernhard Langer	11,482,969	14	Eduardo Romero	7,226,015	23	Mark McNulty	5,366,794
6	Padraig Harrington	11,087,745	15	Michael Campbell	7,067,608	24	Seve Ballesteros	5,328,216
7	Lee Westwood	10,272,269	16	Angel Cabrera	6,124,712	25	Peter O'Malley	4,923,171
8	Ian Woosnam	9,117,040	17	Paul McGinley	6,069,750			
9	Vijay Singh	9,043,024	18	Phillip Price	5,796,696			

Champions Tour

		Earnings			Earnings			Earnings
1	Hale Irwin	$20,329,465	10	Bob Charles	$8,951,920	19	Tom Jenkins	$7,778,606
2	Gil Morgan	14,249,619	11	Isao Aoki	8,917,930	20	Bruce Summerhays	7,681,091
3	Bruce Fleisher	11,873,051	12	Jim Thorpe	8,891,160	21	John Jacobs	7,501,819
4	Larry Nelson	11,708,819	13	Raymond Floyd	8,797,506	22	Tom Kite	7,239,419
5	Jim Colbert	11,302,900	14	Jim Dent	8,641,889	23	Vicente Fernandez	7,197,427
6	Dave Stockton	10,433,865	15	Jay Sigel	8,554,889	24	J.C. Snead	7,145,996
7	Dana Quigley	10,044,993	16	George Archer	8,329,648	25	Doug Tewell	7,145,822
8	Allen Doyle	9,838,091	17	Mike Hill	8,257,545			
9	Lee Trevino	9,758,773	18	Graham Marsh	8,236,554			

LPGA

		Earnings			Earnings			Earnings
1	Annika Sorenstam	$15,064,482	10	Laura Davies	$6,816,525	19	Rachel Teske	$4,255,660
2	Karrie Webb	10,096,940	11	Pat Bradley	5,750,965	20	Grace Park	4,157,215
3	Juli Inkster	9,283,419	12	Kelly Robbins	5,709,625	21	Tammie Green	4,097,260
4	Meg Mallon	8,507,707	13	Patty Sheehan	5,513,409	22	Brandie Burton	4,021,171
5	Beth Daniel	8,213,870	14	Lorie Kane	5,433,284	23	Michele Redman	3,970,115
6	Se Ri Pak	7,985,550	15	Nancy Lopez	5,320,877	24	Jane Geddes	3,805,553
7	Rosie Jones	7,654,780	16	Liselotte Neumann	4,720,207	25	Pat Hurst	3,744,958
8	Betsy King	7,622,549	17	Mi-Hyun Kim	4,620,118			
9	Dottie Pepper	6,827,284	18	Sherri Steinhauer	4,305,838			

Official World Ranking

Begun in 1986, the Official World Golf Ranking (formerly the Sony World Ranking) combines the best golfers on the six pro men's tours which make up the International Federation of PGA Tours. Rankings are based on a rolling two-year period and weighed in favor of more recent results. While annual winners are not announced, certain players reaching No. 1 have dominated each year.

Multiple winners (at year's end): Tiger Woods (7); Greg Norman (6); Nick Faldo (3); Seve Ballesteros (2).

Year		Year		Year		Year	
1986	Seve Ballesteros	1990	Nick Faldo	1994	Nick Price	2000	Tiger Woods
1987	Greg Norman		& Greg Norman	1995	Greg Norman	2001	Tiger Woods
1988	Greg Norman	1991	Ian Woosnam	1996	Greg Norman	2002	Tiger Woods
1989	Seve Ballesteros	1992	Fred Couples	1997	Tiger Woods	2003	Tiger Woods
	& Greg Norman		& Nick Faldo	1998	Tiger Woods		
		1993	Nick Faldo	1999	Tiger Woods		

Annual Awards

PGA of America Player of the Year

Awarded by the PGA of America; based on points scale that weighs performance in major tournaments, regular events, money earned and scoring average. **Note:** As of Oct. 3, Vijay Singh had already clinched the award for 2004.

Multiple winners: Tom Watson (6); Jack Nicklaus and Tiger Woods (5); Ben Hogan (4); Julius Boros, Billy Casper, Arnold Palmer and Nick Price.

Year		Year		Year		Year	
1948	Ben Hogan	1963	Julius Boros	1978	Tom Watson	1993	Nick Price
1949	Sam Snead	1964	Ken Venturi	1979	Tom Watson	1994	Nick Price
1950	Ben Hogan	1965	Dave Marr	1980	Tom Watson	1995	Greg Norman
1951	Ben Hogan	1966	Billy Casper	1981	Bill Rogers	1996	Tom Lehman
1952	Julius Boros	1967	Jack Nicklaus	1982	Tom Watson	1997	Tiger Woods
1953	Ben Hogan	1968	No award	1983	Hal Sutton	1998	Mark O'Meara
1954	Ed Furgol	1969	Orville Moody	1984	Tom Watson	1999	Tiger Woods
1955	Doug Ford	1970	Billy Casper	1985	Lanny Wadkins	2000	Tiger Woods
1956	Jack Burke	1971	Lee Trevino	1986	Bob Tway	2001	Tiger Woods
1957	Dick Mayer	1972	Jack Nicklaus	1987	Paul Azinger	2002	Tiger Woods
1958	Dow Finsterwald	1973	Jack Nicklaus	1988	Curtis Strange	2003	Tiger Woods
1959	Art Wall Jr.	1974	Johnny Miller	1989	Tom Kite	2004	Vijay Singh
1960	Arnold Palmer	1975	Jack Nicklaus	1990	Nick Faldo		
1961	Jerry Barber	1976	Jack Nicklaus	1991	Corey Pavin		
1962	Arnold Palmer	1977	Tom Watson	1992	Fred Couples		

PGA Tour Player of the Year

Award by the PGA Tour starting in 1990. Winner voted on by tour members from list of nominees. Winner receives the Jack Nicklaus Trophy, which originated in 1997.

Multiple winners: Tiger Woods (6); Fred Couples and Nick Price (2).

Year		Year		Year		Year	
1990	Wayne Levi	1994	Nick Price	1998	Mark O'Meara	2002	Tiger Woods
1991	Fred Couples	1995	Greg Norman	1999	Tiger Woods	2003	Tiger Woods
1992	Fred Couples	1996	Tom Lehman	2000	Tiger Woods		
1993	Nick Price	1997	Tiger Woods	2001	Tiger Woods		

PGA Tour Rookie of the Year

Awarded by the PGA Tour in 1990. Winner voted on by tour members from list of first-year nominees.

Year		Year		Year		Year	
1990	Robert Gamez	1994	Ernie Els	1998	Steve Flesch	2002	Jonathan Byrd
1991	John Daly	1995	Woody Austin	1999	Carlos Franco	2003	Ben Curtis
1992	Mark Carnevale	1996	Tiger Woods	2000	Michael Clark II		
1993	Vijay Singh	1997	Stewart Cink	2001	Charles Howell III		

Champions Tour Player of the Year

Awarded by the Champions Tour starting in 1990. Winner voted on by tour members from list of nominees.

Multiple winner: Hale Irwin and Lee Trevino (3); Jim Colbert (2).

Year		Year		Year		Year	
1990	Lee Trevino	1993	Dave Stockton	1997	Hale Irwin	2001	Allen Doyle
1991	George Archer & Mike Hill	1994	Lee Trevino	1998	Hale Irwin	2002	Hale Irwin
1992	Lee Trevino	1995	Jim Colbert	1999	Bruce Fleisher	2003	Tom Watson
		1996	Jim Colbert	2000	Larry Nelson		

European Golfer of the Year

Officially, the Ritz Club Trophy (1985-92), Johnnie Walker Trophy (1993-97) and Asprey Golfer of the Year (1998-present); voting done by panel of European golf writers and tour members.

Multiple winners: Colin Montgomerie (4); Seve Ballesteros, Ernie Els, and Nick Faldo (3); Bernhard Langer and Lee Westwood (2).

Year		Year		Year		Year	
1985	Bernhard Langer	1990	Nick Faldo	1995	Colin Montgomerie	2000	Lee Westwood
1986	Seve Ballesteros	1991	Seve Ballesteros	1996	Colin Montgomerie	2001	Retief Goosen
1987	Ian Woosnam	1992	Nick Faldo	1997	Colin Montgomerie	2002	Ernie Els
1988	Seve Ballesteros	1993	Bernhard Langer	1998	Lee Westwood	2003	Ernie Els
1989	Nick Faldo	1994	Ernie Els	1999	Colin Montgomerie		

Annual Awards (Cont.)
LPGA Player of the Year

Sponsored by Rolex and awarded by the LPGA; based on performance points accumulated during the year.

Multiple winners: Kathy Whitworth (7); Annika Sorenstam (6); Nancy Lopez (4); JoAnne Carner, Beth Daniel and Betsy King (3); Pat Bradley, Judy Rankin and Karrie Webb (2).

Year		Year		Year		Year	
1966	Kathy Whitworth	1976	Judy Rankin	1986	Pat Bradley	1996	Laura Davies
1967	Kathy Whitworth	1977	Judy Rankin	1987	Ayako Okamoto	1997	Annika Sorenstam
1968	Kathy Whitworth	1978	Nancy Lopez	1988	Nancy Lopez	1998	Annika Sorenstam
1969	Kathy Whitworth	1979	Nancy Lopez	1989	Betsy King	1999	Karrie Webb
1970	Sandra Haynie	1980	Beth Daniel	1990	Beth Daniel	2000	Karrie Webb
1971	Kathy Whitworth	1981	JoAnne Carner	1991	Pat Bradley	2001	Annika Sorenstam
1972	Kathy Whitworth	1982	JoAnne Carner	1992	Dottie Mochrie	2002	Annika Sorenstam
1973	Kathy Whitworth	1983	Patty Sheehan	1993	Betsy King	2003	Annika Sorenstam
1974	JoAnne Carner	1984	Betsy King	1994	Beth Daniel		
1975	Sandra Palmer	1985	Nancy Lopez	1995	Annika Sorenstam		

LPGA Rookie of the Year

Sponsored by Rolex and awarded by the LPGA; based on performance points accumulated during the year. Winner receives Louise Suggs Trophy, which originated in 2000. Officially the Louise Suggs Rolex Rookie of the Year.

Year		Year		Year		Year	
1962	Mary Mills	1973	Laura Baugh	1984	Juli Inkster	1995	Pat Hurst
1963	Clifford Ann Creed	1974	Jan Stephenson	1985	Penny Hammel	1996	Karrie Webb
1964	Susie Berning	1975	Amy Alcott	1986	Jody Rosenthal	1997	Lisa Hackney
1965	Margie Masters	1976	Bonnie Lauer	1987	Tammie Green	1998	Se Ri Pak
1966	Jan Ferraris	1977	Debbie Massey	1988	Liselotte Neumann	1999	Mi Hyun Kim
1967	Sharron Moran	1978	Nancy Lopez	1989	Pamela Wright	2000	Dorothy Delasin
1968	Sandra Post	1979	Beth Daniel	1990	Hiromi Kobayashi	2001	Hee-Won Han
1969	Jane Blalock	1980	Myra Van Hoose	1991	Brandie Burton	2002	Beth Bauer
1970	JoAnne Carner	1981	Patty Sheehan	1992	Helen Alfredsson	2003	Lorena Ochoa
1971	Sally Little	1982	Patti Rizzo	1993	Suzanne Strudwick		
1972	Jocelyne Bourassa	1983	Stephanie Farwig	1994	Annika Sorenstam		

National Team Competition
MEN
Ryder Cup

The Ryder Cup was presented by British seed merchant and businessman Samuel Ryder in 1927 for competition between professional golfers from Great Britain and the United States. The British team was expanded to include Irish players in 1973 and the rest of Europe in 1979. The 2001 event was postponed due to the attacks on America, causing the event to switch from an odd- to even-year schedule. The United States leads the series 24-9-2 after 35 matches.

Year		Year		Year		Year	
1927	USA, 9½-2½	1951	USA, 9½-2½	1969	Draw, 16-16	1987	Europe, 15-13
1929	Britain-Ireland, 7-5	1953	USA, 6½-5½	1971	USA, 18½-13½	1989	Draw, 14-14
1931	USA, 9-3	1955	USA, 8-4	1973	USA, 19-13	1991	USA, 14½-13½
1933	Great Britain, 6½-5½	1957	Britain-Ireland, 7½-4½	1975	USA, 21-11	1993	USA, 15-13
1935	USA, 9-3	1959	USA, 8½-3½	1977	USA, 12½-13½	1995	Europe, 14½-13½
1937	USA, 8-4	1961	USA, 14½-9½	1979	USA, 17-11	1997	Europe, 14½-13½
1939-45	Not held	1963	USA, 23-9	1981	USA, 18½-9½	1999	USA, 14½-13½
1947	USA, 11-1	1965	USA, 19½-12½	1983	USA, 14½-13½	2002	Europe, 15½-12½
1949	USA, 7-5	1967	USA, 23½-8½	1985	Europe, 16½-11½	2004	Europe, 18½-9½

Playing Sites

1927—Worcester CC (Mass.); **1929**—Moortown, England; **1931**—Scioto CC (Ohio); **1933**—Southport & Ainsdale, England; **1935**—Ridgewood CC (N.J.); **1937**—Southport & Ainsdale, England; **1939-45**—Not held. **1947**—Portland CC (Ore.); **1949**—Ganton GC, England; **1951**—Pinehurst CC (N.C.); **1953**—Wentworth, England; **1955**—Thunderbird Ranch & CC (Calif.); **1957**—Lindrick GC, England; **1959**—Eldorado CC (Calif.); **1961**—Royal Lytham & St. Annes, England; **1963**—East Lake CC (Ga.); **1965**—Royal Birkdale, England; **1967**—Champions GC (Tex.); **1969**—Royal Birkdale, England; **1971**—Old Warson CC (Mo.); **1973**—Muirfield, Scotland; **1975**—Laurel Valley GC (Pa.); **1977**—Royal Lytham & St. Annes, England; **1979**—The Greenbrier (W.Va.); **1981**—Walton Heath GC, England; **1983**—PGA National GC (Fla.); **1985**—The Belfry, England; **1987**—Muirfield Village GC (Ohio); **1989**—The Belfry, England; **1991**—Ocean Course (S.C.); **1993**—The Belfry, England; **1995**—Oak Hill CC (N.Y.); **1997**—Valderrama, Costa del Sol, Spain; **1999**—The Country Club (Mass.); **2002**— The Belfry, England; **2004**— Oakland Hills CC (Mich.); **2006**— Kildare Hotel & CC, Ireland; **2008**— Valhalla GC (Ky.); **2010**— Celtic Manor, Wales; **2012**— Medinah CC (Ill.); **2014**— Gleneagles, Scotland; **2016**—Hazeltine National GC (Minn.)

Presidents Cup

The Presidents Cup is a biennial event played in non-Ryder Cup years in which the world's best non-European players compete against players from the United States. The U.S. leads the series, 3-1-1. In 2003 the match was called off due to darkness after three sudden-death playoff holes. It was deemed a tie with both teams sharing the Cup until 2005.

Year		Year		Year	
1994	USA, 20-12	1998	International, 20½-11½	2003	Tie, 17-17
1996	USA, 16½-15½	2000	USA, 21½-10½		

Walker Cup

The Walker Cup was presented by American businessman George Herbert Walker in 1922 for competition between amateur golfers from Great Britain, Ireland and the United States. The U.S. leads the series against the combined Great Britain-Ireland team, 31-7-1, after 39 matches.

Year		Year		Year		Year	
1922	USA, 8-4	1947	USA, 8-4	1969	USA, 13-11	1989	Britain-Ireland, 12½-11½
1923	USA, 6½-5½	1949	USA, 10-2	1971	Britain-Ireland, 13-11	1991	USA, 14-10
1924	USA, 9-3	1951	USA, 7½-4½	1973	USA, 14-10	1993	USA, 19-5
1926	USA, 6½-5½	1953	USA, 9-3	1975	USA, 15½-8½	1995	Britain-Ireland, 14-10
1928	USA, 11-1	1955	USA, 10-2	1977	USA, 16-8	1997	USA, 18-6
1930	USA, 10-2	1957	USA, 8½-3½	1979	USA, 15½-8½	1999	Britain-Ireland, 15-9
1932	USA, 9½-2½	1959	USA, 9-3	1981	USA, 15-9	2001	Britain-Ireland, 15-9
1934	USA, 9½-2½	1961	USA, 11-1	1983	USA, 13½-10½	2003	Britain-Ireland, 12½-11½
1936	USA, 10½-1½	1963	USA, 14-10	1985	USA, 13-11		
1938	Britain-Ireland, 7½-4½	1965	Draw, 12-12	1987	USA, 16½-7½		
1940-46	Not held	1967	USA, 15-9				

WOMEN

Solheim Cup

The Solheim Cup was presented by the Karsten Manufacturing Co. in 1990 for competition between women professional golfers from Europe and the United States. The event was switched from even- to odd-numbered years after 2002 so it would not conflict with the men's Ryder Cup event. The U.S. leads the series, 5-3.

Year		Year		Year	
1990	USA, 11½-4½	1996	USA, 17-11	2002	USA, 15½-12½
1992	Europe, 11½-6½	1998	USA, 16-12	2003	Europe, 17½-10½
1994	USA, 13-7	2000	Europe, 14½-11½		

Playing Sites

1990—Lake Nona CC (Fla.); **1992**—Dalmahoy CC, Scotland; **1994**—The Greenbrier (W. Va.); **1996**—Marriott St. Pierre Hotel G&CC, Wales; **1998**—Muirfield Village GC (Ohio); **2000**—Loch Lomond GC, Scotland; **2002**—Interlachen CC (Minn.); **2003**—Barseback G&CC, Sweden; **2005**—Crooked Stick GC (Ind.).

Curtis Cup

Named after British golfing sisters Harriot and Margaret Curtis, the Curtis Cup was first contested in 1932 between teams of women amateurs from the United States and the British Isles.

Competed for every other year since 1932 (except during WWII). The U.S. leads the series, 24-6-3, after 33 matches.

Year		Year		Year		Year	
1932	USA, 5½-3½	1956	British Isles, 5-4	1974	USA, 13-5	1992	British Isles, 10-8
1934	USA, 6½-2½	1958	Draw, 4½-4½	1976	USA, 11½-6½	1994	Draw, 9-9
1936	Draw, 4½-4½	1960	USA, 6½-2½	1978	USA, 12-6	1996	British Isles, 11½-6½
1938	USA, 5½-3½	1962	USA, 8-1	1980	USA, 13-5	1998	USA, 10-8
1940-46	Not held	1964	USA, 10½-7½	1982	USA, 14½-3½	2000	USA, 10-8
1948	USA, 6½-2½	1966	USA, 13-5	1984	USA, 9½-8½	2002	USA, 11-7
1950	USA, 7½-1½	1968	USA, 10½-7½	1986	British Isles, 13-5	2004	USA, 10-8
1952	British Isles, 5-4	1970	USA, 11½-6½	1988	British Isles, 11-7		
1954	USA, 6-3	1972	USA, 10-8	1990	USA, 14-4		

COLLEGES

Men's NCAA Division I Champions

College championships decided by match play from 1897-1964 and stroke play since 1965.

Multiple winners (Teams): Yale (21); Houston (16); Oklahoma St. (9); Stanford (7); Harvard (6); Florida, LSU and North Texas (4); Wake Forest (3); Arizona St., Michigan, Ohio St. and Texas (2).

Multiple winners (Individuals): Ben Crenshaw and Phil Mickelson (3); Dick Crawford, Dexter Cummings, G.T. Dunlop, Fred Lamprecht and Scott Simpson (2).

Year	Team winner	Individual champion	Year	Team winner	Individual champion
1897	Yale	Louis Bayard, Princeton	1905	Yale	Robert Abbott, Yale
1898	Harvard (spring)	John Reid, Yale	1906	Yale	W.E. Clow Jr., Yale
1898	Yale (fall)	James Curtis, Harvard	1907	Yale	Ellis Knowles, Yale
1899	Harvard	Percy Pyne, Princeton	1908	Yale	H.H. Wilder, Harvard
1900	Not held		1909	Yale	Albert Seckel, Princeton
1901	Harvard	H. Lindsley, Harvard	1910	Yale	Robert Hunter, Yale
1902	Yale (spring)	Chas. Hitchcock Jr., Yale	1911	Yale	George Stanley, Yale
1902	Harvard (fall)	Chandler Egan, Harvard	1912	Yale	F.C. Davison, Harvard
1903	Harvard	F.O. Reinhart, Princeton	1913	Yale	Nathaniel Wheeler, Yale
1904	Harvard	A.L. White, Harvard	1914	Princeton	Edward Allis, Harvard

Colleges (Cont.)

Year	Team winner	Individual champion	Year	Team winner	Individual champion
1915	Yale	Francis Blossom, Yale	1961	Purdue	Jack Nicklaus, Ohio St.
1916	Princeton	J.W. Hubbell, Harvard	1962	Houston	Kermit Zarley, Houston
1917-18	Not held		1963	Oklahoma St.	R.H. Sikes, Arkansas
1919	Princeton	A.L. Walker Jr., Columbia	1964	Houston	Terry Small, San Jose St.
1920	Princeton	Jess Sweetser, Yale	1965	Houston	Marty Fleckman, Houston
1921	Dartmouth	Simpson Dean, Princeton	1966	Houston	Bob Murphy, Florida
1922	Princeton	Pollack Boyd, Dartmouth	1967	Houston	Hale Irwin, Colorado
1923	Princeton	Dexter Cummings, Yale	1968	Florida	Grier Jones, Oklahoma St.
1924	Yale	Dexter Cummings, Yale	1969	Houston	Bob Clark, Cal St.-LA
1925	Yale	Fred Lamprecht, Tulane	1970	Houston	John Mahaffey, Houston
1926	Yale	Fred Lamprecht, Tulane	1971	Texas	Ben Crenshaw, Texas
1927	Princeton	Watts Gunn, Georgia Tech	1972	Texas	Ben Crenshaw, Texas
1928	Princeton	Maurice McCarthy, G'town			& Tom Kite, Texas
1929	Princeton	Tom Aycock, Yale	1973	Florida	Ben Crenshaw, Texas
1930	Princeton	G.T. Dunlap Jr., Princeton	1974	Wake Forest	Curtis Strange, W.Forest
1931	Yale	G.T. Dunlap Jr., Princeton	1975	Wake Forest	Jay Haas, Wake Forest
1932	Yale	J.W. Fischer, Michigan	1976	Oklahoma St.	Scott Simpson, USC
1933	Yale	Walter Emery, Oklahoma	1977	Houston	Scott Simpson, USC
1934	Michigan	Charles Yates, Ga.Tech	1978	Oklahoma St.	David Edwards, Okla. St.
1935	Michigan	Ed White, Texas	1979	Ohio St.	Gary Hallberg, Wake Forest
1936	Yale	Charles Kocsis, Michigan	1980	Oklahoma St.	Jay Don Blake, Utah St.
1937	Princeton	Fred Haas Jr., LSU	1981	Brigham Young	Ron Commans, USC
1938	Stanford	John Burke, Georgetown	1982	Houston	Billy Ray Brown, Houston
1939	Stanford	Vincent D'Antoni, Tulane	1983	Oklahoma St.	Jim Carter, Arizona St.
1940	Princeton & LSU	Dixon Brooke, Virginia	1984	Houston	John Inman, N.Carolina
1941	Stanford	Earl Stewart, LSU	1985	Houston	Clark Burroughs, Ohio St.
1942	LSU & Stanford	Frank Tatum Jr., Stanford	1986	Wake Forest	Scott Verplank, Okla. St.
1943	Yale	Wallace Ulrich, Carleton	1987	Oklahoma St.	Brian Watts, Oklahoma St.
1944	Notre Dame	Louis Lick, Minnesota	1988	UCLA	E.J. Pfister, Oklahoma St.
1945	Ohio State	John Lorms, Ohio St.	1989	Oklahoma	Phil Mickelson, Ariz. St.
1946	Stanford	George Hamer, Georgia	1990	Arizona St.	Phil Mickelson, Ariz. St.
1947	LSU	Dave Barclay, Michigan	1991	Oklahoma St.	Warren Schuette, UNLV
1948	San Jose St.	Bob Harris, San Jose St.	1992	Arizona	Phil Mickelson, Ariz. St.
1949	North Texas	Harvie Ward, N.Carolina	1993	Florida	Todd Demsey, Ariz. St.
1950	North Texas	Fred Wampler, Purdue	1994	Stanford	Justin Leonard, Texas
1951	North Texas	Tom Nieporte, Ohio St.	1995	Oklahoma St.	Chip Spratlin, Auburn
1952	North Texas	Jim Vickers, Oklahoma	1996	Arizona St.	Tiger Woods, Stanford
1953	Stanford	Earl Moeller, Oklahoma St.	1997	Pepperdine	Charles Warren, Clemson
1954	SMU	Hillman Robbins, Memphis St.	1998	UNLV	James McLean, Minnesota
1955	LSU	Joe Campbell, Purdue	1999	Georgia	Luke Donald, Northwestern
1956	Houston	Rick Jones, Ohio St.	2000	Oklahoma St.	Charles Howell, Oklahoma St.
1957	Houston	Rex Baxter Jr., Houston	2001	Florida	Nick Gilliam, Florida
1958	Houston	Phil Rodgers, Houston	2002	Minnesota	Troy Matteson, Georgia Tech
1959	Houston	Dick Crawford, Houston	2003	Clemson	Alejandro Canizares, Ariz. St.
1960	Houston	Dick Crawford, Houston	2004	California	Ryan Moore, UNLV

Women's NCAA Division I Champions

College championships decided by stroke play since 1982.

Multiple winners (teams): Arizona St. (6); Arizona, Duke, Florida, San Jose St., Tulsa and UCLA (2).

Year	Team winner	Individual champion	Year	Team winner	Individual champion
1982	Tulsa	Kathy Baker, Tulsa	1994	Arizona St.	Emilee Klein, Ariz. St.
1983	TCU	Penny Hammel, Miami	1995	Arizona St.	K. Mourgue d'Algue, Ariz. St.
1984	Miami-FL	Cindy Schreyer, Georgia	1996	Arizona	Marisa Baena, Arizona
1985	Florida	Danielle Ammaccapane, Ariz.St.	1997	Arizona St.	Heather Bowie, Texas
1986	Florida	Page Dunlap, Florida	1998	Arizona St.	Jennifer Rosales, USC
1987	San Jose St.	Caroline Keggi, New Mexico	1999	Duke	Grace Park, Arizona St.
1988	Tulsa	Melissa McNamara, Tulsa	2000	Arizona	Jenna Daniels, Arizona
1989	San Jose St.	Pat Hurst, San Jose St.	2001	Georgia	Candy Hannemann, Duke
1990	Arizona St.	Susan Slaughter, Arizona	2002	Duke	Virada Nirapathpongporn, Duke
1991	UCLA	Annika Sorenstam, Arizona	2003	USC	Mikaela Parmlid, USC
1992	San Jose St.	Vicki Goetze, Georgia	2004	UCLA	Sarah Huarte, California
1993	Arizona St.	Charlotta Sorenstam, Ariz. St.			

Auto Racing

Driver **Buddy Rice** is flanked by team co-owners **David Letterman**, left, and **Bobby Rahal**, right, after winning the 2004 Indy 500.

AP/Wide World Photos

Chevy's Chase

Chevrolet drivers Dale Earnhardt Jr., Jimmie Johnson and Jeff Gordon made a mad dash for the Nextel Cup title.

Michael Morrison
is co-editor of the ESPN Sports Almanac.

An aura of unfamiliarity hung over NASCAR before a race had even been run in 2004. For the first time since 1970, NASCAR had a title sponsor other than R.J. Reynolds, as wireless communications company Nextel agreed to a 10-year deal before the season began.

So the Winston Cup Series, which was all most NASCAR fans ever knew, gave way to the Nextel Cup Series. Possibly even more jarring than the new name was the introduction of NASCAR's new playoff system starting in 2004 known as the "Chase for the Nextel Cup." With 10 races left in the season, the top 10 drivers in the point standings would have their scores reset and then square off in a proverbial sprint to the finish.

The Nextel era officially began at the Daytona International Speedway in February with President George W. Bush saying, "Gentlemen, start your engines." Five hundred miles later, Dale Earnhardt Jr., running in his No. 8 Budweiser Chevrolet, would not be denied, using a textbook pass to overtake Tony Stewart for his first Daytona 500 victory. It was a bittersweet win for "Little E," racing at the site of his father's death just three years earlier, and just the beginning of an eventful, and at times controversial, season.

In mid-June, during a warmup run for an American Le Mans Series race, Earnhardt crashed into a barrier and his car quickly burst into a fireball. He managed to climb out of the car, escaping with moderate second degree burns on his legs and chin. Three months later during a *60 Minutes* interview with Mike Wallace, Earnhardt suggested he may have made it out of the car with the help of his father.

AP/Wide World Photos

Jeff Gordon, left, and *Dale Earnhardt Jr.* were neck and neck all year as each set their sights on the inaugural Chase for the Nextel Cup .

"I had my PR man by the collar, screaming at him to find the guy that pulled me out of the car," he said. "He was like 'nobody helped you get out.' And I was like, 'That's strange, because I swear somebody had me underneath my arms and was carrying me out of the car.'"

By the end of NASCAR's "regular season," Earnhardt had four race wins and sat in third place as the Chase for the championship began, trailing only Jeff Gordon and Jimmie Johnson. It was yet another banner year for Gordon, who won a season-high five races and five poles by the start of the Chase.

Gordon may never have the love of NASCAR purists like Earnhardt does, as highlighted by the wave of beer cans and debris that rained down on his 24 car as he won the Aaron's 499 under caution at Talladega in April. But his consistency and growing accomplishments have lifted him into the upper echelon of all drivers. He passed the $60 million mark in career earnings in 2004 (tops overall) and while he still has a long way to go before reaching Richard Petty's record of 200 victories, his win at the Brickyard in August (his fourth Brickyard 400 title) gave him 69, good for seventh on the all-time list.

Dale Earnhardt Jr. *celebrates with his team after edging Tony Stewart to win the 2004 Daytona 500 on Feb. 15.*

Where in recent years, the series championship was usually wrapped up by early fall, the Chase changed all that in 2004. Through late October, the championship was still up for grabs. Kurt Busch made a late season charge, while Gordon still remained the odds-on favorite. Earnhardt made a costly mistake after winning the EA Sports 500 at Talladega on Oct. 3, using a forbidden word in a fit of excitement during a TV interview just after the race.

His youthful exuberance cost him $10,000 and a valuable 25 points in the standings. The points removal was an unpopular move by NASCAR officials since drivers and fans would rather see the championship won on the track, but the rules were made crystal clear that no foul language would be tolerated. The precedent had already been set. In March, Busch Series driver Johnny Sauter suffered the same penalty for the same infraction. Regardless, Earnhardt would have an uphill climb to become the first Nextel Cup champion. Much like his father, however, he can never be counted out.

The Ten Biggest Stories
of the Year in Auto Racing

10 Tom Kristensen partners with Rinaldo Capello and Seiji Ara to win the 24 Hours of Le Mans in June, driving an Audi R8. It is Kristensen's fifth Le Mans win in a row and record-tying sixth overall.

9 Open Wheel Racing Series LLC purchases the assets of the Champ Car World Series (formerly CART), ensuring there will in fact be a season in 2004. The series seems to be on better financial footing, having already announced a 2005 schedule with races in new locations, Edmonton, South Korea and California's Silicon Valley. The battle for the 2004 series points championship between Sebastien Bourdais and Bruno Junqueira goes right down to the wire.

8 Dale Earnhardt Jr. suffers moderate second-degree burns to his legs and chin in a scary crash during a practice lap for an American Le Mans race in July. After several weeks of recovery, using a relief driver at Loudan and Pocono, he bounces back to his old form.

7 Tony Kanaan wins the Indy Racing League's IndyCar Series championship and accomplishes something that had never been done in any major series, finishing every lap during the entire season. That's 3,305 laps in 16 races over a nine-month span. "The car never stopped," he says.

6 After winning the EA Sports 500 at Talladega in early October, an enthusiastic Dale Earnhardt Jr. suffers a slip of the tongue, letting a curse word fly during a TV interview. He is fined $10,000, and more importantly, docked 25 points in the standings, weakening his bid for the Nextel Cup points championship.

5 Buddy Rice is victorious at the rain-shortened Indianapolis 500, becoming the first American winner since Eddie Cheever in 1998. The win is the first for co-owners Bobby Rahal (who recently defected from the Champ Car World Series) and television star David Letterman. Brazil's Tony Kanaan finishes in second while England's Dan Wheldon takes third.

4 All of NASCAR mourns in late October after a plane belonging to Hendrick Motorsports crashes in dense fog on its way to the racetrack in Martinsville, Va. Ten people are killed, including the son, brother and two nieces of team owner Rick Hendrick.

3 While many hardcore fans disapprove of NASCAR's brand new playoff system, the Chase for the Nextel Cup certainly succeeds in creating a suspenseful last two months of the year. Unlike in past years, the series points championship is still up for grabs through October.

2 German Michael Schumacher continues to outdo himself, recording the most dominant season in the history of Formula One racing. Of the 17 races through mid-October, Schumacher wins 13 of them and starts from the pole eight times. He puts together streaks of five straight and seven straight wins during his amazing season.

1 Dale Earnhardt Jr. wins the Daytona 500 in February, the first official race of the Nextel Cup era, with an average speed of 156.345. Fellow Chevy driver Tony Stewart finishes runner-up. It is his first victory in NASCAR's biggest race and an emotional one, following the tragic death of his father at Daytona in 2001.

INSIDE the numbers

Like Father, Like Son

With this year's win in the Daytona 500, Dale Earnhardt Jr. and his dad become the third father-son combo to win the Great American Race. They are listed below, along with years won.

Family	Father	Son
Earnhardt	Dale (1998)	Dale Jr. (2004)
Allison	Bobby (1978,82,88)	Davey (1992)
Petty	Lee (1959)	Richard (1964,66, 71,73,74, 79,81)

Burning Up the Track

Dale Earnhardt Jr. motored to his Daytona 500 victory in a average time of 156.345. His speed, however, is nowhere near the top five of all time for winners of the 500.

Year	Driver	Speed
1980	Buddy Baker	177.602
1987	Bill Elliott	176.263
1998	Dale Earnhardt	172.712
1985	Bill Elliott	172.265
1981	Richard Petty	169.651

Source: *Daytona International Speedway*

In 2004, **Buddy Rice** joined **Bobby Unser** (in 1981) as the only drivers in Indy 500 history to record a clean sweep, winning the race, pole and pit crew challenge in the same year.

2003-2004
Season in Review

SPORTS ALMANAC

NASCAR RESULTS
Nextel Cup Series

Results of late 2003 NASCAR Winston Cup races and 2004 Nextel Cup races through Oct. 10 (the series changed sponsorship after the 2003 season). **Note**: Earnings include bonus money. See Updates chapter for later results.

Late 2003

Date	Event	Location	Winner (Pos.)	Avg.mph	Earnings	Pole	Qual.mph
Nov. 2	Checker Auto Parts 500	Phoenix	Dale Earnhardt Jr. (11)	93.984	$203,017	R. Newman	133.675
Nov. 9	Pop Secret 400	North Carolina	Bill Elliott (5)	111.677	207,648	R. Newman	155.577
Nov. 16	Ford 400	Homestead	Bobby Labonte (2)	116.868	331,058	J. McMurray	181.111

Winning cars (entire 2003 season): CHEVROLET (19)—J. Gordon and Johnson (3), Earnhardt Jr., R. Gordon, B. Labonte, Stewart and Waltrip (2), Harvick, T. Labonte and Nemechek; DODGE (9)—Newman (8), Elliott; FORD (7)—Busch (4), Biffle, Jarrett, Kenseth; PONTIAC (1)—Craven.

2004 Season (through Oct. 10)

Date	Event	Location	Winner (Pos.)	Avg.mph	Earnings	Pole	Qual.mph
Feb. 15	**Daytona 500**	Daytona	Dale Earnhardt Jr. (3)	156.345	$1,495,070	G. Biffle	188.387
Feb. 22	Subway 400	North Carolina	Matt Kenseth (23)	112.016	222,303	R. Newman	156.475
Mar. 7	UAW-DaimlerChrysler 400	Las Vegas	Matt Kenseth (25)	128.790	458,828	K. Kahne	174.904
Mar. 14	Golden Corral 500	Atlanta	Dale Earnhardt Jr. (7)	158.679	180,078	R. Newman	193.575
Mar. 21	Dodge Dealers 400	Darlington	Jimmie Johnson (11)	114.001	151,150	K. Kahne	171.716
Mar. 28	Food City 500	Bristol	Kurt Busch (13)	82.607	173,465	R. Newman	128.314
Apr. 4	Samsung/Radio Shack 500	Ft. Worth	Elliott Sadler (19)	138.845	507,733	K. Kahne	193.903
Apr. 18	Advance Auto Parts 500	Martinsville	Rusty Wallace (17)	68.169	170,998	J. Gordon	93.502
Apr. 25	Aaron's 499	Talladega	Jeff Gordon (11)	129.396	320,258	R. Rudd	191.180
May 2	Auto Club 500	Fontana	Jeff Gordon (16)	137.268	318,628	K. Kahne	186.940
May 15	Chevy Amer. Revolution 400	Richmond	Dale Earnhardt Jr. (4)	98.253	285,053	B. Vickers	129.983
May 22@	Nextel All-Star Challenge	Charlotte	Matt Kenseth (3)	91.889	1,044,000	R. Wallace	—@
May 30	**Coca-Cola 600**	Charlotte	Jimmie Johnson (1)	142.763	426,360	J. Johnson	187.052
June 6	MBNA 400 "A Salute to Heroes"	Dover	Mark Martin (7)	97.042	271,900	J. Mayfield	161.522
June 13	Pocono 500	Pocono	Jimmie Johnson (5)	112.129	186,950	K. Kahne	172.533
June 20	DHL 400	Brooklyn	Ryan Newman (4)	139.292	176,367	J. Gordon	190.865
June 27	Dodge/Save Mart 350	Sonoma	Jeff Gordon (1)	77.456	388,103	J. Gordon	94.303
July 3	Pepsi 400	Daytona	Jeff Gordon (1)	145.117	346,703	J. Gordon	188.660
July 11	Tropicana 400	Joliet	Tony Stewart (10)	129.507	336,803	J. Gordon	186.942
July 25	Siemens 300	Loudon	Kurt Busch (32)	97.862	222,225	R. Newman	132.360
Aug. 1	Pennsylvania 500	Long Pond	Jimmie Johnson (14)	126.271	276,950	C. Mears	171.720
Aug. 8	**Brickyard 400**	Indianapolis	Jeff Gordon (11)	115.037	518,053	C. Mears	186.293
Aug. 15	Sirius at The Glen	Watkins Glen	Tony Stewart (4)	92.249	195,288	J. Johnson	—**
Aug. 22	GFS Marketplace 400	Brooklyn	Greg Biffle (24)	139.063	190,180	J. Johnson	—**
Aug. 28	Sharpie 500	Bristol	Dale Earnhardt Jr. (30)	88.538	322,443	J. Gordon	128.520
Sept. 5	Pop Secret 500	Fontana	Elliott Sadler (17)	128.324	279,398	B. Vickers	187.417
Sept. 11	Chevy Rock & Roll 400	Richmond	Jeremy Mayfield (7)	98.946	211,120	R. Newman	128.700

— Chase for the Nextel Cup —

Date	Event	Location	Winner (Pos.)	Avg.mph	Earnings	Pole	Qual.mph
Sept. 19	Sylvania 300	Loudon	Kurt Busch (7)	109.753	237,225	J. Gordon	—**
Sept. 26	MBNA America 400	Dover	Ryan Newman (2)	119.067	195,477	J. Mayfield	159.405
Oct. 3	**EA Sports 500**	Talladega	Dale Earnhardt Jr. (10)	156.929	305,968	J. Nemechek	190.749
Oct. 10	Banquet 400	Kansas City	Joe Nemechek (1)	128.058	279,725	J. Nemechek	180.156

@ A non-points exhibition event, formerly known as The Winston. Qualifying was done over three laps. Wallace won the pole with a time of three laps, 3.998 seconds.
**Qualifying was cancelled due to weather and the pole was awarded to the current Nextel Cup points leader.
Winning Cars: CHEVROLET (17)—Earnhardt Jr. 5, J. Gordon 5, Johnson 4, Stewart 2, Nemechek; FORD (9)—Busch 3, Kenseth 2, Sadler 2, Biffle, Martin; DODGE (4)—Newman 2, Mayfield, Wallace.
Remaining Races (6): UAW-GM Quality 500 in Charlotte (Oct. 16); Subway 500 in Martinsville (Oct. 24); Bass Pro Shops MBNA 500 in Atlanta (Oct. 31); Checker Auto Parts 500 in Phoenix (Nov. 7); Mountain Dew Southern 500 in Darlington (Nov. 14); Ford 400 in Homestead (Nov. 21). See *Updates* for later results.

2004 Daytona 500

Date—Sunday, Feb. 15, 2004, at Daytona International Speedway. **Distance**—500 miles; **Course**—2.5 miles; **Field**—43 cars; **Average speed**—156.345 mph; **Margin of victory**—0.273 seconds; **Time of race**—3 hours, 11 minutes, 53 seconds; **Caution flags**—4 for 23 laps; **Lead changes**—28 among 10 drivers; **Lap leaders**—Stewart (98), Earnhardt Jr. (58), Johnson (16), J. Gordon (8), Harvick (6), Wimmer and Petty (5), Kenseth (2), Andretti and T. Labonte (1).

Pole sitter—Greg Biffle originally earned the pole position with a speed of 188.387 mph. However, after suffering mechanical difficulties that resulted in having to change engines, he was forced to go to the rear of the field during the pace lap. Dale Earnhardt Jr. started the race from the pole.

Attendance—200,000 (estimated). **Rating**—10.6/24 share (NBC). (r) indicates rookie driver.

	Driver (start pos.)	Sponsor	Car	Laps	Ended	Earnings
1	Dale Earnhardt Jr. (3)	Budweiser	Chevrolet	200	Running	$1,495,070
2	Tony Stewart (5)	Home Depot	Chevrolet	200	Running	1,096,160
3	r-Scott Wimmer (26)	Caterpillar	Dodge	200	Running	758,839
4	Kevin Harvick (10)	GM Goodwrench	Chevrolet	200	Running	610,792
5	Jimmie Johnson (6)	Lowe's	Chevrolet	200	Running	472,189
6	Joe Nemechek (14)	U.S. Army	Chevrolet	200	Running	358,839
7	Elliott Sadler (2)	M&M's	Ford	200	Running	358,772
8	Jeff Gordon (39)	DuPont	Chevrolet	200	Running	318,490
9	Matt Kenseth (12)	DeWalt Power Tools	Ford	200	Running	307,917
10	Dale Jarrett (31)	UPS	Ford	200	Running	279,529
11	Bobby Labonte (13)	Interstate Batteries	Chevrolet	200	Running	278,445
12	Greg Biffle (1)	National Guard	Ford	200	Running	249,312
13	John Andretti (29)	Kraft Foods	Chevrolet	200	Running	235,287
14	Casey Mears (25)	Target	Dodge	200	Running	235,087
15	Dave Blaney (23)	Whelen Engineering	Dodge	200	Running	232,762
16	Kurt Busch (15)	Sharpie	Ford	199	Running	236,887
17	Ward Burton (19)	NetZero HiSpeed	Chevrolet	199	Running	218,912
18	Ricky Rudd (16)	Motorcraft Quality Parts	Ford	199	Running	246,020
19	r-Brendan Gaughan (17)	Kodak/Jasper Engines	Dodge	199	Running	225,887
20	Terry Labonte (38)	Kellogg's	Chevrolet	199	Running	245,812
21	Kyle Petty (33)	Georgia Pacific/Brawny	Dodge	199	Running	226,127
22	Mike Skinner (43)	RCR	Chevrolet	198	Running	213,813
23	Ricky Craven (28)	Tide	Chevrolet	198	Running	225,339
24	Jimmy Spencer (40)	Jonny Cat	Dodge	198	Running	223,513
25	Jeremy Mayfield (22)	Dodge Dealers/UAW	Dodge	195	Running	222,889
26	r-Johnny Sauter (21)	America Online	Chevrolet	193	Running	213,687
27	Johnny Benson (24)	Miccosukee Gaming & Resorts	Dodge	177	Accident	210,414
28	Larry Foyt (41)	LPGA	Dodge	176	Running	212,487
29	Rusty Wallace (18)	Miller Lite	Dodge	154	Running	245,572
30	Derrike Cope (42)	Thrifty Rent-a-Car/Melling	Dodge	153	Running	207,962
31	Ryan Newman (20)	ALLTEL	Dodge	149	Running	255,056
32	Kevin Lepage (32)	YokeTV.com	Chevrolet	132	Running	207,488
33	Jeff Green (34)	Cheerios/Betty Crocker	Dodge	110	Accident	232,087
34	r-Scott Riggs (36)	Valvoline	Chevrolet	109	Accident	231,328
35	Robby Gordon (30)	Cingular Wireless	Chevrolet	78	Accident	241,230
36	Jamie McMurray (7)	Texaco/Havoline	Dodge	75	Accident	224,137
37	Sterling Marlin (4)	Coors Light	Dodge	75	Accident	254,714
38	Michael Waltrip (9)	NAPA Auto Parts	Chevrolet	70	Accident	246,193
39	r-Brian Vickers (35)	GMAC Financial Services	Chevrolet	70	Accident	211,888
40	Ken Schrader (37)	Schwan's Home Service	Dodge	59	Accident	203,438
41	r-Kasey Kahne (27)	Dodge Dealers/UAW	Dodge	42	Engine	231,887
42	Jeff Burton (11)	NBA All-Star Game on TNT	Ford	25	Engine	239,554
43	Mark Martin (8)	Viagra	Ford	7	Engine	216,997

Top 5 Finishing Order + Pole

2004 NEXTEL CUP SEASON (through Oct. 10)

No.	Event	Winner	2nd	3rd	4th	5th	Pole
1	Daytona 500	D. Earnhardt Jr.	T. Stewart	S. Wimmer	K. Harvick	J. Johnson	G. Biffle
2	Subway 400	M. Kenseth	K. Kahne	J. McMurray	S. Marlin	D. Earnhardt Jr.	R. Newman
3	UAW-DaimlerChrysler 400	M. Kenseth	K. Kahne	T. Stewart	J. McMurray	M. Martin	K. Kahne
4	Golden Corral 500	D. Earnhardt Jr.	J. Mayfield	K. Kahne	J. Johnson	R. Newman	R. Newman
5	Dodge Dealers 400	J. Johnson	B. Labonte	R. Newman	R. Gordon	E. Sadler	K. Kahne
6	Food City 500	K. Busch	R. Wallace	K. Harvick	S. Marlin	M. Kenseth	R. Newman
7	Samsung/Radio Shack 500	E. Sadler	K. Kahne	J. Gordon	D. Earnhardt Jr.	R. Wallace	B. Labonte
8	Advanced Auto Parts 500	R. Wallace	B. Labonte	D. Earnhardt Jr.	J. Johnson	R. Newman	J. Gordon
9	Aaron's 499	J. Gordon	D. Earnhardt Jr.	K. Harvick	J. Johnson	R. Gordon	R. Rudd
10	Auto Club 500	J. Gordon	J. Johnson	R. Newman	M. Kenseth	B. Labonte	K. Kahne
11	Chevy Amer. Revolution 400	D. Earnhardt Jr.	J. Johnson	B. Labonte	T. Stewart	M. Kenseth	B. Vickers
12	Coca-Cola 600	J. Johnson	M. Waltrip	M. Kenseth	J. McMurray	E. Sadler	J. Johnson
13	MBNA 400	M. Martin	T. Stewart	D. Earnhardt Jr.	J. Burton	S. Riggs	J. Mayfield
14	Pocono 500	J. Johnson	J. Mayfield	B. Labonte	J. Gordon	K. Busch	K. Kahne

No. Event	Winner	2nd	3rd	4th	5th	Pole
15 DHL 400	R. Newman	K. Kahne	D. Jarrett	J. Johnson	E. Sadler	J. Gordon
16 Dodge/Save Mart 350	J. Gordon	J. McMurray	S. Pruett	M. Waltrip	J. Johnson	J. Gordon
17 Pepsi 400	J. Gordon	J. Johnson	D. Earnhardt Jr.	K. Busch	T. Stewart	J. Gordon
18 Tropicana 400	T. Stewart	J. Johnson	D. Jarrett	J. Gordon	J. Mayfield	J. Gordon
19 Siemens 300	K. Busch	J. Gordon	R. Newman	M. Kenseth	T. Stewart	R. Newman
20 Pennsylvania 500	J. Johnson	M. Martin	K. Kahne	G. Biffle	J. Gordon	C. Mears
21 Brickyard 400	J. Gordon	D. Jarrett	E. Sadler	K. Kahne	T. Stewart	C. Mears
22 Sirius at The Glen	T. Stewart	R. Fellows	M. Martin	C. Mears	D. Earnhardt Jr.	J. Johnson
23 GFS Marketplace 400	G. Biffle	M. Martin	D. Jarrett	J. McMurray	K. Kahne	J. Johnson
24 Sharpie 500	D. Earnhardt Jr.	R. Newman	J. Johnson	J. Burton	E. Sadler	J. Gordon
25 Pop Secret 500	E. Sadler	K. Kahne	M. Martin	J. McMurray	R. Newman	B. Vickers
26 Chevy Rock & Roll 400	J. Mayfield	D. Earnhardt Jr.	J. Gordon	M. Bliss	M. Martin	R. Newman

— Chase for the Nextel Cup —

No. Event	Winner	2nd	3rd	4th	5th	Pole
27 Sylvania 300	K. Busch	M. Kenseth	D. Earnhardt Jr.	K. Kahne	J. McMurray	J. Gordon
28 MBNA America 400	R. Newman	M. Martin	J. Gordon	D. Jarrett	K. Busch	J. Mayfield
29 EA Sports 500	D. Earnhardt Jr.	K. Harvick	D. Jarrett	B. Gaughan	K. Busch	J. Nemechek
30 Banquet 400	J. Nemechek	R. Rudd	G. Biffle	E. Sadler	J. Mayfield	J. Nemechek

Point Standings

Official Top 10 NASCAR Winston Cup point leaders for 2003 and unofficial Nextel Cup point leaders for 2004. Points are awarded for all qualifying drivers (winner received 175 in 2003, 180 beginning in 2004) and lap leaders. Earnings include in-season bonuses. Listed are starts (Sts), top-5 finishes (1-2-3-4-5), poles won (PW) and points (Pts).

NASCAR conducted its first playoff system in 2004, known as the "Chase for the Nextel Cup." After the first 26 official races, the top 10 drivers in the point standings (plus anyone within 400 pts. of the leader) were eligible for the "chase" over the final ten races of the season. All drivers in the "chase" had their point totals adjusted, with the first-place driver beginning with 5,050 points, the second with 5,045 and so on in five-point increments. Drivers not in the top 10 still participated in the final ten races, but were not eligible for the championship.

FINAL 2003

		Sts	Finishes 1-2-3-4-5	PW	Pts			Sts	Finishes 1-2-3-4-5	PW	Pts
1	Matt Kenseth	36	1-3-3-4-0	0*	5022	6	Ryan Newman	36	8-1-1-2-5	11	4711
2	Jimmie Johnson	36	3-3-6-1-1	2	4932	7	Tony Stewart	36	2-2-4-2-2	1	4549
3	Dale Earnhardt Jr.	36	2-3-5-2-1	0	4815	8	Bobby Labonte	36	2-4-3-1-2	4	4377
4	Jeff Gordon	36	3-3-2-2-5	4	4785	9	Bill Elliott	36	1-1-0-5-2	0	4303
5	Kevin Harvick	36	1-6-1-2-1	1	4770	10	Terry Labonte	36	1-0-0-1-2	1	4162

*Does not include poles awarded for being points leader when qualification was cancelled.

2004 CHASE FOR THE NEXTEL CUP

"Chase" Qualifiers
(through Sept. 11, Race 26)

		Sts	Finishes 1-2-3-4-5	PW	Old Pts	New Pts
1	Jeff Gordon	26	5-1-2-2-1	6	3602	5050
2	Jimmie Johnson	26	4-4-1-4-2	1*	3542	5045
3	Dale Earnhardt Jr.	26	4-2-3-1-2	0	3541	5040
4	Tony Stewart	26	2-2-1-1-3	0	3410	5035
5	Matt Kenseth	26	2-0-1-2-2	0	3337	5030
6	Elliott Sadler	26	2-0-1-0-4	0	3316	5025
7	Kurt Busch	26	2-0-0-1-1	0	3309	5020
8	Mark Martin	26	1-2-2-0-2	0	3213	5015
9	Jeremy Mayfield	26	1-2-0-0-1	1	3193	5010
10	Ryan Newman	26	1-1-3-0-3	5	3186	5005

Driver Standings
(through Oct. 10)

		Sts	Finishes 1-2-3-4-5	PW	Pts
1	Kurt Busch	30	3-0-0-1-3	0	5685
2	Dale Earnhardt Jr.	30	5-2-4-1-2	0	5656
3	Jeff Gordon	30	5-1-3-2-1	6*	5606
4	Elliott Sadler	30	2-0-1-1-4	0	5542
5	Mark Martin	30	1-3-2-0-2	0	5535
6	Tony Stewart	30	2-2-1-1-3	0	5512
7	Matt Kenseth	30	2-1-1-2-2	0	5505
8	Ryan Newman	30	2-1-3-0-3	5	5453
9	Jimmie Johnson	30	4-4-1-4-2	1*	5438
10	Jeremy Mayfield	30	1-2-0-0-2	2	5428

Drivers 11-15 (after Race 26): **11.** J. McMurray; **12.** K. Kahne; **13.** B. Labonte; **14.** K. Harvick; **15.** D. Jarrett.
*Does not include poles awarded for being points leader when qualification was cancelled.

Money Leaders

FINAL 2003

		Earnings
1	Jimmie Johnson	$5,517,850
2	Tony Stewart	5,227,500
3	Jeff Gordon	5,107,760
4	Kurt Busch	5,020,480
5	Kevin Harvick	4,994,250
6	Dale Earnhardt Jr.	4,923,500
7	Ryan Newman	4,827,380
8	Bobby Labonte	4,745,260
9	Michael Waltrip	4,463,840
10	Bill Elliott	4,321,190

2004 (through Oct. 10)

		Earnings
1	Dale Earnhardt Jr.	$6,211,540
2	Matt Kenseth	5,520,720
3	Jeff Gordon	5,442,910
4	Tony Stewart	5,376,350
5	Jimmie Johnson	4,428,080
6	Elliott Sadler	4,391,880
7	Ryan Newman	4,308,470
8	Kevin Harvick	4,063,670
9	Kasey Kahne	4,019,570
10	Dale Jarrett	3,934,210

CHAMP CAR RESULTS

Schedule and results of Champ Car World Series races from Nov. 2, 2003 through Sept. 25, 2004. Officially the "Bridgestone Presents The Champ Car World Series Powered By Ford" beginning with the 2003 season. Note that Champ Car does not release per-race winnings. See Updates chapter for later results.

Champ Car World Series

Late 2003

Date	Event	Location	Winner (Pos.)	Time	Avg.mph	Pole	Qual.mph
Nov. 2	The 500 presented by Toyota	Fontana	Race canceled due to California wildfires.				

Winning cars (entire 2003 season): FORD-COSWORTH/LOLA (17)—Tracy (7), Bourdais (3), Jourdain and Junqueira (2), Carpentier, Dominguez and Fernandez; FORD-COSWORTH/REYNARD (1)—Hunter-Reay.

2004 Season

Date	Event	Location	Winner (Pos.)	Time	Avg.mph	Pole	Qual.mph
Apr. 13	Toyota GP	Long Beach	Paul Tracy (3)	1:44:12.348	91.785	B. Junqueira	102.808
May 23	Tecate Telmex Monterrey GP	Monterrey	Sebastien Bourdais (1)	1:45:01.498	86.544	S. Bourdais	102.474
June 5	Time Warner 250 Milwaukee Mile	Milwaukee	Ryan Hunter-Reay (1)	1:59:12.397	129.859	R. Hunter-Reay	181.150
June 20	GP of Portland	Portland	Sebastien Bourdais (1)	1:45:50.461	104.923	S. Bourdais	119.678
July 3	U.S. Bank Presents the GP of Cleveland	Cleveland	Sebastien Bourdais (3)	1:48:16.056	113.209	P. Tracy	131.749
July 11	Molson Indy	Toronto	Sebastien Bourdais (1)	1:45:36.930	83.749	S. Bourdais	107.893
July 25	Molson Indy	Vancouver	Paul Tracy (1)	1:34:42.849	95.900	P. Tracy	105.333
Aug. 8	GP of Road America pres. by Chicago Tribune	Elkhart Lake	Alex Tagliani (13)	1:45:07.288	110.903	S. Bourdais	141.420
Aug. 31	Centrix Financial GP of Denver	Denver	Sebastien Bourdais (1)	1:40:25.232	89.103	S. Bourdais	99.516
Aug. 29	Molson Indy	Montreal	Bruno Junqueira (4)	1:39:12.432	113.049	S. Bourdais	122.062
Sept. 12	GP of Monterey	Monterey	Patrick Carpentier (2)	1:45:51.116	100.217	S. Bourdais	116.163
Sept. 25	Bridgestone 400 pres. by Corona	Las Vegas	Sebastien Bourdais (3)	1:29:01.061	167.832	P. Carpentier	206.186

Winning cars (Engine/Chassis): FORD-COSWORTH/LOLA (12)—Bourdais 6, Tracy 2, Carpentier, Hunter-Reay, Junqueira, Tagliani.
Remaining Races (2): Lexmark Indy 300 in Queensland (Oct. 24); Grand Premio Telmex Tecate in Mexico City (Nov. 7).

Top 5 Finishing Order + Pole

2004 SEASON (through Sept. 25)

No.	Event	Winner	2nd	3rd	4th	5th	Pole
1	GP of Long Beach	P. Tracy	B. Junqueira	S. Bourdais	P. Carpentier	M. Dominguez	B. Junqueira
2	Monterrey GP	S. Bourdais	B. Junqueira	M. Dominguez	P. Carpentier	A. Tagliani	S. Bourdais
3	Milwaukee Mile 250	R. Hunter-Reay	P. Carpentier	M. Jourdain Jr.	J. Vasser	A. Allmendinger	R. Hunter-Reay
4	GP of Portland	S. Bourdais	B. Junqueira	P. Tracy	P. Carpentier	J. Wilson	S. Bourdais
5	GP of Cleveland	S. Bourdais	B. Junqueira	A. Tagliani	O. Servia	J. Vasser	P. Tracy
6	Molson Indy Toronto	S. Bourdais	J. Vasser	P. Carpentier	M. Haberfeld	P. Tracy	S. Bourdais
7	Molson Indy Vancouver	P. Tracy	M. Jourdain Jr.	A. Allmendinger	B. Junqueira	S. Bourdais	P. Tracy
8	GP of Road America	A. Tagliani	R. Lavin	S. Bourdais	R. Hunter-Reay	M. Dominguez	S. Bourdais
9	GP of Denver	S. Bourdais	P. Tracy	B. Junqueira	M. Dominguez	A. Allmendinger	S. Bourdais
10	Molson Indy Montreal	B. Junqueira	P. Carpentier	M. Dominguez	P. Tracy	A. Allmendinger	S. Bourdais
11	GP of Monterey	P. Carpentier	B. Junqueira	O. Servia	M. Jourdain Jr.	R. Hunter-Reay	S. Bourdais
12	Bridgestone 400	S. Bourdais	B. Junqueira	P. Carpentier	R. Lavin	J. Vasser	P. Carpentier

Champ Car Point Standings

Official Top 10 Champ Car World Series point leaders for 2003 and unofficial leaders for 2004 (through Sept. 25). Points were awarded for places 1 to 12 in 2003 and 1 to 20 beginning in 2004. Points were also awarded for the pole winner at oval events, fastest driver on each day of qualifying at road/street events, lap leaders and most positions gained. Listed are starts (Sts), top-5 finishes, poles won (PW) and points (Pts). (r) indicates rookie driver.

FINAL 2003

		Sts	Finishes 1-2-3-4-5	PW	Pts
1	Paul Tracy	18	7-2-1-1-0	6	226
2	Bruno Junqueira	18	2-3-4-2-1	2	199
3	Michel Jourdain	18	2-3-1-5-0	1	195
4	r-Sebastien Bourdais	18	3-3-1-1-1	5	159
5	Patrick Carpentier	18	1-1-2-1-3	1	146
6	Mario Dominguez	18	1-1-2-0-3	0	118
7	Oriol Servia	18	0-2-1-1-3	0	108
8	Adrian Fernandez	18	1-1-0-1-1	1	105
9	r-Darren Manning	18	0-1-0-1-1	0	103
10	Alex Tagliani	18	0-0-3-1-1	2	97

2004 (through Sept. 25)

		Sts	Finishes 1-2-3-4-5	PW	Pts
1	Sebastien Bourdais	12	6-0-2-0-1	7	307
2	Bruno Junqueira	12	1-6-1-1-0	1	280
3	Patrick Carpentier	12	1-2-2-3-0	1	241
4	Paul Tracy	12	2-1-1-1-1	2	218
5	Alex Tagliani	12	1-0-1-0-1	0	206
6	Mario Dominguez	12	0-0-2-1-2	0	203
7	r-A.J. Allmendinger	12	0-0-1-0-3	0	184
8	Ryan Hunter-Reay	12	1-0-0-1-1	1	176
9	Oriol Servia	12	0-0-1-1-0	0	174
10	Jimmy Vasser	12	0-1-0-1-2	0	171

Money Leaders

FINAL 2003

		Earnings
1	Paul Tracy	$1,007,000
2	Bruno Junqueira	770,000
3	Michel Jourdain	738,000
4	r-Sebastien Bourdais	709,000
5	Patrick Carpentier	569,000
6	Mario Dominguez	522,750
7	Adrian Fernandez	468,750
8	Oriol Servia	454,250
9	Alex Tagliani	420,250
10	r-Darren Manning	409,250

2004 (through Sept. 25)

		Earnings
1	Sebastien Bourdais	$703,500
2	Bruno Junqueira	598,500
3	Patrick Carpentier	519,000
4	Paul Tracy	502,000
5	Alex Tagliani	437,000
6	Mario Dominguez	410,500
7	Ryan Hunter-Reay	406,500
8	r-A.J. Allmendinger	386,500
9	Jimmy Vasser	385,500
10	Michel Jourdain Jr.	382,500

INDY RACING LEAGUE RESULTS

IndyCar Series

Schedule and results of IndyCar Series events during the 2004 season (through Oct. 3).

2004 Season (through Oct. 3)

Date	Event	Location	Winner (Pos.)	Time	Avg.mph	Pole	Qual.mph
Feb. 29	Toyota 300	Homestead	Sam Hornish Jr. (7)	1:57:56.3961	151.094	B. Rice	217.388
Mar. 21	Copper World 200	Phoenix	Tony Kanaan (2)	1:33:45.8490	127.981	D. Wheldon	174.779
Apr. 17	Japan 300	Motegi	Dan Wheldon (1)	1:49:48.2611	166.114	D. Wheldon	205.762
May 30	**Indianapolis 500**†	Indianapolis	Buddy Rice (1)	3:14:55.2395	138.518	B. Rice	222.024
June 12	Bombardier 500	Ft. Worth	Tony Kanaan (3)	1:53:24.1239	153.965	D. Franchitti	209.609
June 26	SunTrust Challenge	Richmond	Dan Wheldon (20)	1:38:10.6077	114.589	H. Castroneves	171.202
July 4	Argent Mortgage 300	Kansas City	Buddy Rice (1)	1:42:56.6727	177.183	B. Rice	210.141
July 17	Firestone 200	Nashville	Tony Kanaan (5)	1:55:34.6367	134.975	B. Rice	201.231
July 25	Menards A.J. Foyt 225	Milwaukee	Dario Franchitti (7)	1:46:49.4110	128.272	V. Meira	169.338
Aug. 1	Michigan 400	Brooklyn	Buddy Rice (6)	2:11:46.7517	182.123	T. Kanaan	215.871
Aug. 15	Belterra Casino 300	Sparta	Adrian Fernandez (4)	1:38:20.7207	180.588	B. Rice	216.016
Aug 22	Honda 225	Pikes Peak	Dario Franchitti (4)	1:34:56.9156	142.182	T. Kanaan	—**
Aug. 29	Firestone 225	Nazareth	Dan Wheldon (8)	1:46:11.0277	118.874	H. Castroneves	167.396
Sept. 12	Delphi 300	Joliet	Adrian Fernandez (10)	2:09:31.3301	140.825	H. Castroneves	214.759
Oct. 3	Toyota 400	Fontana	Adrian Fernandez (4)	2:14:12.5029	178.826	H. Castroneves	217.479

**Qualifying was canceled due to inclement weather and the pole was awarded based on practice times.

† The Indianapolis 500 was shortened to 450 miles (180 laps) due to inclement weather.

Winning cars (Chassis/Engine): DALLARA/HONDA (8)—Kanaan 3, Wheldon 3, Franchitti 2; PANOZ G FORCE/HONDA (6)—Rice 3, Fernandez 3; DALLARA/TOYOTA (1)—Hornish Jr.

Remaining Race (1): Chevy 500 in Ft. Worth (Oct. 17). See *Updates* for results.

Indy Racing League Results (Cont.)

88th Indianapolis 500

Date—Sunday, May-30, 2004, at Indianapolis Motor Speedway. **Distance**—450 miles (shortened from 500 due to rain); **Course**—2.5 mile oval; **Field**—33 cars; **Winner's average speed**—138.518 mph; **Margin of victory**—under caution; **Time of race**—3 hours, 14 minutes, 55.2395 seconds; **Caution flags**—8 for 56 laps; **Lead changes**—17 by 9 drivers; **Lap leaders**—Rice (91), Kanaan (28), Wheldon (26), Junqueira (16), Hornish Jr. (9), Herta, Barron, Fernandez (3), Franchitti (1); **Pole Sitter**—Buddy Rice at 222.024; **Attendance**—400,000 (est.); **TV Rating**—4.1 (ABC). Note that (r) indicates rookie driver.

	Driver (start pos.)	Country	Car	Laps	Ended	Earnings
1	Buddy Rice (1)	United States	G/H/F	180	Running	$1,761,740
2	Tony Kanaan (5)	Brazil	D/H/F	180	Running	659,240
3	Dan Wheldon (2)	England	D/H/F	180	Running	533,040
4	Bryan Herta (23)	United States	D/H/F	180	Running	366,440
5	Bruno Junqueira (4)	Brazil	G/H/F	180	Running	296,240
6	Vitor Meira (7)	Brazil	G/H/F	180	Running	301,240
7	Adrian Fernandez (6)	Mexico	G/H/F	180	Running	294,740
8	Scott Dixon (13)	New Zealand	G/T/F	180	Running	283,740
9	Helio Castroneves (8)	Brazil	D/T/F	180	Running	311,990
10	Roger Yasukawa (12)	United States	G/H/F	180	Running	261,740
11	r-Kosuke Matsuura (9)	Japan	G/H/F	180	Running	294,740
12	Alex Barron (24)	United States	D/C/F	180	Running	269,240
13	Scott Sharp (20)	United States	D/T/F	180	Running	253,990
14	Dario Franchitti (3)	Scotland	D/H/F	180	Running	255,740
15	Felipe Giaffone (25)	Brazil	D/C/F	179	Running	249,490
16	r-Jeff Simmons (29)	United States	D/T/F	179	Running	224,990
17	Al Unser Jr. (17)	United States	D/C/F	179	Running	220,740
18	Tomas Scheckter (10)	South Africa	D/C/F	179	Running	234,240
19	Tora Takagi (26)	Japan	D/T/F	179	Running	230,740
20	Richie Hearn (30)	United States	G/T/F	178	Running	207,740
21	Sarah Fisher (19)	United States	D/T/F	177	Running	208,740
22	Robby McGehee (33)	United States	D/C/F	177	Running	202,740
23	Buddy Lazier (28)	United States	D/C/F	164	Fuel System	212,240
24	r-Marty Roth (32)	Canada	D/T/F	128	Accident	203,990
25	r-Darren Manning (15)	England	G/T/F	104	Accident	227,490
26	Sam Hornish Jr. (11)	United States	D/T/F	104	Accident	223,240
27	Greg Ray (27)	United States	G/H/F	98	Accident	239,735
28	r-PJ Jones (31)	United States	D/C/F	92	Accident	195,490
29	Robby Gordon* (18)	United States	D/C/F	88	Mechanical	192,420
30	r-Mark Taylor (14)	England	D/C/F	62	Accident	211,990
31	r-Ed Carpenter (16)	United States	D/C/F	62	Accident	212,485
32	r-Larry Foyt (22)	United States	G/T/F	54	Accident	192,485
33	A.J. Foyt IV (21)	United States	D/T/F	26	Handling	215,735

* Jacques Lazier took over for Gordon on a restart after 27 laps.

Car Legend: Chassis/Engine/Tires. D—Dallara, G—Panoz G Force (chassis); C—Chevrolet, H—Honda, T—Toyota (engine); F—Firestone (tires).

Top 5 Finishing Order + Pole

2004 Season (through Oct. 3)

No.	Event	Winner	2nd	3rd	4th	5th	Pole
1	Toyota 300	S. Hornish Jr.	H. Castroneves	D. Wheldon	T. Takagi	T. Scheckter	B. Rice
2	Copper World 300 . .	T. Kanaan	S. Dixon	D. Wheldon	A. Barron	D. Manning	D. Wheldon
3	Japan 300	D. Wheldon	T. Kanaan	H. Castroneves	D. Manning	S. Dixon	D. Wheldon
4	Indy 500	B. Rice	T. Kanaan	D. Wheldon	B. Herta	B. Junqueira	B. Rice
5	Bombardier 500 . . .	T. Kanaan	D. Franchitti	A. Barron	S. Hornish Jr.	A. Fernandez	D. Franchitti
6	SunTrust Challenge .	D. Wheldon	V. Meira	H. Castroneves	B. Herta	T. Kanaan	H. Castroneves
7	Argent Mortgage 300	B. Rice	V. Meira	T. Kanaan	D. Franchitti	B. Herta	B. Rice
8	Firestone 200	T. Kanaan	S. Hornish Jr.	H. Castroneves	D. Manning	T. Bell	B. Rice
9	Menards A.J. Foyt 225	D. Franchitti	B. Rice	S. Hornish Jr.	T. Kanaan	V. Meira	V. Meira
10	Michigan 400	B. Rice	T. Kanaan	D. Wheldon	S. Hornish Jr.	V. Meira	T. Kanaan
11	Belterra Casino 300 .	A. Fernandez	B. Rice	D. Wheldon	K. Matsuura	T. Kanaan	B. Rice
12	Honda 225	D. Franchitti	A. Fernandez	D. Wheldon	D. Manning	T. Kanaan	T. Kanaan
13	Firestone 225	D. Wheldon	T. Kanaan	D. Franchitti	B. Rice	H. Castroneves	H. Castroneves
14	Delphi 300	A. Fernandez	B. Herta	T. Kanaan	D. Wheldon	V. Meira	H. Castroneves
15	Toyota 400	A. Fernandez	T. Kanaan	D. Wheldon	S. Hornish Jr.	B. Rice	H. Castroneves

Indy Racing League Point Standings & Money Leaders

Official top-10 Indy Racing League driver points leaders and money leaders for 2004, through Oct. 3. Points are awarded for places 1 to 33 (winner receives 50) and overall lap leader. Listed are starts (Sts), top-5 finishes, poles won (PW) and points (Pts).

Points

		Sts	Finishes 1-2-3-4-5	PW	Pts
1	Tony Kanaan	15	3-5-2-1-3	2	578
2	Dan Wheldon	15	3-0-7-1-0	2	498
3	Buddy Rice	15	3-2-0-1-1	5	473
4	Adrian Fernandez	14	3-1-0-0-1	0	415
5	Helio Castroneves	15	0-1-3-0-1	4	408
6	Dario Franchitti	15	2-1-1-1-0	1	394
7	Sam Hornish Jr.	15	1-1-1-3-0	0	374
8	Bryan Herta	15	0-1-0-2-1	0	348
9	Vitor Meira	13	0-2-0-0-3	1	344
10	Scott Dixon	14	0-1-0-0-1	0	327

Earnings

		Earnings
1	Buddy Rice	$2,657,140
2	Tony Kanaan	1,825,490
3	Dan Wheldon	1,568,290
4	Helio Castroneves	1,192,290
5	Adrian Fernandez	1,094,140
6	Dario Franchitti	1,063,990
7	Bryan Herta	1,022,040
8	Sam Hornish Jr.	1,007,740
9	Vitor Meira	960,740
10	Scott Dixon	928,790

FORMULA ONE RESULTS

Results of Formula One Grand Prix races in 2004 (through Oct. 10).

2004 Season (through Oct. 10)

Date	Grand Prix	Location	Winner (Pos.)	Time	Avg.mph	Pole
Mar. 7	Australian	Melbourne	Michael Schumacher (1)	1:24:15.757	136.087	M. Schumacher
Mar. 21	Malaysian	Kuala Lumpur	Michael Schumacher (1)	1:31:07.490	126.963	M. Schumacher
Apr. 4	Bahrain	Bahrain	Michael Schumacher (1)	1:28:34.875	129.879	M. Schumacher
Apr. 25	San Marino	Imola	Michael Schumacher (2)	1:26:19.670	131.691	J. Button
May 9	Spanish	Catalunya	Michael Schumacher (1)	1:27:32.841	129.994	M. Schumacher
May 23	Monaco	Monaco	Jarno Trulli (1)	1:45:46.601	90.665	J. Trulli
May 30	European	Nurburgring	Michael Schumacher (1)	1:32:35.101	124.399	M. Schumacher
June 13	Canadian	Montreal	Michael Schumacher (6)	1:28:24.803	128.726	R. Schumacher
June 20	U.S.	Indianapolis	Michael Schumacher (2)	1:40:29.914	113.523	R. Barrichello
July 4	French	Magny-Cours	Michael Schumacher (2)	1:30:18.133	127.431	F. Alonso
July 11	British	Silverstone	Michael Schumacher (4)	1:24:42.700	135.238	K. Raikkonen
July 25	German	Hockenheim	Michael Schumacher (1)	1:23:54.848	134.153	M. Schumacher
Aug. 15	Hungarian	Budapest	Michael Schumacher (1)	1:35:26.131	119.799	M. Schumacher
Aug. 29	Belgian	Spa Francorchamps	Kimi Raikkonen (10)	1:32:35.274	123.589	J. Trulli
Sept. 12	Italian	Monza	Rubens Barrichello (1)	1:15:18.448	151.511	R. Barrichello
Sept. 26	China	Shanghai	Rubens Barrichello (1)	1:29:12.420	127.523	R. Barrichello
Oct. 10	Japan	Suzuka	Michael Schumacher (1)	1:24:26.985	135.184	M. Schumacher

Winning Constructors: FERRARI (15)—M. Schumacher 13, Barrichello 2; RENAULT (1)—Trulli; McLAREN-MERCEDES (1)—Raikkonen.

Remaining Race (1): Brazilian GP in Sao Paolo (Oct. 24). See *Updates* for results.

Top 5 + Pole Finishing Order

2004 Season (through Oct. 10)

No.	Event	Winner	2nd	3rd	4th	5th	Pole
1	Australian	M. Schumacher	R. Barrichello	F. Alonso	R. Schumacher	J. Montoya	M. Schumacher
2	Malaysian	M. Schumacher	J. Montoya	J. Button	R. Barrichello	J. Trulli	M. Schumacher
3	Bahrain	M. Schumacher	R. Barrichello	J. Button	J. Trulli	T. Sato	M. Schumacher
4	San Marino	M. Schumacher	J. Button	J. Montoya	F. Alonso	J. Trulli	J. Button
5	Spanish	M. Schumacher	R. Barrichello	J. Trulli	F. Alonso	T. Sato	M. Schumacher
6	Monaco	J. Trulli	J. Benson	R. Barrichello	J. Montoya	F. Massa	J. Trulli
7	European	M. Schumacher	R. Barrichello	J. Button	J. Trulli	F. Alonso	M. Schumacher
8	Canadian	M. Schumacher	R. Barrichello	J. Button	G. Fisichella	K. Raikkonen	R. Schumacher
9	U.S.	M. Schumacher	R. Barrichello	T. Sato	J. Trulli	O. Panis	R. Barrichello
10	French	M. Schumacher	F. Alonso	R. Barrichello	J. Trulli	J. Button	F. Alonso
11	British	M. Schumacher	K. Raikkonen	R. Barrichello	J. Button	J. Montoya	K. Raikkonen
12	German	M. Schumacher	J. Button	F. Alonso	D. Coulthard	J. Montoya	M. Schumacher
13	Hungarian	M. Schumacher	R. Barrichello	F. Alonso	J. Montoya	J. Button	M. Schumacher
14	Belgian	K. Raikkonen	M. Schumacher	R. Barrichello	F. Massa	G. Fisichella	J. Trulli
15	Italian	R. Barrichello	M. Schumacher	J. Button	T. Sato	J. Montoya	R. Barrichello
16	China	R. Barrichello	J. Button	K. Raikkonen	F. Alonso	J. Montoya	R. Barrichello
17	Japanese	M. Schumacher	R. Schumacher	J. Button	T. Sato	F. Alonso	M. Schumacher

Formula One Results (Cont.)

2004 Formula One Point Standings
(through Oct. 10)

Official top-10 Formula One World Drivers and Constructors Championship point leaders for 2004 (through Oct. 10). Points are awarded for places 1 through 8 only (i.e., 10-8-6-5-4-3-2-1). Listed are starts (Sts), top-8 finishes, poles won (PW) and points (Pts). **Note:** Formula One does not keep money leader standings.

Drivers

		Sts	Finishes 1-2-3-4-5-6-7-8	PW	Pts
1	Michael Schumacher	..17	13-2-0-0-0-0-0-0	8	146
2	Rubens Barrichello	17	2-7-4-1-0-1-0-0	3	108
3	Jenson Button	17	0-4-6-1-2-1-0-1	1	85
4	Fernando Alsonso	17	0-1-3-3-2-1-1-0	1	54
5	Juan Pablo Montoya	...17	0-1-1-2-5-0-1-2	0	48
6	Jarno Trulli	16	1-0-1-4-2-0-1-0	2	46
7	Kimi Raikkonen	17	1-1-1-0-1-2-1-1	1	37
8	Takuma Sato	17	0-0-1-2-2-2-0-1	0	31
9	David Coulthard	17	0-0-0-1-0-4-3-1	0	24
10	Giancarlo Fisichella	...17	0-0-0-1-1-2-2-3	0	22

Other pole won (1): Ralf Schumacher.

Constructors

		Pts
1	Ferrari	254
2	BAR-Honda	116
3	Renault	100
4	Williams-BMW	74
5	McLaren-Mercedes	61
6	Sauber-Petronas	33
7	Jaguar-Cosworth	10
8	Toyota	9
9	Jordan-Ford	5
10	Minardi-Cosworth	1

NHRA RESULTS

Winners of National Hot Rod Association's POWERade Drag Racing events in the Top Fuel, Funny Car and Pro Stock divisions through Oct. 10, 2004. All times are based on two cars racing head-to-head from a standing start over a straight line, quarter-mile course. Differences in reaction time account for apparently faster losing times.

2004 Season (through Oct. 10)

Date	Event	Event	Winner	Time	MPH	2nd Place	Time	MPH
Feb. 22	K&N Filters Winternationals	Top Fuel	Tony Schumacher	4.659	243.55	D. Kalitta (broke before staging)		
		Funny Car	Jerry Toliver	4.821	319.29	G. Densham	4.955	327.11
		Pro Stock	Greg Anderson	6.713	205.76	W. Johnson	6.761	204.23
Mar. 7	Kragen Nationals	Top Fuel	Brandon Bernstein	4.537	326.63	D. Kalitta	5.837	184.85
		Funny Car	Del Worsham	4.970	303.78	T. Pedregon	5.098	251.58
		Pro Stock	Kurt Johnson	6.835	203.49	D. Connolly	6.860	202.39
Mar. 21	Mac Tools Gatornationals	Top Fuel	Tony Schumacher	4.612	312.60	D. Russell	4.981	271.98
		Funny Car	Del Worsham	4.979	296.05	J. Force	4.977	304.36
		Pro Stock	Greg Anderson	6.742	204.91	J. Coughlin	6.790	204.08
Apr. 4	SummitRacing.com Nationals	Top Fuel	Tony Schumacher	4.525	331.53	L. Dixon	4.571	323.97
		Funny Car	Phil Burkart	5.029	264.03	W. Bazemore	5.452	189.50
		Pro Stock	Greg Anderson	6.849	201.31	K. Johnson	6.908	200.08

Major 2004 Endurance Races

24 Hours of Daytona
Jan. 31-Feb. 1, at Daytona Beach, Fla.

Officially the Rolex 24 at Daytona and first held in 1962 (as a 3-hour race). An IMSA Camel GT race for exotic prototype sports cars and contested over a 3.56-mile road course at Daytona International Speedway. Listed are qualifying position, drivers, chassis, class and laps completed.

1 (3) Terry Borcheller, Forest Barber, Andy Pilgrim and Christian Fittipaldi; PONTIAC DORAN (DP); 526 laps (1,872.56 miles) at 77.927 mph; margin of victory—3 laps.

2 (32) Mike Fitzgerald, Joe Policastro, Jay Policastro, Robin Liddell and Johnny Mowlem; PORSCHE GT3 RS, 523 laps.

3 (18) Johannes Van Overbeek, Seth Neiman, Lonnie Pechnik, Peter Cunningham and Mike Rockenfeller; PORSCHE GT3 CUP; 523 laps.

4 (31) Didier Theys, Fredy Lienhard, Jan Lammers and Marc Goosens; LEXUS DORAN (DP); 521 laps.

5 (4) Andy Wallace, Tony Stewart and Dale Earnhardt Jr.; CHEVROLET CRAWFORD (DP); 519 laps.

Top qualifier: Scott Pruett, LEXUS RILEY, 121.154 mph.

24 Hours of Le Mans
June 12-13, at Le Mans, France

Officially the Le Mans Grand Prix d'Endurance and first held in 1923. Contested over the 8.48-mile Circuit de la Sarthe in Le Mans, France. Listed are qualifying position, drivers, car, and laps completed.

1 (4) Tom Kristensen, Rinaldo Capello and Seiji Ara; AUDI R8; 379 laps (3,213.92 miles) at 133.855 mph; margin of victory—41 seconds.

2 (1) Johnny Herbert, Jamie Davies and Guy Smith; AUDI R8; 368 laps.

3 (6) Emmanuele Pirro, Marco Werner and J.J. Lehto; AUDI R8; 368 laps.

4 (11) Soheil Ayari, Erik Comas and Benoit Treluyer; PESCAROLO-JUDD; 361 laps.

5 (2) Frank Biela, Pierre Kaffer and Allan McNish; AUDI R8; 350 laps.

Top qualifier: Johnny Herbert, AUDI R8, 3:32.838 (143.433 mph).

Date	Event	Event	Winner	Time	MPH	2nd Place	Time	MPH
Apr. 18	O'Reilly Spring Nationals . . .	Top Fuel	Brandon Bernstein	4.695	271.79	C. Millican	5.032	238.81
		Funny Car	Tim Wilkerson	4.896	303.30	J. Toliver	5.081	277.03
		Pro Stock	Greg Anderson	6.738	205.57	J. Line	9.466	98.16
May 2	Thunder Valley Nationals . . .	Top Fuel	Tony Schumacher	5.802	283.73	C. Millican	10.446	73.75
		Funny Car	John Force	4.781	322.88	W. Bazemore	13.224	93.50
		Pro Stock	Greg Anderson	6.754	203.12	J. Line	6.790	202.94
May 16	Southern Nationals	Top Fuel	Cory McClenathan	4.651	320.74	C. Millican	4.700	315.93
		Funny Car	Whit Bazemore	5.025	299.80	G. Scelzi	10.847	90.59
		Pro Stock	Greg Anderson	6.812	203.00	L. Morgan	6.850	202.58
May 23	Route 66 Nationals	Top Fuel	Doug Kalitta	4.420	328.22	B. Bernstein (DQ—over centerline)		
		Funny Car	John Force	4.752	325.30	W. Bazemore	8.034	115.06
		Pro Stock	Jason Line	6.840	202.48	G. Anderson	6.826	202.33
May 30	O'Reilly Summer Nationals .	Top Fuel	Brandon Bernstein	4.729	294.43	D. Kalitta	4.874	291.95
		Funny Car	Whit Bazemore	5.168	269.94	E. Medlen	7.795	112.98
		Pro Stock	Greg Anderson	6.833	202.30	K. Johnson	6.845	201.31
June 13	Pontiac Excitement Nationals	Top Fuel	Darrell Russell	4.569	326.00	T. Schumacher	4.602	320.13
		Funny Car	Del Worsham	5.487	254.62	G. Scelzi	5.651	206.95
		Pro Stock	Greg Anderson	6.854	201.73	D. Connolly	6.937	201.55
June 20	K&N Filters SuperNationals .	Top Fuel	Larry Dixon	4.657	318.92	C. McClentahan	4.703	304.39
		Funny Car	Gary Densham	5.004	311.70	J. Force	5.902	175.57
		Pro Stock	Jason Line	6.761	203.58	K. Johnson	6.771	204.29
June 27	Sears Craftsman Nationals . .	Top Fuel	Doug Kalitta	4.535	326.87	D. Grubnic	4.794	304.80
		Funny Car	Gary Scelzi	4.827	325.30	J. Force	5.321	210.28
		Pro Stock	Greg Anderson	6.726	204.98	S. Johns	6.779	205.32
July 18	Mopar Mile-High Nationals .	Top Fuel	Scott Kalitta	4.747	313.58	T. Schumacher	4.814	305.08
		Funny Car	Phil Burkart	5.338	289.69	C. Pedregon	5.715	225.67
		Pro Stock	Greg Anderson	7.194	191.62	L. Morgan	7.199	192.06
July 25	Carquest Auto Parts Nationals	Top Fuel	Tony Schumacher	4.643	320.28	D. Grubnic	4.690	300.20
		Funny Car	John Force	4.896	309.34	C. Pedregon	5.633	194.91
		Pro Stock	Greg Anderson	6.741	205.51	D. Connolly	6.807	203.49
Aug. 1	Fram-Autolite Nationals	Top Fuel	Doug Kalitta	4.678	315.05	D. Grubnic	9.752	86.37
		Funny Car	Tim Wilkerson	5.088	282.72	J. Force	12.254	84.93
		Pro Stock	Greg Anderson	6.728	205.51	D. Connolly	6.758	204.98
Aug. 15	Lucas Oil Nationals	Top Fuel	Tony Schumacher	4.615	321.96	D. Grubnic	4.606	317.49
		Funny Car	Eric Medlen	4.999	302.62	G. Scelzi	5.286	247.66
		Pro Stock	Dave Connolly	6.799	203.31	G. Anderson	6.818	202.97
Aug. 22	O'Reilly Mid-South Nationals	Top Fuel	Larry Dixon	4.660	311.70	S. Kalitta	7.055	121.99
		Funny Car	John Force	4.907	308.00	T. Wilkerson	5.105	252.33
		Pro Stock	Jason Line	6.806	201.58	D. Connolly	6.878	198.85
Sept. 6	Mac Tools U.S. Nationals . .	Top Fuel	Tony Schumacher	4.597	323.66	D. Kalitta	4.621	316.45
		Funny Car	Gary Densham	4.890	317.64	C. Pedregon	6.497	147.15
		Pro Stock	Greg Anderson	6.839	202.09	K. Koretsky	6.870	201.37
Sept. 26	O'Reilly Fall Nationals	Top Fuel	Tony Schumacher	4.575	325.85	D. Grubnic	4.623	323.97
		Funny Car	Del Worsham	4.934	315.56	C. Pedregon	4.948	307.02
		Pro Stock	Dave Connolly	6.810	203.74	B. Allen	6.891	202.79
Oct. 3	Carquest Auto Parts Nationals	Top Fuel	Doug Herbert	4.516	329.75	T. Schumacher	4.527	329.18
		Funny Car	Del Worsham	4.809	329.75	J. Force	6.854	131.11
		Pro Stock	Dave Connolly	#	—	G. Anderson	—	—
Oct. 10	Lucas Oil Nationals	Top Fuel	Tony Schumacher	4.475	329.99	B. Vandergriff	8.206	99.48
		Funny Car	Gary Scelzi	4.853	308.28	J. Force	11.507	86.39
		Pro Stock	Jason Line	6.669	206.23	G. Anderson	6.681	206.67

Connolly's engine blew but won because Anderson red lighted with a .003 reaction time.

Remaining Races (2): ACDelco Las Vegas Nationals (Oct. 31); Automobile Club of Southern California Finals in Pomona (Nov. 14).

NHRA POWERade Point Standings (through Oct. 10)

Top Fuel

		Points
1	Tony Schumacher	1823
2	Doug Kalitta	1493
3	Brandon Bernstein	1444
4	Scott Kalitta	1307
5	David Grubnic	1279
6	Larry Dixon	1176
7	Cory McClenathan	1046
8	Doug Herbert	1015
9	Scott Weis	740
10	Rhonda Hartman-Smith	738

Funny Car

		Points
1	John Force	1672
2	Del Worsham	1412
3	Gary Scelzi	1376
4	Whit Bazemore	1271
5	Eric Medlen	1265
6	Gary Densham	1252
7	Tim Wilkerson	1134
8	Cruz Pedregon	1115
9	Tony Pedregon	1084
10	Phil Burkart	1072

Pro Stock

		Points
1	Greg Anderson	2167
2	Jason Line	1465
3	Dave Connolly	1441
4	Kurt Johnson	1183
5	Larry Morgan	1169
6	Bruce Allen	1026
7	Jeg Coughlin	1023
8	Steve Johns	951
9	Kenny Koretsky	852
10	Rickie Smith	849

1909-2004
Through the Years

SPORTS ALMANAC

NASCAR CIRCUIT
The Crown Jewels

The five biggest races on the NASCAR (National Association for Stock Car Auto Racing) circuit are the Daytona 500, the EA Sports 500, the Coca-Cola 600, the Mountain Dew Southern 500, and the Brickyard 400. They are the Nextel Cup Series' biggest (Daytona), fastest (EA Sports), longest (Coca-Cola), oldest (Southern) and richest (Brickyard) races. The only drivers to win three in one year are Lee Roy Yarbrough (1969), David Pearson (1976), Bill Elliott (1985) Dale Jarrett (1996) and Jeff Gordon (1997-98).

Daytona 500

Held over 200 laps on 2.5-mile oval at Daytona International Speedway in Daytona Beach, Fla. First race in 1959, although stock car racing at Daytona dates back to 1936. Winners who started from pole position are in **bold** type.

Multiple winners: Richard Petty (7); Cale Yarborough (4); Bobby Allison and Dale Jarrett (3); Bill Elliott, Jeff Gordon, Sterling Marlin and Michael Waltrip (2). **Multiple poles:** Buddy Baker and Cale Yarborough (4); Bill Elliott, Dale Jarrett, Fireball Roberts and Ken Schrader (3); Donnie Allison (2).

Year	Winner	Car	Owner	MPH	Pole Sitter	MPH
1959	Lee Petty	Oldsmobile	Petty Enterprises	135.521	Bob Welborn	140.121
1960	Junior Johnson	Chevrolet	Ray Fox	124.740	Cotton Owens	149.892
1961	Marvin Panch	Pontiac	Smokey Yunick	149.601	Fireball Roberts	155.709
1962	**Fireball Roberts**	Pontiac	Smokey Yunick	152.529	Fireball Roberts	156.999
1963	Tiny Lund	Ford	Wood Brothers	151.566	Fireball Roberts	160.943
1964	Richard Petty	Plymouth	Petty Enterprises	154.334	Paul Goldsmith	174.910
1965-a	Fred Lorenzen	Ford	Holman-Moody	141.539	Darel Dieringer	171.151
1966-b	**Richard Petty**	Plymouth	Petty Enterprises	160.627	Richard Petty	175.165
1967	Mario Andretti	Ford	Holman-Moody	149.926	Curtis Turner	180.831
1968	**Cale Yarborough**	Mercury	Wood Brothers	143.251	Cale Yarborough	189.222
1969	Lee Roy Yarbrough	Ford	Junior Johnson	157.950	Buddy Baker	188.901
1970	Pete Hamilton	Plymouth	Petty Enterprises	149.601	Cale Yarborough	194.015
1971	Richard Petty	Plymouth	Petty Enterprises	144.462	A.J. Foyt	182.744
1972	A.J. Foyt	Mercury	Wood Brothers	161.550	Bobby Isaac	186.632
1973	Richard Petty	Dodge	Petty Enterprises	157.205	Buddy Baker	185.662
1974-c	Richard Petty	Dodge	Petty Enterprises	140.894	David Pearson	185.017
1975	Benny Parsons	Chevrolet	L.G. DeWitt	153.649	Donnie Allison	185.827
1976	David Pearson	Mercury	Wood Brothers	152.181	Ramo Stott	183.456
1977	Cale Yarborough	Chevrolet	Junior Johnson	153.218	Donnie Allison	188.048
1978	Bobby Allison	Ford	Bud Moore	159.730	Cale Yarborough	187.536
1979	Richard Petty	Oldsmobile	Petty Enterprises	143.977	Buddy Baker	196.049
1980	**Buddy Baker**	Oldsmobile	Ranier Racing	177.602*	Buddy Baker	194.099
1981	Richard Petty	Buick	Petty Enterprises	169.651	Bobby Allison	194.624
1982	Bobby Allison	Buick	DiGard Racing	153.991	Benny Parsons	196.317
1983	Cale Yarborough	Pontiac	Ranier Racing	155.979	Ricky Rudd	198.864
1984	**Cale Yarborough**	Chevrolet	Ranier Racing	150.994	Cale Yarborough	201.848
1985	**Bill Elliott**	Ford	Melling Racing	172.265	Bill Elliott	205.114
1986	Geoff Bodine	Chevrolet	Hendrick Motorsports	148.124	Bill Elliott	205.039
1987	**Bill Elliott**	Ford	Melling Racing	176.263	Bill Elliott	210.364†
1988	Bobby Allison	Buick	Stavola Brothers	137.531	Ken Schrader	198.823
1989	Darrell Waltrip	Chevrolet	Hendrick Motorsports	148.466	Ken Schrader	196.996
1990	Derrike Cope	Chevrolet	Bob Whitcomb	165.761	Ken Schrader	196.515
1991	Ernie Irvan	Chevrolet	Morgan-McClure	148.148	Davey Allison	195.955
1992	Davey Allison	Ford	Robert Yates	160.256	Sterling Martin	192.213
1993	Dale Jarrett	Chevrolet	Joe Gibbs Racing	154.972	Kyle Petty	189.426
1994	Sterling Marlin	Chevrolet	Morgan-McClure	156.931	Loy Allen	190.158
1995	Sterling Marlin	Chevrolet	Morgan-McClure	141.710	Dale Jarrett	193.498
1996	Dale Jarrett	Ford	Robert Yates	154.308	Dale Earnhardt	189.510
1997	Jeff Gordon	Chevrolet	Rick Hendrick	148.295	Mike Skinner	189.813
1998	Dale Earnhardt	Chevrolet	Richard Childress	172.712	Bobby Labonte	192.415
1999	**Jeff Gordon**	Chevrolet	Rick Hendrick	161.551	Jeff Gordon	195.067
2000	**Dale Jarrett**	Ford	Robert Yates	155.669	Dale Jarrett	191.091
2001	Michael Waltrip	Chevrolet	Dale Earnhardt, Inc.	161.783	Bill Elliott	183.565
2002	Ward Burton	Dodge	Bill Davis	142.971	Jimmie Johnson	185.831
2003-d	Michael Waltrip	Chevrolet	Dale Earnhardt, Inc.	133.870	Jeff Green	186.606
2004	Dale Earnhardt Jr.	Chevrolet	Dale Earnhardt, Inc.	156.345	Greg Biffle	188.387

*Track and race record for winning speed. †Track and race record for qualifying speed.
Notes: a—rain shortened 1965 race to 332.5 miles; **b**—rain shortened 1966 race to 495 miles; **c**—in 1974, race shortened 50 miles due to energy crisis; **d**—rain shortened 2003 race to 272.5 miles. **Also:** Pole sitters determined by pole qualifying race (1959-65); by two-lap average (1966-68); by fastest single lap (since 1969).

EA Sports 500

Held over 188 laps on 2.66-mile tri-oval at Talladega Superspeedway in Talladega, Ala.

Previously known as Winston 500 (1970-93, 1997-2000) and Winston Select 500 (1994-96). It's been EA Sports 500 since 2001. Winners who started from pole position are in **bold** type.

Multiple winners: Dale Earnhardt (4); Bobby Allison, Davey Allison, Buddy Baker, Dale Earnhardt Jr. and David Pearson (3); Mark Martin, Darrell Waltrip and Cale Yarborough (2).

Year		Year		Year		Year	
1970	Pete Hamilton	1979	Bobby Allison	1988	Phil Parsons	1997	Mark Martin
1971	**Donnie Allison**	1980	Buddy Baker	1989	Davey Allison	1998	Dale Jarrett
1972	David Pearson	1981	**Bobby Allison**	1990	**Dale Earnhardt**	1999	Dale Earnhardt
1973	David Pearson	1982	Darrell Waltrip	1991	Harry Gant	2000	Dale Earnhardt
1974	**David Pearson**	1983	Richard Petty	1992	Davey Allison	2001	Dale Earnhardt Jr.
1975	**Buddy Baker**	1984	**Cale Yarborough**	1993	Ernie Irvan	2002	Dale Earnhardt Jr.
1976	Buddy Baker	1985	**Bill Elliott**	1994	Dale Earnhardt	2003	Michael Waltrip
1977	Darrell Waltrip	1986	Bobby Allison	1995	**Mark Martin**	2004	Dale Earnhardt Jr.
1978	**Cale Yarborough**	1987	Davey Allison	1996	Sterling Marlin		

Coca-Cola 600

Held over 400 laps on 1.5-mile oval at Lowe's Motor Speedway in Concord, N.C.

Previously known as World 600 (1960-85). It has been Coca-Cola 600 since 1986 (in 2002, sponsors announced a one-time-only name change to The Coca-Cola Racing Family 600). Winners who started from pole position are in **bold** type.

Multiple winners: Darrell Waltrip (5); Bobby Allison, Buddy Baker, Dale Earnhardt, Jeff Gordon and David Pearson (3); Neil Bonnett, Jeff Burton, Jimmie Johnson, Fred Lorenzen, Jim Paschal and Richard Petty (2).

Year		Year		Year		Year	
1960	Joe Lee Johnson	1972	Buddy Baker	1984	Bobby Allison	1996	Dale Jarrett
1961	David Pearson	1973	**Buddy Baker**	1985	Darrell Waltrip	1997	**Jeff Gordon***
1962	Nelson Stacy	1974	**David Pearson**	1986	Dale Earnhardt	1998	**Jeff Gordon**
1963	Fred Lorenzen	1975	Richard Petty	1987	Kyle Petty	1999	Jeff Burton
1964	Jim Paschal	1976	**David Pearson**	1988	Darrell Waltrip		
1965	**Fred Lorenzen**	1977	Richard Petty	1989	Darrell Waltrip	2000	Matt Kenseth
1966	Marvin Panch	1978	Darrell Waltrip			2001	Jeff Burton
1967	Jim Paschal	1979	Darrell Waltrip	1990	Rusty Wallace	2002	Mark Martin
1968	Buddy Baker*			1991	Davey Allison	2003	Jimmie Johnson*
1969	Lee Roy Yarbrough	1980	Benny Parsons	1992	Dale Earnhardt	2004	**Jimmie Johnson**
		1981	Bobby Allison	1993	Dale Earnhardt		
1970	Donnie Allison	1982	Neil Bonnett	1994	**Jeff Gordon**		
1971	Bobby Allison	1983	Neil Bonnett	1995	Bobby Labonte		

* rain-shortened.

Mountain Dew Southern 500

Held over 367 laps on 1.366-mile oval at Darlington International Raceway in Darlington, S.C.

Previously known as Southern 500 (1950-88); Heinz 500 (1989-91); and Pepsi Southern 500 (1998-2000). It was the Mountain Dew Southern 500 from 1992-97, and since 2001. Winners who started from pole position are in **bold** type.

Multiple winners: Jeff Gordon and Cale Yarborough (5); Bobby Allison (4); Buck Baker, Dale Earnhardt, Bill Elliott, David Pearson and Herb Thomas (3); Harry Gant and Fireball Roberts (2).

Year		Year		Year		Year	
1950	Johnny Mantz	1964	Buck Baker	1978	Cale Yarborough	1991	Harry Gant
1951	Herb Thomas	1965	Ned Jarrett	1979	David Pearson	1992	Darrell Waltrip*
1952	**Fonty Flock**	1966	Darel Dieringer			1993	Mark Martin*
1953	Buck Baker	1967	**Richard Petty**	1980	Terry Labonte	1994	Bill Elliott
1954	Herb Thomas	1968	Cale Yarborough	1981	Neil Bonnett	1995	Jeff Gordon
1955	Herb Thomas	1969	Lee Roy Yarbrough*	1982	Cale Yarborough	1996	Jeff Gordon
1956	Curtis Turner			1983	Bobby Allison	1997	Jeff Gordon*
1957	Speedy Thompson	1970	Buddy Baker	1984	**Harry Gant**	1998	Jeff Gordon
1958	Fireball Roberts	1971	**Bobby Allison**	1985	**Bill Elliott**	1999	Jeff Burton*
1959	Jim Reed	1972	**Bobby Allison**	1986	**Tim Richmond**		
		1973	Cale Yarborough	1987	Dale Earnhardt*	2000	Bobby Labonte*
1960	Buck Baker	1974	Cale Yarborough	1988	**Bill Elliott**	2001	Ward Burton
1961	Nelson Stacy	1975	Bobby Allison	1989	Dale Earnhardt	2002	Jeff Gordon
1962	Larry Frank	1976	**David Pearson**			2003	Terry Labonte
1963	Fireball Roberts	1977	David Pearson	1990	**Dale Earnhardt**	2004	scheduled for Nov. 14

* rain-shortened.

Brickyard 400

Held over 160 laps at 2.5-mile Indianapolis Motor Speedway in Indianapolis, Ind.

Winners who started from pole position are in **bold** type.

Multiple winners: Jeff Gordon (4); Dale Jarrett (2).

Year		Year		Year		Year		Year	
1994	Jeff Gordon	1997	Ricky Rudd	1999	Dale Jarrett	2001	Jeff Gordon	2003	**Kevin Harvick**
1995	Dale Earnhardt	1998	Jeff Gordon	2000	Bobby Labonte	2002	Bill Elliott	2004	Jeff Gordon
1996	Dale Jarrett								

NASCAR Circuit (Cont.)
Nextel Cup Series Champions

Originally the Grand National Championship, 1949-70, then the Winston Cup Series Championship, 1971-2003, and based on official NASCAR records. Note that earnings totals include bonus awards.

Multiple winners: (drivers) Dale Earnhardt and Richard Petty (7); Jeff Gordon (4); David Pearson, Lee Petty, Darrell Waltrip and Cale Yarborough (3); Buck Baker, Tim Flock, Ned Jarrett, Terry Labonte, Herb Thomas and Joe Weatherly (2).

Multiple winners: (cars) Chevrolet (22); Ford (6); Plymouth (5); Dodge, Oldsmobile and Pontiac (4); Buick and Hudson (3); and Chrysler (2).

Year	Car #	Driver	Car	Owner	Sts	Wins	Poles	Earnings
1949	22	Red Byron	Oldsmobile	Raymond Parks	5	2	1	$5,800
1950	60	Bill Rexford	Oldsmobile	Julian Buesink	17	1	0	6,175
1951	92	Herb Thomas	Hudson	Herb Thomas	34	7	4	18,200
1952	91	Tim Flock	Hudson	Ted Chester	33	8	4	20,210
1953	92	Herb Thomas	Hudson	Herb Thomas	37	11	10	27,300
1954	42	Lee Petty	Chrysler	Herb Thomas	34	7	3	26,706
1955	300	Tim Flock	Chrysler	Carl Kiekhaefer	38	18	19	33,750
1956	300B	Buck Baker	Chevrolet	Carl Kiekhaefer	48	14	12	29,790
1957	87	Buck Baker	Chevrolet	Buck Baker	40	10	5	24,712
1958	42	Lee Petty	Oldsmobile	Petty Enterprises	49	7	4	20,600
1959	42	Lee Petty	Plymouth	Petty Enterprises	42	10	2	45,570
1960	4	Rex White	Chevrolet	White-Clements	40	6	3	45,260
1961	11	Ned Jarrett	Chevrolet	W.G. Holloway Jr.	46	1	4	27,285
1962	8	Joe Weatherly	Pontiac	Bud Moore	52	9	6	56,110
1963	8	Joe Weatherly	Mercury	Wood Brothers	53	3	6	58,110
1964	43	Richard Petty	Plymouth	Petty Enterprises	61	9	8	98,810
1965	11	Ned Jarrett	Ford	Bondy Long	54	13	9	77,960
1966	6	David Pearson	Dodge	Cotton Owens	42	14	7	59,205
1967	43	Richard Petty	Plymouth	Petty Enterprises	48	27	18	130,275
1968	17	David Pearson	Ford	Holman-Moody	48	16	12	118,842
1969	17	David Pearson	Ford	Holman-Moody	51	11	14	183,700
1970	71	Bobby Isaac	Dodge	Nord Krauskopf	47	11	13	121,470
1971	43	Richard Petty	Plymouth	Petty Enterprises	46	21	9	309,225
1972	43	Richard Petty	Plymouth	Petty Enterprises	31	8	3	227,015
1973	72	Benny Parsons	Chevrolet	L.G. DeWitt	28	1	0	114,345
1974	43	Richard Petty	Dodge	Petty Enterprises	30	10	7	299,175
1975	43	Richard Petty	Dodge	Petty Enterprises	30	13	3	378,865
1976	11	Cale Yarborough	Chevrolet	Junior Johnson	30	9	2	387,173
1977	11	Cale Yarborough	Chevrolet	Junior Johnson	30	9	3	477,499
1978	11	Cale Yarborough	Oldsmobile	Junior Johnson	30	10	8	530,751
1979	43	Richard Petty	Chevrolet	Petty Enterprises	31	5	1	531,292
1980	2	Dale Earnhardt	Chevrolet	Rod Osterlund	31	5	0	588,926
1981	11	Darrell Waltrip	Buick	Junior Johnson	31	12	11	693,342
1982	11	Darrell Waltrip	Buick	Junior Johnson	30	12	7	873,118
1983	22	Bobby Allison	Buick	Bill Gardner	30	6	0	828,355
1984	44	Terry Labonte	Chevrolet	Billy Hagan	30	2	2	713,010
1985	11	Darrell Waltrip	Chevrolet	Junior Johnson	28	3	4	1,318,735
1986	3	Dale Earnhardt	Chevrolet	Richard Childress	29	5	1	1,783,880
1987	3	Dale Earnhardt	Chevrolet	Richard Childress	29	11	1	2,099,243
1988	9	Bill Elliott	Ford	Harry Meling	29	6	6	1,574,639
1989	27	Rusty Wallace	Pontiac	Raymond Beadle	29	6	4	2,247,950
1990	3	Dale Earnhardt	Chevrolet	Richard Childress	29	9	4	3,083,056
1991	3	Dale Earnhardt	Chevrolet	Richard Childress	29	4	0	2,396,685
1992	7	Alan Kulwicki	Ford	Alan Kulwicki	29	2	6	2,322,561
1993	3	Dale Earnhardt	Chevrolet	Richard Childress	30	6	2	3,353,789
1994	3	Dale Earnhardt	Chevrolet	Richard Childress	31	4	2	3,400,733
1995	24	Jeff Gordon	Chevrolet	Rick Hendrick	31	7	8	4,347,343
1996	5	Terry Labonte	Chevrolet	Rick Hendrick	31	2	4	4,030,648
1997	24	Jeff Gordon	Chevrolet	Rick Hendrick	32	10	1	6,375,658
1998	24	Jeff Gordon	Chevrolet	Rick Hendrick	33	13	7	9,306,584
1999	88	Dale Jarrett	Ford	Robert Yates	34	4	0	6,649,596
2000	18	Bobby Labonte	Pontiac	Joe Gibbs	34	4	2	7,361,387
2001	24	Jeff Gordon	Chevrolet	Rick Hendrick	36	6	6	10,879,757
2002	20	Tony Stewart	Pontiac	Joe Gibbs	36	3	2	9,163,761
2003	17	Matt Kenseth	Ford	Mark Martin	36	1	0	4,038,120

NASCAR Rookie of the Year

Sponsored by Raybestos, the official brake of NASCAR, and presented to rookie driver who accumulates the most Nextel Cup Series Raybestos Rookie of the Year points based on their best 17 finishes.

Year		Year		Year		Year	
1958	Shorty Rollins	1960	David Pearson	1962	Tom Cox	1964	Doug Cooper
1959	Richard Petty	1961	Woodie Wilson	1963	Billy Wade	1965	Sam McQuagg

Year		Year		Year		Year	
1966	James Hylton	1976	Skip Manning	1986	Alan Kulwicki	1996	Johnny Benson
1967	Donnie Allison	1977	Ricky Rudd	1987	Davey Allison	1997	Mike Skinner
1968	Pete Hamilton	1978	Ronnie Thomas	1988	Ken Bouchard	1998	Kenny Irwin
1969	Dick Brooks	1979	Dale Earnhardt	1989	Dick Trickle	1999	Tony Stewart
1970	Bill Dennis	1980	Jody Ridley	1990	Rob Moroso	2000	Matt Kenseth
1971	Walter Ballard	1981	Ron Bouchard	1991	Bobby Hamilton	2001	Kevin Harvick
1972	Larry Smith	1982	Geoff Bodine	1992	Jimmy Hensley	2002	Ryan Newman
1973	Lennie Pond	1983	Sterling Marlin	1993	Jeff Gordon	2003	Jamie McMurray
1974	Earl Ross	1984	Rusty Wallace	1994	Jeff Burton		
1975	Bruce Hill	1985	Ken Schrader	1995	Ricky Craven		

All-Time Leaders

NASCAR's all-time Top 20 drivers in victories, pole positions and earnings based on records through Oct. 10, 2004. Drivers active in 2004 are in **bold** type.

Victories

1	Richard Petty 200	7	**Jeff Gordon** 69	13	Buck Baker 46	19	**Dale Jarrett** 31
2	David Pearson 105	8	Lee Petty 55	14	**Bill Elliott** 44	20	Fred Lorenzen 26
3	Bobby Allison 84		**Rusty Wallace** . . .55	15	Tim Flock 40		Rex White 26
	Darrell Waltrip 84	10	Ned Jarrett 50	16	Bobby Isaac 37		
5	Cale Yarborough 83		Junior Johnson 50	17	**Mark Martin** 34		
6	Dale Earnhardt 76	12	Herb Thomas 48	18	Fireball Roberts 32		

Pole Positions

1	Richard Petty 126	6	**Bill Elliott** 55	11	**Mark Martin** 41	16	**Rusty Wallace** . .36
2	David Pearson . . .113	7	**Jeff Gordon** 52	12	Buddy Baker 40	17	Ned Jarrett 35
3	Cale Yarborough . .70	8	Bobby Isaac 51	13	Tim Flock 39		Fireball Roberts . .35
4	Darrell Waltrip . . .59	9	Junior Johnson 47		Herb Thomas 39		Rex White 35
5	Bobby Allison 57	10	Buck Baker 44	15	**Geoff Bodine** 37	20	Fonty Flock 34

Earnings (unofficial)

1	**Jeff Gordon** $62,453,725	8	Bill Elliott $36,237,263	15	Ken Schrader . . $24,874,731
2	**Dale Jarrett** 45,686,483	9	Ricky Rudd 35,194,727	16	**Ward Burton** 23,655,764
3	**Mark Martin** 43,445,665	10	Jeff Burton 34,262,895	17	**Jeremy Mayfield** .20,561,706
4	**Rusty Wallace** . . .41,951,193	11	Tony Stewart 31,541,571	18	**Kyle Petty** 20,265,891
5	Dale Earnhardt . . .41,742,384	12	Sterling Marlin . .31,506,098	19	Darrell Waltrip 19,416,618
6	**Bobby Labonte** . . .38,753,759	13	Michael Waltrip .26,059,475	20	**Jimmy Spencer** . .19,319,974
7	**Terry Labonte** . . .36,629,692	14	**Dale Earnhardt Jr.** 24,896,592		

CHAMP CAR CIRCUIT

Champ Car Series Champions

Officially the "Bridgestone Presents The Champ Car World Series Powered by Ford" since 2003. Formerly, AAA (American Automobile Assn., 1909-55), USAC (U.S. Auto Club, 1956-78), CART (Championship Auto Racing Teams, 1979-91). CART was renamed IndyCar in 1992 and then lost use of the name in 1997. It was known as the FedEx Championship Series from 1998-2002.

Multiple titles: A.J. Foyt (7); Mario Andretti (4); Jimmy Bryan, Earl Cooper, Ted Horn, Rick Mears, Louie Meyer, Bobby Rahal, Al Unser (3); Tony Bettenhausen, Gil de Ferran, Ralph DePalma, Peter DePaolo, Joe Leonard, Rex Mays, Tommy Milton, Ralph Mulford, Jimmy Murphy, Wilbur Shaw, Al Unser Jr., Bobby Unser, Rodger Ward and Alex Zanardi (2).

AAA

Year		Year		Year		Year	
1909	George Robertson	1920	Tommy Milton	1931	Louis Schneider	1942-45	No racing
1910	Ray Harroun	1921	Tommy Milton	1932	Bob Carey	1946	Ted Horn
1911	Ralph Mulford	1922	Jimmy Murphy	1933	Louie Meyer	1947	Ted Horn
1912	Ralph DePalma	1923	Eddie Hearne	1934	Bill Cummings	1948	Ted Horn
1913	Earl Cooper	1924	Jimmy Murphy	1935	Kelly Petillo	1949	Johnnie Parsons
1914	Ralph DePalma	1925	Peter DePaolo	1936	Mauri Rose	1950	Henry Banks
1915	Earl Cooper	1926	Harry Hartz	1937	Wilbur Shaw	1951	Tony Bettenhausen
1916	Dario Resta	1927	Peter DePaolo	1938	Floyd Roberts	1952	Chuck Stevenson
1917	Earl Cooper	1928	Louie Meyer	1939	Wilbur Shaw	1953	Sam Hanks
1918	Ralph Mulford	1929	Louie Meyer	1940	Rex Mays	1954	Jimmy Bryan
1919	Howard Wilcox	1930	Billy Arnold	1941	Rex Mays	1955	Bob Sweikert

USAC

Year		Year		Year		Year	
1956	Jimmy Bryan	1962	Rodger Ward	1968	Bobby Unser	1974	Bobby Unser
1957	Jimmy Bryan	1963	A.J. Foyt	1969	Mario Andretti	1975	A.J. Foyt
1958	Tony Bettenhausen	1964	A.J. Foyt	1970	Al Unser	1976	Gordon Johncock
1959	Rodger Ward	1965	Mario Andretti	1971	Joe Leonard	1977	Tom Sneva
1960	A.J. Foyt	1966	Mario Andretti	1972	Joe Leonard	1978	A.J. Foyt
1961	A.J. Foyt	1967	A.J. Foyt	1973	Roger McCluskey		

CHAMP CAR Circuit (Cont.)
Champ Car World Series (formerly CART)

Year	Driver	Car	Team	Sts	Wins	Poles	Earnings
1979	**Rick Mears**	Penske Ford	Penske	14	3	2	$408,078
1980	**Johnny Rutherford**	Chaparral Ford	Chaparral	12	5	3	503,595
1981	**Rick Mears**	Penske Ford	Penske	11	6	2	323,670
1982	**Rick Mears**	Penske Ford	Penske	11	4	8	306,454
1983	**Al Unser**	Penske Ford	Penske	13	1	0	500,109
1984	**Mario Andretti**	Lola Ford	Newman/Haas	16	6	8	931,929
1985	**Al Unser**	March Ford	Penske	14	1	1	843,885
1986	**Bobby Rahal**	March Ford	TrueSports	17	6	2	1,488,049
1987	**Bobby Rahal**	Lola Ford	TrueSports	15	3	1	1,261,098
1988	**Danny Sullivan**	Penske Chevrolet	Penske	15	4	9	1,222,791
1989	**Emerson Fittipaldi**	Penske Chevrolet	Patrick	15	5	4	2,166,078
1990	**Al Unser Jr.**	Lola Chevrolet	Galles-Kraco	16	6	1	1,946,833
1991	**Michael Andretti**	Lola Chevrolet	Newman/Haas	17	8	8	2,461,734
1992	**Bobby Rahal**	Lola Chevrolet	Rahal-Hogan	16	4	3	2,235,298
1993	**Nigel Mansell**	Lola Ford	Newman/Haas	15	5	7	2,526,953
1994	**Al Unser Jr.**	Penske Ilmor	Marlboro Team Penske	16	8	4	3,535,813
1995	**Jacques Villeneuve**	Reynard Ford	Team Green	17	4	6	2,996,269
1996	**Jimmy Vasser**	Reynard Honda	Target Chip Ganassi	16	4	4	3,071,500
1997	**Alex Zanardi**	Reynard Honda	Target Chip Ganassi	16	5	4	2,096,250
1998	**Alex Zanardi**	Reynard Honda	Target Chip Ganassi	19	7	0	2,229,250
1999	**Juan Montoya**	Reynard Honda	Target Chip Ganassi	20	7	7	1,973,000
2000	**Gil de Ferran**	Reynard Honda	Marlboro Team Penske	20	2	5	1,677,000
2001	**Gil de Ferran**	Reynard Honda	Marlboro Team Penske	20	2	5	1,761,500
2002	**Cristiano da Matta**	Lola Toyota	Newman/Haas	19	7	7	2,053,000
2003	**Paul Tracy**	Lola Ford-Cosworth	Player's/Forsythe	18	7	6	1,007,000

Champ Car Rookie of the Year

Officially, Jim Trueman Rookie of the Year Award. Named after the late founder of the two-time champion TrueSports Racing Team, it's presented to the rookie who accumulates the most Champ Car Series points among first year drivers.

Year		Year		Year		Year	
1979	Bill Alsup	1986	Dominic Dobson	1993	Nigel Mansell	2000	Kenny Brack
1980	Dennis Firestone	1987	Fabrizio Barbazza	1994	Jacques Villeneuve	2001	Scott Dixon
1981	Bob Lazier	1988	John Jones	1995	Gil de Ferran	2002	Mario Dominguez
1982	Bobby Rahal	1989	Bernard Jourdain	1996	Alex Zanardi	2003	Sebastien Bourdais
1983	Teo Fabi	1990	Eddie Cheever	1997	Patrick Carpentier		
1984	Roberto Guerrero	1991	Jeff Andretti	1998	Tony Kanaan		
1985	Arie Luyendyk	1992	Stefan Johansson	1999	Juan Montoya		

All-Time Champ Car Leaders

Champ Car's all-time Top 20 drivers in victories, pole positions and earnings, based on records through Sept. 25, 2004. Drivers active in 2004 are in **bold** type. Totals include victories, poles and earnings before Champ Car (then CART) was established in 1979. Earnings totals include year-end performance awards. (*) Denotes driver is active, but in Indy Racing League; (†) denotes driver is active, but in Formula One; (**) denotes driver is active, but in NASCAR.

Victories

1 A.J. Foyt 67	7 Rick Mears 29	12 Ralph DePalma 24	17 Earl Cooper 20
2 Mario Andretti ...52	8 **Paul Tracy** 28	Bobby Rahal 24	18 Jimmy Bryan 19
3 Michael Andretti ...42	9 Johnny Rutherford ..27	14 Tommy Milton 23	Jimmy Murphy 19
4 Al Unser 39	10 Rodger Ward 26	15 Tony Bettenhausen .22	20 Ralph Mulford 17
5 Bobby Unser 35	11 Gordon Johncock ..25	Emerson Fittipaldi ..22	Danny Sullivan 17
6 Al Unser Jr.* 31			

Pole Positions

1 Mario Andretti 67	7 Johnny Rutherford ..23	13 Emerson Fittipaldi ..17	19 Parnelli Jones 12
2 A.J. Foyt 53	8 **Paul Tracy** 21	14 Gil de Ferran 16	**Sebastien**
3 Bobby Unser 49	9 Gordon Johncock ..20	15 Tony Bettenhausen .14	**Bourdais** 12
4 Rick Mears 40	10 Rex Mays 19	Don Branson 14	
5 Michael Andretti ..32	Danny Sullivan 19	Tom Sneva 14	
6 Al Unser 27	12 Bobby Rahal 18	Juan Montoya† ...14	

Earnings

1 Al Unser Jr.* $18,828,406	8 **Paul Tracy** $10,334,270	15 Alex Zanardi $5,893,750
2 Michael Andretti ...18,228,119	9 Danny Sullivan 8,884,126	19 Christian Fittipaldi ..5,526,166
3 Bobby Rahal 16,344,008	10 Arie Luyendyk 7,732,188	16 Scott Pruett** 5,440,144
4 Emerson Fittipaldi ..14,293,625	11 Gil de Ferran 7,390,703	17 A.J. Foyt 5,357,589
5 Mario Andretti 11,552,154	12 Adrian Fernandez* ..7,083,015	18 Teo Fabi 5,045,881
6 **Jimmy Vasser** ...11,369,249	13 Raul Boesel 6,971,887	20 Dario Franchitti* 4,935,000
7 Rick Mears 11,050,807	14 Al Unser 6,740,843	

INDY RACING LEAGUE CIRCUIT
Indianapolis 500

Held every Memorial Day weekend; 200 laps around a 2.5-mile oval at Indianapolis Motor Speedway. First race was held in 1911. The Indy Racing League began in 1996 and made the Indianapolis 500 its cornerstone event. Winning drivers are listed with starting positions. Winners who started from pole position are in **bold** type.

Multiple wins: A.J. Foyt, Rick Mears and Al Unser (4); Louis Meyer, Mauri Rose, Johnny Rutherford, Wilbur Shaw and Bobby Unser (3); Helio Castroneves, Emerson Fittipaldi, Gordon Johncock, Arie Luyendyk, Tommy Milton, Al Unser Jr., Bill Vukovich and Rodger Ward (2).

Multiple poles: Rick Mears (6); A.J. Foyt and Rex Mays (4); Mario Andretti, Arie Luyendyk, Johnny Rutherford and Tom Sneva (3); Scott Brayton, Bill Cummings, Ralph DePalma, Leon Duray, Parnelli Jones, Jimmy Murphy, Duke Nalon, Eddie Sachs and Bobby Unser (2).

Year	Winner (Pos.)	Car	MPH	Pole Sitter	MPH
1911	Ray Harroun (28)	Marmon Wasp	74.602	Lewis Strang	–
1912	Joe Dawson (7)	National	78.719	Gil Anderson	–
1913	Jules Goux (7)	Peugeot	75.933	Caleb Bragg	–
1914	Rene Thomas (15)	Delage	82.474	Jean Chassagne	–
1915	Ralph DePalma (2)	Mercedes	89.840	Howard Wilcox	98.90
1916-a	Dario Resta (4)	Peugeot	84.001	John Aitken	96.69
1917-18	Not held	World War I			
1919	Howdy Wilcox (2)	Peugeot	88.050	Rene Thomas	104.78
1920	Gaston Chevrolet (6)	Monroe	88.618	Ralph DePalma	99.15
1921	Tommy Milton (20)	Frontenac	89.621	Ralph DePalma	100.75
1922	**Jimmy Murphy** (1)	Murphy Special	94.484	Jimmy Murphy	100.50
1923	**Tommy Milton** (1)	H.C.S. Special	90.954	Tommy Milton	108.17
1924	L.L. Corum & Joe Boyer (21)	Duesenberg Special	98.234	Jimmy Murphy	108.037
1925	Peter DePaolo (2)	Duesenberg Special	101.127	Leon Duray	113.196
1926-b	Frank Lockhart (20)	Miller Special	95.904	Earl Cooper	111.735
1927	George Souders (22)	Duesenberg	97.545	Frank Lockhart	120.100
1928	Louie Meyer (13)	Miller Special	99.482	Leon Duray	122.391
1929	Ray Keech (6)	Simplex Piston Ring Special	97.585	Cliff Woodbury	120.599
1930	**Billy Arnold** (1)	Miller-Hartz Special	100.448	Billy Arnold	113.268
1931	Louis Schneider (13)	Bowes Seal Fast Special	96.629	Russ Snowberger	112.796
1932	Fred Frame (27)	Miller-Hartz Special	104.144	Lou Moore	117.363
1933	Louie Meyer (6)	Tydol Special	104.162	Bill Cummings	118.530
1934	Bill Cummings (10)	Boyle Products Special	104.863	Kelly Petillo	119.329
1935	Kelly Petillo (22)	Gilmore Speedway Special	106.240	Rex Mays	120.736
1936	Louie Meyer (28)	Ring Free Special	109.069	Rex Mays	119.644
1937	Wilbur Shaw (2)	Shaw-Gilmore Special	113.580	Bill Cummings	123.343
1938	**Floyd Roberts** (1)	Burd Piston Ring Special	117.200	Floyd Roberts	125.681
1939	Wilbur Shaw (3)	Boyle Special	115.035	Jimmy Snyder	130.138
1940	Wilbur Shaw (2)	Boyle Special	114.277	Rex Mays	127.850
1941	Floyd Davis & Mauri Rose (17)	Noc-Out Hose Clamp Special	115.117	Mauri Rose	128.691
1942-45	Not held	World War II			
1946	George Robson (15)	Thorne Engineering Special	114.820	Cliff Bergere	126.471
1947	Mauri Rose (3)	Blue Crown Spark Plug Special	116.338	Ted Horn	126.564
1948	Mauri Rose (3)	Blue Crown Spark Plug Special	119.814	Rex Mays	130.577
1949	Bill Holland (4)	Blue Crown Spark Plug Special	121.327	Duke Nalon	132.939
1950-c	Johnnie Parsons (5)	Wynn's Friction Proofing	124.002	Walt Faulkner	134.343
1951	Lee Wallard (2)	Belanger Special	126.244	Duke Nalon	136.498
1952	Troy Ruttman (7)	Agajanian Special	128.922	Fred Agabashian	138.010
1953	**Bill Vukovich** (1)	Fuel Injection Special	128.740	Bill Vukovich	138.392
1954	Bill Vukovich (19)	Fuel Injection Special	130.840	Jack McGrath	141.033
1955	Bob Sweikert (14)	John Zink Special	128.213	Jerry Hoyt	140.045
1956	**Pat Flaherty** (1)	John Zink Special	128.490	Pat Flaherty	145.596
1957	Sam Hanks (13)	Belond Exhaust Special	135.601	Pat O'Connor	143.948
1958	Jimmy Bryan (7)	Belond AP Parts Special	133.791	Dick Rathmann	145.974
1959	Rodger Ward (6)	Leader Card 500 Roadster	135.857	Johnny Thomson	145.908
1960	Jim Rathmann (2)	Ken-Paul Special	138.767	Eddie Sachs	146.592
1961	A.J. Foyt (7)	Bowes Seal Fast Special	139.130	Eddie Sachs	147.481
1962	Rodger Ward (2)	Leader Card 500 Roadster	140.293	Parnelli Jones	150.370
1963	**Parnelli Jones** (1)	Agajanian-Willard Special	143.137	Parnelli Jones	151.153
1964	A.J. Foyt (5)	Sheraton-Thompson Special	147.350	Jim Clark	158.828
1965	Jim Clark (2)	Lotus Ford	150.686	A.J. Foyt	161.233
1966	Graham Hill (15)	American Red Ball Special	144.317	Mario Andretti	165.899
1967-d	A.J. Foyt (4)	Sheraton-Thompson Special	151.207	Mario Andretti	168.982
1968	Bobby Unser (3)	Rislone Special	152.882	Joe Leonard	171.559
1969	Mario Andretti (2)	STP Oil Treatment Special	156.867	A.J. Foyt	170.568
1970	**Al Unser** (1)	Johnny Lightning Special	155.749	Al Unser	170.221

Indy Racing League Circuit (Cont.)

Year	Winner (Pos.)	Car	MPH	Pole Sitter	MPH
1971	Al Unser (5)	Johnny Lightning Special	157.735	Peter Revson	178.696
1972	Mark Donohue (3)	Sunoco McLaren	162.962	Bobby Unser	195.940
1973-e	Gordon Johncock (11)	STP Double Oil Filters	159.036	Johnny Rutherford	198.413
1974	Johnny Rutherford (25)	McLaren	158.589	A.J. Foyt	191.632
1975-f	Bobby Unser (3)	Jorgensen Eagle	149.213	A.J. Foyt	193.976
1976-g	**Johnny Rutherford** (1) . . .	Hy-Gain McLaren/Goodyear	148.725	Johnny Rutherford	188.957
1977	A.J. Foyt (4)	Gilmore Racing Team	161.331	Tom Sneva	198.884
1978	Al Unser (5)	FNCTC Chaparral Lola	161.363	Tom Sneva	202.156
1979	**Rick Mears** (1)	The Gould Charge	158.899	Rick Mears	193.736
1980	**Johnny Rutherford** (1) . . .	Pennzoil Chaparral	142.862	Johnny Rutherford	192.256
1981-h	**Bobby Unser** (1)	Norton Spirit Penske PC-9B	139.084	Bobby Unser	200.546
1982	Gordon Johncock (5)	STP Oil Treatment	162.029	Rick Mears	207.004
1983	Tom Sneva (4)	Texaco Star	162.117	Teo Fabi	207.395
1984	Rick Mears (3)	Pennzoil Z-7	163.612	Tom Sneva	210.029
1985	Danny Sullivan (8)	Miller American Special	152.982	Pancho Carter	212.583
1986	Bobby Rahal (4) . . . . .˙. . .	Budweiser/Truesports/March	170.722	Rick Mears	216.828
1987	Al Unser (20)	Cummins Holset Turbo	162.175	Mario Andretti	215.390
1988	**Rick Mears** (1)	Pennzoil Z-7/Penske Chevy V-8	144.809	Rick Mears	219.198
1989	Emerson Fittipaldi (3)	Marlboro/Penske Chevy V-8	167.581	Rick Mears	223.885
1990	Arie Luyendyk (3)	Domino's Pizza Chevrolet	185.981*	Emerson Fittipaldi	225.301
1991	**Rick Mears** (1)	Marlboro Penske Chevy	176.457	Rick Mears	224.113
1992	Al Unser Jr. (12)	Valvoline Galmer '92	134.477	Roberto Guerrero	232.482
1993	Emerson Fittipaldi (9)	Marlboro Penske Chevy	157.207	Arie Luyendyk	223.967
1994	**Al Unser Jr.** (1)	Marlboro Penske Mercedes	160.872	Al Unser Jr.	228.011
1995	Jacques Villeneuve (5)	Player's Ltd. Reynard Ford	153.616	Scott Brayton	231.604
1996	Buddy Lazier (5)	Reynard Ford	147.956	Tony Stewart	233.100&
1997	**Arie Luyendyk** (1)	G-Force Olds Aurora	145.827	Arie Luyendyk	218.263
1998	Eddie Cheever Jr. (17)	Dallara Olds Aurora	145.155	Billy Boat	223.503
1999	Kenny Brack (8)	Dallara Olds Aurora	153.176	Arie Luyendyk	225.179
2000	Juan Montoya (2)	G-Force Olds Aurora	167.607	Greg Ray	223.471
2001	Helio Castroneves (11)	Dallara Olds Aurora	153.601	Scott Sharp	226.037
2002-i	Helio Castroneves (13)	Dallara Chevrolet	166.499	Bruno Junqueira	231.342
2003	Gil de Ferran (10)	G-Force Toyota	156.291	Helio Castroneves	231.725
2004-j	**Buddy Rice** (1)	G-Force Honda	138.518	Buddy Rice	222.024

*Track record for winning time.

& Scott Brayton won the pole position with an avg. mph of 233.718 but was killed in a practice run. Stewart was awarded pole position with the next fastest speed.

Notes: a—1916 race scheduled for 300 miles; **b**—rain shortened 1926 race to 400 miles; **c**—rain shortened 1950 race to 345 miles; **d**—1967 race postponed due to rain after 18 laps (May 30), resumed next day (May 31); **e**—rain shortened 1973 race to 332.5 miles; **f**—rain shortened 1975 race to 435 miles; **g**—rain shortened 1976 race to 255 miles; **h**—in 1981, runner-up Mario Andretti was awarded 1st place when winner Bobby Unser was penalized a lap after the race was completed for passing cars illegally under the caution flag. Unser and car-owner Roger Penske appealed the race stewards' decision to the U.S. Auto Club. Four months later, USAC overturned the ruling, saying that the penalty was too harsh and Unser should be fined $40,000 rather than stripped of his championship; **i**—Team Green, runner-up Paul Tracy's team, appealed Castroneves' victory, citing video evidence and driver testimonials that proved Tracy passed Castroneves moments before the caution flag on lap 199. The IRL denied the appeal the following day; **j**—rain shortened 2004 race to 450 miles.

Indy 500 Rookie of the Year

Officially the Bank One Rookie of the Year Award and voted on by a panel of auto racing media. Award does not necessarily go to highest-finishing first-year driver. Graham Hill won the race on his first try in 1966, but the rookie award went to Jackie Stewart, who led with 10 laps to go only to lose oil pressure and finish 6th.

Father and son winners: Mario and Michael Andretti (1965 and 1984); Bill and Billy Vukovich III (1968 and 1988).

Year		Year		Year		Year	
1952	Art Cross	1966	Jackie Stewart	1980	Tim Richmond	1993	Nigel Mansell
1953	Jimmy Daywalt	1967	Denis Hulme	1981	Josele Garza	1994	Jacques Villeneuve
1954	Larry Crockett	1968	Bill Vukovich	1982	Jim Hickman	1995	Christian Fittipaldi
1955	Al Herman	1969	Mark Donohue	1983	Teo Fabi	1996	Tony Stewart
1956	Bob Veith	1970	Donnie Allison	1984	Michael Andretti	1997	Jeff Ward
1957	Don Edmunds	1971	Denny Zimmerman		& Roberto Guerrero	1998	Steve Knapp
1958	George Amick	1972	Mike Hiss	1985	Arie Luyendyk	1999	Robby McGehee
1959	Bobby Grim	1973	Graham McRae	1986	Randy Lanier	2000	Juan Montoya
1960	Jim Hurtubise	1974	Pancho Carter	1987	Fabrizio Barbazza	2001	Helio Castroneves
1961	Parnelli Jones	1975	Bill Puterbaugh	1988	Billy Vukovich III	2002	Alex Barron
	& Bobby Marshman	1976	Vern Schuppan	1989	Bernard Jourdain		& Tomas Scheckter
1962	Jimmy McElreath	1977	Jerry Sneva		& Scott Pruett	2003	Tora Takagi
1963	Jim Clark	1978	Rick Mears	1990	Eddie Cheever	2004	Kosuke Matsuura
1964	Johnny White		& Larry Rice	1991	Jeff Andretti		
1965	Mario Andretti	1979	Howdy Holmes	1992	Lyn St. James		

IRL IndyCar Series Champions

The Indy Racing League (IRL) split from the open-wheel CART series in 1994. Led by Indianapolis Motor Speedway President Tony George, the league's inaugural three-race series began in January 1996 and ended with the league's keystone event—the Indianapolis 500. Past series' sponsors include Pep Boys (1998-99) and Northern Light Technology, Inc., an Internet search engine (2000-01). **Note:** With one race remaining in the 2004 season, Tony Kanaan had unofficially clinched the points title. **Multiple winner:** Sam Hornish Jr. (2).

Year	Driver	Car	Team	Sts	Wins	Poles	Earnings
1996	**Buzz Calkins**	Reynard Ford	A.J. Foyt Enterprises	3	1	0	$345,553
	Scott Sharp	Lola Ford	A.J. Foyt Enterprises	3	0	0	330,303
1997	**Tony Stewart**	Dallara Oldsmobile	Team Menard	10	1	4	1,142,450
1998	**Kenny Brack**	Dallara Oldsmobile	A.J. Foyt Enterprises	11	3	0	2,106,700
1999	**Greg Ray**	Dallara Oldsmobile	Team Menard	10	3	4	2,061,800
2000	**Buddy Lazier**	Dallara Oldsmobile	Hemelgarn Racing	9	2	1	2,176,200
2001	**Sam Hornish Jr.**	Dallara Oldsmobile	Panther Racing	13	3	0	2,477,025
2002	**Sam Hornish Jr.**	Dallara Oldsmobile	Panther Racing	15	5	2	2,470,615
2003	**Scott Dixon**	G-Force Toyota	Target Chip Ganassi	16	3	5	1,481,265

Note: In 1996, Calkins and Sharp were named co-champions after finishing the series tied in drivers' points (246).

IRL Rookie of the Year

Officially the Bombardier Rookie of the Year Award, presented to rookie driver who accumulates the most points in the IRL standings.

Year		Year		Year		Year	
1996	None	1998	Robby Unser	2000	Airton Dare	2002	Laurent Redon
1997	Jim Guthrie	1999	Scott Harrington	2001	Felipe Giaffone	2003	Dan Wheldon

All-Time IRL Leaders

IRL IndyCar Series all-time Top 10 drivers in victories, pole positions and earnings, based on records through Oct. 3, 2004. Earnings totals include season-ending contingency awards. Drivers active in 2004 are in **bold** type. (*) Denotes driver is active, but in NASCAR Nextel Cup Series.

	Victories			Pole Positions			Earnings	
1	**Sam Hornish Jr.**	12	1	**Greg Ray**	13	1	**Buddy Lazier**	$9,132,399
2	**Buddy Lazier**	8	2	Billy Boat	9	2	**Sam Hornish Jr.**	7,808,195
	Scott Sharp	8	3	**Helio Castroneves**	8	3	**Scott Sharp**	6,975,198
4	Eddie Cheever Jr.	5	4	Tony Stewart*	7	4	**Helio Castroneves**	6,774,745
	Greg Ray	5	5	**Scott Sharp**	5	5	Eddie Cheever Jr.	6,265,893
	Helio Castroneves	5		Gil de Ferran	5	6	**Greg Ray**	6,250,690
	Gil de Ferran	5		**Scott Dixon**	5	7	Kenny Brack	5,707,770
8	Kenny Brack	4		**Tony Kanaan**	5	8	**Robbie Buhl**	5,095,158
	Arie Luyendyk	4		Tomas Scheckter	5	9	Billy Boat	4,949,505
	Tony Kanaan	4		**Buddy Rice**	5	10	Jeff Ward	4,586,140

FORMULA ONE CIRCUIT

United States Grand Prix

Federation Internationale Sportive Automobile (FISA) sanctioned two annual U.S. Grand Prix–USA/East and USA/West–from 1976-80 and 1983-84. Phoenix was the site of the U.S. Grand Prix from 1989-91. Indianapolis Motor Speedway has hosted the U.S. Grand Prix since 2000.

Indianapolis 500

Officially sanctioned as Grand Prix race from 1950-60 only. See page 895 for details.

U.S. Grand Prix—East

Held from 1959-80 and 1981-88 at the following locations: Sebring, Fla. (1959); Riverside, Calif. (1960); Watkins Glen, N.Y. (1961-80); and Detroit (1982-88). There was no race in 1981. Race discontinued in 1989.

Multiple winners: Jim Clark, Graham Hill and Ayrton Senna (3); James Hunt, Carlos Reutemann and Jackie Stewart (2).

Year		Car	Year		Car
1959	Bruce McLaren, NZE	Cooper Climax	1974	Carlos Reutemann, ARG	Brabham Ford
1960	Stirling Moss, GBR	Lotus Climax	1975	Niki Lauda, AUT	Ferrari
1961	Innes Ireland, GBR	Lotus Climax	1976	James Hunt, GBR	McLaren Ford
1962	Jim Clark, GBR	Lotus Climax	1977	James Hunt, GBR	McLaren Ford
1963	Graham Hill, GBR	BRM	1978	Carlos Reutemann, ARG	Ferrari
1964	Graham Hill, GBR	BRM	1979	Gilles Villeneuve, CAN	Ferrari
1965	Graham Hill, GBR	BRM	1980	Alan Jones, AUS	Williams Ford
1966	Jim Clark, GBR	Lotus BRM	1981	Not held	
1967	Jim Clark, GBR	Lotus Ford	1982	John Watson, GBR	McLaren Ford
1968	Jackie Stewart, GBR	Matra Ford	1983	Michele Alboreto, ITA	Tyrrell Ford
1969	Jochen Rindt, AUT	Lotus Ford	1984	Nelson Piquet, BRA	Brabham BMW Turbo
1970	Emerson Fittipaldi, BRA	Lotus Ford	1985	Keke Rosberg, FIN	Williams Honda Turbo
1971	Francois Cevert, FRA	Tyrrell Ford	1986	Ayrton Senna, BRA	Lotus Renault Turbo
1972	Jackie Stewart, GBR	Tyrrell Ford	1987	Ayrton Senna, BRA	Lotus Honda Turbo
1973	Ronnie Peterson, SWE	Lotus Ford	1988	Ayrton Senna, BRA	McLaren Honda Turbo

Formula One Circuit (Cont.)

U.S. Grand Prix—West

Held from 1976-83 at Long Beach, Calif. Races also held in Las Vegas (1981-82), Dallas (1984) and Phoenix (1989-91). Race discontinued in 1992.

Multiple winners: Alan Jones and Ayrton Senna (2).

Year		Car	Year		Car
1976	Clay Regazzoni, SWI	Ferrari	1983	John Watson, GBR	McLaren Ford
1977	Mario Andretti, USA	Lotus Ford	1984	Keke Rosberg, FIN	Williams Honda Turbo
1978	Carlos Reutemann, ARG	Ferrari	1985-88	Not held	
1979	Gilles Villeneuve, CAN	Ferrari	1989	Alain Prost, FRA	McLaren Honda
1980	Nelson Piquet, BRA	Brabham Ford	1990	Ayrton Senna, BRA	McLaren Honda
1981	Alan Jones, AUS	Williams Ford	1991	Ayrton Senna, BRA	McLaren Honda
1982	Niki Lauda, AUT	McLaren Ford			

U.S. Grand Prix

Held since 2000 at Indianapolis Motor Speedway.

Multiple winner: Michael Schumacher (3).

Year		Car	Year		Car
2000	Michael Schumacher, GER	Ferrari	2003	Michael Schumacher, GER	Ferrari
2001	Mika Hakkinen, FIN	McLaren Mercedes	2004	Michael Schumacher, GER	Ferrari
2002	Rubens Barrichello, BRA	Ferrari			

World Champions

Officially called the World Championship of Drivers and based on Formula One (Grand Prix) records through the 2003 season.
Note: With one race remaining in the 2004 season, Michael Schumacher had unofficially clinched the World Championship.
Multiple winners: Michael Schumacher (6); Juan-Manuel Fangio (5); Alain Prost (4); Jack Brabham, Niki Lauda, Nelson Piquet, Ayrton Senna and Jackie Stewart (3); Alberto Ascari, Jim Clark, Emerson Fittipaldi, Mika Hakkinen and Graham Hill (2).

Year	Driver	Country	Car	Sts	Wins	Poles	Runner(s)-up
1950	**Guiseppe Farina**	Italy	Alfa Romeo	7	3	2	J.M. Fangio, ARG
1951	**Juan-Manuel Fangio**	Argentina	Alfa Romeo	8	3	4	A. Ascari, ITA
1952	**Alberto Ascari**	Italy	Ferrari	8	6	5	G. Farina, ITA
1953	**Alberto Ascari**	Italy	Ferrari	9	5	6	J.M. Fangio, ARG
1954	**Juan-Manuel Fangio**	Argentina	Maserati/Mercedes	9	6	5	F. Gonzalez, ARG
1955	**Juan-Manuel Fangio**	Argentina	Mercedes	7	4	3	S. Moss, GBR
1956	**Juan-Manuel Fangio**	Argentina	Lancia/Ferrari	8	3	5	S. Moss, GBR
1957	**Juan-Manuel Fangio**	Argentina	Maserati	8	4	4	S. Moss, GBR
1958	**Mike Hawthorn**	Great Britain	Ferrari	11	1	4	S. Moss, GBR
1959	**Jack Brabham**	Australia	Cooper Climax	9	2	1	T. Brooks, GBR
1960	**Jack Brabham**	Australia	Cooper Climax	10	5	3	B. McLaren, NZE
1961	**Phil Hill**	United States	Ferrari	8	2	5	W. von Trips, GER
1962	**Graham Hill**	Great Britain	BRM	9	4	1	J. Clark, GBR
1963	**Jim Clark**	Great Britain	Lotus Climax	10	7	7	G. Hill, GBR & R. Ginther, USA
1964	**John Surtees**	Great Britain	Ferrari	10	2	2	G. Hill, GBR
1965	**Jim Clark**	Great Britain	Lotus Climax	10	6	6	G. Hill, GBR
1966	**Jack Brabham**	Australia	Brabham Repco	9	4	3	J. Surtees, GBR
1967	**Denis Hulme**	New Zealand	Brabham Repco	11	2	0	J. Brabham, AUS
1968	**Graham Hill**	Great Britain	Lotus Ford	12	3	2	J. Stewart, GBR
1969	**Jackie Stewart**	Great Britain	Matra Ford	11	6	2	J. Ickx, BEL
1970	**Jochen Rindt**	Austria	Lotus Ford	13	5	3	J. Ickx, BEL
1971	**Jackie Stewart**	Great Britain	Tyrrell Ford	11	6	6	R. Peterson, SWE
1972	**Emerson Fittipaldi**	Brazil	Lotus Ford	12	5	3	J. Stewart, GBR
1973	**Jackie Stewart**	Great Britain	Tyrrell Ford	15	5	3	E. Fittipaldi, BRA
1974	**Emerson Fittipaldi**	Brazil	McLaren Ford	15	3	2	C. Regazzoni, SWI
1975	**Niki Lauda**	Austria	Ferrari	14	5	9	E. Fittipaldi, BRA
1976	**James Hunt**	Great Britain	McLaren Ford	16	6	8	N. Lauda, AUT
1977	**Niki Lauda**	Austria	Ferrari	17	3	2	J. Scheckter, RSA
1978	**Mario Andretti**	United States	Lotus Ford	16	6	8	R. Peterson, SWE
1979	**Jody Scheckter**	South Africa	Ferrari	15	3	1	G. Villeneuve, CAN
1980	**Alan Jones**	Australia	Williams Ford	14	5	3	N. Piquet, BRA
1981	**Nelson Piquet**	Brazil	Brabham Ford	15	3	4	C. Reutemann, ARG
1982	**Keke Rosberg**	Finland	Williams Ford	16	1	0	D. Pironi, FRA & J. Watson, GBR
1983	**Nelson Piquet**	Brazil	Brabham BMW Turbo	15	3	1	A. Prost, FRA
1984	**Niki Lauda**	Austria	McL. TAG Turbo	16	5	0	A. Prost, FRA
1985	**Alain Prost**	France	McL. TAG Turbo	16	5	2	M. Alboreto, ITA
1986	**Alain Prost**	France	McL. TAG Turbo	16	4	1	N. Mansell, GBR
1987	**Nelson Piquet**	Brazil	Williams Honda Turbo	16	3	4	N. Mansell, GBR

Year	Driver	Country	Car	Sts	Wins	Poles	Runner(s)-up
1988	**Ayrton Senna**	Brazil	McLaren Honda Turbo	16	8	13	A. Prost, FRA
1989	**Alain Prost**	France	McLaren Honda	16	4	2	A. Senna, BRA
1990	**Ayrton Senna**	Brazil	McLaren Honda	16	6	10	A. Prost, FRA
1991	**Ayrton Senna**	Brazil	McLaren Honda	16	7	8	N. Mansell, GBR
1992	**Nigel Mansell**	Great Britain	Williams Renault	16	9	14	R. Patrese, ITA
1993	**Alain Prost**	France	Williams Renault	16	7	13	A. Senna, BRA
1994	**Michael Schumacher**	Germany	Benetton Ford	14	8	6	D. Hill, GBR
1995	**Michael Schumacher**	Germany	Benetton Renault	17	9	4	D. Hill, GBR
1996	**Damon Hill**	Great Britain	Williams Renault	16	8	9	J. Villeneuve, CAN
1997	**Jacques Villeneuve**	Canada	Williams Renault	17	7	10	H.H. Frentzen, GER
1998	**Mika Hakkinen**	Finland	McLaren Mercedes	16	8	9	M. Schumacher, GER
1999	**Mika Hakkinen**	Finland	McLaren Mercedes	16	5	11	E. Irvine, GBR
2000	**Michael Schumacher**	Germany	Ferrari	17	9	9	M. Hakkinen, FIN
2001	**Michael Schumacher**	Germany	Ferrari	17	9	11	D. Coulthard, GBR
2002	**Michael Schumacher**	Germany	Ferrari	17	11	7	R. Barrichello, BRA
2003	**Michael Schumacher**	Germany	Ferrari	16	6	5	K. Raikkonen, FIN

All-Time Leaders

The all-time Top 15 Grand Prix winning drivers, based on records through Oct. 10, 2004. Listed are starts (Sts), poles won (Pole), wins (1st), second place finishes (2nd), and third (3rd). Drivers active in 2004 and career victories in **bold** type.

		Sts	Pole	1st	2nd	3rd			Sts	Pole	1st	2nd	3rd
1	**M. Schumacher**	212	63	**83**	32	19	9	Nelson Piquet	207	24	**23**	20	17
2	Alain Prost	199	33	**51**	35	20	10	Damon Hill	99	20	**22**	15	5
3	Ayrton Senna	161	65	**41**	23	16	11	Mika Hakkinen	163	27	**20**	14	17
4	Nigel Mansell	187	32	**31**	17	11	12	Stirling Moss	66	16	**16**	5	3
5	Jackie Stewart	99	17	**27**	11	5	13	Jack Brabham	126	13	**14**	10	7
6	Jim Clark	72	33	**25**	1	6		Emerson Fittipaldi	144	6	**14**	13	8
	Niki Lauda	171	24	**25**	20	9		Graham Hill	176	13	**14**	15	7
8	Juan-Manuel Fangio	51	28	**24**	10	1							

ENDURANCE RACES

The 24 Hours of Le Mans

Officially, the Le Mans Grand Prix. First run May 22-23, 1923. All subsequent races have been held in June, except in 1956 (July) and 1968 (September). Originally contested on a 10.73-mile track, the circuit was shortened to 8.383 miles in 1932 and has fluxuated around 8.5 miles ever since.

Multiple winners: Jacky Ickx and Tom Kristensen (6); Derek Bell (5); Yannick Dalmas, Oliver Gendebien and Henri Pescarolo (4); Woolf Barnato, Frank Biela, Luigi Chinetti, Hurley Haywood, Phil Hill, Al Holbert, Klaus Ludwig and Emanuele Pirro (3); Sir Henry Birkin, Ivoe Bueb, Rinaldo Capello, Ron Flockhart, Jean-Pierre Jaussaud, Gerard Larrousse, Andre Rossignol, Raymond Sommer, Hans Stuck, Gijs van Lennep and Jean-Pierre Wimille (2).

Year	Drivers	Car	MPH	Year	Drivers	Car	MPH
1923	Andre Lagache & Rene Leonard	Chenard & Walcker	57.21	1935	John Hindmarsh & Louis Fontes	Lagonda	77.85
1924	John Duff & Francis Clement	Bentley	53.78	1936	Not held		
1925	Gerard de Courcelles & Andre Rossignol	La Lorraine	57.84	1937	Jean-Pierre Wimille & Robert Benoist	Bugatti 57G	85.13
1926	Robert Bloch & Andre Rossignol	La Lorraine	66.08	1938	Eugene Chaboud & Jean Tremoulet	Delahaye	82.36
1927	J.D. Benjafield & Sammy Davis	Bentley	61.35	1939	Jean-Pierre Wimille & Pierre Veyron	Bugatti 57G	86.86
1928	Woolf Barnato & Bernard Rubin	Bentley	69.11	1940-48	Not held		
1929	Woolf Barnato & Sir Henry Birkin	Bentley Speed 6	73.63	1949	Luigi Chinetti & Lord Selsdon	Ferrari	82.28
1930	Woolf Barnato & Glen Kidston	Bentley Speed 6	75.88	1950	Louis Rosier & Jean-Louis Rosier	Talbot-Lago	89.71
1931	Earl Howe & Sir Henry Birkin	Alfa Romeo	78.13	1951	Peter Walker & Peter Whitehead	Jaguar C	93.50
1932	Raymond Sommer & Luigi Chinetti	Alfa Romeo	76.48	1952	Hermann Lang & Fritz Reiss	Mercedes-Benz	96.67
1933	Raymond Sommer & Tazio Nuvolari	Alfa Romeo	81.40	1953	Tony Rolt & Duncan Hamilton	Jaguar C	98.65
1934	Luigi Chinetti & Philippe Etancelin	Alfa Romeo	74.74	1954	Froilan Gonzalez & Maurice Trintignant	Ferrari 375	105.13
				1955	Mike Hawthorn & Ivor Bueb	Jaguar D	107.05

ENDURANCE RACES (Cont.)

Year	Drivers	Car	MPH
1956	Ron Flockhart & Ninian Sanderson	Jaguar D	104.47
1957	Ron Flockhart & Ivor Bueb	Jaguar D	113.83
1958	Oliver Gendebien & Phil Hill	Ferrari 250	106.18
1959	Roy Salvadori & Carroll Shelby	Aston Martin	112.55
1960	Oliver Gendebien & Paul Fräre	Ferrari 250	109.17
1961	Oliver Gendebien & Phil Hill	Ferrari 250	115.88
1962	Oliver Gendebien & Phil Hill	Ferrari 250	115.22
1963	Lodovico Scarfiotti & Lorenzo Bandini	Ferrari 250	118.08
1964	Jean Guichel & Nino Vaccarella	Ferrari 275	121.54
1965	Masten Gregory & Jochen Rindt	Ferrari 250	121.07
1966	Bruce McLaren & Chris Amon	Ford Mk. II	125.37
1967	A.J. Foyt & Dan Gurney	Ford Mk. IV	135.46
1968	Pedro Rodriguez & Lucien Bianchi	Ford GT40	115.27
1969	Jacky Ickx & Jackie Oliver	Ford GT40	129.38
1970	Hans Herrmann & Richard Attwood	Porsche 917	119.28
1971	Gijs van Lennep & Helmut Marko	Porsche 917	138.13
1972	Graham Hill & Henri Pescarolo	Matra-Simca	121.45
1973	Henri Pescarolo & Gerard Larrousse	Matra-Simca	125.67
1974	Henri Pescarolo & Gerard Larrousse	Matra-Simca	119.27
1975	Derek Bell & Jacky Ickx	Mirage-Ford	118.98
1976	Jacky Ickx & Gijs van Lennep	Porsche 936	123.49
1977	Jacky Ickx, Jurgen Barth & Hurley Haywood	Porsche 936	120.95
1978	Jean-Pierre Jaussaud & Didier Pironi	Renault-Alpine	130.60
1979	Klaus Ludwig, Bill Wittington & Don Whittington	Porsche 935	108.10
1980	Jean-Pierre Jaussaud & Jean Rondeau	Rondeau-Cosworth	119.23
1981	Jacky Ickx & Derek Bell	Porsche 936	124.94
1982	Jacky Ickx & Derek Bell	Porsche 956	126.85
1983	Vern Schuppan, Hurley Haywood & Al Holbert	Porsche 956	130.70
1984	Klaus Ludwig & Henri Pescarolo	Porsche 956	126.88
1985	Klaus Ludwig, Paolo Barilla & John Winter	Porsche 956	131.75
1986	Derek Bell, Hans Stuck & Al Holbert	Porsche 962	128.75
1987	Derek Bell, Hans Stuck & Al Holbert	Porsche 962	124.06
1988	Jan Lammers, Johnny Dumfries & Andy Wallace	Jaguar XJR	137.75
1989	Jochen Mass, Manuel Reuter & Stanley Dickens	Sauber-Mercedes	136.39
1990	John Nielsen, Price Cobb & Martin Brundle	Jaguar XJR-12	126.71
1991	Volker Weider, Johnny Herbert & Bertrand Gachof	Mazda 787B	127.31
1992	Derek Warwick, Yannick Dalmas & Mark Blundell	Peugeot 905B	123.89
1993	Geoff Brabham, Christophe Bouchut & Eric Helary	Peugeot 905	132.58
1994	Yannick Dalmas, Hurley Haywood & Mauro Baldi	Porsche 962LM	129.82
1995	Yannick Dalmas, J.J. Lehto & Masanori Sekiya	McLaren BMW	105.00
1996	Davy Jones, Manuel Reuter & Alexander Wurz	TWR Porsche	124.65
1997	Michele Alberto, Stefan Johansson & Tom Kristensen	TWR Porsche	126.88
1998	Laurent Aiello, Allan McNish & Stephane Ortelli	Porsche 911 GT1	123.86
1999	Yannick Dalmas, Joachim Winkelhock & Pierluigi Martini	BMW V-12 LMR	129.38
2000	Frank Biela, Tom Kristensen & Emanuele Pirro	Audi R8	128.34
2001	Frank Biela, Tom Kristensen & Emanuele Pirro	Audi R8	129.66
2002	Frank Biela, Tom Kristensen & Emanuele Pirro	Audi R8	131.89
2003	Tom Kristensen, Rinaldo Capello & Guy Smith	Bentley Speed 8	143.43
2004	Tom Kristensen, Rinaldo Capello & Seiji Ara	Audi R8	133.86

The original start to the 24 Hours of Le Mans had drivers sprinting across the track to their unstarted cars. This practice was unsafe, however, as drivers would commonly take off without fastening their safety harnesses.

In 1969, Jacky Ickx took a stand by calmly walking to his car and fastening his harness belt before starting his engine. He went on to win the race...and he made his point. The "Le Mans start" was discontinued in 1970.

The 24 Hours of Daytona

Officially, the Rolex 24 at Daytona. First run in 1962 as a three-hour race and won by Dan Gurney in a Lotus 19 Ford. Contested over a 3.56-mile course at Daytona (Fla.) International Speedway. There have been several distance changes since 1962: the event was a three-hour race (1962-63); a 2,000-kilometer race (1964-65); a 24-hour race (1966-71); a six-hour race (1972) and a 24-hour race again since 1973. The race was canceled in 1974 due to a national energy crisis.

Multiple winners: Hurley Haywood (5); Peter Gregg, Pedro Rodriguez and Bob Wollek (4); Derek Bell, Butch Leitzinger, Rolf Stommelen and Andy Wallace (3); Mauro Baldi, A.J. Foyt, Al Holbert, Ken Miles, John Paul Jr., Brian Redman, Elliott Forbes-Robinson, Lloyd Ruby, Didier Theys and Al Unser Jr. (2).

Year	Drivers	Car	MPH	Year	Drivers	Car	MPH
1962	Dan Gurney	Lotus 19 Ford	104.101	1988	Raul Boesel, Martin Brundle & John Nielsen	Jaguar XJR-9	107.943
1963	Pedro Rodriguez	Ferrari GTO	102.074	1989	John Andretti, Derek Bell & Bob Wollek	Porsche 962	92.009
1964	Pedro Rodriguez & Phil Hill	Ferrari GTO	98.230	1990	Davy Jones, Jan Lammers & Andy Wallace	Jaguar XJR-12	112.857
1965	Ken Miles & Lloyd Ruby	Ford GT	99.944	1991	Hurley Haywood, John Winter, Frank Jelinski, Henri Pescarolo & Bob Wollek	Porsche 962-C	106.633
1966	Ken Miles & Lloyd Ruby	Ford Mk. II	108.020	1992	Masahiro Hasemi, Kazuyoshi Hoshino & Toshio Suzuki	Nissan R-91	112.897
1967	Lorenzo Bandini & Chris Amon	Ferrari 330	105.688	1993	P.J. Jones, Mark Dismore & Rocky Moran	Toyota Eagle	103.537
1968	Vic Elford & Jochen Neerpasch	Porsche 907	106.697	1994	Paul Gentilozzi, Scott Pruett, Butch Leitzinger & Steve Millen	Nissan 300 ZXT	104.80
1969	Mark Donohue & Chuck Parsons	Lola Chevrolet	99.268	1995	Jurgen Lassig, Christophe Bouchut, Giovanni Lavaggi & Marco Werner	Porsche Spyder	102.280
1970	Pedro Rodriguez & Leo Kinnunen	Porsche 917	114.866	1996	Wayne Taylor, Scott Sharp & Jim Pace	Oldsmobile Arness MK-III	103.32
1971	Pedro Rodriguez & Jackie Oliver	Porsche 917K	109.203	1997	Rob Dyson, James Weaver, Butch Leitzinger, Andy Wallace, John Paul Jr., Eliot Forbes-Robinson & John Schneider	Ford R&S MK-III	102.29
1972	Mario Andretti & Jacky Ickx	Ferrari 312P	122.573	1998	Mauro Baldi, Arie Luyendyk, Gianpiero Moretti & Didier Theys	Ferrari 333	105.40
1973	Peter Gregg & Hurley Haywood	Porsche Carrera	106.225	1999	Elliot Forbes-Robinson, Butch Leitzinger & Andy Wallace	Riley & Scott Ford	104.957
1974	Not held			2000	Olivier Beretta, Dominique Dupuy & Karl Wendlinger	Dodge Viper	107.207
1975	Peter Gregg & Hurley Haywood	Porsche Carrera	108.531	2001	Ron Fellows, Franck Freon, Chris Kneifel & Johnny O'Connell	Chevy Corvette	97.293
1976	Peter Gregg, Brian Redman & John Fitzpatrick	BMW CSL	104.040	2002	Mauro Baldi, Fredy Lienhard, Max Papis & Didier Theys	Dallara LMP900	106.143
1977	Hurley Haywood, John Graves & Dave Helmick	Porsche Carrera	108.801	2003	Kevin Buckler, Michael Schrom, Timo Bernhard & Jorg Bergmeister	Porsche GT3 RS	115.969
1978	Peter Gregg, Rolf Stommelen & Antoine Hezemans	Porsche Turbo	108.743	2004	Terry Borcheller, Forest Barber, Andy Pilgrim & Christian Fittipaldi	Pontiac Doran	77.927
1979	Hurley Haywood, Ted Field & Danny Ongais	Porsche Turbo	109.249				
1980	Rolf Stommelen, Volkert Merl & Reinhold Joest	Porsche Turbo	114.303				
1981	Bobby Rahal, Brian Redman & Bob Garretson	Porsche Turbo	113.153				
1982	John Paul Sr., John Paul Jr. & Rolf Stommelen	Porsche Turbo	114.794				
1983	A.J. Foyt, Preston Henn, Bob Wollek & Claude Ballot-Lena	Porsche Turbo	98.781				
1984	Sarel van der Merwe, Tony Martin & Graham Duxbury	March Porsche	103.119				
1985	A.J. Foyt, Bob Wollek, Al Unser Sr. & Thierry Boutsen	Porsche 962	104.162				
1986	Al Holbert, Derek Bell & Al Unser Jr.	Porsche 962	105.484				
1987	Al Holbert, Derek Bell, Chip Robinson & Al Unser Jr.	Porsche 962	111.599				

NHRA DRAG RACING

NHRA Champions

Based on points earned during the NHRA POWERade Drag Racing series. The series, originally sponsored by the R.J. Reynolds Tobacco Company's Winston brand, began for Top Fuel, Funny Car and Pro Stock in 1975. The Coca-Cola Company's POWERade brand soft drink began a five-year sponsorship deal with the series in 2002.

Top Fuel

Multiple winners: Joe Amato (5); Don Garlits, Shirley Muldowney and Gary Scelzi (3); Kenny Bernstein, Larry Dixon and Scott Kalitta (2).

Year		Year		Year		Year	
1975	Don Garlits	1983	Gary Beck	1991	Joe Amato	1999	Tony Schumacher
1976	Richard Tharp	1984	Joe Amato	1992	Joe Amato	2000	Gary Scelzi
1977	Shirley Muldowney	1985	Don Garlits	1993	Eddie Hill	2001	Kenny Bernstein
1978	Kelly Brown	1986	Don Garlits	1994	Scott Kalitta	2002	Larry Dixon
1979	Rob Bruins	1987	Dick LaHaie	1995	Scott Kalitta	2003	Larry Dixon
1980	Shirley Muldowney	1988	Joe Amato	1996	Kenny Bernstein		
1981	Jeb Allen	1989	Gary Ormsby	1997	Gary Scelzi		
1982	Shirley Muldowney	1990	Joe Amato	1998	Gary Scelzi		

Funny Car

Multiple winners: John Force (12); Don Prudhomme, Kenny Bernstein (4); Raymond Beadle (3); Frank Hawley (2).

Year		Year		Year		Year	
1975	Don Prudhomme	1983	Frank Hawley	1991	John Force	1999	John Force
1976	Don Prudhomme	1984	Mark Oswald	1992	Cruz Pedregon	2000	John Force
1977	Don Prudhomme	1985	Kenny Bernstein	1993	John Force	2001	John Force
1978	Don Prudhomme	1986	Kenny Bernstein	1994	John Force	2002	John Force
1979	Raymond Beadle	1987	Kenny Bernstein	1995	John Force	2003	Tony Pedregon
1980	Raymond Beadle	1988	Kenny Bernstein	1996	John Force		
1981	Raymond Beadle	1989	Bruce Larson	1997	John Force		
1982	Frank Hawley	1990	John Force	1998	John Force		

Pro Stock

Multiple winners: Bob Glidden (9); Warren Johnson (6); Lee Shepherd (4); Darrell Alderman, Jeg Coughlin Jr. and Jim Yates (2).

Year		Year		Year		Year	
1975	Bob Glidden	1983	Lee Shepherd	1991	Darrell Alderman	1999	Warren Johnson
1976	Larry Lombardo	1984	Lee Shepherd	1992	Warren Johnson	2000	Jeg Coughlin Jr.
1977	Don Nicholson	1985	Bob Glidden	1993	Warren Johnson	2001	Warren Johnson
1978	Bob Glidden	1986	Bob Glidden	1994	Darrell Alderman	2002	Jeg Coughlin Jr.
1979	Bob Glidden	1987	Bob Glidden	1995	Warren Johnson	2003	Greg Anderson
1980	Bob Glidden	1988	Bob Glidden	1996	Jim Yates		
1981	Lee Shepherd	1989	Bob Glidden	1997	Jim Yates		
1982	Lee Shepherd	1990	John Myers	1998	Warren Johnson		

All-Time Leaders
Career Victories

All-time leaders through Oct. 10, 2004. Drivers active in 2004 are in **bold**.

	Top Fuel			Funny Car			Pro Stock	
1	Joe Amato	52	1	**John Force**	113	1	**Warren Johnson**	92
2	Kenny Bernstein	39	2	Don Prudhomme	35	2	Bob Glidden	85
3	Don Garlits	35	3	Kenny Bernstein	30	3	**Jeg Coughlin**	33
	Larry Dixon	35	4	**Tony Pedregon**	27	4	**Greg Anderson**	29
5	**Cory McClenathan**	28	5	**Cruz Pedregon**	23	5	**Darrell Alderman**	28
							Kurt Johnson	28

Fastest Mile-Per-Hour Speeds

Fastest performances in NHRA major event history through Oct. 10, 2004.

Top Fuel	Funny Car	Pro Stock
MPH	**MPH**	**MPH**
335.57 . . . . . Doug Kalitta, 4/3/2004	333.58 . . . . John Force, 10/3/2004	207.75 . Greg Anderson, 10/2/2004
333.95 . . Scott Kalitta, 10/12/2003	333.25 . Whit Bazemore, 5/23/2004	207.40 . . . . Jason Line, 10/2/2004
333.91 . . Doug Kalitta, 4/11/2004	332.75 . . . . John Force, 10/2/2004	207.30 . . Dave Connolly, 10/2/2004
333.74 . . . . . Scott Kalitta, 4/3/2004	331.28 . Tony Pedregon, 5/22/2004	207.21 . Greg Anderson, 10/2/2004
333.66 . Brandon Bernstein, 4/4/2004	330.55 . . . Gary Scelzi, 5/22/2004	207.18 . Greg Anderson, 5/18/2003

Boxing

*Hard-hitting middleweight **Felix Trinidad** made a triumphant return to boxing in 2004.*

Hopkins Keeps Belts, Wins Purse

In the year's most anticipated bout, Bernard Hopkins cements his place in history, defending his title yet again.

Gerry Brown
is co-editor of the ESPN Sports Almanac.

The biggest fight of the year was a bit of a dud.

Then, quickly, Bernard Hopkins ended it. Defending his home turf in the 160-pound middleweight division, Hopkins put a bigger hurt on Oscar De La Hoya's liver than pounding 160 shots of Mexican tequila would, knocking out the golden boy in the ninth round with a perfect body shot.

"I felt a sense of urgency," Hopkins said. "I wasn't sure if I was winning or not."

He was, at least on two of the three judges' scorecards. But a veteran like Hopkins was taking no chances and spared no expense with the knockout blow, a ferocious left hook that brought the former four-time world champion to his knees.

"I was stuck, just stuck," De La Hoya would say later. "You want to get up, you just can't."

De La Hoya's only consolation could be the fact that he took home $30 million, three times his foe's take. Still with Hopkins' ability to stretch a buck (he's a Costco regular), imagine

what he'll be able to do with the $10 million he was guaranteed for the fight. That will buy a lot of jumbo-sized jars of pickles.

It was, by far, the biggest purse of Hopkins' long career. A career that, despite his continued success and stubborn refusal to grow old, is much closer to its end that its start. Hopkins is 39 years old and made a promise to his late mother before she died that he would not fight beyond age 40.

His mother might have understood his reticence to hang up the gloves if people keep giving him $10 million checks to beat people up. But money has never been the primary motivation for Hopkins and, even if it was, his promise might be easier to keep than some people think. The monster payday he made against De La Hoya (thanks to De La Hoya's broad appeal) will not be easily repeated. There are few fights that could be made in the near future that could approach it.

Former champ Felix Trinidad came out of retirement after more than two years off and looked as if he never

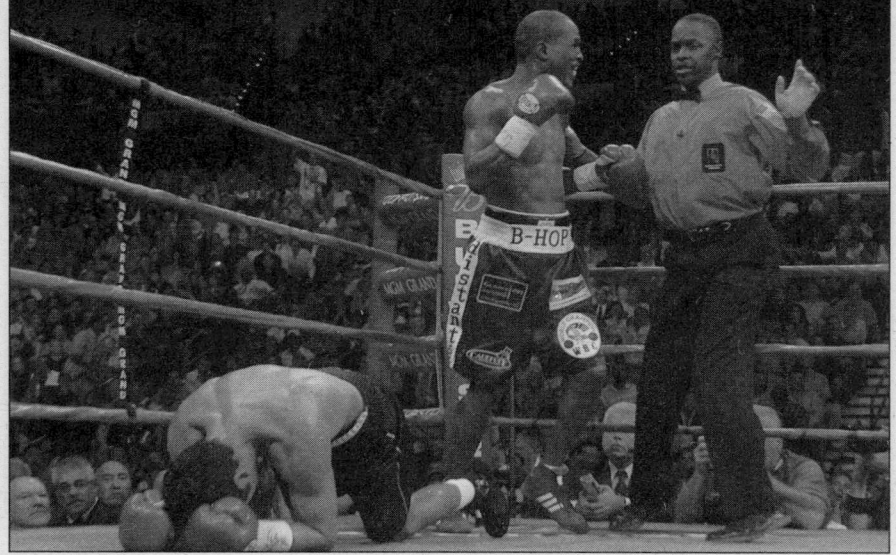

AP/Wide World Photos

Bernard Hopkins floored Oscar De La Hoya with a body shot in their much anticipated 2004 meeting, ending the fight in the ninth round, and keeping his middleweight titles.

left, outgunning Ricardo Mayorga in their October battle.

A rematch of the fight that preceded and largely precipitated Trinidad's first retirement—a knockout loss to Hopkins, the first of Trinidad's career—is a potential mega-money fight but Trinidad's promoter, Don King, whom Hopkins is loathe to do business with, could be the deal breaker.

And if Hopkins tries to forget that fighters can get old fast, he need look no further than the last man to defeat him (in a lopsided decision way back in 1993), Roy Jones Jr.

In search of a new challenge, Jones moved up to heavyweight and took John Ruiz's WBA belt in 2003 before returning to light heavyweight to face Antonio Tarver last November. Jones beat Tarver by majority decision but showed definite signs of mortality. Many observers chalked it up to the detrimental effects of the rapid weight loss that he underwent to shed the 20 pounds of muscle he painstakingly added before facing Ruiz. But a May rematch with Tarver told a different tale.

In that fight, another big left-hook, this one to the jaw, ended things in a jiffy when Tarver caught Jones in the second round. It was a large dose of vindication for Tarver, who all but shouted from the rooftops that he thought he was robbed by the judges in his first fight with Jones, who was, until the Tarver loss, considered by many to be boxing's pound-for-pound champ.

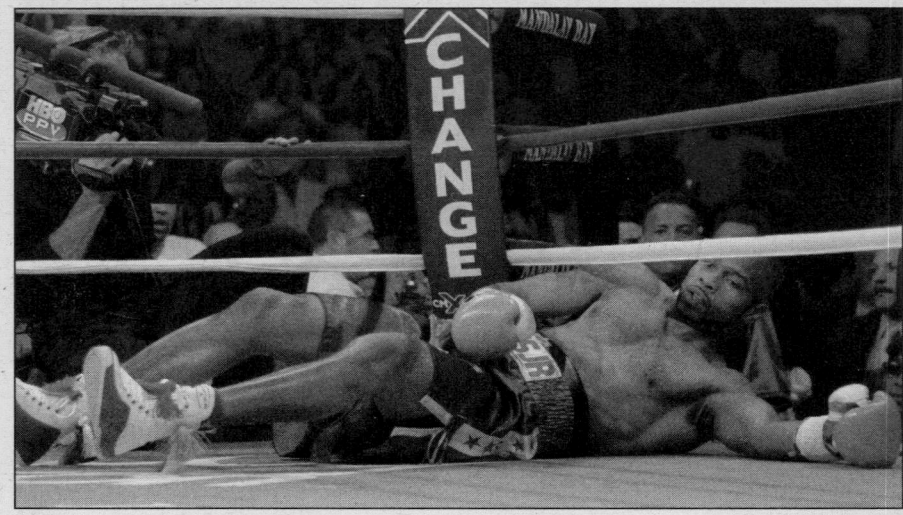

AP/Wide World Photos

Change atop the pound-for-pound rankings was looming when **Roy Jones Jr.** *was knocked out by Antonio Tarver in May 2004.*

Jones, at 35 years old, looked to get his own career back in order (and perhaps line up a third fight with Tarver) when he faced journeyman champion Glen Johnson in September. But all of a sudden Jones looked worse than mortal, he looked dead.

This time, against a much lower regarded opponent than Tarver, it was an accumulation of blows that did in Jones and he fell in the ninth round, perhaps bringing an abrupt end to a Hall of Fame career.

But before he calls it quits, maybe Jones will move down to middleweight in 2005 (or meet at a catch weight) for a rematch with Hopkins, who has now successfully defended the middleweight title 19 times, a record for the division.

Hopkins has plans for a 20th defense to cement his legacy and then has stated he'd be willing to move out of the division for the right opportunity. Furthermore he's made no secret of his long simmering desire for a Jones rematch, one that Jones was never in a hurry to grant, until perhaps now. It could be a fight that—win or lose—ends the careers of two great fighters and one which Hopkins' mother wouldn't blame him for taking.

In the meanwhile, De La Hoya and Trinidad seem destined for a rematch of their own. Trinidad won their first meeting and De La Hoya would love to give him some Tarver-style payback in a fight that could bring him the career-defining satisfaction that Hopkins denied him in 2004.

The Ten Biggest Stories of the Year in Boxing

10 British teenager Amir Khan impresses many seasoned observers and the 17-year-old wins Olympic silver in Athens, falling short against a more experienced opponent— Cuba's 33-year-old Mario Cesar Kindelan—in the lightweight gold medal bout.

9 Despite questions about brain damage, former undisputed heavyweight champ Riddick Bowe undertakes a comeback at age 37, following an eight-year hiatus from the sport. Bowe wins his first bout on a second-round TKO over unknown fighter Marcus Rhode in Shawnee, Oklahoma.

8 Former undisputed heavyweight champion Mike Tyson, once the most feared fighter in the world, loses his latest comeback fight, this time by TKO to unheralded Briton Danny Williams. Tyson's corner later blames a twisted knee as the reason for the fighter's fifth career loss.

7 Former light heavyweight champion Antonio Tarver gets his revenge when he takes back his belt from Roy Jones Jr. in May after losing by majority-decision in November 2003. Tarver does it in dramatic fashion, handing Jones the first knockout loss of his long career with a perfect left hook in the second round.

6 Veteran southpaw and 5-to-2 underdog Ronald "Winky" Wright, after being avoided for years by boxing's biggest names, gets some long-awaited sweet rewards when he wins a unanimous decision over "Sugar" Shane Mosley to unify the junior middleweight belts in Las Vegas.

5 American light heavyweight Andre Ward, fighting in memory of his late father, wins a gold medal in Athens, somewhat salvaging another disappointing Olympics for USA Boxing. It's the first boxing gold for the United States since David Reid's win in 1996.

4 Long-time heavyweight champion Lennox Lewis officially announces his retirement from boxing in February. Lewis leaves a legacy of big wins (over Evander Holyfield and Mike Tyson) and shocking defeats (to Oliver McCall and Hasim Rahman).

3 Ring king Roy Jones Jr., 35, finally starts to show his age, getting knocked out twice (by Antonio Tarver and Glen Johnson) in 2004 after going his entire career without taking a beating. Entering the year, Jones's only official loss was a 1999 disqualification against Montell Griffin for hitting his opponent while he was down.

2 Former middleweight champion Felix "El Tito" Trinidad shakes off more than two years of ring rust and comes out of retirement to face the chain-smoking, Nicaraguan warrior Ricardo Mayorga. Trinidad wins the eight-round slugfest by TKO, knocking "El Matador" to the canvas three times in the final round before the referee steps in and stops the fight.

1 Undisputed middleweight champ Bernard "The Executioner" Hopkins executes his game plan and knocks out golden boy Oscar De La Hoya with a pin-point liver shot in the ninth round to retain his title belts in the most anticipated fight of 2004. Hopkins extends his amazing middleweight division record with his 19th straight successful title defense.

Peaks and Valleys

After his 91-second destruction of Michael Spinks in 1988, Mike Tyson dismissed Kevin Rooney as his trainer. Rooney had been with Tyson since Cus D'Amato took in the troubled youth and served as head trainer when D'Amato died. After that Tyson's downfall in the ring began. Less than two years later, Tyson lost the heavyweight title to Buster Douglas.

	1985-88	1989-present
W-L	34-0	16-5*
W-L Title bouts	9-0	4-4
KO	30	14

*does not include two no-contests.

Most Successful Title Defenses

Bernard Hopkins successfully defended his middleweight title for the 19th time in 2004, beating Oscar De La Hoya. Here is a look at how he stacks up with some of the longest tenured champions in boxing history.

No	Fighter, weight class	Span
25	Joe Louis, heavyweight	1937-49
21	Ricardo Lopez, strawweight	1990-99
20	Larry Holmes, heavyweight	1978-85
19	Bernard Hopkins, middleweight	1995—
19	Henry Armstrong, welterweight	1938-40
19	Eusebio Pedroza, featherweight	1978-85
19	Khaosai Galaxy, jr. bantam.	1984-91

2003-2004
Season in Review

SPORTS ALMANAC

Current Champions
WBA, WBC and IBF Titleholders (through Oct. 31, 2004)

The champions of professional boxing's 17 principal weight divisions, as recognized by the Word Boxing Association (WBA), World Boxing Council (WBC) and International Boxing Federation (IBF). Where applicable, records listed below fighters' names indicate wins-losses-draws-no contest.

	Weight Limit	WBA Champion	WBC Champion	IBF Champion
Heavyweight	—	John Ruiz 40-5-1, 28 KOs	Vitali Klitschko 34-2-0, 33 KOs	Chris Byrd 37-2-1, 20 KOs
Cruiserweight	190 lbs	Jean-Marc Mormeck 30-2-0, 21 KOs	Wayne Braithwaite 21-0-0, 17 KOs	Kelvin Davis 21-2-1, 16 KOs
Light Heavyweight	175 lbs	Fabrice Tiozzo 46-2-0, 30 KOs	Antonio Tarver 22-2-0, 18 KOs	Glen Johnson 41-9-2, 28 KOs
Super Middleweight	168 lbs	Manny Siaca 18-4-0, 16 KOs	Markus Beyer 30-2-0, 12 KOs	Jeff Lacy 17-0-0, 14 KOs
Middleweight	160 lbs	Bernard Hopkins* 45-2-1-1, 32 KOs	Bernard Hopkins 45-2-1-1, 32 KOs	Bernard Hopkins 45-2-1-1, 32 KOs
Jr. Middleweight	154 lbs	Winky Wright* 47-3-0, 25 KOs	Winky Wright 47-3-0, 25 KOs	Kassim Ouma 20-1-1, 13 KOs
Welterweight	147 lbs	Cory Spinks* 34-2-0, 10 KOs	Cory Spinks 34-2-0, 10 KOs	Cory Spinks 34-2-0, 10 KOs
Jr. Welterweight	140 lbs	Vivian Harris 25-1-1, 17 KOs	Kostya Tszyu* 30-1-0-1, 24 KOs	Kostya Tszyu 30-1-0-1, 24 KOs
Lightweight	135 lbs	Juan Diaz 25-0, 12 KOs	Jose Luis Castillo 50-6-1, 45 KOs	Julio Diaz 30-2, 22 KOs
Jr. Lightweight	130 lbs	Acelino Freitas* 43-2-1, 33 KOs	Erik Morales 47-1-0, 34 KOs	Erik Morales 47-1-0, 34 KOs
Featherweight	126 lbs	Juan Manuel Marquez 43-2-1, 33 KOs	Chi In-jin 29-2-1, 18 KOs	Juan Manuel Marquez 43-2-1, 33 KOs
Jr. Featherweight	122 lbs	Mahyar Monshipour 25-2-2, 16 KOs	Oscar Larios 53-3-1, 35 KOs	Israel Vazquez 36-3-0, 26 KOs
Bantamweight	118 lbs	Johnny Bredahl 55-2-0, 26 KOs	Veerapol Sahaprom 45-1-2, 31 KOs	Rafael Marquez 32-3-0, 29 KOs
Jr. Bantamweight	115 lbs	Alexander Munoz 25-0-0, 24 KOs	Katsushige Kawashima 27-3-0, 18 KOs	Luis Perez 22-1-0, 14 KOs
Flyweight	112 lbs	Lorenzo Parra 24-0-0, 17 KOs	Pongsaklek Wonjongkam 53-2-0, 29 KOs	Irene Pacheco 30-0-0, 23 KOs
Jr. Flyweight	108 lbs	Rosendo Alvarez 33-2-2, 21 KOs	Jorge Arce 37-3-1, 27 KOs	Jose Victor Burgos 36-13-3, 21 KOs
Minimumweight	105 lbs	Yutaka Niida 16-1-3, 8 KOs	Eagle Kyowa 13-0-0, 5 KOs	Muhammad Rachman 49-7-3, 21 KOs

Note: The following weight divisions are also known by these names—**Cruiserweight** as Jr. Heavyweight; **Jr. Middleweight** as Super Welterweight; **Jr. Welterweight** as Super Lightweight; **Jr. Lightweight** as Super Featherweight; **Jr. Featherweight** as Super Bantamweight; **Jr. Bantamweight** as Super Flyweight; **Jr. Flyweight** as Light Flyweight; and **Minimumweight** as Strawweight or Mini-Flyweights.

*Bernard Hopkins is the WBA middleweight "super world champion;" Winky Wright is the WBA junior middleweight "super world champion;" Cory Spinks is the WBA welterweight "super world champion;" Kostya Tszyu is the WBC "Champion Emeritus of the World;" Acelino Freitas is the WBA super featherweight "super world champion;"

Major Bouts, 2003-04

Division by division, from Nov. 1, 2003 through Oct. 31, 2004.

WBA, WBC and IBF champions are listed in **bold** type. Note the following Result column abbreviations (in alphabetical order): **Disq.** (won by disqualification); **KO** (knockout); **MDraw** (majority draw); **NC** (no contest); **SDraw** (split draw); **TDraw** (technical draw); **TKO** (technical knockout); **TWm** (won by technical majority decision); **TWs** (won by technical split decision); **TWu** (won by technical unanimous decision); **Wm** (won by majority decision); **Ws** (won by split decision) and **Wu** (won by unanimous decision).

Heavyweights

Date	Winner	Loser	Result	Title	Site
Dec. 6	Vitali Klitschko	Kirk Johnson	TKO 2	—	New York City
Dec. 13	John Ruiz	Hasim Rahman	Wu 12	WBA*	Atlantic City
Apr. 10	Lamon Brewster	Wladimir Klitschko	TKO 5	—	Las Vegas
Apr. 17	**John Ruiz**	Fres Oquendo	TKO 11	**WBA**	New York City
Apr. 17	**Chris Byrd**	Andrew Golota	MDraw 12	**IBF**	New York City
Apr. 24	Vitali Klitschko	Corrie Sanders	TKO 8	**WBC†**	Los Angeles
July 3	Eliseo Castillo	Michael Moorer	Wu 10	—	Miami, Fla.
July 28	Hasim Rahman	Terrence Lewis	KO 2	—	Rochester, N.Y.
July 30	Danny Williams	Mike Tyson	KO 4	—	Louisville, Ky.
Sept. 4	Lamon Brewster	Kali Meehan	Ws 12	—	Las Vegas
Sept. 23	James Toney	Rydell Booker	Wu 12	—	Temecula, Calif.
Sept. 25	Riddick Bowe	Marcus Rhode	TKO 2	—	Shawnee, Okla.
Oct. 2	Wladimir Klitschko	DaVarryl Williamson	TWs 5‡	—	Las Vegas

*John Ruiz won the vacant interim WBA belt. Ruiz lost the real WBA belt to Roy Jones Jr. in March 2003. The interim tag was later dropped when Jones announced he would not be defending his heavyweight title.
†Klitschko won the WBC belt that was left vacant with the retirement of champion Lennox Lewis.
‡The fight went to the scorecards after an accidental clash of heads at the end of the fifth round left a deep gash in Klitschko's forehead. The referee called a halt to the belt on the advice of the ringside physician.

Cruiserweights (190 lbs)
(Jr. Heavyweights)

Date	Winner	Loser	Result	Title	Site
Dec. 13	**Wayne Braithwaite**	Luis Pineda	KO 1	**WBC**	Atlantic City
Apr. 17	**Wayne Braithwaite**	Louis Azille	Wu 12	**WBC**	New York City
May 1	Kelvin Davis	Ezra Sellers	TKO 8	**IBF***	Miami, Fla.
May 22	**Jean-Marc Mormeck**	Virgil Hill	Wu 12	**WBA**	Brakpan, South Africa

*Davis won the IBF title vacated by James Toney when he moved up to heavyweight.

Light Heavyweights (175 lbs)

Date	Winner	Loser	Result	Title	Site
Nov. 7	Glen Johnson	Clinton Woods	Draw 12	**IBF**	Sheffield, England
Nov. 8	**Roy Jones Jr.**	**Antonio Tarver**	Wm 12	**WBA/WBC***	Las Vegas
Feb. 6	Glen Johnson	Clinton Woods	Wu 12	**IBF**	Sheffield, England
Mar. 20	Fabrice Tiozzo	**Silvio Branco**	Wm 12	**WBA**	Lyon, France
May 15	**Antonio Tarver**	**Roy Jones Jr.**	TKO 2	**WBA/WBC**	Las Vegas
Sept. 25	**Glen Johnson**	Roy Jones Jr.	KO 9	**IBF**	Memphis, Tenn.

*When Tarver beat Montell Griffin in April 2003, he won two of the belts (IBF and WBC) Jones vacated in order to move up to heavyweight. However, Tarver gave up his IBF title, saying that a contracted rematch clause would be beat Jones would make him unavailable to make a mandatory defense. Tarver said he didn't want to force a fighter to wait for a title shot the way he did. That meant that the Nov. 7 fight between Clinton Woods and Glen Johnson was for the vacant IBF belt.

On April 24, 2004 Vitali Klitschko defeated Corrie Sanders on an eighth-round TKO in Los Angeles for the vacant WBC Heavyweight title.

Did you know, that by doing so, he became the tallest heavyweight champion in history at 6 feet, 7½ inches.

Super Middleweights (168 lbs)

Date	Winner	Loser	Result	Title	Site
Dec. 13	**Sven Ottke**	Robin Reid	Wu 12	**IBF/WBA**	Nuremberg, Germany
Dec. 13	Jeff Lacy	Donnell Wiggins	TKO 8	—	Manchester, England
Dec. 20	Danny Green	Eric Lucas	TKO 6	WBC*	Montreal, Canada
Jan. 19	Anthony Mundine	Yoshinori Nishizawa	TKO 5	WBA†	Wollongong, Australia
Feb. 28	**Markus Beyer**	Andre Thysse	Wu 12	**WBC**	Desden, Germany
Mar. 27	**Sven Ottke**	Armard Krajnc	Wu 12	**IBF/WBA**	Magdeburg, Germany
May 5	Manny Siaca	Anthony Mundine	Wm 12	WBA‡	Sydney, Australia
June 5	Cristian Sanavia	**Markus Beyer**	Wu 12	**WBC**	Chemnitz, Germany
June 5	Jeff Lacy	Vitali Tsypko	NC	—	Joplin, Mo.
Sept. 8	Anthony Mundine	Sean Sullivan	KO 10	—	Sydney, Australia
Oct. 2	Jeff Lacy	Syd Vanderpool	TKO	IBF	Las Vegas
Oct. 9	Markus Beyer	**Cristian Sanavia**	KO 6	**WBC**	Erfurt, Germany

*Green won the vacant interim WBC super middleweight belt. Markus Beyer holds the official WBC belt. Danny Green was controversially disqualified by the referee for intentional head butting following the fifth round of their Aug. 2003 fight. Green was ahead on all three scorecards at the time.
†Mundine retained the WBA belt but note that Sven Ottke is the WBA super middleweight "super world champion."
‡Siaca won the WBA belt but note that Sven Ottke is the WBA super middleweight "super world champion."

Middleweights (160 lbs)

Date	Winner	Loser	Result	Title	Site
Dec. 5	Hector Camacho	Craig Houk	TKO 3	—	Denver, Colo.
Dec. 13	**Bernard Hopkins**	William Joppy	Wu 12	**IBF/WBA/WBC**	Atlantic City
May 1	Maselino Maseo	Evans Ashira	TKO 2	WBA*	Miami, Fla.
June 5	Oscar De La Hoya	Felix Sturm	Wu 12	—	Las Vegas
June 5	**Bernard Hopkins**	Robert Allen	Wu 12	**IBF/WBA/WBC**	Las Vegas
July 3	Hector Camacho	Clint McNeil	Wu 10	—	Biloxi, Miss.
Sept. 18	**Bernard Hopkins**	Oscar De La Hoya	KO 9	**IBF/WBA/WBC**	Las Vegas
Sept. 24	Howard Eastman	Jerry Elliott	Wu 10	—	Nottingham, England
Oct. 2	Felix Trinidad	Ricardo Mayorga	TKO 8	—	New York City

*Maseo won the vacant WBA title but note that Bernard Hopkins is the WBA middleweight "super world champion."

Junior Middleweights (154 lbs)
(Super Welterweights)

Date	Winner	Loser	Result	Title	Site
Dec. 13	Travis Simms	Alex Garcia	KO 5	WBA*	Atlantic City
Jan. 3	Kassim Candelo	Juan Candelo	TKO 10	—	Mashantucket, Conn.
Mar. 5	Verno Phillips	Julio Garcia	KO 1	—	Pala, Calif.
Mar. 13	"Winky" Wright	Shane Mosely	Wu 12	**IBF/WBA/WBC**	Las Vegas
Apr. 17	Ricardo Mayorga	Eric Mitchell†	Wu 10	—	New York City
June 5	Verno Phillips	Carlos Bojorquez	TKO 6	IBF	Joplin, Missouri
Oct. 2	Kassim Ouma	**Verno Phillips**	Wu 12	IBF‡	Las Vegas
Oct. 2	Travis Simms	Bronco McKart	Wu 12	WBA	New York City

*Simms won Garcia's WBA belt but note that Shane Mosely is the WBA super welterweight "super world champion."
†Mayorga was originally scheduled to fight Jose Rivera for his version of WBA welterweight belt (Cory Spinks is the WBA "super world champion") but Mayorga failed (by 7½ pounds) to make the weight limit of 147 pounds and a deal was made for him to fight Eric Mitchell, who was already on the fight card at Madison Square Garden, at junior middleweight.
‡Phillips won the IBF belt that was stripped from Ronald "Winky" Wright for his failure to fight mandatory challenger Kassim Ouma and instead honor the rematch clause in his Mar. 2004 fight with Shane Mosely. Phillips was scheduled to fight Ouma June 5 but Ouma dropped out four days before the fight with an injury.

Welterweights (147 lbs)

Date	Winner	Loser	Result	Title	Site
Dec. 13	Zab Judah	Jaime Rangel	KO 1	—	Atlantic City
Dec. 13	**Cory Spinks**	**Ricardo Mayorga**	Wm 12	**IBF/WBA/WBC**	Atlantic City
Apr. 10	**Cory Spinks**	Zab Judah	Wu 12	**IBF/WBA/WBC**	Las Vegas
May 15	Zab Judah	Rafael Pineda	Wu 12	—	Las Vegas
Sept. 4	**Cory Spinks**	Miguel Angel Gonzalez	Wu 12	**IBF/WBA/WBC**	Las Vegas
Oct. 2	Zab Judah	Wayne Martell	KO 1	—	New York City

Major Bouts, 2003-04 (Cont.)
Junior Welterweights (140 lbs)
(Super Lightweights)

Date	Winner	Loser	Result	Title	Site
Dec. 13	Ricky Hatton	Ben Tackie	Wu 12	—	Manchester, England
Jan. 24	Arturo Gatti	Gianluca Branco	Wu 12	WBC*	Atlantic City
Feb. 7	Sharmba Mitchell	Lovemore N'Dou	Wu 12	IBF†	Atlantic City
Apr. 3	Sharmba Mitchell	Michael Stewart	Wu 12	IBF	Manchester, England
Apr. 3	Ricky Hatton	Dennis Holbaek Pedersen	TKO 6	—	Manchester, England
Apr. 17	Vivian Harris	Oktay Orkal	Wm 12	WBA‡	Hanover, Germany
Apr. 29	Paul Spadafora	Ruben Galvan	Wu 12	—	Canonsburg, Penn.
May 22	Floyd Mayweather Jr.	DeMarcus Corley	Wu 12	—	Atlantic City
July 18	Paul Spadafora	Francisco Campos	TKO 3	—	Pittsburgh, Penn.
July 24	Arturo Gatti	Leonard Dorin	KO 2	WBC	Atlantic City
Sept. 11	Miguel Cotto	Kelson Pinto	TKO 6	—	San Juan, Puerto Rico
Oct. 1	Ricky Hatton	Michael Stewart	KO 5	—	Manchester, England
Oct. 23	Vivian Harris	Oktay Orkal	TKO 11	WBA	Berlin, Germany

*Gatti won the vacant interim WBC belt but note that Kostya Tszyu is the WBC junior welterweight champion.
†Mitchell won the vacant interim IBF belt but note that Kostya Tszyu is the IBF junior welterweight champion.
‡Harris won the vacant interim WBA belt, Kostya Tszyu was the WBA junior welterweight champion but Harris was elevated to WBA champion in June 2004 when Tszyu was stripped of the belt due to inactivity.

Lightweights (135 lbs)

Date	Winner	Loser	Result	Title	Site
Nov. 1	**Floyd Mayweather Jr.**	Philip N'dou	TKO 7	**WBC**	Grand Rapids, Mich.
Nov. 22	Javier Jauregui	Levander Johnson	TKO 11	IBF*	Los Angeles
Nov. 22	Juan Diaz	Joel Perez	Wu 12	—	Houston, Texas
Jan. 3	Acelino Freitas	Artur Grigorian	Wu 12	—	Mashantucket, Conn.
Apr. 10	Lakva Sim	Miguel Callist	TKO 5	WBA†	Las Vegas
May 13	Julio Diaz	**Javier Jauregui**	Wm 12	IBF	San Diego, Calif.
June 5	Jose Luis Castillo	Juan Lazcano	Wu 12	WBC‡	Las Vegas
July 17	Juan Diaz	**Lakva Sim**	Wu 12	WBA	Houston, Texas
Aug. 7	Diego Corrales	Acelino Freitas	TKO 10	—	Mashantucket, Conn.

*Jauregui won the IBF title that was vacated by Paul Spadafora when he moved up to junior welterweight.
†Sim won the WBA title that was left vacant with the retirement of champion Leonard Dorin.
‡Castillo won the WBC belt that was vacated by Floyd Mayweather Jr. when he moved up to junior welterweight.

Junior Lightweights (130 lbs)
(Super Featherweights)

Date	Winner	Loser	Result	Title	Site
Feb. 8	Yodsanan Nanthachai	Ryuhei Sugita	TKO 7	WBA*	Bangkok, Thailand
Feb. 28	Erik Morales	**Jesus Chavez**	Wu 12	**WBC**	Las Vegas
Mar. 6	Diego Corrales	Joel Casamayor	Ws 12	—	Mashantucket, Conn.
July 3	Joel Casamayor	Daniel Luis Seda	Wu 10	—	Miami, Fla.
July 31	**Erik Morales**	**Carlos Hernandez**	Wu 12	**IBF/WBC**	Las Vegas
Aug. 7	Yodsanan Nanthachai	Steve Forbes	Wu 12	WBA*	Mashantucket, Conn.

*Nanthachai retained with WBA belt but note that Acelino Freitas in the WBA junior lightweight "super world champion."

Featherweights (126 lbs)

Date	Winner	Loser	Result	Title	Site
Nov. 1	**Juan Manuel Marquez**	Derrick Gainer	TWu 7*	**IBF/WBA**	Grand Rapids, Mich.
Nov. 15	Manny Pacquiao	Marco Antonio Barrera	TKO 11	—	San Antonio, Texas
Nov. 22	Rocky Juarez	Hector Velazquez	Wu 12	—	Houston, Texas
Apr. 10	Chi In-Jin	Michael Brodie	KO 7	**WBC†**	Manchester, England
May 8	**Juan Manuel Marquez**	Manny Pacquiao	MDraw 12	**IBF/WBA**	Las Vegas
June 4	Chris John	Osamu Sato	Wu 12	WBA‡	Tokyo
June 19	Marco Antonio Barrera	Paulie Ayala	KO 10	—	Los Angeles
July 24	**Chi In-Jin**	Eiichi Sugama	TKO 10	**WBC**	Seoul, S. Korea
Sept. 18	**Juan Manuel Marquez**	Orlando Salido	Wu 12	**IBF/WBA**	Las Vegas

*Marquez won a technical unanimous decision when the fight went to the scorecards late in the seventh round when Gainer was unable to continue after suffering a deep cut over his left eye from an accidental head butt.
†Chi In-Jin won the vacant WBC belt that was vacated when Erik Morales moved up to junior lightweight.
‡John won the WBA featherweight belt but note that Juan Manuel Marquez is the WBA "super world champion."

Junior Featherweights (122 lbs)
(Super Bantamweights)

Date	Winner	Loser	Result	Title	Site
Nov. 22	**Oscar Larios**	N. Kiatisakchockhai	TKO 10	**WBC**	Los Angeles
Dec. 16	**Mayhar Monshipour**	Jairo Tagliafero	TKO 7	**WBA**	Levallois, France
Mar. 5	**Oscar Larios**	Shigeru Nakazato	Wu 12	**WBC**	Saitma, Japan
Mar. 25	Israel Vazquez	Jose Luis Valbuena	TKO 12	**IBF***	Los Angeles
May 27	**Mahyar Monshipour**	Salim Medjkoune	TKO 8	**WBA**	Clermont, France

*Vazquez captured the IBF belt that was left vacant when Manny Pacquiao moved up to featherweight.

Bantamweights (118 lbs)

Date	Winner	Loser	Result	Title	Site
Oct. 25	**Johnny Bredahl**	David Guerault	Wu 12	**WBA**	Copenhagen, Denmark
Mar. 5	Julio Zarate	Hideki Todaka	Ws12	WBA*	Saitma, Japan
Mar. 5	**Veerapol Sahaprom** . .	Toshiaki Nishioka	Wu 12	**WBC**	Saitma, Japan
Mar. 13	**Johnny Bredahl**	Nobuaki Naka	Wu 12	**WBA**	Copenhagen, Denmark
May 1	**Veerapol Sahaprom** . .	Julio Cesar Avila	TKO 12	**WBC**	Nonkhai, Thailand
July 31	**Rafael Marquez**	Heriberto Ruiz	KO 3	**IBF**	Las Vegas
Sept. 11	**Veerapol Sahaprom** . . .	Cecilio Santos	Wu 12	**WBC**	Chainart, Thailand

*Zarate captured the interim WBA belt but note that Johnny Bredahl is the WBA bantamweight champion.

Junior Bantamweights (115 lbs)
(Super Flyweights)

Date	Winner	Loser	Result	Title	Site
Dec. 13	**Luis Perez**	Felix Machado	Wu 12	**IBF**	Atlantic City
Jan. 3	**Alexander Munoz**	Eija Kojima	TKO 10	**WBA**	Osaka, Japan
Jan. 3	**Masamori Tokuyama**	Dimitri Kirilov	Wu 12	**WBC**	Osaka, Japan
Mar. 6	Mark Johnson	Luis Bolanco	KO 4	—	Mashantucket, Conn.
May 16	Martin Castillo	Hideyasu Ishihara	TKO 11	WBA*	Gifu, Japan
June 28	Katsushige Kawashima	**Masamori Tokuyama**	TKO 1	**WBC**	Yokohama, Japan
Sept. 20	**Katsushige Kawashima**	Raul Juarez	Wu 12	**WBC**	Tokyo

*Castillo won the WBA interim belt but note that Alexander Munoz is the WBA super flyweight champion.

Flyweights (112 lbs)

Date	Winner	Loser	Result	Title	Site
Nov. 14	**P. Wonjongkam**	Hussein Hussein	Wu 12	**WBC**	Bangkok, Thailand
Dec. 6	Lorenzo Parra	**Eric Morel**	Wu 12	**WBA**	Bayamon, Puerto Rico
Jan. 3	**P. Wonjongkam**	Masaki Nakahuma	Wu 12	**WBC**	Yokohama, Japan
June 4	Lorenzo Parra	Takefumi Sakata	Wm 12	**WBA**	Tokyo
July 15	**P. Wonjongkam**	Luis Angel Martinez	TKO 5	**WBC**	Khonkaen, Thailand
Sept. 9	**Lorenzo Parra**	Yosam Choi	Wu 12	**WBA**	Seoul, South Korea

Junior Flyweights (108 lbs)
(Light Flyweights)

Date	Winner	Loser	Result	Title	Site
Nov. 15	Beibis Mendoza	Choi Yosam	Wu 12	WBA*	Yosoo, South Korea
Dec. 13	**Rosendo Alvarez**	**Jose Victor Burgos**	Draw 12	**WBA/IBF**	Atlantic City
Jan. 10	**Jorge Arce**	Joma Gamboa	KO 2	**WBC**	Mexico City
Apr. 24	**Jorge Arce**	Melchor Cob Castro	KO 5	**WBC**	Tuxtla Gutierrrez, Mexico
May 15	**Jose Victor Burgos** . . .	Fahlan Sakkreerin	TKO 6	**IBF**	Las Vegas
July 30	Nelson Dieppa	Ulises Solis	Wm 12	—	Louisville, Ky.
Oct. 2	Rosendo Alvarez	Bebis Mendoza	Ws 12	WBA†	New York City

*Mendoza won the interim WBA belt. Rosendo Alvarez is the WBA light flyweight champion.
†Menoza retained his interim WBA belt despite the loss because Alvarez failed to make the 108-pound weight limit for the fight.

Minimumweights (105 lbs)
(Strawweights or Mini-Flyweights)

Date	Winner	Loser	Result	Title	Site
Jan. 10	Eagle Akakura	**Jose A. Aguirre**	Wu 12	**WBC**	Tokyo, Japan
Jan. 31	Juan Landaeta	Chana Porpaion	Wu 12	WBA*	Caracas, Venezuela
Apr. 10	**Daniel Reyes**	Roberto Leyva	TKO 3	**IBF**	Bolivar, Colombia
May 5	Juan Landeta	Chana Porpaion	MDraw 12	WBA*	Bangkok, Thailand
June 28	Eagle Kyowa†	Satoshi Kogumazaka	TWu 8	**WBC‡**	Yokohama, Japan
July 3	Yutaka Niida	Noel Arambulet	Wu 12	**WBA@**	Tokyo
Oct. 30	**Yutaka Niida**	Juan Landaeta	Ws 12	**WBA**	Tokyo

*Landaeta captured the vacant interim WBA belt but note that Noel Arambulent was the WBA minimumweight champion.
†Eagle Kyowa was formerly known as Eagle Akakura.
‡Kyowa was awarded the technical unanimous decision after the fight was halted in the eighth inning after Kogumazaka suffered a deep cut after a clash of heads. Kyowa was leading on all three judges scorecards at the time.
@Arambulet was stripped of the WBA belt prior to his July 3 fight with Yutaka Niida for failing to make weight, but the fight went on as scheduled and Niida claimed the title with the win. Had Arambulet won, the WBA title would have stayed vacant.

1892-2004
Through the Years

SPORTS ALMANAC

World Heavyweight Championship Fights

Widely accepted world champions in **bold** type. Note following result abbreviations: KO (knockout), TKO (technical knock-out), Wu (unanimous decision), Wm (majority decision), Ws (split decision), Ref (referee's decision), ND (no decision), Disq. (won on disqualification).

Year	Date	Winner	Age	Wgt	Loser	Wgt	Result	Location
1892	Sept. 7	James J. Corbett	26	178	John L. Sullivan	212	KO 21	New Orleans
1894	Jan. 25	**James J. Corbett**	27	184	Charley Mitchell	158	KO 3	Jacksonville, Fla.
1897	Mar. 17	Bob Fitzsimmons	34	167	**James J. Corbett**	183	KO 14	Carson City, Nev.
1899	June 9	James J. Jeffries	24	206	**Bob Fitzsimmons**	167	KO 11	Coney Island, N.Y.
1899	Nov. 3	**James J. Jeffries**	24	215	Tom Sharkey	183	Ref 25	Coney Island, N.Y.
1900	Apr. 6	**James J. Jeffries**	24	NA	Jack Finnegan	NA	KO 1	Detroit
1900	May 11	**James J. Jeffries**	25	218	James J. Corbett	188	KO 23	Coney Island, N.Y.
1901	Nov. 15	**James J. Jeffries**	26	211	Gus Ruhlin	194	TKO 6	San Francisco
1902	July 25	**James J. Jeffries**	27	219	Bob Fitzsimmons	172	KO 8	San Francisco
1903	Aug. 14	**James J. Jeffries**	28	220	James J. Corbett	190	KO 10	San Francisco
1904	Aug. 25	**James J. Jeffries***	29	219	Jack Munroe	186	TKO 2	San Francisco
1905	July 3	Marvin Hart	28	190	Jack Root	171	KO 12	Reno, Nev.
1906	Feb. 23	Tommy Burns	24	180	**Marvin Hart**	188	Ref 20	Los Angeles
1906	Oct. 2	**Tommy Burns**	25	NA	Jim Flynn	NA	KO 15	Los Angeles
1906	Nov. 28	**Tommy Burns**	25	172	Phila. Jack O'Brien	163½	Draw 20	Los Angeles
1907	May 8	**Tommy Burns**	25	180	Phila. Jack O'Brien	167	Ref 20	Los Angeles
1907	July 4	**Tommy Burns**	26	181	Bill Squires	180	KO 1	Colma, Calif.
1907	Dec. 2	**Tommy Burns**	26	177	Gunner Moir	204	KO 10	London
1908	Feb. 10	**Tommy Burns**	26	NA	Jack Palmer	NA	KO 4	London
1908	Mar. 17	**Tommy Burns**	26	NA	Jem Roche	NA	KO 1	Dublin
1908	Apr. 18	**Tommy Burns**	26	NA	Jewey Smith	NA	KO 5	Paris
1908	June 13	**Tommy Burns**	26	184	Bill Squires	183	KO 8	Paris
1908	Aug. 24	**Tommy Burns**	27	181	Bill Squires	184	KO 13	Sydney
1908	Sept. 2	**Tommy Burns**	27	183	Bill Lang	187	KO 6	Melbourne
1908	Dec. 26	Jack Johnson	30	192	**Tommy Burns**	168	TKO 14	Sydney
1909	Mar. 10	**Jack Johnson**	30	NA	Victor McLaglen	NA	ND 6	Vancouver
1909	May 19	**Jack Johnson**	31	205	Phila. Jack O'Brien	161	ND 6	Philadelphia
1909	June 30	**Jack Johnson**	31	207	Tony Ross	214	ND 6	Pittsburgh
1909	Sept. 9	**Jack Johnson**	31	209	Al Kaufman	191	ND 10	San Francisco
1909	Oct. 16	**Jack Johnson**	31	205½	Stanley Ketchel	170¼	KO 12	Colma, Calif.
1910	July 4	**Jack Johnson**	32	208	James J. Jeffries	227	KO 15	Reno, Nev.
1912	July 4	**Jack Johnson**	34	195½	Jim Flynn	175	TKO 9	Las Vegas, Nev.
1913	Dec. 19	**Jack Johnson**	35	NA	Jim Johnson	NA	Draw 10	Paris
1914	June 27	**Jack Johnson**	36	221	Frank Moran	203	Ref 20	Paris
1915	Apr. 5	Jess Willard	33	230	**Jack Johnson**	205½	KO 26	Havana
1916	Mar. 25	**Jess Willard**	34	225	Frank Moran	203	ND 10	NYC (Mad.Sq. Garden)
1919	July 4	Jack Dempsey	24	187	**Jess Willard**	245	TKO 4	Toledo, Ohio
1920	Sept. 6	**Jack Dempsey**	25	185	Billy Miske	187	KO 3	Benton Harbor, Mich.
1920	Dec. 14	**Jack Dempsey**	25	188¼	Bill Brennan	197	KO 12	NYC (Mad. Sq. Garden)
1921	July 2	**Jack Dempsey**	26	188	Georges Carpentier	172	KO 4	Jersey City, N.J.
1923	July 4	**Jack Dempsey**	28	188	Tommy Gibbons	175½	Ref 15	Shelby, Mont.
1923	Sept. 14	**Jack Dempsey**	28	192½	Luis Firpo	216½	KO 2	NYC (Polo Grounds)
1926	Sept. 23	Gene Tunney	29	189½	**Jack Dempsey**	190	Wu 10	Philadelphia
1927	Sept. 22	**Gene Tunney**	30	189½	Jack Dempsey	192½	Wu 10	Chicago
1928	July 26	**Gene Tunney****	31	192	Tom Heeney	203	TKO 11	NYC (Yankee Stadium)

*James J. Jeffries retired as champion on May 13, 1905, then came out of retirement to fight Jack Johnson for the title in 1910.
**Gene Tunney retired as champion in 1928.

Year	Date	Winner	Age	Wgt	Loser	Wgt	Result	Location
1930	June 12	Max Schmeling	24	188	Jack Sharkey	197	Disq. 4	NYC (Yankee Stadium)
1931	July 3	**Max Schmeling**	25	189	Young Stribling	186½	TKO 15	Cleveland
1932	June 21	Jack Sharkey	29	205	**Max Schmeling**	188	Ws 15	Long Island City, N.Y.
1933	June 29	Primo Carnera	26	260½	**Jack Sharkey**	201	KO 6	Long Island City, N.Y.
1933	Oct. 22	**Primo Carnera**	26	259½	Paulino Uzcudun	229¼	Wu 15	Rome
1934	Mar. 1	**Primo Carnera**	27	270	Tommy Loughran	184	Wu 15	Miami
1934	June 14	Max Baer	25	209½	**Primo Carnera**	263¼	TKO 11	Long Island City, N.Y.
1935	June 13	James J. Braddock	29	193¾	**Max Baer**	209	Wu 15	Long Island City, N.Y.
1937	June 22	Joe Louis	23	197¼	**James J. Braddock**	197	KO 8	Chicago
1937	Aug. 30	**Joe Louis**	23	197	Tommy Farr	204¼	Wu 15	NYC (Yankee Stadium)
1938	Feb. 23	**Joe Louis**	23	200	Nathan Mann	193½	KO 3	NYC (Mad. Sq. Garden)
1938	Apr. 1	**Joe Louis**	23	202½	Harry Thomas	196	KO 5	Chicago
1938	June 22	**Joe Louis**	24	198¾	Max Schmeling	193	KO 1	NYC (Yankee Stadium)
1939	Jan. 25	**Joe Louis**	24	200¼	John Henry Lewis	180¾	KO 1	NYC (Mad. Sq. Garden)
1939	Apr. 17	**Joe Louis**	24	201¼	Jack Roper	204¾	KO 1	Los Angeles
1939	June 28	**Joe Louis**	25	200¾	Tony Galento	233¾	TKO 4	NYC (Yankee Stadium)
1939	Sept. 20	**Joe Louis**	25	200	Bob Pastor	183	KO 11	Detroit
1940	Feb. 9	**Joe Louis**	25	203	Arturo Godoy	202	Ws 15	NYC (Mad. Sq. Garden)
1940	Mar. 29	**Joe Louis**	25	201½	Johnny Paychek	187½	KO 2	NYC (Mad. Sq. Garden)
1940	June 20	**Joe Louis**	26	199	Arturo Godoy	201¼	TKO 8	NYC (Yankee Stadium)
1940	Dec. 16	**Joe Louis**	26	202¼	Al McCoy	180¾	TKO 6	Boston
1941	Jan. 31	**Joe Louis**	26	202½	Red Burman	188	KO 5	NYC (Mad. Sq. Garden)
1941	Feb. 17	**Joe Louis**	26	203½	Gus Dorazio	193½	KO 2	Philadelphia
1941	Mar. 21	**Joe Louis**	26	202	Abe Simon	254½	TKO 13	Detroit
1941	Apr. 8	**Joe Louis**	26	203½	Tony Musto	199½	TKO 9	St. Louis
1941	May 23	**Joe Louis**	27	201½	Buddy Baer	237½	Disq. 7	Washington, D.C.
1941	June 18	**Joe Louis**	27	199½	Billy Conn	174	KO 13	NYC (Polo Grounds)
1941	Sept. 29	**Joe Louis**	27	202¼	Lou Nova	202½	TKO 6	NYC (Polo Grounds)
1942	Jan. 9	**Joe Louis**	27	206¾	Buddy Baer	250	KO 1	NYC (Mad. Sq. Garden)
1942	Mar. 27	**Joe Louis**	27	207½	Abe Simon	255½	KO 6	NYC (Mad. Sq. Garden)
1942-45 World War II								
1946	June 9	**Joe Louis**	32	207	Billy Conn	187	KO 8	NYC (Yankee Stadium)
1946	Sept. 18	**Joe Louis**	32	211	Tami Mauriello	198½	KO 1	NYC (Yankee Stadium)
1947	Dec. 5	**Joe Louis**	33	211½	Jersey Joe Walcott	194½	Ws 15	NYC (Mad. Sq. Garden)
1948	June 25	**Joe Louis***	34	213½	Jersey Joe Walcott	194¾	KO 11	NYC (Yankee Stadium)
1949	June 22	**Ezzard Charles**	27	181¾	Jersey Joe Walcott	195½	Wu 15	Chicago
1949	Aug. 10	**Ezzard Charles**	28	180	Gus Lesnevich	182	TKO 8	NYC (Yankee Stadium)
1949	Oct. 14	**Ezzard Charles**	28	182	Pat Valentino	188½	KO 8	San Francisco
1950	Aug. 15	**Ezzard Charles**	29	183¼	Freddie Beshore	184½	TKO 14	Buffalo
1950	Sept. 27	**Ezzard Charles**	29	184½	Joe Louis	218	Wu 15	NYC (Yankee Stadium)
1950	Dec. 5	**Ezzard Charles**	29	185	Nick Barone	178½	KO 11	Cincinnati
1951	Jan. 12	**Ezzard Charles**	29	185	Lee Oma	193	TKO 10	NYC (Mad. Sq. Garden)
1951	Mar. 7	**Ezzard Charles**	29	186	Jersey Joe Walcott	193	Wu 15	Detroit
1951	May 30	**Ezzard Charles**	29	182	Joey Maxim	181½	Wu 15	Chicago
1951	July 18	Jersey Joe Walcott	37	194	**Ezzard Charles**	182	KO 7	Pittsburgh
1952	June 5	**Jersey Joe Walcott**	38	196	Ezzard Charles	191½	Wu 15	Philadelphia
1952	Sept. 23	Rocky Marciano	29	184	**Jersey Joe Walcott**	196	KO 13	Philadelphia
1953	May 15	**Rocky Marciano**	29	184½	Jersey Joe Walcott	197¾	KO 1	Chicago
1953	Sept. 24	**Rocky Marciano**	30	185	Roland LaStarza	184¾	TKO 11	NYC (Polo Grounds)
1954	June 17	**Rocky Marciano**	30	187½	Ezzard Charles	185½	Wu 15	NYC (Yankee Stadium)
1954	Sept. 17	**Rocky Marciano**	31	187	Ezzard Charles	192½	KO 8	NYC (Yankee Stadium)
1955	May 16	**Rocky Marciano**	31	189	Don Cockell	205	TKO 9	San Francisco
1955	Sept. 21	**Rocky Marciano****	32	188¼	Archie Moore	188	KO 9	NYC (Yankee Stadium)
1956	Nov. 30	Floyd Patterson	21	182¼	Archie Moore	187¾	KO 5	Chicago
1957	July 29	**Floyd Patterson**	22	184	Tommy Jackson	192½	TKO 10	NYC (Polo Grounds)
1957	Aug. 22	**Floyd Patterson**	22	187¼	Pete Rademacher	202	KO 6	Seattle
1958	Aug. 18	**Floyd Patterson**	23	184½	Roy Harris	194	TKO 13	Los Angeles
1959	May 1	**Floyd Patterson**	24	182½	Brian London	206	KO 11	Indianapolis
1959	June 26	Ingemar Johansson	26	196	**Floyd Patterson**	182	TKO 3	NYC (Yankee Stadium)
1960	June 20	Floyd Patterson	25	190	**Ingemar Johansson**	194¾	KO 5	NYC (Polo Grounds)

*Joe Louis retired as champion on Mar. 1, 1949, then came out of retirement to fight Ezzard Charles for the title in 1950.

**Rocky Marciano retired as undefeated champion on Apr. 27, 1956.

World Heavyweight Championship Fights (Cont.)

Year	Date	Winner	Age	Wgt	Loser	Wgt	Result	Location
1961	Mar. 13	**Floyd Patterson**	26	194¾	Ingemar Johansson	206½	KO 6	Miami Beach
1961	Dec. 4	**Floyd Patterson**	26	188½	Tom McNeeley	197	KO 4	Toronto
1962	Sept. 25	Sonny Liston	30	214	**Floyd Patterson**	189	KO 1	Chicago
1963	July 22	**Sonny Liston**	31	215	Floyd Patterson	194½	KO 1	Las Vegas
1964	Feb. 25	Cassius Clay**	22	210½	**Sonny Liston**	218	TKO 7	Miami Beach
1965	Mar. 1	Ernie Terrell WBA	25	199	Eddie Machen	192	Wu 15	Chicago
1965	May 25	**Muhammad Ali**	23	206	Sonny Liston	215¼	KO 1	Lewiston, Maine
1965	Nov. 1	Ernie Terrell WBA	26	206	George Chuvalo	209	Wu 15	Toronto
1965	Nov. 22	**Muhammad Ali**	23	210	Floyd Patterson	196¾	TKO 12	Las Vegas
1966	Mar. 29	**Muhammad Ali**	24	214½	George Chuvalo	216	Wu 15	Toronto
1966	May 21	**Muhammad Ali**	24	201½	Henry Cooper	188	TKO 6	London
1966	June 28	Ernie Terrell WBA	27	209½	Doug Jones	187½	Wu 15	Houston
1966	Aug. 6	**Muhammad Ali**	24	209½	Brian London	201½	KO 3	London
1966	Sept. 10	**Muhammad Ali**	24	203½	Karl Mildenberger	194¼	TKO 12	Frankfurt, W. Ger.
1966	Nov. 14	**Muhammad Ali**	24	212¾	Cleveland Williams	210½	TKO 3	Houston
1967	Feb. 6	**Muhammad Ali**	25	212¼	Ernie Terrell WBA	212¼	Wu 15	Houston
1967	Mar. 22	**Muhammad Ali**	25	211½	Zora Folley	202½	KO 7	NYC (Mad. Sq. Garden)
1968	Mar. 4	Joe Frazier NY	24	204½	Buster Mathis	243½	TKO 11	NYC (Mad. Sq. Garden)
1968	Apr. 27	Jimmy Ellis	28	197	Jerry Quarry	195	Wm 15	Oakland
1968	June 24	Joe Frazier NY	24	203½	Manuel Ramos	208	TKO 2	NYC (Mad. Sq. Garden)
1968	Aug. 14	Jimmy Ellis WBA	28	198	Floyd Patterson	188	Ref 15	Stockholm
1968	Dec. 10	Joe Frazier NY	24	203	Oscar Bonavena	207	Wu 15	Philadelphia
1969	Apr. 22	Joe Frazier NY	25	204½	Dave Zyglewicz	190½	KO 1	Houston
1969	June 23	Joe Frazier NY	25	203½	Jerry Quarry	198½	TKO 8	NYC (Mad. Sq. Garden)
1970	Feb. 16	Joe Frazier NY	26	205	Jimmy Ellis WBA	201	TKO 5	NYC (Mad. Sq. Garden)
1970	Nov. 18	**Joe Frazier**	26	209	Bob Foster	188	KO 2	Detroit
1971	Mar. 8	**Joe Frazier**	27	205½	Muhammad Ali	215	Wu 15	NYC (Mad. Sq. Garden)
1972	Jan. 15	**Joe Frazier**	28	215½	Terry Daniels	195	TKO 4	New Orleans
1972	May 26	**Joe Frazier**	28	217½	Ron Stander	218	TKO 5	Omaha, Neb.
1973	Jan. 22	George Foreman	24	217½	**Joe Frazier**	214	TKO 2	Kingston, Jamaica
1973	Sept. 1	**George Foreman**	24	219½	Jose (King) Roman	196½	KO 1	Tokyo
1974	Mar. 26	George Foreman	25	224¾	Ken Norton	212¾	TKO 2	Caracas, Venezuela
1974	Oct. 30	Muhammad Ali	32	216½	**George Foreman**	220	KO 8	Kinshasa, Zaire
1975	Mar. 24	**Muhammad Ali**	33	223½	Chuck Wepner	225	TKO 15	Cleveland
1975	May 16	**Muhammad Ali**	33	224½	Ron Lyle	219	TKO 11	Las Vegas
1975	June 30	**Muhammad Ali**	33	224½	Joe Bugner	230	Wu 15	Kuala Lumpur, Malaysia
1975	Oct. 1	**Muhammad Ali**	33	224½	Joe Frazier	215	TKO 14	Manila, Philippines
1976	Feb. 20	**Muhammad Ali**	34	226	Jean Pierre Coopman	206	KO 5	San Juan, P.R.
1976	Apr. 30	**Muhammad Ali**	34	230	Jimmy Young	209	Wu 15	Landover, Md.
1976	May 24	**Muhammad Ali**	34	220	Richard Dunn	206½	TKO 5	Munich, W. Ger.
1976	Sept. 28	**Muhammad Ali**	34	221	Ken Norton	217½	Wu 15	NYC (Yankee Stadium)
1977	May 16	**Muhammad Ali**	35	221¼	Alfredo Evangelista	209¼	Wu 15	Landover, Md.
1977	Sept. 29	**Muhammad Ali**	35	225	Earnie Shavers	211¼	Wu 15	NYC (Mad. Sq. Garden)
1978	Feb. 15	Leon Spinks	24	197¼	**Muhammad Ali**	224¼	Ws 15	Las Vegas
1978	June 9	Larry Holmes	28	209	Ken Norton WBC††	220	Ws 15	Las Vegas
1978	Sept. 15	Muhammad Ali†	36	221	**Leon Spinks**	201	Wu 15	New Orleans
1978	Nov. 10	Larry Holmes WBC	29	214	Alfredo Evangelista	208¼	KO 7	Las Vegas
1979	Mar. 23	Larry Holmes WBC	29	214	Osvaldo Ocasio	207	TKO 7	Las Vegas
1979	June 22	Larry Holmes WBC	29	215	Mike Weaver	202	TKO 12	NYC (Mad. Sq. Garden)
1979	Sept. 28	Larry Holmes WBC	29	210	Earnie Shavers	211	TKO 11	Las Vegas
1979	Oct. 20	John Tate	24	240	Gerrie Coetzee	222	Wu 15	Pretoria, S. Africa
1980	Feb. 3	Larry Holmes WBC	30	213½	Lorenzo Zanon	215	TKO 6	Las Vegas
1980	Mar. 31	Mike Weaver	27	232	John Tate WBA	232	KO 15	Knoxville, Tenn.
1980	Mar. 31	Larry Holmes WBC	30	211	Leroy Jones	254½	TKO 8	Las Vegas
1980	July 7	Larry Holmes WBC	30	214¼	Scott LeDoux	226	TKO 7	Minneapolis
1980	Oct. 2	Larry Holmes WBC	30	211½	Muhammad Ali	217½	TKO 11	Las Vegas
1980	Oct. 25	Mike Weaver WBA	28	210	Gerrie Coetzee	226½	KO 13	Sun City, S. Africa
1981	Apr. 11	**Larry Holmes**	31	215	Trevor Berbick	215½	Wu 15	Las Vegas
1981	June 12	**Larry Holmes**	31	212½	Leon Spinks	200¼	TKO 3	Detroit
1981	Oct. 3	Mike Weaver WBA	29	215	James (Quick) Tillis	209	Wu 15	Rosemont, Ill.

**After defeating Liston, Cassius Clay announced that he had changed his name to Muhammad Ali. He was later stripped of his title by the WBA and most state boxing commissions after refusing induction into the U.S. Army on Apr. 28, 1967.

† Muhammad Ali retired as champion on June 27, 1979, then came out of retirement to fight Larry Holmes for the title in 1980.

†† WBC recognized Ken Norton as world champion when Leon Spinks refused to meet Norton before Spinks' rematch with Muhammad Ali. Norton had scored a 15-round split decision over Jimmy Young on Nov. 5, 1977 in Las Vegas.

Year	Date	Winner	Age	Wgt	Loser	Wgt	Result	Location
1981	Nov. 6	**Larry Holmes**	32	213¼	Renaldo Snipes	215¾	TKO 11	Pittsburgh
1982	June 11	**Larry Holmes**	32	212½	Gerry Cooney	225½	TKO 13	Las Vegas
1982	Nov. 26	**Larry Holmes**	33	217½	Randall (Tex) Cobb	234¼	Wu 15	Houston
1982	Dec. 10	Michael Dokes	24	216	Mike Weaver WBA	209¾	TKO 1	Las Vegas
1983	Mar. 27	**Larry Holmes**	33	221	Lucien Rodriguez	209	Wu 12	Scranton, Pa.
1983	May 20	Michael Dokes WBA	24	223	Mike Weaver	218½	Draw 15	Las Vegas
1983	May 20	**Larry Holmes**	33	213	Tim Witherspoon	219½	Ws 12	Las Vegas
1983	Sept. 10	**Larry Holmes**	33	223	Scott Frank	211¼	TKO 5	Atlantic City
1983	Sept. 23	Gerrie Coetzee	28	215	Michael Dokes WBA	217	KO 10	Richfield, Ohio
1983	Nov. 25	**Larry Holmes**	34	219	Marvis Frazier	200	TKO 1	Las Vegas
1984	Mar. 9	Tim Witherspoon*	26	220¼	Greg Page	239½	Wm 12	Las Vegas
1984	Aug. 31	Pinklon Thomas	26	216	Tim Witherspoon	217	Wm 12	Las Vegas
1984	Nov. 9	**Larry Holmes** IBF	35	221½	Bonecrusher Smith	227	TKO 12	Las Vegas
1984	Dec. 1	Greg Page	26	236½	Gerrie Coetzee WBA	218	KO 8	Sun City, S. Africa
1985	Mar. 15	**Larry Holmes** IBF	35	223½	David Bey	233¼	TKO 10	Las Vegas
1985	Apr. 29	Tony Tubbs	26	229	Greg Page WBA	239½	Wu 15	Buffalo
1985	May 20	**Larry Holmes** IBF	35	224¼	Carl Williams	215	Wu 15	Las Vegas
1985	June 15	Pinklon Thomas WBC	27	220¼	Mike Weaver	221¼	KO 8	Las Vegas
1985	Sept. 21	Michael Spinks	29	200	**Larry Holmes** IBF	221½	Wu 15	Las Vegas
1986	Jan. 17	Tim Witherspoon	28	227	Tony Tubbs WBA	229	Wm 15	Atlanta
1986	Mar. 22	Trevor Berbick	33	218½	Pinklon Thomas WBC	222¾	Wu 15	Las Vegas
1986	Apr. 19	**Michael Spinks** IBF	29	205	Larry Holmes	223	Ws 15	Las Vegas
1986	July 19	Tim Witherspoon WBA	28	234¾	Frank Bruno	228	TKO 11	Wembley, England
1986	Sept. 6	**Michael Spinks** IBF	30	201	Steffen Tangstad	214¾	TKO 4	Las Vegas
1986	Nov. 22	Mike Tyson	20	221¼	Trevor Berbick WBC	218½	TKO 2	Las Vegas
1986	Dec. 12	Bonecrusher Smith	33	228½	Tim Witherspoon WBA	233½	TKO 1	NYC (Mad. Sq. Garden)
1987	Mar. 7	Mike Tyson WBC	20	219	Bonecrusher Smith WBA	233	Wu 12	Las Vegas
1987	May 30	Mike Tyson	20	218¾	Pinklon Thomas	217¾	TKO 6	Las Vegas
1987	May 30	Tony Tucker**	28	222¼	Buster Douglas	227¼	TKO 10	Las Vegas
1987	June 15	**Michael Spinks†**	30	208¾	Gerry Cooney	238	TKO 5	Atlantic City
1987	Aug. 1	Mike Tyson	21	221	Tony Tucker IBF	221	Wu 12	Las Vegas
1987	Oct. 16	Mike Tyson	21	216	Tyrell Biggs	228¾	TKO 7	Atlantic City
1988	Jan. 22	Mike Tyson	21	215¾	Larry Holmes	225¾	TKO 4	Atlantic City
1988	Mar. 20	Mike Tyson	21	216¼	Tony Tubbs	238¼	KO 2	Tokyo
1988	June 27	Mike Tyson	21	218¼	**Michael Spinks**	212¼	KO 1	Atlantic City
1989	Feb. 25	**Mike Tyson**	22	218	Frank Bruno	228	TKO 5	Las Vegas
1989	July 21	**Mike Tyson**	23	219¼	Carl Williams	218	TKO 1	Las Vegas
1990	Feb. 10	Buster Douglas	29	231½	**Mike Tyson**	220½	KO 10	Tokyo
1990	Oct. 25	Evander Holyfield	28	208	**Buster Douglas**	246	KO 3	Las Vegas
1991	Apr. 19	**Evander Holyfield**	28	208	George Foreman	257	Wu 12	Atlantic City
1991	Nov. 23	**Evander Holyfield**	29	210	Bert Cooper	215	TKO 7	Atlanta
1992	June 19	**Evander Holyfield**	29	210	Larry Holmes	233	Wu 12	Las Vegas
1992	Nov. 13	Riddick Bowe	25	235	**Evander Holyfield**	205	Wu 12	Las Vegas
1993	Feb. 6	**Riddick Bowe**	25	243	Michael Dokes	244	TKO 1	NYC (Mad. Sq. Garden)
1993	May 8	Lennox Lewis WBC‡	27	235	Tony Tucker	235	Wu 12	Las Vegas
1993	May 22	**Riddick Bowe**	25	244	Jesse Ferguson	224	TKO 2	Washington, D.C.
1993	Oct. 1	Lennox Lewis WBC	28	233	Frank Bruno	238	TKO 7	Cardiff, Wales
1993	Nov. 6	Evander Holyfield	31	217	**Riddick Bowe** WBA/IBF	246	Wm 12	Las Vegas
1994	Apr. 22	Michael Moorer	26	214	**Evander Holyfield**	214	Wm 12	Las Vegas
1994	May 6	Lennox Lewis WBC	28	235	Phil Jackson	218	TKO 8	Atlantic City
1994	Sept. 25	Oliver McCall	29	231¼	**Lennox Lewis** WBC	238	TKO 2	London
1994	Nov. 5	George Foreman!	45	250	**Michael Moorer**	222	KO 10	Las Vegas
1995	Apr. 8	Oliver McCall WBC	29	231	Larry Holmes	236	Wu 12	Las Vegas
1995	Apr. 8	Bruce Seldon!	28	236	Tony Tucker	240	TKO 7	Las Vegas
1995	Apr. 22	**George Foreman!**	46	256	Axel Schulz	221	Ws 12	Las Vegas

*WBC recognized winner of Mar. 9, 1984 fight between Tim Witherspoon and Greg Page as world champion after Larry Holmes relinquished title in dispute. IBF then recognized Holmes.

**IBF recognized winner of May 30, 1987 fight between Tony Tucker and James (Buster) Douglas as world champion after Michael Spinks relinquished title in dispute.

†The July 15, 1987 Spinks-Cooney fight was not an official championship bout because it was not sanctioned by any boxing associations, councils or federations.

‡Boxing recognized Lennox Lewis as world champion when Riddick Bowe gave up that portion of his title on Dec. 14, 1992, rather than fight Lewis, the WBC's mandatory challenger.

!George Foreman won WBA and IBF championships when he beat Michael Moorer on Nov. 5, 1994. He was stripped of WBA title on Mar. 4, 1995, when he refused to fight No. 1 contender Tony Tucker, and he relinquished IBF title on June 29, 1995, rather than give Axel Schulz a rematch. Tucker lost to Bruce Seldon in their April 8, 2001 fight for vacant WBA title.

World Heavyweight Championship Fights (Cont.)

Year	Date	Winner	Age	Wgt	Loser	Wgt	Result	Location
1995	Aug. 19	Bruce Seldon WBA	28	234	Joe Hipp	223	TKO 10	Las Vegas
1995	Sept. 2	Frank Bruno	33	248	Oliver McCall WBC	235	Wu 12	London
1995	Dec. 9	Frans Botha*	27	237	Axel Schulz	222	Wu 12	Stuttgart, GER
1996	Mar. 16	Mike Tyson	29	220	Frank Bruno WBC	247	TKO 3	Las Vegas
1996	June 22	Michael Moorer*	28	222	Axel Schulz	223	Ws 12	Dortmund, GER
1996	Sept. 7	Mike Tyson WBC†	30	219	Bruce Seldon WBA	229	TKO 1	Las Vegas
1996	Nov. 9	Evander Holyfield	34	215	**Mike Tyson** WBA	222	TKO 11	Las Vegas
1997	Feb. 7	Lennox Lewis†	31	251	Oliver McCall	237	TKO 5	Las Vegas
1997	Mar. 29	Michael Moorer IBF	29	212	Vaughn Bean	212	Wm 12	Las Vegas
1997	June 28	**Evander Holyfield** WBA‡	34	218	Mike Tyson	218	Disq. 3	Las Vegas
1997	July 12	Lennox Lewis WBC	31	242	Henry Akinwande	237½	Disq. 5	Stateline, Nev.
1997	Oct. 4	Lennox Lewis WBC	32	244	Andrew Golota	244	TKO 1	Atlantic City
1997	Nov. 8	Evander Holyfield WBA	35	214	Michael Moorer IBF	223	TKO 8	Las Vegas
1998	Mar. 28	Lennox Lewis WBC	32	243	Shannon Briggs	228	TKO 5	Atlantic City
1998	Sept. 19	**Evander Holyfield** WBA/IBF	35	217	Vaughn Bean	231	Wu 12	Atlanta
1998	Sept. 26	Lennox Lewis WBC	33	250	Zeljko Mavrovic	220	Wu 12	Uncasville, Conn.
1999	Mar. 13	Lennox Lewis WBC	33	246	**Evander Holyfield** WBA/IBF	215	Draw 12	NYC (Mad. Sq. Garden)
1999	Nov. 13	Lennox Lewis WBC	34	240	**Evander Holyfield** WBA/IBF	218	Wu 12	Las Vegas
2000	Apr. 29	**Lennox Lewis** WBC/IBF!	34	247	Michael Grant	250	KO 2	NYC (Mad. Sq. Garden)
2000	July 15	**Lennox Lewis** WBC/IBF	34	250	Frans Botha	237	TKO 2	London
2000	Aug. 12	Evander Holyfield	37	221	John Ruiz	224	Wu 12	Las Vegas
2000	Nov. 11	**Lennox Lewis** WBC/IBF	35	249	David Tua	245	Wu 12	Las Vegas
2001	Mar. 3	John Ruiz	29	227	Evander Holyfield	217	Wu 12	Las Vegas
2001	Apr. 22	Hasim Rahman	28	237	**Lennox Lewis** WBC/IBF	253	KO 5	Johannesburg, S. Africa
2001	Nov. 17	Lennox Lewis	36	247	**Hasim Rahman** WBC/IBF	236	KO 4	Las Vegas
2001	Dec. 15	**John Ruiz** WBA	29	232	Evander Holyfield	219	Draw 12	Mashantucket, Conn.
2002	June 8	**Lennox Lewis** WBC/IBF@	36	249	Mike Tyson	235	KO 8	Memphis, Tenn.
2002	July 27	**John Ruiz** WBA	30	233	Kirk Johnson	238	Disq. 10	Las Vegas
2002	Dec. 14	Chris Byrd	32	214	Evander Holyfield	220	Wu 12	Atlantic City
2003	Mar. 1	Roy Jones Jr.	34	193	**John Ruiz** WBA	226	Wu 12	Las Vegas
2003	June 21	**Lennox Lewis** WBC	37	257	Vitali Klitschko	248	TKO 6	Los Angeles
2003	Sept. 20	**Chris Byrd** IBF	33	212	Fres Oquendo	224	Wu 12	Uncasville, Conn.
2003	Dec. 13	John Ruiz WBA%	31	241	Hasim Rahman	246	Wu 12	Atlantic City
2004	Apr. 17	**John Ruiz** WBA	32	240	Fres Oquendo	222	TKO 11	NYC (Mad. Sq. Garden)
2004	Apr. 17	**Chris Byrd** IBF	33	210	Andrew Golota	237	Draw 12	NYC (Mad. Sq. Garden)
2004	Apr. 24	Vitali Klitschko WBC^	32	245	Corrie Sanders	236	TKO 8	Los Angeles

*Frans Botha won the vacant IBF title with a controversial 12-round decision over Axel Schulz on Dec. 9, 1995, but after legal sparring, was eventually stripped of the IBF belt for using anabolic steroids. Moorer then claimed the revacated title with his June 22, 1996 win over Schulz.

†Mike Tyson won the WBC belt from Frank Bruno on Mar. 16, 1996 and still held it at the time of his Sept. 7, 1996 win over Bruce Seldon (although it was not at risk for that fight) but was forced to relinquish the title after the bout for not fighting mandatory challenge Lennox Lewis. Tyson also paid Lewis $4 million to step aside and allow the Tyson-Seldon bout to take place. Lewis then fought Oliver McCall for the vacant WBC belt. The fight was stopped 55 seconds into round 5 because, inexplicably, McCall was visibly distraught and stopped throwing punches.

‡Holyfield won the bout by disqualification and retained the WBA belt after Tyson spit out his mouthpiece and bit off a piece of Holyfield's ear. Tyson had received a two-point deduction from referee Mills Lane and after a stern warning and a short delay the fight was allowed to continue. Later in round 3, he bit Holyfield's other ear and Tyson was disqualified.

!Lewis was stripped of the WBA title for choosing to fight Michael Grant instead of John Ruiz, the WBA's #1 challenger. The WBA sanctioned the Evander Holyfield-John Ruiz August 12 bout for its vacant heavyweight belt.

@Lewis effectively sold his IBF title to promoter Don King for $1 million and a Range Rover in September 2002. Lewis stepped aside (in exchange for the car and substantial fee), relinquishing his IBF belt by declining to fight Chris Byrd the mandatory challenger. The IBF sanctioned the Dec. 14, 2002 fight between Byrd and Holyfield for its vacant heavyweight belt.

%Ruiz won the interim WBA title after Roy Jones Jr. declined to defend the title he won from Ruiz on Mar. 1, 2003. The interim tag was later dropped when Jones returned to the light heavyweight division.

^Klitschko won the WBC title vacated by the retirement of Lennox Lewis.

Muhammad Ali's Career Pro Record

Born Cassius Marcellus Clay, Jr. on Jan. 17, 1942, in Louisville; Amateur record of 100-5; won light-heavyweight gold medal at 1960 Olympic Games; Pro record of 56-5 with 37 KOs in 61 fights.

1960

Date	Opponent (location)	Result
Oct. 29	Tunney Hunsaker, Louisville	Wu 6
Dec. 27	Herb Siler, Miami Beach	TKO 4

1961

Date	Opponent (location)	Result
Jan. 17	Tony Esperti, Miami Beach	TKO 3
Feb. 7	Jim Robinson, Miami Beach	TKO 1
Feb. 21	Donnie Fleeman, Miami Beach	TKO 7
Apr. 19	Lamar Clark, Louisville	KO 2
June 26	Duke Sabedong, Las Vegas	Wu 10
July 22	Alonzo Johnson, Louisville	Wu 10
Oct. 7	Alex Miteff, Louisville	TKO 6
Nov. 29	Willi Besmanoff, Louisville	TKO 7

1962

Date	Opponent (location)	Result
Feb. 10	Sonny Banks, New York	TKO 4
Feb. 28	Don Warner, Miami Beach	TKO 4
Apr. 23	George Logan, Los Angeles	TKO 4
May 19	Billy Daniels, Los Angeles	TKO 7
July 20	Alejandro Lavorante, Los Angeles	KO 5
Nov. 15	Archie Moore, Los Angeles	KO 4

1963

Date	Opponent (location)	Result
Jan. 24	Charlie Powell, Pittsburgh	KO 3
Mar. 13	Doug Jones, New York	Wu 10
June 18	Henry Cooper, London	TKO 5

1964

Date	Opponent (location)	Result
Feb. 25	Sonny Liston, Miami Beach	TKO 7

(won World Heavyweight title)

After the fight, Clay announces he is a member of the Black Muslim religious sect and has changed his name to Muhammad Ali.

1965

Date	Opponent (location)	Result
May 25	Sonny Liston, Lewiston, Me	KO 1
Nov. 22	Floyd Patterson, Las Vegas	TKO 12

1966

Date	Opponent (location)	Result
Mar. 29	George Chuvalo, Toronto	Wu 15
May 21	Henry Cooper, London	TKO 6
Aug. 6	Brian London, London	KO 3
Sept. 10	Karl Mildenberger, Frankfurt	TKO 12
Nov. 14	Cleveland Williams, Houston	TKO 3

1967

Date	Opponent (location)	Result
Feb. 6	Ernie Terrell, Houston	Wu 15
Mar. 22	Zora Folley, New York	KO 7
Apr. 28	Refuses induction in U.S. Army and is stripped of world title by WBA and most state commissions the next day.	
June 20	Found guilty of draft evasion in Houston; fined $10,000 and sentenced to 5 years; remains free pending appeals, but is barred from the ring.	

1968-69 (Inactive)

1970

Date	Opponent (location)	Result
Feb. 3	Announces retirement.	
Oct. 26	Jerry Quarry, Atlanta	TKO 3
Dec. 7	Oscar Bonavena, New York	TKO 15

1971

Date	Opponent (location)	Result
Mar. 8	Joe Frazier, New York	Lu 15

(for World Heavyweight title)

June 28	U.S. Supreme Court reverses Ali's 1967 conviction saying he had been drafted improperly.	
July 26	Jimmy Ellis, Houston	TKO 12

(won vacant NABF Heavyweight title)

Nov. 17	Buster Mathis, Houston	Wu 12
Dec. 26	Jurgen Blin, Zurich	KO 7

1972

Date	Opponent (location)	Result
Apr. 1	Mac Foster, Tokyo	Wu 15
May 1	George Chuvalo, Vancouver	Wu 12
June 27	Jerry Quarry, Las Vegas	TKO 7
July 19	Al (Blue) Lewis, Dublin, Ire	TKO 11
Sept. 20	Floyd Patterson, New York	TKO 7
Nov. 21	Bob Foster, Stateline, Nev	TKO 8

1973

Date	Opponent (location)	Result
Feb. 14	Joe Bugner, Las Vegas	Wu 12
Mar. 31	Ken Norton, San Diego	Ls 12

(lost NABF Heavyweight title)

Sept. 10	Ken Norton, Inglewood, Calif	Ws 12

(regained NABF Heavyweight title)

Oct. 20	Rudi Lubbers, Jakarta, Indonesia	Wu 12

1974

Date	Opponent (location)	Result
Jan. 28	Joe Frazier, New York	Wu 12
Oct. 30	George Foreman, Kinshasa, Zaire	KO 8

(regained World Heavyweight title)

1975

Date	Opponent (location)	Result
Mar. 24	Chuck Wepner, Cleveland	TKO 15
May 16	Ron Lyle, Las Vegas	TKO 11
June 30	Joe Bugner, Kuala Lumpur, Malaysia	Wu 15
Oct. 1	Joe Frazier, Manila, Philippines	TKO 14

1976

Date	Opponent (location)	Result
Feb. 20	Jean Pierre Coopman, San Juan	KO 5
Apr. 30	Jimmy Young, Landover, Md	Wu 15
May 24	Richard Dunn, Munich	TKO 5
Sept. 28	Ken Norton, New York	Wu 15

1977

Date	Opponent (location)	Result
May 16	Alfredo Evangelista, Landover	Wu 15
Sept. 29	Earnie Shavers, New York	Wu 15

1978

Date	Opponent (location)	Result
Feb. 15	Leon Spinks, Las Vegas	Ls 15

(lost World Heavyweight title)

Sept. 15	Leon Spinks, New Orleans	Wu 15

(regained World Heavyweight title)

1979

Date		
June 27	Announces retirement.	

1980

Date	Opponent (location)	Result
Oct. 2	Larry Holmes, Las Vegas	TKO by 11

1981

Date	Opponent (location)	Result
Dec. 11	Trevor Berbick, Nassau	Lu 10

(retires after fight)

Major Titleholders

Note the following sanctioning body abbreviations: NBA (National Boxing Association), WBA (World Boxing Association), WBC (World Boxing Council), GBR (Great Britain), IBF (International Boxing Federation), plus other national and state commissions. Fighters who retired as champion are indicated by (*) and champions who abandoned or relinquished their titles are indicated by (†).

Heavyweights

Widely accepted champions in CAPITAL letters. Current champions in **bold** type (as of Oct. 23, 2001).

Note: Muhammad Ali was stripped of his world title in 1967 after refusing induction into the Army (see Muhammad Ali's Career Pro Record). George Foreman was stripped of his WBA and IBF titles in 1995, but remained active as linear champion.

Champion	Held Title
JOHN L. SULLIVAN	1885–92
JAMES J. CORBETT	1892–97
BOB FITZSIMMONS	1897–99
JAMES J. JEFFRIES	1899–1905*
MARVIN HART	1905–06
TOMMY BURNS	1906–08
JACK JOHNSON	1908–15
JESS WILLARD	1915–19
JACK DEMPSEY	1919–26
GENE TUNNEY	1926–28*
MAX SCHMELING	1930–32
JACK SHARKEY	1932–33
PRIMO CARNERA	1933–34
MAX BAER	1934–35
JAMES J. BRADDOCK	1935–37
JOE LOUIS	1937–49*
EZZARD CHARLES	1949–51
JERSEY JOE WALCOTT	1951–52
ROCKY MARCIANO	1952–56*
FLOYD PATTERSON	1956–59
INGEMAR JOHANSSON	1959–60
FLOYD PATTERSON	1960–62
SONNY LISTON	1962–64
CASSIUS CLAY (MUHAMMAD ALI)	1964–67
Ernie Terrell (WBA)	1965–67
Joe Frazier (NY)	1968–70
Jimmy Ellis (WBA)	1968–70
JOE FRAZIER	1970–73
GEORGE FOREMAN	1973–74
MUHAMMAD ALI	1974–78
LEON SPINKS	1978
Ken Norton (WBC)	1978
Larry Holmes (WBC)	1978–80
MUHAMMAD ALI	1978–79*
John Tate (WBA)	1979–80
Mike Weaver (WBA)	1980–82
LARRY HOLMES	1980–85
Michael Dokes (WBA)	1982–83
Gerrie Coetzee (WBA)	1983–84
Tim Witherspoon (WBC)	1984
Pinklon Thomas (WBC)	1984–86
Greg Page (WBA)	1984–85
MICHAEL SPINKS	1985–87
Tim Witherspoon (WBA)	1986
Trevor Berbick (WBC)	1986
Mike Tyson (WBC)	1986–87
James (Bonecrusher) Smith (WBA)	1986–87
Tony Tucker (IBF)	1987
MIKE TYSON (WBC, WBA, IBF)	1987–90
BUSTER DOUGLAS (WBC, WBA, IBF)	1990
EVANDER HOLYFIELD (WBC, WBA, IBF)	1990–92
RIDDICK BOWE (WBA, IBF)	1992–93
Lennox Lewis (WBC)	1992–94
EVANDER HOLYFIELD (WBA, IBF)	1993–94
MICHAEL MOORER (WBA, IBF)	1994
Oliver McCall (WBC)	1994–95
GEORGE FOREMAN (WBA, IBF)	1994–95
Bruce Seldon (WBA)	1995–96
GEORGE FOREMAN	1995–96
Frank Bruno (WBC)	1995–96
Mike Tyson (WBC)	1996†
Mike Tyson (WBA)	1996
Michael Moorer (IBF)	1996–1997
Evander Holyfield (WBA, IBF)	1996–2000
Lennox Lewis (WBC)	1997–2000
LENNOX LEWIS (WBA, WBC, IBF)	2000
Evander Holyfield (WBA)	2000–01
LENNOX LEWIS (WBC, IBF)	2000–01
John Ruiz (WBA)	2001–03
Hasim Rahman (WBC, IBF)	2001
LENNOX LEWIS (WBC, IBF)	2001–02†
LENNOX LEWIS (WBC)	2001–04*
Roy Jones Jr. (WBA)	2003–04
Chris Byrd (IBF)	2003–
John Ruiz (WBA)	2004–
Vitali Klitschko (WBC)	2004–

Note: John L. Sullivan held the Bare Knuckle championship from 1882-85.

Cruiserweights

Current champions in **bold** type.

Champion	Held Title
Marvin Camel (WBC)	1980
Carlos De Leon (WBC)	1980–82
Ossie Ocasio (WBA)	1982–84
S.T. Gordon (WBC)	1982–83
Carlos De Leon (WBC)	1983–85
Marvin Camel (IBF)	1983–84
Lee Roy Murphy (IBF)	1984–86
Piet Crous (WBA)	1984–85
Alfonso Ratliff (WBC)	1985
Dwight Braxton (WBA)	1985–86
Bernard Benton (WBC)	1985–86
Carlos De Leon (WBC)	1986–88
Evander Holyfield (WBA)	1986–88
Ricky Parkey (IBF)	1986–87
Evander Holyfield (WBA/IBF)	1987–88
Evander Holyfield	1988†
Toufik Belbouli (WBA)	1989
Robert Daniels (WBA)	1989–91
Carlos De Leon (WBC)	1989–90
Glenn McCrory (IBF)	1989–90
Jeff Lampkin (IBF)	1990
Massimiliano Duran (WBC)	1990–91
Bobby Czyz (WBA)	1991–92†
Anaclet Wamba (WBC)	1991–95
James Pritchard (IBF)	1991
James Warring (IBF)	1991–92
Alfred Cole (IBF)	1992–96
Orlin Norris (WBA)	1993–95
Nate Miller (WBA)	1995–97
Marcelo Dominguez (WBC)	1996–98
Adolpho Washington (IBF)	1996–97
Uriah Grant (IBF)	1997
Imamu Mayfield (IBF)	1997–98
Arthur Williams (IBF)	1998–99
Fabrice Tiozzo (WBA)	1997–2000
Juan Carlos Gomez (WBC)	1998–2002†
Vassiliy Jirov (IBF)	1999–2003
Virgil Hill (WBA)	2000–02
Jean-Marc Mormeck (WBA)	2002–
Wayne Braithwaite (WBC)	2002–
James Toney (IBF)	2003†
Kelvin Davis (IBF)	2004–

Light Heavyweights

Widely accepted champions in CAPITAL letters. Current champions in **bold** type.

Champion	Held Title
JACK ROOT	1903
GEORGE GARDNER	1903
BOB FITZSIMMONS	1903–05
PHILADELPHIA JACK O'BRIEN	1905–12*
JACK DILLON	1914–16
BATTLING LEVINSKY	1916–20
GEORGES CARPENTIER	1920–22
BATTLING SIKI	1922–23
MIKE McTIGUE	1923–25
PAUL BERLENBACH	1925–26
JACK DELANEY	1926–27†
Jimmy Slattery (NBA)	1927
TOMMY LOUGHRAN	1927-29
JIMMY SLATTERY	1930
MAXIE ROSENBLOOM	1930–34
George Nichols (NBA)	1932
Bob Godwin (NBA)	1933
BOB OLIN	1934–35
JOHN HENRY LEWIS	1935–38
MELIO BETTINA (NY)	1939
Len Harvey (GBR)	1939–42
BILLY CONN	1939–40†
ANTON CHRISTOFORIDIS (NBA)	1941
GUS LESNEVICH	1941–48
Freddie Mills (GBR)	1942–46
FREDDIE MILLS	1948–50
JOEY MAXIM	1950–52
ARCHIE MOORE	1952–62
Harold Johnson (NBA)	1961
HAROLD JOHNSON	1962–63
WILLIE PASTRANO	1963–65
Eddie Cotton (Mich.)	1963–64
JOSE TORRES	1965–66
DICK TIGER	1966–68
BOB FOSTER	1968–74*
Vicente Rondon (WBA)	1971–72
John Conteh (WBC)	1974–77
Victor Galindez (WBA)	1974–78
Miguel A. Cuello (WBC)	1977–78
Mate Parlov (WBC)	1978
Mike Rossman (WBA)	1978–79
Marvin Johnson (WBC)	1978–79
Matthew (Franklin) Saad Muhammad (WBC)	1979–81

Champion	Held Title
Marvin Johnson (WBA)	1979–80
Eddie (Gregory) Mustapha Muhammad (WBA)	1980–81
Michael Spinks (WBA)	1981–83
Dwight (Braxton) Muhammad Qawi (WBC)	1981–83
MICHAEL SPINKS	1983–85†
J.B.Williamson (WBC)	1985–86
Slobodan Kacar (IBF)	1985–86
Marvin Johnson (WBA)	1986–87
Dennis Andries (WBC)	1986–87
Bobby Czyz (IBF)	1986–87
Leslie Stewart (WBA)	1987
Virgil Hill (WBA)	1987–91
Prince Charles Williams (IBF)	1987–93
Thomas Hearns (WBC)	1987
Donny Lalonde (WBC)	1987–88
Sugar Ray Leonard (WBC)	1988
Dennis Andries (WBC)	1989
Jeff Harding (WBC)	1989–90
Dennis Andries (WBC)	1990–91
Jeff Harding (WBC)	1991–94
Thomas Hearns (WBA)	1991–92
Iran Barkley (WBA)	1992†
Virgil Hill (WBA)	1992–97
Henry Maske (IBF)	1993–96
Virgil Hill (WBA/IBF)	1996–97
Mike McCallum (WBC)	1994–95
Fabrice Tiozzo (WBC)	1995–96
Roy Jones Jr. (WBC)	1996
Montell Griffin (WBC)	1996
D. Michaelczewski (WBA/IBF)	1997†
William Guthrie (IBF)	1997–98
Lou Del Valle (WBA)	1997–98
ROY JONES JR. (WBA/WBC)	1997–2003†
Reggie Johnson (IBF)	1998–99
ROY JONES JR. (WBA/WBC/IBF)	1999–2003†
Antonio Tarver (WBC/IBF)	2003
Mehdi Sahnoune (WBA)	2003
ROY JONES JR. (WBC)	2003–04
Silvio Branco (WBA)	2003–04
Antonio Tarver (WBC)	2003–
Glen Johnson (IBF)	2004–
Fabrice Tiozzo (WBA)	2004–

Super Middleweights

Current champions in **bold** type.

Champion	Held Title
Murray Sutherland (IBF)	1984
Chong-Pal Park (IBF)	1984–87
Chong-Pal Park (WBA)	1987–88
Graziano Rocchigiani (IBF)	1988–89
Fugencio Obelmejias (WBA)	1988–89
Ray Leonard (WBC)	1988–90†
In-Chut Baek (WBA)	1989–90
Lindell Holmes (IBF)	1990–91
Christophe Tiozzo (WBA)	1990–91
Mauro Galvano (WBC)	1990–92
Victor Cordova (WBA)	1991
Darrin Van Horn (IBF)	1991–92
Iran Barkley (WBA)	1992
Nigel Benn (WBC)	1992–96
James Toney (IBF)	1992–94
Michael Nunn (WBA)	1992–94
Steve Little (WBA)	1994
Frank Liles (WBA)	1994–99
Roy Jones (IBF)	1994–96
Thulane Malinga (WBC)	1996

Champion	Held Title
Vincenzo Nardiello (WBC)	1996
Robin Reid (WBC)	1996–97
Charles Brewer (IBF)	1997–98
Sven Ottke (IBF)	1998–2004*
Thulane Malinga (WBC)	1997–98
Richie Woodhall (WBC)	1998–99
Byron Mitchell (WBA)	1999–2000
Markus Beyer (WBC)	1999–2000
Glenn Gatley (WBC)	2000
Dingaan Thobela (WBC)	2000
Bruno Girard (WBA)	2000–01†
Dave Hilton (WBC)	2000†
Byron Mitchell (WBA)	2001–03
Eric Lucas (WBC)	2001–03
Sven Ottke (IBF/WBA)	2003–04*
Markus Beyer (WBC)	2003–04
Anthony Mundine (WBA)	2004
Manny Siaca (WBA)	2004–
Cristian Sanavia (WBC)	2004
Jeff Lacy (IBF)	2004–
Markus Beyer (WBC)	2004–

Major Titleholders (Cont.)
Middleweights

Widely accepted champions in CAPITAL letters. Current champions in **bold** type.

Champion	Held Title
JACK (NONPAREIL) DEMPSEY	1884–91
BOB FITZSIMMONS	1891–97
CHARLES (KID) McCOY	1897–98
TOMMY RYAN	1898–1907
STANLEY KETCHEL	1908
BILLY PAPKE	1908
STANLEY KETCHEL	1908–10
FRANK KLAUS	1913
GEORGE CHIP	1913–14
AL McCOY	1914–17
Jeff Smith (AUS)	1914
Mick King (AUS)	1914
Jeff Smith (AUS)	1914–15
Lee Darcy (AUS)	1915–17
MIKE O'DOWD	1917–20
JOHNNY WILSON	1920–23
Wm. Bryan Downey (Ohio)	1921–22
Dave Rosenberg (NY)	1922
Jock Malone (Ohio)	1922–23
Mike O'Dowd (NY)	1922
Lou Bogash (NY)	1923
HARRY GREB	1923–26
TIGER FLOWERS	1926
MICKEY WALKER	1926–31†
GORILLA JONES	1931–32
MARCEL THIL	1932–37
Ben Jeby (NY)	1932–33
Lou Brouillard (NBA, NY)	1933
Vince Dundee (NBA, NY)	1933–34
Teddy Yarosz (NBA, NY)	1934–35
Babe Risko (NBA, NY)	1935–36
Freddie Steele (NBA, NY)	1936–38
FRED APOSTOLI	1937–39
Al Hostak (NBA)	1938
Solly Krieger (NBA)	1938–39
Al Hostak (NBA)	1939–40
CEFERINO GARCIA	1939–40
KEN OVERLIN	1940–41
Tony Zale (NBA)	1940–41
BILLY SOOSE	1941
TONY ZALE	1941–47
ROCKY GRAZIANO	1947–48
TONY ZALE	1948
MARCEL CERDAN	1948–49
JAKE La MOTTA	1949–51
SUGAR RAY ROBINSON	1951
RANDY TURPIN	1951
SUGAR RAY ROBINSON	1951–52*
CARL (BOBO) OLSON	1953–55
SUGAR RAY ROBINSON	1955–57
GENE FULLMER	1957

Champion	Held Title
SUGAR RAY ROBINSON	1957
CARMEN BASILIO	1957–58
SUGAR RAY ROBINSON	1958–60
Gene Fullmer (NBA)	1959–62
PAUL PENDER	1960–61
TERRY DOWNES	1961–62
PAUL PENDER	1962–63
Dick Tiger (WBA)	1962–63
DICK TIGER	1963
JOEY GIARDELLO	1963–65
DICK TIGER	1965–66
EMILE GRIFFITH	1966–67
NINO BENVENUTI	1967
EMILE GRIFFITH	1967–68
NINO BENVENUTI	1968–70
CARLOS MONZON	1970–77*
Rodrigo Valdez (WBC)	1974–76
RODRIGO VALDEZ	1977–78
HUGO CORRO	1978–79
VITO ANTUOFERMO	1979–80
ALAN MINTER	1980
MARVELOUS MARVIN HAGLER	1980–87
SUGAR RAY LEONARD	1987
Frank Tate (IBF)	1987–88
Sumbu Kalambay (WBA)	1987–89
Thomas Hearns (WBC)	1987–88
Iran Barkley (WBC)	1988–89
Michael Nunn (IBF)	1988–91
Roberto Duran (WBC)	1989–90*
Mike McCallum (WBA)	1989–91
Julian Jackson (WBC)	1990–93
James Toney (IBF)	1991–93†
Reggie Johnson (WBA)	1992–93
Roy Jones Jr. (IBF)	1993–94†
Gerald McClellan (WBC)	1993–95†
John David Jackson (WBA)	1993–94
Jorge Castro (WBA)	1994–97
Julian Jackson (WBC)	1995
Bernard Hopkins (IBF)	1995–
Quincy Taylor (WBC)	1995–96
Shinji Takehara (WBA)	1995–96
William Joppy (WBA)	1996–97
Keith Holmes (WBC)	1996–98
Julio Cesar Green (WBA)	1997–98
William Joppy (WBA)	1998–2001
Hassine Cherifi (WBC)	1998–99
Keith Holmes (WBC)	1999–2001
Bernard Hopkins (IBF/WBC)	2001–
Felix Trinidad (WBA)	2001
BERNARD HOPKINS (IBF/WBA/WBC)	2001–

Junior Middleweights

Widely accepted champions in CAPITAL letters. Current champions in **bold** type.

Champion	Held Title
ERNILE GRIFFITH (EBU)	1962–63
DENNIS MOYER	1962–63
RALPH DUPAS	1963
SANDRO MAZZINGHI	1963–65
NINO BENVENUTI	1965–66
KI-SOO KIM	1966–68
SANDRO MAZZINGHI	1968
FREDDIE LITTLE	1969–70
CARMELO BOSSI	1970–71
KOICHI WAJIMA	1971–74
OSCAR ALBARADO	1974–75
KOICHI WAJIMA	1975
Miguel de Oliveira (WBC)	1975–76
JAE-DO YUH	1975–76

Champion	Held Title
Elisha Obed (WBC)	1975–76
KOICHI WAJIMA	1976
JOSE DURAN	1976
Eckhard Dagge (WBC)	1976–77
MIGUEL ANGEL CASTELLINI	1976–77
EDDIE GAZO	1977–78
Rocky Mattioli (WBC)	1977–79
MASASHI KUDO	1978–79
Maurice Hope (WBC)	1979–81
AYUB KALULE	1979–81
Wilfred Benitez (WBC)	1981–82
SUGAR RAY LEONARD	1981–82
Tadashi Mihara (WBA)	1981–82
Davey Moore (WBA)	1982–83

Champion	Held Title
Thomas Hearns (WBC)	1982–84
Roberto Duran (WBA)	1983–84
Mark Medal (IBF)	1984
THOMAS HEARNS	1984–86
Mike McCallum (WBA)	1984–87
Carlos Santos (IBF)	1984–86
Buster Drayton (IBF)	1986–87
Duane Thomas (WBC)	1986–87
Matthew Hilton (IBF)	1987–88
Lupe Aquino (WBC)	1987
Gianfranco Rosi (WBC)	1987–88
Julian Jackson (WBA)	1987–90
Donald Curry (WBC)	1988–89
Robert Hines (IBF)	1988–89
Darrin Van Horn (IBF)	1989
Rene Jacquote (WBC)	1989
John Mugabi (WBC)	1989–90
Gianfranco Rosi (IBF)	1989–94
Terry Norris (WBC)	1990–94
Gilbert Dele (WBA)	1991
Vinny Pazienza (WBA)	1991–92
Julio Cesar Vasquez (WBA)	1992–95
Simon Brown (WBC)	1994

Champion	Held Title
Terry Norris (WBC)	1994–
Vincent Pettway (IBF)	1994–95
Paul Vaden (IBF)	1995
Carl Daniels (WBA)	1995
Terry Norris (WBC)	1995–97
Terry Norris (IBF)	1995–96
Laurent Boudouani (WBA)	1996–99
Raul Marquez (IBF)	1997
Keith Mullings (WBC)	1997–99
Yori Boy Campas (IBF)	1997–98
Fernando Vargas (IBF)	1998–2000
Javier Castillejo (WBC)	1999–2001
David Reid (WBA)	1999–00
Felix Trinidad (WBA/IBF)	2000–01†
Oscar De La Hoya (WBC)	2001–03
Fernando Vargas (WBA)	2001–02
Ronald Wright (IBF)	2001–
Oscar De La Hoya (WBA/WBC)	2002-03
Shane Mosley (WBA/WBC)	2003–04
RONALD WRIGHT (IBF/WBA/WBC)	2004
RONALD WRIGHT (WBA/WBC)	2004–
Kassim Ouma (IBF)	2004–

Welterweights

Widely accepted champions in CAPITAL letters. Current champions in **bold** type.

Champion	Held Title
PADDY DUFFY	1888–90
MYSTERIOUS BILLY SMITH	1892–94
TOMMY RYAN	1894–98
MYSTERIOUS BILLY SMITH	1898–1900
MATTY MATTHEWS	1900
EDDIE CONNOLLY	1900
JAMES (RUBE) FERNS	1900
MATTY MATHEWS	1900–01
JAMES (RUBE) FERNS	1901
JOE WALCOTT	1901–04
THE DIXIE KID	1904–05
HONEY MELLODY	1906–07
Mike (Twin) Sullivan	1907–08†
Harry Lewis	1908–11
Jimmy Gardner	1908
Jimmy Clabby	1910–11
WALDEMAR HOLBERG	1914
TOM McCORMICK	1914
MATT WELLS	1914–15
MIKE GLOVER	1915
JACK BRITTON	1915
TED (KID) LEWIS	1915–16
JACK BRITTON	1916–17
TED (KID) LEWIS	1917–19
JACK BRITTON	1919–22
MICKEY WALKER	1922–26
PETE LATZO	1926–27
JOE DUNDEE	1927–29
JACKIE FIELDS	1929–30
YOUNG JACK THOMPSON	1930
TOMMY FREEMAN	1930–31
YOUNG JACK THOMPSON	1931
LOU BROUILLARD	1931–32
JACKIE FIELDS	1932–33
YOUNG CORBETT III	1933
JIMMY McLARNIN	1933–34
BARNEY ROSS	1934
JIMMY McLARNIN	1934–35
BARNEY ROSS	1935–38
HENRY ARMSTRONG	1938–40
FRITZIE ZIVIC	1940–41
Izzy Jannazzo (Md.)	1940–41
Freddie (Red) Cochrane	1941–46
MARTY SERVO	1946*
SUGAR RAY ROBINSON	1946–51†
Johnny Bratton	1951
KID GAVILAN	1951–54

Champion	Held Title
JOHNNY SAXTON	1954–55
TONY DeMARCO	1955
CARMEN BASILIO	1955–56
JOHNNY SAXTON	1956
CARMEN BASILIO	1956–57†
VIRGIL AKINS	1958
DON JORDAN	1958–60
BENNY (KID) PARET	1960–61
EMILE GRIFFITH	1961
BENNY (KID) PARET	1961–62
EMILE GRIFFITH	1962–63
LUIS RODRIGUEZ	1963
EMILE GRIFFITH	1963–66†
Charlie Shipes (Calif.)	1966–67
CURTIS COKES	1966–69
JOSE NAPOLES	1969–70
BILLY BACKUS	1970–71
JOSE NAPOLES	1971–75
Hedgemon Lewis (NY)	1972–73
Angel Espada (WBA)	1975–76
JOHN H. STRACEY	1975–76
CARLOS PALOMINO	1976–79
Pipino Cuevas (WBA)	1976–80
WILFREDO BENITEZ	1979
SUGAR RAY LEONARD	1979–80
ROBERTO DURAN	1980
Thomas Hearns (WBA)	1980–81
SUGAR RAY LEONARD	1980–82
Donald Curry (WBA)	1983–85
Milton McCrory (WBC)	1983–85
DONALD CURRY	1985–86
LLOYD HONEYGHAN	1986–87
JORGE VACA (WBC)	1987–88
LLOYD HONEYGHAN (WBC)	1988–89
Mark Breland (WBA)	1987
Marlon Starling (WBA)	1987–88
Tomas Molinares (WBA)	1988–89
Simon Brown (IBF)	1988–91
Mark Breland (WBA)	1989–90
MARLON STARLING (WBC)	1989–90
Aaron Davis (WBA)	1990–91
Maurice Blocker (WBC)	1990–91
Meldrick Taylor (WBA)	1991–92
Simon Brown (WBC)	1991
Maurice Blocker (IBF)	1991–93
Buddy McGirt (WBC)	1991–93
Crisanto Espana (WBA)	1992–94

Major Titleholders (Cont.)
Welterweights (Cont.)

Champion	Held Title	Champion	Held Title
Pernell Whitaker (WBC)	1993–97	Andrew Lewis (WBA)	2001–02
Felix Trinidad (IBF)	1993–99	Vernon Forrest (IBF)	2001–02†
Ike Quartey (WBA)	1994–98†	Vernon Forrest (WBC)	2002–03
James Page (WBA)	1998–2000†	Richard Mayorga (WBA)	2002–03
Oscar De La Hoya (WBC)	1997–99	Michele Piccirillo (IBF)	2002–03
Felix Trinidad (WBC/IBF)	1999–2000†	Richard Mayorga (WBA/WBC)	2003
Oscar De La Hoya (WBC)	2000	**Cory Spinks** (IBF)	2003–
Shane Mosley (WBC)	2000–00	**CORY SPINKS** (IBF/WBA/WBC)	2003–

Junior Welterweights

Widely accepted champions in CAPITAL letters. Current champions in **bold** type.

Champion	Held Title	Champion	Held Title
PINKEY MITCHELL	1922–25	Lonnie Smith (WBC)	1985–86
RED HERRING	1925	Patrizio Oliva (WBA)	1986–87
MUSHY CALLAHAN	1926–30	Gary Hinton (IBF)	1986
JACK (KID) BERG	1930–31	Rene Arredondo (WBC)	1986
TONY CANZONERI	1931–32	Tsuyoshi Hamada (WBC)	1986–87
JOHNNY JADICK	1932–33	Joe Louis Manley (IBF)	1986–87
Sammy Fuller	1932–33	Terry Marsh (IBF)	1987
BATTLING SHAW	1933	Juan Coggi (WBA)	1987–90
TONY CANZONERI	1933	Rene Arredondo (WBC)	1987
BARNEY ROSS	1933–35	Roger Mayweather (WBC)	1987–89
TIPPY LARKIN	1946	James McGirt (IBF)	1988
CARLOS ORTIZ	1959–60	Meldrick Taylor (IBF)	1988–90
DUILIO LOI	1960–62	Julio Cesar Chavez (WBC)	1989–94
EDDIE PERKINS	1962	Julio Cesar Chavez (IBF)	1990–91
DUILIO LOI	1962–63	Loreto Garza (WBA)	1990–91
Roberto Cruz	1963	Juan Coggi (WBA)	1991
EDDIE PERKINS	1963–65	Edwin Rosario (WBA)	1991–92
CARLOS HERNANDEZ	1965–66	Rafael Pineda (IBF)	1991–92
SANDRO LOPOPOLO	1966–67	Akinobu Hiranaka (WBA)	1992
PAUL FUJII	1967–68	Pernell Whitaker (IBF)	1992–93†
NICOLINO LOCHE	1968–72	Charles Murray (IBF)	1993–94
Pedro Adigue (WBC)	1968–70	Jake Rodriguez (IBF)	1994–95
Bruno Arcari (WBC)	1970–74	Juan Coggi (WBA)	1993–94
ALFONSO FRAZER	1972	Frankie Randall (WBC)	1994
ANTONIO CERVANTES	1972–76	Frankie Randall (WBA)	1994–96
Perico Fernandez (WBC)	1974–75	Juan Coggi (WBA)	1996
Saensak Muangsurin (WBC)	1975–76	Julio Cesar Chavez (WBC)	1994–96
WILFRED BENITEZ	1976–79	Kostya Tszyu (IBF)	1995–97
Miguel Velasquez (WBC)	1976	Frankie Randall (WBA)	1996–97
Saensak Muangsurin (WBC)	1976–78	Oscar De La Hoya (WBC)	1996–97†
Antonio Cervantes (WBA)	1977–80	Khalid Rahilou (WBA)	1997–98
Sang-Hyun Kim (WBC)	1978–80	Sharmba Mitchell (WBA)	1998–2001
Saoul Mamby (WBC)	1980–82	Vincent Phillips (IBF)	1997–99
Aaron Pryor (WBA)	1980–83	Terronn Millet (IBF)	1999–00†
Leroy Haley (WBC)	1982–83	**Kostya Tszyu** (WBC)	1999–
Aaron Pryor (IBF)	1983–85	Zab Judah (IBF)	2000–01
Bruce Curry (WBC)	1983–84	Kostya Tszyu (WBA/WBC)	2001–04†
Johnny Bumphus (WBA)	1984	KOSTYA TSZYU (IBF/WBA/WBC)	2001–04†
Bill Costello (WBC)	1984–85	**KOSTYA TSZYU** (IBF/WBC)	2004–
Gene Hatcher (WBA)	1984–85	**Vivian Harris** (WBA)	2004–
Ubaldo Sacco (WBA)	1985–86		

Lightweights

Widely accepted champions in CAPITAL letters. Current champions in **bold** type.

Champion	Held Title	Champion	Held Title
JACK McAULIFFE	1886–94	ROCKY KANSAS	1925–26
GEORGE (KID) LAVIGNE	1896–99	SAMMY MANDELL	1926–30
FRANK ERNE	1899–02	AL SINGER	1930
JOE GANS	1902–04	TONY CANZONERI	1930–33
JIMMY BRITT	1904–05	BARNEY ROSS	1933–35†
BATTLING NELSON	1905–06	TONY CANZONERI	1935–36
JOE GANS	1906–08	LOU AMBERS	1936–38
BATTLING NELSON	1908–10	HENRY ARMSTRONG	1938–39
AD WOLGAST	1910–12	LOU AMBERS	1939–40
WILLIE RITCHIE	1912–14	Sammy Angott (NBA)	1940–41
FREDDIE WELSH	1915–17	LEW JENKINS	1940–41
BENNY LEONARD	1917–25*	SAMMY ANGOTT	1941–42
JIMMY GOODRICH	1925	Beau Jack (NY)	1942–43

Champion	Held Title
Slugger White (Md.)	1943
Bob Montgomery (NY)	1943
Sammy Angott (NBA)	1943–44
Beau Jack (NY)	1943–44
Bob Montgomery (NY)	1944–47
Juan Zurita (NBA)	1944–45
IKE WILLIAMS	1947–51
JAMES CARTER	1951–52
LAURO SALAS	1952
JAMES CARTER	1952–54
PADDY DeMARCO	1954
JAMES CARTER	1954–55
WALLACE (BUD) SMITH	1955–56
JOE BROWN	1956–62
CARLOS ORTIZ	1962–65
Kenny Lane (Mich.)	1963–64
ISMAEL LAGUNA	1965
CARLOS ORTIZ	1965–68
CARLOS TEO CRUZ	1968–69
MANDO RAMOS	1969–70
ISMAEL LAGUNA	1970
KEN BUCHANAN	1970–72
Pedro Carrasco (WBC)	1971–72
Mando Ramos (WBC)	1972
ROBERTO DURAN	1972–79†
Chango Carmona (WBC)	1972
Rodolfo Gonzalez (WBC)	1972–74
Ishimatsu Suzuki (WBC)	1974–76
Esteban De Jesus (WBC)	1976–78
Jim Watt (WBC)	1979–81
Ernesto Espana (WBA)	1979–80
Hilmer Kenty (WBA)	1980–81
Sean O'Grady (WBA,WAA)	1981
Alexis Arguello (WBC)	1981–82
Claude Noel (WBA)	1981
Andrew Ganigan (WAA)	1981–82
Arturo Frias (WBA)	1981–82
Ray Mancini (WBA)	1982–84
ALEXIS ARGUELLO	1982–83
Edwin Rosario (WBC)	1983–84
Choo Choo Brown (IBF)	1984
Livingstone Bramble (WBA)	1984–86
Harry Arroyo (IBF)	1984–85
Jose Luis Ramirez (WBC)	1984–85

Champion	Held Title
Jimmy Paul (IBF)	1985–86
Hector Camacho (WBC)	1985–86
Edwin Rosario (WBA)	1986–87
Greg Haugen (IBF)	1986–87
Julio Cesar Chavez (WBA)	1987–88
Jose Luis Ramirez (WBC)	1987–88
JULIO CESAR CHAVEZ (WBC,WBA)	1988–89
Vinny Pazienza (IBF)	1987–88
Greg Haugen (IBF)	1988–89
Pernell Whitaker (IBF,WBC)	1989–90
Edwin Rosario (WBA)	1989–90
Juan Nazario (WBA)	1990
PERNELL WHITAKER (IBF, WBC, WBA)	1990–92†
Joey Gamache (WBA)	1992
Miguel A. Gonzalez (WBC)	1992–96
Tony Lopez (WBA)	1992–93
Dingaan Thobela (WBA)	1993
Fred Pendleton (IBF)	1993–94
Orzubek Nazarov (WBA)	1993–98
Rafael Ruelas (IBF)	1994–95
Oscar De La Hoya (IBF)	1995†
Phillip Holiday (IBF)	1995–97
Jean-Baptiste Mendy (WBC)	1996–97
Stevie Johnston (WBC)	1997–98
Shane Mosley (IBF)	1997–99†
Cesar Bazan (WBC)	1998–99
Jean-Baptiste Mendy (WBA)	1998–99
Julien Lorcy (WBA)	1999
Stevie Johnston (WBC)	1999–00
Stefano Zoff (WBA)	1999
Israel Cardona (IBF)	1999
Paul Spadafora (IBF)	1999–2004†
Gilberto Serrano (WBA)	1999–00
Takanori Hatakeyama (WBA)	2000–01
Jose Luis Castillo (WBC)	2000–02
Julien Lorcy (WBA)	2001
Raul Balbi (WBA)	2001–02
Leonard Dorin (WBA)	2002–03
Floyd Mayweather (WBC)	2002–04†
Javier Jauregui (IBF)	2003-04
Lakva Sim (WBA)	2004
Juan Diaz (WBA)	2004–
Jose Luis Castillo (WBC)	2004–
Julio Diaz	2004–

Junior Lightweights

Widely accepted champions in CAPITAL letters. Current champions in **bold** type.

Champion	Held Title
JOHNNY DUNDEE	1921–23
JACK BERNSTEIN	1923
JOHNNY DUNDEE	1923–24
STEVE (KID) SULLIVAN	1924–25
MIKE BALLERINO	1925
TOD MORGAN	1925–29
BENNY BASS	1929–31
KID CHOCOLATE	1931–33
FRANKIE KLICK	1933–34
SANDY SADDLER	1949–50
HAROLD GOMES	1959–60
GABRIEL (FLASH) ELORDE	1960–67
YOSHIAKI NUMATA	1967
HIROSHI KOBAYASHI	1967–71
Rene Barrientos (WBC)	1969–70
Yoshiaki Numata (WBC)	1970–71
ALFREDO MARCANO	1971–72
Ricardo Arredondo (WBC)	1971–74
BEN VILLAFLOR	1972–73
KUNIAKI SHIBATA	1973
BEN VILLAFLOR	1973–76
Kuniaki Shibata (WBC)	1974–75
Alfredo Escalera (WBC)	1975–78
SAMUEL SERRANO	1976–80
Alexis Arguello (WBC)	1978–80
YASUTSUNE UEHARA	1980–81

Champion	Held Title
Rafael Limon (WBC)	1980–81
Cornelius Boza-Edwards (WBC)	1981
SAMUEL SERRANO	1981–83
Rolando Navarrete (WBC)	1981–82
Rafael Limon (WBC)	1982
Bobby Chacon (WBC)	1982–83
ROGER MAYWEATHER	1983–84
Hector Camacho (WBC)	1983–84
ROCKY LOCKRIDGE	1984–85
Hwan-Kil Yuh (IBF)	1984–85
Julio Cesar Chavez (WBC)	1984–87
Lester Ellis (IBF)	1985
WILFREDO GOMEZ	1985–86
Barry Michael (IBF)	1985–87
ALFREDO LAYNE	1986
BRIAN MITCHELL	1986–91
Rocky Lockridge (IBF)	1987–88
Azumah Nelson (WBC)	1988–94
Tony Lopez (IBF)	1988–89
Juan Molina (IBF)	1989–90
Tony Lopez (IBF)	1990–91
Joey Gamache (WBA)	1991
Brian Mitchell (IBF)	1991
Genaro Hernandez (WBA)	1991–95
James Leija (WBC)	1994
Juan Molina (IBF)	1991–95

Major Titleholders (Cont.)
Junior Lightweights (Cont.)

Champion	Held Title
Gabriel Ruelas (WBC)	1994–95
Eddie Hopson (IBF)	1995
Tracy Patterson (IBF)	1995
Azumah Nelson (WBC)	1995–97
Choi Yong-Soo (WBA)	1995–98
Arturo Gatti (IBF)	1995–98†
Genaro Hernandez (WBC)	1997–98
Floyd Mayweather Jr. (WBC)	1998–2002†
Takanori Hatakeyama (WBA)	1998–99
Roberto Garcia (IBF)	1998–99
Lavka Sim (WBA)	1999

Champion	Held Title
Diego Corrales (IBF)	1999–2001
Baek Jong-Kwon (WBA)	1999–2000
Joel Casamayor (WBA)	2000–02
Steve Forbes (IBF)	2001–02†
Acelino Freitas (WBA)	2002–
Sirimongkol Singmanassak (WBC)	2002–03
Jesus Chavez (WBC)	2003–04
Carlos Hernandez (IBF)	2003–04
Erik Morales (WBC)	2004–
Erik Morales (IBF/WBC)	2004–

Featherweights

Widely accepted champions in CAPITAL letters. Current champions in **bold** type.

Champion	Held Title
TORPEDO BILLY MURPHY	1890
YOUNG GRIFFO	1890–92
GEORGE DIXON	1892–97
SOLLY SMITH	1897–98
Ben Jordan (GBR)	1898–99
Eddie Santry (GBR)	1899–1900
DAVE SULLIVAN	1898
GEORGE DIXON	1898–1900
TERRY McGOVERN	1900–01
YOUNG CORBETT II	1901–04
JIMMY BRITT	1904
ABE ATTELL	1904
BROOKLYN TOMMY SULLIVAN	1904–05
ABE ATTELL	1906–12
JOHNNY KILBANE	1912–23
Jem Driscoll (GBR)	1912–13
EUGENE CRIQUI	1923
JOHNNY DUNDEE	1923–24†
LOUIS (KID) KAPLAN	1925–26†
Dick Finnegan (Mass.)	1926–27
BENNY BASS	1927–28
TONY CANZONERI	1928
ANDRE ROUTIS	1928–29
BATTLING BATTALINO	1929–32†
Tommy Paul (NBA)	1932–33
Kid Chocolate (NY)	1932–33
Freddie Miller (NBA)	1933–36
Baby Arizmendi (MEX)	1935–36
Mike Belloise (NY)	1936–37
Petey Sarron (NBA)	1936–37
HENRY ARMSTRONG	1937–38†
Joey Archibald (NY)	1938–39
Leo Rodak (NBA)	1938–39
JOEY ARCHIBALD	1939–40
Petey Scalzo (NBA)	1940–41
Jimmy Perrin (La.)	1940–41
HARRY JEFFRA	1940–41
JOEY ARCHIBALD	1941
Richie Lemos (NBA)	1941
CHALKY WRIGHT	1941–42
Jackie Wilson (NBA)	1941–43
WILLIE PEP	1942–48
Jackie Callura (NBA)	1943
Phil Terranova (NBA)	1943–44
Sal Bartolo (NBA)	1944–46
SANDY SADDLER	1948–49
WILLIE PEP	1949–50
SANDY SADDLER	1950–57*
HOGAN (KID) BASSEY	1957–59
DAVEY MOORE	1959–63
ULTIMINIO (SUGAR) RAMOS	1963–64
VICENTE SALDIVAR	1964–67*
Howard Winstone (GBR)	1968
Raul Rojas (WBA)	1968
Jose Legra (WBC)	1968–69
Shozo Saijyo (WBA)	1968–71
JOHNNY FAMECHON (WBC)	1969–70

Champion	Held Title
VICENTE SALDIVAR (WBC)	1970
KUNIAKI SHIBATA (WBC)	1970–72
Antonio Gomez (WBA)	1971–72
CLEMENTE SANCHEZ (WBC)	1972
Ernesto Marcel (WBA)	1972–74
JOSE LEGRA (WBC)	1972–73
EDER JOFRE (WBC)	1973–74
Ruben Olivares (WBA)	1974
Bobby Chacon (WBC)	1974–75
ALEXIS ARGUELLO (WBA)	1974–76†
Ruben Olivares (WBC)	1975
David (Poison) Kotey (WBC)	1975–76
DANNY (LITTLE RED) LOPEZ (WBC)	1976–80
Rafael Ortega (WBA)	1977
Cecilio Lastra (WBA)	1977–78
Eusebio Pedroza (WBA)	1978–85
SALVADOR SANCHEZ (WBC)	1980–82
Juan LaPorte (WBC)	1982–84
Wilfredo Gomez (WBC)	1984
Min-Keun Oh (IBF)	1984–85
Azumah Nelson (WBC)	1984–88
Barry McGuigan (WBA)	1985–86
Ki-Young Chung (IBF)	1985–86
Steve Cruz (WBA)	1986–87
Antonio Rivera (IBF)	1986–88
Antonio Esparragoza (WBA)	1987–91
Calvin Grove (IBF)	1988
Jorge Paez (IBF)	1988–91†
Jeff Fenech (WBC)	1988–90†
Marcos Villasana (WBC)	1990–91
Yung-Kyun Park (WBA)	1991–93
Troy Dorsey (IBF)	1991
Manuel Medina (IBF)	1991–93
Paul Hodkinson (WBC)	1991–93
Tom Johnson (IBF)	1993–97
Goyo Vargas (WBC)	1993
Kevin Kelley (WBC)	1993–95
Eloy Rojas (WBA)	1993–96
Alejandro Gonzalez (WBC)	1995
Manuel Medina (WBC)	1995–96
Wilfredo Vasquez (WBA)	1996–98†
Luisito Espinosa (WBC)	1995–99
Naseem Hamed (IBF)	1997†
Hector Lizarraga (IBF)	1997–98
Freddie Norwood (WBA)	1998
Manuel Medina (IBF)	1998–99
Antonio Cermeno (WBA)	1998–99
Cesar Soto (WBC)	1999–00
Paul Ingle (IBF)	1999–2000
Mbuelo Botile (IBF)	2000–01
Guty Espadas (WBC)	2000–01
Freddie Norwood (WBA)	1999–00
Derrick Gainer (WBA)	2000–03
Erik Morales (WBC)	2001–02
Frankie Toledo (IBF)	2001
Manuel Medina (IBF)	2001–02
Johnny Tapia (IBF)	2002†

Champion	Held Title	Champion	Held Title
Erik Morales (WBC)	2002–03†	Juan Manuel Marquez (IBF/WBA)	2003–
Juan Manuel Marquez (IBF)	2003–	**Chi In-jin** (WBC)	2004–

Junior Featherweights

Current champions in **bold** type.

Champion	Held Title	Champion	Held Title
Jack (Kid) Wolfe	1922–23	Jesus Salud (WBA)	1989–90
Carl Duane	1923–24	Welcome Ncita (IBF)	1990–92
Rigoberto Riasco (WBC)	1976	Paul Banke (WBC)	1990
Royal Kobayashi (WBC)	1976	Luis Mendoza (WBA)	1990–91
Dong-Kyun Yum (WBC)	1976–77	Raul Perez (WBA)	1992
Wilfredo Gomez (WBC)	1977–83	Pedro Decima (WBC)	1990–91
Soo-Hwan Hong (WBA)	1977–78	Kiyoshi Hatanaka (WBC)	1991
Ricardo Cardona (WBA)	1978–80	Daniel Zaragoza (WBC)	1991–92
Leo Randolph (WBA)	1980	Tracy Patterson (WBC)	1992–94
Sergio Palma (WBA)	1980–82	Kennedy McKinney (IBF)	1993–94
Leonardo Cruz (WBA)	1982–84	Wilfredo Vasquez (WBA)	1992–95
Jaime Garza (WBC)	1983	Vuyani Bungu (IBF)	1994–99†
Bobby Berna (IBF)	1983–84	Hector Acero Sanchez (WBC)	1994–95
Loris Stecca (WBA)	1984	Antonio Cermeno (WBA)	1995–98†
Seung-Il Suh (IBF)	1984–85	Daniel Zaragoza (WBC)	1995–97
Victor Callejas (WBA)	1984–85	Erik Morales (WBC)	1997–00†
Juan (Kid) Meza (WBC)	1984–85	Enrique Sanchez (WBA)	1998
Ji-Woo Kim (IBF)	1985–86	Nestor Garza (WBA)	1998–00
Lupe Pintor (WBC)	1985–86	Lehlohonolo Ledwaba (IBF)	1999–2001
Samart Payakaroon (WBC)	1986–87	Clarence Adams (WBA)	2000–01†
Seung-Hoon Lee (IBF)	1987–88	Willie Jorrin (WBC)	2000–02
Louie Espinoza (WBA)	1987	Manny Pacquiao (IBF)	2001–04†
Jeff French (WBC)	1987	Yorber Ortega (WBA)	2001–02
Julio Gervacio (WBA)	1987–88	Yoddamrong Sithyodthong (WBA)	2002
Daniel Zaragoza (WBC)	1988–90	Osamu Sato (WBA)	2002
Jose Sanabria (IBF)	1988–90	Salim Medjkoune (WBA)	2002–03
Bernardo Pinango (WBA)	1988	**Oscar Larios** (WBC)	2002–
Juan Jose Estrada (WBA)	1988–89	**Mahyar Monshipour** (WBA)	2003–
Fabrice Benichou (IBF)	1989–90	**Israel Vazquez** (IBF)	2004–

Bantamweights

Widely accepted champions in CAPITAL letters. Current champions in **bold** type.

Champion	Held Title	Champion	Held Title
TOMMY (SPIDER) KELLY	1887	BUD TAYLOR (NBA)	1927–28†
HUGHEY BOYLE	1887–88	Willie Smith (GBR)	1927–28
TOMMY (SPIDER) KELLY	1889	Bushy Graham (NY)	1928–29
CHAPPIE MORAN	1889–90	PANAMA AL BROWN	1929–35
Tommy (Spider) Kelly	1890–92	Sixto Escobar (NBA)	1934–35
GEORGE DIXON	1890–91	BALTAZAR SANGCHILLI	1935–36
Billy Plummer	1892–95	Lou Salica (NBA)	1935
JIMMY BARRY	1894–99	Sixto Escobar (NBA)	1935–36
Pedlar Palmer	1895–99	TONY MARINO	1936
TERRY McGOVERN	1899–1900	SIXTO ESCOBAR	1936–37
HARRY HARRIS	1901–02	HARRY JEFFRA	1937–38
DANNY DOUGHERTY	1900–01	SIXTO ESCOBAR	1938–39*
HARRY FORBES	1901–03	Georgie Pace (NBA)	1939–40
FRANKIE NEIL	1903–04	LOU SALICA	1940–42
JOE BOWKER	1904–05	MANUEL ORTIZ	1942–47
JIMMY WALSH	1905–06†	HAROLD DADE	1947
OWEN MORAN	1907–08	MANUEL ORTIZ	1947–50
MONTE ATTELL	1909–10	VIC TOWEEL	1950–52
FRANKIE CONLEY	1910–11	JIMMY CARRUTHERS	1952–54*
JOHNNY COULON	1911–14	ROBERT COHEN	1954–56
Digger Stanley (GBR)	1910–12	Raul Macias (NBA)	1955–57
Charles Ledoux (GBR)	1912–13	MARIO D'AGATA	1956–57
Eddie Campi (GBR)	1913–14	ALPHONSE HALIMI	1957–59
KID WILLIAMS	1914–17	JOE BECERRA	1959–60*
Johnny Ertle	1915–18	Johnny Caldwell (EBU)	1961–62
PETE HERMAN	1917–20	EDER JOFRE	1961–65
Memphis Pal Moore	1918–19	MASAHIKO FIGHTING HARADA	1965–68
JOE LYNCH	1920–21	LIONEL ROSE	1968–69
PETE HERMAN	1921	RUBEN OLIVARES	1969–70
JOHNNY BUFF	1921–22	CHUCHO CASTILLO	1970–71
JOE LYNCH	1922–24	RUBEN OLIVARES	1971–72
ABE GOLDSTEIN	1924	RAFAEL HERRERA	1972
CANNONBALL EDDIE MARTIN	1924–25	ENRIQUE PINDER	1972–73
PHIL ROSENBERG	1925–27	ROMEO ANAYA	1973
Teddy Baldock (GBR)	1927	Rafael Herrera (WBC)	1973–74

Major Titleholders (Cont.)
Bantamweights (Cont.)

Champion	Held Title	Champion	Held Title
ARNOLD TAYLOR	1973–74	Joichiro Tatsuyoshi (WBC)	1991–92
SOO-HWAN HONG	1974–75	Israel Contreras (WBA)	1991–92
Rodolfo Martinez (WBC)	1974–76	Eddie Cook (WBA)	1992
ALFONSO ZAMORA	1975–77	Victor Rabanales (WBC)	1992–93
Carlos Zarate (WBC)	1976–79	Jorge Julio (WBA)	1992–93
JORGE LUJAN	1977–80	Jung-Il Byun (WBC)	1993
Lupe Pintor (WBC)	1979–83	Junior Jones (WBA)	1993–94
JULIAN SOLIS	1980	Yasuei Yakushiji (WBC)	1993–95
JEFF CHANDLER	1980–84	John M. Johnson (WBA)	1994
Albert Davila (WBC)	1983–85	Daorung Chuvatana (WBA)	1994–95
RICHARD SANDOVAL	1984–86	Harold Mestre (IBF)	1995
Satoshi Shingaki (IBF)	1984–85	Mbuelo Botile (IBF)	1995–97
Jeff Fenech (IBF)	1985	Wayne McCullough (WBC)	1995–96
Daniel Zaragoza (WBC)	1985	Veeraphol Sahaprom (WBA)	1995–96
Miguel (Happy) Lora (WBC)	1985–88	Nana Yaw Konadu (WBA)	1996
GABY CANIZALES	1986	Daorung Chuvatana (WBA)	1996–97
BERNARDO PINANGO	1986–87	Nana Yaw Konadu (WBA)	1997–98
Wilfredo Vasquez (WBA)	1987–88	Sirimongkol Singmanassak (WBC)	1996–97
Kevin Seabrooks (IBF)	1987–88	Tim Austin (IBF)	1997–2003
Kaokor Galaxy (WBA)	1988	Joichiro Tatsuyoshi (WBC)	1997–98
Moon Sung-Kil (WBA)	1988–89	Johnny Tapia (WBA)	1998–99
Kaokor Galaxy (WBA)	1989	**Veerapol Sahaprom** (WBC)	1998–
Raul Perez (WBC)	1988–91	Paulie Ayala (WBA)	1999–2001
Orlando Canizales (IBF)	1988–94†	Eidy Moya (WBA)	2001–02
Luisito Espinosa (WBA)	1989–91	**Johnny Bredahl** (WBA)	2002–
Greg Richardson	1991	**Rafael Marquez** (IBF)	2003–

Junior Bantamweights
Widely accepted champions in CAPITAL letters. Current champions in **bold** type.

Champion	Held Title	Champion	Held Title
Rafael Orono (WBC)	1980–81	Katsuya Onizuka (WBA)	1993–94
Chul-Ho Kim (WBC)	1981–82	Lee Hyung-Chul (WBA)	1994–95
Gustavo Ballas (WBA)	1981	Jose Luis Bueno (WBC)	1993–94
Rafael Pedroza (WBA)	1981–82	Hiroshi Kawashima (WBC)	1994–97
Jiro Watanabe (WBA)	1982–84	Harold Grey (IBF)	1994–95
Rafael Orono (WBC)	1982–83	Alimi Goitia (WBA)	1995–96
Payao Poontarat (WBC)	1983–84	Yokthai Sith-Oar (WBA)	1996–97
Joo-Do Chun (IBF)	1983–85	Carlos Salazar (IBF)	1995–96
JIRO WATANABE	1984–86	Harold Grey (IBF)	1996
Kaosai Galaxy (WBA)	1984	Danny Romero (IBF)	1996–97
Ellyas Pical (IBF)	1985–86	Gerry Penalosa (WBC)	1997–98
Cesar Polanco (IBF)	1986	Johnny Tapia (IBF)	1997–98†
GILBERTO ROMAN	1986–87	Satoshi Iida (WBA)	1997–98
Ellyas Pical (IBF)	1986	Cho In-Joo (WBC)	1998–00
Santos Laciar (WBC)	1987	Jesus Rojas (WBA)	1998–99
Tae-Il Chang (IBF)	1987	Mark Johnson (IBF)	1999–00†
Sugar Rojas (WBC)	1987–88	Hideki Todaka (WBA)	1999–2000
Ellyas Pical (IBF)	1987–89	Masanori Tokuyama (WBC)	2000–04
Gilberto Roman (WBC)	1988–89	Felix Machado (IBF)	2000–03
Juan Polo Perez (IBF)	1989–90	Leo Gamez (WBA)	2000–01
Nana Konadu (WBC)	1989–90	Celes Kobayashi (WBA)	2001–02
Sung-Kil Moon (WBC)	1990–93	**Alexander Munoz** (WBA)	2002–
Robert Quiroga (IBF)	1990–93	**Luis Perez** (IBF)	2003–
Julio Borboa (IBF)	1993–94	**Katsushige Kawashima** (WBC)	2004–

Flyweights
Widely accepted champions in CAPITAL letters. Current champions in **bold** type.

Champion	Held Title	Champion	Held Title
Sid Smith (GBR)	1913	Johnny Hill (GBR)	1928–29
Bill Ladbury (GBR)	1913–14	SPIDER PLADNER (NBA,IBU)	1929
Percy Jones (GBR)	1914	FRANKIE GENARO (NBA,IBU)	1929–31
Joe Symonds (GBR)	1914–16	Willie LaMorte (NY)	1929–30
JIMMY WILDE	1916–23	Midget Wolgast (NY)	1930–35
PANCHO VILLA	1923–25	YOUNG PEREZ (NBA,IBU)	1931–32
FIDEL LaBARBA	1925–27*	JACKIE BROWN (NBA,IBU)	1932–35
FRENCHY BELANGER (NBA,IBU)	1927–28	BENNY LYNCH	1935–38†
Izzy Schwartz (NY)	1927–29	Small Montana (NY,Calif.)	1935–37
Johnny McCoy (Calif.)	1927–28	PETER KANE	1938–43
Newsboy Brown (Calif.)	1928	Little Dado (NBA,Calif.)	1938–40
FRANKIE GENARO (NBA,IBU)	1928–29	JACKIE PATERSON	1943–48

Champion	Held Title	Champion	Held Title
RINTY MONAGHAN	1948–50*	Eleoncio Mercedes (WBC)	1982–83
TERRY ALLEN	1950	Charlie Magri (WBC)	1983
SALVADOR (DADO) MARINO	1950–52	Frank Cedeno (WBC)	1983–84
YOSHIO SHIRAI	1953–54	Soon-Chun Kwon (IBF)	1983–85
PASCUAL PEREZ	1954–60	Koji Kobayashi (WBC)	1984
PONE KINGPETCH	1960–62	Gabriel Bernal (WBC)	1984
MASAHIKO (FIGHTING) HARADA	1962–63	Sot Chitalada (WBC)	1984–88
PONE KINGPETCH	1963	Hilario Zapate (WBA)	1985–87
HIROYUKI EBIHARA	1963–64	Chong-Kwan Chung (IBF)	1985–86
PONE KINGPETCH	1964–65	Bi-Won Chung (IBF)	1986
SALVATORE BURRINI	1965–66	Hi-Sup Shin (IBF)	1986–87
Horacio Accavallo (WBA)	1966–68	Dodie Penalosa (IBF)	1987
WALTER McGOWAN	1966	Fidel Bassa (WBA)	1987–89
CHARTCHAI CHIONOI	1966–69	Choi Chang-Ho (IBF)	1987–88
EFREN TORRES	1969–70	Rolando Bohol (IBF)	1988
Hiroyuki Ebihara (WBA)	1969	Yong-Kang Kim (WBC)	1988–89
Bernabe Villacampo (WBA)	1969–70	Duke McKenzie (IBF)	1988–89
CHARTCHAI CHIONOI	1970	Dave McAuley (IBF)	1989–92
Berkrerk Chartvanchai (WBA)	1970	Sot Chitalada (WBC)	1989–91
Masao Ohba (WBA)	1970–73	Jesus Rojas (WBA)	1989–90
ERBITO SALAVARRIA	1970–73	Yul-Woo Lee (WBA)	1990
Betulio Gonzalez (WBC)	1972	Leopard Tamakuma (WBA)	1990–91
Venice Borkorsor (WBC)	1972–73	Muangchai Kittikasem (WBC)	1991–92
VENICE BORKORSOR	1973	Yong-Kang Kim (WBA)	1991–92
Chartchai Chionoi (WBA)	1973–74	Rodolfo Blanco (IBF)	1992
Betulio Gonzalez (WBC)	1973–74	Yuri Arbachakov (WBC)	1992–97
Shoji Oguma (WBC)	1974–75	Aquiles Guzman (WBA)	1992
Susumu Hanagata (WBA)	1974–75	Phichit Sithbangprachan (IBF)	1992–94†
Miguel Canto (WBC)	1975–79	David Griman (WBA)	1992–94
Erbito Salavarria (WBA)	1975–76	Saen Sor Ploenchit (WBA)	1994–96
Alfonso Lopez (WBA)	1976	Francisco Tejedor (IBF)	1995
Guty Espadas (WBA)	1976–78	Danny Romero (IBF)	1995–96
Betulio Gonzalez (WBA)	1978–79	Mark Johnson (IBF)	1996–99†
Chan-Hee Park (WBC)	1979–80	Jose Bonilla (WBA)	1996–97
Luis Ibarra (WBA)	1979–80	Chatchai Sasakul (WBC)	1997–98
Tae-Shik Kim (WBA)	1980	Hugo Soto (WBA)	1998–99
Shoji Oguma (WBC)	1980–81	Manny Pacquiao (WBC)	1998–99
Peter Mathebula (WBA)	1980–81	**Irene Pacheco** (IBF)	1999–
Santos Laciar (WBA)	1981	Leo Gamez (WBA)	1999
Antonio Avelar (WBC)	1981–82	Medgoen Lukhaoopormasak (WBC)	1999–00
Luis Ibarra (WBA)	1981	Sornpichai Kratindaenggym (WBA)	1999–00
Juan Herrera (WBA)	1981–82	Eric Morel (WBA)	2000–03
Prudencio Cardona (WBC)	1982	Malcolm Tunacao (WBC)	2000–01
Santos Laciar (WBA)	1982–85	**Pongsaklek Wonjongkam** (WBC)	2001–
Freddie Castillo (WBC)	1982	**Lorenzo Parra** (WBA)	2003–

Junior Flyweights

Current champions in **bold** type.

Champion	Held Title	Champion	Held Title
Franco Udella (WBC)	1975	Muangchai Kittikasem (IBF)	1989–90
Jaime Rios (WBA)	1975–76	Humberto Gonzalez (WBC)	1989–90
Luis Estaba (WBC)	1975–78	Michael Carbajal (IBF)	1990–94
Juan Guzman (WBA)	1976	Rolando Pascua (WBC)	1990
Yoko Gushiken (WBA)	1976–81	Melchor Cob Castro (WBC)	1991
Freddy Castillo (WBC)	1978	Humberto Gonzalez (WBC)	1991–93
Netrnoi Vorasingh (WBC)	1978	Hirokia Ioka (WBA)	1991–92
Sung-Jun Kim (WBC)	1978–80	Michael Carbajal (WBC)	1993–94
Shigeo Nakajima (WBC)	1980	Myung-Woo Yuh (WBA)	1993
Hilario Zapata (WBC)	1980–82	Leo Gamez (WBA)	1993–95
Pedro Flores (WBA)	1981	Humberto Gonzalez (WBC/IBF)	1994–95
Hwan-Jin Kim (WBA)	1981	Choi Hi-Yong (WBA)	1995–96
Katsuo Tokashiki (WBA)	1981–83	Saman Sor Jaturong (WBC/IBF)	1995–96
Amado Urzua (WBC)	1982	Carlos Murillo (WBA)	1996
Tadashi Tomori (WBC)	1982	Keiji Yamaguchi (WBA)	1996
Hilario Zapata (WBC)	1982–83	Michael Carbajal (IBF)	1996–97
Jung-Koo Chang (WBC)	1983–88	Saman Sor Jaturong (WBC)	1995–99
Lupe Madera (WBA)	1983–84	Phichit Chor Siriwat (WBA)	1996–00†
Dodie Penalosa (IBF)	1983–86	Mauricio Pastrana (IBF)	1997–98†
Francisco Quiroz (WBA)	1984–85	Will Grigsby (IBF)	1999
Joey Olivo (WBA)	1985	Choi Yo-Sam (WBC)	1999–2002
Myung-Woo Yuh (WBA)	1985–91	Ricardo Lopez (IBF)	1999–2003*
Jum-Hwan Choi (IBF)	1986–88	Beibis Mendoza (WBA)	2000–01
Tacy Macalos (IBF)	1988–89	**Rosendo Alvarez** (WBA)	2001–
German Torres (WBC)	1988–89	**Jorge Arce** (WBC)	2002–
Yul-Woo Lee (WBC)	1989	**Jose Victor Burgos** (IBF)	2003–

Major Titleholders (Cont.)
Strawweights
Current champions in **bold** type.

Champion	Held Title
Franco Udella (WBC)	1975
Jaime Rios (WBA)	1975–76
Luis Estraba (WBC)	1975–78
Juan Guzman (WBA)	1976
Yoko Gushiken (WBA)	1976–81
Freddy Castillo (WBC)	1978
Netrnoi Vorasingh (WBC)	1978
Sung-Jun Kim (WBC)	1978–80
Shigeo Nakajima (WBC)	1980
Hilario Zapata (WBC)	1980–82
Pedro Flores (WBA)	1981
Hwan-Jin Kim (WBA)	1981
Katsuo Tokashiki (WBA)	1981–83
Amado Urzua (WBC)	1982
Tadashi Tomori (WBC)	1982
Hilario Zapata (WBC)	1982–83
Jung-Koo Chang (WBC)	1983–88
Lupe Madera (WBA)	1983–84
Dodie Penalosa (IBF)	1983–86
Francisco Quiroz (WBA)	1984–85
Joey Olivo (WBA)	1985
Myung-Woo Yuh (WBA)	1985–93
Jum-Hwan Choi (IBF)	1986–88
Tacy Macalos (IBF)	1988–89
German Torres (WBC)	1988–89
Yul-Woo Lee (WBC)	1989
Muangchai Kittikasem (IBF)	1989–90

Champion	Held Title
Humberto Gonzalez (WBC)	1989–90
Michael Carbajal (IBF)	1990
Rolando Pascua (WBC)	1990
Melchor Cob Castro (WBC)	1991
Ricardo Lopez (WBC)	1990–98
Ratanapol Voraphin (IBF)	1992–97
Chana Porpaoin (WBA)	1993–95
Rosendo Alvarez (WBA)	1995–98
Ricardo Lopez (WBA/WBC)	1998–99†
Zolani Petelo (IBF)	1997–2001†
Wandee Chor Chareon (WBC)	1999–00
Noel Arambulet (WBA)	1999–00†
Joma Gamboa (WBA)	2000
Keitaro Hoshino (WBA)	2000–01
Jose Antonio Aguirre (WBC)	2000–04
Chana Porpaoin (WBA)	2001
Robert Leyva (IBF)	2001–02
Yutaka Niida (WBA)	2001*
Keitaro Hoshino (WBA)	2002
Noel Arambulent (WBA)	2002–04
Miguel Barrera (IBF)	2002–03
Edgar Cardenas (IBF)	2003
Daniel Reyes (IBF)	2003–04
Eagle Kyowa (WBC)	2004–
Yutaka Niida (WBA)	2004–
Muhammad Rachman (IBF)	2004–

Annual Awards
Ring Magazine Fight of the Year
First presented in 1945 by Nat Fleischer, who started *The Ring* magazine in 1922.

Multiple matchups: Muhammad Ali vs. Joe Frazier, Carmen Basilio vs. Sugar Ray Robinson, Arturo Gatti vs. Micky Ward and Rocky Graziano vs. Tony Zale (2).

Multiple fights: Muhammad Ali (6); Carmen Basilio (5); George Foreman, Arturo Gatti and Joe Frazier (4); Rocky Graziano, Rocky Marciano, Micky Ward and Tony Zale (3); Nino Benvenuti, Bobby Chacon, Ezzard Charles, Marvin Hagler, Thomas Hearns, Evander Holyfield, Sugar Ray Leonard, Floyd Patterson, Sugar Ray Robinson, Jersey Joe Walcott (2).

Year	Winner	Loser	Result		Year	Winner	Loser	Result	
1945	Rocky Graziano	Red Cochrane	KO	10	1975	Muhammad Ali	Joe Frazier	KO	14
1946	Tony Zale	Rocky Graziano	KO	6	1976	George Foreman	Ron Lyle	KO	4
1947	Rocky Graziano	Tony Zale	KO	6	1977	Jimmy Young	George Foreman	W	12
1948	Marcel Cerdan	Tony Zale	KO	12	1978	Leon Spinks	Muhammad Ali	W	15
1949	Willie Pep	Sandy Saddler	W	15	1979	Danny Lopez	Mike Ayala	KO	15
1950	Jake LaMotta	Laurent Dauthuille	KO	15	1980	Saad Muhammad	Yaqui Lopez	KO	14
1951	Jersey Joe Walcott	Ezzard Charles	KO	7	1981	Sugar Ray Leonard	Thomas Hearns	KO	14
1952	Rocky Marciano	Jersey Joe Walcott	KO	13	1982	Bobby Chacon	Rafael Limon	W	15
1953	Rocky Marciano	Roland LaStarza	KO	11	1983	Bobby Chacon	C. Boza-Edwards	W	12
1954	Rocky Marciano	Ezzard Charles	KO	8	1984	Jose Luis Ramirez	Edwin Rosario	KO	4
1955	Carmen Basilio	Tony DeMarco	KO	12	1985	Marvin Hagler	Thomas Hearns	KO	3
1956	Carmen Basilio	Johnny Saxton	KO	9	1986	Stevie Cruz	Barry McGuigan	W	15
1957	Carmen Basilio	Sugar Ray Robinson	W	15	1987	Sugar Ray Leonard	Marvin Hagler	W	12
1958	Sugar Ray Robinson	Carmen Basilio	W	15	1988	Tony Lopez	Rocky Lockridge	W	12
1959	Gene Fullmer	Carmen Basilio	KO	14	1989	Roberto Duran	Iran Barkley	W	12
1960	Floyd Patterson	Ingemar Johansson	KO	5	1990	Julio Cesar Chavez	Meldrick Taylor	KO	12
1961	Joe Brown	Dave Charnley	W	15	1991	Robert Quiroga	Akeem Anifowoshe	W	12
1962	Joey Giardello	Henry Hank	W	10	1992	Riddick Bowe	Evander Holyfield	W	12
1963	Cassius Clay	Doug Jones	W	10	1993	Michael Carbajal	Humberto Gonzalez	KO	7
1964	Cassius Clay	Sonny Liston	KO	7	1994	Jorge Castro	John David Jackson	TKO	9
1965	Floyd Patterson	George Chuvalo	W	12	1995	Saman Sorjaturong	Chiquita Gonzalez	W	7
1966	Jose Torres	Eddie Cotton	W	15	1996	Evander Holyfield	Mike Tyson	TKO	11
1967	Nino Benvenuti	Emile Griffith	W	15	1997	Arturo Gatti	Gabriel Ruelas	KO	5
1968	Dick Tiger	Frank DePaula	W	10	1998	Ivan Robinson	Arturo Gatti	W	10
1969	Joe Frazier	Jerry Quarry	KO	7	1999	Paulie Ayala	Johnny Tapia	W	12
1970	Carlos Monzon	Nino Benvenuti	KO	12	2000	Erik Morales	Marco Antonio Barrera	W	12
1971	Joe Frazier	Muhammad Ali	W	15	2001	Micky Ward	Emanuel Burton	W	10
1972	Bob Foster	Chris Finnegan	KO	14	2002	Micky Ward	Arturo Gatti	W	10
1973	George Foreman	Joe Frazier	KO	2	2003	Arturo Gatti	Micky Ward	W	10
1974	Muhammad Ali	George Foreman	KO	8					

Ring Magazine Fighter of the Year

First presented in 1928 by Nat Fleischer, who started *The Ring* magazine in 1922.

Multiple winners: Muhammad Ali (5); Joe Louis (4); Joe Frazier, Evander Holyfield and Rocky Marciano (3); Ezzard Charles, George Foreman, Marvin Hagler, Thomas Hearns, Ingemar Johansson, Sugar Ray Leonard, Tommy Loughran, Floyd Patterson, Sugar Ray Robinson, Barney Ross, Dick Tiger, James Toney and Mike Tyson (2).

Year		Year		Year	
1928	Gene Tunney	1954	Rocky Marciano	1980	Thomas Hearns
1929	Tommy Loughran	1955	Rocky Marciano	1981	Sugar Ray Leonard
1930	Max Schmeling	1956	Floyd Patterson		& Salvador Sanchez
1931	Tommy Loughran	1957	Carmen Basilio	1982	Larry Holmes
1932	Jack Sharkey	1958	Ingemar Johansson	1983	Marvin Hagler
1933	No award	1959	Ingemar Johansson	1984	Thomas Hearns
1934	Tony Canzoneri	1960	Floyd Patterson	1985	Donald Curry
	& Barney Ross	1961	Joe Brown		& Marvin Hagler
1935	Barney Ross	1962	Dick Tiger	1986	Mike Tyson
1936	Joe Louis	1963	Cassius Clay	1987	Evander Holyfield
1937	Henry Armstrong	1964	Emile Griffith	1988	Mike Tyson
1938	Joe Louis	1965	Dick Tiger	1989	Pernell Whitaker
1939	Joe Louis	1966	No award	1990	Julio Cesar Chavez
1940	Billy Conn	1967	Joe Frazier	1991	James Toney
1941	Joe Louis	1968	Nino Benvenuti	1992	Riddick Bowe
1942	Sugar Ray Robinson	1969	Jose Napoles	1993	Michael Carbajal
1943	Fred Apostoli	1970	Joe Frazier	1994	Roy Jones Jr.
1944	Beau Jack	1971	Joe Frazier	1995	Oscar De La Hoya
1945	Willie Pep	1972	Muhammad Ali	1996	Evander Holyfield
1946	Tony Zale		& Carlos Monzon	1997	Evander Holyfield
1947	Gus Lesnevich	1973	George Foreman	1998	Floyd Mayweather Jr.
1948	Ike Williams	1974	Muhammad Ali	1999	Paulie Ayala
1949	Ezzard Charles	1975	Muhammad Ali	2000	Felix Trinidad
1950	Ezzard Charles	1976	George Foreman	2001	Bernard Hopkins
1951	Sugar Ray Robinson	1977	Carlos Zarate	2002	Vernon Forrest
1952	Rocky Marciano	1978	Muhammad Ali	2003	James Toney
1953	Carl (Bobo) Olson	1979	Sugar Ray Leonard		

Note: Cassius Clay changed his name to Muhammad Ali after winning the heavyweight title in 1964.

All-Time Leaders

Based on rankings compiled by *The Ring Record Book and Encyclopedia.*

Knockouts

	Division		Career	No
1	Archie Moore	Lt. Heavy	1936–63	130
2	Young Stribling	Heavy	1921–33	126
3	Billy Bird	Welter	1920–48	125
4	George Odwel	Welter	1930–45	114
5	Sugar Ray Robinson	Middle	1940–65	110
6	Sandy Saddler	Feather	1944–56	103
7	Sam Langford	Middle	1902–26	102
8	Henry Armstrong	Welter	1931–45	100
9	Jimmy Wilde	Fly	1911–23	98
10	Len Wickwar	Lt. Heavy	1928–47	93

Total Bouts

	Division		Career	No
1	Len Wickwar	Lt. Heavy	1928–47	463
2	Reggie Strickland	Lt. Heavy	1987–	354
3	Jack Britton	Welter	1905–30	350
4	Johnny Dundee	Feather	1910–32	333
5	Billy Bird	Welter	1920–48	318
6	George Marsden	n/a	1928–46	311
7	Maxie Rosenbloom	Lt. Heavy	1923–39	299
8	Harry Greb	Middle	1913–26	298
9	Young Stribling	Lt. Heavy	1921–33	286
10	Battling Levinsky	Lt. Heavy	1910–29	282

Triple Champions

Fighters who have won widely-accepted world titles in more than two divisions. Henry Armstrong is the only fighter listed to hold three titles simultaneously. Note that (*) indicates title claimant.

Sugar Ray Leonard (5) WBC Welterweight (1979-80,80-82); WBA Jr. Middleweight (1981); WBC Middleweight (1987); WBC Super Middleweight (1988-90); WBC Light Heavyweight (1988).

Roy Jones Jr. (4) IBF Middleweight (1993-94); IBF Super Middleweight (1994-96); WBC Light Heavyweight (1996, 1997-2003); WBA Light Heavyweight (1998–); IBF Light Heavyweight (1999-2003); WBA Heavyweight (2003-04).

Oscar De La Hoya (4) IBF Lightweight (1995-96); WBC Super Lightweight (1996-97); WBC Welterweight (1997-99); WBC Jr. Middleweight (2001-03); WBA Jr. Middleweight (2002-03).

Roberto Duran (4) Lightweight (1972-79); WBC Welterweight (1980); WBA Jr. Middleweight (1983-84); WBC Middleweight (1989-90).

Leo Gamez (4) WBA Strawweight (1988-90); WBA Jr. Flyweight (1993-95); WBA Flyweight (1999); WBA Junior Bantamweight (2000-01).

Thomas Hearns (4) WBA Welterweight (1980-81); WBC Jr. Middleweight (1982-84); WBC Light Heavyweight (1987); WBC Middleweight (1987-88); WBA Light Heavyweight (1989-90).

Pernell Whitaker (4) IBF/WBC/WBA Lightweight (1989-92); IBF Jr. Welterweight (1992-93); WBC Welterweight (1993-97); WBC Jr. Middleweight (1995).

Alexis Arguello (3) WBA Featherweight (1974-77); WBC Jr. Lightweight (1978-80); WBC Lightweight (1981-83).

Henry Armstrong (3) Featherweight (1937-38); Welterweight (1938-40); Lightweight (1938-39).

Iran Barkley (3) WBC Middleweight (1988-89); IBF Super Middleweight (1992-93); WBA Light Heavyweight (1992).

Wilfredo Benitez (3) Jr. Welterweight (1976-79); Welterweight (1979); WBC Jr. Middleweight (1981-82).

Tony Canzoneri (3) Featherweight (1928); Lightweight (1930-33); Jr. Welterweight (1931-32,33).

Julio Cesar Chavez (3) WBC Jr. Lightweight (1984-87); WBA/WBC Lightweight (1987-89); WBC/IBF Jr. Welterweight (1989-91); WBC Jr. Welterweight (1991-94, 1994).

Jeff Fenech (3) IBF Bantamweight (1985); WBC Jr. Featherweight (1986-88); WBC Featherweight (1988-90).

Bob Fitzsimmons (3) Middleweight (1891-97); Light Heavyweight (1903-05); Heavyweight (1897-99).

Wilfredo Gomez (3) WBC Super Bantamweight (1977-83); WBC Featherweight (1984); WBA Jr. Lightweight (1985-86).

Emile Griffith (3) Welterweight (1961,62-63,63-66); Jr. Middleweight (1962-63); Middleweight (1966-67,67-68).

Mike McCallum (3) WBA Jr. Middleweight (1984-88); WBA Middleweight (1989-91); WBC Light Heavyweight (1994-95).

Terry McGovern (3) Bantamweight (1889-1900); Featherweight (1900-01); Lightweight* (1900-01).

Erik Morales (3) WBC Jr. Featherweight (1997-2000); WBC Featherweight (2001-02); IBF/WBC Jr. Lightweight (2004—).

Barney Ross (3) Lightweight (1933-35); Jr. Welterweight (1933-35); Welterweight (1934, 35-38).

Johnny Tapia (3) IBF Jr. Bantamweight (1997-98); WBA Bantamweight (1998-99); IBF Featherweight (2002).

James Toney (3) IBF Middleweight (1991-93); IBF Super Middlweight (1992-94); IBF Cruiserweight (2003).

Felix Trinidad (3) IBF/WBC Welterweight (1993-2000); WBA/IBF Jr. Middleweight (2000-01); WBA Middleweight (2001).

Wilfredo Vazquez (3) WBA Bantamweight (1987-88); WBA Jr. Featherweight (1992-95); WBA Featherweight (1996-98).

All-Time Heavyweight Upsets

Buster Douglas was a 42-1 underdog when he defeated previously-unbeaten heavyweight champion Mike Tyson on Feb. 10, 1990. That 10th-round knockout ranks as the biggest upset in boxing history. By comparison, 45-year-old George Foreman was only a 3-1 underdog before he unexpectedly won the title from Michael Moorer on Nov. 5, 1994.

Here are the best-known upsets in the annals of the heavyweight division. All fights were for the world championship except the Max Schmeling-Joe Louis bout.

Date	Winner	Loser	Result	KO Time	Location
9/7/1892	James J. Corbett	John L. Sullivan	KO 21	1:30	Olympic Club, New Orleans
4/5/1915	Jess Willard	Jack Johnson	KO 26	1:26	Mariano Race Track, Havana
9/23/26	Gene Tunney	Jack Dempsey	Wu 10	–	Sesquicentennial Stadium, Phila.
6/13/35	James J. Braddock	Max Baer	Wu 15	–	Mad. Sq.Garden Bowl, L.I. City
6/19/36	Max Schmeling	Joe Louis	KO 12	2:29	Yankee Stadium, New York
7/18/51	Jersey Joe Walcott	Ezzard Charles	KO 7	0:55	Forbes Field, Pittsburgh
6/26/59	Ingemar Johansson	Floyd Patterson	TKO 3	2:03	Yankee Stadium, New York
2/25/64	Cassius Clay	Sonny Liston	TKO 7	*	Convention Hall, Miami Beach
10/30/74	Muhammad Ali	George Foreman	KO 8	2:58	20th of May Stadium, Zaire
2/15/78	Leon Spinks	Muhammad Ali	Ws 15	–	Hilton Pavilion, Las Vegas
9/21/85	Michael Spinks	Larry Holmes	Wu 15	–	Riviera Hotel, Las Vegas
2/10/90	Buster Douglas	Mike Tyson	KO 10	1:23	Tokyo Dome, Tokyo
11/5/94	George Foreman	Michael Moorer	KO 10	2:03	MGM Grand, Las Vegas
11/9/96	Evander Holyfield	Mike Tyson	TKO 11	0:37	MGM Grand, Las Vegas
4/22/01	Hasim Rahman	Lennox Lewis	KO 5	2:32	Johannesburg, South Africa

*Liston failed to answer bell for Round 7.

Miscellaneous Sports

*Alaskan musher **Mitch Seavey** won the Iditarod Trail Sled Dog Race in 2004.*

CHESS

World Champions

Garry Kasparov became the youngest man to win the world chess championship when he beat fellow Russian Anatoly Karpov in 1985 at age 22. In 1993, Kasparov and then-#1 challenger Nigel Short of England broke away from the established International Chess Federation (FIDE) to form the Professional Chess Association (the PCA was disbanded in 1998). FIDE retaliated by stripping Kasparov of the world title and arranging a playoff that was won by Karpov, the former title-holder. Karpov successfully defended the FIDE title several times before failing to show up for the 1999 FIDE World Championship Tournament that was won by Alexander Khalifman. Indian Viswanathan Anand won the 2000 FIDE World Championship.

In his first title defense in five years, Kasparov faced world #2 Vladimir Kramnik for 16 matches in the unofficial (though more widely recognized) world championship from Oct. 8-Nov. 4, 2000 in London. The 25-year-old Kramnik defeated the longtime world champion 8½-6½ in a stunning result. Kasparov failed to win a single game, but despite the loss is still the top-ranked player in the world. Ruslan Ponomariov won the 2002 FIDE title and a plan, known as the Prague agreement, to unify the world chess championship was hatched. FIDE hosted a knockout tournament in 2003 which was won by 18-year-old Ukrainian Ponomariov. Ponomariov was supposed to then play World No. 1 Kasparov. But Ponomariov could not agree to the terms set for his match to play Kasparov and was stripped of his title. Uzbekistan's Rustam Kasimdzhanov won the title in 2004 (however many of the world's top players were absent from the tournament) and was scheduled to play Kasparov at some point in 2005. The winner of that match is supposed to play the winner of the Kramnik-Peter Leko match. ✒

Years		Years		Years	
1866-94	Wilhelm Steinitz, Austria	1957-58	Vassily Smyslov, USSR	1975-85	Anatoly Karpov, USSR
1894-1921	Emanuel Lasker, Germany	1958-59	Mikhail Botvinnik, USSR	1985-2000	Garry Kasparov, RUS
1921-27	Jose Capablanca, Cuba	1960-61	Mikhail Tal, USSR	2000–	Vladimir Kramnik, RUS
1927-35	Alexander Alekhine, France	1961-63	Mikhail Botvinnik, USSR	2002-03	Ruslan Ponomariov, UKR
1935-37	Max Euwe, Holland	1963-69	Tigran Petrosian, USSR	2004–	Rustam Kasimdzhanov, UZB
1937-46	Alexander Alekhine, France	1969-72	Boris Spassky, USSR	*Fischer defaulted the championship
1948-57	Mikhail Botvinnik, USSR	1972-75	Bobby Fischer, USA*	in 1975.

U.S. Champions

Years		Years		Years	
1857-71	Paul Morphy	1957-61	Bobby Fischer	1988	Michael Wilder
1871-76	George Mackenzie	1961-62	Larry Evans	1989	Roman Dzindzichashvili,
1876-80	James Mason	1962-68	Bobby Fischer		Stuart Rachels
1880-89	George Mackenzie	1968-69	Larry Evans		& Yasser Seirawan
1889-90	Samuel Lipschutz	1969-72	Samuel Reshevsky	1990	Lev Alburt
1890	Jackson Showalter	1972-73	Robert Byrne	1991	Gata Kamsky
1890-91	Max Judd	1973-74	Lubomir Kavalek	1992	Patrick Wolff
1891-92	Jackson Showalter		& John Grefe	1993	Alexander Shabalov
1892-94	Samuel Lipschutz	1974-77	Walter Browne		& Alex Yermolinsky
1894	Jackson Showalter	1978-80	Lubomir Kabalek	1994	Boris Gulko
1894-95	Albert Hodges	1980-81	Larry Evans,	1995	Alexander Ivanov
1895-97	Jackson Showalter		& Walter Browne	1996	Alexander Yermolinsky
1897-1906	Harry Pillsbury	1981-83	Walter Browne	1997	Joel Benjamin
1906-09	Vacant		& Yasser Seirawan	1998	Nick de Firmian
1909-36	Frank Marshall	1983	Roman Dzindzichashvili,	1999	Boris Gulko
1936-44	Samuel Reshevsky		Larry Christiansen	2000	Joel Benjamin, Yasser Seirawan & Alex Shabalov
1944-46	Arnold Denker		& Walter Browne	2001	Not held
1946-48	Samuel Reshevsky	1984-85	Lev Alburt	2002	Larry Christiansen
1948-51	Herman Steiner	1986	Yasser Seirawan	2003	Alexander Shabalov
1951-54	Larry Evans	1987	Joel Benjamin		
1954-57	Arthur Bisguier		& Nick DeFirmian		

DOGS

Iditarod Trail Sled Dog Race

Seward, Alaska's Mitch Seavey came from behind to win the 2004 Iditarod. The 43-year-old, racing in his 11th Iditarod, finished the Anchorage-to-Nome race in 9 days, 12 hours, 20 minutes and 22 seconds winning $69,000 and a new $40,000 Dodge pickup truck. Seavey is a second-generation Iditarod musher. His father Dan finished third in the inaugural 1973 race. A record 87 teams began the race and 77 finished the course. Three-time winner Jeff King, of Denali Park, Alaska, finished second, about two hours and 20 minutes behind Seavey. Both Seavey and King passed race leader Kjetil Backen of Norway late in the race.

In even-numbered years the trail follows the 1,151-mile Northern Route, while in odd-numbered years, it takes a slightly different 1,161-mile Southern Route. The Iditarod, the longest sled dog race in the world, commemorates a 674-mile relay race from Nenana to Nome in 1925 when 1925 when mushers and dog teams successfully delivered serum to stave off an outbreak of diphtheria among children.

Multiple winners: Rick Swenson (5); Martin Buser, Susan Butcher and Doug Swingley (4); Jeff King (3).

Year		Elapsed Time	Year		Elapsed Time
1973	Dick Wilmarth	20 days, 00:49:41	1979	Rick Swenson	15 days, 10:37:47
1974	Carl Huntington	20 days, 15:02:07	1980	Joe May	14 days, 07:11:51
1975	Emmitt Peters	14 days, 14:43:45	1981	Rick Swenson	12 days, 08:45:02
1976	Gerald Riley	18 days, 22:58:17	1982	Rick Swenson	16 days, 04:40:10
1977	Rick Swenson	16 days, 16:27:13	1983	Rick Mackey	12 days, 14:10:44
1978	Dick Mackey	14 days, 18:52:24	1984	Dean Osmar	12 days, 15:07:33

Year		Elapsed Time	Year		Elapsed Time
1985	Libby Riddles	18 days, 00:20:17	1996	Jeff King	9 days, 05:43:13
1986	Susan Butcher	11 days, 15:06:00	1997	Martin Buser	9 days, 08:31:45
1987	Susan Butcher	11 days, 02:05:13	1998	Jeff King	9 days, 05:52:26
1988	Susan Butcher	11 days, 11:41:40	1999	Doug Swingley	9 days, 14:31:07
1989	Joe Runyan	11 days, 05:24:34	2000	Doug Swingley	9 days, 00:58:06
1990	Susan Butcher	11 days, 01:53:23	2001	Doug Swingley	9 days, 19:55:50
1991	Rick Swenson	12 days, 16:34:39	2002	Martin Buser	8 days, 22:46:02*
1992	Martin Buser	10 days, 19:17:00	2003	Robert Sorlie	9 days, 15:47:36
1993	Jeff King	10 days, 15:38:15	2004	Mitch Seavey	9 days, 12:20:22
1994	Martin Buser	10 days, 13:02:39	*Race record.		
1995	Doug Swingley	9 days, 02:42:19			

Westminster Kennel Club

Best in Show

The Best in Show prize at the 128th annual All-Breed Dog Show of the Westminster Kennel Club held Feb. 9-10, 2004, went to Ch. Darbydale's All Rise Pouchcove, a big and charismatic black Newfoundland. The four-year-old, 155-pound dog, who answers to the name Josh, was selected among 2,624 dogs in 162 breeds and tied the record (of another Newfie Seaward's Blackbeard who won 1984) for the largest dog ever to win Best in Show at Westminster. The Westminster show is the most prestigious dog show in the country, and one of America's oldest annual sporting events.

Multiple winners: Ch. Warren Remedy (3); Ch. Chinoe's Adamant James, Ch. Comejo Wycollar Boy, Ch. Flornell Spicy Piece of Halleston; Ch. Matford Vic, Ch. My Own Brucie, Ch. Pendley Calling of Blarney, Ch. Rancho Dobe's Storm (2).

Year		Breed	Year		Breed
1907	Warren Remedy	Fox Terrier	1956	Wilber White Swan	Toy Poodle
1908	Warren Remedy	Fox Terrier	1957	Shirkhan of Grandeur	Afghan Hound
1909	Warren Remedy	Fox Terrier	1958	Puttencove Promise	Standard Poodle
1910	Sabine Rarebit	Fox Terrier	1959	Fontclair Festoon	Miniature Poodle
1911	Tickle Em Jock	Scottish Terrier	1960	Chick T'Sun of Caversham	Pekingese
1912	Kenmore Sorceress	Airedale	1961	Cappoquin Little Sister	Toy Poodle
1913	Strathway Prince Albert	Bulldog	1962	Elfinbrook Simon	W. Highland Terrier
1914	Brentwood Hero	Old English Sheepdog	1963	Wakefield's Black Knight	English Springer Spaniel
1915	Matford Vic	Old English Sheepdog	1964	Courtenay Fleetfoot of Pennyworth	Whippet
1916	Matford Vic	Old English Sheepdog	1965	Carmichaels Fanfare	Scottish Terrier
1917	Comejo Wycollar Boy	Fox Terrier	1966	Zeloy Mooremaides Magic	Fox Terrier
1918	Haymarket Faultless	Bull Terrier	1967	Bardene Bingo	Scottish Terrier
1919	Briergate Bright Beauty	Airedale	1968	Stingray of Derryabah	Lakeland Terrier
1920	Comejo Wycollar Boy	Fox Terrier	1969	Glamoor Good News	Skye Terrier
1921	Midkiff Seductive	Cocker Spaniel	1970	Arriba's Prima Donna	Boxer
1922	Boxwood Barkentine	Airedale	1971	Chinoe's Adamant James	E.S. Spaniel
1923	No best-in-show award		1972	Chinoe's Adamant James	E.S. Spaniel
1924	Barberryhill Bootlegger	Sealyham	1973	Acadia Command Performance	Standard Poodle
1925	Governor Moscow	Pointer	1974	Gretchenhof Columbia River	German SH Pointer
1926	Signal Circuit	Fox Terrier	1975	Sir Lancelot of Barvan	Old Eng. Sheepdog
1927	Pinegrade Perfection	Sealyham	1976	Jo Ni's Red Baron of Crofton	Lakeland Terrier
1928	Talavera Margaret	Fox Terrier	1977	Dersade Bobby's Girl	Sealyham
1929	Land Loyalty of Bellhaven	Collie	1978	Cede Higgens	Yorkshire Terrier
1930	Pendley Calling of Blarney	Fox Terrier	1979	Oak Tree's Irishtocrat	Irish Water Spaniel
1931	Pendley Calling of Blarney	Fox Terrier	1980	Sierra Cinnar	Siberian Husky
1932	Nancolleth Markable	Pointer	1981	Dhandy Favorite Woodchuck	Pug
1933	Warland Protector of Shelterock	Airedale	1982	St. Aubrey Dragonora of Elsdon	Pekingese
1934	Flornell Spicy Bit of Halleston	Fox Terrier	1983	Kabik's The Challenger	Afghan Hound
1935	Nunsoe Duc de la Terrace of Blakeen	Stan. Poodle	1984	Seaward's Blackbeard	Newfoundland
1936	St. Margaret Magnificent of Clairedale	Sealyham	1985	Braeburn's Close Encounter	Scottish Terrier
1937	Flornell Spicy Bit of Halleston	Fox Terrier	1986	Marjetta National Acclaim	Pointer
1938	Daro of Maridor	English Setter	1987	Covy Tucker Hill's Manhattan	German Shepherd
1939	Ferry v.Rauhfelsen of Giralda	Doberman	1988	Great Elms Prince Charming II	Pomeranian
1940	My Own Brucie	Cocker Spaniel	1989	Royal Tudor's Wild As The Wind	Doberman
1941	My Own Brucie	Cocker Spaniel	1990	Wendessa Crown Prince	Pekingese
1942	Wolvey Pattern of Edgerstoune	W. Highland Terrier	1991	Whisperwind on a Carousel	Stan. Poodle
1943	Pitter Patter of Piperscroft	Miniature Poodle	1992	Lonesome Dove	Fox Terrier
1944	Flornell Rarebit of Twin Ponds	Welsh Terrier	1993	Salilyn's Condor	E.S. Spaniel
1945	Shieling's Signature	Scottish Terrier	1994	Chidley Willum	Norwich Terrier
1946	Hetherington Model Rhythm	Fox Terrier	1995	Gaelforce Post Script	Scottish Terrier
1947	Warlord of Mazelaine	Boxer	1996	Clussex Country Sunrise	Clumber Spaniel
1948	Rock Ridge Night Rocket	Bedling. Terrier	1997	Parsifal di Casa Netzer	Standard Schnauzer
1949	Mazelaine's Zazarac Brandy	Boxer	1998	Fairewood Frolic	Norwich Terrier
1950	Walsing Winning Trick of Edgerstoune	Scot. Terrier	1999	Loteki's Supernatural Being	Papillon
1951	Bang Away of Sirrah Crest	Boxer	2000	Salilyn 'N Erin's Shameless	E.S. Spaniel
1952	Rancho Dobe's Storm	Doberman	2001	Special Times Just Right	Bichon Frise
1953	Rancho Dobe's Storm	Doberman	2002	Surrey Spice Girl	Miniature Poodle
1954	Carmor's Rise and Shine	Cocker Spaniel	2003	Torums Scarf Michael	Kerry Blue Terrier
1955	Kippax Fearnought	Bulldog	2004	Darbydale's All Rise Pouchcove	Newfoundland

FISHING

IGFA All-Tackle World Records

All-tackle records are maintained for the heaviest fish of any species caught on any line up to 130-lb (60 kg) class and certified by the International Game Fish Association. Records logged through Dec. 31, 2003. **Address:** 300 Gulf Stream Way, Dania Beach, Fla. 33004. **Telephone:** (954) 927-2628.

FRESHWATER FISH

Species	Lbs-Oz	Where Caught	Date	Angler
Barramundi	83-7	N. Queensland, Australia	Sept. 23, 1999	David Powell
Bass, Guadalupe	3-11	Lake Travis, TX	Sept. 25, 1983	Allen Christenson Jr.
Bass, largemouth	22-4	Montgomery Lake, GA	June 2, 1932	George W. Perry
Bass, Roanoke	1-5	Nottoway River, VA	Nov. 11, 1991	Tom Elkins
Bass, rock	3-0	York River, Ontario	Aug. 1, 1974	Peter Gulgin
	3-0	Lake Erie, PA	June 18, 1998	Herbert G. Ratner Jr.
Bass, shoal	8-12	Apalachicola River, FL	Jan. 28, 1995	Carl W. Davis
Bass, smallmouth	10-14	Dale Hollow, TN	Apr. 24, 1969	John T. Gorman
Bass, spotted	10-4	Pine Flat Lake, CA	Apr. 21, 2001	Bryan Shishido
Bass, striped (landlocked)	67-8	O'Neill Forebay, San Luis, CA	May 7, 1992	Hank Ferguson
Bass, Suwannee	3-14	Suwannee River, FL	Mar. 2, 1985	Ronnie Everett
Bass, white	6-13	Lake Orange, VA	July 31, 1989	Ronald L. Sprouse
Bass, whiterock	27-5	Greers Ferry Lake, AR	Apr. 24, 1997	Jerald C. Shaum
Bass, yellow	2-9	Duck River, TN	Feb. 27, 1998	John T. Chappell
Bass, yellow (hybrid)	3-5	Big Cypress Bayou, TX	Mar. 27, 1991	Patrick Collin Myers
Bluegill	4-12	Ketona Lake, AL	Apr. 9, 1950	T.S. Hudson
Bowfin	21-8	Florence, SC	Jan. 29, 1980	Robert L. Harmon
Buffalo, bigmouth	70-5	Bussey Brake, Bastrop, LA	Apr. 21, 1980	Delbert Sisk
Buffalo, black	63-6	Mississippi River, IA	Aug. 14, 1999	Jim Winters
Buffalo, smallmouth	82-3	Athens Lake, AL	June 6, 1993	Randy Collins
Bullhead, black	7-7	Mill Pond, NY	Aug. 25, 1993	Kevin Kelly
Bullhead, brown	6-1	Waterford, NY	Apr. 26, 1998	Bobby Triplett
Bullhead, yellow	4-4	Mormon Lake, AZ	May 11, 1984	Emily Williams
Burbot	18-11	Angenmanelren, Sweden	Oct. 22, 1996	Margit Agren
Carp, bighead	61-15	Old Hickory Lake, TN	Mar. 27, 2002	Rick Richard
Carp, black	40-12	Chiba, Japan	Apr. 1, 2000	Kenichi Hosoi
Carp, common	75-11	St. Cassien, France	May 21, 1987	Leo van der Gugten
Carp, crucian	5-1	Kalterersee, Italy	July 16, 1997	Jorg Marquand
Catfish, blue	116-12	Mississippi River, AR	Aug. 3, 2001	Charles Ashley Jr.
Catfish, channel	58-0	Santee-Cooper Res., SC	July 7, 1964	W.B. Whaley
Catfish, flathead	123-0	Elk City Reservoir, KS	Mar. 14, 1998	Ken Paulie
Catfish, flatwhiskered	16-15	Xingu River, Brazil	Aug. 7, 2001	Ian-Arthur de Sulocki
Catfish, gilded	85-8	Amazon River, Brazil	Nov. 15, 1986	Gilberto Fernandes
Catfish, redtail	97-7	Amazon River, Brazil	July 16, 1988	Gilberto Fernandes
Catfish, sharptoothed	79-5	Orange River, South Africa	Dec. 5, 1992	Hennie Moller
Catfish, white	21-8	East Lyme, CT	Apr. 22, 2001	Thomas Urquahart
Char, Arctic	32-9	Tree River, Canada	July 30, 1981	Jeffery Ward
Crappie, black	4-8	Kerr Lake, VA	Mar. 1, 1981	L. Carl Herring Jr.
Crappie, white	5-3	Enid Dam, MS	July 31, 1957	Fred L. Bright
Dolly Varden	20-14	Wulik River, AK	July 7, 2001	Raz Reid
Dorado	51-5	Corrientes, Argentina	Sept. 27, 1984	Armando Giudice
Drum, freshwater	54-8	Nickajack Lake, TN	Apr. 20, 1972	Benny E. Hull
Gar, alligator	279-0	Rio Grande, TX	Dec. 2, 1951	Bill Valverde
Gar, Florida	10-0	The Everglades, FL	Jan. 28, 2002	Herbert G. Ratner Jr.
Gar, longnose	50-5	Trinity River, TX	July 30, 1954	Townsend Miller
Gar, shortnose	5-12	Rend Lake, IL	July 16, 1995	Donna K. Willmart
Gar, spotted	9-12	Lake Mexia, TX	Apr. 7, 1994	Rick Rivard
Goldfish	6-10	Lake Hodges, CA	Apr. 17, 1996	Florentino M. Abena
Grayling, Arctic	5-15	Katseyedie River, N.W.T.	Aug. 16, 1967	Jeanne P. Branson
Inconnu	53-0	Pah River, AK	Aug. 20, 1986	Lawrence E. Hudnall
Kokanee	9-6	Okanagan Lake, Brit. Columbia	June 18, 1988	Norm Kuhn
Muskellunge	67-8	Hayward, WI	July 24, 1949	Cal Johnson
Muskellunge, tiger	51-3	Lac Vieux-Desert, WI-MI	July 16, 1919	John A. Knobla
Peacock, butterfly	12-9	Chiguao River, Venezuela	Jan. 6, 2000	Antonio Campa G.
Peacock, speckled	27-0	Rio Negro, Brazil	Dec. 4, 1994	Gerald (Doc) Lawson
Perch, Nile	230-0	Lake Nasser, Egypt	Dec. 20, 2000	William Toth
Perch, white	3-1	Forest Hill Park, NJ	May 6, 1989	Edward Tango
Perch, yellow	4-3	Bordentown, NJ	May, 1865	Dr. C.C. Abbot
Pickerel, chain	9-6	Homerville, GA	Feb. 17, 1961	Baxley McQuaig Jr.
Pickerel, grass	1-0	Dewart Lake, IN	June 9, 1990	Mike Berg
Pickerel, redfin	2-4	Gall Berry Swamp, NC	June 27, 1997	Edward C. Davis
Pike, northern	55-1	Lake of Grefeern, Germany	Oct. 16, 1986	Lothar Louis
Redhorse, greater	9-3	Salmon River, Pulaski, NY	May 11, 1985	Jason Wilson

Species	Lbs-Oz	Where Caught	Date	Angler
Redhorse, silver	.11-7	Plum Creek, WI	May 29, 1985	Neal D.G. Long
Salmon, Atlantic	.79-2	Tana River, Norway	1928	Henrik Henriksen
Salmon, chinook	.97-4	Kenai River, AK	May 17, 1985	Les Anderson
Salmon, chum	.35-0	Edye Pass, Brit. Columbia	July 11, 1995	Todd Johansson
Salmon, coho	.33-4	Salmon River, Pulaski, NY	Sept. 27, 1989	Jerry Lifton
Salmon, pink	.14-13	Monroe, WA	Sept. 30, 2001	Alexander Minerich
Salmon, sockeye	.15-3	Kenai River, AK	Aug. 9, 1987	Stan Roach
Sauger	.8-12	Lake Sakakawea, ND	Oct. 6, 1971	Mike Fischer
Shad, American	.11-4	Conn. River, S. Hadley, MA	May 19, 1986	Bob Thibodo
Shad, gizzard	.4-6	Lake Michigan, IN	Mar. 2, 1996	Mike Berg
Sturgeon, lake	.168-0	Georgian Bay, Canada	May 29, 1982	Edward Paszkowski
Sturgeon, white	.468-0	Benicia, CA	July 9, 1983	Joey Pallotta 3rd
Tigerfish, giant	.97-0	Zaire River, Kinshasa, Zaire	July 9, 1988	Raymond Houtmans
Tilapia, spotted	.3-0	Pembroke Pines, FL	Mar. 20, 1999	Jay Wright Jr.
Trout, Apache	.5-3	White Mountain, AZ	May 29, 1991	John Baldwin
Trout, brook	.14-8	Nipigon River, Ontario	July, 1916	Dr. W.J. Cook
Trout, brown	.40-4	Little Red River, AR	May 9, 1992	Rip Collins
Trout, bull	.32-0	Lake Pend Orielle, ID	Oct. 27, 1949	N.L. Higgins
Trout, cutthroat	.41-0	Pyramid Lake, NV	Dec., 1925	John Skimmerhorn
Trout, golden	.11-0	Cooks Lake, WY	Aug. 5, 1948	Charles S. Reed
Trout, lake	.72-0	Great Bear Lake, N.W.T.	Aug. 19, 1995	Lloyd E. Bull
Trout, rainbow	.42-2	Bell Island, AK	June 22, 1970	David Robert White
Trout, tiger	.20-13	Lake Michigan, WI	Aug. 12, 1978	Peter M. Friedland
Walleye	.25-0	Old Hickory Lake, TN	Aug. 2, 1960	Mabry Harper
Warmouth	.2-7	Guess Lake, Holt, FL	Oct. 19, 1985	Tony D. Dempsey
Whitefish, lake	.14-6	Meaford, Ontario	May 21, 1984	Dennis M. Laycock
Whitefish, mountain	.5-8	Elbow River, Manitoba	Aug. 1, 1995	Randy G. Woo
Whitefish, round	.6-0	Putahow River, Manitoba	June 14, 1984	Allan J. Ristori
Zander	.25-2	Trosa, Sweden	June 12, 1986	Harry Lee Tennison

SALTWATER FISH

Species	Lbs-Oz	Where Caught	Date	Angler
Albacore	.88-2	Gran Canaria, Canary Islands	Nov. 19, 1977	Siegfried Dickemann
Amberjack, greater	.155-12	Challenger Bank, Bermuda	Aug. 16, 1992	Larry Trott
Angelfish, gray	.4-0	S.Beach Jetty, Miami, FL	July 12, 1999	Rene G. de Dios
Barracuda, great	.85-0	Christmas Is., Rep. of Kiribati	Apr. 11, 1992	John W. Helfrich
Barracuda, Mexican	.21-0	Phantom Island, Costa Rica	Mar. 27, 1987	E. Greg Kent
Barracuda, pickhandle	.25-5	Scottburgh, South Africa	July 3, 1996	Demetrios Stamatis
Bass, barred sand	.13-3	Huntington Beach, CA	Aug. 29, 1988	Robert Halal
Bass, black sea	.10-4	Virginia Beach, VA	Jan. 1, 2000	Allan P. Paschall
Bass, European	.20-14	Cap d'Agde, France	Sept. 8, 1999	Robert Mari
Bass, giant sea	.563-8	Anacapa Island, CA	Aug. 20, 1968	J.D. McAdam Jr.
Bass, striped	.78-8	Atlantic City, NJ	Sept. 21, 1982	Albert R. McReynolds
Bluefish	.31-12	Hatteras, NC	Jan. 30, 1972	James M. Hussey
Bonefish	.19-0	Zululand, South Africa	May 26, 1962	Brian W. Batchelor
Bonito, Atlantic	.18-4	Faial Island, Azores	July 8, 1953	D. Gama Higgs
Bonito, Pacific	.21-3	Malibu, CA	July 30, 1978	Gino M. Picciolo
Cabezon	.23-0	Juan de Fuca Strait, WA	Aug. 4, 1990	Wesley Hunter
Cobia	.135-9	Shark Bay, W. Australia	July 9, 1985	Peter W. Goulding
Cod, Atlantic	.98-12	Isle of Shoals, NH	June 8, 1969	Alphonse Bielevich
Cod, Pacific	.35-0	Unalaska Bay, AK	June 16, 1999	Jim Johnson
Conger	.133-4	South Devon, England	June 5, 1995	Vic Evans
Dolphinfish	.88-0	Highbourne Cay, Bahamas	May 5, 1998	Richard D. Evans
Drum, black	.113-1	Lewes, DE	Sept. 15, 1975	Gerald M. Townsend
Drum, red	.94-2	Avon, NC	Nov. 7, 1984	David G. Deuel
Eel, American	.9-4	Cape May, NJ	Nov. 9, 1995	Jeff Pennick
Eel, marbled	.36-1	Durban, South Africa	June 10, 1984	Ferdie van Nooten
Flounder, southern	.20-9	Nassau Sound, FL	Dec. 23, 1983	Larenza Mungin
Flounder, summer	.22-7	Montauk, NY	Sept. 15, 1975	Charles Nappi
Grouper, goliath	.680-0	Fernandina Beach, FL	May 20, 1961	Lynn Joyner
Grouper, Warsaw	.436-12	Gulf of Mexico, Destin, FL	Dec. 22, 1985	Steve Haeusler
Haddock	.14-15	Saltraumen, Germany	Aug. 15, 1997	Heike Neblinger
Halibut, Atlantic	.355-6	Valevag, Norway	Oct. 20, 1997	Odd Arve Gunderstad
Halibut, California	.58-9	Santa Rosa Island, CA	June 26, 1999	Roger W. Borrell
Halibut, Pacific	.459-0	Dutch Harbor, AK	June 11, 1996	Jack Tragis
Jack, almaco (Pacific)	.132-0	La Paz, Baja Calif., Mexico	July 21, 1964	Howard H. Hahn
Jack, crevalle	.58-6	Barra do Kwanza, Angola	Dec. 10, 2000	Nuno A.P. da Silva
Jack, horse-eye	.29-8	Ascencion Island, South Atlantic	May 28, 1993	Mike Hanson
Kawakawa	.29-0	Clarion Island, Mexico	Dec. 17, 1986	Ronald Nakamura
Lingcod	.76-9	Gulf of Alaska	Aug. 11, 2001	Antwan D. Tinsley
Mackerel, cero	.17-2	Islamorada, FL	Apr. 5, 1986	G. Michael Mills

FISHING (Cont.)

Species	Lbs-Oz	Where Caught	Date	Angler
Mackerel, king	93-0	San Juan, Puerto Rico	Apr. 18, 1999	Steve Perez Graulau
Mackerel, Spanish	13-0	Ocracoke Inlet, NC	Nov. 4, 1987	Robert Cranton
Marlin, Atlantic blue	1402-2	Vitoria, Brazil	Feb. 29, 1992	Paulo R.A. Amorim
Marlin, black	1560-0	Cabo Blanco, Peru	Aug. 4, 1953	A.C. Glassell Jr.
Marlin, Pacific blue	1376-0	Kaaiwi Point, Kona, HI	May 31, 1982	Jay W. deBeaubien
Marlin, striped	494-0	Tutakaka, New Zealand	Jan. 16, 1986	Bill Boniface
Marlin, white	181-14	Vitoria, Brazil	Dec. 8, 1979	Evandro Luiz Coser
Permit	56-2	Ft. Lauderdale, FL	June 30, 1997	Thomas Sebestyen
Pollack, European	27-6	Salcombe, Devon, England	Jan. 16, 1986	Robert S. Milkins
Pollock	50-0	Salstraumen, Norway	Nov. 30, 1996	Thor-Magnus Lekang
Pompano, African	50-8	Daytona Beach, FL	Apr. 21, 1990	Tom Sargent
Roosterfish	114-0	La Paz, Baja Calif., Mexico	June 1, 1960	Abe Sackheim
Runner, blue	11-2	Dauphin Island, AL	June 28, 1997	Stacey M. Moiren
Runner, rainbow	37-9	Clarion Island, Mexico	Nov. 21, 1991	Tom Pfleger
Sailfish, Atlantic	141-1	Luanda, Angola	Feb. 19, 1994	Alfredo de Sousa Neves
Sailfish, Pacific	221-0	Santa Cruz Is., Ecuador	Feb. 12, 1947	C.W. Stewart
Seabass, white	83-12	San Felipe, Mexico	Mar. 31, 1953	L.C. Baumgardner
Seatrout, spotted	17-7	Ft. Pierce, FL	May 11, 1995	Craig F. Carson
Shark, blue	528-0	Montauk Point, NY	Aug. 9, 2001	Joe Seidel
Shark, great white	2664-0	Ceduna, S. Australia	Apr. 21, 1959	Alfred Dean
Shark, Greenland	1708-9	Trondheimsfjord, Norway	Oct. 18, 1987	Terje Nordtvedt
Shark, hammerhead	991-0	Sarasota, FL	May 30, 1982	Allen Ogle
Shark, shortfin mako	1221-0	Chatham, MA	July 21, 2001	Luke Sweeney
Shark, porbeagle	507-0	Pentland Firth, Scotland	Mar. 9, 1993	Christopher Bennet
Shark, bigeye thresher	802-0	Tutukaka, New Zealand	Feb. 8, 1981	Dianne North
Shark, tiger	1780-0	Cherry Grove, SC	June 14, 1964	Walter Maxwell
Snapper, cubera	121-8	Cameron, LA	July 5, 1982	Mike Hebert
Snapper, red	50-4	Gulf of Mexico, LA	June 23, 1996	Capt. Doc Kennedy
Snook, Pacific black	57-12	Rio Naranjo, Quepos, Costa Rica	Aug. 23, 1991	George Beck
Spearfish, Mediterranean	90-13	Madeira Island, Portugal	June 2, 1980	Joseph Larkin
Swordfish	1182-0	Iquique, Chile	May 7, 1953	Louis Marron
Tarpon	283-4	Sherbro Is., Sierra Leone	Apr. 16, 1991	Yvon Victor Sebag
Tautog	25-0	Ocean City, NJ	Jan. 20, 1998	Anthony R. Monica
Tuna, Atlantic bigeye	392-6	Gran Canaria, Puerto Rico	July 25, 1996	Dieter Vogel
Tuna, blackfin	45-8	Key West, FL	May 4, 1996	Sam J. Burnett
Tuna, bluefin	1496-0	Aulds Cove, Nova Scotia	Oct. 26, 1979	Ken Fraser
Tuna, longtail	79-2	Montague Is., NSW, Australia	Apr. 12, 1982	Tim Simpson
Tuna, Pacific bigeye	435-0	Cabo Blanco, Peru	Apr. 17, 1957	Dr. Russell Lee
Tuna, skipjack	45-4	Flathead Bank, Mexico	Nov. 16, 1996	Brian Evans
Tuna, southern bluefin	348-5	Whakatane, New Zealand	Jan. 16, 1981	Rex Wood
Tuna, yellowfin	388-12	San Benedicto Island, Mexico	Apr. 1, 1977	Curt Wiesenhutter
Tunny, little	35-2	Cap de Garde, Algeria	Dec. 14, 1988	Jean Yves Chatard
Wahoo	158-8	Loreto, Baja Calif., Mexico	June 10, 1996	Keith Winter
Weakfish	19-2	Jones Beach, Long Island, NY	Oct. 11, 1984	Dennis R. Rooney
	19-2	Delaware Bay, DE	May 20, 1989	William E. Thomas

BASSMASTERS Classic

Japanese pro Takahiro Omori reeled in some last-minute heriocs to become the 34th annual CITGO BASSMASTERS Classic champion on the waters of Lake Wylie in Charlotte, N.C. Landing his two biggest bass with under five minutes remaining in the competition, the 33-year-old Tokyo native and Emory, Texas resident won the 2004 title, with his five fish limit weighing in at 39 pounds, 2 ounces to post a 2-pound-12 ounce margin of victory over Californian Aaron Martens. Omori earned $200,000 for the victory and became the first foreign angler to win the Classic.

"This is the best day of my life," said Omori, who pounded the stage repeatedly and cried openly before the 13,200 spectators at the weigh-in at the Charlotte Coliseum. "I've waited 18 years for my dream to come true—since I was 15:"

The CITGO BASSMASTERS Classic, hosted by B.A.S.S. (Bass Anglers Sportsman Society), is professional bass fishing's world championship. Qualifiers for the three-day event include the 40 top pros on the CITGO BASSMASTER Tour and the five top-ranked anglers from each of three CITGO BASSMASTER Open circuits. Anglers may weigh only five bass per day and each bass must be at least 12 inches long. Only artificial lures are permitted. The first Classic, held at Lake Mead, Nev. in 1971, was a $10,000 winner-take-all event.

Multiple winners: Rick Clunn (4); George Cochran, Bobby Murray and Hank Parker (2).

Year		Weight	Year		Weight
1971	Bobby Murray, Hot Springs, Ark	43-11	1979	Hank Parker, Clover, S.C	31-0
1972	Don Butler, Tulsa, Okla	38-11	1980	Bo Dowden, Natchitoches, La	54-10
1973	Rayo Breckenridge, Paragould, Ark	52-8	1981	Stanley Mitchell, Fitzgerald, Ga	35-2
1974	Tommy Martin, Hemphill, Tex	33-7	1982	Paul Elias, Laurel, Miss	32-8
1975	Jack Hains, Rayne, La	45-4	1983	Larry Nixon, Hemphill, Tex	18-1
1976	Rick Clunn, Montgomery, Tex	59-15	1984	Rick Clunn, Montgomery, Tex	75-9
1977	Rick Clunn, Montgomery, Tex	27-7	1985	Jack Chancellor, Phenix City, Ala	45-0
1978	Bobby Murray, Nashville, Tenn	37-9	1986	Charlie Reed, Broken Bow, Okla	23-9

Year		Weight	Year		Weight
1987	George Cochran, N. Little Rock, Ark	15-5	1996	George Cochran, Hot Springs, Ark.	31-14
1988	Guido Hibdon, Gravois Mills, Mo	28-8	1997	Dion Hibdon, Stover, Mo.	34-13
1989	Hank Parker, Denver, N.C.	31-6	1998	Denny Brauer, Camdenton, Mo.	46-3
1990	Rick Clunn, Montgomery, Tex	34-5	1999	Davy Hite, Prosperity, S.C.	55-10
1991	Ken Cook, Meers, Okla	33-2	2000	Woo Daves, Spring Grove, Va.	27-13
1992	Robert Hamilton Jr., Brandon, Miss	59-6	2001	Kevin Van Dam, Kalamazoo, Mich.	32-5
1993	David Fritts, Lexington, N.C.	48-6	2002	Jay Yelas, Tyler, Texas	45-13
1994	Bryan Kerchal, Newtown, Conn	36-7	2003	Michael Iaconelli, Woodbury Heights, N.J.	37-14
1995	Mark Davis, Mount Ida, Ark.	47-14	2004	Takahiro Omori, Emory, Texas	39-2

LITTLE LEAGUE BASEBALL

World Series

Carlos Pineda struck out 11 batters over six innings and Juirckson Profar hit a two-run homer as Willemstad, Curacao beat Thousand Oaks, Calif., 5-2, to win the Little League World Series for the first time. It was the first Little League title for the tiny island in the Netherlands Antilles, and the first for any team from the Caribbean. Teams from Curacao had made it to the international title game in each of the last three years (Willemstad won the third-place game in 2003), but lost each time to a team from Japan. The team from Thousand Oaks was the big favorite but fell behind early, committed three errors and left two runners on base to end the game.

In the third-place game, Richmond, Texas beat Guadalupe, Mexico, 5-0.

Played annually in late August in Williamsport, Penn. at Original Field in Williamsport, Penn. from 1947-1958 and at Howard J. Lamade Stadium since 1959 and also at newly constructed Volunteer Stadium starting in 2001.

In order to be invited to the World Series, teams must first win their regional tournaments. There are eight regions from the U.S. (Great Lakes, Midwest, Mid-Atlantic, New England, Northwest, Southeast, Southwest and West) and eight outside of the U.S. (Asia, Canada, Caribbean, European, Latin America, Mexico, Pacific and Trans-Atlantic). The eight U.S. regions then play each other and the eight international regions play each other and the two winners from each meet in the championship game. This insures that a team from the U.S. will always participate in the final game.

Multiple winners: Taiwan (16); Japan (8); California (5); Connecticut, New Jersey and Pennsylvania (4); Mexico (3); New York, South Korea, Texas and Venezuela (2).

Year	Winner	Score	Loser	Year	Winner	Score	Loser
1947	Williamsport, PA	16-7	Lock Haven, PA	1977	Li-Teh, Taiwan	7-2	El Cajon, CA
1948	Lock Haven, PA	6-5	St. Petersburg, FL	1978	Pin-Tung, Taiwan	11-1	Danville, CA
1949	Hammonton, NJ	5-0	Pensacola, FL	1979	Hsien, Taiwan	2-1	Campbell, CA
1950	Houston, TX	2-1	Bridgeport, CT	1980	Hua Lian, Taiwan	4-3	Tampa, FL
1951	Stamford, CT	3-0	Austin, TX	1981	Tai-Chung, Taiwan	4-2	Tampa, FL
1952	Norwalk, CT	4-3	Monongahela, PA	1982	Kirkland, WA	6-0	Hsien, Taiwan
1953	Birmingham, AL	1-0	Schenectady, NY	1983	Marietta, GA	3-1	Barahona, D. Rep.
1954	Schenectady, NY	7-5	Colton, CA	1984	Seoul, S. Korea	6-2	Altamonte, FL
1955	Morrisville, PA	4-3	Merchantville, NJ	1985	Seoul, S. Korea	7-1	Mexicali, Mex.
1956	Roswell, NM	3-1	Merchantville, NJ	1986	Tainan Park, Taiwan	12-0	Tucson, AZ
1957	Monterrey, Mexico	4-0	La Mesa, CA	1987	Hua Lian, Taiwan	21-1	Irvine, CA
1958	Monterrey, Mexico	10-1	Kankakee, IL	1988	Tai Ping, Taiwan	10-0	Pearl City, HI
1959	Hamtramck, MI	12-0	Auburn, CA	1989	Trumbull, CT	5-2	Kaohsiung, Taiwan
1960	Levittown, PA	5-0	Ft. Worth, TX	1990	Taipei, Taiwan	9-0	Shippensburg, PA
1961	El Cajon, CA	4-2	El Campo, TX	1991	Taichung, Taiwan	11-0	Danville, CA
1962	San Jose, CA	3-0	Kankakee, IL	1992	Long Beach, CA	6-0	Zamboanga, Phil.
1963	Granada Hills, CA	2-1	Stratford, CT	1993	Long Beach, CA	3-2	Panama
1964	Staten Island, NY	4-0	Monterrey, Mex.	1994	Maracaibo, Venezuela	4-3	Northridge, CA
1965	Windsor Locks, CT	3-1	Stoney Creek, Can.	1995	Tainan, Taiwan	17-3	Spring, TX
1966	Houston, TX	8-2	W. New York, NJ	1996	Taipei, Taiwan	13-3	Cranston, RI
1967	West Tokyo, Japan	4-1	Chicago, IL				(called after 5th inn.)
1968	Osaka, Japan	1-0	Richmond, VA	1997	Guadalupe, Mexico	5-4	Mission Viejo, CA
1969	Taipei, Taiwan	5-0	Santa Clara, CA	1998	Toms River, NJ	12-9	Kashima, Japan
				1999	Osaka, Japan	5-0	Phenix City, AL
1970	Wayne, NJ	2-0	Campbell, CA				
1971	Tainan, Taiwan	12-3	Gary, IN	2000	Maracaibo, Venezuela	3-2	Bellaire, TX
1972	Taipei, Taiwan	6-0	Hammond, IN	2001	Tokyo, Japan	2-1	Apopka, FL
1973	Tainan City, Taiwan	12-0	Tucson, AZ	2002	Louisville, KY	1-0	Sendai, Japan
1974	Kao Hsiung, Taiwan	12-1	Red Bluff, CA	2003	Tokyo, Japan	10-1	Boynton Beach, FL
1975	Lakewood, NJ	4-3*	Tampa, FL	2004	Willemstad, Curacao	5-2	Thousand Oaks, CA
1976	Tokyo, Japan	10-3	Campbell, CA				

* Foreign teams were banned from the tournament in 1975, but allowed back in the following year.

Note: In 1992, Zamboanga City of the Philippines beat Long Beach, 15-4, but was stripped of the title a month later when it was discovered that the team had used several players from outside the city limits. Long Beach was then awarded the title by forfeit, 6-0 (one run for each inning of the game).

*Connecticut native **Greg Raymer** won the prestigious No-Limit Texas Hold-'em champions bracelet—and an enormous pile of cash—at the 2004 World Series of Poker in Las Vegas.*

POKER

World Series of Poker

Created by Benny Binion in 1970, the World Series of Poker is held each year at Binion's Horseshoe Casino in Las Vegas, Nev. and brings together the world's greatest poker players. The marquee event is the no-limit Texas hold-'em tournament. The first World Series was a seven-player tournament in which the champion Johnny Moss was chosen by a vote of his peers. The 2004 World Champion was Greg "The Fossilman" Raymer, a patent attorney from Stonington, Conn. who beat out 2,576 entrants over seven days and won a first prize of $5 million—a larger payday than the winner of the Kentucky Derby, Wimbledon, Indianapolis 500 and the Masters combined. Anyone that's over 21 years old and can pay the $10,000 entry fee can compete.

Multiple winners: Johnny Moss and Stu Ungar (3); Doyle Brunson and Johnny Chan (2).

No-Limit Texas Hold-'em Champions

Year	Champion	Prize Money	Year	Champion	Prize Money
1970	Johnny Moss	n/a	1988	Johnny Chan	$ 700,000
1971	Johnny Moss	$ 30,000	1989	Phil Hellmuth Jr.	755,000
1972	"Amarillo Slim" Preston	80,000	1990	Mansour Matloubi	895,000
1973	Puggy Pearson	130,000	1991	Brad Daugherty	1,000,000
1974	Johnny Moss	160,000	1992	Hamid Datsmalchi	1,000,000
1975	Sailor Roberts	210,000	1993	Jim Bechtel	1,000,000
1976	Doyle Brunson	220,000	1994	Russ Hamilton	1,000,000
1977	Doyle Brunson	340,000	1995	Dan Harrington	1,000,000
1978	Bobby Baldwin	210,000	1996	Huck Seed	1,000,000
1979	Hal Fowler	270,000	1997	Stu Ungar	1,000,000
1980	Stu Ungar	385,000	1998	Scotty Nguyen	1,000,000
1981	Stu Ungar	375,000	1999	Noel Furlong	1,000,000
1982	Jack Strauss	520,000	2000	Chris Ferguson	1,500,000
1983	Tom McEvoy	580,000	2001	Carlos Mortensen	1,500,000
1984	Jack Keller	660,000	2002	Robert Varkyoni	2,000,000
1985	Bill Smith	700,000	2003	Chris Moneymaker	2,500,000
1986	Berry Johnston	570,000	2004	Greg Raymer	5,000,000
1987	Johnny Chan	625,000			

POWER BOAT RACING

APBA Gold Cup

Waves of controversy struck as Nate Brown won the APBA Gold Cup, piloting the U-10 Miss Detroit Yacht Club to victory July 18, 2004 on the Detroit River. Brown did not cross the finish line first and it was five-time Gold Cup champ Dave Villwock who had apparently earned his sixth title until about an hour after the race when officials announced that Villwock and Miss Budweiser had been disqualified for infractions (lane violations) that occurred before the start of the race. Video replays backed up a helicopter referee's original call that Miss Budweiser moved into the lane of and struck U-16 Miss Elam Plus.

The American Power Boat Association Challenge Cup for unlimited hydroplane racing is the oldest active motorsports trophy in North America. The first Gold Cup was competed for on the Hudson River in New York in June and September 1904. Since then several cities have hosted the race, led by Detroit (34 times) and Seattle (14). Note that (*) indicates driver was also owner of the winning boat.

Drivers with multiple wins: Chip Hanauer (11); Bill Muncey (8); Dave Villwock and Gar Wood (5); Dean Chenoweth (4); Caleb Bragg, Tom D'Eath, Lou Fageol, Ron Musson, George Reis and J.M. Wainwright (3); Danny Foster, George Henley, Vic Kliesrath, E.J. Schroeder, Bill Schumacher, Zalmon G. Simmons Jr., Joe Taggart, Mark Tate and George Townsend (2).

Year	Boat	Driver	Avg. MPH	Year	Boat	Driver	Avg. MPH
1904	Standard (June)	Carl Riotte*	23.160	1955	Gale V	Lee Schoenith	99.552
1904	Vingt-Et-Un II (Sept.)	W. Sharpe Kilmer*	24.900	1956	Miss Thriftway	Bill Muncey	96.552
				1957	Miss Thriftway	Bill Muncey	101.787
1905	Chip I	J.M. Wainwright*	15.000	1958	Hawaii Kai III	Jack Regas	103.000
1906	Chip II	J.M. Wainwright*	25.000	1959	Maverick	Bill Stead	104.481
1907	Chip II	J.M. Wainwright*	23.903	1960	Not held		
1908	Dixie II	E.J. Schroeder*	29.938	1961	Miss Century 21	Bill Muncey	99.678
1909	Dixie II	E.J. Schroeder*	29.590	1962	Miss Century 21	Bill Muncey	100.710
1910	Dixie III	F.K. Burnham*	32.473	1963	Miss Bardahl	Ron Musson	105.124
1911	MIT II	J.H. Hayden*	37.000	1964	Miss Bardahl	Ron Musson	103.433
1912	P.D.Q. II	A.G. Miles*	39.462	1965	Miss Bardahl	Ron Musson	103.132
1913	Ankle Deep	C.S. Mankowski*	42.779	1966	Tahoe Miss	Mira Slovak	93.019
1914	Baby Speed Demon II	Jim Blackton & Bob Edgren	48.458	1967	Miss Bardahl	Bill Shumacher	101.484
				1968	Miss Bardahl	Bill Shumacher	108.173
1915	Miss Detroit	Johnny Milot & Jack Beebe	37.656	1969	Miss Budweiser	Bill Sterett	98.504
				1970	Miss Budweiser	Dean Chenoweth	99.562
1916	Miss Minneapolis	Bernard Smith	48.860	1971	Miss Madison	Jim McCormick	98.043
1917	Miss Detroit II	Gar Wood*	54.410	1972	Atlas Van Lines	Bill Muncey	104.277
1918	Miss Detroit II	Gar Wood	51.619	1973	Miss Budweiser	Dean Chenoweth	99.043
1919	Miss Detroit III	Gar Wood*	42.748	1974	Pay 'n Pak	George Henley	104.428
1920	Miss America I	Gar Wood*	62.022	1975	Pay 'n Pak	George Henley	108.921
1921	Miss America I	Gar Wood*	52.825	1976	Miss U.S.	Tom D'Eath	100.412
1922	Packard Chriscraft	J.G. Vincent*	40.253	1977	Atlas Van Lines	Bill Muncey*	111.822
1923	Packard Chriscraft	Caleb Bragg	43.867	1978	Atlas Van Lines	Bill Muncey*	100.412
1924	Baby Bootlegger	Caleb Bragg*	45.302	1979	Atlas Van Lines	Bill Muncey*	100.765
1925	Baby Bootlegger	Caleb Bragg*	47.240	1980	Miss Budweiser	Dean Chenoweth	106.932
1926	Greenwich Folly	George Townsend*	47.984	1981	Miss Budweiser	Dean Chenoweth	116.387
				1982	Atlas Van Lines	Chip Hanauer	120.050
1927	Greenwich Folly	George Townsend*	47.662	1983	Atlas Van Lines	Chip Hanauer	118.507
				1984	Atlas Van Lines	Chip Hanauer	130.175
1928	Not held			1985	Miller American	Chip Hanauer	120.643
1929	Imp	Richard Hoyt*	48.662	1986	Miller American	Chip Hanauer	116.523
1930	Hotsy Totsy	Vic Kliesrath*	52.673	1987	Miller American	Chip Hanauer	127.620
1931	Hotsy Totsy	Vic Kliesrath*	53.602	1988	Miss Circus Circus	Chip Hanauer & Jim Prevost	123.756
1932	Delphine IV	Bill Horn	57.775				
1933	El Lagarto	George Reis*	56.260	1989	Miss Budweiser	Tom D'Eath	131.209
1934	El Lagarto	George Reis*	55.000	1990	Miss Budweiser	Tom D'Eath	143.176
1935	El Lagarto	George Reis*	55.056	1991	Winston Eagle	Mark Tate	137.771
1936	Impshi	Kaye Don	45.735	1992	Miss Budweiser	Chip Hanauer	136.282
1937	Notre Dame	Clell Perry	63.675	1993	Miss Budweiser	Chip Hanauer	141.296
1938	Alagi	Theo Rossi*	64.340	1994	Smokin' Joe's	Mark Tate	145.532
1939	My Sin	Z.G. Simmons Jr.*	66.133	1995	Miss Budweiser	Chip Hanauer	149.160
1940	Hotsy Totsy III	Sidney Allen*	48.295	1996	Pico/American Dream	Dave Villwock	149.328
1941	My Sin	Z.G. Simmons Jr.*	52.509				
1942-45	Not held			1997	Miss Budweiser	Dave Villwock	129.366
1946	Tempo VI	Guy Lombardo*	68.132	1998	Miss Budweiser	Dave Villwock	140.704
1947	Miss Peps V	Danny Foster	57.000	1999	Miss Pico	Chip Hanauer	152.591
1948	Miss Great Lakes	Danny Foster	46.845	2000	Miss Budweiser	Dave Villwock	139.416
1949	My Sweetie	Bill Cantrell	73.612	2001	Tubby's Subs	Mike Hanson	140.519
1950	Slo-Mo-Shun IV	Ted Jones	78.216	2002	Miss Budweiser	Dave Villwock	143.093
1951	Slo-Mo-Shun IV	Lou Fageol	90.871	2003	Miss Fox Hills Chrysler Jeep-Sun Coatings	Mitch Evans	144.152
1952	Slo-Mo-Shun IV	Stan Dollar	79.923				
1953	Slo-Mo-Shun IV	Joe Taggart & Lou Fageol	99.108	2004	Miss Detroit Yacht Club	Nate Brown	141.195
1954	Slo-Mo-Shun V	Lou Fageol	92.613				

PRO RODEO

All-Around Champion Cowboy

Trevor Brazile of Decatur, Texas, successfully defended his unofficial title of world's best cowboy and roped in his second straight All-Around Champion Cowboy belt buckle at the 2003 National Finals Rodeo held Dec. 5-14 at the Thomas & Mack Center in Las Vegas. The 27-year-old finished with a near-record earnings total of $294,839. Brazile is just the 10th cowboy to win back-to-back world all-around titles and did so in dominating fashion, specializing in three events (tie-down roping, team roping and steer roping). Tie-down roper, and 2001 all-around champ, Cody Ohl finished second with $222,025.

The Professional Rodeo Cowboys Association (PRCA) title of all-around world champion cowboy goes to the rodeo athlete who wins the most prize money in a single year in two or more events, earning a minimum of $3,000 in each event. Only prize money earned in sanctioned PRCA rodeos is counted. From 1929-44, all-around champions were named by the Rodeo Association of America (earnings for those years are not available).

Multiple winners: Ty Murray (7); Tom Ferguson and Larry Mahan (6); Jim Shoulders (5); Joe Beaver, Lewis Feild and Dean Oliver (3); Everett Bowman, Trevor Brazile, Louis Brooks, Clay Carr, Bill Linderman, Phil Lyne, Gerald Roberts, Casey Tibbs and Harry Tompkins (2).

Year		Year		Year		Year	
1929	Earl Thode	1933	Clay Carr	1937	Everett Bowman	1941	Homer Pettigrew
1930	Clay Carr	1934	Leonard Ward	1938	Burel Mulkey	1942	Gerald Roberts
1931	John Schneider	1935	Everett Bowman	1939	Paul Carney	1943	Louis Brooks
1932	Donald Nesbit	1936	John Bowman	1940	Fritz Truan	1944	Louis Brooks
						1945-46	No award

Year		Earnings	Year		Earnings	Year		Earnings
1947	Todd Whatley	$18,642	1966	Larry Mahan	$40,358	1985	Lewis Feild	$130,347
1948	Gerald Roberts	21,766	1967	Larry Mahan	51,996	1986	Lewis Feild	166,042
1949	Jim Shoulders	21,495	1968	Larry Mahan	49,129	1987	Lewis Feild	144,335
			1969	Larry Mahan	57,726	1988	Dave Appleton	121,546
1950	Bill Linderman	30,715				1989	Ty Murray	134,806
1951	Casey Tibbs	29,104	1970	Larry Mahan	41,493			
1952	Harry Tompkins	30,934	1971	Phil Lyne	49,245	1990	Ty Murray	213,772
1953	Bill Linderman	33,674	1972	Phil Lyne	60,852	1991	Ty Murray	244,231
1954	Buck Rutherford	40,404	1973	Larry Mahan	64,447	1992	Ty Murray	225,992
1955	Casey Tibbs	42,065	1974	Tom Ferguson	66,929	1993	Ty Murray	297,896
1956	Jim Shoulders	43,381	1975	Tom Ferguson	50,300	1994	Ty Murray	246,170
1957	Jim Shoulders	33,299	1976	Tom Ferguson	87,908	1995	Joe Beaver	141,753
1958	Jim Shoulders	32,212	1977	Tom Ferguson	65,981	1996	Joe Beaver	166,103
1959	Jim Shoulders	32,905	1978	Tom Ferguson	83,734	1997	Dan Mortensen	184,559
			1979	Tom Ferguson	96,272	1998	Ty Murray	264,673
1960	Harry Tompkins	32,522				1999	Fred Whitfield	217,819
1961	Benny Reynolds	31,309	1980	Paul Tierney	105,568			
1962	Tom Nesmith	32,611	1981	Jimmie Cooper	105,861	2000	Joe Beaver	225,396
1963	Dean Oliver	31,329	1982	Chris Lybbert	123,709	2001	Cody Ohl	296,419
1964	Dean Oliver	31,150	1983	Roy Cooper	153,391	2002	Trevor Brazile	273,998
1965	Dean Oliver	33,163	1984	Dee Pickett	122,618	2003	Trevor Brazile	294,839

SOAP BOX DERBY

All-American Soap Box Derby

At the 67th annual Soap Box Derby on a rain-soaked track in Akron, Ohio, Hilary Pearson won the Masters division, RickiLea Murphy took the Super Stock division and 10-year-old Tennessean Perrin Norris won the Stock divsion giving Tennessee its first Derby champ.

The All-American Soap Box Derby is a coasting race for small gravity-powered cars built by their drivers and assembled within strict guidelines on size, weight and cost. The Derby was started by Dayton, Ohio newsman Myron Scott after he witnessed several boys racing handmade carts down a hill while on a photographic assignment in 1933. Scott decided to start an organized race for kids and the first All-American Soap Box Derby was held in Dayton in 1934. The race got its name because early on most cars were built from wooden soap boxes. The following year, the race was moved to Akron because of its central location and hilly terrain. In 1936, town leaders saw the need for a permanent site for the growing event and with the help of the Works Progress Administration, Derby Downs was constructed.

Held every summer at Derby Downs in Akron, Ohio, the Soap Box Derby is open to all boys and girls from 8 to 17 years old who qualify. There are three competitive divisions: 1. Stock (ages 8-17)— made up of generic, prefab racers that come from Derby-approved kits and don't exceed 200 pounds with driver, car and wheels are weighed together; 2. Super Stock (ages 10-17)— the same as Stock only with a weight limit of 220 pounds; 3. Masters (ages 11-17)— made up of racers designed by the drivers, but constructed with Derby-approved hardware. The racing ramp at Derby Downs is 989 feet, four inches with an 11 percent grade. In 2004, 483 boys and girls competed.

One champion reigned at the All-American Soap Box Derby each year from 1934-75; Junior and Senior division champions from 1976-87; Kit and Masters champions from 1988-91; Stock, Kit and Masters champions from 1992-94; Stock, Super Stock and Masters champions starting in 1995.

Year		Hometown	Age	Year		Hometown	Age
1934	Robert Turner	Muncie, IN	11	1940	Thomas Fisher	Detroit	12
1935	Maurice Bale Jr.	Anderson, IN	13	1941	Claude Smith	Akron, OH	14
1936	Herbert Muench Jr.	St. Louis	14	1942-45	Not held		
1937	Robert Ballard	White Plains, NY	12	1946	Gilbert Klecan	San Diego	14
1938	Robert Berger	Omaha, NE	14	1947	Kenneth Holmboe	Charleston, WV	14
1939	Clifton Hardesty	White Plains, NY	11	1948	Donald Strub	Akron, OH	13

Year	Hometown	Age
1949 Fred Derks	Akron, OH	15
1950 Harold Williamson	Charleston, WV	15
1951 Darwin Cooper	Williamsport, PA	15
1952 Joe Lunn	Columbus, GA	11
1953 Fred Mohler	Muncie, IN	14
1954 Richard Kemp	Los Angeles	14
1955 Richard Rohrer	Rochester, NY	14
1956 Norman Westfall	Rochester, NY	14
1957 Terry Townsend	Anderson, IN	14
1958 James Miley	Muncie, IN	15
1959 Barney Townsend	Anderson, IN	13
1960 Fredric Lake	South Bend, IN	11
1961 Dick Dawson	Wichita, KS	13
1962 David Mann	Gary, IN	14
1963 Harold Conrad	Duluth, MN	12
1964 Gregory Schumacher	Tacoma, WA	14
1965 Robert Logan	Santa Ana, CA	12
1966 David Krussow	Tacoma, WA	12
1967 Kenneth Cline	Lincoln, NE	13
1968 Branch Lew	Muncie, IN	11
1969 Steve Souter	Midland, TX	12
1970 Samuel Gupton	Durham, NC	13
1971 Larry Blair	Oroville, CA	13
1972 Robert Lange Jr.	Boulder, CO	14
1973 Bret Yarborough	Elk Grove, CA	11
1974 Curt Yarborough	Elk Grove, CA	11
1975 Karren Stead	Lower Bucks, PA	11
1976 JR: Phil Raber	Sugarcreek, OH	11
SR: Joan Ferdinand	Canton, OH	14
1977 JR: Mark Ferdinand	Canton, OH	10
SR: Steve Washburn	Bristol, CT	15
1978 JR: Darren Hart	Salem, OR	11
SR: Greg Cardinal	Flint, MI	13
1979 JR: Russell Yurk	Flint, MI	10
SR: Craig Kitchen	Akron, OH	14
1980 JR: Chris Fulton	Indianapolis	11
SR: Dan Porul	Sherman Oaks, CA	12
1981 JR: Howie Fraley	Portsmouth, OH	11
SR: Tonia Schlegel	Hamilton, OH	13
1982 JR: Carol A. Sullivan	Rochester, NH	10
SR: Matt Wolfgang	Lehigh Val., PA	12
1983 JR: Tony Carlini	Del Mar, CA	10
SR: Mike Burdgick	Flint, MI	14
1984 JR: Chris Hess	Hamilton, OH	11
SR: Anita Jackson	St. Louis	15
1985 JR: Michael Gallo	Danbury, CT	12
SR: Matt Sheffer	York, PA	14
1986 JR: Marc Behan	Dover, NH	9
SR: Tami Jo Sullivan	Lancaster, OH	13

Year		Hometown	Age
1987 JR: Matt Margules		Danbury, CT	11
SR: Brian Drinkwater		Bristol, CT	14
1988 KIT: Jason Lamb		Des Moines, IA	10
MAS: David Duffield		Kansas City	13
1989 KIT: David Schiller		Dayton, OH	12
MAS: Faith Chavarria		Ventura, CA	12
1990 MAS: Sami Jones		Salem, OH	13
KIT: Mark Mihal		Valparaiso, IN	12
1991 MAS: Danny Garland		San Diego, CA	14
KIT: Paul Greenwald		Saginaw, MI	13
1992 MAS: Bonnie Thornton		Redding, CA	12
KIT: Carolyn Fox		Sublimity, OR	11
STK: Loren Hurst		Hudson, OH	10
1993 MAS: Dean Lutton		Delta, OH	14
KIT: D.M. Del Ferraro		Stow, OH	12
STK: Owen Yuda		Boiling Springs, PA	10
1994 MAS: D.M. Del Ferraro		Akron, OH	13
KIT: Joel Endres		Akron, OH	14
STK: Kristina Damond		Jamestown, NY	13
1995 MAS: J. Fensterbush		Kingman, AZ	11
SS: Darcie Davisson		Kingman, AZ	11
STK: Karen Thomas		Jamestown, NY	11
1996 MAS: Tim Scrofano		Conneaut, OH	12
SS: Jeremy Phillips		Charlestown, WV	14
STK: Matt Perez		No. Canton, OH	13
1997 MAS: Wade Wallace		Elk Hart, IN	11
SS: Dolline Vance		Salem, OR	13
STK: Mark Stephens		Waynesboro, VA	13
1998 MAS: James Marsh		Cleveland, OH	12
SS: Stacy Sharp		Kingman, AZ	14
STK: Hailey Simpson		Salem, OR	10
1999 MAS: Allan Endres		Barberton, OH	14
SS: Alisha Ebner		Salem, OR	15
STK: Justin Pillow		Deland, FL	12
2000 MAS: Cody Butler		Anderson, IN	12
SS: Derek Etherington		Anderson, IN	11
STK: Rachel Curran		Medina, OH	14
2001 MAS: Michael Flynn		Harrison Township, MI	12
SS: James Rogers		Hilton, NY	15
STK: Chad Eyerly		Alta Loma, CA	11
2002 MAS: Evan Griffin		Winter Park, FL	15
SS: Roger Youmans Jr.		Spencerport, NY	13
STK: C. Vannatta		Anderson, IN	12
2003 MAS: Anthony Marulli		Rochester, NY	14
SS: Corey Harkins		Chicago	14
STK: Nicholas Sibeto		New Castle, PA	12
2004 MAS: Hilary Pearson		Kansas City, MO	14
SS: RickiLea Murphy		Mantua, OH	12
STK: Perrin Norris		Tullahoma, TN	10

SOFTBALL

Men's and women's national champions since 1933 in Major Fast Pitch, Major Slow Pitch and Super Slow Pitch (men only). Sanctioned by the Amateur Softball Association of America.

MEN
Major Fast Pitch

Multiple winners: Clearwater Bombers (10); Raybestos Cardinals (5); Sealmasters (4); Briggs Beautyware, Decatur Pride, Pay'n Pak and Zollner Pistons (3); Billard Barbell, Farm Tavern, Frontier Players Casino, Hammer Air Field, Kodak Park, Meierhoffer, National Health Care, Penn Corp and Peterbilt Western (2).

Year	Year	Year
1933 J.L. Gill Boosters, Chicago	1943 Hammer Air Field, Fresno, CA	1953 Briggs Beautyware
1934 Ke-Nash-A, Kenosha, WI	1944 Hammer Air Field	1954 Clearwater Bombers
1935 Crimson Coaches, Toledo, OH	1945 Zollner Pistons, Ft. Wayne, IN	1955 Raybestos Cardinals,
1936 Kodak Park, Rochester, NY	1946 Zollner Pistons	1956 Clearwater Bombers
1937 Briggs Body Team, Detroit	1947 Zollner Pistons	1957 Clearwater Bombers
1938 The Pohlers, Cincinnati	1948 Briggs Beautyware, Detroit	1958 Raybestos Cardinals
1939 Carr's Boosters, Covington, KY	1949 Tip Top Tailors, Toronto	1959 Sealmasters, Aurora, IL
1940 Kodak Park	1950 Clearwater (FL) Bombers	1960 Clearwater Bombers
1941 Bendix Brakes, South Bend, IN	1951 Dow Chemical, Midland, MI	1961 Sealmasters
1942 Deep Rock Oilers, Tulsa, OK	1952 Briggs Beautyware	1962 Clearwater Bombers

Softball (Cont.)

Year		Year		Year	
1963	Clearwater Bombers	1980	Peterbilt Western, Seattle	1994	Decatur (IL) Pride
1964	Burch Tool, Detroit	1981	Archer Daniels Midland,	1995	Decatur Pride
1965	Sealmasters		Decatur, IL	1996	Green Bay All-Car,
1966	Clearwater Bombers	1982	Peterbilt Western		Green Bay, WI
1967	Sealmasters	1983	Franklin Cardinals,	1997	Tampa Bay Smokers,
1968	Clearwater Bombers		Stratford, CA		Tampa Bay, FL
1969	Raybestos Cardinals	1984	California Kings, Merced, CA	1998	Meierhoffer-Fleeman,
1970	Raybestos Cardinals	1985	Pay'n Pak, Seattle		St. Joseph, MO
1971	Welty Way, Cedar Rapids, IA	1986	Pay'n Pak	1999	Decatur Pride
1972	Raybestos Cardinals	1987	Pay'n Pak	2000	Meierhoffer
1973	Clearwater Bombers	1988	TransAire, Elkhart, IN	2001	Frontier Players Casino,
1974	Gianella Bros., Santa Rosa, CA	1989	Penn Corp, Sioux City, IA		St. Joseph, MO
1975	Rising Sun Hotel, Reading, PA	1990	Penn Corp	2002	Frontier Players Casino
1976	Raybestos Cardinals	1991	Gianella Bros., Rohnert Park, CA	2003	Farm Tavern, Madison, WI
1977	Billard Barbell, Reading, PA	1992	National Health Care,	2004	Farm Tavern
1978	Billard Barbell		Sioux City, IA		
1979	McArdle Pontiac/Cadillac,	1993	National Health Care		
	Midland, MI				

Super Slow Pitch

Multiple winners: Ritch's/Superior (4); Howard's/Western Steer and Steele's Sports (3); Lighthouse/Worth and Long Haul (2).

Year		Year		Year	
1981	Howard's/Western Steer,	1989	Ritch's Salvage, Harrisburg, NC	1996	Ritch's/Superior
	Denver, NC	1990	Steele's Silver Bullets	1997	Ritch's/Superior
1982	Jerry's Catering, Miami	1991	Sun Belt/Worth, Atlanta	1998	Lighthouse/Worth
1983	Howard's/Western Steer	1992	Ritch's/Superior,	1999	Team Easton, California
1984	Howard's/Western Steer		Windsor Locks, CT	2000	Team TPS, Louisville, KY
1985	Steele's Sports, Grafton, OH	1993	Ritch's/Superior	2001	Long Haul, Albertville, MN
1986	Steele's Sports	1994	Bellcorp., Tampa	2002	Long Haul
1987	Steele's Sports	1995	Lighthouse/Worth, Stone Mt., GA	2003	Not held
1988	Starpath, Monticello, KY				

Major Slow Pitch

Multiple winners: Gatliff Auto Sales, Riverside Paving and Skip Hogan A.C. (3); Campbell Carpets, Hamilton Tailoring, Howard's Furniture, Long Haul TPS and New Construction (2).

Year		Year		Year	
1953	Shields Construction, Newport, KY	1972	Jiffy Club, Louisville, KY	1990	New Construction, Shelbyville, IN
1954	Waldneck's Tavern, Cincinnati	1973	Howard's Furniture, Denver, NC	1991	Riverside Paving, Louisville
1955	Lang Pet Shop, Covington, KY	1974	Howard's Furniture	1992	Vernon's, Jacksonville, FL
1956	Gatliff Auto Sales, Newport, KY	1975	Pyramid Cafe, Lakewood, OH	1993	Back Porch/Destin (FL) Roofing
1957	Gatliff Auto Sales	1976	Warren Motors, J'ville, FL	1994	Riverside Paving, Louisville
1958	East Side Sports, Detroit	1977	Nelson Painting, Okla. City	1995	Riverside Paving
1959	Yorkshire Restaurant, Newport, KY	1978	Campbell Carpets, Concord, CA	1996	Bell II, Orlando, FL
1960	Hamilton Tailoring, Cincinnati	1979	Nelco Mfg. Co., Okla. City	1997	Long Haul TPS, Albertville, MN
1961	Hamilton Tailoring	1980	Campbell Carpets	1998	Chase Mortgage/Easton,
1962	Skip Hogan A.C., Pittsburgh	1981	Elite Coating, Gordon, CA		Wilmington, NC
1963	Gatliff Auto Sales	1982	Triangle Sports, Minneapolis	1999	Gasoline Heaven/Worth,
1964	Skip Hogan A.C.	1983	No.1 Electric & Heating,		Commack, NY
1965	Skip Hogan A.C.		Gastonia, NC	2000	Long Haul TPS
1966	Michael's Lounge, Detroit	1984	Lilly Air Systems, Chicago	2001	New Construction
1967	Jim's Sport Shop, Pittsburgh	1985	Blanton's Fayetteville, NC	2002	Twin States/Worth,
1968	County Sports, Levittown, NY	1986	Non-Ferrous Metals, Cleveland		Montgomery, AL
1969	Copper Hearth, Milwaukee	1987	Stapath, Monticello, KY	2003	New Construction/B&J/Snap-On,
1970	Little Caesar's, Southgate, MI	1988	Bell Corp/FAF, Tampa, FL		Metamora, IL
1971	Pile Drivers, Va. Beach, VA	1989	Ritch's Salvage, Harrisburg, NC	2004	U.S. Vinyl, Houston, TX

WOMEN
Major Fast Pitch

Multiple winners: Raybestos/Stratford Brakettes (24); Orange Lionettes (9); Jax Maids (5); California Commotion (4); Arizona Ramblers and Redding Rebels (3); Hi-Ho Brakettes, J.J. Krieg's, National Screw & Manufacturing and Phoenix Storm (2).

Year		Year		Year	
1933	Great Northerns, Chicago	1958	Raybestos Brakettes, Stratford, CT	1982	Raybestos Brakettes
1934	Hart Motors, Chicago			1983	Raybestos Brakettes
1935	Bloomer Girls, Cleveland	1959	Raybestos Brakettes	1984	Los Angeles Diamonds
1936	Nat'l Screw & Mfg., Cleveland	1960	Raybestos Brakettes	1985	Hi-Ho Brakettes, Stratford, CT
1937	Nat'l Screw & Mfg.	1961	Gold Sox, Whittier, CA	1986	So. California Invasion
1938	J.J. Krieg's, Alameda, CA	1962	Orange Lionettes	1987	Orange County Majestics, Anaheim, CA
1939	J.J. Krieg's	1963	Raybestos Brakettes		
1940	Arizona Ramblers, Phoenix	1964	Erv Lind Florists, Portland, OR	1988	Hi-Ho Brakettes
1941	Higgins Midgets, Tulsa, OK	1965	Orange Lionettes	1989	Whittier (CA) Raiders
1942	Jax Maids, New Orleans	1966	Raybestos Brakettes	1990	Raybestos Brakettes
1943	Jax Maids	1967	Raybestos Brakettes	1991	Raybestos Brakettes
1944	Lind & Pomeroy, Portland, OR	1968	Raybestos Brakettes	1992	Raybestos Brakettes
1945	Jax Maids	1969	Orange Lionettes	1993	Redding (CA) Rebels
1946	Jax Maids	1970	Orange Lionettes	1994	Redding Rebels
1947	Jax Maids	1971	Raybestos Brakettes	1995	Redding Rebels
1948	Arizona Ramblers	1972	Raybestos Brakettes	1996	California Commotion, Woodland Hills
1949	Arizona Ramblers	1973	Raybestos Brakettes		
1950	Orange (CA) Lionettes	1974	Raybestos Brakettes	1997	California Commotion
1951	Orange Lionettes	1975	Raybestos Brakettes	1998	California Commotion
1952	Orange Lionettes	1976	Raybestos Brakettes	1999	California Commotion
1953	Betsy Ross Rockets, Fresno, CA	1977	Raybestos Brakettes	2000	Phoenix Storm, Phoenix, AZ
1954	Leach Motor Rockets,Fresno, CA	1978	Raybestos Brakettes	2001	Phoenix Storm
1955	Orange Lionettes	1979	Sun City (AZ) Saints	2002	Stratford Brakettes, Stratford, CT
1956	Orange Lionettes	1980	Raybestos Brakettes	2003	Stratford Brakettes
1957	Hacienda Rockets, Fresno, CA	1981	Orlando (FL) Rebels	2004	Stratford Brakettes

Major Slow Pitch

Multiple winners: Spooks (5); Dana Gardens (4); Universal Plastics (3); Cannan's Illusions, Bob Hoffman's Dots, Key Ford Mustangs and Marks Brothers Dots (2).

Year		Year		Year	
1959	Pearl Laundry, Richmond, VA	1975	Marks Brothers Dots	1988	Spooks
		1976	Sorrento's Pizza, Cincinnati	1989	Cannan's Illusions, Houston
1960	Carolina Rockets, High Pt., NC	1977	Fox Valley Lassies, St. Charles, IL		
1961	Dairy Cottage, Covington, KY			1990	Spooks
1962	Dana Gardens, Cincinnati	1978	Bob Hoffman's Dots, Miami	1991	Cannan's Illusions, San Antonio
1963	Dana Gardens	1979	Bob Hoffman's Dots	1992	Universal Plastics, Cookeville, TN
1964	Dana Gardens			1993	Universal Plastics
1965	Art's Acres, Omaha, NE	1980	Howard's Rubi-Otts, Graham, NC	1994	Universal Plastics
1966	Dana Gardens			1995	Armed Forces, Sacramento
1967	Ridge Maintenance, Cleveland	1981	Tifton (GA) Tomboys	1996	Spooks
1968	Escue Pontiac, Cincinnati	1982	Richmond (VA) Stompers	1997	Taylor's, Glendale, MD
1969	Converse Dots, Hialeah, FL	1983	Spooks, Anoka, MN	1998	Not held
		1984	Spooks	1999	Lakerettes, Conneaut Lake, PA
1970	Rutenschruder Floral, Cincinnati	1985	Key Ford Mustangs, Pensacola, FL		
1971	Gators, Ft. Lauderdale, FL			2000	Premier Sports, Pittsboro, NC
1972	Riverside Ford, Cincinnati	1986	Sur-Way Tomboys, Tifton, GA	2001	Shooters/Nike, Orlando, FL
1973	Sweeney Chevrolet, Cincinnati	1987	Key Ford Mustangs	2002	Diamond Queens, Nashville, TN
1974	Marks Brothers Dots, Miami			2003	Not held

TRIATHLON
World Championship

Contested since 1989, the Triathlon World Championship consists of a 1.5-kilometer swim, a 40-kilometer bike ride and a 10-kilometer run. The 2004 championship was held May 9 in Madeira, Portugal

Multiple winners: MEN—Simon Lessing (4); Peter Robertson and Spencer Smith (2). WOMEN—Emma Carney, Michellie Jones and Karen Smyers (2).

MEN

Year		Time	Year		Time
1989	Mark Allen, United States	1:58:46	1997	Chris McCormack, Australia	1:48:29
1990	Greg Welch, Australia	1:51:37	1998	Simon Lessing, Great Britain	1:55:31
1991	Miles Stewart, Australia	1:48:20	1999	Dimitry Gaag, Kazakhstan	1:45:25
1992	Simon Lessing, Great Britain	1:49:04	2000	Oliver Marceau, France	1:51:41
1993	Spencer Smith, Great Britain	1:51:20	2001	Peter Robertson, Australia	1:48:01
1994	Spencer Smith, Great Britain	1:51:04	2002	Iván Raña, Spain	1:50:41
1995	Simon Lessing, Great Britain	1:48:29	2003	Peter Robertson, Australia	1:54:13
1996	Simon Lessing, Great Britain	1:39:50	2004	Bevan Docherty, New Zealand	1:41:04

WOMEN

Year		Time	Year		Time
1989	Erin Baker, New Zealand	2:10:01	1997	Emma Carney, Australia	1:59:22
1990	Karen Smyers, United States	2:03:33	1998	Joanne King, Australia	2:07:25
1991	Joanne Ritchie, Canada	2:02:04	1999	Loretta Harrop, Australia	1:55:28
1992	Michellie Jones, Australia	2:02:08	2000	Nicole Hackett, Australia	1:54:43
1993	Michellie Jones, Australia	2:07:41	2001	Siri Lindley, United States	1:58:51
1994	Emma Carney, Australia	2:03:19	2002	Leanda Cave, Wales	2:01:31
1995	Karen Smyers, USA	2:04:58	2003	Emma Snowsill, Australia	2:06:40
1996	Jackie Gallagher, Australia	1:50:52	2004	Sheila Taormina, United States	1:52:17

Ironman Championship

Contested in Hawaii since 1978, the Ironman Triathlon Championship consists of a 2.4-mile swim, a 112-mile bike ride and 26.2-mile run. The race begins at 7 A.M. and continues all day until the course is closed at midnight.

MEN

Multiple winners: Mark Allen and Dave Scott (6); Peter Reid (3); Tim DeBoom, Luc Van Lierde and Scott Tinley (2).

Year	Date	Winner	Time	Runner-up	Margin	Start	Finish	Location
I	2/18/78	Gordon Haller	11:46	John Dunbar	34:00	15	12	Waikiki Beach
II	1/14/79	Tom Warren	11:15:56	John Dunbar	48:00	15	12	Waikiki Beach
III	1/10/80	Dave Scott	9:24:33	Chuck Neumann	1:08	108	95	Ala Moana Park
IV	2/14/81	John Howard	9:38:29	Tom Warren	26:00	326	299	Kailua-Kona
V	2/6/82	Scott Tinley	9:19:41	Dave Scott	17:16	580	541	Kailua-Kona
VI	10/9/82	Dave Scott	9:08:23	Scott Tinley	20:05	850	775	Kailua-Kona
VII	10/22/83	Dave Scott	9:05:57	Scott Tinley	0:33	964	835	Kailua-Kona
VIII	10/6/84	Dave Scott	8:54:20	Scott Tinley	24:25	1036	903	Kailua-Kona
IX	10/25/85	Scott Tinley	8:50:54	Chris Hinshaw	25:46	1018	965	Kailua-Kona
X	10/18/86	Dave Scott	8:28:37	Mark Allen	9:47	1039	951	Kailua-Kona
XI	10/10/87	Dave Scott	8:34:13	Mark Allen	11:06	1380	1284	Kailua-Kona
XII	10/22/88	Scott Molina	8:31:00	Mike Pigg	2:11	1277	1189	Kailua-Kona
XIII	10/15/89	Mark Allen	8:09:15	Dave Scott	0:58	1285	1231	Kailua-Kona
XIV	10/6/90	Mark Allen	8:28:17	Scott Tinley	9:23	1386	1255	Kailua-Kona
XV	10/19/91	Mark Allen	8:18:32	Greg Welch	6:01	1386	1235	Kailua-Kona
XVI	10/10/92	Mark Allen	8:09:08	Cristian Bustos	7:21	1364	1298	Kailua-Kona
XVII	10/30/93	Mark Allen	8:07:45	Paulli Kiuru	6:37	1438	1353	Kailua-Kona
XVIII	10/15/94	Greg Welch	8:20:27	Dave Scott	4:05	1405	1290	Kailua-Kona
XIX	10/7/95	Mark Allen	8:20:34	Thomas Hellriegel	2:25	1487	1323	Kailua-Kona
XX	10/26/96	Luc Van Lierde	8:04:08	Thomas Hellriegel	1:59	1420	1288	Kailua-Kona
XXI	10/18/97	Thomas Hellriegel	8:33:01	Jurgen Zack	6:17	1534	1365	Kailua-Kona
XXII	10/3/98	Peter Reid	8:24:20	Luc Van Lierde	7:37	1487	1379	Kailua-Kona
XXIII	10/23/99	Luc Van Lierde	8:17:17	Peter Reid	5:37	1471	1419	Kailua-Kona
XXIV	10/14/00	Peter Reid	8:21:01	Tim DeBoom	2:09	1525	1426	Kailua-Kona
XXV	10/6/01	Tim DeBoom	8:31:18	Cameron Brown	14:52	1558	1364	Kailua-Kona
XXVI	10/19/02	Tim DeBoom	8:29:56	Peter Reid	3:10	1540	1457	Kailua-Kona
XXVII	10/18/03	Peter Reid	8:22:35	Rutger Beke	5:51	1647	1569	Kailua-Kona
XXVIII	10/16/04	Normann Stadler	8:33:29	Peter Reid	10:11	1728	1579	Kailua-Kona

WOMEN

Multiple winners: Paula Newby-Fraser (8); Natascha Badmann (4); Erin Baker, Lori Bowden and Sylviane Puntous (2).

Year	Winner	Time	Runner-up	Year	Winner	Time	Runner-up
1978	No finishers			1992	Paula Newby-Fraser	8:55:28	Julie Anne White
1979	Lyn Lemaire	12:55.00	None	1993	Paula Newby-Fraser	8:58:23	Erin Baker
1980	Robin Beck	11:21:24	Eve Anderson	1994	Paula Newby-Fraser	9:20:14	Karen Smyers
1981	Linda Sweeney	12:00:32	Sally Edwards	1995	Karen Smyers	9:16:46	Isabelle Mouthon
1982	Kathleen McCartney	11:09:40	Julie Moss	1996	Paula Newby-Fraser	9:06:49	Natascha Badmann
1982	Julie Leach	10:54:08	Joann Dahlkoetter	1997	Heather Fuhr	9:31:43	Lori Bowden
1983	Sylviane Puntous	10:43:36	Patricia Puntous	1998	Natascha Badmann	9:24:16	Lori Bowden
1984	Sylviane Puntous	10:25:13	Patricia Puntous	1999	Lori Bowden	9:13:02	Karen Smyers
1985	Joanne Ernst	10:25:22	Liz Bulman	2000	Natascha Badmann	9:26:17	Lori Bowden
1986	Paula Newby-Fraser	9:49:14	Sylviane Puntous	2001	Natascha Badmann	9:28:37	Lori Bowden
1987	Erin Baker	9:35:25	Sylviane Puntous	2002	Natascha Badmann	9:07:54	Nina Kraft
1988	Paula Newby-Fraser	9:01:01	Erin Baker	2003	Lori Bowden	9:11:55	Natascha Badmann
1989	Paula Newby-Fraser	9:00:56	Sylviane Puntous	2004	Nina Kraft	9:33:25	Natascha Badmann
1990	Erin Baker	9:13:42	P. Newby-Fraser				
1991	Paula Newby-Fraser	9:07:52	Erin Baker				

X GAMES

The ESPN Extreme Games, originally envisioned as a biannual showcase for "alternative" sports, were first held June 24-July 1, 1995 in Newport and Providence, R.I. and Mt. Snow, Vt. The success of the inaugural event prompted organizers to make it an annual competition. Newport would again serve as host for the redubbed X Games in 1996. The X Games has evolved rapidly since its inception and have been held in several cities since. New sports and events have been added while others have been dropped.

Summer X Games sites: 1995-Newport/Providence, R.I. (and Mt. Snow, Vt.); 1996-Newport/Providence, R.I.; 1997-San Diego; 1998-San Diego; 1999-San Francisco; 2000-San Francisco; 2001-Phiadelphia; 2002-Philadelphia; 2003-Los Angeles; 2004-Los Angeles. **Winter X Games sites:** 1997-Snow Summit Mountain Resort, Big Bear Lake, Calif.; 1998-Crested Butte, Colo.; 1999-Crested Butte, Colo.; 2000- Mt. Snow, Vt.; 2001-Mt. Snow, Vt.; 2002-Aspen, Colo.; 2003-Aspen, Colo.; 2004-Aspen, Colo.

Summer X Games
Bicycle Stunt

Year	Vert	Year	Dirt	Year	Street/Stunt Park	Year	Flatland
1995	Matt Hoffman	1995	Jay Miron	1996	Dave Mirra	1997	Trevor Meyer
1996	Matt Hoffman	1996	Joey Garcia	1997	Dave Mirra	1998	Trevor Meyer
1997	Dave Mirra	1997	T.J. Lavin	1998	Dave Mirra	1999	Trevor Meyer
1998	Dave Mirra	1998	Brian Foster	1999	Dave Mirra	2000	Martti Kuoppa
1999	Dave Mirra	1999	T.J. Lavin	2000	Dave Mirra	2001	Martti Kuoppa
2000	Jamie Bestwick	2000	Ryan Nyquist	2001	Bruce Crisman	2002	Martti Kuoppa
2001	Dave Mirra	2001	Stephen Murray	2002	Ryan Nyquist	2003	Simon O'Brien
2002	Dave Mirra	2002	Allan Cooke	2003	Ryan Nyquist	2004	Not held
2003	Jamie Bestwick	2003	Ryan Nyquist	2004	Dave Mirra		
2004	Dave Mirra	2004	Corey Bohan			**Year**	**Downhill**
						2001	Brandon Meadows
						2002	Robbie Miranda
						2003	Brandon Meadows
						2004	Not held

Skateboarding

Year	Vert Singles	Year	Vert Doubles	Year	Street/Park	Year	Women's Park
1995	Tony Hawk	1997	Hawk/Macdonald	1995	Chris Senn	2003	Vanessa Torres
1996	Andy Macdonald	1998	Hawk/Macdonald	1996	Rodil de Araujo Jr.	**Year**	**Women's Street**
1997	Tony Hawk	1999	Hawk/Macdonald	1997	Chris Senn	2004	Elissa Steamer
1998	Andy Macdonald	2000	Hawk/Macdonald	1998	Rodil de Araujo Jr.	**Year**	**Street Best Trick**
1999	Bucky Lasek	2001	Hawk/Macdonald	1999	Chris Senn	2001	Kerry Getz
2000	Bucky Lasek	2002	Hawk/Macdonald	2000	Eric Koston	2002	Rodil de Araujo Jr.
2001	Bob Burnquist	2003	Lasek/Burnquist	2001	Kerry Getz	2003	Chad Muska
2002	Pierre-Luc Gagnon	**Year**	**Vert Best Trick**	2002	Rodil de Araujo Jr.		
2003	Bucky Lasek	2000	Bob Burnquist	**Year**	**Street**	**Year**	**Big Air**
2004	Bucky Lasek	2001	Matt Dove	2003	Eric Koston	2004	Danny Way
Year	**Women's Vert**	2002	Pierre-Luc Gagnon	2004	Paul Rodriguez		
2004	Lyndsey Adams Hawkins	2003	Tony Hawk	**Year**	**Park**		
		2004	Sandro Dias	2003	Ryan Sheckler		

Moto X

Year	Freestyle
1999	Travis Pastrana
2000	Travis Pastrana
2001	Travis Pastrana
2002	Mike Metzger
2003	Travis Pastrana
2004	Nate Adams
Year	**Step Up**
2001	Tommy Clowers
2002	Tommy Clowers
2003	Matt Buyten
2004	Jeremy McGrath
Year	**Big Air**
2001	Kenny Bartman
2002	Mike Metzger
2003	Brian Deegan
2004	Not held
Year	**Super Moto**
2004	Ben Bostrom
Year	**Best Trick**
2004	Chuck Carothers

Bungee Jumping

Year	
1995	Doug Anderson
1996	Peter Bihun
1997	Event discontinued

Big-Air Snowboarding

Year	Men
1997	Peter Line
1998	Kevin Jones
1999	Peter Line
2000	Event discontinued
Year	**Women**
1997	Tina Dixon
1998	Janet Matthews
1999	Barrett Christy
2000	Event discontinued

Skysurfing

Year	
1995	Fradet/Zipser
1996	Furrer/Scmid
1997	Hartman/Pappadato
1998	Rozov/Burch
1999	Fradet/Iodice
2000	Klaus/Rogers
2001	Event discontinued

Surfing

Year	
2003	East Coast
2004	Edst Coast

Note: The X Games surfing event is contested by teams of surfers from the East Coast and the West Coast.

Street Luge

Year	Dual
1995	Bob Pereyra
1996	Shawn Goular
1997	Biker Sherlock
1998	Biker Sherlock
1999	Dennis Derammelaere
2000	Bob Ozman
2001	Event discontinued
Year	**Mass**
1995	Shawn Gilbert
1996	Biker Sherlock
1997	Biker Sherlock
1998	Rat Sult
1999	Event discontinued
Year	**Super Mass**
1997	Biker Sherlock
1998	Rat Sult
1999	David Rogers
2000	Bob Pereyra
2001	Brent DeKeyser
2002	Event discontinued
Year	**King of the Hill**
2001	Dennis Derammelaere
2002	Event discontinued

Sportclimbing

Year	Men's Difficulty
1995	Ian Vickers
1996	Arnaud Petit
1997	Francois Legrand
1998	Christian Core
1999	Chris Sharma
2000	Event discontinued

Year	Women's Difficulty
1995	Robyn Erbersfield
1996	Katie Brown
1997	Katie Brown
1998	Katie Brown
1999	Stephanie Bodet
2000	Event discontinued

Year	Men's Speed
1995	Hans Florine
1996	Hans Florine
1997	Hans Florine
1998	Vladimir Netsvetaev
1999	Aaron Shamy
2000	Vladimir Zakharov
2001	Maxim Stenkovoy
2002	Maxim Stenkovoy
2003	Event discontinued

Year	Women's Speed
1995	Elena Ovtchinnikova
1996	Cecile Le Flem
1997	Elena Ovtchinnikova
1998	Elena Ovtchinnikova
1999	Renata Piszczek
2000	Etti Hendrawati
2001	Elena Repko
2002	Tori Allen
2003	Event discontinued

In-Line Skating

Year	Men's Vert
1995	Tom Fry
1996	Rene Hulgreen
1997	Tim Ward
1998	Cesar Mora
1999	Eito Yasutoko
2000	Eito Yasutoko
2001	Taig Khris
2002	Event discontinued

Year	Women's Vert
1995	Tash Hodgeson
1996	Fabiola da Silva
1997	Fabiola da Silva
1998	Fabiola da Silva
1999	Ayumi Kawasaki
2000	Fabiola da Silva
2001	Fabiola da Silva
2002	Event discontinued

Year	Combined Vert
2002	Takeshi Yasutoko
2003	Eito Yasutoko
2004	Takeshi Yasutoko

Note: In 2002 the men's and women's vert events were combined.

Year	Men's Park
1995	Matt Salerno
1996	Arlo Eisenberg
1997	Arron Feinberg
1998	Jonathan Bergeron
1999	Nicky Adams
2000	Sven Boekhorst
2001	Jaren Grob
2002	Jaren Grob
2003	Bruno Lowe

Year	Women's Park
1997	Sayaka Yabe
1998	Jenny Curry
1999	Sayaka Yabe
2000	Fabiola da Silva
2001	Martina Svobodova
2002	Martina Svobodova
2003	Fabiola da Silva

Year	Vert Triples
1998	Malina/Fogarty/Popa
1999	Khris/Bujanda/ Boekhorst
2000	Event discontinued

Year	Men's Downhill
1995	Derek Downing
1996	Dante Muse
1997	Derek Downing
1998	Patrick Naylor
1999	Event discontinued

Year	Women's Downhill
1995	Julie Brandt
1996	Gypsy Tidwell
1997	Gypsy Tidwell
1998	Julie Brandt
1999	Event discontinued

X-Venture Race

Year	
1995	Team Threadbo
1996	Team Kobeer
1997	Team Presidio
1998	Event discontinued

Watersports

Year	Barefoot Waterski Jumping
1995	Justin Seers
1996	Ron Scarpa
1997	Peter Fleck
1998	Peter Fleck
1999	Event discontinued

Year	Men's Wakeboarding
1996	Parks Bonifay
1997	Jeremy Kovak
1998	Darin Shapiro
1999	Parks Bonifay
2000	Darin Shapiro
2001	Danny Harf
2002	Danny Harf
2003	Danny Harf
2004	Phillip Soven

Year	Women's Wakeboarding
1997	Tara Hamilton
1998	Andrea Gaytan
1999	Meaghan Major
2000	Tara Hamilton
2001	Dallas Friday
2002	Emily Copeland
2003	Dallas Friday
2004	Dallas Friday

Winter X Games

Ice Climbing

Year	Men's Difficulty
1997	Jaren Ogden
1998	Will Gadd
1999	Will Gadd
2000	Event discontinued

Year	Women's Difficulty
1997	Bird Lew
1998	Kim Csizmazia
1999	Kim Csizmazia
2000	Event discontinued

Year	Men's Speed
1997	Jared Ogden
1998	Will Gadd
1999	Event discontinued

Year	Women's Speed
1997	Bird Lew
1998	Kim Csizmazia
1999	Event discontinued

Super-modified Shovel Racing

Year	
1997	Don Adkins
1998	Event discontinued

CrossOver

Year	
1997	Brian Patch
1998	Event discontinued

Snow Mountain Bike Racing

Year	Men's Downhill
1997	Shaun Palmer
1998	Andrew Shandro
1999	Event discontinued

Skiing

Year	Men's Big Air
1999	J.F. Cusson
2000	Candide Thovex
2001	Tanner Hall
2002	Event discontinued

Year	Men's Skier X
1998	Dennis Rey
1999	Enak Gavaggio
2000	Shaun Palmer
2001	Zach Crist
2002	Reggie Crist
2003	Lars Lewen
2004	Casey Puckett

Year	Women's Skier X
1999	Aleisha Cline
2000	Anik Demers
2001	Aleisha Cline
2002	Aleisha Cline
2003	Aleisha Cline
2004	Karin Huttary

Year	SuperPipe
2002	Jon Olsson
2003	Candide Thovex

Year	Men's Slopestyle
2002	Tanner Hall
2003	Not held
2004	Simon Dumont

Year	Women's Downhill
1997	Missy Giove
1998	Marla Streb
1999	Event discontinued

Year	Men's Speed
1997	Phil Tintsman
1998	Jurgen Beneke
1999	Event discontinued

Year	Women's Speed
1997	Cheri Elliott
1998	Elke Brutsaert
1999	Event discontinued

Year	Men's Biker X
1999	Steve Peat
2000	Myles Rockwell
2001	Not held

Year	Women's Biker X
1999	Tara Llanes
2000	Katrina Miller
2001	Not held

Moto X

Year	Big Air
2001	Mike Jones
2002	Brian Deegan
2003	Event discontinued

Year	Best Trick
2004	Caleb Wyatt

Skiboarding

Year	
1998	Mike Nick
1999	Chris Hawks
2000	Neal Lyons
2001	Event discontinued

Snowboarding

Year	Men's Big Air
1997	Jimmy Halopoff
1998	Jason Borgstede
1999	Kevin Sansalone
2000	Peter Line
2001	Jussi Oksanen
2002	Event discontinued

Year	Women's Big Air
1997	Barrett Christy
1998	Tina Basich
1999	Barrett Christy
2000	Tara Dakides
2001	Tara Dakides
2002	Event discontinued

Year	Men's Boarder X
1997	Shaun Palmer
1998	Shaun Palmer
1999	Shaun Palmer
2000	Drew Neilson
2001	Scott Gaffney
2002	Philippe Conte
2003	Ueli Kestenholz
2004	Ueli Kestenholz

Year	Women's Boarder X
1997	Jennie Waara
1998	Tina Dixon
1999	Maelle Ricker
2000	Leslee Olson
2001	Line Oestvold
2002	Ine Poetzl
2003	Lindsey Jacobellis
2004	Lindsey Jacobellis

Year	Men's Halfpipe
1997	Todd Richards
1998	Ross Powers
1999	Jimi Scott
2000	Todd Richards

Year	Men's Superpipe
2001	Dan Kass
2002	J.J. Thomas
2003	Shaun White
2004	Steve Fisher

Year	Women's Halfpipe
1997	Shannon Dunn
1998	Cara-Beth Burnside
1999	Michele Taggart
2000	S. Brun Kjeldaas

Year	Women's Superpipe
2001	Shannon Dunn
2002	Kelly Clark
2003	Gretchen Bleiler
2004	Hannah Teter

Year	Men's Slopestyle
1997	Daniel Franck
1998	Ross Powers
1999	Peter Line
2000	Kevin Jones
2001	Kevin Jones
2002	Travis Rice
2003	Shaun White
2004	Shaun White

Year	Women's Slopestyle
1997	Barrett Christy
1998	Jennie Waara
1999	Tara Dakides
2000	Tara Dakides
2001	Jaime MacLeod
2002	Tara Dakide
2003	Janna Meyen
2004	Janna Meyen

Snomobiling

Year	Snocross
1998	Toni Haikonen
1999	Chris Vincent
2000	Tucker Hibbert
2001	Blair Morgan
2002	Blair Morgan
2003	Not held
2004	Michael Island

Year	Hillcross
2001	Carl Kuster
2002	Carl Kuster
2003	T.J. Kullas
2003	Mike Metzger
2004	Levi LaVallee

Ultracross

Year	
2000	McLain/Lind
2001	Palmer/Takizawa
2002	Wescott/Lind
2003	Delerue/Zackrisson
2004	Holland/Crist

Great Outdoors Games

Playing sites: Lake Placid (2000-02); Reno-Tahoe, Nev. (2003); Madison, Wis. (2004).

Fishing

Year	Flyfishing
2000	Tom Rowland
2001	Chuck Farneth
2002	Peter Erickson
2003	Lance Egan
2004	Lance Egan

Year	Flycasting
2002	Carter Andrews
2003	Mike McFarland
2004	John Wilson

Year	Bass Fishing
2000	Peter Thliveros
2001	Peter Thliveros
2002	Shaw Grigsby
2003	S. Grigsby & G. Klein
2004	M. Gofron & D. Brauer

Target Sports

Year	Rifle
2000	Bob Mastroianni
2001	Jerry Miculek
2002	Jerry Miculek
2003	Doug Koenig
2004	Mike Cumming

Year	Shotgun
2000	Doug Fuller
2001	Dustin Long
2002	Robbie Purser
2003	Scott Robertson
2004	Travis Mears

Year	Archery
2000	Jackie Caudle
2001	Randy Hendrix
2002	Randy Hendrix
2003	Darren Collins
2004	Randy Hendrix

Sporting Dogs

Year	Retriever Trials
2000	Barry Lyons & Skeet
2001	Jerry Day & Super Sue
2002	A. Washburn & Ticket
2003	Chris Akin & Boomer
2004	J.P. Jackson & Achilles

Year	Big Air
2000	Beth Gutteridge & Heidi
2001	Mike Wallace & Jerry
2002	Mike Jackson & Little Morgan
2003	Terry Casey & Skeeter
2004	Mike Jackson & Little Morgan

Year	Agility (large dogs)
2000	D. Bommarito & Lacey
2001	Julie Daniels & Spring
2002	Olga Chaiko & Luz
2003	S. Kluever & Ransom
2004	Marcus Topps & Juice

Year	Superweave (large)
2003	Ken Fairchild & Echo
2004	S. Kluever & Ransom

Year	Agility (small dogs)
2001	Jean LaValley & Taz
2002	Erin Schaefer & Jag
2003	C. Frank & Kimie
2004	Renee King & Hamlet

Year	Superweave (small)
2003	Jean LaValley & Taz
2004	Not held

Year	Disc Drive
2004	Tim Gelb & Lock-Eye Razzle

Timber Events

Year	Endurance (women)
2000	Sheree Taylor
2001	Penny Halvorson
2002	Sheree Taylor
2003	Peg Engasser
2004	Sheree Taylor

Year	Endurance (men)
2000	Jason Wynyard
2001	Jason Wynyard
2002	Matt Bush
2003	Jason Wynyard
2004	Jason Wynyard

Year	Hot Saw
2000	Harry Burnsworth
2001	Mel Lentz
2002	Mike Sullivan
2003	Mike Sullivan
2004	Matt Bush

Year	Springboard
2000	Mitch Hewitt
2001	Mitch Hewitt
2002	Mitch Hewitt
2003	Dave Bolstad
2004	Dale Ryan

Year	Boom Run (men)
2000	J.R. Salzman
2001	J.R. Salzman
2002	Jamie Fischer
2003	Jamie Fischer
2004	J.R. Salzman

Year	Boom Run (women)
2000	Tina Salzman
2001	Mandy Erdmann
2002	Mandy Erdmann
2003	Abbie Hosechler
2004	Mandy Erdmann

Year	Boom Run (mixed)
2003	Jamie Fischer & Tanya Fischer
2004	J.R. Salzman & Shana Martin

Year	Log Rolling (men)
2000	J.R. Salzman
2001	J.R. Salzman
2002	Darren Hudson
2003	Jamie Fischer
2004	J.R. Salzman

Year	Log Rolling (women)
2000	Tina Salzman
2001	Tina Salzman
2002	Tina Bosworth
2003	Tina Bosworth
2004	Tina Bosworth

Year	Speed Climbing
2000	Wade Stewart
2001	Brian Bartow
2002	Brian Bartow
2003	Brian Bartow
2004	Wade Stewart

Year	Tree Topping
2000	Mick Lee
2001	Gregg Hart
2002	Wade Stewart
2003	Greg Hart
2004	Brian Bartow

Year	Team Relay
2001	Team Halvorson
2002	Team Clarke
2003	Team Wynard
2004	Team Zalewski

YACHTING

The America's Cup

International yacht racing was launched in 1851 when England's Royal Yacht Squadron staged a 60-mile regatta around the Isle of Wight and offered a silver trophy to the winner. The 101-foot schooner *America*, sent over by the New York Yacht Club, won the race and the prize. Originally called the Hundred-Guinea Cup, the trophy was renamed The America's Cup after the winning boat's owners deeded it to the NYYC with instructions to defend it whenever challenged.

From 1870-1980, the NYYC successfully defended the Cup 25 straight times; first in large schooners and J-class boats that measured up to 140 feet in overall length, then in 12-meter boats. A foreign yacht finally won the Cup in 1983 when *Australia II* beat defender *Liberty* in the seventh and deciding race off Newport, R.I. Four years later, the San Diego Yacht Club's *Stars & Stripes* won the Cup back, sweeping the four races of the final series off Fremantle, Australia.

Then in 1988, New Zealand's Mercury Bay Boating Club, unwilling to wait the usual three- to four-year period between Cup defenses, challenged the SDYC to a match race, citing the Cup's 102-year-old Deed of Gift, which clearly stated that every challenge had to be honored. Mercury Bay announced it would race a 133-foot monohull. San Diego countered with a 60-foot catamaran. The resulting best-of-three series (Sept. 7-8) was a mismatch as the SDYC's catamaran *Stars & Stripes* won two straight by margins of better than 18 and 21 minutes. Mercury Bay syndicate leader Michael Fay protested the outcome and took the SDYC to court in New York State (where the Deed of Gift was first filed) claiming San Diego had violated the spirit of the deed by racing a catamaran instead of a monohull. N.Y. State Supreme Court judge Carmen Ciparick agreed and on March 28, 1989, ordered the SDYC to hand the Cup over to Mercury Bay. The SDYC refused, but did consent to the court's appointment of the New York Yacht Club as custodian of the Cup until an appeal was ruled on.

On Sept. 19, 1989, the Appellate Division of the N.Y. Supreme Court overturned Ciparick's decision and awarded the Cup back to the SDYC. An appeal by Mercury Bay was denied by the N.Y. Court of Appeals on April 26, 1990, ending three years of legal wrangling. To avoid the chaos of 1988-90, a new class of boat—75-foot monohulls with 110-foot masts—has been used by all competing countries since 1992. Note that (*) indicates skipper was also owner of the boat.

The America's Cup moved to Europe for the first time when the Swiss Alinghi Team beat Team New Zealand, 5-0, in the best-of-nine series in February and March 2003. The dates and location of the next America's Cup races are to be determined.

Schooners And J-Class Boats

Year	Winner	Skipper	Series	Loser	Skipper
1851	America	Richard Brown	—	—	—
1870	Magic	Andrew Comstock	1-0	Cambria, GBR	J. Tannock
1871	Columbia (2-1)	Nelson Comstock	4-0	Livonia, GBR	J.R. Woods
	& Sappho (2-0)	Sam Greenwood			
1876	Madeleine	Josephus Williams	2-0	Countess of Dufferin, CAN	J.E. Ellsworth
1881	Mischief	Nathanael Clock	2-0	Atalanta, CAN	Alexander Cuthbert*
1885	Puritan	Aubrey Crocker	2-0	Genesta, GBR	John Carter
1886	Mayflower	Martin Stone	2-0	Galatea, GBR	Dan Bradford
1887	Volunteer	Henry Haff	2-0	Thistle, GBR	John Barr
1893	Vigilant	William Hansen	3-0	Valkyrie II, GBR	Wm. Granfield
1895	Defender	Henry Haff	3-0	Valkyrie III, GBR	Wm. Granfield
1899	Columbia	Charles Barr	3-0	Shamrock I, GBR	Archie Hogarth
1901	Columbia	Charles Barr	3-0	Shamrock II, GBR	E.A. Sycamore
1903	Reliance	Charles Barr	3-0	Shamrock III, GBR	Bob Wringe
1920	Resolute	Charles F. Adams	3-2	Shamrock IV, GBR	William Burton
1930	Enterprise	Harold Vanderbilt*	4-0	Shamrock V, GBR	Ned Heard
1934	Rainbow	Harold Vanderbilt*	4-2	Endeavour, GBR	T.O.M. Sopwith
1937	Ranger	Harold Vanderbilt*	4-0	Endeavour II, GBR	T.O.M. Sopwith

12-Meter Boats

Year	Winner	Skipper	Series	Loser	Skipper
1958	Columbia	Briggs Cunningham	4-0	Sceptre, GBR	Graham Mann
1962	Weatherly	Bus Mosbacher	4-1	Gretel, AUS	Jock Sturrock
1964	Constellation	Bob Bavier & Eric Ridder	4-0	Sovereign, AUS	Peter Scott
1967	Intrepid	Bus Mosbacher	4-0	Dame Pattie, AUS	Jock Sturrock
1970	Intrepid	Bill Ficker	4-1	Gretel II, AUS	Jim Hardy
1974	Courageous	Ted Hood	4-0	Southern Cross, AUS	John Cuneo
1977	Courageous	Ted Turner	4-0	Australia	Noel Robins
1980	Freedom	Dennis Conner	4-1	Australia	Jim Hardy
1983	Australia II	John Bertrand	4-3	Liberty, USA	Dennis Conner
1987	Stars & Stripes	Dennis Conner	4-0	Kookaburra III, AUS	Iain Murray

60-ft Catamaran vs 133-ft Monohull

Year	Winner	Skipper	Series	Loser	Skipper
1988	Stars & Stripes	Dennis Conner	2-0	New Zealand, NZE	David Barnes

75-ft International America's Cup Class

Year	Winner	Skipper	Series	Loser	Skipper
1992	America [3]	Bill Koch* & Buddy Melges	4-1	Il Moro di Venezia, ITA	Paul Cayard
1995	Black Magic, NZE	Russell Coutts	5-0	Young America, USA	Dennis Conner & Paul Cayard
2000	Black Magic, NZE	Russell Coutts & Dean Barker	5-0	Luna Rossa, ITA	Francesco de Angelis
2003	Alinghi, SWI	Russell Coutts	5-0	New Zealand, NZE	Dean Barker

Deaths

Pat Tillman was killed while deployed with the Army Rangers in Afghanistan.

AP/Wide World Photos

Notable deaths in the world of sports from Nov. 1, 2003-Oct. 30, 2004.

Dan Allen, 48; former head football coach at Holy Cross (six seasons) and Boston University (10 seasons); led BU to the 1-AA playoffs on two occasions; from multiple chemical sensitivities; in Westboro, Mass.; May 16.

George Bamberger, 80; manager for Milwaukee Brewers (1978-80, 1985-86) and New York Mets (1982-83); career managerial record of 458-478, including 377-351 with Brewers; served as pitching coach for Baltimore Orioles from 1968-77 producing 18 20-game winners and four Cy Young awards; of cancer; in North Redington Beach, Fla.; Apr. 4.

Jed Bedford, 21; captain of the Columbus State basketball team who led the nation (NCAA Div. II) with 135 three-pointers made in 2001-02; after collapsing during practice; in Columbus, Ga.; Dec. 14, 2003.

Fanny Blankers-Koen, 85; Dutch housewife and mother of two who won four gold medals (100m, 80m hurdles, 200m, 4x100m relay) in track and field at the 1948 Summer Olympics at the age of 30; two of her wins came after photo finishes, including the 4x100-meter relay in which she ran the anchor leg and went from fourth place to first; also competed at the 1936 (at age 18) and 1952 Summer Games but did not medal; held or shared six world records (100m, 80m hurdles, high jump, long jump, 4x100m and 4x400m); from three golds at the 1950 European championships; from heart problems; in Amsterdam; Jan. 25.

Ray Boone, 81; patriarch of baseball's first three-generation family of major leaguers; father of Bob Boone and grandfather of Aaron and Bret Boone; Boone was an infielder with six teams (Cleveland Indians, Detroit Tigers, Chicago White Sox, Kansas City Athletics, Milwaukee Braves and Boston Red Sox) between 1948-60, hitting .275 with 151 home runs and 737 RBIs; two-time All-Star with the Tigers (1954, 1956); following complications from surgery; in San Diego, Calif.; Oct. 16.

Henry Borowy, 88; right-handed pitcher for several major-league clubs who played in the World Series with the New York Yankees (1942 and 1943) and Chicago Cubs (1945); went 2-2 in 1945 World Series with the Cubs pitching a shutout in Game 1, started and lost Game 5, won as a reliever in Game 6 and then started and lost Game 7, getting knocked out in the first inning; career record of 108-82, with a 3.50 ERA from 1942-51 with Yankees, Cubs, Phillies, Pirates and Tigers; a two-time All-Star, Borowy became the first pitcher in modern history to win at least 10 games in one season for two different teams (10-5 with Yankees and 11-2 with Cubs in 1945); in Brick, N.J.; Aug. 23.

Ken Brett, 55; became the youngest player to pitch in a World Series when he pitched 1 1/3 scoreless innings over two games for the Boston Red Sox in the 1967 World Series against the St. Louis Cardinals just a month after his 19th birthday; left-hander who tied the modern era record for playing for the most teams (10), toiling for Boston, Milwaukee, Philadelphia, New York Yankees, Chicago White Sox, California, Minnesota, Pittsburgh, Los Angeles and Kansas City; was the winning pitcher for the National League in the 1974 All-Star Game while with the Pittsburgh Pirates; set a record for pitchers in 1973 by hitting a home run in four consecutive starts with Philadelphia; was the fourth pick overall in the 1966 amateur draft; brother of Hall of Famer George Brett; following a long battle with brain cancer; in Spokane, Wash.; Nov. 18, 2003.

Rosey Brown, 71; Hall of fame offensive tackle with the New York Giants who was named to nine Pro Bowls and was named to the NFL's 75th Anniversary All-Time Team; not selected until the 27th round of the NFL draft but went on to start at right tackle for 13 seasons, including eight straight All-Pro selections; known as both an outstanding pass and run blocker; of an apparent heart attack; in Mansfield Township, N.J.; June 9.

Ken Caminiti, 41; National League MVP in 1996 with the San Diego Padres, hitting .326 with 40 home runs and 130 RBIs; was a three-time All-Star third baseman in 15 big league seasons with San Diego, Houston Astros, Texas Rangers and Atlanta Braves; admitted to *Sports Illustrated* in 2002 that he used steroids during his MVP season and guessed that half of the players in the majors were also using them (he later distanced himself from those statements); reportedly of a drug overdose; in New York City; Oct. 10.

Alan Cohen, 73; part-owner of Boston Celtics from 1983-93 who was chairman of NBA's Board of Governors from 1985-87 and helped institute NBA's salary cap; previously served as chairman and CEO of Madison Square Garden Corp., owners of the New York Knicks and Rangers; after long battle with idiopathic pulmonary firbrosis; in Boca Raton, Fla.; Aug. 10.

James "Doc" Counsilman, 83; influential and innovative swimming coach at Indiana University, who coached the Hoosiers to six straight NCAA titles (1968-74) and 20 straight Big Ten championships; coached 48 Olympians from nine countries who won 46 medals, including 26 golds; pioneered the use of underwater film for analyzing and improving technique as well as the now widely used pace clocks and markers that separate swimming lanes; set a record when he swam across the English Channel at 58 years old; in his sleep; in Bloomington, Ind.; Jan. 4.

Yinka Dare, 32; 7-foot Nigerian center who was a first-round draft pick in the 1994 NBA draft by the New Jersey Nets; played 110 games over four seasons with the Nets in the NBA, averaging 2.1 points and 2.5 rebounds; played college basketball at George Washington University, leading the Colonials to consecutive NCAA appearances before declaring for the NBA draft following his sophomore year; of a heart attack due to an arrhythmia condition; in Englewood, N.J.; Jan. 9.

Art Devlin, 81; U.S. Olympic ski jumper who competed in two Olympic Games (1952 and 1956); following his ski jumping career he served as television broadcaster for CBS and ABC for more than two decades; also served as vice president of the Lake Placid Olympic Organizing Committee for the 1980 Winter Games; of cancer; in Lake Placid, N.Y.; Apr. 22.

Gertrude Dunn, 72; slick-fielding shortstop who was voted rookie of the year of the All American Girls Professional Baseball League in 1952 after taking the South Bend Blue Sox to the league championship; also a member of the U.S. Field Hockey Hall of Fame, playing on the U.S. national field hockey and lacrosse teams while a student at West Chester University; in a single-engine plane crash; in Avondale, Pa.; Sept. 29.

Gertrude Ederle, 97; American who, for as a teenager, was the most celebrated woman on earth when she became the first woman to swim across the English Channel on Aug. 6, 1926, beating the men's record by more than two hours crossing the treacherous, 21-mile wide waterway going from Cape Griz-Nez, France to Kingsdown, England in 14 hours, 31 minutes; she is estimated to have swam 35 miles across due to

Gertrude Ederle

Indiana
James "Doc" Counsilman

AP/Wide World Photos
Otto Graham

the stormy weather that day; her record was not broken for 24 years until Florence Chadwick swam across in 13 hours, 20 minutes in 1950; also won gold, silver and bronze medals at the 1924 Summer Olympics; of natural causes; in Wyckoff, N.J.; Nov. 30, 2003.

Bruce Edwards, 49; caddie for PGA Tour golfer Tom Watson for 30 years who continued to carry Watson's bag after being diagnosed with Lou Gehrig's disease; his battle with ALS inspired Watson to shoot a 65 at the 2003 U.S. Open, matching his best Open round; was honored in 2004 with the Golf Writers Association of America's Ben Hogan award, given annually to someone who remained active in the game despite a handicap or illness; of Amyoytrophic Lateral Sclerosis commonly known as Lou Gehrig's disease; in Ponte Vedra Beach, Fla.; Apr. 8.

Cotton Fitzsimmons, 72; long-time NBA coach who won 832 games over 21 seasons with five teams: Phoenix (1970-72, 1988-92), Atlanta (1972-76), Buffalo (1977-78), Kansas City (1978-84) and San Antonio (1984-86); career record of 832-775; also coached Kansas State for two seasons before beginning his NBA career; the colorful coach, whose first name is Lowell, worked as a television and radio analyst late in his career; of lung cancer; in Phoenix, Ariz.; July 24.

Charlie Fox, 82; longtime manager and executive with the San Francisco Giants; won the AP National League Manager of the Year Award in 1971, leading the Giants to a 90-72 record and the NL West title before losing to Pittsburgh in the NLCS; career record of 348-327 with Giants; also briefly managed Montreal Expos in 1976 (12-22) and Chicago Cubs in 1983 (17-22) and was Montreal's GM from 1976-78 before ending his baseball career as a scout for the Houston Astros from 1990-93; in Stanford, Calif.; Feb. 16.

Rose Gacioch, 89; All-star outfielder/pitcher for the South Bend Blue Sox and Rockford Peaches of the All-American Girls Baseball League from 1945-54; led the league in triples in 1946 and won 20 games as a pitcher in 1951; had 31 outfield assists in a season from right field twice; threw a no-hitter in 1953; of natural causes; in Clinton Township, Mich.; Sept. 9.

Joe Gold, 82; bodybuilding pioneer and founder of Gold's Gym in Venice Beach, Calif., the beachside gym made famous by Arnold Schwarzenegger in the 1977 documentary Pumping Iron; Gold had already sold the gym in 1970 but returned to the business, founding

World Gym in 1977; following an illness; in Los Angeles; July 11.

Mike Goliat, 78; starting second-baseman on the 1950 Philadelphia Phillies World Series "Whiz Kids" team that lost in four games to the New York Yankees; career batting average of .225 in 249 games over four seasons with the Phillies and St. Louis Browns; of heart failure; in Seven Hills, Ohio; Jan. 14.

Ruben Gomez, 77; major league pitcher who won the first big league regular-season game played on the West Coast while with the San Francisco Giants (the Giants beat the Los Angeles Dodgers, 8-0) on April 15, 1958; Gomez was also the first Puerto Rico native to win a World Series game (Game 3 in 1954 with San Francisco); career record of 76-86 with a 4.09 ERA with Giants, Phillies, Indians and Twins; following a long illness; in San Juan, Puerto Rico; July 26.

Otto Graham, 82; Hall of fame quarterback who led the Cleveland Browns to the league championship every season of his 10-year career (1946-55) winning seven titles (four in the All-American Football Conference and three in the NFL); never missed a game as a professional and amassed an amazing career record of 105-17-4; passed for 23,584 yards and 174 touchdowns; inducted into the Pro Football Hall of Fame in 1965; following diagnosis of a heart condition; in Sarasota, Fla.; Dec. 16, 2003.

C.J. Hart, 93; helped create the country's first commercial drag strip in 1950 at what is now John Wayne Airport; inducted into the International Drag Racing Hall of Fame in 1991 and the Motorsports Hall of Fame of America in 1999; received an "eight-cylinder salute" at his burial when mourners fired up a loud dragster in tribute; following a stroke; in Placentia, Calif., June 25.

Mark Hatley, 54; vice president of football operations for the Green Bay Packers; also served as VP for player personnel with the Chicago Bears from 1997-2001; while in Chicago he drafted back-to-back rookies of the year (Brian Urlacher in 2000 and Anthony Thomas in 2001); cause of death not reported; in Green Bay, Wis.; July 27.

Ivan Hlinka, 54; former Pittsburgh Penguins coach who led the Czech Republic to the gold medal at the 1998 Winter Games; coached the Penguins to the third round of the playoffs in 2001 but was replaced four games into the 2001-02 season; as a player with the Czechoslovakian national team he won world championships in 1972, 1976 and 1977 as well as the bronze medal at the 1972 Winter Olympics and the silver at the 1976 Winter Games; played 137 games in the NHL, scoring 42 goals and 81 assists with the Vancouver Canucks; from injuries sustained in a car crash; in Kralovy Vary, Czech Republic; Aug. 16.

Chuck Hiller, 70; second baseman who played for four teams in eight big-league seasons from 1961-68, batting .243 with 20 homers and 152 RBIs; while with the San Francisco Giants he hit the National League's first World Series grand slam in Game 4 of the 1962 Series against the New York Yankees; worked as a major league coach, minor league manager and adviser in the New York Mets organization for 24 years; following a lengthy illness; in St. Pete Beach, Fla.; Oct. 20.

Elroy Hirsch, 80; Hall of fame NFL running back and receiver who got the nickname "Crazy Legs" for his unorthodox running style; played one season (1942) of college football at Wisconsin, leading the Badgers to an 8-1-1 record and rushing for 786 yards before beginning a pro career with the AAFC's Chicago Rockets; Hirsch joined the NFL's Los Angeles Rams in 1949, leading them to the league championship in 1951; following his playing days, and a brief movie career, he returned to Madison to serve as the Wisconsin athletic director from 1969-87; of natural causes; in Madison, Wisc.; Jan. 28.

Eleanor Holm, 91; two-time swimming gold medalist (100m and 200m backstrokes) at the 1932 Summer Olympics in Los Angeles; also set the world records in both events; she was kicked off the 1936 U.S. Olympic team by USOC chief Avery Brundage after she was caught drinking champagne and shooting dice during the trans-Atlantic voyage to Berlin; following her competitive swimming career she entered show business as a singer and actress; she starred as Jane in the 1938 film *Tarzan's Revenge*, opposite Glenn Morris, the 1936 Olympic decathlon champion; of kidney failure; in Miami, Fla.; Feb. 3.

Paul Hopkins, 99; oldest major league baseball veteran at the time of his death; a right-handed pitcher who made his major league debut in Sept. 1927 at Yankee Stadium, giving up Babe Ruth's record-tying 59th home run of the season with the bases loaded; finished his career in 1929 with a 1-1 record; of natural causes; in Deep River, Conn.; Jan. 2.

Bubba Hyde, 95; fleet-footed star outfielder in the Negro Leagues who played in parts of four decades between 1927-53; among the first players inducted into the Negro Leagues Wall of Fame in Milwaukee's County Stadium; tried to break into the major leagues with the Boston Braves in 1950 but left training camp to be with his pregnant wife and was cut by the team; after a brief illness; in St. Louis; Nov. 20, 2003.

Carl James, 75; former commissioner of the Big Eight Conference (1980-96) who helped bring four Texas schools (Baylor, Texas, Texas A&M and Texas Tech) from the Southwest Conference into the league that would later become the Big 12; also served as athletic director at both his alma mater, Duke, and the University of Maryland; of skin cancer; in Cornelius, N.C.; July 3.

Darrell Johnson, 75; former manager of three major league baseball teams, most notably with the Boston Red Sox (1974-76), winning the American League pennant in 1975 before losing one of the best World Series in history in seven games to Sparky Anderson's Cincinnati Reds; also managed the AL's Seattle Mariners (1977-80) and Texas Rangers (1982); career

managerial record of 472-590; of leukemia; in Fairfield, Calif.; May 3.

Phil Johnson, 78; Hall of Fame horse trainer who won the 2002 Breeders' Cup Classic with 43-1 shot Volponi; of cancer; in Rockville Centre, N.Y.; Aug. 6.

Richard Jones, 21; 6-foot-6 junior forward on the Canisius basketball team who collapsed during a workout with teammates; played 88 games with the Golden Griffins, starting in 47 of them; in Buffalo, N.Y.; May 5.

Jeff Julian, 42; PGA Tour veteran (1996 and 2002 Tours) who was diagnosed with Lou Gehrig's disease in 2001 but continued his playing career; played on the Nationwide Tour in 1990 and from 1997-2000, winning the 1997 Dominion Open; his best finish in 58 starts on the PGA Tour was 16th at the 1996 Buick Classic; of Amyoytrophic Lateral Sclerosis commonly known as Lou Gehrig's disease; in Norwich, Vt.; July 15.

Johnny Kelley, 97; legendary distance runner who ran the Boston Marathon a record 61 times (crossing the finish line 58 times), winning twice (1935 and 1945) and finishing second seven times; was the only American runner to finish the 1936 Olympic Marathon in Berlin placing 18th overall; also competed as a 40-year-old at the 1948 Olympic Marathon in London; ran his final Boston Marathon in 1992 at age 84, finishing in under six hours; of natural causes; on Cape Cod, Mass.; Oct. 6.

Rudy LaRusso, 66; five-time NBA all-star who played alongside Elgin Baylor and helped the Los Angeles Lakers reach the NBA Finals three times (lost all three times to the Boston Celtics); averaged 15.6 points and 9.4 rebounds during his 10-year career; two-time All-Ivy League with Dartmouth College; of Parkinson's disease; in Los Angeles; July 9.

Carl Lipscombe, 89; left-winger who won the Stanley Cup with the Detroit Red Wings in 1943; played for Detroit from 1937-46 scoring 137 goals and 277 points in his career including 36 goals and 73 points in 1944; set the NHL record (since broken) for fastest hat trick, scoring three times in 1:52 against Chicago in 1938; of complications from leukemia; in Wailuku, Hawaii; Feb. 23.

Keith Magnuson, 56; fiery Chicago Blackhawks defenseman from 1969-80, accumulating 14 goals, 125 assists and 1,442 penalty minutes in 589 NHL games; fought plenty on the ice, taking boxing lessons to improve his technique; became a team leader as a player and coached the Blackhawks for two seasons (1980-82) following his playing career, compiling a 49-57-26 record; of injuries sustained in a car accident near Toronto, Canada; Dec. 15, 2003.

Tug McGraw, 59; off-beat, left-handed relief pitcher who won two world championships in 19 seasons (1969 with the New York Mets and 1980 with the Philadelphia Phillies); popularized the catchphrase "You Gotta Believe" during the Mets pennant drive in 1973; traded to Phillies following the 1974 season; struck out Kansas City Royal Willie Wilson to capture the Phillies' only World Series championship in 1980; a two-time All-Star, McGraw went 96-92 in his career with a 3.14 ERA and 180 saves from 1965-1984; once asked if he preferred to play on grass or an artificial surface, he reportedly answered, "I don't know. I never smoked any Astro-Turf."; father of country singer Tim McGraw; outside Nashville, Tenn.; of brain cancer; Feb. 9.

Robert Merrill, 85; Metropolitan Opera star who also became widely known for singing the national

AP/Wide World Photos

Johnny Kelley

NHRA

Darrell Russell

AP/Wide World Photos

Warren Spahn

anthem on opening day at Yankee Stadium for three decades beginning in 1969; of natural causes; in New Rochelle, N.Y.; Oct. 23.

Bob Murphy, 79; Hall of Fame baseball broadcaster who covered the New York Mets since the team's inception in 1962 until his retirement in 2003; started career on radio with the Boston Red Sox in 1954 before moving to the Baltimore Orioles in 1960; with the Mets he joined Lindsey Nelson and Ralph Kiner to form a trio that would work together on radio and television for 17 seasons before Nelson left for San Francisco; received the Ford Frick Award in 1994; brother of famous *San Diego Union* sports editor Jack Murphy; of lung cancer; in West Palm Beach, Fla.; Aug. 3.

Moe Norman, 75; eccentric—possibly autistic—Canadian golfer who has been called the purest ball striker in the history of the sport; nicknamed the "Rain Man of golf," he once hit 356 consecutive drives off a standard wooden tee without even knocking it loose; in his roughly 50 years of playing, he had three sanctioned rounds of 59, nine double eagles, 17 holes in one, won more than 50 tournaments and set over 40 course records; had a tremendous fear of strangers and shunned any kind of media attention; reportedly knew the number of courses he had played in his lifetime (434) and could remember the exact hole yardages of 375 of them; of a heart attack; in Kitchener, Ontario; Sept. 4.

Paul Owens, 79; vice president and director of player development for the Philadelphia Phillies from 1972-85; built the Phillies' only World Series championship team (1980); Philadelphia also won division titles from 1976-1978, reached the playoffs in 1981 and the World Series in 1983, losing to the Orioles; following an illness; in Woodbury, N.J.; Dec. 26, 2003.

Marco Pantani, 34; Italian cyclist who won the 1998 Tour de France, the last Tour before Lance Armstrong's record run; also won the 1998 Giro d'Italia; nicknamed "The Pirate," he was known as a climbing specialist on his bike; his career was tainted by allegations of drug use and he was thrown out of the 1999 Giro d'Italia for failing a blood test; of an overdose of cocaine; in Rimini, Italy; Feb. 14.

Steve Patterson, 56; center on three UCLA national championship teams (1969-71) between the Lew Alcindor (later known as Kareem Abdul-Jabbar) and Bill Walton eras; drafted in the second round of the 1971

NBA draft by the Cleveland Cavaliers and played six seasons in the league; coached Arizona State from 1985-89, compiling a 48-56 record; of lung cancer; in Phoenix, Ariz.; July 29.

David Rickman, 29; professional heavyweight prize fighter who died two days after getting knocked out in a Savannah, Ga. boxing ring; worked as a full-time nurse in Jacksonville, Fla. and had been boxing professionally for less than a year; knocked out after taking several blows to the head during the fourth and final round at Jarrell's Gym and never regained consciousness; Rickman was to be paid $800 for the fight; in Savannah, Ga.; Mar. 29.

Walter Riker, 87; pharmacology professor who later became the first drug adviser to the National Football League helping the league deal with cocaine and steroid use by its players; after he cautioned that steroids could have deleterious health consequences in 1990, the NFL began random testing; cause of death not reported; in New York City; Feb. 20.

James Stillman Rockefeller, 102; former chairman of the National City Bank (which would later become Citigroup) who, at the time of his death, was the oldest-known U.S. Olympic medal winner; he was the captain of the Yale eight that won rowing gold at the 1924 Summer Games in Paris; another member of his gold-medal winning crew was Benjamin Spock, who later became a pediatrician who authored a best-selling book on child rearing; following a stroke; in New Haven, Conn.; Aug. 10.

Mike Rowland, 41; jockey who won nearly 4,000 races in his career; was killed in a pileup of horses at Turfway Park in Florence, Ky.; was thrown from his mount, World Trade, when the horse broke down with a fractured leg while leading the field in the last race of the day; of injuries sustained when kicked in the head by a horse; in Cincinnati, Ohio; Feb. 9.

Darrell Russell, 35; drag racer who died when his Top Fuel car broke apart and burst into flames upon deploying his parachute after crossing the finish line at Madison, Illinois' Gateway International Raceway; Russell was the 2001 NHRA Rookie of the Year becoming just the third driver in NHRA history to win in his first start; had six career Top Fuel wins; of injuries sustained in the accident; in St. Louis, Mo.; June 27.

Marge Schott, 75; controversial, outspoken former owner of the Cincinnati Reds; held a controlling interest in the team from 1984-99; despite her lack of any base-ball experience she took a close hand in team decisions shortly after purchasing the team; her St. Bernard Schottzie was always by her side and under their admin-istration the Reds won the World Series in 1990; was widely criticized and suspended repeatedly after making offensive remarks, including comments praising Hitler, saying he was "good at the beginning" but then "went too far"; under pressure, she sold her controlling interest in the team to Carl Lindner in 1999 for $67 million; cause of death not released; in Cincinnati; Mar. 2.

Norm Sloan, 77; coached N.C. State to the 1974 NCAA basketball national championship and a 30-1 record; started at N.C. State in 1966 and coached the Wolfpack, and star forward David Thompson, to a per-fect 27-0 record in 1973 but the team was excluded from the NCAA tournament and put on probation due to recruiting violations; career record of 624-393 in 37 seasons with four different schools, including N.C. State and two tours of duty with Florida; named AP and USBWA coach of the year in 1974; of pulmonary fibro-sis of the lungs; in Durham, N.C.; Dec. 9, 2003.

Warren Spahn, 82; the winningest left-handed pitcher in baseball history; won 363 games (the sixth highest total ever) over 24 seasons for the Boston and Milwaukee Braves, San Francisco Giants and New York Mets; had 13 20-win seasons, finished 382 of his 665 career starts and recorded 2,583 strikeouts; began his career in 1942 but was reportedly sent down to the minors by manager Casey Stengel for refusing to "brushback" Pee Wee Reese in an exhibition game; joined the army in 1943 and fought in the European the-ater during World War II, receiving the Bronze Star, Pur-ple Heart and a battlefield commission; returned to base-ball in 1945 and went on to have a Hall of Fame career, winning the 1957 Cy Young Award, throwing no-hitters in 1960 (against Philadelphia) and 1961 (against San Francisco), pitching a National League-record 5,243²/₃ innings and hitting 35 home runs; career record of 363-245 and a 3.09 ERA; of natural causes; in Broken Arrow, Okla.; Nov. 24, 2003.

Dernell Stenson, 25; promising young outfielder with the Cincinnati Reds who was found murdered in Chandler, Ariz., where he was playing for the Scottsdale Scorpions in the Arizona Fall League; made his major league debut in 2003, playing in 37 games and hitting .247 with three homers and 13 RBI; of injuries sustained when he was shot and run over during an apparent car-jacking; in Chandler, Ariz.; Nov. 5, 2003.

Shirley Strickland de la Hunty, 78; Australian sprinter/hurdler who won seven Olympic medals, including three golds; the first woman to win back-to-back Olympic titles, winning the 80m hurdles at the 1952 Helsinki Summer Olympics and 1956 Melbourne Summer Games (also won gold in the 4x100 relay and bronze in the 100m in 1956); won three medals at the 1948 London Summer Olympics: silver in the 4x100m relay and bronze in the 100m and 80m hurdles; mem-ber of five Australian relay teams which set or equalled five world records; in Perth, Australia; Feb. 17.

Justin Strzelczyk, 36; former long-time NFL offen-sive lineman who played 137 games (starting 75) from 1990-1998 with the Pittsburgh Steelers; died in a fiery head-on collision with a tanker truck full of acid after leading New York state troopers on a high-speed chase following a hit-and-run during morning rush hour; in Herkimer, N.Y.; Sept. 30.

Travis Tidwell, 79; two-time All-America quarter-back for Auburn; led the nation in total offense twice, including his freshman season in 1946; engineered his-toric upset of archrival Alabama in 1949; taken in the first round of the 1950 NFL draft by the New York Giants and played two seasons in New York before moving to the Canadian Football League; following an illness; in Trussville, Ala.; July 1.

Pat Tillman, 27; safety for the NFL's Arizona Car-dinals who walked away from a $3.6 million contract to join the U.S. Army in the wake of the Sept. 11 terrorist attacks; a specialist in the 75th Ranger Regiment, a light infantry unit out of Fort Benning, Ga.; an All-Pac-10 linebacker at Arizona State, he was named 1997 defen-sive player of the year in the Pac-10; drafted by the Car-dinals in the 7th round of the 1998 draft and broke the team record for tackles (223) in 2000; in 2001, out of loyalty to the Cardinals, he turned down a $9 million, five-year offer sheet from the Super Bowl champion St. Louis Rams; became the first NFL player killed in combat since Buffalo offensive tackle Bob Kalsu died in the Viet-nam War in 1970 (19 NFL players were killed in World War II); was killed in combat in southeastern Afghanistan, apparently from friendly fire; Apr. 22.

Leon Wagner, 69; slugging outfielder who hit 211 home runs in a 12-year major league career with five teams—San Francisco Giants (1958-59), St. Louis Car-dinals (1960), Los Angeles Angels (1961-62), Cleve-land Indians (1964-68) and Chicago White Sox (1968); of natural causes; in Los Angeles; Jan. 3.

Rodger Ward, 83; two-time winner of the Indi-anapolis 500; during a six-year stretch between 1959-64, he finished no lower than fourth and won in 1959 and 1962; finished second in 1960 and 1964 to Jim Rathmann and A.J. Foyt respectively; served as an Air Force fighter and bomber pilot during World War II; of natural causes; in Anaheim, Calif.; July 5.

Max West, 87; major leaguer who, while a player with the Boston Bees (the team would later become known as the Braves), belted a three-run homer in his first All-Star game at-bat, propelling the National League to a 4-0 win over the American League in 1940; his All-Star game home run came off the New York Yankees' Red Ruffing; during WWII he served as part of a B-29 crew, flying missions over the Pacific; after the war West ended his playing career with the Pittsburgh Pirates in 1948 after seven years in the majors and a .254 career batting average; of brain cancer; in Sierra Madre, Calif.; Jan. 5.

Ralph Wiley, 52; outspoken sportswriter who coined the phrase "Billy Ball" while writing for the Oak-land Tribune in 1975 to describe Oakland manager Billy Martin's team's penchant for stealing bases and bunting; also worked as a senior writer for Sports Illus-trated and, most recently, as a columnist for ESPN.com; of heart failure; in Orlando, Fla.; June 13.

George Yardley, 75; Detroit Pistons forward who became first player in NBA history to score 2,000 points in a season (2,001 in 1957-58), breaking Minneapolis Laker George Mikan's single-season record (1,932 in 1950-51); made the all-star team in six of his seven sea-sons in the league with three different teams (Fort Wayne, Detroit and Syracuse) failing to become an all-star in only his rookie season; averaged 20.3 points per game in 46 playoff games; was a star forward at Stan-ford before playing pro ball; of Amyotrophic Lateral Sclerosis a.k.a. Lou Gehrig's disease; in Newport Beach, Calif.; Aug. 12.

RESEARCH MATERIAL

Many sources were used in the gathering of information for this almanac. Day-to-day material was almost always found in copies of *USA Today*, *The Boston Globe*, and *The South Florida Sun-Sentinel* or online at various World Wide Web addresses (see below).

Several weekly and bi-weekly periodicals were also used in the past year's pursuit of facts and figures, among them— *Baseball America*, *ESPN the Magazine*, *FIFA News* (Soccer), *The Hockey News*, *The NCAA News*, *Soccer America*, *Sports Illustrated*, *The Sporting News*, *Street & Smith's Sports Business Journal*, *Track & Field News* and *USA Today Baseball Weekly*.

In addition, the following books provided background material for one or more chapters of the almanac.

Arenas & Ballparks

The Ballparks, by Bill Shannon and George Kalinsky; Hawthorn Books, Inc. (1975); New York.

Diamonds, by Michael Gershman; Houghton Mifflin Co. (1993); Boston.

Green Cathedrals (Revised Edition), by Philip Lowry; Addison-Wesley Publishing Co. (1992); Reading, Mass.

The NFL's Encyclopedic History of Professional Football, Macmillan Publishing Co. (1977); New York.

Take Me Out to the Ballpark, by Lowell Reidenbaugh; The Sporting News Publishing Co. (1983); St. Louis.

24 Seconds to Shoot (An Informal History of the NBA), by Leonard Koppett; Macmillan Publishing Co. (1968); New York.

Auto Racing

Indy: 75 Years of Racing's Greatest Spectacle, by Rich Taylor; St. Martin's Press (1991); New York.

2003 CART FedEx Championship Series Media Guide; Championship Auto Racing Teams; Troy, Mich.

2003 Indy Racing League Media Guide, by IMS Publications; Indianapolis.

2003 NASCAR Winston Cup Series Media Guide, compiled and edited by Sports Marketing Enterprises; NASCAR Winston Cup Series; Winston-Salem, N.C.

Marlboro Grand Prix Guide, 1950-1998 (1999 Edition), compiled by Jacques Deschenaux and Claude Michele Deschenaux; Charles Stewart & Company Ltd; Brentford, England.

NASCAR Online, produced by Turner Sports Interactive, http://www.nascar.com

CART Online, maintained by CART and VFX Digital Solutions, http://www.cart.com

Indy Racing Online, maintained by IRL, http://www.indyracingleague.com

NHRA Online, maintained by NHRA, http://www.nhra.com

Baseball

The All-Star Game (A Pictorial History, 1933 to Present), by Donald Honig; The Sporting News Publishing Co. (1987); St. Louis.

The Baseball Chronology, edited by James Charlton; Macmillian Publishing Co. (1991); New York.

The Baseball Encyclopedia (Ninth Edition), editorial director, Rick Wolff; Macmillan Publishing Co. (1993); New York.

The Complete 2002 Baseball Record Book, edited by Craig Carter; The Sporting News Publishing Co.; St. Louis.

The Scrapbook History of Baseball by Jordan Deutsch, Richard Cohen, Roland Johnson and David Neft; Bobbs-Merrill Company, Inc. (1975); Indianapolis/New York.

2002 Sporting News Official Baseball Guide, edited by Craig Carter and Dave Sloan; The Sporting News Publishing Co.; St. Louis.

2002 Sporting News Official Baseball Register, edited by Jeff Paur, David Walton, John Duxbury; The Sporting News Publishing Co.; St. Louis.

The Sports Encyclopedia: Baseball (1996 Edition), edited by David Neft and Richard Cohen; St. Martin's Press; New York.

Total Baseball (Seventh Edition), edited by John Thorn, Pete Palmer and Michael Gershman; Total Sports Publishing (2001); Kingston, N.Y.

The Official Site of Major League Baseball, produced by Major League Baseball Properties, Inc., http://www.mlb.com

College Basketball

All the Moves (A History of College Basketball), by Neil D. Issacs; J.B. Lippincott Company (1975); New York.

College Basketball, U.S.A. (Since 1892), by John D. McCallum; Stein and Day (1978); New York.

Collegiate Basketball: Facts and Figures on the Cage Sport, by Edwin C. Caudle; The Paragon Press (1960); Montgomery, Ala.

The Encyclopedia of the NCAA Basketball Tournament, written and compiled by Jim Savage; Dell Publishing (1990); New York.

The Final Four (Reliving America's Basketball Classic), compiled by Billy Reed; Host Communications, Inc. (1988); Lexington, Ky.

2000 NCAA Final Four Records Book, compiled by Gary Johnson; edited by Marty Benson; NCAA Books; Indianapolis.

The Modern Encyclopedia of Basketball (Second Revised Edition), edited by Zander Hollander; Dolphins Books (1979); Doubleday & Company, Inc.; Garden City, N.Y.

2000 NCAA Men's Records Book, compiled by Gary Johnson and Sean Straziscar; edited by Marty Benson; NCAA Books; Indianapolis.

2000 NCAA Women's Records Book, compiled by Richard M. Campbell and Jenifer L. Scheibler; edited by Vanessa L. Abell; NCAA Books; Indianapolis.

NCAA Online, produced by National Collegiate Athletic Association, http://www.ncaa.org

Plus many 2003-2004 NCAA Division I conference guides from America East to the WAC.

Pro Basketball

The Official NBA Basketball Encyclopedia (Third Edition), edited by Jan Hubbard; Doubleday (2000); New York.

2002-03 Sporting News Official NBA Guide; edited by Craig Carter and Rob Reheuser; The Sporting News Publishing Co.; St. Louis.

2002-03 Sporting News Official NBA Register, edited by David Walton, John Gardella; The Sporting News Publishing Co.; St. Louis.

NBA Online, produced by NBA Media Ventures, LLC, ESPN Internet Ventures, http://www.nba.com

Bowling

1995 Bowlers Journal Annual & Almanac; Luby Publishing; Chicago.

2001 PWBA Guide, Professional Women's Bowling Association; Rockford, Ill.

2002-03 PBA Tour Media Guide; Professional Bowlers Association; Seattle, Wash.

PBA Online, produced by the Pro Bowlers Association, http://www.pba.com

Boxing

The Boxing Record Book (1996 Edition), edited by Phill Marder; Fight Fax Inc.; Sicklerville, N.J.

The Ring 1985 Record Book & Boxing Encyclopedia, edited by Herbert G. Goldman; The Ring Publishing Corp.; New York.

The Ring: Boxing, The 20th Century, Steven Farhood, editor-in-chief; BDD Illustrated Books (1993); New York.

College Sports

1994-95 National Collegiate Championships, edited by Ted Breidenthal; NCAA Books; Overland Park, Kan.

1999-2000 National Directory of College Athletics, edited by Kevin Cleary; Collegiate Directories, Inc.; Cleveland.

NCAA Online, produced by National Collegiate Athletic Association, http://www.ncaa.org

NAIA.org, produced by National Association of Intercollegiate Athletics, http://www.naia.org

College Football

Football: A College History, by Tom Perrin; McFarland & Company, Inc. (1987); Jefferson, N.C.

Football: Facts & Figures, by Dr. L.H. Baker; Farrar & Rinehart, Inc. (1945); New York.

Great College Football Coaches of the Twenties and Thirties, by Tim Cohane; Arlington House (1973); New Rochelle, N.Y.

2000 NCAA College Football Records Book, compiled by Richard M. Campbell, John Painter and Sean Straziscar; edited by Scott Deitch; NCAA Books; Indianapolis.

Saturday Afternoon, by Richard Whittingham; Workman Publishing Co., Inc. (1985); New York.

Saturday's America, by Dan Jenkins; Sports Illustrated Books; Little, Brown & Company (1970); Boston.

Tournament of Roses, The First 100 Years, by Joe Hendrickson; Knapp Press (1989); Los Angeles.

NCAA Online, produced by National Collegiate Athletic Association, http://www.ncaa.org

Plus numerous college football team and conference guides, especially the 2001 guides compiled by the Atlantic Coast Conference, Big Ten, Big 12 and Southeastern Conference.

Pro Football

2002 Canadian Football League Guide, compiled by the CFL Communications Dept.; Toronto.

The Football Encyclopedia (The Complete History of NFL Football from 1892 to the Present), compiled by David Neft and Richard Cohen; St. Martin's Press (1994); New York.

The Official NFL Encyclopedia, by Beau Riffenburgh; New American Library (1986); New York.

Official NFL 1999 Record and Fact Book, compiled by the NFL Communications Dept. and Seymour Siwoff, Elias Sports Bureau; edited by Chris McCloskey and Matt Marini; produced by NFL Properties, Inc.; Los Angeles.

The Scrapbook History of Pro Football, by Richard Cohen, Jordan Deutsch, Roland Johnson and David Neft; Bobbs-Merrill Company, Inc. (1976); Indianapolis/New York.

2003 Sporting News Football Guide, edited by Craig Carter, Terry Shea and Christen Sager; The Sporting News Publishing Co.; St. Louis.

2003 Sporting News Football Register, edited Brendan Roberts; The Sporting News Publishing Co.; St. Louis.

1995 Sporting News Super Bowl Book, edited by Tom Dienhart, Joe Hoppel and Dave Sloan; The Sporting News Publishing Co.; St. Louis.

Total Football II, edited by Bob Carroll, Michael Gershman, David Neft and John Thorn; HarperCollins; New York.

NFL Online, produced by NFL Enterprises http://www.nfl.com

CFL Online, produced by SLAM! Sports, http://www.cfl.ca

Golf

The Encyclopedia of Golf (Revised Edition), compiled by Nevin H. Gibson; A.S. Barnes and Company (1964); New York.

Guinness Golf Records: Facts and Champions, by Donald Steel; Guinness Superlatives Ltd. (1987); Middlesex, England.

The History of the PGA Tour, by Al Barkow; Doubleday (1989); New York.

The Illustrated History of Women's Golf, by Rhonda Glenn, Taylor Publishing Co. (1991); Dallas.

2003 LPGA Player Guide, produced by LPGA Communications Dept.; Ladies Professional Golf Assn. Tour; Daytona Beach, Fla.

2003 PGA Tour Guide, written and edited by Chuck Adams, James Cramer, Nelson Luis and Lee Patterson; Professional Golfers Assn. Tour; Ponte Vedra, Fla.

Official Guide of the PGA Championships; Triumph Books (1994); Chicago.

The PGA World Golf Hall of Fame Book, by Gerald Astor, Prentice Hall Press (1991); New York.

2003 Champions Tour Guide, written and edited by Dave Senko, Phil Stambaugh and Joan Von Thron-Alexander; Professional Golfers Assn. Tour; Ponte Vedra, Fla.

Pro-Golf 2003, PGA European Tour Media Guide, Virginia Water, Surrey, England.

The Random House International Encyclopedia of Golf, by Malcolm Campbell; Random House (1991); New York.

USGA Record Books (1895-1959, 1960-80 and 1981-90); U.S. Golf Association; Far Hills, N.J.

LPGA Online, produced by the LPGA and Ignite Sports Media LLC., http://www.lpga.com

PGA Online, produced by the PGA of America, http://www.pgaonline.com

PGATour Online, produced by PGA Tour Inc., http://www.pgatour.com

Hockey

Canada Cup '87: The Official History, No.1 Publications Ltd.; Toronto.

The Complete Encyclopedia of Hockey; edited by Zander Hollander; Visible Ink Press (1993); Detroit.

The Hockey Encyclopedia, by Stan Fischler and Shirley Walton Fischler; research editor, Bob Duff; Macmillan Publishing Co. (1983); New York.

Hockey Hall of Fame (The Official History of the Game and Its Greatest Stars), by Dan Diamond and Joseph Romain; Doubleday (1988); New York.

The National Hockey League, by Edward F. Dolan Jr.; W H Smith Publishers Inc. (1986); New York.

The Official National Hockey League 75th Anniversary Commemorative Book, edited by Dan Diamond; McClelland & Stewart, Inc. (1991); Toronto.

2003 Official NHL Guide & Record Book, compiled by the NHL Public Relations Dept.; New York/Montreal/Toronto.

2003 Sporting News Hockey Guide, edited by Craig Carter; The Sporting News Publishing Co.; St. Louis.

2003 Sporting News Hockey Register, edited by David Walton; The Sporting News Publishing Co.; St. Louis.

The Stanley Cup, by Joseph Romain and James Duplacey; Gallery Books (1989); New York.

The Trail of the Stanley Cup (Volumes I-III), by Charles L. Coleman; Progressive Publications Inc. (1969); Sherbrooke, Quebec.

Total Hockey (Second Edition), edited by Dan Diamond, et al.; Total Sports Publishing; Kingston, N.Y.

NHL Online, produced by the NHL Interactive Cyber Enterprises, http://www.nhl.com

Horse Racing

1999 NTRA Media Guide, compiled by the National Thoroughbred Racing Association; New York.

1997 American Racing Manual, compiled by the Daily Racing Form; Hightstown, N.J.

1997 Breeders' Cup Statistics; Breeders' Cup Limited; Lexington, Ky.

1996 Directory and Record Book, Thoroughbred Racing Associations of North America Inc.; Elkton, Md.

2001 Trotting and Pacing Guide, compiled and edited by John Pawlak; United States Trotting Association; Columbus, Ohio.

USTA Online, produced by the USTA, http://www.ustrotting.com

NTRA Online, hosted by Equibase Company LLC, http://www.ntra.com

Equibase.com, hosted by Equibase Company LLC, http://www.equibase.com

International Sports

Athletics: A History of Modern Track and Field (1860-1990, Men and Women), by Roberto Quercetani; Vallardi & Associati (1990); Milan, Italy.

1999 International Track & Field Annual, Association of Track & Field Statisticians; edited by Peter Matthews; SportsBooks Ltd.; Surrey, England.

Track & Field News' Little Blue Book; Metric conversion tables; From the editors of *Track & Field News* (1989); Los Altos, Calif.

US Ski Team Online, produced by US Ski Team and SportsLine USA, http://www.usskiteam.com

Miscellaneous

The America's Cup 1851-1987 (Sailing for Supremacy), by Gary Lester and Richard Sleeman; Lester-Townsend Publishing (1986); Sydney, Australia.

The Encyclopedia of Sports (Fifth Revised Edition), by Frank G. Menke; revisions by Suzanne Treat; A.S. Barnes and Co., Inc. (1975); Cranbury, N.J.

ESPN SportsCentury, edited by Michael McCambridge; Hyperion (1999); New York.

The Great American Sports Book, by George Gipe; Doubleday & Company, Inc. (1978); Garden City, N.Y.

1999 Official PRCA Media Guide, edited by Steve Fleming; Professional Rodeo Cowboys Association; Colorado Springs.

The Sail Magazine Book of Sailing, by Peter Johnson; Alfred A. Knopf (1989); New York.

Ten Years of the Ironman, *Triathlete* magazine; October, 1988; Santa Monica, Calif.

The Ultimate Book of Sports Lists, by Mike Meserole; DK Publishing (1999); New York.

Iditarod Online, produced by the Iditarod Trail Committee and GCI, http://www.iditarod.com

PRCA Online, produced by the Pro Rodeo Cowboys Association, http://www.prorodeo.com

Olympics

All That Glitters Is Not Gold (An Irreverent Look at the Olympic Games); by William O. Johnson, Jr.; G.P. Putnam's Sons (1972); New York.

Barcelona/Albertville 1992; edited by Lisa H. Albertson; for U.S. Olympic Committee by Commemorative Publications; Salt Lake City.

Chamonix to Lillehammer (The Glory of the Olympic Winter Games); edited by Lisa H. Albertson; for U.S. Olympic Committee by Commemorative Publication (1994); Salt Lake City.

The Complete Book of the Olympics (1992 Edition); by David Wallechinsky; Little, Brown and Co.; Boston.

The Games Must Go On (Avery Brundage and the Olympic Movement), by Allen Guttmann; Columbia University Press (1984); New York.

The Golden Book of the Olympic Games, edited by Erich Kamper and Bill Mallon; Vallardi & Associati (1992); Milan, Italy.

Hitler's Games (The 1936 Olympics), by Duff Hart-Davis; Harper & Row (1986); New York/London.

An Illustrated History of the Olympics (Third Edition); by Dick Schaap; Alfred A. Knopf (1975); New York.

The Nazi Olympics, by Richard D. Mandell; Souvenir Press (1972); London.

The Official USOC Book of the 1984 Olympic Games (1984), by Dick Schaap; Random House/ABC Sports; New York.

The Olympics: A History of the Games, by William Oscar Johnson; Oxmoor House (1992); Birmingham, Ala.

Pursuit of Excellence (The Olympic Story), by The Associated Press and Grolier; Grolier Enterprises Inc. (1979); Danbury, Conn.

The Story of the Olympic Games (776 B.C. to 1948 A.D.), by John Kieran and Arthur Daley; J.B. Lippincott Company (1948); Philadelphia/New York.

United States Olympic Books (Seven Editions): 1936 and 1948-88; U.S. Olympic Association; New York.

The USA and the Olympic Movement, produced by the USOC Information Dept.; edited by Gayle Plant; U.S. Olympic Committee (1988); Colorado Springs.

Soccer

The American Encyclopedia of Soccer, edited by Zander Hollander; Everest House Publishers (1980); New York.

The European Football Yearbook (1994-95 Edition), edited by Mike Hammond; Sports Projects Ltd; West Midlands, England.

The Guinness Book of Soccer Facts & Feats, by Jack Rollin; Guinness Superlatives Ltd. (1978); Middlesex, England.

History of Soccer's World Cup, by Michael Archer; Chartwell Books, Inc. (1978); Secaucus, N.J.

The Simplest Game, by Paul Gardner; Collier Books (1994); New York.

The Story of the World Cup, by Brian Glanville; Faber and Faber Limited (1993); London/Boston.

2001 MLS Official Media Guide, edited by the MLS Communications staff; Los Angeles.

1991-92 MSL Official Guide, Major (Indoor) Soccer League; Overland Park, Kan.

FIFA Online, produced by FIFA, http://www.fifa.com

MLSnet, produced by Major League Soccer, http://mlsnet.com

Tennis

Bud Collins' Modern Encyclopedia of Tennis, edited by Bud Collins and Zander Hollander; Visible Ink Press (1994); Detroit.

The Illustrated Encyclopedia of World Tennis, by John Haylett and Richard Evans; Exeter Books (1989); New York.

Official Encyclopedia of Tennis, edited by the staff of the U.S. Lawn Tennis Assn.; Harper & Row (1972); New York.

2004 ATP Tour Player Guide, edited by Greg Sharko; Association of Tennis Professionals Tour Publications; Ponte Vedra Beach, Fla.

2004 WTA Tour Media Guide, compiled by Sanex WTA Public Relations staff; St. Petersburg, Fla.

ATP TourOnline, produced by ATP Tour, Inc., http://www.atptour.com

WTA Tour Online, produced by the WTA Tour, http://www.wtatour.com

Who's Who

The Guinness International Who's Who of Sport, edited by Peter Mathews, Ian Buchanan and Bill Mallon; Guinness Publishing (1993); Middlesex, England.

101 Greatest Athletes of the Century, by Will Grimsley and the Associated Press Sports Staff; Bonanza Books (1987); Crown Publishers, Inc.; New York.

The New York Times Book of Sports Legends, edited by Joseph Vecchione; Simon & Schuster (1991); New York.

Superstars, by Frank Litsky; Vineyard Books, Inc. (1975); Secaucus, N.J.

A Who's Who of Sports Champions (Their Stories and Records), by Ralph Hickok, Houghton Mifflin Co. (1995); Boston.

Other Reference Books/Sites

Facts & Dates of American Sports, by Gorton Carruth & Eugene Ehrlich; Harper & Row, Publishers, Inc. (1988); New York.

Sports Market Place 1997 (January Edition), edited by Kevin J. Myers; Franklin Quest Sports; Phoenix, Ariz.

The World Book Encyclopedia (1988 Edition); World Book, Inc.; Chicago.

The World Book Yearbook (Annual Supplements, 1954-95); World Book, Inc.; Chicago.

ESPN.com, produced by ESPN Internet Ventures., http://espn.com

CBS SportsLine, produced by CBS and SportsLine USA, http://cbs.sportsline.com

Olympics

Winter Games

Year	No.	Host City	Dates
2006	XX	Turin, Italy	Feb. 4-19
2010	XXI	Vancouver, Canada	Feb. 12-28

Summer Games

Year	No.	Host City	Dates
2008	XXIX	Beijing, China	Aug. 8-24

All-Star Games

Baseball

Year	Site	Date
2005	Comerica Park, Detroit	July 6
2006	PNC Park, Pittsburgh	July 11
2007	SBC Park, San Francisco	TBD

NBA Basketball

Year	Site	Date
2005	Pepsi Center, Denver	Feb. 14
2006	Toyota Center, Houston	Feb. 20

NFL Pro Bowl

Year	Site	Date
2005	Aloha Stadium, Honolulu	Feb. 13
2006	Aloha Stadium, Honolulu	Feb. 12

NHL Hockey

Year	Site	Date
2005	Phillips Arena, Atlanta	Feb. 13
2006	Glendale Arena, Phoenix	Jan. 29

Auto Racing

The Daytona 500 stock car race is usually held on the Sunday before the third Monday in February, while the Indianapolis 500 is usually held on the Sunday of Memorial Day weekend in May. The following dates are tentative.

Year	Daytona 500	Indy 500
2005	Feb. 20	May 29
2006	Feb. 19	May 28

NCAA Basketball

Men's Final Four

Year	Site	Dates
2005	Edward Jones Dome, St. Louis	April 2-4
2006	RCA Dome, Indianapolis	April 1-3
2007	Georgia Dome, Atlanta	Mar. 31-April 2
2008	Alamodome, San Antonio	April 5-7
2009	Ford Field, Detroit	Apr. 4-6
2010	RCA Dome, Indianapolis	Apr. 3-5

Women's Final Four

Year	Site	Dates
2005	RCA Dome, Indianapolis	April 3-5
2006	FleetCenter, Boston	April 2-4
2007	Gund Arena, Cleveland	April 1-3
2008	St. Pete Times Forum, Tampa	TBD
2009	Edward Jones Domes, St. Louis	TBD
2010	Alamodome, San Antonio	TBD

Horse Racing

Triple Crown

The Kentucky Derby is always held at Churchill Downs in Louisville on the first Saturday in May, followed two weeks later by the Preakness Stakes at Pimlico Race Course in Baltimore and three weeks after that by the Belmont Stakes at Belmont Park in Elmont, N.Y.

Year	Ky Derby	Preakness	Belmont
2005	May 7	May 21	June 11
2006	May 6	May 20	June 10
2007	May 5	May 19	June 9

NFL Football

Super Bowl

No.	Site	Date
XXXIX	ALLTEL Stadium, Jacksonville	Feb. 6, 2005
XL	Ford Field, Detroit	Feb. 5, 2006
XLI	Pro Player Stadium, Miami	2007
XLII	Glendale, Arizona	2008

Golf

The Masters

Year	Site	Dates
2005	Augusta (Ga.) National GC	April 7-10
2006	Augusta (Ga.) National GC	Apr. 6-9
2007	Augusta (Ga.) National GC	Apr. 5-8

U.S. Open

Year	Site	Dates
2005	Pinehurst (N.C.) Resort & CC	June 16-19
2006	Winged Foot GC, Mamaroneck, N.Y.	June 15-18
2007	Oakmont CC, Oakmont, Pa.	June 14-17
2008	Torrey Pines GC, La Jolla, Ca.	June 12-15

U.S. Women's Open

Year	Site	Dates
2005	Cherry Hills CC, Englewood, Colo.	June 23-26
2006	Newport, R.I. Country Club	June 29-July 2
2007	Pine Needles Lodge and CC, Southern Pines, N.C.	June 28-July 1

U.S. Senior Open

Year	Site	Dates
2005	NCR CC, Kettering, Ohio	July 28-31
2006	Prarie Dunes CC, Hutchinson, Kan.	July 6-9
2007	Whistling Straits, Kohler, Wis.	July 5-8

PGA Championship

Year	Site	Dates
2005	Baltusrol GC, Springfield, N.J.	Aug. 11-14
2006	Medinah CC, Medinah, IL	TBA
2007	Southern Hills CC, Tulsa, OK	TBA
2008	Oakland Hills CC, Bloomfield Hills, Mich	TBA

British Open

Year	Site	Dates
2005	St. Andrews, Scotland	July 14-17
2006	Royal Liverpool GC, England	July 20-23
2007	Carnoustie GC, Scotland	July 19-22

Ryder Cup

Year	Site	Date
2006	Kildare Golf and CC, Ireland	Sept. 22-24
2008	Valhalla GC, Louisville, Ky.	TBA
2010	Celtic Manor, Wales	TBA

Soccer

World Cup

Year	Site	Dates
2006	Germany	June 9-July 9
2010	South Africa	TBD

Women's World Cup

Year	Site	Date
2007	China	TBD

Tennis

U.S. Open

Usually held from the last Monday in August through the second Sunday in Sept., with Labor Day weekend the midway point in the tournament.

Year	Site	Dates
2005	Arthur Ashe Stadium, NYC	Aug. 29-Sept. 11
2006	Arthur Ashe Stadium, NYC	Aug. 28-Sept. 10
2007	Arthur Ashe Stadium, NYC	Aug. 27-Sept. 9
2008	Arthur Ashe Stadium, NYC	Aug. 26-Sept. 8